MW01179042

WHO'S HIRING

2002

NEW THIS YEAR...

- More Employers: Over 5,000 Included
- More HR Contacts and Email Addresses
- More Occupational Categories Ranked
- More Employer Websites and Descriptions
- 100% New Listings

MEDIACORP CANADA INC.
TORONTO

Who's Hiring 2002
Mediacorp Canada Inc.
21 New Street
Toronto, Ontario
M5R 1P7

Telephone   (416) 964-6069
Fax   (416) 964-3202

E-mail   info@mediacorp2.com
Web Site   http://www.mediacorp2.com

© 2002 Mediacorp Canada Inc. All rights reserved. No part of this publication may be reproduced, stored in a retrieval system, or transmitted, in any form or by any means, electronic, mechanical, photocopying, recording, or otherwise, without the prior written permission of the publisher. WHO'S HIRING 2002 is a trade mark of Mediacorp Canada Inc.

To purchase the information in this directory on CD-ROM ($79.95), call (416) 964-6069.

ISBN 1-894450-08-6. Fifth edition: 2002. First edition: 1998.

Printed in Canada by Webcom.

CONTENTS

How to Use This Directory

This is a digest of Canadian employers that have created at least two full-time positions in the past 12 months. *By indexing employers by occupation and city, this book lets you target your job search efforts on the top employers in your field and area.*

The information in this book is drawn from over 50,000 career-level opportunities that were publicized in the past 12 months, as well as research on each employer. The companies and organizations listed in this directory are the fastest-growing employers in 61 major occupations.

To be included in this directory, an employer must meet three criteria:

(a) **The employer has publicized at least two career-level positions in the past 12 months.** Employers publicizing part-time, temporary or seasonal positions are not included, nor are those listing positions with annual salaries under $25,000. 100% of the jobs reported in this directory were created in the past year.

(b) **The employer is a *bona fide* employer, and not a recruitment agency or search firm.** Search firms, recruiters and agencies are not listed in this directory. Information on these firms can be found in the *Canadian Directory of Search Firms* (see p. 600).

(c) **The employer is located in Canada.** Employers outside Canada are not included in this directory.

Employers do not pay to be included in this directory, nor do they decide what is reported about them. We are solely responsible for the rankings and the contents of each listing.

This directory does not include information on unpublicized positions. Even large employers are excluded if they did not publicize two or more jobs in the past year.

To find the top employers in your field:

1. Determine the occupational category that includes your line of work (see page 458).

2. Refer to the appropriate **Occupational Index** for a list of the top employers in your category. (Employers are ranked by the number of positions they publicized in each category.)

3. Then consult the **Employer Listings** at the front of the book for full particulars on each employer that interests you.

You can also use the **Geographic Index** (page 567) to locate the top employers in cities and towns across Canada. Cities are listed in alphabetical order and, within each city, employers are arranged by number of positions publicized.

Employer Listings are shown in alphabetical order according to each employer's most recent business or trade name. In some cases, acronyms are used; readers should take care to check under both forms of an employer's name.

While every effort has been taken to ensure that the information in this directory is accurate and up-to-date, we assume no responsibilty for errors or omissions.

If you find information that is out-of-date or inaccurate, please use the form on page 607 or email us and we will update our records.

Employer Listings

EMPLOYER LISTINGS

01 COMMUNIQUE LABORATORY INC.
Att: Human Resources Manager
1450 Meyerside Drive, Suite 500
Mississauga, ON L5T 2N5
Tel. 905-795-2888
Fax 905-795-0101
Email .... hr@01com.com
Website www.01com.com
Employer Background: 01 Communique Laboratory Inc. is a software publisher. *New Positions Created (9):* Customer Systems Engineer; Marketing Administrative Assistant; Product Marketing Manager; Technical Support Manager; Webmaster / Web Content Developer; Channel Marketing Manager; Marcomm Administrative Assistant; Software Engineers; Technical Support Position.

360 NETWORKS INC.
Att: Human Resources Department
5500 Explorer Drive, 2nd Floor
Mississauga, ON L4W 5C7
Tel. 905-206-5800
Fax 905-206-9019
Email .... careerson@360.net
Website www.360.net
Employer Background: 360 Networks (formerly Ledcor Communications Ltd.) is a broadband network services provider, with an extensive fibre optic network. *New Positions Created (3):* Assistant Project Managers, Local Access Construction (2); Estimating Manager; Network Field Operations Supervisor.

3LOG SYSTEMS INC.
Att: Human Resources Manager
2633 Viking Way, Suite 208
Richmond, BC V6V 1N3
Tel. 604-271-5506
Fax 604-271-5507
Email .... jobs@3log.com
Website www.3log.com
Employer Background: 3LOG Systems Inc. is an enterprise software development firm, specializing in woodlands inventory management systems for the forest industry. *New Positions Created (5):* Database Programmer / Administrator; Delphi Programmer / Analyst; Technical Sales / Marketing Manager; Database Programmer / Administrator; Delphi Programmer / Analyst.

3M CANADA COMPANY
Att: Human Resources Manager
PO Box 5757
London, ON N6A 4T1
Tel. 519-451-2500
Fax 519-452-6502
Email .... 3mcancareers@3m.com
Website www.3m.com
Employer Background: 3M Canada Company manufactures and markets more than 50,000 diverse products. *New Positions Created (6):* Sales Representative, Abrasives; Contract Customer Service Representative, Bilingual; Sales Representatives - Electronic Market Products (2); Bilingual Customer Service Representative; Pre-Press Operator; Marketing Professional, Retail Markets.

45 DEGREES CORP.
Att: Human Resources Manager
99 - 5th Avenue
Suite 11, Fifth Avenue Court
Ottawa, ON K1S 5K4
Tel. 613-230-4545
Fax 613-231-4500
Email .... careers@45degrees.com
Website www.45degrees.com
Employer Background: 45 Degrees Corp. is a marketing communications firm. *New Positions Created (2):* Marketing Positions; Writer.

7-ELEVEN CANADA
Att: Personnel Consultant
3185 Willingdon Green
Burnaby, BC V5G 4P3
Fax 604-293-5660
Website www.7eleven.com
Employer Background: 7-Eleven is the largest convenience store retailer in Canada, with 6,000 employees and 475 stores nationwide. *New Positions Created (2):* District Manager; Store Managers.

7-ELEVEN CANADA
Att: Pat Hopkins, HR Manager
3376 Harvester Road, Suite 201
Burlington, ON L7N 3N2
Tel. 905-634-1711
Fax 905-634-6864
Website www.7eleven.com
Employer Background: 7-Eleven is the largest convenience store retailer in Canada, with 6,000 employees and 475 stores nationwide. *New Positions Created (2):* Store Manager Trainees; Store Manager Trainees.

724 SOLUTIONS INC.
Att: Human Resources Manager
10 York Mills Road, 3rd Floor
Toronto, ON M2P 2G4
Tel. 416-226-2900
Fax 416-226-4456
Email .... hrinfo@724.com
Website www.724.com
Employer Background: 724 Solutions Inc. provides software that connects financial institutions and other online businesses directly to their customers. *New Positions Created (71):* Security Architect; Implementation Architect; Java Developer; Manager, Customer & Device Testing; User Interface Designer / Usability Analyst; Senior Software Developer; Software Developer; Technical Lead / Senior Software Developers (2); Human Resources Generalist; Manager, Financial Reporting; Senior Information Developer; Senior Infrastructure Developer; Treasury Manager; Application Product Support Manager; Intermediate / Senior Software Developers (4); Quality Assurance Analysts (2); Security Architects (2); Senior User Interface Architect; Vendor Coordinator; Intermediate Software Developer; Junior Software Developer; Network Infrastructure Engineer; Technical Lead / Senior Software Developer; Technical Trainer; Tier-2 Support Analyst; Unix Environment Support Specialist; Customer Support Representative; Director, Corporate Communications; Purchasing Clerk; Web Communications Specialist; Accounting Manager; Analyst, Business Solutions; Application Product Support Manager; ClearCase Administrator; Consultant, Internet-Enabled Devices; Environmental Support Specialists (2); Network Systems Engineer; Planning Director, Applications; PLM Product Manager, Banking; Quality Assurance Team Leader; Requirements Manager; Senior Infrastructure Developer; Senior Software Developer, Application Containers; Senior Software Developer, Channel Server Group; Technical Account Manager; User Interface Designer / Usability Analyst; Vendor Manager; Application Development Managers; Business Requirements Analyst; Director of Information Technology; Human Resources Generalist; Intermediate / Senior Software Developers; Intermediate / Senior Software Developers; Internet Application Developers; Planning Analyst, Applications; Planning Manager, Applications; Product Support Specialists; Requirements Coordinator; Security Architect; Security Policy Analyst; Senior Business / Systems Analysts; Senior Product Line Manager; Senior Support Operations Engineer; Software Installation Specialist; Software Quality Assurance Analyst; Support / Operations Engineer; Technology Consultant; Unix C++ Developer, Core Components; Instructional Designer, Learning Development; Manager / Director, Business Development; Technical Trainer.

A. BERGER PRECISION LTD.
Att: Human Resources
28 Regan Road, Unit 1
Brampton, ON L7A 1A7
Tel. 905-840-4207
Fax 905-840-8022
Email ... human.resources@abergercanada.com
Website .... www.aberger.com
Employer Background: A. Berger Precision Ltd. is a global supplier of high-precision screw machine products to the automotive industry. *New Positions Created (5):* Engineer; Estimator / Quotation Position; Machine Operators; Process Engineer / Key Account Representative; Sales Manager.

A.G. SIMPSON CO. LIMITED
Att: Human Resources
560 Conestoga Boulevard
Cambridge, ON N1R 7L7
Tel. 519-621-7953
Fax 519-621-3774
Website .... www.agsimpson.com
Employer Background: A.G. Simpson Co. Limited is an OEM supplier of automotive stampings and assemblies. *New Positions Created (2):* Tooling Specialist; Maintenance Supervisor.

A.L.I. TECHNOLOGIES INC.
Att: Human Resources
10711 Cambie Road, Suite 130
Richmond, BC V6X 3G5

Tel. 604-279-5422
Fax 604-279-5468
Email .... hr@alitech.com
Website .... www.alitech.com

Employer Background: A.L.I. Technologies is a leading provider of digital image network systems for medical applications. *New Positions Created (25):* Hardware Engineer; Java Software Developer; Project Manager, Software Development; Quality Systems Admin Assistant; Remote Systems Administrator and Support Specialist; Visual C++ / COM Software Developer; Imaging Network Systems Analyst; PACS Integration Specialist; Product Mgr, Software Development; Service Software Engineer; Software Test Engineer; Technical Writer; Software Test Engineer; Clinical Applications Specialist, Radiology; Hardware Engineer; Java Software Developer; Product Support Specialist; Quality Systems Admin Assistant; Remote Systems Administrator & Support Specialist; Systems Analyst and UI Designer; Visual C++ / COM Software Developer; Admin Assistant, Quality Systems; Installation Coordinator; Marketing Coordinator; Network Administrator.

A.R. THOMSON GROUP
Att: Valve Product Manager
10030 - 31st Avenue
Edmonton, AB T6N 1G4

Tel. 780-450-8080
Fax 780-450-2021
Email .... edmonton@arthomson.com
Website .... www.arthomson.com

Employer Background: Established in 1967, A.R. Thomson Group manufactures and distributes gaskets and other fluid sealing products. *New Positions Created (3):* Inside Valve Sales Representative; Mechanical Seals Sales Representative; Inside Salesperson.

A.W. MILLER TECHNICAL SALES
Att: Human Resources Manager
5590 McAdam Road
Mississauga, ON L4Z 1P3

Tel. 905-890-8686
Fax 905-890-8611
Email .... hgournias@awmiller.com
Website .... www.awmiller.com

Employer Background: A.W. Miller Technical Sales distributes Mazak and other world-quality CNC machines. *New Positions Created (9):* Machine Tools Sales Representatives; Service / Installer Technician; Technical Sales Positions; Applications Technician / Machinery Installation Positions; Automotive Accounts Specialist; CNC Laser / Fabricating Applications Technician; Fabricating Sales Manager; Machine Tools Sales Representative; Technical Sales Position.

A&B SOUND LTD.
Att: Human Resources
556 Seymour Street
Vancouver, BC V6B 3J5

Tel. 604-687-5837
Fax 604-687-5127
Email .... christa1@netcom.ca
Website .... www.absound.ca

Employer Background: A&B Sound Ltd. is a leading retailer of home and car entertainment products, music and movies, with 21 stores from Victoria to Winnipeg. *New Positions Created (3):* Category Mgr; Field Merchandiser; Director, IT.

AASTRA TELECOM
Att: Human Resources Manager
7648 - 8th Street NE
Calgary, AB T2E 8X4

Tel. 403-262-8202
Fax 403-262-8245
Email .... hr.calgary@aastra.com
Website .... www.aastra.com

Employer Background: Aastra Telecom markets customer-premise telecom equipment that supports services offered by telephone companies. *New Positions Created (17):* Embedded Firmware / DSP Developers; Senior Hardware Engineer; Software Engineer; Embedded Firmware / DSP Developers; Information System Development Engineer; Manufacturing Engineer; OEM / NPI Project Manager; PCB Layout Designer; Senior Hardware Engineer; Software Engineer; Embedded Firmware / DSP Developers; Information System Development Engineer; Manufacturing Engineer; OEM / NPI Project Manager; PCB Layout Designer; Senior Hardware Engineer; Software Engineer.

AASTRA TELECOM
Att: Human Resources Manager
155 Snow Boulevard
Concord, ON L4K 4N9

Tel. 905-760-4200
Fax 905-760-4233
Email .... hr.toronto@aastra.com
Website .... www.aastra.com

Employer Background: Aastra Telecom markets customer-premise telecom equipment that supports services offered by telephone companies. *New Positions Created (7):* Quality Control Technician; Customer Service Representative; Customer Service Representative, Bilingual; Hardware Design Engineers; Manufacturing / Test Engineer; Product Verification and Product Integrity Position; Software / Firmware Design Engineer.

AAVID THERMAL PRODUCTS
Att: Human Resources Department
440 Hanlan Road
Woodbridge, ON L4L 3P6

Tel. 905-850-9595
Fax 905-850-9599
Website .... www.aavid.com

Employer Background: Aavid Thermal Products is a thermal technology and manufacturing company. *New Positions Created (2):* Sales Applications Engineer; Various Trades Positions.

ABB INC.
Att: Dean Duda

1245 - 70th Avenue SE
Calgary, AB T2H 2X8

Tel. 403-253-0271
Email .... dean.g.duda@ca.abb.com
Website .... www.abb.com

Employer Background: ABB Inc. is a technology and engineering company, serving customers in power transmission and distribution, automation, oil, gas and petrochemicals, building technologies and financial services. *New Positions Created (4):* Inside Sales & Marketing Position; Sales Account Manager; Service Representative; Service Representative.

ABBA PARTS AND SERVICE
Att: Human Resources Manager
5370 Munro Court
Burlington, ON L7L 5N8

Tel. 905-333-2720
Fax 905-333-0973
Email .... abba@bserv.com
Website .... www.abbaparts.com

Employer Background: Abba Parts and Service is a leading pump manufacturer. *New Positions Created (2):* Administrative Assistant; Mechanical Engineering Technologist.

ABBEY PACKAGING EQUIPMENT LTD.
Att: Human Resources Manager
975 Fraser Drive, Unit 10
Burlington, ON L7L 4X8

Tel. 905-681-3010
Fax 905-681-3018
Email .... info@abbeytech.com
Website .... www.abbeytech.com

Employer Background: Abbey Packaging Equipment Ltd. is a supplier of high-tech packaging equipment to the food, pharmaceutical and beverage industries across Canada. *New Positions Created (2):* Service Technician; Technical Sales Representative.

ABBOTSFORD, CITY OF
Att: Human Resources Division
32315 South Fraser Way
Abbotsford, BC V2T 1W7

Tel. 604-853-2281
Fax 604-864-5541
Email . employment@city.abbotsford.bc.ca
Website .... www.city.abbotsford.bc.ca

Employer Background: The City of Abbotsford has a population of 117,000. *New Positions Created (5):* Human Resources Advisor; Fire Chief; Real Estate Consultant; Economic Development Manager; Human Resources Manager.

ABC GROUP INC.
Att: Human Resources
2 Norelco Drive
Toronto, ON M9L 2X6

Tel. 416-246-9886
Fax 416-743-8156
Email .... hr@abcgrp.com
Website .... www.abcgroupinc.com

Employer Background: ABC Group Inc. manufactures plastic parts for automotive, packaging and industrial applications. *New Positions Created (82):* CATIA Designer;

MRP / EDI Coordinator; Production Group Leader; Production Manager; Production Team Leader; Project Engineer; QS 9000 Lead Quality Auditor, Corporate Quality Team; Unigraphics Designer; Quality Manager; Blow-Moulding Technician; I-DEAS Designer; Injection Moulding Supervisor; Inventory / MRP Coordinator; Quality Engineer; Account Manager; Engineering Manager; Engineering Technologist; Group Leader; Lead Quality Auditor, TS 16949 / QS 9000; Plant Controller; Applications Engineer, Machine / Fixture Building; Customer Service Position; FEA Engineer; Shift Supervisor; CATIA Designer; Program Manager ; Project Engineer; Secretary; Unigraphics Designer; Administrative Assistant; CATIA / CAD Designer; Customer Service Representative; Engineering Technician; Financial Accountant; Maintenance Mechanic; Manufacturing Engineer, Hydroforming; MRP / ERP Coordinator; Plant Accountant; Production Group Leader, Compounding; Program Manager, Seating; Quality Engineer; Quality Technician, Stamping; Unigraphics / CAD Designer; Plant Controller; Production Manager; Program Manager; Customs / Freight Coordinator; Human Resources Manager; Plant / Production Managers; Project Engineer; Machine Building Manager; MRP Application Specialist; Office Coordinator; Plant Controller; Production Group Leader; Project Engineering Manager; Project / Process Engineer; SDRC I-DEAS / CAD Designer; Senior Project Engineer; TS 16949 / QS 9000 Lead Quality Auditor; Senior Injection Mould Designer; Quality / Delivery Metrics Engineer; Safety / Environmental Engineer; Sales Representative, Japanese / English; Shipper / Customer Service Representative; Accounts Payable Manager; Network Administrator; Quotation / Cost Analyst; Process Engineers; Project Engineers; QS 9000 / ISO 9000 Lead Auditor; Technical Sales Representative; Maintenance Mechanics / Stationary Engineers; MRP Applications / Inventory Control Coordinator; Production / Plant Managers; Quality Managers / Engineers; Delivery Metrics Manager, Corporate Quality Team; Group Leader, Fixture Department; Machine Building Manager, Plastic Machinery Building; Safety / Environmental Engineer; Team Leader, Mould Department; Team Leader, Mould Design.

ABITIBI-CONSOLIDATED INC., MACKENZIE REGION
Att: Nancy Krisko, HR Coordinator
PO Bag 2800, Papermill Division
Mackenzie, BC V0J 2C0
Tel. 250-997-2800
Fax 250-997-6723
Email .... recruit_mack@abicon.com
Website .... www.abicon.com
Employer Background: Abitibi-Consolidated Inc. (formerly Donohue Forest Products Inc.) is a leading manufacturer and global marketer of newsprint and uncoated groundwood papers. *New Positions Created (3):* Maintenance Engineers; Process Engineer; Senior Project Engineers.

ABUGOV KASPAR
Att: Frank Kaspar
601 - 10th Avenue SW
Suite 200, Kipling Square
Calgary, AB T2R 0B2
Tel. 403-237-9227
Fax 403-237-9230
Email .... careers@abugovkaspar.com
Website .... www.abugovkaspar.com
Employer Background: Abugov Kaspar is an architectural, engineering and interior design firm involved in local and international projects. *New Positions Created (4):* Architectural Positions; Architectural / Mechanical AutoCAD Technicians; Design Architects; Interior Designers.

ACADIA UNIVERSITY
Att: Marian Reid, Personnel Officer
Human Resources Department
Acadia University
Wolfville, NS B0P 1X0
Tel. 902-585-1117
Fax 902-585-1075
Email .... marian.reid@acadiau.ca
Website .... www.acadiau.ca
Employer Background: Founded in 1838, Acadia University serves over 3,400 students, with a teaching faculty of 357. *New Positions Created (5):* Biology Instructor; 1st Year Advisor; Director of Athletics; Head Coach, Men's Hockey; University Librarian.

ACADIA UNIVERSITY, JODREY SCHOOL OF COMPUTER SCIENCE
Att: Dr. Andre Trudel,
Chair, Selection Committee
Wolfville, NS B0P 1X0
Tel. 902-585-1331
Fax 902-585-1067
Email .... andre.trudel@acadiau.ca
Website .... www.acadiau.ca
Employer Background: Founded in 1838, Acadia University was ranked Canada's top undergraduate university by Maclean's magazine in 1998. The university serves over 3,400 students, with a teaching faculty of 357. *New Positions Created (2):* Tenure-Track Assistant Professors (2); Assistant Professor, Computer Science.

ACART COMMUNICATIONS
Att: Human Resources Manager
171 Nepean Street, Suite 600
Ottawa, ON K2P 0B4
Tel. 613-230-7944
Fax 613-232-5980
Email .... hitech@psinet.com
Website .... www.acart.com
Employer Background: Acart Communications is a large, full-service marketing and communications agency. *New Positions Created (5):* Mechanical Design Engineers; Power Supply Engineer; Production Coordinator; Proofreader; Sr. Graphic Designer.

ACCELERON
Att: Human Resources Department
5003 Levy Street, Suite 200
St-Laurent, QC H4R 2N9
Tel. 514-331-0007
Fax 514-332-0068
Email .... cv@acceleron.com
Website .... www.acceleron.com
Employer Background: Acceleron (formerly Momentum Business Systems) provides organizations with software that streamlines the travel expense management process. *New Positions Created (4):* Account Managers; Methodology Specialist; Quality Assurance Analyst; Web Application Developers.

ACCELIGHT NETWORKS
Att: Human Resources Manager
26 Auriga Drive
Nepean, ON K2E 8B7
Tel. 613-596-4804
Fax 613-596-2399
Email .... careers@accelight.com
Website .... www.accelight.com
Employer Background: AcceLight Networks develops optical internetworking products, including terabit and wavelength routers. *New Positions Created (27):* CAD Manager; Hardware Integration Prime Position; Layout / PCB Designers; Product Verification Engineer; ASIC / FPGA Design Engineer; ASIC Verification Engineer; Configuration Management and Tools Development Engineer; Digital High-Speed Board Design Engineers; Embedded Real-Time Software Engineer; Fiber Optic Lab Technician; Field System Engineer; Hardware Systems Architect; Junior Office Administrator; Manufacturing Test Engineer; Marketing Manager; MPLS / Traffic Engineering Architect; Network Planning Engineer; Operations Planner; Optical Design Engineer; Opto-Mechanical Engineer; Product Manager; Product Verification Engineer; Public Relations Manager; RF / Analog Design Engineer; Routing Protocol Design Engineer; Senior RF Engineer, Board-Level; Technical Writers.

ACCENT LABELS INC.
Att: Jeff
5690 Boulevard Thimens
St-Laurent, QC H4R 2K9
Tel. 514-335-3505
Fax 514-335-6154
Email .... jeff@accentlabels.com
Employer Background: Accent Labels Inc. specializes in product identification. *New Positions Created (2):* Shipper / Receiver; Sales Representatives.

ACCESS INTERNATIONAL AUTOMOTIVE LTD.
Att: Personnel
2221 - 41st Avenue NE, Unit 15
Calgary, AB T2E 6P2
Tel. 403-291-1005
Fax 403-291-1219
Employer Background: Access International Automotive Ltd. is a national distributor of automotive products. *New Positions Created (2):* Export Sales Professional; Bilingual Sales Professional.

ACCESS MEDICAL INC.
Att: Human Resources
1430 - 28th Street NE, Suite 1
Calgary, AB T2A 7W6
Tel. 403-248-2232
Fax 403-207-4143
Email .... access@accessmedical.com
Website .... www.accessmedical.com
Employer Background: Access Medical Inc.
supplies high-quality emergency medical
supplies and equipment to fire departments,
industry and allied health organizations.
New Positions Created (3): Sales Representa-
tive; Sales Representatives; Regional Sales
Manager.

ACCORD COMMUNICATIONS
Att: Human Resources Department
3200 - 14th Avenue NE, Unit 8
Calgary, AB T2A 6J4
Tel. 403-569-6400
Fax 403-569-6424
Email .... pbalcaen@accordcomm.com
Website .... www.accordcomm.com
Employer Background: Accord Communi-
cations provides design, implementation
and management services to support
telecom infrastructures. *New Positions Cre-
ated (3):* Account Executives; Network Sys-
tems Engineers; Technicians / Designers.

ACCPAC INTERNATIONAL INC.
Att: Human Resources
13700 International Place, Suite 300
Richmond, BC V6V 2X8
Tel. 604-207-9480
Fax 604-207-3602
Email .... canada.jobs@accpac.com
Website .... www.accpac.com
Employer Background: Accpac International
Inc., a subsidiary of Computer Associates
International Inc., offers a broad range of
financial accounting and business manage-
ment software solutions. *New Positions Cre-
ated (7):* Hosting Applications Manager;
Visual Basic Programmers; ColdFusion Pro-
grammers; Telecom Specialist; Business
Partner Account Manager; Business Partner
Recruiting Managers; Web Site Visual Direc-
tor.

ACCPAC INTERNATIONAL INC.
Att: Human Resources Manager
5935 Airport Road
Mississauga, ON L4V 1W5
Tel. 905-676-6700
Fax 905-676-6711
Email .... canada.jobs@accpac.com
Website .... www.accpac.com
Employer Background: Accpac International
Inc., a subsidiary of Computer Associates
International Inc., offers a broad range of
financial accounting and business manage-
ment software solutions. *New Positions Cre-
ated (2):* Business Partner Account Manag-
ers; Business Partner Recruiting Manager.

ACCUBID SYSTEMS LTD.
Att: Human Resources Department
7725 Jane Street, Suite 200
Toronto, ON L4K 1X4

Tel. 905-761-8800
Fax 905-761-1234
Email .... resume@accubid.com
Website .... www.accubid.com
Employer Background: Accubid Systems
provides easy-to-use estimating and billing
software to enhance the productivity of elec-
trical and mechanical contractors. *New Po-
sitions Created (2):* Marketing Specialist;
Product Trainer.

ACCUTEL.COM
Att: Human Resources Coordinator
170 Evans Avenue, Suite 200
Toronto, ON M8Z 1J7
Tel. 416-695-9800
Fax 416-695-9837
Email .... hresources@accutel.com
Website .... www.accutel.com
Employer Background: Accutel.com is Cana-
da's largest independent teleconferencing
provider. *New Positions Created (3):* Bilin-
gual Conference Operators; Inside Sales Su-
pervisor; Reservations Supervisor.

ACD SYSTEMS
Att: Human Resources
PO Box 36
Saanichton, BC V8M 2C3
Tel. 250-544-6700
Fax 250-544-0291
Email .... humanresources@acdnet.com
Website .... www.acdsystems.com
Employer Background: Founded in 1993,
ACD Systems develops and markets digital
imaging and network communication soft-
ware. *New Positions Created (39):* Business
Development Coordinator, OEM; Business
Development Coordinator, SDK and Pane
Extension; European Channel Sales Liaison;
Executive Assistant; Japanese Market Liai-
son; Senior Software Developers (3); Korean
Market Liaison; Director of Marketing; Ger-
man Market Liaison; Product Promotions
Specialist; Software Development Leaders
(2); QA Analyst; Business Development Co-
ordinator - OEM; Business Development
Coordinator - Retail; Business Development
Coordinator - SDK & Pane Extension; Re-
ceptionist; VARS Coordinator; Corporate
Account Developers (3); Japanese Market
Liaison; Junior Software Developers (4);
Mac Programmer; Product Manager; Senior Software Developers (3); Sr Visual Basic
Programmer; Software Development Leaders (2); Advertising Coordinator; Channel
Sales Mgr; Comptroller; Corporate Account
Development Mgrs (3); ESD Business Development Coordinator; Junior Software De-
velopers (4); Mac Programmer; OEM Business Development Specialist; Sr Visual Basic Programmer; Software Development
Leaders (2); Software QA Manager; Translators; Web Programmers (2); Comptroller.

ACI AUTOMATIC CUTTING INC.
Att: Vice-President of Finance
5055 Benson Drive
Burlington, ON L7L 5N7
Tel. 905-335-5750
Fax 905-335-5170
Email .. dbowen@aciautomaticcutting.com

Website .... www.aciautomaticcutting.com
Employer Background: Established in 1968,
ACI Automatic Cutting Inc. specializes in
mechanical tubing parts for the automotive
industry. *New Positions Created (3):* Accountant; Maintenance / Production Supervisor; Plant Superintendent / Manufacturing Manager.

ACKLANDS-GRAINGER INC. / AGI
Att: Logistics Sales Manager
90 West Beaver Creek Road
Richmond Hill, ON L4B 1E7
Tel. 905-731-5516
Fax 905-731-0909
Email .... newboundl@agi.ca
Website .... www.acklandsgrainger.com
Employer Background: AGI is Canada's larg-
est distributor of industrial, fleet and safety
supplies. *New Positions Created (9):* Inside
Sales and Service Representatives; Safety
Supply Sales Specialists (2); Sales Repre-
sentatives; Sales Representatives; Financial
Services Representatives; Inside Sales and
Service Representatives; Credit Manager,
Financial Services; Inside Sales and Service
Representatives (2); Branch Managers.

ACL SERVICES LTD.
Att: Human Resources and Development
575 Richards Street
Vancouver, BC V6B 2Z5
Tel. 604-669-4225
Fax 604-692-1398
Email .... hr@acl.com
Website .... www.acl.com
Employer Background: Founded in 1987,
ACL Services Ltd. provides market-leading
technology and services for data inquiry,
analysis and reporting. *New Positions Cre-
ated (5):* Inventory Clerk / Shipper and Re-
ceiver Position; Bilingual Technical Support
Representative; Technical Support Representatives; Bilingual Technical Support Position; Junior Network Administrator.

ACM AUTOMATION INC.
Att: Human Resources Manager
900 - 6th Avenue SW, Suite 500
Calgary, AB T2C 3Y2
Tel. 403-264-9637
Fax 403-264-6671
Email .... resume@acm.ab.ca
Website .... www.acm.ab.ca
Employer Background: ACM Automation
Inc. is a professional engineering and man-
agement services company specializing in
telecommunications, SCADA and safety
control systems for the oil and gas and utili-
ties industry. *New Positions Created (8):* Risk
Manager / Loss Prevention Engineer; In-
strumentation & Controls Engineer; Public
Affairs & Regulatory Coordinator; Safety
Applications Engineer / Technologist; Sales
Manager; SCADA Engineer; Telecommunications Engineer; Administrative Assistant.

ACNIELSEN COMPANY OF CANADA
Att: Human Resources Department
160 McNabb Street
Markham, ON L3R 4B8

Tel. 905-475-3344
Fax 905-475-8357
Email .... careers@acnielsen.ca
Website .... www.acnielsen.ca

Employer Background: ACNielsen Company is a leading provider of market research information and knowledge-based solutions for retailers, consumer packaged goods manufacturers and advertisers. *New Positions Created (15):* Market Analyst; Sales Consultant; Facility Supervisor; Market Analyst; Computing Positions; QA Specialist; Systems Analyst / Consulting Technical Support Specialist; Technical Coordinator; Technical Writer; Advertising Tracking Services Executive; Computer Industry Services Executive; Intermediate Statistician; Market Analyst; Training Specialist; Business Analyst / Windows Software Developer.

ACOMARIT CANADA INC.
Att: Technical Manager
759 Victoria Square, 6th Floor
Montréal, QC H2Y 2K3

Fax 514-841-6828
Website .... www.acomarit.com

Employer Background: Acomarit Canada Inc. is a Montreal-based ship management company. *New Positions Created (2):* Superintendent Engineer; Technical Assistant.

ACR SYSTEMS INC.
Att: Human Resources Department
12960 - 84th Avenue, Suite 210
Surrey, BC V3W 1K7

Tel. 604-591-1128
Fax 604-591-2252
Email .... acr@acrsystems.com
Website ...., www.acrsystems.com

Employer Background: ACR Systems Inc. is leading designer and manufacturer of portable electronic data logging equipment. *New Positions Created (4):* Hardware Designers; Product Managers; Software Designers; Technical Support / Quality Assurance.

ACRES & ASSOCIATES ENVIRONMENTAL LTD.
Att: Human Resources Department
21 Four Seasons Place, Suite 525
Toronto, ON M9B 6J8

Tel. 416-622-9502
Fax 416-622-6249
Email .... hr@toronto.aae.on.ca
Website .... www.aae.on.ca

Employer Background: Acres & Associates is a professional consulting firm, providing project management, design and environmental science services to clients across Ontario. *New Positions Created (6):* Intermediate and Senior Electrical Engineers; Intermediate and Senior Municipal Engineer; Intermediate Instrumentation and Controls Project Manager; Junior Civil Technologist; Senior Wastewater Project Manager; Senior Water Supply Project Manager.

ACRES INTERNATIONAL LIMITED
Att: Human Resources
845 Cambie Street, 4th Floor
Vancouver, BC V6B 2P4

Tel. 604-683-9141
Fax 604-683-9148
Email .... vancouver@acres.com
Website .... www.acres.com

Employer Background: Founded in 1924, Acres International Limited is a consulting engineering, planning and management company, with a staff of 700. *New Positions Created (6):* Civil Engineer, Transportation; Electrical Engineer, Hydro; Mechanical Engineer, Hydro; Senior Civil / Structural Engineer; Project Manager; Senior Substation Design Engineer.

ACRES INTERNATIONAL LIMITED
Att: Human Resources
1444 Columbia Avenue, Suite 201, Box 700
Castlegar, BC V1N 3K3

Tel. 250-304-2055
Fax 250-304-2277
Email .... castlegar@acres.com
Website .... www.acres.com

Employer Background: Founded in 1924, Acres International Limited is a consulting engineering, planning and management company, with a staff of 700. *New Positions Created (5):* Project Management Staff; Project Manager; Senior Substation Design Engineer; Junior / Intermediate Electrical Designers; Project Management Position.

ACRES INTERNATIONAL LIMITED
Att: Human Resources
500 Portage Avenue, 6th Floor
Winnipeg, MB R3C 3Y8

Tel. 204-786-0171
Fax 204-786-2242
Email .... winnipeg@acres.com
Website .... www.acres.com

Employer Background: Acres International Limited is a leading North American consulting engineering, planning and management company. *New Positions Created (7):* Hydraulic Design Engineers; Instrumentation Design Drafter; Project Manager; Senior Civil / Structural Engineer; Senior Electrical Drafter; Senior Electrical Engineer; Senior Hydraulic Design Engineer.

ACRES INTERNATIONAL LIMITED
Att: Human Resources
1235 North Service Road West
Oakville, ON L6M 2W2

Tel. 905-469-3400
Fax 905-469-3404
Email .... hr@toronto.acres.com
Website .... www.acres.com

Employer Background: Founded in 1924, Acres International Limited is a consulting engineering, planning and management company, with a staff of 700. *New Positions Created (26):* Civil / Structural Engineers; Designers & CAD Operators; Electrical Engineers; Instrumentation and Controls Position; Project Managers; Senior Power Plant Specialists; Engineering Project and Design Professionals; Manager, Planning Division; Nuclear Engineering Project Staff; Engineering Design Technicians & Technologists; Manager, Project Services; Mechanical Engineer 1; Mechanical Engineer 2; Mechanical Engineer 3; Mechanical Project Engineer; Project Managers; Project Secretary; Senior Civil / Structural Engineer; Senior Electrical Engineer; Senior Power Systems Planning Engineer; Senior Transportation Engineer and Project Manager; Manager, Planning Division; Manager, Transmission and Distribution Division; Mechanical Project Engineers; Nuclear Specialists - All Disciplines; Principal Electrical Engineer.

ACRES INTERNATIONAL LIMITED
Att: Human Resources Manager
4342 Queen Street, PO Box 1001
Niagara Falls, ON L2E 6W1

Tel. 905-374-5200
Fax 905-374-1157
Email .... hr@niagarafalls.acres.com
Website .... www.acres.com

Employer Background: Founded in 1924, Acres International Limited is a leading consulting engineering firm in the power, transportation, mining and heavy industrial sectors. *New Positions Created (6):* Jr Electrical Engineer; Project Manager; Computer Scientist, Database Expertise; Junior Mechanical Engineer; Senior Energy Economist; Water Resource Optimization Specialist.

ACRO AEROSPACE INC.
Att: Human Resources
4551 Agar Drive
Richmond, BC V7B 1A4

Tel. 604-276-7600
Fax 604-276-7675
Email .... careers@acro.ca
Website .... www.acro.ca

Employer Background: ACRO Aerospace Inc., a subsidiary of Vector Aerospace, has been Canada's leading helicopter maintenance experts for over 45 years. *New Positions Created (3):* Test Cell Operator; CMM Inspector; Reworks Inspector.

ACTERNA CORPORATION
Att: Human Resources Manager
8644 Commerce Court, Imperial Square
Burnaby, BC V5A 4N6

Tel. 604-415-5917
Fax 604-415-5900
Email .... resume@acterna.com
Website .... www.acterna.com

Employer Background: Acterna Corporation (formerly TTC and WWG) develops customer solutions for telecom networks. *New Positions Created (9):* Office Manager; Product Marketing Manager; Software Developers; Systems Administrator; Engagement Team Leader and Software Designers; Senior Business Analyst; Senior Unix System Administrator; Technical Instructor; Software Test Engineers.

ACTIVE HEALTH MANAGEMENT INC.
Att: Human Resource Manager
1867 Yonge Street, Suite 901
Toronto, ON M4S 1Y5

Tel. 416-481-6851
Fax 416-481-2168
Email .... jobs@activehealth.ca
Website .... www.activehealth.ca

Employer Background: ACTIVE Health Management Inc. is a health claims management company. *New Positions Created (4):* Marketing / Sales Position; Customer Service Representatives; Customer Service Team Position, Kinesiologist; Sales Executive.

ACTIVE PASS PHARMACEUTICALS INC.
Att: Human Resources Manager
2255 Wesbrook Mall
Vancouver, BC V6T 1Z3
Tel. 604-822-7948
Email .... jobs@activepass.com
Website .... www.activepass.com
Employer Background: Active Pass Pharmaceuticals Inc. is a Vancouver-based biotechnology company engaged in genomic-based drug discovery. *New Positions Created (5):* Research Assistant; Research Assistant, Bioinformatics; Administrative Assistant, R&D; Research Assistant; Vice President, Research.

ADACEL INC.
Att: Human Resources Manager
7900 Taschereau Boulevard, Building E
Brossard, QC J4X 1C2
Tel. 450-672-3888
Fax 450-672-4434
Email .... careers@adacelcanada.com
Website .... www.adacel.com
Employer Background: Adacel Inc. is a leading developer of air traffic control systems and training simulators. *New Positions Created (4):* Project Managers; Software Engineers / Developers; System Integration and Installation Specialists; Software Developer.

ADAMS MANUFACTURING
Att: Human Resources Department
40 Bertrand Avenue
Toronto, ON M1L 2P6
Fax 416-701-3023
Email .... to-recruitment@pfizer.com
Website .... www.pfizer.com
Employer Background: Adams Manufacturing, a division of Pfizer Canada Inc., is a manufacturer of quality confectionery products, including Trident, Dentyne, Halls and Certs. *New Positions Created (3):* Production Mechanic; Production Mechanics; Production Electrician.

ADESA CANADA INC.
Att: Human Resources Representative
3365 Highway 7 East
Brampton, ON L6T 5P4
Tel. 905-791-9800
Fax 905-790-0306
Email .... pherbert@adesa.com
Website .... www.adesa.ca
Employer Background: ADESA Canada Inc. is one of North America's largest providers of vehicle remarketing services, with 14 auction sites nationwide. *New Positions Created (2):* Site Administrator; Detail Manager.

ADESA CANADA INC., CORPORATE OFFICE
Att: Human Resources Manager

50 Burnhamthorpe Road West, Suite 800
Mississauga, ON L5B 3C2
Tel. 905-896-4400
Fax 905-896-9627
Website .... www.adesa.ca
Employer Background: ADESA Canada Inc. is one of North America's largest providers of vehicle remarketing services, with 14 auction sites nationwide. *New Positions Created (5):* Administrative Assistant; Key Account Manager; National Reconditioning Manager; Compensation Analyst / Consultant; Health and Safety / Ergonomist Consultant.

ADEXA
Att: Development Centre
20 Queen Street West, Suite 300
Toronto, ON M5H 3R3
Tel. 416-362-1077
Fax 416-362-1076
Email .... careers-yyz-ts@adexa.com
Website .... www.adexa.com
Employer Background: Established in 1994, Adexa is a leading provider of collaborative supply chain planning solutions for e-business. *New Positions Created (17):* Manager, Global Solution Centre; Database Application Programmer; E-Business Services Consultants; Forecasting / Demand Planning Implementation Lead; Integration Services Consultants, ERP; Integration Services Consultants, Internal Applications; Manager, Global Solution Centre; Solution Specialist, Web Client; Supply Chain Consultants; Technical Product Manager, Demand Collaboration; Build Engineers; Information Developers / Technical Writers; Product Support Consultants; Quality Assurance Analysts ; Software Developers; Software Development Managers; User Interface Designers.

ADGA GROUP CONSULTANTS INC.
Att: Recruiting Manager
116 Albert Street, Suite 600
Ottawa, ON K1P 5G4
Tel. 613-237-3022
Fax 613-237-6935
Email .... hr@adga.ca
Website .... www.adga.ca
Employer Background: ADGA Group Consultants Inc. develops mission-critical systems solutions for major government and private sector clients. *New Positions Created (8):* Aviation and Avionics Specialists; ILS Specialists; Systems Engineers; Various Aerospace Positions; Various Aerospace Project Management Positions; Quality Control Analyst; Various IT Positions; Technical Specialist.

ADHEREX TECHNOLOGIES INC.
Att: Human Resources
600 Peter Morand Crescent, Suite 340
Ottawa, ON K1G 5Z3
Tel. 613-738-8000
Fax 613-738-9060
Email .... hr@adherex.com
Website .... www.adherex.com
Employer Background: Adherex Technologies Inc. is a biotechnology company, developing novel therapeutics based on cell ad-

hesion technologies. *New Positions Created (2):* Junior Pharmaceutical R & D Positions; Senior Pharmaceutical R & D Positions.

ADM MILLING COMPANY
Att: Debbie Bell
7585 Danbro Crescent
Mississauga, ON L5N 6P9
Fax 905-819-9768
Email .... info@adm-milling.ca
Website .... www.admworld.com
Employer Background: ADM Milling Company, a division of Archer Daniels Midland Company (ADM), is active in the milling of wheat into flour. *New Positions Created (2):* General Manager, Flour Mill; Senior Account Manager.

ADMINISTRATIVE ASSISTANTS LTD.
Att: Human Resources Department
4480 Harvester Road
Burlington, ON L7L 4X2
Tel. 905-632-0864
Fax 905-632-2605
Email .... sisinfo@admassist.com
Website .... www.admassist.com
Employer Background: AAL develops administration software for the K-12 education field and web-enabled student information systems. *New Positions Created (6):* Senior Programmer Analyst; Systems Analyst; Technical Support Position, Development & Database; Controller; Senior Programmer / Analyst; Client Support / Training Representative(s).

ADP CANADA
Att: Human Resources Consultant
4720 Kingsway, 18th Floor
Burnaby, BC V5H 4N2
Tel. 604-431-2700
Fax 604-431-2766
Website .... www.adp.ca
Employer Background: Established in 1979, ADP Canada provides payroll services and human resource management systems to businesses nationwide. *New Positions Created (3):* Account Manager; Sales Manager; Major Accounts Manager.

ADP CANADA
Att: Human Resources Consultant
6025 - 11th Street SE
Calgary, AB T2H 2Z2
Fax 403-258-5050
Website .... www.adp.com
Employer Background: Established in 1979, ADP Canada provides payroll services and human resource management systems to businesses nationwide. *New Positions Created (9):* Client Services Representative; Sales Professional; Senior Account Manager; Specialist, Technical Support; Major Account Manager; Sales Professional; Payroll Specialist; Sales Professional; Systems Consultant.

ADP CANADA
Att: Human Resources
3250 Bloor Street West, 16th Floor
Toronto, ON M8X 2X9

Fax 416-207-2880
Website .... www.adp.ca
Employer Background: Established in 1979, ADP Canada provides payroll services and human resource management systems to businesses nationwide. *New Positions Created (24):* Collector, NSF Payroll Administration, Accounts Receivable; Financial Analyst; Funding Coordinator; Implementation Specialist; Team Leader, Accounts Receivable; Sales Professionals; Banking Services Coordinator; Major Account District Manager; Product Manager, Payroll; Administrator, Telecommunications; Banking Services Coordinator; Client Financial Services Coordinator (Bilingual); Client Services - National Accounts Position; Client Services Representative (Majors); Director, Production & Operations; Director, Telecommunications; District Manager; District Manager; Payroll Administrator (Bilingual); Payroll Input Representative - Bilingual; Sales Trainee; Trust Accounting, Reconciliation Coordinator; Payroll Manager and Payroll Administrator; Sales Professional.

ADP CANADA
Att: Human Resources
5 Place Ville Marie, 13th Floor
Montréal, QC H3B 2G2
Tel. 514-399-1990
Fax 514-399-1897
Website .... www.adp.com
Employer Background: Established in 1979, ADP Canada provides payroll services and human resource management systems to businesses nationwide. *New Positions Created (5):* Teleservice Representative; District Manager; District Manager Trainee; Major Account District Manager; District Sales Manager.

ADULT MENTAL HEALTH SERVICES OF HALDIMAND-NORFOLK / AMHS
Att: Executive Director
216 West Street, Suite 103
Simcoe, ON N3Y 1S8
Tel. 519-426-3257
Fax 519-426-3257
Email .... amhsnorfolk@primus.ca
Website .... www.hnmentalhealth.com/
.... amhs.htm
Employer Background: AMHS is a multi-disciplinary agency, providing community-based services to adults affected by serious mental health illness. *New Positions Created (3):* Adult Mental Health Program (AMHP) Manager; Crisis Response Clinician; Mental Health Crisis Program (MHCP) Manager.

ADVANCED BUSINESS INTERIORS INC. / ABI
Att: Operations Manager
2160 Thurston Drive
Ottawa, ON K1G 6E1
Tel. 613-738-1003
Fax 613-738-7206
Email .... abi-info@makespacework.com
Website .... www.makespacework.com
Employer Background: ABI is an office furniture dealership. *New Positions Created (3):*

Customer Service Reps; Interior Designers / Space Planners; Project Managers.

ADVANCED MICRO DESIGN
Att: Human Resources
3014 Calgary Trail South
Edmonton, AB T5J 6V4
Tel. 780-414-6775
Fax 780-414-6729
Email ... careers@advancedmicrodesign.com
Website ..... www.advancedmicrodesign.com
Employer Background: Advanced Micro Design is a software development, consulting and training firm. *New Positions Created (15):* Manager of Software Development; Database Programmers; Senior Software Developers; Software Development Program Managers; Web Developer / Designer; Delphi Programmer; Human Resources Manager; Application Analysts; Documentation Coordinator; Quality Assurance Technicians; Senior Architect; Senior Software Developers; Software Development Program Managers (3); Web Developers; Web Developer.

ADVANCED MOTION AND CONTROLS LTD.
Att: Human Resources Manager
56 Churchill Drive, Suite 9
Barrie, ON L4N 8Z5
Tel. 705-726-2260
Fax 705-720-1947
Email .... jobs@advancedmotion.com
Website .... www.advancedmotion.com
Employer Background: Advanced Motion and Controls Ltd. is a Canadian supplier of factory automation products, with offices in Barrie, Kingston, Mississauga, Montreal and Waterloo. *New Positions Created (10):* Customer Service Coordinator; Regional Managers; Technical Sales Representative, Aluminum Structural Framing; Technical Sales Representatives; Customer Service Coordinator / Inside Sales; Regional Managers; Technical Sales Representative, Aluminum Structural Framing; Technical Sales Representatives; Technical Sales Representatives; Technical Support.

ADVANCED RESEARCH TECHNOLOGIES INC. / ART
Att: Human Resources Manager
2300 Alfred Nobel
St-Laurent, QC H4S 2A4
Tel. 514-832-0777
Fax 514-832-0778
Email .... hr@art.ca
Website .... www.art.ca
Employer Background: ART is a Quebec-based laser and thermal imaging firm, developing products for medical and industrial applications. *New Positions Created (2):* Inspector, Quality Control; Senior Manager, Project Management Office.

ADVANTECH ADVANCED MICROWAVE TECHNOLOGIES, INC.
Att: Human Resources
657 Orly Avenue
Dorval, QC H9P 1G1

Tel. 514-420-0045
Fax 514-420-0055
Email .... jobs@advantech.ca
Website .... www.advantech.ca
Employer Background: Advantech Advanced Microwave Technologies, Inc. is a leading manufacturer of microwave communication products for satellite ground stations and wireless base stations. *New Positions Created (7):* Purchasing Manager; Quality Control Manager; QA Assistant; QA Test Technician; QC Inspector; QC Manager; SPC Specialist.

ADVANTERA COMMUNICATIONS INC.
Att: Human Resources Manager
3701 Carling Avenue, Building 4
Ottawa, ON K2H 8S2
Tel. 613-596-9910
Fax 613-596-3058
Employer Background: Advantera Communications Inc. works to deliver more reliable and secure unified networks that bring together voice, video and data services over an optical network. *New Positions Created (5):* Hardware Designer; Network Designer; Network Management Software Designer; Optical Designer; Software Designer.

ADVANTEX MARKETING INTERNATIONAL INC.
Att: Miriam Stamatiou,
Human Resources Manager
491 Eglinton Avenue West, 3rd Floor
Toronto, ON M5N 1A8
Tel. 416-481-5657
Fax 416-481-0715
Email ... miriam.stamatiou@advantex.com
Website .... www.advantex.com
Employer Background: Advantex Marketing International Inc. provides online and offline consumer relationship marketing programs in partnership with international airlines, financial institutions and other North American corporations. *New Positions Created (15):* Client Services Professional; Current Account Manager; Promotions Production Coordinator; Senior Sales Professionals; Client Services Professional; Exec Assistant; Inventory Coordinator; Sales Assistant; Sr Programmer Analyst; Merchant Relationship Manager; New Business Development Position; Research Marketing Analyst; Senior Internet Applications Developer; Administrative Assistant; Sr Recruiter.

AEA TECHNOLOGY ENGINEERING SOFTWARE LTD. / CFX
Att: Human Resources Manager
554 Parkside Drive
Waterloo, ON N2L 5Z4
Tel. 888-827-2356
Fax 519-886-7580
Website .... www.aeat.com
Employer Background: CFX develops and markets Computational Fluid Dynamics (CFD) software and a family of CFD software tools. *New Positions Created (4):* Account Manager; CFD Applications Specialists; Senior Developer; Vice-President, Human Resources.

AEDIFICA
Att: Celine Pilon
4521 Clark
Montréal, QC H2T 2T3

Tel.	514-844-6611
Fax	514-844-7646

Employer Background: AEdifica is an architectural and interior design firm. *New Positions Created (2):* Project Manager, Mechanical Engineering; Designer.

AERO MACHINING LTD.
Att: Human Resources Manager
11400 Albert-Hudon Boulevard
Montréal, QC H1G 3H7

Tel.	514-324-4260
Fax	514-324-9997
Email	marcol@aeromachining.com
Website	www.aeromachining.com

Employer Background: Aero Machining Ltd. is an aerospace manufacturer. *New Positions Created (2):* Deburrer; Inspector.

AEROINFO SYSTEMS INC.
Att: Personnel Manager
13775 Commerce Parkway
Suite 200, 2nd Floor
Richmond, BC V6V 2V4

Tel.	604-214-8700
Fax	604-232-4201
Email	personnel@aeroinfo.com
Website	www.aeroinfo.com

Employer Background: AeroInfo Systems Inc. delivers business process automation solutions to the air transportation industry. *New Positions Created (5):* Quality Assurance Tester; Software Engineers, Product Development and Customer Service; Software Engineers; Account Managers; Software Engineers.

AFFILIATED CUSTOMS BROKERS LIMITED
Att: Human Resources Department
411 des Recollets
Montréal, QC H2Y 1W3

Tel.	514-288-1211
Fax	514-288-1154
Website	www.affiliated.ca

Employer Background: Affiliated Customs Brokers Limited is one of the largest international freight forwarders and customs brokers in North America. *New Positions Created (2):* Export Technician, Ocean Freight; Customs Technicians.

AFFINA
Att: Human Resources
1250 Guy Street, Suite 600
Montréal, QC H3H 2T4

Tel.	514-931-2334
Fax	514-932-8477
Email	employmentmtl@affina.com
Website	www.affina.com

Employer Background: Affina is a customer relationship company, with 8 call centres in North America. *New Positions Created (2):* Assistant Operations Manager; Customer Service Representatives.

AFFINITY FINANCIAL GROUP INC.
Att: Human Resources Manager
195 The West Mall, Suite 500
Toronto, ON M9C 5K1

Tel.	416-622-4575
Fax	416-622-2102
Email	ctchor@affinityfinancial.com
Website	affinityfinancial.com

Employer Background: Affinity Financial Group Inc. is one of Canada's leading strategic advisory groups, specializing in wealth creation, portfolio risk management and tax-efficient investment. *New Positions Created (3):* Investment Services Facilitator, Value Enhancement Services; Investment Services Facilitator, Value Enhancement Services; Manager, Value Enhancement Services.

AFGD GLASS
Att: Human Resources Department
75 Doney Crescent
Concord, ON L4K 1P6

Tel.	905-669-1930
Fax	905-669-6529
Email	afgdhr@istar.ca
Website	www.afgd.com

Employer Background: AFGD Glass, a division of AFG Industries Inc., is a leading Canadian glass manufacturing company. *New Positions Created (2):* Glass Centre Manager; Switchboard / Receptionist.

AGA KHAN FOUNDATION CANADA
Att: Human Resources
360 Albert Street, Constitution Square
Suite 1220
Ottawa, ON K1R 7X7

Tel.	613-237-2532
Fax	613-567-2532
Email	humanresources@akfc.ca
Website	www.akfc.ca

Employer Background: AKFC is a non-denominational, non-profit, international development agency, promoting sustainable and equitable social development in low-income countries in Asia and Africa. *New Positions Created (4):* Information Technology Coordinator; Director of Operations; Manager, Research and Learning; Education Officer.

AGAT LABORATORIES
Att: Human Resources Department
801 - 21st Street NE
Calgary, AB T2E 6T5

Tel.	403-299-2000
Fax	403-299-2005
Email	info@agatlabs.com
Website	www.agatlabs.com

Employer Background: AGAT Laboratories provides analytical and scientific services, including environmental lab services, petroleum-related lab services, soil profiling and air quality monitoring. *New Positions Created (3):* Administrative Positions; Scientific Positions; Laboratory Technicians.

AGERE SYSTEMS
Att: Human Resources Manager

16 Fitzgerald Road, Suite 250
Nepean, ON K2H 8R6

Tel.	613-768-8757
Fax	613-768-8711
Email	careersottawa@agere.com
Website	www.agere.com

Employer Background: Agere Systems (formerly Lucent Technologies Microelectronics Group) is a leading provider of components for communication applications, including optical components and integrated circuits. *New Positions Created (6):* Account Executives; Backend Layout Engineer; Backend Netlist Engineer; CAD Software Developer; Field Application Engineers; Senior ASIC Design Engineer.

AGF MANAGEMENT LTD.
Att: Human Resources Department
PO Box 50, TD Bank Tower
Toronto, ON M5K 1E9

Tel.	416-367-1900
Fax	416-865-4189
Website	www.agf.com

Employer Background: AGF Management Ltd. is a mutual fund and investment management company, with over one million investors and $34 billion in managed assets. *New Positions Created (26):* Business Analysts; Manager, Client Services; Manager, Distributor Services; Programmer / Analyst; Project Leaders, Business Information Services; Supervisor, Securities Cage; Supervisor, Special Projects; Systems Quality Assurance Analysts; Data and Process Architect; Director, Application Architecture; Help Desk Analyst; PC Support Analyst; Programmer / Analyst; Project Manager / Project Director; Senior Computer Operator; Senior Lotus Notes Administrator; Project Leader, BIS; Supervisor, Fund Accounting; User Acceptance Testers; Business Analysts; Business Information Services (BIS) Trainer; User Acceptance Testers; Fund Accountant; Sales Relationship Mgr; Client Administration Reps; Client Service Representatives.

AGFA
Att: Human Resources
77 Belfield Road
Toronto, ON M9W 1G6

Tel.	416-241-1110
Fax	416-245-9053
Email	humanresources.ca.hc@ca.agfa.com
Website	www.agfa.ca

Employer Background: AGFA manufactures photographic and electronic imaging systems, particularly for consumer imaging, graphic arts and medical applications. *New Positions Created (9):* Account Executive; Field Service Technician; Accounts Payable Representative; Customer Support Coordinator; Collections Team Leader; Collectors; Customer Service Representatives; Customer Service Team Leaders; SR. Customer Service Representative.

AGILE SYSTEMS INC.
Att: Human Resources Department
575 Kumpf Drive
Waterloo, ON N2V 1K3

Tel. 519-886-2000
Fax 519-886-2075
Email .... hr@agile-systems.com
Website .... www.agilesys.com
Employer Background: Agile Systems Inc. designs and manufactures electronic products and systems for motion and power control in the robotic, automation, automotive and off-highway vehicle industries. *New Positions Created (26):* IC Design Engineering Specialist; Administrative Assistant; Business Account Manager; Line Operator; Manufacturing Engineering Specialist; Test Technician; Senior IC Design Engineer; Production Supervisor; Applications Engineer; Buyer; Manager, Advanced Manufacturing Research; Manager, Design Engineering; Manager, Test Engineering; Packaging Engineer; PCB Designer; Technical Writer; Test Engineer; Integrated Circuit Development Engineers (2); Manager, Automotive Business Development; Manager, Integrated Circuit Business Development; Program Manager; Business Development Representative; Electronics Technologist / Technician; Product Manager; Project Engineer; Test Engineer.

AGMONT INC.
Att: Human Resources Manager
1501 St. Patrick Street
Montréal, QC H3K 2B7
Tel. 514-939-4000
Fax 514-940-2829
Website .... www.agmont.com
Employer Background: Agmont Inc. is a leading manufacturer of circular knit fabrics. *New Positions Created (4):* Electrotechnician; Assistant to the Vice-President of Sales; Colour Lab Manager; Finishing Manager.

AGRICULTURE AND AGRI-FOOD CANADA
Att: Human Resources Branch
303 Main Street, Suite 401
Winnipeg, MB R3C 3G7
Fax 204-983-1681
Website .... aceis.agr.ca
Employer Background: Agriculture and Agri-Food Canada is the federal department that promotes the development, adaptation and competitiveness of the agriculture and agri-food industry in Canada. *New Positions Created (4):* Biotechnology Lab Technician; Biologist, Cereal Transformation; Entomology Technician; Team Leader / Wheat Breeding Research Scientist.

AGRIUM INC.
Att: Human Resources
Bag 20
Redwater, AB T0A 2W0
Tel. 780-998-6111
Fax 780-998-6140
Email .... agriumhr@agrium.com
Website .... www.agrium.com
Employer Background: Agrium Inc. is a leading North American producer of nitrogen, phosphate, potash and sulphur fertilizers. *New Positions Created (4):* Industrial Chem-

ist; Instrument Technicians; Laboratory Technicians; Senior Piping Draftsperson.

AGTI CONSULTING SERVICES INC.
Att: Russ Hall, Managing Partner
500 - 5th Avenue SW, Suite 400
Calgary, AB T2P 3L5
Email .... russ.hall@agti.ca
Website .... www.agti.ca
Employer Background: AGTI Consulting Services Inc. designs and implements information systems and supporting technologies. *New Positions Created (4):* Management Consultants; Project Managers; Senior Analysts; Strategic Planning Consultant.

AIC LTD.
Att: Human Resources
1375 Kerns Road
Burlington, ON L7R 4X8
Tel. 905-331-4242
Fax 905-319-1985
Email .... resumes@aicfunds.com
Website .... www.aicfunds.com
Employer Background: Founded in 1985, AIC Ltd. is a Canadian mutual fund company, with $14 billion in assets under management. *New Positions Created (11):* Communications Specialist; Manager, Communications; Manager, Media and Public Relations; Senior Graphic Designer; Regional Sales Director; Sales Assistant; Supervisor, National Inside Sales; Sales Associate; Client Service Representative; Accountants; Client Service Representatives.

AIG LIFE OF CANADA
Att: Carl Copeland
145 Wellington Street West
Toronto, ON M5J 2T4
Tel. 416-596-3000
Fax 416-596-0471
Email .... aiglifecahr@aig.com
Website .... www.aiglife.ca
Employer Background: AIG Life of Canada is a member of American International Group Inc., a leading US-based international insurance and financial services organization. *New Positions Created (8):* Assistant Counsel; Accountant; Comptroller; Intermediate Accountant; Tax Specialist; Account Executive; Product Manager; Software Illustration Manager.

AILANTHUS ACHIEVEMENT CENTRE
Att: Human Resources Manager
3000 Commercial Drive
Vancouver, BC V5N 4E2
Tel. 604-876-1366
Fax 604-876-1325
Website .... www.ailanthus.org
Employer Background: Ailanthus Achievement Centre offers a 15-year intensive intervention program, serving 200 inner-city children and youth. *New Positions Created (5):* Manager, Video / Media Literacy; Student Support Coordinators; Counsellor / Advocate; Manager, Video / Media Literacy; Student Support Coordinators.

AILES DE LA MODE, LES
Att: Linda Laporte, HR Department
100 Bayshore Drive
Bayshore Shopping Centre
Nepean, ON K2B 8C1
Fax 613-721-8101
Email .... emploislesailes@lesailes.com
Website .... www.lesailes.com
Employer Background: Les Ailes de la Mode is a retailer of fashion, beauty products and home decor, operated by Les Boutiques San Francisco Inc. *New Positions Created (3):* Fashion Advisors; Various Retail Positions; Various Restaurant Positions.

AILES DE LA MODE, LES
Att: Linda Laporte, HR Department
3035 Le Carrefour Boulevard, Suite E-10A
Laval, QC H7T 1C8
Fax 450-449-9982
Email .... emploislesailes@lesailes.com
Website .... www.lesailes.com
Employer Background: Les Ailes de la Mode is a retailer of fashion, beauty products and home decor, operated by Les Boutiques San Francisco Inc. *New Positions Created (7):* Sales Audit Clerk; Sales Supervisors / Assistants; Service Supervisor; HR Supervisor; Sales Mgrs; Sales Supervisors and Assistant Sales Supervisors; Store Manager.

AIM FUNDS MANAGEMENT INC.
Att: Human Resources Manager
855 - 2nd Street SW, 1930 Bankers Hall
Calgary, AB T2P 4J7
Fax 403-543-7991
Email .... careers@aimfunds.ca
Website .... www.aimfunds.ca
Employer Background: AIM, one of the world's largest mutual fund companies, has more than $34 billion in assets under management and over 1,000 employees in Calgary, Montreal, Toronto and Vancouver. *New Positions Created (4):* Bilingual Client Services Representatives; Content Manager, E-Business; Software Developers; Regional Sales Representatives.

AIM FUNDS MANAGEMENT INC.
Att: Human Resources
5140 Yonge Street, Suite 900
Toronto, ON M2N 6X7
Email .... careers@aimfunds.ca
Website .... www.aimfunds.ca
Employer Background: AIM, one of the world's largest mutual fund companies, has more than $34 billion in assets under management and over 1,000 employees in Calgary, Montreal, Toronto and Vancouver. *New Positions Created (3):* Bilingual Client Service Representatives; Content Manager, E-Business; Software Developers.

AINSWORTH INC.
Att: Bob Crowie
53 Fawcett Road, Suite A
Coquitlam, BC V3K 6V2
Fax 604-525-7081
Email .... bob_crowie@ainsworth.com
Website .... www.ainsworth.com

Employer Background: Ainsworth Inc. installs and services electrical, mechanical, communications and control systems for the industrial, commercial and institutional markets. *New Positions Created (3):* Civil Design / Build Position; Communication Services Supervisor; Mechanical Design / Build Position.

AINSWORTH INC.
Att: Human Resources
131 Bermondsey Road
Toronto, ON M4A 1X4
Tel. 416-751-4420
Fax 416-750-6560
Email .... resumes@ainsworth.com
Website .... www.ainsworth.com
Employer Background: Ainsworth Inc. installs and services electrical, mechanical, communications and control systems for the industrial, commercial and institutional markets. *New Positions Created (9):* Contract Sales Representative; Customer Service Representative; Marketing Specialist; Customer Service Representative, Product Sales; Electrical / Communications Estimators; BAS Account Executive; BAS Systems Specialist; Design / Build Engineer; Telecommunications Account Executive.

AIR CANADA
Att: Employment Services Manager
6001 Grant McConachie Way
Maildrop YVR0284
Richmond, BC V7B 1K3
Tel. 416-207-0247
Fax 604-270-5848
Website .... www.aircanada.ca
Employer Background: Air Canada is a full-service international air carrier, serving over 800 destinations in more than 130 countries. *New Positions Created (3):* Aircraft Avionics Technicians (2); Aircraft Maintenance Technicians (3); Aircraft Structures Technician.

AIR CANADA
Att: Human Resources Manager
PO Box 14000, Zip 1264
Montréal, QC H4Y 1H4
Tel. 514-422-5000
Fax 514-422-5650
Website .... www.aircanada.ca
Employer Background: Air Canada is a full-service international air carrier serving over 800 destinations in more than 130 countries. *New Positions Created (5):* Manager, Reward Management, Aeroplan; Aircraft Avionics Technician; Aircraft Maintenance Technician & Apprentice; Structures & Sheet Metal Technician & Apprentice; Legal Secretary.

AIR NOVA / AIR CANADA REGIONAL INC.
Att: Human Resources Department
310 Goudey Drive
Halifax International Airport
Enfield, NS B2T 1E4
Tel. 902-873-5000
Fax 902-873-5079
Website .... www.airnova.ca

Employer Background: Air Nova Inc. is one of Air Canada's regional carriers. *New Positions Created (2):* Various Aerospace Positions; Aircraft Maintenance Engineers, Category M.

AIR PRODUCTS CANADA LTD.
Att: Human Resources
2090 Steeles Avenue East
Brampton, ON L6T 1A7
Tel. 905-791-2530
Fax 905-791-6797
Email .... hrcanada@apci.com
Website .... www.apci.com
Employer Background: Air Products Canada Ltd. manufactures and distributes industrial gases and related equipment to the manufacturing, process and service industries. *New Positions Created (9):* Communications Coordinator; Industry Specialist, Specialty Gas; Sales Representative; Industry Specialists, Welding (2); Sales Representative, Central Accounts; Sales Representatives (4); Technical Sales Representative; Technical Sales Representatives, Metals or General Industries / Food (2); Zone Managers (4).

AIR TRANSAT
Att: Human Resources Department
11600 Cargo A-1 Street
Montreal International Airport
Mirabel, QC J7N 1G9
Tel. 450-476-1011
Fax 450-476-3821
Email .... rh@airtransat.com
Website .... www.airtransat.com
Employer Background: Air Transat, a subsidiary of Transat AT Inc., specializes in charter flights, with a fleet of 23 aircraft and 2,500 employees, serving 90 destinations in 25 countries. *New Positions Created (2):* Flight Attendants; Flight Attendants.

AIR TRANSAT HOLIDAYS
Att: Human Resources Department
PO Box 2120, Succ. Place du Parc
Montréal, QC H2W 2P6
Fax 514-987-9739
Website .... www.airtransat.com
Employer Background: Air Transat, a subsidiary of Transat AT Inc., specializes in charter flights, with a fleet of 23 aircraft and 2,500 employees, serving 90 destinations in 25 countries. *New Positions Created (3):* Accounting Analyst; Technical Support Agent; Customer Service Agents.

AIRD & BERLIS
Att: Cynthia Van Strien
181 Bay Street
Suite 1800, Box 754, BCE Place
Toronto, ON M5J 2T9
Tel. 416-364-1241
Fax 416-863-1515
Email .... cvanstrien@airdberlis.com
Website .... www.airdberlis.com
Employer Background: Aird & Berlis is a full-service law firm. *New Positions Created (7):* Financial Analyst / Intermediate Accountant; Litigation Legal Secretaries; Com-

mercial Real Estate Legal Assistant; Float Secretary; Intellectual Property Legal Assistant; Municipal Department Legal Assistant; Insolvency Lawyer.

AIRIQ INC.
Att: Human Resources Manager
1099 Kingston Road, Suite 233
Pickering, ON L1V 1B5
Tel. 905-831-6444
Fax 905-831-0567
Email .... people@airiq.com
Website .... www.airiq.com
Employer Background: AirIQ Inc. develops automated wireless vehicle fleet management solutions. *New Positions Created (2):* Account Executives; Marketing Communications Manager.

AISLING DISCOVERIES CHILD AND FAMILY CENTRE
Att: Manager, Residential Services
325 Milner Avenue, Suite 110
Toronto, ON M1B 5N1
Tel. 416-321-5464
Fax 416-321-1510
Email .... aisling@istar.ca
Website .... www.home.istar.ca/~aisling
Employer Background: Aisling Discoveries Child and Family Centre is a non-profit mental health centre, serving children from birth to age 12. *New Positions Created (4):* Child Therapists; Relief Staff, Night Shift; Manager, Residence and Intensive Services; Program Director.

AIT CORPORATION
Att: Human Resources Manager
9 Auriga Drive
Nepean, ON K2E 7T9
Tel. 613-226-7800
Fax 613-226-3066
Email .... jobs@ait.ca
Website .... www.ait.ca
Employer Background: AiT Corporation is a world leader in machine-readable travel document issuance and inspection systems. *New Positions Created (6):* Global Customer Support Representatives; Inventory Assistant; PowerBuilder Developer; Senior Software Engineer; Senior Systems Architect; Web Software Developers.

AIT CORPORATION
Att: Human Resources Department
1545 Carling Avenue, Suite 700
Ottawa, ON K1Z 8P9
Tel. 613-722-2070
Fax 613-722-2063
Email .... jobs@ait.ca
Website .... www.ait.ca
Employer Background: AiT Corporation is a world leader in machine-readable travel document issuance and inspection systems. *New Positions Created (26):* Bench Repair Technologist; Shipper / Receiver; Security Software Specialist; Director, Systems Solutions; Security Software Manager; PowerBuilder Developer; Senior Hardware Engineer; Senior Software Engineer,

Healthcare; Senior Systems Architect, Healthcare; Systems / Business Analyst, Healthcare; Technical Support Representative; Web Software Developers; Bench Repair Technologist; PowerBuilder Developer; Senior Digital Engineer; Senior Software Engineer - Healthcare; Senior Systems Architect - Healthcare; Systems / Business Analyst - Healthcare; Technical Support Representative; Web Software Developer; Global Customer Support Representative; Inventory Assistant; PowerBuilder Developer; Senior Software Engineer; Senior Systems Architect; Web Software Developers.

AJAX, TOWN OF
Att: Human Resources Services
65 Harwood Avenue South
Ajax, ON L1S 2H9

Tel. 905-683-4550
Fax 905-686-8352
Website .... www.townofajax.com
Employer Background: Located 20 minutes east of Toronto, the Town of Ajax is Ontario's first ISO 9001 community, with a population of 67,000. *New Positions Created (3):* Area Supervisor, Works; Director of Planning and Development; Development Engineer.

AKEDA TOOLS
Att: Kevan Lear, President
1027 Davie Street, PO Box 4840
Vancouver, BC V6E 4L2

Tel. 604-685-4840
Fax 604-685-4870
Email .... kevan@eurojig.com
Website .... www.eurojig.com
Employer Background: Akeda Tools develops woodworking jigs for hobbyists and professionals worldwide. *New Positions Created (3):* Corporate Secretary; Creative Director; Sales Representatives.

AKINAI (CALGARY) CANADA INC. / ACI THE IMAGING COMPANY
Att: Cheryl Griffiths
801 - 6th Avenue SW, Suite 150
Calgary, AB T2P 3W2

Tel. 403-280-6482
Fax 403-205-3873
Email .... aci@cadvision.com
Website .... www.acimita.com
Employer Background: Akinai (Calgary) Canada Inc. / ACI The Imaging Company is a large digital imaging company. *New Positions Created (4):* Customer Service Technician; Junior Sales Position / Support Representative; Senior Major Account Manager; Copier and Fax Service Technician.

AKZO NOBEL COATINGS LTD.
Att: Human Resources
110 Woodbine Downs Boulevard, Unit 4
Toronto, ON M9W 5S6

Tel. 416-674-6633
Fax 416-674-0200
Email .... rick.rhodes@akzonobel.com
Website .... www.akzonobel.com
Employer Background: Headquartered in the Netherlands, Akzo Nobel is one of the world's largest chemical companies, with 350 locations in over 50 countries and 70,000 employees. *New Positions Created (3):* Driver / Warehouse Assistant; Operations Finance Manager; Administrative Assistant, Marketing Services.

ALACRIS INC.
Att: Human Resources Manager
45 O'Connor Street, Suite 1400
Ottawa, ON K1P 1A4

Tel. 613-230-9762
Fax 613-237-0314
Email .... careers@alacris.com
Website .... www.alacris.com
Employer Background: Established in 1999, Alacris Inc. builds and deploys next-generation identity management solutions for e-business. *New Positions Created (3):* Senior Software Engineers; Technical Writers / Documentation Specialists; Test Engineers.

ALARMFORCE INDUSTRIES INC.
Att: Margaret Brady
49 Coldwater Road
Toronto, ON M3B 1Y8

Tel. 416-445-2001
Fax 416-445-9381
Email .... mbrady@alarmforce.com
Website .... www.alarmforce.com
Employer Background: Established in 1988, AlarmForce Industries Inc. is Canada's largest installer of two-way voice alarm systems, with 30 offices nationwide. *New Positions Created (8):* Bilingual Customer Care Representative; Shipping / Receiving Clerk; Service Representative; Senior Software Engineer; Inside Sales Representative; Inside Technical Support Position; Service Representative; Software Design Engineer.

ALBERT COLLEGE
Att: Patrick Peotto, Head of School
160 Dundas Street West
Belleville, ON K8P 1A6

Tel. 613-968-5726
Fax 613-968-9651
Email .... ppeotto@albertc.on.ca
Website .... www.albertc.on.ca
Employer Background: Albert College is an independent, co-educational boarding and day school, serving 310 students. *New Positions Created (2):* Assistant Head; Head.

ALBERTA AGRICULTURE, FOOD & RURAL DEVELOPMENT, EDMONTON
Att: Human Resources
7000 - 113th Street, Room 100
Edmonton, AB T6H 5T6

Tel. 780-427-2111
Fax 780-427-3398
Email .... resumes@gov.ab.ca
Website .... www.agric.gov.ab.ca
Employer Background: AAFRD is the provincial department responsible for farming and agribusiness in Alberta. *New Positions Created (43):* Meat Inspector; Communication Officer; Residue Chemist; Senior Manager; Program Assistant; Veterinary Epidemiologist; AESA Water Quality Monitoring Coordinator; Applied Research and Development Coordinator; Dairy Board Auditor; Assistant Quality Officer; Administrative Assistant; Livestock Odour Control Specialist; Soil Management Specialist; Grant & Contract Administrator; Administrative Assistant; Greenhouse Crops Scientist; Industrial Development Officer, Meat Sector; Senior Development Officer; Environmental Management Specialist; Greenhouse Crops Scientist; Processing Technologist; Veterinary Epidemiologist; Conservation Coordinator; Grant Analyst; Program Evaluation Specialist; Plant Breeder, Genetics; Public Lands Specialists (2); Surveillance Veterinarian; Client Service Representative; Food Processing Technologist; Vegetable Technologist; Veterinary Pathologist; Food Scientist, Meat; Assistant to the Chief Provincial Veterinarian; Public Land Specialist; Research Scientist; Surveillance Veterinarian; Plant Breeder, Genetics; Administrative Support Position; Provincial 4-H Media and Marketing Specialist; Veterinary Pathologist; Sustainable Woodlot Specialist; Conservation Technologist.

ALBERTA ALCOHOL AND DRUG ABUSE COMMISSION / AADAC
Att: Human Resources
10909 Jasper Avenue, 6th Floor
Edmonton, AB T5J 3M9

Tel. 780-415-0377
Fax 780-427-1436
Email .... hr@aadac.gov.ab.ca
Website .... www.aadac.com
Employer Background: AADAC is an agency funded by the Government of Alberta, helping citizens achieve lives free from the abuse of alcohol, other drugs and gambling. *New Positions Created (5):* Administrative Assistant II; Nursing Supervisors; Addictions Counsellor; Community Addictions Service Administrator; Community Addictions Service Administrator.

ALBERTA BOILERS SAFETY ASSOCIATION / ABSA
Att: N. Turtle, Human Resources
4208 - 97th Street, Suite 200
Edmonton, AB T6E 5Z9

Tel. 780-427-6859
Fax 780-437-7787
Email .... turtle@albertaboilers.com
Website .... www.albertaboilers.com
Employer Background: ABSA has been designated by the Province of Alberta to deliver all pressure equipment safety services across the province. *New Positions Created (6):* Design Survey Engineer; Inspector; Manager, Education and Certification; Power Engineer Examiner; Systems Analyst; Technical Standards Officer.

ALBERTA CANCER BOARD
Att: Dr. Christine Friedenreich, Research Scientist
1331 - 29th Street NW, Room AE-173
Calgary, AB T2N 4N2

Tel. 403-670-1721
Fax 403-270-8003
Email .... careers@cancerboard.ab.ca

Website .... www.cancerboard.ab.ca
Employer Background: The Alberta Cancer Board provides diagnostic and treatment services, research, education and prevention programs. *New Positions Created (7):* Biostatistician; Cancer Epidemiologist; Help Desk / Support Analyst; Nursing Manager, Outpatients; Patient Education Specialist; Quality Assurance / Quality Improvement Specialist; Computer Support Analyst.

ALBERTA CANCER BOARD / ACB
Att: Human Resources Department
10405 Jasper Avenue, Suite 1220
Edmonton, AB T5J 3N4
Tel. 780-412-6300
Fax 780-412-6326
Email .... careers@cancerboard.ab.ca
Website .... www.cancerboard.ab.ca
Employer Background: Founded in 1940, ACB operates cancer research and treatment facilities throughout Alberta, including the Cross Cancer Institute in Edmonton and the Tom Baker Cancer Centre in Calgary. *New Positions Created (2):* Project Coordinator / Systems Analyst; Provincial Psychosocial Oncology Coordinator.

ALBERTA CHILD AND FAMILY SERVICES AUTHORITY
Att: Bob Ellison, HR Consultant
Alberta Corporate Services Centre
PO Box 326
McLennan, AB T0H 2L0
Tel. 780-324-3261
Fax 780-324-3262
Email .... bob.ellison@gov.ab.ca
Website .... www.acs.gov.ab.ca
Employer Background: Alberta Child and Family Services is the provincial department responsible for developing safe, healthy and strong families, individuals and communities, while protecting and assisting those in need. *New Positions Created (18):* Child Welfare Clerk; Foster Care Workers (2); Child Care Counsellor; Child Welfare Generalists; Houseparent; Community Resource Worker; Manager, Crisis Support and Contract Services; Foster Care Worker; Coordinator, Community Service Centre; Budget Officer; Handicapped Children's Services Worker; Child Welfare Generalist; Child Welfare Generalist; First Nations Program Specialist; Family Therapist; Bilingual Social Worker; Child Care Counselor; Child Welfare Generalist.

ALBERTA CHILDREN'S SERVICES
Att: Human Resources Consultant
10035 - 108th Street
3rd Floor, Centre West Building
Edmonton, AB T5J 3E1
Tel. 780-427-2734
Fax 780-427-1018
Email .... hre-edm@fss.gov.ab.ca
Website .... www.acs.gov.ab.ca
Employer Background: Alberta Children's Services works to enhance the ability of families and communities to develop nurturing and safe environments for children, youth and individuals. *New Positions Cre-*

ated (15): Secretary; Research Officer; Social Work Community Capacity Coordinator; Social Worker; Manager, Fetal Alcohol Syndrome; Social Worker; First Nations Program Specialist; Child and Family Services Workers; Administrative Supervisor; Manager, Strategic HR Planning and Support Systems; Senior Manager; Service Facilitators; Social Worker; Support Facilitator; Manager, Early Childhood Development.

ALBERTA CHILDREN'S SERVICES, NORTHEAST REGION
Att: Pat Murphy, HR Consultant
Alberta Corporate Service Centre
PO Box 1410
Lac La Biche, AB T0A 2C0
Tel. 780-623-5117
Fax 780-623-5313
Email .... hr.laclabiche@gov.ab.ca
Website .... www.gov.ab.ca/cs
Employer Background: Alberta Children's Services works to enhance the ability of families and communities to develop nurturing and safe environments for children, youth and individuals. *New Positions Created (4):* Community Support Worker; Child Welfare Generalist / Foster Care Worker; Manager; Executive Assistant.

ALBERTA COLLEGE OF ART & DESIGN
Att: Human Resources
1407 - 14th Avenue NW
Calgary, AB T2N 4R3
Tel. 403-284-7600
Fax 403-289-6682
Website .... www.acad.ab.ca
Employer Background: ACAD offers studio-based classes in fine art, design and new media, complementary liberal studies and practical theory. *New Positions Created (2):* Teaching Position, Ceramics; Various Faculty Positions.

ALBERTA COLLEGE OF PHARMACISTS
Att: Lynn Paulitsch, Business Manager
10303 Jasper Avenue NW, Suite 1200
Edmonton, AB T5J 3N6
Tel. 780-990-0321
Fax 780-990-0328
Email .... lynn.paulitsch@altapharm.org
Website .... www.altapharm.org
Employer Background: The Alberta College of Pharmacists is responsible for registering and certifying pharmacists and licensing pharmacies. *New Positions Created (3):* Exec Secretary to the Registrar; Executive Assistant to the Registrar; IT Coordinator.

ALBERTA COMMUNITY DEVELOPMENT
Att: Human Resources Branch
10405 Jasper Avenue
Suite 720, Standard Life Centre
Edmonton, AB T5J 3N4
Tel. 780-427-2546
Fax 780-422-3142
Website .... www.gov.ab.ca/mcd
Employer Background: Alberta Community Development works to support community

development and help all Albertans participate fully in the social, cultural and economic life of the province. *New Positions Created (39):* Program Manager; Community Development Officers (2); Human Rights Officer; Intake Administrator; Manager, Financial Reporting; Business Planning Analyst; Business Planning Assistant; Office Coordinator; Secretary; Research and Planning Consultant; Gift Shop Manager; Interpretation Officer; Administrative Coordinator; Facility Manager; Budget Officer; Secretary; Administrative Assistant; Aboriginal Liaison Officer; Housing Policy Advisor; Manager, Planning, Policy Development & Assessment; Special Needs Assessor; Applications Analyst; Webmaster; Administrative Support Position; Senior Investigations Coordinator; Housing Policy Advisor; Manager, Policy and Planning; Restoration Craftsman; Sport Consultant; Program Coordinator; Manager, Operations and Planning; Accountant; Senior Benefit Processors; Manager, Financial Reporting; Team Leader, Seniors Benefits Processing; Writer / Researcher; Archives Technician; Coordinator, Public Programs; Interpretation / Education Officer.

ALBERTA COMMUNITY DEVELOPMENT
Att: Bernie Lefebvre, HR Consultant
10035 - 108th Street
3rd Floor, Centre West Building
Edmonton, AB T5J 3E1
Fax 780-427-1018
Website .... www.gov.ab.ca/mcd
Employer Background: Alberta Community Development works to support community development and help all Albertans participate fully in the social, cultural and economic life of the province. *New Positions Created (4):* Nurses (2); Residential Care Worker; Research Officer; Organizational Business Planner.

ALBERTA CORPORATE SERVICE CENTRE
Att: Kerry Ryan-Cox, HR Consultant
2105 - 20th Avenue, Box 60
Coaldale, AB T1M 1M2
Tel. 403-345-7981
Fax 403-345-4915
Website .... www.gov.ab.ca
Employer Background: The Alberta Corporate Service Centre provides services to help individuals succeed in the workforce. *New Positions Created (10):* Financial Consultant; Financial Benefits Worker; Community Development Specialist; Early Intervention / Family Violence Specialist; Child Welfare Casework Supervisor; Foster Care Support Worker; Quality Services Specialist; Aboriginal Relations Consultant; Welfare Program Supervisor; Auditor.

ALBERTA CORPORATE SERVICES CENTRE
Att: Dana Thompson, HR Consultant
10035 - 108th Street
3rd Floor, Centre West Building
Edmonton, AB T5J 3E1

Tel. 780-427-7280
Fax 780-427-1018
Email .... hre-edm@fss.gov.ab.ca
Website .... www.gov.ab.ca
Employer Background: Alberta Corporate
Services Centre works with partners to as-
sist Albertans to reach their full potential in
society and the economy. *New Positions Cre-
ated (12):* Financial Analyst; Financial Ben-
efit Worker; Manager; Performance Infor-
mation Analyst; Director, Labour Market
Issues; Research Officer; Financial Consultant; Information and Privacy Coordinator;
Nurses (2); Audit Supervisor; Labour Market Economist; Senior Budget & Financial
Analyst.

ALBERTA ECONOMIC DEVELOPMENT
Att: Human Resources
10155 - 102nd Street
6th Floor, Commerce Place
Edmonton, AB T5J 4L6
Tel. 780-427-2571
Fax 780-427-1272
Email .... hr.aed@gov.ab.ca
Website .... www.alberta-canada.com
Employer Background: Alberta Economic
Development provides information and
competitive intelligence on doing business
in Alberta, helping Alberta businesses suc-
ceed in a global economy. *New Positions
Created (14):* Budget Officer II; Trade Devel-
opment Officer; Planning Administrator;
Regional Development Project Officer;
Budget Officer 2; Coordinator, Electronic
Service Delivery; Receptionist; Director, In-
formation Technology Management; Re-
gional Development Support Specialist;
Manager, Regional Alliance Development;
Director, Planning and Analysis; Market
Development Officer; Tourism Business
Development Coordinator; Industrial Devel-
opment Officer.

ALBERTA ENERGY
Att: Human Resources
9945 - 108th Street
10th Floor, North Petroleum Plaza
Edmonton, AB T5K 2G6
Tel. 780-427-6768
Fax 780-422-4299
Email .... resumes.energy@gov.ab.ca
Website .... www.energy.gov.ab.ca
Employer Background: Alberta Energy
manages mineral rights, administers mineral agreements and collects revenue and
royalties for the people of Alberta. *New Positions Created (22):* Senior Manager; Office
and Research Assistant; Technologist; Man-
ager, Management Reporting; Director, Retail and Customer Programs; Mineral Resource Planning Officer, Land Access and
Regulatory Streamlining; Technologist, Resource Land Access; Director, Business
Analysis; Manager, Business Analysis; Manager, Upstream Oil Sands Development;
Analyst, Gas Valuations & Markets; Business
Analyst; Senior Business Architect; Manager, Oil Markets; Administrative Assistant;
Enhanced Oil Recovery Business Analyst;
Director of Markets; Executive Assistant;
Royalty Administrator; Tenure Administra-

tor; Senior Analyst; Acceptance Test Coordinator.

ALBERTA ENERGY AND UTILITIES BOARD / EUB
Att: Human Resources
640 - 5th Avenue SW
Calgary, AB T2P 3G4
Tel. 403-297-6400
Fax 403-297-6917
Email .... human.resources@eub.gov.ab.ca
Website .... www.eub.gov.ab.ca
Employer Background: Created in 1995, EUB
is an independent, quasi-judicial agency of
the Government of Alberta, regulating the
development of Alberta's energy resources.
New Positions Created (16): Human Resources Specialist / Recruitment and Development Leader; Inspector, Field Surveillance
Branch; Technician / Technologist, Air Monitoring; Technical Assistant, Field Surveillance Branch; Technologist, Facilities Applications; Technologist / Technician, Compliance and Operations Branch; Administrative Positions; Economist; Senior Geologist;
Computer Analyst; Regulatory Business
Analyst; Aggregate-Industrial Minerals Geologist; Energy Geologist; Mineral Resources Geologist; Minerals-Oriented
Stratigraphy Sedimentologist Geologist;
Quaternary Geologist.

ALBERTA ENERGY COMPANY LTD.
Att: AEC Oil and Gas Recruiter
421 - 7th Avenue SW, Suite 3900
Calgary, AB T2P 4K9
Tel. 403-266-8111
Fax 403-290-8153
Email .... jobs@aec.ca
Website .... www.aec.ca
Employer Background: AEC is a large oil and
gas company, with interests in exploration,
production, pipelines, natural gas storage
and gas liquids processing. *New Positions
Created (44):* Instrumentation Technician,
Thermal Recovery; Oil & Gas Production
Operators; Drilling Operations Assistant;
Parts and Materials Planner; Drilling Engineer, Southwest Business Unit; Exploration
Geophysicists, Western Region New Ventures; Plant Operator; Production Engineer,
Northeast Gas SBU; Thermal Recovery Operators (3); Administrative Assistant; Administrative Assistant; Exploration Geolo-
gist; Acquisitions Reservoir Engineer; En-
gineering Technologist / Technician, North-
east Business Unit; Instrumentation Technician, Northeast Business Unit; Accountant,
Northwest Business Unit; Exploration Geophysicists; Gas Production Accountant; Area
Land Administrator; Contract Administrator; Land Administrator, Acquisitions &
Divestitures; Mineral Land Administrator;
Surface Land Administrator; Completions
Engineer, NE Gas Team; Drilling Engineer,
NE Gas Team; Engineering Technologist,
NW Business Unit; Group Leader Develop-
ment, NE Oil SBU; Group Leader, NE Gas
Production Accounting; Landman, NE Busi-
ness Unit; Mechanical Technicians, Caribou
Lake, NE Business Unit; Production Coor-
dinator; Reservoir Engineers; Accounting

Assistant; Gas Operators (2); Geophysical
Technician / Technologist; Group Leader;
Group Leader Operations; Office Assistant;
Production Coordinator; Production Tech-
nologist, Thermal Recovery Business Unit;
Project Accountant; Reservoir Engineer;
Administrative Assistant; Project Account-
ant.

ALBERTA ENERGY COMPANY LTD.
Att: Corporate Services Recruiter
421 - 7th Avenue SW, Suite 3900
Calgary, AB T2P 4K9
Tel. 403-266-8180
Fax 403-716-2687
Email .... jobs@aec.ca
Website .... www.aec.ca
Employer Background: AEC is a large oil and
gas company, with interests in exploration,
production, pipelines, natural gas storage
and gas liquids processing. *New Positions
Created (42):* Geological Technologist, Ac-
quisitions; Administrative Assistant, Busi-
ness Development; Information Analyst;
Drilling Engineer, SW Business Unit; Plant
Operator; Senior Information Security Ana-
lyst; Business Analyst; Credit Analyst; Inter-
nal Auditor; Team Leader, Internal Audit;
Human Resources Assistant; Aggregator;
Drilling / Completions Engineer; Procurement Professional, Business Services Group;
Procurement Professional, Thermal Recovery BU; Procurement Professional, West New
Ventures BU; Production Engineer, SE BU;
Production Revenue Accountant; Human
Resources Advisor; Accountant; Accountant,
Financial Reporting; Administrative Assistant, Foster Creek SAGD; Banking and Treasury Position; Evaluations / Reservoir Engi-
neer; Geological Technician, North East Exploration; Instrumentation Technician,
Thermal Recovery Business Unit; Intermediate Environment, Health and Safety Specialist; Landman, Western Region New Ventures Business Unit; Production Coordinator; Property Accountant, SE Business Unit;
Reservoir Engineer, SE Exploration; Senior
Geological Technician, Western New Venture; Thermal Recovery Operator; Group
Leader, Production Engineering; Surface
Land Coordinator; Oil and Gas Counsel;
Geophysical Technologist / Technician; Geophysicists; Gas Facility / Production Engineer; Oil Production Engineer; Reservoir
Engineer; Engineering Technologists / Technicians.

ALBERTA ENVIRONMENT
Att: Human Resource Services
9915 - 108th Street
4th Floor, South Tower, Petroleum Plaza
Edmonton, AB T5K 2G8
Fax 780-427-2513
Email .... ephrresume@gov.ab.ca
Website .... www.gov.ab.ca/env
Employer Background: Alberta Environ-
ment is the provincial Ministry responsible
for enforcing environmental regulations in
Alberta, as well as operating provincial
parks and wildlife management programs.
New Positions Created (33): Research Ana-
lyst; Industrial Approvals Engineer; Senior

Manager; Senior Planner; Regional Inspectors (3); Investigator; Director, Integrated Resource Management; Compliance Analyst; Industrial Approvals Engineer; Geomatics Technologist; Communications Technician; Administrative Assistant; Technologist; Botanist; District Clerk; Enforcement and Monitoring Adviser; Stockkeeper; Air Quality / Plant Physiology Specialist; Regional Inspector; Regional Inspector; Regional Municipal Inspector; Administrative Support Position; Ecological Data Analyst; Senior Operator; Data Management Technologist; Forest Biometrician; Forestry Warehouseman; Investigator; Research Analyst; Resource Information Specialist; Forestry Warehouseman; Field Forester; Area Forest Officer.

ALBERTA ENVIRONMENT
Att: Human Resource Service Centre
3115 - 12th Street NE, Suite 100
Calgary, AB T2E 7J2
Fax 403-297-2902
Email .... ephrresume@gov.ab.ca
Website .... www.gov.ab.ca/env
Employer Background: Alberta Environment is the provincial Ministry responsible for enforcing environmental regulations in Alberta, as well as operating provincial parks and wildlife management programs. *New Positions Created (11):* Investigator; Industrial Approvals Engineer; Finance / Personnel Clerk; Municipal Administrator; Fire Manager; Systems Analyst; Regional Approvals Manager; Engineer; Biologist 3; Administrative Support Position; Engineer.

ALBERTA FAMILY AND SOCIAL SERVICES
Att: Patricia Barnum, HR Services
10035 - 108th Street
3rd Floor, Centre West Building
Edmonton, AB T5J 3E1
Tel. 780-427-2734
Fax 780-427-1018
Email .... hre-edm@fss.gov.ab.ca
Website .... www.gov.ab.ca/fss
Employer Background: Alberta Family and Social Services is the provincial department responsible for developing safe, healthy and strong families, individuals and communities, while protecting and assisting those in need. *New Positions Created (11):* Service Facilitators; Support Facilitators; Child and Family Services Worker; Nurses (2); Executive Director, Strategic and Organizational Development; Manager, Business Planning; Child and Family Services Worker; Project Specialist; Program Planners (2); Child Welfare Social Worker; Research Consultant.

ALBERTA FAMILY AND SOCIAL SERVICES
Att: Kathy Kirbyson, Human Resource Administrator, Michener Services
Box 5002
Red Deer, AB T4N 5Y5
Fax 403-340-7140
Email .... kathykirbyson@gov.ab.ca
Website .... www.health.gov.ab.ca

Employer Background: Alberta Family and Social Services is the provincial department responsible for developing safe, healthy and strong families, individuals and communities, while protecting and assisting those in need. *New Positions Created (9):* Nurse; Dentist; Volunteer Coordinator; Nurse; Dentist; Residential Care Worker; Pay and Benefits Administrator; Residential Care Workers (2); Dentist.

ALBERTA FINANCE
Att: Human Resources
9515 - 107th Street
Room 522, Terrace Building
Edmonton, AB T5K 2C3
Tel. 780-415-9107
Fax 780-422-0421
Website .... www.treas.gov.ab.ca
Employer Background: Alberta Finance is the provincial department responsible for: the management of financial assets and liabilities; fiscal planning and decision-making; accessing financial products and services and pension plans; and administering the regulatory framework to reduce risk for plan members, depositors and policy holders. *New Positions Created (25):* Head, Records & Information Management; Real Estate Accountant; Senior Tax Auditor; Supervisor / Lead Auditor; Correspondence Writer; Investment Management Office Support Position; Systems Analyst; Compliance Officers; Manager, Commodity Tax Audit; Pension Analysts (2); Manager, Objections and Appeals; Business Planning Analyst; Freedom of Information and Protection of Privacy Administrative Support Position; Senior Manager, Strategic Human Resource Services; Tax Policy Analyst; Manager of Compliance; Office Coordinator; Settlement Accountant; Systems Analyst; Tax Assessor; Performance Measurement and Accounting Analyst; Senior Tax Information Officer; Systems Analyst; Commodity Tax Auditors; Corporate Tax Auditors.

ALBERTA GOVERNMENT SERVICES
Att: Human Resources Manager
10155 - 102nd Street
Suite 18D, Commerce Place
Edmonton, AB T5J 4L4
Tel. 780-427-4860
Fax 780-422-0214
Email .... hr.gs@ma.gov.ab.ca
Website www3.gov.ab.ca/gs
Employer Background: Established in 1999, the Ministry of Government Services is responsible for Alberta registries, consumer and corporate services and the Regulatory Review Secretariat. *New Positions Created (18):* Land Titles Examiners; Senior Policy Analyst; Survey Technologists; Municipal Adviser II / FOIP Adviser; Administrative Assistant; Administrative Assistant; Consumer Relations Officer; Financial Analyst; Administrative Assistant; Financial Systems Officer; Land Titles Examiner; Administrative Assistant; Researcher; Policy Analyst; Manager, Business Planning; Consumer Relations Officers (2); Director, Provincial Programs; Consumer and Corporate Services Position.

ALBERTA HEALTH AND WELLNESS
Att: Personnel Administration Office
10011 - 109th Street
5th Floor, Peace Hills Trust Tower
Edmonton, AB T5J 3S8
Tel. 780-408-8460
Fax 780-422-0468
Email .... executivesearch@gov.ab.ca
Website .... www.health.gov.ab.ca
Employer Background: Alberta Health and Wellness works to provide timely access to needed health services. *New Positions Created (2):* Director, Issues Management; Director, Strategy Development.

ALBERTA HEALTH AND WELLNESS
Att: Human Resource Services
10025 Jasper Avenue
17th Floor, Telus Plaza North Tower
Edmonton, AB T5J 2N3
Tel. 780-427-1524
Fax 780-427-5597
Email .... hrresume@health.gov.ab.ca
Website .... www.health.gov.ab.ca
Employer Background: Alberta Health and Wellness works to provide timely access to needed health services. *New Positions Created (42):* Research Officer; Research Claims Officer; Planning Consultant; Project Team Leader; Receptionist / Secretary; Issues Manager; General Team Leader, Communicable Disease (CD); Immunization Team Leader; Information Disclosure Coordinator; Senior Funding Consultant; HIA Information Officer; Financial Analyst; Program Secretary; Supervisor, Flight Coordination; Delivery Manager, Service Delivery; Inventory Management Specialist; Team Leader, IT Service Delivery Management; Nursing Consultant; Senior Planning Advisor; Policy Analyst; Business Analyst; Program Review Specialist; Administrative Assistant; Senior Consultant; Senior Manager, Health Services Funding; Information Coordinator; Legislative Planner; Project Team Leader; Respiratory Consultant; Patient Classification Specialist; Researcher; Branch Communication Liaison; Information Disclosure Coordinator; Manager, Privacy and Security; Executive Director; HIA Information Officer; Auditor; Continuing Care Policy Consultant; HIA Policy & Training Advisor; Ministerial Stenographer; Branch Communication Officer; Information Planning and Dissemination Advisor.

ALBERTA HUMAN RESOURCES AND EMPLOYMENT
Att: Lucie Leduc, HR Services
10030 - 108th Street
3rd Floor, Centre West Building
Edmonton, AB T5J 3E1
Fax 780-427-1018
Website .... www.gov.ab.ca/hre
Employer Background: Alberta Human Resources and Employment helps individuals succeed in the workforce and fosters safe and healthy workplaces. The department has a $1 billion budget and employs over 2,000 people in 71 communities throughout Alberta. *New Positions Created (40):* Call Centre Representative; Manager, Career De-

velopment Services; Team Leader, Labour Market Information Data Mart; Administrative Assistants (2); Performance Coordinator; Program Planner, Skills Development Program; Privacy Impact Coordinator; Administrative Assistant; Regional Communications Manager; Contract Managers; Research Assistant; Administrative Support Position; Facilities Planner; Stockkeeper; Welfare Program Supervisor; Labour Relations Officer; Senior Manager; Manager, Labour Market Analysis; Data and Application Analyst; Facilities Planner; Financial Coordinator; Labour Market Economist; Senior Labour Market Policy Analyst; Welfare Program Supervisors (2); Budget Officer; Manager, Disability Initiatives; Senior Policy Analyst; Financial Analyst; Information and Privacy Coordinator; Information Officer; Budget Officer; Research Analyst; Systems Analyst; Occupational Health and Safety Counsellor; Facilitators, Labour Relations (2); Financial Benefit Worker; Senior Coordinator, Data Services; Career Development Officer; Case Aide / Administrative Support Position; Occupational Health and Safety Officer.

ALBERTA HUMAN RESOURCES AND EMPLOYMENT
Att: Human Resources Manager
4804 - 42nd Avenue, Bay 10
Innisfail, AB T4G 1V2

Fax 403-227-7975
Email .... censssc.jobs@gov.ab.ca
Website .... www.gov.ab.ca/hre
Employer Background: Alberta Human Resources and Employment helps individuals succeed in the workforce and fosters safe and healthy workplaces. The department has a $1 billion budget and employs over 2,000 people in 71 communities throughout Alberta. *New Positions Created (12):* Area Business Manager; EDCI / FM Worker; Area Business Manager; Social Worker; Child Welfare Unit Clerk; Manager, Business Services; Systems Analyst; Program Support Clerk; Financial Unit Clerk; Child Welfare Social Workers; Intake / Financial Benefits / AISH Workers (2); Manager, Finance & Administration.

ALBERTA HUMAN RESOURCES AND EMPLOYMENT
Att: Human Resource Services
855 - 8th Avenue SW
9th Floor, Century Park Place
Calgary, AB T2P 3P1

Tel. 403-297-4511
Fax 403-297-5790
Email .... cal.personnel@gov.ab.ca
Website .... www.gov.ab.ca/hre
Employer Background: Alberta Human Resources and Employment helps individuals succeed in the workforce and fosters safe and healthy workplaces. The department has a $1 billion budget and employs over 2,000 people in 71 communities throughout Alberta. *New Positions Created (17):* Child Welfare Social Workers; Eligibility Review Officer; Administrative Assistant; Contract Assistant; Psychiatric Nurse; Regional

Communications Manager; Career Development Officers; Client Services Coordinator Supervisor; Residential Care Worker; Employment Standards Officer; Human Resource Consultant; Community Development Specialist; Unit Clerk; Career Adviser; Child Welfare Workers; Residential Care Worker; Labour Safety Officer.

ALBERTA HUMAN RESOURCES AND EMPLOYMENT
Att: Bob Ellison, Human Resource Services
Alberta Corporate Services Centre,
Northwest Region
PO Box 326
McLennan, AB T0H 2L0

Tel. 780-324-3285
Fax 780-324-3262
Email .... bob.ellison@gov.ab.ca
Website .... www.gov.ab.ca/hre
Employer Background: Alberta Human Resources and Employment helps individuals succeed in the workforce and fosters safe and healthy workplaces. The department has a $1 billion budget and employs over 2,000 people in 71 communities throughout Alberta. *New Positions Created (16):* Error Detection and Continuous Improvement Worker; Forest Officer; Aboriginal Case Specialist; Occupational Health & Safety Officer; Operations Coordinator / Career Development Officer 2; Child Welfare Program Specialist; Public Guardian Representative; Family Therapist; Project Planning Coordinator; Child Welfare Generalist; Career Development Officer 2; Supports for Independence / Intake Worker; Career Development Officers (2); Social Worker; Bilingual Social Worker / Child Welfare Generalist; Child Welfare Generalist, Aboriginal Liaison.

ALBERTA HUMAN RESOURCES AND EMPLOYMENT
Att: Human Resource Services
Alberta Corporate Service Centre
PO Box 1410
Lac La Biche, AB T0A 2C0

Tel. 780-623-5283
Fax 780-623-5313
Email .... hr.laclabiche@gov.ab.ca
Website .... www.gov.ab.ca/hre
Employer Background: Alberta Human Resources and Employment helps individuals succeed in the workforce and fosters safe and healthy workplaces. The department has a $1 billion budget and employs over 2,000 people in 71 communities throughout Alberta. *New Positions Created (11):* Intake / Family Maintenance Worker; Audit Team Leader; Budget Officer; Child Care Counsellor; Client Service Coordinator; Community Support Worker; Client Service Coordinator; Aboriginal Services Manager; ECSS Worker; Child Welfare Generalist; Career Counsellor.

ALBERTA INFRASTRUCTURE & TRANSPORTATION
Att: Human Resources Branch
6950 - 113th Street, 2nd Floor
Edmonton, AB T6H 5V7

Tel. 780-427-8312

Fax 780-422-5138
Email .... infraresume@gov.ab.ca
Website .... www.infras.gov.ab.ca
Employer Background: Alberta Infrastructure & Transportation contributes to Alberta's economic prosperity and quality of life by providing necessary, effective and safe infrastructure. *New Positions Created (74):* Development & Planning Technologist; Senior Mechanical Engineer; Construction Engineer; Planning Engineer; Secretary to Regional Director; Maintenance Contract Inspector; Architectural Science Specialist; Field Support Technologist; Evaluation Coordinator; Field Support Technologist; Regional Accommodation Planner; Planning Engineer; Administrative Assistant; Field Support Technologist; Field Support Technologist, Construction; Roadway Materials Engineer; Urban / Program Engineer; Construction Manager; Field Support Technologist; Maintenance Contract Inspector; Administrative Assistant; Program Summary Technologist; Senior Purchasing Officer; Field Support Technologist; Structural / Building Envelope Engineer; Traffic Standards Engineer; Field Support Technologist; Human Resource Consultant; Maintenance Contract Inspector; Pay & Benefits Administrator; Assistant Development & Planning Technologist; Field Support Technologist; Operations Engineer; Plumber; Power Plant Engineer, 3rd Class; Administrative Assistant; Operations Supervisor; Project Managers (2); Field Support Technologist; Project Manager; Development and Planning Technologist; Infrastructure Engineer; Project Management Assistant; Technical Webmaster; Facilities Manager Assistant; Senior Business Analyst; Power Plant Supervisor; Senior Manager, Land and First Nations; Stockkeeper; Administrative Assistants (2); Bridge Technologist; Infrastructure Grants Technologist; Property Agent and Appraiser; Senior Purchasing Officers (2); Accommodation Planner; Assistant Development Technologist; Director, Policy, Finance and Information Services; Human Resources Consultant; Facilities Managers (2); Operations Manager; Carpenter; Facilities Assistant; Grants Planning Engineer; Human Resources Assistant; Senior Lease Coordinator; Autocad Technologist; Tender Administration and Claims Specialist; Operations Supervisor; Plumber Apprentice; Policy Manager, Passenger Industry Development; Regional Bridge Manager; Regional Program Support Technologist; Administrative Assistant; Project Manager.

ALBERTA INFRASTRUCTURE & TRANSPORTATION
Att: Human Resources Branch
6950 - 113th Street, 1st Floor
Edmonton, AB T6H 5V7

Tel. 780-427-7310
Fax 780-422-1900
Email .... infraresume@gov.ab.ca
Website .... www.gov.ab.ca
Employer Background: Alberta Infrastructure & Transportation contributes to Alberta's economic prosperity and quality of life by providing necessary, effective and safe

infrastructure. *New Positions Created (22):* Electrical Apprentice; Lease Administrator; Heavy Duty Caretakers; Operations Supervisor; Power Plant Supervisor; Aircraft Maintenance Engineer; Technologist 1; Administrative Assistant; Business Planning Analyst; Manager, Legislative Planning; Area Assistant; Business Planning Analyst; Director, Carrier Services; Secretary; Dangerous Goods Inspector; Technical Resource Officer; Employee Assistance Program Consultant; Survey Systems Technologist; Technologist; Occupational Health and Safety Consultant; Contract and Tender Administration Technologist; Policy Manager, Passenger Industry Development.

ALBERTA INNOVATION & SCIENCE
Att: Human Resources Division
6950 - 113th Street
2nd Floor
Edmonton, AB T6H 5V7
Tel. 780-427-8312
Fax 780-422-5138
Email .... innov.sci.resume@gov.ab.ca
Website .... www.gov.ab.ca/is
Employer Background: Alberta Innovation and Science works to enhance the contribution of science, research and information and communications technology to the sustainable prosperity and quality of life of all Albertans. *New Positions Created (11):* Technology Development Officer; Budget Coordinator; Administrative Assistant; Industrial Development Officer; Radio Operator; Manager, IT; Research Manager; Accounting Analyst; Systems Analyst; Research Officer; Budget Officer.

ALBERTA INTERNATIONAL AND INTERGOVERNMENTAL RELATIONS
Att: Human Resources Services
10155 - 102nd Street
8th Floor, Commerce Place
Edmonton, AB T5J 4L5
Tel. 780-422-1510
Fax 780-422-5362
Email .... hr.learning@gov.ab.ca
Website .... www.iaa.gov.ab.ca
Employer Background: Alberta IIR is a provincial ministry that develops government policy and strategic objectives for Alberta's relations with other governments in Canada and the international community. *New Positions Created (9):* Research Officer; Director, Legal Issues; Research & Development Officer; Director, Claims Policy and Research; Administrative Officer; Research & Development Officer; Manager, Asia / Pacific; Research and Development Officer; Manager, Research Indian Land Claim.

ALBERTA JUSTICE
Att: Human Resources
9833 - 109th Street
1st Floor, Bowker Building
Edmonton, AB T5K 2E8
Tel. 780-427-0320
Fax 780-422-1330
Website .... www.gov.ab.ca/just

Employer Background: Alberta Justice is the government department responsible for ensuring equality and fairness in the administration of justice throughout the province. *New Positions Created (134):* Crown Prosecutor; Legal Manager; Administrative Support Specialist, Judiciary & Administration; Cashier / Court Clerk; Court Clerk Supervisor; Judicial Clerk; Legal Assistant; Assistant Trust Officer; Court Security Officer; Collections Paralegal Officer; Court / Counter Clerks; Crown Prosecutor; Judicial Clerk; Justice's Secretary; Provincial Protection Officer; Crown Prosecutor; Legal Assistant; Management Accountant; Family Intake Clerk; Judicial Clerk; Legal Assistant; Legal Officer; Legal Officer; Administrative Assistant; Junior Program Coordinator; Legal Secretary; Manager, Business Planning; Receptionist; Unit Clerk; Administrative Assistant; Cashier / Counter / Courtroom Clerk; Collection Officers; Nurse; Court Clerk; Judicial Clerk; Judicial Clerk, Divorce Court; Policy and Compliance Analyst; Senior Legal Counsel to the Chief Justice; Court Clerk Supervisor; Court / Counter Clerk; Judicial Clerks; Data Entry Clerk; Legal Assistant; Mediation And Court Services Unit Secretary; Circuit / Docket Clerk; Client Services Assistants (3); Family Court Worker; Legal Officer; Trust Officer; Administrative Assistant; Administrative Assistant; Legal Counsel; Provincial Protection Officer; Receptionist / Clerk; Systems Analyst; Administrative Specialist; Judicial Assistants (2); Administrative Assistant; Crown Prosecutor; Nurse; Administrative Assistant; Judicial Clerk; Nurses (2); Unit Clerks (3); Healthcare Manager / Supervisor; Judicial Clerk; Legal Officer; Correction Officer ; Taxation Administrative Assistant; Administrative Support Position; Court of Appeal / QB Librarian; Court Security Manager; Laboratory Technician; Nurses (2); Policy and Compliance Analyst; Collections Support Clerk; Court Counter Clerk; Judicial Clerk; Legal Officer; Project Manager; Legal Assistant; Registration / Good Payer Clerk; Systems Administrator; Health Records Technician; Webmaster / Web Developer; Data Entry Operator; Mediator; Financial Services Supervisor; Manager, Legislative Security; Special Investigators; Team Leader, Special Investigations; Legal Officer; Legal Officer; Policy and Compliance Analyst; Provincial Protection Officer; Collections Officer; Crown Prosecutor; Legal Assistant; Technical Security Consultant; Judicial Clerk; Psychiatric Nurse; Assistant Trust Officer; Auditor ; Legal Officers (2); Accounts Clerk; Counter Clerk; Team Leaders; Accountant; Collection Officer; Legal Secretaries (2); Crown Prosecutor; Provincial Protection Officer; Correctional Services Workers (2); Crown Prosecutors (2); Data Entry Clerk; Trust Officers (2); Court / Counter Clerk; Judicial Clerk; Duty Driver; Legal Assistant; Records Management Clerks; Sentence Administrative Support Positions (3); Administrative Support Position; Judicial Assistant; Nurses (2); Crown Prosecutor; Family Court Counsellor; Legal Assistant; Records Management Clerk; Cashier / Counter / Courtroom Clerk;

Administrative Support Position; Provincial Protection Officer; Appellate Counsel and Policy Adviser; Crown Prosecutor.

ALBERTA LEARNING
Att: Human Resource Services
11160 Jasper Avenue
5th Floor, Devonian Building
Edmonton, AB T5K 0L2
Tel. 780-427-2058
Fax 780-422-2114
Email .... hr.learning@gov.ab.ca
Website .... ednet.edc.gov.ab.ca
Employer Background: Alberta Learning, the second-largest department of the provincial government, is responsible for education in Alberta and serves over 580,000 students, with a budget exceeding $3 billion. *New Positions Created (14):* Assistant Director, Diploma Examinations Program; Administrative Support Position; Administrative Support Position, Severe Disabilities Funding; Executive Secretary; Assessment Resources Officer; Senior Evaluator; Team Leader, Information Management; Examination Manager, Francais 30 / French Language Arts 30; Senior Systems Analyst; Client Relationship Analysts; Coordinator, Business Intelligence; Coordinator, Data Acquisition; Coordinator, Data Warehouse; Project Coordination Analyst.

ALBERTA LEARNING
Att: Human Resource Services
10155 - 102nd Street
8th Floor, Commerce Place
Edmonton, AB T5J 4L5
Tel. 780-422-4493
Fax 780-422-5362
Website .... www.edc.gov.ab.ca
Employer Background: Alberta Learning, the second-largest department of the provincial government, is responsible for education in Alberta and serves over 580,000 students, with a budget exceeding $3 billion. *New Positions Created (56):* Assistant Director, Achievement Testing Program; Research Officer; Program Coordinator / Group Leader; Examination Clerk; LAC / PAC / OTC Registry Support Assistant; Coordinator, Business Integration; Apprenticeship Analyst, Intern; Trades Qualification Consultant; Director, Aboriginal Policy; German or Japanese Language Administrative Support Position; Research Officer; Management Adviser; Program Manager, Social Studies, K - 12; Senior Data Analyst; Systems Analyst; Research Officer 2; Administrative Coordinator; Program Manager, Health, Career and Life Management; Research Assistant; Senior Data Analysts (2); Director, Alberta Initiative for School Improvement; Market Development Manager; Program Consultant, English Language Arts; Director, Aboriginal Policy Initiative; Manager, Project Coordination; Director, South Region; Senior Systems Analyst; Curriculum Consultant, Social Studies K - 12; Program Manager, Social Studies K - 12; Budget Analyst; Intern, Human Resource Programs; Legislative Intern; Ministerial Stenographer; Legislative Con-

sultant; Research Assistants / Interns (2); Education Manager; Task Group Leader; Research Consultant; Director, Applications and Technology Systems Management; Research Assistant; Research Assistant, Social Sciences; Manager, Public Institutions; Senior Manager; Research Assistant; Senior Consultant; Administrative Support Position; Trades Qualification Consultant; Director, Basic Learning Division; Manager, Designated Trades & Occupations; Trades Qualification Inspector; Trades Qualification Inspector; Research and Policy Analyst; Senior Awards Consultant; Human Resource Consultants; Director, Industry Programs and Standards; Area Manager.

ALBERTA MENTAL HEALTH BOARD
Att: Dr. Pierre Beausejour, Chief of Staff & Director of Provincial Programs, Search and Selection Committees
10025 Jasper Avenue, Box 1360
Edmonton, AB T5J 2N3

Fax 780-422-2472
Email .... trudi.thew@amhb.ab.ca
Website .... www.amhb.ab.ca
Employer Background: AMHB is a provincial health authority, operating 872 beds in 4 mental health facilities: Alberta Hospital Edmonton, Alberta Hospital Ponoka, Claresholm Care Centre and Raymond Care Centre. *New Positions Created (2):* Coordinators of Medical Services (3); Medical Directors (3).

ALBERTA MENTAL HEALTH BOARD, ALBERTA HOSPITAL EDMONTON
Att: Human Resources
17480 Fort Road
PO Box 307
Edmonton, AB T5J 2J7

Tel. 780-472-5333
Fax 780-472-5282
Email .... ahe.hr@amhb.ab.ca
Website .... www.amhb.ab.ca
Employer Background: AMHB is a provincial health authority, operating 872 beds in 4 mental health facilities: Alberta Hospital Edmonton, Alberta Hospital Ponoka, Claresholm Care Centre and Raymond Care Centre. *New Positions Created (12):* Aboriginal Wellness Worker; Central Services Manager; Dietitian; Production Manager; Quality Improvement Coordinator; Physical Therapist; Provincial Eating Disorders Coordinator; Mental Health Therapist; Mental Health Therapist; Mental Health Therapist; Budget Coordinator, Alberta Hospital Edmonton; Budget Technician.

ALBERTA MENTAL HEALTH BOARD, ALBERTA HOSPITAL PONOKA
Att: Human Resources Manager
PO Box 1000
Ponoka, AB T4J 1R8

Tel. 403-783-7672
Fax 403-783-7681
Email .... ahp.hr@amhb.ab.ca
Website .... www.amhb.ab.ca
Employer Background: AMHB is a provincial health authority, operating 872 beds in

4 mental health facilities: Alberta Hospital Edmonton, Alberta Hospital Ponoka, Claresholm Care Centre and Raymond Care Centre. *New Positions Created (27):* Adult Mental Health Therapist; Physical Therapist; Psychiatric Aide; Gardener; Psychologist I; Senior Buyer, Purchasing; Coordinator, Medical Services; Director, Laundry Services; Medical Director, Adult Psychiatry; Medical Director, Geriatric Psychiatry; Medical Director, Provincial Forensic; Mental Health Therapist; Staff Nurses; Administrative Support Position; Clinical Supervisor; PC Support Position; Occupational Therapist I; Social Worker II; Physical Therapist; Quality Improvement Coordinator; Operations Analyst; Psychologist I; Administrative Directors (2), Provincial Programs; Adult (Short-Term) & Seniors Services Manager; Patient Representative; Systems Administrator; Staff Nurse / Admissions Coordinator.

ALBERTA MENTAL HEALTH BOARD, CLARESHOLM AND RAYMOND CARE CENTRES
Att: Human Resources
PO Box 490
Claresholm, AB T0L 0T0

Tel. 403-625-8500
Fax 403-625-8506
Email .... ccc-rcc.hr@amhb.ab.ca
Website .... www.amhb.ab.ca
Employer Background: AMHB is a provincial health authority, operating 872 beds in 4 mental health facilities: Alberta Hospital Edmonton, Alberta Hospital Ponoka, Claresholm Care Centre and Raymond Care Centre. *New Positions Created (18):* Human Resources Assistant; Occupational Health / Infection Control Nurse; Staff Nurses, Adult Psychiatry Program; Patient Care Manager, Geriatric Psychiatry; Administrative Support Position II; Discharge Coordinator; Mental Health Therapist; Mental Health Therapist; Social Worker II; Administrative Support Position; Community Mental Health Nurse; Mental Health Therapist; Staff Nurse; Manager, Student Health Initiative; Mental Health Outreach Therapist; Licensed Practical Nurse; Nursing Coordinator, Geriatric Psychiatry; Mental Health Therapist.

ALBERTA MOTOR ASSOCIATION
Att: Ms T. MacLeod, CHRP
Human Resources Service Manager
PO Box 8180, Station South
Edmonton, AB T6H 5X9

Fax 780-430-5711
Email .... tmacleod@ana.ab.ca
Website .... www.ama.ab.ca
Employer Background: AMA is a non-profit organization, affiliated with CAA and AAA, providing services to over a half-million members across Alberta. *New Positions Created (10):* Wellness Coordinator; Contact Centre Director; Finance Vice-President; Program Facilitator, Traffic Safety Initiatives; Bodily Injury Claims Adjuster; Insurance Agent; Desktop Support Business Analyst; Insurance Agent; Program Facilitator,

Traffic Safety Initiatives; Regional General Managers (2).

ALBERTA MUNICIPAL AFFAIRS
Att: Human Resources Manager
10155 - 102nd Street, Suite 18D
Edmonton, AB T5J 4L4

Tel. 780-427-3744
Fax 780-422-0214
Email .... hr.ama@ma.gov.ab.ca
Website .... www.gov.ab.ca/ma
Employer Background: Alberta Municipal Affairs facilitates the development of good local government in Alberta. *New Positions Created (32):* Legislative Advisor; Municipal Excellence / Municipal Advisor; Policy Analyst; Legal Secretary; Business Planning Analyst; Correspondence Assistant; Senior Records and Disposition Analyst; District Officer; Environmental Engineer / Scientist; Financial Coordinator; Fire Commissioner; Manager, Technical Advisor, Civil; Technical Advisor, Building; Administrative Coordinator; FOIP Coordinator; Municipal Advisor / Planning Officer; Compliance Advisor; Disaster Services Officer; Junior Legal Officer; Financial Analyst; FOIP Adviser; Legislative Adviser; Labour Safety Officer, Building Codes; Fire Commissioner; Administrative Support Position; Financial Assistant; Junior Assessment Auditor; Information Officer; Policy Analyst; Office Administrator; Coordinator of Provincial / Municipal Partnerships; Program / Project Manager.

ALBERTA NEWSPRINT COMPANY
Att: Personnel Services Coordinator
Postal Bag 9000
Whitecourt, AB T7S 1P9

Tel. 780-778-7000
Fax 780-778-7070
Email ...... posting@albertanewsprint.com
Website .... www.altanewsprint.ca
Employer Background: Founded in 1989, Alberta Newsprint operates a 250,000 tonne per year newsprint mill in Whitecourt, Alberta. *New Positions Created (2):* Pulping Production Assistant; Utilities Production Assistant / Steam Chief.

ALBERTA RESEARCH COUNCIL / ARC
Att: Human Resources
250 Karl Clark Road
Edmonton, AB T6N 1E4

Tel. 780-450-5111
Fax 780-450-5195
Email .... human.resources@arc.ab.ca
Website .... www.arc.ab.ca
Employer Background: Founded in 1921, ARC is the largest provincial research agency in Canada, with 500 employees at 4 sites, developing technology for commercial use. *New Positions Created (6):* Various Oil & Gas Positions; Industrial Technology Advisor; Senior Carbohydrate Chemist; Metallurgist; Wildlife Ecologist / Mammologist; Production Engineer.

ALBERTA RESOURCE DEVELOPMENT
Att: Human Resources
9945 - 108th Street

10th Floor, North Petroleum Plaza
Edmonton, AB T5K 2G6
Tel. 780-427-6768
Fax 780-422-4299
Email .... resumes.resdev@gov.ab.ca
Website .... www.gov.ab.ca
Employer Background: The Department of
Resource Development manages mineral
rights, administers mineral agreements and
collects revenue and royalties for the people
of Alberta. *New Positions Created (6):* Payroll and Benefits Administrators (2); Business Analyst / Team Leader; Economists;
Operational Analyst; Data Administrator /
Systems Analyst; Senior Regulatory Analyst.

ALBERTA SCHOOL BOARDS ASSOCIATION / ASBA
Att: Manager, Corporate Services
9925 - 95th Street
Suite 1200
Edmonton, AB T5K 2J8
Tel. 780-451-7123
Fax 780-482-5659
Website .... www.asba.ab.ca
Employer Background: ASBA is a provincial
association of 64 locally elected school
boards. *New Positions Created (4):* Assistant Superintendent; Labour Negotiator;
Staff Lawyer; Assistant Superintendent.

ALBERTA SECURITIES COMMISSION
Att: Manager, Human Resources
10025 Jasper Avenue
20th Floor
Edmonton, AB T5J 3Z5
Tel. 780-422-1498
Fax 780-422-1030
Email ..... humanresources@seccom.ab.ca
Website .... www.albertasecurities.com
Employer Background: ASC, the first industry-funded securities commission in
Canada, plays a leading role in regulating
capital markets. *New Positions Created (3):*
Securities Analyst; Registration Examiner;
Securities Analyst.

ALBERTA SOLICITOR GENERAL
Att: Human Resource Services
9833 - 109th Street
1st Floor, Bowker Building
Edmonton, AB T5K 2E8
Tel. 780-427-0320
Fax 780-422-1330
Website .... www.gov.ab.ca/just
Employer Background: Alberta Solicitor
General works to ensure equality and fairness in the administration of justice
throughout the province. *New Positions Created (7):* Administrative Assistant; Correctional Service Worker; Personnel / Payroll
Clerk; Correctional Service Worker; Psychiatric Nurse; Correction Services Worker;
Provincial Protection Officer.

ALBERTA SUSTAINABLE RESOURCE DEVELOPMENT
Att: Human Resource Services
9915 - 108th Street

4th Floor, South Petroleum Plaza
Edmonton, AB T5K 2G8
Tel. 780-944-0313
Fax 780-427-2513
Email .... ephrresume@gov.ab.ca
Website www3.gov.ab.ca/srd
Employer Background: Alberta Sustainable
Resource Development is responsible for
public lands, fish, wildlife and forest management, including forest industry development. *New Positions Created (13):* Compliance Analyst; Land Surveyor; Forest Management Forester; Land Management Forester; District Clerk; Agricultural Policy and
Issue Management Specialist; Wildland Fire
Prevention Officer; Operations & Maintenance Technologist; Area Forest Officer; Air
Photo Technologist; Forester; Geomatics
Technologist; Land Administrator.

ALBERTA SUSTAINABLE RESOURCE DEVELOPMENT
Att: Human Resource Service Centre
3115 - 12th Street NE
Suite 100
Calgary, AB T2E 7J2
Fax 403-297-2902
Email .... ephrresume@gov.ab.ca
Website www3.gov.ab.ca/srd
Employer Background: Alberta Sustainable
Resource Development is responsible for
public lands, fish, wildlife and forest management, including forest industry development. *New Positions Created (5):* Forest Officers, Land and Resource Management (2);
GIS Technologist; Systems Analyst;
Hydrogeologist; Forest Management Forester.

ALBERTA TEACHERS' ASSOCIATION
Att: Jean Magierowski, Personnel Officer
11010 - 142nd Street NW
Edmonton, AB T5N 2R1
Tel. 780-453-2411
Fax 780-452-3547
Website .... www.teachers.ab.ca
Employer Background: ATA promotes and
advances public education, safeguards professional practice standards and serves as
an advocate for its members. *New Positions
Created (4):* Executive Assistant, Government; Executive Assistant, Member Services; Coordinator; Executive Assistant.

ALBERTA TRANSPORTATION
Att: Human Resources Division
6950 - 113th Street
2nd Floor
Edmonton, AB T6H 5V7
Tel. 780-427-8312
Email .... infraresume@gov.ab.ca
Website .... www.tu.gov.ab.ca
Employer Background: Alberta Transportation is a core business area of Alberta Infrastructure, which contributes to Alberta's
economic prosperity and quality of life
through the provision of necessary, effective
and safe infrastructure. *New Positions Created (9):* Administrative Assistants (2);
Bridge Manager; Property Agent and Ap-

praisers (2); Grants / Planning Engineer;
Office Support Technologist; Infrastructure
Manager; Operations Service Coordinator;
Technologist; Technologist.

ALBERTA TREASURY BRANCHES
Att: Human Resources
9888 Jasper Avenue, ATB Place
Edmonton, AB T5J 1P1
Tel. 780-408-7000
Fax 780-428-0853
Email .... careers@atb.com
Website .... www.atb.com
Employer Background: Established in 1938
by the Government of Alberta, ATB is a full-service financial institution, serving half a
million Albertans in 239 communities. *New
Positions Created (4):* Account Manager;
Marketing Director, Independent Business;
Marketing Director, Retail; Investment Specialist.

ALBI HOMES LTD.
Att: Human Resources Manager
2880 Glenmore Trail SE, Suite 240
Calgary, AB T2C 2E7
Tel. 403-236-4032
Fax 403-236-4038
Website .... www.albihomes.com
Employer Background: Founded in 1982,
Albi Homes Ltd. builds homes in Calgary
communities. *New Positions Created (3):*
Community Manager; Community Manager; Senior Estimator.

ALBIAN SANDS ENERGY INC.
Att: Human Resources Manager
120 - 9521 Franklin Avenue, Suite 420
Fort McMurray, AB T9H 3Z7
Email ..... albian.resumes@albiansands.ca
Website .... www.albiansands.ca
Employer Background: Albian Sands Energy
Inc. is a new company created to construct
and operate the Muskeg River Mine, part of
the $3.5 billion Athabasca Oil Sands Project.
New Positions Created (27): Millwrights (5);
Plant Technologist, Utilities; Steamfitter-Pipefitters / Gasfitters (3); Field Operators,
Plant / Extraction & Tailings Area (24); Field
Operators, Plant / Froth Treatment Area
(20); Plant Maintainers, Plant / Extraction
& Tailings Area (12); Plant Maintainers,
Plant / Froth Treatment (12); Project Controls Manager, Extraction Plant Project;
Control Room Operators, Extraction / Tailings (4); Control Room Operators, Froth
Treatment (4); Control Room Operators, Ore
Preparation (4); Control Room Operators,
Utilities (4); Dispatch Engineer; Electrical
Engineer, Mining Operations; Geotechnical
Engineer; Haulage Team Leader, Mining
Operations; Maintenance Planner, Extraction / Tailings; Maintenance Planner, Ore
Preparation; Maintenance Team Leader,
Utilities; Plant Engineer, Extraction / Tailings; Plant Engineer, Froth Treatment; Plant
Engineer, Ore Preparation; Scheduling Engineer; Services Team Leader, Mining Operations; Shift Team Leader, Extraction /
Tailings (2); Shift Team Leader, Ore Preparation; Short-Range Planning Engineer.

ALCAN PRIMARY METAL GROUP
Att: Alcan Coordinator,
Kitimat Community Skills Centre
676 Mountainview Square, PO Box 1800
Kitimat, BC V8C 2H2

Fax 250-639-8175
Email .... kitimat.recruiter@alcan.com
Website .... www.alcan.com

Employer Background: Alcan Primary Metal Group, a member of Montreal-based Alcan Inc., operates one of the world's largest aluminum smelters. *New Positions Created (17):* Head Planner; Analytical Laboratory Technologist; Millwrights; Commercial Negotiator; Mechanical / Maintenance Engineer / Technologist; Process Engineer; Senior Mechanical Maintenance Engineer; Occupational Health Physician; Chief General Accountant; Financial Analyst; Fisheries Biologist; Human Resources Assistant; Labour Relations Specialist; Labour Relations Supervisor; Maintenance Engineer / Technologist; Occupational Hygiene Supervisor; Safety Supervisor.

ALCATEL CANADA INC., TRANSPORT AUTOMATION
Att: Human Resources
5172 Kingsway, Suite 270
Burnaby, BC V5H 2E8

Tel. 604-434-2455
Fax 604-434-7699
Email .... employment@vansel.alcatel.com
Website .... www.alcatel.ca

Employer Background: Alcatel's Transport Automation Division is one of the world's leading suppliers of railway communications, signaling and control systems. *New Positions Created (6):* Intermediate Software QA Specialist; Senior Systems / Software Designers; Software Analysts; Software Maintenance Specialist; Senior Systems / Software Designers; Various Software Analysts.

ALCATEL CANADA INC., TRANSPORT AUTOMATION
Att: Human Resources
1235 Ormont Drive
Toronto, ON M9L 2W6

Tel. 416-742-3900
Fax 416-742-1543
Email .... hr@torsel.alcatel.com
Website .... www.alcatel.ca

Employer Background: Alcatel's Transport Automation Division is one of the world's leading suppliers of railway communications, signaling and control systems. *New Positions Created (18):* Configuration Management Specialist; Design Engineering Specialist; Installation Planning & Design Specialist; Planner / Scheduler; Product Manager - Data Communication Systems; Project Engineer; Project Manager; Quality Assurance Specialist; Quality Control Inspector; Railway Systems Operations Engineering Specialist; Reliability & Maintainability Engineering Specialist; Software Analyst - Embedded Applications; Software Analyst - Simulator & Tools; Software Analyst - System Management Centre; Software Analyst - Vehicle Control Centre; Systems Design Specialist; Systems Integration & Test Specialist; Systems Safety Engineer.

ALCOA REXDALE PACKAGING
Att: Human Resources Manager
35 City View Drive
Toronto, ON M9W 5A5

Email .... dcdavies@rmc.com
Website .... www.rmc.com

Employer Background: Alcoa Rexdale Packaging is a metal stamping manufacturer, supplying products for the foodservice and consumer markets in North America. *New Positions Created (2):* Materials Planner / Scheduler; Customer Service Representative.

ALCOHOL AND GAMING COMMISSION OF ONTARIO / AGCO
Att: Human Resources Department
20 Dundas Street West, 8th Floor
Toronto, ON M5G 2N6

Tel. 416-326-8700
Fax 416-326-8888
Website .... agco.on.ca

Employer Background: AGCO is a provincial agency responsible for administering the Liquor Licence Act and Gaming Control Act. *New Positions Created (3):* Law Clerk / Legal Secretary; Manager, Customer Services and Administration; Manager, First Nations Gaming.

ALCOS MACHINERY INC.
Att: Human Resources Manager
190 Harry Walker Parkway
Newmarket, ON L3Y 7B4

Tel. 905-836-6030
Fax 905-836-8142
Email .... alcos@alcos.org
Website .... www.alcos.org

Employer Background: Alcos Machinery Inc. designs and manufactures coil processing machinery. *New Positions Created (4):* Application Engineer; Hydraulic System Designer; Project Leader; Design Positions.

ALDATA SOFTWARE MANAGEMENT INC.
Att: Recruiter
211 Pembina Avenue, Suite 206
Hinton, AB T7V 2B3

Tel. 780-817-4040
Fax 780-817-4049
Email .... jobs@aldatasoftware.com
Website .... www.aldatasoftware.com

Employer Background: Established in 1991, Aldata Software Management Inc. offers woodlands business software applications. *New Positions Created (4):* Controller; Embedded Systems Programmer; Software Developer; Support Team Manager.

ALDEN PRINT MANAGEMENT INC.
Att: Human Resources Manager
401 Alden
Markham, ON L3R 4N4

Tel. 905-944-9722
Fax 905-944-9591

Employer Background: Alden Print Management Inc. is a print management company with an internal prepress studio. *New Positions Created (3):* Prepress Production Manager; Print Estimator; Senior and Junior Desktop Operators.

ALDO GROUP INC.
Att: Human Resources Department
905 Hodge Street
St-Laurent, QC H4N 2B3

Tel. 514-747-2536
Fax 514-747-7993
Email ... ressources_humaines@aldogroup.com
Website .... www.aldogroup.com

Employer Background: Aldo Group Inc. is a leading footwear retailer, with 600 stores across North America. *New Positions Created (2):* Executive Assistants; Buyers.

ALDRICHPEARS ASSOCIATES
Att: Gillian Carfra
1455 West Georgia Street, Suite 100
Vancouver, BC V6G 2T3

Tel. 604-669-7044
Email .... jobs@aldrichpears.com
Website .... www.aldrichpears.com

Employer Background: AldrichPears Associates is a 30-member firm, providing planning and design services to an international clientele of museums, science centres, zoos and interpretive centres. *New Positions Created (11):* Design Studio Manager; Exhibit Designer; Graphic Designer; Industrial Designer; Architect; Marketing Coordinator; Writer / Exhibit Developer; Marketing Coordinator; Production Artist / Graphic Designers; Exhibit Designer; Studio Manager.

ALEXANDER HOLBURN BEAUDIN & LANG / AHBL
Att: Bruno De Vita, Managing Partner
700 Georgia Street West
Suite 2700, PO Box 10057
Vancouver, BC V7Y 1B8

Tel. 604-688-1351
Fax 604-669-7642
Website .... www.ahbl.bc.ca

Employer Background: AHBL is a Canadian law firm comprised of nearly 60 lawyers. *New Positions Created (4):* Securities Lawyer; Junior Litigation Lawyer, Commercial Litigation Practice; Junior Litigation Lawyer, Insurance Practice Group; Junior Litigation Lawyer, Professional Liability Practice.

ALFA LAVAL CANADA
Att: Human Resources
101 Milner Avenue
Toronto, ON M1S 4S6

Tel. 416-299-6101
Fax 416-299-3567
Website .... www.alfalaval.ca

Employer Background: Established in 1899, Alfa Laval Canada is a leading provider of fluid handling, heat transfer and separation technologies, with 200 employees nationwide. *New Positions Created (2):* Field Service Representative; General Accountant.

ALFT
Att: Human Resources Manager
189 Deveault Street, Suite 6
Hull, QC J8Z 1S7

Tel. 819-770-0477
Fax 819-770-3862
Email .... alft@alft.com
Website .... www.alft.com

Employer Background: Alft provides x-ray and extreme ultraviolet light sources for semiconductor lithography. *New Positions Created (6):* Electrical Engineer, Power Electronics; Intermediate Electrical / Test Engineers; Materials / Metallurgy Engineer; Mechanical Engineer / Designer; Project Engineers; Senior Technicians.

ALGO GROUP INC.
Att: Human Resources Manager
225 Chabanel Street West, Suite 1100
Montréal, QC H2N 2C9

Tel. 514-382-1240
Fax 514-385-0163
Email .... hralgo@algo.com
Website .... www.algo.com

Employer Background: Algo Group Inc. is an international apparel manufacturer. *New Positions Created (5):* Customer Service Representative / Data Entry Clerk; Picker / Packer; Sales Representative; Production Assistant; Sales / Merchandising Positions.

ALGOMA DISTRICT SCHOOL BOARD
Att: Human Resources Manager
644 Albert Street East
Sault Ste. Marie, ON P6A 2K7

Tel. 705-945-7212
Fax 705-942-2540
Website .... http://www.adsb.on.ca

Employer Background: ADSB consists of 11 secondary and 40 elementary schools in northern Ontario. *New Positions Created (2):* Teachers, Secondary and Elementary; Manager of Information Technology.

ALGONQUIN COLLEGE
Att: Christopher Warburton,
V.P., Student Life & Human Resources
1385 Woodroffe Avenue
Nepean, ON K2G 1V8

Tel. 613-727-4723
Fax 613-727-7785
Website .... www.algonquincollege.com

Employer Background: Algonquin College offers a range of diploma programs, serving 10,500 full-time and 45,000 part-time students from 5 campuses in the Ottawa area. *New Positions Created (8):* English Professor; Chair, Electronics / Telecommunications Department; Dean, School of Business; Technologist, Records Management; Professor, Computer Studies; Professor, Computer Studies; Manager, Technical Services and Energy Conservation; Academic Manager, Electronics / Telecommunications Department, Advanced Technologies Sector.

ALGONQUIN & LAKESHORE CATHOLIC DISTRICT SCHOOL BOARD
Att: Human Resources Department

151 Dairy Avenue
Napanee, ON K7R 4B2

Tel. 613-354-2255
Fax 613-354-5615
Email .... personnel@alcdsb.on.ca
Website .... www.alcdsb.on.ca

Employer Background: The Algonquin and Lakeshore Catholic District School Board serves over 13,000 students in 37 elementary and 6 secondary schools. *New Positions Created (3):* Teachers; Teachers; Teachers.

ALGONQUIN TRAVEL CORPORATION
Att: Human Resources Manager
657 Bronson Avenue
Ottawa, ON K1S 4E7

Tel. 613-233-7713
Fax 613-233-7805
Email .. spatenaude@algonquintravel.com
Website .... www.algonquintravel.com

Employer Background: Founded in 1964, Algonquin Travel operates over 100 franchised travel agencies across Canada. The company has annual revenues exceeding $160 million. *New Positions Created (3):* Junior Counsel; Operations Manager; Marketing Manager.

ALIAS / WAVEFRONT
Att: Human Resources Manager
210 King Street East
Toronto, ON M5A 1J7

Tel. 416-362-9181
Fax 416-369-6142
Email .... careers@aw.sgi.com
Website .... www.aw.sgi.com

Employer Background: Alias / Wavefront develops advanced 3D graphics software for the film and video, games and interactive media, industrial design and visualization markets. The company is a subsidiary of US-based Silicon Graphics, Inc. *New Positions Created (4):* Enterprise Services Project Management Consultant; Industry Marketing Managers (3); Support Product Specialist, Rendering & Compositing; Training Programs & Services Specialist, North America.

ALIRON MARKETING CANADA INC.
Att: Human Resources Manager
261 Trowers Road
Woodbridge, ON L4L 5Z8

Fax 905-264-9411
Email .... aliron@alironmarketing.com
Website .... www.alironmarketing.com

Employer Background: Aliron Marketing, a division of DS-MAX Group, specializes in display marketing in the workplace. *New Positions Created (2):* Marketing Distributor; Marketing Agents.

ALIVE MAGAZINE
Att: Human Resources Manager
7436 Fraser Park Drive
Burnaby, BC V5J 5B9

Tel. 604-435-1919
Email .... financial@axion.net
Website .... www.alivemagazine.com

Employer Background: Alive Magazine is a leading publisher and distributor of natu-

ral health books and magazines to health food stores. *New Positions Created (4):* Assistant Editor; Office Manager; Senior Sales Manager; Editor.

ALL CARE HEALTH SERVICES LTD.
Att: Joanne Browne, RN, Manager
735 Arlington Park Place
Kingston, ON K7M 8M8

Employer Background: All Care Health Services Ltd. is a community homecare agency, serving the counties of Kingston, Frontenac, Lennox and Addington. *New Positions Created (5):* Nurses; Community Nursing Supervisor; Health Care Aides; Registered Nurses and Registered Practical Nurses; Health Care Aides.

ALL NEW MANUFACTURING INC.
Att: Human Resources Manager
4300 - 26th Street NE, Suite 125
Calgary, AB T1Y 7H7

Tel. 403-273-7100
Fax 403-219-3377
Email .... jcleland@allnewmfg.com
Website .... www.allnewmfg.com

Employer Background: All New Manufacturing Inc. is a precision metal fabricator. *New Positions Created (3):* Engineering Manager; Purchasing Manager; Quality Assurance Manager.

ALL WEATHER WINDOWS
Att: Bill Scott, V.P. Sales & Marketing
18550 - 118A Avenue
Edmonton, AB T5S 2L7

Tel. 780-451-0670
Fax 780-447-1997
Website ..... www.allweatherwindows.com

Employer Background: All Weather Windows is one of Canada's largest window and door manufacturers. *New Positions Created (6):* Window and Door Sales Professional; Director, Human Resources; Director, Information Technology; Director, Manufacturing Operations; Senior Accounts Payable Clerk; Environmental Health and Safety Technician.

ALL WEATHER WINDOWS
Att: Warren Martz
8241 - 30th Street SE, Bay 1
Calgary, AB T2C 1H7

Fax 403-720-0050
Website ..... www.allweatherwindows.com

Employer Background: All Weather Windows is one of Canada's largest window and door manufacturers. *New Positions Created (2):* Sales Professional; Receptionist.

ALLCAN ELECTRONIC DISTRIBUTORS
Att: Human Resources Manager
12612 - 124th Street
Edmonton, AB T5L 0N7

Tel. 780-451-2357
Fax 780-451-3052
Email .... careers@allcan.ab.ca
Website .... www.allcan.ab.ca

Employer Background: Allcan Electronic Distributors distributes wireless voice and data communications support products. *New Positions Created (5):* Accounts Payable Specialist; Accounts Receivable Specialist; Inside Sales Position / Order Desk Representative; Outside Sales Representative; Warehouse Position.

ALLENDALE
Att: Carm Cardillo
185 Ontario Street South
Milton, ON L9T 2M4

Tel. 905-878-4141
Fax 905-878-8797
Website .... www.region.halton.on.ca

Employer Background: Allendale is a 300-bed, long-term care facility operated by the Regional Municipality of Halton. *New Positions Created (4):* Healthcare Aides; Mgr, Resident Care; Manager, Resource Development; Manager, Resource Development.

ALLIANCE ATLANTIS COMMUNICATIONS INC.
Att: Human Resources
121 Bloor Street East, Suite 1500
Toronto, ON M4M 3M5

Tel. 416-967-1174
Fax 416-966-7260
Website .... www.allianceatlantis.com

Employer Background: Alliance Atlantis Communications Inc. is Canada's leading independent creator and distributor of TV programs and motion pictures. *New Positions Created (27):* Editor, U8TV; Director, Television Finance; Email Administrator; Content Producer; Executive Assistant to Executive Vice-President, Communications; Executive Assistant to the Vice-President, Sales and Promotions; Producer; Production Coordinator; Intermediate Promotions Editor; Closed Caption Editor; Executive Assistant to President, Motion Picture Distribution; Administrative Assistant, Business & Legal Affairs; Administrative Coordinator, International Television Distribution; Executive Producer, HGTV Canada Interactive; Executive Producer, National Geographic / BBC Canada Interactive; Linear Editor; Marketing Manager; Presentation Producer; Production Executive, Showcase; Project Analyst; Associate Marketing Manager, Financial Networks; Administrative Assistant, Operations and Engineering; Accountant, International Motion Picture Distribution; Accounts Payable Clerk; Studio Assistant; Manager, Business & Legal Affairs; Payroll Analyst.

ALLIANCE STEEL CORP.
Att: Director of Personnel
1060 Boulevard des Laurentides
Laval, QC H7G 2W1

Tel. 450-382-5780
Fax 450-975-9348

Employer Background: Alliance Steel Corp. is a flat-rolled steel service centre. *New Positions Created (3):* Assistant Overhead Crane Operator; Controller; Sales Representative.

ALLIED CLINICAL RESEARCH INC.
Att: Recruiter
4520 Dixie Road
Mississauga, ON L4W 1N2

Tel. 905-569-8255
Fax 905-238-0682
Email .... careers@allied-research.com
Website .... www.allied-research.com

Employer Background: Allied Clinical Research Inc. is a research organization, conducting clinical trials for the pharmaceutical and biotechnology industries. *New Positions Created (2):* Clinical Recruitment Coordinator; QA / QC Associate.

ALLIED DOMECQ, SPIRITS & WINE
Att: Corporate Human Resources
2072 Riverside Drive East
Windsor, ON N8Y 4S5

Tel. 519-561-5800
Fax 519-971-5714
Email .... na_corporate_hr@adsw.com
Website .... www.allieddomecqplc.com

Employer Background: Allied Domecq markets international branded spirits such as Kahlua, Sauza Tequila, Beefeater Gin and Ballantine's Finest. *New Positions Created (7):* Process Manager, Credit and Accounts Receivable; Cognos Support Specialist; Notes Administrator; SAP Basis Administrator; Solutions Architect; Unix Administrator; Project Office Manager.

ALLIED OIL & GAS CORP.
Att: Human Resources Manager
606 - 4th Street SW, Suite 1100
Calgary, AB T2P 1T1

Tel. 403-265-9782
Fax 403-508-2350
Website .... www.alliedoilandgas.com

Employer Background: Allied Oil & Gas Corp. is a junior oil and gas company. *New Positions Created (3):* Intermediate Secretary / Receptionist; Junior Accountant; Senior Accountant.

ALLSTATE INSURANCE COMPANY OF CANADA
Att: John McCullough
5920 Macleod Trail South
Calgary, AB T2H 0K2

Tel. 403-777-3500
Fax 403-248-7767
Website .... www.allstate.ca

Employer Background: Allstate Insurance Company of Canada is a top-tier property and casualty insurance provider, with a team of 1,400 specialists nationwide. *New Positions Created (2):* Auto Field Adjuster; Claim Representative.

ALLSTATE INSURANCE COMPANY OF CANADA
Att: Terry Modesto
1 West Pearce, Suite 207
Richmond Hill, ON L4B 3K3

Tel. 905-771-8026
Fax 905-731-8012
Email .... tmodesto@allstate.ca
Website .... www.allstate.ca

Employer Background: Allstate Insurance Company of Canada is a top-tier property and casualty insurance provider, with a team of 1,400 specialists nationwide. *New Positions Created (2):* Neighbourhood Office Agent; Sales Positions.

ALLSTATE / PEMBRIDGE INSURANCE CLAIMS SERVICES
Att: Ron Van Raalten
4999 - 98th Avenue, Suite 108
Edmonton, AB T6B 2X3

Tel. 780-490-3082
Fax 780-461-7714
Email .... rvanraalten@allstate.ca
Website .... www.allstate.ca

Employer Background: Allstate / Pembridge Insurance Claims Services is a large, multinational insurance company. *New Positions Created (2):* Automobile Adjuster; Bodily Injury Adjuster.

ALLTEMP SENSORS INC.
Att: Human Resources Manager
9328 - 37th Avenue
Edmonton, AB T6E 5K3

Tel. 780-463-7035
Fax 780-469-6751
Email .... hr@alltempsensors.com

Employer Background: Alltemp Sensors Inc., a division of Wika Instruments Ltd., manufactures temperature sensors and distributes industrial instrumentation. *New Positions Created (8):* Inside Sales Representative; Production Planner; Progress Programmer; Project Supervisor; Quality Assurance Manager; CAD Specialist; Inside Sales Representative, Instrumentation; Production Planner / Expeditor.

ALMAC MACHINE WORKS LTD.
Att: Human Resources
9624 - 35th Avenue
Edmonton, AB T6E 5S3

Fax 780-437-3507
Email .... jobs@almacmachine.com
Website .... www.almacmachine.com

Employer Background: Almac Machine Works Ltd. provides services in machinery, steel fabrication, millwright, welding and rotating drum equipment while manufacturing truck, trailer and skid mounted vacuum tank systems and prototype and single purpose production machinery. *New Positions Created (8):* CNC Lathe Operators; Field Service Job Coordinator; Field Superintendent; Journeyman Welders; Millwright Shop Foreman; Parts Sales / Service Representatives; Various Trades Positions; Welding Inspector.

ALMAG ALUMINUM INC.
Att: Human Resources Manager
22 Finley Road
Brampton, ON L6T 1A9

Tel. 905-457-9000
Website .... www.almag.com

Employer Background: Almag Aluminum Inc. is an aluminum extruder. *New Positions Created (3):* Maintenance Technician; Material Handler; Production Worker.

ALNAV PLATINUM GROUP INC.
Att: Human Resources
PO Box 639
Edmonton, AB T5J 2L3
Fax 780-451-2403
Email .... annette.smart@awwfw.com
Website .... www.alnavplatinum.com
Employer Background: ALNAV Platinum Group Inc. is the administrative head office of North American Van Lines and Allied Van Lines. *New Positions Created (6):* General Manager; Claims Manager; Help Desk Analysts; MS Access / VB Developers; Technology Manager; Web Developers.

ALPHA TECHNOLOGIES LTD.
Att: Human Resources Manager
4084 McConnell Court
Burnaby, BC V5A 3N7
Tel. 604-430-1476
Fax 604-430-8908
Email .... careers@alpha.ca
Website .... www.alpha.com
Employer Background: Alpha Technologies Ltd. is a manufacturer of uninterruptable power supplies and power conversion equipment used in cable television, computer and telephone applications. *New Positions Created (17):* Buyer; Corporate Quality Assurance Manager; Materials Manager; Production Supervisor, PCB Shop; Buyer; Director of Sales (Canada); Electronic Manufacturing and Test Engineers; Electronic Technologists; Manager, Human Resources; Marketing Specialist; Power Electronics Design Engineers, Intermediate Level; Product Assurance Engineer; Production Supervisor; Quality Assurance Inspector; Quality Assurance Lead Auditor; Senior Power Electronics Design Engineer; Stores Supervisor.

ALPHAGRAPHICS
Att: Human Resources Manager
128 Queen Street South, PO Box 42266
Mississauga, ON L5M 4Z0
Website .... www.alphagraphics.com
Employer Background: Alphagraphics provides communication services, including web design, custom presentation material and multicolor offset and digital print. *New Positions Created (4):* Customer Service Representatives; Press Position; Production Scheduler; Sales Executive.

ALPNET CANADA
Att: Human Resources Manager
1801 McGill College Avenue, Suite 1450
Montréal, QC H3A 2N4
Tel. 514-844-2577
Fax 514-844-8512
Email .... personnel@ca.alpnet.com
Website .... www.alpnet.com
Employer Background: Alpnet is a supplier of multilingual information management services, with over 650 employees in 15 countries worldwide. *New Positions Created (2):* Senior Project Managers; Specialized Translators.

ALTAGAS SERVICES INC.
Att: Human Resources Department
355 - 4th Avenue SW, Suite 1700
Calgary, AB T2P 0J1
Tel. 403-691-7575
Fax 403-508-7256
Email .... careers@altagas.ca
Website .... www.altagas.ca
Employer Background: AltaGas Services Inc. provides a full range of services needed to move gas from wellhead to market. *New Positions Created (30):* Gas Plant Operator; Production and Revenue Accountant; Surface Land Administrator; Operations Analyst; Accounts Payable Team Leader; Capital Asset Accountant; Financial Accountant, Reporting; Help Desk Analyst; Junior Project Engineer; Supervisor, General Accounting; Enerstream Specialist; Financial Analyst; Production and Revenue Accountants; Treasury Analyst; Gas Controller; Administrative Assistant; Production / Revenue Accountant; Coordinator, Project / Maintenance Engineer; Facilities Engineer / Technologist; Administrative Assistant; Gas Control and Marketing Accountant; Credit Analyst; Systems Analyst, IT; Integration Analyst; Project / Maintenance Engineering Coordinator; Accounts Receivable Clerk; Facilities Engineer; Financial and Tax Accountant; Manager, Business Analysis; Production / Revenue Accountant.

ALTERA CORP.
Att: Human Resources Manager
151 Bloor Street West
Toronto, ON M5S 1S4
Tel. 416-596-5030
Fax 406-926-7488
Email .... results@altera.com
Website .... www.altera.com
Employer Background: Founded in 1983, Altera Corp. supplies programmable logic devices and associated logic development software tools. *New Positions Created (5):* Systems Administrator; Accounting Assistant; Administrative Assistant; Software Engineer, Senior; Office Manager.

ALTERA CORP.
Att: Staffing Coordinator
35 Stafford Road, Unit 1
Nepean, ON K2H 8V8
Tel. 613-596-5030
Fax 613-596-5163
Email .... otc_staffing@altera.com
Website .... www.altera.com
Employer Background: Founded in 1983, Altera Corp. supplies programmable logic devices and associated logic development software tools. The company's Ottawa office specializes in SOPC and optical networking. *New Positions Created (2):* Applications Engineer; Engineering Manger.

ALTERNA TECHNOLOGIES GROUP INC.
Att: Human Resources Director
5970 Centre Street SE, Suite 200
Calgary, AB T2H 0C1
Tel. 403-253-5531
Fax 403-253-5580
Email .... opportunities@alterna.com
Website .... www.alterna.com
Employer Background: Alterna Technologies Group Inc. is a financial technology company, providing advanced solutions for in-house banking, liquidity, cash and treasury management. *New Positions Created (26):* Customer Support Specialist; Implementation Project Manager; Implementation Specialist; Problem Resolution and Change Coordinator; Sales Administration Manager; Software Testing Specialist; Customer Support Specialist; Human Resources Specialist; Implementation Specialist; Senior Accountant; Implementation Project Manager; Marketing Coordinator; Oracle Database Administrator; Performance Specialist; Practices Project Manager; Pre-Sales Support Representative; Product Delivery Manager; Product Manager; Sales Logistics Specialist; Sales Representative; Senior Java Designer / Developer; Senior Product Manager; Senior Technology Specialist; Technical Support Specialist; Vice-President, Marketing; Senior Secretary.

ALTRUCK INTERNATIONAL TRUCK CENTRES
Att: John Van Goethem
2 Arrowsmith Road
Hamilton, ON L8E 4H8
Fax 905-578-7436
Website .... www.altruck.com
Employer Background: Altruck International Truck Centres is a Navistar dealership. *New Positions Created (4):* Service Foreperson and Technicians; Parts Counter Person; Various Transport Positions; Various Transport Positions (2).

ALUDRA INC.
Att: Human Resources Manager
1 Woodborough Avenue
Toronto, ON M6M 5A1
Tel. 416-658-0034
Fax 416-658-0335
Email .... mikec@aludra.com
Website .... www.aludra.com
Employer Background: Aludra Inc. provides digital media and communication solutions for retail and e-business markets. *New Positions Created (6):* New Media Account Executives; Public Relations Specialist; Graphic Designer; Public Relations Manager; Director, Point of Sale; Web Developer.

ALUMABRITE ANODIZING LTD.
Att: Anne Marie Fontainha, Corporate Human Resources Manager
20 Milburn Road
Hamilton, ON L8E 3L9
Tel. 905-561-7773
Fax 905-561-7774
Email .... annemarie.fontainha@kromet.com
Website .... www.kromet.com
Employer Background: Alumabrite Anodizing Ltd. is a major manufacturer of appliance parts. *New Positions Created (3):* Plant Manager; Quality Assurance Technician; Manufacturing Engineer.

AMACO CONSTRUCTION EQUIPMENT
Att: Jim MacDonald
5804 Datsun Road
Mississauga, ON L4W 1H2

Tel. 905-670-3440
Fax 905-670-3446
Employer Background: Amaco Construction Equipment provides construction equipment to the municipal, aggregate and road building sectors. *New Positions Created (2):* Executive Assistant; Territory Sales Manager.

AMAN BUILDING CORP.
Att: Human Resources Manager
41 Broadway Boulevard, Suite 20
Sherwood Park, AB T8H 2C1

Fax 780-467-3513
Email .... amanbldg@telusplanet.net
Employer Background: Aman Building Corp. is a construction company active in the commercial, institutional and industrial sectors. *New Positions Created (2):* Superintendent; Human Resources Manager.

AMC GROUP OF COMPANIES
Att: Human Resources Manager
1414 - 8th Street SW
Suite 530, Mount Royal Place
Calgary, AB T2R 1J6

Tel. 403-244-0468
Fax 403-244-0442
Email .... resumes@albertamining.com
Website ...... www.albertamining.com
Employer Background: The AMC Group of Companies is involved in real estate, manufacturing, financial services and venture capital investing. *New Positions Created (2):* Manager / Supervisor, Marketing Research; Senior Accountant.

AMC TECHNOLOGIES CORP.
Att: Human Resources
8625 - 112th Street, Suite 201
Edmonton, AB T6G 1K8

Email .... jobs@amctechcorp.com
Website .... www.amctechcorp.com
Employer Background: AMC Technologies Corp. uses design tools to develop innovative new electronic products and technologies for the networked industrial controls market. *New Positions Created (4):* Electronic and Computer Technologists; Firmware and Software Design Engineers; Hardware Design Engineers; Sales / Field Applications Engineer.

AMCAN CASTINGS LTD.
Att: Scott Armstrong,
Human Resources Manager
PO Box 446, LCD 1
Hamilton, ON L8L 7X3

Tel. 905-527-9178
Fax 905-681-3372
Email ... humanresources@amcancastings.com
Website .... www.amcancastings.com
Employer Background: Amcan Castings Ltd. is an aluminum die-casting facility and tier-1 supplier to the automotive industry. *New Positions Created (6):* Millwright; Produc-

tion Coordinator; Quality Control Technician; Process Technologist; Tooling Coordinator; Plant Electrician.

AMEC
Att: Human Resources Department
111 Dunsmuir Street, Suite 400
Vancouver, BC V6B 5W3

Tel. 604-664-4300
Fax 604-664-4804
Email .... careers.hr.van@amec.com
Website .... www.amec.com
Employer Background: AMEC is an international provider of services and engineering solutions to the world's infrastructure, manufacturing and process industries. *New Positions Created (11):* Junior / Intermediate Electrical Instrumentation and Control System Designers; Mechanical and Electrical Engineers; Project Service Positions; Senior Mechanical Engineers; Intermediate Port Engineers; Intermediate Project Controls Position; Intermediate / Senior Estimator; Junior / Intermediate Piping and Mechanical Designers; Mechanical Engineers; Process Engineers; Senior Port Engineers.

AMEC E&C SERVICES
Att: Human Resources Manager
PO Box 9600
St. John's, NF A1A 3C1

Email .... careers.na@amec.com
Website .... www.amec.com
Employer Background: AMEC E&C Services is a division of AMEC, an international provider of services and engineering solutions to the world's infrastructure, manufacturing and process industries. *New Positions Created (8):* Construction Engineers; Cost & Planning Engineers; Instrumentation Engineers; Mechanical Engineers; Piping Designers; Piping Engineer; Process Engineers; Telecommunication Engineers.

AMEC EARTH & ENVIRONMENTAL LTD.
Att: Human Resources Manager
4810 - 93rd Street
Edmonton, AB T6E 5M4

Tel. 780-436-2152
Fax 780-435-8425
Email .... recruiting.aee@agra.com
Website .... www.amec.com
Employer Background: AMEC Earth & Environmental Ltd. (formerly AGRA Earth & Environmental) provides engineering, construction, environmental and systems technology services. *New Positions Created (2):* Senior Accountant; Geotechnical Engineering Technologist.

AMEC EARTH & ENVIRONMENTAL LTD.
Att: Human Resources
801 - 6th Avenue SW
Suite 900, Monenco Place
Calgary, AB T2P 3W3

Tel. 403-298-4170
Email .... careers.ee.cgy@amec.com
Website .... www.amec.com

Employer Background: AMEC Earth & Environmental Ltd. (formerly AGRA Earth & Environmental) provides engineering, construction, environmental and systems technology services. *New Positions Created (28):* GIS Specialist; Intermediate Environmental Engineer / Scientist; Intermediate Environmental Engineer / Scientist; Intermediate Geological / Environmental Engineer; Intermediate Geotechnical Engineer; Intermediate / Senior Geotechnical Engineer; Junior / Intermediate AutoCADD Engineer; Junior / Intermediate Fisheries Biologist; Junior / Intermediate Geotechnical Engineering Technologist; Junior / Intermediate Materials Technicians; Lab / Field Technician; Occupational Hygiene Specialist; Occupational Hygiene Technologists; Office Manager / Supervisor; Senior Environmental Consultants; Senior Hydrogeologists; Senior Occupational Hygiene Specialist; Technical Services Coordinator; Controls Engineer; Electrical Engineer; Payroll Manager; Senior Payroll Systems Analyst; Occupational Hygiene Specialists; Senior Environmental Consultants; Engineering Positions; Engineers; Piping and Structural Designers / CAD Operators; Project Managers and Project Engineers.

AMEC INFRASTRUCTURE LTD.
Att: Ken Kozakewich
130 Sioux Road
Sherwood Park, AB T8A 3X5

Tel. 780-464-4553
Fax 780-464-4533
Email .... ken.kozakewich@amec.com
Website .... www.amec.com
Employer Background: AMEC Infrastructure Ltd. is a civil engineering company, providing services for transportation infrastructure projects in the public and private sectors. *New Positions Created (8):* Division Controller; Alberta Land Surveyor; Bridge Engineers and Technologists; Highway Planner; Junior / Intermediate Structural Engineers; Project Managers; Senior Municipal Engineers; Survey Party Crew Chiefs.

AMERICAN APPRAISAL CANADA, INC.
Att: Human Resources
310 Front Street West, Suite 800
Toronto, ON M5V 3B5

Tel. 416-593-4050
Fax 416-593-5168
Email .. kcharles@american-appraisal.com
Website ..... www.american-appraisal.com
Employer Background: American Appraisal Canada, Inc. provides valuation and consulting services to Canada's public and private sectors. *New Positions Created (2):* Senior Industrial Machinery Appraiser; Senior Professional Support Assistant.

AMERICAN EXPRESS CANADA INC.
Att: Human Resources Department
101 McNabb Street
Markham, ON L3R 4H8

Tel. 905-474-8000
Fax 905-474-8004
Email .... crocemployment@aexp.com
Website .... www.americanexpress.ca

Employer Background: Amex Canada is a leading provider of financial and travel-related services. *New Positions Created (14):* On-Site Mgr; Operations Mgr; Print Production Mgr; Sales Mgrs; Team Leaders; Business Analysts; Change Control Administrator; Changeman Specialists; Help Desk Support Position; Production / Testing Support Consultants; Programmer Analysts; Project Leaders; Project Mgrs; Training Co-ordinator.

AMERICAN IRON & METAL COMPANY INC.
Att: Personnel Department
9100 Henri-Bourassa Boulevard East
Montréal, QC H1E 2S4

Tel. 514-494-2000
Fax 514-494-3008
Website .... www.scrapmetal.net
Employer Background: American Iron & Metal Company Inc. recovers and recycles scrap metal byproducts into valuable, reusable raw materials. *New Positions Created (2):* Chemist, Research & Development; Administrative Assistant.

AMICO - ISG
Att: Sales Manager
1080 Corporate Drive
Burlington, ON L7L 5R6

Fax 905-335-4793
Employer Background: Amico - ISG is a leading manufacturer of steel and fiberglass grating. *New Positions Created (3):* Inside Salesperson; Salesperson, Prairie Provinces; Production Planner.

AMITY GOODWILL INDUSTRIES
Att: Sarah-Jane Irvine, Human Resources
225 King William Street
Hamilton, ON L8R 1B1

Tel. 905-526-8481
Fax 905-526-8949
Email .... sirvine@amity.on.ca
Website .... www.amity.on.ca
Employer Background: Amity Goodwill is a non-profit, charitable organization, providing skills training, employment enhancement training programs, community employment services and jobs for people with disabilities or other vocational barriers. *New Positions Created (2):* Career Development Specialist; Worksite Trainer.

AMORE SWEETS CORPORATION
Att: Human Resources
17 Vickers Road
Toronto, ON M9B 1C1

Tel. 416-233-0040
Fax 416-233-9270
Employer Background: Amore Sweets Corporation is a food processing company. *New Positions Created (2):* Credit Officer; Customer Service Representative.

AMPLIFIED LIGHT TECHNOLOGIES CORP. / ALTCO
Att: Human Resources Manager
1195 North Service Road, Unit B3-4
Oakville, ON L6M 2W2

Tel. 905-465-3786
Fax 905-465-3992
Email ...... dbowman@amplifiedlight.com
Employer Background: ALTCO specializes in indoor and outdoor advertising, including a non-traditional form of advertising using laser technology. *New Positions Created (3):* Outside Sales Representatives; Bookkeeper / Administrative Assistant; Inside & Outside Sales Representatives.

AMRAM'S DISTRIBUTING LTD.
Att: Human Resources
18 Parkside Drive
Brampton, ON L6T 5M1

Tel. 905-789-1880
Fax 905-789-1889
Employer Background: Amram's Distributing Ltd., a subsidiary of Russ Berrie & Co. Inc., is a leader in the giftware industry. *New Positions Created (5):* Sales Representative; Bilingual Inventory Correspondence Assistant; Import Clerk; Sales Representative; National Accounts Facilitator.

AMUSEMENT LEISURE WORLDWIDE
Att: Human Resources Manager
1006 - 11th Avenue SW, 2nd Floor
Calgary, AB T2R 0G3

Tel. 403-244-2202
Fax 403-245-6261
Website .... www.amusementleisure.com
Employer Background: Amusement Leisure Worldwide is an international designer and supplier of water theme parks. *New Positions Created (2):* Corporate Controller; Senior Project Manager.

ANADARKO CANADA CORPORATION
Att: Human Resources
425 - 1st Street SW
Suite 400, Box 2595, Station M
Calgary, AB T2P 4V4

Tel. 403-231-0111
Fax 403-231-0028
Email .... hrcanada@anadarko.com
Website .... www.anadarko.com
Employer Background: Anadarko Canada Corporation, a wholly-owned subsidiary of Anadarko Petroleum Corporation, is an exploration and production company focused on the western Canadian sedimentary basin. In Canada, the company employs 650 people. *New Positions Created (20):* Administrative Assistant; Completions & Workover Technician; Drilling and Completions Engineers; Engineering Technologists; Engineers; Exploitation / Reservoir Engineers; Exploration Geologists; Geological Technologist Positions (3); Geologists; Geophysicists; Geophysicists; Landman; Log Data Analyst; MacKenzie Delta Operations Manager; Petrophysicists; Production Engineers; Reservoir Engineering Specialist; Reservoir / Evaluations Engineer; Senior Structural Geologist; Structural Geophysicist.

ANALOG DESIGN AUTOMATION INC.
Att: Human Resources
233 Metcalfe
Ottawa, ON K2P 2C2

Tel. 613-239-3830
Fax 613-239-0104
Email .... jobs@analogsynthesis.com
Website .... www.analogsynthesis.com
Employer Background: ADA develops next-generation analog design systems and novel analog mixed-signal ICs. *New Positions Created (10):* Analog Design Engineer; Field Application Engineer; Senior Analog Design Engineer; Senior Software Designer; Senior Software Designer; Software Designer; Software Designer; Software Quality Manager; Software Verification Engineer; System Administrator.

ANCON INDUSTRIES INC.
Att: Human Resources Manager
842 Farewell Street
Oshawa, ON L1H 6N6

Tel. 905-435-5244
Fax 905-435-0598
Website .... www.ancon-ind.com
Employer Background: Ancon Industries Inc. manufactures custom metal stampings. *New Positions Created (3):* Project Engineer; Various Metals Positions; Production Manager and Production Supervisor.

ANDERSON EXPLORATION LTD. / AXL
Att: Kerri Grabowsky, Administrator, Exploration Department
324 - 8th Avenue SW, Suite 1600
Calgary, AB T2P 2Z5

Tel. 403-232-7100
Email .... hr@axl.ca
Website .... www.axl.ca
Employer Background: AXL is a senior Canadian oil and gas exploration and production company with operations throughout western Canada. *New Positions Created (2):* Seismic Data Mgr; Exploration Geologists.

ANDERSON WATER SYSTEMS LTD.
Att: Mr. D. Freeman
44 Head Street
Dundas, ON L9H 3H3

Tel. 905-627-9233
Fax 905-628-6623
Email .... dfreeman@awsl.com
Website .... www.awsl.com
Employer Background: Anderson Water Systems Ltd. manufactures water treatment systems for use in the power generation, pulp and paper, petrochemical and chemical industries. *New Positions Created (2):* Pipefitter; Industrial Electrician and Mechanic / Pipefitter (2).

ANDREW CANADA INC.
Att: Human Resources
606 Beech Street West
Whitby, ON L1N 5S2

Tel. 905-668-3348
Fax 905-668-8590
Email .... hrcanada@andrew.com
Website .... www.andrew.com
Employer Background: Andrew Canada Inc. is an international supplier of antenna and pedestal systems to the aerospace industry. *New Positions Created (4):* Mechanical En-

gineer; Range Technologist; Structural and Electrical Engineers; Structural / Electrical Technologists and Technicians.

ANDROCAN INC.
Att: Human Resources Manager
50 Bartor Road
Toronto, ON M5M 2G5

Tel. 416-745-3333
Fax 416-745-9884
Email .... androcan@relaymail.net

Employer Background: Androcan Inc. is a privately-held Toronto based holding company with a number of small business subsidiaries active in manufacturing and realty. *New Positions Created (2):* Vice-President, Finance; Vice-President Finance.

ANGLOCOM
Att: Human Resources Manager
343 Saint-Jean
Quebec City, QC G1R 1N8

Tel. 418-529-6928
Fax 418-529-2296
Email .... anglocom@anglocom.com
Website .... www.anglocom.com

Employer Background: Established in 1993, Anglocom is a leading team of English language translators and copywriters, serving ad agencies, government departments, private enterprises and other organizations. *New Positions Created (3):* Senior English Translator / Copywriter; Translator, French-to-English; Technical Translator.

ANGUS CONSULTING MANAGEMENT LTD. / ACML
Att: Grant Hayward
1125 Leslie Street
Toronto, ON M3C 2J6

Tel. 416-443-8300
Fax 416-443-8323
Email .... ghayward@angus-group.com
Website .... www.angus-group.com

Employer Background: ACML specializes in the engineering management, operation and maintenance of mechanical and electrical building systems. *New Positions Created (7):* Building Systems Operation & Maintenance Positions; 2nd-Class Stationary Engineer; Building Systems Operation & Maintenance Positions; 2nd-Class Stationary Engineer; Construction Project Mgrs; 2nd Class Stationary Engineer; Building Operations and Maintenance Position.

ANISHINAABE MINO-AYAAWIN INC.
Att: Search Committee
286 Smith Street, Suite 401
Winnipeg, MB R3C 1K4

Employer Background: AMA is a health organization, serving 7 First Nation communities in the Interlake region of Manitoba. *New Positions Created (3):* Epidemiologist; Chief Financial Officer; Epidemiologist.

ANKARI
Att: Human Resources Manager
3429 Hawthorne Road
Ottawa, ON K1G 4G2

Tel. 613-736-5100
Fax 613-736-1348
Email .... careers@ankari.com
Website .... www.ankari.com

Employer Background: Ankari (formerly American Biometric Company) specializes in data security, multifactor authentication software and hardware, and web and wireless devices. *New Positions Created (4):* Marketing Manager / Coordinator; Various Computing Positions; Various Engineering Positions; Various Sales Positions.

ANORMED INC.
Att: Human Resources
20353 - 64th Avenue, Suite 200
Langley, BC V2Y 1N5

Tel. 604-530-1057
Fax 604-530-0976
Email .... careers@anormed.com
Website .... www.anormed.com

Employer Background: AnorMED Inc. is a publicly-traded biopharmaceutical company dedicated to the discovery of small molecule metal complexes and metal binding drugs for the treatment of life-threatening diseases. *New Positions Created (19):* Accountant; Biochemist / Cell Biologist; Synthetic Organic Chemist; Toxicologist; Vice-President, Business Development; Executive Assistant, CEO / CFO; Manager, Information Technology; Network Assistant; Project Manager; Research Associate / Scientist, Analytical Chemistry; Senior Scientist, Analytical Chemistry; Contract Administrator; Synthetic Organic Chemist; Senior Scientist, Formulations; Research Associate, Process Development; Senior Scientist, Process Development; Business Development Analyst; Director of Investor Relations; Executive Assistant.

ANTARCTI.CA SYSTEMS INC.
Att: Human Resources Manager
1198 Homer Street
Vancouver, BC V6B 2X6

Tel. 604-873-6100
Fax 604-873-6188
Email .... jobs@antarcti.ca
Website .... www.antarcti.ca

Employer Background: Founded in 1999, Antarcti.ca Systems Inc. builds general-purpose network mapping and visualization platforms. *New Positions Created (2):* Integration / Deployment Specialist; Senior Software Developers.

ANTOMAX AUTOMOTIVE TECHNOLOGIES
Att: Human Resources
7405 Tranmere Drive
Mississauga, ON L5S 1L4

Fax 905-676-9468
Email .. dmcculloch@reainternational.com

Employer Background: Antomax Automotive Technologies supplies fluid handling systems to the automotive industry. *New Positions Created (8):* Project Engineer; Quality Assurance Manager; Quality Engineers (2); Industrial Engineers; Industrial Mechanics; Production Supervisors; Tool and Die Makers (10); Engineering Manager.

AON CORPORATION
Att: Joan Fitch,
Executive VP Western Region
900 Howe Street, 5th Floor
Vancouver, BC V6Z 2M4

Tel. 604-688-8591
Fax 604-684-9902
Email .. joan_fitch@aonconsulting.aon.ca
Website .... www.aon.com

Employer Background: Aon Corporation is a leader in insurance brokerage, risk management products and consulting, personal lines, warranties and human resources consulting. *New Positions Created (4):* Health and Benefits Analyst; Retirement Strategies Analysts; Health and Benefits Analyst; Pension Administrators.

APACHE CANADA LTD.
Att: Human Resources Manager
144 - 4th Avenue SW, Suite 2700
Calgary, AB T2P 3N4

Tel. 403-261-1200
Fax 403-298-1252
Website .... www.apachecorp.com

Employer Background: Apache Canada Ltd. is a wholly-owned subsidiary of Apache Corporation, an independent oil and gas exploration and production company. *New Positions Created (2):* Journeyman Instrument Mechanic; Lead Journeyman Instrument Mechanic.

API CONSTRUCTION LTD.
Att: Human Resources Manager
200 Pemberton Avenue
North Vancouver, BC V7P 2R5

Email .... api@uniserve.com

Employer Background: API Construction is a mid-sized residential construction company, specializing in quality homes and renovations. *New Positions Created (4):* Accounting Clerk; Construction Estimator; Construction Mgr; Construction Supervisor.

APLIN & MARTIN CONSULTANTS LTD.
Att: Personnel Manager
12448 - 82nd Avenue, Suite 201
Surrey, BC V3W 3E9

Tel. 604-597-9058
Fax 604-597-9061
Website .... www.aplinmartin.com

Employer Background: Aplin & Martin Consultants Ltd. offers a range of services to public, private and non-profit organizations, from urban and regional planning to civil engineering and landscape architecture. *New Positions Created (4):* Civil Design Engineer / Civil Design Technologist; Project Engineer (Municipal); Urban Planners; Civil Design Engineer.

APOLLO MICROWAVES LTD.
Att: Helen Bitsanis, HR Department
275 Hymus Boulevard
Pointe-Claire, QC H9R 1G6

Tel. 514-426-5959
Website .... www.apollomw.com

Employer Background: Apollo Microwaves Ltd. manufactures satellite communications components and subsystems. *New Positions Created (3):* Sales Account Executive; Accountant; Buyer.

APOTEX INC.
Att: Human Resources Manager
150 Signet Drive
Toronto, ON M9L 1T9

Tel. 416-749-9300
Fax 416-401-3828
Website .... www.apotex.com

Employer Background: Founded in 1974, Apotex Inc. is one of the largest Canadian-owned pharmaceutical companies, producing over 176 generic pharmaceuticals and employing over 3,100 people worldwide. The company has annual worldwide sales of $500 million. *New Positions Created (90):* Domestic Planner A; Medicinal / Organic Chemist, SA Level 4; Associate Consultant; Bioanalytical Chemist, SAS Level I; Building Systems Technician; Buyer, Packaging Components; Clinical Research Associate, Innovative Drug Development (IDD); Document Reviewer, QLS Level II; Electrical Instrumentation Technician; Group Leader, Packaging; Logistics Troubleshooter A; Maintenance Mechanic; Material Handler; Packaging Set-Up Operator; Process Engineer; Production Engineer; Production Technician, Level I; Project Leader, Process Design and Engineering; Regulatory Specialist; Sampler / Material Handler; Set-Up & Maintenance Mechanic, Packaging; Technical Specialist, Material Handling; Technician, Quality Laboratory Services (QLS); Validation Services Coordinator; Administrator, IDD Medicinal Chemistry and Preclinical; Document Reviewer, AR&D; Drug Information Associate; Manufacturing Team Coordinator; Project Leader, Validation Services; Recruiter; Administrator, Quality Assurance; Administrator, Research Planning and Support; Chemist III, International Development Laboratory; Coordinator, Help Desk, Technical Services; QLS Chemist, Level II; Administrator, QLS; Administrator, IDD QA; Production Engineer; Production Technician; Project Leader, Process Design and Engineering; Regulatory Specialist 1; Sampler, Material Handler; Sanitation Worker; Setup & Maintenance Mechanic, Packaging; Technical Specialist, Material Handling; Quality Laboratory Services (QLS); Validation Services Coordinator; Associate Consultant; Associate Pharmacokineticist; Bioanalytical Chemist, SA Level 1; Building Systems Technician; Chemist Level III, Analytical Research Laboratory; Chemist Level V, Analytical Research Laboratory; Clinical Research Associate, Innovative Drug Development; Coordinator, Sanitation / Facilities Help Desk; Electrical Instrumentation Technician; Facility Engineer; Group Leader, Packaging; Logistics Troubleshooter; Maintenance Mechanic; Material Handler; Packaging Setup Operator; Process Engineer; Document Reviewer Level II, QLS; Industrial Electronics Electrician; International Regulatory Affairs Specialist; Method Validation Supervisor ; Order Entry Clerk; Preclinical Screening Operator; Production

Engineer; Project Leader, Innovative Drug Development; Quality Laboratory Chemist, Level III; Quality Laboratory Services Chemist, Level I; Regulatory Affairs Project Leader; Sampler and Material Handler; Technician; Validation Service Coordinator; Administrator, Professional Affairs; Administrator, Quality Laboratory Services (QLS); Associate Consultant; Associate, Project Planning, Innovative Drug Development; Bilingual Marketing Assistant; Building Systems Technician; Chemist Level III; Chemist Level V; Clinical Lab Assistant; Packaging Operator; Set-Up & Maintenance Mechanic, Packaging; Co-ordinator, Process Development; Project Leader, International Regulatory Affairs.

APPAREO SOFTWARE INC.
Att: Human Resources Manager
8988 Fraserton Court, Suite 107
Burnaby, BC V5J 5H8

Tel. 604-439-7355
Fax 604-439-7199
Email .... hr@appareo.com
Website .... www.appareo.com

Employer Background: Appareo Software Inc. is a knowledge management company, with over 90 employees and 4 offices in North America. *New Positions Created (7):* C++ / Java Developers; Data Modelers; Graphic Artist; Lotus Notes Developer CLP; Quality Assurance Manager; User Interface Specialist; Web Designer.

APPENDIX TECHNICAL PUBLISHING GROUP
Att: Human Resources Manager
75 Albert Street, Suite 205
Ottawa, ON K1P 5E7

Tel. 613-234-4849
Fax 613-234-2631
Email .... hr@appendix.ca
Website .... www.appendix.ca

Employer Background: Established in 1989, Appendix Technical Publishing Group is one of Canada's largest independent, full-service technical publications companies, specializing in publications management and production of technical documentation for the aerospace, defence, heavy equipment, manufacturing and high technology industries. *New Positions Created (6):* Human Resources Manager; Desktop Publishers / Technical Illustrators; Quality Assurance Manager; SGML Analysts; Technical Translators; Technical Writers.

APPLANIX CORP.
Att: Human Resources Manager
85 Leek Crescent
Richmond Hill, ON L4B 3B3

Tel. 905-709-4600
Fax 905-709-6027
Email .... hr@applanix.com
Website .... www.applanix.com

Employer Background: Applanix Corp. is a high-tech engineering company that designs, develops and manufactures position orientation systems (POS) for use in the mapping and surveying industry. *New Po-*

sitions Created (9): Customer Support Delegate; Electronics Technician; Hardware Engineer; Navigation Analyst; Project Engineer; Technical Writer; Document Control Administrator; Receptionist; Production Manager.

APPLE AUTO GLASS
Att: Vice-President, Human Resources
4710 Kingsway, 27th Floor
Burnaby, BC V5H 4M2

Fax 604-431-2293
Email .... hr@tcgi.com
Website .... www.tcgi.com

Employer Background: Apple Auto Glass is Canada's largest franchised automotive glass replacement company, with 120 locations across Canada. *New Positions Created (3):* Sales and Marketing Position; Chief Financial Officer; Vice-President, Marketing.

APPLEBY COLLEGE
Att: Guy McLean, Headmaster
540 Lakeshore Road West
Oakville, ON L6K 3P1

Tel. 905-845-4681
Fax 905-845-9301
Email .... info@appleby.on.ca
Website .... www.appleby.on.ca

Employer Background: Founded in 1911, Appleby College is an independent school for 580 young men and women in grades 7 to OAC. *New Positions Created (2):* Head, English Department; Teachers (2).

APW ENCLOSURE SYSTEMS
Att: Tanya Cranford
855 Steeles Avenue East
Milton, ON L9T 5H3

Fax 905-693-8245
Email .... tcranford@apwmilton.com
Website www.apw1.com

Employer Background: APW Enclosure Systems is a global manufacturing company, providing solutions for electronic OEMs, including electronic chassis and enclosures. *New Positions Created (4):* Cost Analyst; Finance Clerk; Junior Supply Chain Clerk; Industrial Electrician.

ARAMARK CANADA LTD.
Att: Human Resources Manager
811 Islington Ave., PO Box 950, Station U
Toronto, ON M8Z 5Y7

Tel. 416-255-1331
Fax 416-255-7640
Website .... www.aramark.ca

Employer Background: Aramark Canada Ltd. is a contract service management company, providing food, catering, cleaning, office management and vending services to over 10,000 Canadian clients. *New Positions Created (32):* Business Analyst, Refreshment Services; Director of Marketing; Director, Support Services; District Supervisor; Food Service Manager; Manager, Food & Nutrition; Marketing Program Trainer; Office Services Manager; Store Managers (2); Assistant Food Services Director; Catering Manager; Food Service Director; Manager,

Support Services; Marketing Manager; Senior Internal Auditor; Special Projects Manager; Supervisor, Housekeeping and Laundry Services; Division Manager, Refreshment Services; Various Hospitality Positions; Financial Systems Manager; Director, Mail Services; Manager, Mail Services; Team Leader, Mail Services; Senior Graphic Designer; Manager, Purchasing Systems; District Supervisor; Internal Audit Manager; Site Supervisor, Office Services; Business-to-Business Systems Analyst; Material Management Team Leader; Internal Audit Manager; Internal Audit Manager.

ARBOR MEMORIAL SERVICES INC.
Att: Human Resources
2 Jane Street
Toronto, ON M6S 4W8

Tel. 416-763-4531
Fax 416-763-8714
Email .... hrdept@arbormemorial.com
Website .... www.arbormemorial.com

Employer Background: Arbor Memorial Services Inc. owns cemetery properties, funeral homes and crematoria across Canada. *New Positions Created (5):* Human Resources Generalist; Payroll Clerk; Marketing Clerk; Payroll Administrator; Administrative Assistant.

ARC'TERYX EQUIPMENT INC.
Att: Jeremy Guard
4250 Manor Street
Burnaby, BC V5G 1B2

Tel. 604-451-7755
Fax 604-451-7705
Email .... bird@arcteryx.com
Website .... www.arcteryx.com

Employer Background: Arc'teryx Equipment Inc. is an outdoor recreational equipment manufacturer with 300 employees. *New Positions Created (3):* VP Sales & Marketing; Outerwear Designer; Controller.

ARCHITECTURAL INSTITUTE OF BRITISH COLUMBIA / AIBC
Att: Dorothy D. Barkley, Executive Director
440 Cambie Street, Suite 100
Vancouver, BC V6B 2N5

Tel. 604-683-8588
Fax 604-683-8568
Email .... dbarkley@aibc.bc.ca
Website .... www.aibc.bc.ca

Employer Background: Founded in 1914, AIBC is the self-disciplinary body for registered architects in British Columbia. *New Positions Created (2):* Communications Generalist; Director of Communications.

ARCHITRAVE DESIGN OFFICE SERVICES
Att: Pamela Aitken
RR 1, Site 17, C-51
Gabriola Island, BC V0R 1X0

Tel. 250-247-8796
Fax 250-247-8764
Email .... parchitrave@home.com
Website .... www.architrave.ca

Employer Background: Architrave Design Office Services is a design firm, specializing in site planning, building design and production of technical drawings. *New Positions Created (4):* Engineers; Office Personnel; Various Bilingual Positions; Various Design Positions.

ARCIS CORPORATION
Att: Human Resources
404 - 6th Avenue SW, Suite 300
Calgary, AB T2P 0R9

Tel. 403-781-1700
Fax 403-269-1966
Email .... hr@arciscorp.com
Website .... www.arciscorp.com

Employer Background: Arcis Corporation is an integrated geophysical service company. *New Positions Created (7):* Director, Sales and Marketing; First Nations / Surface Land Liason; Mgr, Seismic Data Library; Professional Receptionist; Seismic Acquisitions Sales Rep; Intermediate Seismic Data Processors; Intermediate / Senior Technician.

ARGUS TECHNOLOGIES LTD.
Att: Technical Sales Manager
5700 Sidley Street
Burnaby, BC V5J 5E5

Tel. 604-436-8628
Fax 604-638-4070
Email .... sales@argus.ca
Website .... www.argus.ca

Employer Background: Argus Technologies Ltd. provides telecom power systems to wireline and wireless telecom service providers. *New Positions Created (3):* Applications Engineers - Major Projects; Human Resources Manager; Manager, Information Technology.

ARI FINANCIAL SERVICES INC.
Att: Mary Adams, HR Manager
1270 Central Parkway West, Suite 600
Mississauga, ON L5C 4P4

Tel. 905-803-8000
Fax 905-803-8644
Email .... madams@arifleet.ca
Website .... www.arifleet.ca

Employer Background: ARI Financial Services Inc. is a fleet management company. *New Positions Created (4):* Vehicle Maintenance Advisor; Client Service Representatives; Client Service Representative; Electronic Billing Specialist.

ARIUS RESEARCH INC.
Att: Human Resources
55 York Street, 16th Floor
Toronto, ON M5J 1R7

Fax 416-862-9696
Email .... hr@ariusresearch.com
Website .... www.ariusresearch.com

Employer Background: ARIUS Research Inc. is a biotechnology company, developing a unique class of drugs using monoclonal antibodies that will enable oncologists to treat specific tumours for individual cancer patients. *New Positions Created (4):* Research Assistant / Associate, Assay Development; Research Scientist, Assay Development; Senior Scientist / Research Scientist, Molecular Biology; Senior Scientist / Research Scientist, Process Development.

ARIUS3D INC.
Att: Human Resources Manager
4250 Sherwoodtowne Boulevard
Mississauga, ON L4Z 2G6

Tel. 905-270-7999
Fax 905-270-6888
Email .... resume@arius3d.com
Website www.arius3d.com

Employer Background: Arius3D Inc. creates 3D digital content. *New Positions Created (4):* Business Development Associates, Web Solutions; Web Designer; Web Developer; 3D Imaging Specialists (3).

ARK E-TAIL SERVICES INC.
Att: Human Resources Manager
5160 Yonge Street, Suite 300
Toronto, ON M2N 6L9

Tel. 416-640-7300
Fax 416-640-7373
Email .... jobs@arketail.com
Website .... www.arketail.com

Employer Background: ARK e-Tail Services Inc. provides electronic retail services and solutions to the automotive sector. *New Positions Created (6):* Contact Management Centre Supervisor; Outbound Telephone Sales Representatives; Contact Management Centre Supervisor; Outbound Telephone Sales / Service Advisors; Sales / Service Advisors; Telephone Sales Representatives.

ARMBRO CONSTRUCTION LTD.
Att: Human Resources Services
11 Indell Lane
Brampton, ON L6T 3Y3

Tel. 416-754-8735
Fax 416-754-8736
Email .... hr@armbro.ca
Website .... www.armbro.ca

Employer Background: Armbro Construction Ltd. is a division of Armbro Enterprises Inc., Canada's largest publicly-traded construction company. *New Positions Created (2):* Construction Superintendent; Dispatcher.

ARMBRO MATERIALS ENGINEERING CORPORATION / AME
Att: Human Resources Manager
15 Regan Road, Unit 3
Brampton, ON L7A 1E3

Tel. 905-840-5914
Fax 905-840-7859
Email .... materials@armbro.ca
Website .... www.armbro.ca

Employer Background: AME is a growing materials, geotechnical and pavement engineering firm. *New Positions Created (3):* Intermediate Geotechnical Engineer; Intermediate Materials Engineer; Process / Quality Control Technicians.

ARMTEC LTD.
Att: Jan McEwin, CHRP, Human Resources
15 Campbell Road
Guelph, ON N1H 6P2

Tel. 519-822-0210
Fax 519-822-1160
Email .... jmcewin@armtec.com
Website .... www.armtec.com
Employer Background: Armtec Ltd. engineers, manufactures and markets products used in municipal, highway, industrial, mining and water resource construction. *New Positions Created (2):* Design Engineer and Product Development Engineer; Customer Service Representative.

ARRISCRAFT INTERNATIONAL INC.
Att: Human Resource Manager
875 Speedsville Road, PO Box 3190
Cambridge, ON N3H 4S8
Tel. 519-653-3275
Fax 519-653-3275
Email .... solutions@arriscraft.com
Website .... www.arriscraft.com
Employer Background: Founded in 1949, Arriscraft International is a leading marble and stone manufacturer. *New Positions Created (3):* Architectural Technologist; Engineers; Project Management Specialists.

ARROW SPEED CONTROLS LTD.
Att: Engineering Manager
8410 Ontario Street, Suite 111
Vancouver, BC V5X 3E7
Tel. 604-321-4033
Fax 604-321-9415
Employer Background: Arrow Speed Controls Ltd. is a leading supplier of variable frequency drives, PLCs and systems across North America. *New Positions Created (3):* Field Service Technician; Applications Engineer; Field Service Technician.

ART GALLERY OF HAMILTON / AGH
Att: Executive Director
123 King Street West
Hamilton, ON L8P 4S8
Tel. 905-827-6610
Fax 905-577-6940
Website ... www.artgalleryofhamilton.com
Employer Background: AGH is Ontario's third-largest public art gallery, featuring a major collection of historical, modernist and contemporary art. *New Positions Created (2):* Senior Officer, Finance and Administration; Programming Assistant.

ART IN MOTION
Att: Human Resources
2000 Hartley Avenue
Coquitlam, BC V3K 6W5
Tel. 604-525-3900
Fax 604-525-6166
Email ...... recruitment@artinmotion.com
Website .... www.artinmotion.com
Employer Background: Art in Motion is an international publisher and manufacturer of fine art reproductions. *New Positions Created (4):* Director, Manufacturing; Corporate Sales Executive; HR Manager; Art Director.

ARTECH STUDIOS
Att: Human Resources

6 Hamilton Avenue North, Suite 250
Ottawa, ON K1Y 4R1
Tel. 613-728-4880
Email .... human_resources@artech.ca
Website .... www.artech.ca
Employer Background: Artech Studios is a leading developer of interactive entertainment software, with over 15 years experience. *New Positions Created (2):* 3D Animators and Artists; 3D Game Programmers.

ARTITALIA INC.
Att: Human Resources Manager
11755 Rodolphe-Forget
Montréal, QC H1E 7J8
Fax 514-643-4995
Email .... webmaster@artitalia.ca
Website .... www.artitalia.ca
Employer Background: Artitalia Inc. is a large metal and wood fabricating company. *New Positions Created (5):* Customer Service Clerk; Designing Technicians, Junior / Intermediate; Laser Programmers / Operators; Tig Welders / Grinders; Data Entry Clerk.

ARTS UMBRELLA
Att: Executive Assistant to the Director
1286 Cartwright Street, Granville Island
Vancouver, BC V6H 3R8
Tel. 604-681-5268
Fax 604-681-5285
Email ..... avanbuuren@artsumbrella.com
Website .... www.artsumbrella.com
Employer Background: Arts Umbrella is Canada's leading visual and performing arts institute for young people aged 2 to 9, offering over 230 classes to 30,000 children. *New Positions Created (2):* Director, Development; Proposal Writer / Fundraising Coordinator.

ARXX BUILDING PRODUCTS
Att: Human Resources Manager
840 Division Street
Cobourg, ON K9A 5V2
Fax 905-373-8301
Email .... resumes@arxxbuild.com
Website .... www.arxxbuild.com
Employer Background: Arxx Building Products is a $40 million North American supplier of insulated concrete forms for residential and commercial construction. *New Positions Created (4):* Merchandising Manager; Sales Representative; Marketing Manager; Technical Support Representative.

ASA ALLOYS
Att: Human Resources Manager
105 Claireport Crescent
Toronto, ON M9W 6P7
Tel. 416-213-0000
Fax 416-213-9606
Employer Background: ASA Alloys distributes stainless and specialty steels in the North American marketplace. *New Positions Created (4):* Aluminum Sales Specialist; Financial Accountant; Inside / Outside Sales Representatives; Inventory Control Specialist.

ASECO INTEGRATED SYSTEMS LTD.
Att: Human Resources Manager
635 Fourth Line, Unit 16
Oakville, ON L6L 5B3
Tel. 905-339-0059
Fax 905-339-3858
Email .... recruiting@aseco.net
Website .... www.aseco.net
Employer Background: Aseco Integrated Systems Ltd. provides consulting and systems integration services. *New Positions Created (2):* Controls Engineers; Programmer Analyst.

ASH CITY
Att: Human Resources Manager
2111 McCowan Road
Toronto, ON M1S 3Y6
Tel. 416-292-6612
Fax 416-292-9493
Email .... hr@ashcity.com
Website .... www.ashcity.com
Employer Background: Ash City manufactures in-stock, promotional and specialty active wear for the corporate and resort retail markets. *New Positions Created (23):* Assistant to the Design Department; Merchandising Coordinator; New Accounts Administrator; Controller; Designer; Merchandiser; Credit Analyst; Project Manager / Business Analyst; Sales Centre Manager; Logistics Manager; Advertising Catalogue Designer; Golfwear Designer; Junior Merchandising Assistant; Merchandising Manager; Outerwear Designer; Patternmaker, Outerwear and Knits; US Sales Support Customer Service Representative; Assistant Controller; US National Accounts Coordinator; Vice-President of Operations; Apparel Designers, Outerwear and Golfwear (2); Bilingual Customer Service Representative; Marketing Manager.

ASHCROFT HOMES
Att: Human Resources Manager
18 Antares Drive
Ottawa, ON K2E 1A9
Tel. 613-226-7266
Fax 613-226-7161
Website .... www.ashcrofthomes.com
Employer Background: Ashcroft Homes is a leading residential and commercial developer. *New Positions Created (3):* Architect / Project Manager; Architectural Draftsman; Director, Land Development.

ASHLAND CANADA CORP., DREW INDUSTRIAL DIVISION
Att: Brian Danyliw, Regional Manager
1720 - 106th Avenue
Edmonton, AB T6P 1X9
Fax 780-416-2822
Email .... dkirkwood@ashland.com
Website .... www.drewindustrial.com
Employer Background: Ashland Canada, Drew Industrial Division is a major supplier of specialty products and services for industrial water and wastewater treatment. *New Positions Created (2):* Technical Sales Rep, Industrial Water Treatment; Technical Sales Rep, Industrial Water Treatment.

ASHTON COLLEGE
Att: Hiring Committee
1190 Melville Street, Suite 400
Vancouver, BC V6E 3W1
Tel. 604-899-0803
Fax 604-899-0830
Website .... www.ashtoncollege.com
Employer Background: Ashton College provides private business and hospitality education. *New Positions Created (3):* Distance Learning Coordinator; Manager, Executive Education Programs; Manager, Full-Time Programs.

ASPEN REGIONAL HEALTH AUTHORITY NO. 11
Att: Mary Ellen Hoogers,
Human Resource Coordinator
10003 - 100th Street
Westlock, AB T7P 2E8
Tel. 780-349-8705
Fax 780-349-4879
Website .... www.aspenrha.ab.ca
Employer Background: Located in central Alberta, Aspen Regional Health serves 82,595 people in 47 communities. *New Positions Created (3):* Accounts Payable / General Ledger Supervisor; Facility Supervisor; Regional Area Manager, West.

ASSANTE ADVISORY SERVICES
Att: Human Resources Manager
800 Bay Street, Suite 700
Toronto, ON M5S 3A9
Fax 416-645-4394
Email .... recruitment@assante.com
Website .... www.assante.ca
Employer Background: Assante Advisory Services offers financial and life management products and services, with over 200 offices across North America. *New Positions Created (6):* Senior Regional Manager - Finance, Systems & Operations Support; Client Service Representatives; Information Technology System Administrator; Marketing Coordinator; Reconciliation (FAS) Administrators; Trust Accountant.

ASSINIBOINE COMMUNITY COLLEGE
Att: Human Resources Division
1430 Victoria Avenue East
Brandon, MB R7A 2A9
Tel. 204-726-6600
Fax 204-726-7013
Email . humanresources@assiniboinec.mb.ca
Website .... www.assiniboinec.mb.ca
Employer Background: Assiniboine Community College has more than 8,000 full-time, part-time and continuing education students. *New Positions Created (2):* Aboriginal Counsellor / Cultural Consultant; Culinary Arts Instructor.

ASSOCIATED ENGINEERING ALBERTA LTD.
Att: Human Resources
708 - 11th Avenue SW, Suite 200
Calgary, AB T2R 0E4
Tel. 403-262-4500
Fax 403-269-7640

Email .. williamsv@calgary.associated-eng.com
Website .... www.ae.ca
Employer Background: Associated Engineering Alberta Ltd. provides water, wastewater, municipal infrastructure and transportation services to clients in Alberta, BC and Saskatchewan. *New Positions Created (3):* Senior Infrastructure Project Manager; Senior Project Manager, Wastewater Treatment; Senior Project Manager, Water Supply and Treatment.

ASSOCIATED ENGINEERING INDUSTRIAL LTD.
Att: Donna Bonk
10909 Jasper Avenue
Suite 1000, Pacific Plaza
Edmonton, AB T5J 5B9
Fax 780-454-7693
Email .. admin@edmonton.associated-eng.com
Website .... www.associated-eng.com
Employer Background: Associated Engineering Industrial Ltd. is a consulting engineering organization. *New Positions Created (4):* Structural Engineers; Construction Managers; Engineers; Water and Wastewater Specialist.

ASSOCIATION OF CANADIAN TRAVEL AGENTS / ACTA
Att: President / CEO
130 Albert Street, Suite 1705
Ottawa, ON K1P 5G4
Tel. 613-237-3657
Fax 613-237-7052
Email .... rwilliams@acta.ca
Website .... www.acta.ca
Employer Background: Established in 1977, ACTA is a non-profit, national trade association, representing 5,000 retail travel agencies across Canada. *New Positions Created (2):* Administrative Assistant; Program Manager.

ASSOCIATION OF PROFESSIONAL ENGINEERS AND GEOSCIENTISTS OF BC
Att: Wayne Gibson, PEng,
Director, Communications
4010 Regent Street, Suite 200
Burnaby, BC V5C 6N2
Tel. 604-430-8035
Fax 604-430-8085
Website .... www.apeg.bc.ca
Employer Background: APEGBC is an organization responsible for licensing and regulating 18,000 professional engineers and geoscientists in the province. *New Positions Created (3):* Manager, Member and Public Affairs; Mgr, Professional Development; Mgr, Professional Development.

ASSOCIATION OF UNIVERSITIES AND COLLEGES OF CANADA / AUCC
Att: Human Resources Service
350 Albert Street, Suite 600
Ottawa, ON K1R 1B1
Tel. 613-563-1236
Fax 613-563-9745
Email .... careers@aucc.ca
Website .... www.aucc.ca

Employer Background: AUCC represents Canadian universities and degree-granting colleges at home and abroad. *New Positions Created (5):* Translator; Layout and Production Assistant; International Relations Officer; Director, Corporate Services; Director, Research and Policy Analysis.

ASSURE HEALTH MANAGEMENT INC.
Att: Human Resources
5090 Explorer Drive, Suite 1000
Mississauga, ON L4W 4X6
Tel. 905-602-7353
Fax 905-602-7355
Email .... laurie.manser@emergis.com
Website .... www.assureville.com
Employer Background: Assure Health Management Inc. designs and implements occupational health, safety, disease and disability management programs. *New Positions Created (4):* Occupational Health Nurses; Occupational Health Nurses; Occupational Health Nurse; Occupational Health Nurses.

ASTEC ADVANCED POWER SYSTEMS
Att: Human Resources Manager
2280 Alfred-Nobel Boulevard
St-Laurent, QC H4S 2A4
Tel. 514-832-6600
Fax 514-832-6695
Email .... careers@astecaps.com
Website .... www.astecaps.com
Employer Background: Astec Advanced Power Systems, a division of Emerson Electric Co., is a leading supplier of electronic power conversion products. *New Positions Created (11):* Electronic Technologist; Magnetic Designer; Micro-Packager; Power Supply Designer; Prototyper; Testing Team Leader; Designers; Engineer; Hardware Manager; Mechanical Engineer; Product Line Manager.

ASTOUND INC.
Att: Human Resources
304 The East Mall, Suite 800
Toronto, ON M9B 6E2
Tel. 416-207-0605
Fax 416-207-9744
Email .... humanr@astound.com
Website .... www.astound.com
Employer Background: Astound Inc. is a member of Genesys Conferencing, one of the world's leading independent conferencing companies, specializing in virtual group communications. *New Positions Created (4):* Corporate Sales Representative; Inside Sales Associate; Quality Assurance Analyst; Software Developers.

ASTRAZENECA
Att: Human Resources
1004 Middlegate Road
Mississauga, ON L4Y 1M4
Tel. 905-277-7111
Fax 905-275-2950
Email .. humanresources1@astrazeneca.com
Website .... www.astrazeneca.ca
Employer Background: AstraZeneca is a leading pharmaceutical company, with

50,000 employees worldwide. *New Positions Created (33):* Clinical Scientist, Cardiovascular Area; Research Liaison Officer, Medical Department; Administrative Assistant, Manufacturing; Bilingual Regional Sales Coordinator; Disbursements Administrator; Financial Analyst, Tax; Manager, Online Communications; Medical Information Associate; Proofreader; Senior Compensation Consultant; Administrative Assistant, Human Resources; Clinical Data Entry Coordinator; Financial Analyst, Manufacturing Operations; Program Coordinator; Research Monitor; Manager, Research Monitors; Facility Technician; Good Clinical Practices and Training Associate; Manager, Financial Planning; Manager, Therapeutic Area Public Relations; Research Documentation Coordinator; Security and Life Safety Supervisor; Senior Organizational Development Consultant; Supply Management Associate; Translator; Associate Clinical Project Manager; Bilingual Business Partner Coordinator; Clinical Operations Scientist, Gastrointestinal; Manager, Regulatory Affairs, Oncology; Manager, Research Documentation Coordinator; Medical Information Associate; Production Maintenance Coordinator; Sales Training and Development Associate.

ASTRAZENECA
Att: Human Resources
7171 Frederick-Banting
St-Laurent, QC H4S 1Z9
Tel. 514-832-3200
Fax 514-832-3232
Email .... montreal.hr@astrazeneca.com
Website .... www.astrazeneca.com
Employer Background: AstraZeneca is a leading pharmaceutical company, with 50,000 employees worldwide. AstraZeneca R&D Montreal specializes in pain discovery and g-protein coupled receptors. *New Positions Created (3):* Team Leader, Pharmacology, Analgesics; Team Leader, Pharmacology, Animal Behavioural Group; Research Assistant, Pharmacology.

AT&T CANADA
Att: Human Resources Manager
905 King Street West, 4th Floor
Toronto, ON M6K 3G9
Tel. 416-341-5705
Fax 416-341-5725
Email .... careers@attcanada.ca
Website .... www.attcanada.ca
Employer Background: AT&T Canada is Canada's largest voice, data and Internet telecommunications provider. *New Positions Created (19):* Applications Specialist / Analyst; Bilingual Business Customer Support Representative; Bilingual Business Technical Support Manager; Bilingual Customer Support Representative; Bilingual Technical Support Representative; Billing Systems Programmer; Collections Specialist; Core Engineer; Education Specialist; Marketing Channel Manager, Acquisition Focus; Marketing Communications Specialist; Network Administrator, Level I; Network Administrator, Level II; Payment Process Specialist;

Senior Product Manager, E-Business Services, CRM; Unix System Administrator; Web Developers; Bilingual Customer Support Representative; Bilingual Technical Support Representative.

AT&T CANADA
Att: Human Resources
200 Wellington Street West, Suite 820A
Toronto, ON M5V 3G2
Tel. 416-345-2000
Fax 416-345-2481
Email .... careers@attcanada.ca
Website .... www.attcanada.ca
Employer Background: AT&T Canada is Canada's largest voice, data and Internet telecommunications-provider. *New Positions Created (5):* Billing / Collection Analyst; Collectors; Invoice Verification Coordinators; Process Specialists; Senior Manager, Billing.

ATCO ELECTRIC
Att: Human Resources
10035 - 105 Street, PO Box 2426
Edmonton, AB T5J 2V6
Tel. 780-420-7038
Fax 780-420-3847
Email .... humanresources@atcoelectric.com
Website .... www.atcoelectric.com
Employer Background: ATCO Electric provides electricity to 166,000 residential, commercial, industrial and farm customers throughout northern and east-central Alberta. *New Positions Created (3):* Electrical Technologists; Telecom Engineer; Telecom or Electronics Technologist.

ATCO I-TEK
Att: Human Resources Manager
10035 - 105th Street
Edmonton, AB T5J 2V6
Tel. 780-420-7757
Fax 780-420-3737
Email .... careers@atcoitek.com
Website .... www.atcoitek.com
Employer Background: ACTO I-Tek, a division of Canadian Utilities Ltd., operates and supports information systems. *New Positions Created (9):* Senior Network Analyst; Technology Change Management Process Owner; Customer Relations Leader; Customer Representative; Senior Security Analyst; Workstation Support Technician; Field Support Technician; Infrastructure Project Leader; Customer Support Analyst.

ATCO NOISE MANAGEMENT LTD.
Att: Human Resources
1243 McKnight Boulevard NE
Calgary, AB T2E 5T1
Tel. 403-292-7804
Fax 403-292-7816
Email .... info@atconoise.com
Website .... www.atconoise.com
Employer Background: ATCO Noise Management Ltd. designs, supplies and constructs acoustic solutions for industrial customers. *New Positions Created (7):* Acoustical Engineer; Intermediate Structural Engineer; Human Resources Coordinator; Sen-

ior Acoustical Engineer; Chief Draftsperson; Lead Engineer, Structural; Manager, Engineering.

ATCO POWER
Att: Human Resources Manager
10040 - 104th Street
Edmonton, AB T5J 2V6
Fax 780-420-7594
Email .... atcopowerhr@atcopower.ca
Website .... www.atcopower.ca
Employer Background: ATCO Power develops, manages, owns and operates independent power projects in Canada, Great Britain and Australia. *New Positions Created (5):* Engineer-in-Training, Electrical Equipment and Systems; Engineer-in-Training, Instrumentation and Control; Engineer-in-Training, Mechanical; Mechanical Engineer; Senior Mechanical Engineer.

ATCO STRUCTURES INC.
Att: Human Resources
5115 Crowchild Trail SW
Calgary, AB T3E 1T9
Tel. 403-492-7660
Fax 403-292-7603
Website .... www.atcostructures.com
Employer Background: ATCO Structures Inc. manufactures, sells and leases workforce housing and related structures worldwide, from factories in Calgary, Budapest and Santiago, Chile. *New Positions Created (6):* Sales Representatives; Architectural Estimator; Electrical Designer / Estimator; Mechanical Designer / Estimator; Sales Representative; Manager, Corporate Accounting.

ATEN ADVANCE TECH INC.
Att: Human Resources Manager
13091 Vanier Place, Suite 180
Richmond, BC V6V 2J1
Tel. 604-207-0809
Fax 604-207-0812
Email .... helenc@aten-ca.com
Website .... www.aten-ca.com
Employer Background: Aten Advance Tech Inc. is a high-tech R&D company. *New Positions Created (4):* Firmware Design Engineers; Hardware Design Engineers; Hardware Technicians; Software Design Engineers.

ATHABASCA UNIVERSITY
Att: Coordinator, Employment Services
1 University Drive
Athabasca, AB T9S 3A3
Tel. 780-460-3476
Fax 780-675-6135
Email .... resume@athabascau.ca
Website .... www.athabascau.ca
Employer Background: Athabasca University is one of Canada's leading distance-education universities, with operational centres in Calgary and Edmonton serving 25,000 students. *New Positions Created (37):* Director, School of Business; Web and Intranet Coordinator; Canada Research Chair; E-Commerce System Analyst; Reference Services Librarian; NT / Unix Systems Adminis-

trator; Instructional Designer; Assistant / Associate Professor, Management Information Systems; Assistant / Associate Professors, E-Commerce; Institutional Research Analyst; Manager, Information Technology; Systems Analyst / Programmer, Computing Services; Systems Analyst / Programmer, Financial Services; Financial Budget Analyst; Instructional Webspace Designer; Associate Vice-President, Research; Director, Human Resources; University Secretary; Assistant Professor, Counselling Psychology / Applied Psychology; Assistant or Associate Professor, Criminal Justice / Corrections; Multimedia Instructional Design Editor; Coordinator, Academic Records and Examination Services; Coordinator, Registry Services; Assistant / Associate Professor, Communications; Assistant / Associate Professor, Computing and Information Systems; Assistant / Associate Professor, Nursing; Multimedia Instructional Designer; Director, Facilities and Services; Systems Analyst Programmer, Computing Services; Systems Analyst Programmer, Financial Services; Database Analyst; Educational Media Designer; Manager, Marketing and Communications; Course Coordinator, Computers and Management Information Systems; Assistant / Associate Professor, Economics or Finance; Corporate Relations Coordinator; System Analyst / Programmer Computing Services.

ATHLETIC IMAGE
Att: Human Resources Manager
9600 Meilleur Street
Montréal, QC H2N 2E3
Tel. 514-389-1402
Fax 514-389-8088
Employer Background: Athletic Image is a manufacturer and wholesaler of t-shirts and other apparel. *New Positions Created (4):* Accounts Payable Clerk; Data Entry Clerk; Production Clerk; Accounts Payable Clerk.

ATI TECHNOLOGIES INC.
Att: Human Resources Manager
33 Commerce Valley Drive East
Thornhill, ON L3T 7N6
Tel. 905-882-2600
Fax 905-882-2620
Email .... ati@rpc.webhire.com
Website .... www.ati.com
Employer Background: Founded in 1985, ATI Technologies Inc. designs, manufactures and markets multimedia solutions and graphics components for personal computers. *New Positions Created (89):* Director of Sales, Set-Top Box; Director of Software, Set-Top Box; 3D Engineer; BIOS Engineer; Customer Service Representative; Design Verification Engineer; Design-for-Test Engineer; Engineer; Engineer, 9x, 2D; Engineer, Graphics Applications; Financial Planning Manager; HUB Administrator; Inventory Analyst; Manager, Business Development; Manager, Product Qualifications; MPEG System Architect; Patent Law Clerk; PME Software Support Specialist, Mac Team; Product Manager; Product Manger, Desktop Marketing Group; Product Marketing Engi-

neer; Project Team Leader, Production System Support; Senior ASIC Design Engineers; Senior ASIC Designer; Senior Diagnostic Engineer; Senior Group Manager, Desktop Marketing Group; Senior Product Manager; Senior Software Test Engineer; Software Development Manager; Software Engineer; Software Engineer; Software Engineer / Junior Architect; Software Engineer, Mobile Software Group; System Software Architect; Test Engineer; Test Technician; Validation Technologist; ASIC Continuation Engineer; ASIC Test Engineer; Component Engineer; System / Board Designer; Corporate Counsel; Design Verification Engineer; Director, Marketing; Group Marketing Manager; HUB Administrator; Manager, Business Development; Manager, Telecommunications; PME Software Support Specialist; Product Specialist, Computer Operations; Program Manager; Senior ASIC Design Engineers; Senior I / O Designer; Senior Product Manager; Technical Relationship Manager, Game Developers; ASIC Hardware Engineer; Compliance Engineer; Engineer; Engineer, 9x 2D; Engineer, Graphics Applications; Graphics Board Design Engineers; Intermediate Software Engineer; Inventory Analyst; Manager, Multimedia Platforms; Project Team Leader, Graphics Applications; Project Team Leader, Production System Support; Senior Engineer, Physical Design; Senior Engineer, Process & Technology; Senior Interface IC Designer; Senior / Intermediate Board Design Engineer; Senior Memory IC Designer; Software Development Manager; Software Development Manager; Software Engineer; Software Engineer, Convergence Products Group; Software Engineer / Junior Architect; Technology / IP Modelling Engineer; Product Specialist, ASIC Operations; Team Leader, ASIC Operations; ASIC Qualification Engineer / Technician ; Associate Engineer, HW Test Engineering; Customer Service Representatives (10); Embedded DSP Software Engineer; Failure Analysis Engineer; Pricing Analyst; Program Manager; Senior Software Developer ; Senior Software Developer.

ATI TELECOM INTERNATIONAL CO.
Att: Barry Kropielnicki,
Project Staffing Coordinator
10088 - 102nd Avenue
Suite 803, Toronto Dominion Tower
Edmonton, AB T5Y 1C3
Tel. 780-424-9100
Fax 780-424-9777
Email .... bkropiel@altatelecom.com
Website .... www.ciena.com
Employer Background: ATI Telecom International Co. (a subsidiary of CIENA Corporation) provides turn-key services, installation and commissioning, maintenance support, project management and network engineering for the telecom industry. *New Positions Created (2):* Cellular Technicians; DMS 100-500 Technicians.

ATLANTIC HEALTH SCIENCES CORPORATION / AHSC
Att: Recruitment Officer

PO Box 5200
Saint John, NB E2L 4L2
Tel. 506-648-6964
Fax 506-648-6330
Email .... bamli@reg2.health.nb.ca
Website .... www.ahsc.health.nb.ca
Employer Background: AHSC (Health Region 2) operates 12 hospitals and health centres in communities between Sussex and St. Stephen, employing 4,300 people, including 333 physicians. *New Positions Created (3):* Clinical Coordinator; Drug Use Evaluation / Drug Information Pharmacist; Staff Pharmacists.

ATLANTIC PACKAGING PRODUCTS LTD.
Att: Recruiter, Human Resources
111 Progress Avenue
Toronto, ON M1P 2Y9
Tel. 416-298-8101
Fax 416-297-2264
Email .... recruiter@atlantic.ca
Employer Background: Atlantic Packaging Products Ltd. manufactures paper and plastic packaging and recycled paper products. *New Positions Created (4):* Corporate Health & Safety Coordinator; Employee Relations Consultant; Mechanical Technologist; Salesperson.

ATLANTIS SCIENTIFIC INC.
Att: Human Resources Department
20 Colonnade Road, Suite 110
Nepean, ON K2E 7M6
Tel. 613-727-1087
Fax 613-727-5853
Email .... hr@atlsci.com
Website .... www.atlsci.com
Employer Background: Founded in 1981, Atlantis Scientific Inc. provides products and services related to data acquisition, radar remote sensing, image analysis, advanced signal processing applications and interferometric SAR. *New Positions Created (6):* Customer Support and Training Specialist; Scientific Programmer; Administrative Assistant; Scientific Programmer; Business Development Manager; Scientific Programmers.

ATLANTIS SYSTEMS INTERNATIONAL
Att: Human Resources
1 Kenview Boulevard
Brampton, ON L6T 5E6
Tel. 905-792-1981
Fax 905-792-7251
Email .... positions@atlantissi.com
Website .... www.atlantissi.com
Employer Background: Atlantis Systems International is a leading developer of simulation and training devices, performance support software systems and avionics testing equipment. *New Positions Created (19):* Intermediate Electrical Designer; Intermediate Mechanical Designer; Production Planner; Production Technician; Shipper / Receiver; Simulation and Systems Designers; Software Developers; Director, Program Management; Quality Assurance Engineer; Intermediate Electrical Designer; Interme-

diate Mechanical Designer; Production Planner; Production Technician; Proposal Support Manager; Receptionist; Shipper / Receiver; Simulation and Systems Engineer; Simulation and Systems Developers; Software Developers.

ATLAS COLD STORAGE CANADA LTD.
Att. Randy Wagner, HR Manager
5255 Yonge Street, Suite 900
Toronto, ON M2N 5P8
Tel. 416-512-2352
Fax 416-512-2353
Email .... rwagner@atlascold.com
Website .... www.atlascold.com
Employer Background: Atlas Cold Storage Canada Ltd. is a North American temperature-controlled warehouser and distributor, serving the food industry. *New Positions Created (9):* Sales Manager, Ontario; Manager, Safety & Compliance; Senior Team Leader, IT Projects; Controller; Operations Manager; Refrigeration Operator, Class B; General Manager, Transportation; Financial Control Analyst; Refrigeration Operator, Class B.

ATLAS CORPORATION, THE
Att: Human Resources Manager
111 Ortona Court
Concord, ON L4K 3M3
Tel. 905-669-6825
Fax 905-669-4904
Website .... www.atlascorp.com
Employer Background: Founded in the early 1940s, the Atlas Corporation is a general contractor for industrial, commercial, institutional and residential projects. *New Positions Created (7):* Construction Superintendent; Project Manager; Senior Estimator; Junior Estimator / Project Manager; Senior Estimator; Construction Superintendent; Project Manager.

ATLAS VAN LINES (CANADA) LTD.
Att: Human Resources Manager
PO Box 970
Oakville, ON L6J 5M7
Website .... www.atlasvanlines.ca
Employer Background: Atlas Van Lines Canada is a relocation company headquartered in Oakville. *New Positions Created (4):* Credit and Collections Coordinator; Freight Rate Auditor; Operations and Customer Service Clerk; Senior RPG Programmer / Analyst.

ATOMIC ENERGY OF CANADA LTD.
Att: Human Resources
2251 Speakman Drive
Mississauga, ON L5K 1B2
Tel. 905-823-9040
Fax 905-823-9182
Email .... recruit@aecl.ca
Website .... www.aecl.ca
Employer Background: Founded in 1952, AECL sells CANDU nuclear power reactors, MAPLE research reactors and the MACSTOR spent fuel storage system. AECL is owned by the Government of Canada.

New Positions Created (6): Manager, Communications and Community Relations; Manager, Contracting & Project Support; Environmental Assessment / Regulatory Specialist; IT / Communications Specialist; Project Specialists (2); Technical Specialist.

ATREUS SYSTEMS
Att: Human Resources Manager
99 Bank Street, Suite 1201
Ottawa, ON K1P 6B9
Tel. 613-569-8855
Fax 613-569-9397
Email .... hr@atreus-systems.com
Website .... www.atreus-systems.com
Employer Background: Established in 1999, Atreus Systems is a software technology company, developing intelligent broadband service creation and delivery platforms for service providers and carriers. *New Positions Created (3):* Human Experience Architect; Manager, Product Engineering; Senior Software Designers.

ATS AUTOMATION TOOLING SYSTEMS INC.
Att: Human Resources
250 Royal Oak Road
PO Box 32100, Preston Centre
Cambridge, ON N3H 5M2
Tel. 519-653-6500
Fax 519-653-6533
Email .... hr@atsautomation.com
Website .... www.atsautomation.com
Employer Background: ATS Automation Tooling Systems Inc. is a leading designer of automation solutions, with 27 manufacturing and customer support facilities worldwide. *New Positions Created (12):* Mold Designer; Financial Analyst, Reporting; Fluid Power Designer; Manager of Business Development; Motion Control Designer (Hardware); Control Systems Developers; Electrical Designers; PLC Programmers; Senior Mechanical Designers; Systems Integrators; Machine Builder; Senior Mechanical Designer.

ATS TEST SYSTEMS INC.
Att: Human Resources Manager
600 Chrislea Road
Woodbridge, ON L4L 8K9
Tel. 905-850-8600
Fax 905-850-9336
Email . careers.testsystems@atsautomation.com
Website .... www.atstest.com
Employer Background: ATS Test Systems Inc., a division of Automation Tooling Systems Inc., is a leading developer and manufacturer of comprehensive systems for component testing. *New Positions Created (14):* Intermediate Software Developer; Junior and Intermediate Mechanical Designers; Test Systems Technician; Wire Person; Molded Urethane Technician; Wire Person; Test Systems Technician; Electrical Designer; Applications Engineer; Junior and Intermediate Software Developers; Manager, Mechanical Design; Project Manager; Technical Writer / Project Scheduler; Test Systems Technician.

ATTAWAPISKAT FIRST NATION EDUCATION AUTHORITY
Att: Steve Suite, Associate Director
PO Box 15
Attawapiskat, ON P0L 1A0
Tel. 705-997-2114
Fax 705-997-2357
Employer Background: The Attawapiskat First Nation Education Authority serves a community of 1,700 people on the west coast of James Bay. *New Positions Created (2):* Teachers; Principal.

AU PRINTEMPS GOURMET
Att: Lucie Carbonneau
PO Box 388
Prevost, QC J0R 1T0
Tel. 450-224-8221
Fax 450-224-7943
Email .... lucie@printempsgourmet.com
Website ...... www.printempsgourmet.com
Employer Background: Founded in 1978, Au Printemps Gourmet is a specialty food manufacturer, with over 200 employees. *New Positions Created (3):* Plant Manager; Sales Representative; Human Resources Manager.

AUCXIS CORP.
Att: Human Resources Manager
220 King Street West, Suite 200
Toronto, ON M5H 1K4
Tel. 416-214-1587
Fax 416-585-9609
Email .... careers@aucxis.com
Website .... www.aucxis.com
Employer Background: Aucxis Corp. provides real-time trading technologies to e-markets. *New Positions Created (3):* Consultants; Project Mgr; Senior Java Developers.

AUDIO CENTRE
Att: John Mossop
1366 Clyde Avenue
Ottawa, ON K2C 3Z4
Tel. 613-723-2923
Fax 613-228-1787
Email .... sales@audiocentre.com
Website .... www.audiocentre.com
Employer Background: Audio Centre is a leader in high-end, low-voltage, audio, video and home theatre installations. *New Positions Created (4):* Installers; Programmers; Sales Consultants; Service Technician.

AUDIO CENTRE
Att: Sylvain Dufour
9100 Cavendish Boulevard
St-Laurent, QC H4T 1Z8
Tel. 514-731-2772
Fax 514-731-9440
Website .... www.audiocentre.com
Employer Background: Audio Centre is a leader in high-end, low-voltage, audio, video and home theatre installations. *New Positions Created (6):* Accounts Receivable / Billing Clerk; Buyer Assistant; Customer Service Assistant; Installers; Sales Consultants / Commercial Sales Positions; Service Technician.

AUDITOR GENERAL OF ALBERTA
Att: Dale Borrmann, HR Director
9925 - 109th Street, 8th Floor
Edmonton, AB T5K 2J8
Tel. 780-422-6410
Fax 780-422-9555
Email .... dborrmann@oag.ab.ca
Website .... www.oag.ab.ca
Employer Background: The Auditor General of Alberta audits over 100 clients, including government departments and agencies, universities, colleges, regional health authorities, foundations and financial organizations. *New Positions Created (5):* Manager of Audits; Manager of Audits, Business Planning; Manager of Audits; Business Writer; Manager of Audits.

AUTO SENSE
Att: Perry
6060 Burnside Court, U-3
Mississauga, ON L5T 2T5
Tel. 905-564-7800
Fax 905-564-7808
Email .... pshareef@autosense.ca
Website .... www.autosense.ca
Employer Background: Auto Sense is a national auto parts distributor, serving the Canadian automotive aftermarket since 1936. *New Positions Created (3):* Inventory Control Analyst; Material Handlers; Operations Coordinator.

AUTOMATION TOOLING SYSTEMS INC. / ATS
Att: Human Resources Manager
3175 Dundas Street West
Oakville, ON L6J 4Z3
Fax 905-469-6893
Email .... hr@atsautomation.com
Website .... www.atsautomation.com
Employer Background: ATS designs turnkey automated manufacturing and test systems, with 2,400 employees and 19 facilities worldwide. *New Positions Created (3):* Control Systems Designer; Technical Writer; Toolmakers / Machine Builders.

AUTOPRO AUTOMATION CONSULTANTS LTD.
Att: Human Resources Manager
11402 - 100th Street, Suite 202
Grande Prairie, AB T8V 2N5
Tel. 780-539-2450
Fax 780-539-2455
Website .... www.autopro.ca
Employer Background: Autopro Automation Consultants Ltd. is a professional technical services organization, specializing in industrial and business automation systems. *New Positions Created (2):* Electrical Engineer; Intermediate Programmer Analyst.

AVANTAS NETWORKS CORP.
Att: Human Resources Manager
2650 Marie Curie
St-Laurent, QC H4S 2C3
Tel. 514-856-2222
Fax 514-856-2232
Email .... career@avantas.com

Website .... www.avantas.com
Employer Background: Avantas Networks Corp. designs fibre optic telecom test instruments for global service providers and telecom equipment manufacturers. *New Positions Created (6):* ASIC / FPGA Designer; Director of Engineering; Director of Operations; Hardware Engineering; Hardware Test Engineer; Vice President of Engineering.

AVCORP INDUSTRIES INC.
Att: Human Resources Department
10025 River Way
Delta, BC V4G 1M7
Tel. 604-582-4870
Fax 604-587-4845
Email .... careers@avcorp.com
Website .... www.avcorp.com
Employer Background: Founded in 1986, Avcorp Industries Inc. designs, fabricates and assembles metal, composite and plastic components and structures for the global aerospace market. The company has 750 employees. *New Positions Created (3):* Preventative Maintenance Engineers; Payroll / HR Assistants; Various Aerospace Engineering Positions.

AVENTIS PASTEUR LTD.
Att: Human Resources Department
1755 Steeles Avenue West
Toronto, ON M2R 3T4
Tel. 416-667-2701
Fax 416-667-2252
Email ..... recruiting.canada@aventis.com
Website .... www.aventispasteur.com
Employer Background: Aventis Pasteur Ltd. (formerly Pasteur Merieux Connaught) is Canada's premier vaccine company, manufacturing or distributing 30 vaccines and immunotherapeutic products. *New Positions Created (6):* Technologist; Research Technologists; Supervisor; Electricians; HVAC Technologist; Instrumentation & Process Technologist.

AVENTIS PHARMA INC.
Att: Human Resources Department
2150 St. Elzear Boulevard West
Laval, QC H7L 4A8
Fax 514-956-4162
Email .... resume.canada@aventis.com
Website .... www.aventis.com
Employer Background: Aventis Pharma Inc., the Canadian pharmaceutical business of Aventis SA, develops and manufactures innovative pharmaceutical products. *New Positions Created (2):* Clinical Research Associate; Planner, Intercompany Purchases.

AVESTIN INC.
Att: Human Resources Manager
2450 Don Reid Drive
Ottawa, ON K1H 1E1
Tel. 613-736-0019
Fax 613-736-8086
Website .... www.avestin.com
Employer Background: Avestin Inc. manufactures high-pressure homogenizers for the biotechnology industry. *New Positions Created (3):* Accountant; Machinist; Scientist / Engineer.

AVIANOR INC.
Att: Mr. Dolz
2067 Chartier
Dorval, QC H9P 1H3
Tel. 514-631-9075
Fax 514-631-9292
Email .... jdolz@avianor.com
Website .... www.avianor.com
Employer Background: Founded in 1995, Avianor Inc. manufactures aircraft seats and galley equipment. *New Positions Created (2):* Buyer; Quality Control Inspector.

AVID MEDIA INC.
Att: Aldona Satterthwaite,
Editor, Canadian Gardening
340 Ferrier Street, Suite 210
Markham, ON L3R 2Z5
Tel. 905-475-8440
Fax 905-475-9560
Email .. satterthwaite@canadiangardening.com
Website .... www.avidmediainc.com
Employer Background: Avid Media Inc. is a Canadian publisher of special-interest magazines such as Canadian Gardening, Canadian Home Workshop, Outdoor Canada and Snow Goer. *New Positions Created (3):* Managing Editor; Senior Editor, Canada Home Workshop Magazine; Inside Sales Position.

AVMAX GROUP INC.
Att: Kevin McAuley
380 McTavish Road NE
Calgary, AB T2E 7G5
Tel. 403-735-3299
Fax 403-219-0853
Email .... kmcauley@avmaxgrp.com
Website .... www.avmaxgrp.com
Employer Background: Avmax Group Inc. provides global management services and maintenance support for regional-sized aircraft in the areas of mechanics, avionics and structures. *New Positions Created (2):* Aerospace Positions; Accounting Manager.

AVON ENGINEERING LTD.
Att: Human Resources Manager
6th Concession Road East
Suite 381, PO Box 1440
Waterdown, ON L0R 2H0
Tel. 905-689-7994
Fax 905-689-8472
Website .... www.avonengineering.com
Employer Background: Established in 1983, Avon Engineering Ltd. is a leading Canadian supplier of material handling, strip process and press room automation equipment. *New Positions Created (2):* Industrial Machine Painter; Export Agent.

AVS TECHNOLOGIES INC.
Att: Human Resources Manager
2100 Trans Canada Highway South
Dorval, QC H9P 2N4
Tel. 514-683-1771
Fax 514-683-5307

Employer Background: AVS Technologies Inc. is a leading distributor in the Canadian electronics industry. *New Positions Created (3):* Systems Business Analyst, JD Edwards One World; Director of Information Technology, JD Edwards One World; Product Manager.

AWARE MARKETING GROUP
Att: Human Resources
501 Oakdale Road
Toronto, ON M3N 1W7

Tel. 416-742-6846
Fax 416-742-6853
Email .... hr@aware.ca
Website .... www.aware.ca

Employer Background: Aware Marketing Group is an importer of promotional and consumer products. *New Positions Created (7):* Assistant to the President; Arts Department Supervisor; Customer Service Representative; Director, Finance; Graphic Artist / Designer; Graphic Artist, Pre-Press; Outside Print Production Coordinator.

AXA CORPORATE SOLUTIONS
Att: Human Resources Department
1800 McGill College Avenue, Suite 2000
Montréal, QC H3A 3J6

Email ... rhmtl@axa-corporatesolutions.com
Website ... www.axa-corporatesolutions.com

Employer Background: AXA Corporate Solutions is part of the AXA Group, a leading insurance, reinsurance and asset management company. AXA Group has 140,000 employees in 60 countries. *New Positions Created (2):* Claims Analyst; Treaty Underwriter.

AXA PACIFIC
Att: Human Resources Department
1100 Rene-Levesque Boulevard West
Suite 1550
Montréal, QC H3B 4P4

Tel. 514-392-6000
Fax 514-392-6805
Website .... www.axa-insurance.ca

Employer Background: AXA Pacific is a member of the AXA Group, a leading insurance and asset management company. Axa Group, active in 60 countries, serves over 40 million policyholders. *New Positions Created (3):* Sr Underwriter; Senior Programmer-Analysts (3); Sr Programmer-Analysts (5).

AXELSON BIOPHARMA RESEARCH INC. / ABR
Att: Human Resources Manager
4606 Canada Way, Suite 001
Burnaby, BC V5G 1K5

Fax 604-222-3141
Email .... hr@axelson.net
Website .... www.axelson.net

Employer Background: ABR provides analytical laboratory and consultation services in support of animal and human drug studies. *New Positions Created (4):* Data Management Assistant; Executive Assistant; Research Chemist; Research Scientist / Study Director.

AXIA NETMEDIA CORPORATION
Att: Human Resources Department
1040 - 7th Avenue SW, Suite 600
Calgary, AB T2P 3G9

Tel. 403-231-1709
Fax 403-508-7911
Email .... jobs@axia.com
Website .... www.axia.com

Employer Background: Axia NetMedia Corporation uses worldwide computer and telecom networks to develop and implement customer solutions for information exchange, communications and learning. *New Positions Created (7):* Financial Accountant; Intermediate Accountant; Senior Financial Accountant; Data Center Operations Manager; Medical Illustrators; Senior Systems Engineer; Health Knowledge Engineers.

AXIDATA INC.
Att: Human Resources
45 Commander Boulevard
Toronto, ON M1S 3Y3

Fax 416-291-2436
Email .... jobs@axidata.com

Employer Background: Founded in 1998, Axidata Inc., an MCsi company, is a supplier to the computer technology and visual communications industries. *New Positions Created (4):* Customer Service Rep; Desktop Publisher; Marketing Support Coordinator; Technical Advisor, Peripheral Products.

AXIS LOGISTICS INC.
Att: Human Resources
2701 High Point Drive
Milton, ON L9T 5G5

Tel. 905-873-2100
Fax 905-876-2020
Website .... www.axisgrp.com

Employer Background: Axis Logistics Inc. is a temperature-controlled distribution facility, operated by one of the largest suppliers of logistics services in North America. *New Positions Created (2):* Claims Administrator; Various Warehouse Positions.

AXYS ENVIRONMENTAL CONSULTING LTD.
Att: Human Resources
555 - 4th Avenue SW, Suite 600
Calgary, AB T2P 3E7

Tel. 403-269-5150
Fax 403-269-5245
Email .... hr@axys.net
Website .... www.axys.net

Employer Background: Founded in 1974, Axys Environmental Consulting Ltd. is a leading environmental consulting company, with over 100 employees in 4 Canadian offices. *New Positions Created (18):* Various Ecologist Positions; Various Environmental Positions; GIS Analyst / Developer; GIS Technician; Junior / Intermediate Soil Scientists (2); Vegetation Ecologist; Vice-President, Operations; Wildlife Biologist; Chief Editor; Senior Consultants; Botanist; GIS Analyst; GIS Analyst / Developer; GIS Technicians; Intermediate and Senior Environmental Consultants; Soil Scientists; Vice-President, Operations; Wildlife Biologist.

AXYS GROUP
Att: Human Resources Manager
2045 Mills Road, PO Box 2219
Sidney, BC V8L 3S8

Tel. 250-656-0881
Fax 250-658-5811
Email .... hr@axys.net
Website .... www.axys.com

Employer Background: Established in 1974, the Axys Group provides a range of advanced technology products, environmental consulting and analytical services. The company has 115 employees. *New Positions Created (4):* Chemists; Computer Specialist; Entry-Level Chemists; GIS Analyst.

AZURE DYNAMICS INC.
Att: Judy Hillier, HR Manager
3650 Wesbrook Mall
BC Research & Innovation Complex
Vancouver, BC V6S 2L2

Tel. 604-224-4331
Fax 604-224-0540
Email .... careers@azuredynamics.com
Website .... www.azuredynamics.com

Employer Background: Azure Dynamics Inc. is a global supplier of intelligent energy management systems for hybrid electric vehicle technology. *New Positions Created (3):* Electronics / Computer Systems Engineers (2); Mechanical Engineer; Senior and Intermediate Electrical Engineers.

AZURE PUBLISHING INC.
Att: Human Resources Manager
20 Maud Street, Suite 200
Toronto, ON M5V 2M5

Fax 416-203-9842
Email ... humanresources@azureonline.com

Employer Background: Azure Publishing Inc. is a magazine publisher, specializing in design, architecture and art. *New Positions Created (2):* Advertising Sales Representative; Operations Manager.

AZURIX NORTH AMERICA
Att: Human Resources Director
100 King Street West
Suite 2100, PO Box 57159, Jackson Station
Hamilton, ON L8P 4X1

Tel. 905-522-9406
Fax 905-572-5929
Website .... www.azurix.com

Employer Background: Azurix North America delivers management solutions for water and wastewater operations, biosolids, engineering, carbon and underground infrastructures. *New Positions Created (4):* Process Coordinator; Vice-President, Operations, Thermal Technologies; Environmental Compliance Manager; Senior Technical Manager.

AZURIX NORTH AMERICA
Att: Human Resources
700 Woodward Avenue
Hamilton, ON L8H 6P4

Tel. 905-545-4551
Fax 905-545-1540
Website .... www.azurix.com

Employer Background: Azurix North America delivers management solutions for water and wastewater operations, biosolids, engineering, carbon and underground infrastructures. *New Positions Created (14):* Maintenance Operator I; Maintenance Operator II; Maintenance Operator III; Vehicle Operator; Industrial Electrician; Industrial Mechanic / Millwright; Instrumentation Technician; Instrumentation Technician; Maintenance Electrician; Maintenance Mechanic; Maintenance Operator I; Maintenance Operator II; Maintenance Operator III; Millwright.

B.C. DECKER INC.
Att: Human Resources
PO Box 620, LCD 1
Hamilton, ON L8N 3K7

Tel. 905-522-7017
Fax 905-522-3210
Email .... hr@bcdecker.com
Website .... www.bcdecker.com

Employer Background: B.C. Decker Inc. is a health sciences book and journal publisher. *New Positions Created (6):* Publishing Production / Editorial Assistant; Circulation Manager; Distribution Coordinator; Controller; Production Assistant; Production Coordinator.

BA BANKNOTE INC.
Att: Employee & Industrial Relations Dept.
975 Gladstone Avenue
Ottawa, ON K1Y 4W5

Tel. 613-728-5854
Fax 613-728-1688
Website .... www.babanknote.com

Employer Background: BA Banknote Inc., a subsidiary of Giesecke & Devrient, is a leading banknote printer. *New Positions Created (3):* Laboratory / Quality Assurance Technician; Security Officer; Maintenance Machinist A.

BABCO SALES LTD.
Att: Human Resources Manager
8342 - 130th Street, Suite 405
Surrey, BC V3W 8J9

Tel. 604-572-5666
Fax 604-572-6000
Email .... info@babcosales.com
Website .... www.babcosales.com

Employer Background: Babco Sales Ltd. distributes equipment to automotive shops. *New Positions Created (4):* Inside Sales Representatives (2); Office Administrator; Sales and Marketing Manager; Shipper / Receiver.

BABCOCK & WILCOX CANADA
Att: Tom Thomas, Human Resources
581 Coronation Boulevard
Cambridge, ON N1R 5V3

Tel. 519-621-2130
Fax 519-622-6790
Email .... ththomas@babcock.com
Website .... www.babcock.com

Employer Background: Babcock & Wilcox Canada develops nuclear and fossil-fueled steam generation technology. *New Positions Created (19):* Electronic Repairman; Machinist; RT Inspector; District Sales Manager; Industrial / Process Engineer; Procedure Writers / Valve Technicians; Business and Market Planner; Construction Project Manager; Mechanical Designers; Project Engineers; Proposal / Project Manager; Certified Machinists; Certified Pressure Vessel Welders; Fitter / Welders; Layout Person, Tube Assembly / Headers; Maintenance Fitters; Fabrication Inspectors; Machinists; Welders.

BACKYARD PRODUCTS LIMITED
Att: Human Resources Manager
530 Third Street
Collingwood, ON L9Y 3R3

Tel. 705-445-4718
Fax 705-445-4519
Email .... jobs@hedstrom.com

Employer Background: Backyard Products Limited is a manufacturer of wooden play centres for the residential marketplace. *New Positions Created (3):* Industrial Engineer; Production Scheduler; Shift Supervisors.

BAKER GURNEY & MCLAREN PRESS
Att: J.H. Murray
37 Hanna Avenue, Suite 14
Toronto, ON M6K 1W9

Tel. 416-535-3737
Email .... jmurray@bakergraphics.com

Employer Background: Baker Gurney & McLaren Press, a division of Baker Graphics Inc., is a full-service print shop. *New Positions Created (4):* Sales Professionals; Account Executive; Prepress Coordinators; Pressroom Supervisor.

BAKER & MCKENZIE
Att: Dan Malamet
181 Bay Street, Suite 2100, PO Box 874
Toronto, ON M5J 2T3

Tel. 416-863-1221
Fax 416-863-6275
Email .... dan.malamet@bakernet.com
Website .... www.bakernet.com

Employer Background: Baker & McKenzie is a law firm, with over 2,800 lawyers working in 61 offices in 35 countries. *New Positions Created (3):* Corporate / Commercial Lawyer; Financial Services and Commercial Real Estate Lawyers (2); Commercial Litigation Associate.

BALLARD POWER SYSTEMS INC.
Att: Human Resources
9000 Glenlyon Parkway
Burnaby, BC V5J 5J9

Tel. 604-454-0900
Fax 604-412-4747
Email .... careers@ballard.com
Website .... www.ballard.com

Employer Background: Ballard Power Systems Inc. is a leading developer of proton exchange membrane (PEM) fuel cells. *New Positions Created (6):* Investor Relations Associate; Accounts Payable Administrator; Human Resources Advisor; Product Development Engineer, MEA Design; Quality Engineer; Training Specialist.

BALMER PLASTER MOULDING CORPORATION OF AMERICA INC.
Att: Human Resources
271 Yorkland Boulevard
Toronto, ON M2J 1S5

Tel. 416-491-0321
Fax 416-491-0371
Website .... www.balmer-plaster.com

Employer Background: Balmer Plaster Moulding Corporation of America Inc. is an international manufacturer and distributor of interior architectural products. *New Positions Created (5):* Architectural CAD Operator; Project Coordinator; Office Assistant; Accountant, Accounts Receivable; Cost and Inventory Control Accountant.

BANFF CENTRE, THE
Att: Human Resources
PO Box 1020, Station 19
Banff, AB T0L 0C0

Tel. 403-762-7546
Fax 403-762-6677
Email .... jobs@banffcentre.ca
Website .... www.banffcentre.ca

Employer Background: Founded in 1933, The Banff Centre is a learning centre dedicated to the arts, leadership development and mountain culture. *New Positions Created (19):* Administrative Assistant; Business Centre Assistant; Library Clerk; Assistant Supervisor, Custodial Services; Associate Director, Visual Arts; Assistant Supervisor, Aquatics; World Tour Assistant; Diner Cook; Enquiries / Information Officer; Managing Producer, Co-Productions; Associate Director, Core Leadership; Building Service Worker; Pastry Helper; Assistant Housekeeper; Director of Finance; Employee Relations Manager; Director, Creative Electronic Environment; Marketing Coordinator; Associate Director, Development Operations.

BANFF MINERAL SPRINGS HOSPITAL
Att: Sheilah Sommer, CEO
301 Lynx Street, Box 1050
Banff, AB T0L 0C0

Tel. 403-760-7211
Fax 403-760-7220
Email .... ssommer@hha.ab.ca
Website .... www.hha.ab.ca

Employer Background: Banff Mineral Springs Hospital (part of the Headwaters Health Authority) provides medical, surgical, maternity and continuing care, as well as extended services in pre-hospital and emergency care, orthopedic care and plastic surgery. *New Positions Created (3):* Project Coordinator, Human Resources; Manager of Pre-Hospital Care; Surgical Processor, OR / CSR.

BANFF, TOWN OF
Att: Nancy Thornton-Smith, HR Manager
110 Bear Street, PO Box 1260
Banff, AB T0L 0C0

Tel. 403-762-1200
Fax 403-762-1260
Email .... hr@town.banff.ab.ca
Website .... www.town.banff.ab.ca

Employer Background: Located in the heart of Banff National Park, the Town of Banff is home to 7,716 people. *New Positions Created (2):* Deputy Fire Chief; Chief Administration Officer - Banff Housing Corporation.

BANK OF AMERICA CANADA
Att: Human Resources
200 Front Street West, Suite 2500
Toronto, ON M5V 3L2
Tel. 416-349-5389
Fax 416-349-4279
Website .... www.bankofamerica.com
Employer Background: Bank of America Canada is subsidiary of North Carolina-based Bank of America Corporation, one of the largest banks in the world, employing 146,000 people in 38 countries. *New Positions Created (3):* Credit Products Associate; Credit Analyst; Production / Administrative Assistant.

BANK OF CANADA
Att: Human Resources Services
234 Wellington Street
Ottawa, ON K1A 0G9
Tel. 613-782-7201
Fax 613-782-7126
Email .... hr@bankofcanada.ca
Website .... www.bankofcanada.ca
Employer Background: Founded in 1934, the Bank of Canada is a Crown corporation responsible for monetary policy, central banking services, bank notes and the administration of public debt. *New Positions Created (6):* Contract Manager; Cataloguing Librarian; Financial Auditor; Security Officers; Analyst / Senior Analyst, Financial Markets; Economist.

BANK OF CHINA (CANADA)
Att: Manager, Administration & HR
161 Bay Street, PO Box 612
Toronto, ON M5J 2S1
Website .... www.bankofchina.com
Employer Background: The Bank of China (Canada) is China's state-owned bank, striving to meet the changes and challenges of a global market. *New Positions Created (4):* Assistant Accounting Manager; Commercial Account Manager; Marketing Manager; Senior Internal Auditor.

BANK OF MONTREAL
Att: Shane Creamer,
Senior Recruitment Specialist
55 Bloor Street West, 5th Floor
Toronto, ON M4W 3N5
Tel. 416-927-7700
Fax 416-927-3445
Email .... staffing.partners@bmo.com
Website .... www.bmo.com
Employer Background: Founded in 1817, the Bank of Montreal is Canada's oldest bank and has assets of US$101 billion and over 32,000 employees around the world. *New Positions Created (4):* Manager, Customer Service ; Manager, Financial Services; Managers; Sales Associates.

BANK OF MONTREAL
Att: Human Resource Consultants
5555 Turney Drive
Mississauga, ON L5M 1A2
Website .... www.bmo.com
Employer Background: Founded in 1817, the Bank of Montreal is Canada's oldest bank and has assets of US$101 billion and over 32,000 employees around the world. *New Positions Created (6):* Financial Services Manager; Investment Funds Specialist; Financial Services Manager; Investment Funds Specialist; Financial Services Manager; Investment Funds Specialist.

BANK OF MONTREAL, CORPORATE & LEGAL AFFAIRS
Att: Manager, Administration
100 King Street West
21st Floor, First Canadian Place
Toronto, ON M5X 1A1
Tel. 416-867-5000
Website .... www.bmo.com
Employer Background: Founded in 1817, the Bank of Montreal is Canada's oldest bank and has assets of US$101 billion and over 32,000 employees around the world. *New Positions Created (6):* Legal Counsel; Senior Counsel; Legal Counsel; Legal Counsel; Legal Counsel; Legal Counsel.

BANK OF MONTREAL, HARRIS PRIVATE BANKING (TRUST SERVICES)
Att: Gillian Ewing,
Vice-President and Regional Director,
Investment Management
350 - 7th Avenue SW, 3rd Floor, FCC
Calgary, AB T2P 3N9
Email .... gillian.ewing@bmo.com
Website .... www.bmo.com
Employer Background: BMO Harris Private Banking offers integrated wealth management services to high net worth clients. *New Positions Created (4):* Portfolio Management Position; Associate Director, Trust Services; Trust Services Associate / Officer; Portfolio Assistant.

BANTREL INC.
Att: Human Resources
4999 - 98th Avenue, Suite 401, Twin Atria
Edmonton, AB T6B 2X3
Tel. 780-462-5600
Fax 780-462-5635
Email .... mailbox@bantrel.com
Website .... www.bantrel.com
Employer Background: Bantrel Inc. is a large, Canadian engineering, procurement and construction management firm, with over 1,200 employees and extensive refining, oil sands and petrochemical experience. *New Positions Created (9):* Process Engineers; Civil / Structural Engineers or CAD Designers; Control Systems Engineers and Technologists; Electrical Engineers & Technologists; Intermediate / Senior Process Engineer; Mechanical Engineers; Piping Designers; Project Control Specialists; Project Engineers.

BANTREL INC.
Att: Human Resources
700 - 6th Avenue SW, 14th Floor
Calgary, AB T2P 0T8
Tel. 403-290-5000
Fax 403-290-5050
Email .... mailbox@bantrel.com
Website .... www.bantrel.com
Employer Background: Bantrel Inc. is a large, Canadian engineering, procurement and construction management firm, with over 1,200 employees and extensive refining, oil sands and petrochemical experience. *New Positions Created (9):* Network Analyst; Civil / Structural Engineer; Senior / Intermediate Project Engineers; Senior Piping Designers; Process Engineers; Planners / Schedulers; Project Controls Managers; Senior Cost Engineers; Project Accountants.

BANTREL INC.
Att: Human Resources Manager
12 Concorde Place, Suite 200
Toronto, ON M3C 3T1
Fax 416-441-4939
Email .... mailbox@bantrel.com
Website .... www.bantrel.com
Employer Background: Bantrel Inc. is a large, Canadian engineering, procurement and construction management firm, with over 1,200 employees and extensive refining, oil sands and petrochemical experience. *New Positions Created (4):* IS&T Supervisor; Process Engineers; Information Systems & Technology Supervisor; Process / Chemical Engineers.

BARANTI GROUP INC.
Att: Careers
210 Cochrane Drive, Unit 6
Markham, ON L3R 8E6
Tel. 905-479-0148
Fax 905-479-0149
Email .... resumes@baranti.com
Website .... www.baranti.com
Employer Background: Baranti Group is a contract design and manufacturing firm, serving clients in Canada and the USA. *New Positions Created (2):* Analog / Digital Design Engineers; Digital Design Engineers.

BARIATRIX INTERNATIONAL INC.
Att: Human Resources
1125 - 50th Avenue
Lachine, QC H8T 3P3
Tel. 514-380-8383
Fax 514-380-8388
Email .... aszymkowiak@bariatrix.ca
Website .... www.bariatrix.com
Employer Background: Bariatrix International Inc. is a manufacturer of dietary health products, including snacks and meal replacements. *New Positions Created (3):* Technical Maintenance Position; Warehouse Manager; Assistant Sales Manager.

BARMISH INC.
Att: Philip Piccirilli
5555 Thimens Boulevard
St-Laurent, QC H4R 2H4

Fax 514-335-0926
Email .... philip@barmish.com
Employer Background: Barmish Inc. is a leading men's apparel manufacturer and importer. *New Positions Created (3):* IT Technician; Quality Control Specialist; Customer Service Representative.

BARRIE, CITY OF
Att: Director of Human Resources
70 Collier Street, PO Box 400
Barrie, ON L4M 4Z2
Tel. 705-739-4202
Fax 705-739-4233
Email .... hrjobs@city.barrie.on.ca
Website .... www.city.barrie.on.ca
Employer Background: Located 90 km north of Toronto, the City of Barrie is home to over 100,000 residents. *New Positions Created (7):* Solid Waste Supervisor; Water Distribution Operator Class 2; Water Treatment Operator Class 2; Fire Prevention Officer; Policy Planners; Court Services Supervisor; Real Estate Services Agent.

BARRINGER RESEARCH
Att: Human Resources
1730 Aimco Boulevard
Mississauga, ON L4W 1V1
Tel. 905-238-8837
Fax 905-238-3018
Email .... humanresources@barringer.com
Website .... www.barringer.com
Employer Background: Barringer Research is a world leader in high-tech security instrument design and manufacturing. *New Positions Created (2):* Human Resources Administrator; Research Scientist.

BARTIMAEUS INC.
Att: Deanna Pietramala
1009 Scarlett Road
Toronto, ON M9P 2V3
Tel. 416-243-3330
Fax 905-953-0589
Website .... www.bartimaeus.com
Employer Background: Founded in 1988, Bartimaeus Inc. provides rehabilitation support to children, adolescents and adults affected by significant brain injury or other trauma. *New Positions Created (5):* Special Needs Workers; IBI Specialists; Rehabilitation Support Workers; Autism Specialists; Child and Youth Workers / Developmental Services Workers.

BARTLE & GIBSON CO. LTD.
Att: Human Resources Manager
1458 Mustang Place
Port Coquitlam, BC V3C 6L2
Tel. 604-941-7318
Fax 604-945-6534
Email .... mark@bartlegibson.com
Website .... www.bartlegibson.com
Employer Background: Bartle & Gibson Co. Ltd. is a leading plumbing, heating, electrical and industrial distributor. *New Positions Created (4):* Electrical Counter Position; Outside Plumbing Sales Position; Warehousing Position; Branch Manager.

BARTON INSTRUMENT SYSTEMS LTD.
Att: Human Resources Manager
3840 - 11A Street NE
Calgary, AB T2E 6M6
Tel. 403-291-4814
Fax 403-291-5678
Email kkeebler@barton-instruments.com
Website .... www.barton-instruments.com
Employer Background: Barton Instrument Systems Ltd. designs, manufactures and sells measurement and control systems for the oil and gas process control industries. *New Positions Created (4):* Inside Sales Representative; Software Developer; Systems Integration Specialist; Technical Sales Representative.

BARTON PLACE NURSING HOME
Att: Rejane Jones, Administrator
914 Bathurst Street
Toronto, ON M5R 3G5
Tel. 416-533-9473
Fax 416-538-2685
Email .... lborges@responsive.on.ca
Employer Background: Barton Place Nursing Home is a 240-bed, accredited long-term care facility. *New Positions Created (3):* Director of Nursing; Activation Therapist; Activation Aide.

BASF CANADA INC.
Att: Human Resources Department
345 Carlingview Drive
Toronto, ON M9W 6N9
Tel. 416-675-3611
Fax 416-674-2782
Website .... www.basf.ca
Employer Background: BASF Canada Inc. is leader in chemical manufacturing and distribution. *New Positions Created (7):* Bilingual Customer Service / Logistics Representative; Accounts Receivable Coordinator; Junior Lawyer, Corporate and Commercial Law; Legal Assistant; Polyurethane Chemist / Technical Service Representative; Senior Credit Analyst; Sales Representative.

BASIC TECHNOLOGIES CORPORATION
Att: Human Resources Department
490 Prince Charles Drive
Welland, ON L3B 5X7
Fax 905-735-3998
Email .... employment@basic.ca
Website .... www.basic.ca
Employer Background: Basic Technologies Corporation, part of Mannesmann Rexroth, is a leader in innovative drive and drive control solutions. *New Positions Created (2):* Field Service Technicians; Product Mgrs.

BATA RETAIL CANADA
Att: Diane Irvine
59 Wynford Drive
Toronto, ON M3C 1K3
Tel. 416-446-2234
Fax 416-446-2221
Email .... hr@batacanada.com
Website .... www.bata.com
Employer Background: Bata is a large footwear manufacturer and retailer, with over 57,000 employees in 60 countries and 4,458 retail stores worldwide. *New Positions Created (5):* Managers & Assistant Managers; Buyer; Bilingual Customer Services Clerk; Distribution Clerks; Benefits Coordinator.

BATES PROJECT MANAGEMENT INC.
Att: Human Resources Manager
200 Elgin Street, Suite 705
Ottawa, ON K2P 1L5
Tel. 613-567-2060
Fax 613-567-2061
Email .... crabb@bates.ca
Website .... www.bates.ca
Employer Background: Bates Project Management Inc. is a private consulting and training company, specializing in project management. *New Positions Created (2):* Project Managers; Project Coordinators / Administrators.

BATH FITTER / BAIN MAGIQUE
Att: Human Resources
560 Boulevard Industriel
St-Eustache, QC J7R 5V3
Tel. 450-472-0024
Fax 450-472-5023
Email .. ressourceshumaines@bathfitter.com
Website .... www.bathfitter.com
Employer Background: Established in 1984, Bath Fitter / Bain Magique is an international manufacturer of innovative bath renovation products. *New Positions Created (4):* Administrative Assistant; Technical Instructor; Manager of Accounting & Financial Operations; Long Distance Truck Driver.

BATTS CANADA LTD.
Att: Human Resources Department
7020 Allard
Lasalle, QC H8N 1Y8
Fax 514-363-9494
Employer Background: Batts Canada Ltd. is a leading Canadian hanger manufacturer. *New Positions Created (2):* Fashion Industry Sales Position; Fashion Industry Sales Position.

BAUER INDUSTRIES LTD.
Att: Human Resources Manager
187 King Street South, Box 430
Waterloo, ON N2J 4A9
Tel. 519-578-5550
Fax 519-578-1390
Email .... recruiting@bauer.ca
Employer Background: Bauer Industries Ltd. is an established Canadian manufacturer of automotive acoustic insulation. *New Positions Created (2):* Manufacturing Engineer; Process / Project Engineer.

BAUSCH & LOMB CANADA
Att: Human Resources Manager
3762 - 14th Avenue, 2nd Floor
Markham, ON L3R 0G7
Tel. 905-948-7633
Fax 905-948-7657
Email .... hr_canada@bausch.com

Website .... www.bausch.com

Employer Background: Bausch & Lomb Canada is a global eye care company. *New Positions Created (2):* Credit Analyst; Sales Representative.

BAXTER CORPORATION
Att: HR / ED
89 Centre Street South
Alliston, ON L9R 1W7

Tel. 705-435-6261
Fax 705-435-0364
Email .... elizabeth_dow@baxter.com
Website .... www.baxter.ca

Employer Background: Baxter Corporation provides critical therapies for life-threatening conditions. *New Positions Created (8):* Value Stream Manager; Analytical Chemists; Microbiologists; Quality Operations Project Supervisor; Sterilization Technician; Sterilization Supervisor; Purchasing Coordinator; Director of Quality.

BAXTER HEALTHCARE CORPORATION
Att: Human Resources
4 Robert Speck Parkway, Suite 700
Mississauga, ON L4Z 3Y4

Tel. 905-270-1125
Fax 905-281-6440
Website .... www.baxter.ca

Employer Background: For nearly 70 years, Baxter Healthcare has developed and manufactured IV therapy products, technologies and devices. The company employs 42,000 people in over 100 countries. *New Positions Created (6):* Bilingual Contracts Coordinator; Customer Service Manager; Human Resources Representative; Customer Service Representative; Home Patient Representative; Field Service Representative.

BAY ST. DOCUMENT SYSTEMS
Att: Vice-President
145 Wellington Street West, Suite 740
Toronto, ON M5J 1H8

Fax 416-979-8020

Employer Background: Bay St. Document Systems is an authorized Xerox agent. *New Positions Created (2):* Telebusiness Representative; Sales Representatives.

BAYCREST CENTRE FOR GERIATRIC CARE
Att: Employment Services
3560 Bathurst Street
Toronto, ON M6A 2E1

Tel. 416-785-2500
Fax 416-785-2490
Email .... jobopps@baycrest.org
Website .... www.baycrest.org

Employer Background: Baycrest Centre for Geriatric Care, an academic centre affiliated with the University of Toronto, is a leader in gerontology and geriatric care. *New Positions Created (12):* Assistants, Volunteer Programs (2); Behavioural Neurology Program Coordinator; Benefits / Compensation Administrator; Employment Services Adviser; Occupational Therapist; Buyer; Director,

Occupational Health & Safety; Occupational Therapists; Occupational Health Nurse; Print Shop Technician; Exercise Professionals; Building Service Engineer.

BAYER INC.
Att: Human Resources
77 Belfield Road
Toronto, ON M9W 1G6

Tel. 416-248-0771
Fax 416-240-5479
Email .... canada.recruiting@bayer.com
Website .... www.bayer.ca

Employer Background: Bayer Inc. is a part of the Bayer Group, an international research-based company involved in life sciences, polymers and chemicals. *New Positions Created (6):* Area Sales Manager; Pharmaceutical Sales Representatives (12); Procurement Specialist; Clinical Research Associate; Bilingual Support Services Associate; Organization Development Consultant.

BAYMAG
Att: Human Resources
10655 Southport Road SW, Suite 800
Calgary, AB T2W 4Y1

Tel. 403-271-9400
Email .... sales@baymag.com
Website .... www.baymag.com

Employer Background: Baymag specializes in the mining and manufacturing of industrial minerals, specifically magnesium oxide. *New Positions Created (2):* Human Resources Manager; Accountant.

BAYSHORE HEALTHCARE
Att: Terri Glover RN, Recruiter
1227 Barton Street East, Centre Mall
Hamilton, ON L8H 2V4

Tel. 905-544-8282
Fax 905-544-5855
Email .... tglover@bayshore.ca
Website .... www.bayshore.ca

Employer Background: Established in 1966, Bayshore offers health and nursing services to clients in homes and community facilities. *New Positions Created (5):* Nurses; Personal Support Worker / Health Care Aides; Manager of Clinical Practice; Personal Support Worker / Health Care Aides; Nurses.

BAYTEX ENERGY LTD.
Att: Shelley Ward
205 - 5th Avenue SW, Suite 2200
Calgary, AB T2P 2V7

Tel. 403-269-4282
Fax 403-267-0777
Email .... sward@baytex.ab.ca
Website .... www.baytex.ab.ca

Employer Background: Baytex Energy Ltd. is an intermediate oil and gas company. *New Positions Created (4):* Exploitation Engineer; Heavy Oil Production Engineer; Geological Technician; Senior IS Analyst.

BAZAAR & NOVELTY
Att: Human Resources
301 Louth Street
St. Catharines, ON L2S 3V6

Tel. 905-687-1700
Fax 905-687-4129
Email .... jackh@stuartent.com
Website .... www.stuartent.com

Employer Background: Bazaar & Novelty produces break-open tickets, bingo paper, ink markers and related electronic equipment. *New Positions Created (5):* Materials Manager; Accountant; General Counsel; Manager, Cost Accounting; Purchasing Agent.

BBD ELECTRONICS INC.
Att: Human Resources Manager
2 Millcreek Drive, Suite 6685
Mississauga, ON L5N 5M5

Fax 905-821-4541
Email .... resumes@bbd.ca
Website .... www.bbd.ca

Employer Background: BBD Electronics is a leading electronics firm, providing sales, marketing and manufacturing services to OEMs across Canada. *New Positions Created (2):* Communications Architectural Guru; SHARC DSP Technology Specialist.

BBM BUREAU OF MEASUREMENT
Att: Vita Di Serio, HR Manager
1500 Don Mills Road, 3rd Floor
Toronto, ON M3B 3L7

Tel. 416-445-9800
Fax 416-445-5635
Email .... vdiserio@bbm.ca
Website .... www.bbm.ca

Employer Background: BBM Bureau of Measurement supplies ratings information about TV, radio and interactive media users to Canadian broadcasters, advertisers and their agencies. *New Positions Created (3):* Vice-President, Finance / Chief Financial Officer; Panel Administrator; Return to Sample Coordinator.

BC BIOMEDICAL LABORATORIES LTD.
Att: Human Resources Department
7455 - 130th Street
Surrey, BC V3W 1H8

Tel. 604-507-5000
Fax 604-507-5227
Email .... bwong@bcbio.com
Website .... www.bcbio.com

Employer Background: BC Biomedical Laboratories Ltd. is a pathologist-owned laboratory, with over 550 employees, serving 1.2 million people per year. *New Positions Created (4):* Medical Technologist; Medical Technologist; Manager, Materiel Management; Occupational Safety Advisor.

BC CANCER AGENCY
Att: Human Resources
555 - 12th Avenue West
Suite 400, East Tower, City Square
Vancouver, BC V5Z 3X7

Tel. 604-877-6117
Fax 604-708-2015
Email .... hropportunities@bccancer.bc.ca
Website .... www.bccancer.bc.ca

Employer Background: Founded in 1935, the BC Cancer Agency is dedicated to excellence in cancer prevention, research, treatment and care. *New Positions Created (7):* Business Affairs Leader, Cancer Pathology; Section Head, MRI Scan; Section Head, Ultrasound; Clinical Nurse Leader; Registered Nurses; Business Affairs Coordinator, Provincial Systemic Therapy Program; Radiation Therapists.

BC FERRY CORPORATION
Att: Human Resources Advisor
1112 Fort Street, 3rd Floor
Victoria, BC V8V 4V2

Tel. 250-381-1401
Fax 250-978-1225
Website .... www.bcferries.com

Employer Background: BC Ferry Corporation, one of the world's largest ferry systems, provides a safe, reliable and sustainable ferry service to residents of BC. *New Positions Created (7):* Market Research Coordinator; Senior Systems Analyst; Systems Analyst 3, Data Services; Information Systems Positions; Manager, Reservations; Senior Internal Auditor; Senior / Intermediate Systems Analysts (2).

BC GAS UTILITY LTD.
Att: Human Resources Department
1111 West Georgia Street, 12th Floor
Vancouver, BC V6E 4M4

Tel. 604-443-6400
Fax 604-443-6460
Website .... www.bcgas.com

Employer Background: BC Gas Utility Ltd. is a leading provider of energy and utility services in British Columbia, serving 750,000 customers in over 100 communities. *New Positions Created (5):* Intermediate Transmission Planning Engineer; Internal Communications Coordinator; Website Production Manager; ERP Supply Chain Team Leader; Manager, Media Relations.

BC HYDRO
Att: Employment Centre
333 Dunsmuir Street
Vancouver, BC V6B 5R3

Tel. 604-528-3382
Fax 604-623-3811
Email .... hrservices@bchydro.com
Website .... www.bchydro.com

Employer Background: BC Hydro is a provincial Crown corporation and Canada's third-largest electric utility, serving more than 1.5 million customers in over 95% of British Columbia. *New Positions Created (54):* Business Systems Consultant 3; Client Services Manager; Senior Engineer, Contracts; Senior Engineer, Estimating and Scheduling; Mechanical Engineer; Senior Protection and Control Engineer, Generating Plants; Distribution Standards Technologist; Administration Clerk, Work Leader; Environmental / Vegetation Technical Specialist; Manager, Columbia Basin Fish and Wildlife Compensation Program; Senior Engineer, Transmission & Distribution, Substation Design; Financial Analyst 2; Manager, Business Financial Services; Drafter; Engineer, Transmission & Distribution; Environmental & Social Issues Coordinator; Senior Engineer - Cost Estimating

(T&D); Thermal Plant Maintenance Technicians (2); Thermal Plant Operations Technicians (6); Senior Maintenance Engineer; Natural Resource Specialist; Instrumentation Engineer, Civil Surveillance & Dam Safety; Maintenance Program Engineer, Distribution; Manager, Fleet Services; Business Services Specialist; Environmental Research Coordinator, Greenhouse Gas Management; Apparatus Technologist; Electrical Engineering Technologist 2; Equipment Contracts Manager; Financial Analyst; IT Planner & Coordinator; Senior Engineer, Contracts; Senior Engineer, Electrical; Senior Engineer, Operate Assets; Senior Maintenance Engineer; Survey Manager; Senior Engineer / Equipment Specialist; Construction Business Unit Manager; Distribution Design Manager; Distribution Line Manager; Protection & Control Managers (2); Sub-Foreman Power Line Technician; Protection and Control Technologists; Operator / Area Dispatchers; Manager, Aboriginal Relations; Customer Relationship Specialist; Inside Business Account Representative; Intermediate Civil Engineer, Hydroelectric; Maintenance & Operations Services Manager; Maintenance Program Engineer; Senior Account Manager; Senior Rock Engineer; Distribution / Transmission Manager; Intermediate Civil Engineer, Transmission and Distribution Engineering .

BC RAIL LTD.
Att: Human Resources
221 West Esplanade, PO Box 8770
North Vancouver, BC V6B 4X6

Tel. 604-984-5345
Fax 604-984-5471
Email .... jobs@bcrail.com
Website .... www.bcrail.com

Employer Background: BC Rail Ltd. is a provincial Crown corporation, providing seamless transportation and real estate solutions throughout the province. *New Positions Created (5):* Land Development Coordinator; Locomotive Engineers; Supervisor, Yard Operations; Coordinator, Major Accounts and Travel Agent Sales; Coordinator, Product Development.

BC RAPID TRANSIT CO. LTD. / BCRTC
Att: Human Resources
6800 - 14th Avenue
Burnaby, BC V3N 4S7

Fax 604-521-2818
Website .... www.rapidtransit.bc.ca

Employer Background: BCRTC operates the SkyTrain advanced rapid transit system. *New Positions Created (9):* Analyst; Buyer; Vehicle Maintenance Position; Payroll Clerk; Cost Accountant; Elevator / Escalator Technician; Technical Analysts; Storepersons; Vehicle Technicians.

BC RESEARCH INC.
Att: Elizabeth Barnard
3650 Wesbrook Mall
Vancouver, BC V6S 2L2

Tel. 604-224-4331
Fax 604-224-0540
Email .... careers@bcresearch.com

Website .... www.bcresearch.com
Employer Background: BC Research Inc. is an international science and technology company, providing consulting, analytical and research services. *New Positions Created (4):* Document Production Specialist; Accounts Payable Specialist; Human Resources / Payroll Administrator; Senior Ergonomist / Human Factors Specialist.

BC TRANSIT
Att: Human Resources
520 Gorge Road East, PO Box 610
Victoria, BC V8W 2P3

Tel. 250-385-2551
Fax 250-995-5664
Email .... employment_services@bctransit.com
Website .... www.bctransit.com

Employer Background: BC Transit provides public transportation services in the Capital Region of Vancouver Island, serving 1.6 million people with a fleet of 494 conventional buses, 191 vans and minibuses and a staff complement of 650. *New Positions Created (4):* Fleet Training Inspector; Marketing & Communications Coordinator, Municipal Systems; Manager, Transit Fleet Maintenance; Vice-President, Fleet and Facilities.

BC TRANSPLANT SOCIETY / BCTS
Att: Angela Lew, Human Resources
555 - 12th Avenue West
3rd Floor, West Tower
Vancouver, BC V5Z 3X7

Tel. 604-877-2100
Fax 604-877-2122
Website .... www.transplant.bc.ca

Employer Background: BCTS is responsible for the strategic planning, direction and funding of organ transplantation and research in BC. *New Positions Created (3):* Clinical Coordinator; Clinical Research Coordinator; Clinical Trials; Clinical Associate, Renal Transplant.

BC TRANSPORTATION FINANCING AUTHORITY / BCTFA
Att: Donna Alberts
940 Blanshard Street
Suite 300, PO Box 9900, Stn Prov Govt
Victoria, BC V8W 9R1

Tel. 250-387-2664
Fax 250-356-6970
Website .... www.tfa.gov.bc.ca

Employer Background: BCTFA is the provincial Crown corporation responsible for integrated multi-modal transportation planning and the design, costing, financing and construction of approved transportation initiatives. *New Positions Created (2):* Land & Property Administrator; Mgrs, Project Development & Implementation (2).

BCBG MAX AZRIA CANADA INC.
Att: Shelley H.
8158 Devonshire
Montréal, QC H4P 2K3

Fax 514-733-9926
Email .... masons@bcbg.com
Website .... www.bcbg.com

Employer Background: BCBG Max Azria is an international retailer, specializing in high quality fashion for women and men. *New Positions Created (4):* Assistant Store Managers; Sales Specialists; Store Managers; Store Manager.

BCE EMERGIS INC.
Att: Human Resources Manager
1155 Rene-Levesque Boulevard West
Suite 2200
Montréal, QC H3B 4T3
Tel. 514-868-2200
Website .... www.emergis.com
Employer Background: BCE Emergis is a leading provider of business-to-business e-commerce services, positioning companies for growth in the digital economy. *New Positions Created (6):* Bilingual Support Centre Analyst; Business Analyst; Director of Development and Integration; Admin Assistant, Corporate Communications & Investor Relations; Mgr, Payroll & HRIS; R&D Technical Engineer.

BCE EMERGIS INC., ASSURE HEALTH DIVISION
Att: Human Resources Manager
5090 Explorer Drive, Suite 1000
Mississauga, ON L4W 4X6
Tel. 905-602-7350
Fax 905-602-9944
Email .... employment@assure.ca
Website .... www.emergis.com
Employer Background: BCE Emergis Inc., Assure Health Division provides health management services to the Canadian insurance market. *New Positions Created (3):* Pharmacist; Bilingual Client Service Representative; Bilingual Support Centre Analyst.

BCL MAGNETICS
Att: Human Resources
5045 North Service Road
Burlington, ON L7L 5H6
Tel. 905-335-2530
Fax 905-335-9084
Website .... www.tempel.com
Employer Background: BCL Magnetics, a division of the Tempel Steel Company, is a leader in lamination stamping technology. *New Positions Created (4):* Inside Sales Representative; Accounts Payable Clerk; Industrial Electrician; Mechanical Engineer.

BCS ASSOCIATES LTD.
Att: Elizabeth Bowland
121 Dundas Street East, Suite 105
Belleville, ON K8N 1C3
Fax 613-967-7789
Email .... bcs.associates@sympatico.ca
Employer Background: BCS Associates Ltd. designs, builds and programs automation systems for various industries. *New Positions Created (2):* Electrical Engineer; Electrical Engineering Technologist.

BDO DUNWOODY LLP
Att: Donna Russel,
Office Manager / Accountant

800 - 6th Avenue SW, Suite 1500
Calgary, AB T2P 3G3
Tel. 403-266-5608
Fax 403-233-7833
Email .... drussell@bdo.ca
Website .... www.bdo.ca
Employer Background: BDO Dunwoody is an accounting and consulting firm, serving independent business clients and community-based organizations, with 80 offices across Canada. *New Positions Created (2):* Chartered Accountants; Tax Mgr/ Specialist.

BDO DUNWOODY LLP
Att: Susan Williams, National Benefits and Human Resources Coordinator
National Office
33rd Floor, Royal Bank Plaza
Toronto, ON M5J 2J8
Tel. 416-865-0200
Fax 416-367-3912
Email .... swilliams@national.bdo.ca
Website .... www.bdo.ca
Employer Background: BDO Dunwoody is an accounting and consulting firm, serving independent business clients and community-based organizations, with 80 offices across Canada. *New Positions Created (5):* Administrative Assistant; Receptionist / Tax Secretary; Controller; Marketing & Special Services Assistant; Office Services Clerk.

BDO DUNWOODY LLP
Att: L. Neill, Regional HR Manager
19 Front Street North, PO Box 670
Orillia, ON L3V 6K5
Tel. 705-325-7964
Fax 705-325-9203
Email .... lneill@bdo.ca
Website .... www.bdo.ca
Employer Background: BDO Dunwoody, with 80 offices across Canada, is an accounting and consulting firm concentrating on the needs of independent business and community-based organizations. *New Positions Created (3):* Accounting Technology Consultant; Technical Consultant; Trustee in Bankruptcy.

BDO DUNWOODY LLP
Att: Dixie Van Duinen
471 Counter Street, Suite 301
Kingston, ON K7M 8S8
Tel. 613-544-2903
Fax 613-544-6151
Email .... kingston@bdo.ca
Website .... www.kingston.bdo.ca
Employer Background: BDO Dunwoody is an accounting and consulting firm, serving independent business clients and community-based organizations, with 80 offices across Canada. *New Positions Created (2):* Intermediate Accountant; Tax Manager / Specialist.

BEARDEN ENGINEERING CONSULTANTS LTD.
Att: Terry Bearden, PEng
4646 Riverside Drive, Suite 1
Red Deer, AB T4N 6Y5

Tel. 403-343-6858
Fax 403-343-2122
Email ... resumes@beardenengineering.com
Website .... www.beardenengineering.com
Employer Background: Established in 1978, Bearden Engineering Consultants Ltd. is an architectural and engineering consulting firm. *New Positions Created (2):* Architectural Draftsperson and Mechanical Draftsperson; Mechanical Engineer and Structural Engineer.

BEAUFORT-DELTA EDUCATION COUNCIL
Att: Human Resources Officer
Bag Service 12
Inuvik, NT X0E 0T0
Fax 867-777-2469
Email .... lynne_isenor@gov.nt.ca
Website .... www.beaufortdeltaedu.nt.ca
Employer Background: The Beaufort-Delta Education Council serves 1,600 students in 9 schools in Inuvik, Tuktoyaktuk, Paulatuk, Sachs Harbour, Holman, Fort McPherson, Tsiigehtchic and Aklavik. *New Positions Created (6):* Principals; Development / Guidance Counsellor; Educational Psychologist; Junior High / High School Teacher; Teacher; Teachers.

BEAUTY SYSTEMS GROUP (CANADA) INC.
Att: Human Resources Manager,
Jaguar Beauty Systems Division
900B Caledonia Road
Toronto, ON M6B 3Y2
Fax 416-757-7026
Email .... tonybsg@istar.ca
Employer Background: Beauty Systems Group (Canada) Inc. is a large wholesale distributor of professional beauty products. *New Positions Created (3):* Customer Service Representative; Sales Support Administrator; Salon Sales Consultant.

BEAVERS DENTAL
Att: Human Resources
Postal Bag 900
Morrisburg, ON K0C 1X0
Tel. 613-543-3791
Fax 613-543-0176
Email .... morrisburg_hr@sybrondental.com
Website .... www.sybrondental.com
Employer Background: Beavers Dental, a subsidiary of Sybron Dental Specialties / Kerr, manufactures dental rotary instruments. *New Positions Created (3):* Industrial Engineer; Material / Metallurgical Engineer; Product Manager.

BECKER GROUP
Att: Sharon Nichols, Corporate Recruiter
PO Box 7021, Station A
Toronto, ON M5W 1X7
Fax 513-942-7553
Employer Background: Based in Michigan, Becker Group is a supplier of automotive and non-automotive products, including injection molded automotive trim components. *New Positions Created (7):* Assistant

Plant Manager; Human Resource Manager; Materials Manager; Plant Manager; Production Associates; Production Supervisor; Quality Manager.

BECKMAN COULTER CANADA INC.
Att: Human Resources
6755 Mississauga Road, Suite 600
Mississauga, ON L5N 7Y2
Tel. 905-819-9844
Fax 905-819-9713
Email .... purie@beckman.com
Website .... www.beckman.com
Employer Background: Beckman Coulter Canada Inc. is a leading global healthcare company, simplifying and automating clinical laboratory processes. *New Positions Created (4):* Field Service Representative; Application Specialist; Clinical Service Representative ; Field Service Rep - Hematology.

BECO INDUSTRIES LTD.
Att: Director of Human Resources
10900 Colbert Street
Anjou, QC H1J 2H8
Tel. 514-353-9060
Fax 514-354-4442
Email .... mjvalois@becoindustries.com
Website .... www.becoindustries.com
Employer Background: BECO Industries Ltd. manufactures bedding products. *New Positions Created (7):* Administrative Import Assistant; Product Coordinator, Home Fashions; Admin Assistant; Customer Service Representative; Account Coordinator; Product Coordinator; Artist / Illustrator.

BEDO
Att: Human Resources Manager
700 Deslauriers
St-Laurent, QC H4N 1W5
Tel. 514-335-2411
Fax 514-335-0115
Email .... bedoinc@aol.com
Website .... www.bedo.ca
Employer Background: Bedo is a clothing company. *New Positions Created (2):* Designer; Patternmaker.

BELAIR DIRECT
Att: Darryl Weinberg, HR Department
5775 Yonge Street, 17th Floor
Toronto, ON M2M 4J1
Tel. 416-250-7720
Fax 416-590-1695
Email .... ontario_human_resources@
.... belairdirect.com
Website .... www.belair.com
Employer Background: Belair Direct, part of ING Canada, is a progressive insurance company. *New Positions Created (6):* Auto Claims Adjusters; Senior BI Claims Technician; AB Claims Examiner; ADR Specialist / Claims Trainer; Junior / Senior Claims Adjusters; Senior AB Claims Technician.

BELBOIS LTD.
Att: Ressources Humaines
2300 Francis Hughes
Laval, QC H7S 2C1
Tel. 450-975-2000
Fax 450-975-2004
Email .... ress.humaines@belbois.ca
Website .... www.belbois.ca
Employer Background: Established in 1974, Belbois Ltd. is a leading manufacturer of audio-video furniture. *New Positions Created (4):* Furniture Designer, New Products; Furniture Designer, OEM Products; Production Planner; Sourcing Manager.

BELCOR INDUSTRIES INC.
Att: Human Resources
14211 Burrows Road
Richmond, BC V6V 1K9
Tel. 604-270-0811
Fax 604-270-7897
Email .... sales@belcor.com
Website .... www.belcor.com
Employer Background: Belcor Industries Inc. is a manufacturer of high quality packaging machinery. *New Positions Created (2):* Customer Service Representative; Inside Sales Representative.

BELISLE CHEV OLDS CADILLAC
Att: Human Resources Manager
444 Montreal Road
Ottawa, ON K1L 8C5
Tel. 613-749-5941
Fax 613-749-8639
Email .... belisleauto@gmcanada.com
Employer Background: Belisle Chev Olds Cadillac is an automotive dealership. *New Positions Created (3):* Assistant Service Mgr; Sales Administration Assistant; Sales System Coordinator / Leasing Receivable Clerk.

BELL CANADA
Att: Office of the Manager
PO Box 920, Station A
Toronto, ON M5W 1G5
Tel. 416-310-2355
Website .... www.bell.ca
Employer Background: Bell Canada is the country's largest supplier of telecom services. *New Positions Created (3):* Product Development Manager; System Administrator; Professional Accountants.

BELL CANADA, INTELLECTUAL PROPERTY GROUP
Att: Melody Currier
483 Bay Street, Floor 5N
Toronto, ON M5G 2E1
Tel. 416-581-3673
Fax 416-585-2130
Email .... melody.currier@bell.ca
Website .... www.bell.ca
Employer Background: Bell Canada is the country's largest supplier of telecommunications services. *New Positions Created (3):* Director, Business Development / Technology Licencing; Technology Market Analyst; Legal Administrative Assistant.

BELL HELICOPTER TEXTRON CANADA
Att: Recruitment Department
12800 Rue de L'Avenir
Mirabel, QC J7J 1R4
Tel. 450-437-3400
Fax 450-437-0826
Email bhtchr@bellhelicopter.textron.com
Website .. www.bellhelicopter.textron.com
Employer Background: Bell Helicopter Textron is the world's largest producer of vertical lift aircraft. Established in 1986, the Mirabel facility produces over 30% of the world's annual commercial helicopters. *New Positions Created (23):* Airworthiness Specialists; Computer System Administrator; Custom Designer, Avionics; Database Analyst, Oracle; Financial Analyst, Budget and Manpower; Financial Analyst, Planning and Analysis; Intermediate Analyst, ERP; Intermediate Application Analyst, IT; Product Support Representative; Project Control Analyst; Senior Application Analyst, IT; Subcontract Cost Analyst; Tooling CAD Analyst; Airframe Structure Specialists; Avionics Customizing Designer; Continuous Improvement Specialist; Dynamic Structures Specialist; Engineering Designers; Liaison Engineer; Materials and Process Engineer; Product Support Engineer; Projects Engineer; Senior Flight Test Engineer.

BELL & HOWELL LTD.
Att: Human Resources Manager
5650 Yonge Street, Suite 1802
Toronto, ON M2M 4G3
Fax 416-228-2438
Email .... can.resumes@mmt.bellhowell.com
Website .... www.bellhowell.com
Employer Background: Bell & Howell Ltd. (a division of ProQuest Company) manufactures high-speed mail and scanning equipment. *New Positions Created (5):* Customer Service Engineers; Customer Service Engineer; Bilingual Training Specialist; Customer Service Technician; Senior Administrative Assistant.

BELL INTRIGNA
Att: Human Resources Manager
885 Georgia Street West, 20th Floor
Vancouver, BC V6C 3E8
Email .... careers@bellintrigna.com
Website .... www.bellintrigna.com
Employer Background: Owned by Manitoba Telecom Services and Bell Canada, Bell Intrigna provides communication solutions for business clients. *New Positions Created (7):* Future Opportunities Account Executive; Account Executive; Customer Service PBX Technician; Proposal Development Specialist; Manager, Installation, Repair and Central Office; Service Advisor, Norstar / M1 / PBX; Service Advisor, Centrex.

BELL INTRIGNA
Att: Human Resources Manager
10104 - 103rd Avenue, 28th Floor
Edmonton, AB T5J 0H8
Email .... careers@bellintrigna.com
Website .... www.bellintrigna.com
Employer Background: Owned by Manitoba Telecom Services and Bell Canada, Bell Intrigna provides communication solutions for business clients. *New Positions Created (16):* Director, Infrastructure Build, GOA

SuperNet; Director, Partner Alliance, GOA SuperNet; Extended Build Manager, GOA SuperNet; Inter-Carrier Coordinator, GOA SuperNet; Network Architecture and Technology Specialist, GOA SuperNet; Network Implementation Specialist, GOA SuperNet; Network Planning Specialist, GOA SuperNet; Procurement Manager, GOA SuperNet; Project Manager, Centrex Migration; Project Coordinator, GOA, Supernet; Account Executive; Central Office Voice / Data Network Specialists (2); Customer Service PBX Technician; Customer Service Representatives (2); Sales Administrator; Service Advisor, Norstar / M1 / PBX.

BELL INTRIGNA
Att: Human Resources Manager
707 - 7th Avenue SW, 14th Floor
Calgary, AB T2P 3H6

Fax 403-237-9217
Email .... careers@bellintrigna.com
Website .... www.bellintrigna.com
Employer Background: Owned by Manitoba Telecom Services and Bell Canada, Bell Intrigna provides communication solutions for business clients. *New Positions Created (56):* Project Manager, Access and Right of Way; Project Manager, Retail Sales; Proposal Development Specialist; Technical Sales Support Specialist, Retail Sales; Administrative Assistant; Repair Centre Representative; Billing Consultant; Business Analyst, Methods; CPE Technical Support Analyst, Carrier Access; Project Manager, Customer Provisioning; Service Adviser, Centrex or M1; Technical Sales Support Specialist, Retail; Account Executive; Contact Centre Operations Specialist; Customer Care Associate; Human Resources Specialist; National Sales Account Executive, Wholesale; Contact Centre Technology Specialist ; Proposal Development Specialist; Account Support Representative; Administrative Assistant; Application Software Tester; Business Analyst, Service Development; Change Control Coordinator; Cost Analyst; Customer Service Technician; Internal Auditor; Manager, Customer Service; Network Design Specialist / Planner; Segment Manager; Team Leads, Installation & Repair (3); Technical Sales Support Specialist, Wholesale; Technical Sales Support Team Lead; Carrier Access Billing Analyst; CLEC Representative; Credit and Collections Assistant; Customer Quality Agent; Customer Service Representative; Learning Development Specialist; Logistics Agent; Manager, Datamod and Assignment; PIC Care Representative; Project Manager, Service Development; Project Manager, Wholesale; Repair Centre Representative; Sr Accountant; Service Advisors, Centrex / M1; Team Lead, Repair Operations Center; Account Executive, Carrier Services; Account Executives; Billing Consultant; Product Manager; Project Mgr, Internal; Project Mgr, Retail; Repair Operations Centre Technician; Technical Sales Support Specialist.

BELL MOBILITY
Att: Human Resources Manager
2920 Matheson Boulevard East, 8th Floor
Mississauga, ON L4W 5J4

Tel. 905-282-4499
Fax 905-282-3071
Email .... careers@mobility.com
Website .... www.bellmobility.ca
Employer Background: Bell Mobility, a subsidiary of BCE Mobile Communications Inc., provides a complete range of wireless communication services to over 2 million Canadians. *New Positions Created (5):* Manager, Switch Engineering; MTX Translation / Sys tem Support Position; Transport Coordinators; Network Engineer; RF Engineer, CDMA / UMTS.

BELLEVILLE, CITY OF
Att: Human Resources
169 Front Street, City Hall
Belleville, ON K8N 2Y8

Tel. 613-967-3272
Fax 613-967-3225
Email .... hrgeneral@citybelleville.com
Website .... www.city.belleville.on.ca
Employer Background: Located on the sheltered waters of the Bay of Quinte, the City of Belleville is home to 45,000 people. *New Positions Created (2):* Manager of Revenue and Customer Service; Manager of Policy Planning.

BELLWOODS CENTRES FOR COMMUNITY LIVING INC.
Att: David Gibson, HR Director
789 Don Mills Road, Suite 701
Toronto, ON M3C 1T5

Tel. 416-696-9663
Fax 416-696-9481
Email ..... d.gibson@bellwoodscentres.org
Website .... www.bellwoodscentres.org
Employer Background: Bellwoods Centres for Community Living Inc. is a community-based organization, providing services and programs to adults with physical disabilities. *New Positions Created (7):* Occupational Therapist / Program Facilitator; Supervisor, Support Services; Office Clerk; Payroll Clerk; Occupational Therapist / Program Facilitator; Administrative Assistant; Program Facilitator / Occupational Therapist.

BELMONT HOUSE
Att: G. Chiu
55 Belmont Street
Toronto, ON M5R 1R1

Fax 416-964-1448
Email .... gchiu@belmonthouse.com
Employer Background: Belmont House features 140 long-term care beds and 80 retirement suites. *New Positions Created (3):* RN/ RPN; Nurse Mgr; Info Systems Clerk.

BENCHMARK TECHNOLOGIES INC.
Att: Human Resources Manager
1620 - 8th Avenue West, Suite 302
Vancouver, BC V6J 1V4

Tel. 604-731-8584
Fax 604-738-8625
Email .... hr@benchtech.com
Website .... www.benchtech.com
Employer Background: Benchmark Technologies Inc. develops Windows, Internet,

intranet, e-commerce and client-server applications, with offices in Vancouver and Calgary. *New Positions Created (5):* C++ Developers; Application Developers; Internet / Web Developers; Java Developers; Object-Oriented Systems Analysts / Designers.

BENNETT JONES LLP
Att: Human Resources Consultant
855 - 2nd Street SW
Suite 4500, Bankers Hall East
Calgary, AB T2P 4K7

Tel. 403-298-3348
Fax 403-265-7219
Email .... hrdept@bennettjones.ca
Website .... www.bennettjones.ca
Employer Background: Founded in 1897, Bennett Jones is one of Canada's leading law firms, with over 200 lawyers and 400 staff in Calgary, Edmonton and Toronto. *New Positions Created (2):* Assistant, Corporate / Commercial; Lawyer.

BENSON MEDICAL INDUSTRIES INC.
Att: Human Resources Manager
151 Esna Park Drive, Unit 19
Markham, ON L3R 3B1

Tel. 905-475-0401
Fax 905-475-3656
Email .... mail@bensonmedical.ca
Website .... www.bensonmedical.ca
Employer Background: Founded in 1974, Benson Medical Industries Inc. is a supplier of anaesthesia and respiratory products. *New Positions Created (2):* Technical Sales Reps; Technical Service Representative.

BENTALL CORPORATION
Att: Michele Ng, HR Manager
1055 Dunsmuir Street
Suite 1800, PO Box 49001
Vancouver, BC V7X 1B1

Tel. 604-661-5000
Fax 604-661-5652
Email .... careers@bentall.com
Website .... www.bentall.com
Employer Background: Bentall Corporation is a leading real estate, management and development company for properties in Canada and the USA. *New Positions Created (5):* Property Accountants; Chief Engineer; Senior Corporate Accountant; Operations Manager; Real Estate Development Mgr.

BENTLEY LEATHERS
Att: Director, Information Services
3700 Griffith Street, Suite 200
St-Laurent, QC H4T 2B3

Fax 514-341-5619
Email .... bentleyjobs@hotmail.com
Employer Background: Bentley Leathers is a leading retailer of luggage and leather goods. *New Positions Created (4):* Network and PC Support Technician; Secretary; District Sales Manager; District Sales Manager.

BENTLY NEVADA CANADA COMPANY
Att: Human Resources Manager
9403 - 17th Avenue NW
Edmonton, AB T6N 1J1

Tel. 780-439-4000
Fax 780-439-4044
Email ... lorianne.wooldridge@bently.com
Website .... www.bently.com
Employer Background: BTLS Nevada is a leader in machinery protection and management systems, machinery vibrations, diagnostics and rotor dynamic research. *New Positions Created (2):* Application Specialist; Senior Solutions Sales Engineer.

BERLEX CANADA INC.
Att: Manager, Human Resources
2260 - 32nd Avenue
Lachine, QC H8T 3H4
Tel. 514-879-1568
Fax 514-631-7436
Website .... www.berlex.ca
Employer Background: Berlex Canada Inc. is dedicated to excellence in fertility control, oncology, diagnostic imaging and neurology. *New Positions Created (5):* Analyst, Strategic Information Services, Therapeutics; Analyst, Strategic Information Services, Women's Health; Manager, Clinical and Outcomes Research; Drug Safety Officer; Scientific Information Officer.

BERMINGHAMMER FOUNDATION EQUIPMENT
Att: Plant Manager
Wellington St. Marine Terminal
Hamilton, ON L8L 4Z9
Fax 905-528-6187
Employer Background: Berminghammer Foundation Equipment designs and manufactures specialized foundation equipment for the construction industry. *New Positions Created (2):* Journeymen Machinists (2); Mechanical Draftsperson.

BETA MACHINERY ANALYSIS LTD.
Att: John Harvey,
Manager of Design Services
1615 - 10th Avenue SW, Suite 300
Calgary, AB T3C 0J7
Tel. 403-245-5666
Fax 403-245-3257
Email .... jharvey@betamachinery.com
Website .... www.betamachinery.com
Employer Background: Founded in 1967, Beta Machinery Analysis Ltd. is a provider of specialized machinery engineering services. *New Positions Created (3):* Project Analyst; Technical Programmer; Engine / Compressor Analyst.

BETHESDA
Att: Human Resources
2F Tremont Drive, Suite 2
St. Catharines, ON L2T 3B2
Tel. 905-684-6918
Fax 905-684-5866
Email .... work@bethesdaservices.com
Website .... www.bethesdaservices.com
Employer Background: Bethesda is a non-profit agency, serving adults with developmental disabilities. The agency is owned by the Mennonite Brethren Conference of Ontario. *New Positions Created (3):* Behaviour

Therapist; Support Workers; Support Workers.

BETTIS CANADA LTD.
Att: Manager, Human Resources
4112 - 91A Street
Edmonton, AB T6E 5V2
Tel. 780-450-3600
Fax 780-440-8522
Email ...... jescaravage@bettiscanada.com
Website .... www.bettiscanada.com
Employer Background: Bettis Canada Ltd. engineers, manufactures and markets valve automation products and related services. *New Positions Created (10):* Customer Service Representative; Senior Accountant; Field Service / Training Technician; Manufacturing Support Specialist; Plant Maintenance Technician; Mechanical Design Engineers; Sales Representative; Manufacturing Process Coordinator; Purchaser; Mechanical Design Engineer.

BEUTEL GOODMAN REAL ESTATE GROUP INC.
Att: Human Resources
20 Eglinton Avenue West, PO Box 2005
Toronto, ON M4R 1K8
Fax 416-590-1060
Email .... madison@bgreg.com
Website .... www.beutel-can.com
Employer Background: Established in 1988, Beutel Goodman Real Estate Group acquires, develops and manages commercial, retail, industrial, residential and development real estate assets on behalf of Canadian pension funds. *New Positions Created (2):* Building Operator; Building Operator.

BEVERLY CENTRE, THE
Att: Beverley Landry, HR Director
1729 - 90th Avenue SW
Calgary, AB T2V 4S1
Tel. 403-253-8806
Fax 403-252-7771
Website .... www.longtermcare.ab.ca
Employer Background: The Beverly Centre is a 150-bed long-term care and assisted living facility for seniors, slated to open in November 2001. *New Positions Created (5):* Director of Care; Director of Building Services; Director of Food Services; Various Healthcare Positions; Director of Care.

BEYOND 20/20 INC.
Att: Human Resources Department
265 Carling Avenue, Suite 500
Ottawa, ON K1S 2E1
Fax 613-563-7233
Email .... careers@beyond2020.com
Website www.beyond2020.com
Employer Background: Beyond 20/20 Inc. develops, sells and supports numeric data dissemination and publishing products. *New Positions Created (12):* Applications Architect; Customer Support Specialist; Senior Developer (C++, Web, OLAP); Team Leader; Telephone Sales Support Position; Manager, Global Partners Program; Marketing Communications Coordinator; Pre-Sales

Support Consultants; Quality Assurance Specialist; Sales Executives; Software Developer, C++, WEB, OLAP; Webmaster.

BF GOODRICH AEROSPACE
Att: Manager, Human Resources
1303 Aerowood Drive
Mississauga, ON L4W 2P6
Fax 905-602-8141
Website .... www.bfg-aerospace.com
Employer Background: BF Goodrich Aerospace provides essential products and services to the commercial, military, general aviation and space industries. *New Positions Created (3):* CNC Machine Operator; Junior Metallurgist; Shift Supervisor.

BHP DIAMONDS INC.
Att: Human Resources Administrator
4920 - 52nd Street, Suite 1102
Yellowknife, NT X1A 3T1
Tel. 867-669-6144
Fax 867-880-4408
Email .... barb.l.allen@bhpbilliton.com
Website .... www.bhp.com
Employer Background: BHP Diamonds Inc. operates the EKATI diamond mine in the Northwest Territories, which began operation in 1998. *New Positions Created (2):* Blaster; Human Resources Manager.

BIDELL EQUIPMENT INC.
Att: Human Resources Manager
3236 - 50th Avenue SE
Calgary, AB T2B 3A3
Tel. 403-235-5877
Fax 403-272-7749
Email .... bidell@totalenergy.to
Website .... www.totalenergy.to
Employer Background: Bidell Equipment Inc., a division of Total Energy Services Ltd., is a gas compression company. *New Positions Created (4):* Junior Draftsman; Shop Foreman; Intermediate Draftsman; Project Engineer.

BIG SISTERS AND BIG BROTHERS OF CALGARY AND AREA
Att: Human Resources Manager
2411 - 4th Street NW, Suite 106
Calgary, AB T2M 2Z8
Tel. 403-777-3535
Fax 403-777-3525
Email .... bsbbcalgary@cadvision.com
Website .... www.bsbb-calgary.ca
Employer Background: Formed in 1994, Big Sisters and Big Brothers of Calgary and Area is a registered charity, providing adult volunteer support and friendship to children. *New Positions Created (4):* Executive Director; Caseworker; Development Officer, Corporate Giving and Grants; Receptionist / Secretary.

BINKS INSURANCE BROKERS LTD.
Att: Harry S. Binks, President
955 Green Valley Crescent, Suite 270
Ottawa, ON K2C 3V4
Tel. 613-226-1350
Fax 613-226-7029

Email .... h.binks@binks.ca
Website .... www.binks.ca
Employer Background: Established in 1918, Binks Insurance Brokers Ltd. provides a full range of risk management and insurance services to businesses, institutions and individuals. *New Positions Created (4):* Commercial Account Manager; Assistant Commercial Account Manager; Personal Risk Account Manager; Senior Commercial Account Manager.

BIO PED
Att: Human Resources Manager
2150 Winston Park Drive, Unit 2
Oakville, ON L6H 5V1
Tel. 905-829-0505
Fax 905-829-5199
Email .... humanresources@bioped.com
Website .... www.bioped.com
Employer Background: Bio Ped designs and manufactures foot support systems for people affected by foot or lower limb disorders. *New Positions Created (2):* Retail Store Manager; Medical Marketing Representative.

BIO-FORM LABORATORIES
Att: Human Resources
1190 Midway Boulevard, Unit 10
Mississauga, ON L5T 2B9
Fax 905-670-8099
Employer Background: Bio-Form Laboratories develops and manufactures specialty hair and skin products derived from herbal extracts, and prepares them for sale in retail locations across the country. *New Positions Created (3):* Product Manager; R & D Chemist; Sales Manager.

BIO-RAD LABORATORIES (CANADA) LTD.
Att: Life Sciences Sales Manager
5671 McAdam Road
Mississauga, ON L4Z 1N9
Tel. 905-712-2771
Website .... www.biorad.com
Employer Background: Bio-Rad Laboratories (Canada) Ltd. is a leader in biotechnology and life sciences research. *New Positions Created (2):* Technical Representative, Laboratory Products; Service Technician.

BIOGENIE SRDC INC.
Att: Human Resources
350 Franquet Street
Ste-Foy, QC G1P 4P3
Fax 418-653-3583
Email .... quebec@biogenie-env.com
Employer Background: Biogenie SRDC Inc. specializes in the decontamination of polluted sites, serving petroleum, petrochemical and utility companies in North America and Western Europe. *New Positions Created (3):* Environmental Positions; Intermediate / Sr Environmental Technician; Sales Rep.

BIOMIRA INC.
Att: Human Resources Department
2011 - 94th St., Edmonton Research Park
Edmonton, AB T6N 1H1

Tel. 780-450-3761
Fax 780-463-0871
Email .... hr@biomira.com
Website .... www.biomira.com
Employer Background: Biomira Inc. is a biotechnology firm, developing and commercializing products for cancer patients. *New Positions Created (2):* Various Biotechnical Positions; Quality Assurance Specialist.

BIRD CONSTRUCTION COMPANY
Att: Ken Nakagawa, Branch Manager
11780 Hammersmith Way, Suite 220
Richmond, BC V7A 5E3
Fax 604-271-1850
Email .... knakagawa@bird.ca
Website .... www.bird.ca
Employer Background: Established in 1920, Bird Construction Company is a leading general contractor, with operations in Canada and the USA. *New Positions Created (5):* Project Coordinator; Project Manager; Accounts Payable Position; Estimating Assistant; Secretary.

BIRD CONSTRUCTION COMPANY
Att: Meredith Lent
16815 - 117th Avenue
Edmonton, AB T5M 3V6
Tel. 780-452-8770
Fax 780-455-2807
Website .... www.bird.ca
Employer Background: Established in 1920, Bird Construction Company is a leading general contractor with operations in Canada and the USA. *New Positions Created (3):* Various Construction Positions; Safety Manager; Construction Estimators.

BIRD CONSTRUCTION COMPANY
Att: Human Resources
5405 Eglinton Avenue West, Suite 206
Toronto, ON M9C 5K6
Tel. 416-620-7122
Fax 416-620-7121
Website .... www.bird.ca
Employer Background: Established in 1920, Bird Construction Company is a leading general contractor, with operations in Canada and the USA. *New Positions Created (3):* Various Construction Positions; Various Construction Positions; Executive Assistant.

BIRD ON A WIRE NETWORKS / BOAW
Att: Human Resources Manager
55 City Centre Drive, Ground Floor
Mississauga, ON L5B 1M3
Tel. 905-896-6370
Fax 905-896-4865
Email .... recruiting@birdonawire.com
Website .... www.birdonawire.com
Employer Background: BOAW is an Internet services company, providing fully managed, dedicated and ASP hosting services for Internet-based businesses. *New Positions Created (16):* Account Managers; Channel Sales Account Managers; Major Account Managers; Accounts Payable Position / Vendor Support Manager; Accounts Receivable and Customer Support Manager; Adminis-

trative Assistants; Billing Manager; Concierge; Customer Service Representatives; Director of Marketing; Human Resources Administrator; Level 2 Support Technician; Manager, Technical Implementation; Senior Network Engineers; Senior Systems Administrator; Vice President, Strategic Partnerships.

BISHOP & MCKENZIE
Att: B.W. Sarabin
10104 - 103rd Avenue, Suite 2500
Edmonton, AB T5J 1V3
Tel. 780-426-5550
Fax 780-426-1305
Email .... b.sarabin@bishopmckenzie.com
Website .... www.bishopmckenzie.com
Employer Background: Established in 1903, Bishop & McKenzie is a law firm, with offices in Edmonton and Calgary. *New Positions Created (3):* Litigation Lawyers; Personal Services Lawyer; Corporate / Commercial Lawyer.

BISSETT & ASSOCIATES INVESTMENT MANAGEMENT LTD.
Att: Human Resources Manager
350 - 7th Avenue SW, Suite 3100
Calgary, AB T2P 3N9
Tel. 403-266-4664
Fax 403-237-2334
Website .... www.bissett.com
Employer Background: Bissett & Associates Investment Management Ltd. serves institutional, mutual fund and private clients and has $5.7 billion in assets under management. *New Positions Created (2):* Bilingual Mutual Fund Client Service Representative; Equity Analyst.

BITFLASH GRAPHICS, INC.
Att: Human Resources
1410 Blair Place, Suite 700
Ottawa, ON K1J 9B9
Tel. 613-745-3232
Fax 613-745-9202
Email .... hr@bitflash.com
Website .... www.bitflash.com
Employer Background: BitFlash Graphics, Inc. develops Java applets and applications for viewing and publishing technical computer graphics such as maps, schematics and CAD drawings. *New Positions Created (40):* Applied Solutions Developers; Product Manager; Research Developers; Senior Software Developer, Server; SVG / XML Graphics Designer; Applied Solutions Developers; Graphics File Filter Developer; Junior Software Release Engineer; Quality Assurance Specialist; Research Developers; Wireless Industry Specialist; Wireless PDA Developer; Applied Development Specialist; Font / Text Engine Software Developers; Graphics Software Developers; Junior / Intermediate GUI Developer; Junior / Intermediate Server Software Developer; Junior / Intermediate Technical Writer; Quality Assurance Software Developer; Quality Assurance Specialist, Client / Server; Research Developer; Senior Graphics File Filter Software Developers; Senior / Intermediate Software Per-

formance Expert; Senior Software Release Engineer / Server Administrator; SG / XML Graphics Software Developers; Font / Text Engine Software Developers; Intermediate / Junior Graphics File Filter Software Developers; Intermediate / Junior Graphics Software Developers; Intermediate / Junior Graphics Software Developers, Wireless Devices; Intermediate / Junior Server Software Developer; Quality Assurance Software Developer; Quality Assurance Specialists; Quality Assurance Specialists, Client / Server; Quality Assurance Specialists, Databases; Senior Graphics File Filters Software Developers; Senior Graphics Software Developer, Wireless Devices; Senior / Intermediate Research and Applied Development Specialists; Senior Software Performance Expert; Solaris System Administrator / Database Administrator; SVG (XML) Graphics Software Developers.

BITHEADS, INC.
Att: Human Resources Manager
1309 Carling Avenue
Ottawa, ON K1Z 7L3

Tel. 613-722-3232
Fax 613-722-9435
Email .... hr@bitheads.ca
Website .... www.bitheads.ca
Employer Background: bitHeads, Inc. is a systems development company, providing custom software development, object-oriented consulting and in-house commercial product development. *New Positions Created (15):* Quality Control Analyst; Quality Control Engineer; Software Developers, Java, C++, OO; Software Development Managers; C++ / Embedded Software Developer; Quality Assurance Specialist / Manager; Quality Control Analyst; Quality Control Engineer; Receptionist / Administrative Assistant; Senior Business Systems Analyst; Senior Web Developer / Graphic Designer; Software Development Managers; Human Resource Coordinator; Quality Assurance Specialist / Manager; Web Developer / Graphic Designer.

BIZERBA CANADA
Att: Human Resources
6419 Northam Drive
Mississauga, ON L4V 1J2

Tel. 905-405-0820
Fax 905-405-0819
Email .... hr@bizerba.ca
Website .... www.bizerba.ca
Employer Background: Bizerba Canada supplies equipment to the retail and food industries. *New Positions Created (4):* Manager, Finance and Administration; Bilingual Office Clerk; Service Technician; Sales Representative.

BJ PIPELINE INSPECTION SERVICES
Att: Human Resources
4839 - 90th Avenue SE
Calgary, AB T2C 2S8

Fax 403-236-8740
Email .... hr@bjservices.ca
Website .... www.bjservices.ca

Employer Background: BJ Pipeline Inspection Services is a division of BJ Services Company Canada, a leading provider of cementing, stimulation, coiled tubing, nitrogen, pipeline, process and industrial services to the oil and gas industry in Canada. *New Positions Created (7):* Data Analysts; Electronic Engineer; Boom Crane Operator; Data Analyst; Electronic Technologist; Mechanical Engineer; Research Engineer / Scientist.

BJ PROCESS & PIPELINE SERVICES
Att: Dave Wilson, Operations Manager
9010 - 34th Street
Edmonton, AB T6B 2V1

Fax 780-440-0539
Email .... hr@bjservices.ca
Website .... www.bjservices.ca
Employer Background: BJ Process & Pipeline Services, a part of BJ Services Company Canada, supports pipeline construction, commissioning, repair, maintenance and abandonment activities. *New Positions Created (3):* Equipment Operator; Journeyman Heavy Duty Mechanic; Operations Support Engineer.

BJ SERVICES COMPANY CANADA
Att: Human Resources Department
801 - 6th Avenue SW, Suite 1300
Calgary, AB T2P 4E1

Tel. 403-531-5151
Fax 403-296-1575
Email .... hr@bjservices.ca
Website .... www.bjservices.ca
Employer Background: BJ Services Company Canada (formerly Nowsco Well Service Ltd.) is a leading provider of cementing, stimulation, coiled tubing, nitrogen, pipeline, process and industrial services to the oil and gas industry in Canada. *New Positions Created (7):* Technical Specialist, Coiled Tubing Drilling; Facilities Supervisor; Project Engineers; Senior Draftsman; Senior Mechanical Engineer; Fracturing Supervisor; Reservoir Engineer.

BLACK COMMUNITY RESOURCE CENTRE / BCRC
Att: Dr. Horace Goddard
6767 Cote des Neiges, Suite 440
Montréal, QC H3S 2T6

Tel. 514-342-2247
Fax 514-342-2283
Employer Background: BCRC is a non-profit organization, helping young, black, English-speaking individuals residing in Montreal improve their chances of becoming fully functional in mainstream society. *New Positions Created (2):* Coordinator, Internship Program; Executive Director.

BLACK MAX DOWNHOLE TOOLS LTD.
Att: Renee Stacey
1507 - 4th Street
Nisku, AB T9E 7M9

Tel. 780-955-8828
Fax 780-955-3309
Email .... renee.stacey@nql.com
Website .... www.nql.com

Employer Background: Black Max Downhole Tools Ltd. provides downhole tools and technology used primarily in drilling applications in the oil and gas, environmental and utility industries. *New Positions Created (3):* Mechanical Engineer; Mechanical Designer; Mechanical Engineer.

BLACK & MCDONALD LTD.
Att: Human Resources
101 Parliament Street
Toronto, ON M5A 2Y7

Tel. 416-366-2541
Fax 416-366-6032
Email .. mechresume@blackandmcdonald.com
Website ...... www.blackandmcdonald.com
Employer Background: Black & McDonald Ltd. is a major multi-trade contractor, providing electrical, mechanical, utility and maintenance services to Canadian clients. *New Positions Created (8):* Millwrighting and Rigging Sales Estimator; Business Development Representative; Facility Management Implementation Specialist; Service Operations Coordinator; Health, Safety and Environment Manager; Construction Administrative Assistant; Customer Service Coordinator; Lineman.

BLACK, SUTHERLAND, CRABBE LLP
Att: Lorraine Dale, Office Manager
401 Bay Street, Suite 2700, PO Box 101
Toronto, ON M5H 2Y4

Fax 416-361-1674
Email .... lorraine@bsc-law.net
Employer Background: Black, Sutherland, Crabbe LLP is a progressive law firm, with 10 lawyers. *New Positions Created (2):* Litigation Associate; Senior Lawyer.

BLANEY MCMURTRY
Att: Alex Mesbur, QC
20 Queen Street West, Suite 1400
Toronto, ON M5H 2V3

Tel. 416-539-3949
Fax 416-593-5437
Email .... amesbur@blaney.com
Website .... www.blaney.com
Employer Background: Blaney McMurtry is a law firm. *New Positions Created (5):* Intellectual Property Lawyer; Family Law Lawyer; Real Estate Lawyer; Corporate / Commercial Lawyers; Intermediate Litigation Secretary.

BLOCKADE SYSTEMS CORPORATION
Att: Human Resources Manager
2200 Yonge Street, Suite 1400
Toronto, ON M4S 2C6

Tel. 416-482-8400
Fax 416-440-1401
Email .... hr@blockade.com
Website .... www.blockade.com
Employer Background: Blockade Systems Corporation develops data security products for large and med-sized enterprises. *New Positions Created (17):* Intermediate / Senior Security Software Developer; Web Single Sign-On; Intermediate / Senior Software Developer, Remedy / Blockade Integration; Manager, Strategic Alliance; Systems

Engineer; Technical Support Engineer; Manager, Strategic Alliances; Product Developers; Systems Engineer; Technical Support Engineer; Software Developer; Telemarketers; Manager, Strategic Alliances; Outbound Telemarketer, Inside Lead Generation; Product Developers; Quality Assurance Engineer; Systems Engineer; Technical Support Engineer.

BLOCKBUSTER CANADA CO.
Att: Human Resources Partner
1 Bartley Bull Parkway
Brampton, ON L6W 3T7
Tel. 905-457-0035
Fax 905-457-7414
Website .... www.blockbuster.ca
Employer Background: With over 350 stores coast to coast, Blockbuster Canada Co. is Canada's largest provider of rentable home entertainment. *New Positions Created (2):* Store Managers; Store Managers.

BLOCKBUSTER CANADA CO.
Att: Human Resources Department
7760 Sherbrooke Road East
Montréal, QC H1L 1A5
Tel. 514-353-1222
Fax 514-353-8340
Email .... hrcanada.east@blockbuster.com
Website .... www.blockbuster.com
Employer Background: Blockbuster Canada Co. is Canada's largest provider of rentable home entertainment, with over 340 stores nationwide. *New Positions Created (3):* Various Store Positions; Administrative Assistant; Store Management Positions.

BLOORVIEW MACMILLAN CHILDREN'S CENTRE, MACMILLAN SITE
Att: Human Resources
350 Rumsey Road
Toronto, ON M4G 1R8
Tel. 416-425-6220
Fax 416-424-3868
Email .... humanresources@
.... bloorviewmacmillan.on.ca
Website .. www.bloorviewmacmillan.on.ca
Employer Background: Bloorview MacMillan Children's Centre, MacMillan Site provides rehabilitation services for children and young adults with physical disabilities. *New Positions Created (28):* Therapeutic Recreation Specialist; Clinic Secretary; Executive Assistant to the President & CEO; Helpdesk Analyst; Nursing Unit Manager, 24-Hour Client Care Service; Registered Practical Nurse, 24–Hour Client Care Service, Unit 1; Speech-Language Pathologist; Bilingual Receptionist, Family & Community Relations; Communications Disorder Assistant; Human Resources Manager; Physiotherapist; Prosthetist - Musculoskeletal Program, Amputee Team; Registered Nurse - 24 Hour Client Care Service, Unit 2; Registered Nurse, Unit 1; Registered Practical Nurse, 24-Hour Client Care Service, Unit 2; Seating Technician / Upholsterer / Carpenter; Speech Language Pathologist; Speech Language Pathologist; Supervisor, Health Data Resources and Registration Services; Nursing Unit Manager; Registered

Nurses; Bilingual Receptionist, Family and Community Relations; Clinic Secretary; Medical Transcriptionist, Health Data Resources; Supervisor, Health Data Resources and Registration Services; Chief of Medical Staff; Vice-President, Human Resources and Education; Registered Nurses and Registered Practical Nurses.

BLUE HILLS CHILD & FAMILY SERVICES
Att: ELizabeth Burns,
Director of Operations
402 Bloomington Road West
Aurora, ON L4G 3G8
Fax 905-773-8133
Employer Background: Blue Hills Child and Family Services is an accredited provider of children's mental health services throughout York Region. *New Positions Created (2):* Clinical Supervisor / Coordinator; Intensive Intervention Workers.

BLUEWATER DISTRICT SCHOOL BOARD
Att: Michael Forge,
Superintendent of Student Services
351 - 1st Avenue North, PO Box 190
Chesley, ON N0G 1L0
Tel. 514-363-2014
Fax 519-363-3448
Website .... www.bwdsb.on.ca
Employer Background: Bluewater District School Board provides public education in a variety of urban and rural centres in the counties of Grey and Bruce. *New Positions Created (2):* Psychologist / Psychological Associate; Speech Language Pathologists.

BMO HARRIS PRIVATE BANKING
Att: Bruce Harrison
10199 - 101 Street, 5th Floor
Edmonton, AB T5J 3Y4
Email .... d.harrison@bmo.com
Website .... www.bmo.com
Employer Background: BMO Harris Private Banking offers a full spectrum of trust and development products and services to a high net worth clientele. *New Positions Created (2):* Private Banker; Private Banker.

BMO NESBITT BURNS INC.
Att: Human Resources Manager
1 First Canadian Place, PO Box 150
Toronto, ON M5X 1H3
Tel. 416-359-4000
Email .... ia.recruiting@bmonb.com
Website .... www.bmonesbittburns.com
Employer Background: BMO Nesbitt Burns Inc. is a leading full-service investment bank, serving the financial needs of individual, institutional, corporate and government clients. *New Positions Created (3):* Investment Advisor; Life Insurance Marketing Assistant; Investment Advisors.

BMW CANADA INC.
Att: Human Resources
920 Champlain Court
Whitby, ON L1N 6K9

Tel. 905-428-5651
Fax 905-428-5033
Website .... www.bmw.ca
Employer Background: BMW Canada Inc. is an importer of luxury automobiles. *New Positions Created (3):* Operations & Supply Manager; Sales Consultant; Market Area Manager, Western Region.

BMW CANBEC
Att: Human Resources Department
4090 Jean-Talon West
Montréal, QC H4P 1V5
Tel. 514-731-7871
Fax 514-731-5603
Website .... www.bmwcanbec.com
Employer Background: BMW Canbec is a leading BMW dealership in Montreal. *New Positions Created (3):* Sales Consultant; Accounting Clerk; Automobile Sales Manager.

BNT PRODUCTS
Att: Human Resources Manager
2444 Haines Road
Mississauga, ON L4Y 1Y6
Tel. 905-272-1448
Fax 905-272-4401
Email .... bntprod1@resonet.com
Employer Background: BNT Products is a mid-sized tool manufacturer. *New Positions Created (5):* Bookkeeper; Plant Manager; Controller; Front Office Administrator; Production Manager.

BOC CANADA LTD.
Att: Human Resources
5975 Falbourne Street, Unit 2
Mississauga, ON L5R 3W6
Tel. 905-501-2516
Fax 905-501-1641
Email human.resources@boccanada.com
Website .... www.boc.com
Employer Background: BOC Canada Ltd., a member of BOC Group PLC, is a leading distributor of industrial, medical and specialty gases, welding products and industrial vacuum technologies. *New Positions Created (7):* Production Coordinator; Technical Sales Coordinator; Systems Support Analyst; Human Resources Analyst; Assistant Process Operations Manager; Plant Superintendent; Employee Relations Supervisor.

BODY SHOP, THE
Att: Human Resources Manager
33 Kern Road
Toronto, ON M3B 1S9
Fax 416-445-2763
Email .... careers@thebodyshop.ca
Website .... www.thebodyshop.ca
Employer Background: The Body Shop is a leading retailer of high quality cosmetics, skin and hair care products. *New Positions Created (2):* Shop Managers; Promotions Coordinator.

BODYCOTE ORTECH INC.
Att: Human Resources Department
2395 Speakman Drive
Mississauga, ON L5K 1B3

Tel. 905-822-4111
Fax 905-823-1446
Website .... www.bodycote-mt.com
Employer Background: Bodycote Ortech Inc. is a provider of contract research, product and process development, failure analysis, consulting and testing services. *New Positions Created (4):* Manager, Pharmaceutical Chemistry; Computer-Aided Engineer; Chemical Technician / Technologist; Mechanical & Metallurgical Technologist.

BOEHRINGER INGELHEIM (CANADA) LTD.
Att: Human Resources
5150 South Service Road
Burlington, ON L7L 5H4

Tel. 905-639-0333
Fax 905-637-9659
Email .... hr@boehringer-ingelheim.ca
Website .... www.boehringer-ingelheim.ca
Employer Background: Boehringer Ingelheim (Canada) Ltd. is a leader in the field of pharmaceutical products, animal health, nutritional supplements and fine chemicals. *New Positions Created (7):* Sales Representative; Analyst, Business Intelligence / Market Research; Business Intelligence Architect; Electronic Data Interchange Analyst; Manager, Business Intelligence / Market Research; Marketing Assistant; Pharmaceutical Sales Representative.

BOEING CANADA TECHNOLOGY LTD., ARNPRIOR DIVISION
Att: Human Resources Supervisor
107 Baskin Drive East
Arnprior, ON K7S 3M1

Tel. 613-623-4267
Fax 613-623-1720
Email .... arnhr@boeing.com
Website .... www.boeing.com
Employer Background: Boeing Canada, Arnprior Division manufactures parts for all models of Boeing aircraft. *New Positions Created (6):* Automation Development Engineer; Continuous Improvement Engineer; MRB Engineer; Programmer Analyst; Quality Engineer; Sheet Metal Technician.

BOILER INSPECTION & INSURANCE COMPANY OF CANADA, THE
Att: Human Resources Department
18 King Street East
Toronto, ON M5C 1C4

Tel. 416-363-5491
Fax 416-363-0538
Email .... hr@biico.com
Website .... www.biico.com
Employer Background: Established in 1875, BI&I provides the specialized underwriting and technical expertise required for insuring boilers, machinery and electrical equipment. *New Positions Created (7):* Account Executive; Commercial Property Underwriter; Area Manager, Inspection Department; Boiler and Machinery Claims Adjuster; Marketing / Underwriting Position; Maintenance Management Consultant; Manager, Technical Operations.

BOMBARDIER AEROSPACE
Att: Human Resources Department
PO Box 6087, Station Centre-Ville
Montréal, QC H3C 3G9

Tel. 514-861-9481
Email .... hr@aero.bombardier.com
Website .. www.aerospace.bombardier.com
Employer Background: Bombardier Aerospace, a unit of Bombardier Inc., is one of the world's leading manufacturers of business, regional and amphibious aircraft. *New Positions Created (152):* Analyst, Cash Management; Finance Business Analyst; Fly-By-Wire Specialist; Propulsion Technologist / Staff; Senior Specialist, Propulsion; Software Component Specialist; Air Systems Position; Manager of Contracts, Business Aircraft; Intermediate Buyer; Technical Representative, Mechanical; Business Process Reengineering Analyst; Change Agent, Six Sigma; Resource Coordinator; Senior Human Resources Position; Software Application Development Position, Grade 2; Technical Training Coordinator; Application / Data Architect; Change Management Specialist; Financial Analyst, Grade 1; Human Resources Advisor; Senior Process Analyst; Senior Secretary; Software Applications Specialist; Training Coordinator; Airframe Stress Engineer; Business Analyst, Grade 1; Buyer, Grade 3; Change Management Specialist; Coordinator, Customs Compliance; Engineer, Advanced Composites and Chemical Technology; Mechanical Technologist; Senior Financial Analyst; Stress Engineer; Systems Installation Specialist; Web Content Administrator; Administrative Assistant; Financial Analyst, Treasury; Intermediate Structures Design Engineer; Senior Quality Assurance Technician; Specialist, Software Certification; Supervisor, Procurement Quality Assurance; Unix Systems Administrator; Buyer, Grade 2; Coordinator, Special Projects; Flammability Specialist; Network Security Manager; SAP Security Specialist; Senior Secretary; Account Manager; Advanced Design Specialist, Systems; Airworthiness Position; Avionics Specialist, Maintenance Engineering; Buyer, Grade 1; Buyer, Grade 2; Customer Service Representative, Spare Parts Sales; E-Business Analyst; Engineering Specialist, Aircraft Performance; Group Support Equipment Specialist; MSG-3 Coordinator; Program Accounting Supervisor; Program Finance Generalist; Project Controller; Project Team Lead; Propulsion Engineer; Senior Propulsion Controls Engineer; Six Sigma Master Agent; Business Case Analyst; Contract Coordinator; Database Analyst; Engineers, Electrical and Avionics Systems; Failure Analysis Specialist; Flight Control Systems / FBW Position; Human Resources Supervisor; Instrumentation Technician; Material and Processes Specialist; Programmer Analyst; Reliability & Maintainability Position; SAP Basis Administrator; SAP Courseware Developer; SAP Process & System Integrity Specialist; Stress Analysis Position; Systems Stress Specialist; Technologist, Hydro-Mechanical Systems; Weights Engineering Specialist; Business Analyst, Technical Publications; Intermediate Purchasing Agent; Systems Analyst; Advanced Aerodynamics Specialist; Advisor,

Public Relations and Communication; Analyst - Spares Material Planning; Buyer; Contracts Account Executive (Americas); Contracts Account Executive (International); Customer Service Account Manager; Manager, Contracts Support and Services; Program Coordinator BD-100; Programmer Analyst; Programmer Analyst; Programmer Analyst; Project Manager, Aircraft Programs; Senior Financial Analyst; Supervisor; Systems Administrator; Weights and Balance Analyst; ABAP / 4 Developer / Architect; Aircraft Structure Inspectors; Engine Mechanic; Preflight Inspectors; Airframe Design Specialist; Airframe Stress Analyst; Authorization Specialist; Change Management Specialist; Database Administrator, SQL; Database Analyst; Functional Tool Support Specialist; Interior Design Specialist; Network Architect; Project Controller; Project Controller / Senior Clerk; Reliability and Maintainability Specialist; Senior Financial Analyst; Systems Stress Specialist; Analyst / Developer, Lotus Notes; ASIP Engineer; Auditor, Information Technology; Business Analyst; Dashboard Specialist; Human Resources Generalist; Millwright / Machine Repairman; Procedures and Standards Coordinator; Robotic Engineer (Mirabel); Secretary, Legal Department; Supervisor, Airline Security; Tax Specialist; Preflight Avionics Technicians; Preflight Technicians; Simulation Specialist; Maintenance Analyst, Maintenance Management Services; Maintenance Instructors, Regional Aircraft; Inspectors, Structural Assembly; Preflight Avionics Technicians; Preflight Inspectors; Preflight Technicians; Technical Representatives (3); Business Analyst ; Business Analyst; Estimator; Legal Advisors (2); Pilot Instructors; Senior Program Analysts (2); Senior Specialist Architects (2); Supervisor, Technical Publications.

BOMBARDIER AEROSPACE, DEFENSE SERVICES
Att: Human Resources Department
10000, Cargo A-4 Street
Montreal International Airport
Mirabel, QC J7N 1H3

Tel. 450-476-4000
Fax 450-476-4207
Email .... rh@defense.bombardier.com
Website .... www.aerospace.bombardier.com
Employer Background: Bombardier Aerospace, Defense Services offers a range of integrated technical services, including military aircraft fleet management and pilot training for the Canadian and NATO Armed Forces. *New Positions Created (25):* Specialist, Maintenance Engineering and Logistics; CATIA Airframe Designers; Structural Engineer; Business Analyst, Engineering; Business Analyst, General; Business Analyst SAP, Production Planning; Contract Administrators; Coordinator, Procedures and Standards; Engineer, Aircraft Structural Integrated Program; Engineer, Airframe Stress Analysis; Engineer, Electrical and Avionics Systems; Engineer, Robotics; Project Management Analysts; Technical Writers; Avionics Engineer; Business Analyst, Engi-

neering Sector; Business Analyst, ERP System (SAP); Business Analyst, Information System Sector; CF-18 Structural Engineer; Illustrators; Methods Agent; Project Management Analyst; Robotics Engineer; Supervisor, Technical Publications; Technical Writers.

BOMBARDIER AEROSPACE, REGIONAL AIRCRAFT
Att: Employment Office
123 Garratt Boulevard
Toronto, ON M3K 1Y5
Tel. 416-633-7310
Fax 416-375-4519
Email ... humanresources@dehavilland.ca
Website .... www.aero.bombardier.com
Employer Background: Bombardier Aerospace, a unit of Bombardier Inc., is one of the world's leading business, regional and amphibious aircraft manufacturers. *New Positions Created (11):* Buyers, Supply Chain Management; Space Planner; Buyers, Supply Chain Management; Aircraft Services Business Analyst; Change Agent, Six Sigma; Financial Analyst; Environmental Specialist; Human Resources Generalist; Space Planner / Interior Designer; Change Agent, Six Sigma; Aircraft Assemblers.

BOMBARDIER INC., COMPLETION CENTRE MONTREAL
Att: Human Resources Department
200 Cote-Vertu Road West
Dorval, QC H4S 2A3
Tel. 514-420-4155
Fax 514-636-2542
Website .... www.bombardier.com
Employer Background: Bombardier Inc., Completion Centre Montreal specializes in the completion of business aircraft. *New Positions Created (7):* Aircraft Inspectors; Avionics Technicians; Interior Installers; Pre-Flight Technicians; Shop Inspector, Wiring and Final Assembly; Structures Installers; Upholsterers.

BOMBARDIER TRANSPORT, TRANSIT SYSTEMS
Att: Human Resources Manager
3885 Henning Drive, 2nd Floor
Burnaby, BC V5C 6N5
Tel. 604-647-0400
Fax 604-647-0401
Email ....
.... transport.bombardier.com
Website . www.transport.bombardier.com
Employer Background: Bombardier Transport, Transit Systems designs, builds and integrates customized solutions for transportation systems worldwide. *New Positions Created (4):* Installation Coordinator, Electrical Systems; Installation Coordinator; Installation Coordinator; Procurement Agent.

BOMBARDIER TRANSPORTATION
Att: Human Resources Department
125 Judson Street
Toronto, ON M8Z 1A4
Fax 416-253-3729

Email .... jwilliam@
.... transport.bombardier.com
Website .... www.transportation.
.... bombardier.com
Employer Background: Bombardier Transportation develops, designs and manufactures mass transit rail systems and vehicles worldwide. *New Positions Created (2):* Maintenance Technician; Service Workers.

BOMBARDIER TRANSPORTATION
Att: Human Resources Department
PO Box 250, Station A
Kingston, ON K7M 6R2
Tel. 613-384-3100
Fax 613-384-1565
Email .... hrkingst@
.... transport.bombardier.com
Website .... www.transportation.
.... bombardier.com
Employer Background: Bombardier Transportation develops, designs and manufactures mass transit rail systems and vehicles worldwide. *New Positions Created (4):* Manager, Mechanical Engineering; Human Resources Advisor; Legal Counsel; HR / Payroll Technician.

BOMHOFF AEROSPACE CORPORATION
Att: Human Resources Manager
2505 Halpern Street
St-Laurent, QC H4S 1N9
Tel. 514-332-0069
Fax 514-332-4469
Website .... www.bomhoff.com
Employer Background: Bomhoff Aerospace Corporation supplies interior furnishings to the general aviation industry. *New Positions Created (8):* Various Trades Positions; Production Manager; Aircraft Interior Designer; Planner; Human Resources Administrator; Production Manager; Human Resources Position; Project Manager.

BONAR PACKAGING CORP.
Att: Human Resources
2360 McDowell Road
Burlington, ON L7R 4A1
Tel. 905-637-5611
Fax 905-637-1066
Website .... www.lowandbonar.com
Employer Background: Bonar Packaging Corp. is a leading manufacturer of flexible packaging. *New Positions Created (4):* Process Engineer; Machine Operators; Customer Service Coordinator; Quality Assurance Technician.

BONAR PLASTICS
Att: Mary Grace Truchan
423 Highway 36 South, PO Box 88
Lindsay, ON K9V 4R8
Email .... mgtruchan.associates@
.... sympatico.ca
Website .... www.bonarplastics.com
Employer Background: Bonar Plastics is a leader in the field of rotational moulding in plastics, with 14 factories worldwide. The company is a part of Low and Bonar PLC.

New Positions Created (3): Quality Manager; Production Manager; Support Operations Supervisor.

BOND INTERNATIONAL COLLEGE
Att: Derek Patrick, Principal
5 Queenslea Avenue
Toronto, ON M9N 3X9
Tel. 416-248-8191
Fax 416-240-0000
Email .... executive@bondcollege.com
Website .... www.bondcollege.com
Employer Background: Bond International College is an independent residential and day school. *New Positions Created (3):* Head of Student Residence; Project Manager, Primary Education; Residence Supervisor.

BOOMERANG TRACKING INC.
Att: Human Resources Department
9280 Boulevard l'Acadie
Montréal, QC H4N 3C5
Fax 514-385-4719
Website .... www.boomerangtracking.com
Employer Background: Boomerang Tracking Inc. tracks and recovers stolen vehicles using leading-edge technology and a cellular network. *New Positions Created (3):* Marketing Manager; Director of Finance; Director of Operations.

BORDEN LADNER GERVAIS LLP
Att: M. Knoop
40 King Street West, Scotia Plaza
Toronto, ON M5H 3Y4
Tel. 416-367-6000
Fax 416-361-2793
Email .... mknoop@blgcanada.com
Website .... www.blgcanada.com
Employer Background: Borden Ladner Gervais LLP is one of the largest law firms in Canada, with over 600 lawyers, intellectual property agents and other professionals. *New Positions Created (3):* Legal Secretaries / Floaters; Pension and Benefits Law Associate; Junior Litigation Lawyers (2).

BORDEN LADNER GERVAIS LLP
Att: Guy J. Pratte / Peter K. Doody
60 Queen Street, Suite 1000
Ottawa, ON K1P 5Y7
Tel. 613-237-5160
Fax 613-230-8842
Website .... www.blgcanada.com
Employer Background: Borden Ladner Gervais LLP is one of the largest law firms in Canada, with over 600 lawyers, intellectual property agents and other professionals. *New Positions Created (4):* Litigation Lawyer, Administrative and Public Law; Litigation Lawyer, General Commercial / Insurance Litigation; Junior Labour Lawyer; Corporate / Commercial Lawyer.

BORN CANADA
Att: Administration Manager
10333 Southport Road SW, Suite 501
Calgary, AB T2W 3X6
Tel. 403-252-2676
Fax 403-252-2688

Email .... heaters@borncanada.com
Website .... www.borncanada.com
Employer Background: Born Canada is an engineering firm, supplying process equipment to the oil and gas industry. *New Positions Created (3):* Intermediate Purchasing Agent; Project Manager; Small Projects Manager.

BOSCO HOMES
Att: Human Resources
10435 - 76th Street
Edmonton, AB T6A 3B1

Tel. 780-449-3333
Fax 780-440-0760
Email .... employment@boscohomes.ca
Website .... www.bosco-homes.com
Employer Background: Bosco Homes is a leading provider of academic, therapeutic group care and clinical services to children and adolescents with behavioural or psychiatric disorders. *New Positions Created (2):* Aboriginal Program Coordinator; Education Director.

BOT CONSTRUCTION LIMITED
Att: Mike Beatty
1224 Speers Road
Oakville, ON L6L 2X4

Tel. 905-827-4167
Fax 905-827-0458
Email .... position@botconstruction.ca
Website .... www.botconstruction.ca
Employer Background: Bot Construction Limited is active in heavy civil engineering construction and development projects. *New Positions Created (2):* Quality Control Technicians; Surveyor.

BOUCLAIR INC.
Att: Bryan Mansell
1175 Trans Canada Highway North
Dorval, QC H9P 2V3

Tel. 514-685-3700
Fax 514-685-0151
Email .... hr@bouclair.com
Website .... www.bouclair.com
Employer Background: Founded in 1970, BouClair Inc. is a leading retailer of fabrics and home decor, with over 70 big box stores in Quebec and Ontario. *New Positions Created (9):* District Sales Manager; Junior Accountant; Decorators; Merchandising Clerk; Regional Manager; Signage Position; Junior Payroll Clerk; Supplies and Services Coordinator; Data Entry Clerk.

BOULEVARD CLUB, THE
Att: General Manager
1491 Lakeshore Boulevard West
Toronto, ON M6K 3C2

Tel. 416-532-3341
Fax 416-538-9411
Email .... admin@boulevardclub.com
Website .... www.boulevardclub.com
Employer Background: The Boulevard Club is a private, multi-sport family club. *New Positions Created (5):* Director, Membership Sales; Controller; Catering Manager; Food and Beverage Manager; General Manager.

BOULEVARD MEDIA (CANADA) INC.
Att: Human Resources Manager
1190 Hornby Street, 6th Floor
Vancouver, BC V6Z 2K5

Fax 604-639-1772
Email .... hr@blvdmedia.com
Website .... www.blvdmedia.com
Employer Background: Established in 1990, BMC specializes in the "people meeting people" business through interactive voice response technology. *New Positions Created (19):* Advertising Manager; Media Buyer-Planner; Media Financial Services Assistant; Member Services Leader; Staff Accountant; Call Centre Team Manager; Monitor Quality Representative; Senior Systems Specialist; Telecom Facility Coordinator; Telecom Financial Services Coordinator; Web Developer; Advertising Manager; Media Buyer; Junior Media Buyer; Brand Manager; Junior Brand Manager; Marketing Analyst; Media Buyer / Planner; Media Analyst.

BOULEVARD ST-MARTIN AUTO INC.
Att: Human Resources
1430 St. Martin Boulevard West
Laval, QC H7S 1M9

Tel. 450-667-4960
Fax 450-682-1123
Email .... resume@bsmauto.com
Website .... www.bsmauto.com
Employer Background: Established in 1973, BSM operates BMW Laval and Volvo Laval. *New Positions Created (5):* Electrical Diagnostic Technician, BMW; Service Advisers, BMW / Land Rover; Technician, Land Rover; Electrical Diagnostic Technician; Technician.

BOW VALLEY COLLEGE
Att: Human Resources Manager
332 - 6th Avenue SE
Calgary, AB T2G 4S6

Tel. 403-297-4825
Fax 403-297-4867
Email .... careers@bowvalleyc.ab.ca
Website .... www.bowvalleyc.ab.ca
Employer Background: Bow Valley College offers full-time career training programs that are all less than a year long. Each has a work experience component to give students a hands-on feel. *New Positions Created (2):* Dean, English as a Second Language Training; Dean, Health & Community Care.

BPA GROUP OF COMPANIES
Att: Manager, Claims & Administration
PO Box 6020, Station B
Toronto, ON M9W 7A3

Tel. 416-745-6466
Fax 416-745-5163
Website .... www.bpagroup.com
Employer Background: Formed in 1958, the BPA Group of Companies is a leader in multi-employer benefits consulting and administration. *New Positions Created (2):* Entry-Level Benefits Administrator; Senior Health & Dental Claims Examiner.

BPA GROUP OF COMPANIES
Att: Manager, Client Services

135 Queen's Plate Drive, Suite 200
Toronto, ON M9W 6V1

Tel. 416-745-6466
Fax 416-745-5163
Email .... mail@bpagroup.com
Website .... www.bpagroup.com
Employer Background: Formed in 1958, the BPA Group of Companies is a leader in multi-employer benefits consulting and administration. *New Positions Created (2):* Claims Examiner; Health Benefits Administrator.

BRACKNELL TELECOM SERVICES
Att: Engineering Design Manager
20108 Logan Avenue
Langley, BC V3A 4L6

Employer Background: Bracknell Telecom Services provides facilities design, implementation and management services across North America. *New Positions Created (4):* CAD Design Technician; Electrical Engineer; Equipment Installation Technician; Microwave Installation Technician.

**BRADFORD WEST
GWILLIMBURY, TOWN OF**
Att: Juanita Dempster-Evans,
Clerk-Administrator
61 Holland West, PO Box 160
Bradford, ON L3Z 2A8

Tel. 705-775-5366
Fax 705-775-0153
Website
www.town.bradfordwestgwillimbury.on.ca
Employer Background: Located in the County of Simcoe and on the northern fringe of the GTA, the Town of Bradford West Gwillimbury is an urban / rural community of 22,000. *New Positions Created (3):* Director of Engineering; Wastewater System Operators (2); Wastewater System Supervisor.

**BRADON INDUSTRIES LTD. /
HYDRA RIG CANADA**
Att: Human Resources Manager
4910 - 80th Avenue SE
Calgary, AB T2C 2X3

Tel. 403-279-6430
Fax 403-279-7234
Email .... mgraburn@hydrarigcanada.com
Website .... www.hydrarigcanada.com
Employer Background: Bradon Industries Ltd. / Hydra Rig Canada is a leading manufacturer of coiled tubing and nitrogen pumping equipment for the oilfield industry. *New Positions Created (6):* Design Engineers; Draftspersons; Fitters / Welders; Mechanics / Millwrights / Instrumentation Technicians; Project Engineers; Project Planners / Coordinators.

BRAGG PHOTONICS INC.
Att: Mr. D. Cavalieri
2270 St. Francois Road
Dorval, QC H9P 1K2

Tel. 514-421-6766
Fax 514-428-1433
Email .... d.cavalieri@braggphotonics.com
Website .... www.bragg.ca

Employer Background: Bragg Photonics Inc. designs and develops component solutions for high-speed, fibre optic telecom networks. *New Positions Created (18):* Industrial Engineering Technician; Optic Technicians; Process Technicians; Production Supervisor; Training Manager; Technicians; Quality Control Inspector; Senior Inventory Control Clerk; Labview Programmer / Software Developer; CNC Machinist; Operators / Assemblers; Optics Technicians; Production Supervisor; Recruiter; Machinist; Optics Technician; Production Engineering Manager; Production Line Personnel.

BRAKE PRO, LTD.
Att: HR Manager
250 Doney Crescent
Concord, ON L4K 3A8

Tel. 416-213-7169
Fax 905-669-5334
Email .... hrmanager@brakepro.com
Website .... www.brakepro.com

Employer Background: Brake Pro, Ltd. is a manufacturer of heavy-duty brake friction material. *New Positions Created (3):* Production Supervisor; Industrial Engineer; Buyer.

BRAMPTON, CITY OF
Att: Human Resources
2 Wellington Street West
Brampton, ON L6Y 4R2

Tel. 905-874-2150
Fax 905-874-2199
Email .... human.resources@
.... city.brampton.on.ca
Website .... www.city.brampton.on.ca

Employer Background: The City of Brampton, one of Canada's fastest-growing cities, is home to over 325,000 residents. *New Positions Created (40):* Aquatic Staff (10); Manager, Audit and Consulting; Transit Bus Mechanic; Human Resources Advisor; Senior Advisor, Labour Relations; Network Administrator; PC Specialists (2); Buyer; Permit Expediter; Cable & Infrastructure Technologies Coordinator; Facility Programs Supervisor, Fitness; Manager, Marketing Services; PeopleSoft Oracle Database Administrator; PeopleSoft Payroll / HR Analyst; Supervisor of Investments, Insurance & Risk Management; Systems Integrator, PeopleSoft ERP; Chief Information Officer; Director of Economic Development; Manager, Fleet Services; Manager, Roads & Operations; Development Engineer; Financial Planning Analyst; Engineering Technician; Project Coordinators; Manager, Planning & Development Services; Planner 1 Development Position; Manager, Administration & Special Projects; Open Space Planner; PeopleSoft A / P Purchasing Analyst; Communications Officers (2); Gardener II; Treeperson I; Accounts Payable / Purchasing Analyst, PeopleSoft; PeopleSoft A / P - Purchasing Analyst; Environmental Engineer; Corporate Effectiveness Specialist; E-Business Development Manager; GIS Manager; Network Administrator; PC Specialist.

BRAMPTON ENGINEERING INC.
Att: Human Resources

8031 Dixie Road
Brampton, ON L6T 3Y1

Tel. 905-793-3000
Fax 905-793-9244
Email .... hr1@be-ca.com
Website .... www.be-ca.com

Employer Background: Established in 1973, Brampton Engineering Inc. is a custom machinery builder for the global plastics industry, with offices in the USA and overseas. *New Positions Created (2):* Control Systems Designers (2); Project Manager.

BRANDERA.COM INC.
Att: Joanne Alexander, Human Resources
5255 Yonge Street, Suite 705
Toronto, ON M2N 6P4

Tel. 416-226-2800
Email .... hr@brandera.com
Website .... www.brandera.com

Employer Background: BrandEra.com Inc. serves as a business-to-business destination for the marketing communications industry. *New Positions Created (5):* Business Programmer / Analyst; EJB / WebSphere Specialist; JSP Programmer; Oracle Database Administrator; Systems / Network Support Position.

BRANDON REGIONAL HEALTH AUTHORITY
Att: Brad Langston,
Human Resources Director
150 McTavish Avenue East
Brandon, MB R7A 2B3

Tel. 204-726-2246
Fax 204-726-1852
Website .... www.gov.mb.ca/health/rha

Employer Background: Brandon Regional Health Centre is a 326-bed regional referral centre, serving southwestern Manitoba and eastern Saskatchewan. *New Positions Created (3):* Staff Physiotherapists (3); Director, Nuclear Medicine; Staff Pharmacist.

BRANDON UNIVERSITY
Att: Dr. T. Patrick Carrabre,
Vice-President, Academic and Research
270 - 18th Street
Brandon, MB R7A 6A9

Fax 204-728-7340
Website .... www.brandonu.ca

Employer Background: Founded in 1899, Brandon University has over 2,500 students and 170 faculty members. *New Positions Created (2):* Dean, Education; Chief Information Officer / University Librarian.

BRANDT TRACTOR LTD.
Att: Greg Davidson, Branch Manager
10630 - 176th Street
Edmonton, AB T5S 1M2

Tel. 780-484-6613
Fax 780-489-6891
Website .... www.brandttractor.com

Employer Background: Brandt Tractor Ltd. is the John Deere construction and forest equipment dealer for Alberta, Saskatchewan and Manitoba. *New Positions Created (2):* Journeyman Positions; Branch Manager.

BRANKSOME HALL
Att: Karen Murton, Principal
10 Elm Avenue
Toronto, ON M4W 1N4

Tel. 416-920-9741
Fax 416-920-5390
Website .... www.branksome.on.ca

Employer Background: Branksome Hall is an independent day and boarding school for girls, serving 850 students. *New Positions Created (4):* Computer Science Teacher; Director of Admissions and Communications; Residence Dons; Teachers.

BRANS, LEHUN, BALDWIN
Att: Dennis M. Brans
120 Adelaide Street West
Suite 2401, Richmond-Adelaide Centre
Toronto, ON M5H 1T1

Tel. 416-601-1041
Fax 416-601-0655
Email .... dmbrans@blb-law.com
Website .... www.blbcdnlaw.com

Employer Background: Brans, Lehun, Baldwin is a small boutique law firm, specializing in tax, securities, real estate and commercial litigation. *New Positions Created (2):* Commercial Lawyer(s); Corporate / Commercial Lawyer.

BRANT COMMUNITY HEALTHCARE SYSTEM, BRANTFORD GENERAL SITE
Att: Human Resources Department
200 Terrace Hill Street
Brantford, ON N3R 1G9

Tel. 519-751-5526
Fax 519-751-5575
Email .... humanresources@bchsys.org
Website .... www.bchsys.org

Employer Background: Brantford General Hospital, part of the Brant Community Healthcare System, is an acute care facility with over 200 beds. *New Positions Created (38):* Director, Special Programs; Manager, Community Health Services; Manager / Director, Organizational Development; Manager, Human Resources; Pharmacy Manager; Clinical Nurse Educator; Diet Technician; Emergency RN; Health Records Technician / Analyst; Kinesiologist; Laboratory Technical Assistant; Medical Dictatypists; Occupational Therapists and Physiotherapists; Operating Room Technicians; Registered Nurse, Maternal Child Program; Registered Nurses, Day Surgery; Speech Pathologist; Speech Pathologist, Speech-Language Pathology Division; Staff Pharmacists, Hospital and Retail; Hospitalists; Nurse Clinician, Emergency Services; Nurse Clinician, Surgical Services; Internist; Medical Lab Technical Specialist; Refrigeration Mechanic; RNs; RPNs; Staff Pharmacists; Echocardiography Technologist; Registered Respiratory Care Practitioners; Occupational Health and Safety Coordinator; Speech Pathologists; Staff Pharmacists (2); Echocardiography Technologist; Nutrition Services Supervisor; Registered Respiratory Care Practitioners; Echocardiography Technologist; Financial Services Supervisor.

BRANT COMMUNITY HEALTHCARE SYSTEM, WILLETT SITE
Att: Diane Hammer, HRDepartment
28 Grand River Street North
Paris, ON N3L 2N7
Tel. 519-442-2251
Fax 519-442-4793
Email .... dhammer@bchsys.org
Website .... www.bchsys.org
Employer Background: Willett Hospital is a fully-accredited facility, serving people in the town of Paris, Ontario and surrounding rural villages. *New Positions Created (2):* Occupational Therapists and Physiotherapists; Rehabilitation Services Assistants.

BRANT HALDIMAND-NORFOLK CATHOLIC DISTRICT SCHOOL BOARD
Att: Patricia M. Kings, Superintendent of Education (Human Resources)
322 Fairview Drive, PO Box 217
Brantford, ON N3T 5M8
Tel. 519-756-6505
Fax 519-756-9913
Website .... www.bhncdsb.edu.on.ca
Employer Background: BHNCDSB provides Catholic education to 10,400 students in Brant, Haldimand and Norfolk. *New Positions Created (5):* Catholic Secondary School Chaplain; Department Heads; Elementary Catholic Principals; Human Resources Coordinator; French-as-a Second Language Teachers, Elementary Panel.

BRANT TELEPHONE INC.
Att: Human Resources
3190 Harvester Road
Burlington, ON L7N 3T1
Tel. 905-632-0585
Fax 905-333-3445
Email .... hr@branttelephone.com
Website .... www.branttelephone.com
Employer Background: Brant Telephone Inc. is a Lucent Technologies dealer. *New Positions Created (2):* Telecommunications Technician; Customer Service Representative.

BRANTFORD, CORPORATION OF THE CITY OF
Att: Staffing Specialist, HR Department
100 Wellington Square, PO Box 818
Brantford, ON N3T 5R7
Tel. 519-759-4150
Fax 519-752-5719
Email .... resumes@city.brantford.on.ca
Website .... www.city.brantford.on.ca
Employer Background: Located along the Grand River and a 400-series highway, the City of Brantford has a population of over 85,000. *New Positions Created (22):* Director, Building Services; Fire Chief; Coordinator Technical Services, Corporate Buildings; Fire Prevention Officer; Traffic Signal Electrician; Case Worker; Parks Designer; Resource Centre Assistant; Security Coordinator; Technical Services Manager; Economic Development Officer; Horticultural Maintenance Person; Transportation Engineer; Water and Wastewater Engineer; Purchasing and Stores Manager; Fundraising / Corporate Sponsorship Coordinator; Class A

Truck and Coach Mechanic; Director, Property Management Services; Superintendent of Transit Maintenance; Senior Accountant; Small Business Consultant; Property Tax Manager.

BRANTWOOD RESIDENTIAL DEVELOPMENT CENTRE
Att: Manager, Human Resources
25 Bell Lane
Brantford, ON N3T 1E1
Fax 519-753-5639
Email .... bwood@execulink.com
Website ...... www.execulink.com/~bwood
Employer Background: Brantwood Residential Development Centre is a non-profit organization, providing clinical support for individuals with developmental and physical challenges in a group home setting. *New Positions Created (3):* Coordinator, Human Resources; Counsellor 1; Registered Practical Nurse.

BRASCON ARCHITECTURAL PRODUCTS INC.
Att: Human Resources Department
19 Victoria Court
Brampton, ON L6T 1E2
Tel. 905-792-2828
Fax 905-825-5412
Employer Background: Brascon Architectural Products Inc. manufactures and distributes turnstiles, architectural railing systems and other pedestrian control products. *New Positions Created (5):* Mechanical Engineer, Research and Development; Estimator / Inside Sales Coordinator; National Account Manager; Engineers; Regional Sales Managers / Inside Sales Coordinators.

BRENNTAG CANADA INC.
Att: Human Resources Manager
43 Jutland Road
Toronto, ON M8Z 2G6
Tel. 416-259-8231
Fax 416-503-6876
Email .... jmoon@hciww.com
Website .... www.brenntag.ca
Employer Background: Brenntag Canada Inc. (formerly HCI Canada Inc.) is a wholly-owned subsidiary of Holland Chemical International, a global chemicals and plastics distributor with sites in over 29 countries. *New Positions Created (14):* Account Manager; IT Specialist, Basis; Laboratory Supervisor; Corporate Account Manager; Sales Representative; Accounting Manager; Customer Service Supervisor; Regulatory Affairs Assistant; Inside Sales Representative; Logistics Assistant; Product Manager; Sales Representatives (2); Technical Service Coordinator; Inside Sales Representatives.

BRENTWOOD COLLEGE
Att: Andrea Pennells, Head
2735 Mt. Baker Road, Box 1000
Mill Bay, BC V0R 2P0
Tel. 250-743-5521
Fax 250-743-2911
Website .... www.brentwood.bc.ca

Employer Background: Brentwood College is a residential, co-educational university preparatory school, with 420 students. *New Positions Created (5):* American College Placement Counsellor; Director of Music; Houseparent; Mathematics Teacher; Physics Teacher.

BRIDGE BRAND FOOD SERVICES LTD.
Att: Human Resources Department
1802 Centre Avenue NE
Calgary, AB T2E 0A6
Tel. 403-235-8555
Website .... www.bridgebrand.ca
Employer Background: Bridge Brand Food Services Ltd. is a foodservice distributor. *New Positions Created (9):* Seafood / Sales Specialist; Programmer; Operations / LAN Manager; Costing Clerk; Sales Specialists; Credit Collection Specialist; Driver / Service Representative; Purchasing Assistant; Sales Supervisor.

BRIDGESTONE FIRESTONE CANADA INC. / BFCA
Att: Andrea Imanse
5770 Hurontario Street, Suite 400
Mississauga, ON L5R 3G5
Tel. 905-890-1990
Fax 905-712-3907
Employer Background: BFCA, a wholly-owned subsidiary of Bridgestone Firestone Inc. of Nashville, manufactures and markets Bridgestone and Firestone brand tires. *New Positions Created (3):* Manager, Credit and Collections; Purchasing Manager; Central Region Business Manager.

BRIDGESTREET ACCOMMODATIONS
Att: Human Resources Manager
1000 Yonge Street, Suite 301
Toronto, ON M4W 2K2
Tel. 416-923-1000
Fax 416-923-2090
Email .... toronto.hr@bridgestreet.com
Website .... www.bridgestreet.com
Employer Background: BridgeStreet Accommodations is an international provider of furnished corporate housing. *New Positions Created (3):* Accommodation Coordinators (2); Corporate Account Executive; Supervisor, Housekeeping Operations.

BRISBIN & SENTIS ENGINEERING INC.
Att: Human Resources Manager
5403 Crowchild Trail NW
Suite 220, Crowchild Square
Calgary, AB T3B 4Z1
Tel. 403-247-2001
Fax 403-247-2013
Email .... info@brisbin-sentis.com
Website .... www.brisbin-sentis.com
Employer Background: Brisbin & Sentis Engineering Inc. is a consulting firm, providing municipal and environmental engineering services to rural and urban centres, senior government and the private sector. *New Positions Created (3):* CAD Technologist; Intermediate Professional Engineer /

Civil Engineering Technologist; Senior Professional Engineer.

BRISTOL-MYERS SQUIBB PHARMACEUTICAL GROUP
Att: Human Resources Manager
2365 Cote de Liesse
St-Laurent, QC H4N 2M7

Tel. 514-333-3200
Fax 514-333-7943
Website .... www.bms.com

Employer Background: Bristol-Myers Squibb is a diversified worldwide health and personal care company, with principal businesses in medicine, beauty care, nutritional and medical devices. *New Positions Created (2):* Clinical Research Project Manager; Sales Representative.

BRITISH COLUMBIA ASSETS & LAND CORPORATION
Att: Valerie MacMillan
609 Broughton Street
5th Floor, PO Box 9475, Stn Prov Govt
Victoria, BC V8W 9W6

Tel. 250-356-5925
Fax 250-952-6237

Employer Background: British Columbia Assets & Land Corporation manages, develops and markets a diverse portfolio of Crown land. *New Positions Created (5):* Communications Manager; Manager, Aboriginal Relations; Project Manager, Development and Marketing; Senior Business Analyst; Senior Financial Analyst.

BRITISH COLUMBIA AUTOMOBILE ASSOCIATION / BCAA
Att: Human Resources
4567 Canada Way
Burnaby, BC V5G 4T1

Tel. 604-268-5267
Fax 604-268-5564
Email .... hrpersonnel@bcaa.bc.ca
Website .... www.bcaa.com

Employer Background: BCAA is an affiliate of the Canadian Automobile Association, serving members in British Columbia and the Yukon. *New Positions Created (21):* Insurance Agents I and II; Manager, Telecentre; Business Development Strategist; Information Services Administration Coordinator; Insurance Supervisors (2); Manager, ERS Contract Services; Supervisor, ERS Operations; Travel Sales Support Agents; Marketing Database Analyst; Regional Sales Manager; Database Analyst; Intermediate Programmer Analysts (3); System / Data Architects (3); Travel Supervisor; Insurance Agents; Travel Agents; Technical Services Manager; Insurance Agents; Internet Travel and Insurance Agents; Travel Agents; Supervisor, Corporate Records and Mail Systems.

BRITISH COLUMBIA INSTITUTE OF TECHNOLOGY / BCIT
Att: Human Resources
3700 Willingdon Avenue
Burnaby, BC V5G 3H2

Tel. 604-451-6909
Fax 604-434-8462

Email .... hrassist@bcit.ca
Website .... www.bcit.ca

Employer Background: Founded in 1964, BCIT is a post-secondary institution, offering career training in 8 program areas. *New Positions Created (25):* Engineer / Technician, Broadcast Media Communications; Instructor, Power Engineering; Campus Pipeline Coordinator, Team Web; Clinical Assistant Instructor, Medical Radiography Technology; Communications Officer; Jr Systems Analyst, Computer Resources; Mgr, Organizational & People Development; Operations Mgr; Security Supervisors; Director, Finance Dept.; Environmental Health & Safety Coordinator; Mgr, Instructional Media and Delivery Systems; Power Engineering Instructors (2); Assistant Instructor, Electronic Engineering Technology; Instructor, Electronic Engineering Technology; Admin Assistant - IAEAC; Assistant Instructor, Biomedical Engineering Technology; Circulation Assistant, Library; Instructor, Emergency Nursing; Business Manager, BCIT International; Instructor, Electroneurophysiology; Associate Dean, Nursing and Health Engineering; Instructors, Baccalaureate Nursing; Meetings and Events Coordinator; Dean, School of Business.

BRITISH COLUMBIA INVESTMENT MANAGEMENT CORPORATION
Att: Human Resources
2940 Jutland Rd., 3rd Floor, Sawmill Point
Victoria, BC V8T 5K6

Tel. 250-356-0263
Fax 250-953-0453
Email .... hr@bcimc.com
Website .... www.bcimc.com

Employer Background: BCIMC is one of Canada's largest institutional investors, managing assets for 3rd-party trust funds. *New Positions Created (7):* Assistant Portfolio Manager, Equity Investments; Vice-President, Legal Affairs and General Counsel; Assistant Portfolio Manager, Private Placements; Assistant Portfolio Manager, Real Estate; Manager, Policy; Manager, Research; Portfolio Manager, Private Placements.

BRITISH COLUMBIA LOTTERY CORPORATION
Att: Human Resources Manager
74 West Seymour Street
Kamloops, BC V2C 1E2

Tel. 250-828-5638
Fax 250-828-5631
Email .... humanresources@bclc.com
Website .... www.bclc.com

Employer Background: The British Columbia Lottery Corporation is responsible for the conduct and management of lotteries and casino gaming in British Columbia. *New Positions Created (9):* Senior Programmers / Analysts, Casino Gaming; Senior Programmers / Analysts, E-Business / Corporate Systems; Systems Architect, Corporate Applications; Systems Architect, Infrastructure; Manager, Casino Training; Manager, Marketing - Casinos; Manager, Player Relations - Casino; Manager, Slot Development; Manager, Special Projects - Casino.

BRITISH COLUMBIA MARITIME EMPLOYERS ASSOCIATION / BCMEA
Att: Director, Labour Relations
349 Railway Street, Suite 500
Vancouver, BC V6A 1A4

Tel. 604-688-1155
Fax 604-684-2397
Email .... oathwal@bcmea.com
Website .... www.bcmea.com

Employer Background: BCMEA is an unaccredited employers' association, consisting of 74 member companies. *New Positions Created (3):* Labour Relations Manager; Training Officer; Secretaries / Administrative Assistants (2).

BRITISH COLUMBIA MENTAL HEALTH SOCIETY, RIVERVIEW HOSPITAL / BCMHS
Att: Manager, HR Administration
500 Lougheed Highway
Port Coquitlam, BC V3C 4J2

Tel. 604-524-7130
Fax 604-524-7382
Email .... jreid@bcmhs.bc.ca
Website .... www.bcmhs.bc.ca

Employer Background: Riverview Hospital is an 800-bed accredited psychiatric teaching hospital, affiliated with the University of British Columbia and operated by the BCMHS. *New Positions Created (24):* Clinical Neuropsychologist; Clinical Psychologist; Occupational Therapist; Clinical Instructor; Nurses; Vocational Instructor; Occupational Therapist; Nurse Clinician; Nurses; Occupational Therapist; Professional Practice Leader, Dental Officer; Radiology Technologist; Sewing Machine Operator; Manager, Human Resources and Occupational Health and Safety; Administrative Support Position; Health Care Worker; Occupational Therapist; Supervisor, Radiology; Vice-President, Human Resources; Clinical Psychologist; Manager, Food Production; Recreational Therapist; Professional Practice Leader; Tracking Project Research Officer.

BRITISH COLUMBIA PENSION CORPORATION
Att: Brenda Reed, HR Branch
2995 Jutland Road
PO Box 9460, Stn Prov Govt
Victoria, BC V8W 9V8

Tel. 250-356-7967
Fax 250-387-2570
Email ... jobs.pensioncorp@gems7.gov.bc.ca
Website .... www.pensions.gov.bc.ca

Employer Background: BC Pension Corp. is a provincial Crown corporation, administering the college, municipal, public service and teachers' pension plans. *New Positions Created (3):* Desktop Publisher; Communications Planners (2); Financial Analyst.

BRITISH COLUMBIA PHARMACY ASSOCIATION / BCPHA
Att: S. Anthony Toth,
Director of Public Affairs and Marketing
3751 Shell Road, Suite 150
Richmond, BC V6X 2W2

Tel. 604-279-2053

Fax 604-279-2065
Email .... info@bcpharmacy.ca
Website .... www.bcpharmacy.ca
Employer Background: BCPhA is a non-profit, voluntary, professional association of pharmacists, with 2,100 members. *New Positions Created (2):* Marketing Coordinator; Manager, Member Services.

BRITISH COLUMBIA SECURITIES COMMISSION / BCSC

Att: Louise Martin,
Manager, Human Resources
701 West Georgia Street
PO Box 10142, Pacific Centre
Vancouver, BC V7Y 1L2

Tel. 604-899-6522
Fax 604-899-6745
Email .... bcsc-hr@bcsc.bc.ca
Website .... www.bcsc.bc.ca
Employer Background: BCSC is an independent agency of the Government of British Columbia, responsible for regulating trading in securities and exchange contracts. *New Positions Created (3):* Associate Chief Accountant; Librarian; Securities Examiners, Registration Division (2).

BROADCOM CORPORATION

Att: Human Resources Manager
13711 International Place, Suite 200
Richmond, BC V6V 2Z8

Fax 604-233-8501
Email .... jobs_canada@broadcom.com
Website .... www.broadcom.com
Employer Background: Broadband Corporation is a leading provider of highly integrated silicon solutions that enable broadband digital transmission of voice, video and data. *New Positions Created (3):* Design Engineer, Embedded; Major Account Manager; Senior Staff Engineer, Embedded.

BROADTEL CANADA

Att: Human Resources Manager
3700 Griffith Street, Suite 389
St-Laurent, QC H4T 2B3

Fax 514-344-1995
Email .... hr@broadtel.com
Website .... www.broadtel.com
Employer Background: BroadTel Canada, a subsidiary of California-based BroadTel Wireless, offers low-cost broadband wireless Internet access. *New Positions Created (8):* Manager, Wireless Product Development; Modem Design Engineer; Network Engineer; Radio Design Engineer; Software Design Engineer; System Engineer; Modem Design Engineer; Software Design Engineer.

BROCK UNIVERSITY

Att: Human Resources
500 Glenridge Avenue
St. Catharines, ON L2S 3A1

Tel. 905-688-5550
Fax 905-688-8481
Email .... career@www.brocku.ca
Website .... www.brocku.ca
Employer Background: Brock University has over 340 full-time faculty members, 10,800 undergraduate students and 600 graduate students registered in 6 faculties. *New Positions Created (12):* Assistant Registrar, Student Information and Systems Office of the Registrar; Job Creation Program Coordinator, Career Services; Manager, Athletic and Recreation Facilities; Project Manager, Youth Gambling; Coordinator; Research Co-Coordinator; Research Program Assistant / Database Manager; Canada Research Chairs; Coordinator, Mainstream Bachelor of Education in Adult Education Programs; Humanities Reference Librarian; Instruction / Reference Librarian; Associate University Librarian.

BROCKVILLE PSYCHIATRIC HOSPITAL

Att: Human Resources
1804 Highway 2 East, PO Box 1050
Brockville, ON K6V 5W7

Tel. 613-354-1461
Fax 613-345-0881
Email .... bphjobs@rohcg.on.ca
Website .... www.rohcg.on.ca
Employer Background: Established in 1894, Brockville Psychiatric Hospital (part of the Royal Ottawa Health Care Group) provides mental health services in eastern Ontario. *New Positions Created (2):* Various Healthcare Positions; Chief Pharmacist.

BROFORT INC.

Att: Human Resources Manager
7 Noel Street
Ottawa, ON K1M 2A4

Tel. 613-746-8580
Fax 613-749-9930
Employer Background: Brofort Inc. provides new store, renovation and roll-out services to Canadian retailers. *New Positions Created (3):* Merchandisers; Project Mgr, Construction / Fixture Installation; Site Supervisors.

BROGAN INC.

Att: Human Resources Manager
2249 Carling Avenue, Suite 410
Ottawa, ON K2B 7E9

Tel. 613-596-5042
Fax 613-596-5040
Email .... careers@broganinc.com
Website .... www.broganinc.com
Employer Background: Brogan Inc. is an economic research company, specializing in healthcare analysis for pharmaceutical manufacturers, governments, insurers and consultants. *New Positions Created (6):* Sales Assistant; Manager of Programmer Analysts; Regulatory Senior Analyst; Junior Analyst, Pharmaceutical Price Regulation; Market and Health Care Analysts (2); Regulatory Senior Analyst.

BROOKFIELD LEPAGE JOHNSON CONTROLS FACILITY MANAGEMENT SERVICES / BLJC

Att: Human Resources Manager
7400 Birchmount Road
Markham, ON L3R 4E6

Tel. 905-415-3248
Fax 905-415-3299
Email .... jmiller@bljc.ca
Website .... www.bljc.ca
Employer Background: Established in 1992, BLJC provides facility management services for major government and commercial customers. *New Positions Created (13):* Energy Manager; Junior Facility Manager; Insurance / Legal Coordinator; Team Leader, Call Centre; Project Management Team Leader; Project Coordinator; Project Manager; CMMS Support Specialist; Inbound Customer Service Representatives; Team Leader, Customer Service; VisCom Service Coordinator; VisCom Technician; Commissioning Manager NCA 1.

BROOKFIELD LEPAGE JOHNSON CONTROLS FACILITY MANAGEMENT SERVICES / BLJC

Att: Rachel B. Bujold
2141 Thurston Drive, Suite 101
Ottawa, ON K1G 6C9

Tel. 613-736-9211
Fax 613-736-6631
Email .... rbujold@bljc.ca
Website .... www.bljc.ca
Employer Background: Established in 1992, BLJC is a provider of facility management services for major government and commercial customers. *New Positions Created (12):* Property Manager; Technical Support Manager; Project Manager, Architectural; Project Manager, Mechanical; Commissioning Manager; Employee Relations Specialist; Accounting Reporting Assistant; Building Technicians; Maintenance Team Leader; Coordinator, Property Services; Coordinator, Tenant Services; Portfolio Manager.

BROOKFIELD PROPERTIES LIMITED

Att: Joyce Wallace, HR Specialist
181 Bay Street, Suite 4300, PO Box 770
Toronto, ON M5J 2T3

Tel. 416-369-2300
Fax 416-369-2316
Email ... jwallace@brookfieldproperties.com
Website ... www.brookfieldproperties.com
Employer Background: Brookfield Properties Ltd. is a leader in the commercial real estate industry. *New Positions Created (3):* Corporate Hosts; Various Real Estate Positions; Security Supervisor.

BROOKS AUTOMATION SOFTWARE CORPORATION

Att: Human Resources
13777 Commerce Parkway, Suite 100
Richmond, BC V6V 2X3

Tel. 604-214-5000
Fax 604-214-5001
Email .... hrcanada@brooks.com
Website .... www.brooks.com
Employer Background: Brooks Automation supplies equipment control solutions for complex semiconductor processing equipment used to build DRAMs, microprocessors and other devices. *New Positions Created (10):* Product Management Specialist; Project Manager, Customer Solutions; Software Architect; Software Development Engineer, C++ / Java; Software Quality Assur-

ance Team Leader; Technical Writer Training Specialist; Business Mgr; Customer Solutions Engineer; Software Development Engineer; Software QA Test Engineer.

BROOKS, TOWN OF
Att: Neil Hollands, PEng, Director of Engineering and Property Services
PO Bag 800
Brooks, AB T1R 0Z6

Tel. 403-362-3333
Fax 403-362-4787

Employer Background: The Town of Brooks is home to over 11,500 people. *New Positions Created (5):* Manager of Planning Services; Planning Officer; Manager, Administrative Services; Director, Engineering and Property Services; Engineering Technician.

BROWN APPLIED TECHNOLOGY INC.
Att: Engineering Manager
31 Progress Avenue
Toronto, ON M1P 4S6

Tel. 416-298-0560
Fax 416-298-0806

Employer Background: Brown Applied Technology Inc. designs and develops high performance switched mode power supplies. *New Positions Created (5):* Component Engineer; Electronic Engineer; Electronic Technologist; PCB Designers; QA Engineer.

BROWN ECONOMIC ASSESSMENTS INC.
Att: Anne C. Gillespie, CA
340 - 12th Avenue SW, Suite 610
Calgary, AB T2R 1L5

Tel. 403-571-0115
Fax 403-571-0932
Email ... anne.gillespie@browneconomic.com
Website .... www.browneconomic.com

Employer Background: Brown Economic Assessments Inc. is an economic consulting firm, specializing in the calculation of damages in civil litigation. *New Positions Created (2):* Executive Assistant; Legal Assistant, Personal Injury..

BRUNICO COMMUNICATIONS INC.
Att: Effie Rodrigues,
Director of Sales and Marketing
366 Adelaide Street West, Suite 500
Toronto, ON M5V 1R9

Tel. 416-408-2300
Fax 416-408-0870
Email .... erodrigues@brunico.com
Website .... www.brunico.com

Employer Background: Established in 1986, Brunico Communications Inc. is a business communications and publishing company, with offices in Toronto, Montreal and Los Angeles. *New Positions Created (2):* Sales Manager; Editor.

BTI PHOTONICS INC.
Att: Human Resources Manager
2191 Thurston Drive
Ottawa, ON K1G 6C9

Tel. 613-248-9154
Fax 613-248-9156
Email .... hr@btiphotonics.com
Website .... www.btiphotonics.com

Employer Background: BTI Photonics Inc. designs leading-edge optical subsystems and components. *New Positions Created (10):* Inside Sales Representative; Marketing Communications Manager; Optical Amplifier Development Engineer; Product Manager, Optical Amplifiers; Senior Account Manager; Technical Sales Engineer; Director of Marketing; Optical Packaging Engineer; Production Manager; Sales Manager.

BUCHANAN ASSOCIATES
Att: Human Resources Manager
10 Kingsbridge Garden Circle, Suite 301
Mississauga, ON L3R 3K8

Tel. 905-501-0042
Fax 905-501-0068
Email .... career@buchanan.com
Website .... www.buchanan.com

Employer Background: Founded in 1988, Buchanan Associates provides e-business development, network services and end-user services. *New Positions Created (5):* Java Developers; Java Development Team Leader; Microsoft Web Developers; Solution Architects; Sales Postitions.

BUCKMAN LABORATORIES
Att: Shari Guttman, HR Department
351 Joseph-Carrier Boulevard
Vaudreuil, QC J7V 5V5

Tel. 450-424-4404
Fax 450-424-4359
Website .... www.buckman.com

Employer Background: Established in 1945, Buckman Laboratories provides advanced chemical treatment technologies and extensive technical services to solve complex industrial problems. *New Positions Created (2):* Financial Accountant; Manufacturing Support Coordinator.

BUDD CANADA INC.
Att: Human Resources
1011 Homer Watson Boulevard
Kitchener, ON N2C 1L8

Tel. 519-895-1000
Website .... www.buddcanada.com

Employer Background: Budd Canada Inc. is an automotive supplier, specializing in the production of bumpers, chassis components and light truck frames. *New Positions Created (8):* Tool and Die Makers; Electricians; Millwrights; Junior Methods and Standards Technician; Motor Mechanic, Lift Trucks; Electricians; Electricians / Construction and Maintenance Millwrights; Pipefitters.

BUDGET CAR RENTALS TORONTO LTD.
Att: Robert Gearing, HR Specialist
5905 Campus Road
Mississauga, ON L4V 1P9

Tel. 905-676-1240
Fax 905-676-0440
Email .... rgearing@budgettoronto.com
Website .... www.budgettoronto.com

Employer Background: Budget Car Rentals Toronto Ltd. is affiliated with USA-based Budget Group Inc., one of the world's leading vehicle rental companies, with annual revenues of nearly $2.4 billion. *New Positions Created (7):* General Manager; Leasing Account Representatives (2); Airport Manager; Leasing Account Manager; Customer Service / Sales Positions; Management Trainees; Airport Garage Supervisors.

BUILDING BOX, THE
Att: Human Resources
3780 - 14th Avenue, Suite 314
Markham, ON L3R 9Y5

Fax 905-479-2299
Email .... hr@thebuildingbox.com
Website .... www.thebuildingbox.com

Employer Background: The Building Box is a retailer of home improvement products, employing 41,000 people in 500 stores worldwide. *New Positions Created (14):* Corporate Sales Representative; Assistant Store Manager, Night; Department Managers; Front-End Supervisors; Stocking Supervisor, Night; Senior Human Resources Counselor; Human Resources Counsellor; Office Supervisor; Department Manager, Kitchen; Human Resources Counsellor; Senior Human Resources Counsellor; Training Coordinator; Construction Manager; Real Estate Development Manager.

BULK BARN FOODS LTD.
Att: Human Resources Manager
55 Leek Crescent
Richmond Hill, ON L4B 3Y2

Tel. 905-883-3036
Fax 905-886-2722
Website .... www.bulkbarn.ca

Employer Background: Bulk Barn Foods Ltd. is Canada's largest bulk food retailer, carrying over 4,000 products. *New Positions Created (4):* Corporate Controller; Property Accountant / Lease Administrator; Category Manager, Merchandising Department; System Implementer - Point-of-Sale and Store Communications.

BULLDOG GROUP INC., THE
Att: Human Resources
161 Frederick Street
Toronto, ON M5A 4P3

Tel. 416-594-9207
Fax 416-594-9577
Email .... hr@bulldog.com
Website .... www.bulldog.com

Employer Background: Founded in 1991, The Bulldog Group Inc. is a leading provider of digital asset management technologies and services. *New Positions Created (5):* Professional Services Consultants, North America and Europe; Controller; Development Managers; Programmer / Analysts and System Engineers; Software Engineers.

BURGAR, ROWE
Att: Thomas C. Dart
90 Mulcaster Street, PO Box 758
Barrie, ON L4M 4Y5

Tel. 705-721-3377
Fax 705-721-4025
Email .... tdart@burgarrowe.com

Website .... www.burgarrowe.com

Employer Background: Burgar, Rowe is a full-service law firm. *New Positions Created (2):* Senior Litigation Counsel; Lawyer, Family Law.

BURGER KING RESTAURANTS OF CANADA INC.
Att: Human Resources
401 The West Mall, Suite 700
Toronto, ON M9C 5J4

Tel. 416-626-6464
Fax 416-626-6696
Email .... bkjobscanada@whopper.com
Website .... www.burgerking.com

Employer Background: Burger King Restaurants of Canada Inc. is a leading fast food chain. *New Positions Created (3):* Construction and Design Facilitator; Administrative Assistant; Operations Manager.

BURLINGTON, CITY OF
Att: Human Resources Department
426 Brant Street, PO Box 5013
Burlington, ON L7R 3Z6

Tel. 905-335-7602
Fax 905-335-7856
Email .... hr@city.burlington.on.ca
Website .... www.city.burlington.on.ca

Employer Background: The City of Burlington is home to 144,130 people. *New Positions Created (12):* Manager, Accounting; General Manager, Development and Infrastructure; Accountant; Administration Clerks (2); Administration Clerks (8); Courtroom Monitors (2); Prosecution Case Administrator; Prosecutors (2); Supervisor of Court Administration; Mechanic's Helper; Fire Prevention Inspector; General Manager, Community Services.

BURLINGTON RESOURCES CANADA ENERGY LTD.
Att: Human Resources
250 - 6th Avenue SW, Suite 3700
Calgary, AB T2P 3H7

Tel. 403-260-8000
Fax 403-261-5052
Website .... www.br-inc.com

Employer Background: Burlington Resources Canada Energy Ltd. (formerly Poco Petroleum Ltd.) is a Canadian natural gas and crude oil exploration, production and marketing corporation. *New Positions Created (26):* Oil Marketing Accountant; Senior Exploration Engineer; Senior Environment Representative; Compensation Analyst; Production Revenue Accountant; Manager, Operations Accounting; Senior Geophysicist; Reserves Technologist; Joint Venture Accounting Clerk; Senior Geological Technician; Production Engineer; Senior Contract Analyst; Senior Engineering Technologist; Human Resources Representative; Intermediate Exploitation Engineer; Senior Geologist / Intermediate Geologist; Geoscience Technologist; Production Revenue Accountant; Drilling Secretary; Drilling Systems Administrator; Manager, Environment, Health & Safety; Senior Financial Accountant; Senior Engineer, Acquisition

and Divestitures; Accounts Payable Clerk; Planning Technologist; Records Analyst.

BURLINGTON TECHNOLOGIES INC., ALUMETCO DIVISION
Att: Human Resources Manager
150 Garden Avenue
Brantford, ON N3S 7W4

Tel. 519-758-5150
Website .... www.burltech.com

Employer Background: Burlington Technologies Inc., Alumetco Division is a leading supplier of aluminum die casting parts to the automotive industry. *New Positions Created (3):* Industrial Maintenance Electrician, Midnight Shift; Manufacturing Engineering Manager; Industrial Millwright.

BURLINGTON TECHNOLOGIES INC., BURLINGTON DIVISION
Att: Human Resources
3267 Mainway
Burlington, ON L7M 1A6

Tel. 905-335-2742
Fax 905-335-4679
Email .... jar@burltech.com
Website .... www.burltech.com

Employer Background: Established in 1965, Burlington Technologies Inc. manufactures aluminum automobile components for the North American market. *New Positions Created (10):* Electrical Maintenance Supervisor; Machine Development Coordinator; Process Monitoring Technician; Production Control Planner; Quality Assurance Manager; Process Engineer; Licensed Trade / Technician Positions (3); Process Monitoring Technician; Maintenance Manager; Maintenance Supervisor.

BURLINGTON TECHNOLOGIES INC., CENTENNIAL DIVISION
Att: Administrative Manager
920 Century Drive
Burlington, ON L2L 5P2

Tel. 905-632-0435
Fax 905-632-0501
Email .... amhines@burltech.com
Website .... www.burltech.com

Employer Background: Established in 1965, Burlington Technologies Inc. manufactures aluminum automobile components for the North American market. *New Positions Created (3):* Die Assembler / Fitter; General Machinist; QA Inspector.

BURNABY, CITY OF
Att: Human Resources Director
4949 Canada Way
Burnaby, BC V5G 1M2

Tel. 604-294-7313
Fax 604-294-7710
Website .... www.city.burnaby.bc.ca

Employer Background: The City of Burnaby is home to 192,000 residents. *New Positions Created (3):* Assistant Director, Parks and Operations; Assistant Director, Recreation; Manager, Recreation Services.

BURNS INTERNATIONAL SECURITY SERVICES LTD.
Att: Human Resources Manager
1420 Blair Place
Gloucester, ON K1J 9B8

Fax 613-745-5348
Email .... pboucher@burnsintl.com
Website .... www.burnsintl.com

Employer Background: Burns International Security Services Ltd. is a security and protection services firm. *New Positions Created (2):* Various Legal Positions; Human Resources Generalist / Program Coordinator.

BURNTSAND INC.
Att: Human Resources Manager
1075 West Georgia Street, Suite 1500
Vancouver, BC V6E 3C9

Tel. 604-608-6400
Email .... careers@burntsand.com
Website .... www.burntsand.com

Employer Background: Burntsand Inc. is an e-business solutions integrator. *New Positions Created (7):* Database Architect; E-CRM / E-BI Corporate Practice Leader; E-Solutions Developer; Marketing Coordinator; Quality Assurance Manager; Senior Online Branding Specialist; Webmaster.

BURNTSAND INC.
Att: Human Resources Manager
304 The East Mall, Suite 500
Toronto, ON M9B 6E4

Tel. 416-234-3800
Fax 416-234-3900
Email .... careers@burntsand.com
Website .... www.burntsand.com

Employer Background: Burntsand Inc. is an e-business solutions integrator focusing on SellSide, BuySide and InSide strategic Internet-enabled applications. *New Positions Created (10):* Account Executive; Client Support Technician; Database Architect; Director, Sales; E-Solutions Architect; E-Solutions Developer, Open Systems; E-Solutions Strategist; Project Manager; Recruiter; Senior E-Solutions Developer.

BURNTWOOD REGIONAL HEALTH AUTHORITY / BRHA
Att: Jenny Sexton, Human Resources
867 Thompson Drive South
Thompson, MB R8N 1Z4

Tel. 204-677-5353
Fax 204-677-5366
Email .... jsexton@brha.mb.ca
Website .... www.brha.mb.ca

Employer Background: BRHA delivers a broad range of health programs, including 3 community hospitals, in northern Manitoba. *New Positions Created (2):* Midwives (3); President.

BUSINESS DEPOT LTD. / STAPLES
Att: Dan Hill
185 Bunting Road
St. Catharines, ON L2M 3Y2

Tel. 508-870-1111
Fax 905-938-5628
Email .... work@busdep.com

Website .... www.businessdepot.com
Employer Background: Business Depot Ltd. / Staples is Canada's largest supplier of office supplies, business machines, computers, office furniture and business services for small business and home office customers. *New Positions Created (2):* Outside Sales Reps; Outside Sales Representatives.

BUSINESS DEPOT LTD. / STAPLES
Att: Luigi Morabito
3055 Le Carrefour Boulevard
Laval, QC H7T 1C8
Tel. 450-682-9702
Fax 450-666-6502
Email .... luigi.morabito@staples.com
Website .... www.businessdepot.com
Employer Background: Business Depot Ltd. / Staples is Canada's largest supplier of office supplies, business machines, computers, office furniture and business services for small business and home office customers. *New Positions Created (3):* Outside Sales Representatives; Various Retail Positions; Various Retail Positions.

BUSINESS DEVELOPMENT BANK OF CANADA / BDC
Att: Human Resources Department
150 King Street West, Suite 100
Toronto, ON M5H 1J9
Tel. 416-952-6094
Fax 416-954-5002
Email .... careers@bdc.ca
Website .... www.bdc.ca
Employer Background: BDC provides financial and consulting services for entrepreneurs. *New Positions Created (3):* Managers, Consulting Services; Managers, Consulting Services; Account Manager.

BUSINESS DEVELOPMENT BANK OF CANADA / BDC
Att: Human Resources Manager
5 Place Ville-Marie, Suite 400
Montréal, QC H3B 5E7
Tel. 514-496-1738
Fax 514-283-0631
Email .... careers@bdc.ca
Website .... www.bdc.ca
Employer Background: BDC provides financial and consulting services for entrepreneurs. *New Positions Created (12):* Audit Consultant; Senior Advisor, Public Relations and Special Events; Account Manager; Manager, Consulting Services; Account Manager; Business Development Representative; Director, Alliances & Network; E-Commerce & SME Expert; Manager, Business Development; Project Leader, Portals; Business Development Managers; Consultants.

BUSINESS TRAVEL INTERNATIONAL / BTI CANADA
Att: Brigitte Rochon, HR Advisor
407 - 2nd Street SW, Suite 600
Calgary, AB T2P 2Y3
Tel. 403-231-5454
Fax 403-262-7138
Website .... www.bticanada.ca

Employer Background: BTI Canada is a leader in corporate travel management, with 19 years experience, over 850 employees and annual sales of $600 million. *New Positions Created (2):* Senior Corporate Sales Consultant; Senior Team Leader.

BUSINESS TRAVEL INTERNATIONAL / BTI CANADA
Att: Human Resources
370 King Street West, Suite 700
Toronto, ON M5V 1J9
Tel. 416-593-8866
Fax 416-593-7158
Email .... employ@bticanada.ca
Website .... www.bticanada.ca
Employer Background: BTI Canada is a leader in corporate travel management, with 19 years experience, over 850 employees and annual sales of $600 million. *New Positions Created (3):* Hotel and Supplier Program Specialist; BSP Agent; Implementation Mgr.

BUSINESS TRAVEL INTERNATIONAL / BTI CANADA
Att: Human Resources
45 O'Connor Street, Suite 700
Ottawa, ON K1P 1A4
Tel. 613-238-5696
Fax 613-232-1087
Email .... employ@bticanada.ca
Website .... www.bticanada.ca
Employer Background: BTI Canada is a leader in corporate travel management, with 19 years experience, over 850 employees and annual sales of $600 million. *New Positions Created (5):* Executive Assistant; Junior / Intermediate / Senior Travel Counsellors; Ticketing Clerk; TIN / TAN Support Position; Communications Coordinator.

BUTTERWORTHS CANADA LTD.
Att: Human Resources Department
75 Clegg Road, PO Box 1008
Markham, ON L6G 1A1
Tel. 905-479-2665
Fax 905-479-2826
Email .... jobs@butterworths.ca
Website .... www.butterworths.ca
Employer Background: Butterworths Canada Ltd. is a leading publisher of professional and legal reference information. *New Positions Created (3):* Conference Developer; Product Development Editor; Product Development Editor.

BUYSTREAM
Att: Human Resources Manager
340 MacLaren Street
Ottawa, ON K2P 0M6
Tel. 613-563-0303
Email .... jobs@buystream.com
Website .... www.buystream.com
Employer Background: Buystream develops optimization software to monitor, analyze and interpret business-oriented metrics for e-business websites. *New Positions Created (5):* Development Manager; MIS Help Desk Analyst; Quality Assurance Specialist; Sales Engineer; Software Developer.

BYCAST MEDIA SYSTEMS CANADA, INC.
Att: Human Resources Manager
609 West Hastings Street, Suite 700
Vancouver, BC V6B 4W4
Tel. 604-801-5300
Fax 604-801-5309
Email .... careers@bycast.com
Website .... www.bycast.com
Employer Background: Bycast develops streaming solutions to facilitate the delivery of next-generation media services, including personalized content, targeted advertisements and integrated e-commerce. *New Positions Created (5):* Various Computing Positions; Entry-Level Software Developer; Intermediate Software Developer; Internet Researcher; Sr. Software Developer.

BYTOWN LUMBER
Att: General Manager
175 Robertson Road
Nepean, ON K2H 5Z2
Fax 613-726-2698
Employer Background: Bytown Lumber is a major regional player in the building materials field. *New Positions Created (4):* Counter Sales Representative / Estimator; External Sales Representative; Sales Representative; Store Manager.

C-MAC INDUSTRIES INC.
Att: Human Resources Manager
700 Education Road
Cornwall, ON K6H 6B8
Tel. 613-938-6086
Fax 613-930-7380
Email .... cornwallhr@crn.cmac.com
Website .... www.cmac.com
Employer Background: C-MAC Industries Inc. is a designer of integrated electronic manufacturing solutions, with 10,000 employees and 52 facilities worldwide. *New Positions Created (4):* Quality Mgr; Process Engineer; Test Engineer; Engineering Mgr.

C-MAC INDUSTRIES INC.
Att: Human Resources
425 Legget Drive
Kanata, ON K2K 2W2
Fax 613-271-6561
Email .... hr@kan.cmac.com
Website .... www.cmac.ca
Employer Background: C-MAC Industries Inc. is a designer of integrated electronic manufacturing solutions, with 10,000 employees and 52 facilities worldwide. *New Positions Created (13):* Accounting Clerk; Software Engineer; Systems Analyst; Telecom Power Distribution Specialist; ECAD Designer; Electronic Packaging Engineer; Mechanical Technologists; PCB and Back Plane Specialist; Safety Engineer; Controller and Accounting / Payroll Clerk; Intermediate Buyer; Mechanical Technologist; Various Engineering Positions.

C-MAC INVOTRONICS INC.
Att: Human Resources Manager
365 Passmore Avenue
Toronto, ON M1V 4B3

Tel. 416-321-8822
Fax 416-321-1083
Website .... www.invotronics.com

Employer Background: C-MAC Invotronics Inc., a division of C-MAC Industries, engineers and manufactures electronic body controllers, electromechanical systems and intelligent switches for the automotive industry. *New Positions Created (10):* Buyer, Mechanical; Manufacturing Engineers, Process Control; Product Engineer, Electrical; Product Engineer, Software; Production Foreman; Quality Engineers; SMT Technicians / Programmers; Technical Writer; Technician, Electrical; Test Maintenance Technicians.

C-TECH LTD.
Att: Human Resources Department
PO Box 1960
Cornwall, ON K6H 6N7
Tel. 613-933-7970
Fax 613-933-7977
Email .... ctladmin@cnwl.igs.net

Employer Background: Founded in 1969, C-Tech Ltd. is a mid-sized manufacturer of sonar systems for commercial and defense applications worldwide. *New Positions Created (3):* Draftsperson; Engineers; Technologists / Technicians.

C/S CONSTRUCTION SPECIALTIES LTD.
Att: Human Resources
895 Lakefront Promenade
Mississauga, ON L5E 2C2
Tel. 905-274-3611
Fax 905-274-6241
Email .... rsimpson@c-sgroup.com
Website .... www.c-sgroup.com

Employer Background: C/S Construction Specialties Ltd., a member of the C/S Group, has been a supplier of quality aluminum products for almost 40 years. *New Positions Created (6):* Architectural Products Sales Estimator; Bilingual Credit and Collections Associate; Planner / Coordinator; Architectural Draftsperson; Manufacturing Engineer / Technologist; Planner / Coordinator.

C1 COMMUNICATIONS
Att: Human Resources
7111 Syntex Drive
Mississauga, ON L5N 8C3
Email ... careers@c1communications.com
Website www.c1communications.com

Employer Background: C1 Communications provides customized telecom solutions for local, long distance, high-speed data access, Internet products and electronic services. *New Positions Created (8):* Bilingual Client Relations Specialists; Account Manager; PIC Care Administrator; Sales Manager; Network Planner; Technologists; PIC Care Administrator; Sales Trainer.

C2 MEDIA.COM
Att: Human Resources
555 Greenwich Street
Brantford, ON N3T 5T3
Fax 519-759-7979
Website www.c2media.com

Employer Background: C2 Media.com manufactures screen-printed products. *New Positions Created (4):* Customer Service / Account Coordinator; Estimator; Logistics Positions; Print Supervisor.

CAA CENTRAL ONTARIO
Att: Human Resources
60 Commerce Valley Drive East
Thornhill, ON L3T 7P9
Tel. 905-221-4300
Fax 905-771-3447
Email .... jobs@central.on.caa.ca
Website .... www.central.on.caa.ca

Employer Background: CAA Central Ontario provides automobile, insurance and travel-related services. *New Positions Created (9):* Automotive Service Adviser; Emergency Road Services Counsellor; Emergency Road Services Counsellors; Insurance Team Leader, Sales; Locksmith Customer Service Advisor; Insurance Agents; Accident Benefits Adjuster; Service Counsellors; Service Counsellors.

CAA SOUTH CENTRAL ONTARIO
Att: Elizabeth Luhta,
Recruitment Specialist
393 Main Street East
Hamilton, ON L8N 3T7
Tel. 905-525-1210
Fax 905-525-7930
Email .... eluhta@cassco.com
Website .... www.caasco.on.ca

Employer Background: CAA South Central Ontario serves the motoring and travelling needs of 260,000 members. *New Positions Created (7):* Service Rep, New Business Processing; Service Leader; Dispatcher; Customer Service Representatives; Travel Counselling Positions; Manager, Information Systems; Member Services Counsellor.

CABINET OFFICE
Att: Human Resources Manager
99 Wellesley Street West
4th Floor, Whitney Block
Toronto, ON M7A 1A1
Fax 416-325-7646
Website .... www.gov.on.ca

Employer Background: Established by the Executive Council Act, the Cabinet Office consists of the Premier and Ministers and makes all key government policy, financial, resource and statutory decisions. *New Positions Created (7):* Administrative Assistant; Communications Officer; Administrative Services Officer; Communications Administrative Coordinator; Senior Media Analyst / Team Leader; Writers; Issues Analysts.

CABOODLES COSMETICS
Att: Human Resources
1360 Cliveden Avenue
New Westminster, BC V3M 6K2
Fax 604-525-6010
Website .... www.caboodles.com

Employer Background: Caboodles Cosmetics is a manufacturer of cosmetics for the teen market. *New Positions Created (3):* IT

Manager; Purchasing Manager; Marketing and Promotions Coordinator.

CAD RESOURCE CENTRE / CRC
Att: Human Resources Manager
77 Progress Avenue, Suite 201
Toronto, ON M1P 2Y7
Fax 416-321-9721
Email .... hr@cadresource.com
Website .... www.cadresource.com

Employer Background: CRC is a leading provider of PC-based CAD solutions and an integrator of Autodesk design solutions and software technologies. *New Positions Created (3):* Account Mgrs; Application Specialists; Customer Service Representatives.

CADASTRAL GROUP INC., THE
Att: Human Resources Manager
500 - 4th Avenue SW, Suite 400
Calgary, AB T2P 2V6
Tel. 403-263-8200
Fax 403-263-8210
Website .... www.cadastral.org

Employer Background: The Cadastral Group Inc. is a provider of geomatic services for Alberta's energy industry. *New Positions Created (7):* CAD Operator; Land Surveyor; Senior Party Chiefs; Survey Technologists; Equipment Manager; Safety Supervisor; Senior Party Chiefs.

CADBURY TREBOR ALLAN INC.
Att: Human Resource Department
277 Gladstone Avenue
Toronto, ON M6J 3L9
Tel. 416-530-4055
Fax 416-530-4826
Website .... www.ctai.ca

Employer Background: Cadbury Trebor Allan Inc. manufactures premium quality confectionery products. *New Positions Created (4):* Packaging Project Coordinator; Shift Maintenance Manager; Packaging Mechanics; Distribution Supervisors.

CADBURY TREBOR ALLAN INC.
Att: Human Resources Manager
356 Emerald Street
Hamilton, ON L8L 5L6
Website .... www.ctai.ca

Employer Background: Cadbury Trebor Allan Inc. manufactures premium quality confectionery products. *New Positions Created (6):* Project Engineer; Health and Safety Coordinator; Industrial Electrician; Maintenance Mechanic; Maintenance Store Person; Manufacturing Shift Supervisors.

CADENCE DESIGN SYSTEMS, INC.
Att: Human Resources
1130 Morrison Drive, Suite 240
Ottawa, ON K2H 9N6
Tel. 613-828-5626
Email .... hrcanada@cadence.com
Website .... www.cadence.com

Employer Background: Cadence Design Systems, Inc. supplies software tools and professional services for the design of semiconductors, computer systems and networking and telecom equipment. *New Positions Created (8):* Account Manager; Account Manager; Application Engineer, Design Verification; Application Engineers, Synthesis Place and Route (2); Project Manager; Project Manager - Embedded Software; Senior Embedded Software Designer; Senior FPGA / ASIC Designers.

CADESKY AND ASSOCIATES

Att: Ken Brown
2225 Sheppard Avenue East, Suite 1001
Toronto, ON M2J 5C2
Tel. 416-498-9500
Fax 416-498-9501
Email .... kbrown@cadesky.com
Website .... www.cadesky.com
Employer Background: Cadesky and Associates provides Canadian and international tax consulting services. *New Positions Created (2):* Tax Specialist; Tax Specialist.

CADEX ELECTRONICS INC.

Att: Operations Manager
22000 Fraserwood Way
Richmond, BC V6W 1J6
Tel. 604-231-7777
Fax 604-231-7750
Email .... jobs@cadex.com
Website .... www.cadex.com
Employer Background: Founded in 1980, Cadex Electronics Inc. manufactures battery analyzers, chargers and lithium ion batteries. *New Positions Created (2):* Production Mgr; Intermediate Software Developers.

CADILLAC FAIRVIEW CORPORATION LIMITED, THE

Att: Human Resources Department
20 Queen Street West, 5th Floor
Toronto, ON M5H 3R4
Tel. 416-598-8200
Fax 416-598-8578
Email .... staffing@cadillacfairview.com
Website .... www.cadillacfairview.com
Employer Background: Founded in 1953, Cadillac Fairview Corporation Ltd. is one of North America's largest real estate developers and managers. The company has a portfolio of over 100 properties, including many landmark shopping centers. *New Positions Created (11):* General Mgr; Director, Portfolio Marketing; Director, Property Marketing; Embarq Kids Attendant I; Embarq Concierge; Embarq Kids Attendant; Senior Legal Counsel, Ontario Portfolio; Embarq Kids' Supervisor; Head Concierge; Accountant, Parking; Director, Architecture and Design.

CAE INC.

Att: Human Resources Manager
8585 Cote de Liesse, PO Box 1800
St-Laurent, QC H4L 4X4
Tel. 514-341-6780
Fax 514-340-5335
Email .... hr@cae.ca
Website .... www.cae.com
Employer Background: CAE Inc., one of Canada's foremost scientific systems and software enterprises, designs advanced simulation and detection systems. *New Positions Created (39):* Hardware Quality Assurance Analyst; Marketing Manager; Military Systems Specialist; Business Development Managers; Integration Specialists; Simulator Technicians; Junior / Senior Programmer Analysts; Software Programmers / Developers; Administrative Assistant; Analyst, Investor Relations; Database Administrator; Electrical Designer; Electrical Engineer; Electrical Systems Designer; Financial Analyst; Hardware Design Engineer; Hardware Quality Assurance Analyst; Intermediate Buyer; Manufacturing Analyst; Mechanical Designer; Mechanical System Designer; Printed Circuit Board Designer; Senior Hardware Designer; Senior Hardware Technician; Senior Industrial Engineer Analyst; Software Developer; Technical Writer; Integration Specialist, Distance Learning; Military System Specialist; PC Administrator; Project Engineer; Project Manager; Proposal Engineer; Software Developer; Software Specialist; Aircraft Systems Update Specialist; Mechanical Designer; Software Developer; Software Specialist.

CAE MACHINERY LTD.

Att: Roz Leatherdale, Engineering Dept.
3550 Lougheed Highway
Vancouver, BC V5M 2A3
Tel. 604-299-3431
Fax 604-299-4927
Email .... rleather@caemachinery.com
Website .... www.cae.ca
Employer Background: CAE Machinery Ltd., a subsidiary of CAE Inc., is a leading manufacturer of equipment for the engineered wood products industry and a major repair centre for pulp mill machinery. *New Positions Created (4):* Field Service Technician, Electrical / Mechanical; Technical Field Representative; Controller and Company Secretary; Purchaser.

CAISSE DE DEPOT ET PLACEMENT DU QUEBEC / CDP GLOBAL ASSET MANAGEMENT

Att: Human Resources Department
1981 McGill College Avenue
Montréal, QC H3A 3C7
Tel. 514-842-3261
Fax 514-847-5921
Email .... r.humaines@cdpcapital.com
Website .... www.cdpcapital.com
Employer Background: CDP Global Asset Management is a leading Canadian fund and portfolio manager, with $120 billion of assets under management. *New Positions Created (4):* Portfolio Analyst - Manager, Asia; Portfolio Analyst - Technology Sector, Asia; Director, Operations and Trading; Vice-President, International Equity Markets.

CALDWELL RESIDENCES

Att: Human Resources Manager
5750 Lemieux Avenue, Suite 116
Montréal, QC H3W 3G1
Fax 514-737-6365
Employer Background: Caldwell Residences provides subsidized housing to independent, low-income seniors at its four apartment buildings. *New Positions Created (2):* Coordinator of Services; Coordinator of Programs.

CALEA LTD.

Att: Human Resources
2785 Skymark Avenue, Unit 2
Mississauga, ON L4W 4Y3
Tel. 905-624-1234
Fax 905-624-9330
Email .... humanresources@calea.ca
Website .... www.calea.ca
Employer Background: Calea Ltd. (formerly Caremark Ltd.) is a leading provider of community-based healthcare and home intravenous therapies and treatments. *New Positions Created (11):* Buyer; Drug Information Pharmacist; Medical Info Specialists; Nursing Positions; Order Entry Clerk; Palliative Care Project Manager; Payroll Assistant; Pharmacy Assistant, Managed Drugs; Pharmacy Assistant, Pharmacy Services; Purchasing Supervisor; Staff Pharmacists.

CALEDON, TOWN OF

Att: Human Resources
6311 Old Church Road, PO Box 1000
Caledon East, ON L0N 1E0
Tel. 905-584-2272
Fax 905-584-4542
Email .... hr@town.caledon.on.ca
Website .... www.town.caledon.on.ca
Employer Background: Located 20 km northwest of Pearson International Airport, the Town of Caledon is home to 45,000 residents. *New Positions Created (7):* Facility Operator Personnel; Administrative Assistant, Planning & Development; Deputy-Treasurer / Manager, Budgets and Accounts; Manager of Operations; Projects Quality Assurance Inspector; Assistant Director, Capital Projects and Property Management; Senior Plans Examiner.

CALFRAC WELL SERVICES LTD.

Att: Arlene Callsen
513 - 8th Avenue SW, Suite 300
Calgary, AB T2P 1G3
Tel. 403-266-6000
Fax 403-266-7381
Email .... resume@calfrac.com
Website .... www.calfrac.com
Employer Background: Calfrac Well Services Ltd. is an oilfield services company, specializing in fracturing, acidizing, coil tubing, nitrogen and carbon dioxide services. *New Positions Created (4):* Engineering Specialist; Senior Sales Representatives; Health, Safety and Environment Supervisor; Engineering Specialist.

CALGARY AIRPORT AUTHORITY, THE

Att: Sharon Caddigan,
Human Resources Manager
2000 Airport Road NE, Mezzanine Level
Calgary, AB T2E 6W5
Tel. 403-297-0750
Fax 403-717-2216
Email .... sharonc@yyc.com
Website .... www.calgaryairport.com

Employer Background: The Calgary Airport Authority is a non-profit corporation responsible for the safe, secure and efficient operation and development of the Calgary International Airport. *New Positions Created (3):* Manager, Commercial Properties / Air Terminal; Airport Project Manager; Airport Electrical Engineer.

CALGARY BOARD OF EDUCATION, THE
Att: Human Resources, Support Staffing
515 Macleod Trail SE
Calgary, AB T2G 2L9

Tel. 403-294-8134
Fax 403-294-8333
Website .... www.cbe.ab.ca

Employer Background: The Calgary Board of Education operates one of the largest school systems in Canada, with 100,000 students, 9,500 staff members and a budget of $603 million. *New Positions Created (4):* Manager, Property Development; Specialist for Aboriginal Education, School Support Services; Manager, Student Enrolment and Planning; Business Manager.

CALGARY CATHOLIC SCHOOL DISTRICT
Att: Michael Barbero, HR Superintendent
1000 - 5th Avenue SW
Calgary, AB T2P 4T9

Tel. 403-298-1427
Fax 403-298-1382
Website .... www.cssd.ab.ca

Employer Background: The Calgary Catholic School District operates 86 schools in Calgary, Airdrie and Cochrane, serving 42,285 students and employing 4,300 staff members. *New Positions Created (2):* Director, Religious Education; Superintendent of Instructional Services.

CALGARY, CITY OF
Att: Human Resources
800 MacLeod Trail SE
11th Floor, PO Box 2100, Station M
Calgary, AB T2P 2M5

Tel. 403-268-2355
Email .... cityjobs@gov.calgary.ab.ca
Website .... www.gov.calgary.ab.ca

Employer Background: The City of Calgary is home to over 810,000 residents. *New Positions Created (106):* Corporate Records Team Leader; Supervisor, Application Support; Apprentice Signals Electrician; Corporate Reporting / Financial Analyst; Journeyman Signals Electrician; Management Systems Analyst; Construction Engineer; Division Secretary; GIS Data Technician; Senior Project Coordinator; Staff Development Officer; Customer Service Technician; Finance Leader; Preschool Playschool Instructors; Coordinator, Bus Maintenance; Customer Service Representative, Animal Services; Journeyman Construction Electrician; Market Sales Analyst; Technical Analyst; Waste Management Engineer; Assessor Intern; Computer Support Analyst; Database Analyst; Employee Development Coordinator; Library Assistant; LRV Analyst & QA Representative; Operations and Maintenance

Supervisor; Inventory Analyst; Benefits Services Administrator; Project Engineer; Business Analyst; Journeyman 1 Automotive / Heavy Duty Mechanic; Urban Forestry Technician; Business Process Analyst; Engineers, Information Architecture; Subdivision Technician; Vehicle Enquiry Clerk; Engineering Graphic Technologist 1; Engineering Graphic Technologist 2; Supply Management Assistant; Committee Assistant; Planner 2, Development; Planner 2, Subdivision; Leader, Microbiology; Leader, Organic Chemistry; Environmental Specialist, Calgary Roads; Environmental Specialist, Environmental Management; Light Rail Vehicle Analyst; Industrial Sampler; Planning Technician; Safety Advisor; Coordinator, Bus Maintenance; Geomatics Cartographer; Leasing Agent; Customer Coordinator; Equipment Technician; Library Assistant; Manager, Public Engagements; Arts Liaison / Development Coordinator; Coordinator, Business Unit Records; Coordinator, Customer and Business Services; Manager, Community Relations; Manager, Corporate Marketing; Manager, Creative Resources; Manager, Customer Services; Manager, Internal Communications; Marketing and Web Business Analyst; Staff Auditor; Animal Control Officer; Bylaw Clerk; Team Leader, Employee Records; Team Leader, Project Management; Automotive Serviceman; Communications Specialist; Manager, Commercial Planning and Development; Business Analyst; Development Product Analyst; Business Development Analyst; Engineering Graphic Technologist; Engineering Graphic Technologist; Finance Coordinator; Finance Coordinator; Management Systems Analyst, Methodology Support; Manager of Transportation Planning; Coordinator, Strategic Procurement; Financial and Rates Analyst; Junior and Senior Programmers; Laboratory Technician; Payroll Clerk; Traffic Signals Technician; Associate Veterinarian; Utility Line Assignment Technician; Vocational Counsellor; Volunteer Coordinator; Senior Electrical Engineer; Building Grade Technician; M4 Application Business Administrator; Assistant Planners; Chief Subdivision Planner; Planners; Senior Transportation Engineer; Manager, Animal Services, Environmental Management; Supervisor of Concession Operations; By-Law Enforcement Clerk, Environmental Management, Utilities and Environmental Protection; Data Services Analyst; Scanning Process Clerk.

CALGARY CO-OPERATIVE ASSOCIATION LTD.
Att: Human Resources, Recruitment
2735 - 39th Avenue NE
Calgary, AB T1Y 7C7

Tel. 403-219-6025
Fax 403-299-4147
Email humanresources@calgarycoop.com
Website .... www.calgarycoop.com

Employer Background: Calgary Co-operative Association Ltd. is one of Canada's largest retail cooperatives, with 19 centres and annual sales of $600 million. *New Positions Created (11):* Produce Manager; Senior

Travel Consultant; Member and Public Relations Assistant; Gas Bar Manager; Bakery Manager; Pharmacy Manager; Director of Member and Public Relations; Corporate Auditor; Benefits and Compensation Director; Bakery / Deli Manager; Meat Manager.

CALGARY HERALD
Att: Peter Menzies, Editor-in-Chief,
Human Resources
215 - 16th Street SE, Box 2400, Station M
Calgary, AB T2P 0W8

Tel. 403-235-7107
Email ...... resume@theherald.southam.ca
Website .... www.calgaryherald.com

Employer Background: The Calgary Herald, owned by Southam Newspaper Group, is Calgary's largest newspaper. *New Positions Created (5):* Editor, Editorial Pages; Copy Editors (2); Legislature Bureau Chief; Neighbours Editors; Reporters (10).

CALGARY IMMIGRANT AID SOCIETY
Att: Mrs. K. Brace
910 - 7th Avenue SW, Suite 1200
Calgary, AB T2P 3N8

Tel. 403-265-1120
Fax 403-266-2486
Website .... www.cadvision.com/cias

Employer Background: The Calgary Immigrant Aid Society provides resources for immigrants and refugee families. *New Positions Created (3):* Coordinator; Settlement / Integration Counsellor; Youth Program Facilitator.

CALGARY LABORATORY SERVICES
Att: Human Resources
1638 - 10th Avenue SW
Calgary, AB T2C 0J5

Tel. 403-209-5362
Fax 403-209-5296
Email .... jobs@cls.ab.ca

Employer Background: CLS is a public / private partnership between the Calgary Regional Health Authority and MDS Kasper Medical Laboratories. *New Positions Created (6):* Medical Laboratory Technologist; General Pathologists (2); Senior Human Resources Consultant; Accounts Payable Clerk; Applications Analyst; Senior Applications Analysts.

CALGARY REGIONAL HEALTH AUTHORITY / CRHA
Att: Recruitment Service Centre
10101 Southport Road SW
Calgary, AB T2W 3N2

Tel. 403-943-1300
Fax 403-943-1328
Email ...... recruitment@crha-health.ab.ca
Website ...... www.crha-health.ab.ca

Employer Background: CRHA is a provider of community health, acute, tertiary and continuing care services. *New Positions Created (6):* Patient Care Manager, Gynecology Outpatient Clinic; Professional Practice Coordinator, Physiotherapy; Assistant Patient Care Manager, General Surgery / Oncology; Registered Nurse, Internal Medicine, Urgent

Assessment Clinic; Speech-Language Pathologist; Ambulatory Care Manager.

CALGARY REGIONAL HEALTH AUTHORITY / CRHA
Att: Human Resources Department
320 - 17th Avenue SW
PO Box 4016, 5th Floor, Station C
Calgary, AB T2T 5T1
Tel. 403-531-8080
Fax 403-541-6645
Email .... jobs.ch@crha-health.ab.ca
Website .... www.crha-health.ab.ca
Employer Background: CRHA is a provider of community health, acute, tertiary and continuing care services. *New Positions Created (3):* Dental Hygienist; Health Economic / Senior Research Analyst; Health Economic / Senior Research Analyst.

CALGARY REGIONAL HEALTH AUTHORITY / CRHA
Att: Recruitment Consultant
1035 - 7th Avenue SW
Calgary, AB T2P 3E9
Tel. 403-541-2784
Fax 403-541-2710
Email ...... recruitment@crha-health.ab.ca
Website .... www.crha-health.ab.ca
Employer Background: CRHA is a provider of community health, acute, tertiary and continuing care services. *New Positions Created (30):* Nurse Clinician, Thoracic Surgery; Nursing Attendant; Psychologist II; Registered Nurse, CVT Surgery; Respiratory Therapist I; Assistant Patient Care Manager, Neurosciences; Clinic Dentist; Coordinator, Clinical Information Systems; EEG Technologist I; Physiological Lab Technician II; Human Resources Consultant; Medical Teaching Unit Nurse Care Coordinator; Occupational Therapist; Patient Care Manager, Regional Fertility Program; Registered Nurse, Clinical Neurosciences; Registered Nurse, Emergency; Registered Nurse, N Cluster; Architect / Urban Planner; Health Economic Analyst / Senior Research Analyst; Physical Therapist; Occupational Therapist; Psychologist; Clinical Nurse Specialist, Ambulatory Care; Clinical Nurse Specialist, Inpatient and Critical Care; Medical Director, Care in the Community; Senior Compensation Consultant; Human Resources Consultant; Various Healthcare Positions; Management Position, Medicine; Mental Health Specialist Positions.

CALGARY REGIONAL HEALTH AUTHORITY, FOOTHILLS MEDICAL CENTRE / CRHA
Att: Human Resources Manager
1403 - 29th Street NW
Calgary, AB T2N 2T9
Tel. 403-670-1110
Fax 403-670-1041
Email .... jobs.fmc@crha-health.ab.ca
Website .... www.crha-health.ab.ca
Employer Background: CRHA is a provider of community health, acute, tertiary and continuing care services. *New Positions Created (9):* Nurse Practitioners; Academic

Transplant Surgeon / Assistant Professor; Respiratory Therapist; MRI Technologists; Cardiac / Cardiac Surgery Nurse Practitioner; Heart Health Nurses / Technologists; Neuroscience Nurses; Neurosurgical Nurse Practitioner; Patient Care Manager.

CALGARY ZOO, BOTANICAL GARDEN AND PREHISTORIC PARK
Att: Guest Services
1300 Zoo Road NE
Calgary, AB T2E 7V6
Tel. 403-232-9300
Fax 403-237-7582
Website .... www.calgaryzoo.ab.ca
Employer Background: The Calgary Zoo, Botanical Garden and Prehistoric Park is dedicated to environmental education, preservation of endangered species, wildlife research and recreation. *New Positions Created (6):* Catering Supervisor; Banquet Cook; Food Services Team Leaders; Kitchen Assistant; Customer Service Representative; Inventory Coordinator.

CALPINE CANADA RESOURCES LTD.
Att: Human Resources
421 - 7th Avenue SW, Suite 1800
Calgary, AB T2P 4K9
Tel. 403-750-3300
Fax 403-263-4303
Email .... hremploy@calpinecanada.ca
Website .... www.calpinecanada.com
Employer Background: Calpine Canada Resources Ltd. (formerly Encal Energy Ltd.) is an exploration and development company, with core operations in western Canada. *New Positions Created (6):* Production Superintendent; Material Coordinator; Engineering Technologist; Land Administrator; Production Foreman; Production Systems Specialist.

CAMBRIDGE CUSTOM TOOLING
Att: Human Resources
65 Barnes Road
Cambridge, ON N3H 4R7
Tel. 519-740-8071
Fax 519-650-9050
Website .... www.marcelissen.com
Employer Background: Cambridge is a casting tooling supplier for the automotive industry in North America. *New Positions Created (2):* CAD Designers; Shop Supervisors.

CAMBRIDGE MEMORIAL HOSPITAL
Att: Human Resources Services
700 Coronation Boulevard
Cambridge, ON N1R 3G2
Tel. 519-740-4920
Fax 519-740-4907
Email .... jobs@cmh.org
Website .... www.cmh.org
Employer Background: CMH is a full-service facility, providing primary and secondary patient care, education, research and planning services. *New Positions Created (14):* Family and Child Care Nurses, Obstetrics; Haematologist; Oncology Associate; Physiotherapists; Social Workers; Critical

Care Nurses; Psychogeriatric Specialist; Registered Nurses, Telemetry; Ultrasound Technologist; Chief Financial Officer; Program Manager, Critical Care; Program Manager, Diagnostics & Therapeutics; Physiotherapists; Speech Language Pathologist.

CAMBRIDGE PUBLIC LIBRARY
Att: Greg Hayton, Chief Librarian
20 Grand Avenue North
Cambridge, ON N1S 2K6
Website ...... www.library.cambridge.on.ca
Employer Background: The Cambridge Public Library improves community life by providing information, education, research, recreation and culture. *New Positions Created (3):* Children's Services Librarian; Electronic Resources Training Librarian; System Librarian.

CAMCO INC.
Att: Anne Montouri, Human Resources
175 Longwood Road South, PO Box 2094
Hamilton, ON L8N 3Y5
Tel. 905-521-3177
Fax 905-972-7441
Website .... www.ge.com/canada
Employer Background: Camco Inc., GE Canada's appliance affiliate, is the largest manufacturer and servicer of major home appliances in Canada. *New Positions Created (2):* Occupational Health Nurse; Cost Accounting Support Position.

CAMELOT CONTENT TECHNOLOGIES INC.
Att: Human Resources Manager
10 Green Street, Suite 310
Ottawa, ON K2J 3Z6
Tel. 613-825-0899
Email .... careers@camelotcontent.com
Website .... www.camelotcontent.com
Employer Background: Camelot Content Technologies Inc. is a fabless semiconductor company, developing high-speed scalable stream processing engines to recover, manage and present data streams. *New Positions Created (3):* ASIC Designers; ASIC / System Verification Position; Real-Time Software Engineers.

CAMEO CRAFTS GRAPHIC INDUSTRIES LTD.
Att: Cedric Copin, Human Resources
666 Montée de Liesse
St-Laurent, QC H4T 1P2
Fax 514-341-4850
Email .... ccopin@cameocrafts.com
Employer Background: Cameo Crafts Graphic Industries Ltd. is a large specialty label and packaging company, with operations in Canada, the USA and Caribbean. *New Positions Created (2):* Customer Service Representative / Estimator; Corporate Purchasing Manager.

CAMOSUN COLLEGE
Att: Human Resources
3100 Foul Bay Road
Victoria, BC V8P 5J2

Tel. 250-370-3004
Fax 250-370-3664
Email .... personnel@camosun.bc.ca
Website .... www.camosun.bc.ca

Employer Background: Camosun College is a community college, serving the educational needs of the people of Victoria, Southern Vancouver Island, the Gulf Islands and beyond. *New Positions Created (3):* Dean, School of Business; Computer Science Instructors; Electronics and Computer Engineering Instructors.

CAMPBELL FORD SALES LTD.
Att: Mr. Robertson
1500 Carling Avenue
PO Box 3506, Station A
Ottawa, ON K1Y 4K6
Tel. 613-725-3611

Employer Background: Campbell Ford Sales Ltd. is an automotive dealership. *New Positions Created (3):* Accounting Position; Manager, Fast Lane; New Car Sales Manager.

CAMPBELL RIVER / NOOTKA COMMUNITY HEALTH COUNCIL
Att: Human Resources
375 - 2nd Avenue
Campbell River, BC V9W 3V1
Tel. 250-286-7001
Fax 250-286-7090
Email .... jobs@crncare.org
Website .... www.crncare.org

Employer Background: Campbell River / Nootka Community Health Council ensures effective and equitable delivery of quality health services. *New Positions Created (2):* Child & Youth Outreach Worker; Ultrasonographer.

CAMPUS CREW
Att: Human Resources Department
90 Morton Avenue East
Brantford, ON N3R 7J7
Fax 519-759-8415
Email .... hrdept@campuscrew.com
Website .... www.campuscrew.com

Employer Background: Campus Crew is a clothing retailer. *New Positions Created (4):* Retail Positions; District Mgr; Store Mgr; Store Managers & Managers-in-Training.

CAN-AM SURVEYS LTD.
Att: Human Resources Manager
9440 - 49th Street, Suite 111
Edmonton, AB T6B 2M9
Tel. 780-468-5900
Fax 780-466-0476
Email .... careers@canam.com
Website .... www.canam.com

Employer Background: Founded in 1972, Can-Am Surveys Ltd. provides land surveying and geomatics engineering services. *New Positions Created (2):* AutoCAD Operators; Party Chiefs.

CAN-AM SURVEYS LTD.
Att: Human Resources Manager
340 - 12th Avenue SW, Suite 900
Calgary, AB T2R 1I.5
Tel. 403-269-8887
Fax 403-269-8550
Email .... careers@canam.com
Website .... www.canam.com

Employer Background: Founded in 1972, Can-Am Surveys Ltd. provides land surveying and geomatics engineering services. *New Positions Created (2):* AutoCAD Operators; Senior Plan Checker.

CAN-ENG FURNACES LTD.
Att: Human Resources Manager
6800 Montrose Road, PO Box 628
Niagara Falls, ON L2E 6V5
Tel. 905-356-1327
Fax 905-356-3404
Email .... cbowering@can-eng.com
Website .... www.can-eng.com

Employer Background: Can-Eng Furnaces Ltd. is a mid-sized Canadian manufacturer of thermal processing equipment. *New Positions Created (6):* Junior Field Service Technician; Mechanical Engineering Position; Project Leader, Mechanical; Senior Field Service Representative; Field Service Representative; Proposals Coordinator.

CANADA 3000 AIRLINES LTD.
Att: Human Resources Development
27 Fasken Drive
Toronto, ON M9W 1K6
Tel. 416-674-0257
Fax 416-674-7225
Website www.canada3000.com

Employer Background: Canada 3000 Airlines Ltd. is Canada's second-largest scheduled airline, providing affordable air travel for leisure travellers. *New Positions Created (2):* Airport Duty Managers; Scheduled Revenue Accountant.

CANADA 3000 CARGO INC.
Att: Human Resources
6299 Airport Road, Suite 401
Mississauga, ON L4V 1N3
Fax 905-671-3984
Email ...... humanresources@c3cargo.com

Employer Background: Canada 3000 Cargo Inc. operates a dedicated overnight air freighter network in Canada, serving the freight forwarding industry. *New Positions Created (4):* Accounting Positions; Customer Service Representative; Sales Agents and Representatives; Various Cargo Transport Positions.

CANADA BREAD COMPANY LTD.
Att: Jim Curle, Distribution Manager
12151 - 160th Street
Edmonton, AB T5V 1M4
Fax 780-447-6566
Email .... curleji@canadabread.ca
Website .... www.canadabread.ca

Employer Background: Canada Bread Company Ltd., part of Maple Leaf Foods, is a leading producer of fresh and frozen bakery products, fresh pasta and sauces. *New Positions Created (2):* Distribution Supervisors; Customer Service Coordinator, Sales.

CANADA BREAD COMPANY LTD.
Att: Randie Mulligan, Production Manager
4639 - 72nd Avenue SE
Calgary, AB T2C 4H7
Tel. 403-203-3283
Fax 403-203-1676
Email .... hr@canadabread.ca
Website .... www.canadabread.ca

Employer Background: Canada Bread Company Ltd., part of Maple Leaf Foods, is a leading producer of fresh and frozen bakery products, fresh pasta and sauces. *New Positions Created (4):* Maintenance Clerk; Production Supervisor; Production Clerk; Production Supervisor.

CANADA BREAD COMPANY LTD.
Att: Employment Coordinator
10 Four Seasons Place
Toronto, ON M9B 6H7
Tel. 416-622-2040
Fax 416-622-9739
Website .... www.canadabread.ca

Employer Background: Canada Bread Company Ltd., part of Maple Leaf Foods, is a leading producer of fresh and frozen bakery products, fresh pasta and sauces. *New Positions Created (5):* Certified Electrician; Supervisors (3); Class B / Ammonia 3rd Class Stationary Engineer; Maintenance Supervisor; Various Operations Positions.

CANADA BREAD COMPANY LTD.
Att: Madalynn Bates, HR Administrator
144 Viceroy Road
Concord, ON L4K 2L8
Fax 905-738-5056
Email .... camposmx@canadabread.ca
Website .... www.canadabread.ca

Employer Background: Canada Bread Company Ltd., part of Maple Leaf Foods, is a leading producer of fresh and frozen bakery products, fresh pasta and sauces. *New Positions Created (2):* Inventory Control Analyst; A / R Clerk.

CANADA BRICK LTD.
Att: John Black
1570 Yorkton Court
Burlington, ON L7P 5B7
Fax 905-633-7388
Email .... jblack@canadabrick.com
Website .... www.canadabrick.com

Employer Background: Canada Brick Ltd. is one of Canada's largest manufacturers of clay bricks. *New Positions Created (4):* Forklift Operators; Maintenance Mechanics; Material Handlers; Production Operators.

CANADA COLORS AND CHEMICALS LTD. / CCC
Att: Rozi Shamasdin
80 Scarsdale Road
Toronto, ON M3B 2R7
Tel. 416-449-7750
Fax 416-449-3632
Email .... careers@canadacolors.com
Website .... www.canadacolors.com

Employer Background: CCC is a leading manufacturer and distributor of industrial and specialty chemicals, solvents, plastics compounds and additives. *New Positions Created (7):* Product / Sales Manager, Pharmaceuticals and Cosmetics; Inside Sales Representative; Customer Service Representative; Market Manager, Specialty Coatings; Technical Data Coordinator; Market Coordinator - Plastics; Invoicing Clerk.

CANADA COUNCIL FOR THE ARTS, THE
Att: Rachelle Malone, Human Resources
350 Albert Street, PO Box 1047
Ottawa, ON K1P 5V8

Tel. 613-566-4414
Fax 613-566-4323
Email .... rachelle.malone@canadacouncil.ca
Website .... www.canadacouncil.ca
Employer Background: The Canada Council for the Arts is an independent national agency, providing grants and services to professional Canadian artists and arts organizations. *New Positions Created (5):* Program Officer, Dance Section; Records and Information Management Assistant; Program Officer, Canadian Commission for UNESCO; Senior Research Officer, Public Affairs, Research and Communications; Director, Arts Division.

CANADA CUSTOMS AND REVENUE AGENCY / CCRA
Att: Human Resources,
Calgary Tax Services Office
220 - 4th Avenue SE, Room 720
Calgary, AB T2G 0L1

Fax 403-691-7437
Website .... www.ccra-adrc.gc.ca
Employer Background: CCRA is responsible for revenue generation, tax administration, international trade and border services. *New Positions Created (4):* Valuator; Collections Contact Officer; Income Tax / Excise Tax Auditors; Regional Science Advisor.

CANADA CUSTOMS AND REVENUE AGENCY / CCRA
Att: Human Resources Manager
PO Box 980, Station A
Toronto, ON M5W 1G5

Fax 416-954-5170
Website .... www.ccra.gc.ca
Employer Background: CCRA is responsible for revenue generation, tax administration, international trade and border services. *New Positions Created (3):* Tax Auditors; Real Estate Appraiser; Income Tax / Excise Tax Auditors.

CANADA CUSTOMS AND REVENUE AGENCY / CCRA
Att: Human Resources Manager
99 Metcalfe Street, 2nd Floor
Ottawa, ON K1A 0L5

Fax 613-941-0963
Email .... martine.pelletier@ccra.gc.ca
Website .... www.ccra-adrc.gc.ca
Employer Background: CCRA is responsible for revenue generation, tax administration, international trade and border services. *New Positions Created (10):* Actuarial Advisor; Assistant Actuary; Forensic Document Analyst; Customs Inspector; Library Systems Administrator; Secretary, Temporary Replacement Services; Junior Project Officer; Technical Officer; Assistant Commissioner, Communications; Forensic Document Analyst.

CANADA CUSTOMS AND REVENUE AGENCY, IT BRANCH / CCRA
Att: Career Opportunities
875 Heron Road, Room 1025
Ottawa, ON K1A 0L8

Tel. 613-954-9548
Fax 613-990-2518
Website .... www.ccra-adrc.gc.ca
Employer Background: CCRA is responsible for revenue generation, tax administration, international trade and border services. *New Positions Created (3):* Infrastructure Analyst; Systems Integration Analyst; Various Computing Positions.

CANADA CUSTOMS AND REVENUE AGENCY, SAINT JOHN TAX SERVICES OFFICE / CCRA
Att: Human Resources Manager
126 Prince William Street
Saint John, NB E2L 4H9

Fax 506-636-5151
Website .... www.ccra-adrc.gc.ca
Employer Background: CCRA is responsible for revenue generation, tax administration, international trade and border services. *New Positions Created (3):* Excise Tax Auditor; Employee Assistance Program Coordinator / Counsellor; Income Tax / Excise Tax Auditor.

CANADA DEPOSIT INSURANCE CORPORATION / CDIC
Att: Human Resources Department
PO Box 2340, Station D
Ottawa, ON K1P 5W5

Tel. 613-996-2087
Fax 613-943-1994
Email .... hrcdic@cdic.ca
Website .... www.cdic.ca
Employer Background: Created in 1967, CDIC is a Crown corporation responsible for protecting depositors' money in failed financial institutions. *New Positions Created (6):* Communications Advisor; Risk Mgrs; Senior Legal Counsel; Business Analyst; Emerging Issues Analyst; Risk Managers (3).

CANADA LAW BOOK INC.
Att: D. Thompson, Human Resources
240 Edward Street
Aurora, ON L4G 3S9

Tel. 905-841-6472
Fax 905-841-5085
Email .... dthompson@canadalawbook.ca
Website .... www.canadalawbook.ca
Employer Background: Established in 1855, Canada Law Book Inc. is a leading publisher of law reports and legal information. *New Positions Created (4):* Sales Representatives (2); General Sales Managers (2); Sales Representative; Sr Advertising Sales Rep.

CANADA LIFE ASSURANCE COMPANY
Att: Human Resources Department
330 University Avenue
Toronto, ON M5G 1R8

Tel. 416-597-1440
Fax 416-597-6520
Email .... hr@canadalife.com
Website .... www.canadalife.com
Employer Background: Established in 1847, Canada Life Assurance Company provides financial services to over 8 million policyholders throughout Canada, the USA, the UK and Ireland. *New Positions Created (37):* Bilingual Customer Service Representative; Consultant, Knowledge Tools; Customer Service Coordinator; Technical Assistant; Disability Claims Specialist; Disability Claims Specialist I; Senior Marketing Consultant, Reinsurance; Bilingual Individual Savings Product Team Leader; Coordinator, Litigation Law; National Director, Call Centre Development; Manager, Group Savings Client Services; Mortgage Analyst; Senior Project Consultant; Assistant Vice-President; E-Integration Consultants (2); Group / Creditor Medical Underwriter's Assistant; Investment Forecast Consultant; Systems Specialist / Consultant; Administrative Assistant; Customer Account Representative; Customer Account Representative; Group / ASO Accounting Specialist; Group Pricing Analyst, Group Financial Services; Legal Secretary; Litigation Consultant, Group Disability; Senior Financial Analyst, Systems & Financial Services; Commercial / Insurance Lawyers (2); Commercial / Investment Lawyers (2); Securities / Corporate Finance Lawyer; Market Research Specialist; Premium Offset Settlement Coordinators (5); Manager, Corporate Services; Senior Legal Secretaries (3); Corporate Counsel; Customer Service Representative; Manager, Accounting Services; Underwriting Consultant.

CANADA MORTGAGE AND HOUSING CORPORATION / CMHC
Att: Human Resources Department
1661 Duranleau Street, 2nd Floor
Vancouver, BC V6H 3S3

Fax 604-714-3700
Email .... mthomas@cmhc-schl.gc.ca
Website .... www.cmhc-schl.gc.ca
Employer Background: CMHC is the Government of Canada's national housing agency, providing mortgage loan insurance, housing assistance programs and housing information. *New Positions Created (2):* Technical Resource Officer; Information Officer.

CANADA MORTGAGE AND HOUSING CORPORATION / CMHC
Att: Human Resources Manager
100 Sheppard Avenue East, Suite 500
Toronto, ON M2N 6Z1

Website .... www.cmhc-schl.gc.ca
Employer Background: CMHC is the government of Canada's national housing agency, providing mortgage loan insurance, housing assistance programs and housing information. *New Positions Created (3):* Administrative Assistant; Clerk; Manager, Professional Services.

CANADA MORTGAGE AND HOUSING CORPORATION / CMHC
Att: Human Resources
700 Montreal Road
Ottawa, ON K1A 0P7
Tel. 613-748-2461
Website .... www.cmhc-schl.gc.ca
Employer Background: CMHC is the government of Canada's national housing agency, providing mortgage loan insurance, housing assistance programs and housing information. *New Positions Created (18):* Analyst, Costing Systems & Fees / Chargebacks; Senior Analyst, Fixed Income; Residential Underwriters; Senior Financial Operations Analyst; Solicitor; Economist, Market Analyst; Project Officer, Market Analysis and Surveys Analysis; Senior Economist, Capital Markets; Senior Economist / Market Analyst; Senior Officer - Planning and Liaison; Senior Analyst, Fixed Income; Senior Economist, Market Analysis; Senior Researchers, Housing Finance (2); Translator, Linguistic Services; Director, Product and Technology Development; Chief, Default and Claims; Insurance Business Analyst; Insurance Business Analyst.

CANADA POST CORPORATION
Att: Human Resources
2701 Riverside Drive, Suite N0030
Ottawa, ON K1A 0B1
Fax 613-734-7432
Website .... www.canadapost.ca
Employer Background: Canada Post Corporation is a Crown corporation responsible for the delivery of Canada's mail. *New Positions Created (6):* French Revisor / Translator; Officer, Pension Financial Accounting & Reporting; Manager, Graphic Services, External; Manager, Graphic Services, Internal; Officer, Communications (Editor); Officer, Graphic Design.

CANADA SAFEWAY LIMITED
Att: Employment Office
14360 Yellowhead Trail
Edmonton, AB T5L 3C5
Tel. 780-453-6310
Fax 780-453-6379
Email .... donna.marchiel@safeway.com
Website .... www.safeway.com
Employer Background: Canada Safeway Limited is part of California-based Safeway Inc., a leading food and drug retailer, with 1,688 stores in North America. *New Positions Created (2):* Staff Pharmacist; Baker Manager.

CANADA SAFEWAY LIMITED
Att: Human Resources Manager
401 Manitou Road SE
Calgary, AB T2G 4C2
Fax 403-287-4071
Email .... ab.employment@safeway.com
Website .... www.safeway.com
Employer Background: Canada Safeway Limited is a grocery retailer with 1,650 stores across the USA and Canada. *New Positions Created (2):* Pharmacists; Pharmacists.

CANADA SAFEWAY LTD.
Att: Linda Smith,
Employment Coordinator
7280 Fraser Street
Vancouver, BC V5X 3V9
Tel. 604-322-2550
Fax 604-322-2507
Email .... bc.employment@safeway.com
Website .... www.safeway.com
Employer Background: Canada Safeway Ltd. is part of California-based Safeway Inc., a leading food and drug retailer, with 1,688 stores in North America. *New Positions Created (2):* Licensed Pharmacists; Natural Market Specialist.

CANADA SAFEWAY LTD.
Att: Human Resources Department
1020 - 64th Avenue NE, PO Box 864, Stn M
Calgary, AB T2P 2J6
Tel. 403-287-4066
Fax 403-730-3306
Email .... can.employment@safeway.com
Website .... www.safeway.com
Employer Background: Canada Safeway Ltd. is part of California-based Safeway Inc., a leading food and drug retailer, with 1,688 stores in North America. *New Positions Created (2):* Produce Coordinator; Pharmacist.

CANADA SCIENCE AND TECHNOLOGY MUSEUM CORP.
Att: Human Resources Division
PO Box 9724, Station T
Ottawa, ON K1G 5A3
Tel. 613-991-3044
Fax 613-991-9983
Email .... hrd-drh@nmstc.ca
Website .... www.science-tech.nmstc.ca
Employer Background: Canada Science and Technology Museum Corp. aims to improve public knowledge of the ongoing relationships between science, technology and Canadian history. *New Positions Created (2):* Education and Interpretation Officer, Special Events; Visitor Service Officer.

CANADA-NOVA SCOTIA OFFSHORE PETROLEUM BOARD
Att: Administrator, Accounting & HR
1791 Barrington St., 6th Floor, TD Centre
Halifax, NS B3J 3K9
Tel. 902-422-5588
Fax 902-422-1799
Email .... jmcpherson@cnsopb.ns.ca
Website .... www.cnsopb.ns.ca
Employer Background: The Canada-Nova Scotia Offshore Petroleum Board is responsible for regulating petroleum affairs and safe work practices in Nova Scotia's offshore petroleum industry. *New Positions Created (4):* Advisor, Petroleum Process Engineering; Advisor, Regulatory Process; Advisor, Resource Assessment / Exploration; Petroleum / Reservoir Engineer.

CANADIAN 88 ENERGY CORP.
Att: Human Resources
400 - 3rd Avenue SW, Suite 700
Calgary, AB T2P 4H2
Tel. 403-974-8800
Website www.cdn88energy.com
Employer Background: Canadian 88 Energy Corp. is an independent, mid-cap, upstream oil and gas company. *New Positions Created (8):* Construction Foreman; Senior Field Foreman; Intermediate Land Administrator; Accounts Payable Clerk; Fixed Asset Accountant; Intermediate Production and Revenue Accountant; Treasury Clerk; Accounts Payable Clerk.

CANADIAN AMERICAN FINANCIAL CORP. (CANADA) LTD.
Att: Robert I. Plamondon/Norton Solomon
1005 Gold Crescent
Ottawa, ON K2B 8C4
Tel. 613-820-7377
Fax 613-726-8780
Email .... ingrid.norton@sympatico.ca
Website .... www.heritageresp.com
Employer Background: Canadian American Financial Corp. (Canada) Ltd. administers the Heritage Scholarship Trust Plan, one of Canada's leading registered education savings plans. *New Positions Created (3):* Managers / Sales Representatives; Enrollment Officers; Enrollment Officer.

CANADIAN ASSOCIATION OF BROADCASTERS / CAB
Att: Human Resources
350 Sparks Street
Suite 306, Box 627, Station B
Ottawa, ON K1P 5S2
Tel. 613-233-4035
Fax 613-233-6961
Email .... careers@cab-acr.ca
Website .... www.cab-acr.ca
Employer Background: CAB is the collective voice of Canada's private radio and television stations, networks and specialty services. *New Positions Created (2):* Lawyer, Intellectual Property; Mgr, Media Relations.

CANADIAN BANK NOTE COMPANY, LTD.
Att: Doris Couvieau, Human Resources
145 Richmond Road
Ottawa, ON K1Z 1A1
Tel. 613-722-2548
Fax 613-722-4561
Email .... dcouviea@cbnco.com
Website .... www.cbnco.com
Employer Background: Canadian Bank Note Company, Ltd. is an Ottawa-based high-security printer, supplying specialized printed products and related issuance systems to domestic and international markets. *New Positions Created (17):* Letterpress Operators (2); Purchasing Specialist; Senior Accounts Payable Clerk; Database Administrator; Senior Inventory Accountant; Senior Software Developer; Protection Officers; Senior Buyer / Planner; Manufacturing Electronic Technician / Technologist; Offset Press Operator; Project Manager; Database Administrator; QA Coordinator; Senior Software Developer; Manager of Accounting Services; Projects Administrator, Identification Systems; Solutions Engineering Analyst.

CANADIAN BANKERS ASSOCIATION
Att: Human Resources
199 Bay Street, 30th Floor
Toronto, ON M5L 1G2

Tel. 416-362-6092
Fax 416-362-3651
Email .... rallen@cba.ca
Website .... www.cba.ca

Employer Background: Established in 1891, CBA is an industry association, providing information, research, advocacy and operational support services to Canada's banks. *New Positions Created (5):* Advisor, Consumer Affairs; Director, Security; Director, Financial Institutions and Trade Policy; Director, Market and Regulatory Developments; Vice-President, Policy.

CANADIAN BLOOD SERVICES / CBS
Att: Human Resources, Head Office
1800 Alta Vista Drive
Ottawa, ON K1G 4J5

Tel. 613-739-3000
Fax 613-739-2290
Email ... human.resources@bloodservices.ca
Website .... www.bloodservices.ca

Employer Background: CBS is a non-profit, charitable organization mandated to deliver safe and reliable blood services to the health services system. *New Positions Created (16):* Associate Scientist, Molecular Immunology; Quality Systems Professionals; Director, Risk Management; Communications Specialist; Operating Engineer; Administrative Assistant; Coordinator, Occupational Health Safety and Workers' Compensation; SAP HR Operational Support Leader; Technical Team Lead; General Counsel and Corporate Secretary; Manager, Treasury; Quality Systems Associate, Validations; Regulatory Affairs Associates, Audits (4); Manager of Media Relations; Regulatory Affairs Associates, Reporting; Regulatory Affairs Associates, Submissions.

CANADIAN BLOOD SERVICES, EDMONTON CENTRE
Att: Human Resources
8249 - 114th Street
Edmonton, AB T6G 2R8

Tel. 780-431-1122
Fax 780-431-0461
Website .... www.bloodservices.ca

Employer Background: Canadian Blood Services, Edmonton Centre is responsible for meeting the blood transfusion requirements of 100 hospitals in northern Alberta, parts of northern BC and the Northwest Territories. *New Positions Created (2):* Assistant Nursing Manager, Customer Services; Communications Coordinator.

CANADIAN BLOOD SERVICES, TORONTO BLOOD CENTRE / CBS
Att: Human Resources Adviser
67 College Street
Toronto, ON M5G 2M1

Tel. 416-974-9900
Fax 416-596-8305
Email .... human.resources.tor@
.... bloodservices.ca

Website .... www.bloodservices.ca
Employer Background: CBS is a non-profit, charitable organization mandated to deliver safe and reliable blood services to the health services system. *New Positions Created (6):* Medical Laboratory Technologists; Senior Technologists; Biostatistician; Research Assistant; Nurse Mgr; Collections Site Mgr.

CANADIAN BROADCASTING CORPORATION / CBC
Att: Human Resources
PO Box 3220, Station C
Ottawa, ON K1Y 1E4

Tel. 613-724-1200
Fax 613-724-5101
Email .... resume@cbc.ca
Website .... www.cbc.ca

Employer Background: Founded in 1936, CBC is the Crown corporation responsible for public broadcasting in Canada. The company has an annual budget exceeding $750 million and over 7,500 staff members. *New Positions Created (2):* National Fleet Manager; Director, Supply Management.

CANADIAN CANCER SOCIETY / CCS
Att: Human Resources
565 - 10th Avenue West
Vancouver, BC V5Z 4J4

Tel. 604-872-2034
Fax 604-872-4113
Website .... www.cancer.ca

Employer Background: CCS is a national, community-based organization of volunteers working to eradicate cancer and enhance the quality of life for individuals living with cancer. *New Positions Created (23):* Coordinator, South Asian Community; Prevention Coordinator; Quit Specialist; Assistant, Gift Planning and Major Gifts; Manager, Quality Initiatives; Assistant, Program Services and Regions; Manager, Annual Campaign; Program Services Coordinator; Assistant, Finance and Administration; Manager, Gift Planning; Campaign Assistant; Manager, Greater Vancouver Region; Coordinator, Revenue Development; Manager, Cancer Information Service; Quit Specialists (2); Corporate Campaign Manager; Program Services Coordinator; Information Specialist; Assistant, Finance and Administration; Volunteer Resources Coordinator; Manager, Smokers' HelpLine; Prevention Coordinator; Program Services Coordinator.

CANADIAN CANCER SOCIETY / CCS
Att: Ms Wini Stoddart, HR Manager
10 Alcorn Avenue, Suite 200
Toronto, ON M4V 3B1

Tel. 416-961-7223
Fax 416-961-4189
Email .... wstoddar@cancer.ca
Website .... www.cancer.ca

Employer Background: CCS is a national, community-based organization of volunteers working to eradicate cancer and enhance the quality of life for individuals living with cancer. *New Positions Created (4):* Bilingual Communications Specialist; Bilingual Communications Specialist; Senior

Communications and Marketing Officer, Research; National Director, Communications and Marketing.

CANADIAN COPYRIGHT LICENSING AGENCY / CANCOPY
Att: Human Resources
1 Yonge Street, 19th Floor
Toronto, ON M5E 1E5

Tel. 416-868-1620
Fax 416-868-1613
Email .... hr@cancopy.com
Website .... www.cancopy.com

Employer Background: Established in 1988, CANCOPY is a non-profit organization, responsible for administering the reproduction rights of published works on behalf of authors, artists and publishers. *New Positions Created (4):* Accounts Payable Coordinator, Royalties; Accounting / Distribution Manager; Director of Business Development; Corporate Counsel.

CANADIAN COUNCIL ON HEALTH SERVICES ACCREDITATION / CCHSA
Att: Elaine Kinack, Human Resources
1730 St. Laurent Boulevard, Suite 100
Ottawa, ON K1G 5L1

Tel. 613-738-3800
Fax 613-738-1244
Email .... hr@cchsa.ca
Website .... www.cchsa.ca

Employer Background: CCHSA is a national, non-profit organization, helping health organizations improve the quality of care and services provided to clients. *New Positions Created (3):* National Services Specialist, Bilingual; Report Specialists; Research and Development Specialist, Canadian Forces Health Services.

CANADIAN DEPOSITORY FOR SECURITIES LTD. / CDS
Att: Human Resources
85 Richmond Street West
Toronto, ON M5H 2C9

Tel. 416-365-8400
Fax 416-365-0758
Email .... cappelma@cds.ca
Website .... www.cds.ca

Employer Background: The CDS is Canada's national securities depository, clearing and settlement hub, holding nearly $2 trillion on deposit, settling between $100 and $200 billion daily, and handling 57 million securities trades annually for banks. *New Positions Created (11):* Audit Mgr; IT Auditor; Senior Business Analyst; Human Resources Consultant; Sales & Marketing Associate; Senior Corporate Change Analyst; Senior Documentation Specialist; Sr Network Architect; Bilingual CUSIP Administrator; Securities Control Clerk; Transfer Operations Clerk.

CANADIAN EGG MARKETING AGENCY / CEMA
Att: Human Resources
112 Kent Street, Suite 1501
Ottawa, ON K1P 5P2

Tel. 613-238-2514
Fax 613-238-1967

Email .... info@canadaegg.ca
Website .... www.canadaegg.ca
Employer Background: CEMA ensures that Canada's egg producers realize a fair return on their investments and that consumers receive quality eggs at a fair price. *New Positions Created (2):* Trade Analyst; Administrative Coordinator.

CANADIAN FOOD INSPECTION AGENCY / CFIA
Att: Human Resources
59 Camelot Drive
Nepean, ON K1Y 0Y9
Tel. 613-225-2342
Website .... www.inspection.gc.ca
Employer Background: Created in 1997, CFIA is responsible for all federal food, animal and plant health inspection programs. *New Positions Created (4):* Veterinarian; Veterinary Pathologist; Director; TSE Policy Coordinator and National Manager, Animal Health Policy and Standards.

CANADIAN FOOD INSPECTION AGENCY / CFIA
Att: Bonnie Beek, HR Assistant
1081 Main Street, PO Box 1088
Moncton, NB E1C 8R2
Tel. 506-851-7670
Fax 506-851-2064
Email .... beekbl@inspection.gc.ca
Website .... www.inspection.gc.ca
Employer Background: Created in 1997, CFIA is responsible for all federal food, animal and plant health inspection programs. *New Positions Created (2):* Manager, Human Resources; Inspectors.

CANADIAN FORCES EXCHANGE SYSTEM / CANEX
Att: Gérard Étienne, VP Human Resources
245 Cooper Street
Ottawa, ON K2P 0G2
Tel. 613-995-7568
Fax 613-996-5772
Email .... recruiting@cfpsa.com
Website .... www.cfpsa.com
Employer Background: Established in 1968, CANEX operates retail stores, grocery convenience stores and foodservice outlets on military bases throughout Canada. *New Positions Created (4):* Retail Buyer; National Manager, Loss Prevention; Regional Manager; Systems Coordinator.

CANADIAN FORCES PERSONNEL SUPPORT AGENCY / CFPSA
Att: Staffing Officer
245 Cooper Street, 4th Floor
Ottawa, ON K2P 0G2
Tel. 613-995-9590
Fax 613-996-5772
Email .... recruiting@cfpsa.com
Website .... www.cfpsa.com
Employer Background: CFPSA delivers personnel support programs to improve the quality of life for military families. *New Positions Created (10):* Human Resources Coordinator; Human Resources Manager;

Kitchen Services Coordinator; Branch Network Manager; Network Development Specialist; Network Support Manager; Technical Support Specialist (Help Desk); Web Content Administrator; Human Resources Coordinator; Public Relations Coordinator.

CANADIAN FOUNDATION ON COMPULSIVE GAMBLING (ONTARIO)
Att: Jamie Wiebe
505 Consumers Road, Suite 801
Toronto, ON M2J 4V8
Tel. 416-499-9800
Fax 416-499-8260
Email .... jamiew@cfcg.org
Website .... www.responsiblegambling.org
Employer Background: CFCG is a non-profit organization, working to promote responsible gambling through information services, prevention, professional development and research. *New Positions Created (2):* Research Assistant; Project / Events Coordinator.

CANADIAN GENERAL-TOWER LTD.
Att: Human Resources Department
52 Middleton Street
Cambridge, ON N1R 5T6
Tel. 519-623-1630
Fax 519-623-5139
Employer Background: Canadian General-Tower Ltd. manufactures vinyl film and coated fabrics for the automotive, industrial and recreational market. *New Positions Created (7):* Manufacturing Supervisor; Product Development Specialist; Customs and Transportation Technician; Maintenance Planner; Electrician; Millwright; Preventive Maintenance Technician.

CANADIAN GLOBAL FOODS CORPORATION
Att: President
200 Bartor Road
Toronto, ON M9M 2W6
Tel. 416-744-3736
Fax 416-744-7879
Employer Background: Canadian Global Foods Corporation is a leading distributor of biscuits, crackers and snacks with brand names Taste Delight, Nifty and Reale. *New Positions Created (4):* Customer Service Clerk / Order Desk Position; Sales Representative; Customer Service / Order Desk Position; Inventory Manager / Traffic Coordinator.

CANADIAN GOLF & COUNTRY CLUB, THE
Att: Fiona McDonell, HR Coordinator
7842 Highway 7
Ashton, ON K0A 1B0
Tel. 613-253-3290
Fax 613-253-3292
Email .... canadian@magma.ca
Website .... www.canadiangolfclub.com
Employer Background: The Canadian Golf & Country Club is a 27-hole golf facility located minutes west of Kanata. *New Positions Created (3):* Banquet Sous Chef; Payroll /

Accounts Receivable Administrator; Head Chef / Food and Beverage Manager.

CANADIAN GRAIN COMMISSION
Att: Human Resources Branch
303 Main Street, Suite 401
Winnipeg, MB R3C 3G7
Tel. 204-983-2770
Fax 204-983-1681
Website .... www.cgc.ca
Employer Background: Operating under the authority of the Canada Grain Act, CGC is a federal government agency, offering a number of services to the grain industry. *New Positions Created (4):* Program Manager, Plant Molecular Biology; Research Associate, Image Analysis Research - Beans; Research Associate, Image Analysis Research - Cereals; Research Associate, Image Analysis Research - Pulses.

CANADIAN GYPSUM COMPANY / CGC INC.
Att: Barrie Hutchinson, HR Manager
PO Box 99
Hagersville, ON N0A 1H0
Fax 905-768-2020
Email .... bhutchinson@usg.com
Website .... www.cgcinc.com
Employer Background: Founded in 1907, CGC Inc. (a subsidiary of USG Corporation) manufactures, markets and distributes gypsum wallboard, joint treatment and suspended acoustic ceilings. *New Positions Created (5):* HR Supervisor; Industrial Electrician; Industrial Millwright; Mobile Mechanic; Human Resources Supervisor.

CANADIAN HEARING SOCIETY, THE
Att: Human Resources
271 Spadina Road
Toronto, ON M5R 2V3
Tel. 416-964-9595
Fax 416-928-2517
Email .... jobs@chs.ca
Website .... www.chs.ca
Employer Background: The Canadian Hearing Society is a non-profit organization, providing services and counselling for deaf, deafened and hard-of-hearing individuals and their families. *New Positions Created (8):* Manager, Corporate and Foundation Giving; Manager, Staff Development; Administrative Assistant, External Affairs & Employment Development; General Social Services Counsellor; Psychologist / Psychological Associate; Manager of Program Development, Mental Health Services; Project Manager; Regional Directors.

CANADIAN HELICOPTERS LTD.
Att: Director of Maintenance
1215 Montee Pilon
Les Cedres, QC J7T 1G1
Tel. 450-452-3000
Fax 450-452-2483
Email . ebergnach@canadianhelicopters.com
Website ... www.canadianhelicopters.com
Employer Background: Canadian Helicopters Ltd. is Canada's largest helicopter op-

erator, with over 750 employees operating from 51 bases nationwide. *New Positions Created (4):* Aircraft Maintenance Engineers; Maintenance Apprentice Engineers; Pilots; Quality Manager, Maintenance.

CANADIAN IMPERIAL BANK OF COMMERCE / CIBC
Att: Human Resources, Retail Banking
Commerce Court North, 20th Floor
Toronto, ON M5L 1A2
Tel. 416-861-3190
Fax 416-980-3510
Email .... opportunities@cibc.com
Website .... www.cibc.com
Employer Background: CIBC is one of North America's leading financial institutions, offering retail and wholesale products and services through an electronic banking network, branches and offices. *New Positions Created (8):* Financial Adviser; Senior Business Analyst; Finance Positions.; Personal Bankers; Account Manager, Small Business; Branch Manager; Credit Call Centre; Personal Bankers.

CANADIAN IMPERIAL BANK OF COMMERCE, CIBC TECHNOLOGY
Att: Technology Recruitment
750 Lawrence Avenue West, Suite E8
Toronto, ON M6A 1B8
Email .... perc.recruiting@cibc.com
Website .... www.cibc.com
Employer Background: CIBC Technology supports numerous lines of business throughout the Canadian Imperial Bank of Commerce, including card products, the branch network, wealth management and electronic banking. *New Positions Created (4):* Business Analysts; Project Managers; Senior Developers; Systems Architects.

CANADIAN IMPERIAL BANK OF COMMERCE, CIBC WEALTH MANAGEMENT
Att: Ms D. Holroyd,
Imperial Service Resourcing
855 - 2nd Street SW, 8th Floor
Calgary, AB T2P 4J7
Fax 403-221-5565
Email .... hrimperial@cibc.com
Website .... www.cibc.com
Employer Background: CIBC is one of North America's leading financial institutions, offering retail and wholesale products and services through an electronic banking network, branches and offices. *New Positions Created (3):* Financial Advisor; Financial Advisor; Financial Adviser.

CANADIAN IMPERIAL BANK OF COMMERCE, LEGAL DIVISION / CIBC
Att: Leon Dobell, Business Manager
199 Bay Street
Suite 1500, Commerce Court West
Toronto, ON M5L 1A2
Fax 416-368-9826
Email .... leon.dobell@cibc.com
Website .... www.cibc.com
Employer Background: CIBC is one of North America's leading financial institutions, of-

fering retail and wholesale products and services through an electronic banking network, branches and offices. *New Positions Created (4):* Legal Counsel, Junior; Legal Counsel, Retail and Small Business Banking; Legal Counsel, Securities M&A; Legal Counsel, Wealth Management.

CANADIAN IMPERIAL BANK OF COMMERCE, NATIONAL CONTACT CENTRE SUPPORT / CIBC
Att: NCCS Staffing
5650 Yonge Street, 18th Floor
Toronto, ON M2M 4G3
Fax 416-218-9342
Email .... nccs.staffing@cibc.com
Website .... www.cibc.com
Employer Background: CIBC is one of North America's leading financial institutions, offering retail and wholesale products and services through an electronic banking network, branches and offices. *New Positions Created (4):* Contact Centre Representatives; Branch Manager Retail Equity; Manager, Electronic Trading; Supervisors.

CANADIAN INOVATECH INC.
Att: Human Resources
3911 Mt. Lehman Road
Abbotsford, BC V4X 2N1
Tel. 604-857-9080
Fax 604-857-0843
Website .... www.inovatech.ca
Employer Background: Canadian Inovatech processes a variety of dairy, egg, bioproducts and nutraceutical products. *New Positions Created (2):* Vice-President of Finance and Administration; Cost Accountant.

CANADIAN INSTITUTE FOR HEALTH INFORMATION / CIHI
Att: Human Resources
90 Eglinton Avenue East, Suite 300
Toronto, ON M4P 2Y3
Tel. 416-481-2002
Fax 416-481-2950
Email .... careers@cihi.ca
Website .... www.cihi.ca
Employer Background: CIHI is a national, non-profit organization responsible for developing and maintaining Canada's nationwide health information system. *New Positions Created (14):* Consultant, Electronic Health Record; Manager, Classifications; Classification Specialist; Programmers, Senior and Intermediate; Senior Analyst, Trauma Registries; Coordinator, Infostructure Standards; Senior Analyst, Canadian Joint Replacement Registry; Senior Analyst, Data Quality; Senior Analyst, Health Reports and Analysis; Support Services Representative; Coordinator, Research Services; Senior Analyst, Canadian Organ Replacement Register; Senior Analyst, Hospital Morbidity Data; Senior Analyst, Trauma Registries.

CANADIAN INSTITUTE FOR HEALTH INFORMATION / CIHI
Att: Human Resources
377 Dalhousie Street, Suite 200
Ottawa, ON K1N 9N8

Tel. 613-241-7860
Fax 613-241-8120
Email .... careers@cihi.ca
Website .... www.cihi.ca
Employer Background: CIHI is a national, non-profit organization responsible for developing and maintaining Canada's nationwide health information system. *New Positions Created (12):* Analyst, Health Professionals Database; Business / Systems Analyst, Client Relationship Management System; Classification Specialist; Coordinator, Drug Utilization Project; Manager; Policy Analyst, Canadian Population Health Initiative; Senior Analyst; Director, Client Relations; Director, Health Resources Information; Director, Health Services Information; Director, Information Systems; Director, Standards Development.

CANADIAN INSTITUTE, THE
Att: Operations Manager
1329 Bay Street, 3rd Floor
Toronto, ON M5R 2C4
Tel. 416-927-0718
Fax 416-927-1061
Email .... barbara@cicomm.com
Website .... www.canadianinstitute.com
Employer Background: The Canadian Institute is a leading organizer of conferences and workshops for senior business executives, lawyers and other professionals. *New Positions Created (5):* Conference Developer / Team Leader; Conference Producer, Government Group; Conference Coordinator; Legal Position; Legal Position.

CANADIAN INSTITUTES OF HEALTH RESEARCH / CIHR
Att: Robert Rowan, HR Manager
410 Laurier Avenue West
9th Floor, Address Locator 4209A
Ottawa, ON K1A 0W9
Tel. 613-941-2672
Fax 613-954-1800
Email .... hr-rh@cihr.ca
Website .... www.cihr.ca
Employer Background: CIHR is Canada's federal funding agency for health research. *New Positions Created (3):* Director of Secretariat on Research Ethics; Financial Advisor; Institute Liaison Agents (2).

CANADIAN INTERGOVERNMENTAL CONFERENCE SECRETARIAT / CICS
Att: Ronald L. Richer,
Director, Corporate Services
222 Queen Street, 10th Floor
Ottawa, ON K1P 5V9
Tel. 613-995-2341
Fax 613-995-2348
Email .... rricher@scics.gc.ca
Website .... www.scics.gc.ca
Employer Background: CICS provides a complete range of conference support and information services for senior-level intergovernmental meetings. *New Positions Created (3):* Assistant Conference Officer; Conference Assistant; Conference Officers (2).

CANADIAN INTERNET REGISTRATION AUTHORITY / CIRA
Att: Human Resources Manager
350 Sparks Street, Suite 1110
Ottawa, ON K1R 7S8

Tel. 877-860-1411
Email .... hr@cira.ca
Website .... www.cira.ca

Employer Background: Incorporated in 1998, CIRA is the non-profit corporation responsible for operating the .ca domain. *New Positions Created (3):* Call Centre Agent; Customer Support Agent; Technical Writer.

CANADIAN LINEN AND UNIFORM SERVICES
Att: Human Resources
24 Atomic Avenue
Toronto, ON M8Z 5L1

Tel. 416-251-1621
Fax 416-534-6401
Email .... clu.sales@cdnuniforms.org
Website ... www.cdnlinenanduniform.com

Employer Background: Established in 1925, Canadian Linen and Uniform Services is a leading supplier of rental uniforms and related products and services. *New Positions Created (3):* Sales Representative; Apparel Consultant; Major Accounts Executive.

CANADIAN MASS MEDIA INC./CMMI
Att: Human Resources Department
120 Sinnott Road
Toronto, ON M1L 4N1

Tel. 416-752-8720
Fax 416-285-2059
Email .... hr@metronews.org
Website .... www.metronews.org

Employer Background: Canadian Mass Media Inc., a division of Metro News Ltd., is a large value-added reseller of magazines and books. *New Positions Created (7):* Supervisor; Assistant Controller; Audit Supervisor; Administrative Assistant; National Accounts Manager; Regional Sales Manager; Vice President, Business Development.

CANADIAN MEDICAL ASSOCIATION / CMA HOLDINGS INC.
Att: Department of Human Resources
1867 Alta Vista Drive
Ottawa, ON K1G 3Y6

Tel. 613-731-9331
Fax 613-736-7882
Email .... jobapp@cma.ca
Website .... www.cma.ca

Employer Background: Founded in 1867, CMA is the national voice of Canadian physicians, promoting health standards on behalf of 52,000 members. *New Positions Created (3):* Onsite Consultants; Associate Secretary General / Chief Medical Officer; Associate Director, Communications.

CANADIAN MEDICAL PROTECTIVE ASSOCIATION / CMPA
Att: Human Resources Manager
PO Box 8225, Station T
Ottawa, ON K1G 3H7

Tel. 613-725-2000
Fax 613-725-5133
Website .... www.cmpa.org

Employer Background: Established in 1901, CMPA provides 60,000 Canadian physicians with a range of services, including legal defence, indemnification, risk identification and assessment, education programs and general advice. *New Positions Created (15):* Corporate Secretary and Director of Strategic Planning; Communications Supervisor; Legal Assistant; Medical Secretary; Member Service Representative; Member Service Secretary; Research and Education Assistant; Manager, Operational Accounting; Assistant Secretary-Treasurer; Physician Risk Manager; Human Resources Specialist; Medical Analyst; Administrative Services Quality Assistant; Member Service Quality Assistant; Member Service Secretary.

CANADIAN MENTAL HEALTH ASSOCIATION / CMHA
Att: Program Director,
East Metro Connections
1200 Markham Road, Suite 500
Toronto, ON M1H 3C3

Fax 416-289-6285
Email .... cmhascar@sympatico.ca
Website .... www.cmha.ca

Employer Background: Founded in 1918, CMHA is one of the oldest voluntary organizations in Canada and deals with all aspects of mental health and illness, with 135 branches nationwide. *New Positions Created (6):* Case Manager; Case Managers; Housing Support Worker; Nurse Case Manager; Team Leader; Occupational Therapist.

CANADIAN MENTAL HEALTH ASSOCIATION / CMHA
Att: Human Resources Manager
29 Second Street East
Cornwall, ON K6H 1Y2

Fax 613-932-3755
Website .... www.cmha.ca

Employer Background: Founded in 1918, CMHA is one of the oldest voluntary organizations in Canada and deals with all aspects of mental health and illness, with 135 branches nationwide. *New Positions Created (2):* Program Workers, Community Support; Manager, Administration and Human Resources.

CANADIAN MENTAL HEALTH ASSOCIATION, OTTAWA-CARLETON BRANCH / CMHA
Att: Hiring Committee
1355 Bank Street, Suite 301
Ottawa, ON K1H 8K7

Tel. 613-737-7791
Website .... www.ontario.cmha.ca

Employer Background: Founded in 1918, CMHA is one of the oldest voluntary organizations in Canada and deals with all aspects of mental health and illness, with 135 branches nationwide. *New Positions Created (3):* Outreach Workers and Community Support Positions; Outreach and Community Support Workers; Manager, Volunteer Programs.

CANADIAN MENTAL HEALTH ASSOCIATION, PETERBOROUGH BRANCH / CMHA
Att: Human Resources Manager
349A George Street North, Suite 206
Peterborough, ON K9H 3P9

Fax 705-748-2577
Email ..... info@peterborough.cmha.on.ca
Website ... www.peterborough.cmha.on.ca

Employer Background: Founded in 1918, CMHA is one of the oldest voluntary organizations in Canada and deals with all aspects of mental health and illness, with 135 branches nationwide. *New Positions Created (3):* Community Support Workers (4); Community Treatment Order (CTO) Support Worker; Program Manager.

CANADIAN MICROELECTRONICS CORPORATION / CMC
Att: Nancy A. Peters, Secretary-Treasurer
210A Carruthers Hall, Queen's University
Kingston, ON K7L 3N6

Tel. 613-545-2914
Fax 613-548-8104
Email .... peters@cmc.ca
Website .... www.cmc.ca

Employer Background: CMC is an independent, non-profit organization mandated to provide world-class tools and fabrication to support an infrastructure for research and education in microelectronics and microsystems. *New Positions Created (2):* NT System Administrator; Unix System Administrator.

CANADIAN MUSEUM OF CIVILIZATION CORPORATION / CMCC
Att: Ed Richard
100 Laurier Street, PO Box 3100, Station B
Hull, QC J8X 4H2

Tel. 819-776-7000
Fax 819-776-7092
Website .... www.civilization.ca

Employer Background: Founded in 1968, CMCC (formerly the National Museum of Man) is Canada's national museum of human history. *New Positions Created (2):* Various Trades Positions; Director, Collections Management and Planning.

CANADIAN NATIONAL INSTITUTE FOR THE BLIND / CNIB
Att: Helena Lake,
Coordinator of Client Services
15 Colonel Baker Place NE
Calgary, AB T2E 4Z3

Tel. 403-266-8831
Fax 403-265-5029
Website .... www.cnib.org

Employer Background: CNIB is a non-profit organization, providing services to blind, visually impaired and deaf-blind individuals. *New Positions Created (2):* Occupational Therapist; Vision Rehabilitation Counsellor.

CANADIAN NATIONAL INSTITUTE FOR THE BLIND, THE / CNIB
Att: Anthony Futino
1929 Bayview Avenue
Toronto, ON M4G 3E8

Tel. 416-486-2500
Fax 416-480-7453
Email .... roscoem@cnib.ca
Website .... www.cnib.ca

Employer Background: The CNIB is a not-for-profit organization, providing services to blind, visually impaired and deafblind individuals. *New Positions Created (8):* National Director, Fund Development; National Manager, Fund Development Database and Donor Relations; Property Development Manager; National Manager, Technical Aids; Trust Accountant; National Communications Coordinator; Access and Adaptation Consultants (4); Employment Marketing Consultant.

CANADIAN NATURAL RESOURCES LIMITED / CNRL
Att: Human Resources
855 - 2nd Street SW, Suite 2500
Calgary, AB T2P 4J8
Tel. 403-517-7349
Fax 403-517-7352
Email .... careers@cnrl.com
Website .... www.cnrl.com

Employer Background: Established in 1989, CNRL is a senior oil and natural gas exploration, development and production company. *New Positions Created (6):* Business Systems Analyst; Oilsands Mine Geologist; Environmental Field Coordinator; Surface Landman; Environmental Project Leader; Auditor.

CANADIAN NORTHERN SHIELD INSURANCE COMPANY / CNS
Att: Human Resources Department
555 Hastings Street West, Suite 1900
Vancouver, BC V6B 4N6
Tel. 604-662-2911
Fax 604-601-5160
Email .... kduffield@cns.ca
Website .... www.cns.ca

Employer Background: CNS is a leading provider of property and casualty insurance in British Columbia, with over $100 million in gross premiums. *New Positions Created (5):* Senior Finance Manager; Manager, Personal Lines; Supervisor, Telephone Claims; Receptionist; Telephone Adjusters.

CANADIAN NUCLEAR SAFETY COMMISSION / CNSC
Att: Serge Stang, HR Assistant
280 Slater Street, PO Box 1046, Station B
Ottawa, ON K1P 5S9
Tel. 613-955-5894
Fax 613-995-0390
Email .... hr-rh@cnsc-ccsn.gc.ca
Website .... www.nuclearsafety.gc.ca

Employer Background: CNSC (formerly Atomic Energy Control Board) is an independent agency of the Government of Canada, responsible for regulating the use of nuclear energy and materials. *New Positions Created (11):* Licensee Training Program Evaluation Officer; Nuclear Non-Proliferation Officer; Methodology and Standards Officer; Examination and Certification

Officers; Project Officers, Nuclear Generating Division; Admin Assistants; Licence Assessment Specialist; Training Program Evaluation Officer; Environmental Assessment Specialist; Administrative Assistants; Examination and Certification Officers.

CANADIAN NURSES ASSOCIATION
Att: Human Resources Coordinator
50 Driveway
Ottawa, ON K2P 1E2
Fax 613-237-3520
Email .... hr@cna-nurses.ca
Website .... www.cna-nurses.ca

Employer Background: CNA is a federation of 11 provincial and territorial nursing associations, representing over 110,000 registered nurses. *New Positions Created (4):* Corporate Affairs Coordinator; Health Policy Analyst; Team Assistant; Senior Editor.

CANADIAN OLYMPIC ASSOCIATION
Att: Human Resources Department
21 St. Clair Avenue East, Suite 900
Toronto, ON M4T 1L9
Tel. 416-962-0262
Email .... abertoia@coa.ca
Website .... www.coa.ca

Employer Background: COA is Canada's largest private sector funder of amateur sports. *New Positions Created (5):* Executive Assistant; Business Development Team Member; Media Relations Specialist; Senior Financial Officer; Team Captain, Communications and Youth Program.

CANADIAN PACIFIC RAILWAY / CPR
Att: Employment Centre
401 - 9th Avenue SW
Suite 500, Gulf Canada Square
Calgary, AB T2P 4Z4
Tel. 403-218-7000
Fax 403-319-6870
Email .... employment_centre@cpr.ca
Website .... www.cpr.ca

Employer Background: CPR, a subsidiary of Canadian Pacific Limited, operates 25,000 km of track in Canada and the USA. The railway has 19,500 employees. *New Positions Created (4):* Sales Representative, Domestic Intermodal; Manager, Border Strategy; Staff Engineer, Mechanical; Director, Actuarial Services.

CANADIAN PARAPLEGIC ASSOCIATION / CPA
Att: Manager, Rehab Services, Consulting & Vocational Rehabilitation Services
320 - 23rd Avenue SW, Suite 401
Calgary, AB T2S 0J2
Tel. 403-228-3001
Fax 403-229-4271
Website .... www.canparaplegic.org

Employer Background: CPA is a non-profit agency, providing rehabilitation services to individuals with spinal cord injuries and other physical disabilities. *New Positions Created (2):* Occupational Therapist; Vocational Rehabilitation Specialists.

CANADIAN PARAPLEGIC ASSOCIATION ONTARIO / CPA ONTARIO
Att: Human Resources Coordinator
520 Sutherland Drive
Toronto, ON M4G 3V9
Tel. 416-422-5644
Fax 416-422-5943
Email .... aramirez@cpaont.org
Website .... www.cpaont.org

Employer Background: CPA Ontario is a non-profit agency, providing rehabilitation services to individuals with spinal cord injuries and other physical disabilities. *New Positions Created (7):* Director, Attendant Services; Administrative Assistants; Various Disabled Positions; Payroll / Benefits Administrator; Regional Service Coordinator; Accounts Payable / Accounts Receivable Clerk; Director of Rehabilitation Services.

CANADIAN PETCETERA LIMITED PARTNERSHIP
Att: Director of Human Resources
1565 Cliveden Avenue
Delta, BC V3M 6P7
Tel. 604-526-4180
Fax 604-526-4181
Email .... careers@petcetera.ca
Website .... www.petcetera.ca

Employer Background: Canadian Petcetera Limited Partnership is a specialty pet goods and services company, with 29 superstores nationwide. *New Positions Created (7):* Store Management Positions; Advertising Coordinator; Marketing Mgr; Manager, Distribution and Logistics, Toronto; Various Retail Positions; Veterinarians; Retail Managers.

CANADIAN PHARMACISTS ASSOCIATION / CPHA
Att: Jean Hunter
1785 Alta Vista Drive
Ottawa, ON K1G 3Y6
Tel. 613-523-7877
Fax 613-523-0445
Email .... gpa@cdnpharm.ca
Website .... www.cdnpharm.ca

Employer Background: CPhA is a national, non-profit association representing pharmacists in Canada and a major publisher of pharmaceutical information. *New Positions Created (13):* Administrative Assistant; Receptionist / Data Entry Clerk; Director of Practice Development; Director of Research; E-Business Development Manager; Assistant Editor; Project Coordinator / Editor; Director of Government Affairs; E-Business Manager; Manager, Conference and Marketing Administration; Mgr, Marketing Communications; Manager, Membership Development; Director of Government Affairs.

CANADIAN RECREATION PRODUCTS INC.
Att: Human Resources Manager
8515 Place Devonshire
Mount Royal, QC H4P 2K1
Tel. 514-733-4700
Fax 514-733-6352
Email .... gdenman@canadianrec.com
Website .... www.canadianrec.com

Employer Background: Canadian Recreation Products Inc. is a leading sporting goods manufacturer. *New Positions Created (6):* Bilingual Plant Manager; Assistant Sales Manager; Product Manager; Controller; Plant Manager; Sewing Mechanic.

CANADIAN RED CROSS, ONTARIO ZONE
Att: Human Resources
5700 Cancross Court
Mississauga, ON L5R 3E9

Tel. 905-890-1000
Fax 905-712-8814
Email .... nuccia.carbone@redcross.ca
Website .... www.redcross.ca

Employer Background: The Canadian Red Cross is a non-profit organization dedicated to providing safety training, disaster assistance and famine relief. *New Positions Created (3):* Human Resources Assistant; Executive Administrative Assistant; Manager, Homemaker Program.

CANADIAN RESTAURANT AND FOODSERVICES ASSOCIATION / CRFA
Att: Human Resources
316 Bloor Street West
Toronto, ON M5S 1W5

Tel. 416-923-8416
Fax 416-923-1450
Website .... www.crfa.ca

Employer Background: Founded in 1944, CRFA is one of Canada's largest hospitality associations, with over 15,500 members. *New Positions Created (3):* Sales Force Manager; Telemarketing / Sales Position; Trade Show Exhibit Salesperson.

CANADIAN SHAREOWNER
Att: Human Resources Manager
2 Carlton Street, Suite 1317
Toronto, ON M5B 1J3

Tel. 416-595-9600
Fax 416-595-0400
Email .... careers@shareowner.com
Website .... www.shareowner.ca

Employer Background: Established in 1987, Canadian Shareowner specializes in publishing, financial research, securities trading and software development in the financial services industry. *New Positions Created (3):* Database Specialist; Marketing Specialist; Systems Specialist.

CANADIAN SLEEP INSTITUTE / CSI
Att: Office Manager
295 Midpark Way SE, Suite 300
Calgary, AB T2X 2A8

Tel. 403-254-6400
Fax 403-254-6403
Website .... www.csisleep.com

Employer Background: CSI provides clinical care, diagnostic services and consulting in the area of sleep and fatigue disorders. *New Positions Created (3):* Clinical Trial Coordinator; Clinical Trial Coordinator; Senior Sleep Technologist.

CANADIAN SURVEY EQUIPMENT LTD. / CANSEL
Att: Human Resources
3771 Napier Street
Burnaby, BC V5C 3E4

Fax 604-299-1998
Website .... www.cansel.ca

Employer Background: Founded in 1966, Cansel is leading distributor of land-based positioning systems, with over 80 employees and locations across Canada. *New Positions Created (2):* Senior Accountant; Junior Shipper and Receiver.

CANADIAN SURVEY EQUIPMENT LTD. / CANSEL
Att: Don Perrin
4718 - 97th Street NW
Edmonton, AB T6E 5S1

Tel. 780-437-7406
Fax 780-437-4079
Website .... www.cansel.ca

Employer Background: Founded in 1966, Cansel is leading distributor of land-based positioning systems, with over 80 employees and locations across Canada. *New Positions Created (2):* Inside Sales Representative; GPS Mapping Sales Representative.

CANADIAN SURVEY EQUIPMENT LTD. / CANSEL
Att: Brad Smith
2414 Holly Lane
Ottawa, ON K1V 7P1

Tel. 613-731-4703
Fax 613-526-0712
Email .... brad_smith@cansel.ca
Website .... www.cansel.ca

Employer Background: Founded in 1966, Cansel is leading distributor of land-based positioning systems, with over 80 employees and locations across Canada. *New Positions Created (2):* Sales Representatives; GPS Sales Representatives.

CANADIAN TIRE CORPORATION LTD.
Att: Human Resources Manager
2331 - 66th Street NW
Edmonton, AB T6K 4B6

Tel. 780-450-1800
Fax 780-450-2225
Website .... www.canadiantire.com

Employer Background: With 432 associate stores and 204 gasoline outlets, Canadian Tire Corporation Ltd. is a leading retailer of hard goods and petroleum and a provider of financial services. *New Positions Created (3):* Department Manager; Department Manager; Logistics Manager.

CANADIAN TOURISM COMMISSION / CTC
Att: Human Resources
235 Queen Street
8th Floor, CD Howe Building, West Tower
Ottawa, ON K1A 0H6

Tel. 613-954-3959
Fax 613-954-6959
Email .... hr@ctc-cct.ca
Website .... www.canadatourism.com

Employer Background: Created in 1995, CTC is a unique public / private sector partnership, working to promote Canada as a tourist destination. *New Positions Created (7):* Director, E-Marketing; Manager, Board Affairs; Director, Canada Marketing Program; Director, Europe Program; Manager, Communications; Marketing Officer, Meetings, Convention and Incentive Travel Program; Senior Communications Officer.

CANADIAN VENTURE EXCHANGE / CDNX
Att: Paul Chow, Staffing Coordinator
609 Granville Street, PO Box 10333
Vancouver, BC V7Y 1H1

Tel. 604-689-3334
Fax 604-643-6503
Email ....:.............. careers@cdnx.com
Website .... www.cdnx.com

Employer Background: CDNX is Canada's public venture capital marketplace, providing a strong market for emerging companies with 67 member firms and approximately 2,600 listed companies in the resource, technology, industrial and manufacturing sectors. *New Positions Created (5):* Director, E-Business; Trainer; Project Leader; Senior Programmer Analyst; Technical Consultant.

CANADIAN VENTURE EXCHANGE / CDNX
Att: Human Resources Manager
300 - 5th Avenue SW
Calgary, AB T2P 3C4

Fax 403-234-4313
Email .... careers@cdnx.ca
Website .... www.cdnx.ca

Employer Background: CDNX is Canada's public venture capital marketplace, providing emerging companies with access to capital. *New Positions Created (3):* Assistant Analyst; Corporate Maintenance Analyst; Financial Analyst.

CANADIAN WESTERN BANK
Att: Personnel Officer
10303 Jasper Avenue, Suite 2300
Edmonton, AB T5J 3X6

Tel. 780-424-4846
Fax 780-423-8899
Email .... hr@cwbank.com
Website .... www.cwbank.com

Employer Background: Canadian Western Bank is a chartered bank with 27 locations that specializes in commercial loans, real estate financing, equipment lending and leasing and energy loans. *New Positions Created (7):* Internal Auditor; Senior Marketing Position; PC Technician; MIS Programmer; Group Plan Administrator; Branch Mangers and Senior Commercial Lenders; Assistant Vice President, Internal Audit.

CANADIAN WHEAT BOARD / CWB
Att: Human Resources
423 Main Street, PO Box 816, Station Main
Winnipeg, MB R3C 2P5

Tel. 204-983-0239
Fax 204-983-1209

Email .... hrmailbox@cwb.ca
Website .... www.cwb.ca
Employer Background: CWB is a farmer-controlled organization that markets wheat and barley grown by western Canadian producers. *New Positions Created (6):* Coordinator, Purchasing; Research & Planning Coordinator; Treasury Officer, Finance; Agronomist, Market Development; Weather and Crop Analyst; Advisor, Corporate Policy Group.

CANAM MANAC GROUP INC., THE
Att: Human Resources Department
270 Chemin du Tremblay
Boucherville, QC J4B 5X9

Tel. 450-641-4000
Fax 450-641-4001
Email ..... emploi-cmi@canammanac.com
Website .... www.canammanac.com
Employer Background: The Canam Manac Group Inc. is a leading fabricator of steel components and semi-trailers, operating 21 plants worldwide. *New Positions Created (10):* Intermediate Engineer, Structural Steel Connection Design; Senior Engineer, Structural Steel Connection Design; Senior Project Engineer, Structural Steel and Structure; Structural Steel Draftsmen; Internal Auditor; Senior Auditor; Senior Project Engineer, Structural Steel & Structure; Structural Steel Connection Design Senior Engineer; Structural Steel Draftsman - Intermediate Level; Structural Steel Draftsman - Senior Level.

CANAM STEEL WORKS
Att: Nathalie Vincent, Sales Manager
223 - 53rd Avenue SE
Calgary, AB T2H 0N2

Tel. 403-252-7591
Fax 403-252-8824
Email ...... calgary_hr@canammanac.com
Website .... www.canammanac.com
Employer Background: Canam Steel Works is one of the leading manufacturers of steel joists and structural steel components in North America and Europe. *New Positions Created (5):* Deck Manager; Estimator and Estimator Sales Representative; Structural Engineer; Estimators / Sales Representatives (2); Civil Engineer.

CANAMERA FOODS
Att: Personnel Department
PO Box 618, Station A
Hamilton, ON L8N 3K7

Website .... www.canamera.ca
Employer Background: CanAmera Foods manufactures edible oil products and markets oilseed-based products. *New Positions Created (3):* Maintenance Manager; Licensed Industrial Mechanic (Millwright); Licensed Industrial Electrician.

CANAMERA FOODS
Att: Human Resources Department
2190 South Service Road West
Oakville, ON L6L 5N1

Email .... jfrancis@canamerafoods.com
Website .... www.canamerafoods.com

Employer Background: CanAmera Foods manufactures edible oil products and markets oilseed-based products. *New Positions Created (2):* Plant Manager; Packaging Technician.

CANARAIL CONSULTANTS INC.
Att: Elizabeth Tadgell, HR Director
1140 Maisonneuve Blvd. West, Suite 1050
Montréal, QC H3A 1M8

Tel. 514-985-0930
Fax 514-985-0929
Email .... etadgell@canarail.com
Website .... www.canarail.com
Employer Background: Created in 1990, Canarail Consultants Inc. is a railway consulting firm, offering a range of railway engineering, management and operating services worldwide. *New Positions Created (5):* Civil Engineers; Project or Deputy Project Manager(s); Design Engineers; Senior Structures Manager; Senior Track Manager.

CANCABLE INC.
Att: Human Resources Manager
2079 Lakeshore Road
Burlington, ON L7R 1E2

Tel. 905-634-7152
Fax 905-634-1156
Email .... resume@cancable.com
Website .... www.cancable.com
Employer Background: Cancable Inc. offers high-speed Internet access and other computer-related services to individuals, businesses and cable companies. *New Positions Created (4):* Home Technology Technician; Corporate Training Manager; Home Technology Technician; Single Internet Installer.

CANCARE HEALTH SERVICES INC.
Att: Human Resources Manager
45 Sheppard Avenue East, Suite 414
Toronto, ON M2N 5W9

Tel. 416-226-6995
Fax 416-226-6930
Email .... cancare_health@hotmail.com
Website .... www.cancarehealth.com
Employer Background: Established in 1972, CanCare Health Services Inc. is a homecare and personal support organization. *New Positions Created (4):* Client Services Coordinator; Home Support Workers / Personal Support Workers; Scheduling Coordinator; Supervisors.

CANCER CARE ONTARIO, DIVISION OF PREVENTIVE ONCOLOGY / CCO
Att: Robbi Howlett, Manager,
Ontario Cervical Screening Program
620 University Avenue
Toronto, ON M5G 2L7

Tel. 416-971-9800
Fax 416-217-1255
Email ..... robbi.howlett@cancercare.on.ca
Website .... www.cancercare.on.ca
Employer Background: CCO is a provincial government agency responsible for the integration and coordination of cancer control services, and is the Ministry of Health and Long-Term Care's principal adviser on

cancer issues. *New Positions Created (3):* Administrative Secretary, Ontario Cervical Screening Program (OCSP); Senior Research Officer, Breast Cancer Study; Manager, Prevention Programs.

CANCER CARE ONTARIO, PROVINCIAL OFFICE / CCO
Att: Office of the President
620 University Avenue
Toronto, ON M5G 2L7

Tel. 416-971-9800
Website .... www.cancercare.on.ca
Employer Background: CCO is a provincial government agency responsible for the integration and coordination of cancer control services, and is the Ministry of Health and Long-Term Care's principal adviser on cancer issues. *New Positions Created (10):* Bioethicist; Provincial Coordinator, Radiation Treatment Programs; Chief Executive Officer, Windsor Regional Cancer Centre; Bioethicist; Chief Nursing Officer; Health Promotion Specialist; Manager, Ontario Cervical Screening Program; Ontario Cervical Screening Registry Coordinator; Chief Executive Officer; Head, Division of Preventive Oncology.

CANCOIL INTEGRATED SERVICES INC.
Att: Human Resources Manager
633 - 6th Avenue SW, Suite 1550
Calgary, AB T2P 2Y5

Tel. 403-509-0700
Fax 403-509-0701
Email .... employment@cancoil.com
Website .... www.cancoil.com
Employer Background: Cancoil Integrated Services Inc. provides coil tubing services to the oil and gas industry. *New Positions Created (3):* Operations Manager; Fleet Equipment Manager; Various Oil and Gas Positions.

CANEM-HARBOUR
Att: Human Resources Manager
1921 Broadway Street, Unit 1
Port Coquitlam, BC V3C 4Z1

Tel. 604-941-0531
Fax 604-941-4899
Website .... www.canem.com
Employer Background: Canem-Harbour is a division of Canem Systems Ltd., one of western Canada's leading electrical contractors. *New Positions Created (3):* Project Management Assistant; Project Manager, Commercial Construction; Electrical Estimator.

CANGENE CORPORATION
Att: Human Resources
104 Chancellor Matheson Road
Winnipeg, MB R3T 5Y3

Tel. 204-275-4200
Fax 204-269-7003
Email .... hr@cangene.com
Website .... www.cangene.com
Employer Background: Cangene Corporation is a Canadian biopharmaceutical company that develops specialty hyperimmune plasma and biotechnology products. *New*

Positions Created (16): Manager, Regulatory Affairs; Manager, Validation; Clinical Research Scientist; Director, Clinical Research; Laboratory Technician; Laboratory Technician; Laboratory Technicians (4); Manager, Regulatory Affairs; Metrologist; Production Assistants (2); Production Technicians (5); Regulatory Affairs Associate; Project Mgr; Manager, Validation; Plasma Operations Associate; Quality Assurance Associate.

CANJET AIRLINES
Att: Human Resources
693 Barnes Road, Suite 300
Enfield, NS B2T 1K3

Tel. 902-873-2650
Fax 902-873-2622
Email .... hr@canjet.com
Website .... www.canjet.com

Employer Background: CanJet Airlines, a division of IMP Group Limited, is a low-cost scheduled airline. *New Positions Created (11):* Manager, Customer Service; Guest Services Agents; Manager, Sales; Flight Attendants; Aircraft Maintenance Engineer; Maintenance Supervisor; Quality Assurance Inspector; Technical Records Clerks; Aircraft Personnel; Guest Services Agents; Maintenance Supervisor.

CANLIGHT GROUP
Att: Human Resources Manager
48 St. Clair Avenue West, Suite 500
Toronto, ON M4V 3B6

Fax 416-921-5664
Email .... sliao@canlight.com

Employer Background: Canlight Group is a progressive real estate company specializing in condominium and residential property management services. *New Positions Created (2):* Payable Administrator; Property Manager.

CANON CANADA INC.
Att: Human Resources Department
1490 Denison Street
Markham, ON L3R 9T7

Tel. 905-683-9857
Fax 905-305-3913
Email ... hrmarkham@canada.canon.com
Website .... www.canada.ca

Employer Background: Canon Canada Inc. is a leader in professional and consumer imaging equipment and information systems. *New Positions Created (3):* Collector; Senior Account Executive; Supervisor, Technical Support.

CANON CANADA INC.
Att: Human Resources Manager
5990 Cote de Liesse
Montréal, QC H4T 1V7

Fax 514-342-7585
Email ..... hrmontreal@canada.canon.com
Website .... www.canada.canon.com

Employer Background: Canon Canada Inc. is a leader in professional and consumer imaging equipment and information systems. *New Positions Created (2):* Senior Account Executive, National Accounts and Strategic Initiatives; Sales Professionals.

CANPAR INDUSTRIES
Att: Jim Oakes, HR Manager
PO Box 129
Grand Forks, BC V0H 1H0

Fax 250-442-2577
Email ... adavidoff@canparindustries.com
Website .... www.canparindustries.com

Employer Background: Canpar Industries is an established particleboard manufacturing plant with 155 employees. *New Positions Created (3):* Journeyman Industrial Electrician; Journeyman Millwrights; Journeyman Millwrights.

CANRON CONSTRUCTION CORP.
Att: Tanya Edgar
100 Disco Road
Toronto, ON M9W 1M1

Tel. 416-675-6400
Fax 416-675-6522
Website .... www.canron.com

Employer Background: Founded in 1910, Canron Construction Corp. fabricates and erects structural steel. *New Positions Created (2):* Engineers; Sales Administrative Assistant.

CANROOF CORPORATION INC.
Att: Human Resources
560 Commissioners Street
Toronto, ON M4M 1A7

Tel. 416-461-8122
Fax 416-461-2926
Website .... www.ikogroup.com

Employer Background: CanRoof Corporation Inc., part of IKO Group, manufactures and distributes home roofing products. *New Positions Created (7):* Accountant; Production Foreman; Accounts Payable Clerk; Weigh-Scale Operator; Accounts Receivable Clerk; Quality Control Technician; Plant Engineer.

CANTEST LTD.
Att: Human Resources Manager
4606 Canada Way
Burnaby, BC V5G 1K5

Tel. 604-734-7276
Fax 604-731-2386
Email .... resumes@cantest.com
Website .... www.cantest.com

Employer Background: CANTEST Ltd. is a full-service laboratory, specializing in environmental chemistry, food science, industrial hygiene, forensic toxicology and related research. *New Positions Created (6):* Environmental Chemistry Analyst; Information Systems Coordinator; Medical Gas Testing / Inspection Field Representative; Proteomics Director; QA Analyst; Technical Service Representative, Business Development.

CANTEX ENGINEERING & CONSTRUCTION CO. LTD.
Att: V. Neal Davies
780 Okanagan Avenue East
Penticton, BC V2A 3K6

Tel. 250-492-7622
Fax 250-492-0195

Employer Background: Cantex Engineering & Construction Co. Ltd. is an established paving and heavy construction company. *New Positions Created (2):* Mechanical Superintendent; Construction and Paving Superintendents.

CAP GEMINI ERNST & YOUNG / CGEY
Att: Human Resources Manager
222 Bay Street
PO Box 271, Toronto Dominion Centre
Toronto, ON M5K 1J5

Tel. 416-943-3232
Fax 416-943-2075
Email .. consulting.recruiting@ca.cgeyc.com
Website .... www.ca.cgey.com

Employer Background: CGEY is a leading provider of IT consulting services in North America. *New Positions Created (17):* Applications Maintenance and Support Managers; Contact Centre Consultants; CRM Technical Implementation Consultants; Data Centre Managers; Data Warehouse Analyst; Enterprise Application Integration Consultants; Human Resources Managers; Java Application Architects; Network Architects; Oracle Application Consultants; OSS / BSS Technical Implementation Consultants; Project Managers; Sales and Marketing Consultant; SAP Functional Consultants; Senior CRM Strategy and Solutions Specialists; Technical Architects, Network and Infrastructure; Technical Architects, Telecommunications.

CAPERS COMMUNITY MARKETS
Att: Martha Bowen,
West Vancouver Food Service Manager
2496 Marine Drive
Vancouver, BC V7V 1L1

Fax 604-925-9306

Employer Background: Capers Community Markets carries a full range of certified organic and natural foods. *New Positions Created (3):* Cook; Bakers; Kitchen Manager.

CAPILANO CARE CENTRE
Att: Donna Moroz, Administrator
525 Clyde Avenue
Vancouver, BC V7T 1C4

Tel. 604-926-6856
Fax 604-926-9169
Email .... capilano@cplreit.com
Website .... www.cplreit.com

Employer Background: Founded in 1972, Capilano Care Centre, a branch of CPL Long-Term Care Real Estate Investment Trust, provides quality long-term care in a comfortable environment for 217 residents. *New Positions Created (7):* Director of Care; Food and Nutritional Services Manager; Social Workers; Food and Nutritional Services Manager; Licensed Practical Nurses; Nurse Manager; Registered Nurses.

CAPILANO COLLEGE
Att: Dean of Arts
2055 Purcell Way
North Vancouver, BC V7J 3H5

Tel. 604-984-4929
Fax 604-984-1758

Website .... www.capcollege.bc.ca

Employer Background: Capilano College is a post-secondary educational institute, serving 7,000 credit students. *New Positions Created (6):* First Nations Program Developer; Business Relations Manager, Asia Pacific Management Co-operative Program; Deans (2); Special Education Instructor Assistant; Associate Registrar; Human Resources Advisor, Disability and Wellness.

CAPITAL CARE GROUP, THE
Att: Human Resources
9925 - 109th Street, Suite 500
Edmonton, AB T5K 2J8

Tel. 780-413-4719
Fax 780-413-4711
Email .... careers@capitalcare.net
Website .... www.capitalcare.net

Employer Background: In operation since 1964, The Capital Care Group is a publicly-funded continuing care organization. *New Positions Created (3):* Care Managers; Clinical Specialist; Registered Nurses and Licensed Practical Nurses.

CAPITAL CITY SAVINGS
Att: Human Resources Department
8723 - 82nd Avenue, Suite 210
Edmonton, AB T6C 0Y9

Tel. 780-496-2036
Email .... ccscareers@ccscu.ca
Website .... www.capitalcitysavings.ca

Employer Background: Capital City Savings has assets in excess of $1 billion and 24 branches in central and northern Alberta. *New Positions Created (9):* Call Centre Personnel; Investment Specialists & Wealth Management Consultants; Personal Bankers; Retail Branch Management Trainees; Call Centre Personnel; Investment and Wealth Management Specialists; Personal Bankers; Retail Branch Management Trainees; Roving Financial Services Officer.

CAPITAL HEALTH, COMMUNITY CARE AND PUBLIC HEALTH
Att: Human Resources
10216 - 124th Street, Suite 300
Edmonton, AB T5N 4A3

Tel. 780-413-7660
Fax 780-488-0617
Website .... www.cha.ab.ca

Employer Background: Capital Health is an integrated health service organization, employing 16,000 staff members and serving a local community of 800,000. *New Positions Created (4):* Case Manager, Nurse 1; Office Manager, Capital Health Link; Occupational Therapists & Physical Therapists; Speech Language Pathologists.

CAPITAL HEALTH, GLENROSE REHABILITATION HOSPITAL
Att: Human Resources
10230 - 111th Avenue
Edmonton, AB T5G 0B7

Tel. 780-471-7995
Fax 780-471-7996
Website .... www.cha.ab.ca

Employer Background: Glenrose Rehabilitation Hospital is a 244-bed tertiary rehabilitation and geriatric centre for children and adults. *New Positions Created (8):* Clinical Nurse Educator; Psychologist I; Administrative Coordinator; Administrative Secretary; Certified Prosthetist; Clinical Nurse Educator; Patient Care Mgr; Staff Nurse.

CAPITAL HEALTH REGION / CHR
Att: Recruitment Services
1900 Fort Street
Victoria, BC V8R 1J8

Tel. 250-370-8699
Fax 250-370-8570
Email .... jobs@caphealth.org
Website .... www.caphealth.org

Employer Background: CHR provides an integrated network of health services, including prevention, hospital and home healthcare, for residents of southern Vancouver Island and Greater Victoria. *New Positions Created (25):* Registered Nurse, Acute Care; Registered Nurse, Geriatric Assessment Programs; Registered Nurses, Medical / Surgical Relief (7); Registered Nurses, Psychiatric Rehabilitation; Section Head, Core Lab; Unit Coordinators, Resident Care (2); Pharmacists; Section Head, Microbiology; Cardiac Sonographers (2); Director, Clinical Chemistry; Staff Pharmacist Gr. II; Acute Care Pharmacists; Coordinator, Records Management; Operations Coordinators, Residential & Continuing Care; Site Supervisor; Clinical Resource Nurse / Coordinator; Registered Nurse; Registered Nurse, Acute Care; Registered Psychiatric Nurse; Manager, Resident Care; Cardiac Sonographer; Clinical Informatics Coordinator; Various Healthcare Positions; Chief, Nuclear Medicine; Sub-section Supervisor, Cellular Pathology.

CAPITAL HEALTH, ROYAL ALEXANDRA HOSPITAL
Att: Human Resources
10240 Kingsway Avenue
Edmonton, AB T5H 3V9

Tel. 780-477-4250
Fax 780-477-4960
Website .... www.cha.ab.ca

Employer Background: Capital Health is an integrated health service organization, employing 16,000 staff members and serving a local community of 800,000. *New Positions Created (16):* Senior Operating Officer, Diagnostic and Equipment Services; Regional Library Manager; Clinical Nurse Specialist; Pharmacy Assistant; Pharmacy Technicians (2); Regional Manager Acquisitions; Registered Nurse; Unit Manager; Diabetes Nurse; Pharmacy Team Leader; Customer Service Supervisor; Material Management; Research Nurse; Senior Operating Officer, Patient Care; Manager, Respiratory Services; Manager, RIS / PACS; Senior Operating Officer.

CAPITAL HEALTH, UNIVERSITY OF ALBERTA HOSPITAL SITE
Att: Human Resources Services
8440 - 112th Street, CSB 1-161
Edmonton, AB T6G 2B7

Tel. 780-413-4909
Fax 780-407-3084
Website .... www.cha.ab.ca

Employer Background: Capital Health is an integrated health service organization, employing 16,000 staff members and serving a local community of 800,000. *New Positions Created (27):* Advanced Nurse Practitioner; Laboratory Technologist III; Medical Radiology Technologist I; Patient Care Manager; Audiologist; Audiology Team Leader; Clinical Nurse Educator; Clinical Ethicist; Registered Nurse; Audiology Team Leader; Clinical Nurse Specialist; Registered Nurse; Unit Manager; Advanced Nurse Practitioner; Dietitian I; Medical Radiation Technologist I; Medical Radiation Technologist I; Practical Nurse; Registered Nurse; Registered Nurse; Registered Nurse; Respiratory Therapist I; Occupational Therapist / Social Worker; MRI Technologists (2); Senior Director; Pediatric Perioperative Coordinator; Various Healthcare Positions.

CAPITAL METAL INDUSTRIES
Att: Human Resources
61 Milne Avenue
Toronto, ON M1L 1K4

Fax 416-694-3304

Employer Background: Capital Metal Industries, a division of H. Paulin & Co., manufactures and distributes fasteners and automotive parts. *New Positions Created (7):* Production Scheduler; Quality Assurance Technician; Quality Assurance Liaison; Cold Heading & Threading Set-Up Operators; Millwright; Production Schedulers; Supervisor.

CAPITAL REGIONAL DISTRICT / CRD
Att: Human Resources Manager
546 Yates Street, PO Box 1000
Victoria, BC V8W 2S6

Tel. 250-360-3069
Fax 250-360-3076
Email .... hr@crd.bc.ca
Website .... www.crd.bc.ca

Employer Background: CRD governs regional parks, liquid and solid waste treatment, health facilities planning and regional planning. *New Positions Created (2):* Superintendent, Watershed Operations; Senior Planner.

CAPRION PHARMACEUTICALS INC.
Att: Human Resources
5375 Pare Street, Suite 201
Montréal, QC H4P 1P7

Email .... careers@caprion.com
Website .... www.caprion.com

Employer Background: Caprion Pharmaceuticals Inc. is a biotechnology company applying proteomics, the study of proteins, to accelerate the diagnosis and treatment of disease. *New Positions Created (14):* Bioinformatics Research Scientist; Cell Fractionation Specialists, Senior Scientist / Scientist; Database Programmer; Director of Information Technology; Mass Spectrometrists, Senior Scientist / Scientist; Microscopy Technologist; Peptide - Protein

Chemist; Protein Separation Specialists, Senior Scientist / Scientist; Senior Database Administrator; Senior Software Designer; Software Designer; System Administrators & Developers; Web Designers; Web Programmers.

CARA OPERATIONS LTD.
Att: Human Resources
6260 Miller Road, PO Box 23870 APO
Richmond, BC V7B 1Y1
Tel. 604-273-0591
Email .... yvrfkjobs@cara.com
Website .... www.cara.com
Employer Background: Founded in 1883, Cara Operations Ltd. operates branded restaurants (Swiss Chalet and Harvey's) and institutional foodservice operations, and has major shareholdings in other foodservice businesses (Second Cup and Kelsey's). *New Positions Created (4):* Food Assembly Supervisor; Cara Flight Kitchen Buyer; Health and Safety Officer; Purchasing Administrator.

CARA OPERATIONS LTD., HARVEY'S DIVISION
Att: Tom Bushey, Regional Manager
6303 Airport Road
Mississauga, ON L4V 1R8
Tel. 905-405-6500
Fax 905-405-6604
Email .... tbushey@cara.com
Website .... www.cara.com
Employer Background: Founded in 1883, Cara Operations Ltd. operates branded restaurants (Swiss Chalet and Harvey's) and institutional foodservice operations, and has major shareholdings in other foodservice businesses (Second Cup and Kelsey's). *New Positions Created (4):* Project Manager; Real Estate Analyst; Real Estate Manager; Area Manager.

CARE PLUS
Att: Human Resources Manager
2338 Hurontario Street, Suite 100
Mississauga, ON L5B 1N1
Tel. 905-306-0202
Fax 905-306-1709
Employer Background: Care Plus is a progressive healthcare company offering a full range of nursing and therapy services. *New Positions Created (3):* Registered Nurses; Registered Practical Nurses; Registered Nurses.

CAREWEST
Att: Joan Magnussen, Human Resources
1070 McDougall Road NE
Calgary, AB T2E 7Z2
Tel. 403-267-2777
Fax 403-267-2907
Email ... carewest.hr@calgaryhealthregion.ca
Website .... www.carewest.org
Employer Background: Carewest is a non-profit continuing care organization, with 8 locations in Calgary. *New Positions Created (9):* Activity Convenor; Buyer; Program Facilitator; Program Support Coordinator;

Speech-Language Pathologist; Team Leader, Education Services; Occupational Therapists (2); Registered Nurses; Physical Therapists (2).

CARGILL FOODS
Att: Human Resources
PO Bag 3850
High River, AB T1V 1P4
Tel. 403-652-1736
Fax 403-652-4671
Email .... hrd-highriver@cargill.com
Website .... www.cargillfoods.com
Employer Background: Cargill Foods is part of Cargill Inc., an international processor and distributor of agricultural, food, financial and industrial products and services, with 85,000 employees in 60 countries. *New Positions Created (10):* 2nd-Class Steam Engineer; Production Management Trainee; Heavy Duty Mechanics; Journeyman Ticketed Millwrights; Occupational Health Nursing Positions; Maintenance Personnel; Electrical Supervisor; Capital Projects Electrical Supervisor; Journeyman Industrial Electricians; Power Engineers.

CARGILL LIMITED
Att: Human Resources Manager
240 Graham Ave., Suite 300, PO Box 5900
Winnipeg, MB R3C 4C5
Tel. 204-947-0141
Fax 204-947-6222
Email .... canadahr@cargill.com
Website .... www.cargill.com
Employer Background: Cargill Limited is the Canadian subsidiary of Cargill Incorporated, an international marketer, processor and distributor of agricultural, food, financial and industrial products. *New Positions Created (3):* Agronomist; Farm Marketing Representatives (3); Account Manager.

CARIBOO PULP & PAPER COMPANY
Att: Human Resources Superintendent
PO Box 7500
Quesnel, BC V2J 3J6
Tel. 250-992-0200
Fax 250-992-0373
Employer Background: Cariboo Pulp & Paper Company is a 975 tonne-per-day market pulp mill, producing northern bleached softwood pulp. *New Positions Created (2):* Electrical / Instrumentation Engineer; Electrical / Instrumentation Engineer.

CARISTRAP INTERNATIONAL INC.
Att: Human Resources
1760 Fortin Boulevard
Laval, QC H7S 1N8
Tel. 450-667-4700
Fax 450-663-1520
Email .... akarass@caristrap.com
Website .... www.caristrap.com
Employer Background: Founded in 1954, Caristrap International Inc. is a manufacturer of AAR and NATO-approved polyester cord strapping. *New Positions Created (2):* Inside Sales / Customer Service Representative; Technical Sales Representatives.

CARITAS HEALTH GROUP, GREY NUNS COMMUNITY HOSPITAL
Att: Human Resources Services
1100 Youville Drive West
Edmonton, AB T6L 5X8
Tel. 780-482-8423
Fax 780-450-7977
Email .... hr-gn@caritas.ab.ca
Website .... www.caritas.ab.ca
Employer Background: Founded in 1895, Caritas Health Group operates 3 faith-based healthcare facilities in Edmonton. *New Positions Created (3):* Pharmacist I; Registered Nurses; Patient Care Manager.

CARITAS HEALTH GROUP, MISERICORDIA COMMUNITY HOSPITAL
Att: Human Resource Services
16940 - 87th Avenue
Edmonton, AB T5R 4H5
Tel. 780-482-8423
Fax 780-930-5957
Email .... hr-mis@caritas.ab.ca
Website .... www.caritas.ab.ca
Employer Background: Founded in 1895, Caritas Health Group operates 3 faith-based health service facilities in Edmonton. *New Positions Created (8):* Osseointegration Technologist; Physical Therapist I; Dental Assistant II; Pharmacist I; Registered Nurses; Registered Nurses (3); Respiratory Therapists; Anaplastologist.

CARLSON MARKETING GROUP CANADA LTD. / CMG CANADA
Att: Human Resources
3300 Bloor Street West
Centre Tower, 15th Floor
Toronto, ON M8X 2Y2
Tel. 416-236-1991
Fax 416-236-9915
Email .... hr@carlsoncanada.com
Website .... www.cmg.carlson.com
Employer Background: Carlson Marketing Group Canada Ltd. / CMG specializes in helping corporate clients improve their relationships with key customers. *New Positions Created (7):* Account Executive; Account Manager; Bilingual Telemarketing Manager; Director of Marketing; Operations Manager; Project Coordinator; Travel Accounting Position.

CARLTON CARDS LTD.
Att: Enes Nasato, HR Manager
1460 The Queensway
Toronto, ON M8Z 1S7
Tel. 416-255-9131
Fax 416-503-6536
Website .... www.carltoncards.ca
Employer Background: Carlton Cards Ltd. is a leader in the Canadian greeting card and social expression industry. *New Positions Created (3):* Program Administrator; Sales Rep; Mgr, Sales Planning & Analysis.

CARMA FINANCIAL
Att: Sara Bullock
789 Don Mills Road, 4th Floor
Toronto, ON M3C 1T5

Tel. 416-488-3933
Fax 416-488-8658
Email .... sbullock@carmafinancial.com
Website .... www.carmafinancial.com

Employer Background: Carma Financial is an accounts receivable management company. *New Positions Created (2):* Inside and Outside Sales Representatives; Various Administrative Positions.

CARMANAH TECHNOLOGIES INC.
Att: Human Resources Manager
203 Harbour Road, Building 4
Victoria, BC V9A 3S2
Tel. 250-380-0052
Fax 250-380-0062
Email .. humanresources@carmanah.com
Website .... www.carmanah.com

Employer Background: Founded in 1993, Carmanah Technologies Inc. designs and manufactures solar LED lights for navigation, marine, roadway, railway and transportation applications. *New Positions Created (7):* Vice-President, Sales and Marketing; Accounts Payable Administrator; Mechanical Engineer; Product Development Manager; Business Development Manager, Marine Sector; Business Development Manager, Retail Products Sector; Sales Representative, Railway Sector.

CARO RESEARCH
Att: Human Resources Manager
620 Bord du Lac, Suite 305
Dorval, QC H9S 2B6
Fax 514-422-8272

Employer Background: Caro Research is a consulting firm, specializing in pharmacoeconomics and epidemiology. *New Positions Created (3):* Research Assistants; Researchers; Statisticians.

CARPEDIA GROUP INTERNATIONAL INC.
Att: Director of Recruiting
75 Navy Street, Suite 300
Oakville, ON L6J 2Z1
Tel. 905-337-3407
Fax 905-337-1529
Email .... careers@carpedia.com
Website .... www.carpedia.com

Employer Background: Carpedia Group is a management consulting firm, focused on providing significant and measurable improvements in revenue growth, productivity and asset utilization. *New Positions Created (4):* Consultants; Business Analyst; Senior Business Analyst; Consultants.

CARPENTER CANADA LTD.
Att: Manager, Human Resources
500 Hanlan Road
Woodbridge, ON L4L 3P6
Tel. 905-851-6764
Fax 905-856-0339
Website .... www.carpenter.com

Employer Background: Carpenter Canada Ltd. is an international manufacturer of urethane foam products, used primarily in the consumer products, automotive and

medical fields. *New Positions Created (9):* Maintenance Mechanic / Millwright; Production Management Trainee; Human Resources Manager; Industrial Engineer; Electronic Technician; Maintenance Mechanic (Millwright); Afternoon Shift Manager; Maintenance Manager; Foam Manufacturing Manager.

CARRIER CANADA LTD.
Att: Vladimir Konevsky, PEng
15010 - 116th Avenue
Edmonton, AB T5M 3T4
Fax 780-455-4328
Website .... www.carrier.com

Employer Background: Carrier Canada Ltd. sells, distributes and services heating, ventilation, air conditioning and refrigeration systems across Canada. *New Positions Created (2):* Sales Engineers; Territory Manager.

CARRIER CANADA LTD.
Att: General Manager,
Western / Pacific Region
3636 - 7th Street SE, Bay 24
Calgary, AB T2G 2Y8
Fax 403-243-3557
Website .... www.carrier.com

Employer Background: Carrier Canada Ltd. sells, distributes and services heating, ventilation, air conditioning and refrigeration systems across Canada. *New Positions Created (2):* Branch Sales Manager; Sales Engineer.

CARRIER CANADA LTD.
Att: Human Resources
1515 Drew Road
Mississauga, ON L5S 1Y8
Tel. 905-672-0606
Fax 905-405-4003
Email ..... cathy.sciberras@carrier.utc.com
Website .... www.carrier.com

Employer Background: Carrier Canada sells, distributes and services heating, ventilation, air conditioning and refrigeration systems across Canada. *New Positions Created (2):* Buyer; Wholesale Parts Sales Rep.

CARSEN GROUP INC.
Att: Human Resources Manager
151 Telson Road
Markham, ON L3R 1E7
Tel. 905-479-4100
Fax 905-479-2595
Email .... resumes@carsengroup.com
Website .... www.carsengroup.com

Employer Background: Founded in 1946, Carsen Group Inc. is a national distributor of optical imaging products for medical, scientific and industrial applications. *New Positions Created (12):* Endoscope Repair Technicians; Field Service Representative; Sales Representatives, Endotherapy; Sales Representative; Sales Representatives; Surgical / Service Sales Representative; Machine Vision Specialist; Field Service Representative; Technical Sales Representative; Sales Representative, Scientific Imaging Group; Quality Inspection Technician; National Sales Manager.

CARSWELL
Att: Kelly West, Human Resources
2075 Kennedy Road
11th Floor, One Corporate Plaza
Toronto, ON M1T 3V4
Tel. 416-609-8000
Fax 416-298-5094
Email .... kelly.west@carswell.com
Website .... www.carswell.com

Employer Background: Carswell is a leading publisher of specialized information for lawyers, academics, financial executives, accountants and human resource professionals. *New Positions Created (24):* Conversion Editor; Customer Relations Helpline Representative; Order and Credit Processor; Product Writer, Canadian Abridgment; Group Leader; Product Writer; Content Editor; Administrative Assistant, Editorial; CED Legislation Administrator; Conversion Editor; Operations Representative; Research Editors (7); Manager, Order Processing & Billing; Supervisor, Order Processing & Billing; Production Coordinator; Legal Writer; Content Editor; Data Communication / Security Analyst; Product Development Manager; Product Writer - Tax; Product Management Specialist; Technical Support Specialist; Programmer / Analyst; Payroll Consultant.

CASA LOMA
Att: Director of Operations
1 Austin Terrace
Toronto, ON M5R 1X8
Tel. 416-923-1171
Fax 416-923-5734
Email .... info@casaloma.org
Website .... www.casaloma.org

Employer Background: Casa Loma is a 98-room castle and tourist attraction in downtown Toronto. *New Positions Created (3):* Supervisor of Operations; Receptionist / Administrative Assistant; Marketing Manager.

CASCADE
Att: Carol Bent, Human Resource Manager
5570 Timberlea Boulevard
Mississauga, ON L4W 4M6
Tel. 905-629-7777
Fax 905-629-7785
Email .... cbent@cascorp.com
Website .... www.cascorp.com

Employer Background: Cascade is a leading producer of forklift truck attachments and accessories. *New Positions Created (3):* Mechanical Designer; Production Coordinator; Planner / Buyer.

CASCADE AEROSPACE INC.
Att: Human Resources Department
1337 Townline Road
Abbotsford, BC V2T 6E1
Tel. 604-850-7372
Fax 604-855-6649
Email comework@cascadeaerospace.com
Website .... www.cascadeaerospace.com

Employer Background: Cascade Aerospace Inc. (formerly Conair Aerospace) provides aircraft maintenance, repair and overhaul services for commuter aircraft and narrow body jets. *New Positions Created (9):* Aircraft Mechanics; Avionics Technicians; Maintenance Manager; Structures Technicians; Avionics Technicians; Aircraft Maintenance Engineers; Avionics Technicians; Estimator; Sheet Metal Technicians.

CASCO IMPREGNATED PAPERS INC.
Att: Human Resources
56 Willmott Street
Cobourg, ON K9A 4R5

Fax 905-372-3099
Email .... human.resources@
.... cob.cascoprod.com
Website .... www.cascosurf.com
Employer Background: Casco Impregnated Papers Inc. (part of Akzo Nobel) manufactures resin impregnated surfacing materials for woodworking, furniture, flooring and automotive applications. *New Positions Created (3):* Product Engineers & Application Engineers; Research Chemists & Research Scientists; Marketing & Design Coordinator.

CASE CREDIT LTD. / CNH CAPITAL
Att: Human Resources
3350 South Service Road
Burlington, ON L7N 3M6

Tel. 905-632-6251
Fax 905-632-3686
Website .... www.cnh.com
Employer Background: Case Credit Ltd. / CNH Capital is a global provider of financial products and services. *New Positions Created (4):* Customer Service / Collections Representative; Retail Finance Credit Analyst; Customer Service Representative; Dealer Credit Analyst.

CASEWARE INTERNATIONAL INC.
Att: Human Resources Manager
145 King Street East, 2nd Floor
Toronto, ON M5C 2Y8

Tel. 416-867-9504
Fax 416-867-1906
Email .... jobs@caseware.com
Website .... www.caseware.com
Employer Background: CaseWare International Inc. is a leader in auditing and trial balance software, producing workflow and reporting applications for financial, operational and environmental industries. *New Positions Created (14):* Software Engineer; Content Application Developers; Quality Assurance Analyst, CaseView; Quality Assurance Analyst, Working Papers and Time; Quality Assurance Analyst, Working Papers & Web Access; Graphic Artist; Quality Control Analysts; Software Developers; Software Developers, Web Development; Technical Content Manager; Bilingual Sales Representative; Graphic Artist; Receptionist; Various IT Positions (5).

CASEY HOUSE HOSPICE
Att: Manager, Residential Program
9 Huntley Street
Toronto, ON M4Y 2K8

Tel. 416-962-7600
Fax 416-962-5147

Email .. humanresources@caseyhouse.on.ca
Website .... www.caseyhouse.on.ca
Employer Background: Casey House Hospice provides comprehensive residential and community care for people living with HIV / AIDS. *New Positions Created (7):* Food Services Coordinator; Coordinator of Volunteers; Director, Finance and Information Systems; Registered Nurses; Manager, Residential Program; Organizational Development Specialist; Registered Nurses, Community and Residential Program.

CASHCODE
Att: Human Resources Manager
553 Basaltic Road
Concord, ON L4K 4W8

Tel. 905-303-8874
Fax 905-303-8875
Email .... douglasmabee@cashcode.com
Website .... www.cashcode.com
Employer Background: CashCode designs and manufactures banknote verification equipment. *New Positions Created (3):* Technical Service Representatives; Customer Service Rep; Marketing Coordinator.

CASINO NIAGARA
Att: Recruitment
5705 Falls Avenue, PO Box 300
Niagara Falls, ON L2E 6T3

Tel. 905-353-6700
Fax 905-353-7031
Email .... careers@niagaracasino.com
Website .... www.casinoniagara.com
Employer Background: Casino Niagara is one of Ontario's premier gaming and entertainment facilities. *New Positions Created (14):* Programmer Analyst; Advertising Coordinator; Corporate Communications Coordinator; Sales Manager; Senior Buyer; Director of Marketing; Director of Security; Telecommunications Analyst / Technician; Human Resources Executive Director; Database Marketing Manager; Slot Technical Shift Manager; Director of Purchasing; Executive, Player Development; Senior Benefits & Compensation Manager.

CASINO RAMA
Att: Human Resources
Rama Road
Rama, ON L3V 1T4

Tel. 705-329-3325
Fax 705-327-6676
Email .... prattd@casinorama.net
Website .... www.casinorama.net
Employer Background: Casino Rama, a First Nation casino, is a 75,000 square foot gaming complex. *New Positions Created (2):* Executive Director of Hotel Operations; Director, Hotel Sales & Catering.

CASSELS BROCK & BLACKWELL LLP
Att: Deborah Glatter, LLB
40 King Street West
Suite 2100, Scotia Plaza
Toronto, ON M5H 3C2

Tel. 416-869-5369
Fax 416-640-3025

Email .... dglatter@casselsbrock.com
Website .... www.casselsbrock.com
Employer Background: Cassels Brock & Blackwell LLP has been providing quality legal services for over a century. *New Positions Created (4):* Associate, Tax and Trusts; Law Clerk / Trademark Agent; Intellectual Property Law Clerk; Law Clerk / Trade Mark Agent.

CATENA NETWORKS
Att: Human Resources Manager
307 Legget Drive
Kanata, ON K2K 3C8

Tel. 613-599-6430
Fax 613-599-0445
Email .... hr@catena.com
Website .... www.catenatech.com
Employer Background: Founded in 1998, Catena Networks builds new access architecture for converging public networks. *New Positions Created (23):* Field Trials Support Engineer; Human Resources Specialist; Compensation & Policies; PCB Layout Designer; Soldering Specialist; Web Developer; CAE Architecture Support Specialist; Mechanical Application Support Specialist; Mechanical Designer; Silicon Application Support Specialist; Test Automation Engineer; EMS Technical Support Specialist; Financial Analyst; Mechanical Documentation Specialist; Project Manager; Technical Support Engineer; Director, ADSL Standards; EMS Software Engineers; Marketing Communications / Events Manager; Senior Board Level Hardware Designer; Shipper / Receiver and Facilities Administrator; Technical Writer; Vice President, Operations; Webmaster.

CATHOLIC CHILDREN'S AID SOCIETY OF TORONTO / CCAS
Att: Human Resource Services
26 Maitland Street
Toronto, ON M4Y 1C6

Tel. 416-395-1500
Fax 416-395-1551
Email .... hrs@ccas.toronto.on.ca
Website .... www.ccas.toronto.on.ca
Employer Background: CCAS has been protecting children from abuse and neglect for over 100 years. *New Positions Created (14):* Child Protection Supervisors; Senior Child Protection Workers; Associate Child Protection Manager; Child Protection Workers; Health Specialists; Child Protection Workers; Computer Operator / Network Assistant; Human Resource Consultant - Employee Relations; Law Clerks (5); Team Administrative Assistant; Child and Youth Worker; Child Protection Workers, Intake and Ongoing; Health Specialist; Social Services Assistant.

CATHOLIC DISTRICT SCHOOL BOARD OF EASTERN ONTARIO, THE
Att: Barb Renaud, HR Officer
2755 Highway 43, Box 2222
Kemptville, ON K0G 1J0

Tel. 613-258-7757
Fax 613-258-3610

Email .... barb.renaud@cdsbeo.on.ca
Website .... www.cdsbeo.on.ca
Employer Background: The Catholic District School Board of Eastern Ontario operates 48 schools, serving over 14,000 students. *New Positions Created (3):* Communications Officer; Transportation Clerk; Transportation Officer.

CATHOLIC FAMILY SERVICE
Att: Human Resources Manager
707 - 10th Avenue SW, Suite 250
Calgary, AB T2R 0B3
Tel. 403-233-2360
Email .... dianne.federation@cfs-ab.org
Employer Background: Catholic Family Service strengthens people and communities in the pursuit of wellness. *New Positions Created (3):* Early Childhood Educator; Social Worker; Social Worker / Team Supervisor.

CAVIO CORPORATION
Att: Human Resources Manager
1285 Pender Street West, 4th Floor
Vancouver, BC V6E 4B1
Tel. 604-484-4700
Fax 604-484-4701
Email .... careers@cavio.com
Website .... www.cavio.com
Employer Background: Cavio Corporation is an e-commerce company. *New Positions Created (3):* Office Manager; Receptionist; Senior Executive Assistant.

CAYENTA CANADA
Att: Human Resources
9632 Cameron Street, Box 442
Burnaby, BC V3J 1M2
Tel. 604-570-4300
Fax 413-410-9996
Email .... jobs@cayenta.com
Website .... www.cayenta.com
Employer Background: Formed in 1997, Cayenta Canada creates and implements revenue cycle management solutions for utilities and municipal government customers. *New Positions Created (16):* Conversion Analyst; Conversion Manager; Municipal Application Consultant; Project Manager; Report Developer; Utility Application Consultant; Business Analyst; Conversion Analyst; QA Analyst / Manager; QA Testing; Report Developer; Technical Services Consultant; Technical Writers; Software Implementation Consultant, CIS / Billing System; Software Implementation Consultant, Financial Systems; Software Implementation Consultant, Human Resources / Payroll System.

CB ENGINEERING LTD.
Att: Human Resources Manager
5920 - 11th Street SE, Suite 20
Calgary, AB T2H 2M4
Tel. 403-259-6220
Fax 403-259-3377
Email .... resumes@cbeng.com
Website .... www.cbeng.com
Employer Background: CB Engineering Ltd. is a leading manufacturer's representative of industrial automation software and process

control equipment, with 7 offices in Canada. *New Positions Created (4):* Instrumentation Sales Engineer / Technologist; Marketing Assistant; Account Manager, Systems and Automation Products; Inside Sales / Estimating Position, Systems and Automation Products.

CBC / RADIO CANADA
Att: Tony Burman,
Executive Director, CBC News
CBC Television, PO Box 500, Station A
Toronto, ON M5W 1E6
Tel. 416-205-3311
Fax 416-205-3757
Email .... tony_burman@cbc.ca
Website .... www.cbc.ca
Employer Background: CBC / Radio Canada operates Canada's national and international public television and radio networks. *New Positions Created (6):* Director of Current Affairs, CBC Television; Director of Communications; Parliamentary Bureau Chief; Various Media Positions; Producer, CBC Morning; Director of Communications.

CBCL LIMITED
Att: Human Resources
1489 Hollis Street, Box 606, The Brewery
Halifax, NS B3J 2R7
Tel. 902-421-7241
Fax 902-423-3938
Email .... info@cbcl.ca
Website .... www.cbcl.ca
Employer Background: CBCL Limited is a progressive employee-owned multidisciplinary engineering firm. *New Positions Created (4):* Design Technologists; CAD Operators, Mechanical, Structural and Electrical; Engineers, Mechanical, Electrical and Structural; Mechanical, Structural and Electrical Design Technologists.

CC TECHNOLOGIES CANADA LTD.
Att: Jane Poirier, Office Manager
2220 - 39th Avenue NE
Calgary, AB T2E 6P7
Tel. 403-250-9044
Fax 403-250-9141
Website .... www.cctechnologies.com
Employer Background: CC Technologies Canada Ltd. provides engineering, testing and applied research services to the pipeline industry. *New Positions Created (2):* Pipeline Specialist; Senior Corrosion Technologist / Technician.

CCH CANADIAN LTD.
Att: Marianna Abate,
HR Recruiter / Administrator
90 Sheppard Avenue East, Suite 300
Toronto, ON M2N 6X1
Tel. 416-224-2248
Fax 416-224-1067
Email .... marianna_abate@ca.cch.com
Website .... www.ca.cch.com
Employer Background: CCH Canadian Ltd. publishes reference information for tax, financial planning, human resources, business and legal professionals. *New Positions*

Created (2): Senior Editor, Tax and Accounting; Senior Systems Analyst / Developer.

CCI INDUSTRIES LTD.
Att: Human Resources
PO Box 2038
St. Albert, AB T8N 2A3
Tel. 780-447-2122
Fax 780-447-1426
Website .... www.cci-industries.com
Employer Background: CCI Industries Ltd. is a western Canadian manufacturer of concrete products with divisions in Manitoba, Alberta and BC. *New Positions Created (4):* Accounts Receivable Position; Human Resources Assistant; Retail Sales Representative; Human Resources.

CDA INDUSTRIES INC.
Att: Judith Pool, Human Resources
1055 Squires Beach Road
Pickering, ON L1W 4A6
Tel. 905-686-7000
Fax 905-686-1177
Email .... jpool@cda-inc.com
Website .... www.cda-inc.com
Employer Background: CDA Industries Inc. designs and manufactures permanent point-of-purchase displays, trade show exhibits and retail environments. *New Positions Created (8):* Chief Financial Officer; Brake Press Operators; Cabinet Maker; Jig Maker; Traffic Manager; Wire Department Supervisor; Chief Financial Officer; Cost Accountant / Budget Analyst.

CDG BOOKS CANADA INC.
Att: Human Resources Manager
99 Yorkville Avenue, Suite 400
Toronto, ON M5R 3K5
Tel. 416-963-8830
Fax 416-923-4821
Website .... www.cdgbooks.com
Employer Background: CDG Books Canada Inc. publishes a diverse portfolio of technology, business, personal finance, cooking, health and reference books. *New Positions Created (4):* Channel Marketing Coordinator; National Account Manager, Mass Market; Sales Representative; Publicist.

CDL SYSTEMS LTD.
Att: Human Resources Manager
3553 - 31st Street NW, Suite 100
Calgary, AB T2L 2K7
Tel. 403-289-1733
Fax 403-282-1238
Email .... info@cdlsystems.com
Website .... www.cdlsystems.com
Employer Background: CDL Systems Ltd. is an object-oriented software design company, specializing in vehicle control station software. *New Positions Created (3):* Applications Engineer; Real-Time Software Engineer; Technical Office Assistant.

CEDAR ENTERPRISE SOLUTIONS INC.
Att: Human Resources Manager
279 Midpark Way SE, Suite 200
Calgary, AB T2X 1M2

Tel. 403-256-8877
Fax 403-256-8878
Email .... jobs.canada@cedar.com
Website .... www.cedar.com
Employer Background: Cedar Enterprise Solutions Inc. (formerly Cipher Systems Ltd.) is a global enterprise business consulting, technology and solutions company. *New Positions Created (9):* Sales Representative; Executive Assistant; C Programmer for Unix; Programmers / System Analysts; Senior Accountant; Inside Sales Representative; Project Managers; Software Developers; Senior Account Representative.

CEF TECHNOLOGIES LTD., BRITTANIA COMPRESSION
Att: John Ouellette
1437 - 47th Avenue NE, Bay 105
Calgary, AB T2E 6N7
Tel. 403-250-1844
Fax 403-291-2436
Email .... jouellette@cefranklin.com
Website .... www.cefranklin.com
Employer Background: CEF Technologies Ltd., Brittania Compression supplies a range of industrial air, instrument air, gas compression and vapour recovery packages. *New Positions Created (6):* Design Draftsperson; Office Assistant; Receptionist; Project Engineer; Inside Sales Representative, Air Compression; Mechanical Engineering Technologist.

CELESTICA INC.
Att: Human Resources
844 Don Mills Road
Toronto, ON M3C 1V7
Tel. 416-448-5800
Fax 416-448-4699
Email .... apply_toronto@celestica.com
Website .... www.celestica.com
Employer Background: Celestica Inc. provides a broad range of electronics manufacturing services, including design, prototyping, assembly, testing, product assurance, supply chain management, worldwide distribution and after-sales services. *New Positions Created (23):* SAP Consultants; Accounts Receivable Analyst; Intermediate / Senior Contracts Administrator; Programmer Analyst, Intermediate, EAI / B2B; Human Resources Analyst; Business Systems Analyst / Team Leader; Production Support Analyst, i2 / Aspect; Production Support Analyst, i2 / Rhythm; Production Support / System Analyst, AS / 400 and BPCS; SAP Programmer Analyst, ABAP; SAP Programmer Analyst, Basis; Manager, Corporate Business Analysis; Senior Financial Analyst; Business Development Managers; Intermediate / Senior Programmer Analyst (ABAP); Programmer Analyst / Developer, Lotus Notes / Domino; Programmer Analyst or Oracle Developer; Programmer Analyst or Unix Applications Integrator; Programmer / Business Analyst, Lotus Notes; SAP Consultant; Worldwide Information Security Manager; Materials Planners; Supply Buyers.

CELGAR PULP COMPANY
Att: Employment & Benefits Coordinator
PO Box 1000
Castlegar, BC V1N 3H9
Tel. 250-365-7211
Fax 250-365-2652
Website .... www.castlegar.com/celgar
Employer Background: Celgar Pulp Company operates a bleach kraft mill. *New Positions Created (6):* Services Engineer; Mechanical Maintenance Supervisor; Laboratory Technologist; Services Engineer; Engineering Technologist; Project Engineer.

CELLEX POWER PRODUCTS INC.
Att: Human Resources Manager
13155 Delf Place, Suite 220
Richmond, BC V6V 2A2
Tel. 604-270-4300
Fax 604-270-4304
Email .... careers@cellexpower.com
Website .... www.cellexpower.com
Employer Background: Cellex Power Products Inc. develops fuel cell products for use in industrial power applications. *New Positions Created (17):* Reliability Test Engineer; Procurement Specialist; System Design and Integration Engineer; Manufacturing Engineer; Mechanical Designer; Procurement Specialist; Applications Engineer; Fuel Cell Systems Integration Engineer; Chemical Technologist / Engineer; Control Systems Engineer; Energy Systems Test Engineer; Laboratory Test Engineer; Reformer Test Engineer; Senior Safety Engineer; Test Technologist / Engineer; Machinist / Fitter; Metal Fabricator / TIG Welder.

CELSIUS ENERGY RESOURCES LTD.
Att: Glen Heming
500 - 5th Avenue SW, Suite 700
Calgary, AB T2P 3L5
Tel. 403-266-2385
Fax 403-266-2390
Employer Background: Celsius Energy Resources Ltd., an affiliate of Questar Corp., is an oil and gas exploration and production company. *New Positions Created (2):* Production / Operation Engineer; Reservoir Engineer.

CENTENNIAL COLLEGE
Att: Human Resources Department
PO Box 631, Station A
Toronto, ON M1K 5E9
Tel. 416-289-5000
Fax 416-752-5021
Website .... www.cencol.on.ca
Employer Background: Established in 1966, Centennial College offers a wide range of academic programs to 12,000 full-time and 30,000 part-time students in Scarborough and East York. *New Positions Created (3):* Plant Engineer; Vice-President, Student Services and Community Relations; Manager, Compensation and Benefits.

CENTER FOR DIGITAL IMAGING AND SOUND / CDIS
Att: Human Resources Manager

3264 Beta Avenue
Burnaby, BC V5G 4K4
Tel. 604-298-5400
Fax 604-298-5403
Email .... wham@artschool.com
Website .... www.artschool.com
Employer Background: CDIS is a private college, offering programs in new media and entertainment technology, with 3 high-tech campuses and over 600 students. *New Positions Created (8):* Assistant Controller; Instructors; Assistant Dean; Program Advisor; Program Manager; Assistant Program Manager; MIS Architect; Student Services Liaison.

CENTIS (CANADA) INC.
Att: Josee Brunet
150 L.J. Forget, Suite 11
Montréal, QC H1J 2K9
Fax 514-353-4204
Employer Background: Centis (Canada) Inc. manufactures office supplies. *New Positions Created (2):* Sales / Marketing Coordinator; Assistant Controller.

CENTRAL OKANAGAN CHILD DEVELOPMENT ASSOCIATION, THE
Att: Mike Morrill, Executive Director
1546 Bernard Avenue
Kelowna, BC V1Y 6J6
Tel. 250-763-5100
Fax 250-862-8433
Email .... mmorrill@silk.net
Employer Background: The Central Okanagan Child Development Association manages child development programs in a creative partnership between the communities of Penticton, Vernon, Kamloops and Kelowna. *New Positions Created (4):* Behaviour Coordinators; Clinical Director, Autism Project; Occupational Therapists; Speech Language Pathologists.

CENTRAL PARK LODGES LTD.
Att: Regional Director
1813 - 9th Street SW
Calgary, AB T2T 3C2
Tel. 403-244-8994
Fax 403-244-5939
Website .... www.centralparklodges.com
Employer Background: Central Park Lodges Ltd. is a leading health services company, providing long-term care for seniors through 75 retirement homes in North America. *New Positions Created (3):* Occupational Therapist; Director of Quality Improvement; Mgr, Accommodation Services.

CENTRAL PARK LODGES LTD.
Att: Human Resources
175 Bloor Street East
Suite 601, South Tower
Toronto, ON M4W 3R8
Tel. 416-929-5450
Fax 416-929-8695
Email .... hr@cplodges.com
Website .... www.centralparklodges.com
Employer Background: Central Park Lodges Ltd. is a leading health services company,

providing long-term care for seniors through 75 retirement homes in North America. *New Positions Created (2):* Hospital and Community Relations Director; Director of Human Resources.

CENTRAL PRECAST INC.
Att: Human Resource Manager
25 Bongard Avenue
Nepean, ON K2E 6V2
Tel. 613-225-9510
Fax 613-225-5318
Website .... www.centralprecast.com
Employer Background: Central Precast Inc. is a CSA-certified manufacturer of precast concrete products. *New Positions Created (6):* AutoCAD Operator; Quality Assurance Inspector; Structural Engineer; Autocad Operator; Quality Assurance Inspector; Structural Engineer.

CENTRAL REPRODUCTIONS
Att: Shannon Cook
4524 Eastgate Parkway
Mississauga, ON L4W 3W6
Tel. 905-238-1250
Fax 905-238-8162
Employer Background: Central Reproduction is a progressive graphics and printing company. *New Positions Created (4):* Electronic Imposition Operator; Mac Prepress Operator; PC Prepress Operator; Proofreader.

CENTRAL TORONTO COMMUNITY HEALTH CENTRES / CTCHC
Att: Hiring Committee
168 Bathurst Street
Toronto, ON M5V 2R4
Tel. 416-703-8480
Fax 416-703-7832
Email .... hiring@ctchc.com
Website .... www.ctchc.com
Employer Background: CTCHC is a nonprofit health organization that operates 2 inner-city centres, reaching out to individuals at risk from poverty and discrimination. *New Positions Created (2):* Dentist / Dental Coordinator; Program Director.

CENTRE FOR ABILITY, THE
Att: Colleen Pohl
2805 Kingsway
Vancouver, BC V5R 5H9
Tel. 604-451-5511
Fax 604-451-5651
Website .... www.centreforability.bc.ca
Employer Background: The Centre for Ability serves thousands of children and adults with neurological or developmental disabilities, with a staff of 95. *New Positions Created (2):* Early Childhood Education Consultant / Program Assistant; Paediatric Physiotherapist.

CENTRE FOR ADDICTION AND MENTAL HEALTH
Att: Human Resources
1001 Queen Street West
Toronto, ON M6J 1H4
Tel. 416-595-6111
Fax 416-583-4316
Email .... jobs@camh.net
Website .... www.camh.net
Employer Background: The Centre for Addiction and Mental Health is dedicated to improving the lives of people affected by addiction or mental illness through prevention, clinical care, research and education. *New Positions Created (26):* Community Treatment Order Coordinator; Manager, Bed Utilization, Clinical Operations; Occupational Therapist; Registered Nurses; Registered Nurses; Social Workers; Social Workers; Psychologist, Child Psychiatry Program; Nursing Student Supervisor; Community Treatment Order Coordinator; Research Scientist, Neurogenics Research Section; Chart Completion Analysts, IMG & Health Records; Manager, Inpatient Unit & Women's Service; Registered Nurses; Senior Executive Assistant; Molecular Neuroscientist; Research Scientist; Advanced Practice Nurse / Nurse Practitioner; Clinical Nurse Specialist / Advanced Practice Nurse; Neuropsychologist; Outpatient Registered Nurses; Supervisor, Plant Operations and Maintenance; Secretary; Research Technician; Research Associate; Research Scientist.

CENTRE FOR ADDICTION AND MENTAL HEALTH
Att: Human Resources
33 Russell Street
Toronto, ON M5S 2S1
Tel. 416-595-6048
Fax 416-595-6945
Email .... jobs@camh.net
Website .... www.camh.net
Employer Background: The Centre for Addiction and Mental Health is dedicated to improving the lives of people affected by addiction or mental illness through prevention, clinical care, research and education. *New Positions Created (10):* Administrative Secretary; Regional Director, Communications, Education and Community Health; Program Manager; Operations Assistant, Office of the President; Senior Program Consultant, Problem Gambling Project; Registered Nurses; Administrative Assistant, Community Relations; Administrative Assistant, Information Management Group; Director, Decision Support; Psychologist.

CENTRE FOR HEALTH EVALUATION AND OUTCOME SCIENCES / CHEOS
Att: Human Resources Manager
1081 Burrard Street, Suite 620B
Vancouver, BC V6Z 1Y6
Tel. 604-806-8678
Fax 604-806-8674
Email .... jobs@cheos.ubc.ca
Website .... www.cheos.ubc.ca
Employer Background: CHEOS is an interdisciplinary research collective based at St. Paul's Hospital. *New Positions Created (4):* Oracle Programmer Analyst; Academic Secretary; Data Manager; Research Assistants.

CENTRECORP MANAGEMENT SERVICES LTD.
Att: Human Resources
2851 John Street, Suite 1
Markham, ON L3R 5R7
Tel. 905-646-2636
Fax 905-477-1961
Website .... www.centrecorp.com
Employer Background: Founded in 1977, CentreCorp Management Services Ltd. is a property management and leasing company, specializing in neighbourhood and community shopping centres and other retail properties. *New Positions Created (2):* Junior Legal Secretary / Legal Assistant; Lease Administrator.

CENTREPOINT TECHNOLOGIES INC.
Att: Human Resources
1565 Carling Avenue, Suite 510
Ottawa, ON K1Z 8R1
Tel. 613-725-2980
Fax 613-725-2898
Email .... careers@talkswitch.com
Website .... www.talkswitch.com
Employer Background: Centrepoint Technologies Inc. develops Concero desktop phone systems and voice-over IP solutions for small to mid-sized businesses. *New Positions Created (12):* Director, Communications; Director, Marketing; Director, Sales; Firmware Developer; Senior Graphics Designer; Technical Marketing Writer; Director, Communications; Director, Marketing; Director, Sales; Firmware Developer; Senior Graphics Designer; Technical Marketing Writer.

CENTRETOWN COMMUNITY HEALTH CENTRE
Att: Human Resources
420 Cooper Street
Ottawa, ON K2P 2N6
Tel. 613-233-4443
Fax 613-233-3987
Email .... admin@centretownchc.org
Website .... www.centretownchc.org
Employer Background: Centretown Community Health Centre is a non-profit, community-based health and social service organization. *New Positions Created (3):* Physician; Bilingual HR Coordinator; Bilingual Counsellor.

CERIDIAN CANADA LTD.
Att: HR Manager, Head Office
125 Garry Street
Winnipeg, MB R3C 3P2
Tel. 204-946-0770
Fax 204-956-4026
Website .... www.ceridian.ca
Employer Background: Ceridian Canada Ltd. is one of Canada's leading employer services companies, providing payroll and human resource management services to over 135,000 customers in virtually every industry. *New Positions Created (27):* Customer Care Representative; Customer Care Professional ; Security Analyst; Application Developer - Lotus Notes R5 ; Customer Care Representative; HR Product Support Spe-

cialist; Intermediate or Senior C++ Developer; Payroll & HR Administrator; Project Manager, Marketing & Development; Risk Analyst; Senior Security & Network Administrator; Senior Testing Analyst; Team Leader; Account Executive; Director, Information Technology; Customer Care Professionals (3); Account Manager; Business Analysts (2); Crystal Report Writer Specialist; Customer Service Representatives - Payroll (2); Systems Developer; Communications Specialist; Project Specialist; Sales Consultants (2); Senior Risk Analyst; Support Analysts (2); Testing / QA Analyst.

CERIDIAN CANADA LTD.
Att: Human Resources Manager
5600 Explorer Drive, 4th Floor
Mississauga, ON L4W 4Y2
Tel. 905-282-8100
Fax 905-282-8104
Website .... www.ceridian.ca
Employer Background: Ceridian Canada Ltd. is one of Canada's leading employer services companies, providing payroll and human resource management services to over 135,000 customers in virtually every industry. *New Positions Created (5):* Sales Consultant, Small Business Solutions; Product Specialist Trainee; Project Coordinator / Administrative Assistant; Customer Care Representatives; Business Analysts (2).

CERIDIAN CANADA LTD.
Att: Human Resources Manager
675 Cochrane Drive
Markham, ON L3R 0B8
Tel. 905-947-7200
Fax 905-947-7004
Website .... www.ceridian.ca
Employer Background: Ceridian Canada Ltd. is one of Canada's leading employer services companies, providing payroll and human resource management services to over 135,000 customers in virtually every industry. *New Positions Created (8):* Conversion Specialist; Customer Care Coach; Sales Manager; Senior Systems Developer; Conversion / Implementation Officer; Customer Care Representatives; Sales Consultant; Sales Manager.

CERIDIAN CANADA LTD.
Att: Ian Campbell
1111 Prince of Wales Drive, Suite 100
Ottawa, ON K2C 3T2
Tel. 613-228-0222
Email .... ian_campbell@ceridian.ca
Website .... www.ceridian.ca
Employer Background: Ceridian Canada Ltd. is one of Canada's leading employer services companies, providing payroll and human resource management services to over 135,000 customers in virtually every industry. *New Positions Created (2):* Project Specialist; Sales Consultant.

CERIDIAN CANADA LTD.
Att: Human Resources Manager
8777 Trans Canada Highway
St-Laurent, QC H4S 1Z6

Tel. 514-908-3000
Fax 514-908-3111
Website .... www.ceridian.ca
Employer Background: Ceridian Canada Ltd. is one of Canada's leading employer services companies, providing payroll and human resource management services to over 135,000 customers in virtually every industry. *New Positions Created (3):* Account Executive; Customer Care Representative; Team Leader.

CERIDIAN PERFORMANCE PARTNERS LTD.
Att: Human Resources
675 Cochrane Drive
Suite 515, Ceridian Tower
Markham, ON L3R 0B8
Fax 905-947-7396
Email .... hr.lifeworks@ceridian.com
Website .... www.ceridian.ca
Employer Background: Ceridian Performance Partners Ltd. is a leading provider of EAP and work-life services. *New Positions Created (2):* Account Executive; Service Delivery Director.

CERTIFIED GENERAL ACCOUNTANTS ASSOCIATION OF CANADA
Att: Human Resources
1188 West Georgia Street, Suite 700
Vancouver, BC V6E 4A2
Tel. 604-669-3555
Fax 604-689-5845
Email .... hr@cga-canada.org
Website .... www.cga-canada.org
Employer Background: CGA-Canada represents over 60,500 certified general accountants and CGA students in Canada, Bermuda, the Caribbean and Pacific Rim. *New Positions Created (6):* Production Coordinator; Education Development Specialist; Network / Systems Administrator; Oracle Database Programmer; Web Developer; Web Manager.

CGG CANADA SERVICES LTD.
Att: Centre Manager
404 - 6th Avenue SW, Suite 700
Calgary, AB T2P 0R9
Tel. 403-265-7540
Fax 403-264-7054
Website .... www.cgg.com
Employer Background: CGG Canada Services Ltd. is one of the world's largest seismic contractors. *New Positions Created (3):* Geophysical / Geological Technologists; Senior Processing Geophysicists; Senior Reservoir Geophysicists.

CGI GROUP INC.
Att: Karen Savoy
275 Slater Street, 14th Floor
Ottawa, ON K1P 5H9
Tel. 613-234-2155
Fax 613-234-6934
Email .... kate.dickerson@cgi.ca
Website .... www.cgi.ca
Employer Background: CGI Group Inc. provides end-to-end information technology services and business solutions to 2,000 cli-

ents in Canada, the USA and 20 countries around the world. *New Positions Created (2):* Applications Architects; Java Programmers / Web Developers and Analysts.

CGU GROUP CANADA LTD.
Att: Human Resources
1125 Howe Street, Suite 1100
Vancouver, BC V6Z 2Y6
Tel. 604-669-3212
Fax 604-288-9106
Website .... www.cgu.ca
Employer Background: CGU Group Canada Ltd. is one of the leading property and casualty insurers in Canada, with annual premiums exceeding $1.6 billion. *New Positions Created (4):* Bilingual Customer Service Representative; Junior Underwriter; Senior Claims Examiners; Senior Field Adjusters.

CGU GROUP CANADA LTD.
Att: Claims Manager
10250 - 101st Street, Suite 1700
Edmonton, AB T5J 3P4
Tel. 780-428-1822
Fax 780-424-9605
Website .... www.cgu.ca
Employer Background: CGU Group Canada Ltd. is one of the leading property and casualty insurers in Canada, with annual premiums exceeding $1.6 billion. *New Positions Created (7):* Intermediate Service / Field Service Representative; Western Regional Auditor Trainer; Claims Technical Specialist; Injury and Property Field Adjusters; Senior Automobile Underwriter; Regional Claims Investigator; Senior Road Adjuster.

CGU GROUP CANADA LTD.
Att: Human Resources
140 - 4th Avenue SW
Calgary, AB T2P 3N3
Fax 403-263-4972
Website .... www.cgu.ca
Employer Background: CGU Group Canada Ltd. is one of the leading property and casualty insurers in Canada, with annual premiums exceeding $1.6 billion. *New Positions Created (3):* Administrative Assistant; Senior BI / Litigation Claims Supervisor; Senior Field Service Representative.

CGU GROUP CANADA LTD.
Att: Human Resources
2206 Eglinton Avenue East, 3rd Floor
Toronto, ON M1L 4S8
Tel. 416-288-1800
Fax 416-288-9106
Website .... www.cgu.ca
Employer Background: CGU Group Canada Ltd. is one of the leading property and casualty insurers in Canada, with annual premiums exceeding $1.6 billion. *New Positions Created (48):* Administrative Assistant; Claims Financial Analyst; Counsel; Field Service Representative; Manager, National Commercial Lines; System Analyst, Project Documentation; Training and Development Specialist, Head Office Claims; Engineer, Equipment Breakdown; Intermediate AB

Representative; Intermediate Claims Examiner; Intermediate Commercial Underwriter; Intermediate Field Service Representative; Junior Accident Benefits Representatives (3); Loss Control Representative; Manager, Supplier Management; Senior Accountant, Corporate Accounting; Senior Claims Supervisor; Supervisor, Accident Benefits; Supervisor, LAN Technical Service; Support Clerk; Commercial Underwriter (Intermediate); Configuration Analyst; Customer Service Representative; Group Marketing Representative; Intermediate Commercial Lines Property / Casualty Underwriter; Intermediate Commercial Property / Casualty Underwriter; Intermediate Service Representative (Claims); Junior Auto Underwriter - Commercial Lines; Junior Contract Surety Underwriters (2); Junior Service Representative; Large Loss Field Specialist; Liability Specialist; Outbound Sales Position; PC / LAN Analyst; Sales Representative; Senior Bonus Underwriter; Senior Underwriter - CGU Link; Senior Underwriters; Service Representative (Intermediate); Service Representative (Intermediate); Service Reps (Intermediate & Junior); Supervisor - Personal Lines Programmer Analyst; Support Clerk, Senior, CSR Plans and Programs Claims; Underwriter Assistant; Insurance Litigation Lawyer; Western Regional Personal Lines Manager; Communications Manager; Research and Development Analyst.

CH2M HILL CANADA LTD.
Att: Human Resources Manager
475 West Georgia Street, Suite 920
Vancouver, BC V6B 4M9
Tel. 604-684-3282
Fax 604-684-3292
Website www.ch2m.com
Employer Background: CH2M HILL Canada Ltd. (formerly CH2M Gore & Storrie Ltd.) is a consulting engineering company, specializing in transportation, environmental, water and wastewater services. CH2M HILL, their parent company, has 11,000 employees worldwide. *New Positions Created (3):* Design Engineer, Water, Wastewater Treatment and Water Resources; Junior Engineer, Environmental; Project Engineer, Civil.

CH2M HILL CANADA LTD.
Att: Human Resources Coordinator
555 - 4th Avenue SW, Suite 1500
Calgary, AB T2P 3E7
Tel. 403-237-9300
Fax 403-234-7898
Email .... canadiancareers@ch2m.com
Website www.ch2m.com
Employer Background: CH2M HILL Canada Ltd. (formerly CH2M Gore & Storrie Ltd.) is a consulting engineering company, specializing in transportation, environmental, water and wastewater services. CH2M HILL, their parent company, has 11,000 employees worldwide. *New Positions Created (8):* Junior Hydrogeologist; Senior Hydrogeologist; CADD Technicians; Transportation Engineers and Planners; Technical Publications Specialist; Receptionist; Mechanical

Engineers (2); Senior Process Piping Designer.

CH2M HILL CANADA LTD.
Att: Human Resources
255 Consumers Road, Suite 300
Toronto, ON M2J 5B6
Tel. 416-499-9000
Fax 416-499-4687
Email .... careers@ch2m.com
Website www.ch2m.com
Employer Background: CH2M HILL Canada Ltd. (formerly CH2M Gore & Storrie Ltd.) is a consulting engineering company, specializing in transportation, environmental, water and wastewater services. CH2M HILL, their parent company, has 11,000 employees worldwide. *New Positions Created (19):* Human Resources Generalist; Technical Publication Specialists; Engineers, Water / Wastewater; CADD Technicians / Designers; Junior Engineers / EIT; PLC / SCADA Programmer; Professional Engineers; Project Architect; Editor / Writer (2); Building Mechanical Engineers; Civil / Highway Design Technician; Design Manager; Highway / Bridge Engineer; Instrumentation Control Systems Engineers; Process Mechanical Engineers; Project Controls Specialist; Project Manager; Transportation Engineers; Various Engineering Positions.

CHAITON & CHAITON LLP
Att: Office Administrator
185 Sheppard Avenue West
Toronto, ON M2N 1M9
Tel. 416-222-8888
Fax 416-222-8402
Email .... chaiton@chaiton.com
Employer Background: Chaiton & Chaiton LLP is a 25-lawyer firm. *New Positions Created (3):* Lawyers (2); Lawyer; Legal Assistants / Law Clerks.

CHALK NETWORK, THE
Att: Human Resources Manager
4400 Dominion Street, Suite 280
Burnaby, BC V4G 4G3
Tel. 604-684-9399
Fax 604-684-0326
Email .... hr@chalk.com
Website .... www.chalk.com
Employer Background: The Chalk Network is an international new media company, providing information about computers and technology. *New Positions Created (2):* Segment Producer; Chief Financial Officer.

CHALLENGER GEOMATICS LTD.
Att: Human Resources Consultant
6940 Fisher Road SE, Suite 300
Calgary, AB T2H 0W3
Tel. 403-253-8101
Fax 403-253-1985
Email .... calgary@chalsurv.com
Website .... www.chalsurv.com
Employer Background: Challenger Geomatics Ltd. provides survey engineering and geomatics services to the oil and gas, municipal and land development industries.

New Positions Created (8): AutoCAD Technicians; Party Chiefs; AutoCAD Technicians; Mapping Technologist; Party Chiefs; Project Supervisor; Survey Technician; Marketing Representative.

CHALMERS SUSPENSIONS INTERNATIONAL INC. / SCIENTEK
Att: Human Resources Manager
1136 Matheson Boulevard East
Mississauga, ON L4W 2V4
Tel. 905-624-9750
Fax 905-624-9796
Email .. btakhar@chalmerssuspensions.com
Website .. www.chalmerssuspensions.com
Employer Background: Chalmers Suspensions International Inc. / Scientek is a manufacturer and supplier of truck, trailer and bus suspensions to major OEMs. *New Positions Created (3):* Accountant; Engineering Manager; Sales Coordinator.

CHANCELLOR INDUSTRIAL CONSTRUCTION LTD.
Att: Human Resources Manager
2107 - 5th Street
Nisku, AB T9E 7X4
Tel. 780-955-3953
Fax 780-955-3498
Email .... jimclark@chancellor.com
Website .... www.chancellor.com
Employer Background: Chancellor Industrial Construction Ltd. is a mid-sized general industrial contractor and modern pipe fabrication facility. *New Positions Created (4):* Corporate Safety Manager; Estimator / Project Manager; Field Engineer / CET; Project Manager.

CHANCERY SOFTWARE LTD.
Att: Human Resources Manager
3001 Wayburne Drive, Suite 275
Burnaby, BC V5G 4W1
Tel. 604-294-1233
Fax 604-294-2225
Website .... www.chancery.com
Employer Background: Chancery Software is a leading provider of K-12 student information management software. *New Positions Created (18):* Account Coordinator; Crystal Reports Writing Consultant; Data Conversion Specialist; Database Administrator; Director, IS; Director, Program Management; Implementation Account Manager; Implementation Support Analyst; Intermediate Software Engineer; Quality Assurance Specialist; Training and Implementation Coordinator; C++ Developers; Implementation Consultant; Product Manager; Project Manager; Senior Software Architect; Senior Software Engineer, OD; Senior Web Developer.

CHANDOS CONSTRUCTION LTD.
Att: Human Resources Manager
6720 - 104th Street
Edmonton, AB T6H 2L4
Tel. 780-436-8617
Fax 780-436-1797
Website .... www.chandos.com

Employer Background: Chandos Construction Ltd. is a general contractor. *New Positions Created (5):* Sr Construction Estimator; Controller; Sr Estimators (2); Vice-President of Operations; Construction Estimator.

CHANGEPOINT CORPORATION
Att: Human Resources
30 Leek Crescent, Suite 401
Richmond Hill, ON L4B 4N4
Tel. 905-886-7000
Fax 905-886-7023
Email .... careers@changepoint.com
Website .... www.changepoint.com
Employer Background: Changepoint Corporation, an international software company, provides IT business process automation software. *New Positions Created (8):* Financial Analyst; Budget Analyst; International Development Group Localization Specialist; Recruiting Specialist; Segment Marketing Manager; Senior Technical Writer; Web Software Developers; Webmaster.

CHAPLEAU HEALTH SERVICES
Att: Human Resources
6 Broomhead Road, PO Box 757
Chapleau, ON P0M 1K0
Tel. 705-864-1520
Fax 705-864-0449
Email .... mdoyon@hrsrh.on.ca
Website .... www.hrsrh.on.ca
Employer Background: Chapleau Health Services, affiliated with Sudbury Regional and four other hospitals, provides a wide range of health services, including acute, long-term and community-based services. *New Positions Created (3):* Nurse Practitioners (2); Clinical Services Provider; Financial and Corporate Services Officer.

CHAPPELL BUSHELL STEWART
Att: Ross M. Anderson
20 Queen Street West, Suite 3310
Toronto, ON M5H 3R3
Tel. 416-351-0005
Fax 416-351-0002
Website .... www.cbslaw.to
Employer Background: Chappell Bushell Stewart is a law firm. *New Positions Created (2):* Lawyer(s); Lawyers.

CHAPS GROUP INC. / CGS
Att: Human Resources Manager
20 Valleywood Drive, Suite 105
Markham, ON L3R 6G1
Tel. 905-940-2780
Fax 905-940-2904
Website .... chapsgroup.com
Employer Background: Founded in 1985, CGS is an information technology consulting company, specializing in integrated document management. *New Positions Created (2):* Quality Assurance Analyst; Senior System Architects.

CHAPTERS INC. / INDIGO
Att: Human Resources
788 Robson Street
Vancouver, BC V6Z 1A1
Fax 604-633-1316
Email .... resume@chapters.indigo.ca
Website .... www.chapters.indigo.ca
Employer Background: Chapters Inc. / Indigo is Canada's leading book retailer, with stores in every province. *New Positions Created (3):* Merchandising Managers; Operations Managers; Zone Managers.

CHAPTERS INC. / INDIGO BOOKS & MUSIC
Att: Human Resources
90 Ronson Drive
Toronto, ON M9W 1C1
Tel. 416-243-3138
Fax 416-243-5420
Website .... www.chapters.indigo.ca
Employer Background: Chapters Inc. / Indigo Books & Music is Canada's leading book retailer, with stores in every province. *New Positions Created (20):* Assistant Managers; Booksellers; Merchandising Manager; Zone Managers; Cafe Managers; General Managers; Operations / Zone Managers; Regional Director of Operations; Sales Floor Managers; Merchandising Managers, Chapters; Operations Managers and Zone Managers, Chapters; Store Managers, Coles; Store Manager; General Managers; Store Events Coordinator; Store Manager; Booksellers; District Manager; Human Resource Manager; Store Manager.

CHARON SYSTEMS INC.
Att: Human Resources Manager
309 Evans Avenue
Toronto, ON M8Z 1K2
Tel. 416-503-1100
Email .... careers@charon.com
Website .... www.charon.com
Employer Background: Charon Systems Inc., a FutureLink company, is a supplier of networked business solutions. *New Positions Created (4):* Account Managers; Applications Analysts / Programmers; Sales Coordinators; Systems Engineers.

CHARTWELL CARE CORPORATION
Att: Human Resources
2829 Sherwood Heights Drive, Suite 101
Oakville, ON L6J 7R7
Tel. 905-829-1665
Fax 905-829-0943
Email .... admin@chartwellcare.com
Website .... www.chartwellcare.com
Employer Background: Chartwell Care Corporation manages retirement and long-term care facilities. *New Positions Created (2):* General Manager / Nurse, Governor's Walk; Retirement Residence General Managers and Long-Term Care Administrators .

CHATHAM-KENT HEALTH ALLIANCE
Att: Human Resources
519 King Street West, PO Box 2030
Chatham, ON N7M 5L9
Tel. 519-358-3004
Fax 519-352-8094
Email .... employopp@ckha.on.ca
Website .... www.ckha.on.ca
Employer Background: Chatham-Kent Health Alliance operates 250 beds in three hospitals, serving the Municipality of Chatham-Kent. *New Positions Created (2):* Obstetricians / Gynaecologists (2); Nurse Practitioner, Mental Health Services.

CHATHAM-KENT, MUNICIPALITY OF
Att: J.G. Pavlka, PEng,
Chief Administrative Officer
315 King Street West, PO Box 640
Chatham, ON N7M 5K8
Tel. 519-360-1998
Fax 519-436-3237
Website ...... www.city.chatham-kent.on.ca
Employer Background: Created in 1998 by the amalgamation of 23 municipalities, the Municipality of Chatham-Kent covers 2,494 square km and has 110,000 residents. *New Positions Created (2):* Director, Economic Development; Medical Officer of Health.

CHEM SYSTEMS INC.
Att: General Manager
3390 Mainway
Burlington, ON L7M 1A8
Tel. 905-336-7013
Fax 905-336-9443
Email .... info@chemsys.com
Website .... www.chemsys.com
Employer Background: Chem Systems Inc. manufactures water treatment and chemical blending, processing and metering systems for the chemical and pulp and paper industry. *New Positions Created (2):* Mechanical Design Engineer; Mechanical Assembler / Machine Builder.

CHEMQUE INC.
Att: Employee Services
266 Humberline Drive
Toronto, ON M9W 5X1
Tel. 416-679-5676
Fax 416-679-0511
Email .... careers@chemque.com
Website .... www.chemque.com
Employer Background: Chemque Inc. manufactures epoxy polyurethane and silicone polymers for the automotive, construction, industrial and telecom industries. *New Positions Created (13):* Maintenance Manager; Research and Development Chemist; Lab Technician; QA Packaging Manager; Quality Assurance Manager; QA Chemist; QA Technician; Quality Assurance Technician; Accounting Manager; Accounts Payable Clerk; Health and Safety Coordinator; Marketing Coordinator; Product Manager - Trainee.

CHEP CANADA INC.
Att: Human Resources
7400 East Danbro Crescent
Mississauga, ON L5N 8C6
Fax 905-789-4279
Website .... www.chep.com
Employer Background: CHEP Canada Inc. provides global supply chain solutions through their pallet container and pooling network. *New Positions Created (3):* Depot

Operations Coordinator; Warehouse Supervisor; Inside Service Representative.

CHEVRON CANADA LTD.
Att: Nancy Ma
1050 West Pender Street, Suite 1500
Vancouver, BC V6E 3T4

Tel. 604-668-5300
Fax 604-668-5559
Email .... nvma@chevron.com
Website .... www.chevron.ca

Employer Background: Chevron Canada Ltd. is a major refiner and marketer of petroleum products in BC. *New Positions Created (3):* Wholesale Bulk Agency Position; Electrical Engineers; Refinery Operator Trainees.

CHILD'S PLACE, THE
Att: Executive Director
2611 Labelle Street
Windsor, ON N9E 4G4

Tel. 519-966-2211
Fax 519-966-1142

Employer Background: The Child's Place specializes in diagnostic and treatment services for preschool children and their families. *New Positions Created (3):* Occupational Therapists; Psychologist; Speech-Language Pathologists.

CHILDREN'S AID SOCIETY OF HAMILTON-WENTWORTH, THE
Att: Human Resources Department
143 Wentworth Street South
PO Box 1170, Depot 1
Hamilton, ON L8N 4B9

Tel. 905-522-1121
Fax 905-521-1264
Email .... koates@hamiltoncas.com
Website .... www.hamiltoncas.com

Employer Background: The Children's Aid Society of Hamilton-Wentworth provides child protection, placement and adoption services, family education and other programs. *New Positions Created (3):* Child Protection Workers; Child Protection Workers; Child Protection Worker.

CHILDREN'S AID SOCIETY OF OTTAWA-CARLETON / CASOC
Att: Valerie Flynn, Coordinator of Employment Services
1602 Telesat Court
Gloucester, ON K1B 1B1

Tel. 613-745-1893
Fax 613-742-1607
Email .... kchau@casoc.com
Website .... www.casoc.com

Employer Background: CASOC is a non-profit organization, funded by the Government of Ontario and governed by the Child and Family Services Act. *New Positions Created (2):* Legal Counsel; Social Workers; Child Protection.

CHILDREN'S AID SOCIETY OF TORONTO
Att: Human Resources
4211 Yonge Street, Suite 400
Toronto, ON M2P 2A9

Tel. 416-924-4646
Fax 416-324-2375
Email .... hr@torontocas.ca
Website .... www.torontocas.ca

Employer Background: The Children's Aid Society of Toronto is the largest board-operated child welfare agency in North America, serving over 23,000 children per year. *New Positions Created (19):* Administrative Assistants; Legal Secretaries / Legal Clerk Typists; Residential Child and Youth Workers; Training Manager; Child Welfare Supervisors; Front-Line Child Protection Workers; High Risk Infant Nurse; Law Clerk; Front-Line Child Protection Workers; Administrative Support Positions; Child and Youth Workers; Compensation and Benefits Manager; Front Line Workers; High-Risk Infant Nurse; Legal Secretaries / Legal Clerk Typists; Benefits & Compensation Manager; High Risk Infant Nurse; Front Line Workers; Legal Secretaries (2).

CHILDREN'S AND WOMEN'S HEALTH CENTRE OF BRITISH COLUMBIA
Att: Human Resources
4480 Oak Street, Room S213
Vancouver, BC V6H 4C9

Tel. 604-875-2570
Fax 604-875-2599
Email .... careers@cw.bc.ca
Website .... www.cw.bc.ca

Employer Background: Created in 1997 by the merger of three organizations, C&W is a teaching hospital and major provincial resource, providing patient care, education and research. *New Positions Created (55):* Corporate Accountant; Laboratory Scientist, Molecular Diagnostic Laboratory; Registered Nurse, Emergency; Registered Nurse, IV Therapy / Emergency; Confidential Secretary; Laboratory Scientist, Biochemical Geneticist; Physiotherapists; Physiotherapy Section Head; Program Coordinator, High Risk Antepartum; Provincial FAS / NAS Early Intervention Consultant; Child Development & Rehabilitation Manager; Director, Spiritual Care; Pediatric Pathologist; Ultrasonographers; Information Systems Professionals; Registered Nurses; Quality Improvement Consultant; Business Analyst; Program Director, Newborn Care; Public Affairs & Communications Assistant; Senior Practice Leader, Perinatal; Administrative Coordinator, Birthing Program; Clinical Quality Advisors, Child Health (2); Director, Molecular Pathology; Genetic Counsellor, Department of Pathology and Laboratory Medicine; Laboratory Scientist, Molecular Diagnostic Laboratory; Medical Secretary; Medical Technologist, Anatomic & Surgical Pathology; Medical Technologist, Department of Pathology; Operating Room Nurses; Physiotherapists / Occupational Therapists; Registered Nurses, Adolescent Mental Health; Respiratory Therapists; Teaching Orthoptist; Ultrasonographer, Diagnostic Ambulatory Program; Research Program Coordinator; Manager, Dietetic Services; Project Manager; Quality Advisor, Child Development and Rehabilitation; Biomedical Engineer; Biomedical Engineering Technician I; Health Information / Data

Quality Analyst, Pediatrics; Laboratory Scientist; Manager, Customer Services, Cafeteria and Catering; Medical Biochemist; Medical Technologist, Department of Pathology; Operating Room Nurses, Pediatric Peri-Operative Services; Pediatric Echocardiographers; Primary Care Nurse Practitioner; Registered Nurses, Adolescent Mental Health; Teaching Orthoptist; Ultrasonographer, Diagnostic Ambulatory Program; Registered Nurses; Various Registered Nursing Positions; Senior HR Advisor, Nursing Recruitment.

CHILDREN'S HOSPITAL OF EASTERN ONTARIO / CHEO
Att: Employment Services Officer, HR
401 Smyth Road
Ottawa, ON K1H 8L1

Tel. 613-737-7600
Fax 613-738-4233
Email .... personnel@cheo.on.ca
Website .... www.cheo.on.ca

Employer Background: CHEO is an acute care teaching hospital affiliated with the University of Ottawa. *New Positions Created (6):* Psychologist; Speech Language Pathologists (2); Senior Technologist, Blood Transfusion; Health Information Analyst; Clinical Psychologists, Child Development Service; Registered Nurses.

CHILDREN'S REHABILITATION CENTRE OF ESSEX COUNTY
Att: Chair of the Search Committee
3945 Matchette Road
Windsor, ON N9C 4C2

Tel. 519-252-7281
Fax 519-252-5873
Website .... www.childrensrehab.com

Employer Background: The Children's Rehabilitation Centre of Essex County provides comprehensive, family-centered services, including assessment, consultation, treatment design, assistive devices, education, family support and research. *New Positions Created (4):* Executive Director; Occupational Therapists; Physiotherapists; Speech-Language Pathologists.

CHILI'S TEXAS GRILL
Att: Owner and President
17724 - 102nd Avenue
Edmonton, AB T5S 1H5

Email .... chilis@telusplanet.net
Website .... www.chilis.com

Employer Background: Chili's Texas Grill is a leader in the casual dining industry. *New Positions Created (2):* Various Hospitality Positions; Various Restaurant Manager Positions.

CHILLIWACK, CITY OF
Att: Irene Regier, HR Officer
8550 Young Road South
Chilliwack, BC V2P 8A4

Tel. 604-792-9311
Fax 604-793-2715
Email .... regier@chilliwack.com
Website .... www.chilliwack.com

Employer Background: Located one hour east of Vancouver, the City of Chilliwack is home to 70,000 people. *New Positions Created (2):* Manager, Leisure Development; Occupational Health and Safety Officer.

CHINOOK HEALTH REGION
Att: Ms J. Tamayose, Human Resources
960 - 19th Street South
Lethbridge, AB T1J 1W5
Tel. 403-382-6009
Fax 403-382-6016
Email .... humanres@mail.chr.ab.ca
Website .... www.chr.ab.ca
Employer Background: Chinook Health Region provides acute care, continuing care and community-based programs to over 146,000 people, with 3,300 staff members and 200 physicians. *New Positions Created (6):* Clinical Care Coordinator; Nursing Unit Manager; Manager, Occupational Health Services; Regional Director of Pharmacy; Sonographer; Managers, Medical Nursing Unit (2).

CHRIST THE REDEEMER SCHOOL DIVISION
Att: Recruiting Officer
46 Elma Street, PO Bag 3
Okotoks, AB T0L 1T0
Tel. 403-938-4119
Fax 403-938-4575
Website .... www.redeemer.ab.ca
Employer Background: Christ the Redeemer School Division is a publicly-funded Catholic schooling authority. *New Positions Created (3):* Principal; Vice-Principal; Vice-Principal.

CHRISTIAN CHILDREN'S FUND OF CANADA / CCFC
Att: Christine Sanger, HR Consultant
1027 McNicoll Avenue
Toronto, ON M1W 3X2
Fax 416-495-9395
Email .... csanger@ccfcanada.ca
Website .... www.ccfcanada.ca
Employer Background: CCFC is a Christian organization dedicated to helping children of all faiths throughout the world. *New Positions Created (4):* Director of Finance; External Communications Coordinator; Manager, Special Gifts; Receptionist.

CHRISTIE LITES
Att: Tracy Badgerow
15 North Queen Street, Unit 102
Toronto, ON M8Z 6C1
Fax 416-644-0404
Employer Background: Christie Lites is a leader in theatrical and concert lighting. *New Positions Created (3):* Junior Purchasing Clerk; Purchasing and Inventory Control Clerk; Service Manager.

CHRISTINA AMERICA INC.
Att: Agnes Dube
9880 Clark
Montréal, QC H3L 2R3
Tel. 514-381-2365
Fax 514-850-2012
Email .... agnes@christina.ca
Website .... www.christina.ca
Employer Background: Christina America Inc. is a swimwear company. *New Positions Created (3):* Senior Merchandiser; Lab Technician; Office Assistants (2).

CHROMATIC SOFTWARE INC. / CSI
Att: Human Resources Manager
1190 Hornby Street, 6th Floor
Vancouver, BC V6Z 2K5
Tel. 604-257-5583
Fax 604-639-1772
Email .... hr@chromaticsoftware.com
Website ...... www.chromaticsoftware.com
Employer Background: CSI is a leader in enterprise management systems and interactive voice response application development. *New Positions Created (16):* Logistics and Purchasing Manager; IT Positions; IT Positions; Database Administrator; IT Positions (4); Chief Financial Officer; Actuate / Crystal Reports Developer; Database Specialist; Inbound Call Centre Representatives; Intermediate EMS VB / Java Developer; IVR Developer; Network Engineer; Quality Assurance and Testing Position; Systems / Business Analyst; Team Manager, Call Centre; Telecom Technician.

CHRYSALIS-ITS INC.
Att: Human Resources Manager
1688 Woodward Drive
Ottawa, ON K2C 3R7
Fax 613-723-2454
Email .... careers@chrysalis-its.com
Website .... www.chrysalis-its.com
Employer Background: Founded in 1994, Chrysalis-ITS Inc. provides e-business security solutions. *New Positions Created (6):* Director, Software Development; Intermediate / Senior Software Developer; Manager, Middleware Development; Product Manager; Project Manager; Technical Support Specialist.

CHURCHILL REGIONAL HEALTH AUTHORITY INC.
Att: Peter Smith, Human Resources
Churchill, MB R0B 0E0
Tel. 204-675-8307
Fax 204-675-2285
Email .... crhahr@cancom.net
Website .... www.cancom.net/~crhaexec
Employer Background: Churchill RHA Inc. provides health and social services to the residents of Churchill and the Kivalliq Region of Nunavut. *New Positions Created (3):* Chief Pharmacist; Radiology Technologist; Director of Community Services.

CIBA VISION STERILE MANUFACTURING
Att: Human Resources
6515 Kitimat Road
Mississauga, ON L5N 2X5
Tel. 905-821-3661
Fax 905-819-1309
Website .... www.cibavision.com
Employer Background: Established in 1980, CIBA Vision is a leading manufacturer of vision care products, including contact lenses, lens care products, ophthalmic surgical products and ophthalmic pharmaceuticals. The company has over 6,000 employees worldwide. *New Positions Created (11):* Production Mechanic; Quality Control Analyst; Quality Control Stability Analyst; Buyer / Expediter; Intermediate Programmer, Help Desk; Planner; Project Engineer; Quality Control Microbiology Manager; Regulatory Affairs Co-ordinator, Medical Division; Regulatory Affairs Supervisor, Medical Devices; Quality Control Compliance Auditor.

CIBC WOOD GUNDY
Att: Ms J. Eifert, Director, New FC Training
200 King Street West, Suite 1200
Toronto, ON M5H 3W8
Tel. 416-594-8999
Fax 416-594-8908
Website .... www.woodgundy.com
Employer Background: CIBC Wood Gundy offers a broad range of investment advisory services. *New Positions Created (3):* Financial Consultants; Financial Consultants; Financial Consultants.

CIMCO REFRIGERATION
Att: K. Mihay
65 Villiers Street
Toronto, ON M5A 3S1
Tel. 416-465-7581
Fax 416-778-1244
Email .... kmihay@toromont.com
Website ...... www.cimcorefrigeration.com
Employer Background: Cimco Refrigeration, a division of Toromont Industries Ltd., designs and installs industrial refrigeration systems. *New Positions Created (2):* Assistant Credit Manager; Construction Manager.

CIMETRIX SOLUTIONS INC.
Att: Human Resources Manager
50 Acadia Avenue, Suite 120
Markham, ON L3R 0B3
Tel. 905-470-6624
Fax 905-470-6638
Email .... hr@cimetrix.on.ca
Employer Background: Cimetrix Solutions provides industry-leading CAD / CAM / CAE solutions. *New Positions Created (2):* Pre-sales Application Engineer; Technical Instructor.

CIMMETRY SYSTEMS INC. / CSI
Att: Human Resources Manager
6700 Cote de Liesse, Suite 206
St-Laurent, QC H4T 2B5
Tel. 514-735-3219
Fax 514-735-6440
Email .... resumes@cimmetry.com
Website .... www.cimmetry.com
Employer Background: CSI is a leading developer of visualization and collaboration software solutions for web, intranet / extranet, client-server and stand-alone use. *New Positions Created (6):* Marketing Specialist; Marketing Writer; International

Channel Manager; International Sales Co-ordinator; Unix Software Developers; Sales Coordinators.

CIMTEK AUTOMATION SYSTEMS
Att: Human Resources Manager
5328 John Lucas Drive
Burlington, ON L7L 6A6

Tel. 905-331-6338
Fax 905-331-6339
Email .... hr@cimtek.com
Website .... www.cimtek.com

Employer Background: CIMTEK Automation Systems is a supplier of automated test solutions, primarily to the automotive, electronics, telecom and utility industries. *New Positions Created (41):* Internal Stores Assistant; Senior Photonics Test Engineer; Senior Software Systems Integrator; Applications Engineer; Director, Marketing; Intermediate Mechanical Systems Integrator; Intermediate / Senior Software Systems Integrator; Junior Software Systems Integrator; Production Technicians, Electrical Assembly (2); Sales Executive; Senior Datacom / Telecom Test Engineer; Senior Electrical Systems Integrator; Senior Photonics Engineer; Administrative Assistant; Director of Marketing; Engineering Administrator; Intermediate Photonics Engineer; Intermediate / Senior Software Systems Integrators (2); Junior Buyer; Junior Electrical Systems Integrator; Junior Software Systems Integrator; Mechanical Integration Manager; Production Technicians, Electrical Assembly (2); Sales Executive; Senior Electrical Systems Integrators (2); Senior Mechanical Systems Integrator; Senior Mechanical Engineer / Technologist; Senior Electrical Engineer, Software; Electrical Engineer, Software; Senior Electrical Engineer / Technologist, Test and Measurement; Senior Mechanical Engineer / Technologist; Sales Executive; Senior Mechanical Engineer / Technologist; Human Resources Administrative Assistant; Database / Web Programmer; Intermediate / Senior Electrical Engineers / Technologists; Junior / Intermediate Software Engineers; Junior / Senior Mechanical Engineers / Technologists; Engineering Coordinator / Planner; Intermediate / Senior Electrical Test and Measurement Engineers / Technologists; Junior Mechanical Designer / Engineer.

CINAR ANIMATION
Att: Human Resources
1055 Rene-Levesque East
Montréal, QC H2L 4S5

Tel. 514-843-7070
Fax 514-843-7488
Email .... hr@cinar.com
Website .... www.cinar.com

Employer Background: CINAR Animation is an integrated entertainment and education company that develops, produces and distributes non-violent, quality programming and supplemental educational products for children, families and educators. *New Positions Created (2):* Producer, Animation; Producer, Live Action Production.

CINNZEO BAKERY & CINNAMON TREASURES
Att: Norm Swen
6910 Farrell Road SE
Calgary, AB T2H 0T1

Tel. 403-255-4556
Fax 403-259-5124
Website .... www.cinnzeo.com

Employer Background: Cinnzeo Bakery & Cinnamon Treasures is a specialty retail bakery company. *New Positions Created (2):* Managers / Assistant Managers; Training Manager.

CINRAM INTERNATIONAL INC.
Att: Human Resources
2255 Markham Road
Toronto, ON M1B 2W3

Tel. 416-298-8190
Fax 416-298-0627
Email ...... human.resources@cinram.com
Website .... www.cinram.ca

Employer Background: Cinram International Inc. is one of the world's largest independent manufacturers of pre-recorded multimedia products. *New Positions Created (5):* Senior Programmer / Analyst; Controller; EDI Programmer / Analyst; Video Customer Service Representative; Customer Service Representative, Video Services.

CINTAS CANADA LTD.
Att: Nada Cian, Human Resources
6300 Kennedy Road, Unit 3
Mississauga, ON L5T 2X5

Tel. 905-670-4409
Fax 905-670-4435
Email .... shorej@cintas.com
Website .... www.cintas.com

Employer Background: Cintas Canada Ltd. is a leading provider of corporate identity uniform programs. *New Positions Created (4):* Human Resources Manager; Sales Associates; Sales Representatives; Sales Service Representatives.

CIOT MARBLE & GRANITE INC.
Att: Human Resources Manager
8899 Jane Street
Concord, ON L4K 2M6

Tel. 416-739-8000
Fax 905-660-3818
Website .... www.ciot.com

Employer Background: Ciot Marble & Granite Inc. is a leader in the stone industry. *New Positions Created (3):* Sales Manager; Architectural and Designer Sales Representative; Warehouse Manager.

CIRCA COMMUNICATIONS LTD.
Att: Human Resources Manager
1000 - 14th Street West
North Vancouver, BC V7P 3P3

Tel. 604-990-5415
Fax 604-990-5475
Email .... positions@circa.ca
Website .... www.circa.ca

Employer Background: Circa Communications is a leader in voice-over Internet protocol (VoIP) telephone terminal design. *New*

Positions Created (11): Electronics Manufacturing Engineer; Field Applications Engineers; Network and Information Systems Engineer / Administrator; Manufacturing Engineers; Product Managers; Field Applications Engineers / FAE (2); Marketing Administrator; Office Administrative Assistant; Product Managers (2); Senior Software Engineers (2); Software Engineers (4).

CIRCADENCE CORPORATION
Att: Human Resources Manager
1 Adelaide Street East, Suite 2800
Toronto, ON M5C 2V9

Tel. 416-488-8898
Fax 416-488-8141
Email .... careers@toronto.circadence.com
Website .... www.circadence.com

Employer Background: Founded in 1993, Circadence Corporation is a leading provider of Internet business and entertainment quality-of-service applications. *New Positions Created (6):* Development / Project Managers; Network Operation Center Systems Administrators; Quality Assurance Software Testers; Software Developers; Unix Systems Administrators; Wireless Software Architect.

CIRCLE OF CARE
Att: Executive Director
530 Wilson Avenue, 4th Floor
Toronto, ON M3H 1T6

Tel. 416-635-2860
Fax 416-635-1692
Email .... hiring@circleofcare.com
Website .... www.circleofcare.com

Employer Background: Circle of Care is a non-profit, home-based healthcare organization. *New Positions Created (2):* Director of Finance and Administration; Quality Management Specialist.

CIRCON SYSTEMS CORPORATION
Att: Human Resources Manager
6651 Fraserwood Place, Suite 110
Richmond, BC V6W 1J3

Email .... jobs@circon.com
Website .... www.circon.com

Employer Background: Circon Systems Corporation designs control systems for smart buildings. *New Positions Created (8):* Applications Programmer; AutoCAD Technical Support Representative; Contract Marketing Specialist; Engineering Services Representative; Estimator; Hardware Engineer; Junior Technical Support Position; Senior Technical Support.

CIRCUIT GRAPHICS LTD.
Att: Personnel Department
8070 Winston Street
Burnaby, BC V5A 2H5

Tel. 604-420-3313
Fax 604-420-7525
Email .... boards@cirgraph.com
Website .... www.cirgraph.com

Employer Background: Circuit Graphics manufactures printed circuit boards. *New Positions Created (6):* Process Engineer;

Sales Director; Electronics CAD / CAM Technician; Lab Technician; QA Auditor; Technical Documentation Specialist.

CIRQUE DU SOLEIL
Att: HR Manager, Americas Division
1217 Notre-Dame East
Montréal, QC H2L 2R3
Fax 514-522-6362
Email ..... cv@america.cirquedusoleil.com
Website .... www.cirquedusoleil.com
Employer Background: Cirque du Soleil is an international entertainment organization, with operations in artistic creation, production, performance and merchandising. *New Positions Created (9):* Secretary; Tour Assets Management Clerk; Group Insurance Management Adviser; Secretary to the Tour Development Director; Tour Assets Manager; Tour Development Agent; Human Resources Technician; Administration and Tour Services Director; Tour Development Coordinator, North American Tour.

CIRQUE DU SOLEIL
Att: Human Resources Department
8400 - 2nd Avenue
Montréal, QC H1Z 4M6
Tel. 514-722-2324
Fax 514-723-7620
Email .. recru@montreal.cirquedusoleil.com
Website .... www.cirquedusoleil.com
Employer Background: Cirque du Soleil is an international entertainment organization, with operations in artistic creation, production, performance and merchandising. *New Positions Created (48):* External Buyer; Head of Consolidation; Secretary to the Logistical Support Director; Assistant to the Senior Vice-President and Chief Information Officer; Executive Secretary, Creation Service; Internal Audit Technician; Secretary; Senior Human Resources Advisor, Employee Benefits; Technical Analyst / Telephone Support Position; Accountant, Financial Data Structure and Consolidation; Analyst, AutoCAD; Analyst, Macintosh Platform; Artistic Liaison, Production; Business Analyst, IT; Financial Analyst II; IT Systems Analyst; Secretary to the Head of Manufacturing, Costume Shop; Secretary to the Head of Products, Costume Shop; Secretary to the Logistical Support Director; Senior Internal Auditor; ABAP Programmer / Analyst, SAP; Acrobatic Talent Scout; Analyst, Complexes Cirque; Assistant Corporate Tax Advisor; Assistant to Acrobatic Talent Scouts; Budget Analyst, Creation Service; Building Superintendent; Coordinator to the Architectural Team, Complexes Cirque; Corporate Communications Agent; Department Secretary, Public Affairs; Draftsperson; Dyer; Executive Secretary, Creation Service; Financial Data Structure Supervisor, SAP Master Data; Hatmaker; IT Project Supervisor, Marketing; IT Security Architect; Payroll Clerk; Quality Control Supervisor, Advertising And Graphic Design Department; Secretary, Artistic Department; Secretary, Business and Legal Affairs; Secretary, Linguistic Services Team; Shoe Laster; Warehouse Clerk; Corporate Tax Advisor and Assistant Corporate

Tax Advisor; Individual Tax Advisor; Transfer Pricing Tax Advisor; Product Developer, Hard Goods.

CIRQUE ELOIZE
Att: Technical Department
4230 Rue Hogan, 1st Floor
Montréal, QC H2H 2N3
Tel. 514-596-3838
Fax 514-596-3938
Email .... eloize@cirque-eloize.com
Website .... www.cirque-eloize.com
Employer Background: Cirque Eloize is an entertainment company, specializing in theatre, dance, acrobatics, music and circus arts. *New Positions Created (5):* Head Rigger; Light Board Operator; Rigger; Stage Manager; Technical Positions.

CISTEL TECHNOLOGY INC.
Att: Human Resources Manager
210 Colonnade Road, Suite 204
Nepean, ON K2E 7L5
Tel. 613-723-8344
Email .... jobs@cistel.com
Website .... www.cistel.com
Employer Background: Cistel Technology Inc. delivers software and hardware engineering consulting and professional information technology services to the high-tech industry and government sectors. *New Positions Created (4):* Help Desk Technician; Desktop Technician, Inventory; Web Database Developer / Analyst; Web Developer.

CITADEL GENERAL ASSURANCE COMPANY, THE
Att: Robert Kozak
1090 West Georgia Street
Suite 1350, Vancouver Insurance Centre
Vancouver, BC V6E 3V7
Tel. 604-684-6381
Fax 604-684-9195
Website .... www.citadel.ca
Employer Background: The Citadel General Assurance Company provides commercial and personal automobile, property, accident and sickness insurance. *New Positions Created (3):* Receptionist / Typist; Commercial Lines Underwriting Assistant; Senior Commercial Lines Underwriter.

CITADEL GENERAL ASSURANCE COMPANY, THE
Att: Sandy Tantalo
1075 Bay Street
Toronto, ON M5S 2W5
Tel. 416-928-8500
Fax 416-928-1553
Email .... stantalo@citadel.ca
Website .... www.citadel.ca
Employer Background: The Citadel General Assurance Company provides commercial and personal automobile, property, accident and sickness insurance. *New Positions Created (11):* Commercial Lines Underwriting Assistant; Business Development Executive; Senior Personal Lines Underwriter; Accident Benefits Claims Specialist; Bilingual L&H Claims Adjuster; Individual Health Claims

Adjuster; Supervisor, Accident Benefits Claims; Auto Underwriting Specialist, Commercial Lines; Actuarial Student; Administrative Assistant; Automobile Supervisor, Commercial Lines.

CITÉ NISSAN
Att: Human Resources Director
3500 Jean-Talon West
Montréal, QC H3R 2E8
Tel. 514-739-3175
Fax 514-735-1250
Email .... info@citenissan.com
Website .... www.citenissan.com
Employer Background: Cité Nissan is Montreal's largest Nissan dealership. *New Positions Created (6):* Salesperson, New Vehicles; Parks Clerk; Administrative Assistant; Coordinator, Service Department; Customer Service Advisor; Sales Representative, Pre-Owned Vehicles.

CITIBANK CANADA
Att: Human Resources
123 Front Street West, Suite 1900
Toronto, ON M5J 2M3
Tel. 416-947-5500
Fax 416-947-5387
Website .... www.citibank.com/canada
Employer Background: Citibank Canada is the second-largest foreign-owned (Schedule II) bank in Canada, with over 1,500 employees in Toronto, Montreal, Calgary, London and Vancouver. *New Positions Created (5):* Investment Finance (Credit) Specialist; Investment Specialist; Assistant Vice-President, Marketing; Associate, Foreign Exchange; Associate, Global Capital Structuring.

CITIFINANCIAL CANADA INC.
Att: Linda Petty, HR Director
201 Queens Avenue
London, ON N6A 1J1
Fax 519-672-8614
Website .... www.citifinancial.com
Employer Background: CitiFinancial Canada Inc. (formerly Associated Financial Services of Canada Ltd.) is a Fortune 500 company and member of Citicorp. *New Positions Created (2):* Customer Service Representative; Management Trainees.

CITIZENS BANK OF CANADA
Att: Human Relations
815 West Hastings Street, Suite 401
Vancouver, BC V6C 1B4
Tel. 604-682-7171
Fax 604-708-7787
Email .... careers@citizensbank.ca
Website .... www.citizensbank.ca
Employer Background: Citizens Bank of Canada was formed in 1997 by Vancouver City Savings Credit Union (VanCity) as a "branchless" bank, serving customers over the Internet and by telephone. *New Positions Created (3):* Manager, Foreign Exchange Sales; Member Service Specialist; Member Service Specialist.

CITY BUICK PONTIAC CADILLAC LTD.
Att: Human Resources
1900 Victoria Park Avenue
Toronto, ON M1R 1T6

Tel. 416-751-5920
Fax 416-751-3691
Email .... humanresources@citybuick.com
Website .... www.citybuickdirect.com
Employer Background: City Buick Pontiac
Cadillac Ltd. is an automotive dealership.
New Positions Created (2): Leasing Reps; Automotive Sales Professional Position.

CITY CHEVROLET OLDSMOBILE LTD.
Att: Paul Burroughs, President
155 Cannon Street East
Hamilton, ON L8L 2A6

Tel. 905-527-7003
Fax 905-527-3585
Email .... paulb@citychev.com
Website .... www.citychev.com
Employer Background: City Chevrolet
Oldsmobile is a General Motors dealership.
New Positions Created (5): Service Manager;
Body / Collision Mgr; Sales & Leasing Representative / Assistant Business Manager;
Business Mgr; Used Vehicle Sales Manager.

CITYXPRESS.COM CORP.
Att: Human Resources Manager
1727 West Broadway, Suite 200
Vancouver, BC V6J 4W6

Tel. 604-638-3800
Fax 604-638-3808
Email .... info@cityxpress.com
Website .... www.cityxpress.com
Employer Background: CityXpress.com
Corp. develops Internet products to power
local e-commerce. *New Positions Created
(4):* Junior Software Developer; Lead Software Developer; Software Developer; Software Developer.

CIVIL SERVICE CO-OPERATIVE CREDIT SOCIETY / CS CO-OP
Att: Human Resources
400 Albert Street
Ottawa, ON K1R 5B2

Tel. 613-560-0100
Fax 613-560-6385
Email .... query@cscoop.ca
Website .... www.cscoop.ca
Employer Background: CS CO-OP, Ontario's
first credit union, provides innovative financial services to over 143,000 members. *New
Positions Created (14):* Call Centre Associate; Supervisor, Financial Services; Assistant Manager, Marketing; Manager, Applications Development and Support; Manager,
Commercial Credit Products; Manager, Accounting; Community and Public Relations
Officer; Computer Operator; Internal Auditor; Member Services Associates; Procurement Officer; Marketing Manager; Branch
Manager; Member Services Associates.

CJP ARCHITECTS
Att: Human Resources Administrator
301 - 6th Street
New Westminster, BC V3L 3A7

Tel. 604-526-2764
Fax 604-526-6995
Email .... info@cjp.dwg.com
Website .... www.dwg.com/cjp
Employer Background: Established in 1954,
CJP Architects is a multidisciplinary firm,
with offices in New Westminster and
Qualicum Beach. *New Positions Created (3):*
Senior Interior Designer; Contract Administrator; Senior Architects (2).

CLARICA LIFE INSURANCE COMPANY
Att: James Abbott,
Regional Agency Manager
227 King Street South
PO Box 1601, Stn Waterloo
Waterloo, ON N2J 4C5

Tel. 519-888-2290
Fax 519-888-2206
Email .... james.abbott@clarica.com
Website .... www.clarica.com
Employer Background: Clarica Life Insurance Company is one of Canada's fastest
growing financial organizations, specializing in investments, insurance and employee
benefits. *New Positions Created (6):* Mutual
Fund Marketing Manager; Health Insurance
Sales / Marketing Specialist; Assistant Manager, Commercial Mortgages; Manager,
Commercial Mortgages; Manager, Construction Lending; Employee Education and
Communication Manager.

CLARICA LIFE INSURANCE COMPANY
Att: Membership Services
99 Bank Street, Suite 908
Ottawa, ON K1P 5A3

Fax 613-560-7813
Email .... nancy.doran@clarica.com
Website .... www.clarica.com
Employer Background: Established in 1870,
Clarica Life Insurance Company is a leading Canadian financial solutions company,
specializing in investments, insurance and
employee benefits. *New Positions Created
(4):* Bilingual Customer Service Representatives; Bilingual Customer Service Representatives; Benefits Consultant; Bilingual
Customer Service Representatives.

CLARICA LIFE INSURANCE COMPANY
Att: Membership Services
1555 Peel Street
Montréal, QC H3A 3L8

Fax 514-282-9794
Email .... hrjobs@clarica.com
Website .... www.clarica.com
Employer Background: Established in 1870,
Clarica Life is a leading Canadian financial
solutions company, specializing in investments, insurance and employee benefits.
New Positions Created (2): Bilingual Employee Education & Communication Mgr;
Regional Sales Mgr, Health Insurance.

CLARIDGE HOMES
Att: Human Resources
210 Gladstone Avenue, Suite 2001
Ottawa, ON K2P 0Y6

Tel. 613-233-6030

Fax 613-233-8290
Email .... finance@claridgehomes.com
Website .... www.claridgehomes.com
Employer Background: Claridge Homes is
the second-largest homebuilder in Ottawa-Carleton. *New Positions Created (4):* Director, Property Mgmnt; Senior Accountant; Assistant Controller; Site Superintendents.

CLARK BUILDERS
Att: Human Resources Manager
8429 - 24th Street
Edmonton, AB T6P 1L3

Tel. 780-417-6700
Fax 780-449-1048
Email ..... g.clark@edm.clarkbuilders.com
Website .... www.clarkbuilders.com
Employer Background: Founded in 1978,
Clark is a building contractor, specializing
in cold climate, commercial, industrial,
metal and multi-family residential projects.
New Positions Created (2): Intermediate &
Senior Project Managers; Intermediate &
Senior Project Managers.

CLARK, WILSON
Att: Nadia Morrison, HR Manager
885 West Georgia Street, Suite 800
Vancouver, BC V6C 3H1

Tel. 604-687-5700
Fax 604-687-6314
Email .... nem@cwilson.com
Website .... www.cwilson.com
Employer Background: Clark, Wilson is a
business law firm with 60 lawyers. *New Positions Created (2):* Controller; Controller.

CLASS SOFTWARE SOLUTIONS LTD.
Att: Human Resources Manager
6400 Roberts Street
Suite 300, Escom Building
Burnaby, BC V5G 4C9

Tel. 604-438-7361
Fax 604-432-9708
Email .... careers@classinfo.com
Website .... www.classinfo.com
Employer Background: Class Software Solutions Ltd. develops program, facility and
cash management solutions for local government. The company has over 10,000 licensed users. *New Positions Created (11):*
Customer Care Consultants; Solutions /
Sales Consultants; Software Developers;
Customer Care Consultants; Marketing
Team Leader; Software Solution (Sales)
Consultants; Business Unit Manager; Junior
Accounting Clerk; Software Developers;
Software Testers; Vice President, Marketing.

CLASSWAVE WIRELESS INC.
Att: Human Resources Manager
5160 Yonge Street, 12th Floor
Toronto, ON M2N 6L9

Tel. 416-730-8181
Fax 416-730-8448
Website .... www.classwave.com
Employer Background: Founded in 1998,
Classwave Wireless Inc. is a wireless polyphony company, allowing enterprises and
organizations to expand their information

services to a mobile audience. *New Positions Created (19):* Accounts Payable Clerk; Configuration Management Specialist ; Engineering Logistics Prime; Environmental Support Engineer; Intermediate Java Software Developers; Mobile Device Developers; Principal Consultant; Product Manager; Product Specialist ; Project Managers; Quality Assurance Manager; Senior Consultants; Senior Java Developers; Senior Software Developers; Software Developer; Software Development Team Leader / Manager; Systems Engineer; Technical Consultants; User Interface Specialists.

CLAYSON STEEL
Att: Manager, Human Resources
133 East Drive
Brampton, ON L6T 1B5
Tel. 905-790-7100
Fax 905-790-9004
Email .... tkamzol@claysonsteel.com
Website .... www.claysonsteel.com
Employer Background: Clayson Steel is a leading producer of steel parts and components for equipment manufacturers. *New Positions Created (3):* Territory Manager; Inside Sales Trainee; Outside / Inside Sales Representatives.

CLIENTLOGIC CORP.
Att: Human Resources Department
3250 Bloor Street West
East Tower, 10th Floor
Toronto, ON M8X 2X9
Tel. 416-239-4777
Fax 416-207-2814
Email .... hr@clientlogic.com
Website .... www.clientlogic.com
Employer Background: ClientLogic Corp. (formerly North Direct Response), a subsidiary of Onex Corporation, provides customer communications and call centre solutions. *New Positions Created (7):* Call Center Supervisor; Inbound Sales Agents; Level One Technical Support Agents; Bilingual Sales Agent; Bilingual Technical Support Positions; Inbound Sales Customer Service Agent; Level One Technical Support Agents.

CLIFTON ASSOCIATES LTD.
Att: Manager, Human Resources
665 - 8th Street SW, Suite 300
Calgary, AB T2P 3K7
Tel. 403-263-2556
Website .... www.clifton.ca
Employer Background: Clifton Associates Ltd. is a geotechnical and geoenvironmental engineering consulting firm. *New Positions Created (4):* Civil Engineering Technologists; Environmental Engineering Technologists; Junior Engineers / Hydrogeologists; Senior and Intermediate Geotechnical Engineers / Hydrogeologists.

CLIFTON ND LEA CONSULTING INC.
Att: Dan Meidl, PEng, President
665 - 8th Street SW, Suite 720
Calgary, AB T2P 3K7
Tel. 403-263-2499
Fax 403-264-1179

Email .... dmeidl@clifton-ndlea.com
Website .... www.clifton-ndlea.com
Employer Background: Clifton ND Lea Consulting provides services in transportation planning and engineering. *New Positions Created (4):* CAD Designers; Senior and Intermediate Bridge Engineers; Senior and Intermediate Transportation Engineers; Senior Municipal Engineer.

CLIMAN TRANSPORT SERVICES
Att: Marc Belanger
4415 Fairway Street
Lachine, QC H8T 1B5
Tel. 514-639-4210
Fax 514-639-4496
Employer Background: Climan Transport Services is a cross-border transportation company. *New Positions Created (3):* Customer Service Position; Dispatcher; Human Resources Manager.

CLINIDATA
Att: Bev Rezebergs
10 Four Seasons Place, Suite 200
Toronto, ON M9B 6H7
Fax 416-622-2605
Email .... jobs@clinidata.com
Website .... www.clinidata.com
Employer Background: Clinidata, in partnership with provincial governments and private sector clients, provides toll-free telephone triage and health information technology solutions. *New Positions Created (4):* Clinical Services Manager; Director of Operations; Telehealth Nurses; Telehealth Nurses.

CLINTRIALS BIORESEARCH LTD.
Att: Human Resources Manager
87 Senneville Road
Senneville, QC H9X 3R3
Tel. 514-630-8200
Fax 514-630-8234
Email .... hr@ctbr.com
Website .... www.ctbr.com
Employer Background: CTBR provides preclinical research services to pharmaceutical, biopharmaceutical, chemical and medical device companies worldwide. *New Positions Created (7):* Chemists / Analysts, Immunochemistry; Chemists, Analytical Chemistry and Bioanalysis; Scientific Director, Mass Spectrometry; Senior Research Chemists, Mass Spectrometry; Statisticians; Coordinator, Market Research and Sales; Scientist.

CLOAKWARE CORPORATION
Att: Human Resources Manager
260 Hearst Way, Suite 311
Kanata, ON K2L 3H1
Tel. 613-271-9446
Fax 613-271-9447
Email .... jobs@cloakware.com
Website .... www.cloakware.com
Employer Background: Cloakware Corporation develops security technology that converts software into a tamper-resistant form, enabling secure distributed systems and lower security costs. *New Positions Created*

(12): Application Engineer / Software Engineer; Business Development Manager; Compiler Designer; Compiler Testers; Marketing and Communications Manager / Director; Project Manager, Product Development Group; Senior Cryptographer / Mathematician; Application Engineer; Business Development Manager; Compiler Designer; Cryptographer / Mathematician; Marketing Communications Manager.

CLOCKWORK.CA
Att: Human Resources Manager
4950 Yonge Street, Suite 512
Toronto, ON M2N 6K1
Tel. 416-222-8990
Fax 416-222-9066
Email .... resume@clockwork.ca
Website .... www.clockwork.ca
Employer Background: Clockwork.ca is a leader in Internet business framework solutions, serving 500 corporations across Canada. *New Positions Created (2):* Internet Business Framework Consultants; SAP Basis Technology Consultants.

CLSC VERDUN / COTE SAINT-PAUL
Att: Department of Human Resources
400 de L'Eglise
Verdun, QC H4G 2M4
Tel. 514-766-0546
Fax 514-762-4139
Employer Background: CLSC is a public and community health and social services establishment. *New Positions Created (4):* Baccalaureate Nurse; Nurse; Occupational Therapist; Social Services Technicians.

CLUB MONACO INTERNATIONAL
Att: Recruitment Team
430 King Street West
Toronto, ON M5V 1L5
Tel. 416-585-4896
Fax 416-585-4176
Email .... recruitment@clubmonaco.com
Website .... www.clubmonaco.com
Employer Background: Club Monaco International sells clothing for men and women, accessories, cosmetics and items for the home at 76 stores worldwide. *New Positions Created (14):* Accounts Payable Clerk; Production Coordinator; Receptionist; Event / Public Relations Coordinator; Senior Planner, Caban; Manager, Wholesale Merchandising; Regional Manager, Loss Prevention; Account Development and Education Coordinator; Assistant Product Developer - Women's Accessories; Fabric Assistant; Marketing Coordinator, Cosmetics Division; National Education Manager; Receptionist; Regional Account Manager.

CMC ELECTRONICS INC.
Att: Human Resources
415 Legget Drive, PO Box 13330
Kanata, ON K2K 2B2
Tel. 613-592-6500
Website .... www.cmcelectronics.ca
Employer Background: CMC Electronics Inc. (formerly BAE Systems Canada Inc. and

Canadian Marconi Company) is a leader in high-tech electronics for the aerospace and communications markets. *New Positions Created (38):* Contracts Administrator (Customer Support, Repair and Overhaul); Program Manager - Avionics; Human Factors Engineer / Design Specialist; Antenna Specialist; Assistant Manager, Integrated Logistics Support (ILS); Design Specialist / Avionics Systems Engineering; Design Specialist / Human Factors Engineer; Intermediate Design Specialist / Software Quality Assurance; Intermediate Hardware Engineer; Intermediate Level Buyer; Intermediate Software Developer; Junior Hardware Engineer ; Manager, Aviation Electronics Engineering ; Mechanical CAD Design Specialist; Product / Program Manager, Aeronautical Communications; Senior Technical Representative (Customer Support); Software Simulation Engineer; Systems Engineer / Human Factors Engineering; Project Engineer, Avionics; Software Quality Assurance Specialist; Systems Engineer, Avionics; Senior Program Accountant; Avionics Systems Engineers; Design Specialist / Human Factors Engineer; Hardware Engineers; Intermediate Design Specialist; Intermediate Software Developers; Junior Hardware Engineer; Marketing Manager; Product Manager, Airborne Communications Group; Program Manager, Airborne Communications Group; Program Manager, Human Factors Engineering Product; Project Engineer, Airborne Communications Group; RF Engineer; Senior Design Specialist; Senior Technical Representative; Software Quality Assurance Positions; Systems Engineer.

CMC ELECTRONICS INC.
Att: Human Resources
600 Dr. Frederik Philips Boulevard
St-Laurent, QC H4M 2S9
Tel. 514-748-3148
Fax 514-748-3018
Website .... www.cmcelectronics.ca
Employer Background: CMC Electronics Inc. (formerly BAE Systems Canada Inc. and Canadian Marconi Company) is a leader in high-tech electronics for the aerospace and communications markets. *New Positions Created (69):* Antenna Engineer, Aeronautical Communications; Avionics Integration Engineer; Cost Accounting Accountant; Designer, Circuit Packaging; Electrical Engineer (RF, Analog, Digital, Power Supply); Engineer, R&D (Artificial Vision System); Field Service Engineer, Communications; Intermediate Hardware Engineer; Intermediate Software Developers; Junior Hardware Engineer; Mechanical CAD Engineer; Mechanical Engineer; Project Engineer, Avionics; Recruiter / Generalist; RF Design Engineer; Senior Design Specialist, Testing; Software Engineer, Artificial Vision System; Software Engineer, Avionics; Software Engineer, GPS OEM; Software Simulation Engineer; Systems Engineer, Avionics; Systems Engineer, Human Factors Engineering; Systems Engineer, Military Communications; Technical Specialist; Technical Writer; Test Engineer; Manufacturing Manager; Project Manager, Military Communications; De-

signer, Circuit Packaging; Field Service Engineer; Hardware Quality Engineer; International Marketing Position; Mechanical Engineer; Program Manager, Display Group; Program Manager, Mature Products; SMQA Engineer; Software Engineer, Avionics; Software Engineer, GPS / OEM; Technical Specialist, Engineering; Technical Specialist, Production; Technical Specialist, Software; Electrical Engineer; Manufacturing Manager; Project Manager, Military Communications; Software Quality Assurance Engineer; Systems Engineer, Communications Engineering; Test Engineer; Administrative Assistant; Contracts Administrator; Electronic Components Assembly Operator; Electronics Technician; Industrial Methods Analyst, Documentation and Manufacturing; Manufacturing Software Coordinator; Production Inspector; Supervisor, Traffic / Transport / Packing; Designer, Circuit Packaging; Electrical Engineer; Field Service Engineer; International Marketing Position; Manufacturing Manager; Marketing Manager; Master Scheduler; Mechanical Engineer; Software Engineer, Avionics; Software Engineer, GPS OEM; Software Quality Assurance Position; Systems Engineer; Test Engineer; Test Equipment Technician, SSD.

CMC ENGINEERING AND MANAGEMENT LIMITED
Att: Personnel Manager
3683 East Hastings Street, Suite 33
Vancouver, BC V5K 4Z7
Tel. 604-294-6483
Fax 604-294-0457
Email .... info@cmceml.com
Website .... www.cmcengineering.com
Employer Background: CMC Engineering and Management Limited provides multidisciplinary engineering and management services to the civil / structural, mechanical and electrical engineering sectors. *New Positions Created (3):* Drafting Personnel; Intermediate Engineers & Technologists; Senior Engineers & Technologists.

CMD GROUP
Att: Human Resources
280 Yorkland Boulevard
Toronto, ON M2J 4Z6
Email .... m.losier@cmdg.com
Website .... www.cmdg.com
Employer Background: CMD Group is a global provider of product, project, costing and statistical data to the construction industry. *New Positions Created (6):* Client Support Rep; Client Support Rep; Sales Professionals; Customer Support Representative; Customer Technical Support Specialist; Project Management Software Sales Position.

CML ATC TECHNOLOGIES INC.
Att: Human Resources
490 St. Joseph Boulevard, Suite 200
Hull, QC J8Y 3Y7
Email .... hr@cmlatc.com
Website .... www.cmlatc.com
Employer Background: CML ATC Technologies Inc. manufactures and markets state-

of-the-art voice communication systems for the air traffic control and the command, communication and control markets. *New Positions Created (3):* Materials Controller; Sales Support Specialist; Vice-President, Sales & Marketing.

CML EMERGENCY SERVICES, INC.
Att: Human Resources
75 Boulevard de la Technologie
Hull, QC J8Z 3G4
Tel. 819-778-2053
Fax 819-778-3408
Email .... cmlhr@cmles.com
Website .... www.cmles.com
Employer Background: CML Emergency Services, Inc. designs, develops and manufactures hardware and software applications for mission-critical applications such as 911 and radio dispatch. *New Positions Created (12):* Master Scheduler; Senior Buyer; Business and Channel Development Mgr; Director of Sales; Hardware Designer; Repair Technologist; Account Mgr, Business Development; Information Technology Manager; Multimedia and Graphic Artist; Programmer Analyst; Technical Sales Support Specialist; Technical Services Specialist.

CML VERSATEL INC.
Att: Human Resources Manager
80 Jean Proulx Street
Hull, QC J8Z 1W1
Tel. 819-771-0011
Fax 819-771-0031
Email .... careers@cmlversatel.com
Website .... www.cmlversatel.com
Employer Background: CML Versatel Inc. designs open, carrier-grade, programmable switching platforms using leading-edge technology for converged or traditional networks. *New Positions Created (3):* Human Resources Manager; Software Verification Engineer; VP Manufacturing & Quality Processes.

CMP DESIGN
Att: Human Resources Manager
215 Terence Matthews Crescent, Suite 2
Kanata, ON K2M 1X5
Tel. 613-271-2861
Fax 613-271-2862
Email .... careers@cmpdesign.com
Website .... www.cmpdesign.com
Employer Background: CMP Design, part of CMP Group, is a leading electromechanical design engineering firm, specializing in telecom and electronic systems packaging. *New Positions Created (3):* Milling Machine Operator; Network Administrator; Sales Professional.

CO-EX-TEC INDUSTRIES
Att: Human Resources Department
140 Staffern Drive
Concord, ON L4K 2X3
Tel. 416-736-8368
Fax 905-738-1826
Website .... www.magna.ca
Employer Background: Co-Ex-Tec Industries, a division of Magna International, is a

leading supplier of co-extrusion and injection moulded parts to the automotive industry. *New Positions Created (13):* Extrusion Rolling Mill Set-Up Operator; Extrusion Line Operator; Maintenance Line Electrician; Packaging Engineer; Process Improvement Engineer; Set-up Technician, Injection Moulding; Quote Cost Estimator; Industrial Millwright Mechanic; Maintenance Electrician; Maintenance Mechanic; Electrical Technician, Injection Moulding; Mould Maker; Senior Quality Assurance Engineer.

COAST CAPITAL SAVINGS
Att: Human Resource Services
5611 Cooney Road, Suite 300
Richmond, BC V6X 3J5
Tel. 604-273-8138
Fax 604-207-0462
Email .... recruit@richmondsavings.com
Website ..... www.coastcapitalsavings.com
Employer Background: Coast Capital Savings (formerly Richmond Savings and Pacific Coast Savings) is a large credit union. *New Positions Created (2):* Communications Advisor; Advertising and Branding Mgr.

COAST FOUNDATION SOCIETY
Att: Clerk-Typist
293 - 11th Avenue East
Vancouver, BC V5T 2C4
Tel. 604-872-3502
Fax 604-879-2363
Email .... hr@coastfoundation.com
Website .... www.coastfoundation.com
Employer Background: Established in 1974, the Coast Foundation Society provides housing, support and rehabilitation services to individuals recovering from mental illness. *New Positions Created (7):* Community Home Manager; Community Nurses; Program Managers; Employment Specialist; Mental Health Workers; Social Recreation Coordinator; Manager, Supported Housing.

COAST PLAZA HOTEL, THE
Att: Human Resources Department
1316 - 33rd Street NE
Calgary, AB T2A 6B6
Tel. 403-248-8888
Fax 403-235-4548
Email .... mmacleay@calgaryplaza.com
Website .... www.calgaryplaza.com
Employer Background: The Coast Plaza Hotel is one of Calgary's largest hotel catering and conference facilities. *New Positions Created (2):* Catering Manager; Human Resources Manager.

COAST PLAZA SUITE HOTEL, THE
Att: Human Resources Department
1763 Comox Street
Vancouver, BC V6G 1P6
Tel. 604-688-7711
Fax 604-685-7210
Website .... www.coasthotels.com
Employer Background: The Coast Plaza Suite Hotel is a four-star property located in Vancouver's trendy west end, near Stanley Park. *New Positions Created (2):* Chief Engineer; Director of Operations.

COCA-COLA BOTTLING COMPANY
Att: Human Resources Department
3851 - 23rd Street NE
Calgary, AB T2E 6T2
Tel. 403-291-3111
Fax 403-291-9433
Website .... www.cocacola.com
Employer Background: The Coca-Cola Bottling Company bottles and distributes Coca-Cola and other branded soft drink products. *New Positions Created (5):* Warehouse Supervisor; Accounts Receivable Clerk; Sales Professionals; QA Manager; Warehouse Mgr.

COCHRANE GROUP, THE
Att: Sophia Betegh
2150 West Broadway, Suite 200
Vancouver, BC V6K 4L9
Tel. 604-736-5421
Fax 604-736-1519
Email .... reception@cochrane-group.ca
Website .... www.cochrane-group.ca
Employer Background: The Cochrane Group specializes in engineering, applied science, architecture, planning and project management, with over 250 employees in 8 offices across Canada. *New Positions Created (3):* Civil Engineers; Electrical Engineer; Lead Structural Engineers.

COGECO CABLE INC.
Att: Recruitment Services
950 Syscon Rd., Box 5076, Station Main
Burlington, ON L7R 4S6
Tel. 905-333-5522
Fax 905-332-8426
Email .... nbales@internet.cgocable.net
Website .... www.cogeco.ca
Employer Background: Cogeco Cable Canada Inc. is one of Canada's largest cable providers, serving over 850,000 customers nationwide. *New Positions Created (3):* Communications Technician; Circuit Designer; Warehouse Coordinator.

COGENCY SEMICONDUCTOR INC.
Att: Human Resources Manager
144 Front Street West, Suite 600
Toronto, ON M5J 2L7
Tel. 416-217-0250
Fax 416-217-0256
Email .... yourfuture@cogency.com
Website .... www.cogency.com
Employer Background: Cogency Semiconductor Inc. develops high-performance semiconductors for the home networking market. *New Positions Created (11):* Analog IC Designer; ASIC Design Engineer; ASIC Physical Design Engineer; ASIC Test Engineer; Analog IC Designer; ASIC Design Engineer; ASIC Physical Design Engineer; ASIC Test Engineer; Office Assistant / Receptionist; Analog IC Designer; ASIC Physical Design Engineer.

COGENCY SEMICONDUCTOR INC.
Att: Human Resources Manager
362 Terry Fox Drive, Suite 210
Kanata, ON K2K 2P5
Tel. 613-270-9300
Fax 613-270-9995
Email .... yourfuture@cogency.com
Website .... www.cogency.com
Employer Background: Cogency Semiconductor Inc. develops high-performance semiconductors for the home networking market. *New Positions Created (13):* DSP Design Engineer; Hardware Design Engineer; Field Application Engineer; Senior Corporate Field Application Engineer; DSP Design Engineer; Hardware Design Engineer; Digital Design Engineer; DSP Developer; Embedded Software Developer; Field Applications Engineer; Product Verification Engineer; System Architect; Windows Device Driver Developer.

COGNICASE
Att: Recruiting Services
155 University Avenue, 15th Floor
Toronto, ON M5H 3B6
Tel. 416-369-9700
Fax 416-369-1994
Email .... lino.ribeiro@cognicase.ca
Website .... www.cognicase.com
Employer Background: Founded in 1991, Cognicase is an e-commerce consulting firm, with 3,800 employees in 20 branches worldwide. *New Positions Created (2):* Programmer Analyst; Technology Analyst.

COGNICASE
Att: Recruiting Services
1080 Beaver Hall Hill, Suite 2000
Montréal, QC H2Z 1S8
Tel. 514-866-6161
Fax 514-866-6260
Email .... careers3.montreal@cognicase.ca
Website .... www.cognicase.ca
Employer Background: Founded in 1991, Cognicase is an e-commerce consulting firm, with 3,800 employees in 20 branches worldwide. *New Positions Created (4):* Clarify Specialist; GEMMS Analyst / Programmer; Pick Basic Analyst / Programmer; WAVE Technical Support / Integration on MAC OS Positions (3).

COGNIS CANADA CORPORATION
Att: Human Resources
2290 Argentia Road
Mississauga, ON L5N 6H9
Tel. 905-542-7550
Fax 905-542-7566
Website .... www.cognis.com
Employer Background: Cognis Canada Corporation is a leading producer and marketer of specialty chemicals. *New Positions Created (2):* Customer Service Representative; Quality Control Chemist.

COGNOS INC.
Att: Corporate HR Department
3755 Riverside Drive, PO Box 9707
Ottawa, ON K1G 4K9
Tel. 613-738-1440
Email .... jobs@cognos.com
Website .... www.cognos.com
Employer Background: Cognos Inc. supplies business intelligence software, allowing us-

ers to extract critical information through data access, reporting, analysis and forecasting. *New Positions Created (27):* Application Developer, Information Engineering Services; Intermediate / Senior Engineers; Intermediate / Senior Software Engineers; Manager, Compensation and Benefits; Manager, Procurement and Assets; Manager, Server Technology; QC Analyst III, Visualizer; Sales Support Specialist; Senior Quality Control Analyst, Upfront; Software Engineer II; Software Engineer III / IV; Test Team Leader / Analyst; Application Developer; Business Development Representative, Eastern Canada; Consolidation and Reporting Analyst; Customer Support Technical Analyst; Date Warehouse Modeler; German Translator; Human-Computer Interaction Specialist; Manager, Taxation; Marketing Specialist, Internet Marketing; Performance Measurement Developer; Purchasing Analyst; Senior Business Intelligence Lifecycle Advisor; Senior Consultant; Web Developer; Writing Support Specialist, Information Engineering Services.

COHOES FASHIONS INC.
Att: Human Resources Manager
4910 Jean Talon Boulevard West
Montréal, QC H4P 1W9
Fax 514-736-0592
Email .... ami@cohoes.ca
Employer Background: Cohoes Fashions Inc. is a low-cost provider of retail goods and services. *New Positions Created (2):* Chief Operating Officer; Manager, Merchandise Planning.

COHOS EVAMY PARTNERS, THE
Att: Dale Knutson, PEng
10154 - 108th Street
Edmonton, AB T5J 1L3
Tel. 780-429-1580
Fax 780-429-2848
Email .... edmonton@cohos-evamy.com
Website .... www.cohos-evamy.com
Employer Background: The Cohos Evamy Partners is a team of architects, interior designers and engineers working together in Edmonton and Calgary. *New Positions Created (4):* Junior / Intermediate Specification Writer; Architectural Positions (4); Senior Electrical Designer; Senior Electrical Engineer.

COHOS EVAMY PARTNERS, THE
Att: Human Resources Manager
902 - 11th Avenue SW, Suite 200
Calgary, AB T2R 0E7
Tel. 403-229-5501
Fax 403-245-0504
Email .... resumes@cohos-evamy.com
Website .... www.cohos-evamy.com
Employer Background: The Cohos Evamy Partners is a team of architects, interior designers and engineers working together in Edmonton and Calgary. *New Positions Created (6):* 3D Visualizations Position; Electrical Engineer; Receptionist; Electrical Engineer; Project Managers; Senior and Intermediate Architectural Technologists.

COINAMATIC CANADA INC.
Att: Human Resources
6500 Gottardo Court
Mississauga, ON L5T 2A2
Tel. 905-795-1946
Fax 905-795-9622
Email .... syoung@coinamatic.com
Website .... www.coinamatic.com
Employer Background: Coinamatic Canada Inc. is one of Canada's largest suppliers of laundry systems and home appliances to the apartment, multifamily housing and home builder industries. *New Positions Created (6):* Administrative Assistant; Reception / Switchboard Position; Sales Representatives; Sales Manager; Shop / Installation Manager; Retail Manager.

COLDSWITCH TECHNOLOGIES INC.
Att: Human Resources Manager
13155 Delf Place, Suite 250
Richmond, BC V6V 2A2
Tel. 604-274-6866
Fax 604-275-3404
Email .... info@coldswitch.com
Website .... www.coldswitch.com
Employer Background: Founded in 1988, Coldswitch Technologies Inc. has developed a proprietary system of optical switches and sensors for managing light within plastic optical fibres to control electrical loads and instruments. *New Positions Created (4):* Electrical Engineer / Project Engineer; Marketing Coordinator; Mechanical Engineer, Cable Extrusion; Mechanical Engineer / Project Engineer.

COLE VISION CANADA, INC.
Att: Cathy Pelrine
80 Centurian Drive
Markham, ON L3R 8C1
Fax 905-940-2473
Email .... cathy@cvci.com
Website .... www.cvci.com
Employer Background: Operating over 100 stores, Cole Vision Canada, Inc. provides quality eyewear through two retail chains, Sears Optical and Pearle Vision. *New Positions Created (3):* Inventory Controller; Software Support / Training Specialist; Marketing and Advertising Coordinator.

COLEY PHARMACEUTICAL GROUP
Att: Human Resources Manager
11 Holland Avenue, Suite 608, Tower A
Ottawa, ON K1Y 4S1
Tel. 613-761-9454
Fax 613-761-8661
Email .... agriffin@coleycanada.com
Website .... www.coleypharma.com
Employer Background: CPG develops therapeutic and prophylactic products that stimulate the immune system to treat cancer, infectious diseases, allergies and asthma. *New Positions Created (13):* Flow Cytometrist; Admiistrative Assistant II; Administrative Assistant I; Clinical Research Associate; Medical Writer; Research Assistant III; Research Assistants II; Medical Writer; Administrative Assistants; Clinical Research Associate; Human Resources / Fi-

nance Coordinator; Medical Writer; Research Assistants.

COLGATE-PALMOLIVE CANADA INC.
Att: Grace D'Souza, Human Resources
99 Vanderhoof Avenue
Toronto, ON M4G 2H6
Tel. 416-421-6000
Fax 416-421-6913
Email .... consumer_affairs_canada@
.... colpal.com
Website .... www.colgate.ca
Employer Background: Colgate-Palmolive Canada Inc. is a major manufacturer of household goods such as soaps, cleaners, detergents and toiletries. *New Positions Created (6):* Bilingual Consumer Relations Consultant; Team Leader; Quality Assurance Coordinator; Quality Control Technician; Team Leader; Team Leader.

COLLECTIONS ANDRADE INC.
Att: Human Resources Manager
800 Sherbrooke East
Montréal, QC H2L 1K3
Tel. 514-522-4488
Fax 514-524-7619
Email gandrade@collectionsandrade.com
Employer Background: Collections Andrade Inc. specializes in European ladieswear. *New Positions Created (4):* Chief Accountant / Office Manager; Collections & Receivables Position; Customer Service / Traffic Agent; Traffic / Shipping Coordinator, Customer Service.

COLLEGA FOR AVEDA
Att: S. Cozzetto
1800 Birchmount Road
Toronto, ON M1P 2H7
Tel. 416-754-1444
Fax 416-754-2484
Email .... scozzetto@collega.com
Website .... www.aveda.com
Employer Background: Collega for Aveda markets cosmetic products created with organically grown plants and other renewable resources and without animal testing. *New Positions Created (12):* Call Centre Coach; Hair Colour Specialist; Skincare Specialist; General Manager; Retail Positions; Territory Coordinator; Administrative Assistant; District Manager; Management Positions; Senior Accountant; District Manager; Financial Analyst.

COLLEGE OF MASSAGE THERAPISTS OF ONTARIO / CMTO
Att: Dr. Donald Pierson
192 Major Street
Toronto, ON M5S 2L3
Fax 416-929-9312
Email .... donald.pierson@utoronto.ca
Website .... www.cmto.com
Employer Background: CMTO is a regulatory body, working to ensure the competency and quality of services provided by massage therapists. *New Positions Created (2):* Investigations and Complaints Manager; Registration Manager.

COLLEGE OF NEW CALEDONIA
Att: Human Resources Department
3330 - 22nd Avenue
Prince George, BC V2N 1P8
Tel. 250-561-5828
Fax 250-561-5864
Email .... hr@cnc.bc.ca
Website .... www.cnc.bc.ca
Employer Background: The College of New Caledonia is a comprehensive community college with four regional campuses, serving over 6,000 students. *New Positions Created (9):* Dental Hygiene Instructor; Early Intervention Services Occupational Therapist; Dean of Health Sciences; Vice-President, Academic; Instructors, Practical Nursing Program; Public Services Librarian / Coordinator; Dean, Science and Technology; Dean, Health Sciences; Dean of Trades.

COLLEGE OF NURSES OF ONTARIO
Att: Human Resources Department
101 Davenport Road
Toronto, ON M5R 3P1
Tel. 416-928-0900
Fax 416-928-9240
Email .... hr@cnomail.org
Website .... www.cno.org
Employer Background: CNO is committed to the delivery of effective, safe and ethical nursing care in Ontario. *New Positions Created (11):* Practice Consultant, RN; Senior Policy Analyst; Customer Service Representative; Investigators (3); Consultant; Consultant, Marketing & Sales; Data Management Assistant; Education Consultant; Practice Consultant, RN; Program Consultant, Practice Setting Consultation; Decisions Administrator.

COLLEGE OF PHYSICIANS AND SURGEONS OF ONTARIO, THE
Att: Human Resources
80 College Street
Toronto, ON M5G 2E2
Tel. 416-967-2600
Fax 416-967-2608
Email .... hrdept@cpso.on.ca
Website .... www.cpso.on.ca
Employer Background: The College of Physicians and Surgeons of Ontario works to protect the public and promote quality medical care for the citizens of Ontario. *New Positions Created (3):* Quality Management Coordinator; Investigators; Investigators.

COLLEGE OF THE NORTH ATLANTIC, CLARENVILLE CAMPUS
Att: Jennine McDonald
PO Box 3600
Clarenville, NF A0E 1J0
Tel. 709-466-0254
Fax 709-466-2774
Email .... jennine.mcdonald@
.... northatlantic.nf.ca
Website .... www.northatlantic.nf.ca
Employer Background: The College of the North Atlantic is a public post-secondary college, serving over 10,000 full-time students in Newfoundland and Labrador through 18 campus sites and satellite cen-

tres. *New Positions Created (4):* Electrical Instructor; Electrical Instructor; Library Technician; Psychology Instructor.

COLLEGE OF THE NORTH ATLANTIC, STEPHENVILLE CAMPUS
Att: Director of Human Resources
PO Box 5400
Stephenville, NF A2N 2Z6
Tel. 709-643-7706
Fax 709-643-7806
Email .... hq-jobs@northatlantic.nf.ca
Website .... www.northatlantic.nf.ca
Employer Background: The College of the North Atlantic is a public post-secondary college, serving over 10,000 full-time students in Newfoundland and Labrador through 18 campus sites and satellite centres. *New Positions Created (16):* Curriculum Design Specialist, Multimedia; Instructor, IT Enhancement for Office Administration; Instructors, Practical Nursing Program (3); Academic Instructor; Manager, Day Care Centre; Policy, Planning and Research Analyst; Human Resources Clerk; Computer Programmer / Analyst; Graphic Artist; Multimedia Curriculum Design Specialist; Computer Support Specialist; Labour Relations Assistant; Community Liaison Officer; General Counsel and Corporate Secretary; Instructor, Digital Animation; Instructor, Pulp and Paper Engineering Technology Manufacturing Operations.

COLLEGE OF THE ROCKIES
Att: HR Development Department
PO Box 8500
Cranbrook, BC V1C 5L7
Tel. 250-489-2751
Fax 250-489-8206
Email .... hrdd@cotr.bc.ca
Website .... www.cotr.bc.ca
Employer Background: College of the Rockies offers a range of programs and courses, serving over 1,500 students. *New Positions Created (12):* Research Associate; Instructor, Communications and New Media; Instructor, Home Support Attendant and Practical Nursing Programs; Instructor, Economics and Statistics; Nursing Instructors (2); Instructor, Computer Information Systems; Negotiated Income Support & Targeted Wage Subsidy Facilitator; Professional Cook Training Instructor; Manager; Coordinator / Instructor, Local Government Administration Program; Auxiliary Web Technician; President / Chief Executive Officer.

COLLINGWOOD GENERAL & MARINE HOSPITAL / CGMH
Att: Human Resources
459 Hume Street
Collingwood, ON L9Y 1W9
Fax 705-444-8619
Email .... hr@cgmh.on.ca
Website .... www.cgmh.on.ca
Employer Background: Located in a resort community, CGMH provides primary and secondary care to a local population of 40,000 and peak visitor population of 120,000. *New Positions Created (9):* Regis-

tered Nurses, Medical; Registered Nurses, OB / Surgical; Psychogeriatric Consultants; Physiotherapist; Registered Nurse, Emergency Room; Registered Nurse, Medical; Registered Nurse, OB / Surgical; Respiratory Therapist; Senior CT Technologist.

COLLINS & AIKMAN
Att: Employee Relations Coordinator
165 Milner Avenue
Toronto, ON M1S 4G7
Fax 416-298-9050
Email .... resume@colaik.com
Website .... www.colaik.com
Employer Background: Collins & Aikman manufactures and supplies acoustic systems, floor mats and molded plastic interior trim for the automotive industry. *New Positions Created (6):* Dimensional Technician; Production Supervisors (2); Materials Planner; Senior Quality Engineer; Health and Safety Coordinator / Trainer; Supply Quality Representative.

COLT ENGINEERING CORPORATION
Att: Wendy Piper, Human Resources
5008 - 86th Street, Suite 120
Edmonton, AB T6E 5S2
Tel. 780-440-5300
Fax 780-440-5568
Email .... piper.wendy@colteng.com
Website .... www.colteng.com
Employer Background: Established in 1973, Colt Engineering Corporation provides specialized, multidisciplinary EPCM and EPC services for the refinery, pipeline, petrochemical, oil and gas and industrial sectors. *New Positions Created (12):* Civil / Structural Engineers and Designers; Divisional Controller; Electrical Engineers and Designers; Instrumentation / Controls Engineers and Designers; PDS Database Administrators and Designers; Process and Mechanical Engineers; Project Managers; Civil / Structural Engineers; HVAC Designers / Draftspersons; Instrumentation / Controls / Automation Engineers; Project Manager; Recruiter.

COLT ENGINEERING CORPORATION
Att: Human Resources
10201 Southport Road SW, Suite 400
Calgary, AB T2W 4X9
Tel. 403-258-8000
Fax 403-258-5899
Email .... hr.calgary@colteng.com
Website .... www.colteng.com
Employer Background: Established in 1973, Colt Engineering Corporation provides specialized, multidisciplinary EPCM and EPC services for the refinery, pipeline, petrochemical, oil and gas and industrial sectors. *New Positions Created (26):* DCS Specialists; Electrical Designers / Drafters; Electrical Engineers; Inspection Coordinator; Intermediate Estimator; Mechanical Engineers; PLC Programmers; Senior Construction Planner; Senior Accountant; Cost Controllers; DCS Specialist; Electrical Engineers; Estimators; Expediters; PLC Programmers; Schedulers; Human Resources Professional; Business Development Assistant; Electrical

Designer / Drafter; Human Resource Generalist; Intermediate / Senior Contract Administrators; Intermediate / Senior Process Engineers; Mechanical / Electrical Engineers; Project Managers; Senior Buyers; Senior Estimators.

COLT ENGINEERING CORPORATION
Att: Human Resources Manager
90 Tiverton Court, 2nd Floor
Markham, ON L3R 9V2

Tel. 905-940-4774
Fax 905-940-4778
Email .... hr.toronto@colteng.com
Website .... www.colteng.com

Employer Background: Established in 1973, Colt Engineering Corporation provides specialized, multidisciplinary EPCM and EPC services for the refinery, pipeline, petrochemical, and oil and gas and industrial sectors. *New Positions Created (6):* Chief Mechanical Engineer; Senior Mechanical Engineer; Junior Buyer; Senior Controls and Automation Engineer; Senior Instrumentation Engineer; Specifications Accounting Generalist.

COLTIN INTERNATIONAL GROUP
Att: Human Resources
1451 Castlefield Avenue
Toronto, ON M6M 1Y3

Fax 416-656-2021

Employer Background: Coltin International Group is a Canadian manufacturer of bath and linen products. *New Positions Created (2):* Stylist, Home Fashions; Sales Representative.

COLUMBIA HEALTH CARE INC., GRANDE PRAIRIE CENTRE
Att: Nancy Beaton, Director of Operations
9909 - 102nd Street, Suite 200
Grande Prairie, AB T8V 2V4

Fax 780-532-6057

Employer Background: Columbia Health Care Inc. is a privately-owned rehabilitation company. *New Positions Created (3):* Kinesiologist; Occupational Therapist; Physical Therapist.

COLUMBIA HOUSE CANADA
Att: Jan Thompson, CHRP,
Director of Personnel
5900 Finch Avenue East
Toronto, ON M1B 5X7

Tel. 416-299-9400
Fax 416-299-7491
Email .... jan_thompson@chcmail.com
Website www.columbiahousecanada.com

Employer Background: Columbia House Canada is a leading direct marketer of music and video entertainment products. *New Positions Created (8):* Desktop Publishing Artist; Safety and Security Officer; Intermediate Accountant; Manager, E-Commerce; Safety and Security Officer; E-Commerce Manager; SAS Programmer / Analyst; Desktop Publishing Artist.

COLUMBIA INTERNATIONAL COLLEGE
Att: Human Resources Administrator
1033 Main Street West
Hamilton, ON L8S 1B7

Tel. 905-572-7883
Fax 905-572-9332
Email .. human.resources@cic-totalcare.com
Website .... www.cic-totalcare.com

Employer Background: Established in 1979, Columbia International College is the largest private residential high school for international students in Canada. *New Positions Created (5):* School Guidance Counsellor; Student Services Officer / Receptionist; Administrative Assistant; Recreation and Athletics Coordinator; Student Services Officer / Receptionist.

COLUMBIA MANUFACTURING CO. LTD.
Att: H. Kisbee
4575 Tillicum Street
Burnaby, BC V5J 3J9

Tel. 604-437-3377
Fax 604-437-4443
Email .... info@columbia-skylights.com

Employer Background: Columbia Manufacturing Co. Ltd. is a Canadian manufacturer of building materials. *New Positions Created (2):* Account Manager; Marketing Representative.

COLUMBIA MBF
Att: Human Resources
7555 Tranmere Drive
Mississauga, ON L5S 1L4

Tel. 905-678-9191
Fax 905-678-9323

Employer Background: Columbia MBF, a TYCO International Ltd. company, manufactures steel tubes. *New Positions Created (5):* Junior Sales Clerk; Inside Sales Representative; Electrical / Control Technician; Production Manager; Shipping / Warehouse Supervisor.

COLUMBIA REHABILITATION CENTRE
Att: Cathy McFeely, Human Resources
2121 - 29th Street NE
Calgary, AB T1Y 7H8

Fax 403-247-1163

Employer Background: Columbia Rehabilitation Centre provides a range of evaluation and treatment services, with a focus on returning injured individuals to productive lifestyles. *New Positions Created (6):* Kinesiologist; Occupational Therapist; Physical Therapist; Psychologist; Supported Employment Specialist; Vocational Rehabilitation Specialist.

COM DEV INTERNATIONAL
Att: Mickie Churchill, HR Generalist
155 Sheldon Drive
Cambridge, ON N1R 7H6

Tel. 519-622-2300
Fax 519-622-5543
Email ...... spacetech.resumes@comdev.ca
Website .... www.comdev.ca

Employer Background: COM DEV International is a leading manufacturer of products for communications satellites and ground-based wireless communications. *New Positions Created (11):* Manager, Business Development, Surface Acoustic Wave (SAW); MTS / AMTS Supplier Quality Engineer; Test Engineer, Battery Department; AMTS / SMTS Switch Department Specialist; AMTS / SMTS Systems Engineer; New Business Analyst, Finance Department; SAP Systems Developer, MIS Department; Technical Staff Specialist 1, Switch Department; Program Manager, Batteries Department; QC Inspector; Quality Records Coordinator.

COM-NET ERICSSON
Att: Recruitment
5255 Satellite Drive
Mississauga, ON L4W 5E3

Tel. 905-629-6700
Fax 905-282-8302
Email .... com-net.hr@ericsson.ca
Website .... www.ericsson.ca

Employer Background: Com-Net Ericsson offers telecom solutions to land mobile radio customers. *New Positions Created (3):* Billing Coordinator; Cost Analyst; System Engineers.

COMCARE HEALTH SERVICES
Att: Karen MacNeil
3350 Merrittville Highway, Suite 15
Thorold, ON L2V 4Y6

Tel. 905-685-6501
Website .... www.comcarehealth.ca

Employer Background: Comcare Health Services is a community health program and service provider for public, industrial and individual markets. *New Positions Created (3):* Various Healthcare Positions; Branch Manager; Registered Nursing Positions.

COMDA
Att: Human Resources Manager
15 Densley Avenue
Toronto, ON M6M 2P5

Tel. 416-243-8766
Fax 416-243-5391
Email .... humanresources@
.... comdacalendars.com
Website .... www.comdacalendars.com

Employer Background: Comda is an integrated direct marketing company, specializing in promotional calendars. *New Positions Created (3):* Network Manager; Credit Manager; Various Sales Positions.

COMINCO LTD.
Att: Human Resources
Trail, BC V1R 4L8

Tel. 250-364-4328
Fax 250-364-4109
Email .... hrrecruit@trail.cominco.com
Website .... www.cominco.com

Employer Background: Cominco Ltd. is an international mineral exploration, mining, smelting and refining company based in Canada. *New Positions Created (3):* Chemical / Metallurgical Engineers; Electrical Engineers; Mechanical / Maintenance Engineers.

COMMERCIAL SPRING AND TOOL COMPANY LTD.
Att: Human Resources Manager
160 Watline Avenue
Mississauga, ON L4Z 1R1

Tel. 905-568-3899
Fax 905-568-1929
Email .... mis@commercialspring.com
Website .... www.commercialspring.com

Employer Background: Established in 1972, Commercial Spring and Tool Company Ltd. is a tier-2 automotive parts supplier, with 4 facilities and 300 employees. *New Positions Created (6):* Quality Assurance Manager; Senior Buyer; Quality Assurance Manager; Senior Buyer; Senior Production Scheduler; Sales Administrator.

COMMONWEALTH CONSTRUCTION
Att: Human Resources
4599 Tillicum Street
Burnaby, BC V5J 3J9

Tel. 604-431-6000
Fax 604-431-6044
Email .... careers@commonwealth.ca
Website .... www.commonwealth.ca

Employer Background: Commonwealth Construction, part of VECO Corporation, provides construction management, specialty trade contracting and design build solutions for the industrial sector. *New Positions Created (6):* Payroll Supervisor; Construction Managers and Craft Superintendents; Costs Analysts; Project Administration Managers; Project Engineers; Schedulers.

COMMONWEALTH INSURANCE COMPANY
Att: Human Resources Manager
595 Burrard Street
Box 49115, Bental Tower III
Vancouver, BC V7X 1G4

Tel. 604-683-5511
Fax 604-891-6691
Email .... pgibson@commonw.com
Website .... www.commonw.com

Employer Background: Commonwealth Insurance Company specializes in medium / large commercial and industrial risk insurance in Canada, the USA and internationally. *New Positions Created (3):* Assistant Casualty Underwriter; Intermediate Casualty Underwriter; Claims Examiner.

COMMUNICATIONS AND INFORMATION TECHNOLOGY ONTARIO
Att: Human Resources Manager
36 Steacie Drive
Kanata, ON K2K 2A9

Tel. 613-592-9211
Fax 613-591-1288
Email .... accountjob@cito.ca
Website .... www.cito.ca

Employer Background: Formed in 1997, CITO is committed to strengthening Ontario's IT, digital new media and communi-

cations industries through academic and industry research partnerships and networking. *New Positions Created (5):* Director of Finance; Business Development Coordinator; Business Development Representatives; Web Administrator; Accounting Assistant.

COMMUNICATIONS TEST DESIGN, INC. / CTDI
Att: Human Resources
2323 Winston Park Drive, Unit 1
Oakville, ON L6H 6R7

Tel. 905-829-1117
Fax 905-829-3510
Email .... jward@ctdi.com
Website .... www.ctdi.com

Employer Background: Founded in 1975, CTDI provides maintenance service solutions to the telecom industry. *New Positions Created (5):* Electronic Technicians; Forklift Driver; Materials Mgmnt Clerk; Quality Control Inspector; Shipping & Receiving Clerks.

COMMUNITY AIDS TREATMENT INFORMATION EXCHANGE / CATIE
Att: Human Resources Manager
555 Richmond Street West
Suite 505, Box 1104
Toronto, ON M5V 3B1

Tel. 416-203-7122
Fax 416-203-8284
Email .... jobs@catie.ca
Website .... www.catie.ca

Employer Background: CATIE is a community-based, non-profit organization working to improve the lives of individuals with HIV / AIDS. *New Positions Created (2):* Communications Coordinator; Finance Officer.

COMMUNITY CARE ACCESS CENTRE OF PEEL
Att: Human Resources
199 County Court Boulevard
Brampton, ON L6W 4P3

Tel. 905-796-0040
Fax 905-796-7057
Email .... careers@ccacpeel.org
Website .... www.ccacpeel.org

Employer Background: Community Care Access Centre of Peel provides community-based health and long-term care services in the Peel Region. *New Positions Created (6):* Director, Client Services; Director, Corporate Services; Information Analyst; Director, Human Resources; Manager, Client Services; Registered Nurses.

COMMUNITY CARE ACCESS CENTRE OF YORK REGION / CCAC
Att: Recruitment Coordinator
1100 Gorham Street, Unit 1
Newmarket, ON L3Y 7V1

Tel. 905-895-1334
Fax 905-895-7205
Email .... hr@ccacyorkregion.on.ca
Website .... www.ccacyorkregion.on.ca

Employer Background: CCAC is a non-profit organization that provides community care, placement, information and referral serv-

ices for individuals of all ages through a visible, single point of access. *New Positions Created (5):* Client Services Manager; Educator; Quality Improvement Analyst; Case Managers; Contract Manager Coordinator.

COMMUNITY CARE ACCESS CENTRE, RENFREW COUNTY
Att: Confidential, Human Resources
7 International Drive, Suite B
Pembroke, ON K8A 6W5

Tel. 613-732-7007
Fax 613-732-9552
Website .... www.renc.igs.net/~ccacrenc

Employer Background: Community Care Access Centre, Renfrew County is a non-profit organization, providing in-home health and support services. *New Positions Created (3):* Occupational Therapists (3); Speech and Language Pathologists; Occupational Therapist.

COMMUNITY CARE EAST YORK
Att: Human Resources Manager
334 Donlands Avenue
Toronto, ON M4J 3R9

Tel. 416-422-2026
Fax 416-422-1513
Email .... hr@ccey.org
Website .... www.ccey.org

Employer Background: Community Care East York provides a range of services to older adults and persons with disabilities. *New Positions Created (2):* Supervisor, Home Support Services; Director of Finance.

COMMUNITY CARE SERVICES INC.
Att: Human Resources Manager
89 Queensway West, Suite 215
Mississauga, ON L5B 2V2

Tel. 905-275-7098
Fax 905-275-9791

Employer Background: Community Care Services Inc. provides a comprehensive range of home health services. *New Positions Created (3):* Community Healthcare Positions; Home Support Field Supervisor; PSW and HSW positions.

COMMUNITY LIVING MISSISSAUGA
Att: Human Resources Manager
6695 Millcreek Drive, Unit 1
Mississauga, ON L5N 5R8

Tel. 905-542-2694
Fax 905-542-0987
Email .... hr@clmiss.on.ca
Website .... www.clmiss.on.ca

Employer Background: Community Living Mississauga is a non-profit organization that provides services and support to people with intellectual handicaps. *New Positions Created (5):* Accountant; Assistant to the Director of Customer Relations; Respite Provider; Support Worker; Registered Nurse.

COMMUNITY MENTAL HEALTH CLINIC / CMHC
Att: Human Resources Assistant
147 Delhi Street
Guelph, ON N1E 4J3

Tel. 519-821-2060
Fax 519-821-9865
Email ..... mperissinotto@cmhcgwd.on.ca
Website .... www.cmhcgwd.on.ca
Employer Background: CMHC is an accredited community-based agency, providing mental health services to citizens of Wellington and Dufferin counties. *New Positions Created (6):* Intensive Clinical Case Managers; Mental Health Worker; Mental Health Worker, Eating Disorders; Psychogeriatric Education Consultant; Psychiatrists; Psychologists.

COMMUNITY OPTIONS
Att: Lana Sampson, Executive Director
12345 - 121 Street, Suite 200
Edmonton, AB T5L 4Y7
Fax 780-454-6166
Email .... lsampson@compusmart.ab.ca
Employer Background: Community Options is a non-profit community organization providing services to children and their families. *New Positions Created (2):* Paediatric Speech Language Pathologist; Paediatric Speech Language Pathologist.

COMMVESCO LEVINSON-VINER GROUP / CLV GROUP
Att: Debbie Lafleche
1339 Wellington Street
Ottawa, ON K1Y 3B8
Tel. 613-728-2000
Fax 613-728-1107
Email .... debbie.lafleche@clvgroup.com
Website .... www.clvgroup.com
Employer Background: CLV Group is a full-service realty corporation. *New Positions Created (3):* Commercial Property Mgr; Residential Property Mgr; Commercial Property Mgr.

COMPASS GROUP CANADA
Att: Manager, Human Resources
131 Brunel Road
Mississauga, ON L4Z 1X3
Tel. 905-568-4636
Fax 905-568-2964
Email .... human-resources@
.... compass-canada.com
Website .... www.compass-canada.com
Employer Background: Compass Group Canada is a large contract services company. *New Positions Created (2):* Branch Manager; Chef Managers.

COMPCANADA ATLAS
Att: Human Resources Manager
10130 - 103rd Street, Suite 1500
Edmonton, AB T5J 3N9
Tel. 780-426-2667
Fax :....................................... 780-426-2951
Email ...... careers@compcanadaatlas.com
Website .... www.compcanadaatlas.com
Employer Background: CompCanada Atlas provides information technology solutions to mid- and large-sized organizations in western Canada. *New Positions Created (6):* Site Coordinator; LAN Administrators; Operators, Operations Centre; Senior Technicians; Technicians; Inside Sales Rep.

COMPCANADA ATLAS
Att: Human Resources Manager
736 - 6th Avenue SW, Suite 800
Calgary, AB T2P 3T7
Tel. 403-265-2667
Fax 403-265-0652
Email ...... careers@compcanadaatlas.com
Website .... www.compcanadaatlas.com
Employer Background: CompCanada Atlas provides information technology solutions to mid- and large-sized organizations in western Canada. *New Positions Created (3):* Desktop Consultants; Helpdesk Analyst; Team Leader, Help Desk.

COMPCLAIM MANAGEMENT INC.
Att: Steve Carr, Partner
2025 Sheppard Avenue East, Suite 4312
Toronto, ON M2J 1V7
Tel. 416-495-1072
Fax 416-495-8833
Email .... scarr@compclaim.com
Website .... www.compclaim.com
Employer Background: Established in 1988, CompClaim Management Inc. is an employer's resource for workers' compensation claim management and health and safety issues. *New Positions Created (3):* Senior Workers' Compensation Consultant; Claims Manager; Lawyer.

COMPREHENSIVE REHABILITATION AND MENTAL HEALTH SERVICES
Att: Human Resources
700 Lawrence Avenue West, Suite 362
Toronto, ON M6A 3B4
Tel. 416-785-8797
Fax 416-785-9358
Website .... www.cotarehab.on.ca
Employer Background: COTA is an accredited community agency, providing comprehensive rehabilitation and mental health services. *New Positions Created (3):* Project Manager; Community Support Staff; Various Healthcare Positions.

COMPTEC INTERNATIONAL LTD.
Att: Geri Dougall, HR Manager
13145 - 80th Avenue
Surrey, BC V3W 3B1
Tel. 604-597-0681
Fax 604-597-0692
Email .... gdougall@
.... comptec-international.com
Website www.comptec-international.com
Employer Background: Comptec International Ltd. is an ISO 9001-certified manufacturer of custom tools and multi-shot, multi-material, cosmetic plastic parts used in the telecom, automotive and electronic markets. *New Positions Created (5):* Sr Accountant; Plastics Positions; Set-Up Technician; Quality Technician; Tooling Mgr.

COMPUGEN SYSTEMS LTD.
Att: Human Resources Manager
25 Leek Crescent
Richmond Hill, ON L4B 4B3
Tel. 905-707-2000
Fax 905-707-2176

Website .... www.compugen.ca
Employer Background: Compugen Systems Ltd., part of Norigen Communications Group Inc., is a PC-based systems integrator and IT service provider. *New Positions Created (11):* Corporate Account Manager, Public Sector; Pre-Sales Senior System Engineer; Senior Corporate Account Manager; Customer Service Representative; Deployment Manager; Project Managers (2); Java Developer; Web Developer; Data Support Analyst; Configuration Technician; Technical Service Representatives (2).

COMPUGEN SYSTEMS LTD.
Att: Human Resources Manager
1565 Carling Avenue, Suite 712
Ottawa, ON K1Z 8R1
Tel. 613-792-2100
Fax 613-792-1900
Email .... hcarry@compugen.com
Website .... www.compugen.ca
Employer Background: Compugen Systems Ltd., part of Norigen Communications Group Inc., is a PC-based systems integrator and IT service provider. *New Positions Created (6):* Business Technology Consultant; Corporate Account Manager; Enterprise Technology Specialist; Inside Sales Representative; Network Support Specialist; Technical Service Representative.

COMPUGEN SYSTEMS LTD.
Att: Human Resources Manager
333 Graham Boulevard, Suite 302
Mount Royal, QC H3R 3L5
Tel. 514-341-0001
Fax 514-341-0404
Website .... www.compugen.ca
Employer Background: Compugen Systems Ltd., part of Norigen Communications Group Inc., is a PC-based systems integrator and IT service provider. *New Positions Created (2):* Presales Specialist, Data Storage; Sales Specialist, Data Storage.

COMPUSOFT CANADA INC.
Att: Human Resources
9935 - 29A Avenue
Edmonton, AB T6N 1A9
Fax 780-439-3407
Email .... hr@compusoftware.com
Website .... www.compusoftware.com
Employer Background: CompuSoft Canada Inc. is a publicly-held company that develops e-business software solutions for the metals industry. *New Positions Created (14):* Database Analyst; Deployment Services Consultant, Level 1; Deployment Services Consultant, Level 2; Deployment Services Consultant, Level 3; Intermediate Developer; Intermediate Technical Services Position; Senior Developer; Senior Project Manager; Senior Technical Services Position; Database Analyst; Intermediate Developer; Senior Developer; Software Architect; Human Resources Position.

COMPUTALOG LTD.
Att: Maintenance &
Manufacturing Manager

9204 - 37th Avenue
Edmonton, AB T6E 5L4

Tel. 780-462-6300
Fax 780-437-8856
Email .... joe.sajjad@computalog.com
Website .... www.computalog.com

Employer Background: Founded in 1972, Computalog Ltd. (a subsidiary of Precision Drilling Corporation) is an international oilfield service company, specializing in wireline logging and directional and horizontal drilling technologies. *New Positions Created (3):* Mechanical Engineer; Shipping Coordinator; Technical Writer.

COMPUTALOG LTD.
Att: Human Resources Department
150 - 6th Avenue SW, Suite 4500
Calgary, AB T2P 3Y7

Tel. 403-265-6060
Fax 403-218-2424
Email .... resumes@computalog.com
Website .... www.computalog.com

Employer Background: Founded in 1972, Computalog Ltd. (a subsidiary of Precision Drilling Corporation) is an international oilfield service company, specializing in wireline logging and directional and horizontal drilling technologies. *New Positions Created (3):* Network Support Specialist; Operators and Electronics Technicians; Field Engineer Trainees.

COMPUTER SCIENCES CORP. / CSC
Att: Resource Manager
2206 Eglinton Avenue East, Suite 300
Toronto, ON M1L 4S7

Tel. 416-755-7000
Fax 416-755-1848
Website .... www.csc.com

Employer Background: Headquartered in California, CSC is an information technology company, offering consulting, systems integration and outsourcing services. *New Positions Created (18):* Application Developers / Programmer Analysts; Project Control / Administration Position; Quality Assurance / Performance Improvement Consultants; Technology Specialist; Application Developer / Programmer Analysts; Project Manager; Project Manager; Quality Assurance / Performance Improvement Consultants; Transition Manager; Application Developers / Programmer Analysts; Business Architect; Client Services / Help Desk Position; Database Administrator; Financial Manager; Project Manager, EAI; System / Application Architect; Technical Support Technicians; Travel Expense Claims Clerk.

COMPUTER SONICS SYSTEMS INC.
Att: Human Resources Manager
1431 - 40th Avenue NE, Bay 1
Calgary, AB T2E 8N6

Tel. 403-235-6533
Fax 403-235-6737
Email .... rhondah@compsonsys.com
Website .... www.compsonsys.com

Employer Background: CSS is a leading manufacturing and design company for the oilfield service industry. *New Positions Cre-*

ated (2): Electronics Design Engineer; Cased Hole Logging Technical Support Personnel.

COMPUTER WORKWARE INC.
Att: Human Resources Manager
930 The East Mall
Toronto, ON M9B 6J9

Tel. 416-620-1704
Fax 416-620-5692
Email .... hr@computerworkware.com
Website ..... www.computerworkware.com

Employer Background: Computer Workware Inc. is a private Canadian company, developing application software for the insurance and employee benefits industry. *New Positions Created (2):* C++ / COM Programmer; Web Programmer.

COMPUTING DEVICES CANADA LTD.
Att: Human Resources Advisor
1020 - 68th Avenue NE
Calgary, AB T2E 8P2

Tel. 403-295-6700
Fax 403-730-1197
Website .... www.computingdevices.com

Employer Background: CDC is a defence electronics contractor, with over 50 years experience. *New Positions Created (73):* BCOE1 Software Development Engineer; BCOE2 Lead Software Engineer; BOWMAN Land Platforms System Engineer; BOWMAN Senior Contracts Administrators (2); ILS / Training Manager; Tempest Intermediate Engineer; BOWMAN Performance Management Team Leader; Logistics Engineering Manager; Reliability & Maintainability Engineer; Senior Safety Engineer; Technical Documentation / Data Team Lead; Training Team Lead; BCOE Lead System Engineer; BCOE1 System Engineer; BCOE2 COTS Software Engineers; BIDS Hardware Engineering Lead; BIDS Test Software Engineer; BIDS Test Software, Senior Position; Bowman Platform; Cable Design Specialist; DOORS Administrator; Engineering Tools Technologist; Integration and Test Manager; Mechanical Design Specialist; PCB Layout Specialist / Librarian; Radio Frequency Communications Engineer; ARS Lead Hardware Engineer; ARS Test Equipment Developer; ARS Test Lead; BCOE Lab Technologist / Software Specialist; BCOE1 COTS Software Engineer; BCOE1 Lead Software Engineer; BCOE1 Software Development Support Engineer; BCOE2 Software Development Support Engineer; BIDS Firmware Designer; BIDS Firmware Development Engineer; BIDS Firmware Qualification Engineer; BIDS Firmware Senior Engineer; BIDS Test Engineer; BKVMS Engineer; Bowman BIDS Hardware Engineer; Bowman BIDS Technologist; Bowman Cosite Engineer; Bowman Cosite Test Technician; Bowman Cosite Test Technologist; Bowman Date Terminal Software Integration and Build Engineer; Bowman Product QV Lead; Bowman Senior Audio Engineer; Cosite Senior Engineer; External Interfaces Engineer; HIDS Software Engineer; Human Factors Engineer; Integrated Logistics Support (ILS) Manager; Integration Lead Engineer; Iris System Support Lead Hardware Engineer;

Mechanical Engineer; Minder Software Engineering Team Leader; Radio Ancillaries Engineer, GPS and PLGR; Radio Engineer, ADR+ / VHF Net Radio; Radio Engineer, HCDR; Radio Engineer, HF Combat Net Radio; Radio Engineer, VHF Airborne; Senior Human Factors Engineer; Senior Mechanical Engineer; Senior Reliability and Maintainability Engineer; Senior System Engineering Leads; System Engineering Manager; Bowman ILS Manager; Bowman Systems Engineer; Cost / Schedule Analyst II; Cost / Schedule Analyst III; Estimator; Estimator.

COMPUTING DEVICES CANADA LTD.
Att: Human Resources Advisor
3785 Richmond Road
Ottawa, ON K2H 5B7

Tel. 613-596-7000
Fax 613-596-5081
Website .... www.computingdevices.com

Employer Background: CDC is a defence electronics contractor, with over 50 years experience. *New Positions Created (31):* Estimator; Planning and Scheduling Analyst; Executive Assistant; Senior Systems Hardware Engineer; Bowman Data Terminal Hardware Engineer; Bowman External Interfaces Engineer; Bowman Senior Contracts Administrator; Industrial Engineering Technician; Junior Administrator; Manager, Configuration Management; Program Manager; Senior Systems Engineer; Design Drafts Position; Hardware / Systems Engineer, Computer And Display Products; Hardware / Systems Engineer - Lead Engineer; Software Engineer; Contracts Administrator; Manager, Financial and Corporate Accounting; Manufacturing Engineer; Product Engineer, Flat Panel Displays (FPD); Production Program Manager; Project Management Support Office (PMSO) Manager; Software Design Team Manager; Software Test Engineer; Systems Engineer; Configuration Management Administrator; Junior Test Engineer; Senior Systems Analyst; Engineer / Senior Software Engineer; Estimator; Planner / Scheduler.

COMPUTRONIKS INC.
Att: General Manager
6345 Dixie Road, Unit 1
Mississauga, ON L5T 2E6

Tel. 905-564-8868
Fax 905-564-8869
Email .... careers@computroniks.com
Website .... www.computroniks.com

Employer Background: Established in 1983, Computroniks Inc. is a network and systems integration company. *New Positions Created (4):* Inside Sales Representative; Outside Sales Representative; Inside Sales Position; Outside Sales Position.

COMSTOCK CANADA LTD.
Att: Tony Fanelli
10833 - 178th Street
Edmonton, AB T5S 1J6

Tel. 780-483-8803
Fax 780-484-3748
Website .... www.comstockcanada.com

Employer Background: Comstock Canada Ltd. provides a wide range of engineering services, including mechanical and electrical construction, building maintenance, power production and electrical transmission. *New Positions Created (2):* Electrical Manager; Electrical Purchasing Agent.

COMSTOCK CANADA LTD.
Att: Human Resources Manager
3455 Landmark Road
Burlington, ON L7M 1T4
Tel. 905-335-3333
Fax 905-335-4265
Email .... info@comstockcanada.com
Website .... www.comstockcanada.com
Employer Background: Comstock Canada Ltd. provides a wide range of constructor services, including mechanical and electrical construction, building maintenance, power production and electrical transmission. *New Positions Created (2):* Corporate Safety Mgr; Manager, Central Estimating.

COMSTOCK CANADA LTD
Att: Human Resources Department
5805 Kennedy Road
Mississauga, ON L4Z 2G3
Tel. 905-502-9200
Fax 905-568-2773
Website .... www.comstockcanada.com
Employer Background: Comstock Canada Ltd. provides a wide range of engineering services, including mechanical and electrical construction, building maintenance, power production and electrical transmission. *New Positions Created (3):* Maintenance Representative; Project Representative; Service Coordinator.

CON-FORCE STRUCTURES LTD.
Att: Lorina Doyle
4300 - 50th Avenue SE
Calgary, AB T2P 2T7
Tel. 403-248-3171
Fax 403-248-0711
Email .... hr@con-force.com
Website .... www.con-force.com
Employer Background: Established in 1949, Con-Force Structures Ltd. has pioneered the use of precast, prestressed concrete in construction. *New Positions Created (4):* Estimator / Project Planner; Design Engineer / Project Manager; Senior Draftsperson / Checker; Senior Project Manager.

CON-WAY CANADA EXPRESS
Att: Christopher Haworth
99 Howden Road
Toronto, ON M1R 3C7
Tel. 416-285-5399
Fax 416-285-6968
Email .... ccx.jobs@con-way.com
Website .... www.con-way.com
Employer Background: Con-Way Canada Express offers time-definite and day-definite surface freight transportation for commercial, industrial, retail and manufacturing companies throughout North America. *New Positions Created (2):* Account Executive; Account Executive.

CON-WAY CANADA EXPRESS / CON-WAY TRANSPORTATION SERVICE, INC.
Att: Human Resources Manager
5425 Dixie Road, Room 202
Mississauga, ON L4W 1E6
Tel. 905-602-9477
Fax 905-602-9358
Email .... ccx.jobs@con-way.com
Website .... www.con-way.com
Employer Background: Con-Way Canada Express provides time-definite and day-definite surface freight transportation for commercial, industrial, retail and manufacturing companies throughout North America. *New Positions Created (3):* Customer Service Representatives; Supervisors; Freight Operations; Account Manager.

CONAIR CONSUMER PRODUCTS INC.
Att: Human Resources Manager
156 Parkshore Drive
Brampton, ON L6T 5M1
Tel. 905-458-5551
Fax 905-458-6173
Email .. recruitment_canada@conair.com
Website .... www.conair.com
Employer Background: Conair Consumer Products Inc. is a leading distributor of personal care and small kitchen appliances. *New Positions Created (10):* Certified Reach Truck Operators; Shift Supervisor; Various Trade / Technician Positions; National Account Sales Manager; Marketing Assistant; Credit Supervisor; Inventory / Production Planner; Claims / Credit Assistant; Senior Customer Service Representative; Traffic / Imports Coordinator.

CONCORD CONFECTIONS INC.
Att: Human Resources Manager
345 Courtland Avenue
Concord, ON L4K 5A6
Tel. 905-738-9108
Fax 905-660-4591
Email .... jpower@dubblebubble.com
Website .... www.dubblebubble.com
Employer Background: Concord Confections Inc. is a leading manufacturer of bubble gum and pressed dextrose candies, including Dubble Bubble. *New Positions Created (10):* Export Sales Manager; Quality Technologist; Cost Accountant / Accounting Manager; Quality Inspector; Electromechanical Technicians; High-Speed Machine Operators; Licensed Maintenance Mechanics; Production Supervisors; Quality Supervisor; Various Trade / Technician Positions.

CONCORD IDEA CORP.
Att: Human Resources Manager
4118 - 14th Avenue, Unit 4
Markham, ON L3R 0J3
Tel. 905-305-9116
Fax 905-513-9572
Email .... recruit@concordidea.com
Website .... www.concordidea.com
Employer Background: Concord Idea Corp. manufactures PC memory products. *New Positions Created (10):* Account Executive; Customer Service Representative; Internet

Sales Representative; Electronic Engineers; Industrial Engineers; Mechanical Engineers; PCB Designer; Software Engineers; Communication Specialist; Internet Marketing / Sales Specialist.

CONCORDIA UNIVERSITY
Att: Department of Human Resources & Employee Relations
1455 de Maisonneuve Boulevard West
Montréal, QC H3G 1M8
Tel. 514-848-2424
Fax 514-848-2844
Email .... hr-employment@concordia.ca
Website .... www.concordia.ca
Employer Background: Formed in 1974 by the merger of Sir George Williams University and Loyola College, Concordia University offers over 240 undergraduate and graduate programs on two campuses. *New Positions Created (4):* Director, Office of Research Services; Director, Compensation & Benefits / Pension; Planning and Information Officer; Director, Oscar Peterson Concert Hall.

CONCORDIA UNIVERSITY COLLEGE OF ALBERTA
Att: Mary Wagner, HR Director
7128 Ada Boulevard
Edmonton, AB T5B 4E4
Tel. 780-479-9276
Fax 780-479-2793
Email .... mwagner@concordia.ab.ca
Website .... www.concordia.ab.ca
Employer Background: Founded in 1921, Concordia University College of Alberta is an accredited liberal arts university college and academic high school of Lutheran Church (Canada). *New Positions Created (4):* Instructional Technologist, Chemistry; Assistant Dean, Continuing Education; Assistant Professor, Elementary Education; Assistant Professor, Education.

CONEC CORPORATION
Att: Adam Hutchinson,
National Sales Manager
125 Sun Pac Boulevard
Brampton, ON L6S 5Z6
Tel. 905-790-2200
Fax 905-790-2201
Email .... ahutchinson@conec.com
Website .... www.conec.com
Employer Background: Conec Corporation is a manufacturer of quality connector products for the electronic and communications industry. *New Positions Created (2):* Field Sales Applications Engineer; Outside Technical Sales Representative.

CONECO EQUIPMENT INC.
Att: Tom Sanderson, Executive V.P.
16116 - 111th Avenue
Edmonton, AB T5M 2S1
Tel. 780-451-2630
Fax 780-451-2646
Email .... tomsa@coneco.ca
Website .... www.coneco.ca
Employer Background: Coneco Equipment Inc. is a supplier of heavy equipment. *New*

Positions Created (2): Director of Human Resources; Journeyman Parts Person.

CONESTOGA COLLEGE OF APPLIED ARTS & TECHNOLOGY
Att: Recruiting Officer
299 Doon Valley Drive
Kitchener, ON   N2G 4M4

Tel. 519-748-5220
Fax 519-748-3558
Email ... humanresources@conestogac.on.ca
Website .... www.conestogac.on.ca

Employer Background: Conestoga College of Applied Arts & Technology is a community college, with 5 campuses in the Kitchener-Waterloo area. *New Positions Created (14):* Instructor, Business Administration (Accounting); Instructor, Business Administration (Accounting Financial Planning); Instructor, Business Administration (Management Studies); Instructor, Business Administration (Marketing); Instructor, Business Administration (Materials Management); Instructor, Electronics Engineering Technology; Instructor, General Metal Machinist, General Machinist Apprenticeship and Tool & Die Maker Programs; Instructor, Industrial Maintenance Mechanic Program; Instructor, Mechanical Engineering Technology, Robotics & Automation; Instructor, Motive Power Techniques and Automotive Service Technician Programs; Instructor, School of Communications; Instructor, Welding Fitter Apprenticeship; Instructors, Nursing Degree Program (2); Instructors, School of Information Technology (2).

CONESTOGA-ROVERS & ASSOCIATES LIMITED / CRA
Att: Human Resources Department
651 Colby Drive
Waterloo, ON   N2V 1C2

Tel. 519-884-0510
Fax 519-884-0525
Email .... hr@craworld.com
Website .... www.craworld.com

Employer Background: CRA is a multidisciplinary firm, providing scientific and engineering solutions for environmental challenges. The company has over 1,200 employees worldwide. *New Positions Created (18):* Benefits Administrator; Human Resources Assistant B; Intermediate Engineer; Quality Control Officer; Staffing Coordinator; Health & Safety Regulatory Specialist / Technician; Intermediate / Senior Programmer; Junior / Intermediate Air Compliance Engineer; Lab Technician / Technologist; Laboratory Sample Receptionist; GIS Specialist; Junior / Civil Environmental Engineer; Intermediate Engineer; Senior Mechanical Design Engineer; Senior Municipal Engineer; Structural Engineer; Intermediate NT Specialist; Industrial Hygienist / Safety Professional.

CONEX BUSINESS SYSTEMS INC.
Att: Office Manager
18030 - 107th Avenue
Edmonton, AB   T5S 1P4

Tel. 780-484-6116
Fax 780-486-2206
Email .... edmontonjobs@conex.ca
Website .... www.conex.ca

Employer Background: Conex Business Systems Inc., part of the Toshiba Group, is a distributor of Toshiba photocopiers, fax machines, multimedia projects and TEC cash registers. *New Positions Created (6):* Project Coordinator / Customer Service Representative; Telecommunications Sales Mgr; Telecommunications Service Manager; Project Coordinator / Customer Service Representative; Telecommunications Field Technicians; Telecommunications Sales Consultants.

CONFERENCE BOARD OF CANADA, THE
Att: Human Resources
255 Smyth Road
Ottawa, ON   K1H 8M7

Tel. 613-526-3280
Fax 613-526-4857
Email .... recruit@conferenceboard.ca
Website .... www.conferenceboard.ca

Employer Background: The Conference Board of Canada is a private, independent applied research institution, delivering objective public policy and decision-making information to 500 member organizations. *New Positions Created (15):* Vice-President, Marketing; Research Associate, Canadian Centre for Business in the Community; Research Associate, National Forecasting; Research Associate, Compensation Research Centre; Director, Conference Programs; Payroll & Benefits Administrator; Program Manager, Centre of Excellence for Women's Advancement; Administrative Assistant to the Director, Conference Division; Assistant to the V.P., Corporate Services; Conference Program Director, Conference Division; Market Research Analyst, Corporate Marketing; Research Associate, Business Research Group; Research Associate, Innovation and Knowledge Management Practice; Research Associate, Provincial Forecasting; Research Associates, Economic Services.

CONFLUENCE WATERSPORTS CANADA INC.
Att: Human Resources Manager
345 Herbert Street, PO Box 730
Gananoque, ON   K7G 2V2

Tel. 613-382-2531
Fax 613-382-8769

Employer Background: Confluence Watersports Canada Inc. is a distributor of canoes, kayaks, sailboats and related watersports accessories. *New Positions Created (2):* Warehouse Assistant; Warehouse Assistant.

CONRAD C COLLECTION INC.
Att: Dina
9320 St. Laurent Boulevard, Suite 200
Montréal, QC   H2N 1N7

Tel. 514-385-9599
Fax 514-385-9594
Email .... info@conradc.com
Website .... www.conradc.com

Employer Background: Conrad C Collection Inc. is a ladies sportswear company, with over 40 years experience. *New Positions Created (2):* Sr Patternmaker; Design Assistant.

CONSULATE GENERAL OF JAPAN, THE
Att: Robert Davis
Toronto Dominion Centre
PO Box 10, Royal Trust Tower
Toronto, ON   M5K 1A1

Tel. 416-363-5488
Fax 416-367-9392
Email .... access@japancg-toronto.org
Website .... www.embassyjapancanada.org

Employer Background: The Consulate General of Japan oversees official relationships between Japan and Ontario. *New Positions Created (2):* Political / General Affairs Assistant; Teachers.

CONSULTRONICS LTD.
Att: Human Resources Manager
160 Drumlin Circle
Concord, ON   L4K 3E5

Tel. 905-738-3741
Fax 905-738-3712
Email .... resume@consultronics.com
Website .... www.consultronics.com

Employer Background: Consultronics Ltd. designs and manufactures sophisticated telecom test equipment. *New Positions Created (15):* Cost Accountant; Electronic Service / Bench Technician; Hardware Design Engineers; Intermediate / Senior Hardware Designer; Product Manager, Systems; Shipper / Receiver / Stockroom Clerk; Software Design Engineers; Engineering Program Managers; Engineering Technologists; Hardware Design Engineers; Manufacturing Engineer; Product Manager, Systems; Product Support Specialist, Test and Measurement; Software Design Engineers; Marketing Communications Specialist.

CONSUMERS PACKAGING INC.
Att: Human Resources Manager
777 Kipling Avenue
Toronto, ON   M8Z 5Z4

Tel. 416-232-3280
Fax 416-232-3336
Website .... www.consumersglass.com

Employer Background: Consumers Packaging Inc. is an international designer and producer of quality glass containers, with 6 plants in Canada operating under the name Consumers Glass. *New Positions Created (6):* Credit & Collections Analysts (2); Customer Service Representatives (2); Human Resources Specialist; Senior Financial Analysts; Health & Safety Officer; Cost and Budget Analyst.

CONTINENTAL ELECTRIC MOTOR SERVICES (NORTHERN) LTD.
Att: Human Resources Manager
4755 Eleniak Road
Edmonton, AB   T6B 2N1

Fax 780-469-0380

Employer Background: Continental Electric Motor Services (Northern) Ltd. is an electrical motor repair shop. *New Positions Created (3):* Accounting Clerk; Electrical Engineering Technologists / Field Service Technicians; Machinist.

CONTROL-F1
Att: Jennifer Hogan
3510 - 29th Street NE, Suite 125
Calgary, AB T1Y 7E5
Tel. 403-670-0891
Fax 403-668-5183
Email .... jennh@control-f1.com
Website www.control-f1.com
Employer Background: Control-F1 is an e-support software company that markets and hosts technical support delivery solutions. *New Positions Created (7):* Channel Account Manager; Human Resources Manager; Internet Database Developer; Sales Representatives; Senior Software Engineer; Technical Support Agent; Web Designer.

CONVEDIA CORPORATION
Att: Human Resources Manager
4190 Still Creek Drive, Suite 300
Burnaby, BC V5C 6C6
Tel. 604-918-6300
Fax 604-918-6400
Email .... careers@convedia.com
Website .... www.convedia.com
Employer Background: Convedia Corporation supplies next-generation, Softswitch-compliant media servers. *New Positions Created (11):* Director, Marketing; DSP Developers; Product Manager; Component Engineer; DSP Developers; Firmware Developers; Hardware Engineers; Manager, Business Development; Product Manager; Senior Hardware Engineer; Vice-President, Sales.

CONVERGYS CORPORATION
Att: Human Resources
2713 Lancaster Drive
Ottawa, ON K1B 5R6
Tel. 613-260-9616
Fax 613-260-0650
Email .. ottawa.recruitment@convergys.com
Website .... www.convergys.com
Employer Background: Convergys Corporation provides outsourced customer support for a diverse range of clients. *New Positions Created (6):* Financial Analyst; Operations Manager; Technical Project Manager; Technical Support Specialists; Payroll and Benefits Coordinator; Recruitment Coordinator.

CONVERGYS CUSTOMER MANAGEMENT CANADA INC.
Att: Human Resources
120 Millbourne Market Mall
Edmonton, AB T6K 3L6
Tel. 780-485-4010
Fax 780-485-4006
Email .... joe.ngo@convergys.com
Website .... www.convergys.com
Employer Background: Convergys Customer Management Canada Inc. provides inbound customer technical support and billing services. *New Positions Created (11):* Employee Benefits Associate; Payroll Accountant; Technical Support Associates; Employee Benefits Associate; Coordinator, Employee Communications; Manager, Operations; Senior Business Manager; Team Leader; Technical Support Associate; Technical Support Associate; Technical Support Associate.

COOPER LIGHTING
Att: Marc Tigh, HR Manager
5925 McLaughlin Road
Mississauga, ON L5R 1B8
Tel. 905-507-4000
Fax 905-568-7040
Website .... www.cooperlighting.com
Employer Background: Cooper Lighting, a division of Cooper Industries (Canada) Inc., manufactures recessed, trac, fluorescent, high intensity discharge (HID) and emergency lighting fixtures. *New Positions Created (2):* Lighting Quotation Representative; Senior Specification Sales Representative.

COQUITLAM, CITY OF
Att: Human Resources Division
3000 Guildford Way
Coquitlam, BC V3B 7N2
Tel. 604-927-3065
Fax 604-927-3075
Email .... careers@city.coquitlam.bc.ca
Website .... www.city.coquitlam.bc.ca
Employer Background: The City of Coquitlam, the sixth-largest municipality in BC, is home to 110,740 residents. *New Positions Created (5):* Civil Engineer, Development Services; Manager, Economic Development; Planner 2; Manager, Emergency Programs; Manager, Information and Communications.

CORADIANT INC.
Att: Human Resources Manager
4260 Girouard Avenue
Suite 100, Corporate Headquarters
Montréal, QC H4A 3C9
Tel. 514-908-6390
Email .... info@coradiant.com
Website .... www.coradiant.com
Employer Background: Founded in 2000, Coradiant Inc. is an e-business solutions company. *New Positions Created (7):* Account Executive; Documentation Coordinator; Intranet Content Manager; IS Manager; Product Manager; Sales Engineer; Senior Network Operations Specialist.

CORDON BLEU PARIS OTTAWA CULINARY ARTS INSTITUTE, LE
Att: Johanne Diotte
453 Laurier Avenue East
Ottawa, ON K1N 6R4
Tel. 613-236-2433
Fax 613-236-2460
Email .... jdiotte@cordonbleu.net
Website .... www.lcbottawa.com
Employer Background: Le Cordon Bleu Paris Ottawa Culinary Arts Institute is affiliated with one of the world's leading classical French cuisine and pastry schools, established in 1895. *New Positions Created (4):* Cuisine Chef Instructor and Pastry Chef Instructor; Liaison Coordinator; Hospitality Positions; Hospitality Positions.

CORE LABORATORIES CANADA LTD.
Att: Employee Relations
2810 - 12th Street NE
Calgary, AB T2E 7P7
Tel. 403-250-4000
Fax 403-250-4064
Website .... www.corelab.com
Employer Background: Core Laboratories Canada Ltd. provides extensive analytical, consulting and field services for the petroleum industry throughout Canada. *New Positions Created (2):* Project Engineer, Special Core Analysis; Technical Sales Representatives (2).

CORE SOFTWARE CORP.
Att: Human Resources Manager
30 Concourse Gate, Suite 110
Nepean, ON K2E 7V7
Tel. 613-727-5051
Fax 613-727-2603
Email .... jobs@core.ca
Website .... www.core.ca
Employer Background: Core Software Corp. transforms legacy applications into e-business and web portal applications. *New Positions Created (5):* Delivery Support Analyst; Project Leader; VB Developer; Account Manager; VB Developers.

COREL CORPORATION
Att: Human Resources Department
1600 Carling Avenue
Ottawa, ON K1Z 8R7
Tel. 613-728-8200
Fax 613-761-1146
Website .... www.corel.com
Employer Background: Corel Corporation develops graphics and business productivity software applications. *New Positions Created (32):* Builds Engineer; Copy Writer / Copy Editor; HRIS Specialist; International Copy Editor; Systems Analyst, HRIS; Call Centre Agents; Documentation Specialist; Legal Counsel, Corporate / Commercial; Legal Counsel, Sales and Distribution; Manager, Corporate Licensing Programs; Quality Assurance Specialists, Painter; Software Developers, Creative Products Group; Technical Support Specialist; UI Designer, Creative Products Group; Manager, Corporate Licensing Programs; Technical Writers; Certification Program Manager; Channel Reporting Analyst; Documentation Specialist; Editor; Language Specialists; Localization Engineers; Product Management Positions; Quality Assurance Manager, Bryce / KPT / Web; Quality Assurance Specialists; Software Developers; Technical Writer; Training Partner Programs Manager; Brazilian Portuguese Language Specialist; International Copy Editor, Portuguese; Manager, Corporate Licensing Program; Account Manager, Canadian Federal Government.

CORETEC INC.
Att: Human Resources Department
8150 Sheppard Avenue East
Toronto, ON M1B 5K2
Tel. 416-208-2100
Fax 416-208-2189
Email .... hr@coretec-inc.com
Website .... www.coretec-inc.com
Employer Background: Founded in 1980, Coretec Inc. is a leading fabricator of printed

circuit boards. *New Positions Created (7):* Sales Representative; Printed Circuit Board Designers; QA Manager; Process Engineers; QA Professional; Process Engineers; Customer Service Representatives.

CORLAC INDUSTRIES LTD.
Att: Human Resources Manager
6010 - 53rd Avenue
Lloydminster, AB T9V 2T2

Tel. 780-875-5504
Fax 780-875-8584
Email .... corlac@corlac.com
Website .... www.corlac.com
Employer Background: Corlac Industries Ltd. manufactures, assembles and distributes all types of production equipment to the oil and gas industry. *New Positions Created (3):* Pumpjack Mechanic; Trade Positions; Welders.

CORMA INC.
Att: Human Resources
10 McCleary Court
Concord, ON L4K 2Z3

Tel. 905-669-9397
Fax 905-738-4744
Email .... info@corma.com
Website .... www.corma.com
Employer Background: Corma Inc. is a manufacturer of plastic process equipment. *New Positions Created (4):* Industrial Electrician; Quality Control Inspector; Mechanical Designer; Executive Assistant.

CORNWALL GENERAL HOSPITAL
Att: Human Resources
510 - 2nd Street East
Cornwall, ON K6H 1Z6

Tel. 613-932-3300
Fax 613-936-4619
Email .... hr@cornwallgeneralhospital.com
Website .. www.cornwallgeneralhospital.com
Employer Background: Cornwall General Hospital is an accredited, acute care community hospital, with community-based programs in mental health and withdrawal management. *New Positions Created (8):* Psychologist; Health Records Technician; Physiotherapist; Pharmacist; Social Workers, Psychogeriatric Service; Social Worker; Clinical Coordinator; Psychologist.

CORPAV PRESENTATION GROUP
Att: Operations Manager
228 - 7th Avenue West
Vancouver, BC V5Y 1M1

Fax 604-872-4211
Website .... www.corpav.com
Employer Background: CORPAV Presentation Group is a leading supplier of audiovisual equipment to the corporate, educational and video production markets. *New Positions Created (2):* Technical Services Dispatcher; Sales Representative.

CORPORATE EXPRESS
Att: Human Resources Department
2910 - 12th Street NE
Calgary, AB T2E 7P7

Tel. 403-735-2000
Fax 403-735-2137
Website .... www.corporateexpress.com
Employer Background: Corporate Express (a Buhrmann company) is an office products supplier in the business-to-business market, with operations in 28 countries. *New Positions Created (3):* Account Executives, Outside and Inside Sales; Commissioned Account Executives; Customer Service Manager.

CORPORATE RESEARCH GROUP
Att: Brian Card, President
3 Larkspur Drive
Nepean, ON K2H 6K8

Tel. 613-596-2910
Email .... brianc@thecrg.com
Website .... www.thecrg.com
Employer Background: Established in 1982, the Corporate Research Group is an Ottawa-based real estate advisory firm. *New Positions Created (2):* Technical Building Associates; Real Estate Analyst.

CORRECTIONAL SERVICE OF CANADA
Att: Treena Witte, Research Unit
2520 Central Avenue, PO Box 9243
Saskatoon, SK S7K 3X5

Tel. 306-975-4878
Fax 306-975-6024
Email .... wittetd@csc-scc.gc.ca
Website .... www.csc-scc.gc.ca
Employer Background: The Correctional Service of Canada helps offenders become law-abiding citizens, while exercising reasonable, safe, secure and humane control. *New Positions Created (5):* Forensic Psychologists; Staff Nurse; Forensic Psychologists (3); Forensic Psychologists (3); Forensic Psychologists (3).

CORRECTIONAL SERVICE OF CANADA
Att: W.J. Richards, Professional Staffing
2313 Hanselman Place, PO Box 9223
Saskatoon, SK S7K 3X5

Tel. 306-975-4878
Fax 306-975-4435
Email .... richardsjw@csc-scc.gc.ca
Website .... www.csc-scc.gc.ca
Employer Background: The Correctional Service of Canada helps offenders become law-abiding citizens, while exercising reasonable, safe, secure and humane control. *New Positions Created (4):* Psychologists; Psychologists; Psychologist; Psychologist.

CORRECTIONAL SERVICE OF CANADA, REGIONAL HEADQUARTERS (ONTARIO)
Att: Lori Rombough,
Regional Contract Administrator
440 King Street West, PO Box 1174
Kingston, ON K7L 4Y8

Tel. 613-536-6127
Fax 613-536-4571
Email .... romboughlj@csc-scc.gc.ca
Website .... www.csc-scc.gc.ca
Employer Background: The Correctional Service of Canada helps offenders become law-abiding citizens, while exercising reasonable, safe, secure and humane control. *New Positions Created (6):* Teachers, Intermediate and Senior; Teachers, Intermediate and Senior; Pharmacist; Social Worker; Psychologists (2); Teacher.

CORRIDOR PIPELINE LIMITED
Att: Human Resources Manager
PO Box 4006, Stn South
Edmonton, AB T6E 4S8

Tel. 877-275-7473
Fax 780-449-5936
Email .... work@tmpl.ca
Website .... www.corridorpipeline.com
Employer Background: Corridor Pipeline Limited, a wholly-owned subsidiary of BC Gas Inc., manages the Corridor Pipeline System, a 493-kilometre system that will link the 2 major components of the Athabasca Oil Sands Project. *New Positions Created (4):* Industrial Electrician; Instrumentation Technician; Millwright; Supervisor, Pipeline Maintenance.

CORRPRO CANADA, INC. / CORRPOWER
Att: Corrpower Rectifier Division
10848 - 214th Street
Edmonton, AB T5S 2A7

Tel. 780-447-4565
Fax 780-447-4248
Email .... corrpro1@telusplanet.net
Website .... www.corrpro.ca
Employer Background: Corrpro Canada, Inc. / Corrpower is an international leader in cathodic protection technology, corrosion prevention engineering, materials and electronics. *New Positions Created (5):* Mechanical Design Technologist; Product Testing Technologist; Quality Assurance / Quality Control Inspector; Quality Coordinator; Technical Support Technologist.

CORUS ENTERTAINMENT INC.
Att: Human Resources Department
181 Bay Street, Suite 1630
Bay-Wellington Tower, BCE Place
Toronto, ON M5J 2T3

Tel. 416-642-3770
Fax 416-530-5177
Email .... jobs@corusent.com
Website .... www.corusent.com
Employer Background: Corus Entertainment Inc. is one of Canada's leading media companies. *New Positions Created (5):* Database Systems Analyst; Oracle Systems Administrator; Producer, YTV.com; Web Business Manager; Web Programmers.

COSBURN PATTERSON MATHER LTD.
Att: Human Resources Manager
7270 Woodbine Avenue, Suite 300
Markham, ON L3R 4B9

Tel. 905-474-0455
Fax 905-474-9889
Email .... general@cosburn.com
Website .... www.cosburn.com

Employer Background: Cosburn Patterson Mather Ltd. is a consulting engineering firm, specializing in municipal design, water resource engineering, construction administration and project management. *New Positions Created (3):* CAD Technologist; Contract Administrator; Municipal Designer.

COSTCO WHOLESALE CANADA
Att: Bob James, RPh
3550 Brighton Avenue
Burnaby, BC V5A 4W3

Tel. 604-421-8353
Fax 604-444-9929
Email .... bjames@costco.com
Website .... www.costco.com

Employer Background: Costco Wholesale Canada is a leading large format retailer, operating big box superstores under the Costco and Price Club names across Canada. *New Positions Created (4):* Relief Pharmacist; Food Safety Training Coordinator / HACCP Auditor; Pharmacy Operations Manager; Photo Lab Technician.

COSYN TECHNOLOGY
Att: Human Resources Advisor
9405 - 50th Street, Suite 101
Edmonton, AB T6B 2T4

Tel. 780-440-7000
Fax 780-469-4784
Email .... hr.cosyn@colteng.com
Website .... www.colteng.com

Employer Background: CoSyn Technology, a division of Colt Engineering, provides engineering, procurement and construction management services to Syncrude Canada's expanding oil sands operations. *New Positions Created (17):* Intermediate / Senior Civil Engineer; Intermediate / Senior Piping Designers; Intermediate / Senior Structural Designers; Mechanical Engineers; Designers / Engineers, Instrument / Control Automation ; Electrical Designers; Electrical Engineers; Human Resources Leader; ICA Coordinator, CoSyn Site Office; Process Engineers; Sr Instrumentation Technologist, Instrument Control Automation; Senior Process Engineers; Designers / Engineers; Electrical Designers; Electrical Engineers; HR Leader; Process Engineers.

COTTON GINNY LTD.
Att: Sr. District Manager, Power Centres
40 Samor Road
Toronto, ON M6A 1J6

Tel. 416-785-9686
Fax 416-785-9687
Email ...... recruiting@cottonginnyltd.com
Website .... www.cottonginnyltd.com

Employer Background: Cotton Ginny Ltd. is a national ladies' wear retailer, with over 200 stores across Canada. *New Positions Created (5):* Sales Associates; Store Mgrs; Inventory Analyst; Merchandise Allocator; Area Mgr.

COUGAR AUTOMATION TECHNOLOGIES INC.
Att: Human Resources Manager
45 Sheppard Avenue East, Suite 307
Toronto, ON M2N 5W9

Tel. 416-221-6076
Fax 416-221-6498
Email .... hr@cougarautomation.com
Website .... www.cougarautomation.com

Employer Background: Cougar Automation Technologies Inc. is a partnership of electrical engineering professionals, offering services to end-users and other engineering firms in all areas of automation technology. *New Positions Created (6):* Project Manager; Senior Electrical Controls Engineer; Electrical Draftsperson; Junior Electrical Engineers; Marketing Coordinator; SCADA Engineers.

COUGHLIN & ASSOCIATES LTD.
Att: Human Resources Manager
333 Preston Street, Suite 200
Ottawa, ON K1S 5N4

Tel. 613-231-2266
Fax 613-231-2345
Email .... hr@coughlin.ca
Website .... www.coughlin.ca

Employer Background: Coughlin & Associates Ltd. is an employee benefits firm, with offices in Ottawa and Winnipeg. *New Positions Created (4):* Bilingual Group Administrator, Pension Plans; Bilingual Senior Group Benefits Administrator; Bilingual Group Administration Team Leader; Bilingual Group Administrator.

COUNCIL OF ONTARIO UNIVERSITIES / COU
Att: Office of Health Sciences
180 Dundas Street West, Suite 1100
Toronto, ON M5G 1Z8

Tel. 416-979-2165
Fax 416-979-8635
Email .... cgomez@cou.on.ca
Website .... www.cou.on.ca

Employer Background: Formed in 1962, COU works to improve the quality and accessibility of higher education in Ontario, representing the collective interests of 17 member institutions and 2 associate members. *New Positions Created (2):* Project Coordinator; Project Coordinator.

COUNTRY DAY SCHOOL, THE
Att: Paul C. Duckett, Headmaster
13415 Dufferin Street
King City, ON L7B 1K5

Tel. 905-833-1220
Fax 905-833-7049
Website .... www.cds.on.ca

Employer Background: The Country Day School is a university preparatory, co-educational school, serving 700 students from junior kindergarten to OAC. *New Positions Created (5):* Teacher Librarian; Intermediate Science Teacher; Primary / Junior Physical Education Teacher; Teacher / Counsellor, Guidance and Career Education; French Teacher, Primary / Junior.

COVENANT HOUSE TORONTO
Att: Human Resources Coordinator
20 Gerrard Street East
Toronto, ON M5B 2P3

Fax 416-204-7030

Email .... hr@covenanthouse.on.ca
Website .... www.covenanthouse.on.ca

Employer Background: Covenant House is one of Canada's largest youth shelters, providing care services to runaway and homeless young people between the ages of 16 and 24. *New Positions Created (7):* Life Skills Coordinator; Resident Advisors (11); Shift Supervisors (2); Supervisor, Community Support Services; Team Leader, Rights of Passage Program; Youth Workers; Youth Worker.

COVENANT HOUSE VANCOUVER
Att: Human Resources
575 Drake Street
Vancouver, BC V6B 4K8

Fax 604-685-5324
Email .... hr@covenanthousebc.org
Website .... www.covenanthousebc.org

Employer Background: Covenant House Vancouver is a youth-care organization, providing short-term crisis and transitional shelter to runaway, homeless and street youth. *New Positions Created (2):* Client Service Coordinators; Youth Workers.

COWAN GRAPHICS LTD.
Att: Human Resources
9253 - 48th Street
Edmonton, AB T6B 2R9

Tel. 780-468-7220
Fax 780-466-4969
Website .... www.cowan.ca

Employer Background: Cowan Graphics Ltd. manufactures screenprinted graphics. *New Positions Created (2):* Sales Position; Controller.

COWATER INTERNATIONAL INC.
Att: Human Resources Manager
411 Roosevelt Avenue, Suite 400
Ottawa, ON K2A 3X9

Tel. 613-722-6434
Fax 613-722-5893
Email .... jobs@cowater.com
Website .... www.cowater.com

Employer Background: Cowater International Inc. is an international development consulting firm, specializing in government accountability, water, sanitation and social development sectors. *New Positions Created (2):* Marketing Coordinator; Long-Term Advisor.

COWELL AUTO GROUP
Att: Tom Nicholson, Human Resources
13611 Smallwood Place
Richmond Auto Mall
Richmond, BC V6V 1W8

Tel. 604-273-3922
Fax 604-273-0758
Email .... hr@cowellautogroup.com
Website .... www.cowellautogroup.com

Employer Background: Cowell Auto Group is an automotive dealership, with 30 years experience. *New Positions Created (13):* General Sales Manager; Business Manager; Warranty Clerk; Service Technicians; Service Advisor; Parts Advisor; Shipper / Receiver; Sales and Leasing Guide; Audi Brand Specialist; Service Manager; Warranty Clerk; Service Advisor; Parts Advisor.

CPI CANADA INC.
Att: Human Resources Manager
45 River Drive
Georgetown, ON L7G 2J4
Tel. 905-877-0161
Fax 905-877-2658
Email .... denny.foley@cmp.cpii.com
Website .... www.cpii.com
Employer Background: CPI Canada Inc. develops millimeter-wave vacuum electron devices for terrestrial, satcom, broadcast and radar applications, high-voltage power supplies, electronic control systems for semiconductor processing and x-ray generators for medical applications. *New Positions Created (15):* Intermediate Accountant; Contacts Administrator; RF Design Engineers; RF Test Engineer; Software Engineers; Various Engineering Positions; Buyers / Planners; Cost / Operations Accountants; Information Systems Analysts; Mechanical Designers; Microwave Engineers; Senior Contracts Administrator; Technician Positions; Various Engineering Positions; X-Ray Field Service Representative.

CPI PLASTICS GROUP LTD.
Att: Human Resources
979 Gana Court
Mississauga, ON L5S 1N9
Tel. 416-798-9333
Fax 416-798-9229
Email .... careers@cpiplastics.com
Website .... www.cpiplastics.com
Employer Background: CPI Plastics Group Ltd. is a North American supplier of extruded thermoplastic systems, functional components and decorative trims. *New Positions Created (10):* Director, Operations; General Manager; Accounts Receivable Clerk; Marketing Director; Product Designer; Corporate Engineering Manager; Regional Sales Managers (2); Marketing Director; Product Designer; Product Manager, EON.

CPUSED
Att: Human Resources Manager
488 Dupont Street
Toronto, ON M6G 1Y7
Tel. 416-533-2001
Fax 416-533-2887
Email .... sales@cpused.com
Website .... www.cpused.com
Employer Background: CPUsed is a large Macintosh dealer. *New Positions Created (4):* Macintosh Sales and Service Positions; Shipper / Receiver; Sales / Service Position; Shipper / Receiver.

CQUAY INC.
Att: Human Resources Manager
555 - 4th Avenue SW, Suite 300
Calgary, AB T2P 3E7
Tel. 403-262-6141
Fax 403-233-2135
Email .... careers@cquay.com

Website .... www.cquay.com
Employer Background: Cquay Inc. (formerly the TPI Group) is an IT consulting, software engineering and technology company, helping engineering and scientific organizations solve technical, geospatial and geotechnical data, systems and process problems. *New Positions Created (15):* Account Executive; Marketing Communications Manager; Middleware Developers; Oracle Database Administrators; Oracle Developers; Product Manager; Product Marketing Manager; Project Managers; Quality Assurance Specialist; Receptionist / Office Administrator; Technical Team Leader; Technical Writer; Technology Research Scientists; Web Developers; Web Master Designer.

CRANBROOK HEALTH COUNCIL
Att: D. L. Davidson, Director, Corporate Development and Human Resourcees
13 - 24th Avenue North
Cranbrook, BC V1C 3H9
Tel. 250-489-6439
Fax 250-426-5285
Email ...... don.davidson@cchc.hnet.bc.ca
Website www.cranbrookhealthcouncil.org
Employer Background: CHC provides health services to residents of Cranbrook and East Kootenay. *New Positions Created (2):* Director of Health Services; Chemistry Section Head / Medical Technologist.

CRAPE GEOMATICS CORPORATION
Att: Human Resources Manager
640 - 12th Avenue SW, Suite 300
Calgary, AB T2R 0H5
Tel. 403-262-6585
Fax 403-261-9983
Email .... employment@crape.com
Website .... www.crape.com
Employer Background: Crape Geomatics Corporation provides geomatic solutions to the resource industries of Alberta, Saskatchewan and countries worldwide. *New Positions Created (3):* CAD Operator; Party Chief; Survey Assistant.

CRAWFORD HEALTHCARE MANAGEMENT
Att: Ghita Segal, Branch Manager
1 Raymond Street, 2nd Floor
Ottawa, ON K1R 1A2
Fax 613-233-5121
Email .... segalg0@crawco.ca
Website .. www.crawfordandcompany.com
Employer Background: Crawford Healthcare Management is an international disability management company. *New Positions Created (2):* Occupational Therapist; Workers' Compensation Claims Mgmnt Consultant.

CREATION TECHNOLOGIES INC.
Att: Human Resources Administrator
3938 North Fraser Way
Burnaby, BC V5J 5H6
Tel. 604-430-4336
Fax 604-430-4337
Email .... future@creationtech.com
Website .... www.creationtech.com

Employer Background: Creation Technologies Inc. is an independent electronics manufacturing service provider, with plants in British Columbia and Ontario. *New Positions Created (22):* Engineering Support Technicians; IT Support Technician; Project Engineer; Project Managers; Electronic Components Buyer; Senior Process Engineer; Electronic Component Buyers; Program Manager; Project Engineers; Project Managers; Purchasing Manager; RF Test Engineer; Test Engineers; Accounts Receivable Administrator; Afternoon Shift Inspectors; Controller; Electronics Buyers; Financial / Cost Analyst; Human Resources Staff; Maintenance Associate; RF-Test Engineers; RF-Test Technicians.

CREATION TECHNOLOGIES INC.
Att: Human Resources Manager
7075 Financial Drive
Mississauga, ON L5N 6V8
Tel. 905-814-6323
Fax 905-814-6324
Email .... future@creationtech.com
Website .... www.creationtech.com
Employer Background: Creation Technologies Inc. is an independent electronics manufacturing service provider, with plants in British Columbia and Ontario. *New Positions Created (3):* MRP Implementation Specialist; Project Manager / Engineer; Quality Engineer.

CREDENTIAL GROUP
Att: Human Resources
1441 Creekside Drive, 8th Floor
Vancouver, BC V6J 4S7
Fax 604-714-3865
Website .... www.credential.com
Employer Background: Credential Group is one of the fastest growing wealth management providers in Canada, supporting credit unions, investors, advisors and industry participants. *New Positions Created (3):* Research Officer; Finance Positions (4); Sales Assistant.

CREDIT VALLEY CONSERVATION
Att: Karen Brown,
Corporate Services Coordinator
1255 Derry Road West
Meadowvale, ON L5N 6R4
Tel. 905-670-1615
Fax 905-670-2210
Email .... kbrown@creditvalleycons.com
Website .... www.creditvalleycons.com
Employer Background: CVC, a partnership of municipalities in the Credit River Watershed, ensures a clean supply of water for human and environmental needs. *New Positions Created (2):* General Manager; Water Resources Engineer.

CREDIT VALLEY HOSPITAL, THE
Att: Human Resources Department
2200 Eglinton Avenue West
Mississauga, ON L5M 2N1
Tel. 905-813-1573
Fax 905-813-2280

Email .... hr@cvh.on.ca
Website .... www.cvh.on.ca

Employer Background: The Credit Valley Hospital is a 366-bed community hospital, with regional programs in dialysis and genetics, and planned regional programs in cancer treatment, child care and maternal care. *New Positions Created (62):* Nurse Manager, Special Care Nursery; Nurse Manager, Surgery; Nurse Managers, Haemodialysis; Registered Technologist II, MRI; Supervisor, Hematology; Telecommunications Analyst; Autopsy Technologist; Genetics Assistant; Supervisor, Transfusion Medicine; Technologist II, Biochemistry; Director, Volunteer Services; Pharmacist, Nephrology; Project Assistant, Facility Planning; Application Specialist; Music Therapist; Patient Liaison Officer; Risk Management Specialist; Audiologists; Clinical Leader, Oncology Program; Nurse Manager, Haemodialysis; Nurse Manager, Special Care Nursery; Occupational Therapists, Physical Medicine; Physiotherapist; Cardiac Rehabilitation Therapist; Central Service Assistant; Pharmacists; Physiotherapist; Resource Centre Representative; Imaging Supervisor, Computed Radiography; Laboratory Technologist II, Microbiology; Registered Nurses; Echocardiography Technologist; Nuclear Medicine Technologist; Occupational Therapist; Supervisor, Hematology; Application Specialist; Manager, Application Services; Technical Support Specialist; Physician Director, Surgical Oncology; Nurse Educator, Emergency; Nurse Managers; Regional Neonatal Education Coordinator; Medical Secretaries; Social Workers; Clinical Leader, Oncology Program; Diet Clerk / Clerical Support Specialist; Clinical Leader, Inpatient Dietitians; Occupational Therapists; Pharmacists; Registered Nurses; Speech Language Pathologists; Health Information Management Director; Laboratory Technologist II, Histology; Registered Nurse, Imaging / Angiography; Campaign Assistant; Campaign Director; Patient Feedback Representative; Secretary to the Chief Development Officer; Respiratory Therapists, Cardiopulmonary; Laboratory Technologists, Chemistry and Hematology; Supervisor, Hematology; Director, Information Systems and Telecommunications.

CREE BOARD OF HEALTH AND SOCIAL SERVICES OF JAMES BAY
Att: Colette Fink,
Personnel Management Consultant
Chisasibi, QC J0M 1E0
Tel. 819-855-2844
Fax 819-855-2680
Email .... vsnowboy@ssss.gouv.qc.ca

Employer Background: The Cree Board of Health and Social Services of James Bay delivers health and social services to the nine communities of James Bay, Quebec. *New Positions Created (7):* Assistant Executive Director, Services; Health and Safety Officer; Program Manager of Non-Insured Health Benefits; Social Service Worker; Dietitian; Human Relations Officers (2); Occupational Therapist.

CREE SCHOOL BOARD
Att: Personnel Services
203 Main Street
Mistissini, QC G0W 1C0
Tel. 418-923-2764
Fax 418-923-2073
Website .... www.cscree.qc.ca/csb

Employer Background: The Cree School Board operates 9 schools in northern Quebec, providing education to 3,600 Cree students. *New Positions Created (6):* School Principals; School Vice-Principal; Librarian; Teachers; School Vice-Principal; Teachers.

CREOSCITEX
Att: Human Resources
3700 Gilmore Way
Burnaby, BC V5G 4M1
Tel. 604-451-2700
Fax 604-451-2770
Email .... resume@creoscitex.com
Website .... www.creoscitex.com

Employer Background: CreoScitex, a division of Creo Products Inc., is a leading manufacturer of computer-to-plate systems for commercial printers. *New Positions Created (42):* Application Software Developer; First Call Administrator, Response Centre; Project / Product Manager, On-Press Technologies; Remote Support Associate; Software Developer, DOP Technology Team; Software Developer, Service Shell Team; User Interface Software Developer; Mechanical Account Manager; Purchasing Manager; Core Team Leader; Product Support Specialist; Team Leader, Araxi Integration; Product Manager, SYNAPSE Director ; Production Manager, TSVLF / TSVLF AL / Thermoflex; Recruiter, Product Development; Corporate Product Manager, Leasing; Electrical Design Engineer, On-Press Technologies; Intermediate Firmware Developer; Technical Writer; Machine Shop Manager, Imaging & Media; Product Applications Scientist; Production Engineer; Project Manager, Applied Imaging & Media; System Physicists; Lens Designer / Optical Systems Designer; Media Specialist / Scientist; Thermal Imaging Production Integrator; Director, New Business Venture; R&D Manager, Thermal Imaging; Account Manager; Electrical Account Manager; Materials Scientist; Non-Production Procurement Account Manager; Product / Project Manager; Purchasing Manager; R & D Manager; Communications Web Master; Product Marketing Specialist; Facilities Manager; Financial Analyst; Product Marketing Specialist; Executive Assistant - High Tech.

CRESCENT CUSTOM YACHTS
Att: Gary Negrin,
Administration and Resource Manager
11580 Mitchell Road
Richmond, BC V6V 1T7
Tel. 604-301-3900
Fax 604-301-3901
Website . www.crescentcustomyachts.com

Employer Background: Established in 1986, Crescent Custom Yachts builds custom luxury yachts. *New Positions Created (7):* Fairers; Mechanical Equipment Installers; Welders; Trades Positions; Carpenters and Laminators; Electrical and Mechanical Technicians; Draftspersons.

CRESCENT SCHOOL
Att: Human Resources
2365 Bayview Avenue
Toronto, ON M2L 1A2
Tel. 416-449-2556
Fax 416-449-0952
Website .... www.crescentschool.org

Employer Background: Founded in 1913, Crescent School is private day school for boys, offering instruction from grades 3 to 13. The school has 640 students and 53 faculty members. *New Positions Created (4):* Development and Alumni Relations Coordinator; Manager, Major Gifts; Head of Middle School; Teacher, Modern Languages.

CRESTWOOD SCHOOL
Att: Mrs. D. Eisen
411 Lawrence Avenue East
Toronto, ON M3C 1N9
Fax 416-444-2127
Website .... www.crestwoodschool.com

Employer Background: Established in 1980, Crestwood School is a private, co-educational day school for students in junior kindergarten to grade 6. *New Positions Created (2):* Elementary Music Teacher; Teachers.

CRITICAL MASS INC.
Att: Human Resources Manager
805 - 10th Avenue SW, Suite 305
Calgary, AB T2R 0B4
Tel. 403-262-3006
Fax 403-262-7185
Email .... future@criticalmass.com
Website .... www.criticalmass.com

Employer Background: Critical Mass Inc. is an interactive marketing agency. *New Positions Created (8):* Database Administrators; Database Architects; Lead Developers; Sr Software Architects; Sr Systems Administrator; Software Project Managers; Software Testers; Various Advertising Positions (2).

CROMEDICA INC.
Att: Manager, Office of the Chairman
730 View Street, Suite 600
Victoria, BC V8W 3Y7
Tel. 250-480-0818
Fax 250-480-0819
Email .... kdranchuk@cromedica.com
Website .... www.cromedica.com

Employer Background: CroMedica Inc. is a contract research organization, working with pharmaceutical companies to ensure their products are safe and effective. *New Positions Created (8):* Project Management Associate; V.P., Human Resources; Clinical Research Associates; Nurse Manager; Biostatician; Project Manager; Statistical Programmer; Vice President, Biometry.

CROMEDICA INC.
Att: Human Resources
1145 Hunt Club Road, Suite 100
Ottawa, ON K1V 0Y3

Tel. 613-739-8162
Fax 613-739-8163
Email .... hr@cromedica.com
Website .... www.cromedica.com

Employer Background: CroMedica Inc. is a contract research organization, working with pharmaceutical companies to ensure their products are safe and effective. *New Positions Created (27):* Assistant Project Manager; Biostatistician; Clinical Pharmacologist; Clinical Research Associates; Data Manager; Medical Writer; Pharmacovigilance Operations Assistant; Project Managers; Regulatory Affairs Associate; Regulatory Publishing Manager; Senior Clinical Research Associates; Project Management Associate; SAS Programmers; Associate Medical Director; Clinical Data Reviewer; Clinical Research Associate Manager; Medical Monitoring Associate; Assistant Project Managers; Biostatistician; Clinical Operations Assistant; Data Manager; Medical Writer; Regulatory Affairs Associate; Regulatory Publishing Manager; Senior Clinical Research Associate; Clinical Data Reviewers; Assistant Director, Medical Affairs.

CROPAC EQUIPMENT LTD.
Att: Bill Finkle Senior
1007 South Service Road
Oakville, ON L6L 6R3

Tel. 905-825-6377
Fax 905-825-5264
Website .... www.cropac.com

Employer Background: Cropac Equipment Ltd. is a leader in the mobile crane industry. *New Positions Created (4):* Parts Order Desk Clerk; Service Coordinator; Various Trades Positions; Various Trades / Technician Positions.

CROSS CANCER INSTITUTE / CCI
Att: Mrs. L. Bush
11560 University Avenue
Edmonton, AB T6G 1Z2

Tel. 780-432-8411
Fax 780-432-8886
Email .... careers@cancerboard.ab.ca
Website .... www.cancerboard.ab.ca

Employer Background: Operated by the Alberta Cancer Board, CCI is a comprehensive cancer treatment and research facility, serving Edmonton and northern Alberta. *New Positions Created (10):* Director of Rehabilitation; Radiation Safety Officer; Senior Manager, Nursing; Equipment Service Specialist; Clinical Associate; Chief, Oncologic Imaging; Registered Nurses, Inpatient and Outpatient; Registered Nurses; Psychosocial Counsellor; Oncology Nurse.

CROSSEY ENGINEERING LTD.
Att: Human Resources Manager
2255 Sheppard Avenue East, Suite E-331
Toronto, ON M2J 4Y1

Tel. 416-497-3111
Fax 416-497-7210
Email .... cel@cel.ca
Website .... www.cel.ca

Employer Background: Crossey Engineering Ltd. is a progressive consulting engineering firm, providing building services for industrial, commercial and institutional clients. *New Positions Created (7):* Electrical Power Distribution Engineer; CAD Operators; Designers; Engineering Positions; Electrical Engineers; Mechanical Engineers; Senior Designers.

CROSSROADS REGIONAL HEALTH AUTHORITY, CROSSROADS HOSPITAL & HEALTH CENTRE
Att: Anne Brown, HR Assistant
6910 - 47th Street
Wetaskiwin, AB T9A 3N3

Tel. 780-361-4154
Fax 780-361-4107
Email ..... anne.brown@crossroadsrha.net

Employer Background: Crossroads Regional Health Authority provides comprehensive health services to 50,000 residents of a rural region located south of Edmonton. *New Positions Created (3):* Regional Director; Resident Care Services Leader, Continuing Care; Occupational Therapist I.

CROWN CORK & SEAL CANADA INC.
Att: Gary Nichols, HR Manager
7900 Keele Street
Concord, ON L4K 2A3

Tel. 905-669-1401
Fax 905-669-9611
Website .... www.crowncork.com

Employer Background: Crown Cork & Seal Canada Inc. is a leader in the metal packaging business. *New Positions Created (6):* Electrical Supervisor; Machine Shop Supervisor; Electrical Supervisor; Production Scheduler; Statistical Process Control Coordinator; Machine Shop Supervisor.

CROWN WALLPAPER + FABRICS
Att: Manager, Human Resources
88 Ronson Drive
Toronto, ON M9W 1B9

Tel. 416-245-2900
Fax 416-245-9726

Employer Background: Crown Wallpaper + Fabrics is a national distributor of decorative wallcovering and fabric. *New Positions Created (3):* Inside Sales Position; Cost Accountant; CAD Operator.

CROWNE PLAZA TORONTO CENTRE
Att: Human Resources
225 Front Street West
Toronto, ON M5V 2X3

Tel. 416-597-1400
Fax 416-597-8164
Email ... tpierni@crowneplazatoronto.com
Website ..... www.crowneplazatoronto.com

Employer Background: Crowne Plaza Toronto Centre is a 587-room hotel in downtown Toronto. *New Positions Created (2):* Director, Facility Operations; Executive Chef.

CRS ROBOTICS CORPORATION
Att: Al Outhouse
5344 John Lucas Drive
Burlington, ON L7L 6A6

Tel. 905-332-2000

Fax 905-332-1114
Email .... hr@crsrobotics.com
Website .... www.crsrobotics.com

Employer Background: CRS Robotics Corporation manufactures and markets integrated laboratory workstations, laboratory peripheral products and articulated robots for various lab and advanced manufacturing processes. *New Positions Created (3):* Applications Scientist; Product Manager, Drug Discovery; Production Manager, Drug Discovery.

CRYOCATH TECHNOLOGIES INC.
Att: Human Resources
16711 Chemin Ste. Marie
Kirkland, QC H9H 5H3

Tel. 514-694-1212
Fax 514-694-7075
Email .... hr@cryocath.com
Website .... www.cryocath.com

Employer Background: Established in 1994, CryoCath Technologies Inc. develops cost-effective catheter cryotherapy products and support systems for the treatment of cardiovascular disease. *New Positions Created (3):* Design Quality Assurance Technician; Pre-Clinical Coordinator; Research and Development Testing Technician.

CRYOVAC CANADA INC.
Att: Dick Irvine,
Employee Development Manager
2365 Dixie Road
Mississauga, ON L4Y 2A2

Tel. 905-273-5656
Fax 905-273-3572
Website .... www.cryovac.com

Employer Background: Cryovac Canada Inc. is a leading manufacturer of flexible plastic packaging products, packaging machines and art services. *New Positions Created (2):* Analytical Services Technologist; Service Technician, Packaging.

CRYSTAL HOMES
Att: Human Resources Manager
161 Rebecca Street
Hamilton, ON L8R 1B9

Tel. 905-318-7894
Fax 905-318-9503
Website .... www.crystalhomes.com

Employer Background: Crystal Homes is a new home construction company. *New Positions Created (3):* Construction Manager, New Home Construction; Accounting Position; Administrative Assistant / Customer Service Manager Position.

CSA INTERNATIONAL
Att: Julie Johnston
1707 - 94th Street
Edmonton, AB T6N 1E6

Tel. 780-450-2111
Fax 780-461-5322
Email ... julie.johnston@csa-international.org
Website .... www.csa-international.org

Employer Background: CSA International is a leader in the field of standards development through certification, testing programs and quality management systems. *New Positions Created (2):* Certification Specialist, Hazardous Locations; Certification Specialist / Engineer.

CSA INTERNATIONAL
Att: Human Resources
178 Rexdale Boulevard
Toronto, ON M9W 1R3
Tel. 416-747-4000
Fax 416-747-2475
Email .... info@csa-international.org
Website .... www.csagroup.org
Employer Background: CSA International is a leader in the field of standards development through certification, testing programs and quality management systems. *New Positions Created (19):* Editor, Grade II; Executive Assistant; Client Services Specialist; Confidential Secretary; Engineer, Motors & Controls; Engineering Technician / Technologist; Manager, Credit and Collections; Manager, Editorial and Production Services; Quality Assurance Manager; Senior Accounting Clerk; Senior Systems Analyst, Materials Management; Supervisor, Customer Services / Agreements; Engineer, EMC / EMI; Engineer, HVAC; Engineer, Industrial Control; Engineer, Plumbing; Engineer, Wiring Products; Engineers; Engineers and Technologists, Hazardous Locations.

CSB SYSTEMS LTD.
Att: Human Resources Manager
420 Britannia Road East, Suite 200
Mississauga, ON L4Z 3L5
Tel. 905-507-4477
Fax 905-507-4505
Email .... hr@csbsystems.com
Website .... www.csbsystems.com
Employer Background: Established in 1986, CSB Systems Ltd. provides fully integrated information solutions to manufacturers and distributors. *New Positions Created (4):* IMPACT Encore Implementation Specialists; Navision Application Developers; Navision Implementation Specialists; Regional Administrator.

CSI WIRELESS INC.
Att: Human Resources Manager
1200 - 58th Avenue SE
Calgary, AB T2H 2C9
Tel. 403-259-3311
Fax 403-259-8866
Email .... tschmidt@csi-wireless.com
Website .... www.csi-wireless.com
Employer Background: CSI Wireless Inc. provides low-cost, advanced wireless and precision GPS hardware for the automotive, commercial and consumer markets. *New Positions Created (5):* Manufacturing Engineer; Firmware Engineer; Product / Project Managers; Software Test Engineer / Technician; Human Resources Professional.

CTC COMMUNICATIONS CORP.
Att: Human Resources
121 Lakeshore Road East, Suite 203
Mississauga, ON L5G 1E5
Tel. 905-274-3414

Fax 905-274-2954
Employer Background: CTC Communications Corp. is a leading medical publishing and CME event-planning firm. *New Positions Created (4):* Controller / Administration Systems Manager; Medical Advertising Sales Representative; Project Coordinator; Sales Account Manager, Continuing Medical Education.

CTF SYSTEMS INC.
Att: Human Resources Manager
1750 McLean Avenue, Suite 15
Port Coquitlam, BC V3C 1M9
Tel. 604-941-8561
Fax 604-941-8565
Email .... humanresources@ctf.com
Website .... www.ctf.com
Employer Background: CTF Systems Inc. develops and manufactures magneto-encephalographic (MEG) systems to measure magnetic signals from the human brain. *New Positions Created (5):* Electronics Technologist; Hardware-Firmware Design Engineer; Junior Software Technical Writer; Junior Software Tester; Technical Clerk.

CTM BROCHURE DISPLAY LTD.
Att: Human Resources Manager
1011 Haultain Court, Unit 2
Mississauga, ON L4W 1W1
Tel. 905-624-8950
Fax 905-624-2766
Email .... kblack@ctmbd.com
Website ..... www.ctmbrochuredisplay.com
Employer Background: CTM Brochure Display Ltd. is a leading distributor of tourist brochures. *New Positions Created (2):* Account Manager; Sales Manager.

CTS OF CANADA LTD.
Att: Human Resources Department
80 Thomas Street
Streetsville, ON L5M 1Y9
Tel. 905-826-1141
Fax 905-858-9058
Email ..... human.resources@ac.ctscorp.com
Website .... www.ctscorp.com
Employer Background: CTS of Canada Ltd. is a global OEM supplier of electromechanical components. *New Positions Created (7):* Plant Electrician; Design Engineer; Electronics Engineer; Materials Manager; Operations Supervisor, Midnight Shift; Process Engineer; Quality Assurance Engineer.

CUE DATAWEST LTD.
Att: Human Resources Manager
1441 Creekside Drive, Suite 300
Vancouver, BC V6J 4S7
Tel. 604-734-7494
Fax 604-737-8002
Email .... recruit@cuedatawest.com
Website .... www.cuedatawest.com
Employer Background: Cue Datawest Ltd. provides technology solutions for financial services. *New Positions Created (10):* Help Desk Receptionist; Manager, MIS; Project Manager, Operations; Receptionist; Senior Support Specialist; Accountant; Clerical As-

sistant; Product Support Specialist, Loans Team; Senior Business Analyst; Software Developer.

CUMIS GROUP LTD., THE
Att: Human Resources
151 North Service Road, PO Box 5065
Burlington, ON L7R 4C2
Tel. 905-632-1221
Fax 905-639-7641
Email .... hr_resumes@cumis.org
Website .... www.cumis.com
Employer Background: The CUMIS Group Ltd. is a national insurance organization, serving the Canadian cooperative financial system. *New Positions Created (18):* Disability Claims Examiners (3); Accounts Manager; Bilingual Accounts Supervisor; Sales & Service Representative, Group Retirement Services; Executive Assistant; Accounts Supervisor, Fidelity and Professional Liability; Bilingual Claims Manager, Fidelity and Professional Liability; Claims Examiner, Fidelity and Professional Liability.; Retirement Services Sales and Service Representative; Senior Underwriter, Commercial Property and Casualty; Underwriter, Fidelity and Professional Liability; Compliance Officer; Claims Centre Manager; Product / Marketing Actuarial Associate; Director, Personal Lines; Senior Internal Auditor; Regional Sales Consultant; Marketing and Communications Specialist.

CUMMINS INC.
Att: Janice Romanzin-Roy
11751 - 181st Street
Edmonton, AB T5S 2K5
Tel. 780-455-2151
Website .... www.cummins.com
Employer Background: Cummins Inc. manufactures diesel engines and deals with power systems sales and service. *New Positions Created (7):* Technical Sales Representative; Branch Manager; Diesel Electric Technicians; Field Mechanic; Inside Sales Coordinator; Serialized Inventory Accountant; Field Mechanic.

CUMMINS INC.
Att: Human Resources
20 Ashtonbee Road
Toronto, ON M1L 4R5
Fax 416-288-1525
Email ... colleen.a.marostica@cummins.com
Website .... www.cummins.com
Employer Background: Cummins Inc. manufactures diesel engines. *New Positions Created (2):* Materials Manager; Information Technology Leader.

CUNNINGHAM & LINDSEY CANADA LTD.
Att: Human Resources
25 Main Street West, 18th Floor
Hamilton, ON L8P 1H1
Fax 905-667-0117
Email .... hrcanada@
.... na.cunninghamlindsey.com
Website .... www.cunninghamlindsey.com

Employer Background: Cunningham & Lindsey Canada is an insurance adjusting firm. *New Positions Created (8):* Accident Benefits Assistant; Warranty Administrator; Content Administrator; Accident Benefits Adjuster / Examiner; Claims Supervisor; Accident Benefits Assistant; Telephone Claims Adjusters; Delphi Programmer Analyst.

CUSO
Att: Human Resources Department
2255 Carling Avenue, Suite 400
Ottawa, ON K2B 1A6

Tel. 613-829-7445
Fax 613-829-1303
Email .... hrd.srh@cuso.ca
Website .... www.cuso.org

Employer Background: CUSO is a Canadian non-profit organization, with over 35 years experience in international development. *New Positions Created (2):* Executive Director; Regional Directors (2).

CUSTOMER CARE INSURANCE AGENCY LTD. / CCIA
Att: Human Resources Manager
3 Robert Speck Parkway, 4th Floor
Mississauga, ON L4Z 3Z9

Tel. 905-306-3900
Fax 905-306-3148
Email . nicholas.woods@thepersonal.com
Website .... www.thepersonal.com

Employer Background: CCIA provides customer-care telephone services for clients of CIBC Insurance. *New Positions Created (2):* Professional Sales Consultants; Professional Sales Consultants.

CUSTOMS EXCISE UNION DOUANES ACCISE / CEUDA
Att: Serge Charette, National President
1741 Woodward Drive
Ottawa, ON K2C 0P9

Tel. 613-723-8008
Fax 613-723-7895
Email .... legauli@psac.com
Website .... www.ceuda.psac.com

Employer Background: CEUDA represents all GST, excise, and customs employees of the Canada Customs and Revenue Agency. *New Positions Created (2):* Technical Officers (2); Secretary.

CVDS INC.
Att: Human Resources Manager
6900 Trans Canada Highway
Pointe-Claire, QC H9R 1C2

Tel. 514-694-9320
Fax 514-694-0786
Website .... www.cvdsinc.com

Employer Background: CVDS Inc. develops and manufactures telecom and power conversion products. *New Positions Created (4):* Junior Telecom Technologist; Sales Representative; Senior / Intermediate Software Designers; Technical Support Specialist.

CWB GROUP
Att: Valerie Smyth
7250 West Credit Avenue,

Industry Services
Mississauga, ON L5N 5N1

Tel. 905-342-1312
Fax 905-542-1318
Email .... valerie.smyth@cwbgroup.com
Website .... www.cwbgroup.com

Employer Background: CWB Group (formerly the Canadian Welding Bureau) is comprised of 3 operating divisions: Canadian Welding Bureau (CWB), QUASAR and Gooderham Center for Industrial Learning (GCIL). *New Positions Created (6):* Welding Technician; Certification Services Representative; Certified Lead Auditor, QUASAR; Certification Services Representatives; Training Representative; Certified Lead Auditor.

CWD WINDOWS AND DOORS
Att: Human Resources Manager
2008 - 48th Street SE
Calgary, AB T2B 2E5

Tel. 403-272-8871
Fax 403-569-3181
Website .... www.cwdwindows.com

Employer Background: Founded in 1958, CWD Windows and Doors is a leading manufacturer of wood and vinyl windows and entrance systems for the new home construction and renovation markets. *New Positions Created (2):* Glass Shop Manager; Help Desk / PC Support Position.

CYBERSURF CORPORATION
Att: Human Resources Manager
1212 - 31st Avenue NE, Suite 312
Calgary, AB T2E 7S8

Tel. 403-777-2000
Fax 403-777-2003
Email .... jobs@cybersurf.net
Website .... www.cybersurf.net

Employer Background: CyberSurf Corporation develops connectivity and communications software, and operates through two subsidiaries: CyberSurf Technologies and 3web Corporation. *New Positions Created (20):* Interactive Media Account Executive; Intermediate Software Developer; Multimedia Software Developers; Project Coordinator; Senior Macintosh Applications Developer; Unix Administrator; Interactive Media Account Executive; Intermediate Software Developer; Junior Quality Assurance Specialist; Multimedia Software Developers; Senior Database Analyst; Senior Macintosh Applications Developer; Executive Assistant; Advertising Account Executive; Creative Writer; Marketing Facilitator; Sales Liaison; Sales Prospector; Senior Graphic Designer; Recruiter.

CYMBOLIC SCIENCES INC.
Att: Human Resources Manager
13231 Delf Place, Suite 501
Richmond, BC V6V 2C3

Tel. 604-273-7730
Fax 604-273-8646
Email .... hr@cymbolic.com
Website .... www.cymbolic.com

Employer Background: Cymbolic Sciences Inc. (a member of Gretag Group) markets

digital imaging products, including computer-to-plate systems, wide format printers and film recorders. *New Positions Created (8):* Controller; Customer Support Administrator; Human Resources Generalist; Buyer; Electrical Engineer; Mechanical Engineer; Optical Engineer; Software Engineer.

CYPRESS ENERGY INC.
Att: Supervisor, General Accounting
500 - 4th Avenue SW, Suite 2700
Calgary, AB T2P 2V6

Tel. 403-262-8225
Fax 403-750-5488
Website .... www.cypressenergy.com

Employer Background: Cypress Energy Inc. is a publicly-traded Canadian energy company involved in the exploration, development, acquisition and production of crude oil and natural gas in western Canada. *New Positions Created (2):* Operations Accountant; Intermediate Production Revenue Accountant.

CYTEC CANADA INC.
Att: Manager, Human Resources
PO Box 240
Niagara Falls, ON L2E 6T4

Tel. 905-356-9000
Email .... hrdept@we.cytec.com
Website .... www.cytec.com

Employer Background: Cytec Canada Inc. operates the only phosphine and phosphine derivatives plant in North America, manufacturing mining promoters, solvent extraction reagents, catalysts, flame retardants and chemical intermediates. *New Positions Created (7):* Maintenance Engineer; Research Chemist; Research Chemist; Production Engineer; Project Engineer; Financial Analyst; Research Chemist.

CYTOCHROMA INC.
Att: Susanne Whittaker
116 Barrie Street
Suite 2424, Biosciences Complex
Kingston, ON K8L 3N6

Tel. 613-531-9995
Fax 613-531-6580
Email .... susanne@cytochroma.com
Website .... www.cytochroma.com

Employer Background: Cytochroma Inc. is a biotechnology company involved in the discovery and development of new therapeutic agents targeting cytochrome P450s. *New Positions Created (9):* Research Technician, Assay Development; Scientist, Functional Characterization of Novel Cytochrome P450s; Scientist, Target Validation; Director of Research; Post-Doctoral Scientist, Functional Characterization of Novel Cytochrome P450s; Post-Doctoral Scientist, Target Validation; Research Technician, Assay Development; Research Technician, Molecular Biology; V.P., Research and Development.

D. GARY GIBSON & ASSOCIATES REHABILITATION CONSULTANTS, INC.
Att: Frances McCulligh
77 Bloor Street West, Suite 1902
Toronto, ON M5S 1S2

Fax 416-923-2126
Email .. info@gibsonassociates-rehab.com
Website www.gibsonassociates-rehab.com
Employer Background: D. Gary Gibson &
Associates Rehabilitation Consultants, Inc.
is an Ontario-based disability management
and rehabilitation consulting practice serving
automobile insurance and long-term
disability clients. *New Positions Created (2):*
Occupational Therapists; Occupational
Therapists.

DAEDALIAN ESOLUTIONS
Att: Human Resources
4 King Street West, Suite 1700
Toronto, ON M5H 1B6
Tel. 416-862-1401
Fax 416-862-2656
Email .... careers@daedalian.com
Website .... www.daedalian.com
Employer Background: Daedalian eSolutions
is a leader in the delivery of e-solutions
to the mid-market, corporations and
the public sector across North America. *New
Positions Created (4):* Business Director, Network
Infrastructure; Business Director, Solutions
Delivery; Vice-President, Solutions
Delivery; Administrative Assistant / Receptionist.

DAEWOO AUTO CANADA INC.
Att: Maria Hogan, HR Manager
160 Royal Crest Court
Markham, ON L3R 0A2
Tel. 905-415-3500
Fax 905-415-3451
Email .... mhogan@daewooauto.ca
Website .... www.daewooauto.ca
Employer Background: Daewoo Auto
Canada Inc. markets three vehicle models:
Lanos, Nubira and Leganza. Their parent
company sells over a million cars per year
worldwide. *New Positions Created (2):*
Dealer Recruitment Manager; Dealer Development
Manager.

DAILYBREAD
Att: Human Resources Department
3555 Don Mills Road, Suite 18 - 232
Toronto, ON M2H 3N3
Employer Background: Dailybread is a bakery
cafe franchise operating in the Greater
Toronto Area. *New Positions Created (3):*
Administrative / Office Secretary; Baker;
Operation Manager.

DAIMLERCHRYSLER CANADA INC.
Att: Salaried Employment Department
PO Box 1621
Windsor, ON N9A 4H6
Tel. 519-973-2099
Fax 519-561-7043
Email .... hm5@daimlerchrysler.com
Website .... www.daimlerchrysler.ca
Employer Background: DaimlerChrysler
Canada Inc. is a retailer of Chrysler-brand
passenger cars, Dodge minivans and trucks
and Jeep SUVs, with 16,200 employees nationwide.
New Positions Created (2): Financial
Accounting Analyst; District Service
Manager.

DAIRY FARMERS OF ONTARIO
Att: Personnel Department
6780 Campobello Road
Mississauga, ON L5N 2L8
Tel. 905-821-8970
Fax 905-821-3160
Email .... human_resources@milk.org
Website .... www.milk.org
Employer Background: Dairy Farmers of
Ontario is a non-profit marketing organization,
representing over 6,700 dairy farmers
in Ontario. *New Positions Created (2):* Coordinator
Processor, Billings and Receivables;
Assistant Manager, Farm Policies and
Programs.

DAIRY QUEEN CANADA INC.
Att: Human Resources
905 Century Drive, PO Box 430
Burlington, ON L7R 3Y3
Tel. 905-639-1492
Fax 905-681-3623
Website .... www.dairyqueen.com
Employer Background: Dairy Queen Canada
Inc. is a leading quick-service restaurant
franchisor and the operator of Orange Julius
Canada Ltd. *New Positions Created (8):*
Credit Manager; Marketing Coordinator;
Marketing Manager; Field Consultant; Franchise
Development Manager; Paralegal;
Equipment Sales Representative; Marketing
Coordinator.

DAIRYWORLD FOODS INC.
Att: Human Resources
1310 Steeles Avenue East
Brampton, ON L6T 1A2
Tel. 905-451-5335
Fax 905-451-4868
Website .... www.dairyworld.com
Employer Background: Dairyworld Foods
Inc. manufactures Dairyland milk and
cream, Orchard Hill juices and Armstrong
cheeses. *New Positions Created (6):* Maintenance
Supervisor; Plant Accountant; Maintenance
Supervisor; Production Supervisor;
Supply Chain Manager; Warehouse Supervisor.

DAISYTEK CANADA
Att: Rhonda Paris
35 Valleywood Drive
Markham, ON L3R 5L9
Tel. 905-940-9800
Fax 905-940-1220
Website .... www.daisytek.com
Employer Background: Daisytek Canada is
a wholesaler of computer supplies. *New
Positions Created (3):* Inbound Call Centre
Representatives; Inbound Call Centre Representatives;
Warehouse Personnel.

DAITO PRECISION INC.
Att: Human Resources Manager
3901 Sartelon
St-Laurent, QC H4S 2A6
Tel. 514-335-6702
Fax 514-335-6542
Email .... etelka@daitogroup.com
Website .... www.daitogroup.com

Employer Background: Founded in 1975,
Daito Precision Inc. is a precision mechanical
engineering company. *New Positions
Created (6):* Junior Production Planner /
Buyer; CNC Machinists; Junior Mechanical
Engineer; Lathe Operators; Manager; Quality
Assurance.

DALEN DRILLING SERVICES LTD.
Att: Debbie Jennings
PO Box 5358
Airdrie, AB T4B 2B9
Fax 403-912-4609
Email .... mail@dalendrilling.com
Employer Background: Dalen Drilling Services
Ltd. is a coiled tubing and tool service
provider. *New Positions Created (4):* Directional
Drilling Supervisors; MWD Technician;
Sales / Engineering Position; Trainee
Directional Drillers.

DALHOUSIE UNIVERSITY, DEPARTMENT OF CIVIL ENGINEERING
Att: Dr. Farid Taheri, Head
1360 Barrington Street
Halifax, NS B3J 2X4
Tel. 902-494-3960
Fax 902-494-3108
Email .... civil.engineering@dal.ca
Website .... www.dal.ca
Employer Background: Founded in 1818,
Dalhousie is one of Canada's leading institutions
for higher learning and has more
than 13,500 students and 2,500 faculty and
non-academic staff. *New Positions Created
(2):* Assistant Professor, Geotechnical Engineering;
Tenure-Track Faculty Position,
Structural Engineering.

DALHOUSIE UNIVERSITY, FACULTY OF HEALTH PROFESSIONS
Att: Chair, Search Committee
5968 College Street
3rd Floor, Burbidge Building
Halifax, NS B3H 3J5
Tel. 902-494-3327
Fax 902-494-1966
Website .... www.dal.ca
Employer Background: Founded in 1818,
Dalhousie is one of Canada's leading institutions
for higher learning and has more
than 13,500 students and 2,500 faculty and
non-academic staff. *New Positions Created
(2):* Chair, Women's Health and the Environment;
Associate Dean, Research.

DALHOUSIE UNIVERSITY, FACULTY OF LAW
Att: Dawn Russell, Dean
6061 University Avenue
Halifax, NS B3H 4H9
Tel. 902-494-2114
Fax 902-494-1316
Website .... www.dal.ca
Employer Background: Founded in 1818,
Dalhousie is one of Canada's leading institutions
for higher learning and has more
than 13,500 students and 2,500 faculty and
non-academic staff. *New Positions Created*

(4): Associate Director, Health Law Institute; Health Studies Chair; Law Professors (2); Professor, Law and Genomics.

DALIA COLLECTION
Att: Jeff
225 Chabanel West
Montréal, QC H2N 2C9

Tel. 514-381-5393
Fax 514-381-3775
Website .... www.dalia-corwik.com

Employer Background: Dalia Collection, a division of Modes Corwik Inc., is a major importer and manufacturer of ladies' apparel. *New Positions Created (4):* Merchandiser / Designer; Designer; Import Coordinator; Stylist.

DAMINCO INC.
Att: Human Resources Department
2770 Portland Drive
Oakville, ON L6H 6R4

Tel. 905-829-2414
Fax 905-829-8097
Email .... sales@daminco.com
Website .... www.daminco.com

Employer Background: Daminco Inc. is a Canadian manufacturer and distributor of specialty food ingredients. *New Positions Created (3):* Lab Technologist; Technical Sales Representative; Bakery Technologist.

DAN MULROONEY DISPOSAL LTD.
Att: General Manager
1266 McAdoo Lane, RR 1
Kingston, ON K0H 1S0

Tel. 613-548-4428
Fax 613-542-5612
Website .. www.capitalenvironmental.com

Employer Background: Dan Mulrooney Disposal Ltd. is a division of Capital Environmental Resource Inc., a leading provider of solid waste collection, transfer, disposal and recycling services. *New Positions Created (2):* Accounts Receivable / Payroll Clerk; Scale Operator / Relief Dispatcher.

DANA LONG MANUFACTURING LTD.
Att: Tracy Thomson, HR Manager
656 Kerr Street
Oakville, ON L6K 3E4

Tel. 905-849-1200
Fax 905-849-8942
Email .... tracy_thomson@longmfg.com
Website .... www.longmfg.com

Employer Background: Dana Long Manufacturing Ltd. is a leading manufacturer of heat exchangers for the automobile, bus and off-road vehicle markets. *New Positions Created (2):* Commodity Buyer; Human Resources Manager.

DANA LONG MANUFACTURING LTD.
Att: Marilyn Smith, Human Resources
6635 Ordan Drive
Mississauga, ON L5T 1K6

Tel. 905-564-7015
Fax 905-564-7594
Email .... marilyn_smith@longmfg.com
Website .... www.longmfg.com

Employer Background: Dana Long Manufacturing Ltd. is a leading manufacturer of heat exchangers for the automobile, bus and off-road vehicle markets. *New Positions Created (5):* Lab Technician; Manufacturing Engineer; Maintenance Supervisor; Materials Manager; Manufacturing Engineers / Technologists.

DANAPHARM CLINICAL RESEARCH INC. / DCRI
Att: Human Resources
245 Pall Mall Street
London, ON N6A 1P4

Tel. 519-679-1630
Email .... dcri@dcri.com
Website .... www.dcri.com

Employer Background: DCRI provides Phase II - IV clinical research services to the North American pharmaceutical and biotech industry. *New Positions Created (5):* Clinical Research Associate; Clinical Research Associate; Clinical Research Associates; Project Leaders; Clinical Research Monitor.

DANIER LEATHER INC.
Att: Human Resources Manager
2650 St. Clair Avenue West
Toronto, ON M6N 1M2

Website .... www.danier.com

Employer Background: Danier Leather is a Toronto-based international designer, manufacturer and retailer of leather and suede outerwear, sportswear and accessories for women and men. *New Positions Created (5):* Allocator; Internet Content Manager; Visual Merchandisers; Visual Merchandiser; Warehouse Manager.

DANIER LEATHER INC.
Att: Human Resources Department
South Keys, 2210 Bank Street
Ottawa, ON K1V 1J5

Fax 613-730-1921
Email .... jobs@danier.com
Website .... www.danier.com

Employer Background: Since 1972, Danier Leather has been a manufacturer and retailer of leather and suede designs. *New Positions Created (2):* Retail Positions; Retail Positions.

DANIER LEATHER INC.
Att: Anne MacPhail
430 Topsail Road, Unit 101
St. John's, NF A1E 4N1

Fax 902-450-5797
Email .... annem@danier.com
Website .... www.danier.com

Employer Background: Danier Leather is a Toronto-based international designer, manufacturer and retailer of leather and suede outerwear, sportswear and accessories for women and men. *New Positions Created (2):* Tailor; Various Retail Positions.

DANKA CANADA INC.
Att: Human Resources Manager
9 Van Der Graaf Court
Brampton, ON L6T 5E5

Fax 905-458-6127
Website .... www.danka.com

Employer Background: Danka Canada is a supplier of office imaging equipment. *New Positions Created (3):* Service Technicians; Account Executives / Sales Representatives; High-Volume Digital Sales Account Manager.

DARDEN RESTAURANTS, INC.
Att: Human Resources Manager
5045 Orbitor Drive, Suite 400, Building 7
Mississauga, ON L4Y 4Y4

Tel. 905-282-1480
Fax 905-282-1490
Email .... recruit@darden.com
Website .... www.darden.com

Employer Background: Darden Restaurants, Inc. is a large casual dining restaurant company. *New Positions Created (5):* Restaurant Managers; Restaurant Managers; Restaurant Managers; Restaurant Managers; Restaurant Managers.

DARE FOODS LTD.
Att: Nicole Gauvreau, Human Resources
PO Box 1058
Kitchener, ON N2G 4G4

Tel. 519-893-3233
Fax 519-893-4184
Email .... ngauvreau@darefoods.com
Website .... www.darefoodsinc.com

Employer Background: Dare Foods Ltd. is a leading Canadian manufacturer and distributor of quality biscuit, cracker and confectionery products. *New Positions Created (3):* Quality Assurance Coordinator; District Sales Manager; Candy Product Manager.

DATA RESEARCH ASSOCIATES / DRA
Att: Cecilia Galve
500 Place d'Armes, Suite 2420
Montréal, QC H2Y 2W2

Tel. 514-350-4500
Fax 514-350-5299
Email .... cecilia@dra.com
Website .... www.dra.com

Employer Background: DRA is a leading provider of library automation systems and networking services. *New Positions Created (4):* Core Services Developer; Librarian, Customer Service; Librarian, Taos; User Interface Developer.

DATA SYSTEMS MARKETING INC.
Att: Human Resources Manager
345 Wilson Avenue, Suite 100
Toronto, ON M3H 5W1

Tel. 416-398-7855
Fax 416-398-7899
Email .... hr@dsm-corp.com
Website .... www.dsm-corp.com

Employer Background: Data Systems Marketing Inc. is a PC and network systems company. *New Positions Created (3):* Account Managers; Programmers; Windows NT Field Technicians.

DATABEACON INC.
Att: Human Resources Manager

1565 Carling Avenue, Suite 300
Ottawa, ON K1Z 8R1

Tel. 613-729-4480
Fax 613-729-6711
Email .... resume@databeacon.com
Website .... www.databeacon.com

Employer Background: Databeacon Inc. (formerly InterNetivity Inc.) develops Java-based software for business intelligence applications. *New Positions Created (16):* Channel Marketing Manager; Quality Assurance Specialists; Senior Sales Executives; Senior System Integration Consultant; Executive Assistant; Senior Account Managers; Customer Support Specialists; Development Manager; Inside Sales Representative; Professional Services Manager; Quality Assurance Specialist; Senior Java Developers; Senior Sales Executives; System Integration Consultants; UI Designers; Web Development Manager.

DATAHORSE INC.

Att: Human Resources
55 Commerce Valley West, 8th Floor
Thornhill, ON L3T 7V9

Tel. 905-881-1466
Fax 905-882-9916
Email .... hr@datahorse.com
Website .... www.datahorse.com

Employer Background: Formed in 1993, Datahorse Inc. is an IT consulting firm, specializing in SAP products. *New Positions Created (3):* Account Executives; Sales Support Position; Senior / Intermediate ABAP Consultants.

DATAMIRROR CORPORATION

Att: Human Resources Manager
3100 Steeles Avenue East, Suite 1100
Markham, ON L3R 8T3

Tel. 905-415-0310
Fax 905-415-0499
Email .... hr@datamirror.com
Website .... www.datamirror.com

Employer Background: Founded in 1993, Toronto-based DataMirror Corporation develops business data integration software. *New Positions Created (59):* Director of Information Technology; Administrative Assistant; Alliance Manager; Channels Manager; Corporate Counsel; Development Manager, UI; Director, Software Development; Inside Sales Representative, US Markets; Intermediate Quality Assurance Tester; Intermediate / Senior Software Developers (Unix or AS / 400); Intermediate Technical Writer; Java Product Developers; Manager, Marketing & Communications; Marketing Communications Coordinator; Online Marketing Specialist; OS / 390 Administrator / Product Support Specialist; Product Architect; Product Marketing Manager; Quality Assurance Team Leader; Regional Technology Manager; Senior Product Support Specialist (AS / 400 and DB2 / 400); Senior Software Developer, SQL Server; Software Development Manager; Technical Pre-Sales Specialist; Translation Coordinator; Senior Software Developers, UNIX or AS / 400; Channel Marketing Coordinator; Channels Manager; Controller; Credit & Collections Clerk; Director, Sales; General Business Sales Representative, US Markets; Graphic Designer; Intermediate Quality Assurance Tester; Manager, Marketing & Communications; Manager, Training & Education; OS/ 390 Administrator / Technical Support Specialist; Practice Manager, Replication Infrastructure Solutions; Technical Recruiter; Consultants, Constellar Hub Product (2); Consultants, Transformation Server and iDeliver Products (2); Internet Marketing Evangelist; Regional Sales Manager; Sr Software Developer; Software Development Manager; Software Product Developer, Builds and Installs; Technical Pre-Sales Specialist; Territory Account Manager; Administrative Assistant ; Help Desk Administrator; Technical Writer; Training & Education Specialist; Corporate Lawyer; Data Security Officer; General Business Sales Representatives; Intermediate Technical Writer; Product Support Specialist, Oracle / Unix; Sr Java Developer; Territory Account Managers.

DATAWIRE COMMUNICATION NETWORKS INC.

Att: Human Resources Manager
22 Goodmark Place, Suite 22
Toronto, ON M9W 6R2

Tel. 416-798-2226
Fax 416-798-9695
Email .... borntocode@datawire.net
Website .... www.datawire.net

Employer Background: Datawire Communication Networks Inc. is an e-transaction provider, facilitating next-generation commerce for the wireless, wireline and telecom markets. *New Positions Created (6):* Software Engineer; Data Architect; Security Analyst; Senior Database Administrator; Software Developer; Systems Administrator.

DATEX-OHMEDA (CANADA) INC.

Att: Human Resources
1093 Meyerside Drive, Unit 2
Mississauga, ON L5T 1J6

Fax 905-565-8766
Website .... www.datex-ohmeda.com

Employer Background: Datex-Ohmeda (Canada) Inc. supplies and supports anaesthesia, monitoring and infant care equipment. *New Positions Created (2):* Bilingual Customer Service Representative; Bilingual Customer Service Position.

DAVID BROWN UNION PUMPS (CANADA) LTD.

Att: Quality Manager
4211 Mainway
Burlington, ON L7L 5N9

Tel. 905-335-2580
Fax 905-335-8262
Email .... qualitydept@unionpump.ca
Website .... www.unionpump.ca

Employer Background: David Brown Union Pumps (Canada) Ltd. is a manufacturer of engineered fluid handling equipment. *New Positions Created (5):* Junior Quality Control Inspector; Document Control Clerk; Contract Administration Assistant; Intermediate CAD Technician; Project Manager.

DAVID MCMANUS ENGINEERING LTD. / DME

Att: Jean Dowser,
Office & Personnel Manager
39 Camelot Drive, Suite 200
Nepean, ON K2G 5W6

Fax 613-225-7330
Email .... jdowser@dmel.on.ca
Website .... www.dmel.on.ca

Employer Background: David McManus Engineering Ltd. is a civil engineering firm, specializing in municipal and land development and consulting services for public and private sector clients. *New Positions Created (3):* Business Manager; Director of Engineering; Project Managers.

DAVID SCHAEFFER ENGINEERING LTD.

Att: Human Resources Manager
610 Alden Road, Suite 201
Markham, ON L3R 9Z1

Fax 905-475-3081
Email .... dsengineering@home.com

Employer Background: David Schaeffer Engineering Ltd. is a municipal consulting firm, providing engineering services to the land development industry. *New Positions Created (7):* Intermediate Contract Administrator / Construction Manager; Junior Subdivision Designer; Resident Inspector; AutoCAD Operator; Intermediate Municipal Designer; Municipal Design Technician; Water Resources Engineer.

DAVID THOMPSON HEALTH REGION, RED DEER REGIONAL HOSPITAL CENTRE

Att: Human Resource Department
PO Bag 5030
Red Deer, AB T4N 6R2

Tel. 403-343-4588
Fax 403-343-4807
Email .... ccripps@dthr.ab.ca
Website .... www.dthr.ab.ca

Employer Background: Located in central Alberta, the David Thompson Health Region operates 8 hospitals, 12 community health centres and 14 long-term care facilities, serving over 190,000 residents. *New Positions Created (6):* Epidemiologist; Research and Evaluation Associate; Project Manager, Redevelopment Project; Health Statistician; Regional Manager, Corporate Data; Accountant.

DAVIS & COMPANY

Att: Stanley Wong, Administrative Partner
100 King Street West
Suite 5300, PO Box 367, 1 First Canadian Place
Toronto, ON M5X 1E2

Tel. 416-365-6188
Fax 416-365-7886
Website .... www.davis.ca

Employer Background: Established in 1892, Davis & Company is a law firm. *New Positions Created (3):* Business Lawyers; Corporate Commercial Lawyer; Labour and Employment Lawyer.

DAWSON COLLEGE
Att: Andrew Mackay, HR Coordinator
3040 Sherbrooke Street West
Montréal, QC H3Z 1A4

Fax 514-931-3321
Email .... rh@dawsoncollege.qc.ca
Website .... www.dawsoncollege.qc.ca
Employer Background: Dawson College is
an English-language CEGEP, with 7,350 full-
time students and 2,000 continuing education students. *New Positions Created (2):*
Coordinator, Public Relations; Director, Student Services.

**DAY & ROSS TRANSPORTATION
GROUP, THE**
Att: David McNeil, Manager of Staffing
398 Main Street
Hartland, NB E7P 1C6

Tel. 506-375-4401
Fax 506-375-1183
Email .... damcneil@dayandrossinc.ca
Website .... www.dayandross.com
Employer Background: The Day & Ross
Transportation Group is a large trucking
company based in New Brunswick. *New
Positions Created (3):* Trailer Technician;
Regional Operations Manager; Regional
Operations Manager.

DAYS INN
Att: Human Resources Manager
77 Bloor Street West, Suite 2000
Toronto, ON M5S 1M2

Tel. 416-966-3297
Fax 416-923-5424
Website .... www.daysinn.com
Employer Background: Days Inn is a hotel
chain, with over 1,900 hotels worldwide.
New Positions Created (2): Regional Sales
Manager; Franchise Services Manager.

**DAYS INN KINGSTON HOTEL &
CONVENTION CENTRE**
Att: Beth Sproule, HR Manager
33 Benson Street
Kingston, ON K7K 5W2

Tel. 613-546-3661
Fax 613-544-4126
Email ..... daysinnkingston@sympatico.ca
Website .... www.daysinnkingston.com
Employer Background: Built in 1964, the
Days Inn Kingston Hotel & Convention Cen-
tre is a 162-room facility. *New Positions Cre-
ated (5):* Banquet Chef; Night Auditor; Guest
Service Representatives; Various Hospital-
ity Positions; Various Hotel Positions.

**DAYTON / RICHMOND
CONCRETE ACCESSORIES**
Att: Sean van Rassel, Contractor Sales Mgr.
396 Attwell Drive
Toronto, ON M9W 5C3

Tel. 416-798-2000
Fax 416-798-1103
Website .... www.daytonrichmond.com
Employer Background: Dayton / Richmond
Concrete Accessories is a concrete accesso-
ries producer. *New Positions Created (2):*
Territory Mgr; Sales & Marketing Rep.

DBR RESEARCH LTD.
Att: Laboratory Manager
9419 - 20th Avenue
Edmonton, AB T6N 1E5

Tel. 780-463-8638
Fax 780-450-1668
Email .... hnerenberg@drbgroup.com
Website .... www.dbrgroup.com
Employer Background: DBR Research Ltd.
(formerly D.B. Robinson Research Ltd.) provides phase behaviour and fluid property
technology and information to the oil, gas
and petrochemical industries. *New Positions
Created (3):* Project Mgr; Development Engineer; Product Development Technologist.

DCL SIEMENS ENGINEERING LTD.
Att: Human Resources Manager
10305 - 174th Street
Edmonton, AB T5S 1H1

Tel. 780-486-2000
Email .... engineering@dclsiemens.com
Website .... www.dclsiemens.com
Employer Background: DCL Siemens Engineering Ltd. provides municipal engineering services throughout central and northern Alberta. *New Positions Created (3):* Intermediate Engineers, Municipal Engineering; Intermediate Engineers, Municipal Engineering; Senior Engineer, Water and
Wastewater Treatment.

DDK APPAREL INC.
Att: Frank
9500 Meilleur Street, Suite 701-B
Montréal, QC H2N 2C1

Fax 514-381-5837
Employer Background: DDK Apparel Inc. is
a leading North American importer of men's
and women's sportswear and outerwear.
New Positions Created (12): Administrative
Assistant; Sample Room Coordinator; Apparel Positions (2); Computer Graphic Artist; Receptionist / Typist; Vice-President of
Sales; National Sales Manager; International
Traffic Manager; Executive Secretary / Assistant; Import Assistant; Production Assistant; Shipping and Traffic Coordinator.

DDS CANADA
Att: Human Resources Coordinator
210 Wicksteed Avenue
Toronto, ON M4G 2C3

Tel. 416-421-2920
Fax 416-467-3847
Email .... dparsons@ddsltd.com
Website .... www.ddsltd.com
Employer Background: DDS Canada distrib-
utes product support literature and materi-
als for major Canadian businesses. *New
Positions Created (3):* Bilingual Customer
Service Rep; Customer Service Representa-
tive; Receptionist / Switchboard Operator.

DEBIASI GROUP, THE / DBG
Att: Recruiter
1555 Enterprise Road
Mississauga, ON L4W 4L4

Tel. 905-670-1555
Fax 905-670-3415

Email .... starrt@debiasi.com
Website .... www.debiasi.com
Employer Background: DBG is a leading
manufacturer and supplier of high-quality
metal stampings for the automotive, heavy
truck and appliance industries. *New Positions Created (3):* Lean Manufacturing Coordinator; Electrician; Process and Equipment Automation Engineer.

DEBIASI GROUP, THE / DBG
Att: Recruiter
1566 Shawson Road
Mississauga, ON L4W 1N7

Tel. 905-670-1555
Fax 905-670-4005
Email .... sinclairj@debiasi.com
Website .... www.debiasi.com
Employer Background: DBG is a leading
manufacturer and supplier of high-quality
metal stampings for the automotive, heavy
truck and appliance industries. *New Positions Created (4):* Maintenance Team Leader;
Process / Quality Engineering Manager; Tool
and Die Maker; Materials Coordinator.

DECIMA RESEARCH INC.
Att: Human Resources Manager
630 Sherbrooke Street West, Suite 1101
Montréal, QC H3A 1E4

Fax 514-288-0138
Email .... mtljobs@decima.ca
Website .... www.decima.ca
Employer Background: Decima Research
Inc. is a market research firm. *New Positions
Created (5):* Consultants; LAN Administra-
tor; Market Research Field Supervisors;
Market Research Interviewers; Recruitment
Coordinator.

DECOLIN INC.
Att: Human Resources Manager
9150 Park Avenue
Montréal, QC H2N 1Z2

Tel. 514-384-2910
Fax 514-382-1305
Employer Background: Decolin supplies
home furnishings to Canadian and US retailers. *New Positions Created (6):* Jr Merchandiser; Traffic Coordinator; Payroll Clerk; Merchandising Assistant; Traffic Coordinator;
Customer Service Rep / Sales Analyst.

DECOR-REST FURNITURE LTD.
Att: Human Resources
511 Chrislea Road
Woodbridge, ON L4L 8N6

Tel. 905-856-5956
Fax 905-856-8711
Email .... kay@decor-rest.com
Website .... www.decor-rest.com
Employer Background: Established in 1972,
Decor-Rest is a fashion-forward upholstery
company. *New Positions Created (3):* Sys-
tems Administrator; HR Manager; Exporter.

DECOUSTICS LTD.
Att: Human Resources Department
65 Disco Road
Toronto, ON M9W 1M2

Tel. 416-675-3983
Fax 416-675-5546
Email .... resumes@decoustics.com
Website .... www.decoustics.com

Employer Background: Decoustics Ltd. manufactures custom acoustical products. *New Positions Created (6):* Estimator / Sales Coordinator; Production Supervisor; Estimator / Sales Coordinator; Production Supervisor; Project Coordinator; Receptionist.

DEEPMETRIX CORPORATION
Att: Human Resources Manager
15 Gamelin Boulevard, Suite 510
Hull, ON J8Y 1V4
Tel. 819-776-0707
Fax 819-776-5560
Email .... careers@deepmetrix.com
Website .... www.deepmetrix.com

Employer Background: Established in 1992, DeepMetrix Corporation (formerly Mediahouse Software Inc.) develops real-time web statistics and network monitoring software for e-business. *New Positions Created (10):* Inbound / Outbound Technical Sales Representative; Technical Support Specialist; Senior Graphic Designer; Inside Sales Representatives; Content Manager / Senior Webmaster; Marketing Specialist; Perl Programmers; Technical Sales Representative; Technical Support Specialist; Technical Writer.

DEFENCE CONSTRUCTION CANADA
Att: Elaine Warren, HR Manager
112 Kent Street, 17th Floor, Tower B
Ottawa, ON K1P 5P2
Tel. 613-998-9548
Fax 613-998-1004
Email .... warrenel@dcc-cdc.gc.ca
Website .... www.dcc-cdc.gc.ca

Employer Background: Defence Construction Ltd. (known as Defence Construction Canada under the Federal Identity Program) implements construction and related work in the federal public sector. *New Positions Created (3):* Mgr, Contract Services; Environmental Officer; Special Projects Officer.

DEH CHO HEALTH AND SOCIAL SERVICES
Att: Human Resources Coordinator
PO Box 246
Fort Simpson, NT X0E 0N0
Tel. 867-695-3815
Fax 867-695-2920
Email .... vicky_france@gov.nt.ca
Website .... www.hlthss.gov.nt.ca/
.... boards/dehcho.htm

Employer Background: Deh Cho Health and Social Services Board is a regional health board, serving 8 communities in southwestern NT. *New Positions Created (3):* Regional Dental Therapists; Facility Administrator; Community Health Nurse III.

DELCAN CORPORATION
Att: Careers
604 Columbia Street West, Suite 300
New Westminster, BC V3M 1A6
Tel. 604-525-9333
Fax 604-525-9333
Email .... vancouver@delcan.com
Website .... www.delcan.com

Employer Background: Delcan Corporation is an international company engaged in three main fields: the management of major projects; ITS, IT and systems integration; and civil engineering and architecture. *New Positions Created (5):* Intermediate / Senior Transportation Engineers; Municipal / Environmental Engineering Technologist; Intermediate / Sr Transportation Engineers; Intermediate / Senior Municipal Engineers; Junior / Intermediate Structural Engineer.

DELCAN CORPORATION
Att: Steve Brook
1069 Wellington Road South, Suite 214
London, ON N6E 2H6
Fax 519-681-4995
Email .... s.brook@delcan.com
Website .... www.delcan.com

Employer Background: Delcan Corporation is an international company engaged in three main fields: the management of major projects; ITS, IT and systems integration; and civil engineering and architecture. *New Positions Created (7):* Civil Designer; Junior / Intermediate Traffic Technologists; Municipal / Environmental Engineer; Environmental Engineering and Technology Positions; Civil Designer; Junior / Intermediate Traffic Technologists; Municipal / Environmental Engineer.

DELCAN CORPORATION
Att: Human Resources Coordinator
133 Wynford Drive
Toronto, ON M3C 1K1
Tel. 416-441-4111
Fax 416-447-6497
Email .... hr@delcan.com
Website .... www.delcan.com

Employer Background: Delcan Corporation is an international company engaged in three main fields: program and project management; ITS, IT and systems integration; and civil engineering and architecture. *New Positions Created (5):* Senior Transportation Manager; Payroll Administrator; Transportation Engineering Technologist; Civil / Environmental Engineer; Senior Transportation Project Manager.

DELCAN CORPORATION
Att: Nick Palomba
4056 Dorchester Road
Niagara Falls, ON L2E 6M9
Tel. 905-356-7003
Fax 905-356-7008
Email .... n.palomba@delcan.com
Website .... www.delcan.com

Employer Background: Delcan Corporation is an international company engaged in three main fields: the management of major projects; ITS, IT and systems integration; and civil engineering and architecture. *New Positions Created (5):* Junior / Intermediate Traffic Engineers; Junior / Intermediate Traffic Engineers; Intermediate Municipal

Engineers; Traffic Engineers; Traffic Technologists.

DELCAN CORPORATION
Att: David Hearnden, PEng,
Manager Road Design Group
1223 Michael Street, Suite 100
Gloucester, ON K1J 7T2
Tel. 613-738-4160
Fax 613-739-7105
Email .... d.hearnden@delcan.com
Website .... www.delcan.com

Employer Background: Delcan Corporation is an international company engaged in three main fields: the management of major projects; ITS, IT and systems integration; and civil engineering and architecture. *New Positions Created (4):* Environmental Planner; Municipal / Environmental Design Technologists (2); Road Design Engineers / Technologists (2); Structural Engineer.

DELCON DEVELOPMENT GROUP LTD.
Att: Human Resources Manager
10235 - 101st Street, Suite 800
Edmonton, AB T5J 3G1
Tel. 780-944-9994
Fax 780-429-4778
Email .. melissa.hackett@delcongroup.com
Website .... www.delcongroup.com

Employer Background: Delcon Development Group Ltd. (formerly Liquor Depot Corporation) is a leading chain of wine and spirit stores in Alberta. *New Positions Created (3):* Leasing Representative; Managers and Senior Supervisors; Loss Prevention Manager.

DELMAR INTERNATIONAL INC.
Att: Human Resources Department
10636 Cote de Liesse
Lachine, QC H8T 1A5
Tel. 514-636-8800
Fax 514-636-1212
Website .... www.delmar-group.com

Employer Background: Delmar International Inc. is a provider of international freight forwarding and customs brokerage services, with over 35 years experience. *New Positions Created (10):* Accounts Payable Clerk; Import Positions; DataFlex Programmer / Analyst; Java Programmer; Customer Service Positions; Logistics Positions; Accounting Clerk; Customer Service Representative; Customs RMD / Customs Raters; General Manager, Ontario Operations.

DELOITTE CONSULTING
Att: Inga Rugole, Recruiting Manager
121 King Street West, Suite 300
Toronto, ON M5H 3T9
Tel. 416-941-6242
Fax 416-815-2900
Email .... canadaresumes@dc.com
Website .... www.dc.com

Employer Background: Deloitte Consulting is a business consulting firm, providing services ranging from strategy and processes to information technology and human resources. *New Positions Created (5):* Accounts Receivable Clerk; Executive Assistant; Executive Receptionist; Senior Analysts (2); Senior Corporate Accountant.

DELOITTE & TOUCHE
Att: Pamela Cholak, Senior Consultant
10180 - 101st Street
Suite 2000, Manulife Place
Edmonton, AB T5J 4E4

Tel. 780-421-3611
Fax 780-421-3782
Website .... www.deloitte.ca

Employer Background: Deloitte & Touche is a leading professional services firm, providing accounting, auditing, tax and management consulting services throughout the country. *New Positions Created (5):* Business Development Position, Information Technology; Implementation Consultant; Manager, Assurance and Advisory Services; Senior Manager, E-Business; Tax Technician, International Assignment Services.

DELOITTE & TOUCHE
Att: Human Resources Department
181 Bay Street, Suite 1400
Bay Wellington Tower, BCE Place
Toronto, ON M5J 2V1

Tel. 416-601-6150
Fax 416-601-6151
Website .... www.deloitte.ca

Employer Background: Deloitte & Touche is a leading professional services firm, providing accounting, auditing, tax and management consulting services throughout the country. *New Positions Created (7):* Senior Practitioners; Administrative Assistant; Call Centre Dispatcher; Director, Quality Assurance and Technical Resources; Manager, Commodity Tax; Technical Administrator; Real Estate Associate.

DELONGHI
Att: Human Resources Manager
1040 Ronsa Court
Mississauga, ON L4W 3Y4

Tel. 905-238-1495
Fax 905-238-9418
Website .... www.delonghi.com

Employer Background: DeLonghi is a manufacturer of small appliances. *New Positions Created (2):* Customer Service Position / Order Entry Clerk; Junior Receptionist.

DELPHI SOLUTIONS INC.
Att: Human Resources Manager
6101 - 6th Street SE
Calgary, AB T2H 1L9

Tel. 403-258-8800
Email .... will.henderson@
.... delphisolutions.com
Website .... www.delphisolutions.com

Employer Background: Delphi Solutions Inc. is a leading supplier of advanced telecom products, including Mitel, Panasonic and Toshiba telephone and voice messaging systems. *New Positions Created (2):* Customer Service Representative / Trainer; Technician.

DELPHI SOLUTIONS INC.
Att: Human Resources

7550 Birchmount Road, 2nd Floor
Markham, ON L3R 6C6

Tel. 905-513-4600
Fax 905-513-4714
Email .... dhr@delphisolutions.com
Website .... www.delphisolutions.com

Employer Background: Delphi Solutions Inc. is a leading supplier of advanced telecom products, including Mitel, Panasonic and Toshiba telephone and voice messaging systems. *New Positions Created (3):* Sales Professionals; Operations Manager; Sales Managers.

DELTA CONTROLS INC.
Att: Human Resources Manager
17850 - 56th Avenue
Surrey, BC V3S 1C7

Tel. 604-574-9444
Fax 604-574-7793
Email .... jobs@deltacontrols.com
Website .... www.deltacontrols.com

Employer Background: Delta Controls develops and manufactures computerized building automation systems designed to control heating, ventilation and air conditioning (HVAC) systems for various commercial facilities. *New Positions Created (10):* Customer Solutions Technologist; Embedded Systems Developer; Junior Mechanical Designer; Junior Programmers; Marketing Manager; Quality Assurance Software Manager; Quality Assurance Technologists; Regional Sales Manager; Technical Writer; Web Systems Developer.

DELTA HUDSON ENGINEERING LTD.
Att: Staff Human Resources
8500 Macleod Trail South
Suite 400, PO Box 5244, Station A
Calgary, AB T2H 2N7

Tel. 403-258-6411
Fax 403-258-6645
Email .... resume.hr@mcdermott.com
Website .... www.deltahudson.com

Employer Background: Delta Hudson Engineering Ltd. is an engineering, procurement, construction and construction management company. *New Positions Created (46):* Senior Electrical Designer / Checkers; Intermediate Control Systems Engineer / Technologist; Intermediate Cost Engineer / Cost Analyst; Intermediate Electrical Engineers; Intermediate Instrument Engineer / Technologist; Lead Structural Engineer; Mechanical Engineer; Project Managers; Senior Controls Systems Engineer / Technologist; Senior Cost Engineer / Cost Analyst; Senior Electrical Engineer; Senior Electrical Engineer, Cogeneration; Senior Instrument Engineer / Technologists; Senior Mechanical Engineer, Specialized Rotating Equipment; Senior / Principal Project Controls Specialists; Senior Project Engineer, Power Generation; Senior Structural Designer; Senior Electrical Engineer, Cogeneration; Senior Project Engineers, Power Generation; Intermediate / Senior Buyers and Expeditors; Senior Electrical Designer / Checkers; Senior Electrical Engineers; Manager of Quality; Manager, Project Management; Cost Engineers / Cost Analysts, Senior and Inter-

mediate (2); Intermediate and Senior Estimators; Lead Structural Engineer; Mechanical Engineer; Piping AutoCAD Designers; Project Managers; Senior Buyers; Senior Electrical Engineer, Cogeneration; Senior Mechanical Engineer, Rotating Equipment; Senior / Principal Project Controls Specialist; Senior Process Engineers; Senior Project Engineer, Power / Generation; Senior Structural Designer; Subcontract Administrators; Electrical / Instrumentation Designers / Drafters; Junior / Intermediate Control Systems Engineers / Technologists; Junior / Intermediate Electrical Engineers; Junior / Intermediate Instrument Engineers / Technologists; Senior Controls Systems Engineer / Technologist; Senior Electrical Designers; Senior Electrical Engineers; Senior Instrument Engineer / Technologist.

DELTA MEADOWVALE RESORT & CONFERENCE CENTRE
Att: Human Resources
6750 Mississauga Road
Mississauga, ON L5N 2L3

Tel. 905-542-4034
Fax 905-542-6757
Email .... anita_stafford@
.... deltameadowvale.com
Website .... www.deltahotels.com

Employer Background: The Delta Meadowvale Resort & Conference Centre of Mississauga is a full-service hotel, providing accommodation, restaurant, conference and resort facilities. *New Positions Created (2):* Hotel Positions; Hotel Positions (8).

DELTA PINNACLE HOTEL
Att: People Resources
1128 West Hastings Street
Vancouver, BC V6E 4R5

Tel. 604-684-1128
Fax 604-639-4032
Website .... www.deltapinnacle.bc.ca

Employer Background: Located in Vancouver's business district, the Delta Pinnacle Hotel features 434 guest rooms. *New Positions Created (7):* Assistant Show Case Restaurant & Bar Manager; Sales Manager, Group Market; Director of Catering; Engineer Associate; Food and Beverage Outlets Manager; Restaurant Servers; Room Service Servers.

DELTA, THE CORPORATION OF
Att: Human Resources
4500 Clarence Taylor Crescent
Delta, BC V4K 3E2

Tel. 604-946-4141
Fax 604-946-3706
Email .... employment@corp.delta.bc.ca
Website .... www.corp.delta.bc.ca

Employer Background: The Corporation of Delta has a population of 100,000 and serves the communities of Tsawwassen, Ladner and North Delta. *New Positions Created (2):* Facility Operations Supervisor; Manager of Corporate Planning.

DELTA VANCOUVER SUITE HOTEL
Att: General Manager

550 West Hastings Street
Vancouver, BC V6B 1L6

Tel. 604-689-8188
Fax 604-899-3001
Website .... www.deltahotels.com
Employer Background: The Delta Vancouver Suite Hotel is a 225-room facility. *New Positions Created (3):* Director of People Resources; Front Office Manager; Assistant Front Office Manager.

DELTA WHISTLER RESORT
Att: People Resources Manager
4050 Whistler Way
Whistler, BC V0N 1B4

Tel. 604-932-7322
Fax 604-932-7382
Email .... hr-dwr@deltahotels.com
Website .... www.delta-whistler.com
Employer Background: The Delta Whistler Resort is a 288-room, luxury hotel located at the base of North America's top ski destination. *New Positions Created (12):* Various Hospitality Positions; People Resources Manager; Restaurant Manager; Front Office Mgr; Assistant Executive Housekeeper; Assistant Front Office Mgr; Conference Services Mgr; Guest Service Agent; Marketing Manager; Sales Manager; Director, Food and Beverage; Director of Sales and Marketing.

DELUXE LABORATORIES
Att: Human Resources
380 Adelaide Street West
Toronto, ON M5V 1R7

Tel. 416-364-4321
Fax 416-591-2426
Website .... www.bydeluxe.com
Employer Background: Deluxe Laboratories processes, prints and distributes over 2 billion feet of film per year for the motion picture industry. *New Positions Created (3):* Finance Supervisor; Manager, Processing Maintenance; Electronics Technician.

DEMPSEY CORPORATION
Att: Human Resources Manager
47 Davies Avenue
Toronto, ON M4M 2A9

Tel. 416-461-0844
Fax 416-461-7048
Website ... www.dempseycorporation.com
Employer Background: For over 45 years, Dempsey Corporation (formerly Frank E. Dempsey & Sons) has provided quality ingredients and specialty chemicals to manufacturers in the food, industrial coatings, cosmetics and pharmaceutical industries. *New Positions Created (8):* Field Sales Representative; Sales Coordinator; Senior Purchasing Manager; Field Sales Representative; Regulatory Affairs Manager; Sales Coordinator; Assistant Purchasing Coordinator; Technical Field Sales Representative.

DENNISON CHEVROLET OLDSMOBILE LTD.
Att: Dealer Principal
13100 Smallwood Place
Richmond, BC V6V 2B6

Tel. 604-273-4531
Fax 604-273-0648
Email .... genmgr@dennisongm.com
Website .... www.dennisongm.com
Employer Background: Dennison Chevrolet Oldsmobile Ltd. is an automotive dealership. *New Positions Created (2):* Fleet Manager; Sales Associates.

DENSO MANUFACTURING CANADA, INC.
Att: Human Resources
900 Southgate Drive
Guelph, ON N1L 1K1

Fax 519-837-6599
Email .... recruitment_dmcn@
.... denso-diam.com
Website .... www.globaldenso.com
Employer Background: Denso Manufacturing Canada, Inc. (part of Denso Corporation) supplies innovative technology, systems and components to the automotive industry. *New Positions Created (6):* Specialist, OEM Sales; Japanese Translator / Interpreter; After - Market Specialist; Industrial / Maintenance Electrician; Japanese Translator / Interpreter; Production Supervisor.

DENT WIZARD CANADA LTD.
Att: Area Manager
1399 Deerwood Trail
Oakville, ON L6M 2H5

Tel. 905-847-5413
Fax 905-847-9285
Website .... www.dentwizard.com
Employer Background: Dent Wizard Canada Ltd. provides automotive repair services to dealerships, factory fleets and auction accounts. *New Positions Created (4):* Business Development Manager; Reconditioning Inspector / Customer Service Representative; Automotive Trainees / Technicians; Business Development Customer Service Representative.

DENTAL MARKETING INC.
Att: Human Resources
8400-B Jane Street, Suite 6
Vaughan, ON L4K 4L8

Tel. 905-760-9255
Fax 905-760-9163
Website ..... www.dentalmarketinginc.com
Employer Background: Dental Marketing Inc. creates customized patient education and marketing systems using retail concepts. *New Positions Created (3):* Accounting Assistant; Sales Assistant; Multimedia Production Assistant.

DEPARTMENT OF AGRICULTURE, FISHERIES & AQUACULTURE, NEW BRUNSWICK
Att: Christine Mallet
PO Box 6000
Fredericton, NB E3B 5H1

Tel. 506-453-2251
Email .... christine.mallet@gnb.ca
Website .... www.gnb.ca/afa-apa
Employer Background: The Department of Agriculture, Fisheries & Aquaculture facili-

tates the continual growth and development of a viable, competitive and sustainable agrifood system in rural New Brunswick. *New Positions Created (8):* Crop Development Officer; Potato Development Specialist; Potato Development Specialist, Seed; Veterinarian; Manure Nutrient Management Specialist; Crop Development Specialist, Blueberry and Apiculture; Land Development Officers (2); Potato Development Specialist, Pathology.

DEPARTMENT OF EDUCATION, NEW BRUNSWICK
Att: Human Resources Branch
250 King Street, PO Box 6000, Place 2000
Fredericton, NB E3B 5H1

Fax 506-444-4761
Website .... www.gov.nb.ca
Employer Background: The Department of Education monitors educational programs and libraries in New Brunswick. *New Positions Created (3):* Regional Director; Human Resources Officer; Regional Director.

DEPARTMENT OF ENVIRONMENT, NEWFOUNDLAND AND LABRADOR
Att: Human Resources Manager
PO Box 8700
St. John's, NF A1B 4J6

Tel. 709-729-2563
Fax 709-729-2148
Website .... www.gov.nf.ca/env
Employer Background: The Department of Environment protects and promotes healthy, natural environments in Newfoundland and Labrador. *New Positions Created (3):* Engineer; Environmental Biologist; Water Resources Management Engineer.

DEPARTMENT OF EXECUTIVE COUNCIL, NF
Att: Judy Escott, HR Manager
PO Box 8700
St. John's, NF A1B 4J6

Fax 709-729-2156
Email .... rnoseworthy@mail.gov.nf.ca
Website .... www.gov.nf.ca/exec
Employer Background: The Department of Executive Council is responsible for overall operations of the provincial public service, including policy and general development of the province and its resources. *New Positions Created (4):* Communications & Policy Research Analyst; Senior Information Systems Consultant; Staff Relations Specialist; Director of Communications & Consultation.

DEPARTMENT OF EXECUTIVE, NWT
Att: Human Resources Section
5003 - 49th St., Laing Building
5th Floor, PO Box 1320
Yellowknife, NT X1A 2L9

Tel. 867-873-4465
Fax 867-873-0110
Email .... deanna_sartor-pielak@gov.nt.ca
Website .... www.gov.nt.ca
Employer Background: The government of the Northwest Territories provides services

and programs to 39,672 people living in the territory, which covers a land mass of 1,171,918 square kilometres. *New Positions Created (3):* Implementation Negotiator; Assistant Auditors (2); Senior Auditor.

DEPARTMENT OF FINANCE, NEW BRUNSWICK
Att: Department Services
Box 6000, Room 373, Centennial Building
Fredericton, NB E3B 5H1
Fax 506-444-4724
Email ... humanresources.finance@gnb.ca
Website .... www.gnb.ca
Employer Background: The Department of Finance supports and promotes the effective management of the human and financial resources of New Brunswick's government. *New Positions Created (3):* Economists; Manager, Capital Markets; Senior Business Systems Analyst.

DEPARTMENT OF FISHERIES & AQUACULTURE, NF
Att: Human Resources Manager
50 Elizabeth Avenue
PO Box 8700, Natural Resources Building
St. John's, NF A1B 4J6
Fax 709-729-1860
Website .... www.gov.nf.ca/fishaq
Employer Background: The Department of Fisheries & Aquaculture provides a range of services and programs in fisheries development, marketing and aquaculture. *New Positions Created (5):* Aquaculturist, Shellfish; Aquaculturist, Marine Finfish; Laboratory Technician; Manager, Aquaculture Licensing and Administration; Veterinary Specialist / Aquaculture Veterinarian.

DEPARTMENT OF FOREST RESOURCES & AGRIFOODS, NF
Att: Manager, Human Resources
50 Elizabeth Avenue
PO Box 8700, Natural Resources Building
St. John's, NF A1B 4J6
Tel. 709-729-3274
Fax 709-729-1860
Website .... www.gov.nf.ca/forest
Employer Background: The Department of Forest Resources & Agrifoods delivers educational and veterinary programs and services for Newfoundland's forestry, wildlife and agrifoods industries. *New Positions Created (28):* Agriculturist / Drainage Specialist; Agriculturist / Soil Specialist; Departmental Program Coordinator; Departmental Program Coordinator, Agriculture Financial Programs; Agricultural Laboratory Chemist; Agriculturist III; Alternative Feed Coordinator; Assistant Non-Ruminant Specialist; Land Management Specialist; Marketing Specialist; Non-Ruminant Specialist; Pest Management Specialist; Soil Surveyor; Agricultural Laboratory Chemist; Agricultural Technician; Director, Farm Business and Evaluation; Director, Soil & Land Management; Land Use Technician, Soil Survey; Market Development Officer; Policy Planning & Research Analyst; Soil Survey Supervisor; Administrative Officer; Biometrician;

Director, Inland Fish and Wildlife; Resource Protection Specialists (2); Senior Policy, Planning and Research Analyst; Statistician; Wildlife Biologist.

DEPARTMENT OF HEALTH AND COMMUNITY SERVICES, NF
Att: Human Resources Manager
PO Box 8700, Confederation Building, West Block
St. John's, NF A1B 4J6
Fax 709-729-5824
Website .... www.gov.nf.ca/health
Employer Background: The Department of Health and Community Services provides leadership in health and community service programs and provincial policy development. *New Positions Created (24):* Statistician II / Health Information Analyst; LAN Administrator; Information Manager; Network Manager; Manager, Medical Affairs; Program Analyst; Mental Health Program Consultant; Computer Programmer / Analyst; Clerk; Clerk, Public Service and Administration; Clerk Stenographer; Custodial Worker; Manager, Medical Affairs and Training; Medical Claims Assessment Supervisor; Medical Claims Assessors (2); Medical Claims Processing Supervisor; Regional Director; Supervisor, Public Services and Administration; Systems Manager; Claims Processors (2); Computer Programmer / Analyst; Mail and Messenger Clerk; Clerks (3); Data Entry Operator.

DEPARTMENT OF HEALTH AND SOCIAL SERVICES, NWT (POLICY, PLANNING AND HUMAN RESOURCES DIVISION)
Att: Human Resources Unit
Centre Square Tower, 8th Floor, Box 1320
Yellowknife, NT X1A 2L9
Fax 867-873-0281
Website .... www.hlthss.gov.nt.ca
Employer Background: The Government of the Northwest Territories provides services and programs to 39,672 people living in the territory, which covers a land mass of 1,171,918 square kilometres. *New Positions Created (7):* Senior Policy Advisor; Physicians; Senior Health Analyst / Epidemiologist; Various Health Positions; Family / General Practitioners; Various Medical Positions; Nurses and Social Workers.

DEPARTMENT OF HEALTH & WELLNESS, NEW BRUNSWICK
Att: Human Resources Manager
PO Box 5100
Fredericton, NB E3B 5G8
Tel. 405-453-2536
Website .... www.gov.nb.ca/hw-sm/hw
Employer Background: The Department of Health & Wellness works to improve and support the well-being of New Brunswickers through an integrated service network focused on individuals, families and communities. *New Positions Created (10):* Clinical Psychologist; Regional Team Manager; Epidemiologist; Public Health Inspector; Information Architect; Biostatistician; Chief

Medical Officer of Health; Public Health Inspector; Regional Medical Officer of Health; Public Health Inspectors.

DEPARTMENT OF HUMAN RESOURCES, NUNAVUT
Att: Human Resources Manager
PO Bag 002
Rankin Inlet, NU X0C 0G0
Tel. 867-645-3075
Fax 867-645-2870
Email .... rmann@gov.nu.ca
Website .... www.gov.nu.ca
Employer Background: Formed in 1999, the Government of Nunavut provides a wide range of services for 30,000 residents in Canada's eastern arctic. *New Positions Created (17):* Student Financial Assistance Loans Officer; Utilidor Systems Officer; Community Health Representative; Community Monitoring Analyst; Community Probation Officer / Case Manager; Community Social Service Worker III; Community Social Service Workers IV (2); Consumer Affairs Officer; Laboratory Assistant; Cost Accountant; Human Resource Officer; Health Professionals; Manager, Transportation Programs; Municipal Planning Engineer; Municipal Technical Officer; Regional Managers of Wildlife (3); Arts Curriculum Coordinator; Leadership Development Coordinator.

DEPARTMENT OF HUMAN RESOURCES, NUNAVUT
Att: Human Resources Manager
PO Box 2375
Cambridge Bay, NU X0B 0C0
Tel. 867-983-4058
Fax 867-983-4061
Email .... dohokak@gov.nu.ca
Website .... www.gov.nu.ca
Employer Background: Formed in 1999, the Government of Nunavut provides a wide range of services for 30,000 residents in Canada's eastern arctic. *New Positions Created (4):* Career Development Officer / Early Childhood Officer; Career Development Officer / Early Childhood Officer; Computer Technician; Project Officers (2).

DEPARTMENT OF HUMAN RESOURCES, NUNAVUT
Att: Human Resources Manager
PO Box 233
Igloolik, NU X0A 0L0
Tel. 867-934-2024
Fax 867-934-2027
Email .... igloolik_hr@gov.nu.ca
Website .... www.gov.nu.ca
Employer Background: Formed in 1999, the Government of Nunavut provides a wide range of services for 30,000 residents in Canada's eastern arctic. *New Positions Created (4):* Toponymist; Human Resource Officer; Mortgage & Lands Officer; Community Probation Regional Supervisor.

DEPARTMENT OF HUMAN RESOURCES, NUNAVUT
Att: Human Resources Manager

PO Box 1000, Station 430
Iqaluit, NU X0A 0H0

Tel.	867-975-6222
Fax	867-975-6220
Website	www.gov.nu.ca

Employer Background: Formed in 1999, the Government of Nunavut provides a wide range of services for 30,000 residents in Canada's eastern arctic. *New Positions Created (38):* Deputy Minister; Comptroller; Executive Secretary; Reconciliation Accountant; Senior IT Policy Analyst; Survey Manager; Child and Family Services Specialist; Wildlife Biologist II, Carnivore; Correctional Officers; Labour Relations Consultants (3); Legislative Specialist; Manager, Financial Reporting; Manager, Payroll and Benefits; Research Officer; Staffing Consultant; Supervisor, Benefits Administration; Supervisor, Payroll; Transportation Policy Advisor; Director of Policy and Planning; Senior Policy Advisor; Special Research & Communications Advisor; Manager, IT Systems Development; Office Managers (2); Senior IT Policy Analyst; Directors, Health & Social Services Programs (2); Training & Development Consultants (2); Family Support Counsellor; Legal Translator; Assistant Chief Medical Officer of Health; Facilities Planners (2); Senior Facilities Planner; Senior Technical Officer; Assistant Deputy Minister; Data Specialist; Human Resources Officer; Intergovernmental Affairs Advisor; Budget Coordinator, Department of Health and Social Services; Policy Counsel - Special Projects.

DEPARTMENT OF JUSTICE, ALBERTA

Att: Alexis Ford-Ellis, Regional Employment Equity Advisor
10199 - 101 Street
Suite 211, Edmonton Regional Office
Edmonton, AB T5J 3Y4

Tel.	780-495-6608
Fax	780-495-5817
Email	alexis.ford-ellis@justice.gc.ca
Website	www.canada.justice.gc.ca

Employer Background: The Department of Justice works to ensure that Canada is a just and law-abiding society, with an accessible, efficient and fair system of justice. *New Positions Created (5):* Legal Counsel, Criminal Prosecutions; Legal Counsel; Legal Counsel, Criminal Prosecutions; Legal Counsel, Civil Litigation.

DEPARTMENT OF JUSTICE, BC

Att: Lynda Wray
840 Howe Street, Suite 900
Vancouver, BC V6Z 2S9

Tel.	604-666-4729
Fax	604-666-5765
Email	lynda.wray@justice.gc.ca
Website	www.canada.justice.gc.ca

Employer Background: The Department of Justice works to ensure that Canada is a just and law-abiding society, with an accessible, efficient and fair system of justice. *New Positions Created (3):* Legal Counsel, Litigation (FPS); Legal Counsel, Integrated Proceeds of Crime; Legal Counsel.

DEPARTMENT OF JUSTICE, CANADA

Att: Diane Lacroix, HR Directorate
284 Wellington Street, SAT-8060
Ottawa, ON K1A 0H8

Fax	613-957-8381
Website	canada.justice.gc.ca

Employer Background: The Department of Justice works to ensure that Canada is a just and law-abiding society, with an accessible, efficient and fair system of justice. *New Positions Created (3):* Legislative Counsel; Legislative Counsel; Legal Counsel.

DEPARTMENT OF JUSTICE, NOVA SCOTIA (CORPORATE SERVICE UNIT)

Att: Human Resources Division
5151 Terminal Road, PO Box 7, 3rd Floor
Halifax, NS B3J 2L6

Tel.	902-424-4030
Fax	902-424-1782
Website	www.gov.ns.ca/just

Employer Background: The Department of Justice is responsible for administering justice in Nova Scotia, employing 1,452 people in 150 offices and 11 correctional institutions throughout the province. *New Positions Created (6):* Appeal Commissioners; Registered Nurses (3); Accounting Clerk; Cook Helpers (6); Materials Management Clerk; Assistant Probation Officer.

DEPARTMENT OF MINES AND ENERGY, NEWFOUNDLAND

Att: Manager, Human Resources
50 Elizabeth Avenue
PO Box 8700, Natural Resources Building
St. John's, NF A1B 4J6

Tel.	709-729-3247
Fax	709-729-1860
Website	www.gov.nf.ca/mines&en

Employer Background: The Department of Mines and Energy is responsible for managing and developing the province's mineral and energy resources in an efficient and sustainable manner. *New Positions Created (2):* Geological Technicians / Quarry Inspectors (2); Geologist.

DEPARTMENT OF MUNICIPAL AND PROVINCIAL AFFAIRS, NEWFOUNDLAND

Att: HR Manager (Staffing)
PO Box 8700
St. John's, NF A1B 4J6

Fax	709-729-2609
Website	www.gov.nf.ca

Employer Background: The Department of Municipal and Provincial Affairs is responsible for local government, municipal financing, assessment, urban planning, development and coordination of emergency planning for municipalities. *New Positions Created (24):* Senior Policy and Strategic Planning Officer; Environmental Health Officers (4); Director, Commercial Registrations; Agrifoods Sector Development Specialist; Manufacturing Sector Development Specialists (3); Sector Development Specialists (2); Senior Dimension Stone Sector Development Specialist; Senior Manufacturing

Sector Development Specialist; Wood Products Sector Development Specialist; Director, Portfolio Management; Economic Development Officer; Manager, Collections; Manager, Financial Operations; Highway Enforcement Officer; Lands Officer; Manager, Operations; Computer Systems Analyst; Lands Officer; Credit Union Examination Supervisor; Credit Union Examiner; Engineer; Economic Development Officer; Regional Director; Supervisor, Credit Union Stabilization.

DEPARTMENT OF NATIONAL DEFENCE, HEADQUARTERS

Att: Lois Thompson, HR Consultant
305 Rideau Street
DRHRM, 9th Floor, Constitution Building
Ottawa, ON K1A 0K2

Tel.	613-995-2534
Fax	613-996-7063
Email	lois.thompson@drdc-rddc.dnd.ca
Website	www.dnd.ca

Employer Background: The Department of National Defence works to protect Canada and Canadian interests abroad, as well as contribute to world peace. *New Positions Created (3):* Defence Scientist; Defence Scientist / Systems Modelling Scientist; Defence Scientists, Operational Research Division (8).

DEPARTMENT OF PUBLIC SAFETY, NB

Att: Human Resources Manager
PO Box 6000
Fredericton, NB E3B 5H1

Tel.	506-453-3992
Email	paula.trites@gnb.ca
Website	www.gov.nb.ca

Employer Background: The Department of Public Safety is responsible for providing leadership in public order and community safety issues in New Brunswick. *New Positions Created (6):* Electrical Inspector; Programmer / Analyst; Programmers; Technical Resource Specialist, Fire Protection Systems; Administrative Services Position; Correctional Officers.

DEPARTMENT OF TOURISM, CULTURE AND RECREATION, NEWFOUNDLAND AND LABRADOR

Att: Manager of Human Resources
PO Box 8700, Confederation Building
St. John's, NF A1B 4J6

Tel.	709-729-0724
Fax	709-729-2148
Website	www.gov.nf.ca/tcr

Employer Background: The Department of Tourism, Culture and Recreation ensures the preservation of natural and cultural resources and the promotion of resources for economic benefit. *New Positions Created (12):* Park Planner; Program Officer; Museum Curator; Director, Parks and Natural Areas; Manager, Natural Areas Program; Natural Heritage Areas Planner; Planner; Wildlife Biologist; Director of Strategic Tourism Product Development; Museum Technician; Museum Curator; Museum Curator.

DEPARTMENT OF WORKS, SERVICES & TRANSPORTATION, NEWFOUND-LAND / WST NEWFOUNDLAND
Att: Gordon Murphy, HR Director
50 Elizabeth Avenue, PO Box 8700
St. John's, NF A1B 4J6

Fax 709-729-0149
Email .... wstjobs@mail.gov.nf.ca
Website .... www.gov.nf.ca/wst
Employer Background: WST Newfoundland provides transportation infrastructure and meets public sector needs for accommodations, public building facilities and support services. *New Positions Created (9):* Regional Director; Energy Management Technologist / Engineering Technician III; Director, Financial Operations; Ferry Captain II; Computer Support Specialist; Regional Director; Aircraft Dispatchers (3); Avionics Technician; Engineering Technician.

DEPARTMENT OF WORKS, SERVICES & TRANSPORTATION, NEWFOUND-LAND / WST NEWFOUNDLAND
Att: Bob Callahan, Regional Adminstrator, Avalon Region, PO Box 222
McCurdy Complex, Markham Place
Gander, NF A1V 2N9

Tel. 709-256-1003
Fax 709-256-1013
Website .... www.gov.nf.ca/wst
Employer Background: WST Newfoundland provides transportation infrastructure and meets public sector needs for accommodations, public building facilities and support services. *New Positions Created (5):* Project Coordinator; Project Coordinator; Carpenter; Electrician; Power Engineer, 4th Class.

DEPARTMENT OF WORKS, SERVICES & TRANSPORTATION, NEWFOUND-LAND / WST NEWFOUNDLAND
Att: Roxanne Wells, Regional Administrator (Labrador)
PO Box 3014, Station B
Goose Bay, NF A0P 1E0

Fax 709-896-5513
Website .... www.gov.nf.ca/wst
Employer Background: WST Newfoundland ensures a safe, efficient and sustainable transportation system, and meets the needs of the public sector for accommodations, public building facilities and support services. *New Positions Created (2):* Building Manager; Building Manager.

DEPARTMENT OF WORKS, SERVICES & TRANSPORTATION, NEWFOUND-LAND / WST NEWFOUNDLAND
Att: Dana Hynes, Regional Administrator
PO Box 70
Clarenville, NF A0E 1J0

Tel. 709-466-4121
Fax 709-466-3297
Website .... www.gov.nf.ca/wst
Employer Background: WST Newfoundland provides transportation infrastructure and meets public sector needs for accommodations, public building facilities and support services. *New Positions Created (2):* Heavy Equipment Technician; Equipment Operator.

DESCARTES SYSTEMS GROUP
Att: Human Resources Manager
120 Randall Drive
Waterloo, ON N2V 1C6

Tel. 519-746-8110
Website .... www.descartes.com
Employer Background: Descartes Systems Group provides Internet-based logistics solutions, including integrated software applications and collaborative network services. *New Positions Created (7):* Network Analyst; Network / System Administrator; Product Manager, Global Logistics Network; Senior Account Executive, Consumer Packaged Goods; Team Leader, Network Analyst / Administrator; Technical Business Analyst; General Counsel.

DESIGN + COMMUNICATION INC.
Att: Claude Parent
4749 Notre Dame Street West
Montréal, QC H4C 1S9

Tel. 514-932-1428
Fax 514-934-5438
Email .... stremblay@designc.com
Website .... www.designc.com
Employer Background: Design + Communication Inc. is a firm of exhibit designers, specializing in the design and planning of permanent, temporary and travelling museum exhibitions, world fairs, theme parks, interpretation centres and trade shows. *New Positions Created (4):* Receptionist / Secretary; Exhibit Designers / Project Managers; Graphic Designers; Receptionist / Secretary.

DESIGN WORKSHOP
Att: Human Resources Department
7405 Trans Canada Highway, Suite 320
St-Laurent, QC H4T 1Z2

Tel. 514-745-0770
Fax 514-745-6556
Email .... rh@designw.com
Website .... www.designw.com
Employer Background: Founded in 1988, Design Workshop is an established CAD software development company in the microelectronics sector. *New Positions Created (12):* Graphical User Interface Specialist; Library Package Specialist; Microelectronics Application Specialist; Project Manager; Quality Assurance and Software Test Specialist; Software Programmer, Unix; Graphical User Interface Specialist; Library Package Specialist; Microelectronics Application Specialist; Project Manager; Quality Assurance and Software Test Specialist; Software Programmer, Unix (Sun, HP, Linux).

DESTINY WEB DESIGNS INC.
Att: Human Resources Manager
40 Eglinton Avenue East, Suite 501
Toronto, ON M4P 3A2

Tel. 416-480-0500
Email .... hr@destinyweb.com
Website .... www.destinyweb.com
Employer Background: Destiny is an Internet development firm. *New Positions Created (5):* Sales & Marketing Mgr; Sales Associates; Sr Programmer / Team Leader; Web Designer; Sr Web Developer.

DEUTSCHE FINANCIAL SERVICES
Att: Gladys Almeida
90 Burnhamthorpe Road West, Suite 500
Mississauga, ON L5B 3C3

Tel. 905-566-5920
Fax 905-566-5532
Email .... gladys.almeida@db.com
Website .... www.db.com
Employer Background: DFS is a division of Deutsche Bank Canada. *New Positions Created (3):* Credit Analyst; Account Managers; Industrial Sales Manager.

DEVELOPERSNETWORK.COM INC.
Att: Human Resources Manager
133 Richmond Street West, Suite 311
Toronto, ON M5H 2L3

Tel. 416-642-0432
Fax 416-203-9217
Email .... jobs@developersnetwork.com
Website ...... www.developersnetwork.com
Employer Background: DevelopersNetwork.com Inc. is an online business-to-business resource for new media, technology and Internet business solutions, providing tools and guides to develop and manage diverse Internet strategies. *New Positions Created (4):* Database Analyst; Software Developers; System Administrator; Web Developers.

DEVELOPMENTAL DISABILITIES ASSOCIATION / DDA
Att: Human Resources Coordinator
3851 Shell Road, Suite 100
Richmond, BC V6X 2W2

Tel. 604-273-9778
Fax 604-273-9770
Employer Background: DDA provides a wide range of programs and services for individuals with mental disabilities. *New Positions Created (3):* Community Support Worker; Residential Care Workers; Assistant Director, Adult Services.

DEVITT & FORAND CONTRACTORS INC.
Att: Garry Boan
5716 Burbank Crescent SE
Calgary, AB T2H 1Z6

Tel. 403-255-8565
Fax 403-255-8501
Email ...... garry.boan@devitt-forand.com
Website .... www.devitt-forand.com
Employer Background: Devitt & Forand Contractors Inc. is a leading general contractor. *New Positions Created (2):* Senior Project Manager; Project Manager.

DEVRY INSTITUTE OF TECHNOLOGY
Att: Randy Paquette,
Director of Admissions
2700 - 3rd Avenue SE
Calgary, AB T2A 7W4

Tel. 403-235-3450
Fax 403-235-5400
Email .... rpaquette@cal.devry.ca
Website .... www.devry.ca
Employer Background: DeVry is a recognized leader in technology-based education

with institutes in Canada and the USA and a student population of over 30,000. *New Positions Created (3):* Admissions Representative; Education Representatives (3); Educational Sales Positions.

DEVRY, SMITH & FRANK
Att: Sherree R. Mosoff
95 Barber Greene Road, Suite 100
Toronto, ON M3C 3E9
Tel. 416-449-1400
Fax 416-449-7071
Email .... srmosoff@devrylaw.on.ca
Website .... www.devrylaw.on.ca
Employer Background: Founded in 1964, Devry, Smith & Frank provides legal services to a broad range of institutional, corporate and individual clients. *New Positions Created (2):* Litigation Lawyers (2); Associate Lawyer.

DEX BROTHERS CLOTHING LTD.
Att: Jacky, President
433 Chabanel West, Bureau 800
Montréal, QC H2N 2J6
Tel. 514-383-2474
Fax 514-383-6104
Email .... dex@dexclothing.com
Website .... www.dexclothing.com
Employer Background: Founded in 1990, Dex Brothers Clothing Ltd. is an apparel manufacturer. *New Positions Created (15):* Assistant to the President; Ladies Designer; Senior Salesperson; Import Production Assistant; Assistant Controller; Assistant Administrator; Fit Technician; Retail Supervisor; Men's Merchandiser / Designer; Store Manager and Assistant Store Manager; Warehouse Assistant Manager; Credit and Collections Position; Executive Assistant; Graphic Artist; Marketing Director.

DHL INTERNATIONAL EXPRESS LTD.
Att: Customer Service Manager
4871 Miller Road, Suite E109
Richmond, BC V7B 1K8
Fax 604-273-5218
Website .... www.dhl.com
Employer Background: DHL International Express Ltd. provides door-to-door delivery of commercial documents, small packages and air cargo to over 228 countries through more than 5,939 offices worldwide. *New Positions Created (2):* Customer Service Supervisor; Territory Sales Representative.

DHL INTERNATIONAL EXPRESS LTD.
Att: Sales Manager
1435 - 40th Avenue NE, Bay 1
Calgary, AB T2E 8N6
Fax 403-735-6223
Website .... www.dhl.com
Employer Background: DHL International Express Ltd. is a leader in rapid door-to-door delivery of commercial documents, small packages and air cargo to over 228 countries worldwide. *New Positions Created (2):* Air Freight Sales Representative; Courier Sales Representative.

DHL INTERNATIONAL EXPRESS LTD.
Att: Service Center Manager
190 Colonnade Road, Unit 20
Nepean, ON K2E 7J5
Tel. 613-727-8232
Fax 613-727-5623
Email .... jgatenby@ca.dhl.com
Website .... www.dhl.com
Employer Background: DHL International Express Ltd. is a leader in rapid door-to-door delivery of commercial documents, small packages and air cargo to over 228 countries through more than 5,939 offices worldwide. *New Positions Created (2):* Bilingual Customer Service Supervisor; Territory Sales Representative.

DIABETOGEN BIOSCIENCES INC.
Att: Human Resources
100 Collip Circle
Suite 103, UWO Research Park
London, ON N6G 4X8
Fax 519-858-5103
Email .... careers@diabetogen.com
Website .... www.diabetogen.com
Employer Background: Diabetogen Biosciences Inc. is a privately-held biotech company, developing drugs for autoimmune disease. *New Positions Created (5):* Executive Assistant; Lab Manager; Research Associates; Research Associates; Senior Scientist, Immunology.

DIABLO RESEARCH COMPANY
Att: Leilani King
5600 Parkwood Way, Suite 405
Richmond, BC V6V 2M2
Tel. 604-303-1600
Fax 604-231-9555
Email .... hrcanada@cadence.com
Website .... www.cadence.com
Employer Background: Diablo Research Company is part of Cadence Design Systems, a leader in design automation software and engineering services. *New Positions Created (3):* Senior Hardware Designer; Senior Project Manager; Senior Software Design.

DIAGNOSTIC CHEMICALS LIMITED
Att: Human Resources Coordinator
16 McCarville Street
Charlottetown, PE C1E 2A6
Tel. 902-566-1396
Fax 902-566-2498
Email .... employment@dclchem.com
Website .... www.dclchem.com
Employer Background: DCL is a pharmaceutical company that develops innovative biochemical and diagnostic products. *New Positions Created (2):* Chemical Process Operators / Chemical Technologist Operators; Research Biochemist.

DIAMOND WILLOW CHILD AND FAMILY SERVICES AUTHORITY
Att: Human Resource Services, Alberta Corporate Service Centre
4804 - 42nd Avenue, Bay 10
Innisfail, AB T4G 1V2
Fax 403-227-7975
Email .... censssc.jobs@gov.ab.ca
Website .... www.diamondwillow.gov.ab.ca
Employer Background: Diamond Willow Child and Family Services Authority provides special and focused help to children and families. *New Positions Created (8):* Child Welfare Social Workers; Foster Care Support Worker; Social Worker; Child Welfare Unit Clerk; Child Welfare Social Workers; Child Welfare Social Worker; Foster / Adoptions Unit Clerk; Social Worker.

DIBBLEE CONSTRUCTION LTD.
Att: QC Administrator
1600 Westbrook Road
Kingston, ON K7P 2Y7
Tel. 613-389-3232
Fax 613-389-2352
Employer Background: Dibblee Construction Ltd. is a road building, asphalt paving and materials company. *New Positions Created (2):* Laboratory Supervisor; Laboratory Technician.

DIEBOLD COMPANY OF CANADA, THE
Att: Human Resources Manager
2100 Matheson Blvd. East, Suite 102
Mississauga, ON L4W 5E1
Tel. 905-206-7350
Fax 905-206-7381
Email .... hrcanada@diebold.com
Website .... www.diebold.com
Employer Background: The Diebold Company of Canada is a leader in financial technology and manufactures, markets and services security and banking equipment and provides integrated systems solutions. *New Positions Created (2):* Various Trades Positions; Customer Service Technician.

DIGIGRAPHICS
Att: President
16 Bath Road
Kingston, ON K7L 1C4
Tel. 613-548-4546
Fax 613-548-8386
Email .... dburget@digigraphics.on.ca
Website .... www.digigraphics.on.ca
Employer Background: DigiGraphics is a leader in print and digital communications. *New Positions Created (6):* Graphic Designer; IT Systems Support Position; Layout Artist; Presentation Designer; Web Page Designer; Webmaster.

DIGITAL ACCELERATOR CORPORATION
Att: Human Resources Manager
1055 Dunsmuir Street
Suite 904, PO Box 49126, Bentall Centre IV
Vancouver, BC V7X 1J1
Tel. 604-689-1858
Fax 604-689-1758
Email .... hr@daccel.com
Website .... www.daccel.com
Employer Background: Digital Accelerator Corporation is a high-tech computer software and hardware development company. *New Positions Created (4):* Software Engi-

neers (2); Audio Software Developer; DSP Engineers (2); Software Engineer.

DIGITAL DISPATCH SYSTEMS INC.
Att: Human Resources Manager
11920 Forge Place
Richmond, BC V7A 4V9
Tel. 604-241-1441
Fax 604-241-1440
Email .... jobs@digital-dispatch.com
Website .... www.digital-dispatch.com
Employer Background: Digital Dispatch Systems Inc. provides turn-key wireless data systems for the taxi, courier, shuttle, vehicle tracking and airport asset management industries worldwide. *New Positions Created (14):* Project Manager / Engineer; Wireless Network Manager; Intermediate Software Developer; Mechanical Engineer; Product Manager; Software Support; Senior Project Manager; Marketing Director; Vice President, Sales; Business Systems Analyst; Help Desk / Client Support Position; OEM Sales Manager; Software Support / Integrator; Technical Writer.

DIGITAL OILFIELD INC.
Att: Human Resources Manager
530 - 8th Avenue SW, Suite 1910
Calgary, AB T2P 3S8
Tel. 403-205-2550
Fax 403-205-2580
Email .... hr@digitaloilfield.com
Website .... www.digitaloilfield.com
Employer Background: Digital Oilfield Inc. develops e-commerce solutions for the oil and gas industry. *New Positions Created (2):* Java Developers; Senior Java Developers.

DILLON CONSULTING LTD.
Att: Human Resources
495 Richmond Street
London, ON N6A 5A9
Tel. 519-438-6192
Fax 519-672-8209
Email .... london@dillon.ca
Website .... www.dillon.ca
Employer Background: Established in 1946, Dillon Consulting Ltd. provides engineering, facilities development, planning and environmental science services. *New Positions Created (9):* Intermediate / Senior Electrical Engineer; Intermediate / Senior Health & Safety Specialist; Intermediate / Senior Mechanical Engineer; Intermediate Water / Wastewater Treatment Engineer; Junior Architect / Architectural Designer; Intermediate and Sr Municipal Designers; Intermediate Highway Design Engineers; Sr Bridge Engineers; Sr Highway Design Engineers.

DILLON CONSULTING LTD.
Att: Human Resources
235 Yorkland Boulevard, Suite 800
Toronto, ON M2J 4Y8
Tel. 416-229-4646
Fax 416-229-4692
Email .... toronto@dillon.ca
Website .... www.dillon.ca
Employer Background: Established in 1946, Dillon Consulting Ltd. provides engineering,

facilities development, planning and environmental science services. *New Positions Created (10):* Health and Safety Specialist; Highway Design Engineer; Intermediate / Senior Electrical Designers; Land Development / Municipal Engineer; Senior Bridge Design Engineer; Transportation Economist / Policy Planner; Transportation Engineer; Urban Planners; Wastewater Systems Engineer; Water Resources Engineer.

DILLON CONSULTING LTD.
Att: Human Resources
1900 City Park Drive, Suite 500
Ottawa, ON K1J 1A3
Tel. 613-745-2213
Fax 613-745-3491
Email .... ottawa@dillon.ca
Website .... www.dillon.ca
Employer Background: Established in 1946, Dillon Consulting provides engineering, facilities development, planning and environmental science services. *New Positions Created (4):* Intermediate Municipal Engineer; Admin Assistant; Intermediate Road Designer; Microstation Technologist.

DILLON CONSULTING LTD.
Att: Human Resources Manager
348 King Street
Fredericton, NB E3B 1E
Fax 506-444-8821
Email .... fredericton@dillon.ca
Website .... www.dillon.ca
Employer Background: Established in 1946, Dillon Consulting Ltd. provides engineering, facilities development, planning and environmental science services. *New Positions Created (3):* Industrial Hygiene Position; Safety Position; Senior Municipal Engineer.

DILLON ENGINEERING LTD.
Att: Human Resources
895 Waverly Street, Suite 200
Winnipeg, MB R3T 5P4
Fax 204-452-4412
Email .... winnipeg@dillon.ca
Website .... www.dillon.ca
Employer Background: Established in 1946, Dillon Consulting Ltd. provides engineering, facilities development, planning and environmental science services. *New Positions Created (4):* Intermediate Fisheries / Aquatic Biologist; Municipal Engineers; Senior Fisheries / Aquatic Biologist; Senior Transportation Traffic Engineer.

DIMAX CONTROLS INC.
Att: Human Resources Manager
41 International Boulevard
Toronto, ON M9W 6H3
Tel. 416-674-8830
Fax 416-674-9525
Email .... jobs@dimaxcontrols.com
Website .... www.dimaxcontrols.com
Employer Background: Dimax Controls Inc. specializes in multi-site (wide area) systems, integrated power management, security and environmental control systems, and water treatment, air quality management and fab-

rication / biotech plant control systems. *New Positions Created (4):* Accounting Manager; Engineering Manager; Project Manager; Service Technician.

DINERS CLUB INTERNATIONAL / ENROUTE
Att: Human Resources
630 Rene Levesque West, Suite 1400
Montréal, QC H3B 4Z9
Fax 514-394-2565
Email .... doralyn.michel1@citicorp.com
Website .... www.citicorp.com
Employer Background: Diners Club International / enRoute, a part of Citigroup, is a worldwide leader in the credit card business. *New Positions Created (3):* Director, National Accounts and Acquisitions; Credit Analyst, New Accounts; Manager, Sales Development.

DIRECT ENERGY MARKETING LTD.
Att: Human Resources
25 Sheppard Avenue West, Suite 1400
Toronto, ON M2N 6S6
Tel. 905-338-1300
Fax 416-221-1243
Email .... hr@ngwi.com
Website .... www.directenergy.com
Employer Background: Direct Energy Marketing Ltd. provides energy to over 1.5 million residential and commercial customers throughout North America. *New Positions Created (8):* Customer Service Representatives; Senior Collections Officers (2); Processing Administrators (5); Customer Service Representatives; Customer Service Supervisors; Payroll and Processing Administrators; Marketing Analyst; Customer Service Representatives.

DIRECT INTEGRATED TRANSPORATION
Att: Manager, Direct Express
14415 - 128th Avenue
Edmonton, AB T5L 3H3
Tel. 780-453-2244
Fax 780-488-2108
Employer Background: Direct Integrated Transportation is a leader in the transportation industry, with over 53 years experience. *New Positions Created (2):* Operations Supervisor; Driver Supervisor / Recruiter.

DIRECT SERVICE NETWORK LTD.
Att: Audrey Conry
3500 Laird Road, Unit 1 and 2
Mississauga, ON L5L 5Y4
Tel. 905-607-6775
Fax 905-607-8972
Email .... audrey.conry@directservice.com
Website .... www.directservice.com
Employer Background: DSN specializes in transborder transportation for the chemical industry. *New Positions Created (3):* Sales Manager; Controller; Sales Manager.

DIRECTPROTECT
Att: Human Resources Manager
125 - 9th Avenue SE, Suite 1800
Calgary, AB T2G 0P6

Fax 403-264-7955
Email .... lsix@hbgrpins.com
Website .... www.directprotect.com
Employer Background: DirectProtect is a direct insurance service offered by HB Group Insurance Management Ltd. *New Positions Created (4):* Claims Service Advisor; Licensed Insurance Representatives; Field Claims Service Advisor; Coach - Personal Lines Insurance.

DISCOUNT CAR AND TRUCK RENTALS
Att: Human Resources
720 Arrow Road
Toronto, ON M9M 2M1
Tel. 416-744-0123
Fax 416-744-9829
Email .... hr@discountcar.com
Website .... www.discountcar.com
Employer Background: Discount Car and Truck Rentals is at the forefront of the automobile rental industry. *New Positions Created (12):* Accounting Supervisor; Branch Managers; Corporate Truck Rental Manager; Management Trainees; Collector; Management Trainees; Accounting Supervisor; Accounts Receivable Clerk; Central Billing Coordinator; Bilingual Call Centre Agents; Consumer Response Rep; Customer Service Reps.

DISCOVER COMMUNICATIONS INC.
Att: Sandy Tumber
170 Wilkinson Road, Unit 2
Brampton, ON L4L 5M6
Fax 905-459-9633
Email .... stumber@
.... discovercommunications.com
Website .... www.
.... discovercommunications.com
Employer Background: Discover Communications Inc. is one of the premier dealers under the Rogers AT&T name, servicing the GTA with 14 locations. *New Positions Created (3):* Outbound Sales Representative; Controller / Accounting Manager; Outbound Sales Representative.

DISCOVERY FORD SALES
Att: Andy Griggs or Ian Thomas
850 Brant Street
Burlington, ON L7R 2J5
Tel. 905-632-8696
Fax 905-632-0914
Website .... www.discoveryford.com
Employer Background: Discovery Ford Sales is an automotive dealership. *New Positions Created (4):* New Car Sales Positions (2); Back Counter Person and Shipper / Receiver; Technicians; Various Dealership Staff Positions.

DISPLAY DESIGN SYSTEMS LTD.
Att: Human Resources Manager
17306 - 106th Avenue
Edmonton, AB T5S 1H9
Tel. 780-483-6355
Fax 780-489-1132
Email .... displays@displaydesign.com
Website .... www.displaydesign.com

Employer Background: Display Design Systems Ltd. is a screen plant, specializing in large format projects ranging from outdoor advertising to point-of-purchase displays. *New Positions Created (3):* Exhibit and Graphics Sales Consultant; Screen Print Sales Consultant; Sales Consultant.

DISTICAN INC.
Att: Alex Dimoski
35 Fulton Way
Richmond Hill, ON L4B 2N4
Tel. 905-764-0073
Fax 905-764-7090
Website .... www.distican.com
Employer Background: Distican Inc. is the Canadian distributor for Simon & Schuster Inc., a large book publisher. *New Positions Created (7):* Sales and Marketing Assistant; Intermediate Software Developer; Executive Assistant; Human Resources Associate; Senior Accountant; Intermediate Accountant; Customer Service Supervisor.

DISTRICT SCHOOL BOARD OF NIAGARA / DSBN
Att: Wayne Cross, Supt. of Schools
191 Carlton Street
St. Catharines, ON L2R 7P4
Tel. 905-641-1550
Fax 905-685-8511
Website .... www.dsbn.edu.on.ca
Employer Background: DSBN is committed to proving quality education. *New Positions Created (3):* Elementary & Secondary Principals and Vice-Principals; Superintendents (2); Elementary Principals and Vice-Principals.

DIVERSEYLEVER
Att: Human Resources Manager
2401 Bristol Circle
Oakville, ON L6H 6P1
Tel. 905-829-1200
Fax 905-829-4908
Website .... www.diverseylever.com
Employer Background: DiverseyLever manufactures and markets specialized chemicals for cleaning and sanitation purposes. *New Positions Created (2):* Account Representative; Bilingual Representative.

DIVERSICARE CANADA MANAGEMENT SERVICES
Att: Susan Bock, Regional Manager
2121 Argentia Road, Suite 301
Mississauga, ON L5N 2X4
Tel. 905-821-1161
Fax 905-821-2477
Email .... divcan@globalserve.net
Website .... www.diversicare.ca
Employer Background: Diversicare Canada Management Services operates retirement communities and long-term care facilities. *New Positions Created (9):* Administrator; Assistant Directors of Care (2); Directors of Resident Care (2); Environmental Services Supervisor; Health Care Coordinator; Recreation Supervisor; Registered Nurses; Registered Practical Nurses; Administrator.

DIVERSICARE CANADA MANAGEMENT SERVICES, CHELSEY PARK LONG-TERM CARE FACILITY
Att: Alice Grzesiak, Administrator
2250 Hurontario Street
Mississauga, ON L5B 1M8
Tel. 905-270-0411
Fax 905-270-1749
Email .... divcan@globalserve.net
Website .... diversicare.ca/chelseypark
Employer Background: Established in 1970, the Chelsey Park Long-Term Care Facility is a 237-bed nursing home, operated by Diversicare Canada Management Services. *New Positions Created (4):* Recreation Supervisor; Nurses; Various Nursing Home Positions; Recreation Supervisor.

DIVERSICARE CANADA MANAGEMENT SERVICES, ROCKCLIFFE CENTRE
Att: Human Resources Manager
3015 Lawrence Avenue East
Toronto, ON M1P 2V7
Tel. 416-264-3201
Fax 416-264-2914
Email .... divcan@globalserve.net
Website .... www.diversicare.ca
Employer Background: Diversicare Canada Management Services operates retirement communities and long-term care facilities. *New Positions Created (4):* Administrative Assistant, Resident Care; Director of Resident Care; Director of Resident Care; Director of Resident Care.

DIZARO COLLECTION
Att: Human Resources Department
1625 Chabanel West, Suite 603
Montréal, QC H4N 2S7
Tel. 514-381-3313
Fax 514-381-2070
Website .... www.dizaro.com
Employer Background: Dizaro Collection is a manufacturer of junior women's sportswear. *New Positions Created (5):* Patternmaker; Fabric Quality Control Technician; Fabric Swatch Technician; Production Assistant; Purchasing Assistant / Junior Fabric Buyer.

DMC INC.
Att: Human Resources Manager
1 First Canadian Place, 50th Floor
Toronto, ON M5X 1E5
Tel. 416-363-4444
Fax 416-363-0962
Email .... careers@dmc.on.ca
Website .... www.dmc.on.ca
Employer Background: DMC Inc. is an information technology consulting leader, delivering e-commerce applications and enterprise-scale Internet solutions for Canada's leading financial and commercial organizations. *New Positions Created (14):* Client / Server Developer; Data Architect; Data Warehouse Architect / Analyst; Data Warehouse Project Leader; Internet / E-Commerce Developer; Object Specialist; Oracle Database Administrator; Oracle Developer / Analyst; Senior Object Modeller; Sybase

Database Administrator; Technical Architect, Client / Server; Technical Architect, Internet; IT Positions; Internet Computing Positions.

DMR CONSULTING INC.
Att: Human Resources Manager
505 Burrard Street
Suite 510, 1 Bentall Centre
Vancouver, BC V7X 1M4
Email .... bc_recruiting@dmr.ca
Website .... www.dmr.ca
Employer Background: DMR Consulting Inc. is a leading global provider of e-consulting services and business solutions to Fortune 1000 companies and Internet start-ups. *New Positions Created (3):* Business Intelligence Consultant; Project Manager; Senior Business Intelligence Systems.

DMR CONSULTING INC.
Att: Human Resources Manager
606 - 4th Street SW, Suite 1500
Calgary, AB T2P 1T1
Tel. 403-265-6001
Fax 403-237-6856
Website .... www.dmr.ca
Employer Background: DMR Consulting Inc. is a leading global provider of e-consulting services and business solutions to Fortune 1000 companies and Internet start-ups. *New Positions Created (13):* Analyst; Analyst; Analyst; Analyst; Business Analyst / Business Logic Layer Developer; Database Administrator; Enterprise Architect / Data Warehousing Architect; Management Consultant / Network Engineer; Software Developer; Software Developer / Senior Java Developer; System Analyst; System Architect; Technical Specialist.

DMR CONSULTING INC.
Att: Recruiting Coordinator
252 Adelaide Street East
Toronto, ON M5A 1N1
Tel. 416-363-8661
Fax 416-363-4739
Website .... www.dmr.ca
Employer Background: DMR Consulting Inc. is a leading global provider of e-consulting services and business solutions to Fortune 1000 companies and Internet start-ups. *New Positions Created (5):* Accounting Manager / Manager of Financial Reporting; Executive Assistant; Practice Director, Systems Delivery; Senior Management Consultants / Technology Consultants; SAP Consultants.

DMTI SPATIAL INC.
Att: Human Resources Department
625 Cochrane Drive, 3rd Floor
Markham, ON L3R 9R9
Tel. 905-948-2014
Fax 905-948-9404
Email .... jobs@dmtispatial.com
Website .... www.dmtispatial.com
Employer Background: DMTI Spatial Inc. is a leading provider of comprehensive geospatial products and services. *New Positions Created (11):* Administrative Assist-

ant; Data Researchers (4); Data Warehouse Analyst; GIS Specialist; GIS Technician; Product Mgr; Project Leader; Sales and Marketing Coordinator; Senior Account Mgr; Senior Account Mgrs; Senior Account Mgrs.

DOALL INDUSTRIAL SUPPLIES
Att: Plant Manager
10 Meridian Road
Toronto, ON M9W 4Z8
Tel. 416-675-7015
Fax 416-675-6137
Website .... www.doall.com
Employer Background: DoALL Industrial Supplies manufactures bandsaw blades, cut-off saws and production saws, and distributes industrial MRO supplies and cutting tools to customers across North America. *New Positions Created (2):* Junior Buyer; Administrative Assistant.

DOG STAR SYSTEMS INC.
Att: Human Resources Manager
1035 - 64th Avenue South, Suite 30
Calgary, AB T2H 2J7
Fax 403-932-2941
Email .... resume@dogstarsystems.com
Website .... www.dogstarsystems.com
Employer Background: Established in 1996, Dog Star Systems Inc. provides technology consulting and IT outsourcing services. *New Positions Created (2):* Lotus Notes Administrator; Network Administrator.

DOGRIB COMMUNITY SERVICES BOARD / DCSB
Att: Julia Naedzo, Human Resources
PO Bag 5
Rae-Edzo, NT X0E 0Y0
Tel. 867-392-3000
Fax 867-392-3001
Email .... julia.naedzo@dogrib.net
Employer Background: The Dogrib Community Services Board is responsible for educating students in 6 schools. *New Positions Created (5):* Community Health Nurses; Community Health Nurses (2); Manager, Health Programs; Nurse-In-Charge; Junior High Teacher.

DOLCE INTERNATIONAL
Att: Michelle Bordignon
3550 Pharmacy Avenue
Toronto, ON M1W 3Z3
Tel. 416-490-6074
Fax 416-490-4488
Email ...... michelle.bordignon@ifl.bmo.ca
Website .... www.dolce.com
Employer Background: Dolce International specializes in conference centre management. *New Positions Created (5):* Food & Beverage Supervisor; Human Resources Coordinator; Bilingual Conference Desk Attendant; Bilingual Front Office Agent; Food & Beverage Supervisor.

DOLLCO PRINTING
Att: Manager, Human Resources
2340 St. Laurent Boulevard
Ottawa, ON K1G 6E3

Tel. 613-738-9181
Fax 613-738-4655
Email .... jobs@dollco.com
Website .... www.dollco.com
Employer Background: Dollco Printing is one of Canada's largest independently owned commercial printers. *New Positions Created (6):* Customer Service Representative; Various Logistics Positions; Various Printing Positions; Digital Prepress Technicians; Manager, Direct Mail Operations; Mailing Coordinator.

DOME MINE
Att: Laura Michel, HR Coordinator
Box 70
South Porcupine, ON P0N 1H0
Fax 705-235-6551
Email ..... laura_michel@placerdome.com
Website .... www.placerdome.com
Employer Background: Dome Mine, a division of Placer Dome North America, is an underground and open pit gold mining operation. *New Positions Created (2):* Chief Electrician; Compressor and Hoisting Supervisor.

DOMINION COLOUR CORPORATION
Att: Human Resources
515 Consumers Road, 7th Floor
Toronto, ON M2J 4Z2
Tel. 416-791-4200
Fax 416-497-8462
Email .... dccjobs@domcol.com
Website .... www.domcol.com
Employer Background: Dominion Colour Corporation supplies high-quality colour pigments for plastics, paint and ink industry applications. *New Positions Created (9):* General Sales Manager; Group Controller; Programmer / Analyst IT; Customer Service Representative, European Market; Payroll Supervisor; Senior Costing Analyst; Human Resources Representatives; Programmer / Analyst IT; Senior R and D Chemist.

DOMINION CONSTRUCTION COMPANY INC.
Att: Bruce Gilbert, Operations Manager
2256 - 29th Street NE, Suite 90
Calgary, AB T1Y 7G4
Fax 403-269-9211
Email .... bgilbert@calgary.dominion.com
Website .... www.dominionco.com
Employer Background: Established in 1911, Dominion Construction Company Inc. offers design, general contracting, construction and project management services. *New Positions Created (3):* Senior Superintendent / Supervisor; Project Assistant; Divisional Controller.

DOMINION OF CANADA GENERAL INSURANCE COMPANY, THE
Att: Human Resources
1055 West Georgia Street
Suite 2400, Box 11114, Royal Centre
Vancouver, BC V6E 3P3
Tel. 604-684-5811

Fax 604-688-0053
Email .... bcorbett@thedominion.ca
Employer Background: The Dominion of Canada General Insurance Company provides a full range of property and casualty insurance products and services. *New Positions Created (4):* Commercial Lines Underwriter; Portfolio Analyst, Personal Lines Underwriting; Territory Manager, Commercial Lines Underwriting; Manager, Underwriting.

DOMINION OF CANADA GENERAL INSURANCE COMPANY, THE
Att: Manager,
Commercial Lines Underwriting
10060 Jasper Avenue
Suite 601, Tower 2, Scotia Place
Edmonton, AB T5J 3R8
Tel. 780-428-0881
Fax 780-424-2023
Employer Background: The Dominion of Canada General Insurance Company provides a full range of property and casualty insurance products and services. *New Positions Created (2):* Commercial Lines Underwriter; Commercial Lines Underwriter Trainee.

DOMINION OF CANADA GENERAL INSURANCE COMPANY, THE
Att: Darlene Chow, Human Resources
165 University Avenue
Toronto, ON M5H 3B9
Tel. 416-350-3740
Fax 416-362-1602
Email .... dchow@thedominion.ca
Employer Background: The Dominion of Canada General Insurance Company provides a full range of property and casualty insurance products and services. *New Positions Created (14):* Claims Professional, Core Unit; Customer Service Representative; Portfolio Analyst, Personal Lines Underwriting; Senior Claims Professional, Accident Benefits Unit; Sr Claims Professional, Casualty Unit; Sr Claims Professional, Core Unit; Sr Claims Professional, Property Unit; Commercial Lines Underwriter Trainee; Customer Service Representative; Claims Adjuster, Core Unit; Sr Claims Adjuster, Accident Benefit Unit; Sr Claims Adjuster, Casualty Unit; Senior Road Adjuster, Property Unit; Senior Human Resources Manager.

DOMINION SAMPLE LTD.
Att: Human Resources Manager
7945 Viau Boulevard
St-Leonard, QC H1R 3E5
Tel. 514-374-9010
Fax 514-374-9788
Email .... jobs@dominionsample.com
Employer Background: Dominion Sample Ltd. is a manufacturing company. *New Positions Created (3):* Accountant; Sales Representative; Purchasing Position.

DOMINION SPRING INDUSTRIES CORP. / DSI
Att: Human Resources

240 Courtneypark Drive East
Mississauga, ON L5T 2S5
Tel. 905-564-0641
Fax 905-564-3213
Email .... humanresources@
.... dominionspring.com
Website .... www.dominionspring.com
Employer Background: Founded in 1980, DSI is a custom manufacturer of high-quality springs, wire and flat forms, spring washers, metal stampings and value-added light assemblies. *New Positions Created (5):* Machine Operators; Quality Assurance Engineer; Setup Operator; Tool and Die Maker; Quality Clerk.

DOMTAR INC.
Att: Human Resources Department
395 de Maisonneuve Blvd. West, 8th Floor
Montréal, QC H3A 1L6
Tel. 514-848-5400
Fax 514-848-5623
Email .... carole.macphee@domtar.com
Website .... www.domtar.com
Employer Background: Domtar Inc. is one of Canada's largest producers of specialty and fine papers. *New Positions Created (2):* Administrative Technician; Lumber Trader.

DOMTAR INC., COMMUNICATION PAPERS DIVISION
Att: Natalie Kearns, HR Department
PO Box 40
Cornwall, ON K6J 5S3
Fax 613-938-4681
Email .... natalie.kearns@domtar.com
Website .... www.domtar.com
Employer Background: Domtar Inc. is one of Canada's largest producers of specialty and fine papers. *New Positions Created (3):* Electronic Technician; Heavy Equipment and Fork Truck Mechanic; Electrical and Instrumentation Electrical Coordinator.

DOMTAR INC., OTTAWA / HULL MILLS
Att: Superintendent, Employee Services
PO Box 600, Station B
Hull, QC J8X 3Y7
Fax 613-782-2607
Website .... www.domtar.com
Employer Background: Domtar Inc. is one of Canada's largest producers of specialty and fine papers. *New Positions Created (2):* Industrial Electrician; Industrial Millwrights (2).

DON PARK INC.
Att: Human Resources Manager
842 York Mills Road
Toronto, ON M3B 3A8
Tel. 416-449-7275
Fax 416-444-6335
Website .... www.donpark.com
Employer Background: Established in 1972, Don Park Inc. is a large manufacturer and supplier of quality sheet metal and venting products. *New Positions Created (8):* Various Sales Positions; Various Sales Positions; Accounts Payable Clerks (2); Junior Credit Representative; Health and Safety Coordi-

nator / Human Resource Administrator; Branch Manager; Hydronic / HVAC Representative; Purchasing Agent.

DONAHUE ERNST & YOUNG LLP
Att: Michelle Gage
222 Bay Street, Suite 1800, PO Box 197
Ernst & Young Tower, TD Centre
Toronto, ON M5K 1H6
Fax 416-943-2735
Email .... michelle.gage@ca.eyi.com
Website .... www.ey.com
Employer Background: Donahue Ernst & Young LLP is a law firm and member of Ernst & Young International Ltd. *New Positions Created (5):* Associate Lawyer; Junior Associate Lawyer; Associate Lawyer; Corporate / Commercial Lawyer; Intellectual Property Lawyer.

DORAN CONTRACTORS LTD.
Att: Human Resources
3187 Albion Road South
Ottawa, ON K1V 8Y3
Tel. 613-526-2400
Fax 613-526-2880
Website .... www.doran.ca
Employer Background: Doran Contractors Ltd. is involved in general contracting, construction management and design. *New Positions Created (3):* Construction Project Coordinator; Assistant Site Superintendent; Junior Project Manager / Field Engineer.

DOREL INDUSTRIES INC.
Att: Human Resources
1255 Greene Avenue, Suite 300
Montréal, QC H3Z 2A4
Fax 514-323-1522
Email .... carolinem@dorel.com
Website .... www.dorel.com
Employer Background: Dorel Industries Inc. is a global consumer product manufacturer, specializing in three distinct segments: ready-to-assemble furniture, juvenile furniture and accessories / home furnishings. *New Positions Created (5):* Quality Control Inspector; Designer; Customer Service Representative; Tax Specialist; Credit Manager.

DORIGO SYSTEMS LTD.
Att: Human Resources Manager
3885 Henning Drive
Burnaby, BC V5C 6N5
Tel. 604-294-4600
Fax 604-294-4609
Employer Background: Dorigo Systems Ltd. is an electronics manufacturing company. *New Positions Created (3):* Office Secretary; Precision Assemblers; Purchasing Assistant.

DOT COM ENTERTAINMENT GROUP INC. / DCEG
Att: Human Resources Manager
150 Randall Street
Oakville, ON L6J 1P3
Tel. 905-337-8524
Fax 905-337-8630
Email .... staffing@dceg.com
Website .... www.dceg.com

Employer Background: DCEG is an Internet development company, specializing in online gaming. *New Positions Created (6):* Java Developer; Quality Assurance Specialist; Senior Systems Engineer; Systems Administrator; Web Applications Developer; Webmaster.

DOUBLEDAY CANADA LTD.
Att: Kelly Neri
105 Bond Street
Toronto, ON M5B 1Y3

Tel. 416-977-7891
Fax 416-977-7049
Email .... neri.kelly@bookspan.com
Website .... www.randomhouse.ca/
.... about/double.html

Employer Background: Doubleday Canada Ltd. is a leading direct marketer of books. *New Positions Created (5):* Human Resources & Facilities Manager; Marketing Analyst; Customer Service Coordinator; Telemarketing Supervisor; Outbound Sales Representative.

DOUGLAS COLLEGE
Att: Employee Relations Department
PO Box 2503
New Westminster, BC V3L 5B2

Tel. 604-527-5095
Fax 604-527-5549
Website .... www.douglas.bc.ca

Employer Background: Douglas College offers a range of 2-year career and university transfer programs, serving 10,000 credit students through 3 campuses. *New Positions Created (22):* Associate Registrar, Records and Systems; Economics Instructor; Instructor, Philosophy & Humanities; Professional Writing Program Instructor, Print Futures; Professional Writing Program Instructors, Print Futures; College PLAR Service Faculty Liaison; Community and Contract Services Programmer, Health Programs; Instructor, Computer Information Systems; Instructor, Literacy; Instructors, Developmental Studies; Anthropology Instructors; Community and Contract Services Programmer, Health Programs; Sociology Instructors; Faculty Positions, General Nursing; Faculty Positions, Psychiatric Nursing; Faculty Positions, Psychology; Instructors, Communications; Instructors, English; Programmer Analyst; Instructor, Therapeutic Recreation Program; Dean, Humanities and Social Sciences.

DOVER INDUSTRIES LTD.
Att: Division Controller,
Dover Cone Division
4350 Harvester Road
Burlington, ON L7L 5S4

Tel. 905-333-1515

Employer Background: Dover Industries Ltd. is a food products and packaging company. *New Positions Created (6):* Receptionist / Secretary; Accounts Payable Clerk; Health, Safety and Quality Systems Professional; Payroll Clerk; Product Engineer; Product Marketing Manager, Switching.

DOWNTOWN BMW
Att: Human Resources Manager
550 Adelaide Street East
Toronto, ON M5A 1N7

Tel. 416-865-1622
Fax 416-865-1547
Website .... www.downtown.bmw.com

Employer Background: Downtown BMW is an automotive dealership. *New Positions Created (5):* Sales Administrator; Service Advisor; Service Advisor; Service Manager; Accounts Receivable Clerk.

DRAGON PHARMACEUTICALS (CANADA) INC.
Att: Human Resources
543 Granville Street, Suite 1200
Vancouver, BC V6C 1X8

Fax 604-669-4243

Employer Background: Dragon Pharmaceuticals (Canada) Inc. is a biopharmaceutical company, specializing in the discovery, development and marketing of therapies for infectious diseases, cancer and cardiovascular diseases. *New Positions Created (4):* Head, Research and Development; Research Associates; Research Scientists; Research Technicians.

DRECO
Att: Mechanical Drafting Supervisor
6415 - 75th Street
Edmonton, AB T6E 0T3

Fax 780-463-0294
Website .... www.natoil.com

Employer Background: Dreco (part of National Oilwell) designs, manufactures and sells comprehensive systems and components used in oil and gas drilling and production. *New Positions Created (2):* Mechanical Designer; Structural Designer.

DRESSER FLOW CONTROL
Att: Human Resources
5010 North Service Road
Burlington, ON L7L 5R5

Tel. 905-335-3529
Fax 905-335-6147
Website .... www.dresser.com

Employer Background: Dresser Flow Control (part of Dresser Inc. and formerly Dresser Valve) designs, manufactures and supports valves, pumps, actuators and instrumentation for all phases of the energy industry. *New Positions Created (3):* Audit Program Manager; Valve Technicians; Materials Manager.

DRS FLIGHT SAFETY AND COMMUNICATIONS
Att: Human Resource Centre
115 Emily Street
Carleton Place, ON K7C 4J5

Tel. 613-253-3020
Fax 613-253-7218
Email .... hr_cp@drs.ca
Website .... www.drs.com

Employer Background: DRS Flight Safety and Communications designs, manufactures and tests advanced systems for aero-space and defence applications. *New Positions Created (9):* Manufacturing Cost Estimator; Materials Planner; Receptionist; Buyers; Electronic Assemblers; Facilities Leader; Machine Operators; Manufacturing Engineers; Production Manager.

DRUG TRADING COMPANY LTD.
Att: Judy Silverberg, HR Department
131 McNabb Street
Markham, ON L3R 5V7

Tel. 905-943-9499
Fax 905-943-4515
Email .... jsilverberg@pharmassist.ca
Website .... www.pharmassist.ca

Employer Background: Established in 1904, Drug Trading Company Ltd. is a retail pharmacy services company, providing value-added buying, merchandising, marketing programs and logistics solutions to over 1,450 independent pharmacies across Canada. *New Positions Created (4):* Pharmacy Systems Specialist; Point of Sale Product Specialist; Manager, Telemarketing Retail Support; Pharmacy Systems Specialist.

DSC GROUP OF COMPANIES
Att: Reception
95 Bridgeland Avenue
Toronto, ON M6A 1Y7

Website .... www.dscgrp.com

Employer Background: DSC Group of Companies is a specialized manufacturer of security systems for business and residential applications. *New Positions Created (12):* Manufacturing Engineer; Quality Assurance Manager; Manufacturing Engineer; Quality Assurance Manager; Test Engineers (2); Cycle Count Analyst; Midnight Shift Manager; Warehouse Coordinator; Manufacturing Engineering Group Specialist; Production Manager; Senior Planners; Test Engineering Group Specialist.

DSC GROUP OF COMPANIES
Att: Nicole Belperio
3301 Langstaff Road
Concord, ON L4K 4L2

Tel. 905-760-3000
Fax 905-760-3004
Email .... belperin@dscltd.com
Website .... www.dscgrp.com

Employer Background: DSC Group of Companies is a specialized manufacturer of security systems for business and residential applications. *New Positions Created (33):* Customer Service Representative; SQA Specialist, Entry-Level; Accounts Receivable Representative; Financial Analyst; SQL Specialist; Technical Support Representative; Bilingual Product Support Representative; Financial Analyst; Manufacturing Cost Analyst; Customer Service Representative; Data Entry Clerk; Design Team Member; PCB CAD Designer; Wireless and Sensors Design Team Member; Accounts Payable Representative; Credit Analyst; Inside Customer Support Representative; Accounts Receivable Supervisor; Product Support Technician; Financial Analyst; Manufacturing Cost Analyst; Bilingual Technical Support Representative; Hardware Designers (2); International Traffic Coordinator; Senior Electronics Buyer; Senior RF Engineer; Software Developer, Embedded; Software Quality Assurance Technicians; Customer Service Representatives (2); Bilingual Technical Representative; Instrumentation Designer; Software Developer; Systems Administration Specialist, BAAN.

DSI DATOTECH SYSTEMS INC.
Att: Human Resources Manager
905 Pender Street West, Suite 300
Vancouver, BC V6C 1L6

Fax 604-685-9159
Email .... jobs@dato.com
Website .... www.dato.com

Employer Background: DSI Datotech Systems Inc. is a publicly-traded research and development company specializing in human-machine interaction technology for gesture control input and control systems. *New Positions Created (4):* Electronic Engineer; Embedded Software Engineer; Research Scientist; Senior Software Engineer.

DSM BIOLOGICS
Att: Human Resources Department
6000 Royalmount Avenue
Montréal, QC H4P 2T1

Tel. 514-341-9940
Fax 514-847-9075
Email .... allaireguy@sympatico.ca
Website .... www.dsmbiologics.com

Employer Background: DSM Biologics manufactures custom biopharmaceutical products. *New Positions Created (15):* Human Resources Director; Planner; Instrumentation Technician; Mechanical Engineering Technician; Storeman; Warehouse Clerk; Cell Culture Technicians; Downstream Processing Senior Scientist; Quality Assurance Officer Level 1; Quality Control Technicians, Biochemistry; Quality Control Technicians, HPLC; Quality Control Technicians, Raw Materials; Senior Downstream Processing Technician; Senior Scientist, Cell Culture; Validation Specialist.

DSPA SOFTWARE INC.
Att: Human Resources
2050 Dundas Street East, Unit 5
Mississauga, ON L4X 1L9

Tel. 905-279-9993
Fax 905-279-2431
Email .... human.resources@
.... dspasoftware.com
Website .... www.dspasoftware.com

Employer Background: DSPA Software Inc. is a software development company. *New Positions Created (5):* Business Analysts; Project Managers; Client Server Developers; Project Managers; Web Developers.

DUCA FINANCIAL SERVICES CREDIT UNION LTD.
Att: Arnold Denton, Vice-President, Credit
PO Box 1100, Willowdale Station A
Toronto, ON M2N 5W5

Tel. 416-223-8502
Fax 416-223-2575
Email .... adenton@duca.com
Website .... www.duca.com

Employer Background: DUCA Financial Services Credit Union Ltd. is a full-service financial institution, serving the Greater Toronto Area for over 46 years. *New Positions Created (5):* Commercial Lender; Branch Manager; Lender; Member Service Representative; Branch Manager.

DUCKS UNLIMITED CANADA
Att: Richard Walker,
National Director of Development
279 Midpark Way SE, Suite 100
Calgary, AB T2X 1M2

Fax 403-201-5577
Email .... du_development@ducks.ca
Website .... www.ducks.ca

Employer Background: Ducks Unlimited Canada is a private, non-profit company dedicated to the preservation of breeding habitat for waterfowl. *New Positions Created (2):* Major Gift Officers and Development Associates; Manager of Licensing and Royalty Programs.

DUCKS UNLIMITED CANADA
Att: Jean Olsen
PO Box 1160, Stonewall
Oak Hammock Marsh, MB R0C 2Z0

Tel. 204-467-3000
Fax 204-467-9028
Email .... j_olsen@ducks.ca
Website .... www.ducks.ca

Employer Background: Ducks Unlimited Canada is a private, non-profit company dedicated to the preservation of breeding habitat for waterfowl. *New Positions Created (2):* Receptionist; Technologist.

DUECK CHEVROLET OLDSMOBILE CADILLAC LTD.
Att: Ken Elmer or Mike Blaney
86 Marine Drive SE
Vancouver, BC V5X 4P8

Tel. 604-324-7277
Fax 604-324-4414
Email .... sales@dueckgm.com
Website .... www.dueckgm.com

Employer Background: Dueck Chevrolet Oldsmobile Cadillac Ltd. is a large GM dealership. *New Positions Created (3):* Sales Consultant; Office Manager; Body Shop Technician.

DUFFERIN CONSTRUCTION COMPANY
Att: Human Resources Manager
690 Dorval Drive, Suite 200
Oakville, ON L6K 3W7

Tel. 416-798-4912
Fax 905-842-7974
Website ... www.dufferinconstruction.com

Employer Background: Dufferin Construction Company, a division of St. Lawrence Cement Inc., is heavy civil engineering contractor founded in 1912. *New Positions Created (2):* Project Administrator; Quality Control Technologist.

DUFFERIN-PEEL CATHOLIC DISTRICT SCHOOL BOARD, THE
Att: Teacher Personnel
40 Matheson Boulevard West
Mississauga, ON L5R 1C5

Tel. 905-890-1221
Fax 905-501-0182
Website .... www.dpcdsb.org

Employer Background: Dufferin-Peel Catholic District School Board serves 85,000 students in 121 schools. *New Positions Created (20):* Elementary & Secondary Teachers; Itinerant Teachers; Secondary Teacher, Business; Secondary Teacher, Business; Secondary Teacher, Chemistry; Secondary Teacher, Computer Science; Secondary Teacher, Computer Studies; Secondary Teacher, Computer Studies; Secondary Teacher, Guidance; Secondary Teacher, Instrumental Music; Secondary Teacher, Religion; Secondary Teacher, Science; Secondary Teacher, Special Education; Secondary Teacher, Technology; Secondary Teacher, Technology; Secondary Teachers (3); Secondary Teachers, Technology (2); Secondary Teachers, Technology (3); Catholic Elementary Teachers; Secondary Teachers.

DUKE BLAKEY, INC.
Att: Recruiter
3075 - 14th Avenue, Suite 207
Markham, ON L3R 0G9

Tel. 905-513-9400
Fax 905-513-9405
Email .... blakey@dukeengineering.com
Website .... www.dukeengineering.com

Employer Background: Duke Blakey, Inc. (a Duke Energy company) specializes in energy and environmental projects, project planning and execution. *New Positions Created (8):* Design Engineers; Hardware Engineers; Lead Mechanical Engineer; Electrical Engineers; Junior and Senior Draftspersons; Junior and Senior Project Managers; Metallurgical Engineers and Technicians; Senior Contract Managers.

DUMEX MEDICAL
Att: Human Resources Department
104 Shorting Road
Toronto, ON M1S 3S4

Tel. 416-299-4003
Fax 416-299-4912
Email .... feigner@dumex.com
Website .... www.dumex.com

Employer Background: Dumex Medical is a mid-sized manufacturer of medical and pharmaceutical devices. *New Positions Created (8):* Supervisor, QA & RA; Bilingual Customer Service Representative; Scheduler; Accountant / Analyst; Materials Specialist; Customer Service Representative; Accounting and Materials Analyst / Project Specialist; Customer Service Manager.

DUNDEE REALTY MANAGEMENT CORPORATION
Att: Human Resources
390 Bay Street, Suite 1900
Toronto, ON M5H 2Y2

Tel. 416-365-3535

Fax 416-365-5998
Email .... hrrecruit@dundeerealty.com
Website .... www.dundeerealty.com
Employer Background: Dundee Realty Management Corporation is a real estate company. *New Positions Created (8):* Accounts Payable Clerk; Manager, Central Purchasing - Real Estate; Retail Tenant Construction Coordinator; Administrative Assistant; Receptionist; Property Accounting Administrator; Property Administrator; Intermediate Programmer / Analyst.

DUOCOM CANADA

Att: Human Resources Manager
1550 - 16th Avenue
Richmond Hill, ON L4B 3K9
Tel. 905-508-1740
Fax 905-508-4211
Website .... www.duocom.ca
Employer Background: Duocom Canada is a leading audiovisual firm. *New Positions Created (6):* Customer Service Representative; Technical Support Services; A / V Design Engineers; A / V Installation Technician; A / V Project Managers; Staging Video Technicians.

DUPLIUM CORPORATION

Att: Human Resources
35 Minthorn Court
Thornhill, ON L3T 7N5
Tel. 905-709-9930
Fax 905-709-9439
Email .... careers@duplium.com
Website .... www.duplium.com
Employer Background: Duplium Corporation (formerly Media Duplication Corp.) has been providing CD replication services for over 10 years. *New Positions Created (9):* Accountant; Administrative Assistant; Junior Mac Operator / Pre-Flight Technician; Director, Fulfillment and Distribution; Glass Mastering Technicians; Manager, Fulfillment and Distribution; Molding Operators; Shipper / Receiver; Team Leaders.

DUPONT CANADA INC.

Att: Human Resources
7070 Mississauga Road
PO Box 2200, Streetsville Postal Station
Mississauga, ON L5M 2H3
Tel. 905-821-3300
Fax 905-821-5270
Email .... hr.recruiting@can.dupont.com
Website .... www.dupont.ca
Employer Background: DuPont Canada manufactures specialty chemicals and fibres, plastics and polymer films. *New Positions Created (6):* Packaging Development Team Leader; Order Management Resource Position; Purchasing Agent; Cost Accountant; Financial Business Analyst; HR Managers (2).

DUPONT CANADA INC.

Att: Human Resources
455 Front Road, PO Box 2100
Kingston, ON K7L 4Z6
Tel. 613-544-6000
Fax 613-548-5353

Website .... www.dupont.ca
Employer Background: DuPont Canada Inc. manufactures specialty chemicals and fibres, plastics and polymer films. *New Positions Created (2):* Purchasing Agent; Maintenance Mechanics.

DURA-LITE HEAT TRANSFER PRODUCTS LTD.

Att: Human Resources
7041 Farrell Road SE, Bay 3
Calgary, AB T2H 0T3
Tel. 403-259-2691
Fax 403-252-2784
Email .... gerryg@duralite.net
Website .... www.duralite.net
Employer Background: Dura-Lite Heat Transfer Products Ltd. manufactures charged air coolers. *New Positions Created (3):* Plant Superintendent; Senior Mechanical Engineer; Regional Sales Manager.

DURHAM CATHOLIC DISTRICT SCHOOL BOARD

Att: Allan W. Jeffers, HR Manager
650 Rossland Road West
Oshawa, ON L1J 7C4
Tel. 905-576-6150
Fax 905-576-0923
Email .. allan.jeffers@durhamrc.edu.on.ca
Website .... www.durhamrc.edu.on.ca
Employer Background: The Durham Catholic District School Board is dedicated to promoting the gospel of Christ and providing holistic education. *New Positions Created (4):* Coordinator of Psychological Services; Various Teaching Positions; Secondary School Principal; Various Curriculum Chair Positions (11).

DURHAM CHILDREN'S AID SOCIETY

Att: Human Resources Department
555 Rossland Road West
Oshawa, ON L1J 3H3
Fax 905-433-0409
Email .... hrdurhamcas@globalserve.net
Employer Background: The Durham CAS is a child welfare agency serving an expanding, culturally diverse region east of Toronto. *New Positions Created (3):* Children's Services Workers; Family Services Workers; Service Supervisor.

DURHAM COLLEGE

Att: Sandra Bennett,
Director, Staff Services
PO Box 385
Oshawa, ON L1H 7L7
Fax 905-721-3193
Email .... jobs@durhamc.on.ca
Website .... www.durhamc.on.ca
Employer Background: Durham College offers over 50 certificate and diploma programs. *New Positions Created (8):* Technologist B; Technologist B; Graphic Design Professor, School of Design; Human Resources Management Professor, School of Business; Nursing Professor, School of Health; Professor, School of Business; Professor, School of Design; Professor, School of Design.

DURHAM, THE REGIONAL MUNICIPALITY OF

Att: Staffing Advisor
605 Rossland Road East
Whitby, ON L1N 6A3
Tel. 905-668-7711
Fax 905-668-9935
Email ... humanres@region.durham.on.ca
Website .... www.region.durham.on.ca
Employer Background: Located east of Toronto, the Regional Municipality of Durham is home to over 495,000 residents. *New Positions Created (25):* Emergency Measures Coordinator; Employee Relations Officer; Senior Financial Analysts (2); Financial Housing Services Supervisor; Housing Development & Homelessness Initiative Program Manager; Public Health Inspectors; Public Health Nutritionist; Senior Infant Development Consultant; Facilities & Real Estate Manager; Hydrogeologist; Water Pollution Control Superintendent; Project Engineer, Engineering Planning & Studies Division; Project Engineer, Transportation Planning & Design Division; Manager of Public Health Nursing & Nutrition; Administrator, Family Services; Advanced & Primary Care Paramedics; Supervisor, Plant Information Systems; Public Health Nutritionist; Stationary Engineer; Compensation Advisor; Economic Analysts (2); Provincial Offences Collection Coordinator; Senior Financial Analyst; Staffing Advisor; Manager of Employee Relations.

DY 4 SYSTEMS INC.

Att: Human Resources Manager
333 Palladium Drive
Kanata, ON K2V 1A6
Tel. 613-599-9191
Fax 613-599-7777
Email .... jobs@dy4.com
Website www.dy4.com
Employer Background: Founded in 1979, DY 4 Systems Inc. is a leading supplier of single-board computers for defence and aerospace applications. The company has annual revenues of $64 million and 260 employees. *New Positions Created (18):* Project Leader; Technical Support Specialist; Hardware Engineer; Production Planner / Controller; Senior Debug Technician; Senior Quality Engineer; Test Engineering Specialist; Test Operator, Evening Shift; Product Support Specialist; Production Planning / Procurement Manager; Senior Manufacturing Engineer; Administrative Assistant; Project Leaders; QC Final Inspector; Director, Supply Chain Management; Hardware Engineering Specialist; Project Analyst; Technical Support Specialist.

DYNACAST CANADA INC.

Att: Human Resources Department
330 Avro Street
Pointe-Claire, QC H9R 5W5
Tel. 514-694-5740
Fax 514-694-8681
Website .... www.dynacast.com
Employer Background: Dynacast Canada Inc. is a leader in die casting, injection molding and industrial fastening systems.

New Positions Created (14): Die Cleaner; Quality Inspector; Set-Up Person; Tool Maker; Maintenance Mechanic; Quality Technician; Automation Technician; Maintenance Electrician; Tool Maker; Die Cleaner, Preparation; Quality Technician; Network Administrator / Business Systems Analyst; Maintenance Supervisor; Set-Up Person.

DYNAMIC CHOCOLATES INC.
Att: Human Resources Manager
1648 Derwent Way
Annacis Island, BC V3M 6R9

Tel. 604-515-7117
Fax 604-515-7167
Employer Background: Dynamic Chocolates Inc. manufactures fine boxed chocolates. *New Positions Created (2):* Production Supervisor; Shipping Supervisor.

DYNAMIC MUTUAL FUNDS
Att: Human Resources Team
40 King Street West, 55th Floor
Toronto, ON M5H 4A9

Tel. 416-365-5100
Fax 416-363-5850
Website .... www.dynamic.ca
Employer Background: Dynamic Mutual Funds has over $6.5 billion in assets and manages portfolios for more than 350,000 investors. *New Positions Created (3):* Web Production Position; Client Service Representative; Mutual Fund Inside Sales Representatives.

DYNAMIC SOURCE MANUFACTURING INC.
Att: Human Resources Manager
956 - 72nd Avenue NE
Calgary, AB T2E 8V9

Fax 403-516-1892
Email .... hr@dynamicsourcemfg.com
Website ..... www.dynamicsourcemfg.com
Employer Background: Dynamic Source Manufacturing Inc. provides electronics manufacturing services. *New Positions Created (5):* Accounting Clerk; Material Handler; Production Assemblers; Production Manager; SMT Operator.

DYNAPLAS LTD.
Att: Human Resources Manager
380 Passmore Avenue
Toronto, ON M1V 4B4

Fax 416-293-8261
Email .... applications@dynaplas.com
Employer Background: Dynaplas Ltd. is a manufacturing company. *New Positions Created (3):* Production Quality Supervisor; Senior Injection Moulding Process Development Technician; Junior Accountant.

DYNAPRO
Att: Human Resources Manager
800 Carleton Court
Annacis Island, BC V3M 6L3

Tel. 604-521-3962
Fax 604-521-8474

Email .... newjobs_vancouver@dynapro.com
Website .... www.dynapro.com
Employer Background: Dynapro designs and manufactures touch-screen components, touch computers, terminals and monitors. *New Positions Created (5):* Instrumentation Service Technician; Materials Technologist; Senior Analog Design Engineer; Sr Test Engineer; Software Developer.

DYNASTREAM TECHNOLOGIES INC.
Att: Human Resources Manager
206 - 5th Avenue West, Suite 243, Bay 1
Cochrane, AB T4C 1X3

Tel. 403-932-9292
Fax 403-932-6521
Email .... dynastream@dynastream.com
Website .... www.dynastream.com
Employer Background: Dynastream Technologies Inc. develops proprioceptive or "smart" devices using wireless and inertial technology. *New Positions Created (6):* Embedded Software Engineers; PC Software Engineers ; RF Design Engineers; Senior Marketing Manager; Senior Production / Operations Mgr; Senior Project Manager.

DYNASTY MOTORCAR CORP.
Att: Glen Ashdown, VP Engineering
800 McCurdy Road
Kelowna, BC V1X 2P7

Tel. 250-765-4528
Fax 250-765-4187
Email .. gashdown@dynastymotorcar.com
Website .... www.itiselectric.com
Employer Background: Founded in 1998, Dynasty Motorcar Corp. designs and manufactures zero emission, electric low-speed vehicles for urban, recreational and light commercial markets. *New Positions Created (3):* Design Engineer / Technologist; Senior Electrical Design Engineer; Senior Mechanical Design Engineer / Technologist.

E.B. EDDY SPECIALTY PAPERS
Att: S. Ramsay, HR Director
1 Station Road
Espanola, ON P5E 1R6

Tel. 705-869-2020
Fax 705-869-3871
Website .... www.ebeddy.com
Employer Background: E.B. Eddy Specialty Papers (a division of Domtar Inc.) produces pulp and paper products at mills across Canada. *New Positions Created (2):* Wildlife Biologist; Head Filer.

E.S. FOX LTD.
Att: Don Morris, Project Manager
4935 Kent Avenue
Niagara Falls, ON L2H 1J6

Fax 905-734-2929
Employer Background: E.S. Fox Ltd. is a mechanical and electrical contractor. *New Positions Created (2):* Construction Scheduler; Power Plant Operator.

E-CRUITER.COM INC.
Att: Human Resources Manager

45 Sheppard Avenue East, Suite 900
Toronto, ON M2N 5W9

Tel. 416-222-6344
Fax 416-222-9471
Website .... www.ecruiter.com
Employer Background: E-Cruiter.com Inc. develops web-based applications for the online recruiting industry. *New Positions Created (3):* Account Executives; Sales Support Representative; Writer / Communications Specialist.

E-ONE MOLI ENERGY (CANADA) LTD.
Att: Manager, Human Resources
20000 Stewart Crescent
Maple Ridge, BC V2X 9E7

Tel. 604-465-7911
Fax 604-466-6600
Email .... careers@molienergy.com
Website .... www.molienergy.com
Employer Background: E-One Moli Energy (Canada) Ltd. is a high-tech battery manufacturer. *New Positions Created (5):* Development / Manufacturing Engineer; Electronics Technologist; Applications Technologist; Mechanical Engineer; Maintenance Technician - Robotics.

E-SMITH, INC.
Att: Emily Gregory
150 Metcalfe Street
Ottawa, ON K2P 1P1

Tel. 613-564-8000
Fax 613-564-7739
Email .... eeg@e-smith.net
Website .... www.e-smith.com
Employer Background: E-smith, Inc. is a Linux-based, open-source start-up firm that creates cost-effective technologies for small business. *New Positions Created (8):* Chief Information Officer; Director of Quality Assurance; Director of Web Applications; Recruiter; Senior Systems Administrator; Technical Writer; Vice President of Engineering; Vice President of Professional Services.

EAGLE NAVIGATION SYSTEMS INC.
Att: Human Resources
2916B - 19th Street NE
Calgary, AB T2E 6Y9

Tel. 403-291-3959
Fax 403-291-3956
Email ... human_resources@eaglenav.com
Website .... www.eaglenav.com
Employer Background: Eagle Navigation Systems Inc. is a provider of GIS / GPS products. *New Positions Created (2):* Geomatics Engineers & Survey Technologists; Geomatics Engineers and Survey Technologists.

EAGLE PRECISION TECHNOLOGIES INC.
Att: Human Resources
565 West Street, PO Box 786
Brantford, ON N3T 5R7

Tel. 519-756-5223
Fax 519-756-0195
Website .... www.eaglept.com

Employer Background: Eagle Precision Technologies Inc. manufactures high-tech metal tube bending and tube-end forming machinery for automotive and aerospace applications. The company has over $100 million in annual sales. *New Positions Created (6):* CNC Programmer; Hydraulic Controls Designer; Manufacturing Planner; Systems Administrator; Tool Designer; Various Skilled Trades Positions.

EAGLE PUMP & COMPRESSOR LTD.
Att: Human Resources Administration
7025 - 5th Street SE
Calgary, AB T2H 2G2
Tel. 403-253-0100
Fax 403-253-8884
Email .... macphail@eagle-pc.com
Website .... www.eagle-pc.com
Employer Background: Eagle Pump & Compressor Ltd. manufactures and packages air, gas and liquid handling products, including reciprocating air compressors for the construction and automotive industries. *New Positions Created (2):* Sales Representative; Gas Compressor Engineer / Technologist.

EAGLEWEST TRUCK AND CRANE INC.
Att: Operations Manager
PO Box 2304
Abbotsford, BC V2T 4X2
Tel. 604-852-7133
Fax 604-852-4421
Email .... lmackay@eaglewest.bc.ca
Employer Background: Eaglewest Truck and Crane Inc. provides truck and crane units to British Columbia's lower mainland. *New Positions Created (4):* Crane Operators; Freight Truck Operators; Licensed Heavy Duty Mechanics; Sales Representatives.

EARLSCOURT CHILD AND FAMILY CENTRE, THE
Att: Human Resources
46 St. Clair Gardens
Toronto, ON M6E 3V4
Tel. 416-654-8981
Fax 416-654-8996
Email .... mailus@earlscourt.on.ca
Website .... www.earlscourt.on.ca
Employer Background: The Earlscourt Child and Family Centre provides intervention services for youth with aggressive and delinquent behaviours. *New Positions Created (9):* Family and Child Worker; Family Worker, Under 12 Outreach Program; Group Leader / Assistant Camp Director, Under 12 Outreach Program; Residential Worker; Executive Assistant; Family and Child Worker; Manager, Family and School Services; Researcher; Male Residential Staff Position.

EARTH ENERGY UTILITY CORP.
Att: Manager, Human Resources
5420 North Service Road
5th Floor, Provident Tower
Burlington, ON L7L 6C7
Fax 905-634-1333
Employer Background: Earth Energy Utility Corp. is a multi-national private sector utility, exclusively providing renewable energy groundsource geothermal systems. *New Positions Created (3):* Marketing and Media Assistant; Secretary / Office Administrator; Intermediate and Senior Project Managers / Engineers (2).

EARTH SIGNAL PROCESSING LTD.
Att: Brian Wilson
500 - 5th Avenue SW, Suite 600
Calgary, AB T2P 3L5
Tel. 403-264-8722
Website .... www.earthsignal.com
Employer Background: Earth Signal Processing Ltd. is a seismic processing company. *New Positions Created (4):* C / C++ Applications Programmer; Hardware / Systems Administrator; Processing and Programming Geophysicists; Various Computing Positions (2).

EARTH TECH CANADA INC.
Att: Human Resources Manager
105 Commerce Valley Drive West
Markham, ON L3T 7W3
Tel. 905-886-7022
Fax 905-886-9494
Website .... www.earthtech.com
Employer Background: Earth Tech Canada Inc. (a member of Tyco International Ltd.) is an engineering, construction and environmental consulting firm, with over $1 billion in revenues. *New Positions Created (76):* Infrastructure Engineer, Water & Wastewater; Business Practice Manager, Environmental, Remediation and Waste; Data & Communications Engineer / Designer; Process Engineer, Industrial; Project Manager / Director, ASD; Senior Bridge Engineer; Senior Industrial Engineer, Manufacturing; Systems Coordinator, ASD; Junior Engineer, Transportation; Senior Food and Beverage Engineer; Administrative Assistant; Junior Technologist, Water and Wastewater; Project Manager, Water and Wastewater; Trainee Engineer, Water; Senior Project Manager - Water & Wastewater; Senior Project Manger - Water & Wastewater; Senior Water Treatment Engineer - Water & Wastewater; Design Coordinator / Resident Engineer; Intermediate Bridge Engineer; Intermediate Electrical Engineer, Industrial; Intermediate Engineer, Transportation; Intermediate Engineer, Water & Wastewater; Intermediate Mechanical Engineer, Buildings; Intermediate Technologist, Transportation; Municipal Engineering Specialist, Water & Wastewater; Senior Engineer, Industrial; Senior Engineer, Transportation; Senior Municipal Engineer, Water & Wastewater; Senior Project Manager, Water & Wastewater; Junior Environmental Planner; Human Resources Coordinator; Intermediate Structural Engineer - Transportation; Senior Project Manager - Transportation; Traffic Engineer - Transportation; Construction Manager / Superintendent - ASD; Human Resources Coordinator; Instrumentation & Automation Professional - Waste & Wastewater; Intermediate Architectural Technologist - Industrial; Intermediate Bridge Engineer, Transportation; Intermediate Bridge Engineer - Transportation; Intermediate Electrical Engineer - Buildings; Intermediate Engineer - Industrial; Intermediate Engineer - Transportation; Intermediate Engineer - Transportation Design; Intermediate Mechanical Technologist - Industrial; Intermediate Technologist - Industrial; Intermediate Technologist - Transportation Design; Intermediate Technologist - Transportation Planning; Junior Design Technician / Technologist - Transportation; Junior Design Technician / Technologist - Transportation; Junior Technologist - Transportation; Junior Technologist - Transportation; Junior Technologist - Water & Wastewater; Manager, Highways & Roads - Transportation; Manager, Planning & Traffic - Transportation; Project Manager / Director - ASD; Senior Electrical Engineer - Buildings; Senior Electrical Engineer - Buildings; Senior Marine Engineer - Transportation; Senior Mechanical Engineer - Buildings; Senior Process Engineer - Industrial; Senior Project Engineer - Transportation; Senior Project Manager - Industrial; Senior Project Manager - Transportation Design; Senior Project Manger - Water & Wastewater; Senior Water Treatment Engineer - Water & Wastewater; Structural Engineer - Industrial; Systems Coordinator - ASD; Trainee Bridge Engineer - Transportation; Trainee Electrical Engineer - Industrial; Trainee Engineers - Industrial; Waste Design Team Leader - Water & Wastewater; Environmental and Land Use Planners; Project Manager, Land Development; Project Manager, Stormwater Management; Project Managers, Engineers and Technologists.

EAST CENTRAL REGIONAL HEALTH AUTHORITY
Att: Michelle Forest, HR Coordinator
4703 - 53rd Street
Camrose, AB T4V 1Y8
Tel. 780-608-8842
Fax 780-608-8850
Email .... michelle.forest@
.... eastcentralhealth.com
Website .... www.eastcentralhealth.com
Employer Background: East Central Regional Health Authority provides health services to over 100,000 residents in 59 municipalities. *New Positions Created (12):* Nursing Care Coordinator, Acute Care; Pharmacist II; Coordinator, Continuing Care Coordinator; Community Health Coordinator, Home Care; Health Record Technician; Nutritionist; Social Workers; Regional Director, Human Resources; Community Health Coordinator; Health Centre Coordinator; Nursing Care Coordinator, Acute Care.

EAST CENTRAL REGIONAL HEALTH AUTHORITY, ST. MARY'S HOSPITAL SITE
Att: Human Resources
4607 - 53rd Street
Camrose, AB T4V 1Y5
Tel. 780-679-6133
Fax 780-679-6194
Website www.ecrha7.ab.ca

Employer Background: St. Mary's Hospital is a 76-bed acute care facility with multiple regional referral centres. *New Positions Created (4):* Director of Corporate Services; Registered Nurses; Clinical Dietician; Director of Dietetics.

EAST YORK ACCESS CENTRE
Att: Director, Corporate Services
1 Leaside Park Drive, Unit 1
Toronto, ON M4H 1R1
Fax 416-423-7047
Employer Background: One of 43 provincially-funded community care access centres in Ontario, the East York Access Centre provides in-home health, long-term care placement, information and referral services to East York residents. *New Positions Created (2):* Manager, Quality and Contracts; Quality and Contracts Associate.

EASTER SEAL SOCIETY, ONTARIO
Att: Human Resources Department
1185 Eglinton Avenue East, Suite 706
Toronto, ON M3C 3C6
Tel. 416-421-8377
Fax 416-696-1035
Email .... hr@easterseals.org
Website .... www.easterseals.org
Employer Background: Established in 1922, the Easter Seal Society, Ontario helps children and young adults with physical disabilities achieve independence. *New Positions Created (3):* Special Event Coordinator; District Coordinator; District Coordinators (2).

EASTGATE FORD
Att: Tom Carmody
350 Parkdale Avenue North
Hamilton, ON L8H 5Y3
Tel. 905-547-3211
Fax 905-547-8818
Email .... lance.richter@sympatico.ca
Website .... www.ford.ca
Employer Background: Eastgate Ford is Hamilton's largest Ford dealer. *New Positions Created (3):* Automotive Sales Position; Shop Foreperson; Automotive Sales Position.

EASTSIDE DODGE
Att: Mike Csanyi, Service Manager
815 - 36th Street NE
Calgary, AB T2A 4W3
Fax 403-235-0672
Website .... www.eastsidechrysler.com
Employer Background: Eastside Dodge is a Chrysler, Dodge and Jeep dealer. *New Positions Created (4):* Journeyman Technicians (2); Service Advisor; Controller / Secretary-Treasurer; Service Manager.

EBA ENGINEERING CONSULTANTS LTD.
Att: Terry Hillaby
14535 - 118th Avenue
Edmonton, AB T5L 2M7
Tel. 780-451-2121
Fax 780-454-5688
Email .... thillaby@eba.ca
Website .... www.eba.ca
Employer Background: EBA Engineering Consultants Ltd. offers a broad range of engineering and consulting services to clients in domestic and foreign markets. *New Positions Created (39):* Administrative Assistant; Intermediate Geotechnical Engineers; Intermediate / Senior Geotechnical / Materials Engineer; Junior / Intermediate Geotechnical Engineer; Senior Engineer / Hydrogeologist; Senior Engineer / Hydrogeologist; Senior Materials Technologists; Environmental Consultant; Geotechnical / Materials Engineer; Intermediate CADD Designer; Intermediate Design Technologist / Engineer; Intermediate Engineer; Intermediate Environmental Consultant; Intermediate Materials Technicians (5); Intermediate Materials Technologist; Intermediate / Senior Asphalt Technologist; Intermediate Transportation Engineer; Junior Civil Engineer; Junior Engineer; Junior / Intermediate Environmental Technicians / Technologists; Junior / Intermediate Geotechnical Engineer; Junior / Intermediate Hydrogeologist; Junior / Intermediate Materials Engineer; Project Managers; Senior Geotechnical Engineer; Senior Mechanical Technologist; Senior Pavements Engineer; Senior Planner; Survey Party Crew Chief; Intermediate Geotechnical Engineers; Junior Civil Engineers; Junior / Intermediate Geotechnical Engineers; Junior / Intermediate Materials Engineer; Junior / Intermediate Technicians; Senior Asphalt Technologist; Highway Project Managers; Intermediate Transportation Engineer; Survey Party Crew Chiefs; Senior Applied Geophysicist.

EBCO TECHNOLOGIES INC.
Att: Joe Da Silva, HR Department
7851 Alderbridge Way
Richmond, BC V6X 2A4
Tel. 604-278-5578
Fax 604-276-1502
Email .... jdasilva@ebco.com
Website .... www.ebcotech.com
Employer Background: Ebco Technologies Inc. designs and manufactures negative ion cyclotrons, targetry and radiochemical production systems for the medical, commercial and research communities. *New Positions Created (8):* Journeyman Machinists / CNC Operators; Electrical Engineer; Journeyman Machinists / CNC Operators; Machine Shop / Maintenance Technician; Machine Shop Supervisor / Shop Floor Working Foreperson; CNC Programmer; Journeyman Machinists / CNC Operators; Machine Shop Position / Maintenance Position.

ECHO BAY MINES LTD.
Att: Human Resources
9818 Edmonton International Airport
Edmonton, AB T5J 2T2
Fax 780-890-4692
Website .... www.echobay.com
Employer Background: Echo Bay Mines Ltd. owns the Lupin gold mine in Nunavut. *New Positions Created (2):* Human Resources Specialist; Human Resources Manager.

ECOLAB LTD.
Att: Credit and Collections Supervisor
5105 Tomken Road
Mississauga, ON L4W 2X5
Tel. 905-238-0171
Fax 905-238-2096
Website .... www.ecolab.com
Employer Background: Ecolab Ltd. is a provider of cleaning, sanitizing and maintenance products and systems. *New Positions Created (5):* Bilingual Credit Representative; Territory Manager; Sales Service Representative; Production Supervisor; Warehouse Manager.

ECOLAB LTD.
Att: Michael Lloyd
1375 Aimco Boulevard
Mississauga, ON L4W 1B5
Fax 905-238-2093
Website .... www.ecolab.com
Employer Background: Ecolab Ltd. is a provider of cleaning, sanitizing and maintenance products and systems. *New Positions Created (2):* Account Executive; Sales Service Representatives (2).

ECOLE POLYTECHNIQUE DE MONTREAL, DEPARTMENT OF ELECTRICAL AND COMPUTER ENGINEERING
Att: Professor Richard J. Marceau
PO Box 6079, Centre-Ville Station
Montréal, QC H3C 3A7
Email .... recrutement-info@
.... courriel.polymtl.ca
Website .... www.polymtl.ca
Employer Background: Ecole Polytechnique de Montreal is a leader in French-language engineering education and research. *New Positions Created (2):* Professors, Computer Engineering / Software Engineering; Professors, Electrical Engineering.

ECOPLANS LTD.
Att: Human Resources Manager
72 Victoria Street South, Suite 100
Kitchener, ON N2G 4Y9
Tel. 519-741-8850
Fax 519-741-8884
Email .... ecoplans@ecoplans.com
Website .... www.ecoplans.com
Employer Background: Founded in 1970, Ecoplans Ltd. provides consulting services in environmental planning, management and impact assessment. *New Positions Created (4):* Intermediate Municipal Engineer / Technologist; Junior / Intermediate Environmental Planner; Junior / Intermediate Highway Design Engineer; Project Manager, Highway Design.

EDGE NETWORKS CORPORATION
Att: Human Resources Manager
1 Lombard Place, Suite 2620
Winnipeg, MB R3B 0X5
Tel. 204-982-6980
Fax 204-982-6989
Employer Background: Edge Networks Corporation develops and markets products to enable the delivery of services over band-

width-constrained access networks. *New Positions Created (9):* Director of Business Development; Receptionist / Accounts Payable Position; Senior Systems Architects (3); Software Developers (7); Supply Chain Manager; Testing Coordinator; Testing Specialist; Vice President, Marketing; Vice President, Sales.

EDGEFLOW INC.
Att: Human Resources Manager
329 March Road, Suite 104
Kanata, ON K2K 2E1

Tel. 613-270-9279
Fax 613-270-9628
Email .... careers@edgeflow.com
Website .... www.edgeflow.com

Employer Background: Edgeflow Inc. develops cost-effective intelligent optical networking solutions for the carrier and enterprise markets. *New Positions Created (22):* Hardware Design Engineer; Intermediate Software Designer, Network Management; Intermediate Software Engineer, Network Management; Senior Hardware Design Engineer; CAD Librarian; Intermediate Software Designer, Embedded Systems; Hardware Design Engineer; RF / High-Speed Digital Design Engineer; Senior Hardware Design Engineer; Senior Photonics Designer; Senior Software Designer, Embedded Systems; Senior Software Designer, Resource Allocation and Management; Senior Software Designer, Signaling and Routing; Senior Software Engineer, Network Management; DWDM Product Managers and Planners; Intermediate Software Engineer, Network Management; Senior Photonics Network Engineer; RF / High-Speed Digital Design Engineer; Senior Embedded Software Architect; Senior Hardware Design Engineer; Senior Photonics Engineer; Senior Software Designer.

EDM PRODUCTS INC.
Att: Human Resources Manager
736 - 8th Avenue SW, Suite 430
Calgary, AB T2P 1H4

Tel. 403-265-6660
Fax 403-265-5929
Email .... hr@edmp.com
Website .... www.edmp.com

Employer Background: EDM Products Inc. (a division of Seitel Solutions Canada Ltd.) is a software product development company, providing solutions to oil and gas companies. *New Positions Created (13):* AIX System Administrator; Database Administrator; Intermediate Programmer, Facilities-Based Products; Junior Programmer, Facilities-Based Products; Manager, Product Support; SAN Specialist; Senior Team Leader, Web Development; Team Leader, Facilities-Based Products; Application Programmer; Database Developer; Project Leader; Storage Management Specialist; Web Developer.

EDMONTON CATHOLIC SCHOOLS
Att: Paul Gagne,
Employee Services Manager
9807 - 106th Street
Edmonton, AB T5K 1C2

Tel. 780-441-6119
Fax 780-441-6147
Email .... gagnep@ecs.edmonton.ab.ca
Website .... www.ecs.edmonton.ab.ca

Employer Background: Edmonton Catholic Schools is responsible for 32,000 students and 3,000 employees in 84 schools in Edmonton and Vegreville. *New Positions Created (5):* Facilities Technologist; Employee Relations Specialist; Assistant Principal; Principal; Journeyman Electronics Technician.

EDMONTON CELLULAR
Att: Human Resources Manager
14903 - 118th Avenue
Edmonton, AB T5V 1S3

Tel. 780-453-3500
Website .... www.edmontoncellular.com

Employer Background: Edmonton Cellular is a leading cellular dealer. *New Positions Created (4):* Retail Sales Position; Retail Sales Position; Retail Sales Position; Receptionist.

EDMONTON, CITY OF
Att: Employment Office
1 Sir Winston Churchill Square
Main Floor, City Hall
Edmonton, AB T5J 2R7

Tel. 780-496-8178
Fax 780-496-8063
Website .... www.gov.edmonton.ab.ca

Employer Background: The City of Edmonton is the capital of Alberta and home to over 650,000 residents. *New Positions Created (7):* Senior Negotiator; Property & Exhibit Technician 1; Senior Environmental Engineer; Environmental Engineer / Scientist; Database Administrator; General Manager, Planning and Development; Firefighter.

EDMONTON COMMUNITY FOUNDATION
Att: Doug McNally, Chief Executive Officer
10117 Jasper Avenue
Suite 710, Royal Bank Building
Edmonton, AB T5J 1W8

Tel. 780-426-0015
Email .... info@ecfoundation.org
Website .... www.ecfoundation.org

Employer Background: Founded in 1971, the Edmonton Community Foundation specializes in endowment funds for charities involved in social services, arts and culture, education, health and recreation. *New Positions Created (3):* Director of Programs; Director of Communications; Director of Planned Giving.

EDMONTON PUBLIC SCHOOLS
Att: Personnel Recruitment and Staffing
1 Kingsway, Centre for Education
Edmonton, AB T5H 4G9

Tel. 780-429-8000
Fax 780-426-3946
Website .... www.epsb.ca

Employer Background: Edmonton Public Schools offers a wide range of programs to 81,400 students. *New Positions Created (5):* Marketing and Communications Coordinator; Bilingual Teacher, Hebrew; Instrument Mechanic; Principal; Speech Language Pathologists.

EDS CANADA
Att: Calgary Staffing
112 - 4th Avenue SW, 4th Floor
Calgary, AB T2P 0H3

Fax 403-233-8827
Email .... calgary.staffing@eds.com
Website .... www.eds.com

Employer Background: EDS is a leading provider of information technology services, active in Canada since 1985. *New Positions Created (5):* Computer Operators; Database Analyst; HelpDesk Professional; Infrastructure Analyst; Systems Administrator.

EDS INNOVATIONS
Att: Staffing Specialist
5700 Explorer Drive
Mississauga, ON L4W 5J3

Tel. 905-567-3201
Fax 905-282-5740
Email ... edsinnovationscareercent@eds.com
Website .... www.edsinnovations.com

Employer Background: EDS Innovations provides technology infrastructure implementation and support services. *New Positions Created (6):* Senior Field Services Representatives; Technical Support Specialists; Database Administrator, Oracle / SQL Server; Principal Consultant; Senior Programmer Analyst, VAX Applications; Software Architect.

EDS INNOVATIONS
Att: Kimberley Smith, Staffing Consultant
2625 Queensview Drive
Ottawa, ON K2B 8K2

Tel. 613-726-3700
Fax 613-726-3788
Website .... www.edsinnovations.com

Employer Background: EDS Innovations provides technology infrastructure implementation and support services. *New Positions Created (3):* Network Architect; Storage Solutions Specialist; Technological Infrastructure Architect.

EDUCATION ON-LINE / EOL
Att: Human Resources
10709 Jasper Avenue, 6th Floor
Edmonton, AB T5J 3N3

Fax 780-414-5540
Email .... hresources@eol-ca.com
Website .... www.eol-ca.com

Employer Background: EOL is a provider of web-based learning and instructional support, with offices in Canada, the USA and UK. *New Positions Created (5):* Math Teacher / Writer; Language Arts Teacher / Writer; Language Arts Teacher / Writer; Math Teacher / Writer; New Media Editor.

EDWARD JONES
Att: Human Resources
90 Burnhamthorpe Road West
Suite 902, Sussex Centre
Mississauga, ON L5B 3C3

Fax 905-306-8624
Email ..... careeropcan@edwardjones.com
Website .... www.edwardjones.com
Employer Background: Established in 1871, Edward Jones is a full-service brokerage firm, serving the long-term investment needs of individuals. *New Positions Created (9):* Insurance Marketing Specialist; Operations Specialist, Transfer Department; Transfer Broker / Liaison Recruiter; Customer Segments Marketing Specialist; Field Supervision Director; Professional Financial Planning Study Coach; Hiring and Recruiting Administrative Assistant; Payroll Administrative Assistant; Senior Licensing Specialist.

EDWARDS SYSTEMS TECHNOLOGY
Att: Human Resources
625 - 6th Street East
Owen Sound, ON N4K 5P8
Tel. 519-376-2430
Fax 519-376-2066
Email .... hredw@edwards.spx.com
Website .... www.est.net
Employer Background: Edwards Systems Technology (a unit of SPX Canada Inc.) is a leading North American manufacturer of fire alarms, emergency lighting and signaling equipment. *New Positions Created (4):* Various Sales Positions; Various Technical Positions; Service Coordinator; Fire Alarm Service Technicians.

EF EDUCATION
Att: Human Resources
60 Bloor Street West, Suite 405
Toronto, ON M4W 3B8
Tel. 416-323-0330
Fax 416-927-8664
Email .... edtravel@ef.com
Website .... www.ef.com
Employer Background: EF Education is an educational organization, offering student travel, language learning and cultural exchange programs. The company has 15,000 employees in 43 countries. *New Positions Created (4):* Assistant Regional Flights Manager; Educational Tour Consultant; Foundation Regional Manager; International Language Schools Country Product Manager.

EFA SOFTWARE SERVICES LTD.
Att: Human Resources
311 - 6th Avenue SW, Suite 9000
Calgary, AB T2P 3H2
Tel. 403-265-6131
Fax 403-444-3104
Email .... careers@efasoftware.com
Website .... www.efasoftware.com
Employer Background: EFA Software Services Ltd. develops leading-edge applications for securities trading and production revenue accounting systems, as well as providing expert consulting services. *New Positions Created (18):* Market Research Analyst; Programmers; Sales & Marketing Operations Manager; Technical Support Consultant; Intermediate Middleware Architect; Java / C++ Developers; Network Administrator; Receptionist; Senior C Programmer

Analyst; Senior Programmer Analyst; Senior Software Developer; Intermediate Middleware Developer; Java / C++ Developers; Senior Framework Architect; Senior Programmer Analyst; Software Development Manager; Software Quality Assurance Manager; Technical Support Specialist.

EFFIGI INC.
Att: Nathalie Cardinal
1155 Autoroute 13
Laval, QC H7W 5J8
Tel. 450-686-4848
Fax 450-686-2747
Email .... nathaliec@effigi.com
Website .... www.effigi.com
Employer Background: Founded in 1991, Effigi Inc. is an apparel manufacturer. *New Positions Created (8):* Children's Wear Designer; Junior Merchandiser; Sportswear Designer; Children's Wear Designer; Patternmaker; Garment Technician; Designer; Garment Technician, Swimwear and Sportswear.

EFFORT TRUST COMPANY, THE
Att: Theresa Archer
240 Main Street East
Hamilton, ON L8N 1H5
Tel. 905-528-8956
Fax 905-528-8182
Email .... theresa@efforttrust.ca
Website .... www.efforttrust.ca
Employer Background: The Effort Trust Company is a financial intermediary and holding company. *New Positions Created (2):* Mortgage Administration Clerk; Accounting Clerk / Receptionist.

EFOS CORPORATION
Att: Human Resources Manager
2260 Argentia Road
Mississauga, ON L5N 6H7
Tel. 905-821-2600
Fax 905-821-2055
Email .... hrweb@efos.com
Website .... www.efos.com
Employer Background: Founded in 1982, EFOS Corporation is a world leader in light-based technology for advanced manufacturing processes. *New Positions Created (4):* ECO Documentation Coordinator; New Product Introduction Specialist; Production Process Specialist; Warehouse Shipper.

EFX ENERFLEX SYSTEMS LTD.
Att: Human Resources
4700 - 47th Street SE
Calgary, AB T2B 3R1
Tel. 403-236-6800
Fax 403-720-4385
Email .... careers@enerflex.com
Website .... www.enerflex.com
Employer Background: EFX Enerflex Systems Ltd. supplies products and services to the natural gas production and processing industry. *New Positions Created (7):* Project Designers; Project Engineers / Technologists; Various Trades Positions; Quality Inspector; Safety Coordinator; Safety Coordinator; Sales Engineer.

EGAN VISUAL
Att: Human Resources Manager
300 Hanlan Road
Woodbridge, ON L4L 3P6
Tel. 905-851-2826
Fax 905-851-7511
Email .... humanresources@egan.com
Website .... www.egan.com
Employer Background: Egan Visual manufactures meeting room products. *New Positions Created (2):* Receptionist; Office Furniture Installer.

ELCAN OPTICAL TECHNOLOGIES
Att: Human Resources Department
450 Leitz Road
Midland, ON L4R 5B8
Tel. 705-526-5401
Fax 705-528-7122
Email ... kmacmillan@west.raytheon.com
Website .... www.elcan.com
Employer Background: Elcan Optical Technologies designs and manufactures sophisticated optical systems for medical, commercial, industrial, defence and telecom applications. *New Positions Created (15):* Optical Designer; Precision Optician; Product Manager; Assembly Process Planner; Telecommunications Engineer; Calibration Technician; Coating Technician III; Electronic System Repair Person; Marketing Manager; Mechanical Designer; Optical Designer; Precision Optician; Product Manager, Telecommunications; Opto-Electronic Engineer; Electronic Software Designer.

ELCO FINE FOODS INC.
Att: Human Resources Manager
40 West Beaver Creek Road
Richmond Hill, ON L4B 1G5
Tel. 905-731-7337
Fax 905-731-2391
Email .... info@elcofinefoods.com
Employer Background: Elco Fine Foods Inc. is one of Canada's leading importers and distributors of specialty food and beverage products. *New Positions Created (4):* Senior Buyer / Inventory Controller; Regional Sales Manager; Specialty Food Sales Representative; Key Accounts Manager.

ELECTRO SONIC INC.
Att: Human Resources Department
1100 Gordon Baker Road
Toronto, ON M2H 3B3
Tel. 416-494-1666
Fax 416-496-3030
Email .... info@e-sonic.com
Website .... www.e-sonic.com
Employer Background: Electro Sonic Inc. is one of Canada's largest distributors of electronic and electrical components and parts. *New Positions Created (21):* Assigned Inside Sales Representative; Contract Executive Secretary; Data Purchasing Clerk; Product Manager; Purchasing Associate; Unassigned Inside Sales Representative; Product Manager; Quotations Representative; Inside Sales Representative; Receptionist; Account Manager, System Sales; Accounts Payable Clerk; Customer Service Representative;

Data Entry Credit Note Clerk; Product Manager, Product Marketing; Product Marketing Associate; Quotes Representative; Sales Positions; Systems Engineer; Account Manager; Purchasing Manager.

ELECTRONIC ARTS (CANADA) INC.
Att: Human Resources Manager
4330 Sanderson Way,
Electronic Arts Centre
Burnaby, BC V5G 4X1

Tel. 604-451-3600
Fax 604-412-8356
Website .... www.ea.com

Employer Background: Electronic Arts (Canada) Inc. is part of California-based Electronic Arts, a large video game software company founded in 1982. The parent company has annual revenues exceeding $1.2 billion. *New Positions Created (2):* Senior Programmers / Software Architects; Software Engineers.

ELECTRONICS BOUTIQUE
Att: Kylie Jimenez
8995 Airport Road
Brampton, ON L6T 5T2

Tel. 905-790-9262
Fax 905-790-1452
Email .... recruiting@ebworld.com
Website .... www.ebholdings.com

Employer Background: Electronics Boutique is a leading retailer of interactive software and accessories. *New Positions Created (3):* Regional Director; Inventory Planner; Marketing Assistant.

ELECTRONICS MANUFACTURING GROUP / EMG
Att: Production
3805 - 34th Street NE, Suite 7
Calgary, AB T1Y 6Z8

Tel. 403-207-5364
Fax 403-207-5254
Email .... emgjobs@emgplace.com
Website .... www.emgplace.com

Employer Background: EMG provides custom electronics manufacturing and assembly services. *New Positions Created (4):* Junior Electronics Technicians; Manual Insertion Position; Mechanical Assembler; PCB Inspection Positions .

ELECTRONICS WORKBENCH
Att: Human Resources Department
111 Peter Street, Suite 801
Toronto, ON M5V 2H1

Tel. 416-977-5550
Fax 416-977-1818
Email resume@electronicsworkbench.com
Website . www.electronicsworkbench.com

Employer Background: Founded in 1982, Electronics Workbench develops and markets interactive software tools to automate the design of electronics products. *New Positions Created (6):* CSR / Order Desk Position; Inside Software Sales Representative; Information Technology Systems Administrator; Technical Sales Representative; Technical Support Representative; Technical Writer.

ELI LILLY CANADA INC.
Att: Human Resources Manager
3650 Danforth Avenue
Toronto, ON M1N 2E8

Tel. 416-694-3221
Fax 416-693-3811
Email ...... lillycanadarecruiting@lilly.com
Website .... www.lilly.ca

Employer Background: Eli Lilly Canada Inc. is a leading pharmaceutical company. *New Positions Created (2):* Sales Representatives; Analytic Biochemist.

ELIMETAL INC.
Att: Human Resources Manager
1515 Pitfield
St-Laurent, QC H4S 1G3

Fax 514-956-8110
Website .... www.elimetal.com

Employer Background: Elimetal Inc. is a leader in CNC cutting and sinking machined parts for the aerospace industries, as well as intricate tooling for the plastic and metal industries. *New Positions Created (4):* Sales Representative; CNC EDM Sinking Machine Operators; Programmer / Operator; Quality Control Position.

ELK ISLAND PUBLIC SCHOOLS
Att: Human Resources Department
683 Wye Road
Sherwood Park, AB T8B 1N2

Tel. 780-417-8218
Fax 780-467-0820
Email ..... human.resources@ei.educ.ab.ca
Website .... www.ei.educ.ab.ca

Employer Background: Elk Island Public Schools is Alberta's 5th-largest school system, serving 15,500 students in 39 schools. The division employs approximately 1,500 staff members. *New Positions Created (5):* Support Analyst, Technology Services; Speech Language Pathologist; Principal, Chipman School; Principal, Fort Saskatchewan Christian School; Principal, Lamont High School.

ELLETT INDUSTRIES LTD.
Att: Robert D. Gill
1575 Kingsway Avenue
Port Coquitlam, BC V3C 4E5

Tel. 604-941-8211
Fax 604-941-6854
Website .... www.ellet.ca

Employer Background: Ellett Industries Ltd. designs and fabricates heat exchangers, pressure vessels and custom engineered process equipment. *New Positions Created (4):* Pipe Sales / Estimator; Buyer; Pipe Sales / Estimator; Senior Design Engineer.

ELLIS, GOVENLOCK LLP
Att: Human Resources Manager
9363 - 50th Street, Suite 2
Edmonton, AB T6B 2L5

Tel. 780-451-2713
Fax 780-454-0588

Employer Background: Ellis, Govenlock LLP is an accounting firm. *New Positions Created (2):* Accountants; Accounting Positions.

ELYPS DISPATCH SOLUTIONS
Att: Human Resources Manager
4161 Dawson Street
Burnaby, BC V5C 4B3

Tel. 604-293-0107
Fax 604-293-0315
Email .... raitken@elyps.com
Website .... www.elyps.com

Employer Background: Elyps Dispatch Solutions (formerly Group CS) is a leading Canadian supplier of wireless radiocommunication solutions. *New Positions Created (3):* Customer Service Technician; Office Administrator; Sales Representative.

EMANAGE INC.
Att: Human Resources Manager
1565 Carling Avenue, Suite 502
Ottawa, ON K1Z 8R1

Tel. 613-728-5977
Fax 613-728-8566
Email .... info@emanagecorp.com
Website .... www.emanagecorp.com

Employer Background: eManage Inc. is a leading provider of scalable e-solutions, including structured email management, records and knowledge management. *New Positions Created (5):* Customer Support Specialists; Intermediate Marketing Specialists; Marketing Manager; Pre-Sales and Post-Sales Technical Specialists; Senior Software Developers.

EMANATION CONTROL LTD. / EMCON
Att: Human Resources Manager
11 Tristan Court
Nepean, ON K2E 8B9

Tel. 613-723-1838
Fax 613-723-2752
Email .... anita@emcon.com
Website .... www.emcon.com

Employer Background: EMCON develops, certifies and manufactures TEMPEST and rugged data processing equipment and systems. Their products facilitate the secure processing, storage and communication of sensitive or government classified information. *New Positions Created (3):* Computer Technician; Electronic Packaging Designer; Quality Inspector.

EMC GROUP LTD.
Att: Human Resources Manager
7577 Keele Street, Suite 200
Concord, ON L4K 4X3

Employer Background: EMC Group Ltd. is a planning, engineering and project management consulting firm, providing services to the land development industry and government agencies. *New Positions Created (4):* Civil Engineer; Civil Engineering Technician / AutoCAD Operator; Civil Engineering Technologist; Senior Construction Engineer.

EMCO LTD.
Att: Parminder Kalsi
7271 Nelson Road
Richmond, BC V6M 1L3

Tel. 604-233-3701
Fax 604-233-3700
Email .... pkalsi@emcoltd.com

Website .... www.emcoltd.com

Employer Background: Emco Ltd. is one of Canada's leading distributors and manufacturers of building products for the residential, commercial and industrial construction markets. *New Positions Created (2):* Counter Salesperson; Material Handlers.

EMERALD INTERNATIONAL INC.
Att: Recruiting Manager
250 Merton Street, Suite 303
Toronto, ON M4S 1B1
Tel. 416-489-3885
Fax 416-489-3379

Employer Background: Emerald Security, a division of Emerald International, provides mobile alarm response and patrol services in the Greater Toronto Area. *New Positions Created (2):* Mobile Response / Dispatchers; Sales Representative.

EMERALD LAKE LODGE
Att: Craig Chapman,
Assistant Lodge Manager
PO Box 10, Yoho National Park
Field, BC V0A 1G0
Tel. 250-343-6321
Fax 250-343-6724
Email .... emlodge@rockies.net
Website .... www.crmr.com

Employer Background: Built in 1902, the Emerald Lake Lodge is a historic building, offering year-round vacation and conference services. *New Positions Created (5):* Sous Chef; Food and Beverage Manager; Assistant Front Office Manager; Assistant Maintenance Manager; Bell Department Supervisors.

EMERY WORLDWIDE
Att: Sales Manager
6500 Silverdart Drive, PO Box 251
Mississauga, ON L5P 1B1
Tel. 905-676-9970
Fax 905-671-6436
Email ...... resume.west@emeryworld.com
Website .... www.emeryworld.com

Employer Background: Emery Worldwide (part of CNF Transportation Inc.) provides shippers with multi-modal transportation and logistics solutions worldwide. *New Positions Created (2):* Sales Account Manager; Account Manager.

EMI MUSIC CANADA
Att: Human Resources
3109 American Drive
Mississauga, ON L4V 1B2
Tel. 905-677-5050
Fax 905-677-1651
Email .... resumes.canada@emimusic.ca
Website .... www.emimusic.ca

Employer Background: Established in 1949, EMI Music Canada is a major record company, employing 230 people at nine offices across Canada. *New Positions Created (4):* Administrative Assistant; President; Administration Clerk; Royalty Accountant; PC Support Technician.

EMILY CARR INSTITUTE OF ART AND DESIGN
Att: Human Resources
1399 Johnston Street
Vancouver, BC V6H 3R9
Tel. 604-844-3824
Fax 604-844-3885
Email .... hr@eciad.bc.ca
Website .... www.eciad.bc.ca

Employer Background: The Emily Carr Institute of Art and Design is one of Canada's premier art institutions, offering post-secondary, studio-based education. *New Positions Created (8):* Clerk Typist 2, Student Services; Safety and Safety Officer; Instructor, Cultural Studies; Instructor, Integrated Media; Instructor, Integrated Visual Arts; Instructor, Photography; Instructor, Printmaking, Printing and Publishing; Co-ordinator, Writing Centre / English Instructor.

EMPIRE FINANCIAL GROUP
Att: Diane Cooper, HR Manager
259 King Street East
Kingston, ON K7L 3A8
Tel. 613-548-1881
Fax 613-548-8216
Email .... diane.cooper@empire.ca
Website .... www.empire.ca

Employer Background: Empire Financial Group offers a full range of financial products and services, including personal life insurance, critical illness coverage, investment options, group life and health benefits and group RRSP plans. *New Positions Created (10):* Senior Systems Analyst / Lead Programmer; Administrative / Legal Assistant; Team Leader; Bilingual Claims Assessor; Business Analyst; Web Developer; Executive Assistant, Information Systems; Bilingual Customer Service Representative; Project Leader / Senior Programmer Analyst; Technology Security Manager.

EMPOWERED NETWORKS
Att: Human Resources Manager
600 Terry Fox Drive, Suite 202
Kanata, ON K2L 4B6
Tel. 613-271-7970
Fax 613-592-6043
Email .... careers@empowerednetworks.com
Website ... www.empowerednetworks.com

Employer Background: Empowered Networks provides network management and performance solutions for e-business networks through 5 offices across North America. *New Positions Created (5):* Account Manager, Performance Analysis Solutions; Account Manager, Transport Engineering; Business Development Representative; Software Developer; Software Development Manager.

EMPOWERTEL NETWORKS INC.
Att: Janet Clarke, HR Director
1600 Scott Street, Holland Cross Building
Ottawa, ON K1Y 4N7
Tel. 613-722-1772
Fax 613-722-1662
Website .... www.empowertel.com

Employer Background: Empowertel Networks Inc. develops silicon solutions for next-generation IP and media-switching platforms. *New Positions Created (4):* E-commerce Developer; Network Security Specialist; Technical Manager, EMS Development; VoIP Protocol Developers (3).

EMS TECHNOLOGIES CANADA LTD.
Att: Human Resources
1725 Woodward Drive
Ottawa, ON K2C 0P9
Tel. 613-727-1771
Fax 613-727-1200
Email .... resume.ott@ems-t.com
Website .... www.ems-t.com

Employer Background: EMS Technologies Canada Ltd. (part of EMS Technologies, Inc. and formerly CAL Corporation) is a supplier of satellite-based terminals, antennas and systems for terrestrial and aeronautical applications. *New Positions Created (7):* Manager, Product Assurance; Senior Material Controller; Software Engineers; Space Systems Engineer; Assembler; RF Technicians / Technologists; Telecom Engineers.

EMS TECHNOLOGIES CANADA LTD., SPACE AND TECHNOLOGY GROUP
Att: Human Resources
21025 Trans Canada Highway
Ste-Anne-de-Bellevue, QC H9X 3R2
Tel. 514-457-2150
Fax 514-425-3037
Email .... dotation@ems-t.ca
Website .... www.ems-t.com

Employer Background: EMS Technologies Canada Ltd. (part of EMS Technologies, Inc. and formerly CAL Corporation) is a supplier of satellite-based terminals, antennas and systems for terrestrial and aeronautical applications. *New Positions Created (103):* Antenna Engineers; ATM and IP Specialists; Business Administrators; Communication System Designers; Component Engineers; Digital Communications Systems Engineers; Digital Modem Designers; Digital Transmission System Engineers; Electrical Engineering Analysts; Electrical Technicians; Electromechanical Assemblers; Electronic Technicians; FPGA and ASIC Engineer; Modelling and Analysis System Designers; PA Managers; Power Supply Design Engineers; Project Managers; QA Engineers, Electrical; Real-Time Embedded Software Engineers; Real-Time Embedded Software Engineers, Communications; Senior Demodulator Architects; Senior Demodulator Designers; Senior Electronic Packaging Engineers; Senior Material and Process Engineers / Technical Specialists; Senior Project Planning & Control Analysts; SMT Manufacturing Engineers; Software Product Assurance Specialist; System Test Engineers; Thermal Engineers; V&V Engineers, Software Product Assurance; V&V Engineers, Software Product Assurance (Safety); Wireless Access Specialists; Antenna Engineers; ATM / IP Specialists; Business Administrators; Communication System Designers; Component Engineers; Digital Communications Systems Engineers; Digital Modem

Designers; Digital Transmission System Engineers; Electrical Engineering Analysts; Electrical Technicians; Electromechanical Assemblers; Electronic Technicians; FPGA / ASIC Engineers; Modelling and Analysis System Designers; PA Managers; Power Supply Design Engineers; Project Managers; QA Engineers, Electrical; Real-Time Embedded Software Engineers; Real-Time Embedded Software Engineers, Communications; Senior Demodulator Architects; Senior Demodulator Designers; Senior Electronic Packaging Engineers; Senior Material / Process Engineers; Senior Project Planning & Control Analysts; SMT Manufacturing Engineers; Software Product Assurance Specialists; System Test Engineers; Thermal Engineers; V&V Engineers, Software Product Assurance; V&V Engineers, Software Product Assurance (Safety); Wireless Access Specialists; Antenna Engineers; ATM and IP Specialists; Business Administrators; Business Systems Developers; Communication System Designers; Component Engineers; Digital Communications Systems Engineers; Digital Modem Designers; Digital Transmission System Engineers; Electrical Engineering Analysts; Electrical Technicians; Electromechanical Assemblers; Electronic Technicians; FPGA and ASIC Engineers; Manager, Components; Modelling and Analysis System Designers; PA Managers; Plant Operation Coordinator and Civil Draftsman; Power Supply Design Engineers; Project Managers; Quality Assurance Engineers; Real-Time Embedded Software Engineers; Real-Time Embedded Software Engineers, Communications; Reliability Engineer; RF / Microwave Engineers; Secretary; Senior Demodulator Architects; Senior Demodulator Designers; Senior Electronic Packaging Engineers; Senior Project Planning & Control Analysts; SMT Manufacturing Engineers; Software V&V Engineers; System Test Engineers; Technical Associate I; Thermal Engineers; Unix (SUN) Administrators; V&V Engineers, Software Product Assurance; V&V Engineers, Software Product Assurance - Safety; Wireless Access Specialists.

ENBRIDGE CONSUMERS GAS
Att: Human Resources
PO Box 650
Toronto, ON M1K 5E3

Tel. 416-495-5459
Fax 416-495-5739
Email .... recruiting@cgc.enbridge.com
Website .... www.cgc.enbridge.com

Employer Background: Enbridge Consumers Gas is one of the fastest growing natural gas companies in North America, serving 1.5 million residential, commercial and industrial customers. *New Positions Created (2):* Advisor, Labour Relations; Legal Researcher / Law Clerk.

ENBRIDGE PIPELINES INC.
Att: Human Resources Department
PO Box 398
Edmonton, AB T5J 2J9

Tel. 780-420-5210
Fax 780-420-5289

Email .... epicareers@cnpl.enbridge.com
Website .... www.enbridge.com

Employer Background: Enbridge Pipelines Inc., along with US affiliate Lakehead Pipe Line, operates the world's longest crude oil and petroleum products pipeline system. *New Positions Created (5):* Tax Analyst; Tax Specialist; Legal Counsel; Mechanical Technologist; Business Development Representative, Acquisitions.

ENBRIDGE SERVICES
Att: Human Resources
80 Allstate Parkway
Markham, ON L3R 6H3

Tel. 416-758-6565
Fax 905-943-6412
Email .... dpressman@enbridgeservices.com
Website .... www.enbridge.com

Employer Background: Enbridge Services provides energy products and services for commercial and residential customers. *New Positions Created (4):* Manager, Natural Gas Portfolio - Customers; Manager, Natural Gas Portfolio - Value; Manager, Commodity Sales; Manager, Natural Gas Commodity Sales.

ENCON GROUP INC.
Att: Human Resources Department
350 Albert Street, Suite 700
Ottawa, ON K1R 1A4

Tel. 613-786-2000
Fax 613-786-2050
Email .... lily.klassen@encon.ca
Website .... www.encon.ca

Employer Background: Encon Group Inc. is a large underwriter of professional liability and errors and omissions insurance coverage. *New Positions Created (15):* Administrative / File Clerk; Client Service Representative; Underwriter; Account Manager; Bilingual Administrative Assistant; Bilingual Assistant Communications Coordinator; Marketing Specialist; Customer Service Representative; New Business Coordinator; Sales Assistant; Claims Analyst; Software Product Development Manager; Sales Representative; Junior Accountant; System Network Support Specialist.

ENCORE ENERGY INC.
Att: Human Resources Manager
1202 Centre Street South
11th Floor, Center 12
Calgary, AB T2G 5A5

Fax 403-717-4601
Email .... peggyz@encoreenergy.com
Website .... www.encoreenergy.com

Employer Background: Encore Energy Inc., a member of the EPCOR group of companies, provides electricity and energy-based products. *New Positions Created (5):* Natural Gas Supply Rep; Portfolio Analyst; Commodity Services Positions; Energy Operation Positions; Strategic Analyst.

ENERCHEM INTERNATIONAL INC.
Att: Human Resources Manager
1400 - 8th Street
Nisku, AB T9E 7M1

Tel. 780-955-3388
Fax 780-955-8684
Email .... ech@enerchem.com
Website .... www.enerchem.com

Employer Background: Enerchem International Inc. provides chemical solutions and services for oilfield production problems. *New Positions Created (4):* Corrosion Research Chemist; Laboratory Technician; Sales / Service and Contract Representatives; Technical Service Representative.

ENERFLEX SYSTEMS LTD.
Att: Denise Dolph
5049 - 74th Avenue SE
Calgary, AB T2C 3H2

Tel. 403-720-3844
Fax 403-720-4385
Email .... careers@enerflex.com
Website .... www.enerflex.com

Employer Background: Enerflex Systems Ltd. supplies products and services to the natural gas industry. *New Positions Created (4):* Application Engineers; Shop Supervisor; Project Manager; Sales Engineer.

ENERGY INDUSTRIES INC.
Att: Heather Pequin, Human Resources
4303 - 11th Street NE
Calgary, AB T2E 6K4

Tel. 403-250-9415
Fax 403-517-1323
Email .... hpequin@energyindustries.com
Website .... www.energyindustries.com

Employer Background: Energy Industries Inc. is a leader in the custom-engineered design, fabrication and installation of modular reciprocating and rotary screw natural gas compressor packages for the natural gas production and processing industry. *New Positions Created (7):* Draftsperson; Project Engineer; Sales / Applications Engineer; Project Engineer; Sales / Applications Engineer; Various Journeyman Positions; Accountant.

ENERGY SAVINGS CORPORATION
Att: Human Resources Manager
2150 Winston Park Drive, Unit 17
Oakville, ON L6H 5V1

Tel. 905-829-1010
Fax 905-829-3895
Website ...... www.energysavingscorp.com

Employer Background: Energy Savings Corporation is a leader provider of building automation solutions. *New Positions Created (2):* New Systems Salesperson; Owner-Direct Salesperson.

ENERLINE RESTORATIONS INC.
Att: Human Resources Manager
720 Moraine Road NE
Calgary, AB T2A 2P3

Tel. 403-273-8711
Fax 403-273-7433
Website .... www.enerline.com

Employer Background: Enerline Restorations Inc. is an oil and gas service company, specializing in the reduction of lifting costs in oil well applications, corrosion prevention and the lining of pipelines. *New Positions Created (4):* Director, Sales and Marketing; Receptionist; Sales Positions; Manager of Stettler Operations.

ENERSOURCE
Att: Manager, Human Resources
3240 Mavis Road
Mississauga, ON L5C 3K1
Tel. 905-273-9050
Fax 905-566-2704
Website .... www.enersource.com
Employer Background: Founded in 1999, Enersource (formerly Hydro Mississauga) is a utility owned by the City of Mississauga, providing electricity to 150,000 customers. *New Positions Created (7):* Internal Auditor; Occupational Health & Safety Program Supervisor; Power Engineer; Telecom Implementation Specialist; Telecom Internetworking Specialist; Journeyman Lineperson / Cableperson; System Control Operator, Electrical Utility.

ENERSUL INC.
Att: Human Resources Department
7210 Blackfoot Trail SE
Calgary, AB T2H 1M5
Tel. 403-253-5969
Fax 403-259-2771
Email .... lowew@enersul.com
Website .... www.enersul.com
Employer Background: Enersul Inc. provides operating services, products and technology for the safe, efficient and environmentally responsible processing and distribution of sulphur-related products. *New Positions Created (5):* Quality Assurance Coordinator / Director; Quality Assurance Coordinator / Director; Cost Accounting Supervisor; Estimator / Cost Analyst; Intermediate Project Cost Accountant.

ENGAGE ENERGY CANADA, LP
Att: Human Resources Manager
425 - 1st Street SW
Suite 2200, Fifth Avenue Place, East Tower
Calgary, AB T2P 3L8
Tel. 403-297-0333
Fax 403-699-1172
Email .... engageenergycareers@
.... engageenergy.com
Website .... www.engageenergy.com
Employer Background: Engage Energy Canada, LP (a Westcoast Energy Company) is one of the largest Canadian-based players in the North American energy market. *New Positions Created (7):* Junior & Senior Credit Analyst ; Analyst, Commercial Ana-lytics (Power Fundamentals); Client Services Representative; Client Services Representative, Operations; Client Services Representative, Operations (Pacific Northwest / BC); Confirmation Analyst; Power Schedulers.

ENGLISH MONTREAL SCHOOL BOARD / EMSB
Att: Mary Gouskos,
Educational Consultant
6000 Fielding Avenue
Montréal, QC H3X 1T4
Tel. 514-483-7200
Fax 514-483-7530
Email .... mgouskos@emsb.qc.ca
Website .... www.emsb.qc.ca
Employer Background: Founded in 1998, EMSB operates 65 elementary and secondary schools, 7 outreach schools, 10 social affairs institutions and 11 adult and vocational centres, serving a total of 34,327 students. *New Positions Created (6):* Vocational Teaching Positions; Teachers; Computing Support; Teachers; Instructor, Cooking; Teachers, Telecommunications Equipment Installation and Repair; Teachers, Aesthetics Electrolysis.

ENHANCED MARKETING SERVICES CORP. / EMS
Att: Human Resources Manager
1050 West Pender Street, Suite 600
Vancouver, BC V6E 3S7
Tel. 604-257-1200
Fax 604-257-1208
Email .... hr@emsmarketing.com
Website .... www.emsmarketing.com
Employer Background: EMS develops innovative client acquisition and retention marketing programs, fostering collaboration between non-competitive businesses targeting the same customer segments. *New Positions Created (2):* Marketing Assistant; Marketing Manager.

ENMAX CORPORATION
Att: Human Resources
2808 Spiller Road SE
Calgary, AB T2G 4H3
Tel. 403-268-2939
Fax 403-514-2799
Email .... jobs@enmax.com
Website .... www.enmax.com
Employer Background: Established in 1905, ENMAX Corporation is an electrical distribution and transmission utility headquartered in Calgary. *New Positions Created (57):* Apprentice Power System Electrician; Journeyman Power System Electrician; Product Analyst; Design Engineer; Buyers, EPCM & IT; Load Research Analyst; Market Analyst; Pricing Specialist, Natural Gas; Manager of Customer Care, Contact Centre; Manager of Customer Care, Development and Reporting; Manager of Customer Care, Large Accounts; Team Leader, Billing Operations and Support; Team Leader, Customer Care; Electrical Engineering Technologists; Business Development Analyst; IPP Business Manager; Manager, Business Analyst; Manager, New Business Line Development; Mass Market Segment Manager; Assistant Controller, Financial Reporting; Manager, Business Development; Market Manager; Credit Specialist; Apprentice, Power System Electrician; Distribution Engineer; Journeyman, Power Systems Electrician; Billing and Work Order Control Accountant; Financial and Operational Accountant; Operations Supervisor; Manager, Supply Chain; Apprentice Power System Electricians and Journeyman Power System Electricians; Capital Investment Analyst; Manager, Strategic Planning; Pricing and Product Development Analyst; Tax Analyst; Journeyman Power Lineman; Journeyman Power System Electrician; Billing and Support Representative; Control Accountant; Energy Trader; Supervisor, Energy Forecasting; Billing Supervisor; Financial Analyst; Fixed Assets Supervisor; Senior Business Analyst; Senior System Analyst; Senior Wholesale Electricity Marketer; Technical Specialist; Distribution Engineer; Senior Transmission Design Engineer; Specialist Engineer; Manager, Business Development; Senior Business Development Analyst; Senior Energy Marketer; Senior Systems Analyst; Administrative Assistant, Regulatory Affairs; Product Manager and Commercial Product Manager.

ENRON CANADA CORP.
Att: Human Resources
400 - 3rd Avenue SW, Suite 3500
Calgary, AB T2P 4H2
Tel. 403-974-6700
Fax 403-974-6985
Email .... hrcanada@enron.com
Website .... www.enron.com
Employer Background: Enroll Canada Corp. is a leading natural gas and electricity wholesale marketer. *New Positions Created (18):* Engineering Manager; Fundamentals Specialist; Power Volume Management Staff; Gas Scheduler; Desktop Supporter; Systems Administrator; Visual Basic Developer; Natural Gas Marketing Accountant; Specialist, Accounting and Operations; Credit Analyst; Credit Manager; Real-Time Trader; Telecommunications Specialist; Specialist, Power Volume Management; Contract Administrator / Operations Systems Administrator; Deal Clearing / Documentation Specialist; Risk Management Staffer; Accounting Specialist.

ENSEMBLE SYSTEMS INC.
Att: Human Resources Manager
5200 Hollybridge Way, Suite 280
Richmond, BC V7C 4N3
Tel. 604-231-9510
Fax 604-231-9545
Email .... employment@
.... ensemble-systems.com
Website .... www.ensemble-systems.com
Employer Background: Founded in 1995, Ensemble Systems Inc. provides custom software development and consulting services for enterprise solutions using Java, UML and Rational Unified Process. *New Positions Created (2):* Intermediate Software Engineers; Senior Software Engineers.

ENSIGN RESOURCE SERVICE GROUP INC.
Att: Vice-President, Operations
2001 - 4th Street
Nisku, AB T9E 7W6
Tel. 780-955-8808
Fax 780-955-7208
Email .... hr@ensigngroup.com
Website .... www.ensigngroup.com
Employer Background: Ensign Resource Service Group Inc. provides drilling, well

servicing, manufacturing and production services to the oil and natural gas industry. *New Positions Created (8):* Operations Administration Manager; Drilling Safety Coordinator; Drilling Superintendent; Senior Tubular Coordinator; Operations Engineer; Drilling Superintendent; Operations Manager; Mechanical Technologist.

ENSIGN RESOURCE SERVICE GROUP INC.
Att: Human Resources
400 - 5th Avenue SW, Suite 900
Calgary, AB T2P 0L6
Tel. 403-262-1361
Fax 403-266-3596
Email .... hrcgy@ensigngroup.com
Website .... www.ensigngroup.com
Employer Background: Ensign Resource Service Group Inc. provides drilling, well servicing, manufacturing and production services to the oil and natural gas industry. *New Positions Created (5):* Sales Representatives; Technical Sales Representative; Area Manager; Field Safety Coordinators; Safety Coordinator, Field Oilwell Drilling Rigs.

ENSIL INTERNATIONAL
Att: Human Resources Manager
205 Torbay Road
Markham, ON L3R 3W4
Tel. 905-479-6979
Fax 905-479-3185
Email .... hr@ensil.com
Website .... www.ensil.com
Employer Background: Ensil International is a printed circuit board repair organization, serving the defence, aerospace, medical, telecom, mainframe and industrial / robotics industries. *New Positions Created (11):* Technical Sales Position; Technical Sales Position; Sales Professionals; Accounts Receivable Clerk; Component Research and Purchasing Agent; Electronic Technicians / Engineers; Quality Manager; Receptionist; Sales Manager; Senior Application Programmer; Technical Manager.

ENTERO CORPORATION
Att: Human Resources
639 - 5th Avenue SW, Suite 2300
Calgary, AB T2P 0M9
Tel. 403-261-1820
Fax 403-261-2816
Email .... hr@entero.com
Website .... www.entero.com
Employer Background: Founded in 1994, Entero Corporation is a software services and development company. *New Positions Created (3):* Implementation Consultant; Network / Desktop Support Analyst; Web Developer.

ENTERPRISE RENT-A-CAR
Att: Simon Blunden, HR Supervisor
2250 Boundary Road, Suite 210
Burnaby, BC V5M 4L9
Tel. 604-298-9295
Fax 604-298-9244
Website .... www.erac.com

Employer Background: Founded in 1958, US-based Enterprise Rent-A-Car has over 37,000 employees and $5.6 billion in sales. *New Positions Created (2):* Management Trainees; Management Trainees.

ENTERPRISE RENT-A-CAR
Att: Human Resources
1916 Merivale Road, Suite 200
Nepean, ON K2G 1E8
Tel. 613-228-2998
Fax 613-228-1285
Email .... callan@erac.com
Website .... www.enterprise.com
Employer Background: Founded in 1958, US-based Enterprise Rent-A-Car has over 37,000 employees and $5.6 billion in sales. *New Positions Created (3):* Entry-Level Management Trainees; Management Trainees; Management Trainees.

ENTOURAGE TECHNOLOGY SOLUTIONS
Att: Human Resources
2000 Argentia Road, Floor 4, Plaza 2
Mississauga, ON L5N 1V9
Fax 905-542-0614
Email .... hr@entourage.ca
Website .... www.entourage.ca
Employer Background: Founded in 1996, Entourage Technology Solutions is a leading telecom network installation and maintenance services firm, with over 2,900 employees across Canada. *New Positions Created (10):* Accounts Receivable Associate; Budget Mgr; Job Cost Accountant; Control Centre Associate; Forcecom Implementation and Development Mgr; Health & Safety Mgr; Operations Support Associate; Telecommunications Managers; Regional Operations Manager; Regional Operations Manager.

ENTRETEL INC.
Att: Human Resources Manager
1226 White Oaks Boulevard, Unit 7
Oakville, ON L6H 2B9
Tel. 905-842-8588
Fax 905-842-7954
Email .... hr@entretel.com
Website .... www.entretel.com
Employer Background: Entretel Inc. is a call centre training and consulting firm. *New Positions Created (2):* Sales Position; Training Consultant.

ENTRUST TECHNOLOGIES LTD.
Att: Human Resources
750 Heron Road, Suite E080
Ottawa, ON K1V 1A7
Tel. 613-247-3400
Fax 613-248-3040
Email .... hr@entrust.com
Website .... www.entrust.com
Employer Background: Entrust Technologies Ltd. develops and markets software to permit secured transactions over the Internet and private networks. The company has annual sales of $49 million. *New Positions Created (2):* Business Development Manager; Chief Information Officer.

ENVIRONMENTAL ASSESSMENT OFFICE, BC
Att: Human Resource Services Branch
525 Superior Street
1st Floor, PO Box 9420, Stn Prov Govt
Victoria, BC V8W 9V1
Tel. 250-387-2206
Fax 250-387-0694
Website .... www.eao.gov.bc.ca
Employer Background: The Environmental Assessment Office is a neutral provincial agency, coordinating assessments of the impacts of major development proposals in BC. *New Positions Created (2):* Geographical Information Systems Analyst; Administrative Assistant.

ENVIRONMENTAL COMMISSIONER OF ONTARIO, THE
Att: Human Resources Manager
1075 Bay Street, Suite 605
Toronto, ON M5S 2B1
Tel. 416-325-3377
Fax 416-325-3370
Website .... www.eco.on.ca
Employer Background: The Environmental Commissioner of Ontario is an independent officer of the legislature whose duties are set out in the Environmental Bill of Rights (EBR). *New Positions Created (3):* Policy and Decision Analyst; Senior Policy Advisor; Policy and Decision Analyst.

ENVIRONMENTAL WASTE INTERNATIONAL / EWI
Att: Human Resources Manager
283 Station Street
Ajax, ON L1S 1S3
Fax 905-428-8730
Employer Background: EWI produces equipment for medical waste reduction and scrap tire recycling using a patented microwave process. *New Positions Created (3):* Electrical Engineer; Manager, Mechanical Engineering; Vice-President, Manufacturing.

EOTT CANADA LTD.
Att: Human Resources Manager
440 - 2nd Avenue SW, Suite 2401
Calgary, AB T2P 4H2
Tel. 403-266-3688
Fax 403-265-7634
Website .... www.eott.com
Employer Background: EOTT Canada is the Calgary subsidiary of EOTT Energy Partners, a crude oil gathering and marketing organization. *New Positions Created (2):* Accounting Clerk; Crude Oil Marketing Analyst.

EPALS CLASSROOM EXCHANGE
Att: Human Resources Department
353 Dalhousie Street, 3rd Floor
Ottawa, ON K1N 7G1
Tel. 613-562-9847
Fax 613-562-4768
Email .... hr@epalscorp.com
Website .... www.epals.com
Employer Background: ePALS Classroom Exchange is the world's largest online class-

room community, connecting over 2.5 million students and teachers in 182 countries. *New Positions Created (11):* Japanese Tester; Creative Director; Foreign Liaisons; French Translator; Senior Java Developer; Software Developers; Software Engineers; System Administrator; Technical Writer; Web Application Developers; Web Production Designers.

EPCOR UTILITIES INC.
Att: Career Opportunities
10065 Jasper Avenue
Edmonton, AB T5J 3B1

Tel. 780-412-7777
Fax 780-412-7602
Email .... careers@epcor.ca
Website .... www.epcor.ca

Employer Background: EPCOR Utilities Inc. provides electricity, water and gas to customers in western Canada, as well as technology solutions to municipalities across the country. *New Positions Created (59):* Manager, Mechanical Engineering; Business System Analyst; Administrative Assistant; Infrastructure Professionals (5); Manager, Financial Analysis; Settlement Operations Manager; Systems Analyst, Internet / Intranet Support; Purchasing Assistant; Systems Analyst; Power Market Assessment Manager; Business Implementation Analyst; Chemical / Environmental Engineers; Civil / Structural Engineers; Electrical Engineers; Instrumentation & Control Engineers; Mechanical Engineers; Site Civil Engineer; WTP / WWTP Operator; Senior Substations Engineer; Predictive Maintenance Coordinator; Professional Account Managers; Sales Manager, Major Accounts; Operations Accountant; Electrical and Instrument Maintainer; Production Specialist; Senior Mechanical Engineers; Business Development Analyst; Business Systems Analyst; Commodity Risk Manager; Human Resources Consultant; Risk Management Information Manager; Account Managers; Customer Service Manager; GIS / CAD Systems Analyst; Manager, External Communications; Manager, Internal Communications; Payroll Representative / HR Intranet Administrator; Data / Application Architect; Financial Manager; Legal Counsel; Security Analyst; Business Analysts (2); Systems Analysts (2); Administrative Assistant; Database Administrators (2); Project Managers (4); Safety Codes Officer, Building; Safety Codes Officer, Plumbing and Gas; Internal Audit Advisor; Supervisor, Facility Services; Business Systems Analyst; Director, Human Resource Services; Manager, IT Security; Director, Human Resources Services; Graphic Web Designer; Manager, Information Technology Security; Plumbing and Gas Inspector; Systems Analyst; Business Systems Analyst.

EPIC DATA INC.
Att: Human Resources
6300 River Road
Richmond, BC V6X 1X5

Tel. 604-273-9146
Fax 604-273-1830

Email .... hr@epicdata.com
Website .... www.epicdata.com

Employer Background: Epic Data Inc. is a leader in automated data collection solutions for enterprise-wide implementation. *New Positions Created (16):* Data Collection Hardware Specialist; Functional Consultant; Systems Analyst, Baan Practice; Senior Software Team Leader; Software Developer; Systems Support Analyst; Vice-President, North American Sales; Applications Engineer; Software Developer; Systems Support Analyst; Senior Accountant; Senior Software Team Lead; Software Engineer; Senior Accountant; Systems Support Specialist; Office Services Coordinator.

EPSON RESEARCH AND DEVELOPMENT, INC., VANCOUVER DESIGN CENTRE
Att: Human Resources Manager
11120 Horseshoe Way, Suite 320
Vancouver, BC V7A 5E3

Tel. 604-275-5151
Fax 604-271-9765
Email .... vdc.recruiting@erd.epson.com
Website .... www.erd.epson.com

Employer Background: Epson Research and Development, Inc. develops LCD controller-related integrated circuits and software. *New Positions Created (7):* Intermediate / Senior Digital IC Design Engineers; Digital Designers; Application Engineers / Software Developers; Digital Designers; Customer Support Application Engineer; Intermediate / Senior Digital IC Design Engineers; Software Developer.

EQUINOX ENGINEERING LTD.
Att: Human Resources
640 - 12th Avenue SW, Suite 472
Calgary, AB T2R 0H2

Tel. 403-205-3833
Fax 403-205-3818
Email ...... engineering@equinox-eng.com
Website .... www.equinox-eng.com

Employer Background: Equinox Engineering Ltd. is an engineering consulting firm, specializing in facilities design, implementation and operation assistance for the oil and gas industry. *New Positions Created (8):* Engineering Positions; Electrical Designer / Checker; Intermediate Piping Designer; Intermediate / Senior Mechanical Engineer; Intermediate / Senior Process Engineer; Senior Project Manager; Engineering Positions; Engineering Positions.

EQUIPMENT PLANNING ASSOCIATES LTD.
Att: Human Resources Manager
70 East Beaver Creek Road, Suite 202
Richmond Hill, ON L4B 3B2

Fax 905-771-9736
Email .... epa@idirect.com

Employer Background: Equipment Planning Associates Ltd. is a national equipment consulting firm, specializing in healthcare equipment planning. *New Positions Created (3):* Data Coordinator; Equipment Planner / Consultant; Data Coordinator.

EQUITABLE LIFE OF CANADA
Att: Human Resources
1 Westmount Road North
Waterloo, ON N2J 4C7

Tel. 519-886-5210
Fax 519-883-7400
Email .... resumes@equitable.ca
Website .... www.equitable.ca

Employer Background: Equitable Life of Canada is an independent Canadian life insurance company, offering a range of life insurance, annuities and group plans for individuals and businesses. *New Positions Created (3):* Actuarial Associate, Individual Product Development; Actuarial Student, Individual Product Development; Director, Group Sales & Distribution.

ERICSSON CANADA INC.
Att: Human Resources Department
8400 Decarie Boulevard
Mount Royal, QC H4P 2N2

Tel. 514-738-8300
Fax 514-345-6102
Email .... human.resources@lmc.ericsson.se
Website .... www.ericsson.com

Employer Background: Ericsson Canada Inc. is part of Ericsson Communications Inc., a telecom company with over 100,000 employees in 140 countries. *New Positions Created (19):* 3G Packet Core Network Specialist; Correction Assembly Tester; HR Recruiter; Integration & Certification Engineer; JAMBALA Test Plant Support Specialist; Marketing Product Manager; Methods & Tools Engineer; Migration Tool and Strategy Engineer; MSC Marketing Support Specialist; Quality Manager; RPC Developer; Software Designer; System Designer; System Verification Engineer; TelORB Consultant; WAP Designer; IP Network Operator and Manager; IP Systems Architect; Senior Network Manager.

ERICSSON COMMUNICATIONS CANADA
Att: Human Resources
5255 Satellite Drive
Mississauga, ON L4W 5E3

Tel. 905-629-6715
Fax 905-629-6756
Email .... hrjobs@ericsson.ca
Website .... www.ericsson.ca

Employer Background: Ericsson Communications Canada provides Internet consulting services and IP-based business applications and solutions. *New Positions Created (4):* Project Manager; Director of Business Solutions, CDMA; Director of Sales, Central Canada; Product Manager, CDMA.

ERINOAK
Att: Alison Clarke
2277 South Millway
Mississauga, ON L5L 2M5

Tel. 905-820-7111
Fax 905-820-1333
Website .... www.erinoak.org

Employer Background: Erinoak is a children's treatment centre, providing family-centred rehabilitation services to children with physical, developmental and communication disabilities. *New Positions Created (14):* Program Assistants; RNs & RPNs; Occupational Therapists; Physiotherapists; Speech-Language Pathologists; Program Mgr; Psychologists; Audiologists; Psychological Associate; Psychometrists; Occupational Therapist; Speech Language Pathologist; Clinical Coordinator; Physiotherapists.

ERNEST C. DRURY SCHOOL FOR THE DEAF
Att: John Barry, Principal
255 Ontario Street South
Milton, ON L9T 2M5

Fax 905-878-1354

Employer Background: Ernest C. Drury School for the Deaf serves deaf students in a residential school setting. *New Positions Created (3):* Preschool / Home Visiting Teacher; Social Worker; Residence Counsellor Supervisor.

ERNST & YOUNG LLP
Att: Jane McIntosh, Recruiting Manager
222 Bay Street, Ernst & Young Tower
PO Box 251, Toronto-Dominion Centre
Toronto, ON M5K 1J7

Tel. 416-864-1234
Fax 416-943-2207
Website .... www.ey.com/can

Employer Background: Ernst & Young is one of Canada's leading professional services firms, providing consulting, tax, accounting and other services to the nation's leading corporations. *New Positions Created (3):* Tax Professionals; Business Advisors and Auditors; Executive Interviewer.

ERNST & YOUNG LLP
Att: Jessica Goldie, Human Resources Coordinator
55 Metcalfe Street, Suite 1600
Ottawa, ON K1P 6L5

Tel. 613-232-1511
Fax 613-232-5324
Email .... fiscal@ca.eyi.com
Website .... www.ey.com

Employer Background: Ernst & Young is one of Canada's leading professional services firms, providing consulting, tax, accounting and other services to the nation's leading corporations. *New Positions Created (2):* Information Technology Specialists; Technical Writer, Research and Development.

ESBI ALBERTA LTD.
Att: Manager, Human Resources
736 - 8th Avenue SW, Suite 900
Calgary, AB T2P 1H4

Tel. 403-232-0944
Fax 403-266-2959
Email .... resumes@eal.ab.ca
Website .... www.eal.ab.ca

Employer Background: ESBI Alberta Ltd. is an independent transmission administrator responsible for the open access of Alberta's interconnected electric system. *New Positions Created (6):* Senior Commercial Analysts (2); Engineer / Engineering Technologist; Manager, Customer Services; Regulatory Analyst; Customer Account Representative; Transmission Planning Engineer.

ESCENTS AROMATHERAPY
Att: Stephen Hill
1709 Welch Street
North Vancouver, BC V7P 3G9

Fax 604-984-3466
Email .. inquiries@escentsaromatherapy.com
Website ... www.escentsaromatherapy.com

Employer Background: Escents Aromatherapy manufactures and retails bath, body and home fragrance products. *New Positions Created (4):* Co-Manager & Sales Associates; District Sales Manager; Store Manager; Intermediate Accountant.

ESI CANADA INC.
Att: Human Resources
5770 Hurontario Street, 10th Floor
Mississauga, ON L5R 3G5

Tel. 905-712-8008
Fax 905-712-4341
Email ...... hrcanada@express-scripts.com
Website ..... www.esi-canada.com

Employer Background: ESI Canada Inc. (a division of Express Scripts) is a full-service pharmacy benefits management organization. *New Positions Created (6):* Pharmacy Technician; Bilingual Provider Audit Supervisor; Bilingual Training Specialist; Business Analysts; Report Programmer; Bilingual Call Centre Representative.

ESPIAL GROUP INC.
Att: Human Resources Manager
200 Elgin Street, 3rd Floor
Ottawa, ON K2P 1L5

Tel. 613-230-4770
Fax 613-230-8498
Email .... hr@espial.com
Website .... www.espial.com

Employer Background: Espial Group Inc. is a software design and human factors company. *New Positions Created (8):* Manager, Professional Services; Java Developers; Java Infrastructure Developer; Linux Developer; Senior Contracts Administrator; Senior Quality Control Specialist; Software Test Engineers; Software Test Manager.

ESRI CANADA LTD.
Att: Regional Manager, Prairie Region
250 - 6th Avenue SW
Suite 1040, Bow Valley Square 4
Calgary, AB T2P 3H7

Tel. 403-262-3774
Fax 403-263-4023
Email .... dfletcher@esricanada.com
Website .... www.esricanada.com

Employer Background: ESRI Canada Ltd. is leading distributor of geographic information system (GIS) software in Canada. *New Positions Created (2):* Account Managers (2); GIS Consultant.

ESRI CANADA LTD.
Att: Human Resources Department
49 Gervais Drive
Toronto, ON M3C 1Y9

Tel. 416-441-6035
Fax 416-441-6838
Email .... jobs@esri.ca
Website .... www.esricanada.com

Employer Background: ESRI Canada Ltd. is leading distributor of geographic information system (GIS) software in Canada. *New Positions Created (2):* Office Administrator; Human Resources Coordinator.

ESSENTUS INC.
Att: Patricia Di Vincenzo,
Human Resource Specialist
2 Place Alexis Nihon, Suite 1700
Montréal, QC H3Z 3L3

Tel. 514-925-5100
Fax 514-925-5181
Email .... pdivince@essentus.com
Website .... www.essentus.com

Employer Background: Essentus Inc. (formerly Richter Systems International Inc.) is a supplier of business software solutions for the apparel, footwear and softgoods industries. *New Positions Created (6):* Senior Accountant / Controller; EDI Analyst / Designer; Vice-President of Finance; Director of Marketing; Functional / Technical Designers; Sales Account Executives.

ESSLINGER FOODS LTD.
Att: National Sales Manager
5035 North Service Road, Unit A-10
Burlington, ON L7L 5V2

Fax .,..................... 905-332-7574

Employer Background: For over 30 years, Esslinger Foods Ltd. has been providing gourmet products to the Canadian foodservice market. *New Positions Created (2):* Sales Agent, Foodservice Speciality Products; Inside Sales / General Office Duty Position.

ESTEC OILFIELD INC.
Att: Allan Nelson
17510 - 102nd Avenue, 2nd Floor
Edmonton, AB T5S 1K2

Tel. 780-483-3436
Fax 780-489-9557
Email .... arnelson@arneng.ab.ca
Website .... www.oilfield.estec.ca

Employer Background: ESTec Oilfield Inc. (formerly Allan R. Nelson Engineering Ltd.) is a professional engineering group, serving the petrochemical, pulp and paper, power and utilities, mining, transportation, construction and manufacturing industries. *New Positions Created (4):* Mechanical Engineer; Driller; Professional Engineer; Junior Mechanical Engineer / Mechanical Technologist.

ETHAN ALLEN HOME INTERIORS
Att: John Browning
15 Kenview Boulevard
Brampton, ON L6T 5G5

Fax 905-790-2170
Website .... www.ethanallen.com

Employer Background: Ethan Allen Home Interiors is a manufacturer and retailer of fine home furnishings. *New Positions Cre-

ated (3): Drivers; Information Technology Systems Administrator; Intermediate Accounting Clerk.

ETHAN ALLEN HOME INTERIORS
Att: Sue Holland
8134 Yonge Street
Thornhill, ON L4J 1W4
Fax 905-889-7565
Website .... www.ethanallen.com
Employer Background: Ethan Allen Home Interiors is a manufacturer and retailer of fine home furnishings. *New Positions Created (5):* Furniture Touch Up and Repair Specialist; Sales / Designs Consultants; Window Coverings Specialist; Customer Service Receptionists; Soft Goods Specialist.

EUCLID-HITACHI HEAVY EQUIPMENT LTD.
Att: Human Resources Department
200 Woodlawn Road West
Guelph, ON N1H 1B6
Tel. 519-823-2000
Fax 519-837-4220
Website .... www.euclid-hitachi.com
Employer Background: Euclid-Hitachi Heavy Equipment Ltd. manufactures off-highway and mining rigid hauler vehicles. *New Positions Created (2):* Unigraphics CAD Designers (2); Unigraphics CAD Designer.

EUROPEAN SPECIALTY REINSURANCE LTD. / ESG
Att: Human Resources
1 Adelaide Street East, Suite 2610
Toronto, ON M5C 2V9
Tel. 416-864-7443
Fax 416-864-9529
Email .... ana.johnston@esre.on.ca
Website .... www.esre.on.ca
Employer Background: ESG is a publicly-traded reinsurance company, with over 10 offices worldwide. *New Positions Created (3):* Reinsurance Underwriter; Senior Actuarial Analyst; Treaty Wording Specialist.

EVANS CONSOLES INC.
Att: Mina O'Connor
1616 - 27th Avenue NE
Calgary, AB T2E 8W4
Tel. 403-717-3071
Fax 403-543-2957
Email .... moconnor@evansonline.com
Website .... www.evansonline.com
Employer Background: Evans Consoles Inc. designs and manufactures control room products, including modular console furniture and display wall systems. *New Positions Created (22):* Environmental Health & Safety Manager; Design Manager, Engineering; Procurement Specialist; Product Manager, Engineering; Scheduling Coordinator; Installations Supervisor; Mechanical Engineering Tech; Assistant Controller; Audio Visual Specialist; Cabinet Makers; Customer Service Representative; Industrial Engineers and Industrial Engineering Technologists; Intermediate Project Engineering Technologist; Junior Transportation Coordinator;

Maintenance Manager; Manufacturing Engineering Technologist; OEM Product Manager; Project Managers; Quality Assurance Manager; Receiving Inspector; Telesales Professional; Manufacturing Workers.

EVANS & EVANS INC.
Att: Michael A. Evans, Prinicipal
400 Burrard, Suite 1400
Vancouver, BC V6C 3G2
Tel. 604-643-1704
Fax 604-408-2303
Employer Background: Evans & Evans Inc. specializes in corporate finance, valuation-related work and due diligence. *New Positions Created (4):* Analyst; Associate; Junior Analyst; Senior Analyst.

EVERTZ MICROSYSTEMS LTD.
Att: Human Resources Department
5288 John Lucas Drive
Burlington, ON L7L 5Z9
Tel. 905-335-3700
Fax 905-335-0909
Email .... hr@evertz.com
Website .... www.evertz.com
Employer Background: Evertz Microsystems Ltd. designs film production and post-production equipment for the film and television broadcast industry. *New Positions Created (14):* Engineer, Optics Specialist; Executive Assistant; Manufacturing Database Manager; Payroll Coordinator / Junior Accountant; Software Engineers; Technical Sales Representative; Technical Writer; Electronic Components Handler; Executive Assistant / Marketing Assistant; General Accountant; Shipper / Receiver; Engineer - Optics Specialist; PCB Design Engineer; Software Engineers.

EWAZO TECHNOLOGY CORPORATION
Att: Human Resources Manager
239 Menzies Street, Suite 201
Victoria, BC V8V 2G6
Tel. 250-383-6004
Fax 250-381-7977
Email .... careers@ewazo.com
Website .... www.ewazo.com
Employer Background: eWazo Technology Corporation is a global company, focusing on microelectronics and photonics convergence to build leading-edge MPLS, optical ethernet and LAN solutions. *New Positions Created (17):* Director of Human Resources; Hardware Engineer; Hardware Engineer, Verification; High-Speed Design Engineers; Network Engineer, IP Routing; NMS Development Engineer; Sales Engineer; Senior Hardware Engineer; Senior Network Protocol Engineer; Test Engineer; Director of Engineering; Electro-Optic System Designer; Network Standards Engineer; Optical Component Engineer; Senior Network Architect; Senior Optical Engineer; Senior Pre-Production Engineer.

EXCALIBUR-GEMINI GROUP LTD., THE
Att: Human Resource Department
144 - 4th Avenue SW, Suite 1100
Calgary, AB T2P 3N4

Email .... info@teggl.com
Website .... www.teggl.com
Employer Background: The Excalibur-Gemini Group Ltd. is an oil and gas service company. *New Positions Created (3):* Data Analyst; IT Manager; Technical Records and Information Management Specialist.

EXCEL HOMES INC.
Att: Irven Just, General Manager
9705 Horton Road SW, Suite A102
Calgary, AB T2V 2X5
Tel. 403-253-1433
Fax 403-253-1687
Website .... www.excelhomes.com
Employer Background: Excel Homes Inc. is a leading Alberta home builder. *New Positions Created (4):* New Home Sales Area Manager; Estimator; Intermediate Purchaser / Estimator; Home Sales Area Manager.

EXCEL TECH LTD. / XLTEK
Att: Human Resources
2568 Bristol Circle
Oakville, ON L6H 5S1
Tel. 905-829-5300
Fax 905-829-5304
Email .... rsavvis@xltek.com
Website .... www.xltek.com
Employer Background: XLTEK manufactures medical equipment in the fields of neurodiagnostics and electrotherapy. *New Positions Created (14):* Accessories Sales Position; Administrative Assistant, Institution Sales; Assistant to VP; Clinical Support Specialist; CNC / Set-up Operator; DSP Software Developer; Electronic Assemblers; Electronics Test Technicians / Technologists; Graphic and Multimedia Designer; Inside Sales Administrator; MRP Specialist; Printed Circuit Board Layout Specialist; Software Development Position; Warranty Telemarketer.

EXCHANGE SOLUTIONS / ESI
Att: Human Resources Manager
181 University Avenue, Suite 2110
Toronto, ON M5H 3M7
Tel. 416-815-8010
Fax 416-815-1258
Email ... recruiting@exchangesolutions.net
Website ... www.exchangesolutions.net
Employer Background: ESI is an entrepreneurial customer value management firm, with offices in Toronto and Boston. *New Positions Created (3):* Marketing Analyst; Accounting Assistant; Controller.

EXCITE CANADA INC.
Att: Human Resources Manager
156 Front Street West, Suite 303
Toronto, ON M5J 2L6
Tel. 416-642-4700
Fax 416-642-4770
Email .... myexcitecareer@home.com
Website .... www.excite.ca
Employer Background: Excite Canada Inc. (a joint venture of Rogers Media Inc. of Toronto and Excite@Home of Redwood City,

California) is a leader in broadband. *New Positions Created (6):* Database Analyst (DBA); Production Engineer; Software Engineers; Production Engineer; Software Engineer; Digital Media Encoder.

EXCITE@HOME CANADA, INC.
Att: Human Resources Manager
95 King Street East, Suite 300
Toronto, ON M5C 1G4
Email .... toronto-jobs@noc.home.net
Website .... www.excite.ca
Employer Background: Excite@Home Canada, Inc. is a leading provider of residential and commercial broadband access and services. *New Positions Created (12):* Associate Network Engineers; Associate Provisioning Engineers; Associate Systems Administrators; Director of Service Management; Manager of IP Provisioning Operations; Manager of Network Operations; Manager of System Administration; Network Engineers; Oracle Database Administrators; Software Engineers; Technical Project Managers; Unix Systems Administrators.

EXECUTIVE NEEDS INC., THE
Att: Human Resources Manager
67 Yonge Street, Suite 1040
Toronto, ON M5E 1J8
Tel. 416-364-1552
Fax 416-364-0038
Email .... info@sportality.com
Website .... www.sportality.com
Employer Background: The Executive Needs Inc. is a sports marketing and global event management firm. *New Positions Created (4):* Corporate Account Managers / Inside Sales; Office Administrator; Receptionist; Web Developers / Graphic Designers.

EXEL CANADA
Att: Stacey Kowal
PO Box 2334
Sardis, BC V2R 1A7
Email .... stacey.kowal@exel.com
Website .... www.exel.com
Employer Background: Exel Canada is a leading third-party provider of worldwide supply chain management solutions. *New Positions Created (4):* Operations Manager; Project and Implementation Manager; Systems and Inventory Manager; Warehouse Supervisor.

EXEL CANADA
Att: Human Resources
100 Sandalwood Parkway West
Brampton, ON L7A 1A8
Tel. 905-840-7540
Fax 905-840-6831
Website .... www.exel.com
Employer Background: Exel Canada is a leading third-party provider of worldwide supply chain management solutions. *New Positions Created (3):* Receptionist; Operations Supervisor; Bilingual Customer Service Representative.

EXFO ELECTRO-OPTICAL ENGINEERING INC.
Att: Human Resources Department
465 Godin Avenue
Vanier, QC G1M 3G7
Tel. 418-683-0211
Fax 418-683-2170
Email .... resume@exfo.com
Website .... www.exfo.com
Employer Background: EXFO Electro-Optical Engineering Inc. is a leading designer and manufacturer of fibre optic test, measurement and automation equipment for the telecom industry. *New Positions Created (2):* Optical Researcher; Optical Technician.

EXHIBITS INTERNATIONAL
Att: Human Resources
431 Horner Avenue
Toronto, ON M8W 4W3
Tel. 416-252-2818
Fax 416-252-3708
Employer Background: Exhibits International is an exhibit manufacturing company, specializing in custom environments and trade show exhibits. *New Positions Created (7):* Administrative Assistant; Detailing Engineer; Project Manager; Senior Account Manager; Graphic Designer; Buyer / Production Coordinator; Production Manager.

EXI WIRELESS SYSTEMS INC.
Att: Human Resources Manager
13551 Commerce Parkway, Suite 100
Richmond, BC V6V 2L1
Tel. 604-207-7760
Fax 604-207-7765
Email .... jobs@exi.com
Website .... www.exi.com
Employer Background: Established in 1980, EXI Wireless Systems Inc. develops and manufactures RFID / RF transponder systems and technologies. *New Positions Created (10):* Accounting Clerk; Digital / Analog Hardware Designers; Hardware Test Engineer; Industrial / Mechanical Designer; Manufacturing and Materials Manager; Product Manager; Senior Embedded Software / Firmware Engineers; Senior RF Engineer; Systems Architect; Technical Writer.

EXOCOM GROUP INC., THE
Att: Human Resources
400 - 3rd Avenue SW
Suite 500, Canterra Tower
Calgary, AB T2P 4H2
Tel. 403-237-7888
Fax 403-237-7871
Email .... prowan@exocom.com
Website .... www.exocom.com
Employer Background: The Exocom Group Inc. is an IT consulting firm that develops advanced e-business applications for customers in a wide range of industries. *New Positions Created (2):* Systems Architect / Senior Consultant; Systems Architect / Senior Consultant.

EXOCOM GROUP INC., THE
Att: Human Resources Manager

5935 Airport Road, Suite 630
Mississauga, ON L4V 1W5
Tel. 905-405-9171
Fax 905-405-8699
Email .... hr@exocom.com
Website .... www.exocom.com
Employer Background: The Exocom Group Inc. is an IT consulting firm that develops advanced e-business applications for customers in a wide range of industries. *New Positions Created (2):* Project Manager; Technical Architects / Senior Analysts.

EXOCOM GROUP INC., THE
Att: Human Resources Manager
45 O'Connor Street
Suite 1400, World Exchange Plaza
Ottawa, ON K1P 1A4
Tel. 613-237-0257
Fax 613-237-0314
Email .... hr@exocom.com
Website .... www.exocom.com
Employer Background: The Exocom Group Inc., a wholly-owned subsidiary of Manitoba Telecom Services (MTS) Inc., is an IT consulting firm that delivers advanced e-business applications for customers in a wide range of industries. *New Positions Created (45):* Receptionist; IT Management Consultants; Manager, Application Development Services; Project Managers; Security Architect; Security Consultant; Senior Analysts; Senior Software Engineers; Technical Architects / Senior Analysts; Web Developers; E-Business Consultants; IT Enterprise Specialist / WAN Administrator; Knowledge Management Consultants; Performance Management Senior Consultants; E-Business Consultants; Manager, Application Development Services; Project Managers; Security Architect; Security Consultant; Senior Software Engineers; Technical Architects, Senior Analysts; Web Developers; WIN 2000 Internetworking Consultants; IT Management Consultants; Microsoft Web Developers; Senior Analyst; Knowledge Management Consultants; Performance Management Senior Consultants; Accountant; Intermediate Administrative Assistant; Sales Support Specialist; Cisco Internetworking Specialists; E-Business Consultants; Manager, Application Development Services; Manager, Network Infrastructure Services; Project Manager; Security Architect; Security Consultant; Senior IT Recruiter; Senior Software Engineers; Technical Architect, Network Infrastructure; Technical Architects / Senior Analysts; Web Developers; WIN 2000 Internetworking Specialists; IT Management Consultants.

EXOCOM GROUP INC., THE
Att: Human Resources Manager
1969 Upper Water Street, Suite 2200
Tower II Penthouse, Purdy's Wharf
Halifax, NS B3J 3R7
Tel. 902-491-4480
Fax 902-422-8901
Email .... hr@exocom.com
Website .... www.exocom.com
Employer Background: The Exocom Group Inc. is an IT consulting firm that develops

advanced e-business applications for customers in a wide range of industries. *New Positions Created (4):* IT Enterprise Specialist / WAN Administrator; Senior Analyst; E-Business Consultants; Project Manager.

EXPERIAN
Att: Office Administrator
170 University Avenue, Suite 502
Toronto, ON M5H 3B3
Tel. 416-593-7906
Fax 416-593-7909
Email .... contact_us@experian.ca
Website .... www.experian.com
Employer Background: UK-based Experian is a leading supplier of information on consumers, businesses, cars and property. The company has annual sales exceeding $2 billion and 12,000 employees worldwide. *New Positions Created (4):* Application Developer; Credit Scoring Analyst / Consultant; Programmers; Technical Support Position.

EXPLORER HOTEL, THE
Att: Delynn Wannamaker, HR Manager
Postal Service 7000
Yellowknife, NT X1A 2R3
Tel. 867-873-3531
Fax 867-873-3213
Email .... humanresources@
.... explorerhotel.nt.ca
Website .... www.explorerhotel.nt.ca
Employer Background: The Explorer Hotel is a 128-bedroom, full-service facility, located steps away from the commercial and government centre of Yellowknife. *New Positions Created (2):* Sushi Chef / Manager; Hospitality Positions.

EXPLORER SOFTWARE SOLUTIONS LTD.
Att: Arlene Nerrie
734 - 7th Avenue SW, Suite 800
Calgary, AB T2P 3P8
Fax 403-571-5266
Email .. arlenenerrie@explorersoftware.com
Website .... www.explorersoftware.com
Employer Background: Explorer Software Solutions Ltd. supplies computerized property management solutions for the oil and gas industry. *New Positions Created (2):* Implementation Specialist; Enterprise Asset Management (EAM) System Implementer.

EXPORT DEVELOPMENT CORPORATION / EDC
Att: Human Resources Division
151 O'Connor Street
Ottawa, ON K1A 1K3
Tel. 613-598-2500
Fax 613-598-2578
Email .... hrrh@edc-see.ca
Website .... www.edc-see.ca
Employer Background: Founded in 1944, EDC operates as a commercial financial institution, providing trade finance and risk management services to Canadian exporters and investors in 200 markets. *New Positions Created (76):* HR Policy Adviser; Administrator, International Markets (Latin America and Europe); Assistant Director, Real Estate & Facilities; Assistant Director, Recorded Information Management; Project Specialist / Leader, Infrastructure Services; Project Specialist / Network & Server Specialist, Infrastructure Services; Business Analysts, Corporate Business Systems (CBS); Business Analysts, E-Business Team; Business Partner, Business Partners & Recruitment; Financial Services Mgr, Aerospace Team; Financial Services Managers; Human Resources Analysts, Total Compensation (2); Internal Audit Services Specialist; Object-Oriented Software Developer, Application Services; Organizational Development Specialist; Program Mgr, Contract Insurance and Bonding; Project Specialist / Application Support Specialist, Infrastructure Services; Project Specialist / Development DBA, Infrastructure Services; Project Specialist / Mainframe Operating System Specialist, Infrastructure Services; Project Specialist / Microsoft SQL Server DBA, Infrastructure Services; Project Specialist / Network & Server Specialist, Infrastructure Services; Project Specialist / Network Storage and Operating Systems; Project Specialist / Website Administrator, Application Services; Recoveries Services Mgr; Regional Manager, Africa and Middle East; Senior Environmental Adviser, Technical & Environmental Advisory Services; Technical Support Specialist, Helpdesk; Web Developer, Application Services; Web Technical Specialist, Infrastructure Services; Assistant Director, Real Estate & Facilities; Business Development Managers (3); Financial Analyst, Loans Accounting; Financial Standards Mgr; Portfolio Managers, Capital Markets (2); Project Manager, Financial Information Systems; Project Specialist / Lead, Infrastructure Services; Risk Analysts, International (2); Statistical Analyst; Team Leader, Financial Planning; Telemarketing Agent, Emerging Exporters Team; Underwriter, Contract Insurance & Bonding; Underwriters, Short-Term Insurance (4); Administrator, Legal Services; Assistant Underwriter, Base & Semi-Manufactured Goods Team; Corporate Representation Adviser, Ontario Region; Corporate Representation Adviser, Stakeholder Engagement; Administrative Services Technician; Administrator, Emerging Exporters Team; Application Support Specialist, Infrastructure Services; Business Analysts, Corporate Business Systems; Business Analysts, E-Business Team; Business Development Adviser, SME Financial Services; Corporate Analyst; Corporate Policy Officer, Government and International Relations; Data Warehouse Project Manager, Client Services & Telecommunications; IT Project Manager, Application Services; Loan Asset Manager, Asset Management Team; Market Risk Manager; Project Specialist, Network Storage and Operating Systems; Project Specialists, Client Services & Telecommunications (2); Regional Mgr, Africa and Middle East; Specialist, Internal Audit Services; Website Administrator, Application Services; Marketing Mgr; Team Leader, Government Relations; Senior Translator; Human Resources Business Partner; IT Project Managers; Relationship Manager; Business Analyst, Corporate Business Systems; Business Development Coordinator; Financial Software Developer, Application Services; Project Specialist, Infrastructure Services ; Project Specialist, Infrastructure Services; Web Developer, Application Services; Web Technical Specialist, Infrastructure Services.

EXPORT PACKERS COMPANY LTD.
Att: Commodity Divison Manager
107 Walker Drive
Brampton, ON L6T 5K5
Tel. 905-792-9700
Email .... mikel@exportpackers.com
Website .... www.exportpackers.com
Employer Background: Established in 1937, Export Packers is an international food import, export and distribution company. *New Positions Created (3):* Industrial Meat Salesperson; Assistant Trader; Assistant Trader.

EXTENDICARE (CANADA) INC.
Att: Roxanne Adams, Director,
Employment Services
3000 Steeles Avenue East, Suite 700
Markham, ON L3R 9W2
Tel. 905-470-5623
Fax 905-470-5588
Email .... radams@extendicare.com
Website .... www.extendicare.com
Employer Background: Extendicare (Canada) Inc. owns and operates approximately 50 nursing homes across Canada, and provides homecare, hospital management and rehabilitative therapy services. *New Positions Created (13):* Dietary Manager; Canadian Accounting Mgr; Shared Services Mgr; Administrator; Director of Care; Manager; Long-Term Care Administrator; Long-Term Care Consultant; Manager, Financial Reporting; Manager, Employee Benefits; Chief Accountant; Controller; Payroll Supervisor.

EXTRACOMM TECHNOLOGIES INC.
Att: Human Resources Manager
5160 Yonge Street, Suite 1315, PO Box 27
Toronto, ON M2N 6L9
Tel. 416-222-5280
Fax 416-222-7371
Email .... jonathan.mah@extracomm.com
Website .... www.extracomm.com
Employer Background: Extracomm Technologies provides a robust fax server product, allowing customers using Lotus Notes or Domino to integrate fax communications seamlessly and cost-effectively on desktops and with custom business applications. *New Positions Created (10):* Accounting Clerk; Accounts Executive; Lotus Domino Administrator; Business Analyst / Project Mgr; Enterprise Solutions Business Development Manager; Office Clerk / Receptionist; Product Marketing Mgr; Senior Business Development Mgr; Senior Business / System Analyst; Wireless Senior Developer.

EZENET INC.
Att: Human Resources Manager
5160 Yonge Street
11th Floor, North York Centre
Toronto, ON M2N 6L9

Tel. 416-218-2188
Fax 416-218-2189
Email ...., careers@ezenet.com
Website .... www.ezenet.com
Employer Background: Founded in 1995, Ezenet Inc. provides computer software, data centre outsourcing and high-speed Internet communication services to the financial industry. *New Positions Created (8):* Business Systems Analyst; Database Administrator; Graphic Artist / Web Designer; Java Developers; Junior, Intermediate and Senior Developers; Project Mgr; System Testing / Quality Assurance Analysts; Receptionist.

F & K MFG. CO. LIMITED
Att: Human Resources Manager
155 Turbine Drive
Toronto, ON M9L 2S7
Tel. 416-749-3980
Fax 416-749-1814
Employer Background: F & K Mfg. Co. Ltd. is a metal stamping company that manufactures stamping dies, machine tool builders and automation and robotic equipment. *New Positions Created (2):* Purchasing Assistant; Systems Coordinator.

F&P MANUFACTURING, INC.
Att: Human Resources
1 Nolan Road, PO Box 4000
Tottenham, ON L0G 1W0
Tel. 905-936-3435
Fax 905-936-4809
Employer Background: F&P Manufacturing, Inc. is an auto parts manufacturer for Honda North America. *New Positions Created (6):* Occupational Health Specialist / RPN; CMM Technician; Purchasing Engineer; Plant Engineering Coordinator; Hydroforming Technician; Robotics Technician.

FAIRMONT BANFF SPRINGS
Att: Recruitment Office
PO Box 960
Banff, AB T0L 0C0
Tel. 403-762-2211
Fax 403-760-6056
Email .... careers@bsh.cphotels.ca
Website .... www.fairmont.com
Employer Background: Built in 1888, Fairmont Banff Springs is a historic 770-room hotel, operated by Fairmont Hotels and Resorts. *New Positions Created (6):* Assistant Executive Housekeeper; Housekeeping Evening Manager; Various Hospitality Positions; Associate Managers; Group Managers; Sales Associates.

FAIRMONT CHATEAU LAKE LOUISE, THE
Att: Human Resources
111 Lake Louise Drive
Lake Louise, AB T0L 1E0
Tel. 403-522-1854
Fax 403-522-3576
Email .... cll.careers@fairmont.com
Website .... www.fairmont.com
Employer Background: Established in 1890, The Fairmont Chateau Lake Louise is a 488-

room, all-season hotel, operated by Fairmont Hotels and Resorts. *New Positions Created (3):* Assistant Comptroller; Sales Manager, Tour and Travel Market; Systems Coordinator.

FAIRMONT ROYAL YORK
Att: Human Resources
100 Front Street West
Toronto, ON M5J 1E3
Tel. 416-368-2511
Fax 416-860-4560
Email .... recruit2@fairmont.com
Website .... www.fairmont.com
Employer Background: Fairmont Royal York is one of Toronto's premier landmark hotels, with 1,365 luxury rooms. *New Positions Created (3):* Security Officer; Various Hospitality Positions; Various Hospitality Positions.

FAIRMONT VANCOUVER AIRPORT
Att: Human Resources
PO Box 23798
Richmond, BC V7B 1X9
Tel. 604-248-3232
Fax 604-248-3234
Email .... applynow.fva@fairmont.com
Website .... www.fairmont.com
Employer Background: Fairmont Vancouver Airport is a luxury facility, located inside Vancouver International Airport. *New Positions Created (3):* Assistant Outlets Manager; Executive Housekeeper; Various Hospitality Positions.

FAIRVIEW COLLEGE
Att: Carole Arkinstall, HR Assistant
PO Box 3000
Fairview, AB T0H 1L0
Tel. 780-835-6658
Fax 780-835-6790
Email .... carkinstall@fairviewc.ab.ca
Website .... www.fairviewc.ab.ca
Employer Background: Fairview College serves 15 communities, with main campuses in Fairview, Peace River and High Level. *New Positions Created (11):* Executive Assistant, President's Office; Automotive Service Technician / Harley-Davidson Technician Instructor; Harley-Davidson Mechanics Instructor; Marine Service Technician Instructors; Outdoor Power Equipment Technician Instructor; Livestock Instructor; Manager, Enrollment / Registrar; Liaison Officer; E-Commerce Instructor; Partsman Instructor; Business Administration Instructor.

FALCONBRIDGE LTD.
Att: Employment Department,
Mines / Mill Business Unit
Onaping, ON P0M 2R0
Fax 705-966-6577
Email .... jobs@falconbridge.com
Website .... www.falconbridge.com
Employer Background: Falconbridge Limited is a leading low-cost producer of nickel, copper and platinum group metals. *New Positions Created (11):* Designer, Mechanical / Civil / Electrical; Diamond Driller; In-

dustrial Engineering Technician; Maintenance Planner; Mill Process Operator / Mechanic; Millwright; Mine Shift Boss; Miner; Mining Engineering Technician; Mobile Mechanic; Stationary Engineer, 1st-Class.

FALCONBRIDGE LTD.
Att: Patricia Abad,
Supervisor, Employee Relations
95 Wellington Street West, Suite 1200
Toronto, ON M5J 2V4
Tel. 416-956-5700
Fax 416-956-5869
Email .... jobs@falconbridge.com
Website .... www.falconbridge.com
Employer Background: Falconbridge Ltd. is a leading low-cost producer of nickel, copper and platinum group metals. *New Positions Created (6):* Manager, Compensation; Supervisor, Budgets and Forecasting; Geological Computer Specialist; Senior Field Geologist; Senior Tax Advisor; Supply Chain Analyst.

FALCONBRIDGE LTD., SUDBURY SMELTER BUSINESS UNIT
Att: Sheila Laderoute
Falconbridge, ON P0M 1S0
Tel. 705-699-3160
Fax 705-699-3961
Email .... jobs@falconbridge.com
Website .... www.falconbridge.com
Employer Background: Falconbridge Ltd. is a leading low-cost producer of nickel, copper and platinum group metals. *New Positions Created (3):* Engineering Positions, Pyrometallurgy and Mineral Processing; Acid Plant Utilities Supervisor; Smelter Shift Supervisor.

FALCONER CHARNEY MACKLIN
Att: Julian N. Falconer
8 Prince Arthur Avenue
Toronto, ON M5R 1A9
Tel. 416-964-3408
Fax 416-929-8179
Email .... falconerj@globalserve.net
Employer Background: Falconer Charney is a law firm. *New Positions Created (2):* Litigation Lawyer; Litigation Lawyer.

FAM CANADA INC.
Att: J. Weleschuk, Operations Manager
8616 - 51st Avenue, Suite 210
Edmonton, AB T6E 6E6
Tel. 780-481-1177
Fax 780-481-1114
Email ..... joe.weleschuk@famcanada.com
Website .... www.fam.de
Employer Background: FAM Canada Inc. specializes in bulk material handling installations, primarily in the mining and cement manufacturing industries. *New Positions Created (2):* Project Engineer; Controller.

FAMILY AND CHILDREN'S SERVICES NIAGARA
Att: Director of Human Resources
311 Geneva Street, PO Box 24028
St. Catharines, ON L2R 7P7

Tel. 905-937-7731
Fax 905-646-5765
Email .... karolyn_edwards@cas.gov.on.ca
Website .... www.facsniagara.on.ca
Employer Background: Established in 1898, Family and Children's Services Niagara is a child welfare agency committed to protecting children from neglect and abuse. *New Positions Created (12):* Child Welfare Supervisors; Legal Counsel; Child Advocacy Centre Therapist; Family Violence Program Therapist; Child Protection Workers; Assistant Director of Service ; Child Welfare Supervisors; Payroll / Benefits Officer; Clinical Supervisor / Manager; Co-ordinator of Technical Services; Network Administrator; Child Protection Workers.

FAMILY AND CHILDREN'S SERVICES OF RENFREW COUNTY
Att: Jerry Muldoon, Local Director
77 Mary Street, Suite 100
Pembroke, ON K8A 5V4
Tel. 613-735-6866
Fax 613-735-6641
Email .... pem_fcs@webhart.net
Employer Background: Family and Children's Services of Renfrew County is a children's aid society, providing child protection, foster care and adoption services. *New Positions Created (2):* Social Workers; Social Workers (2).

FAMILY CENTRE, THE
Att: Sherran McBrien
9912 - 106th Street, Suite 20
Edmonton, AB T5K 1C5
Tel. 780-917-8228
Fax 780-426-4918
Website .... www.the-family-centre.com
Employer Background: The Family Centre is a non-profit agency dedicated to fostering healthy families and communities. *New Positions Created (3):* Child / Youth Services Workers; Aboriginal Services Coordinator; Therapists.

FAMILY, YOUTH AND CHILD SERVICES OF MUSKOKA
Att: Ivy Joynt
49 Pine Street
Bracebridge, ON P1L 1K8
Tel. 705-645-4426
Fax 705-645-1905
Email .... ivyjoynt@eas.gov.on.ca
Website .... www.cmho.org
Employer Background: Family, Youth and Child Services of Muskoka is an integrated agency, providing children's mental health services. *New Positions Created (3):* Service Team Supervisor; Director of Services; Service Team Supervisor.

FAMOUS PLAYERS INC.
Att: Andrea Rice, HR Department
16061 Macleod Trail SE, Suite 100
Calgary, AB T2Y 3S5
Fax 403-974-0478
Email .... jobs@famousplayers.ca
Website .... www.famousplayers.ca

Employer Background: Famous Players Inc. is one of the largest motion picture exhibitors in North America. *New Positions Created (2):* Theatre Managers; Theatre Managers.

FAMOUS PLAYERS INC.
Att: Human Resources
146 Bloor Street West
Toronto, ON M5S 1P3
Tel. 416-969-7800
Fax 416-964-5839
Email .... jobs@famousplayers.ca
Website .... www.famousplayers.ca
Employer Background: Famous Players Inc. is one of the largest motion picture exhibitors in North America. *New Positions Created (21):* Financial Accountant; Buyer; Computer Operator; Coordinator, Corporate Affairs; Human Resources Benefits Coordinator; Theatre / Food Service Manager; Accounts Payable Supervisor; Accounts Receivable Clerk; Administrative Assistant; Audit Verification Clerk; Theatre / Food Service Managers; Coordinator, Business Planning; Manager, Logistics; Senior Sales & Event Marketing Manager; Accounts Payable Clerk; Assistant Controller; Manager, Accounting Joint Ventures; Sales Accounting Analyst; Payroll Coordinator; Financial Accountant; Theatre / Food Service Managers.

FANSHAWE COLLEGE
Att: Human Resources
1460 Oxford Street East
Room B1056, PO Box 7005
London, ON N5Y 5R6
Tel. 519-452-4246
Fax 519-452-4481
Email .... jobs@fanshawec.on.ca
Website .... www.fanshawec.on.ca
Employer Background: Fanshawe College serves 14,000 full-time and 40,000 part-time students. *New Positions Created (3):* Chair, Health Sciences; Chair, Communication Arts; Manager, Library and Media Services.

FARAH FOODS / HASTY MARKET CORPORATION
Att: Human Resources
879 Cranberry Court
Oakville, ON L6L 6J7
Fax 905-847-7731
Email .... dmarks@farah-hasty.com
Website .... www.farah-hasty.com
Employer Background: Farah Foods / Hasty Market Corporation operates 100 convenience store outlets throughout Ontario. *New Positions Created (3):* Bookkeeper; Administration Assistant; Area Manager.

FARM BUSINESS CONSULTANTS INC.
Att: Mr. Diamond
2748 - 37th Avenue NE
Calgary, AB T1Y 5L3
Tel. 403-735-6105
Fax 403-735-5087
Email .... calgaryjobs@fbc.ca
Website .... www.fbc.ca

Employer Background: FBC is an agriculture tax consulting firm. *New Positions Created (3):* Sales Professional; Service Consultants; Sales Representative.

FARM CREDIT CANADA / FCC
Att: Human Resources
1800 Hamilton Street, PO Box 4320
Regina, SK S4P 4L3
Tel. 306-780-8100
Fax 306-780-5508
Email .... hr-rh@fcc-sca.ca
Website .... www.fcc-sca.ca
Employer Background: FCC is a federal Crown corporation providing financial services to Canada's farming community and agricultural industry. *New Positions Created (4):* General Counsel and Corporate Secretary; Director, Technology Services; Enterprise Architect; Bilingual Communications Consultant.

FASKEN MARTINEAU DUMOULIN LLP
Att: Ms P. Harvie
1075 West Georgia Street, Suite 2100
Vancouver, BC V6E 3G2
Tel. 604-631-3131
Fax 604-632-4757
Email .... pharvie@van.fasken.com
Website .... www.fasken.com
Employer Background: Fasken Martineau DuMoulin LLP is a national business and litigation law firm, with over 500 lawyers worldwide. *New Positions Created (3):* Intellectual Property Lawyer / Patent Agent; Senior Legal Assistant; Legal Secretaries.

FASKEN MARTINEAU DUMOULIN LLP
Att: Anthony F. Baldanza
TD Bank Tower, TD Centre
Suite 4200, PO Box 20
Toronto, ON M5K 1N6
Tel. 416-366-8381
Fax 416-364-7813
Email .... abaldanza@tor.fasken.com
Website .... www.fasken.com
Employer Background: Fasken Martineau DuMoulin LLP is a national business and litigation law firm, with over 500 lawyers worldwide. *New Positions Created (9):* Competition Lawyer; Junior / Intermediate Estates Law Clerk; Pension & Benefits Lawyers (2); Accounts Payable Clerk; Associate, Estate Planning Dept.; Mgr, Professional Personnel; Lawyers; Junior / Intermediate Estates Law Clerk; Trainer, Legal Secretaries.

FAST + EPP
Att: Human Resources Manager
1672 - 1st Avenue West, Suite 201
Vancouver, BC V6J 1G1
Fax 604-731-7620
Email .... mail@fastepp.com
Employer Background: Fast + Epp is a mid-sized structural engineering firm. *New Positions Created (2):* Structural CAD Technician; Structural Engineer.

FAUCHER INDUSTRIES INC.
Att: Human Resources Department

6363 des Grandes-Prairies Boulevard
St-Leonard, QC H1P 1A5

Tel. 514-321-2299
Fax 514-321-2333
Website .... www.faucher.ca

Employer Background: Founded in 1849, Faucher Industries Inc. supplies transportation and industrial hardware to the trucking industry. *New Positions Created (2):* Inside Sales Representative; External Warehouses Manager.

FAURECIA
Att: Human Resources
320 Norfinch Drive
Toronto, ON M3N 1Y4

Tel. 416-661-6995
Fax 416-661-3089
Website .... www.faurecia.com

Employer Background: Faurecia is a leading designer and manufacturer of high-tech seats and other automotive components, with over 150 production sites worldwide and operations in 27 countries. *New Positions Created (5):* Accountant; Millwright Journeyman; Production Supervisor; Scheduler; Tooling Engineers (2).

FCI CANADA INC.
Att: Human Resources Department
245 Renfrew Drive
Markham, ON L3R 6G3

Tel. 905-940-3288
Fax 905-940-0959
Email .... gdipaolo@fciconnect.com
Website .... www.fciconnect.com

Employer Background: FCI Canada Inc. (a division of Framatome Connectors International) is a supplier of electronic and electrical interconnection systems and fibre optic couplers. *New Positions Created (3):* Receptionist / Secretary; Quality Assurance Engineer; Logistics / Warehouse Supervisor.

FCX SPECIALTY VALVES
Att: Vice-President, Industrial Valve Sales
9423 - 41st Avenue NW
Edmonton, AB T6E 5X7

Tel. 780-434-8521
Fax 780-434-4289
Email .... employment@fcx-sv.com
Website . www.fcx-newmanhattersley.com

Employer Background: FCX Specialty Valves (formed by the merger of Newman Hattersley, NH Canada and FC Manufacturing) manufactures flow control solutions for the power and marine industries. *New Positions Created (2):* Valve Specialist; Valve Specialist.

FCX SPECIALTY VALVES
Att: Human Resources
2400 Lucknow Drive, Suite 48
Mississauga, ON L5S 1T9

Tel. 905-678-1240
Fax 905-678-7891
Email .... employment@fcx-sv.com
Website . www.fcx-newmanhattersley.com

Employer Background: FCX Specialty Valves (formed by the merger of Newman

Hattersley, NH Canada and FC Manufacturing) manufactures flow control solutions for the power and marine industries. *New Positions Created (4):* Design Engineer; Supply and Inventory Administrator; Valve Specialist, Atlantic; Vice-President, Specialty Sales.

FDM SOFTWARE LTD.
Att: Human Resources Manager
4681 Highland Boulevard
North Vancouver, BC V7R 3A6

Tel. 604-986-9941
Fax 604-986-7130
Email .... fdm@fdmsoft.com
Website .... www.fdmsoft.com

Employer Background: FDM Software Ltd. provides management and dispatch software solutions for the fire, emergency medical and law enforcement sectors. *New Positions Created (5):* Sales / Distributor Positions; Software Engineers; Support Training Specialist; Receptionist / Administrative Position; Software Support / Training Professionals.

FEDERAL EXPRESS CANADA / FEDEX
Att: Human Resources Manager
5985 Explorer Drive
Mississauga, ON L4W 5K6

Tel. 905-897-9322
Fax 905-212-5653
Email .... jtonna@fedex.com
Website .... www.fedex.com

Employer Background: Federal Express Canada is a subsidiary of the world's largest courier company. In Canada, FedEx operates a domestic air network that includes four Boeing-727s and feeder airlift, providing next-day coast-to-coast service. *New Positions Created (2):* District Fleet Manager; Senior Marketing Specialist, Forecasting.

FEDERATED CO-OPERATIVES LIMITED / FCL
Att: Human Resources Manager
2626 - 10th Avenue NE
PO Box 2599, Station M
Calgary, AB T2P 2P4

Fax 403-531-2275
Email .... hr@fcl.ca
Website .... www.fcl.ca

Employer Background: FCL provides manufacturing, wholesaling and merchandising services to over 300 retail cooperatives. *New Positions Created (4):* Human Resources Officer; Dispatcher, Traffic Department; Warehouse Material Handlers; Warehouse Clerk.

FEDERATED CO-OPERATIVES LIMITED / FCL
Att: Wholesale Recruitment Director
PO Box 1050
Saskatoon, SK S7K 3M9

Tel. 306-244-3311
Fax 306-244-3403
Email .... hr@fcl.ca
Website .... www.fcl.ca

Employer Background: FCL provides manufacturing, wholesaling and merchandising

services to over 300 retail cooperatives. *New Positions Created (8):* Convenience Store Director; Human Resources Officer; Warehouse Supervisor; Maintenance Supervisor; Regional Transportation Supervisor; Bakery Co-ordinator; Regional Meat Sales Coordinator; Regional General Merchandise Sales Coordinator.

FEDERATED INSURANCE COMPANY OF CANADA
Att: Doug Overwater,
Director of Field Operations
2443 Pegasus Road NE
Calgary, AB T2E 8C3

Fax 403-254-8806
Email .... doug.overwater@federated.ca
Website .... www.federated.ca

Employer Background: Federated Insurance Company of Canada (a subsidiary of Fairfax Financial Holdings Ltd.) offers property, automobile, general liability, life and health insurance products. *New Positions Created (3):* Commercial Risk Analyst; Claims Adjuster; Claims Examiner.

FEDERATED INSURANCE COMPANY OF CANADA
Att: Donna Sprague
717 Portage Avenue, PO Box 5800
Winnipeg, MB R3C 3C9

Tel. 204-786-6431
Fax 204-784-6755
Email .... donna.sprague@federated.ca
Website .... www.federated.ca

Employer Background: Federated Insurance Company of Canada (a subsidiary of Fairfax Financial Holdings Ltd.) offers property, automobile, general liability, life and health insurance products. *New Positions Created (4):* In-House Legal Counsel; Field Risk Analyst; Senior Risk Analyst; Claims Adjuster.

FEDERATION CJA
Att: Director of Human Resources
1 Carre Cummings Square
Montréal, QC H3W 1M6

Tel. 514-345-3541
Fax 514-345-6464
Website .... www.federationcja.org

Employer Background: Federation CJA is the central fundraising and community service coordinating body of Montreal's Jewish community. *New Positions Created (6):* Human Resources Associate; Coordinator of Community Services; HVAC Maintenance Person; Fundraiser; Communications & Marketing Director; Planning Associate.

FEDERATION OF CANADIAN MUNICIPALITIES / FCM
Att: Patrick Rosemond, HR Manager
24 Clarence Street
Ottawa, ON K1N 5P3

Tel. 613-241-5221
Fax 613-241-7440
Email .... prosemond@fcm.ca
Website .... www.fcm.ca

Employer Background: Founded in 1901, FCM is Canada's national association of municipal governments. *New Positions Created (6):* Senior Manager, Program Development; Information Manager; Project Officer; Senior Advisor, Communications; Web Editor, Corporate Development Department; Managing Editor, Forum.

FEDNAV INTERNATIONAL LTD.
Att: Human Resources Department
1000 de la Gauchetiere West, Suite 3500
Montréal, QC H3B 4W5
Tel. 514-878-6500
Fax 514-878-6642
Website .... www.fednav.com
Employer Background: Fednav International Ltd. is an international shipping company. *New Positions Created (2):* Chartering Broker Trainee; Fleet Operator.

FEKETE ASSOCIATES INC.
Att: Manager of Geology
540 - 5th Avenue SW, Suite 2000
Calgary, AB T2P 0M2
Tel. 403-213-4200
Fax 403-213-4298
Email .... fast@fekete.com
Website .... www.fekete.com
Employer Background: Fekete Associates Inc. is an independent, international petroleum consulting firm dedicated to total reservoir management. *New Positions Created (5):* Geological Technologist; Petroleum Engineer / Technologist; Senior Engineer; Senior Programmers (2); Well Test Analyst.

FELLFAB LIMITED
Att: Human Resources Manager
2343 Barton Street East
Hamilton, ON L8E 5V8
Tel. 905-560-9230
Fax 905-560-9846
Website .... www.fellfab.com
Employer Background: Fellfab Limited manufactures engineered textile products. *New Positions Created (4):* Material Handler; Plant Manager; Buyer; Production Technologist.

FEMME DE CARRIÈRE
Att: Mylene
225 Chabanel West, Suite 504
Montréal, QC H2N 2C9
Tel. 514-384-6706
Fax 514-384-9533
Employer Background: Femme de Carriere is a women's fashion chain store. *New Positions Created (5):* Various Retail Positions; Sweater Technician; Various Retail Positions; Garment Technicians; Graphic Artist.

FERGUSON SIMEK CLARK / FSC
Att: Sherry-Lynn Lester
10417 Saskatchewan Drive
Edmonton, AB T6E 4R8
Tel. 780-439-0090
Fax 780-439-1158
Website .... www.fsc.ca
Employer Background: FSC is a Yellowknife-based firm of consulting engineers and ar-

chitects specializing in remote, cold regions technology. *New Positions Created (3):* Electrical Engineer; Electrical Engineering Technologists; Mechanical Building System / HVAC Engineer.

FERNLEA FLOWERS LTD.
Att: Human Resources Manager
RR 3, PO Box 126
Delhi, ON N4B 2W9
Fax 519-582-1631
Email .... personnel@fernlea.com
Website .... www.fernlea.com
Employer Background: Established in 1939, Fernlea Flowers Ltd. is a large producer of holiday crops and bedding plants. *New Positions Created (3):* Canadian Sales Account Representative; Corporate Sales Administrator; Logistics Coordinator Assistant.

FERRERO CANADA LTD.
Att: Human Resources
100 Sheppard Avenue East
Toronto, ON M2N 6N5
Tel. 416-590-0747
Fax 416-590-0894
Website .... www.ferrero.ca
Employer Background: Ferrero Canada Ltd. is a leading confectionery company. *New Positions Created (3):* Retail Panel Supervisor; Assistant; Junior A/R and A/P Clerk.

FERSTEN GROUP
Att: Diana Iacobacci
9494 St. Lawrence Boulevard
Montréal, QC H2N 1P4
Tel. 514-384-7462
Fax 514-384-0058
Email .... diana@ferstengroup.com
Website .... www.ferstengroup.com
Employer Background: Fersten Group (formerly Baranda Clothing Company) manufactures children's dresses and sportswear. *New Positions Created (2):* Collections & Receivables Position; Senior Patternmaker.

FESTO INC.
Att: Human Resources Manager
5300 Explorer Drive
Mississauga, ON L4W 5G4
Tel. 905-624-9000
Fax 905-624-9001
Website .... www.festo.com
Employer Background: Festo Inc. is a global manufacturer of industrial automation components and systems. *New Positions Created (5):* Production Supervisor; Assembler; Machine Operator / General Machinist; Outside Technical Sales Representative; Customer Service Representative.

FGI
Att: Ivona Kluza, Human Resources
1599 Hurontario Street, Suite 300
Mississauga, ON L5G 4S1
Tel. 905-278-6065
Fax 905-278-5950
Email .... ikluza@fgiworld.com
Website .... www.fgiworld.com

Employer Background: FGI is a provider of human support services, including employee or family assistance programs, global relocation services, disability intervention and wellness education. *New Positions Created (4):* Generalist, Human Resources; Bilingual Customer Service Representatives; Bilingual Client Care Representatives; Supervisor Clinical Quality EFAP / EAP.

FGI
Att: Human Resources
10 Commerce Valley Drive East, Suite 200
Thornhill, ON L3T 7N7
Tel. 905-886-2157
Fax 905-886-4337
Email .... info@fgiworld.com
Website .... www.fgiworld.com
Employer Background: FGI is a provider of human support services, including employee or family assistance programs, global relocation services, disability intervention and wellness education. *New Positions Created (6):* Associates, Clinical Services; Cross-Cultural Trainers; Account Manager, Employee Assistance Programs; Administrative Positions; Intake Counsellor; Family Care Specialist.

FIBEREX GLASS CORPORATION
Att: Fred A. Atiq, Chairman and CEO
6602 - 45th Street
Leduc, AB T9E 7C9
Tel. 780-980-1300
Fax 780-980-1330
Email .... atiq@fiberexglass.com
Website .... www.fiberexglass.com
Employer Background: Established in 1997, Fiberex Glass Corporation manufactures glass fibres used to manufacture fibreglass products such as boats, tanks, fibre optic cables, construction materials and automotive parts. *New Positions Created (2):* Finance Mgr; Manager, Financial Services.

FIDELITY INVESTMENTS CANADA LIMITED
Att: Human Resources
250 Yonge Street, Suite 700
Toronto, ON M5B 2L7
Tel. 416-307-5300
Fax 416-307-5520
Email .... canada.resumes@fidelity.com
Website .... www.fidelity.ca
Employer Background: Fidelity Investments Canada Limited is Canada's fourth-largest mutual fund company and part of the Fidelity Investments organization of Boston. *New Positions Created (59):* Analyst, Decision Support Systems, FISCo; Application Support Analyst, FISCo; Platform Manager, FISCo Platform; Team Leader, Dealer Services Support; Trust Accountant; Client Manager; Business Systems Analyst, Client Platform; Business Systems Analyst, Client Services; Program Manager, Program Management Office; Senior Project Manager; Senior Software Developer; Systems Analyst, Front-End Development; Dealer Services Representative, FISCo; Dealer Services Specialist, FISCo; Dealer Services Support Rep-

resentative, FISCo; Director, Staffing; Director, Systems Administration and Support; Financial Analyst; Internal Sales Support Coordinator; Manager, Account Administration, FISCo; Manager, Treasury Services; Senior Programmer Analyst, Systems; Senior Unix Administrator; Technical Architect, FISCo; Application Support Analyst; Banking and Payments Representative; Dealer Compensation Representative; Director, Client Projects; Legal Assistant; Manager, Securities Support; Pension Compliance Coordinator; Reconciliations Representative; Regulatory Accountant; Securities Data Coordinator; Settlements Representative; Administrative Assistant, FISCo; Analyst, Product Development; Client Manager; Database Administrator, Sybase; Database Administrator, UDB; Financial Analysts II (2); Internal Sales Support Coordinator; Manager, Cash Operations; Manager, Controls and Reconciliation; Manager, Systems Support; Programmer Analyst, Front-End Development; Project Manager, Front-End Development; Project Manager, Systems Development; Systems Analyst; Bilingual Customer Service Representative; Business Systems Analyst, FISCo Platform; Corporate Actions Project Leader; Director, Investment Management Services; Internet Project Manager, e-Business; Manager, Financial Analysis; Program Officer, Project Management Office; Systems Analyst, Front-End Development; Technical Consultant, Client Systems; Web Administrator, Internet Development and Tech.

FIELD AVIATION WEST LTD.
Att: Elaine Dixon, Personnel Manager
PO Box 3186, Station B
Calgary, AB T2M 4L7

Tel. 403-275-8200
Fax 403-516-8281
Email .... edixon@fieldav.com
Website .... www.fieldav.com

Employer Background: Field Aviation West Ltd., a wholly-owned subsidiary of Hunting PLC, is one of Canada's leading aircraft sales and service organizations. *New Positions Created (11):* Avionics Engineer; Avionics Technologist; Structures / Systems Engineer; Structures / Systems Technologist; Aircraft Inspectors; Aircraft Interior Refinishers; Aircraft Maintenance 'M' Engineers; Aircraft Records Auditors; Composite Technicians, 'S' Licenced; Machinist, Journeyman Level; Maintenance Planners.

FIELDS STORES
Att: Diane Barham
3751 Viking Way
Richmond, BC V6V 1W1

Tel. 604-276-4520
Fax 604-276-4521
Email .... diane.barham@fields.ca
Website .... http:www.hbc.com

Employer Background: Fields Stores, a division of the Hudson's Bay Company, is a chain of value-priced general merchandise stores. *New Positions Created (3):* Fashion Buyer; Intermediate Payroll Associate; Production Layout Artist.

FIELDSTONE DAY SCHOOL / FDS
Att: Mr. D. Butcher, Director
65 Sheldrake Boulevard
Toronto, ON M4P 2B1

Tel. 416-487-7381
Fax 416-487-8190
Website ...... www.fieldstonedayschool.org

Employer Background: FDS is an independent school for boys and girls from kindergarten to grade 10. *New Positions Created (2):* Teachers (4); Teachers.

FIERA FOODS COMPANY
Att: Human Resources
220 Norelco Drive
Toronto, ON M9L 1S4

Tel. 416-744-1010
Fax 416-744-8250
Email .... agunn@fierafoods.com
Website .... www.fierafoods.com

Employer Background: Fiera Foods Company manufactures frozen and fresh bakery products. *New Positions Created (10):* Project Manager; Marketing Coordinator; Vice-President, Operations; Vice-President, Research & Development; Quality Assurance Technical Systems Coordinator / QA Supervisor; Marketing Manager; New Business Developer; Plant Manager, Bakery; Retail Bakery Sales Manager; Human Resources Coordinator.

FIESTA BARBEQUES LIMITED
Att: Human Resources Manager
2 Walker Drive
Brampton, ON L6T 5E1

Tel. 905-791-3200
Fax 905-896-2203
Website .... www.fiestabbq.com

Employer Background: Fiesta Barbeques Limited is one of Canada's leading consumer products companies and one of North America's fastest-growing gas barbeque manufacturers. *New Positions Created (4):* Credit Analyst; Export Coordinator; Materials Manager; Bilingual Customer Service Manager.

FIFTH DIMENSION INFORMATION SYSTEMS INC.
Att: Jennifer McDonald
Suite 500, Merrill Lynch Tower
Edmonton Centre
Edmonton, AB T5J 2Z2

Tel. 780-440-6560
Fax 780-420-6562
Email .... careers@fifthd.ca
Website .... www.fifthd.ca

Employer Background: Fifth Dimension Information Systems Inc. develops, implements and supports biopharmaceutical software. *New Positions Created (4):* Customer Support Team Leader; Software Quality Assurance Specialist; Compliance Specialist; Systems Analyst.

FILAMENT COMMUNICATIONS
Att: Human Resources Manager
126 York Street, Suite 500
Ottawa, ON K1N 5T5

Tel. 613-241-7200
Fax 613-241-7157
Website .... www.filamentinc.com

Employer Background: Filament Communications is a web design agency. *New Positions Created (6):* Art Director; GUI Designer; Interactive Media Developer; Project Manager; Senior Copywriter / Journalist; Web Developer.

FILTEL MICROWAVE INC.
Att: Human Resources Department
342 Aime-Vincent
Vaudreuil-Dorion, QC J7V 5V5

Fax 450-424-5819

Employer Background: Filtel Microwave Inc. manufactures telecom devices. *New Positions Created (6):* CNC Operator; Supervisor, Machine Shop; Quality Assurance Manager; Production Planner; Assembly Line Position; Supervisor.

FILTRAN MICROCIRCUITS INC.
Att: Human Resources Department
2475 Don Reid Drive
Ottawa, ON K1H 1E2

Tel. 613-737-0706
Fax 613-737-0495
Email .... fmi@filtranmicro.com
Website .... www.filtranmicro.com

Employer Background: Filtran Microcircuits Inc. manufactures precision microwave circuitry. *New Positions Created (2):* Human Resources Administrator; Materials Manager.

FINANCIAL INSTITUTIONS COMMISSION / FICOM
Att: Gerry Miss Omness
1050 West Pender Street, Suite 1900
Vancouver, BC V6E 3S7

Tel. 604-660-4809
Fax 604-660-3170
Website .... www.fic.gov.bc.ca

Employer Background: FICOM, an agency of the provincial government, works to safeguard consumers against improper market conduct in the financial services and real estate industries. *New Positions Created (9):* Manager, Investigations; Manager, Credit Unions and Trust Companies; Datapath Designer; Intermediate and Senior Data Test Engineer; Manager, Investigations; Superintendent and Chief Executive Officer; Manager, Mortgage Compliance; Managers, Real Estate (2); Registration Officer.

FINANCIAL SERVICES COMMISSION OF ONTARIO / FSCO
Att: Human Resources Unit
5160 Yonge Street, 16th Floor, Box 85
Toronto, ON M2N 6L9

Fax 416-590-7272
Website .... www.ontarioinsurance.com

Employer Background: FSCO regulates insurance, pensions, credit unions, caisses populaires, cooperatives, mortgage brokers and loan and trust companies. *New Positions Created (23):* Web Editor; Complaints Coordinator; Licensing Clerks; Policy Analyst; Systems Analyst, Telecom; Manager, Business Solutions & Operational Support; Manager, Business Solutions; Senior Actuarial Analyst; Human Resources Coordinator; Senior Policy Analyst; Production Assistant; Coordinator, Administrative & Support Services; Rate Analyst; Licensing Clerks; Mediator; Receptionist; Data Capture Clerks; Mediators; Principal Examiner; Legal Counsel; Manager, Client Operations and Administration; Legal Secretary; Legal Secretary to the Director.

FINANCIAL TRANSACTIONS AND REPORTS ANALYSIS CENTRE OF CANADA / FINTRAC
Att: Human Resources Manager
234 Laurier Avenue West
Ottawa, ON K1P 1H7
Tel. 613-943-3091
Fax 613-943-7931
Email .... jobs-emplois@fintrac.gc.ca
Website .... www.fintrac.gc.ca
Employer Background: FINTRAC is an independent agency with a mandate to collect, analyze, assess and disclose information in order to assist in the detection, prevention and deterrence of money laundering. *New Positions Created (3):* Analysts; Compliance Officers; Liaison Officers.

FINCENTRIC CORP.
Att: IT Recruiter
13571 Commerce Parkway, Suite 200
Richmond, BC V6V 2R2
Tel. 604-278-6470
Fax 604-214-4900
Email .... careers@fincentric.com
Website .... www.fincentric.com
Employer Background: Established in 1984, Fincentric Corp. (formerly Prologic Corp.) develops software solutions for the global financial services industry. Their products are used in over 350 financial institutions worldwide. *New Positions Created (79):* Administrative Assistant, Product Development; Software Tester, Banking; Course Developer; Public Relations Manager, Sales & Marketing; Technical Writer; Applications Programmer, Customer Services; Business Analyst, Product Development; Partner Systems Integration Manager, Product Development; R&D Programmer, Product Development; Applications Developer; Gateway Developers; Load Test Engineer; Product Manager; Investor Relations Manager; Projects Issue Coordinator; Receptionist; Senior Marketing Communications Specialist; Software Engineers, Gateway (3); Wireless Developer; Business Systems Analyst - IT, Product Development; Course Developer (2); i-Wealthview Banking Operations Developer; Marketing Events Specialist; Project Controller, Professional Services; Public Relations Manager; R & D Programmer - IWDK, Product Development; Applications Developer; Applications Programmer; Channel Sales Director; Contracts Manager; Courseware Developer; Gateway Developers; i-WealthView Banking Developer's Kit Maintenance Programmer; i-WealthView Developer's Kit Programmer; iWMS Build

Master; Product Manager; Sales Support Specialist, Product Development; Senior Web Developer; Software Test Engineer; Solutions Architect; Administrative Assistant; i-Wealthview Personal Portal Developer, Product Development; Junior Technical Writer, Product Development; Partner Systems Integration Specialist, Product Development ; Payroll Administrator; Sales Operation Controller; Sales Support, Technical Specialist; Software Engineers, Gateways (3); Technical Business Analyst; Wealth Management Consultant, Account Services; Wireless Developer, Product Development; Technical Writer, Web Applications; Application Programmer (Maintenance); Applications Developer; Applications Programmer (Customer Services); Business Analyst; Channel Sales Director ; Contracts Manager; Courseware / Certification Developer; Customer Support Analyst; Director of Taxation; Gateway Developers; i-Wealthview Developer's Kit Programmer; iWBDK Maintenance Programmer; Partner Marketing Specialist; Senior Web Developer / Architect; Software Test Engineer Lead; Software Tester; Solutions Architect (Applications Integration); Technology Specialist; Tools Implementer; Training Instructor; Banking Application Developers; Product Manager, Wealth Management Systems; Programmer, i-Wealthview Developer's Kit; Project Managers; Software Development Manager, i-Wealthview Banking; Software Development Manager, i-Wealthview Web Portal; Software Engineers, Gateways.

FINNING (CANADA) INTERNATIONAL INC.
Att: Human Resources Manager
16830 - 107th Avenue
Edmonton, AB T5P 4C3
Tel. 780-930-4800
Fax 780-930-4810
Email .... jobline@finning.ca
Website .... www.finning.ca
Employer Background: Finning (Canada) International Inc. is a large heavy equipment dealer. *New Positions Created (2):* Service Management Positions; Associate Human Resources Manager.

FIRECO INC.
Att: Vice-President, Finance and Controller
1280 Courtney Park Drive East
Mississauga, ON L5T 1N6
Tel. 905-670-2790
Fax 905-670-0883
Employer Background: Fireco Inc. is a leading distributor of general merchandise, serving over 4,500 retail outlets. The company has 400 employees. *New Positions Created (4):* Human Resources Manager; Customer Service Supervisor; Inventory Pricing Analyst; Senior Accountant.

FIREFLY BOOKS LTD.
Att: Valerie Hatton
3680 Victoria Park Avenue
Toronto, ON M2H 3K1
Tel. 416-499-8412

Fax 416-499-1142
Email .... valerie@fireflybooks.com
Website .... www.fireflybooks.com
Employer Background: Firefly Books Ltd. is a trade publisher of nature, science and gardening books, children's books and calendars. *New Positions Created (2):* Publicist; Rights and Contracts Manager.

FIREPLACE PRODUCTS INTERNATIONAL / FPI
Att: Susan Milne, HR Manager
6988 Venture Street
Delta, BC V4G 1H4
Tel. 604-946-5155
Fax 604-946-0479
Email .... smilne@regency-fire.com
Website .... www.regency-fire.com
Employer Background: Founded in 1979, FPI develops and manufactures wood fireplaces, gas stoves and fireplace inserts. *New Positions Created (5):* Account Executive; Industrial Engineer; Inventory Control Clerk; Marketing Administrator; Traffic Coordinator.

FIRM TRANSPORTATION & DISTRIBUTION SERVICES
Att: D. Firman
20 Holly Street, Suite 100
Toronto, ON M4S 3B1
Tel. 416-486-3476
Fax 416-486-9981
Email ..... dfirman@firmtransportation.com
Website ...... www.firmtransportation.com
Employer Background: Firm Transportation & Distribution Services is a transportation and freight shipping company. *New Positions Created (6):* Sales Executive / Inside Sales Representative; Customer Service Representative; Dispatcher; Transportation Operations Manager; Customer Service Manager; Dispatcher.

FIRST AIR
Att: Human Resources
3257 Carp Road
Carp, ON K0A 1L0
Tel. 613-839-3340
Fax 613-839-2388
Email .... recruit@firstair.ca
Website .... www.firstair.ca
Employer Background: First Air, Canada's third-largest scheduled airline, specializes in travel throughout Nunavut, the Northwest Territories, northern Quebec and Greenland. *New Positions Created (5):* B727 and B737 SIM Instructors; Director of Organizational Development; Stockkeepers and Driver; Airport Customer Service Agents; Flight Attendants.

FIRST CANADIAN TITLE COMPANY
Att: Human Resources Department
1290 Central Parkway West, Suite 900
Mississauga, ON L5C 4R3
Tel. 905-566-0425
Fax 905-566-5072
Email .... hr.on@firstam.com
Website .... www.firstcanadiantitle.com

Employer Background: First Canadian Title Company, a subsidiary of First American Title Insurance Company, provides title insurance on property transfers. *New Positions Created (27):* Customer Service Specialists; Document Programmers; Law Clerk / Analyst; Law Clerk / Title Underwriter; Legal Counsel; Programmer Analysts; Quality Assurance Testers and Scripters; Help Desk Specialist; Lender Services Administrator; Legal Customer Service Specialists; Document Programmer; Senior Corporate Law Clerk; Supervisor, Operations; Recruitment Specialist; Legal Customer Service Specialist; Administrative Assistant; Account Manager; Commercial Real Estate Lawyer; Senior Law Clerk; Legal Assistants; Administrative Assistant; Human Resources Specialist; Accounts Receivable Clerk; Legal Assistants; Sales Assistant; Receptionist; Senior Title Underwriter / Law Clerk.

FIRST CELLULAR
Att: Human Resources Manager
1566 Carling Avenue
Ottawa, ON K1Z 7M4

Tel. 613-724-1177
Fax 613-761-0437
Website .... www.firstcellular.ca

Employer Background: First Cellular is Bell World's largest Ottawa / Hull agent of cellular telephones. *New Positions Created (2):* Sales Representatives; Controller.

FIRST MEDIA GROUP INC.
Att: Human Resources Manager
536 Kipling Avenue
Toronto, ON M8Z 5E3

Fax 416-252-1644

Employer Background: First Media Group Inc. is a telecom company. *New Positions Created (3):* Call Centre Representatives; Call Centre Supervisors; Marketing Assistants, Media Research and Development.

FIRST PROFESSIONAL MANAGEMENT INC.
Att: Cindy Hogarth, Human Resources
259 Yorkland Road, Suite 300
Toronto, ON M2J 5B2

Tel. 416-493-9112
Fax 416-753-7641
Email .... chogarth@firstpro.com
Website .... www.firstpro.com

Employer Background: First Professional Management Inc. is a national developer of retail shopping centres. *New Positions Created (12):* Associate Counsel; Project Engineer; Senior Engineer; Leasing Representative; Receptionist / Clerical Assistant; Commercial Leasing Lawyer; Leasing Administrative Assistant; Office Administrator; Project Manager, Construction; Development Coordinator; Commercial Real Estate Law Clerk; Commercial Real Estate Lawyer.

FIRST PROFESSIONAL MANAGEMENT INC.
Att: Russ Goto, Director of Construction
2720 Queensview Drive
Ottawa, ON K2B 1A5

Fax 613-721-2201
Email .... rgoto@ott.firstpro.com
Website .... www.firstpro.com

Employer Background: First Professional Management Inc. is a national developer of retail shopping centres. *New Positions Created (2):* Administrative Assistant; Project Manager.

FISHER & LUDLOW
Att: Human Resources
750 Appleby Line, PO Box 5025
Burlington, ON L7R 3Y8

Tel. 905-632-2121
Fax 905-632-6295
Website .... www.fisherludlow.com

Employer Background: Established in 1954, Fisher & Ludlow is manufacturer of steel gratings. *New Positions Created (4):* Cost Accountant; Technical Inside Sales Representative; Cost Accountant; Outside Sales Representative.

FISHER SCIENTIFIC
Att: Human Resources Department
112 Colonnade Road
Nepean, ON K2E 7L6

Tel. 613-226-3273
Fax 613-226-2812
Email .... resume@fishersci.ca
Website .... www.fishersci.ca

Employer Background: Fisher Scientific is a leading distributor of laboratory systems in Canada. *New Positions Created (5):* Account Representative; Account Representatives; Customer Service Representatives; Field Service Representatives; Sales Representatives.

FISKARS CANADA INC.
Att: Human Resources Department
201 Whitehall Drive, Suite 1
Markham, ON L3R 9Y3

Fax 905-940-8469
Email .... hrcanada@fiskars.com
Website .... www.fiskars.com

Employer Background: Fiskars Canada Inc. provides consumer products for the garden, home, office, school, craft and recreational markets. *New Positions Created (3):* Customer Service Supervisor; Product Manager; Sales Administrator / Executive Assistant.

FLIGHT DYNAMICS CORP.
Att: Human Resources Manager
4 Chemin de l'Aeroport
St-Jean-sur-Richelieu, QC J3B 5B7

Tel. 450-357-1992
Fax 450-357-1194
Email .... pepinm@adv-aero.com

Employer Background: Flight Dynamics Corp. is an engineering and composite development company. *New Positions Created (9):* Certified Welder; CNC Machinist; Composite Technician, Lay-Up and Tooling; Test Plan Engineer; CAD Draftsperson; Composite Supervisor; Engineering Manager; Test Plan Writer; Aeronautical Engineers.

FLIGHTSAFETY CANADA
Att: Mike McKenna, Director of Standards
95 Garratt Boulevard
Toronto, ON M3K 2A5

Tel. 416-638-9313
Fax 416-638-3348
Email ...... careers@fsi033.flightsafety.com
Website .... www.flightsafety.com

Employer Background: FlightSafety Canada provides factory-authorized pilot and maintenance technician training for the deHavilland Dash 8, Dash 7 and Twin Otter aircraft. *New Positions Created (3):* Simulator / Ground Instructors; Customer Support Manager; Product Marketing Manager.

FLINT ENERGY SERVICES LTD.
Att: Human Resources Department
2899 Broadmoor Boulevard, Suite 100
Sherwood Park, AB T8H 1B5

Tel. 780-416-3400
Fax 780-416-8078
Email .... hr@flint-energy.com
Website .... www.flint-energy.com

Employer Background: Flint Energy Services Ltd. provides integrated infrastructure services to the energy and resource industries. *New Positions Created (12):* Construction Superintendent; Estimator; Project Manager; Senior Project Manager; Field Safety Personnel; Safety Advisor, MacKay River Project; Aboriginal & Community Affairs Consultant; Estimator; Project Manager / Assistant Project Manager; Site Coordinator; Site Maintenance Coordinator; Site Office Manager.

FLINT ENERGY SERVICES LTD.
Att: Human Resources Manager
7261 - 18th Street
Edmonton, AB T6P 1N1

Fax 780-440-6485
Email .... hr@flint-energy.com
Website .... www.flint-energy.com

Employer Background: Flint Energy Services Ltd. provides integrated infrastructure services to the energy and resource industries. *New Positions Created (3):* Operator / Supervisor, Chemical Cleaning; Job Cost Accountant; Management Accountant.

FLINT ENERGY SERVICES LTD.
Att: Human Resources Department
4747 - 78A Street Close
Red Deer, AB T4P 2G9

Tel. 403-342-6280
Fax 403-309-0737
Email .... reddeer.hr@flint-energy.com
Website .... www.flintenergy.com

Employer Background: Flint Energy Services provides integrated infrastructure services to the energy and resource industries. *New Positions Created (3):* Power Systems Control Technician; High Voltage Testing Technician; Journeyman Trade Positions.

FLOW DRILLING ENGINEERING LTD.
Att: Human Resources Manager
1228 Kingston Road NW, Suite 308
Calgary, AB T2N 3P7

Employer Background: FDEL is an engineering company that offers a unique perspective on applying underbalanced drilling technology. *New Positions Created (3):* HS&E Specialist; Operations Positions; Technical Personnel.

FLOWSERVE INC.
Att: Human Resources
130 Edward Street
St. Thomas, ON N5P 1Z1
Fax 519-631-4609
Email .... canada-hr@flowserve.com
Website .... www.flowserve.com
Employer Background: Flowserve Inc. provides industrial flow management services and produces engineered pumps, mechanical seals, valves and actuators for various industries. *New Positions Created (5):* General Machinist; Sales Engineer; Mechanical Engineer; Millwrights; Sales Engineer.

FLOWSERVE INC.
Att: Human Resources
120 Vinyl Court
Woodbridge, ON L4L 4A3
Tel. 905-856-1140
Fax 905-856-3605
Email .... canada-hr@flowserve.com
Website .... www.flowserve.com
Employer Background: Flowserve Inc. provides industrial flow management services and produces engineered pumps, mechanical seals, valves and actuators. *New Positions Created (2):* Millwright; Welder.

FLUID LIFE CORP.
Att: Human Resources Manager
9321 - 48th Street
Edmonton, AB T6B 2R4
Tel. 780-462-2400
Fax 780-462-2420
Website .... www.fluidlife.com
Employer Background: Established in 1982, Fluid Life Corp. (formerly Industra Lube Testing Laboratories) is one of Canada's leading oil analysis laboratories. *New Positions Created (3):* Controller; Lab Supervisor; Lab Technician.

FLUID MOTION TECHNOLOGIES
Att: Human Resources Manager
2565 Rena Road
Mississauga, ON L4T 1G6
Tel. 905-676-9132
Fax 905-676-0293
Email .... jobs@reainternational.com
Website .... www.reainternational.com
Employer Background: Fluid Motion Technologies, a division of REA International, supplies fluid handling systems to the automotive industry. *New Positions Created (3):* Materials Manager; Production Supervisor; Quality Engineer / Technologist.

FLUOR CANADA LTD.
Att: People Services Department
55 Sunpark Plaza SE
Calgary, AB T2X 3R4
Tel. 403-259-1110

Fax 403-537-5044
Email .... calgary.hr@fluor.com
Website .... www.fluorcanada.ca
Employer Background: Fluor Canada Ltd., the Canadian division of Fluor Corporation, provides complete engineering, procurement, construction management and maintenance services. *New Positions Created (43):* Contracts Managers; Intermediate Programmer / Analyst; Intermediate / Senior Analysts; Design Applications Senior Systems Analyst; Design Applications Support Specialist; Design Applications Systems Analyst; Lead Process Engineer; Sales / Business Development Associate, AMECO; ASME Pressure Welders; Various Trade / Technician Positions (4); Senior Financial Accountant; Citrix Administrator; Peripheral Support Technician; Senior Metallurgist; Senior Metallurgist Engineer; HR Technician; Electrical Design Engineer; IT Planner, Intermediate; Lead Area Coordinator; Intermediate and Senior Estimators; Intermediate and Senior Planners; Materials Handling Engineers; Oilsands Process Engineers; Pressure Vessels Designers; Civil Structural Designers; Civil Structural Engineers; Contracts Managers; Electrical Engineers and Designers; Instrumentation and Controls Engineers and Designers; Intermediate and Senior Process Engineers; Intermediate Desktop Technician; Intermediate Notes 4.6 Administrator; Junior Network Administrator; Material Manager; Pipe Stress Engineers; Piping Designers, 3D PDS; Piping Materials Engineers; Pressure Vessel Engineers; Senior Contracts Administrators; Various Information Technology Positions; Intermediate / Senior Application Developer or Programmer; Senior Project Cost Control Specialists; Intermediate or Senior Process Engineer.

FLUOR CONSTRUCTORS CANADA LTD.
Att: Human Resources
8921 - 50th Street
Edmonton, AB T6B 1E7
Tel. 780-440-6633
Fax 780-440-6813
Email .... fccl.calgary@fluor.com
Website .... www.fluor.com
Employer Background: Fluor Constructors Canada Ltd. is an enterprise of Fluor Corporation, one of the world's largest publicly-owned consulting, engineering, construction, maintenance and diversified business services companies. *New Positions Created (4):* ASME Pressure Welders; Steamfitter / Pipefitter; Instrumentation Mechanics and Technicians; Piping Superintendents.

FOCUS BUSINESS SOLUTIONS INC.
Att: Human Resources Manager
1209 - 59th Avenue SE, Suite 150
Calgary, AB T2H 2P6
Tel. 403-255-5900
Fax 403-253-5944
Email .... hr@focusbusiness.com
Website .... www.focusbusiness.com
Employer Background: Focus Business Solutions Inc. implements technical solutions to address common business problems.

New Positions Created (2): Business System Consultant; Intermediate / Senior Network Analyst.

FOCUS CORPORATION LTD., THE
Att: Brenda Moren, HR Manager
9925 - 109th Street, Suite 1000
Edmonton, AB T5K 2J8
Tel. 780-466-6555
Fax 780-468-6175
Email .... dcarroll@focus.ca
Website .... www.focus.ca
Employer Background: The Focus Corporation Ltd. provides quality geomatics and engineering services to clients throughout Canada and around the world. *New Positions Created (6):* Professional Land Surveyors; GPS & Data Mgmnt Position; Senior Land Development Designer; Senior Survey Layout / Field Inspector; Windows NT Network Administrator; Land Management Staff.

FOCUS FOUNDATION OF BC
Att: Human Resources Manager
1188 West Georgia Street, Suite 1440
Vancouver, BC V6E 4A2
Fax 604-687-8481
Email .... focusbc@telus.net
Employer Background: For over 25 years, Focus Foundation of BC has been researching and developing social practice models by working with youth and their families who suffer from emotional, educational, vocational and justice-related issues. *New Positions Created (4):* Family Workers; Intensive Supervision and Support Workers; Vice-Principal and Teaching Positions; Youth Workers.

FOCUS MICROWAVES INC.
Att: Human Resources Manager
90 Montee de Liesse, Suite 308
St-Laurent, QC H4T 1W7
Tel. 514-335-6227
Fax 514-335-6287
Email .... info@focus-microwaves.com
Website .... www.focus-microwaves.com
Employer Background: Established in 1988, Focus Microwaves Inc. manufactures load-pull and noise measurement systems based on proprietary designs of computer-controlled microwave tuners. *New Positions Created (6):* RF Application Engineer; RF Technician; Software Engineers; Application Engineer; Sales Engineer; RF Technician.

FOCUS ON HEALTH & SAFETY INC.
Att: Human Resources Manager
2100 Matheson Boulevard East, Suite 200
Mississauga, ON L4W 5E1
Tel. 905-602-4522
Fax 905-602-9693
Employer Background: FHS is a leader in occupational health and safety and WSIB employer representation. *New Positions Created (6):* OH & S Consultant; Sales Professionals; WSIB Claims Consultant; WSIB Revenue Consultant; WSIB Claims Consultant; WSIB Revenue Consultant.

FOGLER, RUBINOFF LLP
Att: Human Resources Manager
Suite 4400, PO Box 95, Royal Trust Tower
Toronto Dominion Centre
Toronto, ON M5K 1G8

Tel. 416-864-9700
Fax 416-941-8852
Website .... www.foglerubinoff.com
Employer Background: Fogler, Rubinoff LLP
is a mid-sized law firm, specializing in legal
and business services. *New Positions Created (3):* Intermediate Legal Assistants,
Business Law; Legal Assistants; Law Positions (2).

FONTHILL LUMBER LTD.
Att: Human Resources Manager
105 Highway 20 East, PO Box 340
Fonthill, ON L0S 1E0

Tel. 905-892-2641
Fax 905-892-5626
Email .... truss@fonthill.com
Website .... www.fonthill.com
Employer Background: Founded in 1951,
Fonthill Lumber Ltd. sells wood frame products and employs 75 staff. *New Positions
Created (2):* Roof Truss Estimator; Wood
Truss Salesperson.

FOOTNER FOREST PRODUCTS LTD.
Att: Human Resources Manager
PO Box 1856
High Level, AB T0H 1Z0

Fax 780-841-3662
Email .... shannon.pedlar@footner.ca
Website .... www.ainsworth.ca
Employer Background: Footner Forest Products Ltd. is a partnership between
Ainsworth Lumber Co. Ltd. and Grant Forest Products Inc. *New Positions Created (4):*
Intermediate Accountant; Maintenance and
Engineering Manager; Purchasing Manager;
Shipper / Receiver.

**FORD MOTOR COMPANY OF CANADA
LTD., OAKVILLE ASSEMBLY PLANT**
Att: Human Resources Manager
PO Box 1300
Oakville, ON L6K 5C9

Email .... oakvjobs@ford.com
Website .... www.ford.ca
Employer Background: Established in 1904,
Ford Motor Company of Canada Ltd. is an
auto and truck manufacturer, with over
14,000 employees nationwide. Their
Oakville Assembly Plant is the sole global
producer of the Windstar minivan. *New
Positions Created (3):* Engineering Positions;
Maintenance Supervisors; Production Supervisors.

FORDING COAL LIMITED
Att: Employee Relations
205 - 9th Avenue SE
Suite 1000, Fording Place
Calgary, AB T2G 0R4

Tel. 403-264-1063
Fax 403-269-9863
Email .... jobs@fording.ca
Website .... www.fording.ca

Employer Background: Fording Coal Limited is an export-coal producer, with the
capacity to supply over 20 million tonnes of
metallurgical and thermal coal products to
Canadian and world markets. *New Positions
Created (6):* Visual Basic Contractor; PC
Technical Support Analyst; Programmer
Analyst, E-Commerce; Senior Analyst / Application Developer; Senior Analyst, E-Commerce; Senior Technical Analyst, Engineering Systems.

**FORDING COAL LIMITED, FORDING
RIVER OPERATIONS**
Att: Denis Lehoux, Superintendent,
Employee Relations
PO Box 100
Elkford, BC V0B 1H0

Tel. 250-865-2271
Fax 250-865-5222
Email .... denis_lehoux@fording.ca
Website .... www.fording.ca
Employer Background: Fording Coal Limited is an export-coal producer, with the capacity to supply over 20 million tonnes of
metallurgical and thermal coal products to
Canadian and world markets. *New Positions
Created (6):* Administrative Secretary; Maintenance Engineer; Millwrights; Maintenance Engineer; Industrial Relations Coordinator; Project Design Engineer.

**FORDING COAL LIMITED,
GREENHILLS OPERATIONS**
Att: David Gonnelly,
Administrator, Employee Relations
PO Box 5000
Elkford, BC V0B 1H0

Fax 250-865-3250
Email .... jobs@fording.ca
Website .... www.fording.ca
Employer Background: Fording Coal Limited is an export-coal producer, with the capacity to supply more than 20 million tonnes
of metallurgical and thermal coal products
to world and Canadian markets. *New Positions Created (2):* Electricians; Senior Mining Engineer.

**FORENSIC PSYCHIATRIC SERVICES
COMMISSION, THE / FPSC**
Att: Human Resources
70 Colony Farm Road
Port Coquitlam, BC V3C 5X9

Tel. 604-523-7919
Fax 604-523-7806
Employer Background: FPSC is a 202-bed
facility, providing 24-hour inpatient care
and services for adult forensic patients. *New
Positions Created (8):* Nurses / Direct Caregivers; Nurses; Nurses; Case Mgr, Review
Board; Psychiatric Social Worker; Food Production Services Position; Case Mgr;
Nurses.

FORENSIC TECHNOLOGY INC.
Att: Human Resources Department
5757 Cavendish, Suite 200
Cote St. Luc, QC H4W 2W8

Tel. 514-485-6611
Fax 514-485-9336

Email .... rh_hr@fti-ibis.com
Website .... www.fti-ibis.com
Employer Background: Founded in 1990,
Forensic Technology Inc. markets bullet
image analysis software for firearms examiners and law enforcement agencies. *New
Positions Created (17):* Marketing Researcher; Automation Specialist; Data Base
Administrator; Data Base Developer; Digital
Vision Specialist; Electrical Circuitry Designer; Mechanical Designer; Mechanical
Draftsman / woman; Project Manager, Business Strategy; Scientist; Software Designer;
Software Tester; Systems Administrators;
Customer Support Engineers; Sales Associate; System Administrator; Training Officer.

FOREST PRACTICES BOARD
Att: Human Resources Manager
1675 Douglas Street
3rd Floor, PO Box 9905, Stn Prov Govt
Victoria, BC V8W 9R1

Tel. 250-387-7964
Fax 250-387-7009
Website .... www.fpb.gov.bc.ca
Employer Background: Forest Practices
Board conducts independent audits of forest practices and planning. *New Positions
Created (6):* Forest Practices Audit Specialist; Manager, Special Projects; Assistant Director, Audits; Forest Practices Audit Managers; Senior Communications Officer; Audit Practices Managers (4).

FOREST RENEWAL BC
Att: Leah Brown
727 Fisgard Street
Victoria, BC V8V 1X4

Tel. 250-356-6952
Fax 250-387-4211
Email .... frbc.hr@gems3.gov.bc.ca
Website .... www.forestrenewal.bc.ca
Employer Background: Established in 1994,
Forest Renewal BC is a provincial investment agency, providing funding to help
build a diversified, sustainable forest
economy that supports local communities,
workers and their families. *New Positions
Created (2):* Investment Officer; Corporate
Records and Information Officer.

FORESTRY CORP., THE
Att: Human Resources Manager
11302 - 119th Avenue
Edmonton, AB T5G 2X4

Tel. 780-452-5878
Fax 780-453-3986
Email .... brian_maier@forcorp.com
Website .... www.forcorp.com
Employer Background: Founded in 1993,
The Forestry Corp. is a consulting company,
specializing in forest management services.
New Positions Created (2): Air Photo Interpreter; GIS Analyst.

FORINTEK CANADA CORP.
Att: Human Resources Department
2665 East Mall
Vancouver, BC V6T 1W5

Tel. 604-224-3221

Fax 604-222-5690
Email .... ann@van.forintek.ca
Website .... www.forintek.ca
Employer Background: Founded in 1979, Forintek Canada Corp. is a non-profit institute dedicated to research and development in Canada's forest products industry. *New Positions Created (2):* Industrial Advisor, Wood Products Manufacturing; Industrial Advisor, Wood Products Market Economist.

FORSYS SOFTWARE CORPORATION
Att: Human Resources Manager
340 Ferrier Avenue, Suite 1A
Markham, ON L3R 2Z5

Tel. 905-305-1225
Fax 905-305-1810
Email .... hr@forsyscorp.com
Website .... www.forsyscorp.com
Employer Background: Forsys Software Corporation develops software solutions for the global restaurant and hospitality industry. *New Positions Created (3):* Programmer / Analyst; Technician / Help Desk Position; Trainer.

FORZANI GROUP LTD., THE
Att: Human Resources Department
824 - 41st Avenue NE
Calgary, AB T2E 3R3

Tel. 403-717-1400
Fax 403-717-1491
Email .... hrcorporate@forzani.com
Website .... www.forzanigroup.com
Employer Background: The Forzani Group Ltd. is a leading national sporting goods retailer. *New Positions Created (6):* Intermediate General Accountant; Supervisor, Inventory Integrity; Database Marketing Analyst; Mgr, Process Management; Corporate Trainer; Unix / Network Systems Architect.

FOSTER WHEELER
FIRED HEATERS LTD.
Att: Beryl Cartwright
7330 Fisher Street SE, Suite 450
Calgary, AB T2H 2H8

Tel. 403-255-3447
Website .... www.fwc.com
Employer Background: Foster Wheeler Fired Heaters Ltd. is a leading designer of fired heaters, serving the petrochemical and refinery marketplace. *New Positions Created (3):* Structural Engineer; Project Engineer; Project Proposals Engineer.

FOUND AIRCRAFT CANADA INC.
Att: Human Resources Manager
RR 2, Site 12, Box 10, Georgian Bay Airport
Parry Sound, ON P2A 2W8

Tel. 705-378-0530
Fax 705-378-0594
Email .... foundair@zeuter.com
Website .... www.foundair.com
Employer Background: Found Aircraft Canada Inc. is an aircraft manufacturer, with over 50 employees. *New Positions Created (3):* Licensed AME; Purchasing Agent; Senior Aircraft Assemblers.

FOUNTAIN TIRE
Att: Debbie McKay, HR Manager
PO Box 4530
Edmonton, AB T6E 5G4

Tel. 780-464-3700
Email .... debbie.mckay@fountaintire.com
Website .... www.fountaintire.com
Employer Background: Fountain Tire is one of western Canada's fastest-growing tire and mechanical service retailers. *New Positions Created (4):* Accountant; Call Centre Representative; Off-The-Road (OTR) Coordinator; Instructor.

FOUR SEASONS MOTO-SPORTS
Att: Human Resources Manager
2226 Gregoire Drive
Fort McMurray, AB T9H 4K6

Fax 780-791-4196
Employer Background: Four Seasons Moto-Sports is a full-line Yamaha and Honda recreational products dealership, serving Fort McMurray since 1978. *New Positions Created (5):* Accountant / Bookkeeper; Journeyman Motorcycle Mechanics (2); Parts Positions (3); Sales Positions (2); Service Writer / Administrator.

FOURTH R OF CALGARY LTD., THE
Att: Human Resources Manager
717 - 7th Avenue SW, Suite 200
Calgary, AB T2P 0Z3

Tel. 403-537-5888
Fax 403-537-5885
Website .... www.fourthr.ab.ca
Employer Background: The Fourth R of Calgary Ltd. offers information technology training. *New Positions Created (2):* Account Managers; Instructors.

FOXBORO CANADA INC.
Att: Human Resources Department
4 Lake Road
Dollard-des-Ormeaux, QC H9B 3H9

Tel. 514-421-4210
Fax 514-421-8057
Email .... hr@foxboro.ca
Website .... www.foxboro.com
Employer Background: Foxboro Canada Inc. is a world leader in intelligent automation for total plant management. *New Positions Created (2):* Accountant; Senior Buyer.

FRANK RUSSELL COMPANY
CANADA LIMITED
Att: Human Resources Department
1 First Canadian Place
Suite 5900, PO Box 476
Toronto, ON M5X 1E4

Tel. 416-362-8411
Fax 416-640-6195
Email .... hrcanada@russell.com
Website .... www.russell.com
Employer Background: Frank Russell Company Canada Limited is an international investment management and asset consulting firm. *New Positions Created (2):* Research Analyst; Senior Consulting Analyst, Asset Allocation.

FRANKLIN COVEY CANADA, LTD.
Att: Human Resources Manager
60 Struck Court
Cambridge, ON N1R 8L2

Tel. 519-740-2580
Fax 519-740-8486
Email .... recruiting@franklincovey.ca
Website .... www.franklincovey.ca
Employer Background: Franklin Covey Canada, Ltd. (part of Utah-based Franklin Covey Co.) offers leadership development and productivity services. *New Positions Created (5):* Retail Sales Associates; Retail Store Manager; Senior Sales Consultant, Client Partner; Assistant Retail Store Manager; Retail Sales Associates.

FRANKLIN TEMPLETON
INVESTMENTS
Att: Human Resources Department
1 Adelaide Street East, Suite 2101
Toronto, ON M5C 3B8

Tel. 416-364-4672
Fax 416-364-8320
Email .. resumes-toronto@templeton.com
Website .... www.franklintempleton.ca
Employer Background: Established over 50 years ago, Franklin Templeton Investments is a mutual fund company that manages over \$14 billion in Canadian assets, 2 million unit-holder accounts and 200 pension funds. *New Positions Created (13):* Vice-President, Business Development, Institutional Investment Services; Vice-President, Third Party Alliances, Institutional Investment Services; Vice-President, Institutional Investment Services Business Development; Total Rewards Consultant; Client Service Administrator; Client Service Representative; Client Service Representative; Equity Analyst; Portfolio Accountant; Portfolio Accountant; Tax Compliance Specialist; Vice President, Institutional Client Services; Vice President, Institutional Client Services.

FRASER INSTITUTE, THE
Att: Director of Administration
1770 Burrard Street, 4th Floor
Vancouver, BC V6J 3G7

Tel. 604-688-0221
Fax 604-688-8539
Website .... www.fraserinstitute.ca
Employer Background: Founded in 1974, The Fraser Institute is a leading economic research organization. *New Positions Created (3):* Book Sales Coordinator; Sr Economist; Director of Health Policy Studies.

FRASER MILNER CASGRAIN LLP
Att: Janette Canvin, Director of
Professional Development & Recruitment
100 King St. West, 1 First Canadian Place
Toronto, ON M5X 1B2

Tel. 416-863-4511
Fax 416-863-4592
Email .... janette.canvin@fmc-law.com
Website .... www.fmc-law.com
Employer Background: Fraser Milner Casgrain LLP is a leading Canadian business law firm, with 500 lawyers and six offices across the country. *New Positions Created*

(4): Tax Associate; Various Legal Secretarial Positions; Manager, Student Programs; Commodity Tax Associate.

FRASER SURREY DOCKS LTD.
Att: Peter Jaskiewicz, COO
11060 Elevator Road
Surrey, BC V3V 2R7

Tel. 604-581-2233
Fax 604-581-6488
Email .... peterj@fsd.bc.ca
Website .... www.fsd.bc.ca

Employer Background: Fraser Surrey Docks Ltd. is a shipping terminal that handles forest products, steel and containerized cargo for domestic and international customers, and provides specialized logistics services. *New Positions Created (3):* Marketing Mgr; Assistant to the V.P., Marketing & Customer Service; Assistant Superintendent.

FRASER VALLEY HEALTH REGION
Att: Linda Bendickson,
Regional Director, Employment Services
7324 Hurd Street
Mission, BC V2V 3H5

Tel. 604-814-5153
Fax 604-814-5138
Website .... www.fvhr.org

Employer Background: Fraser Valley Health Region provides health services to 241,000 people in Abbotsford, Mission, Chilliwack, Hope and Agassiz / Harrison. *New Positions Created (17):* Regional Director, Utilization; Regional Risk Management Coordinator; Director, Residential Care Services; Director, Seniors' Health and Community Care; Health Programs Manager, Maternal / Child Program; Health Programs Manager, Surgical Program; Manager, Housekeeping / Laundry Services; Health Programs Manager, Maternal / Child Program; Chief Health Records Administrator; Site Manager; Biomedical Engineering Technologist; Nursing Manager; Physiotherapists; Registered Nurses; Registered Nurses, Operating Room; Bilingual Case Manager, Mental Health Programs (Punjabi / English); Case Manager, Mental Health Programs; Operating Room Booking Nurse.

FRASER VALLEY REGIONAL DISTRICT / FVRD
Att: Suzanne Gresham,
Director of Corporate Administration
8430 Cessna Drive
Chilliwack, BC V2P 7K4

Tel. 604-702-5000
Fax 604-702-5043
Email .... sgresham@fvrd.bc.ca
Website .... www.fvrd.bc.ca

Employer Background: FVRD is comprised of 14,000 square kilometres and 225,000 residents. *New Positions Created (2):* Treaty Advisory Administrator; HR Manager.

FRASER VALLEY REGIONAL LIBRARY
Att: Rob O'Brennan,
Director of Client Services
34589 Delair Road
Abbotsford, BC V2S 5Y1

Fax 604-859-4788
Email .... rob.obrennan@fvrl.bc.ca
Website .... www.fvrl.bc.ca

Employer Background: FVRL provides services to over 600,000 people through 22 community libraries in 15 municipalities and regional districts. *New Positions Created (3):* Library Manager; Manager, Systems; Budget Officer.

FREEBALANCE INC.
Att: People and Teams Department
55 Metcalfe Street, Suite 600
Ottawa, ON K1P 6L5

Tel. 613-236-5150
Fax 613-236-7785
Email .... jobs@freebalance.com
Website .... www.freebalance.com

Employer Background: FreeBalance Inc. creates networks for enterprises and government to collaborate in the global community. *New Positions Created (10):* E-Financial Consultants; Director of Business Solutions; Functional Analyst; Manager, Customer Satisfaction; People Person Position; Product Manager; Project Manager; Quality Assurance / Product Specialist; Senior / Intermediate Java Developers; Web / Graphic Designer.

FREUD WESTMORE TOOLS LTD.
Att: Human Resources
7450 Pacific Circle
Mississauga, ON L5T 2A3

Tel. 905-670-1025
Fax 905-670-0406
Email .. freudwestmore@compuserve.com

Employer Background: Freud Westmore Tools manufactures and wholesales quality woodworking tools and accessories. *New Positions Created (2):* Marketing Assistant / Customer Service; Accounting Assistant.

FRITZ STARBER INC.
Att: Human Resources
6655 Airport Road
Mississauga, ON L4V 1V8

Tel. 800-387-4885
Fax 905-677-6467
Email .... hrcanada@fritz.com
Website .... www.fritz.com

Employer Background: Fritz Starber Inc. is a leader in global integrated logistics, delivering supply chain solutions to its clients worldwide. *New Positions Created (3):* Credit Agent; Credit Supervisor; Customs Raters and Transportation Agents.

FRONTENAC CHILDREN'S AID SOCIETY
Att: Manager of Human Resources
362 Montreal Street
Kingston, ON K7K 3H5

Tel. 613-542-7351
Fax 613-542-4428

Employer Background: Frontenac Children's Aid Society is a child welfare agency, with a staff complement of 85, over 100 volunteers and a budget of $7.2 million. *New Positions Created (9):* Child Protection Workers;

Child-in-Care Workers; Data Analyst; Child Protection Workers; Children In-Care Workers; Statistician / Information Analyst; Staff Legal Counsel; Child In-Care Workers; Child Protection Workers.

FRONTIER
Att: Human Resources Manager
302 - 50th Avenue SE
Calgary, AB T2G 2A9

Fax 403-252-6039

Employer Background: Frontier is a plumbing and heating distribution company. *New Positions Created (2):* Heating Specialist; Purchasing Agent.

FROST FENCE & WIRE PRODUCTS LTD.
Att: Human Resources Manager
250 Lottridge Street
Hamilton, ON L8L 8J8

Tel. 905-547-4303
Fax 905-312-8634
Email .... ventresca@frostfence.com
Website .... www.frostfence.com

Employer Background: Established in 1898, Frost Fence & Wire Products Ltd. manufactures wire fencing. *New Positions Created (6):* Millwrights; Parts Clerk; Bilingual Customer Service Representative; Millwrights; Quality Monitor; Parts Clerk.

FROZEN POND INC.
Att: Human Resources Manager
752 Mount Pleasant Road
Toronto, ON M4S 2N6

Fax 416-488-9430
Email .... frozpond@aol.com
Website .... www.frozenpond.com

Employer Background: Established in 1993, Frozen Pond Inc. is a sports memorabilia marketing company, specializing in autographed hockey collectibles. *New Positions Created (3):* Bookkeeper / Office Manager; Customer Service Personnel; E-Commerce Specialist - Webmaster.

FSONA COMMUNICATIONS CORP.
Att: Human Resources Manager
11120 Horseshoe Way, Suite 140
Richmond, BC V7A 5H7

Tel. 604-664-7772
Fax 604-273-6342
Email .... future@fsona.com
Website .... www.fsona.com

Employer Background: fSONA Communications Corp. develops wireless products for the telecom industry. *New Positions Created (11):* Accounts Payable Clerk; Customer Sales Engineer; Laser Communications Systems Engineer; Optical Engineer; Product Manager; Test Engineer; Electrical Engineers; Network / Software Engineers; Network Diagnostics Technician / Engineer; Product Manager; Shipper / Receiver.

FTI CONSULTING, INC.
Att: Human Resources Manager
4444 Eastgate Parkway, Unit 18
Mississauga, ON L4W 4T6

Fax 847-559-3010
Email .... jsmith@fticonsulting.com
Website .... www.fticonsulting.com
Employer Background: FTI Consulting, Inc. provides expert technical consulting and equipment restoration services to the insurance and legal industries. *New Positions Created (3):* Project Manager, Equipment Restoration; Technical Consultant, Equipment Loss; Business Manager.

FUGRO AIRBORNE SURVEYS
Att: Operations
2270 Argentia Road, Unit 2
Mississauga, ON L5N 6A6
Tel. 905-812-0212
Fax 905-812-1504
Email .... hr@fugroairborne.com
Website .... www.fugroairborne.com
Employer Background: Fugro Airborne Surveys is a leading supplier of airborne geophysical services worldwide. *New Positions Created (3):* Field Operators / Electronic Technicians; Payroll Supervisor; Accountant.

FUGRO AIRBORNE SURVEYS
Att: Manager, Airborne Geophysics
2060 Walkley Road
Ottawa, ON K1G 3P5
Tel. 613-731-9571
Fax 613-731-0453
Email .... hr@fugroairborne.com
Website .... www.fugroairborne.com
Employer Background: Fugro Airborne Surveys is a leading supplier of airborne geophysical services worldwide. *New Positions Created (10):* Aircraft Maintenance Engineers; Electronics Technicians & Technologists; Geophysicists & Data Processors; Survey Pilots; Aircraft Maintenance Engineers; Electronics Technicians / Technologists; Geophysicists & Data Processors; Survey Pilots; Chief Accountant; Sales & Marketing Rep.

FUGRO / SESL GEOMATICS LTD.
Att: Martha Fleming, Human Resources
517 - 10th Avenue SW, Suite 200
Calgary, AB T2R 0A8
Tel. 403-234-9018
Fax 403-266-2919
Email .... mfleming@sesl.com
Website .... www.sesl.com
Employer Background: Fugro / SESL Geomatics Ltd. provides survey services for the petroleum industry. *New Positions Created (4):* AutoCAD / Calculating Technician; Survey Party Chiefs; Surveyor's Assistant; Land Surveyor.

FUJI PHOTO FILM CANADA INC.
Att: Human Resources
275 Britannia Road East
Mississauga, ON L4Z 2E7
Tel. 905-890-6611
Fax 905-890-6446
Email .... careers@fujifilm.ca
Website .... www.fujifilm.ca
Employer Background: Fuji Photo Film Canada Inc. is a leading producer of photo-

graphic, photofinishing, digital and recording media products. *New Positions Created (5):* Environmental, Health & Safety Specialist; Assistant Product Manager, Photofinishing Equipment; Website Communications Specialist; Bilingual Customer Service / Order Desk Representative; Project Manager / Industrial Engineer.

FULL CIRCLE SYSTEMS INC.
Att: Human Resources Manager
2509 Dieppe Avenue SW
Currie Barracks Building B6
Calgary, AB T3E 7J9
Tel. 403-215-0055
Fax 403-215-0058
Email .... jobs2@fullcirclesystems.com
Website .... www.fullcirclesystems.com
Employer Background: Full Circle Systems Inc. is a systems integration and software company that owns and develops DocVue Document Manager, an electronic document management product. *New Positions Created (5):* Quality Assurance Engineer; Technology Consultant; Business Development Manager; Customer Care Manager; Systems Integrator, Electronic Document Management.

FUTURE ELECTRONICS INC.
Att: Lyna Parrino
237 Hymus Boulevard
Pointe-Claire, QC H9R 5C7
Tel. 514-694-7710
Fax 514-694-9376
Email .... lyna.parrino@miromar.com
Website .... www.future.ca
Employer Background: Founded in 1968, Future Electronics Inc. is a global distributor of sophisticated electronic components, operating over 220 offices in 34 countries. *New Positions Created (8):* Customer Service Representatives; Financial Analyst; Interior Designer / Space Planner; Credit Analysts; Account Executives; Customer Service Representative; Account Executives; Customer Service Position.

FUTURE SHOP LTD.
Att: Corporate Human Resources
8800 Glenlyon Parkway
Burnaby, BC V5J 5K3
Tel. 604-435-8223
Fax 604-412-5224
Email .... corp_hr@futureshop.com
Website .... www.futureshop.ca
Employer Background: Established in 1982, Future Shop Ltd. is one of North America's largest computer and electronics retailers, with over 83 stores in Canada. *New Positions Created (2):* Accountant, Level 1; Intermediate Financial Analyst.

FUTURE SHOP LTD.
Att: Human Resources Recruiting
6110 Cantay Road
Mississauga, ON L5R 3W5
Fax 905-501-5677
Email .... ont_hr@futureshop.com
Website .... www.futureshop.com

Employer Background: Established in 1982, Future Shop Ltd. is a large computer and home electronics retailer, with over 83 stores in Canada. *New Positions Created (3):* Photo Lab Managers; Technicians; Various Retail Positions.

FUTURE SHOP LTD.
Att: Human Resources Recruiting
7200 Boulevard des Roseraies
Anjou, QC H1M 2T5
Fax 514-355-0990
Email .... east_hr@futureshop.com
Website .... www.futureshop.com
Employer Background: Established in 1982, Future Shop Ltd. is a large computer and home electronics retailer, with over 83 stores in Canada. *New Positions Created (3):* Customer Service Representatives; Sales Professionals; Human Resources Manager.

FUTURELINK
Att: Human Resources Manager
2 Gibbs Road
Toronto, ON M9B 6L6
Tel. 416-503-1100
Email .... careers@futurelink.net
Website .... www.futurelink.ca
Employer Background: FutureLink is one of the largest application service providers of hosted server-based solutions. *New Positions Created (8):* Account Mgr; Office Administrator; Sales Coordinator; ASP Account Mgrs; ERP Account Mgrs; Account Managers; Sales Coordinators; Systems Engineer.

FUTUREWAY COMMUNICATIONS INC.
Att: Human Resources
45 Vogell Road, Suite 101
Richmond Hill, ON L4B 3P6
Tel. 905-326-1000
Email .... careers@futureway.ca
Website .... www.futureway.ca
Employer Background: Futureway Communications Inc. is a broadband services company, providing business and residential communication solutions. *New Positions Created (6):* Network Surveillance Technician; Account Executives; CAD Drafter; Product Managers; Residential Deployment Manager; Telecom Designer.

G.E. SHNIER CO.
Att: Human Resources Manager
50 Kenview Boulevard
Brampton, ON L6T 5S8
Fax 905-789-3748
Email .... emacisaac@gesco.ca
Website .... www.gesco.ca
Employer Background: G.E. Shnier Co. is one of Canada's largest national floor covering suppliers, distributing to thousands of retailers across Canada. *New Positions Created (3):* Various Sales Positions; National Telesales Manager; Distribution Manager.

G.N. JOHNSTON EQUIPMENT CO. LTD.
Att: Bob Reil
11612 - 170th Street
Edmonton, AB T5S 1J7

Fax 780-483-7236
Website .... www.gnjohnston.com
Employer Background: G.N. Johnston Equipment Co. Ltd. sells and services material handling equipment. *New Positions Created (2):* Customer Service and Sales Representative; Sales Position.

G&K SERVICES
Att: Human Resources Manager
1160 Lola Street
Ottawa, ON K1K 3W9

Fax 613-744-8895
Email .... gkservices@pc.webhire.com
Website .... www.gkservices.com
Employer Background: Founded in 1902, G&K Services is a leader in branded-identity apparel and facilities services, employing over 8,000 people in North America. *New Positions Created (6):* Account Manager; Route Sales Representative; Professional Sales Representative; Route Sales Representative; Professional Sales Consultant / Facility Sales Consultant; Account Manager.

G&K WORK WEAR
Att: Office Manager
940 Warden Avenue
Toronto, ON M1L 4C9

Fax 416-751-9429
Website .... www.gkservices.com
Employer Background: G&K Work Wear is one of North America's leading providers of branded identity apparel and facilities services. *New Positions Created (3):* Accounts Payable / Administrative Assistant; Receptionist; Accounts Receivable Collector.

G&K WORK WEAR
Att: Staffing Manager
6299 Airport Road, Suite 101
Mississauga, ON L4V 1N3

Tel. 905-677-6161
Fax 905-677-6289
Email .... jsimmons@gkservices.com
Website .... www.gkservices.com
Employer Background: Founded in 1902, G&K Work Wear is a leader in branded-identity apparel and facilities services, employing over 8,000 people in North America. *New Positions Created (7):* Bilingual Major Account Representative; Branch Office Administrator; Human Resources Administrative Support Assistant; Regional Engineer; Regional Director of Operations; Branch Manager; Major Account Representative.

G-P FLAKEBOARD COMPANY
Att: Andrew Matchett
PO Box 637
Bancroft, ON K0L 1C0

Tel. 613-332-4200
Fax 613-332-4772
Website .... www.gapac.com
Employer Background: G-P Flakeboard Company is a leading forest products company, specializing in the engineered wood and composite panel industry. *New Positions Created (2):* Electrical Automation Specialist; Mechanical Engineer.

GAD SHAANAN DESIGN
Att: Carmen Canadian, HR - Canada
4480 Cote de Liesse Road, Suite 390
Montréal, QC H4N 2R1

Tel. 514-735-9550
Fax 514-877-3680
Website ...... www.gadshaanandesign.com
Employer Background: Gad Shaanan Design is an international product design, engineering and prototype firm. *New Positions Created (8):* Industrial Designer; Mechanical Designer; Senior Technical Design Verifier; Graphic Designer; Industrial Designers; Mechanical Designer; Project Coordinator; Sales Professional.

GAGE APPLIED, INC.
Att: Human Resources
2000 - 32nd Avenue
Lachine, QC H8T 3H7

Tel. 514-633-7447
Fax 514-633-1414
Email .... hresources@gage-applied.com
Website ...... www.gage-applied.com
Employer Background: Gage Applied, Inc. (part of Tektronix, Inc.) manufactures computer testing hardware and software instruments. *New Positions Created (27):* Analog Design Engineers; Hardware and Software Professionals; Product Managers; Technologist, Group Leader; Analog Design Engineers; Digital Design Engineers; Electronic Technologist; Intermediate Software Engineers, C++; Junior Software Engineers, C++; Network Integration Developers; Electronics Technicians; Firmware Designers / Developers; Manufacturing Engineer; New Product Program Managers; Operations Supervisor; PCB Designers; Senior Analog Design Engineers; Senior Digital Design Engineers; Software Quality Assurance Team Leader; Test Engineers; Applications Engineers; Network Integration Developers; Product Manager; Software Driver Designers / Developers; Software Engineers C++; Technical Writer; Web Developers.

GAGE EDUCATIONAL PUBLISHING
Att: Human Resources Department
164 Commander Boulevard
Toronto, ON M1S 3C7

Tel. 416-293-8141
Fax 416-293-9009
Website .... www.gagelearning.com
Employer Background: Established 1844, Gage Educational Publishing is a leading provider of curriculum support material. *New Positions Created (3):* Copy Editor; Development Editor; Senior Editor, Reference.

GALDOS SYSTEMS INC.
Att: Human Resources Manager
1155 West Pender Street, Suite 200
Vancouver, BC V6E 2P4

Tel. 604-484-2750
Fax 604-484-2755
Email .... careers@galdos.ca
Website .... www.galdosinc.com
Employer Background: Galdos Systems Inc. is focused on the application of XML / Java technology to wide area spatial information

systems and the development of application service providers. *New Positions Created (5):* Manager, Business Development; Manager, Product Development; Integration and Test Engineers; Software Architects; Software Developers.

GALIAN PHOTONICS INC.
Att: Human Resources Manager
1727 West Broadway, Suite 300
Vancouver, BC V6J 4W6

Tel. 604-742-3330
Fax 604-742-3830
Email .... hr@galianphotonics.com
Website .... www.galianphotonics.com
Employer Background: Galian Photonics Inc. (formerly BandGap Photonics Inc.) develops optical component technology. Based on proprietary planar photonic crystal technology, their optical integrated circuit design solutions are designed to boost the capacity of communication networks to carry more data, voice and Internet traffic. *New Positions Created (5):* Office Administration / Accounting Clerk; Research and Development Manager; Senior Scientist, Design; Senior Scientist, Modelling; Senior Scientist, Process.

GALILEO CANADA
Att: Earl Silver, HR Manager (Canada)
330 Front Street West, 7th Floor
Toronto, ON M5V 3B7

Tel. 416-343-6464
Fax 416-581-1701
Email .... earl.silver@galileo.com
Website .... www.galileo.com
Employer Background: Galileo Canada is part of Illinois-based Galileo International, one of the world's leading providers of electronic global distribution services for the travel industry. *New Positions Created (3):* Bilingual Help Desk Positions; Travel Counsellors, Help Desk; Account Manager.

GAMMA-DYNACARE
Att: Human Resources Department
115 Midair Court
Brampton, ON L6T 5M3

Tel. 905-790-3000
Fax 905-790-1287
Email .... hr-toronto@gamma-dynacare.com
Website .... www.dynacare.com
Employer Background: Gamma-Dynacare is one of Canada's largest providers of licensed medical diagnostic laboratory services. *New Positions Created (7):* Dicta-Typists; Venipuncturists; Homecare Supervisor; Homecare Technician; Manager, Patient Services Department; Medical Laboratory Technologists; Venipuncturists.

GANDALF GRAPHICS
Att: Bob Moore, VP Sales and Marketing
260 Bartley Drive
Toronto, ON M4A 1G5

Tel. 416-750-2324
Fax 416-752-0296
Email .... moore@gandalfgraphics.com
Employer Background: Gandalf Graphics is a prepress shop, providing print and finish-

ing services to the large format print, book manufacturing, general commercial print and finishing markets. *New Positions Created (3):* Director of Sales, Book Division; Production Manager; Sales Representative.

GANZ
Att: Human Resources Manager
1 Pearce Road
Woodbridge, ON L4L 3T2
Tel. 905-851-6661
Fax 905-856-4647
Email .... hrcanada@ganz.com
Website .... www.ganz.com
Employer Background: Founded in 1950, Ganz is a Canadian giftware company. *New Positions Created (28):* Assistant Product Manager, Personal Care; Assistant Product Manager, Plush Products; Product Developer; Programmer / Analyst; Purchasing Agent; Quality Control Assistant; Accounts Payable Clerk; Credit / Collections Clerk; Customer Service Representative; Inventory Clerk; Art Director; Credit and Collections Clerk; Intermediate / Senior Graphic Designer; Purchasing Agent; Senior Accountant; Bilingual Customer Service Representative; Cost Accountant; Junior Accounting Clerks; Credit & Collections Representatives; Executive Assistant; Product Development Manager; Accounting Clerks; Credit and Collections Representatives; Payroll & Benefits Specialist; Payroll & Commissions Specialist, US; Senior Accountant; Call Centre Manager; Production Coordinator.

GARRTECH INC.
Att: Human Resources Manager
910 Arvin
Stoney Creek, ON L8E 5Y8
Tel. 905-643-6414
Fax 905-643-6422
Website .... www.garrtech.com
Employer Background: Garrtech Inc. manufactures quality blow molds for the plastics industry. *New Positions Created (3):* Quality Control Position / Inspector; CNC Machine Centre Operators; Mold Makers.

GARTNER LEE LTD.
Att: Human Resources
140 Renfrew Drive, Suite 102
Markham, ON L3R 6B3
Tel. 905-477-8400
Fax 905-477-1456
Email .. humanresources@gartnerlee.com
Website .... www.gartnerlee.com
Employer Background: Gartner Lee Ltd. is a Canadian environmental consulting firm. *New Positions Created (2):* Environmental Approvals Specialist; Waste Management Engineer.

GARY JONAS COMPUTING LTD.
Att: Human Resources Manager
125 Mural Street, Suite 100
Richmond Hill, ON L4B 1M4
Tel. 905-886-0544
Fax 905-763-8324
Email .... jobs@gjonas.com
Website .... beta.gjonas.com

Employer Background: Founded in 1990, Gary Jonas Computing Ltd. is a Canadian business application development firm. *New Positions Created (2):* Project Manager; Senior Development Programmer.

GAS & OIL ACCOUNTING LTD.
Att: Human Resources Manager
734 - 7th Avenue SW, Suite 500
Calgary, AB T2P 0Z1
Tel. 403-234-9202
Fax 403-265-3528
Employer Background: Gas & Oil Accounting Ltd. specializes in petroleum financial and production accounting and gas chart measurement for over 150 companies. *New Positions Created (4):* Accounting Manager; Production Accountant; Financial Accountant; General Manager / Vice-President.

GASTOPS LTD.
Att: Personnel Administrator
1011 Polytek Street
Gloucester, ON K1J 9J3
Tel. 613-744-3530
Fax 613-744-8846
Email .... gtl@gastops.com
Website .... www.gastops.com
Employer Background: GasTOPS Ltd. develops engineering products and services in machinery protection, maintenance and analysis for aerospace, marine and industrial applications. *New Positions Created (3):* Application Engineer; Mechanical Engineer / Analyst; Mechanical Engineer / Designer.

GAVEL & GOWN SOFTWARE INC.
Att: Peggy Lewis, Human Resources
184 Pearl Street, Suite 304
Toronto, ON M5H 1L5
Tel. 416-977-6633
Fax 416-977-6124
Email .... peggy@amicusattorney.com
Website .... www.amicusattorney.com
Employer Background: Gavel & Gown Software Inc. develops practice management software for lawyers and has an installation base of over 165,000 users worldwide. *New Positions Created (3):* Information Systems Supervisor; Marketing Coordinator; Direct Sales Representative.

GAZETTE, THE
Att: Lina Guerra,
Human Resources Manager
250 St. Antoine Street West
Montréal, QC H2Y 3R7
Tel. 514-987-2210
Fax 514-987-2600
Email .... hr@thegazette.southam.ca
Website .... www.montrealgazette.com
Employer Background: Founded in 1778, The Gazette is part of the Southam Newspaper Group, a major Canadian integrated communications enterprise. *New Positions Created (5):* Technical Services Coordinator; Assistant Manager, Payroll; Supervisor, Application Services; Technical Services Coordinator; Controller.

GBC CANADA INC.
Att: Samantha Lock
49 Railside Road
Toronto, ON M3A 1B3
Tel. 416-447-4951
Fax 416-447-4954
Email .... slock@gbc.com
Website .... www.gbccanada.com
Employer Background: GBC Canada Inc. manufactures and markets document finishing, film lamination, visual communications and paper shredder products. *New Positions Created (7):* Inside Sales Representatives; Sales Administration Position; Sales Representative; Sales Support Coordinator; Inbound Customer Service Representatives; Outbound Telesales Representatives; Sales Representative.

GE CANADA
Att: Eric Hotson
2300 Meadowvale Boulevard
Mississauga, ON L5N 5P9
Tel. 905-858-6660
Fax 905-858-5641
Website .... www.ge.com
Employer Background: GE Canada is a diversified technology, manufacturing and services company. *New Positions Created (43):* Account Manager; Marketing Assistant; Bilingual A / P Client Services Representative; University Programs Coordinator; Computer Operator; Sales Consultant, Product; Technical Systems Support Position; Account Manager, Ontario; Black Belt Position; Business Development Manager, HP; Contract Performance Manager; Human Resources Generalist; Human Resources Manager; Regional Sales Manager; Service Sales Specialist; Strategic Account Manager ; Account Executive; Account Manager; Account Manager / Sales Representative; Applications Engineer / Designer; Business Manager; Call Coordinator; Cardiac Ultrasound Sales Specialist; Customer Quality Representative; Financial Analyst; Manager, Human Resources; Pre-Sales Support Specialist, Midrange; Pre-Sales Support Specialist, Midrange; Pre-Sales Support Specialist, Midrange; Pre-Sales Support Specialists, Internetworking; Project Manager; Purchasing Coordinator; Purchasing Coordinator; Regional Sales Manager; Sales Consultant, Financial Services; Sales Manager; Software Developer; Software Programmer; Technical Director; Technical Director; Technical Director; Unix Analyst, Level 2; Unix Analyst, Level 3.

GE CANADA
Att: Sarah Desjardine
107 Park Street North
Peterborough, ON K9J 7B5
Tel. 705-748-7707
Fax 705-748-7352
Website .... www.ge.com
Employer Background: GE Canada is a diversified technology, manufacturing and services company. *New Positions Created (7):* Insulation Engineer; Sourcing Specialist; Electrical Development Engineer; Electrical Requisition Design Engineer; Insula-

tion Development Engineer; Manager, Materials & Sourcing; Manufacturing Engineer.

GE CAPITAL CANADA
Att: Human Resources Manager
1 Place Ville Marie, Suite 1401
Montréal, QC H3B 2B2

Tel. 514-397-5300
Fax 514-397-6780
Website .... www.ge.com

Employer Background: GE Capital Canada is one of the world's largest and most successful diversified financial services companies. *New Positions Created (9):* Assistant Account Manager; Account Manager, Franchise Finance; Account Manager, Aircraft; Account Manager, Corporate Finance Group; Account Manager; Assistant Account Manager; Regional Administration Manager; Account Manager - General Manufacturing; Administrator, National Credit Support.

GE CAPITAL CANADA EQUIPMENT FINANCING INC.
Att: Human Resources
150 York Street, Suite 300
Toronto, ON M5H 3A9

Email .... careers@cefca.capital.ge.com
Website .... www.gecapitalcanada.com

Employer Background: GE Capital Canada Equipment Financing Inc. provides asset-based lending solutions (primarily leases and loans) to businesses operating in a broad range of economic sectors. *New Positions Created (2):* Bilingual Collections Officer; Bilingual Credit Analyst.

GE CAPITAL MODULAR SPACE
Att: Wayne Bichel
5115 Crowchild Trail SW
Calgary, AB T3E 1T9

Tel. 403-292-7664
Fax 403-292-7820
Website .... www.modspace.com

Employer Background: GE Capital Modular Space rents, leases and sells mobile and modular buildings. *New Positions Created (2):* Service Coordinator; Sales and Service Representative.

GE CAPITAL MORTGAGE INSURANCE CANADA
Att: Cheryl Stargratt
2300 Meadowvale Boulevard
Mississauga, ON L5N 5P9

Tel. 905-858-5465
Fax 905-858-5745
Website .... www.ge.com

Employer Background: GE Capital Mortgage Insurance Canada is the only private sector supplier of mortgage default insurance in Canada. *New Positions Created (11):* Customer Process MBB Position; Account Manager; Customer Service Representative; Underwriter; Regional Risk Manager, Prairies; Business Systems Analyst; Loss Mitigation Officer; Underwriter; Risk Manager; Account Manager; Underwriter.

GE CAPITAL SERVICES / GECS
Att: Jill Henn
PO Box 2640
Edmonton, AB T5J 4K9

Tel. 780-990-2300
Fax 780-990-2316
Website .... www.gecapitalcanada.com

Employer Background: GECS is an asset-based lender providing leases, loans and tailored financial products to companies of all sizes. *New Positions Created (2):* Site Communications Manager; Assistant Account Manager.

GE CAPITAL SERVICES / GECS
Att: Human Resources Manager
2300 Meadowvale Boulevard
Mississauga, ON L5N 5P9

Tel. 905-858-5253
Website .... www.ge.com

Employer Background: GECS, a subsidiary of GE, is a diversified financial services company that creates comprehensive solutions to increase client productivity and efficiency. *New Positions Created (6):* Account Manager; Customer Service Representative, Level 2; Inside Sales Consultant, Product Solutions; Pre-Sales Support Specialist; Pre-Sales Support Specialist, Storage; Pre-Sales Support Specialist, Storage.

GE GLEGG WATER TECHNOLOGIES
Att: Leslie Mctaggart
29 Royal Road
Guelph, ON N1H 1G2

Tel. 519-836-0500
Fax 519-836-7831
Website .... www.glegg.com

Employer Background: GE Glegg Water Technologies (formerly Glegg Water Conditioning Inc.) is a leading manufacturer of custom engineered, industrial water treatment equipment. *New Positions Created (3):* Program Manager / Lead Project Manager; Project Manager; Supplier Quality Engineering Technician.

GE INDUSTRIAL SYSTEMS / GEINDSYS
Att: Drew Innes
215 Anderson Avenue
Markham, ON L6E 1B3

Tel. 905-201-2053
Fax 905-201-2114
Website .... www.geindustrial.com

Employer Background: GEINDSYS supplies product and service solutions for commercial and industrial applications, including process automation systems and electric motors. *New Positions Created (3):* Global Sourcing Manager; Staff Accountant; Accounts Payable Specialist.

GE LIGHTING CANADA
Att: Katie Warning
468 South Service Road
Oakville, ON L6J 2X6

Tel. 905-849-2951
Fax 905-849-2911
Website .... www.gelighting.com

Employer Background: GE Lighting manufactures lamp products for the consumer, commercial and industrial markets and employs over 40,000 people at 50 manufacturing facilities worldwide. *New Positions Created (2):* Manager of Finance; Commercial & Industrial Account Manager.

GE MEDICAL SYSTEMS / GEMS
Att: Human Resources
2300 Meadowvale Boulevard
Mississauga, ON L5N 5P9

Fax 905-567-2115
Website .... www.ge.com

Employer Background: GEMS is a global leader in the medical imaging market and manufactures magnetic resonance, computed tomography, x-ray, nuclear imaging, positron emission tomography and ultrasound equipment. *New Positions Created (3):* E-Business Project Leader; Field Service Representative, CT; Field Service Representative, CT / X-Ray.

GE POWER SERVICES
Att: Susan Pancuska
2300 Meadowvale Boulevard
Mississauga, ON L5N 5P9

Fax 905-858-5644
Email .... opportunities@gecareers.com
Website .... www.gepower.com

Employer Background: GE Power Services is a business unit of GE Power Systems, the world's largest third-party provider of high tech services. *New Positions Created (4):* Sales Manager / Technical Director; Service Centre Manager; Field Engineers; Manager Shop Operations.

GE POWER SYSTEMS
Att: Judy Conrad
2728 Hopewell Place NE
Calgary, AB T1Y 7J7

Tel. 403-214-4545
Fax 403-287-9900
Website .... www.gepower.com

Employer Background: GE Power Systems has been supplying the utility industry with advanced monitoring and control systems for over 30 years. *New Positions Created (19):* Sourcing Manager; Marketing Manager; Sales Manager, Aeroderivative & Package Services; Contract Performance Manager; Environmental Health and Safety Specialist; Sales Manager; Manager, Human Resources; Program / Project Manager; Electrical Engineer; Project Manager; Software Developer; Black Belt - ITO Position; Hardware Developer; Manufacturing Engineer; Production Buyer; Program Manager; Proposals Manager; Control Designer; Software Developers.

GE POWER SYSTEMS
Att: Leslie Mctaggart
29 Royal Road
Guelph, ON N1H 1G2

Tel. 519-836-0500
Fax 519-836-7831
Website .... www.gepower.com

Employer Background: GE Power Systems has been supplying the utility industry with advanced monitoring and control systems for over 30 years. *New Positions Created (8):* Services Administrator; Process System Designer; Contract Performance Mgr; Six Sigma Black Belt Program Mgr; Mechanical CADD Designer; Process Control Designer; Buyer; E-Cell Product Engineer.

GE SYPROTEC INC.
Att: Human Resources Manager
179 Brunswick Boulevard
Pointe-Claire, QC H9R 5N2
Tel. 514-694-3637
Fax 514-694-9245
Email ..... syprotecopportunities@ps.ge.com
Website .... www.gepower.com
Employer Background: Founded in 1975, GE Syprotec Inc. manufactures products to monitor oil-filled power transformers, reducing forced outages and increasing system reliability. *New Positions Created (8):* Product Manager; Application Engineer / Inside Sales Specialist; Financial Planning and Analysis Specialist; Manager, Customer Service; Manufacturing Engineer; PLC Programmer; Product Manager, Systems; Research and Development Project Leader.

GEAR CENTRE GROUP OF COMPANIES, THE
Att: Human Resources
14713 - 116th Avenue
Edmonton, AB T5M 3E8
Fax 780-452-9910
Website .... www.gearcentre.com
Employer Background: The Gear Centre Group of Companies is comprised of the Gear Centre, Pat's Driveline and Hydra-Steer. *New Positions Created (4):* Truck and Auto Sales Professionals; Inventory Manager; Junior Buyer; Payroll Administrator.

GEMINI CORPORATION
Att: Human Resources
5940 Macleod Trail SW, Suite 700
Calgary, AB T2H 2G4
Tel. 403-255-2006
Fax 403-252-5338
Email .... hr@geminicorp.ab.ca
Website .... www.geminicorp.ab.ca
Employer Background: Gemini Corporation provides project management, engineering, fabrication, construction, operations and leasing services to a broad range of industrial clients. *New Positions Created (14):* General Manager; Intermediate and Senior Electrical Designers / Engineers; Intermediate and Senior Controls Engineers / Technologists; Intermediate and Senior Piping, Civil or Electrical Designers; Intermediate and Senior Project Engineers; Controls Engineer / Technologist; Design Positions; Engineers; Buyer / Expediter; Controls Engineer / Technologist; Instrumentation Engineer / Technologist; Piping / Civil / Electrical Designers; Project / Process / Electrical Engineers; Project Secretary.

GEMINI POSITIONING SYSTEMS LTD.
Att: Frank Wiskar
6130 - 3rd Street SE, Suite 100
Calgary, AB T2H 1K4
Tel. 403-252-5007
Fax 403-252-5392
Email .... gempos@gps1.com
Website www.gps1.com
Employer Background: Gemini Positioning Systems Ltd. is a distributor of satellite-based positioning systems. *New Positions Created (2):* Canadian Sales Manager; Western Region Sales Representative.

GEN-X SPORTS INC.
Att: Laima J. Dambrauskas,
Human Resources Manager
25 Vanley Crescent
Toronto, ON M3J 2B7
Tel. 416-630-4996
Fax 416-630-6507
Email .... hr@genxsportsinc.com
Website .... www.genxsportsinc.com
Employer Background: Gen-X Sports Inc. is a sporting goods company. *New Positions Created (4):* Accounts Payable Clerk; Bilingual Customer Service Representative; Inventory Control Analyst(s); Legal Assistant.

GENEKA BIOTECHNOLOGY INC.
Att: Human Resources Manager
5445 de Lorimier, Suite 401
Montréal, QC H2H 2S5
Tel. 514-528-9233
Fax 514-528-5447
Email .... info@geneka.com
Website .... www.geneka.com
Employer Background: Geneka Biotechnology Inc. is a world leader in functional genomics and proteomic regulators, which control gene expression. *New Positions Created (4):* Executive Assistant; Accounting Clerk; Human Resources Manager; Telemarketing Representatives.

GENERAL EQUIPMENT LTD.
Att: Bryan Alexander, PEng, Sales Manager
15 - 4th Avenue East
Vancouver, BC V5T 1G1
Tel. 604-876-8881
Fax 604-876-1048
Email .... bryana@generalequipmentltd.com
Website ... www.generalequipmentltd.com
Employer Background: Incorporated in 1928, General Equipment Ltd. is a Vancouver-based manufacturer's agent. *New Positions Created (3):* Industrial Branch Sales Manager; Industrial / Commercial Sales Engineer; Sales Manager.

GENERAL HYDROGEN / GH
Att: Human Resources Manager
555 West Hastings Street, Suite 700
Vancouver, BC V6B 4N5
Tel. 604-878-9009
Fax 604-231-0400
Website .... www.generalhydrogen.com
Employer Background: GH works to ensure a cleaner future through advanced hydrogen-based energy technologies. *New Posi-*

tions Created (19): Engineering Positions; Administrative Assistant; Electrical Group Leader; Electrical Technician / Technologist; Electronics Engineer; Embedded Software Group Leader; Facilities & Safety Manager; General Accountant / Controller; Human Resources Coordinator; Industrial Designer; IP Specialist; Legal Affairs Support / Coordinator; Machinist / Mechanical Technologist; Mechanical Group Leader; Mechanical Technologist / Mechanic; Network Software Group Leader; Payroll and Benefits Coordinator; Purchasing Agent; Systems Engineer.

GENERAL MOTORS OF CANADA LTD., DIESEL DIVISION
Att: Human Resources Department
PO Box 5160
London, ON N6A 4N5
Email .... gmlondon.hr@gm.com
Website .... www.gmcanada.com
Employer Background: General Motor's Diesel Division in London manufactures diesel locomotives and light armoured vehicles. *New Positions Created (6):* Designer, Unigraphics; Electrical Engineer; Logistics Technician; Mechanical Engineer; Senior System Engineering Analyst; Technical Publications Writer.

GENERAL MOTORS OF CANADA LTD., OSHAWA TRUCK ASSEMBLY CENTRE
Att: Engineering and Product Planning, Personnel Department CA1-098-003
1908 Colonel Sam Drive
Oshawa, ON L1H 8P7
Tel. 905-664-5000
Website .... www.gmcanada.com
Employer Background: General Motors of Canada Ltd. is the country's largest manufacturer of passenger cars, light trucks, locomotives and automobile components. The company has 30,000 employees and nine manufacturing plants. *New Positions Created (4):* Lead Project Engineer, Systems Integration; Project Engineer, Antenna / RF; Project Engineer, Computer Platform; Project Engineer, Voice Recognition.

GENERAL PAINT CORP.
Att: Allison Benson, Manager, HR Services
950 Raymur Avenue
Vancouver, BC V6A 3L5
Tel. 604-253-3131
Fax 604-252-9296
Email .... careers@generalpaint.com
Website .... www.generalpaint.com
Employer Background: General Paint Corp. manufactures, distributes and retails paint products and coatings. *New Positions Created (8):* Store Managers; Technical Service Chemist; Document Coordinator; Formulating Chemist; Chemist; Sales Positions; Store Manager; Accountant.

GENESIS MICROCHIP INC.
Att: Human Resources Manager
165 Commerce Valley Drive West
Thornhill, ON L3T 7V8
Tel. 905-889-5400
Fax 905-763-4286

Email .... hr@genesis-microchip.com
Website .... www.genesis-microchip.com
Employer Background: Genesis Microchip Inc. designs and manufactures highly-integrated semiconductors for a variety of video and graphics applications. *New Positions Created (7):* Analog IC Designers; ASIC Designers; Field Application Engineer; Principal Test Design Engineer; Senior Design Automation Engineer; Software Engineer; Field Application Engineer.

GENFAST MANUFACTURING COMPANY

Att: Human Resources
PO Box 1690
Brantford, ON N3T 5V7

Tel. 519-754-4400
Employer Background: Genfast Manufacturing Company produces steel, mechanical and automotive components. *New Positions Created (3):* Quality Systems Analyst; Sales Assistant; Lab Technician.

GENFOOT MANUFACTURING

Att: Marise Chiniara
554 Montee de Liesse
St-Laurent, QC H4T 1P1

Fax 514-341-1861
Website .... www.kamik.com
Employer Background: Genfoot Manufacturing is a North American manufacturer of outdoor footwear, including Kamik brand products. *New Positions Created (3):* International Logistics Specialist; Customer Service Clerk; Office Clerk.

GENNUM CORPORATION

Att: Human Resources
PO Box 489, Station A
Burlington, ON L7R 3Y3

Tel. 905-632-2996
Fax 905-632-2055
Email .... career@gennum.com
Website .... www.gennum.com
Employer Background: Gennum Corporation manufactures components for hearing aids and high-end video broadcast equipment. *New Positions Created (69):* Account Manager, Video Products Division; Applications Engineer, Video / Broadcast Products; Human Resources Generalist; IC Design Engineer, Hearing Instrumentation Products; IC Design Support Engineer, High-Speed Products; Manager, Hybrid Operations; Physical & Mixed-Signal Design Engineer, Video DSP; Product Architect / Product Development Engineer, Video DSP Products; Product Development & Design Engineer; Product Development Engineer; Product Line Specialist; Product Manager, Advanced DSP Hearing Instrument Products; Product Marketing Manager, Video Transport; R&D Video Test Engineer; Senior Process Engineer; System Architect / Algorithm Designer, Video DSP Products; System Circuit Design Engineer, Video DSP Products; Technology Operator; Test Development Engineer; Test Technology Development Engineer; ASIC Design Engineer, Video DSP Products; High-Speed Analog IC Design

Engineer, Video DSP Products; Mgr / Director of Quality Assurance; Mgr, High Speed IC Design; Production Test Support Position; Accounting Mgr; CAD Architect, System-on-a-Chip (SoC); CIS Help Desk Specialist; Corporate Travel Coordinator; Offshore Packaging and Sustaining Engineer; Product Mgr, Multi-GEN; R&D Offshore Packaging and Sustaining Engineer; Recruiter; Manager, ASIC Design; Mgr, Digital IC Design; System Architect / Algorithm Designer - Video DSP Products; Account Mgr - Video Products Division; Applications Engineer - Video & Broadcast Products; CAD Architect; CAD Engineer; Corporate Services Assistant; Digital CAD Architect; Director of Computing & Information Services; Expert Technology Operator; IC Design Engineer - Hearing Instrument Products; IC Design Engineer - Video DSP Products; IC Design Support Engineer - High-Speed Products; Intermediate Technology Operator; Product Development & Design Engineer; Product Development Engineer; Product Line Specialist; Product Mgr - Video & Broadcast Products; Production Planner, Hybrid Operations; R&D Video Test Engineer; Senior Process Engineer; Sr Technology Operator; System Circuit Design Engineer - Video DSP Products; Technology Access Engineer; Test Development Engineer; Test Technology Development Engineer; Video System Architect; Product Architect / Product Development Engineer, Video DSP Products; Project Mgr; Product Development & Design Engineer; Product Mgr, Video and Broadcast Products; Recruiter; Shift Leader / Operator, Night Shifts; Janitor / Maintenance Person; Mechanical Technologist.

GENTEK BUILDING PRODUCTS LTD.

Att: Carole Weir
1001 Corporate Drive
Burlington, ON L7L 5V5

Tel. 905-319-5560
Fax 905-319-5620
Email .... carole_weir@gentek.ca
Website .... www.gentek.ca
Employer Background: Gentek Building Products Ltd. manufactures and distributes vinyl and aluminum siding, windows and other exterior home improvement products. *New Positions Created (2):* Sales Representative; Warehouse Supervisor.

GENTRY KNITTING MILLS LTD.

Att: Joceline Allen, HR Manager
150 Dynamic Drive
Toronto, ON M1V 5A5

Tel. 416-299-5252
Fax 416-299-4007
Email .... joceline@gentryknit.com
Website .... www.gentryknit.com
Employer Background: Gentry Knitting Mills Ltd. produces quality knitted fabric. *New Positions Created (2):* Knitting Machine Operator; Knitting Technician.

GEO GROUP, THE

Att: Rowan
251 Consumers Road, Suite 100
Toronto, ON M2J 4R3

Tel. 416-490-0222
Fax 416-490-0155
Email .... betty@geogrp.com
Website .... www.geoholiday.com
Employer Background: The Geo Group is a vacation club. *New Positions Created (4):* Customer Service Reservationist; Senior Collections Position; Receptionist; Intermediate Accountant.

GEO-X SYSTEMS LTD., ARAM DIVISION

Att: Ian Strang
425 - 1st Street SW, Suite 1501
Calgary, AB T2P 3L8

Tel. 403-298-5600
Fax 403-537-2101
Website .... www.aram.com
Employer Background: Founded in 1971, Geo-X Systems Ltd provides geophysical data processing services to the Canadian oil and gas industry. *New Positions Created (2):* Electronic Technicians; Electronics Technician.

GEOGRAPHIC DYNAMICS CORP. / GDC

Att: Human Resources Manager
10368B - 60th Avenue
Edmonton, AB T6H 1G9

Tel. 780-436-1217
Fax 780-436-4348
Email .... mailbox@gdc-online.com
Website .... www.gdc-online.com
Employer Background: Geographic Dynamics Corp. is a multi-disciplinary company, specializing in ecosystem and resource management consulting. *New Positions Created (4):* Ecologist and Plant Ecologist; Forest Planner; GIS Analyst; Timber Supply Analyst.

GEOLOGIC SYSTEMS LTD.

Att: Human Resources
635 - 6th Avenue SW, Suite 200
Calgary, AB T2P 0T5

Tel. 403-262-1992
Fax 403-262-1987
Email .... opportunities@geologic.com
Website .... www.geologic.com
Employer Background: geoLOGIC Systems Ltd. develops database and software products for the oil and gas industry. *New Positions Created (2):* Sales Position; Software Developers.

GEOMETRIX DATA SYSTEMS INC.

Att: Human Resources
747 Fort Street, 10th Floor
Victoria, BC V8W 3E9

Fax 250-361-9362
Email .... careers@geometrix.bc.ca
Website .... www.geometrix.bc.ca
Employer Background: Founded in 1992, GeoMetrix Data Systems Inc. is a Canadian corporation that develops niche-market learning management software for the Windows environment. *New Positions Created (12):* Account Executive; Assistant Software Engineer; Computer Support Specialist; Office Administrator; Senior Project Imple-

mentation Specialists (2); Senior Implementation Specialist; Account Executive; Assistant Software Engineer; Communications and Marketing Writer; Customer Support Specialist; Office Administrator; Senior Project Implementation Specialist.

GEOMODELING RESEARCH CORP.
Att: Human Resources Manager
633 - 6th Avenue SW, Suite 630
Calgary, AB T2P 2Y5
Tel. 403-262-9172
Fax 403-262-9171
Email .... resume@geomodeling.com
Website .... www.geomodeling.com
Employer Background: Geomodeling Research Corp. is a research-oriented technology company, providing geo-modeling software and services to oil companies worldwide. *New Positions Created (2):* Software Documentation Positions; Software Marketing and Technical Sales Positions.

GEORGE BROWN COLLEGE
Att: Human Resources
PO Box 1015, Station B
Toronto, ON M5T 2T9
Tel. 416-415-4445
Fax 416-415-4795
Email .... hr@gbrownc.on.ca
Website .... www.gbrownc.on.ca
Employer Background: Established by the Government of Ontario in 1967, George Brown College is a non-profit corporation providing quality education through 3 campuses. *New Positions Created (31):* Project Coordinator, Renovations; Associate Director of Development, Asia; Academic Operations Manager, Business & Financial Services; Academic Operations Manager; Graphic Communication; Office Operations Manager; Chairperson, Community Services & Health Sciences; Professor, Building Restoration Technician Program; Professor, Industrial / Construction Millwright and Mechanical Technician Program; Professor, Steamfitter Program; Senior Researcher; Professor of Accounting; Professor of Advertising Design; Professor of Business; Professor of Corporate Design; Professor of Digital Media; Professor of Fashion Technology and Design; Professor of Financial Planning; Professor of Financial Services Management; Professor of Mathematics; Professor of Mathematics and Science; Professor of Visual Arts Fundamentals; Business & Catering Manager; Continuing Education Chairperson, Business and Creative Arts; First Aid Attendant; Human Rights Advisor; Purchasing Agent; Sous Chef; Counsellor; Peer Program; Director, Marketing and Communications; Professors, Faculty of Technology; Chair, Hospitality and Tourism.

GEORGE KELK CORPORATION
Att: Human Resources Manager
48 Lesmill Road
Toronto, ON M3B 2T5
Tel. 416-445-5850
Fax 416-445-5972
Email .... personnel@kelk.com
Website .... www.kelk.com
Employer Background: George Kelk Corporation is a major supplier of force sensors and electro-optical instrumentation to the metals industry. *New Positions Created (24):* Electronics Technician; Applications Specialists; Draftsperson; Electronics Engineers; Laser and Electro-Optics Specialists; Mechanical Optics Specialists; Senior Mechanical Engineer; Technical Salespeople; Applications Specialists; Draftspersons; Electronics Engineers; Electronics Technologists; Laser and Electro-Optics Specialists; Senior Mechanical Engineer; Technical Salesperson; Applications Specialists; Draftspersons; Electronics Engineers; Electronics Technologists; Laser and Electro-Optics Specialists; Laser and Electro-Optics Technologists; Regional Sales Managers; Software Developers; Machinist, Milling / Boring.

GEORGIA-PACIFIC CANADA, CONSUMER PRODUCTS INC.
Att: Human Resources Department
137 Bentworth Avenue
Toronto, ON M6A 1P6
Tel. 416-789-5151
Fax 416-789-2271
Website .... www.gp.com
Employer Background: Georgia-Pacific Canada, Consumer Products Inc. (formerly Fort James Canada Inc.) manufactures and distributes paper and plastic cups, plates and cutlery. *New Positions Created (2):* Extrusion / Thermoprocessing Technician; Maintenance Mechanic.

GEORGIAN COLLEGE
Att: Joyce Goheen,
Human Resource Consultant
1 Georgian Drive
Barrie, ON L4M 3X9
Tel. 705-722-1968
Fax 705-722-1503
Email .... resume@georgianc.on.ca
Website .... www.georgianc.on.ca
Employer Background: Located less than two hours north of Toronto, Georgian College is a community college serving Ontario's fastest-growing region. *New Positions Created (8):* Analyst and Scanning Technician; Residence Manager; Professor, Mechanical Engineering - Automotive Manufacturing; Professor, Mechanical Engineering - Tool & Die; Professor, Computer Programmer / Analyst; Professor, Justice and Public Safety; Professors, Nursing (7); Professor, Literacy Basic Skills Program.

GEOSIGN
Att: Human Resources Manager
727 Speedvale West
Guelph, ON N1K 1E6
Tel. 519-837-4436
Fax 519-837-1288
Email .... jobsTS1121@geosign.com
Website .... www.geosign.com
Employer Background: Geosign is an Internet infrastructure company. *New Positions Created (4):* Spider Utility Development Positions; Team Leader, Data Group; Vice-President, Strategy and Business Development; Windows Development Positions.

GEOTECH COMMUNICATIONS INC.
Att: Debbie
42 Wentworth Court, Unit 1
Brampton, ON L6T 5K6
Tel. 905-790-8887
Fax 905-790-8889
Email .... debbie@geotechcomm.com
Website .... www.geotechcomm.com
Employer Background: Geotech Communications Inc. is a telecom engineering firm. *New Positions Created (3):* AutoCad R14 Technicians; CATV Surveyors; I-MAP Drafters / CAD Technicians.

GERDAU COURTICE STEEL INC.
Att: Human Resources Coordinator
160 Orion Place
Cambridge, ON N1T 1R9
Tel. 905-450-0336
Fax 519-740-2601
Email .... hr@courticesteel.com
Website .... www.courticesteel.com
Employer Background: Gerdau Courtice Steel Inc. is a leader in the steel manufacturing industry, converting 300,000 tons of scrap metal into new products every year. *New Positions Created (5):* Mechanical Process Engineer; Quality Control Technician; Junior Project Engineer; Quality Assurance Coordinator; Sales Representative.

GERMAN ADVERTISING ADVANTAGE INC., THE / TGAA
Att: Human Resources Manager
2750 - 14th Avenue, Unit G2
Markham, ON L3R 0B6
Tel. 905-470-1175
Fax 416-733-8191
Website .... www.tgaa.ca
Employer Background: TGAA is one of the largest distributors of promotional items and business gifts in North America. *New Positions Created (2):* Sales Consultants; Sales Consultant.

GERRIE ELECTRIC WHOLESALE LTD.
Att: Human Resources Department
4104 South Service Road
Burlington, ON L7L 4X5
Tel. 905-681-3656
Fax 905-681-3221
Email .... hr@gerrie.com
Website .... www.gerrie.com
Employer Background: Founded in 1957, Gerrie Electric Wholesale Ltd. is the largest independent electrical distributor in Ontario. *New Positions Created (3):* Account Manager; Counter Sales Position; Electrical Order Desk Position.

GEXEL TELECOM
Att: Human Resources Manager
507 Place d'Armes, 18th Floor
Montréal, QC H2Y 2W8
Tel. 800-263-5161
Fax 514-935-5318
Email .... knoel@gexel.com

Website .... www.gexel.com

Employer Background: Gexel Telecom provides services to optimize customer relationships for companies worldwide. *New Positions Created (2):* Secretary / Administrative and Sales Assistant; Communication Agents, Call Centre.

GFI CONTROL SYSTEMS INC.
Att: Steve Heldman
100 Hollinger Crescent
Kitchener, ON N2K 2Z3
Tel. 519-576-4270
Fax 519-576-6542
Email .... sheldman@gfisystems.com
Website .... www.gfisystems.com

Employer Background: GFI Control Systems Inc. is an automotive system supplier of electronic fuel injection systems and components for natural gas and propane vehicles. *New Positions Created (12):* Product Engineers; Program Managers; Software Developers; Product Design Engineer; Purchasing Agent; Engine Calibrator; Failure Analysis Technician; Junior Product Engineer; Manufacturing Engineer; Materials Manager; Product Design Engineer; Purchasing Agent.

GHI TECHNOLOGIES
Att: Despina Spencer
1550 Enterprise Road, Suite 220
Mississauga, ON L4W 4P4
Tel. 905-564-4955
Fax 905-564-0152
Email ..... dspencer@ghitechnologies.com
Website ... www.ghitechnologies.com

Employer Background: GHl Technologies is a software development firm. *New Positions Created (2):* Bilingual Help Desk Technician; Sales Executive.

GHQ IMAGING INKJET PRODUCTIONS LTD.
Att: K. Riddell
310 Judson Street, Unit 19
Toronto, ON M8Z 5T6
Tel. 416-251-9230
Fax 416-251-6467
Website .... www.ghqimaging.com

Employer Background: GHQ Imaging Inkjet Productions Ltd. is a large international digital printing company for the outdoor advertising industry. *New Positions Created (5):* Printer Trainees; Operations Manager; General Labourer / Material Handler; Printer Trainees; Touch-Up Position.

GIBBS GAGE ARCHITECTS
Att: Human Resources Manager
237 - 8th Avenue SE, Suite 505
Calgary, AB T2G 5C3
Tel. 403-233-2000
Fax 403-264-0879
Email .... careers@gibbsgage.com
Website .... www.gibbsgage.com

Employer Background: Established in 1983, Gibbs Gage Architects is a Calgary-based firm of over 50 architects and technicians. *New Positions Created (3):* Design Architects and Architectural Technicians; Design Architects; Intermediate / Senior Technicians.

GIBRALTAR MORTGAGE LTD.
Att: Darrell Cook
1000 - 9th Avenue SW, Suite 300
Calgary, AB T2P 2Y6
Tel. 403-270-7000
Fax 403-233-8115
Website .... www.gibraltarmortgage.com

Employer Background: Gibraltar Mortgage Ltd. is a private lender, specializing in interim financing and CMHC residential loans. *New Positions Created (2):* Mortgage Representative; Senior Mortgage Underwriter.

GIENOW BUILDING PRODUCTS LTD.
Att: Human Resources
7140 - 40th Street SE
Calgary, AB T2C 2B6
Tel. 403-203-8200
Fax 403-279-2615
Email .... staffing@gienow.com
Website .... www.gienow.com

Employer Background: Gienow Building Products Ltd. is one of Canada's premier manufacturers of custom windows and doors. *New Positions Created (17):* Closing Technician; Receptionist; Order Processing Clerk; Process Engineer; Service Technicians; Order Processing Assistant; Administrative Assistant; Customer Service Representative; Inside Sales Positions, Dealer / New Construction Division; Maintenance Technician; Order Process Clerk; Intermediate Programmer / Analyst; Maintenance Technician; Production Supervisors; Human Resources Manager; Credit Assistant; Inside Sales Positions.

GIFFELS ASSOCIATES LIMITED
Att: Human Resources
30 International Boulevard
Toronto, ON M9W 5P3
Tel. 416-675-5950
Fax 416-675-4620
Email .... jobs@giffels.com
Website .... www.giffels.com

Employer Background: Giffels Associates Limited is a consulting and contracting firm, offering a range of architectural, engineering, management and construction services worldwide. *New Positions Created (25):* Architectural Job Captain; Infrastructure Environmental Planner; Intermediate Transportation Engineer; Infrastructure Project Manager; Junior / Intermediate Planners; Architectural Job Captain; Infrastructure Environmental Planner; Intermediate / Senior Planner / Scheduler; Intermediate Transportation Engineer; Senior Industrial Project Engineer; Infrastructure Project Supervisor; Infrastructure Senior Construction Engineer; Architectural Job Captain; Designers / Drafters; Infrastructure Environmental Planner; Intermediate Specification Writer; Intermediate Traffic Engineer; Intermediate Transportation Engineer; Junior or Intermediate Communications Position / Data Systems Position; Senior Electrical Engineer; Senior Industrial Project Engineer; Intermediate / Senior Mechanical Engineer; Intermediate / Senior Structural Engineer; Supply Chain Specialist; Technical Sales Consultant.

GIFFEN LEE
Att: Kathy Kozlowski
50 Queen Street North, Suite 500
PO Box 2396, Station B, Commerce House
Kitchener, ON N2H 6M3
Tel. 519-578-4150
Fax 519-578-8740
Email .... info@giffenleelaw.com
Website .... www.giffenleelaw.com

Employer Background: Giffen Lee is a 13-lawyer firm. *New Positions Created (2):* Litigation Lawyer; Senior Corporate Commercial Lawyer.

GIFTCRAFT LTD.
Att: Human Resources
95 Walker Drive
Brampton, ON L6T 5H7
Tel. 905-790-2000
Fax 905-790-0738
Email .... hr@giftcraft.com
Website .... www.giftcraft.com

Employer Background: Giftcraft Ltd. is a giftware importer and wholesaler. *New Positions Created (3):* Graphic Designer; Field Sales Manager; Buying Administration Coordinator.

GILBERT, WRIGHT & KIRBY
Att: Sheldon Gilbert
155 University Avenue, Suite 1800
Toronto, ON M5H 3B7
Tel. 416-363-3100
Fax 416-363-1379

Employer Background: Gilbert, Wright & Kirby is a firm of eight lawyers, with a practice restricted to civil litigation with emphasis on insurance and personal injury work. *New Positions Created (2):* Litigation Associate; Litigation Associate.

GILDA'S CLUB GREATER TORONTO
Att: Human Resources Manager
110 Lombard Street
Toronto, ON M5C 1M3
Email ...... jmarino@gildasclubtoronto.org
Website .... www.gildasclubtoronto.org

Employer Background: Gilda's Club Toronto is a charitable organization that provides a non-residential support community for individuals, families and friends touched by cancer. *New Positions Created (3):* Noogieland / Volunteer Coordinator; Program Manager; Program Director.

GILMORE
Att: L. Hind-Smith
130 Bloor Street West, Suite 700
Toronto, ON M5S 1N5
Tel. 416-926-1944
Fax 416-924-5792
Email ..... lhindsmith@gilmore-associates.ca
Website ... www.gilmore-openingminds.com

Employer Background: Gilmore provides transformational training and development initiatives to organizations worldwide. *New Positions Created (9):* Executive Assistant; Training Coordinator; Educational Program Writers; Executive Assistant; Graphic Designers and Desktop Publishers; Project Manager; Vice President, Design & Development; Vice-President, Business Development; Vice-President, Design Operations.

GILMORE GLOBAL LOGISTICS SERVICES / DOCULINK INTERNATIONAL INC.
Att: Human Resources
120 Herzberg Road
Kanata, ON K2K 3B7
Tel. 613-599-6065
Fax 613-271-7475
Email .... hr@gilmore.ca
Website .... www.gilmore.ca
Employer Background: Gilmore Global Logistics Services / DocuLink International Inc. manages and distributes information in multiple media formats, including print, CD-ROM and the Internet. *New Positions Created (4):* Accounting Administrator; Business Operations Manager; Implementation Administrator; Technology Administrator.

GIRL GUIDES OF CANADA, BRITISH COLUMBIA COUNCIL
Att: COO
1476 - 8th Avenue West
Vancouver, BC V6H 1E1
Tel. 604-714-6636
Fax 604-714-6646
Email .... info@bc-girlguides.org
Website .... www.bc-girlguides.org
Employer Background: Established in 1910, the Girl Guides of Canada offers girls and young women the opportunity to develop life skills under the leadership of female role models. *New Positions Created (3):* Administrative Assistant, Events Management; Accountant; Administrative Assistant, Events Management.

GKO ENGINEERING
Att: Milt Webster, HR Manager
4999 - 98th Avenue, Suite 302
Edmonton, AB T6B 2X3
Tel. 780-461-9993
Fax 780-450-9966
Email .... edmonton@gko.com
Website .... www.gko.com
Employer Background: GKO Engineering is an Alberta-based, multi-disciplinary engineering company, providing engineering design and drafting services to the industrial sector. *New Positions Created (21):* Instrumentation / Control Engineers and Designers; Senior Electrical Designers; Senior Materials Handling Designers; Senior Materials Handling Engineers; Senior Process Engineer; Senior Procurement Specialists; C++ Programmer; Instrumentation / Controls & Electrical Engineer; Senior Electrical Engineer; Senior / Intermediate Mechanical Designers; Senior / Intermediate Structural Designers; Senior Project Man-

agers; Senior Structural / Civil Engineers; Civil / Structural Engineers / Designers; Structural Engineer; Instrumentation / Controls & Electrical Engineers; Senior Project Managers; C++ Programmer; Engineers and Designers, Instrumentation / Controls / Electrical; Mechanical / Piping Manager; Senior Mechanical Engineers.

GL&V / DORR-OLIVER CANADA INC.
Att: Human Resources Manager
174 West Street South
Orillia, ON L3V 6L4
Tel. 705-325-6181
Fax 705-325-9884
Email .... dorothy.paavola@glv.com
Website .... www.glv.com
Employer Background: GL&V / Dorr-Oliver Canada Inc. is a supplier of grey and ductile iron castings. *New Positions Created (2):* Sales / Process Engineer; Melt Shop Supervisor.

GLAXOSMITHKLINE
Att: Human Resources
7333 Mississauga Road North
Mississauga, ON L5N 6L4
Tel. 905-819-3000
Fax 905-819-7187
Email .... ca-hr@gsk.com
Website .... ca.gsk.com
Employer Background: GlaxoSmithKline is a research-based pharmaceutical company, fighting disease by developing innovative medicines and services. *New Positions Created (50):* Clinical Data Analysts; Vaccine Sales Representatives; Hospital Sales Representative; Production Project Leader; Auditor, Compliance; Manager, Outsourced Services; Manager, IT Technical Services and Security; Manager, Strategic Change; Pharmaceutics Manager; Pharmaceutics Scientist; Clinical Research Associate; Manager, Media Relations and Corporate Communications; QC Microbiology Manager; Recruitment Specialist; Bilingual Proofreader; Mechanical Team Leader; Project Manager, CMC Regulatory Submissions; Scheduler, Aladdin Project Controls; Senior CMC Submissions Associate; Engineering Specialist; HIV Representatives; Manager, Federal Drug Programs; Manager, Market Research - Strategic Business Services; Manager, Reimbursement Strategy; National Manager, Trade Relations; Performance Consultant, HIV / Oncology / Vaccines; Product Managers; Production Supervisor, Manufacturing and Packaging; Program Development Manager, Continuing Health Education; Sales Manager, Vaccines; Sales Representatives; Project Leader; Bilingual Proofreader; Documentation Associate; Graphics Coordinators; Impact of Change Specialist; Labelling Team Leader; Mechanical Team Leader; Microbiology Analyst; Packaging Technologist; Process Validation Specialist; Project Leader, New Products; Project Manager; Quality Assurance Auditor, Review and Release; Quality Assurance Compliance Specialist; Trainer / Author; Maintenance Mechanic Team Members; Manufacturing Team Members; Packaging

Team Members; Production Compliance Team Members.

GLAXOSMITHKLINE
Att: Human Resources, Quebec
8455 Trans Canada Highway
St-Laurent, QC H4S 1Z1
Fax 514-956-3181
Email .... ca-hr@gsk.com
Website .... ca.gsk.com
Employer Background: GlaxoSmithKline is a research-based company, fighting disease by developing innovative medicines and services. *New Positions Created (4):* Customer Service Representatives; District Sales Manager; Manager, Provincial Reimbursement; Sales Representatives.

GLEN CORPORATION
Att: Human Resources Manager
100 Scarsdale Road
Toronto, ON M3B 2R8
Tel. 416-449-3300
Fax 416-449-0392
Employer Background: Glen Corporation is a real estate company that maintains accounting records for many corporate entities. *New Positions Created (2):* Corporate Accountant; Corporate Accountant.

GLEN GROVE SUITES
Att: President
2837 Yonge Street
Toronto, ON M4N 2J6
Fax 416-440-3073
Website .... www.glengrove.com
Employer Background: Glen Grove Suites provides corporate accommodations for Fortune 500 companies, with over 175 fully furnished suites in Toronto, Ottawa and New York. *New Positions Created (5):* Corporate Sales Manager; In-House Sales Manager; Corporate Sales Manager; Front Desk Sales & Telemarketing Associates; In-House Sales Manager.

GLENBURNIE SCHOOL
Att: Human Resources Manager
2035 Upper Middle Road East
Oakville, ON L6J 4Z2
Tel. 905-338-6236
Fax 905-338-2654
Email hresources@glenburnieschool.com
Website ... www.glenburnieschool.com
Employer Background: Glenburnie School is a private, co-educational day school. *New Positions Created (4):* Teachers (2); Teachers; Grade 4-8 Core French Teacher; Teacher.

GLOBAL CROSSING
Att: Human Resources Manager
1140 de Maisonneuve West, 9th Floor
Montréal, QC H3A 1M8
Tel. 514-843-6177
Email .... kimberly_kloser@
.... globalcrossing.com
Website .... www.globalcrossing.com
Employer Background: Global Crossing offers the world's most extensive IP-based fi-

bre optic network, providing services to 5 continents. *New Positions Created (10):* Network Operations Coach; Network Operations Manager(s); NOC Engineer(s); Telecommunications Technician; Administrative Assistant II; Coach; Manager - Capacity Planning; Senior Technology Manager; Technical Trainer; Technology Support Manager.

GLOBAL EDUCATIONAL TRUST PLAN / GLOBAL EDUCATIONAL MARKETING CORPORATION
Att: Faye W. Slipp
800 Arrow Road, Suite 1100
Toronto, ON M9M 2Z8
Tel. 416-741-7377
Fax 416-741-8987
Email .... fayes@globalresp.com
Website .... www.globalresp.com
Employer Background: Global Educational Trust Plan markets registered educational savings plans. *New Positions Created (7):* Various Financial Sales Positions; Brokerage Manager; Compliance Officer; Marketing Director; Office / Administration Manager; Regional Sales Director; Various Insurance Positions.

GLOBAL GROUP, THE
Att: Bob Ritter, Corporate HR
580 Supertest Road, PO Box 456, Station A
Toronto, ON M3M 3A8
Tel. 416-661-3660
Fax 416-665-2555
Website .... www.globaltotaloffice.com
Employer Background: The Global Group is Canada's largest manufacturer of office furniture. *New Positions Created (12):* Marketing Associate; Field Service Coordinator; Field Services Technician; Marketing Assistant; Quality Technician; CAD Operators; Training / Service Coordinator; District Sales Manager; Machine Operator / Technician; Spray Painters; Maintenance Mechanics; Mechanical Engineer.

GLOBAL STAR SOFTWARE
Att: Human Resources Manager
6225 Kenway Drive
Mississauga, ON L5T 2L3
Tel. 905-795-9880
Fax 905-795-9881
Website .... www.globalstarsoftware.com
Employer Background: Founded in 1995, Global Star Software publishes and sells software products worldwide. *New Positions Created (4):* Salespeople; Production Manager; Marketing Manager; North American Account Manager.

GLOBAL TELEVISION NETWORK INC.
Att: Lori Peever
81 Barber Greene Road
Toronto, ON M3C 2A2
Tel. 416-446-5311
Email .... lpeever@globaltv.ca
Website .... www.globaltv.ca
Employer Background: Global Television Network Inc., a division of Canwest Global

Communications Corp., is one of Canada's premiere television broadcasters. *New Positions Created (14):* Senior Producer, Global News; Program Coordinators; Broadcast Technicians; Graphics Arts, Electronic; Listings Coordinator; Master Control Operators; Non-Linear Production Editors; Producers, On-Air Promotions; Production Coordinators; Production Supervisor, On-Air Promotions; Production VTR Operators; Senior Help Desk Analyst; Traffic Coordinators; VTR Librarians.

GLOBAL THERMOELECTRIC INC.
Att: Manager, Human Resources
4908 - 52nd Street SE
Calgary, AB T2B 3R2
Tel. 403-204-6100
Fax 413-204-6101
Website .... www.globalte.com
Employer Background: Global Thermoelectric Inc. is a leader in the commercialization of solid oxide fuel cell technology, with a focus on residential cogeneration and auxiliary power for automotive applications and small-scale industrial uses. *New Positions Created (81):* Buyer; Electronic Test Engineer; Machinist; Advanced Modeling and Analysis Engineer; Control Systems Specialist; Fluids / Hardware Engineer; Manufacturing Engineer; Accounts Payable Clerk; Assembler; Business Development Manager, Generators; Design Manufacturing Engineer, SOFC; Electronic Technologist, SOFC; Electronics Design Engineer; Manager, Engineering; Manager, Stack Design; Production Member, SOFC; Senior Materials Process Engineer; Stack Test Technician; Test Technician / Technologist, Residential Cogeneration Team; Electronic Technician - SOFC; Facilities Maintenance and Safety Assistant - SOFC; Marketing Analyst; Marketing Manager; Production Manager - Bassano; Stack Design Technologist; Systems Design Engineer - SOFC; Test Engineer - Product Development; Corporate Accounting Manager; Human Resources Advisor; Junior Materials Technologist; Senior Engineer - Codes and Standards; Electronic Design Engineer; Electronic Technologist; Fuel Processing Engineer; Manufacturing Engineer; Power Electronics Engineer; Program Manager, Automotive; Business Development Manager - Generators; Manager, Engineering; Materials Process Engineer; Mechanical Test Technician - Systems; Production Member I - SOFC; Purchasing / Accounting Clerk; Senior Process Engineer; Team Leader - Codes & Standards; Payroll & Benefits Supervisor; Accounts Payable Supervisor / General Accountant; Design Manufacturing Engineer, SOFC; Detail Draftsman; Electronics Design Engineer; Electronics Design Engineer / Group Leader; Fuel Processing Engineer, SOFC; Fuel Processing Specialist, SOFC; IS Support Technician, Corporate; Manager, Government Programs; Manager, Materials (R&D); Manufacturing Engineer, SOFC; Materials Technician, Bassano; Mechanical Laboratory Technician, Automotive (SOFC); Millwright; Power Electronics Engineer, SOFC; Process Engineer, SOFC; Production

Scheduler, Bassano; Program Manager, Automotive (SOFC); Quality Engineer; Sales Administrator, Generator Division; Senior Scientist, Flow Modelling; Test Technician; Electronic Technologist; Electronics Technician; Purchaser; Traffic Coordinator; Accounts Payable Supervisor / General Accountant; Mgr, Cell Manufacturing Research and Development; Mgr, Quality; Manufacturing Engineer; Materials Engineer; Plant Electrician; Process Engineers; Safety and Training Coordinator; Test Technician.

GLOBALSTAR / ONE STOP WIRELESS
Att: Human Resources Manager
55 Chauncey Avenue
Toronto, ON M8Z 2Z2
Tel. 416-231-5333
Fax 416-231-8994
Website .... www.onestopwireless.on.ca
Employer Background: Globalstar / One Stop Wireless provides satellite and wireless communication products. *New Positions Created (2):* Service Manager; Store Manager / Coordinator.

GLOBEL DIRECT MARKETING
Att: National Recruiting
6631 Elmbridge Way, Suite 160
Richmond, BC V7C 4N1
Tel. 604-231-7555
Fax 604-270-7787
Website .... www.globel.ca
Employer Background: Globel Direct Marketing, western Canada's largest direct marketing company, provides customized customer communication solutions, including data-to-mail, digital imaging, call centre services and Internet presentations. *New Positions Created (12):* Manager, New Business Development; Manager, People and Training; Senior Account Manager; Account Manager / Specialist; Applications Programmer; Client Service Specialist; Inside Sales Representative; Integration Specialist; Laser Print Operations Manager; Laser Print Operator; Mail Processing Assistant; Supervisor, Quality Assurance.

GLOBEL DIRECT MARKETING
Att: Human Resources Manager
1324 - 36th Avenue NE
Calgary, AB T2E 8S1
Tel. 403-531-6550
Fax 403-531-6560
Website .... www.globel.ca
Employer Background: Globel Direct Marketing, western Canada's largest direct marketing company, provides customized customer communication solutions, including data-to-mail, digital imaging, call centre services and Internet presentations. *New Positions Created (5):* Applications Programmer; Integration Specialist; Client Service Specialists; Laser Print Operations Manager; Laser Print Operators.

GMB INDUSTRIES
Att: Human Resources
215 Statesman Drive
Mississauga, ON L5S 1X4

Tel. 905-565-0950
Fax 905-565-0951
Email .... jobs@gmbindustries.com
Website .... www.gmbindustries.com
Employer Background: GMB Industries builds custom and semi-custom machinery and automated systems for the packaging, steel mill and automotive markets. *New Positions Created (3):* Accountant; Sr Mechanical Designer; Sr Mechanical Designers.

GN NETTEST (CANADA) INC., NETWORKS DIVISON
Att: Human Resources
55 Renfrew Drive
Markham, ON L3R 8H3
Tel. 905-479-8090
Fax 905-475-6524
Email .... resumes@gnnettest.com
Website .... www.gnnettest.com
Employer Background: GN NetTest (Canada) Inc. manufactures products for testing, monitoring and managing telecom, datacom and fibre optic networks. *New Positions Created (7):* Network Software Engineer, Real-Time Embedded / Device Drivers; Sales Engineer; Senior Applications Engineer; Director, American Support; Hardware Design Engineers (2); Software Development Engineers, Java (2); Inside Sales Representative.

GO TRANSIT / GREATER TORONTO TRANSIT AUTHORITY
Att: Human Resources Office
20 Bay Street, Suite 600
Toronto, ON M5J 2W3
Tel. 416-869-3600
Email .... humanresources@gotransit.com
Website .... www.gotransit.com
Employer Background: GO Transit is Canada's first and Ontario's only interregional public transit system. *New Positions Created (5):* Forms Designer; Rail Operations Coordinator; Performance & Compliance Officer; Equipment Engineer Trainee; Equipment Engineer.

GOLDCARE INDUTIAE INC.
Att: Human Resources Manager
55 Queen Street East
Toronto, ON M5C 1R6
Tel. 416-362-7625
Fax 416-362-7839
Email .... goldcareoffice@goldcare.net
Employer Background: Established in 1995, Goldcare Indutiae Inc. is a consulting firm, providing mentoring forums for chief executives of high-tech companies in Canada and the USA. *New Positions Created (3):* Senior Investment Manager; Senior Vice President; Senior Analyst.

GOLDEN BOY FOODS INC.
Att: Personnel Manager
8820 Northbrook Court
Burnaby, BC V5J 5J1
Email ... goldenboy_foods@bc.sympatico.ca
Employer Background: Golden Boy Foods Inc. is a leading food manufacturer and distributor in western Canada. *New Positions*

Created (3): Maintenance Manager; Quality Assurance Manager, Research and Development; Warehouse Manager.

GOLDEN MILL BAKERY
Att: Human Resources
1275 Rymal Road East
Hamilton, ON L8W 3L3
Fax 905-575-5891
Employer Background: Golden Mill Bakery, part of Weston Bakeries Ltd. and Ready Bake Foods Inc., provides fresh and frozen products. *New Positions Created (2):* Maintenance Mechanic; Production Staff.

GOLDEN WINDOWS LTD.
Att: Human Resources
888 Guelph Street
Kitchener, ON N2H 5Z6
Fax 519-579-8900
Email .... admin@goldenwindows.com
Website .... www.goldenwindows.com
Employer Background: Golden Windows Ltd. is a Canadian manufacturer of windows and doors. *New Positions Created (3):* Architectural Window Builder; Millwright; Tenoner Operator.

GOLDER ASSOCIATES LTD.
Att: Teri Sigmund
4260 Still Creek Drive, Suite 500
Burnaby, BC V5C 6C6
Tel. 604-298-6623
Fax 604-298-5253
Email .... tsigmund@golder.com
Website .... www.golder.com
Employer Background: Founded in 1960, Golder Associates Ltd. is a consulting engineering firm, providing comprehensive civil, geotechnical and environmental consulting services. The company has over 2,000 employees and 80 offices worldwide. *New Positions Created (2):* Junior or Intermediate Solid Waste / Geotechnical Engineer; Regional Coordinator.

GOLDER ASSOCIATES LTD.
Att: Kelly Boyle, HR Administrator
940 - 6th Avenue SW, 10th Floor
Calgary, AB T2P 3T1
Tel. 403-299-5600
Fax 403-299-5606
Email .... kboyle@golder.com
Website .... www.golder.com
Employer Background: Founded in 1960, Golder Associates Ltd. is a consulting engineering firm, providing comprehensive civil, geotechnical and environmental consulting services. The company has over 2,000 employees and 80 offices worldwide. *New Positions Created (16):* Intermediate & Senior Environmental Specialists; Senior Fisheries Biologist; Archaeologist; Fisheries Biologist; Intermediate Air Quality Scientist or Engineer; Intermediate GIS Specialist; Intermediate Vegetation Scientist; Intermediate Wildlife Biologist; Junior Air Quality Scientist or Engineer; Junior GIS Specialist; Junior Hydrogeologist; Junior / Intermediate Water Quality Specialist; Senior Air Quality

Scientist or Engineer; Senior GIS Specialist; Senior Hydrogeologist; Water Resources Engineers.

GOLDWELL COSMETICS (CANADA) LTD.
Att: Human Resources Manager
1100 Courtneypark Drive, Unit 1
Mississauga, ON L5T 1L7
Fax 905-564-0736
Email .... hr@goldwell.ca
Website .... www.goldwell.com
Employer Background: Goldwell Cosmetics (Canada) Ltd. supplies professional haircare products to fine salons worldwide. *New Positions Created (4):* Bilingual Client Services Representative; Receptionist; National Programs Manager; Sales Professionals (2).

GOLF TOWN CANADA INC.
Att: Human Resources Manager
100 Mural Street, Suite 203
Richmond Hill, ON L4B 1J3
Tel. 905-763-1388
Fax 905-763-9257
Email .... careers@golftown.com
Website .... www.golftown.com
Employer Background: Founded in 1999, Golf Town is a large golf retailer in Canada. *New Positions Created (2):* Various Retail Positions; Fashion Buyer.

GOLF-GIG MANAGEMENT SYSTEMS INTERNATIONAL INC. / GMSI INC.
Att: Human Resources
5925 - 12th Street SE, Suite 200
Calgary, AB T2H 2M3
Fax 403-259-5151
Website .... www.golfgig.net
Employer Background: GMSI Inc. provides golf course management software. *New Positions Created (4):* Accountant / Controller; Executive Sales Position; Executive Assistant; Accounting Position.

GOOD SAMARITAN SOCIETY, THE
Att: Recruitment Office
9405 - 50th Street, Suite 200
Edmonton, AB T6B 2T4
Tel. 780-431-3600
Fax 780-431-3795
Website .... www.gss.org
Employer Background: The Good Samaritan Society is a Christian, non-profit caregiving organization, serving individuals who are frail, disabled or chronically ill. *New Positions Created (4):* Physical Therapist; Director of Fund Development and Public Relations; Human Resources Advisors; Team Leader, Labour Relations and Information Services.

GOOD SHEPHERD MINISTRIES
Att: Manager, HR & Administration
412 Queen Street East
Toronto, ON M5A 1T3
Fax 416-869-0510
Email .... resume@goodshepherd.ca
Employer Background: Good Shepherd Ministries provides food, shelter and ancil-

lary services to homeless, disadvantaged and marginalized people. *New Positions Created (3):* Fundraiser; Administrative Assistant; Fundraising Associate.

GOODKEY, WEEDMARK & ASSOCIATES LTD.
Att: Human Resources
1749 Woodward Drive
Ottawa, ON K2C 0P9

Tel. 613-727-5111
Fax 613-727-5115
Email .... gweng@gwal.com
Employer Background: Goodkey, Weedmark & Associates Ltd. is a consulting engineering firm, specializing in the mechanical / electrical engineering of commercial, industrial and institutional building systems. *New Positions Created (4):* Mechanical and Electrical Engineers; Technicians and Site Inspectors; Mechanical and Electrical Site Inspectors; Mechanical / Electrical Engineers and Technicians.

GOODLIFE FOODS
Att: Sherry Freehorn
4830 - 32nd Street SE
Calgary, AB T2B 2S8

Fax 403-215-6099
Email .... jobs@goodlifebrands.com
Employer Background: Goodlife Foods distributes refrigerated products to convenience stores and offers catalogue-based home delivery of high-quality branded frozen foods. *New Positions Created (4):* Accounts Receivable Collector; Payroll Supervisor; Sales Specialist; HR Manager.

GOODMAN PHILLIPS & VINEBERG
Att: Stacy Zosky,
Director, Associate Program
250 Yonge Street, Suite 2400, Box 24
Toronto, ON M5B 2M6

Tel. 416-979-2211
Fax 416-979-1234
Email .... zoskys@tor.gpv.com
Website .... www.gpv.com
Employer Background: Goodman Phillips & Vineberg is a law firm located in downtown Toronto. *New Positions Created (2):* Corporate / Commercial Lawyers; Intermediate and Senior Corporate / Commercial Clerks.

GOODYEAR CANADA INC.
Att: Larry Kimmerly,
Employment and Benefits Manager
PO Box 370
Napanee, ON K7R 3P5

Fax 613-354-7760
Email .... larry.kimmerly@goodyear.com
Website .... www.goodyear.com
Employer Background: Goodyear Canada Inc. is a subsidiary of Ohio-based Goodyear Tire & Rubber Company, the world's largest tire company. The parent company has 97,000 employees and annual revenues of $12.6 billion. *New Positions Created (3):* Accounting Clerk, Finance Department; Electrical Engineers; Mechanical Engineers.

GORE MUTUAL INSURANCE COMPANY
Att: Human Resources
252 Dundas Street North
Cambridge, ON N1R 5T3

Tel. 519-623-1910
Fax 519-623-9473
Email .... careers@goremutual.ca
Website .... www.goremutual.ca
Employer Background: Founded in 1839, Gore Mutual Insurance Company is Canada's oldest federally licensed mutual property and casualty insurance company. *New Positions Created (5):* Personal Lines Underwriters; Claims Representative; Claims Specialist; Senior Field Claims Representatives; Program Manager, Auto Physical Losses.

GOWAY TRAVEL LTD.
Att: Human Resources
3284 Yonge Street, Suite 500
Toronto, ON M4N 3M7

Fax 416-322-9656
Website .... www.goway.com
Employer Background: Established in 1970, Goway Travel Ltd. is one of North America's largest tour operators for travel to the South Pacific. *New Positions Created (7):* Manager, Goway Air; Receptionist; Sales Agents, Goway Air / Wholesale FIT and Tours; Ticketing Agents, Goway Air; Desktop Publisher, Mac; Manager; Ticketing Agents.

GOWLING LAFLEUR HENDERSON LLP
Att: Lisa Wilson, Office Administrator
PO Box 1045, LCD 1
Hamilton, ON L8N 3R4

Tel. 905-540-8200
Fax 905-528-5833
Website .... www.gowlings.com
Employer Background: Gowling Lafleur Henderson LLP specializes in business and technology law, intellectual property and advocacy. *New Positions Created (5):* Legal Real Estate Secretary; Legal Secretary; Corporate / Commercial Legal Secretary; Litigation Law Clerk; Legal Secretary, Real Estate Law.

GOWLING LAFLEUR HENDERSON LLP
Att: Erica Stone
160 Elgin Street, Suite 2600
Ottawa, ON K1P 1C3

Tel. 613-233-1781
Fax 613-563-9869
Website .... www.gowlings.com
Employer Background: Gowling Lafleur Henderson LLP specializes in business and technology law, intellectual property and advocacy. *New Positions Created (6):* Research Lawyer; Tax Lawyer; Intellectual Property Lawyers; Patent Coordinator; Business Law Lawyer; Intellectual Property / Information Technology Lawyer.

GOWLING LAFLEUR HENDERSON LLP
Att: Luc Lissoir, Managing Partner
1 Place Ville-Marie, 37th Floor
Montréal, QC H3B 3P4

Tel. 514-878-9641
Fax 514-878-1450

Email .... luc.lissoir@gowlings.com
Website .... www.gowlings.com
Employer Background: Gowling Lafleur Henderson LLP specializes in business and technology law, intellectual property and advocacy. *New Positions Created (2):* Translators; Various Law Positions (3).

GP CAPITAL MANAGEMENT GROUP
Att: Rick Sprentz
191 The West Mall, Suite 215
Toronto, ON M9W 5K8

Tel. 416-622-9969
Fax 416-622-5040
Website .... www.gpcapital.com
Employer Background: GP Capital Management Group offers customized money management programs. *New Positions Created (2):* Receptionist / Administration Position; Receptionist / Administrative Assistant.

GRAHAM EDMUNDS
Att: Office Administrator
1167 Kensington Crescent NW, Suite 200
Calgary, AB T2N 1X7

Tel. 403-283-7796
Fax 403-283-7779
Email .... lori_rygus@gearch.com
Website .... www.gearch.com
Employer Background: Graham Edmunds is a firm of architects, planners and interior designers working in a collaborative studio environment. *New Positions Created (4):* Architectural Technologist or Architect; Graphic Designer; Intern Architect; Interior Designer.

GRAHAM INDUSTRIAL SERVICES LTD.
Att: Brian Lueken, President
9810 - 60th Avenue
Edmonton, AB T6E 0C5

Tel. 780-430-9600
Fax 780-430-9700
Email .... brianl@graham.ca
Website .... www.graham.ca
Employer Background: Graham Industrial Services Ltd. is one of Canada's leading contractors, providing a range of civil, building and industrial construction services. *New Positions Created (8):* Civil Construction Estimator; Civil Operations Manager; Manager; Mechanical Department Manager; Civil Estimator; Mechanical Department Manager; Various Construction Positions; Various Construction Positions (3).

GRAHAM PACKAGING CANADA
Att: B. O'Neil
4041 North Service Road
Burlington, ON L7L 4X6

Tel. 905-335-0520
Fax 905-335-0357
Website .... www.grahampackaging.com
Employer Background: Graham Packaging manufactures customized blow-molded plastic containers for the branded food and beverage, household, personal care and automotive lubricant markets. *New Positions Created (4):* Industrial Electrician; Sales Service Rep; Maintenance Mechanic; Electrician.

GRAHAM PACKAGING CANADA LTD.
Att: Human Resources Manager
3174 Mavis Road
Mississauga, ON L5C 1T8
Tel. 905-277-1486
Fax 905-275-4255
Email .... nathan.mutch@
.... grahampackaging.com
Website .... www.grahampackaging.com
Employer Background: Graham Packaging
is a leading manufacturer of custom blow-
molded plastic containers, with 4,000 em-
ployees and 57 plants throughout North
America, Europe and Latin America. *New
Positions Created (2):* Production Supervi-
sors; Maintenance Electrician and Maintenance Mechanic.

**GRAND ERIE DISTRICT
SCHOOL BOARD**
Att: Peter Moffatt, Director of Education
349 Erie Avenue
Brantford, ON N3T 5V3
Tel. 519-756-6301
Fax 519-759-0895
Website .... www.gedsb.on.ca
Employer Background: Grand Erie District
School Board is a mid-sized school board,
serving the City of Brantford and Counties
of Brant, Haldimand and Norfolk. *New Po-
sitions Created (2):* Superintendents of
Schools (2); Manager of Human Resources.

GRAND RIVER HOSPITAL
Att: Human Resources Manager
835 King Street West, PO Box 9056
Kitchener, ON N2G 1G3
Tel. 519-749-4300
Fax 519-749-4313
Website ..... www.grandriverhospital.on.ca
Employer Background: Grand River Hospi-
tal is an acute and chronic care facility, serv-
ing a community of over 300,000 residents.
New Positions Created (24): Research & Per-
formance Metrics Analyst; Risk Manage-
ment Coordinator; Hospitalists (6); Mental
Health Clinical Service Coordinator; Clini-
cal Practice Specialist, Central West Eating
Disorder Program; Risk Coordinator; Clini-
cal Director, Complex Continuing Care; Reg-
istered Nurses, Cardiac Care; Registered
Nurses, Intensive Care; Community Treatment Orders Coordinator; Clinical Director;
Human Resources Consultant; Manager,
Payroll Services; Clinical Nurse Specialist;
Nurse Practitioner; Various Medical Posi-
tions; Clinical Dietitian; Community Liaison
/ Education Facilitator; Program Researcher
/ Evaluator; Social Worker; Utilization Clini-
cal Data Analyst; Program Research &
Evaluation Specialist; Manager of Payroll
Services; Registered Technologist, Histology
and Cytology Laboratory.

GRAND RIVER POULTRY FARM LTD.
Att: Sherry Nelson
334 Grand River Street North
Paris, ON N3L 4A5
Tel. 519-442-5453
Fax 519-442-5732
Email .... snelson@grandriverpoultry.com

Website .... www.grandriverpoultry.com
Employer Background: Grand River Poultry Farm Ltd. is a poultry processing company. *New Positions Created (4):* Payroll and
Human Resources Coordinator; Chick
Placement Coordinator; Accounts Receivable Coordinator; Invoicing Coordinator.

GRAND & TOY LTD.
Att: General Sales Manager
11522 - 168th Street
Edmonton, AB T5M 3T9
Fax 780-484-0708
Email .... teod@grandtoy.com
Website .... www.grandtoy.com
Employer Background: Established in 1882,
Grand & Toy Ltd. is Canada's largest com-
mercial office supplies company, with over
90 corporate sales and retail locations and
2,200 employees. *New Positions Created (2):*
Inside Account Mgr; Outside Account Mgr.

GRAND & TOY LTD.
Att: Human Resources Manager
15 Keefer Court
Hamilton, ON L8E 4V8
Fax 905-561-3710
Email .... oddiv@grandtoy.com
Website .... www.grandtoy.com
Employer Background: Established in 1882,
Grand & Toy Ltd. is Canada's largest com-
mercial office supplies company, with over
90 corporate sales and retail locations and
2,200 employees. *New Positions Created (2):*
Account Manager; Furniture Sales Special-
ist.

GRAND & TOY LTD.
Att: Operations Support Coordinator
200 Aviva Park Drive
Vaughan, ON L4L 9C7
Fax 905-264-0257
Website .... www.grandandtoy.com
Employer Background: Established in 1882,
Grand & Toy Ltd. is Canada's largest com-
mercial office supplies company, with over
90 corporate sales and retail locations and
2,200 employees. *New Positions Created (5):*
District Sales Manager, Commercial; Health
& Safety Coordinator; Industrial Mechanic
/ Millwright (2); Transportation Manager;
Inside Sales Coordinator.

GRANDE PRAIRIE, CITY OF
Att: Steve McMinn
9905 - 100th Street, 3rd Floor
PO Bag 4000
Grande Prairie, AB T8V 6V3
Tel. 780-538-0313
Fax 780-539-1056
Email .. smcminn@city.grande-prairie.ab.ca
Website ...... www.city.grande-prairie.ab.ca
Employer Background: Founded in 1881, the
City of Grande Prairie is located in north-
west Alberta and home to over 33,000 resi-
dents. *New Positions Created (4):* Public
Works Director; Financial Services Director;
Enforcement Services Program Manager;
Utilities Director.

**GRANDE PRAIRIE, CITY OF
(TRANSPORTATION SERVICES)**
Att: Darwin Juell, PEng
9905 - 112th Street, City Service Centre
Grande Prairie, AB T8V 6H8
Tel. 780-538-0417
Fax 780-538-3174
Email .... jfurman@city.grande-prairie.ab.ca
Website ..... www.city.grande-prairie.ab.ca
Employer Background: Founded in 1881, the
City of Grande Prairie is home to over 31,000
residents. *New Positions Created (2):* Engi-
neering Technologist; Facility Workers (2).

**GRANDE PRAIRIE PUBLIC
SCHOOL DISTRICT**
Att: Evelyn Seewalt, HR Coordinator
10213 - 99th Street
Grande Prairie, AB T8V 2H3
Tel. 780-532-4491
Fax 780-539-4265
Email .... eseewalt@gppsd.ab.ca
Website .... www.gppsd.ab.ca
Employer Background: The Grande Prairie
Public School District serves the needs of
over 4,900 K-12 students in 9 schools. *New
Positions Created (2):* Educational Psycholo-
gist; Director of Finance.

**GRANDE PRAIRIE
REGIONAL COLLEGE**
Att: Human Resources
10726 - 106th Avenue
Grande Prairie, AB T8V 4C4
Tel. 780-539-2853
Fax 780-539-2854
Email .... humanresources@gprc.ab.ca
Website .... www.gprc.ab.ca
Employer Background: Established in 1966,
Grande Prairie Regional College is a post-
secondary educational institution. *New Po-
sitions Created (6):* Computer Science In-
structors (2); Director, Workforce Develop-
ment; Aboriginal Liaison Advisor, Student
Services; Computer Science Instructor; Eng-
lish / Humanities Instructors; Instructor.

GRANITE CLUB LIMITED
Att: Human Resources Manager
2350 Bayview Avenue
Toronto, ON M2L 1E4
Tel. 416-510-6668
Fax 416-510-6683
Email humanresources@graniteclub.com
Website .... www.graniteclub.com
Employer Background: Granite Club Lim-
ited is one of Canada's premier private so-
cial and athletic clubs. *New Positions Cre-
ated (2):* Casual Dining Server; Formal Din-
ing Server.

GRANT EMBLEMS LTD.
Att: Human Resources Manager
134 Park Lawn Road
Toronto, ON M8Y 3H9
Tel. 416-255-3421
Fax 416-255-4238
Website .... www.grant-emblems.com
Employer Background: Grant Emblems Ltd.
is an embroidery manufacturer. *New Posi-*

tions *Created (4):* Controller; Assistant to Controller; Cost Accountant; Senior Accounts Receivable Position.

GRANT MACEWAN COLLEGE
Att: Human Resources Department
10700 - 104th Avenue
Room 7 - 278, City Centre Campus
Edmonton, AB T5J 4S2

Tel. 780-497-5434
Fax 780-497-5430
Website .... www.gmcc.ab.ca

Employer Background: Grant MacEwan College operates 3 campuses, offering diploma and certificate programs, career-related courses and university transfer programs to 42,000 students. *New Positions Created (3):* Instructional Designer, Computer-Based Instruction; Instructor; Educational Technology Facilitator.

GRANT MACEWAN COLLEGE, JASPER PLACE CAMPUS
Att: Human Resources Department
10045 - 156th Street, Room 430
Edmonton, AB T5P 2P7

Tel. 780-497-5419
Fax 780-497-5430
Email ..... richardsons@admin.gmcc.ab.ca
Website .... www.gmcc.ab.ca

Employer Background: Grant MacEwan College operates 3 campuses, offering diploma and certificate programs, career-related courses and university transfer programs to 42,000 students. *New Positions Created (31):* Human Resources Advisor; Human Resources Assistant; Research Analyst; History Instructor; Instructor, Supply Chain Management; Manager, Information and Registration Services; Production Artist; Instructor; Instructors, Bachelor of Commerce / Bachelor of Management (2); Accounts Receivable Clerk III; Biology Instructor; Chemistry Instructor; Circulation Services Supervisor; Computing Science Instructor; Economics Instructor; Educational Psychology Instructor; Human Resources Assistant; Instructor, Police and Security Program; Philosophy Instructor; Sociology Instructor; Spanish Instructor; Instructor / Curriculum Coordinator, Mental Health Program; Chair, Nursing Program; Instructional Assistant, Nursing Transfer Program; Instructor, Early Childhood Development; Instructor, Nursing; Instructor, Social Work; Instructors, Mental Health; Program Coordinator, Police, Investigation and Security; Chair, Bachelor of Applied Communications in Professional Writing; Instructor, Acupuncture Program.

GRANT STRUCTURAL ENGINEERING LTD.
Att: Human Resources Manager
1721 - 10th Avenue SW, Suite 200
Calgary, AB T3C 0K1

Tel. 403-290-0885
Email .... grantmj@cadvision.com

Employer Background: Grant Structural Engineering Ltd. is a consulting engineering firm specializing in commercial, residential and light industrial building structural design. *New Positions Created (2):* Structural Engineers; Draftsperson.

GRAPHIC CONTROLS CANADA LTD.
Att: Human Resources Assistant
215 Herbert Street
Gananoque, ON K7G 2Y7

Tel. 613-382-4733
Fax 613-382-7134
Website .... www.graphic-controls.com

Employer Background: Graphic Controls manufactures precision charts and markers, thermal paper for POS applications and high-resolution ink jet fluids. *New Positions Created (2):* Production Workers; Toolmaker / Maintenance Mechanic / Machinist.

GRAYBAR ELECTRIC (ONTARIO) LTD.
Att: Human Resources Manager
130 Hayward Avenue
Kitchener, ON N2C 2E4

Tel. 519-576-4121
Fax 519-576-4098
Website .... www.graybar.com

Employer Background: Graybar Electric (Ontario) Ltd. distributes electrical, communication, data and automation products. *New Positions Created (2):* Electrical Order Desk Position; Warehouse Order Selectors.

GREAT ATLANTIC & PACIFIC CO. OF CANADA LTD., THE / A&P CANADA
Att: People Resources and Services
170 The West Mall
Toronto, ON M9C 1C2

Fax 416-626-4907
Email .... gayers@aptea.com
Website .... www.freshobsessed.com

Employer Background: A&P Canada is a food and grocery retailer, operating over 200 stores throughout Ontario. *New Positions Created (3):* Co-ordinators; Maintenance Supervisors; Supervisors.

GREAT ATLANTIC & PACIFIC CO. OF CANADA LTD., THE / A&P CANADA
Att: Human Resources Department
PO Box 68, Station A
Toronto, ON M5W 1A6

Tel. 416-239-7171
Fax 416-234-6583
Email .... canadacareers@aptea.com
Website .... www.freshobsessed.com

Employer Background: A&P Canada is a food and grocery retailer, operating over 200 stores throughout Ontario. *New Positions Created (2):* Senior Planner / Designer; Insight Specialist.

GREAT CANADIAN CASINOS INC.
Att: Director, Human Resources
13775 Commerce Parkway, Suite 350
Richmond, BC V6V 2V4

Tel. 604-303-1000
Fax 604-279-8590
Email .... mnowak@gcgaming.com
Website .... www.gcgaming.com

Employer Background: Great Canadian Casinos Inc. is a large community casino company, with over 1,000 employees and 6 locations throughout British Columbia. *New Positions Created (4):* Human Resources Manager; Purchasing & Inventory Control Manager; Marketing Assistant; Accounts Payable Position.

GREAT CANADIAN RAILTOUR COMPANY LTD.
Att: Human Resources
1150 Station Street, 1st Floor
Vancouver, BC V6A 2X7

Tel. 604-606-7200
Fax 604-606-7219
Email .... hr@rockymountaineer.com
Website .... www.rockymountaineer.com

Employer Background: Great Canadian Railtour Company Ltd. operates seasonal rail tours through the Rocky Mountains between Vancouver, Banff and Calgary. The company has 375 employees. *New Positions Created (2):* Concierge; Human Resources Administrator.

GREAT LAKES POWER LTD.
Att: Kevin Bell,
Manager and Chief Engineer
2 Sackville Road
Sault Ste. Marie, ON P6B 6J6

Tel. 705-759-7600
Fax 705-941-5600
Website .... www.glp.on.ca

Employer Background: Great Lakes Power Ltd. is the largest independent distributor of electric power in Ontario. *New Positions Created (6):* Program Manager, Electrical; Senior Electrical Engineer; Civil Engineer; Electrical Engineer; Program Manager, Electrical; Senior Electrical Engineer.

GREAT LITTLE BOX COMPANY LTD., THE
Att: Human Resources
8330 Chester Street
Vancouver, BC V5X 3Y7

Tel. 604-301-3700
Fax 604-301-3733
Email .... hr@greatlittlebox.com
Website .... www.greatlittlebox.com

Employer Background: The Great Little Box Company Ltd. is a corrugated packaging manufacturer, with 150 employees and 4 locations in British Columbia and Washington. *New Positions Created (3):* Account Manager; Account Manager; Sales Representative.

GREAT-WEST LIFE ASSURANCE COMPANY, THE
Att: Human Resources Department
60 Osborne Street North
Winnipeg, MB R3C 1V3

Tel. 204-946-7693
Fax 204-946-4116
Email .... careers@gwl.ca
Website .... www.gwl.ca

Employer Background: The Great-West Life Assurance Company offers individuals, businesses and organizations a range of life and disability insurance, retirement savings.

investment and employee benefits plans. *New Positions Created (22):* Relationship Manager, Vendor Relations; Actuarial Assistants; Financial Analyst; Leader, Internet Technology Centre; Systems Analyst; Career Leader; Corporate Technology Specialist; Intel Technical Specialist; Performance Management Coordinator; Problem Management Specialist; Project Managers; Systems Architect; Customer Service Representatives; Regional Manager, Retirement & Investment Services; Disability Coordinator; Career Leaders (3); Directors, Career Centre (2); IS Project Managers; Site Leader, Corporate Technology Implementation; Systems Analyst; Systems Architect; WSIB Site Supervisor.

GREATER TORONTO AIRPORTS AUTHORITY / GTAA
Att: Human Resources Department
3111 Convair Drive
PO Box 6031, Lester B. Pearson
International Airport
Toronto, ON L5P 1B2
Tel. 905-676-3000
Fax 905-676-7746
Email .... human_resources@gtaa.com
Website .... www.gtaa.com
Employer Background: GTAA manages the Lester B. Pearson International Airport, Canada's largest and busiest airport. *New Positions Created (12):* Electronic Activation Coordinator; Activation Mgr, Baggage Operations; Activation Mgr, Documentation and Training; Activation Mgr, Ground Side Operations; Activation Manager, Passenger Services; Environmental Technician; Managers, Electronic Systems; Corporate Commercial Lawyer; Payroll Assistant; Deputy Fire Chief; I.T. Analyst; Senior Technologists.

GREATER VANCOUVER COMMUNITY SERVICES SOCIETY / GVCSS
Att: Human Resources
1212 West Broadway, Suite 500
Vancouver, BC V6H 3V2
Tel. 604-737-4900
Fax 604-737-2922
Website .... www.gvcss.bc.ca
Employer Background: GVCSS is a multi-program organization, providing home support assistance, residential care and transportation services to elderly and disabled individuals. *New Positions Created (3):* Chinese-Language Home Support Placement Supervisor; Group Home Supervisor; Supervisor, Community Living Program.

GREATER VANCOUVER REGIONAL DISTRICT / GVRD
Att: Human Resources
4330 Kingsway
Burnaby, BC V5H 4G8
Tel. 604-432-6200
Fax 604-432-6455
Email .... hr@gvrd.bc.ca
Website .... www.gvrd.bc.ca
Employer Background: GVRD is a partnership of the 21 municipalities and one electoral area that make up the metropolitan

area of Greater Vancouver. *New Positions Created (5):* Project Engineer, Geotechnical; Senior Engineer, Civil; Senior Project Engineer, Standards; Senior Project Engineer, Energy Efficiency; Senior Project Engineer, Civil / Structural.

GREEN BELTING INDUSTRIES LTD.
Att: Richard Green
381 Ambassador Drive
Mississauga, ON L5T 2J3
Tel. 905-564-6712
Fax 905-564-6709
Website .... www.greenbelting.com
Employer Background: Green Belting Industries Ltd. is a manufacturer of polymer-coated fibreglass fabrics, belts and tapes. *New Positions Created (3):* Quality Engineer / Technician; Maintenance Supervisor; Second Shift Supervisor.

GREEN LAWN CARE
Att: Human Resources Manager
476 Evans Avenue
Toronto, ON M8W 2T9
Tel. 416-253-6540 ext.4406
Fax 416-201-4425
Email .... service@greenlawncare.com
Website .... www.greenlawncare.com
Employer Background: Founded in 1978, Green Lawn Care is the largest non-franchised lawn care company in Canada. *New Positions Created (2):* Branch Managers (2); Call Centre Manager.

GREENING DONALD CO. LTD.
Att: Human Resources Department
16 Commerce Road
Orangeville, ON L9W 2X7
Tel. 519-941-1920
Fax 519-942-8357
Email ...... human.resources@greendon.com
Website .... www.greendon.com
Employer Background: Greening Donald Co. Ltd. is a North American producer of specialty stainless steel wire products and inflator filters for automotive airbags. *New Positions Created (2):* Sales Manager; MIS Coordinator.

GREENLIGHT POWER TECHNOLOGIES, INC.
Att: R.L. Williamson
9865 West Saanich Road, Suite 210
Sidney, BC V8L 5Y8
Tel. 250-656-2002
Fax 250-656-2060
Email .... bobw@asa.bc.ca
Website .... www.asaautomation.com
Employer Background: Greenlight Power Technologies, Inc. (formerly ASA Automation Systems) is a supplier of testing and diagnostic equipment to the fuel cell industry. *New Positions Created (3):* Electrical Engineer; Mechanical / Chemical Engineer; Senior Software Engineer.

GREENWIN PROPERTY MANAGEMENT INC.
Att: Human Resources

20 Eglinton Avenue West, Suite 1600
Toronto, ON M4R 2H1
Tel. 416-487-3883
Fax 416-487-5344
Email .... hr@greenwinpm.com
Website .... www.greenwinpm.com
Employer Background: Greenwin Property Management Inc. is Canada's largest residential property management firm, with a portfolio of 61,000 suites under management and 3 million square feet of commercial space. *New Positions Created (12):* Rental Administrator; Building Manager, Commercial Operations; Portfolio Administrator, Condominium; Marketing Executive Assistant; Portfolio Administrator; Executive Administrators; Property Managers; Portfolio Administrator; Property Accountant; Property Manager; Property Accountant; Portfolio Administrator - Condominium.

GRENVILLE MANAGEMENT SERVICES
Att: Human Resources Manager
25 Scarsdale Road
Toronto, ON M3B 2R2
Tel. 416-449-2696
Fax 416-449-4119
Website .... www.grenville.com
Employer Background: Grenville Management Services provides outsourced copy centre services to large companies and organizations. *New Positions Created (15):* Receptionist; Site Manager / Copy Operator; Site Floaters; Junior District Manager; Receptionist; Customer Service Representative / Sales Trainee; Shipper / Receiver; Sales Professionals (2); Accounting Clerk; Copy Operator / Administrative Support; Estimator / Coordinator, Copy Centre; Graphic Designer; Mailroom / Back up Receptionist; Site Floater; Site Manager / Copy Operator.

GREY BRUCE HEALTH SERVICES
Att: Ms S. Grimstead, Search Committee
1800 - 8th Street East, PO Box 1800
Owen Sound, ON N4K 6H6
Tel. 519-376-2121
Fax 519-376-4391
Email .... sgrimstead@
.... owensound.healthserv.org
Employer Background: Grey Bruce Health Services serves the communities of Owen Sound, Markdale, Southampton, Meaford, Wiarton, Lion's Head and Tobermory. *New Positions Created (4):* Executive Director; Health Records Technician, Coders; Manager, Nuclear Medicine; Site Director.

GREYHOUND CANADA TRANSPORTATION CORP.
Att: Dennis Tillotson, Manager, Administration Services
877 Greyhound Way SW
Calgary, AB T3C 3V8
Tel. 403-260-0877
Fax 403-218-1230
Email ...... dennis.tillotson@greyhound.ca
Website .... www.greyhound.ca

Employer Background: Greyhound Canada Transportation Corp. is a leader in the transportation business. *New Positions Created (2):* Supervisor, Distribution Centre; Business Development Specialist.

GRIFFITH LABORATORIES LTD.
Att: Human Resources Department
757 Pharmacy Avenue
Toronto, ON M1L 3J8

Tel.	416-288-3050
Fax	416-288-5658
Email	resume@griffithlabs.com
Website	www.griffithlabs.com

Employer Background: Griffith Laboratories Ltd. manufactures and markets custom-designed food ingredients and products. *New Positions Created (3):* Pricing Analyst; Maintenance Electrician; Maintenance Millwright.

GRIFFITH-MCCONNELL RESIDENCE
Att: Director of Nursing & Resident Care
5760 Parkhaven Avenue
Cote St. Luc, QC H4W 1X9

Tel.	514-482-1121
Fax	514-482-1628

Employer Background: Griffith-McConnell Residence is a 300-bed, non-profit residential and long-term care facility for the elderly. *New Positions Created (2):* RNs and RPNs; Director of Nursing and Resident Care Services.

GRIMSBY CUSTOM TOOLING LTD.
Att: Paul Martin
343 Barton Street East
Stoney Creek, ON L8E 2L2

Tel.	905-664-4743
Fax	905-664-1688
Website	www.marcelissen.com

Employer Background: Grimsby Custom Tooling Ltd. is a casting tooling supplier for the North American automotive industry. *New Positions Created (5):* Certified General Machinists; Certified General Machinists; CAD / CAM Designer, Unigraphics; Various Trade Positions; CAD / CAM Designers and Programmers.

GROCERY GATEWAY
Att: Human Resources
3080 Yonge Street
Toronto, ON M4N 3N1

Tel.	416-489-7954
Fax	416-489-9301
Email	careers@grocerygateway.com
Website	www.grocerygateway.com

Employer Background: Grocery Gateway is a grocery shopping and delivery service available over the Internet. *New Positions Created (4):* Database Development Manager; Network Engineer; Senior Database Developer; Web Developer.

GROCERY GATEWAY
Att: Human Resources
6099A Vipond Drive
Mississauga, ON L5T 2B2

Tel.	905-565-5597
Fax	905-670-6016
Email	careers@grocerygateway.com
Website	www.grocerygateway.com

Employer Background: Grocery Gateway is a grocery shopping and delivery service available over the Internet. *New Positions Created (5):* Accounts Receivable Representative; Telesales Representative; HR Data Management Specialists; Inbound / Outbound Tele-Sales Representative; Inventory Control Manager.

GROCERY PEOPLE LTD., THE / TGP
Att: Director, Human Resources
14505 Yellowhead Trail
Edmonton, AB T5L 3C4

Tel.	780-447-5700
Fax	780-452-7759
Email	employment@tgp.ca
Website	www.tgp.ca

Employer Background: Founded in 1960, TGP is a full-service distribution company, providing food products to independent retailers, institutions, restaurants and caterers in western Canada. *New Positions Created (5):* Director of Foodservice; Produce Manager; Produce Manager; Store Manager; Director, Human Resources.

GROIA & COMPANY
Att: Janice Wright
145 King Street West, Suite 1610
Toronto, ON M5H 1J8

Tel.	416-203-2115
Fax	416-203-9231

Employer Background: Groia & Company is law firm, specializing in securities litigation. *New Positions Created (2):* Litigation Lawyer; Securities Lawyer.

GROUP 2 ARCHITECTURE ENGINEERING INTERIOR DESIGN
Att: Connie Casovan, Business Manager
4706 - 48th Avenue, Suite 200
Red Deer, AB T4N 6J4

Tel.	403-340-2200
Fax	403-346-6570
Email	conniec@group2.ab.ca

Employer Background: Group 2 Architecture Engineering Interior Design is a 52-person architectural engineering firm, serving commercial and institutional clients. *New Positions Created (4):* Interior Designer; Architectural Technologists (2); Structural Engineer; Structural Technologist.

GROUP TELECOM
Att: Human Resources Manager
700 West Georgia Street
11th Floor, PO Box 10082, Pacific Centre
Vancouver, BC V7Y 1B6

Tel.	604-484-1000
Fax	604-484-1100
Website	www.gt.ca

Employer Background: Group Telecom is a Canadian local exchange carrier, offering next-generation telecom solutions to small and mid-sized businesses. *New Positions Created (2):* Director, Commercial Sales; Carrier Sales Manager.

GROUP TELECOM
Att: Human Resources Manager
111 - 5th Avenue SW, Petro Canada Centre
Suite 800, East Tower
Calgary, AB T2P 3Y6

Tel.	403-770-5000
Fax	403-770-5202
Email	ioram@gt.ca
Website	www.gt.ca

Employer Background: Group Telecom is a Canadian local exchange carrier, offering next-generation telecom solutions to small and mid-sized businesses. *New Positions Created (7):* Data Usage Specialist; Business Managers; Technical Service Coordinators; Voice / Data Provisioners; Director, Commercial Sales; Field Services Technician; Carrier Sales Manager.

GROUP TELECOM
Att: Human Resources Manager
20 Bay Street, Suite 700
Toronto, ON M5J 2N8

Tel.	416-848-2000
Fax	416-848-2648
Email	resumes.toronto@gt.ca
Website	www.gt.ca

Employer Background: Group Telecom is a Canadian local exchange carrier, offering next-generation telecom solutions to small and mid-sized businesses. *New Positions Created (148):* Business Analyst, Order Management; Cash Specialist; Data Services Provisioner; Director, Market Development; Field Services Technicians, Voice; Recruitment Coordinator; Technical Services Coordinator; Technical Services Project Manger; Transport Provisioner; Voice Services Provisioner; 411 / 911 Specialist; Bilingual LNP Specialist; Data Network Architect; Data Network Planner; Database Administrator, Operations Support; Director, Database Support; Director, Development; Director, Marketing & Sales Support; Metasolv Applications Specialist; Network Engineer; Oracle Applications Specialist; PIC Care Specialist; Programmer Analyst, Development & Implementation; Project Manager / Application Specialist, Daleen; Project Manager / Application Specialist, Mediation; QA Test Manager; Remedy Applications Specialist; Senior Technical Lead; Tools Manager, Development & Implementation; LNP Specialist; Carrier Cost Specialist; Helpdesk Technician; Intermediate Unix Administrator; Senior Unix Administrator; Human Resources Generalist / Advisor; Manager, Development; NMC Technician, IP / Broadband; NMC Technician, Transport; NMC Technician, Voice; Voice Services Product Manager; Intermediate Programmer Analyst; Junior Technology Solutions Specialist; Accounts Payable Administrator; Billing, Audit and Controls Analyst; Financial Systems & Process Trainer; Manager of Capital Asset; Sales Assistant; Purchasing Manager; Billing Coordinator; Change Control / Administrator; Clarify Application Architect; Clarify Application Developer; Intermediate Programmer Analyst; Manager, Billing Operations; Operations Production Support Position; Order Specialist; Process Engineering Specialist; Project Manager; Treasury Analyst;

Programmer Analyst; Regional Performance Analyst; Business Analyst - Marketing; OSS Trainer; Receptionist; Billing Entry and Inquiry Specialist; Business Manager; Business Manager - Commercial Sales; Business Manager - Strategic Sales; Customer Service Trainer; Data Provisioner / Support Technician; Director of Operations; E & D Program Manager - Products, Services & Systems; Inside Sales Assistant; Inside Sales Representative; Payment Services Specialist; Payroll Administrator; Revenue Analyst; SGA Analyst; Technical Solutions Specialist; Voice Services Product Manager; Administrator, National Facilities; Director, Business Operations; Manager, Data Provisioning; Manager, Financial Reporting; Manager, National Facilities Administration; Media Relations Manager; Purchasing Agent; Senior Project Manager; Technical Service Project Manager; Transport Provisioner; Unix System Operator; Voice Services Provisioner; Administrative Assistant; Billing Systems Analyst; BMP / Outlook Programmer / Analyst; Business Systems Analyst; CADD Technician; Carrier Development Manager; Database Architect; Development Architect; Director, Fibre Planning; Director, Network Architecture and Planning; E-Forms Programmer / Analyst; Financial Analyst; General Ledger Accountant; GIS Technician; Help Desk Technician; Internet Engineer; Manager, Accounts Receivable; Manager, Budgeting and Forecasting; Metasolv Applications Specialist; Operation Production Support Specialist; Purchasing Coordinator; Radio Engineer / Wireless Data Network Engineer; Senior Fibre Planner; Service Manager; Site Planner; Switch Engineer; Transport Engineer; Loss Prevention Analyst; Mananger, Occupational Health and Safety; Messaging Services Manager; Regulatory Counsel; Service Development Manager; Webmaster; Applications Portfolio Support Manager; Bilingual Education and Development Assistant / Coordinator; Carrier Account Manager; Carrier Cost Specialist; Carrier Optimization Manager; Carrier Sales Engineer; Data Services Product Manager; Director, Network Architecture and Planning; Director of Marketing; Director, Switching; Education and Development Advisor; Education and Development Program Manager; Hardware Services Product Manager; Leased Service Analyst; Senior Carrier Optimization Analyst; Service Mgr; Technical Trainer / Advisor; Commercial Lawyer; Executive Assistant; Project Mgr; Business Account Mgrs; Regional Directors, Engineering; Technical Solutions Specialist.

GROUPE CONSEIL SAE INC., LE
Att: Human Resources Manager
2695 Paulus Road
St-Laurent, QC M3C 1Z3

Tel. 514-339-1500
Fax 514-339-1599
Email .... resumes@trow.com
Website .... www.trow.com

Employer Background: Le Groupe Conseil Inc. is a member of the Trow Group of Companies, a multidisciplinary engineering firm offering consulting, investigation, testing

and problem-solving services in all fields of engineering. *New Positions Created (4):* Intermediate Project Mgr; Intermediate / Sr Building Science Engineer; Sr Building Science Technician; Senior Environmental Engineer.

GROUPE DYNAMITE INC.
Att: Human Resources Department
5592 Ferrier Street
Mount Royal, QC H4P 1M2

Tel. 514-733-3962
Website .... www.dynamite.ca

Employer Background: Groupe Dynamite Inc. is a women's wear retailer, with over 2,000 employees and 192 locations across Canada. *New Positions Created (32):* Buyer; Intermediate Inventory Control Clerk; Junior Graphic Designer; Junior Helpdesk Technician; Store Managers; Visual Team Leaders; Inventory Control Clerk; Junior Internal Control Clerk; Junior Payroll Clerk; Accounts Payable Clerk; Junior Buyer; Help Desk Technician; Junior Accounting Clerk; Junior Cash Control Clerk; Junior Office Clerk; Junior Payroll Clerks; Human Resources Generalist; Rent & Lease Administrator; Retail Positions; Administrative Assistant; Payroll Clerk; Assistant Analyst, Merchandise / Shuffles; Assistant Buyer; Fit Model / Quality Control Position; Assistant Analyst, Planning and Forecasting; Store Managers, Assistant Managers; Senior Merchandise Manager; Data Entry Clerk; Junior Graphic Designer; Various Apparel Positions; Visual Merchandisers; District Supervisor.

GROUPE ENCORE
Att: Human Resources Manager
6540 Cote de Liesse
Montréal, QC H4T 1E3

Tel. 514-738-7171
Fax 514-738-5582
Website .... www.encore.ca

Employer Background: Founded in 1976, Groupe Encore is a travel management company, with 7 branches across Canada and over 4,000 affiliates worldwide. *New Positions Created (3):* Business Development Mgr, Vacation Experiences; Corporate Travel Specialists; Senior Manager, Client Services.

GROUPE J.S. INTERNATIONAL
Att: Human Resources Department
225 Chabanel Street West, 10th Floor
Montréal, QC H2N 2C9

Tel. 514-384-3551
Fax 514-384-6424
Email .... lbeausejour@jsgroup.com
Website .... www.jsgroup.com

Employer Background: Groupe J.S. International is an apparel manufacturer. *New Positions Created (10):* Patternmakers; Sample Sewers; Patternmaker; Design Assistant; Production Assistant; Floor Supervisor; Shipping Dept.; Patternmakers; Shipper; Design Assistant; System Administrator.

GROWMARK INC.
Att: Lorraine Van Heusden,
Human Resources Manager

2000 Argentia Road
Suite 500, PO Box 634, Plaza 5
Mississauga, ON L5M 2C1

Tel. 905-890-8500
Fax 905-814-4221
Email .... lvanheusden@growmark.com
Website .... www.growmark.com

Employer Background: Growmark Inc. is a large wholesale and service agribusiness, supplying products to over 150 retail store locations. *New Positions Created (3):* General Manager, Retail and Agri-Business; Buyer; Buyer, Lawn and Garden.

GSI LUMONICS INC.
Att: Human Resources
105 Schneider Road
Kanata, ON K2K 1Y3

Tel. 613-592-4375
Email .... gsilumonics@rpc.webhire.com
Website .... www.gsilumonics.com

Employer Background: GSI Lumonics Inc. is a world leader in the development, design, manufacture and marketing of laser-based advanced manufacturing systems. *New Positions Created (3):* Senior Procurement Specialist; Oracle Project Leader; Logistics Planner.

GSI LUMONICS INC.,
TELECOM OPTICS DIVISION
Att: Human Resources
39 Auriga Drive
Nepean, ON K2E 7Y8

Tel. 613-224-4868
Fax 613-224-2043
Email .... nepeanhr@gsilumonics.com
Website .... www.gsilumonics.com

Employer Background: GSI Lumonics Inc., Telecom Optics Division designs and manufactures custom optics for use by the telecom, medical and industrial markets. *New Positions Created (7):* Electrical Engineer and Hardware Engineer; Manufacturing Engineer; Production Activity Coordinator; Software Developer; Documentation Specialist; Senior Buyer; Senior Production Scheduler.

GTR GROUP INC.
Att: Human Resources Manager
8 Kenview Boulevard
Brampton, ON L6T 5E4

Tel. 905-799-4700
Fax 905-799-4799
Email .... hr@gamestraderinc.com
Website .... www.gamestraderinc.com

Employer Background: GTR Group Inc. is North America's leading independent supplier of previously played and value-priced republished video games. *New Positions Created (6):* Account Manager; Accounts Receivable / Collections Clerk; Controller; Customer Service Representative; Key Account Manager; System Administrator.

GUELPH, CITY OF
Att: Employee Resources Department
59 Carden Street
Guelph, ON N1H 3A1

Tel. 519-837-5601
Fax 519-763-2685
Email .... careers@city.guelph.on.ca
Website .... www.city.guelph.on.ca
Employer Background: Situated 100 km west of Toronto, the City of Guelph is home to over 100,000 people. *New Positions Created (15):* Transportation Planning Engineer; Technical Superintendent; Equipment Operator, Grade 4; Licensed Automotive / Truck and Coach Technician; Economic Development Officer; Director, Employee Resources; CAD Operator; Assistant Director of Finance / Deputy City Treasurer; Supervisor, Concrete & Winter Control; Director of Works; Signal and Sign Licensed Electrician; CAD Operator; Manager of Realty Services; Landfill Superintendent; Supervisor, Wastewater Collection.

GUELPH GENERAL HOSPITAL
Att: Human Resources Adviser
115 Delhi Street
Guelph, ON N1E 4J4
Tel. 519-837-6409
Fax 519-837-6468
Email .... recruiting@
.... guelphgeneralhospital.com
Website . www.guelphgeneralhospital.com
Employer Background: Founded in 1875, Guelph General Hospital is 200-bed acute care facility, serving 180,000 people throughout Guelph and Wellington County. *New Positions Created (26):* Physiotherapy Professional Leader; Ultrasound Technologist; Unit Manager, Emergency Department; Unit Manager, Critical Care Unit; Financial Analyst; Financial Applications Specialist; Interim Chaplain; Laboratory Manager; Pharmacist; Physiotherapist; Registered Nurses; Unit Manager, Critical Care; Certified Anesthesiologists (2); Unit Manager, Emergency Room; Chaplain; Financial Analyst; Financial Applications Specialist; Pharmacist; Physiotherapist; Acute Care Nurse Practitioner, Cardiology; Clinical Nurse Specialist, Medical / Surgical; Diabetes Educator; Professional Leader, Physiotherapy; Registered Nurses; Financial Applications Specialist; Registered Nurses.

GULF AND FRASER CREDIT UNION
Att: Kathy Nosella,
Human Resources Department
803 East Hastings Street
Vancouver, BC V6A 1R8
Tel. 604-254-7270
Fax 604-215-8511
Email .... knosella@gafcu.com
Website .... www.gulfandfraser.com
Employer Background: Gulf and Fraser Credit Union is a financial institution, with almost $300 million in assets. *New Positions Created (2):* Financial Services Representative; Financial Services Supervisor.

GUTHRIE PHILLIPS GROUP INC.
Att: Human Resources
1200 - 73rd Avenue West
Suite 340, Airport Square
Vancouver, BC V6P 6G5
Tel. 604-263-9347
Fax 604-261-2336
Email .... careers@guthriephillipsgroup.com
Website ... www.guthriephillipsgroup.com
Employer Background: GPG is a firm of computer specialists, providing customized applications to enhance business systems. *New Positions Created (4):* Documentation Specialist; QA Analyst; Sales Representatives; Systems Development Position.

GUVERNMENT, THE
Att: Human Resources Manager
132 Queens Quay East
Toronto, ON M5A 3Y5
Tel. 416-869-0045
Fax 416-869-0387
Email .... guvern@idirect.com
Website .... www.theguvernment.com
Employer Background: The Guvernment is an entertainment complex that hosts dance nights, concerts and special events. *New Positions Created (2):* Bookkeeper; Accountant / Bookkeeper.

H.B. FENN AND COMPANY LTD.
Att: Debbie Chaulk
34 Nixon Road
Bolton, ON L7E 1W2
Tel. 905-951-6600
Fax 905-951-6601
Email .... debbie.chaulk@hbfenn.com
Website .... www.hbfenn.com
Employer Background: H.B. Fenn and Company Ltd. is a large book publisher and distributor. *New Positions Created (2):* National Key Account Representative; Publicist.

H.H. ANGUS & ASSOCIATES LTD.
Att: Human Resources
1127 Leslie Street
Toronto, ON M3C 2J6
Tel. 416-443-8200
Fax 416-443-8290
Email .... hr@hhangus.com
Website .... www.hhangus.com
Employer Background: H.H. Angus & Associates Ltd. is a mechanical and electrical consulting engineering practice, with operations in Canada and the UK. *New Positions Created (12):* Communications Engineers; Electrical CET; Mechanical / Electrical Junior Project Professional Engineer; Mechanical Site Inspector; Senior HVAC Designer; Commissioning Coordinator; Electrical Designers; Head of Construction Inspection; Prime Consultant, Site Coordinator; Project Electrical Engineer; Senior HVAC Designer; Telecommunications Designers.

H.J. HEINZ COMPANY OF CANADA LTD.
Att: Human Resources Department
5700 Yonge Street, Suite 2100
North American Life Centre
Toronto, ON M2M 4K6
Tel. 416-226-5757
Fax 416-226-3658
Email .... tor.resumes@hjheinz.com
Website .... www.heinz.com
Employer Background: H.J. Heinz Company of Canada Ltd. is a subsidiary of Pittsburgh-based H.J. Heinz Company, one of the world's largest food processors and branded food companies. *New Positions Created (10):* Account Manager; Assistant Product Manager; Financial Analyst; Financial Analyst, Trade Return; Key Account Manager; Senior Product Manager; Product Manager, Foodservice; Territory Sales Manager; District Sales Manager; Credit and Customer Service Manager.

H.J. PFAFF MOTORS INC.
Att: Human Resources Department
17065 Yonge Street
Newmarket, ON L3Y 4V7
Fax 905-853-2517
Email .... hrmanager@hjpfaff.com
Website .... www.hjpfaff.com
Employer Background: H.J. Pfaff Motors Inc. is an import automobile dealership located north of Toronto. *New Positions Created (2):* Office Manager; Sales Associate.

H. PAULIN & CO. LIMITED
Att: Human Resources
55 Milne Avenue
Toronto, ON M1L 1K4
Tel. 416-694-3351
Fax 416-698-3243
Email .... hr@hpaulin.com
Employer Background: H. Paulin & Co. Limited is a large manufacturer and distributor of fasteners and automotive parts. *New Positions Created (9):* Senior Secretary; Executive Secretary / Administrative Assistant; Executive Secretary / Administrative Assistant; Export Administrator; Entry-Level Supervisory Position; Precision Inspection Machine Operators; Production Schedulers; Quality Assurance Technicians; Marketing Desktop Publisher.

H2O ENTERTAINMENT CORP.
Att: Human Resources
570 Granville Street, Suite 1200
Vancouver, BC V6C 3P1
Fax 604-609-0935
Email .... jobs@h2oent.com
Website www.h2oent.com
Employer Background: H2O Entertainment Corp. produces video games. *New Positions Created (3):* Artists; C / C++ Programmers; Java Programmers.

HAAKON INDUSTRIES
Att: Human Resources Manager
993 Princess Street
Kingston, ON K7L 1H3
Tel. 613-548-7101
Fax 613-548-7008
Employer Background: Haakon makes HVAC equipment. *New Positions Created (3):* Painter; Press Brake Operator; Welder.

HALDIMAND-NORFOLK REACH
Att: Human Resources
101 Nanticoke Creek Parkway
Townsend, ON N0A 1S0

Tel. 519-587-4555
Fax 519-587-4798
Website .... www.hnreach.on.ca

Employer Background: Haldimand-Norfolk REACH is a non-profit, multi-service agency that provides 24-hour mobile crisis response services for children and youth in acute crisis. *New Positions Created (2):* Behaviour Management Therapist; Manager of Children's Mental Health Services.

HALEY INDUSTRIES LTD.
Att: Human Resources Manager
634 Magnesium Road
Haley, ON K0J 1Y0

Tel. 613-432-8841
Fax 613-432-2611
Email .... human.resources@haley.on.ca
Website .... www.haley.on.ca

Employer Background: Haley Industries Ltd. produces aluminum and magnesium aerospace sand castings. *New Positions Created (3):* Process Engineer Manager; Environmental Technologist; Human Resources Specialist.

HALIBURTON & WHITE GROUP, THE
Att: Human Resources Manager
2111 St. Regis
Dollard-des-Ormeaux, QC H9B 2M9

Tel. 514-421-1230
Fax 514-421-0466
Email .... bchenier@hw.ca
Website .... www.hw.ca

Employer Background: The Haliburton & White Group is a national sales and service organization, supplying ATM, currency, coin and documents processing equipment. *New Positions Created (3):* Dispatcher / Customer Service Support Position; Parts Coordinator; Technical Manager.

HALIFAX SHIPYARD LIMITED
Att: Employee Relations
PO Box 9110
Halifax, NS B3K 5M7

Tel. 902-423-9271
Fax 902-494-5554
Email conrad_susan@halifaxshipyard.com
Website .... www.halifaxshipyard.com

Employer Background: Halifax Shipyard, a division of Irving Shipbuilding Inc., specializes in new construction, ship repair, conversion and refits on a wide range of commercial and naval vessels. *New Positions Created (3):* Electrical Supervisors; Electrical Tradespeople; Steel Shop Manager.

HALL OF NAMES INTERNATIONAL INC.
Att: Human Resources Manager
480 Bath Road, Suite 100
Kingston, ON K7M 4X6

Tel. 613-548-3409
Website .... www.traceit.com

Employer Background: Established in 1972, Hall of Names International Inc. researches the origins and history of families surnames. *New Positions Created (3):* Computer Programmer; Internet Marketer; Production / Shipping Associate.

HALLIBURTON CANADA INC.
Att: Human Resources Manager
1400 - 5th Street
Nisku, AB T9E 7R6

Fax 780-955-8620
Email .... jobs@halliburton.com
Website .... www.halliburton.com

Employer Background: Halliburton Canada Inc. is one of the world's leading providers of products, services and integrated solutions for oil and gas exploration and production. *New Positions Created (10):* Completion and Service Tool Specialists; Slickline Specialist; Administrative Specialist; Associate Applications Analyst; Directional Drillers; Technical Support Personnel; Engineer; Mechanical Designer; Technical Support Analyst; Technology Engineer.

HALLMARK CANADA
Att: Human Resources Department
501 Consumers Road
Toronto, ON M2J 5E2

Tel. 416-492-1300
Fax 416-492-2301
Email .... hrcanada@hallmark.com
Website .... www.hallmark.com

Employer Background: Hallmark Canada manufactures greeting cards and other personal expression products. *New Positions Created (3):* Manager, Sales and Corporate Training; Systems Programmer; Distribution Secretary.

HALSALL ASSOCIATES LTD.
Att: Janet Tisdall,
Human Resources Manager
2300 Yonge Street, PO Box 2385
Toronto, ON M4P 1E4

Tel. 416-487-5266
Fax 416-487-9766
Email .... jtisdall@halsall.com
Website .... www.halsall.com

Employer Background: Halsall Associates Ltd. provides structural design, assessment and restoration services for new and existing properties. *New Positions Created (5):* Business Manager; Project Engineer; Project Mgr; Building Evaluation and Repair Technologist; Structural Design Technologists.

HALTON ADOLESCENT SUPPORT SERVICES
Att: Executive Director
720 Guelph Line, Suite 301
Burlington, ON L7R 4E2

Tel. 905-639-0025
Fax 905-333-9849

Employer Background: Halton Adolescent Support Services is a non-profit, multi-service agency for youth and families. *New Positions Created (2):* Program Director; Residential Mentor.

HALTON CATHOLIC DISTRICT SCHOOL BOARD
Att: T.J. Fauteux,
Superintendent, Human Resources
802 Drury Lane
Burlington, ON L7R 4L3

Tel. 905-632-6300
Fax 905-632-3435
Website .... www.haltonrc.edu.on.ca

Employer Background: The Halton Catholic District School Board serves over 23,000 students at 32 elementary and 5 secondary schools in Burlington, Halton Hills, Milton and Oakville. *New Positions Created (5):* Elementary Teachers; Secondary Teachers; Research Associate; Elementary and Secondary School Teachers; Elementary and Secondary School Teachers.

HALTON DISTRICT SCHOOL BOARD, THE
Att: Human Resources
2050 Guelph Line, PO Box 5005
Burlington, ON L7R 3Z2

Tel. 905-335-3663
Fax 905-335-9802
Website .... www.haltondsb.on.ca

Employer Background: The Halton District School Board serves 45,000 public school students in Burlington, Halton Hills, Milton and Oakville. *New Positions Created (9):* Teachers; Teachers; Teachers, Adult and Continuing Education; Teacher, Science; Teacher, Technology; Teacher, Technology; Elementary Teachers, FSL; Assistant Superintendents of Schools (2); Superintendent of Business Services.

HALTON HEALTHCARE SERVICES
Att: Human Resources
327 Reynolds Street
Oakville, ON L6J 3L7

Tel. 905-338-4626
Fax 905-338-4137
Email .... hr@haltonhealthcare.on.ca
Website .... www.haltonhealthcare.com

Employer Background: Halton Healthcare Services is a general hospital, formed by the amalgamation of the Oakville-Trafalgar Memorial and Milton District hospitals. *New Positions Created (70):* Community Coordinator & Case Manager; Registered Nurse, Operating Room; Registered Nurses, Intensive Care Unit (2); Registered Practical Nurse, Inpatient Rehabilitation; Senior Administrative Assistant; Case Manager; Diagnostic Imaging Assistant; Intake Coordinator / Office Manager, Central West Eating Disorder Program; Ombudsperson; Pharmacists (2); Professional Practice Clinician, Emergency and Ambulatory Care Program; Registered Nurse, Crisis Response (Mental Health); Registered Nurse, Inpatient Rehabilitation Unit; Registered Nurse, Medical Inpatient Unit / 4C; Registered Nurses, Surgical Inpatient Unit (3); Registered Practical Nurse, Emergency (Observation Room); Researcher; Respiratory Therapist; Speech Language Pathologist; Cardiology Technologist; Chiropodist; Echocardiology Technologist; Emergency Nurse, Emergency / Ambulatory Services; Maternal Child Nurse, Birthing Suite; Maternal Child Nurse, Breastfeeding Clinic; Maternal Child Nurse, Obstetrics; Maternal Child Nurse, Paediatrics / Maternal Child Unit; Maternal Child Nurse, Prenatal Clinic; Maternal Child Nurse, Special Care Nursery; Mental Health

Nurse, Adult Inpatient Psychiatry; Mental Health Nurse, Child and Adolescent Psychiatric Inpatient Unit (CAPIS); Mental Health Nurses, Outpatient Clinics; Occupational Therapists; Pharmacy Technician; Physiotherapists; Registered Imaging Technologist; Registered Nurse, Emergency Room; Registered Nurse, Intensive Care Unit; Registered Nurse, Intensive Care Unit; Registered Nurse, Maternal Child Unit; Registered Nurse, Medical Inpatient Units; Registered Nurse, Medical / Surgical Unit; Registered Nurse, Observation Room; Registered Nurse, Renal Dialysis Unit; Rehabilitation & Geriatric Nurse; Rehabilitation & Geriatric Nurse, Combined Inpatient Rehabilitation / Step Up Unit; Rehabilitation & Geriatric Nurse, Transitional Care Unit; Sonographers; Surgical Nurses, Inpatient Surgical Unit; Surgical Nurses, Operating and Recovery Room; Surgical Nurses, Operating Room; Surgical Nurses, Surgical Day Care (SDC); Intake Coordinator / Office Manager; Regional Coordinator; Therapist, Individual / Family / Group; Hospital Ombud / Quality Coordinator; Pharmacist; Professional Practice Clinician, Surgical Program; Speech Language Pathologist; Senior Financial Analyst; Patient Care Manger, Operating Room and Central Sterilization and Reprocessing; Echocardiography Technologist; Physiotherapist; Professional Practice Clinician, Rehabilitation and Geriatrics; Clinical Performance & Decision Support Leader; Organizational Learning & Professional Development Leader; Echocardiography Technologist; Patient Care Manager, Maternal Child Unit; Professional Practice Clinician, Mental Health Program; Various Registered Nursing Positions.

HALTON HILLS, TOWN OF
Att: Human Resources
1 Halton Hills Drive, PO Box 128
Halton Hills, ON L7G 5G2
Tel. 905-873-2600
Fax 905-873-1431
Website .... www.town.halton-hills.on.ca
Employer Background: Located in the northwestern part of the Greater Toronto Area, the Town of Halton Hills is a rural municipality, with a population of 47,000. *New Positions Created (6):* Building Mechanical Services Inspector; Capital Works Technician; Municipal Law Enforcement Officer; Plans Examiner; Purchasing Agent; Deputy Clerk.

HALTON REGIONAL POLICE SERVICE / HRPS
Att: Human Resource Services
1151 Bronte Road, Box 2700
Oakville, ON L6J 5C7
Tel. 905-825-4747
Fax 905-825-5105
Website .... www.hrps.on.ca
Employer Background: HRPS is responsible for policing the Regional Municipality of Halton, encompassing the City of Burlington and Towns of Oakville, Milton and Halton Hills. *New Positions Created (2):* Crime Analyst; Financial Analyst.

HALTON, THE REGIONAL MUNICIPALITY OF
Att: Human Resource Services
1151 Bronte Road
Oakville, ON L6M 3L1
Tel. 905-825-6000
Fax 905-825-4032
Website .... www.region.halton.on.ca
Employer Background: The Regional Municipality of Halton provides public health, social and community services, planning and public works to a population of 360,000. *New Positions Created (37):* Health Promoter; Program Coordinator; Public Health Nurse; Manager, Financial Services; Assistant Corporate Counsel, Police Services; Supervisor, Children's Health; Supervisors, Community Health (2); Project Manager; Systems Analyst; Administrative Assistant; Board Committee Coordinator; Executive Assistant to the Chairman; Executive Director; Receptionist; Senior Policy Analysts (2); Supervisors, Children's Resource Services (2); Senior Planner / Ecologist; Communications Specialist; Industrial Electrician; Industrial Mechanics / Millwrights (2); Manager, Budgets; Manager, Resident Care; Senior Financial Analyst; Senior Policy Analyst; Executive Assistant to the Chairman; Special Studies and Research Engineers (2); Director, Waste Management Services; Motor Vehicle Mechanic; Community Outreach Worker, Needle Exchange Program; Senior Therapist; Internal Auditor; Manager, Employee Development; Training and Development Specialist; Commissioner, Corporate Services; Director, Community Relations; Regional Clerk; Crewperson, System Operations.

HALTON-PEEL DISTRICT HEALTH COUNCIL / HPDHC
Att: Linda Sullivan, Halton-Peel Addiction System Implementation Committee
6711 Mississauga Road, Suite 600
Mississauga, ON L8N 2W3
Tel. 905-814-5995
Fax 905-814-4835
Email .... linda@hpdhc.com
Website .... www.hpdhc.com
Employer Background: HPDHC provides advice to the Minister of Health and handles local health system planning in Halton and Peel. *New Positions Created (2):* Project Coordinator; Health Planner.

HAMILTON, CITY OF
Att: Recruiter, HR Department
71 Main Street West, City Hall
Hamilton, ON L8P 4Y5
Fax 905-546-2650
Website .... www.city.hamilton.on.ca
Employer Background: The City of Hamilton is an amalgamation of six diverse communities: Ancaster, Dundas, Flamborough, Glanbrook, Hamilton and Stoney Creek. *New Positions Created (19):* Marketing Coordinator, Healthy Lifestyles; Parks Director; Project Manager, Water / Wastewater; Project Manager, Water / Wastewater; Project Manager, Watershed Management; Senior Manager, Emergency Medical Services; Director, Program Policy & Planning; District Super-

intendent, Water Distribution; Legal Counsel; Water Quality Technologists; Project Manager, Capital Programs; Project Manager, Facility Operations; Director, Culture and Recreation; Field Supervisor; Social Worker; Public Health Nurses; Manager, Nutrition & Physical Activity Promotion; Manager, Dental Services; Bus Operators.

HAMILTON, DUNCAN, ARMSTRONG & STEWART
Att: Val Newth, Administrator
13401 - 108th Avenue, Suite 1450
Surrey, BC V3T 5T3
Tel. 604-581-4677
Fax 604-581-5947
Email .... bcd@hdas.com
Website .... www.hdas.com
Employer Background: Hamilton, Duncan, Armstrong & Stewart is a business law firm, serving Surrey since 1974. *New Positions Created (2):* Lawyer; Lawyer.

HAMILTON HEALTH SCIENCES CORPORATION, CHEDOKE CAMPUS
Att: Recruitment, Human Resources
PO Box 2000
Hamilton, ON L8N 3Z5
Tel. 905-521-2100
Fax 905-318-2558
Email .... recruitment@hhsc.ca
Website .. www.hamiltonhealthsciences.ca
Employer Background: HHSC is one of Canada's largest teaching hospitals, employing 10,000 staff members and serving over 2 million people. *New Positions Created (42):* Accounts Payable Specialist; Occupational Health and Safety Coordinator; Social Worker, Addiction Services; Withdrawal Management Counsellors (8); Occupational Therapist, Integrated Stroke Unit; Physiotherapist, Complex Continuing Care; Physiotherapist, Rehabilitation and Seniors; Social Worker, Emergency and Pre-hospital Services; Clinical Manager, Critical Care; Ergonomics Coordinator; Investigator / Patient Fee Specialist; Research Administrative Assistant; Senior Programmer Analyst; Associate Director of Operations, Population Health Institute; Clinical Manager, Cardiac and Vascular Surgical Units; Director of Purchasing and Supply Management; Registered Dietitian; Research Assistant; Behaviour Therapist; Clinical Manager, Peri-Operative Services; Human Resources Representative; Nurse Clinician; Plumbers (2); Psychologist; Public Affairs Coordinator; Speech-Language Pathologist; Driving Instructor; Clinical Audiologist; Coordinator / Social Worker; Pharmacist; Clinical Managers; Health Records Technicians (6); Advanced Practice Nurse; Clinical Manager; Registered Nurses; Cabinet Maker / Carpenter; Program Director, Diagnostic Imaging; Performance Improvement Specialist; Clinical Manager, Oncology Program; Pharmacists; Clinical Director, Psychologist; Registered Nurses.

HAMILTON HEALTH SCIENCES CORPORATION, HAMILTON GENERAL HOSPITAL / HHSC
Att: Recruitment, Human Resources

237 Barton Street East
Hamilton, ON L8L 2X2
Tel. 905-527-4322
Email .... recruitment@hhsc.ca
Website .. www.hamiltonhealthsciences.ca
Employer Background: HHSC is one of Ontario's largest teaching hospitals, providing comprehensive health services to over 2 million people. *New Positions Created (3):* Clinical Care Clinical Assistants; Licenced Physicians; Chief, Department of Nuclear Medicine.

HAMILTON HYDRO INC.
Att: Human Resources Department
55 John Street North
PO Box 2249, Station LCD 1
Hamilton, ON L8N 3E4
Tel. 905-522-6611
Fax 905-522-6570
Email ... gdlepinskie@hamiltonhydro.com
Website .... www.hamiltonhydro.com
Employer Background: Formed in 2000 through the merger of five municipal electric utilities, Hamilton Hydro Inc. is an electricity distributor licensed and regulated by the Ontario Energy Board. *New Positions Created (4):* PC Technician; Assistant Stores Manager; Operator Trainee OP-4; Director, Business Planning and Reporting.

HAMILTON PROGRAM FOR SCHIZOPHRENIA / HPS
Att: Business Administrator
350 King Street East, Suite 102
Hamilton, ON L8N 3Y3
Fax 905-546-0055
Employer Background: HPS is a community mental health program. *New Positions Created (2):* Secretary; Case Manager.

HAMILTON REGION CONSERVATION AUTHORITY
Att: Scott Konkle
838 Mineral Springs Road, PO Box 7099
Ancaster, ON L9G 3L3
Tel. 905-525-2181
Fax 905-648-4622
Website .... www.hamrca.on.ca
Employer Background: The Hamilton Region Conservation Authority is a large environmental management agency dedicated to the conservation of watershed lands and water resources. *New Positions Created (4):* Environmental Technician, Watershed Planning and Engineering; Senior Planner, Watershed Planning and Engineering; Business Systems Analyst; Accounts Receivable Clerk.

HAMILTON REGIONAL CANCER CENTRE / HRCC
Att: Lynn Tessaro,
Manager, Human Resources
699 Concession Street
Hamilton, ON L8V 5C2
Tel. 905-387-9495
Fax 905-575-6338
Email .... human.resources@hrcc.on.ca
Website .... www.hrcc.on.ca

Employer Background: HRCC is one of eight regional offices operated by Cancer Care Ontario, a provincial agency responsible for developing an integrated cancer control system in Ontario. *New Positions Created (16):* General Practitioner, Oncology; Medical Physics Resident; Medical Secretary; Dosimetrist; Research Secretary; Pharmacist; Radiation Therapists; Registered Nurse; Head of Systemic Treatment Program and Medical Oncology; Clinical Trials Department Manager; Manager, Pharmacy Department; Medical Physicist; Head of Nursing and Patient Services; Pharmacists (2); Scientists (2); Senior Social Worker, Supportive Care.

HAMILTON WEB PRINTING
Att: Bob Carver, General Manager
333 Arvin Avenue
Stoney Creek, ON L8E 2M6
Tel. 905-664-2660
Fax 905-664-2994
Email ... bcarver@hamiltonwebprinting.com
Website .. www.hamiltonwebprinting.com
Employer Background: Hamilton Web Printing is a printing services company. *New Positions Created (3):* Pre-Press Digital Systems Technician; Digital Systems Technician; Mac Operator / Film Stripper.

HAMILTON-WENTWORTH DISTRICT SCHOOL BOARD
Att: Deborah Russon,
Manager of Human Resources
100 Main Street West, PO Box 2558
Hamilton, ON L8N 3L1
Tel. 905-527-5092
Website .... www.hwdsb.on.ca
Employer Background: The Hamilton-Wentworth District School Board operates 115 elementary and 18 secondary schools, serving 59,000 students. *New Positions Created (8):* Speech-Language Pathologists; Teacher of Strings; Human Resources Officer; Principals and Vice-Principals; Speech / Language Pathologist; Psychoeducational Consultant; Systems Librarian; Principals and Vice-Principals.

HAMILTON-WENTWORTH, REGIONAL MUNICIPALITY OF
Att: Gwen Marshall, Recruiter
25 Main Street West, City Hall
Hamilton, ON L8N 3A2
Tel. 905-574-8933
Fax 905-546-2650
Website .... www.city.hamilton.on.ca
Employer Background: Located on the Niagara escarpment, the Regional Municipality of Hamilton-Wentworth is composed of 6 diverse communities. *New Positions Created (2):* Adult Day Program Coordinator; Supervisor, Community Traffic Services.

HANOVER MALONEY
Att: Don Ray
8825 Shepard Road SE
Calgary, AB T2C 4N9
Tel. 403-279-5000
Fax 403-279-2068

Email .... hr@maloney-industries.com
Website ..... www.maloney-industries.com
Employer Background: Hanover Maloney (formerly Maloney Industries Inc.) designs and manufactures process equipment for the oil and gas industry. *New Positions Created (3):* Application Specialist / Business Analyst; Account Manager; Application Specialist / Business Analyst.

HARCOURT CANADA LTD.
Att: Human Resources Manager
55 Horner Avenue
Toronto, ON M8Z 4X6
Tel. 416-255-4046
Fax 416-253-9388
Website .... www.harcourt.com
Employer Background: Harcourt Canada Ltd. is a major academic and scholastic publisher. *New Positions Created (2):* Business Development Manager; Database Marketing Analyst.

HARDT EQUIPMENT MANUFACTURING INC.
Att: Human Resources
2025 - 52nd Avenue
Lachine, QC H8T 3C3
Tel. 514-631-7271
Fax 514-631-7273
Email .... hr@hardt.ca
Website .... www.hardtequipment.com
Employer Background: For over 25 years, Hardt Equipment Manufacturing Inc. has been developing food equipment systems for restaurant, deli and supermarket clients worldwide. *New Positions Created (11):* Controller; Director of Technical Services; Mechanical Technologist; Sales Representative; Administrative Assistant; Controller; Director of Marketing; Human Resource Manager; Incoming Products Inspector; Mechanical Designer; Purchasing Agent.

HARRIS COMPUTER SERVICES
Att: Human Resources
2798 Thamesgate Drive, Unit 8
Mississauga, ON L4T 4E8
Tel. 905-672-9070
Fax 905-672-9097
Email .... hr@harriscs.on.ca
Website .... www.harriscs.on.ca
Employer Background: Harris Computer Services is a leading supplier of network and computer services. *New Positions Created (2):* Field Services Printer Technician; Computer Sales Person.

HARRIS COMPUTER SERVICES
Att: Human Resources Manager
16 Fitzgerald Road, Suite 150
Nepean, ON K2H 8R6
Tel. 613-828-1280
Email .... hr@harriscs.on.ca
Website .... www.harriscs.on.ca
Employer Background: Harris Computer Services is a leading supplier of network and computer services. *New Positions Created (3):* Computer Service Manager; Novell / NT Administrator; Computer Service Manager.

HARRIS COMPUTER SYSTEMS
Att: Human Resources Coordinator
117 Centrepointe Drive, Suite 200
Nepean, ON K2G 5X3

Tel. 613-226-5511
Fax 613-226-3377
Email .... hr@harriscomputer.com
Website .... www.harriscomputer.com
Employer Background: Harris Computer Systems develops feature-rich billing and other software for municipal utilities. *New Positions Created (7):* Programmer Analyst; Software Development Manager; Support Analysts (3); Instructors; Project Managers; Software Development Manager; Web Application Developer.

HARRIS CORPORATION, MICROWAVE COMMUNICATIONS DIVISION
Att: Human Resources
6732 - 8th Street NE
Calgary, AB T2E 8M4

Fax 403-295-4675
Email .... hwadhr@harris.com
Website .... www.harris.com
Employer Background: Founded in 1895, US-based Harris Corporation is an international communications equipment company, with 12,000 employees and annual sales of $2.3 billion. *New Positions Created (10):* Product Support Technologist; Hardware Design Engineer; Life Cycle Material Manager; Quality Mgr; Digital Hardware Engineers; DSP Engineer; Java Software Designer; Project Manager / Project Engineer; Senior RF Engineer; Systems Designer.

HART STORES INC.
Att: Marla Orenstein
9001 Louis H. Lafontaine Boulevard
Anjou, QC H1J 2C5

Tel. 514-354-0101
Email .... morenstein@hartco.com
Website .... www.hartco.com
Employer Background: Hart Stores Inc. is an expanding retail chain with over 50 department stores in Canada. *New Positions Created (3):* Jr Merchandising Clerk; Merchandising Assistant; Various Retail Positions.

HARTCO CORPORATION
Att: Human Resources Manager
9393 Louis H. Lafontaine Boulevard
Anjou, QC H1J 1Y8

Tel. 514-354-3810
Fax 514-351-6906
Email .... opportunities@hartco.com
Website .... www.hartco.com
Employer Background: Established in 1976, Hartco is one of the largest franchisors of system integrators, computer resellers and computer retailers in Canada, with over 140 locations and revenues exceeding $650 million. *New Positions Created (3):* Executive Assistant; Payroll Clerk; Senior Translator.

HARTFORD FIBRES LTD.
Att: Human Resources Department
675 Progress Avenue
Kingston, ON K7L 4Y8

Tel. 613-389-4330
Fax 613-389-6794
Email .... cslade@microfibres.com
Website .... www.microfibres.com
Employer Background: Hartford Fibres Ltd. is a leading manufacturer of flocked materials used in the drapery and upholstery industry. *New Positions Created (6):* Operations Manager; Production Supervisor; Quality Control Manager; Accounts Payable / Payroll Clerk; Accounts Payable / Payroll Clerk; Customer Service Clerk.

HARVARD ENERGY
Att: Ann-Marie Soganic
300 - 5th Avenue SW, Suite 2100
Calgary, AB T2P 3C4

Tel. 403-261-2950
Email .... am.soganic@harvardenergy.com
Employer Background: Harvard Energy is a privately-owned oil and gas exploration and production company based in Calgary. *New Positions Created (3):* Controller; Petroleum Engineer; Operations Technologist.

HASTINGS AND PRINCE EDWARD DISTRICT SCHOOL BOARD
Att: Sue Taylor, HR Department
156 Ann Street, Education Centre
Belleville, ON K8N 1N9

Tel. 613-962-8668
Email .... staylor@hpedsb.on.ca
Website .... www.hpedsb.on.ca
Employer Background: The Hastings and Prince Edward District School Board is located in the Quinte region of eastern Ontario. *New Positions Created (2):* Teacher; Psychometrist.

HASTINGS CHILDREN'S AID SOCIETY
Att: Manager, Human Resources
363 Dundas Street West, PO Box 186
Belleville, ON K8P 1B3

Tel. 613-962-9291
Fax 613-966-3868
Email .... hcas@kos.net
Employer Background: The Hastings Children's Aid Society is a mid-sized child welfare agency. *New Positions Created (3):* Intake Supervisor; Protection Supervisors (2); Supervisor.

HATCH ASSOCIATES LTD.
Att: Patricia Caine
128 Pine Street, Suite 103
Sudbury, ON P3C 1X3

Tel. 705-688-0250
Fax 705-688-0244
Email .... pcaine@hatch.ca
Website .... www.hatch.ca
Employer Background: Hatch Associates Ltd. is a consulting firm, providing multidisciplinary engineering services to the process, metallurgical, mineral and transportation industries worldwide. *New Positions Created (5):* Junior Mechanical Engineer; Process Control & Automation Engineers; Junior Mechanical Engineer; Process Control & Automation Engineers; Civil / Structural Technician / Technologist.

HATCH ASSOCIATES LTD.
Att: Human Resources
2800 Speakman Drive
Mississauga, ON L5K 2R7

Tel. 905-855-7600
Fax 905-855-7628
Email .... hr@hatch.ca
Website .... www.hatch.ca
Employer Background: Hatch Associates Ltd. is a consulting firm, providing multi-disciplinary engineering services to the process, metallurgical, mineral and transportation industries worldwide. *New Positions Created (6):* Livelink Developer; Programmer / Analyst; Civil / Structural CADD Technician; Software Developer; Technical Architect; Network Specialist.

HAVERGAL COLLEGE
Att: Human Resources
1451 Avenue Road
Toronto, ON M5N 2H9

Tel. 416-483-3519
Fax 416-483-6796
Email ..... human_resources@havergal.on.ca
Website .... www.havergal.on.ca
Employer Background: Founded in 1894, Havergal College is a private school for girls, offering instruction to over 870 students from kindergarten to university entrance. *New Positions Created (15):* Assistant to Director of Advancement; Leader, After-School Care Program; Head, Resource Centre; English Teacher; Mathematics Teacher, Intermediate / Senior; Mathematics Teacher, Junior / Intermediate; Residential Dons; Teachers; Retail Shop Coordinator; Head, Social Sciences; Middle School Head; Head of Music; Science Teacher, Chemistry; Director of Facilities; Director of Admissions.

HAWTHORNE HOMES
Att: Wayne Prokopetz
7315 - 8th Street NE
Calgary, AB T2E 8A2

Tel. 403-231-8999
Fax 403-231-8960
Email .... wprokopetz@
.... hawthorne-homes.com
Website .... www.hawthorne-homes.com
Employer Background: Hawthorne Homes (formerly Heartland Homes) is the single-family housing division of Carma Developers, one of Calgary's premier land developers. *New Positions Created (6):* Multi-Family Project Manager; Framing Crew Positions; New Home Pre-Occupancy Specialists; Site Carpenters; Residential Estimator; Residential Junior Estimators.

HAY RIVER COMMUNITY HEALTH BOARD
Att: Manager, Human Resources
3 Gaetz Drive
Hay River, NT X0E 0R8

Tel. 867-874-7114
Fax 867-874-7133
Website .... www.hayriver.com
Employer Background: The Hay River Community Health Board operates a 50-bed hospital, 16-bed long-term care facility and

medical clinic, and provides community and social services to a population of 6,000. *New Positions Created (16):* Manager of Ambulatory Care; Occupational Therapist; Physical Therapist; Community Mental Health Therapist Program Coordinator; Gerontology Nurse; Nurse Practitioner; Supervisor, Social Services; Health Records Technician; Environmental Health Officer; Physical and Engineering Services Manager; Clinical Resource Specialist; Executive Assistant; Gerontology Clinic Resource Nurse; Nurse Practitioner; Physical and Engineering Services Manager; Director, Diagnostic and Patient Care Services.

HAYDEN GROUP, THE
Att: Vice-President, Finance
11911 No. 5 Road
Richmond, BC V7A 4E9
Tel. 604-272-0888
Fax 604-448-8616
Website .... www.haydenvac.com
Employer Background: The Hayden Group is a plastic-fitting and central vacuum manufacturing and sales company. *New Positions Created (3):* Cost Accountant; Financial Accountant; Office and Accounting Manager.

HAYES FOREST SERVICE LTD.
Att: Human Resources Manager
7233 Trans Canada Highway
Duncan, BC V9L 6B1
Fax 250-709-6327
Email .... inbox@hayes.bc.ca
Website .... www.hayes.bc.ca
Employer Background: Hayes Forest Service Ltd. provides a broad range of services to the forest industry, including helicopter logging and firefighting, conventional logging, forestry management and engineering, road construction, custom sorting and timber marketing. *New Positions Created (3):* Director, Business Development; S61 Logging Pilots; Purchaser.

HAYWARD GORDON LIMITED
Att: Human Resources Manager
6660 Campobello Road
Mississauga, ON L5N 2L9
Tel. 905-567-6116
Fax 905-567-1706
Email .... jobs@haywardgordon.com
Website .... www.haywardgordon.com
Employer Background: Established in 1952, Hayward Gordon Limited is a Canadian manufacturer of industrial pumps and mixers. *New Positions Created (2):* Sales Engineer; Assistant Operations Manager.

HEALTH CANADA, REGIONAL NURSING
Att: Human Resources Manager
9700 Jasper Avenue, Suite 730
Edmonton, AB T5J 4C3
Fax 780-495-2687
Website .... www.hc-sc.gc.ca
Employer Background: In partnership with provincial and territorial governments,

Health Canada provides national leadership to develop health policy, enforce health regulations, promote disease prevention and enhance healthy living for all Canadians. *New Positions Created (5):* Community Health Nurses; Nurses in Charge; Community Health Nurses; Nurses In Charge; Nurses In Charge.

HEALTH CARE CORPORATION OF ST. JOHN'S, GRACE HOSPITAL SITE
Att: Carolyn Parsons,
Human Resources Officer
Waterford Bridge Road
St. John's, NF A1E 4J8
Tel. 709-778-6222
Fax 709-777-1303
Email .... hcc.parcar@hccsj.nf.ca
Website .... www.hccsj.nf.ca
Employer Background: Grace Hospital is an acute care facility. *New Positions Created (2):* Nurse, Child Health Program; Nurse, Surgery Program.

HEALTH INFORMATION PARTNERSHIP, EASTERN ONTARIO REGION
Att: Heather Wood, Office Administrator
221 Portsmouth Avenue
Kingston, ON K7M 1V5
Fax 613-549-7896
Website .... www.hip.on.ca
Employer Background: HIP provides data and information for planning, education and research related to health services. *New Positions Created (2):* Population Health Researcher; Population Health Research Officer.

HEALTH SCIENCES CENTRE / HSC
Att: Human Resources, Employment Office
60 Pearl Street
2nd Floor, Lennox Bell Lodge
Winnipeg, MB R3E 1X2
Tel. 204-787-3668
Fax 204-787-1376
Email .... employment@hsc.mb.ca
Website .... www.hsc.mb.ca
Employer Background: HSC is an 850-bed comprehensive tertiary care facility and teaching hospital affiliated with the University of Manitoba. *New Positions Created (10):* Staff Occupational Therapist, Child Health; CVT Technologist / Technician, Pediatric Cardiology; Nurse, Cardiovascular Thoracic Surgery; Nurse, Combined Care; Nurse, Medical Oncology / Bone Transplant Unit; Health Information Analyst; Director, Supply and Distribution Services; Discipline Director / Manager - Social Work; Nuclear Medicine Technologist; Staff Pharmacists.

HEALTHCARE BENEFIT TRUST / HBT
Att: Human Resources
1333 West Broadway, Suite 1200
Vancouver, BC V6H 4C1
Tel. 604-736-2087
Fax 604-736-8218
Website .... www.hbt.bc.ca
Employer Background: HBT is a health and welfare trust, managing funds and provid-

ing specified benefits and related services on behalf of participating employers. *New Positions Created (4):* Controller; Rehabilitation Consultant; Occupational Health Psychologist; Benefits Consultants.

HEALTHNET INTERNATIONAL INC.
Att: Human Resources Manager
1201 West Pender Street, Suite 301
Vancouver, BC V6E 2V2
Tel. 604-669-3573
Fax 604-669-1359
Email .... jobs@hlnt.net
Website .... www.hlnt.net
Employer Background: Healthnet International Inc. is a multinational Internet company, serving the health industry and health-minded consumers. *New Positions Created (3):* Programmer; Project Manager; Senior Programmer / Project Manager.

HEALTHTECH INC.
Att: Human Resources
210 Glencairn Avenue
Toronto, ON M4R 1N2
Tel. 416-483-5974
Fax 416-483-9197
Email .... mail@healthtech.on.ca
Website .... www.healthtech.on.ca
Employer Background: Healthtech Inc. is a consulting firm, providing services to the healthcare industry. *New Positions Created (2):* Clinical Consultant; Financial / Administrative Consultant.

HEART AND STROKE FOUNDATION OF ONTARIO
Att: Regional Manager,
Central Ontario, Human Resources
1920 Yonge Street, 4th Floor
Toronto, ON M4S 3E2
Tel. 416-489-7100
Fax 416-482-0948
Email .... resumes@hsf.on.ca
Website .... www.heartandstroke.ca
Employer Background: The Heart and Stroke Foundation of Ontario is the largest non-commercial source of funds for heart disease and stroke research in Canada. *New Positions Created (10):* Area Coordinators (3); Regional Hospital Specialist; Business Analyst; Intermediate Business Analyst; Associate Marketing Manager; Senior Associate Manager, Business Analyst; Senior Associate Manager, New Business Development; Manager, Advertising; Manager, National Corporate Gifts; Manager, Stroke Care Delivery.

HEARTHSTONE CHILD AND FAMILY SERVICES AUTHORITY
Att: Human Resource Services
4804 - 42nd Avenue
Bay 10, Alberta Corporate Service Centre
Innisfail, AB T4G 1V2
Fax 403-227-7975
Email .... censssc.jobs@gov.ab.ca
Website .... www.acs.gov.ab.ca
Employer Background: The Hearthstone Child and Family Services Authority over-

sees a range of services, including child welfare, day care, family violence prevention services, services for children with disabilities, early intervention programs, court services and mediation. *New Positions Created (4):* Community Social Worker; Program Delivery Coordinator; Community Social Worker; Child Welfare Social Workers.

HEARTLAND SHIPPING SUPPLIES INC.
Att: Bruce Chiasson
6420A Kestrel Road
Mississauga, ON L5T 1Z7
Tel. 905-564-9777
Employer Background: Heartland Shipping Supplies Inc. manufactures packaging materials. *New Positions Created (2):* Packaging Supplies Sales Representative; Packaging Supplies Sales Representative.

HEENAN BLAIKIE
Att: Susan Wilson
200 Bay Street, Suite 2600
Box 185, Royal Bank Plaza, South Tower
Toronto, ON M5J 2J4
Tel. 416-360-6336
Fax 416-360-8425
Website .... www.heenanblaikie.com
Employer Background: Heenan Blaikie is one of Canada's premier law firms, with 300 lawyers. *New Positions Created (4):* Legal Assistant, Bilingual; Legal Assistant, Overflow; Intellectual Property Associate; Junior Computer Technician.

HEIDELBERG CANADA
Att: Human Resources Manager
4020 Viking Way, Suite 130
Richmond, BC V6V 2N2
Fax 604-278-4907
Website .... www.heidelberg.ca
Employer Background: Heidelberg Canada manufactures and distributes graphic arts equipment, graphic arts consumables and digital products. *New Positions Created (2):* Secretary; Sales Representative.

HEIDELBERG CANADA
Att: Human Resources
50 Worcester Road
Toronto, ON M9W 5X2
Tel. 416-675-2700
Fax 416-675-0516
Email .... hr@heidelberg.ca
Website .... www.heidelberg.ca
Employer Background: Heidelberg Canada manufactures and distributes graphic arts equipment, graphic arts consumables and digital products. *New Positions Created (6):* Credit and Collections Administrator; Credit and Collections Team Leader; National Prepress Sales Mgr; Bilingual Parts Order Desk; Logistics Manager; Product Manager.

HEIDELBERG CANADA
Att: Human Resources
6265 Kenway Drive
Mississauga, ON L5T 2L3
Tel. 905-362-4400

Fax 905-362-0377
Website .... www.heidelberg.ca
Employer Background: Heidelberg Canada manufactures and distributes graphic arts equipment, graphic arts consumables and digital products. *New Positions Created (25):* Field Press Instructor; Service Manager, Central Region; Digital Solutions Analysts; Sales Representatives; Inventory Auditor; Pressroom Specialist; Reporting Accountant; Field Service Technician; Team Leader, Prepress Demonstration Centre; SAP Business Analyst / Project Manager; Demonstrator, Large Format Presses; National Digital Sales Manager; Electrical / Electronic Service Technician; Sales Representative; National Digital Sales Manager; Bilingual Credit and Collections Clerk; Application Specialist, Pre-Press; Reception Relief / Sales Support Position; Demonstrator, Large Format Presses; Project Coordinator; Field Service Technicians; Sales Professionals; Project Installation Coordinator, Press and Finishing; Product Manager, Digital Imaging and Digital Printing; Project Installation Coordinator, Press and Finishing.

HELLMUTH, OBATA & KASSABAUM, INC. / HOK CANADA
Att: Human Resources Department
207 Queen's Quay West
Suite 802, PO Box 105
Toronto, ON M5J 1A7
Tel. 416-203-9993
Fax 416-203-7263
Email .... patricia.tom@hok.com
Website .... www.hok.com
Employer Background: HOK Canada is a design firm. *New Positions Created (8):* Business Development Manager; Senior Project Architect; Accountant; Graphics Coordinator; Architectural Technologists; Senior Architects; Interior Designers; Technologists.

HEMA-QUEBEC
Att: Human Resources Department
4045 Cote-Vertu Boulevard
St-Laurent, QC H4R 2W7
Tel. 514-832-5000
Fax 514-832-1026
Email .... emploi@hema-quebec.qc.ca
Website .... www.hema-quebec.qc.ca
Employer Background: Established in 1998, Hema-Quebec is Quebec's blood supplier, responsible for recruiting blood donors, organizing blood donor clinics, screening donated blood and preparing blood components. *New Positions Created (9):* Clerk / Attendant; Medical Laboratory Technician; Nurses; Technical Assistant; Nurses; Medical Laboratory Technician; Clerk / Attendant; Drivers; Technical Assistants.

HEMERA TECHNOLOGIES INC.
Att: Human Resources Manager
PO Box 79093
Hull, QC J8Y 6V2
Tel. 819-772-8200
Fax 819-778-6252
Email .... jobs@hemera.com
Website .... www.hemera.com

Employer Background: Hemera Technologies Inc. produces graphics and Internet software for the mass market. *New Positions Created (11):* Account Managers, OEM / Business Development; Application Testing Specialists; Content Acquisitions Manager; Controller; Customer Support Specialists; Digital Imaging Technician; Director of Corporate Communications; Junior Graphic Designer; Junior, Intermediate or Senior Visual C++ / MFC Programmers / Analysts; Macintosh Programmers / Analyst; Vice-President of Marketing.

HEMLOCK PRINTERS LTD.
Att: Human Resources Department
7050 Buller Avenue
Burnaby, BC V5J 4S4
Tel. 604-438-2456
Fax 604-439-5033
Email ....:........ hrd@hemlock.com
Website .... www.hemlock.com
Employer Background: Hemlock Printers Ltd. is a leading commercial sheet-fed printer. *New Positions Created (2):* Production Planner; Sales Representative.

HEMOSOL INC.
Att: Human Resources
2 Meridian Road
Toronto, ON M9W 4Z7
Tel. 416-798-0700
Fax 416-798-0152
Email .... hr@hemosol.com
Website .... www.hemosol.com
Employer Background: Hemosol Inc. is a Canadian biopharmaceutical company, developing a multi-product pipeline based on proprietary technologies in the field of blood cells and proteins. *New Positions Created (11):* Document Control Administrator; Process Automation Technologist; Production Technologist; Quality Assurance Manager, Construction Project; Quality Control Microbiology Sampler; Quality Control Microbiology Tester; Intellectual Property Manger; Facility Construction Auditor; Process Automation Engineer; Production Technologist; Quality Assurance Specialist, Construction Project.

HENDERSON DEVELOPMENT (CANADA) LTD.
Att: Personnel Department
1090 West Pender Street, Suite 803
Vancouver, BC V6E 2N7
Tel. 604-689-8898
Employer Background: Henderson Development (Canada) Ltd. is a property developer and manager, with several large multi-phase residential and commercial projects under development. *New Positions Created (4):* Marketing Manager; Development Manager; Assistant Controller; Development Manager.

HENRY BIRKS & SONS INC.
Att: Human Resources Manager
698 West Hastings Street
Vancouver, BC V6B 1P1
Tel. 604-669-3333

Fax 604-669-3363
Email .... lacassem@birks.com
Website .... www.birks.com
Employer Background: Established in 1879, Henry Birks & Sons Inc. is a leading retailer of high-end jewellery, timepieces, sterling silverware and luxury gift items. *New Positions Created (2):* Sales Coordinator, Corporate Sales Division; Insurance Claims Coordinator.

HENRY BIRKS & SONS INC.
Att: Human Resources
55 Bloor Street West
Manulife Centre, Unit 152
Toronto, ON M4W 1A5
Fax 416-922-8084
Website .... www.birks.com
Employer Background: Established in 1879, Henry Birks & Sons Inc. is a leading retailer of high-end jewellery, timepieces, sterling silverware and luxury gift items. *New Positions Created (2):* Sales Associates; Claims Coordinator.

HENRY BIRKS & SONS INC.
Att: Pauline Lessard, Recruiting Manager
1240 Phillips Square
Montréal, QC H3B 3H4
Tel. 514-397-2511
Fax 514-397-2455
Email .... lessardp@birks.com
Website .... www.birks.com
Employer Background: Established in 1879, Henry Birks & Sons Inc. is a leading retailer of high-end jewellery, timepieces, sterling silverware and luxury gift items. *New Positions Created (18):* Programmer Analyst; Coordinator, Retail Administration; Management Positions; Retail Operations Manager; Administrative Assistant; Benefits and Payroll Supervisor; Loss Prevention Officer; Corporate Sales Account Executive; Shipping and Receiving Clerks; Product Manager; Manager, Training and Performance Management; Store Manager; Marketing Assistant; Accounts Payable Manager; Payroll and Benefits Coordinator; Merchandise Coordinator; Claims Coordinator; Store Manager.

HENRY SCHEIN ARCONA INC.
Att: Human Resources Manager
17 Keefer Road
St. Catharines, ON L2M 6K4
Tel. 905-646-1711
Fax 905-646-9973
Email .... hr@hsa.ca
Website .... www.hsa.ca
Employer Background: Henry Schein Arcona Inc., a subsidiary of Henry Schein Inc., distributes healthcare products to office-based practitioners across Canada. *New Positions Created (11):* Service Technician, Dental Equipment; Administration / Customer Service Assistant; Customer Service Representative; Human Resources Administrator, Western Facility; Dental Laboratory Sales Consultant; Dental Sales Consultant; Veterinarian Field Sales Consultant; Customer Service Position; Dental Laboratory

Sales Consultant; Equipment Coordinator; Dental Sales Consultant.

HENRY TECHNOLOGIES / CHIL-CON PRODUCTS LTD.
Att: Human Resources Manager
36 Craig Street, PO Box 1385
Brantford, ON N3T 5T6
Tel. 519-759-3010
Fax 519-759-1611
Website .... www.henrytech.com
Employer Background: Henry Technologies / Chil-Con Products Ltd. is a leading manufacturer of heat exchangers and pressure vessels for the refrigeration industry. *New Positions Created (3):* Application Engineers (2); Canadian Sales Representative; Project Engineers (2).

HEPCOE CREDIT UNION LTD.
Att: Vice-President, Information Services
777 Bay Street, 26th Floor, PO Box 118
Toronto, ON M5G 2C8
Tel. 416-597-4400
Fax 416-597-5069
Email .... daveh@hepcoe.com
Website .... www.hepcoe.com
Employer Background: Hepcoe Credit Union Ltd. is one of Canada's largest credit unions, with assets exceeding $1 billion. *New Positions Created (7):* HP Unix Programmer; Purchasing Agent; Branch Managers (2); Purchasing Manager; Branch Manager; Financial Services Consultant III; Manager of Training and Development.

HERBON NATURALS, INC.
Att: Human Resources
6691 Elmbridge Way, Suite 160
Richmond, BC V7C 4N1
Tel. 604-214-0705
Fax 604-214-0715
Email .... info@herbon.com
Website .... www.herbon.com
Employer Background: Herbon Naturals, Inc. is a small firm selling herbal cough drops in Canada and overseas. *New Positions Created (3):* Accountant / Bookkeeper; Sales and General Management Position; Shipper / Receiver.

HERCULES INC.
Att: Rose Del Giudice, Terminal Manager
2055 Kennedy Road
Toronto, ON M1T 3G3
Tel. 416-412-7855
Fax 416-412-7853
Employer Background: Hercules Inc. is an LTL carrier, with a focus on US northbound traffic. *New Positions Created (2):* Sales Representative; Sales Position.

HERITAGE FAMILY SERVICES LTD.
Att: Human Resources
4825 - 47th Street, Suite 300
Red Deer, AB T4N 1R3
Tel. 403-343-3422
Fax 403-343-9293
Email ..... hr@heritagefamilyservices.com
Website .. www.heritagefamilyservices.com

Employer Background: Founded in 1975, Heritage Family Services is a privately-owned provider of professional childcare industry services and programs. *New Positions Created (2):* Chartered Psychologist; Therapist / Chartered Psychologist.

HERITAGE PARK
HISTORICAL VILLAGE
Att: Assistant General Manager, HR
1900 Heritage Drive SW
Calgary, AB T2V 2X3
Tel. 403-259-1900
Fax 403-252-3528
Email .... hr@heritagepark.ab.ca
Website .... www.heritagepark.ab.ca
Employer Background: Heritage Park Historical Village features over 66 acres of lush parkland, over 150 historical exhibits, thousands of artifacts and lively interpretive activities. *New Positions Created (2):* Project Manager; Treasury Assistant.

HERO INDUSTRIES LTD.
Att: Drew Gagnier
2719 Lake City Way
Burnaby, BC V5A 2Z6
Tel. 604-420-6543
Fax 604-420-8725
Email .... dgagnier@hero.ca
Website .... www.hero.ca
Employer Background: HERO Industries Ltd. manufactures equipment for the paint industry worldwide. *New Positions Created (2):* Sales Representative; Design Engineer.

HEROUX DEVTEK,
MAGTRON DIVISION
Att: Hans Kleiner, Plant Manager
1480 Birchmount Road
Toronto, ON M1P 2G2
Employer Background: Heroux Devtek is a Canadian manufacturer of aerospace and industrial products. *New Positions Created (4):* CNC Set-Up Operators; Conventional Lathe Operators; Milling Machine Operators; Planner.

HERSHEY CANADA INC.
Att: Employee Relations Department
1 Hershey Drive, PO Box 2100
Smith Falls, ON K7A 4T8
Tel. 613-283-3300
Fax 613-283-8272
Email .... tlucas@hersheys.com
Website .... www.hersheys.com
Employer Background: Hershey Canada Inc. manufactures and markets a variety of grocery and confectionery products. *New Positions Created (9):* Electrical Engineering Technologist; Maintenance Mechanics; Production Supervisors; Shipping / Receiving Supervisor; Electrical Engineering Technologist; Instrumentation Control Specialist; Maintenance Mechanics; Manufacturing Engineer; Production Supervisors.

HERTZ EQUIPMENT RENTAL
Att: Human Resources
35 Claireville Drive
Toronto, ON M9W 5Z7

Tel. 416-674-5000
Fax 416-679-4141
Website .... www.hertzequip.com
Employer Background: Hertz Equipment Rental, a division of the Hertz Corporation, rents, sells and services a full range of construction and industrial equipment. *New Positions Created (4):* Bilingual A / R Administrator; Rental Coordinator; A / R Associate / Collector; Financial Analyst.

HEWITT ASSOCIATES
Att: Christopher Newton
25 Sheppard Avenue West
Toronto, ON M2N 6T1
Tel. 416-225-5001
Fax 416-225-9790
Website .... www.hewitt.com
Employer Background: Hewitt Associates is an international firm of consultants and actuaries. *New Positions Created (13):* Lawyer, Human Resources Consulting; Financial Processor; Health & Group Benefits - Business Analyst, Entry; Technology - Programmer Analyst, Entry; Administrative Assistant, Business Development & Marketing; Administrative / Clerical Assistant, Entry; IS Regional Location Manager; Project Manager, Health & Group Benefits; Bilingual Customer Service Representative; Business Analyst; Business Analyst - Defined Benefit; Compensation Consultant; Technology - Business Systems Analyst.

HEWITT EQUIPMENT LTD.
Att: Personnel Department
5001 Trans Canada Highway
Pointe-Claire, QC H9R 1B8
Tel. 514-630-3100
Fax 514-630-3143
Email .... personnel@hewitt.ca
Website .... www.hewitt.ca
Employer Background: Hewitt Equipment Ltd. is a leading distributor of heavy equipment, lift trucks, truck engines, diesel engines and generator sets. *New Positions Created (7):* Field Technician; Foreman, Shop Department; Representative, Mining Equipment; Sales Representatives; Secretaries (2); Service Foreman; Warranties Coordinator.

HEWLETT-PACKARD (CANADA) LTD.
Att: Human Resources Department
5150 Spectrum Way
Mississauga, ON L4W 5G1
Tel. 905-206-4725
Fax 650-813-3874
Website .... www.canada.hp.com
Employer Background: Established in 1961, Hewlett-Packard (Canada) Ltd. has over 1,300 employees at 21 locations nationwide and annual revenues of $1.9 billion. *New Positions Created (15):* Customer Engineer; IT Management Consultant; Member of IT Technical Staff; Network & Service Provider Practice Manager; Support Agreements Specialist; E-Commerce Solution Consultant; E-Services Manager Architect; Support Agreements Specialist; Business Associate; Employee Communications / Philanthropy Manager; Financial Service Representative;

Principal Consultant; Solution Architect; Exchange Deployment Specialist; Financial Analyst.

HEWSON BRIDGE AND SMITH LTD.
Att: Brigitte Smith
601 Bank Street
Ottawa, ON K1S 3T4
Tel. 613-238-7108
Fax 613-238-7468
Email .... brigitte@hbs.ca
Website .... www.hbs.ca
Employer Background: HBC is a leading marketing communications firm, focused exclusively on the technology sector. *New Positions Created (4):* Designer; HTML Programmer; Media Planner / Buyer; Production Manager.

HFI FLOORING INC.
Att: Rob Burla, V.P., Sales and Marketing
5919 - 5th Street SE
Calgary, AB T2H 1L5
Tel. 403-255-8775
Fax 403-252-8712
Email .... rburla@hfiflooring.com
Website .... www.hfiflooring.com
Employer Background: HFI Flooring Inc. is a leading marketer of specialty wood flooring products based in Calgary. *New Positions Created (3):* Executive Assistant; Junior Purchaser; Product Marketing Manager.

HI-ALTA CAPITAL INC.
Att: Human Resources Manager
309 - 1st Street West, PO Box 5519
High River, AB T1V 1M6
Tel. 403-652-2663
Fax 403-652-2661
Website .... www.hi-alta.com
Employer Background: Hi-Alta Capital Inc. is building a network of rural brokerages in the property and casualty insurance industry in western Canada. *New Positions Created (2):* Financial Accountant; Financial Services Manager.

HICKLING CORPORATION
Att: Human Resource Manager
150 Isabella Street, Penthouse Floor
Ottawa, ON K1S 1V7
Tel. 613-237-2220
Fax 613-237-7347
Email .... dianep@hickling.ca
Website .... www.hickling.ca
Employer Background: Hickling Corporation is a Canadian consulting firm, operating worldwide. *New Positions Created (2):* Advisor, Planning and Budgeting; Advisor, Trade Policy.

HIGHLAND EQUIPMENT LTD.
Att: Human Resources
136 The East Mall
Toronto, ON M8Z 5V5
Tel. 416-236-9610
Fax 416-236-9611
Email .... debbieh@highlandequip.com
Website .... www.highlandequip.com

Employer Background: Highland Equipment Ltd. manufactures and distributes stainless steel process equipment for the food, beverage, dairy and pharmaceutical industries. *New Positions Created (4):* Designer (CAD) / Draftsperson; Estimator; Reception / Administrative Assistant; Inside Sales / Purchasing Agent.

HIGHLAND FARMS INC.
Att: Human Resources Manager
4750 Dufferin Street
Toronto, ON M3H 5S7
Tel. 416-736-6606
Fax 416-736-4795
Email .... franl@highlandfarms.on.ca
Employer Background: Highland Farms Inc. is a high-end, family-owned retailer in the produce and grocery business. *New Positions Created (2):* Manager, Human Resources; Controller.

HIGHLAND TRANSPORT
Att: M. King, Ontario Sales Manager
2815 - 14th Avenue
Markham, ON L3R 0H9
Fax 905-477-0940
Email ..... mking@highlandtransport.com
Website .... www.highlandtransport.com
Employer Background: Founded in 1967, Highland Transport is one of Canada's leading truckload and container carriers. *New Positions Created (4):* Sales Representative; Administrative Assistant; Telemarketing Position; Sales Representative.

HIGHWOOD RESOURCES LTD.
Att: M. Kane, VP Operations
734 - 7th Avenue SW, Suite 715
Calgary, AB T2P 3P8
Fax 403-264-2959
Employer Background: Highwood Resources Ltd. produces ground and micronized industrial minerals. *New Positions Created (2):* Quality Assurance Professional; Accounting Clerk.

HILLEBRAND ESTATES WINERY
Att: Human Resources Manager
1249 Niagara Stone Road
Niagara-on-the-Lake, ON L0S 1J0
Tel. 905-468-7123
Fax 905-468-4789
Email .... info@hillebrand.com
Website .... www.hillebrand.com
Employer Background: Hillebrand Estates Winery is one of Canada's leading producers of premium VQA wines. *New Positions Created (2):* Assistant Manager, Direct Delivery; Various Foodservice Positions.

HILLFIELD-STRATHALLAN COLLEGE
Att: Headmaster
299 Fennell Avenue West
Hamilton, ON L9C 1G3
Fax 905-389-6366
Website .... www.hillstrath.on.ca
Employer Background: Hillfield-Strathallan College is a private, co-educational school

offering instruction from primary to high school. *New Positions Created (6):* Executive Director; Network Administrator; Director of College Administration; Junior School Teacher; Senior School Teacher; Alumni Officer.

HILTI (CANADA) LTD.
Att: Larry Gartley
6790 Century Avenue, Suite 300
Mississauga, ON L5N 2V8
Tel. 905-813-9200
Fax 905-813-9009
Website .... www.hilti.com
Employer Background: Hilti (Canada) Ltd. develops, manufactures and markets construction tools and fastening systems. *New Positions Created (5):* Brushless Motor and Power Electronics Specialist; Embedded Software Specialist; Motor Designer; Sales Representatives; Sales Representatives.

HILTON MONTREAL AEROPORT
Att: Human Resources Department
12505 Cote de Liesse
Dorval, QC H9P 1B7
Tel. 514-631-2411
Fax 514-631-0298
Website .... www.hilton.com
Employer Background: Hilton Montreal Aeroport is a 486-room facilty operated by California-based Hilton Hotels Corporation, a leading hotel company with over 250 hotels and resorts in Canada and the USA. *New Positions Created (3):* Systems Manager; Assistant Controller; Internal Controller.

HISHKOONIKUN EDUCATION AUTHORITY
Att: Jonathan Solomon, Director
430 Riverside Road, PO Box 235
Kashechewan, ON P0L 1S0
Tel. 705-275-4538
Fax 705-275-4515
Employer Background: The Hishkoonikun Education Authority serves the village of Kashechewan, a remote community of 1,500 First Nations people on the coast of James Bay. *New Positions Created (2):* Elementary and Secondary School Teacher; Teachers (2).

HITACHI CANADA, LTD.
Att: Human Resources Manager
6740 Campobello Road
Mississauga, ON L5N 2L8
Tel. 905-821-4545
Fax 905-826-8818
Email .... human.resources@hitachi.ca
Website .... www.hitachi.ca
Employer Background: Hitachi Canada, Ltd. is a leader in consumer electronics. *New Positions Created (3):* Technical Field Representative; Product Manager; National Sales Representative.

HITACHI CANADIAN INDUSTRIES LTD.
Att: Human Resources Manager
826 - 58th Street East
Saskatoon, SK S7K 5Z4
Tel. 306-242-9222

Fax 306-242-9211
Website .... www.hitachi.com
Employer Background: Hitachi Canadian Industries Ltd. (part of Japan-based Hitachi, Ltd.) is a manufacturer of turbine generator equipment, with over 340 employees in Saskatoon. *New Positions Created (7):* Project Engineer; Production Mgr; Assistant Mgr, Planning & Projects; Machine Shop Supervisor; Production Mgr; QA Technologist; QA Engineer.

HITEC SYSTEMS AND CONTROLS INC.
Att: Human Resources Manager
3827 - 98th Street
Edmonton, AB T6E 5V4
Fax 780-435-7496
Website .... www.natoil.com
Employer Background: Hitec Systems and Controls Inc. is part of National Oilwell, a worldwide leader in integrated drilling systems. *New Positions Created (3):* Computer / IT Technician; Intermediate PLC and MMI Programmer; Junior / Senior Instrumentation Technicians.

HITEC SYSTEMS AND CONTROLS INC.
Att: Human Resources Manager
1616 Meridian Road NE
Calgary, AB T2A 2P1
Fax 403-569-2294
Website .... www.natoil.com
Employer Background: Hitec Systems and Controls Inc. is part of National Oilwell, a worldwide leader in integrated drilling systems. *New Positions Created (4):* Information Technologist; Production Coordinators; Production Lead Hands; Various Trade / Technician Positions.

HMS HOST
Att: Human Resources Manager
Vancouver International Airport
Box 23630
Richmond, BC V7B 1X8
Tel. 604-231-3731
Fax 604-231-3732
Website .... www.hmscorp.com
Employer Background: HMS Host (formerly Host Marriott Services) is a leading operator of airport food, beverage and retail concessions. *New Positions Created (3):* Food and Beverage Manager; Retail Store Manager; General Manager.

HMS SOFTWARE
Att: Human Resources Department
1000 St. Jean Boulevard, Suite 711
Pointe-Claire, QC H9R 5P1
Tel. 514-695-8122
Fax 514-695-8121
Email .... hr@hmssoftware.ca
Website .... www.hmssoftware.ca
Employer Background: Founded in 1983, HMS Software is a software publisher, specializing in timesheet control applications. *New Positions Created (4):* Delphi Programmer, Intermediate Level; Sales / Administration Assistant; Sr Java Developer; Technical Associate.

HOFLAND LTD.
Att: Human Resources Manager
6695 Pacific Circle
Mississauga, ON L5T 1V6
Fax 905-670-8257
Email .... careers@hofland.com
Website .... www.hofland.com
Employer Background: Hofland Ltd. is a national floral and giftware distributor. *New Positions Created (8):* Intermediate Buyer; Systems / Software Specialist; Operations Manager; Inside Sales Representative, Floral; Inside Sales Representative, Hard Goods; Class G Driver; Operations Associate; Puller / Packer.

HOLDERBANK GROUP SUPPORT (CANADA) LTD.
Att: Human Resources Manager
2310 Lakeshore Road West
Mississauga, ON L5J 1K2
Tel. 905-822-1693
Fax 905-822-1698
Email .... leeb@holderbank.ca
Website .... www.holderbank.ca
Employer Background: Holderbank Group Support (Canada) Ltd. offers a complete range of engineering services to cement industry producers throughout the Americas. *New Positions Created (2):* Electrical Engineers, Controls Group; Electrical Engineers, Power Group.

HOLIDAY INN BURLINGTON
Att: Human Resources
3063 South Service Road
Burlington, ON L7N 3E9
Tel. 905-639-4443
Fax 905-333-0477
Website ..... www.sixcontinentshotels.com
Employer Background: Holiday Inn Burlington (part of Six Continents Hotels) features 237 guest rooms and 3 suites. *New Positions Created (6):* 2nd Cook; Front Desk Position; Banquet Positions (3); Fitness Club Manager; Controller; Maintenance Assistant.

HOLLAND CHEMICAL INTERNATIONAL (CANADA) / HCI CANADA INC.
Att: Ian Nicholson
777 - 8th Avenue SW, Suite 1900
Calgary, AB T2P 3R5
Fax 403-233-7011
Email .... inicholson@hciww.com
Website .... www.hciww.com
Employer Background: HCI Canada Inc. is a subsidiary of Holland Chemical International, a global chemical and plastics distributor with sites in over 29 countries. *New Positions Created (3):* Sales Representative; Operations Manager; Credit Supervisor.

HOLSTEIN ASSOCIATION OF CANADA, THE / HOLSTEIN CANADA
Att: Human Resources Manager
PO Box 610
Brantford, ON N3T 5R4
Fax 519-756-8202
Email .... jshannon@holstein.ca

Website .... www.holstein.ca
Employer Background: Holstein Canada maintains a genealogical record of the Holstein breed, and promotes the best interests of breeders and owners of Holstein cattle in Canada. *New Positions Created (2):* Holstein Classifiers (2); Intermediate Programmer Analyst.

HOLT RENFREW
Att: Kelly Hadden, HR Manager, Western
633 Granville Street
Vancouver, BC V7Y 1E4
Fax 604-681-9285
Website .... www.holtrenfrew.com
Employer Background: Holt Renfrew is one of Canada's leading fashion and lifestyle retailers. *New Positions Created (3):* Area Sales Manager; Sales Associates / Cosmeticians; General Manager.

HOLT RENFREW
Att: Human Resources Department
50 Bloor Street West
Toronto, ON M4W 1A1
Fax 416-922-9706
Website .... www.holtrenfrew.com
Employer Background: Holt Renfrew is one of Canada's leading fashion and lifestyle retailers. *New Positions Created (2):* Various Retail Positions; Investigators.

HOLT RENFREW
Att: Human Resources Manager
240 Sparks Street, 3rd Floor
Ottawa, ON K1P 6C9
Fax 613-238-6223
Website .... www.holtrenfrew.com
Employer Background: Holt Renfrew is one of Canada's leading fashion and lifestyle retailers. *New Positions Created (3):* Various Retail Positions; Alterations Supervisor; Human Resources / Operations Manager.

HOME DEPOT
Att: Human Resources
7 Curity Avenue
Toronto, ON M4B 3L8
Fax 416-752-3475
Website .... www.homedepot.com
Employer Background: Founded in 1978, Home Depot is the world's largest home improvement retailer, with over 1,000 stores in the USA, Canada, Puerto Rico, Chile and Argentina. *New Positions Created (2):* Cashiers and Sales Associates; Cashiers and Sales Associates.

HOME DEPOT
Att: Recruiting
426 Ellesmere Road
Toronto, ON M1R 4E7
Tel. 416-609-0852
Fax 416-412-4958
Website .... www.homedepot.com
Employer Background: Founded in 1978, Home Depot is the world's largest home improvement retailer, with over 1,000 stores in the USA, Canada, Puerto Rico, Chile and

Argentina. *New Positions Created (3):* Department Supervisors; Associate Development Supervisor; Associate Development Supervisor.

HOME OUTFITTERS
Att: David Hest, Human Resources
401 Bay Street, Suite 1100
Toronto, ON M5H 2Y4
Fax 416-861-4535
Email .... mark.lang@hbc.com
Website .... www.hbc.com
Employer Background: Home Outfitters, a division of the Hudson's Bay Company, is a kitchen, bath and bed superstore. *New Positions Created (3):* Retail Store Managers; Store Manager; Visual Merchandisers.

HOME TRUST CO. CREDIT CARD SERVICES
Att: S. Clarke, Manager, Operations
145 King Street West, Suite 1910
Toronto, ON M5H 1J8
Tel. 416-360-4663
Fax 416-360-6693
Website .... www.hometrust.ca
Employer Background: Home Trust Co. Credit Card Services (formerly Home Savings & Loan Corporation) is an alternative mortgage lender. *New Positions Created (6):* Manager, Mortgage Underwriting; Mortgage Servicing / Collection Administrator; National Manager, Mortgage Marketing; Mortgage Administrator; Mortgage Administrator; Reception / Deposit Clerk.

HOME TRUST COMPANY
Att: M. Ryan
21 King Street West, Suite 800
Hamilton, ON L8P 4W7
Fax 905-522-1888
Email .... ryan@hometrust.ca
Website .... www.hometrust.ca
Employer Background: Home Trust Company (formerly Home Savings & Loan Corporation) is an alternative mortgage lender. *New Positions Created (2):* Mortgage Development Officer; Mortgage Administrator.

HOME TRUST COMPANY
Att: Dinah Henderson, CGA, Controller
15 Church Street, Suite 100, PO Box 1554
St. Catharines, ON L2R 7J9
Tel. 905-688-3131
Fax 905-988-1808
Website .... www.hometrust.ca
Employer Background: Home Trust Company (formerly Home Savings & Loan Corporation) is an alternative mortgage lender. *New Positions Created (2):* Deposit Supervisor; Accounting Clerk.

HOMEOWNER PROTECTION OFFICE
Att: Sandy Branning
PO Box 11132, Royal Centre
Vancouver, BC V6E 3P3
Tel. 604-646-7055
Fax 604-646-7051
Email .... sbrannin@hpo.bc.ca

Website .... www.hpo.bc.ca
Employer Background: The Homeowner Protection Office is a Crown corporation established to strengthen consumer protection and improve the quality of residential construction in BC. *New Positions Created (2):* Licensing Officer; Compliance Officers.

HOMESTAKE CANADA INC., ESKAY CREEK MINE
Att: Human Resources Superintendent
PO Box 3908
Smithers, BC V0J 2N0
Tel. 250-847-4002
Fax 604-515-5241
Email .... lbeitz@homestake.com
Website .... www.homestake.com
Employer Background: Homestake Canada Inc. is one of the largest gold producers in the world, with operations in the USA, South America, Australia and Canada. *New Positions Created (2):* Environmental Coordinator; Mine Accountant.

HOMESTEAD LAND HOLDINGS LTD.
Att: Human Resources Manager
2001 Carling Avenue
Ottawa, ON K2A 3W5
Tel. 613-729-4115
Fax 613-729-5723
Website .... www.homestead.on.ca
Employer Background: Homestead Land Holdings Ltd. builds and manages quality apartments. *New Positions Created (2):* Property Accountant; Building Superintendent.

HONDA CANADA INC.
Att: Mark D'Aliesio, Human Resources
715 Milner Avenue
Toronto, ON M1B 2K8
Tel. 416-284-8110
Fax 416-286-1322
Website .... www.honda.ca
Employer Background: Honda Canada Inc. markets and distributes automobile, motorcycle and power equipment (e.g. lawn mowers) products throughout Canada. *New Positions Created (2):* District Sales Manager; Automotive Product Knowledge Instructor.

HONDA OF CANADA MANUFACTURING
Att: Associate Services
PO Box 5000
Alliston, ON L9R 1A2
Tel. 705-435-5561
Fax 705-435-4116
Website .... www.honda.ca
Employer Background: Honda of Canada Manufacturing's Milton plant has more than 2,000 employees and manufactures over 150,000 Civic and Acura cars each year. *New Positions Created (17):* Mechanical Engineer; Electrical Engineer; Purchasing Position, New Model; Data Analyst; Ergonomist; Cost Analyst; Stationary Engineer; Mechanical / Electrical Engineers; Accounting Cost Analyst; General Accountant; Translator; Accounting Cost Analyst; Purchasing, New

Model; Electrical Engineering Technologist; Mechanical / Electrical Engineers; AIX Technical Support Position; Software Developer.

HONEYWELL IC
Att: Human Resources Manager,
Vancouver Operations
500 Brooksbank Avenue
North Vancouver, BC V7J 3S4
Tel. 604-980-3421
Fax 604-980-9793
Email ..... human.resources@honeywell.com
Website .... www.honeywell.com
Employer Background: Honeywell IC is a leading supplier of measurement and industrial automation systems to unify business and control information throughout a plant or mill. *New Positions Created (5):* Fitter; Health and Safety Specialist; Process Support Engineer; Strategic Sourcing Manager; Transportation Manager.

HONEYWELL INC.
Att: Human Resources
200 Marcel-Laurin Boulevard
Montréal, QC H4M 2L5
Email .... position.montreal@honeywell.com
Website .... www.honeywell.com
Employer Background: Honeywell Inc. is a global leader in aerospace, avionics and engineered material, with over 68 years industry experience and more than 400 employees in Montreal. *New Positions Created (7):* Planner / Buyer, Materials Department; Planner / Buyer; Process Planner; Technicians, Repair and Overhaul; Field Service Representatives (2); Human Resources Coordinator, Training; Human Resources Generalist.

HONEYWELL LTD.
Att: Project Management Leader
3490 Gardner Court, Suite 300
Burnaby, BC V5G 3K4
Tel. 604-654-5678
Fax 604-654-5666
Website .... www.honeywell.ca
Employer Background: Honeywell Ltd. markets building controls to enhance comfort, improve productivity, save energy, protect the environment and increase security. *New Positions Created (2):* Performance Contracting Engineer; Senior Sales Representatives.

HONEYWELL LTD.
Att: Project Management Lead
16240 - 116th Avenue NW
Edmonton, AB T5M 3V4
Fax 780-944-9781
Website .... www.honeywell.ca
Employer Background: Honeywell Ltd. markets building controls to enhance comfort, improve productivity, save energy, protect the environment and increase security. *New Positions Created (3):* Life Safety / Security Control Systems Designer; Senior Automation Technician; Junior Security Sales Representative.

HONEYWELL LTD.
Att: Philip Chow
300 Yorkland Boulevard
Toronto, ON M2J 1S1
Tel. 416-758-2748
Fax 416-758-2690
Email .... philip.chow@honeywell.com
Website .... www.honeywell.ca
Employer Background: Honeywell Ltd. markets building controls to enhance comfort, improve productivity, save energy, protect the environment and increase security. *New Positions Created (3):* Solution Design Centre Coordinator; Junior System Designer; Senior System Designer.

HONEYWELL LTD., INDUSTRIAL AUTOMATION AND CONTROL
Att: Human Resource Manager
5925 Centre Street SW
Calgary, AB T2H 0C2
Tel. 403-320-8866
Fax 403-253-7396
Email .... recruiting.sales@honeywell.com
Website .... www.honeywell.ca
Employer Background: Honeywell Ltd., Industrial Automation and Control is the world's leading supplier of process control systems, services and instrumentation to customers in the hydrocarbon processing and chemical industries. *New Positions Created (3):* Senior Automation Consultant; Senior Application Consultant; Customer Service Representative.

HONG FOOK MENTAL HEALTH ASSOCIATION
Att: Executive Director
1065 McNicoll Avenue, Main Level
Toronto, ON M1W 3W6
Tel. 416-493-2214
Fax 416-493-4242
Email .... hfook@iponline.com
Website .... www.hongfook.ca
Employer Background: Established in 1982, the Hong Fook Mental Health Association works to attain ethno-racial equity in the mental health system for Asian-Canadian communities. *New Positions Created (5):* Administrative Assistant; Administrative Manager; Community Support Worker(s); Mental Health Workers; Team Leader, Housing.

HOPPING KOVACH GRINNELL
Att: Human Resources Manager
81 West Cordova Street
Vancouver, BC V6B 1C8
Fax 604-684-7328
Employer Background: Hopping Kovach Grinnell is a leader in the design industry. *New Positions Created (2):* Design Technicians; Junior and Intermediate Designers.

HORN AND ASSOCIATES
Att: Human Resources Manager
1600 Steeles Avenue West, Suite 412
Concord, ON L4K 4M2
Tel. 905-650-9260
Fax 905-761-8008
Email .... train@horn.com
Website .... www.horn.com
Employer Background: Founded in 1985, Horn and Associates provides sales force training and consulting. *New Positions Created (2):* Sales Trainer; Desktop Publisher.

HORN PLASTICS INC.
Att: Human Resources
4 Cannon Court
Whitby, ON L1N 5V8
Tel. 905-430-7042
Fax 905-430-1605
Email .... hr@hornplastics.com
Website .... www.hornplastics.com
Employer Background: Established in 1979, Horn Plastics Inc. is a leading custom injection moulding and assembly plant. *New Positions Created (4):* Manager, Quality Assurance; Project Engineer; Cost Accountant; Accountant.

HOSPITAL EMPLOYEES' UNION / HEU
Att: Julie Eckert, HR Coordinator
2006 - 10th Avenue West
Vancouver, BC V6J 4P5
Tel. 604-734-3431
Website .... www.heu.org
Employer Background: HEU is the BC Health Services Division of the Canadian Union of Public Employees (CUPE), with 46,000 members in over 400 health facilities and agencies. *New Positions Created (3):* Assistant Office Manager; Controller; Coordinator of Administrative Services.

HOSPITAL FOR SICK CHILDREN, THE
Att: Human Resources
555 University Avenue
Toronto, ON M5G 1X8
Tel. 416-813-6680
Fax 416-813-5671
Email .... hr.recruiter@sickkids.on.ca
Website .... www.sickkids.on.ca
Employer Background: Established in 1875, the Hospital for Sick Children is a major health, teaching and research centre dedicated exclusively to children. *New Positions Created (70):* Registered Nurse, Neurology, Endocrinology and Genetics; Research Administrator / Coordinator, Brain and Behaviour Research; Psychologist, Stroke Program; Child Health Services Director, Cardiac; Quality Analyst; Coordinator, Government Relations / Infrastructure Awards; MRTs; Registered Nurse; Social Worker; Technologist II, DNA Microarray Production and Analysis Facility; Various Health Positions; Health Information Specialist; New Building Project Manager; Child Health Services Directors, Emergency Services / Cardiac; Communications Coordinator, Foundation; Pharmacist / Pharmacy Technicians; Primary Nurse Practitioner, Emergency; Database Manager; Medical Lab Technologist, LIS; Respiratory Therapists; Clinical Nurse Specialist / Nurse Practitioner; Clinical Nurse Specialists / Nurse Practitioners (2); Treasury Analyst; Clinic Nurse, Immunology / Allergy; Administrative Information Specialist; Clinical Phar-

macists; Clinical Research Associates (2); Education Coordinator, Pharmacy Department; Nurse Educator, OR / Anaesthesia; Project Coordinator, Safe Kids Canada; Research Assistant, HIV Risk Reduction Intervention; Senior Secretary; Director, Nursing Education; Research Assistant, Brain and Behaviour; Transfusion Officer; Clinical Leaders; Clinical Nurse Practitioners; Clinical Nurse Specialists, Critical Care / Enterostomal Therapy; Nurse Educators; Registered Nurses; Human Resources Generalist; Clinical Leader, Critical Care; Audiologist; Aural Rehabilitationist; Medical Radiation Technologist; Director, Volunteer Resources; Reference and Instruction Services Librarian; Senior Support Analyst; Occupational Health Nurse; MRI Technologist; Discharge Planner; Neurodiagnostic Technologist; Post-Doctoral Fellow, Brain and Behaviour; Post-Doctoral Fellow, Brain and Behaviour; Senior Secretary; Administrative Coordinator; Research Technologist, Integrative Biology; Senior Secretary; Registered Nurses and Nurse Educator; Respiratory Therapists; Pharmacists; Clinical Nurse Specialist, General Surgery, Orthopedic and Otolaryngology; Nursing Positions; Nurse Practitioners, Haematology / Oncology After Care, Stroke, NICU, General Surgery and Orthopaedic Program; Occupational Health Nurse; Health Records Technician; Nurse Educator, Emergency; Director of Strategy; Health Information Analyst; Staff Scientist, Biological Macromolecular Mass Spectrometry.

HOSPITAL FOR SICK CHILDREN, THE (ADVANCED PROTEIN TECHNOLOGY CENTRE)
Att: Dr. B. Sarkar, Director
555 University Avenue
Toronto, ON M5G 1X8

Tel. 416-813-6680
Fax 416-813-5379
Email .... bsarkar@sickkids.on.ca
Website .... www.sickkids.on.ca

Employer Background: Established in 1875, the Hospital for Sick Children is a major health, teaching and research centre dedicated exclusively to children. *New Positions Created (3):* Manager, Advanced Protein Technology Centre; Staff Scientist, Biological Macromolecular Mass Spectrometry; Various Nursing Positions.

HOTEL DIEU HEALTH SCIENCES HOSPITAL, NIAGARA
Att: Human Resources
155 Ontario Street
St. Catharines, ON L2R 5K3

Tel. 905-682-6411
Fax 905-687-3716
Email .... recruit@hdhsc.org
Website .... www.hoteldieuniagara.org

Employer Background: Hotel Dieu Health Sciences Hospital is a teaching and research hospital affiliated with McMaster University and the University of Western Ontario. *New Positions Created (11):* Manager, ICU & Cardiovascular Risk Factor Clinic and Research Unit; Manager, Inpatient Surgical Unit & Day

Surgery Program; Manager of Pharmacy; Manager, Quality Assurance and Standards; Pharmacists; Physiotherapist; Registered Nurses; Nurse Practitioners, Cardiovascular Clinic and Research Unit Medical / Acute Care; Pastoral Care Associates; Director of Laboratories; Chief of Emergency Medicine.

HOTEL DIEU HOSPITAL
Att: Human Resources
166 Brock Street
Kingston, ON K7L 5G2

Tel. 613-544-3400
Fax 613-547-9331
Email .... resumes@hdh.kari.net
Website .... www.hoteldieu.com

Employer Background: Founded in 1845, Hotel Dieu Hospital is the ambulatory teaching hospital of the Southeastern Ontario Health Sciences Centre, providing health services to 325,000 patients annually. *New Positions Created (10):* Psychologist; Speech Pathologist, Child Development Centre; Nurse Manager; Clinical Dietitian; Social Worker; Child Psychologists (2); Charge Nurse, Inpatient Psychiatry; Chief Technologist, Diagnostic Imaging; Ultrasound Technologist, Diagnostic Imaging; Director, Kingston Regional Ambulance Service.

HOTEL DIEU HOSPITAL
Att: Human Resources Department
840 McConnell Avenue
Cornwall, ON K6H 5S5

Tel. 613-938-4240
Fax 613-938-4074
Email .... jzylstra@hdh.cornwall.on.ca

Employer Background: Hotel Dieu Hospital is part of a health centre composed of 300 beds at 2 locations. *New Positions Created (3):* Coordinator of Pastoral Care Services; Patient Care Coordinator, Operating Suite; Senior Financial Analyst.

HOTEL INTER-CONTINENTAL TORONTO
Att: Human Resources Department
220 Bloor Street West
Toronto, ON M2S 1T8

Fax 416-324-5881
Website .... toronto.interconti.com

Employer Background: Hotel Inter-Continental Toronto is a 208-room facility, located in the fashionable Yorkville district. *New Positions Created (4):* Disbursement / Accounting Clerk; Reservations and Revenue Manager; Director of Sales and Marketing; Public Relations Executive Administrator.

HOTEL-DIEU GRACE HOSPITAL
Att: Director of Human Resources
1030 Ouellette Avenue
Windsor, ON N9A 1E1

Tel. 519-973-4411
Fax 519-973-9382
Email .... mbensona@hdgh.org
Website .... www.hdgh.org

Employer Background: Hotel-Dieu Grace Hospital provides acute care services to the Windsor-Essex County community, with

approximately 400 beds in service at 3 sites. *New Positions Created (17):* Clinical Dietitians (2); Director of Pharmacy; PACS System Administrator, Diagnostic Imaging; MRI Technologists; Decision Support Associates, Health Records; Community Mental Health Service Coordinator; Kinesiologist; Physiotherapists and Occupational Therapist; Speech Language Pathologist; Pharmacists; Health Records Technician; Biomedical Technician; Director, Pastoral Services; Base Hospital Program Manager; MRI Technologist; Acute Care Nurse Practitioner, Neurosurgery; Occupational Therapist.

HOUGHTON BOSTON PRINTERS
Att: Human Resources Manager
709 - 43rd Street East
Saskatoon, SK S7K 0V7

Tel. 306-751-1056
Email .... h.b.admin@sk.sympatico.ca

Employer Background: For over 70 years, Houghton Boston Printing has been providing a full range of printing and book binding services. *New Positions Created (4):* Operators; Operators; Operators; Operators.

HOUSEHOLD FINANCIAL CORPORATION / HFC
Att: Lloyd Ackerman, Branch Manager
9764 - 170th Street, Terra Losa Centre
Edmonton, AB T5T 5L4

Fax 780-489-9761
Website .... www.hfc.com

Employer Background: Founded in 1878, HFC is a leading provider of consumer loans and credit cards in Canada, the USA and UK. *New Positions Created (2):* Management and Management Trainees; Account Executives.

HOUSEHOLD FINANCIAL CORPORATION / HFC
Att: Human Resources
101 Duncan Mills Road, Suite 500
Toronto, ON M3B 1Z3

Fax 416-443-3748
Email .... hfchr@sprint.ca
Website .... www.hfc.com

Employer Background: Founded in 1878, HFC is a leading provider of consumer loans and credit cards in Canada, the USA and the UK. *New Positions Created (3):* Account Executives; Mortgage Underwriters; Account Executives.

HOUSTON FOREST PRODUCTS COMPANY
Att: Human Resources Manager
PO Box 5000
Houston, BC V0J 1Z0

Tel. 250-845-2322
Fax 250-845-5301

Employer Background: Houston Forest Products Company, a joint venture with Weldwood of Canada and West Fraser Timber Co., operates a sawmill and planemill complex and produces 275 million board feet of lumber annually. *New Positions Created (3):* Operational Planning Superintendent; Sawfiler; Head Sawfiler.

HOWE SOUND PULP AND PAPER LTD.
Att: Employment Coordinator
Port Mellon, BC V0N 2S0

Tel. 604-884-5223
Fax 604-884-2182

Employer Background: Howe Sound Pulp and Paper Ltd. (owned by Oji Paper Co. and Canfor Corporation) is a state-of-the-art pulp and paper mill. *New Positions Created (2):* Instrument Mechanic; Millwright.

HSBC BANK CANADA
Att: Laura Suter, HR Manager
885 West Georgia Street, Suite 300
Vancouver, BC V6C 3E9

Tel. 604-685-1000
Fax 604-641-2917
Email .... careers@hsbc.ca
Website .... www.hsbc.ca

Employer Background: Established in 1981, HSBC Bank Canada is a principal member of the HSBC Group, one of the world's largest banking and financial services companies, with over 6,500 offices in 79 countries. *New Positions Created (11):* Assistant Vice-President, Private Trust Services; Account Manager, Commercial Financial Services; Assistant Vice-President, Sales; Manager, Taxation; Vice-President, Private Trust Services; Account Manager, Commercial Financial Services; Personal Financial Services Professionals; Senior Manager, Projects; Senior Manager, Sales Promotions; Senior Manager, Advertising and Promotions; Manager, Securitization Accounting.

HSBC BANK CANADA
Att: Human Resources
3555 Gilmore Way
Burnaby, BC V5G 4S1

Tel. 604-439-5200
Fax 604-453-5220
Email .... careers@hsbc.ca
Website .... www.hsbc.ca

Employer Background: Established in 1981, HSBC Bank Canada is part of the HSBC Group, one of the world's largest financial services companies, with over 6,000 offices in 80 countries. *New Positions Created (2):* Senior System Analysts / Project Leaders; Software Developers.

HSBC BANK CANADA
Att: Michael P. Sooley, Senior Manager, HR
70 York Street, 3rd Floor
Toronto, ON M5J 1S9

Tel. 416-868-8000
Fax 416-868-6930
Email .... careers@hsbc.ca
Website .... www.hsbc.ca

Employer Background: Established in 1981, HSBC Bank Canada is part of the HSBC Group, one of the world's largest financial services companies, with over 6,000 offices in 80 countries. *New Positions Created (2):* Account Mgr, Commercial Financial Services; Personal Financial Services Pros.

HSBC BANK CANADA
Att: Judi Wood,
Head of Corporate & Institutional Banking
70 York Street, 4th Floor
Toronto, ON M5J 1S9

Fax 416-868-3817
Email .... judi_wood@hsbc.ca
Website .... www.hsbc.ca

Employer Background: Established in 1981, HSBC Bank Canada is part of the HSBC Group, one of the world's largest financial services companies, with over 6,000 offices in 80 countries. *New Positions Created (4):* Senior Relationship Manager, Corporate and Institutional Banking; Senior Relationship Manager, Tax Structured Finance; Account Manager, Mortgage Banking Division; Regional Manager, Mortgage Banking Division.

HUBBELL CANADA INC.
Att: Human Resources
870 Brock Road South
Pickering, ON L1W 1Z8

Tel. 905-839-4332
Fax 905-839-7735
Email ...... bjenning@hubbell-canada.com
Website .... www.hubbellonline.com

Employer Background: Hubbell Canada Inc. designs, manufactures and supplies electrical and electronic products for the commercial, industrial and contractor telecom and utilities markets. *New Positions Created (4):* Specified Anchor Project Engineer / Manager; Professional Sales Position; Premise Wiring Sales Representative; Sales Professional, Lighting Division.

HUBER + SUHNER (CANADA) LTD.
Att: Human Resources Manager
50 Hines Road
Kanata, ON K2K 2M5

Tel. 613-271-9771
Fax 613-271-9776
Email .... jobs@hubersuhner.ca
Website .... www.hubersuhner.ca

Employer Background: Huber + Suhner (Canada) Ltd. manufactures cables, connectors, cable assemblies, antennas, lightning protectors and other products for RF, microwave and fibre optic applications. *New Positions Created (2):* Fiberoptic Technician; Assistant Controller.

HUDSON BAY MINING AND SMELTING CO., LTD.
Att: Pat Davidson, Industrial Relations
PO Box 1500
Flin Flon, MB R8A 1N9

Tel. 204-687-2054
Fax 204-687-2770

Employer Background: Hudson Bay Mining and Smelting Co., Ltd. is involved in mining and smelting activities. *New Positions Created (3):* Structural Engineer; Second-Class Power Engineers; Heavy Duty and Industrial Mechanics.

HUDSON & COMPANY
Att: Allan Payne, CA
625 - 11th Avenue SW, Suite 300
Calgary, AB T2R 0E1

Fax 403-265-3142

Email .... staffing@hudsonandco.com
Website .... www.hudsonandco.com

Employer Background: Hudson & Company is a mid-sized accounting firm, serving owner-managed businesses. *New Positions Created (5):* Controller; Accounting Technician; Chartered Accountant; Chartered Accountant; Chartered Accountant.

HUDSON GENERAL AVIATION SERVICES INC.
Att: General Manager
Vancouver International Airport
Box 25012, Airport Postal Outlet
Richmond, BC V7B 1Y4

Tel. 604-278-2118
Website .. www.hudsongeneral-fuelling.bc.ca

Employer Background: Hudson General Aviation Services Inc. is an air transportation ground handling company. *New Positions Created (4):* Operations Manager; Manager, Fuel Services; Ramp Services Supervisor; Manager, Administration.

HUGHES, AMYS
Att: Human Resources Manager
1 First Canadian Place
Suite 5050, PO Box 401
Toronto, ON M5X 1E3

Tel. 416-367-1608
Fax 416-487-1075
Email .... marylavis@home.com
Website .... www.hughesamys.com

Employer Background: Founded in 1918, Hughes, Amys is a 25-lawyer firm, providing litigation and dispute resolution services. *New Positions Created (2):* Civil Litigation Legal Assistant; Associate Lawyer.

HUMANE SOCIETY OF OTTAWA-CARLETON / HSOC
Att: Hiring Committee
101 Champagne Avenue South
Ottawa, ON K1S 4P3

Tel. 613-725-3166
Fax 613-725-5674
Email .... christinae@hsoc.on.ca
Website .... www.hsoc.on.ca

Employer Background: HSOC works to encourage responsible pet ownership and ensure humane treatment of all animals. The organization has 38 staff members and an annual budget of $1.8 million. *New Positions Created (3):* Maintenance Coordinator; Customer Service Representative; Manager, Development.

HUMBER COLLEGE OF APPLIED ARTS AND TECHNOLOGY
Att: Human Resources Department
205 Humber College Boulevard
Toronto, ON M9W 5L7

Tel. 416-675-3111
Fax 416-675-4708
Email .... resumes@admin.humberc.on.ca
Website .... www.humberc.on.ca

Employer Background: Humber College of Applied Arts and Technology is one of Canada's largest and most diversified community colleges. *New Positions Created (7):* Faculty

Positions; Professor and Program Coordinator, Business Administration and Business Management; Professor and Program Coordinator, International Development; Professor, Fashion; Public Relations Professor; Associate Dean, Nursing; Director, Human Resources.

HUMBER RIVER REGIONAL HOSPITAL, FINCH AVENUE SITE
Att: Recruitment & Selection Specialist
2111 Finch Avenue West
Toronto, ON M3N 1N1

Tel. 416-744-2500
Fax 416-747-3758
Email .... recruitment@hrrh.on.ca
Website .... www.hrrh.on.ca

Employer Background: Humber River Regional Hospital is one of Ontario's largest regional community hospitals, with 600 beds, 2,800 staff members and 700 physicians. *New Positions Created (56):* EEG Technician; General Radiology Technologists; Nuclear Medicine Technologists; Pharmacists; Manager, Human Resources; Manager, Payroll; Supervisor, SPD; Financial Consultant; Manager, Dialysis; Clinical Healthcare Professionals; Registered Nurses; Clinical Educators (2); Clinical Educators, Telemetry / Acute Medicine (2); Manager, Inpatient Oncology and Chemotherapy Clinic; Manager, Mental Health; Clinical Information Specialist; Dialysis Technologist; Director, Professional Practice; Infection Control Specialist; Analyst; Director of IS; Project Manager; Technical Specialist; Manager, Dialysis; Manager, Inpatient Medicine Medical Program; Manager, Women and Children's Health Programs; Administrative Assistant; Business Support Specialists; Community Relations Specialist; Dietitians; Mental Health Program Nurses; Nurses, Critical Care; Physiotherapists; Technologists; Diabetic Nurse Educator; Specialist, Recruitment and Selection; Trainers / Instructional Designers (2); Pharmacy Positions; Registered Nurses; Various Healthcare Positions; Various Technologist Positions; Speech Language Pathologists; Clinical Educators (4); Specialist, Recruitment / Selection; Business Analyst; Chaplain; Child and Adolescent Services Coordinator, Mental Health Program; Educators; Speech Language Pathologists; Clinical Educators (2); Managers, Inpatient Medicine; Medical Laboratory Technologist; Occupational Health and Safety Registered Nurse; Physiotherapist, Medical Program; Registered Respiratory Care Practitioner; SPD Training and Development Educator.

HUMMINGBIRD LTD.
Att: Human Resources Manager
1 Sparks Avenue
Toronto, ON M2H 2W1

Tel. 416-496-2200
Fax 416-496-2207
Email .... careers@hummingbird.com
Website .... www.hummingbird.com

Employer Background: Hummingbird Ltd., Canada's third largest software development company, develops enterprise software that provides the ability to access and act upon all business-critical information and resources, aggregated and categorized through a single user interface. *New Positions Created (14):* Collections Clerk; Datacenter Operations Supervisor; Product Architect, CyberDOCS; Product Manager, Host Access Products; Product Marketing Manager, Business Intelligence; Product Marketing Manager, Document and Content Management Solutions; Product Marketing Strategist, Host Access & Network Connectivity Solutions; Senior Collections Clerk; Senior Software Developer, Plug-Ins; Business Development Manager; Junior and Intermediate Software Quality Assurance Analysts; Junior and Senior Software Developers; Senior Business Systems Analyst; Senior Software Developers.

HUNTER AMENITIES INTERNATIONAL LTD.
Att: Jackie Stewart
1205 Corporate Drive
Burlington, ON L7L 5V5

Fax 905-331-2832
Website .... www.hunteramenities.com

Employer Background: Established in 1980, Hunter Amenities International Ltd. provides personal amenity products for the hotel, resort and cruise line industries. *New Positions Created (12):* Packaging Machine Mechanics; Warehouse Position; Junior Traffic Clerk; Compounding Manager; Scheduler; Compounder; Compounding Supervisor; Accounts Receivable / Collections Person; Packaging Machine Mechanics; New Product Coordinator; Junior Buyer; Purchasing Assistant.

HUNTING OILFIELD SERVICES
Att: Human Resources Manager
8815 - 52nd Street SE
Calgary, AB T2C 2R3

Employer Background: Hunting Oilfield Services manufactures various oil industry tubular goods. *New Positions Created (3):* Junior Accountant; Machine Operators; Machinist / Programmer.

HUNTINGTON SOCIETY OF CANADA
Att: Search Committee
151 Frederick Street, Suite 400
Kitchener, ON N2H 2M2

Tel. 519-749-7063
Website .... www.hsc-ca.org

Employer Background: Established in 1973, the Huntington Society of Canada is a national network of volunteers and professionals united in the fight against Huntington disease. *New Positions Created (3):* Development Coordinator; Director of Individual / Family Services; Development Coordinator, Chapter Operations.

HURON, COUNTY OF
Att: Human Resources
Court House
Goderich, ON N7A 1M2

Tel. 519-524-8394
Fax 519-524-2044
Website .... www.hurontourism.on.ca

Employer Background: Located on the west coast of Lake Huron, the County of Huron is an upper-tier municipality, with a population of 65,000. *New Positions Created (4):* Manager, Ambulance Operations; Manager, Housing Services; Manager, Human Resources; Director, Health Unit.

HURRICANE HYDROCARBONS LTD.
Att: Human Resources Manager
300 - 5th Avenue SW, Suite 2700
Calgary, AB T2P 3C4

Tel. 403-221-8435
Fax 403-216-8606
Email .... resumes@hurricane-hhl.com
Website .... www.hurricane-hhl.com

Employer Background: Hurricane Hydrocarbons Ltd. explores, produces, refines and markets oil in the Republic of Kazakhstan in Central Asia. *New Positions Created (3):* Director, Health, Safety and Environment; Field Operations Manager; Field Production Foreman.

HUSH PUPPIES CANADA
Att: Human Resources
4600 Hickmore
St-Laurent, QC H4T 1K2

Tel. 514-344-1219
Fax 514-344-4686
Website .... www.hushpuppies.com

Employer Background: Hush Puppies is a manufacturer and supplier of fashionable comfort footwear. *New Positions Created (4):* Buyer, Imports; Cost Accountant; Account Representative; Warehouse Manager.

HUSKY INJECTION MOLDING SYSTEMS LTD.
Att: Heather Pettitt, Human Resources
500 Queen Street South
Bolton, ON L7E 5S5

Tel. 905-951-5000
Fax 905-951-5323
Email .... hpettitt@husky.ca
Website .... www.husky.ca

Employer Background: Husky Injection Molding Systems Ltd. is a publicly-traded Canadian company that designs and manufactures a comprehensive range of injection molding machines, preform molds, robots and hot runner systems. *New Positions Created (21):* Human Resources Coordinator; Mechanical Designer; FEA Analyst; Mechatronics Engineer, PC-Based Controls; Account Analyst; Finance / Tax Analyst; Mechanical Designer; PeopleSoft Developer; Manager, Construction Management Services; Operations Manager, Robotics; BAAN Software Developer; Controls Engineer, PC-Based Controls; Credit Analyst; Director of Global Sales and Training; Electrical Engineer, PC-Based Control Platform; IT Developer, PeopleSoft; Media Specialist, Photographer; Director of Global Sales Training; Customer Coordinator; Vice-President, Service and Sales; Training Lab Technician.

HUSKY INJECTION MOLDING SYSTEMS LTD.
Att: Human Resources (Index Molds)
530 Queen Street South
Bolton, ON L7E 5S5

Tel.	905-951-5000
Fax	905-951-5359
Website	www.husky.on.ca

Employer Background: Husky Injection Molding Systems Ltd. is a publicly-traded Canadian company that designs and manufactures a comprehensive range of injection molding machines, preform molds, robots and hot runner systems. *New Positions Created (6):* Business Centre Operator / Receptionist; Senior Financial Analyst; Support Technician; Senior Financial Analyst; BAAN Software Developer; IT Developer, PeopleSoft.

HUSKY INJECTION MOLDING SYSTEMS LTD.
Att: Human Resources (Components)
375 Wilton Drive
Bolton, ON L7E 5S5

Tel.	905-951-5000
Fax	905-951-5377
Website	www.husky.on.ca

Employer Background: Husky Injection Molding Systems Ltd. is a publicly-traded Canadian company that designs and manufactures a comprehensive range of injection molding machines, preform molds, robots and hot runner systems. *New Positions Created (6):* Financial Analyst; Assembly Team Leader; CAD Operator; Project Engineer; Senior Mechanical Engineers (2); Unigraphics CAD Operator.

HUSKY INJECTION MOLDING SYSTEMS LTD.
Att: Human Resources (Index Machines)
560 Queen Street South
Bolton, ON L7E 5S5

Tel.	905-951-5000
Fax	905-951-5323
Website	www.husky.ca

Employer Background: Husky Injection Molding Systems Ltd. is a publicly-traded Canadian company that designs and manufactures a comprehensive range of injection molding machines, preform molds, robots and hot runner systems. *New Positions Created (3):* Mechanical Designer; Marketing Managers, Automotive or Thinwall Packaging; Senior Mechanical Designer.

HUSKY LUMBER GROUP / COMMONWEALTH PLYWOOD CO. LTD.
Att: Linda Wylie
1881 Bantree Road
Ottawa, ON K1B 4X3

Tel.	613-747-2725
Fax	613-747-2724
Website	www.commonwealthplywood.com

Employer Background: Husky Lumber / Commonwealth Plywood is a fully-integrated forest products company, with over 35 operations in eastern Canada. *New Positions Created (2):* Sales Rep, Softwood Lumber; Softwood Lumber Sales Rep.

HUSKY OIL OPERATIONS LTD.
Att: Management Services, HR
707 - 8th Avenue SW, Box 6525, Station D
Calgary, AB T2P 3G7

Tel.	403-298-6111
Fax	403-298-6799
Email	careers@huskyenergy.ca
Website	www.huskyenergy.com

Employer Background: Husky Oil Operations Ltd. is an integrated Canadian petroleum company involved in all facets of the industry, from exploration to retail service stations. *New Positions Created (15):* Junior Engineers; Thermal Production Engineering Coordinator; Lubricant Technical Sales Consultant; Treasurer; Document Control / Analytical Services Lab Clerk; Geologists / Technologists; Geophysicists / Technologists; Safety Technician; Administrative Assistant; Account Manager, Commodity Credit Risk; Facility Lead Inspector; Plant Operator; Joint Venture Contracts Analyst; Regulatory Coordinator; Drafting Technologist.

HUSSMANN CANADA INC.
Att: Credit Manager
58 Frank Street, PO Box 550
Brantford, ON N3T 5R2

Tel.	519-756-6351
Fax	519-756-0246
Website	www.hussmann.com

Employer Background: Hussmann Canada Inc. is a leading manufacturer of refrigeration equipment for the supermarket industry. *New Positions Created (4):* Credit and Collections Representative; Sales Coordinator; Research / Refrigeration Engineer; Production Supervisor.

HUTCHINSON ARCHITECTS INC.
Att: Keesa Hutchinson
1029 - 17th Avenue SW, Suite 200
Calgary, AB T2T 0A9

Tel.	403-228-9307
Fax	403-228-4699
Email	keesah@caisnet.com
Website	www.hutchinsonarchitects.com

Employer Background: Hutchinson Architects Inc. is a med-sized firm, specializing in architecture, interior design, planning and programming. *New Positions Created (3):* Design / Project Architects; Intermediate Architectural Technologists; Intermediate and Senior Architectural Technologists.

HYATT REGENCY VANCOUVER
Att: Human Resources Department
655 Burrard Street
Vancouver, BC V6C 2R7

Tel.	604-683-1234
Fax	604-639-4797
Email	cmartins@yvrrvpo.hyatt.com
Website	www.hyatt.com

Employer Background: Hyatt Regency Vancouver is a large convention hotel, with 35,000 square feet of meeting and banquet space. *New Positions Created (2):* MIS Manager; Banquet Captain.

HYD-MECH GROUP LTD.
Att: Human Resources Manager
239 Beards Line
Woodstock, ON N4S 8A4

Tel.	519-537-6751
Fax	519-539-5126
Email	stracy@hydmech.com
Website	www.hydmech.com

Employer Background: Hyd-Mech Group Ltd. manufactures metal cutting band saws. *New Positions Created (3):* Manufacturing Design Technologist; Manufacturing Engineer; Controller.

HYDRO OTTAWA
Att: Human Resources
3025 Albion Road North
Ottawa, ON K1G 3S4

Tel.	613-738-6400
Fax	613-738-5487
Email	jennyj@hydro-ottawa.com
Website	www.hydro-ottawa.com

Employer Background: Hydro Ottawa is the 2nd-largest municipal distributor of electricity in Ontario, serving over 257,000 customers in the amalgamated City of Ottawa. *New Positions Created (9):* System Operator; Travelling Operator; Regulatory Affairs Analyst; Controller; Standards and Records Engineer; Stations Engineer; System Designer; Manager, Energy Services; Mgr, Generation.

HYDROGENICS CORPORATION
Att: Human Resources Manager
5985 McLaughlin Road
Mississauga, ON L5R 1B8

Tel.	905-361-3660
Fax	905-361-3626
Email	careers@hydrogenics.com
Website	www.hydrogenics.com

Employer Background: Hydrogenics Corporation develops fuel cell technologies for clean power generation. *New Positions Created (38):* Electrical Engineering Liaison; Electrical Technician; Mechanical Technician; Test / Installation Technicians (2); Accounting / Administrative Assistant; Embedded Systems Engineer; Senior Mechanical Project Engineer; Senior Process Engineer; Software Developer; Testing / Installation Technician; Administrative Assistant; Electrical Assembler; Electrical Engineer; Embedded Systems Engineer; Manufacturing Engineer; Mechanical Assembler; Senior Mechanical Design Engineer; Senior Process Engineer; Software Developer; Assistant Controller; Mechanical Technician; Accounting / Administrative Assistant; Design Draftsmen; Design Engineer; Electrical Engineer; Electronic Technicians; Mechanical Assembler; Process Engineers; Sales Engineer; Senior Electrochemist; Electrical Assembler; Quality Inspector; Testing Engineer / Customer Service Engineer; Technical Support / Test Technician; Industrial Sales Engineer; Reformer / Chemical Process Engineers (2); Senior Mechanical Designer; Fuel Cell Test Engineer.

HYMARC LTD.
Att: Human Resources Department

35 Antares Drive, Suite 5
Nepean, ON K2E 8B1

Tel. 613-727-1584
Fax 613-727-0441
Email .... info@hymarc.com
Website .... www.hymarc.com

Employer Background: Hymarc Ltd. designs
3D laser digitizing systems for advanced
manufacturing applications. *New Positions
Created (3):* Intermediate Digital Hardware
Designer; Software Engineer; Electronics
Engineering Manager.

HYMOPACK LTD.

Att: Human Resources Manager
41 Medulla Avenue
Toronto, ON M8Z 5L6

Tel. 416-232-1733
Fax 416-232-2194

Employer Background: Hymopack Ltd.
manufactures plastic bags for supermarkets,
department stores and other retailers. *New
Positions Created (4):* Operations Coordinator; Vice President Manufacturing; Scheduling Assistant; Operations Coordinator.

HYPERCHIP

Att: Human Resources Manager
1800 Rene Levesque West
Montréal, QC H3H 2H2

Tel. 514-931-5335
Fax 514-906-2500
Email .... careers@hyperchip.com
Website .... www.hyperchip.com

Employer Background: Hyperchip is a
petabit routing company, creating high-performance carrier-class switches and routers
to support the explosive growth of Internet
traffic. *New Positions Created (4):* EDA Tool
Support Specialist, ASIC / FPGA; Verification
Engineer; PCB Design Manager; Software
Validation Manager.

HYPERTEC SYSTEMS INC.

Att: Human Resources
9275 Trans Canada Highway
St-Laurent, QC H4S 1V3

Tel. 514-745-4540
Fax 514-745-0937
Email .... carrieres@groupe-hypertec.com
Website ... www.groupe-hypertec.com

Employer Background: Hypertec designs
and distributes brand-name computer
products, and provides after-sales service,
technical support, computer assembly, integration and development of complete computer-based solutions. *New Positions Created (4):* Collections Agent; HR Recruiter;
Corporate Controller; Recruiting Agent.

HYPROTECH LTD.

Att: Human Resources
707 - 8th Avenue SW, Suite 800
Calgary, AB T2P 1H5

Tel. 403-520-6000
Fax 403-520-6620
Email .... hr@hyprotech.com
Website .... www.hyprotech.com

Employer Background: Hyprotech Ltd., a
subsidiary of UMA Technology Engineering

Software, specializes in process simulator
development for the petrochemical, oil and
gas and chemical processing industries.
New Positions Created (16): Chemical Engineers; Computational Fluid Dynamics
(CFD) Specialists; Executive Assistant; Quality Assurance Engineers; Quality Control
Engineers; Software Developers; Technical
Writers; Vice-President, Marketing; Inside
Sales Manager; Senior Financial Analyst;
Vice-President, Global Sales; GUI Developer;
Junior Research and Development Engineer;
Senior Commercial Manager; Tax Analyst;
Senior Commercial Manager, Contracts.

HYUNDAI AUTO CANADA

Att: Human Resources
75 Frontenac Drive
Markham, ON L3R 6H2

Tel. 905-477-0202
Fax 905-477-9264
Website .... www.hyundai.com

Employer Background: Hyundai Auto
Canada is one of Canada's leading automobile importers. *New Positions Created (7):*
District Parts & Service Manager; District
Sales Mgr; Warranty Mgr; Bilingual Technical Support Specialist; In-House Legal
Counsel; Bilingual Parts Technical Information Administrator; DCS Support Analyst.

I-STAT CANADA LTD.

Att: Human Resources
436 Hazeldean Road
Kanata, ON K2L 1T9

Tel. 613-831-2725
Fax 613-831-6700
Email .... careers@istat.ca
Website .... www.istat.ca

Employer Background: i-STAT Canada Ltd.
develops, manufactures and markets medical diagnostic products for blood analysis.
New Positions Created (20): Cartridge Assembly / Wafer Fabrication Operators; Clinical Lab Operator; Assembly Team Leader;
Industrial Engineering Engineer / Technologist; Software Technologist, Machine Vision;
Accounting Clerk; Buyer; Documentation
Clerk; Documentation Specialist; Manager,
Cartridge Assembly; Network Architect;
Process Engineer; Programmer Analyst;
Senior R&D Technician; Software Tester;
Clinical Specialist, Research and Development; Human Resources Administrator; Intermediate Accountant; Manager, Purchasing and Production Planning; Research and
Development Scientist.

I-XL INDUSTRIES LTD.

Att: J. W. Drake
612 Porcelain Avenue SE
Medicine Hat, AB T1A 8S4

Tel. 403-526-5901
Fax 403-526-7680
Email .... jdrake@ixlgroup.com
Website .... www.ixlbrick.com

Employer Background: Established in 1912,
I-XL Industries Ltd. is a large manufacturer
and distributor of clay brick and masonry
supplies. *New Positions Created (5):* Controller; Technical Sales Representative; Control-

ler; Technical Sales Representative; Technical Sales Representative.

I2 TECHNOLOGIES

Att: Ray Chesher
80 Whitehall Drive
Markham, ON L3R 0P3

Tel. 905-771-8088
Fax 905-752-4001
Email .... raymond_chesher@i2.com
Website www.i2.com

Employer Background: i2 Technologies (formerly InterTrans Logistics Solutions Ltd.)
provides supply chain planning and electronic business process optimization solutions. *New Positions Created (2):* Business
Development Rep; Payroll Accountant.

IACONO BROWN

Att: Harry Brown
130 Adelaide Street West, 31st Floor
Toronto, ON M5H 3P5

Tel. 416-869-0123
Fax 416-869-0271

Employer Background: Iacono Brown is a
law firm, specializing in insurance defense
litigation. *New Positions Created (4):* Insurance Litigation Lawyers (2); Law Clerk; Secretary; Switchboard / Receptionist.

IBI GROUP

Att: Peter Bull, Associate Director
10405 Jasper Avenue, Suite 1050
Edmonton, AB T5J 3N4

Tel. 780-428-4000
Fax 780-426-3256
Email .... pbull@ibigroup.com
Website .... www.ibigroup.com

Employer Background: Founded in 1974, IBI
Group is a multi-disciplinary consulting
firm, specializing in architecture, engineering and planning, with 450 employees in
Canada, Europe and the USA. *New Positions
Created (4):* Senior Architect; Junior / Intermediate Civil Technologists (2); Junior / Intermediate Municipal Engineers (2); Outside Plant Engineers and Technologists, Fibre Optic Systems.

IBI GROUP

Att: Gayle Thatcher
230 Richmond Street West, 5th Floor
Toronto, ON M5V 1V6

Tel. 416-596-1930
Email .... gthatcher@ibigroup.com
Website .... www.ibigroup.com

Employer Background: Founded in 1974, IBI
Group is a multi-disciplinary consulting
firm, specializing in architecture, engineering and planning, with 450 employees in
Canada, Europe and the USA. *New Positions
Created (4):* Intermediate C / C++ Analyst;
Sr Transportation Design Engineer, Urban
and Rural Freeways / Rapid Transit Systems;
Traffic Analyst; Transportation Planner.

IBM CANADA LTD.

Att: Western Staffing Consultant
400 Ellice Avenue
Winnipeg, MB R3B 3M3

Tel. 204-946-4900
Fax 204-946-6052
Email .... ibmhr@can.ibm.com
Website .... www.can.ibm.com
Employer Background: IBM Canada Ltd. is one of Canada's largest providers of information technology products and services. *New Positions Created (9):* Application Architect, Object-Oriented Design; Enterprise Application Integration Architect / Specialist; Object-Oriented Architects / Websphere Architects; Object-Oriented Project / Websphere Managers; Object-Oriented / Websphere Developers; Project Manager, Integration Services; Technical Solutions Manager; Senior Network Specialist; Senior Network Specialist.

IBM CANADA LTD.
Att: Human Resources Manager
3600 Steeles Avenue East
Markham, ON L3R 9Z7
Tel. 905-316-5000
Website .... www.can.ibm.com
Employer Background: IBM Canada Ltd. is one of Canada's largest providers of information technology products and services. *New Positions Created (81):* Advisory Tax Analyst; Advisory Technical Services Position; Business Integration Services Position; Compiler Developer; Customer Support Representative; Enterprise Architect; Enterprise IT Architects; Field Applications Engineer; Financial Analyst; HSI Customer Support Representative; Management Consultant; Project Manager; Project Manager, Integration Services; Senior Information Technology Architect; Senior Information Technology Specialist; Senior Security Analyst; A / CF Administrator; Application Architect, Integration Services; Assistant Manager; Accountant, Personal Systems Group; Application Architect - Object-Oriented Design; Principal - Business Integration Services, Health Industry; Product Assurance Analyst; Project Manager - Integration Services; Project Manager, Technology Development; Senior IT Architect; Server Sales Specialists; Software Telesales Representative; Staff Financial Analyst - Remarketing; Technical Support Specialist; Associate Operations Specialist; Bilingual Process Specialist, Entry Level Procurement; Inter-Company Agreements Coordinator; Internationalization Specialist; Senior IT Specialist, Lotus Professional Services; Services and Profitability Planner; Advisory Technical Services Professional - Sun Administrator; Networking and Telephony IT Specialist; Business Analyst; Contract Accountant; Directory Services Consultant / Architect; Intermediate Technical Services Professional; IT Architect; Principal Site Services Positions; Project Manager, Application Development / Application Management; Sales Representative, Financial Services; Technical Support Specialist; Assistant Production Operator / Controller; Business Intelligence Architect; Business Intelligence Consultant; CRMS Services; Consultant, Microsoft Technology; Data Management Sales Specialist; Enterprise Application Integration Architect / Specialist; Fulfillment

/ Junior Buyer; IT Architect, Microsoft Technology; IT Specialist; Project Manager, CRMS; Project Manager, Learning Services; Sales Specialists, Tivoli; Senior Market Solutions Specialist, Midrange; Solutions Architects, CRM Services; System Services Representative; Technical and Functional Consultant, JD Edwards; A / CF Administrator; Accountants; Administrative Assistant; Advisory Information Technology Specialist; Domino / Notes Project Manager; Field Sales Engineer; Financial Analysts; Fulfillment / Junior Buyer; Interactive Media Creative Director; Network Architect; Project Manager, Technology Development; Sales Specialist; Sales Specialist, WebServer; Test Analyst; Test Manager; Web Designer; Software Sales Specialist.

ICAM TECHNOLOGIES CORP.
Att: Human Resources
1900 Sources Boulevard
Pointe-Claire, QC H9R 4Z3
Tel. 514-697-8033
Fax 514-697-8621
Email .... mail@icam.com
Website .... www.icam.com
Employer Background: Founded in 1971, ICAM Technologies Corp. is a leading developer and supplier of NC post-processing solutions in the advanced industrial software market. *New Positions Created (2):* CAM NC Specialist; Channel Business Manager (2).

ICEFYRE SEMICONDUCTOR INC.
Att: Human Resources Manager
200 Elgin Street, Suite 602
Ottawa, ON K2P 1L5
Tel. 613-234-2046
Fax 613-234-2049
Email .... hip@icefyre.com
Website .... www.icefyre.com
Employer Background: IceFyre Semiconductor Inc., a fabless semiconductor company, develops highly-integrated silicon solutions to enable high-speed wireless connectivity. *New Positions Created (23):* Applications Engineers; Field Applications Manager; Intermediate RF IC Design Engineer; Manager, Partner Programs; PCB Layout Engineer; Senior Digital ASIC Design Engineer; Strategic Marketing Manager; Verification Engineers; Senior RF IC Designer; Applications Engineers; Applications Team Leader; Digital ASIC Design Engineer; Field Applications Manager; Intermediate Digital ASIC Design Engineer; Intermediate RF-IC Design Engineer; Intermediate Software Design Engineer; Manager, Partner Programs; PCB Layout Engineer; Senior Digital ASIC Design Engineer; Senior Software Design Engineer; Strategic Marketing Manager; Verification Engineer; Verification Team Leader.

ICN CANADA LTD.
Att: Human Resources Department
1956 Bourdon Street
St-Laurent, QC H4M 1V1
Tel. 514-744-6792
Fax 514-744-9734

Website .... www.icncanada.com
Employer Background: ICN Canada Ltd. manufactures and markets a wide range of drugs. *New Positions Created (2):* Laboratory Technician, Quality Assurance; Business Development Manager.

ICP GLOBAL TECHNOLOGIES
Att: Human Resources Manager
6995 Jeanne-Mance
Montréal, QC H3N 1W5
Tel. 514-270-5770
Email .... i-want-in@icpglobal.com
Website .... www.icpglobal.com
Employer Background: ICP Global Technologies develops solar-powered consumer products. *New Positions Created (3):* Director of Sales, Retail Markets; Director of Supply Chain Management; Sales Coordinator.

ICS COURIER SERVICES
Att: Jenny Aguiar-Winter
1243 Islington Avenue
Toronto, ON M8X 1Y9
Fax 416-207-8830
Email .... jwinter@ics-canada.net
Website .... www.ics-canada.net
Employer Background: Established in 1978, ICS Courier Services is one of Canada's largest fixed-route courier companies, with 35 offices and over 1,200 employees nationwide. *New Positions Created (5):* Tracing Clerk; Customer Service Supervisor; Outbound Sales Support Specialist; Account Manager; Central Sales Administration Manager.

ICS COURIER SERVICES
Att: Human Resources
245 Britannia Road East
Mississauga, ON L4Z 2Y7
Tel. 416-259-2353
Fax 416-259-9462
Email .... hr@ics-canada.net
Website .... www.ics-canada.net
Employer Background: Established in 1978, ICS Courier Services is one of Canada's largest fixed-route courier companies, with 35 offices and over 1,200 employees nationwide. *New Positions Created (5):* Central Sales Administrator; Customer Service Representative; Tracing Clerk; Supervisors / Managers; Sales Executive.

IDEAS AND ASSOCIATES
Att: Human Resources Manager
2050 Bleury, Suite 740
Montréal, QC H3A 2J5
Tel. 514-940-2891
Fax 514-940-3675
Email .... info@ideasandassociates.com
Website ...... www.ideasandassociates.com
Employer Background: Ideas and Associates is an information technology company, specializing in Internet applications development. *New Positions Created (4):* Internet Systems Architects / Analysts; Senior / Intermediate Java Programmer Analysts; Senior / Intermediate Perl Programmer Analysts; Web Programmers.

IDEC CANADA, LTD.
Att: Human Resources Manager
151 Brunel Road
Mississauga, ON L4Z 2H6

Tel. 905-890-8561
Fax 305-425-2813
Email .... resume@ca.idec.com
Website .... www.idec.com
Employer Background: IDEC Canada, Ltd. is one of Canada's largest manufacturers of electrical control systems. *New Positions Created (2):* Automation and Control Specialist; Customer Service Representative.

IDMD DESIGN & MANUFACTURING INC.
Att: Human Resources Manager
45 Progress Avenue
Toronto, ON M1P 2Y6

Tel. 416-299-4865
Fax 416-292-9759
Email .... hr@idmd.com
Website .... www.idmd.com
Employer Background: IDMD is a Canadian-owned manufacturer of point-of-purchase displays, with offices in North America and Europe. *New Positions Created (3):* Project Manager; Screen Printer; Store Fixtures Installation Specialist / Supervisor.

IFIRE TECHNOLOGY INC.
Att: Human Resources Manager
15 City View Drive
Toronto, ON M9W 5A5

Tel. 416-246-1030
Fax 416-246-0458
Email .... hr@ifire.com
Website .... www.ifire.com
Employer Background: iFire Technology Inc., a division of Westaim Corporation, is a leader in solid state flat panel display technologies. *New Positions Created (9):* Digital Hardware Engineer; Test Engineer; Process Engineers and Senior Process Engineers; Manager of Human Resources; General Maintenance Position; Junior Administrative / Reception Position; Production Operators; Safety Specialist; Process and Senior Process Engineers.

IHS SOLUTIONS LTD.
Att: Human Resources Manager
1 Antares Drive, Suite 200
Nepean, ON K2E 8C4

Tel. 613-225-2300
Fax 613-225-2304
Email .... hr.ihspsl@ihspsl.com
Website .... www.ihssolutions.com
Employer Background: IHS develops custom information retrieval and electronic publishing applications for organizations with significant investments in information. *New Positions Created (2):* Mgr, Application Development Group; Account Executive.

IKEA CALGARY
Att: Human Resources
555 - 36th Street NE
Suite 15, Northgate Mall
Calgary, AB T2A 6K3

Tel. 403-273-4338
Fax 403-272-6218
Email .... hr37@memo.ikea.com
Website .... www.ikea.com
Employer Background: IKEA Calgary is part of IKEA Group, one of the world's largest home furnishings retailers, with 139 stores in 22 countries. *New Positions Created (6):* Department Managers and Assistant Department Managers; Interior Decorator; Customer Service Department Manager; Receiving Supervisor; Retail Positions; Interior Decorator.

IKEA OTTAWA
Att: Human Resources
2685 Iris Street
Ottawa, ON K2C 3S4

Tel. 613-829-4530
Fax 613-829-0039
Email .... cnew@memo.ikea.com
Website .... www.ikea.com
Employer Background: IKEA Ottawa is part of IKEA Group, one of the world's largest home furnishings retailers, with 139 stores in 22 countries. *New Positions Created (2):* Operations Manager; Sales Manager.

IKO INDUSTRIES LTD.
Att: Human Resources
1600 - 42nd Avenue SE
Calgary, AB T2G 5B5

Tel. 403-265-6022
Fax 403-266-2644
Website .... www.iko.com
Employer Background: Established in 1950, IKO Industries Ltd. is a manufacturer of residential and commercial roofing products. *New Positions Created (3):* AS400 Co-ordinator; AS400 Coordinator; Human Resources Co-ordinator.

IKO INDUSTRIES LTD.
Att: Human Resources Manager
1 Yorkdale Road, Suite 602
Toronto, ON M6A 3A1

Tel. 416-781-5545
Fax 416-781-8411
Email .... bryan.peters@iko.com
Website .... www.iko.com
Employer Background: Established in 1950, IKO Industries Ltd. is a manufacturer of residential and commercial roofing products. *New Positions Created (8):* Business Analyst, ERP Implementation; HR Coordinator; Junior Property Manager; Property Accountant; Plant Manager; Bookkeeper / Receptionist; Manufacturing Manager; Plant Manager.

IKO INDUSTRIES LTD.
Att: MIS Director
40 Hansen Road South
Brampton, ON L6W 3H4

Fax 905-450-3616
Email .... mis.apply@iko.com
Website .... www.iko.com
Employer Background: Established in 1950, IKO Industries Ltd. is a manufacturer of residential and commercial roofing prod-

ucts. *New Positions Created (3):* AS400 Programmer / Analyst; Technical Support Manager, Commercial Roofing; Quality Control Manager.

IKO INDUSTRIES LTD.
Att: Human Resources
87 Orenda Road
Brampton, ON L6W 1V7

Tel. 905-457-5321
Fax 905-457-0955
Website .... www.iko.com
Employer Background: Established in 1950, IKO Industries Ltd. is a manufacturer of residential and commercial roofing products. *New Positions Created (12):* Junior / Intermediate Internal Audit; Administrative Assistant; Scale Operator; Industrial Maintenance Mechanic; Lab Technician; Receiving Department Position; Industrial Maintenance Mechanics (2); Warehouse Coordinator; Internal Auditor; Controller; Manufacturing Manager; Plant Manager.

IKON OFFICE SOLUTIONS
Att: Human Resources Manager
1875 Boundary Road
Vancouver, BC V5M 3Y8

Tel. 604-293-9800
Fax 604-293-9765
Email .... jpross@ikon.com
Website .... www.ikon.com
Employer Background: IKON Office Solutions provides analog and digital copiers, facsimile, printers, color imaging, computers, networking and outsourcing services. *New Positions Created (2):* Account Manager; Office Services Centre Manager.

IKON OFFICE SOLUTIONS, INC.
Att: Human Resources Manager
5200 Orbitor Drive
Mississauga, ON L4W 5B4

Tel. 905-602-1220
Fax 905-602-0858
Website .... www.ikoncdn.com
Employer Background: IKON Office Solutions, Inc. is an office technology solutions company. *New Positions Created (3):* Leasing Coordinator; Bilingual Parts Clerk; Sales Representatives.

ILCO UNICAN INC.
Att: Human Resources Department
7301 Decarie Boulevard
Montréal, QC H4P 2G7

Tel. 514-735-5411
Fax 514-735-5732
Email .... cv@ilcounican.com
Website .... www.ilcounican.com
Employer Background: Ilco Unican Inc. is a world leader in the design and manufacture of key blanks, key machines, mechanical push-button and electronic access controls. *New Positions Created (12):* Engineering Director, New Products Development; Financial Analyst, Cost Accounting; Electronic Technician, Production Support; Credit & Collection Supervisor; Warehouse Coordinator; Graphic Designer; Analyst / Program-

mer; Junior Internal Auditor; Printing Press Operator; Production Support Technologist; Supervisor, Manufacturing Engineering; Technical Writer / Advertising Copy Writer.

ILLUSTRATE INC.
Att: Human Resources Manager
920 The East Mall, Suite 300
Toronto, ON M9B 6K1
Tel. 416-626-6230
Fax 416-626-5302
Email .... friends@illustrateinc.com
Website .... www.illustrateinc.com
Employer Background: Established in 1989, Illustrate Inc. develops illustration software for the life insurance market. *New Positions Created (2):* Intermediate Visual Basic Developers (2); Senior MSVC++ Developers (2).

IMAGE PROCESSING SYSTEMS INC.
Att: Human Resources Manager
221 Whitehall Drive
Markham, ON L3R 9T1
Tel. 905-470-8990
Fax 905-470-8930
Email .... careers@ipsautomation.com
Website .... www.ipsautomation.com
Employer Background: IPS, the Canadian business unit of Photon Dynamics Co., provides electronic vision solutions for the CRT display and glass industries worldwide. *New Positions Created (21):* Administrative Assistant / Receptionist; Analog / Digital Hardware Designer; Director, Customer Service; Engineering Manager, Glass; Junior Hardware Designer; Machine Vision Engineer; Mechanical Engineering Manager; Project Manager; Sales Application Engineer; Software Developer; Customer Service Representative; Production Technician; Project Manager; Research Associate; Software Developer; Engineering Development Manager; Junior Hardware Designer; Optical Engineer; Project Manager; Sales Applications Engineer; Software Developers.

IMAGEWARE SYSTEMS
Att: Human Resources Manager
975 St. Joseph Boulevard, Suite 227
Hull, QC J8Z 1W8
Tel. 819-772-2678
Fax 819-772-7640
Website .... www.iwsinc.com
Employer Background: ImageWare Systems (formerly G&A Imaging) is a global provider of digital identification documents and law enforcement systems. *New Positions Created (7):* Intermediate Quality Assurance Specialist; Intermediate Software Component Engineer; Intermediate Support Specialist; Intermediate Web Developer; Senior Software Component Developer; Senior Support Specialist; Technical Support Manager.

IMAGINEX INC.
Att: Human Resources Manager
1045 Tristar Drive
Mississauga, ON L5T 1W5
Fax 905-795-5550
Website .... www.imaginex.com

Employer Background: Imaginex Inc. is a graphic arts company. *New Positions Created (4):* Mac Operator; Production Coordinator or Customer Service Representative; Mac Operator; Mac Operator.

IMAGING RESEARCH INC.
Att: Human Resources Department
500 Glenridge Avenue, Brock University
St. Catharines, ON L2S 3A1
Tel. 905-688-2040
Email .... careers@imagingresearch.com
Website .... www.imagingresearch.com
Employer Background: Imaging Research Inc. is a software and high-tech instrument developer for the biotechnology and pharmaceutical industries. *New Positions Created (4):* Marketing Associate; Marketing Manager; Product Manager; PC Technical Specialist.

IMI INTERNATIONAL MEDICAL INNOVATIONS INC.
Att: Human Resources Manager
4211 Yonge Street, Suite 300
Toronto, ON M2P 2A9
Tel. 416-222-3449
Fax 416-222-4533
Website .... www.imimedical.com
Employer Background: Founded in 1992, IMI International Medical Innovations Inc. develops innovative tests that detect life-threatening diseases at the earliest possible stage. *New Positions Created (2):* Clinical Research Associate; Product Development Specialists.

IMP GROUP LTD., AEROSPACE DIVISION
Att: Human Resources Department
PO Box 970
Enfield, NS B2T 1L5
Tel. 902-873-2250
Fax 902-873-2292
Email .... hraerospace@impgroup.com
Website .... www.impgroup.com
Employer Background: Founded in 1967, IMP Group Ltd.'s Aerospace Division is Canada's largest military maritime patrol aircraft support contractor. *New Positions Created (21):* Certification Engineer; Electrical / Avionics Engineer / Technologist; Intermediate Aeronautical / Mechanical Engineer; Intermediate Electrical / Avionics Draftsperson; Intermediate EMC Specialist / Engineer; Intermediate / Senior Aeronautical / Mechanical Engineer / Technologist; Logistics Engineering Manager; QA Statistician / Clerk; Senior Aero / Mechanical Draftsperson; Senior Avionics Engineer; Supervisor, Fixed Wing Aeronautical Mechanical Engineering; Supervisor, Materials, Processes and Environmental Engineering; Translator; Various Aerospace Positions; Senior Industrial Engineer; Aeronautical Fatigue Engineer; EMI / EMC Engineer / Technologist; Engineers / Technologists; Manager, Logistics Support Analysis; Manager, Rotary Wing Engineering; Materials & Processes Engineer / Technologist.

IMPACT SERVICES
Att: Human Resources Manager
89 Shorncliffe Road
Toronto, ON M8Z 5K4
Tel. 416-236-7166
Fax 416-236-7168
Employer Background: Impact Services is a renovation and retrofit company. *New Positions Created (2):* Marketing Coordinator; Commercial Construction Coordinator.

IMPATH NETWORKS INC.
Att: Human Resources
1431 Merivale Road
Nepean, ON K2E 1B9
Tel. 613-226-4000
Fax 613-226-4602
Email .... careers@impathnetworks.com
Website .... www.impathnetworks.com
Employer Background: iMPath Networks Inc. is a leading provider of fibre optic telecom solutions for managed video networks. *New Positions Created (3):* Documentation Control Specialist; Product Verification Specialist; Real-Time Embedded Software Designer.

IMPERIAL OIL RESOURCES
Att: Human Resources Department
PO Box 1020
Bonnyville, AB T9N 2J7
Fax 780-639-5102
Website .... www.imperialoil.ca
Employer Background: Founded in 1880, Imperial Oil Resources is the largest integrated petroleum company and a major producer of crude oil, natural gas and natural gas liquids. *New Positions Created (4):* Field Operators; Journeyman Instrument Technicians; Millwright; Plant Operators.

IMPERIAL TOBACCO CANADA LIMITED
Att: Human Resources Department
3810 St. Antoine Street
Montréal, QC H4C 1B5
Tel. 514-932-6161
Fax 514-932-1635
Website .... www.imperialtobacco.com
Employer Background: Imperial Tobacco Canada Limited is the country's largest tobacco enterprise involved in all phases of the industry, from raw leaf to final product. *New Positions Created (2):* Territory Representative; Accounting Analyst.

IMPORT AUTO LEASING
Att: General Manager
1300 Michael Street
Gloucester, ON K1B 3N2
Tel. 613-722-7535
Fax 613-722-6868
Email .... lease@importautoleasing.com
Website .... www.importautoleasing.com
Employer Background: Established in 1982, Import Auto Leasing is an independent leasing company, affiliated with 6 dealerships. *New Positions Created (4):* Controller; Controller; Leasing / Customer Service Representative; Accountant.

IMS HEALTH CANADA LTD.
Att: Human Resources
6100 Trans Canada Highway
Pointe-Claire, QC H9R 1B9
Tel. 514-428-6018
Fax 514-428-6100
Email .... career@ca.imshealth.com
Website .... www.imshealthcanada.com
Employer Background: IMS Health Canada
Ltd. provides healthcare information for
public and private sector clients in the
healthcare industry. *New Positions Created
(3):* Statisticians; Administrative Assistant;
Human Resources Administrator.

IN-TOUCH SURVEY SYSTEMS INC.
Att: Human Resources Manager
2405-C St. Laurent Boulevard
Ottawa, ON K1G 5B4
Tel. 613-247-7222
Fax 613-247-7163
Email .... intouch@intouchsurvey.com
Website .... www.intouchsurvey.com
Employer Background: Established in 1992,
In-Touch Survey Systems Inc. provides full-
service on-site consumer survey and re-
search systems. *New Positions Created (3):*
Regional Vice-President of Sales; Research
Analyst; Project Manager.

INA CANADA INC.
Att: W.E. Becker
2871 Plymouth Drive
Oakville, ON L6H 5S5
Tel. 905-829-2750
Fax 905-829-2563
Email .... beckerwrn@ca.ina.com
Website .... www.ina.com
Employer Background: INA Canada Inc. is a
producer of bearings and precision compo-
nents. *New Positions Created (2):* Account-
ing Manager; Technical Sales Representa-
tive.

INBUSINESS SOLUTIONS INC.
Att: Human Resources Manager
333 Preston Street, Suite 910
Ottawa, ON K1S 5N4
Tel. 613-780-9925
Fax 613-780-9931
Email .... resumes@inbusiness.com
Website .... www.inbusiness.com
Employer Background: InBusiness Solutions
Inc. (formerly NewSys Solutions Inc.) uses
media and information technology to create competitive advantages for clients. The
company has annual revenues of $20 mil-
lion. *New Positions Created (20):* BI Analyst;
Consultants; CRM Developer; Crystal Reports Position; Data Analyst; Data Warehouse Architect; Database Administrator;
Design Team Leader; E-Business Developers; Financial Information Systems Position;
Financial Reporting Systems Position; Oracle Projects Position; PowerPlay / Im-
promptu Consultants; RDIMS Systems Support Position; Senior Java Developers (2);
Senior Sybase Database Analyst; Web Developers; Crystal Reports Positions; DB2 Database Analyst; Senior Programmer / Team
Leader.

INCO LTD.
Att: Human Resources Department
145 King Street West, Suite 1500
Toronto, ON M5H 4B7
Tel. 416-361-7511
Fax 416-361-7716
Email .... phr@inco.com
Website .... www.inco.com
Employer Background: Inco Ltd. is one of
the world's leading producers of nickel, cop-
per, precious metals and cobalt. *New Posi-
tions Created (4):* Director, Project Develop-
ment; Senior Hydrometallurgist; Analytical
Supervisor; Geophysicist.

INCO LTD., MANITOBA DIVISION
Att: Denise Peters,
Employment Coordinator
Thompson, MB R8N 1P3
Tel. 204-778-2211
Fax 204-778-2693
Email .... dpeters@inco.com
Website .... www.inco.com
Employer Background: Inco Ltd. is one of
the world's leading producers of nickel, cop-
per, precious metals and cobalt. *New Posi-
tions Created (8):* Project Metallurgist; Mill
Metallurgist; Heavy Duty Mechanic TQ; In-
dustrial Electrician TQ; Industrial Instrument Mechanic TQ; Machinist TQ; Analytical Chemist; Mine Planning Engineer.

INCO LTD., ONTARIO DIVISION
Att: R.A. Reyburn,
Recruitment and Workforce Planning
Copper Cliff, ON P0M 1N0
Tel. 705-682-4211
Email .. employment_sudbury@inco.com
Website .... www.inco.com
Employer Background: Inco Ltd. is one of
the world's leading producers of nickel, cop-
per, precious metals and cobalt. *New Posi-
tions Created (3):* Design Engineers; Group
Leader; Electrical Design Engineer.

**INDALEX ALUMINUM
SOLUTIONS GROUP**
Att: Human Resources Department
5675 Kennedy Road
Mississauga, ON L4Z 2H9
Tel. 905-890-8821
Fax 905-890-2508
Website .... www.indalex.com
Employer Background: Indalex Aluminum
Solutions Group is the largest independent
producer of soft alloy aluminum products
in North America. *New Positions Created (2):*
Maintenance Mechanic / Industrial Electri-
cian (2); Production Helpers.

INDEKA GROUP, THE
Att: VP Finance & Operations
2120 Bristol Circle
Oakville, ON L6H 5R3
Fax 905-829-5067
Employer Background: The Indeka Group
is one of the largest distributors and mar-
keters of branded footwear in Canada. *New
Positions Created (6):* Distribution Manager;
Vice-President of Finance and Operations;

Administrative Assistant; Bilingual Customer Service Representative; Credit & Collections Representative; Marketing Coordinator.

**INDEPENDENT BROKERAGE
GROUP, THE**
Att: John
1155 Robson Street
Vancouver, BC V6E 1B5
Tel. 604-684-0086
Fax 604-684-9286
Email .... john@ibg.ca
Website .... www.ibg.ca
Employer Background: The Independent
Brokerage Group is a wholesale brokerage
company. *New Positions Created (3):* Branch
Manager / Compliance Officer; Financial
Services / Credit Insurance Assistant; Invest-
ment Products Case Coordinator.

**INDEPENDENT ELECTRICITY
MARKET OPERATOR / IMO**
Att: Human Resources
PO Box 4474, Station A
Toronto, ON M5W 4E5
Tel. 905-855-6100
Fax 905-403-6921
Email .... iemo@rpc.webhire.com
Website .... www.theimo.com
Employer Background: Formerly part of
Ontario Hydro, IMO oversees the safe and
reliable operation of Ontario's bulk electri-
cal system, supplying the needs of over 11
million people. *New Positions Created (4):*
Assistant Exchange Coordinator; Network
and Firewall Administrators; Oracle Data-
base Analyst; Unix Administrator.

**INDEPENDENT ORDER OF
FORESTERS / IOF**
Att: Human Resources
789 Don Mills Road
Toronto, ON M3C 1T9
Tel. 416-429-3000
Fax 416-467-2573
Email .... humanresources@iof.org
Website .... www.iof.org
Employer Background: IOF offers fraternal
benefits, life insurance and financial serv-
ices to over 1 million members. *New Posi-
tions Created (3):* Communications Coordi-
nator; Dialer and Data Administrator, Serv-
ice Centre; Tax Support Technician.

**INDEPENDENT REHABILITATION
SERVICES INC. / IRSI**
Att: Luciana Zazzara,
Director of Therapy Services
2155 Leanne Boulevard, Suite 240
Mississauga, ON L5K 2K8
Tel. 905-823-8895
Fax 905-823-9974
Email .... lou_zazzara@on.aibn.com
Website .... www.irsi.on.ca
Employer Background: IRSI provides qual-
ity, cost-effective rehabilitation manage-
ment services to the insurance industry.
New Positions Created (6): Various Health
Positions; Occupational Therapists; Admin-

istrative Assistants (2); Kinesiologists; Rehabilitation Assistants (2); Occupational Therapists.

INDIGO MANUFACTURING INC.
Att: Human Resources
165 Steelcase Road East
Markham, ON L3R 1G1
Tel. 905-513-9850
Fax 905-513-9849
Email .... hr@bashaudio.com
Website .... www.bashaudio.com
Employer Background: Indigo Manufacturing Inc. engineers audio amplification products and power supplies for the OEM market using patented BASH technology. *New Positions Created (6):* Materials Manager; QA Manager; Auto Insertion Supervisor; Cost Accountant; Junior Buyer; Post Wave Supervisor.

INDUSTRIAL ACCIDENT PREVENTION ASSOCIATION / IAPA
Att: Annie Tsingos
250 Yonge Street, 28th Floor
Toronto, ON M5B 2N4
Tel. 416-506-8888
Fax 416-506-9092
Email .... atsingos@iapa.on.ca
Website .... www.iapa.on.ca
Employer Background: IAPA is a non-profit association dedicated to creating safe, healthy and productive workplaces in Ontario. *New Positions Created (2):* Consultants; Training Materials Coordinator.

INDUSTRIAL EVOLUTION
Att: Recruitment Manager
10080 Jasper Avenue, Suite 1008
Edmonton, AB T5J 1V9
Tel. 780-423-900
Fax 780-423-9051
Email ... contact@industrialevolution.com
Website ...... www.industrialevolution.com
Employer Background: Industrial Evolution provides web-hosting of real-time data and software applications for the process manufacturing industries. *New Positions Created (4):* Administrative Assistant; Chief Web Technologist; Information Technologist; Real-Time Database Administrator.

INDUSTRIAL & FINANCIAL SYSTEMS / IFS NORTH AMERICA, INC.
Att: Trudie Carlesso,
Managing Director, Canada
254 Driftwood Drive
Kitchener, ON N2N 1X6
Tel. 519-744-3298
Fax 519-744-5008
Email .... trudie.carlesso@ifsna.com
Website .... www.ifsworld.com
Employer Background: Founded in 1983, IFS is a leading provider of ERP and e-business solutions, with over 3,600 employees and sales in 43 countries. *New Positions Created (3):* Business Analysts; Sales Representative; Systems Engineer.

INDUSTRIAL RESEARCH AND DEVELOPMENT INSTITUTE / IRDI
Att: Human Resources Manager
649 Prospect Boulevard, PO Box 518
Midland, ON L4R 4L3
Tel. 705-526-2163
Fax 705-526-2701
Email .... jobs@irdi.com
Website .... www.irdi.com
Employer Background: IRDI assists companies in parts design and manufacturing through applied research and development and advanced education services. *New Positions Created (6):* Business Development Manager, Auto Parts Sector; Junior Engineer, Metal Stamping Technologies; Mechanical Engineer, Metal Stamping Technologies; Senior Plastic Part Designer; Technical Sales Engineer, Metal Fabrication Technologies; Technology Manager, Plastics.

INDUSTRIAL-ALLIANCE PACIFIC LIFE INSURANCE SERVICES
Att: Human Resources Department
2165 West Broadway, PO Box 5900
Vancouver, BC V6B 5H6
Tel. 604-737-9385
Fax 604-737-9359
Email .... hr@iapacificlife.com
Website .... www.iapacificlife.com
Employer Background: Industrial-Alliance Pacific Life Insurance Services provides life, accident and sickness insurance in Canada and the USA. *New Positions Created (19):* Life Insurance Administrators; Customer Service Representative, Claims; Customer Service Representative, Investments; Assessor / Claims Service Representative; Customer Service Representative; Agency Administrator; Human Resources Administrator; Customer Service Representative; Marketing Coordinator; Assessor / Claims Service Representative; Real Estate Administrator; Manager, Mortgages and Real Estate; Manager of Marketing and Sales Support; Account Executive, Life Insurance and Investment Products; Senior Administrative Assistant; Customer Service Representative; Assessor / Claims Service Representative; Group Sales Assistant; Assessor / Claims Service Representative.

INDUSTRY CANADA
Att: Carole Sheridan, HR Consultant
50 Victoria Street
Hull, QC K1A 0C9
Fax 819-997-2987
Email .... sheridan.carole@ic.gc.ca
Website .... www.ic.gc.ca
Employer Background: Industry Canada works to improve conditions for investment and innovation performance, increase Canada's share of global trade and build a fair, efficient and competitive marketplace. *New Positions Created (5):* Patent Examiner, Mechanical Engineering; Patent Examiner / Electrical Engineer; Patent Examiner (Organic Chemist); Patent Examiner; Patent Examiner, Biotechnology.

INDUSTRY TRAINING & APPRENTICESHIP COMMISSION
Att: Shirley Caldwell
617 Government Street
3rd Floor, PO Box 9148, Stn Prov Govt
Victoria, BC V8W 9H1
Tel. 250-660-3603
Fax 250-387-6774
Website .... www.itac.gov.bc.ca
Employer Background: ITAC is mandated to develop and expand a system of provincially-recognized credentials for designated trades and occupations that recognize provincial, national and international occupational standards. *New Positions Created (5):* ITAC Counsellor; Administrative Assistant; Events Coordinator; Industry Training and Apprenticeship Commission Counsellor; Area Manager.

INETCO SYSTEMS LTD.
Att: Human Resources Manager
3773 Still Creek Avenue, Suite 201
Burnaby, BC V5C 4E2
Tel. 604-451-1567
Fax 604-451-1565
Email .... careers@inetco.com
Website .... www.inetco.com
Employer Background: Founded in 1984, INETCO Systems Ltd. develops datacom software products and tools for automated teller machines and point-of-sale connectivity solutions. *New Positions Created (6):* Administrative Assistant; Application Programmer; Pre-Sales Engineer; Real-Time Systems Programmer; Regional Sales Manager; Software Release Coordinator.

INEX PHARMACEUTICALS CORP.
Att: Human Resources
8900 Glenlyon Parkway, Suite 100
Burnaby, BC V5J 5J8
Tel. 604-419-3200
Fax 604-419-3201
Email .... careers@inexpharm.com
Website .... www.inexpharm.com
Employer Background: Inex Pharmaceuticals Corp. is a biopharmaceutical company that utilizes proprietary drug delivery systems and therapeutic compounds to increase the effectiveness and reduce the side effects of anti-cancer therapies. *New Positions Created (50):* Clinical Research Associate; Administrative Assistant; Quality Assurance Associate I; Technology Transfer Associate; Document Associate III; Office Services Assistant; Contracts Manager; Facilities Manager; Quality Associate III; Central Records Associate; Word Processor; Financial Analyst; Manager, Central Records; Analytical Research Associate; Associate Director / Senior Manager, Preclinical Regulatory Affairs; Associate Director / Senior Manager, Technical Regulatory Affairs; Database Developer; Director, Clinical Research; Manager, Quality Documentation and Training; Medical Writer; Process Development Scientist; Senior Analytical Chemist; Senior Manager, Quality Control Lab; Senior Manager, Stability; Corporate Communications Specialist; Director, Business Information Systems; Contracts Man-

ager; Facilities Engineer; Facilities Manager; Health and Safety Officer; Help Desk Analyst; Manager, Clinical Research; Technical Writers; Manager, Compensation and Benefits; Manager, Staffing Services; Technical Recruiter; Associate Director / Senior Manager, Preclinical Regulatory Affairs; Associate Director / Senior Manager, Technical Regulatory Affairs; Clinical Research Associate; Controller; Director, Clinical Research; Director, Intellectual Property; Manager, Clinical Research; Medical Writer; Research Associate, Chemistry; Research Associate, Immunology; Research Associate, Preclinical; Research Scientist; Research Scientist, Immunology; Senior Technical Writers (2).

INFLAZYME PHARMACEUTICALS LTD.
Att: Human Resources
5600 Parkwood Way, Suite 425
Richmond, BC V6V 2M2
Tel. 604-279-8511
Fax 604-279-8711
Email .... careers@inflazyme.com
Website .... www.inflazyme.com

Employer Background: Inflazyme Pharmaceuticals Ltd. is a biopharmaceutical company focused on the discovery, development and commercialization of therapies to treat inflammatory diseases. *New Positions Created (6):* Head of HR; Director, Business Development / Licensing; Director, Cellular Biology / Biochemistry; Director, Cellular Biology; Regulatory Affairs Manager; Vice President, Clinical and Regulatory Affairs.

INFOMART DIALOG LTD.
Att: Sales Manager
1450 Don Mills Road
Toronto, ON M3B 2X7
Tel. 416-445-6641
Fax 416-442-2208
Email .... awhite@infomart.ca
Website .... www.infomart.ca

Employer Background: Infomart Dialog Ltd. delivers essential current affairs, business and news / media information to Canadian information and business professionals. *New Positions Created (2):* Account Executive; Senior Account Representative.

INFONEX INC.
Att: Vice-President, Conference Division
35 McCaul Street, Suite 400
Toronto, ON M5T 1V7
Tel. 416-971-4177
Fax 416-971-7295
Email .... hire@infonex.ca
Website .... www.infonex.ca

Employer Background: INFONEX Inc. is a leading provider of business information conferences. *New Positions Created (3):* Conference Program Developer; Conference Administrator; Direct Marketing Director.

INFORETECH WIRELESS TECHNOLOGY INC.
Att: Patti Collins, HR Manager
5500 - 152nd Street, Suite 214
Surrey, BC V3S 8E7
Tel. 604-576-7442
Fax 604-576-7460
Email .... jobs@inforetech.com
Website .... www.inforetech.com

Employer Background: Inforetech Wireless Technology Inc. develops portable recreational devices that use a patented combination of GPS, two-way messaging and Internet technology. *New Positions Created (10):* Senior Windows Developer; Engineering Technician; Manufacturing Technician; Marketing Manager; Accounting Assistant; Administrative Assistant, Engineering Division; Purchasing and Inventory Assistant; Senior Windows Developer; Hardware Engineer; Software Technician.

INFORMATION AND PRIVACY COMMISSIONER, ONTARIO
Att: Human Resources Manager
80 Bloor Street West, Suite 1700
Toronto, ON M5S 2V1
Tel. 416-326-3333
Website .... www.ipc.on.ca

Employer Background: Established in 1988, the Information and Privacy Commissioner is mandated to provide an independent review of government decisions and practices concerning access and privacy. *New Positions Created (4):* Communications Officer; Policy & Information Technology Officer; Mediator; Project Analyst.

INFORMATION SCIENCE AND TECHNOLOGY AGENCY, BC / ISTA
Att: Lori Haggstrom
4000 Seymour Place
PO Box 9412, Stn Prov Govt
Victoria, BC V8W 9V1
Tel. 250-387-1396
Fax 250-356-1576
Email ... lori.haggstrom@gems4.gov.bc.ca
Website .... www.ista.gov.bc.ca

Employer Background: Created in 1995, ISTA is responsible for: strengthening the BC economy through technology; connecting British Columbians through universal, affordable access to networks; and transforming government programs and service delivery through technology. *New Positions Created (4):* Staffing / Development Adviser; Administrative Assistant; Manager, Database Application; Administrative Assistant.

INFORMATION SERVICES CORPORATION OF SASKATCHEWAN
Att: Human Resources Consultant
10 Research Drive, Suite 300
Regina, SK S4P 3V7
Fax 306-798-0682
Email ...... humanresources@isc-online.ca
Website .... www.isc-online.ca

Employer Background: ISC amalgamates responsibility for the province's land survey system and the system of registering ownership of, and interests in, land. *New Positions Created (17):* Project Management Consultant; Director, Business Development; Financial Analyst; Purchasing and Contracts Manager; Web Specialist; Director, GIS Standards and Practices; Informa-

tion Technology Positions (11); Business Policy Analyst, Customer Service; Human Resources Assistant; Director, Sales and Service; GIS Mapping Technicians; GIS Supervisor; Conversion Boundary Analysts; Conversion Data Entry Support Positions; Conversion Workflow Coordinators; Human Resource Administrator; Training Consultants.

INFOSPEC SYSTEMS INC.
Att: Human Resources Manager
3700 North Fraser Way, Suite 180
Burnaby, BC V5J 5H4
Fax 604-430-5748
Website .... www.infospec.com

Employer Background: Founded in 1985, InfoSpec Systems Inc. provides PC-based point-of-sale systems to the hospitality and retail industries. *New Positions Created (6):* Sales Consultant; Systems Support Representatives; Application Software Support / Trainers; Computer Technicians; Programmer Analyst; Receptionist.

INFOSTREAM TECHNOLOGIES INC.
Att: Human Resources Manager
333 Lesmill Road
Toronto, ON M3B 2V1
Tel. 416-449-8919
Fax 416-449-6369
Email .... career@infostream.ca
Website www.infostreamtechnologies.com

Employer Background: Infostream Technologies Inc. plans and designs enterprise e-business solutions. *New Positions Created (4):* Accounts Receivable / Payable Representative; Administrative Assistant / Receptionist; Controller; Accounts Receivable / Payable Representative.

INFOSYS TECHNOLOGIES LTD.
Att: Human Resources Manager
5140 Yonge Street, Suite 1400
Toronto, ON M2N 6L7
Tel. 416-224-7400
Fax 416-224-7449
Email .... careers.canada@infy.com
Website .... www.infy.com

Employer Background: Infosys Technologies Ltd. is a leader in information technology consulting and software services. *New Positions Created (7):* Delivery Manager; Architect, Technical, Application and Infrastructure; Business Analyst; Business Consultant; Program / Account Manager; Project Leader; Project Manager.

INFOWAVE SOFTWARE, INC.
Att: Human Resources Manager
4664 Lougheed Highway, Suite 188
Burnaby, BC V5C 6B7
Tel. 604-473-3600
Fax 604-473-3699
Email .... hr@infowave.com
Website .... www.infowave.com

Employer Background: Founded in 1984, Infowave Software, Inc. builds wireless business solutions that connect mobile workers to critical information. *New Positions Cre-*

ated (17): Director, Business Development; Exchange 2000 Specialist; Lotus Notes Developer; Product Manager; QA Analyst, System Performance; Applied Researcher; Architect; Corporate Counsel; Director, Software Development; Lead, Quality Assurance; Lotus Notes Developer; Manager, Implementation; Performance / Systems Analyst; Senior Manager, IT; Systems Administrator; Mergers and Acquisitions Manager; Operations Director.

INFRASTRUCTURES FOR INFORMATION, INC. / I4I
Att: Human Resources
116 Spadina Avenue, 5th Floor
Toronto, ON M5V 2K6

Tel. 416-920-6489
Fax 416-504-1785
Email .... hrdept@i4i.com
Website www.i-4-i.com

Employer Background: Infrastructures for Information, Inc. is a leader in enterprise-wide software applications. *New Positions Created (7):* Graphic Designer; Intermediate Programmers; Product Manager; Product Specialist; Senior Programmers; Webmaster; XML Consultant.

ING BANK OF CANADA / ING DIRECT
Att: Human Resources
111 Gordon Baker Road, Suite 900
Toronto, ON M2H 3R1

Tel. 416-758-5219
Fax 416-758-5292
Email .... humanresources@ingdirect.ca
Website .... www.ingdirect.ca

Employer Background: ING Bank of Canada (operating under the name ING Direct) is a federally chartered bank and part of the ING Group, an integrated financial services organization. *New Positions Created (5):* Direct Associates; IT Audit Specialist; Team Leader, Human Resources; Technical Support Analyst; Direct Banking Associates.

ING CANADA
Att: Human Resources Manager
181 University Avenue, 7th Floor
Toronto, ON M5H 3M7

Tel. 416-941-5050
Fax 416-941-0014
Website .... www.ingcanada.com

Employer Background: ING Canada is part of the ING Group, an integrated financial services organization. *New Positions Created (3):* Legal Specialists (2); Inside Sales Associates; Regional Vice Presidents, Sales.

ING HALIFAX
Att: Human Resources Consultant, Recruiting
321 - 6th Avenue SW, Suite 1300
Calgary, AB T2P 4W7

Website .... www.inghalifax.com

Employer Background: ING Halifax is a Canadian insurance company and part of the ING Group, an integrated financial services organization. *New Positions Created (3):* Administrative Assistant; Business Develop-

ment Manager; Training and Operations Manager.

ING INTEGRATED FINANCIAL SERVICES
Att: Lana Narowski
321 - 6th Avenue SW, Suite 1300
Calgary, AB T2P 4W7

Tel. 403-231-1313
Fax 403-269-7938
Email .... ifs.alberta@ingcanada.com
Website .... www.inggroup.com

Employer Background: ING Integrated Financial Services is a financial services retailer specializing in investments, insurance and banking solutions. *New Positions Created (2):* Training and Operations Manager; Financial Advisor.

ING WESTERN UNION INSURANCE
Att: Human Resources Department
510 Burrard Street, Suite 800
Vancouver, BC V6C 3H9

Fax 604-899-1075
Website .... www.ingwesternunion.com

Employer Background: ING Western Union Insurance is a property and casualty insurance company and part of the ING Group, an integrated financial services organization. *New Positions Created (7):* Commercial and Personal Insurance Underwriters; Insurance Underwriting Positions; Claims Analyst; Claims Assistant; Inside Claims Representative; Unit Claims Manager; Underwriting Trainees.

ING WESTERN UNION INSURANCE
Att: Human Resources Department
10130 - 103rd Street, Suite 800
Edmonton, AB T5J 3N5

Tel. 780-428-7544
Website .... www.ingwesternunion.com

Employer Background: ING Western Union Insurance is a property and casualty insurance company and part of the ING Group, an integrated financial services organization. *New Positions Created (9):* Claims Casualty Field Representative; Commercial Auto Underwriters; Inside Claims Representative; Senior Personal Insurance Underwriters; Outside Claims Casualty Representative; Claims Assistant; Commercial Auto and Personal Insurance Underwriters; Outside Claims Property Representative; Regional Branch Manager.

ING WESTERN UNION INSURANCE
Att: Human Resources Consultant, Recruiting
321 - 6th Avenue SW, Suite 1300
Calgary, AB T2P 4W7

Tel. 403-269-7961
Fax 403-266-1196
Website .... www.ingwesternunion.com

Employer Background: ING Western Union Insurance is a property and casualty insurance company and part of the ING Group, an integrated financial services organization. *New Positions Created (5):* Commercial Insurance Auto Underwriter; Corporate -

Commercial Insurance Manager; Field Bodily Injury Adjuster; Corporate Personal Insurance Underwriting Manager; Human Resources Advisor, Recruiting.

INGERSOLL-RAND CANADA INC.
Att: Human Resources
51 Worcester Road
Toronto, ON M9W 4K2

Tel. 416-213-4500
Fax 416-213-4527
Email .... resume_ircanada@irco.com
Website .... www.irco.com

Employer Background: Ingersoll-Rand Canada Inc. is a diversified, multinational manufacturer of industrial and commercial equipment and components. *New Positions Created (2):* Office Administrator; Application Engineer.

INGLE LIFE AND HEALTH ASSURANCE COMPANY
Att: Human Resources Department
438 University Avenue, Suite 1200
Toronto, ON M5G 2K8

Tel. 416-340-0100
Fax 416-340-2707
Email .... hr@ingle-health.com
Website .... www.ingle-health.com

Employer Background: Ingle Life and Health Assurance Company provides a full range of individual and group health insurance products, including out-of-country programs, visitor programs and extended health benefits. *New Positions Created (2):* Claims Assessor; Systems Administrator.

INGRAM MICRO INC. (CANADA)
Att: Human Resources
55 Standish Court
Mississauga, ON L5R 4A1

Tel. 905-755-5000
Fax 905-755-1319
Email .... jobs@ingrammicro.ca
Website .... www.ingrammicro.ca

Employer Background: Ingram Micro Inc. (Canada) has been distributing computer hardware and software since 1989, when Ingram Computer Inc. and Micro D Inc. merged their worldwide operations. *New Positions Created (8):* Accounts Payable Representative; Senior Customs Rater; Maintenance Manager; Senior Manager, Process Engineering; Accountant I; Accounts Receivable Supervisor; Credit Representative II; Senior Credit Representative, Key Accounts.

INKRA NETWORKS CANADA
Att: Human Resources Manager
3605 Gilmore Way, Suite 200
Burnaby, BC V5G 4X5

Tel. 604-430-2700
Fax 604-430-2791
Email .... jobs@inkra.com
Website .... www.inkra.com

Employer Background: Founded in 2000, Inkra Networks Canada is a top-tier designer of new carrier systems for Internet data centres. *New Positions Created (17):* Development Test Engineer; Development Test

Leader; Director of Test; Senior Product Manager, Software; Software Engineers, Distributed Systems / HA; Software Engineers, Network Management; System Test Leader; Technical Communications Manager; Distributed Systems / HA Software Engineers; Network Management Software Engineers; Senior Product Manager, Software; Technical Communications Manager; ASIC Design Engineer; Hardware Design Engineer; Layer 4-7 Protocols Software Engineer; Network Management Software Engineer; Networking Software Engineer.

INLAND AGGREGATES LTD.
Att: Human Resources Manager
885 - 42nd Avenue SE
Vintage Park, Building C
Calgary, AB T2G 1Y8

Email ... resumes@inland.lehighcement.com
Website .... www.inlandcanada.com
Employer Background: Inland Aggregates Ltd. (a division of the Inland Group) is a major supplier of screened, crushed, washed and lightweight aggregate products. *New Positions Created (3):* Administrative / Accounting Assistant; Technical Support Analyst, Information Technology; Technical Sales Representatives.

INLAND CEMENT LIMITED
Att: Human Resources Department
Box 3961
Edmonton, AB T5L 4P8

Tel. 780-420-2500
Fax 780-420-2503
Email ... resumes@inland.lehighcement.com
Website .... www.inlandcanada.com
Employer Background: Inland Cement Limited is a major producer of cement, ready-mix concrete, concrete pipe, aggregates and related construction materials and services in western Canada. *New Positions Created (4):* Technical Sales Engineer; Sales & Marketing Representative; Sales and Marketing Representative; Technical Sales Engineer.

INLAND GROUP
Att: Human Resources
17410 - 107th Avenue
Edmonton, AB T5S 1E9

Tel. 780-423-6300
Fax 780-423-6366
Email resumes@inland.lehighcement.com
Website .... www.inlandcanada.com
Employer Background: Inland Group is a subsidiary of Lehigh Portland Cement Company, a leading manufacturer of construction materials throughout North America. *New Positions Created (5):* Technical Support Analyst, Information Technology; Quality Control Laboratory Supervisor; Purchasing Director; General Accountants (2); Human Resources Coordinator.

INLAND GROUP
Att: Human Resources
5340 - 1st Street SW
Calgary, AB T2H 0C8

Tel. 403-255-1131
Fax 403-212-4720

Email ... resumes@inland.lehighcement.com
Website .... www.inlandcanada.com
Employer Background: Inland Group is a subsidiary of Lehigh Portland Cement Company, a leading manufacturer of construction materials throughout North America. *New Positions Created (2):* Shop Superintendent; Project Cost Accountant.

INLINGUA INTERNATIONAL
Att: Human Resources Manager
1238 Melville Street, Suite 2103
Vancouver, BC V6E 4N2

Tel. 604-924-1390
Fax 604-924-1399
Website .... www.inlingua.com
Employer Background: Established in 1968, Inlingua International is one of the largest language training institutions in the world, with over 300 centres in 28 countries. *New Positions Created (3):* English Language Instructor; Head Instructor; Language Instructors.

INNER-TEC SECURITY SERVICES
Att: Winnie Yee
505 Burrard Street
Suite 920, Box 65, 1 Bentall Centre
Vancouver, BC V7X 1M4

Tel. 604-714-3050
Email .... winnieyee@inner-tec.com
Website .... www.inner-tec.com
Employer Background: Inner-Tec Security Services is a leading supplier of security guard services in seven Canadian cities. *New Positions Created (4):* Accounts Payable Clerk; Controller; Office Clerk; Payroll / Office Assistant.

INNOTECH-EXECAIRE AVIATION GROUP, THE
Att: Human Resources Department
10225 Ryan Avenue
Dorval, QC H9P 1A2

Tel. 514-636-7070
Fax 514-636-9659
Email .... human.resources@innotech-execaire.com
Website .... www.innotech-execaire.com
Employer Background: The Innotech-Execaire Aviation Group, a fully-integrated business aircraft service group, is composed of 6 companies. *New Positions Created (6):* Aircraft Line Maintenance Engineer; Avionics Engineer; Programmer Analyst; Aircraft Maintenance Engineers; Avionic Installers; Avionics Technician.

INNOVATIVE COOLING DYNAMICS / STT TECHNOLOGIES INC.
Att: Human Resources Department
6400 Ordan Drive
Mississauga, ON L5T 2H6

Tel. 905-564-9522
Fax 905-564-9523
Email .... hr.stt@tesma.com
Employer Background: Innovative Cooling Dynamics is an automotive parts manufacturer of water and oil pumps. *New Positions Created (4):* Oil Pump Development Engi-

neer; Program Managers; FP & A Analyst; Senior Test Technician.

INNOVATOR ELECTRONIC ASSEMBLY
Att: Human Resources Manager
2530 Alphonse Gariepy
Lachine, QC H8T 3M2

Fax 514-636-7575
Email .... corp@innovator-inc.com
Website .... www.innovator-inc.com
Employer Background: IEA is a contract assembly house for electronic assemblies and sub-assemblies. *New Positions Created (3):* Account Managers (2); Electronic Assemblers; Material Control Personnel (2).

INNOVUS RESEARCH INC.
Att: Human Resources
1016-A Sutton Drive, Suite 200
Burlington, ON L7L 6B8

Tel. 905-331-9911
Fax 905-331-9912
Email .... jobs@innovus.com
Website .... www.innovus.com
Employer Background: Innovus Research Inc. provides clinical, health economic and outcomes research services to the pharmaceutical and biotechnology industries. *New Positions Created (7):* Clinical Research Associates; Project Manager, Health Economics; Senior Manager, Clinical Research; Statistician; Bilingual Clinical Research Associate; Project Coordinator, Clinical Research; Project Manager, Clinical Research.

INO
Att: Human Resources Department
2740 Einstein Street
Quebec Metro High Tech Park
Ste-Foy, QC G1P 4S4

Tel. 418-657-7006
Fax 418-657-7009
Website .... www.ino.ca
Employer Background: INO is Canada's largest optics and photonics R&D centre, with a staff of 140 physicists, engineers and technologists. *New Positions Created (6):* Researchers; Technologists; Project Leader, Optical Communication Products; Researcher, Fiber Sensors; Researcher, Industrial Optics; Researcher, Optical Design.

INPHINITY INTERACTIVE INC.
Att: Julia Ford, Recruiter
1401 - 8th Avenue West, 4th Floor
Vancouver, BC V6H 1C9

Email .... yourfuture@inphinity.com
Website .... www.inphinity.com
Employer Background: Inphinity Interactive Inc. provides advanced software development and product customization services to the Internet entertainment industry. *New Positions Created (5):* Junior Technical Writer; Product Manager, E-Commerce; Product Manager, Pari-Mutuels; Product Manager, Sportsbook; Vice-President, Product Development.

INPHOGENE BIOCOM INC.
Att: Human Resources Administrator

4475 Wayburne Drive, Suite 309
Burnaby, BC V5G 3L1

Fax 604-453-5910
Email .... hr@inphogene.com
Website .... www.inphogene.com
Employer Background: InphoGene BioCom
Inc. is an e-biotechnology company. *New
Positions Created (6):* Database Administrator; Database Architect; IT Manager; Lead
Technologist and Technologist Research
Associate; QA Manager; Systems Manager.

INSIGHT CANADA INC.
Att: Recruiting Department
8600 Decarie Boulevard
Montréal, QC H4P 2N2

Tel. 514-344-3500
Fax 514-344-6945
Email .... icajobs@insight.com
Website .... www.insight.com
Employer Background: Insight Canada Inc.
is a business supplier of computer hardware
and software, with annual sales of over $2
billion. *New Positions Created (5):* Business
Sales Representatives; Accountant; Assistant
Controller; Commercial Credit Representatives; Business Sales Representatives, Outbound.

INSITE COMMUNICATIONS
Att: Human Resources Manager
1020 Bayridge Drive, 2nd Floor
Kingston, ON K7P 2S2

Tel. 613-384-3581
Fax 613-384-1686
Email .... hr@insitecom.com
Website .... www.insitecom.com
Employer Background: inSITE Communications provides complete Internet solutions, including corporate image development, audience-targeted content creation, management of online publications, and web-based marketing and promotion. *New
Positions Created (3):* Junior Systems Administrator; Entry-Level Multimedia Position; Web Experts.

INSPEC-SOL INC.
Att: Human Resources Manager
4600 Cote Vertu, Suite 200
Montréal, QC H4S 1C7

Tel. 514-333-5151
Fax 514-920-0930
Email .... employment@inspecsol.com
Website .... www.inspecsol.com
Employer Background: Founded in 1972,
Inspec-Sol Inc. provides independent
geotechnical engineering, field inspection
and laboratory testing services. *New Positions Created (2):* Intermediate Geotechnical
Engineers, Materials Engineers & Technologists; Various Geotechnical / Civil Engineering Positions.

INSTANTEL INC.
Att: Human Resources
309 Legget Drive
Kanata, ON K2K 3A3

Tel. 613-592-4642
Fax 613-592-4296

Email .... careers@instantel.com
Website .... www.instantel.com
Employer Background: Instantel Inc. is an
advanced technology company, specializing
in vibration monitoring and RF security
products. *New Positions Created (31):* Analog Design Engineer; Electronics Engineer;
Engineering Project Leader; Traffic Coordinator; Firmware Designer; Marketing Manager, Instrumentation; Accountant; Accounts Payable Clerk; Analog Design Engineer; Electronics Engineer; Engineering
Project Leader; Manufacturing Managers
(2); Senior Firmware Designer; Traffic Coordinator; Analog Design Engineer; Bench
Test Technician; Electronics Engineer; Engineering Project Leader; ISO Quality Officer; Manufacturing Test Engineer; Materials Buyer; Production Test Technician;
Senior Firmware Designer; Service Coordinator, Health Care Systems; Engineering
Manager, Healthcare Security; Engineering
Manager, Instrumentation; Engineering
Technologist; Senior Printed Circuit Board
Designer; Senior Technical Support Analyst;
Technical Writer; Test Software Developer.

INSTITUTE FOR CLINICAL
EVALUATIVE SCIENCES / ICES
Att: Patricia Pinfold, Research Manager
2075 Bayview Avenue, G-106
Toronto, ON M4N 3M5

Tel. 416-480-4055
Fax 416-480-6048
Email .... patti@ices.on.ca
Website .... www.ices.on.ca
Employer Background: ICES is a non-profit
organization that conducts research to ensure the effectiveness, equity, quality and
efficiency of health services in Ontario. *New
Positions Created (6):* Research Coordinator;
Controller; Research Coordinator; External
Relations and Policy Advisor; Biostatistician
/ Programmer; Research Coordinators (2).

INSTITUTE FOR
INTERNATIONAL RESEARCH
Att: Human Resources Manager
60 Bloor Street West, Suite 1101
Toronto, ON M4W 3B8

Tel. 416-928-1078
Fax 416-928-3313
Email .... mhouzer@iircanada.com
Website .... www.iir.org
Employer Background: The Institute for International Research is a multimillion dollar conference company, with 36 offices
worldwide. *New Positions Created (2):* Conference Producer; Program Director.

INSTITUTE OF HEALTH
ECONOMICS / IHE
Att: Wanda Draginda
10405 Jasper Avenue, Suite 1200
Edmonton, AB T5J 3N4

Tel. 780-448-4881
Email .... wdraginda@ihe.ab.ca
Website .... www.ihe.ab.ca
Employer Background: IHE is an independent nonprofit organization that delivers
health economics, health outcomes and

health policy research and related services.
New Positions Created (5): Data Analyst;
Administrative Assistant; Director, Corporate and Research Services; Health Services
Research Librarian / Information Scientist;
Health Policy Research Positions.

INSURANCE BUREAU OF CANADA
Att: Human Resources Department
240 Duncan Mill Road, Suite 700
Toronto, ON M3B 1Z4

Tel. 416-445-5912
Fax 416-445-1298
Email .... hrrecruiter@ibc.ca
Website .... www.ibc.ca
Employer Background: Established in 1964,
IBC is the national trade association of non-government property and casualty insurers.
New Positions Created (7): Regional Director, Investigative Services Division; Regional
Director, Investigative Services Division; Bilingual Receptionist; Director, Financial
Project Management; Investigators, Rings /
Accident Benefits & Bodily Injury Claims;
Manager, Health Policy Project; Executive
Director, Government Relations.

INSURANCE CORPORATION OF BC
Att: Human Resources
151 West Esplanade, Room 118
North Vancouver, BC V7M 3H9

Tel. 604-661-2100
Fax 604-661-6450
Website .... www.icbc.com
Employer Background: Established in 1973,
ICBC is a provincial Crown corporation, providing universal auto insurance to BC motorists. *New Positions Created (3):* Manager,
Financial Consulting and Analysis; Regional
Financial Manager; Senior Accountant.

INSYSTEMS TECHNOLOGIES, INC.
Att: Human Resources
19 Allstate Parkway, Suite 400
Markham, ON L3R 5A4

Tel. 905-513-1400
Fax 905-513-1419
Email .... hrdept@insystems.com
Website .... www.insystems.com
Employer Background: InSystems Technologies, Inc. develops relationship management
software for the financial services industry
worldwide. *New Positions Created (44):* Administrative Assistant; Diagnostics Expert;
Architect; Data Administrator; Product Support Representative; Project Manager; Rule
Engine Developer; Senior Architect; Senior
Business Analyst; Senior Consultant; Software Developer; Regional Sales Manager;
Relationship Framework Expert; Architect;
Product Support Representative; Project
Manager; Rule Engine Developer; Senior
Architect; Senior Business Analyst; Senior
Consultant; Software Developer; Director,
Product Support; Java Developer; Regional
Sales Manager; Relationship Framework
Expert; Sales Support Manager; Senior Software Developer, C++ and Com; Administrative Assistant; Senior Developer, Rules Engines; Software QA Engineer; Software
Tester; Architect; Implementation Analyst;

Senior Architect; Software Quality Assurance Engineer; Data Architect; Product Manager; Project Managers (2); Senior Business Analysts (3); Senior Consultant; Senior Technical Writers (2); Software Developers (3); Software Test Engineer; Team Leader.

INTALITE CEILING SYSTEMS
Att: Beverly Cook
255 Montpellier
St-Laurent, QC H4N 2G3

Fax 514-744-2716
Email .... beverly@simplexceilings.com
Website .... www.simplexceilings.com
Employer Background: Intalite Ceiling Systems (formerly Simplex Ceilings) is a North American metal ceiling manufacturer, with over 60 years experience. *New Positions Created (5):* Designer / Draftsperson; Estimators (2); Project Manager; Saw Operators; Trades Positions.

INTEGRA FOUNDATION
Att: Margaret Amerongen, MSW
Clinical Director
25 Imperial Street
Toronto, ON M5P 1B9

Fax 416-486-1282
Email .... ameronge@istar.ca
Employer Background: Integra Foundation is a children's mental health centre, providing services for children and adolescents with learning disabilities. *New Positions Created (3):* Administrative Assistant / Receptionist; Therapist / Case Manager; Psychologist.

INTEGRA NETWORKS CORPORATION
Att: Human Resources Department
2460 Lancaster Road, Suite 102
Ottawa, ON K1B 4S5

Tel. 613-526-4945
Fax 613-526-3641
Email .... hr@integranetworks.com
Website .... www.integranet.com
Employer Background: Integra Networks Corporation is a regional provider of network integration services. *New Positions Created (9):* Account Executives; Inside Sales Representative; Compaq-Certified Service Position; Account Manager; Inside Technical Sales Representative; Lotus Notes Programmer / System Administrator; Network Specialists; Network Consultant and Customer Support Representative; Account Executive.

INTEGRATED PRODUCTION SERVICES LTD. / IPS
Att: Human Resources
840 - 7th Avenue SW, Suite 1500
Calgary, AB T2P 3G2

Fax 403-266-1639
Website .... www.ipsl.ca
Employer Background: IPS is an oil and gas wellbore services company, serving petroleum exploration and production companies in Canada and southeast Asia. *New Positions Created (9):* Reservoir Engineer;

Engineering Marketer; Optimization Engineers and Technologists; Assistant Controller; Technical Field Sales Representative; Field Service Representative; Consulting Engineers / Technologists; Financial Analyst; Rig Supervisors.

INTEGRATIVE PROTEOMICS INC. / IPI
Att: Human Resources Manager
100 College Street, Suite 520
Toronto, ON M5G 1L5

Tel. 416-598-1115
Fax 416-598-1262
Email careers@integrativeproteomics.com
Website . www.integrativeproteomics.com
Employer Background: IPI is a Canadian biotechnology company. *New Positions Created (5):* Controller; Machine Vision and Image Processing Engineer; Mechanical Engineer; Process Engineers; Robotics Software and Controls Engineer.

INTELCAN TECHNOSYSTEMS INC.
Att: Human Resources
69 Auriga Drive
Nepean, ON K2E 7Z2

Tel. 613-228-1150
Fax 613-228-1149
Email .... hr@intelcan.com
Website .... www.intelcan.com
Employer Background: Intelcan Technosystems Inc. is a leading supplier of wireless telecom and air traffic management solutions. *New Positions Created (2):* C++ Programmer; Wireless Systems Engineer.

INTELLITACTICS INC.
Att: Human Resources
305 King Street West, Suite 800
Kitchener, ON N2G 1B9

Tel. 519-743-0144
Fax 519-743-9558
Email .... hr@itactics.com
Website .... www.itactics.com
Employer Background: Intellitactics Inc. develops intelligent technologies for the management and security of large enterprises. *New Positions Created (22):* Intermediate / Senior Java Developers; Sales Support Coordinator; Intermediate / Senior Database Developers; Intermediate Database Developers; Intermediate Java Developers; Lead Java Developers; Integration / Implementation Specialist; National Account Executives; Sales Engineer; Security Solutions Consultants; Senior Java Developers; Senior Technical Writer; National Account Executives; Sales Engineer; Security Solutions Consultants; Senior Software Developers; Technical Trainer; Development Project Manager; Integration / Implementation Specialists; Intermediate / Senior Software Developers; IT Positions; Security Solutions Consultants.

INTERACTIVE CIRCUITS AND SYSTEMS LTD. / ICS
Att: Human Resources
5430 Canotek Road
Gloucester, ON K1J 9G2

Tel. 613-749-9241

Fax 613-749-9461
Email .... jobs@ics-ltd.com
Website .... www.ics-ltd.com
Employer Background: ICS designs, develops and manufactures high-speed data acquisition boards and systems for signal processing applications. *New Positions Created (10):* Hardware Engineer; PCB Designer; Software Engineer; System Engineer; Account Manager, Wireless; Inside Sales Representative; Marketing Representative; Assemblers; Manager, Marketing; Software Engineer.

INTERACTIVE MEDIA GROUP / IMG
Att: Human Resources Manager
905 King Street West, Suite 500
Toronto, ON M6K 3G9

Tel. 416-778-4545
Fax 416-263-6303
Email .... careers@interactivemedia.com
Website .... www.interactivemedia.com
Employer Background: IMG provides user-friendly telephony applications and multimedia web applications. *New Positions Created (9):* HTML Developer; Web Customer Service Team Associate; Desktop Network Support Position; Infrastructure Integrator; Interactive Voice Response Developer; Java Developer; Network Voice Administrator; Senior Web Developer; Technical Specialist, NOC.

INTERALIA INC.
Att: Personnel Director
4110 - 79th Street NW
Calgary, AB T3B 5C2

Tel. 403-288-2706
Fax 403-288-5935
Email .... eng_personnel@interalia.ca
Website .... www.interalia.com
Employer Background: Interalia Inc. is a leading manufacturer of digital voice announcement and call processing equipment. *New Positions Created (3):* Hardware Designer; Technical Support Representative; Product Manager.

INTERAUTOMATION INC.
Att: Human Resources Manager
1115 North Service Road West
Oakville, ON L6M 1N1

Tel. 905-827-7755
Fax 905-827-8162
Email .... jobs@iainc.com
Website .... www.iainc.com
Employer Background: Interautomation Inc. designs and develops automated test systems for automotive companies in North America and Europe. *New Positions Created (5):* Facility Design Engineer; Project Engineers; C++ / Windows Developer; Development Engineers; Service and Installation Engineers / Technologists.

INTERCON SECURITY LTD.
Att: Recruiting Department
40 Sheppard Avenue West, 3rd Floor
Toronto, ON M2N 6K9

Tel. 416-227-4695

Fax 416-229-1207
Email ... recruiting@interconsecurity.com
Website .... www.interconsecurity.com
Employer Background: Intercon Security Ltd. is one of Canada's leading security service providers. *New Positions Created (2):* Installation Technician; Security Officers.

INTERCONTINENTAL MEDICAL STATISTICS / IMS HEALTH
Att: Michael Rozender
6755 Mississauga Road, Suite 200
Mississauga, ON L5N 7Y2
Tel. 905-816-5000
Fax 905-816-5026
Email .... career@ca.imshealth.com
Website .... www.imshealthcanada.com
Employer Background: IMS Health provides critical data, global intelligence and knowledge-based pharmaceutical solutions to the healthcare community, with offices in over 90 countries worldwide. *New Positions Created (2):* Manager, IT Production Support; Operations / Production Manager.

INTERCORP EXCELLE FOODS INC.
Att: Human Resources Manager
1880 Ormont Drive
Toronto, ON M9L 2V4
Tel. 416-744-2124
Fax 416-744-4369
Website .... www.renees.com
Employer Background: Intercorp Excelle Foods Inc. manufactures Renee's Gourmet salad dressings, A1 Sauce and award-winning private label products. *New Positions Created (2):* Research and Development Technologist; Research and Development Manager.

INTERFAST INC.
Att: Human Resources Manager
6360 Cote de Liesse
St-Laurent, QC H4T 1E3
Tel. 514-738-5959
Fax 514-738-6363
Email .... michaelkunz@interfast.ca
Website .... www.interfast.ca
Employer Background: Interfast Inc. distributes aerospace and high-tech fasteners and other hardware. *New Positions Created (3):* Technical Sales Representative; Technical Representative; Project Manager and Quality Manager.

INTERGEN BIOMANUFACTURING CORPORATION
Att: Human Resources Manager
55 Glen Scarlett Road
Toronto, ON M6N 1P5
Tel. 416-763-3600
Fax 416-763-6666
Website .... www.intergenco.com
Employer Background: Intergen Biomanufacturing Corporation manufactures biochemicals from natural sources. *New Positions Created (5):* Chemical Operators; Industrial Mechanic / Millwright; Maintenance Supervisor; Production Supervisor; Production Supervisor.

INTERHOME FURNITURE
Att: Personnel
8400 Woodbine Avenue
Markham, ON L3R 4N7
Tel. 905-475-0705
Fax 905-475-0576
Email .... interhome@sympatico.ca
Employer Background: Interhome Furniture is an independent furniture retailer. *New Positions Created (6):* Warehouse / Logistics Manager; Controller; Director of Customer Relations; Accounting & Data Entry Clerk; Customer Services Manager; Inventory Clerk.

INTERLINK COMMUNITY CANCER NURSES
Att: Jean E. Jackson, Executive Director
620 University Avenue, Suite 701
Toronto, ON M5G 2C1
Fax 416-599-5972
Employer Background: Interlink Community Cancer Nurses is a non-profit, community agency that enables people with cancer and their families to access care and support during all stages of their illness. *New Positions Created (3):* Independent Practice Oncology / Palliative Nurse Consultant; Palliative Care Nurse Consultants; Nurse Consultant, Oncology.

INTERMAP TECHNOLOGIES
Att: Human Resources
2 Gurdwara Road, Suite 200
Nepean, ON K2E 1A2
Tel. 613-226-5442
Fax 613-226-5529
Email .... hr@intermaptechnologies.com
Website ... www.intermaptechnologies.com
Employer Background: Intermap Technologies is a multi-national company, providing services for all aspects of remote sensing, mapping and other geomatics technologies. *New Positions Created (5):* Research Associate / Applications Scientist; Research Associate / Applications Scientist; Cartographic Technician; Manager, Photogrammetry and Image Services; Photogrammetric Technicians.

INTERNATIONAL ACADEMY OF DESIGN AND TECHNOLOGY / IADT OTTAWA
Att: Human Resources Manager
294 Albert Street
Ottawa, ON K1P 6E6
Tel. 613-236-1550
Fax 613-236-7899
Email .... careers@iadtottawa.com
Website .... www.iadtottawa.com
Employer Background: IADT Ottawa is a leading IT institute, offering career training in computer graphics, multimedia, network engineering and software engineering. *New Positions Created (5):* Faculty Member, Computer Graphics; Faculty Member, Multimedia Web Design; Faculty Member, Networking; Faculty Member, Software Engineering; Admissions Representative.

INTERNATIONAL DATACASTING CORPORATION / IDC
Att: Human Resources
2680 Queensview Drive
Ottawa, ON K2B 8H6
Tel. 613-596-4120
Fax 613-596-2335
Email .... hr@intldata.ca
Website .... www.intldata.ca
Employer Background: IDC is a wireless datacasting company that provides advanced systems and services for the broadband satellite distribution of digital data. *New Positions Created (8):* Digital Hardware Engineer; Projects and Systems Engineer; Real-Time Embedded Linux / Software Designer; Vice-President, Manufacturing; Sales Support Representative; Digital Hardware Engineer; Real Time Software Engineer; RF Hardware Engineer.

INTERNATIONAL DATASHARE CORPORATION / IDC
Att: C. Smith
1223 - 31st Avenue NE
Calgary, AB T2E 7W1
Tel. 403-219-7200
Fax 403-291-3894
Email .... jobs@datashare.net
Website .... www.datashare.net
Employer Background: IDC provides well log digitizing and raster imaging services for the oil & gas industry. *New Positions Created (4):* Internet Developer; Software Quality Assurance / Release Mgr; Visual Basic Programmer; Technical Sales Personnel (2).

INTERNATIONAL DEVELOPMENT RESEARCH CENTRE / IDRC
Att: Human Resources
PO Box 8500
Ottawa, ON K1G 3H9
Tel. 613-236-6163
Fax 613-236-5594
Email .... competitions@idrc.ca
Website .... www.idrc.ca
Employer Background: IDRC is a Crown corporation, generating and applying new knowledge to meet the challenges of international development. *New Positions Created (7):* Network Coordinator; Senior Program Officer; Human Resources Development Officer; Senior Program Officer; Project Coordinator; Research Coordinator; Director, Information and Communication Technologies for Development.

INTERNATIONAL FOREST PRODUCTS LIMITED / INTERFOR
Att: D. Hamilton
1055 Dunsmuir Street
Suite 3500, PO Box 49114, 4 Bentall Centre
Vancouver, BC V7X 1H7
Tel. 604-689-6800
Fax 604-520-8506
Email .... itresumes@interfor.com
Website .... www.interfor.com
Employer Background: INTERFOR is one of western Canada's largest logging and sawmilling companies, producing a diversified range of quality wood products for

sale to world markets. *New Positions Created (4):* Database Support Technician; Senior Systems Engineer; Software Trainer; System Support (Customer Service Representative).

INTERNATIONAL GROUP INC., THE
Att: Human Resources Manager
50 Salome Drive
Toronto, ON M1S 2A8

Fax 416-293-5740
Website .... www.igiwax.com
Employer Background: IGI is a petroleum processing plant, specializing in wax refining and blending. *New Positions Created (5):* QC Lab Technician; Quality Control Manager; Maintenance Millwright; Process Operator; Quality Control Lab Technician.

INTERNATIONAL LANGUAGE SCHOOLS OF CANADA, THE / ILSC
Att: Human Resources
1134 St. Catherine Street West, Suite 310
Montréal, QC H3B 1H4

Fax 514-815-0564
Website .... www.ilsc.ca
Employer Background: ILSC offers a full range of general and specialized programs to help people learn the English language in and out of the classroom. *New Positions Created (3):* Bookkeeper; Homestay Coordinator; Instructors, ESL and FSL.

INTERNATIONAL PLAZA HOTEL & CONFERENCE CENTRE
Att: Human Resources Manager
655 Dixon Road
Toronto, ON M9W 1J4

Tel. 416-244-1711
Fax 416-244-0988
Website .... www.internationalplaza.com
Employer Background: The International Plaza Hotel & Conference Centre has 433 guest rooms, meeting and convention space, and dining and entertainment facilities. *New Positions Created (5):* Executive Assistant; Front Desk Supervisor; Assistant Guest Services Manager ; Guest Service Agent; Purchaser / Receiver.

INTERNATIONAL UTILITY STRUCTURES INC.
Att: Human Resources
777 - 8th Avenue SW, Suite 1800
Calgary, AB T2P 3R5

Tel. 403-269-2350
Fax 403-290-0523
Email .... general@iusi.ca
Website .... www.iusi.ca
Employer Background: International Utility Structures Inc. manufactures metal overhead lighting, power line, traffic and telecommunications support structures. *New Positions Created (2):* Civil Engineer; Civil Engineering Technologist.

INTERTAN, INC. / RADIOSHACK
Att: Laura Yourkin, HR Administrator
PO Box 34000
Barrie, ON L4M 4W5

Tel. 705-728-6242
Fax 705-728-2012
Email .... jobs@radioshackcanada.com
Website .... www.intertan.com
Employer Background: InterTAN, Inc. is an international consumer electronics retailer, operating in Canada as RadioShack. *New Positions Created (2):* Manager, Service Centre; Translator.

INTERVISUAL INC.
Att: Human Resources Manager
1812 - 4th Street SW
Calgary, AB T2S 1W1

Tel. 403-264-9199
Fax 403-264-9225
Email .... careers@intervisual.com
Website .... www.intervisual.com
Employer Background: Intervisual Inc. is a corporate Internet developer, delivering solutions to business leaders worldwide. *New Positions Created (6):* Business Development Manager; Account Manager; Quality Control Specialist; Technical Consultant; Web Application Developer; Website Developer.

INTERWORK TECHNOLOGIES LTD.
Att: Human Resources Department
294 Albert Street, Suite 604
Ottawa, ON K1P 6E6

Tel. 613-238-8835
Fax 613-238-6581
Email .... hr@interwork.com
Website .... www.interwork.com
Employer Background: Interwork Technologies Ltd. is a specialty distributor of e-business connectivity and security solutions. *New Positions Created (2):* Channel Sales Manager; Account Manager, USA.

INTESYS NETWORK COMMUNICATIONS LTD.
Att: Human Resources
931 Progress Avenue, Unit 1
Toronto, ON M1G 3V5

Tel. 416-438-0002
Fax 416-438-3704
Email .... hr@intesys-ncl.com
Website .... www.intesys-ncl.com
Employer Background: INTESYS Network Communications Ltd. provides networked solutions to some of Canada's best-known organizations. *New Positions Created (6):* Account Managers; Senior Network Integration Consultants; Telephony Technicians; Account Managers; Inside Sales Representative; Operations Manager.

INTRAWEST CORPORATION
Att: Human Resources
200 Burrard Street, Suite 800
Vancouver, BC V6C 3L6

Tel. 604-669-9777
Fax 604-669-0605
Email .... immobilier@intrawest.com
Website .... www.intrawest.com
Employer Background: Intrawest Corporation is an operator and developer of mountain and golf resorts in North America. *New Positions Created (10):* Can-Ski Supervisor;

Director of Lodging, Blue Mountain; Director of People; Food and Beverage Administrative Assistant; Marketing Manager; Vice-President, Technology Operations; Web Technical Administrator; Destination Sales Manager; Executive Assistant; Web Administrator.

INTRIA-HP
Att: Human Resources Manager
901 King Street West
Toronto, ON M5V 3H5

Fax 416-980-7948
Email .... careers@intria-hp.com
Website .... www.intria-hp.com
Employer Background: INTRIA-HP (a joint venture between CIBC and Hewlett-Packard) provides transaction-intensive, highly-available and secure e-commerce and m-commerce operation services for the financial, retail and manufacturing industries. *New Positions Created (18):* SAP Specialist; Senior Technical Analyst; Senior Technical Analyst; Team Leader, Security Administration; Client Services Manager; High-Availability Technical Leader; Market Research Analyst; Project Managers (4); Senior Unix Consultant; Senior Unix Architect; HP / UX Technical Specialist; Marketing Analyst; SAP Specialist; Security Analyst; Senior Technical Analyst; Senior Technical Analyst, CA7 / Robot Scheduling; Team Leader, Security Administration; Unix Specialist.

INTRINSYC SOFTWARE INC.
Att: Human Resources Manager
700 West Pender Street, 10th Floor
Vancouver, BC V6C 1G8

Tel. 604-801-6461
Fax 604-801-6417
Email .... hr@intrinsyc.com
Website .... www.intrinsyc.com
Employer Background: Intrinsyc Software Inc. develops solutions that allow customers to create, link and manage pervasive networks of servers, computers and devices. *New Positions Created (12):* Embedded Software Developer; Intermediate Software Developer; Senior Account Executive, J-Integra; Senior Software Developer, Enterprise Software; Senior Software Engineer; Customer Support Manager; Embedded Software Developer; Intermediate Software Developer; Senior Account Executive; Senior Hardware Design Engineer; Technical Support, Enterprise Software; Customer Service Engineer.

INTUIT CANADA LIMITED
Att: Human Resources
7008 Roper Road
Edmonton, AB T6B 3H2

Tel. 780-466-9996
Fax 780-450-5885
Email .... canada_resumes@intuit.com
Website .... www.intuit.com/canada
Employer Background: Intuit Canada Limited is Canada's leading developer of personal and small business accounting and tax return software. *New Positions Created (11):* Senior Database Analyst; Senior Unix Sys-

tems Analyst; Telecom Analyst; Accounting Mgr; Financial Planning Mgr; Brand Mgrs; Business Development Specialist; Business Unit Mgr; Retail Services Manager; Software Developer; Telecommunications Analyst.

INTUIT GREENPOINT
Att: Jobs
138 - 4th Street SE, Suite 400
Calgary, AB T2G 4Z6
Tel. 403-205-4848
Fax 403-265-0304
Email .... jobs@greenpointsoftware.com
Website ..... www.greenpointsoftware.com
Employer Background: Founded in 1995, Intuit GreenPoint (formerly GreenPoint Software) develops and markets the ProFile financial application suite for Microsoft Windows. *New Positions Created (14):* Direct Sales and Service Team Leader; Intermediate Software Developer; Tax Analyst; Bilingual Communications Specialist; Bilingual Tax Analyst and Quality Assurance Position; Bilingual Communications Specialist; Bilingual Junior Tax Software Developer; Financial Planning Software Support Provider; Order Entry / Fulfillment Officer; Software Support Provider; Tax and Quality Assurance Analyst; Tax Software Support Provider; Technical Quality Assurance Analyst; Technical Software Support Provider.

INUIT TAPIRISAT OF CANADA / ITC
Att: Chief Operating Officer
170 Laurier Avenue West, Suite 510
Ottawa, ON K1P 5V5
Tel. 613-238-8181
Fax 613-234-1991
Website .... www.tapirisat.ca
Employer Background: ITC is a national, non-profit organization representing the interests of Inuit people in Canada. *New Positions Created (2):* Senior Policy Advisor, Federal Relations; Sr Policy Coordinator.

INUULITSIVIK HEALTH CENTRE
Att: Luc Larouche, Personnel Department
Puvirnituq, QC J0M 1P0
Tel. 819-988-2957
Fax 819-988-2796
Email .... luc.larouche@irc.inuulitsivik.ca
Employer Background: The Inuulitsivik Health Centre provides health and social services to the Inuit population living in 7 villages along the eastern shore of the Hudson Bay. *New Positions Created (3):* Professional Social Worker; Various Healthcare Positions; Pharmacist.

INUVIALUIT CORPORATE GROUP
Att: Ms Otti T. de Kock,
Human Resources Advisor
PO Box 2120
Inuvik, NT X0E 0T0
Tel. 867-777-2737
Fax 867-777-2135
Email .... odekock@irc.inuvialuit.com
Website .... www.inuvialuit.com
Employer Background: Inuvialuit Corporate Group is the parent corporation established by the Inuvialuit Final Agreement (1984) between the Inuvialuit of the western Canadian arctic and the Government of Canada. *New Positions Created (2):* Business Development Officer; Community Economic Development Manager.

INVESTMENT DEALERS ASSOCIATION OF CANADA / IDA
Att: Melissa Smith, Human Resources
650 West Georgia Street, Suite 1325
Vancouver, BC V6B 4N9
Tel. 604-683-6222
Fax 416-943-6766
Email .... msmith@ida.ca
Website .... www.ida.ca
Employer Background: IDA is the national self-regulatory organization and trade association for the Canadian securities industry. *New Positions Created (6):* Regional Director; Enforcement Counsel; Examiner; Sales Compliance Officers; Registration Officer; Investigator.

INVESTMENT DEALERS ASSOCIATION OF CANADA / IDA
Att: Alison Bricker, Human Resources
355 - 4th Avenue SW, Suite 2300
Calgary, AB T2P 0J1
Tel. 403-262-6393
Fax 416-943-6766
Email .... abricker@ida.ca
Website .... www.ida.ca
Employer Background: IDA is the national self-regulatory organization and trade association for the Canadian securities industry. *New Positions Created (3):* Sales Compliance Manager; Sales Compliance Officer; Registration Officer.

INVESTMENT DEALERS ASSOCIATION OF CANADA / IDA
Att: Human Resources
121 King Street West, Suite 1600
Toronto, ON M5H 3T9
Tel. 416-364-6133
Fax 416-943-6766
Email .... humanresources@ida.ca
Website .... www.ida.ca
Employer Background: IDA is the national self-regulatory organization and trade association for the Canadian securities industry. *New Positions Created (15):* Capital Markets Director; Director, Enforcement Litigation; Investigator; Manager, Complaint Inquiries; Public Affairs Specialist; Enforcement Counsel; Director, Sales Compliance; Public Affairs Specialist; Complaint Inquiries Officer; Enforcement Counsel; Financial Compliance Examiners; Investigators; Sales Compliance Officers; Registration Counsel; Legal and Policy Counsel.

INVESTORS GROUP
Att: Human Resources Department
447 Portage Avenue, One Canada Centre
Winnipeg, MB R3C 3B6
Tel. 204-956-8359
Fax 204-942-0967
Email .... careers@investorsgroup.com
Website .... www.investorsgroup.com
Employer Background: Investors Group is one of the leading financial services companies in Canada. *New Positions Created (4):* Area Manager, Ontario East; Insurance Manager; Director, Practice Management; Insurance Sales Manager.

IPC RESISTORS INC.
Att: Human Resources
7615 Kimbel Street, Unit 1
Mississauga, ON L5S 1A8
Tel. 905-673-1553
Fax 905-673-7326
Email .... careers@ipc-resistors.com
Website .... www.ipc-resistors.com
Employer Background: IPC Resistors Inc. manufactures quality power resistors. *New Positions Created (9):* Application Engineer; General Accountant; Materials Coordinator; Regional Sales Representative, Mexico; Vice-President, Engineering; Accountant; Administrative Assistant; Application Engineer; Vice-President of Engineering.

IPSCO INC.
Att: Personnel Department
PO Box 1670
Regina, SK S4P 3C7
Tel. 306-924-7700
Website .... www.ipsco.com
Employer Background: IPSCO Inc. operates steelmaking, coil processing and tubular products facilities in Canada and the USA. *New Positions Created (12):* Research Engineer; Electrician; Millwrights; Assistant Credit Manager; Credit Manager; Mechanical Technologists; Electrical Engineer; Research Engineer; Senior Electrical Engineer; Product Development Engineer; Research Engineer; Senior Electrical Engineer.

IR SECURITY & SAFETY
Att: Human Resources Administrator
1076 Lakeshore Road East
Mississauga, ON L5E 1E4
Tel. 905-278-6128
Fax 905-278-3258
Website ...... www.irsecurityandsafety.com
Employer Background: IR Security & Safety, a sector of Ingersoll-Rand, is a leading manufacturer of door hardware and electronic access control systems. *New Positions Created (6):* Buyer / Planner; Accounting Manager; Credit Mgr; Manufacturing Engineer; Quote Administrator; Salesperson.

IRIS POWER ENGINEERING INC.
Att: Human Resources Manager
1 Westside Drive, Unit 2
Toronto, ON M9C 1B2
Tel. 416-620-5600
Fax 416-620-1995
Email .... admin@irispower.com
Website .... www.irispower.com
Employer Background: Iris Power Engineering Inc. manufactures sensors, electronic instruments and software to monitor the condition of large motors and generators.

New Positions Created (2): Field Service Technicians; Sales Engineers / Specialists.

IRON ORE COMPANY OF CANADA
Att: Human Resources Manager
PO Box 1000
Sept-Iles, QC G4R 4L5

Tel. 418-986-7655
Fax 418-968-7109
Email .... rh@ironore.ca
Website .... www.ironore.ca

Employer Background: Established in 1954, IOC is a leading supplier of quality pellets to the world's steel industry. *New Positions Created (3):* Operations Facilitator and Maintenance Facilitator; Process Manager; Union Maintenance Facilitator.

IRVIN AEROSPACE CANADA LTD.
Att: Human Resources Manager
479 Central Avenue, PO Box 280
Fort Erie, ON L2A 5M9

Tel. 905-871-6510
Fax 905-871-6534

Employer Background: Irvin Aerospace Canada Ltd. is a Six Sigma company, specializing in the defence business. *New Positions Created (3):* Programme Director, NBC; Vice-President, Business Development; Program Director.

IRWIN PUBLISHING LTD.
Att: Manager, Human Resources
325 Humber College Boulevard
Toronto, ON M9W 7C3

Tel. 416-798-0424
Fax 416-445-5967
Website .... www.irwin-pub.com

Employer Background: Established in 1945, Irwin Publishing Ltd. is a Canadian educational book publisher. *New Positions Created (3):* Marketing Manager; Manager, Client Services; Publishers' Coordinator.

IRWIN TOY LIMITED
Att: Lisa Duarte, HR Coordinator
43 Hanna Street
Toronto, ON M6K 1X6

Tel. 416-533-3521
Fax 416-583-4578
Email .... lisa.duarte@irwintoy.com
Website .... www.irwintoy.com

Employer Background: Irwin Toy Limited is a major Canadian manufacturer and distributor of toys and sporting goods. *New Positions Created (4):* Product Development Manager; Sales Representative; Junior / Intermediate Sales Rep; Marketing Position.

IS2 RESEARCH INC.
Att: Human Resources Manager
20 Gurdwara Road, Bay 3-6
Nepean, ON K2E 8B3

Tel. 613-228-8755
Fax 613-228-8228
Email .... vwoodburn@is2research.com
Website www.is2research.com

Employer Background: IS2 Research Inc. specializes in medical imaging used to di-

agnose heart disease and cancer. *New Positions Created (6):* Electronics Technologists; Draftsperson / Mechanical Engineer; Software Engineers; Software Engineers; Service Technician / Regional Service Manager; Software Engineers.

ISB GROUP
Att: Human Resources Manager
2300 Victoria Avenue
Lachine, QC H8S 1Z3

Tel. 514-634-7000
Fax 514-637-4917
Website .... www.isblite.com

Employer Background: Founded in 1972, ISB Group is a multi-division company, specializing in industrial automation and custom lighting fixtures. *New Positions Created (2):* Sales Manager; Salesperson.

ISH ENERGY LTD.
Att: Controller
400 - 3rd Ave. SW, 2450 Canterra Tower
Calgary, AB T2P 4H2

Email .... ish@cadvision.com

Employer Background: ISH Energy Ltd. is a private oil and gas exploration and development company. *New Positions Created (4):* Intermediate Joint Venture Accountant; Intermediate Production Revenue Accountant; Senior Production Revenue Accountant; Controller.

ISLAND KEY COMPUTER LTD. / IKCL
Att: Human Resources Manager
938 Howe Street, Suite 211
Vancouver, BC V6Z 1N9

Tel. 604-669-8178
Fax 604-669-8179
Email .... admin@islandkey.com
Website .... www.islandkey.com

Employer Background: Founded in 1989, IKCL is a value-added reseller of HP, Lexmark, Compaq, NEC, IBM and Autodesk computers. *New Positions Created (4):* Account Executive; Technical Specialist; Inside Sales Rep; Technical Support Technician.

ISLANDS TRUST
Att: Daphne Armstrong
1627 Fort Street, Suite 200
Victoria, BC V8R 1H8

Tel. 250-405-5153
Fax 250-405-5155
Website .... www.islandstrust.bc.ca

Employer Background: Created in 1974, the Islands Trust is a non-profit agency that aims to preserve the beauty, tranquility and unique natural environment of islands in the Strait of Georgia and Howe Sound. *New Positions Created (6):* Regional Planning Coordinator; Communications / Fundraising Specialist; Geographic Information System Coordinator; Regional Planning Coordinator; Planner 2; Mgr, Trust Area Services.

IT CAREER ACCESS OFFICE, BC
Att: Human Resources
4000 Seymour Place, Suite E126
Victoria, BC V8W 9V1

Tel. 250-356-0477
Website .... www.itcareers.gov.bc.ca

Employer Background: ITCAO fills IT employment vacancies in the government of British Columbia. *New Positions Created (43):* Client Manager; Head, Regional Systems; Senior Security Planner; Senior Systems Programmer; Data Analyst; Client Adviser / Project Manager; Senior Programmer Analyst; Senior Electronic Document Management Architect; Senior Programmer Analysts (2); Senior LAN Specialist; Client Support Analyst; Intermediate Communications Specialist; Programmer / Analyst; Project Implementation Analyst; Business Analyst; NT Network Analyst; Client Support Analyst; Corporate Systems Analyst; Junior Programmer Analyst; Senior Project Manager; Technical Analyst; Business Analyst; Systems Trainer; Aggregate Data Administrator; Database Administrator; Electronic Service Delivery Planner; Senior Programmer Analyst; Senior Security Planner; Client Support Analyst; Intermediate Network Support Analysts (2); Technical Analyst; Application Programmer / Analyst; Manager, Information Systems; Aggregate Data Administrator; Client Support Analyst; Data Warehouse Administrator; Database Programmer; Information Systems Analyst; Security Architect; Senior Application Architect; Senior Business Consultants (2); Technology Infrastructure Coordinator; Tier 2 Technical Support Analyst.

IT / NET CONSULTANTS INC.
Att: Human Resources
330 Bay Street, Suite 612
Toronto, ON M5H 2S8

Fax 416-367-8185
Email .... hrtoronto@itnet.ca
Website .... www.itnet.ca

Employer Background: IT / Net Consultants Inc. is a management consulting firm, providing services in all aspects of information management and technology. *New Positions Created (3):* Managing Director; PeopleSoft Positions; SAP Professionals.

IT / NET CONSULTANTS INC.
Att: Human Resources
116 Albert Street, Suite 303
Ottawa, ON K1P 5G3

Tel. 613-234-8638
Fax 613-234-3323
Email .... jobs@itnet.ca
Website .... www.itnet.ca

Employer Background: IT / Net Consultants Inc. is a management consulting firm, providing services in all aspects of information management and technology. *New Positions Created (12):* Bilingual Technical Writers, SAP; Data Analyst; Database Team Leader; DND Practice Leader; Junior & Senior Level Trainers / Coaches, SAP; Management Consulting Practice Leader; SAP - BASIS Consultant; Senior Analyst / Programmer; Senior Data Analyst; Technical Editor; Technical Writer; Windows 2000 Rollout Script Writers.

IT WORLD CANADA
Att: Sonia Singh, HR Manager
55 Town Centre Court, Suite 302
Toronto, ON M1P 4X4
Tel. 416-290-0240
Fax 416-290-0238
Email .... ssingh@itworldcanada.com
Website .... www.itworldcanada.com
Employer Background: IT World Canada is
the Canadian affiliate of International Data
Group (IDG), the world's largest IT informa-
tion provider. IDG publishes over 285 pub-
lications worldwide. *New Positions Created
(2):* Journalists; Sales Representatives.

ITR LABORATORIES CANADA INC.
Att: Human Resources
19601 Clark Graham
Baie d'Urfe, QC H9X 3T1
Tel. 514-457-7400
Fax 514-457-7303
Email .... human_resources@itrlab.com
Website .... www.itrlab.com
Employer Background: ITR Laboratories
Canada Inc. is a contract research laboratory,
performing pre-clinical safety and pharma-
cology evaluations for the pharmaceutical
and biotechnology industries. *New Positions
Created (8):* Clinical Pathology Supervisor;
Director of Pathology; Quality Assurance
Inspector; Technicians; Veterinary Patholo-
gist; Assistant Study Directors; Business
Development Account Managers; Study Di-
rectors.

ITT FLUID PRODUCTS CANADA
Att: Iain Stevenson, Western Manager
19770 - 94A Avenue, C101
Langley, BC V1M 3B7
Tel. 604-513-2330
Fax 604-513-2331
Email .... resume-fpc@fluids.ittind.com
Website .... www.ittfpc.ca
Employer Background: ITT Fluid Products
Canada manufactures and distributes
pumps, heat transfer equipment and fire
protection systems. *New Positions Created
(2):* Marine Sales & Marketing Representa-
tive; Sales & Marketing Representative.

ITT FLUID PRODUCTS CANADA
Att: Bonita Smith, HR Manager
55 Royal Road
Guelph, ON N1H 1T1
Tel. 519-821-1900
Fax 519-821-5316
Email .... resume-fpc@fluids.ittind.com
Website .... www.ittfpc.ca
Employer Background: ITT Fluid Products
Canada manufactures and distributes
pumps, heat transfer equipment and fire
protection systems. *New Positions Created
(2):* Application Engineering Specialist;
Sales Representatives.

ITW CONSTRUCTION PRODUCTS
Att: Human Resources Department
225 Nantucket Boulevard
Toronto, ON M1P 2P2
Tel. 416-750-0557

Fax 416-750-9601
Email .... bhenry@itwconstruction.com
Website .... www.itwconstruction.com
Employer Background: ITW Construction
Products, a subsidiary of Illinois Tool Works,
Inc., is a leading supplier of fastening and
industrial tool products to the construction
and industrial sectors. *New Positions Cre-
ated (2):* Retail Marketing Coordinator; Cus-
tomer Service Representatives.

IVANHOE CAMBRIDGE
Att: Human Resources Manager
95 Wellington Street, Suite 300
Toronto, ON M5J 2R2
Tel. 416-369-1200
Email .... hr@ivanhoecambridge.com
Website ...... www.ivanhoecambridge.com
Employer Background: Ivanhoe Cambridge
(formerly Cambridge Shopping Centres
Limited) is a real estate management, de-
velopment and investment company that
specializes in urban shopping centre prop-
erties. *New Positions Created (8):* Coordina-
tor, Collections & Property Administration;
Senior Collections Administrator; Accounts
Receivable / Collections Clerk; Financial
Analyst; Manager, Property Administration;
Senior Property Accountant; Manager,
Specialty Leasing; Operations Manager.

IVANHOE CAMBRIDGE
Att: Human Resources
413 St. Jacques Street, 7th Floor
Montréal, QC H2Y 3Z4
Tel. 514-841-7600
Fax 514-841-7795
Email .. slaporte@ivanhoecambridge.com
Website ...... www.ivanhoecambridge.com
Employer Background: Ivanhoe Cambridge
(formerly Cambridge Shopping Centres
Limited) is a real estate management, de-
velopment and investment company that
specializes in urban shopping centre prop-
erties. *New Positions Created (3):* Compensation Analyst; Senior Accountant, Joint Ventures; Director, Asset Management.

IVL TECHNOLOGIES LTD.
Att: Human Resources
6710 Bertram Place
Victoria, BC V8M 1Z6
Tel. 250-544-4091
Fax 250-544-4108
Email .... jobs@ivl.com
Website .... www.ivl.com
Employer Background: IVL Technologies
Ltd. designs and manufactures innovative
audio signal processing technology for the
worldwide music recording and entertain-
ment industries. *New Positions Created (12):*
Buyer, Technical; Japanese-Language Prod-
uct Manager, Commercial Applications;
Software Designer; Intermediate Project
Manager; Human Resources Manager; DSP
Engineer; Hardware Engineers; Product
Manager, Commercial Applications; Research Engineers; Senior DSP Audio Engineer; Software Designer; Software Engineers.

J & D SYSTEMS INC.
Att: June Williams
PO Box 1506, Station C
Kitchener, ON N2G 4P2
Tel. 519-748-1177
Fax 519-748-9502
Email .... careers@jdsystems.ca
Website .... www.jdsystems.ca
Employer Background: J & D Systems Inc. is
a leader in integrated voice and data solu-
tions. *New Positions Created (2):* Sales Pro-
fessionals; Receptionist / Administrator.

J & J DISPLAY SALES LTD.
Att: Rob Patten
2455 Meadowvale Boulevard
Mississauga, ON L5N 5S2
Tel. 905-814-5252
Fax 905-814-8147
Employer Background: J & J Display Sales
Ltd. is a store fixture company. *New Posi-
tions Created (3):* Cabinet Maker; Customer
Service Representative; Accounting Man-
ager.

J & S REFRIGERATION LTD.
Att: Human Resources Manager
PO Box 1177
St. Catharines, ON L2R 7A7
Fax 905-684-3919
Email .... jands@vaxxine.com
Website ..... www.jandsheatingandair.com
Employer Background: J & S Refrigeration
Ltd. installs, maintains and services heating,
air conditioning and refrigeration equip-
ment and systems. *New Positions Created
(2):* Air Conditioning, Heating, Refrigeration
Service Mechanic; Residential Installers of
Retrofit Heating and Air Conditioning.

J.S. WATSON & ASSOCIATES LTD.
Att: Paul Foster
50 Acadia Avenue, Suite 207
Markham, ON L3R 0B3
Fax 416-491-7500
Employer Background: J.S. Watson & Asso-
ciates Ltd. is an established project and con-
struction management firm. *New Positions
Created (3):* Senior Construction Managers
/ Superintendents; Senior Estimator / Cost
Consultant; Construction Supervisors.

J. WALTER COMPANY LTD.
Att: Nancy Thiboutot
5977 Trans Canada Highway
Pointe-Claire, QC H9R 1C1
Tel. 514-630-2801
Fax 514-630-2828
Email .... nthiboutot@jwalter.ca
Website .... www.jwalter.ca
Employer Background: J. Walter Company
Ltd. is one of the largest suppliers of indus-
trial abrasives, tools and chemicals in
Canada, with operations in the USA, South
America and Europe. *New Positions Created
(4):* Chemical Engineer; Graphic Artist; In-
dustrial Sales Positions (2); Marketing Co-
ordinator.

JACKMAN MANOR
Att: Dan Levitt, Administrator
27477 - 28th Avenue
Aldergrove, BC V4W 3L9

Fax 604-856-2562
Email .... danlevitt@rocketmail.com

Employer Background: Jackman Manor provides intermediate care to 87 residents, including a 22-bed special care unit. *New Positions Created (2):* Director of Resident Services; Business Manager.

JACQUES WHITFORD ENVIRONMENT LTD.
Att: Human Resources
3771 North Fraser Way, Unit 1
Burnaby, BC V5J 5G5

Fax 604-436-3014
Email ... kmackinn@jacqueswhitford.com
Website .... www.jacqueswhitford.com

Employer Background: Incorporated in 1972, Jacques Whitford Environment Ltd. is a consulting engineering firm, specializing in environmental, geotechnical and risk management services. *New Positions Created (16):* Project Manager, Real Estate Services; Accounting Clerk; Environmental Management Systems Consultant; Group Manager, Real Estate Services; Intermediate Administrative Assistant; Intermediate Aquatic Biologist; Intermediate Environmental Engineer; Junior Environmental Engineers; Manager, Geotechnical Division; Project Manager, Hazardous Materials; Senior Environmental Assessment Biologist; Senior Risk Assessor; Accounting Manager; Environmental Management Consultant; Hazardous Materials Group Manager; LAN Administrator.

JACQUES WHITFORD ENVIRONMENT LTD.
Att: Human Resources
703 - 6th Avenue SW, Suite 500
Calgary, AB T2P 2X6

Tel. 403-263-7113
Fax 403-263-7116
Email ..... kmerrick@jacqueswhitford.com
Website .... www.jacqueswhitford.com

Employer Background: Incorporated in 1972, Jacques Whitford Environment Ltd. is a consulting engineering firm, specializing in environmental, geotechnical and risk management services. *New Positions Created (12):* Terrestrial Biologist; Secretary / File Clerk; Draftsperson; Accounting Clerk; Environmental Consultant; Geotechnical & Materials Consultant; Junior / Intermediate Air Quality Scientists; Senior and Intermediate Geotechnical Engineers; Senior Engineer, Mining / Geoenvironmental; Senior Risk Assessor; Senior Geotechnical Engineer; Air Quality Scientist.

JACQUES WHITFORD ENVIRONMENT LTD.
Att: Human Resources
1200 Denison Street
Markham, ON L3R 8G6

Tel. 905-495-8614
Fax 905-479-9326

Website .... www.jacqueswhitford.com
Employer Background: Incorporated in 1972, Jacques Whitford Environment Ltd. is a consulting engineering firm, specializing in environmental, geotechnical and risk management services. *New Positions Created (8):* Air Quality Positions; Intermediate Environmental Professional; Intermediate Geotechnical Engineer; Petroleum Engineer; Project Manager, Real Estate Services; Senior Geotechnical Engineer / Manager; Executive Assistant; Engineers / Scientists.

JACQUES WHITFORD ENVIRONMENT LTD.
Att: Bruce Fraser
2781 Lancaster Road, Suite 200
Ottawa, ON K1B 1A7

Tel. 613-738-0708
Fax 613-738-0721
Email .... bfraser@jacqueswhitford.com
Website .... www.jacqueswhitford.com

Employer Background: Incorporated in 1972, Jacques Whitford Environment Ltd. is a consulting engineering firm, specializing in environmental, geotechnical and risk management services. *New Positions Created (14):* Intermediate Mechanical Engineer; Asphalt / Aggregate Laboratory Technologist / Technician; Hazardous Materials Consultant; Project Manager, Real Estate Services; Senior Hydrogeologist / Project Manager; Site Inspection & Testing Technologist / Technician, Building Sciences & Materials (2); Engineers / Scientists; Geotechnical / Pavement Technologist / Technician; Intermediate Materials Engineer; Pavement Design / Geotechnical Engineer; Asphalt / Aggregate Laboratory Technologist; Environmental Field Technicians; Environmental Scientist; Site Inspection and Testing Technologists (2).

JACQUES WHITFORD ENVIRONMENT LTD.
Att: Human Resources Manager
711 Woodstock Road, PO Box 1116
Fredericton, NB E3B 5C2

Fax 506-452-7652
Website .... www.jacqueswhitford.com

Employer Background: Incorporated in 1972, Jacques Whitford Environment Ltd. is a consulting engineering firm, specializing in environmental, geotechnical and risk management services. *New Positions Created (4):* Air Quality Consultant; Drafting Technician; Environmental Engineer; Hydrogeologist.

JACQUES WHITFORD ENVIRONMENT LTD.
Att: Human Resources
3 Spectacle Lake Drive
Halifax, NS B3B 1W8

Tel. 902-468-7777
Fax 902-468-0407
Email .... hr@jacqueswhitford.com
Website .... www.jacqueswhitford.com

Employer Background: Incorporated in 1972, Jacques Whitford Environment Ltd. is

a consulting engineering firm, specializing in environmental, geotechnical and risk management services. *New Positions Created (10):* Marine / Aquatic Biologist; Executive Assistant to the President; Environmental Analyst; Corporate Controller; Environmental Engineering / Risk Assessment Position; Field Technicians (2); Manager of Environmental Engineering; Manager, Project Scheduling / Cost Control; Project Manager, Real Estate Services; Senior Geotechnical Engineer.

JAMIESON LABORATORIES LTD.
Att: Marketing Manager
12 St. Clair Avenue East
PO Box 69038, St. Clair Centre
Toronto, ON M4T 3A1

Tel. 416-960-0052
Fax 416-960-4803
Email .... hr@jamiesonvitamins.com
Website .... www.jamiesonvitamins.com

Employer Background: Jamieson Laboratories Ltd. is a leader in the vitamin and herbal products marketplace. *New Positions Created (3):* International Sales Coordinator; Forecaster / Analyst; Forecaster / Analyst.

JANES FAMILY FOODS LTD.
Att: Human Resources
401 Canarctic Drive
Toronto, ON M3J 2P9

Tel. 416-665-1492
Fax 416-665-2401
Website .... www.janesfamilyfoods.com

Employer Background: Janes Family Foods Ltd. manufactures premium frozen boxed meats. *New Positions Created (7):* Production Supervisor; QA Manager; QA Technicians; Accounts Payable Coordinator; Sales Representative; Accounts Receivable Supervisor; Production Supervisor.

JARATECH BUSINESS SOLUTIONS CORP.
Att: Human Resources Director
633 - 6th Avenue SW, Suite 610
Calgary, AB T2P 2Y5

Tel. 403-269-9275
Email .... hrdept@jaratech.com
Website .... www.jaratech.com

Employer Background: Jaratech Business Solutions Corp. offers information technology solutions, ranging from network support and systems consulting to client-server and Internet applications development. *New Positions Created (4):* Ada Developers; ASP / VB / SQL Developer; Windows NT / 95 Technical Support Rep; IT Professionals.

JAYGUR INTERNATIONAL INC.
Att: Human Resources Department
8965 St. Laurent
St-Laurent, QC H2N 1M5

Tel. 514-384-3872
Fax 514-384-8260
Email .... hrjaygur@jaygur.com
Website .... www.jaygur.com

Employer Background: JayGur International Inc. is a leading North American manufacturer and importer of jeans, sportswear, active wear, accessories and handbags. *New Positions Created (16):* Production Assistant; Administrative Assistant; Customer Service / Order Entry Clerk; Junior Style Number Editor; Executive Admin Assistant; Junior Size Spec Technician; Retail Analyst; Sample Maker; Administrative Assistant; Designer / Merchandiser; Fit Technician; Pattern Maker; Sketch Artist; Graphic Designer; Production Assistant; Graphic Artist.

JAYMAN MASTER BUILDER
Att: Harvey Stein, COO
10476 Mayfield Road
Edmonton, AB T5P 4P4
Tel. 780-481-6666
Fax 780-481-7711
Website .... www.jayman.com
Employer Background: Jayman Master Builder is a leader in the home building industry. *New Positions Created (4):* Service Representative; New Home Estimator; Sales and Marketing Manager; Area Manager, New Home Sales.

JAYMAN MASTER BUILDER
Att: Design Manager
9705 Horton Road SW, Suite A203
Calgary, AB T2V 2X5
Tel. 403-258-3772
Fax 403-253-3576
Website .... www.jayman.com
Employer Background: Jayman Master Builder is a leader in the home building industry. *New Positions Created (6):* Intermediate Architectural Drafter; Superintendent, Multi-Family; Project Manager, Multi-Family; Senior New Home Estimator; New Home Estimator; Area Service Manager.

JAYNE INDUSTRIES INC.
Att: Human Resources Administrator
550 Seaman Street
Stoney Creek, ON L8E 3X7
Tel. 905-643-9200
Fax 905-662-1478
Website .... www.jayneindustries.com
Employer Background: Jayne Industries Inc. manufactures refractory hardware and metal products. *New Positions Created (2):* Accountant; Fitter / Welder.

JAZZ MONKEY MEDIA
Att: Human Resources Manager
366 Bay Street, 11th Floor
Toronto, ON M5H 4B2
Tel. 416-815-1771
Fax 416-815-0044
Email .... jobs@jazzmonkey.com
Website .... www.jazzmonkey.com
Employer Background: Jazz Monkey Media specializes in web marketing solutions. *New Positions Created (4):* UNIX / Linux System Administrator; Vice-President, Sales and Marketing; Internet Software Developer; Comptroller.

JDS UNIPHASE CORPORATION
Att: Human Resources

2261 Keating Cross Road, Gateway Park
Saanichton, BC V8M 2A5
Tel. 250-544-2244
Fax 250-544-0758
Email .... hroptics@sdli.com
Website .... www.sdli.com
Employer Background: This location of JDS Uniphase (formerly SDL Optics Inc.) designs and markets fibre optic products for the telecommunications industry. *New Positions Created (24):* MIS Administrator, Manufacturing; Production Supervisor; Trainer, Production; Development Engineers; Equipment Engineers; Facility Mechanical Engineer; Process Development Technicians; Process Engineers; Process Support Technicians; Product Engineers; Quality Engineers; Supplier Quality Engineer; Manager, Compensation and Benefits; Manager, Training; Database Administrator; Industrial Engineer; Manufacturing Manager; Product Support Engineers; Production Control Manager; Project Engineers; Quality Engineers; Manufacturing Assembly Operators; Human Resources Advisors; Recruitment Coordinator.

JDS UNIPHASE CORPORATION
Att: Human Resources Department
570 West Hunt Club
Nepean, ON K2G 5W8
Tel. 613-727-1303
Fax 613-727-3587
Email .... inquiryfpg@ca.jdsuniphase.com
Website .... www.jdsuniphase.com
Employer Background: JDS Uniphase Corporation designs, develops, manufactures and distributes a range of products for the fibre optic communications market. *New Positions Created (34):* Lead Software Architect; Senior Intellectual Property Counsel; Account Manager; Business Systems Analyst, IT; First Aid Coordinator; Global Commodity Manager, Optoelectronic Components; Global Commodity Manager, Optoelectronic Packaging; OA Process Engineer; OA Product Engineer; Optical Designer, Component Switches; Planner; Product Development Engineer; Product Line Manager; Project Manager, IT; R&D Buyer; Senior Business Analyst; Firmware Developers; Material Planner; Mechanical Designers; Optical Design Engineer; Optical Designers; Quality Assurance Process Engineer; Quality Assurance Product Engineer; Research and Development Buyer; Technical Marketing Manager; Corporate Counsel; Process Engineer; Process Engineers; Product Line Manager; Project Coordinator; Quality Engineer; Reliability Engineering Group Leader; Technicians and Technologists; Various Engineering Positions.

JDS UNIPHASE CORPORATION, FIBER-OPTIC PRODUCTS GROUP
Att: Human Resources Manager
2770 - 14th Avenue
Markham, ON L3R 0J1
Tel. 905-946-1336
Fax 905-946-0190
Email .... toronto.resumes@
.... ca.jdsuniphase.com

Website .... www.jdsuniphase.com
Employer Background: This location of JDS Uniphase Corporation (formerly E-TEK ElectroPhotonics Solutions Corp.) specializes in fibre optic components for high-capacity telecommunications networks and fibre optic test equipment. *New Positions Created (17):* Application Engineer; Test Engineer; Application Engineer; Electrical Engineering Technologist; Electronics Engineer; Mechanical Engineer; Optical Engineer, Fiber Grating Technologies; Optical Engineer, Instruments; Quality Control Inspector; Quality Engineer; Software Test Engineer; Grating Production Engineers; Materials Manager; Mechanical Engineer; Process Engineers; Purchasing Associate; Quality Control Inspector.

JEWELSTONE SYSTEMS INC. / JSI
Att: Human Resources
100 King Street West
Suite 2900, 1 First Canadian Place
Toronto, ON M5X 1C8
Tel. 416-364-5800
Fax 416-364-6674
Email .... jobs@jewelstonesystems.com
Website .... www.jewelstonesystems.com
Employer Background: JSI is a leading Canadian software company, providing recordkeeping systems for the investment industry. *New Positions Created (13):* Intermediate Powerhouse Developers; Senior Powerhouse Developers; Manager, Information Services; Business Analysts; Developers; Intermediate Developers; Project Leader; Project Mgr; Relationship Manager; Sales Support Analyst; Senior Developer; User Acceptance Testers; User Support Analysts.

JEWISH COMMUNITY CENTRE OF GREATER VANCOUVER / JCC
Att: Chair, Search Committee
950 - 41st Avenue West, Suite 200
Vancouver, BC V5Z 2N7
Tel. 604-257-5111
Fax 604-257-5110
Website .... www.jfgv.com
Employer Background: JCC provides a full range of recreational, cultural, educational and social programs. *New Positions Created (5):* Executive Director; Assistant Executive Director; Program Director; Lead Hand; Janitorial / Maintenance; Administrative Assistant.

JEWISH ELDERCARE CENTRE, THE
Att: Human Resources Manager
5725 Victoria Street
Montréal, QC H3W 3H6
Fax 514-738-2611
Employer Background: The Jewish Eldercare Centre (formed from the amalgamation of the Jewish Hospital of Hope and Jewish Nursing Home) is a 320-bed long-term care facility committed to providing quality care to an elderly population. *New Positions Created (3):* Director, Financial and Technical Services; Director, Human Resources; Director, Patient Services.

JFB TECHNOLOGIES INC.
Att: Human Resources
96 Steelcase Road West
Markham, ON L3R 3J9

Fax 905-470-0621
Website .... www.jfbtech.com
Employer Background: JFB Technologies Inc. is an electronics manufacturer. *New Positions Created (5):* Accounts Payable Clerk; Material Control Clerk; Electronics Test Engineer; Maintenance Operator / Programming Technician; Receptionist.

JIM PEPLINSKI'S LEASEMASTER NATIONAL
Att: Tracey Martin, HR Representative
3109 Bloor Street West
Toronto, ON M8X 1E2

Fax 403-235-4888
Email .... tmartin@jimplease.com
Website .... www.jimplease.com
Employer Background: Jim Peplinski's Leasemaster National is a national automotive leasing sales, service and finance organization, operating in Canada for over 40 years. *New Positions Created (6):* Accounts Receivable Coordinator; Insurance and Credit Administrator; Leasing Account Executives; Sales Manager; Leasing Account Executives; Sales Manager.

JIRO COMPRESSION LTD.
Att: Human Resources Department
5221 - 46th Street, PO Box 1450
Stettler, AB T0C 2L0

Tel. 403-742-5538
Fax 403-742-5539
Website .... www.jirocompression.com
Employer Background: Jiro Compression Ltd. (formerly Enhanced Energy Services) is a division of ensure Energy Services and the largest manufacturer of small HP gas booster compressors in Canada. *New Positions Created (3):* Mechanical Engineer; Draftsperson; Engineer.

JJ MUGGS GOURMET CATERING
Att: Tony Palermo, Director of Operations
500 Bloor Street West
Toronto, ON M5S 1Y3

Tel. 416-531-8888
Fax 416-531-1404
Website .... www.jjmuggs.com
Employer Background: JJ Muggs Gourmet Catering is a leader in the fine dining industry. *New Positions Created (3):* Service and Beverage Managers; Service and Beverage Managers; General Manager, Catering.

JJM GROUP, THE
Att: Scott D. Jacob, VP Construction
8828 River Road
Delta, BC V4G 1B5

Tel. 604-946-0978
Fax 604-946-9327
Email ..... dvanvliet@jjmconstruction.com
Website .... www.jjmconstruction.com
Employer Background: The JJM Group is a multidisciplinary construction company carrying out heavy construction, road and bridge construction, road maintenance, utilities and marine construction. *New Positions Created (2):* Intermediate Accountant; Various Construction Positions (3).

JL RICHARDS & ASSOCIATES LTD.
Att: Human Resources Manager
11 Princess Street, Suite 301
Kingston, ON K7L 1A1

Fax 613-544-5679
Employer Background: JL Richards & Associates Ltd. is an employee-owned, multi-disciplinary engineering, architectural and land use planning practice. *New Positions Created (3):* Civil / Structural Engineer-in-Training / Junior Engineer; Civil / Structural Inspectors and CAD Operators; Engineering Positions.

JO-VAN DISTRIBUTORS INC.
Att: Human Resources Manager
929 Warden Avenue
Toronto, ON M1L 4C5

Tel. 416-752-7210
Fax 416-752-7282
Website .... www.jovanlock.com
Employer Background: Established in 1982, Jo-Van Distributors Inc. is a supplier of door hardware and security products. *New Positions Created (3):* Inside Sales Representatives (2); General Manager; Operations Manager.

JOHN ABBOTT COLLEGE
Att: Gerald Stachrowski,
Director of Administrative Services
275 Lakeshore Rd., Suite 21, PO Box 2000
Ste-Anne-de-Bellevue, QC H9X 3L9

Tel. 514-457-6610
Email .... hrs@johnabbott.qc.ca
Website .... www.johnabbott.qc.ca
Employer Background: John Abbott College is an English-language, post-secondary institution offering pre-university programs. *New Positions Created (3):* Administrative Assistant; Administrative Assistant; Pipe Mechanic, Plumbing.

JOHN BEAR PONTIAC BUICK CADILLAC LTD.
Att: Jane Wilson
1200 Upper James Street, PO Box 20027
Hamilton, ON L9C 7M5

Tel. 905-575-9400
Fax 905-575-4428
Website .... www.johnbear.com
Employer Background: John Bear Pontiac Buick Cadillac Ltd. is a General Motors dealership. *New Positions Created (9):* Accounting Clerk; GM Service Technicians; Service Advisor; New Vehicle Sales Representatives; Parts Counterperson; Body & Paint Estimator; Automotive Technicians (3); Retail Sales Professionals; Auto Body Person / Prepper.

JOHN CANNINGS, BARRISTERS
Att: Human Resources Manager
425 University Avenue, Suite 400
Toronto, ON M5G 1T6

Tel. 416-591-0703
Fax 416-591-0710
Email .... jcannings@jcannings.com
Website .... www.jcannings.com
Employer Background: Established in 1978, John Cannings specializes in civil litigation with an emphasis on insurance defense litigation, professional liability and personal injury law. *New Positions Created (2):* Litigation Lawyer; Litigation Lawyer.

JOHN DEERE CREDIT INC.
Att: Human Resources Department
1001 Champlain Avenue, Suite 401
Burlington, ON L7L 5Z4

Tel. 905-319-5812
Fax 905-319-2147
Email .... jdccareers@johndeere.com
Website .... www.johndeere.com
Employer Background: John Deere Credit Inc. is one of Canada's leading financial institutions. *New Positions Created (3):* Dealer Service Representative; Dealer Service Representative; Area Sales Manager.

JOHN HOLLAND CHEVROLET OLDSMOBILE LTD.
Att: John Holland
1401 Plains Road East, PO Box 535
Burlington, ON L7R 3Y3

Tel. 905-632-4141
Fax 905-333-4551
Employer Background: John Holland Chevrolet Oldsmobile Ltd. is an automotive dealership. *New Positions Created (3):* Service Manager; Body Shop Prep Position / Body Shop Apprentice; Salespeople (2).

JOHN HOWARD SOCIETY OF CANADA
Att: Hiring Committee
771 Montreal Street
Kingston, ON K7K 3J6

Tel. 613-542-7547
Fax 613-542-6824
Email .... national@johnhoward.ca
Website .... www.johnhoward.ca
Employer Background: John Howard Society of Canada is an organization of societies that attempts to understand and respond to problems of crime and the criminal justice system. *New Positions Created (2):* Policy Project Director; Coordinator, Mentoring Project.

JOHN LOGAN CHEVROLET OLDSMOBILE INC.
Att: Norm Webb / Mike Coughlan
241 Queen Street East
Brampton, ON L6W 2B5

Tel. 905-451-2251
Fax 905-451-7279
Website .... www.autonet.ca/john.logan
Employer Background: John Logan Chevrolet Oldsmobile Inc. is an automotive dealership. *New Positions Created (2):* General Technicians / 4th - 5th Year Apprentices; Sales Manager.

JOHN WILEY & SONS, INC.
Att: Bernadine Galway,
Director of Human Resources

22 Worcester Road
Toronto, ON M9W 1L1

Tel. 416-236-4433
Fax 416-236-0345
Email .... bgalway@wiley.com
Website .... www.wiley.com

Employer Background: John Wiley & Sons, Inc. develops, publishes and sells products in print and electronic media for the educational, professional, scientific, technical, medical and consumer markets worldwide. *New Positions Created (2):* Business Manager; Developmental Editor.

JOHNSON INC.

Att: Supervisor of Human Resources
1595 - 16th Avenue, Suite 400
Richmond Hill, ON L4B 3S5

Tel. 905-764-4949
Fax 905-764-4010
Email .... drusso@johnson.ca
Website .... www.johnson.ca

Employer Background: Johnson Inc. is a leading insurance and benefits company, offering services to over 750,000 members and employees of client associations and employers from 50 branches. *New Positions Created (4):* Bilingual Customer Service Supervisor, Plan Benefits; LTD Claims Examiner; Benefits Analyst; LTD Claims Examiner.

JOHNSON & JOHNSON CONSUMER PRODUCTS INC.

Att: Human Resources Department
7101 Notre-Dame Street East
Montréal, QC H1N 2G4

Tel. 514-251-5151
Fax 514-251-5200
Email .... cv-resume@cpcca.jnj.com
Website .... www.jnj.com

Employer Background: Johnson & Johnson is the world's largest manufacturer of health care products for the consumer, pharmaceutical and professional markets. *New Positions Created (2):* Tax Specialist; Account Manager.

JOHNSON & JOHNSON MEDICAL PRODUCTS

Att: Human Resources Department
200 Whitehall Drive
Markham, ON L3R 0T5

Tel. 905-946-8999
Fax 905-946-2126
Email .... jjmphr@medca.jnj.com
Website .... www.jjmp.ca

Employer Background: Johnson & Johnson Medical Products sells and distributes medical / surgical products and services to the Canadian healthcare industry. *New Positions Created (6):* Inside Sales Representative; Business Process Coordinator; Distribution Supervisor; Traffic and Customs Coordinator; Manager, Quality Systems; PC Technician.

JOSEPH BRANT MEMORIAL HOSPITAL

Att: Human Resources Services

1230 North Shore Boulevard
Burlington, ON L7R 4C4

Tel. 905-336-4129
Fax 905-336-6486
Website .... www.jbmh.com

Employer Background: Joseph Brant Memorial Hospital is 256-bed community hospital providing integrated healthcare services to Burlington and surrounding areas. *New Positions Created (33):* Program Director, Maternal and Child Care; Ultrasound Sonographer; Accounting Supervisor; Family Physicians; Hematologist; Pharmacist; Psychiatrists; Pediatrician; Nurse Manager, Rehabilitation & Geriatric Services; Speech Language Pathologist; Accounting Supervisor; Case Managers (5); Physiotherapists; Registered Nurses; Social Workers, Medicine, Maternal & Child Care; Technical Director, Radiology, Diagnostic Imaging & MDU; Director of Care; Millwright; Manager, Base Hospital Program; Office Supervisor, Radiology; Registered Technologist, Nuclear Medicine; Laboratory Office Supervisor; Pathologist; Pharmacist; Registered Nurses; Supervisor, Health Information; Technical Director, Laboratory Services; Coordinator, Sexual Assault and Domestic Violence Centre; Health Professional / Case Manager; Nurse Manager, Acute Medicine; Nurse Manager, Psychiatric and Mental Health Services; Senior Physiotherapist; Case Manager.

JOSEPH RIBKOFF INC.

Att: Nathalie Robson
2375 de l'Aviation
Dorval, QC H9P 2X6

Tel. 514-685-9191
Fax 514-685-9259
Email .... jrmarketing@ribkoff.com
Website .... www.ribkoff.com

Employer Background: Joseph Ribkoff Inc. is an international dress company. *New Positions Created (3):* Quality Control Person; Patternmaker; Assistant to Division Head.

JP METAL AMERICA INC.

Att: Human Resources Manager
7335 Henri Bourassa East
Montréal, QC H1E 3T5

Tel. 514-648-1042
Fax 514-648-9711
Email ..... imarinho@jpmetalamerica.com
Website ..... www.jpmetalamerica.com

Employer Background: JP Metal America Inc. specializes in the design and manufacturing of high-quality wood and metal store displays. *New Positions Created (4):* Project Managers; Accounts Payable Clerk; Receptionist; Project Manager.

JR LABORATORIES INC.

Att: Human Resources Manager
3871 North Fraser Way, Suite 12
Burnaby, BC V5J 5G6

Tel. 604-432-9311
Fax 604-432-7768
Email .... jrlabs@istar.ca
Website .... www.jrlabs.ca

Employer Background: JR Laboratories Inc. is an ISO 9000, GMP-accredited food, dairy, pharmaceutical and environmental laboratory. *New Positions Created (3):* Inorganic Supervisor; Laboratory Technician; LC / MS / MS Scientist.

JUDICIAL APPOINTMENTS ADVISORY COMMITTEE

Att: Chair
720 Bay Street, Suite 201
Toronto, ON M5G 2K1

Tel. 416-326-4060
Fax 416-326-4065
Website .... www.ontariocourts.on.ca

Employer Background: The Judicial Appointments Advisory Committee advises the Attorney General of Ontario on the appointment of judges to the Ontario Court (Provincial Division). *New Positions Created (5):* Judicial Position, Criminal Court; Judicial Position, Criminal Court; Judicial Vacancy, Family / Criminal Law; Judicial Position; Judicial Vacancy.

JUNEWARREN PUBLISHING LTD.

Att: Dennis McBryan, Sales Director
9915 - 56 Avenue NW
Edmonton, AB T6E 5L7

Tel. 780-944-9333
Fax 780-944-9500
Email .... dmcbryan@junewarren.com
Website .... www.junewarren.com

Employer Background: JuneWarren Publishing Ltd. is a privately-owned, Alberta publishing company specializing in trade publications for the Canadian oil, gas and construction industries. *New Positions Created (3):* Directory Advertising Sales Representative; Microstation / Graphic Digitizer; Senior Graphic Design / Production Artist.

JUNEWARREN PUBLISHING LTD.

Att: Steve Klein, Sales Director, Magazines
1333 - 8th Street SW, Suite 800
Calgary, AB T2R 1M6

Tel. 403-265-3700
Fax 403-265-3706
Email .... sklein@junewarren.com
Website .... www.junewarren.com

Employer Background: JuneWarren Publishing Ltd. is a privately-owned, Alberta publishing company specializing in trade publications for the Canadian oil, gas and construction industries. *New Positions Created (3):* Magazine Advertising Sales Representative; Circulation Manager; Senior Graphic Design / Layout Artist.

JUNGBUNZLAUER CANADA INC.

Att: Human Resources Manager
1555 Elm Street
Port Colborne, ON L3K 5V4

Tel. 905-835-5444
Fax 905-835-0061
Email .... hr@jungbunzlauer.ca
Website .... www.jungbunzlauer.ca

Employer Background: Jungbunzlauer Canada Inc. is part of Swiss-based Jungbunzlauer AG, a producer of natural, biodegradable ingredients for the food, beverage, pharmaceutical and cosmetic industry as well as industrial applications. Their Port Colborne location is a citric acid production facility. *New Positions Created (11):* Control Specialist; Environmental Coordinator; Laboratory Technician; Maintenance and Stores Coordinator; Maintenance Technician, Electrical; Maintenance Technician, Instrumentation; Maintenance Technician, Mechanical; Spore Production Technician; Team Leaders; Utility Coordinator; Utility Technician.

JUSTICE INSTITUTE OF BC / JIBC
Att: Manager, Human Resources
715 McBride Boulevard
New Westminster, BC V3L 5T4

Tel. 604-528-5508
Fax 604-528-5607
Email .... hr@jibc.bc.ca
Website .... www.jibc.bc.ca

Employer Background: Established in 1978, JIBC is a post-secondary educational institution, training personnel in justice and public safety fields. *New Positions Created (6):* Administrative / Research Assistant; Program Assistant, Paramedic Academy; Instructor, HAZMAT Training; Instructor, Marine Emergency Duties Training; Program Developer; Director, Centre for Conflict Resolution.

JVC CANADA INC.
Att: Human Resources Department
21 Finchdene Square
Toronto, ON M1X 1A7

Tel. 416-293-1311
Fax 416-293-8208
Website .... www.jvc.ca

Employer Background: JVC Canada Inc., a subsidiary of the Victor Company of Japan, Ltd., markets consumer and professional electronics, including VCRs, car stereos and large format video projectors. *New Positions Created (5):* Marketing Manager; Sales and Marketing Manager, Mobile Entertainment; Product Specialist; Sales Representative; Electronics Technician.

K-LOR CONTRACTORS SERVICES LTD.
Att: Human Resources Manager
610 - 70th Avenue SE, Suite 210
Calgary, AB T2H 2J6

Tel. 403-255-7303
Fax 403-255-7120
Email .... jobs@k-lor.com
Website .... www.k-lor.com

Employer Background: K-LOR Contractors Services is an established national contractor specializing in environmental remediation, underground site services and demolition. *New Positions Created (3):* Chief Estimator; Estimators; Project Managers.

KAFKO MANUFACTURING LTD.
Att: Human Resources Manager
1231 Kamato Road
Mississauga, ON L4W 2M2

Tel. 905-624-3000

Fax 905-624-5234
Website .... www.kafko.com

Employer Background: Kafko Manufacturing Ltd. is one of North America's largest manufacturers of quality pre-engineered steel and polymer swimming pools, vinyl liners and decorative metal fences. *New Positions Created (2):* Controller; Bilingual Secretary.

KAHN ZACK EHRLICH LITHWICK
Att: Human Resources Manager
10711 Cambie Road, Suite 270
Richmond, BC V6X 3G5

Tel. 604-270-9571
Fax 604-270-8282
Website .... www.kzellaw.com

Employer Background: Kahn Zack Ehrlich Lithwick is a progressive mid-sized law firm. *New Positions Created (2):* Junior Lawyer, Family Law; Junior Litigation Lawyer.

KAM BIOTECHNOLOGY LTD.
Att: Dr. Constantinescu,
V.P., Research and Development
9710 - 187th Street, Suite 101
Surrey, BC V4N 3N6

Tel. 604-888-4336
Fax 604-888-6623
Email ..... admin@kambiotechnology.com
Website .... www.kambiotechnology.com

Employer Background: Kam Biotechnology Ltd. provides custom-designed solutions and products for efficient bioremediation of contaminated systems, system regeneration, protection and maintenance. *New Positions Created (4):* Laboratory Technicians (2); Microbiologists (2); Organic Chemist; Organic Chemist.

KAMLOOPS, CITY OF
Att: Human Resources Department
7 Victoria Street West
Kamloops, BC V2C 1A2

Tel. 250-828-3439
Fax 250-372-1351
Email .... hr@city.kamloops.bc.ca
Website .... www.city.kamloops.bc.ca

Employer Background: The City of Kamloops, located at the junction of the North and South Thompson Rivers, is home to over 76,000 residents. *New Positions Created (5):* Executive Secretary; Administrative Assistant, Property Management; RCMP Front Office Supervisor; Manager, Municipal Support Services; Communications Operators.

KANATA FORD
Att: Wilf Daly
8000 Campeau Drive
Kanata, ON K2K 1X4

Tel. 613-591-9000
Fax 613-591-9191
Website .... www.kanataford.com

Employer Background: Kanata Ford is an automotive dealership. *New Positions Created (2):* Assistant Parts Manager; Service Manager.

KANOTECH INFORMATION SYSTEMS LTD.
Att: Human Resources Manager
17704 - 103rd Avenue, Suite 200
Edmonton, AB T5S 1J9

Tel. 780-455-9197
Fax 780-452-4183
Email .... resume@kanotech.com
Website .... www.kanotech.com

Employer Background: Kanotech Information Systems Ltd. is a value-added reseller of CAD and GIS software. *New Positions Created (3):* Marketing Position; Senior Sales Position; Software Developers.

KASIAN KENNEDY ARCHITECTURE, INTERIOR DESIGN AND PLANNING INC.
Att: Human Resources
1188 West Georgia Street, Suite 980
Vancouver, BC V6E 4A2

Tel. 604-683-4145
Fax 604-683-2827
Email .... kogrodniczuk@kasian.com
Website .... www.kasian.com

Employer Background: Kasian Kennedy Architecture, Interior Design and Planning Inc. is a design practice with offices in Calgary, Edmonton and Vancouver. *New Positions Created (7):* Executive Business Assistant; Senior Executive Assistant; Interior Designers / Team Leaders (2); Contract Administrators; Junior Architect; Sr Architectural Technologist; Senior Project Architects.

KASIAN KENNEDY ARCHITECTURE, INTERIOR DESIGN AND PLANNING INC.
Att: Human Resources
222 Riverfront Avenue SW, Suite 1
Calgary, AB T2P 0A5

Tel. 403-265-2440
Fax 403-233-0013
Email .... jerickson@kasian.com
Website .... www.kasian.com

Employer Background: Kasian Kennedy Architecture, Interior Design and Planning Inc. is a design practice with offices in Calgary, Edmonton and Vancouver. *New Positions Created (3):* Project Manager; Intermediate / Senior Design Architect; Senior Project Architect, Healthcare.

KATIVIK SCHOOL BOARD
Att: Human Resources Department
2055 Oxford Avenue
Montréal, QC H4A 2X6

Tel. 514-482-8220
Fax 514-482-8278
Website .... www.kativik.qc.ca

Employer Background: The Kativik School Board serves the Inuit communities of Nunavik. *New Positions Created (3):* Principals; Vice-Principal; Teachers.

KAWARTHA LAKES, CORPORATION OF THE CITY OF
Att: Recruitment Officer
26 Francis Street, PO Box 9000
Lindsay, ON K9V 5R8

Tel. 705-324-9411
Fax 705-324-5417
Website ..... www.city.kawarthalakes.on.ca
Employer Background: Located one hour northeast of Toronto, the Corporation of the City of Kawartha Lakes is home to 70,000 people. *New Positions Created (13):* RNs; RPNs; Agricultural Development Officer; Financial Analyst, Capital Budgets ; Financial Analyst, Performance Measurement and Cost Accounting ; Labour Relations Coordinator; Manager of Environmental Services; Manager of Library Services; Solicitor / Clerk; Special Events / Sales Officer; Workplace Health & Safety Coordinator; Senior Management Positions (9); Manager, Building Services.

KAWARTHA PINE RIDGE DISTRICT SCHOOL BOARD
Att: Superintendent of Business Services
1994 Fisher Road, PO Box 719
Peterborough, ON K9J 7A1
Tel. 705-742-9773
Fax 705-742-7281
Website .... www.kpr.edu.on.ca
Employer Background: The Kawartha Pine Ridge District School Board operates 85 elementary schools, 15 secondary schools and 6 adult learning centres, serving 41,825 students in Peterborough, Northumberland and Clarington Counties. *New Positions Created (3):* Chief Information Officer; Principal and Vice-Principal; Principal and Vice - Principal.

KAWNEER COMPANY CANADA LTD.
Att: Human Resources
1051 Ellesmere Road
Toronto, ON M1P 2X1
Tel. 416-755-4375
Fax 416-755-7683
Website .... www.kawneer.com
Employer Background: Kawneer Company Canada Ltd. manufactures architectural aluminum products. *New Positions Created (2):* Production Scheduler; Accounts Payable Coordinator.

KAYCAN LTD.
Att: Human Resources
81 Millwick Drive
Toronto, ON M9L 2R4
Tel. 416-747-0887
Fax 416-747-6570
Email .... careers@kaycan.ca
Website .... www.kaycan.com
Employer Background: Founded in 1974, Kaycan Ltd. is a leading manufacturer and distributor of aluminum, wood and vinyl windows, siding and accessories. *New Positions Created (3):* Window Service Technician; Order Desk Clerk; Window Sales Representative.

KAYCAN LTD.
Att: Human Resources
3075 Trans Canada Highway
Pointe-Claire, QC H9R 1B4
Fax 514-694-4423

Email .... careers@kaycan.ca
Website .... www.kaycan.com
Employer Background: Founded in 1974, Kaycan Ltd. is a leading manufacturer and distributor of aluminum, wood and vinyl windows, siding and accessories. *New Positions Created (8):* Inventory Clerk; Sales Representative; Purchasing Agent; Invoice Verification Clerk; Inventory Supervisor; Payroll Administrator; Pricing Clerk; Purchasing Agent.

KAYTRONICS INC.
Att: Human Resources Manager
4585 Canada Way, Suite 306
Burnaby, BC V5G 4L6
Tel. 604-294-2000
Fax 604-294-4585
Email .... infovan@kaytronics.com
Website .... www.kaytronics.com
Employer Background: Kaytronics Inc. provides technical sales services, including product design, application and consultative support. *New Positions Created (3):* Field Applications Engineer; Field Applications Engineer; FPGA / CPLD Designer.

KAYTRONICS INC.
Att: President
5800 Thimens Boulevard
St-Laurent, QC H4S 1S5
Tel. 514-745-5800
Fax 514-745-5858
Email .... infomon@kaytronics.com
Website .... www.kaytronics.com
Employer Background: Kaytronics Inc. provides technical sales services, including product design, application and consultative support. *New Positions Created (2):* Inside Sales / Customer Service Representative; Secretary / Administrative Position.

KAZOOTEK TECHNOLOGIES
Att: Human Resources Manager
1380 Burrard Street, Suite 600
Vancouver, BC V6Z 2H3
Tel. 604-639-3405
Fax 604-639-3401
Email .... careers@kazootek.com
Website .... www.kazootek.com
Employer Background: Kazootek Technologies creates online business models that leverage its proprietary global e-commerce payment system (GePS) and uses multiple channels of distribution including Internet and wireless services. *New Positions Created (10):* Sr Software Engineer; Corporate Development Assistant; Customer Relationship Associate; Data Warehouse Specialist; Sr Project Manager; Sr Software Engineer; Senior Software Engineer; Senior Tester; Web Developer; Web Marketing Administrator.

KB ELECTRONICS LIMITED
Att: Bev Whiteley
150 Bluewater Road
Halifax, NS B4B 1G9
Tel. 902-835-7268
Fax 902-835-6026
Email .... careers@kbe.ns.ca

Employer Background: With 20 years of experience, KB Electronics Limited specializes in designing and manufacturing switchmode power conversion equipment in the low- to medium-power range. *New Positions Created (4):* Electronic Technologists; Mechanical Design Engineer; Project Engineer; Senior Development Engineer / Electronic Design Engineers.

KCI MEDICAL CANADA, INC.
Att: Quality Assurance Department
7170 Edwards Boulevard
Mississauga, ON L5S 1Z1
Tel. 905-565-7187
Fax 905-565-9336
Website www.kci1.com
Employer Background: KCI Medical Canada, Inc. manufactures therapeutic surfaces and vacuum-assisted closure used in the prevention and treatment of complications associated with client immobility, including pressure ulcers. *New Positions Created (7):* Quality Assurance Technician; Junior Shipper / Receiver; Territory Managers (2); Territory Managers (3); Technical Services Representative; Territory Manager; Territory Manager.

KEANALL INDUSTRIES INC.
Att: Human Resources Manager
2695 Meadowvale Boulevard
Mississauga, ON L5N 8A3
Tel. 905-858-8010
Fax 905-858-1165
Email .... careers@keanall.com
Website .... www.keanall.com
Employer Background: Keanall Industries Inc. is a multi-plant, international retail supplier of consumer products. *New Positions Created (2):* Assistant Controller; Assistant Controller.

KEANE CANADA, INC.
Att: Human Resources Representative
2000 Barrington Street
Suite 300, Cogswell Tower
Halifax, NS B3K 3K1
Tel. 902-422-6036
Fax 902-422-6059
Email .... careers.hal@keane.com
Website .... www.keane.com
Employer Background: Founded in 1965, Keane Canada, Inc. is a leader in utilizing the newest technologies to provide business solutions, including application development, outsourcing, operations improvement and e-solutions. *New Positions Created (12):* Application Developer, PeopleSoft; C / C++ / Unix Programmer; DB2 Database Administrator; Developer, HP3000 Cobol Image; Mainframe Professionals; PL / 1 Specialist; Software Developer, Cyborg; Software Developer, Eascl; Software Developer, EDI; Software Developer, JSP / EJB; Software Specialist, Vantage; Programmers & Project Mgrs.

KEEN ENGINEERING CO. LTD.
Att: Tony Grice
10451 - 170th Street, Suite 301
Edmonton, AB T5P 4T2

Tel. 780-444-1630
Fax 780-489-4999
Email .... tony.grice@keen.ca
Website .... www.keen.ca

Employer Background: Keen Engineering Co. Ltd. is an employee-owned mechanical and electrical consulting firm with a strong local and regional presence. *New Positions Created (2):* Technologists and Design / CADD Technicians; Mechanical Engineering Positions.

KEEWEETINOK LAKES REGIONAL HEALTH AUTHORITY / KLRHA
Att: Krista Jenkins
309 - 6th Street NE
Slave Lake, AB T0G 2A2

Tel. 780-805-3437
Fax 780-805-3438
Email .... kjenkins@klrha.ab.ca
Website .... www.klrha.ab.ca

Employer Background: KLRHA serves 26,000 Albertans through a network of community health service sites. *New Positions Created (8):* Community Health Nursing Coordinator; Community Nurse; Northern Communities Service Coordinator; Occupational Therapist; Registered Nurse; Registered Nurse Charge, Acute Care; Registered Nurses (2); Speech / Language Pathologist.

KEEWEETINOK LAKES REGIONAL HEALTH AUTHORITY NO.15 / KLRHA
Att: Human Resource Coordinator
PO Bag 1
High Prairie, AB T0G 1E0

Fax 780-523-6642
Website .... www.klrha.ab.ca

Employer Background: KLRHA serves 26,000 people living in small communities through 3 health facilities, 3 primary health centres and a network of community health service sites. *New Positions Created (6):* Risk & Contracts Manager; Environmental Health Leader; Integrated Rehabilitation Leader; Population Health Researcher; Team Manager, Acute Care Services; Nursing Coordinator.

KELLAM BERG ENGINEERING & SURVEYS LTD.
Att: Ron Kellam, PEng, ACCI
5800 - 1A Street SW
Calgary, AB T2H 0G1

Tel. 403-640-0900
Fax 403-640-0678
Email .... lbailey@kellamberg.com
Website .... www.kellamberg.com

Employer Background: Kellam Berg Engineering & Surveys Ltd. is a consulting firm, providing professional engineering, land surveying and planning services to clientele in Calgary. *New Positions Created (2):* Planner / Planning Technician; AutoCAD Drafting Technologist and Presentation Graphics Technologist.

KELLY HOWARD SANTINI LLP
Att: Pasquale Santini
66 Slater Street, 23rd Floor
Ottawa, ON K1P 5H1

Tel. 613-238-6321
Fax 613-233-4553
Website .... www.khslaw.com

Employer Background: Kelly Howard Santini LLP is a boutique law firm. *New Positions Created (6):* Lawyers (2); Law Clerk; Litigation Lawyer; Litigation Secretary; Legal Secretary; Litigation Secretary.

KELLY PHILLIPS PRODUCTIONS INC.
Att: Human Resources Manager
2792 Halpern
Montréal, QC H4S 1R6

Tel. 514-856-0000
Fax 514-856-0700
Email .... info@kellyphillips.com
Website .... www.kellyphillips.com

Employer Background: Kelly Phillips Productions Inc. is a multimedia company in the healthcare communications industry, which produces original information and education programs. *New Positions Created (4):* Medical Writer; Multimedia Programmers; Multimedia Project Manager; Production Assistant.

KELMAN TECHNOLOGIES INC. / KTI
Att: Human Resources
540 - 5th Avenue SW, Suite 600
Calgary, AB T2P 0M2

Tel. 403-262-5220
Fax 403-263-9525
Email .... hr@kelman.com
Website .... www.kelman.com

Employer Background: KTI services international oil and gas exploration clients with a full suite of geophysical processing and data archiving services. *New Positions Created (7):* Graphics Programmer; Seismic Research and Development; IBM ADSM / TSM Specialist; Junior DBA / Data Management Analyst; Intermediate Programmer Analyst; Senior Programming Analyst; Processing Supervisor; Senior Processing Geophysicist.

KELOWNA, CITY OF
Att: Human Resources Department
1435 Water Street
Kelowna, BC V1Y 1J4

Tel. 250-862-3376
Fax 250-862-3318
Email .... apply@city.kelowna.bc.ca
Website .... www.city.kelowna.bc.ca

Employer Background: The City of Kelowna provides a full range of municipal government services for the community. *New Positions Created (5):* Senior Buyer; Supervisor, Airport Administration; Traffic and Transportation Engineer; Transportation Demand Supervisor; Utilities Design and Construction Engineer.

KELRON LOGISTICS
Att: Human Resources Manager
15290 - 103A Avenue, Suite 201A
Surrey, BC V3B 7A2

Tel. 604-589-5114
Fax 604-589-5123
Website .... www.kelron.com

Employer Background: Kelron Logistics is an international transportation logistics firm. *New Positions Created (3):* Customer Service Representatives; Inside Sales Representative / Account Managers; Logistics Coordinator.

KELSEY'S INTERNATIONAL INC.
Att: Dave Cunningham
1187 Princess Street
Kingston, ON K7M 3E2

Fax 613-546-2928
Website .... www.kelseys.ca

Employer Background: Kelsey's International Inc. is a leader in casual dining, with 80 locations across Canada and the USA. *New Positions Created (2):* Restaurant Manager; Restaurant Managers.

KEN LEWIS GROUP INC.
Att: Human Resource Manager
250 Shields Court, Unit 1
Markham, ON L3R 9W7

Tel. 905-477-1049
Fax 905-477-1043

Employer Background: Ken Lewis Group Inc. is an audiovisual engineering firm. *New Positions Created (5):* AutoCAD Technician; Secretary / Personal Assistant; Hardware / Software Engineer; Installation Technicians; Sales / Marketing Specialists.

KENAIDAN CONTRACTING LTD.
Att: Human Resources Manager
1275 Cardiff Boulevard
Mississauga, ON L5S 1R1

Tel. 905-670-2660
Fax 905-670-9172
Website .... www.kenaidan.com

Employer Background: Kenaidan Contracting Ltd. is a medium-sized employee-owned general contractor specializing in heavy civil structural concrete and waterworks projects. *New Positions Created (13):* Construction Supervisor; Project Coordinator; Project Manager; Purchasing Coordinator; Construction Supervisor; Project Coordinator; Project Manager; Senior Business Development Representative; Construction Cost Auditor; Cost Analyst; Project Administrator; Construction Supervisor; Project Manager.

KENONIC CONTROLS LTD.
Att: Recruiting
7175 - 12th Street SE
Calgary, AB T2H 2S6

Tel. 403-258-6200
Fax 403-258-6201
Email .... recruiting@kenonic.com
Website .... www.kenonic.com

Employer Background: Kenonic Controls Ltd. is a Calgary-based company that specializes in industrial controls, electrical engineering, information systems and automation. *New Positions Created (11):* CADD Drafting Position; Control Systems Specialists; DCS Design Engineer / Technologist; Electrical Engineer; High Voltage Electrical Engineer; Project Mgr; Sr Consultant; Telecommunications / Information System Designer; Control Systems Specialists; Expert System Programmer; Sales Professional.

KENROC BUILDING MATERIALS CO. LTD.
Att: Jerry Spinarski, HR Manager
3030 Saskatchewan Drive
Regina, SK S4T 6P1
Tel. 306-525-8380
Fax 306-352-0911
Email .... spinarski@kenroc.com
Website .... www.kenroc.com
Employer Background: Kenroc distributes wall and ceiling products to contractors in Canada and the USA. *New Positions Created (2):* Manager; Vice-President of Operations.

KENSINGTON HEALTH CENTRE, THE
Att: Human Resources Department
340 College Street, Suite 602
Toronto, ON M5T 3A9
Tel. 416-963-9640
Fax 416-963-8258
Website .... www.tkhc.org
Employer Background: The Kensington Health Centre is a primary healthcare and social service institution and operates The Kensington Health Clinic. *New Positions Created (2):* Director of Resident Care; Manager of Programs and Services.

KENT LINE INTERNATIONAL LIMITED
Att: Human Resources
300 Union Street, PO Box 725
Saint John, NB E2L 4B4
Tel. 506-632-1660
Fax 506-633-5527
Email ...... jennings.gordon@kentline.com
Website .... www.kentline.com
Employer Background: Kent Line International Limited operates an ocean-container shipping service from Eastern / North America to the Caribbean, Central America and South America. *New Positions Created (2):* Logistics Manager; Senior Sales Representative, Ontario and Maritime Region.

KENWOOD ELECTRONICS CANADA INC.
Att: Human Resources Manager
6070 Kestrel Road
Mississauga, ON L5T 1S8
Tel. 905-670-7211
Fax 905-670-7248
Website .... www.kenwood.com
Employer Background: Kenwood Electronics Canada Inc. manufactures and distributes quality consumer electronics. *New Positions Created (2):* Bilingual National Accounts Dealer; Sales Representative.

KERR VAYNE SYSTEMS LTD. / KVS
Att: Human Resources Manager
1 Valleywood Drive, Unit 5A
Toronto, ON L3R 5L9
Tel. 905-475-6161
Fax 905-479-9833
Email .... jobs@kvs.com
Website .... www.kvs.com
Employer Background: KVS designs and develops real-time software for the broadcast industry. *New Positions Created (3):* Real-Time Software Developers; Real-Time Software Developers; Computing Positions.

KERR WOOD LEIDAL ASSOCIATES LTD.
Att: Human Resources Manager
139 - 16th Street West
North Vancouver, BC V7M 1T3
Tel. 604-985-5361
Fax 604-985-3705
Email .... jbroda@kwl.bc.ca
Website .... www.kwl.bc.ca
Employer Background: Kerr Wood Leidal Associates Ltd. is a mid-sized consulting civil engineering firm with offices in North Vancouver, Vernon, Victoria and Castlegar, BC. *New Positions Created (10):* Intermediate Design Engineer; River Engineer; Senior Project Engineer; Senior Water Resources Engineer; Design Technologist; Water / Sewer / Stormwater Engineer; Design Technologists (2); Intermediate Design Engineer; Physical Development Planner; Senior Project Engineer.

KESTREL DATA (CANADA) LIMITED
Att: Manager, Human Resources
4221 - 23B Street NE
Calgary, AB T2E 7V9
Tel. 403-250-1119
Fax 403-291-2921
Email .... mway@kestreldata.net
Website .... www.kestreldata.net
Employer Background: Kestrel Data (Canada) Limited, the Canadian subsidiary of AUSDOC Information Management, provides exploration data management, records management and computer media services. *New Positions Created (2):* Business Development Manager, Business Archives; Operations Manager.

KEY PORTER BOOKS
Att: Lyn Cadence,
Director of Publicity and Promotion
70 The Esplanade
Toronto, ON M5E 1R2
Tel. 416-862-7777
Fax 416-862-2304
Email .... lcadence@keyporter.com
Website .... www.keyporter.com
Employer Background: Founded in 1979, Key Porter is one of the largest independent trade publishers in Canada and produces quality books in various categories. *New Positions Created (2):* Publicist; Publicist.

KEYANO COLLEGE
Att: Human Resources
8115 Franklin Avenue
Fort McMurray, AB T9H 2H7
Tel. 780-791-4800
Fax 780-791-1555
Email .... humanresources@keyano.ca
Website .... www.keyano.ca

Employer Background: Keyano College is a comprehensive community college, with 3 campuses serving northeastern Alberta. *New Positions Created (8):* Process Operator Instructor; Coordinator, Aboriginal Education; Financial Assistant Technician III; Network Administrator; Faculty Position; Teacher Education and Instructional Development; Instructor / Chairperson; Instructors, Gas Field Operations (2); Information Librarian.

KEYBASE FINANCIAL GROUP
Att: Human Resources Manager
100 York Boulevard, Suite 600
Richmond Hill, ON L4B 1J8
Tel. 905-709-7911
Email .... fin-info@keybase.com
Website .... www.keybase.com
Employer Background: Keybase Financial Group is an integrated financial services company. *New Positions Created (4):* Branch Processing Personnel; Data Support Position; Life Insurance Support Position; Trust Accounting Position.

KEYSTONE CHILD AND FAMILY SERVICES AUTHORITY
Att: Human Resource Services
4804 - 42nd Avenue, Bay 10
Innisfail, AB T4G 1V2
Fax 403-227-7975
Email .... censssc.jobs@gov.ab.ca
Website .... www.gov.ab.ca/cs
Employer Background: Keystone Child and Family Services Authority promotes the safety of children and families in a community environment. *New Positions Created (7):* Child Welfare Receptionist / Unit Clerk; Child and Family Services Workers; Child Protection Investigator; Child Welfare Social Workers; Child Welfare Social Workers; Foster Care Support Worker; Community Services Unit Clerk.

KEYSTONE ENVIRONMENTAL LTD.
Att: Office Manager
10691 Shellbridge Way, Suite 250
Richmond, BC V6X 2W8
Tel. 604-273-0898
Fax 604-273-0895
Email .... keyinfo@keystoneenviro.com
Employer Background: Keystone Environmental Ltd. is a leader in environmental consulting, with projects across Canada, the USA and internationally. *New Positions Created (4):* Intermediate Engineers / Geoscientists; Junior Engineers / Geoscientists; Senior Project Managers; Senior Scientist, Risk Assessment.

KFL&A COMMUNITY CARE ACCESS CENTRE
Att: Donna Stephenson, Director, Corporate Services
471 Counter Street, Suite 101
Kingston, ON K7M 8S8
Tel. 613-544-7090
Fax 613-544-0209
Email .... donna.stephenson@kfla-cc.org
Website .... www.kfla-cc.org

Employer Background: The KFL&A Community Care Access Centre manages home healthcare and support services for people in their homes, in schools and other places in the community. *New Positions Created (6):* Care Managers; Planners / Project Managers; Rehabilitation Care Manager; Emergency Room Care Manager; Care Coordinators; Care Managers.

KIA CANADA INC.
Att: Human Resources Manager
5875 Chedworth Way
Mississauga, ON L5R 3L9
Fax 416-352-5608
Email .... hr@kia.ca
Website .... www.kia.com
Employer Background: Kia Canada Inc., a subsidiary of South Korean auto manufacturer Kia Motors Corp., manufactures the Sephia sedan, the Sportage SUV and the Sportage 2-door convertible. *New Positions Created (3):* Warranty Adjuster; District Parts and Service Manager; District Sales Manager.

KIDS CAN PRESS
Att: Karen Boersma
29 Birch Avenue
Toronto, ON M4V 1E2
Tel. 416-925-5437
Fax 416-960-5437
Email .... rights@kidscan.com
Website .... www.kidscanpress.com
Employer Background: Kids Can Press is a children's book publisher. *New Positions Created (6):* Publishing Position; Accounting Assistant; Design Technician; Technical Services Manager; Book Production Coordinator; Contracts Administrator.

KIDS HELP PHONE / PARENT HELP LINE
Att: Human Resources Department
439 University Avenue, Suite 300
Toronto, ON M5G 1Y8
Tel. 416-586-0100
Fax 416-586-0651
Email .... jobs@kidshelp.sympatico.ca
Website .... www.kidshelp.sympatico.ca
Employer Background: Kids Help Phone is Canada's only national, toll-free, 24-hour, bilingual telephone counselling and referral service for children and youth. Parent Help Line is Canada's only national, toll-free, 24-hour, bilingual telephone counselling and referral service for parents. *New Positions Created (4):* Clinical Supervisors; Counsellor, Kids Help Phone; Counsellor, Parent Help Line; Shift Supervisors.

KINAARE NETWORKS CANADA CORPORATION
Att: Staffing, HR Department
2680 Skymark Avenue, Suite 500
Mississauga, ON L4W 5L6
Tel. 905-602-0004
Fax 408-752-0831
Email .... jobs@kinaare.net
Website .... www.kinaare.net

Employer Background: Kinaare Networks Canada Corporation provides broadband access technologies and solutions targeted at telecos, cablecos, ISPs and other service providers offering cable or DSL access. *New Positions Created (10):* MIS / IT Support Engineer; Networking Software Engineers; Senior Software Engineer / Technical Lead; System / Applications Software Engineers; Web Developer; MIS / IT Support Engineer; Networking Software Engineers; Senior Software Engineer / Technical Lead; System / Application Software Engineers; Web Developer.

KINARK CHILD AND FAMILY SERVICES
Att: Margo Wilson, Senior HR Coordinator
240 Duncan Mill Road, Suite 402
Toronto, ON M3B 3B2
Tel. 416-391-3884
Fax 416-444-8896
Email .... info@kinark.on.ca
Website .... www.kinark.on.ca
Employer Background: Kinark Child and Family Services is an accredited children's mental health centre, and one of the largest child and family mental health service providers in Ontario. *New Positions Created (13):* Senior Therapists; Social Workers; Psychologist, Autism Initiative; Assistant Clinical Director; Nurses; Nursing Coordinator; Program Coordinator; Psychologist; Research Assistant; Social Workers; Unit Supervisors; Youth Workers; Crisis and Intensive Services Coordinator.

KINARK CHILD & FAMILY SERVICES
Att: Patty Giles, Administrative Manager
380 Armour Road, Suite 275
Peterborough, ON K9H 7L7
Fax 705-743-4144
Email .... patty.giles@kinark.on.ca
Website .... www.kinark.on.ca
Employer Background: Kinark Child and Family Services is an accredited children's mental health centre, and one of the largest child and family mental health service providers in Ontario. *New Positions Created (2):* Psychologist; Psychologist.

KINECTRICS INC.
Att: Recruitment Supervisor, HR Dept.
800 Kipling Avenue
Toronto, ON M8Z 6C4
Tel. 416-207-6550
Fax 416-207-5875
Email .... hr@kinectrics.com
Website .... www.kinectrics.com
Employer Background: Kinectrics Inc. (formerly Ontario Power Technologies) provides science and engineering services to the energy sector. *New Positions Created (4):* Technologists; Engineer / Scientist, Fuel Channels; Machinist / Tool & Die Maker; Practice Leader, Nondestructive Evaluation.

KINETEK PHARMACEUTICALS INC.
Att: Maureen Gilchrist, HR Director
1779 - 75th Avenue West
Vancouver, BC V6P 6P2

Tel. 604-267-7654
Fax 604-267-7664
Email .... careers@kinetekpharm.com
Website .... www.kinetekpharm.com
Employer Background: Kinetek Pharmaceuticals Inc. is a leading biotechnology company, focused on discovering selective drugs that target the Integrin and PI3 kinase pathways. *New Positions Created (2):* Research Associate; HR Coordinator.

KING PACKAGED MATERIALS COMPANY
Att: Joe Hutter
PO Box 699
Burlington, ON L7R 3Y5
Tel. 905-639-2993
Fax 905-333-3730
Email .... jhutter@kpmindustries.com
Website .... www.kpmindustries.com
Employer Background: Established in 1928, King Packaged Materials Company builds roads and manufactures pre-mixed packaged cement products for the concrete rehabilitation and mining industries. *New Positions Created (4):* Sales / Operations Coordinator; Junior Cost / Inventory Accountant; Junior Technical Representative; Accounting Manager / Divisional Controller.

KING'S HEALTH CENTRE
Att: J. Cathcart, Senior HR Representative
250 University Avenue
Toronto, ON M5H 3E5
Tel. 416-977-5464
Fax 416-979-8511
Email ...... jcathcart@kingshealthcentre.ca
Website .... www.kingshealthcentre.ca
Employer Background: King's Health Centre is an integrated medical practice. *New Positions Created (7):* Certified Building Engineer, Facilities Management; Medical Transcriptionist; Team Leader, Health Records; Medical Secretary, Psychology; Registered Polysomnographic Technologist, Sleep Lab; Rehabilitation Assistant, Physiotherapy Services; Staff Education and Skills Development Facilitator.

KING'S UNIVERSITY COLLEGE, THE
Att: Office of the V.P. Academic
9125 - 50th Street
Edmonton, AB T6B 2H3
Tel. 780-465-8304
Fax 780-465-3534
Email .... skward@kingsu.ab.ca
Website .... www.kingsu.ab.ca
Employer Background: The King's University College is an independently governed Christian institution offering university degree programs. *New Positions Created (4):* Instructors; Business Professor; Computing Science Professor; Theology Professor.

KINGSBURY CANADA INC.
Att: Personnel Department
3385 Mainway
Burlington, ON L7M 1A6
Tel. 905-335-6000
Fax 905-335-3142

Email .... sales@kingsbury-canada.com
Website .... www.kingsbury-canada.com
Employer Background: Kingsbury Canada manufactures high-volume machining and assembly systems for the appliance and automotive industries. *New Positions Created (2):* Sales Engineer; Machine Designers.

KINGSTON AND DISTRICT IMMIGRANT SERVICES / KDIS
Att: Hiring Committee
322 Brock Street
Kingston, ON K7L 1S9
Tel. 613-548-3302
Fax 613-548-3644
Email .... rgodkin@kdis.org
Website .... www.ikweb.com/kdis
Employer Background: KDIS is a non-profit organization that provides assistance to immigrants and refugees. *New Positions Created (2):* Interpreter Program Intake Worker; Executive Director.

KINGSTON, CORPORATION OF THE CITY OF
Att: Human Resources
216 Ontario Street
Kingston, ON K7L 2Z3
Tel. 613-546-4291
Fax 613-546-1607
Email .... hrcity@city.kingston.on.ca
Website .... www.city.kingston.on.ca
Employer Background: Located between Montreal and Toronto, the City of Kingston is home to 112,605 residents. *New Positions Created (13):* Coordinator, Sports Tourism; Fire Chief; Compensation Analyst; Manager, Utility Technical Services and Engineering; Roads Manager; Senior Planner; Secretary, Utilities; Street Light Maintenance Technician; Traffic Technologist; Assistant Leader, Facilities; Taxation & Revenue Manager; Buildings and Properties Manager; Director, Legal Services.

KINGSTON FAMILY YMCA
Att: Gary J. Bissonette, CEO
100 Wright Crescent
Kingston, ON K7L 4T9
Tel. 613-546-2647
Fax 613-546-5799
Website .... www.kingston.ymca.ca
Employer Background: The Kingston Family YMCA is a community-centered Canadian charity where members, volunteers and staff work together to foster the development of spirit, mind and body of individuals and families. *New Positions Created (4):* Director, Health, Fitness & Recreation; Fundraising & Developing Coordinator; Teachers, Child Care Services Dept. (2); Teachers, Child Care Services Department.

KINGSTON FRIENDSHIP HOMES
Att: Ruth Woodman,
ACT Services Coordinator
372 King Street West
Kingston, ON K7L 2X4
Tel. 613-544-1356
Fax 613-544-5804
Employer Background: Kingston Friendship Homes provides community mental health support programs. *New Positions Created (4):* Various Mental Health Positions; Team Leader, New Assertive Community Treatment Team; Assistant Director, Crisis Services; Crisis Workers (7).

KINGSTON, FRONTENAC AND LENNOX & ADDINGTON HEALTH UNIT
Att: Sharon Smith, Admin. Assistant
221 Portsmouth Avenue
Kingston, ON K7M 1V5
Tel. 613-549-1232
Fax 613-549-7896
Website .... www.healthunit.on.ca
Employer Background: KFL&A is an accredited teaching health unit affiliated with Queen's University. *New Positions Created (3):* Speech / Language Assistant; Epidemiologist; Communications Officer.

KINGSTON GENERAL HOSPITAL
Att: Trina McGarvey, HR Consultant
76 Stuart Street
Kingston, ON K7L 2V7
Tel. 613-549-6666
Fax 613-548-1334
Email .... kghhr@kgh.kari.net
Website .... www.kgh.on.ca
Employer Background: Kingston General Hospital is a 452-bed academic health sciences centre affiliated with Queen's University. *New Positions Created (41):* Manager, Distributed Computing; Sleep Laboratory Technologist; Systems Programmer Analyst, 2 PCS; Systems Programmer Analyst, 2 SAP; Program Managers (3); Data Management Coordinator; Financial Analyst, Intermediate, Statistics; Nursing Managers (2); Registered Nurse; Research Assistant, Allergy Unit; Systems Administrator, Unix / SAP Level 2; Coordinator, Drug Distribution; Systems Programmer Analyst; Administrative Secretaries; Biomedical Dialysis Technologist; Clinical Instructor, Surgical Suite Services; Medical Secretaries; Pharmacist; Sleep Laboratory Technologist; Sonographers (2); Manager, Cafeteria & Catering Services; Director, Plant Engineering and Maintenance; Nursing Manager, Cardiac Care; Nursing Manager, Renal Care; Nursing Manager, Surgical Suite; Supervisor, Material Management; Manager, Finance; Social Worker; Financial Analyst, Intermediate Payroll; Intermediate Financial Analyst; Professional Practice Leader, Social Work; Nursing Manager, Renal Care Program; Program Director; Manager, Child Life Program; Secretary / Office Coordinator, Dept. of Obstetrics & Gynaecology; Biostatistician; Clinical Research Nurse; Data Analyst, Strategic Information Development; Manager - Security Services; Program Director, Cardiac Care Program; Sleep Laboratory Technologist.

KINGSTON GENERAL HOSPITAL, RADIATION ONCOLOGY RESEARCH UNIT
Att: Dr. Bill Mackillop, Director
Apps Level 4
Kingston, ON K7L 2V7
Tel. 613-548-6149
Fax 613-548-6150
Website .... www.kgh.on.ca/roru
Employer Background: The Radiation Oncology Unit at Kingston General Hospital is a multidisciplinary research group, engaged in health services research in oncology. *New Positions Created (3):* SAS Programmer / Biostatistician; Research Associate; Research Associate.

KINGSTON PSYCHIATRIC HOSPITAL
Att: Human Resources Branch
752 King Street West, PO Box 603
Kingston, ON K7L 4X3
Tel. 613-548-5573
Fax 613-548-5583
Website .... www.gov.on.ca/health
Employer Background: Kingston Psychiatric Hospital is operated by the Ontario Ministry of Health and Long-Term Care. *New Positions Created (5):* Occupational Therapists; Registered Nurse; Psychiatric Nursing Assistants; Ward Supervisor; Clinical Director, Mood Disorders Service.

KINGSTON REGIONAL CANCER CENTRE
Att: Micki Mulima, HR Administrator
25 King Street West
Kingston, ON K7L 5P6
Tel. 613-544-2630
Fax 613-544-4967
Email .... krcc-employment@krcc.on.ca
Website .... www.krcc.on.ca
Employer Background: The Kingston Regional Cancer Centre supports health promotion activities in cancer control, including education and prevention programs for the public, cancer patients and their families. *New Positions Created (8):* Coordinator, Clinical Trials; Advanced Practice Nurse, Pain and Symptom Management; Health Records Clerk; Radiation Therapist; Palliative Medicine Physician; Human Resources / Finance Assistant; Medical Administrative Secretary; New Patient Referral Clerk.

KINGSWAY COLLEGE SCHOOL
Att: Glen Zederayko, Head of School
4600 Dundas Street West
Toronto, ON M9A 1A5
Tel. 416-234-5073
Fax 416-234-8386
Email .... slittle@kcs.on.ca
Website .... www.kcs.on.ca
Employer Background: Kingsway College School is an independent co-educational elementary school accredited by the Canadian Educational Standards Institute. *New Positions Created (3):* Learning Strategies Teacher; Director of Studies; Primary Classroom Teacher.

KINGSWAY FINANCIAL SERVICES INC.
Att: Manager, Administration & HR
5310 Explorer Drive, Suite 200
Mississauga, ON L4W 5H8
Tel. 905-629-7888
Fax 905-629-9485
Email .... hr@kingsway-financial.com

Website ...... www.kingsway-financial.com

Employer Background: Kingsway Financial Services Inc. is one of the fastest growing property and casualty insurers in North America. *New Positions Created (3):* Legal Counsel; Recruitment and Training Specialist; Underwriting Assistants.

KINGSWAY GENERAL INSURANCE COMPANY

Att: Paula Larter, Alberta Claims Manager
8500 Macleod Tr. SE, 300E Heritage Square
Calgary, AB T2H 2N1

Fax 403-255-9224
Email ...... plarter@kingsway-general.com
Website .... www.kingsway-general.com

Employer Background: Kingsway General Insurance, a subsidiary of Kingsway Financial Services Inc., is a leading property and casualty insurer in Canada. *New Positions Created (3):* Claims Examiners; Supervisor - BI Unit; Telephone Adjuster.

KINROSS GOLD CORP., TIMMINS OPERATION

Att: Len Kutchaw, Manager of HR & Safety
PO Bag 1000
Schumacher, ON P0N 1G0

Fax 705-235-6317
Email .... lkutchaw@kinross.com
Website .... www.kinross.com

Employer Background: Kinross Gold Corp. produces one million ounces of gold per year, with 5 primary operations and 3 flagship gold mines in Canada, Russia and the USA. *New Positions Created (3):* Journeyman Heavy Duty Mechanics; Miners I; Miners IV.

KINSMEN & KINETTE CLUBS OF CANADA

Att: Business Manager
1920 Hal Rogers Drive
Cambridge, ON N3H 5C6

Tel. 519-653-1920
Email .... lshook@kinclubs.ca
Website .... www.kinclubs.ca

Employer Background: Founded in Hamilton in 1920 as a non-profit fraternal organization, Kinsmen & Kinette Clubs of Canada is the country's largest all-Canadian service organization, with over 11,000 members in more than 720 clubs. *New Positions Created (2):* Marketing Coordinator; Membership Development Coordinator.

KITCHEN STUFF PLUS

Att: Human Resources Manager
703 Yonge Street
Toronto, ON M4Y 2B2

Tel. 416-944-2718
Fax 416-944-2768
Email .... jobs@kitchenstuffplus.com

Employer Background: Kitchen Stuff Plus is a leading specialty houseware and giftware retailer. *New Positions Created (2):* Various Retail Positions; Junior Accounting Clerk.

KITCHENER, CITY OF

Att: Employment Officer
200 King Street
Kitchener, ON N2G 4G7

Tel. 519-741-2260
Fax 519-741-2400
Email .... humres@city.kitchener.on.ca
Website .... www.city.kitchener.on.ca

Employer Background: The City of Kitchener provides municipal government services. *New Positions Created (3):* Fire Chief; Vehicle and Equipment Safety Specialist; General Manager, Public Works Department.

KITCHENUHMAYKOOSIB EDUCATION AUTHORITY

Att: Lydia Big George, Education Director
PO Box 53
Big Trout Lake, ON P0V 1G0

Tel. 807-537-2553
Fax 807-537-2316

Employer Background: Kitchenuhmaykoosib Education Authority is a publicly-funded organization. *New Positions Created (2):* Teachers (5); Teachers (5).

KITIMAT, DISTRICT OF

Att: Personnel
270 City Centre
Kitimat, BC V8C 2H7

Tel. 250-632-2161
Fax 250-632-4995
Website .... www.city.kitimat.bc.ca

Employer Background: The District of Kitimat is an industrial centre on British Columbia's North Coast with aluminum, pulp and paper and petrochemical industries. *New Positions Created (3):* Recreation Attendant III; Deputy Municipal Engineer; Director of Planning / Approving Officer.

KLAY INFORMATION MANAGEMENT CONSULTING LTD.

Att: Human Resource Manager
840 - 7th Avenue SW, Suite 1420
Calgary, AB T2P 3G2

Tel. 403-263-6463
Fax 403-263-6537
Email .... work@kimc.com
Website .... www.kimc.com

Employer Background: Klay Information Management Consulting Ltd. provides a range of IT services, ranging from strategic planning and implementation, design and development, and support and management. *New Positions Created (7):* Senior Developer / Project Manager; Senior Network Architect; Application Designer / Developer; Development Specialist; Sales / Account Manager; Senior Developer / Project Manager; Senior Network Architect.

KLEIN LYONS

Att: Andrea Potter
1333 West Broadway, Suite 1100
Vancouver, BC V6H 4C1

Tel. 604-874-7171
Fax 604-874-7180
Email .... apotter@idirect.ca

Website .... www.kleinlyons.com

Employer Background: Klein Lyons is a law firm, specializing in personal injury and consumer class action litigation. *New Positions Created (5):* Lawyer; Legal Assistant; Legal Assistant; Legal Assistant; Legal Secretary.

KLEINFELDT CONSULTANTS LIMITED

Att: Human Resources Manager
2400 Meadowpine Boulevard, Suite 102
Mississauga, ON L5N 6S2

Tel. 905-542-1600
Fax 905-542-2729
Email .... admin@kcl.ca
Website .... www.kcl.ca

Employer Background: Kleinfeldt Consultants Limited is a consulting engineering firm that provides professional services to building owners, property managers and land developers primarily throughout Ontario. *New Positions Created (3):* Administrative Assistant; Building Technologists; Senior Structural Engineer / Architect.

KLICK COMMUNICATIONS INC.

Att: Human Resources Manager
1 First Canadian Place, Suite 2610, Box 5
Toronto, ON M5X 1A9

Tel. 416-410-8581
Fax 416-410-5898
Email .... hr@klickit.com
Website .... www.klickit.com

Employer Background: Klick Communications Inc. is a marketing and communications company, specializing in new media solutions. *New Positions Created (4):* Assistant Project Manager / Administrative Support; Art Director; Senior Designer; Administrative Assistant / Receptionist.

KMH CARDIOLOGY AND DIAGNOSTIC CENTRES

Att: Lynda
9 Robinson Street, Sun Life Building
Hamilton, ON L8P 3A9

Tel. .... 905-570-8781 ext. 238
Fax 905-855-1863
Email .... resume@kmhlabs.com
Website .... www.kmhlabs.com

Employer Background: KMH Cardiology and Diagnostic Centres provides high-quality and caring diagnostic health services. *New Positions Created (5):* ECG Technologists; Nuclear Medicine Technologist; Executive Secretary; Medical Secretary; Nuclear Medicine Technologist / Lab Manager.

KNIGHTHAWK

Att: Gilles Roy, Maintenance Coordinator
100 Airport Road
Ottawa, ON K1V 9B3

Tel. 613-736-0048
Fax 613-736-0789
Website .... www.knighthawk.ca

Employer Background: KnightHawk provides contract transportation services to the North American railway and courier industries. *New Positions Created (3):* Aircraft

Maintenance Engineers; Director of Maintenance; Aircraft Maintenance Engineer.

**KNOLL NORTH AMERICA
CORPORATION**
Att: Human Resources
1000 Arrow Road
Toronto, ON M9M 2Y7
Tel. 416-741-5453
Fax 416-741-7568
Email .... hrjobsto@knoll.com
Website .... www.knoll.com
Employer Background: Knoll North America
Corporation is a manufacturer of wood of-
fice furniture. *New Positions Created (6):*
Junior Process Technologist; Industrial
Maintenance Mechanic; Wood Finishing
Technician; Production Supervisors; Inven-
tory Planner; Inventory Planner.

KOBE INTERIOR PRODUCTS INC.
Att: Human Resources Manager
5380 South Service Road
Burlington, ON L7L 5L1
Tel. 905-639-2730
Fax 905-634-0992
Email .... kobe@kobefabrics.com
Website .... www.kobefabrics.com
Employer Background: Kobe Interior Prod-
ucts Inc. is an established, medium-sized
firm in the textile production business. *New
Positions Created (2):* Warehouse and Pro-
duction Manager; Office Position.

KOCH PETROLEUM CANADA LP
Att: Human Resources Advisor
111 - 5th Avenue SW, Suite 1400
Calgary, AB T2P 3Y6
Tel. 403-298-0600
Fax 403-716-7750
Email .... careers@kochcanada.com
Website .... www.kochcanada.com
Employer Background: Koch Petroleum
Canada LP is involved in heavy oil and gas
exploration and production, crude oil sup-
ply and trading, and crude oil transporta-
tion. *New Positions Created (4):* Environ-
mental Coordinator; Operations Technician;
Operations Technician, Stettler; Payroll Ben-
efits Administrator.

KODAK CANADA INC.
Att: Human Resources Manager
3500 Eglinton Avenue West
Toronto, ON M6M 1V3
Tel. 416-766-8233
Fax 416-760-4462
Email .... hrs@kodak.com
Website .... www.kodak.ca
Employer Background: Established in 1899,
Kodak Canada Inc. is the country's only
major manufacturer of photographic prod-
ucts and a leading supplier of traditional
and digital imaging products for consumer,
commercial, healthcare and motion picture
/ television markets. *New Positions Created
(4):* Fire Prevention Associate; Commodity
Manager, Purchasing; Bilingual Customer
Service Representative; Digital / Minilab
Specialist.

KOHL & FRISCH LIMITED
Att: Human Resources
5040 - 72nd Avenue SE
Calgary, AB T2C 4B5
Tel. 403-203-0303
Fax 403-203-0300
Website .... www.kohlandfrisch.com
Employer Background: Kohl & Frisch is one
of Canada's leading wholesale distributors
of pharmaceuticals, health and beauty aids
and confectionery products. *New Positions
Created (2):* Technical Staff, Pharmaceutical
Distribution; Operations Supervisor.

KOHL & FRISCH LIMITED
Att: Human Resources
7622 Keele Street
Concord, ON L4K 2R5
Tel. 905-660-7622
Fax 905-660-3682
Email .... jobs@kohlandfrisch.com
Website .... www.kohlandfrisch.com
Employer Background: Kohl & Frisch Lim-
ited is one of Canada's leading wholesale
distributors of pharmaceuticals, health and
beauty aids and confectionery products.
New Positions Created (11): Accounts Receiv-
able Clerk; Customer Service Technical Liaison; Financial Services Associate; Controller; Transportation Analyst; Pharmaceutical
Distribution Technical Staff; Junior Accounting Associate; Payment Processing Associate; Senior Accounting Associate; Inventory
Analyst; Senior Accounts Payable Associate.

KOM INC.
Att: Human Resources
4019 Carling Avenue
Kanata, ON K2K 2A3
Tel. 613-599-7205
Fax 613-599-7206
Email .... hr@komnetworks.com
Website .... www.kominc.com
Employer Background: KOM Inc. develops
mass storage and information management
software. *New Positions Created (6):* Human
Resource Mgr; Sr Software Engineer, Stor-
age Mgmnt; Sr Software Engineer, Storage
Management Tools; Software Engineer, Stor-
age Management Tools; Systems Engineer;
Team Leader, Storage Management Tools.

KOMEX INTERNATIONAL LTD.
Att: Lucien Lyness
4500 - 16 Avenue NW, Suite 100
Calgary, AB T3B 0M6
Tel. 403-247-0200
Fax 403-247-4811
Email .... llyness@calgary.komex.com
Website .... www.komex.com
Employer Background: Komex International
Ltd. is a Calgary-based environmental en-
gineering consulting company. *New Posi-
tions Created (2):* Hydrogeologist, Interme-
diate Level; Hydrogeologist, Senior Level.

KOMTECH INC.
Att: Donna Blair, HR Associate
103 Schneider Road
Ottawa, ON K2K 1Y3

Tel. 613-591-3230
Fax 613-591-3734
Email .... dblair@komtech.ca
Website .... www.komtech.ca
Employer Background: Komtech Inc. is an
ISO 9001-registered plastic injection
moulding company. *New Positions Created
(2):* Sales Position; Project Design Engineer.

**KONICA BUSINESS
TECHNOLOGIES CANADA INC.**
Att: Human Resources Manager
1329 Meyerside Drive
Mississauga, ON L5T 1C9
Tel. 905-670-7722
Fax 905-839-1565
Email .... konica@istar.ca
Website .... www.konica.com
Employer Background: Konica Business
Technologies Canada Inc. manufactures in-
novative copier, fax and multi-functional
office equipment. *New Positions Created (2):*
Major Account Sales Executives; Major Ac-
count Sales Manager.

KOOTENAY SAVINGS
Att: Marnie J. Devlin, VP,
HR & Communications
1199 Cedar Avenue, Suite 300
Trail, BC V1R 4B8
Tel. 250-368-6401
Fax 250-368-5203
Email .... marnie.devlin@kscu.com
Website .... www.kscu.com
Employer Background: Kootenay Savings is
the region's leading credit union with more
than 13 branches, over $465 million in as-
sets and 40,000+ members. *New Positions
Created (2):* Sales Manager, Wealth Mgmnt
and Insurance Services; Branch Manager.

KOREX CANADA
Att: Human Resources
104 Jutland Road
Toronto, ON M8Z 2H1
Fax 416-252-6742
Email .... mmacintyre@korex-ca.com
Website .... www.korex-ca.com
Employer Background: Korex Canada man-
ufactures and packages powder detergent
products. *New Positions Created (2):* Manu-
facturing Engineer; Maintenance Engineer.

KOSKIE MINSKY
Att: Louise M. McNeely CGA,
Director of Finance & Administration
20 Queen Street West, Suite 900, Box 52
Toronto, ON M5H 3R3
Tel. 416-977-8353
Fax 416-204-2896
Email .... lmcneely@koskieminsky.com
Website .... www.koskieminsky.com
Employer Background: Koskie Minsky is a
Toronto law firm that specializes in civil liti-
gation, trade union labour law and pensions
and benefits. *New Positions Created (4):* Civil
Litigation Associate; Legal Assistant; Ben-
efits Administrator; Pension and Benefits
Associates (2).

KRAFT CANADA INC., CHEESE OPERATIONS
Att: Human Resources Department
PO Box 220
Ingleside, ON K0C 1M0

Tel. 613-537-2226
Fax 613-537-8045
Email .... knadeau@kraft.com
Website .... www.kraft.com

Employer Background: Kraft Canada Inc. is a subsidiary of USA-based Kraft Foods, Inc., the North American food business of Philip Morris Companies Inc. Their Ingleside plant is a major manufacturer and packager of cheese products. *New Positions Created (2):* Business Consultant; Engineering Manager.

KRAFT FOODS CANADA
Att: Human Resources Department
520 William Street
Cobourg, ON K9A 4L4

Tel. 905-373-3338
Fax 905-373-3332
Website .... www.kraft.com

Employer Background: Kraft Foods Canada is a subsidiary of USA-based Kraft Foods Inc., the North American food business of Philip Morris Companies Inc. Their Cobourg plant produces a wide variety of quality products for the North American market. *New Positions Created (4):* Shift Production Supervisor; Stationary Engineer, 2nd-Class; Maintenance Mechanics; Shift Production Supervisor.

KRETSCHMAR INC.
Att: Michelle O'Brien, HR Supervisor
71 Curlew Drive
Toronto, ON M3A 2P8

Tel. 416-441-1100
Fax 416-441-3386
Email ... michelleobrien@kretschmar.com
Website .... www.kretschmar.com

Employer Background: Kretschmar Inc. is a progressive, quality processor of meat products. *New Positions Created (3):* Cost and Process Analyst; QA Manager; Production Control Assistant.

KRISTOFOAM INDUSTRIES INC.
Att: Human Resources Manager
160 Planchet Road
Concord, ON L4K 2C7

Tel. 905-669-6616
Fax 905-669-6235

Employer Background: KristoFoam Industries Inc. manufactures plastic automotive parts. *New Positions Created (3):* Production Manager; Quality Technician; Junior Buyer / Material Analyst.

KRONOS COMPUTERIZED TIME SYSTEMS
Att: Enid Blanchard
5995 Avebury Road, Suite 804
Mississauga, ON L5R 3P9

Tel. 905-568-0101
Fax 978-256-4550
Email .... eblanchard@kronos.com
Website .... www.kronos.com

Employer Background: Kronos Computerized Time Systems provides solutions for managing employee time and improving labour productivity. *New Positions Created (6):* Field Training Specialist II; Field Training Specialist; Software Trainer; Application Consultant; Software Training Specialist; Application Consultant.

KSR INTERNATIONAL
Att: Human Resources Manager
95 Erie Street South, PO Box 1060
Ridgetown, ON N0P 2C0

Tel. 519-674-5413
Fax 519-674-0290
Website .... www.ksrinternational.on.ca

Employer Background: KSR International is a tier-1 automotive supplier for Ford / Daimler Chrysler / GM. *New Positions Created (2):* Engineering Project / Program Managers; Mechanical Engineers / Technologists.

KUBES STEEL LTD.
Att: Human Resources Manager
930 Arvin Avenue
Stoney Creek, ON L8E 5Y8

Tel. 905-643-1229
Fax 905-643-4003
Website .... www.kubesteel.com

Employer Background: Incorporated in 1974, Kubes Steel Ltd. manufactures custom steel products. *New Positions Created (5):* Fitter, Plate & Structural; Estimator; Technical Sales Representatives; Fitters, Plate and Structural; Machinists.

KUBOTA METAL CORPORATION
Att: Maureen McLean
25 Commerce Road
Orillia, ON L3V 6L6

Tel. 705-325-2781
Fax 705-325-5887
Website .... www.kubotametal.com

Employer Background: Kubota Metal Corporation is a subsidiary of the Kubota Corporation in Japan, specializing in the supply of fabricated lube assemblies for the petrochemical and steel mill markets. *New Positions Created (3):* Fabrication Welder; Supervisor, Fabrication; Sales Manager, Central Region.

KUPER ACADEMY
Att: Human Resource Department
2 Aesop Street
Kirkland, QC H9H 4K7

Tel. 514-426-3426
Fax 514-426-2703

Employer Background: Kuper Academy is a private English school. *New Positions Created (4):* Computer Teachers; English Teachers; French Teachers; Physical Science / Mathematics Teachers.

KVAERNER CHEMETICS
Att: Human Resources Department
1818 Cornwall Avenue
Vancouver, BC V6J 1C7

Tel. 604-737-4400
Fax 604-737-4450

Email .... kci.hr@kvaerner.com
Website ..... www.chemetics.com

Employer Background: Kvaerner Chemetics is a technology and design company that offers engineered systems, proprietary and non-proprietary equipment, fully-erected systems and plants to the pulp and paper, chemical, fertilizer and metal smelting industries worldwide. *New Positions Created (2):* Senior Research Chemist / Engineer; System and Software Engineer.

KVAERNER PROCESS SYSTEMS / KPS
Att: Human Resources
1209 - 59th Avenue SE, Box 19, Suite 200
Calgary, AB T2H 2P6

Tel. 403-640-4230
Fax 403-252-1186
Email .... hr.kpsc@kvaerner.com
Website .... www.kvaerner.com

Employer Background: KPS is a leading international supplier of process systems and complete process trains for oil and gas production. *New Positions Created (20):* Project Manager; Senior Structural Designer; Control Systems Engineer Technologist; Electrical Designer; Electrical Engineer; Mechanical Engineer; Piping Designers; Project Engineers / Technologists; Structural / Civil Designers; Structural / Civil Engineer; Civil / Structural Designers; Civil / Structural Engineer; Controls Systems Engineer / Technologist; Electrical Designer; Electrical Engineer / Technologist; Instrument Engineer / Technologist; Mechanical Engineer; Piping Designers; Project Engineers / Technologists; Project Scheduler.

KVAERNER SNC-LAVALIN OFFSHORE
Att: Elaine Vienot
1660 Hollis Street, 5th Floor
Halifax, NS B3J 1V7

Fax 902-496-3638
Email .... veine@snc-lavalin.com
Website .... www.snc-lavalin.com

Employer Background: KSLO is the Canadian-based joint venture of two prominent engineering and construction management firms. *New Positions Created (7):* Construction Supervisor; Jacket Design Engineers; Mechanical Handling Engineer; Senior Mechanical Rotating Equipment Engineer; Subsea Pipeline Flow Assurance Analysts; Template Design Engineers; Various Oil and Gas Positions.

KVAERNER SNC-LAVALIN OFFSHORE
Att: Michelle Strickland
1133 Topsail Road
Mount Pearl, NF A1N 5G2

Tel. 709-368-0118
Fax 709-368-0158
Email .... strim@snc-lavalin.com
Website .... www.snc-lavalin.com

Employer Background: KSLO is the Canadian-based joint venture of two prominent engineering and construction management firms. *New Positions Created (4):* Design Safety Engineers and Naval Architect; Instrument and Control Engineers; Process Engineers; Telecom Engineers.

KWANTLEN UNIVERSITY COLLEGE
Att: Human Resources Department
12666 - 72nd Avenue
Surrey, BC V3W 2M8
Tel. 604-599-2100
Fax 604-599-2111
Email .... employ@kwantlen.bc.ca
Website .... www.kwantlen.bc.ca

Employer Background: Located in southwestern BC, Kwantlen University College serves over 25,000 students on 4 campuses in Richmond, Langley, Surrey and Newton. *New Positions Created (16):* International Admissions Assistant; Faculty Position, Learning Centre; American Sign Language and Oral Interpreters; CELTA Trainer / ESL Instructor; Horticulture Instructor; Drawing Instructor; Philosophy Instructor; Modern Languages Instructor; Resident Care Attendant Faculty; Counsellor; Faculty Members, Collaborative Nursing Program; Instructors, Administrative Office Systems and Bookkeeping Program; Accounting Instructors; Business Instructors; Economics Instructors; Public Information Assistant.

KYMATA CANADA LTD.
Att: Human Resources Manager
101 Schneider Road
Kanata, ON K2K 1Y3
Tel. 613-270-1090
Fax 613-270-1093
Email .... opportunities@kymata.com
Website .... www.kymata.com

Employer Background: Kymata Canada Ltd. is a leading designer and manufacturer of planar integrated opto-electronic modules and sub-systems to the telecom and datacom markets. *New Positions Created (2):* Customer Engineer; Packaging Position.

LA SENZA LINGERIE
Att: Cathy Audrain, Area Supervisor
1370 Dundas Street East, Suite 210
Mississauga, ON L4Y 4G4
Tel. 905-276-9866
Fax 905-895-2283
Website .... www.lasenza.com

Employer Background: La Senza Lingerie is a leading fashion and lingerie retailer, with over 200 stores throughout Canada, and 80 stores in the UK and Middle East. *New Positions Created (4):* Managers; Managers; Various Management Positions; Various Managerial and Consultant Positions.

LA SENZA LINGERIE
Att: Jennifer Sara, Area Supervisor
1604 St. Regis Boulevard
Dorval, QC H9P 1H6
Tel. 514-684-3651
Fax 514-684-0258
Website .... www.lasenza.com

Employer Background: La Senza Lingerie is a leading fashion and lingerie retailer, with over 200 stores throughout Canada, and 80 stores in the UK and Middle East. *New Positions Created (3):* Assistant Managers / Team Leaders; Store Communications Coordinator; Graphic Designer.

LA-Z-BOY FURNITURE GALLERIES
Att: J. Groff
1220 Brant Street
Burlington, ON L7L 6A3
Tel. 905-331-7600
Fax 905-331-7917
Website .... www.lazboy.com

Employer Background: La-Z-Boy Furniture Galleries is an upholstered and case goods furniture leader. *New Positions Created (2):* Office Personnel; Sales Staff.

LABATT BREWERIES ONTARIO
Att: Human Resources
50 Resources Road
Toronto, ON M9P 3V7
Tel. 416-240-3711
Fax 416-235-2201
Email .... metro.hr@labatt.com
Website .... www.labatt.com

Employer Background: Labatt Breweries Ontario, a subsidiary of Belgian-based Interbrew, operates 8 breweries and employs over 3,700 people. *New Positions Created (7):* Dispatch Manager; Maintenance Manager, Packaging; Distribution Analysts; District Sales Coordinator; Field Sales Training Manager; Quality Resource Manager, Analytical Section; Quality Resource Manager, HACCP.

LABELAD / SANDYLION STICKER DESIGNS
Att: Human Resources Manager
400 Cochrane Drive
Markham, ON L3R 8E3
Tel. 905-943-6623
Fax 905-943-6672
Email .... kschneider@labelad.com
Website .... www.sandylion.com

Employer Background: Labelad / Sandylion Sticker Designs is a leader in the design, manufacturing and marketing of pressure-sensitive labels and novelty stickers. *New Positions Created (2):* Senior Accounts Receivable Representative; Intermediate Production Artist.

LABORIE MEDICAL TECHNOLOGIES INC.
Att: Service Manager
6415 Northwest Drive, Unit 11
Mississauga, ON L4V 1X1
Fax 905-612-9731
Email .... webmaster@laborie.com
Website .... www.laborie.com

Employer Background: Laborie Medical Technologies Inc. develops urodynamic computer applications that are used in urology research and clinics. *New Positions Created (2):* Medical Sales Representative; Technical Customer Service Position.

LAC DE GRAS EXCAVATION INC.
Att: Human Resources Manager
5107 - 48th Street, Suite 104
Yellowknife, NT X1A 1N5
Fax 604-881-8302

Employer Background: Lac de Gras Excavation Inc. is an excavation company involved in the infrastructure and dike construction work at the Diavik diamond mine. *New Positions Created (3):* Crane Operator; Equipment Operator Specialist, Concrete Cut-Off Wall; Heavy Equipment Operators.

LACAILLE ON THE BOW
Att: Human Resources Manager
100 LaCaille Place SW
Calgary, AB T2P 5E2
Fax 403-237-6108
Email .... lacaille@cadvision.com

Employer Background: LaCaille on the Bow is a leader in fine business dining. *New Positions Created (2):* Marketing Coordinator; Reservations Coordinator.

LAFARGE CANADA INC.
Att: Human Resources Manager
7611 No. 9 Road
Richmond, BC V6W 1H4
Tel. 604-244-4300
Fax 604-244-4361
Website .... www.lafargecorp.com

Employer Background: Lafarge Canada Inc. is North America's second largest and Canada's top producer of quality cement, concrete and related specialty products. *New Positions Created (2):* Maintenance Supervisor, Mechanical; Shift Supervisor.

LAFARGE CANADA INC.
Att: Human Resources Manager
PO Box 160
Bath, ON K0H 1G0
Tel. 613-352-7711
Fax 613-352-5109
Email .... greg.krizan@lafarge.ca
Website .... www.lafargecorp.com

Employer Background: Lafarge Canada Inc. is a subsidiary of Lafarge Corporation, one of North America's largest diversified suppliers of cement, aggregate, asphalt, concrete and other construction materials. *New Positions Created (3):* Mechanical Maintenance Inspector; Electrical Coordinator; Predictive / Proactive Maintenance Coordinator.

LAFARGE CANADA INC.
Att: Corporate Technical Services
6150 Royalmount Avenue
Montréal, QC H4P 2R3
Fax 514-739-4915
Email .... hrcts@lafarge.ca
Website .... www.lafargecorp.com

Employer Background: Lafarge Canada Inc. is a subsidiary of Lafarge Corporation, one of North America's largest diversified suppliers of cement, aggregate, asphalt, concrete and other construction materials. *New Positions Created (4):* Automation Engineer; Electrical Engineer; Project Engineer; Project Management Services Manager.

LAFARGE CANADA INC.
Att: Human Resources Manager
606 Cathcart Street, Suite 800
Montréal, QC H3B 1L7
Tel. 514-861-1411
Fax 514-861-1123
Email .... recruitingit@lafarge.ca

Website .... www.lafargecorp.com
Employer Background: Lafarge Canada Inc. is part of the Lafarge Group, a leading producer of construction materials, with over 70,000 employees in more than 65 countries. *New Positions Created (2):* Computing Positions; Administrative Assistant.

LAFARGE CONSTRUCTION MATERIALS
Att: Human Resources Manager
7880 Keele Street, Suite 501
Concord, ON L4K 4G7
Fax 905-738-7080
Email .... jobs@lafarge.ca
Website .... www.lafargecorp.com
Employer Background: Lafarge Construction Materials is North America's second-largest and Canada's top producer of quality cement, concrete and related specialty products. *New Positions Created (4):* Safety Training and Performance Coordinator; Manager, Labour and Employee Relations; Property Coordinator; Purchasing Position.

LAIRD PLASTICS (CANADA) INC.
Att: Human Resources Manager
2600 Drew Road
Mississauga, ON L4T 3M5
Tel. 905-673-8008
Fax 905-673-3147
Email .... toronto@lairdplastics.com
Website .... www.lairdplastics.com
Employer Background: Laird Plastics (Canada) Inc. is a large distributor of plastic sheets, rods, tubing and film. *New Positions Created (2):* Warehouse Labourer; Inside / Outside Sales Representatives.

LAKE ERIE STEEL COMPANY
Att: Human Resources Department
General Delivery
Nanticoke, ON N0A 1L0
Tel. 519-587-4541
Fax 519-587-7716
Website .... www.stelco.com
Employer Background: Lake Erie Steel Company, a division of Stelco Inc., is a growing manufacturer of hot-rolled sheet steel products and employs 1,400 people. *New Positions Created (4):* Project / Construction Engineer; Engineering Positions; Electronics Technicians; Technicians / Electricians.

LAKEFIELD RESEARCH LIMITED
Att: Human Resources Coordinator
185 Concession Street, Box 4300
Lakefield, ON K0L 2H0
Tel. 705-652-2000
Fax 705-652-3529
Email .... hr@lakefield.com
Website .... www.lakefield.com
Employer Background: Lakefield Research provides high-quality analytical services to the global environmental, occupational health, metal recycling, mining and metallurgical industries. *New Positions Created (2):* Health & Safety Supervisor; Manager, Analytical Laboratory Operations.

LAKEHEAD DISTRICT SCHOOL BOARD
Att: Human Resources
2135 Sills Street, 3rd Floor
Thunder Bay, ON P7E 5T2
Tel. 807-625-5100
Fax 807-625-9422
Website .... www.lhbe.edu.on.ca
Employer Background: The Lakehead District School Board operates over 30 schools. *New Positions Created (2):* Elementary and Secondary Core French and Immersion Teachers; Principals and Vice-Principals.

LAKEHEAD UNIVERSITY
Att: Human Resources Manager
955 Oliver Road
Thunder Bay, ON P7B 5E1
Website .... www.lakeheadu.ca
Employer Background: Founded in 1946, Lakehead University offers undergraduate and graduate degrees in a variety of academic disciplines, with a focus on northern studies. *New Positions Created (23):* Vice-President, Research and Development; Executive Assistant; Tenure-Track Position, Aboriginal Education; Tenure-Track Position, Accounting; Tenure-Track Position, Anthropology; Tenure-Track Position, Civil, Environmental or Municipal Engineering; Tenure-Track Position, Computer Science; Tenure-Track Position, Economics; Tenure-Track Position, Educational Psychology and Special Education; Tenure-Track Position, Electrical Engineering; Tenure-Track Position, Geology; Tenure-Track Position, Inorganic or Organic Chemistry; Tenure-Track Position, Natural Resources Management; Tenure-Track Position, Nursing; Tenure-Track Position, Operations Management; Tenure-Track Position, Philosophy; Tenure-Track Position, Physics; Tenure-Track Position, Social Work; Tenure-Track Position, Software Engineering; Tenure-Track Positions, Mathematics (2); Tenure-Track Positions, Outdoor Recreation, Parks and Tourism (3); Tenure-Track Positions, Psychology (2); Dean of Forestry & Forest Environment.

LAKELAND COLLEGE
Att: Human Resources
5707 - 47th Avenue West
Vermilion, AB T9X 1K5
Tel. 780-853-8406
Fax 780-853-8702
Email .... hr@lakelandc.ca
Website .... www.lakelandc.ab.ca
Employer Background: Established in 1913, Lakeland College operates campuses in Vermilion and Lloydminster, providing postsecondary education in apprenticeship trades, business, agriculture, liberal and performing arts, environmental sciences and human services. *New Positions Created (11):* Education Learning Aide; Instructional Web Designer; Technical Writer; Manager, Purchasing; Coordinator, Pesticide Certificate & Business Development; Educational Laboratory Technician; Educational Liaison Assistant; Occupational Health & Safety Officer; Dean, School of Agricultural Sciences;

Instructor, Computer Technology; Vice-President, Finance and Operations.

LAKELAND REGIONAL HEALTH AUTHORITY / LRHA
Att: Human Resources Department
PO Box 248
Smokey Lake, AB T0A 3C0
Tel. 780-656-2030
Fax 780-656-2033
Email .... cprzekop@lrha.ab.ca
Website .... www.lrha.ab.ca
Employer Background: LHRA operates health centres, health units and continuing care (long-term care) facilities, as well as community health services and public health programs. *New Positions Created (2):* Audiologist; Occupational Health, Safety and Wellness Facilitator.

LAKERIDGE HEALTH CORPORATION
Att: Human Resources Department
850 Champlain Avenue, Suite 1
Oshawa, ON L1J 8R2
Tel. 905-576-8711
Fax 905-721-4865
Email recruitment@lakeridgehealth.on.ca
Website .... www.lakeridgehealth.on.ca
Employer Background: Lakeridge Health Corporation has over 4,000 employees and delivers healthcare to over 500,000 people. *New Positions Created (93):* Central Service Reprocessing Team Leader; Charge Registered Technologist; Emergency Physician; Forms Management Coordinator; Health Records Technicians; Occupational Health Nurse; Pharmacists (2); Physiotherapist; Registered Nurse, Cardiopulmonary Program; Registered Nurse, Continuing Care Program; Registered Nurse, Surgical Suite; Registered Nurses, Critical Care; Team Leader, Health Records and Patient Registration; Health Informatics Consultant; Leader, Program Support; Team Leader; Biomedical Registered Technologist; Occupational Therapist; Occupational Therapist; Occupational Therapist; Social Worker, Eating Disorder Program; Financial Analyst, Cost Accounting; Hemodialysis Registered Nurses (2); Social Worker, Adult Mental Health Day Treatment Program; Social Worker, Oncology / Surgery; Clinical Education Leader; Clinical Leader, NICU / Paediatrics; Clinical Nurse Educators (2); Dietitian, Eating Disorders; Echosonographer; Program Leader, Dialysis; Renal Technicians (2); Social Worker, Crisis & Inpatient Services; Speech Language Pathologist; Cardiologist; Cardiopulmonary Services RN; Clinical Psychologist; Coordinator, Management Support; Emergency Physician; Family Physician; Hospitalists (6); Infectious Diseases and Medical Microbiology Specialist; Mental Health Clinician; Pharmacists (3); Physiotherapist; Psychiatrists; Psychologist, Mental Health Day Treatment Program; Radiologist; Registered Nurse, Continuing Care Program; Registered Nurse, Perinatal; Registered Nurse, Special Care Unit; Registered Nurses, Critical Care; Registered Nurses, Emergency Room; Registered Practical Nurses; Registered Respiratory Thera-

pists; Supervisor, Retail Food Court; Team Leader; Transition Coordinator; Chief Operating Officers (2); Clinical Psychologist, Child & Adolescent Program; Mental Health Nurses; Psychologist, Day Hospital & Ambulatory Services; Registered Dietitian, Eating Disorder Program; Social Worker, Crisis & Inpatient Services, Child & Adolescent Program; Social Worker, Intake, Child & Adolescent Program; Biomedical Renal Technologists; Clinical Education Leader, Family and General Medicine; Clinical Education Leader, Perioperative and Surgery; Clinical Leader, NICU / Perinatal Program; Dialysis Program Leader; Dietitian; Kinesiologist / Occupational Therapist; Physiotherapists; Program Leader, Dialysis; Physicians; Physicians; MRI Technologist; Pharmacists (3); Data Analyst, Corporate Planning; Clinical Coordinator, Cardiac Rehabilitation; Renal Technologist; Social Worker; Food Services Supervisor; Health Records Technicians / Manager; Program Leader, Family and General Medicine; Sonographers; Various Healthcare Positions; Clinical Education Leader; Health Records Technicians; Physiotherapists / Occupational Therapists; Registered Nursing Positions; Risk Management Coordinator; Various Healthcare Positions.

LAKERIDGE HEALTH CORPORATION
Att: Human Resources Department
1 Hospital Court
Oshawa, ON L1G 2B9
Tel. 905-576-8711
Fax 905-721-4755
Email ...... tbadour@lakeridgehealth.on.ca
Website .... www.lakeridgehealth.on.ca
Employer Background: Lakeridge Health Corporation Oshawa is an acute care community hospital responding to 70,000 emergency visits and over 20,000 surgeries a year. *New Positions Created (4):* Clinical Education Leader, Staff and Patient Education, Oncology and Supportive Care; Team Leader, Health Records and Patient Registration, Oncology Program; Transition Coordinator, Health Records and Patient Registration, Oncology Program; Program Leader, Family General Medicine.

LAKERIDGE HEALTH CORPORATION
Att: Human Resources
47 Liberty Street South
Bowmanville, ON L1C 2N4
Tel. 905-623-3331
Fax 905-623-4088
Email ...... ctarrant@lakeridgehealth.on.ca
Website .... www.lakeridgehealth.on.ca
Employer Background: Lakeridge Health Corporation serves 500,000 people in Durham Region, with a staff of 3,500. *New Positions Created (2):* Health Records Team Leader; Patient Flow Coordinator.

LAKESHORE GENERAL HOSPITAL
Att: Pierre Jarry
160 Stillview Street
Pointe-Claire, QC H9R 2Y2
Tel. 514-630-2225
Fax 514-630-2371

Email .... pjarry@lgh.qc.ca
Website .... www.lgh.qc.ca
Employer Background: Lakeshore General is a 257-bed community hospital and ambulatory centre, offering health services to a community of over 300,000. *New Positions Created (5):* Head Nurse, Emergency; Head Nurse, Intensive Care; Medical Secretary; Executive Director; Registered Nurses.

LAMBTON HOSPITALS GROUP
Att: Human Resources
89 Norman Street
Sarnia, ON N7T 6S3
Tel. 519-464-4400
Fax 519-464-4479
Email .... lhghr@lhg.on.ca
Website .... www.lhg.on.ca
Employer Background: Lambton Hospitals Group is a partnership of the Charlotte Eleanor Englehart Hospital in Petrolia, the Sarnia General Hospital and St. Joseph's Health Centre in Sarnia. *New Positions Created (5):* Occupational Therapist Rehabilitation Counsellor; Clinical Coordinator, Emergency / Ambulatory Care; Clinical Coordinator, Mental Health Services; Clinical Nurse Educator, Mental Health Services; Clinical Nurse Educators (2).

LANARK COUNTY MENTAL HEALTH
Att: Michael Poulin MSW CSW, Director
88 Cornelia Street West, Unit A2
Smiths Falls, ON K7A 5K9
Tel. 613-283-2170
Fax 613-283-9018
Website .... www.psfdh.on.ca
Employer Background: Sponsored by Perth & Smiths Falls District Hospital, Lanark County Mental Health provides access to rural resources for adults experiencing serious or moderate mental illness. *New Positions Created (3):* Community Mental Health Nurse; Supervisor, MSW; Supervisor, RN.

LANCASTER HOUSE
Att: Human Resources Manager
20 Dundas Street West, PO Box 133
Toronto, ON M5G 2G8
Tel. 416-977-6618
Fax 416-977-5873
Website .... www.lancasterhouse.com
Employer Background: Lancaster House publishes labour, employment and human rights law information. *New Positions Created (3):* Legal Editor / Writer; Legal Editors / Writers; Legal Editors / Writers.

LAND DATA TECHNOLOGIES INC.
Att: Human Resources Manager
11411 - 163rd Street
Edmonton, AB T5M 3Y3
Tel. 780-451-6477
Fax 780-451-3419
Email .... peters@directnet.ab.ca
Website .... www.landdatatech.com
Employer Background: LDT provides mapping and customized GIS and AM / FM solutions to government agencies and private sector businesses. *New Positions Created (3):*

CAD Graphics Operators (2); Mgr, Photogrammetry; Photogrammetrists (2).

LANDCANADA LTD.
Att: Sharon Mooney, President
90 Burnhamthorpe Road, Suite 1004
Mississauga, ON L5B 3C3
Tel. 905-281-4266
Fax 905-281-4278
Email .... smooney@landcanada.ca
Website .... www.landcanada.ca
Employer Background: LandCanada Ltd., affiliated with LandAmerica Financial Group Inc., is a national company offering title insurance and ancillary products to Canadian lenders. *New Positions Created (3):* Commercial Real Estate Lawyer; General Counsel; Lawyer.

LANDMARK GRAPHICS
Att: Human Resources Manager
645 - 7th Avenue SW, Unit 2200
Calgary, AB T2P 4G8
Tel. 403-263-0070
Email .... careers@lgc.com
Website .... www.lgc.com
Employer Background: Founded in 1982, Landmark Graphics is a software company specializing in exploration and production applications for petroleum companies. *New Positions Created (3):* Drilling and Well Services Positions; Geological & Geophysical Support Analyst; Drilling Data Management Support Analyst.

LANDMARK MASTER BUILDER INC.
Att: Bruce Martin
9618 - 42nd Avenue, Suite 301
Edmonton, AB T6E 5Y4
Tel. 780-436-5959
Fax 780-436-4773
Website .. www.landmarkmasterbuilder.com
Employer Background: For over 20 years, Landmark Master Builder Inc. has built classical homes in Edmonton. *New Positions Created (5):* Draftsperson; Residential Construction Superintendent; Residential Construction Superintendent; Estimator; Draftsperson.

LANG MICHENER
Att: Scott Whitley
181 Bay Street, Suite 2500, BCE Place
Toronto, ON M5J 2T7
Tel. 416-360-8600
Fax 416-365-1719
Website .... www.langmichener.ca
Employer Background: Lang Michener provides services in Canadian business law, with 175 dynamic lawyers in Toronto, Vancouver and Ottawa. *New Positions Created (5):* Lending and Commercial Law Associate; Insurance Defense Litigation Lawyer; Commercial Real Estate Lawyer; Legal Secretaries; Employment Law Lawyer.

LANG MICHENER
Att: Dan Leduc
50 O'Connor Street, Suite 300
Ottawa, ON K1P 6L2

Tel. 613-232-7171
Fax 613-231-3191
Website .... www.langmichener.ca

Employer Background: Lang Michener provides services in Canadian business law, with 175 dynamic lawyers in Toronto, Vancouver and Ottawa. *New Positions Created (6):* Commercial Litigation / Construction Lawyer; Commercial Litigation / Construction Lawyer; Junior Legal Secretaries; Law Clerk; Legal Secretary; Office Clerk.

LANGARA COLLEGE
Att: Human Resources
100 - 49th Avenue West
Vancouver, BC V5Y 2Z6

Tel. 604-323-5626
Fax 604-323-5622
Email .... employment@langara.bc.ca
Website .... www.langara.bc.ca

Employer Background: Langara College offers first- and second-year university courses and over 31 career programs to 7,500 students. *New Positions Created (5):* Marketing Coordinator, International Education Department; Financial Aid Advisor; Laboratory Demonstrator, Biology; Physics Instructor; Financial Aid Advisor.

LANGARA ISLAND LODGE
Att: Human Resources Manager
4440 Cowley Crescent, Suite 201
Richmond, BC V5V 3H9

Tel. 604-232-5532
Fax 604-232-5500
Email .... info@langara.com
Website .... www.langara.com

Employer Background: Langara Island Lodge provides fishing and eco-adventure services to guests. *New Positions Created (3):* Lodge Manager; Maintenance Manager; Pastry Chef.

LANGLEY, CITY OF
Att: Darrin Leite, CA, Director of Finance
20399 Douglas Crescent
Langley, BC V3A 4B3

Tel. 604-514-2800
Fax 604-530-4371
Email .... darrinl@city.langley.bc.ca
Website .... www.city.langley.bc.ca

Employer Background: Incorporated in 1955, the City of Langley is home to over 24,000 residents. *New Positions Created (3):* Budget Analyst / IT Support Manager; Deputy Director of Finance; Engineering Technologist.

LANGLEY, CORPORATION OF THE TOWNSHIP OF
Att: Human Resources Department
4914 - 221st Street
Langley, BC V3A 3Z8

Tel. 604-533-6001
Fax 604-533-6129
Email .... resumes@tol.bc.ca
Website .... www.township.langley.bc.ca

Employer Background: Founded in 1873, the Township of Langley is a suburb of Vancouver and home to nearly 90,000 people. *New*

Positions Created (4): Manager of Operations; Senior Water Resources Engineer; Development Planner I; Environmental Coordinator.

LANIER CANADA INC.
Att: District Manager
605 West Kent Avenue, Unit 1
Vancouver, BC V6P 6T7

Tel. 604-323-1011
Fax 604-323-1597
Email .... career@lanier.com
Website .... www.lanier.com

Employer Background: Lanier Canada Inc., a part of the Fortune 200 Harris Corporation, is one of the leading suppliers of document management solutions and services worldwide. *New Positions Created (3):* Vertical Market Representative; Service Technician; Account Representatives.

LANIER CANADA INC.
Att: Mihail Bujor
2735 Matheson Boulevard, Unit 5
Mississauga, ON L4W 4M8

Tel. 905-624-8440
Fax 905-624-9570
Email .... mbujor@lanier.com
Website .... www.lanier.com

Employer Background: Lanier Canada Inc., a part of the Fortune 200 Harris Corporation, is one of the leading suppliers of document management solutions and services worldwide. *New Positions Created (2):* Customer Service Technician; Account Representatives.

LANSDOWNE DODGE CITY LTD.
Att: Human Resources
5900 Minoru Boulevard
Richmond, BC V6X 2A9

Tel. 604-273-8018
Fax 604-273-7234

Employer Background: Lansdowne Dodge City Ltd. is an automotive dealership. *New Positions Created (2):* Switchboard Operator / Receptionist; Auto Technician.

LANSING BUILDALL / REVY HOME CENTRES INC.
Att: Human Resources
1170 Martin Grove Road
Toronto, ON M9W 4X1

Tel. 416-241-5129
Fax 416-241-8847
Email .... hr@lansing.on.ca
Website .... www.lansing.on.ca

Employer Background: Lansing Buildall / Revy Home Centres Inc. is a leading home improvement retailer. *New Positions Created (3):* Sales Representatives, Builder's Hardware; Sales Representatives, Contracting; Sales Representatives, Windows and Doors.

LANTERN COMMUNICATIONS CANADA INC.
Att: Kathy St. Pierre, HR Manager
1642 Merivale Road, Suite 2000
Ottawa, ON K2C 4A1

Tel. 613-727-4343

Fax 613-727-3325
Email .... jobs@lanterncom.ca
Website .... www.lanterncom.ca

Employer Background: Lantern Communications Canada Inc. is developing a new service-aware Ethernet network architecture for operators of metropolitan area networks. *New Positions Created (38):* Intermediate Network Management Software Designer; Product Line Manager, Broadband Optical Switching; Senior ASIC / FPGA Verification Engineer; Senior High-Speed Board Designer; Senior / Intermediate OAM&P Software Designers; Senior Protocol Designer; Senior Switch Architect; ASIC / FPGA Design Manager; Controller; Product Line Manager, Broadband Optical Switching; Senior ASIC / FPGA Designer; Senior OAM&P Architect; Embedded Software Designer; Intermediate Network Management Software Designers; Principal Mechanical Designer; Senior High-Speed Board Designer; Senior / Intermediate OAM&P Software Designers; Senior Protocol Designer; Senior Software Architect; Senior Switching Systems Architect; ASIC Verification Engineers; Build Configuration Manager; Diagnostic Test Engineer; Diagnostics Engineer; ECN Analyst; Embedded Software / Firmware Engineer; Manufacturing Technician; Network Management Software Engineer; Performance Test Engineer; Senior ASIC Design Engineers; Software Architect; Software Design, Verification (Embedded Software); Software Designer, Verification; Software Test Engineers; Test Engineer, Hardware; Test Engineers, Protocols; Test Engineers, SNMP; Tools Development Engineer.

LANZAROTTA WHOLESALE GROCERS LTD.
Att: Human Resources Manager
10 Ronrose Drive
Concord, ON L4K 4R3

Tel. 905-669-9814
Fax 905-669-9570
Email .... theresac@lanzarotta.com
Website .... www.lanzarotta.com

Employer Background: Lanzarotta Wholesale Grocers Ltd. is Ontario's largest independent wholesale food distributor, carrying over 10,000 products. *New Positions Created (3):* Logistics Supervisor; Marketing Assistant; Retail Accountants.

LARCO INDUSTRIAL SERVICES LTD.
Att: Walter Kulakowsky, Service Manager
863 Arvin Avenue
Stoney Creek, ON L8E 5N8

Tel. 905-643-1296
Fax 905-643-7700
Email .... walt.kulakowsky@cmworks.com
Website .... www.larco.ind.com

Employer Background: Larco Industrial Services Ltd. designs, manufactures and services overhead cranes, hoists, industrial doors and other products in the material handling field. *New Positions Created (2):* Field Electricians; Crane Service Technician Apprentices.

**LARLYN PROPERTY
MANAGEMENT LTD.**
Att: S. Martin
540 Wharncliffe Road South
London, ON N5J 2N4
Tel. 519-690-0600
Fax 519-690-1352
Email .... smartin@larlyn.com
Website .... www.larlyn.com
Employer Background: Established in 1975, Larlyn Property Management Ltd. provides professional property and asset management services to owners, investors and institutions. *New Positions Created (2):* Building Manager; Property Manager.

LASIK VISION CORPORATION
Att: Human Resources Manager
4259 Canada Way, Suite 100
Burnaby, BC V5G 1H1
Tel. 604-639-4230
Fax 604-639-4229
Email .... careers@lasik-vision.com
Website .... www.lasik-vision.com
Employer Background: Lasik Vision Corporation is a leader in laser refractive eye surgery. *New Positions Created (3):* Centre Director; National Marketing Director; Accounting Manager.

LAURA CANADA
Att: Director of Sales
1 Yorkdale Road, Suite 509
Toronto, ON M6A 3A1
Fax 416-256-9001
Website .... www.lauracanada.com
Employer Background: Laura Canada operates over 120 retail fashion stores under the names of Laura, Laura Petites, Laura II and Melanie Lyne. *New Positions Created (4):* Store Manager; Public Relations / Special Events Assistant; Regional Manager, Finds Division; Store Manager, Finds Division.

LAURA CANADA
Att: HR Manager
3000 le Corbusier Boulevard
Laval, QC H7L 3W2
Tel. 450-973-6090
Fax 450-973-9141
Website .... www.lauracanada.com
Employer Background: Laura Canada operates over 120 retail fashion stores under the names of Laura, Laura Petites, Laura II and Melanie Lyne. *New Positions Created (8):* Loss Prevention Investigator; Allocator; Assistant Buyer; Merchandise Administrator (Junior Position); Loss Prevention Coordinator; Marketing Coordinator / Graphic Artist; Marketing Manager; Visual Merchandise Trainer.

LAURENTIAN BANK OF CANADA
Att: Rollie Zellmer, Manager
10304 Jasper Avenue
Edmonton, AB T5J 1Y7
Fax 780-429-3775
Website .... www.laurentianbank.com
Employer Background: Laurentian Bank of Canada is a full-service financial institution,

operating 256 branches and serving over one million customers. *New Positions Created (4):* Account Manager, Retail Services; Senior Customer Service Officer; Operations Manager; Senior Customer Service Officer.

LAURENTIAN UNIVERSITY
Att: Manager of Employment & HR
Ramsey Lake Road
Sudbury, ON P3E 2C6
Tel. 705-673-6581
Fax 705-673-6507
Email .... hrd@nickel.laurentian.ca
Website .... www.laurentian.ca
Employer Background: Founded in 1960, Laurentian University is a bilingual postsecondary institution. *New Positions Created (2):* Archives Technician, Library; Director, Computer Services.

LAURYSEN KITCHENS LTD.
Att: Mr. G. Castrucci
2415 Carp Road, PO Box 1235
Stittsville, ON K2S 1B3
Tel. 613-836-5353
Fax 613-836-7511
Employer Background: Laurysen is a kitchen cabinet manufacturer. *New Positions Created (2):* Kitchen Designer / Sales Rep; Kitchen Designer / Sales Rep.

**LAW SOCIETY OF BRITISH
COLUMBIA, THE**
Att: Human Resources Department
845 Cambie Street, 8th Floor
Vancouver, BC V6B 4Z9
Tel. 604-669-2533
Fax 604-443-5747
Email .... personnel@lsbc.org
Website .... www.lawsociety.bc.ca
Employer Background: The Law Society of British Columbia, a self-governing body for lawyers in BC, protects the public interest in the administration of justice. *New Positions Created (2):* Staff Lawyer, Professional Conduct; Staff Lawyer, Policy and Planning.

**LAW SOCIETY OF UPPER CANADA,
THE / LSUC**
Att: Human Resources
130 Queen Street West, Osgoode Hall
Toronto, ON M5G 2N6
Tel. 416-947-3300
Fax 416-947-3448
Email .... mdoyle@lsuc.on.ca
Website .... www.lsuc.on.ca
Employer Background: LSUC is the governing body for Ontario's legal profession. *New Positions Created (43):* Office Assistant, Articling and Placement; Resolution and Compliance Officers (2); Communications Advisor; Program Coordinator, Continuing Legal Education; Human Resources Manager; Auditor, Spot Audit; Website Producer; Counsel, Legal Affairs; Senior Counsel, Legal Affairs; Security Officer; Administrator, Articling and Placement; Bilingual Client Service Representative; Administrative Compliance Representative; Administrator, Spot Audit; Director, Professional Development and Competence; Faculty Position, Bar

Admission Course; Administrative Assistants (5); Coordinator, Spot Audit; Membership Services Representative; Auditor; General Counsel, Investigations; Resolution Services Officer; Administrative Compliance Representative; Academic Services Administrator; Bilingual Call Centre Representative; Administrative Assistants (6); Law Clerk; Membership Administrator; Office Assistant, Regulatory Division; Program Planning Lawyer; Regulatory Membership Services Representatives (2); Resolution and Compliance Officer; Senior Accounts Receivable Clerk; Facility Manager; Administrative Positions; Events Coordinator; Library Assistant; Manager, Advisory & Compliance Services; Discipline Counsel; Investigation Counsels; Policy Advisor; Discipline Counsel; Senior Counsel, Discipline.

**LAWYERS' PROFESSIONAL
INDEMNITY COMPANY / LPIC**
Att: Human Resources Department
1 Dundas Street West, Suite 2200, Box 75
Toronto, ON M5G 1Z3
Tel. 416-598-5899
Fax 416-598-5807
Email .... careers@lpic.ca
Website .... www.lpic.ca
Employer Background: Incorporated in 1990 by the Law Society of Upper Canada, LPIC provides professional liability insurance for lawyers in Ontario. *New Positions Created (8):* TitlePLUS Analyst; Customer Service Representative; Claims Examiner; Underwriter and Customer Service Manager; TitlePLUS Analyst Position; TitlePLUS Consultant; Claims Examiner; Director of practicePRO.

LAYFIELD PLASTICS LTD.
Att: Human Resources Manager
11120 Silversmith Place
Richmond, BC V7A 5E4
Tel. 604-275-5588
Fax 604-275-7867
Email .. bramsbottom@layfieldgroup.com
Website .... www.layfieldplastics.com
Employer Background: Layfield Plastics Ltd. supplies large vinyl liners for landfills, golf courses and other facilities that require geomembranes to insulate groundwater from surface contaminants. *New Positions Created (2):* Customer Service Representative; Materials Manager.

LAZIER HICKEY LANGS O'NEAL
Att: Peter J. Sullivan
25 Main Street West, 17th Floor
Hamilton, ON L8P 1H1
Website .... www.lazierhickey.com
Employer Background: Lazier Hickey Langs O'Neal is a law firm. *New Positions Created (3):* Commercial Litigation Secretary / Law Clerk; Corporate Secretary / Clerk; Corporate Clerk.

LE CHATEAU
Att: Human Resources
5695 Ferrier Street
Mount Royal, QC H4P 1N1

Tel. 514-738-7000
Fax 514-738-3670
Email .... ressources.humaines@lechateau.ca
Website .... www.lechateau.ca

Employer Background: Le Chateau is a leading retailer of apparel, accessories and footwear aimed at young-spirited, fashion-conscious men, women and children. *New Positions Created (8):* Accountant; Chief Accountant; Auditor / Loss Prevention Officer, Eastern Canada; Payroll Manager; General Accountant; Payroll / Benefits Clerk; Lease Administrator; Technical Designer.

LEA CONSULTING LTD.
Att: Human Resource Manager
251 Consumers Road, Suite 1200
Toronto, ON M2J 4R3
Tel. 416-490-8887
Fax 416-490-8376
Email .... humanresources@lea.ca
Website .... www.lea.ca

Employer Background: Lea Consulting Ltd. provides consulting services in transportation planning, traffic operations and highway / bridge design to public and private sector clients across Canada. *New Positions Created (12):* Bridge Engineers; Contract Administrators / Senior Construction Technicians; Highway Planning and Design Positions; Junior / Intermediate Inspector, Municipal; Resident Engineer; Senior Functional Planner / Project Mgr; Senior Inspector, Municipal; Sr Municipal Engineer; Sr Pavement Materials Engineer; Senior Transportation Planner / Traffic Engineer; Team Leader, Senior Resident Engineer; Transportation System Engineers / Technologists.

LEAMINGTON DISTRICT MEMORIAL HOSPITAL
Att: Human Resources Department
194 Talbot Street West
Leamington, ON N8H 1N9
Tel. 519-326-2373
Fax 519-322-2990
Email .... humanresources@ldmh.org
Website ..... www.leamingtonhospital.com

Employer Background: Leamington District Memorial Hospital serves 45,000 residents in South Essex County and surrounding municipalities, including Leamington, Kingsville, Wheatley, Romney, Essex, Harrow, Lakeshore and Pelee Island. *New Positions Created (3):* Assistant Executive Director; Director of Pharmacy; Nurse.

LEASIDE GROUP, INC.
Att: Human Resources Director
49 Wellington Street East
Suite 200, Gooderham Building
Toronto, ON M5E 1C9
Tel. 416-815-8008
Fax 416-815-8009
Email .... hr@leasidegroup.com
Website .... www.leasidegroup.com

Employer Background: Leaside Group, Inc. implements PeopleSoft products for Fortune 500 companies. *New Positions Created (3):* IT Consultants; ERP Consultants; IT Contractors.

LEBLANC LTD.
Att: Vice-President, Human Resources
461 Cornwall Road, PO Box 880
Oakville, ON L6J 5C5
Tel. 905-844-1242
Fax 905-844-8837
Email ..... mmcmeeki@leblanc-group.com
Website .... www.leblanc-group.com

Employer Background: LeBlanc Ltd. designs, manufactures and installs communication towers. *New Positions Created (6):* Aerial Technicians; Safety Mgr; Design Engineers; Installation Mgr / Field Coordinator; Intermediate / Senior Estimator; QC Inspector.

LEBLOND PARTNERSHIP
Att: Robert LeBlond
1000 - 9th Avenue SW, Suite 200
Calgary, AB T2P 2Y6
Fax 403-237-6329

Employer Background: LeBlond Partnership is an architectural firm. *New Positions Created (3):* Design Architects / Senior Architectural Technologists; Design Architects / Senior Architectural Technologists; Various Architectural Technologist Positions.

LEDCOR INDUSTRIES LTD.
Att: R. Hildenbrandt, Branch Manager
1015 - 4th Street SW, Suite 1260
Calgary, AB T2R 1J4
Tel. 403-264-9155
Fax 403-264-9166

Employer Background: Established in 1947, Ledcor Industries Ltd. is a multi-branch general contractor, specializing in design / build, industrial, warehouse, commercial, retail and multi-family residential projects. *New Positions Created (3):* Project Manager; Senior Estimator; Senior Estimator.

LEDCOR INDUSTRIES LTD.
Att: Operations Manager
3930 Nashua Drive, Suite 300
Mississauga, ON L4V 1M5
Tel. 905-673-0009
Fax 905-673-7538
Email .... bernadette.macha@ledcor.com
Website .... www.ledcor.com

Employer Background: Established in 1947, Ledcor Industries Ltd. is a multi-branch general contractor, specializing in design / build, industrial, warehouse, commercial, retail and multi-family residential projects. *New Positions Created (4):* Project Coordinator; Project Manager; Project Superintendent; Intermediate Estimator.

LEDCOR INDUSTRIES LTD.
Att: Branch Manager
555 Legget Drive, Suite 304
Kanata, ON K2K 2X3
Fax 613-271-2129
Website .... www.ledcor.com

Employer Background: Established in 1947, Ledcor Industries Ltd. is a multi-branch general contractor, specializing in design / build, industrial, warehouse, commercial, retail and multi-family residential projects. *New Positions Created (3):* Project Coordi-

nator; Project Manager; Project Superintendent.

LEESTA INDUSTRIES LTD.
Att: Human Resources Manager
6 Plateau Road
Pointe-Claire, QC H9R 5W2
Fax 514-694-3935
Email .... estaub@leesta.com
Website .... www.leesta.com

Employer Background: Leesta Industries Ltd. manufactures precision jet engine, hydraulic and mechanical parts and sub-assemblies for the aircraft industry. *New Positions Created (3):* Buyer; CNC Set-Up Operator Position; Supervisor.

LEGAL AID ONTARIO / LAO
Att: Human Resources
375 University Avenue, Suite 404
Toronto, ON M5G 2G1
Tel. 416-979-1446
Fax 416-979-8946
Email .... murphyj@lao.on.ca
Website .... www.legalaid.on.ca

Employer Background: LAO provides legal services for low-income Ontarians, funding 70 legal clinics in Ontario. *New Positions Created (11):* Civil Law Research Lawyer; Database Administrator; Manager, Technical Services; Programmer / Analyst; Webmaster; Bilingual Staff Lawyer; Project Leader, Clinic Training Coordination; Director of Finance; Supervisors, Criminal Duty Counsel Services; Supervisors, Family and Criminal Duty Counsel Services; Supervisors, Family Duty Counsel Services.

LEGAL AID SOCIETY OF ALBERTA
Att: Senior Counsel,
Human Resources
10320 - 102nd Avenue, Suite 300
Edmonton, AB T5J 4A1
Tel. 780-427-7575
Website .... www.legalaid.ab.ca

Employer Background: The Legal Aid Society of Alberta facilitates equal access to the justice system through the provision of legal services to those in need of financial assistance. *New Positions Created (4):* Staff Counsel; Assistant Senior Counsel (2); Assistant Senior Counsels, Family Law Staff Counsel Pilot Project (2); Senior Counsel.

LEGAL SERVICES SOCIETY
Att: Human Resources Department
1140 West Pender Street, Suite 1500
Vancouver, BC V6E 4G1
Tel. 604-660-4600
Fax 604-682-0725
Email .... lssresume@lss.bc.ca
Website .... www.vcn.bc.ca/lssbc

Employer Background: The Legal Services Society is a non-profit organization, providing legal aid, education and information services. *New Positions Created (2):* Manager, IT; Human Resources Advisors (2).

LEGATO SYSTEMS (CANADA) INC.
Att: Liz Liptrot, Recruiter

1111 International Boulevard
Burlington, ON L7L 6W1
Tel. 905-315-4000
Fax 905-315-4781
Email .... jobs-canada@legato.com
Website .... www.legato.com
Employer Background: Legato Systems
(Canada) Inc. is a leader in data storage
management software. *New Positions Created (4):* Premium Support Account Mgr;
Software Test Engineer; Unix System Administrator; Senior Network Administrator.

**LEGGAT PONTIAC
BUICK CADILLAC LTD.**
Att: Human Resources Manager
2207 Fairview Street
Burlington, ON L7R 3Y3
Tel. 905-333-3700
Fax 905-333-3934
Website .... www.leggatautogroup.com
Employer Background: Leggat Pontiac Buick
Cadillac Ltd. is an automotive dealership.
New Positions Created (2): Sales Manager;
Service Consultant.

**LEGISLATIVE ASSEMBLY OF
ONTARIO, OFFICE OF THE**
Att: Human Resources
Queen's Park, Room 2420, Whitney Block
Toronto, ON M7A 1A2
Fax 416-325-3573
Email .... hr@ontla.ola.org
Website .... www.ontla.on.ca
Employer Background: The Legislative Assembly of Ontario is the seat of the Ontario
government and parliament for the province. *New Positions Created (15):* Clerical
Assistant; Receptionist / Clerical Assistant;
Pay and Benefits Administrator; Supervisor,
Payroll; Broadcast Operator; Director, Permanent Register of Electors for Ontario; Simultaneous Interpreter; Director, Precinct
Properties; Security Officers; Chief Election
Officer; Coordinator, Health Services; Legislative Page Coordinator; Accounts Payable
Representative; Senior Financial Analyst;
Communications Operator.

LEGO CANADA INC.
Att: Louise Ingram, Business Manager
45 Mural Street, Unit 7
Richmond Hill, ON L4B 1J4
Tel. 905-764-5346
Email .. louise.ingram@america.lego.com
Website .... www.lego.com
Employer Background: LEGO Canada Inc.
distributes construction toys. *New Positions
Created (2):* Market / District Manager; National Account Manager.

LEICA GEOSYSTEMS LTD.
Att: Controller
513 McNicoll Avenue
Toronto, ON M2H 2C9
Tel. 416-497-2460
Fax 416-497-3356
Email .... human.resources@leica-lsg.com
Website .... www.leica-geosystems.com

Employer Background: Leica Geosystems
Ltd. is a leader in surveying, mapping and
global positioning systems and software.
New Positions Created (3): Payroll Clerk; Internal Sales Coordinator; Technical Sales
Representatives.

**LEISUREWORLD CAREGIVING
CENTRES**
Att: Human Resources Manager
8500 Warden Avenue
Markham, ON L6G 1A5
Tel. 905-477-4006
Fax 905-415-7623
Email .... lmurray@leisureworld.ca
Website .... www.leisureworld.ca
Employer Background: Leisureworld
Caregiving Centres operates long-term care
facilities throughout Ontario. *New Positions
Created (6):* Administrators; Activation Supervisor; Administrator; Director of Care;
Environmental Services Supervisor; Food
Services Supervisors.

LEITCH TECHNOLOGY CORP.
Att: Human Resources Department
25 Dyas Road
Toronto, ON M3B 1V7
Tel. 416-445-9648
Fax 416-445-7202
Email .... hr@leitch.com
Website .... www.leitch.com
Employer Background: Leitch Technology
Corp. provides innovative technology to television broadcast facilities and the converging communications industry worldwide.
New Positions Created (16): Intermediate
Test Technologist; Audio / Video Systems
Quality Assurance Technologist; Process
Engineering Specialist; Executive Assistant;
Manufacturing Engineering Team Leader;
Software Designer; Embedded Software
Developer; Sr ASIC Designer; Senior Machine Operator, Afternoon Shift; Software
Developer; Trainer Developer; Unix Systems
Analyst; Assistant Inside Sales Manager;
Business Analyst / Programmer; Technical
Clerk; Test Engineering Technologist.

LEN CORCORAN EXCAVATING
Att: Human Resources Manager
2212 Sydenham Road
Elginburg, ON K0H 1M0
Fax 613-548-8616
Employer Background: Len Corcoran Excavating is an excavating, sewer, water and
roadbuilding contractor. *New Positions Created (2):* Pipelayers; Contractor Position.

LENBROOK
Att: Human Resources Manager
633 Granite Court
Pickering, ON L1W 3K1
Tel. 905-831-6333
Fax 905-837-6352
Email .... humanresources@lenbrook.com
Website .... www.lenbrook.com
Employer Background: Lenbrook provides
specialty technology brands through independent national distributors in over 60

countries. *New Positions Created (8):* Audio
/ Visual Technicians; C++ Visual Basic Programmer; CAD Technical Illustrator; Director of Sales and Marketing; Engineer,
Speaker Design; Executive Assistant; Network Administrator; Sales Account Executive.

**LENNOX & ADDINGTON
ADDICTION SERVICES**
Att: Selection Committee
116 John Street, 3rd Floor
Napanee, ON K7R 1R2
Tel. 613-354-7521
Email .... laas@kingston.net
Employer Background: Lennox & Addington
Addiction Services provides community
treatment services to individuals and families with addiction-related problems. *New
Positions Created (2):* Executive Director;
Addiction Counsellor.

LENSCRAFTERS
Att: Recruiting Manager
21 Four Seasons Place, Suite 626
Toronto, ON M9B 6J8
Fax 416-626-2560
Website .... www.lenscrafters.com
Employer Background: LensCrafters is a
large optical retailer. *New Positions Created
(4):* Lab Technicians; Opticians; Retail Associates; Store Retail Manager.

LEON'S FURNITURE LTD.
Att: Human Resources Manager
45 Gordon Mackay Road
PO Box 1100, Station B
Toronto, ON M9L 2R8
Fax 416-243-1922
Website .... www.leonsfurniture.com
Employer Background: Leon's Furniture Ltd.
is a leading retailer of home furnishings,
appliances and electronics. *New Positions
Created (4):* Advertising / Marketing Positions; Merchandising Positions; Sales Positions; Store Managers.

LEONARD KOFFMAN, ARCHITECT
Att: Leonard Koffman
1300 Carling Avenue
Ottawa, ON K1Z 7L2
Fax 613-729-1558
Employer Background: Leonard Koffman,
Architect provides architectural services.
New Positions Created (3): AutoCAD Technologist / Graduate Architect; Autocad Technologist / Graduate Architect; Autocad Technologist / Graduate Architect.

**LESTER B. PEARSON COLLEGE OF
THE PACIFIC / PEARSON COLLEGE**
Att: Deanna Cuthbert, Director's Assistant
650 Pearson College Drive
Victoria, BC V9C 4H7
Fax 250-391-2412
Email .... dcuthbert@pearson-college.uwc.ca
Website .... www.pearson-college.uwc.ca
Employer Background: Pearson College is a
residential school, offering the International

Baccalaureate (IB) program to students from over 80 countries. *New Positions Created (6):* College Nurse; Information Technology Technician; Teacher, French as a Second Language; Faculty Position, Biology / Environmental Systems; Faculty Position, Economics ; Faculty Position, Philosophy.

LESTER B. PEARSON SCHOOL BOARD
Att: Human Resources Manager
257 Beaconsfield Boulevard
Beaconsfield, QC H9W 4A5

Fax 514-422-3006
Email .... advoc@lbpsb.qc.ca
Website .... www.lbpsb.qc.ca
Employer Background: The Lester B. Pearson School Board is responsible for over 65 elementary and secondary schools and centres. *New Positions Created (2):* Teachers, Adult and Vocational Education; Assistant Director General.

LETHBRIDGE COMMUNITY COLLEGE
Att: Barb Nekich, HR Services
3000 College Drive South
Lethbridge, AB T1K 1L6

Tel. 403-320-3207
Fax 403-394-7311
Email .... hr@lethbridgecollege.ab.ca
Website .... www.lethbridgecollege.ab.ca
Employer Background: Founded in 1957, LCC is Canada's first public community college, serving approximately 7,000 students. *New Positions Created (20):* Information Services Librarian; Director, Human Resources; Instructor, Centre for Criminal Justice; Directed Field Studies Instructor; Instructor, Applied Conservation Enforcement; Accounting Instructor; Biology Instructors; Communication Arts Instructor; Computer Applications Instructor; Electrician Apprenticeship Instructor; English Instructors; Geomatics Instructor, Digital Mapping & Geographical Information Systems; Geomatics Instructor, Survey & GPS; Humanities Instructors; Nursing Faculty Positions (3); Office Procedures Instructor; Partsman Apprenticeship Instructor; Psychology Instructors; Speech / Communication Instructors; Dean, Student & Enrolment Services.

LEVELTON ENGINEERING LTD.
Att: Wayne Edwards, PEng
12791 Clarke Place, Suite 150
Richmond, BC V6V 2H9

Tel. 604-278-1411
Fax 604-278-1042
Email .... wedwards@levelton.com
Website .... www.levelton.com
Employer Background: Levelton Engineering Ltd. offers a wide range of engineering and scientific services, from materials engineering to cathodic protection and corrosion prevention. *New Positions Created (2):* Senior Air Quality Specialist; Air Quality Specialists.

LEVI STRAUSS & CO. (CANADA) INC.
Att: Human Resources
70 Easton Road
Brantford, ON N3P 1J5

Tel. 519-756-8770
Fax 519-756-1380
Website .... www.levistrauss.com
Employer Background: Levi Strauss & Co. (Canada) Inc. is a subsidiary of San Francisco-based Levi Strauss & Co. Inc., one of the world's largest brand-name apparel marketers, with sales of $6 billion and 35,000 employees worldwide. *New Positions Created (3):* Industrial Maintenance Mechanic; Data Analyst; Industrial Maintenance Mechanic.

LEVITT-SAFETY
Att: Joan Noble
2872 Bristol Circle
Oakville, ON L6H 5T5

Tel. 905-829-3299
Fax 905-829-5422
Email .... joan.noble@levitt-safety.com
Website .... www.levitt-safety.com
Employer Background: Levitt-Safety is a leading industrial distributor of fire, safety and environmental monitoring equipment. *New Positions Created (2):* Service Manager; Alarm Technician.

LEXCAN LTD.
Att: Human Resources Manager
85 Vulcan Street
Toronto, ON M9W 1L4

Tel. 416-249-8361
Fax 416-249-0253
Email .... sales@lexcan.com
Website .... www.lexcan.com
Employer Background: Lexcan Ltd. manufactures and distributes commercial roofing products. *New Positions Created (2):* Sales Professionals, Roofing & Waterproofing Systems; Architectural Sales Representative.

LGS GROUP INC.
Att: Human Resources Manager
10303 Jasper Avenue
Suite 1650, Metropolitan Place
Edmonton, AB T5J 3N6

Tel. 780-421-8010
Fax 780-421-8077
Email .... lgs_edm_hr@lgs.ca
Website .... www.lgs.ca
Employer Background: Founded in Montreal in 1979, LGS Group Inc. is an international IT and management consulting firm, with over 2,280 employees and 19 offices in Canada, the USA and Europe. *New Positions Created (3):* Intermediate Oracle Designers / Developers; Oracle Database Analyst; Project Manager.

LIBERTY HEALTH
Att: Kim Willhelm, Human Resources
3500 Steeles Avenue East
Markham, ON L3R 0X4

Tel. 905-946-4000
Fax 905-946-4129
Email .... kim_willhelm@health.lmig.com
Website .... www.coverme.com
Employer Background: Liberty Health is one of Canada's largest supplementary health benefits companies. *New Positions Created*

(2): Account Executive; Intermediate Group Underwriter.

LIBERTY MUTUAL GROUP
Att: Human Resources
675 Cochrane Drive, Suite 100
Unionville, ON L3R 0S7

Tel. 905-415-8400
Fax 905-415-9811
Website .. www.libertymutualcanada.com
Employer Background: Liberty Mutual Group is a Fortune 500 financial services organization, with over 23,000 employees and more than 500 offices in North America. *New Positions Created (14):* Claims Representative; Customer Service Representative, Call Centre; Customer Service Representative, Claims; Field Sales Position; Field Service Position; Insurance Sales Counsellors; Support Staff / Personal Assistant Position; Bilingual Underwriter; Call Centre Service Representatives; Personal Sales Representatives; Call Centre Service Reps; Claims Representatives; Accident Benefit Claims Specialist; Bodily Injury Claims Specialist.

LIBURDI ENGINEERING LTD.
Att: Human Resources Manager
400 Highway 6 North
Dundas, ON L9H 7K4

Tel. 905-689-0734
Fax 905-689-0739
Email .... liburdi@liburdi.com
Website .... www.liburdi.com
Employer Background: Liburdi Engineering Ltd. refurbishes turbine engine components and manufactures robotic welding systems and precision welding power supplies for the aerospace industry. *New Positions Created (18):* Machinists; Metal Finishers; Gas Turbine Engineers; Marketing & Sales Order Desk Position; Customer Support / Marketing Position; Machinists; CAD Drafting Position; Computer Systems Position; Electrical Technicians; Materials Buyer, Inventory; Mechanical Engineer; Mechanical Technicians; Metal Finishers / Equipment Operators; Jet Engine Component Repair Technician; Skilled Machinists; Electrical Technicians; Machinists; Mechanical Technologists.

LIFELINE SYSTEMS CANADA INC.
Att: Human Resources Department
95 Barber Greene Road, Suite 105
Toronto, ON M3C 3E9

Tel. 416-445-3387
Fax 416-445-1918
Email .... hrdept@lifelinesys.com
Website .... www.lifelinecanada.com
Employer Background: Established in 1974, Lifeline Systems Canada Inc. provides personal response and support services for elderly individuals residing at home. *New Positions Created (10):* Marketing Representatives (2); Marketing Representative; Program Manager; Response Centre Manager; PC Help Desk Representative; Bilingual Marketing Representative; Marketing Representative; Customer Service Representative; Manager, Regional Sales and Marketing; Response Centre Operator.

LIFESCAN CANADA LTD.
Att: Human Resources Department
4170 Still Creek Drive, Suite 234
Burnaby, BC V5C 6C6
Tel. 604-320-2965
Fax 604-469-7065
Email .... careers@lifescancanada.com
Website .... www.lifescancanada.com
Employer Background: LifeScan Canada Ltd., a subsidiary of Johnson & Johnson, markets blood glucose meters for people with diabetes. *New Positions Created (11):* Associate Product Manager; Director, Human Resources; Manager, Regulatory Affairs; Sales Representatives; Senior Product Manager; Customer Service Representatives; Marketing Communications Specialist; Sales Representative; Marketing Associate; Technical Service Administrator; Financial Planner and Analyst.

LIFESTYLE RETIREMENT COMMUNITIES
Att: Human Resources Manager
2803 - 41st Avenue West
Vancouver, BC V6N 4B4
Tel. 604-263-0921
Fax 604-263-7719
Email .... lisa.kachur@lrc.ca
Website .... www.lrc.ca
Employer Background: Incorporated in 1985, Lifestyle Retirement Communities is a leading operator of upscale retirement residences, serving over 2,000 people across Canada. *New Positions Created (6):* Marketing Manager; Registered Nurses; Office Manager; Director of Care; Registered Nurses; General Manager, Crofton Manor.

LIFESTYLE RETIREMENT COMMUNITIES
Att: Vicki Constantin
50 Burnhamthorpe Road West, Suite 600
Mississauga, ON L5B 3C2
Tel. 905-270-0322
Fax 905-270-3018
Email .... vicki.constantin@lrc.ca
Website .... www.lrc.ca
Employer Background: Incorporated in 1985, Lifestyle Retirement Communities is a leading operator of upscale retirement residences, serving over 2,000 people across Canada. *New Positions Created (4):* Intermediate Accountant; Office Manager; Payroll Coordinator; Retirement Residence Administrator.

LIFESTYLE RETIREMENT COMMUNITIES, FOREST HILL PLACE
Att: Marla Borenstein
645 Castlefield Avenue
Toronto, ON M5N 3A5
Tel. 416-785-1511
Fax 416-785-6228
Email .... fh.rec@lrc.ca
Website .... www.lrc.ca
Employer Background: Incorporated in 1985, Lifestyle Retirement Communities is a leading operator of upscale retirement residences, serving over 2,000 people across Canada. *New Positions Created (5):* Manager,

Resident Care; Service Needs Coordinator; Service Needs Coordinator; Manager, Resident Care; Recreation Assistant.

LIFTKING INDUSTRIES INC.
Att: Bill Mavin
7135 Islington Avenue
Woodbridge, ON L4L 1V9
Tel. 905-851-3988
Fax 905-851-6396
Email .... billm@liftking.com
Website .... www.liftking.com
Employer Background: Established in 1968, Liftking Industries Inc. is a North American manufacturer of rough terrain forklifts, specialized carriers, heavy material handling transporters and steel mill equipment. *New Positions Created (2):* Senior Buyer; Senior Buyer.

LIMESTONE DISTRICT SCHOOL BOARD
Att: Bruce Marchen, HR Services
220 Portsmouth Avenue, Postal Bag 610
Kingston, ON K7L 4X4
Tel. 613-544-6920
Fax 613-544-8501
Website .... www.limestone.edu.on.ca
Employer Background: Limestone District School Board operates 56 elementary schools and 12 secondary schools, serving over 26,000 students. *New Positions Created (6):* Principals and Vice-Principals; Planned Giving and Development Officer; Senior Clerk; Librarian; Secondary Teacher; Superintendent of Education.

LINAMAR CORPORATION, AUTOCOM DIVISION
Att: Recruitment Coordinator
301 Massey Road
Guelph, ON N1K 1B2
Tel. 519-836-7550
Email .... recruiter@linamar.ca
Website .... www.linamar.ca
Employer Background: Founded in 1966, Linamar Corporation is a leader in precision machining for the automotive industry. *New Positions Created (11):* Drivers; General Machinists; Internal Auditor; Maintenance Mechanic; Metallurgist; Process Engineers; Quality Assurance Manager; Quality Engineer; Technical Buyers; Tool Cutter / Grinder; Web Developer.

LINAMAR CORPORATION, ESTON DIVISION
Att: Recruitment Coordinator
287 Speedvale Avenue West
Guelph, ON N1K 1C5
Tel. 519-836-7550
Fax 519-824-4859
Email .... recruiter@linamar.ca
Website .... www.linamar.ca
Employer Background: Founded in 1966, Linamar Corporation is a leader in precision machining for the automotive industry. *New Positions Created (33):* Design Engineer, Clutch Modules; Design Engineer, Small Engines; Drivers; Electrical Engineer; Gen-

eral Machinists; Maintenance Technicians; Manufacturing Technicians; Network Administrator; Planner / Buyer; Process Engineers; Project Engineers; Quality Assurance Manager; Quality Assurance Technician; Quality Engineers; Supplier Quality Engineers; Technical Buyers; Human Resources Manager; Aerospace Process Engineer; Maintenance Mechanics; Materials Manager; Program Managers; Chief Financial Officer; Estimating Engineer; Estimating Manager; Quality Engineer; Design Engineers; Engineering Manager; Estimating Engineer; Metallurgist; Project Engineers; Web Developer; Materials Manager; Project Engineers.

LINCOLN TECHNOLOGY CORPORATION
Att: Aimee Reichert, Office Supervisor
10464 - 172nd Street
Edmonton, AB T5S 1G9
Fax 780-484-1005
Email ...... areichert@lincolntechnology.com
Website .... www.lincolntechnology.com
Employer Background: Lincoln Technology Corporation is a global provider of asset management products and services. *New Positions Created (4):* CMMS Specialists / Trainers; Maintenance Specialists; CMMS Specialist; Technical Facilitator.

LINCOLN, TOWN OF
Att: John Kukalis, CET,
Director of Public Works
4800 South Service Road
Beamsville, ON L0R 1B1
Tel. 905-563-8205
Fax 905-563-6566
Email .... generalinquiries@
.... townoflincoln.com
Website .... www.townoflincoln.com
Employer Background: The Town of Lincoln, one of the fastest-growing municipalities in the Niagara region, has over 20,000 residents. *New Positions Created (2):* Parks and Facilities Foreperson; Roads Services Foreperson.

LINDOR INC.
Att: Human Resources Department
9600 Meilleur Street, Suite 740
Montréal, QC H2N 2E3
Tel. 514-384-5243
Fax 514-384-3487
Employer Background: Lindor Inc. is an established fashion retailer in eastern Canada. *New Positions Created (6):* District Sales Manager; Sales Audit Position; Assistant Manager; Supervisor, Distribution Centre; Administrative Assistant; Inventory Distribution Position.

LINDSAY REHABILITATION HOSPITAL
Att: Eric Vallee, HR Manager
6363 Hudson Road
Montréal, QC H3S 1M9
Fax 514-345-5246
Email .... evallee@ssss.gouv.qc.ca
Website .... www.hopital-lindsay.qc.ca

Employer Background: The Lindsay Rehabilitation Hospital provides intensive functional rehabilitation services to more than 1,100 patients per year in the areas of orthopedics, neurology, amputation and outpatient services. *New Positions Created (3):* Nurses; Occupational Therapists / Physiotherapists; Speech Language Pathologist.

LINEAR TRANSFER SYSTEMS LTD.
Att: Human Resources Manager
75 Hooper Road
Barrie, ON L4N 9S3
Tel. 705-737-9339
Fax 705-737-1689
Email .... linear@bconnex.net
Website .... www.lineartransfer.com
Employer Background: Linear Transfer Systems Ltd. designs, assembles, installs and supports specialized stamping press automation equipment. *New Positions Created (2):* Electrical Engineer; Junior Mechanical Designer.

LINEN CHEST
Att: Human Resources Department
7350 Taschereau Boulevard
Brossard, QC J4W 1M9
Tel. 514-331-5260
Fax 450-622-3052
Email .... aeltagi@linenchest.com
Website .... www.linenchest.com
Employer Background: Linen Chest is a leading retailer of home fashions. *New Positions Created (4):* Decorators; MIS Department Position; Store Manager; Store Manager.

LINMOR TECHNOLOGIES INC.
Att: Human Resources
2270 St. Laurent Boulevard
Ottawa, ON K1G 6C4
Tel. 613-727-2757
Fax 613-727-2627
Email .... hr@linmor.com
Website .... www.linmor.com
Employer Background: Founded in 1994, Linmor Technologies Inc. is a leading developer of network management systems. *New Positions Created (12):* Sales Executives; Customer Service Support Manager; Intermediate and Senior Software Developers; Product Manager; Configuration Management and Build Specialist; Quality Assurance Specialists; Customer Service Manager; Intermediate and Senior Software Developers; Junior Software Developers; Sales Executive; Software Development Manager; Technical Writer.

LIONS GATE HOSPITAL
Att: Frances Carmichael
152 - 15th Street East, 2nd Floor
Vancouver, BC V7L 4N9
Tel. 604-984-5768
Fax 604-984-5770
Email .... frances.carmichael@
.... nshr.hnet.bc.ca
Website .... www.nshr.org
Employer Background: Lions Gate Hospital is 335-bed acute care facility and part of the

North Shore Health Region. *New Positions Created (3):* Administrative Assistant; Registered Nurse; Child and Adult Psychiatrists.

LIPONEX INC.
Att: Dr. Daniel L. Sparks,
Chief Scientific Officer and President
600 Peter Morand Crescent, Suite 250
Ottawa, ON K1G 5Z3
Email .... info@liponex.ca
Website .... www.liponex.ca
Employer Background: Liponex Inc. is a life science R&D company developing novel therapeutics focusing on cholesterol and toxin elimination and the transport of drugs to target tissues. *New Positions Created (3):* Research Associate; Vice-President, Corporate Development; Research Associate.

LIPPMAN LEEBOSH APRIL
Att: Philip Farkas, CA
1 Westmount Square, Suite 1001
Montréal, QC H3Z 2P9
Tel. 514-931-5821
Fax 514-931-3602
Email .... lla@lla.com
Website .... www.lla.com
Employer Background: Lippman Leebosh April is a mid-sized CA firm. *New Positions Created (3):* Chartered Accountants; Bilingual Bookkeeper; Accountant.

LIQUIDATORS CLEARINGHOUSE INC.
Att: Human Resources Manager
3905 - 29th Street NE
Calgary, AB T1Y 6B5
Employer Background: LCI is a full-service liquidation company, using wholesale, retail and auction sales to support the needs of their clients. *New Positions Created (3):* Auction Personnel; Retail Sales Manager; Warehouse Personnel.

LIQUOR CONTROL BOARD OF ONTARIO / LCBO
Att: Human Resource Services
55 Lakeshore Boulevard East, 2nd Floor
Toronto, ON M5E 1A4
Tel. 416-365-5900
Fax 416-864-6849
Email .... jobs@lcbo.com
Website .... www.lcbo.com
Employer Background: LCBO is the largest single purchaser of beverage alcohol in the world, purchasing wine, spirits and beer from over 60 countries for 600 retail stores. *New Positions Created (8):* Economic Policy Analyst; Senior Personal Computer Specialist; Systems Analyst; Coordinator, French Language Services; Accounts Payable Analyst; Retail Accounting Analyst; Labour Lawyer; Process Analyst.

LIQUOR DISTRIBUTION BRANCH, BC
Att: Human Resources Manager
2625 Rupert Street
Vancouver, BC V5M 3T5
Tel. 604-252-3244
Fax 604-252-3250
Email ... darryl.lavalley@bcliquorstores.com

Website .... www.bcliquorstores.com
Employer Background: LDB of British Columbia is the second-largest distributor and retailer of beverage alcohol in Canada, with $1.7 billion in annual sales. *New Positions Created (21):* Performance / Organizational Development Consultant; Manager, Store Support Services; Director, Loss Prevention; Data Warehouse Administrator (IS 11); Database Programmer (IS 9); Technology Infrastructure Coordinator (IS 11); Senior Policy Analyst; Manager, Accounts Payable; Manager, Financial Reporting; Supervisor of Stores Data; Communications Program Officer; Human Resources Advisors (2); Director, Distribution; Project Mgr; Coordinator, Human Resources Information Systems; Senior Operational Auditor; Assistant Manager, Payroll; Director, Information Services; Manager, Social Responsibility; Operational Audit Manager; Manager, Budgets.

LITTLE MOUNTAIN RESIDENTIAL CARE & HOUSING SOCIETY
Att: Angela Johnston, President
330 - 36th Avenue East
Vancouver, BC V5W 3Z4
Tel. 604-325-2298
Fax 604-325-3655
Email .... alzvrds@mindlink.bc.ca
Website .... www.littlemountaincare.org
Employer Background: Little Mountain Residential Care & Housing Society, a nonprofit society, manages a subsidized seniors housing complex, a 117-bed intermediate-care home and a multi-level care facility. *New Positions Created (2):* Executive Director; HR Generalist.

LIVEWIRE DIGITAL IMAGING
Att: Human Resources Department
90 Trowers Road
Woodbridge, ON L4L 7K5
Tel. 905-264-0747
Fax 905-264-0755
Email .... greg@livewiredigital.com
Website .... www.livewiredigital.com
Employer Background: LiveWire Digital Imaging is a prepress house, specializing in digital imaging. *New Positions Created (2):* Proofer; Packaging Print Production Coordinator.

LNB INC.
Att: Human Resources
44B Metropolitan Road
Toronto, ON M1R 2T6
Tel. 416-321-5603
Fax 416-321-6027
Email .... jobs@lnbinc.com
Website .... www.lnbinc.com
Employer Background: LNB Inc. specializes in software and hardware development for card-based access to business equipment and point-of-sale systems. *New Positions Created (9):* Installation / Support Technicians; Production Supervisor; Purchasing and Production Manager; Research and Development Project Manager; Warehouse / Shipping Manager; Purchasing and Productions Manager; Quality Assurance Test-

ers; Service Delivery Manager; Software Developers.

LOADSTAR DISPATCHERS / NORTHERN INDUSTRIAL CARRIERS LTD.
Att: Ernie
7823 - 34th Street
Edmonton, AB T6B 2V5
Fax 780-469-4206
Email .... dmcalpine@nictrucking.com
Employer Background: Loadstar Dispatchers / Northern Industrial Carriers Ltd. provides trucking services, pipe handling and storage. *New Positions Created (3):* General Manager; Purchasing / Administration Manager; Inside Sales Position.

LOBLAW COMPANIES LTD.
Att: Human Resources
6220A Yonge Street
Toronto, ON M2M 3X4
Tel. 416-218-7777
Fax 416-218-7801
Email .... lslhr@ngco.com
Website .... www.loblaw.com
Employer Background: Loblaw Companies Ltd. is a leading grocery retailer, with over 114,000 employees in Canada. *New Positions Created (9):* Photolab Technicians; Non-Food Managers; Assistant Store Managers; Floral Managers; Bilingual Administrative Assistant; Non-Food Manager; Store Manager Trainee; Coffee Bar Technician; Photolab Technician.

LOBLAW COMPANIES LTD.
Att: Human Resources
6100 Freemont Boulevard
Mississauga, ON L5R 3V7
Fax 905-712-6644
Email .... mclimen@ngco.com
Website .... www.loblaw.com
Employer Background: Loblaw Companies Ltd. is a leading grocery retailer, with over 114,000 employees in Canada. *New Positions Created (2):* Operations Mgr; Supervisor.

LOBLAW PROPERTIES LTD. / LPL
Att: Jennifer Kim, HR Department
22 St. Clair Avenue East, Suite 600
Toronto, ON M4T 2S5
Tel. 416-922-8500
Fax 416-967-2541
Website .... www.loblaw.com
Employer Background: LPL is the real estate arm of Loblaw Companies Ltd., the largest food distribution company in Canada. *New Positions Created (3):* Administrative Assistant; Senior Property Administrator; Commercial Real Estate Lawyer.

LOCKERBIE & HOLE CONTRACTING LTD.
Att: Human Resources
PO Box 414
Edmonton, AB T5J 2J6
Tel. 780-452-1250
Fax 780-451-0622
Email .... wbablitz@lockerbiehole.com
Website .... www.lockerbiehole.com

Employer Background: Founded in 1898, Lockerbie & Hole Contracting Ltd. provides construction services to the industrial, municipal, commercial and institutional market sectors. *New Positions Created (3):* Checker Draftsperson, Pipe Fabrication; Chief Draftsperson, Pipe Fabrication; Spooler Draftsperson, Pipe Fabrication.

LOCKERBIE INDUSTRA INC.
Att: Human Resources Manager
401 Salter Street
New Westminster, BC V3M 5Y1
Website .... www.industra.com
Employer Background: Lockerbie Industra Inc. provides engineering, construction, fabrication, manufacturing, thermal and project management services to the pulp and paper, energy and power sectors. *New Positions Created (3):* Senior Piping Estimators; Intermediate Piping Estimator; Piping and Mechanical Designer / Draftsperson.

LOCKHEED MARTIN CANADA INC.
Att: Human Resources Manager
1306 Merril Lynch Tower
Edmonton, AB T5J 2Z2
Fax 780-425-0956
Email ..... recruiting.lmcanada@lmco.com
Website ... www.lockheedmartin.com/canada
Employer Background: Lockheed Martin Canada Inc. is a leading software and systems developer, as well as Canada's leading supplier of electronic defence and sonar systems. *New Positions Created (2):* Accountant; Customer Service Representatives (3).

LOCKHEED MARTIN CANADA INC.
Att: Human Resources Manager
3001 Solandt Road
Kanata, ON K2K 2M8
Tel. 613-599-3270
Email ..... recruiting.lmcanada@lmco.com
Website ... www.lockheedmartin.com/canada
Employer Background: Lockheed Martin Canada Inc. is a leading software and systems integrator, as well as Canada's leading supplier of electronic defence and sonar systems. *New Positions Created (29):* Manufacturing and Training Specialist; Technical Specialist; Acoustics Systems Engineer; Advisory Member, Software Engineering; Application Support Analyst; Data Management Specialist; Development Webmaster; DMS Capture / Program Manager; Electro-Optics System Engineer; Electronic Warfare System Engineer; Facility Coordinator; Hardware Engineers; Head of Engineering, Kanata; Logistics Specialist; Manufacturing and Training Specialist; Process Engineer; Process Owner, Program Management; Programmer Analyst; Quality Process Advisor; Quality Software Engineer; Radar System Engineer; Senior Logistics Specialist; Senior R&D Specialist; Senior Software Engineer; Senior Software Engineer; Software Engineers; Software Specialist; Systems Engineers; Translator.

LOCKHEED MARTIN CANADA INC.
Att: Human Resources Manager

1000 Windmill Road
Suite 20, Burnside Industrial Park
Halifax, NS B3B 1L7
Tel. 902-468-3399
Fax 902-468-3403
Email ..... recruiting.lmcanada@lmco.com
Website ... www.lockheedmartin.com/canada
Employer Background: Lockheed Martin Canada Inc. is a leading software and systems developer, as well as Canada's leading supplier of electronic defence and sonar systems. *New Positions Created (4):* Application Support Analyst; Senior Software Specialist; Software Specialist; Software Specialist.

LODGE AT BROADMEAD, THE
Att: Barb Etherington
4579 Chatterton Way
Victoria, BC V8X 4Y7
Tel. 250-658-3240
Fax 250-658-0948
Employer Background: Operated by the Tillicum and Veterans' Care Society, the Lodge at Broadmead is a 151-bed intermediate care facility, serving elderly residents. *New Positions Created (9):* Coordinator of Rehabilitation Services; Lodge Nurse; Occupational and Physical Therapists; Manager, Client Services; Manager, Client Services; Coordinator, Rehabilitation Services; Systems Analyst; Social Worker; Nurse.

LOEWEN GROUP INC., THE
Att: Human Resources
4126 Norland Avenue
Burnaby, BC V5G 3S8
Tel. 604-299-9321
Email .... careers@loewengroup.com
Website .... www.loewengroup.com
Employer Background: The Loewen Group Inc. is one of North America's largest funeral service corporations, with 1,500 funeral homes and cemeteries and 12,000 employees across Canada, the USA and UK. *New Positions Created (3):* Manager, Advertising; Manager, Employment; Marketing Analyst.

LOEWEN GROUP INC., THE
Att: Human Resources Manager
2225 Sheppard Avenue, Suite 1100
Toronto, ON M2J 5C2
Fax 416-498-2477
Email .... careers@loewengroup.com
Website .... www.loewengroup.com
Employer Background: The Loewen Group Inc. is one of North America's largest funeral service corporations, with 1,500 funeral homes and cemeteries and 12,000 employees across Canada, the USA and UK. *New Positions Created (9):* Administrative Assistant, Finance; Capital Budgeting Analysts; Compensation Analyst; Financial Budgeting Analyst; Merchandising Category Manager; Purchasing Category Mgr; Training Coordinator; Treasury Analyst; Corporate Counsel.

LOFT COMMUNITY SERVICES
Att: Junia Rajapakse
205 Richmond Street, Suite 301
Toronto, ON M5V 1V3

Tel. 416-979-1994
Fax 416-979-3028
Email .... jrajapakse@loftcs.org
Website .... www.loftcs.org
Employer Background: LOFT Community Services offers housing, outreach and support to vulnerable and homeless people in Toronto and York region. *New Positions Created (3):* Project Coordinator; Senior Residential Support Worker; Community Support Worker.

LOGIBRO INC.
Att: Human Resources Department
3500 de Maisonneuve Boulevard West
Suite 1400, 2 Place Alexis-Nihon
Montréal, QC H3Z 3C1
Tel. 514-931-4433
Fax 514-931-4818
Email .... reshum@logibro.com
Website .... www.logibro.com
Employer Background: Founded in 1985, Logibro Inc. designs and markets technology solutions and services for the leisure travel industry. The company employs 200 professionals, with offices in Montreal, Toronto, Portland and Paris. *New Positions Created (16):* Analyst / Programmers, BBX / Basic; Analysts / Programmers; Analysts / Programmers, C; Analysts / Programmers, E-Commerce; Application Specialist; GUI Specialist; Java Developer / Specialist; Network Administrator; Pre-Sale Application Specialist; Programmer / Analysts, C; Programmer / Analysts, Communications; Programmer / Analysts, E-Commerce; Schema Design Database Analyst; Software Support Specialist; Technical Operator; Technician, Application Support.

LOGICAL SOFTWARE CORPORATION
Att: Human Resources Manager
3889 Keith Street, Unit C2
Burnaby, BC V5J 5K4
Tel. 604-419-3939
Fax 604-419-3949
Email .... hr@logicalsoft.com
Website .... www.logicalsoft.com
Employer Background: Logical Software Corporation provides advanced computer telephony integration services to call centres around the world. *New Positions Created (2):* Sales and Marketing Position; Software Developers.

LOMBARD CANADA LTD.
Att: Human Resources Department
105 Adelaide Street West
Toronto, ON M5H 1P9
Tel. 416-350-4389
Fax 416-350-4106
Email ...... human.resources@lombard.ca
Website .... www.lombard.ca
Employer Background: Lombard Canada Ltd. is a mid-sized property and casualty insurance company. *New Positions Created (19):* Business Systems Analyst; Commercial Lines Underwriter, Mass Marketing; Loss Control Representatives (2); Account Director; Market Research Analyst; Researcher; Staff Auditor; Risk Control Representative;

Adjuster II / Senior Adjuster (Inside); Adjuster / Senior Adjuster; Commercial Lines Underwriters / Senior Underwriters; Loss Control Representatives, Boiler and Machinery; Commercial Lines Underwriters / Senior Underwriters; Claims Director; Chief Claims Officer; Chief Underwriting Officer; Director, Actuarial Services; Claims Professionals; Director, Vendor Management.

LONDON BLUES
Att: Human Resources Manager
115 Montpelier Boulevard
St-Laurent, QC H4N 2G3
Tel. 514-727-3701
Fax 514-744-5352
Website .... www.londonbluesjeans.com
Employer Background: London Blues is the newest and fastest-growing label in the W. Green Jeans family of jeans and denim clothing. *New Positions Created (4):* Patternmaker Assistant; Sketcher / Illustrator; Merchandiser; Salesperson.

LONDON, CITY OF
Att: Human Resources Division
300 Dufferin Avenue
Room 508, Box 5035, City Hall
London, ON N6A 4L9
Tel. 519-661-4500
Fax 519-661-5802
Email .... recruit_ads@city.london.on.ca
Website .... www.city.london.on.ca
Employer Background: The City of London is a single-tier municipality, serving 340,000 residents, with approximately 2,200 employees and a budget of $420 million. *New Positions Created (15):* City Clerk; Human Resources Manager; General Manager, Covent Garden Market; General Manager, Tourism London; Manager, Corporate Security; Commissioner of Environmental Services / City Engineer; Administrator, Dearness Services; Administrator, Recreation Services; Manager, Community Planning & Program Development; Manager, Resident Care; Senior Manager, Recreation Programs; Architectural Plans Examiner; Solid Waste / Public Service Representative; Water and Wastewater Control Systems Coordinator; Community Planning and Research Associate.

LONDON GUARANTEE INSURANCE COMPANY
Att: Josie Gallo
650 Georgia Street West
Suite 2500, Box 11542
Vancouver, BC V6B 4N7
Tel. 604-682-2663
Fax 604-682-2664
Email .... jgallo@londonguarantee.com
Website .... www.londonguarantee.com
Employer Background: London Guarantee Insurance Company is a Canadian-owned property and casualty insurer, with expertise in specialty niche insurance products. *New Positions Created (5):* Technical Representative, Residential Construction; Financial Analysts / Underwriters, Contract Surety; Commercial Surety Underwriter; Financial Analysts; Fidelity Underwriter, Corporate Risk.

LONDON GUARANTEE INSURANCE COMPANY
Att: Human Resources Manager
77 King Street West
34th Floor, Royal Trust Tower
Toronto, ON M5K 1K2
Tel. 416-360-8183
Fax 416-360-8267
Website .... www.londonguarantee.com
Employer Background: London Guarantee Insurance Company is a Canadian-owned property and casualty insurer, with expertise in specialty niche insurance products. *New Positions Created (2):* Accounts Payable Clerk; Underwriting Counsel.

LONDON HEALTH SCIENCES CENTRE
Att: Employee Relations Officer, HR
339 Windermere Road, Box 5339
London, ON N6A 5A5
Tel. 519-685-8300
Fax 519-663-3889
Email .... humanres@lhsc.on.ca
Website .... www.lhsc.on.ca
Employer Background: LHSC, one of Canada's largest teaching hospitals, provides a full range of patient care services. *New Positions Created (67):* Social Worker, Children's Care Program; Clinical Dietitian; Clinical Psychologist; Coordinator, Children's Care Paediatric Inpatients; Coordinator, Diagnostic Cardiology; Coordinator, Perioperative Care (Operating Room); Coordinator, Workload Measurement and Resource Team; Echocardiography Technicians (2); Nurse Case Manager, Eating Disorder Treatment Services; Pharmaceutical Care Coordinator; Pharmacist; Professional Practice Leader; Biomedical Engineering Technologist; Compensation Associate; Physiotherapist; Psychometrist; Secretary; Social Worker, Mental Health Care Program; HR Financial Specialist; MRI Registered Technologist; Physiotherapist, Clinical Neuroscience; Regional Field Coordinators; Registered Technologist, Medical Imaging Nuclear Medicine; Professional Practice Leader, Occupational Therapy; Regional Field Coordinator, Ontario Joint Replacement Registry; Vice-President, Human Resources; Coordinator, Workload Measurement and Resource; Nurse Case Manager; Patient Equipment Facilitator; Clinical Dietitian; Clinical Psychologist, Mental Health - Eating Disorder Services; Medical Dicta Typist; Occupational Therapist, Mental Health - Eating Disorder Services; Social Worker, Mental Health - Eating Disorder Services; Registered Nurse, Critical Care, Intensive Care Unit; Employee Relations Officer; Operational Performance Specialists; Coordinator, Children's Care Paediatric Inpatients; Coordinator, Perioperative Care - Operating Room; Coordinator, Perioperative Care - Post-Anesthetic Care Unit; Coordinator, Surgical Care - Chest & Vascular Surgery; Occupational Therapist; Orthoptist; Pharmaceutical Care Coordinator; Pharmacists; Physiotherapist, Clinical Neuroscience Inpatient Unit; Physiotherapist, Surgical Care Orthopaedics; Registered Nurse - 4IP, Rehabilitation; Clinical Coordinator, In-Patient Paediatric Unit; Clinical Coordinator, Paediatric Critical Care Unit

and Extended Role Transport Team; Cardiac Nurses; Coordinator, Diagnostic and Interventional Cardiology; Administrative Dietitian; Auditory - Verbal Therapist; Business / Administrative Coordinator; Business / Administrative Coordinator; CCN - Resource Coordinator; Clinical Educator; Clinical Nurse Specialist; Clinical Psychologist; Echocardiography Technologist; Operational Performance Specialists; Manager, Integrated Strategic Alliances and Networks; Business / Administrative Coordinator; Clinical Educators (2); Patient Care Coordinators (3); Coordinator, General Accounting.

LONDON HYDRO
Att: Nancy Hanlon
111 Horton Street, PO Box 2700
London, ON N6A 4H6

Tel. 519-661-5887
Fax 519-661-5164
Email .... hanlonn@londonhydro.com
Website .... www.londonhydro.com

Employer Background: London Hydro is a utility company, providing electricity for residents and businesses in London, Ontario. *New Positions Created (7):* Substation Maintenance Technician; CIS Trainer; Customer Service Business Analyst; Manager, Customer Care; Business Analysts / Application Developers; Database Administrator; Business Analyst / Application Developer.

LONDON LIFE INSURANCE CO.
Att: Lorie Haugh, Human Resources
255 Dufferin Avenue
London, ON N6A 4K1

Tel. 519-432-2000
Email .... lorie.haugh@londonlife.com
Website .... www.londonlife.com

Employer Background: London Life Insurance Co. provides life insurance and financial services to 1.7 million customers in Canada under the Freedom 55 brand. *New Positions Created (3):* Life Insurance Managers; Account Manager; Director, Account Management.

LONDON REGIONAL CANCER CENTRE / LRCC
Att: Julie Webster, Recruitment Coordinator
790 Commissioners Road East
London, ON N6A 4L6

Tel. 519-685-8600
Fax 519-685-8726
Website .... www.lrcc.on.ca

Employer Background: Founded in 1952, LRCC is one of eight regional cancer centres in Ontario. LRCC is funded by the Ministry of Health and serves a population of 1.8 million in southwestern Ontario. *New Positions Created (3):* Clinical Dietitian; Computer Support Technologist; Medical Physicists (2).

LOOMIS COURIER SERVICE
Att: Director of Sales
3000 - 15th Street NE
Calgary, AB T2E 8V6

Fax 403-531-5970

Website .... www.loomis.com

Employer Background: Loomis Courier Service is Canada's premier provider of secure, time-critical, cash logistics services to financial institutions, commercial customers and government agencies. *New Positions Created (2):* Senior Account Manager; Major Account Service Representatives (2).

LOUIS BRIER HOME AND HOSPITAL
Att: Human Resources
1055 - 41st Avenue West
Vancouver, BC V6M 1W9

Tel. 604-261-9376
Fax 604-266-8712
Email .... jfawcett@louisbrier.com
Website .... www.louisbrier.com

Employer Background: Louis Brier Home and Hospital serves 93 extended care and 124 intermediate care residents. *New Positions Created (3):* Building Services Manager; Director, Resident Care; Manager, Recreation and Volunteer Services.

LOUIS VUITTON OGILVY
Att: Store Manager
1307 St. Catherine Street West, 5th Floor
Montréal, QC H3G 1P7

Tel. 514-849-6520
Fax 514-849-7352
Website .... www.vuitton.com

Employer Background: Louis Vuitton Ogilvy is a fashion retailer. *New Positions Created (2):* Sales Associates; Sales Associates.

LOVAT TUNNEL EQUIPMENT INC.
Att: Human Resources
441 Carlingview Drive
Toronto, ON M9W 5G7

Tel. 416-675-3293
Fax 416-675-6702
Website .... www.lovat.com

Employer Background: Lovat Tunnel Equipment Inc. is a manufacturer of customized tunnel boring machines used in the construction of metro, railway, road, sewer, water, penstock, mine access and telecable tunnels. *New Positions Created (12):* Procurement Manager; Senior Buyer; Technical Writer; Spare Parts Coordinator; Procurement Manager; Spare Parts Coordinator; Intermediate Accountant; Electrical Technicians; Fitters; Fluid Power Technicians and Mechanical Fitter Technicians; Machinists; Welders.

LOWE-MARTIN GROUP, THE
Att: Human Resources
363 Coventry Road, PO Box 9702
Ottawa, ON K1K 2C5

Tel. 613-741-0962
Fax 613-741-2144
Email .... hr@lmgroup.com
Website .... www.lmgroup.com

Employer Background: The Lowe-Martin Group is a full-service commercial printer, with plants in Ottawa, Toronto and California. *New Positions Created (19):* Customer Service Representative; Desktop Publishing Operator; Press Feeder; Press Manager; Sales Representatives; Bilingual Receptionist; Customer Service Representative; Desktop Publishing Operator; Press Feeder; Press Room Manager; Print Estimator; Production Supervisor; Sales Representatives; Shipping Manager; Bindery Supervisors / Team Leaders; Customer Service Representative; Human Resources Manager; Bindery Supervisor; Intermediate Purchasing Clerk.

LOWER CANADA COLLEGE
Att: Elizabeth Neil-Blunden, HR Manager
4090 Royal Avenue
Montréal, QC H4A 2M5

Tel. 514-482-9916
Website .... www.lcc.ca

Employer Background: Founded in 1909, Lower Canada College is an independent, co-educational day school. *New Positions Created (6):* French Teachers, Junior School (2); Kindergarten Teacher / Teaching Assistant, Junior School (2); Teacher, Biology and Chemistry, Senior School; Teacher, English and Drama, Senior School; Teacher, Spanish and French, Middle and Senior School; Director of Advancement.

LOYALIST COLLEGE
Att: Human Resources
Wallbridge-Loyalist Road, Box 4200
Belleville, ON K8N 5B9

Tel. 613-969-1913
Fax 613-962-0937
Email .... humanr@loyalistc.on.ca
Website .... www.loyalistc.on.ca

Employer Background: Loyalist College is a community college, offering diploma programs to over 3,000 students. *New Positions Created (3):* Supervisor of Facilities Services; Nursing Professors; Project Supervisor, Facilities Services.

LOYALIST TOWNSHIP
Att: David C. Thompson, PEng
263 Main Street, Box 70
Odessa, ON K0H 2H0

Tel. 613-386-7351
Fax 613-386-3833
Website .... www.loyalist-township.on.ca

Employer Background: Loyalist Township was incorporated in 1998. *New Positions Created (2):* Engineering Technician; Utilities Operator.

LOYALTY GROUP, THE
Att: Corporate Recruiter, HR
4110 Yonge Street, Suite 200
Toronto, ON M2P 2B7

Tel. 416-228-6500
Fax 416-733-9712
Email .... resumes@loyalty.com
Website .... www.loyalty.com

Employer Background: The Loyalty Group is the owner of the Air Miles rewards program in Canada. *New Positions Created (52):* Web Production Manager; Account Manager, Sponsor Marketing; Business Analyst, Air Miles for Business; Data Modeler; Marketing Coordinator, Consumer Marketing;

Sales Manager, Extra Mile Travel; Solutions Architect, Solutions Consulting; Account Coordinator, Sponsor Marketing; Associate Manager, Marketing; Business Analyst, IT Business Office; Business Analyst, New Business Development; Business Analyst, Solutions Consulting; Corporate Accountant; File Maintenance Position; Solutions Architect, Solutions Consulting; Web Production Manager; Administrative Assistant, Legal; Analyst, Consumer Marketing; Associate Director, Marketing, Consumer Marketing; Associate Manager, Vertically Integrated Businesses; Manager, Graphic Arts; Project Leader, Data Warehouse; Team Leader, Travel Sales; Account Manager, Sponsor Marketing; Administrative Assistant, Reward Services; Associate Manager, Leisure & Entertainment; Bilingual Customer Service Representative; Business Analyst, Sponsor Marketing; Compensation & Benefits Manager; Customer Service Representative; Data Modeler; Java Application Developer, eBusiness; Manager, Analysis; Manager, Flight Rewards; Marketing / GIS Analyst, Business Intelligence; Operations Analyst; Operations Analyst, Summary & Bonusing; Project Manager, Data Warehouse; Reservation Agent; Scheduling Manager, Call Centre; Senior Coordinator, Service Centre Employee Relations; Senior Statistician; Senior Unix Administrator, eBusiness; Solutions Analyst, Quality Assurance; Systems Developer; Team Development Supervisor, Service Centre; Team Leader, Ticketing & Schedule Change; Team Leaders ; Associate Director, Service Centre Operations & Scheduling; Customer Service Representatives; Scheduling Manager, Service Centre; Travel Agents.

LPI COMMUNICATION GROUP INC.
Att: Human Resources Manager
4715 - 13th Street NE, Suite 105
Calgary, AB T2E 6M3

Fax 403-735-0530
Email .... ldutka@lpi-group.com
Website .... www.lpi-group.com

Employer Background: LPI Communication Group Inc. is a leading promotions and marketing agency. *New Positions Created (4):* Account Executive; Account Manager; Production Artist; Senior Art Designer.

LSG SKY CHEFS
Att: Human Resources
2955 Convair Drive, PO Box 184
Mississauga, ON L5P 1B1

Tel. 905-676-4008
Fax 905-676-8471
Email .... ljohnsto@skychefs.com
Website .... www.skychefs.com

Employer Background: LSG Sky Chefs is an airline catering corporation, providing over 390 million in-flight meals per year. *New Positions Created (2):* Operations Supervisor; Purchasing Manager.

LSI LOGIC CORPORATION OF CANADA INC.
Att: Human Resources Manager
260 Hearst Way, Suite 400
Kanata, ON K2L 3H1

Tel. 613-592-1263
Fax 613-592-3253
Website .... www.lsilogic.com

Employer Background: LSI Logic Corporation of Canada Inc. is a global supplier of custom, high-performance semiconductors. *New Positions Created (6):* ASIC Design Engineer; Field Application Engineer; Field Applications Engineer; Integration Engineer; SOC Methodology Engineer; UNIX System Administrator.

LUMBERMEN'S UNDERWRITING ALLIANCE
Att: Human Resources Manager
185 Dorval Avenue, Suite 500
Dorval, QC H9S 5J9

Tel. 514-631-2710
Fax 514-631-0788
Email .... car@mail.ins-lua.com
Website .. www.lumbermensunderwriting.com

Employer Background: Lumbermen's Underwriting Alliance specializes in commercial property insurance for the forest products industry. *New Positions Created (2):* Account Representative; Appraiser Trainee.

LUMENON
Att: Human Resources Department
8851 Trans Canada Highway
St-Laurent, QC H4S 1Z6

Fax 514-331-1272
Email .... resume@lumenon.com
Website .... www.lumenon.com

Employer Background: Lumenon designs, develops and builds integrated optics devices in the form of hybrid glass circuits on silicon chips. *New Positions Created (15):* Account Manager; Advertising Media Specialist; Applications Engineer; Chemical Engineer, Materials Formulation; Marketing Database Specialist; Operators; Photonics Packaging Development Engineer; Planning Manager; Process Engineer - Microfabrication; R & D Coating Scientist; R & D Packaging Specialist; R & D Polymer Chemists; Reliability Engineer; Technician - Materials Formulation; Web / Multimedia Specialist.

LUMIC ELECTRONICS, INC.
Att: Human Resources Manager
18 Antares Drive, Suite 200
Nepean, ON K2E 1A9

Tel. 613-224-9926
Fax 613-224-7330
Email .... careers@lumictech.com
Website .... www.lumictech.com

Employer Background: Lumic Electronics, Inc. develops low-power multimedia processors to enable next-generation wireless multimedia. *New Positions Created (39):* Controller; Market Strategist; MPEG-4 System Specialist; Senior Applications Engineer; Senior DSP Algorithm System Designer; Senior Product Manager; Senior Systems Administrator; DFT Engineer; Board Support and Driver Designer; Hardware Application Engineer; Product Manager; Senior IC Engineer; SOC Architect; Software Application Designer; Software Application Engineer; Test Designers; Market Strategist; Speech and Audio Algorithm Designer; MPEG-4 System Expert ; Senior DSP Algorithm System Designer ; Senior DSP / HW System Architect ; Senior SW System Architect ; Wavelet Expert ; Algorithm Designer; Development Environment Designer; DFT Engineer; Digital IC Verification Engineers; Intermediate Application Engineer; IT Specialist; Senior IC Engineer; Application Designers; Development Environment Designer; SOC Architect; DSP Software Designer; MPEG Architect; Product Manager; SOC Architect; Test / DFT Engineer; Video Software Designer.

LUMSDEN BROTHERS LTD.
Att: Senior Director of Finance
79 Easton Road, PO Box 3100
Brantford, ON N3T 6K2

Tel. 519-751-6000
Fax 519-751-4467
Website .... www.lbl.on.ca

Employer Background: Lumsden Brothers Ltd. (a division of Sobey's Canada) is a major grocery wholesaler, distributing products to independent retailers in Ontario. *New Positions Created (6):* Controller; Merchandiser; Senior Credit and Collection Coordinator; Drivers; Director of Finance; Assistant Cash and Carry Manager.

LUSCAR LTD.
Att: Human Resources Manager
Postal Bag 5000
Edson, AB T7E 1W1

Tel. 780-794-8175
Fax 780-794-8146
Email .... ed_hanley@luscar.com
Website .... www.luscar.com

Employer Background: Luscar Ltd., a large coal producer, operates several open pit mines in Alberta, Saskatchewan and BC. *New Positions Created (3):* Intermediate Mine Engineer; Heavy Duty Mechanics, Electricians & Welders; Trades Positions.

LUTHERWOOD COMMUNITY OPPORTUNITIES DEVELOPMENT ASSOCIATION / CODA
Att: Human Resources
139 Father David Bauer Drive
Waterloo, ON N2L 6L1

Tel. 519-884-7755
Fax 519-884-9071
Website .... www.lwdcoda.org

Employer Background: Lutherwood CODA is non-profit agency based on Christian values, providing social services to 10,000 people. *New Positions Created (2):* Assistant Director, Mental Health Services; Director, Human Resources.

LUXELL TECHNOLOGIES INC.
Att: Director, Human Resources
5170A Timberlea Boulevard
Mississauga, ON L4W 2S5

Tel. 905-206-1708
Fax 905-206-9174
Email .... gschecter@luxell.com
Website .... www.luxell.com

Employer Background: Luxell Technologies Inc. is a leading manufacturer of advanced flat panel displays and systems. *New Positions Created (3):* Hardware Development Engineer; Product Engineer; Project Mgr.

LYRECO OFFICE PRODUCTS
Att: Human Resources Department
875 Middlefield Road
Toronto, ON M1V 4Z5
Tel. 416-754-8485
Fax 416-292-2537
Email .... linda.engelbrecht@lyreco.com
Website .... www.lyreco.ca
Employer Background: Lyreco Office Products is a leading business-to-business distributor of office supplies, office furniture and computer supplies. *New Positions Created (5):* Bilingual Territory Manager; Customer Service Representative; National Account Manager / National Account Rep; Administrative Assistant; Quality Manager.

M.B. FOSTER ASSOCIATES LTD.
Att: Vice-President, Human Resources
82 Main Street South
Chesterville, ON K0C 1H0
Tel. 613-448-2333
Fax 613-448-2588
Email .... hr@mbfoster.com
Website .... www.mbfoster.com
Employer Background: M.B. Foster is a leading developer and reseller of business software tools. *New Positions Created (2):* Sales Executives; Sales Professionals.

M.H. SHAIKH PROFESSIONAL CORPORATION
Att: Mike Shaikh
736 - 6th Avenue SW, Suite 1610
Calgary, AB T2P 3T7
Tel. 403-261-0835
Fax 403-262-4281
Email .... shaikh@cadvision.com
Employer Background: M.H. Shaikh PC is an accounting firm, with 20 years experience. *New Positions Created (3):* Accountant; Chartered Accountant; Accountant.

M.R.S. COMPANY LTD.
Att: VP, Sales & Business Development
700 Matheson Boulevard East
Suite 700, West Tower
Mississauga, ON L4W 4V9
Tel. 905-602-1700
Fax 905-602-0955
Email .... hr@mrscompany.com
Website .... www.mrscompany.com
Employer Background: M.R.S. Company Ltd. provides a wide range of consulting, project management and systems development services to Fortune 1000 companies. *New Positions Created (3):* Corporate Account Sales Representative; Programmer Analysts; Senior Application Developers.

M&R PLASTICS INC.
Att: Manager of Human Resources
109 Lindbergh Street
Laval, QC H7P 2N8
Tel. 450-622-8011
Fax 450-628-3290
Website .... www.mrplastics.com
Employer Background: M&R Plastics Inc. manufactures semi-rigid plastic packaging for the global food industry. *New Positions Created (2):* Buyer; Production Coordinator.

M-CON PRODUCTS INC.
Att: Human Resources
2150 Richardson Side Road
Carp, ON K0A 1L0
Tel. 613-831-1736
Fax 613-831-2048
Email .... walter@mconproducts.com
Website .... www.mconproducts.com
Employer Background: M-Con Products Inc. manufactures precast concrete products. *New Positions Created (2):* Health and Safety Coordinator; Quality Control Position.

M-PERIAL DISPLAY INC.
Att: Human Resources Manager
108 Milvan Drive
Toronto, ON M9L 1Z6
Tel. 416-741-7891
Fax 416-741-8374
Employer Background: Founded in 1945, M-Perial Display Inc. is a point-of-purchase display manufacturer. *New Positions Created (2):* Sales Representative; Account Executive.

M/A-COM
Att: Human Resources Manager
8658 Commerce Court
Burnaby, BC V5A 4N6
Fax 604-415-4001
Email .... shinm@tycoelectronics.com
Website .... www.macom.com
Employer Background: Founded in 1950, M/A-COM (part of Tyco International) manufactures RF and microwave semiconductors, components and IP networks for the wireless telecom and defense-related industries. *New Positions Created (3):* Senior RF Engineer; Software Development Engineers; Systems Engineer - Wireless Networks.

M3I SYSTEMS INC.
Att: Human Resources Manager
1111 St. Charles West
11th Floor, East Tower
Longueuil, QC J4K 5G4
Tel. 450-928-4600
Fax 450-442-5076
Email .... resume@m3isystems.com
Website www.m3isystems.com
Employer Background: M3i Systems Inc. develops, implements and supports integrated software systems for distribution operations and dispatch management. *New Positions Created (2):* Account Manager; Software Demonstration Specialist.

MA'MOWE CAPITAL REGION, CHILD AND FAMILY SERVICES
Att: Child Welfare Selection Committee
10035 - 108th Street
3rd Floor, Centre West Building
Edmonton, AB T5J 3E1
Fax 780-427-1018
Email .... hre-edm@fss.gov.ab.ca
Website .... www.acs.gov.ab.ca/
.... mamowe/us.html
Employer Background: Established in 1999, Ma'mowe Capital Region, Child and Family Services is responsible for providing services to children, youth and families in Edmonton. *New Positions Created (41):* Child and Family Services Trainee / Worker; Foster Care Intake Worker; Social Worker Trainees; Business Manager; Financial / Administrative Review Assistants (5); Assistant Managers (2); Clinical Social Worker; Manager; Psychologist; Psychologist; Child and Family Services Worker; Manager, Foster Care; Child Welfare Trainee; Justice Coordinator; Aboriginal Cross-Cultural Diversity Trainer; Social Worker; Social Worker; Administrative Support Position; Human Resource Design Specialist; Manager, Financial Services; Research Officer; Justice Coordinator; Social Worker; Team Leader; Administrative Support Position; Adoption Workers; Consultant; Senior Consultant; Child Welfare Social Worker; Social Worker; Team Leader; Emotional Behavioural Specialist; Information Coordinator; Casework Supervisor; Consultant, Performance Measures Unit; Justice Coordinator; Manager, Metis Child and Family Services Authority; Social Service Technician; Social Worker; Coordinator, Emotional Behavioral Program; Psychologist / Clinical Social Worker.

MAC'S CONVENIENCE STORES INC.
Att: D. Jensen
807 - 42nd Avenue SE, Suite 119
Calgary, AB T2G 1Y8
Fax 403-278-6137
Website .. www.macsconveniencestores.com
Employer Background: Mac's Convenience Stores Inc. operates Canadian convenience stores under the Mac's, Beckers, Mike's Mart and Winks banners. *New Positions Created (2):* Business Analyst; Operations Manager.

MAC'S CONVENIENCE STORES INC.
Att: Human Resources Manager
10 Commander Boulevard
Toronto, ON M1S 3T2
Tel. 416-291-4441
Fax 416-609-7179
Website .. www.macsconveniencestores.com
Employer Background: Mac's Convenience Stores Inc. operates Canadian convenience stores under the Mac's, Beckers, Mike's Mart and Winks banners. *New Positions Created (4):* Construction Coordinator; Construction Manager; Draftsperson; Franchise Area Representative.

MACDONALD DETTWILER & ASSOCIATES LTD. / MDA
Att: Human Resources Manager
13800 Commerce Parkway
Richmond, BC V6V 2J3
Tel. 604-278-3411
Fax 604-278-2281
Email .... hrinfo@mda.ca
Website .... www.mda.ca

Employer Background: MacDonald, Dettwiler and Associates Ltd. (MDA) provides information products and services for customers around the world. *New Positions Created (33):* International Systems Sales; International Systems Sales Position; Controller; Junior Contracts Specialist; Intermediate Contract / Subcontract Specialist; Research Analyst; Administration Supervisor; Recruiter; HR Advisor; Senior Software Developer / Maintainer; Defense Simulator Software Developer; Image Processing Junior Software Engineers; Junior Operations Accountant; Programmer / Electrical Engineer; Project Accountant II; Receptionist; Research Analyst; Administrative Assistant; Financial Analyst; General Manager; Human Resource Specialist; Maintenance / Service Electrician; Project Accountant, Systems; Project Mgr; Sales Professionals; Software Engineer, Team Lead; Solicitor; Spacecraft Lead Engineer; Systems Engineers; Customer Account Administrator; Software Engineer; Sr Communications Writer; BC Online Solutions Architect.

MACDONALD DETTWILER & ASSOCIATES LTD. / MDA
Att: Human Resources Manager
2060 Walkley Road
Ottawa, ON K1G 3P5

Email .... jobs@ottawa.mda.ca
Website .... www.mda.ca
Employer Background: MDA is a leading Canadian space company and provider of information, products and services, employing over 1,800 people in BC, Ontario, Nova Scotia and overseas. *New Positions Created (7):* Airforce Command and Control Process Analyst; Aviation System, Software and Test Engineers; Research Analyst; Scientists / Software Engineers; Software Engineers, Internet Development; Trainers, Security and Military Police Information System Project (3); Translators.

MACDONALD DETTWILER & ASSOCIATES LTD. / MDA
Att: Human Resources Manager
1000 Windmill Road, Suite 60
Halifax, NS B3B 1L7

Tel. 902-468-3356
Fax 902-468-7795
Email .... jobs@mda.ca
Website .... www.mda.ca
Employer Background: MacDonald, Dettwiler and Associates Ltd. (MDA) provides information products and services for customers around the world. *New Positions Created (5):* Sr Consultant; Signal Processing Engineer; Business Development / Sales Professional; Combat Systems Programmer / Engineer; Senior Acoustic Scientist.

MACDONALD DETTWILER SPACE AND ADVANCED ROBOTICS LTD. / MD ROBOTICS
Att: Manager, Staffing
9445 Airport Road
Brampton, ON L6S 4J3

Tel. 905-790-2800
Fax 905-790-4400

Email .... jobs@mdrobotics.ca
Website .... www.mdrobotics.ca
Employer Background: Formed in 1999, MD Robotics, a subsidiary of MacDonald Dettwiler & Associates, is a leader in space robotics. *New Positions Created (27):* Business Systems Analyst; Electro-Optical Engineer; Senior Accounting Clerk; Business Systems Analyst; Database Administrator; Senior Electrical Engineer / MTS R&D Program; Software Engineer / MTS Database Developer; Senior Contracts Administrator; Senior Software Configuration Mgmnt Technologist; Structural Engineers; Subcontracts Administrator; Digital Design Engineer; Junior / Intermediate Integration and Test Engineers, SRMS; Junior / Intermediate Systems End-to-End Engineers, SPDM; Mechanical Designers; MSS End-to-End System Software Integration Engineers; MSS Sustaining Engineering Systems Engineers; Safety Engineer; Software Developers; Software Product Assurance Engineer; Software Product Assurance Technologist; Software Systems Engineers, RWS Sustaining Engineering; Systems Engineers, Support to Business Development; Mission Operations Engineers; MSS End-to-End Systems Engineers; Simulation and Analysis Software Tool Developers; Software Engineers.

MACDONALD ENGINEERING GROUP LTD. / MEG
Att: Human Resource Administrator
1001 - 1st Street SE
Calgary, AB T2G 5G3

Tel. 403-508-5300
Fax 403-508-5303
Email .... kerrl@meg-cgy.com
Website .... www.meg-cgy.com
Employer Background: Established in 1965, MEG provides engineering, procurement and construction management solutions to the oil and gas industry. *New Positions Created (5):* Engineers, Process / Instrumentation / Mechanical; Intermediate Project Secretary; QA Manager; Intermediate Civil Designers (3); Senior Civil Engineer.

MACGREGORS MEAT & SEAFOOD LTD.
Att: Glenn McNamara
265 Garyray Drive
Toronto, ON M9L 1P2

Tel. 416-749-5951
Fax 416-740-3230
Email .... glenn@macgregors.com
Website .... www.macgregors.com
Employer Background: Established in 1949, MacGregors Meat & Seafood Ltd. is a foodservice supplier. *New Positions Created (2):* Sales Order Desk; Financial Analyst.

MACINNIS ENGINEERING ASSOCIATES LTD. / MEA
Att: Human Resources Manager
11151 Horseshoe Way, Suite 11
Richmond, BC V7A 4S5

Tel. 604-277-3040
Fax 604-277-3020
Email .... employment@maceng.com
Website .... www.maceng.com

Employer Background: Founded in 1982 MEA conducts technical investigations fo cases involving vehicle collisions, fires, per sonal injury, material and mechanical fail ures, slips and falls, product failure and li ability. *New Positions Created (2):* Fire En gineer; Fire Engineer.

MACK CANADA INC.
Att: Manager, Personnel Services
6860 Century Ave., Suite 3000, East Tower
Mississauga, ON L5N 2W5

Tel. .... 905-814-535█
Fax .... 905-814-453█
Email ...... mackhr4515@macktrucks.com
Website ..... www.macktrucks.com/canad█
Employer Background: Mack Canada Inc. i a leader in the trucking industry. *New Posi tions Created (2):* New Truck Sales Repre sentative; Controller.

MACKAY & PARTNERS
Att: Brent Penner, CA
10010 - 106th Street, Suite 705
Edmonton, AB T5J 3L8

Tel. .... 780-420-062█
Fax .... 780-425-878█
Email .... brentpenner@
.... edm.mackayandpartners.com
Website .... www.mackayandpartners.com
Employer Background: MacKay & Partner is a chartered accounting firm, with 6 office in Canada. *New Positions Created (2):* Cli ent Services Specialist; Tax Specialist.

MACKENZIE ART GALLERY
Att: Kate Davis, Director
3475 Albert Street
Regina, SK S4S 6X6

Tel. .... 306-584-426█
Fax .... 306-569-819█
Email .... kate.davis@uregina.c█
Website ... www.mackenzieartgallery.sk.c█
Employer Background: MacKenzie Art Gal lery is a senior art institution and a leade in exhibition, educational and public pro gramming in the visual arts. *New Position Created (2):* Curator; Head Curator.

MACKENZIE FINANCIAL CORPORATION
Att: Human Resources Department
150 Bloor Street West
Toronto, ON M5S 3B5

Tel. .... 416-922-532█
Fax .... 416-922-127█
Email ... service@mackenziefinancial.com
Website ..... www.mackenziefinancial.com
Employer Background: Mackenzie Financia Corporation is one of Canada's leading mu tual fund companies, with over one millio investors across Canada and the USA. *Ne Positions Created (4):* Regional Sales Repre sentative; Client Account Processing an Clerical Positions; Business Analyst - Inter mediate; Internal Regional Sales Rep.

MACKENZIE FINANCIAL CORPORATION
Att: Human Resources Department

777 Bay Street, 29th Floor
Toronto, ON M5G 2N4
Fax 416-934-7014
Website ..... www.mackenziefinancial.com
Employer Background: Mackenzie Financial Corporation is one of Canada's leading mutual fund companies, with over one million investors across Canada and the USA. *New Positions Created (4):* Customer Service Representatives; Fund Accountants; Regional Sales Manager, MRS; Supervisor, Fund Accounting.

MACKIE MOVING SYSTEMS
Att: Human Resources
933 Bloor Street
Oshawa, ON L1J 5Y7
Tel. 905-728-1603
Fax 905-434-4655
Email .... mms.humanresources@
.... mackiegroup.com
Website .... www.mackiegroup.com
Employer Background: Mackie Moving Systems is an ISO 9002-registered company, specializing in transportation and value-added services. *New Positions Created (5):* Vice-President, Finance; Operations Manager; Dispatcher / Planner, Household Goods and High-Value Products; Fleet Supervisor; Operations Manager.

MACLAB HOTELS & RESORTS
Att: Human Resources
10205 - 100th Avenue, Suite 3400
Edmonton, AB T5J 4B5
Tel. 780-420-4040
Fax 780-428-1397
Email .... careers@maclab.ca
Website .... www.maclab.ca
Employer Background: Maclab Hotels and Resorts is part of Maclab Enterprises, the largest privately-held residential rental property holder in Alberta and the Northwest Territories. *New Positions Created (4):* Head Chef; Resort Maintenance Manager; General Manager; General Manager.

MACLACHLAN COLLEGE
Att: Headmaster
337 Trafalgar Road
Oakville, ON L6J 3H3
Tel. 905-844-0372
Fax 905-844-9369
Website .... www.maclachlan.on.ca
Employer Background: MacLachlan College is an independent, co-educational day school, providing education in small class settings for 350 students from junior kindergarten to OAC. *New Positions Created (4):* Teacher, ESL and Language Arts; Teacher, French; Teacher, Math and Information Technology; Teaching Positions.

MACLACHLAN & MITCHELL HOMES INC.
Att: Human Resources Manager
250 Southridge
Edmonton, AB T6H 4M9
Tel. 780-435-9256
Fax 780-436-1373
Website .... www.macmitch-homes.com
Employer Background: MacLachlan & Mitchell Homes Inc. is a new home builder. *New Positions Created (3):* Junior Construction Estimator; Junior - Intermediate Draftsperson; Draftsperson.

MACLEOD DIXON LLP
Att: Darlene Johnston
400 - 3rd Avenue SW, Suite 3700
Calgary, AB T2P 4H2
Tel. 403-267-8222
Fax 403-264-5973
Email .... darlene.johnston@
.... macleoddixon.com
Website .... www.macleoddixon.com
Employer Background: Founded in 1912, Macleod Dixon LLP is an international law firm, with over 450 legal professionals located in 5 offices. *New Positions Created (2):* Manager of Paralegal Services; Business Analyst / Project Coordinator.

MADVAC INC.
Att: Donna
677 Giffard
Longueuil, QC J4G 1Y3
Tel. 450-670-0200
Fax 450-670-0299
Email .... admin@madvac.com
Employer Background: Madvac Inc. is a manufacturer of sweepers. *New Positions Created (2):* Marketing Assistant; Senior Buyer.

MAGIC SPAN FABRICATING LTD.
Att: Jack K. McPherson
5505 - 56th Avenue SE
Calgary, AB T2C 3X6
Fax 403-860-4411
Employer Background: MSF is an oil and gas fabrication company. *New Positions Created (3):* Engineering Manager; Estimator / Buyer; Intermediate / Senior Draftsperson.

MAGMA COMMUNICATIONS LTD.
Att: Human Resources Manager
31 Auriga Drive
Nepean, ON K2E 1C4
Tel. 613-228-3565
Fax 613-228-8313
Email .... careers@magma.ca
Website .... www.magma.ca
Employer Background: Magma Communications Ltd. offers Internet access, hosting and web solutions. *New Positions Created (10):* Client Development Representative; Web Services; Network Administrator; Network Services Manager; Web Developer; Webmaster; Collections Agent; Technical Support Representatives; Web Designers; Computer Services Technician; Corporate Technical Support Position.

MAGNA INTERNATIONAL INC.
Att: Human Resources
55 Confederation Parkway
Concord, ON L4K 4Y7
Tel. 905-760-7666
Fax 905-760-7474
Website .... www.magnaint.com
Employer Background: Established in the 1950s, Magna International Inc. is an automotive parts supplier, with over 62,000 employees worldwide. *New Positions Created (159):* Accounts Payable Assistant; Accounts Payable Specialist; Buyers; Coordinator, Commercial Projects; Coordinator, Specific; Coordinator, Traffic; Cycle Counter; Design / Project Engineers & Managers; Executive Assistant; Forklift Operator; Health and Safety Professionals; Human Resources Generalist; Human Resources Manager; Human Resources Manager; Human Resources Positions; Industrial Electricians; Internal Auditors, Finance; Maintenance Manager; Manufacturing Engineer; Manufacturing Engineers; Manufacturing Manager; Millwright; Millwright Teacher / Instructor; Millwrights; Plant Managers; Process / Environment Engineer; Quality Assurance Technician; Quality Control Engineer; Quality Engineer; Quality Engineer; Quality Engineers; Supervisor, Shipping / Receiving; Tester; Tool & Die Maker; Tool & Die Makers; Compensation Specialist; Administrative Assistants; Human Resources Officer; Inspector, Quality; Maintenance Mechanic; Manager, Network Communications; Administrator, Payroll; Buyer; Communications Specialist; Coordinator, Safety / Environment; Designer; Manager, Plant; Material Handler; Quality Assurance Specialist; Quality Assurance Technician; Supervisor, Production Control; Accounts Payable Assistant; Analyst, Sales / Marketing; Auditor, Internal; CAD Designer; Controller; Coordinator, Health and Safety; Coordinator, Traffic; Customer Liaison; Engineer, Process / Environment; Human Resources Manager; Industrial Electrician; IT Analyst / Programmer; Maintenance Mechanic; Manager, Quality Assurance; Manager, Quality Assurance; Manufacturing Engineer; Materials Manager; Mechanical Designer; Millwright; Plant Manager; PMS and Inventory Control Specialist; Program Manager; Quality Engineer; Quality Engineer; Receptionist / Switchboard Operator; Supervisor, Assembly; Tool and Die Maker; Accounts Receivable Position; Engineer, Tooling; Leader, Warehouse; Manager, Project; Network Analyst; Operator, Forklift; Operator, Punch Press; Sales Representative; Administrative Staff; Analyst, Inventory; Buyer; Leader, Technical Area; Manager, Network; Programmer; Set-Up, Machine Tool Position; Supervisor, Production Control; Supervisor, Quality Control; Supervisor, Toolroom; Accountant; Analyst, Financial / Cost; Assembly Supervisor; Assistant, Payroll & Benefits; CAD Designer; Controller; Coordinator, Safety / Environment; Design Engineer; Design Engineer; Engineer, Assembly Process; Engineer, Process / Environment; Engineer, Process / Environment; Executive Assistant; Executive Assistant; Industrial Electrician; Machine Operator; Maintenance Electrician; Maintenance Electrician; Maintenance Electrician; Maintenance Manager; Maintenance Manager; Maintenance Mechanic; Manufacturing Engineer; Material Handler; Mechanical Designer; Millwright;

Millwright; Millwright; Operations Manager; Plant Manager; Plant Manager; Project Coordinator; Project Engineer; Project Engineer; Project Engineer; Quality Assurance Manager; Quality Engineer; Quality Engineer; Quality Engineer; Rolling Mill Operator; Shift Supervisor; Supervisor, Shipping & Receiving; Tool and Die Maker; Welding Technician; Accounts Payable Position; Buyer; CMM Program Operator; Design Engineer; Human Resources Manager; Human Resources Officer; Industrial Electrician; Maintenance Electrician; Maintenance Mechanic; Maintenance Technician; Millwrights; Process Engineer; Production Supervisor; Program Manager; Project Engineers; Quality Assurance Manager; Quality Inspector; Shipper / Receiver; Tool and Die Maker.

MAGNA INTERNATIONAL INC.
Att: Recruiter, Human Resources
141 Staffern Drive
Concord, ON L4K 2R2
Fax 905-761-5915
Website .... www.magnaint.com
Employer Background: Established in the 1950s, Magna International Inc. is an automotive parts supplier, with over 62,000 employees worldwide. *New Positions Created (21):* Commodity Buyer; Materials Manager; Project Engineer; Software Engineer; Environmental Health and Safety Supervisor; Occupational Health Nurse; Manufacturing Engineer; Master Scheduler; Quality Engineer / Supervisor; Senior Logistics Specialist; Stamping Production Manager; Buyer; Project Engineers; Data Integrity Specialist; Design Engineers; Electrical Engineer; Manufacturing Engineer; Production Planner; Project Engineers, Mechanical; Service Coordinator; Master Scheduler.

MAGNA INTERNATIONAL INC.
Att: Human Resources Manager
337 Magna Drive
Aurora, ON L4G 7K1
Tel. 905-726-2462
Fax 905-726-2603
Website .... www.magnaint.com
Employer Background: Established in the 1950s, Magna International Inc. is an automotive parts supplier, with over 62,000 employees worldwide. *New Positions Created (2):* Corporate Lawyer; Labour Lawyer.

MAGNA IV ENGINEERING LTD.
Att: Roy Chapelsky
4103 - 97th Street NW
Edmonton, AB T6E 6E9
Tel. 780-462-3111
Email .... rchapelsky@magnaiv.com
Website .... www.magnaiv.com
Employer Background: Established in 1982, Magna IV Engineering Ltd. provides electrical consulting, equipment testing and commissioning services to the utility, industrial, commercial and institutional sectors. *New Positions Created (4):* Field Services Rep Technologists; Draftsperson; Electrical Engineer; Senior Mechanical Engineer.

MAGNOKROM INC.
Att: Ms Clarke
3965 Nashua Drive
Mississauga, ON L4V 1P3
Tel. 905-671-2525
Fax 905-671-2888
Website .... www.magnokrom.com
Employer Background: Magnokrom Inc. manufactures a broad range of architectural products. *New Positions Created (2):* Receptionist; Marking and Sales Position.

MAGNUS CHEMICALS LTD.
Att: Sales Manager, IND
964 Westport Crescent, Unit 6
Mississauga, ON L5T 1S3
Tel. 905-670-8121
Fax 905-670-0359
Email .... magnus@magchem.com
Website .... www.magchem.com
Employer Background: Established in 1946, Magnus Chemicals Ltd. manufactures products for the metalworking lubrication, industrial cleaning and water conditioning markets. *New Positions Created (2):* Technical Sales Representative; Technical Sales Representatives (3).

MAGNUS CHEMICALS LTD.
Att: Sales Manager, IND
1271 Ampere
Boucherville, QC J4B 5Z5
Tel. 450-655-1344
Fax 450-655-5428
Email .... magnus@magchem.com
Website .... www.magchem.com
Employer Background: Established in 1946, Magnus Chemicals Ltd. manufactures products for the metalworking lubrication, industrial cleaning and water conditioning markets. *New Positions Created (2):* Junior Representative, Laboratory Technical Support; Technical Sales Representative.

MAILLOT BALTEX INC.
Att: Human Resources
1350 Mazurette, Suite 100
Montréal, QC H4N 1H2
Tel. 514-383-1850
Fax 514-383-7589
Email .... rh@baltex.com
Website .... www.baltex.com
Employer Background: Maillot Baltex Inc. is an international swimwear manufacturer. *New Positions Created (4):* Administrative Sales Assistant; Forecasting Department Personnel; Order Entry Clerk; Fabric Buyer.

MAIN KNITTING INC.
Att: Human Resources
6666 St. Urbain
Montréal, QC H2S 3H1
Tel. 514-274-4403
Fax 514-274-5689
Email .... eric_hr@mainknit.com
Website .... www.mainknit.com
Employer Background: Main Knitting Inc. is a large North American manufacturer of private label underwear for men and boys. *New Positions Created (18):* Account Executive; Office Clerk, Claims; Office Clerk, Claims Department; Assistant Patternmaker; Traffic Clerk / Office Clerk; Assistant Production Coordination Manager; Accounts Payable Clerk; Accounts Receivable Coordinator; Administrative Assistant; Industrial Sewing Machine Mechanics; Assistant Manager, Distribution Centre; Programmer; Technical Coordinator, Quality Assurance; Import Coordinator; Office Clerk; Patternmaker; Programmer; Various Administrative Positions (2).

MAINETTI CANADA
Att: R. Dagenbach, Controller
8272 - 19th Avenue
Montréal, QC H1Z 4J8
Tel. 514-376-1876
Fax 514-376-4296
Email .... rdagenbach@canada.mainetti.com
Website .... www.mainetti.com
Employer Background: Mainetti Canada is a branch of Mainetti, an international company serving the garment industry at the manufacturing and retail levels. *New Positions Created (2):* General Office Assistant; General Office Assistant.

MAINWAY INSURANCE BROKERS LTD.
Att: Sales Manager
154 Main Street East, Suite 202
Hamilton, ON L8N 1G9
Tel. 905-521-3000
Fax 905-577-1023
Website ...... www.mainwayinsurance.com
Employer Background: Founded in 1975, Mainway Insurance Brokers Ltd. is a large brokerage for the distribution of insurance and financial services, with 60 employees serving over 20,000 clients. *New Positions Created (7):* Insurance Sales Broker; Commercial Lines Customer Service Representative; Customer Service Broker; Commercial Lines Customer Service Broker; Life Insurance Sales Broker; Personal Lines Sales Broker; Personal Lines Service Broker.

MAJCO APPAREL INC.
Att: Heidi Majdell
1208 Jules Poitras
St-Laurent, QC H4N 1X7
Tel. 514-956-0322
Fax 514-956-1142
Email .... hmajdell@majco.com
Employer Background: Majco Apparel Inc. manufactures trendy junior and girls' private label sportswear. *New Positions Created (5):* Production Assistant; Assistant Merchandiser; Patternmaker; Designer; Sales Assistant.

MAJESTIC INDUSTRIES LTD.
Att: Human Resources Department
3700 Jean-Rivard
Montréal, QC H1Z 4K3
Tel. 514-727-2000
Fax 514-727-2727
Employer Background: Majestic Industries Ltd. manufactures men's loungewear and active sportswear. *New Positions Created (2):*

Production Planning Manager; Merchandising / Import Assistant.

MAKSTEEL INC.
Att: Human Resources
7615 Torbram Road
Mississauga, ON L4T 4A8

Tel. 905-678-7240
Fax 905-673-4921
Email .... humres@maksteel.com
Website .... www.maksteel.com

Employer Background: Maksteel Inc. is a multi-site supplier of steel products to the automotive industry. *New Positions Created (2):* Purchasing Agent; Millwrights / Industrial Mechanics.

MALASPINA UNIVERSITY-COLLEGE, NANAIMO CAMPUS
Att: Human Resources Department
900 - 5th Street
Nanaimo, BC V9R 5S5

Tel. 250-741-2562
Fax 250-755-8702
Email .... apply@mala.bc.ca
Website .... www.mala.bc.ca

Employer Background: Established in 1969, Malaspina University-College operates 4 campuses on Vancouver Island and offers courses to over 7,500 full-time students. *New Positions Created (10):* Dean, Student Services & Instruction; Psychology Instructor, Neurosciences; Finance Instructor; Management Instructors (2); Mgr, Human Resources; Mathematics Instructor; Dean of Education; Dean of Student Services and Instruction; Instructor, Chemistry Department; Instructor, First Nations Studies.

MAMAC SYSTEMS (CANADA) LTD.
Att: Human Resources
155 McIntosh Drive, Suite 5
Markham, ON L3R 0N6

Tel. 905-474-9215
Fax 905-474-0876
Email .... hr@mamacsys.com
Website .... www.mamacsys.com

Employer Background: Mamac Systems (Canada) Ltd. manufactures HVAC and industrial control instruments. *New Positions Created (6):* General Assembly Position; Manufacturing Engineer; Customer Service Representative; General Light Assembly Workers, Electronics; Customer Service Position; Production Supervisor.

MAMMA.COM
Att: Stuart MacDougall, IT Manager
388 St. Jacques Street West, Suite 900
Montréal, QC H2Y 1S1

Tel. 514-844-2700
Fax 514-844-3532
Email .... stuart@mamma.com
Website .... www.mamma.com

Employer Background: Established in 1996, Mamma.com is a metasearch engine, serving 4.9 million unique users per month. *New Positions Created (2):* Operations Support Specialist; Client Service Representatives.

MANAGEMENT BOARD SECRETARIAT
Att: Human Resources Services Branch
77 Wellesley Street West
8th Floor, Ferguson Block
Toronto, ON M7A 1N3

Tel. 416-327-3812
Fax 416-327-3892
Email .... resumes@mbs.gov.on.ca
Website .... www.gov.on.ca

Employer Background: The Management Board Secretariat carries out the directions of the Management Board, the cabinet committee that manages the government's people, money, technology, information and real estate. *New Positions Created (114):* Administrative Assistant; Administrator & Specialist; Administrator / Specialist, Office Environment; Archives Website Coordinator; Contracts & Services Managers (2); Corporate Compensation Specialist; Manager, I&IT Planning; Pay & Benefits Representatives (4); Real Estate Planners; Manager, Organizational Development & Training; Program and Client Manager, Facility Services; Manager, Technical Services; Senior Lead, Application Maintenance and Enhancement Services; Senior Planners (4); Integrated Operator; Standards Coordinator; Computer Operators; Manager, Services Management; Manager, Solutions Management; Performance Management Analyst; Sr Performance Measurement Analyst; Sr Performance Measurement Analyst; Shift Coordinators, Peripheral Operations; Business / Systems Analyst; Database Coordinator; Change Communications Specialists; Corporate Staff Relations Officers; Forensic Investigator; Senior Operations Analysts; Hardware Support (3); Technical Coordinator; Security Policy Advisers; Administrative Assistant; Benefits Assistant; Change Management Project Leads; Processing Analysts; Project Manager; Team Leader, Collections Management & Development; Senior Analyst; Senior Service Delivery Analysts; Network Access Service Coordinator; RFP Coordinator; Server Storage Analysts; Server Storage Planners; Component Interface Designer; Technology Procurement Officer; Business Office Clerk; Director, Corporate Labour Relations / Negotiations Secretariat; Capital Reporting Coordinator; Customer Service Agents (7); Intermediate Project Managers; Audit Technician; Customer Service Agents; DB2 Systems Software Analyst; Facilities Specialist; Risk and Assurance Consultant; Change Management / Integration Consultants; Corporate Payroll Analyst; Human Resources Consultants (2); Manager, Project Management Office; Process Analyst; Policy Advisor; Senior Procurement Advisors; Methodology Specialist; Administrative Assistant; Senior IT Analysts; Corporate Compensation Specialist; Lead, Performance Management Group; Policy Development Officer; Audit Technician; Business Risk Consultants; Host Software Coordinator; Corporate Staff Relations Officers (2); IT Audit Specialists (4); Regional Leasing Manager; Risk and Assurance Consultants, Audit (14); Senior Technology Procurement Managers; Production Systems Computer Operator; Quality Service Coordinator; Surveys Specialist; Manager, Appraisal Services; Operations Specialist, Facility Services; Program and Client Manager, Facility Services; Senior Marketing Managers (4); Contract and Services Manager; Manager, Operations Support; IT Manager; Audit Manager; Risk and Assurance Consultants (2); Senior Policy Advisers (5); Contract and Liens Specialist; Projects / Contracts Administration Specialists; Specifications Specialist; Systems Software Analyst / CICS; Manager, Shared Service Bureau Contact Centre; Real Estate Planners (3); Business Analysts (3); Coordinator, Data Administration; Financial Systems Administrator; Manager, Customer Relations / Account Management; Manager, Information and Information Technology Planning; Manager, Service Management; Community Events Coordinator; Information Audit Specialists; Information Officer / Editor; Manager, Information Technology Audit; Audit Systems Specialist; Financial Officers (2); Financial Processing Clerk; Senior Infrastructure Analyst, Information Technology Branch; Senior Tax Advisory Specialists (4); Labour Relations and Research Analyst; Manager, Internet Application Development; Manager, Operations; Manager, Risk and Assurance Services.

MANASC ISAAC ARCHITECTS LTD.
Att: Human Resources Manager
10248 - 106th Street
Edmonton, AB T5J 1H7

Fax 780-426-3970
Email .... richard@miarch.com
Website .... www.miarch.com

Employer Background: Manasc Isaac Architects Ltd. is an architectural firm. *New Positions Created (2):* Architect & Intermediate Technologist; Architect / Intermediate Technologist.

MANIA TECHNOLOGIE CANADA INC.
Att: Human Resources Manager
79 Milliken Boulevard, Unit 4
Toronto, ON M1V 1V3

Tel. 416-292-0726
Fax 416-292-3254
Email .... kevins@testerion.com
Website .... www.testerion.com

Employer Background: Mania Technologie Canada Inc. (formerly Testerion Canada Inc.) provides electrical testing services to printed circuit board manufacturers. *New Positions Created (6):* Service Technician; Shift Supervisor; Finance Manager; Shift Supervisor; Service Technician; Test Machine Operators / Assemblers.

MANION, WILKINS & ASSOCIATES LTD.
Att: Human Resources
230 Norseman Street
Toronto, ON M8Z 6A2

Tel. 416-234-5044
Fax 416-234-9147

Employer Background: Manion, Wilkins & Associates Ltd. specializes in providing third-party administration, consulting and actuarial services for employee benefit plans across Canada. *New Positions Created (2):*

Disability Claims Examiner; Pension Benefits Administrator.

MANITOBA ABORIGINAL & NORTHERN AFFAIRS

Att: Human Resources Services
326 Broadway, Suite 500
Winnipeg, MB R3C 0S5
Fax 204-948-3382
Email .... efosty@gov.mb.ca
Website .... www.gov.mb.ca/ana
Employer Background: Established in 1970, Manitoba Aboriginal & Northern Affairs is the provincial department responsible for municipal services and initiatives for building self-reliance in northern communities. *New Positions Created (5):* Development Coordinator; Community Resource Development Consultant; Development Coordinators (2); Municipal Development Consultant; Technical Consultant, Community Public Works.

MANITOBA AGRICULTURE AND FOOD

Att: Human Resources Services
401 York Avenue, Suite 803
Winnipeg, MB R3C 0P8
Tel. 204-945-3308
Fax 204-948-4735
Website .... www.gov.mb.ca/agriculture
Employer Background: Manitoba Agriculture and Food is the provincial department responsible for supporting the economic and personal well-being of participants in the agriculture industry. *New Positions Created (34):* Administrative Secretary; Administrative Secretary; Manager, Field Services Section; Family Living Specialist; Medical Technologist; Agricultural Representative / Manager, Westman Agricultural Diversification; Medical Technologist; Agricultural Representative; Special Crops Agronomist; Accounts and Budgeting Activity Supervisor; Administrative Secretary; Agronomist; Sheep / Goat Specialist; Fruit Crops Specialist; Land Management Specialist; Potato Specialist; Manager, Farm Management Section; Agricultural Meteorologist; Financial Analyst; Administrative Secretary; Agricultural Representative; Plant Pathologist; Regional Crop Specialist; Administrative Secretary; Agricultural Representative; Extension Veterinarian; Weed Specialist; Organic Agriculture Specialist; Forage / Livestock Technician; Agricultural Representative; Land Stewardship Specialist (2); Land Use Planning Specialist; Livestock Environment Engineer; Nutrient Management Specialist.

MANITOBA CIVIL SERVICE COMMISSION

Att: Human Resource Programs Branch
155 Carlton Street, Suite 935
Winnipeg, MB R3C 3H8
Tel. 204-948-2165
Fax 204-945-1486
Website .... www.gov.mb.ca
Employer Background: The Manitoba Civil Service Commission recruits for civil service positions in the provincial government.

New Positions Created (5): Senior Programmer / Analyst; Senior Advisor, French Language Services; Manager, Information Technology; Training Officer; Director, Human Resources Services.

MANITOBA CONSERVATION

Att: Human Resource Services
326 Broadway, Suite 500
Winnipeg, MB R3C 0S5
Fax 204-948-3382
Website .... www.gov.mb.ca/environ
Employer Background: Manitoba Conservation is the provincial department responsible for protecting energy, fisheries, forests, land, parks and natural areas, petroleum, water and wildlife. *New Positions Created (17):* Professional / Technical Trainees; Environment Officer; Planning and Program Analyst; Regional Fisheries Manager; Senior Planning and Program Analyst; Director, Northeast Region; Director, Wildlife Branch; Regional Forester; Regional Fisheries Manager; Senior Legislative Analyst; Regional Fire Clerk; Budget Analysts (2); Environment Officers (4); Manager, Budget Services; Aquifer Capacity Geologist; Director, Aboriginal Relations; Director, Sustainable Resource Management.

MANITOBA CONSUMER & CORPORATE AFFAIRS / CCA

Att: Human Resource Services
1181 Portage Avenue, Suite 407
Winnipeg, MB R3G 0T3
Fax 204-948-2193
Website .... www.gov.mb.ca/cca
Employer Background: CCA works to foster business and consumer confidence in the marketplace and create a system that sustains a competitive Manitoba economy. *New Positions Created (7):* Director, Finance and Systems; Registrar / Coordinator; Administrative Secretary; District Registrar; Manager, Adjudication and Mediation; Manager, Client and Administrative Services; Residential Tenancies Officer.

MANITOBA DEVELOPMENTAL CENTRE

Att: Human Resource Services
840 - 3rd Street NE, Box 1190
Portage la Prairie, MB R1N 3C6
Fax 204-856-4224
Website .... www.gov.mb.ca/fs
Employer Background: The Manitoba Developmental Centre is a 470-bed residential facility dedicated to the care and rehabilitation of adults with mental disabilities. *New Positions Created (5):* Registered Psychiatric / Registered Nurse; Therapeutic Recreation Specialist, Geriatric Program; Physiotherapist; Recreation Facilitators (3); Therapeutic Recreations Therapists (2).

MANITOBA EDUCATION, TRAINING & YOUTH

Att: Amalgamated HR Services Branch
1181 Portage Avenue, Suite 407
Winnipeg, MB R3G 0T3
Fax 204-948-2193

Website .... www.edu.gov.mb.ca
Employer Background: Manitoba Education, Training & Youth is the provincial department responsible for supporting education and job training for children and youth. *New Positions Created (17):* Apprenticeship Counsellor; Systems Librarian; Continuous Submission Clerk; Coordinator, Workplace Education and Prior Learning Assessment; Consultant, Aboriginal Languages Curriculum; Consultant for the Deaf and Hard-Of-Hearing; Financial Analyst, Adult Learning and Literacy; Professional Development Consultant; System Manager; Consultant, Emotional / Behavioural Disorders; Consultant, Special Education (French Immersion); Executive Director; Program Support Clerk; Aboriginal Education Consultant; Distance Learning Consultant; Consultant for the Blind / Visually Impaired; Director, TCE Financial Services.

MANITOBA FAMILY SERVICES AND HOUSING

Att: Human Resource Services
300 Carlton Street, Suite 4089
Winnipeg, MB R3B 3M9
Fax 204-945-0601
Website .... www.gov.mb.ca/fs
Employer Background: Manitoba Family Services and Housing is the provincial department responsible for supporting adults and families in need, as well as keeping children safe and protected. *New Positions Created (51):* Adult Special Needs Workers (2); Behavioural Psychologist / Specialist; Community Service Worker; Financial Systems Administrator; Regional Financial and Administrative Officer; Fetal Alcohol Syndrome Specialist; Child and Family Services Worker; Program Manager, Provincial Special Needs Unit; Agency Relations Specialist; Child and Family Services Worker; Agency Relations Specialist; Lotus Notes / Domino Developer; Clerk; Community Services Worker; Human Resource Consultant; Policy Analyst; Regional Financial and Administrative Officer; Senior Policy Analyst; Community Services Worker; Child and Family Services Worker; Access to Information and Privacy Coordinator; Bilingual Administrative Secretary; Database Administrator; Child and Family Service Worker; Employment & Income Assistance Counsellor; Community Services Worker; Case Coordinator / Intake Specialist; Director, Social Services Advisory Committee; Child and Family Services Worker; Community Services Worker; Regional Psychologist; Child and Family Services Worker; Child Development Counsellor, Bilingual; FAS / FAE Policy and Program Analyst; Manager, Policy, Program Development and Implementation Unit; Family Conciliation Counsellor; Employment and Income Assistance Counsellor; Social Worker; Policy Coordinator; Agency Relations Specialist; Child Development Counsellor; Regional Psychologist; Corporate Support Analyst (2); Program Supervisor, Child And Family Services; Planning and Program Analyst; Senior Planning and Program Analyst; Administrative Officer; Employment Develop-

ment Specialist; Special Programs Coordinator; Technical Officers (2); Verification / Investigation Officers.

MANITOBA FAMILY SERVICES AND HOUSING

Att: Human Resources Services
840 - 3rd Street NE, PO Box 1190
Portage la Prairie, MB R1N 3C6

Fax 204-856-4224
Website .... www.gov.mb.ca/fs

Employer Background: Manitoba Family Services and Housing is the provincial department responsible for supporting adults and families in need, as well as keeping children safe and protected. *New Positions Created (8):* Physiotherapist; Registered Psychiatric Nurse; Supervisor, Housekeeping; Medical Equipment Technician; Clinical Psychologist; Occupational Therapist; Physiotherapist; Pharmacist.

MANITOBA FINANCE

Att: Human Resource Services
379 Broadway Street, Suite 304
Winnipeg, MB R3C 0T9

Fax 204-945-4907
Website .... www.gov.mb.ca/finance

Employer Background: Manitoba Finance is responsible for the treasury and finances of Manitoba. *New Positions Created (32):* Field Audit Supervisor; Tax Auditors (2); Accounts Payable Administrator; Chief Technology Officer; Help Desk / Technical Support Analyst; Labour Relations Officer; Manager, Treasury Board Secretariat; Financial Analyst; Security Technology Analyst; Senior Treasury Officer; Supervisor, Shared Costs & Central Accounts Receivable; Treasury Board Analyst; Administrative Officer; Bilingual Information Specialists (2); Internal Auditor; Payroll System Analyst; Senior Treasury Officer; Bilingual Information Specialist; Bilingual Service Centres Coordinator; Asset Mgmnt Accountant; Senior Analyst / Programmer; System and Audit Supervisor; Director, Corporate Accommodation Planning Branch; Director, Web Services; Webmaster, Web Publishing; Internal Auditor; Tax Auditor; Treasury Officer; Application / Configuration Analyst; Senior Configurer Analyst; Special Investigator; Assistant Director, Legislation and Interpretation.

MANITOBA HEALTH

Att: Human Resources Manager
300 Carlton Street, Suite 4089
Winnipeg, MB R3B 3M9

Tel. 204-945-5900
Fax 204-945-1999
Email .... ccairns@gov.mb.ca
Website .... www.gov.mb.ca/health

Employer Background: Established in 1928, Manitoba Health is the provincial department responsible for developing and administering public and mental health services. *New Positions Created (39):* Chief Technologist; Consultant; Economic Analyst; Financial Analyst; Senior Financial Analyst; Correspondence Writer; Pharmaceutical Consultant; Primary Care Nurse; Finance Of-

ficer; Liaison, Health Programs and Operations; Chief Technologist; Program Policy Consultant; EDS Technicians (2); Pharmaceutical Consultant, EDS; Primary Care Nurse, HSS; Senior Correspondence Officer; Policy Analyst; Primary Care Nurse; Project Manager; Liaison, Health Programs and Operations; Program Consultant, Aboriginal Health; Database Administrator; Director of Primary Health Care; Senior Project Manager; Consultant, Diabetes and Chronic Diseases Unit; Network Operator; Database Administrators (2); Information Standards Architect; Senior Business Analyst; Human Resources Consultant; Program Consultant; Business Analyst; Research Statistical Analyst; Health Services Consultant; Policy Analyst; Laboratory Director; Administrative Assistant; Child Health Program Consultant; Planner.

MANITOBA HEALTH, SELKIRK MENTAL HEALTH CENTRE

Att: Human Resource Services
PO Box 9600
Selkirk, MB R1A 2B5

Tel. 204-482-1620
Fax 204-785-8936
Website .... www.gov.mb.ca/health

Employer Background: Selkirk Mental Health Centre provides services for up to 270 patients suffering from serious and persistent mental illness. *New Positions Created (6):* Staff Nurses; Psychologist; Staff Nurses; Support Service Team Leaders (3); Aboriginal Elder; Staff Nurse.

MANITOBA HIGHWAYS & TRANSPORTATION, ABORIGINAL AND NORTHERN AFFAIRS, NORTHERN REGION

Att: Human Resources Consultant
11 Nelson Road, 2nd Floor
Thompson, MB R8N 0B3

Fax 204-677-6354
Website .... www.gov.mb.ca

Employer Background: Manitoba Highways & Transportation is the provincial department responsible for the maintenance and construction of roads and highways in Manitoba. *New Positions Created (10):* Human Resource / Payroll Assistant; Highways Maintenance Superintendent; Engineering Aides (6); Low-Bed Operator; Safety / Operator Trainer; Administrative Secretary; Engineering Aides (4); Labourer / Operator; Junior Project Supervisor; Regional Project Supervisor.

MANITOBA HYDRO

Att: Human Resource Services,
Transmission & Distribution
PO Box 815
Winnipeg, MB R3C 2P4

Tel. 204-474-4294
Fax 204-474-4985
Email .... employment.td@hydro.mb.ca
Website .... www.hydro.mb.ca

Employer Background: Headquartered in Winnipeg, Manitoba Hydro is a major electric utility, serving over 394,000 customers throughout the province. *New Positions Cre-*

ated (2): Protection Design Engineer; Intellectual Property Officer.

MANITOBA INDUSTRY, TRADES AND MINES / ITM

Att: Human Resource Services
379 Broadway Street, Suite 304
Winnipeg, MB R3C 0T9

Fax 204-945-4907
Website .... www.gov.mb.ca/itt

Employer Background: Manitoba ITM fosters wealth and job creation in industry and trade activities to improve the quality of life for Manitobans. *New Positions Created (9):* Application Developer; Economic Development Officer; Financial Consultant; Geologist; Administrative Secretary; International Trade Development Officer, Mexico; Business Counsellor; Senior Business Investment Officer; Manager, Rural Business Services and Francophone Initiatives.

MANITOBA INTERGOVERNMENTAL AFFAIRS

Att: Human Resources Services
800 Portage Avenue, Suite 600
Winnipeg, MB R3G 0N4

Fax 204-945-3769
Website .... www.gov.mb.ca/ia

Employer Background: Manitoba Intergovernmental Affairs works to facilitate improvement in the economic, social and environmental well-being of Manitoba communities and their citizens. *New Positions Created (15):* Assessment Officers (6); Director; Accounts Payable Clerk; Project Manager; Regional Manager; Assessment Officer; Regional Manager; Policy Planner; Resource Planner; Regional Manager; Manager, Neighbourhood Programs; Financial Analyst; Assessment Officer; Programmer Analyst, Application Development; Community Planner.

MANITOBA JUSTICE / CULTURE, HERITAGE AND TOURISM

Att: Human Resource Services
405 Broadway, Suite 910
Winnipeg, MB R3C 3L6

Tel. 204-945-3739
Fax 204-945-3764
Website .... www.gov.mb.ca

Employer Background: Manitoba Justice / Culture, Heritage and Tourism is a large department responsible for the administration of justice in Manitoba, as well as matters relating to culture, hospitality and tourism. *New Positions Created (73):* Clerk of Court; Administrative Secretary; Bilingual Policy and Program Analyst; Correctional Trade Instructor, Woodworking; Bilingual Administrative Secretary to Judges; Application Developer; Administrative Secretaries / Receptionists (2); Chaplain; Cultural Worker; Departmental Accountant; Development Consultant; Family Conciliation Counselor; Marketing Consultant; Circuit Clerk; Bilingual Policy and Program Analyst; Probation Officer; Senior Application Developer; Aboriginal Probation Officer; Administrative Secretary; Nurses; Probation Officer; Legal Secretaries (2); Director, Information Systems; Administrative Supervisor; Bilingual Arts Consultant; Human Rights Officer; Human Rights Officer; Library Technician; Manager, Investigation and Mediation; Policy Analyst; Manager, Technology Services; Bilingual Administrative Assistant; Nurse; Production Specialist; Accounting Clerk; Manager, Writing Services; Senior Accountant; Analyst / Programmer; Court Clerk / Monitor; Lawyer's Assistant; Advertising Coordinator; Executive Director, Manitoba Seniors Directorate; Library Technician; Archivist; Bilingual Magistrate; Crown Counsel; Probation Officer; Senior Crown Counsel; Director, Maintenance Enforcement; Clerk; Women's Advocacy / Child Victim Support Services Worker; Accounting Clerk; Collection Officers (2); Aboriginal Probation Officers (2); Director, Aboriginal and Community Law Enforcement Services; Manager, Technology Services; Probation Officers; Victim Case Manager; Aboriginal Program Specialist / Probation Officer; Director, Maintenance Enforcement; Tailor / Garment Manager; Lawyer / Mediator; Public Safety Director; Editor; Clerk Typist; Compliance Officer; Legal Counsel; Crown Attorneys; Recreation Consultant; Bilingual Administrative Secretary to Judges; Communications Coordinator; Human Resource Consultant; Manager, Victim Services for Abused Women and Children.

MANITOBA LABOUR & IMMIGRATION
Att: Human Resource Services
1181 Portage Avenue, Room 407
Winnipeg, MB R3G 0T3

Tel. 204-945-6893
Fax 204-948-2193
Website .... www.gov.mb.ca

Employer Background: Manitoba Labour & Immigration is responsible for all matters relating to labour and the workplace in Manitoba. *New Positions Created (39):* Curriculum Development Officer; Worker Advisor; Employment Standards Officer; Residence Counsellor, Girls' Residence; Director, TCE Financial Services; Principal, Manitoba School for the Deaf; Teachers of the Deaf; Manager, Finance and Administration; Registration Clerk; Assistant Fire Commissioner; Codes & Standards Officer; Library Coordinator; Aboriginal Liaison / Consultant; Consultant for the Blind / Visually Impaired; Coordinator, Program Analysis and Development; Assessment and Evaluation Consultant; Employment Services Consultant; Apprenticeship Counsellor; Designation Officer; Consultant, Networking Technologies; Director, International Education; Publications Editor; Bilingual Administrative Officer; Economic Research Analyst; Manager, Finance and Administration; Manager, Adult Learning and Literacy; Provincial Trade Advisory Committee Clerk; Programmer Analyst; Library Coordinator; Training Program Coordinator; Financial Analysts (2); Special Education Consultant; Pre-hospital EMS Training And Development Officer; Consultant, Distance Learning and Information Technology Unit; Director; Di-

rector; Director; Curriculum Consultant; Project Leader, Public Schools Finance Board.

MANITOBA PUBLIC INSURANCE
Att: Human Resources Department
234 Donald Street, Room 704
Winnipeg, MB R3C 4A4

Tel. 204-943-9851
Fax 204-985-8049
Email .... hresources@mpi.mb.ca
Website .... www.mpi.mb.ca

Employer Background: Founded in 1971, Manitoba Public Insurance is an automobile insurer and has 1,200 employees in 13 locations across Manitoba. *New Positions Created (2):* IT Analyst, Databases; IT Analyst, Enterprise Networks.

MANITOBA TRANSPORTATION & GOVERNMENT SERVICES
Att: Human Resource Services
PO Box 690
Dauphin, MB R7N 3B3

Tel. 204-945-3001
Fax 204-638-6696
Website .... www.gov.mb.ca/tgs

Employer Background: Manitoba Transportation & Government Services is the provincial department responsible for roads and highways in Manitoba, as well as government purchasing and real estate. *New Positions Created (8):* Sr Tradesperson; Assistant Works Supervisors (2); Heavy-Duty Mechanic; Works Supervisor; Resident Engineer; Sr Tradesperson; Highways Maintenance Superintendent; Engineering Aids (2).

MANITOBA TRANSPORTATION & GOVERNMENT SERVICES
Att: Human Resources Services
379 Broadway Street, Suite 304
Winnipeg, MB R3C 0T9

Fax 204-945-4907
Website .... www.gov.mb.ca/tgs

Employer Background: Manitoba Transportation & Government Services is the provincial department responsible for roads and highways in Manitoba, as well as government purchasing and real estate. *New Positions Created (34):* Maintenance Assistant; Security Services Officer; Engineering Aid; Power Engineer; Network Operations Analyst; District Property Manager; Business / Technical Analyst; Mechanic; Staff and Organizational Development Consultant; Chief Operating Officer; Manager, Grounds; Clerk Typist; Programmer / Analyst; Property Clerk; Facility Manager; Maintenance Assistant; Maintenance Assistant; Industrial Hygiene Specialist; Industrial Mechanic / Millwright; Tradeshelper; Accounts Receivable Supervisor; Lease Documentation Officer; Planning Analyst; Procurement Manager; Accommodation Consultant; Marketing Coordinator; Planning Officer; Construction Supervisor; Maintenance Assistant; Drafting Technician; Leasing Consultant; Gardener; Technical Engineering Officer; Technical Engineering Officer.

MANITOBA TRANSPORTATION & GOVERNMENT SERVICES
Att: Human Resource Services
326 Broadway, Room 500
Winnipeg, MB R3C 0S5

Fax 204-948-3382
Website .... www.gov.mb.ca/tgs

Employer Background: Manitoba Transportation & Government Services is the provincial department responsible for roads and highways in Manitoba, as well as government purchasing and real estate. *New Positions Created (46):* Contract Technician; Computer Operator; Geotechnical Technician; Bilingual Driver Examiner; Intersection Marker Operator; Policy and Procedures Technician-in-Training; Technical Engineering Officer; Traffic Monitoring Technician; Forms Design and Control / French Language Services Coordinator; Director, Regional Operations; Highway Inventory Technician; Motor Vehicle Inspector; Bilingual Clerk; Bilingual Administrative Secretary; Bridge Maintenance Supervisor; Secretary to the Taxicab Board; Special Operations Technician; Grading & Audit Technician; Assistant Bridge Maintenance Supervisors (2); Assistant Seal Coat Superintendents (2); Engineer-in-Training; Reviewing Officer; Senior Transportation Policy and Development Consultant; Construction Engineer; Administrative Assistant; Compliance Inspectors (2); Engineering Aides (10); Information Technologist; Production Supervisor; Program Analyst; Director, Bridges and Structures; Supervisor, Alcohol and Drug Program; Grading and Audit Inspector; Driver Examiner; Senior Quality Assurance Technician; Bilingual Clerk; Assistant to Contract Engineer; Executive Director; Supervising Technical Engineering Officer; Drafting Technician; Trades Helper; Driver Examiner; Regional Administrative Secretary; Director, Regional Operations; Business Planning Coordinator; Senior Systems Analyst, Information.

MANITOBA TRANSPORTATION & GOVERNMENT SERVICES
Att: Human Resource Services
25 Tupper Street North
Portage la Prairie, MB R1N 3K1

Tel. 204-239-3440
Fax 204-239-3301
Email .... mkrause@gov.mb.ca
Website .... www.gov.mb.ca/tgs

Employer Background: Manitoba Transportation & Government Services is the provincial department responsible for roads and highways in Manitoba, as well as government purchasing and real estate. *New Positions Created (13):* Administrative Secretary; Engineering Aides (2); Heavy Duty Equipment Mechanic; Assistant Works Supervisor; Project Supervisors (2); Regional Human Resource Administrator; Heavy Duty Equipment Mechanic; Engineering Aid; Assistant Works Supervisors (2); Bilingual Administrative Secretary; Area Works Supervisors (3); Regional Design and Materials Technologist; Senior Project Engineer.

MANITOBA TRANSPORTATION & GOVERNMENT SERVICES
Att: Human Resource Administrator
323 Main Street, Suite 316, Box 1028
Steinbach, MB R0A 2A0

Fax 204-326-4852
Website .... www.gov.mb.ca/tgs
Employer Background: Manitoba Transportation & Government Services is the provincial department responsible for roads and highways in Manitoba, as well as government purchasing and real estate. *New Positions Created (10):* Heavy Duty Equipment Mechanic Apprentice; Drafting Technician; Labourer / Operator; Garage Works Supervisor; Heavy Duty Mechanic; Engineering Aid; Engineering Aid; Assistant Works Supervisor; Senior Project Engineer; Technical Engineering Officer.

MANITOBA TRANSPORTATION & GOVERNMENT SERVICES, NORTHERN REGION
Att: Human Resources Manager
59 Elizabeth Drive, Box 23
Thompson, MB R8N 1X4

Fax 204-677-0659
Website .... www.gov.mb.ca/tgs
Employer Background: Manitoba Transportation & Government Services is the provincial department responsible for the maintenance and construction of roads and highways in Manitoba. *New Positions Created (2):* Regional Financial Officer; Labourers / Operators (2).

MANITOBA TRANSPORTATION & GOVERNMENT SERVICES, SOUTH WESTERN REGION
Att: Human Resource
1525 - 1st Street North
Brandon, MB R7C 1B5

Fax 204-726-6836
Website .... www.gov.mb.ca/tgs
Employer Background: Manitoba Transportation & Government Services is the provincial department responsible for roads and highways in Manitoba, as well as government purchasing and real estate. *New Positions Created (12):* Engineering Aide; Works Supervisor; Senior Tradesperson; Crossing Application Technicians; Work Supervisor; Resident Engineer; Heavy Duty Equipment Mechanic; Highways Maintenance Superintendents (2); Technical Engineering Officer; Heavy Duty Equipment Mechanic; Engineering Aid; Regional Utility Co-ordinator.

MANITOULIN TRANSPORT
Att: Human Resources
PO Box 390
Gore Bay, ON P0P 1H0

Tel. 705-282-2640
Fax 705-282-1237
Email .... careers@manitoulintransport.com
Website ... www.manitoulintransport.com
Employer Background: Founded in 1953, Manitoulin Transport is a leading carrier of general commodities, providing premium service throughout North America through a network of 34 terminals. *New Positions*

Created (2): Terminal Manager; Regional Operations Manager.

MANN & GAHTAN
Att: Human Resources Manager
1 First Canadian Place, Suite 5100
Toronto, ON M5X 1K2

Tel. 416-657-4470
Fax 416-645-1410
Email ...... recruitment@manngahtan.com
Website .... www.manngahtan.com
Employer Background: Mann & Gahtan is a law firm involved in information technology, intellectual property, e-commerce and venture law. *New Positions Created (3):* Intermediate / Senior Associates; Lawyers; Patent Agents.

MANSOUR MINING INC.
Att: Human Resources
2578 Lasalle Blvd.
Sudbury, ON P3A 4R7

Tel. 705-566-6463
Fax 705-566-4949
Website .... www.mansourmining.com
Employer Background: Mansour Mining Inc. is a ground support supplier for the mining industry. *New Positions Created (3):* Blacksmith; Industrial Electrician; Rock Mechanics Engineer.

MANTA CORPORATION
Att: Human Resources Department
1430 Blair Place, 2nd Floor
Gloucester, ON K1J 9N2

Tel. 613-744-6111
Fax 613-744-4001
Email .... careers@mantacorp.com
Website .... www.mantacorp.com
Employer Background: Manta Corporation provides e-surveys and e-business consulting services. *New Positions Created (3):* Lotus Notes Developer; Senior Account Executive; Senior Technical Trainer.

MANULIFE FINANCIAL CORPORATION
Att: Human Resources Department
380 Weber Street North, PO Box 1650
Waterloo, ON N2J 4V7

Fax 519-883-5705
Email .... resumes@manulife.com
Website .... www.manulife.com
Employer Background: Manulife Financial Corporation is a leading Canadian-based financial services company, operating in 15 countries and territories worldwide. *New Positions Created (2):* Assistant Counsel; Claims Approver.

MANULIFE FINANCIAL CORPORATION
Att: Canadian Staffing Services
500 King Street North, PO Box 605
Waterloo, ON N2J 4B8

Tel. 519-747-7000
Fax 519-747-6451
Email .... resumes@manulife.com
Website .... www.manulife.com

Employer Background: Manulife Financial Corporation is a leading Canadian-based financial services company, operating in 15 countries and territories worldwide. *New Positions Created (12):* Long-Term Disability Adjudicator; Short-Term Disability Adjudicator; Accounting Administrator; Administrative Assistant; Administrative Secretary; Business Consultant; Database Analyst; Manager, Group Disability Claims; Regional Banking Consultant; Commercial Account Manager; Business Analysts; Systems Designers.

MANULIFE FINANCIAL CORPORATION
Att: Human Resources Manager
200 Bloor Street East
Toronto, ON M4W 1E5

Tel. 416-926-3000
Fax 416-926-6310
Email ... careers_feedback@manulife.com
Website .... www.manulife.com
Employer Background: Manulife Financial Corporation is a leading Canadian-based financial services company, operating in 15 countries and territories worldwide. *New Positions Created (7):* Commissions Coordinator; Project Manager; Senior Actuarial Consultant; Senior Systems Analyst; Service Managers (2); Analyst, Investment Management Services; Cash Management Officer.

MANULIFE FINANCIAL CORPORATION
Att: John Bouchard, Regional Manager
1525 Carling Avenue, Suite 600
Ottawa, ON K1Z 8R9

Fax 613-728-7733
Email ...... john_bouchard@manulife.com
Website .... www.manulife.com
Employer Background: Founded in 1887, Manulife Financial provides financial products in 15 countries, with $122.4 billion under management and more than 28,000 employees and agents worldwide. *New Positions Created (3):* Disability Management Consultant; Rehabilitation Specialist; Regional Compliance Officer.

MANULIFEDIRECT
Att: Human Resources Manager
5650 Yonge Street
Toronto, ON M2M 4G4

Website .... www.manulifedirect.com
Employer Background: ManulifeDirect (a subsidiary of Manulife Financial Corporation) is one of the largest insurers in Canada. *New Positions Created (7):* Senior Actuarial Consultant; Assistant Vice-President and Controller, US Insurance Financial; Actuarial Consultant / Senior; Assistant / Associate Actuary; Associate Actuary; Associate Actuary; Associate Actuary.

MAPINFO CORPORATION
Att: Director, Human Resources
330 Front Street West, Suite 1100
Toronto, ON M5V 3B7

Tel. 416-348-9180
Fax 416-348-9195

Website .... www.mapinfo.com

Employer Background: MapInfo Corporation (formerly Compusearch) is a global software technology organization that provides location-based information to business. *New Positions Created (11):* Contract Analyst; Corporate Account Representatives; Director, Professional Services, Information Technology; Inside Sales Representative; Manager, Corporate Marketing; Professional Services Consultant; Research Analyst, Advanced Site Models; Research Analyst, Custom Research; Senior Database Administrator; Senior Developers; VAR Sales Manager.

MAPLE LEAF CONSUMER FOODS
Att: Human Resources
150 Bartor Road
Toronto, ON M9M 1H1

Tel. 416-741-7181
Fax 416-741-7693
Email .... corridan@mapleleaf.ca
Website .... www.mapleleaf.ca

Employer Background: Maple Leaf Consumer Foods is a major meat processing company and provider of quality food products. *New Positions Created (3):* Licenced Refrigeration Mechanic; Plant Administrator; Millwrights.

MAPLE LEAF CONSUMER FOODS
Att: Human Resources Manager
30 Eglinton Avenue West, Suite 500
Mississauga, ON L5R 3E7

Fax 905-501-3052
Email .... makye@mapleleaf.ca
Website .... www.mapleleaf.ca

Employer Background: Maple Leaf Consumer Foods is a major meat processing company and provider of quality food products. *New Positions Created (6):* Pricing Analyst; Supply Chain Analyst; Cost Accountant; Accounts Payable Manager; Information Systems Coordinator; Regional Sales Manager, Western Canada.

MAPLE LEAF PORK
Att: Employment Coordinator
6355 Richmond Avenue
Brandon, MB R7A 7A3

Tel. 204-571-2500
Fax 204-571-2612
Email .... loregicf@mapleleaf.ca
Website .... www.mapleleaf.ca

Employer Background: Maple Leaf Pork markets fresh pork and processed meats throughout North America, the Caribbean and Pacific Rim. *New Positions Created (2):* 1st-Class Power Engineer; 2nd Class Engineer.

MAPLE LEAF PORK
Att: Plant Employment Coordinator
821 Appleby Line
Burlington, ON L7L 4W9

Tel. 905-637-2301
Fax 905-333-2948
Website .... www.mapleleaf.ca

Employer Background: Maple Leaf Pork markets fresh pork and processed meats throughout North America, the Caribbean and Pacific Rim. *New Positions Created (2):* Occupational Health Nurse; Mechanic B.

**MAPLE LEAF PORK,
CASE REDDI FACILITY**
Att: Cathy Smith, Human Resources
92 Highland Road East
Stoney Creek, ON L8J 2W6

Fax 905-662-3337
Website .... www.mapleleaf.ca

Employer Background: Maple Leaf Pork markets fresh pork and processed meats throughout North America, the Caribbean and Pacific Rim. *New Positions Created (6):* Cost Accountant; Quality Assurance Technician; Distribution Manager; Junior Production Supervisor; Licensed Electrician; Production Planner.

MAPLE LEAF POULTRY
Att: Human Resources
100 Ethel Avenue
Toronto, ON M6N 4Z7

Tel. 416-767-5151
Fax 416-767-2113
Website .... www.mapleleaf.ca

Employer Background: Maple Leaf Poultry is part of Maple Leaf Foods, a major meat processing company and provider of quality food products. *New Positions Created (5):* 4th-Class Stationary Engineer; Health and Safety Attendant; General Shipping Supervisor; Health and Safety Attendant; Shipping Supervisor.

MAPLE LEAF POULTRY
Att: Michael Borden
2626 Argentia Road
Mississauga, ON L5N 5N2

Fax 905-826-4144
Email .... bordenma@mapleleaf.ca
Website .... www.mapleleaf.ca

Employer Background: Maple Leaf Poultry is part of Maple Leaf Foods, a major meat processing company and provider of quality food products. *New Positions Created (4):* Financial Analyst; Customer Service Representative; Sales Representative; Senior Financial Analysts.

MAPLE LODGE FARMS LTD.
Att: Human Resource Coordinator
RR #2
Norval, ON L0P 1K0

Tel. 905-455-8340
Fax 905-455-8370
Email ... tmountford@maplelodgefarms.com
Website .... www.maplelodgefarms.com

Employer Background: Maple Lodge Farms Ltd. is a food processing company primarily involved in poultry processing. *New Positions Created (2):* Industrial Electrician; Security Officer.

MAPLE REINDERS INC.
Att: John Zwaagstra, Manager, Edmonton
4050 - 69th Avenue NW, Suite 200
Edmonton, AB T6B 2V2

Tel. 780-465-5980

Fax 780-465-8927
Email .... johnz@maple.ca
Website .... www.maple.ca

Employer Background: Maple Reinders Inc. is a building and heavy civil construction group, serving the industrial building and water / wastewater treatment construction markets across Canada since 1967. *New Positions Created (6):* Construction Positions; Project Engineer; Superintendent; Estimator; Project Engineer; Superintendent.

MAPLE REINDERS INC.
Att: Harold Reinders
2333 - 18th Avenue NE, Suite 32
Calgary, AB T2E 8T6

Fax 403-216-1459
Email .... harold@maple.ca
Website .... www.maple.ca

Employer Background: Maple Reinders Inc. is a building and heavy civil construction group, serving the industrial building and water / wastewater treatment construction markets across Canada since 1967. *New Positions Created (2):* Senior Superintendent; Site Superintendent.

MAPLE REINDERS INC.
Att: Ray Elgersma
201 County Court Boulevard, Suite 600
Brampton, ON L6W 4L2

Tel. 905-457-6444
Fax 905-457-2498
Email .... raye@maple.ca
Website .... www.maple.ca

Employer Background: Maple Reinders Inc. is a building and heavy civil construction group, serving the industrial building and water / wastewater treatment construction markets across Canada since 1967. *New Positions Created (8):* Accounts Payable Clerk; Labourers (4); Payroll Clerk; Assistant Manager, Buildings Division; Estimator; Project Manager; Various Construction Positions (2); Project Manager.

MAPLE RIDGE, DISTRICT OF
Att: Personnel Department
11995 Haney Place
Maple Ridge, BC V2X 6A9

Tel. 604-467-7352
Fax 604-467-7374
Email .... resumes@mapleridge.org
Website .... www.mapleridge.org

Employer Background: Located 45 km from Vancouver, the District of Maple Ridge is home to 65,000 residents. *New Positions Created (9):* Executive Assistant; Director of Planning; Municipal Engineer; Planner; Draftsperson; Engineering Technologist; Superintendent, Waterworks; General Manager; Youth Recreation Coordinator.

MARCH NETWORKS CORPORATION
Att: Manager, Human Resources
555 Legget Drive, Suite 330, Tower B
Kanata, ON K2K 2X3

Fax 613-591-7337
Email ...... opportunities@telexiscorp.com
Website .... www.telexiscorp.com

Employer Background: March Networks Corporation (formerly Telexis Corporation) is a leading developer of IP multimedia broadband applications and delivery platforms. *New Positions Created (15):* Business Development Analyst; Design Integrity Technologist; Digital Signal Processing Firmware Developer; Intermediate Hardware Developer; Intermediate Software Developers; Inventory Controller; Junior Hardware Developer; Junior Software Developer; Market Research Analyst; Marketing Programs Manager; Product Manager; Senior Hardware Developer; Senior Software Developer; Technical Writer; Test and Verification Specialist.

MARCHESE PHARMACY
Att: Human Resources
316 James Street North
Hamilton, ON L8L 1H2
Fax 905-528-4162
Email .... info@marchesepharmacy.com
Website ..... www.marchesepharmacy.com
Employer Background: Marchese Pharmacy is an independent, community healthcare provider. *New Positions Created (7):* Customer Service Representative; Database Administrator; Dispensary Pharmacist; Infusion Pharmacist; Medical Supplies Assistant; Pharmacy Technicians, Infusion and Dispensary; Purchasing Coordinator.

MARCHON CANADA
Att: Human Resources Department
1865 Trans Canada Highway
Dorval, QC H9P 1J1
Tel. 514-421-1133
Fax 514-421-0811
Website .... www.marchon.com
Employer Background: Marchon Canada is a global manufacturer and distributor of quality fashion eyeglasses, including Calvin Klein, Donna Karan, Nautica, Fendi, Mickey & Co. and Flexon brands. *New Positions Created (3):* Customer Service Representative; General Accountant; Sales and Marketing Coordinator.

MARCONI COMMUNICATIONS
Att: Human Resources
1375 Trans Canada Highway
Dorval, QC H9P 2W8
Fax 514-822-4042
Email ...... cvmtl@na.marconicomms.com
Website .... www.marconicomms.com
Employer Background: Marconi Communications, the optical networks division of Marconi, is a global manufacturer of intelligent communication systems. *New Positions Created (15):* Director; Engineer IV / Lead; Engineering Manager; Hardware Development Engineer; Hardware Development Engineer; Lead Software Engineer; Senior Engineer; Software Development Engineer; Software Development Engineer; Software Development Engineer; Software Development Engineer; Software Development Engineer; Software Development Engineer; Software Development Engineer; Software Quality Assurance Engineer.

MARCONI DATA SYSTEMS CANADA LTD.
Att: National Sales Manager
6500 Viscount Road
Mississauga, ON L4V 1H3
Tel. 905-673-1212
Fax 905-673-8726
Website .... www.marconidata.com
Employer Background: Marconi Data Systems Canada Ltd. (formerly Videojet Canada) manufactures high-speed inkjet coding, marking and imaging systems. *New Positions Created (2):* National Service Manager; Customer Service Position.

MARCUS EVANS
Att: Human Resources Manager
20 Toronto Street, 10th Floor
Toronto, ON M5C 2B8
Tel. 416-955-0375
Fax 416-955-0380
Email .... jobs@marcusevansto.com
Website .... www.marcusevans.com
Employer Background: Founded in 1983, Marcus Evans is a business information company that presents over 1,000 strategic conferences and summits worldwide. *New Positions Created (6):* Inside Sales Executive; Inside Sales Executives; Sales Positions; Administrative Assistant; Corporate Sales Executives; Sales Professionals.

MARCUS EVANS
Att: Human Resources Manager
600 de Maisonneuve Boulevard West
Suite 1700
Montréal, QC H3A 3J2
Tel. 514-289-9700
Fax 514-289-9301
Website .... www.marcusevans.com
Employer Background: Founded in 1983, Marcus Evans is a business information company that presents over 1,000 strategic conferences and summits worldwide. *New Positions Created (2):* Sales Executives; Receptionist / Personnel Manager.

MARITIME HYDRAULICS (CANADA) LTD.
Att: Human Resources Manager
1616 Meridian Road NE
Calgary, AB T2A 2P1
Tel. 403-569-2222
Fax 403-569-2294
Employer Background: Maritime Hydraulics (Canada) Ltd. designs and manufactures oilfield drilling and servicing equipment. *New Positions Created (3):* Electronics Technologist; Electrical Engineers / Technologists; Project Manager.

MARITIME LIFE ASSURANCE COMPANY
Att: Heather M. Hannon, Vice-President, General Counsel and Corporate Secretary
79 Wellington Street West
6th Floor, Box 120, Aetna Tower, TD Centre
Toronto, ON M5K 1N9
Tel. 416-864-8000
Fax 416-864-8549
Email .... cpa@maritimelife.ca
Website .... www.maritimelife.ca
Employer Background: Maritime Life Assurance Company (formerly Aetna Life Insurance Company of Canada) provides group life insurance, group health insurance, individual life and disability insurance. *New Positions Created (3):* In-House Litigation Lawyer; Disability Case Managers; Legal Assistant.

MARK ANTHONY GROUP
Att: Human Resources Manager
1750 - 75th Avenue West, Suite 210
Vancouver, BC V6P 6G2
Tel. 604-263-9994
Fax 604-269-9815
Email .... hr@markanthony.com
Website .... www.markanthony.com
Employer Background: Founded in 1972, Mark Anthony Group is a leading beverage alcohol producer and distributor, with over 300 employees. Their brands include Mike's Hard Lemonade, Corona, California Cooler, Mission Hill and Corbett Canyon. *New Positions Created (5):* Human Resources Assistant; President and COO; Merchandiser; Territory Manager; Art Director.

MARK IV AIR INTAKE SYSTEMS
Att: Human Resources Department
1500 Boucherville Street
Montréal, QC H1N 3V3
Tel. 514-256-6055
Fax 514-256-2055
Email .... julie_hebert@markivauto.com
Website .... www.markivauto.com
Employer Background: Mark IV Air Intake Systems is a leading tier-1 supplier of air intake and engine cooling modules and components. *New Positions Created (2):* Process Engineer; Quality Engineer.

MARKHAM, CORPORATION OF THE TOWN OF
Att: Human Resources
101 Town Centre Boulevard
Markham, ON L3R 9W3
Tel. 905-475-4700
Fax 905-479-7774
Email .... hrinfo@city.markham.on.ca
Website .... www.city.markham.on.ca
Employer Background: The Corporation of The Town of Markham provides municipal government services to residents and businesses in the community. *New Positions Created (22):* Assistant Town Solicitor, Legal Services; Facility Coordinator; Planner II; Applications Engineer; Engineering Technician, Transportation; Structural Engineer; Waterworks Operator II; Arborist; Building Inspector II; Senior Planner, Policy & Research; Transportation Engineer / Coordinator; Zoning Examiner; Manager, Waste Management; Development Technician; Secretary / Treasurer, Committee of Adjustment; Arborist; Manager, Municipal Tax; Employee Relations Advisor; Coordinator Geomatics Group / GIS Advocate; Cultural Development Officer; Planner II / Research & GIS; Roads Technician.

MARKHAM STOUFFVILLE HOSPITAL
Att: Human Resources
381 Church Street
Markham, ON L3P 7P3

Tel.	905-472-7000
Fax	905-472-7055
Email	humanres@msh.on.ca
Website	www.msh.on.ca

Employer Background: Founded in 1990, Markham Stouffville Hospital is a 173-bed, acute care community hospital, with an annual operating budget of $61 million. *New Positions Created (24):* Child Psychologist, Mental Health System; Health Information Analyst; Coordinator, Retail Food Services; Manager, Utilization; Registered Nurses, Childbirth Centre; Dual Certified Radiologist / Nuclear Medicine Physician; Perinatal Nurses; Physiotherapist, Palliative / Complex Care and ALC; Professional Practice Leader / Educator; Registered Nurses, Emergency Department; Registered Nurses, ICU / CCU; Registered Nurses, Medicine / Telemetry; Polysomnographic Technologists; Registered Nurses; Registered Respiratory Care Practitioner; Technical Specialist, Chemistry; Director, Health Records; Pharmacist; Workload Measurement Coordinator; Anaesthesiologist; Manager, Utilization; Speech Language Pathologist; Social Worker, Crisis Team; Health Records Administrator.

MARKS & CLERK
Att: Human Resources Department
280 Slater Street, Suite 1800
Ottawa, ON K1P 1C2

Tel.	613-236-9561
Fax	613-230-8821
Email	hr@markclerk.com
Website	www.markclerk.com

Employer Background: Founded in 1921, UK-based Marks & Clerk is a patent and trademark law firm. *New Positions Created (3):* Formality and Renewal Clerks; Patent Agent; Secretaries.

MARKS SUPPLY INC.
Att: Human Resources
169 Riverbend Drive
Kitchener, ON N2B 2E8

Tel.	519-578-5560
Fax	519-578-1640
Email	hr@markssupply.net
Website	www.markssupply.net

Employer Background: Established in 1962, Marks Supply Inc. is a wholesaler of plumbing, heating, industrial and HVAC products. *New Positions Created (3):* Branch Supervisor; Inside Sales Rep; Warehouse Worker.

MARRIOTT INTERNATIONAL, TORONTO AIRPORT MARRIOTT
Att: Human Resources
901 Dixon Road
Toronto, ON M9W 1J5

Tel.	416-674-9400
Fax	416-674-0429
Email	mhrs.yyzot.dhr@marriott.com
Website	www.marriott.com

Employer Background: Founded in 1927, Marriott International is a leader in the hospitality industry, with nearly 2,100 lodging properties in 59 countries. Their Toronto location is a four-star hotel, with 424 rooms. *New Positions Created (2):* Director of Sales and Marketing; Restaurant Manager.

MARSAN FOODS LTD.
Att: Human Resources
46 Modern Road
Toronto, ON M1R 3B6

Tel.	416-755-9262
Fax	416-755-6790
Website	www.marsanfoods.com

Employer Background: Founded in 1970, Marsan Foods Ltd. prepares and packages quality entrees, sauces and soups. *New Positions Created (3):* Millwright; Product Developer; Purchasing Manager.

MARSHALL MACKLIN MONAGHAN LIMITED
Att: Carolyn Philps, HR Manager
80 Commerce Valley Drive East
Thornhill, ON L3T 7N4

Tel.	905-882-1100
Fax	905-882-0055
Email	hr@mmm.ca
Website	www.mmm.ca

Employer Background: Marshall Macklin Monaghan Limited has been providing comprehensive engineering consulting services to government and private sector clients across Canada and overseas for over 50 years. *New Positions Created (22):* Environmental Engineer; Senior Water Resources Engineer; Civil Design Technologist; Construction Contract Manager; Geomatics Positions; Hydrogeologist; Intermediate Electrical Engineer; Intermediate Structural CAD Technologist; Intermediate Structural Engineer; Landscape and Urban Designer; Municipal Engineers; Project Control Officer; Project Engineer; Project Engineer; Project Engineer / Coordinator; Project Manager; Project / Program Manager; Senior Structural CAD Technologist; Senior Structural Engineer; Traffic Engineer / Transportation Planner; Program / Project Managers; Project Engineer.

MARTIN NEWBY CONSULTING LTD.
Att: Ellen Styner
2139 - 4th Avenue NW
Calgary, AB T2N 0N6

Tel.	403-294-1028
Fax	403-294-1089
Email	ellen@martinnewby.com
Website	www.martinnewby.com

Employer Background: Formed in 1998, Martin Newby is a digital mapping and GIS company, with 18 employees. *New Positions Created (3):* Geomatic Technician; Office Coordinator; Programmer.

MARTIN-BROWER OF CANADA CO.
Att: Human Resources Manager
1109 Derwent Way
New Westminster, BC V3M 5R4

Fax	604-524-5923

Employer Background: Martin-Brower of Canada Co. is a major foodservice distribution and logistics company. *New Positions Created (2):* Warehouse Supervisor, Customized Distribution; Operations Supervisor.

MARTIN-BROWER OF CANADA CO.
Att: Suzana Milovanovic
12 Barton Court
Brampton, ON L6T 5H6

Fax	905-790-0788
Email	smilovanovic@mbcan.com

Employer Background: Martin-Brower of Canada Co. is a major foodservice distribution and logistics company. *New Positions Created (2):* Operations Supervisor; Operations Supervisor.

MASHA KRUPP TRANSLATION GROUP LTD. / MKTG
Att: Human Resources Manager
303 Moodie Drive
Ottawa, ON K2H 9R4

Tel.	613-820-4566
Fax	613-256-4737
Email	brian@mashakrupp.com
Website	www.mashakrupp.com

Employer Background: Founded in 1992, MKTG is an Ottawa-based translation firm, with over 50 full-time staff members. *New Positions Created (3):* Translators (5); Translators; Bilingual Administrative Clerk.

MASTECH CANADA
Att: Toronto Recruiting Department
5800 Explorer Drive, 5th Floor
Mississauga, ON L4W 5L4

Tel.	905-602-7000
Fax	905-602-9801
Email	careers@ca.mastech.com
Website	www.mastcan.com

Employer Background: Mastech Canada is an IT consulting firm. *New Positions Created (33):* Oracle Purchasing Functional Consultants; Programmer Analyst with ABAP; Programmer Analysts with Linux; SAP Functional Consultants; SAP Functional Consultants - SM, SD Modules; Account Manager; Application Development Project Managers; BAAN Developer with Triton; DB2 Database Administrator; Firmware Engineer; Functional Oracle Financials Consultant; Lead Technical Architect; Programmer; Programmer Analyst; Programmer Analyst, Access and Visual Basic; Programmer Analysts; Programmer Analysts, Mainframe; Project Manager, MQ Middle Series; QA Testers; Quality Assurance Testers; Resource Manager; Sales Positions; SAP ABAP Consultant; SAP HR Configuration Consultant; SAP Security Consultant; Security Analyst; Solutions Sales Professional; Team Leader; Test Analysts; Web Administrator; Director, Enterprise Integration; Director, Storage Solutions; Strategic Account Managers.

MASTECH CANADA
Att: Ottawa Recruiting Department
50 O'Connor Street, Suite 1410
Ottawa, ON K1P 6L2

Tel.	613-230-7701
Fax	613-230-9746

Email .... ottcareers@ca.mastech.com
Website .... www.mastcan.com
Employer Background: Mastech Canada is an IT consulting firm. *New Positions Created (7):* Internet Developer - Cold Fusion, SQL Server; Programmer Analyst with C and C++; Data & Process Modellers; Firmware Engineer, Digital Audio / Video; Microprocessor Architect; Network Engineer; Oracle & Sybase Database Analysts.

MASTECH CANADA
Att: Montreal Recruiting Department
2000 McGill College Avenue, Suite 575
Montréal, QC H3A 3H3
Tel. 514-842-8888
Fax 514-842-6235
Email .... mtrlcareers@ca.mastech.com
Website .... www.mastcan.com
Employer Background: Mastech Canada is an IT consulting firm. *New Positions Created (13):* JD Edwards Administrators; Oracle Financials Analyzer Consultant; Oracle Warehouse Builder Consultant; Programmer Analyst, Websphere; Programmer Analyst with Coolgen; Programmer Analysts; Programmer Analysts with Java and Webmethod; SAP Basis Consultant; SAP Consultant; Solutions Mgrs; Team Leader; Technical Trainer; WAN Administrator.

MASTER FLO VALVE INC.
Att: Executive Assistant
4611 - 74th Avenue
Edmonton, AB T6B 2H5
Tel. 780-468-4433
Fax 780-469-9853
Email .... info@masterflo.com
Website .... www.masterflo.com
Employer Background: Master Flo Valve Inc. is a leading manufacturer of oilfield valves and actuators for surface and subsea applications. *New Positions Created (4):* Purchaser; Project / Technical Support Engineers, Junior and Intermediate; Quality Control Supervisor; Quality Control Inspector.

MASTERFILE CORPORATION
Att: Human Resources
175 Bloor Street East
2nd Floor, South Tower
Toronto, ON M4W 3R8
Tel. 416-929-3000
Fax 416-929-2104
Email .... hr@masterfile.com
Website .... www.masterfile.com
Employer Background: Masterfile Corporation is a stock image agency. *New Positions Created (4):* Assistant Client Representative; Imaging Production Artist; Scanner Operator; Executive Assistant.

MATRIKON GROUP
Att: Human Resources Manager
11120 Horseshoe Way, Suite 130
Richmond, BC V7A 5H7
Tel. 604-271-9300
Fax 604-271-9191
Email ...... jobs.vancouver@matrikon.com
Website .... www.matrikon.com

Employer Background: Matrikon Group is an engineering company, specializing in process control and custom real-time software development, with 330 employees and 10 offices worldwide. *New Positions Created (4):* Electrical Engineer / Technologist; Process Control Engineer / Technologist; SAP Consultant; Senior SAP Consultant.

MATRIKON GROUP
Att: Human Resources
10405 Jasper Avenue, Suite 1800
Edmonton, AB T5J 3N4
Tel. 780-448-1010
Fax 780-448-9191
Email .... jobs@matrikon.com
Website .... www.matrikon.com
Employer Background: Matrikon Group is an engineering company, specializing in process control and custom real-time software development, with 330 employees and 10 offices worldwide. *New Positions Created (39):* Project Mgr; Chemical / Petroleum Engineer; Mechanical Engineer; Software Developer / Engineer; Advanced Control Engineer; Intermediate / Sr Network Consultant; Intermediate / Sr Project Mgrs; Lead Programmer; Oracle / SQL Technical Leader; Project Mgrs (2); Account Mgr; Copywriter; Intermediate Software Developer; Process Information Engineer / Technologist; QA Software Lead; SCADA Controls Engineer / Technologist; Applications Consultant; Software Developer / Engineer; Software Tester; Advanced Control Engineer; Intermediate / Senior Project Mgrs; SAP Consultant; Senior SAP Consultant; Graphic Designer; Process Information Engineer / Technologist; QA Software Lead; Receptionist; Scada Controls Engineer / Technologist; Software Developer; Software Quality Assurance Lead; Advanced Control Engineer; Intermediate and Senior Project Managers; Networking Analyst; Process Applications Engineer / Technologist; Process Control Engineer; Project Manager / Software Engineer; Software Developer / Engineer; Software Tester; Test Automation Specialist.

MATRIX CONSULTING GROUP INC.
Att: Stan Gawel, President
8704 - 51st Avenue, Suite 102
Edmonton, AB T6E 5E8
Tel. 780-465-1444
Fax 780-466-8994
Email .... info@matrixconsulting.ab.ca
Website .... www.matrixconsulting.ab.ca
Employer Background: Matrix Consulting Group Inc. is a claims management company, specializing in the control and reduction of workers' compensation and short- or long-term disability premiums. *New Positions Created (5):* Disability Claims Management Specialist; WCB Claims Adjudicator / Case Manager; Claims Adjudicator / Case Manager; Cost Relief Specialist; Disability Management Coordinator.

MATRIX SOLUTIONS INC.
Att: Human Resources
319 - 2nd Avenue SW, Suite 230
Calgary, AB T2P 0C5

Tel. 403-237-0606
Fax 403-263-2493
Email .... info@matrix-solutions.com
Website .... www.matrix-solutions.com
Employer Background: Matrix Solutions Inc. is an environmental consulting firm. *New Positions Created (3):* Senior Hydrogeologist; Senior Soils Expert; Soils Expert.

MATROX ELECTRONIC SYSTEMS LTD.
Att: Human Resources
1055 St. Regis Boulevard
Dorval, QC H9P 2T4
Tel. 514-822-6000
Fax 514-822-6274
Email .... personnel@matrox.com
Website .... www.matrox.com
Employer Background: Matrox Electronic Systems Ltd. designs and manufactures hardware and software for computer graphics, desktop video, PC-based image processing and computer networking applications. *New Positions Created (9):* Corporate Lawyer; Creative Marketing Manager; Senior Legal Counsel; Credit Administrator; Pay Administrator; Corporate Lawyers; Developer Relations Manager (Chief Evangelist); Director of Marketing and Communications; Senior Legal Counsellors.

MATSU MANUFACTURING INC.
Att: Human Resources Manager
1620 Steeles Avenue East
Brampton, ON L6T 1A5
Fax 905-793-1609
Employer Background: Matsu Manufacturing Inc. supplies automotive stampings and assemblies to the mining and agricultural industries. *New Positions Created (6):* Materials Coordinator; Design / Manufacturing Engineer; Manufacturing Services Estimator; Junior Tooling Engineer; Maintenance Supervisor; Process Engineer.

MATTHEW / SCOTT
Att: Human Resources Manager
385 Brunel Road
Mississauga, ON L4Z 1Z5
Tel. 905-890-6959
Fax 905-890-7354
Email .... hr@matthewscott.com
Employer Background: Matthew / Scott is one of North America's fastest-growing customer relationship marketing companies. *New Positions Created (3):* Account Services Manager; Data Processing Systems Administrator (Oracle); Marketing Model Analyst.

MAVERICK SOLUTIONS INC.
Att: Human Resources Manager
5160 Yonge Street
Toronto, ON M2N 6L9
Tel. 416-223-4601
Fax 416-229-0504
Email .... gpendlebury@
.... maverick-solutions.com
Website ..... www.maverick-solutions.com
Employer Background: Maverick Solutions Inc. (formerly Fab Consulting of Canada Inc.) is a leading Canadian CATIA CAD /

CAM specialist. *New Positions Created (4):* CATIA Instructors / Designers; Inside Sales Representative; Senior Sales Representative; Unix / NT System Support Technician.

MAXIM GROUP
Att: Human Resources Manager
703 - 6th Avenue SW, Suite 705
Calgary, AB T2P 0T9

Fax 905-712-8667
Email .... info@webmaxim.com
Website .... www.webmaxim.com
Employer Background: Maxim Group is a leading provider of engineering technical solutions for local and global businesses. *New Positions Created (4):* IT Resourcing Manager; Junior Programmer; Project Manager, Hardware; Technical Writer / Team Lead.

MAXIM MORRISON HERSHFIELD LTD.
Att: Human Resources Manager
17303 - 102th Avenue, Suite 200
Edmonton, AB T5S 1J8

Tel. 780-438-5566
Fax 780-484-3883
Email .... hr@morrisonhershfield.com
Website ..... www.morrisonhershfield.com
Employer Background: Founded in 1946, Maxim Morrison Hershfield Ltd. is a consulting engineering firm, specializing in civil and structural engineering, building science, facilities management, fire / life safety and transportation infrastructure. *New Positions Created (11):* Building Engineering Specialist, Intermediate / Senior; Construction Managers; Mechanical Engineers, Senior; Municipal Engineer, Intermediate / Senior; Project Manager; Municipal Engineer; Building Engineering Specialist (Intermediate / Senior); Construction Manager; Electrical Engineer (Senior); Mechanical Engineer (Senior); Project Manager.

MAXIM MORRISON HERSHFIELD LTD.
Att: Human Resources Manager
4515 Bow Trail SW, Suite 300
Calgary, AB T3C 2G3

Tel. 403-246-4500
Fax 403-246-4220
Email .... hr@morrisonhershfield.com
Website ..... www.morrisonhershfield.com
Employer Background: Founded in 1946, Maxim Morrison Hershfield Ltd. is a consulting engineering firm, specializing in civil and structural engineering, building science, facilities management, fire / life safety and transportation infrastructure. *New Positions Created (3):* Transportation Engineer, Intermediate; Electrical Engineer (Senior); Municipal Engineer (Senior).

MAXIM RENTALS AND LEASING
Att: General Manager
13240 - 170th Street
Edmonton, AB T5V 1M7

Tel. 780-448-3830
Fax 780-453-2458

Email .... lsimmons@maximinc.com
Website .... www.maximinc.com
Employer Background: Maxim Rentals and Leasing is a supplier of straight truck, tractor and trailer transportation, leasing and solution management services. *New Positions Created (5):* Lease Sales Representative; Rental Sales Representative; Transport Trailer Sales Representative; Used Truck Sales Representative; Rental Representative.

MAXXAM ANALYTICS INC.
Att: Human Resources Department
5540 McAdam Road
Mississauga, ON L4Z 1P1

Tel. 905-890-2555
Fax 905-890-0370
Email .... hr@on.maxxam.ca
Website .... www.maxxam.ca
Employer Background: Maxxam Analytics Inc. provides analytical services to the pharmaceutical, environmental, occupational health and food science disciplines. *New Positions Created (5):* Accounting Supervisor; Marketing Coordinator / Specialist; Senior Bioassay Analyst; Technician, Air Quality; Technician, T1.

MAYERTHORPE HEALTHCARE CENTRE
Att: Environmental Services Supervisor
4417 - 45th Street, PO Box 30
Mayerthorpe, AB T0E 1N0

Tel. 780-786-2261
Fax 780-786-2023
Email .... kohm@aspenrha.ab.ca
Website .... www.aspenrha.ab.ca/
.... mayerthorpe.html
Employer Background: Mayerthorpe Healthcare Centre provides nursing and rehabilitation services, including occupational therapy, physical therapy, respiratory therapy, speech-language pathology, audiology, mental health, social work and support services. *New Positions Created (2):* Maintenance Worker III; Physiotherapists (2).

MAYTAG CANADA
Att: S. Vyles, Human Resources
4151 North Service Road
Burlington, ON L7R 4A8

Fax 905-331-5853
Email .... svyles@hoover.com
Website .... www.maytag.com
Employer Background: Maytag Canada is an appliance manufacturer. *New Positions Created (2):* National Account Representative; Customer Service Representative.

MBNA CANADA BANK
Att: Recruitment
1600 James Naismith Drive
Gloucester, ON K1B 5N8

Tel. 613-742-3505
Fax 613-742-3501
Email .... canada@mbnacareers.com
Website .... www.mbna.com
Employer Background: MBNA Canada Bank, a subsidiary of MBNA Corporation, has been marketing affinity credit card programs since 1998. *New Positions Created (6):* Customer Assistance Account Managers; Customer Activation Specialist; Customer Satisfaction Specialists; Auditor; Customer Satisfaction Specialist; Outward Activation Specialists.

MCCAIN FOODS (CANADA)
Att: Human Resources Manager
PO Box 1479
Coaldale, AB T1M 1N3

Fax 403-345-4419
Website .... www.mccain.com
Employer Background: Founded in 1957, McCain Foods produces a wide range of prepared food products. The company has over 16,000 employees and annual revenues of more than $5 billion worldwide. *New Positions Created (3):* First Class Power Engineer, Chief; Production Management Trainees; Programmer / Instrumentation Technician.

MCCARTHY TETRAULT LLP
Att: Manager of Human Resources
777 Dunsmuir Street
Suite 1300, Pacific Centre
Vancouver, BC V7Y 1K2

Tel. 604-643-7100
Fax 604-622-5604
Email .... jkine@mccarthy.ca
Website .... www.mccarthy.ca
Employer Background: McCarthy Tetrault LLP is Canada's largest law firm, with offices in every major Canadian financial and business centre. *New Positions Created (3):* Intermediate Legal Administrative Assistant; Senior Legal Administrative Assistant; Legal Secretaries (2).

MCCARTHY TETRAULT LLP
Att: Christine Tavares,
Recruiting Specialist
TD Bank Tower, Suite 4700
Toronto, ON M5K 1E6

Tel. 416-362-1812
Fax 416-601-7728
Email .... ctavares@mccarthy.ca
Website .... www.mccarthy.ca
Employer Background: McCarthy Tetrault LLP is Canada's largest law firm, with offices in every major Canadian financial and business centre. *New Positions Created (21):* Applications Manager; Executive Receptionist; Legal Secretaries; Business Law Lawyer; Business Law Lawyer; Legal Secretaries; Financial Analyst; Monicord Assistant; Corporate Law Clerks; Energy Lawyers; Information Support Representative; Legal Secretaries; Billing Assistant; Corporate Law Clerks; Intellectual Property Law Clerk; Environmental Law Lawyer; Intellectual Property Secretaries (2); Labour and Employment Lawyer; Corporate Law Clerks; Financial Analyst; Legal Secretaries.

MCCORMICK CANADA INC.
Att: Human Relations Department
316 Rectory Street, PO Box 5788
London, ON N6A 4Z2

Tel. 519-432-1166
Fax 519-432-4648

Email .... london_hr@mccormick.ca
Website .... www.mccormick.ca
Employer Background: McCormick Canada
is an industry leader in the processing, packaging and sale of spices, seasonings and flavourings. *New Positions Created (2):* Product Marketer; Business Development Mgr.

MCCORMICK CANADA INC.

Att: Human Relations Department
3340 Orlando Drive
Mississauga, ON L4V 1C7
Tel. 905-678-1220
Fax 905-678-1229
Email .. mississauga_hr@mccormick.com
Website .... www.mccormick.com
Employer Background: McCormick Canada
Inc. is an industry leader in the processing,
packaging and sale of spices, seasonings and
flavourings. *New Positions Created (2):* Con-
troller; Material Logistics Coordinator.

MCCORMICK RANKIN CORPORATION

Att: Human Resources Manager
2655 North Sheridan Way
Mississauga, ON L5K 2P8
Tel. 905-823-8500
Fax 905-823-8503
Email .... mrc@mrc.ca
Website .... www.mrc.ca
Employer Background: Founded in 1957,
McCormick Rankin Corporation is a leading consulting engineering company, specializing in transportation. The company
has over 200 employees in Canada and Australia. *New Positions Created (8):* Highway
Design Project Managers / Engineers; Intermediate Engineer, Electrical; Intermediate Technologist, Electrical; Junior and Intermediate Structural CAD Technicians;
Junior / Intermediate Engineer, Electrical or
Civil; Senior and Intermediate Bridge Design Engineers; Senior / Intermediate Construction Inspectors; Senior Water Resources Engineer.

MCCORMICK RANKIN CORPORATION

Att: Human Resources Manager
1145 Hunt Club Road, Suite 300
Ottawa, ON K1V 0Y3
Tel. 613-736-7200
Fax 613-736-8710
Email .... mrc-ott@mrc.ca
Website .... www.mrc.ca
Employer Background: Founded in 1957,
McCormick Rankin Corporation is a lead-
ing consulting engineering company, spe-
cializing in transportation. The company
has over 200 employees in Canada and Aus-
tralia. *New Positions Created (4):* Transpor-
tation Planner; CAD Technicians; Highway
Design Engineer; Senior Engineer / Project
Manager.

MCCOY BROS. INC.

Att: S. Johns
14820 - 112th Avenue
Edmonton, AB T5M 2V2
Tel. 780-454-8661
Fax 780-453-8758

Email .... sjohns@mccoybros.com
Website .... www.mccoybros.com
Employer Background: McCoy Bros. Inc. is
a leader in truck and trailer parts, service
and manufacturing. *New Positions Created
(2):* Mechanic; Welders.

MCCREARY CENTRE SOCIETY, THE

Att: Search Committee
401 North Esmond Avenue
Burnaby, BC V5C 1S4
Tel. 604-291-1996
Fax 604-291-7308
Website .... www.mcs.bc.ca
Employer Background: The McCreary Cen-
tre Society is a non-profit, non-government
organization committed to improving youth
health through population health research,
education and youth participation. *New
Positions Created (3):* Executive Director;
Executive Director; Executive Director.

MCCRUM'S OFFICE FURNISHINGS

Att: Sue Banks
5310 - 1st Street SW
Calgary, AB T2H 0C8
Tel. 403-259-4939
Fax 403-253-3230
Email .... info@mccrums.ab.ca
Website .... www.mccrums.ab.ca
Employer Background: Founded in 1972,
McCrum's employs 30 staff and sells office
furnishings from its 28,000 square foot
Calgary showroom. *New Positions Created
(2):* Installation / Service Mgr; Intermedi-
ate Space Planning Consultant.

MCDATA CORPORATION

Att: Human Resources Manager
111 Gordon Baker Road, Suite 200
Toronto, ON M2H 3R1
Fax 416-496-6565
Email .... jim.chiang@mcdata.com
Website .... www.mcdata.com
Employer Background: McData Corporation
is a global leader in open storage network-
ing solutions. *New Positions Created (3):*
Hardware Engineer; Senior Software Engi-
neer Manager; Software Engineer.

MCDONALD'S RESTAURANTS OF CANADA LIMITED

Att: Human Resources Department
McDonald's Place
Toronto, ON M3C 3L4
Tel. 416-433-1000
Fax 416-446-3376
Email .... success@mcdonalds.com
Website .... www.mcdonalds.com
Employer Background: McDonald's is one
of the most recognized brands in the world
and the largest global foodservice retailer.
New Positions Created (2): Bilingual Busi-
ness Analyst; Business Research Mgrs (2).

MCELHANNEY GROUP LTD., THE

Att: Human Resources Department
780 Beatty Street, Suite L100
Vancouver, BC V6B 2M1
Tel. 604-683-8521

Fax 604-683-4350
Email humanresources@mcelhanney.com
Website .... www.mcelhanney.com
Employer Background: The McElhanney
Group Ltd. is an employee-owned company,
specializing in consulting, surveying and
mapping services. The company has 15 of-
fices in BC and Alberta and 2 international
locations. *New Positions Created (57):* Al-
berta Land Surveyor; AutoCAD Operators /
Draftspersons; Intermediate Engineer /
Technologist; Party Chief; Branch Manager;
Civil Engineering Technologist; Draftsper-
son; Engineering Branch Manager; Senior
Structural Engineer; Senior Party Chief;
Survey Assistants; Construction Surveyor;
Engineering Surveyor; Transportation Spe-
cialist; CADD / GIS Technician; Accounts
Payable Clerk; Alberta Land Surveyor;
AutoCAD Operators / Draftspersons;
Draftspersons; Instrument Persons, Pipeline
Construction; Manager, Information Sys-
tems; Party Chief; Accounting / Office Clerk;
BC Land Surveyors; Branch Manager; CAD
Operator / Draftsperson; Civil Engineering
Technologist; Draftsperson; Engineering
Branch Manager; Instrument Specialists;
Operation Manager; Party Chief; Senior
Party Chief; Survey Assistants; Survey Cal-
culators; Construction Surveyor; Municipal
Engineer / Technologist; Alberta Land Sur-
veyor; Accounting / Office Clerk; AutoCAD
Operators / Draftspersons; Branch Manager;
Construction Surveyors; Draftsperson;
Draftspersons; Engineering Branch Man-
ager; Highway Design Engineer / Senior
Highway Design Technologist; Land Devel-
opment / Municipal Design Technician;
Land Surveyors; Municipal Designer; Party
Chief; Party Chief; Secretary; Senior
AutoCAD Operator / Draftsperson; Survey
Assistants; Survey Calculators; Municipal
Designer; Various Transport Positions (2).

MCGILL UNIVERSITY

Att: Staffing, Human Resources
688 Sherbrooke Street West, 15th Floor
Montréal, QC H3A 3R1
Fax 514-398-1023
Website .... www.mcgill.ca
Employer Background: Chartered in 1821,
McGill University offers courses at the undergraduate, graduate and doctoral level to
over 28,000 students. The university has
5,200 faculty and 2,400 support staff members. *New Positions Created (2):* Senior
Project Manager; General Manager, Bookstore.

MCGILL UNIVERSITY, DEPARTMENT OF PATHOLOGY

Att: Professor Gerald J. Prud'homme
3775 University Street
Montréal, QC H3A 2B4
Tel. 514-398-7192
Email .... gprudh@po-box.mcgill.ca
Website .... www.mcgill.ca
Employer Background: Chartered in 1821,
McGill University offers courses at the un-
dergraduate, graduate and doctoral level to
over 28,000 students. The university has
5,200 faculty and 2,400 support staff mem-

bers. *New Positions Created (2):* Post-Doctoral Research Assistant, Immunologic Cancer Therapy Studies; Research Assistant.

MCGILL UNIVERSITY, FACILITIES MANAGEMENT
Att: Area Personnel Office
840 Dr. Penfield
Montréal, QC H3A 1A4
Tel. 514-398-4555
Fax 514-398-2103
Website .... www.mcgill.ca
Employer Background: Chartered in 1821, McGill University offers courses at the undergraduate, graduate and doctoral level to over 28,000 students. The university has 5,200 faculty and 2,400 support staff members. *New Positions Created (2):* Stationary Engineman, Class B; Technician, Automatic Temperature Control System.

MCGILL UNIVERSITY, FACULTY OF MUSIC (DEPARTMENT OF PERFORMANCE)
Att: Professor Gordon Foote, Chair
555 Sherbrooke Street West
Montréal, QC H3A 1E3
Tel. 514-398-4542
Fax 514-398-1540
Email .... foote@music.mcgill.ca
Website .... www.mcgill.ca
Employer Background: Chartered in 1821, McGill University offers courses at the undergraduate, graduate and doctoral level to over 28,000 students. The university has 5,200 faculty and 2,400 support staff members. *New Positions Created (3):* Faculty Position, Composition; Faculty Position, Music Theory; Faculty Position, Piano Performance.

MCGILL UNIVERSITY HEALTH CENTRE, MONTREAL CHILDREN'S HOSPITAL / MUHC
Att: Teri Waldron
2300 Tupper Street, Room A-409
Montréal, QC H3H 1P3
Tel. 514-406-4224
Fax 514-412-4355
Email .... teri.waldron@muhc.mcgill.ca
Website .... www.muhc.mcgill.ca
Employer Background: MUHC represents the first and largest voluntary merger of university teaching hospitals in Canada. *New Positions Created (2):* Nurses; Assistant Professor.

MCGILL UNIVERSITY HEALTH CENTRE / MUHC
Att: Juliet Rogers-Huck
1650 Cedar Avenue
Montréal, QC H3G 1A4
Tel. 514-934-1934
Fax 514-934-8389
Website .... www.muhc.mcgill.ca
Employer Background: MUHC represents the first and largest voluntary merger of university teaching hospitals in Canada. *New Positions Created (5):* Administrative Secretary; Administrative Secretary; Medi-

cal Secretaries; Medical Secretaries (2); Secretary.

MCGILL UNIVERSITY HEALTH CENTRE, ROYAL VICTORIA HOSPITAL
Att: Lucie Delisle
687 Pine Avenue, Room V2.07
Montréal, QC H3A 1A1
Tel. 514-842-1231
Fax 514-843-1561
Email .... lucie.delisle@muhc.mcgill.ca
Website .... www.muhc.mcgill.ca
Employer Background: MUHC represents the first and largest voluntary merger of university teaching hospitals in Canada. *New Positions Created (6):* Manager, Anaesthesia Technology and Pulmonary Function Laboratory; Manager, Respiratory Systems; Site Coordinators; Managers, Call Centre Services; Divisional Director, Cardiothoracic Surgery; Head of Pharmacy Department.

MCGRAW-HILL RYERSON LTD.
Att: Human Resources
300 Water Street
Whitby, ON L1N 9B6
Tel. 905-430-5000
Fax 905-430-5020
Email .... career@mcgrawhill.ca
Website .... www.mcgrawhill.ca
Employer Background: McGraw-Hill Ryerson Ltd. is a leading Canadian publisher of educational textbooks, teaching materials, reference books and general interest books. *New Positions Created (5):* Medical Sales Representative; Business Analyst; Financial Analyst; Publisher's Representative; Sponsoring Editor.

MCKAY-COCKER CONSTRUCTION LTD.
Att: Manager of Construction
1665 Oxford Street East, PO Box 7345
London, ON N5Y 5R9
Tel. 519-451-5270
Fax 519-451-8050
Email .... tfalls@mckaycocker.com
Website .... www.mckaycocker.com
Employer Background: For over half a century, McKay-Cocker Construction Ltd. has been providing construction and pre-construction services in Ontario. *New Positions Created (2):* Estimator and Project Coordinator; Project Manager.

MCMASTER UNIVERSITY
Att: Human Resources Officer
1280 Main Street West
Room 304, Gilmour Hall
Hamilton, ON L8S 4L8
Tel. 905-525-9140
Fax 905-528-6132
Email .... employ@mcmaster.ca
Website .... www.mcmaster.ca
Employer Background: McMaster University is a medium-sized university, offering educational programs through six faculties to over 13,000 students. *New Positions Created (9):* Statistical Information Analyst; Director, Nuclear Operations & Facilities; Business Manager, Dean's Office; Technical Serv-

ice & Maintenance Coordinator; Administrator; Associate Manager; Banquet Supervisor; Buyer, Physical Plant; Electrician.

MCMASTER UNIVERSITY, DEPARTMENT OF ENGINEERING PHYSICS
Att: Dr. Peter Mascher, Professor and Chair
1280 Main Street West
Hamilton, ON L8S 4L7
Fax 905-523-4407
Website .... www.mcmaster.ca
Employer Background: McMaster University is a medium-sized university, offering educational programs through six faculties to over 13,000 students. *New Positions Created (2):* Chair, Optoelectronics; Faculty Positions.

MCMASTER UNIVERSITY, FACULTY OF HEALTH SCIENCES
Att: Human Resources Department
1200 Main Street West, Room 2J5
Hamilton, ON L8N 3Z5
Tel. 905-525-9140
Fax 905-526-6623
Website .... www.mcmaster.ca
Employer Background: McMaster University is a medium-sized university, offering educational programs through six faculties to over 13,000 students. *New Positions Created (10):* Research Assistant; Research Assistant / Chemist; Clinical Department Manager; Research Technician; Medical Secretary; Animal Health Technicians; Academic Department Chair and Chief of Pediatrics; Chair, Department of Biochemistry; Medical Secretary; Biostatistician.

MCMASTER UNIVERSITY, MICHAEL G. DEGROOTE SCHOOL OF BUSINESS
Att: Dr. Vishwanath Baba, Dean
1280 Main Street West
Hamilton, ON L8S 4M4
Fax 905-526-0852
Website .... www.mcmaster.ca
Employer Background: McMaster University is a medium-sized university, offering educational programs through six faculties to over 13,000 students. *New Positions Created (3):* Instructor, Human Resources / Management; Instructor, Management of Innovation and Technology; Instructor, Marketing, Business Policy and International Business.

MCMILLAN & ASSOCIATES
Att: Human Resources Manager
541 Sussex Drive, 3rd Floor
Ottawa, ON K1N 6Z6
Tel. 613-789-1234
Fax 613-789-2255
Email .... hr@thinkup.com
Website .... www.thinkup.com
Employer Background: Founded in 1996, McMillan & Associates is an international advertising agency, developing advertising and marketing strategies for new and traditional media applications. *New Positions Created (9):* Technology Manager; Senior Technology Developer; Art Director; Macromedia FLASH Technician; Senior Ac-

count Executive; Senior Designer; Senior Production Artist; Senior Web Designer; Senior Writer.

MCMILLAN BINCH
Att: Stephanie N. Wilson
Royal Bank Plaza, Suite 3800, South Tower
Toronto, ON M5J 2J7
Tel. 416-865-7947
Fax 416-865-7048
Email .... dpallotta@mcbinch.com
Website .... www.mcbinch.com
Employer Background: McMillan Binch is one of Canada's leading business law firms. *New Positions Created (4):* Commercial Litigation Associate; Legal Secretary Positions; Assistant Director, Student and Associate Programs; Public Markets Lawyers.

MDS AERO SUPPORT CORPORATION
Att: Human Resources Manager
1220 Old Innes Road, Suite 200
Ottawa, ON K1B 3V3
Tel. 613-744-7257
Fax 613-744-8016
Email .... hr@mdsaero.ca
Website .... www.mdsaero.ca
Employer Background: MDS Aero Support Corporation is a leading supplier of engine test facilities and test systems for aviation and industrial gas turbines. *New Positions Created (38):* Application Engineer; Controls Engineers; Mechanical Design Engineer; Mechanical Engineer, Fluids; Project Engineers; Project Managers; Software Project Engineer; Test and Support Engineer; Draftsperson; Expeditor / Buyer; Instrumentation Engineer; Senior Accountant; Contract Administrator / Cost Engineer; Project Engineer; Project Managers; Quality Assurance Representative; Software Project Engineer; Technical Writer; VB / VC++ GUI Developer; Application Engineer; Controls Engineer; Facilities Design Coordinator; Mechanical Design Engineer; Test & Support Engineer, Software; Accounts Payable Clerk; C Unix Programmer; Chief Estimator; Electrical Engineer; Instrumentation Engineer; Contract Administrator / Cost Engineer; Senior Estimator; Senior Facilities Design Coordinator; Software Project Engineer; Applications Engineers; Document Control Technician; Mechanical Design Engineer; Senior Facilities Design Coordinator; Test and Support Representative.

MDS LABORATORIES
Att: Human Resources
75 International Boulevard
Toronto, ON M9W 6L9
Fax 416-213-4241
Email .... bmeloche@mdsintl.com
Website .... www.mdslabs.com
Employer Background: MDS Laboratories (a division of MDS Inc.) is a leading provider of advanced medical diagnostic services, systems and information. *New Positions Created (6):* Supervisor, Customer Care Centre; Microbiology Resource Analyst; Intermediate Lease Administrator; Chemistry Resources Analyst; Medical Laboratory

Technologists; Team Leaders, Chemistry / Microbiology.

MDS LABORATORIES
Att: IRLA Management Team
100 International Boulevard
Toronto, ON M9W 6J6
Fax 416-213-4689
Website .... www.mdslabs.com
Employer Background: MDS Laboratories (a division of MDS Inc.) is a leading provider of advanced medical diagnostic services, systems and information. *New Positions Created (6):* Microbiology Team Leader; Immunohematology Team Leader; Chemistry Specialist, High Volume Team; Immunohematology Team Leader, Technical Response; Medical Laboratory Technologists; Technicians.

MDS METRO LABORATORY SERVICES
Att: Human Resources
3680 Gilmore Way
Burnaby, BC V5G 4V8
Tel. 604-431-5005
Fax 604-412-4448
Email .... careers@mdsmetro.com
Website .... www.mdsmetro.com
Employer Background: MDS Metro Laboratory Services (formerly Metropolitan Bio-Medical Laboratories) provides community-based diagnostic laboratory services throughout British Columbia. *New Positions Created (9):* Medical Technologists; Executive Assistant; Molecular Diagnostic Specialist; Medical Microbiologist / General Pathologist; Human Resources Adviser; Financial Analyst / Accountant; Supervisor, Accounts Payable; Occupational Health Nurse; Quality Resources / Research and Development Technologist, Microbiology.

MDS NORDION
Att: Human Resources Manager
4004 Wesbrook Mall
Vancouver, BC V6T 2A3
Tel. 604-228-1821
Fax 604-222-2724
Email .... careers@mds.nordion.com
Website .... www.mds.nordion.com
Employer Background: MDS Nordion (part of MDS Inc.) designs irradiation systems and manufactures nuclear isotopes for medical applications. *New Positions Created (2):* Manager, Development and Production Support; Technician, Cyclotron Production.

MDS NORDION
Att: Human Resources
447 March Road
Kanata, ON K2K 1X8
Tel. 613-592-2790
Fax 613-592-9117
Email .... careers@mds.nordion.com
Website .... www.mds.nordion.com
Employer Background: MDS Nordion (part of MDS Inc.) designs irradiation systems and manufactures nuclear isotopes for medical applications. *New Positions Created (9):* Environmental Specialist; Purchasing

Agent; Senior Purchasing Agent; Team Leader, Computing Services; Manager, Production Control; Team Leader, Computing Services; Credit and Collections Administrator; Janitor; Lab Assistant.

MDS PHARMA SERVICES INC.
Att: Staffing, Human Resources
2350 Cohen Street
St-Laurent, QC H4R 2N6
Tel. 514-333-0033
Fax 514-335-8340
Email .. employee.recruiting@mdsps.com
Website .... www.mdsps.com
Employer Background: MDS Pharma Services (formerly Phoenix International Life Sciences Inc.) is the 3rd-largest contract research organization in the world, serving the pharmaceutical, generic drug and biotechnology industries. *New Positions Created (5):* Human Resource Specialist; Head, Instrumentation Services; Pharmacist, Clinical Operations; Team Leader, Immunochemistry; Building Manager.

MDS PROTEOMICS
Att: Human Resources Manager
75 International Boulevard
Toronto, ON M9W 6L6
Tel. 416-675-6777
Fax 416-644-5111
Email ... technojobs@mdsproteomics.com
Website .... www.mdsproteomics.com
Employer Background: MDS Proteomics is a privately-held integrated biotechnology company. *New Positions Created (4):* Research Associates and Scientists, HPLC; Research Associates and Scientists, Instrumentation; Research Associates, Process Development; Research Associates, Robotic Group.

MEAD JOHNSON NUTRITIONALS
Att: Human Resources Department
333 Preston Street, Suite 700
Ottawa, ON K1S 5N4
Tel. 613-239-3974
Fax 613-239-3997
Email .... mjnjobs@bms.com
Website .... www.meadjohnson.com
Employer Background: Mead Johnson Nutritionals is a division of Bristol-Myers Squibb, a leader in consumer healthcare products. *New Positions Created (3):* CRM Database Administrator; Adult Medical Nutritionals Specialists; Medical Sales Rep.

MEAD PACKAGING (CANADA) LTD.
Att: Human Resources Manager
281 Fairall Street
Ajax, ON L1S 1R7
Fax 905-683-5032
Email .... jc3@mead.com
Website .... www.mead.com
Employer Background: Mead Packaging (Canada) Ltd., a division of Mead Corporation, is a leader in the North American packaging industry. *New Positions Created (2):* Industrial Mechanic / Millwright; Shift Superintendent.

MEADOWRIDGE SCHOOL
Att: Human Resources
12224 - 240th Street
Maple Ridge, BC V4R 1N1

Fax 604-467-4989
Email .... info@meadowridge.bc.ca
Website .... www.meadowridge.bc.ca
Employer Background: Meadowridge
School is an independent, co-educational,
university preparatory school of 460 stu-
dents from kindergarten to grade 12. *New
Positions Created (4):* Counsellor; Grade 7
Teacher; High School Teachers; Kindergar-
ten Teacher.

MED-ENG SYSTEMS INC.
Att: Human Resources Manager
2400 St. Laurent Boulevard
Ottawa, ON K1G 6C4

Tel. 613-739-9646
Fax 613-739-4536
Email .... hr@med-eng.com
Website .... www.med-eng.com
Employer Background: Med-Eng Systems
Inc. researches, designs and manufactures
systems for personal protection against blast
threats in bomb disposal and mine clear-
ance operations. *New Positions Created (19):*
Controller, Finance; Sales Coordinator; Mar-
keting Communications Specialist; Product
Marketing Specialist; Production Mgr; Mfg/
Industrial Engineer; Quality Engineer;
Quality Mgr; Accounts Payable / Payroll Ad-
ministrator; Quality Engineer; Manufactur-
ing / Industrial Engineer; Materials / Bal-
listic Engineer; Mechanical Design Technologist; Research Engineer, Supervisor;
Marketing Communications Specialist;
Product Mgr; Purchasing Agent; Legal
Counsel; Marketing Specialist.

MEDCOMSOFT INC.
Att: Human Resources Department
1200 Eglinton Avenue East, Suite 900
Toronto, ON M3C 1H9

Tel. 416-499-2888
Fax 416-467-0273
Email .... resumes@medcomsoft.com
Website .... www.medcomsoft.com
Employer Background: MedcomSoft Inc. is
a Canadian software developer for the
healthcare industry. *New Positions Created
(31):* Business / System / Clinical Analysts
(3); Customer Support Representative; Data
Modellers / Miners (3); Receptionist; Software Developers (12); Clinical Systems Analyst; Intermediate Software Developers; Junior Software Developers; Middle-Ware Developers; Research & Development Mgr;
Senior D / W Specialist; Sr Software Developer; Team Managers / Leaders / Product
Mgrs; Technical Training Position; Technical Writer; Executive Assistant; Business /
Systems / Clinical Analysts (3); Software Developers; Middleware Developer; Team
Managers / Leaders; Technical Trainer; Director, Business Development; Customer
Service Rep / Trainer; Data Modeller; Executive Assistant; Junior Database Administrator; Software Developers; Business / Systems
Analyst; Quality Assurance Professionals;
Marketing Director; Controller.

MEDIA WAVE WEB SOLUTIONS
Att: Human Resources
54 Chamberlain Street
Ottawa, ON K1S 1V9

Tel. 613-563-8170
Fax 613-563-8045
Email .... jobs@mediawave.ca
Website .... www.mediawave.ca
Employer Background: Established in 1995,
Media Wave Web Solutions produces ad-
vanced web development projects and in-
teractive media. *New Positions Created (4):*
Account Managers; Microsoft Application
Developer; Oracle Application Developer;
Project Manager.

MEDIAGRIF INTERACTIVE
TECHNOLOGIES INC.
Att: Human Resources Manager
1010 Serigny Road, Suite 400
Longueuil, QC J4K 5G7

Tel. 450-677-8797
Fax 450-677-4612
Email .... recruitment@mediagrif.com
Website .... www.mediagrif.com
Employer Background: Mediagrif Interac-
tive Technologies Inc. develops and operates
B2B vertical marketplaces on the Internet.
New Positions Created (3): Customer Sup-
port Representatives; Product Catalogue
Editors; Technical Development Specialists.

MEDICAL IMAGING CONSULTANTS
Att: Sharon Gray,
Human Resources Manager
11010 - 101st Street, Main Floor
Edmonton, AB T5H 4B9

Tel. 780-428-1121
Fax 780-425-5979
Email .... sgray@mic.ab.ca
Website .... www.mic.ab.ca
Employer Background: Medical Imaging
Consultants is western Canada's largest part-
nership of radiologists. *New Positions Cre-
ated (4):* Electronics Technician; Medical
Radiation Technologists; Medical Sono-
graphers; Nuclear Medicine Technologists.

MEDICINE HAT, CITY OF
Att: Human Resources Department
580 - 1st Street SE
Medicine Hat, AB T1A 8E6

Tel. 403-529-8355
Fax 403-529-8324
Email .... hr@city.medicine-hat.ab.ca
Website .... www.city.medicine-hat.ab.ca
Employer Background: Located 300 km
southeast of Calgary in Alberta's natural gas
heartland, the City of Medicine Hat is home
to over 50,000 people. *New Positions Cre-
ated (18):* Municipal Works Project Engi-
neer; Airport Superintendent; Commis-
sioner, Corporate Services; Laboratory Tech-
nician; Project Supervisor; Water Quality
Controller; Payables Coordinator; Emer-
gency Services Operations Manager; Deputy
Fire Chief; Assistant Shift Engineer, Electric
Utilities; Manager of Engineering Services;
Gas Production Accounting Supervisor;
Municipal Accounting Superintendent;
Technical Analyst I, System Operations;

Technical Analyst II, Technical Services; Labour Relations Officer, Human Resources;
City Assessor; Land Administrator.

MEDICINE HAT COLLEGE
Att: Human Resources
299 College Drive SE
Medicine Hat, AB T1A 3Y6

Tel. 403-504-3685
Email .... spartis@acd.mhc.ab.ca
Website .... www.mhc.ab.ca
Employer Background: Established in 1965
Medicine Hat College operates two campuses and serves over 2,500 full-time credit
students. *New Positions Created (9):* Program Manager, Athletics; Visual Communications Instructor; Academic Advisor / Student Liaison; Dance Instructor; English Instructor; Instructor, Information Technology Program; Instructor, Financial Planning
and Business; Student Work Experience
Manager; Nursing Instructor.

MEDIGAS
Att: Human Resources Manager
470 Lakeshore Boulevard West
Toronto, ON M5V 2V6

Tel. 416-365-1700
Fax 416-365-0092
Email .... careersontario@praxair.com
Website .... www.medigas.com
Employer Background: Medigas, a division
of Praxair Canada Inc., is a leading provider
of home healthcare services in North
America. *New Positions Created (2):* Terri-
tory Mgr, Respiratory Homecare; Territory
Managers, Home Medical Equipment (3).

MEDIS HEALTH &
PHARMACEUTICAL SERVICES LTD.
Att: Human Resources
7510 Bren Road
Mississauga, ON L4T 4H1

Tel. 905-671-4586
Fax 905-671-3025
Website .... www.medis.ca
Employer Background: MEDIS Health &
Pharmaceutical Services Ltd. sells over
30,000 products to major retailers nation-
wide, with 14 distribution centres across
Canada. *New Positions Created (6):* Admin-
istrative Assistant, Distribution; Customer
Service Representatives (4); Shift Opera-
tions Manager; Shift Supervisor; Director of
Operations; Shift Supervisor.

MEDISCA PHARMACEUTIQUE INC.
Att: Human Resources Department
4509 Dobrin
St-Laurent, QC H4R 2L8

Tel. 514-333-7811
Fax 514-338-1693
Email .... medisca@total.net
Employer Background: Medisca Pharma-
ceutique Inc. repackages, wholesales and
distributes chemicals, narcotics and control-
led substances for the pharmaceutical in-
dustry. *New Positions Created (5):* Chemist
/ QPIC; Quality Assurance / Quality Control
Documentalist; Quality Control / Quality

Assurance Assistant; Pharmacy Writer; Senior Advisor, Industrial Pharmaceutical Applications.

MEDISYS HEALTH GROUP INC.
Att: Human Resources Manager
95 St. Clair Avenue West, 16th Floor
Toronto, ON M4V 1N6
Tel. 416-926-2698
Fax 416-730-7699
Email .... clabi@xchg.medisys.ca
Website .... www.medisys.ca
Employer Background: Medisys Health Group Inc. is Canada's largest provider of corporate health services, with over 1,000 employees nationwide. *New Positions Created (3):* Executive Assistant; Director, Sales & Marketing; Directors of Operations (2).

MEDISYS HEALTH GROUP INC.
Att: Suzie Demers, HR Department
500 Sherbrooke West, Suite 1100
Montréal, QC H3A 3C6
Tel. 514-499-2750
Fax 514-499-2796
Email .... info@medisys.ca
Website .... www.medisys.ca
Employer Background: Medisys Health Group Inc. is Canada's largest provider of corporate health services, with over 1,000 employees nationwide. *New Positions Created (2):* Programme Manager / Occupational Health Nurses; Occupational Health Nurse.

MEDTEC MARKETING LIMITED
Att: Human Resources Manager
7946 Winston Street
Burnaby, BC V5A 2H5
Tel. 604-420-4242
Fax 604-420-0324
Employer Background: MedTec Marketing Limited sells medical supplies. *New Positions Created (2):* Customer Service Position; X-Ray Service Engineer.

MEDTRONIC OF CANADA INC.
Att: Human Resources Department
6733 Kitimat Road
Mississauga, ON L5N 1W3
Tel. 905-826-6020
Fax 905-826-6643
Email .... hr.canada@medtronic.com
Website .... www.medtronic.com
Employer Background: Medtronic of Canada Inc. is part of Minnesota-based Medtronic, Inc., a leading provider of medical devices and services for individuals suffering from chronic illness. *New Positions Created (2):* Bilingual Facility Service Team Member; Manager of Regulatory Affairs.

MEGASYS COMPUTER TECHNOLOGIES LTD.
Att: Human Resources Manager
6815 - 8th Street NE
Calgary, AB T2E 7H7
Tel. 403-295-0511
Fax 403-275-2767
Email .... human.resources@megasys.com
Website .... www.megasys.com
Employer Background: MegaSys Computer Technologies Ltd. is a major supplier of advanced network management systems for the telecom market. *New Positions Created (11):* C / C++ Programmers; Model Developer; Senior Multiplatform Developer; Visual Basic Programmers; C / C++ Programmers; Graphics Developer; Model Developer; Product Testers; Project Manager; Technical Support Specialist; Visual Basic Programmers.

MEI
Att: Anne Mazurier,
Director of Human Resources
9001 L'Acadie Boulevard, 7th Floor
Montréal, QC H4N 3H5
Tel. 514-384-6411
Fax 514-384-6410
Email .... resume@mei.ca
Website .... www.meicpg.com
Employer Background: MEI is an international leader in the development of high-end sales force automation software. *New Positions Created (4):* Director of Product Specifications and Quality; Business Analyst; Java Analyst / Developer; Product Specialist, Applications.

MEMBERCARE FINANCIAL SERVICES
Att: Liz Pietrantonio
151 North Service Road, PO Box 5065
Burlington, ON L7R 4C2
Tel. 905-632-1221
Fax 905-631-4995
Email .... liz_pietrantonio@cumis.org
Website .... www.cumis.com
Employer Background: MemberCARE Financial Services, a division of the CUMIS Group, offers financial planning, life insurance and investments to members of credit unions and their communities. *New Positions Created (9):* Insurance Advisor; Analyst, Direct Marketing; Database Analyst, Direct Marketing; Senior Accounting Analyst; Technical Support Representative; Financial Representative; Life Marketing Specialist; Training and Development Consultant; Account Manager.

MEMBERWORKS CANADA CORPORATION
Att: Human Resources Manager
1801 McGill College Avenue, Suite 800
Montréal, QC H3A 2N4
Fax 514-847-8213
Email .... res.hum@memberworks.com
Website .... www.memberworks.com
Employer Background: MemberWorks Canada Corporation designs membership programs that offer services and discounts in healthcare, insurance, travel, fashion, entertainment and personal security. *New Positions Created (5):* Member Services Representatives; E-Business & Systems Security / Business Continuity Specialist; Financial Analyst; Inbound Sales Positions / Call Centre Representatives; Travel Consultants.

MEMORIAL UNIVERSITY OF NEWFOUNDLAND
Att: Dr. Evan Simpson,
Academic Vice-President
St. John's, NF A1C 5S7
Tel. 709-737-8246
Fax 709-737-2074
Email .... vpacad@mun.ca
Website .... www.mun.ca
Employer Background: Founded in 1925, Memorial University of Newfoundland is the largest university in Atlantic Canada, with 16,500 students and four main campuses. *New Positions Created (2):* Junior Canada Research Chair; Senior Canada Research Chair.

MEMORIS, INC.
Att: Human Resources Manager
5220 St. Laurent Boulevard
Montréal, QC H2T 1S1
Tel. 514-490-0699
Fax 514-490-0565
Email .... jobs@memoris.com
Website .... www.memoris.com
Employer Background: Memoris, Inc. develops and markets communications-based productivity tools for the investment industry. *New Positions Created (4):* HTML Designers / Developers; Intermediate Software Developer; Senior and Intermediate Developers; Voice User Interface Developer, Intermediate.

MENTOR ENGINEERING
Att: Human Resources
609 - 14th Street NW, Suite 503
Calgary, AB T2N 2A1
Tel. 403-777-3760
Fax 403-777-3769
Email .... hr@mentoreng.com
Website .... www.mentoreng.com
Employer Background: Founded in 1988, Mentor Engineering develops computer products for the mobile fleet and sales enterprise markets. *New Positions Created (9):* Buyer / Scheduler; Senior Hardware Engineer; Inventory Control Specialist; Junior Accountant; Account Executive; Electronics Technician, Final Assembly; Marketing and Technical Writer; Software Developer; Marketing Communications Writer.

MENU FOODS LTD.
Att: Human Resources Manager
8 Falconer Drive, PO Box 610
Mississauga, ON L5M 2C1
Tel. 905-826-3870
Fax 905-826-1855
Employer Background: Menu Foods is one of the largest pet food manufacturers in North America. *New Positions Created (3):* Database Administrator / Business Analyst; Manager, Network Services; R & D Administrator.

MEOTA RESOURCES CORP.
Att: Human Resources
333 - 7th Avenue SW, Suite 1701
Calgary, AB T2P 2Z1

Tel. 403-781-2440
Fax 403-781-2424
Website .... www.meota.com
Employer Background: Meota Resources Corp. acquires, explores and develops oil, gas and mining properties. *New Positions Created (5):* Reservoir Engineering Technologist; Intermediate Production / Revenue Accountant; Joint Venture Accountant; Drilling and Completions Technical Assistant; Manager of Drilling and Completions.

MERAK PROJECTS LTD.
Att: Hiring Team
322 - 11th Avenue SW, Suite 600
Calgary, AB T2R 0C5
Tel. 403-294-4300
Fax 403-294-4301
Email .... resume@merak.com
Website .... www.merak.com
Employer Background: Merak Projects Ltd. develops and markets software applications and related training and consulting services for the Canadian and international energy markets. *New Positions Created (19):* C++ Software Developer; Field Software Support Analysts; Value Consultant; Value Software Support Analysts; Value Suite Custom Project Programmer; Web Developer; C++ Software Developer; Field Software Support Analysts; Value Consultant; Value Software Support Analysts; Value Suite Custom Project Programmer; Web Developer; Technical Writer, Web Team; Web Developer; C++ Software Developer; Accounts Payable Clerk; Client Technical Service Representative; Quality Assurance Specialist; Senior Software Developer.

MERCEDES-BENZ CANADA INC.
Att: Controller
3650 Charles Street
Vancouver, BC V5K 5A9
Fax 604-639-3275
Email .... humanr@mercedes-benz.ca
Website .... www.mercedes-benz.ca
Employer Background: Established in Canada in 1955, Mercedes-Benz Canada Inc. is a subsidiary of Daimler-Benz AG, the world's oldest car manufacturer. *New Positions Created (2):* Various Automotive Positions; Assistant, Pre-Owned Sales Manager.

MERCEDES-BENZ CANADA INC.
Att: Human Resources Department
849 Eglinton Avenue East
Toronto, ON M4G 2L5
Tel. 416-231-0545
Fax 416-423-5027
Email .... humanr@mercedes-benz.ca
Website .... www.mercedes-benz.ca
Employer Background: Established in Canada in 1955, Mercedes-Benz Canada Inc. is a subsidiary of Daimler-Chrysler, the world's oldest car manufacturer. *New Positions Created (11):* Bilingual Customer Service Representative; Sales Receptionist; Junior Sales Consultant; Service Manager; Parts Technical Specialist; Customer Service Representative; Marketing Services Coordinator; Parts Manager; Customs / Traffic Coordinator; Service Advisor; Parts Manager.

MERCHANT CARD ACCEPTANCE CORP.
Att: Human Resources Manager
3075 - 14th Avenue, Unit 6
Markham, ON L3R 0G9
Tel. 905-305-6171
Fax 905-305-9526
Email .... sales@merchantsales.com
Website .... www.merchantsales.com
Employer Background: Merchant Card Acceptance Corp. is Canada's leading sales agent for Visa, MasterCard and Interac acceptance. *New Positions Created (2):* Business Development Manager; Business Development Manager.

MERCK FROSST CANADA & CO. / MERCK FROSST CANADA LTD.
Att: Human Resources Department
PO Box 1005
Pointe-Claire, QC H9R 4P8
Tel. 514-428-7920
Fax 514-428-4940
Email .... hr_montreal@merck.com
Website .... www.merckfrosst.com
Employer Background: Merck Frosst Canada & Co. / Merck Frosst Canada Ltd. is Canada's largest integrated pharmaceutical company engaged in the discovery, manufacturing, and marketing of medicines for human health. *New Positions Created (6):* Clinical Research Project Manager; Acute Care Specialist; Specialist, Fire Prevention; Technical Specialist, Packaging; Regional Credit Manager; Biologists.

MERCURY FILMWORKS
Att: Human Resources Manager
190 Alexander Street, Suite 500
Vancouver, BC V6A 1B5
Tel. 604-684-9117
Fax 604-684-8339
Email vancouver@mercuryfilmworks.com
Website ...... www.mercuryfilmworks.com
Employer Background: Mercury Filmworks is a service-based digital animation company, with offices in Vancouver and Toronto. *New Positions Created (3):* Production Assistant; Production Coordinator; Senior Network and Systems Administrator.

MERISEL CANADA INC.
Att: Human Resources
200 Ronson Drive
Toronto, ON M9W 5Z9
Tel. 416-240-7012
Fax 416-240-2622
Email .... resumes@merisel.com
Website .... www.merisel.ca
Employer Background: Merisel Canada Inc. distributes over 15,000 hardware and software products to more than 14,000 resellers. *New Positions Created (13):* Bilingual Financial Services Specialist, Credit and Collections; Business Development Representatives; Financial Analyst; Inside Sales Representative; Vendor Price Protection Administrator; Digipath / Report Print Operator; Inventory Analyst; Manager, Facilities and Office Services; Product Manager; Purchasing Supervisor; Retail Marketing Coordina-

tor; Senior Vendor Finance Analyst; Vendor Business Representative.

MERIT KITCHENS
Att: General Manager
12185 - 86th Avenue
Surrey, BC V3W 3H8
Tel. 604-591-3321
Fax 604-591-9141
Email .... meritho@merit-kitchens.com
Website .... www.merit-kitchens.com
Employer Background: Merit Kitchens markets kitchen cabinets throughout North America and Japan. *New Positions Created (3):* Sales Manager, Western Canada; Manager of Finance; Materials Manager.

MERITOR SUSPENSION SYSTEMS COMPANY
Att: Harold MacKinnon,
Manager, Human Resources
150 Steeles Avenue
Milton, ON L9T 2Y5
Email .... mackinhj@meritorauto.com
Website .... www.meritorauto.com
Employer Background: Meritor Suspension Systems is an independent supplier of hot wound coil springs, stabilizer bars and torsion bars to light vehicle manufacturers. *New Positions Created (7):* Accounting Clerk; General Accountant; Logistics Supervisory / Material Planner; Manufacturing Engineer; Maintenance Electrician; Millwright / Electrician; Systems Analyst.

MERLIN CREATIVE GROUP INC.
Att: Human Resources Manager
522 - 11th Avenue SW, Suite 312
Calgary, AB T2R 0C8
Tel. 403-237-7684
Fax 403-237-7745
Email .... merlincg@home.com
Employer Background: Merlin Creative is a leading corporate communications agency, with a blue-chip client list. *New Positions Created (2):* Senior Corporate Designer; Intermediate and Senior Designers.

MERRIAM SCHOOL OF MUSIC
Att: Linda Henderson, Vice-President
2359 Bristol Circle
Oakville, ON L6H 6P8
Tel. 905-829-2020
Fax 905-829-4489
Email .... sales@merriammusic.com
Website .... www.merriammusic.com
Employer Background: Merriam School of Music is one of Canada's most progressive music education centres. *New Positions Created (3):* Assistant Store Manager; Piano Sales Representative; School Enrollment Representatives.

MERRILL LYNCH CANADA INC.
Att: Human Resources Manager
925 Georgia Street West
Vancouver, BC V6C 3L2
Tel. 604-806-5500
Fax 604-806-5517
Website .... www.canada.ml.com

Employer Background: Merrill Lynch Canada Inc. is a full-service brokerage firm and a subsidiary of USA-based Merrill Lynch & Co., Inc. The parent company has operations in 45 countries and manages assets of $1.5 trillion. *New Positions Created (2):* Financial Consultant Assistant; Administrative Sales Assistant.

MERRILL LYNCH CANADA INC.
Att: Human Resources Manager
20 Bay Street, Suite 1402
Toronto, ON M5J 2N8

Fax 416-943-6954
Website .... www.canada.ml.com
Employer Background: Merrill Lynch Canada Inc. (a subsidiary of US-based Merrill Lynch & Co., Inc.) is a full-service brokerage firm. The parent company operates in 44 countries and manages client assets of $2.5 trillion. *New Positions Created (2):* Regional Representatives; Regional Vice-Presidents / Regional Managers.

MESSAGINGDIRECT LTD.
Att: Carol Tymchuk, HR Manager
10117 Jasper Avenue, Suite 900
Edmonton, AB T5J 1W8

Tel. 780-424-4922
Fax 780-424-4925
Email ... recruitment@messagingdirect.com
Website .... www.messagingdirect.com
Employer Background: MessagingDirect Ltd. is one of the world's leading developers of standards-based electronic messaging and directory software for the e-business market. *New Positions Created (9):* Product Marketing Position, Banking; Product Support Representative; Senior Quality Assurance Analysts (2); Senior Software Developer; Web Applications Developer; Developer / Professional Services Position; Quality Assurance Analyst; Senior Software Engineer / Tier III Technical Support Position; Software Engineer.

MESSER CANADA / RESPIRCARE
Att: Human Resources
1000 Thomas Spratt Place
Ottawa, ON K1G 5L5

Tel. 613-737-7711
Fax 613-737-0962
Email .... lisac@messercanada.com
Website .... www.messergroup.com
Employer Background: Messer Canada / Respircare is a supplier of compressed gas products, including home oxygen, asthma and allergy management products, dental gas, veterinary gas, liquid nitrogen and emergency care products. *New Positions Created (5):* Inside Sales Representative; Registered Respiratory Care Practitioner / Registered Nurse; Marketing Representative; Route Sales Representative; Sales Representative, Durable Medical Equipment.

MESSIER-DOWTY INC.
Att: Human Resources Manager
574 Monarch Avenue
Ajax, ON L1S 2G8

Tel. 905-683-3100

Fax 905-683-2863
Email .... human.resources@
.... messier-dowty.on.ca
Website .... www.messier-dowty.on.ca
Employer Background: Messier-Dowty Inc. develops integrated landing gear systems for the aerospace industry. *New Positions Created (3):* Hardware Project Specialist; Manufacturing Engineering Specialist; Software Specialist.

MESSIER-DOWTY INC.
Att: Human Resources
2000 Fisher Drive, PO Box 4525
Peterborough, ON K9J 7B4

Tel. 705-743-6903
Fax 705-745-1394
Email .... human.resources@
.... messier-dowty.on.ca
Website .... www.messier-dowty.on.ca
Employer Background: Messier-Dowty Inc. develops integrated landing gear systems for the aerospace industry. *New Positions Created (5):* Accounting Manager; Program Manager; Hardware Design Specialists; Hardware Technical Lead; Software Design Specialists.

METABO CANADA INC.
Att: General Manager
190 Britannia Road East, Unit 12
Mississauga, ON L4Z 1W6

Tel. 905-755-0608
Email .... hr@metabo.ca
Website .... www.metabo.ca
Employer Background: Metabo Canada Inc. is part of Germany-based Metabo International, a global leader in the field of power tools and accessories. *New Positions Created (3):* Sales Representatives (2); Marketing Manager; Sales Representatives.

METAFORE CORPORATION
Att: Anna Fedele-Di Luigi
333 - 11th Avenue SW, Suite 420
Calgary, AB T2R 1L9

Fax 403-234-7095
Email .... recruiter@metafore.ca
Website .... www.metafore.ca
Employer Background: Metafore Corporation provides e-business solutions. *New Positions Created (3):* Business Unit Leader, Professional Services Network Engineering and Security; Network Engineers; Sales Executives.

METAQUEST SOFTWARE
Att: Human Resources Manager
416 Maisonneuve West, Suite 401
Montréal, QC H3A 1L2

Tel. 514-341-9113
Fax 514-341-4757
Email .... jobs@metaquest.com
Website .... www.metaquest.com
Employer Background: MetaQuest Software markets Census (a defect-tracking system for software development teams) and Triage (a diagnostic software toolset for software developers and publishers). *New Positions Created (18):* Account Manager; Intermedi-

ate Software Developer, Visual C++ / Java; Marketing Manager; Senior Software Developer, Visual Basic / Web Development; Senior Software Developer, Visual C++ / Java; Software Quality Assurance / Technical Support Analyst; Account Manager; Intermediate Software Developer; Marketing Manager; Senior Software Developer (Visual Basic / Web Development); Senior Software Developer (Visual C++ / Java); Software Quality Assurance / Technical Support Analyst; Account Manager; Intermediate Software Developer; Marketing Manager; Senior Software Developer; Senior Software Developer; Software Quality Assurance Position / Technical Support Analyst.

METASOFT SYSTEMS INC.
Att: Human Resources Manager
1080 Howe Street, Suite 203
Vancouver, BC V6Z 2T1

Tel. 604-683-6711
Fax 604-683-6704
Email .... salespositions@bigdatabase.com
Website .... www.bigdatabase.com
Employer Background: Metasoft Systems Inc. is an independent Canadian software company that provides web-based funding information internationally. *New Positions Created (5):* Junior Sales Associate; National Sales Manager, Canada; Sales Representatives (10); Sales Professionals; Sales Representatives.

METCAP LIVING
Att: Vice-President, Human Resources
20 Queen Street West, Suite 2100, Box 36
Toronto, ON M5H 3R3

Fax 416-340-8337
Employer Background: MetCap Living provides quality of life opportunities through services and programs for residents, families and communities. *New Positions Created (3):* Long-Term Care Administrators; Retirement Residence Manager; Resident Services Consultant.

METCON SALES AND ENGINEERING LTD.
Att: Human Resources Manager
15 Connie Crescent, Unit 3
Concord, ON L4K 1L3

Tel. 905-738-2355
Fax 905-738-5520
Email .... metcon@metconeng.com
Website .... www.metconeng.com
Employer Background: Metcon Sales and Engineering Ltd. provides water and wastewater treatment equipment, liquid metering, flow measurement, chemical feed and process control technology. *New Positions Created (3):* Technical Sales Representative; Service Technician; Technical Sales Representative.

METHYLGENE INC.
Att: Human Resources Manager
7220 Frederick Banting Street, Suite 200
St-Laurent, QC H4S 2A1

Tel. 514-337-3333
Email .... info@methylgene.com

Website .... www.methylgene.com
Employer Background: MethylGene Inc. is a biopharmaceutical company engaged in the discovery and development of new drugs. *New Positions Created (6):* Clinical Research Associate; Project Manager, Clinical Research; Analytical / Bioanalytical Chemists; Assistant Scientist, Biochemistry; Medicinal Chemists; Technician, Chemistry.

METRICAN MANUFACTURING CO. INC.
Att: Human Resources Manager
2100 Wyecroft Road West
Oakville, ON L6L 5V6
Tel. 905-825-2222
Fax 905-825-2087
Email .... sales@metrican.com
Website .... www.metrican.com
Employer Background: Founded in 1976, MetriCan Manufacturing Co. Inc. designs and builds progression dies (with in-die tapping capabilities), hand and mechanical transfer dies, and trim, form and blank dies. *New Positions Created (7):* Junior CAD Administrator; QA Technician; Senior Designer; Stamping Press Operators & Material Handlers; Die Maintenance Supervisor; Press Operators; Quality Inspector.

METRO CREDIT UNION / MCU
Att: Human Resources
1173 Brimley Road
Toronto, ON M1P 3G5
Tel. 416-252-5621
Fax 416-439-8881
Email humanresourcesstaff@metrocu.com
Website .... www.metrocu.com
Employer Background: Established in 1949, MCU is a full-service financial institution, cooperatively owned and controlled by 45,000 members. The credit union has 10 branches and over $380 million in assets. *New Positions Created (6):* Business Analyst; Manager, Commercial Loan Administration; Member Service Officers; Members Service Representatives; Manager, Communications; Member Service Officers.

METRO LABEL COMPANY LTD.
Att: Human Resources Manager
74 Shorting Road
Toronto, ON M1S 3S4
Tel. 416-292-6600
Fax 416-321-7862
Email .... cdavis@metrolabel.com
Employer Background: Metro Label Company Ltd. manufactures pressure-sensitive labels. *New Positions Created (3):* Quality Assurance Managers / Technicians; Shift Supervisor; Sales Representative.

METRO TOOL AND DIE LTD. / MTD
Att: Human Resources Manager
1065 Pantera Drive
Mississauga, ON L4W 2X4
Email .... mdmetro@sprint.ca
Employer Background: MTD serves international blue-chip customers in the precision metal stamping industry. *New Positions*
Created (3): Tool Room Mgr; Customer Service Representative; Quality Assurance Mgr.

METROPHOTONICS INC.
Att: Human Resources Manager
3701 Carling Avenue
PO Box 11490, Station H, Building 14
Ottawa, ON K2H 8S2
Tel. 613-828-8717
Fax 613-828-6899
Email .... careers@metrophotonics.com
Website .... www.metrophotonics.com
Employer Background: MetroPhotonics Inc. builds next-generation WDM optical telecom components for optical networks. *New Positions Created (51):* Optical Device Designer, WDM Devices; Assembly Mechanical Engineer; Mgr, Optical Device Design; Marketing Communications Specialist; Material Scientist; Package Seal Engineer; Package Seal Technologist; Photolithography Technician; Process Engineer, Dry-Etch and PECVD; Team Leader, Optical Device Design; Technician, Optical Testing; Automated Assembly Technologists; Automation Software Engineer; Fibre Optics Assembly Process Engineer; Optical Design and Process Engineer; Out-Source Assembly Coordinator; Process Engineer, Photolithography; R&D Engineer / Scientist; Reliability & Endurance Engineer; Die Separation Technologist; Account Mgr; Assembly Process Technologist, Final Assembly; Electronics Technologist; Fiber Optics Assembly Engineer, DeMux Seal; Fiber Optics Assembly Process Technologist; Mask Designer; Optical Designer, WDM Devices; Optoelectronic Assembly Engineer; Technician, Optical Testing; Assembly Process Engineer, Final Assembly; Automated Assembly Technologists; Automation Software Engineer; Die Separation Technologist; Director, VP, R&D; Drafting Technician; Electrical / Electronic Designer, Active & Integrated Devices; Electronics Engineer; Facet Coating Technologist; Fiber Optics Assembly Process Engineer; Industrial Engineer; Marketing Specialist, Communications; Master Scheduler / Production Planner; Optical Design & Process Engineer; Optical Designer, Active & Integrated Devices; Outsource Assembly Coordinator; Process Engineer, Photolithography; Quality Engineer; Reliability and Endurance Engineer; Research Scientist; Semiconductor Heterostructure Design; Technical Marketing Manager; Vice-President, Marketing.

METROPOLITAN HOTEL TORONTO
Att: Human Resources
108 Chestnut Street
Toronto, ON M5G 1R3
Tel. 416-597-6306
Fax 416-597-5480
Website .... www.metropolitan.com
Employer Background: Metropolitan Hotel is a luxury facility, featuring 426 rooms. *New Positions Created (8):* Administrative Assistant, Business Centre; Credit Mgr; Restaurant Supervisor; Administrative Assistant, Engineering; Engineering Coordinator; Hotel Positions; HR Coordinator; Chief Engineer.

METROPOLITAN PREPARATORY ACADEMY
Att: Steven Redding
49 Mobile Drive
Toronto, ON M4A 1H5
Tel. 416-285-0870
Fax 416-285-0873
Email .... sredding@metroprep.com
Website .... www.metroprep.com
Employer Background: Metropolitan Preparatory Academy is a semestered, co-educational day school, serving 500 students in grades 7 to OAC. *New Positions Created (4):* Teachers; Teachers; Teachers; Teacher, Intermediate / Senior Geography.

METSO AUTOMATION (CANADA) LTD.
Att: Human Resources Manager
10333 Southport Road SW, Suite 200
Calgary, AB T2W 3X6
Tel. 403-253-8848
Fax 403-212-3459
Email .... metso.careers@
.... sage.nelesautomation.com
Website .... www.metsoautomation.com
Employer Background: Metso Automation (Canada) Ltd. (formerly Neles Automation) provides real-time automation, simulation and information management solutions for the oil and gas, water and electric utilities worldwide. *New Positions Created (5):* Network Administrator; Programmer Analyst; Project Leader; Senior Systems Analyst / Engineer; Systems Analyst / Engineer.

MEUBLES PRESTIGE FURNITURE
Att: Robert St. Louis
1344 Youville Drive
Orleans, ON K1C 2X8
Tel. 613-824-3300
Fax 613-824-8968
Website .... www.prestigefurniture.com
.... homeappliances.com
Employer Background: Meubles Prestige Furniture is one of Ottawa's largest locally-owned home furnishing stores. *New Positions Created (3):* Sales Associates; Warehouse Associates / Delivery Associates; Sales Professionals.

MEVOTECH INC.
Att: Human Resources Manager
240 Bridgeland Avenue
Toronto, ON M6A 1Z4
Tel. 416-783-7800
Fax 416-783-0904
Email .... sales@mevotech.com
Website .... www.mevotech.com
Employer Background: Mevotech Inc. is an automotive aftermarket manufacturer. *New Positions Created (3):* Administrative Assistant; Customer Service Representative; Warehouse Manager.

MEWS CHEV OLDS
Att: Esther Scott, Human Resources Officer
1875 St. Joseph Boulevard
Orleans, ON K1C 7J2
Fax 613-225-2231
Email .... escott@myerschevolds.com

Website .... www.mewschevolds.com
Employer Background: Mews Chev Olds is an automotive dealership. *New Positions Created (4):* Business Manager; Sales and Leasing Consultants; Licensed Technicians; Service Consultants.

MEXX CANADA INC.
Att: Human Resources Department
9855 Meilleur
Montréal, QC H3L 3J6
Tel. 514-383-5555
Fax 514-387-1590
Email .... cv@mexx-canada.com
Website .... www.mexx.com
Employer Background: Mexx Canada Inc. designs and markets fashion products for young men and women. *New Positions Created (3):* Fitting Coordinator; Production Coordinator; Architectural Technician.

MI GROUP, THE
Att: Lesley-Ann Hayden
6745 Financial Drive
Mississauga, ON L5N 7J7
Tel. 905-813-9600
Fax 905-814-6698
Email ..... mi.recruiting@themigroup.com
Website .... www.themigroup.com
Employer Background: The Ml Group provides international relocation services through 14 offices worldwide. *New Positions Created (5):* Accounts Receivable Coordinator; Training Specialist; Manager of Corporate Communications; Technical Website Manager; Training Specialist.

MIBRO GROUP, THE
Att: Human Resources Consultant
111 Sinnott Road
Toronto, ON M1L 4S6
Tel. 416-285-9000
Fax 416-285-9623
Email .... hrc@mibro.com
Website .... www.mibro.com
Employer Background: The MIBRO Group is an international supplier of hand tools, hardware and power tool accessories. *New Positions Created (4):* Product Developer / Translator; Bilingual Customer Service Representative; Product Planner; Senior Administrative Assistant.

MICHAEL SMITH FOUNDATION FOR HEALTH RESEARCH / MSFHR
Att: Human Resources Manager
4720 Kingsway, Suite 710, Metrotower II
Burnaby, BC V5H 4N2
Tel. 604-436-3573
Fax 604-436-2573
Email .... info@msfhr.org
Website .... www.msfhr.org
Employer Background: Created by the BC government in 2001, MSFHR is a non-profit society, providing leadership and support for the advancement of health research in British Columbia. *New Positions Created (3):* Program Assistant; Senior Advisor; Senior Program Manager.

MICROAGE
Att: Technical Services Manager
1547 Merivale Road, Unit 16B
Nepean, ON K2G 4V3
Tel. 613-228-9798
Fax 613-727-0440
Email ...... nationalsales@microageottawa.ca
Website .... www.microage.ca
Employer Background: MicroAge is a computer systems integrator, marketing products and solutions to government and business accounts. *New Positions Created (3):* Professional Account Manager; Systems Engineer; Professional Account Manager.

MICROCELL CONNEXIONS INC.
Att: Human Resources Manager
20 Bay Street, Suite 1601
Toronto, ON M5J 2N8
Fax 416-368-2106
Email .... hr.toronto@microcell.ca
Website .... www.microcellcnx.com
Employer Background: Microcell Connexions Inc. owns and operates Canada's only coast-to-coast wireless network using GSM technology. *New Positions Created (7):* Director, Product Marketing; Product Managers (2); Director, Project Marketing; Project Managers (2); Senior Account Managers (2); Strategic Market Planner; Webmaster / Writer.

MICROCELL TELECOMMUNICATIONS LTD.
Att: Human Resources
815 West Hastings, Suite 540
Vancouver, BC V6C 1B4
Tel. 604-669-1277
Fax 604-608-9053
Email .... hr.west@microcell.ca
Website .... www.microcell.ca
Employer Background: Microcell is a national provider of personal communication services, with over 1,800 employees across Canada. *New Positions Created (2):* Field Technician; NT Administrator.

MICROLOGIX BIOTECH INC.
Att: Human Resources
3650 Wesbrook Mall,
BC Research Building
Vancouver, BC V6S 2L2
Tel. 604-221-9666
Fax 604-221-9688
Email .... hr@mbiotech.com
Website .... www.mbiotech.com
Employer Background: Micrologix Biotech Inc. is a public biopharmaceutical company, developing and commercializing novel antibiotics to treat infections caused by drug-resistant bacteria. *New Positions Created (6):* Research Associate, Drug Function; Medical Laboratory Technologist, Research; General Services Associate; Research Associate, Molecular Biology; Sr Executive Assistant / Office Manager; VP, Finance / CFO.

MICROSLATE INC.
Att: Human Resources Department
3615-A Isabelle Street
Brossard, QC J4Y 2R2

Fax 450-444-3683
Employer Background: Established in 1989, MicroSlate Inc. designs, manufactures and markets ruggedized microcomputer-based products throughout North America. *New Positions Created (6):* Engineer Support Technician; Master Scheduler / Planner; Microcontroller Software Engineer; Production Engineer; Production Engineering Technicians; Production Technicians.

MICROTIME INC.
Att: Human Resources Manager
275 Slater Street, Suite 801
Ottawa, ON K1P 5H9
Tel. 613-234-2345
Fax 613-234-3600
Email .... hr@microtime-it.com
Website .... www.microtime-it.com
Employer Background: Established in 1972, Microtime Inc. is an Ottawa-based consulting company, specializing in informatics services. *New Positions Created (14):* Account Manager; Human Resources Manager; Senior QA Specialist; Senior Tester; Oracle Database Administrator; Programmer / Analyst, Web Development; Project Administrator; Senior Account Manager; Testers; VB ASP Programmer Analyst; Account Manager; Recruiter / Human Resources Administrator; Web Designer; Web Developer.

MIDDLESEX-LONDON HEALTH UNIT
Att: Manager, Human Resources and Labour Relations
50 King Street
London, ON N6A 5L7
Tel. 519-663-5317
Fax 519-663-5086
Email .... recruit@mlhu.on.ca
Website .... www.healthunit.com
Employer Background: MLHU, a teaching health unit, provides a full range of health promotion, protection and prevention services. *New Positions Created (4):* Air Quality Energy Manager; Program Evaluator; Research Associate; Program Managers.

MIDLAND STEEL LTD.
Att: Human Resources Manager
8550 Ernest Cormier
Anjou, QC H1J 1B4
Email .... cchape@midlandsteel.com
Website .... www.midlandsteel.com
Employer Background: Established in 1951, Midland Steel Ltd. (formerly Acier Midland Ltd.) distributes alloy tool steels, high-speed steels and powder metallurgy steels to Canadian and international markets. *New Positions Created (3):* Assistant Controller; Plant Manager; Senior Sales Representative.

MIELE LTD.
Att: Human Resources Manager
55G East Beaver Creek Road
Richmond Hill, ON L4B 1E5
Tel. 905-707-1171
Fax 905-707-0167
Email .... alam@miele.ca

Website .... www.miele.ca
Employer Background: Established in 1899, Miele Ltd. is a German manufacturer of high-quality electrical appliances, commercial equipment and fitted kitchens. *New Positions Created (2):* Junior Accounting Clerk; National Service Manager.

MIKASA
Att: Human Resources Manager
233 Alden Road
Markham, ON L3R 3W6

Tel. 905-474-0880
Fax 905-474-9663
Email .... mikasajobs@aol.com
Website .... www.mikasa.com
Employer Background: Mikasa is a national distributor of fashionable tabletop and home accessories. *New Positions Created (3):* Accounts Payable / Receivable Assistant; Admin Assistant; Marketing Assistant.

MILESTONE'S GRILL AND BAR
Att: Brian Everett, Regional Executive Chef
1880 - 1st Avenue West, 2nd Floor
Vancouver, BC V6J 1G5

Fax 604-714-6541
Email .... beverett@spectragroup.com
Employer Background: Milestone's is a restaurant chain. *New Positions Created (2):* Chefs; General Managers and Chefs.

MILESTONE'S GRILL AND BAR
Att: Scott Ward, Market Partner
45 Yorkview Drive
Toronto, ON M2N 2R9

Fax 416-222-9341
Email .... sward@spectragroup.com
Employer Background: Milestone's Grill and Bar is a restaurant chain. *New Positions Created (2):* Various Foodservice Positions; Various Hospitality Positions.

MILLENIA RESOURCE CONSULTING
Att: Human Resources Manager
602 - 12th Avenue SW, Suite 100B
Calgary, AB T2R 1J3

Tel. 403-571-0510
Fax 403-571-0514
Website .... www.milleniaresource.com
Employer Background: Millenia Resource Consulting is a full-service EPCM company, with experience in major oil and gas plants and pipelines / pipeline infrastructure. *New Positions Created (4):* Intermediate Project Engineers; Operations Engineers; Project Secretary; Senior and Intermediate Process Engineers.

MILLENIUM BIOLOGIX INC.
Att: Human Resources Manager
785 Midpark Drive, Suite 200, PO Box 744
Kingston, ON K7M 7G3

Tel. 613-389-6565
Fax 613-389-6625
Website ..... www.millenium-biologix.com
Employer Background: Millenium Biologix Inc. is an innovator of bio-active medical devices and tissue engineering systems.

New Positions Created (7): Biomaterials Engineer / Scientist; Cell Culture Technician; Database Technician; Manufacturing Technician; Network Coordinator; Quality Manager; Systems Engineer / Technologist.

MILLER THOMSON LLP
Att: Mr. Pat Hughes, IS Manager
10155 - 102nd Street NW, Suite 2700
Edmonton, AB T5J 4G8

Tel. 780-429-1751
Fax 780-424-5866
Email .... edmonton@millerthomson.ca
Website .... www.millerthomson.ca
Employer Background: Miller Thomson LLP is a full-service law firm, with over 280 lawyers in Toronto, Vancouver, Calgary, Edmonton, Markham, Whitehorse and Washington, DC. *New Positions Created (3):* Help Desk / PC Support Analyst; Help Desk Position / PC Support Analyst; Trainer, Software.

MILLER THOMSON LLP
Att: Manager of Administration
700 - 9th Avenue SW, Suite 3000
Calgary, AB T2P 3V4

Tel. 403-298-2400
Fax 403-262-0007
Email .... calgary@millerthomson.ca
Website .... www.millerthomson.ca
Employer Background: Miller Thomson LLP is a full-service law firm, with over 280 lawyers in Toronto, Vancouver, Calgary, Edmonton, Markham, Whitehorse and Washington, DC. *New Positions Created (6):* Corporate Services Assistant; Legal Assistants; Oil & Gas Lawyer; Securities Lawyer; Civil and Commercial Litigation Lawyer; Commercial and Residential Real Estate Lawyer.

MILLER THOMSON LLP
Att: Human Resources Manager
20 Queen Street West, Suite 2500
Toronto, ON M5H 3S1

Tel. 416-595-8500
Fax 416-595-8695
Website .... www.millerthomson.ca
Employer Background: Miller Thomson LLP is a full-service law firm, with over 280 lawyers in Toronto, Vancouver, Calgary, Edmonton, Markham, Whitehorse and Washington, DC. *New Positions Created (11):* Corporate / Commercial Associate; Senior Corporate / Commercial Practitioner; Trust Lawyer; Associate Lawyer, Insurance Litigation; Securities and Corporate Finance Associates; Accounting Clerk; Accounting Coordinator; Billing Clerk; Corporate Accountant; Secretarial Services Manager; Legal Secretaries.

MILLER WASTE SYSTEMS
Att: Human Resources Administrator
8050 Woodbine Avenue
Markham, ON L3R 2N8

Tel. 905-475-6397
Fax 905-475-6396
Email .... karenh@millergroup.ca
Website .... www.millergroup.ca
Employer Background: Miller Waste Systems operates waste and recycling facilities

and services. *New Positions Created (3):* Senior Dispatcher; Project Supervisor; Sales / Marketing Representative.

MILNE & CRAIGHEAD INC.
Att: Human Resources Manager
112 - 4th Avenue SW, Suite 1980
Calgary, AB T2P 0H3

Tel. 403-263-7856
Fax 403-261-1895
Website ..... www.milneandcraighead.com
Employer Background: Established in 1913, Milne & Craighead Inc. provides trade and logistics solutions to help businesses find more efficient ways to move their products. *New Positions Created (2):* Sales Executive, Air / Ocean Freight-Forwarding; Sales Executive, Customs Brokerage.

MILTON, TOWN OF
Att: Coordinator, Human Resources
43 Brown Street
Milton, ON L9T 5H2

Tel. 905-878-7211
Fax 905-878-4231
Email .... gloday@town.milton.on.ca
Website .... www.town.milton.on.ca
Employer Background: Founded in 1857, the Town of Milton is home to over 32,000 people. *New Positions Created (13):* Building Inspector; Project Engineer; Supervisor of Inspections; Development Administrator; Planner, Development Review; Policy Planner; Property Information Officer; Tax Analyst; Business Analyst; Building / Plumbing Inspectors (3); Development Engineering Technician; Permit Administrator; Plans Examiner.

MINACS WORLDWIDE INC.
Att: Human Resources Manager
2 East Beaver Creek, Building 2
Richmond Hill, ON L4B 2N3

Fax 905-707-8999
Email .... humanresources@minacs.com
Website .... www.minacs.com
Employer Background: Minacs Worldwide Inc. is a customer relationship management company, with over 2,400 employees in 15 facilities worldwide. *New Positions Created (16):* Customer Service Representatives; Project Managers; Solutions Architect; Director of Organizational Learning; Bilingual Customer Service Representatives; Distribution Specialist; Oracle DBA / Architect; Quality Assurance Specialist; Senior Business Consultants; Senior Programmer / Analyst; Telecommunications Manager; Account Manager, Call Centre; Operations Coordinator, Call Centre; Operations Manager, Call Centre; Business Consultant; Senior Project Managers.

MINACS WORLDWIDE INC.
Att: Anthony DiGiulio
505 Cochrane Drive
Markham, ON L3R 8E3

Tel. 905-943-8888
Fax 905-571-5021
Email .... adigiulio@minacs.com
Website .... www.minacs.com

Employer Background: Minacs Worldwide Inc. is a customer relationship management company, with over 2,400 employees in 15 facilities worldwide. *New Positions Created (14):* Application Architect; Java Developer; Oracle Developer; Senior Business Process Engineer; Siebel Developer; SQL Database Administrator; Systems Engineer; Commercial Truck Sales Managers (2); Administration Assistant, Global Compensation; Bilingual Recruiting Specialists (2); Project Coordinator / Assistant; Automotive Service Consultant; Commercial Service Manager; Corporate and Commercial Lawyer.

MINACS WORLDWIDE INC.
Att: Human Resources Department
915 Sandy Beach Road
Pickering, ON L1W 1Z5
Tel. 905-420-0181
Fax 905-420-0180
Email .... hr@minacs.com
Website .... www.minacs.com
Employer Background: Minacs Worldwide Inc. is a customer relationship management company, with over 2,400 employees in 15 facilities worldwide. *New Positions Created (3):* Automotive Training Coordinator; Coordinator; Quality Specialist.

MINDEN GROSS GRAFSTEIN & GREENSTEIN
Att: Manager, Human Resources
111 Richmond Street West, Suite 700
Toronto, ON M5H 2H5
Tel. 416-362-3711
Fax 416-864-9223
Email .... sdimauro@mggg.com
Website .... www.mggg.com
Employer Background: Established in 1950, Minden Gross Grafstein & Greenstein is a law firm in downtown Toronto offering alternate dispute resolution services. *New Positions Created (4):* Accounting Clerk; Law Clerks; Legal Assistants; Civil Litigation Lawyer.

MINDQUAKE SOFTWARE
Att: Human Resources Manager
1168 Hamilton Street, Suite 300
Vancouver, BC V6B 2S2
Tel. 604-685-9229
Fax 604-685-9510
Email .... jobs@mindquake.com
Website .... www.mindquake.com
Employer Background: Mindquake Software creates effective e-business solutions through the strategic use of Internet technologies. *New Positions Created (10):* Development Project Manager; 24 / 7 Application Server Architect; Analyst; Internet Software Developer; Junior Web Graphic Designer; Office Administrator; Senior Java Developers; Software Architect; System Integration Specialist; Web Application Framework Architect.

MINISTRY OF ABORIGINAL AFFAIRS, BC
Att: Jatinder Paul,
Human Resources and Payroll Services

712 Yates Street
6th Floor, PO Box 9899, Stn Prov Govt
Victoria, BC V8W 9T9
Tel. 250-356-6248
Fax 250-356-9532
Website .... www.aaf.gov.bc.ca
Employer Background: The Ministry of Aboriginal Affairs is responsible for treaty negotiations in British Columbia. *New Positions Created (4):* Senior Analyst; Executive Director, Mandates; Assistant Negotiators (2); Records Clerks (2).

MINISTRY OF ADVANCED EDUCATION, TRAINING AND TECHNOLOGY, BC
Att: Teresa Burnett
617 Government Street
3rd Floor, Box 9148, Stn Prov Govt
Victoria, BC V8W 9H1
Tel. 250-356-8382
Fax 250-387-6774
Website .... www.aett.gov.bc.ca
Employer Background: The Ministry of Advanced Education, Training and Technology provides post-secondary and skills development opportunities to British Columbia's youth and adults. *New Positions Created (21):* Research Officer; Coordinator, Research and Accountability; Director; Director, Student Assessment & Program Evaluation; Education Officer; Education Officer; Education Officer; Coordinator, Exams and Assessment - Literacy and Humanities; Coordinator, Exams, Assessment Marking and Reporting; Coordinator, K - 12 Mathematics; Coordinator, Performance Standards; Coordinator, Provincial, National and International Assessments; Manager, K - 12 Field Relations; Education Officer; Manager, Funding Allocation; Director, Special Programs; Director; Research Officer; Coordinator, Provincial K-12 Mathematics; Education Officer; Senior Legislative Analyst.

MINISTRY OF AGRICULTURE, FOOD AND FISHERIES, BC
Att: Gail MacDonald
940 Blanshard Street
Suite 5A, PO Box 9850, Stn Prov Govt
Victoria, BC V8W 9T5
Tel. 250-356-1859
Fax 250-387-5334
Website .... www.gov.bc.ca/agf
Employer Background: The Ministry of Agriculture, Food and Fisheries is dedicated to strengthening, developing and diversifying British Columbia's agrifood and fisheries sectors. *New Positions Created (33):* Grape Specialist; Planning Officer; Senior Small Lakes Biologist; Claims Assistant; Extension Clerk; Livestock Industry Development Specialist; Policy Analyst; Senior Small Lakes Biologist; Coordinator, Grazing Enhancement Fund Program; Senior Claims Verifier; Environmental Soils Specialist; Research Information Specialist; Senior Manager, Business Development; Livestock Industry Development Specialist; Agrologist; Senior Program Analyst; Organic Crop Specialist; Administrative Assistant; Claims Manager; Fish Culture Biologist; Veterinary Microbiol-

ogist; Finfish Aquaculture Specialist; Policy Analyst; Agroforestry Specialist; Assistant Regional Agrologist; Geographic Information Assistant; Grape Specialist; Minor Use Coordinator; Program Reps (2); Extension Clerk; Minor Use Coordinator; Regional Research Officer; Regional Director.

MINISTRY OF AGRICULTURE, FOOD AND RURAL AFFAIRS, ONTARIO (AGRICULTURE AND RURAL DIVISION)
Att: Human Resources Manager
1 Stone Road West, 3rd Floor
Guelph, ON N1G 4Y2
Fax 519-826-3254
Website .... www.gov.on.ca/omafra
Employer Background: The Ministry of Agriculture, Food and Rural Affairs fosters prosperous agriculture and food sectors, and promotes economic development and job creation in rural communities. *New Positions Created (36):* Client Service Representative; IPM Specialist, Specialty Crops; Organization Development Specialist; Agriculture Specialist; Project Analyst; Product Development Specialist; Senior Geographic Information Specialist; Pome Fruit IPM Specialist; Agricultural Specialist; Soybean Specialist; IPM Specialist, Specialty Crops; Manager, Planning & Analysis; On-Farm Food Safety Program Lead; Organic Crop Production Program Lead; Regional Information Coordinator; Project Coordinator; Industrial Development Officer; Swine Nutritionist; Veterinary Scientist, Epidemiology; Soybean Specialist; Antimicrobial Resistance and Biotechnology Specialist; Livestock On-Farm Food Safety Specialist; Vegetable Crop Specialist; Vegetable Crop Specialist; Tender Fruit and Grape IPM Specialist; Marketing and Communications Officers (2); Rural Policy Statistician; Environmental Management Specialists (2); Client Service Representatives; Project Leader, Client Services; Milk Quality Assurance Program Leader; Manager, Veterinary Service; Tobacco Specialist; Manager; Product Development Specialist; Minor Use Co-ordinator.

MINISTRY OF AGRICULTURE, FOOD AND RURAL AFFAIRS, ONTARIO (FOOD INDUSTRY DIVISION)
Att: Brenda McCabe
1 Stone Road West, 5th Floor
Guelph, ON N1G 4Y2
Website .... www.gov.on.ca/omafra
Employer Background: The Ministry of Agriculture, Food and Rural Affairs fosters prosperous agriculture and food sectors, and promotes economic development and job creation in rural communities. *New Positions Created (22):* Inspectors, Food Industry Division (11); Grower Services Officer; Supervisor, Communication, Research and Event Coordination; Regional Veterinarian; Food Safety Advisor, Engineering; Food Safety Advisor, Regulatory / Meat; Quality Program Compliance Auditor; Veterinary Scientist; Policy, Program and Issues Manager; Regulatory and Standards Coordinator; Technical Support Positions (2); Man-

ager, Risk Identification and Management; Coordinator, Information Systems; Risk Management Specialists (4); Data Scientist; Client Account Officer; Compliance and Advisory Officers; Food Safety Adviser, Dairy; Food Safety Advisor, HACCP; Food Scientists (3); Industry Food Safety Advisor, HACCP; Export Marketing Officer.

MINISTRY OF AGRICULTURE, FOOD AND RURAL AFFAIRS, ONTARIO (POLICY AND FARM FINANCE DIVISION)
Att: Cheryl Bustamante
1 Stone Road West, 2nd Floor
Guelph, ON N1G 4Y2
Website .... www.gov.on.ca/omafra
Employer Background: The Ministry of Agriculture, Food and Rural Affairs fosters prosperous agriculture and food sectors, and promotes economic development and job creation in rural communities. *New Positions Created (14):* Economists; Data Management Analysts (3); Statistician; Program Development Coordinator, Fish; Program Development Coordinator, Food Fish Safety; Statisticians (2); Business & Communications Officer; Correspondence and Communication Specialists; Communications Officer; Chemical Food Safety Science Analyst; Coordinator, Food Safety Science Unit; Microbial Food Safety Science Analyst; Surveillance Food Safety Science Analyst; Technical Liaison.

MINISTRY OF AGRICULTURE, FOOD AND RURAL AFFAIRS, ONTARIO (RESEARCH AND CORPORATE SERVICES DIVISION)
Att: Susan Brehaut
1 Stone Road West, 2nd Floor
Guelph, ON N1G 4Y2
Website .... www.gov.on.ca/omafra
Employer Background: The Ministry of Agriculture, Food and Rural Affairs fosters prosperous agriculture and food sectors, and promotes economic development and job creation in rural communities. *New Positions Created (4):* Program Analyst; Director, Financial Management Branch; Contract Manager; Facilities Management Coordinator.

MINISTRY OF CHILDREN AND FAMILY DEVELOPMENT, BC
Att: Regional Human Resource Services
6551 Aulds Road, Suite 203
Nanaimo, BC V9T 6K2
Tel. 250-390-5496
Fax 250-390-6005
Website .... www.gov.bc.ca/mcf
Employer Background: The Ministry of Children and Family Development is responsible for child protection in British Columbia. *New Positions Created (11):* Clinical Child Psychologists; Child and Youth Mental Health Integrated Services Worker; Clinical Child Psychologists (2); Protection Worker / Youth Probation Officer; Mental Health Worker; Integrated Services Coordinator; Youth Probation Officer; Licensed

Psychologists (2); Protection Worker / Youth Probation Officer; Regional Manager, Finance and Administration; Regional Financial Officer, Contracts and Audits.

MINISTRY OF CHILDREN AND FAMILY DEVELOPMENT, BC
Att: Regional Human Resource Services
765 Broughton Street
2nd Floor, PO Box 9703, Stn Prov Govt
Victoria, BC V8W 9S1
Tel. 250-952-6740
Fax 250-952-6725
Email .... mcfrecruit@gems2.gov.bc.ca
Website .... www.gov.bc.ca/mcf
Employer Background: The Ministry of Children and Family Development is responsible for child protection in British Columbia. *New Positions Created (33):* Child Protection Workers; Senior Adoption Consultant; Implementation Consultant; Child Protection Workers; Contract Management Analyst; Senior Security Planner; Provincial Fetal Alcohol Syndrome (FAS) Prevention Consultant; Divisional Financial Coordinators (2); Accounting Policy Analyst; Manager, Employment Equity and Discrimination Prevention; Budget Analyst, Regions and Programs; Performance Management Statistical Analyst; Regional Communications Generalist; Secretary; Manager, Communications Services; Economist; Junior Economist; Planning Officer; Administrative Support Clerk; Senior Budget Officer, Consolidation and Estimates; Policy Analyst, Special Needs; Provincial Fetal Alcohol Syndrome Prevention Consultant; Senior Program Analyst; Budget Analyst; Economist; Implementation Consultant; Project Leader; Child Protection Workers; Child Protection Workers; Practice Analysts (2); Communications Generalist; Administrative Assistant; Accounts Payable Clerk.

MINISTRY OF CHILDREN AND FAMILY DEVELOPMENT, BC
Att: Human Resources
815 Hornby Street, Suite 204
Vancouver, BC V6Z 2E6
Tel. 604-904-4300
Fax 604-660-7177
Email .... mcfrecruit@gems2.gov.bc.ca
Website .... www.gov.bc.ca/mcf
Employer Background: The Ministry of Children and Family Development is responsible for child protection in British Columbia. *New Positions Created (6):* Clinical Supervisor; Regional Financial Officer, Budgets and Accounts; Mental Health Consultant; Regional Guardianship Consultant; Supervisor, Administrative Services; Child and Youth Mental Health Worker.

MINISTRY OF CHILDREN AND FAMILY DEVELOPMENT, BC
Att: Human Resources Manager
1185 West Georgia Street, Suite 1120A
Vancouver, BC V6E 4E6
Tel. 604-660-2213
Fax 604-660-1090
Email .... mcfrecruit@gems2.gov.bc.ca

Website .... www.gov.bc.ca/mcf
Employer Background: The Ministry of Children and Family Development is responsible for child protection in British Columbia. *New Positions Created (2):* Mental Health Consultant; Integrated Services Coordinators.

MINISTRY OF CHILDREN AND FAMILY DEVELOPMENT, BC
Att: Personnel Services
3705 Willingdon Avenue
Burnaby, BC V5G 3H4
Tel. 604-660-4162
Fax 604-775-0063
Website .... www.gov.bc.ca/mcf
Employer Background: The Ministry of Children and Family Development is responsible for child protection in British Columbia. *New Positions Created (3):* Licensed Psychologist; Licensed Psychologist; Licensed Psychologist, Children and Families, Youth Forensic / Youth Court.

MINISTRY OF CHILDREN AND FAMILY DEVELOPMENT, BC
Att: Human Resources
3405 Willingdon Avenue
Burnaby, BC V5G 3H3
Tel. 604-775-0871
Fax 604-660-1273
Email .... mcfrecruit@gems2.gov.bc.ca
Website .... www.gov.bc.ca/mcf
Employer Background: The Ministry of Children and Family Development is responsible for child protection in British Columbia. *New Positions Created (19):* Complex Supervisor; Licenced Psychologist; Licenced Psychologist; Supervisor; Addictions Counsellor; Nurse; Clinic Coordinator; Nurse; Nurse; Nurses; Licensed Psychologists; Shift Supervisor; Nurses; Community Nurses (3); Licensed Psychologists; Psychiatric Social Workers (6); Healthcare Workers (2); Shift Supervisors (2); Child Care Counsellor.

MINISTRY OF CHILDREN AND FAMILY DEVELOPMENT, BC
Att: Regional Personnel Services
3705 Willingdon Avenue, Suite 101
Burnaby, BC V5G 3H2
Tel. 604-660-4162
Fax 604-775-0063
Email .... mcfrecruit@gems2.gov.bc.ca
Website .... www.gov.bc.ca/mcf
Employer Background: The Ministry of Children and Family Development is responsible for child protection in British Columbia. *New Positions Created (3):* Team Leader, Child Protection Services; Child Care Counsellor; Integrated Services Coordinator.

MINISTRY OF CHILDREN AND FAMILY DEVELOPMENT, BC
Att: Regional Human Resource Services
10221 - 153rd Street, Suite 101
Surrey, BC V3R 0L7
Tel. 604-586-4142

Fax 604-589-4261
Website .... www.gov.bc.ca/mcf
Employer Background: The Ministry of Children and Family Development is responsible for child protection in British Columbia. *New Positions Created (11):* Integrated Services Coordinator; Mental Health Worker; Regional Manager, Child Protection; Team Leaders, Mental Health (2); Youth Addictions Specialists (2); Community Nurse; Resources Worker; Team Leaders, Psychology (2); Regional Financial Officer; Child and Youth Therapist, Serious Behaviour Disorders; Intake Child and Youth Therapist.

MINISTRY OF CHILDREN AND FAMILY DEVELOPMENT, BC
Att: Regional Personnel Services
1011 - 4th Avenue, Suite 463
Prince George, BC V2L 3H9
Tel. 250-565-6575
Fax 250-565-4161
Email .... mcfrecruit@gems2.gov.bc.ca
Website .... www.gov.bc.ca/mcf
Employer Background: The Ministry of Children and Family Development is responsible for child protection in British Columbia. *New Positions Created (40):* Team Leaders, Integrated (5); Mental Health Worker; Resources Worker; Team Leaders, Family Services (2); Mental Health Consultant; Community Living Services Workers; Team Leaders, Integrated; Aboriginal Manager; Mental Health Nurses; Team Leader, Child and Youth Mental Health; Community Living Services Worker; Resources / Community Living Services Worker; Resources Worker; Child Protection Workers; Team Leader, Integrated; Guardianship Workers; Team Leader, Addictions Services; Integrated Services Coordinators (4); Mental Health Worker; Mental Health Nurse; Mental Health Worker; Utilization Services Leader; Aboriginal Manager; Youth Probation Officers; Social Program Officer Assistants; Resource Workers; Adoptions Worker; Child Protection Workers; Child Protection Workers; Guardianship Workers; Team Leader, Intake and Investigation; Team Leader, Intake and Investigation; Team Leader, Integrated; Team Leader, Integrated; Team Leader, Integrated; Team Leader, Integrated; Team Leader, Integrated; Data Management Clerk - Civil; Social Program Officer Assistant.

MINISTRY OF CHILDREN AND FAMILY DEVELOPMENT, BC
Att: Carole Popp, Regional HR Services
70 Second Avenue
Kamloops, BC V2C 6W2
Tel. 250-828-4603
Fax 250-828-4730
Email .... mcfrecruit@gems2.gov.bc.ca
Website .... www.gov.bc.ca/mcf
Employer Background: The Ministry of Children and Family Development is responsible for child protection in British Columbia. *New Positions Created (13):* Integrated Services Coordinator; Team Leader; Youth Probation Officer; Integrated Services

Coordinator; Regional Child Protection Consultant; Youth Probation Officers; Regional Financial Officer; Team Leader / Social Program Officer; Integrated Services Coordinators (3); Mental Health Therapists (2); Counsellor, Addiction Services; Counsellor, Addiction Services; Multidisciplinary Team Leader.

MINISTRY OF CHILDREN AND FAMILY DEVELOPMENT, BC
Att: Regional Human Resource Services
167 Lorne Street
Kamloops, BC V2C 1V9
Tel. 250-828-4603
Fax 250-828-4730
Website .... www.gov.bc.ca/mcf
Employer Background: The Ministry of Children and Family Development is responsible for child protection in British Columbia. *New Positions Created (4):* Guardianship Worker; Regional Financial Officer, Budgets & Accounts; Resource Worker; Team Leader, Social Program.

MINISTRY OF CHILDREN AND FAMILY DEVELOPMENT, BC
Att: Human Resources Manager
1726 Dolphin Avenue, Suite 402
Kelowna, BC V1Y 9R9
Tel. 250-470-0868
Fax 250-470-0870
Email .... mcfrecruit@gems2.gov.bc.ca
Website .... www.gov.bc.ca/mcf
Employer Background: The Ministry of Children and Family Development is responsible for child protection in British Columbia. *New Positions Created (5):* Utilization Services Leader; Utilization Services Leader; Integrated Services Coordinator; Regional Financial Officer, Contracts and Audits; Regional Research Analyst.

MINISTRY OF CHILDREN AND FAMILY DEVELOPMENT, BC
Att: Regional Human Resource Services
117 - 10th Avenue South, Room 100
Cranbrook, BC V1C 2N1
Tel. 250-417-4151
Fax 250-426-1609
Website .... www.gov.bc.ca/mcf
Employer Background: The Ministry of Children and Family Development is responsible for child protection in British Columbia. *New Positions Created (12):* Contract and Resources Manager; Regional Community Living Services Manager; Multidisciplinary District Supervisor; Mental Health Nurse; Team Leader, Multidisciplinary; Community Living Services Officer; Community Living Services Worker; Supervisor, Administrative Services; Regional Financial Officer, Contracts and Audits; Child Protection Supervisor; District Supervisor; Supervisor, Child Protection, Youth Probation and Youth Mental Health.

MINISTRY OF CHILDREN AND FAMILY DEVELOPMENT, BC (REGIONAL OPERATING AGENCY)
Att: Regional Personnel Services

712 Yates Street
2nd Fl., Box 9729, Stn Prov Govt
Victoria, BC V8W 9S2
Tel. 250-952-6282
Fax 250-356-0919
Website .... www.gov.bc.ca/mcf
Employer Background: The Ministry of Children and Family Development is responsible for child protection in British Columbia. *New Positions Created (2):* Regional Financial Officer (Contracts and Audits); Regional Financial Officer.

MINISTRY OF CITIZENSHIP, CULTURE AND RECREATION, ONTARIO
Att: Human Resources Branch
400 University Avenue, 2nd Floor
Toronto, ON M7A 2R9
Fax 416-325-6371
Website .... www.gov.on.ca/mczcr
Employer Background: The Ministry of Citizenship, Culture and Recreation is responsible for promoting and developing human rights, equal opportunity, voluntarism, arts and culture. *New Positions Created (24):* Bilingual Communications Officer; Communications Officer; Communications Planner; Consultant; Mgr, Information Systems Development; Secretary to the Executive Director; Area Secretary; Consultants (3); Coordinator, Financial Service; Policy Adviser; Policy Analyst; Secretary; Policy Program Analysts; Sports & Recreation Administrative Coordinator; Director's Secretary; Policy Adviser, Citizenship; Policy Adviser, Tourism, Culture & Recreation; LACAC Adviser; Policy Program Analyst; Library Policy and Program Adviser; Agency Coordinator; Mgr, Heritage Policy and Program Development; Policy Adviser; Internet Specialist.

MINISTRY OF COMMUNITY AND SOCIAL SERVICES, ONTARIO
Att: Doug Noble, HR Consultant
808 Robertson Street, Postal Bag 5400
Kenora, ON P9N 3X9
Fax 807-468-2443
Email .... doug.noble@css.gov.on.ca
Website .... www.gov.on.ca/CSS
Employer Background: The Ministry of Community and Social Services provides income and employment support to 1.1 million Ontario residents in need. *New Positions Created (5):* Program Supervisor; Income Support Specialist; Business Analyst; Program Assistants; Office Managers (2).

MINISTRY OF COMMUNITY AND SOCIAL SERVICES, ONTARIO
Att: James J. Fitzpatrick, HR Consultant
435 James Street South, Suite 111
Thunder Bay, ON P7E 6S9
Website .... www.gov.on.ca/CSS
Employer Background: The Ministry of Community and Social Services provides income and employment support to 1.1 million Ontario residents in need. *New Positions Created (6):* Employment Supports Clerk; Program Assistant; Probation Officer; Program Supervisor; Program Assistant; Income Support Specialist.

**MINISTRY OF COMMUNITY AND
SOCIAL SERVICES, ONTARIO**
Att: NRO Human Resources
199 Larch Street, 10th Floor
Sudbury, ON P3E 5P9
Fax 705-564-3099
Website .... www.gov.on.ca/CSS
Employer Background: The Ministry of
Community and Social Services provides
income and employment support to 1.1 mil-
lion Ontario residents in need. *New Positions
Created (3):* Administrative Clerk; Business
Analyst, Financial Administrative Services;
Program Assistant.

**MINISTRY OF COMMUNITY AND
SOCIAL SERVICES, ONTARIO**
Att: Ron Devost, Acting HR Manager
621 Main Street West
North Bay, ON P1B 2V6
Tel. 705-474-3540
Fax 705-474-5044
Website .... www.gov.on.ca/CSS
Employer Background: The Ministry of
Community and Social Services provides
income and employment support to 1.1 mil-
lion Ontario residents in need. *New Positions
Created (6):* Client Services Representative;
Manager, Administration & Information
Technology Services; Income Support Man-
ager; Finance Analysts; Regional Trainer;
Systems Coordinator.

**MINISTRY OF COMMUNITY AND
SOCIAL SERVICES, ONTARIO**
Att: Human Resources Branch
2 Bloor Street West, 23rd Floor
Toronto, ON M7A 1E9
Fax 416-327-0561
Website .... www.gov.on.ca/css
Employer Background: The Ministry of
Community and Social Services provides
income and employment support to 1.1 mil-
lion Ontario residents who are most vulner-
able and in need. *New Positions Created (14):*
Communications Planners; Manager, Busi-
ness Planning & Allocation; Project Man-
ager, Developmental Services Multi-Year
Plan; Public Affairs Officer; Senior Adviser,
Forecasting / Planning; Senior Policy Ad-
viser; Senior Policy Analysts; HR Analyst;
Program Analysts; Technical Integration
Coordinator; Policy Analysts; Senior Policy
Analyst / Team Leader; Senior Econo-
metrician; Policy / Program Coordinator.

**MINISTRY OF COMMUNITY AND
SOCIAL SERVICES, ONTARIO**
Att: Human Resources Consultant
465 Davis Drive
Newmarket, ON L3Y 8T2
Fax 905-895-4330
Website .... www.gov.on.ca/CSS
Employer Background: The Ministry of
Community and Social Services provides
income and employment support to 1.1 mil-
lion Ontario residents in need. *New Positions
Created (5):* Probation Officer; Probation
Officer; Special Agreements Officer; Pro-
gram Supervisors (3); Income Support
Clerk.

**MINISTRY OF COMMUNITY AND
SOCIAL SERVICES, ONTARIO**
Att: Human Resources Department
10 Rideau Street, 2nd Floor
Ottawa, ON K1N 9J1
Fax 613-787-6001
Website .... www.gov.on.ca/CSS
Employer Background: The Ministry of
Community and Social Services provides
income and employment support to 1.1 mil-
lion Ontario residents in need. *New Positions
Created (9):* Client Service Representatives;
Secretary to Regional Director; Secretary;
Program Supervisors (3); Income Support
Clerks; Community Services Secretaries (2);
Eligibility Review Officer; Income Support
Clerk; Probation Services Secretary.

**MINISTRY OF COMMUNITY AND
SOCIAL SERVICES, ONTARIO (CHILD
& PARENT RESOURCE INSTITUTE)**
Att: Human Resources
600 Sanatorium Road
London, ON N6H 3W7
Tel. 519-858-2774
Fax 519-858-4072
Website .... www.gov.on.ca/CSS
Employer Background: The Child & Parent
Resource Institute is a regional centre, serv-
ing children with behavioural problems and
emotional disturbances or developmental
handicaps. *New Positions Created (7):* Reg-
istered Nurse; Social Worker; Social Worker;
Homeshare Social Worker; Intake Social
Worker; Speech Language Pathologist; Fi-
nancial Analyst.

**MINISTRY OF COMMUNITY AND
SOCIAL SERVICES, ONTARIO (CLIENT
SERVICES UNIT)**
Att: Human Resources Branch
2 Bloor Street West, 23rd Floor
Toronto, ON M4W 3E2
Tel. 416-327-4776
Website .... www.gov.on.ca/CSS
Employer Background: The Ministry of
Community and Social Services provides
income and employment support to 1.1 mil-
lion Ontario residents. *New Positions Cre-
ated (35):* Outreach Coordinator; Sr Com-
munications Consultant; Development Mgr;
Executive Assistant; Executive Secretaries;
Sr Policy Analysts (2); Policy Analyst; Sr
Policy Analyst; Financial Business Analyst;
Program Analyst, Challenge Fund; Project
Coordinator, Challenge Fund; Branch Ad-
ministrative Coordinator; Organizational
Effectiveness Consultant; Senior Policy Development & Fiscal Adviser; Senior Policy
Adviser; Administrative Assistant; Clerical
Assistant; Coordinator, Corporate Issues;
Program Analyst; Senior Consultant, Or-
ganizational Effectiveness; Provincial Train-
ing Coordinator; Business Analysts (3);
Business Support Analysts; French Language Services Officer; Mgr, Development
and Maintenance; Sr Program Analysts (2);
Policy Analyst (4); Assistant Controller; Office Administrator; Business Analysts; Spiritual & Religious Care Co-ordinator; HR
Analyst; Program Analysts; Human Resources Secretary; Training Unit Secretary.

**MINISTRY OF COMMUNITY AND
SOCIAL SERVICES, ONTARIO
(HURONIA REGIONAL CENTRE)**
Att: Manager, Human Resources
700 Memorial Avenue, Box 1000
Orillia, ON L3V 6L2
Fax 705-326-3445
Website .... www.gov.on.ca/CSS
Employer Background: The Ministry of
Community and Social Services provides
income and employment support to 1.1 mil-
lion Ontario residents. *New Positions Cre-
ated (4):* Residential Counsellors; Dietitian;
Physiotherapist; Electrician.

**MINISTRY OF COMMUNITY AND
SOCIAL SERVICES, ONTARIO
(SOUTHWEST REGION)**
Att: Human Resources Unit
217 York Street, Suite 203, PO Box 5217
London, ON N4S 5R1
Fax 519-438-7703
Website .... www.gov.on.ca/CSS
Employer Background: The Ministry of
Community and Social Services provides
income and employment support to 1.1 mil-
lion Ontario residents. *New Positions Cre-
ated (5):* Client Services Representative; In-
come Support Clerk; Receptionist; Financial
Analysts; Administrative Clerk.

**MINISTRY OF COMMUNITY AND
SOCIAL SERVICES, ONTARIO
(SOUTHWESTERN REGIONAL
CENTRE)**
Att: Human Resources Department
RR 1
Blenheim, ON N0P 1A0
Fax 519-676-7710
Website .... www.gov.on.ca/CSS
Employer Background: The Ministry of
Community and Social Services provides
income and employment support to 1.1 mil-
lion Ontario residents. *New Positions Cre-
ated (3):* Switchboard / Dictatypist / Recep-
tionist; Cook; Director of Operations.

**MINISTRY OF COMMUNITY AND
SOCIAL SERVICES, ONTARIO
(THISTLETOWN REGIONAL CENTRE
FOR CHILDREN AND ADOLESCENTS)**
Att: Human Resources
51 Panorama Court
Toronto, ON M9V 4L8
Fax 416-326-9059
Website .... www.gov.on.ca/css
Employer Background: The Ministry of
Community and Social Services provides
income and employment support to 1.1 mil-
lion Ontario residents. *New Positions Cre-
ated (7):* Program Manager, Residential
Services; Groundskeeper; Maintenance
Plumber / Handyman; Clinical Therapist;
Human Resources Consultant; Instructor
Therapists; Senior Instructor Therapist.

**MINISTRY OF COMMUNITY AND
SOCIAL SERVICES, ONTARIO
(TORONTO REGION)**
Att: Human Resources Unit

2195 Yonge Street, 8th Floor
Toronto, ON M7A 1G1

Fax 416-325-9614
Website .... www.gov.on.ca/css
Employer Background: The Ministry of
Community and Social Services provides
income and employment support to 1.1 million Ontario residents. *New Positions Created (8):* Administrative Officer; Employment Support Specialists; Manager, Administration and Information Technology Services; Probation Supervisors; Eligibility Review Officers (2); Licensing Specialist; Business Analyst; Program Secretary.

MINISTRY OF CONSUMER AND BUSINESS SERVICES, ONTARIO

Att: Human Resources Branch
250 Yonge Street, 34th Floor
Toronto, ON M5B 2N5

Fax 416-326-8932
Website .... www.ccr.gov.on.ca
Employer Background: The Ministry of Consumer and Business Services aims to promote a fair, safe and informed marketplace
supporting a competitive economy in Ontario. *New Positions Created (26):* Investigator; Information Coordinator; Systems
Administrator; Information & Referrals
Operator; Receptionist / Clerk; Senior Financial Analyst; Manager, Corporate Analysis & Business Consulting; Team Representative; Administrative Assistants; Systems Administrator; Financial Analyst; Bilingual Business Consultants (2); Business
Consultants (3); Business Relationship Coordinators (4); Senior Business Consultants
(5); Human Resources Strategic Planning
Consultant; Senior Technical Coordinator;
Team Leader, Marketing and Communications; Technical Support Coordinator; Team
Manager; Senior Financial Analyst; Investigator; Director, Quality Customer Service;
Directors, Integrated Service Delivery (4);
Financial Support Analyst; Receptionist /
Clerk.

MINISTRY OF CORRECTIONAL SERVICES, ONTARIO

Att: Human Resources Consultant
171 Judson Street, Building C
Toronto, ON M8Z 1A4

Tel. 416-314-8381
Fax 416-314-9540
Website .... www.sgcs.gov.on.ca
Employer Background: The Ministry of Correctional Services is responsible for the supervision of adults awaiting trial, sentence,
deportation or transfer to a correctional institution. *New Positions Created (8):* Chaplain; Nurses; Probation & Parole Officers (2);
Coordinator, Health Services; Chaplain; Social Worker; Tailor Shop Officer; Plumber.

MINISTRY OF CORRECTIONAL SERVICES, ONTARIO

Att: Human Resources Branch
25 Grosvenor Street, 16th Floor
Toronto, ON M7A 1Y6

Fax 416-327-8807
Website .... www.sgcs.gov.on.ca

Employer Background: The Ministry of Correctional Services is responsible for the supervision of adults awaiting trial, sentence,
deportation or transfer to a correctional institution. *New Positions Created (6):* Contract Compliance Manager; Tailor Shop Officers (2); Regional Director, Community &
Young Offender Services; Project Coordinator / Contract Manager; Director, Leadership
and Development; Regional Director.

MINISTRY OF CORRECTIONAL SERVICES, ONTARIO

Att: Faith Webb, HR
101 Bloor Street West, 12th Floor
Toronto, ON M5S 2Z7

Fax 416-327-8807
Website .... www.sgcs.gov.on.ca
Employer Background: The Ministry of Correctional Services is responsible for the supervision of adults awaiting trial, sentence,
deportation or transfer to a correctional institution. *New Positions Created (3):* Administrative Support Clerk; Trilcor Commodity
Specialist; Group Leaders (2).

MINISTRY OF CORRECTIONAL SERVICES, ONTARIO

Att: Human Resources Consultant
23 Beechgrove Lane, 2nd Floor
Kingston, ON K7M 9A6

Fax 613-531-8496
Website .... www.sgcs.gov.on.ca
Employer Background: The Ministry of Correctional Services is responsible for the supervision of adults awaiting trial, sentence,
deportation or transfer to a correctional institution. *New Positions Created (9):* Chaplain; Welding Trade Instructor; Nurse;
Nurse; Social Worker, Adult and Young Offenders; Social Worker, Young Offenders;
Chaplain; Probation and Parole Officers (4);
Parole and Probation Secretaries (2).

MINISTRY OF CORRECTIONAL SERVICES, ONTARIO (NORTHERN REGION)

Att: Human Resources Branch
200 First Avenue West, 4th Floor
North Bay, ON P1B 9M3

Fax 705-494-3436
Website .... www.sgcs.gov.on.ca
Employer Background: The Ministry of Correctional Services is responsible for the supervision of adults awaiting trial, sentence,
deportation or transfer to a correctional institution. *New Positions Created (12):* Food
Service Officer; Probation & Parole Officer;
Maintenance Supervisor; Senior Psychologist; Supervisor, Psychologist Services; Chief
of Psychology; Psychologist; Manager, Investigations and Security; Probation and Parole
Officers; Probation & Parole Officer; Social
Services Secretary; Psychologist.

MINISTRY OF CORRECTIONAL SERVICES, ONTARIO (WESTERN REGIONAL OFFICE)

Att: Human Resources Manager
150 Dufferin Avenue, Suite 704
London, ON N6A 5N6

Fax 519-661-6182

Website .... www.sgcs.gov.on.ca
Employer Background: The Ministry of Correctional Services is responsible for the supervision of adults awaiting trial, sentence,
deportation or transfer to a correctional institution. *New Positions Created (11):* Chief
Psychologist; Social Worker; Probation and
Parole Officers; Chief Psychologist; Laundry
Officer; General Duty Nurse; Psychometrist;
Chaplaincy Coordinator; Probation and Parole Officer; General Duty Nurse; Secretary.

MINISTRY OF ECONOMIC DEVEL-OPMENT AND TRADE, ONTARIO

Att: Employee Services Branch
900 Bay Street, 3rd Floor, Hearst Block
Toronto, ON M7A 2E1

Tel. 416-325-6666
Fax 416-325-6715
Website .... www.ontario-canada.com
Employer Background: The Ministry of Eco-
nomic Development and Trade aims to
stimulate economic growth, create more
jobs and establish strong competitive ad-
vantages to ensure a more prosperous fu-
ture for Ontario. *New Positions Created (45):*
Investment Sales Consultant; Team Leader,
International Investment Sales; Financial
Analyst; Senior Account Representative;
Senior Business Consultant; Coordinator,
Business Planning & Management Board
Liaison; Senior Policy Adviser, Asia; Man-
ager, Service Sectors & Aerospace; Sector
Team Leaders (3); Senior Policy Adviser,
Environment; Business Development Con-
sultant; Key Account Representatives (2);
Investment Sales Consultant; Investment
Sales Consultants; Senior Economist; Cus-
tomer Service Representative; Key Account
Representative; Marketing Planner; Re-
search & Data Analysis Consultant; Coordi-
nator, Community Export Development;
Senior Economist; Corporate Sales Representative; Intergovernmental Affairs Officers; Manager, Heritage Programs and Operations; Senior Intergovernmental Affairs
Officer; Senior Account Representative,
Stakeholder Communications; Administrative Assistant; Manager, Marketing, Sales &
Corporate Sponsorship; Team Leader, International Investment Sales; Administrative
Assistant; Administrative Assistant; Director, External Relations; Automotive Investment Sales Consultant; Business Development Consultant; Business Practices Analysts; Consultant; Investment Marketing
Consultant; Manager, Product Development
and Client Services; Office Administrator;
Senior Adviser; Senior Development Consultants (3); Team Leader, US Investment
Sales; Business Development Consultant;
Senior Policy Analyst; Senior New Economy
Researcher.

MINISTRY OF EDUCATION / MINISTRY OF TRAINING, COLLEGES AND UNIVERSITIES, ONTARIO

Att: Human Resources Branch
900 Bay Street, 19th Floor, Mowat Block
Toronto, ON M7A 1L2

Tel. 416-327-9045
Fax 416-327-9043

Website .... www.edu.gov.on.ca
Employer Background: The Ministry of Education and the Ministry of Training, Colleges and Universities are responsible for the administration of laws relating to education and skills training in Ontario. *New Positions Created (85):* Administrative Assistant; Coordinators, Special Apprenticeship Programs; Issues Coordinator; Labour Mobility Adviser; Policy Analyst; Program Assistant; Provincial Coordinator; Research Policy Analyst; Secretary; Senior Policy Analyst; Education Officer; Education Officers, Coordinated Services (2); Knowledge Management Coordinator; Literacy & Basic Skills Coordinator; Manager, Performance Systems & Quality Assurance; Manager, Policy Coordination Unit; Secretary; Head, Strategic Business Management; Manager, Performance Systems and Quality Assurance; Administrative Assistant; Assessment Analysts, Data Integrity (3); Coordinator, Field Services; Senior Policy Advisor; Bilingual Program Assistant; Education Officers; Financial Reporting Standards Officer; Policy & Program Consultant; Project Coordinator; Secretary to Project Leader; Information Database Senior Administrator; Administrative Clerk; Secretary; Policy / Program Analyst; Education Counsellor / GED Examiner; Statistics Officer; Senior Policy Advisers (4); Corporate Initiatives & Program Consultant; Assessment Officer, Technical Quality; Coordinator, Operations Planning; Writer / Editor; Program / Policy Analyst; Area Manager; Financial Forecasting Specialist; Learner Services Officers (2); Manager, Performance and Accountability Unit; Senior Forecasting Analyst; Manager, Program Delivery; Training Consultant; Area Manager; Database Administrator; Director, French-Language Education Policy and Programs Branch; Policy Analyst; Policy Analyst; Policy Analyst; Program Coordinator; Senior Policy Analyst; Stakeholder Relations Coordinator; Manager, Cooperative Services Unit; Manager, Policy and Program Support Unit; Administrative Clerk; Manager, Literacy and Basic Skills; Logistics and Procurement Coordinator; Research Analyst; Secretary; Education Officers (2); Coordinator, Business Planning; Manager, Corporate Policy and External Relations; Senior Policy Advisor; District Manager; Manager, Labour Market Information and Research; Senior Policy Adviser; Senior Project Coordinator; Education Officers (7); Executive Assistant; Manager, Performance Systems and Quality Assurance; Manager, Policy and Standards; Manager, Standards and Assessment; Policy Analysts; Senior Policy Advisers (6); Administrative Officer; Executive Secretary; Training Consultant; Analyst; Secretary; Senior Analyst.

MINISTRY OF EDUCATION, ONTARIO (PROVINCIAL SCHOOLS BRANCH)
Att: Hellen Bogie, Director
255 Ontario Street South
Milton, ON L9T 2M5
Tel. 905-878-2851
Website .... www.edu.gov.on.ca

Employer Background: The Ministry of Education is responsible for the administration of laws relating to education in Ontario. *New Positions Created (3):* Principals (2); Prinicpals and Vice-Principals; Teachers of the Deaf.

MINISTRY OF EDUCATION, ONTARIO (SIR JAMES WHITNEY SCHOOL FOR THE DEAF)
Att: Gerard Kennedy, Residential Services
350 Dundas Street West
Belleville, ON K8P 1B2
Fax 613-967-2871
Email ...... gerard.kennedy@edu.gov.on.ca
Website .... www.edu.gov.on.ca

Employer Background: The Ministry of Education's schools for the deaf and hard-of-hearing provide bilingual K-12 educational programs dedicated to the academic, social, emotional and personal development of disabled students. *New Positions Created (9):* Residence Counsellors; Residence Supervisor; Preschool Home-Visiting Teacher; Teacher, Elementary Program; Teacher, Elementary Program; Teacher, Senior English; Teacher, Senior Mathematics; Teacher, Senior Mathematics; Vocational Teacher, Senior Division.

MINISTRY OF EMPLOYMENT AND INVESTMENT, BC
Att: Human Resources Consultant
1810 Blanshard Street
1st Floor, PO Box 9321, Stn Prov Govt
Victoria, BC V8W 9N3
Tel. 250-953-3898
Fax 250-952-0141
Website .... www.ei.gov.bc.ca

Employer Background: The Ministry of Employment and Investment is the provincial agency for job creation and economic development in British Columbia. *New Positions Created (6):* Business Counsellor; Commissioner; Trade Development Officer; Evaluation Analyst; Assistant Director; Senior Policy Advisor, Trade Advisory Service.

MINISTRY OF ENERGY AND MINES, BC
Att: Human Resources Department
1810 Blanshard Street
Suite 1, PO Box 9321, Stn Prov Govt
Victoria, BC V8W 9N3
Tel. 250-952-0109
Fax 250-952-0141
Website .... www.em.gov.bc.ca

Employer Background: The Ministry of Energy and Mines is responsible for managing British Columbia's energy, mineral and petroleum resources to ensure environmental protection and worker safety. *New Positions Created (15):* Mineral Resource Officer; Senior Geotechnical Engineer; Senior Mineral Tax Examiner; Negotiations Research Analyst; Deputy Commissioner, Oil and Gas Commission; Regional Geologist; Inspector of Mines, Occupational Health; Oil and Gas Initiatives Advisor; Senior Policy Adviser; Policy Adviser; Senior Regulatory Advisor; Senior Policy Advisor; Core / Sample Laboratory Assistant; Inspector of Mines, Mechanical; Titles Technician.

MINISTRY OF FINANCE, BC
Att: John Powell
525 Superior Street
1st Floor, PO Box 9420, Stn Prov Govt
Victoria, BC V8W 9V1
Tel. 250-387-1337
Fax 250-387-0694
Website .... www.fin.gov.bc.ca

Employer Background: The Ministry of Finance is responsible for the treasury and finances of British Columbia. *New Positions Created (47):* Deputy Registrar, Corporate and Personal Property; Policy Analyst; Director, Operations; Manager, Technical Support Services; Business Development Officer; Capital Analyst; Treasury Board Analyst; Manager, Consolidated Support and Services; Portfolio Analyst; Administrative Assistant; Tobacco Enforcement Officers (3); Strategic Planning Analyst; Accountants; Auditors; Director, Litigation and Appeals; Chief Economist; Chief Information Officer; Executive Director, Corporate Accounting System; Audit Manager; Manager, Production Services; Project Manager; Senior Project Manager; Manager, Executive Projects and Administrative Planning; Auditor; Manager, Collections; Senior Corporate Taxation Auditor; Senior Policy Advisor; Disposal Agent, Warehousing Services; Senior Economist; Tobacco Enforcement Inspectors (6); Auditors (4); Freedom and Information Analyst; Senior Corporate Taxation Auditor; Senior Income Taxation Auditor; Treasury Board Analyst; Senior Auditor, Property Tax Transfer; Indo-Canadian Media Liaison Officer; Treasury Board Analyst; Program, Policy and Planning Analyst; Communications Officer; Policy Analyst; Taxpayer Services Officer; Technical Analysis Officers (2); Manager, Information Systems Operations and Maintenance; Pharmacist; Accounting Project Analyst; Associate Director, Systems.

MINISTRY OF FINANCE, ONTARIO
Att: Human Resources Branch
56 Wellesley Street West, 6th Floor
Toronto, ON M7A 1C1
Fax 416-325-8299
Website .... www.gov.on.ca/fin

Employer Background: The Ministry of Finance is responsible for managing provincial finances and administering major tax statutes and tax assistance programs. *New Positions Created (42):* Accounting & Financial Reporting Advisor; Economic Specialists (2); Economists (2); Senior Policy Advisor; Senior Policy Analyst; Senior Analyst; Economic Specialists (2); Arbitrators; Economist; Manager, Foreign Exchange; Senior Arbitrator; Senior Policy Analyst / Economist; Senior Economist; Senior Policy Consultant; Senior Legislation Specialist; Transition Management Analysts; Analyst; Financial Reporting Leader; Senior Analysts; Senior Manager, Rates and Classifications; Senior Treasury Specialist; Special Projects Officer, Fiscal Agency / Ontario Savings Bonds; Research Economists (2); Assistant Director, Communications; Communications Team Leader; Education and Training Team Leader; Manager, Derivatives; Registration Specialist; Transition Management Team Leader; Policy Adviser; Senior Policy Advisor; Project Assistant; Accounting and Financial Reporting Adviser; Coordinators, Administrative and Support Services; Director, External Relations; Assistant Pension Officer; Economic Specialist; Policy Analysts (2); Senior Economist; Senior Policy Adviser; Settlement Officers, Debt / Swap Portfolio; Complaint Registrar / Administrative Coordinator.

MINISTRY OF FINANCE, ONTARIO
Att: Human Resources Branch
101 Bloor Street West, 6th Floor
Toronto, ON M7A 1C1
Fax 416-325-8299
Website .... www.gov.on.ca/fin
Employer Background: The Ministry of Finance is responsible for managing provincial finances and administering major tax statutes and tax assistance programs. *New Positions Created (39):* Director, Communications and Corporate Affairs; Economic Specialist; Economic Specialist; Economist; Senior Economist; Senior Financial Analyst; Economic Specialists; Economists (5); Senior Economist; Manager, Revenue Forecasting; Assistant Deputy Minister, Tax Revenue Division; Manager, Fiscal Policy; Policy Analyst; Administrative Coordinator; Economist / Policy Analyst; Director, Risk Control Division; Tax Policy Analysts / Economists; Web Specialist; Communications Analysts; Communications Manager; Economist; ERP Interfaces & Data Conversion Technical Specialists; ERP Workflow and Reporting Technical Specialist; Communications Manager; Project Administration & Quality Assurance Officer; Project Reporting & Risk Management Lead Position; Economic Specialists (2); Health Economists (3); Legislative Design Specialist, Commodity Taxes; Sr Policy Advisor and Policy Advisor; Senior Communications Officer; Accounting & Financial Reporting Adviser; Special Assistant; Sr Accountant; Bank Funding / Fiscal Agency Supervisor; Research Economists (2); Economist; Policy Analyst; Sr Economist.

MINISTRY OF FINANCE, ONTARIO
Att: Human Resources Branch
250 Yonge Street, 27th Floor
Toronto, ON M5B 2N7
Tel. 905-433-6092
Fax 416-325-8299
Website .... www.gov.on.ca/fin
Employer Background: The Ministry of Finance is responsible for managing provincial finances and administering major tax statutes and tax assistance programs. *New Positions Created (3):* Legislative Design Specialist, Commodity Taxes; Administrative Assistant; Sr Fiscal Policy Analysts (2).

MINISTRY OF FINANCE, ONTARIO
Att: Human Resources Branch

33 King Street West, 2nd Floor
Oshawa, ON L1H 8H5
Tel. 416-325-0333
Fax 905-433-6588
Website .... www.gov.on.ca/fin
Employer Background: The Ministry of Finance is responsible for managing provincial finances and administering major tax statutes and tax assistance programs. *New Positions Created (39):* Field Auditors (8); Returns Auditors (10); Field Auditors, Business Programs; Senior Field Auditors; Collection Officers; Driver / Stock Clerk; Customer Service Representative; Filing Clerk; Land Transfer Tax Analysts (4); Service Manager; Collection Officers; Group Managers, Audit; Manager, Post-Assessment Review; Field Auditor, Complex Employer Accounts; Junior Screener; Senior Desk Auditor; Business Systems Analyst; Field Auditor, Employer Accounts; Field Auditor; Collection Officer; Regional Manager, Service and Collections; Security Analyst; Communications Analyst; Training Developers / Writers (2); Transition Management Analysts (2); Administrative Support Clerk; Filing / Mail Clerk; Junior Systems Analyst; Manager, Post-Assessment Review; Manager, Program Planning and Compliance Research; Collection Officers; Learning Consultant; Senior Duplicating Officer; Field Auditors (3); Service Representatives; Field Auditor, Employer Accounts; Senior Appeals Officer; Group Managers, Audit; Group Managers, Field Audit (2).

MINISTRY OF FORESTS, BC
Att: Human Resources Manager
8808 - 72nd Street
Fort St. John, BC V1J 6M2
Tel. 250-787-5600
Fax 250-787-5610
Website .... www.for.gov.bc.ca
Employer Background: The Ministry of Forests is the steward of the timber, range and recreation resources of BC's unreserved public forest land, which covers two-thirds of the province. *New Positions Created (3):* Harvesting Officer; Range Agrologist; Geographic Information Systems Analyst.

MINISTRY OF FORESTS, BC
(CARIBOO REGION)
Att: Theresa Kondor
640 Borland Street, Suite 200
Williams Lake, BC V2G 4T1
Tel. 250-398-4420
Fax 250-398-4853
Email .. heather.botham@gems1.gov.bc.ca
Website .... www.for.gov.bc.ca
Employer Background: The Ministry of Forests is the steward of the timber, range and recreation resources of BC's unreserved public forest land, which covers two-thirds of the province. *New Positions Created (3):* District Manager; Human Resources Manager; Resource Technician.

MINISTRY OF FORESTS, BC
(CHILCOTIN DISTRICT)
Att: Judy Buhler

Stum Lake Road, PO Box 65
Alexis Creek, BC V0L 1A0
Tel. 250-394-4744
Fax 250-394-4515
Website .... www.for.gov.bc.ca
Employer Background: The Ministry of Forests is the steward of the timber, range and recreation resources of BC's unreserved public forest land, which covers two-thirds of the province. *New Positions Created (3):* Tenures Forester; Silviculture Officer; Operations Manager.

MINISTRY OF FORESTS, BC
(FORT ST. JAMES DISTRICT)
Att: Brenda Gougals
Box 100
Fort St. James, BC V0J 1P0
Tel. 250-996-5200
Fax 250-996-5290
Website .... www.for.gov.bc.ca
Employer Background: The Ministry of Forests is the steward of the timber, range and recreation resources of BC's unreserved public forest land, which covers two-thirds of the province. *New Positions Created (7):* Zone Officer; Zone Forester; District Services Technician; Resource Technician; Resource Services Assistant; Aboriginal Liaison Officer; Zone Forester.

MINISTRY OF FORESTS, BC
(KAMLOOPS REGION)
Att: Martin Blake
515 Columbia Street
Kamloops, BC V2C 2T7
Tel. 250-828-4118
Fax 250-371-3747
Website .... www.for.gov.bc.ca
Employer Background: The Ministry of Forests is the steward of the timber, range and recreation resources of BC's unreserved public forest land, which covers two-thirds of the province. *New Positions Created (3):* Corporate Services and Operations Manager; Mapping and Design Supervisor; District Planner.

MINISTRY OF FORESTS, BC
(NELSON DISTRICT)
Att: Shirley Batke
Mile 301, Alaska Highway, RR 1
Fort Nelson, BC V0C 1R0
Tel. 250-774-5511
Fax 250-774-3704
Website .... www.for.gov.bc.ca
Employer Background: The Ministry of Forests is the steward of the timber, range and recreation resources of BC's unreserved public forest land, which covers two-thirds of the province. *New Positions Created (4):* Land Information Management Operator; Operations Manager; Resource Technician; Land Information Management Officer.

MINISTRY OF FORESTS, BC
(NORTH COAST FOREST DISTRICT)
Att: Brian Wesleyson
125 Market Place
Prince Rupert, BC V8J 1B9

Tel. 250-624-7460
Fax 250-624-7479
Website .... www.for.gov.bc.ca
Employer Background: The Ministry of Forests is the steward of the timber, range and recreation resources of BC's unreserved public forest land, which covers two-thirds of the province. *New Positions Created (7):* Small Business Officer; District Planner; District Planning Forester; Special Tenures Forester; Land Information Management Operator; Resource Technician; Zone Forester.

**MINISTRY OF FORESTS, BC
(PRINCE GEORGE DISTRICT)**
Att: Cheryl Marsolais
2000 South Ospika Boulevard
Prince George, BC V2N 4W5

Tel. 250-614-7445
Fax 250-614-7435
Website .... www.for.gov.bc.ca
Employer Background: The Ministry of Forests (also called the "Forest Service") is the steward of the timber, range and recreation resources of BC's unreserved public forest land, which covers two-thirds of the province. *New Positions Created (2):* Aboriginal Liaison Officer; Interior Check Scaler.

**MINISTRY OF FORESTS, BC
(PRINCE GEORGE REGION)**
Att: Betty Basaraba
1011 - 4th Avenue, 5th Floor
Prince George, BC V2L 3H9

Tel. 250-565-6111
Fax 250-565-6671
Website .... www.for.gov.bc.ca
Employer Background: The Ministry of Forests is the steward of the timber, range and recreation resources of BC's unreserved public forest land, which covers two-thirds of the province. *New Positions Created (3):* Revenue Manager; Research Silviculturalist; District Manager.

**MINISTRY OF FORESTS, BC
(PRINCE RUPERT REGION)**
Att: Marilyn Stewart
Bag 5000
Smithers, BC V0J 2N0

Tel. 250-847-7743
Fax 250-847-7707
Website .... www.for.gov.bc.ca
Employer Background: The Ministry of Forests is the steward of the timber, range and recreation resources of BC's unreserved public forest land, which covers two-thirds of the province. *New Positions Created (3):* Audit Accountant; Operations Mgr; Land Information Mgmnt Operations Manager.

**MINISTRY OF FORESTS, BC
(QUESNEL DISTRICT)**
Att: Tia Groves
322 Johnston Avenue
Quesnel, BC V2J 3M5

Tel. 250-992-4483
Fax 250-992-4485

Website .... www.gov.bc.ca/for
Employer Background: The Ministry of Forests is the steward of the timber, range and recreation resources of BC's unreserved public forest land, which covers two-thirds of the province. *New Positions Created (2):* Operations Forester; Liaison Officer, Aboriginal Affairs.

**MINISTRY OF FORESTS, BC
(RESEARCH BRANCH)**
Att: LaVerne Mullane, Human Resources
2957 Jutland Road
PO Box 9503, Stn Prov Govt
Victoria, BC V8W 9C1

Fax 250-387-4816
Email ..... laverne.mullane@gems2.gov.bc.ca
Website .... www.for.gov.bc.ca
Employer Background: The Ministry of Forests is the steward of the timber, range and recreation resources of BC's unreserved public forest land, which covers two-thirds of the province. *New Positions Created (12):* Manager, Fish, Forestry and Watershed Assessment; Strategic Planning Coordinator; Watershed Evaluation Engineer; Forest Biometrician; Research Scientist; Research Scientist; Human Resources Manager; Landscape Modelling Biologist; Manager, Litigation and Issues Analysis; Senior Structure and Roads Engineer; Media Relations Officer; Research Scientist Tree Breeder.

**MINISTRY OF FORESTS, BC
(VANDERHOOF DISTRICT)**
Att: Sylvia Chow
PO Box 190
Vanderhoof, BC V0J 3A0

Tel. 250-567-6363
Fax 250-567-6370
Website .... www.for.gov.bc.ca
Employer Background: The Ministry of Forests is the steward of the timber, range and recreation resources of BC's unreserved public forest land, which covers two-thirds of the province. *New Positions Created (3):* Financial Services Officer; Resource Technicians (3); Financial Services Supervisor.

**MINISTRY OF HEALTH AND LONG-
TERM CARE, ONTARIO**
Att: Mark Momentoff, HR Consultant
850 Highbury Avenue, PO Box 5532,
Terminal B
London, ON N6A 4H1

Tel. 519-455-5110
Fax 519-455-4715
Website .... www.gov.on.ca/health
Employer Background: The Ministry of Health and Long-Term Care is responsible for regulating hospitals and nursing homes, operating psychiatric hospitals and medical labs, and coordinating emergency health services. *New Positions Created (10):* Rehabilitation Officer; Registered Nurse; Capital Consultant, Finance; Registered Nurses (5); Registered Nurses (2); Regional Secretary; Audio Visual Technician; Registered Nurse; Administrative Assistant; Accounting Supervisor.

**MINISTRY OF HEALTH AND LONG-
TERM CARE, ONTARIO**
Att: Human Resources Branch
500 Church Street
Penetanguishene, ON L9M 1G3

Tel. 705-549-3181
Fax 705-549-1549
Website .... www.gov.on.ca/health
Employer Background: The Ministry of Health and Long-Term Care is responsible for regulating hospitals and nursing homes, operating psychiatric hospitals and medical labs, and coordinating emergency health services. *New Positions Created (9):* Bilingual Senior Attendants, Oak Ridge (2); Senior Attendant, Oak Ridge; Systems Officer; Registered Nurses (6); WSIB / Attendance Management Coordinator; Transportation Supervisor; Registered Nurses; Social Worker; Developmental Support Worker.

**MINISTRY OF HEALTH AND LONG-
TERM CARE, ONTARIO**
Att: Rosemary Lutz, Acting Manager
49 Place d'Armes, 4th Floor
Kingston, ON K7L 5J3

Website .... www.gov.on.ca/health
Employer Background: The Ministry of Health and Long-Term Care is responsible for regulating hospitals and nursing homes, operating psychiatric hospitals and medical labs, and coordinating emergency health services. *New Positions Created (16):* Project Analysts; Design and Publication Technician; Operational Statistics Technician; Systems Change Control Analysts; Analyst; Information Management Analyst; Operational Statistics Technician; Senior Project Leader; Senior Business Analysts; Analysts (2); Analysts, Business Operations and Claims; Statistician; Coordinator, Facilities Management Services; Senior Business Analyst / Project Leader; Analysts; Information Management Specialist.

**MINISTRY OF HEALTH AND LONG-
TERM CARE, ONTARIO (CLIENT
SERVICE OFFICE)**
Att: Human Resources Branch,
Client Service Office
5700 Yonge Street, Mezzanine Level
Toronto, ON M2M 4K5

Tel. 416-314-5518
Fax 416-326-4107
Website .... www.gov.on.ca/health
Employer Background: The Ministry of Health and Long-Term Care is responsible for regulating hospitals and nursing homes, operating psychiatric hospitals and medical labs, and coordinating emergency health services. *New Positions Created (124):* Information Management Analyst; Provincial Planners; Regional Addiction & Mental Health Consultant; Rotating Medical Technologists (2); Executive Assistant; Nurse Epidemiologist; Senior Fraud Program Analyst; Divisional Issues Coordinators; Pharmacists; Claims Assessors; Compliance Advisor; Coordinator, Audit and Quality Assurance; Home for Special Care Clerks; Patient Advocate; Regional Addiction and Mental Health Consultants (6); Senior Business

Planning Coordinator; Senior Medical Consultant; Senior Technologist, Medical Mycology; Consultant, Advocacy Services; Program Consultant; Program Coordinator; Rotating Technologist, Microbiology; Contract Mgmnt Consultant; Policy Analysts; Senior Policy & Business Analysts; Compliance Adviser; Financial Coordinator, Healthcare Program; Human Resources Consultant; Compliance Adviser; Program Coordinators (4); Systems Coordinator; Client Support Analyst; Hospital Consultant; Analysts; Audit & Quality Assurance Assistant; Long-Term Care Program Consultants; Program Coordinators; Senior Policy Analyst; Team Leader, Freedom of Information & Protection of Privacy; Compliance Adviser; Enforcement Officer, Nutrition; Policy Analyst; Secretary to the Director; Senior Business Analyst; Senior Program Analysts; Senior Public Health Nursing Consultant, Chronic Disease; Senior Public Health Nursing Consultant, Injury Prevention; Coordinator, Blood System Secretariat; Coordinator, Ontario Hepatitis C Assistance Plan; X-Ray Safety Inspector; Executive Assistant / Program Development Coordinator; Epidemiologist / Senior Policy Analyst; Facili-tators; Senior Medical Consultant; Clerical Assistant; Client Information Clerks; Receptionist / Secretary; Mental Health Consultant; Financial Officer; Secretary; Technical Manger; Clinical Epidemiologist; Senior Policy Advisor; Regional Office Clerk; Senior Policy Analysts (3); Administrative Support Clerk; Claims Assessors; Regional Financial Analyst; Rotating Medical Technologist; Service Manager; Compliance Advisor; Customer Service Clerk; Financial Control Analyst; Project Leader, Call Management; Senior Business Analysts / Project Leaders; Administrative Clerk; CACC Technical Officers; Program Supervisor; Regional Secretaries; Application Architect; Consultant, Speech / Language and Audiology; Rotating Technologists, Clinical Bacteriology; Secretary; Senior Financial Analyst; Administrative Officer; Manager, Financial Services; Aboriginal Health Policy Analyst; Program Consultants (5); Provincial Planning Coordinator; Policy Analyst; Regional Financial Analyst; Coordinator, Distribution & Records Centre; Executive Assistant; Hospital Consultant; Program Analysts; Secretaries; Communication Project Mgrs (2); New Media & Internal Communications Editor; Senior Communications Advisers (2); Senior Policy and Business Analysts; Coordinator, Laboratory Audit Program; Laboratories Auditors; Regional Consultants, Housing; Financial Coordinator; Mgr, Divisional Finance; Mgr, Hospital Operational and Priority Programs; Administrative Support Clerk; Program Coordinators; Technology Support Analyst; Training Coordinators; Manager, Subrogation; Hospital Consultant; Mental Health Consultant; Regional Coordinator; Communications Training Officers; Mgr/ Scientist, Drug Programs Laboratory; Outreach Customer Service Clerk; Senior Economist; Website Coordinator; Fleet Services Co-ordinator; Senior Financial Analyst; Systems Administration Co-ordinator / Analyst; Financial Officer; Compliance Adviser.

MINISTRY OF HEALTH AND LONG-TERM CARE, ONTARIO (HUMAN SERVICES I&IT CLUSTER)
Att: Yasmin Hack
5700 Yonge Street, 9th Floor
Toronto, ON M2M 4K5

Fax 416-327-7089
Website .... www.gov.on.ca/health
Employer Background: The Ministry of Health and Long-Term Care is responsible for regulating hospitals and nursing homes, operating psychiatric hospitals and medical labs, and coordinating emergency health services. *New Positions Created (8):* Sr Business Analyst/Project Leader; Sr Systems Analyst/Lead Programmer; Site Mgr; Sr Business Analyst /Project Leader; Programmer; Sr Systems Analys /Lead Programmer; Receptionist; Sr Systems Analyst /Lead Programmer.

MINISTRY OF HEALTH AND LONG-TERM CARE, ONTARIO (HUMAN SERVICES I&IT CLUSTER)
Att: Sylvia McLaren
49 Place d'Armes, 5th Floor
Kingston, ON K7L 5J3

Fax 613-548-6693
Website .... www.gov.on.ca/health
Employer Background: The Ministry of Health and Long-Term Care is responsible for regulating hospitals and nursing homes, operating psychiatric hospitals and medical labs, and coordinating emergency health services. *New Positions Created (27):* Data Security Analyst; Production Control Officer; Sr Business Analyst / Project Leader; Sr Systems Tester; Systems Testers; Client Support Analysts; Programmers; Senior Business Analyst / Project Leader; Senior Financial / Administrative Clerks ; Mgr, Branch Mgmnt Office; Sr Systems Testing Analyst, Claims & APP; Systems Testers; Sr Project Mgr; Sr Information Technology Project Managers (2); System Tester; Application Architect; Programmers; Sr Business Analyst / Project Leader; Sr Business Analyst / Project Leader; Sr Systems Analyst / Lead Programmer; Sr Systems Tester; Manager, Development & Maintenance; Executive Secretaries; Programmer / Analyst; System Tester; Technology Architects (2); Senior Systems Analyst / Lead Programmer.

MINISTRY OF HEALTH AND LONG-TERM CARE, ONTARIO (LAKEHEAD PSYCHIATRIC HOSPITAL)
Att: Human Resources Branch
580 Algoma Street North
PO Box 2930, Station P
Thunder Bay, ON P7B 5G4

Website .... www.gov.on.ca/health
Employer Background: The Ministry of Health and Long-Term Care is responsible for regulating hospitals and nursing homes, operating psychiatric hospitals and medical labs, and coordinating emergency health services. *New Positions Created (7):* Director of Pharmacy; Occupational Therapist; Public Information Officer; Maintenance Steamfitter; Steam Plant Engineer; Occupational Therapists (2); Psychometrists.

MINISTRY OF HEALTH AND LONG-TERM CARE, ONTARIO (NORTH BAY PSYCHIATRIC HOSPITAL)
Att: Human Resources Branch
PO Box 3010
North Bay, ON P1B 8L1

Website .... www.gov.on.ca/health
Employer Background: The Ministry of Health and Long-Term Care is responsible for regulating hospitals and nursing homes, operating psychiatric hospitals and medical labs, and coordinating emergency health services. *New Positions Created (7):* Nippissing Assertive Community Treatment Team (ACTT) Leader; Social Worker; Psychiatrist, Assertive Community Treatment Team; Social Worker; Occupational Therapist; Social Worker; Bilingual Social Worker.

MINISTRY OF HEALTH AND LONG-TERM CARE, ONTARIO (ORGANIZATIONAL DEVELOPMENT BRANCH)
Att: Executive Services
56 Wellesley Street West, 15th Floor
Toronto, ON M5S 2S3

Fax 416-326-5730
Email ..... executive.services@moh.gov.on.ca
Website .... www.gov.on.ca/health
Employer Background: The Ministry of Health and Long-Term Care is responsible for regulating hospitals and nursing homes, operating psychiatric hospitals and medical labs, and coordinating emergency health services. *New Positions Created (2):* Manager, Health Information Product and Services Unit; Manager, Divisional Finance.

MINISTRY OF HEALTH AND LONG-TERM CARE, ONTARIO (PROVIDER SERVICES BRANCH)
Att: Karen Charlton,
Resources Plan Coordinator
49 Place d'Armes, 2nd Floor
Kingston, ON K7L 5J3

Website .... www.gov.on.ca/health
Employer Background: The Ministry of Health and Long-Term Care is responsible for regulating hospitals and nursing homes, operating psychiatric hospitals and medical labs, and coordinating emergency health services. *New Positions Created (10):* Medical Consultant; Medical Consultant; Senior Analyst; Legal Secretary; Senior Analyst, Monitoring & Control; Research Clerks; Administrative Support Clerical Steno Position; Medical Consultants; Secretary; Human Resource Plan Coordinator.

MINISTRY OF HEALTH AND LONG-TERM CARE, ONTARIO (REGISTRATION AND CLAIMS BRANCH)
Att: Maryann Russell-Dunham
119 King Street West, 10th Floor
Hamilton, ON L8P 4T9

Fax 905-521-7605
Website .... www.gov.on.ca/health
Employer Background: The Ministry of Health and Long-Term Care is responsible for regulating hospitals and nursing homes, operating psychiatric hospitals and medical labs, and coordinating emergency health

services. *New Positions Created (3):* Analyst; Customer Service Clerks; Customer Services Clerk.

MINISTRY OF HEALTH AND LONG-TERM CARE, ONTARIO (REGISTRATION AND CLAIMS BRANCH)

Att: Karen Zanet, HR Consultant
49 Place d'Armes
2nd Floor, Macdonald-Cartier Building
Kingston, ON K7L 5J3

Fax 613-548-6403
Website .... www.gov.on.ca/health
Employer Background: The Ministry of Health and Long-Term Care is responsible for regulating hospitals and nursing homes, operating psychiatric hospitals and medical labs, and coordinating emergency health services. *New Positions Created (6):* Manager, Workforce Planning & Development; Manager, Eligibility Services; Analysts; Senior Policy / Registration Consultants (2); Eligibility Assessment Officers; Analysts (2).

MINISTRY OF HEALTH AND LONG-TERM CARE, ONTARIO (ST. THOMAS PSYCHIATRIC HOSPITAL)

Att: Regional Human Resources Office
467 Sunset Drive, PO Box 2004
St. Thomas, ON N5P 3V9

Fax 519-633-8593
Website .... www.gov.on.ca/health
Employer Background: The Ministry of Health and Long-Term Care is responsible for regulating hospitals and nursing homes, operating psychiatric hospitals and medical labs, and coordinating emergency health services. *New Positions Created (5):* Hospital Consultant; Registered Practical Nurses (16); Therapeutic Recreationist; Clinical Secretary; Social Workers (3).

MINISTRY OF HEALTH AND LONG-TERM CARE, ONTARIO (WORKFORCE PLANNING AND DEVELOPMENT)

Att: Pauline St. Pierre, Manager
199 Larch Street, Suite 801
Sudbury, ON P3E 5R1

Tel. 705-675-4051
Fax 705-675-4015
Website .... www.gov.on.ca/health
Employer Background: The Ministry of Health and Long-Term Care is responsible for regulating hospitals and nursing homes, operating psychiatric hospitals and medical labs, and coordinating emergency health services. *New Positions Created (6):* Outreach Customer Service Clerks; Administrative Support Clerk; Analyst; Outreach Customer Service Clerks; Claims Assessor; On-Call Outreach Customer Service Clerks.

MINISTRY OF HEALTH AND MINISTRY RESPONSIBLE FOR SENIORS, BC

Att: Julie Deveson
1515 Blanshard Street, Suite 5-1
Victoria, BC V8W 3C8

Tel. 250-952-2345
Fax 250-952-2114
Website .... www.hlth.gov.bc.ca

Employer Background: The Ministry of Health and Ministry Responsible for Seniors provide high-quality, accessible and affordable health services for the people of BC. *New Positions Created (49):* Addictions Counsellors; Healthcare Worker, Detox; Nursing Consultant, Integrated Social and Support Services; Executive Director / Registrar, Appeal Board; Regional Manager; Consultant; Senior Manager, Client Services; Senior Manager, Systems Engineering Office; Consultant; Consultant, Speech Language Pathology; Regional Director; Information Analyst; Office Manager; Manager, Information Management Security; Oral Health Consultant; Public Health Consultant; Program Consultant; Public Health Nursing Consultant; Finance and Budget Analyst; Manager, Policy Development for Integrated Social and Support Services; Manager, Policy Development for Public Education and Participation; Finance Analysts (2); Consultant; Quality Assurance Analyst; Program Consultant; Program Coordinator; Information Analyst; Superintendent, Air Ambulance Dispatch; Superintendent, Aviation; Manager, Plan Operations; Nurse Consultant; Consultant, Speech-Language Pathology; Secretary; Program Consultant; Research Analyst; Senior Policy Analyst; Administrative Assistant; Provincial Nutrition Strategy Coordinator; Senior Ministry Investigator; Nurse Consultant; Director, Client Services; Research Officer; Program Adviser, Residential Care; Media Relations Officer; Provincial Management Information System Coordinator; Provincial Nutrition Strategy Coordinator; Manager, Telecommunications; Regional Director, Region 2; Director, Tertiary / Provincial Services.

MINISTRY OF LABOUR, BC (WORKERS' COMPENSATION REVIEW BOARD)

Att: Human Resources Branch
617 Government Street
3rd Floor, Box 9148, Stn Prov Govt
Victoria, BC V8W 9H1

Tel. 250-370-0106
Fax 250-387-6774
Website .... www.labour.gov.bc.ca
Employer Background: The Workers' Compensation Review Board is an independent tribunal that adjudicates appeals to decisions made by the Workers' Compensation Board. *New Positions Created (3):* Gaming Auditor; Administrative Technician; Senior Policy Adviser.

MINISTRY OF LABOUR, ONTARIO

Att: Human Resources Consultant
217 York Street, 5th Floor
London, ON N6A 5P9

Fax 416-642-4316
Email .... ohsijobs@mol.gov.on.ca
Website .... www.gov.on.ca/lab
Employer Background: The Ministry of Labour regulates and promotes safety, health, fairness and equity in the workplace. *New Positions Created (8):* Occupational Health & Safety Inspector, Mining; Occupational

Health & Safety Inspector, Mining - Electrical / Mechanical; Employment Standards Officer; Medical Consultant; Administrative Assistant; Occupational Health and Safety Inspector; Occupational Health and Safety Inspectors, Construction (2); Occupational Health and Safety Inspectors, Industrial (3).

MINISTRY OF LABOUR, ONTARIO

Att: Human Resources Branch
400 University Avenue, 10th Floor
Toronto, ON M7A 1T7

Tel. 416-326-723
Fax 416-326-724
Website .... www.gov.on.ca/la
Employer Background: The Ministry of Labour regulates and promotes safety, health fairness and equity in the workplace. *New Positions Created (38):* Administrative Officer; Facilities Project Coordinator; Manager, Advice Centre & Central Services Writer / Adviser; Program Engineer, Construction; Program Engineer, Industrial Program Engineer, Mining; Intake Counsellor; Account Executives (4); Employer Specialists; Worker Adviser; Provincial Coordinator, Mining; Mediation Administrative Assistant; Senior Communications Officers Policy Advisers; Secretary to the Director Communications Coordinator; Policy Advisors; Policy Advisor; Intake Counsellor; Executive / Legal Secretary; Employee Communications Coordinator; Program Specialists; Operational Assistant; Program Specialist, Toxicology / WHMIS; Provincial Ergonomist; Labour Relations Information Specialists; Desktop Publishing / Distribution Clerk; Provincial Training Specialists Mediators (3); Worker Advisor; Labour Relations Conciliators; Quality Improvement Analysts; Quality Improvement Coordinator; Bilingual Desktop Publishing / Distribution Clerk; Translation Coordinator; Program Assistant; Assistant to Vice-Chairs.

MINISTRY OF LABOUR, ONTARIO

Att: Human Resources Manager
1201 Wilson Avenue, 2nd Floor, Building I
Toronto, ON M3M 1J8

Website .... www.gov.on.ca/la
Employer Background: The Ministry of Labour regulates and promotes safety, health fairness and equity in the workplace. *New Positions Created (6):* Employment Standards Officers (3); Hygiene Consultants (6 Occupational Health and Safety Inspector (2); Occupational Health and Safety Inspectors, Construction (5); Employment Standards Officer; Hygiene Consultant.

MINISTRY OF LABOUR, ONTARIO

Att: Liz Glover
1111 Prince of Wales Drive, Suite 200
Ottawa, ON K2C 3T2

Website .... www.gov.on.ca/la
Employer Background: The Ministry of Labour regulates and promotes safety, health fairness and equity in the workplace. *New Positions Created (8):* Resident Officer; Systems Officer; Occupational Health an Safety Inspectors, Construction (2); Occu

pational Health and Safety Inspectors, Industrial (2); MIS Support Services Clerks; Program Assistant; Systems Officer; Medical Consultant.

MINISTRY OF LABOUR, ONTARIO (NORTHERN REGION)
Att: Human Resources Consultant
159 Cedar Street, Suite 301
Sudbury, ON P3E 6A5
Website .... www.gov.on.ca/lab
Employer Background: The Ministry of Labour regulates and promotes safety, health, fairness and equity in the workplace. *New Positions Created (8):* Systems Officer; Hygiene Consultants (2); Administrative Assistant; Occupational Health and Safety Engineer, Electrical / Mechanical; Occupational Health and Safety Inspector, Industrial; Occupational Health and Safety Inspectors, Mining (2); Human Resources Consultant; Occupational Health and Safety Engineer, Mining.

MINISTRY OF MULTICULTURALISM AND IMMIGRATION, BC
Att: Teresa Switzer
548 Michigan Street
Victoria, BC V8V 1S3
Tel. 250-387-1907
Fax 250-356-8034
Website .... www.gov.bc.ca/mi
Employer Background: Ministry of Multiculturalism and Immigration works to promote multiculturalism and eliminate racism in British Columbia. *New Positions Created (4):* Director, Immigration Program; Manager, Corporate Planning, Evaluation and Systems; Ministry Economist; Program Officers (2).

MINISTRY OF MUNICIPAL AFFAIRS AND HOUSING, ONTARIO
Att: Human Resources Branch
777 Bay Street, 3rd Floor
Toronto, ON M5G 2E5
Tel. 416-585-6670
Fax 416-585-7259
Website .... www.mah.gov.on.ca
Employer Background: The Ministry of Municipal Affairs and Housing aims to make local government less costly and more efficient and provide greater accountability for services delivered at the municipal level. *New Positions Created (53):* Administrative / Event Coordinator; Municipal Adviser; Policy Adviser; Transition Project Manager; Investigator; Senior Policy Adviser; Customer Service Representative; Coordinator, Customer Service; Information Specialists; Senior Policy Adviser; Client Relations Coordinator; Planning Analyst; Senior Human Resources Advisers; Municipal Adviser; Project Manager; Housing Administrators; Financial Officer; Senior Policy Advisor; Business Support Officer; Policy Advisor; Financial Officers (2); Coordinator, Budget Systems and Analysis; Financial Administration Officers; Security Administrative Analyst; Administrative Coordinator; Financial Support Officer; Municipal Services

Analyst; Housing Administrator; Transition Project Manager; Administrative Assistant; Financial Officers; Municipal Adviser; Policy Analyst; Planner; Community Planners; Housing Administrators (2); Senior Financial Consultant, Risk Management; Program Policy Adviser; Senior Policy Advisers (3); Administrative Assistant; Manager, Business Planning and Cabinet Liaison; Receptionist / Information Clerk; Planning Assistants (3); Financial Officer; Administrative Assistant; Business and Resource Planning Analysts (2); Financial Officers (2); Housing Administrator; Financial Team Leader; Hearings Assistant; Investigator; Municipal Planning Adviser; Real Estate Officers (2).

MINISTRY OF MUNICIPAL AFFAIRS, BC
Att: Human Resources Branch
800 Johnson Street
Suite 6, Box 9490, Stn Prov Govt
Victoria, BC V8W 9N7
Tel. 250-387-9176
Fax 250-387-9190
Website .... www.gov.bc.ca/marh
Employer Background: The Ministry of Municipal Affairs works with the people of British Columbia to create and sustain strong, safe and effectively administered local and regional communities. *New Positions Created (2):* Vice-Chair; Registrar.

MINISTRY OF NATURAL RESOURCES, ONTARIO
Att: Human Resources Manager
808 Robertson Street, Box 5080
Kenora, ON P9N 3X9
Fax 807-468-2520
Email .... job.ken1@mnr.gov.on.ca
Website .... www.mnr.gov.on.ca
Employer Background: The Ministry of Natural Resources ensures that Ontario's forests, fish, wildlife, Crown lands and waters, provincial parks and soil resources are managed sustainably to provide environmental, social and economic benefits. *New Positions Created (3):* Management Biologist; IRM Technical Specialist; Management Biologist.

MINISTRY OF NATURAL RESOURCES, ONTARIO
Att: Human Resources
922 Scott Street
Fort Frances, ON P9A 1J4
Fax 807-274-4438
Email .... job.ftfr3@mnr.gov.on.ca
Website .... www.mnr.gov.on.ca
Employer Background: The Ministry of Natural Resources ensures that Ontario's forests, fish, wildlife, Crown lands and waters, provincial parks and soil resources are managed sustainably to provide environmental, social and economic benefits. *New Positions Created (6):* Management Forester; Resource Management Technicians; Land & Waters Technical Specialist; Human Resources Consultant; Resources Liaison Specialist; Park Superintendent.

MINISTRY OF NATURAL RESOURCES, ONTARIO
Att: Pat Earl
479 Government Road, PO Box 730
Dryden, ON P8N 2Z4
Fax 807-223-2580
Email .... pat.earl@mnr.gov.on.ca
Website .... www.mnr.gov.on.ca
Employer Background: The Ministry of Natural Resources ensures that Ontario's forests, fish, wildlife, Crown lands and waters, provincial parks and soil resources are managed sustainably to provide environmental, social and economic benefits. *New Positions Created (3):* GIS / Database Technician; Area Biologist; Assistant Park Superintendent.

MINISTRY OF NATURAL RESOURCES, ONTARIO
Att: Wayne Nakamura
70 Foster Drive
Suite 400, Roberta Bondar Place
Sault Ste. Marie, ON P6A 6V5
Fax 705-945-6667
Email ... wayne.nakamura@mnr.gov.on.ca
Website .... www.mnr.gov.on.ca
Employer Background: The Ministry of Natural Resources ensures that Ontario's forests, fish, wildlife, Crown lands and waters, provincial parks and soil resources are managed sustainably to provide environmental, social and economic benefits. *New Positions Created (12):* Forest Health Technicians; Forest Program Pathologist; Fire Services Program Officer; Forest Fire Management Program Development Coordinator; Business Management Coordinator; Fire Science Specialist; Timber EA Biologist; Timber EA Forester; Program Leader, Fire Science and Technology; Planning Specialist; Flood and Fire Meteorologist; Forest Program Specialist.

MINISTRY OF NATURAL RESOURCES, ONTARIO
Att: Pamela Donnelly, Human Resources
64 Church Street
Sault Ste. Marie, ON P6A 3H3
Tel. 705-949-1231
Fax 705-949-6450
Email .... pamela.donnelly@mnr.gov.on.ca
Website .... www.mnr.gov.on.ca
Employer Background: The Ministry of Natural Resources ensures that Ontario's forests, fish, wildlife, Crown lands and waters, provincial parks and soil resources are managed sustainably to provide environmental, social and economic benefits. *New Positions Created (8):* Conservation Officer; Resource Management Technician; District Biologist; Conservation Officers; Conservation Officer; Information Management Supervisor; Support Services-Licence Issuing Clerk; Client Service Clerks.

MINISTRY OF NATURAL RESOURCES, ONTARIO
Att: Human Resources Manager
PO Box 910
Kirkland Lake, ON P2N 3K4

Fax 705-568-3200
Email .... pauline.suppa@mnr.gov.on.ca
Website .... www.mnr.gov.on.ca
Employer Background: The Ministry of Natural Resources ensures that Ontario's forests, fish, wildlife, Crown lands and waters, provincial parks and soil resources are managed sustainably to provide environmental, social and economic benefits. *New Positions Created (4):* Information Management Supervisor; Resource Liaison Officer; Conservation Officers (2); Resource Management Technician.

MINISTRY OF NATURAL RESOURCES, ONTARIO
Att: District Manager
3301 Trout Lake Road
North Bay, ON P1A 4L7

Fax 705-475-5500
Email .... karen.larabie@mnr.gov.on.ca
Website .... www.mnr.gov.on.ca
Employer Background: The Ministry of Natural Resources ensures that Ontario's forests, fish, wildlife, Crown lands and waters, provincial parks and soil resources are managed sustainably to provide environmental, social and economic benefits. *New Positions Created (6):* District Planner; Aggregate Resource Technician; Client Services Clerk; Resource Management Clerk; Lands and Waters Technical Specialist; Resource Management Clerk.

MINISTRY OF NATURAL RESOURCES, ONTARIO
Att: Administrative Assistant
Highway 101, PO Box 1160
Wawa, ON P0S 1K0

Tel. 705-856-2396
Fax 705-856-7511
Email .... irene.grusys@mnr.gov.on.ca
Website .... www.mnr.gov.on.ca
Employer Background: The Ministry of Natural Resources ensures that Ontario's forests, fish, wildlife, Crown lands and waters, provincial parks and soil resources are managed sustainably to provide environmental, social and economic benefits. *New Positions Created (6):* Administrative Assistant; Forester; Management Biologist; Area Technicians (3); Area Supervisors (2); Land and Waters Technical Specialist.

MINISTRY OF NATURAL RESOURCES, ONTARIO
Att: Chantal Dionne
190 Cherry Street
Chapleau, ON P0M 1K0

Tel. .... 705-864-1710 ext 216
Fax 705-864-1487
Email .... chantal.dionne@mnr.gov.on.ca
Website .... www.mnr.gov.on.ca
Employer Background: The Ministry of Natural Resources ensures that Ontario's forest, fish, wildlife, Crown lands and waters, provincial parks and soil resources are managed sustainably to provide environmental, social and economic benefits. *New Positions Created (4):* Enforcement Supervisor; District Planner; Resource Management Technicians; Ontario Living Legacy (OLL) Planner.

MINISTRY OF NATURAL RESOURCES, ONTARIO
Att: Lynn Alary, Administrative Assistant
613 Front Street, PO Box 670
Hearst, ON P0L 1N0

Tel. 705-372-2223
Fax 705-372-2245
Email .... lynn.alary@mnr.gov.on.ca
Website .... www.mnr.gov.on.ca
Employer Background: The Ministry of Natural Resources ensures that Ontario's forests, fish, wildlife, Crown lands and waters, provincial parks and soil resources are managed sustainably to provide environmental, social and economic benefits. *New Positions Created (4):* Conservation Officer; Conservation Officers; Resource Management Technician; Area Supervisor.

MINISTRY OF NATURAL RESOURCES, ONTARIO
Att: Administrative Assistant
2 - 3rd Avenue, PO Box 730
Cochrane, ON P0L 1C0

Tel. 705-272-7113
Fax 705-272-7183
Email .... chris.clement@mnr.gov.on.ca
Website .... www.mnr.gov.on.ca
Employer Background: The Ministry of Natural Resources ensures that Ontario's forests, fish, wildlife, Crown lands and waters, provincial parks and soil resources are managed sustainably to provide environmental, social and economic benefits. *New Positions Created (6):* Resource Management Technician; Conservation Officer; Management Forester; IRM Technical Specialist; District Planner; District Enforcement Supervisor.

MINISTRY OF NATURAL RESOURCES, ONTARIO
Att: Ernie Habb,
Manager, Petroleum Resources Centre
659 Exeter Road
London, ON N6E 1L3

Fax 519-873-4645
Website .... www.mnr.gov.on.ca
Employer Background: The Ministry of Natural Resources ensures that Ontario's forests, fish, wildlife, Crown lands and waters, provincial parks and soil resources are managed sustainably to provide environmental, social and economic benefits. *New Positions Created (4):* Spatial Data Technician; Administrative Clerk; Assessment Supervisor; Management Biologist / Team Leader.

MINISTRY OF NATURAL RESOURCES, ONTARIO
Att: District Manager
353 Talbot Street West
Aylmer, ON N5H 2S8

Fax 519-773-9014
Email .... sherry.pineo@mnr.gov.on.ca
Website .... www.mnr.gov.on.ca

MINISTRY OF NATURAL RESOURCES, ONTARIO
Employer Background: The Ministry of Natural Resources ensures that Ontario's forests, fish, wildlife, Crown lands and waters, provincial parks and soil resources are managed sustainably to provide environmental, social and economic benefits. *New Positions Created (2):* Biologist; GIS / Database Technician.

MINISTRY OF NATURAL RESOURCES, ONTARIO
Att: District Manager
1 Stone Road West
Guelph, ON N1G 4Y2

Fax 519-826-4929
Email .... linda.freeman@mrn.gov.on.ca
Website .... www.mnr.gov.on.ca
Employer Background: The Ministry of Natural Resources ensures that Ontario's forests, fish, wildlife, Crown lands and waters, provincial parks and soil resources are managed sustainably to provide environmental, social and economic benefits. *New Positions Created (3):* Conservation Officer; Customer Service Technician; Resource Management Technician.

MINISTRY OF NATURAL RESOURCES, ONTARIO
Att: Human Resources Manager
99 Wellesley Street West
Room 3420, Whitney Block
Toronto, ON M7A 1W3

Fax 416-314-2030
Website .... www.mnr.gov.on.ca
Employer Background: The Ministry of Natural Resources ensures that Ontario's forests, fish, wildlife, Crown lands and waters, provincial parks and soil resources are managed sustainably to provide environmental, social and economic benefits. *New Positions Created (4):* Counsel; Senior Communications Officer; Media Approvals Officer; Sr Program Advisers, Geosmart (2).

MINISTRY OF NATURAL RESOURCES, ONTARIO
Att: District Manager
50 Bloomington Road West
Aurora, ON L4G 3G8

Fax 905-713-7415
Email .... linda.mather@mnr.gov.on.ca
Website .... www.mnr.gov.on.ca
Employer Background: The Ministry of Natural Resources ensures that Ontario's forests, fish, wildlife, Crown lands and waters, provincial parks and soil resources are managed sustainably to provide environmental, social and economic benefits. *New Positions Created (2):* Management Forester; Management Biologist.

MINISTRY OF NATURAL RESOURCES, ONTARIO
Att: Louisa Vatri,
Senior Management Group Specialist
300 Water Street, 3rd Floor, South Tower
Peterborough, ON K9J 8M5

Tel. 705-755-2500
Fax 705-755-3108
Website .... www.mnr.gov.on.ca

Employer Background: The Ministry of Natural Resources ensures that Ontario's forests, fish, wildlife, Crown lands and waters, provincial parks and soil resources are managed sustainably to provide environmental, social and economic benefits. *New Positions Created (8):* Manager, Niagara Escarpment Commission; Manager, Fisheries; Manager, Upper Great Lakes Management; Human Resources Analyst; Manager, Lake Erie Management Unit; Manager, Wildlife Section; Director; Director's Secretary.

MINISTRY OF NATURAL RESOURCES, ONTARIO
Att: Human Resources Branch
300 Water Street, 4th Floor, South Tower
Peterborough, ON K9J 8M5
Fax 705-755-1338
Email .... chris.christl@mnr.gov.on.ca
Website .... www.mnr.gov.on.ca
Employer Background: The Ministry of Natural Resources ensures that Ontario's forests, fish, wildlife, Crown lands and waters, provincial parks and soil resources are managed sustainably to provide environmental, social and economic benefits. *New Positions Created (6):* Health & Safety Assistant; Assistant Human Resources Consultant; Programmer / Analyst; Senior Oracle Programmer / Analyst; Manager, Data Warehouse & Distribution Systems; Manager, Geographic Data Maintenance Systems.

MINISTRY OF NATURAL RESOURCES, ONTARIO (AVIATION AND FOREST FIRE MANAGEMENT BRANCH)
Att: Jack J. McFadden, Director
70 Foster Drive, Suite 400
Sault Ste. Marie, ON P6A 6V5
Fax 705-945-5959
Website .... www.mnr.gov.on.ca
Employer Background: The Ministry of Natural Resources ensures that Ontario's forests, fish, wildlife, Crown lands and waters, provincial parks and soil resources are managed sustainably to provide environmental, social and economic benefits. *New Positions Created (2):* Budget Officer; OLL-AFFM Information Management Specialist.

MINISTRY OF NATURAL RESOURCES, ONTARIO (AVIATION SERVICES)
Att: Gail Warner-Smith
475 Airport Road, RR 1, PO Box 2
Sault Ste. Marie, ON P6A 5K6
Fax 705-945-6893
Email ... gail.warnersmith@mnr.gov.on.ca
Website .... www.mnr.gov.on.ca
Employer Background: The Ministry of Natural Resources ensures that Ontario's forests, fish, wildlife, Crown lands and waters, provincial parks and soil resources are managed sustainably to provide environmental, social and economic benefits. *New Positions Created (10):* Aircraft Maintenance Engineer; Aircraft Tracking System Project Manager; Flight Coordinators; Aircraft Maintenance Engineer; Manager, Information & Client Services; Aircraft Maintenance Engineer; King Air Captain; Aircraft Main-

tenance Engineer; Manager, Provincial Coordination Centre; Aircraft Maintenance Engineer.

MINISTRY OF NATURAL RESOURCES, ONTARIO (FIRE MANAGEMENT CENTRE)
Att: Terry Popowich,
Fire Program Manager
Ghost Lake Road, PO Box 850
Dryden, ON P8N 2Z5
Fax 807-937-7282
Email ...... terry.popowich@mnr.gov.on.ca
Website .... www.mnr.gov.on.ca
Employer Background: The Ministry of Natural Resources ensures that Ontario's forests, fish, wildlife, Crown lands and waters, provincial parks and soil resources are managed sustainably to provide environmental, social and economic benefits. *New Positions Created (5):* Equipment Control Clerk; Fire Services Support Clerk; Fire Management Technician; Facility and Warehouse Group Leader; Equipment and Maintenance Specialist.

MINISTRY OF NATURAL RESOURCES, ONTARIO (FISH AND WILDLIFE BRANCH)
Att: Sandra Orsatti,
Lake Ontario Management Unit
300 Water Street, PO Box 7000
Peterborough, ON K9J 8M5
Fax 705-755-1957
Email ...... sandra.orsatti@mnr.gov.on.ca
Website .... www.mnr.gov.on.ca
Employer Background: The Ministry of Natural Resources ensures that Ontario's forests, fish, wildlife, Crown lands and waters, provincial parks and soil resources are managed sustainably to provide environmental, social and economic benefits. *New Positions Created (5):* Enforcement Supervisor; Senior Regional Fisheries Biologist; Fish Culture Coordinator, Fish Health and Aquaculture; Senior Avian Biologist; Senior Regional Wildlife Biologists.

MINISTRY OF NATURAL RESOURCES, ONTARIO (FOREST FIRE MANAGEMENT CENTRE)
Att: Tammie Thibault,
Program Management Assistant
2621 Skead Rd., Sudbury Airport
Unit 14A, Postal Bag 500
Garson, ON P3L 1W3
Fax 705-564-6033
Website .... www.mnr.gov.on.ca
Employer Background: The Ministry of Natural Resources ensures that Ontario's forests, fish, wildlife, Crown lands and waters, provincial parks and soil resources are managed sustainably to provide environmental, social and economic benefits. *New Positions Created (2):* Financial Officer; Warehouse Group Leader.

MINISTRY OF NATURAL RESOURCES, ONTARIO (FOREST RESEARCH INSTITUTE)
Att: Shirley Middleton

1235 Queen Street East
Sault Ste. Marie, ON P6A 2E5
Fax 705-946-2030
Email ...... shirley.middleton@mnr.gov.on.ca
Website .... www.mnr.gov.on.ca
Employer Background: The Ministry of Natural Resources ensures that Ontario's forests, fish, wildlife, Crown lands and waters, provincial parks and soil resources are managed sustainably to provide environmental, social and economic benefits. *New Positions Created (5):* Assistant Boreal Mixed-Wood Scientist; Silviculture Specialist; Biochemistry Lab Technologist; Communications Officer, Forest Science; Forest Research Pathologist.

MINISTRY OF NATURAL RESOURCES, ONTARIO (INDUSTRY RELATIONS BRANCH)
Att: Bill Kissick, Manager,
Forest Business and Economics Section
70 Foster Drive, Suite 400
Sault Ste. Marie, ON P6A 6V5
Fax 705-945-6667
Email .... bill.kissick@mnr.gov.on.ca
Website .... www.mnr.gov.on.ca
Employer Background: The Ministry of Natural Resources ensures that Ontario's forests, fish, wildlife, Crown lands and waters, provincial parks and soil resources are managed sustainably to provide environmental, social and economic benefits. *New Positions Created (4):* Strategic Planning Advisor; Forest Industry Liaison Officer; Forestry Specialist; Supervisor, Forest Industry Unit.

MINISTRY OF NATURAL RESOURCES, ONTARIO (INFORMATION ACCESS SECTION)
Att: Human Resources Manager
300 Water Street, 1st Floor, North Tower
Peterborough, ON K9J 8M5
Fax 705-755-1882
Website .... www.mnr.gov.on.ca
Employer Background: The Ministry of Natural Resources ensures that Ontario's forests, fish, wildlife, Crown lands and waters, provincial parks and soil resources are managed sustainably to provide environmental, social and economic benefits. *New Positions Created (2):* Information and Privacy Coordinator; E-Channel Coordinator.

MINISTRY OF NATURAL RESOURCES, ONTARIO (KEMPTVILLE DISTRICT)
Att: District Manager
Concession Road, PO Bag 2002
Kemptville, ON K0G 1J0
Fax 613-258-9610
Website .... www.mnr.gov.on.ca
Employer Background: The Ministry of Natural Resources ensures that Ontario's forests, fish, wildlife, Crown lands and waters, provincial parks and soil resources are managed sustainably to provide environmental, social and economic benefits. *New Positions Created (4):* District Planner; Stewardship Coordinator; Customer / Client Services Rep; Communications Specialist.

MINISTRY OF NATURAL RESOURCES, ONTARIO (NIPIGON DISTRICT)
Att: Elsa Shepherdson,
Administrative Assistant
208 Beamish Avenue West, PO Box 640
Geraldton, ON P0T 1M0

Email .... elsashepherdson@mnr.gov.on.ca
Website .... www.mnr.gov.on.ca

Employer Background: The Ministry of Natural Resources ensures that Ontario's forests, fish, wildlife, Crown lands and waters, provincial parks and soil resources are managed sustainably to provide environmental, social and economic benefits. *New Positions Created (6):* Area Senior Technicians, Lands and Water / Native Liaisons; Fish and Wildlife Technical Specialist; District Planner; IRM Technical Specialist; Fish and Wildlife Technician; Customer / Client Services Representative.

MINISTRY OF NATURAL RESOURCES, ONTARIO (NORTHEAST REGION PLANNING UNIT)
Att: Human Resources
Highway 101 East, PO Bag 3020
Ontario Government Complex
South Porcupine, ON P0N 1H0

Fax 705-235-1246
Website .... www.mnr.gov.on.ca

Employer Background: The Ministry of Natural Resources ensures that Ontario's forests, fish, wildlife, Crown lands and waters, provincial parks and soil resources are managed sustainably to provide environmental, social and economic benefits. *New Positions Created (5):* Forest Management Planning Specialist; Senior Project Engineer; Senior Project Engineer; Oil Planner; Resource Analyst.

MINISTRY OF NATURAL RESOURCES, ONTARIO (PEMBROKE DISTRICT)
Att: District Planner
31 Riverside Drive, PO Box 220
Pembroke, ON K8A 8R6

Fax 613-732-2972
Website .... www.mnr.gov.on.ca

Employer Background: The Ministry of Natural Resources ensures that Ontario's forests, fish, wildlife, Crown lands and waters, provincial parks and soil resources are managed sustainably to provide environmental, social and economic benefits. *New Positions Created (3):* Integrated Resource Management Technical Specialist, Lands; Planner; Stewardship Coordinator.

MINISTRY OF NATURAL RESOURCES, ONTARIO (SCIENCE AND INFORMATION BRANCH)
Att: Ann Foggia
70 Foster Drive, Suite 400
Sault Ste. Marie, ON P6A 6V5

Fax 705-945-6638
Email .... ann.foggia@mnr.gov.on.ca
Website .... www.mnr.gov.on.ca

Employer Background: The Ministry of Natural Resources ensures that Ontario's forests, fish, wildlife, Crown lands and waters, provincial parks and soil resources are

managed sustainably to provide environmental, social and economic benefits. *New Positions Created (7):* Managers, Systems Development & Maintenance; Information Management Coordinator, Northern Boreal; Programmer / Analyst; Senior Systems Analyst; Application Support Specialist; Systems Analyst; Programmer / Analyst.

MINISTRY OF NATURAL RESOURCES, ONTARIO (SCIENCE AND INFORMATION BRANCH)
Att: Ted Harvey,
Manager, Business Solutions Services
300 Water Street
Peterborough, ON K9J 8M5

Fax 705-755-1640
Email .... edward.harvey@mnr.gov.on.ca
Website .... www.mnr.gov.on.ca

Employer Background: The Ministry of Natural Resources ensures that Ontario's forests, fish, wildlife, Crown lands and waters, provincial parks and soil resources are managed sustainably to provide environmental, social and economic benefits. *New Positions Created (3):* Ecologist / Coordinator; Business Services Manager / Coordinator; Coordinator, Great Lakes Aquatic Biodiversity Conservation Blueprint Project.

MINISTRY OF NATURAL RESOURCES, ONTARIO (SCIENCE DEVELOPMENT AND TRANSFER BRANCH)
Att: Dr. J. Chris Davies, Manager, Wildlife and Natural Heritage Science Section
300 Water Street
PO Box 700, 3rd Floor North
Peterborough, ON K9J 8M5

Fax 705-755-1559
Email .... chris.davies@mnr.gov.on.ca
Website .... www.mnr.gov.on.ca

Employer Background: The Ministry of Natural Resources ensures that Ontario's forests, fish, wildlife, Crown lands and waters, provincial parks and soil resources are managed sustainably to provide environmental, social and economic benefits. *New Positions Created (3):* Wildlife Field Studies Research Scientists; Information Officer; Science Coordinator, Water Power Project.

MINISTRY OF NATURAL RESOURCES, ONTARIO (SUDBURY DISTRICT)
Att: District Manager
3767 Highway 69 South, Suite 5
Sudbury, ON P3G 1E7

Fax 705-564-7879
Email .... donna.paxy@mnr.gov.on.ca
Website .... www.mnr.gov.on.ca

Employer Background: The Ministry of Natural Resources ensures that Ontario's forests, fish, wildlife, Crown lands and waters, provincial parks and soil resources are managed sustainably to provide environmental, social and economic benefits. *New Positions Created (3):* Land & Waters Technical Specialist; Resource Management Technician; Conservation Officer.

MINISTRY OF NATURAL RESOURCES, ONTARIO (WATER RESOURCES INFORMATION PROJECT)
Att: Scott Christilaw, Manager
300 Water Street, 5th Floor, South Tower
Peterborough, ON K9J 3C7

Fax 705-755-1267
Email ...... scott.christilaw@mnr.gov.on.ca
Website .... www.mnr.gov.on.ca/mnr

Employer Background: The Ministry of Natural Resources ensures that Ontario's forests, fish, wildlife, Crown lands and waters, provincial parks and soil resources are managed sustainably to provide environmental, social and economic benefits. *New Positions Created (3):* Sr Systems Analyst; Water Resource Policy Adviser; Hydrologist.

MINISTRY OF NORTHERN DEVELOPMENT AND MINES, ONTARIO
Att: Human Resources Management
159 Cedar Street, Suite 702
Sudbury, ON P3E 6A5

Tel. 705-564-7940
Website .... www.gov.on.ca/mndm

Employer Background: The Ministry of Northern Development and Mines, the only regional ministry in the provincial government, plays a central role in Ontario's northern affairs. *New Positions Created (38):* Administrative Assistant; Client Services Advisers; Financial Officer; General Manager, Northern Ontario Heritage Fund Corporation; Northern Development Adviser, Transportation; Senior Correspondence Coordinator; Divisional Financial Adviser; Northern Development Officer; Senior Human Resources Consultant; Northern Development Officer; Research Analyst; Staff Development & Learning Consultant; Northern Development Adviser, Tourism; Abandoned Mines Specialist; Northern Development Advisers, Natural Resources (5); Senior Business Planner; Area Team Manager; Operations Coordinator / Systems Administrator; Administrative Assistant; Director, Communications Services; Business Consultant and GIS Specialist; Northern Development Advisor; Library Assistant; District Support Geologist; Northern Development Adviser; Senior Manager, Human Resources Management; Administrative Assistant; Bilingual Receptionist / Correspondence Control Clerk; Administrative Assistant; CCM Coordinator; Senior Database / Systems Analyst; Administrative Assistant; District Support Geologist; Northern Development Advisers; Northern Development Officer; Northern Development Adviser; District Support Geologist; Publication Sales Coordinator.

MINISTRY OF SENIORS, ALBERTA
Att: HR & Administration Branch
10405 Jasper Avenue
Suite 720, Standard Life Centre
Edmonton, AB T5J 4R7

Tel. 780-427-2546
Fax 780-422-3142
Website .... www.seniors.gov.ab.ca

Employer Background: The Ministry of Seniors supports the independence and well-being of seniors and supports seniors, family and special-purpose housing needs through 2 divisions: seniors services and housing services. *New Positions Created (3):* Secretary; Alberta Seniors Benefit Processor; Manager, Ministry Business Planning.

MINISTRY OF SMALL BUSINESS, TOURISM AND CULTURE, BC (BC FILM COMMISSION)
Att: Human Resources Manager
7818 - 6th Street
Burnaby, BC V3N 4N8
Tel. 604-660-3764
Fax 604-660-1792
Website ...... www.bcfilmcommission.com
Employer Background: Created in 1978, the BC Film Commission markets BC production, post-production and ancillary service companies to the international film and television industry. *New Positions Created (5):* Librarian / Business Service Officer; Manager, Community Affairs; Manager, Production Location Services; Assistant Photo Librarian; Information Officer.

MINISTRY OF SMALL BUSINESS, TOURISM AND CULTURE, BC (NORTHERN INTERIOR REGION)
Att: Jake van der Merwe
1011 - 4th Avenue, Suite 213
Prince George, BC V2L 3H9
Tel. 250-994-3302
Fax 250-994-3435
Website .... www.gov.bc.ca/sbtc
Employer Background: The Ministry of Small Business, Tourism and Culture stimulates investment and helps provide jobs in small business, tourism, film, culture, heritage, archaeology, sports and recreation. *New Positions Created (3):* Trade Senior Supervisor, Carpenter; Manager, Operations; Business Service Officer.

MINISTRY OF SOCIAL DEVELOPMENT AND ECONOMIC SECURITY, BC
Att: Lee-Anne Dixon
614 Humboldt Street
4th Floor, PO Box 9970, Stn Prov Govt
Victoria, BC V8W 9R5
Tel. 250-356-2204
Fax 250-356-7776
Website .... www.gov.bc.ca/sdes
Employer Background: The Ministry of Social Development and Economic Security provides services and programs to help individuals and families build better futures for their children. *New Positions Created (8):* Senior Policy Analyst; Director, Human Resources Branch; Director, Building Policy; Human Resources Training and Development Officer; Senior Policy Advisor; Occupational Health and Safety Advisor; Communications Planner; Senior Media Relations Officer.

MINISTRY OF SOCIAL DEVELOPMENT AND ECONOMIC SECURITY, BC (EMPLOYMENT AND BENEFITS CENTRE)

Att: Nancy Mix, HR Region 7
299 Victoria Street, Suite 602
Prince George, BC V2L 5B8
Tel. 250-565-7046
Fax 250-565-4370
Email .... nancy.mix@gems5.gov.bc.ca
Website .... www.gov.bc.ca/sdes
Employer Background: The Ministry of Social Development and Economic Security provides services and programs to help individuals and families build better futures for their children. *New Positions Created (3):* Supervisor, Administrative Services; Regional Executive Officer; Supervisor, Administrative Services.

MINISTRY OF SOCIAL DEVELOPMENT AND ECONOMIC SECURITY, BC (PREVENTION COMPLIANCE AND ENFORCEMENT OFFICE)
Att: Human Resources Manager
906 Roderick Avenue, Suite 201
Coquitlam, BC V3K 1R1
Tel. 604-527-1252
Fax 604-527-1255
Website .... www.gov.bc.ca/sdes
Employer Background: The Ministry of Social Development and Economic Security provides services and programs to help individuals and families build better futures for their children. *New Positions Created (2):* Ministry Investigator; Ministry Investigator.

MINISTRY OF THE ATTORNEY GENERAL, BC
Att: Vancouver Metro Personnel Office
815 Hornby Street, Suite 204
Vancouver, BC V6Z 2E6
Tel. 604-660-4100
Fax 604-660-7177
Website .... www.ag.gov.bc.ca
Employer Background: The Ministry of the Attorney General is the government body responsible for the administration of justice in British Columbia. *New Positions Created (5):* Family Justice Counsellor; Judgment Secretary; Judicial Secretary; Legal Secretary; Legal Secretary.

MINISTRY OF THE ATTORNEY GENERAL, BC
Att: Fraser Regional Personnel Services
2881 Garden Street, Suite 220
Abbotsford, BC V2T 4X1
Tel. 604-504-4121
Fax 604-504-4113
Website .... www.ag.gov.bc.ca
Employer Background: The Ministry of the Attorney General is the government body responsible for the administration of justice in British Columbia. *New Positions Created (15):* Nurse; Registered Nurses / Registered Practical Nurses; LPNs; Client Supervisor; Client Supervisor; Nurse; Chaplain; Office Manager; Nurses (2); Regional Personnel Officer; Nurses; Chaplain; Office Manager; Nurse; Nurses.

MINISTRY OF THE ATTORNEY GENERAL, BC (CRIMINAL JUSTICE BRANCH)
Att: Phillip Hadford,
Northern Regional Personnel Services
1011 - 4th Avenue, Suite 463
Prince George, BC V2L 3H9
Tel. 250-525-6515
Fax 250-565-4161
Website .... www.ag.gov.bc.ca
Employer Background: The Ministry of the Attorney General is the government body responsible for the administration of justice in British Columbia. *New Positions Created (7):* Crown Counsel; Crown Victim Witness Services Coordinator; Crown Counsel; Data Management Clerk; Crown Counsels (3); Court Clerk; Adult Probation Officers.

MINISTRY OF THE ATTORNEY GENERAL, BC (CRIMINAL JUSTICE BRANCH)
Att: Marg Johnson
455 Columbia Street, Suite 217
Kamloops, BC V2C 6K4
Tel. 250-828-4021
Fax 250-828-4376
Website .... www.ag.gov.bc.ca
Employer Background: The Ministry of the Attorney General is the government body responsible for the administration of justice in British Columbia. *New Positions Created (3):* Crown Counsel (2); Crown Counsels (2); Crown Counsel.

MINISTRY OF THE ATTORNEY GENERAL, BC (VICTORIA REGIONAL PERSONNEL SERVICES)
Att: Jack Herman
910 Government Street
5th Floor, PO Box 9258, Stn Prov Govt
Victoria, BC V8W 9J4
Tel. 250-586-2644
Fax 250-356-0690
Website .... www.gov.bc.ca/ag
Employer Background: The Ministry of the Attorney General is the government body responsible for the administration of justice in British Columbia. *New Positions Created (33):* Assistant Negotiator; Director, Policy, Planning & Communications; Manager, Financial Services; Personnel Adviser; Senior Analysts, Research (2); Enforcement Hearing Advocate; Liquor Inspector; Regional Manager; Resource Analyst; Staffing Adviser; Director, Family Justice Programs; Legal Secretary; Deputy General Manager; Community Coordinator, Safe Community Initiatives (Nights Alive); Community Coordinator, School and Youth Programs; Legal Assistant; Legal Counsel; Legislative Editor; Regional Youth Coordinator; Complaints Analysts (2); Human Rights Officer; Earthquake Preparedness Engineer; Family Advocate; Regional Youth Coordinators; Legal Secretary; Information Officer; Program Manager; Earthquake Planning Officer; Legal Counsel; Legal Positions (2); Liquor Inspectors; Debtor Advisor; Receptionist / Secretary.

MINISTRY OF THE ATTORNEY GENERAL, ONTARIO

Att: Karen Linsley
PO Box 577
Toronto, ON M3M 3A9

Fax 416-240-2493
Website .. www.attorneygeneral.jus.gov.on.ca

Employer Background: The Ministry of the Attorney General is responsible for the administration of justice in Ontario, including criminal proceedings, court services, drafting legislation and representing government bodies in litigation. *New Positions Created (5):* Trust Fund Manager; Senior Financial Program / Budget Analyst; Executive Assistant; Managers, Client Services; Senior Analyst, Program Planning and Evaluation.

MINISTRY OF THE ATTORNEY GENERAL, ONTARIO (ASSESSMENT REVIEW BOARD)

Att: Manager, Finance and Administration
250 Yonge Street, 29th Floor
Toronto, ON M5B 2L7

Fax 416-326-3121
Website .. www.attorneygeneral.jus.gov.on.ca

Employer Background: The Ministry of the Attorney General is responsible for the administration of justice in Ontario, including criminal proceedings, court services, drafting legislation and representing government bodies in litigation. *New Positions Created (3):* Hearing Schedulers; Systems Analyst / Programmer; Member Services Liaison.

MINISTRY OF THE ATTORNEY GENERAL, ONTARIO (BUSINESS AND FISCAL PLANNING BRANCH)

Att: April Takeda
720 Bay Street, 7th Floor
Toronto, ON M5G 2K1

Fax 416-326-4019
Website .. www.attorneygeneral.jus.gov.on.ca

Employer Background: The Ministry of the Attorney General is responsible for the administration of justice in Ontario, including criminal proceedings, court services, drafting legislation and representing government bodies in litigation. *New Positions Created (4):* Business Consultants; Program Analyst; Coordinator, Aboriginal Alternative Justice Programs; Executive Adviser.

MINISTRY OF THE ATTORNEY GENERAL, ONTARIO (COMMUNICATIONS BRANCH)

Att: Manager, Correspondence and Public Inquiries Unit
720 Bay Street, 11th Floor
Toronto, ON M5G 2K1

Fax 416-326-2451
Website .. www.attorneygeneral.jus.gov.on.ca

Employer Background: The Ministry of the Attorney General is responsible for the administration of justice in Ontario, including criminal proceedings, court services, drafting legislation and representing government bodies in litigation. *New Positions Created (3):* Senior Coordinator, Correspondence and Public Inquiries; Director, Legal Services Branch; Director, Legal Services.

MINISTRY OF THE ATTORNEY GENERAL, ONTARIO (COURT OF APPEAL FOR ONTARIO)

Att: Support Services Coordinator
130 Queen Street West, Osgoode Hall
Toronto, ON M5H 2N5

Fax 416-326-9955
Website .. www.attorneygeneral.jus.gov.on.ca

Employer Background: The Ministry of the Attorney General is responsible for the administration of justice in Ontario, including criminal proceedings, court services, drafting legislation and representing government bodies in litigation. *New Positions Created (4):* Judgment Distribution Release Clerk; Client Service Officers; Criminal / Civil Motions Clerk; Secretary to the Associate Chief Justice of Ontario.

MINISTRY OF THE ATTORNEY GENERAL, ONTARIO (COURT SERVICES DIVISION)

Att: Chris Walpole
720 Bay Street, 2nd Floor
Toronto, ON M5G 2K1

Fax 416-326-4299
Website .. www.attorneygeneral.jus.gov.on.ca

Employer Background: The Ministry of the Attorney General is responsible for the administration of justice in Ontario, including criminal proceedings, court services, drafting legislation and representing government bodies in litigation. *New Positions Created (6):* Senior Systems Consultant; Director, Toronto Courts; Manager, Digital Audio Recording; Policy Planning Adviser; Financial and Statistical Officer; Administrative Secretary.

MINISTRY OF THE ATTORNEY GENERAL, ONTARIO (CRIMINAL LAW DIVISION)

Att: Margaret Dwyer, Director, Divisional Planning and Administration
720 Bay Street, 9th Floor
Toronto, ON M5G 2K1

Fax 416-326-2423
Website .. www.attorneygeneral.jus.gov.on.ca

Employer Background: The Ministry of the Attorney General is responsible for the administration of justice in Ontario, including criminal proceedings, court services, drafting legislation and representing government bodies in litigation. *New Positions Created (3):* Manager, Corporate Services ; Manager, Strategic Business and Project Planning; Correspondence and Issues Officer.

MINISTRY OF THE ATTORNEY GENERAL, ONTARIO (CROWN OPERATIONS)

Att: Thomas Fitzgerald,
Director of Crown Operations
159 Cedar Street, Suite 501
Sudbury, ON P3E 6A5

Tel. 705-671-5900
Fax 705-564-7664
Website .. www.attorneygeneral.jus.gov.on.ca

Employer Background: The Ministry of the Attorney General is responsible for the administration of justice in Ontario, including criminal proceedings, court services, drafting legislation and representing government bodies in litigation. *New Positions Created (6):* Assistant Crown Attorney; Provincial Prosecutor; Assistant Crown Attorney; Assistant Crown Attorney; Legal Secretary; Assistant Crown Attorney.

MINISTRY OF THE ATTORNEY GENERAL, ONTARIO (FACILITIES MANAGEMENT SERVICES BRANCH)

Att: Human Resources
720 Bay Street, Ground Floor
Toronto, ON M5G 2K1

Fax 416-326-4029
Website .. www.attorneygeneral.jus.gov.on.ca

Employer Background: The Facilities Management Services Branch provides strategic facilities planning, programs and services to the Attorney General, Solicitor General and Correctional Services. *New Positions Created (2):* Manager, Capital Works; Manager, Leasing Services.

MINISTRY OF THE ATTORNEY GENERAL, ONTARIO (HUMAN RESOURCES BRANCH)

Att: Marla Macdonald, Office Manager
720 Bay Street, 3rd Floor
Toronto, ON M5G 2K1

Fax 416-326-2298
Website .. www.attorneygeneral.jus.gov.on.ca

Employer Background: The Ministry of the Attorney General is responsible for the administration of justice in Ontario, including criminal proceedings, court services, drafting legislation and representing government bodies in litigation. *New Positions Created (4):* Receptionist; Organizational Development Consultant; Executive Services Coordinator; Human Resources Innovations Consultants (2).

MINISTRY OF THE ATTORNEY GENERAL, ONTARIO (OFFICE OF THE PUBLIC GUARDIAN AND TRUSTEE)

Att: Human Resources Unit
595 Bay Street, 8th Floor
Toronto, ON M5G 2M6

Tel. 416-314-2692
Fax 416-314-2698
Website .. www.attorneygeneral.jus.gov.on.ca

Employer Background: The Ministry of the Attorney General is responsible for the administration of justice in Ontario, including criminal proceedings, court services, drafting legislation and representing government bodies in litigation. *New Positions Created (15):* Client Representative Assistants (2); Manager, Administration Services; Senior Trust Accounting Clerk; Trust Analyst; Trust Accounting Manager; Litigation Secretary; Main Office Receptionist; Securities Cash Control Clerk; Securities Officer; Office Estates Analyst; Client Representative; Financial and Tax Planning Analyst; Administrative Assistant; Legal Assistant; Client Representative Assistants.

MINISTRY OF THE ATTORNEY GENERAL, ONTARIO (PEEL CROWN ATTORNEY'S OFFICE)
Att: Human Resources
7755 Hurontario St., 5th Floor, Suite 100
Brampton, ON L6W 4T6
Website .. www.attorneygeneral.jus.gov.on.ca
Employer Background: The Ministry of the Attorney General is responsible for the administration of justice in Ontario, including criminal proceedings, court services, drafting legislation and representing government bodies in litigation. *New Positions Created (3):* Assistant Victim / Witness Coordinator; Legal Administrative Secretary; Legal Receptionist Secretary.

MINISTRY OF THE ATTORNEY GENERAL, ONTARIO (SPECIAL INVESTIGATIONS UNIT)
Att: Trish Waters, Administrative Manager
5090 Commerce Boulevard
Mississauga, ON L4W 5M4
Fax 416-622-2455
Website .. www.attorneygeneral.jus.gov.on.ca
Employer Background: The Ministry of the Attorney General is responsible for the administration of justice in Ontario, including criminal proceedings, court services, drafting legislation and representing government bodies in litigation. *New Positions Created (2):* Receptionist; Communications Manager.

MINISTRY OF THE ATTORNEY GENERAL, ONTARIO (SUPERIOR COURT OF JUSTICE)
Att: Personnel Liaison Officer
361 University Avenue, Room 410
Toronto, ON M5G 1T3
Fax 416-327-5441
Website .. www.attorneygeneral.jus.gov.on.ca
Employer Background: The Ministry of the Attorney General is responsible for the administration of justice in Ontario, including criminal proceedings, court services, drafting legislation and representing government bodies in litigation. *New Positions Created (6):* Secretaries to the Justices; Documents Clerk; Coordinator; Accounting Clerk; Summary Conviction Appeals Clerk; Secretary to the Justices.

MINISTRY OF THE ATTORNEY GENERAL, ONTARIO (VICTIM / WITNESS ASSISTANCE PROGRAM)
Att: Doman Nandalall
720 Bay Street, 9th Floor
Toronto, ON M5G 2K1
Website .. www.attorneygeneral.jus.gov.on.ca
Employer Background: The Ministry of the Attorney General is responsible for the administration of justice in Ontario, including criminal proceedings, court services, drafting legislation and representing government bodies in litigation. *New Positions Created (4):* Managers (4); Administrative Assistant; Assistant Victim / Witness Coordinator; Victim / Witness Support Worker.

MINISTRY OF THE ENVIRONMENT, ONTARIO
Att: Shirley Aussant, Regional Manager, Administrative Services
435 James Street South, Suite 331
Thunder Bay, ON P7E 6S7
Fax 807-475-1754
Email .... resumes@ene.gov.on.ca
Website .... www.ene.gov.on.ca
Employer Background: The Ministry of the Environment is responsible for improving the quality of air, water and waste management in Ontario. *New Positions Created (9):* Senior Environmental Officer; Senior Environmental Officers; Air Monitoring Technician; Regional Programs Officer; Senior Environmental Officers; GIS Officer; Environmental Assessment Coordinator; Administrative / File Clerk; Permit to Take Water Co-ordinator.

MINISTRY OF THE ENVIRONMENT, ONTARIO
Att: Christine Melvin, HR Consultant
40 St. Clair Avenue West, 5th Floor
Toronto, ON M4V 1M2
Fax 416-314-9313
Email .... resumes@ene.gov.on.ca
Website .... www.ene.gov.on.ca
Employer Background: The Ministry of the Environment is responsible for improving the quality of air, water and waste management in Ontario. *New Positions Created (101):* Bilingual SWAT Inspectors (3); Junior Environmental Officer; Manager, Technical Support; Senior Adviser, Science & Technology; SWAT Inspectors (27); Bilingual Receptionist / Office Assistant; Manager, Business Services; Senior Review Engineers, Air (9); Learning and Development Consultants; Air Policy Advisers; District Manager; Manager, Energy Markets; Senior Environmental Officers (2); Financial Business Analyst; Research and Policy Analysts; Team Leader, Energy Pricing & Competitiveness Analysis; Air Issues Policy Adviser; Issues / Project Coordinator; Senior Adviser; Executive Assistant; Issues Project Coordinator; Receptionist / Clerical Assistant; Senior Program Support Coordinators; Supervisor, Air, Pesticides & Environmental Planning; Administrative Coordinator; Director, Licensing; District Administrative Assistant; Issues Project Coordinators; Secretary; Supervisor, Air & Noise; Deputy Energy Returns Officer / Utility Analyst; Economist; Licensing Analyst; Rates Advisers; Senior Communications Adviser; Business Services Managers (2); Issues Management Coordinator; Manager, Business Planning & Improvement; Business Analyst; District Administrative Assistant; Receptionist; Supervisor, Vehicle Emissions Enforcement Unit; Senior Adviser, Awareness and Innovation; Area Supervisor; Divisional Administrator, Permit-To-Take-Water (PTTW) Program; Administrative Assistant; Assistant FOI Coordinator; Drinking Water Specialist; Manager, Drive Clean Facility Operations; Senior Writer; Regional Project Engineer; SWAT Investigations Supervisor; Coordinator, Workforce Planning; Human Resources Consultant; Senior Advisor; Certification Officer; Ecological Standards Development Specialist; Market Surveillance Advisor; Senior Financial Advisor; Site Manager; Engineer Trainee; Organizational Development Assistant; Senior Evaluations Engineer; Senior Green Industry Program Officer; Senior Program Advisor; SWAT Investigations Supervisor; Review Engineer, Environment; Air Emissions Quality Control and Data Analysis Engineers; Manager, Certificate of Approval Review Section; Special Project Engineer, Air; Administrative Manager; Regional Program Coordinators; Special Project Engineer, Multimedia; SWAT Administrative Assistants; Environmental Program Analysts; Regulatory Officers, Energy Licencing (2); Senior Communications Adviser; Bilingual Junior Environmental Officer; Manager, Client Services; Review Engineers, Air and Water; Senior Engineer, Noise; Senior Engineers, Air; Senior Engineers, Water; Supervisor, Water Resources; Bilingual Administrative Clerk Receptionist; Policy Analyst; Air Issues Policy Advisers; Senior Economist; Coordinator, Writing; Human Resources Consultant; District Manager; Policy Adviser; Water and Wastewater Senior Analysts (2); Manager, Pollution Prevention and Education Programs; Assistant Freedom of Information Co-ordinator / Team Leader; Issues and Briefing Officer; Licensing Analyst; Manager, Issues and Media Relations; Senior Policy Analyst; Administrative Clerk / Receptionist.

MINISTRY OF THE ENVIRONMENT, ONTARIO
Att: Human Resources Manager
133 Dalton Avenue, PO Box 820
Kingston, ON K7L 4X6
Email .... resumes@ene.gov.on.ca
Website .... www.ene.gov.on.ca
Employer Background: The Ministry of the Environment is responsible for improving the quality of air, water and waste management in Ontario. *New Positions Created (3):* Junior Environmental Officer; Junior Environmental Officer; District Engineer.

MINISTRY OF THE ENVIRONMENT, ONTARIO (CENTRAL REGION)
Att: Staffing Assistant
5775 Yonge Street, 8th Floor
Toronto, ON M2M 4J1
Tel. 416-326-3450
Fax 416-325-6345
Email .... crresumes@ene.gov.on.ca
Website .... www.ene.gov.on.ca
Employer Background: The Ministry of the Environment is responsible for improving the quality of air, water and waste management in Ontario. *New Positions Created (10):* Senior Environmental Officers; Financial Assistant; Program Support Clerk; Junior Environmental Officers; Regional Program Coordinator; Senior Environmental Officers; Junior Environmental Officer; Hydrogeologists (2); Investigations Intelligence Officer; Pesticides Control Officer.

MINISTRY OF THE ENVIRONMENT, ONTARIO (COMMUNICATIONS BRANCH)
Att: Human Resources
135 St. Clair Avenue West, 2nd Floor
Toronto, ON M4V 1P5

Fax 416-314-6712
Email .... resumes-cb@ene.gov.on.ca
Website .... www.ene.gov.on.ca
Employer Background: The Ministry of the Environment is responsible for improving the quality of air, water and waste management in Ontario. *New Positions Created (3):* Inquiry Officer; Corporate Web Editor; Publications Officer.

MINISTRY OF THE ENVIRONMENT, ONTARIO (DRIVE CLEAN OFFICE)
Att: Human Resources Manager
40 St. Clair Avenue West, 4th Floor
Toronto, ON M4V 1M2

Fax 416-314-4160
Email .... resumes@ene.gov.on.ca
Website .... www.ene.gov.on.ca
Employer Background: The Ministry of the Environment is responsible for improving the quality of air, water and waste management in Ontario. *New Positions Created (4):* Financial Officer; Technical Specialist; Technical Specialist; Administrative Assistants (2).

MINISTRY OF THE ENVIRONMENT, ONTARIO (ENVIRONMENTAL ASSESSMENT AND APPROVALS BRANCH)
Att: Bev Erratt, Supervisor
2 St. Clair Avenue West, 12A Floor
Toronto, ON M4V 1L5

Fax 416-314-7231
Email .... resumes@ene.gov.on.ca
Website .... www.ene.gov.on.ca
Employer Background: The Ministry of the Environment is responsible for improving the quality of air, water and waste management in Ontario. *New Positions Created (2):* IDS Application Support Officer; Support Services Clerk.

MINISTRY OF THE ENVIRONMENT, ONTARIO (ENVIRONMENTAL MONITORING AND REPORTING BRANCH)
Att: Vilma Sandiford
125 Resources Road, 2nd Floor, West Wing
Toronto, ON M9P 3V6

Fax 416-235-6235
Email .... resumes@ene.gov.on.ca
Website .... www.ene.gov.on.ca
Employer Background: The Ministry of the Environment is responsible for improving the quality of air, water and waste management in Ontario. *New Positions Created (5):* Coordinator, Lake Partner Program; Scientist, Inland Lakes; Scientist, Nutrient and Algal Monitoring; Surface Water Specialist, Water Investigations; Database Administrator.

MINISTRY OF THE ENVIRONMENT, ONTARIO (ENVIRONMENTAL PARTNERSHIPS BRANCH)

Att: Administrative Support Officer
40 St. Clair Avenue West, 14th Floor
Toronto, ON M4V 1M2

Fax 416-327-1506
Email .... resumes@ene.gov.on.ca
Website .... www.ene.gov.on.ca
Employer Background: The Ministry of the Environment is responsible for improving the quality of air, water and waste management in Ontario. *New Positions Created (4):* Program Adviser, Air Quality; Financial Officer; Senior Public Education Adviser; Senior Technology Adviser.

MINISTRY OF THE ENVIRONMENT, ONTARIO (INFORMATION MANAGEMENT AND TECHNOLOGY BRANCH)
Att: Information Management and Technology Branch
40 St. Clair Avenue West, 11th Floor
Toronto, ON M4V 1M2

Fax 416-314-4781
Website .... www.ene.gov.on.ca
Employer Background: The Ministry of the Environment is the provincial department responsible for improving the quality of air, water and waste management in Ontario. *New Positions Created (3):* Senior Business Analysts; Manager, Development and Maintenance; Branch Support Officer.

MINISTRY OF THE ENVIRONMENT, ONTARIO (INTEGRATED ENVIRONMENTAL PLANNING DIVISION)
Att: Manager, Divisional Administration and Finance
135 St. Clair Avenue West, 7th Floor
Toronto, ON M4V 1P5

Fax 416-325-4437
Email .... resumes@ene.gov.on.ca
Website .... www.ene.gov.on.ca
Employer Background: The Ministry of the Environment is responsible for improving the quality of air, water and waste management in Ontario. *New Positions Created (3):* Administrative Assistant; Management Support Coordinator; Senior Policy and Programs Officer, Tires.

MINISTRY OF THE ENVIRONMENT, ONTARIO (INVESTIGATIONS AND ENFORCEMENT BRANCH)
Att: Human Resources Assistant
5775 Yonge Street, 8th Floor
Toronto, ON M2M 4J1

Fax 416-326-5256
Email .... resumes@ene.gov.on.ca
Website .... www.ene.gov.on.ca
Employer Background: The Ministry of the Environment is responsible for improving the quality of air, water and waste management in Ontario. *New Positions Created (9):* Investigations Officer; Regional Administrative Assistant; Smog Patrol Officers; SWAT Investigations Intelligence Officer; Branch Programs Officer; Smog Patrol Officers; Investigations Officers; Regional Administrative Assistant; SWAT Investigations Intelligence Officer.

MINISTRY OF THE ENVIRONMENT, ONTARIO (LABORATORY SERVICES BRANCH)
Att: Manager, Administrative Services
125 Resources Road
Toronto, ON M9P 3V6

Email .... resumes@ene.gov.on.ca
Website .... www.ene.gov.on.ca
Employer Background: The Ministry of the Environment is responsible for improving the quality of air, water and waste management in Ontario. *New Positions Created (5):* ICP-MS Scientist; Exceedance Reporting Clerk; Senior Laboratory Scientist, Mass Spectrometry; Shipping and Receiving Clerk / Group Leader; Data Entry, Reporting and Sample Reception Clerk.

MINISTRY OF THE ENVIRONMENT, ONTARIO (LEGAL SERVICES BRANCH)
Att: Director
135 St. Clair Avenue West, 10th Floor
Toronto, ON M4V 1P5

Email .... resumes@ene.gov.on.ca
Website .... www.ene.gov.on.ca
Employer Background: The Ministry of the Environment is responsible for improving air, water and waste management in Ontario. *New Positions Created (2):* Director's Support Coordinator; Legal Counsel (2).

MINISTRY OF THE ENVIRONMENT, ONTARIO (LONDON REGIONAL OFFICE)
Att: Human Resources Manager
659 Exeter Road, 2nd Floor
London, ON N6E 1L3

Email .... resumes@ene.gov.on.ca
Website .... www.ene.gov.on.ca
Employer Background: The Ministry of the Environment is responsible for improving the quality of air, water and waste management in Ontario. *New Positions Created (10):* Senior Environmental Officer; Senior Environmental Officer; Junior Permit-To-Take-Water (PTTW) Coordinator; Hydrogeologist; Pesticides Officer; Junior Environmental Officer; District Administrative Assistants (4); Surface Water Specialist; Senior Environmental Officer; Hydrogeologist.

MINISTRY OF THE ENVIRONMENT, ONTARIO (STANDARD DEVELOPMENT BRANCH)
Att: Manager, Planning and Coordination
40 St. Clair Avenue West, 7th Floor
Toronto, ON M4V 1M2

Fax 416-327-2936
Email .... resumes@ene.gov.on.ca
Website .... www.ene.gov.on.ca
Employer Background: The Ministry of the Environment is responsible for improving the quality of air, water and waste management in Ontario. *New Positions Created (7):* Sr Pesticides Regulatory Scientist; Sr Pesticides Regulatory Toxicologist; Drinking-Water Treatment Engineering Specialist; Regulatory Toxicologists; Senior Air Toxicology Specialist; Senior Regulatory Toxicologist; Watershed Management Specialist.

MINISTRY OF THE ENVIRONMENT, ONTARIO (WEST CENTRAL REGION)
Att: Manager, Business Support Services
119 King Street West, 12th Floor
Hamilton, ON L8P 4Y7

Fax 905-521-7820
Website .... www.ene.gov.on.ca
Employer Background: The Ministry of the Environment is responsible for improving the quality of air, water and waste management in Ontario. *New Positions Created (5):* Senior Environmental Officers; Regional Program Officer; Pesticides Officer; Junior Environmental Officer; District Administrative Assistant.

MINISTRY OF THE SOLICITOR GENERAL, ONTARIO (CENTRE OF FORENSIC SCIENCES)
Att: Helen McKay
25 Grosvenor Street
Toronto, ON M7A 2G8

Fax 416-314-3258
Website .... www.sgcs.gov.on.ca
Employer Background: The Ministry of the Solicitor General is responsible for policing, public safety and victim services in Ontario. *New Positions Created (11):* Forensic Biologists (8); Senior Forensic Scientists, Gaming Machines; Forensic Technologist; Senior Forensic Scientist, Digital Evidence; Section Head, Firearms and Toolmarks; Senior Forensic Scientists, Chemistry (6); Senior Forensic Scientists, Gaming Machines; Training Assistant; Senior Forensic Scientists, Firearms (2); Forensic Technician, Legal Gaming; Forensic Technologists, Biology.

MINISTRY OF THE SOLICITOR GENERAL, ONTARIO (EMERGENCY MEASURES ONTARIO)
Att: Shirley Chen
25 Grosvenor Street, 19th Floor
Toronto, ON M7A 1Y6

Tel. 416-314-3004
Fax 416-314-3758
Website .... www.sgcs.gov.on.ca
Employer Background: The Ministry of the Solicitor General is responsible for policing, public safety and victim services in Ontario. *New Positions Created (2):* Emergency Measures Officers; Emergency Measures Officers (2).

MINISTRY OF THE SOLICITOR GENERAL, ONTARIO (INTEGRATED JUSTICE INFORMATION TECHNOLOGY DIVISION)
Att: Dorothy Ringwald,
Recruitment Specialist
18 King Street East, 18th Floor
Toronto, ON M5C 2X1

Fax 416-326-6987
Email .... it.recruitment@jus.gov.on.ca
Website .... www.sgcs.gov.on.ca
Employer Background: The Ministry of the Solicitor General is responsible for policing, public safety and victim services in Ontario. *New Positions Created (4):* Systems Administration Analysts; Systems / Business Consulting Specialist; Process Improvement and

Evaluation Analyst; Administrator, Video Court Project.

MINISTRY OF THE SOLICITOR GENERAL, ONTARIO (OFFICE OF THE FIRE MARSHAL)
Att: Kathy Paidock
5775 Yonge Street
Toronto, ON M2M 4J1

Fax 416-325-3126
Website .... www.sgcs.gov.on.ca
Employer Background: The Ministry of the Solicitor General is responsible for policing, public safety and victim services in Ontario. *New Positions Created (6):* Program Specialist, Public Education & Media Relations; Manager, Data Applications & Technical Support; Coordinator / Administrative Assistant; Test Bank Operator; Webmaster; Manager, Field Operations.

MINISTRY OF THE SOLICITOR GENERAL, ONTARIO (ONTARIO POLICE COLLEGE)
Att: Rudy Gheysen, Director
32 County Road, PO Box 1190
Aylmer, ON N5H 2T2

Fax 519-773-5762
Website .... www.sgcs.gov.on.ca
Employer Background: The Ontario Police College provides a variety of training programs designed to prepare police officers to perform their duties safely and professionally, while meeting the policing needs of the province. *New Positions Created (7):* Deputy Director, Patrol Training; Supervisor, Facilities Maintenance; Librarian; Food Services Supervisor; Instructors, Research and Evaluation; Instructor, Senior and Special Courses; Registrar.

MINISTRY OF THE SOLICITOR GENERAL, ONTARIO (ONTARIO PROVINCIAL POLICE)
Att: Josephine Fuller,
Director, Human Resources Branch
777 Memorial Avenue
Orillia, ON L3V 7V3

Tel. 705-329-6900
Fax 705-329-6640
Website .... www.sgcs.gov.on.ca
Employer Background: The Ministry of the Solicitor General is responsible for policing, public safety and victim services in Ontario. *New Positions Created (17):* Senior Systems Administrators, PKI; General Mechanic; Forensic Computer Video Analyst; Assistant Deputy Minister; Receptionist; Coding Analyst; Case Coordinators (2); Fire Protection Adviser; GIS Specialists; Program Specialist, Fire Protection Services; Fire Protection Advisers; Fire Investigation Specialist; Staff Relations Officers; Clerk Stenographer; Forensic Analyst; Forensic Scientists, Toxicology (6); Forensic Technicians (3).

MINISTRY OF TOURISM, CULTURE AND RECREATION, ONTARIO
Att: Human Resources Manager
180 Dundas Street West, 8th Floor
Toronto, ON M7A 2R9

Fax 416-314-4494
Website .... www.tourism.gov.on.ca
Employer Background: Created in 1999, the Ministry of Tourism, Culture and Recreation serves Ontario's tourism industry by enhancing job creation and economic growth and promoting Ontario domestically and internationally. *New Positions Created (4):* Office & Grants Administrator; Policy Advisers; Program Consultants; Sr Business Analyst.

MINISTRY OF TOURISM, CULTURE AND RECREATION, ONTARIO
Att: Human Resources Manager
400 University Avenue, 2nd Floor
Toronto, ON M7A 2R9

Fax 416-325-6371
Website .... www.tourism.gov.on.ca
Employer Background: Created in 1999, the Ministry of Tourism, Culture and Recreation serves Ontario's tourism industry by enhancing job creation and economic growth and supporting the promotion of Ontario domestically and internationally. *New Positions Created (8):* Communications Officer; Consultant; Coordinator, Operations & Maintenance; Policy Adviser; Communications Officer (2); Program Consultant; Manager, Product Development and Client Service; Director's Secretary.

MINISTRY OF TOURISM, CULTURE AND RECREATION, ONTARIO (HURONIA HISTORICAL PARKS)
Att: Human Resources Manager
PO Box 160
Midland, ON L4R 4K8

Fax 705-526-9193
Website .... www.tourism.gov.on.ca
Employer Background: Created in 1999, the Ministry of Tourism, Culture and Recreation serves Ontario's tourism industry by enhancing job creation and economic growth and promoting Ontario domestically and internationally. *New Positions Created (3):* Curator; Heritage Programs Coordinator; Operations and Maintenance Coordinator.

MINISTRY OF TRANSPORTATION, BC
Att: Gail MacDonald
940 Blanshard Street
Suite 5A, PO Box 9850, Stn Prov Govt
Victoria, BC V8W 9T5

Tel. 250-387-7826
Fax 250-387-5334
Website .... www.gov.bc.ca/th
Employer Background: The Ministry of Transportation is responsible for planning, developing and maintaining the provincial highway system, including a marine service that operates 18 inland ferry routes. *New Positions Created (3):* Senior Operations Coordinator; Radio & Electronics Technician; Revenue Officer.

MINISTRY OF TRANSPORTATION, BC
Att: Alina Ring
310 Ward Street, 4th Floor
Nelson, BC V1L 5S4

Fax 250-354-6798

Email .... alina.ring@gems8.gov.bc.ca
Website .... www.gov.bc.ca/th

Employer Background: The Ministry of Transportation is responsible for planning, developing and maintaining the provincial highway system, including a marine service that operates 18 inland ferry routes. *New Positions Created (5):* Marine Engineer; Head Ferry Person; Marine Engineers (2); Bridge Rehabilitation Engineer; Highway Design Engineer.

MINISTRY OF TRANSPORTATION, ONTARIO
Att: Human Resources Manager
615 South James Street
Thunder Bay, ON P7E 6P6
Fax 807-577-0730
Email .... mtojobs-wr@mto.gov.on.ca
Website .... www.mto.gov.on.ca

Employer Background: The Ministry of Transportation is responsible for the construction, maintenance and safety of transportation facilities in Ontario. *New Positions Created (23):* Human Resources Administrative Clerk; Plan / Document Services Technician; Senior Municipal Foreperson; Patrol Maintenance Technician; Transportation Enforcement Officers (4); Financial Analyst; Traffic Field Technician; Systems Network & Security Analyst; Geomatics Plan Technician; Senior Technician, Surveys; Patrol Maintenance Technician; Special Projects Supervisor; Enforcement Services Clerk; Quality Assurance Officer; Foreperson; Aggregates Resource Information Officer; Airport Zone Operator; Assistant Airport Foreman; Warehousing Clerk; Senior Designers (4); Real Estate Officer; Corridor Management Officer; Systems Network and Security Analyst.

MINISTRY OF TRANSPORTATION, ONTARIO
Att: Human Resources
447 McKeown Avenue, Suite 301
North Bay, ON P1B 9S9
Tel. 705-472-7900
Fax 705-497-5531
Email .... mtojobs-nr@mto.gov.on.ca
Website .... www.mto.gov.on.ca

Employer Background: The Ministry of Transportation is responsible for the construction, maintenance and safety of transportation facilities in Ontario. *New Positions Created (20):* Occupational Health and Safety Adviser; Senior Construction Administration Technician; Secretary; Project Soils Engineer; Senior Technician, Survey; Aggregate Resources Information Officer; Head, Quality Assurance; Area Construction Engineer; Geomatics Plan Technician; Head, Construction Administration; Area Engineers (2); Senior Project Engineers; Structural Engineers (2); Secretaries / Clerks; Senior Structural Engineer; Regional Construction Claims Analyst; Geomatics Plan Technicians (2); Project Surveyor; Area Traffic Analysts (2); Area Engineers (2).

MINISTRY OF TRANSPORTATION, ONTARIO
Att: District Engineer
500 Rockley Road, PO Box 1390
New Liskeard, ON P0J 1P0
Email .... mtojobs-nr@mto.gov.on.ca
Website .... www.mto.gov.on.ca

Employer Background: The Ministry of Transportation is responsible for the construction, maintenance and safety of transportation facilities in Ontario. *New Positions Created (8):* Special Project Foreperson; Bridge Crew Foreperson; Bridge Repairer; Municipal Day-Labour Foreperson; Patrol Maintenance Technicians (2); Services Coordinator; Patrol Maintenance Technician; District Engineering Services Supervisor.

MINISTRY OF TRANSPORTATION, ONTARIO
Att: Human Resources Manager
659 Exeter Road
London, ON N6E 1L3
Email .... mtojobs-sr@mto.gov.on.ca
Website .... www.mto.gov.on.ca

Employer Background: The Ministry of Transportation is responsible for the construction, maintenance and safety of transportation facilities in Ontario. *New Positions Created (24):* Maintenance Superintendent; District Engineering Services Officer; Financial Analyst; Senior Network / Client Support Analyst; Traffic Analysts; Transportation Enforcement Officer; Radio Operators; Intermediate Designers; Senior Construction Administration Technician; Transportation Enforcement Officer; Senior Technicians, Surveys (4); Engineering Services Officer; Environmental Planners; Regional Operations Officer; Structural Engineers (4); Geomatics Plan Technicians; Transportation Enforcement Officer; Driver Examiners (2); Head, Financial Services; Inside Examiners (8); Patrol Maintenance Workers (2); Zone Striper Operator; Intermediate Designers (6); Senior Title Processor.

MINISTRY OF TRANSPORTATION, ONTARIO
Att: Human Resource Services Section
1201 Wilson Avenue
1st Floor, Building D, Atrium Tower
Toronto, ON M3M 1J8
Tel. 416-235-5378
Fax 416-235-5287
Email .... mtojobs-ds@mto.gov.on.ca
Website .... www.mto.gov.on.ca

Employer Background: The Ministry of Transportation is responsible for the construction, maintenance and safety of transportation facilities in Ontario. *New Positions Created (42):* Business Analysts; Chemist; Senior Business Analyst; Transportation Enforcement Officer; Administrative Officer; Head, Provincial Sign Shop; Project Assistant; Communications Assistant; Administrative Officer; Communications Coordinators (3); Web Assistant; Senior Technical Consultant; Technical Consultant; Secretaries (2); Head, Highway Services; Senior Safety Research Advisor; Superintendent; Client Services Manager; Customer Service Agents; Sign Maker Improvers; Office Administration Assistant; Writers; Senior Safety Policy Advisers; Quality Assurance Supervisor; Senior Project Engineers; Electrical Project Managers; Inside Examiners; Project Design Engineer; Team Leaders (2); Issues Advisor; Maintenance Operations Planning Engineer; Office Administrative Assistant; Systems Integration Manager; Senior Planner; Drainage Engineer; Client Services Manager; GTA Infrastructure Project Manager; Consultant Acquisition Officers; General Issuing Clerk; Policy and Procedures Writer; Driver Program Administration Clerk; Network Analyst.

MINISTRY OF TRANSPORTATION, ONTARIO
Att: Human Resources Branch
301 St. Paul Street, 5th Floor
St. Catharines, ON L2R 7R4
Tel. 905-704-2000
Fax 905-704-2590
Email .... mtojobs-st@mto.gov.on.ca
Website .... www.mto.gov.on.ca

Employer Background: The Ministry of Transportation is responsible for the construction, maintenance and safety of transportation facilities in Ontario. *New Positions Created (42):* Business Consultant; Senior Evaluation & Inspection Engineer; Senior Technology Consultant; Manager, Customer Information Services; Senior Financial Analyst; Technical / Business Consultant; Database Analyst; Senior Database Analyst; Director, Facilities & Operation Services; Manager, Passenger Policy Office; Director, Carrier Safety and Enforcement Branch; Manager, Best Practices and Service Improvement; Manager, Over-the-Counter Strategy; Branch Administrative Coordinator; Financial Program Analysts; Web Communications Officer; Manager, Traffic Office; Remote Sensing Specialist; Senior Technology Consultant; Facilities Planning Adviser; Senior Design Technician; Coordinator, Municipal Operations and Procedures; Senior Capital Needs Planner; Business Effectiveness Consultant; Claims Analyst; Senior Inventory Planner; Manager, Engineering; Transportation Analyst; Project Engineers, Development (6); Engineer, Safety Design; Estimating Officers; Quality Assurance Supervisor; Secretary; Senior Policy Analyst; Application Planning and Project Coordination Manager; Application Services and Support Manager; Team Leader, Business Planning; Imaging Operator; Systems Analysts / Programmers; Systems Analysts / Programmers (3); Senior Engineering Drafter; IT Quality Assurance Supervisor.

MINISTRY OF TRANSPORTATION, ONTARIO
Att: Human Resources Office
355 Counter Street, PO Bag 4000
Kingston, ON K7L 5A3
Fax 613-545-4848
Website .... www.mto.gov.on.ca

Employer Background: The Ministry of Transportation is responsible for the construction, maintenance and safety of transportation facilities in Ontario. *New Positions Created (14):* Area Equipment Coordinator; Transportation Enforcement Officer; Geomatics Plan Technicians; Structural Engineer; Structural Drafter; Maintenance Superintendents; Intermediate Designer; Senior Title Processor; Transportation Enforcement Officer; Environmental Planner; Senior Designers (2); Patrol Maintenance Technicians (8); Geomatics Plan Technician; Technical Support Analyst.

MINISTRY OF TRANSPORTATION, ONTARIO (DRIVER EXAMINATIONS BRANCH)
Att: Human Resources Manager
1201 Wilson Ave., Room 128, Building C
Toronto, ON M3M 1J8
Fax 416-235-4220
Email .... mtojobs-ds@mto.gov.on.ca
Website .... www.mto.gov.on.ca
Employer Background: The Ministry of Transportation is responsible for the construction, maintenance and safety of transportation facilities in Ontario. *New Positions Created (3):* Driver Examiners (18); Inside Examiners (16); Inside Examiners (14).

MINISTRY OF WATER, LAND AND AIR PROTECTION, BC
Att: Jean van Stigt
2975 Jutland Road, 2nd Floor
PO Box 9345, Stn Prov Govt
Victoria, BC V8W 9M1
Tel. 250-387-9805
Fax 250-356-7286
Website .... www.gov.bc.ca/wlap
Employer Background: The Ministry of Water, Land and Air Protection is the provincial department responsible for protecting and improving the quality of the environment in British Columbia. *New Positions Created (48):* Crown Grant Technician; Production Support Engineer; Senior Policy Adviser; District Resource Officer; Head, Stewardship Initiatives; Information / Administration Clerk; Area Supervisor; Climate Change Economist; Division Services Officer; Area Supervisor; Fisheries Biologist; Head Officer, Assets, Trusts & Special Accounts; Manager, Financial Systems; District Planning Officer; Senior Science Officer; Site Technical Specialists (2); Planning Officer; Pollution Prevention Officer; Section Head, Fisheries Management; Air Quality Analyst; Climate Change Issues Analyst; District Clerk; District Resource Officer; Pollution Prevention Officer; Senior Air Quality Analyst; Senior Science Advisor; Planning Officer; Pollution Prevention Officer; Site Data Technician; Education Assistant; Forest Ecosystem Specialist; Fisheries Stock Assessment Biologist; Senior Advisor, Transportation Issues; Head, Environmental Impact Section; Forest Renewal Section Head; Pollution Prevention Officer; Fisheries Specialist; Air Resources Officer; Planning Assistant; Conservation Officers; Director, Parks Division Services; Forest Renewal Project Coordinator; Human Resources Coordinator; Spatial Data Analysts (2); Geographic Information Systems Coordinator; Geo-

graphic Information Systems Coordinator; Deputy Director; Habitat Protection Officer.

MINOLTA BUSINESS EQUIPMENT (CANADA), LTD.
Att: Human Resources Department
21500 Westminster Highway
Richmond, BC V6V 2V1
Tel. 604-276-1611
Fax 604-276-1612
Email .... hrvancouver@minolta.ca
Website .... www.minolta.ca
Employer Background: Minolta Business Equipment (Canada) Ltd. sells and services business equipment, including photocopiers, facsimile machines and printers. *New Positions Created (9):* Sales Representatives; Software Sales Representative; Digital Imaging / Graphic Specialist; Sales Professionals; Service Technician; Collections Clerk; Customer Service Clerk; Receptionist; Service Technician.

MINOLTA BUSINESS EQUIPMENT (CANADA), LTD.
Att: Human Resources Manager
9651 - 25th Avenue
Edmonton, AB T6N 1H7
Tel. 780-465-6232
Fax 780-465-6225
Email .... edmonton@minolta.ca
Website .... www.minolta.ca
Employer Background: Minolta Business Equipment (Canada) Ltd. sells and services business equipment, including photocopiers, facsimile machines and printers. *New Positions Created (10):* Territory Sales Representative; Business Product Team Sales Representative; Inside Sales Representatives; Peripheral Products Team Sales Representative; Business Product Team Representative; Mailing Systems Team Sales Representatives; Peripheral Products Team Sales Representative; Business Product Team Sales Representative; Inside Sales Representatives; Peripheral Products Team Sales Representative.

MINOLTA BUSINESS EQUIPMENT (CANADA) LTD.
Att: Corporate Manager of HR
369 Britannia Road East
Mississauga, ON L4Z 2H5
Tel. 905-890-6600
Fax 905-890-2339
Email .... careers@minolta.ca
Website .... www.minolta.ca
Employer Background: Minolta Business Equipment (Canada) Ltd. sells and services business equipment, including photocopiers, fax machines and printers. *New Positions Created (2):* Intermediate Accountant; Accounting Training & Support Specialist.

MINOLTA BUSINESS EQUIPMENT (CANADA), LTD.
Att: Tamara Der-Ohanian, CHRM
50 Valleywood Drive, Unit 2
Markham, ON L3R 6E9
Tel. 905-470-2679
Fax 905-470-9213

Email .... tderohanian@minolta.ca
Website .... www.minolta.ca
Employer Background: Minolta Business Equipment (Canada) Ltd. sells and services business equipment, including photocopiers, facsimile machines and printers. *New Positions Created (5):* Commercial Sales Representatives; Digital & Colour Specialists; Fax / Printer Service Technicians; Major Accounts Representatives; MicroPress Account Representative.

MINOLTA BUSINESS EQUIPMENT (CANADA), LTD.
Att: Lee Boville, Inside Sales Manager
1900 City Park Drive, Suite 100
Gloucester, ON K1J 1A3
Tel. 613-749-5588
Fax 613-749-0050
Email .... lboville@minolta.ca
Website .... www.minolta.ca
Employer Background: Minolta Business Equipment (Canada) Ltd. sells and services business equipment, including photocopiers, facsimile machines and printers. *New Positions Created (8):* Associate Account Representatives, Commercial Sales (3); Inside Sales Telemarketing Representative; Sales Coordinator; Colour / Digital Specialist; Administrative Assistant; Inside Sales Telemarketing Representative; Senior Account Representatives (2); Senior Account Representatives (2).

MINOLTA (MONTREAL) INC.
Att: Human Resources Department
2705 Pitfield Boulevard
St-Laurent, QC H4S 1T2
Tel. 514-335-2157
Fax 514-335-2389
Email .... montreal@minolta.ca
Website .... www.minolta.ca
Employer Background: Minolta (Montreal) Inc., part of Japan-based Minolta Co., sells and services business equipment, including photocopiers, facsimile machines and printers. *New Positions Created (5):* Sales Positions; Chief Accountant (CGA); Junior Customer Service Representative; Junior Invoicing Clerk; Sales Professionals.

MINTO COUNSELLING CENTRE
Att: Micheline Gagon, Executive Director
PO Box 2298
Cochrane, ON P0L 1C0
Tel. 705-272-4245
Fax 705-272-6737
Employer Background: Minto Counselling Centre is a community mental health agency, assisting adult clients with acute or severe and persistent mental health issues. *New Positions Created (2):* Aboriginal Services Worker; Community Support Program Worker.

MINTO PLACE SUITE HOTEL
Att: Charles B. Nadeau, General Manager
433 Laurier Avenue West
Ottawa, ON K1R 7Y1
Tel. 613-782-2350

Fax 613-232-6962
Email .... cnadeau@minto.com
Website .... www.minto.com/hotel
Employer Background: Located in downtown Ottawa, the Minto Place Suite Hotel is a large facility, catering to business travellers. *New Positions Created (3):* Human Resources Manager; Hotel Sales Manager; Director, Marketing and Sales.

MIRIAM HOME AND SERVICES
Att: Human Resources Department
4321 Gulmont
Laval, QC H7W 1E7

Tel. 450-681-9256
Fax 450-681-8394
Email .... mdigiaco@ssss.gouv.qc.ca
Employer Background: Miriam Home and Services is a readaptation centre for intellectually handicapped persons. *New Positions Created (2):* Beneficiary Attendants; Educators.

MISCO CANADA INC.
Att: Human Resources
171 Esna Park Drive
Markham, ON L3R 4J1

Fax 905-477-6615
Email .... hr@miscocanada.com
Website .... www.miscocanada.com
Employer Background: Misco Canada Inc. is a leader in business-to-business catalogue marketing of computer supplies and accessories. *New Positions Created (4):* Corporate Sales Representative; Account Manager, Catalogue Marketing; Corporate Sales Representatives; Technical Support Specialist.

MISSION, DISTRICT OF
Att: Human Resources Officer
8645 Stave Lake Street, PO Box 20
Mission, BC V2V 4L9

Tel. 604-820-3700
Fax 604-826-1363
Email .... fran_berube@city.mission.bc.ca
Website .... www.city.mission.bc.ca
Employer Background: Located in the Fraser Valley, the District of Mission is a municipality of 32,500 people. *New Positions Created (2):* Manager of Facilities; Deputy Treasurer / Collector.

MISSION SERVICES OF HAMILTON
Att: Human Resources
50 Murray Street West, PO Box 368
Hamilton, ON L8L 7W2

Tel. 905-528-4211
Fax 905-521-0748
Website .... www.mission-services.org
Employer Background: Mission Services of Hamilton is a Christian charity, serving disadvantaged people. *New Positions Created (10):* Coordinator of Volunteer Development; Assistant Instructor, Food Services; Placement Coordinator; Director of Development; Administrative Assistant; Community Outreach Worker; Women's Group Facilitator; Program Manager; Group Facilitator, Children and Youth; Maintenance Supervisor.

MISSISSAUGA, CITY OF
Att: Human Resources Division
300 City Centre Drive, 5th Floor
Mississauga, ON L5B 3C1

Tel. 905-896-5000
Fax 905-615-4185
Email .... hr.info@city.mississauga.on.ca
Website .... www.city.mississauga.on.ca
Employer Background: The City of Mississauga provides municipal government services to residents and businesses in Canada's sixth-largest city. *New Positions Created (63):* GIS Analyst; Landscape Architect; Community Child and Youth Consultant; Concessions Coordinator; Business Analyst, Information Technology; Manager, Transit Business Development; Senior Buyer; Skilled Tradespersons, HVAC / Plumbing (2); Supervisor, Arts; Prosecutor; Public Affairs Specialist; Taxicab Driver Training Instructor; Fire Prevention Inspectors; Human Resources Consultant; Manager, Collections; Recruitment and Staffing Consultant; GIS / CADD Technician; Bus Mechanic; Client Account Manager; Project Leader, Community Services Applications Support; Project Leader, Enterprise Applications (GIS); Project Leader, Major Projects; Project Leader, Transportation & Works Application Support; Bilingual Customer Service Clerk; Financial Analyst, Capital Budget; Financial Analyst, Financial Services; Manager of Business Planning; Senior Tax Accountant; Tax Collection Coordinator; Concession Coordinator; Building Inspector; Building Plan Examiner; Traffic Operations Technicians (2); Traffic Planning Technicians (2); Traffic Signals Technicians (3); Traffic Signals Technologist; Zoning Plan Examiner; Management Consultant; Planner, Planning and Building; Human Resources Consultant; Prosecutor; Communications Operator, Fire and Emergency Services; Recreation Programmers (2); Senior Financial Analyst; Preventive Maintenance Coordinator; Building Inspector; HVAC Plan Examiner; Plumbing Plan Examiner; Security Officer; Manager of Collections, Office of the City Solicitor; Systems Specialists (3); Webmaster; Development Planners, Planning and Building Department (2); Parks Team Leader; Roadway Programming Technician; Building Inspector; Landscape Architect; Manager, Forestry; Senior Legal Counsel; LRIS Technician; Administrative Officer, Fire and Emergency Services; Prosecutor; Landscape Architect.

MISTAHIA HEALTH REGION
Att: Human Resources
10320 - 99th Street
2nd Floor, Provincial Building
Grande Prairie, AB T8V 6J4

Tel. 780-538-6167
Fax 780-538-6156
Email .... jobs@mhr.ab.ca
Website .... www.mhr.ab.ca
Employer Background: Mistahia Health Region provides health services for 85,000 residents living in Alberta. *New Positions Created (41):* Health Information Consultant; Diabetes Nurse Educator; Pharmacist; Medical Officer of Health; Occupational Therapist; Biomedical Equipment Technologist; Expanded Role Nurse; Instrument Mechanic; Public Health / Home Care Nurse; Site Manager; Licensed Practical Nurse; Maintenance Worker II; Occupational Therapists (2); Physiotherapist; Speech Language Pathologist; Staff Nurses, Acute Care (3); Logistics Manager; Physiotherapists (3); Regional Services Occupational Therapist; Various Health Positions; Nurses; Site Manager; Accounts Analyst; Financial Consultant; Instrument Mechanic; Maintenance Worker II; Occupational Therapists; Pharmacist; Physiotherapist; Public Health Nurse; Site Mgr; Social Worker; Speech Language Pathologist; Staff Nurses, General Float (5); Unit Mgr, Labour & Delivery / Special Care Nursery/Post-Partum/Gynecology; Unit Manager, Pediatrics; Healthcare Positions; Rural Maintenance Manager; Social Worker, Psychiatric Unit; Financial Consultant; Occupational Health Nurse.

MITCHELL & ASSOCIATES CONSULTING ENGINEERING INC.
Att: Human Resources Manager
3455 Harvester Road, Unit 20
Burlington, ON L7N 3P2

Fax 905-631-0444
Email .... genmail@mitchellassoc.com
Employer Background: Mitchell & Associates Consulting Engineering Inc. specializes in project development, project management, process and packaging design and environmental consulting engineering for the consumer product manufacturing industry. *New Positions Created (3):* Design Manager / Senior Designer; Electrical Engineer / Technologist; Mechanical Engineer.

MITCHELL PLASTICS LTD.
Att: Human Resources Manager
100 Washburn Drive
Kitchener, ON N2G 3W5

Fax 519-893-6292
Email . michele.m@mitchellplastics.on.ca
Employer Background: Mitchell Plastics Ltd. manufactures injection molded plastic parts for major automotive and business machine customers. *New Positions Created (3):* Injection Moulding Team Leader; Logistics Manager; Tool Engineer / Program Manager.

MITCHELL'S GOURMET FOODS INC.
Att: Human Resources
3003 - 11th Street West, PO Box 850
Saskatoon, SK S7K 3V4

Tel. 306-382-2210
Fax 306-931-4296
Website .... www.mgf.ca
Employer Background: Mitchell's Gourmet Foods Inc. (formerly Intercontinental Packers Ltd.) is a leading value-added pork processor, with over 1,000 employees. *New Positions Created (2):* Industrial Engineer / Technologist; Mechanical Foreman.

MITEC TELECOM INC.
Att: Human Resources Department
9000 Trans Canada Highway
Pointe-Claire, QC H9R 5Z8

Tel. 514-694-9000
Fax 514-630-8600
Email .. opportunities@mitectelecom.com
Website .... www.mitectelecom.com
Employer Background: Mitec Telecom Inc. designs and manufactures wireless, microwave and satellite communication products. *New Positions Created (19):* Assembler 1; Assembler 2; Manufacturing Test Technician 1; Manufacturing Test Technician II; Manufacturing Tester I; Manufacturing Tester II; Buyer; Documentation Specialist; Master Planner; Purchasing Manager; Receptionist; Test Engineer; Bilingual Administrative Assistant; Assistant Controller; Project Manager; R&D Test Manager; RF Design Engineers, Active and Passive (2); Sales Representative; Marketing Specialist.

MITEL CORPORATION
Att: Human Resources Manager
350 Legget Drive, PO Box 13089
Kanata, ON K2K 2W7
Tel. 613-592-2122
Fax 613-592-4784
Website .... www.mitel.com
Employer Background: Mitel Corporation is an international designer, manufacturer and marketer of semiconductors, subsystems and systems for the communication industries. *New Positions Created (2):* Manufacturing Technologist; Test Developer.

MITRA IMAGING INC.
Att: Human Resources
455 Phillip Street
Waterloo, ON N2L 3X2
Tel. 519-746-2900
Fax 519-746-3745
Email .... hr@mitra.com
Website .... www.mitra.com
Employer Background: Mitra Imaging Inc. develops leading-edge technology that allows hospitals to capture and display medical images throughout their facilities over high-speed networks. *New Positions Created (39):* Marketing Project Mgr; Product Mgr; Software Verification Specialist, Server; Account Mgr; Field Applications Specialist; Object-Oriented Developers; Regulatory Specialist; Client Services Coordinator; Clinical Mgr; Database Component Developers; Helpdesk Coordinator; Junior Accountant; Product Curriculum Training Writer; Software Verification Specialist, Connectivity; Systems Engineer / Analyst; Software Development Team Leaders; Software Verification Specialist; Business Analyst; Client Services Coordinator; Product Mgr; Software Configuration Management Specialist; Unix Systems Administrator; Field Applications Specialist; Image Server Developers; Object-Oriented Developers; Development Team Leaders; Product Template Design & Architecture Team Leader; Product Training Curriculum Writer; Software Verification Specialist; Technical Writer; Business Analyst; Employee Development Specialist; Field Application Specialist; Image Archive Developer; Image Server Developer; Object-Oriented Developer; Product Mgr; Project Mgr; Systems Administrator.

MITSUBISHI CANADA LTD.
Att: Human Resources
200 Granville Street, Suite 2800
Vancouver, BC V6C 1G6
Fax 604-654-8229
Website .... www.micusa.com
Employer Background: Mitsubishi Canada Ltd. is a subsidiary of Japan's Mitsubishi Corporation, one of the world's premier global trading and investment companies. *New Positions Created (4):* Office Mgr; Sales & Marketing Pro; Marketing Mgr; HR Mgr.

MKS INC.
Att: Human Resources
410 Albert Street
Waterloo, ON N2L 3V3
Tel. 519-884-2251
Fax 519-884-8861
Email .... jobs@mks.com
Website .... www.mks.com
Employer Background: Founded in 1984, MKS Inc. develops and markets software to assist programmers in the creation of traditional and web-based software and in the management of the development process. *New Positions Created (12):* Account Manager; Marketing Communications Specialist; Pre-sales System Engineer; Product Implementation Specialist; Sr Consultant, Consulting Services; Software Developer; Software Quality Analyst; Solutions Mgr, Software Solutions; Telequalifier; Applications Support Specialist; Applications Systems Administrator; Technical Writer.

MMMUFFINS CANADA CORP.
Att: Tricia Greco, Director of HR
3300 Bloor Street West, Suite 2900
Toronto, ON M8X 2X3
Tel. 416-236-0055
Fax 416-236-0054
Website .... www.mmmuffins.com
Employer Background: Mmmuffins is one of the most well-known retail bakery concepts in North America, with over 100 locations. *New Positions Created (3):* Sr Accountant; Administrative Assistant; Receptionist.

MOBILE DATA SOLUTIONS INC.
Att: Human Resources Manager
10271 Shellbridge Way
Richmond, BC V6X 2W8
Tel. 604-270-9939
Fax 604-207-6060
Email .... jobs@mdsi.bc.ca
Website .... www.mdsi-advantex.com
Employer Background: MDSI provides mobile workforce management and enterprise-wide mobile connectivity solutions for the utility, telecom, cable, field service, insurance and government sectors. *New Positions Created (3):* Purchasing Coordinator; Project Engineer; Technical Leader.

MOBILIA INC.
Att: Eric Bushell, General Manager
1425 Dundas Street East
Mississauga, ON L4X 2W4
Tel. 905-625-9106

Fax 905-625-6129
Employer Background: Mobilia Inc. is a large, multi-unit retailer of contemporary furniture. *New Positions Created (5):* Store Manager; Sales Associate; Assistant Store Manager; Store Manager; Store Manager.

MOBILIA INC.
Att: Pierre
2525 Boulevard des Sources
Pointe-Claire, QC H9R 5Z9
Tel. 514-685-7557
Fax 514-685-0057
Email .... pierre@mobilia.ca
Employer Background: Mobilia Inc. is a large, multiunit retailer of contemporary furniture. *New Positions Created (18):* Director of Warehousing; Junior Secretary; Order Processing Clerk; Receptionist; General Sales Manager; Sales Consultants; Store Manager; Payroll Clerk; Information Systems Manager; Senior Accounts Payable Clerk; Junior Office Clerk; Sales Consultants; Accounts Payable Clerk; Office Manager; Accounting Clerk; Driver / Installer; Secretary; Order Entry / Price List Coordinator.

MOBILIFT
Att: Vice-President, Marketing and Sales
533 - 71st Avenue SE
Calgary, AB T2H 2Y2
Tel. 403-571-7633
Fax 403-571-7639
Email .... fallprevention@mobilift.com
Website .... www.mobilift.com
Employer Background: Mobilift Inc. is a Calgary-based manufacturer of technology for fall prevention in the rail, transit, aviation and manufacturing markets. *New Positions Created (2):* Product Manager; Regional Sales Manager.

MODATEK SYSTEMS
Att: Human Resources Manager
1 Cosma Court
St. Thomas, ON N5P 4J5
Email ... employment@modateksystems.com
Website .... www.magnaint.com
Employer Background: Modatek is a start-up division of Magna International, a supplier of automotive systems and components. *New Positions Created (5):* Buyers; Department Leaders, Assembly / Manufacturing; Electronic Technicians, Electrical / Controls / Mechanical; Junior Process / Industrial Engineers; Quality Engineers.

MODERN NIAGARA OTTAWA INC.
Att: Tom Hughson,
Technical Services Manager
85 Denzil Doyle Court
Kanata, ON K2M 2G8
Tel. 613-591-7505
Fax 613-591-1523
Email .... resumes@modernniagara.com
Website .... www.modernniagara.com
Employer Background: Modern Niagara Ottawa Inc. (formerly Modern Mechanical Inc.) is a mechanical contracting firm in eastern Ontario. *New Positions Created (4):*

Intermediate Piping / HVAC CAD Technician; Payroll Clerk; Reception / Data Entry Clerk; Junior Project Manager.

MOHAWK COLLEGE OF APPLIED ARTS AND TECHNOLOGY
Att: Human Resources Division
PO Box 2034
Hamilton, ON L8N 3T2

Tel. 905-575-1212
Fax 905-575-2353
Email .... recruit@mail.mohawkc.on.ca
Website .... www.mohawkc.on.ca

Employer Background: Founded in 1947, Mohawk College of Applied Arts and Technology offers diploma programs at six campuses to 7,700 students. *New Positions Created (3):* Chair, Department of Mechanical and Industrial Engineering Technology; Professors, Computer Science and Information Technology; Professor, Computer Engineering and Electronics.

MOLD-MASTERS LTD.
Att: Human Resources
233 Armstrong Avenue
Georgetown, ON L7G 4X5

Tel. 905-877-0185
Fax 905-877-3582
Website .... www.moldmasters.com

Employer Background: Mold-Masters Ltd. is a leader in hot runner technology for the plastics injection molding industry. *New Positions Created (3):* Payroll Administrator; Materials Mgr; Multimedia Coordinator.

MOLECULAR MINING CORPORATION
Att: Human Resources Manager
128 Ontario Street
Kingston, ON K7L 2Y4

Tel. 613-547-9752
Fax 613-547-6835
Website .... www.molecularmining.com

Employer Background: Molecular Mining Corporation is a software company, specializing in the global genomics data mining market. *New Positions Created (6):* Director, Software Development; Software Developers; Quality Assurance Specialist; Software Developers; Statistician / Biostatistician; Technical Writers.

MOMENTOUS.CA CORPORATION
Att: Human Resources Manager
68 Robertson Road, Suite 160
Nepean, ON K2H 8P5

Tel. 613-768-5100
Fax 613-820-0777
Email .... careers@momentous.ca
Website .... www.momentous.ca

Employer Background: Momentous.ca Corporation facilitates the growth of e-business. *New Positions Created (3):* Chief Financial Officer; Public Relations Specialist; Senior Programmers.

MONARCH CONSTRUCTION LTD.
Att: Human Resources
2025 Sheppard Avenue East, Suite 1201
Toronto, ON M2J 1V7

Tel. 416-491-7440
Fax 416-642-0115
Email .... humanresources@
.... monarchgroup.net
Website .... www.monarchgroup.net

Employer Background: Founded in 1917, Monarch Construction Ltd. is a diversified real estate company, specializing in new home construction and residential land development in Ontario. *New Positions Created (8):* Condominium Property Mgr; Production Assistant; Production Coordinator; Condominium Building Administrator; Junior / Intermediate Computer Technician; Director of Land Acquisitions; Junior / Intermediate Technician; Accounts Payable Clerk.

MONDETTA CLOTHING CO.
Att: Human Resources Manager
1109 Winnipeg Avenue
Winnipeg, MB R3E 0S2

Fax 204-786-1840
Email .... jobs@mondetta.com
Website .... www.mondetta.com

Employer Background: Established in 1986, Mondetta develops, designs, subcontracts and imports a wide variety of fashion apparels and accessories. *New Positions Created (2):* Corporate Sales & Marketing Reps; Corporate Sales & Marketing Rep.

MONDIAL ELECTRONICS INC.
Att: Sam Dell'Aquila
960 Begin
St-Laurent, QC H4M 2N5

Tel. 514-956-0056
Fax 514-956-0156
Email .... sam@mondialelectronics.com
Website ..... www.mondialelectronics.com

Employer Background: Mondial Electronics Inc. is one of Canada's leading independent distributors of electronic components. *New Positions Created (2):* Inside Sales Professionals; Salespeople (2).

MONEY'S MUSHROOMS LTD.
Att: Human Resources
7345 Guelph LIne, PO Box 190
Campbellville, ON L0P 1B0

Fax 905-878-7897
Website .... www.moneys.com

Employer Background: Money's Mushrooms Ltd. markets and distributes mushrooms. *New Positions Created (2):* DZ Delivery Drivers; Shipper / Receiver.

MONIT MANAGEMENT LTD.
Att: Human Resources Manager
2155 Guy Street, Suite 1400
Montréal, QC H3H 2R9

Tel. 514-933-3000
Fax 514-939-0334

Employer Background: Monit Management Ltd. is a major commercial property management firm. *New Positions Created (3):* Assistant Accountant; Payroll Clerk; Property Manager.

MONTAGE.DMC EBUSINESS SERVICES
Att: Recruiter
10130 - 103rd Street, Suite 1900
Edmonton, AB T5J 3N9

Tel. 780-423-4553
Fax 780-423-7088
Email .... hr@montage.ca
Website .... www.montage.ca

Employer Background: Montage.dmc eBusiness Services (formerly Montage eIntegration Inc.) is one of Canada's fastest-growing e-business solutions providers, with a focus on e-integration services. *New Positions Created (17):* E-Commerce Project Manager; Information Security Analyst; Java Developers; Oracle Financials Functional Analysts; Oracle Financials Functional Team Leaders; Oracle Financials Technical Consultants; Senior OO / Java Architect; Information Security Analyst; Intermediate / Senior Oracle Financials Technical Consultants; Oracle Financials Functional Analyst; Oracle Financials Functional Team Lead and Manager; Senior Business Development Manager; Senior OO / Java Architect; Business Object Consultant; ETL / Data Mart Consultant; E-Commerce Project Manager; Java Developers.

MONTAGE.DMC EBUSINESS SERVICES
Att: Human Resources Manager
708 - 11th Avenue SW, Suite 350
Calgary, AB T2R 0E4

Tel. 403-303-2000
Fax 403-265-4462
Email .... hr@montage.ca
Website .... www.montage.ca

Employer Background: Montage.dmc eBusiness Services (formerly Montage eIntegration Inc.) is one of Canada's fastest-growing e-business solutions providers, with a focus on e-integration services. *New Positions Created (25):* Java Developers; Senior Java Developers; Senior OO / Java Architect; Intermediate Web Developers; OO Project Manager; Oracle Application Specialists (5); Oracle Developers; Senior Integration Architect; Senior OO Developer; Senior Oracle Analyst; Senior Oracle Developer; Senior Project Management Office (PMO) Leader; Senior Project Manager; Senior Java Developers; Senior Integration Architect; Senior Project Management Office (PMO) Leader; Senior Project Manager; Intermediate Web Developers; Java Developers; OO Project Manager; Oracle Application Specialists (5); Oracle Developers; Senior OO Developer; Senior Oracle Analyst; Senior Oracle Developer.

MONTAGE.DMC EBUSINESS SERVICES
Att: Human Resources Manager
5580 Explorer Drive, Suite 600
Mississauga, ON L4W 4Y1

Tel. 905-602-7700
Fax 905-602-7448
Email .... hr@montage.ca
Website .... www.montage.ca

Employer Background: Montage.dmc eBusiness Services (formerly Montage eIntegration Inc.) is one of Canada's fastest-growing e-business solutions providers, with a focus on e-integration services. *New Positions Created (4):* Data Warehousing Consultants; Oracle Database Administrator; Business Intelligence Application Engineer; Database Administrator.

MONTAGE.DMC EBUSINESS SERVICES
Att: Human Resources Manager
301 Moodie Drive, Suite 200
Nepean, ON K2H 9C4
Tel. 613-820-0080
Fax 613-820-4478
Email .... hr@montage.ca
Website .... www.montage.ca

Employer Background: Montage.dmc eBusiness Services (formerly Montage eIntegration Inc.) is one of Canada's fastest-growing e-business solutions providers, with a focus on e-integration services. *New Positions Created (18):* Java Support Specialists; OO / Java Applications Developers; OO Project Manager; ETL Consultant; Project Leader / Data Architect; 3rd-Level Support Specialists; Account Manager; OO / Java Applications Developers; OO Project Manager; BroadVision Project Manager; Build Management Specialist; Business Objects Consultant; ETL / Data Mart Consultant; Java Support Specialists; OO Application Support Technical Leader; Support Data Analyst; WebObjects Developers; Account Manager.

MONTAGE.DMC EBUSINESS SERVICES
Att: Human Resources Manager
360 Albert Street, Suite 1300
Ottawa, ON K1R 7X7
Tel. 613-232-2760
Fax 613-232-3208
Email .... hr@montage.ca
Website .... www.montage.ca

Employer Background: Montage.dmc eBusiness Services (formerly Montage eIntegration Inc.) is one of Canada's fastest-growing e-business solutions providers, with a focus on e-integration services. *New Positions Created (31):* Global E-Supply Practice Manager; Information Security Analyst; Oracle Financials Functional Analysts; Oracle Financials Functional Team Leader / Manager; Oracle Financials Technical Consultants, Intermediate to Senior; PDM Site Primes Position; Senior Java Developer / Architect; Senior Oracle Financial Technical Analyst; Data Warehousing Consultants; Senior Oracle Architect / Data Warehousing Specialists; System Analysts; Director, Business Development; Information Security Analyst; Oracle Financials Functional Analyst; Oracle Financials Functional Team Leader & Manager; Senior Business Development Manager; Senior Java Developer / Architect; Senior Oracle Financials Technical Analyst; Business Analyst; Data Warehousing Consultants; Global E-Supply Practice Manager; Intermediate

ABAP Developers; Intermediate BASIS Analysts; Intermediate / Senior SAP Functional Analysts; PDM Site Prime Representatives; Programmer Analysts; Project Leaders; Senior Microsoft Developer / Architect; Senior Oracle Architect / Data Warehousing Specialist; Systems Analyst; Business Development Director.

MONTANA'S COOKHOUSE
Att: Pam Ross
450 South Service Road West
Oakville, ON L6K 2H4
Fax 905-842-5603
Email .... pross@hq.kelseys.ca
Website .... www.montanas.ca

Employer Background: Montana's Cookhouse, a division of Kelsey's International, is an old-fashioned western-style barbecue restaurant. *New Positions Created (2):* Restaurant Managers; Kitchen Managers / Assistant Managers.

MONTREAL PORT AUTHORITY / MPA
Att: Personnel Officer
Wing 1, Port of Montreal Building
Cite du Havre
Montréal, QC H3C 3R5
Email .... giardi@port-montreal.com
Website .... www.port-montreal.com

Employer Background: Created in 1999, MPA is an autonomous federal agency, responsible for administering the Port of Montreal and facilitating domestic and international trade. The agency has 325 employees. *New Positions Created (3):* Electrotechnician; Millwright, 1st Class; Technician, Building Maintenance.

MONTRÉAL, VILLE DE
Att: Personnel Services
555 Gosford Street, Gosford Level
Montréal, QC H2Y 3Z1
Website .... www.ville.montreal.qc.ca

Employer Background: Ville de Montreal has a population of over 1 million residents. *New Positions Created (4):* Horticulturist; Welfare Agent; Mechanic, Mechanical Rides; Mechanic, Motorized Equipment and Heavy Machinery.

MONTSHIP INC.
Att: Robert Sakaitis
2700 Matheson Boulevard East
Suite 400, West Tower
Mississauga, ON L4W 4V9
Tel. 905-629-5900
Fax 905-629-5948
Email .... rsakaitis@montship.ca
Website .... www.montship.ca

Employer Background: Founded in 1925, Montship Inc. is one of the oldest shipping agents in Canada. *New Positions Created (3):* Receptionist; Documentation Clerk; Traffic Assistant, MOL Operations Department.

MOODY INTERNATIONAL LTD.
Att: Dean LaRose
10310 - 124th Street, Suite 202
Edmonton, AB T5N 1R2

Tel. 780-482-5911
Fax 780-482-7077
Email ..... deanlarose@moodycanada.com
Website .... www.moodyint.com

Employer Background: Moody International Ltd. offers 3rd-party surveillance, expediting and auditing services in over 50 countries worldwide. *New Positions Created (5):* Cathodic Protection Specialist; Environmental Specialist; Safety Specialist; Manager, Canadian Operations; Marketing Representative.

MOORE CORPORATION LTD.
Att: Human Resources Coordinator
6100 Vipond Drive
Mississauga, ON L5T 2X1
Tel. 416-364-2600
Fax 905-362-1046
Website .... www.moore.com

Employer Background: Moore Corporation Ltd. provides data capture, information design, marketing services, digital communications and print solutions. *New Positions Created (2):* Programmer Analyst; Senior Programmer Analyst.

MOORE PRODUCTS COMPANY (CANADA) INC.
Att: Kevin Hanbury, HR Manager
PO Box 370
Brampton, ON L6V 2L3
Tel. 905-457-9638
Email ... hanburyk@moore-solutions.com
Website .... www.moore-solutions.com

Employer Background: Moore Products Company (Canada) Inc. (formerly Siemens Moore Process Automation Solutions) provides innovative solutions to process control challenges to manufacturers worldwide. *New Positions Created (2):* Account Manager, Control Systems; Account Manager, Control Systems.

MORLEY CONSTRUCTION INC.
Att: Human Resources Manager
135 Walgreen Road
Carp, ON K0A 1L0
Tel. 613-831-5490
Fax 613-831-0067
Website ... www.morley-construction.com

Employer Background: Morley Construction Ltd. is a mid-sized general contractor in eastern Ontario. *New Positions Created (3):* Site Superintendent; Project Assistant; Project Manager.

MORNEAU SOBECO
Att: Human Resources Recruiting
1500 Don Mills Road, Suite 500
Toronto, ON M3B 3K4
Tel. 416-445-2700
Fax 416-445-1858
Email .... hr@morneausobeco.com
Website .... www.morneausobeco.com

Employer Background: Morneau Sobeco provides actuarial, consulting and administrative services for the retirement and benefits programs of over 3,000 organizations across Canada. *New Positions Created (3):*

Junior Pension Lawyers (2); Actuarial Analyst; Pension Analyst.

MORNINGSTAR AIR EXPRESS INC.
Att: Human Resources Manager
29 Airport Road
Box 14, Edmonton City Centre Airport
Edmonton, AB T5G 0W6

Tel.	780-453-3022
Fax	780-453-6057
Website	www.maei.ca

Employer Background: Morningstar Air Express Inc. is an Edmonton-based cargo airline. *New Positions Created (3):* Aircraft Maintenance Engineer; Base Manager; Base Manager.

MORRISON HERSHFIELD
Att: Human Resources Manager
4299 Canada Way, Suite 247
Burnaby, BC V5G 1H3

Tel.	604-454-0402
Fax	604-454-0403
Email	hr@morrisonhershfield.com
Website	www.morrisonhershfield.com

Employer Background: Founded in 1946, Morrison Hershfield is a consulting engineering firm with expertise in civil and structural engineering, building science, facilities management, fire / life safety and transportation infrastructure. *New Positions Created (2):* Administrative Assistant II; Project Engineer.

MORRISON HERSHFIELD
Att: Human Resources Manager
235 Yorkland Boulevard, Suite 600
Toronto, ON M2J 1T1

Tel.	416-499-3110
Fax	416-499-9658
Email	hr@morrisonhershfield.com
Website	www.morrisonhershfield.com

Employer Background: Founded in 1946, Morrison Hershfield is a consulting engineering firm, specializing in civil and structural engineering, building science, facilities management, fire / life safety and transportation infrastructure. *New Positions Created (33):* Building Science Engineer / Technologist; CAD Designers, Intermediate; Civil Engineering Technologists / CAD Designers; Project Manager; Senior Electrical Engineer; Transportation Planner, Intermediate; Webmaster / Programmer; A / R & Collections Officer; USA Payroll Administrator; Accountant and Payroll Supervisor; Accounting Clerk, Junior; Accounts Receivable Clerk; Construction Manager, Junior; Electrical Engineer, Senior, Utilities Division; Payroll Clerk; Project / Construction Managers; Accountant; Accounting Payable Clerk (Junior); Administrative Assistant II; Building Science Engineer / Technologist; CAD Designers (Intermediate); Civil Engineer (Junior); Civil Engineering Technologists and CAD Designers; Electrical Engineer / Designer (Junior); Electrical Engineer (Senior); Electrical Engineer (Senior); Structural Engineers / Designers (Junior); Tower Engineers (Intermediate / Senior); Transportation Planner (Intermediate); Webmaster

/ Programmer; Senior Electrical Engineer; Senior Mechanical Engineer; Structural Engineer.

MORRISON HERSHFIELD
Att: Human Resources
2440 Don Reid Drive
Ottawa, ON K1H 1E1

Tel.	613-739-2910
Fax	613-739-4926
Email	hr@morrisonhershfield.com
Website	www.morrisonhershfield.com

Employer Background: Founded in 1946, Morrison Hershfield is a consulting engineering firm, specializing in civil and structural engineering, building science, facilities management, fire / life safety and transportation infrastructure. *New Positions Created (8):* CAD Designers (Intermediate); Electrical Engineer (Intermediate / Senior); Municipal Engineer (Intermediate); Transportation Roads and Highways Engineer (Intermediate); CAD Designers; Electrical Engineer; CAD Designers; Electrical Engineers.

MORRISON HOMES
Att: Dave B. Yates, Sales Manager
6135 - 10th Street SE
Calgary, AB T2H 2Z9

Tel.	403-279-7600
Fax	403-236-0311
Email	dave@morrisonhomes.com
Website	www.morrisonhomes.com

Employer Background: Morrison Homes is a mid-sized home builder. *New Positions Created (4):* New Home Sales Assistant; Senior Accountant; New Home Sales Person; Senior Accountant.

MOSAICWARES STUDIO
Att: Human Resources Manager
74 Industry Street
Toronto, ON M6M 4L7

Tel.	416-787-5526
Fax	416-787-5424
Website	www.mosaicwares.com

Employer Background: Mosaicwares Studio is a furniture and home accessory manufacturing company. *New Positions Created (2):* Office Manager / Receptionist; Production Manager.

MOSAID TECHNOLOGIES INC.
Att: Human Resources Manager
11 Hines Road
Kanata, ON K2K 2X1

Tel.	613-599-9539
Fax	613-591-8148
Email	hr@mosaid.com
Website	www.mosaid.com

Employer Background: MOSAID Technologies Inc. is a semiconductor company that develops networking products and memory test systems. *New Positions Created (21):* Senior Legal Assistant; ASIC Physical Design Engineer; IC Design Automation Specialist; IC Layout Design Engineers; Senior Networking ASIC Design Engineer; ASIC Design Engineer; Principal Hardware Applica-

tions Engineer; ASIC Design Engineer; Financial Analyst; Full Custom IC Designer Hardware Applications Engineers; IC Place and Route Specialist; IC Program Manager Intermediate Software Engineer; Senior CT$ Applications Engineer; Senior Software Ap plications Engineer; Software Application Engineers; System Architect; Technica Writer; Accounting Assistant; Human Re source Specialist / Compensation Analyst.

MOSS FABRICATION LTD.
Att: Ken Mostowich
6619 - 86th Avenue SE
Calgary, AB T2C 2S4

Tel.	403-279-495(
Fax	403-236-418!
Email	kenmoss@mossfabrication.com
Website	www.mossfabrication.com

Employer Background: Moss Fabricatior Ltd. is a Canadian steel fabrication firm designing facilities for oil and gas produc ers. *New Positions Created (3):* Sr Design Draftsperson; Senior Pressure Vessels & Pip ing Skid Package Designer; Project Manager

MOTOROLA CANADA LIMITED
Att: Human Resources Manager
2 East Beaver Creek Road
Richmond Hill, ON L4B 2N3

Tel.	905-507-7200
Fax	905-709-7220
Email	y17147@email.mot.com
Website	www.motorola.ca

Employer Background: Motorola Canada Limited, a subsidiary of Motorola Inc., is a leading developer of integrated communi cation products and embedded electronic solutions. *New Positions Created (6):* Direc tor of Engineering; Hardware Engineering Manager; Software / Hardware Engineers Component Engineer, Semiconductor Chips; RF Engineer, Circuit Design; Sales Account Manager.

MOUNT PLEASANT GROUP OF CEMETERIES
Att: Human Resources
65 Overlea Boulevard, Suite 500
Toronto, ON M4H 1P1

Tel.	416-696-0049
Fax	416-696-9325
Email	humanresources@
	mountpleasantgroup.com
Website	www.mountpleasantgroup
	ofcemeteries.ca

Employer Background: The Mount Pleasan Group of Cemeteries, one of the largest cem etery organizations in the province, owns and operates 10 cemeteries in the Greater Toronto Area. *New Positions Created (5)* Manager; Pre-Planning Sales Manager; Sen ior and General Accountant; Treasury Super visor; Director of Marketing.

MOUNT ROYAL COLLEGE
Att: Human Resources Department
4825 Richard Road SW
Calgary, AB T3E 6K6

Tel.	403-240-6584
Fax	403-240-6629

Email ..... humanresources@mtroyal.ab.ca
Website .... www.mtroyal.ab.ca
Employer Background: Established in 1910, Mount Royal College is one of Alberta's oldest post-secondary educational institutions, serving 10,000 students per year. *New Positions Created (66):* Administrative Assistant to the Director of Library Services; Registration Assistant; Accounting Clerk; Program Assistant; Secretary; Senior Research Officer; Capital Assets Clerk; Secretary; Dean, Faculty of Arts; Secretarial / Clerical Assistant; Supervisor of Textbook Services, Bookstore; Administrative Assistant; Administrative Assistant; Administrative Assistant; Instructional Assistant, Nursing Studies; Nursing Lab Assistant; Program Director, Business Eduction and Training; Receptionist / Secretary; Coordinator, Work Experience Program; Payroll Assistant; Clerical Assistant; Coordinator, International Projects; Engineering Instructor; Mathematics Instructor; Registered Nurse; Religious Studies Instructor; Faculty Development Consultant; Librarians (2); Shipper / Receiver; Computer Science and Information Systems Instructors; Nursing Instructors; Chemical, Biological and Environmental Sciences Instructor; Counsellor; Justice Studies Instructor; Manager, Security and Public Safety; Faculty Positions, Computer Science and Information Systems; Administrative Assistant; English Instructors (3); Business Information Analyst; Accounting Clerk; Data Centre Supervisor; Human Resources Consultant; Child Studies Instructor; Dean, Faculty of Arts; Information Technology Security Specialist; Programmer Analyst, Internet; Accounting and Finance Instructor; Anthropology / Archaeology Instructor; Aviation Business and Quantitative Methods Instructor; Broadcasting Instructor; Business Communications and Quantitative Methods Instructor; Computer Science Instructors; Education Instructor; Electronic Publishing Instructor; Emergency Nursing Instructor; English Instructors (2); Entrepreneurship Instructor; History Instructor; Journalism Instructor; Music Theory / History Instructor; Nursing Instructors (3); Physical Education, Sport and Recreation Management Instructor; Psychology Instructor; Public Relations Instructor; Sociology Instructor; Strategic Management Studies and Business Generalist Instructor.

MOUNT SAINT VINCENT UNIVERSITY
Att: Human Resources
166 Bedford Highway
Halifax, NS B3M 2J6
Tel. 902-457-6283
Fax 902-457-8801
Email .... tammy.macarthur@msvu.ca
Website .... www.msvu.ca
Employer Background: Established by the Sisters of Charity in 1873, Mount Saint Vincent University serves 4,000 students. *New Positions Created (7):* Assistant Professor, Business Administration and Tourism and Hospitality Management; Assistant Professor, Education - Elementary; Assistant Pro-

fessor, Education - English; Assistant Professor, Education - Mathematics; Assistant Professor, History; Assistant Professor, Philosophy / Religious Studies; Assistant Professors, Psychology (2).

MOUNT SINAI HOSPITAL
Att: Employment Relations Officer
600 University Avenue, Room 301
Toronto, ON M5G 1X5
Tel. 416-586-5040
Fax 416-586-5045
Email .... humanresources@mtsinai.on.ca
Website .... www.mtsinai.on.ca
Employer Background: Mount Sinai Hospital is a fully-accredited, 382-bed tertiary care teaching hospital affiliated with the University of Toronto. *New Positions Created (78):* Ambulatory Coordinator; General Duty Technologist, Computed Tomography; General Technologist; Social Worker, MSW, RSW; Charge Technologist, Angio / Interventional; Human Resources Specialist, Recruitment; Manager, Financial Reporting; Clinical Case Coordinator, Maternal Infant Program; Clinical Nurse Specialist, Oncology / Palliative Care; Geriatric Acute Care Nurse Practitioner, Emergency Services; Nurse Clinician, Post-Anesthetic Care Unit and Surgical Step-Down Unit; Pharmacist; Receptionist; Registered Nurses, Cardiology / CCU; Registered Nurses, Labour and Delivery; Registered Nurses, Medicine; Registered Nurses, Neonatal Intensive Care Unit (NICU); Social Workers; Intermediate Accountant, Research; Physiotherapist; Senior Financial Analyst; Registered Nurses, GI / IBD; Registered Nurses, Surgery; Registered Respiratory Care Practitioner, Core ICU; Registered Respiratory Care Practitioner, Core Neonatal; Registered Respiratory Care Practitioner, Core Operation Room; Application Support / Systems Analyst; Data Quality Officer; General Technologist; General Technologist, Ultrasonography; Nurse Practitioner, Neonatal Intensive Care Unit; Video Technician; Capital Accountant; Administrative Assistant to the Chief of Surgery; Cytogenetics Technologist; Genetic Counsellor; Nurse Clinician, Cardiology / Coronary Care Unit; Program Assistant; Registered Nurse, Operating Room; Registered Nurses, Intensive Care Unit; Risk Manager; Supervisor, Accounts Receivable; Angiography / Intervention / General Technologist; Database Coordinator; Fire Marshal; General Technologist, Ultrasonography; Manager, Planning; Medical Laboratory Technician; Nurse Clinician, Emergency; Nurse Clinician, IBD And Ostomy Program; Registered Nurse, Cardiology / CCU; Registered Nurse, Labour & Delivery; Registered Nurse, Medicine; Registered Nurse, NICU; Registered Nurse, Surgery; Registered Nurse, Surgical Oncology; Registered Nurses, ICU; Registered Respiratory Care Practitioners; Risk Manager; Registered Nurse / Lactation Coordinator; Nursing Clinical Managers; Nursing Unit Administrator, CCU / Cardiology; Nursing Unit Administrator, Medicine; Registered Nurses; Cytogenetics Technologists; LIS Officer; Medical Secretaries; Rapid Response Labo-

ratory Technologists; Clinical Nurse Specialist, Cardiology; Nursing Unit Administrator, CCU / Cardiology; Nursing Unit Administrator, General Medicine; Clinical Case Coordinator, Maternal Infant Program; Registered Nurses, Emergency Program; Registered Nurses, Perioperative Services; Clinical Nurse Specialist, Surgery; Registered Nurses, Critical Care Program; Registered Nurses, General Medicine, Surgery and Perioperative Services; Registered Nurses, Perinatal Program.

MOUNT SINAI HOSPITAL CENTRE
Att: Selection Committee,
Human Resources Administration
5690 Cavendish Boulevard
Cote St. Luc, QC H4W 1S7
Tel. 514-369-2222
Fax 514-369-2225
Website .... www.mountsinaihospital.qc.ca
Employer Background: Mount Sinai Hospital Centre is a 107-bed facility affiliated with McGill University, specializing in respiratory, palliative and long-term care. *New Positions Created (3):* Communication Officer; Director of Administrative Services; Director of Hospital Services.

MOUNTAIN VIEW COUNTY
Att: John Rusling,
Planning and Development Officer
Bag 100
Didsbury, AB T0M 0W0
Tel. 403-335-3311
Fax 403-335-9207
Email .... mvplan@telusplanet.net
Website ... www.mountainviewcounty.net
Employer Background: Located on Highway 2, Mountain View County is a rural municipality, with a population of 12,000. *New Positions Created (2):* Land Use Planner; Land Use Planner.

MOVIEGOODS
Att: Human Resources Director
3600 - 21st Street NE, Suite 9
Calgary, AB T2E 6V6
Email .... jobs@moviegoods.com
Website .... www.moviegoods.com
Employer Background: MovieGoods is a web company, specializing in movie-related consumer products. *New Positions Created (3):* Customer Service Representative; Online Auction Assistants; Online Marketing Assistant.

MOXIE'S CLASSIC GRILL
Att: Manager of Human Resources
11012 Macleod Trail South, Suite 390
Calgary, AB T2J 6A5
Tel. 403-543-2600
Fax 403-543-2646
Email .... admin@moxies.ca
Website .... www.moxies.ca
Employer Background: Moxie's Classic Grill is part of Moxie's Restaurants Inc., a casual dining restaurant chain, with 36 restaurants across Canada. *New Positions Created (8):* Senior Bar Manager; General Managers &

Kitchen Managers; Catering Manager; Senior Kitchen Managers & Assistant Kitchen Managers; General Managers and Kitchen Managers; Kitchen Managers; Controller; General Managers and Kitchen Managers.

MPB TECHNOLOGIES INC.
Att: Sylvie Rousseau, Human Resources
151 Hymus Boulevard
Pointe-Claire, QC H9R 1E9

Tel. 514-694-8751
Fax 514-694-0776
Email .... hr-mpbtech@qc.aibn.com
Website .... www.mpb-technologies.ca
Employer Background: Founded in 1976, MPB Technologies Inc. develops high-tech optical and laser products. The company has over 200 employees. *New Positions Created (2):* Draftsperson; Sales Representative.

MRF GEOSYSTEMS CORPORATION
Att: Human Resources Manager
665 - 8th Street SW, Suite 700
Calgary, AB T2P 3K7

Tel. 403-216-5515
Fax 403-216-5518
Email .... jobs@mrf.com
Website .... www.mrf.com
Employer Background: MRF Geosystems Corporation provides high-end software tools for mapping and GIS. *New Positions Created (9):* GIS Specialist; Office Manager; GIS Sales Manager; GIS Mapping Technician; GIS Marketing Specialist; Web Programmer Analyst; XML Web Developers; Senior Project Leader, Systems Analysts, & Programmer Analysts ; Web Programmer Analysts.

MSAS GLOBAL LOGISTICS
Att: Human Resources
5200 Miller Road, Suite 102
Richmond, BC V7B 1L1

Fax 604-270-3203
Email .... exel.canada@exel.com
Website .... www.exel.com
Employer Background: MSAS Global Logistics, an Exel company, is one of the world's leading cargo managers. *New Positions Created (3):* Account Executives; Operations Supervisor; Station Manager.

MTU MAINTENANCE CANADA LTD.
Att: Human Resources
6001 Grant McConachie Way
Richmond, BC V7B 1K3

Tel. 604-233-5714
Fax 604-233-5701
Email .... mtu_careers@yvr.mtu.de
Website .... www.mtucanada.com
Employer Background: MTU Maintenance Canada Ltd., a DaimlerChrysler company, is one of the largest independent providers of aero-engine services in the country. *New Positions Created (29):* Quality Systems Coordinator; Buyer Analyst; Gas Turbine Engine Mechanic; Manager, Inspection; Material Procurement Specialist; Propulsion Engineer; Shop Engineer; Team Leaders (2); Component Mechanics; Gas Turbine Engine Mechanics; Machinists; Systems Developer; Controller of Logistics / Business Analyst; Customer Support Manager; Manager, Facilities Engineering; Production Process Analyst; Senior Accountant / Analyst; Team Leader; Team Leader, Purchasing; Business Analyst; Customer Support Manager; Customer Support Representative; Head of Logistics; Manager, Engine Production; Manager, Repair Development; Process Reengineer, Logistics; Propulsion Engineer; Repair Development Engineer; Team Leader, Purchasing.

MTW SOLUTIONS ONLINE INC.
Att: Human Resources
235 Yorkland Boulevard, Suite 1200
Toronto, ON M2J 4Y8

Tel. 416-492-3395
Fax 416-490-8741
Website .... www.ioasoftware.com
Employer Background: MTW Solutions Online Inc. is an accounting software developer. *New Positions Created (4):* Accounting Software Support Professionals (2); Accounting Software Trainers (2); Inside Sales / Telemarketers (2); LAN Manager.

MUIR'S CARTAGE LIMITED
Att: Human Resources Department
205 Doney Crescent
Concord, ON L4K 1P6

Tel. 905-761-8251
Fax 905-761-3167
Email ..... ken.harmer@muirscartage.com
Website .... www.muirscartage.com
Employer Background: Muir's Cartage Limited is one of Toronto's largest for-hire trucking fleets, and has been servicing customers for over 110 years. *New Positions Created (4):* Canadian Pricing Manager; City Dispatcher; Dock Foreperson; US Owner-Operators.

MUKI BAUM ASSOCIATION
Att: Human Resources
265 Rimrock Road, Suite 209
Toronto, ON M3J 3C6

Tel. 416-630-2222
Fax 416-630-2236
Email .... jobs@mukibaum.com
Website .... www.mukibaum.com
Employer Background: Muki Baum Association provides educational day treatment and residential care programs to children and adults with developmental disabilities and emotional and psychiatric disorders. *New Positions Created (19):* Clinical Supervisor, Children's Day Treatment Program; Residential Staff; Therapists (5); Administrative Assistant, Fundraising; Classroom Staff / Direct Care Workers; Administrative Assistant, Human Resources; Occupational Therapists, Sensory Integration Project (2); Acting Program Supervisor, Children's Day Program; Clinical Supervisor, Children's Day Program; Direct Care Workers; Occupational Therapists; Direct Care Workers; Clinical Supervisor, Adult Day Program; Expressive Arts Therapists; Residential Supervisor, Adult Residence; Residential Supervisor, Children's Residence; Adult Day Program Worker; Adult Residential Program Worker; Children's Residential Program Worker.

MULTIPAK LTD.
Att: Human Resources Manager
6417 Viscount Road
Mississauga, ON L4V 1K8

Tel. 905-678-2825
Fax 905-678-6563
Employer Background: Multipak Ltd. is a leading North American printer and converter of flexible packaging materials. *New Positions Created (4):* Maintenance Supervisor; Production Supervisor; Production Supervisor; Various Packaging Positions (5).

MULTIPLE SCLEROSIS SOCIETY OF CANADA
Att: Manager, Human Resources
250 Bloor Street East, Suite 1000
Toronto, ON M4W 3P9

Tel. 416-922-6065
Fax 416-922-7538
Email .... maria.collins@mssociety.ca
Website .... www.mssociety.ca
Employer Background: The Multiple Sclerosis Society of Canada is a national voluntary organization dedicated to helping those affected by MS through research, services and education. *New Positions Created (3):* Coordinator, Human Resources; Print Production Coordinator / Merchandise Purchaser; Director, Individual and Family Services.

MULTIPLE SCLEROSIS SOCIETY OF CANADA, BRITISH COLUMBIA DIVISION
Att: Selection Committee
1130 West Pender Street, Suite 1600
Vancouver, BC V6E 4A4

Fax 604-689-0377
Email ... kate-louise.stamford@mssociety.ca
Website .... www.mssociety.ca
Employer Background: The Multiple Sclerosis Society of Canada is a national voluntary organization dedicated to helping those affected by MS through research, services and education. *New Positions Created (2):* Exec Director; Community Services Coordinator.

MULTIVIEW INC.
Att: Sandra Watson
36 Antares Drive, Suite 500
Ottawa, ON K2E 7W5

Tel. 613-225-5050
Fax 613-225-0505
Email .... jobs@multiviewcorp.com
Website .... www.multiviewcorp.com
Employer Background: Multiview Inc. is an independent supplier of full-featured financial applications for the Windows NT, HP Unix and HP 3000 operating systems. *New Positions Created (8):* Controller; Customer Support Team Member; Financial Software Specialist; Internal Technical Support Position; Oracle Application Architect / DBA; Oracle Developers; Quality Assurance Team Members; Visual C++ Developer.

MURCHISON, THOMSON & CLARKE
Att: David Patterson
7565 - 132nd Street, Suite 101
Surrey, BC V3W 1K5
Tel. 604-590-8855
Fax 604-590-2000
Website www.murchinsonthompson.com
Employer Background: Murchison, Thomson & Clarke is a law firm. *New Positions Created (2):* Litigation Lawyers; Junior Litigator.

MURPHY OIL COMPANY LTD.
Att: Human Resources Advisor
PO Box 2721, Station M
Calgary, AB T2P 3Y3
Tel. 403-294-8000
Fax 403-294-8851
Email .... careers_hr@murphyoilcorp.com
Website .... www.murphyoilcorp.com
Employer Background: Murphy Oil Company Ltd. is an integrated oil and gas company. *New Positions Created (2):* Fixed Asset Accountant; Tax Accountant.

MUSCLEMAG INTERNATIONAL
Att: Terry E. Frendo,
Director of Advertising and Marketing
5775 McLaughlin Road
Mississauga, ON L5R 3P7
Fax 905-507-9935
Website .... www.emusclemag.com
Employer Background: MuscleMag International is a leading bodybuilding, health and fitness magazine. *New Positions Created (5):* Retail Marketing Manager; Copy Editor; Editorial Assistant; Junior Graphic Artist, Magazine Design; Junior Graphic Artist, Package Design / Ad Design.

MUSCLETECH RESEARCH AND DEVELOPMENT INC.
Att: Jamie
7050 Telford Way
Mississauga, ON L5S 1V7
Tel. 905-678-3114
Fax 905-678-3121
Website .... www.muscletech.com
Employer Background: MuscleTech Research and Development Inc. is one of the largest developers and marketers of advanced nutritional athletic supplements. *New Positions Created (15):* Customer Service Representative; Data Entry Personnel; Advertising Law Personnel; Copy Editor; Graphic Designers; Marketing Positions; Media Buyer; Research and Development Positions; Webmaster; Food / Flavour Technologist, Product Development; Food Chemist / Product Development Position; Copy Editor; Marketing Personnel; Product Label / Intellectual Property Specialist; Senior Graphic Designer.

MUTTART FOUNDATION, THE
Att: Human Resources Manager
10060 Jasper Avenue
Suite 1150, Scotia Tower 1
Edmonton, AB T5J 3R8
Tel. 780-425-9616
Fax 780-425-0282
Email .... bwyatt@muttart.org
Website .... www.muttart.org
Employer Background: Founded in 1953, the Muttart Foundation helps fund registered Canadian charities. *New Positions Created (2):* Policy Analyst; Grants Officer.

MUTUAL FUND DEALERS ASSOCIATION OF CANADA / MFDA
Att: Dale Pratt, Controller
121 King Street West, Suite 1600
Toronto, ON M5H 3T9
Tel. 416-943-5899
Fax 416-943-1218
Email .... dpratt@mfda.ca
Website .... www.mfda.ca
Employer Background: Incorporated in 1998, MFDA is the mutual fund industry's self-regulatory organization for the distribution side of the industry. *New Positions Created (8):* Compliance Officers; Director of Enforcement; Legal Counsel; Human Resources / Accounting Coordinator; Membership Services / Communications Officer; Compliance Managers (3); Compliance Officers (12); Regional Directors (2).

MYERS CHEV OLDS CADILLAC
Att: Esther Scott, Human Relations Officer
1200 Baseline Road
Ottawa, ON K2C 0A6
Tel. 613-225-1260
Fax 613-225-2231
Email .... escott@myerschevolds.com
Website www.myerschevoldscadillac.com
Employer Background: Myers Chev Olds Cadillac is one of Ottawa's largest automotive dealerships. *New Positions Created (4):* Director of Service; Collision Appraiser / Estimator; Licensed Technicians; Service Advisors.

N.D. LEA CONSULTANTS LTD.
Att: H. Copeland, Office Manager
1455 West Georgia Street
Vancouver, BC V6G 2T3
Tel. 604-685-9381
Fax 604-683-8655
Email .... vancouver@ndlea.com
Website .... www.ndlea.com
Employer Background: N.D. Lea Consultants Ltd. is a consulting engineering firm active in the transportation sector. *New Positions Created (9):* AutoCAD Design Technologists; Bridge Structural Engineers; Construction Inspectors; Drainage Engineer / Hydrologists; Highway Design Technicians; Highway / Infrastructure Engineers; Junior Highway Design Engineers; Structural AutoCAD Operators; Structural Engineers.

NABISCO LTD., LAKESHORE BAKERY
Att: Human Resources Department
2150 Lakeshore Boulevard West
Toronto, ON M8V 1A3
Tel. 416-503-6001
Fax 416-503-6271
Email .... atavares@nabisco.ca
Website .... www.nabisco.ca

Employer Background: Nabisco Ltd. manufactures and markets many of Canada's leading consumer packaged foods, including Oreo, Chips Ahoy!, Arrowroot, Premium Plus and Ritz products. *New Positions Created (2):* Project Engineer; Account Mgr.

NABORS INTERNATIONAL INC.
Att: Human Resources Manager
3545 - 32nd Avenue NE, PO Box 806
Calgary, AB T1Y 6M6
Fax 403-936-3627
Email .... ndfieldjobs@cadvision.com
Website .... www.nabors.com
Employer Background: Nabors International Inc. is a land drilling contractor, conducting oil, gas and geothermal operations around the world (including the Middle East, Central and South America and Africa). *New Positions Created (4):* Drillers; Electricians; Mechanics; Rig Managers / Toolpushers.

NADINE INTERNATIONAL INC.
Att: Human Resources Manager
2570 Matheson Boulevard East, Suite 210
Mississauga, ON L4W 4Z3
Fax 905-602-1853
Employer Background: Nadine International Inc. is a consulting engineering firm, specializing in fire protection, life safety and building code technology. *New Positions Created (3):* Fire Protection Consultant; Code Consultant; Electrical Consultant.

NAL RESOURCES MANAGEMENT LTD.
Att: Angele Mullins
550 - 6th Avenue SW, Suite 600
Calgary, AB T2P 0S2
Tel. 403-294-3600
Fax 403-294-3601
Email .... jobs@nal.ca
Website .... www.nal.ca
Employer Background: NAL Resources Management Ltd. is a mid-sized oil and gas company, operating and managing assets on behalf of the NAL Oil & Gas Trust, as well as for major financial institutions. *New Positions Created (5):* Intermediate / Senior Production Revenue Accountant; Senior Operator; Geologist; Operations Engineer; Surface Land Administrator.

'NAMGIS HEALTH CENTRE
Att: Ian Knipe, Administrator
PO Box 290
Alert Bay, BC V0N 1A0
Tel. 250-974-5522
Fax 250-974-2736
Email .... knipe@namgis.bc.ca
Website .... www.namgis.bc.ca
Employer Background: The 'Namgis Health Centre offers a range of health and social services to the residents of northern Vancouver Island. *New Positions Created (4):* Certified Dental Assistant Level II; Dentist; Community Health Nurse; Physician.

NANAIMO, CITY OF
Att: Human Resources Manager

238 Franklyn Street, Suite 301
Nanaimo, BC V9R 5J6
Fax 250-755-4449
Email .... employmentopportunities@
.... city.nanaimo.bc.ca
Website .... www.city.nanaimo.bc.ca
Employer Background: The City of Nanaimo
is a community of 76,645 residents located
on the east side of Vancouver Island. *New
Positions Created (4):* Municipal Manager,
RCMP; Accounting Assistant; Downtown
Managing Director, Main Street Program;
Supervisor, Revenue and Property.

NANOMETRICS INC.
Att: Human Resources Department
250 Herzberg Road
Kanata, ON K2K 2A1
Tel. 613-592-6776
Fax 613-592-5929
Email .... jobs@nanometrics.ca
Website .... www.nanometrics.ca
Employer Background: Founded in 1986,
Nanometrics Inc. develops equipment and
systems for the study of natural and induced
earthquakes. *New Positions Created (12):*
Assistant, Finance and Administration;
Electronics Engineering Test Technologist;
Field Electronics Engineer; Intermediate or
Senior Electronics Engineer; Intermediate
Software Engineer; Junior Mechanical En-
gineer; R&D Mechanical CAD Technologist;
Manufacturing Electronics Engineer; R & D
and Manufacturing Test Technologists; Sen-
ior Software Engineer; Senior Systems Engineer; Supervisor, Production Testing.

NANOWAVE TECHNOLOGIES INC.
Att: Human Resources
425 Horner Avenue
Toronto, ON M8W 4W3
Tel. 416-252-5602
Fax 416-252-7077
Email .... careers@nanowavetech.com
Employer Background: Nanowave Technolo-
gies Inc. designs and manufactures
broadband wireless and electro-optical
components and subsystems. *New Positions
Created (25):* Administrative Assistant; Cus-
tomer Service Representative; Machine
Shop Supervisor; Manager, Packaging De-
sign / Senior Design Engineer; Purchasing
Assistant; Purchasing Assistant; Stockroom
Supervisor; Advisor, Cost Management; Automation Engineers; Customer Service Representative; Documentation Specialist; Electronic Packaging Engineer; Equipment
Maintenance Technicians; Failure Analysis
Engineers; Industrial Engineer; IS / IT Specialist, Desktop Support; IS / IT Specialist,
IS Strategy; Manager, Infrastructure; Manager, Operations Engineering; Manager, Order Fulfillment; Manager, Quality Assurance; Manager, Strategic Procurement; Process Engineers; Procurement Specialist, Negotiations; Quality Systems Advisor.

NATIONAL ARTS CENTRE / NAC
Att: Natalie Leger
53 Elgin Street, PO Box 1534, Station B
Ottawa, ON K1P 5W1
Tel. 613-947-7000
Fax 613-943-1402
Email .... nleger@nac-cna.ca
Website .... www.nac-cna.ca
Employer Background: Opened in 1969,
NAC produces, co-produces, commissions
and showcases a range of new Canadian
music, theatre and dance in both official lan-
guages. *New Positions Created (10):* Man-
ager of Programming Communications;
Administrative Assistant, Communications
Department; Communications Officer;
Communications Officers; Coordinator,
Dance Programming; Human Resources
Manager; Manager, Finance and Adminis-
tration; Financial Coordinator, Marketing;
Francophone Marketing Officer; Education
Officer, National Arts Centre Orchestra.

NATIONAL BANK OF GREECE / NBG
Att: Human Resources
1170 Place du Frere Andre, 2nd Floor
Montréal, QC H3B 3C6
Tel. 514-954-1522
Fax 514-954-1620
Email .... hr@nbgbank.com
Website .... www.nbgbank.com
Employer Background: NBG, a chartered
bank in Canada since 1982, operates 10 full-
service branches. *New Positions Created
(15):* Branch Supervisor; Legal Counsel;
Manager, Treasury Administration; Commercial Account Managers; Customer Service Assistant; Customer Service Representative; Internal Auditor; Manager, Credit; Marketing Assistant; Personal Banking Officer;
Branch Manager; Customer Service Representatives; Personal Banking Officers; Commercial Account Manager; Regional Manager, Ontario.

NATIONAL BOOK SERVICE / NBS
Att: Human Resources Manager
25 Kodiak Crescent
Toronto, ON M3J 3M5
Tel. 416-630-2950
Fax 416-630-0274
Email .... dwill@nbs.com
Website .... www.nbs.com
Employer Background: Toronto-based NBS
is one of Canada's largest wholesale suppli-
ers of quality books and value-added serv-
ices to schools and public libraries. *New
Positions Created (4):* National Sales and
Marketing Manager; Account Manager; Cus-
tomer Service Assistant; Showroom Coor-
dinator.

NATIONAL CAR RENTAL
Att: Human Resource Manager
280 Attwell Drive
Toronto, ON M9W 5B2
Tel. 416-674-1558
Fax 416-798-9250
Email .... montesanol@nationalcar.com
Website .... www.nationalcar.com
Employer Background: National Car Rental
is a leader in the car rental industry, with
over 3,000 locations in 75 countries and
more than 250,000 vehicles. *New Positions
Created (4):* Administrative Assistant; Main-

tenance & Damage Manager; Truck Fleet
Supervisor; Administrative Assistant Sales.

NATIONAL CHEESE COMPANY LTD.
Att: Human Resources
675 Rivermede Road
Concord, ON L4K 2G9
Tel. 905-669-9393
Fax 905-669-5614
Email .... hr@nationalcheese.com
Website .... www.nationalcheese.com
Employer Background: National Cheese
Company Ltd. is a manufacturer, importer
and distributor of the Tre Stelle brand cheese
and other fine quality food products. *New
Positions Created (2):* Accounting Supervi-
sor; Human Resources Manager.

NATIONAL DIAMOND PUBLIC RELATIONS LTD.
Att: Beth Diamond
322 - 11th Avenue, Suite 210
Calgary, AB T2R 0C5
Tel. 403-531-0331
Fax 403-531-0330
Website .... www.national.ca
Employer Background: National Diamond
Public Relations Ltd. is the Calgary office of
National Public Relations, Canada's largest
public relations consulting firm, with 275
practitioners across the country. *New Posi-
tions Created (2):* Graphic Production Art-
ist; Intermediate Website Designer.

NATIONAL FILM BOARD OF CANADA
Att: Human Resources Branch (A-12)
PO Box 6100, Station Centre-ville
Montréal, QC H4N 2N4
Tel. 514-283-9125
Fax 514-283-5850
Email .... hum@nfb.ca
Website .... www.nfb.ca
Employer Background: Created in 1939, NFB
produces and distributes films and other
audiovisual works showing Canada to Ca-
nadians and the rest of the world. *New Po-
sitions Created (5):* Film Publicist, English
Program; Film Publicist, English Program;
Documentary Producer; Product Manager;
Product Manager.

NATIONAL GROCERS COMPANY LIMITED / LOBLAWS COMPANIES LIMITED
Att: Human Resources
6 Monogram Place
Toronto, ON M9R 4C4
Tel. 416-245-5050
Fax 416-240-3953
Website .... www.loblaw.com
Employer Background: National Grocers
Company Limited / Loblaws Companies
Limited is at the heart of Canada's most suc-
cessful grocery retail and wholesale organi-
zation. *New Positions Created (14):* Analyst;
Software Developer II, Administrative and
Financial Systems; Project Manager, Admin-
istrative & Finance Systems; Pricing Integ-
rity Analyst, Retail Systems; Administrative
Assistant; Database Administrator, Techni-

cal Services; Desktop Coordinator, Desktop Services; Production Coordinator, Operations Services; Project Manager, Desktop Services; Software Developer, Central Reporting; Support Analyst I, Store Systems Support ; Systems Administrator, Technical Services; Systems Analyst II, Merchandising & Retail Systems; Web Content Manager.

NATIONAL INFO-TECH CENTRE / NIC
Att: Human Resources Department
9310 St. Laurent Boulevard, Suite 1120
Montréal, QC H2N 1N4

Tel. 514-381-2772
Fax 514-381-7997
Email .... hr@nitccorp.net
Website .... www.nitccorp.net
Employer Background: NIC provides innovative hardware and software solutions, including network and Internet systems management, integrated custom applications development, structured wire / cabling design and installation, and hardware / software design and support. *New Positions Created (3):* Desktop Support Administrator; Receptionist; Telemarketing Representative.

NATIONAL LIFE ASSURANCE COMPANY OF CANADA
Att: Human Resources Department
522 University Avenue
Toronto, ON M5G 1Y7

Tel. 416-598-2122
Fax 416-598-4574
Email .... hr@nationallife.ca
Website .... www.nationallife.ca
Employer Background: National Life Assurance Company of Canada is one of the country's most trusted names in life insurance, helping Canadians plan their futures with innovative financial products. *New Positions Created (28):* Underwriter; Bilingual Billing Clerk; Financial Analyst; Service Administrator, In-Force; Bilingual Customer Service Representative; Records Clerk; Senior Group Underwriter; Service Administrator, New Business; Director, Communications; Director, Group Underwriting; Disability Specialist; Manager, Group Underwriting; Programmer Analyst; Junior Lawyer; Actuarial Associate, Corporate Actuarial; Administrator, Purchasing and Facilities; Application Specialist; Marketing Associate; Bilingual Disability Specialist; Service Analyst; Bilingual Help Desk Coordinator; Bilingual Service Advisor; Director, Group Underwriting; Actuarial Associate, Corporate Actuarial; Bilingual Annuity Service Administrator; Marketing Associate; Marketing Communications Specialist; Service Advisor.

NATIONAL OILWELL, DOWNHOLE TOOLS DIVISION
Att: Director of Engineering
9118 - 34A Avenue
Edmonton, AB T6E 5P4

Fax 780-430-0760
Employer Background: National Oilwell, Downhole Tools Division is an international designer and manufacturer of oilfield downhole drilling tools. *New Positions Cre-*

 ated (2): Downhole Tool Service Equipment / Hydraulics Specialist; Mechanical Engineering Technologists (2).

NATIONAL PAPER GOODS
Att: Manager of Human Resources
PO Box 2339, LCD 1
Hamilton, ON L8N 4E1

Tel. 905-527-3641
Fax 905-527-0667
Employer Background: National Paper Goods is an envelope manufacturer, with over 89 years experience. *New Positions Created (5):* Sales Service Coordinator; Machine Adjuster; Production Supervisor; Production Control Position; Sales Service Coordinator.

NATIONAL RESEARCH COUNCIL CANADA, CANADA INSTITUTE FOR SCIENTIFIC AND TECHNICAL INFORMATION / NRC
Att: Human Resources Team
Montreal Rd., Room 355A, Building M-55
Ottawa, ON K1A 0R6

Tel. 613-993-7179
Fax 613-941-6283
Email .... hrbcisti@ott.nrc.ca
Website .... www.nrc.ca
Employer Background: NRC is a research and development organization committed to helping Canada realize its potential as an innovative and competitive nation. *New Positions Created (9):* On-Site Services Assistant; Coordinator, Products for Innovation; Information Specialist; Product Support Librarian; Business Systems Programmer / Analyst; Information Specialist; Junior Translator; Product Support Librarian; Cataloguer.

NATIONAL RESEARCH COUNCIL CANADA, INDUSTRIAL MATERIALS INSTITUTE / NRC
Att: Christine Lefebvre
75 de Mortagne Boulevard
Boucherville, QC J4B 6Y4

Tel. 450-641-5005
Fax 450-641-5382
Email .... christine.lefebvre@nrc.ca
Website .... www.nrc.ca
Employer Background: NRC is a research and development organization committed to helping Canada realize its potential as an innovative and competitive nation. *New Positions Created (3):* Research Officer, Optical Techniques; Technical Officer, Polymer Materials Engineering; Technical Officer, Net Shape Metal Forming.

NATIONAL RESEARCH COUNCIL CANADA, INSTITUTE FOR CHEMICAL PROCESS AND ENVIRONMENTAL TECHNOLOGY / NRC
Att: Judy Juneau, Human Resources
1200 Montreal Rd., Rm. 1208, Bldg. M-36
Ottawa, ON K1A 0R6

Tel. 613-991-0879
Fax 613-998-4940
Email .... judy.juneau@nrc.ca

Website .... www.nrc.ca
Employer Background: NRC is a research and development organization committed to helping Canada realize its potential as an innovative and competitive nation. *New Positions Created (7):* Director, Information Resource Management; Research Associate, Energy Materials Group; Research Officer / Coastal Engineer; Technical Officer, Configuration Management Support; Technical Officer, Integrated Logistics Support; Technical Officer, Project Management; Research Officer, Polymers.

NATIONAL RESEARCH COUNCIL CANADA, INSTITUTE FOR MICROSTRUCTURAL SCIENCES / NRC
Att: Annie Toupin
Montreal Road, Building M-50
Ottawa, ON K1A 0R6

Tel. 613-998-7965
Email .... it-&-microstructure.jobs@nrc.ca
Website .... www.nrc.ca/ims
Employer Background: The Institute for Microstructural Sciences aims to develop enabling technologies for information processing, transmission acquisition and display applications. *New Positions Created (2):* Technical Officer, Epitaxy Group; Technical Officer, Quantum Physics Group.

NATIONAL RESEARCH COUNCIL CANADA, INTEGRATED MANUFACTURING TECHNOLOGIES INSTITUTE / NRC
Att: Jannette Fisher,
Human Resource Systems Coordinator
800 Collip Circle
London, ON N6G 4X8

Tel. 519-430-7074
Email .... jannette.fisher@nrc.ca
Website .... www.nrc.ca
Employer Background: NRC is a research and development organization committed to helping Canada realize its potential as an innovative and competitive nation. *New Positions Created (5):* Senior Technical Consultant, Software, VETC; Visualization Specialist, VETC; Technical Officer, Laser Materials Processing; Technical Officer, Pulsed Laser Deposition; Technical Officer, Shape Transfer Processes.

NATIONAL RESEARCH COUNCIL CANADA / NRC
Att: Joey Weir, Human Resources Assistant
435 Ellice Ave., Room W-108, Bldg. M-58
Winnipeg, MB R3B 1Y6

Tel. 204-984-6270
Fax 204-984-6299
Email .... joey.weir@nrc.ca
Website .... www.nrc.ca
Employer Background: NRC is a research and development organization committed to helping Canada realize its potential as an innovative and competitive nation. *New Positions Created (5):* Personal Computer Support Specialist; Scientific Support Worker; Technical Officer, Biosystems; Technical Officer; Finance Officer.

NATIONAL RESEARCH COUNCIL CANADA / NRC
Att: Human Resources Manager
1500 Montreal Rd., Room 210, Bldg. M-50
Ottawa, ON K1A 0R6

Tel. 613-993-5921
Fax 613-998-4643
Website .... www.nrc.ca

Employer Background: NRC is a research and development organization committed to helping Canada realize its potential as an innovative and competitive nation. *New Positions Created (14):* Pay & Benefits Specialist; Research Associate, Quantum Theory Group; Research Officers, E-Business; Systems Support Specialist; Record Systems Clerk; Mechanical and Electrical Engineers; Research Officer, Optics; Financial Analyst; Administrative Support Positions; Director, Atlantic Research Programs; Research Officers; Technical Support Specialists; Compressor Mechanic; Wind Tunnel Mechanical Technologist.

NATIONAL RESEARCH COUNCIL CANADA / NRC
Att: Gisele Elias, HR Assistant
100 Sussex Drive, Room 1152
Ottawa, ON K1A 0R6

Tel. 613-998-7956
Fax 613-990-5143
Email .... gisele.elias@nrc.ca
Website .... www.nrc.ca

Employer Background: NRC is a research and development organization committed to helping Canada realize its potential as an innovative and competitive nation. *New Positions Created (7):* Systems Support Specialist; Research Associate, Quantum Theory Group; Technical Officer, Neutron Program for Materials Research; Research Officer, Acoustics and Signal Processing Group; Research Officers, E-Business; Research Officers, E-Learning; Research Officers, Wireless Networks Software.

NATIONAL RESEARCH COUNCIL CANADA / NRC
Att: Celine Nguyen-Huu
Montreal Road, Room 312, Building M-19
Ottawa, ON K1A 0R6

Tel. 613-993-8682
Fax 613-957-9828
Email .... celine.nguyen-huu@nrc.ca
Website .... www.nrc.ca

Employer Background: NRC is a research and development organization committed to helping Canada realize its potential as an innovative and competitive nation. *New Positions Created (3):* English Writer; Admin. Clerk; Chief Operating Engineer.

NATIONAL RESEARCH COUNCIL CANADA / NRC
Att: Denise Le Vogeur
Montreal Road, Room 226, Building M-2
Ottawa, ON K1A 0R6

Tel. 613-993-5921
Fax 613-990-4148
Email .... denise.levoguer@nrc.ca
Website .... www.nrc.ca

Employer Background: NRC is a research and development organization committed to helping Canada realize its potential as an innovative and competitive nation. *New Positions Created (9):* Research Officer, Optics Group; Communications Officer; Science and Technology Evaluation Officer; Calibration Laboratory Assessment Service Technical Advisor, Mechanical / Dimensional; Research Officer, Photonics; Technical Officer, Electrical Standards; Research Associate, Monte Carlo Techniques; Research Officers, Radiation Dosimetry Standards; SIGMA Data Administrator.

NATIONAL RESEARCH COUNCIL CANADA / NRC
Att: Sylvie Brault, HR Branch
Montreal Road, Room 103, Building M-20
Ottawa, ON K1A 0R6

Tel. 613-993-9504
Fax 613-954-5984
Email .... sylvie.brault@nrc.ca
Website .... www.nrc.ca

Employer Background: NRC is a research and development organization committed to helping Canada realize its potential as an innovative and competitive nation. *New Positions Created (4):* Research Officer, Water Quality Modelling; Technical Advisor, Decision-Making / Investment Planning; Technical Officer, Buried Utilities; Research Officer, Environmental Psychology / Human Factors.

NATIONAL RESEARCH COUNCIL CANADA / NRC
Att: Liette Brazeau
6100 Royalmount Avenue, Room A-17C
Montréal, QC H4P 2R2

Tel. 514-496-2921
Fax 514-496-6277
Email .... liette.brazeau@nrc.ca
Website .... www.nrc.ca

Employer Background: NRC is a research and development organization committed to helping Canada realize its potential as an innovative and competitive nation. *New Positions Created (2):* Travel Clerk; Research Council Officer, Biotech / Bioremediation Processes.

NATIONAL STEEL CAR LTD.
Att: Human Resources Department
PO Box 2450
Hamilton, ON L8N 3J4

Tel. 905-544-3311
Email .... employment@steelcar.com
Website .... www.steelcar.com

Employer Background: National Steel Car Ltd. manufactures railway rolling stock. *New Positions Created (3):* Senior Programmer Analyst; Mechanical Design Engineers; Administrative Assistant.

NATIONAL TRADE CENTRE, THE
Att: Human Resources Department
100 Princess Boulevard, Exhibition Place
Toronto, ON M6K 3C3

Tel. 416-263-3025
Fax 416-263-3019
Website .... www.ntc.on.ca

Employer Background: The National Trade Centre is the largest trade show facility in Canada, with over one million square feet of connected, usable space. *New Positions Created (2):* Building Operations Manager; Executive Chef.

NATREL INC.
Att: Human Resources
1275 Lawrence Avenue East
Toronto, ON M3A 3P9

Tel. 416-442-2300
Website .... www.natrel.ca

Employer Background: Natrel Inc. markets milk and filtered dairy products, with 1,800 employees and 11 plants in Quebec, Ontario and British Columbia. *New Positions Created (6):* Bilingual Call Centre / Customer Service Representative; Bilingual Consumer Response Representative; Bilingual Call Centre / Customer Service Representative; Call Centre / Customer Service Representative; Invoicing Coordinator; Shipping / Production Supervisor.

NATURE CONSERVANCY OF CANADA, THE / NCC
Att: Sara Wilbur
121 Wyndham Street North, Suite 202
Guelph, ON N1H 4E9

Fax 519-826-9206
Email .... ontario@natureconservancy.ca
Website .... www.natureconservancy.ca

Employer Background: NCC is a national, charitable organization dedicated to protecting natural habitats through outright purchase, donations and conservation easements. *New Positions Created (3):* Major Gifts Officer; Director, Development; Mgr., Community & Corporate Relations.

NATURE TRUST OF BRITISH COLUMBIA, THE
Att: Executive Director
1000 Roosevelt Crescent, Suite 260
North Vancouver, BC V7P 1M3

Fax 604-924-9772
Website .... www.mybc.com/groups-naturetrust

Employer Background: Established in 1971, The Nature Trust of British Columbia is a nonprofit conservation organization that has acquired 15,000 hectares of ecologically significant land in 116 BC locations. *New Positions Created (2):* Manager, Financial Administration and Support; Manager, Development and Communication.

NAV CANADA
Att: HR Services & Staffing
PO Box 3411, Station D
Ottawa, ON K1P 5L6

Tel. 613-563-5906
Fax 613-563-4707
Email .... jobs@navcanada.ca
Website .... www.navcanada.ca

Employer Background: NAV Canada provides civil air navigation services, including air traffic control, flight information, weather briefings, airport advisory services and electronic navigation aids. *New Positions Created (7):* Aeronautical Information Services GIS Specialist; Electrical Specialist; Operations Analyst; Real Estate Analyst; Electronic Systems Technologists; Senior Translator / Reviser, English-French; Administrative Assistant.

NAYLOR GROUP INC.
Att: Human Resources Manager
455 North Service Road East
Oakville, ON L6H 1A5
Tel. 905-338-8000
Fax 905-338-1909
Website .... www.naylorgroupinc.com
Employer Background: Naylor Group Inc. is a mid-sized contractor. *New Positions Created (7):* Mechanical Engineer / HVAC Technologist; Sales Representative; Industrial / Commercial Electricians; Industrial / Commercial Electricians; Industrial / Commercial Electricians; Electrical Estimator; Sales Representative.

NBC CLEARING SERVICES INC.
Att: Human Resources
1155 Metcalfe Street, 4th Floor
Montréal, QC H3B 4S9
Tel. 514-879-2222
Fax 514-879-2204
Email .... fbnrh@sympatico.ca
Website .... www.nbfinancial.com
Employer Background: NBC Clearing Services Inc. (a subsidiary of National Bank of Canada) is a full-service broker, providing reconciliation, holding and accounting services for Canadian and foreign securities operations. *New Positions Created (4):* Client Service Agents; Manager, Organization and Productivity; Supervisor, Customer Service; Supervisor, Customer Service.

NCE RESOURCES GROUP INC.
Att: Ms Carolyn Mayrand
444 - 7th Avenue SW, Suite 600
Calgary, AB T2P 0X8
Fax 403-264-5804
Email .... mayrandc@ncecalgary.com
Website .... www.nceresources.com
Employer Background: NCE Resources is a Canadian oil and gas company, focused on acquiring quality producing properties for two publicly-traded royalty trusts. *New Positions Created (2):* Various Oil & Gas Accounting Positions; Senior Landman.

NCH CANADA INC.
Att: Bill McFarlane
20663 - 97B Avenue
Langley, BC V1M 3Y3
Fax 604-882-8097
Website .... www.nch.com
Employer Background: NCH Canada Inc. has been manufacturing and distributing specialty maintenance products to the industrial, commercial, municipal and institutional markets for over 36 years. *New Positions Created (3):* Salespeople; Sales Management Position; Salespeople.

NCOMPASS LABS
Att: Human Resources Manager
321 Water Street, 2nd Floor, Hudson House
Vancouver, BC V6B 1B8
Tel. 604-633-6500
Fax 604-606-0970
Website .... www.ncompasslabs.com
Employer Background: NCompass Labs is a leading vendor of web content management solutions for the Microsoft platform. *New Positions Created (8):* Database Administrator; Intermediate Software Developer, Quick Fix Engineering; Manager, Integration Team; Product Support Analyst; Public Relations Manager; Support Technician Team Lead; User Interface Designer; Web Application Developer / Professional Services Consultant.

NCR CANADA LTD.
Att: Employment Specialist
580 Weber Street North
Waterloo, ON N2J 4G5
Tel. 519-884-1710
Fax 519-883-3668
Website .... www.ncr.com
Employer Background: NCR Canada Ltd. provides point-of-sale equipment, bank machines, data warehousing solutions and related services for financial and retail clients. *New Positions Created (6):* Commodity Manager, Electro-Mechanical; Manager, Order Management; Quality Analyst; Senior Buyer; Supplier Management Technical Support Position; Supply Line Contract Manager.

NEBS BUSINESS PRODUCTS
Att: Susan O'Hearn
330 Cranston Crescent
Midland, ON L4R 4V9
Fax 705-527-9146
Email .... sohearn@nebs.com
Website .... www.nebs.com
Employer Background: For over 24 years, NEBS has been supplying promotional printing, products and services to more than 140,000 small business clients across Canada. *New Positions Created (3):* Outside Sales Account Mgrs; Modelling Analyst; Outside Sales Account Manager.

NECHO SYSTEMS CORP.
Att: Human Resources
10 Kingsbridge Garden Circle, Suite 300
Mississauga, ON L5R 3K6
Tel. 905-501-4800
Fax 905-501-4810
Email .... recruiter@necho.com
Website .... www.necho.com
Employer Background: Necho provides web-enabled travel- and entertainment-expense processing solutions for business. *New Positions Created (3):* Java Developers; Sales Executives; Technical Services Rep.

NEDCO
Att: Manager, Human Resources
4455 - No. 6 Road
Richmond, BC V6Y 1P8
Tel. 604-273-2244

Fax 604-273-0359
Email .... ujobs@nedco.ca
Website .... www.nedco.ca
Employer Background: Nedco distributes electrical equipment and parts, with over 85 branches across Canada. *New Positions Created (7):* Marketing Services Supervisor; Operations Manager; District Operations Manager; Telecom Sales Positions; Branch Manager; Marketing Manager, Western Canada; Outside Sales Representative.

NEILSON DAIRY
Att: Human Resources
279 Guelph Street
Halton Hills, ON L7G 4B3
Tel. 905-702-7242
Fax 905-873-1907
Employer Background: Neilson Dairy manufactures and distributes dairy and related products across Canada. *New Positions Created (4):* Packaging Mechanic; Network Support Technician; Sanitation / QC Supervisor; Packaging Mechanic.

NEILSON DAIRY
Att: Human Resources Manager
861 Clyde Avenue
Ottawa, ON K1Z 5A4
Tel. 613-728-1751
Employer Background: Neilson Dairy manufactures and distributes dairy and related products across Canada. *New Positions Created (3):* Quality Control Technician; Quality Control Technician; Maintenance Engineer.

NELLCOR PURITAN BENNETT (MELVILLE) LTD.
Att: Human Resources Manager
141 Laurier Avenue West, Suite 700
Ottawa, ON K1P 5J3
Fax 613-238-1291
Email .... terri.taylor@mkg.com
Website .... www.mallinckrodt.com
Employer Background: Nellcor Puritan Bennett (Melville) Ltd., a subsidiary of Mallinckrodt Inc., develops medical diagnostic software. *New Positions Created (3):* Software Engineers; Quality Assurance Specialists; Software Engineers.

NELVANA LIMITED
Att: Deborah Fallows,
Director of Recruiting
32 Atlantic Avenue
Toronto, ON M6K 1X8
Tel. 416-588-5571
Fax 416-588-5252
Email .... hr@nelvana.com
Website .... www.nelvana.com
Employer Background: Nelvana Limited is a family entertainment company active in television and film production, distribution, merchandise licensing and publishing. *New Positions Created (13):* 3D Division Lip Sync Animator; Development Artists; Senior Storyboard Artists; 3D Division Layout Artist; 3D Division Modeler; 3D Division Programmer; Character Design Artists; Colour

Stylist; Directors; Overseas Supervisors; Storyboard Artists; Storyboard Revision Artists; Writers & Story Editors.

NEMAK
Att: Salaried Personnel
4600 GN Booth Drive
Windsor, ON N9C 4G8

Email .... hrcanada@nemak.com
Website .... www.nemak.com

Employer Background: Nemak (a joint venture company between Alfa, S.A. de D.V. and Ford Motor Company) manufactures high-tech aluminum components for internal combustion engines. *New Positions Created (3):* Facilities Engineer; Machining Specialist; Tooling Engineer / Analyst.

NEOCORR ENGINEERING LTD.
Att: Human Resources
635 - 8th Avenue SW, Suite 500
Calgary, AB T2P 3M3

Tel. 403-531-1926
Fax 403-531-1927
Email .... resume@neocorr.com
Website .... www.neocorr.com

Employer Background: NeoCorr Engineering Ltd. provides flow assurance and risk-based solutions to the oil and gas industry. *New Positions Created (3):* Business Development Representatives; Corrosion Engineer; Corrosion Technologist.

NEPCAN ENGINEERING LTD.
Att: Human Resources Manager
1770 - 7th Avenue West, Suite 200
Vancouver, BC V6J 4Y6

Tel. 604-736-3273
Fax 604-736-1519
Email .... reception@nepcan.com
Website .... www.cochrane-group.ca

Employer Background: NEPCAN Engineering Ltd., a joint venture company owned by Cochrane Engineering Ltd. and National Energy Production, participates in international energy projects. *New Positions Created (12):* Instrumentation Designers / Engineers; Mechanical Engineers; Piping Designers; Project Managers; Senior and Intermediate Electrical Engineers; Cost Controller; Instrumentation Designers / Engineers; Mechanical Engineer; Piping Designers; Project Manager; Purchasing Manager; Schedulers.

NESTLE CANADA INC.
Att: Human Resources Manager
25 Sheppard Avenue West
Toronto, ON M2N 6S8

Tel. 416-512-9000
Fax 416-218-2612
Email .... human.resources@ca.nestle.com
Website .... www.nestle.ca

Employer Background: Nestle Canada Inc. manufactures and sells a wide variety of food products. *New Positions Created (5):* Customer Service Representatives; Financial Settlement Position; Order Management Position; Shift Leaders; Sales Representatives.

NET SAFETY MONITORING INC.
Att: Corporate Controller
2711 - 39th Avenue NE, 3rd Floor
Calgary, AB T1Y 4T8

Tel. 403-219-0688
Fax 403-219-0694
Email .... netsafe@net-safety.com
Website .... www.net-safety.com

Employer Background: Net Safety Monitoring Inc. designs and manufactures gas and fire monitoring equipment for a wide range of hazardous industrial applications. *New Positions Created (6):* Accounting Technician; Corporate Controller; Test / Repair Technician; Engineering Manager; International Sales Representative; Quality Assurance / Quality Control Coordinator.

NET-LINX AMERICAS, INC.
Att: Human Resources
12420 - 104th Avenue
Edmonton, AB T5N 3Z9

Tel. 780-488-6688
Fax 780-488-1919
Email .... nxa.hr@net-linx.com
Website .... www.net-linx.com

Employer Background: Net-Linx Americas, Inc. (formerly Pre Print Inc.) is an international software developer for the directory and newspaper publishing industries. *New Positions Created (26):* Business Systems Analyst; C++ Software Developer; Data Analyst; Database Administrator; Java Software Developer; Marketing Technical Analyst; Project Manager; Sales Account Manager; Senior Financial Controller; Senior Tester - Test Team Lead; Software Tester; Systems Administrator; Technical Systems Analyst ; Technical Writers / Software Trainer; Visual Basic Developer; VP, Research and Development, Web Solutions; Webmaster; 4D Developers; Business Systems Analyst; C / C++ Software Developers; Customer Support Analysts; Java Software Developers; Project Managers; Software Testers; Technical Systems Analysts; Technical Writers / Software Trainer.

NETACTIVE INC.
Att: Paul Mulligan, HR Manager
1 Antares Drive, Suite 530
Ottawa, ON K2E 8C4

Tel. 613-723-0107
Fax 613-723-1997
Email .... hr@netactive.com
Website .... www.netactive.com

Employer Background: NetActive Inc. (formerly Channelware Inc.) is a leading provider of digital rights management and audience management services. *New Positions Created (2):* Product Test Manager; Visual C++ Software Designer.

NETHERCOTT CHEV OLDS
Att: Sales Manager
1591 Upper James Street
Hamilton, ON L8W 1R9

Tel. 905-388-6555
Fax 905-574-1494
Website ... www.trader.ca/nethercottchevolds

Employer Background: Nethercott Chev Olds is a large GM dealership. *New Positions Created (2):* Business Manager, F & I Automotive; Sales and Leasing Representative.

NETMART INC.
Att: Human Resources Manager
625 Belmont, Ste. 543, AT&T Canada Bldg.
Montréal, QC H3B 2M1

Tel. 514-940-0500
Fax 514-940-0498
Email .... openings@netmart.com
Website .... www.netmart.com

Employer Background: NetMart Inc. is a growing e-commerce development firm that provides custom hosting and data centre solutions, including web hosting. *New Positions Created (3):* Office Assistant; Sales Professionals; Web Designers.

NETNATION COMMUNICATIONS, INC.
Att: Human Resources
555 West Hastings Street, Suite 1410
Vancouver, BC V6B 4N6

Tel. 604-688-8946
Fax 604-688-8934
Email .... resumes@netnation.com
Website .... www.netnation.com

Employer Background: NetNation Communications, Inc. is a leading web hosting and domain name registration company, serving customers in over 90 countries. *New Positions Created (5):* Chief Financial Officer; Human Resources / Recruiter; Java / Oracle Developers; Media Relations Representative; Sales Representative.

NETPCS
Att: Human Resources Manager
232 Herzberg Road
Kanata, ON K2K 2A1

Tel. 613-591-1151
Fax 613-591-3503
Email .... careers@netpcs.com
Website .... www.netpcs.com

Employer Background: NetPCS is a technology development company, specializing in online communication solutions for business portals. *New Positions Created (21):* Human Resources / Office Manager; Corba Component Designer; User Interface Designer; Business Development Officer; E-Marketing Coordinator; Inside Sales Specialist; Net Directory Account Manager; Project Specialist; TCP / IP Application Developer; Web Developer; Database Administrator; Senior Quality Control Engineer; Business Development Officer; CLEC Billing System Domain Specialist; Net Directory Account Manager; Portal Architect; QC Manager; Senior Portal Administrator; Senior System Administrator; TCP / IP Application Developer; Web Developer / Graphics Designer.

NETPCS
Att: Human Resources
105 Hotel de Ville, Suite 302
Hull, QC J8X 4H7

Tel. 819-771-8182
Fax 819-771-5258

Email .... careers@netpcs.com
Website .... www.netpcs.com

Employer Background: NetPCS is a technology development company, specializing in online communication solutions for business portals. *New Positions Created (23):* Corba Component Developer; Corba Component Developer; Help Desk Analyst; Java AWT / Swing User Interface Developer; Network Portal Operations Administrator; Web Developer / Graphic Designer; Windows CE / Palm OS / WAP Developer; Billing System Developer and Integrator; CLEC Billing System Domain Expert; Senior Portal Administrator; Web Developer; Assistant Controller; Business Analyst; Business Development Officer; Portal Architect; Product Documentation Specialist; Product Manager; Quality Control Specialist; Senior Quality Control Engineer; Senior System Administrator; Software Tester; Technology Business Development Manager; Web Developer.

NETWORK BUILDERS INC.
Att: Human Resources Manager
110 Riviera Drive, Suite 14
Toronto, ON L3R 5M1

Tel. 905-947-9201
Fax 905-947-4580
Email .... jobs@networkbuilders.com
Website .... www.networkbuilders.com

Employer Background: Network Builders Inc. designs, builds and supports electronic networks and information systems. *New Positions Created (4):* Account Executive; Administrative Assistant; Inside Sales Representative; Senior Network Architect.

NETWORK DESIGN AND ANALYSIS / NDA CORPORATION
Att: Maureen Tracey
60 Gough Road, 2nd Floor
Markham, ON L3R 8X7

Tel. 905-477-9534
Fax 905-477-9572
Email .... nda@ndacorp.com
Website .... www.ndacorp.com

Employer Background: NDA develops specialized software for telecom network optimization, performance analysis and cost control tools. *New Positions Created (8):* Product Manager; Software Engineers; Account Executives; Product Manager; Software Engineers; Software Developers; Product Manager; Sales Representatives.

NEW AUTOMATION CORPORATION / NAC
Att: Human Resources
5280 South Service Road
Burlington, ON L7L 5H5

Tel. 905-333-3606
Fax 905-333-1477
Email .... hr@newautomation.com
Website .... www.newautomation.com

Employer Background: NAC is an ISO 9001-registered designer and manufacturer of customized manufacturing and material handling systems. *New Positions Created (20):* Administrative Assistant; Mechanical Designer; Manufacturing Manager; Appli-

cations Engineer; Junior Sales Engineer; Controller; Receptionist; Mechanical Designer; Sales and Marketing Assistant; Executive Assistant; Project Manager; Sales & Applications Engineer; Project Manager; Sales and Applications Engineer; Electrician Apprentice, 3rd or 4th Year; Supervisor, Manufacturing Services; Manufacturing Supervisor; Product Manager; Sales and Applications Engineer; Technical Sales Representative.

NEW BRUNSWICK COMMUNITY COLLEGE, DIEPPE CAMPUS / NBCC
Att: Claudine Albert, HR Officer
505 College Street
Dieppe, NB E1A 6X2

Tel. 506-432-4557
Website .... www.dieppe.ccnb.nb.ca

Employer Background: NBCC is a leading adult education facility. The Dieppe campus offers more than 20 French-language programs to over 650 students. *New Positions Created (3):* Computer Technician; Instructor, Teleservice; Instructors, Web Programming Technology (2).

NEW BRUNSWICK COMMUNITY COLLEGE, MIRAMICHI CAMPUS
Att: Human Resources Manager
80 University Avenue, PO Box 1053
Miramichi, NB E1N 3W4

Fax 506-778-6690
Website .... www.miramichi.nbcc.nb.ca

Employer Background: NBCC is a leading adult education facility. The Miramichi campus offers various high-tech programs in multimedia, knowledge engineering, electronic game design and 3D graphics technology. *New Positions Created (3):* Instructor, Learning Technologies Department; Dean; Instructor, French.

NEW BRUNSWICK COMMUNITY COLLEGE, MONCTON CAMPUS / NBCC
Att: Pat Gallagher,
Human Resources Manager
1234 Mountain Road
Moncton, NB E1C 8H9

Tel. 506-856-2220
Fax 506-856-3288
Email .... pat.gallagher@gnb.ca
Website .... www.moncton.nbcc.nb.ca

Employer Background: NBCC is a leading adult education facility. *New Positions Created (3):* Dean of Instruction, Technologies Programs; Instructor, Automotive Service; Instructor, Truck & Transport Service.

NEW BRUNSWICK COMMUNITY COLLEGE, SAINT JOHN CAMPUS
Att: Sandra Maber, HR Manager
PO Box 2270
Saint John, NB E2L 3V1

Tel. 506-643-6109
Fax 506-658-6792
Email .... sandra.maber@gnb.ca
Website .... www.saintjohn.nbcc.nb.ca

Employer Background: NBCC is a leading adult education facility. *New Positions Cre-*

ated (3): Business Information Systems Instructor; Instructor, Mechanical Industrial Department; Coordinator, Quality and Adult / Distance Education.

NEW BRUNSWICK COMMUNITY COLLEGE, ST. ANDREWS CAMPUS
Att: Elaine MacNichol, HR Manager
99 Augustus Street
St. Andrews, NB E5B 2E9

Fax 506-529-5039
Email .... elaine.macnichol@gnb.ca
Website .... www.standrews.nbcc.nb.ca

Employer Background: NBCC is a leading adult education facility. The St. Andrews campus offers programs in specialized areas of hospitality and tourism, marine, refrigeration and air conditioning technologies to 400 students. *New Positions Created (2):* Community College Instructor, Hospitality & Tourism; Manager / Network Technician, Information Technology Services.

NEW BRUNSWICK COMMUNITY COLLEGE, WOODSTOCK CAMPUS
Att: Barbara McKinley, HR Officer
100 Broadway Street
Woodstock, NB E7M 5C5

Tel. 506-453-3641
Email .... barb.mckinley@gnb.ca
Website .... www.woodstock.nbcc.nb.ca

Employer Background: NBCC is a leading adult education facility. *New Positions Created (4):* Custodial Worker; Instructor, Landscaping Program; Instructor, E-Commerce; Building Maintenance Supervisor.

NEW FRONTIERS SCHOOL BOARD
Att: Human Resources Department
214 McLeod Street
Chateauguay, QC J6J 2H4

Tel. 450-691-1440
Fax 450-691-0643
Email .... scaza@csnewfrontiers.qc.ca
Website .... www.csnewfrontiers.qc.ca

Employer Background: The New Frontiers School Board operates 10 elementary schools, 2 secondary schools and 2 career centres in Quebec. *New Positions Created (5):* Welding Teacher; Teacher, French; Teachers (2); Coordinator of Educational Services; Guidance / Career Counsellor.

NEW MEDIA INNOVATION CENTRE / NEWMIC
Att: Human Resources Manager
515 West Hastings Street, Suite 590
Vancouver, BC V6B 5K3

Tel. 604-268-7968
Fax 604-268-7967
Email .... hr@newmic.com
Website .... www.newmic.com

Employer Background: NewMIC is a research centre, bringing universities and industry members together and working to develop the new media sector. *New Positions Created (5):* Applications Programmer; Virtual Reality; Research Associate; Research Positions, E-Lifestyles; Research Scientist, E-Business; Research Scientist.

NEW WESTMINSTER, CITY OF
Att: Human Resources Department
511 Royal Avenue
New Westminster, BC V3L 1H9
Tel. 604-527-4551
Fax 604-527-4619
Website . www.city.new-westminster.bc.ca
Employer Background: Located in the Lower
Mainland, the City of New Westminster is
home to 24,000 residents. *New Positions
Created (2):* Assistant Director of Engineer-
ing; Police Officers.

**NEWFOUNDLAND AND LABRADOR
HYDRO GROUP, THE**
Att: Alan Evans, HR Specialist
PO Box 12400
St. John's, NF A1B 4K7
Tel. 709-737-1400
Fax 709-737-1231
Website .... www.nlh.nf.ca
Employer Background: The Newfoundland
and Labrador Hydro Group generates and
transmits electricity throughout the prov-
ince. *New Positions Created (2):* Network
Services Engineer; Power Systems Applica-
tion Engineer.

NEWHEIGHTS SOFTWARE CORP.
Att: Human Resources
1006 Government Street
Victoria, BC V8W 1X7
Tel. 250-380-0584
Fax 250-380-0404
Website .... www.nh.ca
Employer Background: Founded in 1998,
NewHeights Software Corporation is a pri-
vately-held Canadian company dedicated to
bringing next-generation Internet solutions
to the marketplace. *New Positions Created
(9):* Senior Software Developer; Director of
Product & Solutions Development; Pro-
grammer; Software Architect; HR Recruiter;
Internet Application Developer; Programmer; Software Architect; Software Tester.

NEWMARKET, TOWN OF
Att: Human Resources Division
395 Mulock Drive, Box 328, Stn Main
Newmarket, ON L3Y 4X7
Tel. 905-895-5193
Fax 905-953-5337
Email .... hr@town.newmarket.on.ca
Website ..... www.town.newmarket.on.ca
Employer Background: Located 45 km north
of Toronto, Newmarket is home to 65,000
people. *New Positions Created (3):* Assistant
Solicitor; Manager, Facility & Asset Manage-
ment Services; Building Inspector.

NEWPARK DRILLING FLUIDS
Att: Rick Smith
635 - 6th Avenue SW, Suite 300
Calgary, AB T2P 0T5
Fax 403-263-1760
Website .... www.newpark.ca
Employer Background: Newpark Drilling
Fluids provides integrated site, environmen-
tal and fluid services to the oil and gas ex-
ploration and production industry. *New*

Positions Created (6): QHSE Coordinator;
Distribution / Product Manager; Drilling
Fluids Engineers; Technical Manager; Programmer / Technical Operations Representative; Technical Sales Representative.

NEWS MARKETING CANADA
Att: Director of Human Resources
2400 Skymark Avenue, Suite 6
Mississauga, ON L4W 5L3
Tel. 905-212-3861
Fax 905-602-0153
Email .... recruiting@newsmarketing.ca
Website .... www.newsmarketing.ca
Employer Background: News Marketing
Canada provides top consumer companies
with a single-source marketing solution for
advertising, promotion, sales and market-
ing needs. *New Positions Created (3):* Vice-
President, Media Sales; Sales and Merchan-
dising Supervisor; Sales Associates.

**NEWSPAPER AUDIENCE
DATABANK INC. / NADBANK**
Att: Anne Ruta, Client Services Director
890 Yonge Street, Suite 200
Toronto, ON M4W 3P4
Fax 416-923-4002
Email .... aruta@nadbank.com
Website .... www.nadbank.com
Employer Background: NADbank conducts
research in urban markets to measure news-
paper readership, retail shopping habits,
product consumption and purchase intent.
New Positions Created (2): Research Analyst;
Research Manager.

NEXEN INC.
Att: Corporate Human Resources
635 - 8th Avenue SW, Suite 1500
Calgary, AB T2P 3Z1
Tel. 403-234-6700
Email .... hr_staffing@nexeninc.com
Website .... www.nexeninc.com
Employer Background: Nexen Inc. (formerly
Canadian Occidental Petroleum Ltd.) is a
global energy and chemicals company, and
a major manufacturer of sodium chlorate
and chlor-alkali products. *New Positions
Created (22):* Geophysicist; Geologist, Heavy
Oil; Heavy Oil EOR Reservoir Engineer;
Heavy Oil Reservoir Engineer; Manager,
Completions and Testing; Senior Drilling /
Completions Engineers (2); Senior Reser-
voir Engineer, Coalbed Methane; Vice-Presi-
dent, International Production and Development; Government Relations Analyst;
Staff Facilities Engineer; Human Resources
Position; Procurement Superintendent; Production Engineer; Senior Petrophysicist;
Human Resources Analyst; Taxation Spe-
cialist; Instrumentation / Electrical Techni-
cian; Production Operators; Technical Administrator; Geophysicist; Inventory Control
Supervisor; Procurement Superintendent.

NEXINNOVATIONS
Att: Stacey Marr, Staffing Specialist
112 - 4th Avenue SW, SunLife Plaza
East Tower, 4th Floor, Main Reception
Calgary, AB T2P 0H3

Tel. 403-233-5827
Fax 403-231-5684
Email .... hrwest@nexinnovations.com
Website ..... www.nexinnovations.com
Employer Background: For over 20 years,
NexInnovations has been providing leading
technology consulting, infrastructure, deployment and support expertise to organizations across Canada. *New Positions Created (5):* Deskside Support / Security Position; Project Mgr; Recruiter; Systems Engineer; Technical Services Representative.

NEXINNOVATIONS
Att: Jennifer Roy, Staffing Specialist
5700 Explorer Drive
Mississauga, ON L4W 5J3
Tel. 905-282-5282
Fax 905-282-5740
Email ...... hrcentral@nexinnovations.com
Website ..... www.nexinnovations.com
Employer Background: For over 20 years,
NexInnovations has been providing leading
technology consulting, infrastructure, de-
ployment and support expertise to organi-
zations across Canada. *New Positions Cre-
ated (19):* Commodity Tax Analyst; Exchange Administrator; Principal Consultant;
Project Coordinator; Technical Services
Representative; Collections Specialist; Senior Account Executives (2); Vendor Programs Administrator; Business Unit Accountant; Contracts Manager; Customer
Helpdesk Analyst; Human Resources Coordinator; Product Sales Specialist; Senior
Account Executive; Senior Sales Specialist;
Team Leader / Supervisor; Technical Support Specialist; Technical Writer, B&P; Vendor Programs Administrator.

NEXMEDIA TECHNOLOGIES INC.
Att: Human Resources Manager
5250 Grimmer Street
Burnaby, BC V5H 2H2
Tel. 604-451-3424
Fax 604-454-1545
Email .... hotjobs@nexmedia.com
Website .... www.nexmedia.com
Employer Background: Nexmedia Technolo-
gies Inc. is a software developer that creates
and markets multimedia content-authoring
and delivery applications. *New Positions
Created (2):* Director, Marketing & Business
Development; Senior C++ Programmer.

NEXT ENVIRONMENTAL INC.
Att: Sandra Resendes, Administrator
2550 Boundary Road, Suite 215
Burnaby, BC V5M 3Z3
Tel. 604-419-3800
Fax 604-419-3801
Email .... sresendes@next.bc.ca
Website .... www.next.bc.ca
Employer Background: Next Environmen-
tal Inc. is an environmental consulting firm,
specializing in contaminated site investiga-
tions and remediation for the real estate in-
dustry. *New Positions Created (4):* Interme-
diate Consultant; Senior Consultant; Junior
Consultant; Intermediate Consultant.

NEXTROM LTD.
Att: Human Resources
55 Basaltic Road
Concord, ON L4K 1G4
Tel. 905-761-3000
Fax 905-761-2969
Website .... www.nextrom.com
Employer Background: Nextrom Ltd. manufactures production systems and solutions for the telecom, plastics and energy industries. *New Positions Created (6):* Senior Buyer; Electrical Commissioning Representative; Electricians; Mechanical Design Engineer / Technologist; Mechanical Designer; Mechanical Engineering Manager.

NEXTRON CORPORATION
Att: Len Edwards
6120 - 11th Street NE
Calgary, AB T2H 2L7
Tel. 403-735-9555
Fax 403-735-9559
Email .... ledwards@nextron.ca
Website .... www.nextron.ca
Employer Background: Nextron Corporation is a Calgary-based manufacturer of advanced industrial temperature control devices. *New Positions Created (2):* Manager, Sales and Marketing; Production Manager.

NIAGARA COLLEGE OF APPLIED ARTS & TECHNOLOGY
Att: Recruitment Coordinator
300 Woodlawn Road, PO Box 1005
Welland, ON L3B 5S9
Tel. 905-735-9976
Fax 905-736-6040
Email .... humres@niagarac.on.ca
Website .... www.niagarac.on.ca
Employer Background: Niagara College of Applied Arts & Technology offers diploma programs in a range of technical, tourism-related and computing fields, with campuses in Niagara Falls, Welland and Niagara-on-the-Lake. *New Positions Created (3):* Director, Integrated Manufacturing and Skills Training Division; Professor, Communications and Information Technology Division; Chair, School of Justice Studies, Health and Community Studies Division.

NIAGARA CREDIT UNION LIMITED
Att: Human Resources Department
75 Corporate Park Drive
St. Catharines, ON L2S 3W3
Tel. 905-988-1000
Fax 905-988-1145
Email .... career@niagaracu.com
Website .... www.niagaracu.com
Employer Background: Niagara Credit Union Limited is an innovative full-service financial institution, serving an expanding membership base of over 80,000 Niagara residents and business clients. *New Positions Created (7):* Commercial Account Managers; Manager, Financial Analysis; Financial Planning Specialist; Corporate Secretary; Commercial Account Managers; Branch Manager; Commercial Account Manager.

NIAGARA HEALTH SYSTEM, ST. CATHARINES GENERAL SITE / NHS
Att: Human Resources Department
142 Queenston Street
St. Catharines, ON L2R 7C6
Tel. 905-684-7271
Fax 905-684-7653
Email .... hrrecruit@niagarahealth.on.ca
Website .... www.niagarahealth.on.ca
Employer Background: NHS is a health service organization composed of eight hospitals located in six communities in the Niagara Region. *New Positions Created (10):* Manager, Mental Health Services; Manager, Operating Room / Emergency Room; Registered Nurses; Senior Consultant, Occupational Health & Safety; Pharmacists; Registered Nurses; Regional Director of Corporate and Strategic Planning; Directors of Patient Services (2); Director of Health Programs (2); Registered Nurses & Registered Practical Nurses.

NIAGARA, THE REGIONAL MUNICIPALITY OF
Att: John S. Nicol,
Commissioner of Human Resources
2201 St. David's Road West, PO Box 1042
Thorold, ON L2V 4T7
Tel. 905-685-1571
Fax 905-641-2232
Email .. recruitment@regional.niagara.on.ca
Website .... www.regional.niagara.on.ca
Employer Background: The Regional Municipality of Niagara is an upper-tier municipality, representing 12 local communities and serving 531,872 residents. *New Positions Created (9):* Planner; Case Manager, Ontario Works; General Manager; Projects Manager, Buildings; Manager, Vaccine-Preventable Disease Program; System Maintenance Person; Program Manager, Community Mental Health; Project Manager, Building; Public Health Inspector.

NICE SYSTEMS
Att: Ms M. Lazarus, HR Department
6651 Fraserwood Place, Suite 180
Richmond, BC V6W 1J3
Tel. 604-207-0600
Fax 604-207-5005
Email .... mlazarus@nice.com
Website .... www.nice.com
Employer Background: NICE Systems is a global provider of integrated digital recording and quality management solutions. *New Positions Created (2):* Junior Systems Engineer; Sales Engineering Coordinator.

NICOLA VALLEY HEALTH CARE
Att: Human Resources
3451 Voght Street
Merritt, BC V1K 1C6
Tel. 250-378-3273
Fax 250-378-3240
Employer Background: Nicola Valley Health Care, a member of the Thompson Health Region, is a multi-site facility. *New Positions Created (3):* Nursing Care Coordinator; Nursing Care Coordinator; Nurses.

NIELSEN MEDIA RESEARCH
Att: Human Resources Department
160 McNabb Street, 4th Floor
Markham, ON L3R 4B8
Tel. 905-475-1131
Fax 905-475-7296
Website .... www.nielsenmedia.com
Employer Background: Nielsen Media Research provides television information services for TV networks and affiliates, independent stations, syndicators, cable networks, cable systems, advertisers and their agencies in Canada and the USA. *New Positions Created (3):* Media Field Technicians; Membership Representatives; Media Field Technicians.

NIENKAMPER
Att: Human Resources
257 Finchdene Square, Unit 6
Toronto, ON M1X 1B9
Tel. 416-298-5700
Fax 416-298-9535
Email .... lisas@nienkamper.com
Website .... www.nienkamper.com
Employer Background: Established in 1968, Nienkamper manufactures high-end office furniture. *New Positions Created (5):* Health & Safety Coordinator; Woodworking Positions; Furniture Detailer / CAD Technician; Various Woodworking Positions; Various Woodworking Positions.

NIGHTINGALE HEALTH CARE INC.
Att: Yvonne MacDonald
5001 Yonge Street
Toronto, ON M2N 6P6
Tel. 416-222-6567
Fax 416-222-6949
Email .... lilyanb@nhc.ca
Employer Background: Nightingale Health Care Inc. is a nursing services provider. *New Positions Created (6):* Nursing Positions; Registered Nurses; Registered Nurses; Care Coordinators; Human Resource Coordinator; Nursing Positions.

NIPISSING UNIVERSITY
Att: Human Resources
100 College Drive, Box 5002
North Bay, ON P1B 8L7
Tel. 705-474-3450
Fax 705-495-2601
Email .... hrinfo@unipissing.ca
Website .... www.unipissing.ca
Employer Background: Nipissing University is a small co-educational university, serving 2,165 full-time students. *New Positions Created (5):* Director, Centre for Continuing Business Education / Community Relations Manager, School of Business and Economics; Manager of Research Services; Director, Technology Services; Human Resources Advisor; Dean of Faculty of Arts & Science.

NISKU PRINTERS (1980) LTD.
Att: General Manager
2002 - 8th Street, Suite 7
Nisku, AB T9E 7Y8
Tel. 780-955-8778

Fax 780-955-2270
Employer Background: Nisku Printers (1980) Ltd. is a leading commercial sheet-fed printer. *New Positions Created (2):* Planner / Customer Service Representative; Production Manger.

NISSAN CANADA INC.
Att: Human Resources
5290 Orbitor Drive
Mississauga, ON L4W 4Z5
Tel. 905-629-2888
Email .... human.resources@
.... nissancanada.com
Website .... www.nissancanada.com
Employer Background: Established over 40 years ago, Nissan Canada Inc. is a large automobile and truck manufacturer, marketing the Sentra, Altima, Maxima and PathFinder models. *New Positions Created (3):* Warehouse Supervisor; Extended Service Coordinator; Technical Publications Coordinator.

NISSIN TRANSPORT (CANADA) INC.
Att: Human Resources Manager
42 Voyager Crescent North
Toronto, ON M9W 4Y3
Tel. 416-674-0503
Fax 416-674-0881
Email .... kmiki@nissincda.com
Website .... www.nissincda.com
Employer Background: Nissin Transport (Canada) Inc. is an international freight-forwarder, specializing in warehouse management, JIT, inventory control and related services worldwide. *New Positions Created (3):* Senior Accountant; Human Resource Manager; Warehouse Supervisor.

NITREX METAL INC.
Att: Human Resources Manager
3474 Poirier Boulevard
St-Laurent, QC H4R 2J5
Tel. 514-335-7191
Fax 514-335-4160
Email .... nitrex@nitrex.com
Website .... www.nitrex.com
Employer Background: Nitrex Metal Inc. manufactures industrial heat treating control systems. *New Positions Created (6):* Material Sciences Engineer; Mechanical Engineer; Electrical Engineer; Mechanical Engineer; Control System Assembly Technician; Inside Sales Representative.

NOKIA PRODUCTS LTD.
Att: Human Resources Manager
6651 Fraserwood Place, Suite 250
Richmond, BC V6W 1J3
Fax 604-214-7795
Email ... recruiting.vancouver@nokia.com
Website .... www.nokia.com
Employer Background: Nokia Products Ltd. is the world's largest supplier of mobile phones. Their Vancouver location is a design centre for the next generation of multimedia, Internet-friendly wireless devices. *New Positions Created (8):* Hardware Engineer, Digital Design; Multimedia Developer; Software Engineers; User Interface Designer; RF Engineers, Baseband Engineers and PCB Designer; Software Developers, Applications; Software Developers, Embedded Systems; Test Engineers.

NOKIA PRODUCTS LTD.
Att: Human Resources Department
575 Westney Road South
Ajax, ON L1S 4N7
Tel. 905-427-6654
Fax 905-427-3285
Email .... hr.ajax@nokia.com
Website .... www.nokia.com
Employer Background: Nokia Products Ltd. is the world's largest supplier of mobile phones. Their Ajax location is one of three major technical service centres in North America. *New Positions Created (4):* Quality Assurance Supervisor; Quality Trainer; System / Equipment Leader; Team Leader.

NOR BAKER INC.
Att: Human Resources Department
175 Deerfield Road
Newmarket, ON L3Y 2L8
Tel. 905-895-2308
Fax 905-895-4461
Website .... www.plassein.com
Employer Background: Nor Baker is a Canadian manufacturer and part of Plassein International, a US-based company formed through the merger of several plastic film and packaging companies. *New Positions Created (2):* Director, Financial Control & Analysis; Skilled Machine Operators.

**NORAMPAC INC.,
CONCORD DIVISION**
Att: Human Resources Manager
7700 Keele Street
Concord, ON L4K 2A1
Fax 416-663-9521
Employer Background: Norampac, a joint venture between the packaging divisions of Cascades and Domtar, manufactures corrugated containers, linerboard and corrugating media. *New Positions Created (2):* Production Supervisor; Production Supervisor.

**NORAMPAC INC.,
RED ROCK DIVISION**
Att: Geoff Challinor, Director of HR
Baker Road, Highway 628
Red Rock, ON P0T 2P0
Fax 807-886-2732
Email .... geoff_challinor@norampac.com
Employer Background: Norampac Inc. (a joint venture between Cascades and Domtar) is the 10th-largest North American manufacturer of linerboard, corrugating medium and corrugated packaging products. *New Positions Created (2):* Mechanical Engineer / Planner; Assistant Steam Plant and Recovery Superintendent.

NORANDA INC.
Att: Sylvie Desforges, HR Technician
240 Hymus Boulevard
Pointe-Claire, QC H9R 1G5

Fax 514-630-9478
Email ...... recrutement@ntc.noranda.com
Website .... www.noranda.com
Employer Background: Noranda Inc. is an international mining and metals company. *New Positions Created (6):* Procurement and Stores Supervisor; Automation Technologist; Scientist / Engineer; Scientist / Engineer - Hydrometallurgy; Scientist - Mineral Processing; Assistant Scientist.

NORANDA INC., BRUNSWICK MINE
Att: Human Resources Coordinator
PO Box 3000
Bathurst, NB E2A 3Z8
Tel. 506-547-6084
Fax 506-547-6162
Website .... www.noranda.com
Employer Background: Noranda Inc., Brunswick Mine is a large producer of zinc and lead concentrate, and has an expected operational life of approximately 20 years. *New Positions Created (3):* Junior Mechanical Engineer; Underground Mine Positions; Process Control Engineer.

NORCOM / CDT
Att: Human Resources Manager
700 Gardiners Road
Kingston, ON K7M 3Y1
Tel. 613-549-2100
Fax 613-545-7575
Email .... hr@nordx.com
Website .... www.nordx.com
Employer Background: Norcom / CDT designs, develops and manufactures copper wire and cable products for the telecom market. *New Positions Created (2):* Technical Front Line Manager; Electrical Project Engineer.

NORCOM NETWORKS
Att: Human Resources
3751 North Fraser Way, Unit 1A
Burnaby, BC V5J 5G4
Tel. 604-439-2444
Fax 604-439-2447
Email .... careers@norcomnetworks.com
Website .... www.norcomnetworks.com
Employer Background: Norcom Networks provides wireless datacom solutions to large business clients. *New Positions Created (13):* Data Hub Engineer; Electronic Hardware Engineer; QA / Test Engineer; Senior DSP Engineer; Senior Hardware Engineer; Senior Software Engineer, Modems; Senior Software Engineer, OSS Systems; Senior Software Engineer, Wireless; Senior Systems Engineer; Test Engineer; Intermediate Hardware Designer; Senior RF Engineer; Senior Software Programmer.

NORDIC ACRES ENGINEERING
Att: Human Resources
815 - 8th Avenue SW, Suite 1000
Calgary, AB T2P 3P2
Tel. 403-292-0370
Fax 403-292-0377
Email .... calgary@acres.com
Website .... www.acres.com

Employer Background: Nordic Acres Engineering, a division of Acres International, is an integrated oil and gas EPCM service company that develops creative solutions for a broad range of facility engineering challenges. *New Positions Created (2):* Senior Civil / Structural Design Manager; Senior Thermal Power Engineer / Manager.

NORITSU CANADA LTD.
Att: Human Resources Department
2680 Argentia Road
Mississauga, ON L5N 5V4
Tel. 905-567-8982
Fax 905-567-5044
Email .... careers.canada@noritsu.com
Website .... www.noritsu.com
Employer Background: Noritsu Canada Ltd. manufactures photo processing equipment. *New Positions Created (12):* Technical Service Representative, Level 1; Bilingual Service Dispatcher; Regional Sales Manager; Technical Hotline Representative; Technical Service Representative; Sales Representative; Technical Service Representative; Regional Sales Manager; Administration and Human Resources Mgr; Receptionist / Administrator; Field Support Representative; Bilingual Customer Training Instructor.

NORMERICA
Att: Rob Jonkman
150 Ram Forest Road
Gormley, ON L0H 1G0
Tel. 905-841-3598
Fax 905-841-3594
Email .... r.jonkman@normerica.com
Website .... www.normerica.com
Employer Background: Normerica designs and manufactures post and beam, panelized and timberframe homes for local and export markets. *New Positions Created (2):* Junior Residential Designer; Junior Estimator.

NORQUEST COLLEGE
Att: Human Resources
10215 - 108th Street, Room 121
Edmonton, AB T5J 1L6
Tel. 780-422-2020
Fax 780-427-5476
Email .... jobs@norquest.ab.ca
Website .... www.norquest.ab.ca
Employer Background: Established in 1965, NorQuest College (formerly Alberta Vocational College) offers 37 programs in academic upgrading, career and skills training and language training, serving over 9,000 students. *New Positions Created (8):* Health Careers Instructors; Instructor; Instructor; Instructor; Instructor; Instructor; Facilities Support Technician; Health Instructors.

NORSAT INTERNATIONAL INC.
Att: Human Resources Manager
4401 Still Creek Drive, Suite 100
Burnaby, BC V5C 6G9
Tel. 604-292-9000
Fax 604-292-9007
Email .... careers@norsat.com
Website .... www.norsat.com

Employer Background: Norsat International Inc. designs and distributes products for use in the satellite wireless communications and cable television industries. *New Positions Created (3):* Senior Accountant, Inventory Control; Payroll / Office Administrator; Supply Chain Analyst.

NORSKE SKOG CANADA, ELK FALLS PRINTING PAPERS
Att: Rob Patten,
Staffing and Development Manager
PO Box 2000
Campbell River, BC V9W 5C9
Fax 250-287-5642
Employer Background: Norske Skog Canada, Elk Falls Printing Papers is one of North America's largest producers of quality pulp and paper products. *New Positions Created (4):* Mill IT Managers; Electrical Maintenance Engineer; Process Engineer; Paper Machine Stock Preparation Supervisor.

NORTEL NETWORKS
Att: Human Resources Manager
8200 Dixie Road, Suite 100
Brampton, ON L6T 5P6
Tel. 905-863-0000
Fax 905-863-8483
Email .... resumec@nortelnetworks.com
Website .... www.nortelnetworks.com
Employer Background: Nortel Networks is the world's most diversified provider of digital network solutions, actively shaping the standards for Internet access and high-speed data transmission. *New Positions Created (3):* Collections Specialist; Income Tax Manager; Various Computing Positions.

NORTEL NETWORKS
Att: Human Resources Manager
PO Box 3511, Station C
Ottawa, ON K1Y 4H7
Tel. 613-763-8232
Fax 613-765-3900
Website .... www.nortelnetworks.com
Employer Background: Nortel Networks is the world's most diversified provider of digital network solutions, actively shaping the standards for Internet access and high-speed data transmission. *New Positions Created (37):* Cost Analyst; Product Engineer, Optical Modules; Product Engineer, Optoelectronic; Senior Cost Analyst; Senior Manager, Photonic Systems Architecture; Optical Analysis Engineer; Optical Link Design Engineer; Test Engineer; ECRM Verification Engineer; Product Line Manager, Service Delivery; Applications Engineer - Tunable Lasers; Intellectual Property Counsel; Optical Amplifier Systems Verification Engineer; Optical Components Applications Engineer, Photonics; Optical System Designer; Senior Intellectual Property Manager; Software Designer, Optical Ethernet; Software Designers; Financial Analyst; IC CAD Specialist; IC Design Engineer; Intermediate F / W Designer; RF / Microwave Systems Designers; ClearCase Support Specialist; Facilities Coordinator; Manager, Reliability Studies; Manufacturing Technician;

Product Marketing Position; Real-time Embedded Software Designer, SONET / SDH ; Service Builder Verification Engineer; Software Designer, C++ / Real-Time; Software Designer, Protel, C / C++ and SNMP; Succession Access OAM Software Designer; Succession Customer Support Position; Succession Hardware Designer, RTOS and TCP / IP; Succession Software Designer SNMP; Technical Writer.

NORTH AMERICAN RAILWAY STEEL TIE CORP. / NARSTCO
Att: Human Resources Manager
General Delivery
Squamish, BC V0N 3G0
Tel. 604-892-9822
Fax 604-892-9899
Email .... keightly@direct.ca
Employer Background: NARSTCO is a leading manufacturer of steel sleepers, steel sleeper turnout sets and fastening components. *New Positions Created (2):* Operations Engineer; Project Engineer.

NORTH BAY GENERAL HOSPITAL
Att: Manager of Human Resources
750 Scollard Street, PO Box 2500
North Bay, ON P1B 5A4
Tel. 705-474-8600
Fax 705-495-7977
Website .... www.nbgh.on.ca
Employer Background: North Bay General Hospital is a 207-bed facility, providing a full range of acute and long-term care services. *New Positions Created (2):* Foundation Executive Director; Manager, Laboratory.

NORTH GRENVILLE, TOWNSHIP OF
Att: Christopher Lyon,
Manager of Public Works
275 County Road 44, PO Box 130
Kemptville, ON K0G 1J0
Tel. 613-258-7612
Fax 613-258-1441
Email ..... managerpw@northgrenville.on.ca
Website .... www.northgrenville.on.ca
Employer Background: Located south of Ottawa, the Township of North Grenville is an urban and rural municipality, with a population of 14,000. *New Positions Created (2):* Chief Superintendent of Environmental Services; Economic Development Officer.

NORTH HAMILTON COMMUNITY HEALTH CENTRE
Att: Elizabeth Beader, Executive Director
554 John Street North
Hamilton, ON L8L 4S1
Tel. 905-523-6611
Fax 905-523-5173
Email .... beader@nhchc.mcmaster.ca
Website .... www.fhs.mcmaster.ca
Employer Background: The North Hamilton Community Health Centre promotes better access to health services for the community. *New Positions Created (2):* Information Technology Manager; RN / Nurse Practitioner / Clinic Manager.

NORTH ISLAND COLLEGE / NIC
Att: Office of Human Resources
2300 Ryan Road
Courtenay, BC V9N 8N6
Tel. 250-334-5200
Fax 250-334-5288
Email .... barnes@nic.bc.ca
Website .... www.nic.bc.ca
Employer Background: Founded in 1975, NIC offers a broad range of developmental, university transfer, vocational and career programs to over 7,000 students. *New Positions Created (14):* Support Assistant; Librarian, Collection Development / Reference Services; Administrative Assistant, Human Resources; Instructor, Office Administration; Instructor, Nursing; Instructor, Electronics; Payroll Supervisor; Systems Programmer / Analyst; Administrative Secretary; Instructor, Marine Program; Instructor, Computer Science; Campus Principal; Director, Industrial Mobile Training; Vice - President, Education.

NORTH KINGSTON COMMUNITY HEALTH CENTRE / NKCHC
Att: Chairperson, Hiring Committee
400 Elliott Avenue
Kingston, ON K7K 6M9
Tel. 613-542-2813
Fax 613-542-5486
Email .... nkchc@kingston.net
Website .... www.kingston.org/chc
Employer Background: NKCHC provides holistic and comprehensive care to residents of north Kingston. *New Positions Created (2):* Dietitian / Nutritionist; Community Health Worker, Seniors.

NORTH OKANAGAN HEALTH REGION
Att: Dora Nicinski, Chief Executive Officer
1440 - 14th Avenue
Vernon, BC V1B 2T1
Tel. 250-549-6337
Fax 250-549-6331
Email .... dnicinski@nohr.org
Website .... www.nohr.org
Employer Background: NOHR provides acute, residential and community-based health services to 125,000 people. *New Positions Created (2):* Chief Operating Officer; Regional Medical Director.

NORTH OKANAGAN HEALTH REGION
Att: Jane Carlson, Recruiting Consultant
3800 Haugen Avenue
Armstrong, BC V0E 1B1
Tel. 250-546-2917
Fax 250-546-9943
Email .... careers@nohr.org
Website .... www.nohr.org
Employer Background: NOHR provides acute, residential and community-based health services to 125,000 people. *New Positions Created (18):* Director of Communication & Public Affairs; Human Resources Manager; Nurse Clinician; Organizational Development Consultant; Director, Support Services; Comptroller; Manager of Finance; Manager, Information Services; Patient Care Continuum Coordinator; Operating Room Technician; Coordinator, Community Health Program; Human Resources Consultant; Physiotherapists (2); Chief Human Resources Officer; Manager, Distribution; Residential Care Manager; Occupational Therapist; Physiotherapists / Registered Nurses.

NORTH OKANAGAN, REGIONAL DISTRICT OF
Att: Cara McCurrach, Human Resources
9848 Aberdeen Road
Coldstream, BC V1B 2K9
Tel. 250-545-5368
Fax 250-545-1445
Email .... cara.mccurrach@nord.bc.ca
Employer Background: The Regional District of North Okanagan includes six municipalities and five electoral areas. *New Positions Created (2):* Manager of Budgeting and Finance; Solid Waste Manager.

NORTH SHORE HEALTH REGION
Att: Pat DeCoursey,
Employment Consultant
152 - 15th Street East, 2nd Floor
North Vancouver, BC V7L 4N9
Tel. 604-984-5767
Fax 604-984-5770
Email .... employment@nshr.hnet.bc.ca
Website .... www.nshr.org
Employer Background: North Shore Health Region provides integrated health services to 172,000 residents of North and West Vancouver and neighboring communities. *New Positions Created (6):* Registered Nurse, EGH; Evening Home Care Nurse; RNs; Program Workers; Various Healthcare Positions; Director, Medical Imaging Services.

NORTH VANCOUVER, CITY OF
Att: Brent C. Dunn,
Senior Human Resources Officer
141- 14th Street West
North Vancouver, BC V7M 1H9
Tel. 604-990-4201
Fax 604-985-9149
Email .... hr@cnv.org
Website .... www.cnv.org
Employer Background: The City of North Vancouver is home to 44,000 residents. *New Positions Created (3):* Programmer / Analyst; Fire Prevention Inspector; Systems Analyst.

NORTH VANCOUVER SCHOOL DISTRICT
Att: Dr. Robin Brayne,
Superintendent of Schools
721 Chesterfield Avenue
North Vancouver, BC V7M 2M5
Tel. 604-990-6047
Fax 604-903-3445
Website www.nvsd44.bc.ca
Employer Background: The North Vancouver School District offers educational programs to over 18,000 students in 32 elementary and eight high schools as well as adult continuing education programs, and employs over 2,600 staff. *New Positions Created (2):* Assistant Superintendent of Schools; District Principal, Student Services.

NORTH VANCOUVER, THE DISTRICT OF
Att: Human Resources Department
355 West Queens Road
North Vancouver, BC V7N 4N5
Tel. 604-985-7761
Fax 604-987-9626
Email .... hr@dnv.org
Website .... www.dnv.org
Employer Background: The District of North Vancouver provides services to over 78,000 residents. *New Positions Created (4):* GIS Analyst; Permits Supervisor, Building and Properties; Section Manager, Engineering Services; Payroll Supervisor.

NORTH WEST COMMUNITY HEALTH SERVICES SOCIETY
Att: Sue Samuelson, HR Administrator
3412 Kalum Street
Terrace, BC V8G 4T2
Tel. 250-638-2272
Fax 250-638-2264
Email ... sue.samuelson@nwch.hnet.bc.ca
Employer Background: The North West Community Health Services Society serves nine major communities and some native communities in the region. *New Positions Created (2):* Physiotherapist / Occupational Therapists; Various Healthcare Positions.

NORTH WEST COMPANY, THE
Att: Robert Mader, Manager, Recruitment
77 Main Street, Gibralter House
Winnipeg, MB R3C 2R1
Tel. 204-934-1527
Fax 204-934-1630
Email .... rmader@northwest.ca
Website .... www.northwest.ca
Employer Background: The North West Company is a leading retailer of food, family apparel and general merchandise in northern communities. *New Positions Created (3):* Grocery Mgrs; Meat Mgrs/Meatcutters; Quick Service Restaurant Mgrs.

NORTH YORK COMMUNITY CARE ACCESS CENTRE / NORTH YORK CCAC
Att: Human Resources Department
45 Sheppard Avenue East, 7th Floor
Toronto, ON M2N 5W9
Tel. 416-222-2241
Fax 416-224-1470
Email .... hr@nyccac.on.ca
Website .... www.nyccac.on.ca
Employer Background: North York CCAC is a publicly-funded, non-profit health service organization, working to enhance the health and independence of North York residents. *New Positions Created (5):* Administrative Assistant; Case Managers; Case Managers, Hospital, Float & District; Case Managers, Hospital, Float & District; Executive Assistant / Project Coordinator.

NORTH YORK GENERAL HOSPITAL
Att: Joan White,
Manager of Recruitment and Retention
555 Finch Avenue West
Toronto, ON M2R 1N5
Tel. 416-635-2494

Fax 416-635-2623
Email .... jwhite@nygh.on.ca
Website .... www.nygh.on.ca
Employer Background: North York General Hospital is a community teaching hospital, specializing in genetics, paediatrics, neonatal critical care, geriatric health and ambulatory care services. *New Positions Created (65):* Program Director, Emergency Services; Administrative Assistant; Psychologist; Supervisor, Accounts Payable; Supervisor, Accounts Payable; Supervisor, Environmental Services; Physiotherapists (3); Chinese Language Donor Relations Coordinator; Education Secretary; Payroll Assistants (2); Registered Nurse, Adult Mental Health Department; Registered Nurse, Child & Adolescent Mental Health; Registered Nurse, IV Services; Registered Nurse, Labour & Delivery; Registered Nurse, Pre-Admission / Day Surgery; Registered Nurses, PACU Surgical Services (2); Education Secretary; Registered Dietitian; Unit Secretary; Child & Youth Worker, Child & Adolescent Mental Health; Occupational Therapist, Paediatrics Program - Child Development & Counselling; Psychologist, Child Development & Counselling Services; Registered Dietitian; Administrative Dietician, Corporate Purchasing / Retail / Information Services; Registered Practical Nurse; Child & Youth Workers, Eating Disorder Program; Eating Disorders Coordinator, Eating Disorder Program; Mgr, Child & Adolescent Ambulatory Health Services; Psychologist, Child & Adolescent Mental Health Program; Registered Respiratory Care Practitioner, Community Respiratory Services; Research Associates; Social Worker, Child & Adolescent Mental Health Program; HRIS Specialist; Manager, Labour Relations; Organizational Development Specialist; Donor Relations Coordinator; Charge Respiratory Care Practitioner, Medical Services; Operating Room Technicians, Surgical Services; Polysomnography Technologists; Registered Nurses; Registered Nurses, Critical Care; Respiratory Care Practitioners; Social Workers, Adult Mental Health; Speech Language Pathologist; Healthcare Planning Consultant; Various Health Positions; Child & Adolescent Mental Health Coordinator / Clinical Nurse Specialist; Administrative Coordinators; Nurse Clinicians; Operations / Automated System Applications Coordinator, Pharmacy; Pharmacist; Registered Nurses; Registered Nurses, Rehabilitation Unit; Critical Care Registered Nurses; Healthcare Planning Consultant; Nurse Clinician, Geriatric Services; Nurse Clinician, Medical Services; Physiotherapists, Geriatric Services; Registered Nurses and Nurse Practitioners, Geriatric Services; Registered Nurses, Emergency Department; Unit Administrator, Geriatric Services; Administrative Coordinators; Director of Care; Executive Secretary; Nurse Clinicians.

NORTH YORK GENERAL HOSPITAL, GENERAL DIVISION
Att: Human Resources
4001 Leslie Street
Toronto, ON M2K 1E1

Tel. 416-756-6730
Website .... www.nygh.on.ca
Employer Background: North York General Hospital is a community teaching hospital, specializing in genetics, paediatrics, neonatal critical care, geriatric health and ambulatory care services. *New Positions Created (37):* Manager, Cardio-Respiratory / Sleep Services - Medical Services; Registered Nurse, Adult Mental Health; Registered Nurses, Emergency Program; Registered Nurses, Intensive Care Unit; Registered Nurses, Medical Services Program; Registered Nurses, Paediatric Program; Medical Laboratory Technologist, Cytogenetics; Physiotherapist, Medical / Surgical Programs; General Duty Technologists (3); Public Relations Assistant; Education Secretary; Geriatrics Case Manager; Nurse Clinician, Emergency; Social Worker, Oncology & Palliative Care; Rehabilitation Therapy Assistant, Acute Geriatric Services; Social Worker, Inpatient Oncology - Medical Services; Heart Functions Coordinator; Medical Program; Registered Nurses; Financial Analyst; Senior Financial Analyst; Child & Youth Worker; Coordinator, Eating Disorder Program; Occupational Therapist, Eating Disorder Program; Office Supervisor, Diagnostic Imaging; Psychologist, Child & Adolescent Mental Health Program; Social Worker, Child & Adolescent Mental Health Program; Nurse Clinicians; General Duty Technologists; Medical Laboratory Technologist, Cytogenetics; Registered Nurses; Physiotherapists; Respiratory Care Practitioner; MRI Technologists (2); Registered Nurses, Critical Care; Registered Nurses, Emergency; Registered Nurses, Paediatrics; Registered Nurses, Psychiatric Crisis Team.

NORTHEAST MENTAL HEALTH CENTRE / NEMHC
Att: Recruitment Officer
680 Kirkwood Drive
Sudbury, ON P3E 1X3
Tel. 705-675-9192
Fax 705-675-6817
Email .... ltremblay@nemhc.on.ca
Employer Background: NEMHC is a new organization formed by the Ontario Health Service Restructuring Commission and endorsed by the Ontario Ministry of Health and Long-Term Care. *New Positions Created (8):* Social Workers / Registered Nurses (2); Various Mental Health Positions; Psychiatrist, Assertive Community Treatment Team (ACTT); Director, Information Systems; Registered Nurse Team Leader; Director of Finance; Program Manager, Integrated Services for Northern Children; Manager.

NORTHEASTERN ONTARIO REGIONAL CANCER CENTRE / NEORCC
Att: Human Resources Manager
41 Ramsey Lake Road
Sudbury, ON P3E 5J1
Tel. 705-522-6237
Fax 705-523-7335
Email .... hr@neorcc.on.ca
Website .... www.neorcc.on.ca

Employer Background: NEORCC, one of eight regional offices operated by Cancer Care Ontario, is affiliated with Laurentian University and the University of Ottawa. *New Positions Created (2):* Radiation Oncologist; Pharmacy Manager.

NORTHERN AIRBORNE TECHNOLOGY LTD. / NAT
Att: Tim Reis, Human Resources Manager
1925 Kirschner Road, Suite 14
Kelowna, BC V1Y 4N7
Tel. 250-763-2232
Fax 250-762-3374
Email .... hr@natech.com
Website .... www.northernairborne.com
Employer Background: NAT manufactures specialized airborne communications equipment, used primarily in helicopter and fixed-wing aircraft applications. *New Positions Created (3):* Intermediate Electronics Designer; Intermediate Firmware Designer; Technical Writer / Editor.

NORTHERN ALBERTA DEVELOPMENT COUNCIL / NADC
Att: Allan Geary,
Director of Projects and Research
9621 - 96th Avenue, Suite 206
Provincial Building, Bag 900 - 14
Peace River, AB T8S 1T4
Tel. 780-624-6274
Fax 780-624-6184
Website .... www.gov.ab.ca/nadc
Employer Background: NADC's mandate is to investigate, monitor, evaluate, plan and promote practical measures to foster and advance general development in northern Alberta. *New Positions Created (2):* Northern Development Officer; Senior Northern Development Officer.

NORTHERN ALBERTA INSTITUTE OF TECHNOLOGY, THE / NAIT
Att: Human Resources
11762 - 106th Street
Edmonton, AB T5G 2R1
Tel. 780-491-3000
Fax 780-471-7533
Email .... hrs@nait.ab.ca
Website .... www.nait.ab.ca
Employer Background: Established in 1963, NAIT is a post-secondary institution, with over 54,000 students. *New Positions Created (16):* Cooks; Educational Technology Assistant; Educational Laboratory Technician; Instructor, Computer Engineering Technology; Instructor, Computer Engineering Technology; Instructor, Construction Engineering Technology Program; Instructor, Bachelor of Applied Information Systems ; Instructor, Marketing and E-Commerce; Instructors, Pipetrades; Systems Analyst, Microsoft Exchange ; Instructor, Cytotechnology Program; Instructor, Medical Laboratory Technology Program; Instructors, Instrumentation; Instructors, Telecommunications; Instructor, Electrician Program; Continuing Education Coordinator.

NORTHERN ALBERTA INSTITUTE OF TECHNOLOGY, THE / NAIT
Att: Director, Human Resources
10230 Princess Elizabeth Avenue
Edmonton, AB T5G 0Y2

Tel. 780-471-7466
Fax 780-471-7533
Email .... hrs@nait.ab.ca
Website .... www.nait.ab.ca

Employer Background: Established in 1963, NAIT is a post-secondary institution, with over 54,000 students. *New Positions Created (26):* Power Plant Engineer, 3rd-Class Facilities Engineering; Dean, Business Development; Instructor, Applied Information Systems; New Application Development Analysts (2); Instructors, Pipetrades; Systems Analyst, Microsoft Exchange; Instructor, Computer Engineering Technology; Instructor, Computer Engineering Technology; Instructor, Building Environment Services Technology; Instructor, Interior Design Technology; Assistant Program Head, Instrumentation / Instrument Apprentice; Assistant Program Heads, Telecommunications; Computer Systems Support Technologist II; Instructor, Electrical Engineering Technology; Instructor, Insulator; Instructor, Ironworker Program; Instructor, Sheet Metal; Instructors, Electrician Program; Occupational Health Nurse; Instructor, Cytotechnology Program; Instructor, Medical Laboratory Technology Program; Instructors, Instrumentation; Instructors, Telecommunications; Data Administrator; Continuing Education Program Coordinator; Senior Accountant.

NORTHERN ELEVATOR LTD.
Att: Carol Chiang
270 Finchdene Square
Toronto, ON M1X 1A5

Fax 416-291-4654

Employer Background: Northern Elevator Ltd. is an elevator manufacturer and a member of Thyssen Elevator Worldwide. *New Positions Created (3):* Information Systems Specialist; Human Resources Administrator; Material Manager.

NORTHERN GIFTS LTD.
Att: Human Resources Manager
4585 Canada Way, Suite 300
Burnaby, BC V5G 4L6

Tel. 604-299-5050
Fax 604-299-0808
Email .... marketingassistant@
.... northerngifts.com
Website .... www.northerngifts.com

Employer Background: Founded in 1988, Northern Gifts Ltd. designs and manufactures a unique line of plush animals. *New Positions Created (2):* Marketing / Creative Assistant; Account Executive.

NORTHERN INTERIOR REGIONAL HEALTH BOARD
Att: Jacquie Scobie,
Regional Recruitment Manager
2000 - 15th Avenue, Suite 2000
Prince George, BC V2M 1S2

Tel. 250-565-2722
Fax 250-565-2251
Email .... jscobie@nirhb.bc.ca
Website .... www.nirhb.bc.ca

Employer Background: The Northern Interior Regional Health Board is the governing body responsible for health services in northern BC. *New Positions Created (2):* Child Care Network Mgr / Daycare Manager; Regional Director, Human Resources.

NORTHERN LIGHTS COLLEGE / NLC
Att: Roberta Kuropatwa,
Administrative Assistant
PO Box 1000
Fort St. John, BC V1J 6K1

Tel. 250-785-6981
Fax 250-785-1294
Email .... rkuropat@nlc.bc.ca
Website .... www.nlc.bc.ca

Employer Background: Formed in 1981, NLC provides a range of academic, career, extension, technical and vocational programs through 5 campuses and 3 learning centres in northern British Columbia. *New Positions Created (3):* Counsellor; Land Sciences Instructor; History Instructor.

NORTHERN LIGHTS COLLEGE / NLC
Att: Personnel Administrator,
Regional Administration
11401 - 8th Street
Dawson Creek, BC V1G 4G2

Tel. 250-784-7520
Fax 250-782-5233
Email .... personnel@nlc.bc.ca
Website .... www.nlc.bc.ca

Employer Background: Formed in 1981, NLC provides a range of academic, career, extension, technical and vocational programs through five campuses and three learning centres in northern BC. *New Positions Created (6):* Campus Principal; Power Engineering and Gas Processing Instructor; Assistant Principal; Oil and Gas Field Operations Instructor; Director, Human Resources; Campus Principal.

NORTHERN LIGHTS REGIONAL HEALTH SERVICES / NLRHS
Att: Human Resources Department
7 Hospital Street
Fort McMurray, AB T9H 1P2

Tel. 780-791-6011
Fax 780-791-6281
Email .... employment@nlrha.ab.ca
Website .... www.nlrha.ab.ca

Employer Background: NLRHS provides health services in Fort McMurray, a city of 42,000 people located 435 km northeast of Edmonton. *New Positions Created (9):* Dietary Technologist I; Registered Nurse, Maternal Child; Director, Mental Health Services; Occupational Therapist I; Director, Medicine & Community Services; Children's Mental Health Therapist; Mental Health Working Leader; Occupational Therapist; Emergency Nurses.

NORTHERN ROCKIES REGIONAL DISTRICT
Att: Deb Walker, Corporate Services
Bag Service 399
Fort Nelson, BC V0C 1R0

Tel. 250-774-2541
Fax 250-774-6794
Email .... dwalker@northernrockies.org
Website .... www.northernrockies.org

Employer Background: Situated along the Alaska Highway, the Northern Rockies Regional District includes the Town of Fort Nelson, which has a population of 65,000. *New Positions Created (2):* Grants Coordinator; Public Works Manager.

NORTHERN SCHOOL RESOURCE ALLIANCE
Att: Fred Porter, Chief Executive Officer
101 Syndicate Avenue North
Suite 410, Chapple Building
Thunder Bay, ON P7C 3V4

Tel. 807-475-6989
Fax 807-475-6945
Email .... fporter@resourcenorth.com
Website .... www.resourcenorth.com

Employer Background: Founded in 1977, the Northern School Resource Alliance provides access to products and professional services to smaller educational institutions in northern Ontario. *New Positions Created (3):* FSL Teachers (2); Principal and Teachers; Teachers, English and French.

NORTHERN STAR TRUCKING LTD.
Att: Stan
41 Westside Drive
Toronto, ON M9C 1B3

Tel. 416-695-1060
Fax 416-695-4561
Email .... stan@nst.on.ca
Website .... www.nst.on.ca

Employer Background: Northern Star Trucking Ltd. provides transportation services to domestic and international markets. *New Positions Created (3):* Class A Mechanic; Dispatcher; Junior Dispatcher.

NORTHGATE EXPLORATION LTD., KEMESS MINE
Att: Human Resources
PO Box 3519
Smithers, BC V0J 2N0

Tel. 250-847-5667
Fax 604-881-8401
Email .... jstrain@kemess.com
Website .... www.kemess.com

Employer Background: Northgate Exploration Ltd. is a mid-tier gold mining company, with investments in North and South America. Their Kemess Mine produces 260,000 ounces of gold and 74 million pounds of copper per year. *New Positions Created (2):* Accounting Technician; Mine Accountant.

NORTHLAND SYSTEMS TRAINING INC.
Att: Steve Shivkumar,
Director of Business Development

255 Albert Street, Suite 600
Ottawa, ON K1P 6A9

Tel. 613-566-7044
Fax 613-566-7001
Email .... hr@northlandinc.com
Website .... www.northlandinc.com

Employer Background: Established in 1997, Northland Systems Training Inc. is a Canadian technology company, specializing in the outsourced delivery of vendor-specific hardware and software training programs for the IT sectors. *New Positions Created (10):* Consultants; Instructors, Internetworking, Security or Wireless; Subject Matter Expert; Wireless Engineer, ATM; Consultants, Internetworking, Security and Wireless Technology; Instructors, Internetworking; Graphic Designers; Instructional Designers; Technical Writers; Telecom Instructors.

NORTHWEST CATHOLIC DISTRICT SCHOOL BOARD, THE
Att: G. Rousseau, Chair of the Board
555 Flinders Avenue
Fort Frances, ON P9A 3L2

Fax 807-274-8792
Website .... www.tncdsb.on.ca

Employer Background: The Northwest Catholic District School Board is committed to providing an education based on gospel values, in partnership with home, church and community. *New Positions Created (2):* Director of Education and Secretary to the Board; French Immersion Teachers.

NORTHWEST DIGITAL
Att: Human Resources Manager
1985 Michelin Road
Laval, QC H7L 5B7

Tel. 450-973-6678
Fax 450-973-9588
Email .... ppalmieri@mtl.nwd.ca
Website .... www.nwd.com

Employer Background: Established in 1980, Northwest Digital is a national computer integrator. *New Positions Created (2):* Customer Service Representative; Inside Sales Support Representatives.

NORTHWEST HYDRAULIC CONSULTANTS LTD. / NHC
Att: Human Resources Manager
4823 - 99th Street
Edmonton, AB T6E 4Y1

Tel. 780-436-5868
Fax 780-436-1645
Email .... bevans@nhc-edm.com
Website .... www.nhcweb.com

Employer Background: NHC is a leading water resources engineering consulting firm. *New Positions Created (3):* Principal Engineer; Senior Engineer; Water Resources Technologists.

NORTHWEST TERRITORIES POWER CORPORATION / NTPC
Att: Human Resources
4 Capital Drive
Hay River, NT X0E 1G2

Tel. 867-874-5200

Fax 867-874-5229
Email .... dmunro@ntpc.com
Website .... www.ntpc.com

Employer Background: NTPC is responsible for generating and distributing electricity throughout the Northwest Territories. *New Positions Created (12):* Group Leader, Financial Planning & Coordination; Treasurer; Group Leader, Financial Planning and Coordination; Treasurer; Mechanical Design Drafting Technologist; Mechanical Technologist; Planning and Budgets Officer; Power Lineperson; Director; Group Leader, Planning; Mechanical Design Drafting Technologist; Mechanical Engineer.

NORTHWESTEL INC.
Att: Human Resources
PO Box 2727
Whitehorse, YT Y1A 4Y4

Tel. 867-668-5300
Fax 867-668-3236
Email .... recruitment@nwtel.ca
Website .... www.nwtel.ca

Employer Background: Northwestel Inc. provides a range of telecommunications solutions to 110,000 people across the Yukon, Northwest Territories and northern British Columbia. *New Positions Created (4):* Manager, Business Development and Implementation; Information Systems Program Manager; Mgr, Settlements; Director, Operations.

NORTHWESTERN HEALTH SERVICES REGION
Att: Human Resources,
Regional Administration
10106 - 100th Avenue
Suite 200, Provincial Building
High Level, AB T0H 1Z0

Tel. 780-926-4391
Fax 780-926-4379
Email .... hr@nwhsr.com
Website .... www.nwhsr.com

Employer Background: The Northwestern Health Services Region is a regional health authority, employing over 270 people and serving a population of 19,000. *New Positions Created (13):* Community Health Nurses; Environmental Services Officer; Patient Services Leader; Healthcare Positions; Nursing Positions; Combined Laboratory and X-ray Technician; Community Health Nurse; Director, Communications and Planning; General Duty Nurses; Mgr, Information Services; Physiotherapist; Psychologist; Manager, Information Services.

NORTHWESTERN HEALTH UNIT
Att: Phyllis Anderson,
Health Promotion Team Leader
75-D Van Horne Avenue
Dryden, ON P8N 2B2

Tel. 807-223-3301
Fax 807-223-5754
Website .... www.nwhu.on.ca

Employer Background: The Northwestern Health Unit provides a range of health services to promote an optimal lifestyle. *New Positions Created (2):* Speech Language Pathologist; Speech-Language Pathologist.

NORTHWOOD TECHNOLOGIES INC.
Att: Human Resources Department
43 Auriga Drive
Nepean, ON K2E 7Y8

Tel. 613-224-2020
Fax 613-224-1696
Email .... careers@northwoodtec.com
Website .... www.northwoodtec.com

Employer Background: Northwood Technologies Inc. develops software solutions for the wireless telecom industry. *New Positions Created (21):* Documentation Specialist; E-Business Manager; Marketing Manager; Product Manager, deciBel Planner; Product Specialist; Sales Engineer; Software Developer; Software Engineer; Telecommunications Account Manager; Director of Product Management; Network Administrator; Software Developer; Test Engineer; Project Leaders; Project Mgrs; RF Engineers; Executive Assistant; Product Mgr, Data; Sales Engineer; Technical Editor; Test Engineer.

NOVA CHEMICALS CORPORATION, RESEARCH AND TECHNOLOGY CENTRE
Att: People Services
2928 - 16th Street NE
Calgary, AB T2E 7K7

Tel. 403-250-4700
Fax 403-250-0633
Email .... resumes@novachem.com
Website .... www.novachem.com

Employer Background: NOVA Chemicals Corporation is a petrochemicals company that operates two commodity chemicals businesses, olefins / polyolefins and styrenics. *New Positions Created (2):* Research Scientist, Product Development; Research Scientist.

NOVA SCOTIA COLLEGE OF ART AND DESIGN / NSCAD
Att: Vice-President, Academic
5163 Duke Street
Halifax, NS B3J 3J6

Fax 902-425-4664
Website .... www.nscad.ns.ca

Employer Background: Founded in 1887, NSCAD provides undergraduate and graduate programs in art, craft and design to over 900 students. *New Positions Created (5):* Instructors, Computer and Digital Media; Assistant Professor, Communication Design Program; Assistant Professor, History of Craft and Decorative Arts; Assistant Professor, Sculpture; Dean.

NOVARTIS PHARMACEUTICALS CANADA INC.
Att: Human Resources Department
385 Bouchard Boulevard
Dorval, QC H9S 1A9

Tel. 514-631-6775
Fax 514-631-1867
Email .... pharmops@
.... recruitmentsolutions.com
Website .... www.novartis.com

Employer Background: Novartis Pharmaceuticals Canada Inc., a subsidiary of Novartis Pharma AG, develops and provides a broad range of innovative prescription medicines to medical professionals and patients. *New Positions Created (6):* Engineering Project Manager (3); Product Manager, Oncology; Director, Sales Training and Development; District Sales Managers (4); Medical Representatives, Primary Care (30); Product Managers (7).

NOVATEL INC.
Att: Human Resources Department
1120 - 68th Avenue NE
Calgary, AB T2E 8S5

Tel. 403-295-4500
Fax 403-730-4627
Email .... hr@novatel.ca
Website .... www.novatel.ca

Employer Background: Novatel Inc. designs, markets and supports a broad range of products using the Global Positioning System (GPS). *New Positions Created (4):* Manufacturing Engineer; RF Engineer; Software Quality Assurance Engineer; Systems Engineer.

NOVATEL WIRELESS TECHNOLOGIES LTD.
Att: Human Resources Manager
6715 - 8th Street NE, Suite 200
Calgary, AB T2E 7H7

Tel. 403-295-4800
Fax 403-295-4803
Email .... hr@novatelwireless.com
Website .... www.novatelwireless.com

Employer Background: Novatel Wireless Technologies Ltd. develops and manufactures wireless Internet solutions, providing access to mission-critical information in fixed and mobile environments. *New Positions Created (9):* CDMA Engineers; Project Manager, CDMA Wireless Modems; Hardware Engineer, Electronic Design; Hardware Engineer, Product Design; Project Manager; Reliability Engineer; Software Engineers, Quality Assurance; Software Systems Engineers; Engineers.

NOVATOR SYSTEMS LTD.
Att: Recruiting
444 Yonge Street, Suite 203
Toronto, ON M5B 2H4

Tel. 416-260-5131
Fax 416-260-5121
Email .... careers@novator.com
Website .... www.novator.com

Employer Background: Founded in 1994, Novator Systems Ltd. is an e-commerce services and software company. *New Positions Created (8):* Director, Web Development; Product Manager; Quality Assurance Analyst; Senior E-Commerce Sales Executives; Senior Project Manager; Senior Software Developer; Telemarketing Representative; Web Developer.

NOVATRONICS INC.
Att: Human Resources Department
677 Erie Street
Stratford, ON N5A 6V6

Tel. 519-271-3880
Fax 905-271-6133

Email .... hrm@novatronics.com
Website .... www.novatronics.com

Employer Background: Novatronics Inc. manufactures custom precision electromechanical and electromagnetic devices for the aerospace industry. *New Positions Created (3):* Design Engineer; Quality Assurance Manager; Professional Engineer.

NOVEX PHARMA
Att: Human Resources
380 Elgin Mills Road East
Richmond Hill, ON L4C 5H2

Tel. 905-884-0470
Fax 905-884-8385
Website .... www.apotex.ca

Employer Background: Novex Pharma (part of Apotex Group) develops, manufactures and distributes a broad line of quality pharmaceuticals. *New Positions Created (2):* Process Engineer; Information Technology Consultant.

NOVOPHARM LTD.
Att: Chandra Ramnarain,
Human Resources Administrator
30 Novopharm Court
Toronto, ON M1B 2K9

Tel. 416-291-8876
Fax 416-291-1148

Employer Background: Novopharm (part of TEVA Pharmaceutical) has manufactured branded generic drugs for over 35 years. *New Positions Created (11):* GLP Compliance Auditor; Inventory Control Clerk; Patent Lawyer; Bioanalytical Chemists; Business Development Analyst; Director, Clinical Research; Mgr, Engineering Compliance; Mgr, Research and Development GMP Compliance; Organic Chemist; Research Chemists; Senior MS / MS Research Scientist.

NOWTV
Att: VP, Television Broadcasting
Box 2010
Winnipeg, MB R3C 3R3

Email .... jobs@nowtv.ca
Website .... www.nowtv.ca

Employer Background: NOWTV (a division of Trinity Television Inc.) is a new Christian television station, serving the people of the Fraser Valley / Greater Vancouver Area starting fall 2001. *New Positions Created (10):* Bandwith Host / Producer; Big Event Movie Host; Executive Assistant; Host / Producer, NOW Online; Host / Producer, World NOW; Manager, Creative Services; Manager, On-Air Promotions; Production Manager; Sales Manager; Television Sales Representative.

NPD GROUP CANADA, CORP., THE
Att: Human Resources
240 Duncan Mill Road, Suite 200
Toronto, ON M3B 3R6

Tel. 416-445-1804
Fax 416-445-2876
Email ..... caren_healyjones@ipsos-npd.com
Website .... www.npd.com

Employer Background: The NPD Group Canada, Corp. provides consumer-based in-

formation for the development of effective marketing strategies. *New Positions Created (2):* Account Mgr; Vice President, Finance.

NPS PHARMACEUTICALS INC.
Att: Human Resources
6850 Goreway Drive
Mississauga, ON L4V 1V7

Tel. 905-677-0831
Fax 905-677-9595
Email .... jobs@npsp.com
Website .... www.npsp.com

Employer Background: NPS Pharmaceuticals Inc. (formerly NPS Allelix Corporation) is a public pharmaceutical company, developing novel therapeutics for the treatment of hyperparathyroidism, osteoporosis, stroke, pain and other debilitating diseases and disorders. *New Positions Created (13):* Information Services Technician; Research Associate; Receptionist; Scientist, Molecular Biology, Drug Development; Process Development Associate II; Research Information Specialist; Research Scientist; Process Development Associate; Receptionist; Competitive Intelligence Specialist; Shipping and Receiving Clerk / Maintenance; Oracle DBA and NT Systems Administrator; Executive Assistant.

NRB INC.
Att: Duncan Alexander
115 South Service Road West
Grimsby, ON L3M 4G3

Tel. 905-945-9622
Fax 905-945-2003
Email ..... duncanalexander@nrb-inc.com
Website .... www.nrb-inc.com

Employer Background: Established in 1979, NRB Inc. is a manufacturer of modular buildings. *New Positions Created (7):* Plant Mgr; Carpenters/Carpenter Helpers; Carpenter Subcontractors; Welder/Fitter; CAD Operator; Shipper / Receiver; Estimator.

NRCS INC.
Att: Michelle Primeau, Supervisor
240 Catherine Street, Suite 406
Ottawa, ON K2P 2G8

Tel. 613-566-4500
Fax 613-566-4511

Employer Background: NRCS Inc. is a disability management firm offering medical assessment, disability / injury management and WSIB services. *New Positions Created (4):* Kinesiologists; Occupational Therapist; Registered Nurse; Vocational Consultants.

NRNS INC.
Att: Human Resources Manager
300 March Road, Suite 205
Kanata, ON K2K 2E2

Tel. 613-599-7860
Fax 613-599-7739
Email .... careers@nrnsinc.on.ca
Website .... www.nrnsinc.on.ca

Employer Background: NRNS Inc. designs, implements and maintains IT infrastructure and associated network services. *New Positions Created (6):* LDAP Programmer;

Mail / Messaging Specialist; Network Operations Engineer; Programmer, Business-to-Business / MQSeries; Public Key Infrastructure Specialist; X.500 Directory Specialist.

NRX GLOBAL CORP.
Att: Human Resources Manager
150 York Street, 14th Floor
Toronto, ON M5H 3S5

Tel.	416-368-4567
Fax	416-368-9844
Email	careers@nrx.com
Website	www.nrx.com

Employer Background: NRX Global Corp. is a B2B software and business solutions provider, focused on the industrial maintenance, repair and operations market. *New Positions Created (4):* Implementation Specialist; Manager, Finance and Accounting; Recruiter, Technology; Technical Infrastructure Specialist.

NSI COMMUNICATIONS
Att: Human Resources Manager
6900 Trans Canada Highway
Pointe-Claire, QC H9R 1C2

Tel.	514-694-2244
Fax	514-694-5288
Email	jobs.emplois@nsicomm.com
Website	www.nsicomm.com

Employer Background: NSI Communications designs, manufactures and markets state-of-the-art satellite-based telecommunications equipment and services worldwide. *New Positions Created (34):* Bilingual Accounts Payable Clerk; Applications Engineer; Digital Modem Designer; DSP Designer; Embedded Software Designer, C / C++; Engineering Technologist; FPGA Designer; PCB Designer; Project Manager; RF Designer; Senior Field Engineer; Senior Systems Engineer; System Architect; Technician; DSP Designer; Embedded Software Designer; Engineering Technologist; FPGA Designer; PCB Designer; RF Designer; Technician; Applications Engineer; Digital Modem Designer; Project Manager; Senior Field Engineer; Senior Systems Engineer; System Architect; CM / Document Control Specialist; Director, Business Development; Computing Positions (3); Director, Project Management; Software Architect; Senior Systems Engineer; Technical Trainer.

NSTEIN TECHNOLOGIES
Att: Human Resources Manager
3090 le Carrefour Boulevard, Suite 700
Laval, QC H7T 2J7

Tel.	514-908-5406
Fax	514-908-5407
Email	careers@nstein.com
Website	www.nstein.com

Employer Background: NStein specializes in linguistic engineering, processing information into relevant web content for easy retrieval. *New Positions Created (11):* Computational Linguist; Linguist; Programmer Analyst, C++; Business Development Exec; C++ Programmer / Analyst; Functional Analyst; HR Coordinator; Marketing Coordinator; Object-Oriented Architect; Technical Writer; Technology Specialist.

NTG CLARITY NETWORKS INC.
Att: Human Resources Manager
90 Nolan Court, Suite 1A
Markham, ON L3R 4L9

Tel.	905-305-1325
Fax	905-305-8993
Email	hr-tor@ntgclarity.com
Website	www.ntgclarity.com

Employer Background: NTG Clarity Networks Inc. (formerly Clarity Telecom Networking Inc.) offers network, IT and infrastructure solutions to telecom service providers. *New Positions Created (3):* Telecom Voice and Data Installation Technicians, Junior and Senior; Graphic / Website Designer; Various Telecom Positions.

NUANCE GLOBAL TRADERS (CANADA) INC.
Att: Human Resources
5200 Hollybridge Way, Unit 180
Richmond, BC V7C 4N3

Fax	604-270-0324
Website	www.thenuancegroup.com

Employer Background: Nuance Global Traders, a division of SwissAir, is part of a global network of premier, duty-free department stores and retail outlets. *New Positions Created (6):* Flight Operations Position; Japanese Language Sales & Promotions Staff; Retail Positions; Retail Positions; Various Retail Positions; Warehouse Persons.

NUBASE TECHNOLOGIES INC.
Att: Human Resources Manager
5075 Yonge Street, 6th Floor
Toronto, ON M2N 6C6

Tel.	416-512-2727
Fax	416-512-2726
Email	hr@nubase.com
Website	www.nubase.com

Employer Background: Nubase Technologies is an enterprise e-business enabler and application service provider for the financial services industry. *New Positions Created (3):* Corporate Account Execs; Business Analyst; Software Developers / Architects.

NUCON SYSTEMS INC.
Att: Estimating Manager
498 Markland Street, Unit 7
Markham, ON L6C 1Z6

Tel.	416-213-5556
Fax	416-213-5577
Website	www.nuconsystems.com

Employer Background: Nucon Systems Inc. (a division of Wittmann) designs and manufactures pneumatic conveying and robotics equipment. *New Positions Created (6):* Project Estimator; Secretary / Receptionist; Parts Order / Customer Service Coordinator; Project Estimator; Service Technician; Project Estimator.

NUHC INC.
Att: Ken Johnston, Regional Manager
3800 Steeles Avenue West, Suite 100E
Woodbridge, ON L4L 4G9

Tel.	905-850-6806
Fax	905-850-6839

Email	kjohnston@nuhorizons.com
Website	www.nuhorizons.com

Employer Background: NUHC Inc. is the Canadian subsidiary of Nu Horizons Electronics Corp., a major distributor of electronic components in the USA. *New Positions Created (5):* Field Application Engineers; General Manager; Field Application Engineers; Field Sales Reps; Inside Sales Reps.

NUNA LOGISTICS LTD.
Att: Leah Sheck
5107 - 48th Street, Suite 104
Yellowknife, NT X1A 1N5

Tel.	867-766-3001
Fax	867-766-3005
Email	nuna@theedge.ca
Website	www.nunasi.com

Employer Background: Nuna Logistics Ltd. is an arctic construction and contract mining company, operating in the Northwest Territories and Nunavut. *New Positions Created (3):* Site Administrator; Heavy Equipment Trainer; Project Manager / Assistant Project Manager.

NXTPHASE CORPORATION
Att: Human Resources
3040 East Broadway
Vancouver, BC V5M 1Z4

Tel.	604-215-9822
Fax	604-215-9833
Email	careers@nxtphase.com
Website	www.nxtphase.com

Employer Background: NxtPhase Corporation is dedicated to improving the way electric power is measured and controlled in the electric power industry. *New Positions Created (5):* Electronics Engineer; Electronics Technician; Firmware / DSP Engineer; High Voltage Test Engineer; Manufacturing Manager.

O&Y CB RICHARD ELLIS FACILITIES MANAGEMENT
Att: Joanne Herbert
Manager, Products & Services
21 Melinda Street, 4th Floor, PO Box 367
Toronto, ON M5L 1G4

Email	joanne_herbert@oycbre.com
Website	www.oyp.com

Employer Background: O&Y CB Richard Ellis Facilities Management, a division of O&Y Properties Inc., is a corporate real estate services company. *New Positions Created (2):* Coordinator, Products and Services; Real Estate Analyst.

O&Y ENTERPRISE
Att: Allan Drummond,
Director, Facilities Management
555 Burrard Street, Suite 1455
Vancouver, BC V7X 1M9

Tel.	604-669-3511
Fax	604-689-0738
Email	adrummond@oyp.com
Website	www.oyp.com

Employer Background: O&Y Enterprise, a division of O&Y Properties Inc., manages nearly 105 million square feet of office, retail, residential, mixed-use and industrial properties in Canada. *New Positions Created (3):* Facilities Administration Representative; Regional Premises Officer; Facilities / Property Management Executive.

O&Y ENTERPRISE

Att: Maureen MacMillan, Controller
18 King Street East, Suite 1500
Toronto, ON M5C 1C4

Tel. 416-862-6100
Fax 416-862-6163
Email .... mmacmillan@oyp.com
Website .... www.oyp.com

Employer Background: O&Y Enterprise, a division of O&Y Properties Inc., manages nearly 105 million square feet of office, retail, residential, mixed-use and industrial properties in Canada. *New Positions Created (14):* Accounts Payable Clerk; Property Manager; Property Accountant; Property Coordinator; Amicus Project Coordinator; Facilities Services Representative; Manager, Facilities Coordination; Premises Officer; Leasing Administrative Assistant; Accounts Payable Administrator; Premises Officers (2); Executive Assistant; Property Manager; Revenue Control Accountant.

O&Y ENTERPRISE

Att: Mark Barszczewski,
Life / Safety & Technical Manager
Place de Ville, PO Box 69009
Ottawa, ON K1R 1A7

Tel. 613-236-3600
Fax 613-567-7809
Email .... mbarszczewski@oyp.com
Website .... www.oyp.com

Employer Background: O&Y Enterprise, a division of O&Y Properties Inc., manages nearly 105 million square feet of office, retail, residential, mixed-use and industrial properties in Canada. *New Positions Created (3):* Maintenance Electrician; Third-Class Stationary Engineer; Third-Class Stationary Engineer.

O'BRIEN INSTALLATIONS LTD.

Att: Controller
14 Garden Avenue
Stoney Creek, ON L8E 2Y9

Tel. 905-662-4979
Fax 905-662-3214
Website .... www.obrieninstall.com

Employer Background: O'Brien Installations Ltd. is a leader in the overhead crane and hoist industry. *New Positions Created (4):* Accounts Payable / Billing Specialist; Inside Sales Rep; Mechanical Design Engineer; Industrial Engineering Technician.

O'HARA TECHNOLOGIES INC.

Att: Human Resources Manager
20 Kinnear Court
Richmond Hill, ON L4B 1K8

Tel. 905-707-3286
Fax 905-707-3304
Email .... suzanne@oharatech.com
Website .... www.oharatech.com

Employer Background: O'Hara Technologies Inc. manufactures process equipment for the food, pharmaceutical and confectionery industries. *New Positions Created (4):* Engineering Manager; Electrical Panel / Machine Builder; PLC Programmer; Manufacturing / Plant Manager.

OAK BAY LODGE

Att: Personnel Office
2251 Cadboro Bay Road
Victoria, BC V8R 5H3

Tel. 250-370-6647
Fax 250-370-6601

Employer Background: Oak Bay Lodge is an accredited, licensed, 273-bed intermediate care facility operated by a non-profit society. *New Positions Created (2):* Coordinator, Housekeeping and Laundry Services; Nurses.

OAKRUN FARM BAKERY LTD.

Att: Human Resources
58 Carluke Road West
Ancaster, ON L9G 3L1

Tel. 905-648-1818
Fax 905-648-0679
Website .... www.oakrun.com

Employer Background: Oakrun Farm Bakery Ltd. is a high-volume manufacturer of fresh and frozen baked goods. *New Positions Created (11):* Production Supervisor; Customer Service Representative; Licensed Electrician; Shipper; Sanitation Supervisor; Accounting Clerk; Maintenance Engineer; Accounts Payable Clerk; Quality Assurance Technician; Cost Accountant; Electrician / Millwrights.

OAKVILLE, CORPORATION OF THE TOWN OF

Att: Human Resources Department
1225 Trafalgar Road, PO Box 310
Oakville, ON L6J 5A6

Tel. 905-845-6601
Fax 905-338-4425
Email .... humanresources@
.... town.oakville.on.ca
Website .... www.town.oakville.on.ca

Employer Background: The Corporation of the Town of Oakville is home to over 140,000 people. *New Positions Created (7):* Director, Parks and Recreation; Planner, Site Plan; Manager of Works; Planner / Analyst; Traffic Engineer; Fire Chief; Draftsperson.

OAKWOOD ASSOCIATES

Att: Managing Director
840 - 6th Avenue SW, Suite 220
Calgary, AB T2P 3E5

Tel. 403-264-8020
Fax 403-263-8020
Email .... sarahk@oakwood.ca
Website .... www.oakwood.ca

Employer Background: Oakwood Associates is a corporate capital management group. *New Positions Created (4):* Legal Assistant; Multimedia Graphics Specialist; Lawyer; Marketing Coordinator.

OAKWOOD RETIREMENT COMMUNITIES INC.

Att: James Schiegel, V.P. Operations
460 Frederick Street
Kitchener, ON N2H 2P5

Employer Background: Oakwood Retirement Communities Inc. operates long-term care facilities for the elderly in Ontario. *New Positions Created (7):* Administrators (2); Directors, Food Services (2); Directors, Nursing Care (2); Directors, Recreation Services (2); Administrator; Director of Food Services; Director of Nursing Care.

OAO TECHNOLOGY SOLUTIONS

Att: Human Resources Manager
100 Tempo Avenue
Toronto, ON M2H 3S5

Tel. 416-491-2112
Fax 416-491-9163
Email .... apply@oaot.com
Website .... www.oaot.com

Employer Background: OAOT is a publicly-traded, global provider of information technology and e-business solutions. *New Positions Created (11):* Analysts / Consultants; Programmers / Analysts; E-Business Project Manager; Human Resources Manager; Senior E-Business Architect; Programmers; MQ Series Certified Specialist; Quality Coordinator; Senior Database Analyst; Software Developers / Team Leaders; Intermediate / Senior Developers and Team Leaders.

OBJECT TECHNOLOGY INTERNATIONAL INC. / OTI

Att: Human Resources Manager
2670 Queensview Drive
Ottawa, ON K2B 8K1

Tel. 613-820-1200
Fax 613-820-1202
Email .... hr@oti.com
Website .... www.oti.com

Employer Background: OTI, a subsidiary of IBM, is an advanced software engineering company and leader in object-oriented technology. *New Positions Created (3):* Contract Administrator; Facilities Coordinator; Switchboard / Receptionist.

OBJEXIS CORPORATION

Att: Human Resources Department
1635 Sherbrooke West, Suite 405
Montréal, QC H3H 1E2

Tel. 514-932-3295
Fax 514-932-4639
Email .... jobs@objexis.com
Website .... www.objexis.com

Employer Background: Objexis Corporation (formerly Future Strategy International, Inc.) is a leading developer of web-based team portals for collaborative strategic management. *New Positions Created (8):* Marketing Communications Manager; Account Manager / Account Executive; Coordinator of Administrative Services; Customer Support Representative; Software Engineer, Web; Tester, Software Quality Assurance; Vice-President of Sales; Web Programmer / Programmer-Analyst.

OCCUPATIONAL HEALTH AND SAFETY AGENCY FOR HEALTHCARE IN BC
Att: Edward P. McCormick,
Associate Director
1195 West Broadway, Suite 301
Vancouver, BC V6H 3X5
Tel. 604-775-4034
Fax 604-775-4031
Website .... www.ohsah.bc.ca
Employer Background: Funded by the Ministry of Health, OHSAH is a non-profit organization dedicated to providing care for caregivers. *New Positions Created (3):* Occupational Health Positions; Office Manager; Social Science Researcher.

OCEAN CONSTRUCTION SUPPLIES LTD.
Att: Rob Slarks
PO Box 2300
Vancouver, BC V6B 3W6
Tel. 604-261-2211
Fax 604-261-7537
Email ..... rslarks@tilbury.lehighcement.com
Website .... www.lehighcement.com
Employer Background: Ocean Construction Supplies Ltd. is part of Tilbury Cement Ltd., a major producer of cement, concrete building products, concrete and aggregates. *New Positions Created (2):* Ready-Mix Concrete Dispatcher; Order Taker / Relief Ready Mix Concrete Dispatcher.

OERLIKON AEROSPACE INC.
Att: Staffing Counsellor
225 Boulevard du Seminaire Sud
St-Jean-sur-Richelieu, QC J3B 8E9
Tel. 450-358-2000
Fax 450-358-1744
Email .... recrutement@oerlikon.ca
Website .... www.oerlikon.ca
Employer Background: Oerlikon Aerospace Inc. is a systems integrator, specializing in the design, assembly, integration, testing and delivery of complete systems solutions. *New Positions Created (22):* Electrical / Electronics Technician; Integrated Logistics Support Specialist; Project Coordinator; Project Engineer; Project Manager, Protected Weapon Station; Reliability Availability Maintainability Durability (RAMD) Specialist; Test Engineer; Accounts Receivable Clerk; Program Manager, Power Electronics; Project Manager, SES / R & O; Satellite Controller; Satellite Operations Planner; Design Engineer; Electrical / Electronics Technician; Estimator; Intermediate Technical Buyer; Power Electronics Engineer; RAMD Specialist; Senior Software Engineer; Software Engineer; Technical Writer; Test Engineer.

OFFICE OF THE AUDITOR GENERAL, BC (CORPORATE SERVICES)
Att: Ielean Spanos
8 Bastion Square
Victoria, BC V8V 1X4
Tel. 250-387-6803
Fax 250-387-1230
Website .... bcauditor.com

Employer Background: The Office of the Auditor General provides independent assessments of government accountability and performance. *New Positions Created (3):* Coordinator, Professional Development and Student Services; Senior Financial Auditor; Manager, Human Resources.

OFFICE OF THE AUDITOR GENERAL OF CANADA
Att: Human Resources
240 Sparks Street
Ottawa, ON K1A 0G6
Tel. 613-995-3708
Email .... emplo@oag-bvg.gc.ca
Website .... www.oag-bvg.gc.ca
Employer Background: The Office of the Auditor General of Canada conducts independent audits and examinations that provide objective information, advice and assurance to Parliament. *New Positions Created (9):* Legal Counsel; Director, INAC Audit Team; Director, Results Measurement; Financial Audit Professionals; VFM Audit Professionals; Programmer / Analyst; VFM Audit Professionals; Director of Communications; Legislative Auditor.

OFFICE OF THE CHILD, YOUTH & FAMILY ADVOCATE, BC
Att: Lynell Anderson
595 Howe Street, Suite 600, Box 6
Vancouver, BC V6C 2T5
Tel. 604-775-3433
Fax 604-775-3205
Website .... www.advokids.org
Employer Background: The Office of the Child, Youth and Family Advocate is an independent officer of the British Columbia legislature, responsible for protecting the rights of children, youth and their families. *New Positions Created (3):* Executive Coordinator; Intake Officer; Research Officer.

OFFICE SPECIALTY
Att: Human Resources Manager
1865 Birchmount Road
Toronto, ON M1P 2J5
Tel. 416-293-5666
Fax 416-293-9975
Email .... recruiting@officespecialty.com
Website .... www.officespecialty.com
Employer Background: Office Specialty (a business unit of Inscape) is a leading manufacturer of contract office furniture and filing systems. *New Positions Created (3):* Marketing Communications Coordinator; Product Manager; Production Planner.

OGILVIE LLP
Att: Bette Podgurny, General Manager
10303 Jasper Avenue, Suite 1400
Edmonton, AB T5J 3N6
Tel. 780-421-1818
Fax 780-429-4453
Email .... bpodgurny@ogilvielaw.com
Website .... www.ogilvielaw.com
Employer Background: Founded in 1920, Ogilvie LLP is a mid-sized law firm, with offices in Edmonton, Calgary, Whitecourt

and Regina. *New Positions Created (3):* Litigation Assistant; Litigation Lawyer; Litigation Lawyers (2).

OGILVY RENAULT
Att: Lioba Reeves-Bet
77 King St. W., Royal Trust Tower
Suite 2100, Box 141, TD Centre
Toronto, ON M5K 1H1
Tel. 416-216-4000
Email ..... torontojobs@ogilbyrenault.com
Website .... www.ogilvyrenault.com
Employer Background: Ogilvy Renault is a national law firm, with five offices in Canada and an office in London, England. *New Positions Created (2):* Life Sciences Lawyers; Labour and Employment Lawyer.

OIL AND GAS COMMISSION, BC
Att: Human Resources Branch
1810 Blanchard Street
Suite 1, PO Box 9321, Stn Prov Govt
Victoria, BC V8W 9N3
Tel. 250-952-0109
Fax 250-952-0141
Website .... www.ogc.gov.bc.ca
Employer Background: The Oil and Gas Commission regulates crude oil, natural gas and pipeline activities in British Columbia. *New Positions Created (8):* Heritage Conservation Program Manager; Senior Aboriginal Program Specialist; Manager, Northern Operations; Stakeholder Relations Advisor; Geographic Information System Coordinator; Oil and Gas Initiatives Advisor; Oil and Gas Resource Officer; Senior Aboriginal Program Specialist.

OIS-FISHER INC.
Att: Human Resources Manager
1 Duffy Place, 2nd Floor
St. John's, NF A1B 4M6
Tel. 709-758-4950
Fax 709-722-8730
Email .... hres@oisfisher.com
Website .... www.oisfisher.com
Employer Background: OIS-Fisher Inc. supplies inspection management and associated services to onshore and offshore assets in the oil and gas, power, nuclear and mining industries. *New Positions Created (2):* NDT Technicians; Vendor Inspectors.

OK TRANSPORTATION LTD.
Att: Administration
91 Melford Drive
Toronto, ON M1B 2G6
Fax 416-321-5547
Website .... www.oktransportation.com
Employer Background: Established in 1919, OK Transportation Ltd. has over 50 owner-operators, offering services in Ontario, Quebec and the US eastern seaboard. *New Positions Created (2):* Recruiter; Junior Office Clerk.

OKANAGAN SIMILKAMEEN HEALTH REGION, KELOWNA GENERAL HOSPITAL
Att: Human Resources

250 Harvey Avenue, Suite 101
Kelowna, BC V1Y 7S5
Fax 250-979-4575
Email .... human.resources@oshr.org
Website .... www.oshr.org
Employer Background: The Okanagan
Similkameen Health Region provides health
services to 226,000 people, with over 5,000
employees and an annual operating budget
of $283 million. *New Positions Created (14):*
ICU Nurse; Public Health Nursing Manager;
Regional Director, Infection Prevention &
Control; Manager, Emergency Care Services;
Manager, Renal Services; Registered Nurses;
Registered Nurses; Registered Nurses; Reg-
istered Nurses; Registered Nurses; Regis-
tered Nurses, Residential Care; Residential
Services Positions; Regional Director, Pharmacy Services; Registered Nurses.

OKANAGAN SIMILKAMEEN HEALTH REGION, PENTICTON REGIONAL HOSPITAL
Att: Human Resources Service Centre
550 Carmi Avenue
Penticton, BC V2A 3G6
Tel. 250-492-9024
Fax 250-492-9025
Email .... human.resources@oshr.org
Website .... www.oshr.org
Employer Background: The Okanagan
Similkameen Health Region provides health
services to 226,000 people, with over 5,000
employees and an annual operating budget
of $283 million. *New Positions Created (4):*
Assistant Director, Plant & Maintenance
Services; Corporate Nursing Recruitment /
Retention Consultant; Various Healthcare
Positions; Registered Nurses.

OKANAGAN UNIVERSITY COLLEGE
Att: Employee Relations Division
1000 K.L.O. Road
Kelowna, BC V1Y 4X8
Tel. 250-862-5464
Fax 250-862-5475
Email .... erapplicants@okanagan.bc.ca
Website .... www.ouc.bc.ca
Employer Background: OUC is a compre-
hensive, multi-campus institution, with
7,000 students enrolled in vocational, devel-
opmental, applied and academic programs.
New Positions Created (50): College Profes-
sor, Electronic Engineering Technology;
Practice Placement Coordinator, Nursing;
Writer / Publications Assistant; Counsellor;
Associate Dean, Health and Social Develop-
ment; Manager of Institutional Research,
Finance and Analysis; Assistant to the Dean;
College Professor, English; College Professor,
Modern Languages; Assistant to the Director; College Professor, Biology; Manager,
Human Resources; Instructor, Practical
Nursing; Admissions Clerk; College Profes-
sor, Mechanical Engineering Technology;
Records and Registration Data Entry Clerk;
Accounting Assistant; Career Tech Achievement Assistant; Maintenance Engineer; College Professor, Social Work; College Professor, Geography; Instructor, Adult Basic Education; Programmer / Analyst; College Professor, Business Administration; College

Professor, History; College Professor, Net-
work Engineering Technology; Laboratory
Instructor, Nursing; College Professor, Civil
Engineering Technology; College Professor,
Education; College Professor, Education;
College Professor, Fine Arts; Counsellor,
Counselling Services, Vernon Centre; Re-
search Officer; College Professor, Biology;
College Professor, Microbiology; Laboratory
Instructor, Biology; College Professor, Nurs-
ing; Financial Awards Assistant; Associate
Vice-President, Campus Development and
Facilities Management; College Professor,
Earth and Environmental Science; College
Professor, English; College Professor, Social
Work; College Professor, Sociology; Profes-
sors, Watershed Management (2); College
Professor, Chemistry; College Professor,
Chemistry; College Professor, Mathematics;
College Professors (2); College Professor,
Computer Science; College Professor, Earth
and Environmental Science.

OLD MILL, THE
Att: Human Resources
21 Old Mill Road
Toronto, ON M8X 1G5
Tel. 416-236-2641
Fax 416-239-9587
Email .... jobsoldmill@yahoo.ca
Website .... www.oldmilltoronto.com
Employer Background: The Old Mill is a
Toronto landmark, featuring restaurant,
banquet and wedding facilities. *New Posi-
tions Created (3):* Guest Services Manager
and Concierge; Human Resources Coordi-
nator / Payroll Clerk; Banquet Captain.

OLDS COLLEGE
Att: Human Resources,
Development Department
4500 - 50th Street
Olds, AB T4H 1R6
Tel. 403-556-8362
Fax 403-556-4794
Email ... employop@admin.oldscollege.ab.ca
Website .... www.oldscollege.ab.ca
Employer Background: Founded in 1913,
Olds College offers programs in agriculture,
horticulture, land and environmental man-
agement, agribusiness and rural entrepre-
neurship, serving 1,300 full-time students.
New Positions Created (9): Vice-President,
Student & Support Services; Director, Busi-
ness Development Extension Services; Man-
ager, Business Development Extension Serv-
ices; Greenhouse Instructor, Production
Horticulture Program; Landscape Design,
Contracting and Construction Instructor;
Animal Health Technology Instructional
Assistants, Animal Health Technology Program; Animal Health Technology Instruc-
tor, Animal Health Technology Program;
Medical Lab Technology Instructional As-
sistant, Animal Health Technology Program;
Vice-President, Academic Services.

OLSON LEMONS
Att: Human Resources Manager
734 - 7th Avenue SW, Suite 602
Calgary, AB T2P 3P8
Tel. 403-974-3400

Fax 403-974-3427
Email .... joanne@olsonlemons.com
Employer Background: Olson Lemons (formerly Olson Reid) is a tax planning organization. *New Positions Created (2):* Tax Analyst; Accountant.

OMNEX CONTROL SYSTEMS INC.
Att: Human Resources Manager
1833 Coast Meridian Road, Building 74
Port Coquitlam, BC V3C 6G5
Tel. 604-944-9247
Fax 604-944-9267
Email .... jobs@omnexcontrols.com
Website .... www.omnexcontrols.com
Employer Background: OMNEX Control
Systems Inc. designs and manufactures fre-
quency-hopping spread spectrum radio
products for the global market. *New Posi-
tions Created (4):* Hardware Designer; Serv-
ice Technician; Test Engineer; Manufactur-
ing; Hardware Designer.

OMNI DIRECTIONAL TECHNOLOGIES INC.
Att: Human Resources Manager
1015 - 4th Street SW, Suite 1230
Calgary, AB T2R 1J4
Tel. 403-265-9992
Fax 403-265-2601
Website .... www.omnidd.ca
Employer Background: Omni Directional
Technologies Inc. provides horizontal and
directional drilling solutions to exploration
companies. *New Positions Created (4):* Di-
rectional Driller; MWD Coordinator; MWD
Operator; Sales & Marketing Position.

OMNIMARK TECHNOLOGIES CORPORATION
Att: Human Resources Generalist
1400 Blair Place, 4th Floor
Ottawa, ON K1J 9B8
Tel. 613-745-4242
Fax 613-745-5560
Email .... hr@omnimark.com
Website .... www.omnimark.com
Employer Background: OmniMark Tech-
nologies Corporation is an IT consulting
firm that provides innovative solutions for
enterprise-wide website management. *New
Positions Created (3):* Consultant, Profes-
sional Services; Software Developers, R&D;
Writer / Programmer.

OMNISALES
Att: Human Resources Manager
2520 St. Laurent Boulevard
Ottawa, ON K1H 1B1
Tel. 613-248-9000
Fax 613-248-8577
Email .... careers@osi3.com
Website www.osi3.com
Employer Background: OmniSales inte-
grates telephony, multimedia communica-
tions and performance management solu-
tions to help businesses deliver optimum
customer service. *New Positions Created (3):*
Director of Technical Support; Senior Ac-
count Managers (2); Controller.

OMYA (CANADA) INC.
Att: Human Resources Department
PO Box 245
Perth, ON K7H 3E4

Tel. 613-267-5367
Fax 613-267-5408
Website .... www.omya.com
Employer Background: OMYA (Canada) Inc. manufactures calcium carbonate products for industrial use. *New Positions Created (2):* Plant Administrator; Environmental / Safety Engineer.

ONCOMMAND CANADA INC.
Att: Patricia Bertrand
292 Walker Drive, Unit 1
Brampton, ON L6T 4Z1

Tel. 905-458-0200
Fax 905-458-7787
Email .... pbertran@ocv.com
Website .... www.ocv.com
Employer Background: OnCommand Canada Inc. provides interactive in-room entertainment, information and business services to the lodging industry. *New Positions Created (2):* Project Accountant; Financial Accountant.

ONLINE BUSINESS SYSTEMS
Att: Personnel Manager
115 Bannatyne Avenue, Suite 200
Winnipeg, MB R3B 0R3

Tel. 204-982-0200
Fax 204-982-0201
Email .... personnel@online.mb.ca
Website .... www.online-can.com
Employer Background: Online Business Systems develops industrial e-business applications and services for IS strategic planning, IT infrastructure, applications development, packaged software and training solutions. *New Positions Created (4):* Intermediate Java Developer; Intermediate PowerBuilder Developers; Junior PowerBuilder Developers; Senior Java Developer.

ONTARIO ASSOCIATION OF ARCHITECTS / OAA
Att: Human Resources Manager
111 Moatfield Drive
Toronto, ON M3B 3L6

Tel. 416-449-6898
Fax 416-449-5756
Website .... www.oaa.on.ca
Employer Background: OAA is the licensing body and professional association for architects in Ontario. *New Positions Created (2):* Administrative Assistant, IndPlan; Executive Assistant.

ONTARIO BAR ASSOCIATION / OBA
Att: Douglas Simpson, Executive Director
20 Toronto Street, Suite 200
Toronto, ON M5C 2B8

Tel. 416-869-1047
Fax 416-869-1390
Email .... dsimpson@oba.org
Website .... www.oba.org
Employer Background: OBA is a voluntary membership organization, representing

14,000 lawyers, judges and law students. *New Positions Created (3):* Advocacy Director, Government Relations & Communications; Membership & Member Support Director; Professional Development Director.

ONTARIO CLEAN WATER AGENCY, NORTHWESTERN ONTARIO HUB
Att: Betty Pengelly
105 Park Street, PO Box 819
Longlac, ON P0T 2A0

Fax 807-876-2402
Website .... www.ocwa.com
Employer Background: Created in 1993, OCWA is a provincial Crown corporation, providing environmentally responsible, cost-efficient water and wastewater services. *New Positions Created (2):* Operator / Mechanic; Operator / Mechanics (2).

ONTARIO CLEAN WATER AGENCY
Att: Human Resources Manager
3508 Wonderland Road South
London, ON N6L 1A7

Fax 519-652-7020
Website .... www.ocwa.com
Employer Background: Created in 1993, OCWA is a provincial Crown corporation, providing environmentally responsible, cost-efficient water and wastewater services. *New Positions Created (3):* Maintenance Foreperson / Operator; Assistant Operations Manager; Operators / Mechanics (3).

ONTARIO CLEAN WATER AGENCY
Att: Human Resources
1 Yonge Street, Suite 1700
Toronto, ON M5E 1E5

Fax 416-314-4615
Website .... www.ocwa.com
Employer Background: Created in 1993, OCWA is a provincial Crown corporation, providing environmentally responsible, cost-efficient water and wastewater services. *New Positions Created (8):* Proposal and Reports Coordinator; Water and Wastewater Instrumentation Technician Specialist; Compliance and QA / QC Advisor; Accounting Manager; Client Services Representatives; Applications Programmer; Administrative Assistant; Manager of Compliance.

ONTARIO CLEAN WATER AGENCY
Att: Anne Thornton
593 Norris Court
Kingston, ON K7P 2R9

Fax 613-634-1942
Website .... www.ocwa.com
Employer Background: Created in 1993, OCWA is a provincial Crown corporation, providing environmentally responsible, cost-efficient water and wastewater services. *New Positions Created (2):* Operations Manager; Operations Manager.

ONTARIO CLEAN WATER AGENCY, QUINTE HUB / OCWA
Att: Robin Hollywood, Admin. Assistant
PO Box 20157
Belleville, ON K8N 5V1

Fax 613-962-1966
Website .... www.ocwa.com
Employer Background: Created in 1993, OCWA is a provincial Crown corporation that provides environmentally responsible, cost-efficient water and wastewater services. *New Positions Created (7):* Assistant Operations Manager; Electrician / Operator; Maintenance Foreperson / Operator; Mechanic / Operators (2); Process Technician; Senior Operator / Mechanics; Operators / Mechanics.

ONTARIO COLLEGE OF ART AND DESIGN / OCAD
Att: Human Resources
100 McCaul Street
Toronto, ON M5T 1W1

Tel. 416-977-6000
Fax 416-977-3034
Website .... www.ocad.on.ca
Employer Background: OCAD is a post-secondary institution, specializing in advanced art and design education. *New Positions Created (8):* Counsellor, Writing and Learning Centre; Building Systems Operator; Building Operations Attendant; Building Systems Operator; College Purchasing Agent; Manager, Plant Operations; Head, Registrarial Services; Dean, Faculty of Liberal Studies.

ONTARIO COLLEGE OF PHARMACISTS
Att: Lisa Baker, HR Administrator
483 Huron Street
Toronto, ON M5R 2R4

Tel. 416-962-4861
Fax 416-703-3114
Email .... lbaker@ocpharma.com
Website .... www.ocpharma.com
Employer Background: The Ontario College of Pharmacists is the licensing and regulatory body for pharmacists in Ontario. *New Positions Created (3):* Practice Advisory Assistant; Field Representative; Manager, Patient Relations.

ONTARIO COLLEGE OF TEACHERS
Att: Human Resources
121 Bloor Street East, 6th Floor
Toronto, ON M4W 3M5

Tel. 416-961-8800
Fax 416-961-8822
Email .... hr@oct.on.ca
Website .... www.oct.on.ca
Employer Background: The Ontario College of Teachers licenses, governs and regulates Ontario's teaching profession. *New Positions Created (2):* Coordinator of Professional Affairs; Deputy Registrar.

ONTARIO COUNCIL OF ALTERNATIVE BUSINESSES / OCAB
Att: Human Resources Manager
761 Queen Street West, Suite 307
Toronto, ON M6J 1G1

Tel. 416-504-1693
Fax 416-504-8063
Email .... ocab@icomm.ca
Website .... www.icomm.ca/ocab

Employer Background: OCAB is a provincial organization committed to developing economic / employment opportunities for psychiatric survivors in Ontario. *New Positions Created (3):* Community Developer; Administrative Assistant; Kitchen Manager.

ONTARIO ENGLISH CATHOLIC TEACHERS' ASSOCIATION / OECTA
Att: Kathy McVean, President
65 St. Clair Avenue East, Suite 400
Toronto, ON M4T 2Y8

Tel. 416-925-2493
Fax 416-925-6940
Website .... www.oecta.on.ca
Employer Background: OECTA is a union representing 34,000 English-speaking teachers in publicly-funded Roman Catholic schools in Ontario. *New Positions Created (4):* Deputy General Secretary; Office Mgr; Executive Assistant; Executive Assistant.

ONTARIO HERITAGE FOUNDATION, CORPORATE SERVICES BRANCH
Att: Human Resources Manager
10 Adelaide Street East
Toronto, ON M5C 1J3

Fax 416-325-0838
Website .... www.heritagefdn.on.ca
Employer Background: The Ontario Heritage Foundation (a non-profit agency of the Ontario Ministry of Citizenship, Culture and Recreation) preserves, protects and promotes Ontario's built, cultural and natural heritage. *New Positions Created (6):* Architectural Conservation Technician; Property Administrator, Easements; Coordinator, Information Technology; Coordinator, Media Relations and Marketing; Heritage Customer Service and Research Assistant; Marketing and Customer Service Assistant.

ONTARIO HIV TREATMENT NETWORK / OHTN
Att: Administrative Coordinator
1300 Yonge Street, Suite 308
Toronto, ON M4T 1X3

Tel. 416-642-6486
Fax 416-640-4245
Email .... info@ohtn.on.ca
Website .... www.ohtn.on.ca
Employer Background: OHTN is a non-profit incorporated agency, working to ensure excellence in the treatment and care of people living with HIV in Ontario. *New Positions Created (7):* Administrative Assistant; Research Coordinator; Project Mgr; Program Assistant; Communications Coordinator; Program Director; Program Assistant.

ONTARIO HOSPITAL ASSOCIATION
Att: Sarah Vanderputten,
Human Resources Assistant
200 Front Street West, Suite 2800
Toronto, ON M5V 3L1

Tel. 416-205-1300
Fax 416-205-1392
Email .... recruit@oha.com
Website .... www.oha.com
Employer Background: OHA is a non-profit, voluntary organization of hospitals in Ontario. *New Positions Created (2):* Administrative Assistant; Public Affairs Specialist.

ONTARIO HUMAN RIGHTS COMMISSION / OHRC
Att: Human Resources
180 Dundas Street West, 8th Floor
Toronto, ON M7A 2R9

Tel. 416-314-4500
Fax 416-314-4494
Website .... www.ohrc.on.ca
Employer Background: OHRC is committed to eliminating discrimination by effectively enforcing the Human Rights Code. *New Positions Created (4):* Investigations Manager; Mediation Manager; Human Rights Mediation Officer; Disclosure Clerks (2).

ONTARIO INSTITUTE FOR STUDIES IN EDUCATION / OISE
Att: Madalaine Panoulias,
Human Resource Generalist
252 Bloor Street West, 8th Floor, Room 117
Toronto, ON M5S 1A2

Tel. 416-923-6641
Fax 416-971-2801
Website .... www.oise.utoronto.ca
Employer Background: OISE, part of the University of Toronto since 1996, offers undergraduate and graduate studies for teachers. *New Positions Created (17):* Assistant Dean, Alumni and Development; Communication Officer; Admissions Counsellor and Administrative Assistant; Secretary; Campaign Secretary; Development Secretary; Teaching Positions; Tenure-Stream Position, Child Study and Education; Tenure-Stream Position, Community College Studies; Tenure-Stream Position, Mathematics Education; Tenure-Stream Position, Multicultural Counselling; Tenure-Stream Position, Science Education; Tenure-Stream Position, Special Education and Adaptive Instruction; Various Tenure-Stream Positions (5); Director, Institute of Child Study; Assistant to the Registrar; Production Assistant.

ONTARIO LOTTERY AND GAMING CORPORATION, BRANTFORT CHARITY CASINO / OLGC
Att: Tom Millar, Human Resources
251 Colborne Street
Brantford, ON N3T 2H3

Fax 519-753-8380
Email .... tmillar@olgc.on.ca
Website .... www.gov.on.ca
Employer Background: OLGC provides controlled gaming entertainment and supports provincial government initiatives with its revenues. *New Positions Created (2):* Restaurant Mgr; Food & Beverage Manager.

ONTARIO LOTTERY AND GAMING CORPORATION / OLGC
Att: Human Resources
70 Foster Drive, Suite 800
Sault Ste. Marie, ON P6A 6V2

Fax 705-946-6404
Email .... humanresourcesssm@olgc.on.ca
Website .... www.gov.on.ca

Employer Background: OLGC provides controlled gaming entertainment and supports provincial government initiatives with its revenues. *New Positions Created (18):* Applications Specialists, ERM; Security Architect; Technology Specialist, Application; Technology Specialist, Direct Gaming; Technology Specialist, Network; Resource Planner; Senior Project Consultant; Accounts Payable Manager; Application Specialists; Coordinator, Documentation, Training & Communications; Manager, Shared Services Development; Manager, Support; Project Leader; Project Manager; Solution Delivery Analyst; Audit Specialist; Corporate Insurance and Claims Specialist; Brand Manager.

ONTARIO LOTTERY AND GAMING CORPORATION / OLGC
Att: Human Resources
555 Rexdale Boulevard, PO Box 250, Station B
Toronto, ON M9W 5L1

Fax 416-213-9616
Email .... humanresources@olgc.on.ca
Website .... www.olgc.on.ca
Employer Background: OLGC provides controlled gaming entertainment and supports provincial government initiatives with its revenues. *New Positions Created (4):* Audit Supervisor; Audit Manager; Slot Supervisor; Security Manager.

ONTARIO LOTTERY AND GAMING CORPORATION / OLGC
Att: Human Resources
4120 Yonge Street, Suite 420
Toronto, ON M2P 2B8

Fax 416-224-7077
Email .... humanresources@olgc.on.ca
Website .... www.gov.on.ca
Employer Background: OLGC provides controlled gaming entertainment and supports provincial government initiatives with its revenues. *New Positions Created (28):* Employee Programs Coordinator; Executive Assistant; Manager, Loyalty Marketing; Marketing Managers (2); Director of E-Business; Corporate Planning Manager; Regional Manager, Facilities Maintenance; Regional Group Sales Coordinators; Casino Manager; General Manager; Contract Manager; Project Analyst, Facilities Management; Executive Assistant; Network Analyst, Level I; Network Analyst, Level II; Director, Commercial Casinos Operations; Senior Financial Analyst; Human Resource Generalist; Woodbine Racetrack Slots; Human Resources Consultant, Charity Casinos; Project Leader, Information Technology; Team Leader, Computer Operations; Procurement Director; Distribution Assistant / Courier; Distribution Operations Supervisor; Project Coordinator, Internet Development; Administrative Assistant; District Sales Manager; Communications Assistant.

ONTARIO MARCH OF DIMES
Att: Human Resources Department
10 Overlea Boulevard
Toronto, ON M4H 1A4

Tel. 416-425-3463

Fax 416-425-1920
Email .... hr@dimes.on.ca
Website .... www.dimes.on.ca
Employer Background: Ontario March of Dimes is a multi-service, charitable organization that delivers a wide range of programs to people with physical disabilities. *New Positions Created (6):* Financial Services Coordinator; Vocational Evaluator; Provincial Independent Living Assistant; Provincial Web Information Services Coordinator; Management Information Systems Coordinator; Regional Director.

ONTARIO MARCH OF DIMES
Att: Judy Regis
303 Bagot Street, 5th Floor
Kingston, ON K7K 5W7
Tel. 613-549-4141
Fax 613-549-6321
Email .... hr@dimes.on.ca
Website .... www.dimes.on.ca
Employer Background: Ontario March of Dimes is a multi-service, charitable organization that delivers a wide range of programs to people with physical disabilities. *New Positions Created (3):* Community Placement Developer; Job Finding Club Instructor; Case Manager II.

ONTARIO MUNICIPAL EMPLOYEES RETIREMENT SYSTEM / OMERS
Att: Human Resources Division
1 University Avenue, Suite 1000
Toronto, ON M5J 2P1
Tel. 416-369-2400
Fax 416-363-6723
Email .... careers@omers.com
Website .... www.omers.com
Employer Background: OMERS is a multi-employer pension plan. *New Positions Created (12):* Analyst, Application / Server Support; Client Applications Analyst; Senior Analyst, Private Placement / Merchant Banking; Team Leader, Service Management; Vice-President, Pension Services; Administrative Positions (2); Senior Analyst, External Funds; Senior Analyst, Pension Accounting Operations; Team Leader, Training and Quality Assurance; Pension Specialists; Senior Business Analyst, Pension Systems; Pension Specialists.

ONTARIO NATIVE AFFAIRS SECRETARIAT / ONAS
Att: Doug Carr, Negotiations Branch
720 Bay Street, 4th Floor
Toronto, ON M5G 2K1
Fax 416-326-4017
Website ... www.nativeaffairs.jus.gov.on.ca
Employer Background: ONAS works with public and private sector partners to promote Aboriginal self-reliance and economic development. *New Positions Created (6):* Administrative Coordinator; Deputy Director; Program & Community Liaison Assistant; Legal Counsel; Aboriginal Program Adviser; Senior Co-ordinator, Issues and Media Relations.

ONTARIO NON-PROFIT HOUSING ASSOCIATION / ONPHA
Att: Human Resources
489 College Street, Suite 400
Toronto, ON M6G 1A5
Tel. 416-927-9144
Fax 416-927-8401
Email .... karen.fisher@onpha.org
Website .... www.onpha.org
Employer Background: ONPHA is a membership organization of non-profit housing corporations providing housing to the homeless and low income people. *New Positions Created (2):* Communications & Marketing Position; Communications Assistant.

ONTARIO PENSION BOARD
Att: Human Resources Section
1 Adelaide Street East, Suite 1100
Toronto, ON M5C 2X6
Tel. 416-364-8558
Fax 416-364-7578
Website .... www.opb.on.ca
Employer Background: The Ontario Pension Board provides pension-related services to 25,000 active members and 40,000 pensioners. *New Positions Created (9):* Administrative Services Officer; Pension Policy Research Analyst; Administrative Services Officer; Senior Benefits Specialist; Senior Analyst, Treasury and Finance; Senior Investment Accountant; Junior Pension Analysts; Pension Analysts; Records Clerk.

ONTARIO PHARMACISTS' ASSOCIATION / OPA
Att: Chief Executive Officer
23 Lesmill Road, Suite 301
Toronto, ON M3B 3P6
Tel. 416-444-1500
Fax 416-441-9566
Employer Background: OPA is the voluntary professional association for pharmacists in Ontario. *New Positions Created (2):* Director of Education; Drug Information Pharmacists.

ONTARIO PLACE CORPORATION
Att: Employee Services
955 Lakeshore Boulevard West
Toronto, ON M6K 3B9
Tel. 416-314-9900
Fax 416-314-9994
Email .. employeeservices@ontarioplace.com
Website .... www.ontarioplace.com
Employer Background: Ontario Place Corporation operates an internationally-acclaimed leisure and entertainment complex on Toronto's waterfront. *New Positions Created (2):* Manager, Finance and Administration; Chief Financial Officer.

ONTARIO POWER GENERATION
Att: Human Resources Manager
700 University Avenue
Toronto, ON M5G 1X6
Tel. 416-592-1701
Email .... careers@
.... ontariopowergeneration.com
Website .... www.opg.com
Employer Background: Ontario Power Generation, the fifth-largest generating company in North America, supplies 85% of all electricity consumed in Ontario. *New Positions Created (29):* Control Technician; Chemical Technicians; IT Program / Service Manager; Occupational Health Nurse; Protection and Control Engineer; Chemical Technologist; Stationary Engineer - 4th Class; Building Maintenance Advisor; Senior Business Development Advisor; Technical Engineer, Software Programming; Thermal Station Engineer; Nuclear Safety Analysis and Support Positions; Steam Plant Operator; Steam Plant Production Supervisor; IT Security Advisor; Occupational Health Nurse; Protection and Control Technologist; Station Technologist; Training Specialist - Nuclear Operations; Section Manager, Components Analysis; Team Leader, Information Management; Information Technology Security Advisor; Senior Security Policy Specialist; Nuclear Security Liaison Coordinator; Nuclear Security Officer; Security Support Advisors; Control Maintainer Trainees; Mechanical Maintainer Trainees; Power Plant Operator Trainees.

ONTARIO POWER GENERATION, BRUCE NUCLEAR STATION
Att: Human Resources Manager
Location B29, Box 1000
Tiverton, ON N0G 2T0
Email .... careers@
.... ontariopowergeneration.com
Website .... www.opg.com
Employer Background: Ontario Power Generation, the fifth-largest generating company in North America, supplies 85% of all electricity consumed in Ontario. *New Positions Created (4):* Steam Plant Operators; Human Resources Professional; Control Technicians; Electrical Draftsperson.

ONTARIO POWER GENERATION INC., OTTAWA AND ST. LAWRENCE PLANT GROUP
Att: Human Resources
2 Innovation Drive, PO Box 950
Renfrew, ON K7V 4H4
Fax 613-433-9678
Email .... careers@
.... ontariopowergeneration.com
Website .... www.opg.com
Employer Background: Ontario Power Generation, the fifth-largest generating company in North America, supplies 85% of all electricity consumed in Ontario. *New Positions Created (3):* Electrical Maintainer Apprentices; Mechanical Maintainer Apprentices; Site Project Manager.

ONTARIO SCIENCE CENTRE / OSC
Att: Human Resources
770 Don Mills Road
Toronto, ON M3C 1T3
Tel. 416-696-3213
Fax 416-696-3221
Email .... jobs@osc.on.ca
Website .... www.ontariosciencecentre.ca
Employer Background: OSC (an agency of the Ontario Ministry of Citizenship, Culture

and Recreation) features a wide variety of permanent and temporary exhibits devoted to science. *New Positions Created (16):* Campaign Director; Human Resources Consultant; Senior Marketing and Communications Officer; Senior Associate, Corporate & Foundation Partnerships; Human Resources Manager; Marketing Promotions Officer; Project Consultants, International Sales; Marketing Coordinator; Group Leader, 2D Design; Science Educators; Electronic Engineers/Technologists; Group Leader, 3D Design; Researcher/Programmer, Astronomy and Space Sciences; Senior Scientist, Physics; Drafter / Detailer; Exhibit Designer.

ONTARIO SECURITIES COMMISSION
Att: Human Resources
20 Queen Street W., Suite 1900, PO Box 55
Toronto, ON M5H 3S8

Tel. 416-593-8121
Fax 416-593-8348
Email .... hr@osc.gov.on.ca
Website .... www.osc.gov.on.ca
Employer Background: OSC is a self-funded agency responsible for enforcing securities legislation and fostering fair capital markets. *New Positions Created (10):* Information Technology Project Manager; Litigation Counsel; Manager, Market Regulation; Accountant, Corporate Finance; Investigator, Case Assessment; Legal Counsel, Corporate Finance; Legal Counsel, Market Regulation; Legal Counsel; Investigation Counsel, Case Assessment; Investigation Counsel, Investigations Unit.

ONTARIO SERVICE SAFETY ALLIANCE / OSSA
Att: Human Resources Manager
4950 Yonge Street, Suite 1500
Toronto, ON M2N 6K1

Tel. 416-250-9111
Website .... www.ossa.com
Employer Background: Founded in 1998, OSSA delivers health and safety consulting, education and assistance to their members in the Ontario service sector. *New Positions Created (2):* Consultants (3); Consultant.

ONTARIO STORE FIXTURES INC. / OSF
Att: Kelly Schellenberg,
Human Resources Manager
650 Barmac Drive
Toronto, ON M9L 2X8

Tel. 416-749-7700
Fax 416-644-6365
Email .... kschellenberg@osfinc.com
Website .... www.osfinc.com
Employer Background: OSF is a leading North American manufacturer of complete retail store interiors. *New Positions Created (3):* Detailer; Estimator; Product Data Administrator.

ONTARIO STORE FIXTURES INC. / OSF
Att: Human Resources
400 Fenmar Drive
Toronto, ON M9L 1M6

Tel. 416-745-4687
Fax 416-740-5191

Email .... kamaral@osfinc.com
Website .... www.osfinc.com
Employer Background: OSF is a leading North American manufacturer of complete retail store interiors. *New Positions Created (2):* Mailroom Clerk; Manager, Safety & Environment.

ONTARIO TEACHERS' PENSION PLAN BOARD
Att: Human Resources Specialist
5650 Yonge Street
Toronto, ON M2M 4H5

Tel. 416-226-2700
Fax 416-730-5346
Email .... human_resources@otpp.com
Website .... www.otpp.com
Employer Background: The Ontario Teachers' Pension Plan Board is responsible for the retirement income of 328,000 teachers and administers assets in excess of $70 billion. *New Positions Created (13):* Accounts Receivable Administrator; Administrative Assistant, Equity Trading; Associate Technical Team Leader, Web Development; Lotus Notes Developer / Analyst; Quantitative Investment Analyst; Web and Publications Writer; Website Technical Writer; Financial Analyst; Portfolio Administrator, Merchant Banking; Project Manager, Member Services; Technical Analyst; Software Developer; Legal Counsel, Investments.

ONTARIO TRILLIUM FOUNDATION, THE
Att: Human Resources
45 Charles Street East, 5th Floor
Toronto, ON M4Y 1S2

Tel. 416-963-4927
Website .... www.trilliumfoundation.org
Employer Background: Established in 1982, Ontario Trillium Foundation is Canada's largest public foundation, mandated to provide funding to the arts and culture, environmental, sports and recreation, and human and social service sectors in Ontario. *New Positions Created (4):* Coordinator of Administration; Senior Policy / Research Analyst; Bilingual Area Manager, Province-Wide Program; Bilingual Program Manager, Central Ontario Region.

ONVIA.COM
Att: Human Resources Manager
948 Homer Street, Suite 330
Vancouver, BC V6B 2W7

Tel. 604-647-1400
Fax 604-647-1499
Website .... www.onvia.com
Employer Background: Onvia.com (formerly MegaDepot.com) is an e-commerce site for small business. *New Positions Created (2):* VP Finance & Administration; VP Market Development.

OOLAGEN COMMUNITY SERVICES
Att: Ruth Pluznick,
Director of Clinical Services
65 Wellesley Street East, Suite 500
Toronto, ON M4Y 1G7

Tel. 416-395-0660

Fax 416-395-0666
Email .... ana_oolagen@hotmail.com
Website .... www.oolagen.org
Employer Background: Oolagen Community Services is a children's mental health centre that has been providing programs for adolescents, youth and their families for over 30 years. *New Positions Created (3):* Wraparound Worker; Family Workers (2); Intensive Child Workers (2).

OP PUBLISHING LTD.
Att: Human Resources Manager
780 Beatty Street, Suite 300
Vancouver, BC V6B 2M1

Tel. 604-687-1581
Fax 604-687-1925
Website .... www.oppublishing.com
Employer Background: OP Publishing Ltd. is western Canada's leading publisher of outdoor lifestyle magazines. *New Positions Created (3):* Associate Publisher; Account Manager; Assistant Promotion Manager.

OPEN LEARNING AGENCY / OLA
Att: Human Resources Department
4355 Mathissi Place
Burnaby, BC V5G 4S8

Tel. 604-431-3000
Fax 604-431-3384
Email .... hrinfo@ola.bc.ca
Website .... www.ola.bc.ca
Employer Background: OLA is a non-profit, fully-accredited educational institution. *New Positions Created (13):* Budget Analyst; Project Coordinator, Delivery Support Systems; Employment Consultant, Skills Centre Operations; Coordinator, Practical Nursing Programs; Credit Review Coordinator; Employment Consultant; Employment Consultant; Human Resources Advisors (2); Vice-President, Business Affairs; Senior Business Analyst; Academic Credit Review Coordinator; Associate Dean; Director, Marketing and Communications.

OPEN STORAGE SOLUTIONS, INC.
Att: Mike Curran
2 Castleview Drive, Unit 1
Brampton, ON L6T 5S9

Tel. 905-790-0660
Fax 905-790-0712
Website .... www.openstore.com
Employer Background: Open Storage Solutions, Inc. markets high-capacity storage products and servers for high-performance computing applications. *New Positions Created (3):* Office Assistant; Sales Representatives; Storage Solutions Architect.

OPEN TEXT CORPORATION
Att: Human Resources
185 Columbia Street West
Waterloo, ON N2L 5Z5

Tel. 519-888-7111
Email .... careers@opentext.com
Website .... www.opentext.com
Employer Background: Open Text Corporation provides collaborative intranets, extranets and e-business applications. *New*

Positions Created (13): Bilingual Customer Service Representative; Business Systems Analyst; Business Systems Analyst, Financial Systems; Site Administrator; Vice-President of Human Resources; Web Developer; Purchasing Coordinator; Senior Buyer; Account Executive; Corporate Accountant; Financial Analyst, Sales / Services; Product Specialists (2); Software Quality Analyst.

OPISYSTEMS INC.
Att: Human Resources Manager
1216 - 36th Avenue NE
Calgary, AB T2E 6M8
Fax 403-219-3123
Email .... opisystm@opisystems.com
Employer Background: OPIsystems Inc. is a leading supplier of grain storage management solutions. *New Positions Created (4):* Purchasing / Materials Management Position; Sales Position; Service Technician; Manager, Electronics Lab.

OPSCO ENERGY INDUSTRIES LTD.
Att: Wireline Manager
2601 Centre Avenue East
Calgary, AB T2A 2L1
Tel. 403-272-2206
Fax 403-569-2419
Website .... www.ensigngroup.com
Employer Background: Opsco Energy Industries Ltd. (a division of the Ensign Group) is an oilfield service and manufacturing company. *New Positions Created (3):* Wireline Specialist; Senior Production Testing Supervisors; Wireline Specialist.

OPTECH INC.
Att: Human Resources
100 Wildcat Road
Toronto, ON M3J 2Z9
Tel. 416-661-5904
Fax 416-661-4168
Email .... resume@optech.on.ca
Website .... www.optech.on.ca
Employer Background: Optech Inc. is a leading developer of laser range finder instrumentation for industrial and scientific applications. *New Positions Created (61):* ALTM Salesperson, Terrestrial Division; Electronics Technologist, Marine Division; Product Manager / Specialist, Industrial Products Division; Senior Electronics Engineer, Marine Division; Software Engineer, Terrestrial Division; Test Technologist, Terrestrial Division; Accounts Payable / Accounts Receivable Assistant; Receptionist / General Support Clerk; Financial and Accounting Manager; Technology Specialist / Technologist; Electrical Engineer, Marine Division; Electronics Technician; Receptionist, Accounts Payable / Accounts Receivable Assistant; Senior Software Designer / RTOS, Laser Imaging Division; Software Developer, Laser Imaging Division; Technical Sales Specialist, Laser Imaging Division; Data Processing Software Programmer, Marine Division; Electro-Mechanical Engineer, Marine Division; Integrated Logistics Support (ILS) Manager, Marine Division; Junior Technical Writer; Laser Scientist / Engi-

neer, Marine Division; Technical Specialist / Technologist, Corporate Manufacturing Division; Daycare Instructor; Manufacturing Manager, Terrestrial Division; Sales Administrator, Repair Department; ALTM Salesperson, Terrestrial Division; Applications Software Specialist, Laser Imaging Division; Document Coordinator, Marine Division; Electronics Technologist, Marine Division; Junior Software Designer / RTOS, Laser Imaging Division; Product Manager / Specialist, Industrial Products Division; Senior Electronics Engineer, Marine Division; Software Engineer, Terrestrial Division; Technical Field Sales Specialist, Laser Imaging Division; Test Technologist, Terrestrial Division; Data Manager, Marine Division; Date Processing Software Programmer, Marine Division; Division Manager; Electro-Mechanical Engineer, Marine Division; Integrated Logistics Support Manager, Marine Division; Junior Software Designer / RTOS, Terrestrial Division; Junior Systems / Electronics Engineer, Terrestrial Division; Laser Scientist / Engineer, Marine Division; Senior Software Designer / RTOS, Terrestrial Division; Senior Systems / Electronics Engineer, Terrestrial Division; Software Engineer, Marine Division; Test Manager, Marine Division; ALTM Sales Specialist; Applications Software Specialist; Customer Account Manager; Electronics Procurement Technician; Electronics Technologist; Project Accountant; Senior Electronics Engineer; Senior Scientist / Engineer; Senior Windows Program Developer; Software Programmer; Systems Engineer; Technical Field Sales Specialist; Test Technologist; Division Manager.

OPTICAL SYSTEMS
Att: Human Resources Manager
67 Iber Road
Stittsville, ON K2S 1E7
Tel. 613-831-0697
Fax 613-836-8895
Email .... allison@opticalsystems.ca
Website .... www.opticalsystems.ca
Employer Background: Optical Systems provides quality inspection equipment for the high-tech sector. *New Positions Created (2):* Sales Representative; Client Services Position.

OPTIMAL ROBOTICS CORP.
Att: Human Resources
4700 de la Savane, Suite 101
Montréal, QC H4P 1T7
Tel. 514-738-8885
Fax 514-738-2284
Email .... jobs@opmr.com
Website .... www.optimal-robotics.com
Employer Background: Founded in 1991, Optimal Robotics Corp. is a leader in the development and implementation of automated self-checkout systems for retail applications. *New Positions Created (30):* Accounts Receivable Clerks (4); Accounts Receivable Supervisor; Collection Clerks (2); Quality Control Developer, Quality Control; Software / Hardware Tester, Quality Control; C++ Developers; Hardware Tester, Quality Control; Technical Support Assistants, Sup-

port Centre (2); Coordinator, Marketing; Human Resources Assistant; Intermediate Software Developer; System Administrator, Information Technology; Accounting Clerk; Multimedia Configuration Support Analyst; Graphic Artist, Multimedia; System Support Specialist, Support Center; Technical Support Specialist, Support Centre (2); Technical Writer; Project Manager; Quality Control Developer; Technical Support Assistant; Quality Control Developers; Software Developers; Software Research and Development Analyst; Team Leader, Quality Control Development; Clerk, Project Management; Senior Developer, Software R&D; Support Centre Specialists; U-Scan System Trainers; Accounts Receivable Clerk.

OPTOTEK LTD.
Att: Personnel Administrator
62 Steacie Drive
Kanata, ON K2K 2A9
Tel. 613-591-0336
Fax 613-591-0584
Email .... dgirard@optotek.com
Website .... www.optotek.com
Employer Background: Optotek Ltd. designs and manufactures light-emitting diode display systems, including drive and interface electronics, associated optics and test equipment. *New Positions Created (6):* Mechanical Engineer / Technologist; Processing Engineer / Technologist; Software Engineer; Electro - Mechanical Technologist; Quality Control Technician; Wafer Process Operator.

OPTX CORPORATION
Att: Michele Hodge
287 Broadway, Suite 100
Winnipeg, MB R3C 0R9
Tel. 204-987-8770
Fax 204-987-8772
Email .... hr@healthierpractices.com
Website .... www.healthierpractices.com
Employer Background: Optx is a healthcare service and technology company, specializing in oncology. *New Positions Created (3):* Manager, Integration Services; Systems Analyst / Developer; Clinical Analyst .

ORACLE CORPORATION CANADA INC.
Att: Ian Collyer, Human Resources
110 Matheson Boulevard West, Suite 100
Mississauga, ON L5R 3P4
Tel. 905-890-8100
Fax 905-890-0263
Email .... ian.collyer@oracle.com
Website .... www.oraclecanada.com
Employer Background: Founded in 1984, Oracle Corporation Canada Inc. is a developer of customized, fully-integrated computing solutions, with over 1,000 employees and 13 offices nationwide. *New Positions Created (4):* CRM Sales Consultants; Field Technical Analyst; Account Manager; Account Managers.

ORBITAL TECHNOLOGIES INC.
Att: Human Resources Manager
1090 Homer Street, Suite 200
Vancouver, BC V6B 2W9

Tel. 604-681-7237
Fax 604-681-7247
Email .... resumes@orbitaltech.com
Website .... www.orbitaltech.com
Employer Background: Orbital Technologies Inc. develops custom software solutions, specializing in database technologies, web integration, file format analysis and conversion and cross-platform development. *New Positions Created (3):* Computer Scientists; Quality Assurance Engineers; Customer Support Technologist.

ORENDA AEROSPACE CORPORATION
Att: Human Resources Department
3160 Derry Road East
Mississauga, ON L4T 1A9
Tel. 905-677-3250
Fax 905-673-5304
Website .... www.orenda.com
Employer Background: Orenda Aerospace Corporation, an operating division of Magellan Aerospace Corporation, has been advancing power and propulsion technologies for over 50 years. *New Positions Created (3):* Quality Control Planner; Process Planner; Design Engineer.

ORIGENIX TECHNOLOGIES INC.
Att: Linette Grey, HR Department
230 Bernard-Belleau, Suite 210
Laval, QC H7V 4A9
Tel. 450-688-8588
Fax 450-688-8018
Email .... lgrey@origenix.com
Website .... www.origenix.com
Employer Background: Origenix Technologies Inc. is a pre-IPO biotechnology company, discovering and developing novel nucleic acid-based drugs for the treatment of infectious diseases. *New Positions Created (9):* Associate Director, Computational Chemistry; Computational Chemist; Post-Doctoral Scientists; Research Associate, Synthetic Chemistry; Research Scientist, Analytical Chemistry; Research Scientist, Combinatorial Chemistry; Research Scientist, Medicinal Chemistry; Research Scientist, Process Chemistry; Corporate Accounting Manager.

ORIGINAL CAKERIE LTD.
Att: Human Resources
1345 Cliveden Avenue
Delta, BC V3M 6C7
Tel. 604-515-4555
Fax 604-515-4569
Email .... smp@cakerie.com
Website .... www.cakerie.com
Employer Background: Original Cakerie Ltd. manufactures high-quality frozen desserts. *New Positions Created (2):* Production Supervisor; Maintenance Manager.

ORILLIA SOLDIERS' MEMORIAL HOSPITAL / OSMH
Att: Human Resources Department
170 Colborne Street West
Orillia, ON L3V 2Z3
Tel. 705-327-9120
Fax 705-327-9170

Email .... humanresources@osmh.on.ca
Website .... www.osmh.on.ca
Employer Background: OSMH is a 176-bed facility, with over 25 outpatient clinics and 45,000 emergency care visits per year. *New Positions Created (2):* Radiology Technologists; Registered Dietitian, Regional Dialysis Program.

ORION BUS INDUSTRIES LTD.
Att: Human Resources Department
350 Hazelhurst Road
Mississauga, ON L5J 4T8
Tel. 905-403-1111
Fax 905-403-8806
Email .... recruiting@orionbus.com
Website .... www.freightliner.com/
.... products/orion.html
Employer Background: Orion Bus Industries Ltd., a division of Western Star Trucks Inc., manufactures transit vehicles. *New Positions Created (8):* Cost Accountant; Bid Analyst / Coordinator; Contracts Administrator / Project Manager; Demand Planner; Payroll & Benefits Administrator; Quality Assurance Supervisor; Senior Design Engineer; Bid Analyst.

ORIX FINANCIAL SERVICES CANADA LTD. / OFS CANADA
Att: Executive Vice-President
300 The East Mall, Suite 200
Toronto, ON M9B 6B7
Fax 416-236-3010
Email .... csc@orix-cac.com
Website ... www.orixfinancialservices.com
Employer Background: OFS Canada has been providing financing and leasing products for over 30 years. *New Positions Created (3):* Collection Officers; Credit Officers; Sales Representatives.

ORLICK INDUSTRIES LTD.
Att: Employee Services
411 Parkdale Avenue North
PO Box 5190, LCD 1
Hamilton, ON L8L 8G1
Tel. 905-544-1997
Fax 905-544-9612
Email .... hr@orlick.on.ca
Website .... www.orlick.on.ca
Employer Background: Orlick Industries Ltd. is a leader in high-pressure die casting and machining of aluminum parts for the automotive industry. *New Positions Created (35):* Environmental Services Assistant; Production Control Supervisor; CNC Operator; Industrial Electrician; Maintenance Millwright; Tool & Die Maker; Trim Press Operator; Senior Manufacturing Technician; CNC Operator; Gauge Control Technician; Industrial Electrician; Maintenance Millwright; Screw Machine Trainee; SPC Coordinator; Tool & Die Maker; Trim Press Operator; Internal Systems Auditor, QS9000 / ISO14001; Production Control Manager; Junior Buyer; Project Engineer; Senior Manufacturing Technician; Project Coordinator; Technical Costing Estimator; QA Auditor; Accountant; Technical Costing Coordinator; Tier 1 / Tier 2 Automotive Sales Pro-

fessionals; Health and Safety Coordinator; SPC Coordinator; Tool and Die Maker; Training Coordinator; Production Control Manager; CNC Maintenance Supervisor; Tool Setter; Facilities Engineer.

OSHAWA, CITY OF
Att: Employment Coordinator
50 Centre Street South
Oshawa, ON L1H 3Z7
Tel. 905-725-7351
Fax 905-436-5698
Email ..... employment@city.oshawa.on.ca
Website .... www.city.oshawa.on.ca
Employer Background: Located 40 minutes east of Toronto, the City of Oshawa is home to 142,000 people. *New Positions Created (8):* Senior Solicitor; Traffic Operations Technician; Transportation & Parking Support Technician; Director of Recreation and Culture Services; Traffic Engineering Technicians (2); Intermediate Draftsperson; Manager of Parking & Transportation Support Services; Transportation Planner / Engineer.

OSITECH COMMUNICATIONS INC.
Att: Human Resources Manager
679 Southgate Drive
Guelph, ON N1G 4S2
Tel. 519-836-8063
Fax 519-836-6156
Email .... resume@ositech.com
Website .... www.ositech.com
Employer Background: Founded in 1989, Ositech Communications Inc. designs, manufactures and markets voice and data communications products for personal computers. *New Positions Created (7):* Corporate Accounts Manager; Hardware Engineer; Junior Hardware Engineer; Junior / Intermediate Software Engineer; Senior Hardware Engineer; Senior Software Engineer; Technician / Technologist.

OSLER, HOSKIN & HARCOURT LLP
Att: Human Resources
333 - 7th Avenue SW
Suite 1900, Dome Tower, TD Square
Calgary, AB T2P 2Z1
Tel. 403-260-7000
Fax 403-260-7024
Website .... www.osler.com
Employer Background: Osler, Hoskin & Harcourt LLP is one of Canada's largest law firms, with 325 lawyers and offices in Toronto, Ottawa, Calgary and New York. *New Positions Created (2):* Securities, M & A and General Corporate Lawyer; Legal Assistant, Real Estate.

OSLER, HOSKIN & HARCOURT LLP
Att: Marie Huxter,
Director, Associate Program
1 First Canadian Place, PO Box 50
Toronto, ON M5X 1B8
Tel. 416-362-2111
Fax 416-862-6666
Email .... mhuxter@osler.com
Website .... www.osler.com
Employer Background: Osler, Hoskin & Harcourt LLP is one of Canada's largest law

firms, with 325 lawyers and offices in Toronto, Ottawa, Calgary and New York. *New Positions Created (10):* Insolvency and Restructuring Lawyer; Senior Corporate Law Clerk; Pension & Benefits Lawyer; Labour & Employment Lawyer; Environmental Litigation Lawyer; Litigation Lawyer, Construction and Infrastructure; Litigation Lawyer, Intellectual Property / Information Technology; Pensions and Benefits Lawyer; Senior Corporate Law Clerk; Research Lawyer.

OTTAWA CHILDREN'S TREATMENT CENTRE / OCTC
Att: Director of Human Resources
395 Smyth Road
Ottawa, ON K1H 8L2
Tel. 613-820-4222
Fax 613-738-4304
Email .... octchr@cheo.on.ca
Website .... www.cheo.on.ca
Employer Background: OCTC provides family-centred rehabilitative care for children and youth with physical and developmental disabilities. *New Positions Created (3):* Speech Language Pathologist; Program Administrator, Clinic for Augmentative Communication; Program Administrator, Pediatric Rehabilitation.

OTTAWA, CITY OF
Att: Client Service Centre
110 Laurier Avenue West, 1st Floor
Ottawa, ON K1P 1J1
Fax 613-580-4762
Email .... citystaffing@city.ottawa.on.ca
Website .... www.city.ottawa.on.ca
Employer Background: The City of Ottawa provides essential programs and services for 800,000 citizens. *New Positions Created (14):* Manager of Marketing; Manager of Public Affairs; Manager of Sponsorship & Special Events; Property Mgr, OC Transpo Campus Portfolio; Advanced Care Paramedics; Human Rights Consultants; Mgr, French Language Services; Labour Relations Consultants (2); Business Analysts, HRIS; Compensation Analysts; Job Evaluation Consultants; Performance Mgmnt Consultants; Planning, Policy & Program Development Consultants; Sr Labour Relations Consultants.

OTTAWA, CITY OF
Att: Human Resources Service Bureau
800 Green Creek Drive
RO Pickard Environmental Centre
Gloucester, ON K1J 1A6
Fax 613-560-1294
Email .... sbropec@city.ottawa.on.ca
Website .... www.city.ottawa.on.ca
Employer Background: The City of Ottawa provides essential programs and services for 800,000 citizens. *New Positions Created (6):* Documentation Technologist; Program Analyst; Technical Analyst; Wastewater Collection Mgr; Maintenance Management Engineers (2); Wastewater Collection Manager.

OTTAWA HEALTH RESEARCH INSTITUTE / OHRI
Att: Human Resources Manager

725 Parkdale Avenue
Ottawa, ON K1Y 4E9
Tel. 613-761-4395
Website .... www.ohri.ca
Employer Background: OHRI, one of the largest hospital-based research institutes in Canada, is the research arm of the Ottawa Hospital and part of the University of Ottawa. *New Positions Created (5):* Junior Health Economist; Research Assistant; Research Assistant; Research Coordinator; Research Coordinator.

OTTAWA HOSPITAL, THE
Att: Human Resources Department
1053 Carling Avenue
Ottawa, ON K1Y 4E9
Tel. 613-798-5555
Fax 613-761-5374
Email .... jobs@ottawahospital.on.ca
Website .... www.ottawahospital.on.ca
Employer Background: The Ottawa Hospital, Canada's largest acute care teaching hospital, is affiliated with the University of Ottawa. *New Positions Created (45):* Registered Nurse, Neurosurgery; Registered Nurse, Cardiac Surgery; Clinical Scientist, Nursing Research; Senior Orthopaedic Technician; Clinical Manager, Critical Care / Emergency / Trauma; Technologist I; Programmer Analyst; Senior Programmer Analyst; Senior Systems Analyst; Registered Nurse, Emergency; Registered Nurse, Intensive Care Unit; Chief Clinical Pharmacist; Staff Educator, Supply, Processing and Distribution; Education Coordinator; Official Languages Officer; Pharmacist; Senior Orthopaedic Technician; Associate Radiation Safety Officer; Research Administrative Assistant; Health Records Administrator; Chaplain I; Clinical Leader; Director, Admitting / Patient Registration; Director, Palliative Care; Manager, Processing Services; Occupational Health Nurse; Plumber; Registered Nurses; Senior Clerk, Accounts Payable; Supervisor, Health Records; Supervisor, Security and Parking; Technologist II; Clinical Managers (2); Coordinator, Library Services; Genetic Research Technician; Geriatric Nurse Specialists (2); Construction Site Supervisor; Operations Team Manager; Chief of Occupational Therapy and Recreation Therapy; Clinical Manager; Systems Specialists; Chief Physiotherapist; Chief Respiratory Therapist; Chief, Speech Language Pathologist; Clinical Manager, Coronary Care Unit / Nephrology / Renal Transplant / Cardiology.

OTTAWA HOUSING CORPORATION
Att: Human Resources Manager
2197 Riverside Drive, 6th Floor
Ottawa, ON K1H 1A9
Tel. 613-731-7223
Fax 613-731-4463
Employer Background: The Ottawa Housing Corporation is a large residential property management organization that administers rent-geared-to-income housing. *New Positions Created (2):* District Landscape Manager; Property Manager.

OTTAWA MOULD CRAFT LTD.
Att: Human Resources
2600 Lancaster Road
Ottawa, ON K2B 4Z4
Tel. 613-521-6402
Fax 613-521-6178
Email .... hr@ottawamould.com
Website .... www.ottawamould.com
Employer Background: Ottawa Mould Craft Ltd. is a plastic injection custom moulder, with over 25 years experience. *New Positions Created (5):* Production Planning / Customer Service Coordinator; Lead Hand / Team Leaders; Machine Operators; Machine Set Up Technicians; Quality Control Inspectors.

OTTAWA REGIONAL CANCER CENTRE FOUNDATION
Att: Executive Director
503 Smyth Road
Ottawa, ON K1H 1C4
Tel. 613-797-7700
Fax 613-247-3526
Website .... www.orcc.on.ca
Employer Background: The Ottawa Regional Cancer Centre Foundation is the fundraising arm of an outpatient cancer treatment facility. *New Positions Created (2):* Manager of Communications; Director, Clinical Research.

OTTAWA SALUS CORPORATION
Att: Human Resources Manager
945 Wellington
Ottawa, ON K1Y 2X5
Tel. 613-729-0123
Fax 613-729-7800
Employer Background: Ottawa Salus Corporation is a non-profit mental health agency, providing housing and support services. *New Positions Created (7):* Front-Line Workers; Manager; Service Coordinator; Community Developer; Manager; Occupational Therapist; Finance Manager.

OTTAWA SENATORS HOCKEY CLUB
Att: Human Resources
1000 Palladium Drive, Corel Centre
Kanata, ON K2V 1A5
Tel. 613-599-0250
Fax 613-599-0226
Website .... www.ottawasenators.com
Employer Background: The Ottawa Senators Hockey Club supports the Ottawa Senators hockey team. *New Positions Created (5):* Database Coordinator; Manager, Retail Operations; Senior Accountant; Payroll Administrator; Account Manager.

OTTAWA-CARLETON CATHOLIC SCHOOL BOARD / OCCSB
Att: Staffing Officer, HR Department
140 Cumberland Street
Ottawa, ON K1N 7G9
Tel. 613-241-3161
Fax 613-241-5532
Website .... www.occdsb.on.ca
Employer Background: OCCSB operates 78 schools, serves 40,000 students and employs over 2,400 qualified teachers. *New Positions*

Created (4): Secretary; Principals and Vice-Principals; Chaplains; Teachers.

OTTAWA-CARLETON DISTRICT SCHOOL BOARD / OCDSB
Att: Human Resources Department, Administrative and Support Staff
133 Greenbank Road
Nepean, ON K2H 6L3
Tel. 613-596-8246
Fax 613-596-8776
Website .... www.ocdsb.edu.on.ca
Employer Background: OCDSB serves public school students in the Ottawa-Carleton area. *New Positions Created (8):* Electricians (2); Plumbers (2); Supervisor, Design & Construction Services; Elementary Principals; Business and Learning Technologies Technician; Speech Language Pathologists; Vice-Principals; Transportation Coordinator.

OTTAWA-CARLETON TRANSIT COMMISSION / OC TRANSPO
Att: Manager,
Employment & Services Department
1500 St. Laurent Boulevard
Ottawa, ON K1G 0Z8
Tel. 613-842-3636
Fax 613-742-7303
Website .... www.octranspo.com
Employer Background: OC Transpo has over 2,000 employees, 825 buses and ridership of 75 million. *New Positions Created (2):* Bus Operator; Materials and Equipment Safety Instructor.

OTTER FARM & HOME CO-OPERATIVE
Att: Chair, Search Committee
3600 - 248th Street, RR 4, PO Box 4200
Aldergrove, BC V4W 2V1
Tel. 604-607-6907
Fax 604-856-2674
Website .... www.otter-coop.com
Employer Background: The Otter Farm & Home Co-operative sells food, general merchandise, petroleum and feed products to over 30,000 members. *New Positions Created (2):* General Manager, Retailing; Feed Marketing / Mill Manager.

OVERSEAS COURIER SERVICE LTD.
Att: Ian Price, Branch Manager
3280 Caroga Drive
Mississauga, ON L4V 1L4
Tel. 905-673-0108
Fax 905-673-2429
Email .... iprice@ocs.ca
Website .... www.ocs.ca
Employer Background: OCS is a global express courier and air cargo company, operating in Canada since 1963. *New Positions Created (2):* Account Exec; Account Exec.

OVERSEAS EXPRESS CONSOLIDATORS INC. / OEC
Att: Human Resources Manager
10500 Cote de Liesse, Suite 200
Montréal, QC H8T 1A4
Fax 514-633-6044
Email ... humanresources@oecymx.oecgroup.ca

Website .... www.oecgroup.ca
Employer Background: OEC is an international freight forwarder and logistics provider, with offices in Montreal, Calgary and Vancouver. *New Positions Created (7):* Accounts Payable Clerk; Ocean Import Clerks; Accounts Payable Coordinator; Shipment Coordinators, Ocean Import; Account Executive, Sales; Administrative Assistant; Customer Service Representative.

OVERWAITEA FOOD GROUP
Att: Human Resources
PO Box 7200
Vancouver, BC V6B 4E4
Tel. 604-888-1213
Fax 604-888-8580
Email .... employment@owfg.com
Website .... www.owfg.com
Employer Background: Overwaitea Food Group, one of western Canada's largest food and consumer goods organizations, operates Overwaitea Foods, Save-On-Foods and Urban Fare. *New Positions Created (10):* Pharmacists; Project Managers; Senior Database Architects; Senior Software Engineers; Senior System Architects; Senior Systems Database Administrator; Systems Administrator; Systems Administrator, NT; Web Application Architect; Pharmacists.

OWEN SOUND, CITY OF
Att: Human Resources Manager
808 - 2nd Avenue East
Owen Sound, ON N4K 2H4
Fax 519-371-8190
Website .... www.city.owen-sound.on.ca
Employer Background: The City of Owen Sound is a progressive community located on the southern shore of Georgian Bay. *New Positions Created (5):* Director, Financial Services; Firefighter / Paramedic; Water / Wastewater Superintendent; Tourism Manager; Intermediate Planner.

OWENS CORNING CANADA
Att: Human Resources Manager
247 York Road, PO Box 3603
Guelph, ON N1H 6P6
Fax 519-823-7204
Website .... www.owenscorning.com
Employer Background: Owens Corning Canada is one of the largest manufacturers of glass fibre insulation products for the Canadian market. *New Positions Created (2):* Industrial Electricians (2); Industrial Maintenance Mechanics (3).

OWENS CORNING CANADA
Att: Human Resources
3450 McNicoll Avenue
Toronto, ON M1V 1Z5
Tel. 416-292-4000
Fax 416-292-5014
Email ... richard.fink@owenscorning.com
Website .... www.owenscorning.com
Employer Background: Owens Corning Canada is one of the largest manufacturers of glass fibre insulation products for the Canadian market. *New Positions Created (2):*

Occupational Health Nurse; Human Resources Manager.

OWENS, WRIGHT
Att: Grace Albiez
20 Holly Street, Suite 401
Toronto, ON M4S 3B1
Tel. 416-486-9800
Fax 416-486-3309
Email .... galbiez@owenswright.com
Employer Background: Owens, Wright is a law firm, specializing in commercial real estate. *New Positions Created (3):* Legal Secretary; Commercial Leasing Lawyer; Commercial Real Estate Lawyer.

OXFORD, COUNTY OF
Att: Human Resources Office
415 Hunter Street, PO Box 397
Woodstock, ON N4S 7Y3
Tel. 519-539-9800
Fax 519-537-3024
Email .... hr@county.oxford.on.ca
Website .... www.county.oxford.on.ca
Employer Background: Located between London and Kitchener, the County of Oxford is home to 100,000 people. *New Positions Created (2):* Water / Wastewater Engineer; Water / Wastewater Technologist.

OXFORD PROPERTIES GROUP INC.
Att: Human Resources Manager
2000 Merrill Lynch Tower,
Edmonton Centre
Edmonton, AB T5J 2Z2
Tel. 780-426-8400
Fax 780-424-9949
Email .... hrrecruit@oxfordproperties.com
Website .... www.oxfordproperties.com
Employer Background: Oxford Properties Group Inc. is one of North America's leading real estate corporations. *New Positions Created (4):* Maintenance and Cleaning Inspector / Parkade Patroller; Leasing Representative; Marketing Manager, Retail; Administrative Assistant.

OXFORD PROPERTIES GROUP INC.
Att: Human Resources
120 Adelaide Street West, Suite 1700
Toronto, ON M5H 1T1
Tel. 416-865-8300
Fax 416-868-1802
Email ... hrrecruit@oxfordproperties.com
Website ... www.oxfordproperties.com
Employer Background: Oxford Properties Group Inc. is one of North America's leading real estate corporations. *New Positions Created (5):* 4th Class Stationary Shift Engineer; Acquisitions Analyst; General Manager; Manager, Development; Director, Operations and Financial Control.

OZ OPTICS LTD.
Att: Human Resources Manager
219 Westbrook Road
Carp, ON K0A 1L0
Tel. 613-831-0981
Fax 613-836-5089
Email .... hr@ozoptics.com

Website .... www.ozoptics.com
Employer Background: Established in 1985, OZ Optics Ltd. is a leading manufacturer of fibre optic components, with 500 employees worldwide. *New Positions Created (106):* Coating Technician; Manager, Marketing and Communications; Manager, Thin Film Deposition; Senior Network Systems Engineer; Tool and Die Maker; Fibre Optic Engineers; Manager, Communications; Manager, Server Operations; Manufacturing Engineers; Electronics Engineer; Customer Service and Order Desk Coordinator; Documentation Control Supervisor; Document Control Clerks (3); Electronic Technician; Expediter; Fibre Optic Engineers; Inside Sales Representatives (4); Project Manager, Information Technology; Purchasing Manager; QA Calibration Specialist; Security Officer; Senior Systems Engineer; Vice-President, Engineering; Trade Show and Sponsorship Specialist; Accounts Receivable Supervisor; Occupational Health Nurse; Design Engineers; International Accountant / Analyst; Electronics Technologist; Manufacturing Engineer; Product Managers (3); Production Controller; Senior Buyer / Planner; Technical Writer; Purchasing Manager; Senior Machinist / Tool and Die Maker; Administrative Assistant; Fibre Optic Engineers; Mechanical Engineer; Clerical Support / Travel Coordinator; Quality Assurance Calibration Specialist; Quality Assurance Project Manager; Controller, International Operations; Document Control Clerks (3); ERP Implementation Manager; Fibre Optic Assemblers (10); Graphic Designer; Inside Sales Representative ; Manufacturing Process Engineers ; Optical Technicians (2); Payroll Manager; Production Controller ; Production Planners (2); Quality Assurance Inspector, Machine Shop; Travel / Meeting Coordinator; Vice-President, Engineering; Buyer / Planner; Draftsperson; Expeditor; Project Manager, Test Equipment; Regional Sales Manager; A / R Clerk; Administrative Assistant; Help Desk Position; Marketing Administrative Assistant; Order Department Administrative Assistant; Payroll Manager; Physical Distribution Manager; Product Manager; Reception / Event Coordinator; Fiber Optic Assemblers; Accounting Manager; Document Control Clerks; Electro-mechanical Assemblers; Electronics Assemblers; Electronics Technicians; Executive Administrators; Fiber Optic Engineer; Fiber Optic Technicians; Inside Sales / Customer Service Representative; Machine Shop Foreman; Machinists (2); Manager, Marketing Communications; Manufacturing Process Engineer; Office Manager; Product Manager / Process Manager; Senior Circuit Designers; Senior Human Resource Generalist; Senior Reliability Engineer; Senior Sales Coordinator; Software Programmers; Trade Show Manager; Bookkeeper and Office Administration; Mechanical Engineer; Database Administrator; Human Resources Administrative Assistant; Human Resources Generalists; Executive Administrators (2); Financial Analyst; Investor Relations Position; Junior Clerk, Document Control; Marketing Manager / Trade Show Manager; Order Desk Position; Quality Engineer; Senior Clerk, Document Control; Executive Administrators (2).

P.J. WHITE HARDWOODS LTD.
Att: Lawrence Tetreault, Manager
14604 - 124th Avenue
Edmonton, AB T5L 3B3
Tel. 780-454-6561
Fax 780-455-9289
Email .... pjwed@telusplanet.net
Website .... www.pjwhitehardwoods.com
Employer Background: Established in 1949, P.J. White Hardwoods Ltd. is a Canadian-owned wholesale hardwood distributor, with branches in Victoria, Vancouver, Calgary and Edmonton. *New Positions Created (4):* Specifications Representative; Inside Sales Position; Outside Sales Representative; Sales Position.

P&H MINEPRO SERVICES
Att: Graham Brown, Human Resources
7326 - 10th Street NE, Suite 300
Calgary, AB T2E 8W1
Tel. 403-730-9851
Fax 403-730-9872
Website .... www.pandhcanada.com
Employer Background: P&H MinePro Services supplies heavy equipment to the surface mining industry in Canada. *New Positions Created (4):* Director of Distribution and Logistics; Field Service Representative; Service Technician Trainee; Marketing Mgr.

PACCAR FINANCIAL SERVICES LTD.
Att: Mike Rome
6711 Mississauga Road North, Suite 500
Mississauga, ON L5N 4J8
Tel. 905-858-7000
Fax 905-858-7015
Email .... michael.rome@paccar.com
Website .... www.paccar.com
Employer Background: PACCAR Financial Services Ltd. offers truck financing services to Kenworth and Peterbilt dealerships in Canada. *New Positions Created (3):* Credit Administrator; Contract Administrator; Director of Credit.

PACCAR INC.
Att: Human Resources Manager
6711 Mississauga Road North, 5th Floor
Mississauga, ON L5N 4J8
Email .... plcjobs@paccar.com
Website .... www.paccar.com
Employer Background: PACCAR Inc. is the world's 2nd-largest independent heavy-duty truck manufacturer. *New Positions Created (2):* Corporate Financial Accounting Manager; Sr Financial Analyst / Tax Accountant.

PACE, JOHNSON
Att: Human Resources Manager
5110 Dundas Street West
Toronto, ON M9A 1C2
Tel. 416-236-3060
Fax 416-236-1809
Employer Background: Pace, Johnson is a personal injury law firm. *New Positions Created (3):* Personal Injury Lawyer; Secretary / Receptionist; Senior Litigation Lawyer.

PACESETTER HOMES LTD.
Att: General Manager
10520 - 178th Street, Suite 202
Edmonton, AB T5S 2J1
Tel. 780-483-2653
Fax 780-483-4691
Website ... www.pacesetterhomes-edm.com
Employer Background: Pacesetter Homes Ltd. is a large-volume home builder. *New Positions Created (2):* Estimator; Warranty Technician.

PACIFIC BLUE CROSS / BC LIFE
Att: Human Resources
PO Box 7000
Vancouver, BC V6B 4E1
Tel. 604-419-2000
Email .. human_resources@pac.bluecross.ca
Website .... www.pac.bluecross.ca
Employer Background: Pacific Blue Cross / BC Life was formed by the merger of CU&C Health Services Society and Medical Services Association. *New Positions Created (11):* Data Entry Operator; Payroll Administrator; Programmer / Analyst; Retention / Research Analyst; Benefit Claims Examiner; Customer Retention & Research Analyst; Customer Service Representative; Dental Benefit Examiner; Disability Specialist; General Finance Clerk; Member Administrator.

PACIFIC INSTITUTE OF CULINARY ARTS
Att: Walter Messiah, Executive Chef
1505 - 2nd Avenue West
Vancouver, BC V6H 3Y4
Tel. 604-734-4488
Fax 604-734-4408
Website .... www.picularts.bc.ca
Employer Background: The Pacific Institute of Culinary Arts is a private culinary institute, with an on-site training restaurant and bake shop. *New Positions Created (2):* Chef Instructors; Chef Instructors.

PACIFIC LANGUAGE INSTITUTE / PLI
Att: President
1030 West Georgia Street, Suite 300
Vancouver, BC V6E 2Y3
Tel. 604-688-7223
Fax 604-688-7242
Email .... headoffice@pli.ca
Website .... www.pli.ca
Employer Background: PLI is a private ESL school. *New Positions Created (2):* Marketing Manager; Academic Director.

PACIFIC NATIONAL AQUACULTURE
Att: Human Resources Manager
1001 Wharf Street, Suite 300
Victoria, BC V8W 1T6
Tel. 250-386-0866
Fax 250-386-0860
Website .... www.pacificnational.ca
Employer Background: Pacific National Aquaculture (a division of Ewos Canada)

specializes in fresh salmon products, with farms in Canada, Scotland and Chile. *New Positions Created (5):* Data and Inventory Control Analyst; Finance and Budget Manager; Licensing Administrator; Sales and Logistics Coordinator; Reporting Manager.

PACIFIC SAFETY PRODUCTS INC.
Att: Human Resources
2821 Fenwick Road
Kelowna, BC V1X 5E4
Fax 250-491-0930
Email .... lpinkney@pacsafety.com
Website .... www.pacsafety.com
Employer Background: PSP manufactures high-performance safety products, including protective armour and apparel. *New Positions Created (2):* Director, Manufacturing; Territory Sales Representative, Law Enforcement Products.

PACKAGING GROUP, THE
Att: Human Resources Manager
360 Spinnaker Way
Concord, ON L4K 4W1
Tel. 905-761-7040
Fax 905-761-7463
Email .. recruiting@thepackaginggroup.com
Website ..... www.thepackaginggroup.com
Employer Background: The Packaging Group manufactures flexible packaging for the food industry. *New Positions Created (2):* Assistant Technical Support; Senior Accountant.

PAGING NETWORK OF CANADA, INC. / PAGENET CANADA
Att: Human Resources Manager
4180 Lougheed Highway, Suite 300
Vancouver, BC V5C 6A7
Fax 604-415-2001
Email .... careers@pagenet.ca
Website .... www.pagenet.ca
Employer Background: PageNet Canada offers paging and messaging services in areas covering 75% of Canada's population. The company is a subsidiary of US-based PageNet Inc., the world's largest paging company. *New Positions Created (3):* Administrative Assistant; Customer Service Representative; Inventory Supervisor.

PAGING NETWORK OF CANADA, INC. / PAGENET CANADA
Att: Human Resources Manager
3250 Bloor Street West, Suite 700
Toronto, ON M8X 2X9
Tel. 416-490-3100
Fax 416-233-1424
Email .... careers@pagenet.ca
Website .... www.pagenet.ca
Employer Background: PageNet Canada (formerly Madison Telecommunications) offers paging and messaging services in areas covering 75% of Canada's population. The company is a subsidiary of USA-based PageNet Inc., the world's largest paging company. *New Positions Created (2):* A / P Representatives; General Accountant.

PAGING NETWORK OF CANADA, INC. / PAGENET CANADA
Att: Direct Marketing Manager
2001 Sheppard Avenue East, Suite 100
Toronto, ON M2J 4Z8
Tel. 416-490-3100
Fax 416-490-3149
Email .... careers@pagenet.ca
Website .... www.pagenet.ca
Employer Background: PageNet Canada offers paging and messaging services in areas covering 75% of Canada's population. The company is a subsidiary of US-based PageNet Inc., the world's largest paging company. *New Positions Created (6):* Direct Marketing Representatives; Corporate Sales Representatives; Customer Service Representatives; Direct Marketing Representatives; Direct Marketing Representatives; Sales Representatives.

PAISLEY PRODUCTS OF CANADA
Att: Human Resources
40 Upton Road
Toronto, ON M1L 2B8
Fax 416-751-3882
Email .... peter@paisley.ca
Website .... www.paisley.ca
Employer Background: Paisley Products converts and distributes adhesives, pressure-sensitive tapes and dispensing systems to the electronics and electrical market. *New Positions Created (2):* Associate Product Mgr; Specialty Tape Sales Rep, Graphic Arts.

PALFINGER INC.
Att: Human Resources Manager
7942 Dorchester Road, PO Box 846
Niagara Falls, ON L2E 6V6
Tel. 905-374-3363
Fax 905-374-3032
Website .... www.palfinger.com
Employer Background: Palfinger Inc. is a German-based manufacturer and distributor of truck-mounted cranes and forklifts. *New Positions Created (2):* Shop Mechanic; NetWare Administrator.

PALLETT VALO LLP
Att: Denise Collins, Accounting Manager
90 Burnhamthorpe Road West, Suite 1600
Mississauga, ON L5B 3C3
Tel. 905-273-3300
Fax 905-897-0267
Email .... dcollins@pallettvalo.com
Website .... www.pallettvalo.com
Employer Background: Founded in 1948, Pallett Valo LLP is one of the largest law firms in Peel Region, with 19 lawyers specializing in business law, real estate and litigation. *New Positions Created (7):* Commercial Litigation Lawyers; Construction Lawyers; Corporate / Business Lawyers; Litigation Legal Administrator; Jr Litigation Secretary; Labour / Employment / Administrative Lawyer; Sr Litigation Administrator.

PALLISER FURNITURE LTD.
Att: Louise Boucher, Towne Hall Division
705 East Lake Road
Airdrie, AB T4B 2B7
Tel. 204-988-0827
Fax 204-988-5657
Email .... wewantyou@palliser.ca
Website .... www.palliser.com
Employer Background: Palliser Furniture Ltd.'s Airdrie location manufactures upholstered motion furniture. *New Positions Created (2):* Purchaser / Buyer; Cost Analyst / Project Analyst.

PALLISER FURNITURE LTD.
Att: Employment Services,
Corporate Human Resources
80 Furniture Park
Winnipeg, MB R2G 1B9
Tel. 204-988-0827
Fax 204-988-5657
Email .... wewantyou@palliser.ca
Website .... www.palliser.com
Employer Background: Palliser Furniture Ltd. is Canada's largest furniture manufacturer specializing in upholstery and casegoods products. *New Positions Created (5):* Divisional Accounting Manager; Export Sales Managers; Industrial / Manufacturing / Mechanical Engineer; Manufacturing Engineers; Product Engineering Manager.

PALLISER HEALTH AUTHORITY
Att: Human Resources Manager
666 - 5th Street SW
Medicine Hat, AB T1A 4H6
Tel. 403-502-8272
Fax 403-502-7272
Email .... rmattson@pha.ab.ca
Website .... www.pha.ab.ca
Employer Background: The Palliser Health Authority was established to serve the area from the Alberta-Saskatchewan border to Bassano in the west, and from the Canadian-American border in the south to Oyen in the north. *New Positions Created (7):* Site Supervisor, Diagnostic Imaging; Medical Radiation Technologists (3); Paramedics; Medical Radiation Technologist; Occupational Therapist; Physical Therapist; Respiratory Therapist.

PANALPINA INC.
Att: Human Resources
6350 Cantay Road
Mississauga, ON L5R 4E2
Fax 905-755-4613
Email .... panalpina.jobs@
.... yyz-dt.panmail.com
Website .... www.panalpina.com
Employer Background: Panalpina Inc. provides airfreight and seafreight forwarding and logistics services, with 312 branches in 65 countries. *New Positions Created (3):* Accounting Positions; Logistics Positions; Accounting Analyst.

PANCANADIAN PETROLEUM LTD.
Att: Human Resources Department
150 - 9th Avenue SW, PO Box 2850
Calgary, AB T2P 2S5
Tel. 403-290-2000
Fax 403-290-3309
Email .... recruit@pancanadian.ca
Website .... www.pancanadian.ca

Employer Background: PanCanadian Petroleum Ltd. is an exploration, production and marketing company in the oil and natural gas industry. *New Positions Created (57):* Business Partner, Supply Management Facilities; Drilling Partner, Supply Management Business; Senior Business Partner, Human Resources; Software Development Infrastructure Lead; Development Engineer; Risk Analyst, Gas Marketing; Senior / Staff Reservoir Engineer; Senior Production Accountant; Software Developer; Coordinator, Commercial Ventures; Drilling Engineer; Tradesperson / Mechanic; Analyst; Director, Media Relations; Exploration Technologist; IT Business Analyst; Land Administrator; Marketing Accountant; Senior Production Engineer; Sour Gas Operator; TerraDeck Visualization Pilot; US Tax Specialist; Senior Engineer; Production Engineer; Administrative Assistant; Geologist; Production Measurement Auditor; Senior Administrative Assistant; Senior Instrument Electrician; Senior Plant Electrician; Technologist / Petroleum Technician; Business Analyst; Exploration Technologist; Facilities Engineer; Petroleum Technician; Steam Assisted Gravity Drainage (SAGD) Chief Stationary Engineer; Steam Assisted Gravity Drainage (SAGD) Plant Operator; Steam Assisted Gravity Drainage (SAGD) Shift Stationary Engineer; Well Operators (3); Administrative and Technical Assistant; Electronic Messaging Administrator; Firewall / Web / Security Administrator; Junior Knowledge Management Analyst; Senior Contracts Administrator; Operations Coordinator; Production Foreman; Senior Testing / Completion Supervisor; Gas Marketing Accountant; Gas Supply Analyst; Senior Gas Supply Analyst; Senior / Staff Land Negotiator or Lawyer; Senior Human Resources Analyst; Capital / Joint Venture Accountant; Communications Analyst; Production / Revenue Accountant; Senior Production Revenue Accountant; Senior Tax Analyst.

PANELX.COM / PANELX TECHNICAL SERVICES
Att: Human Resources Manager
239 Church Street, Suite 300
Oakville, ON L6J 1N4
Tel. 905-337-1287
Fax 905-337-3975
Email .... jobs@panelx.com
Website .... www.panelx.com
Employer Background: PanelX develops web and embedded device technology for the flat panel display industry. *New Positions Created (4):* PHP / Perl Developer, North America; Systems Administrator, North America; Web Graphic Artist, North America; Office Administrator.

PANGAEA SYSTEMS INC.
Att: Human Resources Manager
10080 Jasper Avenue
4th Floor, Empire Building
Edmonton, AB T5J 1V9
Tel. 780-488-6119
Fax 780-482-0931
Email .... careers@pangaeainc.com
Website .... www.pangaeainc.com

Employer Background: Pangaea Systems Inc. is an Internet business solutions provider. *New Positions Created (11):* Internet Application Developer; Internet Project & Technical Sales Leader; Network Administrator; Project Mgrs; Senior Business Analysts; Web Developers; Account Executives; Internet Application Developer; Project Mgrs; Senior Analysts; Web Designers.

PANGAEA SYSTEMS INC.
Att: Human Resources Manager
308 - 11th Avenue SE
Suite 200, Louise Block
Calgary, AB T2G 0Y2
Tel. 403-262-7888
Email .... careers@pangaeainc.com
Website .... www.pangaeainc.com
Employer Background: Pangaea Systems is an Internet business solutions provider. *New Positions Created (5):* Director; Internet Application Developers; Project Mgrs; Sr Business Analysts; Web Developers.

PANORAMA BUSINESS VIEWS
Att: Gae Pitman
77 Peter Street, Suite 300
Toronto, ON M5V 2G4
Tel. 416-537-0921
Fax 416-537-8298
Email .... gpitman@pbviews.com
Website .... www.pbviews.com
Employer Background: Panorama Business Views develops performance management software for all types of organizations. *New Positions Created (2):* Administrative Assistant; Implementation Director.

PAR-PAK LTD.
Att: Human Resources
26 Victoria Crescent
Brampton, ON L6T 1E5
Tel. 905-792-3000
Fax 905-792-3330
Email .... resume@parpak.com
Website .... www.parpak.com
Employer Background: Par-Pak Ltd. designs and manufactures rigid plastic containers for the foodservice and bakery industries. *New Positions Created (3):* Machine Shop Helper; Maintenance Electrician; Human Resources Coordinator.

PARADATA SYSTEMS INC.
Att: Human Resources Manager
1080 Millar Creek Road, Suite 102
Whistler, BC V0N 1B0
Tel. 604-905-5546
Fax 604-905-3818
Email .... careers@paradata.com
Website .... www.paradata.com
Employer Background: Paradata Systems Inc. provides secure, easy-to-implement payment solutions for financial institutions and their merchants. *New Positions Created (20):* Client Project Manager; Merchant Services Technical Support; Software Development Technical Writer; Strategic Alliance Developer; Business Developer; Market Business Analyst; Senior Systems Architect; Software Developer; Strategic Alliance

Leader; Webmaster; Project Managers; User / Network Support Specialists; Financial Analysts; In-House Corporate Counsel; Merchant Services Sales Support, National; Quality Assurance Leader; Senior Software Developers; Senior Systems Architect; Technical Project Manager; Merchant Services Technical Support / Configuration Team Member.

PARADIGM ELECTRONICS
Att: Human Resources Manager
205 Annagem Boulevard
Mississauga, ON L5T 2V1
Fax 905-564-8726
Website .... www.paradigm.ca
Employer Background: Paradigm Electronics is a manufacturer of amplifiers and speakers. *New Positions Created (7):* Junior Customer Service Representative; Injection Moulding Supervisor; Purchaser; Accountant; Data Entry Clerk; Amplifier Production Manger; Production Manager.

PARADIGM GEOPHYSICAL
Att: Human Resources Manager
520 - 5th Avenue SW, Suite 700
Calgary, AB T2P 3R7
Tel. 403-750-3535
Fax 403-750-3536
Email .... mduffy@paradigmgeo.com
Website .... www.paradigmgeo.com
Employer Background: Paradigm Geophysical provides seismic data analysis for the oil and gas industry. *New Positions Created (7):* Geological / Geophysical Technician; Intermediate Petrophysicist; Inversion Specialist; Vice-President, Reservoir Services; Vice-President, Sales; Seismic Data Processor; Seismic Data Processors.

PARAMED HOME HEALTH CARE
Att: Administration Manager
1508 West Broadway
Vancouver, BC V6J 1W8
Fax 604-737-7325
Employer Background: ParaMed Home Health Care, a division of Extendicare Inc., has been providing home health services since 1974. *New Positions Created (2):* Client Service Supervisors; Registered Nurse, Home Support.

PARAMED HOME HEALTH CARE
Att: Regional Manager
601 Broadway West, Suite 721
Vancouver, BC V5Z 1G6
Fax 604-730-1024
Website .... www.extendicare.com
Employer Background: ParaMed Home Health Care, a division of Extendicare (Canada) Inc., is a leader in community healthcare. *New Positions Created (2):* Manager, Human Resources System; Educational Consultant / Registered Nurse.

PARAMED HOME HEALTH CARE
Att: Human Resources Manager
375 Select Drive
Kingston, ON K7M 8R1

Website .... www.extendicare.com
Employer Background: ParaMed Home Health Care, a division of Extendicare Inc., has been providing home health services since 1974. *New Positions Created (3):* Home Support Workers / Personal Support Workers; Registered Nurse and Registered Practical Nurses; Registered Nurses.

PARAMOUNT RESOURCES LTD.
Att: Human Resources Department
888 - 3rd Street SW, Suite 4700
Calgary, AB T2P 5C5

Tel. 403-290-3600
Fax 403-262-7994
Email .... resumes@paramountres.com
Website .... www.paramountres.com
Employer Background: Founded in 1978, Paramount Resources is a Canadian energy company, focusing on natural gas sales and exploration. *New Positions Created (4):* Area Engineering Manager; Junior Engineer; Junior Geologist; Senior Exploration / Exploitation Geologist.

PARASUCO JEANS INC.
Att: Sandra
128 Deslauriers Street
St-Laurent, QC H4N 1V8

Tel. 514-334-0888
Fax 514-334-9833
Email .... sandra@parasuco.com
Website .... www.parasuco.com
Employer Background: Parasuco Jeans Inc. is a leading denim manufacturer. *New Positions Created (20):* Traffic Manager and Assistant; Inventory Analyst; Technical Designer; Assistant Designer; Quality Control Position; Production Merchandiser; Assistant to Traffic Manager; Junior Duty Drawback Clerk; Quality Control Supervisor; Collection Officer; Distribution Analyst; Fashion Designers; Regional Supervisors; Sample Developers; Vice-President of Merchandising, Kids and Teens Division; Graphic Artist; Pattern Maker; Art Director / Image Creator; Import Traffic Position; Director, Public Relations / Marketing.

PARISELLA, VINCELLI ASSOCIATES CONSULTING GROUP INC. / PVA
Att: Human Resources Department
2540 Daniel-Johnson Boulevard, Suite 500
Laval, QC H7T 2S3

Tel. 450-686-8606
Fax 450-686-7446
Website .... www.pva.ca
Employer Background: PVA is a consulting firm, specializing in management training and productivity improvement. *New Positions Created (5):* Management Consultant; VP Regional Sales Representative; Regional Sales Representative; V.P. / Regional Sales Representative; Management Consultant.

PARK HYATT TORONTO
Att: Human Resources
4 Avenue Road
Toronto, ON M5R 2E8

Fax 416-929-4031
Website .... www.hyatt.com

Employer Background: Park Hyatt Toronto is a luxury hotel. *New Positions Created (5):* Administrative Assistant; Assistant Executive Steward; Sous-Chef; Various Spa Positions; Various Hospitality Positions.

PARKER HANNIFIN (CANADA) INC.
Att: Kevin Kinsella, Division Human Resources Manager
255 Hughes Road
Orillia, ON L3V 2M3

Fax 705-330-0210
Website .... www.parker.com
Employer Background: Parker Hannifin (Canada) Inc. develops, manufactures and distributes hose, fittings, flexible connectors, instrumentation products and associated components for all hydraulic and pneumatic markets. *New Positions Created (3):* Inside Sales Position; Sales Manager; Salesperson.

PARKER HANNIFIN (CANADA) INC.
Att: Kathy Caswell
4635 Durham Road South, PO Box 158
Grimsby, ON L3M 4G4

Tel. 905-945-2274
Fax 905-945-2112
Email .... kathy_caswell@parker.com
Website .... www.parker.com
Employer Background: Parker Hannifin develops, manufactures and distributes hose, fittings, flexible connectors, instrumentation products and associated components for hydraulic and pneumatic markets. *New Positions Created (6):* Customs Compliance Coordinator; Accountant; Programmer / Analyst; Construction Sales Coordinator; Customs & Traffic Coordinator; PC Specialist.

PARKHURST KNITWEAR
Att: Peggy Thompson
20 Research Road
Toronto, ON M4G 2G6

Tel. 416-421-3773
Fax 416-421-4799
Email ...... peggythompson@parkhurst.ca
Employer Background: Parkhurst Knitwear is an established knitwear manufacturer. *New Positions Created (3):* Bilingual Customer Service Representative; Stockroom Supervisor; Apparel Foreperson.

PARKHURST PUBLISHING LTD.
Att: Susan Usher
400 McGill Road
Montréal, QC H2Y 2G1

Tel. 514-397-9065
Fax 514-397-0228
Email .... usher@parkpub.com
Website .... www.parkpub.com
Employer Background: Parkhurst Publishing Ltd. is involved in health-related publications. *New Positions Created (2):* Managing Editor and Project Coordinator; Editor.

PARKLAND REGIONAL HEALTH AUTHORITY
Att: Human Resources Manager
Box 448
Swan River, MB R0L 1Z0

Tel. 204-734-5529
Fax 204-734-5954
Email .... eileen-hr@prha.mb.ca
Website .... www.prha.mb.ca
Employer Background: The Parkland Regional Health Authority provides health services to 44,000 residents. *New Positions Created (8):* Audiologist; Clinical Service Managers; Medical / Lab Technologists; Occupational Therapists; Physiotherapists; RNs and RPNs; Site Mgrs; Physiotherapist.

PARKS CANADA AGENCY
Att: Joanne Veillette, HR Manager
25 Eddy Street, 6th Floor, Room 71
Hull, QC K1A 0M5

Fax 819-997-5285
Email .... parks_webmaster@pch.gc.ca
Website .... parkscanada.pch.gc.ca
Employer Background: The Parks Canada Agency provides professional and technical expertise to support national parks, national historic sites and national marine conservation areas. *New Positions Created (4):* Manager, Collective Bargaining; Ethnoarchaeologist; Research Manager, Archaeological and Aboriginal Heritage; Audit and Review Manager.

PARKVALLEY CONSULTING LTD.
Att: Human Resources Manager
808 - 4th Avenue SW, Suite 1050
Calgary, AB T2P 3E8

Email .... operations@parkvalley.net
Employer Background: Parkvalley Consulting Ltd. is a project management firm, serving the resource sector for over 25 years. *New Positions Created (5):* Constructions Managers / Supervisors; Environmental Technicians (Intermediate / Senior); Inspectors; Project Managers; Reclamation Supervisors.

PARMALAT CANADA
Att: Human Resources Manager
25 Rakely Court
Toronto, ON M9C 5G2

Fax 416-622-4180
Website .... www.parmalat.ca
Employer Background: Parmalat Canada is a leading provider of fine cheeses, butter and processed dairy ingredients. *New Positions Created (2):* Route Sales Representative; Maintenance Millwright Mechanic.

PARTICIPATION HOUSE
Att: Human Resources
2080 Trinity Church Road, RR 1
Binbrook, ON L0R 1C0

Tel. 905-692-4465
Fax 905-692-4622
Website .... www.participationhouse.
.... hamilton.on.ca
Employer Background: Established in 1978, Participation House is a non-profit agency that provides community-based attendant services, homemaking, life skills instruction and housing to adults with physical disabilities. *New Positions Created (6):* Managers; Evening Supervisor; Project Coordinators

(2); Registered Nurse; Maintenance Worker and Driver; Assistant Supervisor.

PARTNERS IN PLANNING FINANCIAL SERVICES LTD.
Att: Terry Ford,
National Compliance Officer
2330 - 15th Avenue
Regina, SK S4P 1A2

Tel.	306-347-4462
Fax	306-359-7442
Email	tford@pipfs.com
Website	www.pipfs.com

Employer Background: Established in 1986, Partners in Planning Financial Services Ltd. is a securities and mutual fund dealer registered in the four western provinces. *New Positions Created (3):* Provincial Trading Officer; Securities Compliance Officer; Securities Compliance Officer.

PARTY PACKAGERS
Att: Operations Manager
1225 Finch Avenue West
Toronto, ON M3J 2E8

Tel.	416-631-7688
Fax	416-631-6621

Employer Background: Party Packagers is a retail outlet. *New Positions Created (3):* Receiver; Store Mgr and Assistant Mgr; Inventory Control Manager / Systems Analyst.

PASON SYSTEMS CORP.
Att: Human Resources Manager
6130 - 3rd Street SE
Calgary, AB T2H 1K4

Tel.	403-255-3158
Fax	403-253-9681
Email	resumes@pason.com
Website	www.pason.com

Employer Background: Pason Systems Corp. is an oilfield service technology company, providing instrumentation and communication systems for drilling rigs. *New Positions Created (2):* Quality Assurance Analyst; Senior Hardware Design Engineer.

PASSBAND DOWNHOLE COMMUNICATIONS INC.
Att: Dr. P. Camwell, CTO
263 Midvalley Drive SE
Calgary, AB T2X 1M1

Employer Background: PDC is developing a communications device to transpond drilling data from well to surface. *New Positions Created (5):* Electrical Engineer; Lab Technician / Drafter / PCB Layout Person; Mechanical Engineer; Software Engineer, Embedded; Software Engineer, High Level.

PATELLA MANUFACTURING INC.
Att: Human Resources Department
161 Stirling Avenue
Lasalle, QC H8R 3P3

Tel.	514-364-1964
Fax	514-364-1906
Email	humanresources@patella.com
Website	www.patella.com

Employer Background: Established in 1960, Patella Manufacturing Inc. produces pre-mium grade architectural woodwork, with over 350 employees worldwide. *New Positions Created (9):* Cabinetmakers; CAD Technician; CNC Operators and Programmers; Estimators; Shippers; Draftsperson; Administrative Assistant; Receptionist / Accounting Assistant; Controller.

PATHEON INC.
Att: Human Resources Department
865 York Mills Road
Toronto, ON M3B 1Y5

Tel.	416-443-9030
Fax	416-443-2200
Email	hr@patheon.com
Website	www.patheon.com

Employer Background: Patheon Inc. provides drug development services to the pharmaceutical and biotechnology industries. *New Positions Created (22):* Manufacturing Operators; Quality Assurance Chemists; Senior Component Development Specialist; Technical Writer; Building Service Operator; Document Reviewer; Manufacturing Operators; Senior Manufacturing Operators; Document Reviewer; Quality Assurance Chemists; Quality Assurance Specialists; Technical Writer; Building Service Operator; Equipment Specialist; GMP Training Coordinator; Manufacturing Operators; Master Scheduler; Manufacturing Supervisor / Manager; Packaging Mechanic; Senior Buyer; Senior Manufacturing Operators; Technical Project Manager.

PATHEON INC.
Att: Human Resources Department
977 Century Drive
Burlington, ON L7L 5J8

Tel.	905-639-5254
Fax	905-639-2506
Email	hr@patheon.com
Website	www.patheon.com

Employer Background: Patheon provides drug development services to the pharmaceutical and biotechnology industries. *New Positions Created (8):* Packaging Line Operator; Packaging Mechanic; QC Analyst I; QC Analyst II; Packaging Line Operator; Packaging Mechanic; Quality Control Analyst I; Quality Control Analyst II.

PATHEON INC.
Att: Human Resources Department
2100 Syntex Court
Mississauga, ON L5N 7K9

Tel.	905-821-4001
Fax	905-812-6709
Email	hr@patheon.com
Website	www.patheon.com

Employer Background: Patheon Inc. provides drug development services to the pharmaceutical and biotechnology industries. *New Positions Created (97):* Analytical Development Managers; Data Reviewer, PDS; Documentation Coordinator, SOP; Group Leader, PDS Lab; HR Associate; Materials Coordinator; Process Development Scientist; Processing Technologist; Scientific Technical Writer, Analytical; Senior Formulation Scientist; Validation Assistant; For-mulation Development Scientist; Pre-Formulation Manager; Processing Operator; Research Chemists; Senior Manufacturing Operators, Commercial Manufacturing; Technical Transfer Specialist / Process Engineer; Validation Engineer; Manufacturing Operator; Processing Group Leaders; Processing Supervisors; Quality Assurance Chemists; Senior Component Development Specialists; Technical Writer; Human Resources Assistant; Project Managers, PDS; Validation / Calibration Specialist; Documentation Reviewer; Operations SOP Specialist / Trainer; Packaging Mechanic; Pharmaceutical Manufacturing Operators; Senior Pharmaceutical Manufacturing Operators; Analytical Development Managers; Market Research Analyst; Materials Coordinator; Process Development Scientist; Senior Formulation Scientist; Technical Writer, Analytical; Technical Writer, PDS Formulation Development; Validation / Calibration Specialist; Industrial Hygienist; Formulation Development Scientist; Human Resources Administrator; IT Application Specialist; Pre-Formulation Manager; Processing Operator; QA PDS Documentation Reviewer; Group Leader; Research Chemists; Senior Manufacturing Operators, Commercial Manufacturing; Technical Transfer Specialist / Process Engineer; Validation Engineer; Documentation Reviewer; PDS Project Managers; Analytical Development Managers; Clinical Formulation Development Technologists; Component Development Specialist; Environmental, Health & Safety Compliance Officer ; Material Manager; Process Development Scientists; Process Engineer; Senior Formulation Scientists; System Administrator; Technical Administrative Assistant; Technical Writer, Analytical; Validation / Calibration Specialist; Data Reviewer; Environmental Health and Safety Assistant; Financial Analyst; Formulation Development Specialist; Packaging Manager; Pre-Formulation Manager; Process Engineers, Drug Development; Processing Operator; Project Engineer; Project Managers, Drug Development; Quality Assurance Supervisor; Research Chemists; Senior Manufacturing Operators, Commercial Manufacturing; Technical Transfer Specialist / Process Engineer; Validation Engineer; Project Engineer; Front-Line Production Supervisor; Manufacturing Operator; Middle Management Position, Production; Packaging Operator; Pharmaceutical Manufacturing Operators; Manufacturing Supervisor / Manager; Packaging Mechanic; Pre-Formulation Manager, Pre-Formulation Unit; Process Engineers, Clinical Manufacturing Unit; Project Managers, Business Unit; Senior Buyer; Senior Formulation Development Scientists, Formulation Development Unit; Senior Manufacturing Operators, Commercial Manufacturing; Technical Project Managers; Operations Standard Operating Procedures Specialist / Trainer; Senior Processing Operators.

PATHEON INC.
Att: Human Resources Department
333 Jarvis Street, PO Box 158
Fort Erie, ON L2A 5M9

Tel. 905-871-1870
Fax 905-871-7758
Email .... hr@patheon.com
Website .... www.patheon.com
Employer Background: Patheon Inc. provides drug development services to the pharmaceutical and biotechnology industries. *New Positions Created (3):* Validation Assistant; Validation Assistant; Packaging Supervisor.

PATHEON INC.
Att: Human Resources Department
111 Consumers Drive
Whitby, ON L1N 5Z5
Tel. 905-668-3368
Fax 905-668-2747
Website .... www.patheon.com
Employer Background: Patheon provides drug development services to the pharmaceutical and biotechnology industries. *New Positions Created (7):* Payroll Administrator; Auditors; Information Technology Technical Services Supervisor; Validation Technicians; Project Engineer; Industrial Engineer; Production Supervisor, Powders.

PAVEY, LAW
Att: Brian R. Law
19 Cambridge Street, PO Box 1707
Cambridge, ON N1R 3R8
Tel. 519-621-7260
Fax 519-621-1304
Email .... law@paveylaw.com
Website .... www.paveylaw.com
Employer Background: Pavey, Law is a family and commercial litigation law firm. *New Positions Created (2):* Litigation Lawyer; Corporate / Commercial and Real Estate Lawyer.

**PAVILION FAMILY
RESOURCE CENTRE / PFRC**
Att: Selection Committee
PO Box 37
Haileybury, ON P0J 1K0
Tel. 705-672-2128
Fax 705-672-5922
Employer Background: PFRC is a non-profit, 10-bed shelter that provides support, counseling, public education and a 24-hour crisis line for survivors of domestic violence and sexual assault. *New Positions Created (2):* Executive Director; Historical Abuse Counselor.

PBB GLOBAL LOGISTICS
Att: Manager
5000 Miller Road, Suite 2010
Richmond, BC V7B 1K6
Tel. 604-717-1500
Fax 604-270-8661
Email .... vancouverregional@pbb.com
Website .... www.pbb.com
Employer Background: Established in 1946, PBB Global Logistics is an integrated global logistics provider. *New Positions Created (2):* Customs Broker; Customs Brokerage Supervisor.

PC WORLD
Att: Human Resources
250 Finchdene Square
Toronto, ON M1X 1A5
Tel. 416-299-4000
Fax 416-299-9055
Email .... info@circtwrld.com
Website .... www.circtwrld.com
Employer Background: PC World, a division of Circuit World Corp., manufactures high-tech printed circuit boards for the North American and European electronics industry. *New Positions Created (4):* Production Control Manager; Analog / Digital Designer; Midnight Shift Supervisor; Junior Buyer.

PCL CONSTRUCTORS CANADA INC.
Att: Lisa J. Cooke
2085 Hurontario Street, Suite 400
Mississauga, ON L5A 4G1
Tel. 905-276-7600
Fax 905-803-4525
Email .... ljcooke@pcl.com
Website .... www.pcl.ca
Employer Background: PCL Constructors Canada Inc. is one of Canada's largest general contracting organizations. *New Positions Created (3):* Estimators; Project Managers; Superintendents.

PCL CONSTRUCTORS INC.
Att: Tina K. Young
5410 - 99th Street
Edmonton, AB T6E 3P4
Tel. 780-435-9711
Fax 780-436-2247
Email .... tkyoung@pcl.com
Website .... www.pcl.com
Employer Background: PCL Constructors Inc. is one of North America's largest general contractors. *New Positions Created (8):* Civil Estimator; Tradesperson Champion; Financial Accountant; Quality Inspector; Business Systems Analyst; Quality Engineer / Quality Technician; Pipe Spoolers; Project Managers and Estimators.

PCSUPPORT.COM, INC.
Att: Human Resources Manager
3605 Gilmore Way, Suite 300
Burnaby, BC V5G 4X5
Fax 604-419-4494
Email .... jobs@pcsupport.com
Website .... www.pcsupport.com
Employer Background: PCsupport.com, Inc. provides outsourced helpdesk solutions to the corporate market. *New Positions Created (12):* Administrative Coordinator; E-Support Analysts, PC and Mac; Helpdesk Supervisor; HR Generalist; Support Analyst; eSupport Analyst; Help Desk Supervisor; MarCom Specialist; Network Administrator; Online Tech Support Position; Senior Developer in COM / DCOM Development; Software Project Managers.

**PEACE HILLS GENERAL
INSURANCE COMPANY**
Att: Pat White, Claims Manager
140 - 4th Avenue SW, Suite 1950
Calgary, AB T2P 3N3

Tel. 403-262-7600
Fax 403-266-7266
Email ... pwhite@peacehillsinsurance.com
Website ..... www.peacehillsinsurance.com
Employer Background: The Peace Hills General Insurance Company is a multi-line property and casualty insurer in western Canada. *New Positions Created (4):* Bodily Injury Field Adjuster; Section B Adjuster; Telephone Adjuster; Claims Manager.

PEACE LIARD HEALTH
Att: Gwyneth Pelster,
Director, Continuing Care
1001 - 110th Avenue
Dawson Creek, BC V1G 4X3
Tel. 250-784-2400
Fax 250-784-2413
Employer Background: Peace Liard Health provides health services to residents of Fort St. John, Fort Nelson and Dawson Creek. *New Positions Created (3):* Health Positions (2); Health Positions (2); Home Nursing Care Nurse.

**PEACE RIVER
CORRECTIONAL CENTRE**
Att: Carlotta Culbert
PO Bag 900 - 40
Peace River, AB T8S 1T4
Fax 780-624-5807
Website .... www.gov.ab.ca/just
Employer Background: The Peace River Correctional Centre is operated by Alberta Justice, the government department responsible for policing, victim services, legal services for vulnerable persons, corrections, prosecutions and courts. *New Positions Created (3):* Correction Officer; Correction Officer; Correction Officer.

PEACE RIVER REGIONAL DISTRICT
Att: Gary Williams, Search Consultant
1981 Alaska Avenue, PO Box 810
Dawson Creek, BC V1G 4H8
Tel. 250-825-9586
Email .... garyw@netidea.com
Website .... www.pris.bc.ca/prrd
Employer Background: PRRD provides local government services to seven incorporated municipalities and four electoral areas, with a rural and urban population of 60,000. *New Positions Created (2):* Director, Field Services; Assistant Treasurer.

PEACOCK INC.
Att: P. Edwards, Human Resources
4737 - 97th Street NW
Edmonton, AB T6E 5W2
Tel. 780-438-1122
Fax 780-439-0752
Email .... pedwards@peacock.ca
Website .... www.peacock.ca
Employer Background: Peacock Inc. supplies Canadian industry with a wide range of industrial products and services. *New Positions Created (3):* Sales and Marketing Manager; Senior Outside Technical Sales Representative; Inside Technical Sales Representative, Instrumentation.

PEACOCK INC.
Att: Human Resources Department
8600 St. Patrick Street
Montréal, QC H8N 1V1

Tel.	514-366-5900
Fax	514-366-9804
Email	cvhr@peacock.ca
Website	www.peacock.ca

Employer Background: Peacock Inc. supplies Canadian industry with a wide range of industrial products and services. *New Positions Created (2):* Inside Sales Representative; Outside Sales Representative.

PEAK ENERGY SERVICES LTD.
Att: Matt J. Huber, VP Finance
421 - 7th Avenue SW, Suite 2100
Calgary, AB T2P 4K9

Fax	403-543-7320

Employer Background: Peak Energy Services Ltd. is a publicly-listed corporation in the oil and gas services sector, with business units thoroughout Canada. *New Positions Created (2):* Corporate Controller; Vice-President, Operations.

PEARSON PEACEKEEPING CENTRE
Att: Administration Manager
Cornwallis Park, PO Box 100
Clementsport, NS B0S 1E0

Tel.	902-638-8611
Fax	902-638-8888
Email	dtrimper@
	ppc.cdnpeacekeeping.ns.ca
Website	www.cdnpeacekeeping.ns.ca

Employer Background: Established by the Government of Canada in 1994, PPC is dedicated to the education and training of individuals participating in global peacekeeping initiatives. *New Positions Created (2):* Exercise Development Officer; Marketing Manager.

PECHINEY PLASTIC PACKAGING (CANADA) INC.
Att: Human Resources
180 Walker Drive
Brampton, ON L6T 4V8

Fax	905-458-0741
Website	www.
	pechineyplasticpackaging.com

Employer Background: Pechiney Plastic Packaging (Canada) Inc., part of the Pechiney Group, manufactures packaging for food and personal products. *New Positions Created (3):* Electricians and Millwright; Production Line Mechanics; Laminator Operators.

PEEL CHILDREN'S AID SOCIETY / PEEL CAS
Att: Human Resources
8 Nelson Street West, Suite 204
Brampton, ON L6X 4J2

Tel.	905-796-2121
Fax	905-796-2293
Email	rharoon@peelcas.org
Website	www.peelcas.org

Employer Background: Peel CAS provides child protection services as mandated by the Child and Family Services Act in Mississauga, Brampton and Caledon. *New Positions Created (14):* Legal Counsel (2); Intake and Family Service Workers; Residential Supervisor; Legal Counsel; Latency Aged Program; Residential Services Position; Support Program; Compensation and Benefits Specialist; Residential Services Supervisor; Intake, Family Services and Residential Services Supervisors; Child and Youth Workers; Residential Program Supervisor; Social Workers, Intake and Family Services; Information Analyst.

PEEL CHILDREN'S CENTRE
Att: Recruitment & Training Coordinator
101 Queensway West, Suite 500
Mississauga, ON L5B 2P7

Tel.	905-273-3193
Fax	905-273-7487
Email	hr@peelcc.org
Website	www.peelcc.org

Employer Background: Peel Children's Centre is an accredited mental health centre that provides treatment services to children and their families. *New Positions Created (17):* Development Assistant; Development Coordinator; Intake / Telephone Crisis Response Workers; Mobile Crisis Workers; Residential Counsellors; Residential Night Staff; Residential Relief; Child & Family Clinicians; Clinical Coordinators; Manager, Clinical Services; Nexus Youth Services Community Worker; Psychologist; Child & Family Clinicians (3); Crisis Response Workers (5); Manager of Crisis Services; Mobile Crisis Workers (6); Child & Family Clinician, Intensive Outreach Services.

PEEL DISTRICT SCHOOL BOARD
Att: David Pedwell, Superintendent of School Services and Staff Development
5650 Hurontario Street
H.J.A. Brown Education Centre
Mississauga, ON L5R 1C6

Tel.	905-890-1099
Fax	905-890-3110
Website	www.peelschools.org

Employer Background: The Peel District School Board operates 187 schools, serves over 111,000 students, employs over 10,000 staff members and has an annual budget of $661.2 million. *New Positions Created (10):* Elementary & Secondary Principal & Vice-Principal; Elementary & Secondary Teachers; Associate Director, Educational Services; Speech / Language Pathologists; Library Automation Systems Analyst; Various Education Positions (3); Research Coordinator; Media Technology Specialist; WSIB Officer; Speech / Language Pathologists.

PEEL HALTON ACQUIRED BRAIN INJURY SERVICES
Att: Elisabeth Martin, HR Administrator
151 City Centre Drive, Suite 403
Mississauga, ON L5B 1M7

Fax	905-949-4019
Email	lizmartin@phabis.com

Employer Background: Peel Halton Acquired Brain Injury Services is a community ABI rehabilitation leader. *New Positions Created (2):* Client Programme Facilitators; Client Programme Facilitators.

PEEL LUMBER
Att: Human Resources Manager
281 Alliance Road
Milton, ON L9T 3M6

Tel.	905-693-9663
Fax	905-693-9475
Email	jbrown@peellumber.com
Website	www.peellumber.com

Employer Background: Peel Lumber is a lumber distribution centre specializing in framing materials for commercial and home builders. *New Positions Created (4):* Estimator; Forklift Operators; Site Customer Service Position; Yard Supervisor.

PEEL, THE REGIONAL MUNICIPALITY OF
Att: Human Resources
10 Peel Centre Drive
Brampton, ON L6T 4B9

Tel.	905-791-7800
Fax	905-791-6118
Email	jobline@region.peel.on.ca
Website	www.region.peel.on.ca

Employer Background: The Regional Municipality of Peel provides various municipal programs and services to 985,000 residents and a thriving business community. *New Positions Created (49):* Manager, Engineering Technical Services; Manager, Plant Operations; Manager, Public Works Business Unit; Purchasing Professional; Supervisor, Existing Program Enhancement; Technical Analyst, Waste Program Planning; Public Affairs Associate; Systems Analyst; Real Estate Clerk; Epidemiologist; File Clerks; PeopleSoft Technical Analyst; Public Health Nurses; Communication Specialist; Nutritionist; Public Health Inspectors; Early Childhood Educators; Planner; Director, Water and Wastewater Treatment; Financial Analyst; Project Manager; Risk Management Analyst; Senior Financial Analysts; Senior Internal Auditor; Supervisor, Document & File Support; Nutritionist; Public Health Inspectors; Manager of Environmental Control; Manager, Technical Services; Project Manager, Corporate GIS; Paramedic Quality Assurance, Program Assistant; Planner I; Public Affairs Associate, Public Works; Technical Analyst, Traffic Signals and Systems; Chemical Analyst, Laboratory; Community Developer / Policy Analyst; Nutritionist; Public Health Dietitian; Hydrogeologist; Early Childhood Educators; Appraiser / Negotiator II; Purchasing Professional; Capital Projects Manager - Energy Deregulation; Development Manager; Housing Administrator; Housing & Facilities Business Development Manager; Housing Policy Program Manager; Project Leader, Powerbuilder / Oracle; Property Manager - Residential.

PEERLESS CLOTHING INC.
Att: Marie-Michele Gelinas
8888 Pie IX Boulevard
Montréal, QC H1Z 4J5

Tel. 514-593-9300
Fax 514-593-1281
Email .... marie-micheleg@
.... peerless-clothing.com
Employer Background: Peerless Clothing Inc. is a large manufacturer of men's clothing, including brands such as Chaps, Ralph Lauren, DKNY and Peerless Man. *New Positions Created (7):* Facility Maintenance Technician; Sewing Machine Mechanic; Accountant; Claims and Collections Officer; Credit Officer; Maintenance Engineer; Time Study Technician.

PEGASUS HEALTHCARE INTERNATIONAL
Att: Human Resources Manager
1456 Sherbrooke Street West
Passage du Musée
Montréal, QC H3G 1K4
Tel. 514-284-1138
Fax 514-284-0415
Website .... www.pegasus.ca
Employer Background: Pegasus Healthcare International, a division of PCI Group, specializes in medical communications. *New Positions Created (3):* Client Services Manager; Copy Editor / Proofreader; Senior Editor.

PELOTON PETROLEUM SOFTWARE SOLUTIONS
Att: Human Resources Manager
Box 20055 BVPO
Calgary, AB T2P 4H3
Tel. 403-263-2915
Email .... resumes@peloton.com
Website ...., www.peloton.com
Employer Background: Established in 1992, Peloton Petroleum Software Solutions provides software to the oil and gas industry. *New Positions Created (2):* Technical Writer; Software Support Analyst.

PEMBROKE GENERAL HOSPITAL
Att: Director of Human Resources
705 Mackay Street
Pembroke, ON K8A 1G8
Tel. 613-732-2811
Fax 613-732-6348
Email .... lmoss@pemgenhos.org
Website .... www.pemgenhos.org
Employer Background: Pembroke General Hospital is a 110-bed acute care community hospital, with an ambulatory clinic service, a regional acute mental health program and a regional rehabilitation program. *New Positions Created (3):* Physiotherapist / Occupational Therapist; Rehabilitation Assistants; Speech Language Pathologist.

PENGROWTH MANAGEMENT LTD.
Att: Human Resources
112 - 4th Avenue SW
Suite 700, East Tower, Sun Life Plaza
Calgary, AB T2P 0H3
Tel. 403-233-0224
Fax 403-265-6251
Email ..... humanresources@pengrowth.com
Website .... www.pengrowth.com

Employer Background: PML manages the Pengrowth Energy Trust, a large energy royalty trust in Canada, with stakes in over 60 producing oil and gas wells. *New Positions Created (15):* Petroleum Evaluations Engineer, Oil & Gas Property Acquisition / Dispositions; Field Operator; Journeyman Millwright; Senior Geologist; Facilities / Project Engineer; Senior Buyer; Senior Marketing Representative; Senior Reservoir Engineer; Assistant Corporate Secretary; Geologist; Manager, Investor Relations; Community Relations Coordinator; Environmental Technologist; Production Revenue Accountant; Supervisor, Joint Venture Accounting.

PENGUIN BOOKS CANADA LTD.
Att: Director, Human Resources
10 Alcorn Avenue, Suite 300
Toronto, ON M4V 3B2
Tel. 416-925-2249
Fax 416-925-0068
Website .... www.penguin.ca
Employer Background: Penguin Books Canada Ltd. is one of the foremost book publishers in North America. *New Positions Created (5):* Desktop Typesetter; Publicist; Designer, Internet / Production; Senior Marketing And Production Associate; Senior Advertising and Production Associate.

PENN WEST PETROLEUM LTD.
Att: Alan R. Montgomery
425 - 1st Street SW, Suite 2000
Calgary, AB T2P 3L8
Tel. 403-777-2500
Fax 403-777-3397
Website .... www.pennwest.com
Employer Background: Penn West Petroleum Ltd. is an senior oil and natural gas company. *New Positions Created (4):* Joint Venture Accountant; Production and Revenue Accountant; Facilities Engineer; Construction Manager.

PENNSYLVANIA LIFE INSURANCE COMPANY
Att: Human Resources Manager
55 Superior Boulevard
Mississauga, ON L5T 2X9
Email .... jobs@penncorp.ca
Website .... www.penncorp.ca
Employer Background: Pennsylvania Life Insurance Company, a member of the Universal American Financial Corporation, is a publicly-traded company with $1.2 billion in assets. *New Positions Created (4):* Group Leader, Policy Owner Services; Life Claims Adviser; Policy Owner Services Coordinator; Vice-President, Claims.

PENNSYLVANIA LIFE INSURANCE COMPANY
Att: Human Resources
90 Dundas Street West, 4th Floor
Mississauga, ON L5B 2T5
Tel. 905-272-0210
Fax 905-272-3797
Email .... jobs@penncorp.ca
Website .... www.penncorp.ca

Employer Background: Pennsylvania Life Insurance Company (a member of the Universal American Financial Corporation) is a publicly-traded company, with $1.2 billion in assets. *New Positions Created (2):* Client Services Position; Disability Claims Advisors (5).

PENTALIFT EQUIPMENT CORP.
Att: Human Resources
PO Box 1060
Guelph, ON N1H 6N1
Tel. 519-763-3625
Fax 519-763-2894
Email .... hr@pentalift.com
Website .... www.pentalift.com
Employer Background: Pentalift Equipment Corp. manufactures loading dock products and in-plant positioning equipment. *New Positions Created (2):* Sales Representative, Loading Dock Products; Estimating / Customer Service Manager.

PENTAX CANADA INC.
Att: National Sales & Marketing Manager
3131 Universal Drive
Mississauga, ON L4X 2E5
Tel. 905-625-4930
Fax 905-625-8550
Email .... amcneil@pentaxcanada.ca
Website .... www.pentaxcanada.ca
Employer Background: Pentax Canada Inc. is a leading distributor of quality photographic equipment, binoculars, CCTV lenses and survey equipment. *New Positions Created (2):* Territory Manager, Photographic Products; Inside Sales Position.

PENTICTON, CITY OF
Att: Human Resources Department
171 Main Street, City Hall
Penticton, BC V2A 5A9
Tel. 250-490-2470
Fax 250-490-2471
Email .... hr@city.penticton.bc.ca
Website .... www.city.penticton.bc.ca
Employer Background: The City of Penticton is the 3rd-largest city in the Okanagan, with a population of 33,000. *New Positions Created (2):* Administration Manager, RCMP; Fire Chief.

PEPSI BOTTLING GROUP (CANADA)
Att: Human Resources Department
5900 Falbourne Street
Mississauga, ON L5R 3M2
Tel. 905-568-7883
Fax 905-568-7889
Website .... www.pepsi.com
Employer Background: Pepsi Bottling Group (Canada) markets soft drinks and beverage products. *New Positions Created (3):* Area Sales Representatives; Bilingual Customer Equipment Service Representatives; Telephone Customer Representative.

PERCEPTA
Att: Human Resources
5775 Yonge Street, Suite 1002
Toronto, ON M2M 4J1

Tel. 416-228-6200
Fax 416-228-6340
Website .... www.percepta-crm.com
Employer Background: Percepta is a North American customer relationship centre, serving the automobile industry. *New Positions Created (12):* Customer Service Representatives; Business Analyst; Workforce Planner; Customer Service Representatives; Team Leaders; IT Positions (2); Bilingual Customer Service Representative, French / Spanish; IT Corporate Help Desk Manager; IT Help Desk Analysts; Network Administrators (2); Team Leaders; Various Computing Positions (2).

PERCEPTRON INC., FOREST PRODUCTS DIVISION
Att: Human Resources Manager
501 Standford Avenue, Suite 1, PO Box 666
Parksville, BC V9P 2G7
Tel. 250-954-1566
Fax 250-954-3657
Email .... wpotter@nanoose.com
Website .... www.perceptron.com
Employer Background: Perceptron Inc., Forest Products Division is a world leader in 3D laser scanning and high-performance real-time process optimization for sawmills in North and South America, Europe and Australia. *New Positions Created (2):* Programmers; Project Managers.

PEREGRINE SYSTEMS, INC.
Att: Human Resources Manager
955 Green Valley Crescent, Suite 210
Ottawa, ON K2C 3V4
Tel. 613-723-7505
Fax 613-723-7209
Email .... ottawa-hr@peregrine.com
Website .... www.peregrine.com
Employer Background: Peregrine Systems, Inc. is a leading provider of employee self-service, infrastructure management and e-business connectivity solutions. *New Positions Created (10):* Bilingual Territory Account Manager; C++ Developer; Delphi / C++ Developer; Inventory Clerk; LAN Administrator; Multilingual Application Librarian; Senior Product Manager; Software Developers; Software Quality Assurance Engineers; Technical Support.

PERENNIAL DESIGN COMPANY
Att: Human Resources Manager
14 Dorchester Avenue
Toronto, ON M8Z 4W3
Tel. 416-251-2180
Fax 416-251-3560
Employer Background: Perennial Design is a retail design and marketing firm, specializing in building and revitalizing great brands. *New Positions Created (2):* Designers, Environments; Graphic Designers.

PERFORMANCE TECHNOLOGIES, INC.
Att: Human Resources Manager
150 Metcalfe Street, Suite 1300
Ottawa, ON K2P 1P1
Email .... myjobrocks@pt.com
Website .... www.pt.com

Employer Background: Performance Technologies, Inc. is a global provider of telecom and networking products. *New Positions Created (16):* Field Applications Engineer; Intermediate Software Engineer; Network Management Software Engineers; Senior Product Mgrs; Senior Software Engineers; Test Engineers; Lab Technicians; Market Managers; Product Communication Specialists; Product Marketing Mgrs; Project Managers; Release Engineer; Software Engineers, Intermediate; Software Engineers, Senior; Technical Recruiter; Test Engineers.

PERI FORMWORK SYSTEMS INC.
Att: Cora Olszewski
63B Progress Court
Brampton, ON L6S 5X2
Tel. 905-792-8000
Fax 905-792-9942
Email .... colszewski@peri.ca
Employer Background: PERI Formwork Systems Inc. is a leader in construction equipment, with over 2,200 employees in 40 countries. *New Positions Created (4):* Receptionist / Secretary; Accounting Clerk; Customer Service Representative; Scaffolding Sales Rep / Customer Service Representative.

PERIMIS PROPERTIES
Att: Human Resources
350 Albert Street, Suite 200
Ottawa, ON K1R 1A4
Email .... hrrecruit@oxfordproperties.com
Website .... www.oxfordproperties.com
Employer Background: Perimis Properties, a division of Oxford Properties Group, is a new facilities management company. *New Positions Created (2):* Property Administrator; Building Superintendent.

PERKINELMER OPTOELECTRONICS INC.
Att: Human Resources Manager
22001 Dumberry Road
Vaudreuil, QC J7V 8P7
Tel. 450-424-3300
Fax 450-424-3413
Email ...... optocan.hr@perkinelmer.com
Website .... www.opto.perkinelmer.com
Employer Background: PerkinElmer Optoelectronics Inc. (formerly EG&G, Inc.) develops a range of optoelectronic products and applications, including high-volume specialty lighting sources, detectors, imaging devices, emitters and receivers. *New Positions Created (18):* Application Support Specialist; Business Development and Sales Specialist, Eastern North America; Electrical Engineer, Automated Production; Process Engineer, Diffusion III - V Materials; Process Engineer, Metalization III - V Materials; Process Engineer, Photolithography III - V Materials; Process Engineer, Thin Film III - V Materials; Process Engineer, Wafer / Chip Test; Process Engineer, Wafer Saw / Scribe, III - V Materials; Product Line Engineer; Quality Control Engineer; Quality Leader, Sensor Products; Senior Electrical RF Design Engineer; Senior Hybrid Circuit Design Engineer; Senior Planner Analyst; Senior Technicians, III - V Process Department; Telecom Business Planner / Analyst; Wafer Fab Equipment Maintenance Technician.

PERLEY AND RIDEAU VETERANS' HEALTH CENTRE / PRVHC
Att: Human Resources Services
1750 Russell Road
Ottawa, ON K1G 5Z6
Tel. 613-526-7170
Fax 613-526-7190
Email .... jobs@prvhc.com
Website .... www.prvhc.com
Employer Background: PRVHC is a 450-bed facility and leading regional resource in resident-centred long-term, respite and convalescent care. *New Positions Created (2):* Manager, Nursing Practice; Financial Analyst.

PERTH AND SMITHS FALLS DISTRICT HOSPITAL
Att: Human Resources Manager
60 Cornelia Street West
Smiths Falls, ON K7A 2H9
Tel. 613-283-2330
Fax 613-283-8990
Email .... lmontgomery@psfdh.on.ca
Website .... www.psfdh.on.ca
Employer Background: The Perth and Smiths Falls District Hospital is an accredited 100-bed facility, serving a catchment population of 40,000 residents. *New Positions Created (4):* Physiotherapist; Human Resources Manager; Laboratory Manager; Registered Ultrasound Technologist.

PET VALU CANADA INC.
Att: Human Resources Department
121 McPherson Street
Markham, ON L3R 3L3
Tel. 905-946-1200
Fax 905-946-1860
Email .... hr@petvalu.com
Website .... www.petvalu.com
Employer Background: Pet Valu Canada Inc. is a retailer of specialty pet products. *New Positions Created (11):* Business / Operations Analyst, Real Estate; Help Desk Support Specialist; Inventory Analyst; Pricing and Promotions Assistant; Trainer, Retail Section; Import / Export Administrator; Purchasing Expeditor / Coordinator; Payables Clerk; Internal Auditor; Manager, Store Accounting; Secretary.

PETER HALL SCHOOL INC.
Att: Human Resources Department
1455 Rochon Street
St-Laurent, QC H4L 1W1
Tel. 514-748-6727
Fax 514-748-5122
Email .... mvachon@peterhall.qc.ca
Website .... www.peterhall.qc.ca
Employer Background: Subsidized by the Ministry of Education, Peter Hall School Inc. is a private school for intellectually handicapped students, with or without associated physical handicaps. *New Positions Created (5):* Teachers, Special Education; Various

Health Positions; Nurse; Psychologists (2); Special Education Teachers.

PETER KIEWIT SONS CO. LTD.
Att: John Gazankas
11211 - 215th Street
Edmonton, AB T5S 2B2

Tel. 780-447-3509
Fax 780-447-3202
Website .... www.kiewit.com
Employer Background: Established in 1884, Peter Kiewit Sons Co. Ltd. is a major industrial contractor. *New Positions Created (4):* Various Construction Positions; Mechanical / Piping Superintendents; Mechanical Superintendent and Field Engineers; Mechanical Estimator.

PETERBOROUGH, COUNTY OF
Att: Michael Rutter,
Chief Administrative Officer
470 Water Street
Peterborough, ON K9H 3M3

Tel. 705-743-0380
Fax 705-743-2405
Email .. mrutter@county.peterborough.on.ca
Website www.county.peterborough.on.ca
Employer Background: The County of Peterborough represents nine local communities and serves 57,000 residents. *New Positions Created (2):* Director of Human Resources; Chief Administrative Officer / Treasurer.

PETERBOROUGH REGIONAL HEALTH CENTRE
Att: Corporate Director, HR Division
1 Hospital Drive
Peterborough, ON K9J 7C6

Tel. 705-743-2121
Fax 705-876-5015
Email .... jparr@prhc.on.ca
Website .... www.prhc.on.ca
Employer Background: The Peterborough Regional Health Centre is a 483-bed regional referral centre, with two sites, over 300 physicians and 1,800 staff members. *New Positions Created (7):* Nephrologist; Kinesiologist; New Hospital Contract Coordinator, Materials Management; Physiotherapists; Surgical Services Director; Social Worker / Occupational Therapist; Renal Dialysis Unit Director.

PETERBOROUGH UTILITIES COMMISSION
Att: Human Resources Manager
1867 Ashburnham Drive
PO Box 4125, Stn Main
Peterborough, ON K9J 6Z5

Tel. 705-748-6900
Fax 705-748-4358
Email .... cmccaw@puc.org
Website .... www.puc.org
Employer Background: Founded in 1914, the Peterborough Utilities Commission provides electricity and water services to residents of Peterborough. *New Positions Created (2):* Distribution Engineer; Water Treatment Plant Relief Operator.

PETERBOROUGH, VICTORIA, NORTHUMBERLAND & CLARINGTON CATHOLIC DISTRICT SCHOOL BOARD
Att: Manager of Human Resources
1355 Lansdowne Street West
Peter L. Roach Catholic Education Centre
Peterborough, ON K9J 7M3

Tel. .... 705-748-4861 ext 240
Fax 705-748-3819
Email .... hrdept@pvnccdsb.on.ca
Website .... www.pvnccdsb.on.ca
Employer Background: The Board serves 14,330 students in 37 schools, employs 1,800 teaching and support staff and has an operating budget in excess of $79 million. *New Positions Created (4):* Communicative Disorders Assistants (2); Pastoral Care Worker; Speech Language Pathologist; Core French Teachers (3).

PETO MACCALLUM LTD.
Att: Alnoor Nathoo, BSc, PEng,
V.P., Greater Toronto Operations
165 Cartwright Avenue
Toronto, ON M6A 1V5

Tel. 416-785-5110
Fax 416-785-5120
Email .... pacig@petomac.on.ca
Website .... www.petomac.on.ca
Employer Background: Peto MacCallum Ltd. is a Canadian specialist consulting engineering company. *New Positions Created (2):* Technicians; Geotechnical Engineers.

PETRO PLAN SAFETY LTD.
Att: Managing Director
924 - 6th Avenue SW, Suite 200
Calgary, AB T2P 0V5

Tel. 403-261-7064
Fax 403-261-7853
Email .... brent@petroplansafety.com
Website .... www.petroplansafety.com
Employer Background: Petro Plan Safety Ltd. is a consulting company that provides support to petroleum industry clientele in emergency response planning, safety management, technical services and regulatory processes. *New Positions Created (3):* Drafting / Mapping Technician; Petroleum / Emergency Planning Technician; Receptionist / Administrative Assistant.

PETRO-CANADA
Att: Human Resources Manager
150 - 6th Avenue SW, 14th Floor West
Calgary, AB T2P 3E3

Tel. 403-296-8000
Fax 403-296-7747
Email .... hrwest@petro-canada.ca
Website .... www.petro-canada.ca
Employer Background: Petro-Canada is one of Canada's largest oil and gas companies, operating in the exploration and retail sectors of the industry. Petro-Canada is 82%-owned by institutional and individual investors. *New Positions Created (4):* SAP Technical Specialist, ABAP; Gas Plant Operator; Senior Supply Chain Advisor; Senior Offshore Drilling Supervisor.

PETRO-CANADA
Att: Employment Coordinator
3275 Rebecca Street
Suite 184, Central Region Business Centre
Oakville, ON L6L 6N5

Tel. 905-525-9040
Fax 905-469-3610
Email .... tataryn@petro-canada.ca
Website .... www.petro-canada.ca
Employer Background: Petro-Canada is one of Canada's largest oil and gas companies, operating in the exploration and retail sectors of the industry. Petro-Canada is 82%-owned by institutional and individual investors. *New Positions Created (2):* Advisor, Commodity Taxes; Senior Advisor, Benchmarking Analysis and Capital.

PETSMART
Att: Human Resources
23 Lesmill Road, Head Office
Toronto, ON M3B 3P6

Tel. 416-383-0520
Fax 416-383-0524
Website .... www.petsmart.com
Employer Background: PetsMart is a leader in the pet products and services industry. *New Positions Created (3):* Department Managers; Department Managers; Assistant Store Director.

PFB CORPORATION
Att: Human Resources Manager
3015 - 5th Avenue NE, Suite 270
Calgary, AB T2A 6T8

Tel. 403-569-4300
Fax 403-569-4075
Email .... mailbox@pfbcorp.com
Website .... www.pfbcorp.com
Employer Background: PFB Corporation is a public plastic foam company that manufactures building products for the construction industry. *New Positions Created (3):* Administrative Assistant; Laboratory Chemist; Financial Accountant.

PFIZER CANADA INC.
Att: Human Resources Department
PO Box 800
Pointe-Claire, QC H9R 4V2

Tel. 514-426-6888
Fax 514-426-6972
Email .... cv@pfizer.ca
Website .... www.pfizer.ca
Employer Background: Pfizer Canada Inc. is a subsidiary of New York-based Pfizer Inc., the world's second-largest pharmaceutical company. The parent company was founded in 1849 and employs nearly 50,000 people worldwide. *New Positions Created (4):* Biostatistician; Specialist Pharmaceutical Representative; Business Information Analyst; Data Quality Analyst.

PHANTOM MANUFACTURING (INTERNATIONAL) LTD. / PHANTOM SCREENS
Att: Human Resources Manager
30451 Simpson Road
Abbotsford, BC V2T 6C7

Tel. 604-855-3654
Fax 604-855-7834
Email .... phantom@phantomscreens.com
Website .... www.phantomscreens.com

Employer Background: Phantom Screens provides retractable screen solutions for doors and windows. *New Positions Created (4):* Customer Service Manager; Materials Manager; National Accounts Representative; Product Manager.

PHARMACIA ANIMAL HEALTH
Att: Human Resources
40 Centennial Road
Orangeville, ON L9W 3T3

Fax 519-941-1074
Email .... m.d.cowen@pharmacia.com
Website .... www.pharmacia.com

Employer Background: Pharmacia Animal Health, a division of Pharmacia Corporation, is a first-tier global pharmaceutical company. *New Positions Created (2):* Bilingual Inside Sales Representative; Sales Positions.

PHARMACIA CANADA INC.
Att: Human Resources Manager
3500 Steeles Avenue East
4th Fl., Tower 4, Liberty Centre
Markham, ON L3R 0X1

Fax 905-755-3120
Website .... www.pharmacia.com

Employer Background: Created through the merger of Pharmacia & Upjohn and Monsanto / Searle, Pharmacia Canada Inc. is a first-tier global pharmaceutical company. *New Positions Created (6):* Clinical Data Management Specialist; Clinical Data Validation Specialist; Junior / Intermediate Biostatistician; SAS Programmer; Senior Biostatistician; Unix Administrator.

PHASE TECHNOLOGY
Att: Sandi Smith
11960 Hammersmith Way, Suite 135
Richmond, BC V7A 5C9

Tel. 604-241-9568
Fax 604-241-9569
Email .... info@phase-technology.com
Website .... www.phase-technology.com

Employer Background: Phase Technology researches, develops and manufactures automatic analyzers for the detection of phase transitions. *New Positions Created (2):* Marketing Communications Assistant; Research Scientist / Engineer.

PHH VEHICLE MANAGEMENT SERVICES INC.
Att: Dyanne Oleszkowicz
350 Burnhamthorpe Road West, Suite 700
Mississauga, ON L5B 3P9

Tel. 905-270-8250
Fax 905-896-6322
Website .... www.phh.com

Employer Background: PHH Vehicle Management Services Inc. provides fleet and vehicle management services. *New Positions Created (5):* District Sales Manager, Vehicle Management; Manager, New Business Development and Client Services, Asset Management; Bilingual Client Services Administrator; Client Consultants; Client Services Representative.

PHILIP SERVICES CORPORATION
Att: Human Resources
5555 North Service Road
Burlington, ON L7L 5H7

Tel. 905-332-8788
Fax 905-548-8444
Email .... azappia@contactpsc.com
Website .... www.contactpsc.com

Employer Background: PSC is one of North America's leading integrated service providers of ferrous scrap processing, brokerage and industrial outsourcing services. *New Positions Created (10):* Analytical Chemists; AZ Drivers; Client Account Managers; General Office Assistant; Laboratory Positions; Laboratory Technicians; Sales Representatives; Facility Operations Manager; Payroll Specialist; AZ / DZ Company Drivers.

PHILIPS ANALYTICAL
Att: Human Resources
101 Randall Drive
Waterloo, ON N2V 1C5

Tel. 519-746-6260
Fax 519-746-8270
Email .... paw.hr@philips.com
Website .... www.philips.com

Employer Background: Philips Analytical is a high-tech company, designing and manufacturing metrology equipment for the semiconductor industry. *New Positions Created (5):* Senior Mechanical Design Engineer; Service Specialist; Software Development Manager; Applications Scientist; Electrical Designer.

PHILIPS ENGINEERING LTD.
Att: Personnel Director
3215 North Service Road
PO Box 220, Stn LCD 1
Burlington, ON L7R 3Y2

Tel. 905-335-2353
Fax 905-335-1414
Email .... admin@philipseng.com
Website .... www.philipseng.com

Employer Background: Philips Engineering Ltd. (formerly Philips Planning and Engineering Ltd.) is a consulting and civil engineering firm. *New Positions Created (13):* CAD Technician; Intermediate Municipal Engineer, Level B; Intermediate Water Resources Engineer, Level B; Municipal Engineering Technologist; Structural / Building Technologist; Water Resources Engineering Technologist; CAD Technician; Intermediate Municipal Engineer; Intermediate Municipal Engineer; Municipal Engineering Technologist; Structural / Building Technologist; Water Resources Engineering Technologist; Water Resources Engineer.

PHILLIPS, HAGER & NORTH INVESTMENT MANAGEMENT LTD.
Att: Debbie Bennett, HR Manager
200 Burrard Street, 21st Floor
Vancouver, BC V6C 3N5

Tel. 604-408-6100
Fax 604-685-5712
Email .... jobs@phn.com
Website .... www.phn.com

Employer Background: Phillips, Hager & North is one of Canada's largest independent investment management firms. *New Positions Created (3):* Advisor, Investment Funds; Manager, Communications; Global Equity Analysts (2).

PHILLIPS PETROLEUM RESOURCES, LTD.
Att: Human Resources Manager
144 - 4th Avenue SW, Suite 2700
Calgary, AB T2P 3N4

Tel. 403-298-1266
Fax 403-298-1252
Email .... resumes@ppco.com
Website www.phillips66.com

Employer Background: Phillips Petroleum Resources, Ltd. is a subsidiary of a multinational company. *New Positions Created (2):* Maintenance Mechanic; Procurement / Inventory Representative.

PHOENIX CONTACT LTD.
Att: Ms Tuyet Tran
235 Watline Avenue
Mississauga, ON L4Z 1P3

Tel. 905-890-2820
Fax 905-890-0180
Email .... ttran@phoenixcontact.ca
Website .... www.phoenixcontact.ca

Employer Background: Phoenix Contact Ltd. is a leader in industrial connection, automation technology and electronic interface systems. *New Positions Created (3):* Interface Product Manager; Technical Customer Service Representative; Business Development Professional, Western Canada.

PHOENIX HYDRAULICS GROUP
Att: Robert Martin
1805 - 4th Street, Niksu Industrial Park
Nisku, AB T9E 7T9

Tel. 780-955-3575
Fax 780-955-3572
Email .... robertm@phoenixreman.com
Website .... www.phoenixreman.com

Employer Background: Phoenix Hydraulics Group supplies remanufactured hydraulic components to machine OEMs and mining companies throughout North America, South America and Australia. *New Positions Created (3):* Systems Analyst; Web Development; Quality Assurance and Services Clerk; Materials Control Manager.

PHOENIX TECHNOLOGY SERVICES LP
Att: Mike Buker, Sales Manager
640 - 8th Avenue SW, Suite 500
Calgary, AB T2P 1G7

Tel. 403-543-4466
Fax 403-543-4485
Email .... mbuker@phoenixcan.com
Website .... www.phoenixcan.com

Employer Background: Established in 1985, Phoenix Technology Services LP is a Calgary-based directional and horizontal drilling company. *New Positions Created (8):* Senior Technical Sales Representative; Well Planner; Engineers (2); Directional Driller; Electrical Technician; Measurement While Drilling Field Operators; Shop Hand; Electronics Engineer.

PHYTODERM INC.
Att: Human Resources
8355 Bougainville
Montréal, QC H4P 2G5
Tel. 514-735-1531
Fax 514-735-8460
Employer Background: PhytoDerm Inc. is a professional skin care company, serving the aesthetics and spa industry. *New Positions Created (5):* Sales Representative / Technical Trainer; Administrative Assistant; National Sales and Key Account Manager; Product Manager, Skin Care; Executive Secretary.

PIASETZKI & NENNIGER
Att: Gregory A. Pizsetzki
120 Adelaide Street West, Suite 2308
Toronto, ON M5H 1T1
Tel. 416-955-0050
Fax 416-955-0053
Website .... www.pia-nenn.ca
Employer Background: Piasetzki & Nenniger is a law firm, specializing in patent, trademark and copyright litigation, licensing and prosecution. *New Positions Created (2):* Associate Lawyer, Intellectual Property; Associate Lawyer, Intellectual Property.

PICARD TECHNOLOGIES INC.
Att: B. Ferris
170 Evans Avenue, Suite 304
Toronto, ON M8Z 1J7
Tel. 416-259-2611
Fax 416-259-0582
Email .... bferris@picardtech.com
Website .... www.picardtech.com
Employer Background: Picard is a systems integration and project management company, serving the pharmaceutical industry. *New Positions Created (2):* Regulatory Specialist; Pharmaceutical Specialists.

PICKERING COLLEGE
Att: Selection Committee
16945 Bayview Avenue
Newmarket, ON L3Y 4X2
Tel. 905-895-1700
Fax 905-895-9076
Email ...... selcom@pickeringcollege.on.ca
Website .... www.pickeringcollege.on.ca
Employer Background: Founded in 1842, Pickering College is a non-denominational, co-educational private college for students in junior kindergarten to OAC. *New Positions Created (3):* Admissions Officer; Assistant Head of School; Faculty Assistant.

PIKA TECHNOLOGIES INC.
Att: Human Resources Manager
20 Cope Drive
Kanata, ON K2M 2V8
Tel. 613-591-1555

Fax 613-591-9295
Email .... careers@pikatech.com
Website .... www.pikatech.com
Employer Background: Pika Technologies Inc. designs and manufactures computer telephony solutions for Fortune 500 customers worldwide. *New Positions Created (14):* Head of Product Line Management; Travel / Administrative Coordinator; Webmaster; Credit and Collections Administrator; DSP Firmware Test Engineer; Intermediate / Senior DSP Software Design Engineer; Intermediate / Senior Hardware Development Engineer; Junior Hardware Development Engineer; Media Relations Manager; Payroll and Financial Analysis Manager; Product Verification Software Tester; Quality Coordinator; Senior Product Manager; Software Designer.

PILLER SAUSAGES & DELICATESSENS LTD.
Att: Director, Human Resources
443 Wismer Street, PO Box 338
Waterloo, ON N2H 4A4
Tel. 519-743-1412
Fax 519-743-7111
Email .... hr@pillers.com
Website .... www.pillers.com
Employer Background: Founded in 1957, Piller Sausages & Delicatessens Ltd. supplies over 13 million pounds of cooked and smoked meats to 1,700 stores across Canada. The company has 250 employees. *New Positions Created (2):* Account Manager, Food Service; Manager, Maintenance Technical Services.

PILLSBURY CANADA LIMITED
Att: Human Resources Manager
111 Pillsbury Drive
Midland, ON L4R 4L4
Fax 705-526-6311
Website .... www.pillsbury.com
Employer Background: Pillsbury Canada Limited is a subsidiary of the Pillsbury Company, a major US consumer products company that markets brands such as Häagen-Dazs, Old El Paso and Green Giant. *New Positions Created (4):* Maintenance Millwright; Project Engineer; Quality Assurance Process Technologist; Quality Control Technician / Team Leader.

PILOT INSURANCE COMPANY, THE
Att: Brian Hall
90 Eglinton Avenue West
Toronto, ON M4R 2E4
Tel. 416-487-5141
Fax 416-487-7604
Email .... jobs@pilot.ca
Website .... www.pilot.ca
Employer Background: Established in 1927, the Pilot Insurance Company is a leading provider of personalized insurance services, with 440,000 policyholders in Ontario. *New Positions Created (3):* Senior Claims Examiner; Personal Property Supervisor; Accident Benefits Adjuster.

PINACLE STAINLESS STEEL INC.
Att: Philip Hebert
22 Huddersfield Road
Toronto, ON M9W 5Z6
Tel. 416-798-9700
Fax 416-798-9321
Website .... www.pinacle.ca
Employer Background: Pinacle Stainless Steel Inc. is a national distributor of stainless steel fluid handling products, valves and fasteners. *New Positions Created (2):* Bookkeeper Assistant; Field and Inside Sales Representatives.

PINK ELEPHANT INC.
Att: Human Resources
5575 North Service Road
Burlington, ON L7L 6M1
Tel. 905-331-5060
Fax 905-331-5070
Email .... resume@pinkelephant.com
Website .... www.pinkelephant.com
Employer Background: Pink Elephant Inc. is an information technology service management provider in the areas of consulting, education and outsourcing. *New Positions Created (10):* Receptionist; Process Consultants, IT Service Management; Receptionist / Office Support Position; Trainers, IT Service Management; Client Care Sales Representatives; Accounting Manager; Technical Consultants; Process Consultants, Information Technology Service Management; Trainers, Information Technology Service Management; Client Care Sales Representative.

PINK TRIANGLE PRESS
Att: Ken Popert, Executive Director
491 Church Street, Suite 200
Toronto, ON M4Y 2C6
Fax 416-925-6503
Email .... ken.popert@xtra.ca
Website .... www.xtra.ca
Employer Background: Established in 1971, Pink Triangle Press is a national gay and lesbian media group. The company publishes Xtra, Xtra West and Capital Xtra. *New Positions Created (2):* IT Administrator; Production Manager / Senior Designer.

PIPING RESOURCES
Att: Michael Ulmer
3691 - 98th Street
Edmonton, AB T6E 5N2
Fax 780-944-8909
Email .... mulmer@cefranklin.com
Website .... www.cefranklin.com
Employer Background: Piping Resources, a division of CE Franklin Ltd., distributes supplies to the oil and gas drilling and production industry. *New Positions Created (3):* Document Control Specialist; Expeditor; Inside Sales Position.

PITNEY BOWES MANAGEMENT SERVICES CANADA INC.
Att: Human Resources
2200 Yonge Street, 9th Floor
Toronto, ON M4S 3E1
Tel. 416-484-3915

Fax 416-484-3916
Email .... careers@pitneybowes.ca
Website .... www.pitneybowes.ca
Employer Background: Pitney Bowes Management Services Canada Inc. is a provider of business support services. *New Positions Created (8):* Customer Service Associate / Lead; Graphics Designer; Channel Manager, Canada; Corporate Account Managers; Customer Service Associates; Copy Operators; Site Managers / Supervisors; Strategic Account Development Manager.

PITNEY BOWES OF CANADA LTD.
Att: M. Jonasson, Area Service Manager
5600 Parkwood Way, Suite 520
Richmond, BC V6V 2M2
Tel. 604-231-9353
Fax 604-303-9235
Email .. marno.jonasson@pitneybowes.ca
Website .... www.pitneybowes.ca
Employer Background: Pitney Bowes offers integrated solutions for complex messaging needs through copier, mailing and facsimile systems and software. *New Positions Created (2):* Service Technician, Production Mail; Production Mail Service Technician.

PIZZA PIZZA LIMITED
Att: Human Resources
580 Jarvis Street
Toronto, ON M4Y 2H9
Tel. 416-967-1010
Fax 416-967-3566
Email .... hire_me@pizzapizza.ca
Website .... www.pizzapizza.ca
Employer Background: Pizza Pizza Limited is one of Canada's leading pizza restaurant chains. *New Positions Created (13):* Call Centre Scheduler / Planner; Event Coordinator; Bilingual Franchising Manager; Location Research Analyst; Payroll and Benefits Assistant; Customer Service / Order Takers; Market Managers; Store Managers; Accounting Assistant; Accounts Receivable; Territory Managers; Quality Assurance Specialist; Architectural Technologist.

PLACER DOME INC.
Att: Human Resources Manager
1055 Dunsmuir Street
Suite 1600, Box 49330, Bentall Station
Vancouver, BC V7X 1P1
Tel. 604-682-7082
Fax 604-602-3811
Website .... www.placerdome.com
Employer Background: Established in 1910, Placer Dome is an international gold mining company, with 8,400 employees. *New Positions Created (3):* Financial Analyst; Exec Assistant; Contracts Administrator.

PLAINS PERFORATING LTD.
Att: Production Logging Manager
150 - 6th Avenue SW, Suite 4100
Calgary, AB T2P 3Y7
Tel. 403-262-6306
Fax 403-266-3960
Email .... phuber@plainschal.com
Employer Background: Founded in 1972, Plains Perforating Ltd. serves the oil and gas industry in Alberta, Saskatchewan and BC, with 23 logging and perforating units and 85 employees. *New Positions Created (3):* Cased Hole Wireline Operator; Drivers; Production Logging Operator / Engineer.

PLANNED PARENTHOOD OF TORONTO
Att: Hiring Committee
36 Prince Arthur Avenue, Suite B
Toronto, ON M5R 1A9
Tel. 416-961-3200
Fax 416-961-2512
Email .... ppt@ppt.on.ca
Website .... www.ppfc.ca
Employer Background: Planned Parenthood of Toronto is a community-based organization committed to promoting and supporting healthy sexuality, and advocating for sexual and reproductive health rights. *New Positions Created (2):* Primary Healthcare Nurse; Program Manager.

PLANTECH CONTROL SYSTEMS INC.
Att: Human Resources Manager
3466 South Service Road
Vineland, ON L0R 2E0
Fax 905-562-5958
Email .... plantech@plantech.ca
Website .... www.plantech.ca
Employer Background: Plantech Control Systems Inc. designs and installs greenhouse electrical systems. *New Positions Created (3):* Construction Electrician; Purchasing / Control Assistant; Job Co-ordinator.

PLATON CONSULTING LTD.
Att: Lorne Drozdowski
566 Lougheed Highway, Suite 302
Coquitlam, BC V3K 3S3
Tel. 604-933-1212
Fax 604-933-1200
Email .... ldrozdow@groupwest.ca
Website ..... www.groupwestsolutions.com
Employer Background: Platon Consulting Ltd., a Group West company, provides business applications software development and systems support services. *New Positions Created (3):* Programmer / Analyst; Technical Support Specialists; Programmer.

PLAYDIUM ENTERTAINMENT CORP.
Att: Human Resources Manager
355 King Street West, 6th Floor
Toronto, ON M5V 1J6
Tel. 416-593-9703
Fax 416-260-3560
Email .... careers@playdium.com
Website .... www.playdium.com
Employer Background: Playdium Entertainment Corporation operates large-scale entertainment centres, featuring state-of-the-art interactive computer-based attractions. *New Positions Created (2):* Assistant General Manager; Group Sales Professionals.

PLAZA GROUP, THE
Att: Human Resources Manager
90 Morgan Road, Suite 200
Baie d'Urfe, QC H9X 3A8
Tel. 514-457-0751
Fax 514-457-0220
Employer Background: The Plaza Group develops and manages shopping centres. *New Positions Created (2):* Architectural Technician; Operations Manager, Shopping Center.

PLEASE MUM
Att: Michelle Preszacator,
Director of Retail Career Development
1121 William Street
Vancouver, BC V6A 2J1
Tel. 604-254-1998
Fax 604-254-0831
Email .... michellep@pleasemum.com
Website .... www.pleasemum.com
Employer Background: Founded in 1986, Please Mum designs and manufactures children's clothing. The company has over 800 employees. *New Positions Created (2):* Assistant Mgrs (2); Director of Marketing.

PMC-SIERRA, INC.
Att: Human Resources Manager
8555 Baxter Place, Suite 105
Burnaby, BC V5A 4V7
Tel. 604-415-6000
Fax 604-415-6209
Email .... careers@pmc-sierra.com
Website .... www.pmc-sierra.com
Employer Background: PMC-Sierra, Inc. designs semiconductors for high-speed data transmission and networking applications. *New Positions Created (17):* Design Engineers; Applications Engineer, Customer Support; Business Development Engineer; Communications Analyst, Collaboration; Communications Analyst, Messaging; Communications Analyst, Telephony; Communications Analyst, Video Streaming; Director, Communications Services; DSP Design Engineer; Financial Accountant; Financial Analyst; IC Package Designer; Network Analyst, Communications Services; Systems Software Developer; Technology Access Engineer; Production and Materials Planner; Shipper / Receiver.

PMC-SIERRA, INC.
Att: Employment Services Team
555 Legget Drive, Suite 834, Office Tower B
Kanata, ON K2K 2X3
Tel. 613-271-7001
Fax 613-271-7007
Email .... careers@pmc-sierra.com
Website .... www.pmc-sierra.com
Employer Background: PMC-Sierra, Inc. designs semiconductors for high-speed data transmission and networking applications. *New Positions Created (6):* Mixed Signal Design Engineer; Leader, Product Development; Leader, Product Validation; Mixed Signal Design Engineer; Product Research Engineer; Software Design Engineer.

POLAR COMPLETIONS ENGINEERING INC.
Att: Human Resources Manager
555 - 4th Avenue SW, Suite 450
Calgary, AB T2P 3E7

Tel. 403-219-0626
Fax 403-262-4076
Website .... www.polareng.com

Employer Background: Polar Completions Engineering Inc. (a subsidiary of Precision Drilling Corp.) is an oil and gas service / manufacturing company, supplying downhole completions and workover equipment to the national and international energy sectors. *New Positions Created (2):* Operations Manager; Technical Sales Representative.

POLY-PACIFIC INTERNATIONAL INC.

Att: Human Resources Manager
8918 - 18th Street
Edmonton, AB T6P 1K6

Tel. 780-467-3612
Fax 780-464-1852
Email .... poly@poly-pacific.com
Website .... www.poly-pacific.com

Employer Background: Poly-Pacific International Inc. manufactures MultiCut plastic blasting media, an environmentally-friendly and technologically-advanced alternative for removing paint and coatings from any surface. *New Positions Created (7):* Account Manager; Assistant Chief Financial Officer; Assistant Plant Manager; Account Manager; Chief Financial Officer; Account Manager; Plant Manager.

POLYAIR INTER PACK INC.

Att: Human Resources Manager
258 Attwell Drive
Toronto, ON M9W 5B2

Tel. 416-740-2687
Fax 416-740-7356
Website .... www.polyair.com

Employer Background: Polyair Inter Pack Inc. is a large supplier of packaging and pool products. *New Positions Created (2):* Executive Assistant; Customer Service Representatives (2).

POLYCOM CANADA INC.

Att: Human Resources
1000 - 14th Street West
North Vancouver, BC V7P 3P3

Fax 604-990-5475
Email ...... heather.holland@polycom.com
Website .... www.polycom.com

Employer Background: Polycom Canada Inc. provides high-quality, easy-to-use communications equipment. *New Positions Created (4):* Director of Development; Senior Engineer; Senior Software Engineer; Systems Analyst, Networks.

POLYGON INTERIOR DESIGN LTD.

Att: Patricia Ng
1800 Spyglass Place
Vancouver, BC V5Z 4K8

Tel. 604-877-1131
Website .... www.polyhomes.com

Employer Background: Established in 1980, Polygon Interior Design Limited has built over 9,500 homes throughout the Lower Mainland of BC. *New Positions Created (5):* Customer Service Manager Trainee; Residential Development Manager; Assistant

Land Manager; Construction Administrator; Interior Designer.

POLYTAINERS INC.

Att: Human Resources Department
197 Norseman Street
Toronto, ON M8Z 2R5

Tel. 416-239-7311
Fax 416-239-7220

Employer Background: Polytainers Inc. has been producing rigid plastic packaging for the North American food and dairy industries for over 30 years. *New Positions Created (13):* Industrial Electrical Technician; Production Mechanics; Production Operator; Injection Molders; Industrial Maintenance Mechanic; Plant Maintenance Electrician; Production Mechanic; Industrial Electrical Technician; Production Engineer / Continuous Improvement Coordinator; Injection Molders; Production Mechanics; Pre-Press Printing Quality Technician; Printing Quality Supervisor.

POON MCKENZIE ARCHITECTS

Att: Human Resources Manager
209 - 8th Avenue SW, Suite 400
Calgary, AB T2P 1B8

Tel. 403-264-4000
Fax 403-269-7215

Employer Background: Poon McKenzie Architects is a Calgary-based architectural firm. *New Positions Created (3):* AutoCAD & Information Technology Manager; Design Architect; Project Technical Coordinators.

POPSTAR COMMUNICATIONS CANADA, INC.

Att: Human Resources Manager
107 - 3rd Avenue East
Vancouver, BC V5T 1C7

Tel. 604-872-6608
Fax 604-872-6601
Website .... www.pop-star.net

Employer Background: POPstar Communications Canada, Inc. provides Internet messaging services to the world. *New Positions Created (5):* Account Manager, The Americas; Junior Software Development Engineers; Media Writer; Software Development Positions (3); UNIX System Administration Position.

PORT COLBORNE, CITY OF

Att: Sue McIntyre, HR Coordinator
66 Charlotte Street
Port Colborne, ON L3K 3C8

Tel. 905-835-2900
Website .... www.portcolborne.com

Employer Background: The City of Port Colborne is located on the shore of Lake Erie. *New Positions Created (3):* Fire Chief; Public Works Superintendent; Public Works Superintendent.

PORT MOODY, CITY OF

Att: Human Resources Department
100 Newport Drive, Box 36
Port Moody, BC V3H 3E1

Tel. 604-469-4511

Fax 604-469-4664
Email .... jobs@cityofportmoody.com
Website .... www.cityofportmoody.com

Employer Background: Located 25 minutes east of downtown Vancouver, the City of Port Moody is home to 23,000 residents. *New Positions Created (8):* Bylaw Inspector 1; City Clerk; Financial Accountant; Plumbing / Building Inspector; Planner; Manager, Human Resources; Systems and Technical Services Assistant; Operations Engineer.

PORTAGE COLLEGE

Att: Human Resources
PO Box 417
Lac La Biche, AB T0A 2C0

Tel. 780-623-5598
Fax 780-623-5721
Email .... hr@portagec.ab.ca
Website .... www.portagec.ab.ca

Employer Background: Portage College (formerly Alberta Vocational College) has been providing quality education to northeastern Alberta for over 30 years. *New Positions Created (10):* Administrative Support Position; Learning Assistance Centre Coordinator / Psychologist; Instructor, Business Programs; Instructor, Academic Preparation; Dean, Career Programs; Instructor, Academic Upgrading; Instructors, Practical Nurse Program; Vice-President, Student and College Services; Instructor, Educational Assistant Program; Instructor, Office Administration Program.

PORTER-CABLE DELTA

Att: Human Resources Manager
505 Southgate Drive, PO Box 848
Guelph, ON N1H 6M7

Tel. 519-836-2840
Fax 519-836-9352
Website .... www.portercable.com

Employer Background: Porter-Cable Delta provides quality woodworking products worldwide. *New Positions Created (2):* Accounting Manager; Retail Sales Rep.

POSITRON PUBLIC SAFETY SYSTEMS INC.

Att: Human Resources
5101 Buchan Street
Montréal, QC H4P 2R9

Tel. 514-345-2200
Fax 514-345-2258
Email .... hr@positron911.com
Website www.positron911.com

Employer Background: Positron Public Safety Systems Inc. manufactures telecom equipment for high-reliability, critical service applications. *New Positions Created (22):* Business Development Manager; Marketing Assistant; Staging Technician; Project Manager, Integration; Embedded Software Developer; Project Manager, Integration; Senior Cost Analyst; Quality Analyst; Quality Assurance Manager; Manager, Technical Communications; Senior Compensation Counsellor; Software Developer; Systems Architect; Technical Leader, Software Development; Accounting Manager; Engineering Technical Leader; Human Resources Professionals; Senior Financial Analyst; Components Specialist; Software Developers; Technical Leader, MIS Products; Technical Support Specialist.

POSS & HALFNIGHT
Att: Sheila McKinlay
1 Queen Street East, Suite 2000
Toronto, ON M5C 2W5
Tel. 416-361-3200
Fax 416-361-1405
Email .... sheila@posshalfnight.com
Employer Background: Poss & Halfnight is a law firm, specializing in insurance litigation and advice for property, casualty and fidelity insurers. *New Positions Created (2):* Junior Associate / Litigation Lawyer; Litigation Lawyer.

POST IMPRESSIONS SYSTEMS INC.
Att: Human Resources Manager
4398 St. Laurent Boulevard, Suite 102
Montréal, QC H2W 1Z5
Tel. 514-842-0903
Fax 514-842-0491
Email .... jobs_montreal@
.... postimpressions.com
Website .... www.postimpressions.com
Employer Background: Post Impressions Systems Inc. designs and manufactures high-quality products used in the television and film industries. *New Positions Created (2):* Applications Programmer; Audio Applications Programmer.

POSTAL PROMOTIONS LIMITED
Att: Human Resources Department
1100 Birchmount Road
Toronto, ON M1K 5H9
Tel. 416-752-8100
Fax 416-752-8239
Website .... www.postalpro.com
Employer Background: Postal Promotions provides direct mail advertising services. *New Positions Created (2):* Letter-Shop Maintenance Mechanic; Project Coordinator.

POTENTIA TELECOM POWER
Att: Human Resources Manager
4043 Carling Avenue
Kanata, ON K2K 2A3
Tel. 613-592-0027
Fax 613-592-1686
Email .... info@potentia.ca
Website .... www.potentia.ca
Employer Background: Potentia Telecom Power designs power systems and components for telecom equipment manufacturers. *New Positions Created (3):* Hardware Designer; Program Manager; Power Supply Designers.

POTTRUFF & SMITH TRAVEL INSURANCE BROKERS INC.
Att: Virginia DeSouza, HR Manager
8001 Weston Road, Suite 300
Woodbridge, ON L4L 9C8
Tel. 416-798-8001
Fax 905-264-5177
Email .... vdesouza@pottruffsmith.com

Website .... www.pottruffsmith.com
Employer Background: Pottruff & Smith Travel Insurance Brokers Inc. is a multi-line insurance brokerage. *New Positions Created (8):* Nurses; Bilingual Assistance Coordinators; Bilingual Medical Assistance Coordinators; Commercial Lines Broker / Marketer; Group Benefit Specialist; Personal Lines Brokers; Bilingual Assistance Coordinators; Bilingual Customer Service Representative.

POUNDMAKER'S LODGE
Att: Geraldine Potts, Executive Assistant
PO Box 34007, Kingsway Mall PO
Edmonton, AB T5G 3G4
Tel. 780-458-1884
Fax 780-459-1876
Website .... www.poundmaker.org
Employer Background: Founded in 1973, Poundmaker's Lodge is a non-profit organization and the oldest Aboriginal-oriented inpatient alcoholism program in Canada. *New Positions Created (2):* Addictions Counsellor; Clinical Supervisor.

POWELL RIVER COMMUNITY HEALTH COUNCIL / PRCHC
Att: Cynthia Stevens, HR Supervisor
5000 Joyce Avenue
Powell River, BC V8A 5R3
Tel. 604-485-3207
Fax 604-485-3245
Email .... cynthia.joy@prchc.hnet.bc.ca
Employer Background: PRCHC consists of a modern 45-bed hospital, 75-bed extended care unit, 81-bed intermediate care residence, home support services and the Texada Island Health Centre. *New Positions Created (6):* Pharmacist, Grade I; Registered Nurse; Registered Nurses; Nurse Manager, Acute Care; Surgical Care Coordinator; Medical Radiation / Ultrasound Technician.

POWELL RIVER, DISTRICT OF
Att: Ian Fremantle,
Chief Administrative Officer
6910 Duncan Street
Powell River, BC V8A 1V4
Tel. 604-485-6291
Fax 604-485-2913
Website .... www.prcn.org
Employer Background: The District of Powell River is located 80 miles north of Vancouver. *New Positions Created (2):* Manager of Human Resources; Director, Recreation and Community Services.

POWER MEASUREMENT LTD.
Att: Human Resources Manager
2195 Keating Cross Road
Victoria, BC V8M 2A5
Tel. 250-652-7100
Fax 250-652-7107
Email .... personnel@pml.com
Website .... www.pml.com
Employer Background: Power Measurement Ltd. supplies enterprise energy management systems. *New Positions Created (3):* BOM Coordinator / Purchasing Technical

Support; Database Support Administrator; Surface Mount Technicians.

POWERLASERS LTD.
Att: Human Resources
55 Confederation Parkway
Concord, ON L4K 4Y7
Tel. 905-761-1525
Fax 905-761-1527
Email .... hr@powerlasers.com
Website .... www.powerlasers.com
Employer Background: Powerlasers Ltd. specializes in laser-welded automotive blanks and related components. *New Positions Created (3):* Industrial Electrician; General Accountant; Maintenance Millwright / Mechanic.

POWERPLUS SYSTEMS CORPORATION
Att: Wolfgang Wenk
100 - 4th Avenue SW, Suite 900
Calgary, AB T2P 3N2
Tel. 403-294-0102
Fax 403-294-0182
Email .... wolfgang.wenk@
.... powerplussystems.com
Website .... www.powerplussystems.com
Employer Background: PowerPlus Systems Corporation provides front-end system consulting services and training using the GBR system analysis approach. *New Positions Created (4):* Account Executive, Consulting Sales; Sales Associate; Senior and Intermediate Consultants; Account Executive.

POWERTECH LABS INC.
Att: Personnel
12388 - 88th Avenue
Surrey, BC V3W 7R7
Tel. 604-590-7500
Fax 604-590-5347
Email ...... personnel@powertechlabs.com
Website .... www.powertechlabs.com
Employer Background: Powertech Labs Inc. is a wholly-owned subsidiary of BC Hydro, the principal electric utility of British Columbia. *New Positions Created (11):* Gas Storage System Engineer; Mechanical Engineer; Nondestructive Testing Engineer; Seismic Engineer; Civil Engineering Technologist; Gas Storage System Engineer; Mechanical Engineer; Mechanical Technologist; Nondestructive Technologist; Nondestructive Testing Engineer; Seismic Engineer.

PPD DEVELOPMENT CANADA, LTD.
Att: Peter Spiliotopoulos
2700 Matheson Boulevard East
Suite 203, East Tower
Mississauga, ON L4W 4V9
Tel. 905-625-3400
Fax 905-625-0814
Website .... www.ppddevelopment.com
Employer Background: PPD Development Canada, Ltd. is a global provider of discovery research and development services for pharmaceutical and biotechnology companies. *New Positions Created (2):* Clinical Research Associate; Clinical Research Associate.

PPM 2000 INC.
Att: Human Resources Manager
10405 Jasper Avenue, Suite 1400
Edmonton, AB T5J 3N4

Tel. 780-448-0616
Fax 780-448-0618
Email .... personnel@ppm2000.com
Website www.ppm2000.com

Employer Background: Founded in 1988, PPM 2000 Inc. develops and distributes software solutions for the security and loss prevention industry. *New Positions Created (2):* Technical Support Supervisor; Software Quality Assurance Specialist.

PRAIRIE MALT LTD.
Att: Human Resources
602 - 4th Avenue East, PO Box 1150
Biggar, SK S0K 0M0

Tel. 306-948-3500
Fax 306-948-3969

Employer Background: Prairie Malt Ltd. processes high-quality malt barley for customers worldwide. *New Positions Created (2):* Plant Engineer; Quality Assurance Manager.

PRATT & WHITNEY CANADA CORPORATION / P&WC
Att: Human Resources
1000 Marie-Victorin Boulevard
Longueuil, QC J4G 1A1

Tel. 450-647-9966
Fax 450-647-7516
Email .... hronline@pwc.ca
Website .... www.pwc.ca

Employer Background: Pratt & Whitney Canada Corporation (P&WC) is one of the world's leading manufacturers of gas turbine engines for helicopters and airplanes. *New Positions Created (5):* Marketing Manager, Industrial Engine Division; Commercial Support Representative; Financial Auditor; Industrial Radiographer; Business Planning Analyst.

PRAXAIR CANADA INC.
Att: Recruiting Manager
1470 Derwent Way
Delta, BC V3M 6H9

Tel. 604-527-0744
Fax 604-540-1700
Email .... careerswest@praxair.com
Website .... www.praxair.com

Employer Background: Praxair Canada Inc. is a leading supplier of industrial, medical and specialty gases. *New Positions Created (5):* Sales Position; Distribution / Fleet Supervisor; Respiratory Therapist; Quality Control Specialist, Gas Operations; Logistics Supervisor.

PRAXAIR CANADA INC.
Att: Ken Davis, Human Resources Director
1 City Centre Drive, Suite 1200
Mississauga, ON L5B 1M2

Tel. 905-803-1600
Fax 905-803-1693
Email .... ken_davis@praxair.com
Website .... www.praxair.com

PRECIDIA TECHNOLOGIES
Att: Human Resources Manager
10A Hearst Way
Kanata, ON K2L 2P4

Tel. 613-592-7557
Fax 613-592-0944
Email .... careers@precidia.com
Website .... www.precidia.com

Employer Background: Precidia Technologies is a leader in IP-enabling technologies for e-commerce. *New Positions Created (6):* Systems Administrator; Director, Wireless Business Development; Gateway Product Development Manager; Product Manager, New Products; Senior ASIC Designer and ASIC Verification Engineer; Wireless Network Support Specialist.

PRECISE SOFTWARE TECHNOLOGIES INC.
Att: Personnel Department
301 Moodie Drive, Suite 308
Nepean, ON K2H 9C4

Tel. 613-596-2251
Fax 613-596-6713
Email .... jobs@psti.com
Website .... www.psti.com

Employer Background: Precise Software Technologies Inc. builds embedded software components and development tools for over 500 clients. *New Positions Created (6):* Applications Engineer; Embedded Device Protocols Developer; Embedded Internet Protocol Developer; Embedded Software Tools Developer; Field Application Engineer; Real-Time Operating System Developer.

PRECISION DRILLING CORPORATION
Att: Jacquie Stahl, HR Coordinator
150 - 6th Avenue SW, Suite 4200
Calgary, AB T2P 3Y7

Tel. 403-716-4500
Fax 403-716-4949
Email .... jstahl@precisiondrilling.com
Website .... www.precisiondrilling.com

Employer Background: Precision Drilling Corporation is an integrated oilfield and industrial service contractor that provides land drilling services. *New Positions Created (3):* Directional Drilling Well Planner; Community Relations Manager; Drilling Engineering Manager, International.

PREFERRED HEALTH CARE INC.
Att: Corporate Office
111 Avenue Road
Toronto, ON M5R 3J8

Tel. 416-924-8800
Fax 416-924-8755
Email .... rgratton@prefhealthcare.com
Website .... www.prefhealthcare.com

Employer Background: Founded in 1987, Preferred Health Care Inc. provides nursing and personal support services in the Greater Toronto Area. *New Positions Created (3):* RNs & RPNs; Registered Nurses / Registered Practical Nurses; PSWs / HCAs / HSWs III.

PREMIER FASTENERS
Att: Carole Gendron, HR Manager
271 Attwell Drive
Toronto, ON M9W 5B9

Tel. 416-675-2020
Fax 416-675-2115
Website .... www.premierind.com

Employer Background: Premier Fastener markets cutting tools, cap screws, specialty fasteners and shop supplies designed for the maintenance and repair of heavy equipment. *New Positions Created (2):* Bilingual Customer Care Representative; Field Sales Representatives.

PREMIER SALONS INTERNATIONAL
Att: Donna Reeve, V.P., Operations
3780 - 14th Avenue, Suite 106
Markham, ON L3R 9Y5

Tel. 905-470-2887
Fax 905-470-0278
Email .... dreeve@premiersalons.com
Website .... www.premiersalons.com

Employer Background: Premier Salons International operates over 400 hair salons in department stores across North America. *New Positions Created (2):* Spa Manager; Regional Director of Operations.

PRESCIENT NEUROPHARMA INC.
Att: Donna Coulson
96 Skyway Avenue
Toronto, ON M9W 4Y9

Tel. 416-674-8047
Fax 416-674-8060
Email ..... donnac@prescientneuropharma.com
Website www.prescientneuropharma.com

Employer Background: Prescient Neuro-Pharma Inc. (formed by the merger of Neurotrophic Bioscience Inc. and IGT Pharma Inc.) is leading the discovery of neuroprotectants to slow or reverse acute and chronic diseases of the brain. *New Positions Created (5):* Research Chemists; Research Associate, Cell Biology; Scientist, Cell Biology; Scientist, Molecular Biology; Senior Technician, Molecular Biology.

PRICEWATERHOUSECOOPERS, BUSINESS PROCESS OUTSOURCING SOLUTIONS INC.
Att: Recruiting Team
240 - 4th Avenue SW
Calgary, AB T2P 4H4

Email ...... krista.m.weir@ca.pwcglobal.com
Website .... www.pwcglobal.com

Employer Background: Pricewaterhouse-Coopers is a leading professional services organization. *New Positions Created (4):* Production Revenue Accountants; Senior Gas Marketing Accountants; Business Analysts; Information Technology Professionals.

PRICEWATERHOUSECOOPERS LLP
Att: Human Resources
21 King Street West, Main Floor
Hamilton, ON L8P 4W7

Tel. 905-777-7000
Fax 905-777-7060
Email .... pwc.hamilton.recruiting@
.... ca.pwcglobal.com
Website .... www.pwcglobal.com
Employer Background: Pricewaterhouse-Coopers LLP is an accounting and professional services firm that occasionally does search work. *New Positions Created (4):* Succession and Strategic Planning Specialist; Accounting Positions; Quality Systems Engineer and Coordinator; Administrative Assistant.

PRIME MINISTER'S OFFICE
Att: Director of Appointments
80 Wellington Street
Room 406, Langevin Block
Ottawa, ON K1A 0A2
Tel. 613-992-4211
Fax 613-957-5743
Website .... pm.gc.ca
Employer Background: The Prime Minister's Office is responsible for recommending appointments to the Prime Minister and handling other policy and administrative responsibilities. *New Positions Created (4):* Superintendent, Office of the Superintendent of Financial Institutions; Executive Director, Telefilm Canada; Executive Director; Government Film Commissioner and Chairperson.

PRIME RESTAURANT GROUP INC.
Att: Manager, Recruitment & Selection
10 Kingsbridge Garden Circle, Suite 600
Mississauga, ON L5R 3K6
Tel. 905-568-0000
Fax 905-568-9308
Email ... recruiter@primerestaurants.com
Website .... www.primerestaurants.com
Employer Background: Prime Restaurant Group Inc. operates 115 restaurants across Canada, including Pat & Mario's and Casey's. The company has annual sales exceeding $200 million and 8,000 employees. *New Positions Created (2):* Accounting Assistant; Restaurant Manager Positions (3).

PRIMERICA FINANCIAL SERVICES (CANADA) LTD.
Att: V.P., General Counsel & Secretary
2000 Argentia Road, Suite 300, Plaza V
Mississauga, ON L5N 2R7
Tel. 905-812-2900
Fax 905-813-5310
Website .... www.primerica.com
Employer Background: Primerica Financial Services (Canada) Ltd. is a member of Citicorp, one of North America's largest financial services marketing organizations. *New Positions Created (7):* In-House Legal Counsel; Inquiry Analyst; Director, Compliance; Underwriter; PC Support Position; Bilingual Customer Service Representatives; Financial Accountant.

PRIMETECH ELECTRONICS INC.
Att: Director of Human Resources
18107 Trans Canada Highway
Kirkland, QC H9J 3K1

Tel. 514-693-1030
Fax 514-697-0085
Email .... hrcv@primetech.ca
Website .... www.primetech.ca
Employer Background: Primetech Electronics Inc. provides contract manufacturing services to the telecom, computer and consumer electronics industries. *New Positions Created (6):* Test Engineer; Industrial Engineer; Industrial Engineer; Process Engineer; Product Engineer; Test Engineer.

PRIMEWEST ENERGY TRUST
Att: Human Resources Coordinator
150 - 6th Avenue SW, Suite 4700
Calgary, AB T2P 3Y7
Tel. 403-234-6600
Fax 403-699-7266
Email .... anned@primewestenergy.com
Website .... www.primewestenergy.com
Employer Background: PrimeWest Energy Trust is one of Canada's largest conventional oil and gas royalty trusts. The company acquires, develops, produces and sells crude oil, natural gas and natural gas liquids. *New Positions Created (31):* Acquisition & Divestiture Specialists (2); Land Analysts (2); Surface Landman; Intermediate Production Revenue Accountant; Marketing Representative; Manager, Risk Management and Marketing; Accounts Payable Team Leader; Business Development Engineer; Gas Plant Operator, 2nd Class; Land Manager / Landman; Capital Accountant; Environmental Specialist; Exploitation Engineer; Gas Controller; Investor Relations and Communications Practitioner; Marketing Accountant; Production Revenue Accountant; Senior Marketing Rep; Maintenance Craftsman; Instrument Electrical Lead; Intermediate Production Revenue Accountant; Reservoir Engineer; Non-Operated Joint Venture Accountant; Production Revenue Accountant; Acquisition Specialist; Environmental, Health and Safety Mgr; Exploitation Engineers; Joint Venture Engineer; Reservoir Engineer; Revenue Receivable Accountant; Land Administrator, Mineral.

PRINCE EDWARD, COUNTY OF
Att: Brian McComb,
Commissioner of Planning
332 Main Street, 1st Floor
Drawer 1550, Shire Hall
Picton, ON K0K 2T0
Tel. 613-476-2148
Fax 613-476-8356
Website .... www.pec.on.ca
Employer Background: The County of Prince Edward is a unique island community in southeastern Ontario. *New Positions Created (4):* Chief Building Official/By-Law Enforcement Officer; Planner; Planner; Chief Building Official / By-Law Enforcement Officer.

PRINCE GEORGE, CITY OF
Att: Service Centre
1100 Patricia Boulevard
Prince George, BC V2L 3V9
Tel. 250-561-7626
Fax 250-561-7719

Email .... rcaston@city.pg.bc.ca
Website .... www.city.pg.bc.ca
Employer Background: Incorporated in 1915, the City of Prince George is located in northern British Columbia and home to 80,000 residents. *New Positions Created (15):* Financial Operations Analyst; Planner I; Manager, Financial Planning; Senior Planner; Property Assistant; Health & Safety Facilitator; Coordinator, Fleet Acquisitions; Manager, Budgets and Accounting; Deputy City Clerk; Manager, Budgets and Accounting; Planner 1; GIS Technologist; City Clerk; GIS Technologist; Property Agent.

PRINTERON CORPORATION
Att: Human Resources
221 McIntyre Drive
Kitchener, ON N2R 1G1
Tel. 519-748-2462
Fax 519-748-9457
Email .... hr@printeron.com
Website .... www.printeron.net
Employer Background: PrinterON Corporation provides secure, easy-to-use, innovative Internet printing products and solutions to mobile professionals and businesses worldwide. *New Positions Created (80):* Advanced Formats Software Developer; Application Product Manager; Applications Project Manager; Business Development Representative; Call Centre Representative; Change Management and Production Analyst; Client Product C / C++ Developers; Java Client Developers; Java Middleware Developer; Lead Developer, Applications; Marketing Coordinator; Marketing Writer; Print Driver C / C++ Developers; Process Analyst; Quality Assurance Specialist; Senior 3D Developer; Senior Database Analyst; Senior Integration Developer; Software Architect; Software Developer, Interfaces; Software Developer, Java; Software Development Project Managers; Software Team Leaders; Technical Product Implementation Specialist; Vice-President, Research & Development; Web Developers; Wireless C / C++ Developers; Affiliate Program Manager; Public Relations Manager; Sales Manager; Marketing Coordinator; Marketing Writer; Senior 3D Developer; Software Developer, Interfaces; Technical Writer / Communicator; Advanced Formats Software Developer; Application Product Manager; Applications Project Manager; Business Development Representative; Lead Developer, Applications; Senior Database Analyst; Senior Integration Developer; Software Developers, Java; Software Development Project Managers; Technical Printer Support Specialist; Technical Product Implementation Specialist ; Translation / Localization Specialist; Call Center Representative; Change Management and Production Analyst; Client Product C / C++ Developers; Java Client Developers; Java Middleware Developers; Print Driver C / C++ Developers; Process Analyst; Quality Assurance Specialist; Software Architects; Software Team Leaders; Unix Administrator; Vice-President, Research and Development; Web Developers; Wireless C / C++ Developers; Graphic Designer; Marketing Coordinator; Senior 3D Developer; Software

Developer, Interfaces; Technical Writer / Communicator; Trade Show Coordinator; Process Analyst; Software Development Project Managers; Application Product Manager; Call Centre Representative / Technical Support; Driver Software Developer; Java Software Developer; Senior Database Analyst; Web Design / Producer Lead; Web Technical Specialist; Quality Assurance Specialist; Technical Writer; Web Graphic Designer; Web Producer.

PRISM CENTRE, THE
Att: Human Resources
355 Lark Street
Chatham, ON N7L 5B2

Tel. 519-354-0520
Fax 519-354-7355
Website .... www.prismcentre.ca

Employer Background: The Prism Centre is an accredited, community-based health service centre that provides audiology and children's rehabilitation services. *New Positions Created (7):* Communication Disorders Assistants; Speech Language Pathologists (2); Physiotherapist; Audiologist; Communication Disorders Assistant; Occupational Therapist; Speech Language Pathologists.

PRISZM BRANDZ INC.
Att: Human Resources
500 Hood Road
Markham, ON L3R 0P6

Fax 905-332-8577
Email .... hr@priszm.com
Website .... www.priszm.com

Employer Background: Priszm Brandz Inc. operates KFC, Pizza Hut and Taco Bell franchises. *New Positions Created (2):* Assistant Mgrs; WSIB / WCB Claims Coordinator.

PRIVA INC.
Att: Human Resources Manager
9100 Ray Lawson Boulevard
Montréal, QC H1J 1K8

Tel. 514-356-8881
Fax 514-356-0055
Email .... piv@priva-inc.com
Website .... www.priva-inc.com

Employer Background: Priva Inc. specializes in innovative textile products, including reusable waterproof and absorbent products for personal protection. *New Positions Created (2):* Customer Service Representative; Production Assistant.

PRIVATE RECIPES LTD.
Att: Rae Aust
12 Indell Lane
Brampton, ON L6T 3Y3

Tel. 905-799-1022
Fax 905-799-2666
Email .... raust@privaterecipes.com

Employer Background: Private Recipes Ltd. is a food manufacturer. *New Positions Created (4):* Cook and Kitchen Helper; Plant Manager; Senior Accountant; Controller.

PRO-BEL ENTERPRISES, LTD.
Att: Manny Mameri, Engineering Manager
765 Westney Road South
Ajax, ON L1S 6W1

Tel. 905-427-0616
Fax 905-427-2545
Email .... careers@pro-bel.ca
Website .... www.pro-bel.ca

Employer Background: Pro-Bel Enterprises, Ltd. is an international designer, manufacturer and installer of mid- to high-rise suspended access equipment and safety systems. *New Positions Created (4):* Engineering Designers / CAD Operators; Administrative Assistant; Various Construction Positions; Project Coordinators.

PRO-CAD SOFTWARE LTD.
Att: Human Resources Manager
37 Richard Way SW, Suite 300
Calgary, AB T3E 7M8

Tel. 403-216-3375
Fax 403-216-3378
Email .... resume@procad-software.com
Website .... www.procad-software.com

Employer Background: Pro-Cad Software Ltd. develops piping and electrical CAD applications for AutoCAD. *New Positions Created (2):* Senior Programmers; Software Developers.

PRO-SPEC INC.
Att: Human Resources Manager
9 Pinelands Avenue
Stoney Creek, ON L8E 3A4

Tel. 905-664-8280
Fax 905-664-8310

Employer Background: Pro-Spec Inc. is a custom metalworking machine shop. *New Positions Created (4):* Various Trades Positions; Programmers, Gibbs; Set-up Operators; Maintenance Person.

PROCECO LTD.
Att: Human Resources Department
7300 Tellier Street
Montréal, QC H1N 3T7

Tel. 514-254-8494
Fax 514-254-8184
Website .... www.proceco.com

Employer Background: Proceco Ltd. designs and manufactures water-based parts cleaning systems. *New Positions Created (8):* Engineering Projects Coordinator; Technical Writer; Customer Service Manager; Electrical Foreperson; Mechanical Designer; Project Coordinator; Technical Buyer; Technical Writer.

PROCO MACHINERY INC.
Att: Human Resources Manager
1111 Brevik Place
Mississauga, ON L4W 3R7

Tel. 905-206-9392
Fax 905-206-9776
Website .... www.procomachinery.com

Employer Background: Proco Machinery Inc. manufactures automated / robotic machinery for the blow molding industry. *New Positions Created (6):* Sales / Marketing Secretary; Accountant / Bookkeeper; Technical Sales & Marketing Manager; Service Tech-

nician; Electrical Technician; Inventory Control / Stores Clerk.

PROCOR LTD.
Att: Human Resources Department
2001 Speers Road
Oakville, ON L6J 5E1

Tel. 905-827-4111
Fax 905-827-7735
Email .... jobs@procor.com
Website .... www.procor.com

Employer Background: Procor Ltd. manufactures rail cars. *New Positions Created (9):* Aluminum Welders; Plate Fitters or Fitter Welders; Smalltalk / Java Programmers (3); Programmer Analyst; Senior CAD Operator; Plate Fitters / Fitter Welders; Pressure Vessel Welders; Administrative Assistant, Marketing; Computer Operator.

PROCTER & GAMBLE INC.
Att: Shanti Raktoe
PO Box 355, Station A
Toronto, ON M5W 1C5

Tel. 416-730-4711
Website .... www.pg.com/canada

Employer Background: Procter & Gamble Inc. is a recognized leader in the development and marketing of a broad range of consumer products. *New Positions Created (3):* Bilingual Drug Information & Safety Specialist; Bilingual Drug Information & Safety Specialist; French Translator.

PROCURON INC.
Att: Recruiting Centre
105 Commerce Valley Drive W., Suite 400
Thornhill, ON L3T 7W3

Tel. 905-707-8849
Fax 905-707-2443
Email .... careers@procuron.com
Website .... www.procuron.com

Employer Background: Procuron Inc. is one of Canada's largest business-to-business e-marketplaces for indirect goods. *New Positions Created (25):* Manager, Maintenance, Repair and Operations; Executive Assistant; Account Executive; Application Architect; Business Development Manager; Catalogue Analyst; Customer Care Manager; Director of Marketing; Director of Sales; Director of Vertical Markets; Human Resources Manager; Information Technology Procurement Specialist; Manager, Payment Solutions; Marketing Manager; Portal Content Specialist; Pricing Analyst; Procurement Analyst; Procurement Specialist; Product Manager; Quality Assurance Manager; Senior Network Administrator; Senior Recruiter; Team Leader, Office Supplies; Team Leader, Real Estate; Webmaster.

PRODUCTIVITY IMPROVEMENT CENTER / PIC
Att: Debra White
1610 Champlain Avenue
Whitby, ON L1N 6A7

Fax 905-720-2778
Email .... debra.white@durhamc.on.ca
Website .... www.productivity
.... improvementcenter.com

Employer Background: Established in 1984, PIC is a leading trainer in quality system standards. *New Positions Created (3):* Quality Inspectors; Trainers / Consultants; Project Manager, Automotive Quality.

PROFAC FACILITIES MANAGEMENT SERVICES INC.
Att: Human Resources
304 The East Mall, Suite 900
Toronto, ON M9B 6E2
Tel. 416-207-4700
Fax 416-207-4780
Email .... spopescu@profac-group.com
Website .... www.profac-group.com

Employer Background: ProFac Facilities Management Services Inc., through its partnership with SNC-Lavalin, manages an inventory of 55 million square feet and more than 4,000 buildings. *New Positions Created (7):* Technician, Building Operations; National Director, Project Management; Facility Manager; Property Manager; JD Edwards Team Leader; Senior Systems Developer; Contract Manager.

PROFACE INDE ELECTRONICS INC.
Att: Human Resource Manager
8700 North Fraser Way, Suite 220
Burnaby, BC V5J 5H4
Tel. 604-430-1446
Fax 604-430-1332
Email .... careers@inde.bc.ca
Website .... www.profaceinde.com

Employer Background: Proface Inde Electronics Inc. creates innovative graphics software for industrial human-machine interface markets worldwide. *New Positions Created (13):* Real-Time Software Developer; Sr Developer / Project Leader; Software Developer; Windows Software Developer; Control Ladder Logic Engineers; Windows CE / Real Time Embedded Developers; Japanese Technical Translator; QA Software Tester; Real-Time Software Developer; Software Developer; Software Project Manager; Technical Writer; Windows Software Developer.

PROFESSIONAL ENGINEERS ONTARIO / PEO
Att: Human Resources
25 Sheppard Avenue West, Suite 1000
Toronto, ON M2N 6S9
Tel. 416-224-1100
Fax 416-224-8168
Website .... www.peo.on.ca

Employer Background: PEO is the 64,000-member association responsible for licensing Ontario's professional engineers and setting the standards for engineering in the province. *New Positions Created (3):* Manager, Information Systems; Admissions Representative; Investigator, Complaints, Discipline and Enforcement.

PROFESSIONAL INSTITUTE OF THE PUBLIC SERVICE OF CANADA / PIPSC
Att: Sue Baribeau, Staffing and Administration Officer
43 Auriga Drive
Nepean, ON K2E 8C3
Tel. 613-228-6310
Fax 613-224-2294
Website .... www.pipsc.ca

Employer Background: Founded in 1920, PIPSC represents 40,000 public service professionals in Canada. *New Positions Created (4):* Bilingual Research Officers / Compensation Analysts (2); Bilingual Information Officer; Bilingual Negotiator; Bilingual Universal Classification Standard (UCS) Administrative Coordinator.

PROFESSIONAL PHARMACEUTICAL CORP.
Att: Human Resources Manager
9200 Cote de Liesse
Lachine, QC H8T 1A1
Tel. 514-631-7710
Fax 514-631-2867
Email .... hr@ppc.ca
Website .... www.ppc.ca

Employer Background: Professional Pharmaceutical Corp. manufactures Marcelle, Caroline and Annabelle cosmetic products. *New Positions Created (6):* Sales Representative; Regional Sales Manager; Merchandiser; Data Entry & Payables Clerk; Receptionist; Junior Buyer.

PROFIT RECOVERY GROUP CANADA, INC. / PRG
Att: Human Resources
15 Sheldon Drive, Unit 4
Cambridge, ON N1R 6R8
Tel. 519-740-7471
Fax 519-740-9348
Email .... cambridgeoffice@prgx.com
Website .... www.prgx.com

Employer Background: PRG provides recovery auditing services to Fortune 1000 companies worldwide. *New Positions Created (6):* Senior Auditor; Accounts Payable Auditor; Auditor; Staff Auditor; Inside Sales Representative; Recovery Auditing Position.

PROGESTIC INTERNATIONAL INC.
Att: Human Resources Department
310 Broadway, Suite 600
Winnipeg, MB R3C 0S6
Tel. 204-925-7610
Fax 204-925-7620
Email .... hr-wpg@progestic.com
Website .... www.progestic.com

Employer Background: Founded in 1982, Progestic International Inc. is an IT consulting and technology solutions firm. *New Positions Created (4):* Powerbuilder Experts; Systems Administrator; Java Developer; PowerBuilder Developer.

PROGESTIC INTERNATIONAL INC.
Att: Human Resource Manager
222 Queen Street, Suite 400
Ottawa, ON K1P 5V9
Tel. 613-230-7522
Fax 613-230-5739
Email .... hr@progestic.com
Website .... www.progestic.com

Employer Background: Founded in 1982, Progestic International Inc. is an IT consult-

ing and technology solutions firm. *New Positions Created (26):* Recruiting Officer; Senior Developers; Data Modeller; Senior Analyst, GOL; Senior Object-Oriented Specialists; Senior Oracle Database Administrator; Reception and Administrative Support Position; Intermediate / Senior Developer, Interactive Voice Response; Senior Business Technical Architect; Oracle Financials Specialists; Director, Audit Consulting Services; Senior IT Analyst; Technical Proposal Writer; Senior Developers; Senior Systems Analyst; Visual Software Specialists; Database Architect / Designer; Senior Business Analyst; Senior Developer / Analyst; Senior IT System Analyst, Project Leaders; Senior IT Technical Architect, Web Design; Technical Proposal Writer, Information Technology; Account Executive, Information Technology; Senior Auditor, Information Technology; Senior Auditor, Value-for-Money Auditing; Web Developer.

PROGRESSIVE ENGINEERING LTD.
Att: Human Resources Manager
7220 Fisher Street SE, Suite 375
Calgary, AB T2H 2H8
Tel. 403-509-3030
Fax 403-509-3035

Employer Background: Progressive Engineering Ltd. is a growing consulting firm specializing in land development and municipal engineering projects. *New Positions Created (3):* Design Engineer; Design Technologists; Design Engineers / Technologists.

PROGRESSIVE SOLUTIONS INC.
Att: Human Resources Manager
2601 Highway 6, Unit 8
Vernon, BC V1T 5G4
Tel. 250-545-0626
Fax 250-545-0767
Email ...... hr@progressive-solutions.com
Website .. www.progressive-solutions.com

Employer Background: Progressive Solutions Inc. is an established company providing software business solutions to large corporate clients in the forest products industry. *New Positions Created (3):* Application Developers; Implementation Specialist; Application Developers.

PROPAK SYSTEMS LTD.
Att: S. Thexton
440 East Lake Road, Postal Bag 2, Stn. M
Airdrie, AB T4B 2C3
Tel. 403-948-2001
Fax 403-912-7095
Email .... sthexton@propaksystems.com
Website .... www.propaksystems.com

Employer Background: Propak Systems Ltd. engineers, fabricates and constructs gas compression and processing facilities for the energy industry. *New Positions Created (8):* Electrical / Control Engineers; Intermediate Civil / Structural Engineer; Mechanical Engineer; Senior Electrical Designers; Technical Positions; Software / Database Support and Customization Position; Compressor Controls Technologist; Electrical / Controls Engineer.

PROTECH CHEMICALS LTD.
Att: Human Resources
7600 Henri-Bourassa Boulevard West
St-Laurent, QC H4S 1W3
Tel. 514-745-0200
Fax 514-745-5774
Email .... protech@generation.net
Website .... www.protechpowder.com
Employer Background: Established in 1976, Protech Chemicals Ltd. manufactures powder coatings for industrial use. *New Positions Created (3):* Administrative Secretary; Executive Administrative Assistant; Order Desk Customer Service Representative.

PROVANCE TECHNOLOGIES INC.
Att: Human Resources Manager
85 Bellehumeur Street, 3rd Floor
Gatineau, QC J8T 8B7
Tel. 819-568-8787
Fax 819-568-1453
Email .... careers@provance.com
Website .... www.provance.com
Employer Background: Provance Technologies Inc. creates and delivers leading-edge asset management solutions for IT outsourcing providers. *New Positions Created (19):* Communications Adviser; Database Analyst; Executive Assistant; Software Engineer; Technical Writer; Web Developer; Director, Information Systems; Communications Advisor; Project Manager; Business Consultant; Web Developer; Database Analyst; Senior Quality Control Analyst; Director, Sales; C++ Programmer; Database Analyst; Project Manager; Quality Control Manager; Senior Quality Control Analyst.

PROVENANCE SYSTEMS INC.
Att: Human Resources Manager
1525 Carling Avenue, Suite 110
Ottawa, ON K1Z 8R9
Tel. 613-792-1150
Fax 613-792-1750
Email .... jobs@provsys.com
Website .... www.provsys.com
Employer Background: Provenance Systems Inc. develops electronic records management software. *New Positions Created (5):* Network Administrator; Customer Support Specialist; Database Administrator; Senior Software Developers; Software Quality Assurance Engineers.

PROVIDENCE CENTRE
Att: Diane Lobo, HR Generalist
3276 St. Clair Avenue East
Toronto, ON M1L 1W1
Tel. 416-759-9321
Fax 416-285-3756
Email .... hr@providence.on.ca
Website .... www.providence.on.ca
Employer Background: Founded in 1857, Providence Centre is a 280-patient complex continuing care and rehabilitation hospital, as well as a 288-resident home for the aged. *New Positions Created (10):* Gift Shop / General Store Manager; Patient Care Managers (3); Systems Analyst; Clinical Nurse Specialists / Nurse Practitioners (2); Occupational Therapist; Physiotherapist; Social Worker;

Pharmacist; Evening Coordinator; Patient Care Manager.

PROVIDENCE CHILDREN'S CENTRE
Att: Human Resources Manager
5332 - 4th Street SW
Calgary, AB T2V 0Z4
Fax 403-255-1254
Email .. general@providencechildren.com
Website ..... www.providencechildren.com
Employer Background: Established in 1943, Providence Children's Centre is a non-profit development centre for children with special needs. *New Positions Created (2):* Teachers; Speech - Language Pathologists.

PROVIDENCE CONTINUING CARE CENTRE / PCCC
Att: Cindy Tindal, Human Resources
340 Union Street, PO Box 3600
Kingston, ON K7L 5A2
Tel. 613-544-5220
Fax 613-544-6036
Email .... tindalc@pccc.kari.net
Website .... www.pccconline.com
Employer Background: PCCC is a Catholic provider of long-term palliative, geriatric and rehabilitative health services. *New Positions Created (11):* Director, Rehabilitation Services; Service Coordinator; Administrative Applications Coordinator; Clinical Applications Coordinator; PC Support / Help Desk Positions (2) ; Service Coordinator; Financial Analyst; Financial Manager; Human Resource Consultant; Human Resource Managers (2); Speech Language Pathologist.

PROVIDENCE CONTINUING CARE CENTRE / PCCC
Att: J. Raven
PO Box 603
Kingston, ON K7L 4X3
Fax 613-548-5583
Email .... ravenj@pccc.kari.net
Website .... www.pccconline.com
Employer Background: PCCC is a Catholic provider of long-term palliative, geriatric and rehabilitative health services. *New Positions Created (5):* Social Worker, Homes for Special Care Program; Health Service and Education Research Evaluator; Psychologist; Registered Nurses (5); Registered Practical Nurses (4).

PROVIDENCE CONTINUING CARE CENTRE, ST. VINCENT DE PAUL HOSPITAL SITE
Att: Human Resources Manager
42 Garden Street
Brockville, ON K6V 2C3
Tel. 613-342-4461
Fax 613-342-1656
Email .... davisc@pccc.kari.net
Website .... www.pccconline.com
Employer Background: St. Vincent de Paul Hospital is a complex continuing care, palliative care and rehabilitation hospital. *New Positions Created (2):* Physiotherapists; Coordinator, Palliative Care, Pain and Symptom Management.

PROVIDENCE HEALTH CARE, MOUNT ST. JOSEPH HOSPITAL
Att: Human Resources Department
3080 Price Edward Street
Vancouver, BC V5T 3N4
Tel. 604-877-8306
Fax 604-875-8733
Website .... www.providencehealthcare.org
Employer Background: Providence Health Care is a Catholic health service organization comprised of multiple hospitals and care facilities. *New Positions Created (2):* Pastoral Care Associate; 4th Class Engineer

PROVIDENCE HEALTH CARE, ST. PAUL'S HOSPITAL
Att: Human Resources
1081 Burrard Street, Room 541
Vancouver, BC V6Z 1Y6
Tel. 604-806-8007
Fax 604-806-8144
Website .... www.providencehealthcare.org
Employer Background: Opened in 1894, St Paul's Hospital is an acute academic and research hospital, providing quaternary, tertiary and secondary care services. *New Positions Created (37):* Clinical Nurse Specialist, Mental Health; Nurse Specialist, Education; Health Records Administrator; Organizational Development Consultant; Secretary to Chair, Emergency Medicine; Executive Assistant to the President and CEO; Nursing Positions; Secretary to the Chair of Emergency Medicine; Classification Consultant, Human Resources; Clinical Nurse Specialist, Palliative Care; Clinical Pastoral Education Teaching Supervisor; Infrastructure Leader, Corporate Information Technology; Nurse Educator, Intensive Care Unit RNs; Team Leader, Client Services (Information Systems); Health Record Technicians; Health Records Administrators; Medical Laboratory Technologists; Medical Radiation Technologists; Pharmacists; Transcriptionists; Staffing Clerk; Patient Care Leader Ambulatory Care Program; Classification Consultant - Human Resources; Clinical Nurse Specialist - Palliative Care; Clinical Pastoral Education Teaching Supervisor; Infection Control Nurse; Infrastructure Leader, Corporate Information Technology; Medical Transcriptionist - Health Records Services; Nurse Educator - Intensive Care Unit; Registered Nurses; Registered Nurses Renal Program; RN / RPN; Team Leader Client Services - Information Systems; Clinical Pathway Consultant; Employee Services Advisor; Labour Relations Officer.

PROVIDENCE HEALTH CARE, ST. VINCENT'S HOSPITAL (HEATHER SITE)
Att: Human Resources Department
749 - 33rd Avenue West
Vancouver, BC V5Z 2K4
Tel. 604-877-3081
Fax 604-877-3185
Website .... www.providencehealthcare.org
Employer Background: Providence Health Care is a Catholic health service organization comprised of multiple hospitals and care facilities. *New Positions Created (10):* Pastoral Care Associate; Registered Nurse

Surgical Unit; Registered Nurses, Intensive Care Unit (2); Leader, Diversity; Leader, Health Records; Medical Secretary; Registered Nurse, Surgical Unit; Registered Nurses, Intensive Care Unit (2); Leader, Diversity; Leader, Health Record Services.

PROVINCIAL AUDITOR OF ONTARIO, OFFICE OF THE / OPA

Att: Manager, Human Resources
20 Dundas Street West
PO Box 105, 15th Floor
Toronto, ON M5G 2C2

Tel. 416-327-2381
Fax 416-327-9862
Email .... resumes@opa.gov.on.ca
Website .... www.gov.on.ca/opa

Employer Background: The mission of the OPA is to report to the legislative assembly objective information and recommendations resulting from independent audits of the government's programs, its crown agencies and corporations. *New Positions Created (3):* Audit Professionals; Auditor; Communications Officer.

PROVINCIAL AUDITOR'S OFFICE, MANITOBA

Att: Human Resource Services
379 Broadway Street, Suite 304
Winnipeg, MB R3C 0T9

Fax 204-945-4907
Website .... www.pao.mb.ca

Employer Background: The Provincial Auditor's Office works with members of the legislature to build an environment of trust between citizens and public institutions. *New Positions Created (4):* Compliance Auditor; Network and User Support Specialist; Quality Assurance and Project Coordinator; Value-for-Money Auditor.

PROVINCIAL STORE FIXTURES LTD.

Att: Human Resources Manager
895 Meyerside Drive
Mississauga, ON L5T 1R8

Tel. 905-564-6700
Fax 905-564-6711
Website .... www.psfltd.com

Employer Background: Provincial Store Fixtures Ltd. produces custom millwork, loose fixtures, showcases and promotional, POP and display fixturing. *New Positions Created (2):* Woodworkers; Materials and Transportation Coordinator.

PROXIMI-T INFORMATION TECHNOLOGY INC.

Att: Human Resources Manager
5800 Explorer Drive, Suite 1
Mississauga, ON L4W 5K9

Tel. 905-602-8282
Fax 905-602-8209
Email .... career@proximi-t.com
Website .... www.proximi-t.com

Employer Background: Founded in 1984, Proximi-T Information Technology Inc. is an IT consulting firm, with offices in Toronto and Montreal. *New Positions Created (2):* Business Intelligence Architect; Business Intelligence Developer.

PSC ANALYTICAL LTD.

Att: Human Resources Manager
5735 McAdam Road
Mississauga, ON L4Z 1N9

Tel. 905-890-8566
Fax 905-890-8575
Email .... jmccarthy@contactpsc.com
Website .... www.pscanalytical.com

Employer Background: PSC Analytical Ltd. specializes in the environmental testing of solid waste, effluent, receiving waters, ground waters, soil, sediment, stack emissions, ambient air and plant, animal and fish tissues. *New Positions Created (3):* Analytical Chemists & Laboratory Technicians; Client Account Managers & Sales Representatives; Client Account Managers.

PSINAPTIC COMMUNICATIONS INC.

Att: Human Resources Manager
200 Riverside Drive SE, Suite 216
Calgary, AB T2C 2X5

Tel. 403-720-2531
Fax 403-720-2537
Email .... sbrache@psinaptic.com
Website .... www.psinaptic.com

Employer Background: PsiNaptic Communications Inc. is a digital communications technology company. *New Positions Created (3):* Intermediate Hardware Engineers / Technologists; Intermediate Software Engineer; Senior Software Engineer.

PSION TEKLOGIX INC.

Att: Human Resources
2100 Meadowvale Boulevard
Mississauga, ON L5N 7J9

Tel. 905-813-9900
Email .... hr@teklogix.com
Website .... www.psionteklogix.com

Employer Background: Psion Teklogix Inc. is a leading global supplier of wireless data communication systems for industrial applications. *New Positions Created (25):* Junior / Intermediate Test Engineer / Technologist; Senior Hardware Design Engineer; Senior Process Auditor; Software Developer, Level 2; Software Developer, Level 3; Application Support Specialist; Consolidation Analyst; Draftsperson; Financial Analyst; Industrial Engineer; Marketing Research Associate; Product Specialist; Quality Engineer; Regional Sales Manger; Senior Buyer; Senior Program Manager; Software Developer Level 4; Technical Support Analyst; Technical Trainer; Test Engineer / Technologist; Warehouse Manager; Buyer; Consolidations Analyst; Financial Analyst; Product Support Analyst.

PTI GROUP INC.

Att: Alan Konkin, Director, HR
3050 Parsons Road
Edmonton, AB T6N 1B1

Tel. 780-463-8872
Fax 780-462-6784
Email .... akonkin@ptigroup.com
Website .... www.ptigroup.com

Employer Background: PTI Group Inc. provides catering and camp services to remote work sites in the oilfield, mining and construction industries. *New Positions Created (8):* System Support Analyst; Purchasing Coordinator; Transportation / Maintenance Coordinator; Manager, Housing and Food Services; Area Managers; Accountant; Service Manger; Accounts Payable Supervisor.

PUBLIC GUARDIAN AND TRUSTEE OF BRITISH COLUMBIA

Att: Sandy Tordiffe
808 West Hastings Street, Suite 700
Vancouver, BC V6C 3L3

Tel. 604-660-4475
Fax 604-660-0374
Email ...... humanresources@trustee.bc.ca
Website .... www.trustee.bc.ca

Employer Background: The Public Guardian and Trustee of British Columbia operates independently to protect the legal and financial interests of children and adults, and administers the estates of deceased and missing persons. *New Positions Created (11):* Healthcare Decisions Consultant; Client Services Financial Assistant; Administrative Assistant / Legal Secretary; Committee Review Officer; Database Administrator; Senior Legal Secretaries (2); Director, Finance, Administration and Systems; Health Care Decisions Consultant (2); Human Resources Advisor; Regional Financial Officer; Legal Secretary.

PUBLIC INTEREST ADVOCACY CENTRE / PIAC

Att: Human Resources Manager
1 Nicholas Street, Suite 1204
Ottawa, ON K1N 7B7

Tel. 613-562-4002
Fax 613-562-0007
Email .... piac@piac.ca
Website .... www.piac.ca

Employer Background: PIAC is a non-profit organization engaged in regulatory intervention, policy research and advocacy on behalf of consumers of public services. *New Positions Created (3):* Researcher; Researcher; Researcher.

PUBLIC SERVICE ALLIANCE OF CANADA / PSAC

Att: Human Resources
233 Gilmour Street
Ottawa, ON K2P 0P1

Tel. 613-560-4237
Fax 613-248-4885
Email .... careers@psac.com
Website .... www.psac.com

Employer Background: PSAC, one of Canada's largest unions, works to secure fair treatment, employment security, better pay and safe working conditions for 150,000 members. *New Positions Created (4):* Facilities Technician; Coordinator, Information Technology; Human Resources / Classification Advisor; Bilingual Negotiator.

PUBLIC SERVICE COMMISSION OF CANADA, ALBERTA & NWT / PSC

Att: Human Resources
9700 Jasper Ave., Room 830, Canada Place
Edmonton, AB T5J 4G3

Tel. 780-495-3130
Fax 780-495-2098
Website .... www.psc-cfp.gc.ca

Employer Background: PSC, an independent agency, appoints qualified persons to and within the Canadian Federal Public Service and develops corporate learning opportunities for professional communities.
New Positions Created (47): Support Geophysicist; Team Leader, Information Technology Operations; Engineer, Drilling / Production; Engineers; Health System Analyst; Institution Clerk; Pipeline Engineering Specialist, Pipeline Integrity; Regional Director, Policy and Intergovernmental Affairs; Regulatory Financial Analyst; Senior Surveyor; Socio-Economic Specialist; Surveyor; Electromagnetic Compatibility Evaluation Engineer; Geochemistry Technician; Property Managers (2); Regional Communications Director; Development Officer; Organic Synthesis and Analysis Research Technologist; Communications Officer; Electrical and Controls Services Supervisor; Fish Habitat Biologist; Market Analyst; Forestry Research Field Coordinator; Clinical Nurses; Outreach Officer; Geographic Information Systems Technician; Laboratory Technologist; Senior Maintenance Management Specialist, Electrical; Legal Secretaries; Office Assistant; Senior Surveyor, Land Claims; Service Delivery Specialist; Head, Laboratory Sciences; Communications Officers; Junior Project Manager, Developmental Engineer; Water Treatment and Environmental Services Technician; Junior Legal Counsel; Project Geologist, Mineral; Project Geologist, Petroleum; Seabird Biologist; Research Scientist, Organic Geochemist; Environmental Scientist; Electrical Engineer; Mechanical Engineer - Maintenance Management Specialist; Environmental Assessment Specialist; Electromagnetic Compatibility Evaluation Engineer; Finance Clerk.

PUBLIC SERVICE COMMISSION OF CANADA, BC / PSC
Att: Human Resources Manager
1230 Government Street, 5th Floor
Victoria, BC V8W 3M4
Tel. 250-363-8120
Fax 250-363-0558
Website .... www.psc-cfp.gc.ca

Employer Background: PSC, an independent agency, appoints qualified persons to and within the Canadian Federal Public Service and develops corporate learning opportunities for professional communities.
New Positions Created (18): Research Scientist; Research Scientist, Organic Pollution Chemist / Toxicologist; Data Systems Geophysicist; Integrated Coastal Management Coordinator; Senior Biologist; Research Scientist, Ocean Climate Modeler; Fish Health and Research Veterinarian; Computer Scientist, Software Developer; Physical Scientist, Carbon Budget Modelling; Physical Scientist, Spatial C Budget Modelling; Research Scientist, Quantitative Stock Assessment; Mechanical Engineering Officer; Risk Management Research Scientist; Employment Equity and Aboriginal Liaison Officer; Analytical Technologist; Production Manager;

Electrical Engineer; Research Scientist, Ocean Climate Modeller.

PUBLIC SERVICE COMMISSION OF CANADA, BC / PSC
Att: Human Resources Manager
757 West Hastings Street
Suite 210, Sinclair Centre
Vancouver, BC V6C 3M2
Tel. 604-666-0696
Fax 604-666-6808
Website .... www.psc-cfp.gc.ca

Employer Background: PSC, an independent agency, appoints qualified persons to and within the Canadian Federal Public Service and develops corporate learning opportunities for professional communities.
New Positions Created (21): Hydrological Applications Specialist; Environmental Health Officer; Lab Technician; Water Quality Biologist; Bilingual Library Manager; Program Delivery Officer; Architect; Environmental Scientist; Habitat Management Biologist; Information Services Officer; Fishery Officer; Electrical Engineer; Regional Manager, Appraisals; Food Research Scientist; Civil CADD Specialist; Translator / Language Advisor; Electrical Technologist; Legal Secretary; Electrical Engineer; Dental Therapists (2); Salmon Stock Assessment Biologist.

PUBLIC SERVICE COMMISSION OF CANADA, EXECUTIVE PROGRAMS
Att: Pierette Renaud, Data Information Assistant, Centralized Processing Unit
300 Laurier Ave. W., Room B2163
L'Esplanade Laurier, West Tower
Ottawa, ON K1A 0M7
Tel. 613-992-8646
Fax 613-995-1099
Website .... www.psc-cfp.gc.ca

Employer Background: PSC, an independent agency, appoints qualified persons to and within the Canadian Federal Public Service and develops corporate learning opportunities for professional communities.
New Positions Created (9): Director General, Sport Canada; Director General, Finance Division; Director General, Information Management Project Delivery; Director, Northwest Territories; Director General, Social Policy; Director, Communications; Director, Contract Claims Resolution Board; Director of Programs, Industry, Economics and Programs Branch; Executive Director, Aboriginal Business Canada.

PUBLIC SERVICE COMMISSION OF CANADA, MANITOBA / PSC
Att: Human Resources Manager
344 Edmonton Street, Room 100
Winnipeg, MB R3B 2L4
Fax 204-983-8188
Website .... jobs.gc.ca/winnipeg

Employer Background: PSC, an independent agency, appoints qualified persons to and within the Canadian Federal Public Service and develops corporate learning opportunities for professional communities.
New Positions Created (22): Program Man-

ager, Home and Community Care; Program Manager, Northern Infrastructure Implementation; Regional Nursing Officer; Structural Engineer; Laboratory Technologist; Director of Rehabilitation; Research Scientist; Staff Pharmacist; Regional Engineer, Railway; Research Scientist, Arctic Marine Mammal Populations; Laboratory Technologist; Arctic Contaminants Research Scientist; Director of Rehabilitation; Laboratory Technologist; Fisheries Research Biologist; Regional Psychologist; Technician; Environmental Health Officer; Regional Programs Medical Officer; Deputy Chief, Safety and Environmental Services; Technician; Technician.

PUBLIC SERVICE COMMISSION OF CANADA, NEW BRUNSWICK / PSC
Att: Human Resources Manager
777 Main Street, 7th Floor
Moncton, NB E1C 1E9
Fax 506-851-2336
Website .... www.psc-cfp.gc.ca

Employer Background: PSC, an independent agency, appoints qualified persons to and within the Canadian Federal Public Service and develops corporate learning opportunities for professional communities.
New Positions Created (22): Librarian; Forest Sociologist; Realty Asset Planning Officer; Audit Managers / Team Leaders; Registered Nurses; Nurse, Quality Assurance; Environmental Analytical Chemists (2); Spatial Data Analyst; Stock Assessment Biologist, Project Leader; Sr Investment Officer; Senior Marketing & Trade Officer; Development Officers (2); Project Mgr, Developmental; Project Manager, Developmental; Research Scientist, Salmonid Aquaculture; Strategic Development Officers; Account Manager; Nurse; Assistant to Warden, Deputy Warden & Psychologist; Hazardous Materials Officer; General Manager, Atlantic Region; Administrative Assistant.

PUBLIC SERVICE COMMISSION OF CANADA, NEWFOUNDLAND & LABRADOR / PSC
Att: Human Resources Manager
PO Box 8700
St. John's, NF A1B 4J6
Tel. 709-729-5840
Fax 709-729-6234
Website .... www.psc-cfp.gc.ca

Employer Background: PSC, an independent agency, appoints qualified persons to and within the Canadian Federal Public Service and develops corporate learning opportunities for professional communities.
New Positions Created (22): Director of Human Resources; Accounting Clerk; Administrative Officer; Administrative Officer; Assistant Manager; Clerk; Clerk, Human Resources; Clerk / Typist; Clerk / Typist; Clerk / Typist; Data Entry Operators (2); Director, Financial Operations; Director, Information Technology; Director, Regional Services; Division Manager; Executive Director; LAN Administrator; Library Technician; Library Technicians (2); Payroll Clerk; Storekeeper; Associate Director, Human Resources.

PUBLIC SERVICE COMMISSION OF CANADA, NOVA SCOTIA / PSC
Att: Human Resources Manager
1505 Barrington Street
17th Floor, PO Box 1664, CRO
Halifax, NS B3J 3V3

Tel. 902-426-2900
Fax 902-426-0507
Website .... www.psc-cfp.gc.ca

Employer Background: PSC, an independent agency, appoints qualified persons to and within the Canadian Federal Public Service and develops corporate learning opportunities for professional communities.
New Positions Created (12): Command Decision Aid Technology (COMDAT) Systems Engineer; Bilingual Marine Navigation Instructor; Bilingual Secretary, Civil Litigation and Advisory Group; Compliance Promotion Officer; Senior Economic Analyst; Fishery Officers; Acoustic Research Technologists (2); Detachment Assistant; Manager, Program Operations and Implementation; Junior Informatics Analyst (Oracle); Area Aboriginal Programs Coordinator; Manager, Program Operations and Implementations.

PUBLIC SERVICE COMMISSION OF CANADA, NWT / PSC
Att: Human Resources Manager
4914 - 50th Street
3rd Floor, Bellanca Building
Yellowknife, NT X1A 2R1

Fax 867-669-2448
Website .... www.psc-cfp.gc.ca

Employer Background: PSC, an independent agency, appoints qualified persons to and within the Canadian Federal Public Service and develops corporate learning opportunities for professional communities.
New Positions Created (3): IT Help Desk Technicians; Assistant Land Negotiator; Sr Environmental Scientist.

PUBLIC SERVICE COMMISSION OF CANADA, ONTARIO / PSC
Att: Human Resources Manager
1 Front Street West
Toronto, ON M5J 2X5

Tel. 416-973-4636
Fax 416-973-1883
Website .... www.psc-cfp.gc.ca

Employer Background: PSC, an independent agency, appoints qualified persons to and within the Canadian Federal Public Service and develops corporate learning opportunities for professional communities.
New Positions Created (33): Environmental Contaminants Officer; Project Officer; Bilingual Customer Service Representative; Head, Finance and Administration; Head, Central Registry; Pest Management Technician; Electronic Resources Librarian; Grain Inspector; Senior Program Officer; Electrical Engineer; Field Laboratory Technician; Ecosystems Status and Trends Monitoring Specialist; Knowledge Manager; Cloud Physics Support and Data Analyst; Organization Development Consultant; Housing and Property Managers; Tomato Germplasm and Molecular Biology Technician; Translator; Electronic Installation Technolo-

gist; Head, Library Services; Research Scientist, Nematode-Crop Interactions; Senior Science Advisor, Ground Level Ozone; Chief, Cloud Physics Research Division; Civilian Ammunition Technician; Food Microbiologist / Research Scientist; Occupational Health Nurse; Plant Pathologist / Research Scientist; Wastewater Management Research Scientist; Comptroller; Manager, Library and Information Services; Public Affairs Officer; Head, Wildlife Outreach and Liaison; Model Applications Specialist.

PUBLIC SERVICE COMMISSION OF CANADA, ONTARIO / PSC
Att: Human Resources Manager
66 Slater Street, 3rd Floor
Ottawa, ON K1A 0M7

Tel. 613-996-8436
Fax 613-996-8048
Website .... www.psc-cfp.gc.ca

Employer Background: PSC, an independent agency, appoints qualified persons to and within the Canadian Federal Public Service and develops corporate learning opportunities for professional communities.
New Positions Created (140): Deputy Project Manager, Aurora; Research Scientist; Chief, Aircraft Registration and Leasing; International Affairs Specialists; Lead Engineer, Metal and Fibre Communications; Lead Engineer, Sensor Systems; Maritime Helicopter Project (MHP) Certification Engineering Project Manager; Medical Officer; Research Scientist; Senior Nuclear Specialists (2); Senior Specialist / Subject Matter Expert Engineer; Director, Field Epidemiology Training Program; Human Factors Engineering Certification Engineer; Project Managers, Architectural & Engineering Services; Research Analyst; Senior Naval Simulation Engineer; Above-Water Warfare Engineer; Aerospace Electronic Warfare Engineer; Aerospace Weapons Systems Engineer; C41SR Engineer; Land Systems Simulation Engineer; Land Tactical Vehicles Engineer; Manager, Special Initiatives Unit; Quality Assurance Representative / Occupational Development Trainee; Registration Specialist, Quality Management Systems Auditor; Radio Frequency Qualification Facilities Engineer; Aero Mechanical Systems Specialist; Electrical System Certification Specialist; Environmental Protection Officer; Manager and Senior Specialist / Subject Matter Expert; Project Managers, Architectural & Engineering Services; Senior Crossing Engineer; Senior Realty Adviser; Senior Research Officer; Chief, Division of Immunization; Senior Track Engineer; Financial Policy and Systems Officer; Project Managers, Architectural & Engineering Services; Thermal / Structure Qualification Facilities Technologist; Manager, Canadian Explosive Research Laboratory; Senior Methodologist; Avionics System Certification Engineer; Communications System Certification Engineer; Flight Control / Instrument / Electrical System Certification Engineer; Software Certification Engineer; Systems Integration Certification Engineer; Evaluator; Senior Avionics & Electrical Systems Engineer; Senior Evaluator; Senior

Software Certification Engineers (2); Director, Legal Services, General Counsel; Research Scientist / Engineer, Audio Signal Processing; CH146 Health and Usage Monitoring System (HUMS) Engineer; Manager, Conformity Assessment; Manager, Supply (Standards); Manager, Supply (Strategic Standardization); Senior Researcher and Policy Adviser; Biomedical Evaluators; Medical Devices Evaluators; Project Managers, Architectural and Engineering Services; Compliance Officer; Consumer Education Officer; Optical Communications Engineer; Optical Communications Researcher; Public Affairs Officers (2); Research Scientist; Senior Advisor, Compliance; Foreign Service Electronic Technologists; Head, Clinical Unit; Medical Advisor / Evaluators; Program Scientist, Space Environment; Research Engineer; Research Scientist; Aircraft Maintenance Engineer, Avionics Systems; Broadband Wireless Engineer; Business Manager; Historian; Economist; Electrical Engineer; Manager, Spectrum Engineering; Agriculture Specialist; Project Managers, Architectural and Engineering Services; Transportation Accident Investigator, Rail / Pipeline; Senior Project Managers (2); Communications Specialist; Manager, Communications and Marketing; Senior Communications Specialists; Senior Human Resources Advisor; Senior Human Resources Advisor; Chief, Engineering Maintenance Program; Economist; Foreign Service Electronic Technologist; IM Business Manager; Program Scientist, Space Astronomy; Project Manager, Architectural and Engineering Services; Actuarial Analyst; Aircraft Maintenance Engineer, Avionics Systems; Airport Pavement Engineer; Architect; Biologist; Coastal Engineer; Director, Food Services Division; Geotechnical Engineer; Indoor Air Quality Specialist; Medical Advisors / Evaluators; Physicians (6); Senior Bridge Engineer; Senior Financial Managers and Officers, Inventory; Structural Engineer, Conservation; Structural Engineer Team Leader; Asset Manager; Scientific Officer; Flight Simulation Technologist; Client Services Officers; Commissioning and Guidelines Manager; Program Scientist, Space Life Sciences; Realty Manager; Supply Specialist; Business Specialist; Negotiation / Audit Specialist; Economic Policy Analyst; Chief, Emotional Health Programs; Project Manager, Architectural and Engineering Services; Security Education Project Manager; Senior Economist; Supply Team Leaders; Senior Financial Policy and Systems Officer; Biological and Associated Products Evaluator; Pharmaceutical Product Evaluator; Strategic Investment Analysis Advisor; Human Resources Advisor, Employment Equity Groups; Physical Scientist; Research Economist; Senior Policy Advisor, Motor Carrier Safety; Group Leader; Field Epidemiologist; French Language Teachers; Psychologists; Senior Systems Engineer, Voice Telecommunications; Systems Engineer, Voice Telecommunications.

PUBLIC SERVICE COMMISSION OF CANADA, QUEBEC / PSC
Att: Human Resource Manager

200 Rene-Levesque Boulevard West
8th Fl., East Tower, Complexe Guy-Favreau
Montréal, QC H2Z 1X4

Tel. 514-283-2467
Fax 514-496-2404
Website .... www.psc-cfp.gc.ca

Employer Background: PSC, an independent agency, appoints qualified persons to and within the Canadian Federal Public Service and develops corporate learning opportunities for professional communities. *New Positions Created (35):* Real-Time Engineer, Robotics; Senior Systems Analyst; Financial Technician; Manager, International Space Station Commercial Development; Manager, Technology Development (Telecommunications & GNSS); Occupational Health Medical Officer; Optical Design Engineer; Mission Planner; Architect / Junior Project Manager; Database Administrator, Oracle; Flight Surgeon; Ground Segment Project Engineer; Optical Design Engineer; Applied Spectroscopy / Instrumentation Researcher; Earth Observation Application Development Project Officer; Manager, Technology Development (Generic Technology for Satellites and Spacecraft); Manager, Technology Development (Remote Sensing Payload); Manager, Technology Development (Telecommunications & GNSS); Research Scientist; Systems Engineers; Ground Segment Project Engineer; Systems Engineer; Paralegal; Head, Mission Planning; Project Risks and Standards Engineer; Real-Time Robotics Mission Planner; Junior Building Electrical Engineer; Engineer / Research Scientist, Food Biotechnology; Instrumentation and Control Technician; Mechanical Engineer; MSS Flight Software Operations Senior Analyst; Senior Analyst, MSS Operations and Analysis; Head, Mission Planning; Project Risks and Standards Engineer; Signalling Inspector, Department of Transport.

PUBLIC SERVICE COMMISSION OF CANADA, QUEBEC / PSC
Att: Human Resources Manager
901 du Cap Diamant
Room 349, Champlain Harbour Station
Quebec City, QC G1K 4K1

Tel. 418-648-3230
Fax 418-648-4575
Website .... www.psc-cfp.gc.ca

Employer Background: PSC, an independent agency, appoints qualified persons to and within the Canadian Federal Public Service and develops corporate learning opportunities for professional communities. *New Positions Created (26):* Advisor, Conservation of Marine Ecosystems; Biologist, Fish Habitat; Biologist, Native Fisheries Stock Assessment; Specialist, Aerodynamic Studies; Specialist, Electro-Optics And Optronics Sciences; Specialist, Modeling & Simulation; Specialist, Spectral Remote Sensing; Specialist, Exploitation of Hyperspectral Data; Specialist, Spectral Remote Sensing; Spectral-Image Processing Specialist; Workshop Supervisor; Heavy Truck Mechanic; Architect / Assistant Project Manager; Client Services Officers (3); Defence Scientist; Research Scientist, Physical Oceanography; Quality As-

surance Representative; Scientific Coordinator, Aquaculture; Defence Scientist; Halieutic Sciences Statistician; Manager, Marine (Regional Operations); Principal Marine Inspector; Multidisciplinary Hydrographer; Civil and Marine Engineer, Marine Hydraulics; Junior Civil Engineer; Research Scientist, Ecosystems Approach.

PUBLIC SERVICE COMMISSION OF CANADA, SASKATCHEWAN / PSC
Att: Human Resources Manager
1955 Smith Street, Suite 400
Regina, SK S4P 2N8

Tel. 306-780-8851
Fax 306-780-5723
Website .... www.jobs.gc.ca

Employer Background: PSC, an independent agency, appoints qualified persons to and within the Canadian Federal Public Service and develops corporate learning opportunities for professional communities. *New Positions Created (15):* Regional Budget Officer; Silviculture Technician; Branch Administrative Officer; Program Delivery Officer; Operations Inspector, Railway; Regional Project Coordinator; Managers, Funding Services or Transfer Payments; Associate Program Director; Research Officer, Fill Mechanics; Service Centre Director; Agronomy Technician; Bilingual Service Delivery Representative; Firefighter; Maintenance Equipment Labourer; Financial Control Officer.

PUBLIC SERVICE COMMISSION OF CANADA, YUKON / PSC
Att: Human Resources Manager
300 Main Street, Suite 400
Whitehorse, YT Y1A 2B5

Tel. 867-667-3900
Fax 867-668-5033
Website .... www.psc-cfp.gc.ca

Employer Background: PSC, an independent agency, appoints qualified persons to and within the Canadian Federal Public Service and develops corporate learning opportunities for professional communities. *New Positions Created (9):* District Clerks (3); Program Consultant, Aboriginal Head Start; Regional Mgr, Information Mgmnt; Manager, Project Assessment; Environmental Assessment Officer; Land Use Planner; Mgr, Financial Services; Senior Biological Technicians (2); Air Attack Officer.

PUBLIC SERVICE COMMISSION, PEI
Att: Human Resources Manager
PO Box 2000
Charlottetown, PE C1A 7N8

Tel. 902-368-4080
Fax 902-368-4383
Website .... www.gov.pe.ca

Employer Background: The Public Service Commission of PEI manages the human resource needs of the provincial government. *New Positions Created (60):* Liquor Store Clerk; Plumber; Bilingual Speech-Language Pathologist; Director, Business Expansion; Diagnostic Ultrasonographer; Elementary Coordinator; Acute Care Worker; Child Wel-

fare Worker; Critical Care Float Nurse; Director, Patient Services; Medical / University Student Clinical Instructor; Psychologist; Registered Nurse; Speech Language Pathologist; Director, Child and Family Services; Elementary Communication & Information Technology Consultant; Potato Virologist; Registered Nurses; Cook; Programmer Analyst; Teachers, French as a Second Language; Technical Services / Systems Librarian; Manager, Georgetown / Tyne Valley Youth Centres; Regional Services Manager; Social Worker, Child Protection Team; Clinical Dentist; Coordinator, Clinical Services; Director, English Programs; Social Worker; Project Leader / Business Technologist; Provincial Planner; Senior Tax Auditor; Children's Mental Health Clinician; Medical / University Student Clinical Instructor; Critical Care Float Nurse; Nurses; Registered Nurse; Registered Nurses; Social Workers, Child Welfare; Correction / Special Education Coordinator; Grade 6 - 9 Math and Science Consultant; Social Workers, Child Welfare; Chief Librarian; Speech Language Pathologist; Critical Care Float Nurse; Medical / Surgical Float Nurses; Pharmacist; Registered Nurse; Registered Nurse; Clinical Dentist; Diabetes Coordinator / Educator, Provincial Diabetes Program; Irrigation Technician; Registered Nurse; Speech Language Pathologist; Social Workers, Child Welfare; Chief Librarian; Radiation Therapist; Clinical Dentist; Registered Nurses; Auditor.

PUBLIC SERVICE EMPLOYEE RELATIONS COMMISSION, BC / PSERC
Att: Teresa Switzer, Corporate Services
548 Michigan Street
Victoria, BC V8V 1S3

Tel. 250-387-0430
Fax 250-356-8034
Email ..... teresa.switzer@gems3.gov.bc.ca
Website .... www.pserc.gov.bc.ca

Employer Background: PSERC is the central human resources agency for the Government of British Columbia. *New Positions Created (11):* Manager, Human Resources Application Planning; Occupational Health Nurse; Director, Information Management; Assistant Medical Director / Occupational Health Physician; Corporate Business Trainers (2); Executive Director; Financial Operations Clerk; Branch Secretary; Project Consultant; Rehabilitation and Benefits Clerks (2); Administrative Assistant.

PUBLISHING PLUS LTD.
Att: Human Resources Manager
1280 Old Innes Road, Unit 805
Ottawa, ON K1B 5M7

Tel. 613-744-2617
Fax 613-744-7461
Website .... www.publishingplus.com

Employer Background: Established in 1990, Publishing Plus Ltd. is a technical publishing service bureau, serving government and private sector clients. *New Positions Created (6):* Customer Service Representatives; Desktop Publisher; Layout Proofreader; Print Shop Manager; Sales Representatives; Senior Graphic Designer.

PULP & PAPER RESEARCH INSTITUTE OF CANADA / PAPRICAN
Att: Joanne Bacher
570 St. Jean Boulevard
Pointe-Claire, QC H9R 3J9
Tel. 514-630-4100
Fax 514-630-4110
Email .... jbacher@paprican.ca
Website .... www.paprican.ca
Employer Background: Paprican is a pulp and paper research and education organization, operating laboratories and pilot plants in Quebec and British Columbia. The organization has 340 employees. *New Positions Created (4):* Vice-President, Administration and Secretary-Treasurer; Vice-President, Research and Education; Vice-President of Business Development; Postdoctoral Position, Molecular Genetics.

PURATOS CANADA, INC.
Att: Operations Manager
5690 Timberlea Boulevard
Mississauga, ON L4W 4M6
Tel. 905-624-7500
Fax 905-624-2085
Website .... www.puratos.com
Employer Background: Puratos develops and produces quality ingredients for the baking, confectionery and chocolate industries. *New Positions Created (2):* Production Supervisor; Purchasing Coordinator.

PURCELL ENERGY LTD.
Att: Lossie Cavero
250 - 6th Avenue SW, Suite 950
Calgary, AB T2P 3H7
Tel. 403-269-5803
Fax 403-264-1336
Email .... info@purcellenergy.com
Website .... www.purcellenergy.com
Employer Background: Purcell Energy Ltd. is a natural gas and crude oil exploration company. *New Positions Created (3):* Engineering / Operations Assistant; Controller; Production / Revenue Accountant.

PURDY'S CHOCOLATES
Att: Human Resources
2777 Kingsway
Vancouver, BC V5R 5H7
Fax 604-454-2701
Email .... resumes@purdys.com
Website .... www.purdys.com
Employer Background: Purdy's Chocolates manufactures and retails premium chocolates. *New Positions Created (8):* Store Managers; Warehouse Manager; Retail Direct Manager; CFO; Production Supervisor; Production / Inventory Coordinator; Store Managers; Administration Clerk.

PURE TECHNOLOGIES INC.
Att: Lindsay Staniforth
340 - 12th Avenue SW, Suite 1050
Calgary, AB T2R 1L5
Tel. 403-266-6794
Fax 403-266-6570
Email ... lindsay.staniforth@soundprint.com
Website .... www.soundprint.com

Employer Background: Pure Technologies Inc. manufactures, installs and operates computer-based continuous structural monitoring systems for buildings, parking structures, bridges, pipelines and other structures. *New Positions Created (9):* Data Processor; Operations and Marketing Assistant; Project Engineer / Technologist; Senior Electronic / Design Engineer or Technologist; Project Manager; Project Engineer; Data Processor, Geophysical / Engineering; Network Analyst; Software Developer.

PUREEDGE SOLUTIONS INC.
Att: Human Resources
4396 West Saanich Road
Victoria, BC V8Z 3E9
Tel. 250-479-8334
Fax 250-708-8010
Email .... jobs@pureedge.com
Website .... www.pureedge.com
Employer Background: PureEdge Solutions Inc. is an e-commerce security software development firm. *New Positions Created (7):* Project Analyst; Senior Software Developer; Customer Support Manager; Quality Assurance Officer; Quality Assurance Programmer; Technical Writer; Software Developers.

PUROLATOR COURIER LTD.
Att: Senior Human Resources Manager
424 Aviation Road NE
Calgary, AB T2E 8H6
Fax 403-730-4215
Email .... careers@purolator.com
Website .... www.purolator.com
Employer Background: Purolator Courier Ltd., a subsidiary of Canada Post Corp., is one of Canada's largest overnight courier companies. *New Positions Created (2):* Regional Sales Manager; Sales Executive.

PUROLATOR COURIER LTD.
Att: Human Resources
62 Vulcan Street
Toronto, ON M9W 1L2
Tel. 416-241-4496
Fax 416-241-8955
Email .... tcousins@purolator.com
Website .... www.purolator.com
Employer Background: Purolator Courier Ltd., a subsidiary of Canada Post Corp., is one of Canada's largest overnight courier companies. *New Positions Created (9):* Control Room Representative; Data Entry Assistant; Loss Prevention Professionals; Electrician; Garage Foreperson; Industrial Millwright; Truck and Coach Technician; Loss Prevention Assistant Manager; Loss Prevention Professionals.

PUROLATOR COURIER LTD.
Att: Debbie Kamino, Human Resources
5995 Avebury Road
Mississauga, ON L5R 3T8
Tel. 905-712-1084
Fax 905-712-6741
Email .... dkamino@purolator.com
Website .... www.purolator.com
Employer Background: Purolator Courier Ltd., a subsidiary of Canada Post Corp., is

one of Canada's largest overnight courier companies. *New Positions Created (7):* Accountants; Communications Manager; Direct Marketing Manager; Finance Manager; Financial Analysts; Industrial Engineers; Senior Buyer.

PYROGENESIS INC.
Att: Human Resources Manager
1744 William Street, Suite 200
Montréal, QC H3J 1R4
Tel. 514-937-0002
Fax 514-937-5757
Email .... personnel@pyrogenesis.com
Website .... www.pyrogenesis.com
Employer Background: Founded in 1992, PyroGenesis Inc. designs and fabricates waste treatment systems and produces high-performance materials related to thermal spraying technology. *New Positions Created (3):* Marketing and Sales Analyst; Materials Engineer; Mechanical Engineer.

Q-MEDIA SERVICES CORPORATION
Att: Susan Kopeschny, Assistant
13566 Maycrest Way
Richmond, BC V6V 2J7
Tel. 604-303-6630
Fax 604-232-5299
Email .... skopeschny@qmedia.ca
Website .... www.qmedia.ca
Employer Background: Q-Media Services Corporation is a $200 million supply chain management company. *New Positions Created (3):* Account Manager; Internet Services Manager; Fulfillment Supervisor.

Q-TRON LTD.
Att: Human Resources Manager
3855 - 64th Avenue SE
Calgary, AB T2C 2V5
Tel. 403-279-0805
Fax 403-236-2555
Email .... qtncareers@wabtec.com
Website .... www.q-tron.com
Employer Background: Founded in 1974, Q-Tron Ltd. (a division of Wabtec Corporation) designs and manufactures electronic equipment for railroads. *New Positions Created (4):* QA Supervisor; Quality Assurance Technician; HR Generalist; Buyer / Planner.

QCA SYSTEMS LTD.
Att: Human Resources Manager
7355 - 72nd Street, Suite 16
Delta, BC V4G 1L5
Tel. 604-940-0868
Fax 604-940-0869
Website .... www.qca-systems.com
Employer Background: QCA Systems Ltd. is an industrial systems integrator. *New Positions Created (2):* PLC Automation Specialist; PLC Automation Specialists.

QDESIGN CORPORATION
Att: Human Resources Manager
1035 Cambie Street
Vancouver, BC V6B 5L7
Tel. 604-688-1525
Fax 604-688-1524

Email .... jobs@qdesign.com
Website .... www.qdesign.com
Employer Background: Established in 1995, QDesign Corporation provides advanced digital audio compression technologies. *New Positions Created (8):* DSP Engineer, Audio Coding Algorithms; Software Engineer, Cross Platform Development; Software Engineer, Mac Applications; Software Engineer, Plug - In Technology; Software Engineer, Windows Application; Technical Lead, Application Development; Technical Lead, Audio Coding Algorithms; Technical Support and Systems Coordinator.

QJUNCTION TECHNOLOGY INC.
Att: Human Resources Manager
405 King Street North
Waterloo, ON N2J 2Z4
Tel. 519-725-8621
Fax 519-885-7954
Email .... resumes@qjunction.com
Website .... www.qjunction.com
Employer Background: QJunction Technology Inc. is a voice portal infrastructure provider, developing proprietary patent-pending speech engine suites. *New Positions Created (6):* GUI Software Developers; Intermediate Software Developers; QA Specialist; Quality Assurance Leader; Senior Software Developers; System Administrator.

QLT INC.
Att: Human Resources Department
887 Great Northern Way
Vancouver, BC V5T 4T5
Tel. 604-707-7000
Fax 604-707-7308
Email .... hr@qltinc.com
Website .... www.qltinc.com
Employer Background: QLT Inc. is a leader in photodynamic therapy and the emerging field of light-activated drug treatments. *New Positions Created (52):* Associate II; Central Stores Operator; Technical Writer; Manager, Clinical Archive; Document Management Coordinator; Manager, Commercial Operations ERP Support; Senior Manager / Associate Director; Administrative Assistant, Investor Relations; Analyst III, Quality Control Laboratories; ERP - Finance Sustainment Analyst; Clinical Archive Document Coordinator; Clinical Archivist; Compensation Analyst; Computer Systems Validation Associate; Senior Clinical Quality Associate; Analyst II, Quality Control Laboratories; Biostatistician; Clinical Data Associate; Compliance Manager; Manager, Technical Services; Scientist I, Formulation Sciences; Senior Manager / Associate Director, API; Training Coordinator, ERP; Administrative Assistant, Corporate Development; Administrative Assistant, Preclinical Pharmacology; Associate Director, API Process Sciences; Calibration & Validation Technician I; Calibration & Validation Technician III; Clinical Data Manager; Director, Director, Analytical Development; Director, Formulation Sciences; Health & Safety Coordinator; Human Resources Information Coordinator; Manager, Formulation Process Sciences; Manager / Senior Manager, Global

Market Research & Evaluation; Mechanical Technician III; Research Associate I-II, Ocular; Scientist I, Formulation Process Sciences; SCM - MM Consultant; SCM - PP Consultant; Tax Analyst; Technician III / Research Associate I; Quality Assurance Associate; Administrative Assistant; FI / CO Consultant; Calibration and Validation Technician III; Director of Information Technology; Director, Preclinical Pharmacology; Scientist, Ocular; Senior Quality Assurance Associate, Analytical; Senior Quality Assurance Associate, Microbiology.

QUACK.COM
Att: Human Resources Manager
450 Phillip Street
Waterloo, ON N2L 5J2
Tel. 519-883-0222
Email .... hr@quack.com
Website .... www.quack.com
Employer Background: Quack.com develops voice-to-web technology. *New Positions Created (7):* C++ DAS Engineer; Communication Engineer; Executive Producer / Director of Speech Production; Senior Software QA; Senior UNIX System Administrator; Speech Designers; Speech Tool Designer.

QUADRA CHEMICALS LTD.
Att: Human Resources Manager
370 Joseph Carrier
Vaudreuil-Dorion, QC J7V 5V5
Fax 450-424-9458
Website .... www.quadra.ca
Employer Background: Quadra Chemicals Ltd. is a national distribution company. *New Positions Created (4):* Logistics Coordinator; Lotus Notes Programmer; Network Administrator; Warehouse Positions.

QUADRUS DEVELOPMENT INC.
Att: Human Resources Manager
3553 - 31st Street NW
Suite 200, Alistair Ross Technology Centre
Calgary, AB T2L 2K7
Tel. 403-257-0850
Fax 403-720-2610
Website .... www.quadrus.com
Employer Background: Quadrus Development Inc. specializes in custom software development and IT consulting and training. *New Positions Created (6):* Data Warehousing Specialist; Software Engineers; Systems Administrator; Communications Manager; Data Warehousing Specialist; Software Engineers.

QUAKE TECHNOLOGIES INC.
Att: Human Resources
1335 Carling Avenue, Suite 101
Ottawa, ON K1Z 8N8
Tel. 613-724-6651
Fax 613-724-6683
Email .... careers@quaketech.com
Website .... www.quaketech.com
Employer Background: Quake Technologies Inc. develops physical layer chips for high-speed optical networks. *New Positions Created (11):* CAD Specialist; Device Engineer;

Electro-Optical Interface Design Engineer; IC Product Manager; Senior MarComm / Public Relations Specialist; Digital ASIC Design Engineers; IC Layout Design Engineers; Mixed Signal IC Design Engineers; IC Applications Engineers; IC Product Test Engineers; Mixed Signal IC Design Engineers.

QUAKER OATS COMPANY OF CANADA LIMITED
Att: Manager, Human Resources
Quaker Park
Peterborough, ON K9J 7B2
Tel. 705-743-6330
Fax 705-876-4141
Website .... www.quakeroats.ca
Employer Background: The Quaker Oats Company of Canada Limited manufactures and markets oat-based food products and Gatorade beverages for retail and foodservice industries. *New Positions Created (5):* Plant Accountant and Cost Accountant; Human Resource Manager; Electrical Systems Coordinator; Labour Relations Manager; Occupational Health Nurse.

QUALITY GOODS IMD INC.
Att: Allan
235 Migneron Street
St-Laurent, QC H4T 1W8
Tel. 514-733-8285
Fax 514-342-7773
Email .... allan@qualitygoods.net
Employer Background: Quality Goods IMD Inc. supplies products to destination resorts. *New Positions Created (13):* Freelance Artists; Sales Executive; Inside / Outside Sales Position; Customer Service; Patternmaker / Markermaker; Regional Sales Manager; Clerk; Contractor Coordinator; Quality Control Position; Artist; Credit and Collections Manager; Warehouse / Distribution Manager; Customer Support Representative.

QUEBEC STUDENT HEALTH ALLIANCE / ASEQ
Att: Human Resources Coordinator
2045 Stanley
Montréal, QC H3A 2V4
Tel. 514-844-4423
Fax 514-221-4882
Employer Background: ASEQ provides health services to over 150,000 university students. *New Positions Created (4):* Controller; Customer Service Receptionist; Database / Network Administrator; Executive Administrative Assistant.

QUEBECOR WORLD PRINTPAK
Att: Human Resources
3500 - 19th Street NE, Unit 5
Calgary, AB T2E 8B9
Fax 403-250-1273
Email .... careers@quebecor-printpak.com
Website ...... www.quebecor-printpak.com
Employer Background: Quebecor World Printpak is a leading digital print-on-demand company. *New Positions Created (4):* Customer Service Representative; Database

and Applications Support Specialist; Inventory Analyst; Quality Manager.

QUEEN ELIZABETH II HEALTH SCIENCES CENTRE / QEII
Att: Human Resources
1278 Tower Road
1st Floor, Bethune Building West
Halifax, NS B3H 2Y9
Tel. 902-473-5757
Fax 902-473-8499
Email .... opportunities@cdha.nshealth.ca
Website www.qe2-hsc.ns.ca
Employer Background: QEII is a major adult referral hospital for the Maritime provinces, with 1,100 beds and 6,500 staff members. *New Positions Created (17):* Director, Cancer Care Program; Registered Nurse, CCU/ IMCU; Registered Nurse, Orthopaedics; Registered Nurses, General Medicine (4); Registered Nurse, Ophthalmology OR; Registered Nurses, Emergency (2); Registered Nurses, Family Medicine Centre; Laboratory Technologist II, Laboratory Shared Services; LIS Database Coordinator, Pathology & Laboratory Medicine; Registered Nurse (2), Urology; Registered Nurse (6), Medicine; Registered Nurse, Stroke Unit; Registered Nurse, Transitional Care Unit; Registered Nurses (2), Medical Surgical ICU; Registered Nurses (2), Vascular/Surgery; Registered Nurses (3), Medical/Surgical / Neuro ICU; Staff Pharmacist.

QUEEN'S UNIVERSITY, CANCER RESEARCH LABORATORIES
Att: John Singleton,
Administrative Assistant
3rd Floor, Botterell Hall
Kingston, ON K7L 3N6
Fax 613-533-6830
Email .... singletn@post.queensu.ca
Website .... www.queensu.ca
Employer Background: Founded in 1841, Queen's University has over 13,000 full-time students and 2,950 faculty and staff members. *New Positions Created (3):* Research Technician; Business Assistant; Research Technician.

QUEEN'S UNIVERSITY, DEPARTMENT OF HUMAN RESOURCES
Att: Employment &
Employee Relations Officer
Kingston, ON K7L 3N6
Tel. 613-533-6000
Fax 613-533-6196
Email .... hradmin@post.queensu.ca
Website .... www.queensu.ca
Employer Background: Founded in 1841, Queen's University has over 13,000 full-time students and 2,950 faculty and staff members. *New Positions Created (3):* Assistant Manager, Grounds; Director of Environmental Health and Safety; Residence Life Coordinators (5).

QUEEN'S UNIVERSITY, FACULTY OF EDUCATION
Att: Susan Lloyd, Acting Coordinator of Continuing Teacher Education
Kingston, ON K7L 3N6

Tel. 613-533-6210
Fax 613-533-6307
Website .... www.educ.queensu.ca
Employer Background: Founded in 1841, Queen's University has over 13,000 full-time students and 2,950 faculty and staff members. *New Positions Created (4):* Instructors, Online / On-site; Assistant Professor, Educational Policy Studies; Assistant Professor, Elementary Social Studies; Instructor, Outdoor and Experiential Education.

QUEEN'S UNIVERSITY, JOSEPH S. STAUFFER LIBRARY
Att: Paul Wiens, University Librarian
Kingston, ON K7L 5C4
Fax 613-533-6362
Website .... www.queensu.ca
Employer Background: Founded in 1841, Queen's University has over 13,000 full-time students and 2,950 faculty and staff members. *New Positions Created (2):* Outreach Services Librarian, Bracken Health Sciences Library; Law Librarian & Professor of Law.

QUEEN'S UNIVERSITY, NATIONAL CANCER INSTITUTE OF CANADA (CLINICAL TRIALS GROUP) / NCIC
Att: Operations Manager
84 Barrie Street, Suite 82
Kingston, ON K7L 3N6
Tel. 613-545-2070
Website .... www.ncic.cancer.ca
Employer Background: NCIC provides support for cancer research and related programs undertaken at Canadian universities, hospitals and research institutions. *New Positions Created (3):* Study Coordinator; Biostatistician; SAS / Oracle Programmer.

QUEENSWAY-CARLETON HOSPITAL
Att: Director of Human Resources
3045 Baseline Road
Nepean, ON K2H 8P4
Tel. 613-721-4702
Fax 613-721-4737
Email .... jobs@qch.on.ca
Website .... www.qch.on.ca
Employer Background: Queensway-Carleton Hospital offers a broad range of programs and services to the communities of Ottawa-Carleton and the West Ottawa Valley. *New Positions Created (4):* Business Analyst, Nursing Informatics; Safety / Disability Management Coordinator; Manager of Financial Services; Manager, Processing and Quality Control, SPD Department.

QUESTAIR TECHNOLOGIES INC.
Att: Human Resources Manager
6961 Russell Avenue
Burnaby, BC V5J 4R8
Tel. 604-454-1134
Fax 604-454-1137
Email .... jobs@questairinc.com
Website .... www.questairinc.com
Employer Background: QuestAir Technologies Inc. is a manufacturer of compact gas separation systems. *New Positions Created (45):* Buyer; Lab Hand; Sales Representative;

IT Manager; Materials Scientist / Mechanical Engineer; Mechanical Engineer; Production Technician; Leader, Manufacturing Design; Engineering Technologist, Test / Calibration; Human Resources Coordinator; Manufacturing Technologist; Mechanical Technologist, Compact Gas Systems; Test / Calibration Engineer; Test Engineer, Compact Gas Systems; Test Technologist, Compact Gas Systems; Process Engineer, Industrial Gas Systems; Quality Assurance Inspector; Payroll and Benefits Administrator; Product Engineer, Compact Gas; Senior Design Engineer, PSA Machine Design; Test Equipment Design Engineer; Assembly Lead Hand, Industrial Gas; Junior Test Technician; Quality Assurance Inspector; Administrative Assistant; Assembly Lead Hand, Industrial Gas; Design Engineer; Process Engineer; Receptionist; Business Development and Product Manager, Compact Gas Systems; Test / Calibration Engineer; Compression Leader, Industrial Gas Systems; Design Engineer, Industrial Hydrogen; Facilities Manager; Laminate Engineer; Laminate Packaging Engineer; Laminate Technologist; Mechanical Engineer, Compact Gas Systems; Process Engineer, Industrial Gas Systems; Project Engineer, Industrial Gas Systems; Senior Engineering Leader; Senior Mechanical Engineer; Test Engineer; Test Equipment Design Engineer; Test Technologist, Compact Gas Systems.

QUICK LINK COMMUNICATIONS LTD.
Att: Human Resources
311 - 6th Avenue SW, Suite 1505
Calgary, AB T2P 3H2
Tel. 403-265-5558
Fax 403-265-4411
Email .... careers@qlccom.com
Website .... www.qlccom.com
Employer Background: QLC is a satellite-based telecom company. *New Positions Created (9):* Sales Engineer; Sales Professional; Application Engineer; Marketing Assistant; Process Analyst; Director of Marketing and Corporate Development; Sales Engineer; Sales Positions; Director of Sales.

QUICKMILL INC.
Att: Controller
760 Rye Street, Suite 11
Peterborough, ON K9J 6W9
Tel. 705-745-2961
Fax 705-745-8130
Email .... hr@quickmill.com
Website .... www.quickmill.com
Employer Background: Quickmill Inc. designs and manufactures 3-axis, large-area, CNC gantry machining centres. *New Positions Created (4):* Accountant / Analyst; Electrical and Mechanical Assemblers; Electrical and Mechanical Customer Service Advisors; Electrical Engineer.

QUINTE & DISTRICT REHABILITATION INC.
Att: Human Resources Manager
11 Bayridge Road
Suite 106, Harbourview Business Centre
Belleville, ON K8P 3P6

Tel. 613-966-5015
Fax 613-966-6695
Email .... qdrehab@reach.net

Employer Background: Quinte & District Rehabilitation Inc. is a therapist-owned company, providing health services to clients throughout Hastings and Prince Edward Counties. *New Positions Created (4):* Social Workers; Various Healthcare Positions; Healthcare Positions; Social Workers.

QUINTE HEALTHCARE CORPORATION / QHC
Att: Linda Mitchell, CHRP, HR Director
265 Dundas Street East
Belleville, ON K8N 5A9
Tel. 613-969-5511
Fax 613-969-1451
Email .... lmitchell@qhc.on.ca
Website .... www.qhc.on.ca

Employer Background: QHC consists of four fully-accredited hospitals southeastern Ontario. *New Positions Created (9):* Physiotherapists; Coordinator, Rehabilitation Therapies; Speech Language Pathologist; Echocardiography Technologist; Manager - Medicine; Manager - Rehabilitation Services; Physiotherapists (4); Registered Nurses; Social Worker.

QUORUM INFORMATION SYSTEMS INC.
Att: Human Resources Manager
2451 Dieppe Avenue, Suite 100
Calgary, AB T3E 7K1
Tel. 403-777-0035
Email .... hr@quorumis.com
Website .... www.quorumis.com

Employer Background: Quorum Information Systems Inc. is an IT company, providing computer solutions to vehicle dealerships. *New Positions Created (7):* Network Technicians; Accounting / Business Software Implementer; Intermediate Systems Support Technician; Branch Manager; IT Sales Representative; IT Technician, Team Leader; IT Technicians (3).

R. CARMICHAEL LTD.
Att: Jean Desautels, HR Director
3822 Courtrai Avenue
Montréal, QC H3S 1C1
Tel. 514-735-4361
Fax 514-735-2300
Email .... jdesautels@carmichael-eng.ca
Website .... www.carmichael-eng.ca

Employer Background: Founded in 1922, R. Carmichael Ltd. employs over 100 specialists and provides technical services for the air conditioning, refrigeration, ventilation, mechanical piping, natural gas and heating industries. *New Positions Created (2):* Sales Representative; Human Resource Generalist.

R.J. BURNSIDE & ASSOCIATES LTD.
Att: Human Resources Manager
8500 Torbram Road, Suite 56
Brampton, ON L6T 5C6
Tel. 905-793-9239
Fax 905-793-5018

Email .... bds@rjburnside.com
Website .... www.rjburnside.com

Employer Background: Established in 1970, R.J. Burnside & Associates Ltd. is a consulting engineering firm, specializing in municipal design, water supply, wastewater treatment, stormwater management, land development, transportation, bridges and structures. *New Positions Created (3):* Building Sciences Positions; CADD Technicians; Design Engineer / Technologist.

R.J. MCKEE ENGINEERING LTD.
Att: Francois Dussault, PEng, Vice-President and Electrical Section Head
1785 Woodward Drive
Ottawa, ON K2C 0P9
Tel. 613-723-9585
Fax 613-723-9584
Email .... francoisd@rjmeng.com
Website .... www.rjmeng.com

Employer Background: Established in 1975, R.J. McKee Engineering Ltd. provides mechanical and electrical engineering design services for commercial facilities and building systems. *New Positions Created (2):* Senior Electrical Engineer; Mechanical and Electrical Field Inspectors.

R.L. BREWS LTD.
Att: Personnel Department
10810 - 119th Street
Edmonton, AB T5H 3P2
Tel. 780-452-3730
Fax 780-455-4422
Email .... rlbrews@rlbrews.com
Website .... www.rlbrews.com

Employer Background: R.L. Brews Ltd. is a mid-sized supplier of industrial electrical products, with 60 employees. *New Positions Created (3):* Technical Representatives, Electrical Control and Automation; Electrical Engineers; Inside Sales Supervisor.

R.L. BREWS LTD.
Att: C. Macgregor
4910 Builders Road SE
PO Box 5340, Station A
Calgary, AB T2H 1X6
Tel. 403-243-1144
Fax 403-243-2975
Email .... rlbrews@rlbrews.com
Website .... www.rlbrews.com

Employer Background: R.L. Brews Ltd. is a mid-sized supplier of industrial electrical products, with 60 employees. *New Positions Created (2):* Industrial Electrical Inside Salesperson; Inside Sales Representative.

R. NICHOLLS DISTRIBUTORS INC.
Att: Human Resources Department
2475, de la Province
Longueuil, QC J4G 1G3
Tel. 450-442-9300
Fax 450-442-9581
Email .... ressourcesh@rnicholls.com
Website .... www.rnicholls.com

Employer Background: Founded in 1980, R. Nicholls Distributors Inc. supplies law enforcement products to Canadian police and

security agencies. *New Positions Created (2):* Customer Service Representative; Sales Representative.

R.V. ANDERSON ASSOCIATES LTD.
Att: Human Resources
2001 Sheppard Avenue East, Suite 400
Toronto, ON M2J 4Z8
Tel. 416-497-8600
Fax 416-497-0342
Email .... hresources@rvanderson.com
Website .... www.rvanderson.com

Employer Background: R.V. Anderson Associates Limited is a consulting engineering and technology management firm. *New Positions Created (12):* Billing Coordinator; Intermediate Environmental Engineer / Project Manager; Instrumentation and Control Technologist; Professional Engineer; Bridge Engineer; Chief Structural Engineer; CAD Designers; CAD Designers; Land Development Designer; Transportation Project Manager; Senior Electrical Engineer; Senior Environmental Engineers (2).

RADARSAT INTERNATIONAL
Att: Human Resources
13800 Commerce Parkway
MacDonald Dettwiler Building
Richmond, BC V6V 2J3
Tel. 604-231-5000
Fax 604-231-4999
Email .... jobs@rsi.ca
Website .... www.rsi.ca

Employer Background: Radarsat International provides data products, information services and national information networks based on satellite imagery. *New Positions Created (2):* Geo-Spatial Project Specialist; Market Analyst.

RADIANT COMMUNICATIONS
Att: Human Resources Manager
885 West Georgia Street, Suite 1660
Vancouver, BC V6C 3E8
Tel. 604-257-0500
Fax 604-608-0999
Email .... vancouver@radiant.net
Website .... www.radiant.net

Employer Background: Established in 1996, Radiant Communications offers Internet services, including high-speed access, web hosting and e-commerce applications, to over 7,500 businesses and government agencies throughout North America. *New Positions Created (8):* Office Manager; Receptionist; French Tech Support Representative; Bilingual Technical Support Representative; Marketing Manager; Web Applications Developer; Account Manager; Accounts Receivable Collections Team Leader.

RADIANT COMMUNICATIONS
Att: Human Resources Manager
125 - 9th Avenue SE, Suite 1810
Calgary, AB T2G 0P8
Tel. 403-303-2729
Fax 403-303-2723
Email .... calgary@radiant.net
Website .... www.radiant.net

Employer Background: Established in 1996, Radiant Communications offers Internet services, including high-speed access, web hosting and e-commerce applications, to over 7,500 businesses and government agencies throughout North America. *New Positions Created (20):* Channel Manager; Applications Developer; Account Manager, Channel Partners; Administrative Assistant; Network Technician; Sales Coordinator; Senior Account Manager; Senior Sales Engineer; Account Executive; Business Development Manager; Marketing Coordinator; Media Planner / Buyer; Product Delivery Manager; Product Manager; Project Manager; Senior Account Manager; Senior Sales Engineer; Technical Service Specialist; Unix Systems Administrator; Web Application Developer.

RADIANT COMMUNICATIONS
Att: Human Resources Manager
3650 Victoria Park Avenue, Suite 102
Toronto, ON M2H 3P7
Tel. 416-490-8770
Fax 416-490-8976
Email .... toronto@radiant.net
Website .... www.radiant.net
Employer Background: Established in 1996, Radiant Communications offers Internet services, including high-speed access, web hosting and e-commerce applications to over 7,500 businesses and government agencies throughout North America. *New Positions Created (5):* Receptionist / Office Administrator; Account Mgr; Channel Mgr; Receptionist; Bilingual Sales Coordinator.

RADICAL ENTERTAINMENT
Att: Human Resources Manager
369 Terminal Avenue, 8th Floor
Vancouver, BC V6A 4C4
Tel. 604-688-0606
Fax 604-685-0298
Email .... resumes@radical.ca
Website .... www.radical.ca
Employer Background: Radical Entertainment is a leading developer of interactive video games, with 160 employees. *New Positions Created (27):* 3D Modeler / Texture Artist; Lead Animator; Texture Artist; PS2 Graphics Library Programmer; Recruiter / HR Generalist; Business Development Manager; Game Project Manager; AI Programmer; Animator; Research Programmer; Art Director; Content Pipeline Programmer; Game Designer; Gamecube Game Programmer; Lead Game Programmer; Platform Specialist Graphics Programmer; Playstation 2 Game Programmer; Technical Director; Technical Project Manager; XBox Game Programmer; Character Modeler; Embedded Systems Software Developer; Graphics Programmer, Tools; Intermediate / Senior Programmer; Producer; Senior Animator; Texture Artist.

RAM COMPUTER GROUP INC.
Att: Human Resources Manager
3280 Langstaff Road
Vaughan, ON L4K 5B6
Tel. 905-760-7559

Fax 905-760-7970
Email .... hr@ramco.ca
Website .... www.ramco.ca
Employer Background: RAM Computer Group Inc. is a supplier of computer products and integration services, with over 300 employees in twelve cities nationwide. *New Positions Created (6):* Purchasing Assistant; Collections Officer; Inside Sales Representatives; Junior Purchaser / Operations Assistant; Marketing Services Manager; Senior Client Manger.

RAMADA PLAZA HOTEL HARBOURFRONT
Att: Victor Clementino, Executive Chef
1 Johnson Street
Kingston, ON K7L 5H7
Tel. 613-549-8100
Website .... www.ramada.ca
Employer Background: The Ramada Plaza Hotel Harbourfront is a 127-room facility. *New Positions Created (3):* Banquet Chef; Sous Chef; Maintenance Helper.

RAMCO ELECTRICAL CONSULTING LTD.
Att: Karen Wilson, Office Administrator
744 - 4th Avenue SW, 5th Floor
Calgary, AB T2P 3T4
Email .... wilson@optimaepc.com
Website .... www.ramcoelectrical.com
Employer Background: Ramco Electrical Consulting Ltd. is an electrical and instrumentation engineering and inspection company. *New Positions Created (4):* Control Systems Personnel; Energy Management Personnel; Inspections Personnel; Power Engineering and Design Personnel.

RAMCOR GROUP
Att: Personnel Department
55 Innovation Drive
Flamborough, ON L9H 7L8
Fax 905-689-0133
Employer Background: The Ramcor Group includes Arcor Windows Inc., Valcor Inc., Icor Installations Inc. and Innovacor Manufacturing Inc. *New Positions Created (3):* Inside Sales Representative; Production Workers; Truck Driver.

RATIONAL SOFTWARE CORPORATION
Att: Human Resources Manager
555 Legget Drive, Suite 222
Kanata, ON K2K 2X3
Tel. 613-599-8581
Fax 613-599-7147
Email .... kevinm@rational.com
Website .... www.rational.com
Employer Background: Rational Software Corporation is an e-development company, helping organizations develop and deploy software for e-business, e-infrastructure and e-devices. *New Positions Created (14):* Sales Engineer; Software Development Manager; Suite Product Manager; Technical Documentation Expert; Senior Software Engineer; Senior Software Engineering Spe-

cialist; Senior Software Quality Engineer; Software Tester / Engineer; Account Executive; Build Engineer; Program Manager; Software Engineers; Technical Support Engineers (2); Technical Writer.

RAVEN TOURS
Att: Human Resources Manager
PO Box 2435
Yellowknife, NT X1A 2P8
Tel. 867-873-4776
Fax 867-873-4856
Email ..... humanresources@raventours.yk.com
Website .... www.raventours.yk.com
Employer Background: Established in 1981, Raven Tours specializes in Northern Lights tours in the Canadian north, as well as summer tours and cruise programs in the western arctic. *New Positions Created (2):* Comptroller; Manager, Accounting Services.

RAYLO CHEMICALS INC.
Att: Human Resources
1021 Hayter Road
Edmonton, AB T6S 1A1
Fax 780-472-8189
Email .... resumes@raylo.laporteplc.com
Website .... www.laporteplc.com
Employer Background: Raylo Chemicals Inc., a Laporte Fine Chemicals company, manufactures pharmaceutical actives and intermediates for international markets. *New Positions Created (7):* Chemical Plant Operators; Laboratory Technologists; Chemical Plant Operators; Laboratory Technologists, Laboratory Manufacturing / Quality Control; Senior Analytical Chemist; Commercial Officer; Purchasing Assistant.

RAYMARK INTEGRATED RETAIL SOLUTIONS
Att: Human Resources
8375 Mayrand
Montréal, QC H4P 2E2
Tel. 514-737-0941
Fax 514-737-0041
Email .... careers@raymarkx.com
Website .... www.raymarkx.com
Employer Background: Raymark Integrated Retail Solutions offers retailers and e-tailers an integrated, scalable and modular software suite through partnerships with bluechip companies, including Microsoft, IBM, NCR and Wincor-Nixdorf. *New Positions Created (4):* Customer Service Technician; Database Administrator; Programmer Clippers (2); Systems Architect, E-Commerce.

RAYMOND JAMES LTD.
Att: Human Resources
601 West Hastings Street, Suite 1000
Vancouver, BC V6B 5E2
Tel. 604-654-1111
Fax 604-654-7362
Email .... resumes@raymondjames.ca
Website .... www.raymondjames.ca
Employer Background: Raymond James Ltd. is a full-service investment dealer, with branches across Canada. *New Positions Created (8):* Accounting Clerk; Portfolio Serv-

ices Administrator; Financial Analyst; Systems Support Assistant; Administrative Assistant; Mutual Fund Administrator; Executive Assistant; Registration Clerk.

RAYTHEON SYSTEMS CANADA LTD.
Att: Human Resources Manager
13951 Bridgeport Road
Richmond, BC V6V 1J6
Tel. 604-279-5600
Fax 604-821-5100
Email .... rmd_hr@raytheon.com
Website .... www.raytheon.ca
Employer Background: Raytheon Systems Canada Ltd. provides technological solutions to the defence and commercial electronics, business aviation and special mission aircraft sectors. *New Positions Created (7):* Manager, Engineering Programs; Manager 1, Financial Accounting; Lotus Notes Administrator; PeopleSoft Technical Support Representative; Software Engineers; System Engineers; Technical Support Specialist.

RAYTHEON SYSTEMS CANADA LTD.
Att: Human Resources
919 - 72nd Avenue NE
Calgary, AB T2E 8N9
Tel. 403-295-6900
Fax 403-295-6690
Email .... hr@raytheon-ssd.com
Website .... www.raytheon.ca
Employer Background: Raytheon Systems provides technological solutions to the defence and commercial electronics, business aviation and special mission aircraft sectors. *New Positions Created (2):* Contract Administrator; Radar Engineer.

RAYTHEON SYSTEMS CANADA LTD.
Att: Human Resources Department
400 Phillip Street
Waterloo, ON N2J 4K6
Tel. 519-885-0110
Fax 519-885-8601
Email .... wlo_hr@res.raytheon.com
Website .... www.raytheon.ca
Employer Background: Raytheon Systems Canada Ltd. provides technological solutions to the defence and commercial electronics, business aviation and special mission aircraft sectors. *New Positions Created (26):* ATC Systems Support Technician; Components, Materials and Processes Engineer; Computer Network Analyst; Design Engineering Mgr; Engineering Technologist (Digital Design); Program Manager; Project Engineer (DASR); Project Engineering Mgr; RF Analog Engineer; Senior Contracts Administrator; Senior Financial Analyst; Systems Engineers (2); Technical Support Specialist; Business Capture Mgr; Hardware Systems Engineer; Transmitter Design Engineer; Business Development Manager; Mgr - Systems Engineering; Quality Assurance Manager; Senior Electrical Engineer; Senior Electrical Engineer (Support Services); Senior Mechanical Engineer; Senior Systems Engineer; Program Mgr; RF Analog Design Engineers; Mechanical / Process Technician.

RBC DOMINION SECURITIES INC.
Att: Stephen Dupuis
181 Bay St., Bay Wellington Tower
Suite 700, PO Box 831
Toronto, ON M5J 2T3
Tel. 416-842-2000
Fax 416-842-7242
Email .... stephen.dupuis@rbcinvestments.com
Website .... www.rbcds.com
Employer Background: Founded in 1901, RBC Dominion Securities Inc. (a member of the Royal Bank Financial Group) is a leading corporate and investment bank. *New Positions Created (3):* Investment Advisors and Sales Professionals; Investment Advisors / Sales Positions; Finance Positions.

RBC DOMINION SECURITIES INC.
Att: Ian Glover, VP, Branch Manager
5140 Yonge Street, Suite 2120, Box 28
Toronto, ON M2N 6L7
Tel. 416-733-5200
Fax 416-733-5258
Email ..... ian.glover@rbcinvestments.com
Website .... www.rbcds.com
Employer Background: Founded in 1901, RBC Dominion Securities Inc. (a member of the Royal Bank Financial Group) is a leading corporate and investment bank. *New Positions Created (3):* Investment Advisor; Investment Advisor; Investment Advisor.

RBC INSURANCE
Att: Christine D. Binder, Branch Manager
555 - 8th Avenue West, Suite 500
Vancouver, BC V5Z 1C6
Tel. 604-875-9866
Email .... cbinder@rbcinsurance.ca
Website .... www.rbcinsurance.ca
Employer Background: RBC Insurance, a member of the Royal Bank Financial Group, provides insurance products and services to 2 million customers across Canada. *New Positions Created (2):* Associate Branch Manager; Group Sales Representative.

RBC INSURANCE
Att: Colleen Ham, ERC
335 - 8th Avenue SW, 4th Floor
Calgary, AB T2P 1C9
Tel. 403-292-2304
Fax 403-292-2670
Email .... jobapp.cal@rb-erc.com
Website .... www.rbcinsurance.ca
Employer Background: RBC Insurance, a member of the Royal Bank Financial Group, provides insurance products and services to 2 million customers across Canada. *New Positions Created (9):* Account Manager, Aboriginal Markets; Branch Administrators; Customer Service Assistant; New Business Clerk; Regional Advanced Sales Manager; Personal Financial Advisor; Commercial Mortgage Originator; Territory Sales Manager, Managed Investments and Trusts; Trust Officer, Estates and Trusts.

RBC INSURANCE
Att: Nicole Jack, Coordinator,
Recruiting & Selection

6880 Financial Drive, West Tower
Mississauga, ON L5N 7Y5
Fax 905-813-4788
Email .... rbci@rb-erc.com
Website .... www.rbcinsurance.ca
Employer Background: RBC Insurance, a member of the Royal Bank Financial Group, provides insurance products and services to 2 million customers across Canada. *New Positions Created (4):* Branch Manager; Licensed Insurance Advisors; Associate Branch Managers; Branch Manager.

RBC INSURANCE
Att: Ben Joshan, Branch Manager
6715 Airport Road, Suite 101
Mississauga, ON L4V 1W7
Fax 905-672-5566
Email .... bjoshan@rbcinsurance.ca
Website .... www.rbcinsurance.ca
Employer Background: RBC Insurance, a member of the Royal Bank Financial Group, provides insurance products and services to 2 million customers across Canada. *New Positions Created (2):* Insurance Sales Representative; Branch Manager.

RCI CAPITAL GROUP INC.
Att: Human Resources Manager
1030 West Georgia Street, Suite 919
Vancouver, BC V6E 2Y3
Tel. 604-689-0113
Fax 604-602-9883
Email .... hr@rcicapitalgroup.com
Employer Background: RCI Capital Group Inc. operates in the financial services, hotel and real estate, immigration and international trading businesses. *New Positions Created (2):* Asia-Pacific Marketing Manager; Administration & HR Manager.

RCM TECHNOLOGIES CANADA
Att: Human Resources Manager
360 Albert Street, Suite 1640
Ottawa, ON K1R 7Z7
Tel. 613-232-9616
Fax 613-232-7831
Email .... hr.ottawa@rcmt.com
Website .... www.rcmt.com
Employer Background: RCM Technologies Canada provides business, information technology and engineering solutions to the high-tech, corporate and government sectors. *New Positions Created (2):* Aerospace Engineers; Avionics Engineers.

RCP INC.
Att: Human Resources
2891 Langstaff Road
Concord, ON L4K 4Z2
Tel. 905-660-7274
Fax 905-660-3282
Email .... jobs@rcpcanada.com
Website .... www.rcpcanada.com
Employer Background: RCP Inc. is a mid-sized aftermarket manufacturer and wholesaler of rotating automotive electrical products. *New Positions Created (6):* Export Traffic Coordinator; Accounting Analyst / Receptionist; Receptionist / Switchboard Opera-

tor; Inventory Analyst; Customer Service Rep; Customs and Traffic Clerk.

REA INTERNATIONAL INC.
Att: Vice-President, Engineering
2533 Rena Road
Mississauga, ON L4T 3X4
Tel. 905-676-9132
Fax 905-676-9724
Email .... jobs@reainternational.com
Website .... www.reainternational.com
Employer Background: Rea International Inc. supplies tubing components and fluid handling systems to the automotive industry. *New Positions Created (4):* Product Designer; Program Coordinator; Senior Mechanical Designer; CNC Operator.

READ JONES CHRISTOFFERSEN LTD.
Att: Doug Clark
1285 West Broadway, 3rd Floor
Vancouver, BC V6H 3X8
Tel. 604-738-0048
Fax 604-738-1107
Email .... dclark@rjc.ca
Website .... www.rjc.ca
Employer Background: Founded in 1948, Read Jones Christoffersen Ltd. is a national firm of consulting engineers, specializing in the structural design and restoration of buildings. *New Positions Created (3):* Entry-Level Engineers; Intermediate / Senior Engineers; Structural Field Representative.

READ JONES CHRISTOFFERSEN LTD.
Att: Ted Stone, Practice Leader
14904 - 123rd Avenue, Suite 101
Edmonton, AB T5V 1B4
Fax 780-455-7516
Email .... tstone@rjc.ca
Website .... www.rjc.ca
Employer Background: Founded in 1948, Read Jones is a national firm of consulting engineers, specializing in the structural design and restoration of buildings. *New Positions Created (2):* Entry-Level Engineers; Intermediate / Senior Engineers.

REAL CANADIAN SUPERSTORE, THE
Att: Human Resources Department
1792 Trans Canada Highway
Medicine Hat, AB T1B 1C6
Tel. 403-528-5735
Fax 403-291-6340
Employer Background: The Real Canadian Superstore (an operating division of Westfair Foods Ltd.) has 50 locations in western Canada. *New Positions Created (3):* Bakery Sales Supervisor; Grocery Supervisor; Apparel Supervisor.

REBER INC. / R-2000 INC.
Att: Human Resources Manager
9150 Maurice Duplessis Boulevard
Riviere-des-Prairies, QC H1E 7C2
Fax 514-494-8324
Email .... mail@reberinc.com
Website .... www.reberinc.com
Employer Background: Reber Inc. / R-2000 Inc. is an architectural millwork company.

New Positions Created (6): Buyer; Cabinetwork Technicians; Drafting Technician; Estimator; Project Mgr; Millwork Positions.

RECYCLAGE CAMCO INC.
Att: Human Resources Manager
20500 Clark Graham Avenue
Baie d'Urfe, QC H9X 4B6
Fax 514-457-0544
Website .... www.recyclagecamco.com
Employer Background: Recyclage Camco Inc. is a recycling company. *New Positions Created (3):* Supervisor; Team Leader / Operator; Transport Coordinator.

RED CADDY
Att: Wayne Mitchell
1050 Baxter Road
Ottawa, ON K2C 3P1
Tel. 613-820-8779
Fax 613-820-6813
Website .... www.redcaddy.com
Employer Background: Red Caddy is in the design and web architecture industry. *New Positions Created (4):* Web Designer; Graphic Designer; Internet Programmer; Web Designer.

RED CARPET FOOD SERVICES
Att: Human Resources Manager
515 Consumers Road, Suite 401
Toronto, ON M2J 4Z2
Tel. 416-490-8552
Fax 416-490-8714
Website .... www.redcarpetcoffee.com
Employer Background: Red Carpet Food Services is an office coffee and vending services supplier. *New Positions Created (5):* Accountant; Controller; Sales & Marketing Coordinator; Payroll Coordinator; Receptionist.

RED CARPET FOOD SERVICES
Att: Branch Manager
428 Millen Road, Units 16 & 17
Stoney Creek, ON L8E 3N9
Tel. 905-662-4323
Fax 905-662-4079
Website .... www.redcarpetcoffee.com
Employer Background: Red Carpet Food Services is an office coffee and vending services supplier. *New Positions Created (4):* Service Technician; Warehouse Person; Accounting Clerk; Vending Route Representative.

RED DEER, CITY OF
Att: Personnel Department
PO Box 5008
Red Deer, AB T4N 3T4
Tel. 403-342-8156
Fax 403-342-8378
Email .... personnel@city.red-deer.ab.ca
Website .... www.city.red-deer.ab.ca
Employer Background: The City of Red Deer is home to over 65,000 people. *New Positions Created (8):* Electrical Utility Distribution Engineer; Journeyman Auto Body Mechanic; Traffic Analysis Technician; Distribution Engineer; Distribution Engineer; Firefighter /

Paramedic; Director of Corporate Services; Land & Economic Development Mgr.

RED DEER COLLEGE
Att: Human Resources Department
Box 5005
Red Deer, AB T4N 5H5
Tel. 403-342-3273
Fax 403-342-3161
Email .... hro@rdc.ab.ca
Website .... www.rdc.ab.ca
Employer Background: Established in 1963, Red Deer College offers a range of certificate, diploma, apprenticeship, university transfer and collaborative degree completion programs. *New Positions Created (35):* Prospective Student Consultant 7; Budget Assistant VII; Library Assistant II; Campus Card Manager; Technical Support Analyst; Kinesiology and Sport Studies Instructor; Collaborative BSc Nursing Instructors; Dean of Leadership Development & Learning Effectiveness; Dean of Research & Technology Integration; BA Program and Advising Assistant; Chemistry Instructor; Executive Director, Advancement; Assistant Microcomputer Technician; English Instructor; Instructor, Educational Information Technology; Kinesiology Instructor / Women's Basketball Coach; Foundation / Alumni Coordinator; Instructor, Computer Systems Technology; Instructor, Educational Psychology and Family Studies; Instructor, Hospitality & Tourism; Instructor, Rehabilitation Services; Instructors, Business Administration And Commerce; Instructors, Theatre Studies; Librarian; Music Instructor; Music Instructor; Collaborative Nursing Instructors; Economics Instructor; French Instructor; Philosophy Instructor; Practical Nursing Program Instructors; Psychology Instructors; Sociology Instructors; Steamfitter Instructor; Extension Services Coordinator.

**RED DEER REGIONAL
HOSPITAL CENTRE / RDRHC**
Att: Human Resources
PO Bag 5030
Red Deer, AB T4N 6R2
Tel. 403-343-4588
Fax 403-343-4807
Email .... dthrhr1@rttinc.com
Website .... www.dthr.ab.ca
Employer Background: RDRHC is a 285-bed acute care facility, offering 24-hour emergency services. The hospital is part of the David Thompson Health Region. *New Positions Created (4):* Physical Therapists; Payroll Supervisor; Planning Coordinator; Regional Mgr, Food Production & Purchasing.

REDBACK NETWORKS
Att: Human Resources Manager
8988 Fraserton Court, Suite 305
Burnaby, BC V5J 5H8
Tel. 604-433-0597
Fax 604-433-0257
Email .... recruiting@redback.com
Website .... www.redback.com
Employer Background: Founded in 1998, Redback Networks develops next-genera-

tion telecom solutions to move high-speed IP packets over SONET networks. The company has 97 employees. *New Positions Created (3):* GUI Software Engineer; Network Management Software Manager; SONET Software Engineers.

REEBOK CANADA
Att: Jeff Sherwood
201 Earl Stewart Drive
Aurora, ON L4G 3H1
Tel. 905-727-0704
Fax 905-713-4961
Email .... jeff.sherwood@reebok.com
Website .... www.reebok.com
Employer Background: Reebok Canada is a subsidiary of Massachusetts-based Reebok International Ltd., a global marketer of sports, fitness and casual footwear, apparel and equipment. The company has worldwide revenues of $3.2 billion. *New Positions Created (2):* Retail Management Position; Market Development Representative.

REGENT HOLIDAYS LIMITED
Att: Linda Johnston, HR Manager
6205 Airport Road, Suite 200, Building A
Mississauga, ON L4V 1E1
Tel. 905-673-0777
Fax 905-673-1717
Email .... general@regentholidays.com
Website .... www.regentholidays.com
Employer Background: Regent Holidays Limited places travel reservations and bookings from travel agents. *New Positions Created (3):* Junior Entertainer / Animator; Reception Assistant; Secretary.

REGINA, CITY OF
Att: Human Resources Department
PO Box 1790, 11th Floor, City Hall
Regina, SK S4P 3C8
Tel. 306-777-7550
Fax 306-777-6825
Website .... www.cityregina.com
Employer Background: The City of Regina provides municipal government services to over 185,000 residents in Saskatchewan's capital city. *New Positions Created (9):* Assistant Mechanic; Systems Integration Analyst; Financial Systems Analyst; Aboriginal Program Specialist; Waste Diversion Officer; Superintendent, Parks & Open Maintenance; Coordinator, Assessment Administration; Research Technician; Tradesperson / Industrial Mechanic.

REGINA HEALTH DISTRICT
Att: Human Resources
2180 - 23rd Avenue
Regina, SK S4S 0A5
Tel. 306-766-5208
Fax 306-766-5147
Email .... jobs@reginahealth.sk.ca
Website .... www.reginahealth.sk.ca
Employer Background: The Regina Health District provides health services to residents of southern Saskatchewan. *New Positions Created (4):* Medical Physicist, Nuclear Medicine; Staff Pharmacists; Manager, Di-

agnostic Imaging / Services; Assistant Manager, Laboratory Services.

REGIONAL DOORS AND HARDWARE
Att: Ted Van Geest, General Manager
44 Scott Street West, Box 2187
St. Catharines, ON L2M 6P6
Tel. 905-684-8161
Employer Background: Regional Doors and Hardware is a wholesale distributor of wood and metal doors, frames, architectural and builders' hardware and wood mouldings. *New Positions Created (3):* Assistant to Welder; Project Co-ordinator; Truck Driver.

REGIONAL HEALTH AUTHORITY 5
Att: Position Control Clerk, HR Dept.
PO Box 429
Drumheller, AB T0J 0Y0
Tel. 403-820-6009
Fax 403-823-5418
Website www.ha5.ab.ca
Employer Background: Regional Health Authority 5 provides health services to residents of southeast Alberta. *New Positions Created (3):* Director of Financial Services; Team Leader, Acute Care; Information Technology Director.

REGISTERED NURSES ASSOCIATION OF ONTARIO / RNAO
Att: Human Resources
438 University Avenue, Suite 1600
Toronto, ON M5G 2K8
Tel. 416-599-1925
Fax 416-599-1926
Website .... www.rnao.org
Employer Background: RNAO is the professional association that represents registered nurses in Ontario. *New Positions Created (5):* Project Coordinators (2); Conference Coordinator; Director of Membership; Administrative Assistant; Director of Communications.

REHABILITATIVE ERGONOMICS INC.
Att: Human Resources Manager
109 Rocky Lake Drive, Unit 8
Halifax, NS B4A 2T3
Fax 902-835-0886
Email .... jharatsis@rehabergo.com
Website .... www.rehabergo.com
Employer Background: Established in 1993, Rehabilitative Ergonomics Inc. provides a full range of rehabilitative and injury management consulting services. *New Positions Created (3):* Account Manager; Manager, Rehabilitation Services; Occupational Therapists and Kinesiologists.

REIMER EXPRESS LINES LTD.
Att: Human Resources
1400 Inkster Boulevard
Winnipeg, MB R2X 1R1
Email .... reimerhr@reimerexpress.com
Website .... www.reimerexpress.com
Employer Background: Reimer Express Lines Ltd. is a member of the Roadway Express Inc. transportation system, a leading

less-than-truckload motor carrier in North America, serving 65 countries worldwide. *New Positions Created (2):* Operations Supervisor; Sales Representative.

REITMANS (CANADA) LIMITED
Att: Employment Coordinator
250 Sauve Street West
Montréal, QC H3L 1Z2
Tel. 514-384-1140
Fax 514-385-2699
Email .... careers@reitmans.com
Website .... www.reitmans.ca
Employer Background: Reitmans (Canada) Limited is Canada's largest women's specialty retailer, with about 600 stores operating under five divisions: Reitmans, Smart Set, Dalmys, RW & Co. and Penningtons Superstore. *New Positions Created (3):* Rent Administrator; Technical Coordinators; Planning and Allocation Manager.

REKAI CENTRE, THE
Att: Human Resources
345 Sherbourne Street
Toronto, ON M5A 2S3
Tel. 416-964-1599
Fax 416-964-3907
Website .... www.rekaicentre.com
Employer Background: The Rekai Centre is Canada's first multicultural, multilingual, non-profit long-term care facility, providing care to elderly citizens who have difficulty communicating in English. *New Positions Created (5):* Activation Aides; RNs and RPNs; Programs Manager; Director of Resident Care; Director of Resident Programs.

RELIABLE LIFE INSURANCE COMPANY
Att: Human Resources
Box 557
Hamilton, ON L8N 3K9
Tel. 905-523-5587
Fax 905-523-5899
Employer Background: The Reliable Life Insurance Company, part of the Old Republic Insurance Group, provides life, health, creditor, travel and student accident insurance. *New Positions Created (3):* Claims Manager; Customer Service Representative; Staff Accountant.

RELIZON CANADA INC.
Att: Human Resources Manager
4259 Canada Way, Suite 215
Burnaby, BC V5G 1H1
Tel. 604-454-9545
Fax 604-454-9262
Email .... careers@relizon.ca
Website .... www.relizon.ca
Employer Background: Relizon Canada Inc. (formerly Crain-Drummond Inc.) is a leading provider of business communication services and customer relationship management solutions. *New Positions Created (2):* Sales Rep; Major Account Sales Rep.

RELIZON CANADA INC.
Att: Human Resources Department

200 Yorkland Boulevard, Suite 710
Toronto, ON M2J 5C1
Tel. 416-756-0774
Fax 416-756-0617
Email .... careers@relizon.ca
Website .... www.relizon.ca
Employer Background: Relizon Canada Inc. (formerly Crain-Drummond Inc.) is a leading provider of business communication services and customer relationship management solutions. *New Positions Created (6):* AIS Systems Specialists; Business Analyst; Customer Service Representative; Inside Sales Representative; Major Account Sales Representative; Project Manager.

REMINGTON DEVELOPMENT CORPORATION
Att: Human Resources Manager
30 Glendeer Circle SE, Suite 200
Calgary, AB T2H 2Z7
Tel. 403-255-7003
Fax 403-255-7530
Employer Background: Remington Development Corporation is a commercial real estate developer. *New Positions Created (2):* Project Manager; Site Superintendent.

RENAISSANCE LEARNING OF CANADA
Att: Human Resources Manager
15 Capella Court, Suite 128
Nepean, ON K2E 7X1
Tel. 613-225-4824
Fax 613-225-1670
Email .... jobs@ottawa.advlearn.ca
Website .... www.advlearn.com
Employer Background: Renaissance Learning of Canada builds educational software used in schools. *New Positions Created (6):* Software Developers; Software Development Manager; Senior Software Development Leader; Software Developers; Software Quality Assurance Developers and Testers; Software Development Manager.

RENFREW EDUCATIONAL SERVICES
Att: Kim LaCourse
2050 - 21st Street NE
Calgary, AB T2E 6S5
Tel. 403-291-5038
Fax 403-291-2499
Email ...... renfrew@renfreweducation.org
Website .... www.renfreweducation.org
Employer Background: Renfrew Educational Services is a multi-location provider of individualized programming for all students, as well as speech therapy, occupational therapy, physiotherapy and psychology services for children with special needs. *New Positions Created (2):* Physical Therapist; Speech Language Pathologist.

RENO-DEPOT
Att: Human Resources Department
7240 Waverly Street
Montréal, QC H2R 2Y8
Tel. 514-270-8111
Fax 514-270-8141
Website .... www.renodepot.com

Employer Background: Founded in 1933, Reno-Depot is a leader in the renovation warehouse store sector. *New Positions Created (4):* Print Advertising Director, Quebec and Ontario; Assistant Buyer, Lumber and Building Materials; Marketing Planner; Telephone Operators.

RENTOKIL INITIAL HEALTHCARE (CANADA) LTD.
Att: David McLenachan
7280 Victoria Park Avenue
Markham, ON L3R 2M5
Fax 905-940-2196
Email .. dmclenachan@rentokilinitial.com
Website .... www.rentokilinitial.com
Employer Background: Rentokil Initial Healthcare (Canada) Ltd. is part of Rentokil Initial PLC, the world's largest international business services company. *New Positions Created (2):* Sales Professional; Sales Professional.

REPLICON INC.
Att: Human Resources Manager
910 - 7th Avenue SW, Suite 830
Calgary, AB T2P 3N8
Tel. 403-262-6519
Fax 403-233-8046
Email .... careers@replicon.com
Website .... www.replicon.com
Employer Background: Replicon Inc. develops web-based solutions to optimize workforce productivity, including time tracking products. *New Positions Created (7):* Junior and Senior Account Executives; Website / Public Relations Coordinator; Customer Support Representative; Inside Sales Representative; Receptionist; Senior Database Developer; Senior Software Engineer.

RESEARCH IN MOTION LIMITED
Att: Human Resources Manager
295 Phillip Street
Waterloo, ON N2L 3W8
Tel. 519-888-7465
Fax 519-888-7884
Email .... careers@rim.net
Website .... www.rim.net
Employer Background: RIM is a leading designer, manufacturer and marketer of wireless solutions for the mobile communications market. *New Positions Created (188):* Team Leader, Knowledge Management; Blackberry Systems Administrator, Email Systems; Billing Operations Manager; Project Implementation Director, Revenue Readiness; SAP FI Team Member; SAP Project Manager; IT Site Manager; Mechanical Designer; Mechanical Engineering Support Specialist; Senior Project Manager; Test Engineer; Test Engineering Manager; Wireless Protocol Developers; Blackberry Sales and Service Consultant; Channel Program Manager; Contact Centre Representative, Customer Master Records; Facilities Coordinator; Marketing Program Manager, ISVs; Optical Display Engineer; Project Implementation Director, Revenue Readiness; SAP Project Manager; Blackberry Solutions Consultant; Channel Development Special-

ist; Channel Program Manager, Carrier; Channel Program Manager, Distributor; Configuration Management Engineer; Database Program Manager; DSP Software Developers; Embedded O / S Developers; Financial Analyst, Reporting and Metrics ; Industrial Designer; Inside Sales Account Manager; Manager, Billing Operations; Manager, Network Forecasting; Manager, Special Assignments; Market Development Manager; Mechanical Design Engineer; Sales Trainer; Senior Manager, Training; Shift Coordinator; Technical Program Administrator; Executive Assistant; Infrastructure Support Specialist; Product Configuration Coordinator; Receptionist; Senior Technical Writer; Technical Writer / Researcher; Software Architecture; Beta Program Team Leader; Buyer / Planner, Packaging; Customer Forums Manager; Customer Support Specialist; Electro-Acoustic Engineer; Internal Communications Manager; Intranet Content Developers; Mechanical Engineering Support Position; Metallurgical Technologist; National Account Manager; Payroll and Benefits Administrator; Process and Performance Manager; Product Test Engineer; Project Manager, Process Design; Senior Project Manager; Software Quality Team Leader; Software Quality Tester; Tooling Project Engineer; Administrative Assistant - Organizational Development; Antenna Technologist; BlackBerry Enterprise Software Developers; BlackBerry System Operators; Business Development Manager; Desktop Developer; Engineering Development Manager (BlackBerry); Engineering Development Manager (Radio Modems); Livelink System Administrator; Market Research Specialist; Material Planner; Mechanical Draftsperson; PDM Applications Specialist; Production Engineering Technologists / Technicians; Senior Buyer / Planner; Senior Product Manager; Strategic Account Manager - Indirect Channels; Unix System Developers; Web-Based Training Developer; Certification Analyst / Technician; Manufacturing Engineer; Regulatory Approval Coordinator / Engineer; RF Technologist / Technician; Technical Editor; Test Engineer; Test Engineering Manager; Executive Assistant; SAP Training Coordinator ; Senior Accounts Payable Clerk; Marketing Alliance Manager; National Account Manager; Unix System Administrator; ABAP Developer; Administrative Assistant, Software; Configuration Management Specialist; Interop Test Specialists; Project Manager, Interface Solutions; Public Relations Manager; Recruitment Manager; Repair Production Manager; Lotus Notes Technical Support; Master Scheduler; Web Site Designer; Administrative Assistant; Network Infrastructure Engineer; Network Operators; Operations Manager; Program / Project Manager; Quality Assurance Manager / Team Leader; Quality Assurance Specialist; Software Developers; Technical Recruiter; Technical Writer; Blackberry Enterprise Software Developers; Blackberry Solutions Consultant; Channel Program Manager; Component Engineer; Consumer Marketing Specialist; Document Coordinator / Administrative Assistant; DSP Software Developers; Embedded Application Developers; Embedded Operating System Developers; Engineering Development Manager, Blackberry; Engineering Development Manager, Radio Modems; ESD Engineer; Inside Sales Account Manager; Market Development Manager; Marketing Product Managers; Marketing Program Managers; Organizational Development Assistant; Plant Accountant; Product Manager / Coordinator; Quality Assurance Technologists; Quality Engineer; Receiving Inspector; Senior Product Manager; Senior Reliability Engineer; Unix System Developers; Escalation Manager; Blackberry System Operators; Desktop Developers; Facilities Coordinator; Facilities Technician; Material Planner; MS Exchange Developers ; Notes / Domino Developers ; Oracle Database Administrator; Payroll and Benefits Administrator; SAP Basis Administrator; SAP Security Administrator; Technical Writer; Web Content Developer; Wireless Protocol Developers; Assistant Shift Coordinators; Electronic Assemblers; Government Channel Manager; Senior Business Development Manager; Special Projects Manager, Indirect Channels; Strategic Account Manager; Enterprise Storage Specialist; Market Demand Planner; Production Planning and Control Manager; RF Repair Technician; Shift Coordinator; SMT Process Operator; Technical Training Specialist; Project Managers; System Engineers; Lotus Notes System Developers; Product Configuration Analyst; Software Developers; Special Project Manager, Indirect Channels; Production Manager; Regulatory Approval Coordinator / Engineer; Senior Buyer / Planner; Test Engineering Manager; Senior Battery Systems Engineer; Accounts Payable Clerk; Administrative Assistant / Receptionist; BlackBerry Technical Facilitator; ERP Team Member, Finance; Networking Specialist; Receiving Inspector.

RESEARCH IN MOTION LIMITED
Att: Human Resources Manager
600 Terry Fox Drive, Suite 100
Kanata, ON K2L 4B6

Tel. 613-599-7465
Fax 613-599-5109
Email .... careers@rim.net
Website .... www.rim.net

Employer Background: RIM is a leading designer, manufacturer and marketer of wireless solutions for the mobile communications market. *New Positions Created (54):* Facilities Building Operator; Baseband ASIC Architect; Design Architect, Digital Hardware Development; Design Architect, RF Hardware Development; Design Architect, Software Development; Digital Hardware Designers; DSP ASIC Designers; DSP Designers; Embedded Software Designers; Enterprise Application Software Developers; Interoperability and Field Trial Engineer; Manager / Team Leader, RF Hardware Development; Manager / Team Leader, Software Development; Networking Software Engineer; RF Hardware Designers; RF Hardware Systems Designers; Senior RFIC Designers; Systems Software Designers; Test Software Designer; Design Architect, Digital

Hardware Development; Design Architect, RF Hardware Development; Design Architect, Software Development; Digital ASIC Design Engineers; Digital Hardware Designers; Director, Product Development; DSP Designers; Embedded Software Designers; Interoperability and Field Trial Engineer; Manager / Team Leader, Digital Hardware Development; Manager / Team Leader, RF Hardware Development; Manager / Team Leader, Software Development; Project Coordinator, Product Development; Project Engineer, Product Development; RF Calibration Designer; RF Hardware Designers; RF Hardware System Designers; RF Test Automation Engineer; RF Test Technician; System Performance Test Engineer; System Software Designers; Test Software Designer; Blackberry System Operators; Desktop Developers; MS Exchange Developers; Notes / Domino Developers; Oracle Database Administrator; Technical Writer; IC Development Manager; RFIC Layout Engineer; Project Co-ordinator(; Project Engineer; Recruiter / HR Generalist; RF Hardware Systems Designer; Test Software Designer.

RESERVEAMERICA
Att: Human Resources Manager
401 Wheelabrator Way
Milton, ON L9T 4B7

Tel. 905-875-1158
Fax 905-875-2612
Email .... humanresources@
.... reserveamerica.com
Website .... www.reserveamerica.com

Employer Background: Established in 1984, ReserveAmerica (a subsidiary of Ticketmaster) provides technological solutions to meet the reservation, registration and reporting needs of the recreation industry. *New Positions Created (48):* Development Manager; Marketing Coordinator; Product Support Specialist; Senior Software Development Specialist; Senior Technical Consultant; Development Team Leader; Director, Project Management Office; Java / OO Programmer; Senior Analyst, Budgets / Cost Accounting; Product Support & Help Desk Manager; Human Resources Generalist; Marketing Coordinator; Product Manager, Financial and Reporting Systems; Product Support & Help Desk Manager; Senior Technical Consultant; Intermediate Product Building Specialist; Java / OO Programmer; Project Administrator; Senior Software Development Specialist; Technical Implementation Team Leader; User Interface Developer; Development Manager; Development Team Leader; Accounts Payable Administrator; Application Support Specialists (2); Director, Project Management Office; Product Manager - Financial Reporting; Product Manager - New Products; Product Manager - Web Services; Project Managers; Senior Account Manager, Government Sales; Director, Client Management; Director, Solutions Development; Project Administrator; Senior Analyst, Budget / Cost Accounting; Application Support Specialist; Director, Program Office; Help Desk Analysts; Java OO Programmer; Project Managers; Quality Assurance Specialist; Senior Accountants

(2); Senior Sales Support Specialist; Technical Development Manager; Technical Implementation Specialist / Team Leader; Training Specialist; User Interface Developer; Webmaster.

RESONANCE PHOTONICS INC.
Att: Human Resources Manager
505 Apple Creek Boulevard, Unit 3
Markham, ON L3R 5B1

Tel. 905-947-8722
Fax 905-947-8727
Email .... careers@resonance-photonics.com
Website ... www.resonance-photonics.com

Employer Background: Resonance Photonics Inc. designs and manufactures photonics components for use in next-generation fibre amplifier and laser modules. *New Positions Created (25):* Lead Scientist, Fibre Amplifier Development; Lead Scientist, Fibre Laser Development; Lead Scientist, Raman / Brillouin Fibre Laser Development; Fibre Optic Assembly and Test Associates; Fibre Optic Component Applications Specialist, Telecom; Fibre Optic Materials / Process Engineer; Fibre Optic Reliability Engineer; Market Analyst; Sales Engineer, Telecom; Test Technologist, Component Reliability; Accounting Specialist; Customer Service Manager; Fibre Optic Assembly and Test Associates; Fibre Optic Development Engineer - Test Instrumentation; Fibre Optic Materials / Process Engineer; Fibre Optic Reliability Engineer; Fibre Optics Patent Research Analyst; Field Applications Engineer, Telecom; Lead Scientist - Fibre Amplifier Development; Lead Scientist - Fibre Laser Development; Lead Scientist - Raman Brillouin Fibre Laser Development; Manufacturing Manager; Test Technologist - Component Reliability; Vice-President, Marketing & Sales; Test Technologist, Component Reliability.

RESORTS OF THE CANADIAN ROCKIES INC. / RCR
Att: Human Resources Manager
1505 - 17th Avenue SW
Calgary, AB T2T 0E2

Tel. 403-244-6665
Fax 403-244-3774

Employer Background: RCR owns and operates eight ski resorts in Canada. *New Positions Created (2):* Controller; Resort Development Manager.

RESOURCE INFORMATION SYSTEMS INC. / RIS
Att: Human Resources Manager
400 - 3rd Avenue SW
Suite 2601, Canterra Tower
Calgary, AB T2P 4H2

Tel. 403-263-2272
Fax 403-266-4281
Email .... recruit.calgary@ris.ca
Website .... www.ris.ca

Employer Background: Established in 1979, RIS is an information technology consulting company. *New Positions Created (3):* PeopleSoft HRMS Analyst; Intermediate Visual Basic Developers; Oracle Architect / Developer.

RESPONSE BIOMEDICAL CORP.
Att: Human Resources Department
8855 Northbrook Court
Burnaby, BC V5J 5J1
Tel. 604-681-4101
Fax 604-412-9830
Email .... jobs@responsebio.com
Website .... www.responsebio.com
Employer Background: Response Biomedical Corp. develops point-of-care quantitative diagnostic systems. *New Positions Created (2):* Manager, Clinical and Regulatory Affairs; Research and Production Development Assistants.

RESPONSIVE HEALTH MANAGEMENT
Att: Administrator
429 Walmer Road
Toronto, ON M5P 2X9
Tel. 416-967-6949
Fax 416-928-1965
Email .... lcalbre@responsive.on.ca
Website .... www.responsive.on.ca
Employer Background: Responsive Health Management (formerly Lincoln Place Nursing Home) operates a 248-bed nursing home for the aged. *New Positions Created (3):* Bookkeeper; Director of Nursing; Nurse Managers (2).

RETAIL READY FOODS INC.
Att: Human Resources Manager
2420 Meadowpine Boulevard, Suite 105
Mississauga, ON L5N 6S2
Tel. 905-812-8555
Fax 905-812-7101
Email .... hr@retailready.com
Website .... www.retailready.com
Employer Background: Retail Ready Foods Inc. distributes refrigerated food products to independent retailers across Ontario. *New Positions Created (4):* Assistant to Product Mgr; Junior Sales Representative; Logistics Coordinator; Retail Account Manager.

REVOLVE MAGNETIC BEARINGS INC.
Att: Human Resources Department
707 - 10th Avenue SW, Suite 300
Calgary, AB T2R 0B3
Tel. 403-232-9292
Fax 403-232-9255
Email .... sshane@revolve.com
Website .... www.revolve.com
Employer Background: Revolve Magnetic Bearings Inc., an SKF company, develops magnetic bearing technologies for the semiconductor, industrial equipment and machine tool markets. *New Positions Created (5):* Shipper / Receiver and Inventory Clerk; C++ Programmer; DSP Programmer, Software; Marketing Coordinator; Mechanical / Electrical Engineer.

REXCAN CIRCUITS INC.
Att: Human Resources Department
PO Box 949
Belleville, ON K8N 5B6
Employer Background: RexCan manufactures multi-layer printed circuit boards for the telecom and computer industries. *New*

Positions Created (4): Electronic Technologist / Electrician; Production Mgr; Production Planner; Senior Process Engineers.

REXEL CANADA INC.
Att: Human Resources Manager
1810 Ironstone Drive
Burlington, ON L7L 5V3
Fax 905-331-2184
Email .... lara.stewart@westburne.ca
Website .... www.westburne.ca
Employer Background: Rexel Canada Inc. (formerly Westburne Inc.) is one of Canada's largest plumbing and industrial distributors. *New Positions Created (2):* Sales Manager; Warehouse / Yard Person.

RGO OFFICE PRODUCTS
Att: Human Resources
229 - 33rd Street NE, Suite 100
Calgary, AB T2A 4Y6
Tel. 403-569-4400
Fax 403-569-4550
Email .... hr@rgo.ab.ca
Website .... www.rgo.ab.ca
Employer Background: RGO Office Products is a Calgary-based office environment resource company. *New Positions Created (11):* After Market Sales Representative; Showroom Sales Representative; Customer Care Team Lead; Showroom Sales Representatives; Business Systems Analyst; Junior Service Technician; Installers; Accounting Analyst; Administrative Assistant; Sales Professionals; Space Planning Consultant.

RIBSTONE CHILD & FAMILY SERVICES AUTHORITY
Att: Patricia Barnum, HR Services
10035 - 108 Street
3rd Floor, Centre West Building
Edmonton, AB T5J 3E1
Fax 780-427-1018
Website .... www.ribstone.ab.ca
Employer Background: Formed in 1999, Ribstone Child & Family Services Authority is a Crown agency, promoting the development and well-being of children, youth and families. *New Positions Created (3):* Service Facilitator; Social Worker / Service Facilitator; Social Worker/Support Facilitator.

RIBSTONE CHILD AND FAMILY SERVICES AUTHORITY
Att: Human Resource Services
4804 - 42nd Avenue, Bay 10
Innisfail, AB T4G 1V2
Fax 403-227-7975
Website .... www.ribstone.ab.ca
Employer Background: Formed in 1999, the Ribstone Child and Family Services Authority is a Crown agency, promoting the development and well-being of children, youth and families. *New Positions Created (5):* Administrative Support Position; Auditor; Service Facilitator; Support Facilitator; Family Maintenance / Intake Worker.

RICE BRYDONE LTD.
Att: Beth Christiani

553 Richmond Street West
Toronto, ON M5V 1Y6
Tel. 416-504-9094
Fax 416-504-2008
Employer Background: Rice Brydone Ltd. is an architecture and interior design company. *New Positions Created (3):* Facilities Management Position / Project Coordinator; Residential Interior Designer, Corporate and Condominium; Interior Designer / Architect.

RICH PRODUCTS OF CANADA LTD.
Att: Assistant Human Resources Manager
PO Box 1008
Fort Erie, ON L2A 5N8
Tel. 905-871-2605
Fax 905-871-0148
Email .... forterierecruiting@rich.com
Website .... www.richs.com
Employer Background: Rich Products of Canada Ltd. manufactures frozen non-dairy, bakery and dessert products. *New Positions Created (3):* Group Product Manager; Regional Key Account Manager, Bakery; Marketing Manager.

RICHMOND, CITY OF
Att: Human Resources Department
6911 No. 3 Road
Richmond, BC V6Y 2C1
Tel. 604-276-4100
Fax 604-276-4169
Email .... humanresources@
.... city.richmond.bc.ca
Website .... www.city.richmond.bc.ca
Employer Background: The City of Richmond provides municipal government services to residents and businesses in one the country's most rapidly changing cities. *New Positions Created (7):* Budget and Accounting Clerk I; Business Systems Analyst; Records Clerk; Lifeguard / Instructors 2; Director, Land Assets and Property; General Manager, Community Safety; General Manager, Parks, Recreation and Cultural Services.

RICHMOND HEALTH SERVICES
Att: Human Resources Department
7000 Westminster Highway
Richmond, BC V6X 1A2
Tel. 604-244-5208
Fax 604-244-5228
Website .... www.rhss.bc.ca
Employer Background: Richmond Health Services is the umbrella employer for the Richmond Hospital, Richmond Health Department, Minoru Residence, Richmond Lion's Manor, Richmond Mental Health Team, Richmond School Mental Health Program and Blundell Therapeutic and Educational Services. *New Positions Created (7):* Clinical Nurse Specialist, Acute Treatment; Site Manager, Clinical Services; Cardiac Ultrasonographer; Clinical Practice Improvement Leader; Consumer Relations Specialist; Quality Improvement Coordinator; Emergency Services and Utilization Manager.

RICHMOND HILL PUBLIC LIBRARY
Att: Denise Petri, Executive Assistant
1 Atkinson Street
Richmond Hill, ON L4C 0H5

Fax 905-770-0312
Website ...... www.rhpl.richmondhill.on.ca
Employer Background: The Richmond Hill Public Library is one of Canada's large urban library system, serving a community of 136,000. *New Positions Created (3):* Library Systems Manager; Library Systems Project Manager; Manager of Information Systems.

RICHMOND HILL, TOWN OF
Att: Human Resources
225 East Beaver Creek, PO Box 300
Richmond Hill, ON L4C 4Y5

Tel. 905-771-8800
Fax 905-771-5435
Email ..... jobs@town.richmond-hill.on.ca
Website ... www.town.richmond-hill.on.ca
Employer Background: Incorporated in 1872 and situated just north of Toronto, the Town of Richmond Hill is one of Canada's fastest-growing municipalities. *New Positions Created (10):* Mechanical Engineer; Senior Plans Examiner; Deputy Fire Chief, Support Services; Human Resources Adviser; Programmer Analyst; Systems Analyst; Manager, Parks Planning and Development; Treasurer / Commissioner of Finance; Parks Planner; Director of Council Support Services / Town Clerk.

RICHMOND HONDA
Att: Glen Goldhawk
13600 Smallwood Place
Richmond, BC V6V 1W8

Tel. 604-207-1888
Fax 604-207-1924
Website .... www.richmondhonda.com
Employer Background: Richmond Honda is an automotive dealership. *New Positions Created (4):* Warranty Clerk / Work Order Booker; Business Manager; Service Receptionist; Customer Care Coordinator.

RICHMOND SUZUKI SUBARU
Att: Garry Yu / Mike Yu
2511 No. 3 Road
Richmond, BC V6X 2B8

Fax 604-273-0317
Employer Background: Richmond Suzuki Subaru is an automotive dealership. *New Positions Created (2):* Service Receptionist / Warranty Administrator; Parts Advisor.

RICOH / SAVIN CANADA INC.
Att: Kevin Small, HR Director
4100 Yonge Street, Suite 414
Toronto, ON M2P 2B5

Tel. 416-218-4360
Email .... ksmall@ricoh.ca
Website .... www.ricoh.ca
Employer Background: Ricoh / Savin Canada Inc. (and its related company, Document Direction Ltd.) is a leader in the fast-growing color copier market and major supplier of copiers and facsimile products, digital duplicators and management services.

New Positions Created (3): Junior Accountant; Marketing Communications Manager; Solutions Manager, Digital Document Management.

RICOH / SAVIN CANADA INC.
Att: Hugh Douglas
1550 Enterprise Road, Suite 310
Mississauga, ON L4W 4P4

Fax 905-796-5719
Email .... resume@ricoh.ca
Website .... www.ricoh.ca
Employer Background: Ricoh / Savin Canada Inc. (and its related company, Document Direction Ltd.) is a leader in the fast-growing color copier market and major supplier of copiers and facsimile products, digital duplicators and management services. *New Positions Created (2):* Copier Field Service Technician; Facsimile Field Service Technician.

RIDGEWOOD INDUSTRIES
Att: Human Resources
3305 Loyalist Street
Cornwall, ON K6H 6W6

Tel. 613-937-0711
Fax 613-837-3446
Website .... www.dorel.com
Employer Background: Founded in 1969, Ridgewood Industries (formerly Ameriwood Industries) is a leading manufacturer of ready-to-assemble furniture and a division of Dorel Industries Inc. *New Positions Created (5):* Quality Assurance Analyst; Product Engineer; Industrial Electrician; Purchasing Manager; Supervisor, Cost Accounting.

RIDLEY COLLEGE
Att: Bryan A. Auld, Middle School Director
PO Box 3013
St. Catharines, ON L2R 7C3

Tel. 905-684-8193
Fax 905-684-8100
Email .... bryan_auld@ridley.on.ca
Website .... www.ridley.on.ca
Employer Background: Ridley College is an independent, co-educational residential school, offering an advanced academic program for 600 students in grades 5 through OAC. *New Positions Created (5):* Teachers (3); Development Officer; Head of Drama; Teacher, Mathematics; Teacher-Housemaster, Boys' Residence.

RIDOUT & MAYBEE LLP
Att: Kathy Murphy, Director of Operations
1 Queen Street East, Suite 2400
Toronto, ON M5C 3B1

Tel. 416-868-1482
Fax 416-362-0823
Email .... kmurphy@ridoutmaybee.com
Website .... www.ridoutmaybee.com
Employer Background: Established in 1893, Ridout & Maybee LLP is a firm of intellectual property lawyers and patent and trademark agents, with offices in Ottawa, Mississauga and Toronto. *New Positions Created (3):* Controller; Patent Agents / Lawyers; Patent Agents / Lawyers.

RIO ALTO EXPLORATION LTD.
Att: Human Resources
205 - 5th Avenue SW, Suite 2500
Calgary, AB T2P 2V7

Tel. 403-716-6214
Fax 403-261-7626
Email .... careers@rioalto.com
Website .... www.rioalto.com
Employer Background: Rio Alto Exploration Ltd. is an oil and gas production company based in Calgary. *New Positions Created (7):* Surface Land Administrator; Contract Operators, Heavy Oil; Exploitation Engineer, International; Facilities Engineer; Lead Geophysicist; Production Engineer; Surface Landman.

RIOCAN REAL ESTATE INVESTMENT TRUST
Att: Danny Kissoon, VP Operations
130 King St. West, Suite 700, PO Box 378
Toronto, ON M5X 1E2

Fax 416-646-8136
Email .... lnaik@riocan.com
Website .... www.riocan.com
Employer Background: RioCan Real Estate Investment Trust is one of Canada's largest retail real estate investment trust companies. *New Positions Created (3):* Assistant Vice-President, Finance; Assistant Vice-President, Operations; Director of Human Resources.

RITTAL SYSTEMS LTD.
Att: Ruth Lancaster, HR Manager
7320 Pacific Circle
Mississauga, ON L5T 1V1

Tel. 905-795-0777
Fax 905-795-0535
Website .... www.rittal.ca
Employer Background: Rittal Systems Ltd. is the Canadian subsidiary of Rittal International, a leading manufacturer of enclosures and enclosure climate control solutions. *New Positions Created (18):* National Sales Manager, Industrial Enclosures (IE); National Sales Manager, IT; Modification Lead Hand; Branch Manager; Western Regional Sales Manager; Industrial Sales Project Coordinator; Inside Sales Representative; Marketing Coordinator; Shipper / Receiver; Electronic Marketing Coordinator; Inventory Controller; Outside Sales Representative; Customs Coordinator; Receiver; Receptionist; IT Project Coordinator; Inside Sales Rep; Junior Accounting Clerk.

RIVERDALE HOSPITAL, THE
Att: Human Resources
14 St. Matthews Road
Toronto, ON M4M 2B5

Tel. 416-461-8251
Fax 416-461-9972
Email .... careers@trh.on.ca
Website .... www.trh.on.ca
Employer Background: The Riverdale Hospital is a 547-bed facility, specializing in complex continuing care and rehabilitation services. *New Positions Created (23):* Acting Manager, Volunteer Resources; Coordinator, Clinical Informatics; Registered Nurses; Evening Patient Care Manager;

Nurse Clinicians (4); Project Director, Planning, Construction and Site Redevelopment; Financial Analyst; Occupational Health Nurse; Occupational Therapy / Physiotherapy Assistant; Physiotherapist; Social Worker; Registered Nurses; Executive Assistant; Occupational Therapist, Cognitive Support; Occupational Therapy / Physiotherapy Assistants; Physiotherapist, Neuro-Rehabilitation; Social Worker; Evening Patient Care Mgr; Nurse Clinicians (4); Occupational Health Nurse; Patient Relations & Cultural Interpreter Coordinator; Registered Nurses; Nurse Educator, Dialysis.

RIVERSIDE SCHOOL BOARD
Att: Mrs. Francis Weiser, HR Director
299 Sir Wilfred Laurier Boulevard
St-Lambert, QC J4R 2V7

Tel. 450-672-4010
Fax 450-465-8809
Website .... www.rsb.qc.ca

Employer Background: Founded in 1998, the Riverside School Board (one of nine English-language school boards in Quebec) serves 11,200 students. *New Positions Created (3):* Career Education Consultant; Finance Officer; HR Coordinator.

RIVTOW MARINE LTD.
Att: Marjorie Lee, HR Manager
PO Box 3650
Vancouver, BC V6B 3Y8

Fax 604-251-0213
Website .... www.rivtow.com

Employer Background: Rivtow Marine Ltd. is involved in all types of marine transportation, including ship docking, chip and log barging and general freight and log towing. *New Positions Created (3):* Marine Shift Dispatcher; Accounting / Purchasing Clerk; Barge Repair Foreman.

RJL PACKAGING & LABELLING INDUSTRIES INC.
Att: Philip Lassner
8230 Mayrand Avenue
Montréal, QC H4P 2C6

Tel. 514-344-5122
Fax 514-344-9717
Email .... info@rjlindustries.com
Website .... www.rjlindustries.com

Employer Background: RJL Packaging & Labelling Industries Inc. sells point-of-sale product identifiers to private and national brand manufacturers and retailers. *New Positions Created (4):* Junior Bookkeeper; Sales Representatives; Marketing Position; Sales Representatives.

RLG INTERNATIONAL
Att: Human Resources Manager
375 Water Street, Suite 750
Vancouver, BC V6B 5C6

Tel. 604-669-7178
Fax 604-669-0814
Email .... vitae@rlginternational.com
Website .... www.rlginternational.com

Employer Background: RLG International specializes in the on-site implementation of measurable performance improvement

projects. *New Positions Created (2):* Project Managers; Project Managers.

RMH TELESERVICES INTERNATIONAL INC.
Att: Cindee Torba
1 Market Street
Brantford, ON N3T 6C8

Fax 519-757-1844
Email .... cdibartolomeo@
.... rmhteleservices.com
Website .... www.rmhteleservices.com

Employer Background: RMH Teleservices International Inc. is a leading provider of outsourced customer relationship management services. *New Positions Created (5):* Supervisor; Operations Analyst; Competitive Analyst I; Reporting Specialist; Benefits Administrator.

RMH TELESERVICES INTERNATIONAL INC.
Att: Human Resources Manager
180 Crown Street
Saint John, NB E2L 2X7

Fax 506-638-5250
Email .... pgallagher@rmhteleservices.com
Website .... www.rmhteleservices.com

Employer Background: RMH Teleservices International Inc. is a leading provider of outsourced customer relationship management services. *New Positions Created (2):* Technical Support Specialists; Operations Manager.

RNG GROUP INC.
Att: Human Resources Manager
181 Bay Street, BCE Place
Suite 2040, Box 825, Bay Wellington Tower
Toronto, ON M5J 2T3

Tel. 416-364-0611
Fax 416-364-8949
Email .... ksmith@rng.com
Website .... www.rng.com

Employer Background: RNG Group Inc. supplies and services fuel delivery systems in Canada and the USA. *New Positions Created (3):* Accountant; Accounts Payable Position; Accounts Receivable Position.

ROBERTSON INC.
Att: Human Resources
97 Bronte Street
Milton, ON L9T 2N8

Tel. 905-878-2861
Fax 905-878-2299
Email .. dbaldassari@robertsonscrew.com
Website .... www.robertsonscrew.com

Employer Background: Robertson Inc. is a fastener manufacturer. *New Positions Created (5):* Programmer / Systems Analyst; Sales Representative; Territory Manager; Programmer / System Administrator; AutoCad Operator.

ROBIN HOOD MULTIFOODS INC., BICK'S PLANT
Att: Human Resources Department
701 Broad Street East
Dunnville, ON N1A 1H2

Fax 905-774-5145

Employer Background: Robin Hood Multifoods Inc. manufactures and markets quality foods. *New Positions Created (3):* Maintenance Electrician; Maintenance Supervisor; Plant Purchasing Coordinator.

ROBINS, APPLEBY & TAUB
Att: Admin
130 Adelaide Street West, Suite 2500
Toronto, ON M5H 2M2

Tel. 416-868-1080
Fax 416-868-0306
Email .... roborn@robapp.com
Website .... www.robapp.com

Employer Background: Robins, Appleby & Taub is a commercial litigation firm. *New Positions Created (3):* Senior Corporate Law Clerk; Corporate / Commercial Lawyer; Lawyer.

ROBINSON CONSULTANTS INC.
Att: Human Resources Manager
350 Palladium Drive
Kanata, ON K2V 1A8

Tel. 613-592-6060
Fax 613-592-5995
Email .... imckinnon@rcii.com
Website .... www.rcii.com

Employer Background: Robinson Consultants Inc. provides consulting engineering services in the areas of municipal infrastructure, water resources, transportation and environmental engineering. *New Positions Created (4):* Junior / Intermediate Civil Draftspersons (2); Construction Technician / Inspector; Project Managers; Water Resources Engineer.

ROCKWELL AUTOMATION CANADA
Att: Rob Page, Human Resources Department
135 Dundas Street
Cambridge, ON N1R 5X1

Tel. 519-740-4100
Fax 519-740-4111
Email .... racambhumanresources@
.... ra.rockwell.com
Website ... www.automation.rockwell.com

Employer Background: Rockwell Automation Canada creates automation solutions for companies worldwide. *New Positions Created (30):* Account Development Sales Manager; Motor Technical Specialist; Packaged Control Products, Medium Voltage Specialist; Engagement Manager, Engineering Services; PCP / MV Specialist; Quality System Specialist; Regional Manager, Quebec Global Manufacturing Solutions Group; Development Engineering Project Manager; Distributor Response Centre Representative; Marketing / Application Specialist; Motor Technical Specialist; Safety Engineering Specialist; Canadian Asset Management Business Manager; Technical Sales Representative; Regional Manager; Applications Engineer; Project Manager; Accounting Analyst; Field Service Analyst; Field Support Representatives; Sales Account Manager; Technical Field Support Instructor; Technical Sales Account Manager; Commercial

Support Specialist; Technical Assistant Representative, Motors; Engineering Services Manager; Manager, Human Resources - Sales; Technical Support Manager; Manufacturing Engineering Specialist; Product Marketing Manager, Presence Sensing and Safety Products.

ROCKY MOUNTAIN INSTRUMENTS INC. / RMI
Att: Human Resources Manager
4755 - 76th Avenue
Edmonton, AB T6B 0A3

Tel. 780-496-7754
Fax 780-438-9093
Email .... rmi@rmiwireless.com
Website .... www.rmiwireless.com
Employer Background: RMI manufactures and services remote, wireless monitoring systems. *New Positions Created (11):* Manager of Engineering Services; Assistant Production Manager; Field Service Technician Personnel; Sales Manager; Wireless Digital Services Manager; Embedded Software Engineer; US Sales Representatives Manager; Information Processing Technician; Plant Manager; Receptionist; Salesperson.

ROCKY VIEW NO. 44, MUNICIPAL DISTRICT OF
Att: Director of Transportation and Field Services
911 - 32nd Avenue NE
Calgary, AB T2E 6X6

Tel. 403-230-1401
Fax 403-277-3113
Email .... transportationjobs@
.... gov.mdrockyview.ab.ca
Website .... www.gov.mdrockyview.ab.ca
Employer Background: The Municipal District of Rocky View No. 44 is a growing municipality near Calgary. *New Positions Created (4):* Director of Planning and Development; Human Resource Coordinator; Economic Development Officer; Fire Prevention Officer.

ROE LOGISTICS
Att: Human Resources Manager
474 McGill Street, Suite 300
Montréal, QC H2Y 2H2

Tel. 514-396-0000
Fax 514-221-2185
Email .... gary@roelogistics.com
Website .... www.roelogistics.com
Employer Background: Founded in 1979, Roe Logistics is a freight forwarder and customs broker, with offices in Montreal, Toronto, Calgary and Vancouver. *New Positions Created (3):* Account Specialist; Junior Freight Position; Marketing Coordinator.

ROGERS AT&T WIRELESS
Att: Human Resources
4710 Kingsway, Suite 1600
Burnaby, BC V5H 4M5

Tel. 604-436-1111
Fax 604-431-1138
Email .... hrwest@rci.rogers.com
Website .... www.rogers.com

Employer Background: Rogers AT&T Wireless is the trade name of Rogers Wireless Inc., Canada's largest mobile communications provider. *New Positions Created (4):* Customer Service Consultants; Dealer Sales Manager; Customer Service Representative; In-Home Representatives.

ROGERS AT&T WIRELESS
Att: Human Resources Department
6815 - 8th Street NE, Suite 340
Calgary, AB T2E 7H7

Fax 403-730-2656
Email .... jbeaven@rci.rogers.com
Website .... www.rogers.com
Employer Background: Rogers AT&T Wireless is the trade name of Rogers Wireless Inc., Canada's largest mobile communications provider. *New Positions Created (3):* Network Technician; Network Technician, Civil Coordinator; Project Manager.

ROGERS AT&T WIRELESS
Att: Human Resources Manager
1 Mount Pleasant Road, 7th Floor
Toronto, ON M4Y 2Y5

Tel. 416-935-1100
Fax 416-935-7651
Website .... www.rogers.com
Employer Background: Rogers AT&T Wireless is the trade name of Rogers Wireless Inc., Canada's largest mobile communications provider. *New Positions Created (9):* Sales Manager, Enterprise Applications; Sales Manager, Field Force Automation; Analyst, Revenue; Analyst, Sales; Director, Business Performance Reporting; Manager, Analysis; Manager, Business Performance Reporting; Manager, Development; Senior Analyst, Marketing.

ROGERS AT&T WIRELESS
Att: HR, National Recruitment
333 Bloor Street East, 3rd Floor
Toronto, ON M4W 1G9

Tel. 416-935-1100
Fax 416-935-3111
Email ...... wirelesscareers@rci.rogers.com
Website .... www.rogers.com
Employer Background: Rogers AT&T Wireless is the trade name of Rogers Wireless Inc., Canada's largest mobile communications provider. *New Positions Created (79):* Operations Manager, Information & Analysis; Administrative Assistant II; Manager, Finance, Sales & Marketing; Manager, Financial Reporting; Corporate Sales Executive; National Retail Account Manager; Technical Service Consultants; Global Account Manager; Segment Manager; Manager Finance, Ontario Region; Contract Coordinator, Roamer Services; Roamer Settlement Analyst; Senior Systems Analyst; Wireless NOC Specialists, GSM Testing; Manager, Guest Relations; Communications Consultant; Corporate Sales Executive; Human Resources Specialist; Market Analyst, Business; Market Analyst, Consumer Products; Market Analyst, Youth Products; Network Technicians, Data Control; Project Lead, Enterprise Products; Senior Financial Analyst;

Treasury Accountant; Administrative Assistant; Business Account Specialist; Customer Service Consultants; Desktop Analyst; Equipment Engineering Specialists; Field Technician, Telecommunications; Inside Sales Representative; Integrated Retail Customer Service Representative; Integrated Retail Territory Manager; Inventory Coordinator, Fulfillment; IP Network Analyst; Manager, Advertising & Marketing; Manager, Advertising / Youth Segment; Manager, Direct Marketing and Print; Manager, IT Plans; Network Technician, Civil Coordinator; Network Technician, Transport; Product Manager; Programmer; Programmer Analyst; Project Manager; Retail Sales Representative; Senior QA Analyst; Senior QA Analyst, eBusiness ; Senior Sales Trainer; Senior Systems Analyst, Q & P; Shipper / Receiver; Wireless NOC Specialist; Corporate Sales Executive; Human Resources Advisor; Human Resources Specialist; Senior Financial Analyst; Developer - Internet / eBusiness Applications; Project Manager - Internet / eBusiness Applications; Senior Technology Architect - Desktop and Internet Applications; Systems Analyst - Desktop and Internet; Administrative Assistant II; Business Development - Account Executive; Content Support Analyst; Corporate Partnerships Coordinator; Market Analyst, Business; Market Analyst, Consumer Products; Market Analyst, Youth Products; Network Technicians, Data Control; Operations Manager, Telemessaging; Project Leader, Enterprise Products; Senior Accountant; Senior Architect; Senior Engineer, Strategic Industry Planning; Senior Programmer Analyst; Senior Quality Assurance Analyst - Internet / e-Business Applications; Technical Support Analyst; Technical Support Specialist - Devices; Treasury Accountant.

ROGERS CABLE INC.
Att: Cindy Rakic, HR Coordinator
85 Grand Crest Place, PO Box 488
Kitchener, ON N2G 4A8

Fax 519-893-7857
Email .... crakic@rci.rogers.com
Website .... www.rogers.com
Employer Background: Rogers Cable Inc. is Canada's largest cable television company, serving more than two million customers in Ontario and British Columbia. *New Positions Created (6):* Sales Coordinator, Rogers@Home; Work Order Control Clerk; Inside Plant Engineering Specialist; Technical Service Consultants; NFL Sunday Ticket & NHLCI Sales Representative; Home Entertainment Specialists.

ROGERS CABLE INC.
Att: Tara Kerr, Human Resources Advisor
333 Bloor Street East, 7th Floor
Toronto, ON M4W 1G9

Tel. 416-935-7777
Fax 416-935-4723
Email .... tkerr1@rci.rogers.com
Website .... www.rogers.com
Employer Background: Rogers Cable Inc. is Canada's largest cable television company, serving more than two million customers in

Ontario and British Columbia. *New Positions Created (32):* Finance Director; Network Performance Specialist; Web Producer; Account Executives, Retail (3); IPE Specialist / Planner; Manager, Technology Support; SMC TAC Network Service Specialist; Account Executive, Retail; Human Resources Manager, Call Centres; Administrative Assistant; Administrative Assistant IV; Business Analyst; Business Solutions Representatives; Customer Service Consultants; Engineering Associate; Financial Analyst; HR Consultant, National Programs; Manager, eBusiness Development; Manager, Product Development; Product Manager, Rogers @ Home; Project Manager, Internet Development; Receptionist / Facilities Coordinator; Rogers @ Home Sales Process Analyst; Senior Project Leader, Mid-Range Systems; Business Development Manager; Product Development Manager; Program Manager, Interactive Television Services; Program Manager, Interactive Television Services; Project Manager, Internet Service Operations; Manager, Commercial Operations; Manger, Technical Operations; Process Analyst.

ROGERS CABLE INC.
Att: Human Resources Manager
855 York Mills Road
Toronto, ON M3B 1Z1

Tel. 416-466-6500
Fax 416-446-0250
Website .... www.rogers.com

Employer Background: Rogers Cable Inc. is Canada's largest cable television company, serving more than two million customers in Ontario and British Columbia. *New Positions Created (20):* Maintenance Technician; Producer; Service Technician; Technical Support Consultant; Accounts Receivable Consultant; Sales Coordinator, Rogers@ Home; Support Services Coordinator; Team Manager, Budgeting CCOS; Team Manager, Reporting CCOS; Process Analyst; Process Analyst, IVR Process; Network Performance Specialist; Bilingual Customer Care Team Manager; Support Service Coordinator; Administrative Assistant IV; HR Advisor; Producer - Plugged IN ; Publicist; New Product Sales Specialist; Sales Coordinator.

ROGERS CABLE INC.
Att: Shamai Silcott-Graham,
HR Administrator
244 Newkirk Road
Richmond Hill, ON L4C 3S5

Tel. 905-884-8111
Fax 905-884-8151
Email .... ssilcot2@rci.rogers.com
Website .... www.rogers.com

Employer Background: Rogers Cable Inc. is Canada's largest cable television company, serving more than two million customers in Ontario and British Columbia. *New Positions Created (7):* Home Entertainment Specialists; Direct Sales Representative; Sales Coordinator, Rogers@Home; Construction Technician; Customer Service Consultant; Human Resources Administrator; Senior Producer.

ROGERS CABLE INC.
Att: Joe Brooks, HR Manager
199 Chesley Drive
Saint John, NB E2K 4S9

Fax 506-649-7111
Email .... jbrooks@rci.rogers.com
Website .... www.rogers.com

Employer Background: Rogers Cable Inc. is Canada's largest cable television company, serving more than two million customers in Ontario and British Columbia. *New Positions Created (7):* Material Handler; Master Control Operator; Team Leader, Eastern Region; Team Leader, Western Region; Field Supervisor; Bilingual Publicity & Promotions Officer; Bilingual Regional Coordinator, Volunteer Services.

ROGERS CABLE INC.
Att: Tracey O'Toole, Human Resources
22 Austin Street, PO Box 8596
St. John's, NF A1B 4M1

Fax 709-722-8384
Email .... totoole@cableatlantic.nf.ca
Website .... www.rogers.com

Employer Background: Rogers Cable Inc. is Canada's largest cable television company. *New Positions Created (4):* Account Executive; Community Relations & Promotions Coordinator; Administrative Assistant; Television Producer.

ROGERS CABLE INC., CALGARY DISTRIBUTION CENTER
Att: Linda Smith
4816 - 52nd Street SE
Calgary, AB T2B 3R2

Fax 403-252-4836
Email .... lsmith@rci.rogers.com
Website .... www.rogers.com

Employer Background: Rogers Cable Inc. is Canada's largest cable television company, serving more than two million customers in Ontario and British Columbia. *New Positions Created (3):* Assistant Store Manager; Freight Coordinator; Shipper and Receiver.

ROGERS COMMUNICATIONS INC.
Att: Pamela Leslie
1 Mount Pleasant Road
Toronto, ON M4Y 2Y5

Fax 416-935-7620
Email .... pleslie@rci.rogers.com
Website .... www.rogers.com

Employer Background: Rogers Communications is Canada's national communications company, with wireless, cable and media divisions. *New Positions Created (5):* Manager, Planning & Projects; Network Management Analyst; Administrative Assistant III; Learning Centre Administrator; Real Estate Analyst.

ROGERS COMMUNICATIONS INC.
Att: HR Director, Customer Care
333 Bloor Street East
Toronto, ON M4W 1G9

Tel. 416-935-1100
Fax 416-935-7951
Website .... www.rogers.com

Employer Background: Rogers Communications Inc. is Canada's leading provider of communication, entertainment and information services. *New Positions Created (44):* Bilingual Receptionist; Mgr, Purchasing, Sales & Marketing; Administrative Assistant II; Contract Negotiator; Capacity Planning Analyst, National; National Scheduling Analyst; National Scheduling Team Manager; Senior Buyer; Unix Database Administrator; HR Coordinator; Administrative Assistant; Construction Specialist; Director, Marketing; Telecom Technician; Zoning Specialist; Associate Analyst; Benefits & Pension Analyst; Executive Assistant; Facilities Manager, Ontario; Mgr, Brand Administration; Manager, Operations; Marketing Analyst; Program Manager; Senior Programmer Analyst; System Operator; Construction Specialist; Consultant, Mgmnt Development; Coordinator, Telecom & Infrastructure; Customer Care Information Database Analyst; Human Resources Advisor, Customer Care Call Centre; Manager, Customer Care Finance; Manager, Sales Planning; Senior Database Programmer / Analyst; Senior Information Technology Auditor; Zoning Specialist; Administrative Assistant ; Group Leader, Wireless Production Control; Human Resources Manager, Projects; Manager, Recruitment, Customer Care; Senior Financial Analyst; Corporate Partnerships Coordinator; Receptionist; National HR Project Manager; National Recruitment Manager.

ROGERS COMMUNICATIONS INC.
Att: Human Resources Manager
475 Richmond Road
Ottawa, ON K2A 3Y8

Tel. 613-725-3581
Fax 613-759-8681
Email .... mallevat@rci.rogers.com
Website .... www.rogers.com

Employer Background: Rogers Communications Inc. is Canada's leading provider of communication, entertainment and information services. *New Positions Created (9):* Dispatch / Work Order Control Clerk ; Sales Representatives; Territory Field Sales Representative; Bilingual Publicity & Promotions Officer; Executive Assistant, Government Relations; Mobile Sports Producer; Territory Field Sales Representative; Bilingual Telephone Service Representatives; Work Order Control Administrator.

ROGERS IMEDIA
Att: Human Resources
156 Front Street West, Suite 400
Toronto, ON M5J 2L6

Tel. 416-340-7242
Fax 416-642-4888
Email .... careers@imedia.rogers.com
Website .... www.rogers.com

Employer Background: Rogers iMedia develops and markets Canadian content for some of North America's most popular Internet properties, including Quicken.ca, Bid.com, Electric Library and Rogers@ Home. *New Positions Created (5):* Assistant Editor; Controller; XML Production Specialist; Applications Developers; Project Mgr.

ROGERS MEDIA, PUBLISHING
Att: Human Resources
777 Bay Street, 9th Floor
Toronto, ON M5W 1A7

Tel. 416-596-5270
Fax 416-596-5967
Website .... www.rogers.com
Employer Background: Rogers Media, Publishing is Canada's largest publisher of magazines and communication products. *New Positions Created (49):* Account Representative; Associate Art Director; Bilingual Credit Service Representative; District Sales Manager; Inside Sales Representative, New Business Development; Marketing Analyst; Sales Representative; Supervisor of Corporate Accounting; Account Manager; Business Manager; Sales Representative; Associate Editor; Creative Services Specialist; Managing Editor, Conferences; Sales Manager; Web Sales and Marketing Director; Healthcare Writer / Editor; Publisher / Manager; Publisher; Account Manager, New Business Development; Administrative Assistant; Editorial & Administrative Manager; Group Accountant; Sales Representative; Web Manager / Editor; Website Coordinator; Postscript Operator; Senior Editor; Senior Sales Representative; Senior Writer, Canadian Business; Staff Writer, Pharmacy Post; Web Account Manager, Chatelaine; Insert & Supplement Supervisor; Editorial Secretary / Production Coordinator; Publisher, Account Executive; Marketing Analyst; Administrative Assistant, Consumer Marketing Division; Assistant Editor; News Editor; Assistant, Information Systems; Assistant Editor; Editorial Producer; Project Coordinator, Marketing Information Systems; Account Manager; Junior Bilingual Credit Representative ; Manager, Recruitment and Human Resources; Account Executive; Classified Sales Representative; Website Customer Administrator.

ROGERS MEDIA, TELEVISION
Att: Human Resources Manager
545 Lakeshore Boulevard West
Toronto, ON M5V 1A3

Fax 416-260-3655
Website .... www.rogers.com
Employer Background: Rogers Media, Television is a local television station that provides coverage of local entertainment, lifestyle, sports and information programming. *New Positions Created (14):* Broadcast Facility Technician; Master Control Switcher; Administrative Assistant; Camera Pre-Production Position; Intermediate Traffic Coordinator; Receptionist; Assistant Coordinator of Library Service; Library and Interstitial Services Coordinator; Library & Broadcast Services Coordinator; Master Control Switchers (8); National Language Sales Account Executive; Accountant; Intermediate Traffic Coordinators (3); Receptionist.

ROGERS & PARTNERS SECURITIES INC.
Att: Controller
777 - 8th Avenue SW, Suite 2300
Calgary, AB T2P 3R5

Tel. 403-531-6800

Fax 403-265-6039
Email ...... llattery@rogers-securities.com
Website .... www.rogers-securities.com
Employer Background: Rogers & Partners Securities Inc. provides retail brokerage services to over 12,000 clients. *New Positions Created (3):* Accounting / Office Assistant; RRSP Administrator; Vice President, Finance.

ROGERS SHARED SERVICES
Att: Donna Dunne, Human Resources
45 Esna Park Drive
Markham, ON L3R 1C9

Fax 905-513-5330
Email .... ddunne@rci.rogers.com
Website .... www.rogers.com
Employer Background: Rogers Shared Services (part of Rogers Communications Inc.) provides IT infrastructure and business solutions to Rogers operating companies. *New Positions Created (19):* Senior Project Manager; Bilingual Receptionist; Message Processing System Analyst; Database Administrator; Program Manager; Senior Network Architect; Storage Technical Analyst; Technical Architect; Unix Systems Administrator; Real Estate Coordinator; Senior Application (Web) Developer ; Systems Administrator (NT); Technical Planner; Contract Negotiator; Property Administrator; Manager, Real Estate; Real Estate Analyst; Real Estate Coordinator; Facilities Planner.

ROGERS VIDEO
Att: Sam Sidhu, Manager, Recruitment, Training & Development, Western Canada
10100 Shellbridge Way, Suite 100
Richmond, BC V6X 2W7

Tel. 604-270-9200
Fax 604-270-4530
Email .... ssidhu@rci.rogers.com
Website .... www.rogersvideo.ca
Employer Background: Rogers Video is a large Canadian-owned video retailer, operating over 240 video retail stores in British Columbia, Alberta, Saskatchewan, Manitoba and Ontario. *New Positions Created (15):* Payroll Administrator; Category Assistant; Financial Analyst; Human Resources Assistant; Staff Accountant, Shows to Go; Assistant Store Manager; Junior Analyst / Programmer, Store Systems; Print Production Coordinator; Regional Marketing Coordinator; Assistant Store Manager; Store Managers; Advertising and Marketing Coordinator; Accounts Payable Clerk; Area Manager - Burnaby Area 21; Senior Financial Analyst.

ROHDE & SCHWARZ CANADA INC.
Att: Human Resources
555 March Road
Kanata, ON K2K 2M5

Tel. 613-592-8000
Fax 613-592-8009
Website .... www.rohde-schwarz.com
Employer Background: Rohde & Schwarz Canada Inc., a subsidiary of German-based Rohde & Schwarz GmbH, manufactures communications and measuring equipment. The parent company was founded in

1933 and has 4,400 employees worldwide. *New Positions Created (2):* Customer Service Coordinator; Service Technologists.

ROHIT GROUP, THE
Att: Human Resources Manager
9644 - 54th Avenue, Suite 200
Edmonton, AB T6E 5V1

Tel. 780-436-9015
Fax 780-437-6226
Email .... rohit@rohithomes.com
Website .... www.rohithomes.com
Employer Background: Rohit is a real estate investment development and management company. *New Positions Created (7):* New Home Sales Professional; Multifamily Sales Professional; Draftsperson; General Manager; New Home Salesperson; Sales & Marketing Manager; Project Manager.

ROHM AND HAAS CANADA INC.
Att: Mr. P. Berner, HR Manager
2 Manse Road
Toronto, ON M1E 3T9

Tel. 416-284-4711
Fax 416-287-4486
Website .... www.rohmandhaas.com
Employer Background: Rohm and Haas Canada Inc. manufactures specialty chemical products. *New Positions Created (2):* Chemical Engineer; Communications and PC Support Specialist.

ROLLS-ROYCE CANADA LTD.
Att: Human Resources Department
9500 Cote de Liesse
Lachine, QC H8T 1A2

Tel. 514-631-3541
Fax 514-828-1626
Email .... cv@rolls-royce.ca
Website .... www.rolls-royce.com
Employer Background: Rolls-Royce Canada Ltd. is a subsidiary of UK-based Rolls-Royce, the world's largest manufacturer of jet engines and energy turbines. *New Positions Created (14):* Aerodynamics Analysts; Applications Engineers; Combustion Analysts; Development Engineers; Industrial Engineers; Integrated Logistics Support Specialist; Non-Destructive Testing Technicians; Performance Analysts; Production Manager; Program Managers; Project Controllers; Project Quality Manager; Proposal Engineers; Financial Analyst.

RONALDS PRINTING
Att: Customer Service Manager
2626 - 12th Street NE
Calgary, AB T2E 7K3

Tel. 403-250-0400
Fax 403-250-2574
Employer Background: Ronalds Printing is a large sheet-fed printer. *New Positions Created (2):* Customer Service Representative; Estimator.

RONCO PROTECTIVE PRODUCTS
Att: Human Resources
146 St. Regis Crescent South
Toronto, ON M3J 1Y8

Tel. 416-663-0061
Fax 416-663-0149
Email .... ronco@ronco.ca
Website .... www.ronco.org

Employer Background: Ronco Protective Products manufactures and distributes safety / protective products, including gloves, aprons, sleeves, beard covers and bouffant caps. *New Positions Created (3):* Accountant; Customer Service / Inside Sales Representative; Sales Representative.

ROOFMART ALBERTA INC.
Att: General Manager
6125 - 11th Street SE, Suite 250
Calgary, AB T2H 2L6
Fax 403-265-3845
Email .... roofmart@telusplanet.net

Employer Background: Roofmart Alberta Inc. distributes building products. *New Positions Created (6):* Branch Manager; Inside Sales Position / Order Desk Warehouse Position; Truck Driver; Sales Representative; Field Technical Representative; Accountant.

ROOMBLOCK INC.
Att: Human Resources Manager
372 Bay Street, 17th Floor, Sterling Tower
Toronto, ON M5H 2W9
Tel. 416-203-2800
Fax 416-352-0099
Email .... hr@roomblock.com
Website .... www.roomblock.com

Employer Background: RoomBlock Inc. is a new business-to-business e-commerce company that provides accommodations for attendees of meetings and conventions. *New Positions Created (4):* Various Sales Management Positions (3); Billing Services Coordinator; Convention Services Manager; Team Assistant.

ROOMS INTERNATIONAL
Att: Allan Nolan
1230 Old Innes Road, Unit 413
Ottawa, ON K1B 3V3
Tel. 613-744-3340
Fax 613-744-1719

Employer Background: Rooms International is a retailer of home furnishings. *New Positions Created (2):* Floor Display Coordinator; Interior Designer.

ROOTS CANADA LTD.
Att: Mr. Baker
1168 Caledonia Road
Toronto, ON M6A 2W5
Tel. 416-781-8284
Fax 416-484-4306
Email .... hr@roots.com
Website .... www.roots.com

Employer Background: Founded in 1973, Roots Canada Ltd. manufactures and retails high-quality leather products and casual clothing. The company has over 119 stores in Canada, the USA and Asia. *New Positions Created (7):* Pattern Maker / Product Development Manager; Various Garment Manufacturing Positions; Buyers (2); Men's and Baby's; Design Technicians (2), Men's and

Accessories; Director, Human Resources; Financial Controller; Senior Merchandise Design Director, Kids and Babies.

ROPAK CANADA INC.
Att: Human Resources Manager
1081 Cliveden Avenue
Annacis Island, BC V3M 5V1
Tel. 604-526-9947
Fax 604-526-8929
Website .... www.ropak.ca

Employer Background: Ropak Canada Inc. manufactures plastic containers used in the packaging of dairy, food and industrial products. *New Positions Created (2):* Injection Moulding Processor; Maintenance Mechanic.

ROPAK CANADA INC.
Att: Human Resources Department
2240 Wyecroft Road
Oakville, ON L6L 6M1
Tel. 905-827-9340
Fax 905-827-8841
Website .... www.ropak.ca

Employer Background: Ropak Canada Inc. manufactures plastic containers used in the packaging of dairy, food and industrial products. *New Positions Created (6):* Warehouse Supervisor; Quality Assurance Manager; Injection Moulder; Lead Hand; Maintenance Mechanic; Regional Sales Manager.

ROSEDALE GOLF CLUB
Att: Robert Burrows, Course Manager
1901 Mount Pleasant Road
Toronto, ON M4N 2W3
Tel. 416-485-9321
Fax 416-485-7087
Email ... burrowsofrosedale@hotmail.com

Employer Background: Established in 1893, the Rosedale Golf Club is one of Canada's most prestigious year-round private clubs. *New Positions Created (2):* Horticulturist / Gardener; Bartenders and Foodservice.

ROSEDALE TRANSPORT LTD.
Att: Human Resources
6845 Invader Crescent
Mississauga, ON L5T 2B7
Tel. 905-670-0057
Fax 905-670-7271
Email .... humanresources@rosedale.ca
Website .... www.rosedale.ca

Employer Background: Rosedale Transport Ltd. is an international transportation company. *New Positions Created (4):* Customer Service Representative; Operations Manager; Linehaul / Logistics Position; General LTL Freight Sales Representative.

ROSS VIDEO LTD.
Att: Troy English
8 John Street, PO Box 220
Iroquois, ON K0E 1K0
Tel. 613-652-4886
Fax 613-228-0464
Email .... troye@rossvideo.com
Website .... www.rossvideo.com

Employer Background: Ross Video Ltd. makes equipment for television broadcasters. *New Positions Created (3):* Senior CAD PCB Designers; Software Quality Assurance; Video Product Software Developers.

ROTHENBERG GROUP, THE
Att: Human Resource
4420 St. Catherine Street West
Westmount, QC H3Z 1R2
Tel. 514-934-0586
Fax 514-934-4685
Email .... corrigan@rothenberg.ca
Website .... www.rothenberg.ca

Employer Background: The Rothenberg Group provides investment advice on stocks, bonds, RRSPs, RIFFs and mutual funds. *New Positions Created (5):* Customer Service Position; Financial Planner; Customer Rep; Financial Planner; Stockbroker.

ROUGE VALLEY HEALTH SYSTEM, AJAX & PICKERING HEALTH CENTRE
Att: Human Resources Department
580 Harwood Avenue South
Ajax, ON L1S 2J4
Tel. 905-683-2320
Fax 905-428-5208
Email .... hr@rougevalley.ca
Website .... www.excellentcare.com

Employer Background: The Ajax and Pickering Health Centre is a community hospital, serving residents of west Durham since 1954. *New Positions Created (5):* Registered Nurses, Child Health Unit; Various Medical Professionals; Patient Flow Facilitator; Manager, Diagnostic Imaging; Manager, Intensive Care Unit.

ROUGE VALLEY HEALTH SYSTEM, CENTENARY HEALTH CENTRE
Att: Human Resources Department
2867 Ellesmere Road
Toronto, ON M1E 4B9
Tel. 416-281-7271
Fax 416-281-7289
Email .... hr@rougevalley.ca
Website .... www.excellentcare.com

Employer Background: The Rouge Valley Health System is a two-site system, with Centenary Health Centre serving east Toronto, and the Ajax and Pickering Health Centre serving west Durham. *New Positions Created (42):* Registered Nurses; Various Medical Professionals; Clinical Practice Leaders (2); Manager of Operations, Maternal / Newborn Services; Various Clinical Practice Leader Positions; Manager, Inpatient Medicine / Chemotherapy Clinic; Clinical Informatics Specialists; Medical Laboratory Technologist, Core Lab; Pharmacists; Social Worker, Continuing Care Rehabilitation; Adult Psychiatrists (3); Child Psychiatrists (3); Manager, Inpatient Surgical Unit; Neurologists (2); Oncologists (2); Respirologist; Clinical Practice Leader, Mental Health; Radiology Technologist; Registered Nurses, IV Team; Registered Nurses, Medical / Telemetry; Registered Technologist, Nuclear Medicine; Social Worker, Continuing Care Rehabilitation; Cardiac Technicians; Clinical Practice Leaders; ECG Technicians; Physiotherapists; Registered Nurses, CCU; Registered Nurses, Children's Health; Registered Nurses, Emergency; Registered Nurses, ICU; Registered Nurses, Inpatient Medicine; Registered Nurses, Mental Health Unit; Registered Nurses, Neonatal ICU; Registered Nurses, Operating Room; Registered Nurses, Surgical; Registered Nurses, Women's Health; Registered Technologists, Ultrasound; Human Resources Practitioner; Anaesthesiologists (2); Associate Chief, Paediatrics; Chief, Paediatrics; Otolaryngologists (2).

ROUNDHEAVEN COMMUNICATIONS CANADA INC.
Att: Human Resources Manager
595 Burrard St., 3 Bentall Ctr.
Suite 2323, PO Box 49336
Vancouver, BC V7X 1L4
Tel. 604-687-7757
Website .... www.roundheaven.com
Employer Background: RoundHeaven Communications Canada Inc. provides web hosting services for business clients. *New Positions Created (20):* Client Manager; Employee Services Manager; Sales Engineer; Director of Finance; Employee Services Manager; Facility Manager; Information Systems Security Officer; Oracle Database Administrator; Purchasing Manager; Recruiter; Regional Sales Manager; Sales Engineer; Security Engineer; Senior Network Engineer; Senior Project Manager; Senior SQL Specialist; Senior Systems Engineer; Senior UNIX Engineer; Senior Web-Server Specialist; Technician, Network Operations Centre.

ROUTES ASTROENGINEERING LTD.
Att: Human Resources Manager
303 Legget Drive
Kanata, ON K2K 1B1
Tel. 613-592-0748
Fax 613-592-6553
Email .... staff@routes.com
Website .... www.routes.com
Employer Background: Routes AstroEngineering Ltd. is a Canadian advanced engineering company that designs and builds space science instrumentation. *New Positions Created (3):* Electrical Designer 1; Electrical Designer 2; Mechanical Designer 1.

ROWAN WILLIAMS DAVIES & IRWIN
Att: Human Resources Coordinator
650 Woodlawn Road West
Guelph, ON N1K 1B8
Tel. 519-823-1311
Fax 519-823-1316
Email .... recruiting@rwdi.com
Website .... www.rwdi.com
Employer Background: RWDI specializes in wind / environmental engineering, microclimates, industrial process flows, noise, vibration and acoustics analysis. *New Positions Created (5):* Air Quality Modellers; Environmental Wind Engineer; Noise / Acoustics Engineer; Project Manager, Noise / Acoustics; Urban Airshed Modeller.

ROYAL ALLIANCE INC.
Att: Human Resources
7200 Martin Grove Road
Woodbridge, ON L4L 9J3
Fax 905-264-3720
Website .... www.royalgrouptech.com
Employer Background: Royal Alliance Inc. manufactures consumer household products, including patio furniture. *New Positions Created (4):* Manager, Production Planning & Logistics; Customer Service Representative; Receptionist; Accounts Receivable Clerk.

ROYAL ARCH MASONIC HOME
Att: Diane Miller, Director of Resident Care
7850 Champlain Crescent
Vancouver, BC V5S 4C7
Tel. 604-437-7343
Fax 604-437-7373
Employer Background: The Royal Arch Masonic Home is an intermediate care facility in Vancouver, with space for 151 residents. *New Positions Created (2):* Nurse Clinician; Nurse Clinician, Geriatrics.

ROYAL BANK FINANCIAL GROUP
Att: Human Resources Manager
1055 West Georgia Street
Vancouver, BC V6E 3S5
Tel. 604-665-5189
Fax 604-665-5956
Email .... jobapp.van@rb-erc.com
Website .... www.royalbank.com
Employer Background: Royal Bank Financial Group is Canada's premier financial services group. *New Positions Created (4):* Account Manager, Personal Financial Services; Branch Administrator, Career Sales; Customer Care Associates; Territory Sales Manager, Mortgage Specialists.

ROYAL BANK FINANCIAL GROUP
Att: Adele Selby
335 - 8th Avenue SW, 6th Floor
Calgary, AB T2P 1C9
Tel. 403-292-3493
Fax 403-292-3017
Email .... jobapp.cal@rb-erc.com
Website .... www.royalbank.com
Employer Background: Royal Bank Financial Group is Canada's largest financial services group, with 60,000 employees who serve 10 million clients. *New Positions Created (11):* Lending Services Officer; Manager, Documentation; Investment and Retirement Planners; Income Tax Officer; Team Leader, Agriculture; Account Managers, Business Banking; Assistant Manager, Personal Financial Services Training Program; Manager, Personal Financial Services Training Program; Parcel Preparation Clerk; Personal Financial Services Representative; Manager, Personal Financial Services.

ROYAL BANK FINANCIAL GROUP
Att: Employment Resource Centre
970 Lawrence Avenue West, Suite 110
Toronto, ON M6A 3B6
Tel. 416-256-0088

Fax 416-256-0169
Email .... emp@rb-erc.com
Website .... www.royalbank.com
Employer Background: Royal Bank Financial Group is Canada's premier financial services group. *New Positions Created (165):* Director, Mergers and Acquisitions; Marketing Database Analyst; Operations and Relief Officer; Account Representative; Data Input Position, Dealer Services; Dealer Services Representatives; Derivative Specialists; Fund Accountants; Manager, Performance and Learning Strategies; Sales Proposal Writer; Supervisor, Dealer Services; Trust Accountant, Dealer Services; Actuarial Assistant; Customer Assistance Officer; Accident Benefits Specialist; Assistant Manager, Costing MIS, Products and Service Delivery Finance; Claims Manager, Cancellation Unit; Inside Claims Advisors; Investment and Retirement Planners; Manager, Closing; Manager, Custody; Manager, Recruiting and Selection; Road Claims Advisors; Senior Manager, Accounting Advisory Services; Account Manager, Personal Financial Services; Assistant Manager, Personal Financial Services; Liaison Officer, Accounts Payable; Licenced Insurance Advisor; Manager, Group Risk Management; Account Manager, Personal Financial Services; Director, Performance and Learning Strategies; Manager, Risk Policy, Securities Lending; Marketing Coordinator; Senior Compensation Advisor; Senior Technical Systems Analyst; Actuarial Analyst; Alliance and Online Service Assistant, North American Markets; Auditors; Corporate Actuary; Group Manager, e-Procurement; Personal Financial Services Trainees (2); Senior Analyst, GIS; Senior Auditors; Senior Manager; Manager, Nostro Reconciliation and Investigations; Marketing Manager, Retail Support; Project Manager; Senior Business / Technical Analyst; Senior Telecom Analyst; Telecommunication Analyst; Business Systems Analysts; Consultant; Distribution Analyst; IT Architect, Information Management, Technology Architecture; Program Manager; Project Manager; Project Manager, Software Distribution; Senior Developer, Web Solutions; Senior Programmers / Analysts; Senior Programmers / Analysts, Client / Server Systems; Senior Technical Analyst; Senior Technical Specialist, Client Management Technologies; Senior Technical Systems Analyst; Senior Technical Systems Analyst; Senior Technical Systems Analyst; Systems Auditors; Technical Systems Analyst; Technical Systems Analyst; Technical Systems Analyst; Technical Systems Analyst; Technical Systems Analyst, Production Support; Account Manager, Business Banking; Account Representatives; Actuarial Analyst; Associate, Debt Products, Corporate Banking Group; Bilingual Account Representative; Bilingual Customer Assistance Officer; Bilingual Customer Service Representative; Bilingual Technical Support Representative; Client Management Analyst; Copywriter; Corporate Actuarial Position; Corporate Compliance Analyst; Customer Assistance Officer; Customer Assistance Officer; Customer Service Representative; Customer Service Representative; Customer Service

Representative; Derivative Specialists; Director, Service Delivery; Executive Account Manager, Asian; Fund Accountants; Graphic Designer; Insurance Sales Advisor; Legal and Regulatory Officer; Manager, Business Implementation & Client Transition; Mortgage Service Representative Batcher; Pension Administrator; Personal Financial Service Rep, Mortgage Assistance Program; Personal Financial Service Rep Trainees; Personal Financial Service Rep Trainees; Personal Financial Services Rep; Personal Financial Services Rep; Personal Financial Services Rep; Personal Financial Services Rep; Personal Financial Services Representative; Personal Financial Services Representative; Personal Financial Services Representative Trainees; Product Development Coordinator; Product Management Positions; Senior Account Representative, Mutual Fund Recordkeeping; Senior Analyst, Interest Rate Risk Analysis; Senior Financial Analyst; Senior Manager, Marketing Public Relations; Senior Manager, Portfolio Management Research; Senior Product Manager, Core Transactional Services; Senior Product Manager, Fund Management Services; Tax Administrator; Web Developer; Claims Advisors - Home and Auto Division; Inside Service Advisor - Claims; Manager - Design and Space Standards; Registered Nurse; Territory Sales Manager, Managed Investments and Trusts; Managers, Internal Audit Services; Project Manager, Recruitment; Recruitment Advisor, Attracting & Sourcing; Senior Technical Analyst; Tax Administrator; Insurance Advisors; Team Manager, Call Centre Operations; Personal Financial Services Representatives; Senior IT Security Consultant; Account Service Officers; Administrative Positions; Product Manager; Road Claims Advisor; SAP Specialists; Senior Analyst, Software Asset Management; Technical Systems Analyst; Unit Manager, Claims Road Operations; Senior Financial Planning Consultant; Senior Manager, Audit Development; Manager / Analyst, Industry Risk; Senior Technical Systems Analyst; Senior Technology Architect; Technical Systems Analysts; Accident Benefits Specialist; Inside Service Advisor; Process Analyst; Risk Management and Compliance Specialists; Insurance Advisors; Trade Manager, Global Integrated Solutions; Manager, Credit and Compliance; Manager, Customer Service Centre; Sales Proposal Writer; Various Financial Positions; Business Systems Analysts; Senior Programmer / Analysts, Client / Server Systems; Systems Auditors; Analyst; Insurance Sales Advisor; Mortgage Specialist; Senior Account Manager, Real Estate.

ROYAL BANK FINANCIAL GROUP
Att: Employment Resource Centre
1 Place Ville Marie, 10th Floor, West Wing
Montréal, QC H3B 4S6
Tel. 514-874-7222
Fax 514-874-5453
Email .... jobapp.mtl@rb-erc.com
Website .... www.royalbank.com
Employer Background: Royal Bank Financial Group is Canada's premier financial services group. *New Positions Created (11):*

Personal Financial Service Representative; Executive Assistant, Global Banking; Branch Managers; Administrative Assistant; Contracting Administrator; Operations Officers / Operations Assistants; Regional Advanced Sales Director; Regional Supervisor; Regional Agency Coordinator; Business Banking Account Manager; Customer Service Representative, RBC Insurance.

ROYAL BRITISH COLUMBIA MUSEUM
Att: Terry Lawrence, Personnel Services
675 Belleville Street
Victoria, BC V8W 9W2
Tel. 250-387-2263
Fax 250-953-4336
Email .. tlawrence@royalbcmuseum.bc.ca
Website .... www.royalbcmuseum.bc.ca
Employer Background: The Royal British Columbia Museum is dedicated to preserving British Columbia's cultural and natural heritage. *New Positions Created (6):* Marketing Coordinator; Heritage Resource Officer, Curator of Botany; Manager, Anthropology; Director, Customer & Corporate Services; Manager; Group Sales and Services Supervisor.

ROYAL BUILDING SYSTEMS (CDN) LTD. / RBS
Att: Human Resources Department
1 Royal Gate Boulevard
Woodbridge, ON L4L 8Z7
Tel. 905-264-0701
Fax 905-264-0699
Email .... pdefrancesco@rbsdirect.com
Website .... www.rbsdirect.com
Employer Background: RBS (a member of Royal Group Technologies Ltd.) manufactures polymer-based home improvement, consumer and construction products. *New Positions Created (5):* Engineer / Designer; Administrative Assistant; Designer; Project Manager; Various Accounting Positions.

ROYAL CANADIAN GOLF ASSOCIATION / RCGA
Att: Human Resources
1333 Dorval Drive, Golf House
Oakville, ON L6J 4Z3
Tel. 905-849-9700
Fax 905-845-7040
Email .... gaskin@rcga.org
Website .... www.rcga.org
Employer Background: Founded in 1895, RCGA is the governing body of men's amateur golf in Canada. *New Positions Created (3):* Bilingual Sponsorship Mgr; Communications Coordinator; Publications Editor.

ROYAL CANADIAN MINT / RCM
Att: Alex Tremblay, Human Resources
320 Sussex Drive
Ottawa, ON K1A 0G8
Tel. 613-993-3500
Fax 613-998-0272
Email .... careers@rcmint.ca
Website .... www.rcmint.ca
Employer Background: RCM is a profit-making Crown corporation involved in all aspects of coin design, production and mar-

keting. *New Positions Created (6):* Programmer / Analyst; Communications Manager; Senior Buyers (2); Director of Purchasing; Electrician; Quality Systems Engineer.

ROYAL COLLEGE OF DENTAL SURGEONS OF ONTARIO / RCDSO
Att: Paul Harrison,
CMA, Treasurer / Director
6 Crescent Road, 5th Floor
Toronto, ON M4W 1T1
Fax 416-961-5814
Email .... pharrison@rcdso.org
Website .... www.rcdso.org
Employer Background: The RCDSO is the regulatory or governing body established by the provincial government to regulate the practice of dentistry in Ontario. *New Positions Created (2):* Claims Examiner / Adjuster; Office Services Assistant.

ROYAL DOULTON COMPANY, THE
Att: Human Resources
850 Progress Avenue
Toronto, ON M1H 3C4
Tel. 416-431-4202
Fax 416-431-6512
Email .... careers@royaldoulton.ca
Employer Background: The Royal Doulton Company manufactures ceramic tableware and giftware. *New Positions Created (5):* Key Account Manager; National Sales Manager; Account Manager; Account Manager; Human Resources / ISO 9002 Coordinator.

ROYAL GROUP TECHNOLOGIES INC.
Att: Human Resources Manager
1 Royal Gate Boulevard
Woodbridge, ON L4L 8Z7
Tel. 905-264-0701
Fax 905-850-3017
Email .... recruiting@royplas.com
Website .... www.royalgrouptech.com
Employer Background: Royal Group Technologies Inc. manufactures technologically advanced, polymer-based home improvement, consumer and construction products. *New Positions Created (16):* Accounting Clerk; Customer Service Representative; Maintenance Technician; Paint Line Set-Up Technician; Process / Application / Manufacturing Technicians (2); Quality Analyst; Receptionist; Receptionist / Administrator; Replacement Parts Shipper; Lead Hand; Production Coordinators (3); Quality Control Inspector; Quality Control Technician; Shipper / Receiver; Supervisor; Technical Support Person.

ROYAL INLAND HOSPITAL
Att: Human Resources Department
311 Columbia Street
Kamloops, BC V2C 2T1
Tel. 250-314-2720
Fax 250-314-2337
Email .... isobel.lamarche@ex.thr.bc.ca
Employer Background: Royal Inland Hospital, a member of the Thompson Health Region, is a 285-bed regional facility. *New Positions Created (2):* Tech III Pathology Assistant; EEG Technologist.

ROYAL LEPAGE COMMERCIAL INC.
Att: Sandra Seeley
2235 Sheppard Avenue East, Suite 1600
Toronto, ON M2J 5B8

Tel. 416-494-9500
Fax 416-494-9444
Email .... sseeley@royallepage.com
Website .... www.royallepage.com
Employer Background: Royal LePage Commercial Inc. is a diversified commercial real estate services company. *New Positions Created (4):* Senior Word Processor; Administrative Assistant; Executive Assistant; Sales Trainee.

ROYAL ONTARIO MUSEUM / ROM
Att: Human Resources Department
100 Queen's Park
Toronto, ON M5S 2C6

Tel. 416-586-5543
Fax 416-586-5827
Email .... info@rom.on.ca
Website .... www.rom.on.ca
Employer Background: Established in 1912, the ROM has over 700,000 visitors per year and more than 500 employees. *New Positions Created (5):* Associate Curator, Ancient Near Eastern Art and Archaeology; Associate Curator, European Decorative Arts; Associate Curator, Molecular Systematics of Fungi; Associate Curator, South Asian Civilizations; Project Manager, Exhibits, Cultural Innovations.

ROYAL OTTAWA HEALTH CARE GROUP / ROHCG
Att: Human Resources
1145 Carling Avenue
Ottawa, ON K1Z 7K4

Tel. 613-722-6521
Fax 613-798-2970
Email .... recruit@rohcg.on.ca
Website .... www.rohcg.on.ca
Employer Background: ROHCG provides specialized physical rehabilitation and mental health services. *New Positions Created (12):* Clinical Psychologist, Anxiety Disorders; Foundation Director; Pharmacy Manager; General Accountant; Geriatric Psychiatric Nurse; Psychogeriatric Nurse; Psychogeriatric Nurse; Team Manager, Dual Diagnosis; Payroll Accountant; Psychogeriatric Outreach Nurse; Service Coordinator, Addictions Program; Clinical Nurse Consultant.

ROYAL ROADS UNIVERSITY
Att: HR Career Opportunities
2005 Sooke Road
Victoria, BC V9B 5Y2

Tel. 250-391-2511
Fax 250-391-2500
Email .... rru-career-opportunities@
.... royalroads.ca
Website .... www.royalroads.ca
Employer Background: Royal Roads University offers degree programs in sustainable development, entrepreneurship, empowering leadership and conflict management. *New Positions Created (10):* Faculty Position; Faculty Position; Director, MA Leadership

and Training Program; Executive Assistant to the President / Secretary to the Board of Governors; Faculty Member, Knowledge Management Programs; Faculty Positions, Environmental Programs; Communications Manager; Program Coordinator, Executive Leadership Program; Programmer Analyst; Senior Database Administrator.

ROYAL ST. GEORGE'S COLLEGE
Att: Hal Hannaford, Principal
120 Howland Avenue
Toronto, ON M5R 3B5

Tel. 416-533-9481
Fax 416-533-5879
Email .... hhannaford@rsgc.on.ca
Website .... www.rsgc.on.ca
Employer Background: Royal St. George's College is an independent day school of 430 boys. *New Positions Created (3):* Teacher, Grade 6 Core; Teacher, Intermediate / Senior Languages; Teacher, Intermediate / Senior Mathematics.

ROYAL & SUNALLIANCE CANADA
Att: Tina Jones
10 Wellington Street East
Toronto, ON M5E 1L5

Tel. 416-366-7511
Fax 416-366-8615
Email ..... tina_jones@royalsunalliance.ca
Website .... www.royalsunalliance.ca
Employer Background: Royal & SunAlliance Canada is a subsidiary of British-based Royal & Sun Alliance Insurance Group PLC. Founded in 1710, the parent company is the world's third-largest insurer. *New Positions Created (5):* Production Underwriters; Corporate Commercial Lawyers (2); Human Resources Operations Leader; Senior Human Resources Leader; Senior Underwriter.

ROYAL & SUNALLIANCE CANADA
Att: Human Resources Manager
360 Albert Street, Suite 400
Ottawa, ON K1R 7X7

Tel. 613-236-0501
Fax 613-236-3525
Email barb_groenke@royalsunalliance.ca
Website .... www.royalsunalliance.ca
Employer Background: Royal & SunAlliance Canada is a subsidiary of British-based Royal & Sun Alliance Insurance Group PLC. Founded in 1710, the parent company is the world's third-largest insurer. *New Positions Created (2):* Casualty Adjuster, Claims; Claims Trainees.

ROYAL ULTRAFRAME LTD.
Att: Human Resources
470 Signet Drive
Toronto, ON M9L 1R4

Fax 416-740-2654
Employer Background: Royal Ultraframe Ltd. manufactures vinyl conservatory roofing systems. *New Positions Created (3):* Structural Engineer; Technical Support Advisor, Sunrooms / Conservatories; Sales Administrator.

ROYAL VICTORIA HOSPITAL / RVH
Att: Human Resources
201 Georgian Drive
Barrie, ON L4M 6M2

Tel. 705-728-9802
Fax 705-739-5616
Email .... careers@rvh.on.ca
Website .... www.rvh.on.ca
Employer Background: RVH provides health services to the residents of Simcoe County, Muskoka and Parry Sound. *New Positions Created (30):* Internists, Internal Medicine; Registered Polysomnographers; Pharmacists (3); Anesthesiologist; Collections Specialist; Preschool Speech Language Pathologist; Social Worker, Cancer Care Program; Coordinator, Outpatient Mental Health Services; Clinical Nurse Educator; Coordinator of Spiritual Care; Mental Health Clinicians & Registered Dietitians; Clinical Nurse Specialist, Cancer Care; Medical Oncologists; Pharmacists; Preschool Speech Language Pathologists; Registered Dietitian, Eating Disorders Program; RNs and RPNs; Health Record Technician / Administrator; Coordinator, Eating Disorders; Social Worker; Labour Relations Manager; Registered Practical Nurses, Operating Room; Radiology Technologists; Clinical Nurse Specialists, Cancer Care Program; Clinical Nurse Specialists, Gerontology Program; Pharmacist; Oncology Pharmacist; Health Record Technician / Administrator; Clinical Nurse Educator, Mental Health; Registered Respiratory Therapist.

RSC GROUP, THE
Att: Human Resources Manager
999 West Broadway, Suite 250
Vancouver, BC V5Z 1K5

Tel. 604-737-8570
Fax 604-737-8572
Email .... jobs@rsc.com
Website .... www.rsc.com
Employer Background: The RSC Group is a leader in financial and business software consulting, implementation and development. *New Positions Created (2):* Receptionist; Telemarketer.

RSL COM CANADA INC.
Att: Human Resources
PO Box 2130
Vancouver, BC V6B 3T5

Tel. 604-689-9377
Fax 604-990-2143
Email .... hr@rslcom.ca
Website .... www.rslcom.ca
Employer Background: RSL COM Canada Inc. is a subsidiary of RSL Communications Ltd., a large telecommunications company. *New Positions Created (26):* Customer Service Consultant; Production Control Coordinator; Supply Management Assistant; Systems Administrator; Inside Sales Representative; Purchasing Coordinator; Accounting Assistant, Accounts Payable; Business Systems Analyst; Systems Analyst; Account Executives; Data Services Specialist; Sales Engineers; Senior Provisioning Coordinator; Senior Trainer, Customer Programs; Customer Service Consultant; Manager, Human

Resources; Telecom Technician; Account Executives; Billing Operations Supervisor; Customer Activation Representative, Internet Services; IS Analyst; Manager, Customer Marketing; Network Support Representative, DSL; Project Manager; Sales Engineers; Technician, Network Operations.

RTO ENTERPRISES INC.
Att: Human Resources
170 Robert Speck Parkway, Suite 201
Mississauga, ON L4Z 3G1
Tel. 905-272-2788
Fax 905-272-9886
Website .... www.rto.ca
Employer Background: RTO Enterprises Inc. is a rental-purchase company, with 130 retail locations in Canada. *New Positions Created (5):* Marketing Manager; Planning Manager; Rental Specialist; Store Manager Trainees; Administrative Assistant.

RTP PHARMA INC.
Att: Human Resources
1000 Chemin du Golf, Ile des Soeurs
Verdun, QC H3E 1H4
Tel. 514-362-9818
Fax 514-362-1172
Website .... www.rtp-pharma.com
Employer Background: RTP Pharma Inc. is a research-based pharmaceutical company, specializing in the development of insoluble drugs. *New Positions Created (2):* Formulation Scientist; Particle Surface Characterization Scientist.

RUFFNECK HEATERS
Att: Human Resources
2827 Sunridge Boulevard NE
Calgary, AB T1Y 6G1
Tel. 403-291-5488
Fax 403-735-9181
Email .... careers@ruffneck.com
Website .... www.ruffneckheaters.com
Employer Background: Ruffneck Heaters manufactures explosion-proof electric air heaters, heat-exchanger unit heaters, explosion-proof thermostats and accessories. *New Positions Created (25):* Production Assistant; Service Technician; Accounting Assistant; Assembly Workers; Product Development Supervisor; Engineering Technologist; Human Resources Assistant; Corporate Typist; Graphic Designer; Quality Mgr; Regional Account Manager; Assembly Workers; Assistant to the Vice-President, Strategic And Corporate Planning; Product Development Supervisor; Assembly Worker; Draftsperson; Facilities Coordinator; Market Researcher; Marketing Coordinator; Systems Analyst; Systems Analyst; Marketing Coordinator; HR Generalist; Junior Graphic Designer; Market Researcher.

RUNNYMEDE CHRONIC CARE HOSPITAL
Att: Human Resources
274 St. Johns Road
Toronto, ON M6P 1V5
Tel. 416-762-7316
Fax 416-762-3836

Email .... humanres@rcch.on.ca
Website .... www.rcch.on.ca
Employer Background: Runnymede Chronic Care Hospital provides care to patients with progressive neurological diseases, including Huntington's and multiple sclerosis. *New Positions Created (7):* Nurse Manager, Hospital-Wide; Occupational Health / Infection Control Coordinator; Occupational Therapy / Physiotherapy Assistant; Occupational Health / Infection Control Co-Coordinator; Continuous Quality Improvement / Education Manager; Executive Secretary; Clinical Nurse Manager.

RUSSEL METALS INC.
Att: General Manager
1031 Cliveden Avenue, Annacis Island
New Westminister, BC V3M 5V1
Fax 604-521-4364
Website .... www.russelmetals.com
Employer Background: Russel Metals Inc. is involved in the processing, warehousing and distribution of steel. *New Positions Created (2):* Distribution / Logistics Coordinator; Manager, Plant Operations.

RUSSEL METALS INC.
Att: Inside Sales Manager
7016 - 99th Street
Edmonton, AB T6E 4T2
Tel. 780-439-2051
Fax 780-439-0147
Email .... jwilson@russelmetals.com
Website .... www.russelmetals.com
Employer Background: Russel Metals Inc. processes and distributes metals and metal products to the North American market. *New Positions Created (2):* Inside Sales Representative; Outside Sales Representative.

RUSSEL METALS INC.
Att: Corporate Human Resources
1900 Minnesota Court, Suite 210
Mississauga, ON L5N 3C9
Tel. 905-567-8500
Fax 905-819-7292
Email .... hrdept@russelmetals.com
Website .... www.russelmetals.com
Employer Background: Russel Metals Inc. is one of the largest metal distribution and processing companies in North America. *New Positions Created (2):* Regional Credit Manager; Vice-President, Purchasing.

RUSSELL A. FARROW LIMITED
Att: Sandra Coelho, Manager, HR & Payroll
106 Earl Thompson Road, PO Box 1177
Ayr, ON N0B 1E0
Tel. 519-740-9866
Fax 519-740-9663
Email .... sandraco@farrow.com
Website .... www.farrow.com
Employer Background: Russell A. Farrow Limited is a leading provider of logistics solutions, including customs brokerage, through offices across Canada and the USA. *New Positions Created (2):* Sales Professional; Director of Sales.

RYAN ENERGY TECHNOLOGIES INC.
Att: Human Resources Manager
505 - 2nd Street SW, Suite 700
Calgary, AB T2P 1N8
Tel. 403-269-5981
Fax 403-263-2031
Email .... hr@ryancdn.com
Website .... www.ryanenergy.com
Employer Background: Ryan Energy Technologies Inc. provides horizontal and directional drilling equipment and services to the oil and gas industry. *New Positions Created (17):* Mechanical Technologist; MWD Field Engineer / Technologist; MWD Operators; Directional Drilling Coordinator; Directional Drilling Supervisor; Mechanical Technologist / Technician; MWD Field Engineer / Technologist; MWD Operators; Senior Drilling Engineer; Direction Drilling Coordinator; Mechanical Technologist / Technician; MWD Field Engineer / Technologist; MWD Operators; Senior Drilling Engineer; Senior Electronics Engineer; Senior Mechanical Engineer; Assistant Controller.

RYAN, LAMONTAGNE & ASSOCIATES
Att: Marc Lamontagne
2249 Carling Avenue, Suite 304
Ottawa, ON K2B 7E9
Tel. 613-596-3353
Fax 613-596-2441
Email .... info@ryanlamontagne.com
Employer Background: Ryan, Lamontagne & Associates is a professional, fee-for-service financial planning and accounting firm, serving individual, corporate and government clients. *New Positions Created (4):* Accounting and Tax Assistant; Reception / Administration Position; Financial Planning / Tax Assistant; Receptionist / Administrative Assistant.

RYDER TRANSPORTATION SERVICES
Att: Al Grant, Senior HR Manager
4308 Village Centre Court
Mississauga, ON L4Z 1S2
Tel. 905-276-4392
Fax 905-276-7486
Email .... al_grant@ryder.com
Website .... www.ryder.com
Employer Background: Ryder Transportation Services provides transportation solutions for both small and large businesses. *New Positions Created (2):* Director, Business Development; Director, Sales Development.

RYERSON POLYTECHNIC UNIVERSITY
Att: Human Resources
350 Victoria Street
Toronto, ON M5B 2K3
Tel. 416-979-5076
Fax 416-979-5163
Website .... www.ryerson.ca
Employer Background: Ryerson Polytechnic University is one of Canada's leading universities for applied education, offering over 40 career-oriented programs. *New Positions Created (28):* Development Secretary; Gift Processing Clerk; Customer Service Clerk; Mentoring Program Assistant; Educational

Equity Adviser; Employment Equity Adviser; Financial Assistance Associate; Scheduler; Research Analyst; Learning Disabilities Specialist; Departmental Secretary, Corporate and Professional Training ; Disability Services Coordinator; Development Assistant; Human Resources Planning Analysts; Research Analyst; Technologist; Program Assistant; Treasury Officer; Housing Assistant; Intermediate Distributed Systems Specialist; Junior Fitness Specialist; Technical Officer, Mechanical Engineering; Multimedia Production Specialist; Special Advisor to the Associate Vice President, Academic; Employment and Educational Equity Advisor; Financial Aid Advisors (2); Computer and Communications Support Specialist; Junior Systems Programmer.

RYERSON POLYTECHNIC UNIVERSITY
Att: Dr. Errol Aspevig, V.P. Academic
350 Victoria Street
Toronto, ON M5B 2K3
Fax 416-979-5279
Website .... www.ryerson.ca
Employer Background: Ryerson Polytechnic University is one of Canada's leading universities for applied education, offering over 40 career-oriented programs. *New Positions Created (2):* Secretary of Academic Council; Dean, Faculty of Arts.

RYERSON POLYTECHNIC UNIVERSITY, DEPARTMENT OF ARCHITECTURAL SCIENCE AND LANDSCAPE ARCHITECTURE
Att: Michael Miller, Chair
350 Victoria Street
Toronto, ON M5B 2K3
Fax 416-979-5353
Website .... www.ryerson.ca
Employer Background: Ryerson Polytechnic University is one of Canada's leading universities for applied education, offering over 40 career-oriented programs. *New Positions Created (2):* Faculty Position, Project Management; Faculty Positions, Architectural Science (2).

RYERSON POLYTECHNIC UNIVERSITY, FACULTY OF APPLIED ARTS
Att: Dr. Ira Levine, Dean
350 Victoria Street
Toronto, ON M5B 2K3
Tel. 416-979-5000
Fax 416-979-5226
Email .... ilevine@ryerson.ca
Website .... www.ryerson.ca
Employer Background: Ryerson Polytechnic University is one of Canada's leading universities for applied education, offering over 40 career-oriented programs. *New Positions Created (9):* Chair, School of Interior Design; Educator, Film / Video Craft and Technology Studies; Educator, Printing Processes; Educator, School of Fashion Design; Educator, Technical Television Production; Educator, Video and Sound Production; Educators, School of Interior Design (2); Educators, School of Journalism (2); Theatre Professional / Theatre Educator.

RYERSON POLYTECHNIC UNIVERSITY, SCHOOL OF BUSINESS MANAGEMENT
Att: Lee Maguire, Associate Dean
350 Victoria Street
Toronto, ON M5B 2K3
Tel. 416-979-5061
Email .... lmaguire@ryerson.ca
Website .... www.ryerson.ca
Employer Background: Ryerson Polytechnic University is one of Canada's leading universities for applied education, offering over 40 career-oriented programs. *New Positions Created (4):* Assistant Professor, Entrepreneurship, Innovation and Strategy; Assistant Professors, Accounting (3); Assistant Professors, Marketing (2); Assistant Professors, Finance (2).

RYKA BLOW MOLDS LTD.
Att: Human Resources Manager
1608 Bonhill Road
Mississauga, ON L5T 1C7
Tel. 905-670-1450
Fax 905-670-2621
Email .... rykabm@aol.com
Website .... www.rykabm.com
Employer Background: Established in 1972, Ryka Blow Molds Ltd. supplies high-performance molds to the blow molding industry. *New Positions Created (2):* CNC Operators; Tool Room Crib Attendant.

S.A. ARMSTRONG LTD.
Att: Human Resources Department
23 Bertrand Avenue
Toronto, ON M1L 2P3
Tel. 416-755-2291
Fax 416-759-9101
Email .... hrcanada@armlink.com
Website .... www.armstrongpumps.com
Employer Background: S.A. Armstrong Ltd. is a multi-national manufacturer of centrifugal pumps, valves, heat exchangers and other fluid flow equipment. *New Positions Created (20):* Director of Procurement; Industrial Engineering Manager; Marketing Manager, High-Volume Hydronics; Marketing Manager, Strategic Products; Product Development Engineer; Product Development Engineer, Heat Transfer; Pump Testing Technician; Senior Quality Assurance Specialist; Technical Marketing Specialist; Customer Service Representatives; Heat Exchanger Supervisor; Mgr, Strategic Product Development; Product Development Engineer; Senior Quality Assurance Specialist; Director, Purchasing; Industrial Engineering Manager; Marketing Manager, Strategic Projects; Product Development Engineer, Heat Transfer; Technical Marketing Specialist; Warehouse Logistics Supervisor.

S&C ELECTRIC CANADA LTD.
Att: Human Resources
90 Belfield Road
Toronto, ON M9W 1G4
Tel. 416-249-9171
Email .... cfoster@scelectric.ca
Website .... www.sandc.com
Employer Background: S&C Electric Canada Ltd. is a leading manufacturer of high-volt-

age switching and protection equipment for the electric power industry. *New Positions Created (2):* CNC Amada Punch Press Operator; Power Systems Project Engineer.

SACKS PARTNERSHIP, THE
Att: Howard Colton CA
23 Lesmill Road, Suite 418
Toronto, ON M3B 3P6
Tel. 416-444-1500
Fax 416-444-2121
Website .... www.sackspartnership.com
Employer Background: The Sacks Partnership is a chartered acccounting firm. *New Positions Created (2):* Controller; Controller / Accountant.

SAFETY-KLEEN LTD.
Att: Operations Manager
PO Box 390
Ryley, AB T0B 4A0
Tel. 780-663-3828
Fax 780-663-3539
Website .... www.safety-kleen.com
Employer Background: Safety-Kleen Ltd. (formerly Laidlaw Environmental Services Inc.) is an environmental waste management company. *New Positions Created (2):* Plant Operator; TFS Account Specialist.

SAFETYSMART.COM
Att: Human Resources Manager
1111 - 11th Avenue SW, Suite 206
Calgary, AB T2R 0G5
Fax 403-802-0338
Email .... phil@bongarde.com
Website .... www.safetysmart.com
Employer Background: SafetySmart.com, a division of Bongarde Communications Ltd., is a leader in safety compliance and communications. *New Positions Created (3):* B2B Call Centre Representatives; Sales Team Leader; Safety Professional.

SAGEBRUSH CORPORATION
Att: Mary Campenot
10130 - 103rd Street, Suite 1750
Edmonton, AB T5J 3N9
Email .... resumes@sagebrushcorp.com
Website .... www.sagebrushcorp.com
Employer Background: Sagebrush Corporation develops and markets library automation software. *New Positions Created (4):* Telephone Support Analysts; Help Desk Analysts; Quality Assurance Analyst; Help Desk Analysts, Software Support.

SAHTU DIVISIONAL EDUCATION COUNCIL, THE
Att: Steve Rose, Supervisor of Schools
PO Box 64
Norman Wells, NT X0E 0V0
Tel. 867-587-3453
Fax 867-587-3467
Employer Background: The Sahtu Divisional Education Council is responsible for delivering K-12 education in the Sahtu region of the Northwest Territories. *New Positions Created (3):* Teachers; Teachers (3); Comptroller.

SAINT ELIZABETH HEALTH CARE
Att: Human Resources Department
20 Hughson Street South, Suite 908
Hamilton, ON L8N 2A1

Tel. 905-972-0800
Fax 905-972-8788
Email ...... hresources@saintelizabeth.com
Website .... www.saintelizabeth.com

Employer Background: Founded in 1908, Saint Elizabeth Health Care provides in-home health services to over 100,000 patients across Ontario. *New Positions Created (3):* Community RNs and RPNs; Nurse Continence Advisor; Various Registered Nursing Positions.

SAINT ELIZABETH HEALTH CARE
Att: Human Resources Department
90 Allstate Parkway, Suite 300
Markham, ON L3R 6H3

Tel. 905-940-9655
Fax 905-940-8977
Email ...... hresources@saintelizabeth.com
Website .... www.saintelizabeth.com

Employer Background: Founded in 1908, Saint Elizabeth Health Care provides in-home health services to over 100,000 patients across Ontario. *New Positions Created (11):* Health and Safety Specialist; RNs & RPNs; Financial Manager / Controller; Healthcare Managers; Supportive Care Supervisors; Community Occupational Therapists and Physiotherapists; Accounting Analyst; Help Desk and PC Support Position; Payroll Analyst; Programmers (2); RNs, RPNs & Community Crisis Workers.

SAINT MARY'S HOSPITAL
Att: Deborah Smalley, HR Advisor
220 Royal Avenue
New Westminster, BC V3L 1H6

Tel. 604-527-3313
Fax 604-527-3316
Email . deborah_smalley@sfhr.hnet.bc.ca
Website .... www.saintmaryshospital.org

Employer Background: Saint Mary's Hospital is a mid-sized acute care facility affiliated with the Simon Fraser Health Region. *New Positions Created (6):* Patient Care Mgr; Patient Care Mgr, Medicine & Palliative Care Services; Patient Care Mgr, Geriatric Program; Anesthesiologists; Licensed Practical Nurses; Registered Nurses.

SAKO RENT-A-CAR
Att: Human Resources Department
2350 Manella
Montréal, QC H4P 2P4

Tel. 514-735-3701
Fax 514-735-6724
Email .... dwoods@sako.com
Website .... www.sako.com

Employer Background: Sako Rent-A-Car is a car rental agency. *New Positions Created (2):* Customer Service Agents (2); Customer Service Agent.

SALESCENTRIX.COM INC.
Att: Human Resources Manager
605 Robson Street, Suite 1360
Vancouver, BC V6B 5J3

Tel. 604-687-1877
Fax 604-687-1837
Email .... careers@salescentrix.com
Website .... www.salescentrix.com

Employer Background: SalesCentrix.com Inc. develops Internet-hosted applications to automate the sales and distribution process for small manufacturers and their channel partners. *New Positions Created (4):* Software Developers; Senior Test Engineer; Software Developers; Unix Systems Engineers.

SALIT STEEL
Att: Human Resources Manager
7771 Stanley Avenue, Box 837
Niagara Falls, ON L2E 6V6

Tel. 905-356-3820
Fax 905-356-0809
Email .... jstokes@salitsteel.com
Website .... www.salitsteel.com

Employer Background: Salit Steel (a division of Myer Salit Ltd.) is a diversified steel service centre and rebar fabricator, serving clients in southern Ontario. *New Positions Created (4):* Reinforcing Steel Detailers; Reinforcing Steel Estimators; Senior Operations Manager; Truck Driver.

SAMAC ENGINEERING LTD.
Att: Human Resources Manager
6107 - 6th Street SE
Calgary, AB T2H 1L9

Tel. 403-261-0888
Fax 403-243-2270
Email .... samac@samaceng.com
Website .... www.samaceng.com

Employer Background: Samac Engineering Ltd. is a mechanical failure analysis and vehicle accident consulting firm. *New Positions Created (2):* Accident Reconstruction Engineer; Mechanical Engineer, Industrial.

SAMSON CANADA LTD.
Att: Jill Radiff
605 - 5th Avenue SW, Suite 2200
Calgary, AB T2P 3H5

Tel. 403-233-0724
Fax 403-233-0874
Email .... jradiff@samson.com
Website .... www.samson.com

Employer Background: Samson Canada Ltd. is an independent energy company involved in the exploration, acquisition and production of oil and natural gas. *New Positions Created (2):* Records Administrator; Senior Land Contracts Analyst.

SAMSON CONTROLS INC.
Att: Human Resources
105 Riviera Drive, Unit 1
Markham, ON L3R 5J7

Tel. 905-474-0354
Fax 905-474-0998
Email .... admin@samsoncontrols.com
Website .... www.samsoncontrols.com

Employer Background: Samson Controls Inc. is a subsidiary of German-based Samson AG, a leader in valve manufacturing for over 90 years. *New Positions Created (3):* Inside Sales Representative; Outside / Inside Sales Representative; Technician, Control Valves.

SAMTACK
Att: Human Resources
385 Bentley Street
Toronto, ON L3R 9T2

Tel. 905-940-1880
Fax 905-940-0331
Email .... hr@samtack.com
Website .... www.samtack.com

Employer Background: Samtack is a Canadian distributor of computer systems, components and multimedia products. *New Positions Created (5):* Financial Controller; Accounts Payable Clerks; Accounts Receivable Clerk; Financial Analyst; Technical Support Personnel.

SAMUEL, SON & CO., LTD.
Att: Human Resources
2360 Dixie Road
Mississauga, ON L4Y 1Z7

Tel. 905-279-5460
Fax 905-281-6036
Email .... humanresources@samuel.com
Website .... www.samuel.com

Employer Background: Samuel, Son & Co., Ltd. is one of the largest steel and aluminum service centers in North America, with over 40 locations. *New Positions Created (2):* Human Resources Assistant; Inside Sales Representatives (2).

SAN FRANCISCO GROUP
Att: Human Resources Department
50 de Lauzon
Boucherville, QC J4B 1E6

Fax 450-449-9924
Email .... careers@bsf.ca
Website .... www.bsf.ca

Employer Background: Established in 1978, San Francisco Group is a leading apparel company, with 3,000 employees. *New Positions Created (18):* Assistant Designer; Stylist; Stylist, Product Development; Transportation and Customs Clerk; Patternmaker; Sales Consultant; Store Manager & Assistant Manager; Buyer, Product Development; Assistant Buyer, Men's Accessories; Patternmaker; Stylist; Buyer, Lingerie; Translator; Stylist; Patternmaker; Manager Accounting / Planning and Distribution; Merchandiser, Stock Management; Various Retail Positions.

SANDER GEOPHYSICS LTD. / SGL
Att: Human Resources Manager
260 Hunt Club Road
Ottawa, ON K1V 1C1

Tel. 613-521-9626
Fax 613-521-0215
Email .... info@sgl.com
Website .... www.sgl.com

Employer Background: SGL is an airborne geophysical exploration company, specializing in airborne magnetometer and gamma-ray spectrometer surveys for the mining and oil industries. *New Positions Created (11):* Aircraft Maintenance Engineers / AME Apprentices; Computer Field Technicians; Geophysicists; Pilots; Scientific Programmer; Aircraft Maintenance Engineers and AME Apprentices; Computer Field Technician; Geophysicists; Pilots; Scientific Programmer; Inventory Manager / Purchaser.

SANDWELL ENGINEERING INC.
Att: Keith Land, HR Manager
1045 Howe Street, Suite 700
Vancouver, BC V6Z 2A9

Tel. 604-684-9311
Fax 604-688-5913
Email .... hr@sandwell.com
Website .... www.sandwell.com

Employer Background: Sandwell is an international engineering company that specializes in marine, bulk material handling, rail and general transportation applications. *New Positions Created (27):* Electrical Engineer; Electrical Engineers / Designers; Intermediate Structural Engineers; Mechanical Project Engineers; Piping Group Leaders; Power & Recovery Plant Specialists; Senior Instrumentation Engineer; Structural Engineers; Wood Products Specialist; Electrical Engineers; Intermediate Structural Engineers; Mechanical Project Engineers; Piping Group Leaders; PLC Programmers; Power & Recovery Plant Specialists; Senior Instrumentation Engineer; Structural Engineers; Wood Products Specialist; On-Site Project Engineers; Electrical Designers; Electrical Engineers; Mechanical Designers; Materials Handling; Process Control Engineer; Intermediate Piping Designers; Piping Group Leaders; Power and Recovery Plant Specialists; Wood Products Specialist.

SANDWELL EPC INC.
Att: Sylvie Baril, HR Manager
620 Rene-Levesque Boulevard West
Montréal, QC H3B 4V8

Tel. 514-866-1221
Fax 514-866-0804
Email .... hr@sandwell.com
Website .... www.sandwell.com

Employer Background: Sandwell EPC is an international engineering company specializing in marine, bulk material handling, rail and general transportation applications. *New Positions Created (2):* Senior Project Manager; Senior Project Manager.

SANDY HILL COMMUNITY HEALTH CENTRE / SHCHC
Att: Karen Patzer, Executive Director
221 Nelson Street
Ottawa, ON K1N 1C7

Tel. 613-789-1500
Fax 613-789-7962
Website .... www.sandyhillchc.on.ca

Employer Background: Established in 1973, SHCHC is a private, non-profit, community-based health and social service organization. *New Positions Created (2):* Director, Addictions Assessment Services; Executive Director.

SANJEL CORPORATION
Att: HR Department

639 - 5th Avenue SW, Suite 2400
Calgary, AB T2P 0M9

Tel. 403-269-1420
Fax 403-716-0333
Email .... hr@sanjel.com
Website .... www.sanjel.com

Employer Background: Sanjel Corporation is one of Canada's largest privately-owned oilfield services companies. *New Positions Created (4):* Accounts Payable Clerk; Accounts Receivable Clerk; Applications Developer; Technical Services Programming & Design Supervisor.

SANMAR CANADA
Att: Human Resources Manager
13741 Crestwood Place
Richmond, BC V6V 2G4

Tel. 604-273-9088
Fax 604-279-9406
Website ...... www.sanmarcanada.com

Employer Background: SanMar Canada is a leading national wholesale distributor of printable apparel. *New Positions Created (2):* Purchasing Manager; System Analyst.

SANMINA ENCLOSURE SYSTEMS
Att: Human Resources Department
1385 Huntingwood Drive
Toronto, ON M1S 3J1

Tel. 416-754-2133
Fax 416-754-4846
Email .. recruiting@sanminaenclosures.com
Website ..... www.sanminaenclosures.com

Employer Background: Sanmina Enclosure Systems, a division of Sanmina Corporation, supplies state-of-the-art enclosures for the electronics industry. *New Positions Created (11):* Inside Sales Manager, Standard Products Division; Document Control Coordinator; Estimator; Manufacturing Engineer / NC Programmer; Receiver; Shipping Supervisor; Planners; Proposal Mgr; Quality Engineer; Quality Inspectors; Quality Manager.

SANOFI-SYNTHELABO CANADA INC.
Att: People Development
15 Allstate Parkway
Markham, ON L3R 5B4

Fax 905-513-4564
Email .. people.development@ca.sanofi.com
Website .... www.sanofi-synthelabo.com

Employer Background: Sanofi-Synthelabo Canada Inc. is a pharmaceutical company. *New Positions Created (3):* Continuing Health Education and Clinical Research Positions; Marketing Positions; Primary Care and Specialty Sales Representatives.

SAPUTO INC.
Att: Human Resources Services
6869 Metropolitain Boulevard East
St-Leonard, QC H1P 1X8

Tel. 514-328-6662
Fax 514-328-3095
Email .... cv@saputo.com
Website .... www.saputo.com

Employer Background: Saputo Inc. is a leading producer and distributor of dairy and grocery products. *New Positions Created (4):*

HR Advisor; Coordinator, Quality Assurance; Attorney; Legal Assistant.

SAPUTO INC., MILK DIVISION
Att: Colin Harris, HR Director
PO Box 9100
Vancouver, BC V6B 4G4

Fax 604-420-9700
Website .... www.saputo.com

Employer Background: Saputo Inc. is a leading producer and distributor of dairy and grocery products. *New Positions Created (2):* Sales Distribution Supervisor; Engineering Manager, Western Canada.

SAS INSTITUTE (CANADA) INC.
Att: Human Resources Manager
181 Bay St., BCE Place
Suite 2220, PO Box 819
Toronto, ON M5J 2T3

Tel. 416-363-4424
Fax 416-363-5399
Email .... recruiting@sas.com
Website .... www.sas.com

Employer Background: SAS Institute (Canada) Inc. is a subsidiary of SAS Institute Inc., one of the world's largest privately-held software companies. SAS develops and markets leading-edge data warehousing and decision support software. *New Positions Created (19):* Account Executives; Business Solutions Specialist, Performance Management; Consultant, Data Warehouse Architect; Consultant, Technical; Manager, Facilities and Office Services; Sales Associate; Senior Consultant, Project Manager; Consultant, Data Mining; Project Manager / Business Analyst; Sales Associate; Performance Management Software Specialist; Financial Software Solutions Specialist; Manager, Facilities & Office Services; Regional Sales & Marketing Manager; Solution Practices Manager, Customer Business, CRM; Technical Training Specialist; Account Executive; Account Executive, Ottawa; Data Warehouse Architect / Consultant.

SAS INSTITUTE (CANADA) INC.
Att: Human Resources Manager
1000 Sherbrooke Street West, Suite 2100
Montréal, QC H3B 3G4

Tel. 514-395-8922
Fax 514-395-8962
Email .... recruiting@sas.com
Website .... www.sas.com

Employer Background: SAS Institute (Canada) Inc. is a subsidiary of SAS Institute Inc., one of the world's largest privately-held software companies. SAS develops and markets leading-edge data warehousing and decision support software. *New Positions Created (4):* Account Executives; Consultant, Data Mining; Account Executives; Business Relationship Manager.

SASKATCHEWAN INSTITUTE OF APPLIED SCIENCE AND TECHNOLOGY, PALLISER CAMPUS / SIAST
Att: Human Resources Manager
PO Box 1420
Moose Jaw, SK S6H 4A2

Tel. 306-694-3231
Fax 306-694-3457
Email .... palliserjobs@siast.sk.ca
Website .... www.siast.sk.ca
Employer Background: SIAST is the largest post-secondary institution in Saskatchewan, serving over 44,000 students. *New Positions Created (4):* Instructor, Automotive Service Technician; Instructor, Basic Education; Instructor, Computer Information Systems; Instructor, Electronics Engineering.

SASKATCHEWAN INSTITUTE OF APPLIED SCIENCE AND TECHNOLOGY
Att: Human Resources
119 - 4th Ave. S., Suite 400, PO Box 1520
Saskatoon, SK S7K 5X2
Tel. 306-933-7897
Fax 306-933-7334
Email .... jobs@siast.sk.ca
Website .... www.siast.sk.ca
Employer Background: SIAST is the largest post-secondary institution in Saskatchewan, serving over 44,000 students. *New Positions Created (9):* Registrar; Instructor, Mechanical Engineering Technology Program; Program Head / Instructor, Chemical Technology Program; Instructor, Heavy Equipment Mechanics Program; Instructors, Computer Systems Technology (2); Campus Director; Director of Communications; Clerk Typist 2; Instructor, Industrial Mechanics.

SASKATCHEWAN INSTITUTE OF APPLIED SCIENCE AND TECHNOLOGY, WOODLAND CAMPUS
Att: Human Resources
PO Box 3003
Prince Albert, SK S6V 6G1
Tel. 306-953-7198
Fax 306-953-7068
Email .... woodlandjobs@siast.sk.ca
Website .... www.siast.sk.ca
Employer Background: SIAST is the largest post-secondary institution in Saskatchewan, serving over 44,000 students. *New Positions Created (2):* Instructor, Forestry; Instructors, Forest Ecosystem Technology (2).

SASKATCHEWAN LIQUOR AND GAMING AUTHORITY / SLGA
Att: Human Resources Branch
2500 Victoria Avenue, PO Box 5054
Regina, SK S4P 3M3
Tel. 306-787-4213
Website .... www.slga.gov.sk.ca
Employer Background: SLGA is responsible for the regulation and control of gaming and liquor activities throughout Saskatchewan. *New Positions Created (6):* Supervisor, Technical Operations; Executive Secretary; Director of Communications; Manager of Organizational Development; Senior Gaming Policy Analyst; Executive Assistant.

SASKATCHEWAN POST-SECONDARY EDUCATION AND SKILLS TRAINING / SASKATCHEWAN EDUCATION
Att: Romila Chetty, HR Branch
2220 College Avenue, 4th Floor
Regina, SK S4P 3V7

Tel. 306-787-8431
Fax 306-787-7149
Website .... www.sasked.gov.sk.ca
Employer Background: Saskatchewan Post-Secondary Education and Skills Training / Saskatchewan Education ensures the availability of relevant post-secondary, skills-training and labour market programs. *New Positions Created (4):* Prior Learning Assessment Recognition / Credit Transfer Analyst; Financial Development Coordinator; Administrative Support Position; Director, Loan Management and Accounting.

SASKATCHEWAN RESEARCH COUNCIL / SRC
Att: Wendy Lawrence,
Staff Resource Services
15 Innovation Boulevard
Saskatoon, SK S7N 2X8
Tel. 306-933-5400
Fax 306-933-5479
Email .... lawrence@src.sk.ca
Website .... www.src.sk.ca
Employer Background: SRC is a Crown corporation, helping the people of Saskatchewan strengthen the economy with quality jobs and a secure environment. *New Positions Created (5):* Hydrogeologist; Senior Research Engineer; Director, Petroleum Branch; Senior Hydrogeologist / Quaternary Geologist; Senior Research Engineer.

SASKATCHEWAN WHEAT POOL
Att: Human Resources Division
2625 Victoria Avenue
Regina, SK S4T 7T9
Tel. 306-569-4411
Fax 306-569-5070
Email .... employment@swp.com
Website .... www.swp.com
Employer Background: Founded in 1923, the Saskatchewan Wheat Pool is Canada's largest agricultural cooperative, with 70,000 farmer members. *New Positions Created (2):* Manager, Field Evaluation and Cereal Research; Senior Buyer, Rail.

SASKATCHEWAN WORKERS' COMPENSATION BOARD / SASKATCHEWAN
Att: Human Resources
1881 Scarth Street, Suite 200
Regina, SK S4P 4L1
Tel. 306-787-4370
Email .... employment@wcbsask.com
Website .... www.wcbsask.com
Employer Background: Created in 1930, Saskatchewan WCB administers a system of no-fault insurance for workers funded by employers. *New Positions Created (3):* Director, Claims Entitlement; Director of Safety, Prevention and Return-To-Work; Directors, Case Management (2).

SASKATOON CREDIT UNION
Att: Karen Macooh
309 - 22nd Street East, Suite 201
Saskatoon, SK S7K 0G7
Tel. 306-934-4000
Fax 306-934-4019

Email .... karen.macooh@saskatoon.cu.sk.ca
Website ..... www.saskatooncreditunion.com
Employer Background: The Saskatoon Credit Union offers a complete range of financial products and services. *New Positions Created (2):* Vice-President, Retail Branch Operations; Vice-President, Sales and Member Services.

SASKATOON DISTRICT HEALTH
Att: Human Resources
103 Hospital Drive
Saskatoon, SK S7N 0W8
Tel. 306-655-2428
Fax 306-655-2444
Email .... jobs@sdh.sk.ca
Website .... www.sdh.sk.ca
Employer Background: Established in 1992, Saskatoon District Health is the largest of 33 community-managed health districts in Saskatchewan, serving 212,000 residents. The organization has over 8,000 staff members. *New Positions Created (29):* Mental Health Therapist / Senior Marriage and Family Therapist; Senior Occupational Therapist; Manager of Inventory, Materials Management; Pharmacists; Director; Manager, Clinical Nutrition Services; Infection Prevention and Control Practitioner; Assistant Manager; Manager of Occupational Therapy; Coordinator of Physician Recruitment, Retention and Remuneration; Nursing Positions; Primary Health Care Nurses (2); Clinical Engineering Technologist; Health Records Technician; Occupational Therapist, Senior; Occupational Therapist, Staff; Physical Therapist, Senior; Physical Therapist, Staff; Social Worker, Mental Health Services - Child & Youth; Speech Language Pathologist; Speech Language Pathologist; Speech Language Pathologist; Speech Language Pathologist; Manager of Coordinated Assessment Unit; Emergency Physicians; Podiatrist; Professional Leader - Social Work; Speech Language Pathologists; Physician Specialists.

SASKPOWER
Att: Recruitment & Selection
2025 Victoria Avenue
Regina, SK S4P 0S1
Tel. 306-566-2121
Fax 306-566-2087
Email .... hr@saskpower.com
Website .... www.saskpower.com
Employer Background: SaskPower delivers electricity throughout the province of Saskatchewan. *New Positions Created (6):* Chemical Laboratory Technician; Meter Reader; Business Assistant / Secretary; Communication Services Coordinator; Risk and Insurance Analyst; Journeyman Powerline Technician.

SASKTEL
Att: Selection and Staffing Manager
2121 Saskatchewan Drive, 13th Floor
Regina, SK S4P 3Y2
Tel. 306-777-4117
Fax 306-777-3277
Email ..... human.resources@sasktel.sk.ca

Website .... www.sasktel.com
Employer Background: SaskTel provides a complete range of communication services to customers in Saskatchewan and around the world. *New Positions Created (7):* Business Analysts; Marketing Research Assistant; Engineers; Business Analysts; Client Technology Manager; Marketing Research Assistants; Mobility Engineer.

SATCHEL SHOP, THE
Att: V. Matches
117 - 5th Avenue West
Vancouver, BC V5Y 1H9

Fax 604-873-5211
Email .... vmatches@satchelshop.ca
Website .... www.satchelshop.ca
Employer Background: The Satchel Shop is a retailer of quality leather products, handbags and luggage. *New Positions Created (3):* Manager & Assistant Manager; Store Manager; Store Manager.

SATISFIED BRAKE PRODUCTS INC.
Att: Human Resources Department
805 Education Road
Cornwall, ON K6H 6C7

Tel. 613-933-3300
Fax 613-933-8128
Email .... hr@satisfied.ca
Website .... www.satisfied.ca
Employer Background: Satisfied Brake Products Inc. is an independent, QS 9000-certified brake manufacturer, with over 20 years experience. *New Positions Created (3):* Certified Industrial Mechanics / Millwrights; Millwright; Human Resources Manager / Payroll Administrator.

SAULT AREA HOSPITALS
Att: President
969 Queen Street East
Sault Ste. Marie, ON P6A 2C4

Fax 705-759-3640
Email .... malkanim@sah.on.ca
Website .... www.sah.on.ca
Employer Background: Sault Area Hospitals, composed of Sault Ste. Marie General Hospital Inc. and Plummer Memorial Public Hospital, has 328 beds and an annual budget of $95 million. *New Positions Created (7):* Vice-President, Finance; Vice-President, Public Affairs; Chaplain; Clinical Nurse Specialist, Psychiatry; Nurse Practitioner, Emergency Department; Occupational Therapist; Staff Pharmacists.

SAVAGE SOFTWARE
Att: Human Resources Manager
1050 Homer Street
Vancouver, BC V6B 2W9

Tel. 604-684-7793
Fax 604-684-0298
Email .... jobs@savagesoftware.com
Website .... www.savagesoftware.com
Employer Background: Savage Software is an Internet graphics company that develops and markets scalable, high-performance rich-media content serving products. *New Positions Created (8):* Lead QA Developer;

Technical Documentation Writer; Lead QA Developer; Product Development Manager; Software Developer; Technical Documentation Writer; Web Developer; Biotechnology Product Manager.

SBR INTERNATIONAL
Att: Human Resources Manager
14 College Street, Suite 300
Toronto, ON M5G 1K2

Tel. 416-962-7500
Fax 416-962-7503
Email .... hr@sbr-global.com
Website .... www.sbr-global.com
Employer Background: SBR International is a growing management consulting firm for Fortune 500 clients. *New Positions Created (4):* Controller; Financial Analysts; Office Manager; Senior Project Manager.

SCANCODE LOGISTICS
Att: Human Resources Manager
2560 Matheson Boulevard East, Suite 223
Mississauga, ON L4W 4Y9

Tel. 905-602-0441
Email .... jobs@scancode.com
Website .... www.scancode.com
Employer Background: Scancode Logistics is a software company, specializing in complete solutions for transportation and warehouse management systems. *New Positions Created (3):* Admin Assistant; Diagnostics Software Support Position; Project Manager.

SCARBOROUGH COMMUNITY CARE ACCESS CENTRE / SCARBOROUGH CCAC
Att: Cristina Amiana, HR Specialist
1940 Eglinton Avenue East, 3rd Floor
Toronto, ON M1L 4R1

Tel. 416-750-2444
Fax 416-750-4116
Email ... cristina.amiana@scarbccac.on.ca
Website .... www.scarbccac.org
Employer Background: Scarborough CCAC is a community-based, non-profit organization, providing a wide range of home health and support services. *New Positions Created (12):* Client Services Coordinator; In-Home / Placement Service & Hospital Coordinators; Coordinator, Statistical Reporting; Accountant; Communications Manager; Coordinator, Statistical Reporting; In-home / Placement Service Coordinators; Information and Referral Assistant; Manager, Client Services; Educator; Float In-home Services Coordinators and Hospital Coordinators; Mental Health Coordinator.

SCARBOROUGH HOSPITAL, GENERAL DIVISION
Att: Human Resources Consultant
3050 Lawrence Avenue East
Toronto, ON M1P 2V5

Tel. 416-431-8126
Fax 416-431-8186
Email .... sghhr@tsh.to
Website .... www.tsh.to
Employer Background: Scarborough Hospital, General Division is a teaching hospital

affiliated with the University of Toronto and a regional centre for MRP, renal dialysis, pacemaker and vascular surgery programs. *New Positions Created (46):* Payroll Manager; Registered Nurse, 3 Central Medicine; Physiotherapy Assistant, Physiotherapy; Registered Nurse, Oncology; Registered Technologist, X-Ray; Applications Analysts; Medical Radiation Technologists; Registered Nurses, Emergency; Registered Nurses, ICU; Registered Nurses, Nephrology; Registered Nurses, OR; Social Worker; Cardiologists / Endocrinologists / Rheumatologists; Geriatrician; HVAC Mechanic; Journeyman Electrician; Journeyman Plumber; Psychogeriatric Resource Consultant; Registered Nurse, Medicine Float; Registered Nurse, Special Care Nursery; Registered Nurse, T9 / CCU; Physiotherapists; Registered Technologists; Speech Language Pathology Practice Leader; Registered Nurse, ER; Application Analyst; Registered Nurses, CCU / Telemetry; Registered Nurses, ICU; Social Workers, Emergency / Cardiology; Speech Language Pathologists; Registered Nurses, Emergency; Social Workers; Transcription Specialist; Registered Technologist; Physiotherapists (2); Occupational Therapists; Nurse Educator / Clinician, Medicine; Health Information Professionals; Speech Language Pathologists, Grace Division (2); Cardio-Respiratory / Critical Care Practitioners; Case Manager, Substance Abuse Specialist; Occupational Therapist, Vocational Specialist; Registered Nurses; Registered Nurses; Registered Nurses; Registered Nurses .

SCARBOROUGH HOSPITAL, GRACE DIVISION
Att: Human Resources Manager
3030 Birchmount Road
Toronto, ON M1W 3W3

Tel. 416-495-2416
Fax 416-495-2560
Email .... hrgrace@tsh.to
Website .... www.tsh.to
Employer Background: Scarborough Hospital, Grace Division is part of the Scarborough Hospital (TSH), formed through the amalgamation of the former Scarborough General and Salvation Army Scarborough Grace hospitals. *New Positions Created (34):* Occupational Therapist; Registered Nurse, Family Birth Place / MNCC; Registered Nurse, Intensive Care Unit; Registered Nurse, SCN and Paediatrics; Registered Technologist, Radiology; Registered Technologists, Nuclear Medicine (2); Applications Analysts; Medical Radiation Technologists; Registered Nurse; Senior Medical Laboratory Technologist; Speech Language Pathologists; Health Records Technician; Pharmacists (2); Registered Nurse, 4B / SCN; Registered Nurses, Emergency (2); Registered Technologist, Ultrasound; Transcription Specialist; Speech Language Pathologists; Ultrasound Sonographer, Diagnostic Imaging; Application Analyst; Registered Technologists, Radiology; Registered Technologist, Nuclear Medicine; Registered Technologist, Ultrasound; Speech-Language Pathologists; Data Specialist; Pharmacy

Manager; Physiotherapist, Ortho-Rehab; Physiotherapists, Amputee and Lymphedema Team; Specialist, Organizational Development; Applications Analyst; Patient Care Manager, ICU / CCU; Pharmacists; Social Workers; Manager of Diagnostic Imaging.

SCHAEFFER & ASSOCIATES LTD.
Att: Human Resources Manager
54 Jardin Drive
Concord, ON L4K 3P3
Tel. 905-738-6100
Fax 905-738-6875
Email .... general@schaeffers.com
Website .... www.schaeffers.com
Employer Background: Schaeffer & Associates Ltd., a Canadian-owned company, provides civil engineering services to land developers and government agencies. *New Positions Created (2):* Various Engineering Positions; Various Engineering Positions.

SCHIFFENHAUS CANADA INC. / SCI
Att: Human Resources
5591 Kitimat Road, Unit 2
Mississauga, ON L5N 3T4
Tel. 905-858-8855
Fax 905-858-7808
Website .... www.schiffenhaus.com
Employer Background: Schiffenhaus Canada Inc. supplies flexographic printing to the corrugated packaging industry. *New Positions Created (2):* Internal Sales Coordinator; Internal Sales Coordinator.

SCHLUMBERGER CANADA LIMITED
Att: Technical Manager
3087 - 54th Street SE
Calgary, AB T2C 4R7
Tel. 403-509-4000
Fax 403-509-4321
Website .... www.slb.com
Employer Background: Schlumberger Canada Limited provides engineering services to the energy industry through three business segments: oilfield services, resource management services and test and transactions. *New Positions Created (11):* Mud Motor / Down Hole Drilling Tool Technicians; Software Support Geophysicist; Tax Accountant; Logistics and Procurement Coordinator; Overseas Oil & Gas Positions; Personnel Manager; Directional Driller; Field Specialist, Measurement While Drilling; Equipment Operators; Exploration Services Assistant; Various Geology Positions.

SCHLUMBERGER COMPLETION SYSTEMS
Att: Human Resources
5616 - 80th Avenue SE
Calgary, AB T2C 4N5
Fax 403-509-2380
Website .... www.slb.com
Employer Background: Schlumberger Completion Systems, a division of Schlumberger Canada Ltd., provides engineering services to the energy industry. *New Positions Created (5):* Computer Technician; Manufactur-

ing Engineer; Senior Buyer; Machinists; IT Supervisor.

SCHLUMBERGER RESOURCE MANAGEMENT SERVICES
Att: Human Resources
7275 West Credit Avenue
Mississauga, ON L5N 5M9
Tel. 905-858-4211
Fax 905-858-0428
Website .... www.slb.com
Employer Background: Schlumberger Resource Management specializes in water meter service and installation programs. *New Positions Created (2):* Apprentices / Certified Plumbers; Certified Plumbers.

SCHNEIDER ELECTRIC
Att: Human Resources
19 Waterman Avenue
Toronto, ON M4B 1Y2
Tel. 416-752-8020
Website .... www.schneider-electric.ca
Employer Background: Schneider Electric is a leading Canadian equipment manufacturer and supplier of electrical distribution, control, and automation equipment. *New Positions Created (5):* Bilingual Project Manager, Large & Complex Quotations Order Team; Process Engineer; Corporate Accountant; Ready-To-Serve / Design Manufacturing Engineer; Industrial Sales Representative.

SCHNEIDER ELECTRIC
Att: Craig Smith, Human Resources
255 Orenda Road
Bramalea, ON L6T 1E6
Tel. 905-459-8805
Fax 905-459-1377
Email .... smithc10@squared.com
Website .... www.schneider-electric.ca
Employer Background: Schneider Canada is a leading Canadian equipment manufacturer and supplier of electrical distribution, control and automation equipment. *New Positions Created (2):* Cost Analyst; Mechanical Designers (2).

SCHNEIDER ELECTRIC SERVICES
Att: Nicole Grosz, Human Resources
6675 Rexwood Road
Mississauga, ON L4V 1V1
Tel. 905-678-7000
Fax 905-678-0145
Email .... groszn@squared.com
Website .... www.schneider-electric.ca
Employer Background: Schneider Electric Services is a Canadian manufacturer and supplier of electrical distribution, control and automation equipment. *New Positions Created (6):* Operations Supervisor; Project Engineer; Service Technician; Business Development Rep; Service Technicians (2); Project Supervisor and Service Technician.

SCHNEIDER FOODS INC.
Att: Human Resources
5523 - 176th Street
Surrey, BC V3S 4C2

Tel. 604-576-1191
Fax 604-576-6762
Email .... careers@schneiderfoods.ca
Website .... www.schneiderfoods.ca
Employer Background: Schneider Foods Inc. is one of Canada's largest producers of premium quality meat and European-style products. *New Positions Created (6):* Maintenance Technicians; Account Manager, Food Service; Refrigeration Mechanic and Millwright; Maintenance Technician; Process Manager; Maintenance Shift Leader.

SCHNEIDER FOODS INC.
Att: Human Resources
321 Courtland Avenue East, PO Box 130
Kitchener, ON N2G 3X8
Tel. 519-741-5000
Fax 519-749-7414
Email .... careers@schneiderfoods.ca
Website .... www.schneiderfoods.ca
Employer Background: Schneider Foods Inc. is one of Canada's largest producers of premium quality meat and European-style products. *New Positions Created (27):* 4th-Class Stationary Engineer, Night Shift; Administrative Assistant; Apprentice Truck & Coach Technician; Business Process Analysis Manager; Cost Accountant; Senior Internal Auditor; Senior Programmer Analyst; Senior Information Systems Auditor; Account Manager, Foodservice; Demand Planning Manager; Maintenance Mechanic; Production Supervisors; Project Manager; Quality Assurance Supervisor; Customer Sales Representative; Marketing Manager, Sliced Meats; Senior Accounts Payable Clerk; Translation Assistant; Accounts Payable Clerk; Industrial Electrician; Inventory / Replenishment Analyst; Maintenance Mechanic; Millwright; Senior Information Systems Auditor; Industrial Engineer; Health & Safety Coordinator / Plant Nurse; Director, Information Services.

SCHNEIDER FOODS INC.
Att: Human Resources
15350 Old Simcoe Road
Port Perry, ON L9L 1A6
Tel. 905-985-7373
Fax 905-985-7289
Email .... careers@schneiderfoods.ca
Website .... www.schneiderfoods.ca
Employer Background: Schneider Foods Inc. is one of Canada's largest producers of premium quality meat and European-style products. *New Positions Created (3):* Maintenance Electrician; Maintenance Mechanic; Production Supervisors.

SCHNEIDER FOODS INC.
Att: Human Resources Manager
2233 Argentia Road, Suite 300
Mississauga, ON L5N 2X7
Fax 905-819-0328
Email .... careers@schneiderfoods.ca
Website .... www.schneiderfoods.ca
Employer Background: Schneider Foods Inc. is one of Canada's largest producers of premium quality meat and European-style products. *New Positions Created (6):* De-

mand Planning Manager; Industrial Electrician; Millwright; Corporate Sales Specialists; Customer Service Representative; Bilingual Customer Service Representatives.

SCHNEIDER NATIONAL
Att: Human Resource Manager
7475 McLean Road East
Guelph, ON N1H 6H9
Tel. 519-826-7300
Fax 519-826-7024
Email .... stonek@schneider.com
Website .... www.schneider.com
Employer Background: Schneider National is one of the largest truckload carriers in Canada, with over 750 driver associates to support inbound, outbound and domestic freight moves. *New Positions Created (2):* Team Leader; Transport Positions (2).

SCHOLARSHIP CONSULTANTS OF NORTH AMERICA LTD. / SCONA
Att: Joanne McMahon, Vice-President, HR
50 Burnhamthorpe Road West, Suite 1500
Mississauga, ON L5B 4A5
Tel. 905-270-8777
Fax 905-270-3551
Email .... mcmahon@resp-usc.com
Website .... www.resp-usc.com
Employer Background: SCONA is a large group RESP organization with over $1.2 billion under administration and the exclusive distributor / administrator of USC Education Savings Plan. *New Positions Created (3):* Vice-President, Finance; Manager, Accounting; Special Events Coordinator.

SCHOLASTIC CANADA LTD.
Att: Human Resources Coordinator
175 Hillmount Road
Markham, ON L6C 1Z7
Tel. 905-887-7323
Fax 905-887-3639
Email .... scefala@scholastic.ca
Website .... www.scholastic.ca
Employer Background: Scholastic Canada Ltd. is a publisher and distributor of children's books. *New Positions Created (5):* Assistant Product Manager; Marketing Graphics Manager; Warehouse Clerk; Branch Manager; Marketing Manager.

SCHOOL DISTRICT #06 (ROCKY MOUNTAIN)
Att: Len G. Luders, HR Director
PO Box 70
Kimberly, BC V1A 2Y5
Tel. 250-427-2245
Fax 250-427-2044
Website www.sd6.bc.ca
Employer Background: School District #6 (Rocky Mountain) serves 4,350 students in 27 schools. *New Positions Created (2):* Superintendent, Schools; HVAC Journeyman.

SCHOOL DISTRICT #35 (LANGLEY)
Att: Cynthia Bosch, HR Department
4875 - 222nd Street
Langley, BC V3A 3Z7
Tel. 604-534-7891

Fax 604-532-1403
Email .... cbosch@sd35.bc.ca
Website www.sd35.bc.ca
Employer Background: School District #35 (Langley) operates 44 public schools and 4 post-secondary educational institutes, serves 20,790 students and employs 2,313 staff members. *New Positions Created (2):* Manager, Custodial and Transportation Services; Principals and Vice-Principals.

SCHOOL DISTRICT #36 (SURREY)
Att: Human Resources Department
14225 - 56th Avenue
Surrey, BC V3X 3A3
Tel. 604-599-7400
Fax 604-596-8695
Website www.sd36.surrey.bc.ca
Employer Background: School District #36 (Surrey) operates 95 elementary schools, 19 secondary schools and 5 learning centres, serving over 60,000 students. *New Positions Created (11):* Assistant Manager, Front of House; Assistant Manager / Technical Director; Secondary School Positions; Director, Information Management Services; Manager, Grounds Maintenance; District Principal, Human Resources; Assistant Superintendents (2); Administrative Officers (4); Vice Principal / Principal, Secondary; Vice Prinicpal / Principal, Elementary; Associate Director, Internal Audit and Fiscal Accountability.

SCHOOL DISTRICT #40 (NEW WESTMINSTER)
Att: Human Resource Services
821 - 8th Street
New Westminster, BC V3M 3S9
Fax 514-517-6319
Website www.sd40.bc.ca
Employer Background: School District #40 (New Westminster) has 6,400 students and 600 employees. *New Positions Created (5):* Secretary Treasurer; Elementary Principal; Middle School Vice-Principal; Secondary Vice-Principal; Manager, HR Services.

SCHOOL DISTRICT #41 (BURNABY)
Att: Sheila Rooney,
Superintendent of Schools
5325 Kincaid Street
Burnaby, BC V5G 1W2
Tel. 604-664-8389
Fax 604-664-8382
Website www.sd41.bc.ca
Employer Background: School District #41 (Burnaby) is an urban district, with 53 schools and sites, 18,000 students and 3,000 staff members. *New Positions Created (4):* Principal, B.C. Provincial School for the Deaf; Principals & Vice-Principals; Comptroller; Maintenance Supervisor.

SCHOOL DISTRICT #43 (COQUITLAM)
Att: Keith Denley,
Human Resources Department
550 Poirier Street
Coquitlam, BC V3J 6A7
Tel. 604-939-9201

Fax 604-937-6798
Email .... kdenley@sd43.bc.ca
Website www.sd43.bc.ca
Employer Background: School District #43 (Coquitlam) is the third-largest school district in BC, with over 33,000 students at 69 schools, 3,500 employees and a budget of $181 million. *New Positions Created (6):* Manager of Payroll; Manager, Information Services; Director of Financial Services; Director, Personnel and Employee Relations; Secretary / Treasurer; Assistant Superintendent of Schools.

SCHOOL DISTRICT #57 (PRINCE GEORGE)
Att: Shari Dionne, HR Officer
1894 - 9th Avenue
Prince George, BC V2M 1L7
Tel. 250-561-6800
Fax 250-561-6801
Website www.schdist57.bc.ca
Employer Background: School District #57 (Prince George) is the largest urban and rural school district in B.C., with 64 schools over 18,000 students and 2,000 employees. *New Positions Created (2):* Speech Language Pathologist; Superintendent / CEO.

SCHOOL DISTRICT #59 (PEACE RIVER SOUTH)
Att: Yvonne Becotte
10105 - 12A Street, 1st Floor
Dawson Creek, BC V1G 3V7
Tel. 250-782-8571
Fax 250-782-3204
Email .... ybecotte@mail.sd59.bc.ca
Website www.sd59.bc.ca
Employer Background: School District #59 (Peace River South) serves the northeastern communities of Dawson Creek, Chetwynd, Tumbler Ridge and surrounding areas. *New Positions Created (4):* Speech / Language Pathologist; French Immersion Teacher Drama / Theatre Teacher; Various Teaching Positions.

SCHOOL DISTRICT #60 (PEACE RIVER NORTH)
Att: Leslie Lahaye,
Director of Student Support Services
10112 - 105th Avenue
Fort St. John, BC V1J 4S4
Tel. 250-262-6018
Fax 250-262-6046
Website .... www.prn.bc.ca
Employer Background: School District #60 (Peace River North) serves 5,600 students in 20 schools. *New Positions Created (17):* Grade 3 / 4 Teacher; Primary / Intermediate Teacher; Automotive, Technology Education / CAPP Teacher; French, Science, CAPP Teacher; Physical Education / Outdoor Recreation and CAPP Teacher; Science, CAPP Teacher; Science Teacher; Special Education (Skills Class) Teacher; Teacher; Teacher; Teacher; Teacher; Desktop Publishing / Information Technology Teacher; Library Secretary; Technology Education Teacher; Technology Education Teacher; Woodwork / Construction / Drafting / CAPP Teacher.

SCHOOL DISTRICT #74 (GOLD TRAIL)
Att: Fred Benallick,
Assistant Superintendent of Schools
PO Bag 250
Ashcroft, BC V0K 1A0
Tel. 250-453-9101
Fax 250-453-2425
Website minto.sd74.bc.ca
Employer Background: School District #74
(Gold Trail) serves the south-central interior of British Columbia. *New Positions Created (6):* Intermediate Teacher; Secondary
School Teacher; Secondary School Teachers;
Secondary School Teachers; Speech-Language Pathologists; Teachers.

SCHOOL DISTRICT #81
(FORT NELSON)
Att: Diana Samchuck,
Acting Superintendent of Schools
Box 87
Fort Nelson, BC V0C 1R0
Tel. 250-774-2591
Fax 250-774-2598
Email .... dsamchuck@husky.sd81.bc.ca
Website www.sd81.bc.ca
Employer Background: School District #81
(Fort Nelson) has 1,200 students and 130
staff members. *New Positions Created (2):*
Secondary Counsellor; Superintendent.

SCHOOL DISTRICT #82
(COAST MOUNTAINS)
Att: Don MacPherson,
Director of HR & Labour Relations
3211 Kenney Street
Terrace, BC V8G 3E9
Tel. 250-638-4441
Fax 250-638-4461
Website .... www.cmsd.bc.ca
Employer Background: School District #82
(Coast Mountains) operates 27 schools,
serving 8,000 students in Kitimat, Terrace,
Thornhill, Hazelton, Kitwanga, Moricetown
and Stewart. *New Positions Created (2):*
Teacher; Principal.

SCI BROCKVILLE CORP.
Att: Betty Salmon, HR Manager
100 Strowger Boulevard
Brockville, ON K6V 5W8
Tel. 613-342-6621
Fax 613-498-3608
Email .... betty.salmon@sci.com
Website .... www.sci.com
Employer Background: SCI Brockville Corp.
is part of SCI Systems, a leading provider of
electronics manufacturing services, with
facilities in 19 countries and over 34,000
employees worldwide. *New Positions Created (4):* Technology Development Leader;
Electromechanical Technician - Robotics;
Electronic Technicians; Industrial Maintenance Electrician.

SCICAN
Att: Human Resources Manager
1440 Don Mills Road
Toronto, ON M3B 3P9
Tel. 416-445-1600

Fax 416-445-2727
Email .... resumes@scican.com
Website .... www.scican.com
Employer Background: Founded in 1957,
SciCan manufactures and distributes dental and medical equipment. *New Positions
Created (3):* International Customer Service
Representative; Product Manager; Director,
Product Service.

SCIEMETRIC INSTRUMENTS INC.
Att: Human Resources Manager
27 Northside Road
Nepean, ON K2H 8S1
Tel. 613-596-3995
Fax 613-820-3746
Email .... scinfo@sciemetric.com
Website .... www.sciemetric.com
Employer Background: Founded in 1981,
Sciemetric Instruments Inc. develops industrial computer-based data acquisition and
control systems. *New Positions Created (6):*
Design Quality Assurance Technologist;
Senior Product Line Manager; Applications
Engineers; Marketing Communications
Specialist; System Administrator / QWX Installer; Test Technician.

SCIENCE ALBERTA FOUNDATION
Att: Human Resources Manager
3523 - 33rd Street NW
Suite 260
Calgary, AB T2L 2A6
Tel. 403-220-0077
Fax 403-284-4132
Website .... www.sciencealberta.org
Employer Background: Science Alberta
Foundation is a non-profit, charitable organization that creates programs and services to promote science and technology. *New
Positions Created (3):* Director of Finance
and Administration; Director, Communications ; Director of Science Networks.

SCINTREX LTD.
Att: Ed Quinton, HR Department
222 Snidercroft Road
Concord, ON L4K 1B5
Tel. 905-669-2280
Fax 905-669-6403
Email .... equinton@scintrexltd.com
Website .... www.scintrexltd.com
Employer Background: Scintrex manufactures precision geophysical instrumentation
used in mineral and oil and gas exploration.
New Positions Created (3): Buyer; Manufacturing Engineer; Quality Assurance Mgr.

SCINTREX TRACE CORP.
Att: Human Resources
152 Cleopatra Drive
Ottawa, ON K2G 5X2
Tel. 613-224-1061
Fax 613-224-2603
Email .... hr@tracedetection.com
Website .... www.tracedetection.com
Employer Background: Scintrex Trace Corp.
develops and manufactures trace chemical
detection devices for military, security and
law enforcement agencies. *New Positions*

Created (9): Accounts Receivable Clerk; Controller / Assistant Controller; Electronics
Technologists (2); Purchaser; Sales Executive; Senior Scientist; Calibration Technician; Materials Supervisor; Test Technicians.

SCOR CANADA
REINSURANCE COMPANY
Att: Administration Manager
161 Bay Street, BCE Place
PO Box 615, Canada Trust Tower
Toronto, ON M5J 2S1
Tel. 416-869-3670
Fax 416-365-9393
Email .... lmcclelland@scor.com
Website .... www.scor.com
Employer Background: SCOR Canada
Reinsurance Company is part of Paris-based
SCOR Group, one of the world's largest
reinsurers. *New Positions Created (5):* Executive Assistant; Event Coordinator / Receptionist; Senior Treaty Account Manager;
Technical Reinsurance Accountant; Technical Underwriting Assistant.

SCOTIAMCLEOD
Att: ISS Human Resources Department
40 King Street West
PO Box 4085
Toronto, ON M5W 2X6
Tel. 416-866-6161
Fax 416-863-3089
Website .... www.scotiabank.ca
Employer Background: ScotiaMcLeod is one
of Canada's leading full-service investment
dealers, serving clients in over 70 branches
across the country. *New Positions Created
(2):* Financial Analysts; Branch Administrator, Private Client Financial Services.

SCOTT BUILDERS INC.
Att: Ralph Ward, President
8105 - 49th Avenue Close
Red Deer, AB T4P 2V5
Tel. 403-343-7270
Fax 403-346-4310
Email .... ralphw@scottbuilders.com
Website .... www.scottbuilders.com
Employer Background: Founded in 1971,
Scott Builders Inc. is a leading design / build
construction firm, with offices in Calgary,
Red Deer and Edmonton. *New Positions Created (2):* Intermediate / Senior Project Managers; Project Superintendents.

SCOTT CONSTRUCTION LTD.
Att: Human Resources Manager
620 - 8th Avenue West
Suite 200
Vancouver, BC V5Z 1C8
Tel. 604-874-8228
Fax 604-874-0273
Email .... headoffice@scottcanada.com
Website .... www.scottconstructionltd.com
Employer Background: Scott Construction
Ltd. is a leading general contractor, specializing in high-rise residential, commercial
and institutional projects. *New Positions
Created (2):* Senior Project Managers;
Project Managers.

SCOTT LAND & LEASE LTD.
Att: Human Resources Manager
202 - 6th Avenue SW
Suite 900
Calgary, AB T2P 2R9
Fax 403-264-7997
Email .... lgabora@scottland.ca
Website .... www.scottland.ca
Employer Background: Scott Land & Lease Ltd. is a land service company that operates over western and northern Canada. *New Positions Created (3):* Surface Land Administrators; Surface Manager; Various Real Estate Positions.

SCOTT PAPER LTD.
Att: Human Resources Department
PO Box 760
New Westminster, BC V3L 4Z9
Fax 604-520-9250
Website .... www.scottpaper.ca
Employer Background: Scott Paper Ltd. manufactures paper products for household, industrial and commercial use. *New Positions Created (5):* Power Engineer, 3rd-Class; Third-Class Power Engineer; Occupational Health and Safety Supervisor; Paper Mill Supervisor; Utilities Supervisor.

SCOTT PAPER LTD.
Att: Human Resources Department
20 Laurier Street
Hull, QC J8X 4H3
Tel. 819-595-5302
Fax 819-595-5396
Website .... www.scottpaper.ca
Employer Background: Scott Paper Ltd. manufactures paper products for household, industrial and commercial use. *New Positions Created (4):* Electrical Technician; Technical Control Supervisor; Stores Supervisor; Production Supervisor.

SCOTT SPRINGFIELD MANUFACTURING INC.
Att: Marketing Manager
2234 Portland Street SE
Calgary, AB T2G 4M6
Tel. 403-236-1212
Fax 403-236-9093
Email .... rmuzeen.ssm@nucleus.com
Website .... www.scottspringfield.com
Employer Background: Founded in 1970, Scott Springfield Manufacturing Inc. is a leading supplier of custom-designed air handlers. *New Positions Created (2):* Customer Service Rep; Inside Sales Position.

SCP SCIENCE
Att: Human Resources Manager
21800 Clark Graham
Baie d'Urfe, QC H9X 4B6
Tel. 514-457-0701
Fax 514-457-4499
Email .... mbox@scpscience.com
Website .... www.scpscience.com
Employer Background: SCP Science manufactures and distributes atomic spectroscopy standards, supplies and instruments

for analytical chemistry laboratories. *New Positions Created (14):* Technical Sales Representative; Electromechanical Engineer; Inside Sales Representatives (2); Sales Representatives (5); Chemical Lab Technician; Customer Service Representative; Human Resources Position; Sales Representative; US Sales Manager; Catalogue Technical Writer; Sales Representative; Graphics Coordinator; Catalogue Layout Assistant; Chemical Sales Representatives (3).

SEACOR ENVIRONMENTAL ENGINEERING INC.
Att: Human Resources Manager
13251 Delf Place
Suite 406
Richmond, BC V6V 2A2
Tel. 604-244-2266
Fax 604-244-1184
Website .... www.seacorcanada.com
Employer Background: Seacor Environmental Engineering Inc. specializes in a full range of environmental consulting services. *New Positions Created (6):* Intermediate Environmental Engineer / Scientist; Junior Environmental Engineer / Scientist; Sr Environmental Consultant; Intermediate Environmental Engineer / Scientist; Junior Environmental Engineer / Scientist; Sr Environmental Engineer / Scientist.

SEACOR ENVIRONMENTAL ENGINEERING INC.
Att: Human Resources Manager
200 Rivercrest Drive SE
Suite 185
Riverbend Atrium
Calgary, AB T2C 2X5
Tel. 403-266-2030
Fax 403-263-7906
Email .... hduff@seacorcanada.com
Website .... www.seacorcanada.com
Employer Background: Seacor Environmental Engineering Inc. specializes in a full range of environmental consulting services. *New Positions Created (3):* Intermediate Environmental Engineer / Scientist; Junior Environmental Engineer / Scientist; Senior Environmental Consultant.

SEARS TRAVEL SERVICE
Att: Pierre Raymond,
Customer Contact Centre
1200 St. Laurent Boulevard
Ottawa, ON K1K 4K9
Fax 613-748-6497
Website .... www.searstravel.com
Employer Background: Sears Travel Service has been helping Canadians plan their vacations since 1972. *New Positions Created (5):* Telephone Sales Consultant; Central Processing Agent; Branch Travel Consultant; Telephone Sales Consultant; Travel Processing Agent.

SEAWIND
Att: Human Resources Manager
315 MacDonald Street

Suite 301
St-Jean-Iberville, QC J3B 8J3
Fax 450-359-0994
Email .... cldhr.industriel@netc.net
Employer Background: Seawind is an aircraft manufacturing company. *New Positions Created (3):* Human Resources / Business Manager; Production Leaders; Production Manager.

SECURICOR CASH SERVICES
Att: Patricia Moretti
365 Bloor Street East
Suite 400
Toronto, ON M4W 3L4
Tel. 416-645-5447
Fax 416-645-5406
Email .... hr@securicor.ca
Website .... www.securicor.ca
Employer Background: Securicor Cash Services provides secure cash logistics services to financial institutions in Canada. *New Positions Created (4):* Regional Administrator; Human Resource Manager; Customer Service Representatives, Corporate Accounts; Account Manager.

SECURITEX INC.
Att: Gaetane Savard
4200 St. Laurent
6th Floor
Montréal, QC H2W 2R2
Tel. 514-282-0503
Fax 514-282-8871
Website .... www.securitex.com
Employer Background: Securitex Inc. is a leader in protective clothing technology. *New Positions Created (2):* Samples Operators; Sewing Machine Operators.

SECURITIES VALUATION CO. / SVC
Att: Human Resources Manager
5255 Orbitor Drive
Mississauga, ON L4W 4Y8
Tel. 905-602-1044
Fax 905-602-6040
Email .... svccareers@svco.com
Website .... www.svco.com
Employer Background: Established in 1992, SVC is a global supplier of securities data. *New Positions Created (2):* Client Service Representative; Data Specialist.

SECURITYLINK AMERITECH
Att: Human Resources Manager
1501 Bank Street
1st Floor
Ottawa, ON K1H 7Z1
Tel. 613-736-8888
Fax 416-745-9294
Email .... pbeard@securitylink.com
Website .... www.securitylink.ca
Employer Background: SecurityLink Ameritech is an electronic security company, with over 1.2 million monitored security systems across North America. *New Positions Created (2):* Field Technicians & Project Coordinators; Service Technicians.

SED SYSTEMS
Att: Human Resources Manager
18 Innovation Boulevard
PO Box 1464
Saskatoon, SK S7K 3P7
Tel. 306-931-3425
Fax 306-933-1582
Email .... hr@sedsystems.ca
Website .... www.sedsystems.ca
Employer Background: SED Systems, a division of Calian Ltd., develops hardware and software applications for space and satellite communications. *New Positions Created (3):* RF Engineers; Software Developers; Telecommunication Engineers.

SEDBERGH SCHOOL
Att: Jeremy McLean, Headmaster
810 Cote Azelie
Montebello, QC J0V 1L0
Tel. 819-423-5523
Fax 819-423-5769
Email .... info@sedbergh.com
Website .... www.sedbergh.com
Employer Background: Founded in 1939, Sedbergh School is an independent, co-educational boarding school of 100 students, offering instruction from grades 4-12. *New Positions Created (5):* Teacher, English; Teacher, Mathematics & Science; Teacher, Second Languages; Academic Dean; Teachers.

SEDONA NETWORKS
Att: Human Resources
308 Legget Drive
Kanata, ON K2K 1Y6
Tel. 613-599-3114
Fax 613-599-3040
Employer Background: Sedona Networks designs and builds an infrastructure-neutral access network architecture, enabling service providers to deliver integrated voice and data services to customers on demand. *New Positions Created (29):* Board Support Package Software Designer; Carrier Signaling Protocol Developer; Customer Technical Support Engineer; Element Management Developers; Embedded System OAM Developer; IP QoS Management Designer; Principal IP Networking Software Engineer; Product Support Software Designers; Senior ATM Software Design Engineer; Signaling Software Developer; Software Designer; Systems Architect; Tools Designer; Voice Networking Manager; Voice Over IP Protocol Developer; Voice Verification / Test Engineer; Customer Technical Support Engineer; Director of Customer Technical Services; Director of Product Management; Hardware Manager; Hardware Project Leader; Hardware Sustaining / Integration Engineers; Hardware Technician; Junior and Intermediate Hardware Design Engineers; Project Manager; Research and Development Alliances Manager; Senior Hardware Design Engineers; Senior Product Manager; Test Engineer.

SEIDEN HEALTH MANAGEMENT INC.
Att: Human Resources
145 Front Street East
Toronto, ON M5A 1E3
Fax 416-362-8925
Email ... humanresources@seidenhealth.com
Employer Background: Seiden Health Management Inc. provides objective, independent impairment evaluation, disability assessment and related services to corporate clients. *New Positions Created (7):* Customer Service / Order Entry Assistant; Bilingual Receptionist; Executive Assistant; Health Professionals; Intake Personnel; Office / IT Mgr; Photoshop / Graphic Arts Specialist.

SELDRUM CORPORATION
Att: Sales Manager
1370 Artisans Court
Burlington, ON L7L 5Y2
Tel. 905-335-2766
Fax 905-335-5986
Email .... lifecareer@hotmail.com
Website .... www.seldrum.com
Employer Background: Seldrum Corporation is a major distributor of office supplies and equipment. *New Positions Created (2):* Inside Sales Rep; Inside Sales Rep.

SELJAX INTERNATIONAL INC.
Att: Human Resources Manager
5013 - 48th Street
Suite 104, PO Box 2117
Stony Plain, AB T7Z 1X6
Tel. 780-963-1717
Fax 780-963-3290
Email .... careers@seljax.com
Website .... www.seljax.com
Employer Background: Seljax International Inc. (formerly Bjornson Concepts Inc.) provides software solutions for the building materials industry. *New Positions Created (3):* Customer Service Specialists; Outside Sales Account Representatives; Webmaster / E-Commerce Developer.

**SELKIRK COLLEGE,
CASTLEGAR CAMPUS**
Att: Human Resources Department
301 Frank Beinder Way, Box 1200
Castlegar, BC V1N 3J1
Tel. 250-365-1283
Fax 250-365-3929
Email .... postings@selkirk.bc.ca
Website .... www.selkirk.bc.ca
Employer Background: Selkirk College is a multi-campus community college. *New Positions Created (2):* Director of Human Resources; Fine Woodworking Instructor.

**SELKIRK FINANCIAL
TECHNOLOGIES, INC.**
Att: Human Resources Manager
1055 West Hastings Street
17th Floor
Vancouver, BC V6E 2E9
Tel. 604-682-2862
Fax 604-682-1059
Email .... hr@selkirkfinancial.com
Website .... www.selkirkfinancial.com
Employer Background: Selkirk Financial Technologies, Inc. is a software developer

that develops financial management applications for large companies. *New Positions Created (13):* Communications Specialist; Director, Information Technology; Marketing Operations Manager; Product Manager; Professional Services Business Analyst; Professional Services Implementation Consultant, ICS; Reception / Administration Assistant; Senior Administrator; Senior Software Engineer, Applications; Senior Software Systems Engineer; Software Engineer; Software Quality Assurance Analyst; Vice President, Business Development.

SEMBIOSYS GENETICS INC.
Att: Human Resources Manager
2985 - 23rd Avenue NE
Calgary, AB T1Y 7L3
Tel. 403-250-5424
Fax 403-250-3886
Email .... jobs@sembiosys.ca
Website .... www.sembiosys.ca
Employer Background: SemBioSys Genetics is a biotechnology company focused on the development of natural oil body-based products and recombinant proteins from plants. *New Positions Created (7):* Physical Organic Chemist; Analytical Chemist; Biochemist; Molecular Biologist/Research Associate; Molecular Biologist/Research Associate; Molecular Biologist/Research Associate; Plant Growth Facilities Manager.

SEMICONDUCTOR INSIGHTS INC.
Att: Human Resources Department
3000 Solandt Road
Kanata, ON K2K 2X2
Tel. 613-599-6500
Fax 613-599-6501
Email .... hr@semiconductor.com
Website .... www.semiconductor.com
Employer Background: Semiconductor Insights provides microelectronics services and products to major corporations worldwide. *New Positions Created (4):* Account Managers / Patent Analysis Engineers; Design Analysis Engineer; Electrical Lab and Test Supervisor; Process Analysis Engineer.

SEMOTUS SYSTEMS CORPORATION
Att: Human Resources Manager
1500 West Georgia Street, Suite 1800
Vancouver, BC V6G 2Z6
Tel. 604-257-2700
Fax 604-602-0817
Email .... hr.van@semotus.com
Website .... www.semotus.com
Employer Background: Semotus Systems Corporation (formerly Datalink Systems Corporation) has been a leading wireless application service provider since 1993. *New Positions Created (2):* Customer Support Representative, Financial Services; Senior Software Developers.

SEN COMMUNITY HEALTH CARE
Att: President / CEO
698 King Street West, Cathedral Square
Hamilton, ON L8P 1C7
Tel. 905-522-6887
Fax 905-522-6918

Email .... sen@sen.on.ca
Website .... www.sen.on.ca
Employer Background: SEN Community Health Care provides in-home nursing, supportive housing and volunteer visiting services to the communities of Hamilton-Wentworth and Halton. *New Positions Created (3):* Manager, Financial Services; Visiting Nurses; Registered Nurses / Registered Practical Nurses.

SEN5ES
Att: Human Resources
801 West Georgia Street
Vancouver, BC V6C 1P7

Tel. 604-633-0138
Fax 604-633-0304
Email .... tvt@senses.ca
Website www.sen5es.com
Employer Background: Sen5es is a leading gourmet food retail, restaurant and catering company. *New Positions Created (3):* 1st, 2nd and 3rd Cooks; Sous-Chef; Catering Sales Manager.

SEN5ES
Att: Human Resources Manager
108 Chestnut Street, Metropolitan Hotel
Toronto, ON M5G 1R3

Fax 416-935-0047
Website www.sen5es.com
Employer Background: Sen5es is a leading gourmet food retail, restaurant and catering company. *New Positions Created (2):* Retail Mangers; Controller.

SENECA COLLEGE OF APPLIED ARTS & TECHNOLOGY
Att: Jane Wilson, Personnel Officer
1750 Finch Avenue East
Toronto, ON M2J 2X5

Tel. 416-491-5050
Fax 905-479-4162
Email ..... employee.relations@senecac.on.ca
Website .... www.senecac.on.ca
Employer Background: Seneca College is the largest multi-campus college in Canada, with 15,000 full-time and 90,000 part-time students. *New Positions Created (3):* Director, Employee Relations; Director, Facilities Mgmnt; Manager, General Accounting.

SENSTAR-STELLAR CORPORATION
Att: Human Resources
119 John Cavanagh Road
Carp, ON K0A 1L0

Tel. 613-839-5572
Fax 613-839-5830
Email .... ndunn@senstarstellar.com
Website .... www.senstarstellar.com
Employer Background: Senstar-Stellar supplies outdoor perimeter intrusion detection products and security control systems. *New Positions Created (11):* Engineering Data Coordinator; Field Service Rep; Graphic Designer; Systems Project Engineer; Test Technician; Quality Assurance Mgr; Buyer; Product Information Specialist; Product Line Supervisor, Cable Facility; Software Engineers; Systems Project Engineer.

SERCA FOODSERVICE INC., WESTERN DIVISION
Att: Human Resources Manager
14404 - 128th Avenue
Edmonton, AB T5L 3H6

Tel. 780-451-3550
Fax 780-451-0742
Email .... hr_western@serca.com
Website .... www.serca.com
Employer Background: Serca Foodservice Inc. supplies food and non-food products to the hospitality and institutional sectors. *New Positions Created (3):* District Sales Representative and Trainees; Key Account Representative; Product Manager.

SERCO FACILITIES MANAGEMENT INC.
Att: Human Resources Manager
PO Box 1012, Station C
Goose Bay, NF A0P 1C0

Fax 709-896-6929
Email .... hr@serco-goosebay.com
Website .... www.serco-goosebay.com
Employer Background: Serco Facilities Management Inc. provides facilities management and aviation services to government and industry clients. *New Positions Created (2):* Manager of Finance and Administration; Planning and Works Control Manager.

SERNAS GROUP INC., THE
Att: Human Resources Manager
110 Scotia Court, Unit 41
Whitby, ON L1N 8Y7

Tel. 905-686-6402
Fax 905-432-7877
Email .... hr@sernas.com
Website .... www.sernas.com
Employer Background: The Sernas Group Inc. provides consulting services in specialized fields of engineering and urban planning in southern Ontario. *New Positions Created (2):* Urban Planner; Civil Drafter.

SETON
Att: Elaine Moulton
56 Leek Crescent
Richmond Hill, ON L4B 1H1

Tel. 905-764-1122
Fax 905-764-3138
Email ... elaine_moulton@bradycorp.com
Website .... www.seton.com
Employer Background: Seton is a world leader in industrial, safety and identification products. *New Positions Created (2):* Account Manager; Telemarketer.

SEWER-MATIC SERVICES INC.
Att: Kyle Peori
4140 Belgreen Drive
Ottawa, ON K1G 3N2

Tel. 613-739-1449
Fax 613-739-1955
Website .... www.sewer-matic.com
Employer Background: Sewer-Matic Services Inc. provides utility maintenance and environmental services. *New Positions Created (11):* Assistant Helpers; Drain Technicians; DZ Drivers; Licensed or Apprentice Plumbers; Waste Transfer Manager / Supervisor; Dispatcher; Assistant Helpers (10); Bilingual Customer Service Representative; Drain Technicians (4); DZ Drivers (5); Licensed Plumbers (4).

SEYLER ELECTRIC LTD.
Att: Jason
410 Richardson Road
Orangeville, ON L9W 4W8

Tel. 519-941-0025
Fax 519-941-6509
Email .... jculver@seylerelectric.com
Website .... www.seylerelectric.com
Employer Background: Seyler Electric Ltd. is a leading electric motor repair and servicing technology company. *New Positions Created (3):* Electric Motor Technicians (2); Electrician; Millwright.

SHABEN INTERNATIONAL INC.
Att: Deanna Carlson
14735 - 124th Avenue
Edmonton, AB T5L 3B2

Tel. 780-452-3830
Fax 780-455-8500
Email .... dcarlson@shaben.com
Employer Background: Shaben markets and distributes toys, stationery and giftware. *New Positions Created (2):* Marketing / Inside Sales Position; Controller.

SHADE-O-MATIC
Att: Human Resources Manager
550 Oakdale
Toronto, ON M3N 1W6

Tel. 416-742-1524
Fax 416-742-4310
Email .... cathy@shade-o-matic.on.ca
Employer Background: Shade-O-Matic manufactures vertical and horizontal blinds, pleated and cellular shades, wood and roller blinds and poly-satin shutters. *New Positions Created (3):* Sales Representative; Key-Account Sales Rep; Territory Sales Rep.

SHALOM VILLAGE
Att: Ms Pat Morden, CEO
60 Macklin Street North
Hamilton, ON L8S 3S1

Tel. 905-529-1613
Fax 905-529-7542
Website .... www.shalomvillage.on.ca
Employer Background: Shalom Village is a long-term care provider, licensed by the Ontario Ministry of Health and affiliated with McMaster University. *New Positions Created (3):* Hospitality Director / Food Services Supervisor; Health Professional, Adult Day Program; Registered Nurses / Personal Support Workers.

SHANA CORPORATION
Att: Human Resources
9744 - 45th Avenue
Edmonton, AB T6E 5C5

Tel. 780-433-3690
Fax 780-437-4381
Email .... careers@shana.com
Website .... www.shana.com

Employer Background: Shana Corporation is a leading software company, providing e-business solutions to industries across North America. *New Positions Created (13):* Accounting Supervisor; Development Group Leader; Development Team Leader; Principal Consultant; Product Manager; QA Analyst; Support Analyst; Technical Writer; Demand Generation Specialist; Graphic Designer, Marketing; Java Programmer, Development; Sales Account Managers (3); Vice-President, Marketing.

SHANE HOMES
Att: Human Resources
5661 - 7th Street NE
Calgary, AB T2E 8V3
Tel. 403-571-8844
Fax 403-571-8855
Email .... info@shanehomes.com
Website .... www.shanehomes.com
Employer Background: Founded in 1979, Shane Homes is Calgary's second largest builder. *New Positions Created (2):* Professional New Homes Salespeople; New Home Estimator.

SHARED SERVICES WEST, REGIONAL MATERIALS MANAGEMENT
Att: Human Resources Manager
150 Sherway Drive
Trillium Health Centre, Queensway Site
Toronto, ON M9C 1A5
Fax 416-521-4003
Employer Background: Shared Services West, Regional Materials Management serves the materials sourcing, purchasing and management needs of the Trillium Health Centre, Credit Valley Hospital, Halton Healthcare Services and William Osler Health Centre. *New Positions Created (8):* Buyer Assistants; Data Management Specialists; Inventory Analyst; Logistics Manager; Meditech Systems Analyst; Process Review & System Trainer; Regional Purchasing Manager; Senior Buyers.

SHARP'S AUDIO-VISUAL LTD.
Att: John Will, Branch Manager
10552 - 106th Street
Edmonton, AB T5H 2X6
Fax 780-426-0724
Employer Background: Sharp's Audio-Visual Ltd. is western Canada's leader in presentation services. *New Positions Created (3):* Audio-Visual Technicians; Sales Representatives; Systems Installers.

SHAW COMMUNICATIONS INC.
Att: Human Resources Manager
4710 Kingsway Avenue, Suite 1600
Burnaby, BC V5H 4M5
Tel. 604-629-3000
Fax 604-629-3371
Website .... www.shaw.ca
Employer Background: Shaw Communications Inc. has been a cable television operator in Canada for over 35 years. *New Positions Created (6):* Inside Sales Representative; Shaw@Home Technical Field Representative; Customer Service Representatives; In-Home Representatives; Shaw@ Home Sales Representatives; Technical Field Representative.

SHAW PIPE PROTECTION LTD.
Att: Human Resources Department
10275 - 21st Street
Edmonton, AB T6P 1P3
Tel. 780-467-5501
Fax 780-467-0898
Email .... hrrecruitment.office@bredero.com
Website .... www.bredero.com
Employer Background: Shaw provides corrosion coating to the energy industry. *New Positions Created (2):* EHS Coordinator; Quality Control Technician.

SHAW PIPE PROTECTION LTD.
Att: Human Resources
630 - 3rd Avenue SW, Suite 1200
Calgary, AB T2P 4L4
Tel. 403-264-2255
Fax 403-261-9078
Email .... hrrecruitment.office@bredero.com
Website .... www.bredero.com
Employer Background: Shaw Pipe Protection Ltd. provides corrosion coating to the energy industry. *New Positions Created (7):* Senior Account Representative; Customer Service Representative; Customer Service Representative; Intermediate Accountant; Senior Product Development Engineer; Secretary; Plant Accountant.

SHAWCOR LTD.
Att: Human Resources
25 Bethridge Road
Toronto, ON M9W 1M7
Tel. 416-743-7111
Fax 416-743-8194
Website .... www.shawcor.com
Employer Background: ShawCor Ltd. (formerly Shaw Industries Ltd.) is an energy services company focusing on technology-based products and services for exploration and production, pipeline, and petrochemical and industrial markets worldwide. *New Positions Created (11):* Benefits and Compensation Analyst; Administrative Assistant, Compensation and Benefits; Junior Research Scientist; Senior Financial Analyst; Benefits and Compensation Analyst; Manufacturing Engineer; Manufacturing Engineering Manager; Marketing Coordinator; Quality Engineer; Customer Service Representative; Lab Technician.

SHAWNIGAN LAKE SCHOOL
Att: David Robertson, Headmaster
1975 Renfrew Road
Shawnigan Lake, BC V0R 2W0
Tel. 250-743-5516
Fax 250-743-6230
Email .... dbr@sls.bc.ca
Website .... www.sls.bc.ca
Employer Background: Shawnigan Lake School is a co-educational boarding school, with 400 students in grades 8 to 12. *New Positions Created (2):* Teacher, Mathematics; Weekend Activities Coordinator.

SHEEHAN'S TRUCK CENTRE INC.
Att: Service Manager
4320 Harvester Road
Burlington, ON L7L 5S4
Tel. 905-632-0300
Fax 905-632-4557
Website .... www.heavytrux.com
Employer Background: Sheehan's Truck Centre Inc. is a heavy truck dealership. *New Positions Created (6):* Diesel Mechanics; Warranty Administrator; Service Manager; Diesel Mechanics / Foreperson; Tire Repair Technician / Diesel Mechanics; Parts Counterperson.

SHELL CANADA LIMITED
Att: Human Resources
Range Road 214, Bag 23, Scotford Complex
Fort Saskatchewan, AB T8L 3T2
Fax 780-992-3448
Email .... scotford.hr@shell.ca
Website .... www.shell.ca
Employer Background: Shell Canada Limited is one of the largest integrated petroleum companies in Canada. *New Positions Created (2):* Business Manager; Organizational Effectiveness Coordinator.

SHELL CANADA LIMITED
Att: Louise Loiselle
400 - 4th Avenue SW
Calgary, AB T2P 2H5
Tel. 403-269-2586
Fax 403-691-2500
Email .... louise.loiselle@shell.ca
Website .... www.shell.ca
Employer Background: Shell Canada Limited is one of the largest integrated petroleum companies in Canada. *New Positions Created (29):* Bilingual Customer Support Representative; Bilingual National Systems Support Representative; Bilingual Commercial Selling Customer Service Representative; Environmental Specialist; Senior Geologist and Geophysicist; Advisor, Brand and Advertising; Senior Geologists and Geophysicists; Senior Geologists and Geophysicists; Senior Geologists and Geophysicists; Quantitative Interpretation Geophysicist; Senior Exploration Geologists; Bilingual Credit Representative; Bilingual Customer Support Rep; Bilingual National Systems Support Representative; Extraction / Tailings Engineer; Extraction / Tailings Shift Team Leaders (3); Froth Treatment Shift Team Leaders (4); Health / Safety / Environment (HSE) Coordinator, Utilities; Maintenance Coordinator, Extraction / Tailings; Maintenance Coordinator, Ore Preparation; Maintenance Coordinator, Utilities; Maintenance Team Leader, Utilities; Ore Preparation Engineer; Ore Preparation Shift Team Leaders (2); Plant Technologist, Ore Preparation; Utilities Control Room Operators (4); Utilities Engineer; Utilities Shift Team Leaders (4); Thermal Reservoir Engineer.

SHELL CANADA LIMITED
Att: Florence Marino
90 Sheppard Avenue East, Suite 600
Toronto, ON M2N 6Y2

Fax 416-227-7194
Email .... florence.marino@shell.ca
Website .... www.shell.ca
Employer Background: Shell Canada Limited is one of the largest integrated petroleum companies in Canada. *New Positions Created (2):* Fluids Program Manager, Industrial Services; Fluids Program Manager.

SHERATON CAVALIER HOTEL
Att: Director of Human Resources
2620 - 32nd Avenue NE
Calgary, AB T1Y 6B8

Tel. 403-291-0107
Fax 403-291-2834
Website .... www.sheraton-calgary.com
Employer Background: The Sheraton Cavalier Hotel is a 306-room facility. *New Positions Created (2):* Corporate Sales Account Executive; Sales Account Executive.

SHERATON PARKWAY HOTEL, TORONTO NORTH
Att: Human Resources
600 Highway 7 East
Richmond Hill, ON L4B 1B2

Tel. 905-881-2121
Fax 905-882-3112
Email .... humanresources@
.... sheratonparkway.com
Website .... www.sheraton.com
Employer Background: Sheraton Parkway Hotel, Toronto North is a 450-room, 4-diamond hotel that provides accommodation, food and beverage and convention services to tourists, corporations and associations. *New Positions Created (8):* Director, Sales & Marketing; Front Office Manager; Various Hotel Positions; Revenue Manager; Various Hospitality Positions; Various Fitness Positions (2); Manager, Parkway Racquet & Fitness Club; Night Manager.

SHERIDAN COLLEGE
Att: Human Resources Department
1430 Trafalgar Road
Oakville, ON L6H 2L1

Tel. 905-845-9430
Fax 905-815-4054
Email .... human.resources@sheridanc.on.ca
Website .... www.sheridanc.on.ca
Employer Background: Founded in 1967, Sheridan College is the 5th-largest community college in Ontario, with 10,000 full-time post-secondary students and 42,000 continuing education students. *New Positions Created (11):* Professor, Pharmacy Technician Program; Dean, Continuing Education & Corporate Training; Director of Development; Director of Research Administration; Major Gift Officer; Dean, School of Community & Liberal Studies; Vice-President, Academic; Finance / Registration Clerk; Manager, Accounting Services; Pharmacy Technician; Professor, Mechanical and Electro-Mechanical Engineering Technology.

SHERIDAN NURSERIES LTD.
Att: David Court
12302 - 10th Line, RR 4
Georgetown, ON L7G 4S7

Tel. 905-798-7970
Fax 905-873-2478
Email ...... gcsm@sheridan-nurseries.com
Website ...... www.sheridan-nurseries.com
Employer Background: Sheridan Nurseries Ltd. is a leading retailer in the horticulture industry. *New Positions Created (6):* Patio and Gift Department Supervisor; Store Accountant; Hardgoods Supervisor; Nursery and Seasonal Plant Supervisor; Seasonal Products Supervisor; Trade Sales Assistant.

SHERRITT INTERNATIONAL CORP.
Att: Human Resources
PO Box 3388
Fort Saskatchewan, AB T8L 2T3

Tel. 780-992-7000
Fax 780-992-7575
Email .... scampbell@sherrittoil.com
Website .... www.sherritt.com
Employer Background: Sherritt International Corp. is a public Canadian company, with business interests in nickel and cobalt mining and refining, oil and gas, engineering and metallurgical technologies, fertilizer production, tourism and agriculture. *New Positions Created (3):* Senior Geological Technologist; Technologist, Process Technology; Senior Geologist.

SHERWIN-WILLIAMS COMPANY, THE
Att: Jack Singh, District Manager
7047 Venture Street
Delta, BC V4G 1H8

Fax 604-526-9898
Email ... vancouver.district@sherwin.com
Website .... www.sherwin.com
Employer Background: The Sherwin-Williams Company is a national leader in the home improvement and coatings industry. *New Positions Created (3):* Store Manager; Store Manager; Sales Representative.

SHIBLEY RIGHTON LLP
Att: Sandra E. Dawe, Managing Partner
401 Bay Street, Suite 1900
Toronto, ON M5H 2Z1

Tel. 416-363-9381
Fax 416-214-5480
Website .... www.shibleyrighton.com
Employer Background: Shibley Righton LLP is a real estate and litigation law firm. *New Positions Created (4):* Corporate / Commercial Lawyer; Employment and Public Law Lawyer; Intermediate Real Estate Assistant; Senior Litigation Assistants (2).

SHIKATRONICS INC.
Att: Human Resources
30 Taschereau Boulevard, Suite 204
La Prairie, QC J5R 5H7

Tel. 450-444-4200
Fax 450-659-1000
Website .... www.shikatronics.com
Employer Background: Established in 1989, Shikatronics Inc. manufactures memory solutions for high-end servers, workstations, telecom devices, desktop PCs, notebooks and handheld digital devices. *New Positions Created (2):* Senior Account Manager and

Inside Sales Representative; Sales Representatives.

SHIP.COM, INC.
Att: Human Resources Manager
191 Lombard Avenue, 14th Floor
Winnipeg, MB R3B 0X1

Tel. 204-940-7447
Fax 204-940-7440
Email .... jobs@ship.com
Website .... www.ship.com
Employer Background: Ship.com, Inc. aims to create the world's most comprehensive web-based supply chain platform. *New Positions Created (7):* Customer Relationship Management - i2, Kana Communications and Siebel Implementation Specialists; E-Commerce Solution Designers; EDI Specialists; i2, Oracle, PeopleSoft, and Manugistics Supply Chain Application Sales Professionals; i2, Oracle, PeopleSoft, Manugistics and Descartes Implementation Specialists; i2, Oracle, PeopleSoft, Manugistics, and Descartes Integration Specialists; Platform Architects; Technical Project Manager.

SHIRMAX FASHIONS LTD.
Att: Human Resources Department
3901 Jarry Street East
Montréal, QC H1Z 2G1

Tel. 514-729-3333
Fax 514-729-3018
Email .... hr@shirmax.com
Website .... www.shirmax.com
Employer Background: Shirmax Fashions Ltd. is a leading retailer of maternity and plus-size women's fashions. *New Positions Created (26):* Printer; Architectural Technicians; Senior Marketing Specialist; Supervisor, Marketing; Manager; Head of Loss Prevention; Payroll Clerk; Assistant Managers and Visual Specialist; Administrative Assistant; Office Supervisor; Buyer; Fashion Coordinator / Product Developer; Administrative Assistant; Store Planner; Grader, Marker and Patternmaker; Inventory Analyst; Loss Prevention Administrator; Merchandise Planner; Computer Operator; Intermediate Programmer-Analyst; Office Supervisor; Computer Technician; Director of Marketing; Graphic Artists; Visual Specialists; Human Resources Consultant.

SHISEIDO (CANADA) INC.
Att: Human Resources Manager
60A Leek Crescent
Richmond Hill, ON L4B 1H1

Tel. 905-763-1250
Fax 905-763-8636
Website .... www.shiseido.com
Employer Background: Shiseido (Canada) Inc. is a leading cosmetics company. *New Positions Created (2):* Counter Mgr; Trainer.

SHOPPERS DRUG MART
Att: Heather Grossman
225 Yorkland Boulevard
Toronto, ON M2J 4Y7

Tel. 416-493-1220
Fax 416-490-2685
Email .... hgrossman@shoppersdrugmart.ca

Website .... www.shoppersdrugmart.ca

Employer Background: Shoppers Drug Mart (Pharmaprix in Quebec) is Canada's largest drugstore group, with 824 locations and sales of $4.2 billion. *New Positions Created (34):* Senior Marketing Assistant; Business Development Manager; Category Assistant; Marketing Support Representative; Role Development Coordinator; Graphic Designer; Communications Analyst; Customer Loyalty Analyst ; Junior Leasing Lawyer; LAN Analyst; Legal Counsel; Pricing Analyst; Programmer Analyst; Translator, Marketing Communications; Web Page Designer; Communications Analyst; Customer Loyalty Analyst; LAN Analyst; Manager, Logistics Operations ; Revisor, Marketing Communications; Role Development Coordinator; Senior Systems Analyst; Translator, Marketing Communications; Business Development Manager; Cosmetic Managers; Front Store Managers; Senior Designer / Team Leader; Central Support Representative; Conference Coordinator; Retail Accounting Manager; Cosmetic Managers; Front Store Managers; Pharmacy Marketing Assistant; Advertising Distribution Coordinator.

SHOPPERS HOME HEALTH CARE
Att: Human Resources
753 Main Street East
Hamilton, ON L8M 1L2

Fax 905-547-7927
Website .... www.shoppersdrugmart.ca

Employer Background: Shoppers Home Health Care, a division of Shoppers Drug Mart Inc., is a leading home healthcare retailer. *New Positions Created (2):* Seating Technician; Service Technician.

SHOPPING CHANNEL, THE / TSC
Att: Human Resources Department
1400 Castlefield Avenue
Toronto, ON M6B 4H8

Tel. 416-785-3500
Email .... tschr@rci.rogers.com
Website .... www.tsc.ca

Employer Background: TSC produces a Canadian televised home shopping service, providing products ranging from fashions to jewellery to household appliances, and has over 500 employees. *New Positions Created (30):* Assistant Manager, Off-Air Outlet; Duty Manager; Jewellery Sales Associates; Merchandise Assistant, Fine Jewellery; Operations Manager, Customer Care Centre; Shipper / Receiver; Logistics & Marketing Coordinator; Recruitment Coordinator; Retail Sales Manager; Customer Service Manager; Customer Service Representative, E-mail ; Customer Service Representative; Assistant Buyer; Associate Buyer, Fashion Jewellery; Web Graphic Designer; Accounting Manager; Accounts Payable Clerk; Accounts Receivable Clerk; Help Desk Representative; Help Desk Representative, E-mail; Marketing Coordinator; Master Control Operator; Director, Call Centre Operations; Human Resources Generalist; Intermediate Graphic Designer; Web Producer; Junior Computer Operator; Payroll / Human Resources Coor-

dinator; Various Merchandising Positions; Key Account Sales Representative.

SHOPPING CHANNEL, THE / TSC
Att: Human Resources Department
59 Ambassador Drive
Mississauga, ON L5T 2P9

Fax 416-785-0493
Email .... tschr@rci.rogers.com
Website .... www.tsc.ca

Employer Background: TSC produces a Canadian televised home shopping service, providing products ranging from fashions to jewellery to household appliances, and has over 500 employees. *New Positions Created (9):* Duty Manager; Shipper / Receiver; General Operator; Showroom Assistant; Camera Operator; Inventory Analyst ; Merchandising Assistant; Associate Buyers and Inventory Analysts, Housewares / Fashions; Merchandise Programmers, Health, Beauty and Fashions.

SHOREWOOD PACKAGING CORPORATION
Att: Human Resources Department
2220 Midland Avenue, Unit 50
Toronto, ON M1P 3E6

Tel. 416-292-3990
Fax 416-292-7823
Website .... www.shorepak.ca

Employer Background: Shorewood Packaging Corporation is a leading manufacturer of value-added folding cartons. *New Positions Created (4):* General Accountant; Customer Service Representative; Folding Carton Planner; Administrative Assistant.

SHRED-IT
Att: Human Resouces
2794 South Sheridan Way
Oakville, ON L6J 7T4

Tel. 905-829-2794
Fax 905-829-1999
Email .... hr@shredit.com
Website .... www.shredit.com

Employer Background: Shred-it is a leading on-site, mobile paper shredding and recycling company. *New Positions Created (18):* Service Manager; Director of Marketing; Director of Sales, Industrial Products Group; Internal Auditor; Customer Service Representative; Diesel Mechanic; Field Trainer; Accounts Receivable Clerical Position; Branch Accountant; Coordinator, Financial Services; Fleet Manager, Industrial Shredding Systems; General Manager; Internal Auditor, Financial Services; Senior Accounts Payable Administrator; Business Consultant; Director, Strategic Partnerships; General Manager, Toronto Branch; Vice-President, Sales and Marketing.

SIBLEY & ASSOCIATES INC.
Att: Janet Lynden
3027 Harvester Road, Suite 401
Burlington, ON L7N 3G7

Tel. 905-633-7800
Fax 905-633-7900
Email .... janet_lynden@sibley.ca
Website .... www.sibley.ca

Employer Background: Sibley & Associates Inc. is a national disability management consulting firm. *New Positions Created (4):* Health Positions; Occupational Therapists; Future Care Cost Specialists; Administrative Assistant.

SICHT-PACK HAGNER INC.
Att: Human Resources Manager
3478 Ashby Avenue
St-Laurent, QC H4R 2C1

Tel. 514-335-1775
Fax 514-335-0179
Email .... info@sicht-pack-hagner.com
Website .... www.sicht-pack-hagner.com

Employer Background: Sicht-Pack Hagner Inc. is a manufacturer of clear packaging folding cartons. *New Positions Created (2):* Department Foreman; Gluing Machine Operators.

SIEMENS AUTOMOTIVE
Att: Human Resources Manager
1020 Adelaide Street South
London, ON N6E 1R6

Tel. 519-680-5382
Fax 519-680-5789
Email .... siemensat@rpc.webhire.com
Website .... www.siemensauto.com

Employer Background: Siemens Automotive is a global supplier of automotive electronics. *New Positions Created (13):* Maintenance Supervisor; Production Supervisor; Supervisor of Logistics; Supplier Quality Representative; Electronics Development Engineer; Financial Analyst; Process Engineer; Senior Financial Analyst; Electronics Development Engineer; Production Scheduler; CAD Designer - SolidWorks; Quality Engineer; Senior Buyer - Capital.

SIEMENS BUILDING TECHNOLOGIES LTD.
Att: Human Resources Manager
2435 Holly Lane
Ottawa, ON K1V 7P2

Tel. 613-733-9781
Fax 613-737-4985
Email .... caottfaxes@sbt.siemens.com
Website .... www.sbt.siemens.com

Employer Background: Siemens Building Technologies Ltd. provides facility performance solutions to improve the comfort, life safety, security and energy efficiency of buildings. *New Positions Created (4):* Service Coordinator; Automation Technical Representative; Building Systems Operator; Sales Representative.

SIEMENS BUILDING TECHNOLOGIES LTD., CERBERUS DIVISION
Att: W. Holman
3671 Viking Way, Unit 1
Richmond, BC V6V 2J5

Tel. 604-273-7733
Fax 604-273-1373
Website .... www.sbt.siemens.com

Employer Background: Siemens Building Technologies Ltd., Cerberus Division is a leader in fire detection technology. *New*

Positions Created (6): Fire Alarm Technician; Project Manager; Service Coordinator; System Sales Representative; Warehouse Position; Mechanical Sales Services Account Executive.

SIEMENS BUILDING TECHNOLOGIES LTD., CERBERUS DIVISION
Att: Diana Szeller, HR Manager
50 East Pearce Street
Richmond Hill, ON L4B 1B7
Tel. 905-764-8384
Fax 905-731-3056
Email ...... diana.szeller@sbt.siemens.com
Website .... www.siemens.ca
Employer Background: Siemens Building Technologies Ltd., Cerberus Division is a leader in fire detection technology. *New Positions Created (2):* Human Resources / Payroll Representative; Systems Sales Representative / Service Sales Representative.

SIEMENS BUILDING TECHNOLOGIES LTD., LANDIS DIVISION
Att: Cherie Arrigo
5462 Timberlea Boulevard
Mississauga, ON L4W 2T7
Tel. 905-602-1959
Fax 905-602-1920
Email ...... cherie.arrigo@sbt.siemens.com
Website ...... www.sbt.siemens.com
Employer Background: Siemens Building Technologies Ltd. provides facility performance solutions to improve the comfort, life safety, security and energy efficiency of buildings. *New Positions Created (4):* Project Coordinator II; Systems Designer II; Systems Specialist II; Security Technicians.

SIEMENS CANADA LTD.
Att: Human Resources
2185 Derry Road West
Mississauga, ON L5N 7A6
Tel. 905-819-8000
Fax 905-819-5788
Email .... jobs@siemens.ca
Website .... www.siemens.ca
Employer Background: Established in 1912, Siemens Canada Ltd. specializes in innovative high-tech products. *New Positions Created (51):* Customs Administrator; National Service Manager; Business Manager; Senior Technical Sales Representative; Senior Technical Sales Representative; Manager, Management Development; Tax Analyst II; Strategic Planning Analyst; Vice-President, Telecom Innovation Centre; Manager, Purchasing & Logistics; Senior Strategic Buyers (3); Account Manager, Nuclear Medicine / PET Equipment; Customs Administrator; National Sales Manager; Product Manager, Industrial Control Products / Low-Voltage Motor Control; Benefits and Compensation Administrator; Human Resources Key Account Manager; Human Resources Project Specialist; Senior Business Analyst; Telecommunications Specialist; Business Development Manager, Industrial; Business Development Manager, Public Sector; Manager, Management Development and Training; Administrative Assistant; Technical

Sales Representative; Technical Sales Representative; Product Specialist, Shelf Goods; Specialist, Real Estate and Facility Management; Manager, Web Communications; Product Specialist, Industrial Control Products; Financial Accountant; Intermediate Assistant; Service Logistics Manager; Benefits Specialist; Environmental Health and Safety Specialist; Industrial Solutions Specialist; Senior Technical Service Representative; Technical Training Instructor; Administrative Assistant; Commercial Administrator; PeopleSoft Analyst; Technical Sales Representative; Configurator, Switchboards; Coordinator, Education Services; Business Analyst, Corporate IT Division; Database Administrator; Specialists, Business Development Industrial Control Products (2); Project Manager; District Manager, Sales; Facility Project Administrator; Internal Auditor.

SIEMENS CANADA LTD., MEDICAL SYSTEMS DIVISION
Att: Human Resources
7300 Trans Canada Highway
Pointe-Claire, QC H9R 4R6
Tel. 514-695-7300
Fax 514-426-6101
Email .... jobs@siemens.ca
Website .... www.siemens.ca
Employer Background: Established in 1912, Siemens Canada Ltd. specializes in innovative high-tech products. *New Positions Created (2):* Engineer, Technical Services; Account Manager.

SIEMENS CANADA LTD., PRODUCTION AND LOGISTICS SYSTEMS DIVISION
Att: Human Resources Manager
167 Hunt Street
Ajax, ON L1S 1P6
Fax 905-683-0186
Email .... ajax@siemens.ca
Website .... www.siemens.ca
Employer Background: Established in 1912, Siemens Canada Ltd. specializes in innovative high-tech products. *New Positions Created (2):* Computer Systems Analysts; Junior Software Quality Specialist.

SIEMENS CANADA LTD., TELECOM INNOVATION CENTRE
Att: Human Resources Manager
505 March Road
Kanata, ON K2K 2M5
Tel. 613-591-8730
Fax 613-591-8731
Email ... recruitment@innovation.siemens.ca
Website .... www.tic.siemens.ca
Employer Background: The Telecom Innovation Centre is the Canadian research and development facility for Siemens AG Information and Communication Mobile, a leader in wireless IP-based communications. *New Positions Created (37):* Manager, Network & Service Management (SW Development); Senior Software Architect; Senior Software Designer; Senior Software Designer, Internet Security; Senior Software

Developer, Diameter; Senior Software Developer, Network Management; Senior Software Designer; Project Assistant; Intermediate Software Configuration Management Designer; Project Assistant; Intermediate Software Configuration Management (SCM) Designer; Junior Software Developer; Senior Software Architect; Software CM Developer; Intermediate Diameter Software Developer; Intermediate Diameter Software Developer; Intermediate Software Designer; Junior Software Designer; Manager, Network and Service Management; Manager Network and Service Management, SW Development; Senior Diameter Software Developer; Senior Diameter Software Developer; Senior Software Architect; Senior Software Architect, IP and NM; Senior Software Architect, IP and NM; Senior Software Designer; Sr Software Designer, Internet Security; Sr Software Designer, Internet Security; Senior Software Network Management Developer; Senior Software Network Manager; Senior Software Tester; Software Configuration Mgmnt Developer; Software Configuration Mgmnt Developer; Software Network Management Developer; Software Network Management Developer; Senior Software Architect; Senior Software Tester.

SIEMENS DEMATIC LTD., RAPISTAN DIVISION
Att: Human Resources Department
7300 Rapistan Court
Mississauga, ON L5N 5S1
Tel. 905-567-7300
Fax 905-567-0585
Email .... canada@rapistan.com
Website .... www.rapistan.com
Employer Background: Siemens Dematic Ltd., Rapistan Division supplies material handling solutions. *New Positions Created (6):* Inside Sales Coordinator; Mechanical Designer; Mechanical Estimator; Mechanical Project Engineer; Territory Sales Manager; Manufacturing Foreperson.

SIEMENS HEARING INSTRUMENTS INC.
Att: Human Resources Manager
320 Pinebush Road, Unit 7
Cambridge, ON N3C 2V3
Tel. 519-622-5200
Fax 519-622-2460
Email .... jquinn@siemens-hearing.com
Website ...... www.siemens-hearing.com
Employer Background: Siemens Hearing Instruments Inc. designs, engineers and manufactures hearing-aids. *New Positions Created (2):* Audiologist, In-House; Intermediate Accountant.

SIEMENS MILLTRONICS PROCESS INSTRUMENTS INC.
Att: Human Resources Department
1954 Technology Drive, PO Box 4225
Peterborough, ON K9J 7B1
Tel. 705-745-2431
Fax 705-741-0037
Email .... cahr@milltronics.com
Website .... www.milltronics.com

Employer Background: Siemens Milltronics Process Instruments Inc. (formerly Milltronics Ltd.) designs and manufactures advanced, electronics-based instrumentation and sensors for customers in 93 countries. *New Positions Created (15):* Buyer; Mechanical Designer, Radar Technology; Cost Analyst; Electronics Design Engineer; Industrial Communication Device Description Specialist; Embedded Software Designer; Senior Human Resources Adviser; Senior Product Manager, Marketing; R & D Technologist, Mechanical; RF Design Engineer; Mechanical Approval Specialist; Financial Analyst; Mechanical Designer, Radar Technology; Technical Customer Support Representative; Embedded Software Designer.

SIEMENS MILLTRONICS PROCESS INSTRUMENTS INC., SHERREX SYSTEMS DIVISION
Att: R&D Manager
4130 – 93rd Street
Edmonton, AB T6E 5PE
Tel. 780-462-4085
Fax 780-450-8369
Email .... waynes@milltronics.com
Website .... www.milltronics.com
Employer Background: Siemens Milltronics Process Instruments Inc., Sherrex Systems Division provides various liquid flow application solutions, from intrinsically-safe rate totalizers to a complete line of turbine meters. *New Positions Created (3):* Embedded Software Designer; Mechanical Engineer; Mechanical Engineering Technologist.

SIEMENS TECHNICAL SERVICES
Att: Bob Stait, Key Account Manager
717 Woodward Ave., 1st Floor, Box 1080
Hamilton, ON L8N 4B3
Tel. 905-545-1151
Fax 905-545-0921
Email .... bob.stait@siemens.ca
Website .... www.siemens.ca
Employer Background: Siemens Technical Services is part of Siemens Canada Ltd., a leader in innovative high-tech products. *New Positions Created (5):* Service Manager; Service Manager; Service Manager; Field Service Representative; Mechanical Service Representative.

SIEMENS WESTINGHOUSE
Att: Human Resources
30 Milton Avenue, PO Box 2510
Hamilton, ON L8N 3K2
Tel. 905-528-8811
Fax 905-577-0275
Email .... resumes@swpc.siemens.com
Website .... www.siemens.com
Employer Background: Siemens Westinghouse, a division of Siemens Canada Ltd., is a leader in gas and steam turbine technology, manufacturing and sales service. *New Positions Created (44):* Mechanical Engineer; Electrical Specialist / Electrical Engineer; Mechanical Engineer / Senior Mechanical Engineer ; Marketing Engineer; Maintenance Electrical / Electronic Special-

ists; Millwrights; Production Controller; Welding Engineer; Configuration Specialist; Consultant, Organization Development & Process; Electrical Field Service Engineer; Inventory Coordinator; Manager, Quality Assurance Engineering Services; Millwright / Industrial Mechanic; Inspectors; Production Coordinator; Manufacturing Engineering Analyst; Mechanical Engineer; Shift Supervisors; Millwright / Industrial Mechanic; Configuration Engineer; Factory Engineers; Field Service Engineers; Inventory Order Coordinator; Marketing Engineer; Mechanical / Electrical Field Service Engineers and Technologists, Steam; Order Manager; Procurement Technical Engineer; Program Manager; Senior Buyer; Welding Engineer; Senior Software Engineer; Maintenance Engineer; Marketing Engineers; Mechanical / Electrical Field Service Engineers; Millwrights; Production Controller; Quality Assurance Engineers; Electrical Engineer; Mechanical Engineer; Site Service Supervisor, Electrical; Site Service Supervisor, Mechanical; Sales Representative, Automation Engineering and Services; Technical Sales Representative.

SIERRA SYSTEMS
Att: Recruiting
10104 - 103rd Avenue
Suite 1300, Canada Trust Tower
Edmonton, AB T5J 0H8
Tel. 780-424-0852
Fax 780-426-0281
Email .... edmontonresume@
.... sierrasystems.com
Website .... www.sierrasystems.com
Employer Background: Sierra Systems is one of North America's leading management consulting and systems integration firms and has 14 offices. *New Positions Created (9):* Data Architect; Developer / Technical Architect; Intermediate Business Analyst; Intermediate Microsoft Web Applications Developer; Microsoft Web Applications Architect; Oracle Developer; Senior Business Analysts; Senior Intermediate Architect; Senior Programmer.

SIERRA SYSTEMS GROUP INC.
Att: Wendy Duross
130 Slater Street, Suite 800
Ottawa, ON K1P 6E2
Tel. 613-236-7888
Fax 613-236-9333
Email .... wendyduross@sierrasys.com
Website .... www.sierrasys.com
Employer Background: Sierra Systems Group Inc. is a full-service IT consulting company, with 900 employees and 14 locations across North America. *New Positions Created (9):* Analyst / Team Leader; Business Analyst; Directory Specialist; Electronic Commerce Integrators and Developers; PeopleSoft Implementation Analysts; Senior Technical Architect; Systems Analysts / Developers; Systems Developer; Windows 2000 Specialist.

SIERRA WIRELESS INC.
Att: Human Resources Manager

13811 Wireless Way
Richmond, BC V6V 3A4
Tel. 604-231-1100
Fax 604-233-6322
Email .... careers@sierrawireless.com
Website .... www.sierrawireless.com
Employer Background: Sierra Wireless Inc. is a leading wireless enabler for laptops and Personal Digital Assistants (PDAs), providing wireless access to the Internet. *New Positions Created (12):* Antenna Designer; Communications Engineer; Digital ASIC Design Engineer; Director, Indirect Distribution; Principal Software Engineer; Receptionist; Senior Project Manager; Technical Training Consultant; Operations Support Manager; Product Line Manager; Real-time Embedded Software Developers; RF Design Engineers.

SIFTO CANADA INC.
Att: Human Resources
47A Harbour Square, PO Box 81014
Toronto, ON M5J 2V3
Email .... siftohr@imcsalt.com
Website .... www.siftocanada.com
Employer Background: Sifto Canada Inc., a division of IMC Global, manufactures salt for industrial and consumer use. *New Positions Created (2):* Controller; Consumer / Industrial Sales Rep.

SIGEM INC.
Att: Human Resources Manager
84 Hines Road, Suite 240
Kanata, ON K2K 3G3
Tel. 613-271-1601
Fax 613-271-9827
Email .... careers@sigem.com
Website .... www.sigem.ca
Employer Background: Sigem Inc. develops world-class GPS and satellite communication products. *New Positions Created (14):* Communication System Software Designers; Data RF Communication Technologist; Embedded System Engineer; Graphic Artist; Hardware Designer; Internet Application Designer; Junior Test Software Developer; Mechanical Designer; Process Engineer; Product Design Engineer / Senior Technologist; Senior Computer Hardware Designer; Senior RF Engineer; Software Designer; Test Engineer / Technologist.

SIGMA SYSTEMS GROUP INC.
Att: Human Resources Manager
55 York Street, Suite 1100
Toronto, ON M5J 1R7
Tel. 416-943-9696
Fax 416-365-9227
Email .... resumes@sigma-systems.com
Website .... www.sigma-systems.com
Employer Background: Sigma Systems Group Inc. is a leading provider of operations support systems and business support systems for communications service providers worldwide. *New Positions Created (27):* Configuration Manager; Delivery Engineers; Domain Architect; Pre-Sales Engineers; Product Managers; Project Managers; Configuration Manager; Delivery Engineers /

Team Leaders; Domain Architect; Sales Proposal Manager; Project Manager; C++ Developers or Programmers / Analysts, Intermediate and Senior; Quality Control Analyst; Systems Analyst; Technical Team Leader; Data Modeller / Data Architect; Intermediate / Senior C++ Developers; Java / GUI Developers; Project Managers; Sales Engineers; C++ Developers, Intermediate and Senior; Data Modeller / Data Architect; Help Desk Representative; Java Developer; Sales Engineers (4); Senior Systems Architects (2); Software Development Manager.

SIGNALSOFT CANADA
Att: Human Resources
57 Cadillac Avenue
Victoria, BC V8Z 1T3
Tel. 250-920-4111
Fax 250-475-4701
Email .... hr@signalsoftcorp.com
Website .... www.signalsoftcorp.com
Employer Background: SignalSoft Canada develops software that allows wireless network operators to provide location-based services to their subscribers. *New Positions Created (3):* Development Mgr; Internet Application Developer; Product Manager.

SIGNATURE VACATIONS INC.
Att: Human Resources
160 Bloor Street East, Suite 400
Toronto, ON M4W 1B9
Tel. 416-967-1510
Fax 416-969-2698
Email .... hr@signature.ca
Website ...... www.signaturevacations.com
Employer Background: Signature Vacations Inc. is one of Canada's leading tour operators. *New Positions Created (3):* Customer Service Representatives; Manager, Customer Relations; Product Building Coordinator.

SILANIS TECHNOLOGY INC.
Att: Human Resources
398 Isabey
St-Laurent, QC H4T 1V3
Tel. 514-337-5255
Fax 514-337-5258
Email .... hr@silanis.com
Website .... www.silanis.com
Employer Background: Silanis Technology Inc. develops the ApproveIt family of electronic signature products. *New Positions Created (4):* Digital Media and Print Designer; Marketing / Communications Specialist; Marketing Writer; Web Coordinator.

SILENTEC LTD.
Att: Human Resources Manager
785 Plymouth, Suite 304
Montréal, QC H4P 1B2
Tel. 514-731-3397
Fax 514-731-1282
Website .... www.silentec.com
Employer Background: Silentec Ltd. manufactures aero-acoustic equipment for gas turbines and fans, used by the aviation, power generation and other industries worldwide. *New Positions Created (2):* Op-

erations Administration Manager; Project and Contract Managers.

SILEX DESIGN INC.
Att: Human Resources Manager
7850 Tranmere Drive
Mississauga, ON L5S 1L9
Tel. 905-612-4001
Fax 905-612-0076
Email .... hr@silex.com
Website .... www.silex.com
Employer Background: Silex Design Inc. is a division of Silex Inc., an environmental products company specializing in the design and manufacture of exhaust systems and related noise and environmental control products. *New Positions Created (11):* Accounting Clerks; Accounting Supervisors; Cost Accountants; Design Engineers; Engineering Managers; General / Plant Managers; Inside Sales Engineers; Manufacturing Engineer Mgrs; Project Mgrs; Quality Assurance Coordinators; Territory Managers.

SILEX INC.
Att: Human Resources
6659 Ordan Drive
Mississauga, ON L5T 1K6
Tel. 905-612-4000
Fax 905-612-8999
Email .... hr@silex.com
Website .... www.silex.com
Employer Background: Silex Inc. is an environmental products company that designs and manufactures exhaust systems and related noise and environmental control products, including acoustic housing, blankets and enclosures for diesel and gas engines and other industrial applications. *New Positions Created (20):* Territory Account Manager, Western Canada; Engineering Manager; Manager, Corporate Procurement; Inside Sales Representative; Cost Accountant; Design Engineer; Manager, Corporate Procurement; Manager, Information Systems; Manager, Inside Sales; Manager, Quality Assurance; Project Manager, Electrical Systems; Territory Managers; Manufacturing Engineers; Project Managers; Welding Engineer; Senior Design Engineers; Senior Designers; Account Manager; Engineering Manager; General Manager.

SILICON ACCESS NETWORKS LTD.
Att: Human Resources Manager
1600 Scott Street, 3rd Floor, Tower B
Ottawa, ON K1Y 4N7
Tel. 613-728-4483
Fax 613-728-7858
Email ..... careers-ottawa@siliconaccess.com
Website .... www.siliconaccess.com
Employer Background: Silicon Access Networks Ltd. is a network semiconductor company that provides high-performance components for terabit routers. *New Positions Created (11):* Hardware / Software Applications Engineer; Technical Writer; Network Architect; Network Processor, ASIC Verification; Network Processors, ASIC Designers; Senior Network ASIC Architect; Senior Network Processor / ASIC Designers; Senior

Network Processor, ASIC Verification; Senior Network Software Engineers; Senior Network Systems Hardware Engineer; Senior Software Tools Engineers.

SILICON VIDEO
Att: Human Resources Manager
2005 Sheppard Avenue East, Suite 100
Toronto, ON M2J 5B4
Tel. 416-490-7779
Fax 416-490-0344
Email .... hr_can@silicon-video.com
Website .... www.silicon-video.com
Employer Background: Silicon Video is a fabless semiconductor start-up, targeting the digital image and video processing markets. *New Positions Created (11):* Embedded Software Design Engineers; Marketing Director / Marketing Specialist (2); ASIC Architecture Engineer; ASIC Design Engineers; ASIC Lead Engineer / Design Manager; ASIC Modelling / Verification Engineer; DSP Algorithm and Application Software Position; Field Application Engineers; Hardware Design Engineers; Marketing Positions; Product Engineering Manager.

SILLIKER CANADA
Att: Human Resources Manager
90 Gough Road, Unit 4
Markham, ON L3R 5V5
Tel. 905-479-5255
Fax 905-479-4645
Website .... www.silliker.com
Employer Background: Silliker Canada is part of Silliker Laboratories, a worldwide network of 25 accredited labs serving the food industry in Europe and North America. *New Positions Created (3):* Client Service Representative; Quality Control Specialist; Staff Accountant.

SIMARK CONTROLS LTD.
Att: Human Resources
7725 - 46th Street SE
Calgary, AB T2C 2Y5
Tel. 403-236-0580
Fax 403-279-6553
Website .... www.simarkcontrols.com
Employer Background: Simark Controls Ltd. sells and services a wide range of high-quality electrical and instrumentation products. *New Positions Created (2):* Information Technology Mgr; Draftsperson / Designer.

SIMCOE, CORPORATION OF THE COUNTY OF
Att: Human Resources Office
1110 Highway 26
Midhurst, ON L0L 1X0
Tel. 705-726-9300
Fax 705-725-1285
Email .... hr@county.simcoe.on.ca
Website .... www.county.simcoe.on.ca
Employer Background: Located north of the Greater Toronto Area, the Corporation of the County of Simcoe is home to over 330,000 people. *New Positions Created (2):* Manager of Land Ambulance and Emergency Services; Manager of Labour Relations.

SIMCOE COUNTY CHILDREN'S AID SOCIETY / SIMCOE CAS
Att: Director, Human Resources
60 Bell Farm Road, Unit 7
Barrie, ON L4M 5G6
Tel. 705-726-6587
Fax 705-726-9788
Website .... www.simcoecas.com
Employer Background: Founded in 1894, the Simcoe CAS works to strengthen families and protect children from abuse and neglect. *New Positions Created (2):* Family Service Workers; Legal Counsel.

SIMCOE COUNTY DISTRICT HEALTH UNIT
Att: Human Resources Coordinator
15 Sperling Drive
Barrie, ON L4M 6K9
Tel. 705-721-7330
Fax 705-721-1495
Email .... lpighin@simcoehealth.org
Website .... www.simcoehealth.org
Employer Background: The Simcoe County District Health Unit is a public health agency, serving over 350,000 residents in Simcoe County. *New Positions Created (3):* Early Years Project Coordinator; Physical Activity Coordinator; Public Health Dietitian.

SIMCOE COUNTY DISTRICT SCHOOL BOARD
Att: Sharon Bate, Director of Education
1170 Highway 26
Midhurst, ON L0L 1X0
Tel. 705-728-7570
Fax 705-737-6996
Website .... www.scdsb.on.ca
Employer Background: The Simcoe County District School Board is one of the largest schools boards in Canada, with over 54,000 students, more than 4,000 staff members, 100 schools and 5 adult learning centres. *New Positions Created (5):* Superintendent of Schools; Librarian; Librarian; Psychologist; Elementary and Secondary Principals and Vice-Principals.

SIMCOE MUSKOKA CATHOLIC DISTRICT SCHOOL BOARD
Att: Human Resources
46 Alliance Boulevard
Barrie, ON L4M 5K3
Tel. 705-722-3555
Fax 705-737-1297
Email .... hr@smcdsb.edu.on.ca
Website .... www.smcdsb.edu.on.ca
Employer Background: The Simcoe Muskoka Catholic District School Board serves 20,000 students in 40 elementary schools and 8 secondary schools. *New Positions Created (2):* Capital Projects Officer; Human Resources Generalist Position.

SIMMONS DA SILVA & SINTON LLP
Att: Helen Elliott
201 County Court Boulevard, Suite 200
Brampton, ON L6W 4L2
Tel. 905-457-1660
Fax 905-457-5641
Website .... www.lawcan.com

Employer Background: Established in 1969, Simmons Da Silva & Sinton LLP is a full-service law firm. *New Positions Created (3):* Family Law Lawyer & Junior Family Law Lawyer; Accounting Assistant; Lawyer, Family Law.

SIMON FRASER HEALTH REGION, BURNABY HOSPITAL
Att: Human Resources Services
3935 Kincaid Street
Burnaby, BC V5G 2X6
Tel. 604-412-6228
Fax 604-412-6178
Website .... www.sfhr.com
Employer Background: Burnaby Hospital is a 445-bed facility, with over 55,000 emergency visits per year. *New Positions Created (24):* Health Record Administrator; Physiotherapist; Registered Nurse, Emergency; Coordinator, Major Gifts; Health Record Administrator; Registered Nurse, Coronary Care Cardiac Stepdown; Rehabilitation Therapist, LTC; Resident Care Nurse Clinician, Long-Term Care; Nurse Clinicians, Queen's Park Care Centre; Resident Care Manager, Cascade Residence; Assistant Manager, Admitting / Switchboard; Health Records Technical Supervisor; Technical Supervisor, Health Records; Internal Medicine Specialist; Neurologist; Medical Oncologist; Clinical Nurse Educator, Operating Room; Nurse Clinician; Coordinator, Health Records; Manager, Volunteer Services; Critical Nurse Educators; Business Systems Coordinator, Continuing Care Portfolio; Chaplain / Manager of Pastoral Services; Housekeeping Supervisor.

SIMON FRASER HEALTH REGION
Att: Human Resource Services
33 Blackberry Drive
New Westminster, BC V3L 5S9
Tel. 604-517-8633
Fax 604-517-8652
Website .... www.sfhr.com
Employer Background: SFHR provides health services to 500,000 residents, with 8,000 employees working in over 30 locations. *New Positions Created (36):* Clerk / Secretary, Quality Improvement Program; Manager, Pastoral Care and Social Work Services; Nurse Clinician; Program Leaders, Palliative Care Program; Human Resources Consultant; Clinical Supervisor Physiotherapist, Grade IV; Physiotherapist; Rehabilitation Therapist; Community Nurse Adult Community Support Services; Mental Health Therapist, Adult Short Term & Assessment, Tri-Cities Mental Health Centre; Nursing Support Services Coordinator; Occupational Therapist I, Maple Ridge Home Health Care; Occupational Therapist I, Tri-Cities Home Health Care; Occupational Therapist, Schools; Public Health Nursing Supervisor, New Westminster Preventive Services; Social Worker (ASTAT) / Social Worker, Outpatient Team; Supervisor, Adult Day Program; Director, Mental Health Services; Confidential Secretary; Human Resources Assistant; Secretary, Human Resource Services; Director, Home Health Care

Services; Clinical Supervisor / Physiotherapist; Mentoring Coordinator; Public Health Inspector; Speech-Language Pathologists; Coordinator, Quality Improvement; Nurse Clinician; Resident Care Manager; Medical Records Supervisor; Confidential Secretary; Community Education Coordinator, Preventive Health Services; Preventive Health Services Position; Resident Care Manager; Technical Coordinator.

SIMON FRASER HEALTH REGION
Att: Verna Campbell, HR Services
475 Guildford Way
Port Moody, BC V3L 5S9
Tel. 604-524-2845
Fax 604-469-3245
Email ... verna_campbell@sfhr.hnet.bc.ca
Website .... www.sfhr.com
Employer Background: SFHR provides health services to over 500,000 residents, with more than 8,000 employees working in over 30 locations. *New Positions Created (10):* Manager, Patient Care Services; Registered Nurses, ICU / CCU / CIU; RN, Intensive Care Unit; Manager, Patient Care Services; Manager, Resident Care Services; Clinical Educators; Clinical Nurse Educator, OR; Clinical Resource Nurse, Home Support; Coordinator, Clinical Products; Nurse Clinician.

SIMON FRASER HEALTH REGION
Att: Employment Services
260 Sherbrooke Street
New Westminster, BC V3L 3M2
Tel. 604-524-2845
Fax 604-520-4827
Website .... www.sfhr.com
Employer Background: SFHR provides health services to 500,000 residents, with 8,000 employees working in over 30 locations. *New Positions Created (23):* Cardiac Ultrasound Technician; Cardiovascular Perfusionist; Consultant Vascular Surgeon; Clinical Nurse Specialist, Trauma Program; Manager, Patient Care Services; Manager, Patient Care Services; Manager, Patient Care Services; Manager, Resident Care Services; Cardiology Technologist; Catheterization Cardiology Technologist; Manager, Planning & Budgeting; Management Accounting Analyst; Coordinator, Claims Mangement; Facilities Planner; Cardiovascular Technologist; Various Nursing Positions; Director, Patient Documentation; Physiological Laboratory Technologist; Inventory Analyst; Employment Consultants; Manager, Financial Planning; Payroll Clerk; Perfusionist and Cardiac Ultrasound Technologist.

SIMON FRASER HEALTH REGION
Att: Jane Mason, HR Services
11666 Laity Street, Box 5000
Maple Ridge, BC V2X 7G5
Tel. 604-524-2845
Fax 604-463-1832
Email .... jane_mason@sfhr.hnet.bc.ca
Website .... www.sfhr.com
Employer Background: SFHR provides health services to 500,000 residents, with

8,000 employees working in over 30 locations. *New Positions Created (11):* Respiratory Therapist, IV (Manager); Occupational Therapist, Mental Health Services; Pharmacists II; Physiotherapist, Acute Care; Physiotherapists / OTs, Home Healthcare; Physiotherapists, Residential Care Services; Respiratory Therapists; Site Administrators (2); Social Worker, Long Term Care; Assistant Manager, Sterile Processing; Pharmacist.

SIMON FRASER UNIVERSITY
Att: Human Resources
8888 University Drive
Burnaby, BC V5A 1S6

Tel.	604-291-3237
Fax	604-291-4381
Email	job_postings@sfu.ca
Website	www.sfu.ca

Employer Background: Simon Fraser University is a mid-sized Canadian university, with 17,000 students and over 100 programs. *New Positions Created (10):* Instructional Developer; Women's Basketball Head Coach; Men's Soccer Head Coach, SFU Clan; Dean, Faculty of Business Administration; Dean of Applied Sciences; Director, Instructional Development Centre; Learning Skills Counsellor; Director, Cooperative Education; Manager, Media Resources and IMC Administration; Research Grants Facilitator.

SIMON FRASER UNIVERSITY, DEPARTMENT OF BIOLOGICAL SCIENCES
Att: Dr. Norbert H. Haunerland, Chair
8888 University Boulevard
Burnaby, BC V5A 1S6

Tel.	604-291-4475
Fax	604-291-4312
Website	www.biol.sfu.ca

Employer Background: Simon Fraser University is a mid-sized Canadian university, with 17,000 students and over 100 programs. *New Positions Created (2):* Assistant Professor, Plant Physiology; Assistant Professor, Computational Biology.

SIMON FRASER UNIVERSITY, FACULTY OF BUSINESS ADMINISTRATION
Att: Dr. Lawrence T. Pinfield, Chair
8888 University Drive
Burnaby, BC V5A 1S6

Fax	604-291-4920
Email	pinfield@sfu.ca
Website	www.bus.sfu.ca

Employer Background: Simon Fraser University is a mid-sized Canadian university, with 17,000 students and over 100 programs. *New Positions Created (2):* Canada Research Chair, Management of Technology; Faculty Positions.

SIMON FRASER UNIVERSITY, SCHOOL OF ENGINEERING SCIENCE
Att: Dr. John D. Jones, Director
8888 University Drive
Burnaby, BC V5A 1S6

Email	jones@cs.sfu.ca
Website	www.sfu.ca

Employer Background: Simon Fraser University is a mid-sized Canadian university, with 17,000 students and over 100 programs. *New Positions Created (2):* PMC-Sierra Senior Chair, Communications; Sierra Wireless Chair, Communications.

SIMPLEXGRINNELL
Att: Human Resources
1485 Lindsey Place
Delta, BC V3M 6V1

Fax	604-241-9554
Email	hkennedy@tycoint.com
Website	www.tycoint.com

Employer Background: SimplexGrinnell offers fire protection, life safety, healthcare communications, integrated sound, telephone / intercom and workforce management services to clients throughout North America. *New Positions Created (3):* Designers; System Sales Reps; Technicians.

SIMPLEXGRINNELL
Att: Human Resources Manager
2400 Skymark Avenue
Mississauga, ON L4W 5K5

Fax	905-212-4405
Website	www.simplexgrinnell.com

Employer Background: SimplexGrinnell offers fire protection, life safety, healthcare communications, integrated sound, telephone / intercom and workforce management services to clients throughout North America. *New Positions Created (3):* Associate Project Manager; Building Systems Sales Representative; Service Sales Representatives.

SIMPLOT CANADA LIMITED
Att: Human Resources Administrator
1400 - 17th Street East
Brandon, MB R7A 7C4

Tel.	204-729-2900
Fax	204-729-2944
Website	www.simplot.com

Employer Background: Simplot Canada Limited is a world-class fertilizer and industrial chemical manufacturing complex employing 250 employees. *New Positions Created (4):* Journeyperson Steamfitter / Pipefitter; Major Gift Coordinator; Site Services Mgr; Process / Production Engineers.

SIMS MOELICH ASSOCIATES LTD.
Att: Richard Dernowski, VP
277 Lakeshore Road East, Suite 408
Oakville, ON L6J 1H9

Tel.	905-849-1833
Fax	905-849-9734
Email	employment@simsmoelich.com
Website	www.simsmoelich.com

Employer Background: Sims Moelich Associates Ltd. provides professional project and construction management services. *New Positions Created (3):* Project Coordinators; Project Manager and Assistant Project Managers; Project Superintendents.

SIR CORP.
Att: Recruitment, Human Resources

5360 South Service Road, Suite 200
Burlington, ON L7L 5L1

Tel.	905-681-2997
Fax	905-681-5201
Email	jobs@sircorp.com
Website	www.sircorp.com

Employer Background: SIR Corp. operates several popular branded restaurants, including Jack Astor's Bar and Grill, Alice Fazooli's and Al Frisco's. *New Positions Created (5):* Manager, Kitchen Operations; Various Managerial Positions; Restaurant Managers; Restaurant Managers; Various Management Positions.

SIR MORTIMER B. DAVIS - JEWISH GENERAL HOSPITAL
Att: Department of Human Resources
3755 Cote Ste. Catherine Road
Montréal, QC H3T 1E2

Tel.	514-739-7761
Fax	514-340-7545
Website	www.jgh.mcgill.ca

Employer Background: Sir Mortimer B. Davis - Jewish General Hospital is a 637-bed facility affiliated with McGill University, providing tertiary care to a multi-cultural clientele. *New Positions Created (4):* Director of Communications; Physiotherapists (2); Chief of Biomedical Engineering; Foundation Chief Executive Officer.

SIR WILFRID LAURIER SCHOOL BOARD
Att: Francois Badin, HR Director
235 Montée Lesage
Rosemere, QC J7A 4Y6

Fax	450-621-7968
Email	fbadin@swlauriersb.qc.ca
Website	www.cfpsa.com

Employer Background: The Sir Wilfrid Laurier School Board is the third-largest English school board in Quebec, covering the City of Laval, the Laurentians, and the Lanaudiere Regions. *New Positions Created (3):* Speech-Language Pathologists; Principal, Secondary; Data Processing Technician.

SISIP FINANCIAL SERVICES
Att: Human Resources Coordinator
National Defence Headquarters
MGen George R. Pearkes Building
Ottawa, ON K1A 0K2

Fax	613-233-5907
Email	castonguay.anick@cfpsa.com
Website	www.cfpsa.com

Employer Background: SISIP Financial Services is a non-public funds entity, providing the Canadian Forces and their families with insurance products and personal financial programs. *New Positions Created (5):* Branch Mgr; Financial Counsellor; Financial Planner; Insurance Rep; National Financial Counselling Systems Mgr.

SISTERS OF CHARITY OF OTTAWA HEALTH SERVICE / SCO HEALTH SERVICE, ELISABETH BRUYERE HEALTH CENTRE
Att: Kelly Babcock, Director of Pharmacy

43 Bruyere Street
Ottawa, ON K1R 5C8

Tel. 613-562-0050
Fax 613-562-4245
Email .... kbabcock@scohs.on.ca
Website .... www.scohs.on.ca

Employer Background: The SCO Health Service provides long-term care, complex continuing care, palliative care and rehabilitation at 3 main sites: the Elisabeth Bruyere Health Centre; the Saint-Vincent Hospital; and the Residence Saint-Louis. *New Positions Created (4):* Clinical Pharmacist; Medical Communication Officers; Supervisor, Food Service; Director of Payroll.

SISU ENTERPRISES CO. INC.
Att: Director of Human Resources
3430 Brighton Avenue, Suite 104A
Burnaby, BC V5A 3H4

Tel. 604-420-6610
Fax 604-420-4892
Email .... hr@sisuhealth.com
Website .... www.sisuhealth.com

Employer Background: SISU Enterprises Co. Inc. is a leading natural healthcare company. *New Positions Created (2):* Regional Sales Manager; Account Manager.

SITEL CANADA INC.
Att: Pamela Taraday
350 Bloor Street East, 5th Floor
Toronto, ON M4W 1H4

Tel. 416-932-2000
Fax 416-964-8966
Email .... pamela.taraday@sitel.com
Website .... www.sitel.com

Employer Background: SITEL Canada Inc. is one of Canada's leading providers of outsourced customer relationship management services. *New Positions Created (9):* Call Traffic Controller; Employment Specialists; Human Resources Manager; Operations Manager; Quality Assurance Representatives; Trainers; Team Managers; Customer Service Professionals; Customer Service Professionals.

SITEL CANADA INC.
Att: Human Resources Manager
5252 De Maisonneuve Boulevard West
Suite 400
Montréal, QC H4A 3S5

Tel. 514-482-6188
Fax 514-482-3463
Website .... www.sitel.com

Employer Background: SITEL Canada Inc. is one of Canada's leading providers of outsourced customer relationship management services. *New Positions Created (6):* Customer Service Agents; Facility Manager; Human Resources Manager; Operations Manger; Recruiter; Call Centre Agents.

SITRAKA MOBILITY
Att: Human Resources Manager
90 Richmond Street East, Suite 400
Toronto, ON M5C 1P1

Tel. 416-366-6425
Fax 416-214-1235

Email .... jobs@sitraka.com
Website .... www.sitraka.com

Employer Background: Sitraka Mobility develops innovative solutions to help enterprises achieve a competitive advantage in a wireless world. *New Positions Created (22):* J2EE Performance Consultants; Java Performance Instructor / Mentor; Mobile Applications Team Leaders (2); Quality Assurance and Release Engineering Manager; Sales Engineer; Technical Consultant, Level 1; Technical Consultant, Level 2; Mobile Applications Developers (5); Server Infrastructure Developer; Product Manager; Quality Assurance Manager; Server Infrastructure Team Lead; Technical Writers (3); Executive Administrator; Marketing Communications Manager; Marketing Communications Specialist; Public Relations Manager; Strategic Partners Manager; Director of Sales; Java Mobile Applications Developer; Java Server Developer; Mobile Applications Implementation Specialist.

SITRAKA SOFTWARE INC.
Att: Human Resources Manager
260 King Street East
Toronto, ON M5A 4L5

Tel. 416-594-1026
Fax 416-591-1919
Email .... jobs@sitraka.com
Website .... www.sitraka.com

Employer Background: Sitraka Software Inc. (formerly KL Group) is a leader in advanced Java development, deployment and management solutions. *New Positions Created (54):* Associate Product Manager, New Products; German, Spanish or French Language Technical Support Engineers (2); J2EE Performance Consultants; Java Performance Instructor / Mentor; Development Support Manager; Manager, Technical Publications; Software Products Developer, Java Tools Products; Team Leader, Performance Tools Development; Team Leader / Software Tools Developer, Performance Tools Testing; Technical Writers; Applications Engineer; Business Applications Developer; Configuration Management and Tools Developers (2); Implementation Specialists (2); Java Trainer; Marketing Copywriter; Marketing Programs Specialist; Porting Specialist - Java Developer Tools; Java Web Developer / Webmaster; Manager, Public Relations; Office Assistant; Product Manager and Associate Product Manager; Senior Unix Systems Administrator; Development Support Manager, Software Products; Software Products Developers, Java Performance Tools; Software Tools Developer, J2EE / WebLogic / WebSphere; Software Tools Developer, Performance Tools Testing; Team Lead, Performance Tools Development; Manager, Technical Publications; Product Manager, New Products; Product Release Manager; Recruitment Consultant; Sales Administrator; Configuration Management and Tools Developers (2); Development Support Manager; Human Resources Coordinator; Market Research Associate; Platform Technology Manager; Technical Writer and Tools Specialist; Applications Engineer; Customer Support Engineers; Java Trainer; Porting

Specialist; Recruitment Consultant; Research and Development Systems Administrator ; Configuration Manager and Tools Developers (2); Evaluation Support Specialist; Implementation Specialists (2); Java Mobile Application Developers (2); Mobility Telemarketing Representative; Partner Manager; Porting Specialist - Java Developer Tools; Product Mgr - New Product; Windows Mobile Application Developers (2).

SKD AUTOMOTIVE GROUP
Att: Human Resources Department
375 Wheelabrator Way
Milton, ON L9T 3C1

Tel. 905-875-1427
Fax 905-875-9974
Email .... skdhr@skdmilton.com
Website .... www.skdautomotive.com

Employer Background: SKD Automotive Group, a subsidiary of National Material L.P., supplies metal stamping and modular assemblies to the automotive industry. *New Positions Created (4):* Production Supervisors; Superintendent, Manufacturing; Superintendent, Technical Services; Welding / Robotic Technicians.

SKILLSCAPE
Att: Human Resources Manager
3318 Oak Street, Suite 19
Victoria, BC V8X 1R1

Tel. 250-475-7525
Fax 250-475-7511
Website .... www.skillscape.com

Employer Background: SkillScape is a software provider specializing in intranet applications related to skills management. *New Positions Created (6):* Administrative Assistant / Support; Competency Management Consultants; Internal Sales Representative; Java Developers; Skills Dictionary Developer; Software Testers.

SKJODT-BARRETT FOODS
Att: Human Resources
2395 Lucknow Drive
Mississauga, ON L5S 1H9

Tel. 905-671-2884
Fax 905-671-2885
Email .... ronbudenas@skjodt-barrett.com
Website .... www.skjodt-barrett.com

Employer Background: Skjodt-Barrett Foods manufactures quality fruit fillings, icings, and specialty products. *New Positions Created (3):* Research & Development Assistant; Research & Development Coordinator; Salesperson / Territory Manager.

SKY EYE AMERICA
Att: Geoff Salter, Director of Engineering
455 Fenelon Boulevard, Suite 120
Dorval, QC H9S 5T8

Tel. 514-633-8892
Fax 514-633-5359
Email .... geoff.s@sky-eye.com
Website .... www.sky-eye.com

Employer Background: Founded in 1996, Sky Eye America provides global remote monitoring and information services to railway and intermodal companies. *New Positions Created (3):* Electronics Hardware Engineer; Electronics Hardware Technician; Software Programmer / Engineer.

SKYLINK TECHNOLOGIES INC.
Att: Human Resources Manager
2213 Dunwin Drive
Mississauga, ON L5L 1X1

Tel. 905-608-9223
Fax 905-608-8744
Email .... copyresume@yahoo.com
Website .... www.skylinkhome.com

Employer Background: Skylink Technologies Inc. manufactures garage door remote-control devices and home security products. *New Positions Created (4):* Sales & Marketing Secretary; Bilingual Customer Service Representative; General Sales Manager; Sales Manager.

SKYSERVICE AIRLINES INC.
Att: Human Resources
5501 Electra Road
Mississauga, ON L5P 1B1

Tel. 905-677-3300
Fax 905-678-5719
Website .... www.skyservice.com

Employer Background: Skyservice Airlines Inc. provides commercial airline, air ambulance and business aviation operations. *New Positions Created (5):* Operations Supervisor; Customer Relations Coordinators and Customer Relations Lead Agent; Operations Duty Manager; Revenue Accounting Manager; Controller.

SKYWAY BUSINESS MACHINES
Att: Austin Williams
5155 Spectrum Way, Building #6
Mississauga, ON L4W 5A1

Fax 905-624-1295
Email .... skyway@on.aibn.com

Employer Background: Skyway Business Machines has been in office equipment sales and service for over 25 years. *New Positions Created (3):* Receptionist; Service Technician; Territory Sales.

SLAVE LAKE PULP
Att: Troy Anderson, Technical Coordinator
PO Box 1790
Slave Lake, AB T0G 2A0

Tel. 780-849-7777
Email .... slpjobs@westfrasertimber.ca
Website .... www.westfrasertimber.ca

Employer Background: Slave Lake Pulp, a division of West Fraser Mills Ltd., produces high-yield market pulp from Aspen hardwood logs. *New Positions Created (2):* Environmental Technologist; Instrumentation Journeyman Tradesperson.

SLOCAN GROUP, TACKAMA DIVISION
Att: Derek Stewart, General Manager, Fort Nelson Operations
Mile 294 Alaska Highway
Fort Nelson, BC V0C 1R0

Tel. 250-233-6500
Fax 250-233-6565

Website .... www.slocan.com

Employer Background: Slocan Group, Tackama Division is an integrated stud lumber and plywood mill. *New Positions Created (2):* Divisional Controller; Woodlands Manager.

SMART TECHNOLOGIES INC.
Att: Human Resources
1177 - 11th Avenue SW, Suite 600
Calgary, AB T2R 1K9

Tel. 403-245-0333
Fax 403-228-2500
Email .... hr@smarttech.com
Website .... www.smarttech.com

Employer Background: Founded in 1987, Smart Technologies Inc. markets high-tech "roomware" products, including interactive whiteboards, multimedia cabinets and group collaboration software. The company is partly owned by Intel Corp. and employs over 280 people. *New Positions Created (26):* Industrial Designers, Mechanical Engineers and Mechanical Technologists; Internal PC Support Specialist; Public Relations Position; Return Materials Authorization Coordinator; Web Programmer; Customer Contact Specialist; Product Manager; Systems Integration Specialist; Project Manager; Software Development; Senior Software Developer; Electronics Engineer; Programmer / Analyst; IS Support Specialist / Analyst; Project Manager; Customer Contact Specialist; Electronics Engineer; Marketing Editor; Senior Electronics Engineer; Software Developers; Technical Support Specialist; Help Desk; Senior Optical Engineer; Product Manager; Senior Software Developer; Channel Marketing Specialist; Public Relations Position; Software Developers.

SMART TECHNOLOGIES INC.
Att: Human Resources
3 Iber Road
Stittsville, ON K2S 1E6

Tel. 613-836-2110
Fax 613-836-6707
Email .... info@ottawa.smarttech.com
Website .... www.smarttech.com

Employer Background: Founded in 1987, Smart Technologies Inc. markets high-tech "roomware" products, including interactive whiteboards, multimedia cabinets and group collaboration software. The company is partly owned by Intel Corp. and employs over 280 people. *New Positions Created (7):* Configuration Management and Documentation Control Team Leader; Process Engineer; Senior Electronics Engineer; Buyer; Drafting and Configuration Management Supervisor; Materials Engineer; Supplier Engineer.

SMARTFORCE CORPORATION
Att: Human Resources Manager
10 Knowledge Park Drive
Fredericton, NB E3B 2M7

Tel. 506-457-1285
Fax 506-489-2382
Email .... careers@smartforce.com
Website .... www.smartforce.com

Employer Background: SmartForce provides e-learning solutions to their customers. *New Positions Created (5):* Database Administrator; Network Engineer; Project Mgr - Web Development; Team Leader, Customer Service; Technical Specialist.

SMC PNEUMATICS (CANADA) LTD.
Att: Regional Manager
730 Eaton Way, Unit 2
Annacis Business Park
Delta, BC V3M 7J6

Email .... bdavis@mail.smcusa.com
Website .... www.smcpneumatics.ca

Employer Background: SMC Pneumatics (Canada) Ltd. manufactures pneumatic components. *New Positions Created (2):* Junior Account Representatives (2); Senior Account Representatives (2).

SMED INTERNATIONAL INC.
Att: Human Resources Department
10 Smed Lane SE
Calgary, AB T2C 4T5

Tel. 403-203-6000
Fax 403-203-6537
Email .... resumes@smednet.com
Website .... www.smed.com

Employer Background: SMED International Inc. manufactures and markets creative office environments. *New Positions Created (10):* Occupational Health Nurse; Agency Coordinator; Facility Support Position; Programmer / Analyst; Product Definition Technician; Team Drivers; Team Lease Operators; Oracle Developer / Analyst; Engineer / Technologist, Moveable Wall Division; Engineer, Wood Division.

SMITH CAGEORGE PERRY
Att: John W. Perry
340 - 12th Avenue SW, Suite 300
Calgary, AB T2R 1L5

Tel. 403-261-7779
Fax 403-262-3917
Email .... jperry@scp-ca.com
Website .... www.scp-ca.com

Employer Background: Smith Cageorge Perry, a chartered accounting firm, provides accounting, auditing, taxation and business advisory services to small and medium-sized enterprises. *New Positions Created (2):* Manager, Assurance and Accounting; Manager, Tax.

SMITH LYONS LLP
Att: Carol McGrath, HR Director
40 King Street West
Suite 5800, Scotia Plaza
Toronto, ON M5H 3Z7

Tel. 416-369-7200
Fax 416-369-7250
Email .... cmcgrath@smithlyons.ca
Website .... www.smithlyons.ca

Employer Background: Founded in 1962, Smith Lyons is a large law firm with offices in Toronto, Ottawa and the Ukraine. *New Positions Created (3):* Banking and Finance Clerk; Corporate Services Clerk; Director of Associates and Students.

SMURFIT-MBI
Att: Human Resources Department
747 Appleby Line
Burlington, ON L7L 2Y6
Fax 905-634-4420
Email .... mikwit@smurfit-mbi.com
Website .... www.smurfit-mbi.com
Employer Background: Smurfit-MBI manufactures corrugated packaging products. *New Positions Created (3):* Industrial Millwright; Industrial Millwrights; Industrial Millwrights.

SNAP-ON TOOLS OF CANADA LTD.
Att: Jennifer Gordon, Human Resources
2325 Skymark Avenue
Mississauga, ON L4W 5A9
Fax 905-624-9237
Email .... jennifer.l.gordon@snapon.com
Website .... www.snapon.com
Employer Background: Snap-On Tools of Canada Ltd. is a leading automotive and industrial equipment company. *New Positions Created (14):* Assistant Store Managers; Store Associates; Store Manager; Industrial Sales Representative; Technical Sales Representative; Bilingual Customer Service Representative; Credit Coordinator; Customer Service Manager; Warehouse Supervisor; Field Service Technicians; Installers; Supply Chain Analyst; Industrial Sales Representative; Supervisor, Repair Centre.

SNAP-ON TOOLS OF CANADA LTD.
Att: Victor Somkuti
1500 Riverside Drive, Suite 1106
Ottawa, ON K1G 4J4
Fax 613-837-7879
Email .... vstrain1@home.com
Website .... www.snapon.com
Employer Background: Snap-On Tools of Canada Ltd. is a leading automotive and industrial equipment company. *New Positions Created (2):* Service Technician; Technical Sales Representatives.

SNC-LAVALIN INC.
Att: Human Resources
1075 West Georgia Street, Suite 1800
Vancouver, BC V6E 3C9
Tel. 604-662-3555
Fax 604-605-5926
Email .... langm4@snc-lavalin.com
Website .... www.snc-lavalin.com
Employer Background: SNC-Lavalin Inc. is one of the largest Canadian engineering-construction firms, with expertise in engineering-construction, procurement, project management and project financing services. *New Positions Created (7):* Business Development Manager; Electrical Engineers; Estimator; Lead Mechanical Engineer; Project Engineer, Civil; Project Engineers, Mechanical / Electrical; Electrical Engineers.

SNC-LAVALIN INC.
Att: Human Resources
10235 - 101st Street, Suite 608
Edmonton, AB T5J 3G1
Tel. 780-422-6288
Fax 780-412-6288

Email .... cvedm@snc-lavalin.com
Website .... www.snc-lavalin.com
Employer Background: SNC-Lavalin Inc. is one of the largest Canadian engineering-construction firms, with expertise in engineering-construction, procurement, project management and project financing services. *New Positions Created (12):* Civil / Structural Designers; Civil / Structural Engineers; Contracts Administrator; Mechanical Engineers; Piping Designers, PDS; Piping Draftsperson; Senior Mechanical Engineers; Marketing Account Mgr; Project Managers; Junior Process Engineers; Senior Process Engineers; Marketing Account Manager.

SNC-LAVALIN INC.
Att: Human Resources Department
455 Rene-Levesque Blvd. West, 16th Floor
Montréal, QC H2Z 1Z3
Tel. 514-393-1000
Fax 514-866-3118
Email .... cv-corp@snc-lavalin.com
Website .... www.snc-lavalin.com
Employer Background: SNC-Lavalin Inc. is one of the largest Canadian engineering-construction firms, with expertise in engineering-construction, procurement, project management and project financing services. *New Positions Created (12):* AutoCAD Operator / Junior Designer, Mechanical or Electrical; Electrical Engineer; Mechanical Engineer; Project Manager, Design and Construction; Accountant; Construction Site Inspector, Telecommunications Project; Contract Administrator; Document Controllers, Telecommunications Project; Material Expediting and Warehouse Coordinator, Telecommunications Project; Planners / Schedulers; Project Controls Manager, Telecommunications Project; Project Managers / Senior Engineers, Various Positions.

SNC-LAVALIN INC., CHEMICALS & PETROLEUM BUSINESS UNIT
Att: Human Resources Manager
909 - 5th Avenue SW
Calgary, AB T2P 3G5
Tel. 403-294-2100
Email ... human.resources2@snclavalin.com
Website .... www.snc-lavalin.com
Employer Background: SNC-Lavalin Inc. is one of the largest Canadian engineering-construction firms, with expertise in engineering-construction, procurement, project management and project financing services. *New Positions Created (12):* DCS Position; Electrical Position; Instrumentation Position; Piping Position; SCADA Position; Contracts Managers and Administrators; Procurement Position; Project Controls Position; Project Engineers; Process Engineers; Senior / Principal Metallurgists; Business Development Manager.

SNIDERMAN, DYKSTRA & FORD
Att: Human Resources Manager
3365 Harvester Road, Suite 1010
Burlington, ON L7N 3N2
Tel. 905-634-4747
Fax 905-634-5995

Email .... search@sdfca.com
Website .... www.sdfca.com
Employer Background: Sniderman, Dykstra & Ford is a chartered accounting firm. *New Positions Created (2):* Accounting Technician; Chartered Accountant.

SOBERMAN ISENBAUM & COLOMBY LLP
Att: P.J. Lowry
2 St. Clair Avenue East
Toronto, ON M4T 2T5
Tel. 416-964-7633
Fax 416-964-6454
Email .... pjlowry@soberman.com
Website .... www.soberman.com
Employer Background: Soberman Isenbaum & Colomby LLP is a mid-sized accounting firm. *New Positions Created (4):* Chartered Accountants; Managers, Audit and Accounting Group; Accountants - CA; Accountants - CGA.

SOBEYS CANADA INC.
Att: Director of Recruitment and Selection
115 King Street
Stellarton, NS B0K 1S0
Tel. 902-752-8371
Fax 902-928-1621
Email .... resumes@sobeys.com
Website .... www.sobeys.ca
Employer Background: Sobeys Canada Inc. is a major food retailer, wholesaler and food service distributor. *New Positions Created (2):* Vice-President, Applications; Vice-President, Technical Infrastructure.

SOBEYS INC.
Att: Bill Dawson, VP Human Resources
6355 Viscount Road
Mississauga, ON L4V 1W2
Tel. 905-671-5032
Fax 905-671-5009
Email .... barbara_wilczura@sobeys.net
Website .... www.sobeys.ca
Employer Background: Founded in 1905, Sobeys Inc. operates 120 grocery stores in six provinces and has annual revenues of over $3 billion. *New Positions Created (7):* Product Manager, Retail Brands; Vice-President, Finance; Graphic Production Desktop Publisher; Various Retail Positions; Pharmacist Manager and Pharmacists; Pharmacists; Project Manager.

SOBEYS INC., WESTERN DIVISION
Att: Manager, Employment Services
17220 Stony Plain Road, Suite 200
Edmonton, AB T5S 1K6
Fax 780-444-3438
Website .... www.sobeys.ca
Employer Background: Founded in 1905, Sobeys Inc. operates 120 grocery stores in six provinces and has annual revenues of over $3 billion. *New Positions Created (6):* Retail Food Managers; Produce and Meat Specialists; Field Coordinator; Manager, Labour Relations; Retail Food Managers; Sanitation and Food Safety Specialist.

SOBOTEC LTD.
Att: Human Resources Manager
67 Burford Road
Hamilton, ON L8E 3C6

Tel. 905-578-1278
Fax 905-578-1446
Website .... www.sobotec.com

Employer Background: Sobotec Ltd. manufactures architectural wall panel systems. *New Positions Created (7):* Estimator; Project Manager; Salesperson; Senior Architectural Draftspersons; Architectural Draftspersons; Construction Coordinator; Project Manager.

SOCIAL RESEARCH AND DEMONSTRATION CORPORATION / SRDC
Att: Director of Human Resources
50 O'Connor Street, Suite 1400
Ottawa, ON K1P 6L2

Tel. 613-237-4311
Fax 613-237-5045
Website .... www.srdc.org

Employer Background: Established in 1991, SRDC is a non-profit, social policy research organization. *New Positions Created (6):* Executive Assistant; Project Director, Community Development; Project Director, Income Security; Research Associates, Income Security; Director of Finance; Payroll / Accounting Clerk.

SOCIETY OF ENERGY PROFESSIONALS, THE
Att: Human Resources
525 University Avenue, Suite 630
Toronto, ON M5G 2L3

Tel. 416-979-2709
Website .... www.society.on.ca

Employer Background: The Society of Energy Professionals is a multi-employer union representing 5,500 engineers, scientists and other professionals in the electrical industry. *New Positions Created (3):* Office Assistant; Staff Officer, Labour Relations (2); Technical Support Analyst.

SODEMA / TRANSCONTINENTAL TECHNOLOGY
Att: Human Resources Manager
1501 McGill College, Suite 1000
Montréal, QC H3A 3M8

Tel. 514-287-3236
Fax 514-285-8005
Email .... ejob@transcontinental.ca
Website .... www.transcontinental.ca

Employer Background: Sodema / Transcontinental Technology is a Canadian telemarketing call centre. *New Positions Created (4):* Telemarketing Agents (30); Personal Insurance Counsellors; Call Centre Agents (40); Technical Support Agents (30).

SODEXHO MARRIOTT SERVICES CANADA, INC. / SMSC
Att: D. MacMillan, Recruiting Manager
3350 South Service Road
Burlington, ON L7N 3M6

Tel. 905-632-8592
Fax 905-632-7114
Email .... dmacmillan@sodexhoca.com

Website .... www.sodexhoca.com
Employer Background: SMSC is one of Canada's leading providers of outsourced food and facilities management services. *New Positions Created (7):* Regional Purchasing Manager; Food Service Manager; Housekeeping Manager, Health Care; Foodservice Manager, Retail; Director of Foodservice, Healthcare; Foodservice Director; Food Service Managers and Directors.

SOFT TRACKS
Att: Human Resources Manager
13351 Commerce Parkway, Suite 1258
Richmond, BC V6V 2X7

Tel. 604-214-6641
Fax 604-214-6631
Email .... jobs@softtracks.com
Website .... www.softtracks.com

Employer Background: Soft Tracks provides leading-edge technology to the mobile transaction industry. *New Positions Created (9):* Office Clerk; Product Mgr; Senior Software Developer; Systems Engineer / Analyst; Verification Specialist; Call Centre Support Technician; Development Project Manager; Systems Engineer; Technical Writer.

SOLECT TECHNOLOGY GROUP
Att: Human Resources Manager
55 University Avenue, Suite 1500
Toronto, ON M5J 2H7

Tel. 416-363-7844
Fax 416-363-1011
Email .... jobs@solect.com
Website .... www.solect.com

Employer Background: Select Technology Group provides IP billing software for Internet service providers. *New Positions Created (41):* Quality Assurance Analyst; Database Administrator; Senior Product Manager, CRM and Broadband (2); Business Consultant; Documentation Specialist; Project Manager / Office Administrator; Senior Integration Specialist; Senior Java / C++ Developer; Senior Java GUI Developer; AES Project Manager; Business Manager; C++ Developer, Advanced Engineering Sales; Corporate Accountant; Managers, Product Integration and Product Software Infrastructure; Marketing Operations Analyst; Network Systems Administrator; Product Analyst; Product Architect; Product Development Coordinator; Product Manager, Billing and Rating; Product Manager, Generalist; Product Marketing Analyst, Broadband Markets; Quality Assurance Analyst; Release Program Manager; Research Analyst; Software Developer; Software Development Manager; ADS Software Developer; Application Support Specialist; Business Analyst; Business Operations Coordinator; Database Administrator; Director, Information Technology; Engineering Laboratory Systems Administrator; Hardware Design Engineer; Manager, Product Maintenance; Procurement Services Specialist; Senior Java Developer; Voice Services Support Specialist; Administrative Assistant; Facility / Administrative Assistant.

SOLECTRON
Att: Human Resources
5550 Skyline Way NE
Calgary, AB T2E 7Z7

Fax 403-516-4285
Email .... laurelsatter@solectron.com
Website .... www.solectron.com

Employer Background: Solectron provides fully-integrated outsourcing solutions to the electronics industry with 51,000 employees at over 39 manufacturing facilities worldwide. *New Positions Created (13):* PCB Layout Designers; Customer Service Supply Chain Manager; Director of Engineering Materials Director; Materials Manager, New Product Introduction / NPI; Program Managers; Senior CIM Engineer; Senior Manager, Program Management; Senior Procurement Analyst; Test Engineers; Section Managers; Technicians; Buyers, Circuit Pack Manufacturing.

SOLID CADDGROUP INC.
Att: Human Resources Manager
3575 - 14th Avenue, Unit 7
Markham, ON L3R 0H6

Fax 905-474-1899
Email .... pforman@solidcadcam.com
Website .... www.solidcadcam.com

Employer Background: Solid Caddgroup Inc is a leader in CAD / CAM and architectural software and hardware implementation. *New Positions Created (3):* CAD / CAM Application Engineer; CAD Sales Associate; Marketing Manager.

SOLINET SYSTEMS INC.
Att: Human Resources Manager
180 Elgin Street, Suite 1200
Ottawa, ON K2P 2K3

Tel. 613-230-6628
Fax 613-230-1362
Email .... careers@solinetsystems.com
Website .... www.solinetsystems.com

Employer Background: Solinet Systems Inc. provides network and service management products that enable service providers to achieve cost-effective, optical core networks. *New Positions Created (34):* Director, Product Line Management (Hardware); Director, Supply Chain Management; Hardware Design Engineer; NMS Software Engineer, GUI; Senior Optical Amplifier Engineer; Senior Optical Control Architect; Senior Optical Systems Engineer; Senior Photonics Engineer; Senior Product Verification Engineer ; System Specialist (Protocol); Development Lab Technician; Facilities Manager; Network Element Software Design Engineer; OAM&P Software Architect; Optical Network Architect; Optical Network Planner; RF Design Engineer; Senior Microcode Designer; Senior Optical Control Architect; Senior Photonics Engineer; Senior Product Verification Engineer; Senior Software Designer, Embedded Datacom; Senior Systems Engineer; Software Loadbuild and Source Control Specialist; Test Automation Software Designer; Director, Software OAM; Broadband RF Design Engineers; Real-time Embedded Software Engineer; Senior Hardware Design Engineer; Senior Mechanical

Engineer; Senior Optical Amplifier Engineer; Senior Optical Component Engineer; Senior Optical Systems Engineer; Senior Product Integrity Engineer.

SOLINST CANADA LTD.
Att: Jim Pianosi, Sales Manager
35 Todd Road
Georgetown, ON L7G 4R8
Tel. 905-873-2255
Fax 905-873-1992
Email .... jim.pianosi@solinst.com
Website .... www.solinst.com
Employer Background: Founded in 1980, Solinst Canada Ltd. is a manufacturer of groundwater monitoring instruments. *New Positions Created (2):* Technical & Computer Support Position; Marketing Assistant.

SOLOWAY WRIGHT
Att: John Moss / Richard McNevin
366 King Street East, Suite 440
Kingston, ON K7K 6Y3
Tel. 613-544-7334
Fax 613-544-6689
Email .... mossj@soloways.com
Website .... www.soloways.com
Employer Background: Soloway Wright is a 21-lawyer firm, with over 60 years experience. *New Positions Created (2):* Junior Lawyer; Real Estate / Commercial Secretary.

SOLVAY PHARMA INC.
Att: Human Resources
50 Venture Drive
Toronto, ON M1B 3L6
Tel. 416-284-7666
Fax 416-284-6895
Email .... hr.canada@solvay.com
Website .... www.solvay.com
Employer Background: Solvay Pharma Inc. is a Canadian pharmaceutical division of Solvay, an international chemical and pharmaceutical group based in Brussels, Belgium that deals with chemicals, plastics, processing and pharmaceuticals. *New Positions Created (7):* Manager, Marketing Research; Medical Sales Rep; Senior Administrative Coordinator; Medical Sales Representative; Product Manager; Sales Trainer; Medical Sales Reps, Nationwide.

SONITROL SECURITY SYSTEMS
Att: Human Resources
238 Britannia Road East
Mississauga, ON L4Z 1S6
Tel. 905-890-7727
Fax 905-890-8391
Email .... ttopps@sonitrolcanada.com
Website .... www.sonitrol.com
Employer Background: Sonitrol Security Systems is an international company providing security systems. *New Positions Created (2):* Emergency Dispatcher / Customer Service; Customer Service Representatives.

SONY MUSIC CANADA
Att: Human Resources Manager
1121 Leslie Street
Toronto, ON M3C 2J9
Tel. 416-391-3311
Fax 416-391-7969
Website .... www.sonymusic.ca
Employer Background: Sony Music Canada produces, manufactures, markets, sells and distributes recorded music. *New Positions Created (13):* Administrative Assistant, Music Publishing; Artist Marketing Manager; Bindery Operator; Cost Analyst; Intermediate Programmer Analyst ; Law Clerk; Manager, E-Business Solutions; Purchasing Representative; Bilingual Content and Promotions Coordinator; Director, New Media; Graphic Artist; Payroll & Benefits Coordinator; Talent Financial Analyst.

SOROC TECHNOLOGY INC.
Att: Human Resources
607 Chrislea Road
Woodbridge, ON L4L 8A3
Tel. 905-265-8000
Fax 905-265-8008
Website .... www.soroc.com
Employer Background: Established in Canada in 1981, Soroc Technology Inc. distributes, manufactures and custom designs Soroc computer-based terminals for IBM, DEC, Basic Four and Tandem systems. *New Positions Created (13):* Senior Project Manager; Unix Support Specialist; Bilingual Call Centre Support Representative; Senior Project Manager; PC Field Technician; Project Manager, Deployments; Senior Business Analyst; Senior Network Project and Support Analyst; C++ / Cobol / HTML Analyst ; IT / Finance Project Manager; Point-of-Sale Helpdesk Representative; Technical Resource Manager; Unix Operator.

SOTA GLAZING INC.
Att: Human Resources
443 Railside Drive
Brampton, ON L7A 1E1
Tel. 905-846-3177
Fax 905-846-3530
Email .... juan@sotawall.com
Website .... www.sotawall.com
Employer Background: Founded in 1986, Sota Glazing Inc. manufactures engineered curtainwall systems. *New Positions Created (3):* Assembly Manager; Project Manager; Senior Designer / Draftsperson.

SOURCE MEDICAL CORPORATION
Att: Human Resources Manager
1330 Meyerside Drive
Mississauga, ON L5T 1C2
Fax 905-565-2298
Email .... careers@sourcemedical.com
Website .... www.sourcemedical.com
Employer Background: Source Medical Corporation is one of Canada's leading distributors of medical and surgical products and services. *New Positions Created (2):* Distribution Leader, Nights; QIC Analyst.

SOUTH FRASER HEALTH REGION
Att: Elaine Ivancic, Recruitment
13750 - 96th Avenue
Surrey, BC V3V 1Z2
Tel. 604-585-5671
Fax 604-585-5670
Email .... recruitment@sfvhr.hnet.bc.ca
Website .... www.southfraserhealth.com
Employer Background: SFHR is the 2nd-largest health region in British Columbia, serving a population of 588,600. *New Positions Created (7):* Clinical Resource Nurse, OR; Patient Services Coordinator, Extended Care; Chief Therapist, Respiratory Therapy; Registered Nurses, Emergency; Ultrasound Technologist; Antepartum Coordinator; Nurse, Post-Anaesthetic Care Unit.

SOUTH LAKE REGIONAL HEALTH CENTRE
Att: Human Resources Department
596 Davis Drive
Newmarket, ON L3Y 2P9
Tel. 905-895-4521
Fax 905-853-2218
Email .... careers@southlakeregional.org
Website .... www.southlakeregional.org
Employer Background: South Lake Regional Health Centre (formerly York County Hospital) is a 292-bed full-service facility, located 30 minutes north of Toronto. *New Positions Created (56):* Medical Radiation, X-Ray and Ultrasound Technologists; Occupational Therapist, Assertive Community Treatment Team (ACTT); Registered Practical Nurses, OR; Clinical Trials Assistant; Educator / Pain Management Resource Provider; Project Manager, Continuous Improvement; Registered Nurses, Cardiac Cath Lab; Registered Nurses, Cardiology; Manager, Regional Paediatrics Program; Emergency Manager; Manager, HCIS Applications; Manager, Radiology; Respiratory Care Practitioners; Social Worker; Data & Information Clerk, Cancer Care; Film File Clerk, Diagnostic Imaging; Medical Radiation Technologist, Mammography; Registered Practical Nurses; Advanced Practice Nurse, Geriatrics / Psychogeriatrics; Nurse Educators, Cancer; Nurse Educators, NICU; Project Manager, Continuous Improvement; Registered Nurses; Medical Radiation Technologists; Sonographer; Cardiac Sonographer; Manager, Pharmacy Services; RN Cardiac Pacemaker Program Specialist; NICU Nurse Educator; Emergency Manager; Manager, Radiology; Social Worker; Cytotechnologists; Manager, HCIS Applications; Manager, Regional Paediatrics Program; Project Manager, Clinical Informatics; Registered Nurses; Director, Cancer Care / Ambulatory Care; Discharge Planner; Emergency Manager; Human Resources Recruiter; Nurse Educators; Registered Nurses, Surgery; Respiratory Care Practitioners; Advanced Practice Nurse, Geriatrics / Psychogeriatrics; Physiotherapist; Clinical Dietitian; X-Ray Technologists; Clinical Support Coordinators; Nurse Educators; Registered Nurses; Cytotechnologist; Food Services Supervisors; Registered Nurses; Registered Nurses; Social Worker.

SOUTH MUSKOKA MEMORIAL HOSPITAL
Att: Human Resources
75 Ann Street
Bracebridge, ON P1L 2E4

Tel. 705-645-4404
Fax 705-645-4594
Email .... hr@muskoka.com

Employer Background: The South Muskoka Memorial Hospital is an 80-bed rural acute care hospital. *New Positions Created (3):* Technical Director, Laboratory Services; Registered Nurses; Chief Nursing Officer.

SOUTH PEACE HEALTH COUNCIL
Att: Norene Hawkins, Human Resources
11100 - 13th Street
Dawson Creek, BC V1G 3W8

Tel. 250-784-7350
Fax 250-784-7301
Email .... hr@spchc.hnet.bc.ca
Website .... www.sphc.bc.ca

Employer Background: South Peace Health Council serves the communities of Dawson Creek, Chetwynd, Tumbler Ridge and Pouce Coupe. *New Positions Created (10):* Combined X-Ray / Lab Technicians; Diagnostic Imaging Manager; Diagnostic Imaging Technologists; Laboratory Services Manager; Diagnostic Imaging Manager; Nurses; Laboratory Services Manager; Manager, Nursing Services; Pharmacists; LPN-OR Technician.

SOUTHERN ALBERTA INSTITUTE OF TECHNOLOGY / SAIT
Att: Heather Ravlich, Human Resources
1301 - 16th Avenue NW
Calgary, AB T2M 0L4

Tel. 403-284-8780
Fax 403-284-7223
Email .... heather.ravlich@sait.ab.ca
Website .... www.sait.ab.ca

Employer Background: SAIT is an established post-secondary technical institute, offering 72 certificate and diploma programs, 3 applied degrees and 25 apprenticeship programs to over 67,000 students. *New Positions Created (53):* Director of International Training; Manager, International Centre; Database Administration Instructors; Dean of Information and Communication Technologies; Food Service Worker; Instructor, Network Technician Program; Educational Counsellor; Customer Services Representative; Food Operations Supervisors (2); Prehospital Care Instructor; Manager of Employee Services, Human Resources; Vice-President, Academic; Academic Coordinator, Diagnostic Imaging Programs; Occupational Health Safety and Environment Coordinator; Senior Purchasing Officer; Computer Technology Instructor; Electrical Apprenticeship Instructor; Environmental Technology Program Academic Coordinator; Geophysics / Geology Instructor; Information and Communications Technologies Instructor; Software Engineering Instructors; Financial Analyst; Public / Community Relations Specialist; Student Recruitment and Employment Specialist; Electronic Technician; Supervisor, Corporate Reporting; Graphic Artist; Instructor, Civil Engineering Technology; Instructor, Health Record Technician; Instructor, Pre-Hospital Care ; Computer Controls Technology Instructors; Curriculum Developer; Electron-

ics Engineering Technology Instructors; Network Engineering Technology Instructors; Personal Computer Support Specialist; Pre-Hospital Care Instructor; Director, Fund Development; Academic Coordinator, Computer Engineering Technologies; Academic Coordinator, Energy Department; Academic Coordinator, Journalism, Digital Communication and Library Information Technology; Automation Systems Instructor, Manufacturing and Automation; Computer Technology Instructor; Instructor, Applied Information Systems Technology; Key Account Mgr, Continuing Education; Personal Computer Support Specialist, Information Systems; Manager, Academic Departments; Director, Innovation and Technology; Computer Control Technology Instructor; Computer Engineering Technology Instructor; Database Administration Instructors; Electronic Engineering Technology Instructor; Network Engineering Technology Instructor; Object-Oriented Programming Instructors.

SOUTHMOUNT CABLE LTD.
Att: Human Resources
1074 Upper Wellington Street
Hamilton, ON L9A 3S6

Tel. 905-574-6464
Fax 905-574-4909
Website .... www.southmount.com

Employer Background: Southmount Cable Ltd. is a medium-sized communications company, deploying digital and high-speed data services. *New Positions Created (2):* Field Installation Technician; Field Maintenance Technician.

SOUTHRIDGE SCHOOL
Att: William Jones, Head of School
2656 - 160th Street
Surrey, BC V3S 0B7

Fax 604-535-3676
Email .... sduckwor@southridge.bc.ca
Website .... www.southridge.bc.ca

Employer Background: Southridge School is a K - 12 independent, non-denominational co-educational day school. *New Positions Created (3):* Head of Senior School; Director of Academics; Teachers.

SPACEBRIDGE NETWORKS CORPORATION
Att: Human Resources Manager
115 Champlain Street
Hull, QC J8X 3R1

Tel. 819-776-2848
Fax 819-776-4179
Email .... hr@spacebridge.com
Website .... www.spacebridge.com

Employer Background: SpaceBridge Networks Corporation specializes in the development of semiconductors for broadband wireless access systems. *New Positions Created (32):* RF IC Designer / Technical Leader; Senior ASIC Designer; Senior Modem Architect; Senior Systems Engineer; Financial Analyst; Director, ASIC Design and Development; Senior Product Engineer; Senior Quality Engineer; Senior Software Designer; ASIC Manager; RF IC Designer, Technical

Leader; Senior ASIC Designer; Senior Modem Architect; Senior Software Architect; Senior Systems Engineer; Purchasing Specialist; Senior Hardware Designer; Accounts Payable Clerk; ASIC Development Manager; HR Administrator; Purchasing Specialist; Senior Manufacturing Engineer; Account Executive; Application Engineer; ASIC Designer; ASIC Manager; CAD Tools Manager; Documentation Specialists; DSP Designer; Product Manager / Director; Senior Modem Architect; Senior Research Engineer.

SPAETGENS SYMONS EVANS ARCHITECTS / SSE ARCHITECTS
Att: Todd Hutton
1400 Kensington Road NW, Suite 100
Calgary, AB T2N 3P9

Tel. 403-283-6955
Fax 403-283-6941
Email .... thutton@sse.ab.ca
Website .... www.sse.ab.ca

Employer Background: Established in 1994, SSE Architects is a multi-disciplinary design firm providing services in architecture, interior design and urban planning. *New Positions Created (6):* Computer-Aided Facility Mgmnt Technologist; Design Architects; Intermediate & Senior Architectural Technologists; Executive Assistant; Design Architect; Designer / Intern Architect.

SPAFAX CANADA INC
Att: Josée Roberge
355 St. Catherine Street West, Suite 400
Montréal, QC H3B 1A5

Tel. 514-844-2001
Fax 514-844-6001
Website .... www.spafax.com

Employer Background: Spafax is an international media management firm with offices in Montreal, Toronto, London, Singapore, Los Angeles and New York. *New Positions Created (2):* Sr Editor; Editor-in-Chief.

SPAN MANUFACTURING LTD.
Att: Human Resources Manager
7100 Warden Avenue
Markham, ON L3R 8B5

Tel. 905-479-1327
Fax 905-479-0297
Email .... hr@spanltd.com
Website .... www.spanltd.com

Employer Background: Span Manufacturing Ltd. is an electronics assembly company. *New Positions Created (4):* Manufacturing Engineer; QA Inspectors; Senior Test Engineer; Various Technician Positions.

SPAR AEROSPACE LIMITED
Att: Human Resources
Edmonton International Airport,
PO Box 9864
Edmonton, AB T5J 2T2

Tel. 780-890-6495
Fax 780-890-6544
Email .... edmhr@spar.ca
Website .... www.spar.ca

Employer Background: Spar Aerospace Limited provides repair, overhaul, logistics, upgrades and maintenance services in support of military and civil aviation customers. *New Positions Created (55):* Aircraft Mechanics, Sheet Metal Technicians; Customer Services Coordinator, Edmonton International Airport Facility; Planners; Training Developer / Instructors (Maintenance); Training Developer / Instructors (Operator); Aircraft Interiors Technicians (3); Avionics / Electrical Systems Analysts and Testers; Avionics / Electrical Systems Designers; Avionics Technician; Avionics Test Engineer; Mechanical / Electrical Design Drafters; Painter / Cleaner; Structural Analysts; Structural Designers; Technical Writers; Aircraft Maintenance Supervisors (2); Aircraft Mechanics (20); Avionics Certification Engineer; Avionics Engineers; Liaison Engineer Specialist; Manager, Integrated Logistics Support; Planner; Program Manager, HAF C-130 Avionics Upgrade Program; Quality Systems Manager; Senior Buyers (2); Senior / Principal Structures Engineer; Structures Engineer; Structures Technicians (20); Aircraft Maintenance Supervisors (3); Aircraft Mechanics (15); Airworthiness Controllers; Avionics Certification Engineer; Avionics Engineer; Avionics Engineers; Avionics Technicians (2); Design Draftspersons; Editor; Lead Training Developer / Instructors; Liaison Engineers / Specialists; Manager, Integrated Logistics Support; Manager of Environment, Health and Safety; Manager, Quality Systems; Material Supply Chain Analyst; Planners; Program Managers; Senior Structures Engineer; Structures Engineers / Specialists; Structures Technicians (20); Technical Illustrators; Technical Writers; Training Coordinator; Data Entry Clerk; Customer Services Coordinator; Structures Engineer / Specialist; Program Accountant.

SPAR AEROSPACE LIMITED
Att: David Bucsis, HR Manager
7785 Tranmere Drive
Mississauga, ON L5S 1W5
Tel. 905-671-5868
Fax 905-671-5809
Email .... tranhr@spar.ca
Website .... www.spar.ca
Employer Background: Spar Aerospace Limited provides repair, overhaul, logistics, upgrades and maintenance services in support of military and civil aviation customers. *New Positions Created (17):* Mechanical Repair and Overhaul Technician; Operations Engineer (S61/H3 Helicopter Dynamic Components); Treasury Analyst; Mechanical Repair & Overhaul Technicians; Buyer / Planner; Mgr, Supply Chain; Marketing Mgr, Commercial; Marketing Mgr, Department of Defense; Material Supply Chain Analyst; Operations Engineer, S61/H3 Helicopter Dynamic Components; Quality Analyst; Team Leader, Material Planning; Treasury Mgr; Planner / Buyer; Supply Chain Mgr; Environment, Health & Safety Specialist.

SPECTRA ALUMINUM PRODUCTS INC.
Att: President
127 Aviva Park Drive
Woodbridge, ON L4L 9C1
Tel. 905-856-5992
Fax 905-856-9568
Website .... www.spectraaluminum.com
Employer Background: Spectra Aluminum Products Inc. is an ISO-9002 certified international supplier of aluminum products specializing in extrusions, fabrication, anodizing, painting and polishing. *New Positions Created (5):* Operations Manager; Quality & Training Manager; Plant Chemist; Project Coordinator; Senior Plant Engineer.

SPECTRAL DIAGNOSTICS INC.
Att: Dr. Paul Hemmes
2 The West Mall, Suite 135
Toronto, ON M9C 1C2
Fax 416-626-3651
Email ... phemmes@spectraldiagnostics.com
Website ..... www.spectraldiagnostics.com
Employer Background: Spectral Diagnostics Inc. is a TSE-listed company specializing in the development and marketing of cardiac diagnostic products for healthcare professionals. *New Positions Created (4):* Manufacturing Engineer; Research Scientist, Protein Chemistry; Biomedical Technical Support and Marketing; Technical Support Provider.

SPECTRUM HEALTH CARE
Att: Human Resources
180 Bloor Street West, Suite 1000
Toronto, ON M5S 2V6
Tel. 416-964-0322
Fax 416-964-0912
Email .... admin-spectrum@
.... spectrumhealthcare.com
Website .... www.spectrumhealthcare.com
Employer Background: Spectrum Health Care provides community nursing and home support services. *New Positions Created (2):* Home Support Workers; Various Health Care Positions.

SPECTRUM HEALTH CARE
Att: Human Resources Manager
48 Village Centre Place, Upper Level
Mississauga, ON L4Z 1V9
Tel. 905-272-2271
Fax 905-272-1116
Email ..... stewart@spectrumhealthcare.com
Website .... www.spectrumhealthcare.com
Employer Background: Spectrum Health Care provides community nursing and home support services. *New Positions Created (3):* Nurses; RN Clinical Supervisor; Nurses.

SPECTRUM INVESTMENT MANAGEMENT LTD.
Att: Human Resources Department
PO Box 160, Station A
Toronto, ON M5W 1B2
Tel. 416-352-3000
Fax 416-352-3233
Email .... tpur@spectrum.com
Website .... www.spectrum.com
Employer Background: Established in 1987, Spectrum Investment Management Limited

is a growing force in the Canadian mutual fund industry with over $7 billion in assets under management. *New Positions Created (3):* Vice-President, National Accounts; Bilingual Regional Sales Manager; Regional Sales Manager.

SPECTRUM SIGNAL PROCESSING INC.
Att: Careers
2700 Production Way
One Spectrum Court, Suite 200
Burnaby, BC V5A 4X1
Tel. 604-421-5422
Fax 604-421-1764
Email .... jobs@spectrumsignal.com
Website .... www.spectrumsignal.com
Employer Background: Spectrum Signal Processing Inc. designs and manufactures high-density signal processing technology and subsystems that acquire, process and transmit signals for wireless and Voice-over-Packet (VoP) applications. *New Positions Created (20):* DSP Algorithm Team Leader; Inside Sales Engineer; Senior Software Architect; Senior High-Speed Digital Hardware Engineer; Senior Real-Time / Embedded Software Engineer; Senior Telecommunications Hardware Engineer; Telecommunications Systems Engineer; Senior ASIC Engineer; Manager, Product Marketing; Senior High-Speed Digital Hardware Engineer; Senior Real-Time / Embedded Software Engineer; Senior Software Engineers, Embedded; Test Technologist; Senior High-Speed Digital Hardware Engineer; Senior Real-Time / Embedded Software Engineer; ASIC Designer; ASIC Technical Lead; Director, Research and Development; Hardware Design Engineer; Senior ASIC Engineer.

SPEECHWORKS INTERNATIONAL, INC.
Att: Human Resources Manager
1800 McGill College, Suite 1930
Montréal, QC H3A 3J6
Tel. 514-843-4844
Fax 514-843-6872
Email .. montreal.jobs@speechworks.com
Website .... www.speechworks.com
Employer Background: SpeechWorks International, Inc. provides speech recognition solutions that allow consumers to obtain information and complete transactions by speaking over the phone. *New Positions Created (4):* Applications Software Developers; Loadbuild Engineer; Product Software Developer; Quality Assurance Engineer.

SPEED-I-COM INC. / SCI
Att: Human Resources Manager
4195 Dundas Street West, Suite 229
Toronto, ON M8X 1Y4
Tel. 416-232-2657
Fax 905-232-2619
Email .... jobs@scicanada.com
Website .... www.scicanada.com
Employer Background: SCI is a national deployer of ATM and POS equipment. *New Positions Created (4):* Administrative Assistant / Receptionist; Administrative Assistant / Bookkeeper; Customer Service Representatives; Software Developer.

SPEEDY AUTO & WINDOW GLASS
Att: M. Welsh
360 Applewood Crescent
Concord, ON L4K 4V2

Fax 905-669-7706
Website .... www.speedyglass.com
Employer Background: Speedy Auto & Window Glass is a large automotive glass replacement company. *New Positions Created (2):* Sales Rep; Sales Rep.

SPENCE DIAMONDS
Att: Human Resources
17010 - 90th Avenue
Edmonton, AB T5T 1L6

Tel. 780-484-1709
Fax 780-484-5952
Website .... www.spencediamonds.com
Employer Background: Founded in 1978, Spence Diamonds is a specialized retailer of diamond jewellery. *New Positions Created (3):* Sales Mgr; Regional Mgr; Sales Mgr.

SPIDERCACHE
Att: Human Resources Manager
1661 Duranleau Street, 2nd Floor
Granville Island, BC V6H 3S3

Tel. 604-637-0200
Fax 604-637-0205
Email .... hr@spidercache.com
Website .... www.spidercache.com
Employer Background: SpiderCache is an Internet performance software company. *New Positions Created (3):* Pre-Sales / Technical Support Engineer; Sales Representatives; Software Engineers / Programmers.

SPIELO GAMING INTERNATIONAL
Att: Human Resources Manager
654 Malenfant Boulevard
Dieppe, NB E1A 5V8

Tel. 506-859-7598
Fax 506-852-7640
Email .... jobs@spielo.ca
Website .... www.spielo.ca
Employer Background: Spielo Gaming International is a world leader in the lottery industry. *New Positions Created (34):* Game Designer; Accounts Payable Clerk; Database Specialist, Internet Gaming; Documentation Control Clerk; Electronics Technician; Senior Software Developer; Team Leader, Software; Team Leader, Video Gaming Division; Budget Analyst; QA Tester; Communications / Marketing Coordinator; Corporate Marketing Assistant; Game Designer; Game Designer, Internet Group; Lead Web Application Developer; Product Manager; Programmer; Project Manager, Internet Gaming Group; Project Manager, Software Development; Senior Account Executive; Software Designer, C++; Software Manager; Team Leader; Team Leader, Software; Telecommunication Network Engineer; Client Service Team Manager; Game Designer; Graphic Artists; Payroll Manager; Programmer; Project Manager, Software Development; Software Technical Writer; Web Application Developers ; Web Security and Technology Specialist.

SPIN MASTER TOYS
Att: Human Resources Manager
250 The Esplanade, Suite 400
Toronto, ON M5A 1J2

Fax 416-364-8005
Email .... jobs@spinmaster.com
Website .... www.spinmaster.com
Employer Background: Established in 1993, Spin Master Toys develops, designs, manufactures and markets toy products, including novelty, die cast and air pressure items. *New Positions Created (3):* Brand Managers and Marketing Directors; Executive Assistant; Recruiter.

SPINELLI LEXUS TOYOTA
Att: Sales Manager
561 St. Joseph Boulevard
Lachine, QC H8S 2K9

Tel. 514-634-7171
Fax 514-637-7407
Website .... www.spinelliauto.com
Employer Background: Founded in 1922, Spinelli Lexus Toyota is an automotive dealership. *New Positions Created (3):* Leasing and Renewal Representative; Sales Representatives; Sales Representative.

SPIRENT COMMUNICATIONS
Att: Human Resources Manager
169 Colonnade Road
Ottawa, ON K2E 7J4

Tel. 613-225-6087
Fax 613-225-6315
Website .... www.spirentcom.com
Employer Background: Spirent Communications offers a comprehensive range of tests to ensure the functionality, reliability, performance and conformance to standards of networks and network devices. *New Positions Created (14):* Master Production Scheduler; Public Relations Specialist; Software Tester; Digital Analog Designer; DSP Engineer; ERP Project Leader; Facilities Coordinator; Modem Design Engineer; Product Managers (2); Product Marketing Manager; Project Scheduler; Senior Purchasing Hi-Tech Specialist; Software Production Engineer; Systems Engineer.

SPLENTEC LTD.
Att: Human Resources Manager
15 Wertheim Court, Unit 309
Richmond Hill, ON L4B 3H7

Tel. 905-707-1954
Fax 905-707-1974
Email .... careers@splentec.com
Website .... www.splentec.com
Employer Background: Splentec Ltd. develops leading-edge networking, backup and network attached storage software and hardware. *New Positions Created (3):* Senior Software Engineer, Linux; Senior Hardware Design Engineer; Sr Software Engineer.

SPM / UNITED PLASTICS GROUP
Att: Human Resources Manager
16817 Hymus Boulevard
Kirkland, QC H9H 3L4

Fax 514-426-5682

Employer Background: SPM / United Plastics Group is a leader in the production of precision plastic components. *New Positions Created (2):* Process Technician; Setup Technician.

SPORTING LIFE INC.
Att: Human Resources Manager
2665 Yonge Street
Toronto, ON M4P 2J6

Tel. 416-485-1611
Fax 416-485-7825
Email .... hr@sportinglife.ca
Website .... www.sportinglife.ca
Employer Background: Sporting Life Inc. is an upscale sporting goods and fashion retailer. *New Positions Created (2):* Various Retail Positions; Various Retail Positions.

SPORTS CLUBS OF CANADA, THE / BALLY TOTAL FITNESS
Att: Jason Freeland
110 Eglinton Avenue East
Toronto, ON M4P 2Y1

Tel. 416-485-0343
Fax 416-485-9838
Email .... jfree@sportsclubs.com
Website .... www.ballyfitness.com
Employer Background: Bally Total Fitness is the largest and only nationwide commercial operator of fitness centres with over 4 million members and hundreds of clubs across the USA and Canada. *New Positions Created (2):* Personal Training Managers; Personal Trainers.

SPRINT CANADA INC.
Att: Human Resources
2235 Sheppard Avenue East, Suite 600
Toronto, ON M2J 5G1

Tel. 416-496-1644
Website .... www.sprintcanada.ca
Employer Background: Sprint Canada Inc. is a leading alternative long-distance telecommunications company, offering voice and data services nationwide. *New Positions Created (47):* Customer Care Associate; Customer Care Specialist; Data / Voice Customer Care Specialist; Manager, Credit & Accounts Receivable; Senior Business Analyst; Revenue Analyst; Senior National Director of Sales, E-Solutions; Accounts Receivables Associate; Credit Analyst; Product Manager, Frame Relay and Managed Network Services; Account Support Representative; Account Support Representative, GBM; Corporate Services Coordinator; Help Desk Technician; Manager, Tax and Treasury; Manager, Touchpoint Communications; Product Analyst; Product Manager, ASP Services, Enterprise Applications; Product Manager, ASP Services, Portal Applications; Senior Financial Analyst; Senior Project Manager, Field Services; Senior Risk Analyst; Account Support Representative; Carrier Cost Analyst; Carrier Relations Manager; Financial Analyst; Manager, Professional Services; Migration Specialist; Network Analyst; Product Manager, Customer Premise Equipment; Project Manager; Records Management Clerk & Office Administrator; Regional Data

Coordinator; Senior Database Developer; Senior Programmer / Analyst, Java; Senior Programmer / Analyst, PowerBuilder or VB; Senior Technical Analyst; Technical Implementation Coordinator; Voice Services Activation Analyst; Cash Administration Associate; List Coordinator; Customer Care Associate; Director, Call Centre Operations; Executive Assistant; Marketing Analyst; Product Manager, Local; Product Marketing Analyst.

SPROULE ASSOCIATES LIMITED
Att: Shelley Paulson
140 - 4th Avenue SW
Suite 900, North Tower, Sun Life Plaza
Calgary, AB T2P 3N3
Tel. 403-294-5500
Fax 403-294-5590
Email .... shelley.paulson@sproule.com
Website .... www.sproule.com
Employer Background: Sproule Associates is a Canadian, privately-owned consulting company specializing in economic evaluations of oil and gas reserves and resource assessments. *New Positions Created (6):* Geological Technologist / Technician; Network Technician; Reservoir Evaluation Engineers; Reservoir Geologist; Intermediate Geologist; Intermediate Reservoir Engineer.

SPRUCE GROVE, CITY OF
Att: Neil Riley, HR Advisor
315 Jespersen Avenue
Spruce Grove, AB T7X 3E8
Tel. 780-962-2611
Fax 780-962-2526
Email .... nriley@sprucegrove.ca
Website .... www.sprucegrove.ca
Employer Background: The City of Spruce Grove is located west of Edmonton and is home to over 14,000 residents. *New Positions Created (2):* Managing Director; Fire Chief.

SQUAMISH-LILLOOET REGIONAL DISTRICT / SLRD
Att: Susan Gimse, Chair
Box 219
Pemberton, BC V0N 2L0
Tel. 604-894-6371
Fax 604-894-6526
Email .... admin@slrd.bc.ca
Website .... www.slrd.bc.ca
Employer Background: Located north of Vancouver, the SLRD is the fastest growing regional district in BC and includes the municipalities of Lillooet, Pemberton, Whistler and Squamish. *New Positions Created (3):* Administrator / Secretary - Treasurer; Manager of Utilities / Community Services; Planning Assistant.

SQUARE PEG COMMUNICATIONS INC.
Att: Recruiting
4017 Carling Avenue, Suite 200
Kanata, ON K2K 2A3
Tel. 613-271-0044
Fax 613-271-3007
Email .... jobs@squarepeg.ca
Website .... www.squarepeg.ca

Employer Background: SPCI develops and manufactures DSP-based ground and airborne communications products, from audio to L-band, including satellite modems, Turbo decoders and complete channel units. *New Positions Created (2):* Mechanical / PCB Designer; Real-Time / Windows NT Programmer.

SR TELECOM INC.
Att: Human Resources Manager
425 Legget Drive
Kanata, ON K2K 2W2
Fax 613-599-2254
Email .... cv@srtelecom.com
Website .... www.srtelecom.com
Employer Background: Established in 1981, SR Telecom Inc. is a leader in fixed wireless access solutions. *New Positions Created (3):* Hardware Engineer; RF Engineers; Wireless IP Software Engineers.

SRI STRATEGIC RESOURCES INC.
Att: Human Resources Manager
4720 Kingsway, Suite 1920
Burnaby, BC V5H 4N2
Tel. 604-435-0627
Fax 604-435-2782
Email .... hr@sri.bc.ca
Website .... www.sri.bc.ca
Employer Background: Founded in 1986 as a subsidiary of BC Telecom, SRI Strategic Resources Inc. provides technology integration solutions, consulting and application development services to public and private sector clients. *New Positions Created (9):* Software Developers; Senior Software Engineers / Architects; Software Developers; Business Analysts; Project Managers; Project Managers, ERP Projects; Senior Software Engineers / Architects; Software Developers; Software Engineers / Analysts.

SS8 NETWORKS INC.
Att: Human Resources
495 March Road
Ottawa, ON K2K 3G1
Tel. 613-592-2100
Fax 613-592-9634
Email .... jobs@ss8.com
Website www.ss8.com
Employer Background: SS8 Networks Inc. provides an innovative IP telephony signaling and services platform. *New Positions Created (10):* Element Management System Designers; GUI Designer; Product Marketing Specialist; Real-Time Embedded System Software Designers; Service Control Point Software Designers; WAP / Wireless Services Software Designers; Manufacturing Specialist; Order Management Position; Software Developer; Technical Support Technician.

SSI EQUIPMENT INC.
Att: Human Resources Manager
5470 Harvester Road
Burlington, ON L7L 5N5
Tel. 905-333-6440
Fax 905-333-5235
Website .... www.ssiequipment.com

Employer Background: SSI Equipment Inc. manufactures strainers, pressure vessels and piping components. *New Positions Created (3):* TSSA Certified Welders; Weld Fitter; Customer Service / Documentation Representative.

SST
Att: Human Resources
50 Northland Road
Waterloo, ON N2V 1N3
Tel. 519-725-5136
Fax 519-743-3610
Email .... hrmanager@mysst.com
Website .... www.mysst.com
Employer Background: SST is a member company of Woodhead Connectivity, a leader in communication technology for the industrial world. *New Positions Created (8):* Engineering Project Manager; Firmware Engineer; Hardware Engineers; Junior Technical Writer; Payroll / Benefits Administrator; Product Marketing Manager; Software Engineer; Web Developer.

ST. ALBERT, THE CITY OF
Att: Human Resource Services
5 St. Anne Street
St. Albert, AB T8N 3Z9
Tel. 780-459-1500
Fax 780-459-1729
Website .... www.city.st-albert.ab.ca
Employer Background: Located just outside Edmonton, The City of St. Albert has 50,000 residents and Alberta's second-highest per capita income. *New Positions Created (3):* Aquatics Program Supervisor; Solicitor, Legal Services; City Solicitor.

ST. ANDREW'S COLLEGE
Att: Selection Committee
15800 Yonge Street
Aurora, ON L4G 3H7
Tel. 905-727-3178
Fax 905-841-6911
Email .... st.andrews@sac.on.ca
Website .... www.sac.on.ca
Employer Background: Founded in 1899, St. Andrew's College is a private boarding and day school for boys from grade 6 to university entrance. *New Positions Created (2):* Head, Music; History Teacher.

ST. BONIFACE GENERAL HOSPITAL
Att: Staffing Officer, Human Resources
409 Tache Avenue
Winnipeg, MB R2H 2A6
Tel. 204-233-8563
Fax 204-235-3695
Email .... staffing@sbgh.mb.ca
Website .... www.sbgh.mb.ca
Employer Background: Established in 1871 by the Sisters of Charity (Grey Nuns), St. Boniface General Hospital is a tertiary care facility affiliated with the University of Manitoba. *New Positions Created (4):* General Duty Technologists (3); Audiologist; Occupational Therapist / Clinical Specialist; Senior Physiotherapist.

ST. CATHARINES, CITY OF

Att: Kenneth R. Todd,
Director, Corporate Support Services
50 Church Street, PO Box 3012, City Hall
St. Catharines, ON L2R 7C2

Tel. 905-688-5601
Fax 905-682-3631
Website .... www.city.stcatharines.on.ca

Employer Background: With a population of almost 130,000, the City of St. Catharines is the commercial centre of the Niagara Peninsula. It is surrounded by one the most productive agricultural areas in the world. *New Positions Created (3):* Assistant City Solicitor; Manager, Human Resources ; Planner I, Policy.

ST. CLEMENT'S SCHOOL

Att: Patricia D. Parisi
21 St. Clements Avenue
Toronto, ON M4R 1G8

Tel. 416-483-4414
Website .... www.scs.on.ca

Employer Background: Founded in 1901, St. Clement's is a private school for girls offering classes from grade one to university entrance for 425 students. *New Positions Created (3):* Teacher, Geography; Teacher, Music; Administrative Assistant.

ST. FRANCIS XAVIER UNIVERSITY

Att: Human Resources Services
PO Box 5000
Antigonish, NS B2G 2W5

Tel. 902-867-2452
Fax 902-867-2177
Website .... www.stfx.ca

Employer Background: St. Francis Xavier University is a liberal arts university, with a student body of 4,100 and a staff of 500. *New Positions Created (3):* High School Liaison Officers (4); Manager of Recruitment and Admissions; Vice-President, Advancement.

ST. GEORGE'S SCHOOL

Att: Lee Laxton, Office Manager
4175 - 29th Avenue West
Vancouver, BC V6S 1V6

Tel. 604-224-1304
Fax 604-224-7066
Email .... llaxton@stgeorges.bc.ca
Website .... www.stgeorges.bc.ca

Employer Background: Founded in 1930, St. George's School is a university preparation school for grades 1 - 12, with an enrolment of 1,070 students. *New Positions Created (5):* Counsellor; Head of Department, Mathematics; Senior Academic Positions (3); Teacher, Drama; Teacher, Information Technology.

ST. JOHN'S REHABILITATION HOSPITAL

Att: Terry McMahon, Director HR
285 Cummer Avenue
Toronto, ON M2M 2G1

Tel. 416-226-6780
Fax 416-226-1598
Email .... careers@stjohnsrehab.com
Website .... www.stjohnsrehab.com

Employer Background: St. John's Rehabilitation Hospital provides quality short-term rehabilitation services to adolescent and adult populations on an outpatient and inpatient basis. *New Positions Created (22):* Occupational Therapists; Occupational Therapy Assistants; Registered Practical Nurses; Executive Assistant; Administrative Assistant; Clinical Nurse Specialist; Kinesiologist; Physiotherapist; Physiotherapists, Amputee / Cardiovascular Program; Registered Nurses; Speech-Language Pathologist; Chaplaincy Services Coordinator and Teaching Supervisor; Project Manager, Capital Development; Manager, Cardiac Prevention and Rehabilitation; Program Director, Ambulatory Care and Complex Musculoskeletal Programs; Corporate Planner; Occupational Therapists; Occupational Therapy Assistants; Social Worker, Amputee / Cardiovascular Program; Registered Nurses; Physical / Occupational Therapists, In-Patient / Out-Patient Programs; Physical / Occupational Therapists, Private Clinic.

ST. JOSEPH'S HEALTH CARE, PARKWOOD HOSPITAL SITE

Att: Human Resources Consultant
801 Commissioners Road East
London, ON N6C 5J1

Tel. 519-685-4292
Fax 519-685-4084
Website .... www.sjhc.london.on.ca

Employer Background: Parkwood Hospital is a regional rehabilitation institute affiliated with the University of Western Ontario. *New Positions Created (4):* Registered Nurses; Staff Chaplains; Physiotherapist; Registered Nurses.

ST. JOSEPH'S HEALTH CARE, ST. JOSEPH'S HOSPITAL SITE

Att: Human Resources
895 Richmond Street
London, ON N6C 3J1

Tel. 519-646-6100
Fax 519-646-6122
Email .... kim.fowler@sjhc.london.on.ca
Website .... www.sjhc.london.on.ca

Employer Background: St. Joseph's Health Care, London is a full-service, teaching and research hospital affiliated with the University of Western Ontario and Fanshawe College in London. *New Positions Created (3):* Director, Perinatal Program; Clinical Nurse Specialist / Program Coordinator, Osteoporosis; Clinical Pathway Facilitator, Ambulatory and Surgical Care.

ST. JOSEPH'S HEALTH CENTRE

Att: Human Resource Services
30 The Queensway
Toronto, ON M6R 1B5

Tel. 416-530-6460
Fax 416-530-6034
Email .... hrjob@stjoe.on.ca
Website .... www.sjhc.london.on.ca

Employer Background: Founded in 1921, St. Joseph's Health Centre is a community teaching hospital sponsored by the Catholic Health Corporation of Ontario and affiliated with the University of Toronto. *New Positions Created (24):* Administrative Director; Clinical Care Leader, ICU; Patient Care Manager, Cardiology / CCU; Patient Care Manager, Oncology / Palliative Care; Professional Practice Leaders; Registered Nurse, Emergency; Registered Nurses, ICU; Ultrasound Technologist; Education Coordinator, Mental Health; Patient Care Manager, Renal Therapy Centre; Manager, Diagnostic Imaging & Cardio-Respiratory Services; Director of Professional Practice and Chief Nursing Officer; Nurse Educator, Emergency Department; Nurse Practitioner, Pre-Admission Centre; Construction Project Manager; Maintenance Positions (2); Manager, Protection Services and Life Safety; Supervisor, Engineering Services; Human Resources Employment Coordinators; Allied Health Professionals; Patient Care Managers (3); Registered Nurses; Utilization Manager; Employment Coordinators (3).

ST. JOSEPH'S HEALTHCARE HAMILTON

Att: Human Resources
50 Charlton Avenue East
Hamilton, ON L8N 4A6

Tel. 905-522-1155
Fax 905-521-6027
Email .... recruit@stjosham.on.ca
Website .... www.stjosham.on.ca

Employer Background: St. Joseph's Healthcare Hamilton is a multi-site teaching hospital and academic health science centre affiliated with McMaster University and Mohawk College. *New Positions Created (48):* Social Worker; Vice-President, Medical Services and Clinical Programs; Nurse Manager, Maternal Child Program; Director, Health Information Services; Educator, Kidney & Urinary Program; Educator, Perioperative; Health Records Technician; Manager, Health Records; Mental Health Workers, Crisis Outreach & Support Team (2); Non-Registered Nephrology Technician; Operations Coordinator, Sterile Room; Pharmacy Technicians (2); Technical Specialist, Operations - Transfusion Medicine; Perioperative Nurse; Pharmacists; Administrative Coordinator; Clinical Coordinator / Instructor; Occupational Therapist; Pharmacotherapy Specialist; Physiotherapists (2); Pulmonary Function Technologist; Respiratory Care Practitioners (2); Secretary I; Secretary, Volunteer and Pastoral Services; Speech Language Pathologist; Staff Pharmacist; Redevelopment Administrative Coordinator; Registered Nurses; Recreational Therapist, Geriatric Services; Clinical Nurse Specialist, Palliative Care; Diagnostic Medical Sonographer; Social Worker; Nurse Manager, Chest / Head & Neck Program; Nurse Practitioner, Chest / Head & Neck Program; Educator, Emergency Services; Occupational Health and Safety Coordinator; Administrative Director; Physiotherapists; Mental Health Worker; Educator, Kidney and Urinary Program; Registered Nurses; Administrative Director; Pharmacist, Outpatient Pharmacy; Respiratory Care Practitioners; Director, Financial Services; Social Worker; Various Registered Nursing Positions; Acute Care Nurse Practitioner.

ST. JOSEPH'S HEALTHCARE HAMILTON, CENTRE FOR MOUNTAIN HEALTH SERVICES
Att: Human Resources
100 - 5th Street West, Box 585
Hamilton, ON L8N 3K7
Fax 905-381-5609
Email .... recruit@stjosham.on.ca
Website .... www.stjosham.on.ca
Employer Background: St. Joseph's Healthcare Hamilton is a 600-bed, acute care, academic health centre affiliated with the Faculty of Health Sciences at McMaster University and Mohawk College. *New Positions Created (5):* Coordinator, Mental Health Services; Manager, Inpatient Services; Team Coordinator, Assertive Community Treatment; Case Manager; Psychogeriatric Consulting Resource Position.

ST. JOSEPH'S VILLA
Att: Human Resources
56 Governor's Road
Dundas, ON L9H 5G7
Tel. 905-627-3541
Fax 905-627-2012
Email .... lduncan@sjv.on.ca
Website .... www.sjv.on.ca
Employer Background: St. Joseph's Villa is a fully-accredited 378-bed long-term care facility for the aged. *New Positions Created (4):* Human Resources Specialist; Finance Secretary; Registered Nurses; Therapeutic Recreationists (2).

ST. LAWRENCE COLLEGE
Att: Human Resources
King & Portsmouth Avenue, PO Box 6000
Kingston, ON K7L 5A6
Tel. 613-544-5532
Fax 613-544-4902
Email .... employ@sl.on.ca
Website .... www.sl.on.ca
Employer Background: Founded in 1967, St. Lawrence College is a community college offering diploma and certificate programs from 3 campuses in Kingston, Brockville and Cornwall. *New Positions Created (4):* Professor, Human Resources; Professor, Child and Youth Worker Program; Professor, Electronics Engineering Technology; Academic Director, School of Engineering, Technology and Trades.

ST. LAWRENCE PARKS COMMISSION
Att: Human Resources
RR #1
Morrisburg, ON K0C 1X0
Tel. 613-543-3704
Fax 613-543-2847
Website .... www.parks.on.ca
Employer Background: SLPC is an agency of the Ontario Ministry of Tourism, Culture and Recreation, and manages recreational areas from Kingston to near the Quebec border. *New Positions Created (2):* Recreational Programming Officer; Supervisor, Visitor Services, Retail and Special Events.

ST. LAWRENCE SEAWAY MANAGEMENT CORPORATION, THE
Att: Human Resources Services
508 Glendale Avenue, PO Box 370
St. Catharines, ON L2R 6V8
Tel. 905-641-1932
Fax 905-641-4554
Website .... www.greatlakes-seaway.com
Employer Background: The St. Lawrence Seaway Management Corporation is a non-profit corporation responsible for the safe and efficient movement of marine traffic through Canadian seaway facilities. *New Positions Created (3):* Maintenance Analyst; Electronics Technician; Mechanical Technical Officer.

ST. MARY'S GENERAL HOSPITAL
Att: Jack Borman, HR Director
911 Queen's Boulevard
Kitchener, ON N2M 1B2
Tel. 519-749-6556
Fax 519-749-6766
Email .... jborman@stmaryshosp.on.ca
Website .... www.stmaryshosp.on.ca
Employer Background: St. Mary's General Hospital, a member of St. Joseph's Health Care System, is a fully-accredited 168-bed facility. *New Positions Created (12):* Program Manager, Musculoskeletal / Rehabilitation; Care Path & Research Coordinator; Program Manager; Health Records Technicians; Medical Transcriptionists; Manager, Cardiac Prevention & Rehabilitation; Program Director; Program Managers; Corporate Care Path & Research Coordinator; Health Records Technicians; Utilization and Quality Management Specialist; Clinical Nurse Educator.

ST. MARY'S HOSPITAL CENTER
Att: Human Resources Department
3830 Lacombe Avenue
Montréal, QC H3T 1M5
Tel. 514-345-3390
Fax 514-734-2633
Website .... www.smhc.qc.ca
Employer Background: St. Mary's Hospital Center is a community hospital affiliated with McGill University. *New Positions Created (3):* Clinical Nurse Specialist; Clinical Educator; Nurse.

ST. MARYS PAPER LTD.
Att: Human Resources Department
75 Huron Street
Sault Ste. Marie, ON P6A 5P4
Tel. 705-942-6070
Fax 705-541-2440
Email .... rasla_r@stmarys-paper.com
Website .... www.stmarys-paper.com
Employer Background: St. Marys Paper Ltd. operates a three-machine super-calendered paper mill producing over 660 tons per day and employs 400 people. *New Positions Created (2):* Steam Plant Superintendent; Technical Assistant - No. 5 Paper Machine.

ST. MICHAEL'S HOSPITAL
Att: Human Resources Department
30 Bond Street
Toronto, ON M5B 1W8
Tel. 416-867-7460
Fax 416-867-7488
Email .... resume@smh.toronto.on.ca
Website .... www.smh.toronto.on.ca
Employer Background: St. Michael's Hospital, a Catholic teaching hospital affiliated with the University of Toronto, specializes in six clinical areas: diabetes comprehensive care; heart and vascular disease; inner city health; minimal access therapeutics and diseases of the digestive system; neurology-musculoskeletal; and trauma and neurosurgery. *New Positions Created (35):* Various Healthcare Positions; Clinical Specialist, Occupational Therapy; Physiotherapists (7); Social Worker, Trauma & Neurosurgery Program; Clinical Educator; Clinical Nurse Specialist / Nurse Practitioner; Manager, Blood Bank and Haematology; Nuclear Medicine Technologist; Pathology Technologist; Physiotherapists; Registered Nurses, Mental Health Service; Registered Nurses, Psychiatry; Team Leader, Medical Imaging Informatics; Technical Specialists (2); Ultrasonographer; Manager, Health Information Security; Healthcare Positions; Acute Care Nurse Practitioners and Clinical Nurse Specialists; Critical Care Nurses; Health Laboratory Positions; Nurse Managers; Registered Nurses; Coordinator, Community Outreach; Crisis Worker, Crisis Intervention Team; Registered Nurse, CONTACT Mental Health Outreach Service; Registered Nurse, Psychiatry / In-Patient Care; Coding and Abstracting Technician; Dialysis Technologist, Haemodidalysis Unit; Registered Nurse, Medical Imaging; Registered Respiratory Care Practitioner; Team Leader, Nuclear Medicine; Technologist - CT / Angiography; Technologists, MRI and Research; Clinical Leader / Manager, Central Processing; Clinical Leader / Manager, Pre-Admission, Day Surgery and Post-Anaesthetic Care.

ST. MICHAELS UNIVERSITY SCHOOL
Att: Robert Snowden
3400 Richmond Road
Victoria, BC V8P 4P5
Tel. 250-592-2411
Fax 250-592-2812
Website .... www.smus.bc.ca
Employer Background: St. Michaels University School is a co-educational, independent, day and boarding school of 850 students, from kindergarten to grade 12. *New Positions Created (2):* Teacher, Senior English; Teacher, Senior Physics.

ST. PAUL JOURNAL
Att: Clare Gauvreau, Publisher
4813 - 50th Avenue, Box 159
St. Paul, AB T0A 3A0
Tel. 780-645-3342
Fax 780-645-2346
Email ...... cgauvreau@stpaul.greatwest.ca
Website .... www.spjournal.com
Employer Background: St. Paul Journal is a weekly newspaper in northeastern Alberta. *New Positions Created (2):* Editor; Sports / General News Reporter.

ST. PAUL'S HOSPITAL, DEPARTMENTS OF MEDICINE AND FAMILY MEDICINE

Att: Ramona Gomes
1081 Burrard Street, Suite 667
Vancouver, BC V6Z 1Y6

Fax 604-806-8527
Website .... www.providencehealthcare.org

Employer Background: St. Paul's Hospital, part of Providence Health Care, is an academic and research hospital, providing quaternary, tertiary and secondary care services. *New Positions Created (2):* Clinical Associates, HIV / AIDS Care; Medical Secretary.

ST. PAUL'S L'AMOREAUX SENIORS' CENTRE

Att: Human Resources Coordinator
3333 Finch Avenue East
Toronto, ON M1W 2R9

Tel. 416-493-3333
Fax 416-493-3391
Email .... loletta@stpaulscentre.com
Website .... www.stpaulscentre.com

Employer Background: St. Paul's L'Amoreaux Seniors' Centre is a multicultural centre providing quality housing, home support, health and wellness and recreation services. *New Positions Created (2):* Greek Language Case Manager / Social Worker; Accounting Manager.

ST. PETER'S HEALTH SERVICES

Att: Mrs. V. Baird
88 Maplewood Avenue
Hamilton, ON L8M 1W9

Tel. 905-549-6525
Fax 905-549-4237
Website ... www.stpetershealthsystem.com

Employer Background: St. Peter's Health Services provides care for older adults and chronically ill individuals. *New Positions Created (5):* Nurse Manager; Licensed Maintenance Tradesperson; Speech Language Pathologist; Physiotherapist; Clinical Leader, Nursing.

STACKPOLE LIMITED, AUTOMOTIVE GEAR DIVISION

Att: Andrea DeMichele
2430 Royal Windsor Drive
Mississauga, ON L5J 1K7

Tel. 905-822-6015
Fax 905-855-4591
Website .... www.stackpole.on.ca

Employer Background: Stackpole Limited is a leading manufacturer and assembler of technologically-advanced powder metal components and assemblies for the North American automotive industry. *New Positions Created (4):* Thermal Process Specialist; Industrial Electrician; Industrial Millwright; Quality Assurance Manager.

STACKPOLE LTD., ENGINEERED PRODUCTS DIVISION

Att: Human Resources
2400 Royal Windsor Drive
Mississauga, ON L5J 1K7

Tel. 905-403-0550
Fax 905-403-0557
Email .... jfretz@stackpole.on.ca
Website .... www.stackpole.on.ca

Employer Background: Stackpole Ltd., Engineered Products Division designs, develops and manufactures OEM automotive pumps and pump components. *New Positions Created (8):* Automation / Tool Designer; Development Project Manager; Manufacturing Engineering Technician; Manufacturing Project Engineer / Manager; Manufacturing Systems Technician; Product Engineer; Automation / Tool Designer; Manufacturing Systems Technician.

STACKTECK SYSTEMS INC.

Att: Human Resources
27 Leading Road
Toronto, ON M1H 2V5

Tel. 416-749-0880
Fax 416-749-8206
Website .... www.tradesco.com

Employer Background: StackTeck Systems Inc. is one of the world's largest mould manufacturers. *New Positions Created (6):* EDM Team Leader; Project Engineer; Project Manager; Estimator; Mould Designer; Quality Technician.

STANDARD LIFE ASSURANCE COMPANY, THE

Att: Human Resources Department
1245 Sherbrooke Street West
Montréal, QC H3G 1G3

Tel. 514-499-8855
Email .... recruitment@standardlife.ca
Website .... www.standardlife.ca

Employer Background: The Standard Life Assurance Company specializes in life insurance and financial services. *New Positions Created (50):* Analyst, Planning; Consultant, Sales Support; Corporate Auditor; Customer Service Representative, Customer Service Centre; Money Market Assistant; Programmer / Analyst; Rehabilitation Specialist; Senior Building Operator, Con-Vista; Specialist, Trust and Securities Administration; Fund Administrator; Management Associate, Print Production; Marketing Specialist, Standard Life Investments; Planning Analyst, Sales; Programmer / Analyst, Information Technology; Specialist, Real Estate Accounting; Systems Analyst; Associate, Life New Business; Associate, Operations Support; Customer Service Representative (Group Savings and Retirement); Manager, Architecture and Planning; Senior Administrative Assistant; Group Underwriter; Junior Commercial Mortgage Negotiator / Appraiser; Legal Counsel; Management Associate, Group Savings and Retirement; Administrative Assistant, Building; Commercial Mortgage Negotiator / Appraiser; Consultant, Employee Communications; Coordinator, Public Relations; Customer Service Representative (Group Savings & Retirement); Paralegal Lease Specialist; Programmer / Analyst; Security Administrator; Senior Building Operator; Analyst, Planning; Consultant, Internet Branding; Consultant, Sales Support; Disability Claims Examiner; Rehabilitation Specialist; Building Operator; Corporate Auditor; Corporate IT Auditor; Customer Service Representatives; Service Representative; Commercial Mortgage Negotiator / Appraiser; Analyst, Financial Reporting; Associate, Financial Controls; Consultant, Portfolio Strategy; Help Desk Analyst; Underwriter, Insurance.

STANDARD PAPER BOX

Att: Human Resources Manager
1065 Kamato Road
Mississauga, ON L4W 2L3

Tel. 905-625-7420
Fax 905-625-9933

Employer Background: Standard Paper Box supplies and prints corrugated containers, POP displays and set-up boxes enhanced by high-quality graphics using flexographic, lithographic and silkscreen printing processes. *New Positions Created (2):* Printing Plates Buyer; Sales Representative.

STANDARD PAPER BOX

Att: Human Resources Manager
340 University Avenue, PO Box 217
Belleville, ON K8N 4Y8

Tel. 613-968-3581
Fax 613-966-0397

Employer Background: Standard Paper Box supplies and prints corrugated containers, POP displays and set-up boxes, enhanced by high-quality graphics using flexographics and lithographic printing processes. *New Positions Created (2):* Maintenance Electrician; Maintenance Mechanic.

STANDARD & POOR'S

Att: Manager, Human Resources
130 King St. W., Exchange Tower
27th Floor, PO Box 486
Toronto, ON M5X 1E5

Tel. 416-364-8580
Fax 416-364-5336
Email .... sp_recruitmentcanada@
.... standardandpoors.com
Website .... www.standardandpoors.com

Employer Background: Standard & Poor's is an international financial service provider delivering products and services to the global financial community. *New Positions Created (3):* Copy Editor; Financial Analyst; Copy Editor.

STANDARDS COUNCIL OF CANADA

Att: Human Resources Manager
270 Albert Street, Suite 200
Ottawa, ON K1P 6N7

Tel. 613-238-3222
Fax 613-569-7808
Email .... info@scc.ca
Website .... www.scc.ca

Employer Background: SCC is a federal Crown corporation with a mandate to promote efficient and effective standardization. *New Positions Created (6):* Administrative Officer, Environmental & Quality Management Systems (E&QMS); Policy Analyst; Program Officer, International Organization for Standardization; Senior Policy Analyst; Senior Program Officer, Laboratories; Program Officer, Laboratories.

STANDENS LIMITED
Att: Human Resources
1222 - 58th Ave. SE, PO Box 67, Station T
Calgary, AB T2H 2G7
Tel. 403-258-7000
Fax 403-258-7808
Email .... employment@standens.com
Website .... www.standens.com
Employer Background: Established in 1924,
Standens Limited manufactures leaf springs
and other industrial, automotive and agri-
cultural machinery parts. *New Positions
Created (6):* Facilities Coordinator; Interme-
diate Accounts Receivable Representative;
Manufacturing Engineer; Quality / Manu-
facturing Engineer; Intermediate Accounts
Receivable Rep; Occupational Health Nurse.

STANLEY DOOR SYSTEMS
Att: Human Resources
10 Walker Drive
Brampton, ON L6T 4H6
Fax 905-791-9604
Email .... cearle@stanleyworks.com
Website .... www.stanleyworks.com
Employer Background: Stanley Door Sys-
tems, a division of Stanley Works, manufac-
tures closet doors and hardware. *New Posi-
tions Created (3):* Engineering Technician;
Maintenance Mechanic; Operators, Die
Punch Press Machines.

STANPAC INC.
Att: Erika Zelenyt
Spring Creek Road, RR 3
Smithville, ON L0R 2A0
Tel. 905-957-3326
Fax 905-957-3616
Email .... info@stanpacnet.com
Website .... www.stanpacnet.com
Employer Background: Stanpac Inc. manu-
factures packaging products and systems for
the food and dairy industries. *New Positions
Created (2):* Customer Service Representa-
tive; Graphic Artist.

STANTEC CONSULTING LTD.
Att: Paul Blanchard
1985 West Broadway, Suite 100
Vancouver, BC V6J 4Y3
Tel. 604-731-4921
Fax 604-742-8080
Email .... pblanchard@stantec.com
Website .... www.stantec.com
Employer Background: Established in 1954,
Stantec Consulting Ltd. is a professional con-
sulting firm offering a range of planning,
engineering, technical and design services
to public and private sector clients. *New
Positions Created (7):* Intermediate Electri-
cal Technologist / Engineer, Power Systems
Design; Intermediate Electrical Technolo-
gist / Engineer; Municipal and Drainage
Engineers; Wastewater Treatment Engineers
; Water Treatment Engineers; Marketing
Coordinator; Engineer / Junior Designer.

STANTEC CONSULTING LTD.
Att: Reno Fiorante
7445 - 132 Street, Suite 1007
Surrey, BC V3W 1J8

Tel. 604-597-0422
Fax 604-591-1856
Email .... surrey@stantec.com
Website .... www.stantec.com
Employer Background: Established in 1954,
Stantec Consulting Ltd. is a professional con-
sulting firm offering a range of planning,
engineering, technical and design services
to public and private sector clients. *New
Positions Created (3):* Municipal and Drain-
age Engineers; Wastewater Treatment Engi-
neers; Water Treatment Engineers.

STANTEC CONSULTING LTD.
Att: Kathy Greenough, Human Resources
1122 - 4th Street SW, Suite 200
Calgary, AB T2R 1M1
Tel. 403-716-8000
Fax 403-716-8059
Email .... kgreenough@stantech.com
Website .... www.stantec.com
Employer Background: Established in 1954,
Stantec Consulting Ltd. is a professional con-
sulting firm, offering a range of planning,
engineering, technical and design services
to public and private sector clients. *New
Positions Created (19):* Junior / Intermedi-
ate CAD Technician; Landscape Architec-
tural Technologist; Resident Inspectors;
Rodmen; Intermediate / Sr Architectural
Technologist; Sr / Intermediate Landscape
Architectural Technologist; CAD Technolo-
gist; Intermediate Land Development Resi-
dent Field Supervisors; Graphic Designer,
Landscape Architecture; Senior Landscape
Architect; Sr Land Development Engineer;
Environmental Engineer, Remediation;
Electrical Inspector; Intermediate Drafts-
person; Intermediate Engineering Tech-
nologist; Junior Landscape Architectural
Technologist; Sr / Intermediate Land Devel-
opment Engineer; Sr Project Manager, Solid
Waste Mgmnt; Survey Draftsperson.

STANTEC CONSULTING LTD.
Att: Chris Van Gerwen, PEng
871 Victoria Street North
Kitchener, ON N2B 3S4
Tel. 519-579-4410
Fax 519-579-6733
Email .... cvangerwen@stantec.com
Website .... www.stantec.com
Employer Background: Established in 1954,
Stantec Consulting Ltd. is a professional con-
sulting firm, offering a range of planning,
engineering, technical and design services
to public and private sector clients. *New
Positions Created (9):* Mechanical & Electri-
cal Design Technician / Technologists; Me-
chanical & Electrical Project Engineers; IT
Professional, Support Desk; Data Manage-
ment / GIS Specialist; Intermediate
Hydrogeologist / Environmental Engineer;
Junior Hydrogeologist / Environmental
Technician; Senior Hydrogeologist,
Groundwater Resource Management; CAD
Technologist; PC Manager.

STANTEC CONSULTING LTD.
Att: Chris Overholt, Senior Associate
1400 Rymal Road
Hamilton, ON L8W 3N9

Tel. 905-385-3234
Fax 905-385-3534
Email .... coverholt@stantec.com
Website .... www.stantec.com
Employer Background: Established in 1954,
Stantec Consulting Ltd. is a professional con-
sulting firm, offering a range of planning,
engineering, technical and design services
to public and private sector clients. *New
Positions Created (2):* Intermediate Land
Development Engineer / Technologist; Sen-
ior Electrical Engineer.

STANTEC CONSULTING LTD.
Att: Richard Waite,
Manager, Environmental
7070 Mississauga Road, Suite 160
Mississauga, ON L5N 7G2
Tel. 905-858-4424
Fax 905-858-4426
Email .... rwaite@stantec.com
Website .... www.stantec.com
Employer Background: Established in 1954,
Stantec Consulting Ltd. is a professional con-
sulting firm, offering a range of planning,
engineering, technical and design services
to public and private sector clients. *New
Positions Created (2):* Project Engineer; Sen-
ior Project Manager.

STANTEC CONSULTING LTD.
Att: Duane Aubie, Principal, Urban Land
1700 Langstaff Road, Suite 2002
Concord, ON L4K 3S3
Tel. 905-761-6100
Fax 905-761-6101
Email .... daubie@stantec.com
Website .... www.stantec.com
Employer Background: Established in 1954,
Stantec Consulting Ltd. is a professional con-
sulting firm, offering a range of planning,
engineering, technical and design services
to public and private sector clients. *New
Positions Created (2):* Land Development
Project Manager; Land Development Tech-
nologist / Draftsperson.

STANTEC CONSULTING LTD.
Att: Marc Rivard, PEng
1505 Laperriere Avenue, 4th Floor
Ottawa, ON K1Z 7T1
Tel. 613-722-4420
Fax 613-722-2799
Email .... mrivard@stantec.com
Website .... www.stantec.com
Employer Background: Established in 1954,
Stantec is a professional consulting firm of-
fering a range of planning, engineering,
technical and design services to public and
private sector clients. *New Positions Created
(2):* Senior Electrical Engineer; Senior Me-
chanical Engineer.

STANTEC GEOMATICS LTD.
Att: Lisa McLaughlin
10160 - 112th Street
Edmonton, AB T5K 2L6
Tel. 780-917-7000
Fax 780-917-7425
Email .... lmclaughlin@stantec.com
Website .... www.stantec.com

Employer Background: Established in 1954, Stantec Geomatics Ltd. is a professional consulting firm, offering a range of planning, engineering, technical and design services to public and private sector clients. *New Positions Created (25):* CAD Operators / Survey Technicians & Technologists; Corporate Legal Assistant; Senior Electrical Engineer / Senior Electrical Project Manager; Project Manager, Environmental Assessments; Senior Project Managers; Business Development Coordinator; Compensation and Benefits Assistant; Corporate Financial Accountant; Intermediate Hydrogeologist; Regional Controller, Canada West; Intermediate Bridge Engineering Technologist; Senior Bridge Engineering Technologist; Senior / Intermediate Structural Engineering Technologist; Support Analyst; Systems Administrator; Application Developer; Human Resources Advisor; Highway / Roadway Engineers and Technologists; Transportation Engineers and Technologists; Intermediate Structural Engineer; Junior Engineer / Intermediate Designer, Electrical Power and Control; Junior Engineer / Intermediate Designer, Instrumentation; Senior Pipeline Specialist / Mechanical Engineer; Senior Power Specialist / Mechanical Engineer; Chief Technology Officer.

STANTON REGIONAL HEALTH BOARD
Att: HR Department, Employee Services
PO Box 10
Yellowknife, NT X1A 2N1
Tel. 867-669-4113
Fax 867-669-4209
Email ... srh_human_resources@gov.nt.ca
Website .... www.gov.nt.ca
Employer Background: Stanton Regional Health Board provides acute and long-term care to residents of the western Northwest Territories. *New Positions Created (3):* Telehealth Coordinator; Coordinator, Planning; Manager, Rehabilitation Services.

STAPLES BUSINESS DEPOT LTD.
Att: Wally Beaupre
4265 Lougheed Highway
Burnaby, BC V5C 3Y6
Tel. 604-320-6800
Fax 604-298-3481
Email .... careers@staples.ca
Website .... www.staples.ca
Employer Background: Staples Business Depot Ltd. is one of Canada's fastest-growing retailers of office supplies, operating over 180 locations nationwide. *New Positions Created (2):* Retail Positions; Retail Mgrs.

STAPLES BUSINESS DEPOT LTD.
Att: Ellen Sachs, Human Resources
30 Centurian Drive, Suite 106
Markham, ON L3R 8B9
Tel. 905-513-6116
Fax 905-513-7194
Email .... corpjobs@busdep.com
Website .... www.businessdepot.com
Employer Background: Staples Business Depot Ltd. is one of Canada's fastest-growing retailers of office supplies, operating over

180 locations nationwide. *New Positions Created (50):* Category Specialist; Help Desk Team Leader; Manager, Application Development; Receptionist; HRIS Specialist; Advertising Production Manager; Public Relations Manager; Management Position; Outside Sales Representative; Regional Sales Manager; Corporate Customer Service Representative; Treasury Analyst; HR Assistant; Manager, Application Development; Senior Programming Analyst; Category Manager; Category Specialist; Loss Prevention Administrative Assistant; Operations Administrative Assistant; Assistant Managers; General Ledger Analyst; Help Desk Analyst; Store System Support Associate; Catalogue Marketing Specialist; Dot.Com Marketing Specialist; Marketing Manager; Merchandising Manager; Help Desk Team Leader; Inventory Control Analyst; Manager, Technical Services; Marketing Coordinator; Production Artist; Repair and Maintenance Coordinator; Telecom Support Analyst; Recruiter; Retail Store Management Positions; Accounts Payable Trade Analyst; Help Desk Team Leader; Import Specialist; Payroll Analyst; Category Specialist; Lease Administration Assistant; Various Managerial Positions; Broadcast Media Buyer; Category Specialist; Compensation Analyst; Human Resources Generalist; Inventory Control Analyst; Senior Network Team Leader; Telecom Support Analyst.

STAR DATA SYSTEMS INC.
Att: Organization and
Professional Development
7030 Woodbine Avenue, 8th Floor
Markham, ON L3R 1A2
Tel. 905-479-7827
Fax 905-479-0736
Email .... resumes@stardata.ca
Website .... www.stardata.com
Employer Background: Star Data Systems Inc. provides high-tech delivery of online, real-time financial information systems, solutions and data to over 16,000 wealth managers in Canada. *New Positions Created (3):* Product Analyst; Service Delivery Manager; Programmer Analysts, Unix / C++ or HTML / Java.

STARLINE INDUSTRIES
Att: Human Resources Department
37 Staffern Drive
Concord, ON L4K 2X2
Fax 905-738-1410
Website .... www.starline.com
Employer Background: Starline Industries is a leading manufacturer of promotional products across North America. *New Positions Created (2):* Regional Sales Representative; Building Maintenance Technician.

STARTECH BUSINESS SYSTEMS LTD.
Att: Frank Faria
1725 - 30th Avenue NE, Suite 27
Calgary, AB T2E 7P6
Tel. 403-291-5507
Fax 403-291-0736
Email .... sales@startech.ab.ca
Website .... www.startech.ab.ca

Employer Background: Established in 1986, Startech Business Systems Ltd. is an information systems company, with 7 employees. *New Positions Created (2):* Account Manager; Systems Engineer.

STATE FARM INSURANCE COMPANIES
Att: Nicole Harrison
100 Consilium Place, Suite 102
Toronto, ON M1H 3G9
Tel. 416-290-4100
Fax 416-290-4716
Email ..... jobopps.canada@statefarm.com
Website .... www.statefarm.com
Employer Background: State Farm Insurance Companies provides automobile, life and homeowner's insurance. *New Positions Created (7):* Agency Field Consultant / Mutual Funds Compliance Officer; Claim Service Receptionist; Injury Claim Trainer; Claim Service Representative; Mutual Fund Administrator; Claim Service Representative; Estimator, Automobile Damage.

STATE INDUSTRIAL PRODUCTS
Att: Bob Elgin, Vice-President Canada
1745 Meyerside Drive, Unit 1
Mississauga, ON L5T 1C6
Tel. 905-670-4669
Fax 905-670-7202
Website .... www.stateindustrial.com
Employer Background: State Industrial Products provides a complete line of industrial maintenance products for the hospitality, manufacturing, institutional, automotive, construction and transportation industries. *New Positions Created (3):* Sales Manager; District Manager; Industrial Sales Representative.

STATE STREET CANADA
Att: Human Resources
100 King Street West, Suite 3100
Toronto, ON M5X 1A9
Tel. 416-956-2400
Fax 416-594-4001
Email .... hr-canada@statestreet.com
Website .... www.statestreet.com
Employer Background: State Street Canada is a subsidiary of State Street Corporation, a leading provider of financial services for institutional investors, with over $5.8 trillion in assets under custody. *New Positions Created (5):* Financial Positions; Financial Positions; Income and Tax Administrators; Various Finance Positions; Various Financial Positions.

STATE STREET CANADA
Att: Human Resources Manager
770 Sherbrooke Street West, Suite 1100
Montréal, QC H3A 1G1
Tel. 514-282-2400
Fax 514-282-2498
Website .... www.statestreet.com
Employer Background: State Street Canada is a subsidiary of State Street Corporation, a leading provider of financial services for institutional investors, with over $5.8 tril-

lion in assets under custody. *New Positions Created (4):* Corporate Action Accountant; Investment Accountants; Senior Investment Accountants; Investment Administrator.

STATESMAN CORPORATION
Att: Office Manager
7370 Sierra Morena Boulevard SW
Calgary, AB T3H 4H9
Tel. 403-256-4151
Fax 403-256-6100
Website .... www.statesmancorporation.com
Employer Background: Statesman Corporation is a builder-developer and has marketed homes for over 6,000 residents. *New Positions Created (2):* Sales Associate; Design Consultant.

STATICON LTD.
Att: Personnel Manager
390 Tapscott Road, Unit 5
Toronto, ON M1B 2Y9
Tel. 416-291-3723
Fax 416-291-3871
Email .... sales@staticon.ca
Website .... www.staticon.ca
Employer Background: Established in 1964, Staticon Ltd. specializes in the design, manufacture and application of DC and AC power equipment and has 80 employees. *New Positions Created (3):* Sales Engineer; Electrical Engineer; Magnetics Design Engineer.

STEEL ART SIGNS CORP.
Att: Operations Manager
37 Esna Park Drive
Markham, ON L3R 1C9
Tel. 905-474-1678
Fax 905-474-0976
Website .... www.steelart.com
Employer Background: Founded in 1949, Steel Art Signs Corp. manufactures custom and corporate signs. *New Positions Created (3):* Permit / Project Coordinator; Senior Accountant; Draftsperson (2).

STEELCASE CANADA LTD.
Att: Human Resources
1 Steelcase Road West
Markham, ON L3R 0T3
Tel. 905-475-6333
Fax 905-475-6073
Website .... www.steelcase.com
Employer Background: Steelcase is a leading designer and manufacturer of high-performance work environments. *New Positions Created (4):* Millwright; Network Analyst; Product Engineer; Production Workers.

STEEPLEJACK SERVICES GROUP
Att: Human Resources Manager
8925 - 62nd Avenue
Edmonton, AB T6E 5L2
Tel. 780-465-9016
Fax 780-466-8584
Email .... info@steeplejack.ca
Website .... www.steeplejack.ca
Employer Background: Steeplejack Services Group provides industrial and commercial

scaffolding, industrial maintenance and general plant maintenance. *New Positions Created (3):* Accounting Manager; Manager, Industrial Insulation Division; Controller.

STEEVES & ROZEMA ENTERPRISES LTD.
Att: Human Resources Manager
265 North Front Street, Suite 200
Sarnia, ON N7T 7X1
Tel. 519-344-8829
Fax 519-344-8518
Email .... lisa_brush@snr.on.ca
Website .... www.snr.on.ca
Employer Background: Steeves & Rozema Enterprises Ltd. is a fully-integrated real estate company involved in residential, commercial and healthcare properties. *New Positions Created (4):* Director, Resident Care; Division Mgr, Long Term Care Positions; Registered Nurses; Senior Property Mgr.

STELLATE SYSTEMS
Att: Human Resources Manager
345 Victoria Avenue, Suite 300
Westmount, QC H3Z 2N2
Tel. 514-486-1306
Fax 514-486-0694
Email .... hr@stellate.com
Website .... www.stellate.com
Employer Background: Stellate Systems develops and manufactures medical software and integrated systems for the recording and analysis of brain waves. *New Positions Created (3):* Analyst Programmer; Electrical or Computer Engineer; Salesperson.

STERIS CANADA INC.
Att: Human Resources
6280 Northwest Drive
Mississauga, ON L4V 1J7
Tel. 905-677-0863
Fax 905-677-1886
Website .... www.steris.com
Employer Background: Steris Canada Inc. provides infection prevention, contamination control and surgical support systems and services to healthcare, scientific research and industrial customers worldwide. *New Positions Created (2):* Field Service Technician; Field Service Technician.

STERLING HALL SCHOOL, THE
Att: Director of Academics
99 Cartwright Avenue
Toronto, ON M6A 1V4
Tel. 416-785-3410
Fax 416-785-6616
Website .... www.sterlinghall.com
Employer Background: Founded in 1987, The Sterling Hall School is an independent school for boys from junior kindergarten to grade 8. *New Positions Created (2):* Grade 8 Homeroom Teacher; Teachers.

STERLING HOMES
Att: Design Manager
5709 - 2nd Street SE, Suite 200
Calgary, AB T2H 2W4
Tel. 403-253-7476

Fax 403-212-6305
Website .... www.sterlinghomes.ab.ca
Employer Background: Sterling Homes, one of Alberta's largest home builders, has been building homes in the Calgary area for three decades. *New Positions Created (2):* Architectural Technologists; Sales Professionals.

STEWART TITLE
GUARANTY COMPANY
Att: Personnel
200 Bay St., Royal Bank Plaza
Suite 2200, North Tower
Toronto, ON M5J 2J2
Tel. 416-307-3300
Fax 416-307-3305
Email .... rcoburn@stewart.com
Website .... www.stewart.com
Employer Background: Established in 1893 in the USA, Stewart Title Guaranty Company provides title insurance and real estate-related services with over 5,000 offices worldwide. *New Positions Created (3):* Real Estate Lawyer; Marketing & Underwriting; Real Estate Lawyer; Marketing & Sales Manager.

STEWART, WEIR & CO. LTD.
Att: Wayne Thom, PEng
11405 - 163 Street
Edmonton, AB T5M 3Y3
Tel. 780-451-6465
Fax 780-452-2316
Email .... swcl@swg.ca
Website .... www.swg.ca
Employer Background: Stewart, Weir & Co. Ltd. is an engineering and surveying company providing a wide range of services to the public and private sectors throughout western Canada. *New Positions Created (5):* Central Laboratory Supervisor; Legal & Engineering Survey Party Chiefs; Resident Inspector; Senior CAD Operator; Senior Municipal Design Engineer.

STIKEMAN ELLIOT
Att: Manager, Human Resources
666 Burrard Street, Suite 1700, Park Place
Vancouver, BC V6C 2X8
Tel. 604-631-1300
Fax 604-681-1825
Email .... hpez@van.stikeman.com
Website .... www.van.stikeman.com
Employer Background: Founded in 1952, Stikeman Elliott is a leading Canadian business law firm, with over 300 lawyers in offices across Canada and around the world. *New Positions Created (2):* Legal Assistant, I-II Securities; Senior Real Estate Secretary.

STIKEMAN ELLIOTT
Att: Director of Administration
888 - 3rd Street West
4300 Bankers Hall West
Calgary, AB T2P 5C5
Tel. 403-266-9000
Fax 403-266-9034
Website .... www.stikeman.com
Employer Background: Founded in 1952, Stikeman Elliott is a leading Canadian business law firm, with over 300 lawyers in of-

fices across Canada and around the world. *New Positions Created (3):* Legal Assistant; Commercial Real Estate Associates; Corporate / Commercial Associates.

STIKEMAN ELLIOTT
Att: Cathy Bleakley
199 Bay Street
Suite 5300, Commerce Court West
Toronto, ON M5L 1B9
Tel. 416-869-5203
Fax 416-947-0866
Email .... cbleakley@tor.stikeman.com
Website .... www.stikeman.com
Employer Background: Founded in 1952, Stikeman Elliott is a leading Canadian business law firm, with over 300 lawyers in offices across Canada and around the world. *New Positions Created (14):* Purchasing Coordinator; Employment and Labour Associate; Human Resources Trainer; Intermediate / Senior Corporate Law Clerks (2); Junior Corporate Securities Law Clerk; Legal Project Manager; Financial Analyst; Legal Secretaries; Marketing Relationship Coordinator; Corporate / Commercial Associates; Corporate / IT and Corporate / IP Associate; Employment and Labour Associate; Project Coordinator; Legal Secretaries.

STIKINE HEALTH COUNCIL
Att: Edith Carrier, Council Chair
PO Box 386
Dease Lake, BC V0C 1L0
Tel. 250-771-4444
Fax 250-771-3911
Email .... edith.carrier@gems6.gov.bc.ca
Employer Background: The Stikine Health Council operates the Stikine Health Centre, a well-equipped diagnostic and treatment centre. *New Positions Created (3):* Chief Executive Officer; Chief Executive Officer; Registered Nurse.

STIRLING PRINT-ALL
Att: Valerie Clark
374 King Street East
Hamilton, ON L8N 1C3
Tel. 905-525-5467
Fax 905-529-5215
Email .... valeriec@stirlingprint-all.com
Website ...... www.stirlingprint-all.com
Employer Background: Stirling Print-All provides an array of traditional and digital print services. *New Positions Created (2):* Digital Print Production and Preflight Specialist; Mac / PC Artist.

STMICROELECTRONICS
Att: Human Resources Manager
185 Corkstown Road
Nepean, ON K2H 8V4
Tel. 613-768-9000
Fax 613-768-2778
Email .... hr.ottawa@st.com
Website .... www.st.com
Employer Background: STMicroelectronics is a global independent company that designs and manufactures semiconductor integrated circuits for use in microelectronic applications. *New Positions Created (3):* Failure Analyst; Manager - New Business Development; Facilities Operations Manager.

STOCK TRANSPORTATION LIMITED
Att: Human Resources
320 Bloomington Road West, PO Box 732
Aurora, ON L4G 4J9
Tel. 905-713-6900
Fax 905-713-6901
Email .... cindyk@stock-transport.com
Website .... www.stock-transport.com
Employer Background: Stock Transportation Limited is a leader in school bus transportation. *New Positions Created (5):* Operations Manager; Dispatchers / Assistant Route Coordinators; Operations Manager; Assistant Route Coordinator / Dispatcher; Payroll / Benefits Administrator.

STOCKERYALE CANADA INC.
Att: Human Resources Department
275 Kesmark Street
Dollard-des-Ormeaux, QC H9B 3J1
Tel. 514-685-1005
Fax 514-685-6139
Email .... desparois@lasiris.com
Website .... www.stockeryale.com
Employer Background: StockerYale Canada Inc. (formerly Lasiris Inc.) is a manufacturing company, specializing in lasers and telecom components. *New Positions Created (13):* Automation Engineer; Incoming Inspection Technician; Optical Components Packaging Engineer; Optics and Laser Systems Engineer; Optics Application Engineer; Optics Measurement Systems Engineer; Optics / Physics Technologists; Optics Researcher; Optics Testing and Measurement Engineer; Opto-Mechanical Engineer; R&D Electronics Technician; Sales Engineer, Lasers; Sales Assistant.

STOCKERYALE CANADA INC.
Att: Human Resources Department
3549 Ashby Street
St-Laurent, QC H4R 2K3
Tel. 514-335-1005
Fax 514-335-4576
Email .... desparois@lasiris.com
Website .... www.lasiris.com
Employer Background: StockerYale Canada Inc. (formerly Lasiris Inc.) is a manufacturing company, specializing in lasers and telecom components. *New Positions Created (11):* Automation Engineer; Engineer, Optical Components Packaging; Engineers, Optical Measurement and Testing (2); Optics Application Engineer; Optics Researcher; Optomechanical Engineer; Research & Development Electronics Technicians (3); Systems Engineers, Optics and Laser (3); Technician, Incoming Inspection; Technologists, Optics-Physics (10); Mechanical Engineer.

STOCKSCAPE.COM TECHNOLOGIES INC.
Att: Human Resources Manager
325 Howe Street, Suite 407
Vancouver, BC V6C 1Z7
Tel. 604-688-3386
Fax 604-681-4170
Email .... jobs@stockscape.com
Website .... www.stockscape.com
Employer Background: Stockscape.com Technologies Inc. is a financial Internet company providing extensive investor information. *New Positions Created (2):* Investor Relations Salesperson; Cold Fusion Programmer.

STONCOR GROUP
Att: Human Resources Manager
1585 Cliveden Avenue, Unit 11
Delta, BC V3M 6M1
Tel. 604-777-1225
Fax 604-777-1226
Email .... gdramalis@home.com
Website .... www.stoncor.com
Employer Background: StonCor Group is a Fortune 500 company and a world leader in concrete and steel protection finishes. *New Positions Created (2):* Sales Professionals (2); Sales Professional.

STONCOR GROUP
Att: Human Resources
95 Sunray Street
Whitby, ON L1N 9C9
Tel. 905-430-3333
Fax 905-430-3056
Email .... cwhite@stoncor.com
Website .... www.stoncor.com
Employer Background: StonCor Group is a Fortune 500 company and a world leader in concrete and steel protection finishes. *New Positions Created (14):* Sales Manager; Coatings Sales Specialists; Senior Territory Manager; Sales Professionals; Bilingual Sales Professional; Sales Manager; Coatings Sales Specialists; Sales Professionals; A&E Sales Specialist; Bilingual Account Manager; Senior Account Manager; Field Engineer; Sales Professional; Senior Account Manager.

STONE & WEBSTER CANADA LIMITED
Att: Human Resources
2300 Yonge Street
Toronto, ON M4P 2W6
Tel. 416-932-4400
Fax 416-932-4380
Email .... swcl.hr@stoneweb.com
Website .... www.stoneweb.com
Employer Background: Stone & Webster Canada Limited, part of the Shaw Group of companies, is a full-service engineering, procurement and construction management firm employing 13,000 people worldwide. *New Positions Created (22):* Cost Engineers / Analysts; Project Services; Designers / Drafters, Civil / Structural Engineering; Designers / Drafters, Electrical, Instrumentation and Controls Engineering; Designers, Mechanical Engineering, Intermediate and Senior; Junior Engineer, Project Services; Mechanical Engineers; Mechanical Engineers, Intermediate and Senior; Mechanical Engineers, Intermediate and Senior; Process Engineers, Intermediate and Senior; Project Engineers; Quality Control Inspectors, Procurement; Resident Engi-

neers; Senior Planner / Scheduler, Project Services; Site Managers; Various Engineering Positions, Intermediate and Senior; Chief Mechanical Engineer; Heat Balance Specialist; Lead Mechanical Engineers, Fossil; Lead Mechanical Engineers, Nuclear; Process Engineers; Project Engineers; Project Managers, Power.

STONEY CREEK MACK
Att: Joe Palermo, Service Manager
330 South Service Road
Stoney Creek, ON L8E 2R4
Tel. 905-561-4565
Fax 905-664-9200
Email .... jpalermo@mack.on.ca
Website ...... www.mack.on.ca/stoneycreek
Employer Background: Stoney Creek Mack offers a variety of truck products and services. *New Positions Created (2):* Truck Mechanics; Truck Mechanic.

STONHARD LTD.
Att: Human Resources
95 Sunray Street
Whitby, ON L1N 9C9
Tel. 905-430-3333
Fax 905-430-3056
Email .... cwhite@stoncor.com
Website .... www.stonhard.com
Employer Background: Stonhard Ltd., part of the StonCor Group, is the only worldwide manufacturer and installer of polymer floors. *New Positions Created (4):* Coating Sales Specialists; Senior Territory Mgr; Coating Sales Specialists; Sales Pros.

STORKCRAFT BABY
Att: E. Konorti
11511 - 5th Road
Richmond, BC V7A 4E8
Tel. 604-275-4242
Fax 604-274-9727
Email .... eli@storkcraft.com
Website .... www.storkcraft.com
Employer Background: Storkcraft Baby (formerly Stork Craft Manufacturing Inc.) manufactures cribs and other baby supplies. *New Positions Created (2):* Quality Supervisor; Shipping Coordinator.

STOTHERT ENGINEERING LTD.
Att: Human Resources Manager
609 Granville Street, 14th Floor, Box 10355
Vancouver, BC V7Y 1G5
Tel. 604-681-8165
Fax 604-687-3589
Email .... engineering@stothert.com
Website .... www.stothert.com
Employer Background: Stothert Engineering Ltd. provides technologies and multidiscipline engineering and management services for industrial projects in North America and overseas. *New Positions Created (3):* Designers / CAD Drafters; Mechanical, Electrical & Structural Engineers; Senior Mechanical & Process Engineers.

STRATEGY FIRST
Att: Human Resources Manager

147 St. Paul West, Suite 300
Montréal, QC H2Y 1Z5
Fax 514-844-4337
Email .... emps@strategyfirst.com
Website .... www.strategyfirst.com
Employer Background: Strategy First is a team of programmers, artists and animators creating entertainment software for personal computers. *New Positions Created (3):* Associate Producer; Production Assistant; Quality Assurance Manager.

STRATEGY INSTITUTE
Att: Human Resources Manager
40 King Street West, Suite 4900
Toronto, ON M5H 4A2
Tel. 416-944-8833
Fax 416-944-0403
Email .... hr@strategyinstitute.com
Website .... www.strategyinstitute.com
Employer Background: The Strategy Institute is a leading provider of business conferences for North American executives and professionals. *New Positions Created (2):* Conference Developers; Conference Developers.

STRATFORD GENERAL HOSPITAL
Att: Regional Coordinator,
Human Resources
46 General Hospital Drive
Stratford, ON N5A 2Y6
Tel. 519-272-8210
Fax 519-271-1177
Email .... humanresources@
.... sgh.stratford.on.ca
Website .... www.sgh.stratford.on.ca
Employer Background: Stratford General Hospital is a 134-bed facility. *New Positions Created (4):* Pharmacist; Physiotherapists; Various Healthcare Positions; Various Healthcare Positions (2).

STREAM DATA SYSTEMS LTD.
Att: Human Resources Manager
2880 Glenmore Trail SE, Suite 265
Calgary, AB T2C 2E7
Tel. 403-720-0900
Fax 403-720-0940
Email .... bonnie@streamdata.com
Website .... www.streamdata.com
Employer Background: Established in 1984, Stream Data Systems Ltd. is an IS consulting company, specializing in systems integration, software development, e-commerce and project management. *New Positions Created (2):* Analysts / Programmers; Systems Analyst.

STREAM INTERNATIONAL
Att: Recruiting
2319 Old Highway 2
Belleville, ON K8P 1B8
Tel. 613-961-5400
Fax 613-961-1761
Website .... www.stream.com
Employer Background: Stream International provides customer care services over the phone and Internet. *New Positions Created (27):* Customer Information Agent, Techni-

cal Support; Customer Service Representative; Employment Assistant; Human Resource Manager; Human Resource Representative; Human Resources Assistant; Information Technology Analyst; Information Technology Coordinator; Manager, Facility Services; Operations Manager; Operations Planning Analyst; Quality Analysts; Quality Manager I; Recruiter; Resource Planner; Site Financial Analyst; Team Managers; Telecommunications Coordinator; Training Manager; Human Resources Manager; Service Delivery Manager; Operations Planning Manager; Service Delivery Manager; Support Service Representatives; Team Manager; Telecom Coordinator; Trainers.

STREET HEALTH
Att: Susan Bender
338 Dundas Street East
Toronto, ON M5A 2A1
Tel. 416-921-8668
Fax 416-921-5233
Employer Background: Street Health provides a range of services for homeless individuals. *New Positions Created (3):* Project Coordinator; Conference Coordinator; Mental Health Workers (3).

STRESSGEN BIOTECHNOLOGIES CORP.
Att: Human Resources
4243 Glanford Avenue, Suite 350
Victoria, BC V8Z 4B9
Tel. 250-744-2811
Fax 250-744-3331
Email .... jobs@stressgen.com
Website .... www.stressgen.com
Employer Background: StressGen Biotechnologies Corp. is a growing biopharmaceutical company with a focus on utilizing stress proteins as immunomodulatory agents in therapeutic applications. *New Positions Created (4):* Research Associate; Quality Control / Quality Assurance Associate; Senior Research Scientist; Research Assistant / Research Associate (2).

STRONCO AUDIO-VISUALS
Att: Human Resources Manager
45 Fima Crescent, Suite 43
Toronto, ON M8W 3R1
Tel. 416-255-5511
Fax 416-255-0052
Email .... group@stronco.com
Website .... www.stronco.com
Employer Background: Founded in 1953, Stronco Audio-Visuals is a Canadian-owned trade show and convention contractor. Stronco provides equipment rentals, exhibit design, and trade show set-up / dismantling services. *New Positions Created (2):* Accounting Clerk; Project Coordinator.

STRONGCO EQUIPMENT
Att: Human Resources Manager
54 Iber Road
Stittsville, ON K2S 1E8
Fax 613-836-2614
Website .... www.strongco.com

Employer Background: Strongco Equipment is a leading North American multi-line equipment company, with approximately 1100 employees, over 65 branches and an expanding range of customers throughout Canada. *New Positions Created (3):* Customer Service Representative; Service Clerk; Service Technician.

STS SYSTEMS
Att: Human Resources Department
2800 Trans Canada Highway
Pointe-Claire, QC H9R 1B1
Tel. 514-426-2413
Fax 514-426-0824
Email .... hr@stssystems.com
Website .... www.stssystems.com

Employer Background: Founded in 1972, STS Systems is part of the NSB Group, a global supplier of software solutions for the retail industry. *New Positions Created (4):* POS Support Analysts; Financial Analyst; Internal Auditor; Chief Financial Officer.

STUART ENERGY SYSTEMS
Att: Donna Carlson, Human Resources
5101 Orbitor Drive
Mississauga, ON L4W 4V1
Tel. 905-282-7700
Fax 905-282-7705
Email .... dcarlson@stuartenergy.com
Website .... www.stuartenergy.com

Employer Background: Stuart Energy Systems is a hydrogen fuel company. *New Positions Created (2):* Quality Engineer; Proposal Engineer.

STUART OLSON CONSTRUCTION
Att: Human Resources Department
1211 Centre Street NW, Suite 360
Calgary, AB T2E 7K6
Tel. 403-520-6565
Fax 403-230-3577
Email .... webmaster@stuartolson.com
Website .... www.stuartolson.com

Employer Background: Stuart Olson Construction is one of western Canada's largest construction management and general contracting firms. *New Positions Created (6):* Intermediate Accountant; Branch Accountant; Senior Estimators; Information Systems and Technology Coordinator; Marketing Coordinator; Office Manager / Executive Assistant.

STURGEON COUNTY
Att: Human Resources, Sturgeon County
9613 - 100 Street
Morinville, AB T8R 1L9
Tel. 780-939-4321
Fax 780-939-3003
Email .... dgalay@sturgeoncounty.ab.ca
Website .... sturgeoncounty.ab.ca

Employer Background: Sturgeon County is located close to Edmonton and includes the municipalities of Bon Accord, Gibbons, Legal, Morinville and Redwater. The County has approximately 18,000 residents. *New Positions Created (2):* Assessor; Planning Technician.

SUDBURY & DISTRICT HEALTH UNIT
Att: Elsie Lindsay, HR Manager
1300 Paris Street
Sudbury, ON P3E 3A3
Tel. 705-522-9200
Fax 705-522-5182
Email .... lindsaye@sdhu.moh.gov.on.ca
Website .... www.sdhu.com

Employer Background: As one of six provincially designated teaching health units in Ontario, SDHU is a progressive, accredited agency committed to the concepts of workplace wellness. *New Positions Created (4):* Director, Health Protection; Epidemiologist; Health Promoters (4); Public Health Inspectors (3).

SUDBURY NEUTRINO OBSERVATORY
Att: Dr. J.D. Hepburn
PO Box 159
Lively, ON P3Y 1M3
Tel. 705-692-7000
Fax 705-692-7001
Email .... hepburn@surf.sno.laurentian.ca
Website .... www.sno.phy.queensu.ca

Employer Background: SNO is a research lab for the collaborative study of neutrino particles by 80 scientists from Canada, the USA and UK. *New Positions Created (4):* Site Manager; Operations Engineer; Operator Assistants; Water Systems Operators.

SUITES HOTEL, LES
Att: Controller
130 Besserer Street
Ottawa, ON K1N 9M9
Tel. 613-232-2000
Fax 613-232-3646
Email .... lvizzari@les-suites.com
Website .... www.les-suites.com

Employer Background: Located in downtown Ottawa, Les Suites Hotel features business, leisure and meeting facilities. *New Positions Created (4):* Assistant Controller; Front Office Manager; Rooms Division Manager; Executive Assistant.

SULZER MITROFLOW CORP.
Att: Human Resources
11220 Voyageur Way, Suite 1
Richmond, BC V6X 3E1
Tel. 604-270-7751
Fax 604-270-6308
Website .... www.mitroflow.com

Employer Background: Sulzer Mitroflow Corp. is a world leader in the manufacturing and development of tissue heart valves. *New Positions Created (8):* Research & Development Manager; Quality Control Manager; Engineer; Engineering Supervisor / Manager; Information Systems Coordinator / Supervisor; Quality Assurance Engineer; Validation Engineer; Validation Technician.

SUMMIT FOOD SERVICE DISTRIBUTORS INC.
Att: Human Resources
580 Industrial Road
London, ON N5V 1V1
Fax 519-453-4945
Email .... employme@summitfoods.com

Website .... www.summitfoods.com

Employer Background: Summit Food Service Distributors Inc. is a major food supplier to hotels, the healthcare sector, restaurants and various commercial outlets in Canada. *New Positions Created (2):* Distribution & Warehouse Supervisors; Branch Manager.

SUMMIT FOOD SERVICE DISTRIBUTORS INC.
Att: Office Manager
100 Legacy Road
Ottawa, ON K1G 5T8
Tel. 613-737-7000
Fax 613-737-4678
Website .... www.summitfoods.com

Employer Background: Summit Food Service Distributors Inc. is a major food supplier to hotels, the healthcare sector, restaurants and various commercial outlets in Canada. *New Positions Created (2):* Customer Service Representative; Secretary.

SUMMO MANUFACTURING
Att: Human Resources
1200 Burloak Drive
Burlington, ON L7L 6B3
Tel. 905-336-3306
Fax 905-336-0863
Email .... susanf@summo.com
Website .... www.summo.com

Employer Background: Summo Manufacturing is QS 9000-registered supplier of tubular and welded products to the automotive industry. *New Positions Created (2):* Quality Manager; Engineering Manager.

SUN CHEMICAL INK LIMITED
Att: Patricia Beveridge, HR Manager
10 West Drive
Brampton, ON L6T 4Y4
Tel. 905-796-2222
Fax 905-796-6821
Email .... beveridgep@sunchem.com
Website .... www.sunchemicalink.com

Employer Background: Sun Chemical Ink Limited is one of the world's largest manufacturers of high-performance printing inks and graphic arts coatings. *New Positions Created (3):* Formulator; Office Clerk, Accounts Receivable; In-Plant Ink Technicians.

SUN LIFE FINANCIAL
Att: Jeff Douwes, Leasing Manager
1100 Melville Street, Suite 700
Vancouver, BC V6E 4A6
Tel. 604-689-9578
Fax 604-682-3199
Website .... www.sunlife.ca

Employer Background: Sun Life is a large Canadian financial institution, offering retirement and insurance products, trust services, investment funds and mortgages. *New Positions Created (3):* Lease Administrator; Mortgage Underwriter; Property Manager.

SUN LIFE FINANCIAL
Att: Human Resources
225 King Street West, 8th Floor
Toronto, ON M5V 3C5

Tel. 416-408-7585
Fax 416-595-1587
Email ... can_hrnetjobs@mail.sunlife.com
Website .... www.sunlife.com
Employer Background: Sun Life Financial is a large Canadian financial institution, offering retirement and insurance products, trust services, investment funds and mortgages. *New Positions Created (55):* Expense Management Director; Lease Administrator; Group Disability Claims Positions; Investment Officer; Senior Actuarial Analyst; Property Manager; Actuarial Opportunities; Actuary, Consulting Group; Compliance Consultants; Director, Marketing Communications; Programmer; Programmer Analyst; Group Technical Assistant; Group Underwriting Clerk; Assistant Vice-President, Information Security; Programmer / Analyst; Rehabilitation Specialists; Senior Claims Operations Analyst; Senior Information Architect; Group Disability Claims Positions; Manager, Internet Technologies Group; Programmer / Analyst; Senior Business Analyst; Data Quality Analyst; Bilingual Account Administrator; Business Analyst; Business Process Specialist; Business System Coordinator; Director, Accounting; Document Production Services Operator; IT Asset Management Specialist; Manager, Customer Care; Manager, E-Commerce; Pension Benefits Administrator; Programmer; Project Manager; Quality Assurance Specialist; Real Estate Investment Officer; Senior Auditor; Senior Contract Specialist; Senior Financial Analyst; Service Representative; Sun Affinity Project Manager; Systems Administrator; Systems Analyst / Senior Systems Analyst; Technical Support Specialist; Universal Life Specialist; Buyer; Strategic Sourcing Director; Group Disability Claims Positions; Real Estate Analyst; Investment Product Manager; Facility Manager; Financial Planner; Pension Account Representative.

SUN LIFE FINANCIAL
Att: Human Resources
1155 Metcalfe Street, Suite 760
Montréal, QC H3B 2V9
Tel. 514-866-6411
Fax 514-866-6503
Email ... can_hrnetjobs@mail.sunlife.com
Website .... www.sunlife.ca
Employer Background: Sun Life Financial is a large Canadian financial institution, offering retirement and insurance products, trust services, investment funds and mortgages. *New Positions Created (54):* General Inventory Clerk; Support Administrator; Disability Management Manager; Disability Management Team Leader; Specialists, Group Client Services (2); Group Disability Claims Assistant; Plan Administrator; Claims Examiner; Customer Support Administrator; Data Entry Operator; Disability Claims Administrator; NB Production Administrator; Rehabilitation Specialist; Customer Service Representative; Dental Claims Manager; Regional Tax Planning Consultant; Claims Assistants; Secretary-Receptionist; Contract Writer; Customer Service Representative; Disability Claims

Adjudicator; Senior Medical Underwriter; Senior Underwriter; Short-Term Disability Adjudicator; Support Clerk; Underwriter; Accountant; Administrative Assistant, Group Underwriting; Asset Manager; Manager, Large Accounts; Call Centre Representative; Client Services Specialist; Accounting Analyst; Disability Management Client Consultant; Disability Management Specialist; Secretary; Senior Administrator; Senior Producer Payroll Administrator; Telephone Inquiry Clerk; Underwriter Support Position; Underwriting Client Manager; Mortgage Underwriter; Account Administrators; Bilingual Customer Service Representatives; Claims Examiners; Contract Writers; Group Underwriters; Team Leader, Administrative Support; Team Leader, Group Client Services; Underwriting Claims Manager; Life Wholesaler; Bilingual Call Centre Representative, Group Retirement Client Services; Bilingual Customer Service Representative, Group Insurance; Supervisor, Mail and Filing Services.

SUN RICH FRESH FOODS INC.
Att: Leanne Johnson, HR Manager
22151 Fraserwood Way
Richmond, BC V6W 1J5
Tel. 604-244-8800
Fax 604-244-8811
Email .... leannej@sun-rich.com
Website .... www.sun-rich.com
Employer Background: Sun Rich Fresh Foods Inc. processes high-quality fresh fruit products, with three production facilities in Canada and the USA. *New Positions Created (6):* QC Assistant; QC Technician; Receptionist; Vice-President / General Manager; Vice-President / General Manager; Director of Marketing.

SUNCOR ENERGY INC.
Att: Human Resources
112 - 4th Avenue SW, PO Box 38
Calgary, AB T2P 2V5
Tel. 403-269-8100
Fax 403-269-6202
Email .... calgaryresumes@suncor.com
Website .... www.suncor.com
Employer Background: Suncor Energy Inc., a world leader in oil sands development, is a high-performing oil and gas producer and one of the top petroleum refiners and marketers in the country. *New Positions Created (29):* Manager Income Tax; Corporate Accountant; Manager of Diesel Supply; Business Process Analyst; CAD Coordinator; Construction Controls Manager; Construction Manager; Contracts Manager; Field Procurement Manager; Lead Electrical / Instrumentation Engineer; Lead Mechanical Engineer; Lead Piping Design Specialist; Manager, Engineering; Piping Layout Specialist; Process Engineers; Procurement Manager; Project Engineers; Project Scheduler; Manager, Operations (Firebag); Executive Administrator / Paralegal; Pricing and Contract Analyst; Surface Land Administrator; Deskside Support Technicians; Manager, Environment, Loss Control and Quality; Support Analyst, Client Support;

Support Analyst, Information Technology Performance Measurement; Senior Advisor, External Communications; Manager, Income Tax; Employee Communications Advisor.

SUNCOR ENERGY INC., OIL SANDS
Att: Human Resources
PO Box 4001
Fort McMurray, AB T9H 3E3
Tel. 780-743-6411
Email .... osemploy@suncor.com
Website .... www.suncor.com
Employer Background: Suncor Energy Inc., a world leader in oil sands development, is a high-performing oil and gas producer and one of the top petroleum refiners and marketers in the country. *New Positions Created (87):* Area Manager, Upgrading Maintenance; Business Analyst; Senior Planner; Emergency Response Officer; Procurement Manager; Buyer; Construction Manager; Lead Electrical Engineer; Lead Instrument Engineer; Lead Mechanical Engineer; Manager, Engineering; Manager, Finance; Mechanical Engineers (3); Senior Inspectors (2); Electrical Specialist; Electronic Technician (Radio); Lead Refinery Inspector; Senior Cost Engineer; Senior Estimator; Day Shift Supervisor / Project Engineer; Instrument Engineer; Labour Relations Specialist; Maintenance Supervisor; Performance Analyst; Rotating Equipment Technologist; Senior Engineer / Manager, Mining Technical Development; Senior Planner; Staff Process Engineers; Environmental Engineer / Scientist; Senior Analyst; Senior Mechanical Engineer; Industrial Hygienist; Consolidated Tailings / Offplots Contact Engineer; Dual Ticket Instrument Mechanics / Electricians; Emergency Response Officer; Emergency Services Maintenance Technicians (2); Estimators / Cost Specialists; Intermediate / Senior / Staff Process Engineers; Intermediate Workstation Maintenance Technicians (2); Internal Control Analyst; Mechanical Engineer; Operations Supervisors; Performance Analyst; Process Control Engineer; Process Operators; Project Engineers / Managers; Quality Assurance Representative; Refinery Inspectors; Senior Engineer / Manager Mining Technical Development; Senior Programmer Analyst; Senior Programmer Analyst; Senior Programmer Analyst; Shift Supervisors - Maintenance (4); Williams Energy Contracts Advisor; Planning and Logistics Coordinator; Applications Specialist; Senior Support Analyst; Manager, Operations - Primary Extractions; Senior Mechanical Engineer; Instrument Engineer; Mechanical Engineer; Planners / Senior Planner, Mechanical; Rotating Equipment Engineer; Internal Control Analyst; Managerial Accountant / Accounting Associate; Senior Programmer Analyst; Applications Specialist; Manager, Energy Coordination; Planner; Technologist; Electronic Technician, Radio; Estimator / Cost Specialist; Laboratory Supervisor; Mechanical Engineers; Project Engineer; Quality Assurance Representative; Senior Staff Electrical Power Engineer; Senior Staff Instrumentation & Control Engineer; Sen-

ior Staff Mechanical Engineer; Buyers; Day Shift Supervisor / Project Engineer; Applications Engineer; Instrument Mechanic / Electrician; Lead Refinery Inspector; Mechanical Engineers; Planners / Senior Planners - Mechanical; Process Engineers.

SUNDOG PRINTING LTD.
Att: Ken Mateshaytis
1311 - 9th Avenue SW
Calgary, AB T3C 0H9
Tel. 403-264-8450
Fax 403-294-1496
Email .... kenmat@sundogprint.com
Website .... www.sundogprint.com
Employer Background: Sundog Printing Ltd. is one of Calgary's largest printing companies. *New Positions Created (5):* Account Manager; Bindery Operator; Press Operator; Print Estimator; Sales Associate.

SUNNYBROOK & WOMEN'S COLLEGE HEALTH SCIENCES CENTRE, ORTHOPAEDIC & ARTHRITIC INSTITUTE
Att: Human Resources
43 Wellesley Street East
Toronto, ON M4Y 1H1
Tel. 416-967-8647
Fax 416-967-8782
Email .... career.opportunities@
.... swchsc.on.ca
Website ..... www.sunnybrookandwomens.
.... on.ca
Employer Background: The Orthopaedic & Arthritic Institute is a 96-bed acute care facility, specializing in the treatment of musculoskeletal disorders. *New Positions Created (7):* Executive Assistant, Foundation; Physiotherapists, Musculoskeletal & Related Disorders Clients; Hospital Coordinator; Human Resources Associates (2); Registered Nurses; Social Worker; Managing Director, Rehabilitation and Working Condition Program Operations.

SUNNYBROOK & WOMEN'S COLLEGE HEALTH SCIENCES CENTRE, SUNNYBROOK CAMPUS
Att: Human Resources
2075 Bayview Avenue
Toronto, ON M4N 3M5
Tel. 416-480-4169
Fax 416-480-5492
Email ... career.opportunities@swchsc.on.ca
Website .... www.swchsc.on.ca
Employer Background: Sunnybrook & Women's College Health Sciences Centre is a teaching hospital, specializing in women's health, family and community medicine, dermatology and perinatal services. *New Positions Created (62):* Patient Care Manager, Cardiovascular ICU; Assistant Professor / Anesthesiologist; Health Records Clerk; Transgenic Technologist; Cardiology Positions; Cardiovascular Surgery Positions; Coronary Care Positions; Nursing Professional Practice Leader / Educator, Trauma Program; Registered Nurses; Registered Nurses, Cath Lab; Pacemaker Technician, Arrhythmia Services; Clinical Nurse Specialist / Nurse Practitioner, Cardiovascular

Surgery; Professional Practice Leader, Cardiovascular; Professional Practice Leader, Critical Care; Patient Care Manager, Cardiovascular Surgery; Registered Nurses, Occupational Health & Safety (2); Speech Language Pathologist - Acute Medicine / Stroke; Physiotherapists; Physiotherapists, General Medicine / Acute Geriatric / Stroke Rehab Unit; Professional Practice Leader, Critical Care & Emergency; Registered Nurses, Cardiology; Registered Nurses, Coronary Care; Registered Nurses, Medicine; Return-to-Work Program Coordinator; Technologist, Echo Lab; Coordinator; Nursing Shift Managers; Professional Practice Leader / Educator, Trauma Program; Registered Nurses, Neurosurgery / Trauma / Plastics, Trauma Program; Registered Nurses, Neurosurgical Intensive Care Unit, Trauma; Registered Nurses, Physical Support Unit, Aging Program; Research Associate, Ultrasound Research; Research Engineers (4); Pacemaker Technician, Arrhythmia Services; Registered Nurses, Acute Medical; Registered Nurses, Cognitive Support PSU; Administrative Assistant; Clinical Nurse Specialist / Nurse Practitioner, Arrhythmia Services; Decision Support Consultant; Patient Care Manager, Cardiovascular Surgery; Registered Nurses; Clinical Nurse Specialist / Nurse Practitioners, Acute Medicine; Educator, Aging Program; Patient Flow Specialist; Professional Practice Leader / Educator, General Medicine; Professional Practice Leader / Educator, Physical Support PSU; Registered Nurses, Aging Program; Registered Nurses, Behavioural Unit; Registered Nurses, Cath Lab; Registered Nurses, Emergency; Registered Nurses, Post-Anaesthetic Care / Flow-Through Unit; Cardiovascular Patient Liaison Position; Patient Care Manager, Acute Medical Unit; Lab Manager, Clinical Pathology; Research Technician; Accountants (2); Registered Nurse, Home Dialysis Program; High Frequency Instrumentation Engineer; Signal and Image Processing Engineer; Transducer Development Engineer; Patient Care Manager, Cardiovascular; Registered Nurses.

SUNNYBROOK & WOMEN'S COLLEGE HEALTH SCIENCES CENTRE, WOMEN'S COLLEGE CAMPUS
Att: Human Resources
76 Grenville Street
Toronto, ON M5S 1B2
Tel. 416-323-6050
Fax 416-323-6177
Email .... wcrecruitment@swchsc.on.ca
Website ..... www.sunnybrookandwomens.
.... on.ca
Employer Background: Sunnybrook & Women's College Health Sciences Centre is a teaching hospital, specializing in women's health, family and community medicine, dermatology and perinatal services. *New Positions Created (15):* Bilingual Web Community Coordinator; Administrative Assistant, Chief of Obstetrics / Gynaecology and VP Women's Health; Cytology Technician, Anatomic Pathology Lab; Endocrinologist, Department of Medicine; Registered Technologists, Medical Imaging; Secretary to

Epidemiologist - Microbiology; Sonographers, Ultrasound (2); Coordinator, Medical Education; HVAC Technician; Registered Technologist, Radiology / Nuclear Medicine; Administrative Assistant, Medicine / Respirology; Development Coordinator; Medical Imaging Department Positions; Social Worker, Women Recovering from Abuse Program; Professional Leader, Social Work.

SUNOCO INC.
Att: Human Resources
36 York Mills Road
Toronto, ON M2P 2C5
Tel. 416-733-7000
Fax 416-733-2251
Email .... resumes@suncor.com
Website .... www.sunoco.ca
Employer Background: Sunoco Inc., a subsidiary of Suncor Energy Inc., is a publicly-owned, Canadian integrated oil and gas company. *New Positions Created (6):* Business Development Adviser; Manager, Business Analysis; Programmer Analyst; Senior Accounting Coordinator; Retail Field Merchandiser; Truck Driver.

SUNRISE ASSISTED LIVING
Att: M. McCammont
350 Burnhamthorpe Road West, Suite 210
Mississauga, ON L5B 3J1
Fax 905-281-8895
Email .. marie.mccammont@sunrise-al.com
Website ... www.sunriseassistedliving.com
Employer Background: Sunrise Assisted Living is an international provider of personalized elder support, with 165 assisted living communities in Canada, the USA and Great Britain. *New Positions Created (3).* Director, Sales; Executive Director; Regional Business Manager.

SUNSHINE COAST COMMUNITY HEALTH COUNCIL / SCCHC
Att: Human Resources
PO Box 133
Sechelt, BC V0N 3A0
Tel. 604-885-2261
Fax 604-885-7909
Website ... www.sunshinecoastcommunity
.... healthcouncil.com
Employer Background: SCCHC manages health services for Sunshine Coast residents. *New Positions Created (2):* Site Manager, Shorncliffe Intermediate Care; Development Control Planner.

SUPERCOM CANADA LTD.
Att: Human Resources
4011 - 14th Avenue
Markham, ON L3R 0Z9
Tel. 905-415-1166
Fax 905-944-3819
Website .... www.supercom.ca
Employer Background: Established in 1989 Supercom Canada Ltd. is a leading distributor of personal computers, components and peripherals, with offices in Montreal, Vancouver and the USA. *New Positions Created (7):* Inside Sales Representatives; Operations

Manager; Developer, Lotus Notes and Domino Application; Human Resources Generalist; Operations Manager; Senior Product Manger; Service Manager.

SUPERINTENDENT OF FINANCIAL INSTITUTIONS OF CANADA, OFFICE OF THE / OSFI
Att: Human Resources Manager
225 Albert Street, 14th Floor
Ottawa, ON K1A 0H2
Tel. 613-990-7788
Fax 613-990-9017
Email .... hr.ottawa@osfi-bsif.gc.ca
Website .... www.osfi-bsif.gc.ca
Employer Background: OSFI supervises and regulates all federally-chartered banks, incorporated or registered trust and loan companies, insurance companies, cooperative credit associations, fraternal benefit societies and pension plans. *New Positions Created (3):* Senior Supervisor, Credit Risk Financial Institutions Group; Data Architect; Web and IT Security Specialist.

SUPERIOR CABINETS ALBERTA LTD.
Att: Human Resources Manager
6920 - 76th Avenue
Edmonton, AB T6B 2R2
Tel. 780-468-4242
Fax 780-463-0243
Website .... www.superiormillwork.com
Employer Background: Superior Cabinets Alberta Ltd. is leading manufacturer of residential kitchen cabinets and commercial millwork. *New Positions Created (6):* Installation Coordinator; Installers; Service Professional; Cabinet Sales Professionals; Installation Coordinator; Installers.

SUPERIOR EMERGENCY VEHICLES LTD.
Att: Gloria Derksen, HR Manager
6430 Golden West Avenue
Red Deer, AB T4P 1A6
Tel. 403-341-5187
Fax 403-341-3523
Email ... gderksen@superiorfirevehicles.com
Website ..... www.superiorfirevehicles.com
Employer Background: Superior Emergency Vehicles Ltd. manufactures firefighting and rescue vehicles. *New Positions Created (3):* Purchasing and Materials Manager; General Manager; Plant Manager.

SUPERIOR MEDICAL LTD.
Att: Human Resources Manager
520 Champagne Drive
Toronto, ON M3J 2T9
Tel. 416-635-9797
Fax 416-635-8931
Email .... info@superiormedical.com
Website .... www.superiormedical.com
Employer Background: Superior Medical Ltd. distributes medical equipment, surgical instrumentation and related systems. *New Positions Created (2):* Medical Sales Representative; Technical Sales Representative.

SUPERIOR NORTH CATHOLIC DISTRICT SCHOOL BOARD
Att: Leonard A. Bishop,
Director of Education
PO Box 610
Terrace Bay, ON P0T 2W0
Tel. 807-825-3209
Fax 807-825-9401
Website .... www.superiornorth
.... catholicdsb.on.ca
Employer Background: The Superior North Catholic District School Board operates elementary Catholic school systems in 9 communities. *New Positions Created (2):* Elementary Teaching Positions; Elementary Principals.

SUPERIOR PROPANE INC.
Att: Branch Manager
PO Box 70
Smithville, ON L0R 2A0
Fax 905-945-0577
Email .... careers@superiorpropane.com
Website .... www.superiorpropane.com
Employer Background: Superior Propane Inc. is a large retail propane marketer. *New Positions Created (2):* Service Apprentice; Service Technician.

SUPPORTIVE HOUSING COALITION OF METROPOLITAN TORONTO
Att: Hiring Committee
761 Queen Street West, Suite 301
Toronto, ON M6J 1G1
Tel. 416-703-9266
Fax 416-703-9265
Website .... www.supportivehousing.ca
Employer Background: The Supportive Housing Coalition of Metropolitan Toronto provides affordable and accessible housing for consumer / survivors and people with special needs. *New Positions Created (3):* Housing Access Coordinator; Supervisor, Tenant & Member Services; Supportive Housing Workers.

SUPPORTIVE HOUSING IN PEEL FOUNDATION, THE / SHIP
Att: Brenda M. Elias, Executive Director
1035 Windsor Hill Boulevard, Suite 3
Mississauga, ON L5V 1Z3
Employer Background: SHIP is a not-for-profit community agency that provides mental health services to individuals in need of housing and support. *New Positions Created (5):* Bookkeeper; Community Support Worker; Director of New Initiatives; Executive Assistant / Communications Coordinator; Housing Directors (2).

SUPREME TOOLING GROUP
Att: Human Resources
2 Norelco Drive
Toronto, ON M9L 1R9
Tel. 416-742-9600
Fax 416-742-8422
Email .... hr.stg@abcgrp.com
Website .... www.abcgroupinc.com
Employer Background: Supreme Tooling Group, an ABC Group Company, manufac-

tures plastic moulding equipment for the automotive industry. *New Positions Created (13):* Applications Engineer; Electrical Engineer / Designer; Technical Administrator; Administrative Assistant, Engineering; Senior Mechanical Designers; Accounting and Payroll Coordinator; CAM Programmer; Fixture Design Position; Industrial Electrician; Buyer; Engineering Clerk; Mould Surfacer; Senior Mechanical Designer.

SUREFIRE COMMERCE INC.
Att: Human Resources
3500 de Maisonneuve Blvd. West
7th Floor, 2 Place Alexis Nihon
Westmount, QC H3Z 3C1
Tel. 514-380-2700
Fax 514-380-2760
Email .... personnel@sfcommerce.com
Website .... www.sfcommerce.com
Employer Background: SureFire Commerce Inc. (formerly Micro Tempus) specializes in e-commerce solutions for transaction processing and merchant enablement activities. *New Positions Created (32):* Manager, Financial Analysis; Manager, Financial Operations; Senior Accountant; Treasurer; Technical Writer; Technical Team Lead; Accounts Payable Coordinator; Senior Creative Designer; Java Developer; Project Management Assistant; System Administrator, Unix; Technical Project Manager; Office Services Manager; Human Resources Representative; Architect; Bank Reconciliations Assistants; Call Centre Agents; Chargebacks / Refunds Assistant; Client Reconciliations Assistants; Lead Developer; Network Administrator; NT System Administrator; Oracle Database Developer; Project Manager, MIS; Sales Agents, Call Centre; Senior System Administrator; Software Developer; Team Leader, Technical Support; Technical Project Manager; Financial Analyst; Accounting Assistants; Accounting Coordinators.

SURFACE MOUNT TECHNOLOGY CENTRE INC. / SMTC
Att: Human Resources Manager
635 Hood Road
Markham, ON L3R 4N6
Tel. 905-479-1810
Fax 905-479-1877
Website .... www.smtc.com
Employer Background: STMC Manufacturing Corporation provides contract electronic manufacturing services to the global electronics industry. *New Positions Created (6):* Business Analysts; Commodity Mgrs; Director, Commodity Mgmnt; Director, Supplier Relations; Supplier Relations Mgrs; Team Test Engineers.

SURREY, CITY OF
Att: George Siudut, HR Division
14245 - 56th Avenue
Surrey, BC V3X 3A2
Tel. 604-591-4117
Fax 604-591-4517
Email . humanresources@city.surrey.bc.ca
Website .... www.city.surrey.bc.ca
Employer Background: The City of Surrey provides local government services to

340,000 residents in one of Canada's fastest-growing municipalities. *New Positions Created (29):* Community Services Coordinator; IT Manager; Parks and Recreation Planner; Section Manager, Community & Leisure Services; Electrical Inspector; Building Engineer; Manager, Community and Leisure Services; Cemetery Supervisor; Community Development Section Manager; Manager, Commercial Section; Landscape Maintenance Crew Chief; Fire Chief; General Manager, Community Protective Services; Drainage / Building Engineer; Network Analyst; Clerk Typist; Graphic Designer; Manager, Commercial Section; Manager, Traffic Operations; Park Operation Coordinators (2); Assistant Manager, Victim Services; Building Engineer; Section Manager, Community and Leisure Services; Applications Specialist, Integration Planning; Assistant Manager, RCMP Victim Services; Project Manager / Business Analyst; Traffic Engineer; Traffic Technologist; Traffic Technologist.

SURREY METRO SAVINGS
Att: Human Resources Manager
15117 - 101st Avenue
Surrey, BC V3R 8P7
Tel. 604-583-8198
Fax 604-517-7465
Email .... hr@metrosavings.com
Website .... www.metrosavings.com
Employer Background: Surrey Metro Savings is a large credit union with over 700 employees at 17 branches. *New Positions Created (3):* Customer Service Representative; Financial Service Representative; Retail Loans Officer.

SURREY PLACE CENTRE
Att: Human Resources
2 Surrey Place, Surrey Place Centre
Toronto, ON M5S 2C2
Tel. 416-925-5141
Fax 416-925-5645
Website .... www.surreyplace.on.ca
Employer Background: Surrey Place Centre is dedicated to improving the quality of life for people with developmental disabilities. *New Positions Created (6):* Clinical Psychologist; Senior Behaviour Therapist; Service Coordinator; Speech Language Pathologist; Instructor-Therapists; Health Records Technician.

SUSS WOODCRAFT INTERNATIONAL
Att: Human Resources Manager
9585 Wanklyn Street
Lasalle, QC H8R 1Z1
Tel. 514-367-7206
Fax 514-363-8501
Website .... www.susswoodcraft.com
Employer Background: Founded in 1964, Suss Woodcraft International manufactures store fixtures for such retail giants as Barnes & Noble, Saks Fifth Avenue and Macy's. They have a 140,000 square foot plant and 200 employees. *New Positions Created (3):* Accountant; Detail Design Draftsperson; Estimator.

SUTTON PLACE HOTEL, THE
Att: Director of Human Resources
955 Bay Street
Toronto, ON M5S 2A2
Tel. 416-924-9221
Fax 416-934-4394
Website .... www.suttonplace.com
Employer Background: The Sutton Place Hotel is a luxury hotel located in the heart of downtown Toronto. *New Positions Created (3):* Hotel Positions; Human Resources Coordinator; Night Auditor.

SUTTON PLACE HOTEL VANCOUVER, THE
Att: Constance Gorlach,
Director of Human Resources
845 Burrard Street
Vancouver, BC V6Z 2K6
Tel. 604-682-5511
Fax 604-642-2953
Website .... www.suttonplace.com
Employer Background: The Sutton Place Hotel Vancouver is a 5-diamond facility, with 397 guest rooms. *New Positions Created (5):* Financial Controller; Reservation Agent; Security Officer; Assistant Director, HR; Executive Administrative Assistant.

SWI SYSTEMWARE INC.
Att: Hiring Coordinator
2300 Yonge Street, Suite 1800, Box 2418
Toronto, ON M4P 1E4
Tel. 416-932-4700
Fax 416-932-4710
Website .... www.swi.com
Employer Background: SWI Systemware Inc. is a software engineering consulting firm that develops and integrates large mission-critical systems for Fortune 500 companies. *New Positions Created (4):* Receptionist / Office Assistant; Sales Administrator; Software Positions; Sales Account Manager.

SWISS HERBAL REMEDIES LTD.
Att: Human Resources Department
35 Leek Crescent
Richmond Hill, ON L4B 4C2
Tel. 905-886-9500
Fax 905-886-5434
Website .... www.swissherbal.ca
Employer Background: Swiss Herbal Remedies Ltd. is a leading distributor of vitamin and mineral supplements. *New Positions Created (9):* Junior Chemist, Quality Control; Quality Control Nutritionist; Sales Supervisor; Sales Representative; Entry-Level Sales Position; Key Account Coordinator; Key Account Coordinator; Purchasing Manager; Regional Sales Manager.

SWISS REINSURANCE COMPANY CANADA
Att: Kamla Bhim
150 King Street West, Suite 2200, Box 50
Toronto, ON M5H 1J9
Tel. 416-408-0272
Fax 416-364-2449
Email .... srlna_hrca@swissre.com
Website .... www.swissre.ca

Employer Background: Swiss Reinsurance Company Canada has served the Canadian market for over 45 years as the domestic arm of the worldwide Swiss Re Group. *New Positions Created (2):* Business Analyst; Reinsurance Underwriter.

SWL CRANE & HOIST 2000 LTD.
Att: Larry Gordon
170 Wilkinson Road, Unit 12
Brampton, ON L6T 4Z5
Tel. 905-450-1331
Fax 905-450-0026
Website .... www.swl-crane.com
Employer Background: Founded in 1987, SWL Crane & Hoist 2000 Ltd. designs and manufactures overhead industrial hoists, cranes and crane components. *New Positions Created (2):* Telemarketing Position; Overhead Crane Technician.

SYBRIDGE TECHNOLOGIES INC.
Att: Human Resources Manager
36 Antares Drive, Suite 200
Nepean, ON K2E 7W5
Tel. 613-274-0002
Fax 613-274-0162
Email .... hr@sybridge.com
Website .... www.sybridge.com
Employer Background: Sybridge Technologies Inc. is an e-commerce company. *New Positions Created (6):* Intermediate Programmer / Developer; Security Architect; Senior Software Architect (2); Senior Software Developers (5); Technical Applications Engineer; Technical Applications Engineer.

SYCHOWSKI COMMUNICATIONS INC.
Att: Human Resources Manager
1751 Richardson, Suite 3505
Montréal, QC H3K 1G6
Tel. 514-931-4434
Fax 514-931-7267
Employer Background: Sychowski Communications Inc. is an advertising agency. *New Positions Created (2):* Graphic Designer; Sales Position.

SYLVAN LEARNING CENTRE
Att: Kristi Ash
2 Orchard Heights
Aurora, ON L4G 3W3
Tel. 905-726-3666
Fax 905-898-8062
Website .... www.educate.com
Employer Background: Sylvan Learning Centre is a leader in supplemental educational services. *New Positions Created (2):* Director of Education; Call Centre Manager.

SYMAGERY MICROSYSTEMS INC.
Att: Human Resources Department
3026 Solandt Road
Kanata, ON K2K 2A5
Tel. 613-592-2592
Fax 613-592-6778
Email .... hr@symagery.com
Website .... www.symagery.com

Employer Background: Symagery Microsystems Inc. develops and supplies intelligent imaging solutions based on CMOS technology. *New Positions Created (13):* Applications Engineer; Evaluation Engineer / Technologist; Engineering Services Technologist; Hardware Verification Engineer; Manager, Applications Engineering; Manager, Hardware Engineering; Mixed Signal Designers; New Product Introduction Engineer; Product and Test Engineer; Senior Digital Designer; Analog Designers; Applications Engineers; Digital Designers.

SYN X PHARMA INC.
Att: Director of Clinical
and Regulatory Affairs
6354 Viscount Road
Mississauga, ON L4V 1H3
Tel. 905-677-1944
Fax 905-677-1674
Email .... vectra@canada.com
Website .... www.synxpharma.com
Employer Background: Syn X Pharma Inc. is an established proteomics research and development company focused on cardiovascular and central nervous system diseases. *New Positions Created (3):* Laboratory Project Manager; Manager, Clinical Affairs; Research Scientists.

SYNAVANT INC.
Att: Human Resources Manager
2210 Markham Road
Toronto, ON M1B 5V6
Tel. 416-298-4631
Fax 416-298-9358
Email .... bdelville@synavant.com
Website .... www.synavant.com
Employer Background: Synavant Inc. supplies integrated marketing and information solutions to the pharmaceutical industry. *New Positions Created (4):* Market Research Consultant; Quantitative Analyst; Bilingual HelpDesk Analyst; Senior Technical Analyst / Project Leader.

SYNCHROPOINT WIRELESS INC.
Att: Human Resources Manager
1333 Johnston Street, Suite 200
Vancouver, BC V6H 3R9
Tel. 604-685-7962
Fax 604-685-7969
Email .... careers@synchropoint.com
Website .... www.synchropoint.com
Employer Background: SynchroPoint Wireless Inc. is a leading software developer for a new category of Face-to-Face (F2F) computing, enabling people connected by short-range wireless networks to work together using portable computing devices. *New Positions Created (17):* Business Development Manager; Intermediate / Junior Software Engineers; Project Leaders; Project Manager; QA Tester; Senior Software Engineers; Software Developer, GUI & Applications; Software Developers, Networking; Human Resources Manager; Product Manager; Product Manager; Development Support Technician; Project Leaders; Senior Software Engineer; Software Developer - GUI and Applications; Software Developers, Junior and Intermediate; Software Developers - Networking.

SYNCOR BUSINESS ENVIRONMENTS LTD.
Att: Niles Spiro, Design Director
1050 West Pender Street, Suite 800
Vancouver, BC V6E 3S7
Tel. 604-688-0052
Fax 604-682-1850
Email .... nspiro@syncorsolutions.com
Website .... www.syncorsolutions.com
Employer Background: Established in 1984, Syncor Business Environments Ltd. provides office interior planning services. *New Positions Created (2):* Intermediate Architectural Technologist; Senior Interior Designer.

SYNCRUDE CANADA LTD.
Att: Recruitment Department
PO Bag 4023, MD 3200
Fort McMurray, AB T9H 3H5
Tel. 780-790-6403
Fax 780-790-6186
Email .... recruitment@syncrude.com
Website .... www.syncrude.com
Employer Background: Syncrude Canada Ltd. is the operator of the Syncrude Project and the world's largest producer of crude oil from the oil sands. *New Positions Created (29):* Hydrotransport Process Engineer; Junior / Intermediate Metallurgical Engineer; Mine Planning Engineers (2); Senior Systems Analyst; Accounting Positions; Intermediate Equipment Inspector; Pipefitters / Steamfitters / Welders; Senior Mechanical Inspector; Administrative Resource / Assistants; Boilermakers; Chemical / Process / Control Engineers / Technologists; Chemists; Civil / Structural Designers; Electrical Engineers / Technologists; Electricians; Geotechnical Engineers; Health & Wellness Advisors; Heavy Equipment Operators / Technicians; Instrument & Process Control Engineers; Instrument Technicians / Instrumentation Technologists; Materials / Metallurgical Engineers; Mechanical Engineers / Technologists; Piping Designers; Process Operators / Power Engineers; Health and Wellness Advisor; Human Resources Representative; Leader, Employee and Family Assistance Program; Senior Civil / Structural Engineer; Senior Pressure Vessel Inspector.

SYNDESIS LIMITED
Att: Human Resources Manager
30 Fulton Way
Richmond Hill, ON L4B 1E6
Tel. 905-886-7818
Fax 905-886-9076
Email .... hr@syndesis.com
Website .... www.syndesis.com
Employer Background: Syndesis Limited develops and markets advanced service creation systems to automate the deployment of data-centric telecommunications services. *New Positions Created (8):* Legal Counsel; Accounts Payable Clerk; Financial Analyst; Human Resources Administrator; Human Resources Generalist; Legal Counsel; Payroll and Benefits Administrator; Receptionist.

SYNDESIS LIMITED
Att: Human Resources Manager
1150 Morrison Drive, Suite 400
Ottawa, ON K2H 8S9
Tel. 613-820-0015
Fax 613-820-3307
Email .... hr.ottawa@syndesis.com
Website .... www.syndesis.com
Employer Background: Syndesis Limited develops and markets advanced service creation systems to automate the deployment of data-centric telecommunications services. *New Positions Created (8):* Account Manager; Manager, Software Product Development; Intermediate Software Engineers; Junior Software Engineers; Manager, Software Product Development; Product Manager; Professional Services Consultant; Senior Software Engineer.

SYNOPSYS INC.
Att: Human Resources Manager
155 Queen Street, Suite 900, Heritage Place
Ottawa, ON K1P 6L1
Tel. 613-751-6653
Fax 613-751-4452
Email .... jobs-ca@synopsys.com
Website .... www.synopsys.com
Employer Background: Founded in 1986, Synopys Inc. is a technology leader in complex integrated circuit design solutions, employing 3,100 people at 79 locations worldwide. *New Positions Created (4):* Senior Account Manager; Professional Consultant; Senior Professional Consultant; Target Account Manager.

SYNREVOICE TECHNOLOGIES INC.
Att: Human Resources Manager
200 Cochrane Drive, Unit 1A
Markham, ON L3R 8E7
Tel. 905-946-8500
Fax 905-940-1545
Email .... jobs@synrevoice.com
Website .... www.synrevoice.com
Employer Background: SynreVoice Technologies Inc. develops state-of-the-art and cost effective computer / telephone integration (CTI) and automated voice processing systems. *New Positions Created (4):* Communication Software Major Account Managers; Sales Representatives; Major Account Managers; Senior Sales Manager.

SYNSORB BIOTECH INC.
Att: Human Resource Specialist
1204 Kensington Road NW, Suite 201
Calgary, AB T2N 3P5
Tel. 403-283-5900
Fax 403-283-5907
Email .... twoods@synsorb.com
Website .... www.synsorb.com
Employer Background: Synsorb Biotech Inc. is a publicly-traded pharmaceutical company specializing in the discovery and development of carbohydrate-based therapeu-

tic products. *New Positions Created (2):* Quality Control Technician; Scientist, Analytical Methods Development.

SYSCO FOOD SERVICES OF ONTARIO
Att: Human Resources Department
PO Box 6000
Peterborough, ON K9J 7B1
Tel. 705-748-6701
Fax 705-748-0244
Email .... adams.keri@ont.sysco.com
Website .... www.sysco.com
Employer Background: Sysco Food Services of Ontario is a full-line foodservice distributor. *New Positions Created (3):* Class A Resident Drivers; Customer Service Representative; Marketing Associates / Sales Representatives (2).

SYSCO I & S FOODSERVICES
Att: Director of Sales
PO Box 7185
Edmonton, AB T5E 5S9
Tel. 780-478-3451
Fax 780-472-2026
Website .... www.isfoodservices.com
Employer Background: Sysco I & S Foodservices is a major foodservice distributor. *New Positions Created (2):* Sales Marketing Associate; Sales Representative.

SYSCO / KONINGS
Att: Human Resources
1346 Kingsway Avenue
Port Coquitlam, BC V3C 6G4
Tel. 604-944-4410
Fax 604-945-1411
Email .... careers@syscokonings.com
Website .... www.syscokonings.com
Employer Background: Founded in 1976, Sysco / Konings is a distributor of food and related products to the restaurant, healthcare and hospitality industries. *New Positions Created (2):* Outside Sales Position; Purchasing Positions.

SYSCOM CONSULTING INC. / SCI
Att: Human Resources
1090 Georgia Street West, Suite 1000
Vancouver, BC V6E 3V7
Tel. 604-684-5344
Fax 604-684-5322
Email .... careers@sci-syscom.com
Website .... www.sci-syscom.com
Employer Background: SCI, owned by Telus Enterprise Solutions, is an IT consulting firm that provides technical support services to a wide variety of legal clients. *New Positions Created (3):* Corporate Sales Associates; Technical Support Specialists; Windows Software Developers.

SYSTEMCORP ALG LTD.
Att: Human Resources
6969 Trans Canada Highway, Suite 225
Montréal, QC H4T 1V8
Tel. 514-339-1067
Fax 514-339-9776
Email .... careers@systemcorp.com
Website .... www.systemcorp.com

Employer Background: Systemcorp ALG Ltd. is a leading worldwide developer and provider of global web-based enterprise program management systems. *New Positions Created (13):* Business Development Manager; Business Consultant; Delphi Developers / Programmers; Graphic Designers; Intermediate Java Programmers / Developers; Junior Seminar Coordinator; Marketing Writer; Public Relations Executive; Public Relations / Web Researcher; Public Relations Writer; Senior C++ Programmer / Developer; Senior Customer Relations Developer; Senior Java Programmers / Developers.

SYTEK ENTERPRISES INC.
Att: Human Resources
980 - 1st Street West, Suite 116
North Vancouver, BC V7P 3N4
Tel. 604-988-1125
Fax 604-988-0299
Email .... hr@sytek-ent.com
Website .... www.sytek-ent.com
Employer Background: Sytek Enterprises Inc. is a leader in electronic product interfacing. *New Positions Created (6):* Sales Manager; Incoming Quality Inspector; Technicians / Engineers (2); Sales Manager; Purchaser; QA Manager / Technician.

TALISMAN ENERGY INC.
Att: Human Resources Advisor
888 - 3rd Street SW, Suite 3400
Calgary, AB T2P 5C5
Tel. 403-237-1234
Fax 403-237-1601
Email .... careers-can@talisman-energy.com
Website .... www.talisman-energy.com
Employer Background: Talisman Energy Inc. is a senior oil and gas company active domestically and internationally. *New Positions Created (3):* Legal Counsel; Interpretive Geophysicists; Operations Engineers.

TALITY CORP.
Att: Human Resources Manager
1130 Morrison Drive
Ottawa, ON K2H 9N6
Tel. 613-828-5626
Fax 613-828-7606
Email .... hrcanada@tality.com
Website .... www.tality.com
Employer Background: Tality Corp. is an independent provider of engineering services and intellectual property for the design of complex electronic systems and integrated circuits, with over 1,100 engineers and 14 locations worldwide. *New Positions Created (9):* Lead ASIC Designer; Board Designer; Business Manager; PCB Designer; Senior Embedded Software Designer; Senior Software Verification Specialist; SONET / ATM / Frame Relay Designers; FPGA / ASIC Designers; Senior Systems Architect.

TALON SYSTEMS INC.
Att: Human Resources Manager
6200 Cantay Road
Mississauga, ON L5R 3Y9
Tel. 905-501-9350
Fax 905-501-9355

Employer Background: Talon Systems Inc. is a high-volume woodworking plant. *New Positions Created (5):* Accounts Payable Position / General Office Clerk; Equipment Maintenance Mechanic; Production Coordinator; Packaging Positions; Quality Control Technician.

TALSTRA & COMPANY
Att: Maria
3219 Eby Street, Suite 101
Terrace, BC V8G 4R3
Tel. 250-638-1137
Fax 250-638-1306
Employer Background: Talstra & Company is an established law firm. *New Positions Created (2):* Lawyer; Associate Barrister.

TANTALUS SYSTEMS CORP.
Att: Rob Mielcarski
4224 Manor Street
Burnaby, BC V5G 1B2
Tel. 604-299-0458
Email .... careers@tantalus-systems.com
Website ... www.tantalus-systems.com
Employer Background: Established in 1989, Tantalus Systems Corp. designs and manufactures narrowband two-way wireless telemetry products for the utility industry. *New Positions Created (7):* Application Software Developer; Bookkeeper; Buyer; DSP Firmware Developer; Field Engineer; RF Design Engineers; RF Design Team Leader.

TAP VENTURES, INC.
Att: Human Resources Manager
1140 Homer Street, Suite 305
Vancouver, BC V6B 2X6
Tel. 604-609-6253
Email .... recruiting@tap.ca
Website .... www.tap.ca
Employer Background: Founded in 1990, TAP provides professional services in the areas of web-enabled service delivery, web-accessible business intelligence, web-based knowledge management and employee portals. *New Positions Created (2):* Senior Sales Consultant; Director, New York Office.

TARGRAY TECHNOLOGY INTERNATIONAL INC.
Att: Personnel Manager
195 Labrosse Avenue
Pointe-Claire, QC H9R 5Y9
Tel. 514-695-8095
Fax 514-695-0593
Email .... careers@targray.com
Website .... www.targray.com
Employer Background: Targray Technology International Inc. is a leading supplier and distributor of consumables and services for the CD and DVD manufacturing industry. *New Positions Created (4):* Area Sales Manager; Director of Operations; Intermediate Accountant; Administrative Assistant.

TARIAN SOFTWARE INC.
Att: Human Resources Manager
1701 Woodward Drive, LL20
Ottawa, ON K2C 0R4

Tel. 613-274-7700
Fax 613-274-7608
Email .... jobs@tariansoftware.com
Website .... www.tariansoftware.com
Employer Background: Tarian Software Inc. specializes in electronic records management solutions and technology for business. *New Positions Created (5):* Documentation / Technical Writers; Records Management Consultants; Senior DBMS Programmers; Software Quality Assurance Engineers; Web Application Developers.

TARO PHARMACEUTICALS INC.
Att: Human Resources
130 East Drive
Bramalea, ON L6T 1C3
Tel. 905-791-8276
Fax 905-791-8670
Email .... hr@tarocan.com
Website .... www.taro.ca
Employer Background: Founded in Israel in 1950, Taro Pharmaceuticals Inc. is a multinational, science-based pharmaceutical company that discovers, develops, manufactures and markets healthcare products. *New Positions Created (27):* Computer Validation Specialist; Line Mechanics; Packaging Line Operators; Pilot Plant Technologist; QC Calibration Chemist; QC Document Reviewer; Quality Assurance Inspector; Quality Control Group Leader; R&D Analytical Chemists; Regulatory Affairs Associate (2); Systems Analyst; Accounting Manager; Director, MIS; Financial Analyst; Laboratory Steward; Line Mechanics; Market Research Analyst; Packaging Line Operators; Pilot Plant Group Leader; Pilot Plant Technologist; Product Development Formulator; Regulatory Affairs Associates (2); Research and Development Project Manager; Research & Development Analytical Chemists; Sales Representatives, Branded Dermatology; Systems Analyst; Technical Documentation & Compliance Specialist.

TARTAN ENGINEERING LTD.
Att: Human Resources Manager
800 - 6th Avenue SW, Suite 1700
Calgary, AB T2P 3G3
Tel. 403-232-8288
Fax 403-232-8298
Email .... hr@tartaneng.com
Website .... www.tartaneng.com
Employer Background: Tartan Engineering Ltd. is an established engineering consulting firm that provides EPCM services to clients in the oil, gas and petrochemical industries. *New Positions Created (7):* Mechanical Draftspersons; Mechanical / Project Engineers; Process Engineers; Intermediate / Senior Process Engineers; Mechanical / Project Engineers; Intermediate Control Systems Engineers; Mechanical and Project Engineers, Intermediate / Senior.

TAS DESIGNBUILD
Att: Human Resources Manager
1 Valleybrook Drive, Suite 300
Toronto, ON M3B 2S7
Tel. 416-510-8181
Fax 416-510-1516

Email .... hr@tasdesignbuild.com
Website .... www.tasdesignbuild.com
Employer Background: For 15 years, TAS Designbuild has been providing services in 3 core aspects of home-building: architecture, interior design and construction. *New Positions Created (6):* Project Managers, Design; Senior Studio Manager; Site Supervisors, Construction; Designers, Architecture & Interiors; Project Managers, Construction; Receptionist.

TAXSAVE CONSULTANTS LIMITED
Att: Human Resources Manager
7100 Woodbine
Toronto, ON L3R 5J2
Tel. 905-305-8900
Fax 905-305-8905
Email .... hartnoll@taxsave.ca
Website .... www.taxsave.ca
Employer Background: TaxSave Consultants Limited is a national commodity tax recovery firm. *New Positions Created (4):* Commodity Tax Consultants; Sales Tax Consultants; Sales Tax Consultants; Sales Representative.

TAYLOR STEEL INC.
Att: Human Resources Department
PO Box 3366, Station C
Hamilton, ON L8H 7L4
Fax 905-662-7660
Email .... hr@taylorsteel.com
Website .... www.taylorsteel.com
Employer Background: Founded in 1967, Taylor Steel Inc. is a flat-rolled steel service centre with state-of-the art processing equipment and facilities. *New Positions Created (2):* Certified Industrial Electrician; Field / Inside Sales Representatives.

TAYMOR INDUSTRIES
Att: Human Resources
1655 Derwent Way
Delta, BC V3M 6K8
Tel. 604-540-9525
Fax 604-540-2153
Email .... builders@taymor.com
Website .... www.taymor.com
Employer Background: Taymor Industries is a Canadian company supplying quality hardware to the builder / decorative hardware industry. *New Positions Created (2):* Product Coordinator; Sales Representative.

TCT DAILY MOTOR FREIGHT
Att: Director of Sales and Marketing
1100 Haultain Court
Mississauga, ON L4W 2T1
Tel. 905-602-1782
Fax 905-602-1750
Email .... blindley@daily.ca
Employer Background: Daily Motor Freight is an expanding LTL transportation company. *New Positions Created (6):* Customer Service / Dispatch Support Clerk; Sales Representatives; Comptroller; Dispatcher; Account Manager; Inside Sales Position.

TCT LOGISTICS INC.
Att: Human Resources
1100 Haultain Court
Mississauga, ON L4W 2T1
Tel. 905-602-1782
Fax 905-671-9036
Email .... dbradford@tctlogistics.com
Website .... www.tctlogistics.com
Employer Background: TCT Logistics Inc. provides transportation, storage and distributive services for grocery products, specializing in temperature-sensitive freight. *New Positions Created (6):* A/P Clerk; Dock Supervisors; Payroll Clerk; Freight Bill Auditors; A/P Clerk; Customer Service Rep.

TDL GROUP LTD., THE
Att: Human Resources
874 Sinclair Road
Oakville, ON L6K 2Y1
Tel. 905-845-6511
Fax 905-845-0265
Email .... tdlgroup_hr@timhortons.com
Website .... www.timhortons.com
Employer Background: The TDL Group Ltd., operators of Tim Hortons restaurants, is a leader in the quick service industry. *New Positions Created (12):* Counsel, Real Estate and Franchising; Project Manager, Special Projects; Bilingual Operations Services Representatives; District Manager; General Ledger Analyst; Legal Assistant; District Manager; Marketing Coordinator; District Managers; Building Maintenance Clerk; Real Estate Assistant; Corporate Counsel.

TDL GROUP LTD., THE
(DISTRIBUTION CENTRE)
Att: Human Resources Department
226 Wyecroft Road
Oakville, ON L6K 3X7
Tel. 905-845-6511
Fax 905-845-0265
Email .... tdlgroup_hr@timhortons.com
Website .... www.timhortons.com
Employer Background: The TDL Group Ltd., operators of Tim Hortons restaurants, is a leader in the quick service industry. *New Positions Created (2):* Truck Driver; Truck Driver.

TEAM INC.
Att: Human Resources Manager
4105 Cousens Street
St-Laurent, QC H4S 1V6
Tel. 514-745-1600
Email .... sales@teaminc.ca
Website .... www.teaminc.ca
Employer Background: TEAM Inc., a Chelton Group Company, is actively involved in aeronautics, with a strong commitment to remain at the highest technical level. *New Positions Created (4):* QA Manager; Sales & Customer Support Mgr; QA Manager; Secretary / Receptionist.

TECHMIRE LTD.
Att: Systems Engineering Department
7535 M.B. Jodoin
Anjou, QC H1J 2H9

Tel. 514-354-6110
Fax 514-352-0028
Email .... apollak@techmire.com
Website .... www.techmire.com
Employer Background: Techmire Ltd. designs and manufactures multiple-slide die casting machines for high-precision components. *New Positions Created (3):* Die Casting Process Engineer or Technologist; Industrial Machine Design Engineer / Designer; Metallurgist Engineer or Technologist.

TECHNICAL STANDARDS & SAFETY AUTHORITY / TSSA
Att: Human Resources
3300 Bloor Street West
4th Floor, West Tower
Toronto, ON M8X 2X4

Tel. 416-325-2000
Fax 416-326-1497
Email .... humanresources@tssa.org
Website .... www.tssa.org
Employer Background: TSSA is a risk-based, prevention-oriented organization that provides a variety of safety services, including public education, training and certification, engineering review and inspection, and safety management consultation. *New Positions Created (12):* Quality Assessors, Fuels; General Accounting Manager; Human Resource Advisor; Information Systems Manager; Audit Inspector, Fuels Safety ; Technical Services Specialist; Assistant General Counsel; Elevator Safety Inspectors; Audit Inspectors, Fuels Safety (2); Inspectors, Elevating and Amusement Devices Safety; Inspectors, Fuels Safety (2); Inspectors, Boilers and Pressure Vessels Safety.

TECHNICAL UNIVERSITY OF BRITISH COLUMBIA / TECHBC
Att: Human Resources
2400 Surrey Place
Surrey, BC V3T 2W1

Tel. 604-586-5225
Fax 604-586-5233
Email .... opportunities2b@techbc.ca
Website .... www.techbc.ca
Employer Background: Founded in 1997, TechBC is a Canadian university focusing on applied programs and innovative learning technologies. *New Positions Created (34):* Coordinator, Facilities Services; Director, Office of Institutional Research; Facilities Support Assistant; Finance & Purchasing Assistant; Learning Systems Technologist; Online Course Editor; Coordinator, Recruitment & Liaison; Director, Educational Technology and Learning; Human Resources Assistant; Research Programs Administrative Assistant; Administrative Assistant, Faculty; Director, University Facilities; Information Services Support Specialist; Instructional Designer; Organizational Development Consultant; Admissions Officer; Communication Engineering Faculty Position; Computer Engineering Faculty Position; Computer Science Faculty Position; Coordinator, Co-Op / Internship Programs; Learning Support Associate; Mailroom / Shipping & Receiving Assistant; Learner & Informa-

tion Services Assistant; Systems Analyst; TechLife Assistant II; Faculty Positions, School of Information Technology (3); Faculty Positions, School of Interactive Arts; Faculty Positions, School of Management & Technology; Manager, Production & Delivery; Research Services Officer; Graduate Program Services Coordinator; Graduate Programs Coordinator; Administrative Assistant, Information Resource Services; Course Delivery Coordinator.

TECHNISONIC INDUSTRIES LIMITED
Att: Human Resources Manager
250 Watline Avenue
Mississauga, ON L4Z 1P4

Tel. 905-890-2113
Fax 905-890-5338
Employer Background: Technisonic Industries Limited manufactures aeronautical AM and airborne FM communications equipment. *New Positions Created (3):* Senior Purchaser; Electronics Technologist / Electronic Engineer; QA Manager.

TECO PRECISION INC.
Att: Human Resources Manager
5841 St. Francois Street
St-Laurent, QC H4S 1B6

Tel. 514-332-4212
Fax 514-332-8326
Employer Background: TECO Precision Inc. performs CNC and conventional machining of precision components. *New Positions Created (6):* Mechanical Engineer; Computer Engineers; Electronics Engineers; Mechanical Engineer; Electronics Engineer; Electronics Technician.

TEEKAY SHIPPING CORP.
Att: Human Resources Manager
505 Burrard Street
Suite 1400, One Bentall Centre
Vancouver, BC V7X 1M5

Tel. 604-683-3529
Fax 604-844-6665
Email .... hr.info@teekay.com
Website .... www.teekay.com
Employer Background: Teekay Shipping Corp. provides international crude oil and petroleum product transportation services and owns a large fleet of medium-sized tankers. *New Positions Created (3):* Manager, Project Office; Project Manager; Financial Analyst.

TELAV AUDIO VISUAL SERVICES
Att: Operations Department
1475 East Georgia Street
Vancouver, BC V5L 2A9

Tel. 604-255-1151
Fax 604-255-0225
Email .... careers@telav.com
Website .... www.telav.com
Employer Background: TELAV Audio Visual Services specializes in audiovisual and simultaneous interpretation services, providing audio, visual and staging support for more than 65,000 events per year. *New Positions Created (3):* Audio Visual Operators; Account Executive; Service Technician.

TELAV AUDIO VISUAL SERVICES
Att: Human Resources
2916 - 5th Avenue NE, Box 17
Calgary, AB T2A 6K4

Tel. 403-235-1563
Fax 403-235-1564
Email .... careers@telav.com
Website .... www.telav.com
Employer Background: TELAV Audio Visual Services specializes in audiovisual and simultaneous interpretation services, providing audio, visual and staging support for more than 65,000 events per year. *New Positions Created (2):* General Manager; Account Executive.

TELAV AUDIO VISUAL SERVICES
Att: Operations Department
124 The East Mall
Toronto, ON M8Z 5V5

Tel. 416-234-5444
Fax 416-234-2781
Email .... careers@telav.com
Website .... www.telav.com
Employer Background: TELAV Audio Visual Services specializes in audiovisual and simultaneous interpretation services, providing audio, visual and staging support for more than 65,000 events per year. *New Positions Created (9):* Audio Visual Operators; Intermediate / Senior Audio Visual Operators; Rental and Staging Account Executive; Warehouse Personnel; Audio Visual Operators; Rental and Staging Account Executive; Account Executive; Systems Design Specialists; Installation and Service Technicians.

TELAV AUDIO VISUAL SERVICES
Att: Operations Department
2295 St. Laurent Boulevard
Ottawa, ON K1G 4H6

Tel. 613-526-3121
Fax 613-526-0850
Email .... careers@telav.com
Website .... www.telav.com
Employer Background: TELAV Audio Visual Services specializes in audiovisual and simultaneous interpretation services, providing audio, visual and staging support for more than 65,000 events per year. *New Positions Created (9):* Client Service Representative; Audio Visual Operators, Entry-Level; Audio Visual Operators, Intermediate and Senior; Warehouse Personnel; Audio Visual Operators, Entry Level; Audio Visual Operators, Intermediate and Senior; Audio Visual Operators; Intermediate / Senior Audio Visual Operators; Receptionist.

TELAV AUDIO VISUAL SERVICES
Att: Human Resources
1930 Onesime-Gagnon
Lachine, QC H8T 3M6

Fax 514-631-2695
Email .... careers@telav.com
Website .... www.telav.com
Employer Background: TELAV Audio Visual Services specializes in audiovisual and simultaneous interpretation services, providing audio, visual and staging support for more than 65,000 events per year. *New Po-*

sitions Created (21): Programmer / Analyst; Director, System Sales Division; Account Executives; Senior Accounting Clerk; Electronic Technicians; Administrative Assistant; Junior Payroll Clerk; Accounts Payable Clerk; Audio Visual Operators; Audio Visual Operators, Entry-Level; Installation and Service Technicians; Systems Design Specialists (2); Project Coordinator; Accounting Clerk; Human Resources Counsellor; Project Co-ordinator; Electronic Technicians; Service Coordinator; Payroll Manager; Purchasing Agent; Junior Accounting Clerk.

TELAV AUDIO VISUAL SERVICES
Att: Human Resources Department
90 Montée de Liesse
Montréal, QC H4T 1N4

Tel. 514-340-1821
Fax 514-340-9646
Email .... careers@telav.com
Website .... www.telav.com
Employer Background: TELAV Audio Visual Services specializes in audiovisual and simultaneous interpretation services, providing audio, visual and staging support for more than 65,000 events per year. *New Positions Created (3):* Director of Sales; Audio Visual Operators, Entry-Level; Audio Visual Operators, Intermediate / Senior.

TELDON INTERNATIONAL INC.
Att: Human Resources
3500 Viking Way
Richmond, BC V6V 1N6

Tel. 604-273-4500
Fax 604-273-6100
Website .... www.teldon.com
Employer Background: Teldon International Inc. is one of North America's leading advertising and commercial printing companies. *New Positions Created (12):* Production Coordinator; Graphic Designer / Coordinator; Pre-Press Manager; Electrician; Production Coordinator; Shipper / Receiver; Production Coordinator; Business Systems Coordinator; Motorsports Photo Editor; Customer Service Supervisor; Pressman; Inside Sales Representative.

TELEFLEX (CANADA) LTD.
Att: Employee Services
3831 No. 6 Road
Richmond, BC V6V 1P6

Tel. 604-270-6899
Fax 604-303-2899
Email .... hrcan@teleflex.bc.ca
Website .... www.teleflexcanada.com
Employer Background: Teleflex (Canada) Ltd., a subsidiary of Teleflex Inc., manufactures hydraulic steering for boats, coolant heaters for buses and trucks, and specialty industrial controls. *New Positions Created (2):* Technical Service Representative; Design Engineers.

TELEMATIC CONTROLS INC.
Att: General Manager
3364 - 114th Avenue SE
Calgary, AB T2Z 3V6

Tel. 403-253-7939
Fax 403-255-0042
Email .... careers@telematic.ab.ca
Website .... www.telematic.ca
Employer Background: Telematic Controls Inc. is a leader in the western Canadian industrial instrumentation and process control marketplace. *New Positions Created (4):* Technical Sales Representative; Technical Sales Representative; Accountant; Inside Sales Representative.

TELEPERFORMANCE CANADA INC.
Att: Human Resources Manager
365 Bloor Street East
Toronto, ON M4W 3L4

Tel. 416-922-3519
Fax 416-922-7830
Email .... recruiting@
.... teleperformancecanada.net
Website .... www.teleperformance.com
Employer Background: TPCAN is an international call centre service. *New Positions Created (11):* Systems Administrator, Call Centre Services; HR Manager; Account Mgr; Director of Operations; Director; IT Project Manager; Director, CRM New Business Development & Marketing, Contact Centre; Telesales Reps; IT Project Mgrs; Supervisors; Telesales Representatives.

TELESAT CANADA
Att: Human Resources
1601 Telesat Court
Gloucester, ON K1B 5P4

Tel. 613-748-0123
Fax 613-748-8865
Email .... resumes@telesat.ca
Website .... www.telesat.ca
Employer Background: Founded in 1969, Telesat Canada operates a fleet of satellites that provide broadcast distribution and telecommunications services, and is a consultant and partner in satellite ventures around the world. *New Positions Created (29):* Customer Service Engineer; Quality Assurance / Technical Trainer; Satellite Engineer; Spacecraft Bus Engineer, Mechanical; Bus Engineer / Specialist, Mechanical; Customer Service Engineer; Programmer / Analyst; R&D Lab Technologist; Satellite Engineer; SNOC Technologist; Spacecraft Bus Engineer; Technologist; Technologist; Electronics Technologists; Mgr, Eastern Sales; Senior Market Planners (2); Senior Payload Engineer; Spacecraft Bus Engineer; Systems Engineer; Technologist; Human Resources Manager; Mgr, Eastern Sales; Senior Market Planners (2); Senior Payload Engineer; Spacecraft Bus Engineer; Systems Engineer; Technologist; Technologist; Database / System Administrator.

TELESPECTRUM CANADA INC.
Att: Human Resources Generalist
1 Concorde Gate, 9th Floor
Toronto, ON M3C 3N6

Fax 416-443-6857
Email .... hr@telespectrum.com
Website .... www.telespectrum.com
Employer Background: TeleSpectrum Canada (formerly S&P Data) is one of North

America's leading teleservices firms. *New Positions Created (7):* Call Centre Professionals; Senior Telecom Administrator; Shift Manager; Commercial Banking Telephone Sales Representatives; Internet Sales / Customer Service Positions; Bilingual Call Centre Professionals; Internet Sales / Customer Service Positions.

TELETECH CANADA
Att: Human Resources Manager
100 Sheppard Avenue East, Suite 200
Toronto, ON M2N 6N5

Tel. 416-228-7530
Fax 416-228-7399
Website .... www.teletech.com
Employer Background: TeleTech Canada is one of the leading telephone services and call centre operators in North America. *New Positions Created (7):* Bilingual Supervisor; Customer Interaction Centre Manager; Human Resources Manager; Recruiter; Training Manager; Customer Service Representatives; Technical Support Representative.

TELLABS TTG INC.
Att: Human Resources Manager
1420 Blair Place, 3rd Floor
Gloucester, ON K1J 9L8

Fax 514-736-1468
Email .... ttg.hr@tellabs.com
Website .... www.tellabs.com
Employer Background: Tellabs TTG Inc. provides the communications industry with optical networking, switching, broadband access and service solutions. *New Positions Created (4):* Telecom Positions; Senior EMS Software Engineer; Senior Software Engineers; System Engineer.

TELLABS TTG INC.
Att: Human Resources Department
3403 Griffith Street
St-Laurent, QC H4T 1W5

Fax 514-736-1468
Email .... ttg.hr@tellabs.com
Website .... www.tellabs.com
Employer Background: Tellabs TTG Inc. provides the communications industry with optical networking, switching, broadband access and service solutions. *New Positions Created (3):* Telecom Positions; Senior Software Engineers; System Engineer.

TELLAMON PHOTONIC NETWORKS INC.
Att: Human Resources Manager
2280 Walkley Road
Ottawa, ON K1G 6B1

Tel. 613-731-6513
Fax 613-731-1013
Email .... hr@tellamon.com
Website .... www.tellamon.com
Employer Background: Tellamon Photonic Networks Inc. develops and manufactures optical networking products for long-haul, metro and access optical networks. *New Positions Created (26):* High Speed Electronic Designer; Lab Technician; Integrated Optics Process Engineer; Integrated Optics

Senior Process Engineer; Materials Manager; Optical Networking Industry Analyst; Photonics Engineer; Advisor, New Product Introduction; Field Applications Engineer; Head of Sales, Major Accounts; Product Manager; Receptionist; Sr Buyer; Senior HR Manager; Technical Support Technician; Test Technician; Optical Networking Engineer; Electrical / Photonics Engineer; High Speed Electronic Designer; Manufacturing Documentation Specialist; Materials Manager; Optical Amplifier Designer; Quality Engineer; Technical Writer; Telecommunications System Engineer; Test Engineer.

TELOS TECHNOLOGY INC.
Att: Human Resources
13120 Vanier Place, Suite 110
Richmond, BC V6V 2J2

Tel.	604-276-0055
Fax	604-276-0501
Email	jobs@telostech.com
Website	www.telostech.com

Employer Background: TELOS Technology Inc. develops wireless telecom systems, including 3G and IP telephony networks. *New Positions Created (32):* Administrative Assistant, Operations; Facilities Assistant; Network Administrator; Oracle Developer, IP, Telephony, Wireless Telecom; System Test Specialist; Executive Assistant; Software Architect; Software Requirements Analyst; Software Project Manager; Technical Trainer; Contracts Manager; Oracle Software Developer; Software Quality Assurance Specialist; Technical Writer; Inside Sales / Sales Support Position; Quality Assurance Manager; Sales Account Managers; Software Developer / Engineer, IP Telephony / Wireless; System Test Specialist; Systems Administrator; Technical Sales Engineer; Wireless Network Engineer; Software Developer, Network Management; Contracts Administrator; Project Assistant, Technology; Software Project Manager; System Test Specialists; Wireless Telecom Engineers; Administrative Assistant; Engineering Specialists; Marketing Manager; Software Developers.

TELTECH ASSETS.COM LTD.
Att: Human Resources Manager
3220 - 5th Avenue NE, Suite 14
Calgary, AB T2A 5L7

Fax	403-569-9192
Email	hrd@teltechassets.com
Website	www.teltechassets.com

Employer Background: TelTech Assets.Com Ltd. is a global source for low-cost computer products. *New Positions Created (7):* Corporate Account Representative; Operations Manager; Retail Sales Position; Senior Accountant; Technicians; Warehouse Personnel; Wholesale Account Representatives.

TELUS CORPORATION
Att: Human Resources Manager
3777 Kingsway, 6th Floor
Burnaby, BC V5H 3Z7

Tel.	604-432-4435
Fax	604-435-5530
Email	human.resources@telus.com
Website	www.telus.com

Employer Background: Telus Corporation is a leading telecommunications company, providing a full range of communications products and services that connect Canadians to the world. *New Positions Created (24):* Help Desk Analysts; Engagement Manager; Account Executive, Business Solutions; Advisor, Corporate Development & Strategy; Advisor, Corporate Research; Business Analyst; Executive Assistant, Emerging Operators; Manager, Corporate Client Support; Senior Communications Professional; Business Continuity Planner; Clerical Positions; CO Technician - Network Operations Centre; Compensation Consultant; Data Coordinator Centre Manager; Installation Wiring Assistant; National Customer Support Centre Manager; Senior Network Consultant; Tax Advisor; Business Account Manager, Enterprise Management; Consulting Analysts (2); Service Management Coordinator; Programmer Analyst, Business Systems; System Analyst; Sales and Service Manager.

TELUS ENTERPRISE SOLUTIONS
Att: Human Resource Manager
4720 Kingsway, 24th Floor, Metrotower II
Burnaby, BC V5H 4N2

Tel.	604-451-2595
Fax	604-451-2165
Email	recruit@ismbc.com
Website	www.ismbc.com

Employer Background: Telus Enterprise Solutions (formerly ISM-BC Corporation) is one of Canada's premier providers of information system management services. *New Positions Created (5):* Computer Scheduling Supervisor; E-Commerce Systems Specialist; Mainframe Database Administrator; Siebel Implementation Specialists; Systems Administrators, Unix.

TELUS INTEGRATED COMMUNICATIONS
Att: Human Resources
222 Bay Street, 10th Floor, PO Box 226
Toronto, ON M5K 1A1

Fax	416-304-0943
Email	tic.hr@telus.com
Website	www.telus.com

Employer Background: Telus Integrated Communications is Canada's second-largest full-service telecom company, with expansion plans in Canada and internationally. *New Positions Created (27):* Design Engineer (Core); Design Engineer (Service Delivery); Client Billing Consultant; Network Surveillance Specialist; Reporting and Analysis Manager; Sales Operations Performance Manager; Training Performance and Coordination Manager; Alliance Manager, Telus Enterprise Solutions; Change Management Specialist; Director of Sales; Director, Sales Client Solutions; E-Business - Project Manager, Internet Data Centre; Project Manager - Operations, Internet Data Centre; Recruitment Manager; Supplier Performance Manager; Billing Analyst; Client Project Manager; Client Project Manager; Client Service Manager; Client Service Manager; Consulting Analyst OSS; Data & IP Account Manager; Data & IP Account Manager, Ontario Government Account; Director, Client Service Manager; IP Solutions Architect / Technical Solutions Architect; Project Financials Coordinator; Sr Client Product Manager.

TELUS MOBILITY
Att: Human Resources
200 Consilium Place, Suite 1600
Toronto, ON M1H 3J3

Tel.	416-279-2532
Fax	416-279-3137
Email	hr@clearnet.com
Website	www.telusmobility.com

Employer Background: Telus Mobility (formerly Clearnet Communications Inc.) is a leading provider of wireless communication services. *New Positions Created (127):* Sales Representative; Telecom Applications Analyst; Business Reporting Analyst; Client Management Analyst; Dealer Services Manager, Channel Services; IT Billing Operator; National Translations Specialist; Production Systems Analyst / Team Lead; Assistant Store Manager; Dealer Services Manager, Channel Services; Inventory and Repair Coordinator; Loyalty and Retention Analyst; Manager, Client Risk Management (A / R Inbound); Manager, Shared Network Support Systems; Network Engineer, Power Engineering; Payment Processing Administrator; Sales Representative; Store Manager; Store Manager; Account Manager; Store Manager; Store Manager; Account Manager; Assistant Store Manager; Assistant Manager; Executive Assistant; Manager, Billing Operations; Manager, Client Care; Manager, RF TD, Non-Core Systems; Peripherals Engineer TD; RF Engineer, RF TD, Core Systems; RF Engineer, RF TD, Non-Core Systems; RF Network Engineer; RF Specialist; RF Specialist; Sales Representatives (2); Security Specialist, Policy and Planning; Senior Account Manager; Subscriber Equipment Engineer; Subscriber Equipment Specialist; Switching Technology Development Engineer; System Analyst; Telecom Analyst; Web Developer; Wireless Data Network Engineer; Account Manager; Administration Support Position; Business Analyst, Web Services; Decision Support Programmer / Analyst; Director, Network Services; Fixed Network Engineer; Market Analyst, Competitive Intelligence; Sales Representative; Sales Representatives (2); Senior Internet Application Developer; Area Managers (4); Business Analyst, Strategic Analysis CRM; Communications Specialist, External; Communications Specialist, Internal; Disbursements Administrator; Sales Representatives (2); Store Manager; Account Manager; Account Manager; Assistant Manager; Business Systems Analyst; Change Management Analyst; Commissioning Specialist; Data Analyst; Data Architect; Database Administrator; Director, Transmission Planning; Engineering Budget Analyst; Engineering Budgets and Metric Analyst; Executive Assistant; Field Analyst; Financial Support Analyst; iDEN Engineer; Integration Analyst; Internet Application Developer; Manager, Incident Management and Performance Tuning; Manager, Maintenance Operations; Manager, Research & Development;

Market Leadership Council Coordinator; Marketing Specialist; Production Development Specialist, Wireless Web; Quality Assurance Analyst; Retail Field Sales Trainer; Retail Sales Rep; Retail Sales Rep; Sales Rep; Sales Rep; Sales Rep; Sales Rep; Sales Rep; Sales Rep; Sales Rep; Sales Rep; Sales Rep; Security Specialist; Senior Network Support Specialist; Store Manager; Store Manager; Store Manager; Store Manager; Store Manager; Store Manager; Store Manager; Systems Analyst; Team Lead, Quality Assurance; Vice-President, Technology Operations; Wireless Data Network Engineer; Account Executives; Account Representatives; Bilingual Client Business Analyst; Commissioning Specialist; IP Network Specialist; Manager, Field Support and Compliance; Network OSS Specialist; PCS Translations Engineer; Programmer / Analyst; RF Engineer; RF Specialist; Account Executives; Dealer Sales Representatives (24); Retail Sales Representatives, Channel Marketing.

TEN STAR FINANCIAL SERVICES / TEN STAR INSURANCE BROKERS
Att: Controller
95 Hamilton Street North
Suite 2, PO Box 1490
Waterdown, ON L0R 2H0
Tel. 905-689-7911
Fax 905-689-3246
Website .... www.tenstar.ca
Employer Background: Ten Star Financial Services is the trading name of four integrated financial service companies, serving Canadians for over 25 years. *New Positions Created (2):* Administrative Assistant; Marketing Co-ordinator.

TENAQUIP LTD.
Att: Human Resources Department
20701, chemin Ste-Marie
Ste-Anne-de-Bellevue, QC H9X 5X5
Tel. 514-457-7122
Fax 514-457-4815
Email .... cv@tenaquip.com
Website .... www.tenaquip.com
Employer Background: Tenaquip Ltd. is a national distributor of industrial equipment and supplies. *New Positions Created (4):* Accounts Payable Supervisor; Associate Product Manager; Buyer; Inside Sales Representatives, Fasteners.

TENARISNETWORK
Att: Human Resources
855 - 2nd Street SW, Suite 3450
Calgary, AB T2P 4J8
Website .... www.techintgroup.com
Employer Background: TenarisNetwork manufactures seamless pipes and has over 48,000 employees worldwide. *New Positions Created (4):* Line Pipe Sales Position; Marketing Analyst; New Product and Services Manager; OCTG Sales Position.

TENCORR PACKAGING INC.
Att: Teresa Nagy
188 Cartwright Avenue
Toronto, ON M6A 1V6
Tel. 416-787-1687
Fax 416-787-0741
Employer Background: Tencorr Packaging Inc. is a paper converter. *New Positions Created (2):* Manager, Customer Service; Quality Assurance Manager.

TENG & ASSOCIATES INC.
Att: Human Resources
1450 Meyerside Drive, Suite 502
Mississauga, ON L5T 2N5
Tel. 905-670-1770
Fax 905-670-1775
Employer Background: Teng & Associates is a multi-disciplinary engineering company with a primary focus on providing professional engineering services to petroleum / petrochemical and pharmaceutical clients. *New Positions Created (2):* Electrical Design Technologist; Electrical Engineer.

TENNANT COMPANY
Att: Brian Levins
1329 Cardiff Boulevard
Mississauga, ON L5S 1R2
Fax 905-670-8547
Email .... brian.levins@tennantco.com
Website .... www.tennantco.com
Employer Background: Founded in 1870, Minneapolis-based Tennant Company manufactures non-residential floor maintenance equipment, floor coatings and related products. *New Positions Created (3):* Field Service Technician; Mechanic; Area Commercial Service Representative.

TERAGO NETWORKS INC.
Att: Human Resources Manager
300 Manning Road NE, Suite 300
Calgary, AB T2E 8K4
Tel. 403-668-5300
Fax 403-668-5344
Website .... www.terago.ca
Employer Background: TeraGo Networks Inc. is a new facilities-based Internet and data communications carrier that utilizes wireless broadband technologies. *New Positions Created (6):* Director of Marketing Communications; Field Service Managers; Field Service Technicians; Network Engineer; Product Marketing Managers; Regional Sales Managers.

TERAXION
Att: Human Resources Manager
360 Franquet, Suite 20
Ste-Foy, QC G1P 4N3
Tel. 418-658-9500
Fax 418-658-9595
Email .... jobs1@teraxion.com
Website .... www.teraxion.com
Employer Background: Teraxion designs, researches and manufactures leading-edge optical components for high-performance fibre-optic networks. *New Positions Created (6):* Optomechanical Engineer; Product Manager; Production Engineer; Production Technologist; Sales Director, North America; Technical Assistants / Operators.

TERMINAL FOREST PRODUCTS LIMITED
Att: Manager, Log Supply
12180 Mitchell Road
Richmond, BC V6V 1M8
Fax 604-321-4223
Employer Background: Terminal Forest Products Limited is a privately-owned company with harvesting, sawmilling and dryland sorting operations. *New Positions Created (2):* Log Trader; Log Quality Control Supervisor.

TERRA GROUP OF COMPANIES
Att: Human Resources
1245 - 7th Avenue East
Vancouver, BC V5T 1R1
Tel. 604-874-1245
Fax 604-874-2358
Email .... resumes@terra.ca
Website .... www.terra.ca
Employer Background: The Terra Group of Companies offers services in geotechnical engineering, forest industry consulting and materials engineering. *New Positions Created (2):* Administrative Assistants; Construction Materials Testing Technician.

TERRACE FORD LINCOLN SALES
Att: Chris Krawczyk
900 Walkers Line
Burlington, ON L7N 2G2
Tel. 905-632-6252
Fax 905-632-9643
Email .... jobs@terracefordlincoln.com
Website .... www.terracefordlincoln.com
Employer Background: Terrace Ford Lincoln Sales is an automotive dealership with annual volumes of 1100+ and an inventory of 300+ units. *New Positions Created (3):* Vehicle Clerk; Trim Technician; Automobile Sales Position.

TERRAFIX GEOSYNTHETICS INC.
Att: Sales Manager
178 Bethridge Road
Toronto, ON M9W 1N3
Tel. 416-674-0363
Fax 416-674-1159
Email .... terrafix@terrafixgeo.com
Website .... www.terrafixgeo.com
Employer Background: Terrafix Geosynthetics Inc. is a leader in geosynthetics and polyethylene pipes. *New Positions Created (3):* Product Engineer; Inside Sales Position; Technical Sales Position.

TESMA INTERNATIONAL INC.
Att: Heidi Garcia, Human Resources
PO Box 895
Maple, ON L6A 3M3
Tel. 905-303-2300
Fax 905-303-9792
Email .... resumes@tesma.com
Website .... www.tesma.com
Employer Background: Tesma International Inc. is a global supplier of die cast, machined and assembled automotive parts. *New Positions Created (4):* CNC Programmer / Operator; Engineering Manager; Industrial

Maintenance Mechanic / Millwright; Production Supervisor.

TESTFORCE
Att: Human Resources Manager
5990 Vanden Abeele
St-Laurent, QC H4S 1R9
Tel. 514-856-0970
Fax 514-856-6983
Website .... www.testforce.com
Employer Background: Testforce supplies test and measurement equipment and integrated systems. *New Positions Created (6):* Assembler Technician; Inside Sales Representative; Intermediate Sales Representative; Intermediate Sales Representative; Senior Sales Rep; Secretary, Sales Support.

TEXTILES HUMAN RESOURCES COUNCIL
Att: Julia Miles
66 Slater Street, Suite 1720
Ottawa, ON K1P 5H1
Tel. 613-230-7217
Fax 613-230-1270
Email .... julia.miles@thrc-crhit.org
Website .... www.thrc-crhit.org
Employer Background: Established in 1994, Textiles Human Resources Council is a non-profit, union management partnership mandated to assist the industry develop training and education solutions. *New Positions Created (2):* Project Coordinators; Director of Operations & Communications.

TEXTRON FASTENING SYSTEMS
Att: Human Resources Manager
875 Stone Street North
Gananoque, ON K7G 3E4
Tel. 800-544-6117
Fax 613-382-5805
Email .... gcoburn@tfsa.textron.com
Website .... www.camcar.textron.com
Employer Background: Textron Fastening Systems, a division of Textron Canada Ltd., manufactures cold formed fasteners and screw products. *New Positions Created (2):* Secondary (Threader) Operators; Maintenance Machinist.

THALES AVIONICS CANADA INC.
Att: Human Resources Department
7190 Frederick Banting Street, Suite 100
St-Laurent, QC H4S 2A1
Tel. 514-832-0911
Fax 514-832-0929
Website .... www.ravl.co.uk
Employer Background: Thales Avionics Canada Inc. develops electronics for aerospace, defense and information technology and services, and has 65,000 employees worldwide. *New Positions Created (2):* Buyer; Regional Service Manager.

THALES OPTRONICS CANADA INC.
Att: Human Resources Manager
4868 Levy Street
St-Laurent, QC H4R 2P1
Email .... hr@tcoc.thomson-csf.ca
Website .... www.thalesgroup.com

Employer Background: Thales Optronics Canada Inc. specializes in the design and manufacture of electro-optic equipment for airborne, naval and land military applications. *New Positions Created (3):* Intermediate Production Engineer; Senior and Intermediate Designers; Technicians, Production, Repair and Overhaul.

THAMES VALLEY DISTRICT SCHOOL BOARD
Att: Linda Peck,
Superintendent, HR Services
1250 Dundas Street, PO Box 5888
London, ON N6A 5L1
Tel. 519-452-2000
Fax 519-452-2395
Website .... www.tvdsb.on.ca
Employer Background: The Thames Valley District School Board is the third-largest board in Ontario, operating 30 secondary schools and 160 elementary schools. *New Positions Created (3):* Principal, Elementary and Secondary Schools; Vice-Principal, Elementary and Secondary Schools; Manager - Business Services.

THEMEDIA
Att: Human Resources Department
1008 Homer Street, Suite 208
Vancouver, BC V6B 2X1
Tel. 604-687-1268
Fax 604-687-2826
Email .... hr@themediaco.com
Website .... www.themediaco.com
Employer Background: THEmedia is an advertising agency that delivers multimedia and creative print design to help businesses with their marketing needs. *New Positions Created (2):* Sales Position; Sales Rep.

THERAPIST'S CHOICE MEDICAL SUPPLIES INC.
Att: Human Resources Manager
944 Lawrence Avenue West
Toronto, ON M5A 1C4
Tel. 416-781-7210
Fax 416-781-8406
Website .... www.therapistschoice.com
Employer Background: Established in 1990, Therapist's Choice Medical Supplies Inc. is a leading supplier of quality medical equipment, services and rentals. *New Positions Created (5):* Customer Service / Inside Sales Position; Data Entry / Accounts Receivable Clerk; Purchasing Agent; Collections / Accounts Receivable Position; Inside Sales / Customer Service Representative.

THERMADYNE CANADA
Att: Glenn Smith,
Regional Business Manager
2070 Wyecroft Road
Oakville, ON L6L 5V6
Tel. 905-827-1111
Fax 506-388-3101
Email .... gssmith@nbnet.nb.ca
Website .... www.thermadyne.com
Employer Background: Thermadyne Canada is a leader in the welding and cut-

ting hard goods industry. *New Positions Created (3):* District Manager; District Manager; District Manager.

THERMAL ENERGY INTERNATIONAL INC.
Att: Human Resources Manager
34 Bentley Avenue
Nepean, ON K2E 6T8
Tel. 613-723-6776
Fax 613-723-7286
Email .... careers@thermalenergy.com
Website .... www.thermalenergy.com
Employer Background: Thermal Energy International Inc. is an Ottawa-based leader in air pollution control and energy recovery solutions. *New Positions Created (7):* Intermediate Chemical Engineers; Manager of Engineering; Piping Designers; Project Leaders and Design Engineers; Project Managers; Sales Engineers and Managers; Junior Accounting Position.

THERMO DESIGN ENGINEERING LTD.
Att: Human Resources Manager
Box 5557, SECSC
Edmonton, AB T6C 6P8
Tel. 780-440-6064
Fax 780-440-1657
Email .... hr@thermodesign.com
Website .... www.thermodesign.com
Employer Background: Thermo Design Engineering Ltd. is one of Canada's leading suppliers of oil and gas production and process equipment systems. *New Positions Created (5):* Control Systems Technologists / Engineers; Electrical Designers; Instrumentation Technologist; Project Designers / Draftspersons; Project / Process Engineers.

THIINC INFORMATION MANAGEMENT INC.
Att: Cindy Draycott, Executive Director, Clinical Information Services
6 Adelaide Street East, Suite 500
Toronto, ON M5C 1H6
Tel. 416-203-1168
Fax 416-203-1148
Email .... cindy.draycott@thiincimi.com
Website .... www.thiincimi.com
Employer Background: THiiNC Information Management Inc. provides a broad range of health information services. *New Positions Created (3):* Client Services Mgr; Health Record Coders & Data Quality Reviewers; Mgr, Training, Recruitment & Development.

THOMAS & BETTS LIMITED
Att: Human Resources Department
700 Thomas Avenue
Iberville, QC J2X 2M9
Tel. 450-347-5318
Fax 450-357-3521
Email .... hr_canada@tnb.com
Website .... www.tnb.com
Employer Background: Thomas & Betts Limited is a leading North American manufacturer of electrical connectors, components, accessories and electronic systems, including emergency lighting. *New Positions*

Created (5): Documentation Control Specialist; Electronic Design Engineer; Materials Manager; Production Manager; Senior Buyer, Electronic Components.

THOMAS COOK TRAVEL
Att: Joe Newell
7 Court House Avenue
Brockville, ON K6V 4T3
Tel. 613-342-1412
Fax 613-342-1754
Email .... jnewell@thomascook.ca
Website .... www.thomascook.ca
Employer Background: Thomas Cook Travel provides retail travel services, markets travellers cheques, and trades foreign currencies and precious metals. *New Positions Created (2):* Intermediate / Senior Travel Sales Consultants; Intermediate / Senior Travel Sales Consultants.

THOMPSON HEALTH REGION
Att: Michael D. Wolfman, Acting CEO
311 Columbia Street
Kamloops, BC V2C 2T1
Tel. 250-314-2780
Fax 250-314-2765
Employer Background: The Thompson Health Region encompasses nine communities, serves a regional population of approximately 125,000, employs in excess of 2,000 employeees and has an annual budget of over $138 million. *New Positions Created (2):* Executive Director, Human Resources; Executive Director, Mental Health Services.

THOMSON TECHNOLOGY INC.
Att: Human Resources Manager
9087A - 198th Street
Langley, BC V1M 3B1
Tel. 604-888-0110
Fax 604-888-3381
Email .. lmoore@thomsontechnology.com
Website ..... www.thomsontechnology.com
Employer Background: Established in 1973, Thomson Technology Inc. is an ISO-certified manufacturer of power generation controls and switchgear. *New Positions Created (6):* Electrical Power and Control Designers; Electrical Wireperson / Mechanical Assembler; Electrical Designer; Mechanical Designer; Component Assembler; Electrical Wireperson / Assembler.

THOMSON-CSF OPTRONIQUE CANADA INC.
Att: Human Resources
4868 Levy Street
St-Laurent, QC H4R 2P1
Fax 514-337-1104
Email .... hr@tcoc.thomson-csf.ca
Website .... www.thomson-csf.ca
Employer Background: Thomson-CSF Optronique Canada Inc. specializes in the design, manufacture and after-sales support of electro-optic equipment for air, naval and land military applications. *New Positions Created (3):* Intermediate Material Planner / Buyer; Designers; Quality Engineer.

THORBURN EQUIPMENT INC.
Att: Marie Valin
173 Oneida Drive
Pointe-Claire, QC H9R 1A9
Tel. 514-695-8714
Fax 514-695-1321
Email .... mvalin@thorburnflex.com
Website .... www.thorburnflex.com
Employer Background: Thorburn Equipment Inc. manufactures and designs ultra high-quality flexible piping products. *New Positions Created (4):* Accounts Payable / Accounting Clerk; Contract Administrator / Assistant to the President; Mechanical Design Engineer; Project Planner.

THRIFTY CANADA, LTD.
Att: Human Resources
6050 Indian Line
Mississauga, ON L4V 1G5
Tel. 905-612-1881
Fax 905-612-1893
Website .... www.thrifty.com
Employer Background: Thrifty Canada, Ltd. is a car rental company, operating in 62 countries and territories throughout the world. *New Positions Created (3):* Customer Service Representatives; Administrative Assistant; Accounts Payable Clerk.

THRIFTY CAR RENTAL
Att: Hans Verbeek
3860 Macdonald Road South
Richmond, BC V7B 1L8
Tel. 604-606-1666
Fax 604-606-1672
Website .... www.thrifty.
Employer Background: Thrifty Car Rental is a car rental company, operating in 62 countries and territories throughout the world. *New Positions Created (5):* Airport Manager; Customer Service / Telephone Service Representatives; Sales Executive; Airport Manager; Customer Service Representatives / Telephone Service Representatives.

THRIFTY FOODS
Att: Bonnie A. Campbell, HR Department
6649 Butler Crescent
Saanichton, BC V8M 1Z7
Tel. 250-544-1122
Fax 250-544-6751
Email .... bcampbell@thriftyfoods.com
Website .... www.thriftyfoods.com
Employer Background: Founded in 1977, Thrifty Foods is a leading grocery retailer, with 17 locations, over 2,300 employees and annual sales exceeding $340 million. *New Positions Created (2):* Chief Financial Officer; Pharmacists.

THRIVE MEDIA
Att: Human Resources
856 Homer Street, Suite 500
Vancouver, BC V6B 2W5
Tel. 604-681-2858
Fax 604-681-2869
Email .... hr@thrivemedia.com
Website .... www.thrivemedia.com

Employer Background: Thrive Media is a technology development company focusing on Internet-based entertainment applications, Internet-enabled commercial transaction systems and Internet-oriented marketing / advertising. *New Positions Created (8):* Director of Marketing; Senior Java Programmer; Technical Researcher; Business Development Representative; Advertising Manager; Web Designer; Business Development / Sales Director; Office Manager.

THUNDER BAY, CITY OF
Att: Human Resources Department
141 South May Street, PO Box 800
Thunder Bay, ON P7E 1A9
Tel. 807-346-2000
Fax 807-625-3585
Email .. recruitment@city.thunder-bay.on.ca
Website .... www.city.thunder-bay.on.ca
Employer Background: Thunder Bay is Ontario's 10th-largest city, with a metropolitan population of over 120,000 people and a regional trading population exceeding 260,000. *New Positions Created (2):* Mgr, Accounting; Network Planning Engineer.

THURBER GROUP
Att: Dimitri Papanicolas, PEng, Edmonton Operation Manager
9636 - 51st Avenue, Suite 200
Edmonton, AB T6E 6A5
Tel. 780-438-1460
Fax 780-437-7125
Website .... www.thurbergroup.com
Employer Background: Established in 1957, Thurber Group is a geo-engineering and environmental consulting firm, with offices in British Columbia, Alberta and Ontario. *New Positions Created (3):* Intermediate Geotechnical Engineer; Intermediate Hydrogeologist; Senior Environmental Consultants.

TIERCON INDUSTRIES INC.
Att: Human Resources Department
565 Arvin Avenue
Stoney Creek, ON L8E 5N7
Tel. 905-643-4176
Fax 905-643-3431
Email .... edebiasi@tierconcdn.com
Website .... www.tierconcdn.com
Employer Background: Tiercon Industries Inc. produces plastic injection molded parts, including painted body side moldings, rocker panels, interior moldings, decorative trim and enclosure applications. *New Positions Created (10):* Area Mgrs; Plant Mgrs; Executive Assistant; Receptionist; Process Set-up Technicians; Packaging Engineer; Process Engineer; Quality Engineer; Inventory Control Analyst; Warehouse Supervisor.

TIERONE OSS TECHNOLOGIES INC.
Att: Human Resources
5945 Airport Rd., Suite 185, Airway Centre
Mississauga, ON L4V 1R9
Tel. 905-677-4228
Fax 905-677-4296
Email .... hr@tieroneoss.com
Website .... www.tieroneoss.com

Employer Background: TierOne OSS Technologies Inc. provides strategy consulting, product deployment, integration and custom software development to communication service providers worldwide. *New Positions Created (3):* Business Analysts (2); Software Developers (2); System Tester.

TILBURY CEMENT LTD.
Att: Maintenance Superintendent
7777 Ross Road, PO Box 950
Delta, BC V4K 3S6

Tel. 604-946-0411
Email .... dthillman@
.... tilbury.lehighcement.com
Website .... www.lehighcement.com
Employer Background: Tilbury Cement Ltd. (part of Lehigh Portland Cement Company) is an integrated cement manufacturing and building materials company, with operations in British Columbia, Washington and Oregon. *New Positions Created (2):* Maintenance Millwright; Purchasing Director.

TILLEY ENDURABLES
Att: Sandi Furtado, Human Resources
900 Don Mills Road
Toronto, ON M3C 1V6

Fax 416-444-3860
Email .... sandif@tilley.com
Website .... www.tilley.com
Employer Background: Tilley Endurables manufactures travel clothing. *New Positions Created (2):* Inventory Control Clerk; Sales Associates.

TILLSONBURG DISTRICT MEMORIAL HOSPITAL
Att: Human Resources
167 Rolph Street
Tillsonburg, ON N4G 3Y9

Tel. 519-842-3611
Fax 519-842-6733
Email .... tdmh@oxford.net
Employer Background: Tillsonburg District Memorial Hospital is a community hospital located in southwestern Ontario. *New Positions Created (2):* Executive Leader, Specialty Areas; Physiotherapist.

TIM OFFICE SOLUTIONS
Att: General Manager
50 Ronson Drive, Unit 190
Toronto, ON M9W 1B3

Fax 416-245-0398
Employer Background: Tim Office Solutions is a distributor for Kyocera Mita Canada Ltd., a leading imaging solutions manufacturer. *New Positions Created (4):* Sales Consultants; Account Representatives; Receptionist; Service Technicians.

TIMBERFIELD ROOF TRUSS
Att: Human Resources Manager
2016 Oxford Street East
London, ON N5V 2Z8

Fax 519-659-2714
Employer Background: Timberfield Roof Truss manufactures and distributes building components and pre-engineered wood products. *New Positions Created (5):* Estimator; Roof Truss Designers; Roof Truss Designers; Estimator; Roof Truss Designers.

TIME ICR INC.
Att: Human Resources Coordinator
1600 Laperriere Avenue, Suite 102
Ottawa, ON K1Z 8P5

Tel. 613-798-1500
Fax 613-798-1595
Email .... jobs@timeicr.ca
Website .... www.timeicr.ca
Employer Background: Time iCR Inc. provides complex call processing solutions, with a focus on custom speech recognition and interactive voice response applications. *New Positions Created (6):* Various Programming Positions; Account Managers; Administrative Support Positions; Implementation Support Associate; Implementation Technical Support Position; Systems Analyst.

TIMES FIBER CANADA LIMITED
Att: Human Resources
580 O'Brien Road
Renfrew, ON K7V 4A6

Tel. 613-432-8566
Fax 613-432-9373
Employer Background: Times Fiber Canada Limited produces cable products for video, telephony, high-speed data transmission and system powering. *New Positions Created (2):* Assistant Accountant; Plant Controller.

TIMMINS & DISTRICT HOSPITAL
Att: Brenda Corbeil, HR Officer
700 Ross Avenue East
Timmins, ON P4N 8P2

Tel. 705-267-6371
Fax 705-360-6008
Email .... jobs@tadh.com
Website www.timminsanddistricthosp.org
Employer Background: TDH is a modern, 160-bed acute care facility. *New Positions Created (2):* Obstetricians / Gynecologists; Clinical Nurse Specialist, Mental Health.

TIMOTHY'S WORLD COFFEE
Att: Human Resources
400 Steeprock Drive
Toronto, ON M3J 3B1

Tel. 416-638-3333
Fax 416-638-5603
Email .... careers@timothys.com
Website .... www.timothys.com
Employer Background: Timothy's World Coffee is a leading retail specialty coffee company. *New Positions Created (9):* Payroll Administrator; Sales & Marketing Assistant; Order Desk Administrator; Quality Assurance Assistant; Database Technician; District Manager; Machine Operator; Mechanic; Receptionist.

TIRECRAFT AUTO CENTERS LTD.
Att: Ross Kelly, Corporate Office
68 Chippewa Road
Sherwood Park, AB T8A 3Y1

Tel. 780-449-3700
Fax 780-449-6159

Website .... www.tirecraft.com
Employer Background: Tirecraft Auto Centers Ltd. is a full-service tire retailer. *New Positions Created (2):* Credit Manager; Assistant Advertising Coordinator.

TITANIUM LTD.
Att: Ms S. Polud
5055 Levy Road
St-Laurent, QC H4R 2N9

Tel. 514-334-5781
Fax 514-334-3410
Employer Background: Titanium Ltd. is a large fabricator of titanium process equipment. *New Positions Created (4):* Breakperson; CNC Drill Operator; Fitters (2); Machine Shop Workers (2).

TIW WESTERN
Att: Recruitment Department
7770 - 44th Street SE
Calgary, AB T2C 2L5

Tel. 403-279-8310
Fax 403-279-0120
Email .... hakim@telusplanet.net
Website .... www.tiwwestern.com
Employer Background: TIW Western provides engineered products and services to the oil and gas and pulp and paper industries. *New Positions Created (2):* Chief Draftsperson; Draftspersons (2).

TLC LASER EYE CENTERS
Att: Human Resources Manager
5280 Solar Drive
Mississauga, ON L4W 5M8

Tel. 905-602-2020
Fax 905-602-6697
Email .... carole.fortier@tlcvision.com
Website .... www.tlcvision.com
Employer Background: TLC is a leading provider of laser vision correction services. *New Positions Created (5):* Accounts Payable Accountants; Junior Accountant; Sales and Customer Service Representatives; Financial Budgets & Forecasting Manager; Public Relations Manager.

TOA CANADA CORPORATION
Att: Human Resources Manager
6150 Kennedy Road, Unit 3
Mississauga, ON L5T 2J4

Tel. 905-564-3570
Fax 905-564-3569
Website .... www.toacanada.com
Employer Background: TOA Canada Corporation is a leading international manufacturer of commercial and engineered sound products. *New Positions Created (4):* Coordinator of Accounts Receivable; Regional Sales Manager; AV Technical Support Position; Marketing Analysts.

TOA INC.
Att: Human Resources Manager
90 Richmond Street East, Suite 102
Toronto, ON M5C 1P1

Tel. 416-368-0308
Fax 416-368-3381

Email .... ccrewe@calltoa.com
Website .... www.calltoa.com

Employer Background: TOA Inc. is a rapidly growing leader in the office equipment industry with offices in Richmond Hill, Toronto, Rexdale, Burlington and Hamilton. *New Positions Created (2):* Copier Sales Representative; Telecommunication / Copier Technical Service Representative.

TOLKO INDUSTRIES LTD.
Att: Vyvian Burton, HR Coordinator
PO Box 39
Vernon, BC V1T 6M1

Tel. 250-545-4411
Fax 250-549-5331
Email .... human_resources@tolko.com
Website .... www.tolko.com

Employer Background: Tolko Industries Ltd. is a forest products company with marketing and manufacturing facilities throughout western Canada and Washington State. *New Positions Created (3):* Manager, Kraft Paper Logistics; Financial Accountant; Tax Accountant.

TOMMY HILFIGER CANADA INC.
Att: Deborah Bassenden
7077 Park Avenue, Suite 502
Montréal, QC H3N 1X7

Tel. 514-278-6000
Fax 514-278-3066
Email .... jobs@tommyhilfiger.ca
Website .... www.tommy.com

Employer Background: Tommy Hilfiger Canada Inc. markets designer men's and women's sports wear, jeans wear and children's wear under the "Tommy Hilfiger" brand. *New Positions Created (4):* Merchandise Coordinator; User Support Assistant; Senior Programmer Analyst; Traffic Department Director.

TOONBOOM TECHNOLOGIES
Att: Human Resources Manager
7 Laurier Street East
Montréal, QC H2T 1E4

Tel. 514-278-8666
Fax 514-278-2666
Email .... hrgen@toonboom.com
Website .... www.toonboom.com

Employer Background: ToonBoom Technologies develops leading-edge animation software. *New Positions Created (4):* Product Manager; Product Support Manager; New Internet Products; Software Design Engineers; Testing and Quality Assurance Specialist .

TOP PRODUCER SYSTEMS INC.
Att: Personnel Manager
10651 Shellbridge Way, Suite 155
Richmond, BC V6X 2W8

Tel. 604-270-8819
Fax 604-270-8218
Email .... careers@topproducer.com
Website .... www.topproducer.com

Employer Background: Founded in 1982, Top Producer Systems Inc. provides leads management and marketing software for

the real estate industry. *New Positions Created (12):* Multimedia Department Manager; Project Managers; Senior Developers; Database Architect; Director of Product Management, Customer Management Products; HR Manager; Senior Developers; Software Test Engineers; Computing Positions; Multimedia Positions; Project Manager; Technical Support Engineers.

TOP TAPE & LABEL LTD.
Att: Human Resources Manager
1259 Sandhill Drive
Ancaster, ON L9G 4V5

Tel. 905-648-0774
Fax 905-648-1139
Email .... cwd@toptape.com
Website .... www.toptape.com

Employer Background: Top Tape & Label Ltd. is a manufacturer of industrial identification products. *New Positions Created (2):* Silk Screen Printer; Customer Service Representative / Order Entry Clerk.

TORCAN CHEMICAL LTD.
Att: Human Resources
110 Industrial Parkway North
Aurora, ON L4G 3H4

Tel. 905-727-9417
Fax 905-727-7545
Website .... www.torcanchemical.on.ca

Employer Background: Torcan Chemical Ltd. is a research, development and manufacturing organization, specializing in active pharmaceutical ingredients and new chemical entities. *New Positions Created (4):* Technology Transfer Associate, Process Chemistry; Maintenance Technician; Process / Project Engineer in Training; Synthetic Organic Chemists.

TOROMONT CAT
Att: Human Resources
3131 Highway 7 West, PO Box 5511
Concord, ON L4K 1B7

Tel. 416-667-5511
Fax 416-667-5725
Email .... hradmin@toromont.com
Website .... www.toromont.com

Employer Background: Toromont CAT is the authorized dealer and distributor of Caterpillar heavy equipment, engines, power generator units and components in Ontario, Manitoba, Nunavut, Newfoundland and Labrador. *New Positions Created (10):* Field Service Dispatcher; HR / HRIS Analyst; Senior Payroll Administrator; Warehouse Parts Person; Customer Support Specialist; Parts Counter Position; Various Technician Positions; Shop Manager; IT Buyer; Technical Training Instructor.

TOROMONT PROCESS SYSTEMS, DIVISION OF TOROMONT INDUSTRIES
Att: Human Resources Manager
3615 - 34th Street NE
Calgary, AB T1Y 6Z8

Tel. 403-291-3438
Fax 403-291-3443
Email .... sjones@toromontprocess.com
Website .... www.toromontprocess.com

Employer Background: Toromont is a leading designer and manufacturer of gas processing systems, including gas compression packages, process refrigeration systems and cryogenic gas processing plants for domestic and international clients. *New Positions Created (4):* Production Planner; Draftsperson; Senior Project Engineers; Intermediate / Senior Application Engineers.

TORONTO BLUE JAYS BASEBALL CLUB
Att: Human Resources
1 Blue Jays Way, Suite 3200
Toronto, ON M5V 1J1

Tel. 416-341-1000
Website .... www.bluejays.com

Employer Background: Toronto Blue Jays is a major league baseball club in the American League East division. The Blue Jays were the World Series Champions in 1992 and 1993. *New Positions Created (3):* General Accounting Coordinator; Payroll & Benefits Assistant; Ticket Office Receivable Coordinator.

TORONTO CATHOLIC DISTRICT SCHOOL BOARD
Att: Mr. Ashleigh Molloy,
Continuing Ed Dept.
80 Sheppard Avenue East
Toronto, ON M2N 6E8

Tel. 416-222-8282
Fax 416-512-3047
Website .... www.tcdsb.on.ca

Employer Background: The Toronto Catholic District School Board operates 222 Catholic schools and serves over 102,000 students. The Board has a teaching staff of over 5,700 and 1,400 support staff. *New Positions Created (5):* Secondary School Teachers, Continuing Education Program, Tamil; Non-Academic Music Instructors; Building Automation System & Controls Technician; Security Technician; Safety Officer, Occupational Health and Safety Personnel Issues.

TORONTO, CITY OF
Att: Employment Services, HR
55 John Street, Metro Hall, 5th Floor
Toronto, ON M5V 3C6

Tel. 416-392-8665
Fax 416-397-9818
Website .... www.city.toronto.on.ca

Employer Background: The City of Toronto has an annual operating budget of over $5.6 billion and employs over 45,000 people. *New Positions Created (17):* Supervisor, General Ledger and Financial Reporting; Director, Urban Design; Director, Urban Design; Director, Information and Technology Planning; Social Service Caseworker; Executive Director, Technical Services; Lawyer, Labour and Employment Law; Lawyers, Municipal Law; Lawyers, Real Estate; Supervisor, Operations; Manager, Communicable Disease Surveillance Unit; Senior Epidemiologist, Communicable Disease Control; Labour and Employment Lawyer; Children's Services Consultant, Financial; Children's Services Consultant, Service Planning and Support; Social Services Caseworker; Director, Budget Services.

TORONTO.COM
Att: Human Resources Manager
80 Peter Street
Toronto, ON M5V 2G5

Tel.	416-596-4300
Fax	416-596-4350
Email	resumes@toronto.com
Website	www.toronto.com

Employer Background: Toronto.com is an Internet-based guide to the Greater Toronto Area, with a complete online directory of businesses, community groups and events. *New Positions Created (3):* Accounting Manager; New Media Sales Position; Telemarketing Representative.

TORONTO COMMUNITY CARE ACCESS CENTRE
Att: Human Resources
250 Dundas St. West, Unit 5, Ground Floor
Toronto, ON M5T 2Z5

Tel.	416-506-9888
Fax	416-506-1629
Website	www.torontoccac.com

Employer Background: Toronto Community Care Access Centre is a non-profit organization providing quality in-home health and social support services. *New Positions Created (3):* Care Coordinators; Care Coordinators; Service Quality Associate.

TORONTO CRICKET, SKATING AND CURLING CLUB
Att: Paul Cadieux, Assistant GM
141 Wilson Avenue
Toronto, ON M5M 3A3

Tel.	416-487-4581
Fax	416-487-7595
Email	pcadieux@torcricketclub.org
Website	www.torcricketclub.org

Employer Background: The Toronto Cricket, Skating and Curling Club is a year-round facility for sports and social activities. *New Positions Created (4):* Various Hospitality Positions; Sous Chef; Club Controller; Food and Beverage Coordinator.

TORONTO DISTRICT SCHOOL BOARD
Att: Elementary Recruitment Centre
155 College Street, 4th Floor
Toronto, ON M5T 1P6

Tel.	416-397-3726
Fax	416-397-3605
Email	applications.submissions@ tdsb.on.ca
Website	www.tdsb.on.ca

Employer Background: The Toronto District School Board serves almost 1.6 million electors of the City of Toronto. They are the largest school board in Canada and fourth largest in North America. *New Positions Created (4):* Elementary Teachers; Supervisory Officer; Elementary Teaching Positions; District Supervisor, Nutrition Services.

TORONTO EAST GENERAL & ORTHOPAEDIC HOSPITAL INC. / TEGH
Att: Human Resources
825 Coxwell Avenue
Toronto, ON M4C 3E7

Tel.	416-469-6326
Fax	416-469-7982
Email	hr@tegh.on.ca

Employer Background: TEGH is a 500-bed acute care community teaching hospital. *New Positions Created (37):* General Pathologist; Registered Nurses; Psychiatrist, Adult Services; Psychiatrist, Child and Adolescent; Clinical Nurse Specialist / Nurse Practitioner; Registered Nurses; Ultrasound Technologist; X-Ray Technologists; Coordinator, Psychogeriatric Case Management Program; Coordinator, Recruitment & Employee Records; Perinatal Nurse Educator; Registered Nurses; Patient Care Coordinator, Cardiac Catheterization Lab; Patient Care Coordinator, Emergency; Child & Adolescent Crisis Workers; Child & Adolescent Program Coordinator; Child & Adolescent Psychiatrists; Psychiatrists, Adult Outpatient Services; Clinical Manager, Pharmacy; Educators, Perinatal / Neonatal / Paediatrics; Manager, Hemodialysis; Nuclear Medicine Technologist; Occupational Therapists; Pharmacists; Physiotherapists; Registered Nurses; Senior MRI Technologist; Social Workers; Speech Language Pathologists; Ultrasound Technologist; Audiologist; Coordinator, Staffing Office and Float Pool; Manager, Health Record Services; Occupational Therapists; Physiotherapists; Social Workers; Speech Language Pathologist.

TORONTO FRENCH SCHOOL / TFS
Att: Office of Human Resources
296 Lawrence Avenue East
Toronto, ON M4N 1T7

Tel.	416-484-6533
Fax	416-488-2937
Email	ilavoie@tfs.on.ca
Website	www.tfs.on.ca

Employer Background: TFS is one of the largest independent schools in Canada, offering a broad, internationally-based academic curriculum to over 1,200 students. *New Positions Created (8):* Directors of Lower School Studies (2); Math & Science Teacher; Primary / Junior Teachers; Teachers; Vice-Principals (2); Bilingual Human Resources Coordinator; Biology Teacher, Senior Levels; Bilingual Assistant Director.

TORONTO GRACE HOSPITAL, THE SALVATION ARMY
Att: Human Resources
650 Church Street
Toronto, ON M4Y 2G5

Tel.	416-925-2251
Fax	416-925-3211
Website	www.sallynet.org

Employer Background: The Salvation Army Toronto Grace Hospital is a 119-bed chronic and palliative care centre. *New Positions Created (8):* Program Director, Palliative Care; Physiotherapist; Social Worker; GRASP Project Manager; Registered Nurses; Physiotherapist; Registered Nurses; Rehabilitation Practice Leader.

TORONTO HUMANE SOCIETY
Att: Manager, Executive Department

11 River Street
Toronto, ON M5A 4C2

Tel.	416-392-2273
Fax	416-392-9978
Email	info@torontohumanesociety.com
Website	www.torontohumanesociety.com

Employer Background: The Toronto Humane Society provides animal protection services. *New Positions Created (7):* Junior Administrative Assistant; Animal Shelter Supervisor; Accounts Payable Clerk; Administrative Assistant; Investigator, OSPCA; Coordinator, Volunteer Resources; Systems Support Representative.

TORONTO HYDRO
Att: Human Resources Department
14 Carlton Street
Toronto, ON M5B 1K5

Tel.	416-599-0400
Fax	416-542-2682
Email	recruit@torontohydro.com
Website	www.torontohydro.com

Employer Background: Toronto Hydro maintains power lines in the city of Toronto. *New Positions Created (2):* Manager, Taxation; Legal Secretary.

TORONTO MARRIOTT BLOOR YORKVILLE
Att: Gail Loder, HR Manager
90 Bloor Street East
Toronto, ON M4W 1A7

Tel.	416-961-8000
Fax	416-961-9581
Email	gail@marriottbloor.com
Website	www.marriott.com

Employer Background: Toronto Marriott Bloor Yorkville is a 258-room hotel. *New Positions Created (3):* Night Manager and Group Coordinator; Front Office Manager; Various Hotel Positions.

TORONTO MICROELECTRONICS INC.
Att: Human Resources Department
5149 Bradco Boulevard
Mississauga, ON L4W 2A6

Tel.	905-625-3203
Fax	905-625-3717
Email	thinhnguyen@tme-inc.com
Website	www.tme-inc.com

Employer Background: Founded in 1989, TME designs industrial single board computers and industrial computer system products for OEM applications and industrial systems integrators. *New Positions Created (7):* CAD Technologist; Mechanical Design Engineer; Electronic Packaging; Senior Electronics Design Engineers (2); Accounts Manager (2); CAD Technologist; Junior Engineer / Technologist; Senior Electronics Design Engineer (2).

TORONTO MONTESSORI SCHOOLS
Att: Development Office
8569 Bayview Avenue
Richmond Hill, ON L4B 3M7

Tel.	905-889-9201
Fax	905-886-6516
Website	www.toronto-montessori.on.ca

Employer Background: Toronto Montessori Schools is a private school offering a unique education program to students. *New Positions Created (5):* Assistant; Art Teacher; French Teachers; Middle School Teacher; Physical Education Teacher.

TORONTO POLICE SERVICE
Att: Employment Unit
40 College Street, 2nd Floor
Toronto, ON M5G 2J3
Tel. 416-808-7150
Fax 416-808-7152
Email .... careers@torontopolice.on.ca
Website .... www.torontopolice.on.ca
Employer Background: The Toronto Police Service is dedicated to delivering police services, in partnership with communities. *New Positions Created (2):* Civilian Staffing Officer; Communication Operators.

TORONTO REAL ESTATE BOARD
Att: Linda MacAndrew
1400 Don Mills Road
Toronto, ON M3B 3N1
Tel. 416-443-8102
Fax 416-443-9153
Email .... lmacandrew@trebnet.com
Website .... www.realestate.ca/toronto
Employer Background: TREB is an industry association, representing over 17,000 realtors. *New Positions Created (3):* Director of Membership Development; Computer Operator; Network Specialist.

TORONTO REHABILITATION INSTITUTE
Att: Human Resources Manager
550 University Avenue
Toronto, ON M5G 2A2
Tel. 416-597-3422
Fax 416-597-6626
Email .... hr.resume@torontorehab.on.ca
Website .... www.torontorehab.com
Employer Background: Formed in 1998, Toronto Rehabilitation Institute is a 530-bed teaching, adult rehabilitation and complex continuing care hospital. *New Positions Created (76):* Cardiac Rehabilitation Supervisor; Cardiopulmonary Exercise Technician; Clerk / Receptionist; Clinical Pharmacist; Computer Support Specialist; Database Coordinator; Database Coordinator, Neuro Rehabilitation Program; Human Resources Assistant; Infection Prevention and Control Manager; Manager, Program Services; Manager, Program Services (Spinal Cord Rehabilitation Program); Secretary, Operations Director and Medical Director; Technical Specialist; Therapeutic Recreationist; Biostatisticians; Programmers; Research Coordinators; Director, Pharmacy; Medical Secretary; Nurse Clinician, Geriatric Rehabilitation Program; Occupational Therapists, Geriatric Psychiatry; Outpatient Secretary; Physiotherapist, Spinal Cord Rehab; Research Administrative Coordinator; Research Assistant; Research Grant Analyst / Accountant; Scientists; Secretary, Social Work and Psychology; Social Worker; Unit Secretary; Occupational Therapist; Psychogeriatric Resource Consultant; Operations Director, Cardiac Rehabilitation; Physiotherapist, Seating Clinic; Pilot Site Coordinator, Cardiac Rehabilitation; Secretaries / Administrative Assistants; Occupational Therapy Assistants; Physiotherapists; Physiotherapy Assistants; Registered Nurses; Behavioural Therapists; Speech Language Pathologists; Clinical Nurse Specialists; Health Records Technician; Staffing Office Supervisor; Workload Measurement Coordinator; Community Resource Workers; Physiotherapists, Neuro Rehabilitation and Spinal Cord Rehabilitation Programs; Registered Nurses, Neuro Rehabilitation and Spinal Cord Rehabilitation Programs; Rehabilitation Therapists, Neuro Rehabilitation and Spinal Cord Rehabilitation Programs; Therapeutic Recreationists, Neuro Rehabilitation and Spinal Cord Rehabilitation Programs; Social Workers; Speech Language Pathologists; Occupational Therapists; Pharmacist; Physiotherapists; Registered Nurses; Registered Practical Nurses; Clinical Nurse Specialist; Registered Nurses; Registered Nurses; Clinical Pharmacist; Health Records Technician; Occupational Therapy Assistant; Physiotherapist Assistants; Psychologist; Pharmacist; Physiotherapist; Therapeutic Recreation Programmer; Physicians; Human Resource / Payroll Computer Application Specialist; Secretaries; Various Rehabilitation Positions; Therapeutic Positions (2); Technical Support Specialist; Director of Information Management.

TORONTO STAR NEWSPAPERS LTD.
Att: Human Resources Department
1 Yonge Street
Toronto, ON M5E 1E6
Tel. 416-367-2000
Fax 416-869-4762
Email .... mmoxnes@thestar.ca
Website .... www.thestar.com
Employer Background: Toronto Star Newspapers Ltd. publishes Canada's largest daily newspaper, The Toronto Star, and several other dailies in southwestern Ontario, including the Hamilton Spectator, the Kitchener-Waterloo Record and the Cambridge Reporter. *New Positions Created (2):* Pension / Benefits Administrator; Pre-Flight / Digital Ad Technician.

TORONTO STAR NEWSPAPERS LTD., PRESS CENTRE
Att: George Donaldson,
Maintenance Manager
1 Century Place, Press Centre
Woodbridge, ON L4L 8R2
Website .... www.thestar.ca
Employer Background: Toronto Star Newspapers Ltd. operates a 660,00 square foot printing facility in the township of Vaughan. *New Positions Created (3):* Apprentice Maintenance Machinist; Industrial Mechanic / Millwright; Building Operator.

TORONTO TRANSIT COMMISSION
Att: Human Resources Department,
Placement Services
1138 Bathurst Street
Toronto, ON M5R 3H2
Tel. 416-393-4564
Fax 416-397-8307
Email .... jobs@ttc.ca
Website .... www.ttc.ca
Employer Background: TTC operates Canada's largest public transit system, offering subway, bus and light rail transit transportation. *New Positions Created (41):* Transit Special Constable; Drivers; Assistant Designer, Traction Power; Fire Prevention Inspector, Safety Department; Superintendent, Bus Maintenance and Shops Department; Supervisor, Procedures; Senior Industrial Engineer, Bus Maintenance and Shops; Service Coordinator, IT Services Department; Marketing Research Director; Occupational Health Nurse; Senior Superintendent, Heavy Maintenance; Construction Engineer; Design Engineer, Track Maintenance; Foreperson, Machine Shop; Quality Assurance Officer; General Automotive Machinist, Duncan Shops; Instructor, Surface Maintenance Training; Senior Database Analyst; Senior Technical Assistant; Drivers; Vehicle Engineer, Electrical; Senior Electrical Engineer; Assistant Design Engineer, Signals; Assistant Designers, Electrical and Traction Power; Project Scheduler; Technical Assistant, Mechanical; Work Method Writer; Design Engineer, Mechanical; Audit Project Manager; Leak Remediation Engineer; Foreperson, Surface Track; Auditor; Change and Configuration Coordinator; Database Analyst; Director, Technical Services; Fleet Supervisor; Project Controls Coordinator; Project Manager; Senior Technical Assistant; Operational Test Coordinator; Quality Assurance Specialist.

TORONTO ZOO
Att: Ms P. Scott-Bovens, Human Resources
361A Old Finch Avenue
Toronto, ON M1B 5K7
Tel. 416-392-5900
Fax 416-392-5934
Email .... hr@zoo.metrotor.on.ca
Website .... www.torontozoo.ca
Employer Background: Toronto Zoo is a major tourist attraction in the southern Ontario market, providing unique educational and recreational opportunities for over 1.1 million guests annually. *New Positions Created (9):* Craftsperson; Maintenance Helper; Security & Safety Officer; Marketing Manager; Membership & Guest Services Manager; Senior Human Resources Manager; Exhibit Design Technician; Curatorial Gardener; Gardener.

TORONTO-SUNNYBROOK REGIONAL CANCER CENTRE
Att: Human Resources Department
2075 Bayview Avenue
Toronto, ON M4N 3M5
Tel. 416-480-5000
Fax 416-480-6102
Email .... hr@tsrcc.on.ca
Website .... www.tsrcc.on.ca
Employer Background: The Toronto-Sunnybrook Regional Cancer Centre, a partnership between Sunnybrook and Women's Health Sciences and Cancer Care Ontario,

provides a comprehensive cancer control program. *New Positions Created (8):* Health Records Technician; Clinical Practice Leader; Supervisor Nursing, General Treatment Services; Administrative Coordinator; Regional Administrator, OBSP; Health Records Clerk; Health Records Technicians; Registered Nurses, Chemotherapy Unit.

TORPHARM
Att: Human Resources
50 Steinway Boulevard
Toronto, ON M9W 6Y3
Fax 416-675-8386
Website .... www.apotex.ca
Employer Background: TorPharm, a member of the Apotex Group of Companies, produces pharmaceutical products. *New Positions Created (3):* Building Systems Technician; Maintenance Mechanics; Manufacturing Operators.

TOSHIBA BUSINESS SYSTEMS INC.
Att: Office Manager
5905 Centre Street SW
Calgary, AB T2H 0C2
Tel. 403-273-5200
Fax 403-273-2622
Email .... calgaryjobs@conex.ca
Website .... www.conex.com
Employer Background: Toshiba Business Systems Inc., a Toshiba Group Company, offers telephone systems, copiers and faxes for the Calgary market. *New Positions Created (5):* Project Coordinator / Customer Service Representative; Telecom Sales Manager; Telecommunications Service Manager; Telecommunications Field Technicians; Telecommunications Sales Consultants.

TOSHIBA OF CANADA LIMITED
Att: Human Resources
191 McNabb Street
Markham, ON L3R 8H2
Tel. 905-470-3500
Fax 905-470-3521
Email .... resumes@toshiba.ca
Website .... www.toshiba.ca
Employer Background: Toshiba of Canada Limited is a leading manufacturer and distributor of home entertainment, business and medical equipment. *New Positions Created (7):* Electronics Technician, Office Products; Technical Trainer / Dealer Support Position; Warehouse Supervisor; Customer Service Representative; Channel and Industry Marketing Manager; Product Manager; Intermediate Accountant.

TOTAL CARE TECHNOLOGIES INC.
Att: Human Resources Director
1708 Dolphin Avenue, Suite 500
Kelowna, BC V1Y 9S4
Tel. 250-763-0034
Fax 250-763-0039
Email .... tctcareers@total-care.com
Website .... www.total-care.com
Employer Background: Total Care Technologies Inc. develops leading-edge staff scheduling software for healthcare organizations.

New Positions Created (7): Senior Software Engineer; Business Analyst; Product Designers; Regional Sales Manager, Eastern Canada; Senior Software Engineer; Product Designer; User Interface Manager.

TOTAL COMMUNICATIONS
Att: Human Resources Department
1400 Upper James Street
Hamilton, ON L9B 1K3
Tel. 905-387-6464
Fax 905-383-1799
Website .... www.rogers.com
Employer Background: Total Communications is an authorized Rogers, Cantel and AT&T dealer, with 10 stores located throughout southwestern Ontario. *New Positions Created (3):* Administrative Assistant; Purchasing / Inventory Clerk; Bookkeeper / Accountant.

TOTAL CREDIT RECOVERY / TRC
Att: Human Resources
225 Yorkland Boulevard
Toronto, ON M2J 4Y7
Tel. 416-774-4000
Fax 416-774-4293
Email .... hr@totalcrediting.com
Website .... www.totalcrediting.com
Employer Background: TRC is a call centre and collection company that provides collection services to a range of governments and major Canadian corporations. *New Positions Created (3):* Collection Officers; Auditor / Analyst; Call Centre Team Leader.

TOTTEN SIMS HUBICKI ASSOCIATES
Att: Tanya Currie, Recruiting Coordinator
300 Water Street
Whitby, ON L1N 9J2
Tel. 905-668-9363
Fax 905-668-0221
Email .... tcurrie@tsh.ca
Website .... www.tsh.ca
Employer Background: Founded in 1962, TSH is a multidisciplinary engineering and architectural firm providing consulting services to the private and public sectors. The firm has 10 offices across Ontario. *New Positions Created (74):* Architectural Technologist; Drainage Engineer; Intermediate / Senior Environmental Engineer; Project Engineer, Environmental; Project Manager, Environmental; Traffic and Transportation Analyst; Electrical Engineer-in-Training; Desktop Publisher; Intermediate Architect; Intermediate Structural Engineer; Junior CAD Operator; Manager, Transportation Planning; Mechanical Designer; Project Manager, Civil Engineering; Structural Engineer; Transportation Planner; Transportation Project Engineer; Transportation / Traffic Technologist; Branch Manager; Civil Technologist; Drainage Engineer; Electrical AutoCAD Drafter; Environmental Engineer; Environmental Engineering Trainee; Highway Designer; Intermediate Electrical Engineer; Intermediate Environmental Engineer; Intermediate / Senior Environmental Engineer; Junior CAD Operator, Highways; Junior CAD Operator, Structures; Manager,

Environmental Science; Municipal Engineer; Municipal / Environmental Technologist; Project Manager, Highways Group Roads Designer; Senior Electrical Designer Senior Environmental Engineer; Senior Mechanical Engineer; Senior Structural Inspector; Structural Engineers; Transportation Technologist; Water Resources Engineer / Technologist; Drainage Engineer Highways Designer; Intermediate Architect Manager, Environmental Science; Municipal Engineers; Roads Designer; Senior & Intermediate Environmental Engineers; Senior Transportation Planner; Structural Engineer; Transportation Engineers; Water Resources Engineer / Technologist; CADD Operators; Environmental / Municipal Engineers; Highway / Road Designers; Senior Project Managers / Project Managers; Structural Engineers; Transportation / EA Planner; Civil Technologist; Project Manager Civil Engineering; Roads Designer; Structural Engineer / Project Manager; Transportation / Traffic Technologist; Water Resources Engineer / Technologist; Electrical Engineer, Buildings Group; Electrical Engineer, Highways Group; Environmental Engineers; Highway Designers; Project Manager, Highway Engineering; Senior Environmental Engineer; Solid Water Management Engineer; Structural Engineers, Bridge Design; Transportation Project Engineer.

TOWER GROUP INTERNATIONAL CANADA INC.
Att: Human Resources Department
5915 Airport Road, Suite 1100
Mississauga, ON L4V 1T1
Tel. 905-678-2644
Fax 905-677-6814
Email .... jobs_tor@towergrp.com
Website .... www.towergroupintl.com
Employer Background: Tower Group International Canada Inc. provides logistics, international freight forwarding and customs brokerage services. *New Positions Created (2):* Release and Classification Specialist Senior Rater.

TOWER GROUP INTERNATIONAL CANADA INC.
Att: Human Resources
420 Notre Dame Street West, Suite 300
Montréal, QC H2Y 2G6
Tel. 514-845-3171
Fax 514-845-7423
Email .... jobs_mtl@towergrp.com
Website .... www.towergroupintl.com
Employer Background: Tower Group International Canada Inc. provides logistics, international freight forwarding and customs brokerage services. *New Positions Created (5):* Regional Manager North American Transportation; Junior Accounting Analyst Refunds Specialist; Manager, Transportation; Release and Classification Specialist.

TOWN + COUNTRY BMW
Att: Arthur Madjarian
7200 Yonge Street
Thornhill, ON L4J 1V8
Tel. 905-886-3100

Fax 905-886-0408
Email .... arthur@tcbmw.com
Website .... www.tcbmw.com
Employer Background: Town + Country BMW is one of Canada's top selling BMW dealerships. *New Positions Created (3):* New Car & Pre-Owned Specialists; Licensed Technician; Pre-Owned Specialist.

TOWN PUBLISHING INC.
Att: Sheryl Humphreys
875 Main Street West
Hamilton, ON L8S 4R1
Tel. 905-522-6117
Fax 905-529-2242
Email .... sheryl@townpublishing.com
Website .... www.townpublishing.com
Employer Background: Town Publishing Inc. is an integrated media company, specializing in magazine publishing and consumer and trade shows and one of the region's largest periodic publisher of magazines. *New Positions Created (5):* Financial Accountant; Advertising Representative; Assistant Show Manager; General Manager, Publishing; Advertising Representative.

TOWNE CHEVROLET OLDSMOBILE INC.
Att: Pino Smith, Service Manager
547 Trafalgar Road
Oakville, ON L6J 3J1
Tel. 905-844-2320
Fax 905-844-1497
Email .... pinos@townechev.com
Website .. www.towne chev.gmcanada.com
Employer Background: Towne Chevrolet Oldsmobile Inc. is an automotive dealership, offering sales and parts services for over 30 years. *New Positions Created (5):* Cashier / Warranty Clerk; General & Transmission Technicians; Service Adviser; New Vehicle Sales Manager; Customer Service Reps.

TOYOTA CANADA INC.
Att: Human Resources
1 Toyota Place
Toronto, ON M1H 1H9
Tel. 416-438-6320
Fax 416-431-1871
Website .... www.toyota.ca
Employer Background: Toyota Canada Inc. is the exclusive importer and distributor of Toyota cars (including Lexus), trucks, industrial equipment, replacement parts and accessories. *New Positions Created (9):* Specialist, Technical Assistance; Bilingual Coordinator, Warranty Claims; Customer Loyalty Consultant; Manager, Training Administration; Manager, Customer Loyalty; Coordinator, Forklift Division; Technical Service Manager; Consultant, Parts and Service; Technical Assistance Consultant.

TOYS R US (CANADA) LTD.
Att: HR Manager, Western Canada
2929 - 32nd Avenue
Calgary, AB T1Y 6J1
Fax 403-291-2706
Website .... www.tru.com

Employer Background: Toys R Us (Canada) Ltd. is a specialty retailer for children. *New Positions Created (2):* Retail Store Manager; Retail Store Manager.

TRACER INDUSTRIES CANADA LTD.
Att: Human Resources
11004 - 174th Street
Edmonton, AB T5S 2P3
Tel. 780-455-8111
Fax 780-455-8115
Email .... careers@tracer-ind.com
Website .... www.tracer-ind.com
Employer Background: Tracer Industries Canada Ltd. (a division of Tyco Thermal Controls) is a specialty engineering, procurement and construction contractor. *New Positions Created (35):* Project Accounting Assistant; Plant Controller; QA / QC Inspector; Document Control Administrator; Project Engineer; Project Manager; Design Engineers & Technologists; Engineering Managers; Executive Assistant; Materials Manager; Procurement Manager; Project Controls Manager; Project Engineers; Project Managers; Site Construction Manager; Site Field Engineer; Site Project Controls Manager; Site Quality Assurance Managers; Site Senior Cost Control Specialist; Site Senior Planner; Site Turnover Engineer / Technologist; QA / QC Personnel; Clerical Position; Construction Managers; Cost Control Position; Design / Drafting Position; Document Control Lead; Instrumentation Technologist; Planner / Scheduler; Project Accountant; Project Engineers; Project Reporting Position; Superintendents; Materials Coordinator; QA / QC Specialists.

TRACTEL LTD., SWINGSTAGE DIVISION
Att: Human Resources Manager
1615 Warden Avenue
Toronto, ON M1R 2T3
Tel. 416-298-8822
Fax 416-298-1053
Website .... www.tractel.com
Employer Background: Tractel Ltd. manufactures material handling and access equipment, building maintenance machines, safety equipment, and fall arrest systems. *New Positions Created (7):* Project Engineer / Group Leader; Billing Clerk; Sales Coordinator; Accountant; Draftsperson; Project Engineer / Group Leader; Administrative and Financial Vice-President.

TRADER.COM
Att: Human Resources
14101 - 128th Avenue
Edmonton, AB T5L 3H3
Fax 780-452-9161
Email .... resume@trader.com
Website .... www.trader.com
Employer Background: Trader.com is a global facilitator of consumer-to-consumer and business-to-consumer transactions, with a portfolio of 292 print and 61 online classified advertising properties. *New Positions Created (14):* District Sales Manager; Accountant; Internet Sales Executive; Ex-

ecutive Assistant; Graphic Artist; Account Executive; New Media Specialist; Accounts Receivable Clerk; Business Analyst; JD Edwards One World Applications Support Position; Payroll Supervisor; New Media Specialist; New Media Specialist; Sales Supervisor.

TRADER.COM
Att: District Sales Manager
3401 - 19th Street NE, Bay 9
Calgary, AB T2E 6S8
Fax 403-250-2188
Email .... resume@trader.com
Website .... www.trader.com
Employer Background: Trader.com is a global facilitator of consumer-to-consumer and business-to-consumer transactions, with a portfolio of 292 print and 61 online classified advertising properties. *New Positions Created (2):* Sales Supervisor; Account Executive.

TRADER.COM
Att: Human Resources
625 Church Street, 6th Floor
Toronto, ON M4Y 2G1
Fax 416-923-3931
Email .... hr.toronto@trader.com
Website .... www.trader.com
Employer Background: Trader.com is a global facilitator of consumer-to-consumer and business-to-consumer transactions, with a portfolio of 292 print and 61 online classified advertising properties. *New Positions Created (4):* Account Manager; Director, Financial Planning; Director, Treasury Operations; Financial Analyst.

TRAIL APPLIANCES LTD.
Att: Pat Broderick
5400 Minoru Boulevard
Richmond, BC V6X 2A9
Tel. 604-278-6133
Fax 604-821-0631
Email .... patbroderick@trailappliances.com
Website .... www.trailappliances.com
Employer Background: Trail Appliances Ltd. sells quality brand-name appliances. *New Positions Created (2):* Assistant Controller; Payroll / Accounting Clerk.

TRAIL APPLIANCES LTD.
Att: Human Resources Manager
5716 - 1st Street SE, Suite 4
Calgary, AB T2H 1H8
Fax 403-253-5849
Website .... www.trailappliances.com
Employer Background: Trail Appliances Ltd. sells quality brand-name appliances. *New Positions Created (7):* Credit Associate; Payroll and Benefits Adminstrator; Project Coordinator; Service Department Dispatcher; Service Technicians - Major Appliances; Accounting Supervisor; Project Coordinator.

TRAKONIC
Att: Human Resources Manager
PO Box 594
Sydney, NS B1P 6H4

Fax 902-539-1651
Email .... jobs@trakonic.com
Website .... www.trakonic.com

Employer Background: Founded in 1997, Trakonic is a leading provider of web-enabled security products and services. *New Positions Created (4):* Product Manager; Intermediate Software Developers; Java Server Developers; Programmers, C++, Linux, Delphi and Java.

TRAMMELL CROW CORPORATE SERVICES CANADA, LTD.
Att: Pam Rogacki
100 Sheppard Avenue East, Suite 940
Toronto, ON M2N 6N5
Tel. 416-229-5771
Fax 416-229-4410
Email .... progacki@trammellcrow.com
Website .... www.trammellcrow.com

Employer Background: Trammell Crow Corporate Services Canada, Ltd. is one of the largest commercial real estate services companies in North America, and a leading provider of facilities management services to corporate clients. *New Positions Created (3):* Mechanical Engineer; AutoCAD Operator; Tenant Coordinators.

TRANE CENTRAL ONTARIO
Att: Human Resources
4051 Gorden Baker Road
Toronto, ON M1W 2P3
Tel. 416-499-3600
Fax 416-499-3615
Email .... kmathur@trane.com
Website .... www.trane.com

Employer Background: Trane makes heating, ventilation and air conditioning (HVAC) systems for residential and commercial customers. *New Positions Created (4):* Customer Service Coordinator; Inside Parts Salesperson; Account Exec, Existing Building Sales; Dispatcher / Resource Coordinator.

TRANGO SOFTWARE CORPORATION
Att: Human Resources
45 Vogell Road, Suite 201
Richmond Hill, ON L4B 3P6
Tel. 905-737-6388
Fax 905-737-0622
Email .... hr@trangosoft.com
Website .... www.trangosoft.com

Employer Background: Trango Software Corporation develops and markets computer telephony integration products, as well as development and integration services. *New Positions Created (7):* Application Developers, C++ and VB; Sales Representative; QA Specialist; Technical Support Specialist; Technical Writer; Application Developers; Software Tester.

TRANS MOUNTAIN PIPE LINE COMPANY LTD.
Att: Human Resources Department
300 - 5th Avenue SW
Suite 2700, Stock Exchange Tower
Calgary, AB T2P 5J2
Tel. 403-514-6400

Fax 403-514-6580
Email .... work@tmpl.ca
Website .... www.transmountain.com

Employer Background: Trans Mountain Pipe Line Company Ltd. operates a 1,260 kilometre pipeline that transports petroleum products from Alberta to Canada's west coast and Washington state. *New Positions Created (21):* Systems Administrator; Quality Control Technician; Intermediate Pipeline Engineer; Senior Pipeline Engineer; Electrical & Instrumentation Draftsperson and Project Analyst; Executive Assistant - Legal; General Services Coordinator; Pipeline Engineer - Electrical; Production Coordinator; Safety Personnel; Accounts Payable Personnel; Application Support Personnel; Benefits Administrator; Emergency Response Planner; Facilities / General Services Personnel; Information System and Technology Professionals; Network Support Personnel; Oil Accountant; Pipeline Scheduler; Pipeline Simulation Analyst; Senior Finance Positions.

TRANSALTA CORPORATION
Att: Human Resources Manager
PO Box 4001
Fort McMurray, AB T9H 3E3
Fax 780-791-8394
Website .... www.transalta.com

Employer Background: Founded in 1911, TransAlta is a leading producer of power in Canada, New Zealand, Australia and the USA, with $5 billion in assets. *New Positions Created (3):* Environmental Specialist / Technologist; Mechanical Engineer; Process Engineer.

TRANSALTA CORPORATION
Att: Human Resources
110 - 12th Avenue SW, PO Box 1900,
Station M
Calgary, AB T2P 2M1
Tel. 403-267-7110
Fax 403-267-2131
Website .... www.transalta.com

Employer Background: Founded in 1911, TransAlta is a leading producer of power in Canada, New Zealand, Australia and the USA, with $5 billion in assets. *New Positions Created (48):* Business Analyst; Field Coordinator, Substation; Field Coordinators, Telecom (2); Operations Land Clerk; Project Leaders (2); Relay Technologists (2); Senior Equipment Engineer; Senior Substation Design Engineer; Substation Design Engineers (4); Supervisor, Asset Engineering; Telecom Design Engineer; Cycle Chemist; Turbine / Condensate Project Leaders (2); Electrical Project Leader; Plant Training Supervisor; Assistant Training Coordinator, Maintenance; Environmental Specialist / Technologist; Plant Clerk 2; Thermal Electrical / Instrumentation Maintenance Positions; Assistant Plant Manager, Mississauga Cogeneration Plant; Demand Specialist; Fleet Specialist; Plant Manager; Senior Commodity Specialist; Senior HR Advisor; Senior Inventory Analyst; Senior Investment Analyst; Turnaround Services Mechanical Maintenance Position; Administrative As-

sistant; Manager, Poplar Creek Power Station; Boiler Maintenance - Pressure Welders and Fitters; Market Analyst; Administrative Assistant; Administrative Assistant - IPP Financial Group; Senior Financial Analyst; Senior Mechanical Engineer; Senior Process Engineer; Administrative Assistant, Corporate Secretary; Chemical Project Leader; Director, Strategic Sourcing; Group Leader - Chemical Engineering; Legal Administrative Assistant; Plant Accounting Assistant; Real-Time Trader; Senior Analyst, eBusiness; Senior Labour Relations Supervisor; Supervisor, Electrical / Implementation; Transmission Power System Engineers.

TRANSALTA CORPORATION
Att: Paul Patenaude
2655 North Sheridan Way, Suite 230
Mississauga, ON L5K 2P8
Fax 905-829-7261
Website .... www.transalta.com

Employer Background: Founded in 1911, TransAlta is a leading producer of power in Canada, New Zealand, Australia and the USA, with $5 billion in assets. *New Positions Created (2):* Assistant Plant Manager; Plant Manager.

TRANSALTA CORPORATION, SUNDANCE GENERATING STATION
Att: Human Resources Manager
Site 4, Box 1, RR 1
Duffield, AB T0E 0N0
Tel. 780-797-3062
Fax 780-960-7916
Website .... www.transalta.com

Employer Background: Founded in 1911, TransAlta is a leading producer of power in Canada, New Zealand, Australia and the USA, with $5 billion in assets. *New Positions Created (2):* Power Engineer; Operations Planning Coordinator.

TRANSAMERICA LIFE CANADA
Att: Julia Garreffa, Senior HR Consultant
300 Consilium Place
Toronto, ON M1H 3G2
Tel. 416-290-6221
Fax 416-290-2911
Email ... julia.garreffa@transamerica.com
Website .... www.transamerica.com

Employer Background: Transamerica Life Canada provides financial security services and affordable life insurance and annuity products. *New Positions Created (3):* Assistant Vice-President, Corporate Actuarial Department; Corporate Commercial Lawyer; Corporate Commercial Lawyer.

TRANSCONTINENTAL MEDIA
Att: Jenny Pruegger, HR Coordinator
25 Sheppard Avenue West, Suite 100
Toronto, ON M2N 6S7
Fax 416-218-3637
Email .... pruegger@transcontinental.ca
Website .... www.transcontinental.ca

Employer Background: Transcontinental Media is one of Canada's largest publishers of consumer magazines, including TV

Guide, Canadian Living, Style at Home and Elle Canada. *New Positions Created (3):* Account Manager; Bilingual Receptionist / Switchboard Operator; Production Manger.

TRANSCONTINENTAL PUBLICATIONS G.T. INC.
Att: Maryse Lalonde
555 - 12th Avenue West
Suite 300, East Tower
Vancouver, BC V5Z 4L4
Fax 604-877-4849
Email ..... vanreception@transcontinental.ca
Website .... www.transcontinental-gtc.ca
Employer Background: Created in 1979, Transcontinental Publications G.T. Inc. is a leader in publications for targeted markets. *New Positions Created (2):* Sales Manager; Executive Sales Assistant.

TRANSOFT SOLUTIONS
Att: Human Resources Manager
4311 Viking Way, Suite 240
Richmond, BC V6V 2K9
Tel. 604-244-8387
Fax 604-244-1770
Email .... ct@transoftsolutions.com
Website .... www.transoftsolutions.com
Employer Background: Transoft Solutions is a transportation software firm. *New Positions Created (3):* Order Desk Position; Account Manager; Administrative Assistant.

TRAPEZE SOFTWARE INC.
Att: Human Resources Manager
2800 Skymark Ave., 2nd Floor, Building 1
Mississauga, ON L4W 5A6
Tel. 905-629-8727
Fax 905-238-8408
Email .... careers@trapezesoftware.com
Website .... www.trapezesoftware.com
Employer Background: Trapeze Software Inc. is a leading provider of advanced transportation software systems. *New Positions Created (9):* Account Rep; Contract Administrator; HR Coordinator; Implementation Specialist; Programming Analyst; Contract Administrator; Call Centre Operator; Lotus Notes Developer; Sales Consultant.

TRAVEL GUARD CANADA
Att: D.G. Stefak, Director of Operations
405 The West Mall, Suite 600
Toronto, ON M9C 5J1
Fax 416-621-4806
Email .... dstefak@travelguard.ca
Website .... www.travelguard.ca
Employer Background: Travel Guard Canada is a division of Travel Guard International, America's largest travel insurance company. *New Positions Created (8):* Bilingual Customer Service Representative; Lead Nurse; Bilingual Customer Service Representatives; Claims Administrative Support Specialist; Claims Analysts; Customer Service Trainer; IT Consultant; Registered Nurses.

TRAVEL UNDERWRITERS GROUP OF COMPANIES, THE
Att: Human Resources Manager

6081 No. 3 Road, Suite 1101
Richmond, BC V6Y 2B2
Tel. 604-276-9900
Fax 604-276-9409
Email .... jobs@travelunderwriters.com
Website ...... www.travelunderwriters.com
Employer Background: The Travel Underwriters Group of Companies has been a leading North American travel insurance provider for over 35 years. *New Positions Created (3):* Claims Representatives; Call Centre Reps.; Regional Account Manager.

TRAVELACTIVE.COM MARKETING INC.
Att: Human Resources Manager
74 Queen Street East
Cambridge, ON N3C 2B1
Tel. 519-651-1400
Fax 519-651-1800
Email .... jobs@travelactive.com
Website .... www.travelactive.com
Employer Background: TravelActive.com Marketing Inc. is a developing e-commerce and web portal applications company that provides online marketing for the travel industry. *New Positions Created (3):* Customer Support and System Administrator; Director of Sales and Marketing; HTML / ASP Developer.

TRAVELERS LEASING CORPORATION
Att: Kane Mah, Credit Manager
6450 Roberts Street, Suite 375
Burnaby, BC V5G 4E1
Fax 604-473-3816
Email .... kmah@travelersfinancial.com
Website .... www.travelersfinancial.com
Employer Background: Travelers Leasing Corporation is one of western Canada's leading independent vehicle leasing companies. *New Positions Created (2):* Vehicle Credit Analyst; Vehicle Leasing Specialist.

TREBOR ALLAN INC.
Att: Human Resources
45 Ewen Road
Hamilton, ON L8S 3C3
Fax 905-529-6999
Website .... www.treborallan.com
Employer Background: Trebor Allan Inc. is one of Canada's leading confectionery companies. *New Positions Created (5):* Electrical Maintenance Technician; Maintenance Mechanic; Electronic Technician; Maintenance Mechanic; Maintenance Mechanic.

TRENDEX INFORMATION SYSTEMS INC.
Att: Human Resources Manager
4100 Steinberg
St-Laurent, QC H4R 2G7
Tel. 514-333-6373
Fax 514-333-5705
Email .... sales@trendexsys.com
Website .... www.trendexsys.com
Employer Background: Trendex Information Systems Inc. develops welding / compressed gas, distribution and manufacturing software. *New Positions Created (3):* Program-

mer / Analyst; Software Support Position; Customer Support Representative.

TRENDS INTERNATIONAL CORPORATION
Att: Human Resources
3345 Laird Road
Mississauga, ON L5L 5R6
Tel. 905-569-8500
Fax 905-569-8507
Employer Background: Trends International Corporation is a national company manufacturing toy and stationery products. *New Positions Created (5):* Warehouse Manager; Customer Service / Sales Clerk; Sales Representative; Marketing Assistant; Sales Representative.

TRENT UNIVERSITY
Att: Associate Vice-President, HR
1600 West Bank Drive, Symons Campus
Peterborough, ON K9J 7B8
Tel. 705-748-1011
Fax 705-748-1276
Website .... www.trentu.ca
Employer Background: Trent University is a small university committed to liberal undergraduate education. *New Positions Created (3):* Senior Project Manager; Pension Coordinator; Director of Financial Services.

TRESCO INDUSTRIES
Att: Sales Manager
2235 Blackfoot Trail SE
Calgary, AB T2G 5C5
Tel. 403-237-0882
Fax 403-262-3420
Email .... ydahl@trescoconsoles.com
Website .... www.trescoconsoles.com
Employer Background: Tresco Industries designs and manufactures functional console systems for control centres around the world. *New Positions Created (3):* Account Executive; Cabinet Maker / Installer; Account Executive.

TRI OCEAN ENGINEERING LTD.
Att: Human Resources Manager
727 - 7th Avenue SW, Suite 1400
Calgary, AB T2P 0Z5
Tel. 403-266-4400
Fax 403-266-5525
Email .... personnel@tri-ocean.com
Website .... www.tri-ocean.com
Employer Background: Founded in 1976, Tri Ocean Engineering Ltd. is a consulting engineering firm providing comprehensive engineering, procurement and project management services to the production and drilling sectors of the petroleum industry worldwide. *New Positions Created (18):* Intermediate Process / Systems Engineer; Junior Instrumentation Technologists (2); Senior Instrumentation / Controls Technologist; Senior Mechanical Engineer; Senior Process Engineer; Senior Project Engineer, Offshore Front-End Studies; Senior Project Engineer, Offshore Projects; Senior Project Engineer, Onshore Projects; Senior Project Planner; Systems Engineer; Facilities and

Pipelines Regulatory Coordinator; Instrumentation and Control Systems Positions; Intermediate Buyer; Intermediate Process Engineer; Intermediate / Senior Mechanical Engineers and Project Engineers; Offshore Engineers and Designers; Quality Assurance Position; Senior Process Engineer.

TRI-AD GRAPHIC COMMUNICATIONS LTD.
Att: Human Resources Manager
2 Dorchester Avenue
Toronto, ON M8Z 4W3

Tel.	416-252-9331
Fax	416-252-3043
Website	www.triad-graphics.com

Employer Background: Tri-ad Graphic Communications Ltd. is a prepress graphics company. New Positions Created (6): Certified CMA; Electronics Pre-Press Film Output Technician; Production Coordinators; Proofreader; Accounting Position; Accounting Position.

TRI-ED LTD.
Att: Human Resources Manager
3688 Nashua Drive, Units A-F
Mississauga, ON L4V 1Z5

Tel.	905-677-8997
Fax	905-760-3004
Email	hr@dscltd.com
Website	www.tri-ed.com

Employer Background: Tri-Ed Ltd. is a Canadian wholesale distributor of low voltage, life safety and security systems. New Positions Created (3): A/R Administrator; Administrative Assistant; Buyer.

TRI-MEDIA MARKETING & PUBLICITY INC.
Att: Human Resources Department
517 Niagara Street
Welland, ON L3C 1L7

Tel.	905-732-6431
Fax	905-732-3028
Email	career@tri-media.com
Website	www.tri-media.com

Employer Background: Established in 1986, Tri-Media Marketing & Publicity Inc. is an integrated marketing communications firm. New Positions Created (8): Communications Manager; Copywriter; E-Commerce Programmers, Level 2; Graphic Designer; Art Director; Account Managers; Communications Manager; Media Planner.

TRIANGULUM CORPORATION
Att: Human Resources
6444 - 12th Street SE
Calgary, AB T2H 2X2

Tel.	403-640-9002
Fax	403-640-9005
Email	jobs@triangulum.org
Website	www.triangulum.org

Employer Background: TriAngulum provides systems integration services, wireless data and Internet solutions, including fleet management, asset tracking, vehicle reporting and CAD. New Positions Created (7): Lead Developer; Technical Support Rep; VB Developer; Account Mgr; Technical Sales Support; VB Developer; Web Developer.

TRIATHLON
Att: Human Resources Manager
13800 Commerce Parkway
Richmond, BC V6V 2J3

Fax	604-233-5043
Email	hr@triathloninc.com

Employer Background: Triathlon, a subsidiary of MacDonald, Dettwiler and Associates, is a large image scanning, photogrammetric mapping and digital orthophoto company. New Positions Created (4): Map Finishing Technician; Orthophoto Technician; Photogrammetrist; Project Accountant.

TRIBAL SPORTSWEAR INC.
Att: Michel Chong, CA
9030 Pie IX
Montréal, QC H1Z 4M7

Tel.	514-322-5337
Fax	514-322-4717
Email	mchong@tribal-inc.com
Website	www.tribal-inc.com

Employer Background: Tribal Sportswear Inc. is a ladies' wear manufacturer and importer. New Positions Created (8): Senior Accountant; Systems Administrator; Customer Service Position; Patternmaker; Director, Information Systems; Import Technician; Controller; Merchandising and Product Development Position.

TRIBUTE PUBLISHING
Att: Human Resources Manager
71 Barber Greene Road
Toronto, ON M3C 2A2

Tel.	416-445-0544
Fax	416-445-2894
Email	eblomkwist@tribute.ca
Website	www.tribute.ca

Employer Background: Tribute Publishing publishes Tribute Magazine, a free movie and entertainment magazine available in theatres. New Positions Created (3): Circulation Manager; Intermediate / Senior Graphic Designer; Production Coordinator.

TRICAN WELL SERVICE LTD.
Att: Controller
645 - 7th Avenue SW, Suite 2900
Calgary, AB T2P 4G8

Tel.	403-266-0202
Fax	403-237-7716
Email	finance@trican.ca
Website	www.trican.ca

Employer Background: Trican Well Service Ltd. is a well service company providing specialized products, equipment and technology for the drilling, completion and production stages of oil and gas wells. New Positions Created (4): Accountant; AFE / Fixed Asset Clerk; Fracturing Engineer; Technical Assistant, Fracturing Services.

TRICOM TECHNOLOGIES
Att: Human Resources Manager
6535 Millcreek Drive, Unit 34
Mississauga, ON L5N 2N2

Tel.	905-858-8917
Fax	905-858-8927
Email	jobs@tricom-tech.com
Website	www.tricom-tech.com

Employer Background: Founded in 1995, Tricom Technologies is a leading supplier of affordable aircraft simulations to the aviation industry. New Positions Created (11): Intermediate Mechanical Designer; Intermediate / Senior Electrical Engineer; Intermediate / Senior Software Development Engineer; Junior Software Development Engineer; Electrical Engineers (2); Junior Software Development Engineer; Intermediate / Senior Simulation Development Engineer; Intermediate / Senior Software Development Engineer; Junior Electronic Technician / Technologist; Junior Simulation Development Engineer; Program Manager.

TRILLIUM DIGITAL SYSTEMS CANADA, LTD.
Att: Human Resources Manager
4260 Still Creek Drive, Suite 320
Burnaby, BC V5C 6C6

Tel.	604-320-7338
Fax	604-320-7358
Email	recruiting_vancouver@trillium.com
Website	www.trillium.com

Employer Background: Trillium Digital Systems Canada, Ltd. is a leading provider of communications software solutions for computer and communications equipment manufacturers. New Positions Created (4): Engineering Project Manager; Software Engineer; Software Engineer / Senior Software Engineer; Technical Architect.

TRILLIUM HEALTH CARE PRODUCTS
Att: Human Resources
2337 Parkedale Avenue
Brockville, ON K6V 5W5

Tel.	613-342-4436
Fax	613-342-5330
Email	careers@trillium.ca
Website	www.trilliumhealthcare.com

Employer Background: Trillium Health Care Products manufactures health and beauty products, including a number of national brand and retail products, for Canadian and US clients. New Positions Created (3): Maintenance Electrician; Production Maintenance Supervisor; Human Resources Manager.

TRILLIUM HEALTH CENTRE
Att: Staffing Solutions (Recruiting)
150 Sherway Drive, Queensway Site
Toronto, ON M9C 1A5

Tel.	416-521-4060
Fax	416-521-4003
Email	dorrico@thc.on.ca
Website	www.trilliumhealthcentre.com

Employer Background: Trillium Health Centre was formed in 1998 through the merger of Mississauga Hospital and Queensway General Hospital. New Positions Created (95): Case Manager; Clinical Leaders, Complex Continuing Care (2); Corporate Training Consultant; Electronic Imaging Application Specialist; Manager, Neurosurgery; Paediatric / Emergency Registered Nurses; Systems Administrator; Acute Care Nurse Practitioner / Clinical Nurse Specialist; Child Psychologist; Clinical Educators; Coordinator, Nursing Informatics; Director, Pharmaceutical Services; Occupational Therapist; Emergency Preparedness Coordinator; Mental Health Case Managers; Benefits and Compensation Consultant; Ergonomics Consultant; Recruiter; WSIB / Return-to-Work Consultant; Case Managers, Assertive Community Treatment Team (ACTT); Clinical Educator, Inpatient Psychiatry; Clinical Leader, Relinc South; Community Treatment Order Coordinator; Psychogeriatric Consultants, Community Mental Health Services (2); Registered Nurses, Assertive Community Treatment Team (ACTT); Registered Nurses, Psychiatry; Endocrinology & Metabolism Specialist; Physiotherapist, Continuing Care Services; Physiotherapist, Neurosurgery, Neuroscience and MSK Health System ; Clinical Leader, Pharmacy; Diagnostic Informatics Specialist; Pharmacists; Registered Technologists, Neurodiagnostics; Registered Ultrasound Technologists; Registered Vascular Technologist, Vascular Lab; Resource Leader, Diagnostic Imaging; Team Leader, Film Library; Utilization Coordinator, Pharmacy; Director, Medical Health System; Manager, Diagnostic Imaging; Manager, Neurosciences / Musculoskeletal Health System; Manager, Pharmaceutical Services; Managers, Surgical Health System (2); Team Leader, Facility Services; Team Leader, Hospitality / Environmental; Coordinator, Health Information and Wellness Centre; Director - Operations, Corporate Services; Senior Specialist, Organizational Development; Acute Care Nurse Practitioner / Clinical Nurse Specialist; Clinical Educators; Registered Nurses; Director, Corporate Services; Director, Diagnostic Imaging; Director, Neurosciences / Musculoskeletal Health System; Director, Staffing Solutions; Director, Surgical Health System; Project Managers (2); Registered Nurses, Mental Health; Public Relations Manager; Clinical Leader, Continuing Care Service; Manager, Logistics and Processing; Registered Nurses; Clinical Leaders; Nurse Educators; Buyer Assistants; Contract Specialists; Data Management Specialists; Inventory Analyst; Logistics Manager; Manager, Financial Planning and Analysis; Meditech Systems Analyst; Process Review and System Trainer; Regional Contracts Manager; Regional Purchasing Manager; Senior Buyers; Manager, Surgical Health System; Manager, Women's and Children's Health System; Occupational Hand Therapist, WSIB Hand Program; Occupational Therapist, Day Hospital; Physiatrist, Rehabilitation Unit; Physiotherapists and Occupational Therapists; Registered Practical Nurses; Coding Specialist; Financial Analyst; Child and Adolescent Psychologist, Mental Health; Clinical Leader, Oncology; Geriatrician; Manager, Emergency Services; Registered Nurses; Registered Nurses, Emergency; RNs, Assertive Community Treatment Team (ACTT); Clinical Leader, Angioplasty; Registered Nurses, Angioplasty; Various Registered Nursing Positions; Refrigeration / HVAC Mechanic.

TRILLIUM HEALTH CENTRE
Att: Denis MacDougall, Special Consultant
100 Queensway West
Mississauga, ON L5B 1B8
Tel. 905-848-7100
Fax 905-848-5598
Website ...... www.trilliumhealthcentre.org
Employer Background: Trillium Health Centre is a major healthcare facility serving Peel Region and was created through the 1998 amalgamation of The Mississauga Hospital and the Queensway General Hospital. *New Positions Created (3):* Vice-President, Information Services; Director, Project Management; Vice-President, Planning.

TRILLIUM LAKELANDS DISTRICT SCHOOL BOARD / TLDSB
Att: Paul Doiron, Superintendent of Schools, Elementary Operations
76 Pine Street
Bracebridge, ON P1L 1N4
Website .... www.tldsb.on.ca
Employer Background: TLDSB operates 44 elementary schools located across the former districts of Haliburton, Muskoka and Victoria. *New Positions Created (3):* Special Education Teachers; Teachers; Teachers.

TRILLIUM PHOTONICS
Att: Human Resources
1500 Montreal Road, Suite M50
Ottawa, ON K1A 0R6
Tel. 613-742-1011
Fax 613-742-8900
Email .... jobs@trilliumphotonics.com
Website .... www.trilliumphotonics.com
Employer Background: Trillium Photonics designs, develops and manufactures fibre optical amplifiers. *New Positions Created (14):* Electronics Engineer, Digital / Analog; Electronics Technologist; Photonics Technologist; Product Manager; Sr Optical Assembler; Test Engineer; Embedded Software Engineer; Fiber-Optic Packaging Engineer; PCB Layout Designer ; Electronics Engineer, Digital / Analog; Electronics Technologist; Fiber Optic Packaging Engineer; Photonics Engineers; Photonics Technologist.

TRINITY COLLEGE SCHOOL
Att: David E. McCart,
Executive Director of Development
190 Ward Street
Port Hope, ON L1A 3W2
Tel. 905-885-4565
Fax 905-885-9690
Email .... dmccart@tcs.on.ca
Website .... www.tcs.on.ca
Employer Background: Founded in 1865, Trinity College School is a co-educational boarding school serving over 440 students from grades 7 to 13. The school has 50 faculty members and an annual budget of $9.8 million. *New Positions Created (2):* Publications / Communications Officer; Associate Director of Admissions.

TRINITY WESTERN UNIVERSITY
Att: Dr. Dennis Jameson,
Vice-President (Academic)

7600 Glover Road
Langley, BC V2Y 1Y1
Tel. 604-513-2037
Fax 604-513-2010
Email .... jameson@twu.ca
Website .... www.twu.ca
Employer Background: Trinity Western University is a Christian liberal arts university affiliated with the Evangelical Free Church of Canada. *New Positions Created (2):* Dean, School of Business; Faculty Position, School of Business.

TRIO SELECTION INC.
Att: Human Resources Manager
353 Chabanel West
Montréal, QC H2N 2G1
Fax 514-387-3034
Email .... frank@trio-selection.com
Employer Background: Trio Selection Inc. is a sportswear importer. *New Positions Created (5):* Customer Service Coordinator; Import Production Assistant; Merchandise Manager, Accessories Division; Graphic Artist / Designer / Merchandiser; Specification Specialist / Garment Fit Technician.

TRIOS COLLEGE OF INFORMATION TECHNOLOGY
Att: Human Resources Manager
6711 Mississauga Road, Suite 400
Mississauga, ON L5N 2W3
Tel. 905-542-0656
Fax 905-542-7380
Email .... hrmanager@trios.ca
Website .... www.trios.ca
Employer Background: Trios College of Information Technology is an IT technical education centre. *New Positions Created (5):* Admissions Sales Representatives; Admissions Sales Reps; Career Placement Coach; Instructors; Marketing Program Manager.

TRIPLE-C INC.
Att: Curt Russell
8 Burford Road
Hamilton, ON L8E 5B1
Tel. 905-573-7900
Fax 905-573-7877
Email .... crussell@triple-c-candy.com
Website .... www.triple-c-candy.com
Employer Background: For over 40 years, Triple-C Inc. has been a leading importer and distributor of confectionery products. *New Positions Created (3):* Assistant Buyer / Repackaging Coordinator; Traffic Clerk; Head Buyer.

TRISTAN & AMERICA
Att: Human Resources
20, des Seigneurs
Montréal, QC H3K 3K3
Tel. 514-937-4601
Fax 514-935-1233
Website .... www.tristan-america.com
Employer Background: Tristan & America is a clothing retailer, with 70 boutiques in Quebec, Ontario and the USA. *New Positions Created (3):* Assistant Manager; Store Manager; Visual Presentation Specialist.

**TRIUMF MESON
RESEARCH FACILITY**
Att: Human Resources
4004 Westbrook Mall
Vancouver, BC V6T 2A3

Tel. 604-222-1047
Fax 604-222-1074
Website .... www.triumf.ca

Employer Background: TRIUMF Meson
Research Facility is a national research labo-
ratory for nuclear and particle physics. *New
Positions Created (3):* Programer / Systems
Manager; Cyclotron Operator / Technologist;
Mechanical Technician.

TRIUMPH TOOL LTD.
Att: Sales Manager
91 Arrow Road
Guelph, ON N1K 1S8

Tel. 519-836-4811
Fax 519-836-7903
Email .... ttg@triumphtool.com
Website .... www.triumphtool.com

Employer Background: Triumph Tool Ltd.
distributes high-quality metal cutting tools
and related niche products. *New Positions
Created (2):* Cutting Tool Technical Sales
Representative; Cutting Tool Technical Sales
Representatives.

TRIVALENCE MINING CORPORATION
Att: AVP, Human Resources
815 Hornby Street, Suite 502
Vancouver, BC V6Z 2E6

Tel. 604-684-2401
Fax 604-684-2407
Email .... ochoudhry@trivalence.com
Website .... www.trivalence.com

Employer Background: Trivalence Mining
Corporation is a mineral exploration and
development company focusing on diamonds. *New Positions Created (4):* Investor
Relations Manager; Electrical Maintenance
Supervisor; Heavy Duty Mechanic; Warehouse Controller.

TRIVERSITY INC.
Att: Human Resources Manager
3550 Victoria Park Avenue, Suite 400
Toronto, ON M2H 2N5

Tel. 416-791-7100
Fax 416-791-7101
Email .... triversity@rpc.webhire.com
Website .... www.triversity.com

Employer Background: Triversity Inc. is a
leading provider of complete "click-and-
mortar" software solutions to traditional
and Internet retailers. *New Positions Created
(9):* Director, Support Services; Java Developer; Manager, Call Centre; Project Manager;
Quality Assurance Specialist; Team Leader,
Call Centre Support; Legal / General Counsel; Business Development Consultant; Human Resources Manager.

TRIVU INTERACTIVE CORPORATION
Att: Human Resources Manager
3250 Ridgeway Drive, Unit 7
Mississauga, ON L5L 5Y6

Tel. 905-607-0410

Fax 905-607-2219
Email .... barb@trivu.ca
Website .... www.trivu.ca

Employer Background: TriVu Interactive
Corporation provides TV and Internet sys-
tems for hotels. *New Positions Created (3):*
Inside Sales Position; Movie / TV / Internet
Programming Content Person; Sales Ac-
count Executive.

TRIZECHAHN
Att: Human Resources
181 Bay Street, Suite 3900, BCE Place
Toronto, ON M5J 2T3

Fax 416-601-4879
Website .... www.trizechahn.com

Employer Background: TrizecHahn is an
international, commercial real estate developer / owner. *New Positions Created (4):*
Cooks; Reservations Agents; Manager, Leisure Sales; Regional Sales Representative.

TRK ENGINEERING LTD.
Att: Human Resources Manager
17700 Highway 10
Surrey, BC V3S 1C7

Tel. 604-574-6432
Fax 604-574-6431
Email .... mail@trkeng.com
Website .... www.trkeng.com

Employer Background: TRK Engineering
Ltd. designs infrastructure for wireless
broadband and telecom carriers across
North America. *New Positions Created (3):*
Designer / Draftsperson; Electrical Engi-
neer; Structural Engineer.

TRM TECHNOLOGIES, INC.
Att: Human Resources Manager
370 Churchill Avenue, Suite 301
Ottawa, ON K1Z 5C2

Tel. 613-722-8843
Fax 613-722-8574
Email .... hr@trm.ca
Website .... www.trm.ca

Employer Background: TRM Technologies
Inc. is an information technology, systems
engineering and consulting firm with
strengths in communications and network
architecture. *New Positions Created (13):*
Director, Management Consulting; Management Consulting Professionals; Network
Analyst; Network Architect; Network Engineer; Practice Manager, Professional Services; Security Consultant; Senior Account
Executives; Consulting Practice Manager;
Director of Management Consulting; Network Architects; Senior Account Executives;
Systems Engineers .

TROJAN TECHNOLOGIES INC.
Att: Human Resources
3020 Gore Road
London, ON N5V 4T7

Tel. 519-457-3400
Fax 519-457-0447
Email .... hr@trojanuv.com
Website .... www.trojanuv.com

Employer Background: Trojan Technologies
Inc. designs and manufactures water and

wastewater disinfection systems and air
pollutant control systems that use ultraviolet light to destroy unwanted particles. *New
Positions Created (6):* CFD Engineer / Scientist; Electrical Engineering Manager;
Field Operations Team Leader; Senior Controls Engineer; Senior Mechanical Engineer;
Technical Trainer, Client Services.

TROPHY FOODS INC.
Att: Human Resources Manager
71 Admiral Boulevard
Mississauga, ON L5T 2T1

Tel. 905-670-8050
Fax 905-670-4256
Email .... hr@trophyfoods.com
Website .... www.trophyfoods.com

Employer Background: Established in 1967,
Trophy Foods Inc. markets nut, confectionery and bulk food products. *New Positions
Created (6):* Customer Service Representative; Order Pickers; Shipper / Receiver; Assistant Controller; Machine Operators; Territory Sales Representative.

TROPIC NETWORKS INC.
Att: Human Resources Manager
135 Michael Cowpland Drive
Kanata, ON K2M 2E9

Tel. 613-270-9660
Fax 613-270-9667
Email .... jobs@tropicnetworks.com
Website .... www.tropicnetworks.com

Employer Background: Tropic Networks Inc.
is an optical networking company that provides carriers with high bandwidth Inter-
net- and Ethernet-based services in metropolitan area networks. *New Positions Created (9):* Director / AVP, Operations; Hardware Designer; Optical Component Engineer; Optical Software Manager; Optical
System Engineer; Sr Network Management
Software Designer; Senior Optical Software
Designer; Software Designer; Systems Administrator.

**TROTTER & MORTON
TECHNICAL SERVICES LTD.**
Att: Penny Masear,
Human Resources Director
5711 - 1st Street SE
Calgary, AB T2H 1H9

Tel. 403-255-7535
Fax 403-640-0767
Email ..... masear-p@trotterandmorton.com
Website .... www.trotterandmorton.com

Employer Background: Founded in 1927,
Trotter & Morton Technical Services Ltd. is
a mechanical and electrical contractor, providing economical solutions for owners with
difficult building problems. *New Positions
Created (2):* General Manager; Sales Rep.

TROW CONSULTING ENGINEERS LTD.
Att: Human Resources Manager
807 Harold Crescent
Thunder Bay, ON P7C 5H8

Tel. 807-623-9495
Fax 807-623-8070
Email .... resumes@trow.com
Website .... www.trow.com

Employer Background: Founded in 1957, Trow Consulting Engineers Ltd. is a multidisciplinary engineering firm offering consulting, investigation, testing and problem-solving services in all fields of engineering. *New Positions Created (3):* Intermediate / Senior Geotechnical Engineers; Building Science and Abatement Engineers; Intermediate / Senior Hydrogeologist.

TROW CONSULTING ENGINEERS LTD.
Att: Human Resources Manager
15 Cuddy Boulevard
London, ON N5V 3Y3
Tel. 519-453-1480
Fax 519-453-1551
Email .... resumes@trow.com
Website .... www.trow.com
Employer Background: Founded in 1957, Trow Consulting Engineers Ltd. is a multidisciplinary engineering firm offering consulting, investigation, testing and problem-solving services in all fields of engineering. *New Positions Created (5):* Intermediate Structural Bridge Engineer; Geotechnical Engineer; Geotechnical Technician; Intermediate Building Science Technologist; Intermediate Structural Bridge Engineer.

TROW CONSULTING ENGINEERS LTD.
Att: Human Resources Manager
1000C Lang's Drive
Cambridge, ON N1R 6Z7
Tel. 519-622-2470
Fax 519-622-5720
Email .... resumes@trow.com
Website .... www.trow.com
Employer Background: Founded in 1957, Trow Consulting Engineers Ltd. is a multidisciplinary engineering firm offering consulting, investigation, testing and problem-solving services in all fields of engineering. *New Positions Created (7):* Electrical Engineer; Inspection / Testing Technician; Intermediate Geoenvironmental Engineer; Junior / Intermediate Building Science Engineer; Electrical Engineer; Inspection / Testing Technician; Intermediate Geoenvironmental Engineer.

TROW CONSULTING ENGINEERS LTD.
Att: Human Resources Manager
1595 Clark Boulevard
Brampton, ON L6T 4V1
Tel. 905-793-9800
Fax 905-793-0641
Email .... resumes@trow.com
Website .... www.trow.com
Employer Background: Founded in 1957, Trow Consulting Engineers Ltd. is a multidisciplinary engineering firm offering consulting, investigation, testing and problem-solving services in all fields of engineering. *New Positions Created (40):* Building Environmental Engineer; Building Science Engineering Trainee; Division Manager; Transportation; Senior Highway Design Engineer; Senior Structural Engineer, Transportation; Building Science Engineer; Engineering Trainee; Geotechnicians; Intermediate Administrative Assistant; Intermedi-

ate Municipal Designer; Intermediate / Senior Engineer, Solid Waste Management; Junior / Intermediate Engineer, Solid Waste Management; Mechanical / Electrical Engineers; Senior Fire Protection Engineer; Senior Laboratory Supervisor; Senior Project Manager, Solid Waste Management; Intermediate Geotechnical Engineer; Building Science Engineering Trainee; Intermediate / Senior Building Science Technician; Satellite Office Manager; Transportation Planners / Traffic Engineers; Building Environment Engineer; Building Science and Abatement Personnel; Building Science Engineer; Engineering Trainee; Engineering Trainee, Geotechnical; Engineers, Control, Safety, Mechanical; Field / Lab Technician; Geotechnical / Geoenvironmental Engineers; Hydrogeologist / Environmental Engineers; Intermediate Building Science Technologist; Intermediate Draftsperson / Designer; Intermediate Municipal Designer; Intermediate / Senior Fire Protection Engineer; Intermediate / Senior Geotechnical Engineer; Intermediate Structural Engineer; Mechanical / Electrical Engineers; Planner; Senior Civil Engineer; Senior Environmental Engineer.

TROW CONSULTING ENGINEERS LTD.
Att: Human Resources Manager
154 Colonnade Road South
Nepean, ON K2E 7J5
Tel. 613-723-2411
Fax 613-225-7337
Email .... resumes@trow.com
Website .... www.trow.com
Employer Background: Founded in 1957, Trow Consulting Engineers Ltd. is a multidisciplinary engineering firm offering consulting, investigation, testing and problem-solving services in all fields of engineering. *New Positions Created (9):* Intermediate / Senior Building Science Engineer; Intermediate / Senior Building Science Technologist; Mechanical / Electrical Engineer; Building Science Engineer; Field Technician; Intermediate / Senior Forensic Engineer; Junior / Intermediate Environmental Engineer / Scientist; Materials Testing Lab Technician; Senior Civil Engineer.

TROY MANUFACTURING LTD.
Att: D. Hodgkinson, PEng
PO Box 1269
Brockville, ON K6V 5W2
Tel. 613-345-1306
Fax 613-345-1257
Email .... dhodgkinson@troymfg.com
Website .... www.troymfg.com
Employer Background: Troy Manufacturing Ltd. is one of North America's leading fabricators of corrosion-resistant fibre glass equipment. *New Positions Created (2):* Vessel Design FEA Engineer; President / CEO.

TRUDELL MEDICAL INTERNATIONAL
Att: Human Resources
725 - 3rd Street
London, ON N5V 5G4
Tel. 519-455-7060
Fax 519-455-9053

Email .... hr@trudellmed.com
Website .... www.trudellmed.com
Employer Background: Established in 1922, TMI is a leading developer and manufacturer of aerosol drug delivery devices and asthma management products. *New Positions Created (3):* Instrumentation and Testing Technologist; Mechanical Product Development Engineer; Product Development Engineer.

TRUSTMARQUE CANADA LTD.
Att: Human Resources Manager
9900 Cavendish Boulevard, Suite 406
St-Laurent, QC H4M 2V2
Tel. 514-336-4949
Fax 514-336-0239
Email .... careers@trustmarque.ca
Website .... www.trustmarque.ca
Employer Background: TrustMarque Canada Ltd. provides a range of e-commerce applications and services to support online businesses in a secure and trusted environment. *New Positions Created (4):* Account Manager / Executive; Engineers / Developers; Senior Database Developer / DBA; Software Tester.

TRYLON TSF
Att: Human Resources Manager
21 South Field Drive, PO Box 186
Elmira, ON N3B 2Z6
Tel. 519-669-5421
Fax 519-669-8912
Email .... jobs@trylon.com
Website .... www.trylon.com
Employer Background: Established in 1932, Trylon TSF is a leading Canadian designer, manufacturer and installer of world-class communication towers and related technical services. *New Positions Created (10):* Antenna Installation Specialists; Design Engineers; Riggers; Telecom Technicians; Sales Manager; Antenna Installation Experts; Installation Foremen and Riggers; Regional Manager; Riggers; Technicians.

TRYLON - TSF
Att: Human Resources
872 Cité des Jeunes Boulevard
St-Lazare, QC J7T 2B5
Tel. 450-455-4545
Fax 450-455-2882
Email .... jobs@trylon.com
Website .... www.trylon.com
Employer Background: Trylon - TSF is a leader in the design, fabrication and installation of communications towers and related structures. *New Positions Created (2):* Senior Telecommunications Technician / Coordinator; Telecommunications Technician.

TTG SYSTEMS INC.
Att: Human Resources Manager
4220 - 98th Street, Suite 202
Edmonton, AB T6E 6A1
Tel. 780-462-6365
Fax 780-450-0186
Email .... jobs@ttg-inc.com
Website .... www.ttg-inc.com

Employer Background: TTG Systems Inc. designs, develops and implements e-learning management systems. *New Positions Created (11):* Internet Applications Developer; Sales Support and Coordination Position; Application Software Tester, Quality Assurance; Business Development Liaison Position; C++ Programmer / Analyst; Internet Application Developer; Internet Graphics / Media Design Specialist; Internet Network Programming Specialist; Internet Page Assembler; Technical Writer / Editor; Word Processor Technologist.

TUBE-FAB LTD.
Att: Human Resources
6845 Davand Drive
Mississauga, ON L5T 1L4
Tel. 905-565-0223
Fax 905-565-0065
Employer Background: Tube-Fab Ltd. manufactures aerospace, tubular and machined products. *New Positions Created (7):* Quality Control Inspector; Welder / Fitter; Quality Assurance Manager; Production Coordinator; Quality Control Inspector, Aircraft Parts and Welding; Welder / Fitter; Quality Assurance Manager.

TUBULAR STEEL INC.
Att: Human Resources Department
285 Raleigh Avenue
Toronto, ON M1K 1A5
Tel. 416-261-2089
Fax 416-261-9517
Email .... tubular@idirect.ca
Employer Background: Tubular Steel Inc. is a tier-1 automotive supplier. *New Positions Created (3):* Maintenance Millwrights; Tube Mill Crew Member; Tube Mill Operators.

TUNDRA ENGINEERING LTD.
Att: Michelle Maxwell,
Manager of Administration
250 - 6th Avenue SW, Suite 1800
Calgary, AB T2P 3H7
Tel. 403-777-2477
Fax 403-777-2479
Email .... michelle@tundraeng.com
Employer Background: Tundra Engineering Ltd. is an established full-service oil and gas facilities engineering firm. *New Positions Created (3):* Intermediate Project Engineer; Intermediate Project Engineer; Intermediate / Senior Electrical Designer.

TURBOCOR INC.
Att: Human Resources Manager
1850 Trans Canada Highway
Dorval, QC H9P 2N4
Fax 514-421-4277
Email .... slefebvre@turbocor.com
Website .... www.turbocor.com
Employer Background: Turbocor Inc. is a leading compressor technology company, enabling significant reductions in HVACR power consumption. *New Positions Created (10):* Precision Mechanics / Assemblers; Air Conditioning / Refrigeration Mechanic; Precision Mechanics; Mechanical Designer; Air Conditioning / Refrigeration Mechanic; Precision General Machinists / Mechanics; Information Technology Technician; Precision General Machinists; Precision Mechanics; Senior Accounting Clerk.

TVONTARIO / TVO
Att: Human Resources
PO Box 200, Station Q
Toronto, ON M4T 2T1
Tel. 416-484-2600
Email .... resume@tvo.org
Website .... www.tvo.org
Employer Background: TVO is a public broadcaster providing educational programming. *New Positions Created (2):* Producers / Directors; Story Producer.

TWF LOGISTICS GROUP INC.
Att: Manager, Central Dispatch
6801 Columbus Road
Mississauga, ON L5T 2G9
Tel. 905-795-1272
Fax 905-795-9655
Email .... ed@twflog.com
Website .... www.twflog.com
Employer Background: TWF Logistics Group Inc. is a logistics company, providing transportation, warehousing and fulfillment services to a North American client base. *New Positions Created (3):* Logistics Transportation Dispatchers; Logistics Transportation Dispatcher; Transportation Customer Service Clerk.

TY-CROP MANUFACTURING LTD.
Att: Human Resources Department
9880 McGrath Road
Rosedale, BC V0X 1X0
Tel. 604-794-7078
Fax 604-794-3446
Website .... www.tycrop.com
Employer Background: Ty-Crop is a medium-sized manufacturer of chip trailers and walking floor trailers. *New Positions Created (3):* Design Engineer; Manufacturing Engineer; Software Engineer.

TYCO ELECTRONICS CANADA LTD.
Att: Bryan Peters
20 Esna Park Drive
Markham, ON L3R 1E1
Tel. 905-475-6222
Fax 905-474-5556
Website .... www.tycoelectronics.com
Employer Background: Tyco Electronics Canada Ltd. (formerly AMP of Canada Ltd.) produces a wide variety of electrical and electronic connectors for industries such as automotive, power and energy, communications and computers. *New Positions Created (2):* Technical Sales Representative; Account Representative.

**TYCO HEALTHCARE
GROUP CANADA INC.**
Att: Director of Operations
4490 Garand Street
St-Laurent, QC H4R 2A2
Fax 514-334-8371
Website .... www.tyco.com
Employer Background: Tyco Healthcare Group Canada Inc., part of Tyco International Ltd., is a diversified global manufacturer and supplier of medical supplies. *New Positions Created (8):* Customer Service Representative; Programmer Analyst; Bilingual Accounting Clerk; Bilingual Administrative Clerk; Bilingual Sales Contract Analyst; Bilingual Business Analyst; Bilingual Credit and Collection Agent; Bilingual Customer Service / Order Desk Representative.

UMA ENGINEERING LTD.
Att: Human Resources Manager
3030 Gilmore Diversion
Burnaby, BC V5G 3B4
Tel. 604-438-5311
Fax 604-438-5587
Email .... careers@umagroup.com
Website .... www.umagroup.com
Employer Background: UMA Engineering Ltd. is part of the UMA Group, a Canadian employee-owned company that provides engineering consulting services worldwide. UMA Group has over 1,500 employees, including 600 engineers, planners and other professionals. *New Positions Created (5):* Administrative Assistant; Accounts Payable / Invoicing Administrator; CADD Technicians; Administrative Assistant; CADD Technicians.

UMA ENGINEERING LTD.
Att: Human Resources Manager
1835 - 56th Street, Suite 25
Delta, BC V4L 2L9
Tel. 604-943-7704
Fax 604-943-7706
Email .... careers@umagroup.com
Website .... www.umagroup.com
Employer Background: UMA Engineering Ltd. is part of the UMA Group, a Canadian employee-owned company that provides engineering consulting services worldwide. UMA Group has over 1,500 employees, including 600 engineers, planners and other professionals. *New Positions Created (3):* Lead Structural Draftsperson; Structural Design and Drafting Technologists; Structural Engineer.

UMA ENGINEERING LTD.
Att: Human Resources
17007 - 107th Avenue
Edmonton, AB T5S 1G3
Tel. 780-486-7000
Fax 780-486-7070
Website .... www.umagroup.com
Employer Background: UMA Engineering Ltd. is part of the UMA Group, a Canadian employee-owned company that provides engineering consulting services worldwide. UMA Group has over 1,500 employees, including 600 engineers, planners and other professionals. *New Positions Created (27):* Business Development Manager; Drafting and Design / Drafting Technologists; Intermediate Planning Technologist; Geo-Environmental Engineers / Scientists; Geotechnical Engineer / Scientist, Senior; Land De-

velopment Engineers, Intermediate or Senior; Landscape Architects, Intermediate; Landscape Architectural Technologists, Intermediate; Municipal Engineers, Intermediate or Senior; Planning Technologist, Intermediate; Senior Drafting Technologist; Water Resources Engineer, Urban Drainage; Land Development / Municipal Design / Drafting Technologists; Senior Planner / Scheduler; Senior QA Manager; Accounts Payable Administrator; Assistant Controller; CADD Design Draftsperson, Transportation; CADD Draftsperson, Earth & Water; Geotechnical Engineers; Payroll Administrator; Senior Construction Project Manager; Senior Planner / Scheduler; Senior Project Manager; Senior QA Manager; Land Development / Municipal Design Drafting Technologist; Municipal Engineer.

UMA ENGINEERING LTD.
Att: Human Resources
2540 Kensington Road NW
Calgary, AB T2N 3S3
Tel. 403-270-9200
Fax 403-270-2865
Email .... careers@umagroup.com
Website .... www.umagroup.com
Employer Background: UMA Engineering Ltd. is part of the UMA Group, a Canadian employee-owned company that provides engineering consulting services worldwide. UMA Group has over 1,500 employees, including 600 engineers, planners and other professionals. *New Positions Created (29):* Airport Engineer; Planners; Senior Water Resources Engineer, Urban Drainage; Environmental Engineer / Scientist; Water / Wastewater Treatment Engineer; Administrative Assistant; Billing / Invoice Administrator; Geotechnical Engineers; Municipal and Land Development Engineers; Water Resources Engineer, Hydro Power; Water Resources Engineer, Urban Drainage; Airport Engineer; Project Coordinator, Airport Redevelopment; Project & Construction Managers; Survey Technicians / Technologists; Civil / Structural Draftspersons; Mechanical Engineers; Municipal and Land Development Engineers; Project Managers; Regional Municipal Engineering Leader; Airport Engineer; Geotechnical Engineers; Municipal & Land Development Engineer; Transportation Technologist; Civil / Structural Draftspersons; Electrical and Structural Engineers; Mechanical Engineers; Piping & Electrical Designers; Project Managers.

UMA ENGINEERING LTD.
Att: Human Resources Manager
2100 - 8th Street East, Suite 200
Saskatoon, SK S7H 0V1
Fax 306-955-0044
Email .... careers@umagroup.com
Website .... www.umagroup.com
Employer Background: UMA Engineering Ltd. is part of the UMA Group, a Canadian employee-owned company that provides engineering consulting services worldwide. UMA Group has over 1,500 employees, including 600 engineers, planners and other

professionals. *New Positions Created (2):* Municipal Engineer; Municipal Engineer.

UMA ENGINEERING LTD.
Att: Human Resources Manager
1479 Buffalo Place
Winnipeg, MB R3T 1L7
Tel. 204-284-0580
Fax 204-475-3646
Email .... careers@umagroup.com
Website .... www.umagroup.com
Employer Background: UMA Engineering Ltd. is part of the UMA Group, a Canadian employee-owned company that provides engineering consulting services worldwide. UMA Group has over 1,500 employees, including 600 engineers, planners and other professionals. *New Positions Created (5):* Mechanical Engineer; Application Developer; Municipal Design Engineer; Application Developer; Municipal Design Engineer.

UMA ENGINEERING LTD.
Att: Human Resources Manager
50 Gervais Drive, 4th Floor
Toronto, ON M3C 1Z3
Tel. 416-445-4844
Fax 416-445-7107
Email .... careers@umagroup.com
Website .... www.umagroup.com
Employer Background: UMA Engineering Ltd. is part of the UMA Group, a Canadian employee-owned company that provides engineering consulting services worldwide. UMA Group has over 1,500 employees, including 600 engineers, planners and other professionals. *New Positions Created (4):* Project Engineer / Designer; Architectural Technologist / Intermediate Project Manager; Managing Director, Industrial; Project Engineer / Designer.

UMBRA LTD.
Att: Human Resources
40 Emblem Court
Toronto, ON M1S 1B1
Tel. 416-299-0088
Fax 416-299-0481
Email .... jobs@umbra.com
Website .... www.umbra.com
Employer Background: Umbra Ltd. manufactures, imports and distributes a collection of consumer products. *New Positions Created (2):* Receptionist; Controller.

UNDERWRITERS ADJUSTMENT BUREAU LTD. / UAB
Att: Carole Kane-Moore,
Human Resources Manager
18 King Street East, Suite 800
Toronto, ON M5C 1C4
Fax 416-601-1220
Email .... employment@iao.ca
Website .... www.uab.ca
Employer Background: UAB is a leading insurance adjuster, handling all classes of insurance claims. *New Positions Created (5):* Director, IAO School; General Counsel; Property Casualty Manager; Quality Control Manager; Accident Benefit Road Adjuster.

UNDERWRITERS ADJUSTMENT BUREAU LTD. / UAB
Att: Gay Fletcher, HR Administrator
90 Allstate Parkway
Toronto, ON L3R 6H3
Fax 905-474-5856
Email .... gfletcher@iao.ca
Website .... www.uab.ca
Employer Background: UAB is a leading insurance adjuster, handling all classes of insurance claims. *New Positions Created (3):* Accident Benefits Adjuster; All Lines Road Adjuster; Quality Control Manager, P&C Claims.

UNDERWRITERS' LABORATORIES OF CANADA / ULC
Att: Manager, Employee Relations
7 Crouse Road
Toronto, ON M1R 3A9
Tel. 416-757-5250
Fax 416-757-3948
Website .... www.ulc.ca
Employer Background: ULC is a non-profit Canadian safety, certification, testing, quality registration and standards organization. *New Positions Created (6):* Management System Auditors; Engineers; Lead Auditor, Automotive; Lead Auditor, Telecommunications; Laboratory Services Manager; Team Leader, Electrical.

UNI-RAM CORPORATION LTD.
Att: Human Resources Manager
381 Bentley Street
Toronto, ON L3R 9T2
Tel. 905-477-5911
Fax 905-477-8922
Email .... salescan@uniram.com
Website .... www.uniram.com
Employer Background: Uni-Ram Corporation Ltd. is an industrial / automotive equipment manufacturer with a worldwide market. *New Positions Created (3):* Mechanical Design Engineer; Mechanical Design Engineer; Sales Coordinator.

UNICCO FACILITY SERVICES
Att: Dan Williams, Chief Engineer
PO Box 195
Napanee, ON K7R 3M3
Tel. 613-354-7818
Fax 613-354-9377
Email .... sbrown@unicco.com
Website .... www.unicco.com
Employer Background: Founded in 1949, Unicco provides integrated facility services to commercial, industrial and institutional clients in North America. *New Positions Created (3):* 2nd-Class Stationary Engineer; 2nd-Class Stationary Engineer; HVAC Technician / Controls Technician.

UNIFIRST CANADA LTD.
Att: Human Resources
3514 - 78th Avenue
Edmonton, AB T6B 2X9
Tel. 780-423-0384
Fax 780-466-2146
Website .... www.unifirst.com

Employer Background: UniFirst Canada Ltd. supplies industrial uniforms to Canadian businesses in all industries. *New Positions Created (2):* Customer Service Representative; Route Service Representative.

UNIFIRST CANADA LTD.
Att: Sales Manager
5728 - 35th Street SE
Calgary, AB T2C 2G3
Tel. 403-531-1155
Fax 403-279-2801
Website .... www.unifirst.com
Employer Background: UniFirst Canada Ltd. supplies industrial uniforms to Canadian businesses in all industries. *New Positions Created (2):* Sales Representatives; Maintenance Manager.

UNIGROUP ARCHITECTURE & INTERIOR DESIGN INC.
Att: Human Resources Manager
10408 - 124th Street, Suite 202
Edmonton, AB T5N 1R5
Tel. 780-488-7271
Fax 780-482-7159
Email .... unigroup@planet.eon.net
Employer Background: Founded in 1975, Unigroup Architecture & Interior Design Inc. is a small architectural firm specializing in shopping centres, churches, offices, retail, hotels and education facilities. *New Positions Created (3):* Architectural Technologist; Interior Designers; Interior Designer.

UNION FINANCIAL
Att: General Manager
2 Lansing Square, 12th Floor
Toronto, ON M2J 4P8
Fax 416-756-8925
Email .... careers@union-financial.com
Website .... www.union-financial.com
Employer Background: Union Financial, a division of Union Energy and member of Westcoast Energy Inc. group, is a retail / commercial leasing and finance organization. *New Positions Created (4):* Account Manager; Business Analyst; Business Development Manager; Credit Officer.

UNION GAS LIMITED
Att: Human Resources
50 Keil Drive North
Chatham, ON N7M 5M1
Tel. 519-352-3100
Fax 519-436-5319
Email .... hrservices@uniongas.com
Website .... www.uniongas.com
Employer Background: Union Gas Limited is a major Canadian natural gas utility, serving 1.1 million residential, commercial and industrial customers in over 400 communities throughout Ontario. *New Positions Created (7):* Coordinator, Upstream Regulation; Industrial Account Representatives (2); Product and Service Posting Analyst; Senior Advisor, End Use Codes and Standards; Senior Analyst, Finance; Senior Energy Demand Forecaster; Senior Market Advisor.

UNION OF CANADIAN TRANSPORTATION EMPLOYEES
Att: National President
233 Gilmour Street, Suite 702
Ottawa, ON K2P 0P1
Fax 613-236-0379
Email .... careers@psac.com
Website .... www.psac.com
Employer Background: UCTE is a member of the Public Service Alliance of Canada, one of Canada's largest unions. The union works to secure member rights to fair treatment and respect in the workplace, employment security, better pay and safe working conditions. *New Positions Created (4):* Assistant to the National President; Bilingual Membership Clerk / Receptionist; Communications & Research Officer; Finance & Administrative Officer.

UNIONVILLE HOME SOCIETY / UHS
Att: Sara O'Donnell, HR Coordinator
4300 Highway 7
Unionville, ON L3R 1L8
Tel. 905-477-2822
Fax 905-477-5938
Email .... sara@uhs.on.ca
Website .... www.uhs.on.ca
Employer Background: UHS is a charitable organization, providing long-term care and retirement housing for seniors. *New Positions Created (5):* President and CEO; Director of Care; Director of Care; Registered Practical Nurses; Registered Nurses / Registered Practical Nurses.

UNIQUE BROADBAND SYSTEMS, INC.
Att: Human Resources
300 Edgeley Boulevard
Concord, ON L4K 3Y3
Tel. 905-669-8533
Fax 905-669-8516
Email .... careers@uniquesys.com
Website .... www.uniquesys.com
Employer Background: UBS designs and manufactures high-speed fixed and mobile wireless transmission solutions. *New Positions Created (22):* Modem Design Engineer; Senior DSP Engineer; Senior Systems Architect; Field Service Engineer / Technician; Manufacturing Engineer; Patent Agent; QA Technician / Inspector; Senior PCB Designer; Embedded Software Developer; Hardware Engineer; RF Test Engineer; Sales Engineer; Senior Network Administrator; Director, Staffing and Human Resources; Windows Database Developer; Windows Developers (2); Windows Software Group Leader; Hardware Development Manager; Product Manager; Project Manager; System Engineer; Test Engineer.

UNISEARCH ASSOCIATES INC.
Att: Human Resource Manager
96 Bradwick Drive
Concord, ON L4K 1K8
Tel. 905-669-3547
Fax 905-669-8652
Website ... www.unisearch-associates.com
Employer Background: Founded in 1980, Unisearch Associates Inc. is a manufacturer of optical air cleaning systems. *New Positions Created (3):* Software Engineer; Controller; Field Service and Installation Technicians (2).

UNITED NATIONS CHILDREN'S FUND / UNICEF CANADA
Att: Human Resources
443 Mount Pleasant Road
Toronto, ON M4S 2L8
Tel. 416-482-4444
Fax 416-482-8035
Email .... careers@unicef.ca
Website .... www.unicef.ca
Employer Background: Established in 1946, UNICEF Canada works to help children in developing countries. The organization has 75 employees and 40,000 volunteers. *New Positions Created (13):* Administrative Assistant, Marketing & Development; Area Manager, Ottawa-Carleton; Bilingual Customer Service Representatives; Direct Mail Assistant; Direct Mail Specialist, Catalogues; Finance / HR Assistant; Greeting Card Sales Representative, Ontario Region; Inventory and Logistics Coordinator; Manager, Call & Customer Service Centre; National Account Manager; Public Relations Specialist, Ontario Region; Regional Director, Ontario Region; Inventory & Logistics Coordinator.

UNITED OIL & GAS CONSULTING LTD.
Att: Human Resources Manager
777 - 8th Avenue SW, Suite 500
Calgary, AB T2P 3R5
Tel. 403-265-0111
Fax 403-294-9544
Email .... info@uogc.com
Website .... www.uogc.com
Employer Background: United Oil & Gas Consulting provides quality reservoir engineering and geological services to the oil and gas industry. *New Positions Created (4):* Geologists; Production & Reservoir Engineers; Geologists; Oil & Gas Positions (2).

UNITED PARCEL SERVICE CANADA LTD. / UPS
Att: Stuart Leatherdale
790 Belgrave Way
Delta, BC V3M 5R9
Fax 604-528-4211
Website .... www.ups.com
Employer Background: Established in 1907, UPS is the world's largest package distribution and courier company, with over 359,000 employees worldwide. *New Positions Created (3):* Account Executive; Security Associate; Account Executive.

UNITED PARCEL SERVICE CANADA LTD. / UPS
Att: Human Resources
3650 - 12th Street NE
Calgary, AB T2E 6N1
Fax 403-291-1627
Email .... can1cck@ups.com
Website .... www.ups.com
Employer Background: Established in 1907, UPS is the world's largest package distribu-

tion and courier company, with over 359,000 employees worldwide. *New Positions Created (3):* Premium Sales Associate; Premium Sales Associate; Account Executive.

UNITED PARCEL SERVICE CANADA LTD./ UPS
Att: Human Resources
1221 - 32nd Avenue
Lachine, QC H8T 3H2
Tel. 514-633-4921
Fax 514-633-4811
Email .... mtlemploy@ups.com
Website .... www.ups.com
Employer Background: Established in 1907, UPS is the world's largest package distribution and courier company, with over 359,000 employees worldwide. *New Positions Created (6):* Account Executives; Automotive Mechanic; Internal Sales Representative; Mechanics; Human Resources Supervisor; Account Executives.

UNITED SAFETY LTD.
Att: Manager, Human Resources
2135 - 32nd Avenue NE, Bay 1
Calgary, AB T2E 6Z3
Tel. 403-273-7774
Fax 403-273-0963
Email .... info@unitedcalgary.com
Employer Background: United Safety Ltd. is an integrated global safety service company that provides hydrogen sulfide protection and safety services during drilling, production and well-servicing operations. *New Positions Created (3):* Oilfield Personnel; Emergency Response Planner; Oil Field Safety Positions.

UNITED SYNAGOGUE DAY SCHOOL
Att: Head
3072 Bayview Avenue
Toronto, ON M2N 5L3
Tel. 416-225-5928
Fax 416-225-9108
Employer Background: The United Synagogue Day School has 1,350 students. *New Positions Created (2):* Teachers; Judaic Studies Coordinator.

UNITED VAN LINES (CANADA) LTD.
Att: Human Resources
1024 Westport Crescent
Mississauga, ON L5T 1G1
Tel. 905-670-4400
Fax 905-670-9139
Email .... jennifer@armmove.com
Website .... www.uvl.ca
Employer Background: United Van Lines (Canada) Ltd. is the only Canadian-owned and controlled van line, with 75% of its private shares held by its Canadian member companies. *New Positions Created (3):* Senior Accountant; Traffic Mgr; Leasing Mgr.

UNITED WAY / CENTRAIDE OTTAWA
Att: Valerie Parker,
HR & Volunteer Coordinator
106 Colonnade Road, Suite 100
Nepean, ON K2E 7P4
Tel. 613-228-6700
Fax 613-228-6730
Email .... parker@unitedwayottawa.ca
Website .... www.unitedwayottawa.ca
Employer Background: Since 1933, United Way / Centraide has distributed over $228 million to charitable organizations in the Ottawa-Carleton Region. *New Positions Created (3):* Evaluation Coordinator; Manager, Communications and Marketing; Campaign Division Director.

UNIVERSITY COLLEGE OF THE CARIBOO / UCC
Att: Irene Bazell, HR Officer
PO Box 3010
Kamloops, BC V2C 5N3
Tel. 250-828-5000
Fax 250-828-5338
Email .... jobops@cariboo.bc.ca
Website .... www.cariboo.bc.ca
Employer Background: UCC is a regional institution, serving 8,500 students in south-central British Columbia. *New Positions Created (27):* Director of Human Resources; Faculty Member, English and Modern Languages; Faculty Member, School of Education; Instructional Assistant, Adventure Guide Program; Faculty Member, Natural Resource Sciences; Faculty Member, Accounting and Business; Faculty Member, Anthropology; Faculty Member, Computing Science; Faculty Member, Instructor / Practica Coordinator; Faculty Members, Psychology (2); Human Resources Officer; Assistant Director, Building Operations; Faculty Member, Adventure Guide; Faculty Member, Journalism; Faculty Member, Management and Marketing; Faculty Member, Mathematics / Economics or Mathematics / Computing; Faculty Member, Physics; Faculty Member, School of Nursing; Associate Dean and Director, School of Social Work and Human Service; Cooperative Education Coordinator; Faculty Member, Socio-Cultural Anthropology; Faculty Member, Chemistry; Faculty Member, Social Work and Human Services; Dean, Williams Lake Campus; Instructors, Cook Training (2); Faculty Position, Computing Science; Dean, Williams Lake Campus.

UNIVERSITY COLLEGE OF THE FRASER VALLEY / UCFV
Att: Human Resources Manager
33844 King Road
Abbotsford, BC V2S 7M8
Tel. 604-854-4554
Fax 604-854-1538
Email .... erinfo@ucfv.bc.ca
Website .... www.ucfv.bc.ca
Employer Background: UCFV is a multi-campus institution, offering undergraduate degree programs to 6,000 students in Abbotsford, Chilliwack, Mission and Hope. *New Positions Created (29):* Assistant Supervisors, Child Care Centre; Budget Analyst; Library Technician; Department Assistants (2); Scheduling and Records Assistant; PC Lan Administrator; Programmer Analyst; Systems Analyst; Website Administrator; Department Assistant, Math and Psychol-

ogy; Biology Lab Instructor; Faculty Position, Entrepreneurship / Small Business; Faculty Position, Financial Accounting; Faculty Position, Human Resources and Organization Studies; Faculty Position, Marketing; Faculty Position, Operations Management; Laboratory Instructor, Kinesiology & Physical Education; Supervisor, Registration and Information Centre; Nursing Instructors (3); Faculty Position, Entrepreneurship / Small Business; Faculty Position, Financial Accounting; Faculty Position, Human Resources and Organization Studies; Faculty Position, Marketing; Faculty Position, Operations Management; Psychology Instructors (2); Graphic Design Instructor; Math Instructor; Oracle Database Administrator; Systems Analyst.

UNIVERSITY HEALTH NETWORK, MEDICAL AFFAIRS / UHN
Att: Dr. John R. Wright, Vice-President
190 Elizabeth Street
1S-404, 1st Floor, NNSB
Toronto, ON M5G 2C4
Fax 416-340-3537
Email .... john.wright@uhn.on.ca
Website .... www.uhn.on.ca
Employer Background: UHN is an acute-care teaching institution with over 1,000 beds in three sites: Toronto General Hospital; Toronto Western Hospital; and Princess Margaret Hospital. *New Positions Created (3):* Director, Emergency Medicine; Opthalmologist-In-Chief; Psychiatrist-In-Chief.

UNIVERSITY HEALTH NETWORK, SHARED INFORMATION MANAGEMENT SERVICES / SIMS
Att: SIMS Recruiting
190 Elizabeth Street, 2nd Floor
Toronto, ON M5G 2C4
Fax 416-340-3818
Website .... www.uhn.on.ca
Employer Background: University Health Network is an acute-care teaching institution with over 1,000 beds in three sites: Toronto General Hospital; Toronto Western Hospital; and Princess Margaret Hospital. *New Positions Created (6):* Director, Cardiac IT; Switchboard Operator; Analyst, Telecommunications; Manager, E-Chart; Manager, Resource Management & Scheduling; Operator, Technical & Support Services.

UNIVERSITY HEALTH NETWORK
Att: Staffing Solutions
190 Elizabeth Street, 2nd Floor
Toronto, ON M5G 2C4
Fax 416-597-2742
Email .... careers@uhn.on.ca
Website .... www.uhn.on.ca
Employer Background: UHN is an acute-care teaching institution with over 1,000 beds in three sites: Toronto General Hospital; Toronto Western Hospital; and Princess Margaret Hospital. *New Positions Created (30):* Clinical Dietitian; Communication Disorders Assistant; Occupational Therapist; Occupational Therapy Assistant; Phar-

macy Technician; Physiotherapist; Physiotherapy Assistants; Respiratory Technician; Respiratory Therapist; Social Worker; Speech-Language Pathologist; Staff Pharmacist; Clinician II, Multicultural Program; Coordinator; Intensive Case Managers (4); Medical Secretary; Nurses; Registered Nurses; Chief Nursing Officer; Research Assistant II; Research Assistant III; Research Ethics Coordinator; Special Events Coordinator; Staff Physiotherapist; Director of Nursing; Associate Director, Planning & Design; CAD Operator, Planning & Design; Project Mgr, Planning & Design; Registered Dietitian; Social Worker / Psychometrist.

UNIVERSITY HEALTH NETWORK
Att: Katherine Wyslobocki
101 College Street, CW2 - 335
Toronto, ON M5G 1L7
Tel. 416-340-4141
Fax 416-340-3476
Email .... careers@uhn.on.ca
Website .... www.uhealthnet.on.ca
Employer Background: UHN is an acute-care teaching institution with over 1,000 beds in three sites: Toronto General Hospital; Toronto Western Hospital; and Princess Margaret Hospital. *New Positions Created (17):* Secretary, Portuguese and Mental Health Addictions; Registered Nurses, Emergency; Registered Nurses, Intensive Care; Registered Nurses, Transplantation; Registered Nurses, Thoracic Surgery (3); Medical Laboratory Technologists / Technicians; Various Nursing Positions; Director of Nursing; Hemodialysis Coordinator; Manager, Project Planning and Redevelopment; Program Manager, Outpatient, MSK Physiotherapy; Operations Supervisor, Environmental Management Services; Registered Nurse, Dentistry; Administrative Director; Medical Lab Technologist - Cancer Cytogenetics; Medical Lab Technologist - Molecular Diagnostics; Pathologist Assistant.

UNIVERSITY OF ALBERTA
Att: Employment Services
40 Assiniboia Hall, Room 2
Edmonton, AB T6G 2E7
Tel. 780-492-5201
Fax 780-492-0371
Email .... hrs.recruitment@ualberta.ca
Website .... www.ualberta.ca
Employer Background: Founded in 1908, the University of Alberta is one of Canada's five largest research-intensive universities, serving over 29,000 students with 200 undergraduate programs and over 170 graduate programs. *New Positions Created (2):* Financial Analyst / Gift Processing Manager; Student Advisor, Faculty of Nursing.

UNIVERSITY OF ALBERTA,
ACADEMIC STAFF ADMINISTRATION
Att: Donna Herman, Director
10 University Hall, Suite 2
Edmonton, AB T6G 2J9
Tel. 780-492-1918
Fax 780-492-9671
Email .... donna.herman@ualberta.ca
Website .... www.ualberta.ca

Employer Background: Founded in 1908, the University of Alberta is one of Canada's five largest research-intensive universities. Over 29,000 students are served by 200 undergraduate programs and over 170 graduate programs. *New Positions Created (3):* Executive Assistant to the Vice-President (Finance & Administration) & Vice-President (Facilities & Operations); Mgr, Individual & Organizational Effectiveness; Mgr, Pension Policy.

UNIVERSITY OF ALBERTA,
DEPARTMENT OF PHYSICAL PLANT
Att: Facilities Management Personnel
General Services Building, Room 420
Edmonton, AB T6G 2J7
Fax 780-492-7582
Website .... www.ualberta.ca
Employer Background: Founded in 1908, the University of Alberta is one of Canada's five largest research-intensive universities. Over 29,000 students are served by 200 undergraduate programs and over 170 graduate programs. *New Positions Created (3):* Manager, Operations and Energy Management; Senior Engineer, Operations & Engineering; Communications Control Centre Operator.

UNIVERSITY OF ALBERTA,
FACULTY OF NURSING
Att: Human Resources Advisor
Clinical Sciences Building, Room 3-114
Edmonton, AB T6G 2G3
Fax 780-492-2551
Email .... susan.kavanagh@ualberta.ca
Website .... www.ualberta.ca
Employer Background: Founded in 1908, the University of Alberta is one of Canada's five largest research-intensive universities. Over 29,000 students are served by 200 undergraduate programs and over 170 graduate programs. *New Positions Created (4):* Exec Assistant; HR Assistant; Research Administration Officer; Sessional Clinical Instructors.

UNIVERSITY OF ALBERTA,
FACULTY OF PHYSICAL EDUCATION
AND RECREATION
Att: Dr. Michael J. Mahon, Dean
Edmonton, AB T6G 2H9
Tel. 780-492-3364
Fax 780-492-1008
Email .... mike.mahon@ualberta.ca
Website .... www.ualberta.ca
Employer Background: University of Alberta's Faculty of Physical Education and Recreation offers several degree programs, a combined BPE / BED program and an MSc Health Promotion Studies program for approximately 1,000 undergraduate and graduate students. *New Positions Created (2):* Clinical Teaching Position; Lecturer, Health / Exercise Psychology.

UNIVERSITY OF BRITISH COLUMBIA,
DEPARTMENT OF COMPUTER
SCIENCE / UBC
Att: Nick Pippenger,
Chair, Recruiting Committee
2366 Main Mall, Room 201
Vancouver, BC V6T 1Z4

Tel. 604-822-3061
Fax 604-822-5485
Email .... nicholas.pippenger@ubc.ca
Website .... www.ubc.ca
Employer Background: Founded in 1908, UBC is one of Canada's largest universities, with over 1,800 faculty and 12,000 staff members, serving over 35,000 students. *New Positions Created (2):* Faculty Positions, Computer Science; Tenure-Track Teaching Position.

UNIVERSITY OF BRITISH COLUMBIA,
FACULTY OF APPLIED SCIENCE / UBC
Att: Donna Shultz
2324 Main Mall, Suite 2006
Vancouver, BC V6T 1Z4
Tel. 604-822-6412
Fax 604-822-7006
Website .... www.ubc.ca
Employer Background: Founded in 1908, UBC is one of Canada's largest universities, with over 1,800 faculty and 12,000 staff members, serving over 35,000 students. *New Positions Created (2):* Instructor, Technical Communication; Director, School of Nursing.

UNIVERSITY OF BRITISH COLUMBIA,
FACULTY OF COMMERCE
Att: Nancy Hogan,
Manager of Administration
2053 Main Mall, Room 753
Vancouver, BC V6T 1Z2
Fax 604-822-8468
Website .... www.commerce.ubc.ca
Employer Background: UBC Commerce is a world leader in business research and education. *New Positions Created (3):* Assistant Dean & Director, Master's Program; Business Development Mgr; Sessional Lecturers.

UNIVERSITY OF BRITISH COLUMBIA,
FACULTY OF LAW
Att: Pitman B. Potter, Secretary,
Appointments Committee
1822 East Mall
Vancouver, BC V6T 1Z1
Tel. 604-822-5653
Fax 604-822-8108
Email .... potter@law.ubc.ca
Website .... www.law.ubc.ca
Employer Background: Founded in 1908, UBC is one of Canada's largest universities, with over 1,800 faculty and 12,000 staff members, serving over 35,000 students. *New Positions Created (2):* Assistant Law Professors (3); Director, Legal Research and Writing.

UNIVERSITY OF BRITISH COLUMBIA,
SCHOOL OF NURSING
Att: Acting Director
2211 Wesbrook Mall, Room T201
Vancouver, BC V6T 2B5
Tel. 604-822-7748
Fax 604-822-7423
Website .... www.nursing.ubc.ca
Employer Background: UBC School of Nursing is Canada's oldest university nursing

education institution, offering Baccalaureate, Master's and Doctoral-level nursing programs. *New Positions Created (3):* Sessional Clinical Faculty; Nursing Research Consultant; Tenure-Track Positions (2).

UNIVERSITY OF BRITISH COLUMBIA

Att: Human Resources
2075 Wesbrook Mall, Suite 350
Vancouver, BC V6T 1Z1

Tel. 604-822-8111
Fax 604-822-8134
Email .... itsadmin@itservices.ubc.ca
Website .... www.ubc.ca

Employer Background: Founded in 1908, UBC is one of Canada's largest universities, with over 1,800 faculty and 12,000 staff members, serving over 35,000 students. *New Positions Created (9):* Administrative Secretary; Presentation and Communications Coordinator; Associate Registrar; Counselling Psychologist; Assistant Director; Voice Services Manager; Course Designer / Developer; Systems Administrator; Counselling Psychologist.

UNIVERSITY OF CALGARY

Att: Human Resources
2500 University Drive NW
Room 3340, Murray Fraser Hall
Calgary, AB T2N 1N4

Tel. 403-220-5932
Fax 403-284-5753
Email .... hr@ucalgary.ca
Website .... www.ucalgary.ca

Employer Background: The University of Calgary has 16 faculties and 60 academic departments, employing 1,900 academic and 2,400 support staff and serving 30,000 degree students. *New Positions Created (131):* Cashier Leader; Competition / Tech Shop Coordinator; Customer Service Associate; Departmental Administrative Assistant; Distribution Clerk; Lead Alberta Room Chef; Programmer Analyst; Scurfield Hall Supervisor; Administrative Assistant; Administrative Secretary; Business Systems Application Technician; Career Advisors (3); Classroom Services Assistant; Hazardous Materials Assistant; Loans and Awards Assistant; Registration Clerk; Research / Communications Specialist; Store Assistant; Administrative Secretary, Clinical and Research; Administrative Secretary, Joint Arthritis & Injury Research Group; Administrative Secretary, Research; Computer Operator; Coordinator, Graduate Program Services; Front Office Customer Service Representative; Information Technology Coordinator; Registration Clerk, Access Desk; Telecom Services Advisor; Transcriptionist; Administrative Secretary, Information Systems Group; Bilingual Administrative Assistant, Teacher Preparation; Capital Projects Secretary; Coordinator, Meetings and Events; Information Commons Night Assistant; Instructor, English Language Foundation Program; Library Facilities Services Assistant; Office Assistant; Public Affairs Manager; Reception / Data Entry Position; Receptionist; Consultant; Customer Service Agent; Academic Support Specialist; Account Administrator, Research and Trust Accounting; Administration Clerk; Administrative Assistant / Records Coordinator; Administrative Secretary, Cardiovascular Research Group; Administrative Secretary, Neuroscience Research Group; Assistant Supervisor, Intramural Sports and Sport Club; Associate Director, Capital Projects; Board of Governors Specialist; Core Support Technicians; Department Administrator, Sociology; Departmental Office Assistant, Department of French, Italian and Spanish; Engineering Internship Coordinator / Assistant Director; Front Office Receptionist; Graduate Program Officer; Manager, Event Marketing; Manager, Intellectual Property Development and Research Transition Facility; Media Assistant; Office Administrator; Program Advisor; Receptionist; Registration Clerk, Access Desk; Research Assistant; Residence Facilities Coordinator; Secretary / Scholarship Assistant; Shift Engineer; Sport Services Assistant; Technical Manager; Administrative Assistant; Administrative Secretary, Cancer Biology Research Group; Recruitment and Retention Project Coordinator; Technology Manager; Communications / Athlete Services Coordinator; Junior Accountant; Administrative Secretary; Clinical Administrative Assistant; Computer Operator; Course Coordinators (2); Desktop Support Technician; Graduate and Research Secretary; Instructor, Mathematics and Statistics; Maintenance Worker Leadhand; Program Planner; Residence Life Coordinators (2); Secretary; Administrative Assistant; Chair Secretary; Maintenance Contract and Service Planner; Administrative Secretary / Receptionist; Apprentice; Assistant Head Cashier; Head, Department of Computer Science; Instrumentation Technician; Long Track Speed Skating - Training Centre Coach; Manager, Financial Reporting; Short Track Speed Skating - Training Centre Coach; Special Project Accountant; Account Administrator - Research & Trust Accounting; Core Support Technician - Central Wash Up; Document Delivery Services / Circulation Assistant; Exchanges and Study Abroad Advisor; Human Resources Analyst; Human Resources Consultant; Manager, Systems Programming; Records Analyst / Archivist; Senior Systems Administrator, Mathematics & Statistics; Supervisor - Retail Operations, Residence Services; Administrative Assistant - Development & External Relations; Administrative Assistant - Food Services; Administrative Secretary - Clinical; Administrative Secretary - Communications & Fund Development; Assistant to the Program Director; Manager, Information Systems; Program Officer; Accounts Payable Processor; Administrative Assistant; Administrative Assistant / Engineering Internship Program; Administrative Secretaries - Department of Community Health Sciences (2); Administrative Secretary - Mucosal Inflammation Research Group; Construction Estimator; Customer Service Associates (2); Director of Administration; Order / Returns Coordinator; Residence Assistant; System Support / Database Administrator; Technician; Undergraduate Student Advisor; Director, Alumni Relations / Executive Director, U of C Alumni Association; OS / 390 Specialist; Senior UNIX Specialist.

UNIVERSITY OF CALGARY, DEPARTMENT OF COMPUTER SCIENCE

Att: Dr. K. Loose, Head
2500 University Drive NW
Calgary, AB T2N 1N4

Email .... search@cpsc.ucalgary.ca
Website .... www.ucalgary.ca

Employer Background: The University of Calgary has 16 faculties and 60 academic departments, employing 1,900 academic and 2,400 support staff and serving 30,000 degree students. *New Positions Created (2):* Instructor, Computer Science; Assistant, Associate and Full Professors, Computer Science.

UNIVERSITY OF CALGARY, DEPARTMENT OF HISTORY

Att: Dr. D.B. Marshall, Head
2500 University Drive NW
Calgary, AB T2N 1N4

Tel. 403-220-3837
Fax 403-289-8566
Email .... marshall@ucalgary.ca
Website .... www.ucalgary.ca

Employer Background: The University of Calgary has 16 faculties and 60 academic departments, employing 1,900 academic and 2,400 support staff and serving 30,000 degree students. *New Positions Created (2):* Assistant Professor, History; Assistant Professor, History.

UNIVERSITY OF CALGARY, FACULTY OF EDUCATION

Att: Dr. Annette LaGrange, Dean
2500 University Drive NW
Calgary, AB T2N 1N4

Fax 403-282-5849
Website .... www.ucalgary.ca

Employer Background: The University of Calgary has 16 faculties and 60 academic departments, employing 1,900 academic and 2,400 support staff and serving 30,000 degree students. *New Positions Created (7):* Assistant / Associate Professor, Educational Technology; Assistant Professor, Secondary School Science Education; Assistant Professors, Educational Leadership and Multicultural Education; Tenure-Track Position, Counselling Psychology; Tenure-Track Position, School Psychology; Tenure-Track Position, Secondary School Science Education; Associate Dean, Division of Applied Psychology.

UNIVERSITY OF CALGARY, FACULTY OF MANAGEMENT

Att: Allen Ponak, Chair, Human Resources and Organizational Dynamics
2500 University Drive NW
Calgary, AB T2N 1N4

Tel. 403-220-5932
Fax 403-220-0095
Email .... ponak@mgmt.ucalgary.ca
Website .... www.ucalgary.ca

Employer Background: The Faculty of Management, an AACSB-accredited institution, offers programs at the undergraduate, MBA and PhD levels. *New Positions Created (5):* University Teaching Position, Human Resources and Organizational Dynamics; Chair, Management; Professor, Management; Professor, Management; Professor, Management.

UNIVERSITY OF CALGARY, FACULTY OF SOCIAL WORK
Att: Dr. Gayla Rogers, Dean
2500 University Drive NW
Calgary, AB T2N 1N4

Tel.	403-220-5945
Fax	403-284-1391
Website	www.fsw.ucalgary.ca

Employer Background: The University of Calgary has 16 faculties and 60 academic departments, employing 1,900 academic and 2,400 support staff and serving 30,000 degree students. *New Positions Created (7):* Assistant and Associate Professor, Social Work; Instructor, Social Work; Administrative Assistant; Associate Director of Field Education, Social Work; Professor, Social Work; Assistant Professor, Social Work; Research and Development Administrator.

UNIVERSITY OF GUELPH
Att: Human Resources
University Centre, Level 5
Guelph, ON N1G 2W1

Tel.	519-824-4120
Fax	519-763-2780
Website	www.uoguelph.ca

Employer Background: Founded in 1964, the University of Guelph serves over 11,000 students in a variety of undergraduate and graduate programs. The university is best known for its agricultural studies program. *New Positions Created (40):* Intramural Coordinator, On-Campus Programs; Laboratory Technician, Animal Health Lab; Learner Services Representative; Senior Construction Coordinator; Veterinary Technician, Large Animal Clinic; Assistant Cook; Cook; Library Assistant, Document Delivery / Interlibrary Loan, Access Services; Nursing Manager, Small Animal Clinic; Scientist, Trace Organics and Pesticides; Secretary to the Chair, Department of Zoology; Technician, Drug Residue Lab; Veterinary Technician, Specialty Services, Small Animal Clinic; Associate Registrar, Student Recruitment; Intellectual Property Assistant; Lab Instructor / Coordinator; Out-of-Hours Laboratory Technician, Central Services; Pharmacy Manager, Veterinary Teaching Hospital; Research Technician, Plant Metabolism Laboratory; Residence Manager, Student Housing Services; Staff Auditor; College Senior Lecturer, Farm Business Management; Nuclear Magnetic Resonance Technician; Staff Pharmacist, Veterinary Teaching Hospital; Teaching Laboratory Technician; Child Care Cook; Laboratory Technician, Mammalian Virology; Pharmacy Technician; Residence and Recreation Assistant; Administrative Assistant; Agricultural Technician; Laboratory Technician;

Agricultural Assistant; Analyst II, Academic Services, Computing and Communications Services; Analyst II, Campus Services, Computing and Communications Services; Analyst III, Departmental Services, Computing and Communications Services; Associate Director, News Service; Police Sergeant; Special Constable; Director, Student Housing Services.

UNIVERSITY OF GUELPH, DEPARTMENT OF FAMILY RELATIONS AND APPLIED NUTRITION
Att: Dr. Joseph Tindale,
Co-Chair, Joint Selection Committee
Guelph, ON N1G 2W1

Fax	519-766-0691
Email	jtindale@uoguelph.ca
Website	www.uoguelph.ca/family

Employer Background: The Department of Family Relations & Applied Nutrition is a research-intensive department offering strong undergraduate, MSc and PhD programs in applied human nutrition, child and youth, gerontology, and couple and family therapy (CFT). *New Positions Created (3):* Assistant/ Associate Professor, College of Social & Applied Human Sciences; Lecturer/Assistant Professor, Couple & Family Therapy; Lecturer / Assistant Professor, Gerontology.

UNIVERSITY OF GUELPH, DEPARTMENT OF PATHOBIOLOGY
Att: Dr. Patricia E. Shewen, Chair
Guelph, ON N1G 2W1

Fax	519-824-5930
Email	pshewen@uoguelph.ca
Website	www.uoguelph.ca/family

Employer Background: The Department of Pathobiology offers instructional and research programs in animal research, including mammalian and comparative pathology, veterinary infectious disease and immunology. *New Positions Created (3):* Assistant / Associate Professor, Fish Pathobiologist; Assistant / Associate Professor, Laboratory Animal Medicine; Assistant / Associate Professor, Veterinary Clinical Pathology.

UNIVERSITY OF GUELPH, OFFICE OF THE VICE-PRESIDENT (RESEARCH)
Att: Dr. Alan Wildeman,
Chair of the Search Committee
University Centre - Level 4
Guelph, ON N1G 2W1

Fax	519-837-1639
Email	wildeman@uoguelph.ca
Website	www.uoguelph.ca

Employer Background: Founded in 1964, the University of Guelph serves over 11,000 students in a variety of undergraduate and graduate programs. The university is best known for its agricultural studies program. *New Positions Created (2):* Associate Vice-President, Agri-Food and Partnerships; Associate Vice-President, Research.

UNIVERSITY OF LETHBRIDGE
Att: Human Resources Manager
4401 University Drive
Lethbridge, AB T1K 3M4

Tel.	403-329-2201
Fax	403-329-2224
Email	human.resources@uleth.ca
Website	www.uleth.ca

Employer Background: University of Lethbridge has approximately 5,500 undergraduate and 200 graduate students, and a faculty and staff complement of 1,200. *New Positions Created (5):* General Manager; Manager, Capital Projects; Project Technician; Manager, Caretaking Services; Journeyman Electrician.

UNIVERSITY OF LETHBRIDGE, DEPARTMENT OF MODERN LANGUAGES
Att: Professor Barbara Dickinson, Chair
4401 University Drive
Lethbridge, AB T1K 3M4

Tel.	403-329-2560
Fax	403-329-5187
Email	erickson@uleth.ca
Website	www.uleth.ca

Employer Background: The University of Lethbridge has approximately 5,500 undergraduate and 200 graduate students, and a faculty and staff complement of 1,200. *New Positions Created (3):* Assistant Professor; Assistant Professor, French; Lecturer, Japanese.

UNIVERSITY OF MANITOBA, DEPARTMENT OF CHEMISTRY
Att: Dr. Harry W. Duckworth,
Search Committee Chair
Winnipeg, MB R3T 2N2

Tel.	204-474-9265
Fax	204-474-7608
Email	hdckwth@cc.umanitoba.ca
Website	www.umanitoba.ca

Employer Background: Founded in in 1877, the University of Manitoba is western Canada's oldest university. The University serves a student population of 21,800 with a faculty and staff of 5,726. *New Positions Created (2):* Assistant Professor; Instructor II.

UNIVERSITY OF MANITOBA, DEPARTMENT OF MECHANICAL AND INDUSTRIAL ENGINEERING
Att: Professor S. Balakrishnan,
Chair of Search Committee
Winnipeg, MB R3T 5V6

Tel.	204-474-9803
Fax	204-275-7507
Email	vyas@ms.umanitoba.ca
Website	www.umanitoba.ca

Employer Background: Founded in in 1877, the University of Manitoba is western Canada's oldest university. The University serves a student population of 21,800, with a faculty and staff of 5,726. *New Positions Created (3):* Assistant Professor, Fluids; Assistant Professor, Manufacturing and Production Engineering; Assistant Professor, Thermofluids.

UNIVERSITY OF MANITOBA LIBRARIES
Att: Carolynne Presser, Director
Winnipeg, MB R3T 2N2

Tel.	204-474-8749

Fax 204-474-7583
Website .... www.umanitoba.ca
Employer Background: Founded in 1877, the University of Manitoba is western Canada's oldest university, serving a student population of 21,800 with a faculty and staff of 5,726. *New Positions Created (3):* Head; Section Head; Section Head, DS Woods Education Library, Elizabeth Dafoe Library.

UNIVERSITY OF NEW BRUNSWICK, DEPARTMENT OF BIOLOGY / UNB
Att: Professor T.G. Dilworth, Chair
Bag Service 45111
Fredericton, NB E3B 6E1
Tel. 506-453-4583
Fax 506-453-3583
Email .... biology@unb.ca
Website .... www.unb.ca
Employer Background: UNB has 17,000 students, over 1,500 employees and annual revenues of $170 million. *New Positions Created (3):* Assistant Professor, Algal Research; Assistant Professor, Quantitative (Animal) Ecology; Biology Instructor.

UNIVERSITY OF NEW BRUNSWICK, FACULTY OF BUSINESS / UNB
Att: Dean
PO Box 5050
Saint John, NB E2L 4L5
Tel. 506-648-5695
Fax 506-648-5574
Website .... www.unb.ca
Employer Background: UNB has 17,000 students, over 1,500 employees and annual revenues of $170 million. *New Positions Created (3):* Director of Hospitality and Tourism; Instructors, Accounting; Professors, Faculty of Business.

UNIVERSITY OF NEW BRUNSWICK, FACULTY OF SCIENCE, APPLIED SCIENCE & ENGINEERING
Att: Dr. Keith DeBell, Dean
PO Box 5050
Saint John, NB E2L 4L5
Tel. 506-648-5671
Fax 506-648-5650
Email .... sci-eng@unbsj.ca
Website .... www.unb.ca
Employer Background: The University of New Brunswick has 17,000 students, over 1,500 employees and annual revenues of $170 million. *New Positions Created (2):* Chemistry Instructor; Faculty Positions, Department of Nursing.

UNIVERSITY OF NEW BRUNSWICK
Att: Human Resources & Organizational Development
PO Box 4400
Fredericton, NB E3B 5A3
Tel. 506-453-4648
Fax 506-453-4611
Email .... hrandod@unb.ca
Website .... www.unb.ca
Employer Background: UNB has 17,000 students, over 1,500 employees and annual revenues of $170 million. *New Positions Created (7):* Assistant Director; Community Coordinators (2); Executive Director, Alumni Association; Secretary; Preschool Teacher; Assistant Comptroller, Operations; Assistant Director of Campus Recreation.

UNIVERSITY OF NORTHERN BRITISH COLUMBIA / UNBC
Att: Dr. Deborah Poff,
Vice-President (Academic) and Provost
3333 University Way
Prince George, BC V2N 4Z9
Tel. 250-960-5521
Fax 250-960-7300
Website .... www.unbc.ca
Employer Background: UNBC is a Canadian university established in 1994. *New Positions Created (26):* Chair of Nursing; Assistant / Associate / Full Professors, Business Program (3); Assistant / Associate Professor, Geomorphology; Assistant Professor, Economics Program; Assistant Professor, Human Geography; Senior Laboratory Instructor, GIS Lab; Senior Laboratory Instructor, Mathematics and Computer Science Program; Deputy Registrar, Systems; Assistant Professor, Social and Cultural Anthropology; Assistant Professor, Forestry Program / Silviculture; Assistant Professors, Social Work (3); Assistant Professor, Computer Science; Dean of Graduate Studies; Coordinator, First Nations Centre; Assistant Professor, English Program; Assistant Professor, Political Science Program; Director of Computing and Telecommunication Services; Assistant / Associate Professor, Environmental Science Program; Biology Instructors (2); Chair of Social Work; Medical Geographer, Geography Program; Operating System Support; Assistant / Associate Professor; Chair, Disability Management; Faculty Positions, Accounting and Finance (2); Tenure Track Position, Economics Program.

UNIVERSITY OF OTTAWA
Att: Human Resources Service
550 Cumberland Street
Room 046, PO Box 450, Station A
Ottawa, ON K1N 6N5
Tel. 613-562-5809
Fax 613-562-5206
Website .... www.uottawa.ca
Employer Background: Established in 1848, the University of Ottawa is North America's largest bilingual university, with 200 staff members and 25,000 students. *New Positions Created (2):* Assistant to the Manager, Payroll Systems; Manager, Classification, Compensation and Pay Equity.

UNIVERSITY OF OTTAWA, FACULTY OF ADMINISTRATION
Att: Douglas E. Angus,
Vice-Dean Faculty of Administration
VNR 150, PO Box 450, Station A
Ottawa, ON K1N 6N5
Tel. 613-562-5815
Fax 613-562-5165
Email .... angus@admin.uottawa.ca
Website .... www.uottawa.ca
Employer Background: Established in 1848, the University of Ottawa is one of North America's largest bilingual university, with 200 staff members and 25,000 students. *New Positions Created (3):* Various Teaching Positions; Professors; Business Professors.

UNIVERSITY OF OTTAWA HEART INSTITUTE
Att: Heather Sherrard,
Vice-President of Clinical Services
40 Ruskin Street
Ottawa, ON K1Y 4W7
Tel. 613-761-4604
Fax 613-761-5323
Website .... www.ottawaheart.ca
Employer Background: The University of Ottawa Heart Institute is a bilingual, academic healthcare institution dedicated to the promotion of cardiovascular health. *New Positions Created (5):* Clinical Scientist, Nursing Research; Research Associate / Assistant; Clinical Services Manager, Cardiac Operating Rooms and Catheterization Labs; Clinical Services Program Analyst; Nuclear Medicine Technologist.

UNIVERSITY OF REGINA
Att: Ray Smith, HR Manager
3737 Wascana Parkway, Room 206
Administration - Humanities Building
Regina, SK S4S 0A2
Tel. 306-585-4808
Fax 306-585-5232
Email .... uofr.recruitment@uregina.ca
Website .... www.uregina.ca
Employer Background: The University of Regina offers a variety of degree programs to over 11,500 students. The university has an annual operating budget of $85 million. *New Positions Created (6):* Chief Engineer, Heating Plant; Faculty of Arts Position; Faculty of Physical Activity Studies Position; International Recruitment Officer, Latin America & Europe Language Institute; Internal Auditor; International Recruitment Officer.

UNIVERSITY OF REGINA, FACULTY OF EDUCATION
Att: Dr. Margaret McKinnon, Dean
University of Regina
Regina, SK S4S 0A2
Tel. 306-585-4500
Fax 306-525-5330
Website .... education.uregina.ca
Employer Background: The University of Regina offers a variety of degree programs to over 11,500 students. The university has an annual operating budget of $85 million. *New Positions Created (3):* Director, Vocational / Technical Education and Human Resource Development Program; Assistant Professors, Education; Assistant Professors, Special Education and Social Studies.

UNIVERSITY OF REGINA, FACULTY OF ENGINEERING
Att: Dr. Paitoon (P.T.) Tontiwachwuthikul, PEng, Dean
University of Regina
Regina, SK S4S 0A2
Tel. 306-585-4159

Fax 306-585-4556
Email .... paitoon@uregina.ca
Website .... www.uregina.ca/engg
Employer Background: The University of Regina offers a variety of degree programs to over 11,500 students. The university has an annual operating budget of $85 million. *New Positions Created (8):* Laboratory Instructor; Tenure-Track Appointment, Environmental Systems Engineering; Laboratory Instructor, Faculty of Engineering; Laboratory Instructor; Tenure-Track Faculty Position, Electronic Systems Engineering; Tenure-Track Faculty Position, Industrial Systems Engineering; Tenure-Track Faculty Position, Petroleum Systems Engineering; Tenure-Track Faculty Position, Software Systems Engineering.

UNIVERSITY OF REGINA, LANGUAGE INSTITUTE
Att: Dr. A. Lalonde, Director
Regina, SK S4S 0A2
Tel. 306-585-4093
Fax 306-525-5183
Website .... www.uregina.ca/langinst
Employer Background: The University of Regina offers a variety of degree programs to over 11,500 students. The Language Institute was established in 1991. *New Positions Created (2):* Spanish Instructor; Instructor, English as a Second Language.

UNIVERSITY OF SASKATCHEWAN, COLLEGE OF EDUCATION
Att: Dr. K.G. Jacknicke, Dean
28 Campus Drive
Saskatoon, SK S7N 0X1
Tel. 306-966-7634
Fax 306-966-7624
Website .... www.usask.ca/education
Employer Background: The College of Education at the University of Saskatchewan serves 1,300 undergraduate students and 450 graduate students in PhD, MEd and diploma programs. *New Positions Created (4):* Assistant Professor, Curriculum Studies; Assistant Professor, Educational Administration; Assistant Professors, Educational Psychology and Special Education; Head, Department of Educational Psychology and Special Education.

UNIVERSITY OF TORONTO
Att: Tina Ferrari, HR Generalist
214 College Street, Room 310
Toronto, ON M5T 2Z9
Tel. 416-978-2011
Fax 416-971-2019
Website .... www.utoronto.ca
Employer Background: Founded in 1827, U of T has over 42,000 students and is Canada's largest university. *New Positions Created (10):* Billing Services Coordinator; Divisional Controller; Senior Auditors (2); Accountant; Business Analyst; Career Development Officer; Grants Officer; Labour Relations Specialist; Financial Analyst; Assistant Catering Coordinator.

UNIVERSITY OF TORONTO
Att: Edith Sinclair, Personnel Generalist
130 St. George Street
Room 2005, Robarts Library
Toronto, ON M5S 1A5
Fax 416-946-5543
Website .... www.utoronto.ca
Employer Background: Founded in 1827, U of T has over 42,000 students and is Canada's largest university. *New Positions Created (4):* Technology Assistant; Courseware Support Specialist; System Administrator, Centre for Academic and Adaptive Technology; System Analyst / Technical Support, TCard Administration Office.

UNIVERSITY OF TORONTO AT SCARBOROUGH / UTSC
Att: Marilyn Kwan, HR Generalist
1265 Military Trail
Toronto, ON M1C 1A4
Fax 416-287-7078
Website .... www.utsc.utoronto.ca
Employer Background: Established in 1964, UTSC is a constituent college of the University of Toronto, with 5,500 students and over 200 faculty members. *New Positions Created (5):* Co-op Assistant; Manager, Health and Wellness Services; Associate Coordinator, Cooperative Education; Computer Graphics and E-Publishing Assistant, Centre for Instructional Technology Development and CITDPress; Registration and Financial Aid Assistant.

UNIVERSITY OF TORONTO, DEPARTMENT OF IMMUNOLOGY
Att: Search Committee
1 King's College Circle
Medical Science Building
Toronto, ON M5S 1A8
Tel. 416-978-6382
Fax 416-978-1938
Website ... www.immune.med.utoronto.ca
Employer Background: Founded in 1827, U of T has over 42,000 students and is Canada's largest university. *New Positions Created (2):* Assistant Professors, Human Immunology (2); Endowed Chair, Human Immunology.

UNIVERSITY OF TORONTO, FACULTY OF ARTS & SCIENCE
Att: Helen Givelas,
Faculty Personnel Office
100 St. George Street, Room 2007
Toronto, ON M5S 3G3
Tel. 416-946-5477
Fax 416-971-2881
Email .... helen.givelas@artsci.utoronto.ca
Website .... www.utoronto.ca
Employer Background: Founded in 1827, U of T has over 42,000 students and is Canada's largest university. *New Positions Created (4):* Petitions Assistant; Manager, Physics Computing Services; Physics Instrumentation Specialist; Information Technology Administrator, Departments of Economics and Sociology.

UNIVERSITY OF TORONTO, FACULTY OF MEDICINE
Att: Dean David Naylor
c/o Leslie Bush, Executive Assistant
1 King's College Circle
Room 2109, Medical Sciences Building
Toronto, ON M5S 1A8
Tel. 416-978-8313
Fax 416-978-1774
Email .... leslie.bush@utoronto.ca
Website .... www.utoronto.ca
Employer Background: Founded in 1827, U of T has over 42,000 students and is Canada's largest university. *New Positions Created (7):* Chair, Department of Biochemistry; Administrative Assistant, Rehabilitation Sciences; Administrative Assistant, Faculty of Medicine; Assistant Director, CIHR Institute of Human Development, Child and Youth Health; Assistant Director, Institute of Aboriginal Peoples' Health; Assistant Director, Institution of Population and Public Health; Department Secretary.

UNIVERSITY OF TORONTO, OPERATIONS & SERVICES
Att: Lynne Fitton,
Human Resource Services
215 Huron Street, 6th Floor
Toronto, ON M5S 1A2
Fax 416-946-7047
Website .... www.utoronto.ca
Employer Background: Founded in 1827, U of T has over 42,000 students and is Canada's largest university. *New Positions Created (7):* HVAC Engineer; Business Officer; Human Resources Generalist; Communications Operator; Chief Engineer; Second Class Constable Positions; Manager, Construction.

UNIVERSITY OF TORONTO PRESS INC. / UTP
Att: Kathryn Laub
10 St. Mary Street, Suite 700
Toronto, ON M4Y 2W8
Tel. 416-978-8651
Fax 416-978-4738
Website .... www.utpress.utoronto.ca
Employer Background: Established in 1901, UTP is a major publisher of scholarly books and journals, a full-service printer, book distributor and campus retailer. *New Positions Created (2):* Production Manager; Assistant, Manufacturing Services and Purchasing.

UNIVERSITY OF TORONTO, PROFESSIONAL FACULTIES SOUTH
Att: Alina Balosin, HR Manager
203 College Street, 5th Floor
Toronto, ON M5T 1P9
Tel. 416-978-2011
Fax 416-978-0381
Website .... www.utoronto.ca
Employer Background: Founded in 1827, U of T has over 42,000 students and is Canada's largest university. *New Positions Created (6):* Office Assistant / Receptionist; Program Administrative Assistant; Research Office Coordinator, Faculty of Nursing; Director, Development and Alumni Relations; Labo-

ratory Support Engineer; Senior Development Officer, Faculty of Pharmacy.

UNIVERSITY OF VICTORIA
Att: Human Resources Advisor
Sedgewick B Wing, PO Box 1700
Victoria, BC V8W 2Y2
Tel. 250-721-7211
Fax 250-721-8094
Website .... www.uvic.com
Employer Background: University of Victoria is one of Canada's highest-ranked comprehensive universities. *New Positions Created (3):* Senior Laboratory Instructor; Unix Systems Administrator; Director, Institutional Planning and Analysis.

UNIVERSITY OF WATERLOO
Att: Alfrieda Swainston, Human Resources
200 University Avenue West
Waterloo, ON N2L 3G1
Tel. 519-885-1211
Fax 519-746-3242
Website .... www.uwaterloo.ca
Employer Background: Founded in 1957, the University of Waterloo serves a population of over 22,000 students, with a faculty of 1,426 and staff of 2,027. *New Positions Created (8):* Senior Development Officers, Office of Development; Software Specialist and Hardware Specialist; Information Systems Specialists, Senior and Intermediate; Chief Stationary Engineer, Plant Operations; Materials Characterization Specialist; Associate Director, Education and Administration; Commercialization Associate, Technology Transfer and Licensing Office ; Field Coordinator, Chartered Accounting Cooperative Education and Career Services.

UNIVERSITY OF WESTERN ONTARIO
Att: Associate Vice-President
Stevenson-Lawson Building, Room 206
London, ON N6A 5B8
Tel. 519-661-2194
Fax 519-661-2079
Website .... www.uwo.ca
Employer Background: Founded in 1878, the University of Western Ontario is a leading post-secondary educational institution, with over 22,900 students and 1,250 faculty members. *New Positions Created (3):* Director, Alumni Relations; Director, Medicine & Dentistry Campaign; Director of Bookstore, Computer Store and Graphics Services.

UNIVERSITY OF WESTERN ONTARIO, DEPARTMENT OF ECONOMICS
Att: Chair
1151 Richmond Street
London, ON N6A 5C2
Tel. 519-661-3500
Website .... www.uwo.ca
Employer Background: Founded in 1878, the University of Western Ontario is a leading post-secondary educational institution, with over 22,900 students and 1,250 faculty members. *New Positions Created (4):* Assistant Professor and Associate Professor; Associate Professor or Professor of Macroeconomics; Lecturer; Professor.

UNIVERSITY OF WESTERN ONTARIO, FACULTY OF HEALTH SCIENCES
Att: Dr. Angelo N. Belcastro, Dean
Health Sciences Addition, Room H124
London, ON N6A 5C1
Tel. 519-661-4249
Website .... www.uwo.ca/fhs
Employer Background: Founded in 1878, the University of Western Ontario is a leading post-secondary educational institution, with over 22,900 students and 1,250 faculty members. *New Positions Created (3):* Director, School of Occupational Therapy; Tenure-Track Positions, School of Nursing (3); Director, School of Kinesiology.

UNIVERSITY OF WESTERN ONTARIO, FACULTY OF MEDICINE AND DENTISTRY (DEPARTMENT OF FAMILY MEDICINE)
Att: Dr. Carol Herbert, Dean
Health Sciences Addition
London, ON N6A 5C1
Fax 519-850-2357
Website .... www.uwo.ca
Employer Background: Founded in 1878, the University of Western Ontario is a leading post-secondary educational institution, with over 22,900 students and 1,250 faculty members. *New Positions Created (3):* Chair, Department of Family Medicine; Chair, Department of Pharmacology and Toxicology; Chair, Department of Physiology.

UNLEASH CORPORATION
Att: Larry Kistner, President
5935 Airport Road, Suite 410
Mississauga, ON L4V 1W5
Tel. 905-405-9405
Fax 905-405-9404
Website .... www.unleashcorp.com
Employer Background: Unleash Corporation develops software for the integration of sales force automation, accounting and distribution systems. *New Positions Created (18):* Business Systems Analyst / Team Leader; Developer / Integrator; Junior Developer / Integrator; Junior Systems Engineer; Project Management / Senior Consultant; Systems Engineer; Business Systems Analyst / Team Leader; Developer / Integrator; Junior Developer / Integrator; Junior Systems Engineer; Project Manager / Senior Consultant; Systems Engineer; Business Systems Analyst / Team Leader; Developer / Integrator; Junior Developer / Integrator; Junior Systems Engineer; Project Manager / Senior Consultant; Systems Engineer.

UNUMPROVIDENT CORPORATION
Att: Danyah Qadir, Human Resources
5420 North Service Road, PO Box 5044
Burlington, ON L7R 4C1
Tel. 416-594-1601
Fax 905-319-8476
Email .... dqadir@unum.com
Website .... www.unum.com
Employer Background: UnumProvident Corporation is a leading provider of disability insurance, with 150 years experience in the industry. *New Positions Created (10):*

Bilingual Account Specialists; Bilingual Call Centre Representatives; Legal Counsel; Translators; Underwriting Specialists; Account Analysts; Contract Administrators; Supervisor, Customer Service Call Centre; Supervisor, Individual New Business; Compliance Officer.

UPPER CANADA COLLEGE, PREPARATORY SCHOOL
Att: Human Resources
200 Lonsdale Road
Toronto, ON M4V 2X8
Fax 416-484-8617
Website .... www.ucc.on.ca
Employer Background: Upper Canada College is one of Canada's leading independent schools for boys. *New Positions Created (5):* Teacher, Outdoor Education; Teachers (2); Teachers (2); Science / Technology and Math Teacher; Teaching Assistant, Physical Education, Athletics and Games.

UPPER CANADA COLLEGE, UPPER SCHOOL
Att: Human Resources
200 Lonsdale Road
Toronto, ON M4V 1W6
Tel. 416-488-1125
Fax 416-484-8657
Website .... www.ucc.on.ca
Employer Background: Upper Canada College is one of Canada's leading independent schools for boys. *New Positions Created (5):* Coordinators; Residence Dons; Educators, Mathematics / Economics; Head Coach - Rowing Team; Manager, Database Administration.

UPPER CANADA DISTRICT SCHOOL BOARD
Att: Eleanor Newman, Superintendent
25 Central Avenue West
Brockville, ON K6V 5X1
Tel. 613-342-0371
Fax 613-342-9459
Website .... www.ucdsb.on.ca
Employer Background: The Upper Canada School Board serves over 40,000 students at 110 elementary and secondary schools. The Board has a budget of $244.5 million and employs 4,000 staff. *New Positions Created (7):* Executive Assistants (2); Public Relations Officer; Human Resources Information Systems Specialist; Human Resources Officer; Junior Staffing Officer; Drawing Database and Project Coordinator; Various Principalship Positions (4).

UPS LOGISTICS GROUP CANADA LIMITED
Att: Corporate Human Resources
1453 Cornwall Road
Oakville, ON L6J 7T5
Fax 905-845-4330
Email ... careerscanada@upslogistics.com
Website .... www.upslogistics.ca
Employer Background: UPS Logistics Group Canada Limited (formerly Livingston Healthcare Services Inc.) provides custom-

ized logistics solutions for the healthcare, consumer packaged goods and high-technology markets. *New Positions Created (14):* Business Development Managers, High-Tech and Telecom (2); Senior Client Partnering Manager; Branch Manager, Operations; Business Development Manager, Healthcare; Logistics Engineer; Manager, Client Care; Manager, Client Care; Manager, Transportation - Carriers; Manager, Transportation - Partnership Clients; Operations Manager; Senior Client Partnering Manager; Transportation Analyst; Various Logistics Positions (2); Manager, Human Resources.

UPSIDE ENGINEERING LTD.
Att: Human Resources Manager
100 - 8th Avenue SW, Suite 200
Calgary, AB T2P 3T9

Fax 403-299-0949
Email ..... human.resources@upsideeng.com
Website .... www.upsideeng.com

Employer Background: Upside Engineering Ltd. is an EPCM company working on pipeline, facilities, power generation and co-generation projects. *New Positions Created (3):* Mechanical Engineer; PLC Programmer; Power System Electrical Engineer.

URBANDALE CORPORATION
Att: Human Resources Manager
2193 Arch Street
Ottawa, ON K1G 2H5

Tel. 613-731-6331
Fax 613-731-7835
Website .... www.urbandale.com

Employer Background: Urbandale Corporation is an established real estate developer and landlord in the Ottawa-Carleton region. *New Positions Created (6):* Sales Representative(s); Site Superintendent; Sales Assistants; Construction Accounts Payable Clerk; Construction Co-ordinator Assistant; Construction Accountant.

URS COLE, SHERMAN
Att: Human Resources
75 Commerce Valley Drive East
Thornhill, ON L3T 7N9

Tel. 905-882-4401
Fax 905-882-4399
Email .... colesherman@urscorp.com
Website .... www.colesherman.com

Employer Background: Established in 1954, URS Cole, Sherman (formerly Cole, Sherman & Associates Ltd.) provides consulting engineering, architectural and planning services to government and private-sector clients. *New Positions Created (28):* Executive Assistant; Senior Bridge Engineer; Site Representative; Environmental Engineer; Environmental Scientist / Engineer; Hydrogeologist / Remediation Engineer; Junior Environmental Technologist; Municipal Engineer; Proposals and Marketing Position; Structural Engineer, Intermediate; Water Resources Engineers, Intermediate / Junior; Administrative Assistant; Architectural Graduate; Bridge Engineers; Building Science Engineer; CADD Operator; Intermediate Project Manager; Intermediate / Sen-

ior Project Manager; Junior / Intermediate Highway Designer; Project Engineer, Transportation; Senior Architect / Marketing Manager; Senior Bridge Engineer; Senior Mechanical Engineer / Department Manager; Structural Technologist; Word-Processing Position; Administrative Assistant; Structural Technologist; Word Processor.

URS CORPORATION
Att: Human Resources
734 - 7th Avenue SW, Suite 1610
Calgary, AB T2P 3P8

Fax 403-777-4150
Email .... hralberta@urscorp.com
Website .... www.urscorp.com

Employer Background: URS Corporation (formerly NDM Radian Inc.) is one of the largest environmental and engineering service firms in the world. *New Positions Created (2):* Project Hydrogeologists; Senior Hydrogeologist.

USCO LOGISTICS
Att: Human Resources Department
2200, chemin St-François
Dorval, QC H9P 1K2

Fax 514-818-8122
Email .... aelkaim@usco.com
Website .... www.usco.com

Employer Background: USCO Logistics, a full service provider of integrated logistics solutions and information systems, manages over 11 million square feet of shared and dedicated distribution space for some of the world's largest companies. *New Positions Created (5):* Administrative Assistant; Distribution Centre Manager; Inventory Control Specialist; Warehouse Associates; Warehouse Supervisors.

USFILTER / WALLACE & TIERNAN PRODUCTS CANADA
Att: Human Resources Department
250 Royal Crest Court
Markham, ON L3R 3S1

Tel. 905-944-2800
Fax 905-474-1752
Email .... wtcmarketing@usfilter.com
Website .... www.wallaceandtiernan.
.... usfilter.com

Employer Background: USFilter / Wallace & Tiernan Products Canada manufactures water and wastewater treatment products and services. *New Positions Created (2):* Technical Salesperson; Applications Engineering / Service Representative.

UTEX CORPORATION
Att: Human Resources Manager
845 Plymouth
Montréal, QC H4P 1B2

Tel. 514-737-4300
Fax 514-737-8560
Website .... www.utexcorp.com

Employer Background: Utex Corporation is a leading apparel manufacturer. *New Positions Created (2):* Assistants, Merchandising Department (2); Stylist, Men's Outerwear.

VA TECH FERRANTI-PACKARD TRANSFORMERS LTD.
Att: Richard Atamanyk, HR Manager
189 Dieppe Road, PO Box 548
St. Catharines, ON L2R 6W9

Tel. 905-685-6551
Fax 905-685-7351
Email .... atamanyk.richard@vatech.fpt.ca
Website .... www.vatech.co.at

Employer Background: A member of the VA Tech group of transformer companies, VA Tech Ferranti-Packard Transformers Ltd. manufactures liquid-filled transformers. *New Positions Created (6):* Industrial Electrician; Product Controller, Purchasing and Planning; Contract Manager; Financial Analyst; Fitter / Welders; Transformer Winders.

VALADEO TECHNOLOGIES CORP.
Att: Human Resources Manager
95 Trinity Street
Toronto, ON M5A 3C7

Tel. 416-350-2111
Fax 416-350-2137
Email .... jobs@valadeo.com
Website .... www.valadeo.com

Employer Background: Founded in 1996, Valadeo Technologies Corp. develops Internet software designed to meet web creation, publishing and management needs. *New Positions Created (10):* Graphic Artist; Technical Writer; C++ Developer; E-Services Developer; Java Developer; Localization Developer; Manager, Desktop Applications; Unix System Developer; VB Developer; Web Application Developer.

VALCOM LIMITED (OTTAWA)
Att: Technical Recruiter
85 Albert Street, Suite 300
Ottawa, ON K1P 6A4

Tel. 613-594-5206
Fax 613-233-0009
Email .... hr@valcom.ca
Website .... www.valcom-ottawa.com

Employer Background: Valcom Limited (Ottawa) provides consulting, project management and professional services to government and industry clients. *New Positions Created (30):* Administrative Assistant; Senior ITIL Release Management Practitioner; Administrative Assistant; IM Training Officer; Windows 2000 Pro Instructor; Database Analyst / Programmer; Electronic Technologist; Web Developer; Avionics Specialist, Communications; Engineer, Aerospace; Project Manager; Senior Financial Analyst; System Engineers (2); Data Entry Positions (2); Engineer / Project Manager, Military Automated Air Traffic Control System; Engineer Technologist, Radioactive Material; Engineering Specialist, Configuration Management; Integrated Logistics Support Positions (2); IT Support Position; Procurement Specialist; Project Manager; Senior Engineer, Aerospace; Senior Engineer, Aerospace / Software; Senior Engineer, Avionics; Senior Engineer, Mechanical / Automotive; Senior Engineer, Tactical Command Control and Communications System; Senior Technician, Automotive; Senior Technician, Tactical Command Control and

Communications System; Supply Specialist; Technologist, Aerospace.

VALLEY CITY MANUFACTURING COMPANY LIMITED
Att: Andrew Steele, Factory Manager
64 Halt Street, PO Box 8578
Dundas, ON L9H 5G2

Tel. 905-628-2253
Fax 905-628-4470
Website .... www.valleycity.com

Employer Background: Valley City Manufacturing Company is a custom woodworking manufacturer, providing architect-designed laboratory furniture, courthouse architectural woodwork, specialty furniture and church furniture. *New Positions Created (2):* Industrial Woodworkers; Project Manager.

VALUE DRUG MART ASSOCIATES LTD.
Att: Human Resources Manager
16504 - 121A Avenue
Edmonton, AB T5V 1J9

Tel. 780-453-1701
Email .... careers@valuedrugmart.com
Website .... www.valuedrugmart.com

Employer Background: Value Drug Mart Associates Ltd. operates Value Drug Mart and Apple Drugs pharmacy companies. *New Positions Created (3):* Technology Systems Manager; Retail Technology Coordinator; AS400 / RPG Programmer.

VALUE VILLAGE
Att: Betty Schoemaker
3003 St. Johns Street, Suite 200
Port Moody, BC V3H 2C4

Tel. 604-461-7000
Fax 604-461-7001
Email .... bcbetty@home.com
Website .... www.valuevillage.com

Employer Background: Value Village, one of the largest thrift department store chains in the world, owns and operates 176 stores in North America and Australia. *New Positions Created (3):* Store Mgrs; Bilingual Recruiter; Regional Loss Prevention Mgr.

VALUE VILLAGE
Att: Regional Human Resources Manager
45 Woodbine Downs Boulevard
Toronto, ON M9W 6N5

Fax 416-675-6469
Website .... www.valuevillage.com

Employer Background: Value Village, one of the largest thrift department store chains in the world, owns and operates 176 stores throughout North America and Australia. *New Positions Created (3):* Manager Trainees / Department Supervisors; Managers; Managers.

VALVOLINE CANADA LTD.
Att: Human Resources
905 Winston Churchill Boulevard
Mississauga, ON L5J 4P2

Tel. 905-823-4701
Fax 905-823-2488
Website .... www.valvoline.com

Employer Background: Valvoline Canada, a division of Ashland Canada Inc., manufactures and markets lubricants, automotive chemicals and antifreeze. *New Positions Created (3):* Corporate Accountant; Financial Manager; Bilingual Customer Service Representative.

VAN DER GRAAF INC.
Att: Human Resources
2 Van der Graaf Court
Brampton, ON L6T 5R6

Tel. 905-793-8100
Fax 905-793-8129
Website .... www.vandergraaf.com

Employer Background: Van der Graaf Inc. manufactures precision drum motors. *New Positions Created (2):* Production Scheduler / Inventory Analyst; Receiver / Shipper.

VAN-KAM FREIGHTWAYS LTD.
Att: Bill Henry, VP Sales & Marketing
2355 Madison Avenue
Burnaby, BC V5C 4Z3

Tel. 604-299-7451
Fax 604-299-2469
Website .... www.vankam.com

Employer Background: Established in 1947, Van-Kam Freightways Ltd. provides quality transportation services. *New Positions Created (2):* Territory Manager; Inside Account Manager.

VAN-ROB STAMPINGS INC.
Att: Human Resources
200 Vandorf Sideroad
Aurora, ON L4G 3G8

Tel. 905-764-0334
Fax 905-727-2689
Email .... hr@van-rob.com
Website .... www.van-rob.com

Employer Background: Van-Rob Stampings Inc. manufactures and supplies high-quality metal stamping and assemblies to the OEM automotive industry. *New Positions Created (5):* License Industrial Maintenance Millwrights; Licensed Industrial Maintenance Electrician; Licensed Tool and Die Makers; Machinist; Customer Service Coordinator.

VANCITY INSURANCE SERVICES
Att: Personnel Department
Box 2120, Stn Terminal
Vancouver, BC V6B 5R8

Tel. 604-877-4961
Fax 604-877-7243
Website .... www.vancity.com

Employer Background: VanCity Insurance Services Ltd. has 18 Lower Mainland locations offering a range of insurance products and services. *New Positions Created (3):* Sales Representatives; Customer Service and Sales Positions; Sales Representatives.

VANCOUVER ABORIGINAL CHILD & FAMILY SERVICES SOCIETY
Att: Carol Patrick, President
210 West Broadway, 4th Floor
Vancouver, BC V5Y 1R8

Tel. 604-872-6723
Fax 604-872-5274
Website .... www.vacfss.com

Employer Background: The Vancouver Aboriginal Child & Family Services Society offers support and preventative services to Aboriginal children and families in the Lower Mainland. *New Positions Created (8):* Addictions Specialist; Family Advancement Worker; Mental Health Workers (2); Family Support Workers; Executive Director; Assistant Executive Director; Family Support Workers; Clinical Supervisor.

VANCOUVER ART GALLERY
Att: Personnel Officer
750 Hornby Street
Vancouver, BC V6Z 2H7

Tel. 604-662-4700
Fax 604-682-8287
Website .... www.vanartgallery.bc.ca

Employer Background: Founded in 1931, the Vancouver Art Gallery houses a permanent collection of 7,000 works of art valued at approximately $100 million. *New Positions Created (3):* Associate Director; Development Director; Registrar Collections Position.

VANCOUVER, CITY OF
Att: Human Resource Services
453 - 12th Avenue West, 2nd Floor
Vancouver, BC V5Y 1V4

Tel. 604-873-7011
Fax 604-873-7696
Email ...... city_jobs@city.vancouver.bc.ca
Website .... www.city.vancouver.bc.ca

Employer Background: The City of Vancouver is home to 560,000 residents. *New Positions Created (18):* Civil Engineers; Transportation Engineers; Assistant to City Councillors; Budget Manager; Senior Internal Auditor; Human Resources Consultant; Human Resources Consultant / Compensation Analyst; Return-to-Work Coordinator; Cultural Planner II; Mapping and CAD Analyst; Programmer / Analyst; Engineering Assistant; Help Centre Specialists; Neighbourhood Transportation Engineer; Human Resources Consultant; Human Resources Consultant; Human Resources Consultant, Compensation Analyst; Project Manager - Architect.

VANCOUVER, CITY OF
Att: Equipment Branch,
Engineering Services
250 - 70th Avenue West
Vancouver, BC V5X 2X1

Fax 604-323-7770
Website .... www.city.vancouver.bc.ca

Employer Background: The City of Vancouver is home to 560,000 residents. *New Positions Created (3):* Fabricators and Machinists; Journeyman Steel Fabricators and Machinists; Heavy Duty Mechanics.

VANCOUVER CITY SAVINGS CREDIT UNION / VANCITY
Att: Personnel Department
PO Box 2120, Station Terminal
Vancouver, BC V6B 5R8

Tel. 604-877-8298

Fax 604-877-8299
Email ...... personnel_resumes@vancity.com
Website .... www.vancity.com

Employer Background: Established in 1946, VanCity is Canada's largest credit union, with $6.4 billion in assets, 262,000 members and 39 branches throughout British Columbia. *New Positions Created (14):* Leasing Administration Officer; Purchasing Buyer / Administrator; Corporate Communications Specialist; Manager, IT Security; Investment and Retirement Advisor / Branch Compliance Manager; Operations Coordinator; Account Manager; Risk Manager; Programmer Analysts; Assistant Manager, Trust Services; Financial Services Advisors; Financial Services Officers; Investment Manager, Non-Profit; Chief Internal Auditor.

VANCOUVER COMMUNITY COLLEGE

Att: Human Resources Manager
250 West Pender Street
Vancouver, BC V6B 1S9

Tel. 604-443-8300
Fax 604-443-8588
Website .... www.vcc.bc.ca

Employer Background: Founded in 1965, VCC offers a wide range of programs and courses, combining theory and practical, hands-on training. *New Positions Created (3):* Practical Nursing Instructors; Instructor, Computer Technology; Instructor, Dental Hygiene.

VANCOUVER COMMUNITY COLLEGE

Att: Human Resources
1155 East Broadway,
PO Box 24620, Station F
Vancouver, BC V5N 5T9

Tel. 604-871-7000
Fax 604-871-7445
Email .... kkelly@vcc.bc.ca
Website .... www.vcc.bc.ca

Employer Background: Founded in 1965, VCC offers a wide range of programs and courses, combining theory and practical, hands-on training. *New Positions Created (7):* Computer Support Analyst; Director of Marketing and Communications; Program Assistant; Telephone Operator / Receptionist; Vice-President, Finance and Administration; Department Head and Instructor, Practical Nursing; Instructors, ESL Division.

VANCOUVER GENERAL HOSPITAL, PROSTATE CENTRE

Att: Dr. Paul S. Rennie,
Director of Laboratory Research
2660 Oak Street
Vancouver, BC V6H 3Z6

Fax 604-875-5654
Website .... www.vanhosp.bc.ca

Employer Background: The Prostate Center combines basic laboratory research, clinical research, education and treatment programs, with an exclusive focus on prostate cancer. *New Positions Created (2):* Post-doctoral Fellow; Senior Post-doctoral Fellow / Research Associate.

VANCOUVER HOSPITAL AND HEALTH SCIENCES CENTRE

Att: Human Resources Department
855 - 12th Avenue West
Vancouver, BC V5Z 1M9

Tel. 604-875-5123
Fax 604-875-4761
Email .... careers@vanhosp.bc.ca
Website .... www.vanhosp.bc.ca

Employer Background: Vancouver Hospital and Health Sciences Centre is an adult tertiary care, teaching and research facility affiliated with the University of British Columbia. *New Positions Created (38):* Neuroscience Nurses; Nurses; Registered Nurse, Emergency; Registered Nurse, ICU; Registered Nurses, Operating Room; Diagnostic Neurophysiology Technician; Human Resources Advisor; Pharmacists; Physical Therapist, Level 1, Vascular Surgery; Physical Therapist, Level 3, Clinical Specialist; Physical Therapists, Cardiac Sciences (2); Radiology Service Technologist; Respiratory Therapists; Senior Planner; Neurotechnician; Capital Equipment Manager, Radiology; Construction Coordinator, CAD; Patient Services Manager; Senior Medical Transcriptionist; Work Design Specialist; Registered Nurse, Stroke Program; Clinical Assistants, Multidisciplinary ICU; Stroke Program Manager; Access Director; Data Collector / Analyst; Health Record Technicians; Labour Relations Officer; Mechanical Systems Field Engineer; Medical Transcriptionist; Pharmacists; Physical Therapist, Cardiac Sciences; Practical Nurse; Receptionist; Respiratory Therapists; Sleep Lab Technicians; Sterile Supply Technician; Critical Care Nurses; Medical Transcriptionists.

VANCOUVER INTERNATIONAL AIRPORT AUTHORITY

Att: Human Resources
PO Box 23750 APO
Richmond, BC V7B 1Y7

Tel. 604-276-6506
Fax 604-276-6538
Email .... careers@yvr.ca
Website .... www.yvr.ca

Employer Background: Vancouver International Airport Authority is an independent, non-governmental, non-profit corporation that operates the Vancouver International Airport under a 60-year ground lease with the government of Canada. *New Positions Created (16):* Coordinator, Aviation Security Programs; Jr Accountant; Superintendent, Landside Operations; Expenditure Analyst; Technical Analyst; Airfield Operations Specialists; Corporate Financial Analyst; Buyer; Credit and Collections Officer; Employment Advisor; Manager, Employee Services; Millwrights; Property Management Representative; Shift Superintendent, Airport Operations; Superintendent, Landside Operations; Supervisor, Airside Operations.

VANCOUVER RESOURCE SOCIETY

Att: Human Resources
2150 West Broadway, Suite 310
Vancouver, BC V6K 4L9

Tel. 604-731-1020
Fax 604-731-4003
Email .... vanres@vrs.org
Website .... www.vrs.org

Employer Background: Founded in 1972, Vancouver Resource Society provides opportunities for people with disabilities to integrate their lives in the community. *New Positions Created (2):* Licenced Practical Nurses (LPN); Supervisor.

VANCOUVER / RICHMOND HEALTH BOARD

Att: Human Resources
520 - 6th Avenue West
Vancouver, BC V5Z 4H5

Tel. 604-730-7632
Fax 604-736-7389
Email .... abatt@vrhb.bc.ca
Website .... www.vrhb.bc.ca

Employer Background: The Vancouver / Richmond Health Board is the governing body responsible for coordinating and delivering health services in Vancouver and Richmond, with 28,000 staff members and 55 sites. *New Positions Created (28):* Housing Partnership Pilot Project Coordinator; Technician, Health Records Department; Child Care Counsellors; Community Health Nursing Position, Maternal / Child Program; Community Health Nursing Position, Safe Babies Program; Vice-President, Communications and Public Affairs; Occupational Therapist; Clinical Educator, Adult & Older Adult Program; Clinical Educator, Infant, Child & Youth Program; Healthy Beginnings & Early Childhood Nurse; Home Care Nurses; Paediatric Physiotherapist; Registered Nurses; Wound Clinician; Community Developers; Community Health Nurse I; Coordinator, Diversity and Equity Initiatives; Director, Audiology; Hospital / Community Liaison Nurses; Quality Improvement Facilitator; Director, Aboriginal Health Service Development; Caregiver Support Coordinator; Home Care Nurses; Hospital / Community Liaison Nurses; Coordinator, Diversity, Human Rights and Equity Initiatives; ESL Teacher; Clinical Nurse Specialist, Hospice / Palliative Care Program; Coordinator, Financial Processing.

VANCOUVER SCHOOL BOARD / VSB

Att: Noelle Hart, Human Resources
1580 West Broadway
Vancouver, BC V6J 5K8

Tel. 604-713-5095
Email .... humanresources@vsb.bc.ca
Website .... www.vsb.bc.ca

Employer Background: VSB serves over 56,000 students at 73 elementary, 18 primary and 18 secondary schools. The Board has a budget of $350 million and employs 3,200 teachers. *New Positions Created (4):* School and Student Support Workers, Braille; Maintenance Support Supervisor; Elementary French Immersion Teachers; Manager of Purchasing.

VANDERWELL CONTRACTORS (1971) LTD.

Att: Chris Schischikowsky, Plant Manager
PO Box 415
Slave Lake, AB T0G 2A0

Tel. 780-849-3824
Fax 780-849-2530
Email ..... cschischikowsky@vanderwell.com
Website .... www.vanderwell.com

Employer Background: Vanderwell Contractors (1971) Ltd. is a forest products company. *New Positions Created (2):* Health & Safety Coordinator; Human Resources Coordinator.

VANSCO ELECTRONICS LTD.

Att: Human Resources
1305 Clarence Avenue
Winnipeg, MB R3T 1T4

Tel. 204-452-6776
Fax 204-478-1749
Email .... humanres@vansco.mb.ca
Website .... www.vansco.mb.ca

Employer Background: Vansco Electronics Ltd. is an electronics and wire harness manufacturing company that provides innovative custom solutions for original equipment manufacturers in 3 continents. *New Positions Created (18):* Accounts Payable Team Leader; Financial Analyst; Hardware Designers; Manager, Manufacturing Engineering; Manufacturing Engineers; Occupational Health Nurse; Senior ABAP Programmer; Senior Hardware Designer; Hardware Designers, Product Development Technologies; Design Technologist; Hardware Designers; Manager, Manufacturing Engineering ; Manufacturing Engineers; Mechanical Designer; Program Manager; Software Developers; Customer Service Representative; Electronic Technologist.

VARIAN CANADA INC.

Att: Human Resources Manager
6705 Millcreek Drive
Mississauga, ON L5N 5R9

Tel. 905-819-8181
Fax 905-819-8348
Website .... www.varianinc.com

Employer Background: Varian Canada Inc. manufactures research and analytical instrumentation used in the chemical and biochemical fields. *New Positions Created (3):* Customer Service Representative, Chromatography; Sales Representative; Chromatography Applications Chemist.

VAUGHAN, CITY OF

Att: Human Resources Department
2141 Major Mackenzie Drive
Vaughan, ON L6A 1T1

Tel. 905-832-2281
Fax 905-832-8575
Email .... resume@city.vaughan.on.ca
Website .... www.city.vaughan.on.ca

Employer Background: The City of Vaughan, one of Canada's fastest growing urban municipalities, is home to 180,000 residents. *New Positions Created (6):* Building Inspector; Plans Examiner, Buildings; Supervisors, Park Operations (2); Engineering Assistant; Fitness Programmer; GIS Technician.

VECO CANADA LTD.

Att: Joanne Jaege, HR Manager
4599 Tillicum Street
Burnaby, BC V5J 3J9

Tel. 604-659-3335
Fax 604-659-3345
Email .... veco.hr@veco.com
Website .... www.veco.com

Employer Background: VECO Canada Ltd. is a multi-disciplinary consulting engineering firm, specializing in EPCM projects for the resource industries, primarily oil and gas and petrochemical industries. *New Positions Created (11):* CADD Support Technologist; Instrumentation Designer / Technologist; Intermediate Process Engineer; Junior Mechanical Engineer; Senior / Principal Piping Designers; Principal Piping Designer; Process Engineer; Senior Mechanical Engineer; Structural Engineer; Intermediate Environmental Planner; Various Oil and Gas Positions.

VECO CANADA LTD.

Att: Carolyn Leonard
401 - 9th Avenue SW, Suite 1200
Calgary, AB T2P 3C5

Tel. 403-232-9800
Fax 403-232-9840
Email .... alberta.careers@veco.com
Website .... www.veco.com

Employer Background: VECO Canada Ltd. is a multi-disciplinary consulting engineering firm, specializing in EPCM projects for the resource industries, primarily oil and gas and petrochemical industries. *New Positions Created (15):* Senior Project Accountant; Senior Designer, Piping; Senior Process Engineer; Document Control Engineer; Intermediate Mechanical / Project Engineer; Piping Designers; CAD Designers; Intermediate and Senior Civil / Structural Engineers; Intermediate and Senior Piping Designers; Intermediate and Senior Process Engineers; Manager of Electrical Engineering; Manager of Instrumentation and Controls Engineering; Project Engineers; Senior Mechanical Engineers; Senior Process Engineers.

VEGREVILLE HEALTH UNIT

Att: Human Resources Manager
5318 - 50th Street, Box 99
Vegreville, AB T9C 1R1

Tel. 780-632-3331
Fax 780-632-4334
Website .... www.lrha.ab.ca

Employer Background: Vegreville Health Unit is part of Lakeland Regional Health Authority. *New Positions Created (2):* Various Healthcare Jobs; Healthcare Jobs.

VELAN INC.

Att: Human Resources Department
7007 Cote-de-Liesse
Montréal, QC H4T 1G2

Tel. 514-748-7743
Fax 514-908-0179
Email .... hr.ca@velanvalve.com
Website .... www.velan.com

Employer Background: Velan Inc. is a leading manufacturer of industrial valve lines, with over \$300 million in annual revenues. *New Positions Created (38):* Programmer; Project Engineer, Quotations; Machine Shop Foreman; Material Planner; Mechanical Draftsman; Quotations Administrator; Shipper; Calibration Technician; Field Service Technician; Planner; Programmers; Company Driver; Plant Engineering Manager; Tool Designer; Engineering LAN Systems Administrator; Administrative Assistant, Purchasing; NDT Inspector; Office Clerk; Receptionist; Welding Engineer; Applications Specialist; Expeditors; Planner; Planning Manager; Quotations Administrator; Vice-President, Production; Applications Engineer; Buyer; Engineer / Designer; Order Administrator - Export; Programmer; Project Engineer; Support Technician; Accounts Receivable Clerk; Vice President, Information Technology; Administrative Assistant; Product Sales Manager; Quotations Administrator.

VENETOR EQUIPMENT RENTAL INC.

Att: Vice-President, Operations
420 Grays Road
Hamilton, ON L8E 4H6

Tel. 905-664-5007
Fax 905-561-4062
Website .... www.venetor.com

Employer Background: Venetor Equipment Rental Inc. is an equipment rental company that specializes in hydraulic mobile cranes and aerial work platforms. *New Positions Created (7):* Heavy Duty Mechanic; Junior Accounts Receivable Clerk; Tractor Trailer Drivers; Receptionist / Office Assistant; Safety Awareness Trainer; Heavy Duty Mechanic; Parts Coordinator.

VENTURE COMMUNICATIONS LTD.

Att: Human Resources
720 - 11th Avenue SW
Calgary, AB T2R 0E3

Tel. 403-237-2388
Fax 403-265-4562
Email .... careers@openminds.ca
Website .... www.openminds.ca

Employer Background: Established in 1984, Venture Communications Ltd. is a full-service, integrated marketing communications firm, with 3 offices in Canada. *New Positions Created (3):* Office Administrator; Accountant; Account Supervisor.

VEONNEL INC.

Att: Human Resources Manager
1390 Clyde Avenue, Suite 201
Nepean, ON K2G 3H9

Tel. 613-225-9339
Fax 613-225-1939
Website .... www.veonnel.com

Employer Background: Veonnel Inc. offers off-site project-based software development services. *New Positions Created (2):* Network Management Developers; Network Management Team Leaders.

VERDIROC DEVELOPMENT CORPORATION

Att: Human Resources Manager

20 Eglinton Avenue West, Suite 1500
Toronto, ON M4R 1K8
Fax 416-486-4272
Website .... www.verdiroc.com
Employer Background: Verdiroc Development Corporation is a construction company. *New Positions Created (4):* Construction Coordinator; Estimator; Project Manager; Regional Hotel Project Manager.

VERI TRANSPORT LOGISTICS
Att: Sandro Caccaro,
Director, Sales & Marketing
245 McConnell Street
Exeter, ON N0M 1S3
Fax 519-235-4474
Email .... scaccaro@veritrucking.com
Website .... www.veritrucking.com
Employer Background: Established in 1985, Veri Transport Logistics operates a large fleet of modern air ride trucks, temperature-controlled trailers and dry van equipment. *New Positions Created (2):* Transportation Sales Professionals; Tractor Trailer Drivers.

VERIDIAN CORPORATION
Att: Human Resources Manager
55 Taunton Road East
Ajax, ON L1T 3V3
Tel. 905-427-9870
Fax 905-619-0210
Email ... humanresources@veridian.on.ca
Website .... www.veridian.on.ca
Employer Background: Veridian Corporation is an energy company serving over 60,000 electric customers in central-eastern Ontario. *New Positions Created (4):* HR Administrator; Manager, Customer Care; Settlements Officer; Systems Analyst.

VERITAS GEOSERVICES
Att: Supervisor,
Technical Training and Recruitment
715 - 5th Avenue SW, Suite 2200
Calgary, AB T2P 5A2
Tel. 403-205-6100
Fax 403-205-6404
Email .... bob_parker@veritasdgc.com
Website .... www.veritasdgc.com
Employer Background: Veritas GeoServices is an international processing and seismic acquisition company. *New Positions Created (4):* Mgr, Exploration Data Mgmnt; Senior Database Analyst; Marine Seismic Processors; Senior Processing Support Analyst.

VERTEFEUILLE KASSAM
Att: Human Resources Manager
304 - 8th Avenue SW, Suite 401
Calgary, AB T2P 1C2
Tel. 403-294-0733
Fax 403-294-0734
Email .... mkassam@vertkassam.com
Website .... www.vertkassam.com
Employer Background: Vertefeuille Kassam is a chartered accounting firm providing accounting, assurance, financial advisory, tax planning and consulting services. *New Positions Created (3):* Accounting Technicians (2); Controller; Supervisor.

VERTICAL BUILDER
Att: Human Resources Manager
255 - 5th Avenue SW
15th Floor, Bow Valley 3
Calgary, AB T2P 3T6
Tel. 403-705-7500
Fax 403-705-7555
Email .... jobs@verticalbuilder.com
Website .... www.verticalbuilder.com
Employer Background: Vertical Builder is a technology application company that manages and incubates a network of e-business companies. *New Positions Created (6):* Customer Support Centre Mgr; Customer Support Reps (2); Digital Media Designer; Implementation Coordinators (2); Quality Assurance Tester; Software Developer.

VESTSHELL INC.
Att: Human Resources Manager
10378 Pelletier Avenue
Montréal, QC H1H 3R3
Tel. 514-326-1280
Fax 514-326-6140
Email .... rh@vestshell.com
Website .... www.vestshell.com
Employer Background: Vestshell Inc. is a well-established investment casting manufacturer. *New Positions Created (2):* Production Supervisor; Production Planner.

VFC INC.
Att: Human Resources
25 Booth Avenue, Suite 101
Toronto, ON M4M 2M3
Tel. 416-463-4422
Fax 416-463-5459
Email .... mshaw@vfc.ca
Employer Background: VFC Inc. provides vehicle financing for retail customers through a dealer network. *New Positions Created (11):* Administrative Assistant; Area Manager; Collection Specialists; Customer Service Reps; Customer Service Representative; Collection Officer; Area Manager; Credit Underwriter; Inside Area Manager; Inside Area Manager; Insurance Clerk.

VHA HEALTH AND HOME SUPPORT
Att: Carla Frazzoni-Canoy, RPR
880 Wellington Street, Suite 700
Ottawa, ON K1R 6K7
Tel. 613-238-8420
Fax 613-238-1306
Website .... www.vha.com
Employer Background: Established in 1955, VHA Health and Home Support is a non-profit, registered charity that provides quality home support, personal support and healthcare services. *New Positions Created (5):* Registered Nurses; RN Supervisor; Scheduling Coordinator; Director, Business Development; Field Supervisor.

VHA HOME HEALTHCARE
Att: Human Resources
170 Merton Street
Toronto, ON M4S 1A1
Tel. 416-489-2500
Fax 416-489-7533

Email .... hr@vha.on.ca
Website .... www.vha.ca
Employer Background: VHA Home HealthCare is a charitable, non-profit nursing services organization, and one of the largest providers of in-home services in Toronto. *New Positions Created (9):* Program Support Workers / Reception Positions (2); Business Development Associate; Supervisor; Support Worker; Director, Finance & Administration; After-Hours Unit Supervisor; Support Workers; Registered Nurses; Health Services Manager.

VIASYSTEMS CANADA INC.
Att: Human Resources Manager
205 Brunswick Boulevard
Pointe-Claire, QC H9R 1A5
Fax 514-694-4416
Email .... alain.riberdy@viasystems.com
Website .... www.viasystems.com
Employer Background: Viasystems Canada Inc. is a leading EMS solutions provider to the telecommunications and networking industries, with 34 manufacturing facilities worldwide. *New Positions Created (3):* CAD Database Technicians (2); CAD Inspection Technicians (2); CAD Technician.

VICONICS ELECTRONICS INC.
Att: Human Resources Manager
9245 Langelier Boulevard
St-Leonard, QC H1P 3K9
Tel. 514-321-5660
Fax 514-321-4150
Email .... job@viconics.com
Website .... www.viconics.com
Employer Background: Viconics Electronics Inc. is a division of Viconics Inc., a manufacturer of electronic controls for the heating, ventilation and air conditioning industry. *New Positions Created (11):* Bilingual Receptionist; Electrical Technician; Patent Engineer; Programmer / Design Engineer; Test Technician; Bilingual Receptionist; Electrical Technician; Patent Engineer; Production Manager; Programmer / Design Engineer; Test Technician.

VICTORIA, CITY OF
Att: Human Resources Department
627 Pandora Avenue
Victoria, BC V8W 1N8
Tel. 250-361-0391
Fax 250-361-0238
Website .... www.city.victoria.bc.ca
Employer Background: Founded in 1843, the City of Victoria is the capital of British Columbia and home to over 300,000 residents. *New Positions Created (3):* PC and Network Administrator; Manager, Recreation Services; Director of Finance.

VICTORIA PARK COMMUNITY HOMES
Att: Harry Popiluk, Property Manager
155 Queen Street North
Hamilton, ON L8R 2V7
Fax 905-527-3181
Website .... www.vpch.com
Employer Background: Victoria Park Community Homes is a property management

company. *New Positions Created (2):* Assistant Resident Manager; Resident Manager.

VICTORIAN ORDER OF NURSES, TORONTO-YORK REGION BRANCH
Att: Pat Hoover, HR Department
3190 Steeles Avenue East, Suite 300
Markham, ON L3R 1G9
Tel. 416-499-2009
Fax 416-499-8460
Email ..... opportunities@vontoryork.com
Website .... www.von.ca
Employer Background: VON is a charitable, non-profit organization providing nursing visits, shift care, home support, adult day care and complementary therapies to the community. *New Positions Created (17):* Assistant Director, Client Services; Dietitians; Homemakers; Registered Practical Nurses; Director, Human Resources; Manager, Education, Quality Initiatives and Professional Practice; Volunteer Coordinator; Occupational Health Professional; Customer Service Reps; Manager, Health Services; Manager, Hospice Scarborough; Director of Client Services; Executive Assistant; Client Services Manager; Dietitians; RNs & RPNs; Switchboard / Receptionist.

VICTORIAN ORDER OF NURSES / VON BRITISH COLUMBIA
Att: Executive Director
1525 - 7th Avenue West
Vancouver, BC V6J 1S1
Tel. 604-733-6614
Fax 604-733-6698
Email .... vonbc@bc.von.ca
Website .... www.von.ca
Employer Background: VON British Columbia is a charitable, non-profit organization providing nursing visits, shift care, home support, adult day care and complementary therapies to the community. *New Positions Created (2):* Director, Corporate Health Services; Director Community Health Services.

VICTORIAN ORDER OF NURSES / VON CANADA
Att: Human Resources
5 Blackburn Avenue
Ottawa, ON K1N 8A2
Tel. 613-233-5694
Fax 613-230-4376
Email .... hr@von.ca
Website .... www.von.ca
Employer Background: VON Canada is a charitable, non-profit organization providing nursing visits, shift care, home support, adult day care and complementary therapies to the community. *New Positions Created (5):* Branch Director, New Brunswick; Payroll/Accounts Receivable Administrator; Executive Assistant / Proposal Writer; Exec Director; Sr Administrative Assistant.

VICTORIAN ORDER OF NURSES , EASTERN LAKE ONTARIO BRANCH
Att: Elizabeth Campbell,
Manager, Human Resources & Operations
737 Arlington Park Place
Kingston, ON K7M 8M8

Tel. 613-634-0130
Fax 613-634-0125
Email .... campbele@elo.von.ca
Website .... www.von.ca
Employer Background: VON is a charitable, non-profit organization providing nursing visits, shift care, home support, adult day care and complementary therapies to the community. *New Positions Created (5):* Registered Nurses; Registered Nurses; Clerk / Caseload Planner; On-Call Registered Nurses; Payroll / Accounting Clerk.

VICTORIAN ORDER OF NURSES / VON HALTON BRANCH
Att: People in Crisis Program
2370 Speers Road
Oakville, ON L6L 5M2
Tel. 905-827-8800
Fax 905-827-3390
Website .... www.von.ca
Employer Background: VON Halton is an innovative, charitable organization that has provided community health and support services to residents of Halton Region since 1930. *New Positions Created (2):* Registered Nurses; HCA, PSW & HSW Positions.

VICTORIAN ORDER OF NURSES / VON HAMILTON-WENTWORTH BRANCH
Att: Human Resources Manager
414 Victoria Avenue North
Hamilton, ON L8L 5G8
Tel. 905-529-0700
Fax 905-527-1919
Email .... hwvon@hw.von.ca
Website .... www.von.ca
Employer Background: VON Hamilton-Wentworth is a charitable healthcare organization that has been providing health and supportive services to Hamilton-Wentworth for 100 years. *New Positions Created (3):* Registered Nurses; Nurse Continence Advisor; Nursing Client Service Supervisor.

VICTORIAN ORDER OF NURSES / VON OTTAWA-CARLETON
Att: Human Resources
1200 St. Laurent Boulevard, Box 205
Ottawa, ON K1K 3B8
Tel. 613-749-7557
Fax 613-749-4002
Email .... von@vonottawa.on.ca
Website .... www.von.ca
Employer Background: VON Ottawa-Carleton is a charitable, non-profit organization providing nursing visits, shift care, home support, adult day care and complementary therapies to the community. *New Positions Created (2):* Manager, Program Development; Registered Nurses.

VIDEOSCOPE
Att: Mike Spear, General Manager
31 Prince Andrew Place
Toronto, ON M3C 2H2
Tel. 416-449-3030
Fax 416-449-5230
Website .... www.videoscope.com
Employer Background: Videoscope supplies audiovisual equipment to the corporate,

educational and video production markets. *New Positions Created (5):* Audiovisual Staging Technician; Rental and Staging Marketing Representative; Rental and Staging Sales Consultant; Camera Technician; Junior Order Desk Clerk.

VIDEOSPHERES INC.
Att: Human Resources Manager
329 March Road
Kanata, ON K2K 2E1
Tel. 613-270-9646
Fax 613-271-1896
Website .... www.videospheres.com
Employer Background: VideoSpheres Inc. is a leading developer of infrastructure for the delivery of managed digital video services over IP networks. *New Positions Created (12):* Account Managers; Intermediate Software Designer; IT Specialist; Junior Software Designer; Manager, Product Verification; Operations Manager; Product Managers; Product Testers; Senior Research and Development Manager; Senior Software Designer; Vice President, Sales and Marketing; Video Compression Developer.

VILLA COLOMBO SERVICES FOR THE AGED INC.
Att: John Nardi, Human Resources Advisor
40 Playfair Avenue
Toronto, ON M6B 2P9
Tel. 416-789-2113
Fax 416-789-5435
Employer Background: Villa Colombo Services for the Aged Inc. is a 268-bed long-term care facility for Italian-speaking seniors. *New Positions Created (2):* RNs & RPNs; Nurses.

VILLA MARCONI
Att: Jill Hart
1026 Baseline Road
Nepean, ON K2C 0A6
Tel. 613-727-6201
Fax 613-727-9352
Website .... www.villamarconi.com
Employer Background: Founded in 1989, Villa Marconi is a non-profit, charitable organization, providing health and social services for Italian-Canadian seniors. *New Positions Created (4):* Cook and Dietary Aides; Director of Nursing Care; Nurses; Personal Care Aides.

VIPSWITCH INC.
Att: Human Resources Manager
7005 Taschereau Boulevard, 3rd Floor
Montréal, QC J4Z 1A7
Tel. 450-923-4040
Fax 450-923-4882
Email .... jobs@vipswitch.com
Website .... www.vipswitch.com
Employer Background: VIPswitch Inc. manufactures optical metropolitan area network solutions for residential and corporate customers. *New Positions Created (35):* Change Administrator; High-Speed Board Designer; Integration Leader; Mathematician Trainee; Optical Component Specialist; Optical System Designer; Protocol Engineer,

BGP; Protocol Engineer, LDP / RSVP-TE; Software Engineer, EMS; Software Engineer, Forwarding Support; Software Engineer, Layer 2 Support; Software Engineer, MPLS MIBs; Software Engineer, MPLS Support; Software Engineer, Network Management; Software Engineer, VCEMS Interface; Software & High-Availability Architect; Software V&V Test Group Leader; System Engineering and Software Development Director; VHDL / Board Designer; Hardware Designers; Hardware / Software Manager; Production Director; Software Architect; ASIC Designers; Hardware Engineers; Optical Designers; Patent Writers; Product Manager; Product Marketing Manager; Sales Engineers; Senior Quality Engineers; Senior Reliability Engineers; Software Engineers; System / Test Engineers, Intermediate and Senior; Technical Writer.

VIRIDAE CLINICAL SCIENCES INC.
Att: Human Resources
1134 Burrard Street
Vancouver, BC V6Z 1Y8

Tel. 604-689-9159
Fax 604-689-5153
Website .... www.viridae.com
Employer Background: Viridae Clinical Sciences Inc. is a clinical and laboratory research company focusing on management and treatment of chronic viral diseases including studies of antiviral medications and vaccines. *New Positions Created (3):* Preclinical Project Assistant; Clinical Trials Research Nurse; Project Assistant.

VIRTUAL PROTOTYPES INC. / VPI
Att: Human Resources
4700 de la Savane, Suite 300
Montréal, QC H4P 1T7

Tel. 514-341-3874
Fax 514-341-8554
Email .. human.resources@virtualprototypes.ca
Website .... www.virtualprototypes.ca
Employer Background: VPI is a leading supplier of software tools for the development of real-time, interactive graphical applications and real-time simulations. *New Positions Created (8):* Assistant Controller; Applications Software Developer; Business Marketing Mgr, Esterel Studio; Inside Sales Specialist; Intermediate Technical Writer; Technical Recruiter; Technical Support Specialist / Trainer; Third Party Product Mgr.

VISIBLE GENETICS INC.
Att: Human Resources Manager
700 Bay Street, Suite 1000, PO Box 333
Toronto, ON M5G 1Z6

Tel. 416-255-0256
Fax 416-813-3289
Email .... jobs@visgen.com
Website .... www.visgen.com
Employer Background: Visible Genetics, a leader in the emerging field of molecular diagnostics, is committed to advancing the treatment of HIV, hepatitis and infectious diseases. *New Positions Created (3):* Manufacturing Engineer; Quality Engineer; MicroCel Production; Sr Quality Inspector, Instruments.

VISION2HIRE SOLUTIONS
Att: Human Resources Manager
1107 Homer Street, Suite 200
Vancouver, BC V6B 2Y1

Tel. 604-648-2400
Fax 604-408-5973
Website www.vision2hire.com
Employer Background: Vision2Hire Solutions (formerly Spintopia.com) designs web-based business solutions. *New Positions Created (6):* Sales Account Managers; Senior Java Applications Developer; Applications Developer (Java, JSP); Telesales Associate; Channel Sales Manager; Sales Account Manager.

VISIONS ELECTRONICS
Att: General Sales Manager
6009 - 1A Street SW
Calgary, AB T2C 0G5

Fax 403-255-6471
Email .... david.watson@telusplanet.net
Website .... www.visionselectronics.com
Employer Background: Incorporated in 1981, Visions Electronics is an electronics company, with 26 locations and 320 employees in western Canada. *New Positions Created (2):* Manager, Corporate Wireless Sales; Advertising Manager.

VISIONWALL CORPORATION
Att: Jocelyne April, Executive Assistant
14904 - 123rd Avenue, Suite 110
Edmonton, AB T5V 1B4

Tel. 780-451-4000
Fax 780-451-4745
Email .... apriljd@visionwall.com
Website .... www.visionwall.com
Employer Background: Visionwall Corporation custom engineers and manufactures commercial window and curtain wall systems that are marketed throughout Canada, the USA and southeast Asia. *New Positions Created (2):* Production Planner; Manager, Project Management.

VISITING HOMEMAKERS ASSOCIATION / VHA
Att: Human Resources Manager
393 Rymal Road West, Suite 105
Hamilton, ON L9B 1V2

Tel. 905-389-1970
Fax 905-389-2449
Website .... www.vha-ham.on.ca
Employer Background: VHA is a not-for-profit provider of home support services in the community of Hamilton-Wentworth. *New Positions Created (2):* Home Support Workers / Nursing Students; Scheduling Coordinator.

VISTAR TELECOMMUNICATIONS INC.
Att: Ellen Simpson,
Employment Opportunities
427 Laurier Avenue West, Suite 1410
Ottawa, ON K1G 3J4

Tel. 613-230-4848
Fax 613-230-4940
Email .... jobs@vistartelecom.com
Website .... www.vistar.ca

Employer Background: Vistar Telecommunications Inc. develops wireless and satellite communications systems and integrates satellite and terrestrial communications networks. *New Positions Created (7):* DSP Developers; Manufacturing Manager; Manufacturing Specialist; Mechanical Engineers; Mixed Signal Board Designer; RF Technologist; Software Developers.

VISTEK LTD.
Att: Human Resources Manager
1015 - 11th Avenue SW
Calgary, AB T2R 0G1

Tel. 403-244-0333
Fax 403-245-1662
Email .... hr@vistek.net
Website .... www.vistek.ca
Employer Background: Founded in 1977, Vistek Ltd. is a large Canadian retailer of professional cameras, digital photo equipment, scanners and printers. *New Positions Created (2):* Sales Professionals / Assistant Manager; Video Sales Representative.

VISTEK LTD.
Att: Human Resources
496 Queen Street East
Toronto, ON M5A 4G8

Tel. 416-365-1777
Fax 416-365-7776
Email .... hr@vistek.ca
Website .... www.vistek.ca
Employer Background: Founded in 1977, Vistek Ltd. is a large Canadian retailer of professional cameras, digital photo equipment, scanners and printers. *New Positions Created (13):* Photo Retail Department Manager; Executive Assistant; Film and Supplies Sales Representatives; Photo Retail Buyer; Pro-Photo Rental Representatives; AV Specialist; Digital Photo Equipment Sales Representative; Inventory Control Specialist; Programmer; Video Specialist; Sales Representative; Service Manager; Sales Position.

VITALAIRE HEALTHCARE
Att: Human Resources
2000 Argentia Road, Suite 200, Plaza 2
Mississauga, ON L5N 1V8

Tel. 905-855-0440
Email .... hr.vitalaire@airliquide.com
Website .... www.vitalaire.ca
Employer Background: VitalAire Healthcare is a leading provider of respiratory care products and services. *New Positions Created (5):* Director of Information Technology; Health & Safety Officer; Receptionist; Regional Managers; Respiratory Therapists.

VITANA CORPORATION
Att: Human Resources Manager
2500 Don Reid Drive
Ottawa, ON K1H 1E1

Tel. 613-247-1211
Fax 613-247-2001
Email .... hr@vitana.com
Website .... www.vitana.ca
Employer Background: Vitana Corporation designs and manufactures imaging prod-

ucts for industrial and commercial clients. *New Positions Created (5):* Business Development Manager; Field Application Engineer; Hardware Engineer; Manufacturing Engineer; Product Marketing Manager.

VIVONET CANADA INC.

Att: Human Resources Manager
750 Pacific Boulevard
Suite 301, Plaza of Nations
Vancouver, BC V6B 3E7

Tel. 604-408-4306
Fax 604-408-4307
Email .... careers@vivonet.com
Website .... www.vivonet.com

Employer Background: Vivonet Canada Inc. is a software development company that has created an enabling technology to leverage the power of the Internet as a vehicle for moving and gathering business data and intelligence. *New Positions Created (8):* C++ Programmers; Database Programmers; Internet Programmers; Java Programmers; Junior Oracle Administrator; Quality Assurance Specialist; Quality Assurance Team Leader; Technical Writer.

VK BRUNETTE LTD.

Att: Personnel Manager
330 Edworthy Way
New Westminster, BC V3L 5G5

Tel. 604-522-3977
Fax 604-522-6806
Website .... www.vkb.com

Employer Background: VK Brunette Ltd. is a leading designer of high-speed debarkers. *New Positions Created (3):* Purchasing Manager; Senior Mechanical Designer; Senior Mechanical Designer.

VOCATIONAL AND REHABILITATION RESEARCH INSTITUTE / VRRI

Att: Human Resources
3304 - 33rd Street NW
Calgary, AB T2L 2A6

Fax 403-284-1146
Website .... www.vrri.org

Employer Background: The VRRI is a non-profit, research and service agency that supports people with disabilities to live, learn and work in their community. *New Positions Created (3):* Support Workers; Support Workers; Health Care Instructor.

VOCATIONAL PATHWAYS INC.

Att: Albert Soulis
1 Yorkdale Crescent
Toronto, ON M9M 1B9

Tel. 416-784-9541
Fax 416-784-9633
Website .... www.vocpathways.com

Employer Background: Vocational Pathways Inc. provides programs in vocational evaluation, career and return-to-work planning, and job placement service. *New Positions Created (3):* Employment Facilitator; Vocational Case Manager; Vocational Evaluator.

VOGUE BRASSIERE INCORPORATED

Att: Tony Gonsalves, HR Director

225 Sparks Avenue
Toronto, ON M2H 2S5

Tel. 416-497-8802
Fax 416-497-5322
Email .... tony.gonsalves@voguebra.com

Employer Background: Vogue Brassiere Inc. is a leader in the branded intimate apparel industry. *New Positions Created (8):* Quality Control Technician; Product Manager; Patternmaker, Private Label; Technical Design Associate; Administrative Assistant; Corporate Accounts, Department Mgr; Purchasing Mgr; Quality Control Technician.

VOICE MOBILITY INC.

Att: Human Resources Manager
13777 Commerce Parkway, Suite 180
Richmond, BC V6V 2X3

Tel. 604-482-0000
Fax 604-482-0002
Email .... jburton@voicemobility.com
Website .... www.voicemobility.com

Employer Background: Voice Mobility Inc. markets unified communications software. *New Positions Created (2):* Software Professionals; Business Development Associate.

VOICE-WAVE MEDICAL TRANSCRIPTION

Att: David Urquhart
205 - 9th Avenue SE, Suite 199
Calgary, AB T2G 0R3

Tel. 403-266-6056
Fax 403-266-5829
Email ... david.urquhart@voice-wave.com
Website .... www.voice-wave.com

Employer Background: Voice-wave Medical Transcription is a private Alberta-based company providing medical transcription to doctors, clinics and hospitals using the latest digitalized voice and Internet technology. *New Positions Created (2):* Client Services Coordinator; Medical Transcriptionists.

VOICEGENIE.COM

Att: Human Resources Manager
1120 Finch Avenue West, 8th Floor
Toronto, ON M3J 3H7

Tel. 416-736-0905
Fax 416-736-1551
Email .... contact@voicegenie.com
Website .... www.voicegenie.com

Employer Background: VoiceGenie.com is a voice portal infrastructure company. *New Positions Created (15):* Speech Technology Specialist; Systems and Technical Support Engineer; Voice User Interface Designer; Voice XML Applications Developer; Voice XML Gateway Platform Developer; Business Development Channel Manager; Sales Associate; Director, Public Relations; Human Resources Generalist; Marketing Specialist; Software Test Engineer; Software Test Manager; System Engineers; Technical Support Engineers; Technical Support Manager.

VOICEIQ INC.

Att: Rod Graham
240 Riviera Drive
Markham, ON L3R 5M1

Tel. 905-948-8266

Fax 905-948-8276
Email .... rgraham@voiceiq.com
Website .... www.voiceiq.com

Employer Background: VoiceIQ Inc. (formerly BCB Voice Systems Inc.) is a leading designer and manufacturer of hardware and software technology for recording and transcription systems in the courtroom and medical environments. *New Positions Created (2):* Intermediate Software Development Programmers; Software Developers.

VOLEX CANADA INC.

Att: Human Resources
360 Terry Fox Drive
Kanata, ON K2K 2P5

Tel. 613-591-6500
Fax 613-591-3806
Email .... human_resources@volexna.com
Website .... www.volex.com

Employer Background: Volex Canada Inc. supplies cable and harness assemblies to international telecommunications companies. *New Positions Created (9):* Accountant; Applications Engineer, Fiber Optics; Applications Engineer, Plastics Moulding; Applications Engineer, RF; Inside Sales Representative; Manufacturing Engineer; Quality Engineer; Quality Supervisor; Systems Administrator.

VOLKSWAGEN CANADA INC. / VCI

Att: Human Resources
777 Bayly Street West
Ajax, ON L1S 7G7

Tel. 905-428-5806
Fax 905-428-5837
Website .... www.vw.ca

Employer Background: VCI provides wholesale, retail and lease financing for qualified Volkswagen and Audi dealerships. *New Positions Created (3):* Warranty Auditor; Area Executive; Business Development Mgrs (2).

VOLVO LAVAL

Att: Human Resources Manager
1436 St. Martin Boulevard West
Laval, QC H7S 1M9

Tel. 450-667-4960
Fax 450-667-3146
Website .... www.bsmauto.com

Employer Background: Established in 1973, Volvo Laval is an authorized Volvo and BMW dealer. *New Positions Created (3):* Night Receptionist; Parts Clerk; Shipper / Receiver.

VOLVO MOTOR GRADERS

Att: Michael J. O'Brien, HR Manager
PO Box 10
Goderich, ON N7A 3Y6

Tel. 519-524-2601
Fax 519-524-3015
Email .... jobs@volvograders.com
Website .... www.volvograders.com

Employer Background: Volvo Motor Graders (formerly Champion Road Machinery Limited) is an equipment supplier and manufacturer of a comprehensive line of industry-leading motor graders. *New Positions Created (4):* Global Buyer; Operational

Buyer; Paint Process Specialist; Supplier Development Specialist.

VOPAK CANADA LTD.
Att: Mary-Ann McCann
16911 - 118th Avenue
Edmonton, AB T5V 1H3
Fax 780-451-1027
Email .... maryann.mccann@
.... vopakcanada.com
Website .... www.vopakcanada.com
Employer Background: Vopak Canada Ltd. (formerly Van Waters & Rogers Ltd.) is a leading chemical distributor. *New Positions Created (4):* Buyer; Office Services Supervisor; Customer Service Representative; Credit Assistant.

VOPAK CANADA LTD.
Att: Human Resources Department
64 Arrow Road
Toronto, ON M9M 2L9
Tel. 416-740-5300
Fax 416-747-3190
Website .... www.vopakcanada.com
Employer Background: Vopak Canada Ltd. is an industrial chemical distributor. *New Positions Created (4):* Safety, Health and Environment Representative; Warehouse Supervisor; Warehouse Supervisor; Marketing Assistant.

VORUM RESEARCH CORPORATION
Att: Human Resources
8765 Ash Street, Suite 6
Vancouver, BC V6P 6T3
Tel. 604-321-7277
Fax 604-321-5345
Email .... jobs@vorum.com
Website .... www.vorum.com
Employer Background: Vorum Research Corporation develops interactive 3D CAD / CAM software and systems to the prosthetics, orthotics and custom footwear industries. *New Positions Created (3):* Software Developers; Product Support Technician; Software Development Technician.

VOXDATA SOLUTIONS INC.
Att: Susan St. Marseille
4101 Yonge Street
Toronto, ON M2P 1N6
Fax 416-226-1530
Email .... info@voxdata.ca
Employer Background: Voxdata Solutions Inc., a call centre company, provides outsourced consumer contact management solutions. *New Positions Created (2):* Account Manager, Client Services; Customer Service Representatives.

VOYUS CANADA INC.
Att: Human Resources Manager
3602 Gilmore Way, Suite 302
Burnaby, BC V5G 4W9
Tel. 604-320-6566
Fax 604-320-6577
Email .... careers@voyus.com
Website .... www.voyus.com

Employer Background: Established in 1998, Voyus Canada Inc. provides complete IT management and support solutions, with over 155 professionals serving more than 3,500 clients. *New Positions Created (33):* Customer Relationship Manager; Network Engineer; Network / IT Support Engineer; Network / IT Support Engineer; Account Executive; Accounts Receivable Clerk; Helpdesk Analyst; Logistics Coordinator; Senior Systems Consulting Engineer; Account Executive; Office Coordinator; Network / IT Support Engineer; Network / IT Support Engineer; Technical Consulting Engineer; Account Executives; Network Engineer; Regional Vice-President; Director of Eastern Operations; Sales Manager; Senior Project Engineer; Technical Consulting Engineer; Account Manager; Customer Relationship Manager; Logistics Coordinator; Network Engineer; Platform Specialist; Sales Manager; Senior Project Engineer; Account Executive; Customer Relationship Manager; Field / Network Engineer; General Manager; Office Manager.

VQUIP INC.
Att: Doug Burke
4430 Mainway Drive
Burlington, ON L7L 5Y5
Tel. 800-567-0103
Fax 905-336-3035
Email .... doug.burke@vquip.com
Website .... www.vquip.com
Employer Background: VQuip Inc. manufactures and distributes equipment for environmental collection, industrial plant and commercial floor cleaning, airport de-icing fluid recovery and recycling and waste transfer. *New Positions Created (4):* Parts Manager; Road Service and Installation Technicians; Road Service Technicians (2); Parts & Service Manager.

VULCAIN INC.
Att: Guy Gervais
3, boul. Industrielle
Delson, QC J0L 1G0
Tel. 450-632-2967
Fax 450-632-9938
Email .... guy@vulcaininc.com
Website .... www.vulcaininc.com
Employer Background: Founded in 1968, Vulcain Inc. designs and manufactures gas detection equipment. *New Positions Created (3):* Technical Customer Service Position; Inside Sales Rep; Regional Sales Rep.

W.I. VILLAGER LTD. / MARSHLANDS CANADA
Att: Human Resources Manager
598 Norris Court
Kingston, ON K7P 2R9
Tel. 613-384-3930
Fax 613-384-4932
Website ..... www.marshlands.canada.com
Employer Background: W.I. Villager Ltd. / Marshlands Canada is manufactures Marshlands Canada apparel and design. *New Positions Created (2):* Accountant; Inside Sales Representative.

WAINBEE LIMITED
Att: Garry Rodger, Sales Manager - Central
5789 Coopers Avenue
Mississauga, ON L4Z 3S6
Tel. 905-568-1700
Fax 905-568-0083
Email .... grodger@toronto.wainbee.ca
Website .... www.wainbee.ca
Employer Background: Established in 1957, Wainbee Limited manufactures and sells pneumatics, hydraulics, air tools, machine tool elements, electro-motion actuators and controllers, and electronic controls. *New Positions Created (2):* Hydraulic Sales Representative; Inside Sales Representative.

WAJAX INDUSTRIES LIMITED
Att: Joe Bilodeau
17604 - 105th Avenue
Edmonton, AB T5S 1G4
Tel. 780-483-6641
Fax 780-484-4378
Website .... www.wilwest.wajax.com
Employer Background: Wajax Industries Limited is a national leader in the construction and forestry equipment industry. *New Positions Created (2):* Product Support Representative; Heavy Duty Resident Field Mechanics.

WAJAX INDUSTRIES LIMITED
Att: Robert Ruff, Parts Manager
3280 Wharton Way
Mississauga, ON L4X 2C5
Tel. 905-624-5611
Fax 905-624-8403
Email .... rruff@wajax.com
Website .... www.wilwest.wajax.com
Employer Background: Wajax Industries Limited is a $1 billion organization specializing in the distribution of mobile equipment for the forestry, mining, construction and manufacturing industries. *New Positions Created (4):* Warehouse Person; E-Commerce Database Analyst; E-Commerce Web Analyst; JD Edwards One World Specialist.

WAL-MART CANADA INC.
Att: Gary Chan, District Manager
1940 Argentia Road
Mississauga, ON L5N 1P9
Tel. 905-821-2111
Fax 905-821-6372
Email .... dcmille@wal-mart.com
Website .... www.wal-mart.com
Employer Background: Walmart Canada Inc., a subsidiary of Arkansas-based Wal-mart Stores, Inc., operates 144 retail superstores and employs 32,500 associates. *New Positions Created (2):* Staff Pharmacist or Pharmacy Manager; Financial Planning Analyst.

WALKER, HEAD
Att: Allan Rowsell
1305 Pickering Parkway, Suite 200
Pickering, ON L1V 3P2
Tel. 905-839-4484
Fax 905-420-1073

Email .... arowsell@walkerhead.com
Website .... www.walkerhead.com
Employer Background: Walker, Head is a law firm. *New Positions Created (2):* Real Estate Lawyer; Real Estate Lawyer.

WALSH AUTOMATION / VALIDATION TECHNOLOGIES
Att: Human Resources Department
3300 Cavendish Boulevard, Suite 670
Montréal, QC H4B 2M8
Tel. 514-485-6611
Fax 514-485-6617
Email .... rh_hr@walshautomation.com
Website .... www.walshautomation.com
Employer Background: Walsh Automation / Validation Technologies (formerly a member of the Walsh Group) is a part of Invensys, a global leader in automation software and control systems. *New Positions Created (13):* Advanced Control Specialists; Automation Engineers / Electrical Engineers; Computer Engineers; Computer Systems Specialists; Contract Administrators; Design Engineers, Machine Vision Systems; Electrodynamics Technicians; Industrial Engineers; Laboratory Systems Specialists; Machinery Designers / Draftspersons; Mechanical Engineers; Service Engineers / Technicians; Validation Engineers.

WALTER CUMBRIA ENGINEERING LTD. / WCEL
Att: Human Resources
17511 - 107th Avenue, Suite 202
Edmonton, AB T5S 1E5
Tel. 780-444-9534
Fax 780-444-8653
Email ... ncumbria.wcel@interbaun.com
Employer Background: WCEL is a consulting firm, providing plant engineering services to power generation plants. *New Positions Created (5):* Engineering Technicians, Electrical / Instrumentation; Piping / Mechanical Designers; Project Engineers; Piping / Mechanical Designers; Project Engineers, Mechanical.

WALTERS INC.
Att: Tim Verhey,
Engineering & Production Manager
1318 Rymal Road East
Hamilton, ON L8W 3N1
Tel. 905-388-7111
Fax 905-575-7747
Email .... tverhey@waltersinc.com
Website .... www.waltersinc.com
Employer Background: Established in 1956, Walters Inc. is a structural steel fabricator. *New Positions Created (3):* Production Assistant; CNC Operators / Programmers; Structural Steel Engineers / Designers.

WANN CONNECTION DEVICES INC.
Att: Michelle Kostiuk, CBN Group
18 Auriga Drive
Nepean, ON K2E 7Y9
Tel. 613-225-9266
Fax 613-226-1089
Email .... jobs@wann.com
Website .... www.wann.com

Employer Background: WANN Connection Devices Inc. (a division of Canadian Bank Note Company Ltd.) designs and manufactures analog and digital communication devices, POS terminals, lottery terminals and OCR passport readers. *New Positions Created (6):* Hardware Engineer; Intermediate Software Designer; Senior Hardware Designer / Manager; Senior Software Designer; Electronics Technologist; Lab Technologists (2).

WARDROP ENGINEERING INC.
Att: Human Resources Department
725 Hewitson Street
Thunder Bay, ON P7B 6B5
Tel. 807-345-5453
Fax 807-345-8708
Email .... thunderbay@wardrop.com
Website .... www.wardrop.com
Employer Background: Wardrop Engineering Inc. is a multidisciplinary engineering, environmental and information technology consulting firm. *New Positions Created (7):* Civil / Municipal Design Engineer; Electrical / Instrumentation Design Drafter; Intermediate / Senior Electrical Engineer; Intermediate / Senior Mechanical Engineer; Lotus Notes Administrator; Municipal Engineers; Transportation Engineer.

WARDROP ENGINEERING INC.
Att: Human Resources Department
6725 Airport Road, 6th Floor
Mississauga, ON L4V 1V2
Tel. 905-673-3788
Fax 905-673-8007
Email .... toronto@wardrop.com
Website .... www.wardrop.com
Employer Background: Wardrop Engineering Inc. is a multidisciplinary engineering, environmental and information technology consulting firm. *New Positions Created (11):* Geoenvironmental Engineer / Geoscientist; Lead Electrical Engineer; Mechanical Designer - Unigraphics; Project Manager; Technical Lead; Civil / Structural Designer; Civil / Structural Engineer; Quality Manager; Senior Electrical Engineer; Senior Mechanical Engineer, Nuclear; Visual Basic Programmer.

WAREHOUSE ONE
Att: Human Resources Manager
590 Moray Street
Winnipeg, MB R3J 3V9
Fax 204-897-4860
Email .... terrys@warehouseone.com
Website .... www.warehouseone.com
Employer Background: Founded in 1977, Warehouse One operates 37 clothing and jeans stores across Manitoba, Saskatchewan and northwestern Ontario. *New Positions Created (3):* Merchandisers (2); Sales Associates; Store Mgrs/ Assistant Mgrs.

WARNER MUSIC CANADA
Att: Controller
3751 Victoria Park Avenue
Toronto, ON M1W 3Z4
Website .... www.warnermusic.ca

Employer Background: Warner Music Canada is a major music label. *New Positions Created (3):* Intermediate Accountant; PowerBuilder Developer; Powerbuilder Developer.

WARNER-LAMBERT CANADA INC.
Att: Recruitment Co-ordinator
2200 Eglinton Avenue East
Toronto, ON M1L 2N3
Tel. 416-288-2200
Fax 416-288-2156
Email .... careers@pfizer.com
Website .... www.warner-lambert.com
Employer Background: Warner-Lambert Canada Inc., a division of Pfizer Canada Inc., develops, manufactures and markets quality pharmaceutical, consumer healthcare and confectionery products. *New Positions Created (3):* Territory Manager; Regulatory Affairs Manager; Sales Force Automation Administrator.

WARREN SHEPELL CONSULTANTS CORP.
Att: Human Resources Department
170 Bloor Street West, Suite 600
Toronto, ON M5S 1T9
Tel. 416-961-0023
Fax 416-961-4339
Email .... hr@warrenshepell.com
Website .... www.warrenshepell.com
Employer Background: Established over 20 years ago, Warren Shepell Consultants Corp. provides employee assistance program services. *New Positions Created (14):* Counsellors, Central Clinical Services; Facilitator / Mediation Network Position; National Quality and Accreditation Mgr; National Trauma Response Mgr; Product Development Mgr; Regional Clinical Managers; EAP Counsellors; Clinical Counsellor; Clinical & Tele-Counsellors; EAP Counsellors; Bilingual Clinical Intake Counsellors; Bilingual Service Counsellors; Bilingual Telecounsellors; Bilingual Trauma Response Counsellors.

WATCHFIRE
Att: Human Resources Manager
1 Hines Road
Kanata, ON K2K 3C7
Tel. 613-599-3888
Fax 613-599-4661
Website .... www.watchfire.com
Employer Background: Watchfire is a leading web experience management software firm. *New Positions Created (14):* Senior Software Developer, Server Components; Senior Software Developer, Web Applications; Customer Support Representative; Integration Consultant; Intermediate / Senior Technical Writer; Legal and Investor Relations Administrator; Product Manager; Public Relations Specialist; Senior Quality Assurance Specialist; Senior Web Architect; GUI Designer; Product Managers (3); Senior Software Developer; Web Designer.

WATERLOO CATHOLIC DISTRICT SCHOOL BOARD, THE
Att: Patricia Kelly

Human Resource Services Administrator
91 Moore Avenue, PO Box 91116
Kitchener, ON N2G 4G2

Tel. 519-578-3660
Fax 519-578-3020
Website .... www.wcdsb.edu.on.ca

Employer Background: The Waterloo Catholic District School Board provides educational programs and services to 29,895 young and adult learners. *New Positions Created (6):* Secondary School Program Heads; Program Consultant, Visual / Performing Arts; Special Education & FSL Teachers; Vice-Principal; Itinerant Resource Teacher; Vice Principals.

WATERLOO, CITY OF
Att: Human Resources
100 Regina Street South
Waterloo, ON N2J 4A8

Tel. 519-747-8709
Fax 519-747-8511
Email .... bpayne@city.waterloo.on.ca
Website .... www.city.waterloo.on.ca

Employer Background: The City of Waterloo provides municipal government services to businesses and residents in Waterloo. *New Positions Created (4):* Policy Planner; Clerks, Administration/Customer Service (4); Zoning Clerk; Organizational Leader, Communications, Marketing & Programming.

WATERLOO NORTH HYDRO INC.
Att: Mrs. E.J. Allen, Executive Assistant
300 Northfield Drive East, PO Box 640
Waterloo, ON N2J 4A3

Tel. 519-886-5090
Fax 519-886-8592
Website .... www.wnhydro.on.ca

Employer Background: Waterloo North Hydro Inc. serves approximately 41,750 customers in the city of Waterloo and the townships of Wellesley and Woolwich. *New Positions Created (4):* Director, Finance; Linesperson; Lineperson; Engineering Technician.

WATERLOO REGION DISTRICT SCHOOL BOARD
Att: Elementary and Secondary Staffing
51 Ardelt Avenue
Kitchener, ON N2C 2R5

Tel. 519-570-0300
Fax 519-742-1364
Website .... www.wrdsb.edu.on.ca

Employer Background: The Waterloo Region District School Board provides public education to the 7 municipalities of Waterloo region and serves over 59,000 students in 121 schools, with a staff of over 4,800. *New Positions Created (3):* Teachers; Financial Analyst; Speech Pathologist.

WATERLOO, THE REGIONAL MUNICIPALITY OF
Att: Wendy Ryan, Staffing Coordinator
150 Frederick Street, 3rd Floor
Kitchener, ON N2G 4J3

Tel. 519-575-4400
Fax 519-575-4454

Email .... rywendy@region.waterloo.on.ca
Website .... www.region.waterloo.on.ca

Employer Background: Located 100 km west of Toronto, the Regional Municipality of Waterloo is a unique urban / rural area, with a population of 431,000. *New Positions Created (21):* Manager, Waterloo Regional Airport; Bus Operators; Public Health Nurses; Manager, Waterloo Region Emergency Services Training and Research Complex; Senior Project Manager, Transportation Engineering; Project Manager, Transportation Infrastructure; Project Manager, Environmental Engineering; Surveys Supervisor; Hydrogeologist; Family Health Manager; Health and Safety Advisor; Public Health Nurses; Senior Planning Engineer, Water Services; Emergency Measures Specialist; Project Manager, Transportation Engineering; Senior Project Manager, Environmental Engineering; Manager, Engineering and Programs; Senior Project Manager, Transportation Engineering; Head, Environmental Engineering; Senior Project Manager; Executive Assistant.

WATERMARK ADVERTISING DESIGN LTD.
Att: Search Committee
1333 - 8th Street SW, Suite 417
Calgary, AB T2R 1M6

Tel. 403-228-7949
Fax 403-245-5443
Email .... careers@watermark.ab.ca
Website .... www.watermarkadvertising.com

Employer Background: Watermark Advertising Design Ltd. is an integrated marketing communications company. *New Positions Created (4):* Project Manager; Senior Designer; Senior Art Director; Senior Copywriter.

WATSON GOEPEL MALEDY
Att: Mr. T.J. Maledy, Partner
1075 West Georgia Street, Suite 1700
Vancouver, BC V6E 3C9

Tel. 604-688-1301
Fax 604-688-8193
Email .... tmaledy@wgmlaw.com
Website .... www.wgmlaw.com

Employer Background: Founded in 1984, Watson Goepel Maledy is a law firm with 21 lawyers practising in almost all areas of law. *New Positions Created (3):* Lawyers; Lawyers; Lawyers.

WAVEMAKERS RESEARCH INC.
Att: Human Resources Manager
134 Abbot Street, Suite 404
Vancouver, BC V6B 2K4

Tel. 604-639-9990
Fax 604-639-9991
Email .... jobs@wavemakers.com
Website .... www.wavemakers.com

Employer Background: Founded in 1993, WaveMakers Research Inc. develops state-of-the-art technologies that enable computing devices to listen. *New Positions Created (7):* Administrative Assistant, Sales & Marketing ; Application Engineer; Embedded Linux / WinCE C++ Developer ; QA Ana-

lyst; Marketing Manager; Software Application Engineer; Vice-President, Software Development.

WAVESAT TELECOM INC.
Att: Human Resources Manager
4600 Cousens Street, 2nd Floor
St-Laurent, QC H4S 1X3

Tel. 514-956-6300
Fax 514-956-8587
Email .... careers@wavesat.com
Website .... www.wavesat.com

Employer Background: Founded in 1993, Wavesat Telecom Inc. is a leading developer of commercialized high-power, linear, efficient RF and microwave solid-state power amplifiers (SSPA). *New Positions Created (17):* Channels Programs Manager; Digital Hardware Design Engineers; Direct Sales Executives; Director, Engineering (RF Microwave); DSP Engineers; Electronic Assemblers; Embedded Software Designers; FPGA / ASIC Design Engineers; Human Resources Manager; Operations Manager; Process Engineer; Product Marketing Manager; RF Technicians; Senior Embedded Software Architect; Senior RF / Microwave Manager; Senior Telecommunications Engineer; Vice-President, Sales / Marketing.

WAWANESA MUTUAL INSURANCE COMPANY, THE
Att: Bev Moyan, Personnel Department
Box 2680
Edmonton, AB T5J 1K7

Tel. 780-469-5700
Fax 403-469-5777
Website .... www.wawanesa.com

Employer Background: Founded in 1896, The Wawanesa Mutual Insurance Company provides a range of insurance products in Canada and California. The company has assets of over $2.3 billion and over 1,300 employees. *New Positions Created (8):* Jr Auto Underwriter; Sr Commercial Underwriter; Personnel Assistant; Auto & Property Underwriters (2); Senior Claims Adjuster; Sr Telephone Adjuster; Junior Personal Lines Underwriter; Sr Commercial Underwriter.

WAWANESA MUTUAL INSURANCE COMPANY, THE
Att: Human Resources
4110 Yonge Street, Suite 100
Toronto, ON M2P 2B7

Tel. 416-440-3335
Fax 416-228-7858
Email .... seekingjobsintoronto@
.... wawanesa.com
Website .... www.wawanesa.com

Employer Background: Founded in 1896, The Wawanesa Mutual Insurance Company provides a range of insurance products in Canada and California. The company has assets of over $2.3 billion and over 1,300 employees. *New Positions Created (2):* Accident Benefits Claims Adjusters (2); Junior Auto Underwriters (2).

WD-40 PRODUCTS (CANADA) LTD.
Att: Human Resources Manager

PO Box 220
Toronto, ON M9C 4V3

Tel. 416-622-9881
Fax 416-622-8096
Email .... gencan@wd40.com
Website www.wd40.com

Employer Background: For over 40 years, WD-40 Products (Canada) Ltd. has provided top-quality, multipurpose lubrication products. *New Positions Created (2):* Marketing / Sales Manager; Regional Sales Representative.

WE CARE HOME HEALTH SERVICES INC.
Att: Human Resources Department
151 Bloor Street West, Suite 602
Toronto, ON M5S 1S4

Tel. 416-922-7601
Fax 416-239-1234
Email .... wecare1@interlog.com
Website .... www.wecare.ca

Employer Background: Founded in 1984, We Care Home Health Services Inc. is an independent health services provider, with 60 franchised locations across Canada. *New Positions Created (8):* RN Supervisors; RNs and RPNs; Various Healthcare Positions; Accounting Manager; Regional Manager; Care Coordinators; Care Manager; Administrative Assistants.

WEATHERFORD CANADA LTD.
Att: Human Resources
1306 - 5th Street
Nisku, AB T9E 7R6

Tel. 780-955-8070
Fax 780-955-6394
Email .... hr.cos-dis@weatherford.com
Website .... www.weatherford.com

Employer Background: Weatherford Canada Ltd. provides an extensive range of oilfield products, services and technologies. *New Positions Created (21):* Quality Control Technologist; Assistant, Tubular Supervisor; Service Technician, BOP; Operations Manager, East Coast; Calgary Sales Representative; Wireline Operators (Slickline); Branch Manager; Payroll Administrator; Senior Payroll Coordinator; Fishing Tool Technician; Wireline Operators; Field Operators / Technicians / Mechanics; Pipeline Testing Operators; Production Testing Operators; Senior Payroll Coordinator; Controller; Manager, Service Department; Engineering Assistant; Cased Hole Unit Supervisors; Equipment Operators; Field Sales Representatives.

WEATHERFORD / MCALLISTER
Att: Human Resouces
7920 - 42nd Street SE
Calgary, AB T2C 2T5

Tel. 403-279-9300
Fax 403-279-9220
Website .... www.weatherford.com

Employer Background: Weatherford / McAllister is a major manufacturer of inflatable packing products for the global marketplace. *New Positions Created (2):* Machinists; Intermediate / Senior Buyer.

WEB KREW INC.
Att: Human Resources Manager
87 Mowat Avenue
Toronto, ON M6K 3E3

Fax 416-534-7655
Email .... hr@webkrew.com
Website .... www.webkrew.com

Employer Background: Web Krew Inc. is an international web developer specializing in turnkey affiliate programs and e-commerce solutions. *New Positions Created (4):* International Marketing Manager; IT Project Manager; Programmer; Web Developer.

WEBER MARKING SYSTEMS OF CANADA
Att: D. Gilbert
6180 Danville Road
Mississauga, ON L5T 2H7

Tel. 905-564-6881
Fax 905-564-6886
Email .... dgilbert@webermarking.ca
Website .... www.webermarking.ca

Employer Background: Weber Marking Systems of Canada is an ISO-certified manufacturer of labels and coding systems. *New Positions Created (4):* Administrative Assistant; Marketing Coordinator; Bilingual Sales Representative; Sales Representative, Labelling Industry.

WEBGAIN INC.
Att: Human Resources Manager
100 Metcalfe Street, 18th Floor
Ottawa, ON K1P 5M1

Tel. 613-786-0700
Fax 613-569-9397
Email .... ottawa.careers@webgain.com
Website .... www.webgain.com

Employer Background: WebGain Inc. creates open standards-based solutions for enterprise-class e-business applications. *New Positions Created (12):* QA Manager; Software Engineers; SQA Engineers; SQA Manager; Business Consultant; Inside Sales Representative; Principal and Senior Consultants; Sales Engineers; Software Developer; Technical Support Engineers; Technical Support Manager; Insider Sales.

WEBHANCER CORPORATION
Att: Human Resources Manager
2255 Carling Avenue, 3rd Floor
Ottawa, ON K2P 7E9

Tel. 613-721-7747
Fax 613-721-1118
Email .... jobs@webhancer.com
Website .... www.webhancer.com

Employer Background: WebHancer pioneers new ways of looking at Internet performance. *New Positions Created (5):* Director, Consulting Engineering; Manager, Quality Assurance; Mgr, Research & Development; Product Mgr; Product Marketing Manager.

WEBPLAN INC.
Att: Human Resources Manager
700 Silver Seven Road
Ottawa, ON K2V 1C3

Tel. 613-592-5780

Fax 613-592-0584
Email .... hr@webplan.com
Website .... www.webplan.com

Employer Background: Webplan Inc. is an e-business company that provides an e-platform for high-velocity supply chains. *New Positions Created (64):* Business Algorithm Developers; Integration Consultant; Product Marketing Managers; Senior Application Developer; Senior NT Server Developer; Supply Chain Consultant; Test & Quality Assurance Manager; Administrative Accountant; Director, Product Marketing; Software Test Engineer; Business Algorithm Developers; Client Advocate; Database Specialist; Globalization Test Engineer; Integration Consultant; Intermediate Windows 2000 Server Developers; Junior / Intermediate NT Server Developers; Manager, Applications Development, E-Supply Chain; Marketing Specialist; Networking Specialist; Project Manager; Quality Analyst; Quality Assurance Testers; Senior LAN Administrator; Senior NT Server Developer; Software Quality Analyst; Supply Chain Architect; Supply Chain Consultant; Test Engineer; Vertical Product Marketing Managers; Web Application Developers; Web Tools Architect; Web Tools Developers; Workshop Consultant; Administrative Accountant; Applications Developer; Database Technical Architect; Junior / Intermediate NT Server Developers; Project Manager; Quality Assurance Testers; Senior LAN Administrator; Software Quality Analyst; Software Test Engineer; Supply Chain Architect; Supply Chain Consultant; Test Manager; Web Tools Developer; Account Executives; Business Algorithms Developers; Client Account Manager; Customer Integration Consultant; Junior / Intermediate NT Server Developers; Partner Manager; Sales Support Specialist; Senior Accountants; Senior NT Server Developer; Senior Web Applications Developer; Senior Windows MFC Developer; Software Verification / Testing Specialist; Strategic Alliances Manager; Supply Chain Consultants; Technical Support Manager; Web Application Developers; Web Tools Architect.

WEBSTORM MEDIA
Att: Human Resources Manager
121 Saint-Pierre Street, Suite 300
Montréal, QC H2Y 2L6

Tel. 514-392-7722
Fax 514-875-6138
Email .... sales@webstormmedia.com
Website .... www.webstormmedia.com

Employer Background: Webstorm specializes in online gaming and gambling resources. *New Positions Created (3):* Sales Rep; Internet Marketers; Media Planners / Buyers & Traffic Coordinators; Web Developer.

WEEKENDERS CANADA INC.
Att: Human Resources Department
29 East Wilmot Street
Richmond Hill, ON L4B 1A3

Tel. 905-886-5995
Fax 905-886-8016
Email .... hr-canada@weekenders.com
Website .... www.weekenders.com

Employer Background: Weekenders Canada Inc. is a leader in the direct sales industry, specializing in high-quality ladieswear. *New Positions Created (2):* Manager, Sales Support and Promotions; Bilingual Customer Service Representatives.

WEIDMULLER LTD.
Att: Human Resources Manager
10 Spy Court
Markham, ON L3R 5H6

Tel. 905-475-1507
Fax 905-475-8796
Email .... hr@weidmuller.ca
Website .... www.weidmuller.ca

Employer Background: Established in 1975, Weidmuller Ltd. is a leading supplier of terminal blocks, DIN rail-mounted power supplies and signal interface products. *New Positions Created (7):* Switched Mode Power Supply Design Engineer; Technical Sales Rep; Oracle Database Administrator; Web Developer; Technical Sales Rep; Programmer / Analyst; Senior Web Developer.

WEIGHPACK PAXIOM
Att: Human Resources Department
2525 Louis Amos
Lachine, QC H8T 1C3

Tel. 514-422-0808
Fax 514-422-0834
Email .... hr@paxiom.com
Website .... www.paxiom.com

Employer Background: Weighpack Paxiom is a leading manufacturer of packaging machinery. *New Positions Created (4):* Draftsperson; Planner / Buyer; Territory Sales Manager; Production Manager.

WEIRFOULDS LLP
Att: Dee Nevett, General Manager
130 King St. W., Exchange Tower
Suite 1600, PO Box 480
Toronto, ON M5X 1J5

Tel. 416-365-1110
Fax 416-365-1876
Website .... www.weirfoulds.com

Employer Background: WeirFoulds LLP is a medium-sized downtown law firm. *New Positions Created (4):* Tax Practitioner; Commercial Real Estate Associate; Litigation Associate; Litigation Secretaries.

WEISER LOCK
Att: Human Resources
3980 North Fraser Way
Burnaby, BC V5J 5K5

Tel. 604-419-4300
Fax 604-419-4383
Website .... www.weiserlock.com

Employer Background: Weiser Lock is a lock security company. *New Positions Created (2):* Independent Product Detail and Service Representative; Product Detail and Service Representative.

WEISHAUPT CORPORATION
Att: Human Resources Manager
6280 Danville Road
Mississauga, ON L5T 2H7

Tel. 905-564-0946
Fax 905-564-1676
Email .... weishaupt@weishaupt-corp.com
Website .... www.weishaupt-corp.com

Employer Background: Weishaupt Corporation is a world leader in the combustion technology industry. *New Positions Created (5):* Systems Support Specialist; Engineering / Combustion Trainee; Logistics Coordinator; Project Coordinator; Stockkeeper.

WELCH & COMPANY
Att: Human Resources Manager
151 Slater Street, 12th Floor
Ottawa, ON K1P 5H3

Tel. 613-236-9191
Fax 613-236-8258
Email .... jspencer@welchandco.ca
Website .... www.welchandco.ca

Employer Background: Welch & Company provides comprehensive accounting services to a wide spectrum of clients in eastern Ontario and western Quebec. The firm consists of 11 offices and employs 220 people across Canada. *New Positions Created (4):* Certified Business Valuator; Marketing Manager; QA Manager; Tax Manager.

WELDWOOD OF CANADA LIMITED
Att: Director, Employee Relations
1055 West Hastings Street, PO Box 2179
Vancouver, BC V6B 3V8

Tel. 604-687-7366
Fax 604-662-2807
Website .... www.weldwood.com

Employer Background: Weldwood of Canada Limited has over 50 years experience in forestry operations. *New Positions Created (2):* Materials Coordinator, Fleet Assets; GIS Technical Analyst.

WELLAND COUNTY GENERAL HOSPITAL
Att: Human Resources Service Consultant
65 Third Street
Welland, ON L3B 4W6

Tel. 905-732-6111
Fax 905-714-9473
Website .... www.wcgh.on.ca

Employer Background: Welland County General Hospital is a 300-bed acute and continuing care community hospital. *New Positions Created (2):* Registered Physiotherapist; Manager, Rehabilitation Services.

WENTWORTH MOLD INC.
Att: Bob Israni
58 Bigwin, PO Box 4520, Station D
Hamilton, ON L8V 4S7

Tel. 905-574-0010
Fax 905-574-0018
Email .... bisrani@wentworthmold.com

Employer Background: Wentworth Mold Inc. is an international manufacturer of blow moulds for the plastics packaging industry. *New Positions Created (11):* Plant Controller; Blow Mould Design Engineer; Injection / Extrusion Mould Design Engineer; Engravers; Lead Position, CNC Machining Centres; Benchers / Polishers; CNC Lathe Operators; CNC Machining Centre Set-up Operators; Engravers; Mould Designers; Toolmakers.

WERNER HAAG
Att: Human Resources Manager
1210 - 8th Street SW, Suite 400
Calgary, AB T2R 1L3

Fax 403-228-2476

Employer Background: Werner Haag is a progressive accounting firm, serving owner-managed businesses. *New Positions Created (2):* Accounting Technicians (2); Chartered Accountant.

WESCAM
Att: Human Resources Department
649 North Service Road West
Burlington, ON L7P 5B9

Tel. 905-633-4000
Fax 905-633-4044
Email .... hr.canada@wescam.com
Website .... www.wescam.com

Employer Background: Wescam is a leading manufacturer of stabilized camera and microwave transmission systems, providing real-time images as information and entertainment to government and commercial clients worldwide. *New Positions Created (44):* Electro-Optical Technologist; Electronic Assemblers; Inventory Auditor; Manufacturing Engineer; Mechanical Technicians; Real-Time Software Engineers; Test Engineering Technician; Marketing Communications Specialist; Intermediate Contracts Administrator; Mechanical In-Process Inspector / Trainer; IT Analyst; Inventory Auditor; Division Controller; Electro-Optical Technologist; Electronic Assemblers; Electronic Technicians / Technologists; General Manager; Integration and Test Technician; Mechanical Technicians; Real Time Software Engineers; Test Engineer; Test Room Technician; Senior Payroll Specialist; Electrical Engineer; Electro-Optical Engineer; Manufacturing Engineers; Market Research Manager; Real-Time Software Engineer; Systems Engineer; Buyer; Electro-Optical Technologist; Electronic Assemblers; Electronic Technicians / Technologists; Integration and Test Technician; Manufacturing Engineer; Mechanical Technicians; Project Engineer; Quality Assurance Product Line Coordinator; Real Time Software Engineer; Sales Account Manager; Test Engineer; Test Room Technician; Corporate Lawyer; Quality Assurance Vendor Coordinator.

WESCAST INDUSTRIES INC.
Att: Tanya Buchanan, Human Resources
799 Powerline Road West, PO Box 1930
Brantford, ON N3T 5W5

Tel. 519-759-0452
Fax 519-759-8535
Email .... tanya.buchanan@wescast.com
Website .... www.wescast.com

Employer Background: Wescast Industries Inc. is a large independent manufacturer of iron exhaust manifolds for cars and light trucks in North America. *New Positions Cre-*

ated (2): Human Resources Leader; Industrial Maintenance Electrician.

WESCO DISTRIBUTION CANADA INC.
Att: Human Resources Department
6000 Lougheed Highway
Burnaby, BC V5B 4V6
Tel. 604-299-5566
Fax 604-299-5547
Email .... ddodge@wescodist.com
Website .... www.wesco.ca
Employer Background: Wesco Distribution Canada Inc. (part of Wesco International, Inc.) is a leading distributor of electrical products, with over 50 branches and 700 employees nationwide. *New Positions Created (3):* Automation Application Technologist; Credit and Collections Representative; Credit Manager.

WESCO DISTRIBUTION CANADA INC.
Att: Branch Manager
11641 - 151st Street
Edmonton, AB T5M 4E6
Tel. 780-452-7920
Fax 780-451-2195
Email .... mtotino@wescodist.com
Website .... www.wescodist.com
Employer Background: Wesco Distribution Canada Inc. (part of Wesco International, Inc.) is a leading distributor of electrical products, with over 50 branches and 700 employees nationwide. *New Positions Created (3):* Account Specialist, Datacom; Inside Sales Associate; Inside Sales Associate.

WESCO DISTRIBUTION CANADA INC.
Att: Tony Vacca
475 Hood Road
Markham, ON L3R 0S8
Tel. 905-415-6100
Fax 905-415-8724
Email .... tvacca@wescodist.com
Website .... www.wescodist.com
Employer Background: Wesco Distribution Canada Inc. (part of Wesco International, Inc.) is a leading distributor of electrical products, with over 50 branches and 700 employees nationwide. *New Positions Created (3):* Intermediate Financial Services Associate; Contract Administrator; Trainee.

WEST COAST APPAREL INC.
Att: Human Resources
611 Alexander Street
Vancouver, BC V6A 1E1
Fax 604-251-8602
Email .... jobopportunities@jax.ca
Website .... www.jax.ca
Employer Background: West Coast manufactures Jax, a leading designer label. *New Positions Created (8):* Planning Manager; Garment Costing Analyst; Patternmaker; Industrial Engineering Assistant; Garment Costing Analyst; Head Mechanic; Import Coordinator; Sewing Supervisor.

WEST LINCOLN MEMORIAL HOSPITAL
Att: Human Resources

169 Main Street East
Grimsby, ON L3M 1P3
Tel. 905-945-2253
Fax 905-945-0504
Employer Background: West Lincoln Memorial Hospital is a 60-bed acute care facility. *New Positions Created (2):* Director of Finance and Human Resources; Echocardiology Technologist.

WEST PARK HEALTHCARE CENTRE
Att: Employee Services
82 Buttonwood Avenue
Toronto, ON M6M 2J5
Tel. 416-243-3600
Fax 416-243-3422
Email .... hr@westpark.org
Website .... www.westpark.org
Employer Background: West Park Healthcare Centre is a regional adult rehabilitation centre providing local complex continuing and long-term care services. *New Positions Created (44):* Advanced Practice Nurse, Neurology and Complex Continuing Care; Clinical Practice Leader, Occupational Therapy; Financial Analyst; Health Records Technician; Human Resources Partner, Organizational Development; Manager, Neurological Rehabilitation Service; Occupational Therapist, MSK and Geriatric Rehabilitation; Physiotherapist; Speech-Language Pathologist; Biomedical Engineering Technologist; Care Coordinator, Tuberculosis (TB) Service; Development Officer; Exercise Specialist; Occupational Therapist; Speech Language Pathologist; DBA / System Administrator; Advanced Practice Nurse, Neurology / Gerontology; Client Services Coordinator; Clinical Practice Leader, Physiotherapy; Physiotherapist, Complex Continuing Care; Research Assistant, Clinical Evaluation and Research Unit; Sleep / Pulmonary Function Technologist; Special Procedures Technologist, Respiratory Diagnostic & Evaluation Service; Financial Analyst; Manager of Accounting; Payroll Officer; Buyer; Corporate Performance Coordinator; Research Officer; Advanced Practice Clinician, Physiotherapy; Advanced Practice Nurse, Neurology and Gerontology; Chef Supervisor; Director, Program Operations; Manager, Ambulatory Care Services; Nurse Practitioner, TB Services; Registered Nurses; Director of Financial Services; Biomedical Engineering Technologist; Clinical Practice Leader, Occupational Therapy; Clinical Practice Leader, Physiotherapy; Clinical Practice Leader, Respiratory Therapy; Acute Care Nurse Practitioner, TB Services; Physiotherapist, Rotating; Registered Nurses.

WEST POINT GREY ACADEMY
Att: Clive S.K. Austin, Headmaster
4125 - 8th Avenue West
Vancouver, BC V6R 4P9
Tel. 604-222-8750
Fax 604-222-8756
Email .... headmaster@wpga.bc.ca
Website .... www.wpga.bc.ca
Employer Background: West Point Grey Academy is a co-educational university preparatory school with over 500 students from

pre-kindergarten to grade 11. *New Positions Created (2):* Skills Development Centre Coordinator; Various Teaching Positions.

WESTBAY SEMICONDUCTOR INC.
Att: Human Resources Manager
1333 Broadway West, Suite 688
Vancouver, BC V6H 4C1
Tel. 604-639-1188
Fax 604-639-1185
Email .... jobs@westbaysemi.com
Website .... www.westbaysemi.com
Employer Background: WestBay Semiconductor Inc. designs and markets semiconductors for SONET / SDH optical communication networks. *New Positions Created (6):* CAD Engineers; Intermediate ASIC Design Engineers; Product Marketing Mgr; Product Verification Engineers; Senior ASIC Design Engineers; Systems Architect.

WESTCAN WIRELESS
Att: Human Resources Manager
12618 - 124th Street
Edmonton, AB T5L 0N7
Tel. 780-451-2355
Fax 780-452-2080
Email .... careers@westcanwireless.com
Website .... www.westcanwireless.com
Employer Background: Founded in 1977, Westcan Wireless is a wireless communications provider. *New Positions Created (16):* Mike / Cellular Phone Sales Representative; Two-Way Radio Rental Coordinator; Two-Way Radio Sales Representative; Bench Technicians; Field Technicians; Radio Installer / Repairman; Accounts Receivable Specialist; Bench Technicians; Field Technicians; Inside Sales Representative / Telemarketer; Installer; Office Administrator; Rental Coordinator; Shipper / Receiver; Two-Way Radio / Data Sales Representative; Warehouse Supervisor.

WESTCOAST POWER INC.
Att: Human Resources Consultant
300 - 5th Ave. SW, Suite 1600, PO Box 61
Calgary, AB T2P 3C4
Fax 403-262-3510
Email .... resumes_wbd@wei.org
Website .... www.wei.org
Employer Background: Westcoast Power Inc., a subsidiary of Westcoast Energy, a gas-fired power generation company. *New Positions Created (2):* Plant Manager, Island Cogeneration Plant; Project Manager.

WESTECH INFORMATION SYSTEMS INC.
Att: Human Resources
401 West Georgia Street, 9th Floor
Vancouver, BC V6B 5R3
Tel. 604-663-3550
Fax 604-663-3554
Email .... careers.westech@
.... westechinfosys.com
Website .... www.westechinfosys.com
Employer Background: A subsidiary of BC Hydro, Westech Information Systems Inc. is a consulting firm with expertise in electric

and gas utility systems. *New Positions Created (18):* Business Consultant; Business Systems Analyst; Business Systems Analyst, Infrastructure; Data Warehouse Consultant; Database Analyst; Geospatial Information System Developers; Oracle Database Administrator; PeopleSoft Application Administrator; Senior Java Architect; System Developer; System Developer, Call Centre Technology; System Developer, PeopleSoft; System Development Consultant; System Development Consultant; System Development Consultant; Systems Development Consultant; Technical Analyst, Infrastructure; e-Business Developer.

WESTEINDE CONSTRUCTION LTD.
Att: Human Resources
17 Fitzgerald Road, Suite 101
Nepean, ON K2H 9G1
Tel. 613-820-9600
Fax 613-820-5861
Email .... dianne@westeinde.ca
Website .... www.westeinde.ca
Employer Background: Westeinde Construction Ltd. is a contractor and developer. *New Positions Created (2):* Accountant; Project Manager.

WESTERN ASSURANCE COMPANY
Att: Human Resources Manager
230 Westney Road South, 7th Floor
Ajax, ON L1S 7J5
Tel. 905-686-8326
Fax 905-686-4542
Website .... www.westernassurance.com
Employer Background: Western Assurance Company, a provider of personal insurance services since 1851, is part of the Royal & SunAlliance Group PLC. The company services a portfolio of approximately $120 million represented by 200 independent brokers. *New Positions Created (3):* Claims Team Leader; Accident Benefit Claims Representative; Claims Representative.

WESTERN PULP LIMITED PARTNERSHIP, PORT ALICE OPERATION
Att: Industrial Relations Department
PO Box 2000
Port Alice, BC V0N 2N0
Tel. 250-284-3331
Fax 250-284-7788
Email .... employment@alicepulp.com
Website .... www.westernpulp.bc.ca
Employer Background: Western Pulp Limited Partnership produces bleached softwood kraft pulp for fine paper making and dissolving sulphite pulp for the manufacture of various specialty products. *New Positions Created (6):* Maintenance Supervisor; Machinist; Systems Technician; Instrument Mechanic; Millwright; Industrial Relations Supervisor.

WESTERNGECO
Att: K. Fehr
2720 - 5th Avenue NE
Calgary, AB T2A 4V4
Fax 403-509-4217
Website .... www.westerngeco.com

Employer Background: WesternGeco is a leader in integrated exploration and reservoir imaging services, providing worldwide seismic acquisition, processing and multiclient surveys. *New Positions Created (2):* Payables Clerks; Payroll Administrator.

WESTFAIR FOODS LTD.
Att: Industrial Relations Manager
4700 Kingsway, Suite 1105
Burnaby, BC V5H 4M1
Fax 604-439-4465
Employer Background: Westfair Foods Ltd. is a leading retail and wholesale distributor of groceries, perishables and general merchandise. *New Positions Created (6):* Pharmacy Managers & Pharmacists; Assistant Industrial Relations Mgr; Warehouse Supervisor; Assistant Industrial Relations Mgr; Pharmacy Technician; Produce Manager.

WESTFAIR FOODS LTD.
Att: Industrial Relations Department
PO Box 280
Edmonton, AB T5J 2J5
Tel. 780-452-5411
Fax 780-451-7383
Employer Background: Westfair Foods Ltd. is a leading retail and wholesale distributor of groceries, perishables and general merchandise. *New Positions Created (3):* Grocery Supervisor; Loss Prevention Officer; Trailer Maintenance Supervisor.

WESTFAIR FOODS LTD.
Att: Human Resources Department
PO Box 300, Station M
Calgary, AB T2P 2H9
Tel. 403-291-7700
Fax 403-291-6340
Email .... resume@westfair.ca
Employer Background: Westfair Foods Ltd. is a leading retail and wholesale distributor of groceries, perishables and general merchandise. *New Positions Created (26):* Assistant Category Managers; Quality Control Auditor; Advertising Coordinator; Entry Level Accounting Position; Telecommunications Analyst; Assistant Manager, WCB and Safety; Category Manager; Accountant; Senior Telecommunications Analyst; Assistant Category Managers; Assistant Produce Buyer; Assistant Apparel Supervisor; Intermediate Accountant; Programmer / Analyst; Technical Support Representative; Accounting Position; Desktop Support Position; Voice Communications Specialist; Assistant Buyer; Assistant Category Manager; Assistant Transportation Coordinators; Staff Coordinator; Computer Operator; Photo Lab Supervisor; Programmer / Analysts; Assistant Category Manager.

WESTFAIR PROPERTIES LTD.
Att: Director, Store Planning, Engineering & Construction Department
3189 Grandview Highway
Vancouver, BC V5M 2E9
Fax 604-439-8704
Employer Background: Westfair Properties develops The Real Canadian Superstores in

western Canada as a large Canadian food distributor. *New Positions Created (3):* Store Designer; Construction / Fixturing Project Manager; Store Designer.

WESTIN BAYSHORE RESORT & MARINA, THE
Att: Human Resources Department
1601 Bayshore Drive
Vancouver, BC V6G 2V4
Tel. 604-682-3377
Fax 604-691-6986
Website .... www.westin.com
Employer Background: The Westin Bayshore Resort & Marina is Vancouver's only downtown resort property. *New Positions Created (2):* Banquet Management Positions; Food and Beverage Manager.

WESTIN OTTAWA, THE
Att: Human Resources Manager
11 Colonel By Drive
Ottawa, ON K1N 9H4
Tel. 613-560-7000
Fax 613-569-4557
Website .... www.westin.com
Employer Background: The Westin Ottawa is a 487-room hotel. *New Positions Created (2):* Sales & Catering Positions (3); Restaurant Manager.

WESTIN PRINCE TORONTO
Att: Director of Human Resources
900 York Mills Road
Toronto, ON M3B 3H2
Tel. 416-444-2511
Fax 416-444-9597
Website .... www.westin.com
Employer Background: The Westin Prince Toronto is a full-service hotel. *New Positions Created (2):* Assistant Controller; Chef Saucier / Sous Chef.

WESTIN RESORT & SPA, THE
Att: Karen Wilhelm, HR Director
4090 Whistler Way
Whistler, BC V0N 1B4
Tel. 604-935-4377
Fax 604-935-4351
Email .... karen@westinwhistler.net
Website .... www.westinwhistler.com
Employer Background: The Westin Resort & Spa is a four-star, luxury resort and conference centre. *New Positions Created (7):* Director of Sales and Marketing; Assistant Controller; Day Auditor; Sales Manager; Manager on Duty; Assistant Housekeeping Manager; Banquet Manager.

WESTJET AIRLINES LTD.
Att: Human Resources
5055 - 11th Avenue NE
Calgary, AB T2E 8N4
Tel. 403-444-2600
Fax 403-444-2577
Email .... greatjobs@westjet.com
Website .... www.westjet.com
Employer Background: WestJet Airlines Ltd. is Canada's leading discount fare airline.

New Positions Created (5): Senior Revenue Analyst; Administrator; Aircraft Maintenance Engineers (5); Avionics Technicians (2); Various Airline Positions.

WESTMAR CONSULTANTS INC.
Att: Human Resources Manager
233 - 1st Street West, Suite 400
North Vancouver, BC V7M 1B3

Tel. 604-985-6488
Fax 604-985-2581
Email .... info@westmar.com
Website .... www.westmar.com

Employer Background: Founded in 1988, Westmar Consultants Inc. is an international engineering consulting firm specializing in the design and project management of Maritime and industrial facilities and bulk materials handling systems. *New Positions Created (6):* Intermediate Electrical and Controls Designers; Electrical Division Manager; Electrical Controls Engineer; Lead Mechanical Engineer; Project Engineer; Project Manager.

WESTMINSTER SAVINGS CREDIT UNION
Att: Human Resources Manager
960 Quayside Drive, Suite 108
New Westminster, BC V3M 6G2

Tel. 604-525-7384
Fax 604-519-4210
Website .... www.betterbanking.com

Employer Background: Westminster Savings Credit Union has six branches in the Lower Mainland region of British Columbia. *New Positions Created (5):* Advertising and Promotions Officer; Financial Planner; Financial Planner; Marketing Manager; Senior Manager, Wealth Management.

WESTON BAKERIES LTD.
Att: Krista Baldwin, Human Resources
1425 The Queensway
Toronto, ON M8Z 1T3

Tel. 416-252-7323
Fax 416-252-0863
Email ..... kbaldwin@westonbakeries.com
Website .... www.weston.ca

Employer Background: Weston Bakeries Ltd. is one of Canada's largest bakery operations. *New Positions Created (2):* Bilingual File Maintenance Clerk; Product Developer.

WESTPORT INNOVATIONS INC.
Att: Human Resources
1691 - 75th Avenue West
Vancouver, BC V6P 6P2

Tel. 604-718-2016
Fax 604-718-2001
Email .... careers@westport.com
Website .... www.westport.com

Employer Background: Westport Innovations Inc. develops technologies to reduce pollutant emissions from heavy-duty diesel engines. *New Positions Created (68):* CAD Draftsperson; Calibration Engineer; Compressor Systems Design Engineer; Controls Engineers; Electrical and Instrumentation Technologists; Electronic Manufacturing Engineer / Technologist; Engine Test Cell Engineers, Product Development; Engine Test Technologist; Field Service Technician, Power Generation; Injector Design Engineer; Integration / Field Service Engineer; Power Generation; LNG Fuel Systems Design Engineer; Mechanical Project Engineer; Mechanical Technician; Senior Engine Development Engineers; Simulation Engineer; Software Application Engineer; Test Technician, Fuel Injection; Test Technologist, Fuel Systems; Mechanical Design Engineer; Pressure Vessel Design Engineer; CAD Design Draftsperson; Calibration Engineer; Compressor Systems Design Engineer; Controls Engineers; Electrical and Instrumentation Technologists; Electronic Manufacturing Engineer / Technologist; Engine Test Cell Engineers; Engine Test Technologist; Field Service Technician, Power Generation; Injection Design Engineer; Integration / Field Service Engineer, Power Generation; LNG Fuel Systems Design Engineer; Mechanical Project Engineer; Mechanical Technician; Senior Engine Development Engineers; Simulation Engineer; Software Applications Engineer; Test Technician, Fuel Injection; Test Technologist, Fuel Systems; Exchange Network Administrator; Facilities Services Assistant; Corporate Communications Manager; Intellectual Property Lawyer and Patent Agents; Design Engineers, Compressor; Director of Corporate Communications; Document Controller / Librarian; Electrical / Instrumentation Engineer; LNG Design Engineer; Mechanical Test Engineers, Injector; Network Administrator; Industrial Electrician; Mechanical Technician; Compressor Technicians; Controls Engineers; Engine Development Engineers; Hardware Test Engineer; Integration Engineer, Power Generation; Intellectual Property Lawyer / Patent Agent; Manufacturing Engineers; Technical Recruiter; Mechanical Technicians and Mechanics; Compressor Design Engineers; Design Engineers, LNG and Diesel Fuel Systems; Engine Test Engineers; Instrumentation Technologist and Electrician; Mechanical Test Engineers; Test Technologists.

WESTPOWER EQUIPMENT LTD.
Att: Lorie Price
3015 - 58th Avenue SE
Calgary, AB T2C 0B4

Tel. 403-720-3300
Fax 403-720-3175
Email .... lorie@westpwr.com

Employer Background: Westpower Equipment Ltd. is a major supplier of engineered centrifugal and reciprocating pumps to the oil and gas industry. *New Positions Created (4):* Engineer / Contract Administrator; Application Engineer; Sales Engineer; Pump Parts and Service Sales Representative.

WESTPRO CONSTRUCTORS GROUP LTD.
Att: Laura Seto
91 Golden Drive
Coquitlam, BC V3K 6R2

Tel. 604-942-5156
Fax 604-942-6877
Email .... info@westprocon.com
Website .... www.westprocon.com

Employer Background: Established in 1993, Westpro Constructors Group Ltd. is a general contractor, serving the commercial, industrial and institutional construction industry. *New Positions Created (2):* Estimator; Project Manager.

WESTVIEW REGIONAL HEALTH AUTHORITY / WRHA
Att: Human Resources
4605 - 48th Street
Stony Plain, AB T7Z 2J6

Tel. 780-968-3210
Fax 780-963-7641
Email .... hr@westviewrha.ab.ca
Website .... www.westviewrha.ab.ca

Employer Background: WRHA serves 89,500 residents and employs 850 staff members. *New Positions Created (4):* Acute Care Nurse; Public Health Inspectors (2); Acute Care Manager; Budget Officer / Accountant.

WEXFORD RESIDENCE INC., THE
Att: Human Resources Manager
1860 Lawrence Avenue East
Toronto, ON M1R 5B1

Tel. 416-752-8877
Fax 416-752-4350
Email .... information@thewexford.org

Employer Background: The Wexford Residence is an accredited, non-profit charitable long-term facility, that has been serving the community for 25 years. *New Positions Created (3):* Administrative Assistant; Registered Nurse Team Leader; Director of Care.

WEXXAR PACKAGING MACHINERY LTD.
Att: Human Resources Department
10101 Nordel Court
Delta, BC V4G 1J8

Tel. 604-930-9300
Fax 604-930-8605
Website .... www.wexxar.com

Employer Background: Wexxar Packaging Machinery Ltd. manufactures a comprehensive line of innovative automated equipment for corrugated container packaging. *New Positions Created (5):* Electrical Designer; Product Engineer / Technologist; Purchasing Manager; Electrical Designer; Product Engineer / Technologist.

WEYERHAEUSER COMPANY LIMITED
Att: Recruitment & Staffing
925 West Georgia Street, 5th Floor
Vancouver, BC V6C 3L2

Tel. 604-661-8000
Fax 604-688-8256
Email .... hrcntrex@weyerhaeuser.com
Website .... www.weyerhaeuser.com

Employer Background: Founded in 1900, Weyerhaeuser Company Limited is one of North America's largest producers of forest products, with 47,000 employees worldwide. *New Positions Created (3):* Financial / Analytical Support Leaders; Sales / Marketing Position; Corporate Security Manager.

**WEYERHAEUSER
COMPANY LIMITED**
Att: Mr. Armin B. Pyde,
Employee Relations
1850 Mission Flats Road, PO Box 800
Kamloops, BC V2C 5M7
Tel. 250-828-7310
Fax 250-828-7496
Email .... resume@weyerhaeuser.com
Website .... www.weyerhaeuser.com
Employer Background: Founded in 1900,
Weyerhaeuser Company Limited is one of
North America's largest producers of forest
products, with 47,000 employees worldwide.
New Positions Created (2): Shift Engineer;
Customer Relationship Manager, Informa-
tion Technology.

**WEYERHAEUSER
COMPANY LIMITED**
Att: Sherrie Colpitts
11553 - 154th Street
Edmonton, AB T5M 3N7
Tel. 780-452-5395
Fax 780-454-2961
Email ... sherrie.colpitts@weyerhaeuser.com
Website .... www.weyerhaeuser.com
Employer Background: Founded in 1900,
Weyerhaeuser Company Limited is one of
North America's largest producers of forest
products, with 47,000 employees worldwide.
New Positions Created (2): Sales Manager;
Warehouse Supervisor.

**WEYERHAEUSER
COMPANY LIMITED**
Att: Angele Quenneville,
Administrative Assistant
Cache Bay Road
Sturgeon Falls, ON P0H 2G0
Fax 705-753-4154
Email .... angele.quenneville@
.... weyerhaeuser.com
Website .... www.weyerhaeuser.com
Employer Background: Weyerhaeuser Com-
pany Limited, Sturgeon Falls is a 100% re-
cycled fiber mill producing corrugating
cardboard for the central Canada and Great
Lakes states market. *New Positions Created
(3):* Electrical Engineer; Steam Plant Superintendent; Mechanical Supervisor / Planner.

**WEYERHAEUSER COMPANY
LIMITED, DRYDEN MILL**
Att: Employment Coordinator
175 West River Road, Mail Bag 4004
Dryden, ON P8N 3J7
Tel. 807-223-9281
Fax 807-223-9388
Email ... don.forsythe@weyerhaeuser.com
Website .... www.weyerhaeuser.com
Employer Background: Weyerhaeuser Com-
pany Limited's Dryden Mill produces a va-
riety of papers including photocopier paper,
commercial printing paper and business
forms. *New Positions Created (5):* Project
and Investment Evaluation Analyst; Pulp
Finance and Planning Superintendent;
Forestland Area Managers; Maintenance
Supervisor; Financial Team Leader.

WHEELTRONIC LTD.
Att: Marilyn D. Johnson, HR Manager
6500 Millcreek Drive
Mississauga, ON L5N 2W6
Tel. 905-826-8600
Fax 905-826-7800
Email .. marilyn.d.broderick@snapon.com
Website .... www.wheeltronic.com
Employer Background: Wheeltronic Ltd., a
subsidiary of Snap-On Tools of Canada Ltd.,
manufactures and supplies mechanical lifts
to the automotive and transportation mar-
ket. *New Positions Created (8):* A / R Clerk;
Accounting Clerk, General; Junior Buyer;
Millwright Mechanic; Production Supervi-
sor; Technical Representative; Production
Shift Supervisor; QA Manager.

**WHISTLER BLACKCOMB /
INTRAWEST**
Att: Karen Bauckham, Recruiting Manager
4545 Blackcomb Way
Whistler, BC V0N 1B4
Tel. 604-932-3141
Fax 604-938-7527
Website www.wework2play.com
Employer Background: Whistler Blackcomb
/ Intrawest is a leading developer and op-
erator of village-centered destination resorts
across North America. *New Positions Cre-
ated (7):* A / P Data Entry Clerk; Sales Pro-
fessionals; Application Services Manager;
Executive Assistant; Financial Analyst; Sys-
tems Support Position; Marketing Manager.

**WHISTLER,
RESORT MUNICIPALITY OF**
Att: Human Resources
4325 Blackcomb Way
Whistler, BC V0N 1B4
Tel. 604-932-5535
Fax 604-935-8179
Email .... humanresources@
.... rmow.whistler.bc.ca
Website .... www.whistler.com/rmow
Employer Background: The Resort Munici-
pality of Whistler was established as a mu-
nicipal district by the Government of Brit-
ish Columbia to provide municipal services
and development control in the Whistler
area. *New Positions Created (4):* Manager of
Transportation and Drainage; Special
Project Coordinator; Utilities Manager; Senior Planner.

WHITBY MENTAL HEALTH CENTRE
Att: Human Resources
700 Gordon Street, PO Box 613
Whitby, ON L1N 5S9
Tel. 905-430-4002
Fax 905-430-4036
Website .... www.whitbymental
.... healthcentre.com
Employer Background: Opened in 1996, the
Whitby Mental Health Centre is a 325-bed
treatment facility with a staff of 35 serving
the residents of Haliburton, Kawartha, Pine
Ridge and Durham. *New Positions Created
(13):* Manager, Vocational Rehabilitation &
Recreation; Maintenance Mechanic; Psy-
chiatrists; Clinical Dietitian; Registered

Nurses; Social Workers; Psychologists; Clinical Service Coordinator, Psychiatric Rehabilitation Program; Gardener; Leisure / Life
Skills Instructor; Manager, Housekeeping
and Laundry Services; Staff Pharmacist;
Heating and Ventilation Engineers (2).

WHITBY, TOWN OF
Att: Human Resources Department
575 Rossland Road East
Whitby, ON L1N 2M8
Tel. 905-430-4303
Fax 905-686-5696
Email .... jobs@town.whitby.on.ca
Website .... www.town.whitby.on.ca
Employer Background: The Town of Whitby
is located 15 miles east of Toronto on Lake
Ontario and is home to over 74,000 resi-
dents. *New Positions Created (6):* Seniors'
Programmer; Manager of Development
Services; Desktop Support Specialist; Super-
visor, Seniors' Programs; Fire Chief; Man-
ager, Recreation.

**WHITE ROSE
HOME AND GARDEN CENTRES**
Att: Manager, Human Resources
4038 Highway 7 East
Unionville, ON L3R 2L5
Tel. 905-477-3330
Fax 905-477-1105
Email .... hr@whiterose.ca
Website .... www.whiterose.ca
Employer Background: White Rose Home
and Garden Centres is the largest retailer of
nursery, home decor and craft-related items
in Canada. *New Positions Created (5):* Store
and Department Managers; Director of
Home Decor; Buyer, Home Decor; Loss Pre-
vention / Risk Management Manager; Retail Facilities Coordinator.

WHITE SPOT LIMITED
Att: Human Resources
1126 Marine Drive SE
Vancouver, BC V5X 2V7
Tel. 604-321-6631
Fax 604-325-1499
Email .... carinah@whitespot.ca
Website .... www.whitespot.ca
Employer Background: White Spot Limited
is a leading Canadian hospitality organiza-
tion with over 80 retail units in BC and Al-
berta. *New Positions Created (4):* Marketing
Coordinator; Director of Finance; Kitchen
Manager; Restaurant Managers.

WHITECOURT OIL CORP.
Att: Mary
101 Spinnaker Way
Vaughan, ON L4K 2T2
Tel. 905-738-9008
Fax 905-738-9310
Email .... whitecourt.oil@sympatico.ca
Employer Background: Whitecourt Oil Corp.
is a leading proponent of long-life metal
working fluids. *New Positions Created (2):*
Accounts Payable / Receivable Clerk; Tech-
nical Sales Position.

WHITEHALL-ROBINS INC.
Att: Shirley Shikaze, HR Director
5975 Whittle Road
Mississauga, ON L4Z 3M6

Tel. 905-507-7000
Fax 905-507-7110
Website .... www.whitehall-robins.com
Employer Background: Whitehall-Robins
Inc. is a leading nonprescription pharma-
ceutical company. The company manufac-
tures Centrum, Advil, Dimetapp, Robitussin
and other quality healthcare products. *New
Positions Created (4):* Scientific Services
Manager; Sales Merchandiser; Medical
Service Representative; Sales Merchandiser.

WHITEHORSE, CITY OF
Att: Human Resources Department
2121 - 2nd Avenue
Whitehorse, YT Y1A 1C2

Tel. 867-668-8619
Fax 867-668-8384
Email .... humanresources@
.... city.whitehorse.yk.ca
Website .... www.city.whitehorse.yk.ca
Employer Background: The City of
Whitehorse provides municipal government
services to over 23,000 people spread over a
wide geographical area. *New Positions Created (2):* Manager, Transit Services; Director of Community Services.

WHITESELL CANADA INC.
Att: Controller
590 Basaltic Road
Vaughan, ON L4K 5A2

Tel. 905-879-0433
Fax 905-879-0458
Website .... www.whitesell.ca
Employer Background: Whitesell Canada
Inc. manufactures and distributes industrial
fasteners. *New Positions Created (2):* Ac-
counting Clerk; Bilingual Inside Sales Rep-
resentative.

WI-LAN INC.
Att: Human Resources Manager
801 Manning Road SE, Suite 300
Calgary, AB T2E 8J5

Tel. 403-273-9133
Fax 403-273-5100
Email .... info@wi-lan.com
Website .... www.wi-lan.com
Employer Background: Wi-LAN Inc. is an
innovator in the development of high-speed
wireless communications products, specializing in high-speed Internet access, LAN /
WAN extension and broadband wireless access. *New Positions Created (36):* ASIC Engineer; Channel and Programs Manager;
DSP Engineer; Embedded Real-Time Software Engineers; Intermediate / Senior RF /
Microwave Hardware Engineer; Intermediate Systems Engineers; Market Development
Analyst; Product Manager; Senior Electronics Designer; Senior Quality Engineer; Senior Systems Engineers; Systems Integration
& Verification Engineers or Technologists;
Intermediate / Senior ASIC Engineer; Intermediate / Senior DSP Engineer; Intermediate / Senior RF Design Engineers; Project

Manager; Senior Hardware Designer; Sen-
ior PCB Designer; Software Test Engineer;
Accounting Manager; Director, Hardware
Development; Hardware Design Technolo-
gist / Technician; Intermediate / Senior RF
Design Engineers; Manager, Radio Develop-
ment; Senior Hardware Designer; Senior
Mechanical Design Draftsperson; Senior
PCB Designer; ASIC Engineer; Design Prime
Position; DSP Engineer, Advanced Technol-
ogy; DSP Engineer, Core Technology and
ASIC; Hardware Designer; Senior RF Design
Engineer; System Integration and Verifica-
tion Engineers; Technical Writer; Writing
Assistant.

WILFRID LAURIER UNIVERSITY
Att: Human Resources Department
75 University Avenue West
Waterloo, ON N2L 3C5

Tel. 519-884-1970
Fax 519-884-4203
Email .... mdalsilva@wlu.ca
Website .... www.wlu.ca
Employer Background: Founded in 1910,
Wilfrid Laurier is a liberal arts university
with a faculty of 290 teaching professionals.
New Positions Created (2): Manager, Envi-
ronmental / Occupational Health & Safety;
Marketing Manager.

WILKINSON STEEL AND METALS
Att: Product Manager,
Non-Ferrous Products
9525 - 60th Avenue
Edmonton, AB T6E 0C3

Tel. 780-434-8441
Fax 780-435-8134
Email dmcammond@wilkinsonsteel.com
Website .... www.wilkinsonsteel.com
Employer Background: Wilkinson Steel and
Metals is one of the largest metal processors
and distributors in western Canada. *New
Positions Created (2):* Inside Salesperson,
Non-Ferrous Products; CAD / Programming
Operator.

**WILLARD MEATS
INTERNATIONAL LTD.**
Att: Human Resources Manager
2455 Cawthra Road, Suite 77
Mississauga, ON L5A 3P1

Tel. 905-566-9855
Fax 905-566-9163
Email .... kathyp@willardmeats.com
Website .... www.willardmeats.com
Employer Background: Willard Meats International Ltd. is a leading global meat trading company that buys and sells beef, pork,
poultry and sheep meat and meat
byproducts for a variety of industries including packinghouses, processors, food
service and pet food manufacturers. *New
Positions Created (2):* Accounting Clerk; Logistics Coordinator.

WILLIAM M. MERCER LIMITED
Att: Laurie Filice
161 Bay Street, PO Box 501, BCE Place
Toronto, ON M5J 2S5

Tel. 416-868-2000

Fax 416-868-2865
Email .... laurie.filice@wmmercer.com
Website .... www.wmmercer.com
Employer Background: Established in 1945,
William M. Mercer Limited is a global consulting firm, specializing in employee ben-
efits, compensation, communication and
actuarial services. The company has 13,000
employees in over 130 cities. *New Positions
Created (18):* Bilingual Help Desk Analyst;
Regional Information Security Administra-
tor; Senior Technical Analyst; Compensation
Survey Analyst; Actuarial Analysts; Project
Administrator; Retirement Consultants; Investment Analyst; Investment Analyst, Defined Contribution Plans; Benefits State-
ment Coordinator (English); Bilingual Help
Desk Analyst; Manager, Technology Operations; National Technical Architect; Senior
Project Manager, Global IT Projects Office;
Senior Human Capital Consultants; Project
Coordinator / Administrative Assistant; Pension & Benefits Lawyer; Administrative Assistant.

WILLIAM M. MERCER LIMITED
Att: Human Resources Manager
70 University Avenue, 10th Floor, PO Box 5
Toronto, ON M5J 2M4

Fax 416-351-5900
Email ...... linkwithus@ca.wmmercer.com
Website .... www.wmmercer.com
Employer Background: Established in 1945,
William M. Mercer Limited is a global con-
sulting firm, specializing in employee ben-
efits, compensation, communication and
actuarial services. The company has 13,000
employees in over 130 cities. *New Positions
Created (8):* Senior Analyst / Consultant;
Senior Consultant; Assistant Director and
Team Leader, Pension Administration; Man-
ager, Special Projects; Pension Administrators; Project Managers; Senior Defined Benefit Plan Implementers; Team Leader, Data
Management.

WILLIAM M. MERCER LIMITED
Att: Celine Karla
275 Slater Street, Suite 1100
Ottawa, ON K1P 5H9

Tel. 613-230-9348
Fax 613-230-9357
Email ..... celine.kalra@ca.wmmercer.com
Website .... www.wmmercer.com
Employer Background: Established in 1945,
William M. Mercer Limited is a global con-
sulting firm, specializing in employee ben-
efits, compensation, communication and
actuarial services. The company has 13,000
employees in over 130 cities. *New Positions
Created (3):* Actuarial Analysts; Consulting
Assistant; Writer, Communication Practice.

WILLIAM MORRIS LAW OFFICES
Att: Jill Trites
151 John Street South
Hamilton, ON L8N 2C3

Tel. 905-526-8080
Fax 905-521-1927
Email .... jtrites@morrislawyers.com
Website .... www.morrislawyers.com

Employer Background: William Morris Law Offices is a personal injury law firm. *New Positions Created (2):* Rehabilitation Services Advisor; Senior Litigation Law Clerk.

WILLIAM OSLER HEALTH CENTRE, BRAMPTON MEMORIAL HOSPITAL CAMPUS
Att: Human Resources Department
20 Lynch Street
Brampton, ON L6W 2Z8
Tel. 905-796-4066
Fax 905-451-9888
Email ...... human_resources@oslerhc.org
Website .... www.williamoslerhc.on.ca
Employer Background: William Osler Health Centre is Ontario's largest community hospital, employing over 3,800 people at three locations in Etobicoke, Georgetown and Brampton. *New Positions Created (52):* Corporate Clinical Educator, Special Care Nursery; General Duty Technologist; Dietitian; Patient Care Manager, Adult Mental Health Services; Physiotherapist; Psychologist; Social Worker, Central West Eating Disorder Program; Social Worker, Obstetric / Paediatric Program; Technical Specialist, Histology; Corporate Manager, Safety / Wellness; Occupational Therapist; Pharmacy Manager, Distribution Services; Corporate Clinical Educator, Pediatrics; Corporate Clinical Nurse Specialist, Special Care Nursery; Echocardiography Technologists; Emergency Medicine Positions; Health Records Technicians; Mammographer; Occupational Therapist; Patient Process Facilitator; Radiologists; Registered Nurses, Integrated Care Float Team; Registered Nurses, Labour and Delivery; Social Worker; Infection Prevention & Control Practitioner; Speech Language Pathology Professional Leader, Acute Medicine; Clinical Educator, Paediatrics; Clinical Nurse Specialist, Special Care Nursery; Director, Process Improvement; Registered Dietitian, Paediatrics / NICU; Registered Nurses; Addiction Crisis Workers; Counsellor, Problem Gambling Program; Employee Relations Manager; Professional Leader, Speech Language Pathology; Registered Respiratory Care Practitioners; Pathologist; Manager, Health Records & Patient Registration, Coding; Echocardiography Technologist; Integrated Care Float Team Nurses; Resource Nurses, Medicine; Clinical Educator; Dietitian; Infection Prevention & Control Practitioner; Occupational Therapists; Pharmacists; Physiotherapists; Social Workers; Speech Language Pathologists; Renal Technologist; Supervisor, Environmental Services; Various RN Positions.

WILLIAMS ENERGY CANADA INC.
Att: Human Resources
237 - 4th Avenue SW, Suite 2800
Calgary, AB T2P 4K3
Tel. 403-444-4500
Email .... hrcanada@williams.com
Website .... www.williams.com
Employer Background: Williams Energy Canada Inc. delivers reliable products and services through extensive networks of en-ergy-distributed pipelines and high-speed fibre optic cables. *New Positions Created (5):* Controls Technology Specialist / Engineer; Contract Specialist; Engineer; NGL Marketing Representative; Senior Attorney.

WILLIAMS MACHINERY LTD.
Att: Human Resources Department
2071 Viceroy Place
Richmond, BC V6V 1Y9
Tel. 604-273-1411
Fax 604-273-4277
Website ...... www.williamsmachinery.com
Employer Background: Williams Machinery Ltd. is a full-service forklift dealership. *New Positions Created (6):* Electric Forklift Technician; Parts Manager; Warranty Analyst; Senior Accountant; Parts Supervisor; Rental Manager.

WILLMAR WINDOWS
Att: Sales Manager
3687 Nashua Drive, Unit 10
Mississauga, ON L4V 1V5
Tel. 905-673-1997
Fax 905-673-8589
Website .... www.willmar.ca
Employer Background: Willmar Windows is a national leader in the production of wood and PVC windows and doors. *New Positions Created (2):* Inside Sales Support Position; Outside Sales Representative.

WILLSON INTERNATIONAL LTD.
Att: Human Resources
6725 Airport Road, Suite 101
Mississauga, ON L4V 1V2
Tel. 905-677-4844
Fax 905-677-4721
Email .... resume@willson1918.com
Website www.willson1918.com
Employer Background: Founded in 1918, Willson is an ISO 9002-certified supplier of logistic services for inbound and outbound freight. *New Positions Created (2):* International Ocean Freight Coordinator; Sr Rater.

WILSONART CANADA
Att: Human Resources
380 Courtneypark Drive East, Unit A
Mississauga, ON L5T 2S4
Fax 905-565-1883
Email .... hovent@wilsonart.com
Website .... www.wilsonart.com
Employer Background: Wilsonart Canada, a division of Premark Canada Inc., sells and distributes laminate and solid surfacing materials for countertops, cabinets, fixtures and flooring. *New Positions Created (3):* DZ Driver; Customer Service Representative; Accounting Manager.

WILTON INDUSTRIES CANADA LTD.
Att: Director of Human Resources
98 Carrier Drive
Toronto, ON M9W 5R1
Tel. 416-679-0790
Fax 416-679-1728
Email .... humanresources@wilton.ca
Website .... www.wilton.com
Employer Background: Wilton Industries Canada Ltd. is a national housewares distributor. *New Positions Created (5):* EDI Assistant / Analyst; Marketing Communications Manager; Intermediate Accountant; Staff Accountant; Executive Assistant.

WIND RIVER SYSTEMS, INC.
Att: Human Resources Manager
6815 - 8th Street NE, Suite 180
Calgary, AB T2E 7H7
Tel. 403-730-7550
Fax 403-730-4403
Email .... wrc-hr@windriver.com
Website .... www.windriver.com
Employer Background: Wind River Systems, Inc. (formerly AudeSi Technologies Inc.) develops technology that connects household appliances to the Internet. *New Positions Created (11):* Customer Satisfaction Application Developer; Embedded Firmware Developer; Java Software Developers; Marketing Manager; Product Champion; Senior Java Software Engineer; Senior Systems Administrator; Software Engineering Manager; Intermediate Java Software Developer; Marketing Manager, Internet Appliances; Senior Systems Administrator.

WINDIGO EDUCATION AUTHORITY
Att: Director of Education
PO Box 299
Sioux Lookout, ON P8T 1A3
Tel. 807-737-1064
Fax 807-737-3452
Email .... windigo@
.... sioux-lookout.lakeheadu.ca
Website ...... www.windigoeducation.on.ca
Employer Background: Windigo Education Authority schools emphasize the importance of retaining Native language and culture in traditional academic education. *New Positions Created (3):* Teachers; Teachers and Principals; Teachers (2).

WINDSOR CASINO LIMITED
Att: Team Centre
250 Windsor Avenue
Windsor, ON N9A 6V9
Tel. 519-258-7878
Fax 519-258-6043
Website .... www.casinowindsor.com
Employer Background: Windsor Casino Limited operates Casino Windsor, Ontario's first permanent casino complex. Casino Windsor features a 4-diamond hotel, 9 restaurants, live entertainment and gaming facilities. *New Positions Created (10):* Assistant to Materials Manager; Beverage Manager; Casino Auditor; Employment Services Supervisor; Executive Office Receptionist; Labour Relations Specialist; Programmer / Analyst; Sous Chef; Director of Surveillance; Purchasing Manager.

WINDSOR REGIONAL HOSPITAL
Att: Diane Cortina, HR Department
1453 Prince Road
Windsor, ON N9C 3Z4
Tel. 519-257-5159
Fax 519-252-4565

Email .... dcortina@wrh.on.ca
Website .... www.wrh.on.ca
Employer Background: Formed in 1994 through the merger of Windsor Western Hospital Centre and Metropolitan General Hospital, Windsor Regional Hospital is an 800-bed community hospital with an annual budget of $135 million. *New Positions Created (7):* Program Manager, Operating Room, PACU / CSR; Psychologist; Social Workers; Laboratory Management Position / Technical Coordinator; Clinical Practice Coordinator, Emergency; Laboratory / Technical Coordinator; Program Manager, Operating Room / PACU / CSR.

WINNERS MERCHANTS INC.
Att: Helen Cordeiro
6715 Airport Road, Suite 500
Mississauga, ON L4V 1Y2
Tel. 905-405-8000
Fax 905-405-7581
Email .... jobs_hr@winners.ca
Website .... www.tjx.com
Employer Background: Winners Merchants Inc. (formerly Winners Apparel Ltd.) is a leading off-price retailer of brand name and designer label apparel and home fashions. *New Positions Created (10):* District Managers; Store Managers; Merchandise Buyers; Store Design Coordinator; Management Positions; District Managers; Store Managers; Allocation Analysts; Assistant Planners; Planning Managers.

WINNERS MERCHANTS INC.
Att: Recruitment Services
6900 Decarie Boulevard, Suite 3105
Cote St. Luc, QC H3X 2T8
Tel. 514-733-4200
Fax 514-733-0785
Website .... www.tjx.com
Employer Background: Winners Merchants Inc. (formerly Winners Apparel Ltd.) is a leading off-price retailer of brand name and designer label apparel and home fashions. *New Positions Created (2):* Store Coordinators; Store Manager.

WINNIPEG, CITY OF (PLANNING, PROPERTY AND DEVELOPMENT SERVICES DEPARTMENT)
Att: Competition Coordinator
65 Garry Street, 3rd Floor
Winnipeg, MB R3C 4K4
Website .... www.city.winnipeg.mb.ca
Employer Background: Located at the geographic centre of North America, the City of Winnipeg is home to over 636,000 residents. *New Positions Created (4):* Senior Negotiator; Accredited Appraiser III; Planner; Senior Planner.

WINNIPEG, CITY OF (PUBLIC WORKS DEPARTMENT)
Att: Brian Laurin,
Coordinator of Payroll & Recruitment
2000 Portage Avenue
Winnipeg, MB R3J 0K1
Tel. 204-986-3452
Website .... www.city.winnipeg.mb.ca

Employer Background: Located at the geographic centre of North America, the City of Winnipeg is home to over 636,000 residents. *New Positions Created (6):* Building Servicer 2; Financial Analyst; Supervisor, Financial Services; Manager, Human Resources; Superintendent of Park Services; Chief Operating Officer of Fleet Management Services.

WINNIPEG, CITY OF (WATER AND WASTE DEPARTMENT)
Att: Staffing Clerk,
Coordinator of Human Resource Services
1155 Pacific Avenue, Suite 101
Winnipeg, MB R3E 3P1
Website .... www.city.winnipeg.mb.ca
Employer Background: Located at the geographic centre of North America, the City of Winnipeg is home to over 636,000 residents. *New Positions Created (6):* Waste Minimization Coordinator; Design and Construction Engineer; Design and Specification Coordinator; Senior Project Engineer; Water Planning Engineer; Supervisor of Disposal, Water and Waste Department.

WINNIPEG REGIONAL HEALTH AUTHORITY / WRHA
Att: Felicity Chappell,
Assistant Director, Human Resource
155 Carlton Street, Suite 1800
Winnipeg, MB R3C 4Y1
Tel. 204-926-7081
Fax 204-926-7107
Email .... mpanos@wrha.mb.ca
Website .... www.wrha.mb.ca
Employer Background: WRHA provides overall planning and integration of services on a program-managed model of healthcare delivery. *New Positions Created (5):* Audiologists (2); Nursing Director, Child Health; Medical Director, Transfusion Medicine; Pathologists (2); Mental Health Cross Cultural Specialist.

WINPAK TECHNOLOGIES INC.
Att: Human Resources
85 Laird Drive
Toronto, ON M4G 3T8
Tel. 416-421-1750
Fax 416-421-2350
Website .... www.winpak.com
Employer Background: Winpak Technologies Inc. is a leader in the design and manufacture of machines that produce sophisticated flexible packaging materials in roll and bag formats. *New Positions Created (9):* Mechanical Engineer; Scheduler; Quality Assurance Coordinator; Sales Coordinator; Traffic Coordinator; Production Supervisor; Business Development Coordinator; Intermediate Secretary; Millwright Mechanic / Machinist.

WINTERS INSTRUMENTS
Att: Marketing Manager
121 Railside Road
Toronto, ON M3A 1B2
Tel. 416-444-2345
Fax 416-444-8979
Email .... sfrancella@winters.ca

Website .... www.winters.ca
Employer Background: Established in 1953, Winters Instruments manufactures and supplies industrial instrumentation to customers in over 60 countries. *New Positions Created (5):* Marketing Coordinator; Industrial Sales Position; Receptionist / Administrative Position; Marketing Coordinator; Purchasing Supervisor.

WMA SECURITIES OF CANADA INC.
Att: Chief Compliance Officer
3100 Steeles Avenue West, Suite 500
Concord, ON L4K 4Y4
Tel. 905-761-5306
Fax 905-761-6757
Website .... www.wmas.com
Employer Background: WMA Securities of Canada Inc. is a mutual fund dealer. *New Positions Created (4):* Alberta Compliance Officer; BC Compliance Officer; Compliance Officer; Provincial Trading Officer.

WOCO AUTOMOTIVE INC.
Att: Human Resources
289 Courtland Avenue
Concord, ON L4K 4W9
Tel. 905-738-4288
Fax 905-738-7933
Website .... www.wocoautomotive.com
Employer Background: Woco Automotive Inc. is an international tier-1 and tier-2 manufacturer and supplier of rubber components to the automotive industry. *New Positions Created (8):* Millwright / Mechanic; Payroll Clerk; Millwright / Mechanic; Health and Safety / Environmental Coordinator; Logistics Manager; General Accountant; Receptionist / Accounting Clerk; Quality Inspector.

WOLFE MERCHANDISING
Att: Human Resources
6 Dohme Avenue
Toronto, ON M4B 1Y8
Tel. 416-752-5599
Fax 416-752-8746
Email .... employment@wolfe-intl.com
Website .... www.wolfe-intl.com
Employer Background: Wolfe Merchandising is a leading supplier of advertising displays and merchandising systems. *New Positions Created (2):* Project Manager; Warehouse Coordinator.

WOLVERINE RATCLIFFS INC.
Att: Mary Cushing, HR Manager
865 Gartshore Street, PO Box 100
Fergus, ON N1M 2W7
Fax 519-843-6202
Email .... cushingm@wlv.com
Website .... www.wlv.com
Employer Background: Wolverine Ratcliffs Inc. is a non-ferrous strip metal manufacturing plant in southwestern Ontario. *New Positions Created (6):* Electrician; Machine Operators & Helpers; Millwright; Technical Manager; Technical Sales Manager; Engineering Manager.

WOODBINE ENTERTAINMENT GROUP

Att: Human Resources Services
555 Rexdale Boulevard, PO Box 156
Toronto, ON M9W 5L2

Tel. 416-675-7223
Fax 416-213-2129
Email jobs@woodbineentertainment.com
Website www.woodbineentertainment.com

Employer Background: Founded in 1881, Woodbine Entertainment Group (formerly The Ontario Jockey Club) is a sports entertainment organization and a respected player in Canada's horse racing heritage. *New Positions Created (6):* Buyer; Human Resources Associate; Human Resources Generalist; Programmer / Analyst; Beverage Shift Supervisor; Food & Beverage Shift Supervisor.

WORKDYNAMICS TECHNOLOGIES INC.

Att: Human Resources Department
1379 Bank Street
Ottawa, ON K1H 8N3

Tel. 613-260-1441
Fax 613-260-1551
Email .... hr@work-dynamics.com
Website .... www.work-dynamics.com

Employer Background: WorkDynamics Technologies Inc. develops and supports information tracking and workflow management software products. *New Positions Created (6):* Intermediate Web Application Developers; LAN / Database Administrator; Junior Sales Position; Senior Quality Assurance Analyst; Senior Software Developer; Technical Analyst.

WORKERS' COMPENSATION BOARD, ALBERTA

Att: Human Resources
PO Box 2415
Edmonton, AB T5J 2S5

Tel. 780-498-4000
Fax 780-498-8618
Email ..... career.opportunities@wcb.ab.ca
Website .... www.wcb.ab.ca

Employer Background: Workers' Compensation Board, Alberta is a non-profit mutual insurance corporation funded by employers. *New Positions Created (4):* Team Leader, Systems Management / Information Management; Director, Finance; Health Care Auditor; Senior Database Analyst.

WORKERS' COMPENSATION BOARD OF BC

Att: Human Resources
PO Box 5350
Vancouver, BC V6B 5L5

Tel. 604-664-7800
Fax 604-276-3291
Email .... careers@wcb.bc.ca
Website .... www.worksafebc.ca

Employer Background: The Workers' Compensation Board of BC is a provincial statutory agency committed to prevention of workplace injury and occupational disease. *New Positions Created (12):* Manager, Information Technology Financial Services; Policy Analyst, Policy and Regulation Development Bureau; Psychologist; Medical Secretary; Financial Analyst; Quality Assurance Supervisor, Physiotherapy; Vocational Evaluator; Vocational Rehabilitation Consultants; Manager, Financial Systems; Industry Specialists; Programmer Analysts; Occupational Hygiene Officer.

WORKGROUP DESIGNS INC.

Att: Human Resources Manager
70 Silton Road, Unit 9
Vaughan, ON L4L 8B9

Tel. 905-264-0262
Fax 905-264-0636
Email .... careers@workgroupdesigns.com
Website .... www.workgroupdesigns.com

Employer Background: Founded in 1994, WorkGroup Designs Inc. is an information technology and professional consulting firm that specializes in customized application development, software products for business, technical support and business consulting. *New Positions Created (3):* IT Developers; Management Consultants; Senior Business Analysts.

WORKPLACE SAFETY & INSURANCE APPEALS TRIBUNAL / WSIAT

Att: Human Resources
505 University Avenue, 2nd Floor
Toronto, ON M5G 2P2

Tel. 416-314-8800
Fax 416-326-0115
Website .... www.wsiat.on.ca

Employer Background: WSIAT is the final level of appeal to which workers and employers may bring disputes regarding workplace safety and insurance matters in Ontario. *New Positions Created (5):* Legal Worker; Registrar Information Officer; Information Clerk; Translator / Reviser; Manager, Finance.

WORKPLACE SAFETY & INSURANCE BOARD / WSIB

Att: Karima Karmali,
Professional Practice Branch
200 Front Street West, 4th Floor
Toronto, ON M5V 3J1

Tel. 416-344-1000
Fax 416-344-4684
Email .... wsibresumes@wsib.on.ca
Website .... www.wsib.on.ca

Employer Background: WSIB administers Ontario's no-fault workplace insurance for employers and workers, and oversees the province's system of workplace safety education and training. *New Positions Created (3):* Nurse Case Managers; Nurse Case Managers; Nurse Case Managers.

WORLD FEDERATION OF HEMOPHILIA

Att: Human Resources Manager
1425 Rene-Levesque Boulevard West
Suite 1010
Montréal, QC H3G 1T7

Tel. 514-875-7944
Fax 514-875-8916
Email .... wfh@wfh.org
Website .... www.wfh.org

Employer Background: The World Federation of Hemophilia is an international non-profit organization working to improve care for persons with hemophilia. *New Positions Created (3):* Director, Major Gifts and Foundations; Program Officer, Asia; Program Officers (2).

WORLD HEART CORPORATION

Att: Judy Carvish
1 Laser Street
Ottawa, ON K2E 7V1

Tel. 613-226-4278
Fax 613-226-4744
Email .... hr@worldheart.com
Website .... www.worldheart.com

Employer Background: World Heart Corporation is a global medical device company focused on the development and commercialization of pulsatile ventricular assist devices. *New Positions Created (8):* Manufacturing Engineer; Materials Manager; Senior Accountant; Senior Mechanical ProE Engineer; Manager, Investor Relations; Electronic Design Engineers; Mechanical Engineers; Process Development Engineer.

WORLDPROFIT INC.

Att: Human Resources Manager
17505 - 107th Avenue, Suite 205
Edmonton, AB T5S 1E5

Tel. 780-444-7477
Fax 780-483-8672
Email .... customerservice@worldprofit.com
Website .... www.worldprofit.com

Employer Background: Worldprofit Inc. is an international company offering domain hosting, website design, software applications and services. *New Positions Created (2):* Website Designers; Graphic Designer / Website Designer.

WORLDWIDE IMMIGRATION CONSULTANCY SERVICES CANADA INC.

Att: Senior Director
7025 Tomken Road, Suite 231
Mississauga, ON L5S 1R6

Tel. 905-564-7797
Fax 905-564-8309
Email .... parvinder@wwicscanada.com
Website .... www.wwicscanada.com

Employer Background: WWICS, a large Canadian immigration and settlement firm, operates in conjunction with over 30 offices and business associates worldwide. *New Positions Created (3):* Account Manager; Immigration Lawyer; Information Technology Recruitment Manager.

WRIGLEY CANADA INC.

Att: Human Resources Department
1123 Leslie Street
Toronto, ON M3C 2K1

Tel. 416-442-3253
Fax 416-442-3299
Email .... wccareers@wrigley.ca
Website .... www.wrigley.com

Employer Background: Wrigley Canada Inc. is a subsidiary of Chicago-based William R. Wrigley Company, one of the world's largest manufacturers of confectionery products. *New Positions Created (3):* Packaging Team Leaders; QA / Regulatory Affairs Manager; Bilingual Territory Manager.

WURTH CANADA LIMITED
Att: Human Resources
6330 Tomken Road
Mississauga, ON L5T 1N2
Tel. 905-564-6225
Fax 905-564-6227
Email .... hfurlotte@wurthcanada.com
Website .... www.wurthcanada.com
Employer Background: Wurth Canada Limited is a large fastener company, servicing the automotive, industrial maintenance and MRO trades. *New Positions Created (5):* Sales Professionals (2); Bilingual Accounts Receivable Representative; Bilingual Executive Assistant; Marketing Assistant; Sales Representative.

WYETH-AYERST CANADA INC.
Att: Human Resources
88 McNabb Street
Toronto, ON L3R 6E6
Fax 905-470-3904
Email .... waci-mh-hr@wai.wyeth.com
Website .... www.wyeth.com
Employer Background: Wyeth-Ayerst Canada Inc. is a leading pharmaceutical organization. *New Positions Created (10):* Pharmaceutical Sales Representative; Research Scientist I; Research Scientist II; Research Scientist III; Communications Coordinator; Pharmaceutical Sales Representatives; Market Research Analyst; Legal Assistant; Pharmaceutical Sales Representatives; Continuing Health Education Associate.

WYNDHAM BRISTOL PLACE TORONTO AIRPORT
Att: Human Resources Director
950 Dixon Road
Toronto, ON M9W 5N4
Tel. 416-675-9444
Fax 416-675-2053
Website .... www.wyndham.com
Employer Background: Wyndham Bristol Place Toronto Airport is a 4-diamond hotel, with 287 rooms and 6 suites. *New Positions Created (2):* Hotel Positions; Director of Human Resources.

WYSDOM INC.
Att: Human Resources Manager
30 West Beaver Creek Road, Suite 111
Richmond Hill, ON L4B 3K1
Tel. 905-763-6979
Fax 905-763-6932
Email .... hotjobs@wysdom.com
Website .... www.wysdom.com
Employer Background: Wysdom Inc. is a wireless software and infrastructure company, enabling companies to offer user-centric mobile products and services. *New Positions Created (5):* Senior Project Manager; Solutions Architect; Public Relations Manager; Senior Software Developer; Product Manager.

WYSDOM INC.
Att: Human Resources Manager
3 Place Ville Marie
Bureau 12350, Niveau Plaza
Montréal, QC H3B 5J9
Tel. 514-395-6060
Fax 514-395-6080
Email .... hotjobs@wysdom.com
Website .... www.wysdom.com
Employer Background: Wysdom Inc. is a wireless software and infrastructure company, enabling companies to offer user-centric mobile products and services. *New Positions Created (7):* Project Administrator; Senior Consultant; Senior Software Developer; Senior Web Developer; Software Quality Analyst; System Administrator; Training Specialist.

X.EYE INC.
Att: Human Resources Manager
130 King Street West
Suite 1310, The Exchange Tower
Toronto, ON M5W 1E4
Tel. 416-601-9833
Fax 416-601-9491
Email .... hr@xeye.com
Website .... www.xeye.com
Employer Background: X.eye Inc. is a software firm that builds and delivers products and consulting services for the wealth management industry. *New Positions Created (13):* Financial Software Engineer; Financial Systems Analyst; Implementation Consultant; Project Manager; Requirements / Systems Analyst; Customer Service Manager; Financial Software Engineer; Financial Systems Analyst; Project Manager; Systems Analyst; Implementation Project Manager / Consultant; Oracle / Unix Systems Engineer; Software Build Manager.

XANTREX TECHNOLOGY INC.
Att: Employee Development Manager
8999 Nelson Way
Burnaby, BC V5A 4B5
Tel. 604-422-8595
Fax 604-415-4674
Email .... careers@xantrex.com
Website .... www.xantrex.com
Employer Background: Xantrex Technology Inc. is a power conversion specialist pioneering breakthrough technology for a wide range of local and international organizations, including large electronics and telecommunications companies. *New Positions Created (8):* Manufacturing Engineer; Mechanical Designer; PCB Designer; Regulatory Engineer; Senior Project Buyer; Senior Software Engineer; Technical Communicator; Technologist, Electrical.

XCELLSIS
Att: Human Resources Manager
3900 North Fraser Way
Burnaby, BC V5J 5G1
Fax 604-419-6396
Email ..... human_resources@fcengines.com
Website .... www.xcellsis.com
Employer Background: XCELLSiS, a joint venture between DaimlerChrysler, Ballard

Power Systems and Ford, is focused on the development and manufacture of fuel cell engines for buses, cars and trucks. *New Positions Created (7):* Pro Engineer Designers / Engineers, Mechanical (2); Pro Engineer / Pro Intralink Administrator; Pro Engineer Technologist; Systems Engineering Manager; Heavy Duty Mechanic; Operations Data Coordinator; Sheet Metal Fabricator.

XCERT INTERNATIONAL INC.
Att: Human Resources Department
505 Burrard Street
Bentall Centre 1, Suite 300
Vancouver, BC V7X 1M3
Tel. 604-640-6210
Fax 604-640-6220
Email .... careers@xcert.com
Website .... www.xcert.com
Employer Background: Xcert International Inc. develops e-commerce security software, such as their public key infrastructure products, to enable secure communications and business over the Internet. *New Positions Created (6):* Support Manager; Software Test Manager; Project Manager; Quality Assurance Engineers and Testers; Software Developers; Quality Assurance Manager.

XEBEC IMAGING SERVICES INC.
Att: Human Resources Manager
2255 St. Laurent Boulevard, Suite 200
Ottawa, ON K1G 4K3
Tel. 613-739-9901
Fax 613-526-1496
Email .... jobs@ottawa.xebec.ca
Website .... www.xebec.ca
Employer Background: Xebec Imaging Services Inc. offers a full range of integrated document management and business communication solutions. *New Positions Created (4):* Microfilming Camera Operator; Data Entry Operators; Account Manager; Various Administrative Positions (3).

XENTEL DM INC.
Att: David Smith
10 Kodiak Crescent
Toronto, ON M3J 3G5
Tel. 416-633-4646
Fax 416-633-4643
Email .... davids@xentel.com
Website .... www.xentel.com
Employer Background: Xentel DM Inc. provides integrated event planning, marketing and production services, with over 300 clients, 30 offices and 2,500 employees in Canada and the USA. *New Positions Created (2):* Accounts Payable Positions; Various Accounting Positions.

XEROX CANADA LTD.
Att: Human Resources
5650 Yonge Street
Toronto, ON M2M 4G7
Tel. 416-229-3769
Fax 416-733-6802
Email .... mfulton77@home.com
Website .... www.xerox.ca
Employer Background: Founded in 1953, Xerox Canada Ltd. manufactures document

processing products and systems, and has revenues of $1.2 billion and over 4,600 employees in Canada. *New Positions Created (4):* Sales Representative; Sales Agent Representative; Channel Manager, Laser Cartridges; Sales Representatives.

XEROX CANADA LTD.
Att: Alison Dobson, HR Specialist
3060 Caravelle Drive
Mississauga, ON L4V 1L7

Tel. 905-672-4600
Fax 905-678-1721
Email ..... alison.dobson@cmot.xerox.com
Website .... www.xerox.ca
Employer Background: Founded in 1953, Xerox Canada Ltd. is a leading manufacturer of document processing products and systems, with revenues of $1.2 billion and over 4,278 employees in Canada. *New Positions Created (3):* Accounting Analyst; Project Leader, Mechanical Design Engineering; Financial Analyst.

XEROX CANADA, SUPPLIES DEVELOPMENT CENTRE
Att: Heather Power, HR Specialist
2660 Speakman Drive
Mississauga, ON L5K 2L1

Tel. 905-823-7091
Fax 905-823-0380
Email .... heather.power@crt.xeroc.com
Website .... www.xerox.ca
Employer Background: Founded in 1953, Xerox Canada manufactures document processing products and systems, and has revenues of $1.2 billion and over 4,278 employees in Canada. *New Positions Created (5):* Chemical Engineer; Chemical Technologist; Electrical Engineer; Maintenance and Facilities Technologist (2); Quality Control Engineer.

XILLIX TECHNOLOGIES CORP.
Att: Human Resources Manager
13775 Commerce Parkway, Suite 100
Richmond, BC V6V 2V4

Tel. 604-278-5000
Fax 604-278-5111
Email .... hr@xillix.com
Website .... www.xillix.com
Employer Background: Xillix Technologies Corp. is a medical device company engaged in the research, development and commercialization of imaging products. *New Positions Created (6):* Electronics Engineering Group Leader; Software Developers; Systems Engineer; Technical Writer; Group Leader, Electronics Engineering; Project Manager.

XTRA LEASE
Att: Operations Manager
1111, rue Courval
Lachine, QC H8T 3P4

Tel. 514-633-5717
Fax 514-633-0343
Website .... www.xtralease.com
Employer Background: Founded in 1992, Xtra Lease is a national leader in truck trailer leasing and a division of Xtra Corpo-

ration. In Canada, the company has 5 branch locations. *New Positions Created (3):* Mechanic; Assistant Operations Manager; Assistant Operations Manager.

XWAVE SOLUTIONS INC.
Att: Human Resources Manager
777 - 8th Avenue SW, Suite 600
Calgary, AB T2P 3R5

Tel. 403-263-7533
Fax 403-266-3594
Email .... albertacareers@xwave.com
Website .... www.xwave.com
Employer Background: Formed in 1999, Xwave Solutions Inc. (formerly Prior Data Science Ltd.) is an IT consulting company serving clients in the telecom, oil and gas and public sectors. *New Positions Created (10):* C / C++ Software Specialists; Embedded Validation and Verification Testers; Software Build and Release Specialist; Telecommunications Software Specialists; Application Architects; Intermediate Web Developers; Senior Developers; Senior Project Managers; Senior Quality Assurance Testers; System Analysts.

XWAVE SOLUTIONS INC.
Att: Human Resources Manager
1550 Enterprise Road, Suite 120
Mississauga, ON L4W 4P4

Tel. 905-670-1225
Fax 905-670-1344
Email .... torontojobs@xwave.com
Website .... www.xwave.com
Employer Background: Formed in 1999, Xwave Solutions Inc. (formerly Prior Data Science Ltd.) is an IT consulting company serving clients in the telecom, oil and gas and public sectors. *New Positions Created (6):* Data Architect; Director, E-Business Solutions; Embedded Validation and Verification Team Leader; Internet Software Security Architect; J2EE Websphere Solution Architect; Real-Time Embedded Ada Developers.

XWAVE SOLUTIONS INC.
Att: Human Resources
65 Iber Road
Ottawa, ON K2S 1E7

Tel. 613-831-0888
Fax 613-831-1836
Email .... jobs@xwave.com
Website .... www.xwave.com
Employer Background: Formed in 1999, Xwave Solutions Inc. (formerly Software Kinetics) is an IT consulting company serving clients in the telecom, oil and gas and public sectors. *New Positions Created (8):* Director, eBusiness Solutions; Marketing Events Coordinator; Account Executive / Sales Manager; Human Resources Generalist; Java Developers; Real-Time / Embedded Software Developers; Software Developers; Technical Architect.

XWAVE SOLUTIONS INC.
Att: Human Resources Manager
1255 Trans Canada Highway, Suite 330
Dorval, QC H9P 2V4

Tel. 514-685-3817
Fax 514-685-7940
Email .... montreal@xwave.com
Website .... www.xwave.com
Employer Background: Formed in 1999, Xwave Solutions Inc. is an IT consulting company serving clients in the telecom, oil and gas and public sectors. *New Positions Created (12):* Account Executive / Sales Executives; Avionics Software Developer; BSP Software Specialist; Communications Software Specialists; Embedded Software Developer; Project Manager; Real-Time Software Developers; Satellite Communication Software Developer; Senior & Intermediate Development Engineers; SNMP Specialist; Software Coders & Testers; Wireless Communications Software Developer.

XXL ENGINEERING LTD.
Att: Cindy Szott
811 Manning Road NE, Suite 106
Calgary, AB T2E 7L4

Email .... cszott@xxleng.com
Employer Background: XXL Engineering Ltd. is a facility engineering consulting firm that provides EPCM services to clients within the oil and gas industry. *New Positions Created (3):* Intermediate Mechanical Engineers; Intermediate Piping Draftsmen; Senior Mechanical Engineers.

XXXY
Att: Store Manager
1176 Robson Street
Vancouver, BC V6E 1B2

Fax 604-632-9970
Email .... xxxyjobs@dylex.com
Employer Background: XXXY is a clothing retailer. *New Positions Created (3):* Assistant Mgr; Sales Associates; Store Manager.

YACHIYO OF ONTARIO MANUFACTURING INC. / YOM
Att: Associate Services
120 Mapleview Drive West
Barrie, ON L4N 9H6

Tel. 705-734-1688
Fax 705-734-1209
Email .... resumes@yachiyo.on.ca
Employer Background: YOM is a leading manufacturer of automotive parts. *New Positions Created (3):* Industrial Electrician; Press Technician; Welding Technician.

YAMAHA MOTOR CANADA LTD.
Att: Adina Ingram
480 Gordon Baker Road
Toronto, ON M2H 3B4

Tel. 416-498-1911
Fax 416-491-3517
Website .... www.yamaha-motor.ca
Employer Background: Yamaha Motor Canada Ltd. is a leader in the leisure vehicle industry. *New Positions Created (7):* Accessory Development Coordinator; Bilingual Dealer Service Support Coordinator; Product Manager, Marine and OPE; Inside Sales Coordinator; Bilingual Retail Finance Coordinators (3); Accounting Assistant; Dealer Sales Support Coordinator.

YASKAWA MOTOMAN CANADA LTD.
Att: Human Resources Department
2280 Argentia Road
Mississauga, ON L5N 6H8

Tel. 905-858-5556
Fax 905-813-5938
Website .... www.motoman.com

Employer Background: Yaskawa Motoman Canada Ltd. is dedicated to delivering high-quality, innovative automation solutions. *New Positions Created (5):* Senior Accounting Assistant; Controller; Field Service Technician; Regional Sales Manager; Robotics Instructor.

YEE HONG COMMUNITY WELLNESS FOUNDATION
Att: President
2319 McNicoll Avenue
Toronto, ON M1V 5L2

Tel. 416-321-6333
Fax 416-321-1849
Email .... foundation@yeehong.com
Website .... www.yeehong.com

Employer Background: The Yee Hong Community Wellness Foundation develops culturally and linguistically appropriate services for seniors of Chinese origin. *New Positions Created (5):* Communications and Public Relations Coordinator; Executive Assistant; Receptionist; Special Events Coordinator; Volunteer Coordinator.

YELLOWKNIFE CATHOLIC SCHOOLS
Att: Kern Von Hagen, Superintendent
5124 - 49th Street, PO Box 1830
Yellowknife, NT X1A 2P4

Tel. 867-873-2200
Fax 867-873-2701
Website .... www.ycs.nt.ca

Employer Background: Yellowknife Catholic Schools operates three schools in the Yellowknife area: St. Patrick High School; Weledah Catholic School; and Ecole St-Joseph. *New Positions Created (2):* Assistant Principal; Teaching Positions.

YM INC.
Att: Sabrina
50 Dufflaw Road
Toronto, ON M6A 2W1

Fax 416-789-8984
Email .... sabrinas@stitches.ca
Website .... www.stitchesonline.com

Employer Background: YM Inc. is a fashion retailer, catering to teens and youth under the Sirens, Urban Planet, Stitches and Siblings banners. *New Positions Created (8):* District Manager; District Manager; Visual Merchandising Manager; Store Management Visual Merchandiser; Young Men's Buyer; Junior Clerks (2); Junior Field Administrators (2); District Manager.

YM - YWHA, BEN WEIDER JEWISH COMMUNITY CENTRE
Att: Executive Director
5500 Westbury Avenue
Montréal, QC H3W 2W8

Tel. 514-737-6551

Website .... www.ymywha.com

Employer Background: Founded in 1910, YM - YWHA provides of social, cultural, recreational, fitness and sports activities. The organization has 5 branches and serves over 35,000 members. *New Positions Created (4):* Assistant; Director of Housekeeping and Maintenance Services; Director of Marketing and Public Relations; Graphic Designer.

YMCA OF GREATER VANCOUVER
Att: Manager, Child Care
4970 Canada Way
Burnaby, BC V5G 1M4

Fax 604-294-9414
Website .... www.vanymca.org

Employer Background: YMCA of Greater Vancouver is a charitable association dedicated to the development of people in spirit, mind and body as well as the improvement of local, national and international communities. *New Positions Created (2):* Supervisors; Supervisors.

YMCA OF OAKVILLE
Att: Human Resources Manager
410 Rebecca Street
Oakville, ON L6K 1K7

Tel. 905-845-3417
Fax 905-842-6792
Website .... www.ymcaofoakville.com

Employer Background: YMCA is one of the largest and most active charitable organizations in Canada, serving over 200 communities nationwide. *New Positions Created (2):* Early Childhood Educators; School Age Child Care Supervisors and Assistants.

YMCA-YWCA, NATIONAL CAPITAL REGION
Att: VP, Human Resources
180 Argyle
Ottawa, ON K2P 1B7

Tel. 613-788-5000
Fax 613-788-5036
Website .... educom.on.ca/ymca-ywca

Employer Background: The National Capital Region YMCA-YWCA is a charitable community-based association dedicated to improving the lives of children, youth, adults and families. *New Positions Created (3):* Business Consultant; Program Delivery Assistant; Supervisor, Food Services.

YORK CATHOLIC DISTRICT SCHOOL BOARD
Att: Josephine Fazzari, HR Administrator
320 Bloomington Road West
Aurora, ON L4G 3G8

Tel. 905-713-2711
Fax 905-713-1809
Email .... fazzarj@ycdsb.edu.on.ca
Website .... www.ycdsb.edu.on.ca

Employer Background: The York Catholic District School Board serves over 43,000 students through 70 elementary and 11 secondary schools. *New Positions Created (9):* Department Heads; Secondary School Teachers; Secondary School Teachers, Business Studies; Secondary School Teachers,

Computer Studies; Supervisor, Speech Language Services; Human Resources Coordinator; Superintendent of Schools; Supervisor, Attendance Counselling Services; Elementary and Secondary School Teachers.

YORK CENTRAL HOSPITAL
Att: Human Resource Services
10 Trench Street
Richmond Hill, ON L4C 4Z3

Tel. 905-883-2250
Fax 905-883-2273
Email .... resumes@yorkcentral.on.ca
Website .... www.yorkcentral.on.ca

Employer Background: York Central Hospital is one of Ontario's fastest-growing hospitals. *New Positions Created (104):* Administrative Coordinator, Operating Room / PACU; Biomedical Engineering Technologist, Facility & Environmental Services; Clinical Nurse Specialist, Medicine (Cardiac Rehab); Coordinator, Pastoral Services; Environmental Leader; Instructor Therapist, Behaviour Management; Patient Care Coordinator, Emergency Medicine Program; Patient Care Coordinator, Vascular Access (Dialysis Program); Project Coordinator, Redevelopment; Recreation Therapist, Continuing Care Program; Technical Specialist, X-Ray (Diagnostic Imaging); Administrative Coordinators, Medicine Ambulatory Clinic / Diabetes / Endoscopy; Administrative Coordinators, Mental Health Program; Patient Care Coordinator, Medicine Program (Respiratory); Pharmacist; Social Worker, Complex Continuing Care; Registered Nurses, Complex Continuing Care; Registered Nurses, Dialysis; Registered Nurses, Emergency Medicine; Registered Nurses, Emergency Medicine (Domestic Violence); Registered Nurses, Emergency Medicine (Sexual Assault); Registered Nurses, Medicine Program (Critical Care); Registered Nurses, Medicine Program (Diabetes Education); Registered Nurses, Medicine Program (Oncology / Neurology / Nephrology); Registered Nurses, Medicine Program (Respiratory / General); Registered Nurses, Medicine Program (Telemetry / Stepdown); Registered Nurses, Medicine / Surgery Program (Ambulatory Care); Registered Nurses, Rehabilitation; Registered Nurses, Surgery Program (General Surgery and Orthopaedic); Registered Nurses, Surgery Program (Operating Room); Registered Nurses, Woman & Child Program (Labour and Delivery); Registered Nurses, Woman & Child Program (Paediatrics); Registered Nurses, Woman & Child Program (Post-Partum); Administrative Coordinator, Ambulatory Care, Surgery; Instructor Therapist, Autism Program; Pharmacist, Pharmacy Services; Budget Analyst, Financial Services; Administrative Coordinator, Mental Health Program; Occupational Therapist / MSW; Social Worker, Medicine Program; Physicians, Emergency Medical Program; Registered Nurse, Complex Continuing Care; Registered Nurse, Dialysis; Registered Nurse, Emergency Medicine; Registered Nurse, Emergency Medicine - Domestic Violence; Registered Nurse, Emergency Medicine - Sexual Assault; Registered Nurse, Medicine Program - Critical Care; Registered Nurse, Medicine Program - Diabetes Education; Registered Nurse, Medicine Program - Oncology / Neurology / Nephrology; Registered Nurse, Medicine Program - Respiratory / General; Registered Nurse, Medicine Program - Telemetry / Stepdown; Registered Nurse, Medicine / Surgery Program - Ambulatory Care; Registered Nurse, Rehabilitation; Registered Nurse, Surgery Program - General Surgery and Orthopaedic; Registered Nurse, Surgery Program - Operating Room; Registered Nurse, Woman & Child Program - Labour & Delivery; Registered Nurse, Woman & Child Program - Paediatrics; Registered Nurse, Woman & Child Program - Post-Partum; Construction Coordinator; Department Secretary; Shift Engineer; Administrative Dietitian; EEG Technologist; Nuclear Medicine, MRT & X-Ray Technologist; Patient Care Coordinator, Cardiology; Patient Care Coordinator, Respiratory; Pharmacist; Psychological Associate, Mental Health Program; Psychological Associates, Child and Family Services Program; Registered Nurses; Utilization Data Analyst; Dialysis Technician; Director, HR Development; Nephrology Social Worker; Patient Care Coordinator, Hemodialysis; Technical Specialist; Ultrasonographer; Administrative Coordinator; Clinical Dietitian; Coordinator, Volunteer and Community Resources; Medical Radiation Technologist; Nurse Educator, Medicine Program; Patient Care Coordinator, Medicine Program; Pharmacists; Registered Respiratory Therapists; Drug Utilization Pharmacist; Infection Control Coordinator; Nurse Educator, Surgery Program; Registered Nurses; Director, Organizational Development; Budget and MIS Coordinator; Clinical Nurse Specialist, Continuing Care Program; Drug Utilization Pharmacist; Health Records Technician; Instrument Technician, Supply and Distribution; Technical Specialist, Nuclear Medicine; Accounts Receivable Analyst; Administrative Assistant; Clinical Educator, OR / PACU; Environmental Services Coordinator; Nuclear Medicine Technologist; Pharmacist; Program Secretary; Registered Nurses.

YORK COMMUNITY CARE ACCESS CENTRE / CCAC
Att: Human Resources
1400 Castlefield Avenue
Toronto, ON M6B 4C4
Tel. 416-780-1919
Fax 416-780-0940
Email .... debbie.macaskill@yccac.on.ca
Website .... www.yccac.on.ca
Employer Background: CCAC provides information, in-home healthcare and long-term care facility placement and support services enabling people to live independently. *New Positions Created (7):* Coordinator; Manager, Client Services; Team Assistant; Coordinators (2); Senior Secretary; Co-ordinators; Team Support Personnel.

YORK COMMUNITY SERVICES / YCS
Att: Chair, Ad Hoc Hiring Committee
1651 Keele Street
Toronto, ON M6M 3W2
Tel. 416-653-5400
Fax 416-653-1696
Employer Background: YCS is an accredited community health centre, community legal clinic and community support organization. *New Positions Created (3):* Executive Director; Adult Protective Service Workers; Counsellor, Crisis Intervention.

YORK HOUSE SCHOOL
Att: Eve Hunnings, Director of Personnel
4176 Alexandra Street
Vancouver, BC V6J 2V6
Tel. 604-736-6551
Fax 604-736-6530
Website .... www.yorkhouse.bc.ca
Employer Background: Founded in 1932, York House School is a Canadian independent day school for girls from kindergarten through grade 12. *New Positions Created (7):* Clothing and Textiles Teacher; Art Teacher, Senior School; Classroom Teacher, Junior School (2); English Teacher, Senior School; Information Technology Teacher, Senior School; Kindergarten Teacher; Science Teacher, Senior School (2).

YORK REGION CHILDREN'S AID SOCIETY / YORK REGION CAS
Att: Julie Lee,
Director of Corporate Services
85 Eagle Street West, PO Box 358
Newmarket, ON L3Y 4X7
Tel. 905-895-2318
Fax 905-954-1861
Email .... jlee@neptune.on.ca
Website .... www.yorkcas.on.ca
Employer Background: York Region CAS is a child welfare agency, providing assistance to abused and neglected children. *New Positions Created (5):* Child Protection Workers; Director of Services; Managers; Social Workers; Director of Services.

YORK REGION DISTRICT SCHOOL BOARD
Att: Human Resources Manager
60 Wellington Street West
Aurora, ON L4G 3H2
Tel. 905-727-3141
Fax 905-841-3943
Website .... www.yrdsb.edu.on.ca
Employer Background: York Region District School Board operates more than 125 schools, with an enrolment of 78,000 students served by 6,000 staff members. *New Positions Created (20):* Elementary Teachers; Project Leader, Student & Classroom Systems; Recruiting Officer; Secondary Teachers; Speech-Language Pathologist; Assistant Head of Special Education; Department Heads; Head of Geography; Special Education Teachers; Special Education Teachers; Teacher, Business Studies and Computer Science; Teacher, Computer Science; Teacher, Instrumental Music; Teacher, Special Education; Teachers (2); Teachers, French; Teachers of the Deaf and Hard of Hearing; Teachers of the Visually Impaired; Elementary and Secondary School Teachers (9); Public Affairs Officer.

YORK SCHOOL, THE
Att: Barbara K. Goodwin-Zeibots, Head
1320 Yonge Street
Toronto, ON M4T 1X2
Tel. 416-926-1325
Fax 416-926-9592
Website .... www.yorkschool.com
Employer Background: The York School is an independent, non-denominational, co-educational elementary and secondary school offering the International Baccalaureate (IB) program. *New Positions Created (2):* Teachers; Teachers.

YORK, THE REGIONAL MUNICIPALITY OF
Att: Human Resource Services
17250 Yonge Street
Newmarket, ON L3Y 6Z1
Tel. 905-895-1231
Fax 905-895-4232
Email .... yrkhr@region.york.on.ca
Website .... www.region.york.on.ca
Employer Background: Founded in 1971, York Region is comprised of 9 urban and rural communities, with a total population of 730,065. *New Positions Created (25):* Fleet Coordinator; Solicitor, Generalist; Solicitor, Generalist; Business Support Analysts, ERP; Senior Network Analyst; Support Analyst / Help Desk Operator; Support Analyst / Help Desk Second-Level Support Position; Technical Specialist, ERP; Business Administrator; Planner; Policy & Project Development Specialist; Policy & Project Development Specialist; Director, Court Administration; General Manager, Emergency Medical Services; Project Manager; Resource Coordinator; Policy Advisor; Registered Dental Hygienist; Dental Assistants (2); Manager, Design; Senior Project Manager; Export Development Consultant; Tourism Promotion Coordinator; Librarian / Resource Centre Coordinator; Director, Internal Audit and Management Effectiveness.

YORK UNIVERSITY
Att: Human Resource Services
4700 Keele Street
Toronto, ON M3J 1P3
Tel. 416-736-5005
Fax 416-736-5703
Email .... clarkep@yorku.ca
Website .... www.yorku.ca
Employer Background: York University is Canada's third-largest university, with approximately 40,000 students in 10 faculties. *New Positions Created (3):* Sr Coordinator, Enrolment Mgmnt & Resource Planning; Security Officers; Laboratory Technician.

YORK UNIVERSITY, FACULTY OF EDUCATION
Att: Dr. Terry Piper, Dean
4700 Keele Street, S853 Ross Building
Toronto, ON M3J 1P3
Tel. 416-736-5002
Fax 416-736-5913
Website .... www.edu.yorku.ca
Employer Background: York University, Faculty of Education offers undergraduate

(BEd) and graduate (MEd) degrees, as well as a deaf education program, and field development programs offered cooperatively with area school boards. *New Positions Created (4):* Tenure Track Position, Aboriginal / First Nations Teacher Education; Tenure Track Position, Health Education; Tenure Track Position, Mathematics Education; Tenure Track Position, Pedagogy of Technology.

YORKTOWN SHELTER FOR WOMEN / YORKTOWN CHILD AND FAMILY CENTRE
Att: Program Manager
2468 Eglinton Avenue West
Toronto, ON M6M 5E2
Tel. 416-394-2999
Fax 416-394-2942
Email .... ycfc@istar.ca
Website .... www.interlog.com/~yrkchfam
Employer Background: Yorktown provides a safe haven for women and children living in abusive relationships. *New Positions Created (3):* Children's Program / Volunteer Coordinator; Children's Program / Volunteer Coordinator; Transitional Support Worker.

YOTTA YOTTA INC.
Att: Human Resources Manager
10328 - 81st Avenue, Suite 301
Edmonton, AB T6E 1X2
Tel. 780-439-9000
Fax 780-989-6868
Email .... careers@yottayotta.com
Website .... www.yottayotta.com
Employer Background: Yotta Yotta Inc. develops the "Net Storage Cube", which allows users to store large amounts of data over the Internet. *New Positions Created (36):* Customer Support Engineer ; Intermediate Java Developer; Junior and Intermediate Technical Communicator; Product Manager, Storage Management; Product Manager, Storage Security; Program Manager; Senior Customer Support Engineer; Senior Software Architect / Developer; Senior Software Developer; Software Integration Lead; System Performance Principal; Test Developer; Wide Area Data Networking Engineer; Hardware Designer / Developer; Product Manager; Product Marketing Position; Software Developer; Software Tester; Technical Recruiter / Staffing Specialist; Test Lead Position; Internal Technical Support Position; Java Software Developer; Office Manager; Advanced Networking Specialist; Customer Liaison Position; Distributed Storage API Architect; Hardware Design / Development Position; Hardware Product Manager; Linux / Unix Administrator; Product Requirements Specialist; SAN Specialist; Software Developers; Software Product Manager; Storage Management API Architect; Storage Performance Specialist; Support Software Liaison Specialist.

YOUTHDALE TREATMENT CENTRES
Att: Dr. Andrew Bennett
227 Victoria Street
Toronto, ON M5B 1T8
Tel. 416-368-4896

Fax 416-368-3192
Email .... clinics@youthdale.ca
Website .... www.youthdale.ca
Employer Background: Youthdale Treatment Centres is a leading children's mental health centre, offering outpatient day and residential treatment, mobile crisis response and intensive psychiatric inpatient treatment. *New Positions Created (5):* Family Therapist; Clinical Psychologist; Director of Mobile Crisis Services; Mobile Crisis Counsellor; Youth Workers.

YOUVILLE HOME
Att: Human Resources Manager
9 St. Vital Avenue
St. Albert, AB T8N 1K1
Tel. 780-460-6900
Fax 780-459-4139
Website .... www.greynuns.ab.ca
Employer Background: Youville Home is a 162-bed continuing care facility, founded in 1863 by the Grey Nuns (Sisters of Charity) of St. Albert. *New Positions Created (3):* Resource Management Coordinator; Education / Mission Integration Coordinator; Resource Management Coordinator.

YUKON COLLEGE
Att: Human Resources Services
PO Box 2799
Whitehorse, YT Y1A 5K4
Tel. 867-668-8706
Fax 867-668-8896
Email .... personnel@yukoncollege.yk.ca
Website .... www.yukoncollege.yk.ca
Employer Background: Yukon College is a northern college that serves adult educational and training needs. *New Positions Created (2):* Director, Student Services; Instructor, Psychology.

YUKON PUBLIC SERVICE COMMISSION
Att: Human Resources Manager
2071 - 2nd Avenue, PO Box 2703
Whitehorse, YT Y1A 2C6
Tel. 867-667-5653
Fax 867-667-5755
Email .... resume@gov.yk.ca
Website .... www.gov.yk.ca
Employer Background: The Yukon Public Service Commission provides recruitment services for the government of Yukon. *New Positions Created (11):* Clinical Dietitian; Classification Analyst; Coordinator, Therapeutic Caregiver Program; Director, Government Audit Services; Community Nutritionist; Social Worker; Social Worker, Mobile; Audiometric Technician; Clinical Dietitian; Registered Nurse; Speech Language Consultants (2).

ZARPAC INC.
Att: Personnel Department
476 Morden Road
Oakville, ON L6K 3W4
Tel. 905-338-8880
Fax 905-338-3521
Email .... zarpac@zarpac.com
Website .... www.zarpac.com

Employer Background: Zarpac Inc. is an international engineering company specializing in the design and project management of highly-automated assembly and packaging systems for multinational consumer goods companies. *New Positions Created (4):* Electrical Project Engineer; Mechanical Project Engineer; Electrical Project Engineer; Mechanical Project Engineer.

ZED.I SOLUTIONS
Att: Human Resources Department
9650 - 20th Avenue
Suite 211, Advanced Technology Centre
Edmonton, AB T6N 1G1
Tel. 780-462-3400
Fax 780-463-1567
Email .... careers@zedisolutions.com
Website .... www.zedisolutions.com
Employer Background: Zed.i Solutions is a technology-based company serving the upstream oil and gas industry. *New Positions Created (26):* Database Administrator; Electronic Technologist; Manufacturing Engineering Manager; Network Administrator; Senior Active Server Pages (ASP) Developer; Senior Network Administrator / Security Administrator; Systems Analyst; ASP Developer; Electronics / Electrical Engineer; Embedded Programmer / Analyst; Field Technician; Firmware Engineer; ISO Manager; R & D Technologist; Senior Electronic Design Engineer; System Designer; Administrative Assistant / Secretary; ASP Developer; Electronics / Electrical Engineer; Embedded Programmer / Analyst; Firmware Programmer / Engineer; ISO Manager; R&D Technologist; Security Administrator; Software Architect; System Designer.

ZED.I SOLUTIONS
Att: Human Resources Manager
555 - 4th Avenue SW, Suite 500
Calgary, AB T2P 3E7
Tel. 403-444-1100
Fax 403-444-1101
Email .... careers@zedisolutions.com
Website .... www.zedisolutions.com
Employer Background: Zed.i Solutions is a technology-based company serving the upstream oil and gas industry. *New Positions Created (9):* ASP Developer; Electronics / Electrical Engineer; Firmware Engineer; Information Technology System Designer; Mechanical Technologist; Research and Development Technologist; Senior Electronic System Designer; Senior Mechanical Designer; Technical Writer.

ZELLERS
Att: Steve Wowk, Pharmacy Recruiting
8925 Torbram Road
Brampton, ON L6T 4G1
Tel. 905-792-5773
Fax 905-792-6310
Website .... www.hbc.com/zellers
Employer Background: Founded in 1931, Zellers is a leading chain of discount department stores, with over 350 locations across Canada. The retailer is a subsidiary of the Hudson Bay Company. *New Positions Created (2):* Pharmacists; Pharmacists.

ZENASTRA PHOTONICS INC.
Att: Human Resources
120 Colonnade Road, 2nd Floor
Ottawa, ON K2E 7J5

Tel. 613-736-8777
Fax 613-731-4558
Email .... hr@zenastra.com
Website .... www.zenastra.com

Employer Background: Founded in 1999, Zenastra Photonics Inc. (formerly Nu-Wave Photonics) is a leader in integrated optical components for high-performance networking systems. *New Positions Created (68):* Account Managers; Assembly Process Engineers; CAD Photomask Specialist; Component Engineers; Electronic / ASIC Design Engineers; Equipment Technicians; Fabrication Process Development Specialists; Field Application Engineers; Manager, Intellectual Property; Manufacturing Engineers; Market Analyst; Material Development Specialists; Mechanical Design Engineers; Photonic Grating Specialists; Photonic Product Design Specialists; Photonic Research Scientists; Photonic Simulation Tool Developers; Photonic Systems Architects; Process / Industrial Engineers; Product Managers, Optical Componentry; Product Managers, Optical Networking; Reliability Engineers; Software Engineer; Vendor Quality Engineers / Specialists; CAD Photomask Specialist; Customer Service Supervisor; Equipment Technicians; Field Application Engineers; Manager, Intellectual Property; Manufacturing Engineer; Process / Industrial Engineers; Regional Sales Managers; Vendor Quality Engineers / Specialists; Account Managers; Assembly Process Engineers; Customer Service Manager; Customer Service Representative; Electronic / ASIC Design Engineers; Fabrication Process Development Specialists; Market Analyst; Material Development Specialists; Photonic Grating Specialists; Photonic Product Design Specialists; Photonic Research Scientists; Photonic Simulation Tool Developers; Photonic Systems Architects; Planner / Buyer; Product Managers, Optical Networking / Componentry; Reliability Engineers; Sales Engineers; Test / Verification Engineers; Accounts Payable Clerk; Buyers; Component Engineers; Custom / Traffic Specialists; Documentation Control Specialists; Equipment Technicians; Manufacturing Engineers; Mechanical Design Engineers; Process / Industrial Engineers; Product Engineers; Production Planner; Project Managers; Purchasing Administrative Assistant; Purchasing Associates (2); Software Engineer; Technical Writers; Vendor Quality Engineers / Specialists.

ZERO-KNOWLEDGE SYSTEMS INC.
Att: People Department
888 de Maisonneuve East, 6th Floor
Montréal, QC H2L 4S8

Tel. 514-286-2636
Fax 514-287-0967
Email .... jobs@zeroknowledge.com
Website .... www.zeroknowledge.com

Employer Background: Zero-Knowledge Systems Inc. is a leading provider of privacy-enabling technologies and services for consumers and business. *New Positions Created (3):* Senior Accountant; Executive Assistant; Administrative Assistant.

ZI CORPORATION OF CANADA INC.
Att: Human Resources Manager
500 - 4th Avenue SW, Suite 300
Calgary, AB T2P 2V6

Tel. 403-233-8875
Fax 403-233-8878
Email .... careers@zicorp.com
Website .... www.zicorp.com

Employer Background: Zi is a software developer of Chinese character-based language applications and Internet products and services. Zi has developed a unique Chinese character-based input system for computers and other electronic devices. *New Positions Created (4):* Junior Software Developer; Legal Assistant; Senior Software Developer; Software Developer.

ZIFF ENERGY GROUP
Att: Human Resources Manager
1117 Macleod Trail SE
Calgary, AB T2G 2M8

Tel. 403-265-0600
Fax 403-261-4631
Email .... employment@ziffenergy.com
Website .... www.ziffenergy.com

Employer Background: Ziff Energy Group is a large energy consulting organization that combines corporate analysis, natural gas strategies and regulatory support for governments and energy companies worldwide. *New Positions Created (3):* Senior Gas Analyst; Marketing and Communications Coordinator; Data Analyst.

ZIRCATEC PRECISION INDUSTRIES INC. / ZPI
Att: Director, Human Resources
200 Dorset Street East
Port Hope, ON L1A 3V4

Fax 905-885-7457
Email .... alan.mayes@zircatec.ca

Employer Background: ZPI is Canada's leading manufacturer of nuclear fuel and reactivity control mechanisms for CANDU reactors. *New Positions Created (6):* Quality Assurance Specialist; Manufacturing Process Engineering Specialist; Materials Management Specialist; Quality Assurance Engineer; Quality Verification / Inspection Supervisor; Training Specialist.

ZIVEX IT UTILITY COMPANY
Att: Human Resources Manager
495 March Road, Suite 300
Kanata, ON K2K 3G1

Tel. 613-270-8525
Fax 613-236-9819
Email .... opportunity@zivex.com
Website .... www.zivex.com

Employer Background: Zivex IT Utility Company is a pre-IPO technology firm that markets new IT utility services. *New Positions Created (3):* Help Desk Coordinator; Marketing Manager; Sales Account Executive .

ZOX TECHNOLOGIES INC.
Att: Human Resources Manager
5001 Yonge Street, Suite 1900
Toronto, ON M2N 6P6

Tel. 416-218-2100
Fax 416-218-2127
Email .... hr@zox.net
Website .... www.zox.net

Employer Background: ZOX Technologies develops and distributes software designed to optimize business-to-business, business-to-consumer and personal interaction over the Internet. *New Positions Created (7):* Product Architect; Product Support Technician; Senior Java Developer; Senior Process Analyst; Senior Software Developer; Technical Consulting Manager; Senior Java Developers.

ZTR CONTROL SYSTEMS INC.
Att: Human Resources Assistant
PO Box 2543, Station B
London, ON N6A 4G9

Tel. 519-452-1233
Fax 519-452-7764
Email .... resumes@ztr.com
Website .... www.ztr.com

Employer Background: ZTR Control Systems Inc. designs and develops monitoring and control systems for use in a range of industries. *New Positions Created (3):* Railway Sales Representative; Technical Service Representative; Technical Service Supervisor, Railway Division.

ZUCOTTO WIRELESS INC.
Att: Human Resources Manager
130 Slater Street, Suite 1300
Ottawa, ON K1P 6E2

Tel. 613-789-0090
Fax 613-789-0050
Email .... jobs@zucotto.com
Website .... www.zucotto.com

Employer Background: Zucotto Wireless Inc. develops Java-based native processors, with complementing cores, software and development tools for the handheld wireless device industry. *New Positions Created (12):* ASIC Technician; Senior IC Packaging Design Engineer; Wireless Event Manager; Embedded Software Validation Engineer; FPGA / ASIC Lead; Intermediate ASIC Validation Engineer; Microprocessor Architect; Performance Architect; Senior ASIC Designers; Software Manager; Validation Lead / Manager; Event Manager.

ZURICH CANADA
Att: Recruitment
311 - 6th Avenue SW, Suite 1800
Calgary, AB T2P 3H2

Tel. 403-691-7000
Fax 403-691-7071
Website .... www.zurichcanada.com

Employer Background: Zurich Canada is a leading provider of home, auto and life insurance products. *New Positions Created (5):* Claims Assistant; Claims File Manager 1, Accident Benefits; Closed File Review Auditor; Claims File Manager, Liability; Team Manager, Property.

ZURICH CANADA
Att: Recruitment
400 University Avenue
Toronto, ON M5G 1S7

Tel. 416-586-3000
Website .... www.zurichcanada.com

Employer Background: Zurich Canada is a leading provider of home, auto and life insurance products. *New Positions Created (75):* Bilingual Customer Account Representative; Broker Distribution Administrator; Casualty Underwriting Specialist; Claim File Manager 3, Auto / Liability; Junior Business Analyst, CIT; Senior Underwriter, Preeminence; Underwriting Assistant; Junior Underwriter; Accountant, Reinsurance; Claims Assistant; Life Broker Services Administrator; Senior Actuarial Analyst; Claim File Manager 2, Accident Benefits; Imaging Associate; Intermediate Property / Casualty Underwriter; Manager, Contact Centre Business Services; Team Manager, Accident Benefits; Workforce Manager Specialist; Employee Relations & Policy Consultant; Technical Support Analyst, Level I; Loss Control Fleet Specialist; Senior Accounting Assistant; Senior Underwriter, Commercial (Auto / Fleet); Subrogation / Salvage File Manager; Underwriting Specialist, Property; Casualty Underwriter; Coordinator / Technical Assistant, International Programs; Investigative Services Specialist; Manager, Underwriting, Commercial Insurance; Bilingual Customer Account Representative; Casualty Underwriting Specialist; Customer Account Representative, PeoplePlus; Financial Analyst; Health Counsellors (2); Intermediate Auto / Fleet Underwriter; Junior Accounting Assistant; Senior Accounting Assistant, Reinsurance; Senior Commercial Property / Casualty Underwriter; Senior Reinsurance Consultant; Senior Underwriter, Preeminence; Underwriters (2); Underwriting Assistant; Actuarial Analyst, P & C; Claim File Manager 3, Auto / Liability; Claim File Manager 3, Liability; Claims Assistant; Customer Service Assistants (2); Intranet Content Manager; Major Case Unit Specialist; Relationship Representative, Express Claims; Subrogation Manager; Underwriting Assistant; Bilingual Billing Customer Payment Representative; Bilingual Registered Nurse; Employment Consultant; Senior Commercial Auto Underwriter; Senior Commercial Property / Casualty Underwriter; Team Manager, Property; Traffic & Production Manager; Underwriter; Bilingual Billing / Collection Customer Service Representative; Commercial Lines Underwriting Consultant; Mechanical Claims Adjuster; Team Manager, Accident Benefits; Vice-President, Life Sales; Bilingual Customer Service Representatives, PeoplePlus; Bilingual Customer Service Representatives, World Travel Protection; Bilingual Customer Service Representatives, Zurich Assist; Bilingual Assistance Coordinators; Bilingual Customer Service Representatives; Registered Nurse; Manager, Claims; Claims File Manager; Bilingual Claims File Managers; Policy Service Representatives.

ZURICH CANADA
Att: Recruitment
1155 Metcalfe Street
Montréal, QC H3B 4V1

Tel. 514-393-7222
Website .... www.zurichcanada.com

Employer Background: Zurich Canada is a leading provider of home, auto and life insurance products. *New Positions Created (5):* Bilingual Customer Account Representative; Senior Commercial Property / Casualty Underwriter; Senior Fleet / Commercial Auto Underwriter; Senior Underwriter, Preeminence; Underwriting Assistant, Commercial Auto .

Occupational Index

ABOUT THE OCCUPATIONAL CATEGORIES
USED IN THIS DIRECTORY...

Here are more detailed descriptions of the occupational categories used in this directory. To locate the top employers in your field, find the category that best describes your occupation, then refer to the appropriate index page.

Accounting (p. 461) includes chartered accountants (CAs, CGAs, CMAs), controllers, comptrollers, auditors, cost accountants, tax specialists, accounting supervisors, bookkeepers and students in professional training programs. *See also: Finance, Actuarial, Consulting.*

Actuarial (p. 466) includes actuaries, statisticians, statistical process control (SPC) personnel, biostatisticians, epidemiologists and other positions requiring actuarial or statistical training. *See also: Insurance, Quality Control.*

Administrative (p. 467) includes executive assistants, office managers, secretarial staff, call centre personnel, data entry staff, receptionists, collectors and clerks.

Advertising (p. 473) includes creative directors, advertising managers, media buyers, copy writers and advertising sales representatives. *See also: Graphic Arts, Public Relations, Marketing, Publishing/Media.*

Aerospace (p. 474) includes aerospace engineers, propulsion engineers, avionics technicians, aircraft maintenance engineers, simulator engineers, airport managers, airworthiness inspectors, pilots and airline staff. *See also: Engineering, Transport, Trades/Technicians.*

Agriculture/Fisheries (p. 475) includes agricultural scientists, agronomists, botanists, veterinarians, crop insurance managers, feed sales personnel, farm equipment personnel and farm managers. *See also: Biotech/Biology, Scientific.*

Apparel (p. 475) includes buyers, designers and marketers of clothing and footwear. *See also: Retail, Design.*

Architecture (p. 476) includes architects, architectural technologists, interior designers, landscape architects and structural technologists. *See also: Construction, Real Estate, Design, Trades/Technicians.*

Arts & Culture (p. 477) includes anyone working for a museum, gallery, theatre company, orchestra or other cultural organization. *See also: Govt./Nonprofit, Hospitality, Public Relations.*

Automotive (p. 477) includes automotive engineers, designers and technologists, tooling engineers, leasing managers, parts managers, service managers, car rental managers, warranty administrators and dealership staff. *See also: Engineering, Transport, Trades/Technicians.*

Banking (p. 478) includes anyone working for a bank, credit union or trust company, including branch managers, loan officers, mortgage specialists, private banking representatives, credit analysts, RRSP administrators and customer service representatives. *See also: Finance, Insurance, Accounting.*

Bilingual (p. 478) includes translators, interpreters and other positions where the ability to speak a second language is a principal requirement of the position. *See also: International, Education, Administrative.*

Biotech/Biology (p. 480) includes biologists, biomedical engineers, biotechnology developers, biological scientists and other positions relating to the commercial development of biological, life sciences and genetic technologies. *See also: Pharmaceutical, Scientific, Health/Medical.*

Computing (p. 481) includes programmers, analysts, software developers, hardware engineers, MIS directors, CIOs, LAN administrators, database administrators, software testers, technical support personnel, quality control positions requiring knowledge of software applications and other information technology positions. *See also: Multimedia, Engineering, Telecom, Design.*

Construction (p. 489) includes project managers, site supervisors, surveyors, occupational health and safety inspectors, building inspectors, builders and other personnel required for construction projects. Also includes salespeople for building supplies. *See also: Real Estate, Architecture, Trades/Technicians.*

Consulting (p. 491) includes management consultants, policy advisors and personnel working for management consulting firms. Does not include consulting and contract positions in information technology, which are listed under "Computing". *See also: Management, Computing, Human Resource, Govt./Nonprofit.*

Design (p. 491) includes positions requiring a creative or artistic component such as draftspersons, designers, product designers, circuit designers, electrical designers, mechanical designers, design technicians and technologist positions requiring specialized CAD, AUTOCad or ProEngineer training. *See also: Architects, Engineering, Graphic Arts, Publishing/Media.*

Direct Mktng. (p. 493) includes direct mail managers, call centre supervisors, telemarketing managers and all senior positions that involve marketing by direct mail, telephone, television (infomercials), fax or email. Does not include call centre representatives, which are included in "Administrative". *See also: Sales, Marketing, Advertising, Graphic Arts, Printing.*

Disabled (p. 494) includes all positions working with physically or mentally challenged people. *See also: Health/Medical, Education, Govt./Nonprofit.*

Education (p. 495) includes teachers, principals, instructors, superintendents, school inspectors, professors, deans, education directors, ESL teachers, ECE (early childhood education) positions, admission directors and administrative positions at schools, universities and colleges. Does not include training positions, which are listed under "Human Resource". *See also: Librarians, Govt./Nonprofit.*

Engineering (p. 497) includes electrical engineers, mechanical engineers, structural engineers, civil engineers, chemical engineers, packaging engineers, engineering managers and other positions requiring a university engineering degree or membership in a provincial engineering association. Does not include engineering technologists and non-university trained engineers (see "Trades/Technicians") or software engineers (see "Computing"). *See also: Aerospace, Automotive, Design, Quality Control, Telecom.*

Environmental (p. 501) includes environmental compliance specialists, environmental engineers, hydrogeologists, wastewater technicians, environmental technicians, pollution control officers, conservation officers. *See also: Engineering, Agriculture/Fisheries, Govt/Nonprofit.*

Finance (p. 502) includes finance directors, CFOs, treasurers, budget directors, financial analysts, investment bankers, investment advisors, credit managers, collection managers, economists, stockbrokers, traders, securities regulators, compliance officers, portfolio managers, mutual fund administrators and any position requiring a CFA or completion of a securities course. *See also: Accounting, Banking.*

Forestry (p. 506) includes foresters, lumber traders, forest practices officers, arborists and other positions relating to tree planting, harvesting and sawmills. Does not include positions in papermaking, which are listed separately under "Pulp & Paper". *See also: Pulp & Paper, Govt./Nonprofit.*

Franchising (p. 507) includes franchise recruiters, territory managers and all other positions involved in developing new retail franchises. Does not include positions in franchisees' stores, which are listed separately under "Retail". *See also: Retail, Hospitality, Real Estate.*

Geology/Geography (p. 507) includes geologists, geophysicists, geodesists, geotechnical engineers, geological technicans and GIS personnel. *See also: Mining, Oil & Gas, Engineering, Scientific.*

Govt./Nonprofit (p. 508) includes deputy ministers, executive directors of nonprofit organizations, town administrators, city planners, economic development officers, fundraisers and other positions working for government bodies, charities or nonprofit organizations. Does not include healthcare positions, which are listed under "Health/Medical", or arts opportunities, which are listed under "Arts & Culture". *See also: Education, Health/Medical, International, Arts & Culture.*

Graphic Arts (p. 510) includes artists, graphic designers, creative directors, art directors, illustrators, medical illustrators, Mac artists, prepress operators, imaging technicians and other positions requiring knowledge of graphic design software such as QuarkXpress, Photoshop, Illustrator or PageMaker. Does not include website designers, which are listed separately under "Multimedia". *See also: Multimedia, Printing, Advertising, Publishing/Media, Packaging.*

Health/Medical (p. 511) includes nurses, therapists, medical doctors, health officers, hospital administrators, physiotherapists, rehabilitation counsellors, occupational therapists, kinesiologists, anaesthesiologists, ultrasound technicians, epidemiologists, dietitians, ophthalmologists, dentists, dental hygienists, pathologists, psychologists, psychiatrists, mental health workers, social workers, health data analysts, medical sales representatives, nursing assistants, medical technologists and medical secretaries. *See also: Pharmaceutical, Biotech/Biology, Govt./Nonprofit.*

Hospitality (p. 516) includes anyone working in the tourism, foodservice, entertainment or travel industries, including hotel managers, catering managers, film theater managers, travel agents, lodge and resort managers, fitness club staff, chefs, food and beverage directors, vending salespeople, nightclub managers and restaurant managers. *See also: Retail, Franchising, Govt./Nonprofit.*

Human Resource (p. 517) includes human resource managers, personnel managers, compensation and benefits specialists, labour relations officers, HRIS specialists, pension administrators, payroll officers, career counsellors, outplacement consultants, employee development personnel, trainers, recruiters, executive search staff. *See also: Public Relations.*

Insurance (p. 522) includes underwriters, adjusters, brokers, risk management professionals, treaty negotiators, claims supervisors, WCB claims personnel, investigators and insurance sales representatives. *See also: Actuarial, Banking, Govt./Nonprofit.*

International (p. 523) includes positions based outside Canada or requiring significant international experience, foreign language skills or travel outside Canada. *See also: Consulting, Oil & Gas, Govt./Nonprofit, Bilingual.*

Law (p. 523) includes lawyers, prosecutors, general counsel positions, in-house lawyers and corporate secretaries, barristers and solicitors, judges, arbitrators, mediators, law professors, patent and trade mark agents, law office administrators, articling clerks, paralegals, legal secretaries, court reporters, police officers, correctional officers and law enforcement personnel. *See also: Govt./Nonprofit.*

Librarians (p. 526) includes librarians, archivists and health record technicians. *See also: Education, Health/Medical.*

Logistics (p. 527) includes material managers, distribution managers, inventory supervisors, traffic managers, material resource planning (MRP) specialists, Crown assets disposal agents, production schedulers, supply chain managers, order administrators, shippers, customs brokers, import/export staff and warehouse supervisors. *See also: Purchasing, Transport, Operations, Actuarial.*

Management (p. 530) includes executive and managerial positions not otherwise classified including presidents, CEOs, managing directors, vice-presidents, general managers. Managerial positions in particular occupations are listed under the occupation (e.g. a Vice President of Marketing would be found under "Marketing" not "Management"). *See also: Consulting.*

Marketing (p. 530) includes positions where there is rarely any contact with customers such as marketing managers, product managers, brand managers, marketing analysts, merchandisers, competitive analysts and market researchers. *See also: Sales, Direct Mktng., Advertising, Public Relations.*

Metals (p. 533) includes metallurgists, metallurgical engineers, metal traders, foundry supervisors, metallurgical technologists, metal fabricators, sheet metal personnel and metal stamping staff. *See also: Mining, Trades/Technicians, Automotive.*

Mining (p. 533) includes mine superintendents, prospectors, underground shift bosses, mine inspectors and all positions requiring specialized knowledge of mines and minerals. *See also: Geology/Geography, Metals, Oil & Gas, Engineering.*

Multimedia (p. 533) includes positions requiring a creative or artistic component such as website designers, webmasters, Internet content developers, new media specialists, audio visual technicians, CD-ROM designers, HTML programmers and games programmers. *See also: Graphic Arts, Computing, Publishing/Media, Printing.*

Oil & Gas (p. 535) includes exploration engineers, drilling engineers, reservoir engineers, pipeline engineers, petroleum chemists, crude oil marketing analysts, gas marketing specialists, oil and gas traders, gas plant personnel and wellhead operators. *See also: Geology/Geography, Engineering, International, Trades/Technicians.*

Operations (p. 536) includes plant managers, operations managers, production managers, manufacturing managers, shift supervisors, maintenance supervisors, line supervisors and production-related technologists. *See also: Logistics, Quality Control, Trades/Technicians.*

Packaging (p. 538) includes positions in the packaging industry, including packaging engineers, label designers, packaging line supervisors, pressmen, label machine operators, box specialists and packaging technicians. *See also: Graphic Arts, Printing, Trades/Technicians.*

Pharmaceutical (p. 539) includes pharmacists, pharmaceutical sales representatives, medicinal chemists, clinical trial administrators, toxicology study managers, clinical research associates, regulatory affairs specialists and drug approval officers. Does not include pure research positions (see "Scientific") or life science opportunities outside the drug industry (see "Biotech/Biology"). *See also: Biotech/Biology, Health/Medical, Scientific.*

Plastics (p. 540) includes all positions in the plastics industry, including plant managers, project engineers, line managers, injection molding personnel, mold makers, fixture builders and plastics traders. *See also: Operations, Engineering, Trades/Technicians.*

Printing (p. 540) includes all positions in the printing industry, including plant managers, press operators, pre-press printers, printing sales representatives and bindery operators. *See also: Publishing/Media, Graphic Arts, Packaging, Trades/Technicians.*

Public Relations (p. 540) includes public relations officers, communications managers, media relations managers, public affairs managers, community relations officers, corporate writers, lobbyists and government affairs consultants. *See also: Advertising, Marketing, Govt./Nonprofit.*

Publishing/Media (p. 542) includes publishers, writers, editors, journalists, reporters, publication managers, editorial assistants, technical writers and copy writers. *See also: Printing, Multimedia, Graphic Arts, Advertising.*

Pulp & Paper (p. 544) includes all positions in the papermaking industry, including pulp mill managers, woodyard superintendents, pulp chemists, pulp line personnel, pulp sales representatives, pulp transport specialists, paper mill supervisors and paper sales personnel. *See also: Forestry, Printing, Engineering.*

Purchasing (p. 544) includes purchasing managers, buyers, purchasing agents, procurement managers, contract administrators, estimators, quotation administrators, commodity traders, category managers and any position requiring a Certified Professional Purchaser (CPP) designation or completion of the PMAC course. *See also: Logistics, Operations.*

Quality Control (p. 546) includes quality engineers, quality auditors, statistical process control (SPC) coordinators, test engineers, reliability managers, quality assurance technicians, TQM consultants, continuous improvement coordinators, testers and ISO 9000 inspectors. *See also: Actuarial, Logistics, Operations, Engineering.*

Real Estate (p. 548) includes leasing managers, land development engineers, land administrators, facilities managers, landmen, real estate agents, brokers, new home sales representatives, rental agents, zoning inspectors, shopping mall managers, property managers, building maintenance managers, superintendents, building security staff and space planners. *See also: Construction, Franchising, Architecture.*

Religious (p. 550) includes chaplains, clergy, ministers, pastoral care workers and religious educators. *See also: Education.*

Retail (p. 550) includes store managers, retail analysts, store planners, loss prevention specialists, assistant managers, management trainees and store sales associates. *See also: Sales, Franchising, Apparel, Hospitality.*

Sales (p. 552) includes positions where there is direct contact with the customer, such as sales managers, account executives, area supervisors, territory managers, sales representatives and customer service representatives. *See also: Marketing, Direct Mktng.*

Scientific (p. 556) includes scientists, chemists, research associates, anthropologists, physicists, ecologists, regulatory affairs associates, laboratory managers and any position requiring a BSc, MSc or PhD in science. *See also: Biotech/Biology, Pharmaceutical, Health/Medical.*

Telecom (p. 557) includes network managers, telecommunications engineers, telephony analysts, switch technicians, network engineers, WAP engineers, SONET software engineers, fibre optic engineers and technicians, network support analysts, TCP/IP engineers and ATM/Frame Relay engineers. *See also: Engineering, Computing, Trades/Technicians.*

Trade Shows (p. 559) includes trade show managers, exhibit sales representatives, exhibit designers, convention organizers, exposition staff and conference producers. *See also: Marketing, Sales, Hospitality.*

Trades/Technicians (p. 559) includes millwrights, stationary engineers, mechanics, tool and die makers, electricians, welders, machinists and other skilled trades requiring an apprentice, journeyman or master tradesman designation. Also includes technologists, technicians and technical staff with associate's and community college diplomas. Does not include university-trained engineers, which are listed under "Engineering". *See also: Operations, Engineering.*

Transport (p. 564) includes transportation managers, transit planners, highway planners and designers, transport analysts, traffic study engineers, marine engineers, terminal managers, fleet managers, rail traffic coordinators, dispatchers, tractor-trailer drivers, coach drivers, ship's pilots and AZ drivers. *See also: Logistics, Operations, Aerospace, Automotive.*

OCCUPATIONAL INDEX

ACCOUNTING

See also: Finance, Actuarial, Consulting.

Ministry of Finance, ON (16 positions) .... Oshawa ON
AltaGas Services Inc. (14) .... Calgary AB
Alberta Finance (12) .... Edmonton AB
Ministry of Finance, BC (11) .... Victoria BC
Magna International Inc. (10) .... Concord ON
Management Board Secretariat (10) .... Toronto ON
ENMAX Corporation (9) .... Calgary AB
Famous Players Inc. (9) .... Toronto ON
Manitoba Finance (9) .... Winnipeg MB
PanCanadian Petroleum Ltd. (9) .... Calgary AB
PrimeWest Energy Trust (9) .... Calgary AB
ABC Group Inc. (7) .... Toronto ON
Burlington Resources Canada Energy Ltd. (7) .... Calgary AB
Cirque du Soleil (7) .... Montréal QC
Alberta Energy Company Ltd. / AEC (6) .... Calgary AB
Group Telecom (6) .... Toronto ON
Kohl & Frisch Limited (6) .... Concord ON
Royal Bank Financial Group (6) .... Toronto ON
Alberta Energy Company Ltd. / AEC (5) .... Calgary AB
DSC Group of Companies (5) .... Concord ON
Ganz (5) .... Woodbridge ON
Hudson & Company (5) .... Calgary AB
IBM Canada Ltd. (5) .... Markham ON
Morrison Hershfield (5) .... Toronto ON
Office of the Auditor General of Canada (5) .... Ottawa ON
Profit Recovery Group Canada, Inc. / P (5) .... Cambridge ON
TELAV Audio Visual Services (5) .... Lachine QC
AIG Life of Canada (4) .... Toronto ON
Aramark Canada Ltd. (4) .... Toronto ON
Auditor General of Alberta (4) .... Edmonton AB
Canadian 88 Energy Corp. (4) .... Calgary AB
Global Thermoelectric Inc. (4) .... Calgary AB
Grant Emblems Ltd. (4) .... Toronto ON
Ingram Micro Inc. (Canada) (4) .... Mississauga ON
ISH Energy Ltd. (4) .... Calgary AB
MacDonald Dettwiler & Associates Ltd. / (4) .... Richmond BC
Manitoba Justice / Culture, Heritage an (4) .... Winnipeg MB
Ministry of Health and Long-Term Care, O (4) .... Toronto ON
Mount Royal College (4) .... Calgary AB
Multiview Inc. (4) .... Ottawa ON
NexInnovations (4) .... Mississauga ON
O&Y Enterprise (4) .... Toronto ON
Optimal Robotics Corp. (4) .... Montréal QC
OZ Optics Ltd. (4) .... Carp ON
ReserveAmerica (4) .... Milton ON
Schneider Foods Inc. (4) .... Kitchener ON
Shred-it (4) .... Oakville ON
Siemens Canada Ltd. (4) .... Mississauga ON
Soberman Isenbaum & Colomby LLP (4) .... Toronto ON
Standard Life Assurance Company, The (4) .... Montréal QC
Suncor Energy Inc., Oil Sands (4) .... Fort McMurray AB
SureFire Commerce Inc. (4) .... Westmount QC
Tracer Industries Canada Ltd. (4) .... Edmonton AB
University of Calgary (4) .... Calgary AB
University of Toronto (4) .... Toronto ON
Westfair Foods Ltd. (4) .... Calgary AB
ADP Canada (3) .... Toronto ON
Alberta Health and Wellness (3) .... Edmonton AB
Alberta Justice (3) .... Edmonton AB
Axia NetMedia Corporation (3) .... Calgary AB
Bird On a Wire Networks / BOAW (3) .... Mississauga ON
Canadian Bank Note Company, Ltd. (3) .... Ottawa ON
Creation Technologies Inc. (3) .... Burnaby BC
Department of Human Resources, Nunavut (3) .... Iqaluit NU
Discount Car and Truck Rentals (3) .... Toronto ON
Enron Canada Corp. (3) .... Calgary AB
Extendicare (Canada) Inc. (3) .... Markham ON
Gas & Oil Accounting Ltd. (3) .... Calgary AB
Groupe Dynamite Inc. (3) .... Mount Royal QC
Guelph General Hospital (3) .... Guelph ON
Hamilton Health Sciences Corporation, C (3) .... Hamilton ON
Hayden Group, The (3) .... Richmond BC
Honda of Canada Manufacturing (3) .... Alliston ON
Hydrogenics Corporation (3) .... Mississauga ON
Import Auto Leasing (3) .... Gloucester ON
Intuit GreenPoint (3) .... Calgary AB
Law Society of Upper Canada, The / LSUC (3) .... Toronto ON
Le Chateau (3) .... Mount Royal QC
Liquor Distribution Branch, BC / LDB (3) .... Vancouver BC
M.H. Shaikh Professional Corporation (3) .... Calgary AB
McElhanney Group Ltd., The (3) .... Vancouver BC
Medicine Hat, City of (3) .... Medicine Hat AB
Miller Thomson LLP (3) .... Toronto ON
Ministry of Finance, Ontario (3) .... Toronto ON
Ministry of the Attorney General, Ontari (3) .... Toronto ON
Mount Sinai Hospital (3) .... Toronto ON
Oakrun Farm Bakery Ltd. (3) .... Ancaster ON
Optech Inc. (3) .... Toronto ON
Research in Motion Limited / RIM (3) .... Waterloo ON
Rogers AT&T Wireless (3) .... Toronto ON
Samtack (3) .... Toronto ON
Shopping Channel, The / TSC (3) .... Toronto ON
Silex Design Inc. (3) .... Mississauga ON
Staples Business Depot Ltd. (3) .... Markham ON
State Street Canada (3) .... Montréal QC
TaxSave Consultants Limited (3) .... Toronto ON
Tri-ad Graphic Communications Ltd. (3) .... Toronto ON
Vancouver International Airport Authori (3) .... Richmond BC
Vertefeuille Kassam (3) .... Calgary AB
Webplan Inc. (3) .... Ottawa ON
Zurich Canada (3) .... Toronto ON
ACD Systems (2) .... Saanichton BC
Allcan Electronic Distributors (2) .... Edmonton AB
Alliance Atlantis Communications Inc. (2) .... Toronto ON
Allied Oil & Gas Corp. (2) .... Calgary AB
APW Enclosure Systems (2) .... Milton ON
Ash City (2) .... Toronto ON
Athletic Image (2) .... Montréal QC
Balmer Plaster Moulding Corporation of A (2) .... Toronto ON
Bank of China (Canada) (2) .... Toronto ON
Bazaar & Novelty (2) .... St. Catharines ON
BDO Dunwoody LLP (2) .... Calgary AB
BDO Dunwoody LLP (2) .... Orillia ON
BDO Dunwoody LLP (2) .... Kingston ON
Bell Intrigna (2) .... Calgary AB
Bentall Corporation (2) .... Vancouver BC
BNT Products (2) .... Mississauga ON
Bombardier Aerospace (2) .... Montréal QC
BouClair Inc. (2) .... Dorval QC
Boulevard Media (Canada) Inc. / BMC (2) .... Vancouver BC
Brantford, Corporation of the City of (2) .... Brantford ON
Bulk Barn Foods Ltd. (2) .... Richmond Hill ON
Burlington, City of (2) .... Burlington ON
C-MAC Industries Inc. (2) .... Kanata ON
Cadesky and Associates (2) .... Toronto ON
Canada Customs and Revenue Agency / CCRA (2) .... Toronto ON
Canada Customs and Revenue Agency, Sa (2) .... Saint John NB
Canada Life Assurance Company (2) .... Toronto ON
Canadian Copyright Licensing Agency / CA (2) .... Toronto ON
Canadian Depository for Securities Ltd. (2) .... Toronto ON
Canadian Mass Media Inc. (2) .... Toronto ON
Canam Manac Group Inc., The (2) .... Boucherville QC
CanRoof Corporation Inc. (2) .... Toronto ON
CaseWare International Inc. (2) .... Toronto ON
Chemque Inc. (2) .... Toronto ON
Civil Service Co-operative Credit Society (2) .... Ottawa ON
Claridge Homes (2) .... Ottawa ON
Clark, Wilson (2) .... Vancouver BC
Colt Engineering Corporation (2) .... Calgary AB
Com-Net Ericsson (2) .... Mississauga ON
Computing Devices Canada Ltd. / CDC (2) .... Calgary AB
CPI Canada Inc. (2) .... Georgetown ON
Cypress Energy Inc. (2) .... Calgary AB
Delmar International Inc. (2) .... Lachine QC
Deloitte Consulting (2) .... Toronto ON
Deloitte & Touche (2) .... Edmonton AB
Deloitte & Touche (2) .... Toronto ON
Department of Executive, NWT (2) .... Yellowknife NT
Distican Inc. (2) .... Richmond Hill ON
Dominion Colour Corporation (2) .... Toronto ON
Dumex Medical (2) .... Toronto ON
Ellis, Govenlock LLP (2) .... Edmonton AB
Enbridge Pipelines Inc. (2) .... Edmonton AB

ACCOUNTING (Cont.)

Enersul Inc. (2) .... Calgary AB
Entourage Technology Solutions (2) .... Mississauga ON
EPCOR Utilities Inc. (2) .... Edmonton AB
Epic Data Inc. (2) .... Richmond BC
Evertz Microsystems Ltd. (2) .... Burlington ON
Falconbridge Ltd. (2) .... Toronto ON
Fidelity Investments Canada Limited (2) .... Toronto ON
Fincentric Corp. (2) .... Richmond BC
Fisher & Ludlow (2) .... Burlington ON
Flint Energy Services Ltd. (2) .... Edmonton AB
Forest Practices Board (2) .... Victoria BC
Forzani Group Ltd., The (2) .... Calgary AB
Franklin Templeton Investments (2) .... Toronto ON
Future Shop Ltd. (2) .... Burnaby BC
GE Industrial Systems / GEINDSYS (2) .... Markham ON
Glen Corporation (2) .... Toronto ON
Golf-Gig Management Systems Internationa (2) .... Calgary AB
Greenwin Property Management Inc. (2) .... Toronto ON
GTR Group Inc. (2) .... Brampton ON
Guvernment, The (2) .... Toronto ON
Hardt Equipment Manufacturing Inc. (2) .... Lachine QC
Hartford Fibres Ltd. (2) .... Kingston ON
Hertz Equipment Rental (2) .... Toronto ON
Hilton Montreal Aeroport (2) .... Dorval QC
Horn Plastics Inc. (2) .... Whitby ON
Hospital Employees' Union / HEU (2) .... Vancouver BC
Husky Injection Molding Systems Ltd. (2) .... Bolton ON
I-XL Industries Ltd. (2) .... Medicine Hat AB
IKO Industries Ltd. (2) .... Toronto ON
IKO Industries Ltd. (2) .... Brampton ON
Inner-Tec Security Services (2) .... Vancouver BC
Insight Canada Inc. (2) .... Montréal QC
Instantel Inc. (2) .... Kanata ON
Insurance Corporation of BC / IC (2) .... North Vancouver BC
Investment Dealers Association of Canada (2) .... Toronto ON
IPC Resistors Inc. (2) .... Mississauga ON
Ivanhoe Cambridge (2) .... Toronto ON
Jacques Whitford Environment Ltd. (2) .... Burnaby BC
Janes Family Foods Ltd. (2) .... Toronto ON
Joseph Brant Memorial Hospital (2) .... Burlington ON
Keanall Industries Inc. (2) .... Mississauga ON
King Packaged Materials Company (2) .... Burlington ON
Legislative Assembly of Ontario, Office (2) .... Toronto ON
Lippman Leebosh April (2) .... Montréal QC
Liquor Control Board of Ontario / LCBO (2) .... Toronto ON
MacKay & Partners (2) .... Edmonton AB
Mackenzie Financial Corporation (2) .... Toronto ON
Main Knitting Inc. (2) .... Montréal QC
Maple Leaf Consumer Foods (2) .... Mississauga ON
MDS Aero Support Corporation (2) .... Ottawa ON
Meota Resources Corp. (2) .... Calgary AB
Meritor Suspension Systems Company (2) .... Milton ON
Milton, Town of (2) .... Milton ON
Mobilia Inc. (2) .... Pointe-Claire QC
Morrison Homes (2) .... Calgary AB
MTW Solutions Online Inc. (2) .... Toronto ON
Murphy Oil Company Ltd. (2) .... Calgary AB
Nanaimo, City of (2) .... Nanaimo BC
Net Safety Monitoring Inc. (2) .... Calgary AB
North York General Hospital (2) .... Toronto ON
Northgate Exploration Ltd., Kemess Mine (2) .... Smithers BC
Olson Lemons (2) .... Calgary AB
OnCommand Canada Inc. (2) .... Brampton ON
Ontario Lottery and Gaming Corp (2) .... Sault Ste. Marie ON
Overseas Express Consolidators Inc. / O (2) .... Montréal QC
PACCAR Inc. (2) .... Mississauga ON
Pacific National Aquaculture (2) .... Victoria BC
Paging Network of Canada, Inc. / PageNet (2) .... Toronto ON
Panalpina Inc. (2) .... Mississauga ON
Pengrowth Management Ltd. / PML (2) .... Calgary AB
Penn West Petroleum Ltd. (2) .... Calgary AB
Pet Valu Canada Inc. (2) .... Markham ON
Pizza Pizza Limited (2) .... Toronto ON
Positron Public Safety Systems Inc. (2) .... Montréal QC
PricewaterhouseCoopers, Business Process (2) .... Calgary AB
Private Recipes Ltd. (2) .... Brampton ON
Provincial Auditor of Ontario, Office of (2) .... Toronto ON
Provincial Auditor's Office, Manitoba (2) .... Winnipeg MB

PTI Group Inc. (2) .... Edmonton AB
Public Service Commission of Canada, New (2) .... Moncton NB
Public Service Commission of Canada, Onta (2) .... Ottawa ON
Public Service Commission, PEI (2) .... Charlottetown PE
Purcell Energy Ltd. (2) .... Calgary AB
Raven Tours (2) .... Yellowknife NT
Red Carpet Food Services (2) .... Toronto ON
Rogers Media, Publishing (2) .... Toronto ON
Rogers Video (2) .... Richmond BC
RSL COM Canada Inc. (2) .... Vancouver BC
Sacks Partnership, The (2) .... Toronto ON
Sanjel Corporation (2) .... Calgary AB
Scintrex Trace Corp. (2) .... Ottawa ON
Shaw Pipe Protection Ltd. (2) .... Calgary AB
Skyservice Airlines Inc. (2) .... Mississauga ON
Smith Cageorge Perry (2) .... Calgary AB
Sniderman, Dykstra & Ford (2) .... Burlington ON
Standens Limited (2) .... Calgary AB
Stantec Geomatics Ltd. (2) .... Edmonton AB
Steeplejack Services Group (2) .... Edmonton AB
Stuart Olson Construction (2) .... Calgary AB
Sun Life Financial (2) .... Toronto ON
Sun Life Financial (2) .... Montréal QC
Suncor Energy Inc. (2) .... Calgary AB
Times Fiber Canada Limited (2) .... Renfrew ON
TLC Laser Eye Centers (2) .... Mississauga ON
Tolko Industries Ltd. (2) .... Vernon BC
Toronto Blue Jays Baseball Club (2) .... Toronto ON
Toronto Transit Commission / TTC (2) .... Toronto ON
Trader.com (2) .... Edmonton AB
Trail Appliances Ltd. (2) .... Richmond BC
Trail Appliances Ltd. (2) .... Calgary AB
Tribal Sportswear Inc. (2) .... Montréal QC
Trican Well Service Ltd. (2) .... Calgary AB
UMA Engineering Ltd. (2) .... Edmonton AB
University College of the Fraser Vall (2) .... Abbotsford BC
Urbandale Corporation (2) .... Ottawa ON
Welch & Company (2) .... Ottawa ON
Werner Haag (2) .... Calgary AB
Westin Resort & Spa, The (2) .... Whistler BC
Wheeltronic Ltd. (2) .... Mississauga ON
Wilton Industries Canada Ltd. (2) .... Toronto ON
Xentel DM Inc. (2) .... Toronto ON
Yaskawa Motoman Canada Ltd. (2) .... Mississauga ON
724 Solutions Inc. (1) .... Toronto ON
ACI Automatic Cutting Inc. (1) .... Burlington ON
Administrative Assistants Ltd. / AAL (1) .... Burlington ON
AGF Management Ltd. (1) .... Toronto ON
AIC Ltd. (1) .... Burlington ON
Ailes de la Mode, Les (1) .... Laval QC
Air Transat Holidays (1) .... Montréal QC
Aird & Berlis (1) .... Toronto ON
Alberta Agriculture, Food & Rural Devel (1) .... Edmonton AB
Alberta Community Development (1) .... Edmonton AB
Alberta Corporate Service Centre (1) .... Coaldale AB
Alberta Corporate Services Centre (1) .... Edmonton AB
Alberta Environment (1) .... Calgary AB
Alberta Government Services (1) .... Edmonton AB
Alberta Human Resources and Employm (1) .... Lac La Biche AB
Alberta Innovation & Science (1) .... Edmonton AB
Alberta Mental Health Board, Alberta Ho (1) .... Edmonton AB
Alberta Mental Health Board, Alberta Hosp (1) .... Ponoka AB
Alberta Municipal Affairs (1) .... Edmonton AB
Alcan Primary Metal Group (1) .... Kitimat BC
Aldata Software Management Inc. (1) .... Hinton AB
Alfa Laval Canada (1) .... Toronto ON
All Weather Windows (1) .... Edmonton AB
Alliance Steel Corp. (1) .... Laval QC
Altera Corp. (1) .... Toronto ON
Alterna Technologies Group Inc. (1) .... Calgary AB
AMC Group of Companies (1) .... Calgary AB
AMEC Earth & Environmental Ltd. (1) .... Edmonton AB
AMEC Infrastructure Ltd. (1) .... Sherwood Park AB
Amusement Leisure Worldwide (1) .... Calgary AB
AnorMED Inc. (1) .... Langley BC
API Construction Ltd. (1) .... North Vancouver BC
Apollo Microwaves Ltd. (1) .... Pointe-Claire QC
Arc'Teryx Equipment Inc. (1) .... Burnaby BC
ASA Alloys (1) .... Toronto ON
Aspen Regional Health Authority No. 11 (1) .... Westlock AB
Assante Advisory Services (1) .... Toronto ON
AstraZeneca (1) .... Mississauga ON

For descriptions of the occupational categories used in this index, see page 458.

OCCUPATIONAL INDEX 463

ACCOUNTING (Cont.)

AT&T Canada (1) .... Toronto ON
AT&T Canada (1) .... Toronto ON
ATCO Structures Inc. (1) .... Calgary AB
Atlas Cold Storage Canada Ltd. (1) .... Toronto ON
Audio Centre (1) .... St-Laurent QC
Avestin Inc. (1) .... Ottawa ON
Avmax Group Inc. (1) .... Calgary AB
B.C. Decker Inc. (1) .... Hamilton ON
Ballard Power Systems Inc. (1) .... Burnaby BC
Bantrel Inc. (1) .... Calgary AB
BASF Canada Inc. (1) .... Toronto ON
Bath Fitter / Bain Magique (1) .... St-Eustache QC
Baymag (1) .... Calgary AB
BC Ferry Corporation (1) .... Victoria BC
BC Rapid Transit Co. Ltd. / BCRTC (1) .... Burnaby BC
BC Research Inc. (1) .... Vancouver BC
BDO Dunwoody LLP (1) .... Toronto ON
Bell Canada (1) .... Toronto ON
Bell Helicopter Textron Canada (1) .... Mirabel QC
Bettis Canada Ltd. (1) .... Edmonton AB
Bird Construction Company (1) .... Richmond BC
BMW Canbec (1) .... Montréal QC
Boulevard Club, The (1) .... Toronto ON
Brampton, City of (1) .... Brampton ON
Brenntag Canada Inc. (1) .... Toronto ON
Bridge Brand Food Services Ltd. (1) .... Calgary AB
British Columbia Securities Commission (1) .... Vancouver BC
Brookfield LePage Johnson Controls Facili (1) .... Ottawa ON
Buckman Laboratories (1) .... Vaudreuil QC
Bulldog Group Inc., The (1) .... Toronto ON
Burntsand Inc. (1) .... Toronto ON
Business Development Bank of Canada / B (1) .... Montréal QC
Cadillac Fairview Corporation Limited, T (1) .... Toronto ON
CAE Machinery Ltd. (1) .... Vancouver BC
Calgary, City of (1) .... Calgary AB
Calgary Co-operative Association Ltd. (1) .... Calgary AB
Calgary Laboratory Services / CLS (1) .... Calgary AB
Camco Inc. (1) .... Hamilton ON
Campbell Ford Sales Ltd. (1) .... Ottawa ON
Canada 3000 Cargo Inc. (1) .... Mississauga ON
Canada Bread Company Ltd. (1) .... Concord ON
Canada Customs and Revenue Agency / CCRA (1) .... Calgary AB
Canadian Inovatech Inc. (1) .... Abbotsford BC
Canadian Medical Protective Association / (1) .... Ottawa ON
Canadian Natural Resources Limited / CNR (1) .... Calgary AB
Canadian Recreation Products Inc. (1) .... Mount Royal QC
Canadian Survey Equipment Ltd. / Cansel (1) .... Burnaby BC
Canadian Western Bank (1) .... Edmonton AB
Canlight Group (1) .... Toronto ON
Carmanah Technologies Inc. (1) .... Victoria BC
CCH Canadian Ltd. (1) .... Toronto ON
CCI Industries Ltd. (1) .... St. Albert AB
CDA Industries Inc. (1) .... Pickering ON
Cedar Enterprise Solutions Inc. (1) .... Calgary AB
Celestica Inc. (1) .... Toronto ON
Center for Digital Imaging and Sound / C (1) .... Burnaby BC
Centis (Canada) Inc. (1) .... Montréal QC
Ceridian Canada Ltd. (1) .... Winnipeg MB
Certified General Accountants Associat (1) .... Vancouver BC
CGU Group Canada Ltd. (1) .... Toronto ON
Chalmers Suspensions International I (1) .... Mississauga ON
Chandos Construction Ltd. (1) .... Edmonton AB
Changepoint Corporation (1) .... Richmond Hill ON
Chapleau Health Services (1) .... Chapleau ON
Children's and Women's Health Centre o (1) .... Vancouver BC
Cinram International Inc. (1) .... Toronto ON
Cirque du Soleil (1) .... Montréal QC
Class Software Solutions Ltd. (1) .... Burnaby BC
Club Monaco International (1) .... Toronto ON
CMC Electronics Inc. (1) .... Kanata ON
CMC Electronics Inc. (1) .... St-Laurent QC
Coca-Cola Bottling Company (1) .... Calgary AB
Cognos Inc. (1) .... Ottawa ON
Collections Andrade Inc. (1) .... Montréal QC
Collega for Aveda (1) .... Toronto ON
Colt Engineering Corporation (1) .... Edmonton AB
Colt Engineering Corporation (1) .... Markham ON
Columbia House Canada (1) .... Toronto ON
Communications and Information Technology (1) .... Kanata ON
Community Living Mississauga (1) .... Mississauga ON
Comptec International Ltd. (1) .... Surrey BC
Concord Confections Inc. (1) .... Concord ON
Conestoga College of Applied Arts & Te (1) .... Kitchener ON
Consultronics Ltd. (1) .... Concord ON
Continental Electric Motor Services (No (1) .... Edmonton AB
Corel Corporation (1) .... Ottawa ON
Cowan Graphics Ltd. (1) .... Edmonton AB
CPI Plastics Group Ltd. (1) .... Mississauga ON
Crown Wallpaper + Fabrics (1) .... Toronto ON
Crystal Homes (1) .... Hamilton ON
CSA International (1) .... Toronto ON
CTC Communications Corp. (1) .... Mississauga ON
Cue Datawest Ltd. (1) .... Vancouver BC
CUMIS Group Ltd., The (1) .... Burlington ON
Cummins Inc. (1) .... Edmonton AB
Cymbolic Sciences Inc. (1) .... Richmond BC
DaimlerChrysler Canada Inc. (1) .... Windsor ON
Dairy Farmers of Ontario (1) .... Mississauga ON
Dairyworld Foods Inc. (1) .... Brampton ON
Dan Mulrooney Disposal Ltd. (1) .... Kingston ON
DataMirror Corporation (1) .... Markham ON
David Thompson Health Region, Red Deer (1) .... Red Deer AB
Dental Marketing Inc. (1) .... Vaughan ON
Department of Human Resources, Nuna (1) .... Rankin Inlet NU
Department of Justice, Nova Scotia (Corp (1) .... Halifax NS
Dex Brothers Clothing Ltd. (1) .... Montréal QC
Dimax Controls Inc. (1) .... Toronto ON
Direct Service Network Ltd. / DSN (1) .... Mississauga ON
Discover Communications Inc. (1) .... Brampton ON
DMR Consulting Inc. (1) .... Toronto ON
Dominion Construction Company Inc. (1) .... Calgary AB
Dominion Sample Ltd. (1) .... St-Leonard QC
Dorel Industries Inc. (1) .... Montréal QC
Downtown BMW (1) .... Toronto ON
Dueck Chevrolet Oldsmobile Cadillac Lt (1) .... Vancouver BC
Dufferin Construction Company (1) .... Oakville ON
Dundee Realty Management Corporation (1) .... Toronto ON
Duplium Corporation (1) .... Thornhill ON
DuPont Canada Inc. (1) .... Mississauga ON
Durham, The Regional Municipality of (1) .... Whitby ON
Dynamic Source Manufacturing Inc. (1) .... Calgary AB
Dynaplas Ltd. (1) .... Toronto ON
Eastside Dodge (1) .... Calgary AB
Electro Sonic Inc. (1) .... Toronto ON
EMI Music Canada (1) .... Mississauga ON
Encon Group Inc. (1) .... Ottawa ON
Energy Industries Inc. (1) .... Calgary AB
Enersource (1) .... Mississauga ON
Engage Energy Canada, LP (1) .... Calgary AB
EOTT Canada Ltd. (1) .... Calgary AB
Ernst & Young LLP (1) .... Toronto ON
Escents Aromatherapy (1) .... North Vancouver BC
Essentus Inc. (1) .... Montréal QC
Ethan Allen Home Interiors (1) .... Brampton ON
Evans Consoles Inc. (1) .... Calgary AB
Exchange Solutions / ESI (1) .... Toronto ON
EXI Wireless Systems Inc. (1) .... Richmond BC
Exocom Group Inc., The (1) .... Ottawa ON
Export Development Corporation / EDC (1) .... Ottawa ON
Extracomm Technologies Inc. (1) .... Toronto ON
Fairmont Chateau Lake Louise, The (1) .... Lake Louise AB
FAM Canada Inc. (1) .... Edmonton AB
Farah Foods / Hasty Market Corporation (1) .... Oakville ON
Fasken Martineau DuMoulin LLP (1) .... Toronto ON
Faurecia (1) .... Toronto ON
Ferrero Canada Ltd. (1) .... Toronto ON
Fersten Group (1) .... Montréal QC
Financial Transactions and Reports Analys (1) .... Ottawa ON
Fireco Inc. (1) .... Mississauga ON
First Canadian Title Company (1) .... Mississauga ON
First Cellular (1) .... Ottawa ON
Fluid Life Corp. (1) .... Edmonton AB
Fluor Canada Ltd. (1) .... Calgary AB
Footner Forest Products Ltd. (1) .... High Level AB
Fountain Tire (1) .... Edmonton AB
Four Seasons Moto-Sports (1) .... Fort McMurray AB
Foxboro Canada Inc. (1) .... Dollard-des-Ormeaux QC
Freud Westmore Tools Ltd. (1) .... Mississauga ON
Frozen Pond Inc. (1) .... Toronto ON
fSONA Communications Corp. (1) .... Richmond BC
Fugro Airborne Surveys (1) .... Mississauga ON

ACCOUNTING (Cont.)

Fugro Airborne Surveys (1) .... Ottawa ON
G&K Work Wear (1) .... Toronto ON
Galian Photonics Inc. (1) .... Vancouver BC
Gazette, The (1) .... Montréal QC
Gen-X Sports Inc. (1) .... Toronto ON
Geneka Biotechnology Inc. (1) .... Montréal QC
General Hydrogen / GH (1) .... Vancouver BC
General Paint Corp. (1) .... Vancouver BC
Gennum Corporation (1) .... Burlington ON
Geo Group, The (1) .... Toronto ON
George Brown College (1) .... Toronto ON
Gilmore Global Logistics Services / DocuL (1) .... Kanata ON
Girl Guides of Canada, British Columbi (1) .... Vancouver BC
GMB Industries (1) .... Mississauga ON
Goodyear Canada Inc. (1) .... Napanee ON
Grand River Poultry Farm Ltd. (1) .... Paris ON
Grant MacEwan College, Jasper Place Cam (1) .... Edmonton AB
Great Canadian Casinos Inc. (1) .... Richmond BC
Grenville Management Services (1) .... Toronto ON
Grocery Gateway (1) .... Mississauga ON
Halton, The Regional Municipality of (1) .... Oakville ON
Hamilton Hydro Inc. (1) .... Hamilton ON
Harvard Energy (1) .... Calgary AB
Healthcare Benefit Trust / HBT (1) .... Vancouver BC
Heidelberg Canada (1) .... Mississauga ON
Hellmuth, Obata & Kassabaum, Inc. / HOK (1) .... Toronto ON
Hemera Technologies Inc. (1) .... Hull QC
Henderson Development (Canada) Ltd. (1) .... Vancouver BC
Henry Birks & Sons Inc. (1) .... Montréal QC
Herbon Naturals, Inc. (1) .... Richmond BC
Heritage Park Historical Village (1) .... Calgary AB
Hi-Alta Capital Inc. (1) .... High River AB
Highland Farms Inc. (1) .... Toronto ON
Highwood Resources Ltd. (1) .... Calgary AB
Holiday Inn Burlington (1) .... Burlington ON
Home Trust Company (1) .... St. Catharines ON
Homestake Canada Inc., Eskay Creek Mine (1) .... Smithers BC
Homestead Land Holdings Ltd. (1) .... Ottawa ON
Hospital for Sick Children, The (1) .... Toronto ON
Hotel Inter-Continental Toronto (1) .... Toronto ON
HSBC Bank Canada (1) .... Vancouver BC
Huber + Suhner (Canada) Ltd. (1) .... Kanata ON
Hudson General Aviation Services Inc. (1) .... Richmond BC
Hunting Oilfield Services (1) .... Calgary AB
Hush Puppies Canada (1) .... St-Laurent QC
Hyd-Mech Group Ltd. (1) .... Woodstock ON
Hydro Ottawa (1) .... Ottawa ON
Hypertec Systems Inc. (1) .... St-Laurent QC
Hyprotech Ltd. (1) .... Calgary AB
i-STAT Canada Ltd. (1) .... Kanata ON
Ilco Unican Inc. (1) .... Montréal QC
Imperial Tobacco Canada Limited (1) .... Montréal QC
INA Canada Inc. (1) .... Oakville ON
Indeka Group, The (1) .... Oakville ON
Independent Order of Foresters / IOF (1) .... Toronto ON
Indigo Manufacturing Inc. (1) .... Markham ON
Inforetech Wireless Technology Inc. (1) .... Surrey BC
Infostream Technologies Inc. (1) .... Toronto ON
ING Bank of Canada / ING Direct (1) .... Toronto ON
Inland Aggregates Ltd. (1) .... Calgary AB
Inland Group (1) .... Edmonton AB
Inland Group (1) .... Calgary AB
Innovative Cooling Dynamics / STT Te (1) .... Mississauga ON
Institute for Clinical Evaluative Scienc (1) .... Toronto ON
Integrated Production Services Ltd. / IP (1) .... Calgary AB
Integrative Proteomics Inc. / IPI (1) .... Toronto ON
Interhome Furniture (1) .... Markham ON
International Language Schools of Canad (1) .... Montréal QC
Intuit Canada Limited (1) .... Edmonton AB
Investment Dealers Association of Cana (1) .... Vancouver BC
IR Security & Safety (1) .... Mississauga ON
Ivanhoe Cambridge (1) .... Montréal QC
J & J Display Sales Ltd. (1) .... Mississauga ON
Jacques Whitford Environment Ltd. (1) .... Calgary AB
Jacques Whitford Environment Ltd. (1) .... Halifax NS
Jayne Industries Inc. (1) .... Stoney Creek ON
Jazz Monkey Media (1) .... Toronto ON
JFB Technologies Inc. (1) .... Markham ON

Jim Peplinski's Leasemaster National (1) .... Toronto ON
JJM Group, The (1) .... Delta BC
John Bear Pontiac Buick Cadillac Ltd. (1) .... Hamilton ON
Johnson & Johnson Consumer Products Inc (1) .... Montréal QC
JP Metal America Inc. (1) .... Montréal QC
Kafko Manufacturing Ltd. (1) .... Mississauga ON
Kawneer Company Canada Ltd. (1) .... Toronto ON
Kenaidan Contracting Ltd. (1) .... Mississauga ON
Keyano College (1) .... Fort McMurray AB
Keybase Financial Group (1) .... Richmond Hill ON
Kids Can Press (1) .... Toronto ON
Kingston General Hospital (1) .... Kingston ON
Kitchen Stuff Plus (1) .... Toronto ON
Kobe Interior Products Inc. (1) .... Burlington ON
Kretschmar Inc. (1) .... Toronto ON
Kwantlen University College (1) .... Surrey BC
Labelad / Sandylion Sticker Designs (1) .... Markham ON
Lakehead University (1) .... Thunder Bay ON
Lantern Communications Canada Inc. (1) .... Ottawa ON
Lanzarotta Wholesale Grocers Ltd. (1) .... Concord ON
Lasik Vision Corporation (1) .... Burnaby BC
Lethbridge Community College / LCC (1) .... Lethbridge AB
Lifestyle Retirement Communities (1) .... Vancouver BC
Lifestyle Retirement Communities (1) .... Mississauga ON
Linamar Corporation, Autocom Division (1) .... Guelph ON
Lindor Inc. (1) .... Montréal QC
Lockheed Martin Canada Inc. (1) .... Edmonton AB
Lombard Canada Ltd. (1) .... Toronto ON
London Health Sciences Centre / LHSC (1) .... London ON
Lovat Tunnel Equipment Inc. (1) .... Toronto ON
Loyalty Group, The (1) .... Toronto ON
Lumic Electronics, Inc. (1) .... Nepean ON
Lumsden Brothers Ltd. (1) .... Brantford ON
Ma'mowe Capital Region, Child and Famil (1) .... Edmonton AB
MacDonald Dettwiler Space and Advanced (1) .... Brampton ON
Mack Canada Inc. (1) .... Mississauga ON
Manitoba Agriculture and Food (1) .... Winnipeg MB
Manitoba Family Services and Housing (1) .... Winnipeg MB
Manitoba Intergovernmental Affairs (1) .... Winnipeg MB
Manitoba Transportation & Government Se (1) .... Winnipeg MB
Manulife Financial Corporation (1) .... Waterloo ON
Maple Leaf Pork, Case Reddi Facilit (1) .... Stoney Creek ON
Maple Reinders Inc. (1) .... Brampton ON
Marchon Canada (1) .... Dorval QC
Markham, Corporation of the Town of (1) .... Markham ON
Maxxam Analytics Inc. (1) .... Mississauga ON
MBNA Canada Bank (1) .... Gloucester ON
McCormick Canada Inc. (1) .... Mississauga ON
Med-Eng Systems Inc. (1) .... Ottawa ON
MedcomSoft Inc. (1) .... Toronto ON
MemberCARE Financial Services (1) .... Burlington ON
Mentor Engineering (1) .... Calgary AB
Merak Projects Ltd. (1) .... Calgary AB
Merisel Canada Inc. (1) .... Toronto ON
Messier-Dowty Inc. (1) .... Peterborough ON
MI Group, The (1) .... Mississauga ON
Midland Steel Ltd. (1) .... Anjou QC
Miele Ltd. (1) .... Richmond Hill ON
Mikasa (1) .... Markham ON
Minden Gross Grafstein & Greenstein (1) .... Toronto ON
Ministry of Community and Social Services (1) .... Kenora ON
Ministry of Community and Social Service (1) .... Toronto ON
Ministry of Energy and Mines, BC (1) .... Victoria BC
Ministry of Finance, Ontario (1) .... Toronto ON
Ministry of Forests, BC (Vanderhoof D (1) .... Vanderhoof BC
Ministry of Health and Long-Term Care, On (1) .... London ON
Ministry of Labour, BC (Workers' Compen (1) .... Victoria BC
Ministry of the Attorney General, BC (1) .... Abbotsford BC
Ministry of the Attorney General, Ontari (1) .... Toronto ON
Ministry of Transportation, BC (1) .... Victoria BC
Minolta Business Equipment (Canada) (1) .... Mississauga ON
Minolta (Montreal) Inc. (1) .... St-Laurent QC
Mississauga, City of (1) .... Mississauga ON
Mistahia Health Region (1) .... Grande Prairie AB
Mitec Telecom Inc. (1) .... Pointe-Claire QC
Mitra Imaging Inc. (1) .... Waterloo ON
Mmmuffins Canada Corp. (1) .... Toronto ON
Monit Management Ltd. (1) .... Montréal QC
MOSAID Technologies Inc. (1) .... Kanata ON
Mount Pleasant Group of Cemeteries (1) .... Toronto ON
Moxie's Classic Grill (1) .... Calgary AB
NAL Resources Management Ltd. (1) .... Calgary AB

For descriptions of the occupational categories used in this index, see page 458.

ACCOUNTING (Cont.)

ACCOUNTING (Cont.)

Sutton Place Hotel, The (1) .... Toronto ON
Sutton Place Hotel Vancouver, The (1) .... Vancouver BC
Syncrude Canada Ltd. (1) .... Fort McMurray AB
Syndesis Limited (1) .... Richmond Hill ON
Tantalus Systems Corp. (1) .... Burnaby BC
Targray Technology International I (1) .... Pointe-Claire QC
Taro Pharmaceuticals Inc. (1) .... Bramalea ON
TCT Daily Motor Freight (1) .... Mississauga ON
TCT Logistics Inc. (1) .... Mississauga ON
TDL Group Ltd., The (1) .... Oakville ON
Technical Standards & Safety Authority / (1) .... Toronto ON
Telematic Controls Inc. (1) .... Calgary AB
TelTech Assets.Com Ltd. (1) .... Calgary AB
Telus Mobility (1) .... Toronto ON
Tenaquip Ltd. (1) .... Ste-Anne-de-Bellevue QC
Therapist's Choice Medical Supplies Inc. (1) .... Toronto ON
Thermal Energy International Inc. (1) .... Nepean ON
Thorburn Equipment Inc. (1) .... Pointe-Claire QC
Thrifty Canada, Ltd. (1) .... Mississauga ON
Thunder Bay, City of (1) .... Thunder Bay ON
TOA Canada Corporation (1) .... Mississauga ON
Toronto.com (1) .... Toronto ON
Toronto Cricket, Skating and Curling Clu (1) .... Toronto ON
Toronto Humane Society (1) .... Toronto ON
Toronto Hydro (1) .... Toronto ON
Toronto Rehabilitation Institute (1) .... Toronto ON
Toshiba of Canada Limited (1) .... Markham ON
Total Communications (1) .... Hamilton ON
Total Credit Recovery / TRC (1) .... Toronto ON
Tower Group International Canada Inc. (1) .... Montréal QC
Town Publishing Inc. (1) .... Hamilton ON
Tractel Ltd., Swingstage Division (1) .... Toronto ON
Trans Mountain Pipe Line Company Ltd. (1) .... Calgary AB
TransAlta Corporation (1) .... Calgary AB
Tri-Ed Ltd. (1) .... Mississauga ON
Triathlon (1) .... Richmond BC
Trophy Foods Inc. (1) .... Mississauga ON
Turbocor Inc. (1) .... Dorval QC
UMA Engineering Ltd. (1) .... Burnaby BC
Umbra Ltd. (1) .... Toronto ON
Unisearch Associates Inc. (1) .... Concord ON
United Van Lines (Canada) Ltd. (1) .... Mississauga ON
University College of the Cariboo / UCC (1) .... Kamloops BC
University of Guelph (1) .... Guelph ON
University of New Brunswick, Faculty (1) .... Saint John NB
University of New Brunswick / UNB (1) .... Fredericton NB
University of Regina (1) .... Regina SK
University of Waterloo (1) .... Waterloo ON
Valvoline Canada Ltd. (1) .... Mississauga ON
Vancouver, City of (1) .... Vancouver BC
Vancouver City Savings Credit Union / (1) .... Vancouver BC
Vancouver / Richmond Health Board (1) .... Vancouver BC
Vansco Electronics Ltd. (1) .... Winnipeg MB
VECO Canada Ltd. (1) .... Calgary AB
Venetor Equipment Rental Inc. (1) .... Hamilton ON
Venture Communications Ltd. (1) .... Calgary AB
Victorian Order of Nurses / VON Canada (1) .... Ottawa ON
Victorian Order of Nurses / VON, Easter (1) .... Kingston ON
Virtual Prototypes Inc. / VPI (1) .... Montréal QC
Volex Canada Inc. (1) .... Kanata ON
Voyus Canada Inc. (1) .... Burnaby BC
W.I. Villager Ltd. / Marshlands Canada (1) .... Kingston ON
Warner Music Canada (1) .... Toronto ON
We Care Home Health Services Inc. (1) .... Toronto ON
Wentworth Mold Inc. (1) .... Hamilton ON
West Park Healthcare Centre (1) .... Toronto ON
Westcan Wireless (1) .... Edmonton AB
Westeinde Construction Ltd. (1) .... Nepean ON
WesternGeco (1) .... Calgary AB
Westin Prince Toronto (1) .... Toronto ON
WestView Regional Health Authority / (1) .... Stony Plain AB
Whitecourt Oil Corp. (1) .... Vaughan ON
Wi-LAN Inc. (1) .... Calgary AB
Willard Meats International Ltd. (1) .... Mississauga ON
Williams Machinery Ltd. (1) .... Richmond BC
Wilsonart Canada (1) .... Mississauga ON
Windsor Casino Limited (1) .... Windsor ON
Woco Automotive Inc. (1) .... Concord ON

Workers' Compensation Board, Alberta (1) .... Edmonton AB
World Heart Corporation (1) .... Ottawa ON
Xerox Canada Ltd. (1) .... Mississauga ON
Yamaha Motor Canada Ltd. (1) .... Toronto ON
York Central Hospital (1) .... Richmond Hill ON
York, The Regional Municipality of (1) .... Newmarket ON
Zenastra Photonics Inc. (1) .... Ottawa ON
Zero-Knowledge Systems Inc. (1) .... Montréal QC

ACTUARIAL
See also: Insurance, Quality Control.

Canadian Institute for Health Informatio (7) .... Toronto ON
ManulifeDirect (6) .... Toronto ON
Alberta Human Resources and Employment (5) .... Edmonton AB
Pharmacia Canada Inc. (5) .... Markham ON
Royal Bank Financial Group (5) .... Toronto ON
Alberta Learning (4) .... Edmonton AB
Public Service Commission of Canada, Onta (4) .... Ottawa ON
Brock University (3) .... St. Catharines ON
CroMedica Inc. (3) .... Victoria BC
CroMedica Inc. (3) .... Ottawa ON
Ministry of Health and Long-Term Care, (3) .... Kingston ON
Sun Life Financial (3) .... Toronto ON
Alberta Cancer Board (2) .... Calgary AB
Anishinaabe Mino-Ayaawin Inc. / AMA (2) .... Winnipeg MB
Canada Customs and Revenue Agency / CCRA (2) ...... Ottawa ON
College of the Rockies (2) .... Cranbrook BC
David Thompson Health Region, Red Deer (2) .... Red Deer AB
Department of Forest Resources & Agri (2) .... St. John's NF
Equitable Life of Canada (2) .... Waterloo ON
Frontenac Children's Aid Society (2) .... Kingston ON
Health Information Partnership, Eastern (2) .... Kingston ON
Loyalty Group, The (2) .... Toronto ON
MapInfo Corporation (2) .... Toronto ON
Ministry of Agriculture, Food and Rural A (2) .... Guelph ON
Ministry of Community and Social Service (2) .... Toronto ON
National Life Assurance Company of Canad (2) .... Toronto ON
Public Service Commission of Canada, BC (2) .... Victoria BC
Queen's University, National Cancer Ins (2) .... Kingston ON
Scarborough Community Care Access Centre (2) .... Toronto ON
Toronto Rehabilitation Institute (2) .... Toronto ON
VIPswitch Inc. (2) .... Montréal QC
William M. Mercer Limited (2) .... Toronto ON
Zurich Canada (2) .... Toronto ON
ACNielsen Company of Canada (1) .... Markham ON
Alberta Children's Services (1) .... Edmonton AB
Alberta Environment (1) .... Edmonton AB
Alberta Learning (1) .... Edmonton AB
Aon Corporation (1) .... Vancouver BC
British Columbia Mental Health So (1) .... Port Coquitlam BC
Brogan Inc. (1) .... Ottawa ON
Calgary, City of (1) .... Calgary AB
Canadian Blood Services, Toronto Blood C (1) .... Toronto ON
Canadian Foundation on Compulsive Gambli (1) .... Toronto ON
Canadian Institute for Health Information (1) .... Ottawa ON
Canadian Pacific Railway / CPR (1) .... Calgary AB
Caro Research (1) .... Dorval QC
Children's and Women's Health Centre o (1) .... Vancouver BC
Children's Hospital of Eastern Ontario / (1) .... Ottawa ON
Citadel General Assurance Company, The (1) .... Toronto ON
ClinTrials BioResearch Ltd. / CTBR (1) .... Senneville QC
College of Nurses of Ontario / CNO (1) .... Toronto ON
College of the North Atlantic, Step (1) .... Stephenville NF
Conference Board of Canada, The (1) .... Ottawa ON
CUMIS Group Ltd., The (1) .... Burlington ON
Department of Health and Community Se (1) .... St. John's NF
Department of Health and Social Serv (1) .... Yellowknife NT
Department of Health & Wellness, New (1) .... Fredericton NB
Department of Human Resources, Nunavut (1) .... Iqaluit NU
ENMAX Corporation (1) .... Calgary AB
European Specialty Reinsurance Ltd. / ES (1) .... Toronto ON
Experian (1) .... Toronto ON
Export Development Corporation / EDC (1) .... Ottawa ON
Frank Russell Company Canada Limited (1) .... Toronto ON
Georgian College (1) .... Barrie ON
Grand River Hospital (1) .... Kitchener ON
Great-West Life Assurance Company, The (1) .... Winnipeg MB
Honda of Canada Manufacturing (1) .... Alliston ON

For descriptions of the occupational categories used in this index, see page 458.

ACTUARIAL (Cont.)

ADMINISTRATIVE

ADMINISTRATIVE (Cont.)

Groupe Dynamite Inc. (3) .... Mount Royal QC
H. Paulin & Co. Limited (3) .... Toronto ON
Halton, The Regional Municipality of (3) .... Oakville ON
Henry Birks & Sons Inc. (3) .... Montréal QC
Inex Pharmaceuticals Corp. (3) .... Burnaby BC
Infostream Technologies Inc. (3) .... Toronto ON
Maillot Baltex Inc. (3) .... Montréal QC
McGill University Health Centre / MUHC (3) .... Montréal QC
MedcomSoft Inc. (3) .... Toronto ON
Ministry of Community and Social Services (3) .... London ON
Ministry of Consumer and Business Servic (3) .... Toronto ON
Ministry of Health and Ministry Respons (3) .... Victoria BC
Ministry of Natural Resources, Ontario (3) .... North Bay ON
Ministry of the Attorney General, Ontari (3) .... Toronto ON
Ministry of the Solicitor General, Ontar (3) .... Orillia ON
Ministry of Water, Land and Air Protect (3) .... Victoria BC
Minolta Business Equipment (Canada), Lt (3) .... Richmond BC
National Life Assurance Company of Canad (3) .... Toronto ON
New Automation Corporation / NAC (3) .... Burlington ON
North Island College / NIC (3) .... Courtenay BC
North York General Hospital (3) .... Toronto ON
NPS Pharmaceuticals Inc. (3) .... Mississauga ON
Ontario HIV Treatment Network / OHTN (3) .... Toronto ON
Ontario Lottery and Gaming Corporation / (3) .... Toronto ON
Optimal Robotics Corp. (3) .... Montréal QC
Paging Network of Canada, Inc. / PageNet (3) .... Toronto ON
PanCanadian Petroleum Ltd. (3) .... Calgary AB
Pink Elephant Inc. (3) .... Burlington ON
Providence Health Care, St. Paul's Hos (3) .... Vancouver BC
Rogers Cable Inc. (3) .... Toronto ON
Rogers Communications Inc. (3) .... Ottawa ON
Royal Alliance Inc. (3) .... Woodbridge ON
Royal Bank Financial Group (3) .... Toronto ON
Royal Group Technologies Inc. (3) .... Woodbridge ON
Royal LePage Commercial Inc. (3) .... Toronto ON
Seiden Health Management Inc. (3) .... Toronto ON
Shirmax Fashions Ltd. (3) .... Montréal QC
Solect Technology Group (3) .... Toronto ON
St. Joseph's Healthcare Hamilton (3) .... Hamilton ON
Standard Life Assurance Company, The (3) .... Montréal QC
Toronto Humane Society (3) .... Toronto ON
Tracer Industries Canada Ltd. (3) .... Edmonton AB
University College of the Fraser Vall (3) .... Abbotsford BC
University of Toronto, Faculty of Medici (3) .... Toronto ON
01 Communique Laboratory Inc. (2) .... Mississauga ON
ACD Systems (2) .... Saanichton BC
Advantex Marketing International Inc. (2) .... Toronto ON
Alberta Children's Services (2) .... Edmonton AB
Alberta College of Pharmacists (2) .... Edmonton AB
Alberta Economic Development (2) .... Edmonton AB
Alberta Environment (2) .... Calgary AB
Alberta Human Resources and Employment (2) .... Calgary AB
Alberta Innovation & Science (2) .... Edmonton AB
Alberta Solicitor General (2) .... Edmonton AB
AltaGas Services Inc. (2) .... Calgary AB
Altera Corp. (2) .... Toronto ON
AnorMED Inc. (2) .... Langley BC
Applanix Corp. (2) .... Richmond Hill ON
Aramark Canada Ltd. (2) .... Toronto ON
Arbor Memorial Services Inc. (2) .... Toronto ON
ARK e-Tail Services Inc. (2) .... Toronto ON
Artitalia Inc. (2) .... Montréal QC
AstraZeneca (2) .... Mississauga ON
BECO Industries Ltd. (2) .... Anjou QC
Bellwoods Centres for Community Living I (2) .... Toronto ON
Boulevard Media (Canada) Inc. / BMC (2) .... Vancouver BC
Business Travel International / BTI Canad (2) .... Ottawa ON
Canada Colors and Chemicals Ltd. / CCC (2) .... Toronto ON
Canada Mortgage and Housing Corporation (2) .... Toronto ON
Canadian Internet Registration Authority (2) .... Ottawa ON
Canadian Nuclear Safety Commission / CNSC (2) .... Ottawa ON
Canadian Nurses Association / CNA (2) .... Ottawa ON
Canadian Paraplegic Association Ontario (2) .... Toronto ON
Canadian Pharmacists Association / CPhA (2) .... Toronto ON
Capital City Savings (2) .... Edmonton AB
CEF Technologies Ltd., Brittania Compres (2) .... Calgary AB
Ceridian Canada Ltd. (2) .... Mississauga ON
CGU Group Canada Ltd. (2) .... Toronto ON

Children's Aid Society of Toronto (2) .... Toronto ON
Circa Communications Ltd. (2) .... North Vancouver BC
Cité Nissan (2) .... Montréal QC
ClientLogic Corp. (2) .... Toronto ON
Club Monaco International (2) .... Toronto ON
Coinamatic Canada Inc. (2) .... Mississauga ON
Computing Devices Canada Ltd. / CDC (2) .... Ottawa ON
Conair Consumer Products Inc. (2) .... Brampton ON
Consumers Packaging Inc. (2) .... Toronto ON
Credit Valley Hospital, The (2) .... Mississauga ON
CSA International (2) .... Toronto ON
David Brown Union Pumps (Canada) Ltd. (2) .... Burlington ON
DDS Canada (2) .... Toronto ON
Deloitte Consulting (2) .... Toronto ON
DeLonghi (2) .... Mississauga ON
Department of Human Resources, Nunavut (2) ......,, Iqaluit NU
Design + Communication Inc. (2) .... Montréal QC
Diamond Willow Child and Family Servic (2) .... Innisfail AB
Discount Car and Truck Rentals (2) .... Toronto ON
DMTI Spatial Inc. (2) .... Markham ON
Dover Industries Ltd. (2) .... Burlington ON
Dundee Realty Management Corporation (2) .... Toronto ON
Effort Trust Company, The (2) .... Hamilton ON
EMI Music Canada (2) .... Mississauga ON
Ensil International (2) .... Markham ON
Entourage Technology Solutions (2) .... Mississauga ON
EPCOR Utilities Inc. (2) .... Edmonton AB
Evertz Microsystems Ltd. (2) .... Burlington ON
Excel Tech Ltd. / XLTEK (2) .... Oakville ON
Executive Needs Inc., The (2) .... Toronto ON
Exocom Group Inc., The (2) .... Ottawa ON
Financial Services Commission of Ontario (2) .... Toronto ON
First Professional Management Inc. (2) .... Toronto ON
G&K Work Wear (2) .... Toronto ON
Genfoot Manufacturing (2) .... St-Laurent QC
Geo Group, The (2) .... Toronto ON
GeoMetrix Data Systems Inc. (2) .... Victoria BC
Gexel Telecom (2) .... Montréal QC
Girl Guides of Canada, British Columbi (2) .... Vancouver BC
GP Capital Management Group (2) .... Toronto ON
Greenwin Property Management Inc. (2) .... Toronto ON
Grocery Gateway (2) .... Mississauga ON
Hema-Quebec (2) .... St-Laurent QC
Henry Schein Arcona Inc. (2) .... St. Catharines ON
Hewitt Associates (2) .... Toronto ON
Hewlett-Packard (Canada) Ltd. (2) .... Mississauga ON
Highland Transport (2) .... Markham ON
Home Trust Co. Credit Card Services (2) .... Toronto ON
Hospital for Sick Children, The (2) .... Toronto ON
Husky Oil Operations Ltd. (2) .... Calgary AB
i-STAT Canada Ltd. (2) .... Kanata ON
IBM Canada Ltd. (2) .... Markham ON
Information Science and Technology Agen (2) .... Victoria BC
Information Services Corporation of Saska (2) .... Regina SK
InSystems Technologies, Inc. (2) .... Markham ON
Intuit GreenPoint (2) .... Calgary AB
John Abbott College (2) .... Ste-Anne-de-Bellevue QC
Justice Institute of BC / JIBC (2) .... New Westminster BC
Kasian Kennedy Architecture, Interior (2) .... Vancouver BC
Kaycan Ltd. (2) .... Pointe-Claire QC
Kaytronics Inc. (2) .... St-Laurent QC
Keystone Child and Family Services Aut (2) .... Innisfail AB
Kingston General Hospital (2) .... Kingston ON
Klick Communications Inc. (2) .... Toronto ON
Kohl & Frisch Limited (2) .... Concord ON
Legislative Assembly of Ontario, Office (2) .... Toronto ON
Loyalty Group, The (2) .... Toronto ON
Lyreco Office Products (2) .... Toronto ON
Ma'mowe Capital Region, Child and Famil (2) .... Edmonton AB
Mainetti Canada (2) .... Montréal QC
Manitoba Labour & Immigration (2) .... Winnipeg MB
Manitoba Transportation & Government Se (2) .... Winnipeg MB
Manulife Financial Corporation (2) .... Waterloo ON
Masterfile Corporation (2) .... Toronto ON
MDS Metro Laboratory Services (2) .... Burnaby BC
MEDIS Health & Pharmaceutical Servic (2) .... Mississauga ON
Mercedes-Benz Canada Inc. (2) .... Toronto ON
Metropolitan Hotel Toronto (2) .... Toronto ON
Minacs Worldwide Inc. (2) .... Markham ON
Ministry of Community and Social Service (2) .... Toronto ON
Ministry of Finance, Ontario (2) .... Toronto ON
Ministry of Health and Long-Term Care, On (2) .... London ON

ADMINISTRATIVE (Cont.)

Ministry of Health and Long-Term Care, (2) .... Kingston ON
Ministry of Health and Long-Term Care, (2) .... Kingston ON
Ministry of Health and Long-Term Care, (2) .... Hamilton ON
Ministry of Health and Long-Term Care, O (2) .... Sudbury ON
Ministry of Labour, Ontario (2) .... Ottawa ON
Ministry of Seniors, Alberta (2) .... Edmonton AB
Ministry of Social Development and (2) .... Prince George BC
Ministry of the Environment, Ontario (Ce (2) .... Toronto ON
Ministry of the Environment, Ontario (In (2) .... Toronto ON
Ministry of the Environment, Ontario (La (2) .... Toronto ON
Ministry of the Solicitor General, Ontar (2) .... Toronto ON
Minolta Business Equipment (Canada), (2) .... Gloucester ON
Mmmuffins Canada Corp. (2) .... Toronto ON
Monarch Construction Ltd. (2) .... Toronto ON
Morrison Hershfield (2) .... Toronto ON
Mount Sinai Hospital (2) .... Toronto ON
Nanowave Technologies Inc. (2) .... Toronto ON
National Car Rental (2) .... Toronto ON
Nestle Canada Inc. (2) .... Toronto ON
North York General Hospital, General Div (2) .... Toronto ON
Nucon Systems Inc. (2) .... Markham ON
O&Y Enterprise (2) .... Toronto ON
Okanagan University College / OUC (2) .... Kelowna BC
Ontario Association of Architects / OAA (2) .... Toronto ON
Ottawa Hospital, The (2) .... Ottawa ON
Pacific Blue Cross / BC Life (2) .... Vancouver BC
Paging Network of Canada, Inc. / PageN (2) .... Vancouver BC
Paradigm Electronics (2) .... Mississauga ON
Patella Manufacturing Inc. (2) .... Lasalle QC
Pet Valu Canada Inc. (2) .... Markham ON
PhytoDerm Inc. (2) .... Montréal QC
Polyair Inter Pack Inc. (2) .... Toronto ON
Protech Chemicals Ltd. (2) .... St-Laurent QC
Public Service Commission of Canada, New (2) .... Moncton NB
Public Service Commission of Canada, (2) .... St. John's NF
Public Service Employee Relations Commi (2) .... Victoria BC
Quality Goods IMD Inc. (2) .... St-Laurent QC
Quebec Student Health Alliance / ASEQ (2) .... Montréal QC
QuestAir Technologies Inc. (2) .... Burnaby BC
Radiant Communications (2) .... Vancouver BC
Radiant Communications (2) .... Toronto ON
Raymond James Ltd. (2) .... Vancouver BC
RCP Inc. (2) .... Concord ON
RGO Office Products (2) .... Calgary AB
RNG Group Inc. (2) .... Toronto ON
Rogers Cable Inc. (2) .... Kitchener ON
Rogers Communications Inc. (2) .... Toronto ON
Royal Bank Financial Group (2) .... Montréal QC
RSC Group, The (2) .... Vancouver BC
Ruffneck Heaters (2) .... Calgary AB
Ryan, Lamontagne & Associates (2) .... Ottawa ON
SCOR Canada Reinsurance Company (2) .... Toronto ON
Securicor Cash Services (2) .... Toronto ON
Selkirk Financial Technologies, Inc. (2) .... Vancouver BC
Sitraka Software Inc. (2) .... Toronto ON
Smart Technologies Inc. (2) .... Calgary AB
Sodema / Transcontinental Technology (2) .... Montréal QC
Speed-i-Com Inc. / SCI (2) .... Toronto ON
Stream International (2) .... Belleville ON
Sun Life Financial (2) .... Toronto ON
Supreme Tooling Group (2) .... Toronto ON
Telus Corporation (2) .... Burnaby BC
Tiercon Industries Inc. (2) .... Stoney Creek ON
Time iCR Inc. (2) .... Ottawa ON
Timothy's World Coffee (2) .... Toronto ON
Trans Mountain Pipe Line Company Ltd. (2) .... Calgary AB
Transoft Solutions (2) .... Richmond BC
UMA Engineering Ltd. (2) .... Burnaby BC
UMA Engineering Ltd. (2) .... Calgary AB
University of Alberta, Faculty of Nursi (2) .... Edmonton AB
University of Toronto at Scarborough / U (2) .... Toronto ON
University of Toronto, Professional Facu (2) .... Toronto ON
Vancouver Community College / VCC (2) .... Vancouver BC
VHA Home HealthCare (2) .... Toronto ON
Victorian Order of Nurses, Toronto-York (2) .... Markham ON
Victorian Order of Nurses / VON Canada (2) .... Ottawa ON
Vopak Canada Ltd. (2) .... Edmonton AB
Voyus Canada Inc. (2) .... Burnaby BC
We Care Home Health Services Inc. (2) .... Toronto ON

Whistler Blackcomb / Intrawest (2) .... Whistler BC
William M. Mercer Limited (2) .... Toronto ON
Xebec Imaging Services Inc. (2) .... Ottawa ON
Yee Hong Community Wellness Foundation (2) .... Toronto ON
York Central Hospital (2) .... Richmond Hill ON
York Community Care Access Centre / CCAC (2) .... Toronto ON
Zenastra Photonics Inc. (2) .... Ottawa ON
Zero-Knowledge Systems Inc. (2) .... Montréal QC
724 Solutions Inc. (1) .... Toronto ON
A.L.I. Technologies Inc. (1) .... Richmond BC
Aastra Telecom (1) .... Concord ON
Abba Parts and Service (1) .... Burlington ON
ABC Group Inc. (1) .... Toronto ON
AcceLight Networks (1) .... Nepean ON
ACM Automation Inc. (1) .... Calgary AB
Acomarit Canada Inc. (1) .... Montréal QC
Acres International Limited (1) .... Oakville ON
Acterna Corporation (1) .... Burnaby BC
ADESA Canada Inc., Corporate Office (1) .... Mississauga ON
Advanced Motion and Controls Ltd. (1) .... Barrie ON
AFGD Glass (1) .... Concord ON
AGAT Laboratories (1) .... Calgary AB
Agile Systems Inc. (1) .... Waterloo ON
Agmont Inc. (1) .... Montréal QC
Akeda Tools (1) .... Vancouver BC
Akzo Nobel Coatings Ltd. (1) .... Toronto ON
AlarmForce Industries Inc. (1) .... Toronto ON
Alberta Alcohol and Drug Abuse Commissi (1) .... Edmonton AB
Alberta Child and Family Services Autho (1) .... McLennan AB
Alberta Children's Services, Northe (1) .... Lac La Biche AB
Alberta Energy and Utilities Board / EUB (1) .... Calgary AB
Alberta Energy Company Ltd. / AEC (1) .... Calgary AB
Alberta International and Intergovernme (1) .... Edmonton AB
Alberta Mental Health Board, Alberta Hosp (1) .... Ponoka AB
Alberta Sustainable Resource Developmen (1) .... Edmonton AB
Alberta Transportation (1) .... Edmonton AB
Aldo Group Inc. (1) .... St-Laurent QC
AldrichPears Associates (1) .... Vancouver BC
Algo Group Inc. (1) .... Montréal QC
Alive Magazine (1) .... Burnaby BC
All Weather Windows (1) .... Calgary AB
Allied Oil & Gas Corp. (1) .... Calgary AB
Alterna Technologies Group Inc. (1) .... Calgary AB
Amaco Construction Equipment (1) .... Mississauga ON
American Appraisal Canada, Inc. (1) .... Toronto ON
American Iron & Metal Company Inc. / AI (1) .... Montréal QC
Amore Sweets Corporation (1) .... Toronto ON
Amplified Light Technologies Corp. / AL (1) .... Oakville ON
Anadarko Canada Corporation (1) .... Calgary AB
Architrave Design Office Service (1) .... Gabriola Island BC
Arcis Corporation (1) .... Calgary AB
ARI Financial Services Inc. (1) .... Mississauga ON
Ash City (1) .... Toronto ON
Association of Canadian Travel Agents / A (1) .... Ottawa ON
AT&T Canada (1) .... Toronto ON
Athletic Image (1) .... Montréal QC
Atlantis Scientific Inc. (1) .... Nepean ON
Atlantis Systems International (1) .... Brampton ON
Atlas Van Lines (Canada) Ltd. (1) .... Oakville ON
Audio Centre (1) .... St-Laurent QC
Aware Marketing Group (1) .... Toronto ON
Axelson BioPharma Research Inc. / ABR (1) .... Burnaby BC
Babco Sales Ltd. (1) .... Surrey BC
Balmer Plaster Moulding Corporation of A (1) .... Toronto ON
Bank of America Canada (1) .... Toronto ON
Barmish Inc. (1) .... St-Laurent QC
Bath Fitter / Bain Magique (1) .... St-Eustache QC
Baxter Healthcare Corporation (1) .... Mississauga ON
BC Hydro (1) .... Vancouver BC
BC Research Inc. (1) .... Vancouver BC
BCE Emergis Inc. (1) .... Montréal QC
BCL Magnetics (1) .... Burlington ON
Beauty Systems Group (Canada) Inc. (1) .... Toronto ON
Bell & Howell Ltd. (1) .... Toronto ON
Bell Intrigna (1) .... Edmonton AB
Belmont House (1) .... Toronto ON
Bennett Jones LLP (1) .... Calgary AB
Bentley Leathers (1) .... St-Laurent QC
Bettis Canada Ltd. (1) .... Edmonton AB
Bird Construction Company (1) .... Richmond BC
Bird Construction Company (1) .... Toronto ON
Bird On a Wire Networks / BOAW (1) .... Mississauga ON

ADMINISTRATIVE (Cont.)

bitHeads, Inc. (1) .... Ottawa ON
Black & McDonald Ltd. (1) .... Toronto ON
Blockbuster Canada Co. (1) .... Montréal QC
Bloorview MacMillan Children's Centre, M (1) ..... Toronto ON
BNT Products (1) .... Mississauga ON
Boehringer Ingelheim (Canada) Ltd. (1) .... Burlington ON
BouClair Inc. (1) .... Dorval QC
BPA Group of Companies (1) .... Toronto ON
Bridge Brand Food Services Ltd. (1) .... Calgary AB
British Columbia Automobile Association (1) ...... Burnaby BC
British Columbia Institute of Technology (1) .... Burnaby BC
British Columbia Maritime Employers As (1) ..... Vancouver BC
British Columbia Mental Health So (1) ...... Port Coquitlam BC
Brogan Inc. (1) .... Ottawa ON
Brookfield LePage Johnson Controls Facil (1) .... Markham ON
Buckman Laboratories (1) .... Vaudreuil QC
Building Box, The (1) .... Markham ON
Burger King Restaurants of Canada Inc. (1) .... Toronto ON
C2 Media.com (1) .... Brantford ON
CAA Central Ontario (1) .... Thornhill ON
CAD Resource Centre / CRC (1) .... Toronto ON
CAE Inc. (1) .... St-Laurent QC
Calea Ltd. (1) .... Mississauga ON
Caledon, Town of (1) .... Caledon East ON
Canada 3000 Cargo Inc. (1) .... Mississauga ON
Canada Customs and Revenue Agency / CCRA (1) ...... Ottawa ON
Canada Life Assurance Company (1) .... Toronto ON
Canadian Bank Note Company, Ltd. (1) .... Ottawa ON
Canadian Blood Services / CBS (1) .... Ottawa ON
Canadian Egg Marketing Agency / CEMA (1) .... Ottawa ON
Canadian Global Foods Corporation (1) .... Toronto ON
Canadian Imperial Bank of Commerce, Nati (1) .... Toronto ON
Canadian Mass Media Inc. (1) .... Toronto ON
Canadian Northern Shield Insurance Com (1) .... Vancouver BC
Canadian Olympic Association / COA (1) .... Toronto ON
Canadian Red Cross, Ontario Zone (1) .... Mississauga ON
Cancer Care Ontario, Division of Prevent (1) .... Toronto ON
Canon Canada Inc. (1) .... Markham ON
CanRoof Corporation Inc. (1) .... Toronto ON
Capital Health, Community Care and Publ (1) .... Edmonton AB
Capital Health, Glenrose Rehabilitation (1) .... Edmonton AB
Carma Financial (1) .... Toronto ON
Casa Loma (1) .... Toronto ON
Case Credit Ltd. / CNH Capital (1) .... Burlington ON
CaseWare International Inc. (1) .... Toronto ON
Catholic Children's Aid Society of Toron (1) .... Toronto ON
CDL Systems Ltd. (1) .... Calgary AB
Cedar Enterprise Solutions Inc. (1) .... Calgary AB
Centre for Addiction and Mental Health (1) .... Toronto ON
Centre for Health Evaluation and Outco (1) ...... Vancouver BC
Ceridian Canada Ltd. (1) .... Winnipeg MB
CGU Group Canada Ltd. (1) .... Calgary AB
CH2M HILL Canada Ltd. (1) .... Calgary AB
Chancery Software Ltd. (1) .... Burnaby BC
Christian Children's Fund of Canada / CC (1) .... Toronto ON
Christie Lites (1) .... Toronto ON
Christina America Inc. (1) .... Montréal QC
CIMTEK Automation Systems (1) .... Burlington ON
Citadel General Assurance Company, The (1) .... Vancouver BC
Citadel General Assurance Company, The (1) .... Toronto ON
Civil Service Co-operative Credit Society (1) .... Ottawa ON
Classwave Wireless Inc. (1) .... Toronto ON
CMC Electronics Inc. (1) .... St-Laurent QC
CMD Group (1) .... Toronto ON
Cogency Semiconductor Inc. (1) .... Toronto ON
Cognis Canada Corporation (1) .... Mississauga ON
Cohos Evamy Partners, The (1) .... Calgary AB
Collections Andrade Inc. (1) .... Montréal QC
Collega for Aveda (1) .... Toronto ON
College of Nurses of Ontario / CNO (1) .... Toronto ON
College of the North Atlantic, Step (1) .... Stephenville NF
Colt Engineering Corporation (1) .... Calgary AB
Columbia MBF (1) .... Mississauga ON
Communications and Information Technology (1) .... Kanata ON
Community Living Mississauga (1) .... Mississauga ON
Compugen Systems Ltd. (1) .... Richmond Hill ON
Computer Sciences Corp. / CSC (1) .... Toronto ON
Con-Way Canada Express / Con-Way Tra (1) .... Mississauga ON

Concord Idea Corp. (1) .... Markham ON
Conference Board of Canada, The (1) .... Ottawa ON
Cordon Bleu Paris Ottawa Culinary Arts In (1) .... Ottawa ON
Corel Corporation (1) .... Ottawa ON
Corma Inc. (1) .... Concord ON
Cquay Inc. (1) .... Calgary AB
CreoScitex (1) .... Burnaby BC
Cropac Equipment Ltd. (1) .... Oakville ON
Crystal Homes (1) .... Hamilton ON
CSB Systems Ltd. (1) .... Mississauga ON
CTF Systems Inc. (1) .... Port Coquitlam BC
CUMIS Group Ltd., The (1) .... Burlington ON
Customs Excise Union Douanes Accise / CEU (1) .... Ottawa ON
CyberSurf Corporation (1) .... Calgary AB
Cymbolic Sciences Inc. (1) .... Richmond BC
Daedalian eSolutions (1) .... Toronto ON
Dailybread (1) .... Toronto ON
Daisytek Canada (1) .... Markham ON
Databeacon Inc. (1) .... Ottawa ON
Decoustics Ltd. (1) .... Toronto ON
Deloitte & Touche (1) .... Toronto ON
Department of Forest Resources & Agri (1) .... St. John's NF
Department of Public Safety, NB (1) .... Fredericton NB
DHL International Express Ltd. (1) .... Richmond BC
Diabetogen Biosciences Inc. (1) .... London ON
Dillon Consulting Ltd. (1) .... Ottawa ON
Distican Inc. (1) .... Richmond Hill ON
Diversicare Canada Management Services, (1) .... Toronto ON
DMR Consulting Inc. (1) .... Toronto ON
DoALL Industrial Supplies (1) .... Toronto ON
Dominion Spring Industries Corp. / D (1) .... Mississauga ON
Domtar Inc. (1) .... Montréal QC
Don Park Inc. (1) .... Toronto ON
Dorigo Systems Ltd. (1) .... Burnaby BC
Doubleday Canada Ltd. (1) .... Toronto ON
DRS Flight Safety and Communicati (1) .... Carleton Place ON
Ducks Unlimited Canada (1) .... Oak Hammock Marsh MB
Dumex Medical (1) .... Toronto ON
Duplium Corporation (1) .... Thornhill ON
DY 4 Systems Inc. (1) .... Kanata ON
Earlscourt Child and Family Centre, The (1) .... Toronto ON
Earth Energy Utility Corp. (1) .... Burlington ON
Earth Tech Canada Inc. (1) .... Markham ON
East Central Regional Health Authority (1) .... Camrose AB
East York Access Centre (1) .... Toronto ON
EBA Engineering Consultants Ltd. (1) .... Edmonton AB
Edge Networks Corporation (1) .... Winnipeg MB
Edmonton Cellular (1) .... Edmonton AB
Edward Jones (1) .... Mississauga ON
EFA Software Services Ltd. (1) .... Calgary AB
Egan Visual (1) .... Woodbridge ON
Electronics Workbench (1) .... Toronto ON
Elyps Dispatch Solutions (1) .... Burnaby BC
Emily Carr Institute of Art and Design (1) .... Vancouver BC
Empire Financial Group (1) .... Kingston ON
EMS Technologies Canada Ltd (1) .... Ste-Anne-de-Bellevue QC
Encon Group Inc. (1) .... Ottawa ON
Enerline Restorations Inc. (1) .... Calgary AB
Enhanced Marketing Services Corp. / EM (1) .... Vancouver BC
ENMAX Corporation (1) .... Calgary AB
Environmental Assessment Office, BC (1) .... Victoria BC
Epic Data Inc. (1) .... Richmond BC
Equipment Planning Associates Ltd. (1) .... Richmond Hill ON
ESRI Canada Ltd. (1) .... Toronto ON
Ethan Allen Home Interiors (1) .... Thornhill ON
Exel Canada (1) .... Brampton ON
Exhibits International (1) .... Toronto ON
Extracomm Technologies Inc. (1) .... Toronto ON
Ezenet Inc. (1) .... Toronto ON
Fairview College (1) .... Fairview AB
Famous Players Inc. (1) .... Toronto ON
Farah Foods / Hasty Market Corporation (1) .... Oakville ON
FCI Canada Inc. (1) .... Markham ON
FDM Software Ltd. (1) .... North Vancouver BC
Federated Co-operatives Limited / FCL (1) .... Calgary AB
Ferrero Canada Ltd. (1) .... Toronto ON
FGI (1) .... Thornhill ON
Fidelity Investments Canada Limited (1) .... Toronto ON
First Professional Management Inc. (1) .... Ottawa ON
Fiskars Canada Inc. (1) .... Markham ON
FlightSafety Canada (1) .... Toronto ON
Flint Energy Services Ltd. (1) .... Sherwood Park AB

For descriptions of the occupational categories used in this index, see page 458.

ADMINISTRATIVE (Cont.)

Fording Coal Limited, Fording River Oper (1) .... Elkford BC
Fountain Tire (1) .... Edmonton AB
Fraser Surrey Docks Ltd. (1) .... Surrey BC
Freud Westmore Tools Ltd. (1) .... Mississauga ON
Fritz Starber Inc. (1) .... Mississauga ON
Future Electronics Inc. (1) .... Pointe-Claire QC
FutureLink (1) .... Toronto ON
G&K Work Wear (1) .... Mississauga ON
Gamma-Dynacare (1) .... Brampton ON
GE Canada (1) .... Mississauga ON
Gemini Corporation (1) .... Calgary AB
Geneka Biotechnology Inc. (1) .... Montréal QC
General Hydrogen / GH (1) .... Vancouver BC
General Paint Corp. (1) .... Vancouver BC
Gennum Corporation (1) .... Burlington ON
George Brown College (1) .... Toronto ON
Gilmore Global Logistics Services / DocuL (1) .... Kanata ON
GlaxoSmithKline (1) .... St-Laurent QC
Global Crossing (1) .... Montréal QC
Global Educational Trust Plan / Global E (1) .... Toronto ON
Global Thermoelectric Inc. (1) .... Calgary AB
Goldwell Cosmetics (Canada) Ltd. (1) .... Mississauga ON
Golf-Gig Management Systems Internationa (1) .... Calgary AB
Good Shepherd Ministries (1) .... Toronto ON
Goodlife Foods (1) .... Calgary AB
Goway Travel Ltd. (1) .... Toronto ON
Grand River Poultry Farm Ltd. (1) .... Paris ON
Great-West Life Assurance Company, The (1) .... Winnipeg MB
H.J. Pfaff Motors Inc. (1) .... Newmarket ON
Halliburton Canada Inc. (1) .... Nisku AB
Hallmark Canada (1) .... Toronto ON
Halton Healthcare Services (1) .... Oakville ON
Hamilton Program for Schizophrenia / HP (1) .... Hamilton ON
Hamilton Region Conservation Authority (1) .... Ancaster ON
Hamilton Regional Cancer Centre / HRCC (1) .... Hamilton ON
Hardt Equipment Manufacturing Inc. (1) .... Lachine QC
Hartco Corporation (1) .... Anjou QC
Havergal College (1) .... Toronto ON
Hay River Community Health Board (1) .... Hay River NT
Heidelberg Canada (1) .... Richmond BC
Heidelberg Canada (1) .... Mississauga ON
Hemera Technologies Inc. (1) .... Hull QC
Hewitt Equipment Ltd. (1) .... Pointe-Claire QC
HFI Flooring Inc. (1) .... Calgary AB
Highland Equipment Ltd. (1) .... Toronto ON
Hong Fook Mental Health Association (1) .... Toronto ON
Hospital Employees' Union / HEU (1) .... Vancouver BC
Humber River Regional Hospital, Finch Av (1) .... Toronto ON
Hummingbird Ltd. (1) .... Toronto ON
Hunter Amenities International Ltd. (1) .... Burlington ON
Husky Injection Molding Systems Ltd. (1) .... Bolton ON
Hussmann Canada Inc. (1) .... Brantford ON
Hydrogenics Corporation (1) .... Mississauga ON
Hypertec Systems Inc. (1) .... St-Laurent QC
Hyprotech Ltd. (1) .... Calgary AB
Iacono Brown (1) .... Toronto ON
ICS Courier Services (1) .... Toronto ON
iFire Technology Inc. (1) .... Toronto ON
IKO Industries Ltd. (1) .... Toronto ON
IKO Industries Ltd. (1) .... Brampton ON
Image Processing Systems Inc. / IPS (1) .... Markham ON
IMS Health Canada Ltd. (1) .... Pointe-Claire QC
Indeka Group, The (1) .... Oakville ON
Independent Rehabilitation Services (1) .... Mississauga ON
Industrial Evolution (1) .... Edmonton AB
Industrial-Alliance Pacific Life Insur (1) .... Vancouver BC
Industry Training & Apprenticeship Comm (1) .... Victoria BC
INETCO Systems Ltd. (1) .... Burnaby BC
Inforetech Wireless Technology Inc. (1) .... Surrey BC
InfoSpec Systems Inc. (1) .... Burnaby BC
ING Bank of Canada / ING Direct (1) .... Toronto ON
ING Halifax (1) .... Calgary AB
ING Western Union Insurance (1) .... Vancouver BC
Ingersoll-Rand Canada Inc. (1) .... Toronto ON
Ingram Micro Inc. (Canada) (1) .... Mississauga ON
Inner-Tec Security Services (1) .... Vancouver BC
Insight Canada Inc. (1) .... Montréal QC
Instantel Inc. (1) .... Kanata ON
Institute of Health Economics / IHE (1) .... Edmonton AB
Integra Foundation (1) .... Toronto ON
Interactive Media Group / IMG (1) .... Toronto ON
Interhome Furniture (1) .... Markham ON
International Academy of Design and Techn (1) .... Ottawa ON
International Plaza Hotel & Conference C (1) .... Toronto ON
Intrawest Corporation (1) .... Vancouver BC
IPC Resistors Inc. (1) .... Mississauga ON
J & D Systems Inc. (1) .... Kitchener ON
J & J Display Sales Ltd. (1) .... Mississauga ON
Jacques Whitford Environment Ltd. (1) .... Burnaby BC
Jacques Whitford Environment Ltd. (1) .... Calgary AB
Jacques Whitford Environment Ltd. (1) .... Markham ON
Jacques Whitford Environment Ltd. (1) .... Halifax NS
Jayman Master Builder (1) .... Edmonton AB
Jewish Community Centre of Greater Van (1) .... Vancouver BC
JFB Technologies Inc. (1) .... Markham ON
Jim Peplinski's Leasemaster National (1) .... Toronto ON
Joseph Brant Memorial Hospital (1) .... Burlington ON
JP Metal America Inc. (1) .... Montréal QC
Kamloops, City of (1) .... Kamloops BC
Kaycan Ltd. (1) .... Toronto ON
Kazootek Technologies (1) .... Vancouver BC
Ken Lewis Group Inc. (1) .... Markham ON
Kingston, Corporation of the City of (1) .... Kingston ON
Kingston Regional Cancer Centre (1) .... Kingston ON
Kleinfeldt Consultants Limited (1) .... Mississauga ON
KMH Cardiology and Diagnostic Centres (1) .... Hamilton ON
Kwantlen University College (1) .... Surrey BC
La-Z-Boy Furniture Galleries (1) .... Burlington ON
Labatt Breweries Ontario (1) .... Toronto ON
Laborie Medical Technologies Inc. (1) .... Mississauga ON
Lafarge Canada Inc. (1) .... Montréal QC
Lakeridge Health Corporation (1) .... Oshawa ON
Lang Michener (1) .... Ottawa ON
Lansdowne Dodge City Ltd. (1) .... Richmond BC
Layfield Plastics Ltd. (1) .... Richmond BC
Lazier Hickey Langs O'Neal (1) .... Hamilton ON
Leitch Technology Corp. (1) .... Toronto ON
Lenbrook (1) .... Pickering ON
Lethbridge Community College / LCC (1) .... Lethbridge AB
Liberty Mutual Group (1) .... Unionville ON
Liburdi Engineering Ltd. (1) .... Dundas ON
LifeScan Canada Ltd. (1) .... Burnaby BC
Lifestyle Retirement Communities (1) .... Mississauga ON
Limestone District School Board (1) .... Kingston ON
Lindor Inc. (1) .... Montréal QC
Lions Gate Hospital (1) .... Vancouver BC
Loblaw Properties Ltd. / LPL (1) .... Toronto ON
Lockheed Martin Canada Inc. (1) .... Edmonton AB
Loewen Group Inc., The (1) .... Toronto ON
London Guarantee Insurance Company (1) .... Toronto ON
London Health Sciences Centre / LHSC (1) .... London ON
Macdonald Engineering Group Ltd. / MEG (1) .... Calgary AB
Mackenzie Financial Corporation (1) .... Toronto ON
Mackenzie Financial Corporation (1) .... Toronto ON
Magma Communications Ltd. (1) .... Nepean ON
Magnokrom Inc. (1) .... Mississauga ON
Mamma.com (1) .... Montréal QC
Manitoba Conservation (1) .... Winnipeg MB
Manitoba Consumer & Corporate Affairs / (1) .... Winnipeg MB
Manitoba Education, Training & Youth (1) .... Winnipeg MB
Manitoba Finance (1) .... Winnipeg MB
Manitoba Health (1) .... Winnipeg MB
Manitoba Highways & Transportation, Abo (1) .... Thompson MB
Manitoba Industry, Trades and Mines / I (1) .... Winnipeg MB
Manitoba Transportation & Government Se (1) .... Winnipeg MB
Manitoba Transportation & Gov (1) .... Portage la Prairie MB
Maple Ridge, District of (1) .... Maple Ridge BC
Marchon Canada (1) .... Dorval QC
Marconi Data Systems Canada Ltd. (1) .... Mississauga ON
Marcus Evans (1) .... Toronto ON
Marcus Evans (1) .... Montréal QC
Martin Newby Consulting Ltd. (1) .... Calgary AB
Matrikon Group (1) .... Edmonton AB
Maytag Canada (1) .... Burlington ON
McCarthy Tetrault LLP (1) .... Toronto ON
McElhanney Group Ltd., The (1) .... Vancouver BC
Med-Eng Systems Inc. (1) .... Ottawa ON
Mediagrif Interactive Technologies Inc (1) .... Longueuil QC
Medisys Health Group Inc. (1) .... Toronto ON
MemberWorks Canada Corporation (1) .... Montréal QC
Menu Foods Ltd. (1) .... Mississauga ON

ADMINISTRATIVE (Cont.)

Mercury Filmworks (1)	Vancouver BC
Mevotech Inc. (1)	Toronto ON
MIBRO Group, The (1)	Toronto ON
Michael Smith Foundation for Health Rese (1)	Burnaby BC
Micrologix Biotech Inc. (1)	Vancouver BC
Mikasa (1)	Markham ON
Millenia Resource Consulting (1)	Calgary AB
Miller Thomson LLP (1)	Toronto ON
Minacs Worldwide Inc. (1)	Richmond Hill ON
Mindquake Software (1)	Vancouver BC
Ministry of Agriculture, Food and Rural A (1)	Guelph ON
Ministry of Children and Family Develo (1)	Vancouver BC
Ministry of Children and Family Develo (1)	Cranbrook BC
Ministry of Community and Social Services (1)	Kenora ON
Ministry of Community and Social Ser (1)	Thunder Bay ON
Ministry of Community and Social Service (1)	Sudbury ON
Ministry of Community and Social Servi (1)	Newmarket ON
Ministry of Community and Social Servic (1)	Blenheim ON
Ministry of Correctional Services, Ontar (1)	Toronto ON
Ministry of Correctional Services, Onta (1)	Kingston ON
Ministry of Correctional Services, Ont (1)	North Bay ON
Ministry of Correctional Services, Ontari (1)	London ON
Ministry of Finance, Ontario (1)	Toronto ON
Ministry of Forests, BC (Fort St. (1)	Fort St. James BC
Ministry of Health and Long-Term Care, O (1)	Toronto ON
Ministry of Labour, Ontario (1)	London ON
Ministry of Labour, Ontario (Northern Re (1)	Sudbury ON
Ministry of Natural Resources, (1)	Sault Ste. Marie ON
Ministry of Natural Resources, Ontario (1)	Wawa ON
Ministry of Natural Resources, Ontario (1)	London ON
Ministry of Natural Resources, Onta (1)	Peterborough ON
Ministry of Natural Resources, Ontario (F (1)	Dryden ON
Ministry of Natural Resources, Ontario (1)	Geraldton ON
Ministry of the Attorney General, BC (1)	Abbotsford BC
Ministry of the Attorney General, Ontari (1)	Toronto ON
Ministry of the Attorney General, Ontari (1)	Toronto ON
Ministry of the Attorney General, Ontari (1)	Toronto ON
Ministry of the Attorney General, On (1)	Mississauga ON
Ministry of the Environment, Ontario (1)	Thunder Bay ON
Ministry of the Environment, Ontario (Co (1)	Toronto ON
Ministry of the Environment, Ontario (Dr (1)	Toronto ON
Ministry of the Environment, Ontario (En (1)	Toronto ON
Ministry of the Environment, Ontario (In (1)	Toronto ON
Ministry of the Environment, Ontario (In (1)	Toronto ON
Ministry of the Environment, Ontario (Lon (1)	London ON
Ministry of the Environment, Ontario (W (1)	Hamilton ON
Ministry of the Solicitor General, Ontar (1)	Toronto ON
Ministry of Tourism, Culture and Recreat (1)	Toronto ON
Ministry of Transportation, Ontario (1)	Thunder Bay ON
Ministry of Transportation, Ontario (1)	North Bay ON
Ministry of Transportation, Ontario (1)	London ON
Ministry of Transportation, Ontar (1)	St. Catharines ON
Ministry of Transportation, Ontario (Dri (1)	Toronto ON
Minolta (Montreal) Inc. (1)	St-Laurent QC
Mission Services of Hamilton (1)	Hamilton ON
Mitec Telecom Inc. (1)	Pointe-Claire QC
Mitra Imaging Inc. (1)	Waterloo ON
Mitsubishi Canada Ltd. (1)	Vancouver BC
Modern Niagara Ottawa Inc. (1)	Kanata ON
Montship Inc. (1)	Mississauga ON
Morrison Hershfield (1)	Burnaby BC
Mosaicwares Studio (1)	Toronto ON
MRF Geosystems Corporation (1)	Calgary AB
MuscleTech Research and Development (1)	Mississauga ON
National Arts Centre / NAC (1)	Ottawa ON
National Book Service / NBS (1)	Toronto ON
National Grocers Company Limited / Lobla (1)	Toronto ON
National Info-Tech Centre / NIC (1)	Montréal QC
National Research Council Canada / NRC (1)	Ottawa ON
National Research Council Canada / NRC (1)	Ottawa ON
National Steel Car Ltd. (1)	Hamilton ON
Natrel Inc. (1)	Toronto ON
NAV Canada (1)	Ottawa ON
NetMart Inc. (1)	Montréal QC
Network Builders Inc. (1)	Toronto ON
NexInnovations (1)	Mississauga ON
Noritsu Canada Ltd. (1)	Mississauga ON
Nortel Networks (1)	Brampton ON
North York Community Care Access Centre (1)	Toronto ON
Northern Alberta Institute of Technolog (1)	Edmonton AB
Northwood Technologies Inc. (1)	Nepean ON
Novator Systems Ltd. (1)	Toronto ON
NOWTV (1)	Winnipeg MB
Oakrun Farm Bakery Ltd. (1)	Ancaster ON
Object Technology International Inc. / OT (1)	Ottawa ON
Objexis Corporation (1)	Montréal QC
Occupational Health and Safety Agency (1)	Vancouver BC
Office of the Child, Youth & Family Ad (1)	Vancouver BC
OK Transportation Ltd. (1)	Toronto ON
Ontario Clean Water Agency / OCWA (1)	Toronto ON
Ontario Council of Alternative Businesse (1)	Toronto ON
Ontario Hospital Association / OHA (1)	Toronto ON
Ontario Human Rights Commission / OHRC (1)	Toronto ON
Ontario Municipal Employees Retirement S (1)	Toronto ON
Ontario Store Fixtures Inc. / OSF (1)	Toronto ON
Ontario Trillium Foundation, The (1)	Toronto ON
Open Storage Solutions, Inc. (1)	Brampton ON
Optech Inc. (1)	Toronto ON
ORIX Financial Services Canada Ltd. / OF (1)	Toronto ON
Ottawa-Carleton Catholic School Board / O (1)	Ottawa ON
Overseas Express Consolidators Inc. / O (1)	Montréal QC
Oxford Properties Group Inc. (1)	Edmonton AB
Pace, Johnson (1)	Toronto ON
PanelX.com / PanelX Technical Services (1)	Oakville ON
Panorama Business Views (1)	Toronto ON
Parasuco Jeans Inc. (1)	St-Laurent QC
Park Hyatt Toronto (1)	Toronto ON
Patheon Inc. (1)	Mississauga ON
PCsupport.com, Inc. (1)	Burnaby BC
Peel, The Regional Municipality of (1)	Brampton ON
Peerless Clothing Inc. (1)	Montréal QC
Percepta (1)	Toronto ON
PERI Formwork Systems Inc. (1)	Brampton ON
Petro Plan Safety Ltd. (1)	Calgary AB
PFB Corporation (1)	Calgary AB
Philip Services Corporation / PSC (1)	Burlington ON
Piping Resources (1)	Edmonton AB
Pitney Bowes Management Services Canada (1)	Toronto ON
Pizza Pizza Limited (1)	Toronto ON
Placer Dome Inc. (1)	Vancouver BC
Portage College (1)	Lac La Biche AB
PricewaterhouseCoopers LLP (1)	Hamilton ON
Priva Inc. (1)	Montréal QC
Pro-Bel Enterprises, Ltd. (1)	Ajax ON
Proco Machinery Inc. (1)	Mississauga ON
Procor Ltd. (1)	Oakville ON
Procuron Inc. (1)	Thornhill ON
Professional Engineers Ontario / PEO (1)	Toronto ON
Professional Pharmaceutical Corp. (1)	Lachine QC
Progestic International Inc. (1)	Ottawa ON
Provance Technologies Inc. (1)	Gatineau QC
Public Service Commission of Canada, Al (1)	Edmonton AB
Public Service Commission of Canada, Nov (1)	Halifax NS
Public Service Commission of Canada, (1)	Quebec City QC
Public Service Commission of Canada, Sask (1)	Regina SK
Purdy's Chocolates (1)	Vancouver BC
Pure Technologies Inc. (1)	Calgary AB
Purolator Courier Ltd. (1)	Toronto ON
Queen's University, Cancer Research Lab (1)	Kingston ON
Quick Link Communications Ltd. / QLC (1)	Calgary AB
R. Nicholls Distributors Inc. (1)	Longueuil QC
R.V. Anderson Associates Limited (1)	Toronto ON
Radiant Communications (1)	Calgary AB
RAM Computer Group Inc. (1)	Vaughan ON
Red Carpet Food Services (1)	Toronto ON
Red Deer College (1)	Red Deer AB
Registered Nurses Association of Ontario (1)	Toronto ON
Reliable Life Insurance Company (1)	Hamilton ON
Replicon Inc. (1)	Calgary AB
ReserveAmerica (1)	Milton ON
Ribstone Child and Family Services Aut (1)	Innisfail AB
Richmond Honda (1)	Richmond BC
Rittal Systems Ltd. (1)	Mississauga ON
Riverdale Hospital, The (1)	Toronto ON
Rocky Mountain Instruments Inc. / RMI (1)	Edmonton AB
Rogers Cable Inc. (1)	St. John's NF
RoomBlock Inc. (1)	Toronto ON
Royal Bank Financial Group (1)	Vancouver BC
Royal Building Systems (Cdn) Ltd. / R (1)	Woodbridge ON
Royal College of Dental Surgeons of Onta (1)	Toronto ON

For descriptions of the occupational categories used in this index, see page 458.

ADMINISTRATIVE (Cont.)

Royal Roads University (1) .... Victoria BC
Royal Ultraframe Ltd. (1) .... Toronto ON
Royal Victoria Hospital / RVH (1) .... Barrie ON
RSL COM Canada Inc. (1) .... Vancouver BC
RTO Enterprises Inc. (1) .... Mississauga ON
Runnymede Chronic Care Hospital (1) .... Toronto ON
SafetySmart.com (1) .... Calgary AB
SAS Institute (Canada) Inc. (1) .... Toronto ON
Saskatchewan Institute of Applied Scie (1) .... Saskatoon SK
Saskatchewan Liquor and Gaming Authority (1) .... Regina SK
Saskatchewan Post-Secondary Education and (1) .... Regina SK
SaskPower (1) .... Regina SK
SBR International (1) .... Toronto ON
Scancode Logistics (1) .... Mississauga ON
Seton (1) .... Richmond Hill ON
Shaw Communications Inc. (1) .... Burnaby BC
Shaw Pipe Protection Ltd. (1) .... Calgary AB
Shoppers Drug Mart (1) .... Toronto ON
Shopping Channel, The / TSC (1) .... Mississauga ON
Shorewood Packaging Corporation (1) .... Toronto ON
Shred-it (1) .... Oakville ON
Sibley & Associates Inc. (1) .... Burlington ON
Siemens Building Technologies Ltd. (1) .... Ottawa ON
Siemens Building Technologies Ltd., Cer (1) .... Richmond BC
Siemens Canada Ltd., Telecom Innovation C (1) .... Kanata ON
Sierra Wireless Inc. (1) .... Richmond BC
SITEL Canada Inc. (1) .... Toronto ON
SITEL Canada Inc. (1) .... Montréal QC
Sitraka Mobility (1) .... Toronto ON
SkillScape (1) .... Victoria BC
Skylink Technologies Inc. (1) .... Mississauga ON
Skyway Business Machines (1) .... Mississauga ON
SMED International Inc. (1) .... Calgary AB
Social Research and Demonstration Corpora (1) .... Ottawa ON
Society of Energy Professionals, The (1) .... Toronto ON
Soft Tracks (1) .... Richmond BC
Solvay Pharma Inc. (1) .... Toronto ON
Sony Music Canada (1) .... Toronto ON
Southern Alberta Institute of Technology (1) .... Calgary AB
Spaetgens Symons Evans Architects / SSE (1) .... Calgary AB
Spar Aerospace Limited (1) .... Edmonton AB
Spin Master Toys (1) .... Toronto ON
St. Clement's School (1) .... Toronto ON
St. John's Rehabilitation Hospital (1) .... Toronto ON
St. Joseph's Villa (1) .... Dundas ON
Stanpac Inc. (1) .... Smithville ON
State Farm Insurance Companies (1) .... Toronto ON
StockerYale Canada Inc. (1) .... Dollard-des-Ormeaux QC
Stronco Audio-Visuals (1) .... Toronto ON
Strongco Equipment (1) .... Stittsville ON
Stuart Olson Construction (1) .... Calgary AB
Suites Hotel, Les (1) .... Ottawa ON
Summit Food Service Distributors Inc. (1) .... Ottawa ON
Sun Chemical Ink Limited (1) .... Brampton ON
Sun Rich Fresh Foods Inc. (1) .... Richmond BC
Sunnybrook & Women's College Health Scie (1) .... Toronto ON
Sunnybrook & Women's College Health Scie (1) .... Toronto ON
Supportive Housing in Peel Foundatio (1) .... Mississauga ON
Surrey, City of (1) .... Surrey BC
Sutton Place Hotel Vancouver, The (1) .... Vancouver BC
SWI Systemware Inc. (1) .... Toronto ON
SWL Crane & Hoist 2000 Ltd. (1) .... Brampton ON
Syncrude Canada Ltd. (1) .... Fort McMurray AB
Syndesis Limited (1) .... Richmond Hill ON
Talon Systems Inc. (1) .... Mississauga ON
Targray Technology International I (1) .... Pointe-Claire QC
TAS Designbuild (1) .... Toronto ON
TCT Logistics Inc. (1) .... Mississauga ON
TEAM Inc. (1) .... St-Laurent QC
TELAV Audio Visual Services (1) .... Ottawa ON
TELAV Audio Visual Services (1) .... Lachine QC
Teleperformance Canada Inc. / TPCAN (1) .... Toronto ON
TeleSpectrum Canada Inc. (1) .... Toronto ON
Tellamon Photonic Networks Inc. (1) .... Ottawa ON
Ten Star Financial Services / Ten Star (1) .... Waterdown ON
Terra Group of Companies (1) .... Vancouver BC
Testforce (1) .... St-Laurent QC
Therapist's Choice Medical Supplies Inc. (1) .... Toronto ON
Thorburn Equipment Inc. (1) .... Pointe-Claire QC
Thrifty Canada, Ltd. (1) .... Mississauga ON
Thrifty Car Rental (1) .... Richmond BC
Thrive Media (1) .... Vancouver BC
Tim Office Solutions (1) .... Toronto ON
TLC Laser Eye Centers (1) .... Mississauga ON
Top Tape & Label Ltd. (1) .... Ancaster ON
Toronto Montessori Schools (1) .... Richmond Hill ON
Toronto Police Service (1) .... Toronto ON
Total Communications (1) .... Hamilton ON
Total Credit Recovery / TRC (1) .... Toronto ON
Towne Chevrolet Oldsmobile Inc. (1) .... Oakville ON
Tractel Ltd., Swingstage Division (1) .... Toronto ON
Trader.com (1) .... Edmonton AB
Transcontinental Publications G.T. Inc (1) .... Vancouver BC
Travel Guard Canada (1) .... Toronto ON
Travel Underwriters Group of Companies, (1) .... Richmond BC
Tri-Ed Ltd. (1) .... Mississauga ON
Tribal Sportswear Inc. (1) .... Montréal QC
Trophy Foods Inc. (1) .... Mississauga ON
Trow Consulting Engineers Ltd. (1) .... Brampton ON
TTG Systems Inc. (1) .... Edmonton AB
Umbra Ltd. (1) .... Toronto ON
UniFirst Canada Ltd. (1) .... Edmonton AB
Union of Canadian Transportation Employee (1) .... Ottawa ON
United Nations Children's Fund / UNICEF (1) .... Toronto ON
University Health Network, Shared Inform (1) .... Toronto ON
University of British Columbia / UBC (1) .... Vancouver BC
University of Calgary, Faculty of Social (1) .... Calgary AB
University of New Brunswick / UNB (1) .... Fredericton NB
Upper Canada District School Board (1) .... Brockville ON
USCO Logistics (1) .... Dorval QC
Vancouver, City of (1) .... Vancouver BC
Vancouver City Savings Credit Union / (1) .... Vancouver BC
Vancouver Hospital and Health Sciences (1) .... Vancouver BC
Venetor Equipment Rental Inc. (1) .... Hamilton ON
Venture Communications Ltd. (1) .... Calgary AB
Victorian Order of Nurses / VON, Easter (1) .... Kingston ON
Videoscope (1) .... Toronto ON
Vistek Ltd. (1) .... Toronto ON
VitalAire Healthcare (1) .... Mississauga ON
Vogue Brassiere Incorporated (1) .... Toronto ON
Volvo Laval (1) .... Laval QC
Waterloo, City of (1) .... Waterloo ON
Waterloo, The Regional Municipality of (1) .... Kitchener ON
WaveMakers Research Inc. (1) .... Vancouver BC
Weber Marking Systems of Canada (1) .... Mississauga ON
Wesco Distribution Canada Inc. (1) .... Burnaby BC
Westcan Wireless (1) .... Edmonton AB
WestJet Airlines Ltd. (1) .... Calgary AB
Wexford Residence Inc., The (1) .... Toronto ON
Whitesell Canada Inc. (1) .... Vaughan ON
Wi-LAN Inc. (1) .... Calgary AB
Williams Machinery Ltd. (1) .... Richmond BC
Wilton Industries Canada Ltd. (1) .... Toronto ON
Windsor Casino Limited (1) .... Windsor ON
Winpak Technologies Inc. (1) .... Toronto ON
Winters Instruments (1) .... Toronto ON
Woco Automotive Inc. (1) .... Concord ON
YM Inc. (1) .... Toronto ON
YM - YWHA, Ben Weider Jewish Community (1) .... Montréal QC
Yotta Yotta Inc. (1) .... Edmonton AB
Zed.i Solutions (1) .... Edmonton AB
Zurich Canada (1) .... Calgary AB

ADVERTISING

See also: Graphic Arts, Public Relations, Marketing, Publishing/Media.

Rogers Media, Publishing (11 positions) .... Toronto ON
Boulevard Media (Canada) Inc. / BMC (7) .... Vancouver BC
Trader.com (5) .... Edmonton AB
Tri-Media Marketing & Publicity Inc. (5) .... Welland ON
Watermark Advertising Design Ltd. (3) .... Calgary AB
Amplified Light Technologies Corp. / AL (2) .... Oakville ON
CTM Brochure Display Ltd. (2) .... Mississauga ON
Display Design Systems Ltd. (2) .... Edmonton AB
German Advertising Advantage Inc., The / (2) .... Markham ON
LPI Communication Group Inc. (2) .... Calgary AB
McMillan & Associates (2) .... Ottawa ON

ADVERTISING (Cont.)

MuscleTech Research and Development (2) .... Mississauga ON
NOWTV (2) .... Winnipeg MB
Rogers AT&T Wireless (2) .... Toronto ON
Staples Business Depot Ltd. (2) .... Markham ON
THEmedia (2) .... Vancouver BC
Town Publishing Inc. (2) .... Hamilton ON
Trader.com (2) .... Calgary AB
45 Degrees Corp. (1) .... Ottawa ON
Acart Communications (1) .... Ottawa ON
ACD Systems (1) .... Saanichton BC
ACNielsen Company of Canada (1) .... Markham ON
Advantex Marketing International Inc. (1) .... Toronto ON
Akeda Tools (1) .... Vancouver BC
Azure Publishing Inc. (1) .... Toronto ON
Calgary, City of (1) .... Calgary AB
Canada Law Book Inc. (1) .... Aurora ON
Canadian Petcetera Limited Partnership (1) .... Delta BC
Casino Niagara (1) .... Niagara Falls ON
Cloakware Corporation (1) .... Kanata ON
Coast Capital Savings (1) .... Richmond BC
Corel Corporation (1) .... Ottawa ON
Corus Entertainment Inc. (1) .... Toronto ON
Critical Mass Inc. (1) .... Calgary AB
CTC Communications Corp. (1) .... Mississauga ON
CyberSurf Corporation (1) .... Calgary AB
Dex Brothers Clothing Ltd. (1) .... Montréal QC
Filament Communications (1) .... Ottawa ON
George Brown College (1) .... Toronto ON
Global Television Network Inc. (1) .... Toronto ON
Heart and Stroke Foundation of Ontario (1) .... Toronto ON
Hewson Bridge and Smith Ltd. / HBS (1) .... Ottawa ON
HSBC Bank Canada (1) .... Vancouver BC
Ilco Unican Inc. (1) .... Montréal QC
IT World Canada (1) .... Toronto ON
JuneWarren Publishing Ltd. (1) .... Edmonton AB
JuneWarren Publishing Ltd. (1) .... Calgary AB
Leon's Furniture Ltd. (1) .... Toronto ON
Loewen Group Inc., The (1) .... Burnaby BC
Manitoba Justice / Culture, Heritage an (1) .... Winnipeg MB
Mentor Engineering (1) .... Calgary AB
Misco Canada Inc. (1) .... Markham ON
News Marketing Canada (1) .... Mississauga ON
OP Publishing Ltd. (1) .... Vancouver BC
Parasuco Jeans Inc. (1) .... St-Laurent QC
Penguin Books Canada Ltd. (1) .... Toronto ON
Radiant Communications (1) .... Calgary AB
Reno-Depot (1) .... Montréal QC
Rogers Media, Television (1) .... Toronto ON
Royal Bank Financial Group (1) .... Toronto ON
Shell Canada Limited (1) .... Calgary AB
Shoppers Drug Mart (1) .... Toronto ON
Shopping Channel, The / TSC (1) .... Mississauga ON
Starline Industries (1) .... Concord ON
Sychowski Communications Inc. (1) .... Montréal QC
Thrive Media (1) .... Vancouver BC
Tirecraft Auto Centers Ltd. (1) .... Sherwood Park AB
Toronto.com (1) .... Toronto ON
Trader.com (1) .... Toronto ON
Transcontinental Media (1) .... Toronto ON
Transcontinental Publications G.T. Inc (1) .... Vancouver BC
Venture Communications Ltd. (1) .... Calgary AB
Visions Electronics (1) .... Calgary AB
Webstorm Media (1) .... Montréal QC
Westfair Foods Ltd. (1) .... Calgary AB
Westminster Savings Credit Union (1) .... New Westminster BC
Whistler Blackcomb / Intrawest (1) .... Whistler BC

AEROSPACE

See also: Engineering, Transport, Trades/Technicians.

Bombardier Aerospace (75 positions) .... Montréal QC
Spar Aerospace Limited (48) .... Edmonton AB
EMS Technologies Canada Ltd (30) .... Ste-Anne-de-Bellevue QC
Public Service Commission of Canada, Onta (25) .... Ottawa ON
CMC Electronics Inc. (23) .... Kanata ON
Public Service Commission of Canada, Qu (22) .... Montréal QC
IMP Group Ltd., Aerospace Division (18) .... Enfield NS
MTU Maintenance Canada Ltd. (18) .... Richmond BC
MacDonald Dettwiler Space and Advanced (17) ...... Brampton ON
Bell Helicopter Textron Canada (12) .... Mirabel QC
Bombardier Aerospace, Defense Services (12) .... Mirabel QC
CMC Electronics Inc. (12) .... St-Laurent QC
Field Aviation West Ltd. (11) .... Calgary AB
Spar Aerospace Limited (11) .... Mississauga ON
CAE Inc. (10) .... St-Laurent QC
CanJet Airlines (10) .... Enfield NS
Ministry of Natural Resources, (10) .... Sault Ste. Marie ON
Cascade Aerospace Inc. (9) .... Abbotsford BC
MDS Aero Support Corporation (9) .... Ottawa ON
Telesat Canada (9) .... Gloucester ON
Tricom Technologies (8) .... Mississauga ON
Valcom Limited (Ottawa) (8) .... Ottawa ON
Raytheon Systems Canada Ltd. (7) .... Waterloo ON
Rolls-Royce Canada Ltd. (7) .... Lachine QC
Bombardier Inc., Completion Centre Montre (6) .... Dorval QC
Oerlikon Aerospace Inc. (6) .... St-Jean-sur-Richelieu QC
ADGA Group Consultants Inc. (5) .... Ottawa ON
Bomhoff Aerospace Corporation (5) .... St-Laurent QC
Innotech-Execaire Aviation Group, The (5) .... Dorval QC
Sander Geophysics Ltd. / SGL (5) .... Ottawa ON
Air Canada (4) .... Montréal QC
Boeing Canada Technology Ltd., Arnprior (4) .... Arnprior ON
Canadian Helicopters Ltd. (4) .... Les Cedres QC
Flight Dynamics Corp. (4) .... St-Jean-sur-Richelieu QC
Fugro Airborne Surveys (4) .... Ottawa ON
Greater Toronto Airports Authority / GTA (4) .... Toronto ON
Marshall Macklin Monaghan Limited (4) .... Thornhill ON
UMA Engineering Ltd. (4) .... Calgary AB
Vancouver International Airport Authori (4) .... Richmond BC
ACRO Aerospace Inc. (3) .... Richmond BC
Air Canada (3) .... Richmond BC
First Air (3) .... Carp ON
Honeywell Inc. (3) .... Montréal QC
Hudson General Aviation Services Inc. (3) .... Richmond BC
KnightHawk (3) .... Ottawa ON
Liburdi Engineering Ltd. (3) .... Dundas ON
MacDonald Dettwiler & Associates Ltd. / (3) .... Richmond BC
MacDonald Dettwiler & Associates Ltd. / M (3) .... Ottawa ON
Messier-Dowty Inc. (3) .... Peterborough ON
Ministry of Transportation, Ontario (3) .... Thunder Bay ON
Morningstar Air Express Inc. (3) .... Edmonton AB
Orenda Aerospace Corporation (3) .... Mississauga ON
Routes AstroEngineering Ltd. (3) .... Kanata ON
Skyservice Airlines Inc. (3) .... Mississauga ON
TEAM Inc. (3) .... St-Laurent QC
Wescam (3) .... Burlington ON
WestJet Airlines Ltd. (3) .... Calgary AB
Aero Machining Ltd. (2) .... Montréal QC
Air Nova / Air Canada Regional Inc. (2) .... Enfield NS
Air Transat (2) .... Mirabel QC
Alberta Infrastructure & Transportation (2) .... Edmonton AB
Avcorp Industries Inc. (2) .... Delta BC
Bombardier Aerospace, Regional Aircraft (2) .... Toronto ON
Canada 3000 Airlines Ltd. (2) .... Toronto ON
COM DEV International (2) .... Cambridge ON
Computing Devices Canada Ltd. / CDC (2) .... Ottawa ON
Department of Works, Services and Tra (2) .... St. John's NF
EMS Technologies Canada Ltd. (2) .... Ottawa ON
FlightSafety Canada (2) .... Toronto ON
Found Aircraft Canada Inc. (2) .... Parry Sound ON
Harris Corporation, Microwave Communicat (2) .... Calgary AB
Irvin Aerospace Canada Inc. (2) .... Fort Erie ON
NAV Canada (2) .... Ottawa ON
Novatronics Inc. (2) .... Stratford ON
Optech Inc. (2) .... Toronto ON
Pratt & Whitney Canada Corporation / P (2) .... Longueuil QC
Public Service Commission of Canada, (2) .... Quebec City QC
Raytheon Systems Canada Ltd. (2) .... Richmond BC
RCM Technologies Canada (2) .... Ottawa ON
Thales Avionics Canada Inc. (2) .... St-Laurent QC
Thales Optronics Canada Inc. (2) .... St-Laurent QC
Thomson-CSF Optronique Canada Inc. (2) .... St-Laurent QC
Tube-Fab Ltd. (2) .... Mississauga ON
Adacel Inc. (1) .... Brossard QC
AeroInfo Systems Inc. (1) .... Richmond BC
Air Transat Holidays (1) .... Montréal QC
Andrew Canada Inc. (1) .... Whitby ON

AEROSPACE (Cont.)

Appendix Technical Publishing Group (1) .... Ottawa ON
Atlantis Systems International (1) .... Brampton ON
Avmax Group Inc. (1) .... Calgary AB
CML ATC Technologies Inc. (1) .... Hull QC
Duke Blakey, Inc. (1) .... Markham ON
EBA Engineering Consultants Ltd. (1) .... Edmonton AB
GE Capital Canada (1) .... Montréal QC
Hayes Forest Service Ltd. (1) .... Duncan BC
Heroux Devtek, Magtron Division (1) .... Toronto ON
Interfast Inc. (1) .... St-Laurent QC
Linamar Corporation, Eston Division (1) .... Guelph ON
Lockheed Martin Canada Inc. (1) .... Kanata ON
MacDonald Dettwiler & Associates Ltd. / (1) .... Halifax NS
Medicine Hat, City of (1) .... Medicine Hat AB
Ministry of Health and Ministry Respons (1) .... Victoria BC
Mount Royal College (1) .... Calgary AB
Northern Airborne Technology Ltd. / NAT (1) .... Kelowna BC
Nuance Global Traders (Canada) Inc. (1) .... Richmond BC
Waterloo, The Regional Municipality of (1) .... Kitchener ON
Xwave Solutions Inc. (1) .... Mississauga ON
Xwave Solutions Inc. (1) .... Dorval QC

AGRICULTURE/FISHERIES

See also: Biotech/Biology, Scientific.

Alberta Agriculture, Food & Rural Devel (29 positions)Edmonton AB
Ministry of Agriculture, Food and Rural A (28) .... Guelph ON
Manitoba Agriculture and Food (27) .... Winnipeg MB
Ministry of Agriculture, Food and Fishe (25) .... Victoria BC
Department of Forest Resources & Agri (20) .... St. John's NF
Ministry of Agriculture, Food and Rural A (15) .... Guelph ON
Department of Agriculture, Fisheries (8) .... Fredericton NB
University of Guelph (8) .... Guelph ON
Public Service Commission of Canada, Ont (7) .... Toronto ON
Department of Fisheries & Aquaculture (5) .... St. John's NF
Canadian Wheat Board / CWB (4) .... Winnipeg MB
Ministry of Water, Land and Air Protect (4) .... Victoria BC
Olds College (4) .... Olds AB
Public Service Commission of Canada, New (4) .... Moncton NB
Public Service Commission of Canada, (4) .... Quebec City QC
Agriculture and Agri-Food Canada (3) .... Winnipeg MB
Axys Environmental Consulting Ltd. (3) .... Calgary AB
Canadian Food Inspection Agency / CFIA (3) .... Nepean ON
Canadian Grain Commission / CGC (3) .... Winnipeg MB
Lakeland College (3) .... Vermilion AB
Manitoba Conservation (3) .... Winnipeg MB
Ministry of Agriculture, Food and Rural A (3) .... Guelph ON
Ministry of Natural Resources, Onta (3) .... Peterborough ON
Ministry of Natural Resources, Onta (3) .... Peterborough ON
Public Service Commission of Canada, B (3) .... Vancouver BC
Sheridan Nurseries Ltd. (3) .... Georgetown ON
Sun Rich Fresh Foods Inc. (3) .... Richmond BC
University of Guelph, Department of Patho (3) .... Guelph ON
BC Hydro (2) .... Vancouver BC
Cargill Limited (2) .... Winnipeg MB
Farm Business Consultants Inc. / FBC (2) .... Calgary AB
Golder Associates Ltd. (2) .... Calgary AB
Manitoba Transportation & Government Se (2) .... Winnipeg MB
Ministry of Natural Resources, Ontari (2) .... Kemptville ON
Public Service Commission of Canada, BC (2) .... Victoria BC
Public Service Commission of Canada, Nov (2) .... Halifax NS
Public Service Commission of Canada, Sask (2) .... Regina SK
Toronto Zoo (2) .... Toronto ON
Alberta Environment (1) .... Edmonton AB
Alberta Mental Health Board, Alberta Hosp (1) .... Ponoka AB
Alberta Sustainable Resource Developmen (1) .... Edmonton AB
AMEC Earth & Environmental Ltd. (1) .... Calgary AB
BASF Canada Inc. (1) .... Toronto ON
Brampton, City of (1) .... Brampton ON
Brantford, Corporation of the City of (1) .... Brantford ON
Calgary, City of (1) .... Calgary AB
Canadian Food Inspection Agency / CFIA (1) .... Moncton NB
Canadian Petcetera Limited Partnership (1) .... Delta BC
Dairy Farmers of Ontario (1) .... Mississauga ON
Dairyworld Foods Inc. (1) .... Brampton ON
Department of Municipal and Provincia (1) .... St. John's NF

Dillon Engineering Ltd. (1) .... Winnipeg MB
E.B. Eddy Specialty Papers (1) .... Espanola ON
Fairview College (1) .... Fairview AB
Fernlea Flowers Ltd. (1) .... Delhi ON
Grand River Poultry Farm Ltd. (1) .... Paris ON
Growmark Inc. (1) .... Mississauga ON
Henry Schein Arcona Inc. (1) .... St. Catharines ON
Holstein Association of Canada, The / (1) .... Brantford ON
ITR Laboratories Canada Inc. (1) .... Baie d'Urfe QC
Kawartha Lakes, Corporation of the City (1) .... Lindsay ON
Kwantlen University College (1) .... Surrey BC
Loblaw Companies Ltd. (1) .... Mississauga ON
McMaster University, Faculty of Health (1) .... Hamilton ON
Ministry of Forests, BC (1) .... Fort St. John BC
Ministry of Natural Resources, Ontario (1) .... London ON
Ministry of Natural Resources, Ontario (1) .... Geraldton ON
Ministry of the Environment, Ontario (W (1) .... Hamilton ON
Mississauga, City of (1) .... Mississauga ON
Montréal, Ville de (1) .... Montréal QC
Neilson Dairy (1) .... Ottawa ON
Northern Lights College / NLC (1) .... Fort St. John BC
Otter Farm & Home Co-operative (1) .... Aldergrove BC
Pacific National Aquaculture (1) .... Victoria BC
Pharmacia Animal Health (1) .... Orangeville ON
Public Service Commission of Canada, Al (1) .... Edmonton AB
Public Service Commission of Canada, Onta (1) .... Ottawa ON
Public Service Commission, PEI (1) .... Charlottetown PE
Queen's University, Department of Human (1) .... Kingston ON
Regina, City of (1) .... Regina SK
Rosedale Golf Club (1) .... Toronto ON
Royal Bank Financial Group (1) .... Calgary AB
Saskatchewan Wheat Pool (1) .... Regina SK
SemBioSys Genetics Inc. (1) .... Calgary AB
Skjodt-Barrett Foods (1) .... Mississauga ON
University of Calgary (1) .... Calgary AB
Whitby Mental Health Centre (1) .... Whitby ON

APPAREL

See also: Retail, Design.

Parasuco Jeans Inc. (13 positions) .... St-Laurent QC
Ash City (12) .... Toronto ON
San Francisco Group (12) .... Boucherville QC
JayGur International Inc. (9) .... St-Laurent QC
Effigi Inc. (8) .... Laval QC
Dex Brothers Clothing Ltd. (7) .... Montréal QC
Groupe J.S. International (7) .... Montréal QC
Main Knitting Inc. (7) .... Montréal QC
West Coast Apparel Inc. (7) .... Vancouver BC
DDK Apparel Inc. (6) .... Montréal QC
Groupe Dynamite Inc. (6) .... Mount Royal QC
Quality Goods IMD Inc. (6) .... St-Laurent QC
Dizaro Collection (5) .... Montréal QC
Majco Apparel Inc. (5) .... St-Laurent QC
Roots Canada Ltd. (5) .... Toronto ON
Winners Merchants Inc. (5) .... Mississauga ON
Cirque du Soleil (4) .... Montréal QC
Club Monaco International (4) .... Toronto ON
Dalia Collection (4) .... Montréal QC
Shirmax Fashions Ltd. (4) .... Montréal QC
Trio Selection Inc. (4) .... Montréal QC
Agmont Inc. (3) .... Montréal QC
Algo Group Inc. (3) .... Montréal QC
Joseph Ribkoff Inc. (3) .... Dorval QC
Laura Canada (3) .... Laval QC
London Blues (3) .... St-Laurent QC
Tribal Sportswear Inc. (3) .... Montréal QC
Vogue Brassiere Incorporated (3) .... Toronto ON
Ailes de la Mode, Les (2) .... Laval QC
Batts Canada Ltd. (2) .... Lasalle QC
BECO Industries Inc. (2) .... Anjou QC
Bedo (2) .... St-Laurent QC
Canadian Recreation Products Inc. (2) .... Mount Royal QC
Christina America Inc. (2) .... Montréal QC
Conrad C Collection Inc. (2) .... Montréal QC
Femme de Carrière (2) .... Montréal QC
Gentry Knitting Mills Ltd. (2) .... Toronto ON
Majestic Industries Ltd. (2) .... Montréal QC
Mexx Canada Inc. (2) .... Montréal QC

APPAREL (Cont.)

Mondetta Clothing Co. (2) .... Winnipeg MB
Securitex Inc. (2) .... Montréal QC
Utex Corporation (2) .... Montréal QC
Aldo Group Inc. (1) .... St-Laurent QC
Arc'Teryx Equipment Inc. (1) .... Burnaby BC
Athletic Image (1) .... Montréal QC
Barmish Inc. (1) .... St-Laurent QC
Bata Retail Canada (1) .... Toronto ON
British Columbia Mental Health So (1) .... Port Coquitlam BC
Canadian Linen and Uniform Services (1) .... Toronto ON
Collections Andrade Inc. (1) .... Montréal QC
Coltin International Group (1) .... Toronto ON
Cotton Ginny Ltd. (1) .... Toronto ON
Danier Leather Inc. (1) .... St. John's NF
Essentus Inc. (1) .... Montréal QC
Fersten Group (1) .... Montréal QC
Fields Stores (1) .... Richmond BC
George Brown College (1) .... Toronto ON
Golf Town Canada Inc. (1) .... Richmond Hill ON
Holt Renfrew (1) .... Ottawa ON
Humber College of Applied Arts and Techn (1) .... Toronto ON
Indeka Group, The (1) .... Oakville ON
Le Chateau (1) .... Mount Royal QC
Louis Vuitton Ogilvy (1) .... Montréal QC
Maillot Baltex Inc. (1) .... Montréal QC
Manitoba Justice / Culture, Heritage an (1) .... Winnipeg MB
Ministry of Correctional Services, Ontar (1) .... Toronto ON
Ministry of Correctional Services, Ontar (1) .... Toronto ON
Parkhurst Knitwear (1) .... Toronto ON
Peerless Clothing Inc. (1) .... Montréal QC
Real Canadian Superstore, The (1) .... Medicine Hat AB
Reitmans (Canada) Limited (1) .... Montréal QC
Tommy Hilfiger Canada Inc. (1) .... Montréal QC
Tristan & America (1) .... Montréal QC
Westfair Foods Ltd. (1) .... Calgary AB
YM Inc. (1) .... Toronto ON
York House School (1) .... Vancouver BC

ARCHITECTURE

*See also: Construction, Real Estate, Design, Trades/
Technicians.*

Public Service Commission of Canada, (8 positions) ..... Ottawa ON
Alberta Infrastructure & Transportation (6) .... Edmonton AB
Hellmuth, Obata & Kassabaum, Inc. / HOK (6) .... Toronto ON
Kasian Kennedy Architecture, Interior (5) .... Vancouver BC
Spaetgens Symons Evans Architects / SSE (5) .... Calgary AB
Stantec Consulting Ltd. (5) .... Calgary AB
UMA Engineering Ltd. (5) .... Edmonton AB
URS Cole, Sherman (5) .... Thornhill ON
Group 2 Architecture Engineering Interi (4) .... Red Deer AB
Mississauga, City of (4) .... Mississauga ON
Surrey, City of (4) .... Surrey BC
Abugov Kaspar (3) .... Calgary AB
Gibbs Gage Architects (3) .... Calgary AB
Giffels Associates Limited (3) .... Toronto ON
Graham Edmunds (3) .... Calgary AB
Hutchinson Architects Inc. (3) .... Calgary AB
Kasian Kennedy Architecture, Interior De (3) .... Calgary AB
LeBlond Partnership (3) .... Calgary AB
Leonard Koffman, Architect (3) .... Ottawa ON
Timberfield Roof Truss (3) .... London ON
Totten Sims Hubicki Associates / TSH (3) .... Whitby ON
Unigroup Architecture & Interior Design (3) .... Edmonton AB
AldrichPears Associates (2) .... Vancouver BC
Ashcroft Homes (2) .... Ottawa ON
Balmer Plaster Moulding Corporation of A (2) .... Toronto ON
Bombardier Aerospace, Regional Aircraft (2) .... Toronto ON
C/S Construction Specialties Ltd. (2) .... Mississauga ON
CJP Architects (2) .... New Westminster BC
Cohos Evamy Partners, The (2) .... Edmonton AB
Cohos Evamy Partners, The (2) .... Calgary AB
Department of Human Resources, Nunavut (2) .... Iqaluit NU
Earth Tech Canada Inc. (2) .... Markham ON
Fast + Epp (2) .... Vancouver BC

Henderson Development (Canada) Ltd. (2) .... Vancouver BC
IKEA Calgary (2) .... Calgary AB
Management Board Secretariat (2) .... Toronto ON
Manasc Isaac Architects Ltd. (2) .... Edmonton AB
Niagara, The Regional Municipality of (2) .... Thorold ON
Ontario Science Centre / OSC (2) .... Toronto ON
Polygon Interior Design Limited (2) .... Vancouver BC
Poon McKenzie Architects (2) .... Calgary AB
Rice Brydone Ltd. (2) .... Toronto ON
Richmond Hill, Town of (2) .... Richmond Hill ON
Ryerson Polytechnic University, Departme (2) .... Toronto ON
Syncor Business Environments Ltd. (2) .... Vancouver BC
TAS Designbuild (2) .... Toronto ON
Acres & Associates Environmental Ltd. (1) .... Toronto ON
Advanced Business Interiors Inc. /ABI (1) .... Ottawa ON
AEdifica (1) .... Montréal QC
Ainsworth Inc. (1) .... Coquitlam BC
Alberta Community Development (1) .... Edmonton AB
Algonquin College (1) .... Nepean ON
Architrave Design Office Service (1) .... Gabriola Island BC
Arriscraft International Inc. (1) .... Cambridge ON
Arxx Building Products (1) .... Cobourg ON
Bantrel Inc. (1) .... Edmonton AB
Brampton, City of (1) .... Brampton ON
Brantford, Corporation of the City of (1) .... Brantford ON
Brookfield LePage Johnson Controls Facili (1) .... Ottawa ON
Burger King Restaurants of Canada Inc. (1) .... Toronto ON
Cadillac Fairview Corporation Limited, T (1) .... Toronto ON
Calgary Regional Health Authority / CRHA (1) .... Calgary AB
Central Precast Inc. (1) .... Nepean ON
CH2M HILL Canada Ltd. (1) .... Toronto ON
Ciot Marble & Granite Inc. (1) .... Concord ON
Cirque du Soleil (1) .... Montréal QC
Cosburn Patterson Mather Ltd. (1) .... Markham ON
David Thompson Health Region, Red Deer (1) .... Red Deer AB
Decoustics Ltd. (1) .... Toronto ON
Delta Hudson Engineering Ltd. (1) .... Calgary AB
Department of Tourism, Culture and Re (1) .... St. John's NF
Dillon Consulting Ltd. (1) .... London ON
Edmonton Catholic Schools (1) .... Edmonton AB
EMS Technologies Canada Ltd (1) .... Ste-Anne-de-Bellevue QC
Future Electronics Inc. (1) .... Pointe-Claire QC
Great Atlantic & Pacific Co. of Canada L (1) .... Toronto ON
Halsall Associates Ltd. (1) .... Toronto ON
Halton Hills, Town of (1) .... Halton Hills ON
Hatch Associates Ltd. (1) .... Mississauga ON
Hopping Kovach Grinnell (1) .... Vancouver BC
IBI Group (1) .... Edmonton AB
IDMD Design & Manufacturing Inc. (1) .... Toronto ON
Jayman Master Builder (1) .... Calgary AB
JL Richards & Associates Ltd. (1) .... Kingston ON
Landmark Master Builder Inc. (1) .... Edmonton AB
Laurysen Kitchens Ltd. (1) .... Stittsville ON
Linen Chest (1) .... Brossard QC
London, City of (1) .... London ON
Loyalist College (1) .... Belleville ON
Mac's Convenience Stores Inc. (1) .... Toronto ON
MacLachlan & Mitchell Homes Inc. (1) .... Edmonton AB
Marshall Macklin Monaghan Limited (1) .... Thornhill ON
Maxim Morrison Hershfield Ltd. (1) .... Edmonton AB
McCrum's Office Furnishings (1) .... Calgary AB
MDS Aero Support Corporation (1) .... Ottawa ON
Mexx Canada Inc. (1) .... Montréal QC
Milton, Town of (1) .... Milton ON
Morrison Hershfield (1) .... Toronto ON
New Brunswick Community College, Woods (1) .... Woodstock NB
Normerica (1) .... Gormley ON
Northern Alberta Institute of Technolog (1) .... Edmonton AB
Oakville, Corporation of the Town of (1) .... Oakville ON
Olds College (1) .... Olds AB
Ontario Heritage Foundation, Corporate S (1) .... Toronto ON
Patella Manufacturing Inc. (1) .... Lasalle QC
Perennial Design Company (1) .... Toronto ON
Pizza Pizza Limited (1) .... Toronto ON
Plaza Group, The (1) .... Baie d'Urfe QC
Public Service Commission of Canada, B (1) .... Vancouver BC
Public Service Commission of Canada, Qu (1) .... Montréal QC
Public Service Commission of Canada, (1) .... Quebec City QC
Regional Doors and Hardware (1) .... St. Catharines ON
RGO Office Products (1) .... Calgary AB
Rohit Group, The (1) .... Edmonton AB
Rooms International (1) .... Ottawa ON

For descriptions of the occupational categories used in this index, see page 458.

ARCHITECTURE (Cont.)

Royal Bank Financial Group (1) .... Toronto ON
Ryerson Polytechnic University, Faculty (1) .... Toronto ON
Shirmax Fashions Ltd. (1) .... Montréal QC
Shoppers Drug Mart (1) .... Toronto ON
Sobotec Ltd. (1) .... Hamilton ON
Stantec Geomatics Ltd. (1) .... Edmonton AB
Statesman Corporation (1) .... Calgary AB
Sterling Homes (1) .... Calgary AB
Suss Woodcraft International (1) .... Lasalle QC
Toronto, City of (1) .... Toronto ON
Trent University (1) .... Peterborough ON
Trow Consulting Engineers Ltd. (1) .... Brampton ON
UMA Engineering Ltd. (1) .... Delta BC
UMA Engineering Ltd. (1) .... Calgary AB
UMA Engineering Ltd. (1) .... Toronto ON
University of Toronto, Operations & Serv (1) .... Toronto ON
Upper Canada District School Board (1) .... Brockville ON
Valley City Manufacturing Company Limited (1) .... Dundas ON
Vancouver, City of (1) .... Vancouver BC
Westfair Properties Ltd. (1) .... Vancouver BC
Winners Merchants Inc. (1) .... Mississauga ON

ARTS & CULTURE

See also: Govt./Nonprofit, Hospitality, Public Relations.

Alberta Community Development (7 positions) .... Edmonton AB
Cirque Eloize (5) .... Montréal QC
Department of Tourism, Culture and Re (5) .... St. John's NF
Emily Carr Institute of Art and Design (5) .... Vancouver BC
National Arts Centre / NAC (5) .... Ottawa ON
Royal British Columbia Museum (5) .... Victoria BC
Royal Ontario Museum / ROM (5) .... Toronto ON
Canada Council for the Arts, The (4) .... Ottawa ON
Banff Centre, The (3) .... Banff AB
Cirque du Soleil (3) .... Montréal QC
McGill University, Faculty of Music (De (3) .... Montréal QC
Red Deer College (3) .... Red Deer AB
Arts Umbrella (2) .... Vancouver BC
Canada Science and Technology Museum Corp (2) ...... Ottawa ON
MacKenzie Art Gallery (2) .... Regina SK
Medicine Hat College (2) .... Medicine Hat AB
Ministry of Citizenship, Culture and Rec (2) .... Toronto ON
Ministry of Tourism, Culture and Recreat (2) .... Midland ON
Nova Scotia College of Art and Design / (2) .... Halifax NS
Parks Canada Agency (2) .... Hull QC
School District #36 (Surrey) (2) .... Surrey BC
Vancouver Art Gallery (2) .... Vancouver BC
Alberta College of Art & Design / ACAD (1) .... Calgary AB
AldrichPears Associates (1) .... Vancouver BC
Art Gallery of Hamilton / AGH (1) .... Hamilton ON
Art in Motion (1) .... Coquitlam BC
Brentwood College (1) .... Mill Bay BC
Calgary, City of (1) .... Calgary AB
Canadian Museum of Civilization Corporation (1) .... Hull QC
Cirque du Soleil (1) .... Montréal QC
Concordia University (1) .... Montréal QC
Crestwood School (1) .... Toronto ON
Dufferin-Peel Catholic District Scho (1) .... Mississauga ON
Halton, The Regional Municipality of (1) .... Oakville ON
Hamilton, City of (1) .... Hamilton ON
Hamilton-Wentworth District School Boar (1) .... Hamilton ON
Havergal College (1) .... Toronto ON
Kwantlen University College (1) .... Surrey BC
Manitoba Justice / Culture, Heritage an (1) .... Winnipeg MB
Markham, Corporation of the Town of (1) .... Markham ON
Ministry of Economic Development and Tra (1) .... Toronto ON
Mississauga, City of (1) .... Mississauga ON
Mount Royal College (1) .... Calgary AB
Oil and Gas Commission, BC (1) .... Victoria BC
Okanagan University College / OUC (1) .... Kelowna BC
Ontario Institute for Studies in Educati (1) .... Toronto ON
Prime Minister's Office (1) .... Ottawa ON
Public Service Commission of Canada, Onta (1) .... Ottawa ON
Quality Goods IMD Inc. (1) .... St-Laurent QC
Ridley College (1) .... St. Catharines ON
School District #59 (Peace River So (1) .... Dawson Creek BC

Sony Music Canada (1) .... Toronto ON
St. Clement's School (1) .... Toronto ON
St. George's School (1) .... Vancouver BC
Toronto Catholic District School Board (1) .... Toronto ON
Toronto Montessori Schools (1) .... Richmond Hill ON
Toronto Zoo (1) .... Toronto ON
Vancouver, City of (1) .... Vancouver BC
Waterloo Catholic District School Boar (1) .... Kitchener ON
York House School (1) .... Vancouver BC
York Region District School Board (1) .... Aurora ON

AUTOMOTIVE

See also: Engineering, Transport, Trades/Technicians.

Magna International Inc. (35 positions) .... Concord ON
ABC Group Inc. (20) .... Toronto ON
Westport Innovations Inc. (15) .... Vancouver BC
Cowell Auto Group (12) .... Richmond BC
John Bear Pontiac Buick Cadillac Ltd. (8) .... Hamilton ON
Linamar Corporation, Eston Division (8) .... Guelph ON
Orlick Industries Ltd. (8) .... Hamilton ON
Budget Car Rentals Toronto Ltd. (7) .... Mississauga ON
Toyota Canada Inc. (7) .... Toronto ON
Mercedes-Benz Canada Inc. (6) .... Toronto ON
Siemens Automotive (6) .... London ON
Boulevard St-Martin Auto Inc. / BSM (5) .... Laval QC
City Chevrolet Oldsmobile Ltd. (5) .... Hamilton ON
GFI Control Systems Inc. (5) .... Kitchener ON
Hewitt Equipment Ltd. (5) .... Pointe-Claire QC
Sheehan's Truck Centre Inc. (5) .... Burlington ON
Cité Nissan (4) .... Montréal QC
Dent Wizard Canada Ltd. (4) .... Oakville ON
Discount Car and Truck Rentals (4) .... Toronto ON
Discovery Ford Sales (4) .... Burlington ON
Downtown BMW (4) .... Toronto ON
Four Seasons Moto-Sports (4) .... Fort McMurray AB
Jim Peplinski's Leasemaster National (4) .... Toronto ON
Magna International Inc. (4) .... Concord ON
Mews Chev Olds (4) .... Orleans ON
Modatek Systems (4) .... St. Thomas ON
Myers Chev Olds Cadillac (4) .... Ottawa ON
Towne Chevrolet Oldsmobile Inc. (4) .... Oakville ON
Belisle Chev Olds Cadillac (3) .... Ottawa ON
Calgary, City of (3) .... Calgary AB
Dynasty Motorcar Corp. (3) .... Kelowna BC
Eastgate Ford (3) .... Hamilton ON
Eastside Dodge (3) .... Calgary AB
F&P Manufacturing, Inc. (3) .... Tottenham ON
Global Thermoelectric Inc. (3) .... Calgary AB
Honda of Canada Manufacturing (3) .... Alliston ON
Hyundai Auto Canada (3) .... Markham ON
Innovative Cooling Dynamics / STT Te (3) .... Mississauga ON
John Holland Chevrolet Oldsmobile Ltd (3) .... Burlington ON
Kia Canada Inc. (3) .... Mississauga ON
Richmond Honda (3) .... Richmond BC
SKD Automotive Group (3) .... Milton ON
Spinelli Lexus Toyota (3) .... Lachine QC
Terrace Ford Lincoln Sales (3) .... Burlington ON
Town + Country BMW (3) .... Thornhill ON
VFC Inc. (3) .... Toronto ON
Volkswagen Canada Inc. / VCI (3) .... Ajax ON
Woco Automotive Inc. (3) .... Concord ON
A. Berger Precision Ltd. (2) .... Brampton ON
ADESA Canada Inc., Corporate Office (2) .... Mississauga ON
Agile Systems Inc. (2) .... Waterloo ON
Altruck International Truck Centres (2) .... Hamilton ON
BMW Canada Inc. (2) .... Whitby ON
BMW Canbec (2) .... Montréal QC
British Columbia Automobile Association (2) .... Burnaby BC
CAA Central Ontario (2) .... Thornhill ON
Campbell Ford Sales Ltd. (2) .... Ottawa ON
City Buick Pontiac Cadillac Ltd. (2) .... Toronto ON
Daewoo Auto Canada Inc. (2) .... Markham ON
Dana Long Manufacturing Ltd. (2) .... Mississauga ON
Dueck Chevrolet Oldsmobile Cadillac Lt (2) .... Vancouver BC
Enterprise Rent-A-Car (2) .... Burnaby BC
Enterprise Rent-A-Car (2) .... Nepean ON
Fairview College (2) .... Fairview AB
Ford Motor Company of Canada Ltd., Oakv (2) .... Oakville ON

AUTOMOTIVE (Cont.)

General Hydrogen / GH (2) .... Vancouver BC
Honda Canada Inc. (2) .... Toronto ON
John Logan Chevrolet Oldsmobile Inc. (2) .... Brampton ON
Kanata Ford (2) .... Kanata ON
KSR International (2) .... Ridgetown ON
Leggat Pontiac Buick Cadillac Ltd. (2) .... Burlington ON
Matsu Manufacturing Inc. (2) .... Brampton ON
Mercedes-Benz Canada Inc. (2) .... Vancouver BC
Minacs Worldwide Inc. (2) .... Markham ON
Nemak (2) .... Windsor ON
Nethercott Chev Olds (2) .... Hamilton ON
Nissan Canada Inc. (2) .... Mississauga ON
Richmond Suzuki Subaru (2) .... Richmond BC
Sako Rent-A-Car (2) .... Montréal QC
Snap-On Tools of Canada Ltd. (2) .... Mississauga ON
Snap-On Tools of Canada Ltd. (2) .... Ottawa ON
Speedy Auto & Window Glass (2) .... Concord ON
Stackpole Ltd., Engineered Products (2) .... Mississauga ON
Stoney Creek Mack (2) .... Stoney Creek ON
Tesma International Inc. (2) .... Maple ON
Thrifty Car Rental (2) .... Richmond BC
Tiercon Industries Inc. (2) .... Stoney Creek ON
Wheeltronic Ltd. (2) .... Mississauga ON
Williams Machinery Ltd. (2) .... Richmond BC
Yamaha Motor Canada Ltd. (2) .... Toronto ON
A.W. Miller Technical Sales (1) .... Mississauga ON
Access International Automotive Ltd. (1) .... Calgary AB
ADESA Canada Inc. (1) .... Brampton ON
Alberta Motor Association / AMA (1) .... Edmonton AB
Amcan Castings Ltd. (1) .... Hamilton ON
Antomax Automotive Technologies (1) .... Mississauga ON
ARI Financial Services Inc. (1) .... Mississauga ON
Auto Sense (1) .... Mississauga ON
Bauer Industries Ltd. (1) .... Waterloo ON
BC Rapid Transit Co. Ltd. / BCRTC (1) .... Burnaby BC
Brampton, City of (1) .... Brampton ON
Bridgestone Firestone Canada Inc. / (1) .... Mississauga ON
Budd Canada Inc. (1) .... Kitchener ON
Burlington Technologies Inc., Burling (1) .... Burlington ON
C-MAC Invotronics Inc. (1) .... Toronto ON
Canadian Gypsum Company / CGC Inc. (1) .... Hagersville ON
Carsen Group Inc. (1) .... Markham ON
Chalmers Suspensions International I (1) .... Mississauga ON
Co-Ex-Tec Industries (1) .... Concord ON
Collins & Aikman (1) .... Toronto ON
Commercial Spring and Tool Company L (1) .... Mississauga ON
Conestoga College of Applied Arts & Te (1) .... Kitchener ON
DaimlerChrysler Canada Inc. (1) .... Windsor ON
Day & Ross Transportation Group, The (1) .... Hartland NB
Debiasi Group, The / DBG (1) .... Mississauga ON
Debiasi Group, The / DBG (1) .... Mississauga ON
Dennison Chevrolet Oldsmobile Ltd. (1) .... Richmond BC
Denso Manufacturing Canada, Inc. (1) .... Guelph ON
Dufferin-Peel Catholic District Scho (1) .... Mississauga ON
Fountain Tire (1) .... Edmonton AB
Gear Centre Group of Companies, The (1) .... Edmonton AB
General Motors of Canada Ltd., Diesel Div (1) .... London ON
Georgian College (1) .... Barrie ON
Giffels Associates Limited (1) .... Toronto ON
Guelph, City of (1) .... Guelph ON
H.J. Pfaff Motors Inc. (1) .... Newmarket ON
Halton, The Regional Municipality of (1) .... Oakville ON
Import Auto Leasing (1) .... Gloucester ON
Industrial Research and Development Inst (1) .... Midland ON
Lansdowne Dodge City Ltd. (1) .... Richmond BC
Mack Canada Inc. (1) .... Mississauga ON
Mark IV Air Intake Systems (1) .... Montréal QC
Mevotech Inc. (1) .... Toronto ON
Minacs Worldwide Inc. (1) .... Pickering ON
Ministry of Economic Development and Tra (1) .... Toronto ON
Ministry of the Solicitor General, Ontar (1) .... Orillia ON
Mississauga, City of (1) .... Mississauga ON
National Research Council Canada, Institu (1) .... Ottawa ON
New Brunswick Community College, Moncton (1) .... Moncton NB
Northern Star Trucking Ltd. (1) .... Toronto ON
Percepta (1) .... Toronto ON
Productivity Improvement Center / PIC (1) .... Whitby ON
Public Service Commission of Canada, (1) .... Quebec City QC

Purolator Courier Ltd. (1) .... Toronto ON
Red Deer, City of (1) .... Red Deer AB
Regina, City of (1) .... Regina SK
Saskatchewan Institute of Applied Scie (1) .... Moose Jaw SK
School District #60 (Peace River N (1) .... Fort St. John BC
Toronto Transit Commission / TTC (1) .... Toronto ON
Travelers Leasing Corporation (1) .... Burnaby BC
Tyco Electronics Canada Ltd. (1) .... Markham ON
Underwriters' Laboratories of Canada / U (1) .... Toronto ON
United Parcel Service Canada Ltd. / UPS (1) .... Lachine QC
Valcom Limited (Ottawa) (1) .... Ottawa ON
Volvo Laval (1) .... Laval QC
VQuip Inc. (1) .... Burlington ON
Wurth Canada Limited (1) .... Mississauga ON
XCELLSiS (1) .... Burnaby BC
Xtra Lease (1) .... Lachine QC

BANKING
See also: Finance, Insurance, Accounting.

Royal Bank Financial Group (56 positions) .... Toronto ON
National Bank of Greece / NBG (12) .... Montréal QC
HSBC Bank Canada (9) .... Vancouver BC
Business Development Bank of Canada / B (8) .... Montréal QC
Royal Bank Financial Group (7) .... Calgary AB
Canadian Imperial Bank of Commerce / CIB (6) .... Toronto ON
Vancouver City Savings Credit Union / (6) .... Vancouver BC
DUCA Financial Services Credit Union Ltd (5) .... Gloucester ON
MBNA Canada Bank (5) .... Gloucester ON
Niagara Credit Union Limited (5) .... St. Catharines ON
Bank of Montreal (4) .... Toronto ON
Civil Service Co-operative Credit Society (4) .... Ottawa ON
HSBC Bank Canada (4) .... Toronto ON
Laurentian Bank of Canada (4) .... Edmonton AB
Metro Credit Union / MCU (4) .... Toronto ON
Bank of Montreal (3) .... Mississauga ON
Bank of Montreal, Harris Private Banking (3) .... Calgary AB
Capital City Savings (3) .... Edmonton AB
Citibank Canada (3) .... Toronto ON
Royal Bank Financial Group (3) .... Montréal QC
Surrey Metro Savings (3) .... Surrey BC
Westminster Savings Credit Union (3) .... New Westminster BC
Bank of America Canada (2) .... Toronto ON
Bank of China (Canada) (2) .... Toronto ON
BMO Harris Private Banking (2) .... Edmonton AB
Canadian Western Bank (2) .... Edmonton AB
Citizens Bank of Canada (2) .... Vancouver BC
Department of Municipal and Provincia (2) .... St. John's NF
Deutsche Financial Services / DFS (2) .... Mississauga ON
Gulf and Fraser Credit Union (2) .... Vancouver BC
Hepcoe Credit Union Ltd. (2) .... Toronto ON
Home Trust Co. Credit Card Services (2) .... Toronto ON
HSBC Bank Canada (2) .... Toronto ON
Manulife Financial Corporation (2) .... Waterloo ON
RBC Insurance (2) .... Calgary AB
Saskatoon Credit Union (2) .... Saskatoon SK
Business Development Bank of Canada / BD (1) .... Toronto ON
Canadian Bankers Association / CBA (1) .... Toronto ON
Canadian Imperial Bank of Commerce, CIBC (1) .... Toronto ON
Cue Datawest Ltd. (1) .... Vancouver BC
Fincentric Corp. (1) .... Richmond BC
Gibraltar Mortgage Ltd. (1) .... Calgary AB
Home Trust Company (1) .... Hamilton ON
Household Financial Corporation / HFC (1) .... Toronto ON
ING Bank of Canada / ING Direct (1) .... Toronto ON
Kootenay Savings (1) .... Trail BC
NBC Clearing Services Inc. (1) .... Montréal QC
Procuron Inc. (1) .... Thornhill ON
Royal Bank Financial Group (1) .... Vancouver BC

BILINGUAL
See also: International, Education, Administrative.

Zurich Canada (11 positions) .... Toronto ON
Manitoba Justice / Culture, Heritage an (7) .... Winnipeg MB
AT&T Canada (6) .... Toronto ON

For descriptions of the occupational categories used in this index, see page 458.

BILINGUAL (Cont.)

Ministry of the Environment, Ontario (6) ... Toronto ON
National Life Assurance Company of Canad (6) ... Toronto ON
Shell Canada Limited (6) ... Calgary AB
Tyco Healthcare Group Canada Inc. (6) ... St-Laurent QC
ACD Systems (5) ... Saanichton BC
AstraZeneca (4) ... Mississauga ON
Corel Corporation (4) ... Ottawa ON
Coughlin & Associates Ltd. (4) ... Ottawa ON
Intuit GreenPoint (4) ... Calgary AB
Manitoba Transportation & Government Se (4) ... Winnipeg MB
Pottruff & Smith Travel Insurance Bro (4) ... Woodbridge ON
Professional Institute of the Public Serv (4) ... Nepean ON
Royal Bank Financial Group (4) ... Toronto ON
Warren Shepell Consultants Corp. (4) ... Toronto ON
ADP Canada (3) ... Toronto ON
Anglocom (3) ... Quebec City QC
Clarica Life Insurance Company (3) ... Ottawa ON
DSC Group of Companies (3) ... Concord ON
ESI Canada Inc. (3) ... Mississauga ON
Manitoba Finance (3) ... Winnipeg MB
Masha Krupp Translation Group Ltd. / MKTG (3) ... Ottawa ON
Ministry of Consumer and Business Servic (3) ... Toronto ON
Natrel Inc. (3) ... Toronto ON
Procter & Gamble Inc. (3) ... Toronto ON
Shoppers Drug Mart (3) ... Toronto ON
Sun Life Financial (3) ... Montréal QC
UnumProvident Corporation (3) ... Burlington ON
3M Canada Company (2) ... London ON
ABC Group Inc. (2) ... Toronto ON
ACL Services Ltd. (2) ... Vancouver BC
Alpnet Canada (2) ... Montréal QC
BCE Emergis Inc., Assure Health Divi (2) ... Mississauga ON
Bloorview MacMillan Children's Centre, M (2) ... Toronto ON
Canada Life Assurance Company (2) ... Toronto ON
Canadian Cancer Society / CCS (2) ... Toronto ON
Centretown Community Health Centre (2) ... Ottawa ON
ClientLogic Corp. (2) ... Toronto ON
CUMIS Group Ltd., The (2) ... Burlington ON
Datex-Ohmeda (Canada) Inc. (2) ... Mississauga ON
Denso Manufacturing Canada, Inc. (2) ... Guelph ON
Dolce International (2) ... Toronto ON
Empire Financial Group (2) ... Kingston ON
Encon Group Inc. (2) ... Ottawa ON
FGI (2) ... Mississauga ON
GE Capital Canada Equipment Financing In (2) ... Toronto ON
GlaxoSmithKline (2) ... Mississauga ON
Group Telecom (2) ... Toronto ON
Hyundai Auto Canada (2) ... Markham ON
Law Society of Upper Canada, The / LSUC (2) ... Toronto ON
Manitoba Family Services and Housing (2) ... Winnipeg MB
MIBRO Group, The (2) ... Toronto ON
Ministry of Education / Ministry of Trai (2) ... Toronto ON
Ministry of Labour, Ontario (2) ... Toronto ON
Noritsu Canada Ltd. (2) ... Mississauga ON
Ontario Trillium Foundation, The (2) ... Toronto ON
Peregrine Systems, Inc. (2) ... Ottawa ON
Public Service Commission of Canada, B (2) ... Vancouver BC
Public Service Commission of Canada, Nov (2) ... Halifax NS
Public Service Commission of Canada, Ont (2) ... Toronto ON
Public Service Commission, PEI (2) ... Charlottetown PE
Radiant Communications (2) ... Vancouver BC
Rogers Cable Inc. (2) ... Saint John NB
Rogers Communications Inc. (2) ... Ottawa ON
StonCor Group (2) ... Whitby ON
Travel Guard Canada (2) ... Toronto ON
University of Calgary (2) ... Calgary AB
Viconics Electronics Inc. (2) ... St-Leonard QC
William M. Mercer Limited (2) ... Toronto ON
Wurth Canada Limited (2) ... Mississauga ON
Yamaha Motor Canada Ltd. (2) ... Toronto ON
Aastra Telecom (1) ... Concord ON
Access International Automotive Ltd. (1) ... Calgary AB
Accutel.com (1) ... Toronto ON
AIM Funds Management Inc. (1) ... Calgary AB
AIM Funds Management Inc. (1) ... Toronto ON
AlarmForce Industries Inc. (1) ... Toronto ON
Alberta Child and Family Services Autho (1) ... McLennan AB
Alberta Human Resources and Employment (1) ... McLennan AB
Alberta Learning (1) ... Edmonton AB
Amram's Distributing Ltd. (1) ... Brampton ON
Apotex Inc. (1) ... Toronto ON
Appendix Technical Publishing Group (1) ... Ottawa ON
Architrave Design Office Service (1) ... Gabriola Island BC
Ash City (1) ... Toronto ON
Association of Universities and Colleges (1) ... Ottawa ON
ATI Technologies Inc. (1) ... Thornhill ON
BASF Canada Inc. (1) ... Toronto ON
Bata Retail Canada (1) ... Toronto ON
Baxter Healthcare Corporation (1) ... Mississauga ON
Bayer Inc. (1) ... Toronto ON
BCE Emergis Inc. (1) ... Montréal QC
Bell & Howell Ltd. (1) ... Toronto ON
Bissett & Associates Investment Manageme (1) ... Calgary AB
Bizerba Canada (1) ... Mississauga ON
Business Travel International / BTI Canad (1) ... Ottawa ON
C/S Construction Specialties Ltd. (1) ... Mississauga ON
C1 Communications (1) ... Mississauga ON
Canada Mortgage and Housing Corporation / (1) ... Ottawa ON
Canada Post Corporation (1) ... Ottawa ON
Canadian Depository for Securities Ltd. (1) ... Toronto ON
Canadian Recreation Products Inc. (1) ... Mount Royal QC
Carlson Marketing Group Canada Ltd. / CM (1) ... Toronto ON
CaseWare International Inc. (1) ... Toronto ON
CGU Group Canada Ltd. (1) ... Vancouver BC
Citadel General Assurance Company, The (1) ... Toronto ON
Clarica Life Insurance Company (1) ... Montréal QC
Cognos Inc. (1) ... Ottawa ON
Colgate-Palmolive Canada Inc. (1) ... Toronto ON
DataMirror Corporation (1) ... Markham ON
DDS Canada (1) ... Toronto ON
Department of Human Resources, Nunavut (1) ... Iqaluit NU
DHL International Express Ltd. (1) ... Nepean ON
Discount Car and Truck Rentals (1) ... Toronto ON
DiverseyLever (1) ... Oakville ON
Dumex Medical (1) ... Toronto ON
Ecolab Ltd. (1) ... Mississauga ON
Edmonton Public Schools (1) ... Edmonton AB
ePALS Classroom Exchange (1) ... Ottawa ON
Exel Canada (1) ... Brampton ON
Export Development Corporation / EDC (1) ... Ottawa ON
Farm Credit Canada / FCC (1) ... Regina SK
Fidelity Investments Canada Limited (1) ... Toronto ON
Fiesta Barbeques Limited (1) ... Brampton ON
Fraser Valley Health Region (1) ... Mission BC
Frost Fence & Wire Products Ltd. (1) ... Hamilton ON
Fuji Photo Film Canada Inc. (1) ... Mississauga ON
G&K Work Wear (1) ... Mississauga ON
Galileo Canada (1) ... Toronto ON
Ganz (1) ... Woodbridge ON
GE Canada (1) ... Mississauga ON
Gen-X Sports Inc. (1) ... Toronto ON
GHI Technologies (1) ... Mississauga ON
Goldwell Cosmetics (Canada) Ltd. (1) ... Mississauga ON
Gowling Lafleur Henderson LLP (1) ... Montréal QC
Grant MacEwan College, Jasper Place Cam (1) ... Edmonton AB
Greater Vancouver Community Services S (1) ... Vancouver BC
Hartco Corporation (1) ... Anjou QC
Heidelberg Canada (1) ... Mississauga ON
Hertz Equipment Rental (1) ... Toronto ON
Hewitt Associates (1) ... Toronto ON
Honda of Canada Manufacturing (1) ... Alliston ON
IBM Canada Ltd. (1) ... Markham ON
IKON Office Solutions, Inc. (1) ... Mississauga ON
IMP Group Ltd., Aerospace Division (1) ... Enfield NS
Indeka Group, The (1) ... Oakville ON
Inlingua International (1) ... Vancouver BC
Innovus Research Inc. (1) ... Burlington ON
Insurance Bureau of Canada / IBC (1) ... Toronto ON
InterTAN, Inc. / RadioShack (1) ... Barrie ON
IT / Net Consultants Inc. (1) ... Ottawa ON
IVL Technologies Ltd. (1) ... Victoria BC
Johnson Inc. (1) ... Richmond Hill ON
Kafko Manufacturing Ltd. (1) ... Mississauga ON
Kenwood Electronics Canada Inc. (1) ... Mississauga ON
Kodak Canada Inc. (1) ... Toronto ON
Kuper Academy (1) ... Kirkland QC
Kwantlen University College (1) ... Surrey BC
Legal Aid Ontario / LAO (1) ... Toronto ON
Legislative Assembly of Ontario, Office (1) ... Toronto ON
Liberty Mutual Group (1) ... Unionville ON
Lifeline Systems Canada Inc. (1) ... Toronto ON

BILINGUAL (Cont.)

Lippman Leebosh April (1) .... Montréal QC
Liquor Control Board of Ontario / LCBO (1) .... Toronto ON
Loblaw Companies Ltd. (1) .... Toronto ON
Lockheed Martin Canada Inc. (1) .... Kanata ON
Lowe-Martin Group, The (1) .... Ottawa ON
Loyalty Group, The (1) .... Toronto ON
Lyreco Office Products (1) .... Toronto ON
MacDonald Dettwiler & Associates Ltd. / M (1) .... Ottawa ON
MacLachlan College (1) .... Oakville ON
Manitoba Civil Service Commission (1) .... Winnipeg MB
Manitoba Education, Training & Youth (1) .... Winnipeg MB
Manitoba Industry, Trades and Mines / I (1) .... Winnipeg MB
Manitoba Labour & Immigration (1) .... Winnipeg MB
Manitoba Transportation & Gov (1) .... Portage la Prairie MB
McDonald's Restaurants of Canada Limited (1) .... Toronto ON
Medtronic of Canada Inc. (1) .... Mississauga ON
Mercedes-Benz Canada Inc. (1) .... Toronto ON
Merisel Canada Inc. (1) .... Toronto ON
Minacs Worldwide Inc. (1) .... Richmond Hill ON
Minacs Worldwide Inc. (1) .... Markham ON
Ministry of Citizenship, Culture and Rec (1) .... Toronto ON
Ministry of Community and Social Service (1) .... Toronto ON
Ministry of Finance, BC (1) .... Victoria BC
Ministry of Health and Long-Term (1) .... Penetanguishene ON
Ministry of Health and Long-Term Care, (1) .... North Bay ON
Ministry of Northern Development and Min (1) .... Sudbury ON
Ministry of Transportation, Ontario (1) .... North Bay ON
Mississauga, City of (1) .... Mississauga ON
Mitec Telecom Inc. (1) .... Pointe-Claire QC
National Research Council Canada, Canada (1) .... Ottawa ON
NAV Canada (1) .... Ottawa ON
New Brunswick Community College, Miram (1) .... Miramichi NB
New Frontiers School Board (1) .... Chateauguay QC
North York General Hospital (1) .... Toronto ON
Northwest Catholic District School (1) .... Fort Frances ON
NSI Communications (1) .... Pointe-Claire QC
Nuance Global Traders (Canada) Inc. (1) .... Richmond BC
Okanagan University College / OUC (1) .... Kelowna BC
Open Text Corporation (1) .... Waterloo ON
Optech Inc. (1) .... Toronto ON
Ottawa, City of (1) .... Ottawa ON
Ottawa Hospital, The (1) .... Ottawa ON
Parkhurst Knitwear (1) .... Toronto ON
Pepsi Bottling Group (Canada) (1) .... Mississauga ON
Percepta (1) .... Toronto ON
Pharmacia Animal Health (1) .... Orangeville ON
PHH Vehicle Management Services Inc. (1) .... Mississauga ON
Pizza Pizza Limited (1) .... Toronto ON
Premier Fasteners (1) .... Toronto ON
Primerica Financial Services (Canada (1) .... Mississauga ON
Proface Inde Electronics Inc. (1) .... Burnaby BC
Public Service Alliance of Canada / PSAC (1) .... Ottawa ON
Public Service Commission of Canada, Sask (1) .... Regina SK
Radiant Communications (1) .... Toronto ON
Red Deer College (1) .... Red Deer AB
Riverdale Hospital, The (1) .... Toronto ON
Rogers Cable Inc. (1) .... Toronto ON
Rogers Communications Inc. (1) .... Toronto ON
Rogers Media, Publishing (1) .... Toronto ON
Rogers Shared Services (1) .... Markham ON
Royal Canadian Golf Association / RCGA (1) .... Oakville ON
San Francisco Group (1) .... Boucherville QC
Schneider Electric (1) .... Toronto ON
Schneider Foods Inc. (1) .... Kitchener ON
Schneider Foods Inc. (1) .... Mississauga ON
School District #59 (Peace River So (1) .... Dawson Creek BC
Sedbergh School (1) .... Montebello QC
Seiden Health Management Inc. (1) .... Toronto ON
Sewer-Matic Services Inc. (1) .... Ottawa ON
Sitraka Software Inc. (1) .... Toronto ON
Skylink Technologies Inc. (1) .... Mississauga ON
Snap-On Tools of Canada Ltd. (1) .... Mississauga ON
Sony Music Canada (1) .... Toronto ON
Soroc Technology Inc. (1) .... Woodbridge ON
Spectrum Investment Management Ltd. (1) .... Toronto ON
St. Paul's L'Amoreaux Seniors' Centre (1) .... Toronto ON
Sun Life Financial (1) .... Toronto ON
Sunnybrook & Women's College Health Scie (1) .... Toronto ON
Superior North Catholic District Sch (1) .... Terrace Bay ON

Synavant Inc. (1) .... Toronto ON
TDL Group Ltd., The (1) .... Oakville ON
TeleSpectrum Canada Inc. (1) .... Toronto ON
TeleTech Canada (1) .... Toronto ON
Telus Mobility (1) .... Toronto ON
Toronto Catholic District School Board (1) .... Toronto ON
Toronto Montessori Schools (1) .... Richmond Hill ON
Toyota Canada Inc. (1) .... Toronto ON
Transcontinental Media (1) .... Toronto ON
Union of Canadian Transportation Employee (1) .... Ottawa ON
United Nations Children's Fund / UNICEF (1) .... Toronto ON
University Health Network / UHN (1) .... Toronto ON
Value Village (1) .... Port Moody BC
Valvoline Canada Ltd. (1) .... Mississauga ON
Weber Marking Systems of Canada (1) .... Mississauga ON
Weekenders Canada Inc. (1) .... Richmond Hill ON
Weston Bakeries Ltd. (1) .... Toronto ON
Whitesell Canada Inc. (1) .... Vaughan ON
Workplace Safety & Insurance Appeals Tri (1) .... Toronto ON
Wrigley Canada Inc. (1) .... Toronto ON
York Region District School Board (1) .... Aurora ON
Zurich Canada (1) .... Montréal QC

BIOTECH/BIOLOGY

See also: Pharmaceutical, Scientific, Health/Medical.

DSM Biologics (9 positions) .... Montréal QC
Cytochroma Inc. (7) .... Kingston ON
Inex Pharmaceuticals Corp. (6) .... Burnaby BC
SemBioSys Genetics Inc. (5) .... Calgary AB
ARIUS Research Inc. (4) .... Toronto ON
Dragon Pharmaceuticals (Canada) Inc. (4) .... Vancouver BC
Integrative Proteomics Inc. / IPI (4) .... Toronto ON
Okanagan University College / OUC (4) .... Kelowna BC
Prescient NeuroPharma Inc. (4) .... Toronto ON
Public Service Commission of Canada, Ma (4) .... Winnipeg MB
StressGen Biotechnologies Corp. (4) .... Victoria BC
Active Pass Pharmaceuticals Inc. (3) .... Vancouver BC
Cangene Corporation (3) .... Winnipeg MB
Millenium Biologix Inc. (3) .... Kingston ON
Ministry of Water, Land and Air Protect (3) .... Victoria BC
University of Guelph (3) .... Guelph ON
AstraZeneca (2) .... Mississauga ON
Bio-Rad Laboratories (Canada) Ltd. (2) .... Mississauga ON
Caprion Pharmaceuticals Inc. (2) .... Montréal QC
Diabetogen Biosciences Inc. (2) .... London ON
Hospital for Sick Children, The (2) .... Toronto ON
Hospital for Sick Children, The (Advance (2) .... Toronto ON
i-STAT Canada Ltd. (2) .... Kanata ON
Industry Canada (2) .... Hull QC
ITR Laboratories Canada Inc. (2) .... Baie d'Urfe QC
Kam Biotechnology Ltd. (2) .... Surrey BC
MDS Laboratories (2) .... Toronto ON
MDS Laboratories (2) .... Toronto ON
MDS Pharma Services Inc. (2) .... St-Laurent QC
MDS Proteomics (2) .... St-Laurent QC
MethylGene Inc. (2) .... St-Laurent QC
Micrologix Biotech Inc. (2) .... Vancouver BC
Ministry of Health and Long-Term Care, O (2) .... Toronto ON
Ministry of Natural Resources, Ontario (2) .... Kenora ON
Ministry of Natural Resources, Onta (2) .... Peterborough ON
Ministry of the Solicitor General, Ontar (2) .... Toronto ON
National Research Council Canada / NRC (2) .... Winnipeg MB
Public Service Commission of Canada, Onta (2) .... Ottawa ON
University of New Brunswick, Departm (2) .... Fredericton NB
Vancouver General Hospital, Prostate C (2) .... Vancouver BC
Acadia University (1) .... Wolfville NS
Agriculture and Agri-Food Canada (1) .... Winnipeg MB
Alberta Environment (1) .... Calgary AB
Alberta Research Council / ARC (1) .... Edmonton AB
Alcan Primary Metal Group (1) .... Kitimat BC
AnorMED Inc. (1) .... Langley BC
Apotex Inc. (1) .... Toronto ON
Avestin Inc. (1) .... Ottawa ON
Baxter Corporation (1) .... Alliston ON
Beckman Coulter Canada Inc. (1) .... Mississauga ON
Biomira Inc. (1) .... Edmonton AB
British Columbia Institute of Technology (1) .... Burnaby BC
Canadian Blood Services / CBS (1) .... Ottawa ON

BIOTECH/BIOLOGY (Cont.)

Canadian Grain Commission / CGC (1) .... Winnipeg MB
Carsen Group Inc. (1) .... Markham ON
ClinTrials BioResearch Ltd. / CTBR (1) .... Senneville QC
Coley Pharmaceutical Group / CPG (1) .... Ottawa ON
CRS Robotics Corporation (1) .... Burlington ON
Department of Forest Resources & Agri (1) .... St. John's NF
Department of Tourism, Culture and Re (1) .... St. John's NF
Diagnostic Chemicals Limited / DCL (1) .... Charlottetown PE
Dufferin-Peel Catholic District Scho (1) .... Mississauga ON
Fraser Valley Health Region (1) .... Mission BC
GlaxoSmithKline (1) .... Mississauga ON
Grant MacEwan College, Jasper Place Cam (1) .... Edmonton AB
Hemosol Inc. (1) .... Toronto ON
Hotel-Dieu Grace Hospital (1) .... Windsor ON
IMI International Medical Innovations In (1) .... Toronto ON
Inflazyme Pharmaceuticals Ltd. (1) .... Richmond BC
InphoGene BioCom Inc. (1) .... Burnaby BC
Langara College (1) .... Vancouver BC
Lethbridge Community College / LCC (1) .... Lethbridge AB
Liponex Inc. (1) .... Ottawa ON
MDS Metro Laboratory Services (1) .... Burnaby BC
Medtronic of Canada Inc. (1) .... Mississauga ON
Merck Frosst Canada & Co. / Merck (1) .... Pointe-Claire QC
Ministry of Forests, BC (Research Branc (1) .... Victoria BC
Ministry of Natural Resources, Ontario (1) .... Dryden ON
Ministry of Natural Resources, Ontario (1) .... London ON
Ministry of Natural Resources, Ontario (1) .... Aylmer ON
Ministry of Natural Resources, Ontario (1) .... Aurora ON
Ministry of Natural Resources, Onta (1) .... Peterborough ON
Ministry of Natural Resources, Onta (1) .... Peterborough ON
Mount Royal College (1) .... Calgary AB
National Research Council Canada / NRC (1) .... Montréal QC
North York General Hospital, General Div (1) .... Toronto ON
Northern Alberta Institute of Technolog (1) .... Edmonton AB
Ottawa Health Research Institute / OHRI (1) .... Ottawa ON
Ottawa Hospital, The (1) .... Ottawa ON
Public Service Commission of Canada, Al (1) .... Edmonton AB
Public Service Commission of Canada, BC (1) .... Victoria BC
Public Service Commission of Canada, B (1) .... Vancouver BC
Public Service Commission of Canada, Qu (1) .... Montréal QC
Public Service Commission of Canada, (1) .... Quebec City QC
Public Service Commission of Canada, (1) .... Whitehorse YT
Queen's University, Cancer Research Lab (1) .... Kingston ON
Response Biomedical Corp. (1) .... Burnaby BC
Savage Software (1) .... Vancouver BC
Simon Fraser University, Department of (1) .... Burnaby BC
Spectral Diagnostics Inc. (1) .... Toronto ON
Sulzer Mitroflow Corp. (1) .... Richmond BC
Sunnybrook & Women's College Health Scie (1) .... Toronto ON
University College of the Fraser Vall (1) .... Abbotsford BC
University Health Network (1) .... Toronto ON
Viridae Clinical Sciences Inc. (1) .... Vancouver BC
West Park Healthcare Centre (1) .... Toronto ON
York Central Hospital (1) .... Richmond Hill ON

COMPUTING

See also: Multimedia, Engineering, Telecom, Design.

PrinterON Corporation (54 positions) .... Kitchener ON
IBM Canada Ltd. (52) .... Markham ON
724 Solutions Inc. (50) .... Toronto ON
Fincentric Corp. (48) .... Richmond BC
Management Board Secretariat (45) .... Toronto ON
ATI Technologies Inc. (44) .... Thornhill ON
Research in Motion Limited / RIM (44) .... Waterloo ON
IT Career Access Office, BC / ITCAO (42) .... Victoria BC
InSystems Technologies, Inc. (40) .... Markham ON
DataMirror Corporation (39) .... Markham ON
Webplan Inc. (37) .... Ottawa ON
Exocom Group Inc., The (36) .... Ottawa ON
Royal Bank Financial Group (35) .... Toronto ON
Sitraka Software Inc. (35) .... Toronto ON
Bombardier Aerospace (34) .... Montréal QC
ReserveAmerica (32) .... Milton ON
Mastech Canada (31) .... Mississauga ON
Yotta Yotta Inc. (29) .... Edmonton AB

Group Telecom (28) .... Toronto ON
Montage.dmc eBusiness Services (27) .... Ottawa ON
Export Development Corporation / EDC (26) .... Ottawa ON
Solect Technology Group (26) .... Toronto ON
Computing Devices Canada Ltd. / CDC (25) .... Calgary AB
Ministry of Health and Long-Term Care, (25) .... Kingston ON
Mitra Imaging Inc. (25) .... Waterloo ON
Matrikon Group (24) .... Edmonton AB
Montage.dmc eBusiness Services (24) .... Calgary AB
Lumic Electronics, Inc. (23) .... Nepean ON
Net-Linx Americas, Inc. (23) .... Edmonton AB
BitFlash Graphics, Inc. (22) .... Ottawa ON
MedcomSoft Inc. (22) .... Toronto ON
ACD Systems (20) .... Saanichton BC
Fidelity Investments Canada Limited (20) .... Toronto ON
Intellitactics Inc. (20) .... Kitchener ON
Sun Life Financial (20) .... Toronto ON
A.L.I. Technologies Inc. (18) .... Richmond BC
AiT Corporation (18) .... Ottawa ON
EPCOR Utilities Inc. (18) .... Edmonton AB
InBusiness Solutions Inc. (18) .... Ottawa ON
Progestic International Inc. (18) .... Ottawa ON
University of Calgary (18) .... Calgary AB
Unleash Corporation (18) .... Mississauga ON
Voyus Canada Inc. (18) .... Burnaby BC
Alterna Technologies Group Inc. (17) .... Calgary AB
Cognos Inc. (17) .... Ottawa ON
Montage.dmc eBusiness Services (17) .... Edmonton AB
Montage.dmc eBusiness Services (17) .... Nepean ON
Southern Alberta Institute of Technology (17) .... Calgary AB
Westech Information Systems Inc. (17) .... Vancouver BC
Classwave Wireless Inc. (16) .... Toronto ON
INTRIA-HP (16) .... Toronto ON
Optimal Robotics Corp. (16) .... Montréal QC
MetaQuest Software (15) .... Montréal QC
NetPCS (15) .... Hull QC
SureFire Commerce Inc. (15) .... Westmount QC
Zed.i Solutions (15) .... Edmonton AB
AGF Management Ltd. (14) .... Toronto ON
Celestica Inc. (14) .... Toronto ON
Chancery Software Ltd. (14) .... Burnaby BC
Databeacon Inc. (14) .... Ottawa ON
DMC Inc. (14) .... Toronto ON
EFA Software Services Ltd. (14) .... Calgary AB
Rogers AT&T Wireless (14) .... Toronto ON
Sigma Systems Group Inc. (14) .... Toronto ON
Telus Mobility (14) .... Toronto ON
Blockade Systems Corporation (13) .... Toronto ON
Cayenta Canada (13) .... Burnaby BC
CompuSoft Canada Inc. (13) .... Edmonton AB
Computer Sciences Corp. / CSC (13) .... Toronto ON
Epic Data Inc. (13) .... Richmond BC
Logibro Inc. (13) .... Montréal QC
Optech Inc. (13) .... Toronto ON
Paradata Systems Inc. (13) .... Whistler BC
RoundHeaven Communications Canada Inc. (13) ..... Vancouver BC
Spielo Gaming International (13) .... Dieppe NB
VIPswitch Inc. (13) .... Montréal QC
X.eye Inc. (13) .... Toronto ON
Athabasca University (12) .... Athabasca AB
DMR Consulting Inc. (12) .... Calgary AB
EDM Products Inc. (12) .... Calgary AB
Fluor Canada Ltd. (12) .... Calgary AB
Gage Applied, Inc. (12) .... Lachine QC
Intrinsyc Software Inc. (12) .... Vancouver BC
Keane Canada, Inc. (12) .... Halifax NS
Loyalty Group, The (12) .... Toronto ON
Mastech Canada (12) .... Montréal QC
Merak Projects Ltd. (12) .... Calgary AB
Ontario Lottery and Gaming Corp (12) .... Sault Ste. Marie ON
Provance Technologies Inc. (12) .... Gatineau QC
Research in Motion Limited / RIM (12) .... Kanata ON
Sitraka Mobility (12) .... Toronto ON
Smart Technologies Inc. (12) .... Calgary AB
Adexa (11) .... Toronto ON
Calgary, City of (11) .... Calgary AB
GE Canada (11) .... Mississauga ON
Great-West Life Assurance Company, The (11) ...... Winnipeg MB
Ministry of Transportation, Ontar (11) .... St. Catharines ON
NexInnovations (11) .... Mississauga ON
SAS Institute (Canada) Inc. (11) .... Toronto ON
Soroc Technology Inc. (11) .... Woodbridge ON

COMPUTING (Cont.)

Brampton, City of (10) ... Brampton ON
CAE Inc. (10) ... St-Laurent QC
Ceridian Canada Ltd. (10) ... Winnipeg MB
Chromatic Software Inc. / CSI (10) ... Vancouver BC
Cloakware Corporation (10) ... Kanata ON
CMC Electronics Inc. (10) ... St-Laurent QC
Compugen Systems Ltd. (10) ... Richmond Hill ON
Computing Devices Canada Ltd. / CDC (10) ... Ottawa ON
Design Workshop (10) ... St-Laurent QC
EMS Technologies Canada Ltd (10) ... Ste-Anne-de-Bellevue QC
Infowave Software, Inc. (10) ... Burnaby BC
Inkra Networks Canada (10) ... Burnaby BC
Microtime Inc. (10) ... Ottawa ON
National Grocers Company Limited / Lobla (10) ... Toronto ON
Proface Inde Electronics Inc. (10) ... Burnaby BC
Rational Software Corporation (10) ... Kanata ON
Staples Business Depot Ltd. (10) ... Markham ON
WebGain Inc. (10) ... Ottawa ON
Wind River Systems, Inc. (10) ... Calgary AB
Advanced Micro Design (9) ... Edmonton AB
American Express Canada Inc. / Amex (9) ... Markham ON
Beyond 20/20 Inc. (9) ... Ottawa ON
bitHeads, Inc. (9) ... Ottawa ON
Cap Gemini Ernst & Young / CGEY (9) ... Toronto ON
Excite@Home Canada, Inc. (9) ... Toronto ON
IT / Net Consultants Inc. (9) ... Ottawa ON
Linmor Technologies Inc. (9) ... Ottawa ON
Lockheed Martin Canada Inc. (9) ... Kanata ON
MacDonald Dettwiler & Associates Ltd. / (9) ... Richmond BC
MKS Inc. (9) ... Waterloo ON
Nortel Networks (9) ... Ottawa ON
OAO Technology Solutions / OAOT (9) ... Toronto ON
PCsupport.com, Inc. (9) ... Burnaby BC
Rogers Shared Services (9) ... Markham ON
Sierra Systems (9) ... Edmonton AB
Sierra Systems Group Inc. (9) ... Ottawa ON
SRI Strategic Resources Inc. (9) ... Burnaby BC
Analog Design Automation Inc. / ADA (8) ... Ottawa ON
ATCO I-Tek (8) ... Edmonton AB
Caprion Pharmaceuticals Inc. (8) ... Montréal QC
Corel Corporation (8) ... Ottawa ON
Cquay Inc. (8) ... Calgary AB
CyberSurf Corporation (8) ... Calgary AB
DSC Group of Companies (8) ... Concord ON
Forensic Technology Inc. (8) ... Cote St. Luc QC
GeoMetrix Data Systems Inc. (8) ... Victoria BC
Hewlett-Packard (Canada) Ltd. (8) ... Mississauga ON
Hummingbird Ltd. (8) ... Toronto ON
Jewelstone Systems Inc. / JSI (8) ... Toronto ON
Ministry of Health and Long-Term Care, O (8) ... Toronto ON
NetPCS (8) ... Kanata ON
Siemens Canada Ltd., Telecom Innovation C (8) ... Kanata ON
Standard Life Assurance Company, The (8) ... Montréal QC
Suncor Energy Inc., Oil Sands (8) ... Fort McMurray AB
Alcatel Canada Inc., Transport Automatio (7) ... Toronto ON
Canadian Bank Note Company, Ltd. (7) ... Ottawa ON
CIMTEK Automation Systems (7) ... Burlington ON
Cirque du Soleil (7) ... Montréal QC
Class Software Solutions Ltd. (7) ... Burnaby BC
Critical Mass Inc. (7) ... Calgary AB
Espial Group Inc. (7) ... Ottawa ON
IBM Canada Ltd. (7) ... Winnipeg MB
Infosys Technologies Ltd. (7) ... Toronto ON
Manitoba Health (7) ... Winnipeg MB
MessagingDirect Ltd. (7) ... Edmonton AB
Minacs Worldwide Inc. (7) ... Markham ON
Ministry of Natural Resources, (7) ... Sault Ste. Marie ON
NewHeights Software Corporation (7) ... Victoria BC
Overwaitea Food Group (7) ... Vancouver BC
Performance Technologies, Inc. (7) ... Ottawa ON
Shana Corporation (7) ... Edmonton AB
Ship.com, Inc. (7) ... Winnipeg MB
Top Producer Systems Inc. (7) ... Richmond BC
VideoSpheres Inc. (7) ... Kanata ON
Vivonet Canada Inc. (7) ... Vancouver BC
Wysdom Inc. (7) ... Montréal QC
Xwave Solutions Inc. (7) ... Calgary AB
Xwave Solutions Inc. (7) ... Dorval QC
Zucotto Wireless Inc. (7) ... Ottawa ON
Alberta Learning (6) ... Edmonton AB
Alcatel Canada Inc., Transport Automatio (6) ... Burnaby BC
Allied Domecq, Spirits & Wine (6) ... Windsor ON
Burntsand Inc. (6) ... Toronto ON
CaseWare International Inc. (6) ... Toronto ON
Compugen Systems Ltd. (6) ... Ottawa ON
CreoScitex (6) ... Burnaby BC
Datawire Communication Networks Inc. (6) ... Toronto ON
DY 4 Systems Inc. (6) ... Kanata ON
Extracomm Technologies Inc. (6) ... Toronto ON
Ezenet Inc. (6) ... Toronto ON
Fording Coal Limited (6) ... Calgary AB
ImageWare Systems (6) ... Hull QC
Kinaare Networks Canada Corporation (6) ... Mississauga ON
Kingston General Hospital (6) ... Kingston ON
Klay Information Management Consulting L (6) ... Calgary AB
Kronos Computerized Time Systems (6) ... Mississauga ON
MacDonald Dettwiler Space and Advanced (6) ... Brampton ON
Manitoba Finance (6) ... Winnipeg MB
Manitoba Justice / Culture, Heritage an (6) ... Winnipeg MB
MDS Aero Support Corporation (6) ... Ottawa ON
MegaSys Computer Technologies Ltd. (6) ... Calgary AB
Ministry of Health and Long-Term Care, O (6) ... Toronto ON
Ministry of Health and Ministry Respons (6) ... Victoria BC
Ministry of Transportation, Ontario (6) ... Toronto ON
Mississauga, City of (6) ... Mississauga ON
NCompass Labs (6) ... Vancouver BC
Northern Alberta Institute of Technolog (6) ... Edmonton AB
Objexis Corporation (6) ... Montréal QC
Open Text Corporation (6) ... Waterloo ON
OZ Optics Ltd. (6) ... Carp ON
Pangaea Systems Inc. (6) ... Edmonton AB
Peregrine Systems, Inc. (6) ... Ottawa ON
QLT Inc. (6) ... Vancouver BC
Quack.com (6) ... Waterloo ON
Quorum Information Systems Inc. (6) ... Calgary AB
Radiant Communications (6) ... Calgary AB
Red Deer College (6) ... Red Deer AB
Renaissance Learning of Canada (6) ... Nepean ON
Rogers Communications Inc. (6) ... Toronto ON
Soft Tracks (6) ... Richmond BC
Spectrum Signal Processing Inc. (6) ... Burnaby BC
Syndesis Limited (6) ... Ottawa ON
Trango Software Corporation (6) ... Richmond Hill ON
University College of the Fraser Vall (6) ... Abbotsford BC
Valadeo Technologies Corp. (6) ... Toronto ON
Vansco Electronics Ltd. (6) ... Winnipeg MB
Velan Inc. (6) ... Montréal QC
William M. Mercer Limited (6) ... Toronto ON
Acterna Corporation (5) ... Burnaby BC
Administrative Assistants Ltd. / AAL (5) ... Burlington ON
AiT Corporation (5) ... Nepean ON
Bell Helicopter Textron Canada (5) ... Mirabel QC
Bombardier Aerospace, Defense Services (5) ... Mirabel QC
Brooks Automation Software Corporation (5) ... Richmond BC
Buystream (5) ... Ottawa ON
Chrysalis-ITS Inc. (5) ... Ottawa ON
Circadence Corporation (5) ... Toronto ON
Control-F1 (5) ... Calgary AB
Convedia Corporation (5) ... Burnaby BC
DeepMetrix Corporation (5) ... Hull ON
Department of Health and Community Se (5) ... St. John's NF
Descartes Systems Group (5) ... Waterloo ON
Digital Dispatch Systems Inc. (5) ... Richmond BC
E-smith, Inc. (5) ... Ottawa ON
EDS Canada (5) ... Calgary AB
eManage Inc. (5) ... Ottawa ON
First Canadian Title Company (5) ... Mississauga ON
FreeBalance Inc. (5) ... Ottawa ON
Galdos Systems Inc. (5) ... Vancouver BC
GE Capital Services / GECS (5) ... Mississauga ON
Harris Computer Systems (5) ... Nepean ON
Hyprotech Ltd. (5) ... Calgary AB
Image Processing Systems Inc. / IPS (5) ... Markham ON
Interactive Media Group / IMG (5) ... Toronto ON
Kazootek Technologies (5) ... Vancouver BC
KOM Inc. (5) ... Kanata ON
Leitch Technology Corp. (5) ... Toronto ON
London Hydro (5) ... London ON
Magma Communications Ltd. (5) ... Nepean ON
Marconi Communications (5) ... Dorval QC

For descriptions of the occupational categories used in this index, see page 458.

COMPUTING (Cont.)

Metso Automation (Canada) Ltd. (5) ... Calgary AB
Ministry of Finance, BC (5) ... Victoria BC
Ministry of Health and Long-Term Care, (5) ... Kingston ON
MOSAID Technologies Inc. (5) ... Kanata ON
Mount Royal College (5) ... Calgary AB
NRNS Inc. (5) ... Kanata ON
NStein Technologies (5) ... Laval QC
Ontario Power Generation (5) ... Toronto ON
Ontario Teachers' Pension Plan Board (5) ... Toronto ON
Psion Teklogix Inc. (5) ... Mississauga ON
PureEdge Solutions Inc. (5) ... Victoria BC
QDesign Corporation (5) ... Vancouver BC
Quadrus Development Inc. (5) ... Calgary AB
Selkirk Financial Technologies, Inc. (5) ... Vancouver BC
SmartForce Corporation (5) ... Fredericton NB
Sprint Canada Inc. (5) ... Toronto ON
SST (5) ... Waterloo ON
Stream International (5) ... Belleville ON
SynchroPoint Wireless Inc. (5) ... Vancouver BC
Technical University of British Columbia (5) ... Surrey BC
TELOS Technology Inc. (5) ... Richmond BC
Telus Enterprise Solutions (5) ... Burnaby BC
Toronto Transit Commission / TTC (5) ... Toronto ON
TriAngulum Corporation (5) ... Calgary AB
Unique Broadband Systems, Inc. / UBS (5) ... Concord ON
Valcom Limited (Ottawa) (5) ... Ottawa ON
Vertical Builder (5) ... Calgary AB
Watchfire (5) ... Kanata ON
WaveMakers Research Inc. (5) ... Vancouver BC
Wescam (5) ... Burlington ON
Westfair Foods Ltd. (5) ... Calgary AB
Xwave Solutions Inc. (5) ... Ottawa ON
York, The Regional Municipality of (5) ... Newmarket ON
ZOX Technologies Inc. (5) ... Toronto ON
01 Communique Laboratory Inc. (4) ... Mississauga ON
3LOG Systems Inc. (4) ... Richmond BC
ACNielsen Company of Canada (4) ... Markham ON
AeroInfo Systems Inc. (4) ... Richmond BC
AGTI Consulting Services Inc. (4) ... Calgary AB
Alberta Learning (4) ... Edmonton AB
Aten Advance Tech Inc. (4) ... Richmond BC
Atlantis Scientific Inc. (4) ... Nepean ON
BC Ferry Corporation (4) ... Victoria BC
Benchmark Technologies Inc. (4) ... Vancouver BC
Bird On a Wire Networks / BOAW (4) ... Mississauga ON
Buchanan Associates (4) ... Mississauga ON
Bulldog Group Inc., The (4) ... Toronto ON
Bycast Media Systems Canada, Inc. (4) ... Vancouver BC
Canada Life Assurance Company (4) ... Toronto ON
Canadian Forces Personnel Support Agency (4) ... Ottawa ON
Cedar Enterprise Solutions Inc. (4) ... Calgary AB
CGU Group Canada Ltd. (4) ... Toronto ON
Circon Systems Corporation (4) ... Richmond BC
CityXpress.com Corp. (4) ... Vancouver BC
CMC Electronics Inc. (4) ... Kanata ON
Cognicase (4) ... Montréal QC
CompCanada Atlas (4) ... Edmonton AB
Computroniks Inc. (4) ... Mississauga ON
Convergys Customer Management Canada In (4) ... Edmonton AB
Core Software Corp. (4) ... Nepean ON
Credit Valley Hospital, The (4) ... Mississauga ON
Cue Datawest Ltd. (4) ... Vancouver BC
Dot Com Entertainment Group Inc. / DCEG (4) ... Oakville ON
Edge Networks Corporation (4) ... Winnipeg MB
EDS Innovations (4) ... Mississauga ON
ePALS Classroom Exchange (4) ... Ottawa ON
Exocom Group Inc., The (4) ... Halifax NS
Full Circle Systems Inc. (4) ... Calgary AB
Genesis Microchip Inc. (4) ... Thornhill ON
Geosign (4) ... Guelph ON
Hatch Associates Ltd. (4) ... Mississauga ON
Humber River Regional Hospital, Finch Av (4) ... Toronto ON
Husky Injection Molding Systems Ltd. (4) ... Bolton ON
Inforetech Wireless Technology Inc. (4) ... Surrey BC
Infrastructures for Information, Inc. / (4) ... Toronto ON
InphoGene BioCom Inc. (4) ... Burnaby BC
Integra Networks Corporation (4) ... Ottawa ON
Interactive Circuits and Systems Ltd. (4) ... Gloucester ON
International Forest Products Limited (4) ... Vancouver BC
Island Key Computer Ltd. / IKCL (4) ... Vancouver BC
IVL Technologies Ltd. (4) ... Victoria BC
Jaratech Business Solutions Corp. (4) ... Calgary AB
Kelman Technologies Inc. / KTI (4) ... Calgary AB
Lantern Communications Canada Inc. (4) ... Ottawa ON
Legato Systems (Canada) Inc. (4) ... Burlington ON
Liquor Distribution Branch, BC / LDB (4) ... Vancouver BC
Lockheed Martin Canada Inc. (4) ... Halifax NS
Magna International Inc. (4) ... Concord ON
Manitoba Transportation & Government Se (4) ... Winnipeg MB
MapInfo Corporation (4) ... Toronto ON
Mastech Canada (4) ... Ottawa ON
MEI (4) ... Montréal QC
MicroSlate Inc. (4) ... Brossard QC
Minacs Worldwide Inc. (4) ... Richmond Hill ON
Mindquake Software (4) ... Vancouver BC
Ministry of Consumer and Business Servic (4) ... Toronto ON
Ministry of Education / Ministry of Trai (4) ... Toronto ON
Molecular Mining Corporation (4) ... Kingston ON
Montage.dmc eBusiness Services (4) ... Mississauga ON
MRF Geosystems Corporation (4) ... Calgary AB
Multiview Inc. (4) ... Ottawa ON
NexInnovations (4) ... Calgary AB
Northern Alberta Institute of Technolog (4) ... Edmonton AB
Online Business Systems (4) ... Winnipeg MB
Ositech Communications Inc. (4) ... Guelph ON
Ottawa Hospital, The (4) ... Ottawa ON
PanCanadian Petroleum Ltd. (4) ... Calgary AB
Pangaea Systems Inc. (4) ... Calgary AB
Peel, The Regional Municipality of (4) ... Brampton ON
Percepta (4) ... Toronto ON
Pink Elephant Inc. (4) ... Burlington ON
POPstar Communications Canada, Inc. (4) ... Vancouver BC
Positron Public Safety Systems Inc. (4) ... Montréal QC
Precise Software Technologies Inc. (4) ... Nepean ON
Progestic International Inc. (4) ... Winnipeg MB
Provenance Systems Inc. (4) ... Ottawa ON
Pure Technologies Inc. (4) ... Calgary AB
QJunction Technology Inc. (4) ... Waterloo ON
Raymark Integrated Retail Solutions (4) ... Montréal QC
Raytheon Systems Canada Ltd. (4) ... Richmond BC
Raytheon Systems Canada Ltd. (4) ... Waterloo ON
Replicon Inc. (4) ... Calgary AB
Rogers Cable Inc. (4) ... Toronto ON
SalesCentrix.com Inc. (4) ... Vancouver BC
Savage Software (4) ... Vancouver BC
Schneider Foods Inc. (4) ... Kitchener ON
Sedona Networks (4) ... Kanata ON
Shoppers Drug Mart (4) ... Toronto ON
Stantec Geomatics Ltd. (4) ... Edmonton AB
Surrey, City of (4) ... Surrey BC
Sybridge Technologies Inc. (4) ... Nepean ON
Systemcorp ALG Ltd. (4) ... Montréal QC
Taro Pharmaceuticals Inc. (4) ... Bramalea ON
Trakonic (4) ... Sydney NS
Trapeze Software Inc. (4) ... Mississauga ON
Triversity Inc. (4) ... Toronto ON
TTG Systems Inc. (4) ... Edmonton AB
University of Northern British Col (4) ... Prince George BC
University of Toronto (4) ... Toronto ON
Virtual Prototypes Inc. / VPI (4) ... Montréal QC
Westport Innovations Inc. (4) ... Vancouver BC
WorkDynamics Technologies Inc. (4) ... Ottawa ON
Xcert International Inc. (4) ... Vancouver BC
Xwave Solutions Inc. (4) ... Mississauga ON
Accpac International Inc. (3) ... Richmond BC
ACR Systems Inc. (3) ... Surrey BC
Adacel Inc. (3) ... Brossard QC
Alberta Finance (3) ... Edmonton AB
Alberta Human Resources and Employment (3) ... Edmonton AB
Aldata Software Management Inc. (3) ... Hinton AB
ALNAV Platinum Group Inc. (3) ... Edmonton AB
AMC Technologies Corp. (3) ... Edmonton AB
Apotex Inc. (3) ... Toronto ON
Appareo Software Inc. (3) ... Burnaby BC
AT&T Canada (3) ... Toronto ON
Atlantis Systems International (3) ... Brampton ON
Atreus Systems (3) ... Ottawa ON
Aucxis Corp. (3) ... Toronto ON
BrandEra.com Inc. (3) ... Toronto ON
British Columbia Automobile Association (3) ... Burnaby BC
British Columbia Lottery Corporation (3) ... Kamloops BC

COMPUTING (Cont.)

For descriptions of the occupational categories used in this index, see page 458.

OCCUPATIONAL INDEX 485

COMPUTING (Cont.)

Certified General Accountants Associat (2) .... Vancouver BC
Changepoint Corporation (2) .... Richmond Hill ON
Charon Systems Inc. (2) .... Toronto ON
Cinram International Inc. (2) .... Toronto ON
Circa Communications Ltd. (2) .... North Vancouver BC
Civil Service Co-operative Credit Society (2) .... Ottawa ON
Clockwork.ca (2) .... Toronto ON
CML Emergency Services, Inc. (2) .... Hull QC
Cogency Semiconductor Inc. (2) .... Toronto ON
Cognicase (2) .... Toronto ON
College of the North Atlantic, Step (2) .... Stephenville NF
Colt Engineering Corporation (2) .... Calgary AB
Computer Workware Inc. (2) .... Toronto ON
Conestoga-Rovers & Associates Limited / (2) .... Waterloo ON
Consultronics Ltd. (2) .... Concord ON
Convergys Corporation (2) .... Ottawa ON
Corus Entertainment Inc. (2) .... Toronto ON
Creation Technologies Inc. (2) .... Burnaby BC
CVDS Inc. (2) .... Pointe-Claire QC
Data Research Associates / DRA (2) .... Montréal QC
Data Systems Marketing Inc. (2) .... Toronto ON
Delmar International Inc. (2) .... Lachine QC
Delta Controls Inc. (2) .... Surrey BC
Department of Public Safety, NB (2) .... Fredericton NB
Digital Oilfield Inc. (2) .... Calgary AB
Dog Star Systems Inc. (2) .... Calgary AB
Dominion Colour Corporation (2) .... Toronto ON
Douglas College (2) .... New Westminster BC
DSI Datotech Systems Inc. (2) .... Vancouver BC
EDS Innovations (2) .... Ottawa ON
Electronic Arts (Canada) Inc. (2) .... Burnaby BC
Empowered Networks (2) .... Kanata ON
Encon Group Inc. (2) .... Ottawa ON
Ensemble Systems Inc. (2) .... Richmond BC
Entero Corporation (2) .... Calgary AB
Epson Research and Development, Inc., (2) .... Vancouver BC
Ericsson Canada Inc. (2) .... Mount Royal QC
ESI Canada Inc. (2) .... Mississauga ON
Essentus Inc. (2) .... Montréal QC
Evertz Microsystems Ltd. (2) .... Burlington ON
Excel Tech Ltd. / XLTEK (2) .... Oakville ON
Exocom Group Inc., The (2) .... Calgary AB
Exocom Group Inc., The (2) .... Mississauga ON
Explorer Software Solutions Ltd. (2) .... Calgary AB
Family and Children's Services Ni (2) .... St. Catharines ON
Farm Credit Canada / FCC (2) .... Regina SK
Financial Services Commission of Ontario (2) .... Toronto ON
Forsys Software Corporation (2) .... Markham ON
Gary Jonas Computing Ltd. (2) .... Richmond Hill ON
Gavel & Gown Software Inc. (2) .... Toronto ON
General Hydrogen / GH (2) .... Vancouver BC
GKO Engineering (2) .... Edmonton AB
Globel Direct Marketing (2) .... Richmond BC
Groupe Dynamite Inc. (2) .... Mount Royal QC
H2O Entertainment Corp. (2) .... Vancouver BC
Halton, The Regional Municipality of (2) .... Oakville ON
Hanover Maloney (2) .... Calgary AB
Healthnet International Inc. (2) .... Vancouver BC
Hewitt Associates (2) .... Toronto ON
Honda of Canada Manufacturing (2) .... Alliston ON
Hospital for Sick Children, The (2) .... Toronto ON
HSBC Bank Canada (2) .... Burnaby BC
Hydrogenics Corporation (2) .... Mississauga ON
IHS Solutions Ltd. (2) .... Nepean ON
IKO Industries Ltd. (2) .... Calgary AB
Illustrate Inc. (2) .... Toronto ON
Inex Pharmaceuticals Corp. (2) .... Burnaby BC
International Academy of Design and Techn (2) .... Ottawa ON
International Datacasting Corporation / I (2) .... Ottawa ON
Interwork Technologies Ltd. (2) .... Ottawa ON
Intrawest Corporation (2) .... Vancouver BC
Jazz Monkey Media (2) .... Toronto ON
Kanotech Information Systems Ltd. (2) .... Edmonton AB
Lenbrook (2) .... Pickering ON
Lincoln Technology Corporation (2) .... Edmonton AB
Liquor Control Board of Ontario / LCBO (2) .... Toronto ON
London Life Insurance Co. (2) .... London ON
M.R.S. Company Ltd. (2) .... Mississauga ON
MacDonald Dettwiler & Associates Ltd. / M (2) .... Ottawa ON
MacDonald Dettwiler & Associates Ltd. / (2) .... Halifax NS
Main Knitting Inc. (2) .... Montréal QC
Manitoba Civil Service Commission (2) .... Winnipeg MB
Manitoba Family Services and Housing (2) .... Winnipeg MB
Manitoba Intergovernmental Affairs (2) .... Winnipeg MB
Manitoba Labour & Immigration (2) .... Winnipeg MB
Manitoba Public Insurance (2) .... Winnipeg MB
McCarthy Tetrault LLP (2) .... Toronto ON
McMillan & Associates (2) .... Ottawa ON
MDS Nordion (2) .... Kanata ON
Media Wave Web Solutions (2) .... Ottawa ON
Medicine Hat, City of (2) .... Medicine Hat AB
MemberCARE Financial Services (2) .... Burlington ON
Menu Foods Ltd. (2) .... Mississauga ON
Metafore Corporation (2) .... Calgary AB
MetroPhotonics Inc. (2) .... Ottawa ON
MicroAge (2) .... Nepean ON
Miller Thomson LLP (2) .... Edmonton AB
Ministry of Agriculture, Food and Rural A (2) .... Guelph ON
Ministry of Agriculture, Food and Rural A (2) .... Guelph ON
Ministry of Finance, Ontario (2) .... Toronto ON
Ministry of Labour, Ontario (2) .... Ottawa ON
Ministry of Municipal Affairs and Housin (2) .... Toronto ON
Ministry of Northern Development and Min (2) .... Sudbury ON
Ministry of the Solicitor General, Ontar (2) .... Toronto ON
Ministry of the Solicitor General, Ontar (2) .... Toronto ON
Ministry of Transportation, Ontario (2) .... Thunder Bay ON
Mobile Data Solutions Inc. / MDSI (2) .... Richmond BC
Monarch Construction Ltd. (2) .... Toronto ON
Moore Corporation Ltd. (2) .... Mississauga ON
Morrison Hershfield (2) .... Toronto ON
Nanometrics Inc. (2) .... Kanata ON
Nanowave Technologies Inc. (2) .... Toronto ON
National Life Assurance Company of Canad (2) .... Toronto ON
National Research Council Canada, Integra (2) .... London ON
Nellcor Puritan Bennett (Melville) Ltd. (2) .... Ottawa ON
NetActive Inc. (2) .... Ottawa ON
Network Builders Inc. (2) .... Toronto ON
New Brunswick Community College, Dieppe C (2) .... Dieppe NB
New Media Innovation Centre / NewMIC (2) .... Vancouver BC
North Island College / NIC (2) .... Courtenay BC
North Vancouver, City of (2) .... North Vancouver BC
Northwestern Health Services Region (2) .... High Level AB
Northwood Technologies Inc. (2) .... Nepean ON
NRX Global Corp. (2) .... Toronto ON
Oerlikon Aerospace Inc. (2) .... St-Jean-sur-Richelieu QC
Open Storage Solutions, Inc. (2) .... Brampton ON
Optx Corporation (2) .... Winnipeg MB
Orbital Technologies Inc. (2) .... Vancouver BC
PanelX.com / PanelX Technical Services (2) .... Oakville ON
Parker Hannifin (Canada) Inc. (2) .... Grimsby ON
Passband Downhole Communications Inc. / (2) .... Calgary AB
Patheon Inc. (2) .... Mississauga ON
Polycom Canada Inc. (2) .... North Vancouver BC
Precidia Technologies (2) .... Kanata ON
Pro-Cad Software Ltd. (2) .... Calgary AB
ProFac Facilities Management Services In (2) .... Toronto ON
Proximi-T Information Technology Inc (2) .... Mississauga ON
Public Service Commission of Canada, (2) .... St. John's NF
Public Service Commission of Canada, Qu (2) .... Montréal QC
Public Service Commission, PEI (2) .... Charlottetown PE
QCA Systems Ltd. (2) .... Delta BC
Quadra Chemicals Ltd. (2) .... Vaudreuil-Dorion QC
Revolve Magnetic Bearings Inc. (2) .... Calgary AB
Richmond Hill, Town of (2) .... Richmond Hill ON
Rittal Systems Ltd. (2) .... Mississauga ON
Robertson Inc. (2) .... Milton ON
Ross Video Ltd. (2) .... Iroquois ON
Royal Roads University (2) .... Victoria BC
Ruffneck Heaters (2) .... Calgary AB
Saint Elizabeth Health Care (2) .... Markham ON
Saskatchewan Institute of Applied Scie (2) .... Moose Jaw SK
Scancode Logistics (2) .... Mississauga ON
Scarborough Hospital, General Division (2) .... Toronto ON
Schlumberger Completion Systems (2) .... Calgary AB
Siemens Canada Ltd. (2) .... Mississauga ON
Siemens Canada Ltd., Production and Logisti (2) .... Ajax ON
SignalSoft Canada (2) .... Victoria BC
Silicon Access Networks Ltd. (2) .... Ottawa ON
SMED International Inc. (2) .... Calgary AB
Sobeys Canada Inc. (2) .... Stellarton NS
Sony Music Canada (2) .... Toronto ON

COMPUTING (Cont.)

South Lake Regional Health Centre (2) ... Newmarket ON
SpeechWorks International, Inc. (2) ... Montréal QC
SpiderCache (2) ... Granville Island BC
Splentec Ltd. (2) ... Richmond Hill ON
Startech Business Systems Ltd. (2) ... Calgary AB
Stream Data Systems Ltd. (2) ... Calgary AB
Superintendent of Financial Institutions (2) ... Ottawa ON
Tarian Software Inc. (2) ... Ottawa ON
Teekay Shipping Corp. (2) ... Vancouver BC
Teleperformance Canada Inc. / TPCAN (2) ... Toronto ON
Telesat Canada (2) ... Gloucester ON
Thrive Media (2) ... Vancouver BC
Tommy Hilfiger Canada Inc. (2) ... Montréal QC
Toronto Real Estate Board / TREB (2) ... Toronto ON
TravelActive.com Marketing Inc. (2) ... Cambridge ON
Tribal Sportswear Inc. (2) ... Montréal QC
UMA Engineering Ltd. (2) ... Winnipeg MB
University College of the Cariboo / UCC (2) ... Kamloops BC
University Health Network, Shared Inform (2) ... Toronto ON
University of British Columbia / UBC (2) ... Vancouver BC
University of Calgary, Department of Com (2) ... Calgary AB
University of Toronto, Faculty of Arts & (2) ... Toronto ON
University of Waterloo (2) ... Waterloo ON
Value Drug Mart Associates Ltd. (2) ... Edmonton AB
Vancouver, City of (2) ... Vancouver BC
Vancouver City Savings Credit Union / (2) ... Vancouver BC
Veonnel Inc. (2) ... Nepean ON
Vision2Hire Solutions (2) ... Vancouver BC
Vitana Corporation (2) ... Ottawa ON
VoiceGenie.com (2) ... Toronto ON
VoiceIQ Inc. (2) ... Markham ON
Vorum Research Corporation (2) ... Vancouver BC
Wajax Industries Limited (2) ... Mississauga ON
WANN Connection Devices Inc. (2) ... Nepean ON
Wardrop Engineering Inc. (2) ... Mississauga ON
Warner Music Canada (2) ... Toronto ON
Web Krew Inc. (2) ... Toronto ON
Weidmuller Ltd. (2) ... Markham ON
Whistler Blackcomb / Intrawest (2) ... Whistler BC
Wi-LAN Inc. (2) ... Calgary AB
William M. Mercer Limited (2) ... Toronto ON
Workers' Compensation Board, Alberta (2) ... Edmonton AB
Workers' Compensation Board of BC (2) ... Vancouver BC
York Region District School Board (2) ... Aurora ON
Zivex IT Utility Company (2) ... Kanata ON
Zurich Canada (2) ... Toronto ON
A&B Sound Ltd. (1) ... Vancouver BC
ABC Group Inc. (1) ... Toronto ON
Acadia University, Jodrey School of Co (1) ... Wolfville NS
Acres International Limited (1) ... Niagara Falls ON
ADESA Canada Inc. (1) ... Brampton ON
ADP Canada (1) ... Calgary AB
Advantera Communications Inc. (1) ... Ottawa ON
Aga Khan Foundation Canada / AKFC (1) ... Ottawa ON
Agere Systems (1) ... Nepean ON
AGFA (1) ... Toronto ON
Agile Systems Inc. (1) ... Waterloo ON
AIM Funds Management Inc. (1) ... Calgary AB
AIM Funds Management Inc. (1) ... Toronto ON
Ainsworth Inc. (1) ... Toronto ON
Air Transat Holidays (1) ... Montréal QC
Alacris Inc. (1) ... Ottawa ON
Alberta Boilers Safety Association / AB (1) ... Edmonton AB
Alberta Cancer Board / ACB (1) ... Edmonton AB
Alberta College of Pharmacists (1) ... Edmonton AB
Alberta Community Development (1) ... Edmonton AB
Alberta Energy (1) ... Edmonton AB
Alberta Energy and Utilities Board / EUB (1) ... Calgary AB
Alberta Energy Company Ltd. / AEC (1) ... Calgary AB
Alberta Environment (1) ... Calgary AB
Alberta Human Resources and Employment (1) ... Innisfail AB
Alberta Infrastructure & Transportation (1) ... Edmonton AB
Alberta Mental Health Board, Alberta Hosp (1) ... Ponoka AB
Alberta Motor Association / AMA (1) ... Edmonton AB
Alberta Resource Development (1) ... Edmonton AB
Alberta Sustainable Resource Development (1) ... Calgary AB
Algoma District School Board / (1) ... Sault Ste. Marie ON
All Weather Windows (1) ... Edmonton AB
Alltemp Sensors Inc. (1) ... Edmonton AB
Ankari (1) ... Ottawa ON
Appendix Technical Publishing Group (1) ... Ottawa ON
Aramark Canada Ltd. (1) ... Toronto ON
Argus Technologies Ltd. (1) ... Burnaby BC
Ash City (1) ... Toronto ON
Assante Advisory Services (1) ... Toronto ON
Atlas Cold Storage Canada Ltd. (1) ... Toronto ON
Atlas Van Lines (Canada) Ltd. (1) ... Oakville ON
Atomic Energy of Canada Ltd. / AECL (1) ... Mississauga ON
Audio Centre (1) ... Ottawa ON
Autopro Automation Consultants Lt (1) ... Grande Prairie AB
Axys Group (1) ... Sidney BC
Azure Dynamics Inc. (1) ... Vancouver BC
Barmish Inc. (1) ... St-Laurent QC
Barton Instrument Systems Ltd. (1) ... Calgary AB
Baytex Energy Ltd. (1) ... Calgary AB
BDO Dunwoody LLP (1) ... Orillia ON
Bell Canada (1) ... Toronto ON
Bentley Leathers (1) ... St-Laurent QC
Beta Machinery Analysis Ltd. (1) ... Calgary AB
BJ Pipeline Inspection Services (1) ... Calgary AB
Bloorview MacMillan Children's Centre, M (1) ... Toronto ON
BOC Canada Ltd. (1) ... Mississauga ON
Boeing Canada Technology Ltd., Arnprior (1) ... Arnprior ON
Boulevard Media (Canada) Inc. / BMC (1) ... Vancouver BC
Branksome Hall (1) ... Toronto ON
Brenntag Canada Inc. (1) ... Toronto ON
British Columbia Assets & Land Corporat (1) ... Victoria BC
Brogan Inc. (1) ... Ottawa ON
Business Development Bank of Canada / B (1) ... Montréal QC
Business Travel International / BTI Cana (1) ... Calgary AB
CAA South Central Ontario (1) ... Hamilton ON
Caboodles Cosmetics (1) ... New Westminster BC
Cadex Electronics Inc. (1) ... Richmond BC
Canada Deposit Insurance Corporation / CD (1) ... Ottawa ON
Canadian Blood Services / CBS (1) ... Ottawa ON
Canadian Depository for Securities Ltd. (1) ... Toronto ON
Canadian Forces Exchange System / CANEX (1) ... Ottawa ON
Canadian Medical Protective Association / (1) ... Ottawa ON
Canadian Natural Resources Limited / CNR (1) ... Calgary AB
CANTEST Ltd. (1) ... Burnaby BC
Carlson Marketing Group Canada Ltd. / CM (1) ... Toronto ON
Casino Niagara (1) ... Niagara Falls ON
Catholic Children's Aid Society of Toron (1) ... Toronto ON
CCH Canadian Ltd. (1) ... Toronto ON
Center for Digital Imaging and Sound / C (1) ... Burnaby BC
Centre for Health Evaluation and Outco (1) ... Vancouver BC
Ceridian Canada Ltd. (1) ... Markham ON
CGI Group Inc. (1) ... Ottawa ON
CH2M HILL Canada Ltd. (1) ... Toronto ON
Chaps Group Inc. / CGS (1) ... Markham ON
Children's and Women's Health Centre o (1) ... Vancouver BC
CIBA Vision Sterile Manufacturing (1) ... Mississauga ON
Cirque du Soleil (1) ... Montréal QC
ClientLogic Corp. (1) ... Toronto ON
CMD Group (1) ... Toronto ON
CMP Design (1) ... Kanata ON
Cole Vision Canada, Inc. (1) ... Markham ON
College of the Rockies (1) ... Cranbrook BC
Colt Engineering Corporation (1) ... Edmonton AB
Columbia House Canada (1) ... Toronto ON
COM DEV International (1) ... Cambridge ON
Comda (1) ... Toronto ON
Community Care Access Centre of Peel (1) ... Brampton ON
Computalog Ltd. (1) ... Calgary AB
Conestoga College of Applied Arts & Te (1) ... Kitchener ON
Coquitlam, City of (1) ... Coquitlam BC
Coradiant Inc. (1) ... Montréal QC
Cougar Automation Technologies Inc. (1) ... Toronto ON
CSA International (1) ... Toronto ON
CSI Wireless Inc. (1) ... Calgary AB
CTF Systems Inc. (1) ... Port Coquitlam BC
Cummins Inc. (1) ... Toronto ON
Cunningham & Lindsey Canada Ltd. (1) ... Hamilton ON
CWD Windows and Doors (1) ... Calgary AB
Cymbolic Sciences Inc. (1) ... Richmond BC
Daedalian eSolutions (1) ... Toronto ON
Decima Research Inc. (1) ... Montréal QC
Decor-Rest Furniture Ltd. (1) ... Woodbridge ON
Deloitte & Touche (1) ... Edmonton AB
Deloitte & Touche (1) ... Toronto ON

For descriptions of the occupational categories used in this index, see page 458.

COMPUTING (Cont.)

COMPUTING (Cont.)

MemberWorks Canada Corporation (1) .... Montréal QC
Memoris, Inc. (1) .... Montréal QC
Mentor Engineering (1) .... Calgary AB
Mercury Filmworks (1) .... Vancouver BC
Merisel Canada Inc. (1) .... Toronto ON
Meritor Suspension Systems Company (1) .... Milton ON
Messier-Dowty Inc. (1) .... Ajax ON
Messier-Dowty Inc. (1) .... Peterborough ON
Metasoft Systems Inc. (1) .... Vancouver BC
Microcell Telecommunications Ltd. (1) .... Vancouver BC
Millenium Biologix Inc. (1) .... Kingston ON
Milton, Town of (1) .... Milton ON
Ministry of Citizenship, Culture and Rec (1) .... Toronto ON
Ministry of Community and Social Servi (1) .... North Bay ON
Ministry of Community and Social Service (1) .... Toronto ON
Ministry of Correctional Services, Ontar (1) .... Toronto ON
Ministry of Labour, Ontario (1) .... Toronto ON
Ministry of Labour, Ontario (Northern Re (1) .... Sudbury ON
Ministry of Natural Resources, (1) .... Sault Ste. Marie ON
Ministry of Natural Resources, Onta (1) .... Peterborough ON
Ministry of the Attorney General, Ontari (1) .... Toronto ON
Ministry of the Attorney General, Ontari (1) .... Toronto ON
Ministry of the Environment, Ontario (1) .... Toronto ON
Ministry of the Environment, Ontario (En (1) .... Toronto ON
Ministry of the Environment, Ontario (En (1) .... Toronto ON
Ministry of the Solicitor General, Ontar (1) .... Toronto ON
Ministry of the Solicitor General, Ontar (1) .... Orillia ON
Ministry of Transportation, Ontario (1) .... London ON
Ministry of Transportation, Ontario (1) .... Kingston ON
Minolta Business Equipment (Canada), Lt (1) .... Richmond BC
Minolta Business Equipment (Canada) (1) .... Mississauga ON
Misco Canada Inc. (1) .... Markham ON
Mitel Corporation (1) .... Kanata ON
Mobilia Inc. (1) .... Pointe-Claire QC
Mohawk College of Applied Arts and Tech (1) .... Hamilton ON
Momentous.ca Corporation (1) .... Nepean ON
MTU Maintenance Canada Ltd. (1) .... Richmond BC
MTW Solutions Online Inc. (1) .... Toronto ON
National Info-Tech Centre / NIC (1) .... Montréal QC
National Research Council Canada, Canada (1) .... Ottawa ON
National Research Council Canada / NRC (1) .... Winnipeg MB
National Research Council Canada / NRC (1) .... Ottawa ON
National Steel Car Ltd. (1) .... Hamilton ON
Neilson Dairy (1) .... Halton Hills ON
NetNation Communications, Inc. (1) .... Vancouver BC
New Brunswick Community College, Sain (1) .... Saint John NB
New Brunswick Community College, St. (1) .... St. Andrews NB
New Brunswick Community College, Woods (1) .... Woodstock NB
Nexmedia Technologies Inc. (1) .... Burnaby BC
Nextrom Ltd. (1) .... Concord ON
Nipissing University (1) .... North Bay ON
Nokia Products Ltd. (1) .... Richmond BC
Norcom Networks (1) .... Burnaby BC
NorQuest College (1) .... Edmonton AB
Nortel Networks (1) .... Brampton ON
North Hamilton Community Health Centre (1) .... Hamilton ON
North Okanagan Health Region / NOHR (1) .... Armstrong BC
North Vancouver, The District of (1) .... North Vancouver BC
Northeast Mental Health Centre / NEMHC (1) .... Sudbury ON
Northern Airborne Technology Ltd. / NAT (1) .... Kelowna BC
Northern Elevator Ltd. (1) .... Toronto ON
Novatel Inc. (1) .... Calgary AB
Novex Pharma (1) .... Richmond Hill ON
NPS Pharmaceuticals Inc. (1) .... Mississauga ON
Nubase Technologies Inc. (1) .... Toronto ON
O'Hara Technologies Inc. (1) .... Richmond Hill ON
Office of the Auditor General of Canada (1) .... Ottawa ON
OmniSales (1) .... Ottawa ON
Ontario Clean Water Agency / OCWA (1) .... Toronto ON
Ontario Heritage Foundation, Corporate S (1) .... Toronto ON
Ontario March of Dimes (1) .... Toronto ON
Ontario Securities Commission / OSC (1) .... Toronto ON
Open Learning Agency / OLA (1) .... Burnaby BC
Oracle Corporation Canada Inc. (1) .... Mississauga ON
Ottawa Senators Hockey Club (1) .... Kanata ON
Ottawa-Carleton District School Board / O (1) .... Nepean ON
Pacific Blue Cross / BC Life (1) .... Vancouver BC
Packaging Group, The (1) .... Concord ON
Palfinger Inc. (1) .... Niagara Falls ON
Patheon Inc. (1) .... Whitby ON
PCL Constructors Inc. (1) .... Edmonton AB
Perceptron Inc., Forest Products Divi (1) .... Parksville BC
Pet Valu Canada Inc. (1) .... Markham ON
Petro-Canada (1) .... Calgary AB
Pharmacia Canada Inc. (1) .... Markham ON
Philips Analytical (1) .... Waterloo ON
Phoenix Hydraulics Group (1) .... Nisku AB
Pika Technologies Inc. (1) .... Kanata ON
Pink Triangle Press (1) .... Toronto ON
PMC-Sierra, Inc. (1) .... Burnaby BC
PMC-Sierra, Inc. (1) .... Kanata ON
Post Impressions Systems Inc. (1) .... Montréal QC
Power Measurement Ltd. (1) .... Victoria BC
PowerPlus Systems Corporation (1) .... Calgary AB
PPM 2000 Inc. (1) .... Edmonton AB
PricewaterhouseCoopers, Business Process (1) .... Calgary AB
Primerica Financial Services (Canada (1) .... Mississauga ON
Professional Engineers Ontario / PEO (1) .... Toronto ON
Propak Systems Ltd. (1) .... Airdrie AB
Providence Centre (1) .... Toronto ON
Provincial Auditor's Office, Manitoba (1) .... Winnipeg MB
PTI Group Inc. (1) .... Edmonton AB
Public Guardian and Trustee of British (1) .... Vancouver BC
Public Service Alliance of Canada / PSAC (1) .... Ottawa ON
Public Service Commission of Canada, Al (1) .... Edmonton AB
Public Service Commission of Canada, BC (1) .... Victoria BC
Public Service Commission of Canada, B (1) .... Vancouver BC
Public Service Commission of Canada, Exec (1) .... Ottawa ON
Public Service Commission of Canada, Nov (1) .... Halifax NS
Public Service Commission of Canada, (1) .... Yellowknife NT
Public Service Commission of Canada, Onta (1) .... Ottawa ON
Public Service Commission of Canada, (1) .... Whitehorse YT
Public Service Employee Relations Commi (1) .... Victoria BC
Quake Technologies Inc. (1) .... Ottawa ON
Quebec Student Health Alliance / ASEQ (1) .... Montréal QC
Quebecor World Printpak (1) .... Calgary AB
QuestAir Technologies Inc. (1) .... Burnaby BC
Radiant Communications (1) .... Vancouver BC
Raymond James Ltd. (1) .... Vancouver BC
Redback Networks (1) .... Burnaby BC
Regina, City of (1) .... Regina SK
Regional Health Authority 5 (1) .... Drumheller AB
RGO Office Products (1) .... Calgary AB
Richmond, City of (1) .... Richmond BC
RMH Teleservices International Inc. (1) .... Saint John NB
Rocky Mountain Instruments Inc. / RMI (1) .... Edmonton AB
Rogers AT&T Wireless (1) .... Toronto ON
Rogers iMedia (1) .... Toronto ON
Rogers Video (1) .... Richmond BC
Rohm and Haas Canada Inc. (1) .... Toronto ON
Royal Building Systems (Cdn) Ltd. / R (1) .... Woodbridge ON
Royal Canadian Mint / RCM (1) .... Ottawa ON
Sagebrush Corporation (1) .... Edmonton AB
Samtack (1) .... Toronto ON
Sander Geophysics Ltd. / SGL (1) .... Ottawa ON
Sanjel Corporation (1) .... Calgary AB
SanMar Canada (1) .... Richmond BC
Saskatchewan Institute of Applied Scie (1) .... Saskatoon SK
Saskatchewan Liquor and Gaming Authority (1) .... Regina SK
Saskatchewan Post-Secondary Education and (1) .... Regina SK
School District #36 (Surrey) (1) .... Surrey BC
School District #43 (Coquitlam) (1) .... Coquitlam BC
Sciemetric Instruments Inc. (1) .... Nepean ON
SED Systems (1) .... Saskatoon SK
Seiden Health Management Inc. (1) .... Toronto ON
Semotus Systems Corporation (1) .... Vancouver BC
Senstar-Stellar Corporation (1) .... Carp ON
Shared Services West, Regional Materials (1) .... Toronto ON
Shikatronics Inc. (1) .... La Prairie QC
Shopping Channel, The / TSC (1) .... Toronto ON
Siemens Milltronics Process Instruments (1) .... Edmonton AB
Siemens Westinghouse (1) .... Hamilton ON
Sierra Wireless Inc. (1) .... Richmond BC
Silex Inc. (1) .... Mississauga ON
Simark Controls Ltd. (1) .... Calgary AB
Simon Fraser Health Region, Burnaby Hosp (1) .... Burnaby BC
Sir Wilfrid Laurier School Board (1) .... Rosemere QC
Sky Eye America (1) .... Dorval QC
Society of Energy Professionals, The (1) .... Toronto ON

For descriptions of the occupational categories used in this index, see page 458.

COMPUTING (Cont.)

Sodema / Transcontinental Technology (1) .... Montréal QC
Solectron (1) .... Calgary AB
Solinst Canada Ltd. (1) .... Georgetown ON
SpaceBridge Networks Corporation (1) .... Hull QC
Speed-i-Com Inc. / SCI (1) .... Toronto ON
Sproule Associates Limited (1) .... Calgary AB
Square Peg Communications Inc. / SPCI (1) .... Kanata ON
SS8 Networks Inc. (1) .... Ottawa ON
St. George's School (1) .... Vancouver BC
Stantec Consulting Ltd. (1) .... Kitchener ON
Steelcase Canada Ltd. (1) .... Markham ON
Stellate Systems (1) .... Westmount QC
Strategy First (1) .... Montréal QC
STS Systems (1) .... Pointe-Claire QC
Stuart Olson Construction (1) .... Calgary AB
Sulzer Mitroflow Corp. (1) .... Richmond BC
Sunoco Inc. (1) .... Toronto ON
Synavant Inc. (1) .... Toronto ON
Syncrude Canada Ltd. (1) .... Fort McMurray AB
Synopsys Inc. (1) .... Ottawa ON
Tantalus Systems Corp. (1) .... Burnaby BC
TAP Ventures, Inc. (1) .... Vancouver BC
Technical Standards & Safety Authority / (1) .... Toronto ON
TECO Precision Inc. (1) .... St-Laurent QC
TELAV Audio Visual Services (1) .... Lachine QC
TeleTech Canada (1) .... Toronto ON
Tellabs TTG Inc. (1) .... Gloucester ON
TelTech Assets.Com Ltd. (1) .... Calgary AB
TierOne OSS Technologies Inc. (1) .... Mississauga ON
Time iCR Inc. (1) .... Ottawa ON
Timothy's World Coffee (1) .... Toronto ON
Toronto, City of (1) .... Toronto ON
Tracer Industries Canada Ltd. (1) .... Edmonton AB
Trader.com (1) .... Edmonton AB
Trail Appliances Ltd. (1) .... Calgary AB
TransAlta Corporation (1) .... Calgary AB
Travel Guard Canada (1) .... Toronto ON
Tri-Media Marketing & Publicity Inc. (1) .... Welland ON
Tricom Technologies (1) .... Mississauga ON
Trillium Health Centre (1) .... Mississauga ON
Trillium Photonics (1) .... Ottawa ON
Trios College of Information Technol (1) .... Mississauga ON
TRIUMF Meson Research Facility (1) .... Vancouver BC
TRM Technologies, Inc. (1) .... Ottawa ON
Tropic Networks Inc. (1) .... Kanata ON
Turbocor Inc. (1) .... Dorval QC
Ty-Crop Manufacturing Ltd. (1) .... Rosedale BC
Tyco Healthcare Group Canada Inc. (1) .... St-Laurent QC
Unisearch Associates Inc. (1) .... Concord ON
University of British Columbia, Depar (1) .... Vancouver BC
University of Regina, Faculty of Engineer (1) .... Regina SK
University of Victoria (1) .... Victoria BC
Upper Canada College, Upper School (1) .... Toronto ON
Vancouver Community College / VCC (1) .... Vancouver BC
Vancouver Community College / VCC (1) .... Vancouver BC
Vancouver International Airport Authori (1) .... Richmond BC
Veridian Corporation (1) .... Ajax ON
Victoria, City of (1) .... Victoria BC
Vistar Telecommunications Inc. (1) .... Ottawa ON
Vistek Ltd. (1) .... Toronto ON
VitalAire Healthcare (1) .... Mississauga ON
Voice Mobility Inc. (1) .... Richmond BC
Volex Canada Inc. (1) .... Kanata ON
Walsh Automation / Validation Technolog (1) .... Montréal QC
Wardrop Engineering Inc. (1) .... Thunder Bay ON
Weishaupt Corporation (1) .... Mississauga ON
West Park Healthcare Centre (1) .... Toronto ON
Weyerhaeuser Company Limited (1) .... Kamloops BC
Whitby, Town of (1) .... Whitby ON
Windsor Casino Limited (1) .... Windsor ON
Woodbine Entertainment Group (1) .... Toronto ON
Xantrex Technology Inc. (1) .... Burnaby BC
Xillix Technologies Corp. (1) .... Richmond BC
York Catholic District School Board (1) .... Aurora ON
York House School (1) .... Vancouver BC

CONSTRUCTION

See also: Real Estate, Architecture, Trades/Technicians.

Trow Consulting Engineers Ltd. (15 positions) .... Brampton ON
Kenaidan Contracting Ltd. (11) .... Mississauga ON
McElhanney Group Ltd., The (11) .... Vancouver BC
StonCor Group (10) .... Whitby ON
Tracer Industries Canada Ltd. (10) .... Edmonton AB
Flint Energy Services Ltd. (9) .... Sherwood Park AB
Graham Industrial Services Ltd. (8) .... Edmonton AB
Atlas Corporation, The (6) .... Concord ON
Maple Reinders Inc. (6) .... Edmonton AB
UMA Engineering Ltd. (6) .... Edmonton AB
Colt Engineering Corporation (5) .... Calgary AB
Giffels Associates Limited (5) .... Toronto ON
Hawthorne Homes (5) .... Calgary AB
Maple Reinders Inc. (5) .... Brampton ON
Ministry of Transportation, Ontario (5) .... North Bay ON
Calgary, City of (4) .... Calgary AB
Chandos Construction Ltd. (4) .... Edmonton AB
Commonwealth Construction (4) .... Burnaby BC
Earth Tech Canada Inc. (4) .... Markham ON
Inland Cement Limited (4) .... Edmonton AB
Jacques Whitford Environment Ltd. (4) .... Ottawa ON
Jayman Master Builder (4) .... Calgary AB
Ledcor Industries Ltd. (4) .... Mississauga ON
Morrison Hershfield (4) .... Toronto ON
Rogers Communications Inc. (4) .... Toronto ON
Sobotec Ltd. (4) .... Hamilton ON
Stantec Consulting Ltd. (4) .... Calgary AB
Stonhard Ltd. (4) .... Whitby ON
Trow Consulting Engineers Ltd. (4) .... Nepean ON
Verdiroc Development Corporation (4) .... Toronto ON
Alberta Municipal Affairs (3) .... Edmonton AB
API Construction Ltd. (3) .... North Vancouver BC
ATCO Structures Inc. (3) .... Calgary AB
Bird Construction Company (3) .... Richmond BC
Bird Construction Company (3) .... Edmonton AB
Black & McDonald Ltd. (3) .... Toronto ON
Bytown Lumber (3) .... Nepean ON
Doran Contractors Ltd. (3) .... Ottawa ON
Groupe Conseil SAE Inc., Le (3) .... St-Laurent QC
Hemosol Inc. (3) .... Toronto ON
J.S. Watson & Associates Ltd. (3) .... Markham ON
K-LOR Contractors Services Ltd. (3) .... Calgary AB
Landmark Master Builder Inc. (3) .... Edmonton AB
Lansing Buildall / Revy Home Centres Inc (3) .... Toronto ON
Ledcor Industries Ltd. (3) .... Calgary AB
Ledcor Industries Ltd. (3) .... Kanata ON
Maxim Morrison Hershfield Ltd. (3) .... Edmonton AB
Milton, Town of (3) .... Milton ON
Morley Construction Inc. (3) .... Carp ON
Nadine International Inc. (3) .... Mississauga ON
NRB Inc. (3) .... Grimsby ON
PCL Constructors Canada Inc. (3) .... Mississauga ON
Pro-Bel Enterprises, Ltd. (3) .... Ajax ON
Roofmart Alberta Inc. (3) .... Calgary AB
Royal Group Technologies Inc. (3) .... Woodbridge ON
Sims Moelich Associates Ltd. (3) .... Oakville ON
SNC-Lavalin Inc. (3) .... Montréal QC
Stewart, Weir & Co. Ltd. (3) .... Edmonton AB
TAS Designbuild (3) .... Toronto ON
360 Networks Inc. (2) .... Mississauga ON
Acres & Associates Environmental Ltd. (2) .... Toronto ON
Alberta Infrastructure & Transportation (2) .... Edmonton AB
Armbro Materials Engineering Corporatio (2) .... Brampton ON
Arxx Building Products (2) .... Cobourg ON
BC Hydro (2) .... Vancouver BC
Bird Construction Company (2) .... Toronto ON
Brampton, City of (2) .... Brampton ON
Brofort Inc. (2) .... Ottawa ON
Brookfield LePage Johnson Controls Facili (2) .... Ottawa ON
Building Box, The (2) .... Markham ON
Canam Steel Works (2) .... Calgary AB
Canem-Harbour (2) .... Port Coquitlam BC
Cantex Engineering & Construction Co. (2) .... Penticton BC
Chancellor Industrial Construction Ltd. (2) .... Nisku AB
Clark Builders (2) .... Edmonton AB
CMD Group (2) .... Toronto ON
Columbia Manufacturing Co. Ltd. (2) .... Burnaby BC

CONSTRUCTION (Cont.)

Con-Force Structures Ltd. (2) .... Calgary AB
Dayton / Richmond Concrete Accessories (2) .... Toronto ON
Department of Works, Services and Transpo (2) .... Gander NF
Devitt & Forand Contractors Inc. (2) .... Calgary AB
Dillon Consulting Ltd. (2) .... Fredericton NB
Dominion Construction Company Inc. (2) .... Calgary AB
EBA Engineering Consultants Ltd. (2) .... Edmonton AB
Excel Homes Inc. (2) .... Calgary AB
General Paint Corp. (2) .... Vancouver BC
George Brown College (2) .... Toronto ON
Gienow Building Products Ltd. (2) .... Calgary AB
H.H. Angus & Associates Ltd. (2) .... Toronto ON
Hilti (Canada) Ltd. (2) .... Mississauga ON
Homeowner Protection Office (2) .... Vancouver BC
I-XL Industries Ltd. (2) .... Medicine Hat AB
Intalite Ceiling Systems (2) .... St-Laurent QC
Jacques Whitford Environment Ltd. (2) .... Burnaby BC
Kaycan Ltd. (2) .... Toronto ON
Kenroc Building Materials Co. Ltd. (2) .... Regina SK
King Packaged Materials Company (2) .... Burlington ON
LeBlanc Ltd. (2) .... Oakville ON
Len Corcoran Excavating (2) .... Elginburg ON
Lexcan Ltd. (2) .... Toronto ON
Mac's Convenience Stores Inc. (2) .... Toronto ON
Maple Reinders Inc. (2) .... Calgary AB
Markham, Corporation of the Town of (2) .... Markham ON
Marshall Macklin Monaghan Limited (2) .... Thornhill ON
McKay-Cocker Construction Ltd. (2) .... London ON
Ministry of Labour, Ontario (2) .... London ON
Ministry of Labour, Ontario (2) .... Toronto ON
Mississauga, City of (2) .... Mississauga ON
Pacesetter Homes Ltd. (2) .... Edmonton AB
Parkvalley Consulting Ltd. (2) .... Calgary AB
PCL Constructors Inc. (2) .... Edmonton AB
Peel Lumber (2) .... Milton ON
Peel, The Regional Municipality of (2) .... Brampton ON
PERI Formwork Systems Inc. (2) .... Brampton ON
Peter Kiewit Sons Co. Ltd. (2) .... Edmonton AB
Polygon Interior Design Limited (2) .... Vancouver BC
Reber Inc. / R-2000 Inc. (2) .... Riviere-des-Prairies QC
Remington Development Corporation (2) .... Calgary AB
Scott Builders Inc. (2) .... Red Deer AB
Scott Construction Ltd. (2) .... Vancouver BC
Stantec Geomatics Ltd. (2) .... Edmonton AB
Stone & Webster Canada Limited (2) .... Toronto ON
Stuart Olson Construction (2) .... Calgary AB
Superior Cabinets Alberta Ltd. (2) .... Edmonton AB
Timberfield Roof Truss (2) .... London ON
Toromont CAT (2) .... Concord ON
Trow Consulting Engineers Ltd. (2) .... Cambridge ON
University of Calgary (2) .... Calgary AB
Urbandale Corporation (2) .... Ottawa ON
Vancouver Hospital and Health Sciences (2) .... Vancouver BC
Vaughan, City of (2) .... Vaughan ON
Vulcain Inc. (2) .... Delson QC
Westpro Constructors Group Ltd. (2) .... Coquitlam BC
Willmar Windows (2) .... Mississauga ON
York Central Hospital (2) .... Richmond Hill ON
Acres International Limited (1) .... Vancouver BC
Acres International Limited (1) .... Castlegar BC
AFGD Glass (1) .... Concord ON
Ainsworth Inc. (1) .... Toronto ON
Alberta Infrastructure & Transportation (1) .... Edmonton AB
Albian Sands Energy Inc. (1) .... Fort McMurray AB
All Weather Windows (1) .... Calgary AB
Amaco Construction Equipment (1) .... Mississauga ON
Aman Building Corp. (1) .... Sherwood Park AB
AMEC (1) .... Vancouver BC
AMEC Infrastructure Ltd. (1) .... Sherwood Park AB
Amusement Leisure Worldwide (1) .... Calgary AB
Angus Consulting Management Ltd. / ACML (1) .... Toronto ON
Armbro Construction Ltd. (1) .... Brampton ON
Arriscraft International Inc. (1) .... Cambridge ON
Associated Engineering Industrial Ltd. (1) .... Edmonton AB
Babcock & Wilcox Canada (1) .... Cambridge ON
Bot Construction Limited (1) .... Oakville ON
Brandt Tractor Ltd. (1) .... Edmonton AB
Calgary Airport Authority, The (1) .... Calgary AB

Canada Mortgage and Housing Corporatio (1) .... Vancouver BC
Canadian Survey Equipment Ltd. / Cansel (1) .... Edmonton AB
Canron Construction Corp. (1) .... Toronto ON
Cara Operations Ltd., Harvey's Divis (1) .... Mississauga ON
Cimco Refrigeration (1) .... Toronto ON
Circon Systems Corporation (1) .... Richmond BC
CJP Architects (1) .... New Westminster BC
Claridge Homes (1) .... Ottawa ON
Comstock Canada Ltd. (1) .... Burlington ON
Coquitlam, City of (1) .... Coquitlam BC
Corporate Research Group (1) .... Nepean ON
Cosburn Patterson Mather Ltd. (1) .... Markham ON
Crystal Homes (1) .... Hamilton ON
David McManus Engineering Ltd. / DME (1) .... Nepean ON
David Schaeffer Engineering Ltd. (1) .... Markham ON
Delta Hudson Engineering Ltd. (1) .... Calgary AB
Department of Human Resources, Nunavut (1) .... Iqaluit NU
Department of Municipal and Provincia (1) .... St. John's NF
Department of Public Safety, NB (1) .... Fredericton NB
Dillon Consulting Ltd. (1) .... Toronto ON
Dimax Controls Inc. (1) .... Toronto ON
Dufferin Construction Company (1) .... Oakville ON
Duke Blakey, Inc. (1) .... Markham ON
Dundee Realty Management Corporation (1) .... Toronto ON
E.S. Fox Ltd. (1) .... Niagara Falls ON
Earth Energy Utility Corp. (1) .... Burlington ON
EMC Group Ltd. (1) .... Concord ON
Emco Ltd. (1) .... Richmond BC
Enersource (1) .... Mississauga ON
EPCOR Utilities Inc. (1) .... Edmonton AB
Fiera Foods Company (1) .... Toronto ON
First Professional Management Inc. (1) .... Toronto ON
First Professional Management Inc. (1) .... Ottawa ON
Fluor Canada Ltd. (1) .... Calgary AB
Fonthill Lumber Ltd. (1) .... Fonthill ON
General Hydrogen / GH (1) .... Vancouver BC
Gentek Building Products Ltd. (1) .... Burlington ON
Goodkey, Weedmark & Associates Ltd. (1) .... Ottawa ON
Greater Toronto Airports Authority / GTA (1) .... Toronto ON
Guelph, City of (1) .... Guelph ON
Halsall Associates Ltd. (1) .... Toronto ON
Halton Hills, Town of (1) .... Halton Hills ON
Heritage Park Historical Village (1) .... Calgary AB
Hertz Equipment Rental (1) .... Toronto ON
Hospital for Sick Children, The (1) .... Toronto ON
Husky Injection Molding Systems Ltd. (1) .... Bolton ON
IBI Group (1) .... Edmonton AB
IKO Industries Ltd. (1) .... Brampton ON
Impact Services (1) .... Toronto ON
Ingersoll-Rand Canada Inc. (1) .... Toronto ON
Inland Group (1) .... Calgary AB
IR Security & Safety (1) .... Mississauga ON
ITW Construction Products (1) .... Toronto ON
Jacques Whitford Environment Ltd. (1) .... Halifax NS
JJM Group, The (1) .... Delta BC
Kaycan Ltd. (1) .... Pointe-Claire QC
Kellam Berg Engineering & Surveys Ltd. (1) .... Calgary AB
Lafarge Canada Inc. (1) .... Montréal QC
Lake Erie Steel Company (1) .... Nanticoke ON
Lea Consulting Ltd. (1) .... Toronto ON
London Guarantee Insurance Company (1) .... Vancouver BC
MacLachlan & Mitchell Homes Inc. (1) .... Edmonton AB
Management Board Secretariat (1) .... Toronto ON
Manitoba Health (1) .... Winnipeg MB
Manitoba Transportation & Government Se (1) .... Winnipeg MB
Manitoba Transportation & Government Se (1) .... Winnipeg MB
McCormick Rankin Corporation (1) .... Mississauga ON
McGill University (1) .... Montréal QC
Medicine Hat, City of (1) .... Medicine Hat AB
Miller Waste Systems (1) .... Markham ON
Ministry of Labour, Ontario (1) .... Toronto ON
Ministry of Labour, Ontario (1) .... Ottawa ON
Ministry of the Attorney General, Ontari (1) .... Toronto ON
Ministry of Transportation, Ontario (1) .... London ON
Monarch Construction Ltd. (1) .... Toronto ON
Moody International Ltd. (1) .... Edmonton AB
Naylor Group Inc. (1) .... Oakville ON
Newmarket, Town of (1) .... Newmarket ON
Normerica (1) .... Gormley ON
Northern Alberta Institute of Technolog (1) .... Edmonton AB
Novartis Pharmaceuticals Canada Inc. (1) .... Dorval QC
Ocean Construction Supplies Ltd. (1) .... Vancouver BC

For descriptions of the occupational categories used in this index, see page 458.

CONSTRUCTION (Cont.)

Ontario Power Generation Inc., Ottawa an (1) .... Renfrew ON
Ontario Store Fixtures Inc. / OSF (1) .... Toronto ON
Ottawa Hospital, The (1) .... Ottawa ON
Ottawa-Carleton District School Board / O (1) .... Nepean ON
P.J. White Hardwoods Ltd. (1) .... Edmonton AB
Parker Hannifin (Canada) Inc. (1) .... Grimsby ON
Penn West Petroleum Ltd. (1) .... Calgary AB
Philips Engineering Ltd. (1) .... Burlington ON
Port Moody, City of (1) .... Port Moody BC
ProFac Facilities Management Services In (1) .... Toronto ON
Public Service Commission of Canada, New (1) .... Moncton NB
R.J. McKee Engineering Ltd. (1) .... Ottawa ON
Read Jones Christoffersen Ltd. (1) .... Vancouver BC
Riverdale Hospital, The (1) .... Toronto ON
Robinson Consultants Inc. (1) .... Kanata ON
Royal Ultraframe Ltd. (1) .... Toronto ON
Seljax International Inc. (1) .... Stony Plain AB
Sherwin-Williams Company, The (1) .... Delta BC
Siemens Building Technologies Ltd., Cer (1) .... Richmond BC
Siemens Canada Ltd. (1) .... Mississauga ON
Simcoe Muskoka Catholic District School B (1) .... Barrie ON
SNC-Lavalin Inc. (1) .... Vancouver BC
SNC-Lavalin Inc., Chemicals & Petroleum (1) .... Calgary AB
Sobeys Inc. (1) .... Mississauga ON
St. John's Rehabilitation Hospital (1) .... Toronto ON
St. Joseph's Health Centre (1) .... Toronto ON
Steeplejack Services Group (1) .... Edmonton AB
StonCor Group (1) .... Delta BC
Suncor Energy Inc. (1) .... Calgary AB
Suncor Energy Inc., Oil Sands (1) .... Fort McMurray AB
Surrey, City of (1) .... Surrey BC
TDL Group Ltd., The (1) .... Oakville ON
Terra Group of Companies (1) .... Vancouver BC
Terrafix Geosynthetics Inc. (1) .... Toronto ON
Toronto Transit Commission / TTC (1) .... Toronto ON
Trow Consulting Engineers Ltd. (1) .... Thunder Bay ON
Trow Consulting Engineers Ltd. (1) .... London ON
UMA Engineering Ltd. (1) .... Calgary AB
University Health Network / UHN (1) .... Toronto ON
University of Guelph (1) .... Guelph ON
University of Lethbridge (1) .... Lethbridge AB
URS Cole, Sherman (1) .... Thornhill ON
Venetor Equipment Rental Inc. (1) .... Hamilton ON
Visionwall Corporation (1) .... Edmonton AB
Wajax Industries Limited (1) .... Edmonton AB
Waterloo, The Regional Municipality of (1) .... Kitchener ON
Wesco Distribution Canada Inc. (1) .... Markham ON
Westcoast Power Inc. (1) .... Calgary AB
Westeinde Construction Ltd. (1) .... Nepean ON
Westfair Properties Ltd. (1) .... Vancouver BC
Weyerhaeuser Company Limited (1) .... Edmonton AB
Wilsonart Canada (1) .... Mississauga ON

CONSULTING

See also: Management, Computing, Human Resource, Govt./
Nonprofit.

Parisella, Vincelli Associates Consulting (5 positions) ...... Laval QC
TRM Technologies, Inc. (5) .... Ottawa ON
Carpedia Group International Inc. (3) .... Oakville ON
Ministry of Consumer and Business Servic (3) .... Toronto ON
Business Development Bank of Canada / BD (2) .... Toronto ON
Management Board Secretariat (2) .... Toronto ON
Ministry of Economic Development and Tra (2) .... Toronto ON
Ontario Service Safety Alliance / OSSA (2) .... Toronto ON
RLG International (2) .... Vancouver BC
Alberta Learning (1) .... Edmonton AB
British Columbia Institute of Technology (1) .... Burnaby BC
Business Development Bank of Canada / B (1) .... Montréal QC
Daedalian eSolutions (1) .... Toronto ON
David McManus Engineering Ltd. / DME (1) .... Nepean ON
Deloitte & Touche (1) .... Edmonton AB
Ernst & Young LLP (1) .... Toronto ON
Exocom Group Inc., The (1) .... Ottawa ON
Export Development Corporation / EDC (1) .... Ottawa ON
GlaxoSmithKline (1) .... Mississauga ON

Halsall Associates Ltd. (1) .... Toronto ON
IBM Canada Ltd. (1) .... Markham ON
Industrial Accident Prevention Associati (1) .... Toronto ON
Manitoba Industry, Trades and Mines / I (1) .... Winnipeg MB
McDonald's Restaurants of Canada Limited (1) .... Toronto ON
Ministry of Employment and Investment, (1) .... Victoria BC
PowerPlus Systems Corporation (1) .... Calgary AB
PricewaterhouseCoopers LLP (1) .... Hamilton ON
Research in Motion Limited / RIM (1) .... Waterloo ON
Ryerson Polytechnic University, School o (1) .... Toronto ON
SBR International (1) .... Toronto ON
Siemens Westinghouse (1) .... Hamilton ON
Suncor Energy Inc. (1) .... Calgary AB
Toronto, City of (1) .... Toronto ON
Westech Information Systems Inc. (1) .... Vancouver BC
ZOX Technologies Inc. (1) .... Toronto ON

DESIGN

See also: Architects, Engineering, Graphic Arts, Publishing/
Media.

McElhanney Group Ltd., The (10 positions) .... Vancouver BC
Global Thermoelectric Inc. (7) .... Calgary AB
Totten Sims Hubicki Associates / TSH (7) .... Whitby ON
CIMTEK Automation Systems (6) .... Burlington ON
Gad Shaanan Design (6) .... Montréal QC
Westport Innovations Inc. (6) .... Vancouver BC
Sandwell Engineering Inc. (5) .... Vancouver BC
Stantec Consulting Ltd. (5) .... Calgary AB
Alcos Machinery Inc. (4) .... Newmarket ON
ATS Automation Tooling Systems Inc. (4) .... Cambridge ON
CAE Inc. (4) .... St-Laurent QC
Calgary, City of (4) .... Calgary AB
Catena Networks (4) .... Kanata ON
Delta Hudson Engineering Ltd. (4) .... Calgary AB
Fluor Canada Ltd. (4) .... Calgary AB
Gennum Corporation (4) .... Burlington ON
H.H. Angus & Associates Ltd. (4) .... Toronto ON
Kvaerner Process Systems / KPS (4) .... Calgary AB
ABC Group Inc. (3) .... Toronto ON
AcceLight Networks (3) .... Nepean ON
Astec Advanced Power Systems (3) .... St-Laurent QC
ATS Test Systems Inc. (3) .... Woodbridge ON
C-MAC Industries Inc. (3) .... Kanata ON
Canam Manac Group Inc., The (3) .... Boucherville QC
Computing Devices Canada Ltd. / CDC (3) .... Calgary AB
Crossey Engineering Ltd. (3) .... Toronto ON
Forensic Technology Inc. (3) .... Cote St. Luc QC
George Kelk Corporation (3) .... Toronto ON
GKO Engineering (3) .... Edmonton AB
Husky Injection Molding Systems Ltd. (3) .... Bolton ON
Hydrogenics Corporation (3) .... Mississauga ON
Kerr Wood Leidal Associates Ltd. (3) .... North Vancouver BC
Lockerbie & Hole Contracting Ltd. (3) .... Edmonton AB
Magna International Inc. (3) .... Concord ON
Marshall Macklin Monaghan Limited (3) .... Thornhill ON
Morrison Hershfield (3) .... Ottawa ON
NEPCAN Engineering Ltd. (3) .... Vancouver BC
Nextram Ltd. (3) .... Concord ON
Progressive Engineering Ltd. (3) .... Calgary AB
Research in Motion Limited / RIM (3) .... Waterloo ON
Silex Inc. (3) .... Mississauga ON
SNC-Lavalin Inc. (3) .... Edmonton AB
Total Care Technologies Inc. (3) .... Kelowna BC
Velan Inc. (3) .... Montréal QC
Viasystems Canada Inc. (3) .... Pointe-Claire QC
Wexxar Packaging Machinery Ltd. (3) .... Delta BC
XCELLSiS (3) .... Burnaby BC
Zenastra Photonics Inc. (3) .... Ottawa ON
Acres International Limited (2) .... Winnipeg MB
Acres International Limited (2) .... Oakville ON
Alcatel Canada Inc., Transport Automatio (2) .... Toronto ON
Analog Design Automation Inc. / ADA (2) .... Ottawa ON
ATCO Structures Inc. (2) .... Calgary AB
Atlantis Systems International (2) .... Brampton ON
Belbois Ltd. (2) .... Laval QC
Bettis Canada Ltd. (2) .... Edmonton AB
Bidell Equipment Inc. (2) .... Calgary AB
CAD Resource Centre / CRC (2) .... Toronto ON

DESIGN (Cont.)

CBCL Limited (2) .... Halifax NS
CEF Technologies Ltd., Brittania Compres (2) .... Calgary AB
CH2M HILL Canada Ltd. (2) .... Calgary AB
CH2M HILL Canada Ltd. (2) .... Toronto ON
Cirque du Soleil (2) .... Montréal QC
CMC Electronics Inc. (2) .... Kanata ON
CMC Electronics Inc. (2) .... St-Laurent QC
Colt Engineering Corporation (2) .... Calgary AB
Corrpro Canada, Inc. / Corrpower (2) .... Edmonton AB
David Schaeffer Engineering Ltd. (2) .... Markham ON
Decoustics Ltd. (2) .... Toronto ON
Design Workshop (2) .... St-Laurent QC
Dreco (2) .... Edmonton AB
DSC Group of Companies (2) .... Concord ON
Duocom Canada (2) .... Richmond Hill ON
Euclid-Hitachi Heavy Equipment Ltd. (2) .... Guelph ON
Ferguson Simek Clark / FSC (2) .... Edmonton AB
Geotech Communications Inc. (2) .... Brampton ON
GMB Industries (2) .... Mississauga ON
Grimsby Custom Tooling Ltd. (2) .... Stoney Creek ON
Guelph, City of (2) .... Guelph ON
Hilti (Canada) Ltd. (2) .... Mississauga ON
Husky Injection Molding Systems Ltd. (2) .... Bolton ON
Kvaerner SNC-Lavalin Offshore / KSLO (2) .... Halifax NS
Lantern Communications Canada Inc. (2) .... Ottawa ON
Magna International Inc. (2) .... Concord ON
MetriCan Manufacturing Co. Inc. (2) .... Oakville ON
Morrison Hershfield (2) .... Toronto ON
Moss Fabrication Ltd. (2) .... Calgary AB
New Automation Corporation / NAC (2) .... Burlington ON
Nokia Products Ltd. (2) .... Richmond BC
Northwest Territories Power Corporatio (2) .... Hay River NT
O'Brien Installations Ltd. (2) .... Stoney Creek ON
OZ Optics Ltd. (2) .... Carp ON
Philips Engineering Ltd. (2) .... Burlington ON
QuestAir Technologies Inc. (2) .... Burnaby BC
R.J. Burnside & Associates Ltd. (2) .... Brampton ON
R.V. Anderson Associates Limited (2) .... Toronto ON
S.A. Armstrong Ltd. (2) .... Toronto ON
Solid Caddgroup Inc. (2) .... Markham ON
Stackpole Ltd., Engineered Products (2) .... Mississauga ON
Stantec Consulting Ltd. (2) .... Kitchener ON
Stantec Geomatics Ltd. (2) .... Edmonton AB
Steel Art Signs Corp. (2) .... Markham ON
Supreme Tooling Group (2) .... Toronto ON
Thomson Technology Inc. (2) .... Langley BC
TIW Western (2) .... Calgary AB
Toronto MicroElectronics Inc. / TME (2) .... Mississauga ON
Tracer Industries Canada Ltd. (2) .... Edmonton AB
Trow Consulting Engineers Ltd. (2) .... Brampton ON
UMA Engineering Ltd. (2) .... Delta BC
UMA Engineering Ltd. (2) .... Calgary AB
Uni-Ram Corporation Ltd. (2) .... Toronto ON
Vansco Electronics Ltd. (2) .... Winnipeg MB
VECO Canada Ltd. (2) .... Calgary AB
VK Brunette Ltd. (2) .... New Westminster BC
Walsh Automation / Validation Technolog (2) ...... Montréal QC
Walter Cumbria Engineering Ltd. / WCEL (2) .... Edmonton AB
Wardrop Engineering Inc. (2) .... Mississauga ON
Wi-LAN Inc. (2) .... Calgary AB
Xantrex Technology Inc. (2) .... Burnaby BC
Zed.i Solutions (2) .... Edmonton AB
Zed.i Solutions (2) .... Calgary AB
724 Solutions Inc. (1) .... Toronto ON
Aastra Telecom (1) .... Calgary AB
Agile Systems Inc. (1) .... Waterloo ON
Agrium Inc. (1) .... Redwater AB
Ainsworth Inc. (1) .... Coquitlam BC
Alberta Environment (1) .... Edmonton AB
Alberta Infrastructure & Transportation (1) ..... Edmonton AB
AldrichPears Associates (1) .... Vancouver BC
Alltemp Sensors Inc. (1) .... Edmonton AB
AMEC (1) .... Vancouver BC
AMEC Earth & Environmental Ltd. (1) .... Calgary AB
Arriscraft International Inc. (1) .... Cambridge ON
Artitalia Inc. (1) .... Montréal QC
ATCO Noise Management Ltd. (1) .... Calgary AB
Babcock & Wilcox Canada (1) .... Cambridge ON

BC Hydro (1) .... Vancouver BC
Bearden Engineering Consultants Ltd. (1) .... Red Deer AB
Berminghammer Foundation Equipment (1) .... Hamilton ON
BJ Services Company Canada (1) .... Calgary AB
Black Max Downhole Tools Ltd. (1) .... Nisku AB
Bracknell Telecom Services (1) .... Langley BC
Bradon Industries Ltd. / Hydra Rig Canad (1) ...... Calgary AB
Brake Pro, Ltd. (1) .... Concord ON
Brisbin & Sentis Engineering Inc. (1) .... Calgary AB
Brown Applied Technology Inc. (1) .... Toronto ON
C-Tech Ltd. (1) .... Cornwall ON
Cadastral Group Inc., The (1) .... Calgary AB
Cambridge Custom Tooling (1) .... Cambridge ON
Can-Am Surveys Ltd. (1) .... Edmonton AB
Cascade (1) .... Mississauga ON
Celgar Pulp Company (1) .... Castlegar BC
Cellex Power Products Inc. (1) .... Richmond BC
Central Precast Inc. (1) .... Nepean ON
Chem Systems Inc. (1) .... Burlington ON
Circon Systems Corporation (1) .... Richmond BC
Circuit Graphics Ltd. (1) .... Burnaby BC
CMC Engineering and Management Limited (1) ...... Vancouver BC
CML Emergency Services, Inc. (1) .... Hull QC
Cohos Evamy Partners, The (1) .... Edmonton AB
Colt Engineering Corporation (1) .... Edmonton AB
Computing Devices Canada Ltd. / CDC (1) .... Ottawa ON
Con-Force Structures Ltd. (1) .... Calgary AB
Concord Idea Corp. (1) .... Markham ON
Coretec Inc. (1) .... Toronto ON
Cosburn Patterson Mather Ltd. (1) .... Markham ON
CoSyn Technology (1) .... Edmonton AB
Cougar Automation Technologies Inc. (1) .... Toronto ON
CPI Canada Inc. (1) .... Georgetown ON
Crescent Custom Yachts (1) .... Richmond BC
Cymbolic Sciences Inc. (1) .... Richmond BC
Daito Precision Inc. (1) .... St-Laurent QC
David Brown Union Pumps (Canada) Ltd. (1) .... Burlington ON
Delta Controls Inc. (1) .... Surrey BC
Dillon Consulting Ltd. (1) .... Toronto ON
Dillon Consulting Ltd. (1) .... Ottawa ON
Dorel Industries Inc. (1) .... Montréal QC
Duke Blakey, Inc. (1) .... Markham ON
Eagle Pump & Compressor Ltd. (1) .... Calgary AB
EFX Enerflex Systems Ltd. (1) .... Calgary AB
Elcan Optical Technologies (1) .... Midland ON
Emanation Control Ltd. / EMCON (1) .... Nepean ON
EMC Group Ltd. (1) .... Concord ON
Energy Industries Inc. (1) .... Calgary AB
Evans Consoles Inc. (1) .... Calgary AB
Evertz Microsystems Ltd. (1) .... Burlington ON
Excel Tech Ltd. / XLTEK (1) .... Oakville ON
EXI Wireless Systems Inc. (1) .... Richmond BC
Flight Dynamics Corp. (1) .... St-Jean-sur-Richelieu QC
Futureway Communications Inc. (1) .... Richmond Hill ON
GasTOPS Ltd. (1) .... Gloucester ON
GE Power Systems (1) .... Calgary AB
GE Power Systems (1) .... Guelph ON
GE Syprotec Inc. (1) .... Pointe-Claire QC
Gemini Corporation (1) .... Calgary AB
General Hydrogen / GH (1) .... Vancouver BC
General Motors of Canada Ltd., Diesel Div (1) ..... London ON
Giffels Associates Limited (1) .... Toronto ON
Global Group, The (1) .... Toronto ON
Grant Structural Engineering Ltd. (1) .... Calgary AB
Greenlight Power Technologies, Inc. (1) .... Sidney BC
Group Telecom (1) .... Toronto ON
Hardt Equipment Manufacturing Inc. (1) .... Lachine QC
Hatch Associates Ltd. (1) .... Sudbury ON
HERO Industries Ltd. (1) .... Burnaby BC
Highland Equipment Ltd. (1) .... Toronto ON
Hopping Kovach Grinnell (1) .... Vancouver BC
Husky Injection Molding Systems Ltd. (1) .... Bolton ON
Husky Oil Operations Ltd. (1) .... Calgary AB
ICAM Technologies Corp. (1) .... Pointe-Claire QC
IceFyre Semiconductor Inc. (1) .... Ottawa ON
Instantel Inc. (1) .... Kanata ON
Intalite Ceiling Systems (1) .... St-Laurent QC
Interactive Circuits and Systems Ltd. (1) .... Gloucester ON
Irwin Toy Limited (1) .... Toronto ON
IS2 Research Inc. (1) .... Nepean ON
Jacques Whitford Environment Ltd. (1) .... Calgary AB
Jacques Whitford Environment Ltd. (1) .... Fredericton NB

For descriptions of the occupational categories used in this index, see page 458.

DESIGN (Cont.)

Jiro Compression Ltd. (1) .... Stettler AB
JuneWarren Publishing Ltd. (1) .... Edmonton AB
KB Electronics Limited (1) .... Halifax NS
Keen Engineering Co. Ltd. (1) .... Edmonton AB
Kellam Berg Engineering & Surveys Ltd. (1) .... Calgary AB
Ken Lewis Group Inc. (1) .... Markham ON
Kenonic Controls Ltd. (1) .... Calgary AB
Kingsbury Canada Inc. (1) .... Burlington ON
Landmark Master Builder Inc. (1) .... Edmonton AB
LeBlanc Ltd. (1) .... Oakville ON
Lenbrook (1) .... Pickering ON
Liburdi Engineering Ltd. (1) .... Dundas ON
Linear Transfer Systems Ltd. (1) .... Barrie ON
Lockerbie Industra Inc. (1) .... New Westminster BC
Macdonald Engineering Group Ltd. / MEG (1) .... Calgary AB
MacLachlan & Mitchell Homes Inc. (1) .... Edmonton AB
Magic Span Fabricating Ltd. / MSF (1) .... Calgary AB
Magna IV Engineering Ltd. (1) .... Edmonton AB
Manitoba Transportation & Government Se (1) .... Winnipeg MB
Manitoba Transportation & Government Se (1) .... Winnipeg MB
Maple Ridge, District of (1) .... Maple Ridge BC
Maritime Hydraulics (Canada) Ltd. (1) .... Calgary AB
Matsu Manufacturing Inc. (1) .... Brampton ON
Maverick Solutions Inc. (1) .... Toronto ON
McCormick Rankin Corporation (1) .... Mississauga ON
McCormick Rankin Corporation (1) .... Ottawa ON
MDS Aero Support Corporation (1) .... Ottawa ON
Med-Eng Systems Inc. (1) .... Ottawa ON
MetroPhotonics Inc. (1) .... Ottawa ON
Milton, Town of (1) .... Milton ON
Ministry of Transportation, Ontar (1) .... St. Catharines ON
Modern Niagara Ottawa Inc. (1) .... Kanata ON
MOSAID Technologies Inc. (1) .... Kanata ON
MPB Technologies Inc. (1) .... Pointe-Claire QC
N.D. Lea Consultants Ltd. (1) .... Vancouver BC
Nanometrics Inc. (1) .... Kanata ON
National Research Council Canada, Institu (1) .... Ottawa ON
Nienkamper (1) .... Toronto ON
Nortel Networks (1) .... Ottawa ON
NRB Inc. (1) .... Grimsby ON
Oakville, Corporation of the Town of (1) .... Oakville ON
Oerlikon Aerospace Inc. (1) .... St-Jean-sur-Richelieu QC
OMNEX Control Systems Inc. (1) .... Port Coquitlam BC
Ontario Power Generation, Bruce Nuclear (1) .... Tiverton ON
Ontario Science Centre / OSC (1) .... Toronto ON
Ontario Store Fixtures Inc. / OSF (1) .... Toronto ON
Orion Bus Industries Ltd. (1) .... Mississauga ON
Oshawa, City of (1) .... Oshawa ON
Ottawa, City of (1) .... Gloucester ON
Passband Downhole Communications Inc. / (1) .... Calgary AB
Patella Manufacturing Inc. (1) .... Lasalle QC
PC World (1) .... Toronto ON
Poon McKenzie Architects (1) .... Calgary AB
Proceco Ltd. (1) .... Montréal QC
Procor Ltd. (1) .... Oakville ON
Psion Teklogix Inc. (1) .... Mississauga ON
Public Service Commission of Canada, B (1) .... Vancouver BC
Pure Technologies Inc. (1) .... Calgary AB
Quake Technologies Inc. (1) .... Ottawa ON
Ramco Electrical Consulting Ltd. (1) .... Calgary AB
Rea International Inc. (1) .... Mississauga ON
Reber Inc. / R-2000 Inc. (1) .... Riviere-des-Prairies QC
Ridgewood Industries (1) .... Cornwall ON
Rittal Systems Ltd. (1) .... Mississauga ON
Robertson Inc. (1) .... Milton ON
Robinson Consultants Inc. (1) .... Kanata ON
Ross Video Ltd. (1) .... Iroquois ON
Royal Building Systems (Cdn) Ltd. / R (1) .... Woodbridge ON
Ruffneck Heaters (1) .... Calgary AB
Schneider Electric (1) .... Bramalea ON
Sernas Group Inc., The (1) .... Whitby ON
Siemens Automotive (1) .... London ON
Siemens Dematic Ltd., Rapistan Divis (1) .... Mississauga ON
Siemens Milltronics Process Instrum (1) .... Peterborough ON
Sigem Inc. (1) .... Kanata ON
Simark Controls Ltd. (1) .... Calgary AB
Smart Technologies Inc. (1) .... Calgary AB
Smart Technologies Inc. (1) .... Stittsville ON
SNC-Lavalin Inc. (1) .... Montréal QC

Sobotec Ltd. (1) .... Hamilton ON
Solectron (1) .... Calgary AB
Sota Glazing Inc. (1) .... Brampton ON
SpaceBridge Networks Corporation (1) .... Hull QC
Square Peg Communications Inc. / SPCI (1) .... Kanata ON
Stantec Consulting Ltd. (1) .... Vancouver BC
Steelcase Canada Ltd. (1) .... Markham ON
Stewart, Weir & Co. Ltd. (1) .... Edmonton AB
Stothert Engineering Ltd. (1) .... Vancouver BC
Suncor Energy Inc. (1) .... Calgary AB
Suss Woodcraft International (1) .... Lasalle QC
Tality Corp. (1) .... Ottawa ON
Techmire Ltd. (1) .... Anjou QC
TELAV Audio Visual Services (1) .... Toronto ON
Thermal Energy International Inc. (1) .... Nepean ON
Thermo Design Engineering Ltd. (1) .... Edmonton AB
Thomas & Betts Limited (1) .... Iberville QC
Thorburn Equipment Inc. (1) .... Pointe-Claire QC
Toromont Process Systems, Division of To (1) .... Calgary AB
Toronto Transit Commission / TTC (1) .... Toronto ON
Tractel Ltd., Swingstage Division (1) .... Toronto ON
Trammell Crow Corporate Services Canada, (1) .... Toronto ON
Trillium Photonics (1) .... Ottawa ON
TRK Engineering Ltd. (1) .... Surrey BC
Troy Manufacturing Ltd. (1) .... Brockville ON
Turbocor Inc. (1) .... Dorval QC
Ty-Crop Manufacturing Ltd. (1) .... Rosedale BC
UMA Engineering Ltd. (1) .... Edmonton AB
University Health Network / UHN (1) .... Toronto ON
URS Cole, Sherman (1) .... Thornhill ON
Vorum Research Corporation (1) .... Vancouver BC
Walters Inc. (1) .... Hamilton ON
Wardrop Engineering Inc. (1) .... Thunder Bay ON
Weatherford Canada Ltd. (1) .... Nisku AB
Weidmuller Ltd. (1) .... Markham ON
Weighpack Paxiom (1) .... Lachine QC
WestBay Semiconductor Inc. (1) .... Vancouver BC
Westfair Properties Ltd. (1) .... Vancouver BC
Westmar Consultants Inc. (1) .... North Vancouver BC
Westpower Equipment Ltd. (1) .... Calgary AB
Wilkinson Steel and Metals (1) .... Edmonton AB
World Heart Corporation (1) .... Ottawa ON
Xillix Technologies Corp. (1) .... Richmond BC

DIRECT MKTNG.

*See also: Sales, Marketing, Advertising, Graphic Arts,
Printing.*

Shopping Channel, The / TSC (7 positions) .... Toronto ON
Stream International (7) .... Belleville ON
Teleperformance Canada Inc. / TPCAN (7) .... Toronto ON
Minacs Worldwide Inc. (6) .... Richmond Hill ON
SITEL Canada Inc. (6) .... Toronto ON
ENMAX Corporation (4) .... Calgary AB
Loyalty Group, The (4) .... Toronto ON
Staples Business Depot Ltd. (4) .... Markham ON
Aramark Canada Ltd. (3) .... Toronto ON
Brookfield LePage Johnson Controls Facil (3) .... Markham ON
Convergys Customer Management Canada In (3) .... Edmonton AB
Globel Direct Marketing (3) .... Richmond BC
Percepta (3) .... Toronto ON
RMH Teleservices International Inc. (3) .... Brantford ON
Rogers AT&T Wireless (3) .... Toronto ON
Rogers Communications Inc. (3) .... Toronto ON
SITEL Canada Inc. (3) .... Montréal QC
TeleSpectrum Canada Inc. (3) .... Toronto ON
United Nations Children's Fund / UNICEF (3) .... Toronto ON
Accutel.com (2) .... Toronto ON
Affina (2) .... Montréal QC
American Express Canada Inc. / Amex (2) .... Markham ON
ARK e-Tail Services Inc. (2) .... Toronto ON
Blockade Systems Corporation (2) .... Toronto ON
Chromatic Software Inc. / CSI (2) .... Vancouver BC
ClientLogic Corp. (2) .... Toronto ON
Corporate Express (2) .... Calgary AB
Decima Research Inc. (2) .... Montréal QC
Dollco Printing (2) .... Ottawa ON
First Media Group Inc. (2) .... Toronto ON
GBC Canada Inc. (2) .... Toronto ON

DIRECT MKTNG. (Cont.)

Global Crossing (2) .... Montréal QC
Globel Direct Marketing (2) .... Calgary AB
Hofland Ltd. (2) .... Mississauga ON
Lifeline Systems Canada Inc. (2) .... Toronto ON
Minolta Business Equipment (Canada), Lt (2) .... Edmonton AB
NetPCS (2) .... Kanata ON
Sitraka Software Inc. (2) .... Toronto ON
Sprint Canada Inc. (2) .... Toronto ON
TeleTech Canada (2) .... Toronto ON
Telus Corporation (2) .... Burnaby BC
Triversity Inc. (2) .... Toronto ON
Voxdata Solutions Inc. (2) .... Toronto ON
Zurich Canada (2) .... Toronto ON
Alberta Motor Association / AMA (1) .... Edmonton AB
Babco Sales Ltd. (1) .... Surrey BC
BC Hydro (1) .... Vancouver BC
Bell Intrigna (1) .... Calgary AB
Beyond 20/20 Inc. (1) .... Ottawa ON
Boulevard Media (Canada) Inc. / BMC (1) .... Vancouver BC
British Columbia Automobile Association (1) .... Burnaby BC
C1 Communications (1) .... Mississauga ON
Canadian Imperial Bank of Commerce / CIB (1) .... Toronto ON
Canon Canada Inc. (1) .... Markham ON
Cap Gemini Ernst & Young / CGEY (1) .... Toronto ON
Carlson Marketing Group Canada Ltd. / CM (1) .... Toronto ON
Cedar Enterprise Solutions Inc. (1) .... Calgary AB
Ceridian Canada Ltd. (1) .... Markham ON
Citizens Bank of Canada (1) .... Vancouver BC
Collega for Aveda (1) .... Toronto ON
Comda (1) .... Toronto ON
Convergys Corporation (1) .... Ottawa ON
CreoScitex (1) .... Burnaby BC
Daisytek Canada (1) .... Markham ON
DataMirror Corporation (1) .... Markham ON
Deloitte & Touche (1) .... Toronto ON
Direct Energy Marketing Ltd. (1) .... Toronto ON
Doubleday Canada Ltd. (1) .... Toronto ON
Drug Trading Company Ltd. (1) .... Markham ON
Dumex Medical (1) .... Toronto ON
Empire Financial Group (1) .... Kingston ON
EPCOR Utilities Inc. (1) .... Edmonton AB
Ernst & Young LLP (1) .... Toronto ON
Evans Consoles Inc. (1) .... Calgary AB
Excel Tech Ltd. / XLTEK (1) .... Oakville ON
Exchange Solutions / ESI (1) .... Toronto ON
Executive Needs Inc., The (1) .... Toronto ON
Export Development Corporation / EDC (1) .... Ottawa ON
Forzani Group Ltd., The (1) .... Calgary AB
G.E. Shnier Co. (1) .... Brampton ON
Ganz (1) .... Woodbridge ON
GE Canada (1) .... Mississauga ON
Geneka Biotechnology Inc. (1) .... Montréal QC
Grant MacEwan College, Jasper Place Cam (1) ...... Edmonton AB
Green Lawn Care (1) .... Toronto ON
Group Telecom (1) .... Toronto ON
ICS Courier Services (1) .... Toronto ON
Independent Order of Foresters / IOF (1) .... Toronto ON
INFONEX Inc. (1) .... Toronto ON
London Hydro (1) .... London ON
McGill University Health Centre, Royal (1) .... Montréal QC
MDS Laboratories (1) .... Toronto ON
MemberCARE Financial Services (1) .... Burlington ON
Minacs Worldwide Inc. (1) .... Pickering ON
Ministry of Municipal Affairs and Housin (1) .... Toronto ON
Ministry of the Attorney General, Ontari (1) .... Toronto ON
MKS Inc. (1) .... Waterloo ON
MTW Solutions Online Inc. (1) .... Toronto ON
National Info-Tech Centre / NIC (1) .... Montréal QC
New Brunswick Community College, Dieppe C (1) .... Dieppe NB
Paging Network of Canada, Inc. / PageNet (1) .... Toronto ON
Pepsi Bottling Group (Canada) (1) .... Mississauga ON
Pink Elephant Inc. (1) .... Burlington ON
Pizza Pizza Limited (1) .... Toronto ON
Postal Promotions Limited (1) .... Toronto ON
Procuron Inc. (1) .... Thornhill ON
Purolator Courier Ltd. (1) .... Mississauga ON
Reno-Depot (1) .... Montréal QC
Research in Motion Limited / RIM (1) .... Waterloo ON

RMH Teleservices International Inc. (1) .... Saint John NB
Rocky Mountain Instruments Inc. / RMI (1) .... Edmonton AB
Royal Bank Financial Group (1) .... Toronto ON
Sun Life Financial (1) .... Toronto ON
Sylvan Learning Centre (1) .... Aurora ON
Teldon International Inc. (1) .... Richmond BC
TelTech Assets.Com Ltd. (1) .... Calgary AB
Telus Mobility (1) .... Toronto ON
Toronto.com (1) .... Toronto ON
Total Credit Recovery / TRC (1) .... Toronto ON
Trapeze Software Inc. (1) .... Mississauga ON
UnumProvident Corporation (1) .... Burlington ON
Veridian Corporation (1) .... Ajax ON
Virtual Prototypes Inc. / VPI (1) .... Montréal QC
Vision2Hire Solutions (1) .... Vancouver BC
Westcan Wireless (1) .... Edmonton AB

DISABLED
See also: Health/Medical, Education, Govt./Nonprofit.

Muki Baum Association (12 positions) .... Toronto ON
Manitoba Family Services and Housing (9) .... Winnipeg MB
Ministry of Education, Ontario (Sir J (9) .... Belleville ON
British Columbia Mental Health So (8) .... Port Coquitlam BC
Canadian Hearing Society, The (6) .... Toronto ON
Alberta Human Resources and Employment (5) .... Calgary AB
Halton Healthcare Services (5) .... Oakville ON
Participation House (5) .... Binbrook ON
Simon Fraser Health Region / SFH (5) .... New Westminster BC
Trillium Health Centre (5) .... Toronto ON
Aisling Discoveries Child and Family Cen (4) .... Toronto ON
Bellwoods Centres for Community Living I (4) .... Toronto ON
Canadian Paraplegic Association Ontario (4) .... Toronto ON
Manitoba Developmental Centre (4) .... Portage la Prairie MB
Manitoba Labour & Immigration (4) .... Winnipeg MB
Ministry of Children and Family De (4) .... Prince George BC
Ministry of Community and Social Service (4) .... Toronto ON
Surrey Place Centre (4) .... Toronto ON
Toronto East General & Orthopaedic Hospi (4) .... Toronto ON
York Region District School Board (4) .... Aurora ON
Adult Mental Health Services of Haldimand (3) .... Simcoe ON
Alberta Community Development (3) .... Edmonton AB
Alberta Family and Social Services (3) .... Edmonton AB
Alberta Human Resources and Employm (3) .... Lac La Biche AB
Bartimaeus Inc. (3) .... St. Catharines ON
Bethesda (3) .... St. Catharines ON
Bloorview MacMillan Children's Centre, M (3) .... Toronto ON
Canadian National Institute for the Blin (3) .... Toronto ON
Coast Foundation Society (3) .... Vancouver BC
Developmental Disabilities Association (3) .... Richmond BC
Erinoak (3) .... Mississauga ON
Ernest C. Drury School for the Deaf (3) .... Milton ON
Kingston Friendship Homes (3) .... Kingston ON
Lanark County Mental Health (3) .... Smiths Falls ON
Manitoba Education, Training & Youth (3) .... Winnipeg MB
Manitoba Family Services and (3) .... Portage la Prairie MB
Ministry of Children and Family Developm (3) .... Nanaimo BC
Ministry of Children and Family Develo (3) .... Cranbrook BC
Ministry of Community and Social Services (3) .... London ON
Ministry of Community and Social Service (3) .... Toronto ON
Ministry of Education, Ontario (Provincia (3) .... Milton ON
Ministry of Health and Long-Term Care, (3) .... North Bay ON
Ministry of Health and Ministry Respons (3) .... Victoria BC
Ottawa Salus Corporation (3) .... Ottawa ON
Peter Hall School Inc. (3) .... St-Laurent QC
South Lake Regional Health Centre (3) .... Newmarket ON
Vocational and Rehabilitation Research I (3) .... Calgary AB
Whitby Mental Health Centre (3) .... Whitby ON
Alberta Family and Social Services (2) .... Red Deer AB
Alberta Human Resources and Employment (2) .... McLennan AB
Amity Goodwill Industries (2) .... Hamilton ON
Canadian National Institute for the Blin (2) .... Calgary AB
Canadian Paraplegic Association / CPA (2) .... Calgary AB
Capital Health Region / CHR (2) .... Victoria BC
Central Okanagan Child Development Assoc (2) .... Kelowna BC
Children's and Women's Health Centre o (2) .... Vancouver BC
Community Living Mississauga (2) .... Mississauga ON
Grand River Hospital (2) .... Kitchener ON

For descriptions of the occupational categories used in this index, see page 458.

DISABLED (Cont.)

Greater Vancouver Community Services S (2) .... Vancouver BC
Hospital for Sick Children, The (2) .... Toronto ON
Ma'mowe Capital Region, Child and Famil (2) .... Edmonton AB
Manitoba Health, Selkirk Mental Health C (2) .... Selkirk MB
Ministry of Community and Social Servi (2) .... North Bay ON
Ministry of Community and Social Service (2) .... Toronto ON
Miriam Home and Services (2) .... Laval QC
Northeast Mental Health Centre / NEMHC (2) .... Sudbury ON
Northern Lights Regional Health Se (2) .... Fort McMurray AB
Ryerson Polytechnic University (2) .... Toronto ON
St. Joseph's Healthcare Hamilton, Centr (2) .... Hamilton ON
St. Michael's Hospital (2) .... Toronto ON
Sunnybrook & Women's College Health Scie (2) .... Toronto ON
Alberta Child and Family Services Autho (1) .... McLennan AB
Alberta Community Development (1) .... Edmonton AB
Alberta Corporate Service Centre (1) .... Coaldale AB
Alberta Corporate Service Centre (1) .... Edmonton AB
Alberta Human Resources and Employment (1) .... Edmonton AB
Alberta Human Resources and Employment (1) .... Innisfail AB
Alberta Mental Health Board, Alberta Hosp (1) .... Ponoka AB
Brantwood Residential Development Cent (1) .... Brantford ON
Canadian Mental Health Association / CMH (1) .... Toronto ON
Canadian Mental Health Association / CM (1) .... Cornwall ON
Capital Health, Glenrose Rehabilitation (1) .... Edmonton AB
Centre for Ability, The (1) .... Vancouver BC
Chatham-Kent Health Alliance (1) .... Chatham ON
Columbia Rehabilitation Centre (1) .... Calgary AB
Community Mental Health Clinic / CMHC (1) .... Guelph ON
Crawford Healthcare Management (1) .... Ottawa ON
Credit Valley Hospital, The (1) .... Mississauga ON
Dufferin-Peel Catholic District Scho (1) .... Mississauga ON
Easter Seal Society, Ontario (1) .... Toronto ON
Healthcare Benefit Trust / HBT (1) .... Vancouver BC
Humber River Regional Hospital, Finch Av (1) .... Toronto ON
Integra Foundation (1) .... Toronto ON
Kinark Child and Family Services (1) .... Toronto ON
Kwantlen University College (1) .... Surrey BC
Markham Stouffville Hospital (1) .... Markham ON
Ministry of Children and Family Develo (1) .... Vancouver BC
Ministry of Children and Family Developm (1) .... Burnaby BC
Ministry of Children and Family Developm (1) .... Burnaby BC
Ministry of Children and Family Developme (1) .... Surrey BC
Ministry of Community and Social Servi (1) .... Newmarket ON
Ministry of Community and Social Services (1) .... Ottawa ON
Ministry of Community and Social Service (1) .... Toronto ON
Ministry of Community and Social Service (1) .... Orillia ON
Ministry of Community and Social Services (1) .... London ON
Ministry of Education / Ministry of Trai (1) .... Toronto ON
Ministry of Health and Long-Term Care, O (1) .... Toronto ON
Ministry of Health and Long-Term Car (1) .... Thunder Bay ON
Ministry of the Attorney General, Ontari (1) .... Toronto ON
North York General Hospital (1) .... Toronto ON
NRCS Inc. (1) .... Ottawa ON
Ontario March of Dimes (1) .... Toronto ON
Ontario March of Dimes (1) .... Kingston ON
Ottawa Children's Treatment Centre / OCTC (1) .... Ottawa ON
Public Service Employee Relations Commi (1) .... Victoria BC
Red Deer College (1) .... Red Deer AB
Rekai Centre, The (1) .... Toronto ON
Rouge Valley Health System, Centenary He (1) .... Toronto ON
Royal Victoria Hospital / RVH (1) .... Barrie ON
Saskatoon District Health (1) .... Saskatoon SK
School District #41 (Burnaby) (1) .... Burnaby BC
School District #60 (Peace River N (1) .... Fort St. John BC
Sibley & Associates Inc. (1) .... Burlington ON
Siemens Hearing Instruments Inc. (1) .... Cambridge ON
St. John's Rehabilitation Hospital (1) .... Toronto ON
St. Joseph's Healthcare Hamilton (1) .... Hamilton ON
Supportive Housing in Peel Foundatio (1) .... Mississauga ON
Trillium Lakelands District School B (1) .... Bracebridge ON
University of Calgary (1) .... Calgary AB
University of Northern British Col (1) .... Prince George BC
Vancouver / Richmond Health Board (1) .... Vancouver BC
Vancouver School Board / VSB (1) .... Vancouver BC
Winnipeg Regional Health Authority / WR (1) .... Winnipeg MB
York Central Hospital (1) .... Richmond Hill ON
York Community Services / YCS (1) .... Toronto ON

EDUCATION
See also: Librarians, Govt./Nonprofit.

Ministry of Education (29 positions) .... Toronto ON
Okanagan University College / OUC (20) .... Kelowna BC
Ministry of Advanced Education, Trainin (19) .... Victoria BC
Alberta Learning (17) .... Edmonton AB
Mount Royal College (17) .... Calgary AB
University of Calgary (15) .... Calgary AB
Lakehead University (12) .... Thunder Bay ON
Manitoba Labour & Immigration (12) .... Winnipeg MB
University College of the Cariboo / UCC (12) .... Kamloops BC
Douglas College (11) .... New Westminster BC
Ontario Institute for Studies in Educati (11) .... Toronto ON
Technical University of British Columbia (11) .... Surrey BC
Havergal College (10) .... Toronto ON
Red Deer College (10) .... Red Deer AB
Southern Alberta Institute of Technology (10) .... Calgary AB
University of Northern British Col (10) .... Prince George BC
Athabasca University (9) .... Athabasca AB
Dufferin-Peel Catholic District Scho (9) .... Mississauga ON
Grant MacEwan College, Jasper Place Cam (9) .... Edmonton AB
York Region District School Board (9) .... Aurora ON
Ryerson Polytechnic University, Faculty (8) .... Toronto ON
School District #60 (Peace River N (8) .... Fort St. John BC
Simon Fraser University (8) .... Burnaby BC
Halton District School Board, The (7) .... Burlington ON
Portage College (7) .... Lac la Biche AB
Toronto French School / TFS (7) .... Toronto ON
University of Calgary, Faculty of Educat (7) .... Calgary AB
York Catholic District School Board (6) .... Aurora ON
Cree School Board (5) .... Mistissini QC
George Brown College (5) .... Toronto ON
Grande Prairie Regional College (5) .... Grande Prairie AB
Halton Catholic District School Board (5) .... Burlington ON
Kwantlen University College (5) .... Surrey BC
Lethbridge Community College / LCC (5) .... Lethbridge AB
Lower Canada College (5) .... Montréal QC
Mount Saint Vincent University (5) .... Halifax NS
Peel District School Board (5) .... Mississauga ON
Public Service Commission, PEI (5) .... Charlottetown PE
Royal Roads University (5) .... Victoria BC
School District #36 (Surrey) (5) .... Surrey BC
School District #74 (Gold Trail) (5) .... Ashcroft BC
Sheridan College (5) .... Oakville ON
Upper Canada College, Preparatory School (5) .... Toronto ON
Waterloo Catholic District School Boar (5) .... Kitchener ON
Alberta Learning (4) .... Edmonton AB
Alberta Teachers' Association / ATA (4) .... Edmonton AB
Algonquin College (4) .... Nepean ON
Beaufort-Delta Education Council (4) .... Inuvik NT
Brentwood College (4) .... Mill Bay BC
Capilano College (4) .... North Vancouver BC
Center for Digital Imaging and Sound / C (4) .... Burnaby BC
Crescent School (4) .... Toronto ON
Education On-Line / EOL (4) .... Edmonton AB
Glenburnie School (4) .... Oakville ON
Malaspina University-College, Nanaimo Ca (4) .... Nanaimo BC
Manitoba Education, Training & Youth (4) .... Winnipeg MB
Metropolitan Preparatory Academy (4) .... Toronto ON
NorQuest College (4) .... Edmonton AB
North Island College / NIC (4) .... Courtenay BC
Olds College (4) .... Olds AB
Queen's University, Faculty of Educatio (4) .... Kingston ON
Ryerson Polytechnic University (4) .... Toronto ON
Sedbergh School (4) .... Montebello QC
University College of the Fraser Vall (4) .... Abbotsford BC
University of Calgary, Faculty of Manage (4) .... Calgary AB
University of Saskatchewan, College of (4) .... Saskatoon SK
Upper Canada College, Upper School (4) .... Toronto ON
York University, Faculty of Education (4) .... Toronto ON
Acadia University (3) .... Wolfville NS
Algonquin & Lakeshore Catholic District (3) .... Napanee ON
Bond International College (3) .... Toronto ON
Branksome Hall (3) .... Toronto ON
Brant Haldimand-Norfolk Catholic Distr (3) .... Brantford ON
British Columbia Institute of Technology (3) .... Burnaby BC
Cadillac Fairview Corporation Limited, T (3) .... Toronto ON
Camosun College (3) .... Victoria BC
Christ the Redeemer School Division (3) .... Okotoks AB

EDUCATION (Cont.)

College of the North Atlantic, Step (3) ... Stephenville NF
Concordia University College of Alberta (3) ... Edmonton AB
Correctional Service of Canada, Regiona (3) ... Kingston ON
Country Day School, The (3) ... King City ON
DeVry Institute of Technology (3) ... Calgary AB
District School Board of Niagara (3) ... St. Catharines ON
Durham Catholic District School Board (3) ... Oshawa ON
Elk Island Public Schools (3) ... Sherwood Park AB
English Montreal School Board / EMSB (3) ... Montréal QC
Hillfield-Strathallan College (3) ... Hamilton ON
Kativik School Board (3) ... Montréal QC
Keyano College (3) ... Fort McMurray AB
King's University College, The (3) ... Edmonton AB
Kingsway College School (3) ... Toronto ON
Lakeland College (3) ... Vermilion AB
Langara College (3) ... Vancouver BC
Limestone District School Board (3) ... Kingston ON
MacLachlan College (3) ... Oakville ON
Meadowridge School (3) ... Maple Ridge BC
Medicine Hat College (3) ... Medicine Hat AB
Nipissing University (3) ... North Bay ON
Northern Lights College / NLC (3) ... Dawson Creek BC
Northern School Resource Alliance (3) ... Thunder Bay ON
Ontario College of Art and Design / OCAD (3) ... Toronto ON
Ontario English Catholic Teachers' Assoc (3) ... Toronto ON
Open Learning Agency / OLA (3) ... Burnaby BC
Pickering College (3) ... Newmarket ON
Ridley College (3) ... St. Catharines ON
Royal St. George's College (3) ... Toronto ON
School District #40 (New Westmin (3) ... New Westminster BC
Southridge School (3) ... Surrey BC
Toronto District School Board (3) ... Toronto ON
University of British Columbia, Facult (3) ... Vancouver BC
University of Guelph (3) ... Guelph ON
University of Lethbridge, Department (3) ... Lethbridge AB
University of New Brunswick / UNB (3) ... Fredericton NB
University of Ottawa, Faculty of Administ (3) ... Ottawa ON
University of Regina, Faculty of Educatio (3) ... Regina SK
University of Toronto, Professional Facu (3) ... Toronto ON
Windigo Education Authority (3) ... Sioux Lookout ON
York House School (3) ... Vancouver BC
Albert College (2) ... Belleville ON
Alberta School Boards Association / ASB (2) ... Edmonton AB
Appleby College (2) ... Oakville ON
Ashton College (2) ... Vancouver BC
Attawapiskat First Nation Education (2) ... Attawapiskat ON
College of New Caledonia (2) ... Prince George BC
College of the Rockies (2) ... Cranbrook BC
Columbia International College (2) ... Hamilton ON
Concordia University (2) ... Montréal QC
Dalhousie University, Faculty of Health (2) ... Halifax NS
Department of Human Resources, Nuna (2) ... Rankin Inlet NU
Edmonton Catholic Schools (2) ... Edmonton AB
Fairview College (2) ... Fairview AB
Fieldstone Day School / FDS (2) ... Toronto ON
Group Telecom (2) ... Toronto ON
Hamilton-Wentworth District School Boar (2) ... Hamilton ON
Hishkoonikun Education Authority (2) ... Kashechewan ON
Inlingua International (2) ... Vancouver BC
Justice Institute of BC / JIBC (2) ... New Westminster BC
Kawartha Pine Ridge District School (2) ... Peterborough ON
Kingston Family YMCA (2) ... Kingston ON
Kitchenuhmaykoosib Education Auth (2) ... Big Trout Lake ON
Kuper Academy (2) ... Kirkland QC
Lakehead District School Board (2) ... Thunder Bay ON
Lester B. Pearson College of the Pacifi (2) ... Victoria BC
Lester B. Pearson School Board (2) ... Beaconsfield QC
New Frontiers School Board (2) ... Chateauguay QC
North Vancouver School District (2) ... North Vancouver BC
Northern Alberta Institute of Technolog (2) ... Edmonton AB
Northern Lights College / NLC (2) ... Fort St. John BC
Ontario College of Teachers (2) ... Toronto ON
Ottawa-Carleton Catholic School Board / O (2) ... Ottawa ON
Ottawa-Carleton District School Board / O (2) ... Nepean ON
Peel, The Regional Municipality of (2) ... Brampton ON
Public Service Commission of Canada, Onta (2) ... Ottawa ON
Ryerson Polytechnic University (2) ... Toronto ON
Sahtu Divisional Education Council, (2) ... Norman Wells NT
Saskatchewan Institute of Applied Scie (2) ... Saskatoon SK
School District #81 (Fort Nelson) (2) ... Fort Nelson BC
School District #82 (Coast Mountains) (2) ... Terrace BC
Shawnigan Lake School (2) ... Shawnigan Lake BC
Simcoe County District School Board (2) ... Midhurst ON
Simon Fraser University, Faculty of Busi (2) ... Burnaby BC
St. Andrew's College (2) ... Aurora ON
St. Francis Xavier University (2) ... Antigonish NS
St. George's School (2) ... Vancouver BC
St. Lawrence College (2) ... Kingston ON
St. Michaels University School (2) ... Victoria BC
Sterling Hall School, The (2) ... Toronto ON
Thames Valley District School Board (2) ... London ON
Toronto Montessori Schools (2) ... Richmond Hill ON
Trillium Lakelands District School B (2) ... Bracebridge ON
Trinity Western University (2) ... Langley BC
University of Alberta, Faculty of Physi (2) ... Edmonton AB
University of British Columbia / UBC (2) ... Vancouver BC
University of Calgary, Department of His (2) ... Calgary AB
University of Guelph, Office of the Vice- (2) ... Guelph ON
University of Regina (2) ... Regina SK
University of Regina, Language Institute (2) ... Regina SK
West Point Grey Academy (2) ... Vancouver BC
Yellowknife Catholic Schools (2) ... Yellowknife NT
YMCA of Oakville (2) ... Oakville ON
York School, The (2) ... Toronto ON
724 Solutions Inc. (1) ... Toronto ON
Acadia University, Jodrey School of Co (1) ... Wolfville NS
Alberta College of Art & Design / ACAD (1) ... Calgary AB
Algoma District School Board / (1) ... Sault Ste. Marie ON
Association of Professional Engineers an (1) ... Burnaby BC
Bosco Homes (1) ... Edmonton AB
Bow Valley College (1) ... Calgary AB
Brandon University (1) ... Brandon MB
Brock University (1) ... St. Catharines ON
Calgary Board of Education, The (1) ... Calgary AB
Calgary Catholic School District (1) ... Calgary AB
Calgary, City of (1) ... Calgary AB
Catholic Family Service (1) ... Calgary AB
Centennial College (1) ... Toronto ON
Cogency Semiconductor Inc. (1) ... Kanata ON
Conestoga College of Applied Arts & Te (1) ... Kitchener ON
Consulate General of Japan, The (1) ... Toronto ON
Crestwood School (1) ... Toronto ON
Dawson College (1) ... Montréal QC
Department of Human Resources, Nun (1) ... Cambridge Bay NU
Dogrib Community Services Board / DCSB (1) ... Rae-Edzo NT
Durham College (1) ... Oshawa ON
Edmonton Public Schools (1) ... Edmonton AB
Emily Carr Institute of Art and Design (1) ... Vancouver BC
Fanshawe College (1) ... London ON
Focus Foundation of BC (1) ... Vancouver BC
Fountain Tire (1) ... Edmonton AB
Georgian College (1) ... Barrie ON
Gilmore (1) ... Toronto ON
Grand Erie District School Board (1) ... Brantford ON
Grant MacEwan College (1) ... Edmonton AB
Hastings and Prince Edward District S (1) ... Belleville ON
Humber College of Applied Arts and Techn (1) ... Toronto ON
International Language Schools of Canad (1) ... Montréal QC
McMaster University (1) ... Hamilton ON
McMaster University, Michael G. DeGroot (1) ... Hamilton ON
Ministry of the Environment, Ontario (En (1) ... Toronto ON
Ministry of the Solicitor General, Ontari (1) ... Aylmer ON
Mohawk College of Applied Arts and Tech (1) ... Hamilton ON
New Brunswick Community College, Miram (1) ... Miramichi NB
New Brunswick Community College, Moncton (1) ... Moncton NB
New Brunswick Community College, Sain (1) ... Saint John NB
Niagara College of Applied Arts & Techno (1) ... Welland ON
Northern Interior Regional Health (1) ... Prince George BC
Northland Systems Training Inc. (1) ... Ottawa ON
Northwest Catholic District School (1) ... Fort Frances ON
Nova Scotia College of Art and Design / (1) ... Halifax NS
Ontario Science Centre / OSC (1) ... Toronto ON
Optech Inc. (1) ... Toronto ON
Pacific Language Institute / PLI (1) ... Vancouver BC
Peterborough, Victoria, Northumberl (1) ... Peterborough ON
Providence Children's Centre (1) ... Calgary AB
Public Service Employee Relations Commi (1) ... Victoria BC
Queen's University, Department of Human (1) ... Kingston ON
Richmond, City of (1) ... Richmond BC
Ryerson Polytechnic University, School o (1) ... Toronto ON

For descriptions of the occupational categories used in this index, see page 458.

EDUCATION (Cont.)

Saskatchewan Institute of Applied Scie (1) .... Moose Jaw SK
Saskatchewan Post-Secondary Education and (1) .... Regina SK
Scarborough Community Care Access Centre (1) .... Toronto ON
School District #06 (Rocky Mountain) (1) .... Kimberly BC
School District #35 (Langley) (1) .... Langley BC
School District #41 (Burnaby) (1) .... Burnaby BC
School District #43 (Coquitlam) (1) .... Coquitlam BC
School District #57 (Prince George) (1) .... Prince George BC
School District #59 (Peace River So (1) .... Dawson Creek BC
Simon Fraser University, Department of (1) .... Burnaby BC
Sir Wilfrid Laurier School Board (1) .... Rosemere QC
Sunnybrook & Women's College Health Scie (1) .... Toronto ON
Superior North Catholic District Sch (1) .... Terrace Bay ON
Sylvan Learning Centre (1) .... Aurora ON
Trinity College School (1) .... Port Hope ON
Trios College of Information Technol (1) .... Mississauga ON
Trojan Technologies Inc. (1) .... London ON
United Synagogue Day School (1) .... Toronto ON
University of Alberta (1) .... Edmonton AB
University of Alberta, Academic Staff A (1) .... Edmonton AB
University of British Columbia, Depar (1) .... Vancouver BC
University of British Columbia, Facult (1) .... Vancouver BC
University of Calgary, Faculty of Social (1) .... Calgary AB
University of Lethbridge (1) .... Lethbridge AB
University of New Brunswick, Faculty (1) .... Saint John NB
University of Regina, Faculty of Engineer (1) .... Regina SK
University of Toronto at Scarborough / U (1) .... Toronto ON
University of Toronto, Faculty of Arts & (1) .... Toronto ON
University of Toronto, Faculty of Medici (1) .... Toronto ON
University of Victoria (1) .... Victoria BC
University of Waterloo (1) .... Waterloo ON
University of Western Ontario, Faculty of (1) .... London ON
Upper Canada District School Board (1) .... Brockville ON
Vancouver Community College / VCC (1) .... Vancouver BC
Vancouver / Richmond Health Board (1) .... Vancouver BC
Vancouver School Board / VSB (1) .... Vancouver BC
Waterloo Region District School Board (1) .... Kitchener ON
York University (1) .... Toronto ON
Yukon College (1) .... Whitehorse YT

ENGINEERING

See also: Aerospace, Automotive, Design, Quality Control, Telecom.

Gennum Corporation (38 positions) .... Burlington ON
Global Thermoelectric Inc. (26) .... Calgary AB
Siemens Westinghouse (26) .... Hamilton ON
BC Hydro (22) .... Vancouver BC
Westport Innovations Inc. (21) .... Vancouver BC
Acres International Limited (20) .... Oakville ON
Computing Devices Canada Ltd. / CDC (18) .... Calgary AB
QuestAir Technologies Inc. (18) .... Burnaby BC
Stone & Webster Canada Limited (18) .... Toronto ON
ATI Technologies Inc. (17) .... Thornhill ON
Totten Sims Hubicki Associates / TSH (15) .... Whitby ON
Earth Tech Canada Inc. (14) .... Markham ON
GKO Engineering (14) .... Edmonton AB
Hydrogenics Corporation (14) .... Mississauga ON
Public Service Commission of Canada, Onta (14) .... Ottawa ON
CIMTEK Automation Systems (13) .... Burlington ON
CMC Electronics Inc. (13) .... St-Laurent QC
Optech Inc. (13) .... Toronto ON
Agile Systems Inc. (12) .... Waterloo ON
Symagery Microsystems Inc. (12) .... Kanata ON
TransAlta Corporation (12) .... Calgary AB
Instantel Inc. (11) .... Kanata ON
MDS Aero Support Corporation (11) .... Ottawa ON
Cellex Power Products Inc. (10) .... Richmond BC
George Kelk Corporation (10) .... Toronto ON
Research in Motion Limited / RIM (10) .... Waterloo ON
Sandwell Engineering Inc. (10) .... Vancouver BC
Wescam (10) .... Burlington ON
EPCOR Utilities Inc. (9) .... Edmonton AB
MOSAID Technologies Inc. (9) .... Kanata ON
CSA International (8) .... Toronto ON
Lockheed Martin Canada Inc. (8) .... Kanata ON

Siemens Canada Ltd. (8) .... Mississauga ON
Canadian Nuclear Safety Commission / CNSC (7) .... Ottawa ON
CH2M HILL Canada Ltd. (7) .... Toronto ON
Delta Hudson Engineering Ltd. (7) .... Calgary AB
Image Processing Systems Inc. / IPS (7) .... Markham ON
JDS Uniphase Corporation (7) .... Saanichton BC
Morrison Hershfield (7) .... Toronto ON
OZ Optics Ltd. (7) .... Carp ON
PerkinElmer Optoelectronics Inc. (7) .... Vaudreuil QC
Silicon Video (7) .... Toronto ON
UMA Engineering Ltd. (7) .... Calgary AB
Alpha Technologies Ltd. (6) .... Burnaby BC
AMEC Earth & Environmental Ltd. (6) .... Calgary AB
CAE Inc. (6) .... St-Laurent QC
Cogency Semiconductor Inc. (6) .... Toronto ON
Computing Devices Canada Ltd. / CDC (6) .... Ottawa ON
EMS Technologies Canada Ltd (6) .... Ste-Anne-de-Bellevue QC
ENMAX Corporation (6) .... Calgary AB
Gage Applied, Inc. (6) .... Lachine QC
GE Canada (6) .... Peterborough ON
JDS Uniphase Corporation, Fiber-Optic Pr (6) .... Markham ON
Kenonic Controls Ltd. (6) .... Calgary AB
Linamar Corporation, Eston Division (6) .... Guelph ON
Lumic Electronics, Inc. (6) .... Nepean ON
Matrikon Group (6) .... Edmonton AB
Ontario Power Generation (6) .... Toronto ON
Primetech Electronics Inc. (6) .... Kirkland QC
Raytheon Systems Canada Ltd. (6) .... Waterloo ON
Rockwell Automation Canada (6) .... Cambridge ON
StockerYale Canada Inc. (6) .... St-Laurent QC
Suncor Energy Inc., Oil Sands (6) .... Fort McMurray AB
Zenastra Photonics Inc. (6) .... Ottawa ON
ATCO Power (5) .... Edmonton AB
Babcock & Wilcox Canada (5) .... Cambridge ON
GE Canada (5) .... Mississauga ON
GE Power Systems (5) .... Calgary AB
Giffels Associates Limited (5) .... Toronto ON
Hydro Ottawa (5) .... Ottawa ON
LSI Logic Corporation of Canada Inc. (5) .... Kanata ON
Lumenon (5) .... St-Laurent QC
Magna International Inc. (5) .... Concord ON
Nanometrics Inc. (5) .... Kanata ON
Nanowave Technologies Inc. (5) .... Toronto ON
NEPCAN Engineering Ltd. (5) .... Vancouver BC
Public Service Commission of Canada, Al (5) .... Edmonton AB
Tracer Industries Canada Ltd. (5) .... Edmonton AB
Velan Inc. (5) .... Montréal QC
Wardrop Engineering Inc. (5) .... Mississauga ON
Westmar Consultants Inc. (5) .... North Vancouver BC
Acres International Limited (4) .... Vancouver BC
Agere Systems (4) .... Nepean ON
Alft (4) .... Hull QC
AMEC (4) .... Vancouver BC
Canam Manac Group Inc., The (4) .... Boucherville QC
Cogency Semiconductor Inc. (4) .... Kanata ON
CPI Canada Inc. (4) .... Georgetown ON
Creation Technologies Inc. (4) .... Burnaby BC
Crossey Engineering Ltd. (4) .... Toronto ON
Duke Blakey, Inc. (4) .... Markham ON
EBA Engineering Consultants Ltd. (4) .... Edmonton AB
Epson Research and Development, Inc., (4) .... Vancouver BC
Fluor Canada Ltd. (4) .... Calgary AB
General Hydrogen / GH (4) .... Vancouver BC
Great Lakes Power Ltd. (4) .... Sault Ste. Marie ON
IVL Technologies Ltd. (4) .... Victoria BC
Med-Eng Systems Inc. (4) .... Ottawa ON
Novatel Wireless Technologies Ltd. (4) .... Calgary AB
R.V. Anderson Associates Limited (4) .... Toronto ON
Rolls-Royce Canada Ltd. (4) .... Lachine QC
Rowan Williams Davies & Irwin / RWDI (4) .... Guelph ON
S.A. Armstrong Ltd. (4) .... Toronto ON
Siemens Milltronics Process Instrum (4) .... Peterborough ON
SNC-Lavalin Inc. (4) .... Vancouver BC
SNC-Lavalin Inc. (4) .... Edmonton AB
Sunnybrook & Women's College Health Scie (4) .... Toronto ON
Testforce (4) .... St-Laurent QC
Toronto MicroElectronics Inc. / TME (4) .... Mississauga ON
Trojan Technologies Inc. (4) .... London ON
Trow Consulting Engineers Ltd. (4) .... Brampton ON
Vansco Electronics Ltd. (4) .... Winnipeg MB
World Heart Corporation (4) .... Ottawa ON
ABC Group Inc. (3) .... Toronto ON

ENGINEERING (Cont.)

Acres International Limited (3) ... Castlegar BC
Acres International Limited (3) ... Winnipeg MB
Acres International Limited (3) ... Niagara Falls ON
Alberta Infrastructure & Transportation (3) ... Edmonton AB
Alcatel Canada Inc., Transport Automatio (3) ... Toronto ON
AMEC E&C Services (3) ... St. John's NF
Aplin & Martin Consultants Ltd. (3) ... Surrey BC
Astec Advanced Power Systems (3) ... St-Laurent QC
ATCO Noise Management Ltd. (3) ... Calgary AB
Atlantis Systems International (3) ... Brampton ON
Bombardier Aerospace, Defense Services (3) ... Mirabel QC
Brooks Automation Software Corporation (3) ... Richmond BC
C-MAC Industries Inc. (3) ... Cornwall ON
CMC Electronics Inc. (3) ... Kanata ON
Cochrane Group, The (3) ... Vancouver BC
Colt Engineering Corporation (3) ... Calgary AB
Concord Idea Corp. (3) ... Markham ON
CreoScitex (3) ... Burnaby BC
CTS of Canada Ltd. (3) ... Streetsville ON
DCL Siemens Engineering Ltd. (3) ... Edmonton AB
Dynapro (3) ... Annacis Island BC
Environmental Waste International / EWI (3) ... Ajax ON
EXI Wireless Systems Inc. (3) ... Richmond BC
Gemini Corporation (3) ... Calgary AB
Genesis Microchip Inc. (3) ... Thornhill ON
GFI Control Systems Inc. (3) ... Kitchener ON
Goodkey, Weedmark & Associates Ltd. (3) ... Ottawa ON
Honda of Canada Manufacturing (3) ... Alliston ON
Honeywell Ltd. (3) ... Toronto ON
Husky Injection Molding Systems Ltd. (3) ... Bolton ON
Hyprotech Ltd. (3) ... Calgary AB
iFire Technology Inc. (3) ... Toronto ON
Industry Canada (3) ... Hull QC
Interautomation Inc. (3) ... Oakville ON
IPSCO Inc. (3) ... Regina SK
Jacques Whitford Environment Ltd. (3) ... Ottawa ON
Kaytronics Inc. (3) ... Burnaby BC
Kvaerner Process Systems / KPS (3) ... Calgary AB
Lafarge Canada Inc. (3) ... Bath ON
Lafarge Canada Inc. (3) ... Montréal QC
Lakehead University (3) ... Thunder Bay ON
Lantern Communications Canada Inc. (3) ... Ottawa ON
Leitch Technology Corp. (3) ... Toronto ON
Luxell Technologies Inc. (3) ... Mississauga ON
Magna International Inc. (3) ... Concord ON
March Networks Corporation (3) ... Kanata ON
Maxim Morrison Hershfield Ltd. (3) ... Edmonton AB
McElhanney Group Ltd., The (3) ... Vancouver BC
Mitchell & Associates Consulting Engi (3) ... Burlington ON
Morrison Hershfield (3) ... Ottawa ON
National Research Council Canada / NRC (3) ... Ottawa ON
Northwest Territories Power Corporatio (3) ... Hay River NT
Oerlikon Aerospace Inc. (3) ... St-Jean-sur-Richelieu QC
Okanagan University College / OUC (3) ... Kelowna BC
Palliser Furniture Ltd. (3) ... Winnipeg MB
Patheon Inc. (3) ... Mississauga ON
Philips Engineering Ltd. (3) ... Burlington ON
Powertech Labs Inc. (3) ... Surrey BC
QDesign Corporation (3) ... Vancouver BC
Red Deer, City of (3) ... Red Deer AB
Semiconductor Insights Inc. (3) ... Kanata ON
Silex Inc. (3) ... Mississauga ON
Smart Technologies Inc. (3) ... Calgary AB
Solectron (3) ... Calgary AB
Stantec Geomatics Ltd. (3) ... Edmonton AB
Staticon Ltd. (3) ... Toronto ON
Sulzer Mitroflow Corp. (3) ... Richmond BC
TECO Precision Inc. (3) ... St-Laurent QC
University of Manitoba, Department of M (3) ... Winnipeg MB
Valcom Limited (Ottawa) (3) ... Ottawa ON
Viconics Electronics Inc. (3) ... St-Leonard QC
VIPswitch Inc. (3) ... Montréal QC
Walsh Automation / Validation Technolog (3) ... Montréal QC
Xillix Technologies Corp. (3) ... Richmond BC
Acart Communications (2) ... Ottawa ON
AiT Corporation (2) ... Ottawa ON
Andrew Canada Inc. (2) ... Whitby ON
Applanix Corp. (2) ... Richmond Hill ON
Associated Engineering Industrial Ltd. (2) ... Edmonton AB
Azure Dynamics Inc. (2) ... Vancouver BC
Azurix North America (2) ... Hamilton ON
Bantrel Inc. (2) ... Edmonton AB
Bantrel Inc. (2) ... Calgary AB
Bantrel Inc. (2) ... Toronto ON
Baranti Group Inc. (2) ... Markham ON
Bently Nevada Canada Company (2) ... Edmonton AB
BJ Services Company Canada (2) ... Calgary AB
Black Max Downhole Tools Ltd. (2) ... Nisku AB
Born Canada (2) ... Calgary AB
Brascon Architectural Products Inc. (2) ... Brampton ON
Brisbin & Sentis Engineering Inc. (2) ... Calgary AB
Brown Applied Technology Inc. (2) ... Toronto ON
Burlington Technologies Inc., Burling (2) ... Burlington ON
C-MAC Industries Inc. (2) ... Kanata ON
C-MAC Invotronics Inc. (2) ... Toronto ON
Cadence Design Systems, Inc. (2) ... Ottawa ON
Carmanah Technologies Inc. (2) ... Victoria BC
Central Precast Inc. (2) ... Nepean ON
Cohos Evamy Partners, The (2) ... Calgary AB
Coldswitch Technologies Inc. (2) ... Richmond BC
Colt Engineering Corporation (2) ... Edmonton AB
Colt Engineering Corporation (2) ... Markham ON
Conestoga College of Applied Arts & Te (2) ... Kitchener ON
Cougar Automation Technologies Inc. (2) ... Toronto ON
Crown Cork & Seal Canada Inc. (2) ... Concord ON
Cymbolic Sciences Inc. (2) ... Richmond BC
David Schaeffer Engineering Ltd. (2) ... Markham ON
Delcan Corporation (2) ... New Westminster BC
DY 4 Systems Inc. (2) ... Kanata ON
E-One Moli Energy (Canada) Ltd. (2) ... Maple Ridge BC
Eagle Precision Technologies Inc. (2) ... Brantford ON
EFOS Corporation (2) ... Mississauga ON
Energy Industries Inc. (2) ... Calgary AB
Ensil International (2) ... Markham ON
ESBI Alberta Ltd. (2) ... Calgary AB
Evans Consoles Inc. (2) ... Calgary AB
FCX Specialty Valves (2) ... Edmonton AB
FCX Specialty Valves (2) ... Mississauga ON
First Professional Management Inc. (2) ... Toronto ON
Flowserve Inc. (2) ... St. Thomas ON
Foster Wheeler Fired Heaters Ltd. (2) ... Calgary AB
General Equipment Ltd. (2) ... Vancouver BC
GlaxoSmithKline (2) ... Mississauga ON
Goodyear Canada Inc. (2) ... Napanee ON
Greater Vancouver Regional District / GV (2) ... Burnaby BC
GSI Lumonics Inc., Telecom Optics Divisio (2) ... Nepean ON
H.H. Angus & Associates Ltd. (2) ... Toronto ON
Hatch Associates Ltd. (2) ... Sudbury ON
Henry Technologies / Chil-Con Product (2) ... Brantford ON
Hitachi Canadian Industries Ltd. (2) ... Saskatoon SK
Holderbank Group Support (Canada) Lt (2) ... Mississauga ON
Husky Injection Molding Systems Ltd. (2) ... Bolton ON
Hymarc Ltd. (2) ... Nepean ON
IBM Canada Ltd. (2) ... Markham ON
Ilco Unican Inc. (2) ... Montréal QC
Inkra Networks Canada (2) ... Burnaby BC
International Datacasting Corporation / I (2) ... Ottawa ON
IPC Resistors Inc. (2) ... Mississauga ON
JL Richards & Associates Ltd. (2) ... Kingston ON
KB Electronics Limited (2) ... Halifax NS
MacDonald Dettwiler & Associates Ltd. / (2) ... Richmond BC
MacDonald Dettwiler & Associates Ltd. / (2) ... Halifax NS
MacInnis Engineering Associates Ltd. / (2) ... Richmond BC
Magna IV Engineering Ltd. (2) ... Edmonton AB
Marconi Communications (2) ... Dorval QC
Marshall Macklin Monaghan Limited (2) ... Thornhill ON
Messier-Dowty Inc. (2) ... Ajax ON
MetroPhotonics Inc. (2) ... Ottawa ON
Ministry of Natural Resources, O (2) ... South Porcupine ON
Motorola Canada Limited (2) ... Richmond Hill ON
National Research Council Canada, Integra (2) ... London ON
National Research Council Canada / NRC (2) ... Ottawa ON
New Automation Corporation / NAC (2) ... Burlington ON
Newfoundland and Labrador Hydro Group (2) ... St. John's NF
Niagara College of Applied Arts & Techno (2) ... Welland ON
Nordic Acres Engineering (2) ... Calgary AB
Nortel Networks (2) ... Ottawa ON
Northwest Hydraulic Consultants Ltd. / (2) ... Edmonton AB
NUHC Inc. (2) ... Woodbridge ON
NxtPhase Corporation (2) ... Vancouver BC

For descriptions of the occupational categories used in this index, see page 458.

OCCUPATIONAL INDEX 499

ENGINEERING (Cont.)

Orlick Industries Ltd. (2) ..... Hamilton ON
Patheon Inc. (2) ..... Whitby ON
Philips Analytical (2) ..... Waterloo ON
Public Service Commission of Canada, B (2) ..... Vancouver BC
Public Service Commission of Canada, New (2) ..... Moncton NB
Public Service Commission of Canada, Qu (2) ..... Montréal QC
PyroGenesis Inc. (2) ..... Montréal QC
Quake Technologies Inc. (2) ..... Ottawa ON
Rea International Inc. (2) ..... Mississauga ON
Read Jones Christoffersen Ltd. (2) ..... Vancouver BC
Read Jones Christoffersen Ltd. (2) ..... Edmonton AB
Research in Motion Limited / RIM (2) ..... Kanata ON
Robinson Consultants Inc. (2) ..... Kanata ON
Ruffneck Heaters (2) ..... Calgary AB
Samac Engineering Ltd. (2) ..... Calgary AB
Sandwell EPC Inc. (2) ..... Montréal QC
Saskatchewan Institute of Applied Scie (2) ..... Saskatoon SK
Schaeffer & Associates Ltd. (2) ..... Concord ON
Seacor Environmental Engineering Inc. (2) ..... Richmond BC
Senstar-Stellar Corporation (2) ..... Carp ON
Siemens Automotive (2) ..... London ON
Silex Design Inc. (2) ..... Mississauga ON
Smart Technologies Inc. (2) ..... Stittsville ON
Stantec Consulting Ltd. (2) ..... Vancouver BC
Stantec Consulting Ltd. (2) ..... Ottawa ON
Synopsys Inc. (2) ..... Ottawa ON
Thermal Energy International Inc. (2) ..... Nepean ON
Toromont Process Systems, Division of To (2) ..... Calgary AB
Tractel Ltd., Swingstage Division (2) ..... Toronto ON
Tricom Technologies (2) ..... Mississauga ON
TRK Engineering Ltd. (2) ..... Surrey BC
Trow Consulting Engineers Ltd. (2) ..... Nepean ON
Trudell Medical International / TMI (2) ..... London ON
UMA Engineering Ltd. (2) ..... Edmonton AB
UMA Engineering Ltd. (2) ..... Saskatoon SK
UMA Engineering Ltd. (2) ..... Winnipeg MB
University of Calgary (2) ..... Calgary AB
University of Regina, Faculty of Engineer (2) ..... Regina SK
URS Cole, Sherman (2) ..... Thornhill ON
Walter Cumbria Engineering Ltd. / WCEL (2) ..... Edmonton AB
WANN Connection Devices Inc. (2) ..... Nepean ON
Wardrop Engineering Inc. (2) ..... Thunder Bay ON
Waterloo, The Regional Municipality of (2) ..... Kitchener ON
Wavesat Telecom Inc. (2) ..... St-Laurent QC
Westpower Equipment Ltd. (2) ..... Calgary AB
Williams Energy Canada Inc. (2) ..... Calgary AB
Xerox Canada, Supplies Development C (2) ..... Mississauga ON
Zed.i Solutions (2) ..... Edmonton AB
Aastra Telecom (1) ..... Calgary AB
Aavid Thermal Products (1) ..... Woodbridge ON
Acres & Associates Environmental Ltd. (1) ..... Toronto ON
AEA Technology Engineering Software Ltd (1) ..... Waterloo ON
Ainsworth Inc. (1) ..... Toronto ON
Air Products Canada Ltd. (1) ..... Brampton ON
Ajax, Town of (1) ..... Ajax ON
Alberta Energy and Utilities Board / EUB (1) ..... Calgary AB
Alberta Innovation & Science (1) ..... Edmonton AB
Alfa Laval Canada (1) ..... Toronto ON
Algonquin College (1) ..... Nepean ON
Altera Corp. (1) ..... Nepean ON
Alumabrite Anodizing Ltd. (1) ..... Hamilton ON
AMEC Infrastructure Ltd. (1) ..... Sherwood Park AB
Ankari (1) ..... Ottawa ON
Antomax Automotive Technologies (1) ..... Mississauga ON
Apotex Inc. (1) ..... Toronto ON
Architrave Design Office Service (1) ..... Gabriola Island BC
Armtec Ltd. (1) ..... Guelph ON
Arrow Speed Controls Ltd. (1) ..... Vancouver BC
Ashland Canada Corp., Drew Industrial D (1) ..... Edmonton AB
Associated Engineering Alberta Ltd. (1) ..... Calgary AB
ATS Automation Tooling Systems Inc. (1) ..... Cambridge ON
ATS Test Systems Inc. (1) ..... Woodbridge ON
Automation Tooling Systems Inc. / ATS (1) ..... Oakville ON
Autopro Automation Consultants Lt (1) ..... Grande Prairie AB
Ballard Power Systems Inc. (1) ..... Burnaby BC
Bauer Industries Ltd. (1) ..... Waterloo ON
BCL Magnetics (1) ..... Burlington ON
BCS Associates Ltd. (1) ..... Belleville ON
Bearden Engineering Consultants Ltd. (1) ..... Red Deer AB
Beavers Dental (1) ..... Morrisburg ON
Bell Helicopter Textron Canada (1) ..... Mirabel QC
Beta Machinery Analysis Ltd. (1) ..... Calgary AB
Bettis Canada Ltd. (1) ..... Edmonton AB
Bidell Equipment Inc. (1) ..... Calgary AB
BJ Pipeline Inspection Services (1) ..... Calgary AB
Bodycote Ortech Inc. (1) ..... Mississauga ON
Boiler Inspection & Insurance Company of (1) ..... Toronto ON
Bombardier Transport, Transit Systems (1) ..... Burnaby BC
Bracknell Telecom Services (1) ..... Langley BC
Bradford West Gwillimbury, Town of (1) ..... Bradford ON
Bragg Photonics Inc. (1) ..... Dorval QC
Brampton, City of (1) ..... Brampton ON
Brooks, Town of (1) ..... Brooks AB
BTI Photonics Inc. (1) ..... Ottawa ON
Burlington Technologies Inc., Alumetco (1) ..... Brantford ON
C-Tech Ltd. (1) ..... Cornwall ON
Cadbury Trebor Allan Inc. (1) ..... Hamilton ON
Calfrac Well Services Ltd. (1) ..... Calgary AB
Calgary Airport Authority, The (1) ..... Calgary AB
Calgary, City of (1) ..... Calgary AB
Camelot Content Technologies Inc. (1) ..... Ottawa ON
Canam Steel Works (1) ..... Calgary AB
CanRoof Corporation Inc. (1) ..... Toronto ON
Carpenter Canada Ltd. (1) ..... Woodbridge ON
Carrier Canada Ltd. (1) ..... Calgary AB
Catena Networks (1) ..... Kanata ON
CBCL Limited (1) ..... Halifax NS
CH2M HILL Canada Ltd. (1) ..... Vancouver BC
CH2M HILL Canada Ltd. (1) ..... Calgary AB
Chalmers Suspensions International I (1) ..... Mississauga ON
CIBA Vision Sterile Manufacturing (1) ..... Mississauga ON
Circa Communications Ltd. (1) ..... North Vancouver BC
Circon Systems Corporation (1) ..... Richmond BC
Circuit Graphics Ltd. (1) ..... Burnaby BC
Clifton ND Lea Consulting Inc. (1) ..... Calgary AB
Cohos Evamy Partners, The (1) ..... Edmonton AB
Colgate-Palmolive Canada Inc. (1) ..... Toronto ON
Cominco Ltd. (1) ..... Trail BC
Comstock Canada Ltd (1) ..... Mississauga ON
Con-Force Structures Ltd. (1) ..... Calgary AB
Conestoga-Rovers & Associates Limited / (1) ..... Waterloo ON
Consultronics Ltd. (1) ..... Concord ON
Convedia Corporation (1) ..... Burnaby BC
Coretec Inc. (1) ..... Toronto ON
Creation Technologies Inc. (1) ..... Mississauga ON
CSA International (1) ..... Edmonton AB
CTF Systems Inc. (1) ..... Port Coquitlam BC
Cytec Canada Inc. (1) ..... Niagara Falls ON
Dalhousie University, Department of Civi (1) ..... Halifax NS
Dana Long Manufacturing Ltd. (1) ..... Mississauga ON
David Brown Union Pumps (Canada) Ltd. (1) ..... Burlington ON
David McManus Engineering Ltd. / DME (1) ..... Nepean ON
DBR Research Ltd. (1) ..... Edmonton AB
Debiasi Group, The / DBG (1) ..... Mississauga ON
Delcan Corporation (1) ..... Niagara Falls ON
Department of Environment, Newfoundla (1) ..... St. John's NF
Department of Human Resources, Nuna (1) ..... Rankin Inlet NU
Department of National Defence, Headquart (1) ..... Ottawa ON
Department of Works, Services and Tra (1) ..... St. John's NF
Dillon Consulting Ltd. (1) ..... London ON
Dillon Consulting Ltd. (1) ..... Ottawa ON
Dover Industries Ltd. (1) ..... Burlington ON
DSC Group of Companies (1) ..... Toronto ON
DSI Datotech Systems Inc. (1) ..... Vancouver BC
Dura-Lite Heat Transfer Products Ltd. (1) ..... Calgary AB
Ebco Technologies Inc. (1) ..... Richmond BC
Ecole Polytechnique de Montreal, Depart (1) ..... Montréal QC
Elcan Optical Technologies (1) ..... Midland ON
Electro Sonic Inc. (1) ..... Toronto ON
Ellett Industries Ltd. (1) ..... Port Coquitlam BC
EMC Group Ltd. (1) ..... Concord ON
Enerline Restorations Inc. (1) ..... Calgary AB
Enersource (1) ..... Mississauga ON
Enersul Inc. (1) ..... Calgary AB
Enron Canada Corp. (1) ..... Calgary AB
ESTec Oilfield Inc. (1) ..... Edmonton AB
FAM Canada Inc. (1) ..... Edmonton AB
Ferguson Simek Clark / FSC (1) ..... Edmonton AB
Fireplace Products International / FPI (1) ..... Delta BC
FTI Consulting, Inc. (1) ..... Mississauga ON
G&K Work Wear (1) ..... Mississauga ON

ENGINEERING (Cont.)

G-P Flakeboard Company (1) ... Bancroft ON
GasTOPS Ltd. (1) ... Gloucester ON
GE Power Services (1) ... Mississauga ON
GE Power Systems (1) ... Guelph ON
GE Syprotec Inc. (1) ... Pointe-Claire QC
General Motors of Canada Ltd., Diesel Div (1) ... London ON
General Motors of Canada Ltd., Oshawa Tru (1) ... Oshawa ON
Gienow Building Products Ltd. (1) ... Calgary AB
Global Group, The (1) ... Toronto ON
Grant Structural Engineering Ltd. (1) ... Calgary AB
Greenlight Power Technologies, Inc. (1) ... Sidney BC
Guelph, City of (1) ... Guelph ON
Halsall Associates Ltd. (1) ... Toronto ON
Harris Corporation, Microwave Communicat (1) ... Calgary AB
Heidelberg Canada (1) ... Mississauga ON
Hemosol Inc. (1) ... Toronto ON
Honeywell Ltd. (1) ... Burnaby BC
Honeywell Ltd. (1) ... Edmonton AB
Honeywell Ltd., Industrial Automation an (1) ... Calgary AB
Hussmann Canada Inc. (1) ... Brantford ON
Hyd-Mech Group Ltd. (1) ... Woodstock ON
IBI Group (1) ... Edmonton AB
IceFyre Semiconductor Inc. (1) ... Ottawa ON
IMP Group Ltd., Aerospace Division (1) ... Enfield NS
Inco Ltd., Ontario Division (1) ... Copper Cliff ON
International Utility Structures Inc. (1) ... Calgary AB
IR Security & Safety (1) ... Mississauga ON
Irvin Aerospace Canada Ltd. (1) ... Fort Erie ON
J. Walter Company Ltd. (1) ... Pointe-Claire QC
Jacques Whitford Environment Ltd. (1) ... Burnaby BC
JDS Uniphase Corporation (1) ... Nepean ON
Jiro Compression Ltd. (1) ... Stettler AB
Keen Engineering Co. Ltd. (1) ... Edmonton AB
Kerr Wood Leidal Associates Ltd. (1) ... North Vancouver BC
Kinectrics Inc. (1) ... Toronto ON
Kingsbury Canada Inc. (1) ... Burlington ON
Kingston, Corporation of the City of (1) ... Kingston ON
Kitchener, City of (1) ... Kitchener ON
Kitimat, District of (1) ... Kitimat BC
Kleinfeldt Consultants Limited (1) ... Mississauga ON
Kvaerner SNC-Lavalin Offshore / KSLO (1) ... Halifax NS
Kymata Canada Ltd. (1) ... Kanata ON
Langley, Corporation of the Township of (1) ... Langley BC
Lea Consulting Ltd. (1) ... Toronto ON
Lenbrook (1) ... Pickering ON
Liburdi Engineering Ltd. (1) ... Dundas ON
LNB Inc. (1) ... Toronto ON
MacDonald Dettwiler Space and Advanced (1) ... Brampton ON
Manitoba Hydro (1) ... Winnipeg MB
Manitoba Transportation & Government Se (1) ... Winnipeg MB
Maple Ridge, District of (1) ... Maple Ridge BC
Maritime Hydraulics (Canada) Ltd. (1) ... Calgary AB
Markham, Corporation of the Town of (1) ... Markham ON
Mastech Canada (1) ... Ottawa ON
Master Flo Valve Inc. (1) ... Edmonton AB
Maxim Group (1) ... Calgary AB
Maxim Morrison Hershfield Ltd. (1) ... Calgary AB
McMaster University, Department of Engi (1) ... Hamilton ON
MDS Nordion (1) ... Vancouver BC
Medicine Hat, City of (1) ... Medicine Hat AB
Mentor Engineering (1) ... Calgary AB
Meritor Suspension Systems Company (1) ... Milton ON
Metafore Corporation (1) ... Calgary AB
Metropolitan Hotel Toronto (1) ... Toronto ON
MicroSlate Inc. (1) ... Brossard QC
Millenium Biologix Inc. (1) ... Kingston ON
Ministry of Labour, Ontario (1) ... Toronto ON
Ministry of Labour, Ontario (Northern Re (1) ... Sudbury ON
Ministry of Transportation, Ontario (1) ... London ON
Ministry of Transportation, Ontario (1) ... Toronto ON
Modern Niagara Ottawa Inc. (1) ... Kanata ON
Mohawk College of Applied Arts and Tech (1) ... Hamilton ON
Moss Fabrication Ltd. (1) ... Calgary AB
Mount Royal College (1) ... Calgary AB
Nabisco Ltd., Lakeshore Bakery (1) ... Toronto ON
National Research Council Canada, Institu (1) ... Ottawa ON
National Research Council Canada, Institu (1) ... Ottawa ON
NCR Canada Ltd. (1) ... Waterloo ON
Net Safety Monitoring Inc. (1) ... Calgary AB
New Brunswick Community College, Sain (1) ... Saint John NB
New Westminster, City of (1) ... New Westminster BC
NICE Systems (1) ... Richmond BC
Noranda Inc., Brunswick Mine (1) ... Bathurst NB
Norcom / CDT (1) ... Kingston ON
Norske Skog Canada, Elk Falls Pri (1) ... Campbell River BC
North American Railway Steel Tie Corp. (1) ... Squamish BC
Novatel Inc. (1) ... Calgary AB
Novatronics Inc. (1) ... Stratford ON
Novopharm Ltd. (1) ... Toronto ON
O'Hara Technologies Inc. (1) ... Richmond Hill ON
Ontario Science Centre / OSC (1) ... Toronto ON
Optimal Robotics Corp. (1) ... Montréal QC
PanCanadian Petroleum Ltd. (1) ... Calgary AB
Peerless Clothing Inc. (1) ... Montréal QC
Peterborough Utilities Commission (1) ... Peterborough ON
Piller Sausages & Delicatessens Ltd. (1) ... Waterloo ON
Pillsbury Canada Limited (1) ... Midland ON
Port Moody, City of (1) ... Port Moody BC
Positron Public Safety Systems Inc. (1) ... Montréal QC
Potentia Telecom Power (1) ... Kanata ON
Pratt & Whitney Canada Corporation / P (1) ... Longueuil QC
Proface Inde Electronics Inc. (1) ... Burnaby BC
Professional Engineers Ontario / PEO (1) ... Toronto ON
Psion Teklogix Inc. (1) ... Mississauga ON
Public Service Commission of Canada, BC (1) ... Victoria BC
Public Service Commission of Canada, Ma (1) ... Winnipeg MB
Public Service Commission of Canada, Nov (1) ... Halifax NS
Public Service Commission of Canada, Ont (1) ... Toronto ON
Public Service Commission of Canada, (1) ... Quebec City QC
Purolator Courier Ltd. (1) ... Mississauga ON
Quickmill Inc. (1) ... Peterborough ON
R.J. McKee Engineering Ltd. (1) ... Ottawa ON
Raytheon Systems Canada Ltd. (1) ... Calgary AB
Revolve Magnetic Bearings Inc. (1) ... Calgary AB
Richmond Hill, Town of (1) ... Richmond Hill ON
Rocky Mountain Instruments Inc. / RMI (1) ... Edmonton AB
Rogers Cable Inc. (1) ... Toronto ON
RoundHeaven Communications Canada Inc. (1) ... Vancouver BC
Royal Building Systems (Cdn) Ltd. / R (1) ... Woodbridge ON
Royal Ultraframe Ltd. (1) ... Toronto ON
Ryerson Polytechnic University (1) ... Toronto ON
S&C Electric Canada Ltd. (1) ... Toronto ON
Saputo Inc., Milk Division (1) ... Vancouver BC
Schlumberger Completion Systems (1) ... Calgary AB
Schneider Electric (1) ... Toronto ON
Schneider Electric Services (1) ... Mississauga ON
Schneider Foods Inc. (1) ... Kitchener ON
SCI Brockville Corp. (1) ... Brockville ON
SciCan (1) ... Toronto ON
Sciemetric Instruments Inc. (1) ... Nepean ON
Scintrex Ltd. (1) ... Concord ON
SCP Science (1) ... Baie d'Urfe QC
Sedona Networks (1) ... Kanata ON
Sheridan College (1) ... Oakville ON
Siemens Building Technologies Ltd. (1) ... Richmond Hill ON
Siemens Canada Ltd., Medical Syste (1) ... Pointe-Claire QC
Siemens Dematic Ltd., Rapistan Divis (1) ... Mississauga ON
Siemens Milltronics Process Instruments (1) ... Edmonton AB
Siemens Technical Services (1) ... Hamilton ON
Sigem Inc. (1) ... Kanata ON
Simplot Canada Limited (1) ... Brandon MB
Sky Eye America (1) ... Dorval QC
SMED International Inc. (1) ... Calgary AB
SNC-Lavalin Inc. (1) ... Montréal QC
Southern Alberta Institute of Technology (1) ... Calgary AB
SpaceBridge Networks Corporation (1) ... Hull QC
Span Manufacturing Ltd. (1) ... Markham ON
Spectral Diagnostics Inc. (1) ... Toronto ON
Spectrum Signal Processing Inc. (1) ... Burnaby BC
Spirent Communications (1) ... Ottawa ON
Splentec Ltd. (1) ... Richmond Hill ON
SS8 Networks Inc. (1) ... Ottawa ON
Stackpole Ltd., Engineered Products (1) ... Mississauga ON
StackTeck Systems Inc. (1) ... Toronto ON
Standens Limited (1) ... Calgary AB
Stanley Door Systems (1) ... Brampton ON
Stantec Consulting Ltd. (1) ... Calgary AB
Stantec Consulting Ltd. (1) ... Kitchener ON
Stantec Consulting Ltd. (1) ... Hamilton ON
Stellate Systems (1) ... Westmount QC

For descriptions of the occupational categories used in this index, see page 458.

ENGINEERING (Cont.)

ENVIRONMENTAL

See also: Engineering, Agriculture/Fisheries, Govt/Nonprofit.

ENVIRONMENTAL (Cont.)

Ministry of Natural Resources, Ontario (2) .... Geraldton ON
Ministry of Natural Resources, Ontario (2) .... Pembroke ON
Ministry of Natural Resources, Onta (2) .... Peterborough ON
Ministry of the Environment, Ontario (Dr (2) .... Toronto ON
Ministry of the Environment, Ontario (En (2) .... Toronto ON
Okanagan University College / OUC (2) .... Kelowna BC
Ontario Clean Water Agency, Northwestern (2) .... Longlac ON
Oxford, County of (2) .... Woodstock ON
Public Service Commission of Canada, New (2) .... Moncton NB
Public Service Commission of Canada, Onta (2) .... Ottawa ON
Public Service Commission of Canada, (2) .... Quebec City QC
Public Service Commission of Canada, (2) .... Whitehorse YT
Safety-Kleen Ltd. (2) .... Ryley AB
Silex Design Inc. (2) .... Mississauga ON
Stantec Consulting Ltd. (2) .... Calgary AB
Stantec Consulting Ltd. (2) .... Mississauga ON
Stantec Geomatics Ltd. (2) .... Edmonton AB
Thermal Energy International Inc. (2) .... Nepean ON
Trow Consulting Engineers Ltd. (2) .... Nepean ON
URS Corporation (2) .... Calgary AB
Wardrop Engineering Inc. (2) .... Thunder Bay ON
Whistler, Resort Municipality of (2) .... Whistler BC
Acres International Limited (1) .... Oakville ON
Acres International Limited (1) .... Niagara Falls ON
Ajax, Town of (1) .... Ajax ON
Alberta Energy and Utilities Board / EUB (1) .... Calgary AB
Alberta Energy Company Ltd. / AEC (1) .... Calgary AB
Alberta Municipal Affairs (1) .... Edmonton AB
Alberta Sustainable Resource Developmen (1) .... Edmonton AB
Alberta Sustainable Resource Development (1) .... Calgary AB
Ashland Canada Corp., Drew Industrial D (1) .... Edmonton AB
Associated Engineering Industrial Ltd. (1) .... Edmonton AB
Atlas Corporation, The (1) .... Concord ON
Bombardier Aerospace, Regional Aircraft (1) .... Toronto ON
Brampton, City of (1) .... Brampton ON
Brantford, Corporation of the City of (1) .... Brantford ON
Burlington Resources Canada Energy Ltd. (1) .... Calgary AB
Canadian Nuclear Safety Commission / CNSC (1) .... Ottawa ON
Capital Regional District / CRD (1) .... Victoria BC
CH2M HILL Canada Ltd. (1) .... Toronto ON
Clifton Associates Ltd. (1) .... Calgary AB
CSA International (1) .... Toronto ON
Delcan Corporation (1) .... New Westminster BC
Delcan Corporation (1) .... Toronto ON
Department of Human Resources, Nunavut (1) .... Iqaluit NU
Dillon Consulting Ltd. (1) .... Fredericton NB
Ecoplans Ltd. (1) .... Kitchener ON
Export Development Corporation / EDC (1) .... Ottawa ON
Geographic Dynamics Corp. / GDC (1) .... Edmonton AB
Grande Prairie, City of (1) .... Grande Prairie AB
Greater Toronto Airports Authority / GTA (1) .... Toronto ON
Groupe Conseil SAE Inc., Le (1) .... St-Laurent QC
Guelph, City of (1) .... Guelph ON
Haley Industries Ltd. (1) .... Haley ON
Hay River Community Health Board (1) .... Hay River NT
Hemosol Inc. (1) .... Toronto ON
Homestake Canada Inc., Eskay Creek Mine (1) .... Smithers BC
International Development Research Centre (1) .... Ottawa ON
Jungbunzlauer Canada Inc. (1) .... Port Colborne ON
Kawartha Lakes, Corporation of the City (1) .... Lindsay ON
Kelowna, City of (1) .... Kelowna BC
Koch Petroleum Canada LP (1) .... Calgary AB
Lester B. Pearson College of the Pacifi (1) .... Victoria BC
Loyalist Township (1) .... Odessa ON
Manitoba Intergovernmental Affairs (1) .... Winnipeg MB
Maple Ridge, District of (1) .... Maple Ridge BC
Maxim Morrison Hershfield Ltd. (1) .... Calgary AB
McCormick Rankin Corporation (1) .... Mississauga ON
McElhanney Group Ltd., The (1) .... Vancouver BC
MDS Nordion (1) .... Kanata ON
Miller Waste Systems (1) .... Markham ON
Ministry of Agriculture, Food and Fishe (1) .... Victoria BC
Ministry of Natural Resources, Ontario (1) .... Kenora ON
Ministry of Natural Resources, Ontario (1) .... Dryden ON
Ministry of Natural Resources, Ont (1) .... Kirkland Lake ON
Ministry of Natural Resources, Ontario (1) .... Cochrane ON
Ministry of Natural Resources, Ontario (1) .... Guelph ON
Ministry of Natural Resources, Ontari (1) .... Kemptville ON

Ministry of Natural Resources, O (1) .... South Porcupine ON
Ministry of Natural Resources, Onta (1) .... Peterborough ON
Ministry of Natural Resources, Onta (1) .... Peterborough ON
Ministry of Northern Development and Min (1) .... Sudbury ON
Ministry of the Environment, Ontario, (In (1) .... Toronto ON
Ministry of Transportation, Ontario (1) .... London ON
Ministry of Transportation, Ontar (1) .... St. Catharines ON
Ministry of Transportation, Ontario (1) .... Kingston ON
Moody International Ltd. (1) .... Edmonton AB
Morrison Hershfield (1) .... Ottawa ON
National Research Council Canada / NRC (1) .... Ottawa ON
North Grenville, Township of (1) .... Kemptville ON
North Okanagan, Regional District of (1) .... Coldstream BC
Northwest Hydraulic Consultants Ltd. / (1) .... Edmonton AB
Northwestern Health Services Region (1) .... High Level AB
OMYA (Canada) Inc. (1) .... Perth ON
Ontario Clean Water Agency / OCWA (1) .... Kingston ON
Ontario Power Generation (1) .... Toronto ON
Orlick Industries Ltd. (1) .... Hamilton ON
Pacific National Aquaculture (1) .... Victoria BC
Parkvalley Consulting Ltd. (1) .... Calgary AB
Patheon Inc. (1) .... Mississauga ON
Peace River Regional District / PRR (1) .... Dawson Creek BC
Pengrowth Management Ltd. / PML (1) .... Calgary AB
Philip Services Corporation / PSC (1) .... Burlington ON
PrimeWest Energy Trust (1) .... Calgary AB
Public Service Commission of Canada, Ma (1) .... Winnipeg MB
Public Service Commission of Canada, Nov (1) .... Halifax NS
Public Service Commission of Canada, (1) .... Yellowknife NT
R.V. Anderson Associates Limited (1) .... Toronto ON
Regina, City of (1) .... Regina SK
Rocky Mountain Instruments Inc. / RMI (1) .... Edmonton AB
Rohm and Haas Canada Inc. (1) .... Toronto ON
Rowan Williams Davies & Irwin / RWDI (1) .... Guelph ON
Royal Roads University (1) .... Victoria BC
Saskatchewan Research Council / SRC (1) .... Saskatoon SK
Shell Canada Limited (1) .... Calgary AB
Siemens Canada Ltd. (1) .... Mississauga ON
Silex Inc. (1) .... Mississauga ON
Southern Alberta Institute of Technology (1) .... Calgary AB
Spar Aerospace Limited (1) .... Edmonton AB
Squamish-Lillooet Regional District / (1) .... Pemberton BC
Standards Council of Canada / SCC (1) .... Ottawa ON
Suncor Energy Inc., Oil Sands (1) .... Fort McMurray AB
TransAlta Corporation (1) .... Fort McMurray AB
TransAlta Corporation (1) .... Calgary AB
Trojan Technologies Inc. (1) .... London ON
Trow Consulting Engineers Ltd. (1) .... Thunder Bay ON
Trow Consulting Engineers Ltd. (1) .... Cambridge ON
UMA Engineering Ltd. (1) .... Winnipeg MB
University College of the Cariboo / UCC (1) .... Kamloops BC
University of New Brunswick, Departm (1) .... Fredericton NB
University of Regina, Faculty of Engineer (1) .... Regina SK
VECO Canada Ltd. (1) .... Burnaby BC
Wilfrid Laurier University (1) .... Waterloo ON

FINANCE

See also: Accounting, Banking.

Fidelity Investments Canada Limited (31 positions) ...... Toronto ON
Ministry of Finance, Ontario (30) .... Toronto ON
Ministry of Finance, Ontario (23) .... Toronto ON
Ministry of Finance, BC (20) .... Victoria BC
Royal Bank Financial Group (16) .... Toronto ON
Standard Life Assurance Company, The (16) .... Montréal QC
Group Telecom (15) .... Toronto ON
Export Development Corporation / EDC (13) .... Ottawa ON
ENMAX Corporation (12) .... Calgary AB
Ministry of Health and Long-Term Care, O (12) .... Toronto ON
Ministry of Municipal Affairs and Housin (12) .... Toronto ON
Bombardier Aerospace (11) .... Montréal QC
Franklin Templeton Investments (10) .... Toronto ON
Ministry of the Environment, Ontario (10) .... Toronto ON
AGF Management Ltd. (9) .... Toronto ON
Canada Mortgage and Housing Corporation / (9) .... Ottawa ON
Ministry of Children and Family Develop (9) .... Victoria BC
Ministry of Economic Development and Tra (9) .... Toronto ON
Public Service Commission of Canada, Onta (9) .... Ottawa ON
Ministry of Finance, Ontario (8) .... Oshawa ON

For descriptions of the occupational categories used in this index, see page 458.

FINANCE (Cont.)

Sprint Canada Inc. (8) .... Toronto ON
Sun Life Financial (8) .... Toronto ON
Calgary, City of (7) .... Calgary AB
Canada Life Assurance Company (7) .... Toronto ON
Department of Municipal and Provincia (7) .... St. John's NF
Manitoba Finance (7) .... Winnipeg MB
Mississauga, City of (7) .... Mississauga ON
AIC Ltd. (6) .... Burlington ON
Enron Canada Corp. (6) .... Calgary AB
EPCOR Utilities Inc. (6) .... Edmonton AB
IBM Canada Ltd. (6) .... Markham ON
Ministry of Education / Ministry of Trai (6) .... Toronto ON
724 Solutions Inc. (5) .... Toronto ON
Alberta Energy (5) .... Edmonton AB
Alberta Human Resources and Employment (5) .... Edmonton AB
BC Hydro (5) .... Vancouver BC
British Columbia Investment Management (5) .... Victoria BC
Canadian Depository for Securities Ltd. (5) .... Toronto ON
Clarica Life Insurance Company (5) .... Waterloo ON
Edward Jones (5) .... Mississauga ON
Financial Institutions Commission / FI (5) .... Vancouver BC
GE Capital Canada (5) .... Montréal QC
Global Educational Trust Plan / Global E (5) .... Toronto ON
Investment Dealers Association of Canada (5) .... Toronto ON
Jewelstone Systems Inc. / JSI (5) .... Toronto ON
Manitoba Labour & Immigration (5) .... Winnipeg MB
Northwest Territories Power Corporatio (5) .... Hay River NT
Rogers AT&T Wireless (5) .... Toronto ON
Rothenberg Group, The (5) .... Westmount QC
TransAlta Corporation (5) .... Calgary AB
ADP Canada (4) .... Toronto ON
Alberta Finance (4) .... Edmonton AB
AltaGas Services Inc. (4) .... Calgary AB
Caisse de Depot et Placement du Quebec (4) .... Montréal QC
Capital City Savings (4) .... Edmonton AB
Cirque du Soleil (4) .... Montréal QC
Conference Board of Canada, The (4) .... Ottawa ON
DSC Group of Companies (4) .... Concord ON
Durham, The Regional Municipality of (4) .... Whitby ON
Evans & Evans Inc. (4) .... Vancouver BC
Management Board Secretariat (4) .... Toronto ON
Manitoba Family Services and Housing (4) .... Winnipeg MB
Manitoba Health (4) .... Winnipeg MB
Ministry of Consumer and Business Servic (4) .... Toronto ON
Mutual Fund Dealers Association of Canad (4) .... Toronto ON
Ontario Teachers' Pension Plan Board (4) .... Toronto ON
Psion Teklogix Inc. (4) .... Mississauga ON
Raymond James Ltd. (4) .... Vancouver BC
Research in Motion Limited / RIM (4) .... Waterloo ON
SISIP Financial Services (4) .... Ottawa ON
State Street Canada (4) .... Toronto ON
Suncor Energy Inc., Oil Sands (4) .... Fort McMurray AB
SureFire Commerce Inc. (4) .... Westmount QC
Telus Mobility (4) .... Toronto ON
Union Financial (4) .... Toronto ON
University of Western Ontario, Department (4) .... London ON
WMA Securities of Canada Inc. (4) .... Concord ON
Alberta Community Development (3) .... Edmonton AB
Alberta Corporate Services Centre (3) .... Edmonton AB
Alberta Energy Company Ltd. / AEC (3) .... Calgary AB
Alberta Human Resources and Employment (3) .... Innisfail AB
Alberta Justice (3) .... Edmonton AB
Alberta Learning (3) .... Edmonton AB
Alberta Municipal Affairs (3) .... Edmonton AB
Alberta Securities Commission / ASC (3) .... Edmonton AB
Assante Advisory Services (3) .... Toronto ON
AstraZeneca (3) .... Mississauga ON
Bank of Canada (3) .... Ottawa ON
Bank of Montreal (3) .... Mississauga ON
Canada Deposit Insurance Corporation / CD (3) .... Ottawa ON
Canadian American Financial Corp. (Canada (3) .... Ottawa ON
Canadian Bankers Association / CBA (3) .... Toronto ON
Canadian Imperial Bank of Commerce, CIBC (3) .... Calgary AB
Canadian Imperial Bank of Commerce, Nati (3) .... Toronto ON
Canadian Venture Exchange / CDNX (3) .... Calgary AB
Case Credit Ltd. / CNH Capital (3) .... Burlington ON
CIBC Wood Gundy (3) .... Toronto ON
Credential Group (3) .... Vancouver BC
Encore Energy Inc. (3) .... Calgary AB

Fincentric Corp. (3) .... Richmond BC
Goldcare Indutiae Inc. (3) .... Toronto ON
H.J. Heinz Company of Canada Ltd. (3) .... Toronto ON
Halton, The Regional Municipality of (3) .... Oakville ON
Hewitt Associates (3) .... Toronto ON
Hewlett-Packard (Canada) Ltd. (3) .... Mississauga ON
Investment Dealers Association of Cana (3) .... Vancouver BC
Investment Dealers Association of Canada (3) .... Calgary AB
Liquor Distribution Branch, BC / LDB (3) .... Vancouver BC
Loewen Group Inc., The (3) .... Vancouver BC
Loyalty Group, The (3) .... Toronto ON
Manitoba Industry, Trades and Mines / I (3) .... Winnipeg MB
Merisel Canada Inc. (3) .... Toronto ON
Ministry of Community and Social Service (3) .... Toronto ON
Ministry of the Attorney General, BC (V (3) .... Victoria BC
Ministry of the Attorney General, Ontari (3) .... Toronto ON
Ministry of Transportation, Ontar (3) .... St. Catharines ON
MTU Maintenance Canada Ltd. (3) .... Richmond BC
NBC Clearing Services Inc. (3) .... Montréal QC
Nortel Networks (3) .... Ottawa ON
Ontario Municipal Employees Retirement S (3) .... Toronto ON
Ontario Pension Board (3) .... Toronto ON
Partners in Planning Financial Services L (3) .... Regina SK
Peel, The Regional Municipality of (3) .... Brampton ON
Phillips, Hager & North Investment Man (3) .... Vancouver BC
Prince George, City of (3) .... Prince George BC
Public Guardian and Trustee of British (3) .... Vancouver BC
Public Service Commission of Canada, Sask (3) .... Regina SK
RBC Dominion Securities Inc. (3) .... Toronto ON
RBC Dominion Securities Inc. (3) .... Toronto ON
Rogers AT&T Wireless (3) .... Toronto ON
Rogers Cable Inc. (3) .... Toronto ON
Rogers Communications Inc. (3) .... Toronto ON
SAS Institute (Canada) Inc. (3) .... Toronto ON
Sun Life Financial (3) .... Montréal QC
Telus Integrated Communications (3) .... Toronto ON
Toronto, City of (3) .... Toronto ON
Trader.com (3) .... Toronto ON
VFC Inc. (3) .... Toronto ON
West Park Healthcare Centre (3) .... Toronto ON
Weyerhaeuser Company Limited, Dryden Mill (3) .... Dryden ON
Acklands-Grainger Inc. / AGI (2) .... Richmond Hill ON
Affinity Financial Group Inc. (2) .... Toronto ON
AIM Funds Management Inc. (2) .... Calgary AB
Alberta Economic Development (2) .... Edmonton AB
Alberta Health and Wellness (2) .... Edmonton AB
Alberta Innovation & Science (2) .... Edmonton AB
Alberta Treasury Branches / ATB (2) .... Edmonton AB
Alterna Technologies Group Inc. (2) .... Calgary AB
American Express Canada Inc. / Amex (2) .... Markham ON
Androcan Inc. (2) .... Toronto ON
Aramark Canada Ltd. (2) .... Toronto ON
ATI Technologies Inc. (2) .... Thornhill ON
ATS Automation Tooling Systems Inc. (2) .... Cambridge ON
Bell Helicopter Textron Canada (2) .... Mirabel QC
Bell Intrigna (2) .... Calgary AB
BMO Nesbitt Burns Inc. (2) .... Toronto ON
Brampton, City of (2) .... Brampton ON
CAE Inc. (2) .... St-Laurent QC
Canada Customs and Revenue Agency / CCRA (2) ..... Calgary AB
CDA Industries Inc. (2) .... Pickering ON
Celestica Inc. (2) .... Toronto ON
Ceridian Canada Ltd. (2) .... Winnipeg MB
Citibank Canada (2) .... Toronto ON
Computer Sciences Corp. / CSC (2) .... Toronto ON
Consumers Packaging Inc. (2) .... Toronto ON
CreoScitex (2) .... Burnaby BC
Delta Hudson Engineering Ltd. (2) .... Calgary AB
Department of Finance, New Brunswick (2) .... Fredericton NB
Department of Human Resources, Nuna (2) .... Rankin Inlet NU
Diners Club International / enRoute (2) .... Montréal QC
Dufferin-Peel Catholic District Scho (2) .... Mississauga ON
Dynamic Mutual Funds (2) .... Toronto ON
Engage Energy Canada, LP (2) .... Calgary AB
Fiberex Glass Corporation (2) .... Leduc AB
GE Canada (2) .... Mississauga ON
GE Capital Mortgage Insurance Canada (2) .... Mississauga ON
George Brown College (2) .... Toronto ON
Great-West Life Assurance Company, The (2) .... Winnipeg MB
Guelph General Hospital (2) .... Guelph ON
Heidelberg Canada (2) .... Toronto ON
Home Trust Co. Credit Card Services (2) .... Toronto ON

FINANCE (Cont.)

Humber River Regional Hospital, Finch Av (2) ... Toronto ON
Husky Injection Molding Systems Ltd. (2) ... Bolton ON
Husky Oil Operations Ltd. (2) ... Calgary AB
Ilco Unican Inc. (2) ... Montréal QC
InBusiness Solutions Inc. (2) ... Ottawa ON
Inex Pharmaceuticals Corp. (2) ... Burnaby BC
ING Halifax (2) ... Calgary AB
ING Integrated Financial Services (2) ... Calgary AB
Inuvialuit Corporate Group (2) ... Inuvik NT
IPSCO Inc. (2) ... Regina SK
John Deere Credit Inc. (2) ... Burlington ON
Kawartha Lakes, Corporation of the City (2) ... Lindsay ON
Keybase Financial Group (2) ... Richmond Hill ON
Kingston General Hospital (2) ... Kingston ON
Liquor Control Board of Ontario / LCBO (2) ... Toronto ON
Lumsden Brothers Ltd. (2) ... Brantford ON
Mackenzie Financial Corporation (2) ... Toronto ON
Manitoba Conservation (2) ... Winnipeg MB
Manitoba Education, Training & Youth (2) ... Winnipeg MB
Manulife Financial Corporation (2) ... Toronto ON
Maple Leaf Poultry (2) ... Mississauga ON
McCarthy Tetrault LLP (2) ... Toronto ON
McGraw-Hill Ryerson Ltd. (2) ... Whitby ON
Merrill Lynch Canada Inc. (2) ... Vancouver BC
Merrill Lynch Canada Inc. (2) ... Toronto ON
Ministry of Agriculture, Food and Rural A (2) ... Guelph ON
Ministry of Agriculture, Food and Rural A (2) ... Guelph ON
Ministry of Children and Family Developm (2) ... Nanaimo BC
Ministry of Children and Family Develop (2) ... Victoria BC
Ministry of Employment and Investment, (2) ... Victoria BC
Ministry of Health and Ministry Respons (2) ... Victoria BC
Ministry of Northern Development and Min (2) ... Sudbury ON
Ministry of Small Business, Touris (2) ... Prince George BC
Ministry of the Attorney General, Ontari (2) ... Toronto ON
Ministry of Transportation, Ontario (2) ... London ON
Ministry of Water, Land and Air Protect (2) ... Victoria BC
Mistahia Health Region (2) ... Grande Prairie AB
Mount Sinai Hospital (2) ... Toronto ON
North York General Hospital, General Div (2) ... Toronto ON
Nubase Technologies Inc. (2) ... Toronto ON
Ontario Lottery and Gaming Corporation / (2) ... Toronto ON
Ontario Place Corporation (2) ... Toronto ON
Open Learning Agency / OLA (2) ... Burnaby BC
ORIX Financial Services Canada Ltd. / OF (2) ... Toronto ON
OZ Optics Ltd. (2) ... Carp ON
PACCAR Financial Services Ltd. (2) ... Mississauga ON
PanCanadian Petroleum Ltd. (2) ... Calgary AB
Poly-Pacific International Inc. (2) ... Edmonton AB
PrimeWest Energy Trust (2) ... Calgary AB
Providence Continuing Care Centre / PCC (2) ... Kingston ON
Public Service Commission of Canada, Al (2) ... Edmonton AB
Purolator Courier Ltd. (2) ... Mississauga ON
RBC Insurance (2) ... Calgary AB
ReserveAmerica (2) ... Milton ON
Rogers & Partners Securities Inc. (2) ... Calgary AB
Rogers Video (2) ... Richmond BC
Ryerson Polytechnic University (2) ... Toronto ON
School District #43 (Coquitlam) (2) ... Coquitlam BC
ScotiaMcLeod (2) ... Toronto ON
Securities Valuation Co. / SVC (2) ... Mississauga ON
Selkirk Financial Technologies, Inc. (2) ... Vancouver BC
Siemens Automotive (2) ... London ON
Siemens Milltronics Process Instrum (2) ... Peterborough ON
Simon Fraser Health Region / SFH (2) ... New Westminster BC
Sony Music Canada (2) ... Toronto ON
Spar Aerospace Limited (2) ... Mississauga ON
Spectrum Investment Management Ltd. (2) ... Toronto ON
Spielo Gaming International (2) ... Dieppe NB
State Farm Insurance Companies (2) ... Toronto ON
STS Systems (2) ... Pointe-Claire QC
Trillium Health Centre (2) ... Toronto ON
Union Gas Limited (2) ... Chatham ON
University of Calgary (2) ... Calgary AB
University of Northern British Col (2) ... Prince George BC
University of Toronto (2) ... Toronto ON
William M. Mercer Limited (2) ... Toronto ON
Winnipeg, City of (Public Works Departm (2) ... Winnipeg MB
Workers' Compensation Board of BC (2) ... Vancouver BC
York Central Hospital (2) ... Richmond Hill ON
Zurich Canada (2) ... Toronto ON
Acres International Limited (1) ... Niagara Falls ON
Akzo Nobel Coatings Ltd. (1) ... Toronto ON
Alberta Child and Family Services Autho (1) ... McLennan AB
Alberta Corporate Service Centre (1) ... Coaldale AB
Alberta Energy and Utilities Board / EUB (1) ... Calgary AB
Alberta Government Services (1) ... Edmonton AB
Alberta Human Resources and Employm (1) ... Lac La Biche AB
Alberta Infrastructure & Transportation (1) ... Edmonton AB
Alberta Mental Health Board, Alberta Ho (1) ... Edmonton AB
Alberta Motor Association / AMA (1) ... Edmonton AB
Alcan Primary Metal Group (1) ... Kitimat BC
Alliance Atlantis Communications Inc. (1) ... Toronto ON
Allied Domecq, Spirits & Wine (1) ... Windsor ON
Amore Sweets Corporation (1) ... Toronto ON
Anishinaabe Mino-Ayaawin Inc. / AMA (1) ... Winnipeg MB
AnorMED Inc. (1) ... Langley BC
Apple Auto Glass (1) ... Burnaby BC
ARI Financial Services Inc. (1) ... Mississauga ON
Art Gallery of Hamilton / AGH (1) ... Hamilton ON
Ash City (1) ... Toronto ON
Association of Universities and Colleges (1) ... Ottawa ON
Athabasca University (1) ... Athabasca AB
Atlas Cold Storage Canada Ltd. (1) ... Toronto ON
Atlas Van Lines (Canada) Ltd. (1) ... Oakville ON
Atomic Energy of Canada Ltd. / AECL (1) ... Mississauga ON
Aware Marketing Group (1) ... Toronto ON
Ballard Power Systems Inc. (1) ... Burnaby BC
Banff Centre, The (1) ... Banff AB
Bank of Montreal, Harris Private Banking (1) ... Calgary AB
BASF Canada Inc. (1) ... Toronto ON
Bausch & Lomb Canada (1) ... Markham ON
BBM Bureau of Measurement (1) ... Toronto ON
BCE Emergis Inc. (1) ... Montréal QC
Belleville, City of (1) ... Belleville ON
Bissett & Associates Investment Manageme (1) ... Calgary AB
Bizerba Canada (1) ... Mississauga ON
Bombardier Aerospace, Regional Aircraft (1) ... Toronto ON
Boomerang Tracking Inc. (1) ... Montréal QC
Boulevard Media (Canada) Inc. / BMC (1) ... Vancouver BC
Brant Community Healthcare System, Bra (1) ... Brantford ON
Brantford, Corporation of the City of (1) ... Brantford ON
Bridgestone Firestone Canada Inc. / (1) ... Mississauga ON
British Columbia Assets & Land Corporat (1) ... Victoria BC
British Columbia Automobile Association (1) ... Burnaby BC
British Columbia Institute of Technology (1) ... Burnaby BC
British Columbia Pension Corporation (1) ... Victoria BC
British Columbia Securities Commission (1) ... Vancouver BC
Burlington Resources Canada Energy Ltd. (1) ... Calgary AB
Caledon, Town of (1) ... Caledon East ON
Calgary Board of Education, The (1) ... Calgary AB
Cambridge Memorial Hospital / CMH (1) ... Cambridge ON
Canada Post Corporation (1) ... Ottawa ON
Canadian Blood Services / CBS (1) ... Ottawa ON
Canadian Imperial Bank of Commerce / CIB (1) ... Toronto ON
Canadian Inovatech Inc. (1) ... Abbotsford BC
Canadian Institutes of Health Research / (1) ... Ottawa ON
Canadian National Institute for the Blin (1) ... Toronto ON
Canadian Northern Shield Insurance Com (1) ... Vancouver BC
Canadian Olympic Association / COA (1) ... Toronto ON
Canadian Venture Exchange / CDNX (1) ... Vancouver BC
Canadian Wheat Board / CWB (1) ... Winnipeg MB
Carlton Cards Ltd. (1) ... Toronto ON
Carpedia Group International Inc. (1) ... Oakville ON
Casey House Hospice (1) ... Toronto ON
Catena Networks (1) ... Kanata ON
Chalk Network, The (1) ... Burnaby BC
Changepoint Corporation (1) ... Richmond Hill ON
Children's and Women's Health Centre o (1) ... Vancouver BC
Christian Children's Fund of Canada / CC (1) ... Toronto ON
Chromatic Software Inc. / CSI (1) ... Vancouver BC
Cimco Refrigeration (1) ... Toronto ON
Circle of Care (1) ... Toronto ON
CitiFinancial Canada Inc. (1) ... London ON
Civil Service Co-operative Credit Society (1) ... Ottawa ON
Cognos Inc. (1) ... Ottawa ON
Collega for Aveda (1) ... Toronto ON
COM DEV International (1) ... Cambridge ON
Comda (1) ... Toronto ON
Commonwealth Construction (1) ... Burnaby BC
Communications and Information Technology (1) ... Kanata ON

FINANCE (Cont.)

Community AIDS Treatment Information Exc (1) ... Toronto ON
Community Care Access Centre of Peel (1) ... Brampton ON
Community Care East York (1) ... Toronto ON
Computing Devices Canada Ltd. / CDC (1) ... Ottawa ON
Conair Consumer Products Inc. (1) ... Brampton ON
Conestoga College of Applied Arts & Te (1) ... Kitchener ON
Convergys Corporation (1) ... Ottawa ON
Coquitlam, City of (1) ... Coquitlam BC
CSA International (1) ... Toronto ON
Cue Datawest Ltd. (1) ... Vancouver BC
Cytec Canada Inc. (1) ... Niagara Falls ON
Daedalian eSolutions (1) ... Toronto ON
Dairy Queen Canada Inc. (1) ... Burlington ON
Deloitte Consulting (1) ... Toronto ON
Deloitte & Touche (1) ... Edmonton AB
Deloitte & Touche (1) ... Toronto ON
Deluxe Laboratories (1) ... Toronto ON
Department of Human Resources, Nunavut (1) ... Iqaluit NU
Department of Works, Services and Tra (1) ... St. John's NF
Deutsche Financial Services / DFS (1) ... Mississauga ON
Don Park Inc. (1) ... Toronto ON
Dorel Industries Inc. (1) ... Montréal QC
Douglas College (1) ... New Westminster BC
DuPont Canada Inc. (1) ... Mississauga ON
DY 4 Systems Inc. (1) ... Kanata ON
East Central Regional Health Authority, (1) ... Camrose AB
Enbridge Pipelines Inc. (1) ... Edmonton AB
Entourage Technology Solutions (1) ... Mississauga ON
EOTT Canada Ltd. (1) ... Calgary AB
ESBI Alberta Ltd. (1) ... Calgary AB
Essentus Inc. (1) ... Montréal QC
Exchange Solutions / ESI (1) ... Toronto ON
Extendicare (Canada) Inc. (1) ... Markham ON
Extracomm Technologies Inc. (1) ... Toronto ON
Federation of Canadian Municipalities / F (1) ... Ottawa ON
Fiesta Barbeques Limited (1) ... Brampton ON
Financial Services Commission of Ontario (1) ... Toronto ON
Financial Transactions and Reports Analys (1) ... Ottawa ON
Forest Renewal BC (1) ... Victoria BC
Frank Russell Company Canada Limited (1) ... Toronto ON
Fraser Institute, The (1) ... Vancouver BC
Fraser Valley Regional Library / FVRL (1) ... Abbotsford BC
FreeBalance Inc. (1) ... Ottawa ON
Fritz Starber Inc. (1) ... Mississauga ON
Future Electronics Inc. (1) ... Pointe-Claire QC
Ganz (1) ... Woodbridge ON
GE Capital Services / GECS (1) ... Edmonton AB
GE Lighting Canada (1) ... Oakville ON
GE Syprotec Inc. (1) ... Pointe-Claire QC
Gienow Building Products Ltd. (1) ... Calgary AB
Global Thermoelectric Inc. (1) ... Calgary AB
Grande Prairie, City of (1) ... Grande Prairie AB
Grande Prairie Public School Dist (1) ... Grande Prairie AB
Grant MacEwan College, Jasper Place Cam (1) ... Edmonton AB
Griffith Laboratories Ltd. (1) ... Toronto ON
Guelph, City of (1) ... Guelph ON
Halton Healthcare Services (1) ... Oakville ON
Halton Regional Police Service / HRPS (1) ... Oakville ON
Heart and Stroke Foundation of Ontario (1) ... Toronto ON
Hepcoe Credit Union Ltd. (1) ... Toronto ON
Hi-Alta Capital Inc. (1) ... High River AB
Holland Chemical International (Canada) (1) ... Calgary AB
Home Trust Company (1) ... Hamilton ON
Home Trust Company (1) ... St. Catharines ON
Hotel Dieu Hospital (1) ... Cornwall ON
Hotel Inter-Continental Toronto (1) ... Toronto ON
Household Financial Corporation / HFC (1) ... Edmonton AB
Household Financial Corporation / HFC (1) ... Toronto ON
Hummingbird Ltd. (1) ... Toronto ON
Husky Injection Molding Systems Ltd. (1) ... Bolton ON
Husky Injection Molding Systems Ltd. (1) ... Bolton ON
Hyprotech Ltd. (1) ... Calgary AB
IKO Industries Ltd. (1) ... Brampton ON
Indeka Group, The (1) ... Oakville ON
Independent Brokerage Group, The (1) ... Vancouver BC
Information Services Corporation of Saska (1) ... Regina SK
Infowave Software, Inc. (1) ... Burnaby BC
ING Canada (1) ... Toronto ON
Insurance Bureau of Canada / IBC (1) ... Toronto ON
Insurance Corporation of BC / IC (1) ... North Vancouver BC
Integrated Production Services Ltd. / IP (1) ... Calgary AB
Intuit Canada Limited (1) ... Edmonton AB
Intuit GreenPoint (1) ... Calgary AB
Investors Group (1) ... Winnipeg MB
IR Security & Safety (1) ... Mississauga ON
Ivanhoe Cambridge (1) ... Toronto ON
Ivanhoe Cambridge (1) ... Montréal QC
Jewish Eldercare Centre, The (1) ... Montréal QC
John Wiley & Sons, Inc. (1) ... Toronto ON
Kenaidan Contracting Ltd. (1) ... Mississauga ON
Kingston, Corporation of the City of (1) ... Kingston ON
Kwantlen University College (1) ... Surrey BC
Lakeridge Health Corporation (1) ... Oshawa ON
Langley, City of (1) ... Langley BC
Legal Aid Ontario / LAO (1) ... Toronto ON
Lester B. Pearson College of the Pacifi (1) ... Victoria BC
LifeScan Canada Ltd. (1) ... Burnaby BC
Linamar Corporation, Eston Division (1) ... Guelph ON
London Guarantee Insurance Company (1) ... Vancouver BC
Ma'mowe Capital Region, Child and Famil (1) ... Edmonton AB
Mac's Convenience Stores Inc. (1) ... Calgary AB
MacDonald Dettwiler & Associates Ltd. / (1) ... Richmond BC
MacGregors Meat & Seafood Ltd. (1) ... Toronto ON
Mackenzie Financial Corporation (1) ... Toronto ON
Mackie Moving Systems (1) ... Oshawa ON
Macleod Dixon LLP (1) ... Calgary AB
Magna International Inc. (1) ... Concord ON
Malaspina University-College, Nanaimo Ca (1) ... Nanaimo BC
Mania Technologie Canada Inc. (1) ... Toronto ON
Manitoba Agriculture and Food (1) ... Winnipeg MB
Manitoba Consumer & Corporate Affairs / (1) ... Winnipeg MB
Manitoba Intergovernmental Affairs (1) ... Winnipeg MB
Manitoba Transportation & Government Se (1) ... Thompson MB
Manulife Financial Corporation (1) ... Waterloo ON
ManulifeDirect (1) ... Toronto ON
Mastech Canada (1) ... Mississauga ON
Matrox Electronic Systems Ltd. (1) ... Dorval QC
MDS Metro Laboratory Services (1) ... Burnaby BC
MDS Nordion (1) ... Kanata ON
Med-Eng Systems Inc. (1) ... Ottawa ON
Medicine Hat College (1) ... Medicine Hat AB
MemberCARE Financial Services (1) ... Burlington ON
MemberWorks Canada Corporation (1) ... Montréal QC
Merck Frosst Canada & Co. / Merck (1) ... Pointe-Claire QC
Merit Kitchens (1) ... Surrey BC
MessagingDirect Ltd. (1) ... Edmonton AB
Metro Credit Union / MCU (1) ... Toronto ON
Metropolitan Hotel Toronto (1) ... Toronto ON
Micrologix Biotech Inc. (1) ... Vancouver BC
Ministry of Advanced Education, Trainin (1) ... Victoria BC
Ministry of Agriculture, Food and Rural A (1) ... Guelph ON
Ministry of Children and Family Develo (1) ... Vancouver BC
Ministry of Children and Family Developme (1) ... Surrey BC
Ministry of Children and Family Develop (1) ... Kamloops BC
Ministry of Children and Family Develop (1) ... Kamloops BC
Ministry of Children and Family Developm (1) ... Kelowna BC
Ministry of Children and Family Develo (1) ... Cranbrook BC
Ministry of Citizenship, Culture and Rec (1) ... Toronto ON
Ministry of Community and Social Service (1) ... Sudbury ON
Ministry of Community and Social Servi (1) ... North Bay ON
Ministry of Community and Social Service (1) ... Toronto ON
Ministry of Community and Social Services (1) ... London ON
Ministry of Community and Social Services (1) ... London ON
Ministry of Community and Social Service (1) ... Toronto ON
Ministry of Energy and Mines, BC (1) ... Victoria BC
Ministry of Finance, Ontario (1) ... Toronto ON
Ministry of Forests, BC (Vanderhoof D (1) ... Vanderhoof BC
Ministry of Health and Long-Term Care, On (1) ... London ON
Ministry of Health and Long-Term Care, O (1) ... Toronto ON
Ministry of Health and Long-Term Care, O (1) ... Toronto ON
Ministry of Multiculturalism and Immigr (1) ... Victoria BC
Ministry of Natural Resources, (1) ... Sault Ste. Marie ON
Ministry of Natural Resources, Ontario (F (1) ... Garson ON
Ministry of the Attorney General, Ontari (1) ... Toronto ON
Ministry of the Attorney General, Ontari (1) ... Toronto ON
Ministry of the Environment, Ontario (Dr (1) ... Toronto ON
Ministry of the Environment, Ontario (En (1) ... Toronto ON
Ministry of Tourism, Culture and Recreat (1) ... Toronto ON
Ministry of Transportation, Ontario (1) ... Thunder Bay ON
Mission, District of (1) ... Mission BC
Momentous.ca Corporation (1) ... Nepean ON

FINANCE (Cont.)

MOSAID Technologies Inc. (1) .... Kanata ON
Mount Pleasant Group of Cemeteries (1) .... Toronto ON
Nanometrics Inc. (1) .... Kanata ON
Nanowave Technologies Inc. (1) .... Toronto ON
National Arts Centre / NAC (1) .... Ottawa ON
National Life Assurance Company of Canad (1) .... Toronto ON
National Research Council Canada / NRC (1) .... Winnipeg MB
National Research Council Canada / NRC (1) .... Ottawa ON
Nature Trust of British Columbia (1) .... North Vancouver BC
NetNation Communications, Inc. (1) .... Vancouver BC
Niagara Credit Union Limited (1) .... St. Catharines ON
Nor Baker Inc. (1) .... Newmarket ON
North Grenville, Township of (1) .... Kemptville ON
North Okanagan Health Region / NOHR (1) .... Armstrong BC
North Okanagan, Regional District of (1) .... Coldstream BC
Northeast Mental Health Centre / NEMHC (1) .... Sudbury ON
Northwestel Inc. (1) .... Whitehorse YT
NPD Group Canada, Corp., The (1) .... Toronto ON
NRX Global Corp. (1) .... Toronto ON
Office of the Auditor General of Canada (1) .... Ottawa ON
Okanagan University College / OUC (1) .... Kelowna BC
Ontario Lottery and Gaming Corporation / (1) .... Toronto ON
Ontario March of Dimes (1) .... Toronto ON
Ontario Securities Commission / OSC (1) .... Toronto ON
Onvia.com (1) .... Vancouver BC
Open Text Corporation (1) .... Waterloo ON
Optech Inc. (1) .... Toronto ON
Ottawa Salus Corporation (1) .... Ottawa ON
Owen Sound, City of (1) .... Owen Sound ON
Oxford Properties Group Inc. (1) .... Toronto ON
Patheon Inc. (1) .... Mississauga ON
Peerless Clothing Inc. (1) .... Montréal QC
Perley and Rideau Veterans' Health Centre (1) ...... Ottawa ON
Peterborough, County of (1) .... Peterborough ON
Petro-Canada (1) .... Oakville ON
Pika Technologies Inc. (1) .... Kanata ON
Placer Dome Inc. (1) .... Vancouver BC
PMC-Sierra, Inc. (1) .... Burnaby BC
Positron Public Safety Systems Inc. (1) .... Montréal QC
PricewaterhouseCoopers, Business Process (1) .... Calgary AB
Prime Minister's Office (1) .... Ottawa ON
Primerica Financial Services (Canada) (1) .... Mississauga ON
Progestic International Inc. (1) .... Ottawa ON
Provincial Auditor's Office, Manitoba (1) .... Winnipeg MB
Public Service Commission of Canada, B (1) .... Vancouver BC
Public Service Commission of Canada, Exec (1) .... Ottawa ON
Public Service Commission of Canada, (1) .... St. John's NF
Public Service Commission of Canada, Nov (1) ...... Halifax NS
Public Service Commission of Canada, Ont (1) .... Toronto ON
Public Service Commission of Canada, Qu (1) .... Montréal QC
Public Service Commission of Canada, (1) .... Whitehorse YT
Purdy's Chocolates (1) .... Vancouver BC
QLT Inc. (1) .... Vancouver BC
Quality Goods IMD Inc. (1) .... St-Laurent QC
Queensway-Carleton Hospital (1) .... Nepean ON
Raytheon Systems Canada Ltd. (1) .... Waterloo ON
RCI Capital Group Inc. (1) .... Vancouver BC
Red Deer, City of (1) .... Red Deer AB
Red Deer College (1) .... Red Deer AB
Regina, City of (1) .... Regina SK
Regional Health Authority 5 (1) .... Drumheller AB
Richmond Hill, Town of (1) .... Richmond Hill ON
RioCan Real Estate Investment Trust (1) .... Toronto ON
Riverdale Hospital, The (1) .... Toronto ON
Riverside School Board (1) .... St-Lambert QC
Rogers Cable Inc. (1) .... Toronto ON
Rogers Media, Publishing (1) .... Toronto ON
Rolls-Royce Canada Ltd. (1) .... Lachine QC
Roots Canada Ltd. (1) .... Toronto ON
RoundHeaven Communications Canada Inc. (1) ...... Vancouver BC
Royal Bank Financial Group (1) .... Vancouver BC
Russel Metals Inc. (1) .... Mississauga ON
Ryan, Lamontagne & Associates (1) .... Ottawa ON
Saint Elizabeth Health Care (1) .... Markham ON
Samtack (1) .... Toronto ON
Sault Area Hospitals (1) .... Sault Ste. Marie ON
SBR International (1) .... Toronto ON

Scholarship Consultants of North Ame (1) .... Mississauga ON
School District #40 (New Westmin (1) .... New Westminster BC
Science Alberta Foundation (1) .... Calgary AB
Semotus Systems Corporation (1) .... Vancouver BC
SEN Community Health Care (1) .... Hamilton ON
Serco Facilities Management Inc. (1) .... Goose Bay NF
ShawCor Ltd. (1) .... Toronto ON
Shred-it (1) .... Oakville ON
Siemens Canada Ltd. (1) .... Mississauga ON
Snap-On Tools of Canada Ltd. (1) .... Mississauga ON
Sobeys Inc. (1) .... Mississauga ON
Social Research and Demonstration Corpora (1) .... Ottawa ON
Soroc Technology Inc. (1) .... Woodbridge ON
Southern Alberta Institute of Technology (1) .... Calgary AB
SpaceBridge Networks Corporation (1) .... Hull QC
St. Joseph's Healthcare Hamilton (1) .... Hamilton ON
Standard & Poor's (1) .... Toronto ON
Staples Business Depot Ltd. (1) .... Markham ON
State Street Canada (1) .... Montréal QC
Stikeman Elliott (1) .... Toronto ON
Stream International (1) .... Belleville ON
Sun Life Financial (1) .... Vancouver BC
Suncor Energy Inc. (1) .... Calgary AB
Superintendent of Financial Institutions (1) .... Ottawa ON
Syndesis Limited (1) .... Richmond Hill ON
Taro Pharmaceuticals Inc. (1) .... Bramalea ON
Teekay Shipping Corp. (1) .... Vancouver BC
Telus Corporation (1) .... Burnaby BC
Thrifty Foods (1) .... Saanichton BC
Tirecraft Auto Centers Ltd. (1) .... Sherwood Park AB
TLC Laser Eye Centers (1) .... Mississauga ON
Tractel Ltd., Swingstage Division (1) .... Toronto ON
Trail Appliances Ltd. (1) .... Calgary AB
Trans Mountain Pipe Line Company Ltd. (1) .... Calgary AB
Trent University (1) .... Peterborough ON
Union of Canadian Transportation Employee (1) ...... Ottawa ON
University College of the Fraser Vall (1) .... Abbotsford BC
University of Alberta (1) .... Edmonton AB
University of Toronto, Operations & Serv (1) .... Toronto ON
University of Waterloo (1) .... Waterloo ON
VA Tech Ferranti-Packard Transfor (1) .... St. Catharines ON
Valcom Limited (Ottawa) (1) .... Ottawa ON
Valvoline Canada Ltd. (1) .... Mississauga ON
Vancouver, City of (1) .... Vancouver BC
Vancouver City Savings Credit Union / (1) .... Vancouver BC
Vancouver Community College / VCC (1) .... Vancouver BC
Vancouver International Airport Authori (1) .... Richmond BC
Vansco Electronics Ltd. (1) .... Winnipeg MB
VHA Home HealthCare (1) .... Toronto ON
Victoria, City of (1) .... Victoria BC
Wal-Mart Canada Inc. (1) .... Mississauga ON
Waterloo North Hydro Inc. (1) .... Waterloo ON
Waterloo Region District School Board (1) .... Kitchener ON
Weatherford Canada Ltd. (1) .... Nisku AB
Wescam (1) .... Burlington ON
Wesco Distribution Canada Inc. (1) .... Burnaby BC
Wesco Distribution Canada Inc. (1) .... Markham ON
West Lincoln Memorial Hospital (1) .... Grimsby ON
WestJet Airlines Ltd. (1) .... Calgary AB
Weyerhaeuser Company Limited (1) .... Vancouver BC
Whistler Blackcomb / Intrawest (1) .... Whistler BC
White Spot Limited (1) .... Vancouver BC
Workers' Compensation Board, Alberta (1) .... Edmonton AB
Workplace Safety & Insurance Appeals Tri (1) .... Toronto ON
World Heart Corporation (1) .... Ottawa ON
Xerox Canada Ltd. (1) .... Mississauga ON
York, The Regional Municipality of (1) .... Newmarket ON
Yukon Public Service Commission (1) .... Whitehorse YT

FORESTRY

See also: Pulp & Paper, Govt./Nonprofit.

Ministry of Natural Resources (9 positions) ..... Sault Ste. Marie ON
Alberta Environment (6) .... Edmonton AB
Ministry of Forests, BC (North Coa (6) .... Prince Rupert BC
Alberta Sustainable Resource Developmen (5) .... Edmonton AB
Ministry of Forests, BC (Fort St. (5) .... Fort St. James BC
Ministry of Forests, BC (Nelson Dist (4) .... Fort Nelson BC

For descriptions of the occupational categories used in this index, see page 458.

FORESTRY (Cont.)

Ministry of Forests, BC (Research Branc (4) .... Victoria BC
Ministry of Natural Resources, (4) .... Sault Ste. Marie ON
Ministry of Natural Resources, (4) .... Sault Ste. Marie ON
Forest Practices Board (3) .... Victoria BC
Houston Forest Products Company (3) .... Houston BC
Ministry of Forests, BC (Chilcotin (3) .... Alexis Creek BC
Ministry of Forests, BC (Prince Ge (3) .... Prince George BC
Ministry of Forests, BC (Prince Rupert (3) .... Smithers BC
Ministry of Water, Land and Air Protect (3) .... Victoria BC
Alberta Sustainable Resource Development (2) .... Calgary AB
Footner Forest Products Ltd. (2) .... High Level AB
Forintek Canada Corp. (2) .... Vancouver BC
Geographic Dynamics Corp. / GDC (2) .... Edmonton AB
Hayes Forest Service Ltd. (2) .... Duncan BC
Husky Lumber Group / Commonwealth Plywood (2) ...... Ottawa ON
Markham, Corporation of the Town of (2) .... Markham ON
Ministry of Forests, BC (Cariboo R (2) .... Williams Lake BC
Ministry of Forests, BC (Kamloops Regio (2) .... Kamloops BC
Ministry of Forests, BC (Prince Ge (2) .... Prince George BC
Ministry of Forests, BC (Quesnel Distric (2) .... Quesnel BC
Ministry of Natural Resources, Ontario (2) .... Cochrane ON
Public Service Commission of Canada, BC (2) .... Victoria BC
Sandwell Engineering Inc. (2) .... Vancouver BC
Saskatchewan Institute of Applied (2) .... Prince Albert SK
Terminal Forest Products Limited (2) .... Richmond BC
Alberta Agriculture, Food & Rural Devel (1) .... Edmonton AB
Alberta Environment (1) .... Calgary AB
Alberta Human Resources and Employment (1) ...... McLennan AB
Brampton, City of (1) .... Brampton ON
Calgary, City of (1) .... Calgary AB
Canpar Industries (1) .... Grand Forks BC
Department of Municipal and Provincia (1) .... St. John's NF
Forestry Corp., The (1) .... Edmonton AB
Lakehead University (1) .... Thunder Bay ON
Manitoba Conservation (1) .... Winnipeg MB
Ministry of Forests, BC (1) .... Fort St. John BC
Ministry of Forests, BC (Vanderhoof D (1) .... Vanderhoof BC
Ministry of Natural Resources, Onta (1) .... Fort Frances ON
Ministry of Natural Resources, Ontario (1) .... Wawa ON
Ministry of Natural Resources, Ontario (1) .... Aurora ON
Ministry of Natural Resources, Ontario (F (1) .... Dryden ON
Ministry of Natural Resources, O (1) .... South Porcupine ON
Mississauga, City of (1) .... Mississauga ON
Mitsubishi Canada Ltd. (1) .... Vancouver BC
P.J. White Hardwoods Ltd. (1) .... Edmonton AB
Peel Lumber (1) .... Milton ON
Perceptron Inc., Forest Products Divi (1) .... Parksville BC
Public Service Commission of Canada, Al (1) .... Edmonton AB
Public Service Commission of Canada, Exec (1) .... Ottawa ON
Public Service Commission of Canada, New (1) .... Moncton NB
Public Service Commission of Canada, Sask (1) .... Regina SK
Public Service Commission of Canada, (1) .... Whitehorse YT
Slocan Group, Tackama Division (1) .... Fort Nelson BC
SMED International Inc. (1) .... Calgary AB
Surrey, City of (1) .... Surrey BC
University of Northern British Col (1) .... Prince George BC
Weyerhaeuser Company Limited (1) .... Vancouver BC
Weyerhaeuser Company Limited, Dryden Mill (1) ..:..... Dryden ON

FRANCHISING

See also: Retail, Hospitality, Real Estate.

Dairy Queen Canada Inc. (3 positions) .... Burlington ON
TDL Group Ltd., The (3) .... Oakville ON
Apple Auto Glass (1) .... Burnaby BC
Canada Bread Company Ltd. (1) .... Edmonton AB
Dailybread (1) .... Toronto ON
Days Inn (1) .... Toronto ON
Mac's Convenience Stores Inc. (1) .... Calgary AB
Mac's Convenience Stores Inc. (1) .... Toronto ON

GEOLOGY/GEOGRAPHY

See also: Mining, Oil & Gas, Engineering, Scientific.

EBA Engineering Consultants Ltd. (9 positions) .... Edmonton AB
McElhanney Group Ltd., The (9) .... Vancouver BC
Anadarko Canada Corporation (7) .... Calgary AB
Alberta Energy and Utilities Board / EUB (6) .... Calgary AB
AMEC Earth & Environmental Ltd. (6) .... Calgary AB
Arcis Corporation (6) .... Calgary AB
DMTI Spatial Inc. (6) .... Markham ON
Optech Inc. (6) .... Toronto ON
Alberta Energy Company Ltd. / AEC (5) .... Calgary AB
Axys Environmental Consulting Ltd. (5) .... Calgary AB
Challenger Geomatics Ltd. (5) .... Calgary AB
Fugro Airborne Surveys (5) .... Ottawa ON
Sander Geophysics Ltd. / SGL (5) .... Ottawa ON
Shell Canada Limited (5) .... Calgary AB
Trow Consulting Engineers Ltd. (5) .... Brampton ON
Alberta Energy Company Ltd. / AEC (4) .... Calgary AB
Burlington Resources Canada Energy Ltd. (4) .... Calgary AB
Cadastral Group Inc., The (4) .... Calgary AB
Ministry of Northern Development and Min (4) .... Sudbury ON
Ministry of Water, Land and Air Protect (4) .... Victoria BC
MRF Geosystems Corporation (4) .... Calgary AB
PanCanadian Petroleum Ltd. (4) .... Calgary AB
Veritas GeoServices (4) .... Calgary AB
Alberta Energy (3) .... Edmonton AB
Alberta Environment (3) .... Edmonton AB
Calgary, City of (3) .... Calgary AB
CGG Canada Services Ltd. (3) .... Calgary AB
Crape Geomatics Corporation (3) .... Calgary AB
Golder Associates Ltd. (3) .... Calgary AB
Information Services Corporation of Saska (3) .... Regina SK
Intermap Technologies (3) .... Nepean ON
Jacques Whitford Environment Ltd. (3) .... Calgary AB
Kelman Technologies Inc. / KTI (3) .... Calgary AB
Land Data Technologies Inc. / LDT (3) .... Edmonton AB
Ministry of Transportation, Ontario (3) .... Thunder Bay ON
Ministry of Transportation, Ontario (3) ·:.............. North Bay ON
Mississauga, City of (3) .... Mississauga ON
Paradigm Geophysical (3) .... Calgary AB
Powertech Labs Inc. (3) .... Surrey BC
Schlumberger Canada Limited (3) .... Calgary AB
Sproule Associates Limited (3) .... Calgary AB
Trow Consulting Engineers Ltd. (3) .... Cambridge ON
UMA Engineering Ltd. (3) .... Calgary AB
University of Northern British Col (3) .... Prince George BC
Alberta Sustainable Resource Developmen (2) .... Edmonton AB
Anderson Exploration Ltd. / AXL (2) .... Calgary AB
Applanix Corp. (2) .... Richmond Hill ON
BC Hydro (2) .... Vancouver BC
Brampton, City of (2) .... Brampton ON
Clifton Associates Ltd. (2) .... Calgary AB
Department of Mines and Energy, Newfo (2) .... St. John's NF
Eagle Navigation Systems Inc. (2) .... Calgary AB
ESRI Canada Ltd. (2) .... Calgary AB
Falconbridge Ltd. (2) .... Toronto ON
Geomodeling Research Corp. (2) .... Calgary AB
Husky Oil Operations Ltd. (2) .... Calgary AB
Inspec-Sol Inc. (2) .... Montréal QC
Jacques Whitford Environment Ltd. (2) .... Markham ON
Jacques Whitford Environment Ltd. (2) .... Ottawa ON
Leica Geosystems (2) .... Toronto ON
Lethbridge Community College / LCC (2) .... Lethbridge AB
Markham, Corporation of the Town of (2) .... Markham ON
Ministry of Energy and Mines, BC (2) .... Victoria BC
Ministry of Transportation, Ontario (2) .... Kingston ON
Paramount Resources Ltd. (2) .... Calgary AB
Pengrowth Management Ltd. / PML (2) .... Calgary AB
Prince George, City of (2) .... Prince George BC
Public Service Commission of Canada, Al (2) .... Edmonton AB
Public Service Commission of Canada, Onta (2) .... Ottawa ON
Sherritt International Corp. (2) .... Fort Saskatchewan AB
Trow Consulting Engineers Ltd. (2) .... London ON
UMA Engineering Ltd. (2) .... Edmonton AB
United Oil & Gas Consulting Ltd. (2) .... Calgary AB
Alberta Government Services (1) .... Edmonton AB
Alberta Municipal Affairs (1) .... Edmonton AB
Alberta Sustainable Resource Development (1) .... Calgary AB
Albian Sands Energy Inc. (1) .... Fort McMurray AB

GEOLOGY/GEOGRAPHY (Cont.)

AMEC Earth & Environmental Ltd. (1) .... Edmonton AB
Armbro Materials Engineering Corporatio (1) .... Brampton ON
Atlantis Scientific Inc. (1) .... Nepean ON
Axys Group (1) .... Sidney BC
Baytex Energy Ltd. (1) .... Calgary AB
Calgary Board of Education, The (1) .... Calgary AB
Canadian Natural Resources Limited / CNR (1) .... Calgary AB
Canadian Survey Equipment Ltd. / Cansel (1) .... Edmonton AB
Canadian Survey Equipment Ltd. / Cansel (1) .... Ottawa ON
Conestoga-Rovers & Associates Limited / (1) .... Waterloo ON
Dalhousie University, Department of Civi (1) .... Halifax NS
Department of Human Resources, Nunavut (1) .... Igloolik NU
Earth Signal Processing Ltd. (1) .... Calgary AB
Environmental Assessment Office, BC (1) .... Victoria BC
EPCOR Utilities Inc. (1) .... Edmonton AB
Fekete Associates Inc. (1) .... Calgary AB
Focus Corporation Ltd., The (1) .... Edmonton AB
Forestry Corp., The (1) .... Edmonton AB
Geographic Dynamics Corp. / GDC (1) .... Edmonton AB
Greater Vancouver Regional District / GV (1) .... Burnaby BC
Group Telecom (1) .... Toronto ON
Hubbell Canada Inc. (1) .... Pickering ON
Inco Ltd. (1) .... Toronto ON
Islands Trust (1) .... Victoria BC
Jacques Whitford Environment Ltd. (1) .... Burnaby BC
Jacques Whitford Environment Ltd. (1) .... Halifax NS
Kestrel Data (Canada) Limited (1) .... Calgary AB
Lafarge Construction Materials (1) .... Concord ON
Lakehead University (1) .... Thunder Bay ON
Landmark Graphics (1) .... Calgary AB
Manitoba Conservation (1) .... Winnipeg MB
Manitoba Industry, Trades and Mines / I (1) .... Winnipeg MB
Manitoba Transportation & Government Se (1) .... Winnipeg MB
Marshall Macklin Monaghan Limited (1) .... Thornhill ON
Martin Newby Consulting Ltd. (1) .... Calgary AB
Ministry of Agriculture, Food and Fishe (1) .... Victoria BC
Ministry of Agriculture, Food and Rural A (1) .... Guelph ON
Ministry of Forests, BC (1) .... Fort St. John BC
Ministry of Forests, BC (Kamloops Regio (1) .... Kamloops BC
Ministry of Forests, BC (North Coa (1) .... Prince Rupert BC
Ministry of Natural Resources, Ontario (1) .... Dryden ON
Ministry of Natural Resources, (1) .... Sault Ste. Marie ON
Ministry of Natural Resources, Ontario (1) .... Aylmer ON
Ministry of Natural Resources, Ontario (1) .... Toronto ON
Ministry of Natural Resources, Onta (1) .... Peterborough ON
Ministry of Natural Resources, Onta (1) .... Peterborough ON
Ministry of the Attorney General, BC (V (1) .... Victoria BC
Ministry of the Environment, Ontario (1) .... Thunder Bay ON
Ministry of the Solicitor General, Ontar (1) .... Orillia ON
Ministry of Transportation, Ontar (1) .... St. Catharines ON
NAL Resources Management Ltd. (1) .... Calgary AB
Nexen Inc. (1) .... Calgary AB
Novatel Inc. (1) .... Calgary AB
Oil and Gas Commission, BC (1) .... Victoria BC
Okanagan University College / OUC (1) .... Kelowna BC
Peel, The Regional Municipality of (1) .... Brampton ON
Peto MacCallum Ltd. (1) .... Toronto ON
Pizza Pizza Limited (1) .... Toronto ON
Public Service Commission of Canada, BC (1) .... Victoria BC
Public Service Commission of Canada, New (1) .... Moncton NB
Pure Technologies Inc. (1) .... Calgary AB
Radarsat International (1) .... Richmond BC
Rio Alto Exploration Ltd. (1) .... Calgary AB
Royal Bank Financial Group (1) .... Toronto ON
Saskatchewan Research Council / SRC (1) .... Saskatoon SK
Southern Alberta Institute of Technology (1) .... Calgary AB
St. Clement's School (1) .... Toronto ON
Stantec Consulting Ltd. (1) .... Kitchener ON
Sturgeon County (1) .... Morinville AB
Suncor Energy Inc., Oil Sands (1) .... Fort McMurray AB
Syncrude Canada Ltd. (1) .... Fort McMurray AB
Talisman Energy Inc. (1) .... Calgary AB
Triathlon (1) .... Richmond BC
Trow Consulting Engineers Ltd. (1) .... Thunder Bay ON
Trow Consulting Engineers Ltd. (1) .... Nepean ON
Vancouver, City of (1) .... Vancouver BC
Vaughan, City of (1) .... Vaughan ON
Wardrop Engineering Inc. (1) .... Mississauga ON
Weldwood of Canada Limited (1) .... Vancouver BC

GOVT./NONPROFIT

See also: Education, Health/Medical, International, Arts & Culture.

Ministry of Community and Social Service (16 positions) Toronto ON
Alberta Municipal Affairs (14) .... Edmonton AB
Ministry of Municipal Affairs and Housin (14) .... Toronto ON
Ministry of Education / Ministry of Trai (13) .... Toronto ON
Ministry of the Environment, Ontario (13) .... Toronto ON
Ministry of Northern Development and Min (12) .... Sudbury ON
Calgary, City of (11) .... Calgary AB
Ministry of Citizenship, Culture and Rec (11) .... Toronto ON
Ministry of the Attorney General, BC (V (11) .... Victoria BC
Ministry of Economic Development and Tra (10) .... Toronto ON
Ministry of Health and Long-Term Care, O (10) .... Toronto ON
Alberta Government Services (9) .... Edmonton AB
Canadian Cancer Society / CCS (9) .... Vancouver BC
Management Board Secretariat (9) .... Toronto ON
Public Service Commission of Canada, Onta (8) .... Ottawa ON
Surrey, City of (8) .... Surrey BC
Alberta Community Development (7) .... Edmonton AB
Department of Human Resources, Nunavut (7) .... Iqaluit NU
Halton, The Regional Municipality of (7) .... Oakville ON
Manitoba Family Services and Housing (7) .... Winnipeg MB
Alberta Learning (6) .... Edmonton AB
Manitoba Intergovernmental Affairs (6) .... Winnipeg MB
Mississauga, City of (6) .... Mississauga ON
Alberta Economic Development (5) .... Edmonton AB
Alberta International and Intergovernme (5) .... Edmonton AB
Brantford, Corporation of the City of (5) .... Brantford ON
Department of Municipal and Provincia (5) .... St. John's NF
Heart and Stroke Foundation of Ontario (5) .... Toronto ON
Ministry of Transportation, Ontar (5) .... St. Catharines ON
Prince George, City of (5) .... Prince George BC
York, The Regional Municipality of (5) .... Newmarket ON
Alberta Corporate Services Centre (4) .... Edmonton AB
Alberta Health and Wellness (4) .... Edmonton AB
Credit Valley Hospital, The (4) .... Mississauga ON
Islands Trust (4) .... Victoria BC
Manitoba Aboriginal & Northern Affairs (4) .... Winnipeg MB
Manitoba Justice / Culture, Heritage an (4) .... Winnipeg MB
Manitoba Transportation & Government Se (4) .... Winnipeg MB
Maple Ridge, District of (4) .... Maple Ridge BC
Medicine Hat, City of (4) .... Medicine Hat AB
Ministry of Children and Family Develop (4) .... Victoria BC
Ministry of Community and Social Ser (4) .... Thunder Bay ON
Ministry of Consumer and Business Servic (4) .... Toronto ON
Ministry of the Solicitor General, Ontar (4) .... Orillia ON
Ministry of Tourism, Culture and Recreat (4) .... Toronto ON
Ministry of Water, Land and Air Protect (4) .... Victoria BC
Ontario Native Affairs Secretariat / ONA (4) .... Toronto ON
Public Service Commission of Canada, Exec (4) .... Ottawa ON
Alberta Energy (3) .... Edmonton AB
Alberta Justice (3) .... Edmonton AB
Big Sisters and Big Brothers of Calgary (3) .... Calgary AB
Brampton, City of (3) .... Brampton ON
Brooks, Town of (3) .... Brooks AB
Burlington, City of (3) .... Burlington ON
Calgary Immigrant Aid Society (3) .... Calgary AB
Export Development Corporation / EDC (3) .... Ottawa ON
Federation CJA (3) .... Montréal QC
Jewish Community Centre of Greater Van (3) .... Vancouver BC
London, City of (3) .... London ON
Manitoba Conservation (3) .... Winnipeg MB
Markham, Corporation of the Town of (3) .... Markham ON
McCreary Centre Society, The (3) .... Burnaby BC
Ministry of Aboriginal Affairs, BC (3) .... Victoria BC
Ministry of Community and Social Service (3) .... Toronto ON
Ministry of Energy and Mines, BC (3) .... Victoria BC
Ministry of Finance, BC (3) .... Victoria BC
Ministry of Finance, Ontario (3) .... Toronto ON
Ministry of Finance, Ontario (3) .... Toronto ON
Ministry of Health and Long-Term Care, (3) .... Kingston ON
Ministry of Health and Long-Term Care, (3) .... Kingston ON
Ministry of Multiculturalism and Immigr (3) .... Victoria BC
Ministry of Tourism, Culture and Recreat (3) .... Toronto ON
Mission Services of Hamilton (3) .... Hamilton ON
Nature Conservancy of Canada, The / NCC (3) .... Guelph ON
Peel, The Regional Municipality of (3) .... Brampton ON
Prince Edward, County of (3) .... Picton ON

For descriptions of the occupational categories used in this index, see page 458.

GOVT./NONPROFIT (Cont.)

Public Interest Advocacy Centre / PIAC (3) .... Ottawa ON
Public Service Commission of Canada, Al (3) .... Edmonton AB
Richmond Hill, Town of (3) .... Richmond Hill ON
Rocky View No. 44, Municipal District of (3) .... Calgary AB
Social Research and Demonstration Corpora (3) .... Ottawa ON
Standards Council of Canada / SCC (3) .... Ottawa ON
United Nations Children's Fund / UNICEF (3) .... Toronto ON
Vancouver Aboriginal Child & Family Se (3) .... Vancouver BC
Abbotsford, City of (2) .... Abbotsford BC
Alberta Agriculture, Food & Rural Devel (2) .... Edmonton AB
Alberta Corporate Service Centre (2) .... Coaldale AB
Alberta Human Resources and Employment (2) .... Edmonton AB
Alberta Infrastructure & Transportation (2) .... Edmonton AB
Alberta Infrastructure & Transportation (2) .... Edmonton AB
Alberta Innovation & Science (2) .... Edmonton AB
Allendale (2) .... Milton ON
Barrie, City of (2) .... Barrie ON
Caledon, Town of (2) .... Caledon East ON
Canada Customs and Revenue Agency / CCRA (2) ...... Ottawa ON
Canadian National Institute for the Blin (2) .... Toronto ON
Conference Board of Canada, The (2) .... Ottawa ON
Coquitlam, City of (2) .... Coquitlam BC
Durham, The Regional Municipality of (2) .... Whitby ON
Easter Seal Society, Ontario (2) .... Toronto ON
Edmonton, City of (2) .... Edmonton AB
Edmonton Community Foundation (2) .... Edmonton AB
Financial Services Commission of Ontario (2) .... Toronto ON
Focus Foundation of BC (2) .... Vancouver BC
Good Shepherd Ministries (2) .... Toronto ON
Hillfield-Strathallan College (2) .... Hamilton ON
Hospital for Sick Children, The (2) .... Toronto ON
Humane Society of Ottawa-Carleton / HSOC (2) .... Ottawa ON
Huntington Society of Canada (2) .... Kitchener ON
Information Services Corporation of Saska (2) .... Regina SK
Kamloops, City of (2) .... Kamloops BC
Kingston and District Immigrant Service (2) .... Kingston ON
Legislative Assembly of Ontario, Office (2) .... Toronto ON
Ministry of Agriculture, Food and Fishe (2) .... Victoria BC
Ministry of Agriculture, Food and Rural A (2) .... Guelph ON
Ministry of Employment and Investment, (2) .... Victoria BC
Ministry of Labour, Ontario (2) .... Toronto ON
Ministry of Natural Resources, (2) .... Sault Ste. Marie ON
Ministry of Natural Resources, Ont (2) .... Kirkland Lake ON
Ministry of Natural Resources, Ontario (2) .... Cochrane ON
Ministry of Natural Resources, Ontario (2) .... Guelph ON
Ministry of Natural Resources, Ontario (2) .... Geraldton ON
Ministry of the Attorney General, Ontari (2) .... Toronto ON
Ministry of the Attorney General, Ontari (2) .... Toronto ON
Ministry of the Environment, Ontario (In (2) .... Toronto ON
Ministry of the Solicitor General, Ontar (2) .... Toronto ON
Ministry of the Solicitor General, Ontar (2) .... Toronto ON
Ministry of Transportation, Ontario (2) .... Toronto ON
Muttart Foundation, The (2) .... Edmonton AB
Nanaimo, City of (2) .... Nanaimo BC
Northern Alberta Development Council (2) .... Peace River AB
Northern Rockies Regional District (2) .... Fort Nelson BC
Oakville, Corporation of the Town of (2) .... Oakville ON
Ontario HIV Treatment Network / OHTN (2) .... Toronto ON
Ontario Human Rights Commission / OHRC (2) .... Toronto ON
Peel Children's Centre (2) .... Mississauga ON
Port Colborne, City of (2) .... Port Colborne ON
Port Moody, City of (2) .... Port Moody BC
Public Service Commission of Canada, New (2) .... Moncton NB
Public Service Commission of Canada, Nov (2) .... Halifax NS
Public Service Commission of Canada, Sask (2) .... Regina SK
Public Service Commission of Canada, (2) .... Whitehorse YT
Public Service Commission, PEI (2) .... Charlottetown PE
Red Deer College (2) .... Red Deer AB
Regina, City of (2) .... Regina SK
Saskatchewan Liquor and Gaming Authority (2) .... Regina SK
Sheridan College (2) .... Oakville ON
Squamish-Lillooet Regional District / (2) .... Pemberton BC
Supportive Housing in Peel Foundatio (2) .... Mississauga ON
Toronto, City of (2) .... Toronto ON
Toronto Humane Society (2) .... Toronto ON
United Way / Centraide Ottawa (2) .... Nepean ON
University of Western Ontario (2) .... London ON
Waterloo, City of (2) .... Waterloo ON
Waterloo, The Regional Municipality of (2) .... Kitchener ON

West Park Healthcare Centre (2) .... Toronto ON
Whitby, Town of (2) .... Whitby ON
Winnipeg, City of (Planning, Property a (2) .... Winnipeg MB
Yee Hong Community Wellness Foundation (2) .... Toronto ON
YMCA of Greater Vancouver (2) .... Burnaby BC
YMCA-YWCA, National Capital Region (2) .... Ottawa ON
Aga Khan Foundation Canada / AKFC (1) .... Ottawa ON
Alberta Alcohol and Drug Abuse Commissi (1) .... Edmonton AB
Alberta Community Development (1) .... Edmonton AB
Alberta Energy and Utilities Board / EUB (1) .... Calgary AB
Alberta Environment (1) .... Edmonton AB
Alberta Family and Social Services (1) .... Edmonton AB
Alberta Family and Social Services (1) .... Red Deer AB
Alberta Human Resources and Employment (1) .... Innisfail AB
Alcohol and Gaming Commission of Ontario (1) .... Toronto ON
Association of Universities and Colleges (1) .... Ottawa ON
Athabasca University (1) .... Athabasca AB
Banff, Town of (1) .... Banff AB
Bank of Canada (1) .... Ottawa ON
Baycrest Centre for Geriatric Care (1) .... Toronto ON
BC Hydro (1) .... Vancouver BC
Belleville, City of (1) .... Belleville ON
Black Community Resource Centre / BCRC (1) .... Montréal QC
Bosco Homes (1) .... Edmonton AB
British Columbia Assets & Land Corporat (1) .... Victoria BC
British Columbia Pharmacy Association / (1) .... Richmond BC
Brock University (1) .... St. Catharines ON
Burnaby, City of (1) .... Burnaby BC
Cabinet Office (1) .... Toronto ON
Canadian Foundation on Compulsive Gambli (1) .... Toronto ON
Canadian Hearing Society, The (1) .... Toronto ON
Canadian Medical Protective Association / (1) .... Ottawa ON
Canadian Pharmacists Association / CPhA (1) .... Ottawa ON
Casey House Hospice (1) .... Toronto ON
Chatham-Kent, Municipality of (1) .... Chatham ON
Children's Rehabilitation Centre of Esse (1) .... Windsor ON
Christian Children's Fund of Canada / CC (1) .... Toronto ON
College of the Rockies (1) .... Cranbrook BC
Consulate General of Japan, The (1) .... Toronto ON
Covenant House Vancouver (1) .... Vancouver BC
Cree Board of Health and Social Servic (1) .... Chisasibi QC
Delta, The Corporation of (1) .... Delta BC
Department of Executive, NWT (1) .... Yellowknife NT
Department of Forest Resources & Agri (1) .... St. John's NF
Department of Health and Community Se (1) .... St. John's NF
Department of Health and Social Serv (1) .... Yellowknife NT
Department of Human Resources, Nuna (1) .... Rankin Inlet NU
Department of Human Resources, Nun (1) ...... Cambridge Bay NU
Department of Tourism, Culture and Re (1) .... St. John's NF
Dillon Consulting Ltd. (1) .... Toronto ON
Ducks Unlimited Canada (1) .... Calgary AB
Federation of Canadian Municipalities / F (1) .... Ottawa ON
Fraser Valley Regional District / FVR (1) .... Chilliwack BC
Good Samaritan Society, The (1) .... Edmonton AB
Grande Prairie, City of (1) .... Grande Prairie AB
Greater Toronto Airports Authority / GTA (1) .... Toronto ON
Grey Bruce Health Services (1) .... Owen Sound ON
Guelph, City of (1) .... Guelph ON
Halton Adolescent Support Services (1) .... Burlington ON
Halton Hills, Town of (1) .... Halton Hills ON
Hamilton, City of (1) .... Hamilton ON
Information and Privacy Commissioner, On (1) .... Toronto ON
Insurance Bureau of Canada / IBC (1) .... Toronto ON
Inuit Tapirisat of Canada / ITC (1) .... Ottawa ON
John Howard Society of Canada (1) .... Kingston ON
Kawartha Lakes, Corporation of the City (1) .... Lindsay ON
Kingston, Corporation of the City of (1) .... Kingston ON
Kingston Family YMCA (1) .... Kingston ON
Kinsmen & Kinette Clubs of Canada (1) .... Cambridge ON
Kitchener, City of (1) .... Kitchener ON
Kitimat, District of (1) .... Kitimat BC
Kodak Canada Inc. (1) .... Toronto ON
Langley, City of (1) .... Langley BC
Langley, Corporation of the Township of (1) .... Langley BC
Legal Aid Ontario / LAO (1) .... Toronto ON
Limestone District School Board (1) .... Kingston ON
Liquor Distribution Branch, BC / LDB (1) .... Vancouver BC
LOFT Community Services (1) .... Toronto ON
Ma'mowe Capital Region, Child and Famil (1) .... Edmonton AB
Manitoba Labour & Immigration (1) .... Winnipeg MB
Manitoba Transportation & Government Ser (1) .... Brandon MB
Milton, Town of (1) .... Milton ON

GOVT./NONPROFIT (Cont.)

Ministry of Agriculture, Food and Rural A (1) .... Guelph ON
Ministry of Children and Family Developme (1) .... Surrey BC
Ministry of Children and Family Develo (1) .... Cranbrook BC
Ministry of Community and Social Services (1) .... Kenora ON
Ministry of Community and Social Servi (1) .... North Bay ON
Ministry of Community and Social Servi (1) .... Newmarket ON
Ministry of Community and Social Services (1) .... Ottawa ON
Ministry of Correctional Services, Ontar (1) .... Toronto ON
Ministry of Health and Long-Term Care, (1) .... Hamilton ON
Ministry of Health and Long-Term Care, O (1) .... Sudbury ON
Ministry of Health and Ministry Respons (1) .... Victoria BC
Ministry of Natural Resources, Onta (1) .... Fort Frances ON
Ministry of Natural Resources, (1) .... Sault Ste. Marie ON
Ministry of Natural Resources, Ontario (1) .... North Bay ON
Ministry of Natural Resources, Ontario (1) .... Chapleau ON
Ministry of Natural Resources, Ontario (1) .... Hearst ON
Ministry of Natural Resources, Ontario (F (1) .... Dryden ON
Ministry of Natural Resources, Onta (1) .... Peterborough ON
Ministry of Natural Resources, Ontario (1) .... Pembroke ON
Ministry of Seniors, Alberta (1) .... Edmonton AB
Ministry of Social Development and Econ (1) .... Victoria BC
Ministry of Social Development and (1) .... Prince George BC
Ministry of the Attorney General, Ontari (1) .... Toronto ON
Ministry of the Attorney General, Ontari (1) .... Toronto ON
Ministry of the Environment, Ontario (Ce (1) .... Toronto ON
Ministry of the Environment, Ontario (In (1) .... Toronto ON
Ministry of the Environment, Ontario (Lon (1) .... London ON
Ministry of the Solicitor General, Ontari (1) .... Aylmer ON
Montréal, Ville de (1) .... Montréal QC
Mountain View County (1) .... Didsbury AB
Muki Baum Association (1) .... Toronto ON
Multiple Sclerosis Society of Canada (1) .... Toronto ON
Multiple Sclerosis Society of Canada, (1) .... Vancouver BC
National Research Council Canada / NRC (1) .... Ottawa ON
Niagara, The Regional Municipality of (1) .... Thorold ON
North Bay General Hospital (1) .... North Bay ON
North Vancouver, City of (1) .... North Vancouver BC
North York General Hospital (1) .... Toronto ON
Oil and Gas Commission, BC (1) .... Victoria BC
Ontario Bar Association / OBA (1) .... Toronto ON
Ontario Clean Water Agency / OCWA (1) .... Toronto ON
Ontario Council of Alternative Businesse (1) .... Toronto ON
Ontario Heritage Foundation, Corporate S (1) .... Toronto ON
Ontario Lottery and Gaming Corporation / (1) .... Toronto ON
Ontario March of Dimes (1) .... Toronto ON
Ontario Municipal Employees Retirement S (1) .... Toronto ON
Ontario Science Centre / OSC (1) .... Toronto ON
Ontario Trillium Foundation, The (1) .... Toronto ON
Open Learning Agency / OLA (1) .... Burnaby BC
Owen Sound, City of (1) .... Owen Sound ON
Pavilion Family Resource Centre / PFR (1) .... Haileybury ON
Pearson Peacekeeping Centre / PPC (1) .... Clementsport NS
Penticton, City of (1) .... Penticton BC
Prime Minister's Office (1) .... Ottawa ON
Providence Health Care, St. Vincent's (1) .... Vancouver BC
Public Service Commission of Canada, BC (1) .... Victoria BC
Public Service Commission of Canada, Ma (1) .... Winnipeg MB
Registered Nurses Association of Ontario (1) .... Toronto ON
Richmond, City of (1) .... Richmond BC
Ridley College (1) .... St. Catharines ON
Riverdale Hospital, The (1) .... Toronto ON
Royal Ottawa Health Care Group / ROHCG (1) .... Ottawa ON
Science Alberta Foundation (1) .... Calgary AB
Simcoe, Corporation of the County of (1) .... Midhurst ON
Simon Fraser Health Region, Burnaby Hosp (1) .... Burnaby BC
Simplot Canada Limited (1) .... Brandon MB
Sir Mortimer B. Davis - Jewish General (1) .... Montréal QC
Southern Alberta Institute of Technology (1) .... Calgary AB
Spruce Grove, City of (1) .... Spruce Grove AB
St. Catharines, City of (1) .... St. Catharines ON
Street Health (1) .... Toronto ON
Sunnybrook & Women's College Health Scie (1) .... Toronto ON
Sunshine Coast Community Health Council (1) .... Sechelt BC
Trow Consulting Engineers Ltd. (1) .... Brampton ON
UMA Engineering Ltd. (1) .... Calgary AB
University of Alberta, Faculty of Nursi (1) .... Edmonton AB
University of Northern British Col (1) .... Prince George BC

University of Toronto (1) .... Toronto ON
Vancouver Art Gallery (1) .... Vancouver BC
Vancouver / Richmond Health Board (1) .... Vancouver BC
Vaughan, City of (1) .... Vaughan ON
Victorian Order of Nurses, Toronto-York (1) .... Markham ON
Victorian Order of Nurses / VON Canada (1) .... Ottawa ON
Whistler, Resort Municipality of (1) .... Whistler BC
Whitehorse, City of (1) .... Whitehorse YT
Winnipeg, City of (Public Works Departm (1) .... Winnipeg MB
Workers' Compensation Board of BC (1) .... Vancouver BC
World Federation of Hemophilia (1) .... Montréal QC
York Central Hospital (1) .... Richmond Hill ON
York Community Services / YCS (1) .... Toronto ON

GRAPHIC ARTS

See also: Multimedia, Printing, Advertising, Publishing/Media, Packaging.

Nelvana Limited (8 positions) .... Toronto ON
Ganz (4) .... Woodbridge ON
Aware Marketing Group (3) .... Toronto ON
Canada Post Corporation (3) .... Ottawa ON
George Brown College (3) .... Toronto ON
Imaginex Inc. (3) .... Mississauga ON
McMillan & Associates (3) .... Ottawa ON
AldrichPears Associates (2) .... Vancouver BC
CaseWare International Inc. (2) .... Toronto ON
Centrepoint Technologies Inc. (2) .... Ottawa ON
Columbia House Canada (2) .... Toronto ON
Durham College (2) .... Oshawa ON
Groupe Dynamite Inc. (2) .... Mount Royal QC
Hemera Technologies Inc. (2) .... Hull QC
JayGur International Inc. (2) .... St-Laurent QC
Klick Communications Inc. (2) .... Toronto ON
Lowe-Martin Group, The (2) .... Ottawa ON
LPI Communication Group Inc. (2) .... Calgary AB
Masterfile Corporation (2) .... Toronto ON
MuscleMag International (2) .... Mississauga ON
MuscleTech Research and Development (2) .... Mississauga ON
Rogers Media, Publishing (2) .... Toronto ON
Ruffneck Heaters (2) .... Calgary AB
Teldon International Inc. (2) .... Richmond BC
Acart Communications (1) .... Ottawa ON
AIC Ltd. (1) .... Burlington ON
AIG Life of Canada (1) .... Toronto ON
Aludra Inc. (1) .... Toronto ON
Appareo Software Inc. (1) .... Burnaby BC
Appendix Technical Publishing Group (1) .... Ottawa ON
Aramark Canada Ltd. (1) .... Toronto ON
Arius3D Inc. (1) .... Mississauga ON
Ash City (1) .... Toronto ON
Association of Universities and Colleges (1) .... Ottawa ON
Axia NetMedia Corporation (1) .... Calgary AB
Axidata Inc. (1) .... Toronto ON
BECO Industries Ltd. (1) .... Anjou QC
BouClair Inc. (1) .... Dorval QC
British Columbia Pension Corporation (1) .... Victoria BC
Central Reproductions (1) .... Mississauga ON
CINAR Animation (1) .... Montréal QC
Cirque du Soleil (1) .... Montréal QC
Cohos Evamy Partners, The (1) .... Calgary AB
College of the North Atlantic, Step (1) .... Stephenville NF
Crown Wallpaper + Fabrics (1) .... Toronto ON
CyberSurf Corporation (1) .... Calgary AB
DataMirror Corporation (1) .... Markham ON
DDK Apparel Inc. (1) .... Montréal QC
Design + Communication Inc. (1) .... Montréal QC
Dex Brothers Clothing Ltd. (1) .... Montréal QC
DigiGraphics (1) .... Kingston ON
Douglas College (1) .... New Westminster BC
Exhibits International (1) .... Toronto ON
Femme de Carrière (1) .... Montréal QC
Fields Stores (1) .... Richmond BC
Gad Shaanan Design (1) .... Montréal QC
Giftcraft Ltd. (1) .... Brampton ON
Gilmore (1) .... Toronto ON
Global Television Network Inc. (1) .... Toronto ON

GRAPHIC ARTS (Cont.)

GO Transit / Greater Toronto Transit Aut (1) .... Toronto ON
Goway Travel Ltd. (1) .... Toronto ON
Graham Edmunds (1) .... Calgary AB
Grant MacEwan College, Jasper Place Cam (1) .... Edmonton AB
Grenville Management Services (1) .... Toronto ON
H. Paulin & Co. Limited (1) .... Toronto ON
H2O Entertainment Corp. (1) .... Vancouver BC
Heidelberg Canada (1) .... Mississauga ON
Hellmuth, Obata & Kassabaum, Inc. / HOK (1) .... Toronto ON
Hewson Bridge and Smith Ltd. / HBS (1) .... Ottawa ON
Ilco Unican Inc. (1) .... Montréal QC
Industrial Accident Prevention Associati (1) .... Toronto ON
J. Walter Company Ltd. (1) .... Pointe-Claire QC
JuneWarren Publishing Ltd. (1) .... Edmonton AB
JuneWarren Publishing Ltd. (1) .... Calgary AB
Kwantlen University College (1) .... Surrey BC
La Senza Lingerie (1) .... Dorval QC
Labelad / Sandylion Sticker Designs (1) .... Markham ON
Laura Canada (1) .... Laval QC
LiveWire Digital Imaging (1) .... Woodbridge ON
London Blues (1) .... St-Laurent QC
Marconi Data Systems Canada Ltd. (1) .... Mississauga ON
Mark Anthony Group (1) .... Vancouver BC
Matrikon Group (1) .... Edmonton AB
MegaSys Computer Technologies Ltd. (1) .... Calgary AB
Merlin Creative Group Inc. (1) .... Calgary AB
Ministry of Health and Long-Term Care, (1) .... Kingston ON
Ministry of Transportation, Ontario (1) .... Toronto ON
National Diamond Public Relations Ltd. (1) .... Calgary AB
Northern Gifts Ltd. (1) .... Burnaby BC
Northland Systems Training Inc. (1) .... Ottawa ON
Nova Scotia College of Art and Design / (1) .... Halifax NS
Ontario Science Centre / OSC (1) .... Toronto ON
Optimal Robotics Corp. (1) .... Montréal QC
OZ Optics Ltd. (1) .... Carp ON
Parasuco Jeans Inc. (1) .... St-Laurent QC
Penguin Books Canada Ltd. (1) .... Toronto ON
Perennial Design Company (1) .... Toronto ON
Pitney Bowes Management Services Canada (1) .... Toronto ON
PrinterON Corporation (1) .... Kitchener ON
Publishing Plus Ltd. (1) .... Ottawa ON
Red Caddy (1) .... Ottawa ON
Royal Bank Financial Group (1) .... Toronto ON
Scholastic Canada Ltd. (1) .... Markham ON
SCP Science (1) .... Baie d'Urfe QC
Seiden Health Management Inc. (1) .... Toronto ON
Shana Corporation (1) .... Edmonton AB
Shirmax Fashions Ltd. (1) .... Montréal QC
Shoppers Drug Mart (1) .... Toronto ON
Shopping Channel, The / TSC (1) .... Toronto ON
Sobeys Inc. (1) .... Mississauga ON
Sony Music Canada (1) .... Toronto ON
Southern Alberta Institute of Technology (1) .... Calgary AB
Spar Aerospace Limited (1) .... Edmonton AB
Stanpac Inc. (1) .... Smithville ON
Stantec Consulting Ltd. (1) .... Calgary AB
Staples Business Depot Ltd. (1) .... Markham ON
Stirling Print-All (1) .... Hamilton ON
SureFire Commerce Inc. (1) .... Westmount QC
Surrey, City of (1) .... Surrey BC
Sychowski Communications Inc. (1) .... Montréal QC
Totten Sims Hubicki Associates / TSH (1) .... Whitby ON
Trader.com (1) .... Edmonton AB
Trans Mountain Pipe Line Company Ltd. (1) .... Calgary AB
Trends International Corporation (1) .... Mississauga ON
Tri-ad Graphic Communications Ltd. (1) .... Toronto ON
Tri-Media Marketing & Publicity Inc. (1) .... Welland ON
Triathlon (1) .... Richmond BC
Tribute Publishing (1) .... Toronto ON
University College of the Fraser Vall (1) .... Abbotsford BC
University of Calgary (1) .... Calgary AB
Vistek Ltd. (1) .... Toronto ON
Watermark Advertising Design Ltd. (1) .... Calgary AB
YM - YWHA, Ben Weider Jewish Community (1) .... Montréal QC
Zurich Canada (1) .... Toronto ON

HEALTH/MEDICAL
See also: Pharmaceutical, Biotech/Biology, Govt./Nonprofit.

Lakeridge Health Corporation (79 positions) .... Oshawa ON
York Central Hospital (78) .... Richmond Hill ON
Mount Sinai Hospital (64) .... Toronto ON
Halton Healthcare Services (60) .... Oakville ON
Trillium Health Centre (59) .... Toronto ON
London Health Sciences Centre / LHSC (56) .... London ON
Toronto Rehabilitation Institute (53) .... Toronto ON
Ministry of Health and Long-Term Care, O (52) .... Toronto ON
Sunnybrook & Women's College Health Scie (50) .... Toronto ON
North York General Hospital (49) .... Toronto ON
Credit Valley Hospital, The (46) .... Mississauga ON
William Osler Health Centre, Brampton M (46) .... Brampton ON
South Lake Regional Health Centre (45) .... Newmarket ON
Hospital for Sick Children, The (44) .... Toronto ON
Children's and Women's Health Centre o (40) .... Vancouver BC
Rouge Valley Health System, Centenary He (39) .... Toronto ON
Scarborough Hospital, General Division (39) .... Toronto ON
Humber River Regional Hospital, Finch Av (38) .... Toronto ON
Public Service Commission, PEI (37) .... Charlottetown PE
Ministry of Children and Family De (34) .... Prince George BC
St. Joseph's Healthcare Hamilton (33) .... Hamilton ON
St. Michael's Hospital (32) .... Toronto ON
North York General Hospital, General Div (31) .... Toronto ON
West Park Healthcare Centre (30) .... Toronto ON
Brant Community Healthcare System, Bra (29) .... Brantford ON
Hamilton Health Sciences Corporation, C (29) .... Hamilton ON
Mistahia Health Region (29) .... Grande Prairie AB
Toronto East General & Orthopaedic Hospi (29) .... Toronto ON
Ma'mowe Capital Region, Child and Famil (28) .... Edmonton AB
Ministry of Health and Ministry Respons (28) .... Victoria BC
Capital Health, University of Alberta H (27) .... Edmonton AB
Calgary Regional Health Authority / CRHA (26) .... Calgary AB
Joseph Brant Memorial Hospital (26) .... Burlington ON
Ottawa Hospital, The (26) .... Ottawa ON
Vancouver Hospital and Health Sciences (26) .... Vancouver BC
Scarborough Hospital, Grace Division (25) .... Toronto ON
University Health Network / UHN (25) .... Toronto ON
Saskatoon District Health (24) .... Saskatoon SK
Simon Fraser Health Region / SFH (22) .... New Westminster BC
Alberta Health and Wellness (21) .... Edmonton AB
Kingston General Hospital (21) .... Kingston ON
Manitoba Family Services and Housing (20) .... Winnipeg MB
Providence Health Care, St. Paul's Hos (20) .... Vancouver BC
Royal Victoria Hospital / RVH (20) .... Barrie ON
Vancouver / Richmond Health Board (20) .... Vancouver BC
Alberta Mental Health Board, Alberta Hosp (19) .... Ponoka AB
Manitoba Health (19) .... Winnipeg MB
Markham Stouffville Hospital (18) .... Markham ON
Ministry of Children and Family Developm (18) .... Burnaby BC
Riverdale Hospital, The (18) .... Toronto ON
St. John's Rehabilitation Hospital (18) .... Toronto ON
St. Joseph's Health Centre (18) .... Toronto ON
Alberta Mental Health Board, Claresho (17) .... Claresholm AB
Capital Health Region / CHR (17) .... Victoria BC
Centre for Addiction and Mental Health (17) .... Toronto ON
Grand River Hospital (17) .... Kitchener ON
Guelph General Hospital (17) .... Guelph ON
Bloorview MacMillan Children's Centre, M (16) .... Toronto ON
Queen Elizabeth II Health Sciences Centr (16) .... Halifax NS
Peel Children's Centre (15) .... Mississauga ON
Simon Fraser Health Region, Burnaby Hosp (15) .... Burnaby BC
University Health Network / UHN (15) .... Toronto ON
Alberta Child and Family Services Autho (14) .... McLennan AB
Simon Fraser Health Region / SFH (14) .... New Westminster BC
Cambridge Memorial Hospital / CMH (13) .... Cambridge ON
Fraser Valley Health Region (13) .... Mission BC
Okanagan Similkameen Health Region, Kelo (13) .... Kelowna BC
Kinark Child and Family Services (12) .... Toronto ON
Victorian Order of Nurses, Toronto-York (12) .... Markham ON
Erinoak (12) .... Mississauga ON
Hay River Community Health Board (11) .... Hay River NT
Hotel-Dieu Grace Hospital (11) .... Windsor ON
Public Service Commission of Canada, Ma (11) ...... Winnipeg MB
Public Service Commission of Canada, Onta (11) .... Ottawa ON
Sunnybrook & Women's College Health Scie (11) .... Toronto ON
Alberta Children's Services (10) .... Edmonton AB

HEALTH/MEDICAL (Cont.)

British Columbia Mental Health So (10) .... Port Coquitlam BC
Cancer Care Ontario, Provincial Office / (10) .... Toronto ON
Capital Health, Royal Alexandra Hospita (10) .... Edmonton AB
Catholic Children's Aid Society of Toron (10) .... Toronto ON
Children's Aid Society of Toronto (10) .... Toronto ON
Department of Health and Community Se (10) .... St. John's NF
Hamilton Regional Cancer Centre / HRCC (10) .... Hamilton ON
Hotel Dieu Hospital (10) .... Kingston ON
Ministry of Children and Family Develop (10) .... Victoria BC
Ministry of Children and Family Develop (10) .... Kamloops BC
Peel Children's Aid Society / Peel CAS (10) .... Brampton ON
Simon Fraser Health Region / SFHR (10) .... Port Moody BC
St. Mary's General Hospital (10) .... Kitchener ON
Alberta Mental Health Board, Alberta Ho (9) .... Edmonton AB
Calgary Regional Health Authority, Footh (9) .... Calgary AB
Canadian Cancer Society / CCS (9) .... Vancouver BC
Collingwood General & Marine Hospita (9) .... Collingwood ON
Cross Cancer Institute / CCI (9) .... Edmonton AB
Diversicare Canada Management Servic (9) .... Mississauga ON
Niagara Health System, St. Cathar (9) .... St. Catharines ON
North Okanagan Health Region / NOHR (9) .... Armstrong BC
Northwestern Health Services Region (9) .... High Level AB
Quinte Healthcare Corporation / QHC (9) .... Belleville ON
Simon Fraser Health Region / SFHR (9) .... Maple Ridge BC
South Peace Health Council (9) .... Dawson Creek BC
Warren Shepell Consultants Corp. (9) .... Toronto ON
Yukon Public Service Commission (9) .... Whitehorse YT
Alberta Justice (8) .... Edmonton AB
Department of Health & Wellness, New (8) .... Fredericton NB
Earlscourt Child and Family Centre, The (8) .... Toronto ON
East Central Regional Health Authority (8) .... Camrose AB
Family and Children's Services Ni (8) .... St. Catharines ON
Halton, The Regional Municipality of (8) .... Oakville ON
Hotel Dieu Health Sciences Hospit (8) .... St. Catharines ON
Keeweetinok Lakes Regional Health Aut (8) .... Slave Lake AB
Lodge at Broadmead, The (8) .... Victoria BC
Ministry of Children and Family Developme (8) .... Surrey BC
Ministry of the Attorney General, BC (8) .... Abbotsford BC
Mount Royal College (8) .... Calgary AB
Parkland Regional Health Authority (8) .... Swan River MB
Royal Ottawa Health Care Group / ROHCG (8) .... Ottawa ON
Toronto Grace Hospital, The Salvation Ar (8) .... Toronto ON
Alberta Family and Social Services (7) .... Edmonton AB
Alberta Human Resources and Employment (7) .... McLennan AB
Canadian Institute for Health Information (7) .... Ottawa ON
Capilano Care Centre (7) .... Vancouver BC
Carewest (7) .... Calgary AB
Caritas Health Group, Misericordia Comm (7) .... Edmonton AB
Centre for Addiction and Mental Health (7) .... Toronto ON
College of Nurses of Ontario / CNO (7) .... Toronto ON
Covenant House Toronto (7) .... Toronto ON
Durham, The Regional Municipality of (7) .... Whitby ON
Forensic Psychiatric Services Com (7) .... Port Coquitlam BC
Grant MacEwan College, Jasper Place Cam (7) .... Edmonton AB
Hamilton, City of (7) .... Hamilton ON
Health Sciences Centre / HSC (7) .... Winnipeg MB
Northern Lights Regional Health Se (7) .... Fort McMurray AB
Palliser Health Authority (7) .... Medicine Hat AB
Peel, The Regional Municipality of (7) .... Brampton ON
Prism Centre, The (7) .... Chatham ON
Providence Centre (7) .... Toronto ON
Richmond Health Services (7) .... Richmond BC
Scarborough Community Care Access Centre (7) .... Toronto ON
South Fraser Health Region / SFHR (7) .... Surrey BC
Windsor Regional Hospital (7) .... Windsor ON
Alberta Human Resources and Employment (6) ...... Edmonton AB
Baycrest Centre for Geriatric Care (6) .... Toronto ON
BC Cancer Agency (6) .... Vancouver BC
British Columbia Institute of Technology (6) .... Burnaby BC
Calgary Regional Health Authority / CRHA (6) .... Calgary AB
Capital Health, Glenrose Rehabilitation (6) .... Edmonton AB
Cornwall General Hospital (6) .... Cornwall ON
Cree Board of Health and Social Servic (6) .... Chisasibi QC
CroMedica Inc. (6) .... Ottawa ON
Diamond Willow Child and Family Servic (6) .... Innisfail AB
Frontenac Children's Aid Society (6) .... Kingston ON
KFL&A Community Care Access Centre (6) .... Kingston ON
Kingston Regional Cancer Centre (6) .... Kingston ON

Ministry of Children and Family Develo (6) .... Cranbrook BC
Ministry of Correctional Services, Ont (6) .... North Bay ON
Ministry of Correctional Services, Ontari (6) .... London ON
North Shore Health Region (6) .... North Vancouver BC
Peterborough Regional Health Centre (6) .... Peterborough ON
Providence Health Care, St. Vincent's (6) .... Vancouver BC
Runnymede Chronic Care Hospital (6) .... Toronto ON
Saint Elizabeth Health Care (6) .... Markham ON
Saint Mary's Hospital (6) .... New Westminster BC
Workers' Compensation Board of BC (6) .... Vancouver BC
Alberta Corporate Service Centre (5) .... Coaldale AB
Alberta Family and Social Services (5) .... Red Deer AB
All Care Health Services Ltd. (5) .... Kingston ON
Bayshore HealthCare (5) .... Hamilton ON
Canadian Medical Protective Association / (5) .... Ottawa ON
Canadian Mental Health Association / CMH (5) .... Toronto ON
Children's Hospital of Eastern Ontario / (5) .... Ottawa ON
Chinook Health Region (5) .... Lethbridge AB
College of New Caledonia (5) .... Prince George BC
Columbia Rehabilitation Centre (5) .... Calgary AB
Community Mental Health Clinic / CMHC (5) .... Guelph ON
Correctional Service of Canada (5) .... Saskatoon SK
Department of Health and Social Serv (5) .... Yellowknife NT
Douglas College (5) .... New Westminster BC
Extendicare (Canada) Inc. (5) .... Markham ON
Gamma-Dynacare (5) .... Brampton ON
Health Canada, Regional Nursing (5) .... Edmonton AB
Independent Rehabilitation Services (5) .... Mississauga ON
Keeweetinok Lakes Regional Health A (5) .... High Prairie AB
Kingston Psychiatric Hospital (5) .... Kingston ON
Lakeshore General Hospital (5) .... Pointe-Claire QC
Lambton Hospitals Group (5) .... Sarnia ON
Ministry of Children and Family Developm (5) .... Nanaimo BC
Ministry of Health and Long-Term Care, On (5) .... London ON
Ministry of Health and Long-Term (5) .... Penetanguishene ON
Ministry of Health and Long-Term Care, (5) .... Kingston ON
Ministry of Health and Long-Term Care (5) .... St. Thomas ON
Muki Baum Association (5) .... Toronto ON
Nightingale Health Care Inc. (5) .... Toronto ON
Okanagan University College / OUC (5) .... Kelowna BC
Powell River Community Health Counc (5) .... Powell River BC
Providence Continuing Care Centre / PCC (5) .... Kingston ON
Public Service Commission of Canada, Al (5) .... Edmonton AB
Rouge Valley Health System, Ajax & Pickerin (5) .... Ajax ON
Southern Alberta Institute of Technology (5) .... Calgary AB
Sunnybrook & Women's College Health Scie (5) .... Toronto ON
Toronto-Sunnybrook Regional Cancer Centr (5) .... Toronto ON
Unionville Home Society / UHS (5) .... Unionville ON
University of Calgary, Faculty of Social (5) .... Calgary AB
Vancouver Aboriginal Child & Family Se (5) .... Vancouver BC
VHA Health and Home Support (5) .... Ottawa ON
VHA Home HealthCare (5) .... Toronto ON
We Care Home Health Services Inc. (5) .... Toronto ON
Whitby Mental Health Centre (5) .... Whitby ON
York Community Care Access Centre / CCAC (5) .... Toronto ON
York Region Children's Aid Society / Y (5) .... Newmarket ON
York, The Regional Municipality of (5) .... Newmarket ON
Youthdale Treatment Centres (5) .... Toronto ON
Alberta Human Resources and Employm (4) .... Lac La Biche AB
Assure Health Management Inc. (4) .... Mississauga ON
Canadian Blood Services / CBS (4) .... Ottawa ON
Canadian Blood Services, Toronto Blood C (4) .... Toronto ON
CanCare Health Services Inc. (4) .... Toronto ON
Clinidata (4) .... Toronto ON
CLSC Verdun / Cote Saint-Paul (4) .... Verdun QC
Community Care Access Centre of York R (4) .... Newmarket ON
Correctional Service of Canada (4) .... Saskatoon SK
Department of Human Resources, Nuna (4) .... Rankin Inlet NU
Department of Human Resources, Nunavut (4) .... Iqaluit NU
Dogrib Community Services Board / DCSB (4) .... Rae-Edzo NT
Hema-Quebec (4) .... St-Laurent QC
Henry Schein Arcona Inc. (4) .... St. Catharines ON
Institute for Clinical Evaluative Scienc (4) .... Toronto ON
KCI Medical Canada, Inc. (4) .... Mississauga ON
Keystone Child and Family Services Aut (4) .... Innisfail AB
Kids Help Phone / Parent Help Line (4) .... Toronto ON
King's Health Centre (4) .... Toronto ON
KMH Cardiology and Diagnostic Centres (4) .... Hamilton ON
Leisureworld Caregiving Centres (4) .... Markham ON
Lifeline Systems Canada Inc. (4) .... Toronto ON
LifeScan Canada Ltd. (4) .... Burnaby BC
Lifestyle Retirement Communities, Forest (4) .... Toronto ON

For descriptions of the occupational categories used in this index, see page 458.

HEALTH/MEDICAL (Cont.)

Manitoba Justice / Culture, Heritage an (4) .... Winnipeg MB
McMaster University, Faculty of Health (4) .... Hamilton ON
MDS Laboratories (4) .... Toronto ON
Medical Imaging Consultants (4) .... Edmonton AB
Middlesex-London Health Unit / MLHU (4) .... London ON
Ministry of Children and Family Develo (4) .... Vancouver BC
Ministry of Correctional Services, Onta (4) .... Kingston ON
'Namgis Health Centre (4) .... Alert Bay BC
North York Community Care Access Centre (4) .... Toronto ON
Northeast Mental Health Centre / NEMHC (4) .... Sudbury ON
Oakwood Retirement Communities Inc. (4) .... Kitchener ON
Providence Continuing Care Centre / PCC (4) .... Kingston ON
Quinte & District Rehabilitation Inc. (4) .... Belleville ON
Red Deer College (4) .... Red Deer AB
Rekai Centre, The (4) .... Toronto ON
St. Boniface General Hospital (4) .... Winnipeg MB
St. Peter's Health Services (4) .... Hamilton ON
Sudbury & District Health Unit / SDHU (4) .... Sudbury ON
Suncor Energy Inc., Oil Sands (4) .... Fort McMurray AB
Toronto, City of (4) .... Toronto ON
University College of the Cariboo / UCC (4) .... Kamloops BC
University of Calgary (4) .... Calgary AB
University of Ottawa Heart Institute (4) .... Ottawa ON
Waterloo, The Regional Municipality of (4) .... Kitchener ON
Winnipeg Regional Health Authority / WR (4) .... Winnipeg MB
Ailanthus Achievement Centre (3) .... Vancouver BC
Alberta Alcohol and Drug Abuse Commissi (3) .... Edmonton AB
Alberta Children's Services, Northe (3) .... Lac La Biche AB
Alberta Human Resources and Employment (3) .... Calgary AB
Barton Place Nursing Home (3) .... Toronto ON
BC Biomedical Laboratories Ltd. (3) .... Surrey BC
BC Transplant Society / BCTS (3) .... Vancouver BC
Beverly Centre, The (3) .... Calgary AB
Calea Ltd. (3) .... Mississauga ON
Calgary Regional Health Authority / CRHA (3) .... Calgary AB
Canadian Mental Health Association, Ottaw (3) .... Ottawa ON
Canadian Mental Health Association, (3) .... Peterborough ON
Capital Care Group, The (3) .... Edmonton AB
Capital Health, Community Care and Publ (3) .... Edmonton AB
Care Plus (3) .... Mississauga ON
Casey House Hospice (3) .... Toronto ON
Child's Place, The (3) .... Windsor ON
Children's Aid Society of Hamilton-Went (3) .... Hamilton ON
Children's Rehabilitation Centre of Esse (3) .... Windsor ON
Coast Foundation Society (3) .... Vancouver BC
Columbia Health Care Inc., Grande (3) .... Grande Prairie AB
Comcare Health Services (3) .... Thorold ON
Community Care Access Centre of Peel (3) .... Brampton ON
Community Care Access Centre, Renfrew C (3) .... Pembroke ON
Community Care Services Inc. (3) .... Toronto ON
Comprehensive Rehabilitation and Mental (3) .... Toronto ON
Crossroads Regional Health Authority, (3) .... Wetaskiwin AB
Deh Cho Health and Social Services (3) .... Fort Simpson NT
Diversicare Canada Management Services, (3) .... Toronto ON
Durham Children's Aid Society / CAS (3) .... Oshawa ON
East Central Regional Health Authority, (3) .... Camrose AB
Family Centre, The (3) .... Edmonton AB
Family, Youth and Child Services of (3) .... Bracebridge ON
FGI (3) .... Thornhill ON
Gilda's Club Greater Toronto (3) .... Toronto ON
Hamilton Health Sciences Corporation, H (3) .... Hamilton ON
Hamilton-Wentworth District School Boar (3) .... Hamilton ON
Hastings Children's Aid Society (3) .... Belleville ON
Hearthstone Child and Family Services (3) .... Innisfail AB
Hong Fook Mental Health Association (3) .... Toronto ON
Interlink Community Cancer Nurses (3) .... Toronto ON
Kwantlen University College (3) .... Surrey BC
Lakehead University (3) .... Thunder Bay ON
Lifestyle Retirement Communities (3) .... Vancouver BC
Lindsay Rehabilitation Hospital (3) .... Montréal QC
Manitoba Family Services and (3) .... Portage la Prairie MB
Manitoba Health, Selkirk Mental Health C (3) .... Selkirk MB
McGill University Health Centre, Royal (3) .... Montréal QC
MDS Metro Laboratory Services (3) .... Burnaby BC
Messer Canada / Respircare (3) .... Ottawa ON
MetCap Living (3) .... Toronto ON
Ministry of Children and Family Developm (3) .... Burnaby BC
Ministry of Children and Family Develop (3) .... Kamloops BC
Ministry of Children and Family Developm (3) .... Kelowna BC

Ministry of Community and Social Services (3) .... London ON
Ministry of Correctional Services, Ontar (3) .... Toronto ON
Ministry of Health and Long-Term Care, (3) .... Kingston ON
Ministry of Health and Long-Term Care, (3) .... North Bay ON
Ministry of Labour, Ontario (3) .... Toronto ON
Mission Services of Hamilton (3) .... Hamilton ON
Mitra Imaging Inc. (3) .... Waterloo ON
Niagara, The Regional Municipality of (3) .... Thorold ON
Nicola Valley Health Care (3) .... Merritt BC
Northern Alberta Institute of Technolog (3) .... Edmonton AB
Okanagan Similkameen Health Region, Pe (3) .... Penticton BC
Oolagen Community Services (3) .... Toronto ON
Ottawa Health Research Institute / OHRI (3) .... Ottawa ON
Ottawa Salus Corporation (3) .... Ottawa ON
ParaMed Home Health Care (3) .... Kingston ON
Peace Liard Health (3) .... Dawson Creek BC
Pembroke General Hospital (3) .... Pembroke ON
Perth and Smiths Falls District Hos (3) .... Smiths Falls ON
Preferred Health Care Inc. (3) .... Toronto ON
Public Service Commission of Canada, New (3) .... Moncton NB
Public Service Commission of Canada, Sask (3) .... Regina SK
Queensway-Carleton Hospital (3) .... Nepean ON
Rehabilitative Ergonomics Inc. (3) .... Halifax NS
Ribstone Child and Family Services Auth (3) .... Edmonton AB
Ribstone Child and Family Services Aut (3) .... Innisfail AB
Saint Elizabeth Health Care (3) .... Hamilton ON
Sault Area Hospitals (3) .... Sault Ste. Marie ON
Simcoe County District Health Unit (3) .... Barrie ON
South Muskoka Memorial Hospital (3) .... Bracebridge ON
Spectrum Health Care (3) .... Mississauga ON
St. Joseph's Health Care, Parkwood Hospit (3) .... London ON
St. Joseph's Health Care, St. Joseph's Ho (3) .... London ON
St. Joseph's Healthcare Hamilton, Centr (3) .... Hamilton ON
St. Mary's Hospital Center (3) .... Montréal QC
Stanton Regional Health Board (3) .... Yellowknife NT
Stikine Health Council (3) .... Dease Lake BC
Stratford General Hospital (3) .... Stratford ON
Syncrude Canada Ltd. (3) .... Fort McMurray AB
Toronto Community Care Access Centre (3) .... Toronto ON
University College of the Fraser Vall (3) .... Abbotsford BC
University Health Network, Medical Affai (3) .... Toronto ON
University of British Columbia, School (3) .... Vancouver BC
University of British Columbia / UBC (3) .... Vancouver BC
University of Guelph, Department of Famil (3) .... Guelph ON
University of Toronto, Faculty of Medici (3) .... Toronto ON
University of Western Ontario, Faculty of (3) .... London ON
Victorian Order of Nurses / VON, Easter (3) .... Kingston ON
Victorian Order of Nurses / VON Hamilto (3) .... Hamilton ON
Villa Marconi (3) .... Nepean ON
VitalAire Healthcare (3) .... Mississauga ON
WestView Regional Health Authority / (3) .... Stony Plain AB
Workplace Safety & Insurance Board / WSI (3) .... Toronto ON
Yorktown Shelter for Women / Yorktown Ch (3) .... Toronto ON
Youville Home (3) .... St. Albert AB
A.L.I. Technologies Inc. (2) .... Richmond BC
Active Health Management Inc. (2) .... Toronto ON
Alberta Cancer Board (2) .... Calgary AB
Alberta Health and Wellness (2) .... Edmonton AB
Alberta Human Resources and Employment (2) .... Innisfail AB
Alberta Infrastructure & Transportation (2) .... Edmonton AB
Alberta Mental Health Board / AMHB (2) .... Edmonton AB
Alcan Primary Metal Group (2) .... Kitimat BC
Allendale (2) .... Milton ON
AMEC Earth & Environmental Ltd. (2) .... Calgary AB
Aspen Regional Health Authority No. 11 (2) .... Westlock AB
Athabasca University (2) .... Athabasca AB
Banff Mineral Springs Hospital (2) .... Banff AB
Bartimaeus Inc. (2) .... Toronto ON
Baxter Healthcare Corporation (2) .... Mississauga ON
Belmont House (2) .... Toronto ON
Blue Hills Child and Family Services (2) .... Aurora ON
Bluewater District School Board (2) .... Chesley ON
Brandon Regional Health Authority (2) .... Brandon MB
Brant Community Healthcare System, Willett (2) .... Paris ON
Brogan Inc. (2) .... Ottawa ON
Burntwood Regional Health Authority / B (2) .... Thompson MB
Calgary, City of (2) .... Calgary AB
Calgary Laboratory Services / CLS (2) .... Calgary AB
Campbell River / Nootka Community (2) .... Campbell River BC
Canadian Council on Health Services Accre (2) .... Ottawa ON
Canadian Institutes of Health Research / (2) .... Ottawa ON
Canadian Medical Association / CMA Holdin (2) .... Ottawa ON

HEALTH/MEDICAL (Cont.)

Cancer Care Ontario, Division of Prevent (2) .... Toronto ON
Caritas Health Group, Grey Nuns Communi (2) .... Edmonton AB
Catholic Family Service (2) .... Calgary AB
Central Okanagan Child Development Assoc (2) .... Kelowna BC
Central Toronto Community Health Centres (2) .... Toronto ON
Chapleau Health Services (2) .... Chapleau ON
Chartwell Care Corporation (2) .... Oakville ON
Churchill Regional Health Authority In (2) .... Churchill MB
College of Massage Therapists of Ontario (2) .... Toronto ON
College of Physicians and Surgeons of On (2) .... Toronto ON
College of the Rockies (2) .... Cranbrook BC
Community Options (2) .... Edmonton AB
Conestoga-Rovers & Associates Limited / (2) .... Waterloo ON
Correctional Service of Canada, Regiona (2) .... Kingston ON
Council of Ontario Universities / COU (2) .... Toronto ON
Cranbrook Health Council / CHC (2) .... Cranbrook BC
D. Gary Gibson & Associates Rehabilitati (2) .... Toronto ON
David Thompson Health Region, Red Deer (2) .... Red Deer AB
Diversicare Canada Management Servic (2) .... Mississauga ON
Equipment Planning Associates Ltd. (2) .... Richmond Hill ON
Excel Tech Ltd. / XLTEK (2) .... Oakville ON
Family and Children's Services of Renfr (2) .... Pembroke ON
GE Medical Systems / GEMS (2) .... Mississauga ON
George Brown College (2) .... Toronto ON
Grey Bruce Health Services (2) .... Owen Sound ON
Griffith-McConnell Residence (2) .... Cote St. Luc QC
Haldimand-Norfolk REACH (2) .... Townsend ON
Halton-Peel District Health Council (2) .... Mississauga ON
Health Care Corporation of St. John's (2) .... St. John's NF
Healthtech Inc. (2) .... Toronto ON
Heart and Stroke Foundation of Ontario (2) .... Toronto ON
Heritage Family Services Ltd. (2) .... Red Deer AB
Humber College of Applied Arts and Techn (2) .... Toronto ON
Innovus Research Inc. (2) .... Burlington ON
Inuulitsivik Health Centre (2) .... Puvirnituq QC
Kawartha Lakes, Corporation of the City (2) .... Lindsay ON
Kensington Health Centre, The (2) .... Toronto ON
Kinark Child and Family Services (2) .... Peterborough ON
Lakeland Regional Health Authority / (2) .... Smokey Lake AB
Lakeridge Health Corporation (2) .... Oshawa ON
Lasik Vision Corporation (2) .... Burnaby BC
Leamington District Memorial Hospital (2) .... Leamington ON
Lennox & Addington Addiction Services (2) .... Napanee ON
Lethbridge Community College / LCC (2) .... Lethbridge AB
Lions Gate Hospital (2) .... Vancouver BC
LOFT Community Services (2) .... Toronto ON
London, City of (2) .... London ON
Magna International Inc. (2) .... Concord ON
Magna International Inc. (2) .... Concord ON
Maple Leaf Poultry (2) .... Toronto ON
McGill University Health Centre, Montre (2) .... Montréal QC
McGill University Health Centre / MUHC (2) .... Montréal QC
MDS Laboratories (2) .... Toronto ON
Medigas (2) .... Toronto ON
Medisys Health Group Inc. (2) .... Montréal QC
Michael Smith Foundation for Health Rese (2) .... Burnaby BC
Ministry of Children and Family Developm (2) .... Burnaby BC
Ministry of Community and Social Services (2) .... Kenora ON
Ministry of Community and Social Service (2) .... Orillia ON
Ministry of Community and Social Service (2) .... Toronto ON
Ministry of Health and Long-Term Car (2) .... Thunder Bay ON
Ministry of Health and Long-Term Care, (2) .... Kingston ON
Ministry of Health and Long-Term Care, O (2) .... Sudbury ON
Ministry of Labour, Ontario (2) .... Toronto ON
Minto Counselling Centre (2) .... Cochrane ON
Mount Sinai Hospital Centre (2) .... Cote St. Luc QC
MuscleTech Research and Development (2) .... Mississauga ON
NorQuest College (2) .... Edmonton AB
North Kingston Community Health Centre (2) .... Kingston ON
North Okanagan Health Region / NOHR (2) .... Vernon BC
North West Community Health Services Soc (2) .... Terrace BC
Northern Alberta Institute of Technolog (2) .... Edmonton AB
Northwestern Health Unit (2) .... Dryden ON
NRCS Inc. (2) .... Ottawa ON
Occupational Health and Safety Agency (2) .... Vancouver BC
Ontario Power Generation (2) .... Toronto ON
Orillia Soldiers' Memorial Hospital / OS (2) .... Orillia ON
Ottawa Children's Treatment Centre / OCTC (2) .... Ottawa ON

ParaMed Home Health Care (2) .... Vancouver BC
Peel District School Board (2) .... Mississauga ON
Peel Halton Acquired Brain Injury Se (2) .... Mississauga ON
Peter Hall School Inc. (2) .... St-Laurent QC
Peterborough, Victoria, Northumberl (2) .... Peterborough ON
Planned Parenthood of Toronto (2) .... Toronto ON
Portage College (2) .... Lac La Biche AB
Poundmaker's Lodge (2) .... Edmonton AB
Providence Continuing Care Centre, St (2) .... Brockville ON
Public Guardian and Trustee of British (2) .... Vancouver BC
Public Service Commission of Canada, B (2) .... Vancouver BC
Public Service Commission of Canada, Qu (2) .... Montréal QC
Red Deer Regional Hospital Centre / RDR (2) .... Red Deer AB
Regina Health District (2) .... Regina SK
Renfrew Educational Services (2) .... Calgary AB
Responsive Health Management (2) .... Toronto ON
Royal Arch Masonic Home (2) .... Vancouver BC
Royal Inland Hospital (2) .... Kamloops BC
Sandy Hill Community Health Centre / SHCH (2) .... Ottawa ON
SEN Community Health Care (2) .... Hamilton ON
Shalom Village (2) .... Hamilton ON
Shared Services West, Regional Materials (2) .... Toronto ON
Sibley & Associates Inc. (2) .... Burlington ON
Siemens Canada Ltd. (2) .... Mississauga ON
Sir Mortimer B. Davis - Jewish General (2) .... Montréal QC
Spectrum Health Care (2) .... Toronto ON
St. Joseph's Villa (2) .... Dundas ON
St. Paul's Hospital, Departments of Me (2) .... Vancouver BC
Steeves & Rozema Enterprises Ltd. (2) .... Sarnia ON
Superior Medical Ltd. (2) .... Toronto ON
Therapist's Choice Medical Supplies Inc. (2) .... Toronto ON
Tillsonburg District Memorial Hospit (2) .... Tillsonburg ON
Timmins & District Hospital / TDH (2) .... Timmins ON
Travel Guard Canada (2) .... Toronto ON
Trillium Health Centre (2) .... Mississauga ON
University Health Network, Shared Inform (2) .... Toronto ON
University of Northern British Col (2) .... Prince George BC
Vancouver Community College / VCC (2) .... Vancouver BC
Vancouver Resource Society (2) .... Vancouver BC
Vegreville Health Unit (2) .... Vegreville AB
Victorian Order of Nurses / VON Britis (2) .... Vancouver BC
Victorian Order of Nurses / VON Halton (2) .... Oakville ON
Victorian Order of Nurses / VON Ottawa-Ca (2) .... Ottawa ON
Villa Colombo Services for the Aged Inc. (2) .... Toronto ON
Viridae Clinical Sciences Inc. (2) .... Vancouver BC
Visiting Homemakers Association / VHA (2) .... Hamilton ON
Voice-wave Medical Transcription (2) .... Calgary AB
Welland County General Hospital (2) .... Welland ON
Wexford Residence Inc., The (2) .... Toronto ON
Access Medical Inc. (1) .... Calgary AB
ADESA Canada Inc., Corporate Office (1) .... Mississauga ON
AGFA (1) .... Toronto ON
Alberta Cancer Board / ACB (1) .... Edmonton AB
Alberta Community Development (1) .... Edmonton AB
Alberta Motor Association / AMA (1) .... Edmonton AB
Alberta Solicitor General (1) .... Edmonton AB
All Weather Windows (1) .... Edmonton AB
Allied Clinical Research Inc. (1) .... Mississauga ON
Assiniboine Community College (1) .... Brandon MB
Axia NetMedia Corporation (1) .... Calgary AB
Bausch & Lomb Canada (1) .... Markham ON
Beaufort-Delta Education Council (1) .... Inuvik NT
Beckman Coulter Canada Inc. (1) .... Mississauga ON
Benson Medical Industries Inc. (1) .... Markham ON
Berlex Canada Inc. (1) .... Lachine QC
Big Sisters and Big Brothers of Calgary (1) .... Calgary AB
Bio Ped (1) .... Oakville ON
Bow Valley College (1) .... Calgary AB
Brampton, City of (1) .... Brampton ON
Brantwood Residential Development Cent (1) .... Brantford ON
Brock University (1) .... St. Catharines ON
Brockville Psychiatric Hospital (1) .... Brockville ON
Cadastral Group Inc., The (1) .... Calgary AB
Cadbury Trebor Allan Inc. (1) .... Hamilton ON
Caldwell Residences (1) .... Montréal QC
Camco Inc. (1) .... Hamilton ON
Canada Customs and Revenue Agency, Sa (1) .... Saint John NB
Canadian Blood Services, Edmonton Cent (1) .... Edmonton AB
Canadian Nurses Association / CNA (1) .... Ottawa ON
Canadian Red Cross, Ontario Zone (1) .... Mississauga ON
Canadian Sleep Institute / CSI (1) .... Calgary AB
Capital Regional District / CRD (1) .... Victoria BC

For descriptions of the occupational categories used in this index, see page 458.

HEALTH/MEDICAL (Cont.)

Cara Operations Ltd. (1) .... Richmond BC
Cargill Foods (1) .... High River AB
Carsen Group Inc. (1) .... Markham ON
Central Park Lodges Ltd. (1) .... Calgary AB
Central Park Lodges Ltd. (1) .... Toronto ON
Centre for Ability, The (1) .... Vancouver BC
Centretown Community Health Centre (1) .... Ottawa ON
Chancellor Industrial Construction Ltd. (1) .... Nisku AB
Chatham-Kent Health Alliance (1) .... Chatham ON
Chatham-Kent, Municipality of (1) .... Chatham ON
Chemque Inc. (1) .... Toronto ON
Children's Aid Society of Ottawa-Carl (1) .... Gloucester ON
Chilliwack, City of (1) .... Chilliwack BC
Coley Pharmaceutical Group / CPG (1) .... Ottawa ON
College of the North Atlantic, Clare (1) .... Clarenville NF
College of the North Atlantic, Step (1) .... Stephenville NF
Collins & Aikman (1) .... Toronto ON
Community Care East York (1) .... Toronto ON
Community Living Mississauga (1) .... Mississauga ON
Conestoga College of Applied Arts & Te (1) .... Kitchener ON
Consumers Packaging Inc. (1) .... Toronto ON
Covenant House Vancouver (1) .... Vancouver BC
CroMedica Inc. (1) .... Victoria BC
Department of Justice, Nova Scotia (Corp (1) .... Halifax NS
Department of Municipal and Provincia (1) .... St. John's NF
Dillon Consulting Ltd. (1) .... London ON
Durham Catholic District School Board (1) .... Oshawa ON
Durham College (1) .... Oshawa ON
East York Access Centre (1) .... Toronto ON
Edmonton Public Schools (1) .... Edmonton AB
EFX Enerflex Systems Ltd. (1) .... Calgary AB
Elk Island Public Schools (1) .... Sherwood Park AB
Entourage Technology Solutions (1) .... Mississauga ON
Evans Consoles Inc. (1) .... Calgary AB
F&P Manufacturing, Inc. (1) .... Tottenham ON
Fanshawe College (1) .... London ON
FGI (1) .... Mississauga ON
Fraser Institute, The (1) .... Vancouver BC
Fuji Photo Film Canada Inc. (1) .... Mississauga ON
GE Canada (1) .... Mississauga ON
GE Power Systems (1) .... Calgary AB
Georgian College (1) .... Barrie ON
Global Thermoelectric Inc. (1) .... Calgary AB
Good Samaritan Society, The (1) .... Edmonton AB
Grande Prairie Public School Dist (1) .... Grande Prairie AB
Group Telecom (1) .... Toronto ON
Halton Adolescent Support Services (1) .... Burlington ON
Hamilton Program for Schizophrenia / HP (1) ...... Hamilton ON
Hastings and Prince Edward District S (1) .... Belleville ON
Healthcare Benefit Trust / HBT (1) .... Vancouver BC
Honeywell IC (1) .... North Vancouver BC
Hospital for Sick Children, The (Advance (1) .... Toronto ON
Hotel Dieu Hospital (1) .... Cornwall ON
Huntington Society of Canada (1) .... Kitchener ON
Huron, County of (1) .... Goderich ON
Hurricane Hydrocarbons Ltd. (1) .... Calgary AB
iFire Technology Inc. (1) .... Toronto ON
IMI International Medical Innovations In (1) .... Toronto ON
Inex Pharmaceuticals Corp. (1) .... Burnaby BC
Institute of Health Economics / IHE (1) .... Edmonton AB
Insurance Bureau of Canada / IBC (1) .... Toronto ON
Integra Foundation (1) .... Toronto ON
International Development Research Centre (1) .... Ottawa ON
Inuit Tapirisat of Canada / ITC (1) .... Ottawa ON
IS2 Research Inc. (1) .... Nepean ON
Jackman Manor (1) .... Aldergrove BC
JDS Uniphase Corporation (1) .... Nepean ON
Jewish Eldercare Centre, The (1) .... Montréal QC
Kingston Friendship Homes (1) .... Kingston ON
Kingston, Frontenac and Lennox & Adding (1) .... Kingston ON
Kingston General Hospital, Radiation On (1) .... Kingston ON
Laborie Medical Technologies Inc. (1) .... Mississauga ON
Lakefield Research Limited (1) .... Lakefield ON
Lakeland College (1) .... Vermilion AB
Lakeridge Health Corporation (1) .... Bowmanville ON
Legislative Assembly of Ontario, Office (1) .... Toronto ON
LensCrafters (1) .... Toronto ON
Lester B. Pearson College of the Pacifi (1) .... Victoria BC

Little Mountain Residential Care & Hou (1) .... Vancouver BC
London Regional Cancer Centre / LRCC (1) .... London ON
Louis Brier Home and Hospital (1) .... Vancouver BC
Loyalist College (1) .... Belleville ON
Lutherwood Community Opportunities Deve (1) ...... Waterloo ON
Malaspina University-College, Nanaimo Ca (1) ..... Nanaimo BC
Manitoba Developmental Centre (1) .... Portage la Prairie MB
Manitoba Labour & Immigration (1) .... Winnipeg MB
Manitoba Transportation & Government Se (1) .... Winnipeg MB
Maple Leaf Pork (1) .... Burlington ON
Mayerthorpe Healthcare Centre (1) .... Mayerthorpe AB
Meadowridge School (1) .... Maple Ridge BC
MedcomSoft Inc. (1) .... Toronto ON
Medicine Hat College (1) .... Medicine Hat AB
Medisys Health Group Inc. (1) .... Toronto ON
MethylGene Inc. (1) .... St-Laurent QC
Ministry of Children and Family Develo (1) .... Vancouver BC
Ministry of Community and Social Service (1) .... Sudbury ON
Ministry of Health and Long-Term Care, O (1) ...... Toronto ON
Ministry of Labour, Ontario (1) .... London ON
Ministry of Labour, Ontario (1) .... Ottawa ON
Ministry of Labour, Ontario (Northern Re (1) .... Sudbury ON
Ministry of Natural Resources, Onta (1) .... Peterborough ON
Ministry of Social Development and Econ (1) .... Victoria BC
Ministry of the Solicitor General, Ontar (1) .... Orillia ON
Ministry of Transportation, Ontario (1) .... North Bay ON
Mississauga, City of (1) .... Mississauga ON
Mount Saint Vincent University (1) .... Halifax NS
Multiple Sclerosis Society of Canada, (1) .... Vancouver BC
Nienkamper (1) .... Toronto ON
North Bay General Hospital (1) .... North Bay ON
North Hamilton Community Health Centre (1) ..... Hamilton ON
North Island College / NIC (1) .... Courtenay BC
Northeastern Ontario Regional Cancer Cen (1) ..... Sudbury ON
Oak Bay Lodge (1) .... Victoria BC
Office of the Child, Youth & Family Ad (1) .... Vancouver BC
Ontario Store Fixtures Inc. / OSF (1) .... Toronto ON
Open Learning Agency / OLA (1) .... Burnaby BC
Optx Corporation (1) .... Winnipeg MB
Orlick Industries Ltd. (1) .... Hamilton ON
Ottawa, City of (1) .... Ottawa ON
Ottawa Regional Cancer Centre Foundation (1) ..... Ottawa ON
Ottawa-Carleton District School Board / O (1) .... Nepean ON
Owen Sound, City of (1) .... Owen Sound ON
Owens Corning Canada (1) .... Toronto ON
OZ Optics Ltd. (1) .... Carp ON
ParaMed Home Health Care (1) .... Vancouver BC
Patheon Inc. (1) .... Mississauga ON
Pavilion Family Resource Centre / PFR (1) .... Haileybury ON
Pegasus Healthcare International (1) .... Montréal QC
Perley and Rideau Veterans' Health Centre (1) ...... Ottawa ON
Pottruff & Smith Travel Insurance Bro (1) ..... Woodbridge ON
Praxair Canada Inc. (1) .... Delta BC
Prince George, City of (1) .... Prince George BC
Providence Children's Centre (1) .... Calgary AB
Public Service Commission of Canada, Ont (1) .... Toronto ON
Public Service Commission of Canada, (1) .... Whitehorse YT
Public Service Employee Relations Commi (1) .... Victoria BC
QLT Inc. (1) .... Vancouver BC
Quaker Oats Company of Canada Limit (1) ...... Peterborough ON
Queen's University, Department of Human (1) ...... Kingston ON
Red Deer, City of (1) .... Red Deer AB
Regional Health Authority 5 (1) .... Drumheller AB
Registered Nurses Association of Ontario (1) .... Toronto ON
Response Biomedical Corp. (1) .... Burnaby BC
Royal Bank Financial Group (1) .... Toronto ON
SafetySmart.com (1) .... Calgary AB
Sanofi-Synthelabo Canada Inc. (1) .... Markham ON
Schneider Foods Inc. (1) .... Kitchener ON
School District #57 (Prince George (1) .... Prince George BC
School District #59 (Peace River So (1) ...... Dawson Creek BC
School District #74 (Gold Trail) (1) .... Ashcroft BC
Scott Paper Ltd. (1) .... New Westminster BC
Seiden Health Management Inc. (1) .... Toronto ON
Simcoe County Children's Aid Society / Si (1) .... Barrie ON
Simcoe County District School Board (1) .... Midhurst ON
Simon Fraser University (1) .... Burnaby BC
Sir Wilfrid Laurier School Board (1) .... Rosemere QC
Sisters of Charity of Ottawa Health Servi (1) .... Ottawa ON
SMED International Inc. (1) .... Calgary AB
Standens Limited (1) .... Calgary AB
Stellate Systems (1) .... Westmount QC

HEALTH/MEDICAL (Cont.)

Street Health (1) .... Toronto ON
Sun Life Financial (1) .... Toronto ON
Sunrise Assisted Living (1) .... Mississauga ON
Sunshine Coast Community Health Council (1) .... Sechelt BC
Surrey Place Centre (1) .... Toronto ON
Thompson Health Region (1) .... Kamloops BC
Toronto Catholic District School Board (1) .... Toronto ON
Toronto Transit Commission / TTC (1) .... Toronto ON
Tyco Healthcare Group Canada Inc. (1) .... St-Laurent QC
University of Alberta, Faculty of Nursi (1) .... Edmonton AB
University of British Columbia, Facult (1) .... Vancouver BC
University of New Brunswick, Faculty (1) .... Saint John NB
University of Toronto at Scarborough / U (1) .... Toronto ON
University of Waterloo (1) .... Waterloo ON
University of Western Ontario, Faculty of (1) .... London ON
Vancouver Community College / VCC (1) .... Vancouver BC
Vanderwell Contractors (1971) Ltd. (1) .... Slave Lake AB
Vansco Electronics Ltd. (1) .... Winnipeg MB
Victorian Order of Nurses / VON Canada (1) .... Ottawa ON
Waterloo Region District School Board (1) .... Kitchener ON
West Lincoln Memorial Hospital (1) .... Grimsby ON
William Morris Law Offices (1) .... Hamilton ON
York Catholic District School Board (1) .... Aurora ON
York Community Services / YCS (1) .... Toronto ON
York Region District School Board (1) .... Aurora ON
Yukon College (1) .... Whitehorse YT
Zurich Canada (1) .... Toronto ON

HOSPITALITY

See also: Retail, Franchising, Govt./Nonprofit.

Aramark Canada Ltd. (14 positions) .... Toronto ON
Delta Whistler Resort (11) .... Whistler BC
Loyalty Group, The (11) .... Toronto ON
Sheraton Parkway Hotel, Toronto No (8) .... Richmond Hill ON
Moxie's Classic Grill (7) .... Calgary AB
Delta Pinnacle Hotel (6) .... Vancouver BC
Ministry of Economic Development and Tra (6) .... Toronto ON
Sodexho Marriott Services Canada, Inc (6) .... Burlington ON
Banff Centre, The (5) .... Banff AB
British Columbia Lottery Corporation (5) .... Kamloops BC
Calgary Zoo, Botanical Garden and Prehis (5) .... Calgary AB
Darden Restaurants, Inc. (5) .... Mississauga ON
Days Inn Kingston Hotel & Convention Ce (5) .... Kingston ON
Glen Grove Suites (5) .... Toronto ON
Goway Travel Ltd. (5) .... Toronto ON
Sears Travel Service (5) .... Ottawa ON
SIR Corp. (5) .... Burlington ON
University of Calgary (5) .... Calgary AB
University of Guelph (5) .... Guelph ON
Westin Resort & Spa, The (5) .... Whistler BC
Boulevard Club, The (4) .... Toronto ON
British Columbia Automobile Association (4) .... Burnaby BC
CAA South Central Ontario (4) .... Hamilton ON
Emerald Lake Lodge (4) .... Field BC
Holiday Inn Burlington (4) .... Burlington ON
Intrawest Corporation (4) .... Vancouver BC
Maclab Hotels & Resorts (4) .... Edmonton AB
Ontario Lottery and Gaming Corporation / (4) .... Toronto ON
Park Hyatt Toronto (4) .... Toronto ON
Pizza Pizza Limited (4) .... Toronto ON
TrizecHahn (4) .... Toronto ON
BridgeStreet Accommodations (3) .... Toronto ON
Business Travel International / BTI Cana (3) .... Toronto ON
Canadian Tourism Commission / CTC (3) .... Ottawa ON
Capers Community Markets (3) .... Vancouver BC
Cordon Bleu Paris Ottawa Culinary Arts In (3) .... Ottawa ON
EF Education (3) .... Toronto ON
Fairmont Banff Springs (3) .... Banff AB
Fairmont Vancouver Airport (3) .... Richmond BC
Famous Players Inc. (3) .... Toronto ON
George Brown College (3) .... Toronto ON
Groupe Encore (3) .... Montréal QC
H.J. Heinz Company of Canada Ltd. (3) .... Toronto ON
International Plaza Hotel & Conference C (3) .... Toronto ON

JJ Muggs Gourmet Catering (3) .... Toronto ON
London, City of (3) .... London ON
Manitoba Justice / Culture, Heritage an (3) .... Winnipeg MB
PTI Group Inc. (3) .... Edmonton AB
Regent Holidays Limited (3) .... Mississauga ON
Sen5es (3) .... Vancouver BC
Signature Vacations Inc. (3) .... Toronto ON
Toronto Cricket, Skating and Curling Clu (3) .... Toronto ON
Toronto Marriott Bloor Yorkville (3) .... Toronto ON
Algonquin Travel Corporation (2) .... Ottawa ON
Apotex Inc. (2) .... Toronto ON
BC Rail Ltd. (2) .... North Vancouver BC
Burnaby, City of (2) .... Burnaby BC
Business Travel International / BTI Canad (2) .... Ottawa ON
Cadillac Fairview Corporation Limited, T (2) .... Toronto ON
Canadian Golf & Country Club, The (2) .... Ashton ON
Casino Niagara (2) .... Niagara Falls ON
Casino Rama (2) .... Rama ON
Chili's Texas Grill (2) .... Edmonton AB
Collega for Aveda (2) .... Toronto ON
Compass Group Canada (2) .... Mississauga ON
Crowne Plaza Toronto Centre (2) .... Toronto ON
Delta Meadowvale Resort & Conference (2) .... Mississauga ON
Delta Vancouver Suite Hotel (2) .... Vancouver BC
Diversicare Canada Management Servic (2) .... Mississauga ON
Dolce International (2) .... Toronto ON
Esslinger Foods Ltd. (2) .... Burlington ON
Explorer Hotel, The (2) .... Yellowknife NT
Fairmont Royal York (2) .... Toronto ON
Famous Players Inc. (2) .... Calgary AB
Galileo Canada (2) .... Toronto ON
Granite Club Limited (2) .... Toronto ON
Hillebrand Estates Winery (2) .... Niagara-on-the-Lake ON
HMS Host (2) .... Richmond BC
Kelsey's International Inc. (2) .... Kingston ON
LaCaille on the Bow (2) .... Calgary AB
Langara Island Lodge (2) .... Richmond BC
Marriott International, Toronto Airport (2) .... Toronto ON
McMaster University (2) .... Hamilton ON
Metropolitan Hotel Toronto (2) .... Toronto ON
Milestone's Grill and Bar (2) .... Vancouver BC
Milestone's Grill and Bar (2) .... Toronto ON
Minto Place Suite Hotel (2) .... Ottawa ON
Mississauga, City of (2) .... Mississauga ON
Montana's Cookhouse (2) .... Oakville ON
Oakwood Retirement Communities Inc. (2) .... Kitchener ON
Old Mill, The (2) .... Toronto ON
Ontario Lottery and Gaming Corporation (2) .... Brantford ON
Ontario Science Centre / OSC (2) .... Toronto ON
Pacific Institute of Culinary Arts (2) .... Vancouver BC
Playdium Entertainment Corporation (2) .... Toronto ON
Ramada Plaza Hotel Harbourfront (2) .... Kingston ON
Sheraton Cavalier Hotel (2) .... Calgary AB
Southern Alberta Institute of Technology (2) .... Calgary AB
Sports Clubs of Canada, The / Bally Tota (2) .... Toronto ON
St. Lawrence Parks Commission / SLPC (2) .... Morrisburg ON
Suites Hotel, Les (2) .... Ottawa ON
Sysco I & S Foodservices (2) .... Edmonton AB
Sysco / Konings (2) .... Port Coquitlam BC
Thomas Cook Travel (2) .... Brockville ON
Toronto Zoo (2) .... Toronto ON
Westin Bayshore Resort & Marina, The (2) .... Vancouver BC
Westin Ottawa, The (2) .... Ottawa ON
Whitby, Town of (2) .... Whitby ON
White Spot Limited (2) .... Vancouver BC
Windsor Casino Limited (2) .... Windsor ON
Woodbine Entertainment Group (2) .... Toronto ON
York Central Hospital (2) .... Richmond Hill ON
Ailes de la Mode, Les (1) .... Nepean ON
Alberta Economic Development (1) .... Edmonton AB
Alberta Mental Health Board, Alberta Ho (1) .... Edmonton AB
Alberta Mental Health Board, Alberta Hosp (1) .... Ponoka AB
Alcohol and Gaming Commission of Ontario (1) .... Toronto ON
American Express Canada Inc. / Amex (1) .... Markham ON
Ashton College (1) .... Vancouver BC
Assiniboine Community College (1) .... Brandon MB
Association of Canadian Travel Agents / A (1) .... Ottawa ON
BC Ferry Corporation (1) .... Victoria BC
Beverly Centre, The (1) .... Calgary AB
Bird On a Wire Networks / BOAW (1) .... Mississauga ON
Brampton, City of (1) .... Brampton ON
Bridge Brand Food Services Ltd. (1) .... Calgary AB

For descriptions of the occupational categories used in this index, see page 458.

HOSPITALITY (Cont.)

HUMAN RESOURCE

See also: Public Relations.

HUMAN RESOURCE (Cont.)

OZ Optics Ltd. (5) .... Carp ON
Providence Health Care, St. Paul's Hos (5) .... Vancouver BC
Public Service Commission of Canada, (5) .... St. John's NF
University of Calgary (5) .... Calgary AB
ADP Canada (4) .... Montréal QC
Alberta Human Resources and Employment (4) .... Calgary AB
Alberta Infrastructure & Transportation (4) .... Edmonton AB
Durham, The Regional Municipality of (4) .... Whitby ON
EPCOR Utilities Inc. (4) .... Edmonton AB
Export Development Corporation / EDC (4) .... Ottawa ON
Fincentric Corp. (4) .... Richmond BC
GE Canada (4) .... Mississauga ON
Group Telecom (4) .... Toronto ON
Groupe Dynamite Inc. (4) .... Mount Royal QC
Hewitt Associates (4) .... Toronto ON
JDS Uniphase Corporation (4) .... Saanichton BC
Liquor Distribution Branch, BC / LDB (4) .... Vancouver BC
London Health Sciences Centre / LHSC (4) .... London ON
Manitoba Family Services and Housing (4) .... Winnipeg MB
Manitoba Labour & Immigration (4) .... Winnipeg MB
North Okanagan Health Region / NOHR (4) .... Armstrong BC
North York General Hospital (4) .... Toronto ON
Open Learning Agency / OLA (4) .... Burnaby BC
Public Service Commission of Canada, Onta (4) .... Ottawa ON
Public Service Employee Relations Commi (4) .... Victoria BC
Rogers AT&T Wireless (4) .... Toronto ON
Ryerson Polytechnic University (4) .... Toronto ON
Southern Alberta Institute of Technology (4) .... Calgary AB
724 Solutions Inc. (3) .... Toronto ON
ADP Canada (3) .... Burnaby BC
Alberta Corporate Services Centre (3) .... Edmonton AB
Alcan Primary Metal Group (3) .... Kitimat BC
Arbor Memorial Services Inc. (3) .... Toronto ON
AstraZeneca (3) .... Mississauga ON
Calgary Regional Health Authority / CRHA (3) .... Calgary AB
Canadian Forces Personnel Support Agency (3) .... Ottawa ON
Ceridian Canada Ltd. (3) .... Mississauga ON
Ceridian Canada Ltd. (3) .... St-Laurent QC
Children's Aid Society of Toronto (3) .... Toronto ON
Conestoga-Rovers & Associates Limited / (3) .... Waterloo ON
Convergys Customer Management Canada In (3) .... Edmonton AB
Extendicare (Canada) Inc. (3) .... Markham ON
Gennum Corporation (3) .... Burlington ON
Grand River Hospital (3) .... Kitchener ON
Grant MacEwan College, Jasper Place Cam (3) .... Edmonton AB
Henry Birks & Sons Inc. (3) .... Montréal QC
Inex Pharmaceuticals Corp. (3) .... Burnaby BC
Ma'mowe Capital Region, Child and Famil (3) .... Edmonton AB
MacDonald Dettwiler & Associates Ltd. / (3) .... Richmond BC
Manitoba Education, Training & Youth (3) .... Winnipeg MB
Ministry of Health and Long-Term Care, O (3) .... Toronto ON
Ministry of Northern Development and Min (3) .... Sudbury ON
Ministry of the Attorney General, Ontari (3) .... Toronto ON
Mississauga, City of (3) .... Mississauga ON
Okanagan University College / OUC (3) .... Kelowna BC
Ontario Lottery and Gaming Corporation / (3) .... Toronto ON
Ontario Municipal Employees Retirement S (3) .... Toronto ON
Patheon Inc. (3) .... Mississauga ON
RoundHeaven Communications Canada Inc. (3) .... Vancouver BC
ShawCor Ltd. (3) .... Toronto ON
Shopping Channel, The / TSC (3) .... Toronto ON
Simon Fraser Health Region / SFH (3) .... New Westminster BC
Simon Fraser Health Region / SFH (3) .... New Westminster BC
Sitraka Software Inc. (3) .... Toronto ON
Syndesis Limited (3) .... Richmond Hill ON
Technical University of British Columbia (3) .... Surrey BC
TeleTech Canada (3) .... Toronto ON
TransAlta Corporation (3) .... Calgary AB
University College of the Cariboo / UCC (3) .... Kamloops BC
Upper Canada District School Board (3) .... Brockville ON
Vancouver Hospital and Health Sciences (3) .... Vancouver BC
Vocational Pathways Inc. (3) .... Toronto ON
Weatherford Canada Ltd. (3) .... Nisku AB
William M. Mercer Limited (3) .... Toronto ON
Abbotsford, City of (2) .... Abbotsford BC
Alberta Children's Services (2) .... Edmonton AB
Alberta Community Development (2) .... Edmonton AB
Alberta Energy Company Ltd. / AEC (2) .... Calgary AB

Alberta Human Resources and Employm (2) .... Lac La Biche AB
Alberta Learning (2) .... Edmonton AB
AMEC Earth & Environmental Ltd. (2) .... Calgary AB
Aon Corporation (2) .... Vancouver BC
Atlantic Packaging Products Ltd. (2) .... Toronto ON
Ballard Power Systems Inc. (2) .... Burnaby BC
Baycrest Centre for Geriatric Care (2) .... Toronto ON
Bell Intrigna (2) .... Calgary AB
Bloorview MacMillan Children's Centre, M (2) .... Toronto ON
BOC Canada Ltd. (2) .... Mississauga ON
Bombardier Aerospace, Regional Aircraft (2) .... Toronto ON
Bombardier Transportation (2) .... Kingston ON
Bomhoff Aerospace Corporation (2) .... St-Laurent QC
Bragg Photonics Inc. (2) .... Dorval QC
Brampton, City of (2) .... Brampton ON
Brant Community Healthcare System, Bra (2) .... Brantford ON
Brantford, Corporation of the City of (2) .... Brantford ON
British Columbia Maritime Employers As (2) .... Vancouver BC
British Columbia Mental Health So (2) .... Port Coquitlam BC
Burlington Resources Canada Energy Ltd. (2) .... Calgary AB
Canadian Gypsum Company / CGC Inc. (2) .... Hagersville ON
Casino Niagara (2) .... Niagara Falls ON
CCI Industries Ltd. (2) .... St. Albert AB
Celestica Inc. (2) .... Toronto ON
Ceridian Canada Ltd. (2) .... Ottawa ON
Ceridian Performance Partners Ltd. (2) .... Markham ON
Cirque du Soleil (2) .... Montréal QC
Cirque du Soleil (2) .... Montréal QC
College of the North Atlantic, Step (2) .... Stephenville NF
Colt Engineering Corporation (2) .... Calgary AB
Conference Board of Canada, The (2) .... Ottawa ON
Convergys Corporation (2) .... Ottawa ON
Corel Corporation (2) .... Ottawa ON
CoSyn Technology (2) .... Edmonton AB
DataMirror Corporation (2) .... Markham ON
Dominion Colour Corporation (2) .... Toronto ON
Earth Tech Canada Inc. (2) .... Markham ON
Echo Bay Mines Ltd. (2) .... Edmonton AB
Famous Players Inc. (2) .... Toronto ON
Fidelity Investments Canada Limited (2) .... Toronto ON
First Canadian Title Company (2) .... Mississauga ON
Ganz (2) .... Woodbridge ON
General Hydrogen / GH (2) .... Vancouver BC
George Brown College (2) .... Toronto ON
Gilmore (2) .... Toronto ON
GlaxoSmithKline (2) .... Mississauga ON
Global Thermoelectric Inc. (2) .... Calgary AB
Good Samaritan Society, The (2) .... Edmonton AB
Goodlife Foods (2) .... Calgary AB
Halton, The Regional Municipality of (2) .... Oakville ON
Home Depot (2) .... Toronto ON
Honeywell Inc. (2) .... Montréal QC
Hypertec Systems Inc. (2) .... St-Laurent QC
Information Services Corporation of Saska (2) .... Regina SK
Kawartha Lakes, Corporation of the City (2) .... Lindsay ON
Lafarge Construction Materials (2) .... Concord ON
Le Chateau (2) .... Mount Royal QC
Legislative Assembly of Ontario, Office (2) .... Toronto ON
Loewen Group Inc., The (2) .... Toronto ON
Loyalty Group, The (2) .... Toronto ON
Manitoba Civil Service Commission (2) .... Winnipeg MB
Manitoba Finance (2) .... Winnipeg MB
Matrix Consulting Group Inc. (2) .... Edmonton AB
MI Group, The (2) .... Mississauga ON
Microtime Inc. (2) .... Ottawa ON
Ministry of Finance, Ontario (2) .... Toronto ON
Ministry of Labour, Ontario (2) .... Toronto ON
Ministry of Social Development and Econ (2) .... Victoria BC
Ministry of the Attorney General, BC (V (2) .... Victoria BC
Ministry of the Environment, Ontario (2) .... Toronto ON
Morrison Hershfield (2) .... Toronto ON
Mount Royal College (2) .... Calgary AB
Nexen Inc. (2) .... Calgary AB
North Island College / NIC (2) .... Courtenay BC
Office of the Auditor General, BC (Corp (2) .... Victoria BC
Ontario March of Dimes (2) .... Kingston ON
Ontario Pension Board (2) .... Toronto ON
Ontario Science Centre / OSC (2) .... Toronto ON
Optimal Robotics Corp. (2) .... Montréal QC
PanCanadian Petroleum Ltd. (2) .... Calgary AB
Positron Public Safety Systems Inc. (2) .... Montréal QC
Procuron Inc. (2) .... Thornhill ON

For descriptions of the occupational categories used in this index, see page 458.

OCCUPATIONAL INDEX 519

HUMAN RESOURCE (Cont.)

Providence Continuing Care Centre / PCC (2) .... Kingston ON
QLT Inc. (2) .... Vancouver BC
Quaker Oats Company of Canada Limit (2) .... Peterborough ON
QuestAir Technologies Inc. (2) .... Burnaby BC
ReserveAmerica (2) .... Milton ON
Riverside School Board (2) .... St-Lambert QC
Rogers Cable Inc. (2) .... Toronto ON
Rogers Video (2) .... Richmond BC
Royal & SunAlliance Canada (2) .... Toronto ON
Ruffneck Heaters (2) .... Calgary AB
Saskatchewan Workers' Compensation Board (2) .... Regina SK
School District #43 (Coquitlam) (2) .... Coquitlam BC
Shirmax Fashions Ltd. (2) .... Montréal QC
Shoppers Drug Mart (2) .... Toronto ON
SITEL Canada Inc. (2) .... Toronto ON
SITEL Canada Inc. (2) .... Montréal QC
St. Joseph's Health Centre (2) .... Toronto ON
Stantec Geomatics Ltd. (2) .... Edmonton AB
Stikeman Elliott (2) .... Toronto ON
Suncor Energy Inc., Oil Sands (2) .... Fort McMurray AB
TELAV Audio Visual Services (2) .... Lachine QC
Telus Integrated Communications (2) .... Toronto ON
Textiles Human Resources Council (2) .... Ottawa ON
Toromont CAT (2) .... Concord ON
Toronto Rehabilitation Institute (2) .... Toronto ON
University College of the Fraser Vall (2) .... Abbotsford BC
University of Alberta, Academic Staff A (2) .... Edmonton AB
University of Ottawa (2) .... Ottawa ON
University of Toronto (2) .... Toronto ON
Vancouver International Airport Authori (2) .... Richmond BC
Vancouver / Richmond Health Board (2) .... Vancouver BC
West Park Healthcare Centre (2) .... Toronto ON
Westfair Foods Ltd. (2) .... Burnaby BC
Westfair Foods Ltd. (2) .... Calgary AB
Windsor Casino Limited (2) .... Windsor ON
Woodbine Entertainment Group (2) .... Toronto ON
Worldwide Immigration Consultancy Se (2) .... Mississauga ON
York Central Hospital (2) .... Richmond Hill ON
Zurich Canada (2) .... Toronto ON
ABC Group Inc. (1) .... Toronto ON
ADESA Canada Inc., Corporate Office (1) .... Mississauga ON
Advanced Micro Design (1) .... Edmonton AB
Advantex Marketing International Inc. (1) .... Toronto ON
AEA Technology Engineering Software Ltd (1) .... Waterloo ON
Ailes de la Mode, Les (1) .... Laval QC
Alberta Energy and Utilities Board / EUB (1) .... Calgary AB
Alberta Family and Social Services (1) .... Red Deer AB
Alberta Finance (1) .... Edmonton AB
Alberta Justice (1) .... Edmonton AB
Alberta Mental Health Board, Claresho (1) .... Claresholm AB
Alberta Resource Development (1) .... Edmonton AB
Alberta School Boards Association / ASB (1) .... Edmonton AB
All Weather Windows (1) .... Edmonton AB
Alpha Technologies Ltd. (1) .... Burnaby BC
Alterna Technologies Group Inc. (1) .... Calgary AB
Aman Building Corp. (1) .... Sherwood Park AB
Apotex Inc. (1) .... Toronto ON
Appendix Technical Publishing Group (1) .... Ottawa ON
Argus Technologies Ltd. (1) .... Burnaby BC
Art in Motion (1) .... Coquitlam BC
Association of Professional Engineers an (1) .... Burnaby BC
AT&T Canada (1) .... Toronto ON
ATCO Noise Management Ltd. (1) .... Calgary AB
Athabasca University (1) .... Athabasca AB
Au Printemps Gourmet (1) .... Prevost QC
Avcorp Industries Inc. (1) .... Delta BC
Axis Logistics Inc. (1) .... Milton ON
Banff Centre, The (1) .... Banff AB
Banff Mineral Springs Hospital (1) .... Banff AB
Barringer Research (1) .... Mississauga ON
Bata Retail Canada (1) .... Toronto ON
Baxter Healthcare Corporation (1) .... Mississauga ON
Bayer Inc. (1) .... Toronto ON
Baymag (1) .... Calgary AB
BC Rapid Transit Co. Ltd. / BCRTC (1) .... Burnaby BC
BC Research Inc. (1) .... Vancouver BC
BCE Emergis Inc. (1) .... Montréal QC
Beaufort-Delta Education Council (1) .... Inuvik NT
Becker Group (1) .... Toronto ON
Bellwoods Centres for Community Living I (1) .... Toronto ON
BHP Diamonds Inc. (1) .... Yellowknife NT
Bird On a Wire Networks / BOAW (1) .... Mississauga ON
bitHeads, Inc. (1) .... Ottawa ON
Black Community Resource Centre / BCRC (1) .... Montréal QC
Brant Haldimand-Norfolk Catholic Distr (1) .... Brantford ON
Brantwood Residential Development Cent (1) .... Brantford ON
British Columbia Institute of Technology (1) .... Burnaby BC
Brock University (1) .... St. Catharines ON
Brookfield LePage Johnson Controls Facili (1) .... Ottawa ON
Burns International Security Services (1) .... Gloucester ON
Burntsand Inc. (1) .... Toronto ON
C1 Communications (1) .... Mississauga ON
Calea Ltd. (1) .... Mississauga ON
Calgary Co-operative Association Ltd. (1) .... Calgary AB
Calgary Laboratory Services / CLS (1) .... Calgary AB
Canada Customs and Revenue Agency / CCRA (1) .... Ottawa ON
Canadian Blood Services / CBS (1) .... Ottawa ON
Canadian Depository for Securities Ltd. (1) .... Toronto ON
Canadian Food Inspection Agency / CFIA (1) .... Moncton NB
Canadian Golf & Country Club, The (1) .... Ashton ON
Canadian Hearing Society, The (1) .... Toronto ON
Canadian Medical Protective Association / (1) .... Ottawa ON
Canadian Mental Health Association / CM (1) .... Cornwall ON
Canadian Paraplegic Association Ontario (1) .... Toronto ON
Canadian Red Cross, Ontario Zone (1) .... Mississauga ON
Canadian Venture Exchange / CDNX (1) .... Vancouver BC
Canadian Western Bank (1) .... Edmonton AB
Cancable Inc. (1) .... Burlington ON
Cap Gemini Ernst & Young / CGEY (1) .... Toronto ON
Capilano College (1) .... North Vancouver BC
Carpenter Canada Ltd. (1) .... Woodbridge ON
Carswell (1) .... Toronto ON
Casey House Hospice (1) .... Toronto ON
Catena Networks (1) .... Kanata ON
Catholic Children's Aid Society of Toron (1) .... Toronto ON
Centennial College (1) .... Toronto ON
Central Park Lodges Ltd. (1) .... Toronto ON
CH2M HILL Canada Ltd. (1) .... Toronto ON
Changepoint Corporation (1) .... Richmond Hill ON
Chapters Inc. / Indigo Books & Music (1) .... Toronto ON
Children's and Women's Health Centre o (1) .... Vancouver BC
CIMTEK Automation Systems (1) .... Burlington ON
Cintas Canada Ltd. (1) .... Mississauga ON
Climan Transport Services (1) .... Lachine QC
Club Monaco International (1) .... Toronto ON
CMC Electronics Inc. (1) .... St-Laurent QC
CML Versatel Inc. (1) .... Hull QC
Coast Foundation Society (1) .... Vancouver BC
Coast Plaza Hotel, The (1) .... Calgary AB
Cognos Inc. (1) .... Ottawa ON
Coley Pharmaceutical Group / CPG (1) .... Ottawa ON
College of the Rockies (1) .... Cranbrook BC
Colt Engineering Corporation (1) .... Edmonton AB
Commonwealth Construction (1) .... Burnaby BC
Community Care Access Centre of Peel (1) .... Brampton ON
CompClaim Management Inc. (1) .... Toronto ON
CompuSoft Canada Inc. (1) .... Edmonton AB
Computer Sciences Corp. / CSC (1) .... Toronto ON
Computing Devices Canada Ltd. / CDC (1) .... Calgary AB
Concordia University (1) .... Montréal QC
Coneco Equipment Inc. (1) .... Edmonton AB
Consumers Packaging Inc. (1) .... Toronto ON
Control-F1 (1) .... Calgary AB
Country Day School, The (1) .... King City ON
Crawford Healthcare Management (1) .... Ottawa ON
Creation Technologies Inc. (1) .... Burnaby BC
CreoScitex (1) .... Burnaby BC
CroMedica Inc. (1) .... Victoria BC
CSI Wireless Inc. (1) .... Calgary AB
Customs Excise Union Douanes Accise / CEU (1) .... Ottawa ON
CyberSurf Corporation (1) .... Calgary AB
Cymbolic Sciences Inc. (1) .... Richmond BC
Dana Long Manufacturing Ltd. (1) .... Oakville ON
Decima Research Inc. (1) .... Montréal QC
Decolin Inc. (1) .... Montréal QC
Decor-Rest Furniture Ltd. (1) .... Woodbridge ON
Delcan Corporation (1) .... Toronto ON
Delta Vancouver Suite Hotel (1) .... Vancouver BC
Delta Whistler Resort (1) .... Whistler BC
Department of Education, New Brunswi (1) .... Fredericton NB
Department of Executive Council, NF (1) .... St. John's NF

HUMAN RESOURCE (Cont.)

Department of Health and Community Se (1) ... St. John's NF
Department of Human Resources, Nuna (1) ... Rankin Inlet NU
Department of Human Resources, Nun (1) ... Cambridge Bay NU
Department of Human Resources, Nunavut (1) ... Igloolik NU
Direct Energy Marketing Ltd. (1) ... Toronto ON
Distican Inc. (1) ... Richmond Hill ON
Dolce International (1) ... Toronto ON
Dominion of Canada General Insurance Com (1) ... Toronto ON
Don Park Inc. (1) ... Toronto ON
Doubleday Canada Ltd. (1) ... Toronto ON
Dover Industries Ltd. (1) ... Burlington ON
DSM Biologics (1) ... Montréal QC
DuPont Canada Inc. (1) ... Mississauga ON
Durham College (1) ... Oshawa ON
E-smith, Inc. (1) ... Ottawa ON
East Central Regional Health Authority (1) ... Camrose AB
Edmonton Catholic Schools (1) ... Edmonton AB
Edmonton, City of (1) ... Edmonton AB
Edward Jones (1) ... Mississauga ON
EFX Enerflex Systems Ltd. (1) ... Calgary AB
Enbridge Consumers Gas (1) ... Toronto ON
Entretel Inc. (1) ... Oakville ON
Ericsson Canada Inc. (1) ... Mount Royal QC
ESRI Canada Ltd. (1) ... Toronto ON
eWazo Technology Corporation (1) ... Victoria BC
Exocom Group Inc., The (1) ... Ottawa ON
Fairview College (1) ... Fairview AB
Falconbridge Ltd. (1) ... Toronto ON
Family and Children's Services Ni (1) ... St. Catharines ON
Fasken Martineau DuMoulin LLP (1) ... Toronto ON
Federated Co-operatives Limited / FCL (1) ... Calgary AB
Federated Co-operatives Limited / FCL (1) ... Saskatoon SK
Federation CJA (1) ... Montréal QC
FGI (1) ... Mississauga ON
FGI (1) ... Thornhill ON
Fields Stores (1) ... Richmond BC
Fiera Foods Company (1) ... Toronto ON
Filtran Microcircuits Inc. (1) ... Ottawa ON
Financial Services Commission of Ontario (1) ... Toronto ON
Finning (Canada) International Inc. (1) ... Edmonton AB
Fireco Inc. (1) ... Mississauga ON
First Air (1) ... Carp ON
Fluor Canada Ltd. (1) ... Calgary AB
Fording Coal Limited, Fording River Oper (1) ... Elkford BC
Forensic Technology Inc. (1) ... Cote St. Luc QC
Forsys Software Corporation (1) ... Markham ON
Forzani Group Ltd., The (1) ... Calgary AB
Franklin Templeton Investments (1) ... Toronto ON
Fraser Milner Casgrain LLP (1) ... Toronto ON
Fraser Valley Regional District / FVR (1) ... Chilliwack BC
FreeBalance Inc. (1) ... Ottawa ON
Fugro Airborne Surveys (1) ... Mississauga ON
Future Shop Ltd. (1) ... Anjou QC
G&K Work Wear (1) ... Mississauga ON
Gazette, The (1) ... Montréal QC
GE Power Systems (1) ... Calgary AB
Gear Centre Group of Companies, The (1) ... Edmonton AB
Geneka Biotechnology Inc. (1) ... Montréal QC
Gienow Building Products Ltd. (1) ... Calgary AB
Global Group, The (1) ... Toronto ON
Globel Direct Marketing (1) ... Richmond BC
Grand Erie District School Board (1) ... Brantford ON
Grand River Poultry Farm Ltd. (1) ... Paris ON
Grand & Toy Ltd. (1) ... Vaughan ON
Great Canadian Casinos Inc. (1) ... Richmond BC
Great Canadian Railtour Company Ltd. (1) ... Vancouver BC
Greater Toronto Airports Authority / GTA (1) ... Toronto ON
Grocery Gateway (1) ... Mississauga ON
Grocery People Ltd., The / TGP (1) ... Edmonton AB
Guelph, City of (1) ... Guelph ON
Haley Industries Ltd. (1) ... Haley ON
Hallmark Canada (1) ... Toronto ON
Hamilton Health Sciences Corporation, C (1) ... Hamilton ON
Hamilton-Wentworth District School Boar (1) ... Hamilton ON
Hardt Equipment Manufacturing Inc. (1) ... Lachine QC
Harris Computer Systems (1) ... Nepean ON
Hartco Corporation (1) ... Anjou QC
Healthcare Benefit Trust / HBT (1) ... Vancouver BC
Hearthstone Child and Family Services (1) ... Innisfail AB
Henry Schein Arcona Inc. (1) ... St. Catharines ON
Hepcoe Credit Union Ltd. (1) ... Toronto ON
Highland Farms Inc. (1) ... Toronto ON
Holt Renfrew (1) ... Ottawa ON
Hong Fook Mental Health Association (1) ... Toronto ON
Horn and Associates (1) ... Concord ON
Hospital for Sick Children, The (1) ... Toronto ON
Humber College of Applied Arts and Techn (1) ... Toronto ON
Huron, County of (1) ... Goderich ON
Husky Injection Molding Systems Ltd. (1) ... Bolton ON
i-STAT Canada Ltd. (1) ... Kanata ON
i2 Technologies (1) ... Markham ON
iFire Technology Inc. (1) ... Toronto ON
IKO Industries Ltd. (1) ... Calgary AB
IKO Industries Ltd. (1) ... Toronto ON
IMS Health Canada Ltd. (1) ... Pointe-Claire QC
Industrial-Alliance Pacific Life Insur (1) ... Vancouver BC
Industry Training & Apprenticeship Comm (1) ... Victoria BC
Inflazyme Pharmaceuticals Ltd. (1) ... Richmond BC
Information Science and Technology Agen (1) ... Victoria BC
ING Bank of Canada / ING Direct (1) ... Toronto ON
ING Western Union Insurance (1) ... Calgary AB
Inland Group (1) ... Edmonton AB
Inner-Tec Security Services (1) ... Vancouver BC
International Development Research Centre (1) ... Ottawa ON
Intrawest Corporation (1) ... Vancouver BC
Investors Group (1) ... Winnipeg MB
Ivanhoe Cambridge (1) ... Montréal QC
IVL Technologies Ltd. (1) ... Victoria BC
Jewish Eldercare Centre, The (1) ... Montréal QC
Kaycan Ltd. (1) ... Pointe-Claire QC
Kinetek Pharmaceuticals Inc. (1) ... Vancouver BC
King's Health Centre (1) ... Toronto ON
Kingston, Corporation of the City of (1) ... Kingston ON
Kingston General Hospital (1) ... Kingston ON
Kingsway Financial Services Inc. (1) ... Mississauga ON
Koch Petroleum Canada LP (1) ... Calgary AB
KOM Inc. (1) ... Kanata ON
Koskie Minsky (1) ... Toronto ON
Labatt Breweries Ontario (1) ... Toronto ON
Law Society of Upper Canada, The / LSUC (1) ... Toronto ON
Legal Services Society (1) ... Vancouver BC
Leica Geosystems Ltd. (1) ... Toronto ON
Leitch Technology Corp. (1) ... Toronto ON
Lethbridge Community College / LCC (1) ... Lethbridge AB
LifeScan Canada Ltd. (1) ... Burnaby BC
Lifestyle Retirement Communities (1) ... Mississauga ON
Linamar Corporation, Eston Division (1) ... Guelph ON
Little Mountain Residential Care & Hou (1) ... Vancouver BC
Loewen Group Inc., The (1) ... Burnaby BC
London, City of (1) ... London ON
Lowe-Martin Group, The (1) ... Ottawa ON
Lutherwood Community Opportunities Deve (1) ... Waterloo ON
M-Con Products Inc. (1) ... Carp ON
Malaspina University-College, Nanaimo Ca (1) ... Nanaimo BC
Manion, Wilkins & Associates Ltd. (1) ... Toronto ON
Manitoba Health (1) ... Winnipeg MB
Manitoba Highways & Transportation, Abo (1) ... Thompson MB
Manitoba Justice / Culture, Heritage an (1) ... Winnipeg MB
Manitoba Transportation & Government Se (1) ... Winnipeg MB
Manitoba Transportation & Gov (1) ... Portage la Prairie MB
Maple Leaf Consumer Foods (1) ... Toronto ON
Maple Reinders Inc. (1) ... Brampton ON
Mark Anthony Group (1) ... Vancouver BC
Markham, Corporation of the Town of (1) ... Markham ON
Matrox Electronic Systems Ltd. (1) ... Dorval QC
Maxim Group (1) ... Calgary AB
McMaster University, Michael G. DeGroot (1) ... Hamilton ON
MDS Metro Laboratory Services (1) ... Burnaby BC
MDS Pharma Services Inc. (1) ... St-Laurent QC
Medicine Hat, City of (1) ... Medicine Hat AB
Medicine Hat College (1) ... Medicine Hat AB
MemberCARE Financial Services (1) ... Burlington ON
Metropolitan Hotel Toronto (1) ... Toronto ON
Miller Thomson LLP (1) ... Edmonton AB
Miller Thomson LLP (1) ... Toronto ON
Minacs Worldwide Inc. (1) ... Richmond Hill ON
Ministry of Children and Family Develop (1) ... Victoria BC
Ministry of Community and Social Servi (1) ... North Bay ON
Ministry of Community and Social Service (1) ... Toronto ON
Ministry of Community and Social Service (1) ... Toronto ON

For descriptions of the occupational categories used in this index, see page 458.

OCCUPATIONAL INDEX 521

HUMAN RESOURCE (Cont.)

Ministry of Consumer and Business Servic (1) .... Toronto ON
Ministry of Correctional Services, Ontar (1) .... Toronto ON
Ministry of Finance, Ontario (1) .... Oshawa ON
Ministry of Forests, BC (Cariboo R (1) .... Williams Lake BC
Ministry of Forests, BC (Research Branc (1) .... Victoria BC
Ministry of Health and Long-Term (1) .... Penetanguishene ON
Ministry of Health and Long-Term Care, (1) .... Kingston ON
Ministry of Health and Long-Term Care, (1) .... Kingston ON
Ministry of Labour, BC (Workers' Compen (1) .... Victoria BC
Ministry of Labour, Ontario (1) .... London ON
Ministry of Labour, Ontario (Northern Re (1) .... Sudbury ON
Ministry of Municipal Affairs and Housin (1) .... Toronto ON
Ministry of Natural Resources, Onta (1) .... Fort Frances ON
Ministry of Natural Resources, Onta (1) .... Peterborough ON
Ministry of Natural Resources, Onta (1) .... Peterborough ON
Ministry of the Attorney General, BC (1) .... Abbotsford BC
Ministry of the Solicitor General, Ontar (1) .... Orillia ON
Ministry of Transportation, Ontar (1) .... St. Catharines ON
Ministry of Water, Land and Air Protect (1) .... Victoria BC
Minto Place Suite Hotel (1) .... Ottawa ON
Mission Services of Hamilton (1) .... Hamilton ON
Mitra Imaging Inc. (1) .... Waterloo ON
Mitsubishi Canada Ltd. (1) .... Vancouver BC
Mobilia Inc. (1) .... Pointe-Claire QC
Modern Niagara Ottawa Inc. (1) .... Kanata ON
Mold-Masters Ltd. (1) .... Georgetown ON
Monit Management Ltd. (1) .... Montréal QC
Morneau Sobeco (1) .... Toronto ON
MOSAID Technologies Inc. (1) .... Kanata ON
Mount Sinai Hospital (1) .... Toronto ON
Muki Baum Association (1) .... Toronto ON
Multiple Sclerosis Society of Canada (1) .... Toronto ON
Mutual Fund Dealers Association of Canad (1) .... Toronto ON
National Arts Centre / NAC (1) .... Ottawa ON
National Cheese Company Ltd. (1) .... Concord ON
National Research Council Canada / NRC (1) .... Ottawa ON
NetNation Communications, Inc. (1) .... Vancouver BC
NetPCS (1) .... Kanata ON
New Frontiers School Board (1) .... Chateauguay QC
NewHeights Software Corporation (1) .... Victoria BC
NexInnovations (1) .... Calgary AB
NexInnovations (1) .... Mississauga ON
Niagara, The Regional Municipality of (1) .... Thorold ON
Nightingale Health Care Inc. (1) .... Toronto ON
Nipissing University (1) .... North Bay ON
Nissin Transport (Canada) Inc. (1) .... Toronto ON
Noritsu Canada Ltd. (1) .... Mississauga ON
Norsat International Inc. (1) .... Burnaby BC
North Vancouver, The District of (1) .... North Vancouver BC
Northern Elevator Ltd. (1) .... Toronto ON
Northern Interior Regional Health (1) .... Prince George BC
Northern Lights College / NLC (1) .... Dawson Creek BC
NRCS Inc. (1) .... Ottawa ON
NRX Global Corp. (1) .... Toronto ON
NStein Technologies (1) .... Laval QC
OAO Technology Solutions / OAOT (1) .... Toronto ON
OK Transportation Ltd. (1) .... Toronto ON
Old Mill, The (1) .... Toronto ON
OMYA (Canada) Inc. (1) .... Perth ON
Ontario Bar Association / OBA (1) .... Toronto ON
Ontario English Catholic Teachers' Assoc (1) .... Toronto ON
Ontario Lottery and Gaming Corp (1) .... Sault Ste. Marie ON
Ontario March of Dimes (1) .... Toronto ON
Ontario Power Generation, Bruce Nuclear (1) .... Tiverton ON
Open Text Corporation (1) .... Waterloo ON
Orion Bus Industries Ltd. (1) .... Mississauga ON
Orlick Industries Ltd. (1) .... Hamilton ON
Ottawa Senators Hockey Club (1) .... Kanata ON
Ottawa-Carleton Transit Commission / OC T (1) .... Ottawa ON
Owens Corning Canada (1) .... Toronto ON
Pacific Blue Cross / BC Life (1) .... Vancouver BC
Par-Pak Ltd. (1) .... Brampton ON
ParaMed Home Health Care (1) .... Vancouver BC
Parks Canada Agency (1) .... Hull QC
Patheon Inc. (1) .... Whitby ON
PCL Constructors Inc. (1) .... Edmonton AB
PCsupport.com, Inc. (1) .... Burnaby BC
Peel Children's Aid Society / Peel CAS (1) .... Brampton ON
Peel District School Board (1) .... Mississauga ON
Percepta (1) .... Toronto ON
Performance Technologies, Inc. (1) .... Ottawa ON
Perth and Smiths Falls District Hos (1) .... Smiths Falls ON
Pet Valu Canada Inc. (1) .... Markham ON
Peterborough, County of (1) .... Peterborough ON
Philip Services Corporation / PSC (1) .... Burlington ON
Pika Technologies Inc. (1) .... Kanata ON
Pink Elephant Inc. (1) .... Burlington ON
Pizza Pizza Limited (1) .... Toronto ON
Port Moody, City of (1) .... Port Moody BC
Powell River, District of (1) .... Powell River BC
Priszm Brandz Inc. (1) .... Markham ON
Progestic International Inc. (1) .... Ottawa ON
Public Guardian and Trustee of British (1) .... Vancouver BC
Public Service Alliance of Canada / PSAC (1) .... Ottawa ON
Public Service Commission of Canada, BC (1) .... Victoria BC
Public Service Commission of Canada, Exec (1) .... Ottawa ON
Public Service Commission of Canada, Ont (1) .... Toronto ON
Q-Tron Ltd. (1) .... Calgary AB
R. Carmichael Ltd. (1) .... Montréal QC
Radical Entertainment (1) .... Vancouver BC
RCI Capital Group Inc. (1) .... Vancouver BC
Red Carpet Food Services (1) .... Toronto ON
Red Deer Regional Hospital Centre / RDR (1) .... Red Deer AB
Research in Motion Limited / RIM (1) .... Kanata ON
Richmond Hill, Town of (1) .... Richmond Hill ON
RioCan Real Estate Investment Trust (1) .... Toronto ON
RMH Teleservices International Inc. (1) .... Brantford ON
Rockwell Automation Canada (1) .... Cambridge ON
Rocky View No. 44, Municipal District of (1) .... Calgary AB
Rogers Cable Inc. (1) .... Toronto ON
Rogers Cable Inc. (1) .... Richmond Hill ON
Rogers Media, Publishing (1) .... Toronto ON
Roots Canada Ltd. (1) .... Toronto ON
Rouge Valley Health System, Centenary He (1) .... Toronto ON
Royal Doulton Company, The (1) .... Toronto ON
Royal Ottawa Health Care Group / ROHCG (1) .... Ottawa ON
Royal Victoria Hospital / RVH (1) .... Barrie ON
RSL COM Canada Inc. (1) .... Vancouver BC
Saint Elizabeth Health Care (1) .... Markham ON
Samuel, Son & Co., Ltd. (1) .... Mississauga ON
Saputo Inc. (1) .... St-Leonard QC
Saskatchewan Liquor and Gaming Authority (1) .... Regina SK
Saskatoon District Health (1) .... Saskatoon SK
Satisfied Brake Products Inc. (1) .... Cornwall ON
Scarborough Hospital, General Division (1) .... Toronto ON
Scarborough Hospital, Grace Division (1) .... Toronto ON
Schlumberger Canada Limited (1) .... Calgary AB
Schneider Foods Inc. (1) .... Kitchener ON
School District #36 (Surrey) (1) .... Surrey BC
School District #40 (New Westmin (1) .... New Westminster BC
SCP Science (1) .... Baie d'Urfe QC
Seawind (1) .... St-Jean-Iberville QC
Securicor Cash Services (1) .... Toronto ON
Selkirk College, Castlegar Campus (1) .... Castlegar BC
Seneca College of Applied Arts & Technol (1) .... Toronto ON
Shell Canada Limited (1) .... Fort Saskatchewan AB
Shred-it (1) .... Oakville ON
Siemens Building Technologies Ltd. (1) .... Richmond Hill ON
Siemens Milltronics Process Instrum (1) .... Peterborough ON
Simcoe, Corporation of the County of (1) .... Midhurst ON
Simcoe Muskoka Catholic District School B (1) .... Barrie ON
Sisters of Charity of Ottawa Health Servi (1) .... Ottawa ON
SkillScape (1) .... Victoria BC
Sobeys Inc., Western Division (1) .... Edmonton AB
Society of Energy Professionals, The (1) .... Toronto ON
Sony Music Canada (1) .... Toronto ON
South Lake Regional Health Centre (1) .... Newmarket ON
SpaceBridge Networks Corporation (1) .... Hull QC
Spar Aerospace Limited (1) .... Mississauga ON
Spielo Gaming International (1) .... Dieppe NB
Spin Master Toys (1) .... Toronto ON
SST (1) .... Waterloo ON
St. Catharines, City of (1) .... St. Catharines ON
St. Francis Xavier University (1) .... Antigonish NS
St. George's School (1) .... Vancouver BC
St. Joseph's Villa (1) .... Dundas ON
St. Lawrence College (1) .... Kingston ON
Stock Transportation Limited (1) .... Aurora ON
Sun Life Financial (1) .... Toronto ON
Sun Life Financial (1) .... Montréal QC
Sunnybrook & Women's College Health Scie (1) .... Toronto ON

HUMAN RESOURCE (Cont.)

Sunnybrook & Women's College Health Scie (1) .... Toronto ON
Supercom Canada Ltd. (1) .... Markham ON
SureFire Commerce Inc. (1) .... Westmount QC
Sutton Place Hotel, The (1) .... Toronto ON
Sutton Place Hotel Vancouver, The (1) .... Vancouver BC
SynchroPoint Wireless Inc. (1) .... Vancouver BC
Syncrude Canada Ltd. (1) .... Fort McMurray AB
TCT Logistics Inc. (1) .... Mississauga ON
Technical Standards & Safety Authority / (1) .... Toronto ON
Teleperformance Canada Inc. / TPCAN (1) .... Toronto ON
Telesat Canada (1) .... Gloucester ON
Tellamon Photonic Networks Inc. (1) .... Ottawa ON
Telus Corporation (1) .... Burnaby BC
Thompson Health Region (1) .... Kamloops BC
Timothy's World Coffee (1) .... Toronto ON
Top Producer Systems Inc. (1) .... Richmond BC
Toronto Blue Jays Baseball Club (1) .... Toronto ON
Toronto East General & Orthopaedic Hospi (1) .... Toronto ON
Toronto French School / TFS (1) .... Toronto ON
Toronto Police Service (1) .... Toronto ON
Toronto Star Newspapers Ltd. (1) .... Toronto ON
Toronto Zoo (1) .... Toronto ON
Toyota Canada Inc. (1) .... Toronto ON
Trader.com (1) .... Edmonton AB
Trail Appliances Ltd. (1) .... Calgary AB
Trans Mountain Pipe Line Company Ltd. (1) .... Calgary AB
Trapeze Software Inc. (1) .... Mississauga ON
Trent University (1) .... Peterborough ON
Trillium Health Care Products (1) .... Brockville ON
Trios College of Information Technol (1) .... Mississauga ON
Triversity Inc. (1) .... Toronto ON
UMA Engineering Ltd. (1) .... Edmonton AB
Unique Broadband Systems, Inc. / UBS (1) .... Concord ON
United Parcel Service Canada Ltd. / UPS (1) .... Lachine QC
University of Calgary, Faculty of Manage (1) .... Calgary AB
University of Toronto, Operations & Serv (1) .... Toronto ON
UPS Logistics Group Canada Limited (1) .... Oakville ON
Vanderwell Contractors (1971) Ltd. (1) .... Slave Lake AB
Veridian Corporation (1) .... Ajax ON
Victorian Order of Nurses, Toronto-York (1) .... Markham ON
Virtual Prototypes Inc. / VPI (1) .... Montréal QC
VoiceGenie.com (1) .... Toronto ON
Wavesat Telecom Inc. (1) .... St-Laurent QC
Wawanesa Mutual Insurance Company, The (1) .... Edmonton AB
Wescam (1) .... Burlington ON
Wescast Industries Inc. (1) .... Brantford ON
Western Pulp Limited Partnership, Por (1) .... Port Alice BC
WesternGeco (1) .... Calgary AB
Westport Innovations Inc. (1) .... Vancouver BC
William M. Mercer Limited (1) .... Ottawa ON
William Osler Health Centre, Brampton M (1) .... Brampton ON
Winnipeg, City of (Public Works Departm (1) .... Winnipeg MB
Woco Automotive Inc. (1) .... Concord ON
Workers' Compensation Board of BC (1) .... Vancouver BC
Wyndham Bristol Place Toronto Airport (1) .... Toronto ON
Xwave Solutions Inc. (1) .... Ottawa ON
York Catholic District School Board (1) .... Aurora ON
York Region District School Board (1) .... Aurora ON
Yotta Yotta Inc. (1) .... Edmonton AB
Yukon Public Service Commission (1) .... Whitehorse YT
Zircatec Precision Industries Inc. / Z (1) .... Port Hope ON

INSURANCE

See also: Actuarial, Banking, Govt./Nonprofit.

Zurich Canada (43 positions) .... Toronto ON
CGU Group Canada Ltd. (37) .... Toronto ON
Sun Life Financial (26) .... Montréal QC
Royal Bank Financial Group (16) .... Toronto ON
Lombard Canada Ltd. (15) .... Toronto ON
Industrial-Alliance Pacific Life Insur (14) .... Vancouver BC
Dominion of Canada General Insurance Com (13) .... Toronto ON
CUMIS Group Ltd., The (12) .... Burlington ON
Liberty Mutual Group (12) .... Unionville ON
National Life Assurance Company of Canad (11) .... Toronto ON

Canada Life Assurance Company (10) .... Toronto ON
Standard Life Assurance Company, The (10) .... Montréal QC
ING Western Union Insurance (9) .... Edmonton AB
Citadel General Assurance Company, The (8) .... Toronto ON
Encon Group Inc. (8) .... Ottawa ON
GE Capital Mortgage Insurance Canada (8) .... Mississauga ON
CGU Group Canada Ltd. (7) .... Edmonton AB
Mainway Insurance Brokers Ltd. (7) .... Hamilton ON
Wawanesa Mutual Insurance Company, The (7) ...... Edmonton AB
Belair Direct (6) .... Toronto ON
Cunningham & Lindsey Canada Ltd. (6) .... Hamilton ON
Export Development Corporation / EDC (6) .... Ottawa ON
ING Western Union Insurance (6) .... Vancouver BC
Royal Bank Financial Group (6) .... Montréal QC
Sun Life Financial (6) .... Toronto ON
Boiler Inspection & Insurance Company of (5) .... Toronto ON
British Columbia Automobile Association (5) .... Burnaby BC
Canada Mortgage and Housing Corporation / (5) .... Ottawa ON
Financial Services Commission of Ontario (5) .... Toronto ON
Gore Mutual Insurance Company (5) .... Cambridge ON
RBC Insurance (5) .... Calgary AB
Binks Insurance Brokers Ltd. (4) .... Ottawa ON
CAA Central Ontario (4) .... Thornhill ON
DirectProtect (4) .... Calgary AB
Dominion of Canada General Insurance C (4) .... Vancouver BC
ING Western Union Insurance (4) .... Calgary AB
Pacific Blue Cross / BC Life (4) .... Vancouver BC
Peace Hills General Insurance Company (4) .... Calgary AB
Pennsylvania Life Insurance Company (4) .... Mississauga ON
RBC Insurance (4) .... Mississauga ON
State Farm Insurance Companies (4) .... Toronto ON
UnumProvident Corporation (4) .... Burlington ON
Zurich Canada (4) .... Calgary AB
Zurich Canada (4) .... Montréal QC
Alberta Motor Association / AMA (3) .... Edmonton AB
Canadian Northern Shield Insurance Com (3) .... Vancouver BC
CGU Group Canada Ltd. (3) .... Vancouver BC
Commonwealth Insurance Company (3) .... Vancouver BC
Federated Insurance Company of Canada (3) .... Calgary AB
Federated Insurance Company of Canada (3) .... Winnipeg MB
Insurance Bureau of Canada / IBC (3) .... Toronto ON
Johnson Inc. (3) .... Richmond Hill ON
Kingsway General Insurance Company (3) .... Calgary AB
London Guarantee Insurance Company (3) .... Vancouver BC
Manulife Financial Corporation (3) .... Waterloo ON
Matrix Consulting Group Inc. (3) .... Edmonton AB
MemberCARE Financial Services (3) .... Burlington ON
Pilot Insurance Company, The (3) .... Toronto ON
Pottruff & Smith Travel Insurance Bro (3) .... Woodbridge ON
SCOR Canada Reinsurance Company (3) .... Toronto ON
Underwriters Adjustment Bureau Ltd. / UA (3) .... Toronto ON
Underwriters Adjustment Bureau Ltd. / UA (3) .... Toronto ON
VanCity Insurance Services (3) .... Vancouver BC
Western Assurance Company (3) .... Ajax ON
AIG Life of Canada (2) .... Toronto ON
Allstate Insurance Company of Canada (2) .... Calgary AB
Allstate Insurance Company of Cana (2) .... Richmond Hill ON
Allstate / Pembridge Insurance Claims S (2) .... Edmonton AB
AXA Corporate Solutions (2) .... Montréal QC
BPA Group of Companies (2) .... Toronto ON
CGU Group Canada Ltd. (2) .... Calgary AB
Citadel General Assurance Company, The (2) .... Vancouver BC
Customer Care Insurance Agency Ltd. (2) .... Mississauga ON
Dominion of Canada General Insurance Co (2) .... Edmonton AB
European Specialty Reinsurance Ltd. / ES (2) .... Toronto ON
Independent Brokerage Group, The (2) .... Vancouver BC
Investors Group (2) .... Winnipeg MB
Lawyers' Professional Indemnity Company (2) .... Toronto ON
Liberty Health (2) .... Markham ON
Lumbermen's Underwriting Alliance (2) .... Dorval QC
Manulife Financial Corporation (2) .... Ottawa ON
Ministry of Finance, Ontario (2) .... Toronto ON
Ministry of Health and Long-Term Care, O (2) .... Toronto ON
Pennsylvania Life Insurance Company (2) .... Mississauga ON
Primerica Financial Services (Canada) (2) .... Mississauga ON
RBC Insurance (2) .... Vancouver BC
RBC Insurance (2) .... Mississauga ON
Royal & SunAlliance Canada (2) .... Toronto ON
Royal & SunAlliance Canada (2) .... Ottawa ON
Swiss Reinsurance Company Canada (2) .... Toronto ON
Travel Underwriters Group of Companies, (2) .... Richmond BC
Wawanesa Mutual Insurance Company, The (2) .... Toronto ON

INSURANCE (Cont.)

ALNAV Platinum Group Inc. (1) .... Edmonton AB
Aon Corporation (1) .... Vancouver BC
AXA Pacific (1) .... Montréal QC
BMO Nesbitt Burns Inc. (1) .... Toronto ON
BPA Group of Companies (1) .... Toronto ON
CAA South Central Ontario (1) .... Hamilton ON
Canadian Blood Services / CBS (1) .... Ottawa ON
CitiFinancial Canada Inc. (1) .... London ON
Clarica Life Insurance Company (1) .... Waterloo ON
Clarica Life Insurance Company (1) .... Ottawa ON
Clarica Life Insurance Company (1) .... Montréal QC
CompClaim Management Inc. (1) .... Toronto ON
DSPA Software Inc. (1) .... Mississauga ON
Edward Jones (1) .... Mississauga ON
Empire Financial Group (1) .... Kingston ON
Equitable Life of Canada (1) .... Waterloo ON
First Canadian Title Company (1) .... Mississauga ON
GE Canada (1) .... Mississauga ON
Gibraltar Mortgage Ltd. (1) .... Calgary AB
Global Educational Trust Plan / Global E (1) .... Toronto ON
Henry Birks & Sons Inc. (1) .... Vancouver BC
Henry Birks & Sons Inc. (1) .... Toronto ON
Henry Birks & Sons Inc. (1) .... Montréal QC
Ingle Life and Health Assurance Company (1) .... Toronto ON
Keybase Financial Group (1) .... Richmond Hill ON
Kingsway Financial Services Inc. (1) .... Mississauga ON
Kootenay Savings (1) .... Trail BC
London Life Insurance Co. (1) .... London ON
Manion, Wilkins & Associates Ltd. (1) .... Toronto ON
Manulife Financial Corporation (1) .... Waterloo ON
Manulife Financial Corporation (1) .... Toronto ON
Maritime Life Assurance Company (1) .... Toronto ON
Ministry of Health and Long-Term Care, O (1) .... Sudbury ON
Ontario Lottery and Gaming Corp (1) .... Sault Ste. Marie ON
Peel, The Regional Municipality of (1) .... Brampton ON
Reliable Life Insurance Company (1) .... Hamilton ON
Royal Bank Financial Group (1) .... Vancouver BC
Royal College of Dental Surgeons of Onta (1) .... Toronto ON
Saskatchewan Workers' Compensation Board (1) .... Regina SK
SaskPower (1) .... Regina SK
SISIP Financial Services (1) .... Ottawa ON
Sodema / Transcontinental Technology (1) .... Montréal QC
Travel Guard Canada (1) .... Toronto ON
VFC Inc. (1) .... Toronto ON

INTERNATIONAL

See also: Consulting, Oil & Gas, Govt./Nonprofit, Bilingual.

Computing Devices Canada Ltd. / CDC (3 positions) .... Calgary AB
International Development Research Centre (3) .... Ottawa ON
Aga Khan Foundation Canada / AKFC (2) .... Ottawa ON
Alberta Economic Development (2) .... Edmonton AB
Alberta International and Intergovernme (2) .... Edmonton AB
Cowater International Inc. (2) .... Ottawa ON
CUSO (2) .... Ottawa ON
Export Development Corporation / EDC (2) .... Ottawa ON
Hickling Corporation (2) .... Ottawa ON
MacDonald Dettwiler & Associates Ltd. / (2) .... Richmond BC
Ministry of Economic Development and Tra (2) .... Toronto ON
Public Service Commission of Canada, Onta (2) .... Ottawa ON
University of Regina (2) .... Regina SK
World Federation of Hemophilia (2) .... Montréal QC
ACD Systems (1) .... Saanichton BC
Association of Universities and Colleges (1) .... Ottawa ON
Canadian Egg Marketing Agency / CEMA (1) .... Ottawa ON
Capilano College (1) .... North Vancouver BC
Concord Confections Inc. (1) .... Concord ON
FGI (1) .... Thornhill ON
Focus Corporation Ltd., The (1) .... Edmonton AB
GE Industrial Systems / GEINDSYS (1) .... Markham ON
George Brown College (1) .... Toronto ON
Humber College of Applied Arts and Techn (1) .... Toronto ON
IPC Resistors Inc. (1) .... Mississauga ON
Manitoba Industry, Trades and Mines / I (1) .... Winnipeg MB
Manitoba Labour & Immigration (1) .... Winnipeg MB
Mount Royal College (1) .... Calgary AB

Pacific Language Institute / PLI (1) .... Vancouver BC
PMC-Sierra, Inc. (1) .... Burnaby BC
Positron Public Safety Systems Inc. (1) .... Montréal QC
Public Service Commission of Canada, New (1) .... Moncton NB
Thrive Media (1) .... Vancouver BC
Tri Ocean Engineering Ltd. (1) .... Calgary AB
TriVu Interactive Corporation (1) .... Mississauga ON

LAW

See also: Govt./Nonprofit.

Alberta Justice (95 positions) .... Edmonton AB
Manitoba Justice / Culture, Heritage an (28) .... Winnipeg MB
Law Society of Upper Canada, The / LSUC (25) .... Toronto ON
McCarthy Tetrault LLP (16) .... Toronto ON
Ministry of the Attorney General, BC (V (14) .... Victoria BC
First Canadian Title Company (10) .... Mississauga ON
Osler, Hoskin & Harcourt LLP (10) .... Toronto ON
Stikeman Elliott (9) .... Toronto ON
Canada Life Assurance Company (8) .... Toronto ON
Fasken Martineau DuMoulin LLP (7) .... Toronto ON
Ministry of the Attorney General, (7) .... Prince George BC
Ontario Securities Commission / OSC (7) .... Toronto ON
Pallett Valo LLP (7) .... Mississauga ON
Aird & Berlis (6) .... Toronto ON
Bank of Montreal, Corporate & Legal Affa (6) .... Toronto ON
Burlington, City of (6) .... Burlington ON
Financial Services Commission of Ontario (6) .... Toronto ON
Gowling Lafleur Henderson LLP (6) .... Ottawa ON
Investment Dealers Association of Canada (6) .... Toronto ON
Kelly Howard Santini LLP (6) .... Ottawa ON
Lawyers' Professional Indemnity Company (6) .... Toronto ON
Miller Thomson LLP (6) .... Calgary AB
Miller Thomson LLP (6) .... Toronto ON
Ministry of the Attorney General, Ontari (6) .... Sudbury ON
Blaney McMurtry (5) .... Toronto ON
Department of Justice, Alberta (5) .... Edmonton AB
Donahue Ernst & Young LLP (5) .... Toronto ON
Gowling Lafleur Henderson LLP (5) .... Hamilton ON
Judicial Appointments Advisory Committee (5) .... Toronto ON
Klein Lyons (5) .... Vancouver BC
Lang Michener (5) .... Toronto ON
Lang Michener (5) .... Ottawa ON
Ministry of the Attorney General, BC (5) .... Vancouver BC
Mississauga, City of (5) .... Mississauga ON
Alberta Solicitor General (4) .... Edmonton AB
Alexander Holburn Beaudin & Lang / AHB (4) .... Vancouver BC
Borden Ladner Gervais LLP (4) .... Ottawa ON
Canadian Imperial Bank of Commerce, Lega (4) .... Toronto ON
Cassels Brock & Blackwell LLP (4) .... Toronto ON
Children's Aid Society of Toronto (4) .... Toronto ON
Dalhousie University, Faculty of Law (4) .... Halifax NS
First Professional Management Inc. (4) .... Toronto ON
Legal Aid Ontario / LAO (4) .... Toronto ON
Legal Aid Society of Alberta (4) .... Edmonton AB
Matrox Electronic Systems Ltd. (4) .... Dorval QC
McMillan Binch (4) .... Toronto ON
Ministry of the Attorney General, Ontari (4) .... Toronto ON
Ministry of the Attorney General, Ontari (4) .... Toronto ON
Ministry of the Attorney General,, Ontari (4) .... Toronto ON
Ontario Power Generation (4) .... Toronto ON
Shibley Righton LLP (4) .... Toronto ON
Toronto, City of (4) .... Toronto ON
WeirFoulds LLP (4) .... Toronto ON
Alberta Municipal Affairs (3) .... Edmonton AB
Baker & McKenzie (3) .... Toronto ON
Bell Canada, Intellectual Property Group (3) .... Toronto ON
Bishop & McKenzie (3) .... Edmonton AB
Borden Ladner Gervais LLP (3) .... Toronto ON
Carswell (3) .... Toronto ON
Chaiton & Chaiton LLP (3) .... Toronto ON
Davis & Company (3) .... Toronto ON
Department of Human Resources, Nunavut (3) .... Iqaluit NU
Department of Justice, BC (3) .... Vancouver BC
Department of Justice, Canada (3) .... Ottawa ON
Fasken Martineau DuMoulin LLP (3) .... Vancouver BC
Fogler, Rubinoff LLP (3) .... Toronto ON
Fraser Milner Casgrain LLP (3) .... Toronto ON
Heenan Blaikie (3) .... Toronto ON

LAW (Cont.)

Iacono Brown (3) .... Toronto ON
Koskie Minsky (3) .... Toronto ON
Lancaster House (3) .... Toronto ON
LandCanada Ltd. (3) .... Mississauga ON
MacDonald Dettwiler & Associates Ltd. / (3) .... Richmond BC
Mann & Gahtan (3) .... Toronto ON
Marks & Clerk (3) .... Ottawa ON
McCarthy Tetrault LLP (3) .... Vancouver BC
Minden Gross Grafstein & Greenstein (3) .... Toronto ON
Ministry of Correctional Services, Ont (3) .... North Bay ON
Ministry of Finance, BC (3) .... Victoria BC
Ministry of the Attorney General, BC (C (3) .... Kamloops BC
Ministry of the Attorney General, Ontari (3) .... Toronto ON
Ministry of the Attorney General, Ontar (3) .... Brampton ON
Ministry of the Solicitor General, Ontar (3) .... Orillia ON
Ogilvie LLP (3) .... Edmonton AB
Owens, Wright (3) .... Toronto ON
Peace River Correctional Centre (3) .... Peace River AB
Public Guardian and Trustee of British (3) .... Vancouver BC
Purolator Courier Ltd. (3) .... Toronto ON
Robins, Appleby & Taub (3) .... Toronto ON
Smith Lyons LLP (3) .... Toronto ON
Stikeman Elliott (3) .... Calgary AB
TDL Group Ltd., The (3) .... Oakville ON
Watson Goepel Maledy (3) .... Vancouver BC
York, The Regional Municipality of (3) .... Newmarket ON
Alberta Community Development (2) .... Edmonton AB
Alberta Environment (2) .... Edmonton AB
Alberta Government Services (2) .... Edmonton AB
Alberta Human Resources and Employment (2) .... Calgary AB
Alberta Infrastructure & Transportation (2) .... Edmonton AB
Alberta Learning (2) .... Edmonton AB
Alliance Atlantis Communications Inc. (2) .... Toronto ON
Athabasca University (2) .... Athabasca AB
ATI Technologies Inc. (2) .... Thornhill ON
BASF Canada Inc. (2) .... Toronto ON
Black, Sutherland, Crabbe LLP (2) .... Toronto ON
Bombardier Aerospace (2) .... Montréal QC
Brans, Lehun, Baldwin (2) .... Toronto ON
Brown Economic Assessments Inc. (2) .... Calgary AB
Burgar, Rowe (2) .... Barrie ON
Calgary, City of (2) .... Calgary AB
Canadian Institute, The (2) .... Toronto ON
CGU Group Canada Ltd. (2) .... Toronto ON
Chappell Bushell Stewart (2) .... Toronto ON
Corel Corporation (2) .... Ottawa ON
DataMirror Corporation (2) .... Markham ON
Department of Justice, Nova Scotia (Corp (2) .... Halifax NS
Devry, Smith & Frank (2) .... Toronto ON
Enron Canada Corp. (2) .... Calgary AB
Export Development Corporation / EDC (2) .... Ottawa ON
Falconer Charney Macklin (2) .... Toronto ON
Fincentric Corp. (2) .... Richmond BC
General Hydrogen / GH (2) .... Vancouver BC
Giffen Lee (2) .... Kitchener ON
Gilbert, Wright & Kirby (2) .... Toronto ON
Goodman Phillips & Vineberg (2) .... Toronto ON
Groia & Company (2) .... Toronto ON
Group Telecom (2) .... Toronto ON
Hamilton, Duncan, Armstrong & Stewart (2) .... Surrey BC
Hughes, Amys (2) .... Toronto ON
Investment Dealers Association of Cana (2) .... Vancouver BC
JDS Uniphase Corporation (2) .... Nepean ON
John Cannings, Barristers (2) .... Toronto ON
Kahn Zack Ehrlich Lithwick (2) .... Richmond BC
Law Society of British Columbia, The (2) .... Vancouver BC
Lazier Hickey Langs O'Neal (2) .... Hamilton ON
Legislative Assembly of Ontario, Office (2) .... Toronto ON
Ma'mowe Capital Region, Child and Famil (2) .... Edmonton AB
Magna International Inc. (2) .... Aurora ON
Maritime Life Assurance Company (2) .... Toronto ON
Ministry of Children and Family De (2) .... Prince George BC
Ministry of Children and Family Develop (2) .... Kamloops BC
Ministry of Community and Social Servi (2) .... Newmarket ON
Ministry of Consumer and Business Servic (2) .... Toronto ON
Ministry of Correctional Services, Ontar (2) .... Toronto ON
Ministry of Correctional Services, Ontari (2) .... London ON
Ministry of Finance, Ontario (2) .... Toronto ON

Ministry of Health and Ministry Respons (2) .... Victoria BC
Ministry of Labour, Ontario (2) .... Toronto ON
Ministry of Municipal Affairs, BC (2) .... Victoria BC
Ministry of Social Development and Eco (2) .... Coquitlam BC
Ministry of the Attorney General, BC (2) .... Abbotsford BC
Ministry of the Attorney General, Ontari (2) .... Toronto ON
Ministry of the Attorney General, Ontari (2) .... Toronto ON
Ministry of the Attorney General, Ontari (2) .... Toronto ON
Ministry of the Environment, Ontario (In (2) .... Toronto ON
Ministry of the Environment, Ontario (Le (2) .... Toronto ON
Ministry of the Solicitor General, Ontari (2) .... Aylmer ON
Murchison, Thomson & Clarke (2) .... Surrey BC
Mutual Fund Dealers Association of Canad (2) .... Toronto ON
Nortel Networks (2) .... Ottawa ON
Oakwood Associates (2) .... Calgary AB
Ogilvy Renault (2) .... Toronto ON
Osler, Hoskin & Harcourt LLP (2) .... Calgary AB
Pace, Johnson (2) .... Toronto ON
Pavey, Law (2) .... Cambridge ON
Peel Children's Aid Society / Peel CAS (2) .... Brampton ON
Piasetzki & Nenniger (2) .... Toronto ON
Poss & Halfnight (2) .... Toronto ON
Public Service Commission of Canada, Al (2) .... Edmonton AB
Public Service Commission of Canada, Onta (2) .... Ottawa ON
Ridout & Maybee LLP (2) .... Toronto ON
Saputo Inc. (2) .... St-Leonard QC
Shoppers Drug Mart (2) .... Toronto ON
Simmons Da Silva & Sinton LLP (2) .... Brampton ON
St. Albert, The City of (2) .... St. Albert AB
Standard Life Assurance Company, The (2) .... Montréal QC
Stewart Title Guaranty Company (2) .... Toronto ON
Stikeman Elliot (2) .... Vancouver BC
Surrey, City of (2) .... Surrey BC
Syndesis Limited (2) .... Richmond Hill ON
Talstra & Company (2) .... Terrace BC
Transamerica Life Canada (2) .... Toronto ON
University of British Columbia, Facul (2) .... Vancouver BC
University of Guelph (2) .... Guelph ON
University of Toronto, Operations & Serv (2) .... Toronto ON
UnumProvident Corporation (2) .... Burlington ON
Walker, Head (2) .... Pickering ON
Westport Innovations Inc. (2) .... Vancouver BC
Workplace Safety & Insurance Appeals Tri (2) .... Toronto ON
Zenastra Photonics Inc. (2) .... Ottawa ON
AIG Life of Canada (1) .... Toronto ON
Air Canada (1) .... Montréal QC
Alberta Energy Company Ltd. / AEC (1) .... Calgary AB
Alberta Energy Company Ltd. / AEC (1) .... Calgary AB
Alberta Health and Wellness (1) .... Edmonton AB
Alberta International and Intergovernme (1) .... Edmonton AB
Alberta School Boards Association / ASB (1) .... Edmonton AB
Alberta Sustainable Resource Developmen (1) .... Edmonton AB
Alcohol and Gaming Commission of Ontario (1) .... Toronto ON
Algonquin Travel Corporation (1) .... Ottawa ON
AnorMED Inc. (1) .... Langley BC
Bank of Canada (1) .... Ottawa ON
Barrie, City of (1) .... Barrie ON
Bazaar & Novelty (1) .... St. Catharines ON
Bennett Jones LLP (1) .... Calgary AB
Bombardier Transportation (1) .... Kingston ON
British Columbia Institute of Technology (1) .... Burnaby BC
British Columbia Investment Management (1) .... Victoria BC
Brookfield LePage Johnson Controls Facil (1) .... Markham ON
Burns International Security Services (1) .... Gloucester ON
Butterworths Canada Ltd. (1) .... Markham ON
Cadillac Fairview Corporation Limited, T (1) .... Toronto ON
Canada Deposit Insurance Corporation / CD (1) .... Ottawa ON
Canada Mortgage and Housing Corporation / (1) .... Ottawa ON
Canada-Nova Scotia Offshore Petroleum Bo (1) .... Halifax NS
Canadian Association of Broadcasters / CA (1) .... Ottawa ON
Canadian Bankers Association / CBA (1) .... Toronto ON
Canadian Blood Services / CBS (1) .... Ottawa ON
Canadian Copyright Licensing Agency / CA (1) .... Toronto ON
Canadian Medical Protective Association / (1) .... Ottawa ON
Casino Niagara (1) .... Niagara Falls ON
Catholic Children's Aid Society of Toron (1) .... Toronto ON
CentreCorp Management Services Ltd. (1) .... Markham ON
Children's Aid Society of Ottawa-Carl (1) .... Gloucester ON
Cirque du Soleil (1) .... Montréal QC
College of Nurses of Ontario / CNO (1) .... Toronto ON
College of Physicians and Surgeons of On (1) .... Toronto ON
College of the North Atlantic, Step (1) .... Stephenville NF

For descriptions of the occupational categories used in this index, see page 458.

LAW (Cont.)

Columbia House Canada (1) .... Toronto ON
CompClaim Management Inc. (1) .... Toronto ON
Computing Devices Canada Ltd. / CDC (1) .... Ottawa ON
CUMIS Group Ltd., The (1) .... Burlington ON
Dairy Queen Canada Inc. (1) .... Burlington ON
Delcon Development Group Ltd. (1) .... Edmonton AB
Department of Human Resources, Nuna (1) .... Rankin Inlet NU
Department of Human Resources, Nunavut (1) .... Igloolik NU
Department of Municipal and Provincia (1) .... St. John's NF
Department of Public Safety, NB (1) .... Fredericton NB
Descartes Systems Group (1) .... Waterloo ON
Edmonton, City of (1) .... Edmonton AB
Emily Carr Institute of Art and Design (1) .... Vancouver BC
Empire Financial Group (1) .... Kingston ON
Enbridge Consumers Gas (1) .... Toronto ON
Enbridge Pipelines Inc. (1) .... Edmonton AB
EPCOR Utilities Inc. (1) .... Edmonton AB
Fairmont Royal York (1) .... Toronto ON
Family and Children's Services Ni (1) .... St. Catharines ON
Farm Credit Canada / FCC (1) .... Regina SK
Federated Insurance Company of Canada (1) .... Winnipeg MB
Fidelity Investments Canada Limited (1) .... Toronto ON
Financial Institutions Commission / FI (1) .... Vancouver BC
Financial Transactions and Reports Analys (1) .... Ottawa ON
Focus Foundation of BC (1) .... Vancouver BC
Frontenac Children's Aid Society (1) .... Kingston ON
Gen-X Sports Inc. (1) .... Toronto ON
Georgian College (1) .... Barrie ON
Gowling Lafleur Henderson LLP (1) .... Montréal QC
Grande Prairie, City of (1) .... Grande Prairie AB
Grant MacEwan College, Jasper Place Cam (1) .... Edmonton AB
Greater Toronto Airports Authority / GTA (1) .... Toronto ON
Halton Hills, Town of (1) .... Halton Hills ON
Halton Regional Police Service / HRPS (1) .... Oakville ON
Halton, The Regional Municipality of (1) .... Oakville ON
Hamilton, City of (1) .... Hamilton ON
Hewitt Associates (1) .... Toronto ON
Holt Renfrew (1) .... Toronto ON
Hyprotech Ltd. (1) .... Calgary AB
Hyundai Auto Canada (1) .... Markham ON
Inex Pharmaceuticals Corp. (1) .... Burnaby BC
Information and Privacy Commissioner, On (1) .... Toronto ON
Infowave Software, Inc. (1) .... Burnaby BC
ING Canada (1) .... Toronto ON
Intercon Security Ltd. (1) .... Toronto ON
John Howard Society of Canada (1) .... Kingston ON
Justice Institute of BC / JIBC (1) .... New Westminster BC
Kamloops, City of (1) .... Kamloops BC
Kawartha Lakes, Corporation of the City (1) .... Lindsay ON
Keystone Child and Family Services Aut (1) .... Innisfail AB
Kingston, Corporation of the City of (1) .... Kingston ON
Kingston General Hospital (1) .... Kingston ON
Kingsway Financial Services Inc. (1) .... Mississauga ON
Lethbridge Community College / LCC (1) .... Lethbridge AB
Liquor Control Board of Ontario / LCBO (1) .... Toronto ON
Liquor Distribution Branch, BC / LDB (1) .... Vancouver BC
Loblaw Properties Ltd. / LPL (1) .... Toronto ON
Loewen Group Inc., The (1) .... Toronto ON
Lombard Canada Ltd. (1) .... Toronto ON
London, City of (1) .... London ON
London Guarantee Insurance Company (1) .... Toronto ON
Loyalty Group, The (1) .... Toronto ON
MacDonald Dettwiler & Associates Ltd. / M (1) .... Ottawa ON
Macleod Dixon LLP (1) .... Calgary AB
Management Board Secretariat (1) .... Toronto ON
Manitoba Conservation (1) .... Winnipeg MB
Manitoba Consumer & Corporate Affairs / (1) .... Winnipeg MB
Manitoba Finance (1) .... Winnipeg MB
Manitoba Hydro (1) .... Winnipeg MB
Manitoba Transportation & Government Se (1) .... Winnipeg MB
Manulife Financial Corporation (1) .... Waterloo ON
Manulife Financial Corporation (1) .... Ottawa ON
Maple Lodge Farms Ltd. (1) .... Norval ON
Markham, Corporation of the Town of (1) .... Markham ON
Med-Eng Systems Inc. (1) .... Ottawa ON
Minacs Worldwide Inc. (1) .... Markham ON
Ministry of Advanced Education, Trainin (1) .... Victoria BC
Ministry of Children and Family Developm (1) .... Nanaimo BC
Ministry of Children and Family Develop (1) .... Victoria BC

Ministry of Community and Social Ser (1) .... Thunder Bay ON
Ministry of Community and Social Services (1) .... Ottawa ON
Ministry of Community and Social Service (1) .... Toronto ON
Ministry of Correctional Services, Ontar (1) .... Toronto ON
Ministry of Correctional Services, Onta (1) .... Kingston ON
Ministry of Finance, Ontario (1) .... Toronto ON
Ministry of Forests, BC (Research Branc (1) .... Victoria BC
Ministry of Health and Long-Term Care, O (1) .... Toronto ON
Ministry of Health and Long-Term Care, (1) .... Kingston ON
Ministry of Labour, Ontario (1) .... Ottawa ON
Ministry of Municipal Affairs and Housin (1) .... Toronto ON
Ministry of Natural Resources, Ontario (1) .... Cochrane ON
Ministry of Natural Resources, Ontario (1) .... Toronto ON
Ministry of the Attorney General, Ontari (1) .... Toronto ON
Ministry of the Environment, Ontario (Ce (1) .... Toronto ON
Ministry of Water, Land and Air Protect (1) .... Victoria BC
Morneau Sobeco (1) .... Toronto ON
MOSAID Technologies Inc. (1) .... Kanata ON
Mount Royal College (1) .... Calgary AB
MuscleTech Research and Development (1) .... Mississauga ON
National Bank of Greece / NBG (1) .... Montréal QC
National Life Assurance Company of Canad (1) .... Toronto ON
New Westminster, City of (1) .... New Westminster BC
Newmarket, Town of (1) .... Newmarket ON
Niagara Credit Union Limited (1) .... St. Catharines ON
Novopharm Ltd. (1) .... Toronto ON
Object Technology International Inc. / OT (1) .... Ottawa ON
Office of the Auditor General of Canada (1) .... Ottawa ON
Ontario Human Rights Commission / OHRC (1) .... Toronto ON
Ontario Lottery and Gaming Corporation / (1) .... Toronto ON
Ontario Native Affairs Secretariat / ONA (1) .... Toronto ON
Ontario Teachers' Pension Plan Board (1) .... Toronto ON
Oshawa, City of (1) .... Oshawa ON
OZ Optics Ltd. (1) .... Carp ON
PanCanadian Petroleum Ltd. (1) .... Calgary AB
Paradata Systems Inc. (1) .... Whistler BC
Peel, The Regional Municipality of (1) .... Brampton ON
Pengrowth Management Ltd. / PML (1) .... Calgary AB
Port Moody, City of (1) .... Port Moody BC
Praxair Canada Inc. (1) .... Mississauga ON
Primerica Financial Services (Canada (1) .... Mississauga ON
Prince George, City of (1) .... Prince George BC
Public Service Commission of Canada, B (1) .... Vancouver BC
Public Service Commission of Canada, Qu (1) .... Montréal QC
Public Service Commission, PEI (1) .... Charlottetown PE
Queen's University, Joseph S. Stauffer (1) .... Kingston ON
Research in Motion Limited / RIM (1) .... Waterloo ON
Royal Bank Financial Group (1) .... Calgary AB
Royal Bank Financial Group (1) .... Toronto ON
Royal & SunAlliance Canada (1) .... Toronto ON
Ruffneck Heaters (1) .... Calgary AB
Ryerson Polytechnic University (1) .... Toronto ON
Simcoe County Children's Aid Society / Si (1) .... Barrie ON
Soloway Wright (1) .... Kingston ON
Sony Music Canada (1) .... Toronto ON
St. Catharines, City of (1) .... St. Catharines ON
St. Joseph's Health Centre (1) .... Toronto ON
Stantec Geomatics Ltd. (1) .... Edmonton AB
Suncor Energy Inc. (1) .... Calgary AB
Sutton Place Hotel Vancouver, The (1) .... Vancouver BC
Talisman Energy Inc. (1) .... Calgary AB
Technical Standards & Safety Authority / (1) .... Toronto ON
Toronto Humane Society (1) .... Toronto ON
Toronto Hydro (1) .... Toronto ON
Toronto Transit Commission / TTC (1) .... Toronto ON
Toronto Zoo (1) .... Toronto ON
Trans Mountain Pipe Line Company Ltd. (1) .... Calgary AB
TransAlta Corporation (1) .... Calgary AB
Triversity Inc. (1) .... Toronto ON
Underwriters Adjustment Bureau Ltd. / UA (1) .... Toronto ON
Unique Broadband Systems, Inc. / UBS (1) .... Concord ON
United Parcel Service Canada Ltd. / UPS (1) .... Delta BC
University of Calgary (1) .... Calgary AB
Value Village (1) .... Port Moody BC
Watchfire (1) .... Kanata ON
Wescam (1) .... Burlington ON
Weyerhaeuser Company Limited (1) .... Vancouver BC
William M. Mercer Limited (1) .... Toronto ON
William Morris Law Offices (1) .... Hamilton ON
Williams Energy Canada Inc. (1) .... Calgary AB
Windsor Casino Limited (1) .... Windsor ON
Worldwide Immigration Consultancy Se (1) .... Mississauga ON

LAW (Cont.)

Wyeth-Ayerst Canada Inc. (1) .... Toronto ON
York University (1) .... Toronto ON
Zi Corporation of Canada Inc. (1) .... Calgary AB

LIBRARIANS

See also: Education, Health/Medical.

Public Service Commission of Canada (11 positions) St. John's NF
National Research Council Canada, Canada (7) .... Ottawa ON
Lakeridge Health Corporation (6) .... Oshawa ON
Canadian Institute for Health Informatio (5) .... Toronto ON
Hospital for Sick Children, The (5) .... Toronto ON
Public Service Commission of Canada, Ont (5) .... Toronto ON
Simon Fraser Health Region, Burnaby Hosp (5) .... Burnaby BC
Calgary, City of (4) .... Calgary AB
QLT Inc. (4) .... Vancouver BC
Toronto Rehabilitation Institute (4) .... Toronto ON
Alberta Justice (3) .... Edmonton AB
Brock University (3) .... St. Catharines ON
Cambridge Public Library (3) .... Cambridge ON
Markham Stouffville Hospital (3) .... Markham ON
Ottawa Hospital, The (3) .... Ottawa ON
Providence Health Care, St. Paul's Hos (3) .... Vancouver BC
Public Service Commission, PEI (3) .... Charlottetown PE
Richmond Hill Public Library (3) .... Richmond Hill ON
St. Joseph's Healthcare Hamilton (3) .... Hamilton ON
THiiNC Information Management Inc. (3) .... Toronto ON
Toronto-Sunnybrook Regional Cancer Centr (3) .... Toronto ON
University of Calgary (3) .... Calgary AB
University of Manitoba Libraries (3) .... Winnipeg MB
William Osler Health Centre, Brampton M (3) .... Brampton ON
Bloorview MacMillan Children's Centre, M (2) .... Toronto ON
Canadian Institute for Health Information (2) .... Ottawa ON
Data Research Associates / DRA (2) .... Montréal QC
Department of Education, New Brunswi (2) .... Fredericton NB
Export Development Corporation / EDC (2) .... Ottawa ON
Inex Pharmaceuticals Corp. (2) .... Burnaby BC
Lakeridge Health Corporation (2) .... Oshawa ON
Manitoba Education, Training & Youth (2) .... Winnipeg MB
Manitoba Justice / Culture, Heritage an (2) .... Winnipeg MB
Manitoba Labour & Immigration (2) .... Winnipeg MB
Ministry of Small Business, Tourism and (2) .... Burnaby BC
Mount Royal College (2) .... Calgary AB
NPS Pharmaceuticals Inc. (2) .... Mississauga ON
Providence Health Care, St. Vincent's (2) .... Vancouver BC
Red Deer College (2) .... Red Deer AB
Research in Motion Limited / RIM (2) .... Waterloo ON
Royal Victoria Hospital / RVH (2) .... Barrie ON
Sagebrush Corporation (2) .... Edmonton AB
Scarborough Hospital, Grace Division (2) .... Toronto ON
Simcoe County District School Board (2) .... Midhurst ON
South Lake Regional Health Centre (2) .... Newmarket ON
St. Mary's General Hospital (2) .... Kitchener ON
Trillium Health Centre (2) .... Toronto ON
Vancouver Hospital and Health Sciences (2) .... Vancouver BC
York Central Hospital (2) .... Richmond Hill ON
Acadia University (1) .... Wolfville NS
Alberta Community Development (1) .... Edmonton AB
Alberta Energy Company Ltd. / AEC (1) .... Calgary AB
Alberta Finance (1) .... Edmonton AB
Alberta Municipal Affairs (1) .... Edmonton AB
Apotex Inc. (1) .... Toronto ON
AstraZeneca (1) .... Mississauga ON
Athabasca University (1) .... Athabasca AB
Banff Centre, The (1) .... Banff AB
Bank of Canada (1) .... Ottawa ON
Brandon University (1) .... Brandon MB
Brant Community Healthcare System, Bra (1) .... Brantford ON
British Columbia Automobile Association (1) .... Burnaby BC
British Columbia Institute of Technology (1) .... Burnaby BC
British Columbia Securities Commission (1) .... Vancouver BC
Burlington Resources Canada Energy Ltd. (1) .... Calgary AB
Canada Council for the Arts, The (1) .... Ottawa ON
Canada Customs and Revenue Agency / CCRA (1) ...... Ottawa ON
Capital Health Region / CHR (1) .... Victoria BC

Capital Health, Royal Alexandra Hospita (1) .... Edmonton AB
Centre for Addiction and Mental Health (1) .... Toronto ON
Children's and Women's Health Centre o (1) .... Vancouver BC
College of New Caledonia (1) .... Prince George BC
College of the North Atlantic, Clare (1) .... Clarenville NF
Cornwall General Hospital (1) .... Cornwall ON
Country Day School, The (1) .... King City ON
Credit Valley Hospital, The (1) .... Mississauga ON
Cree School Board (1) .... Mistissini QC
CroMedica Inc. (1) .... Ottawa ON
East Central Regional Health Authority (1) .... Camrose AB
Excalibur-Gemini Group Ltd., The (1) .... Calgary AB
Fanshawe College (1) .... London ON
Financial Services Commission of Ontario (1) .... Toronto ON
Forest Renewal BC (1) .... Victoria BC
Fraser Valley Health Region (1) .... Mission BC
Fraser Valley Regional Library / FVRL (1) .... Abbotsford BC
GlaxoSmithKline (1) .... Mississauga ON
Global Television Network Inc. (1) .... Toronto ON
Grand River Hospital (1) .... Kitchener ON
Grant MacEwan College, Jasper Place Cam (1) .... Edmonton AB
Grey Bruce Health Services (1) .... Owen Sound ON
Hamilton Health Sciences Corporation, C (1) .... Hamilton ON
Hamilton-Wentworth District School Boar (1) .... Hamilton ON
Havergal College (1) .... Toronto ON
Hay River Community Health Board (1) .... Hay River NT
Health Sciences Centre / HSC (1) .... Winnipeg MB
Hemosol Inc. (1) .... Toronto ON
Hotel-Dieu Grace Hospital (1) .... Windsor ON
Institute of Health Economics / IHE (1) .... Edmonton AB
Joseph Brant Memorial Hospital (1) .... Burlington ON
Kawartha Lakes, Corporation of the City (1) .... Lindsay ON
Keyano College (1) .... Fort McMurray AB
King's Health Centre (1) .... Toronto ON
Kingston General Hospital (1) .... Kingston ON
Kingston Regional Cancer Centre (1) .... Kingston ON
Lakeridge Health Corporation (1) .... Bowmanville ON
Lantern Communications Canada Inc. (1) .... Ottawa ON
Laurentian University (1) .... Sudbury ON
Law Society of Upper Canada, The / LSUC (1) .... Toronto ON
Legislative Assembly of Ontario, Office (1) .... Toronto ON
Lethbridge Community College / LCC (1) .... Lethbridge AB
Limestone District School Board (1) .... Kingston ON
Lockheed Martin Canada Inc. (1) .... Kanata ON
Management Board Secretariat (1) .... Toronto ON
MDS Aero Support Corporation (1) .... Ottawa ON
Ministry of Aboriginal Affairs, BC (1) .... Victoria BC
Ministry of Citizenship, Culture and Rec (1) .... Toronto ON
Ministry of Municipal Affairs and Housin (1) .... Toronto ON
Ministry of Natural Resources, Ont (1) .... Kirkland Lake ON
Ministry of Northern Development and Min (1) .... Sudbury ON
Ministry of the Solicitor General, Ontari (1) .... Aylmer ON
Ministry of Transportation, Ontario (1) .... Thunder Bay ON
National Research Council Canada, Institu (1) .... Ottawa ON
National Research Council Canada / NRC (1) .... Ottawa ON
North Island College / NIC (1) .... Courtenay BC
Ontario HIV Treatment Network / OHTN (1) .... Toronto ON
Ontario Pension Board (1) .... Toronto ON
Optech Inc. (1) .... Toronto ON
Peel District School Board (1) .... Mississauga ON
Peel, The Regional Municipality of (1) .... Brampton ON
Port Moody, City of (1) .... Port Moody BC
Public Service Commission of Canada, New (1) .... Moncton NB
Queen's University, Joseph S. Stauffer (1) .... Kingston ON
Richmond, City of (1) .... Richmond BC
Samson Canada Ltd. (1) .... Calgary AB
Sanmina Enclosure Systems (1) .... Toronto ON
Saskatoon District Health (1) .... Saskatoon SK
Scarborough Hospital, General Division (1) .... Toronto ON
School District #60 (Peace River N (1) .... Fort St. John BC
Senstar-Stellar Corporation (1) .... Carp ON
Simon Fraser Health Region / SFH (1) .... New Westminster BC
Simon Fraser Health Region / SFH (1) .... New Westminster BC
SNC-Lavalin Inc. (1) .... Montréal QC
Southern Alberta Institute of Technology (1) .... Calgary AB
Spielo Gaming International (1) .... Dieppe NB
Sprint Canada Inc. (1) .... Toronto ON
St. Michael's Hospital (1) .... Toronto ON
Sunnybrook & Women's College Health Scie (1) .... Toronto ON
Surrey Place Centre (1) .... Toronto ON
Tarian Software Inc. (1) .... Ottawa ON
Technical University of British Columbia (1) .... Surrey BC

For descriptions of the occupational categories used in this index, see page 458.

LIBRARIANS (Cont.)

Thomas & Betts Limited (1) .... Iberville QC
Toronto East General & Orthopaedic Hospi (1) .... Toronto ON
Tracer Industries Canada Ltd. (1) .... Edmonton AB
University College of the Fraser Vall (1) .... Abbotsford BC
University of Guelph (1) .... Guelph ON
Vancouver / Richmond Health Board (1) .... Vancouver BC
West Park Healthcare Centre (1) .... Toronto ON
Westport Innovations Inc. (1) .... Vancouver BC
Workplace Safety & Insurance Appeals Tri (1) .... Toronto ON
York, The Regional Municipality of (1) .... Newmarket ON
Zenastra Photonics Inc. (1) .... Ottawa ON

LOGISTICS

See also: Purchasing, Transport, Operations, Actuarial.

Magna International Inc. (12 positions) .... Concord ON
UPS Logistics Group Canada Limited (10) .... Oakville ON
ABC Group Inc. (8) .... Toronto ON
Apotex Inc. (8) .... Toronto ON
ATI Technologies Inc. (7) .... Thornhill ON
OZ Optics Ltd. (7) .... Carp ON
Velan Inc. (7) .... Montréal QC
Webplan Inc. (7) .... Ottawa ON
Magna International Inc. (5) .... Concord ON
Research in Motion Limited / RIM (5) .... Waterloo ON
Atlantis Systems International (4) .... Brampton ON
Delmar International Inc. (4) .... Lachine QC
Exel Canada (4) .... Sardis BC
JDS Uniphase Corporation (4) .... Nepean ON
LNB Inc. (4) .... Toronto ON
Rittal Systems Ltd. (4) .... Mississauga ON
Siemens Canada Ltd. (4) .... Mississauga ON
Surface Mount Technology Centre Inc. / S (4) .... Markham ON
USCO Logistics (4) .... Dorval QC
Adexa (3) .... Toronto ON
Carswell (3) .... Toronto ON
Computing Devices Canada Ltd. / CDC (3) .... Ottawa ON
DSC Group of Companies (3) .... Toronto ON
DSM Biologics (3) .... Montréal QC
Duplium Corporation (3) .... Thornhill ON
EMS Technologies Canada Ltd (3) .... Ste-Anne-de-Bellevue QC
Evans Consoles Inc. (3) .... Calgary AB
Johnson & Johnson Medical Products (3) .... Markham ON
MSAS Global Logistics (3) .... Richmond BC
Patheon Inc. (3) .... Mississauga ON
RCP Inc. (3) .... Concord ON
Sanmina Enclosure Systems (3) .... Toronto ON
Siemens Westinghouse (3) .... Hamilton ON
Solectron (3) .... Calgary AB
Spar Aerospace Limited (3) .... Mississauga ON
Tellamon Photonic Networks Inc. (3) .... Ottawa ON
TransAlta Corporation (3) .... Calgary AB
Affiliated Customs Brokers Limited (2) .... Montréal QC
AiT Corporation (2) .... Ottawa ON
Alpha Technologies Ltd. (2) .... Burnaby BC
Auto Sense (2) .... Mississauga ON
Backyard Products Limited (2) .... Collingwood ON
Bartle & Gibson Co. Ltd. (2) .... Port Coquitlam BC
Bombardier Aerospace (2) .... Montréal QC
Canada Bread Company Ltd. (2) .... Calgary AB
Capital Metal Industries (2) .... Toronto ON
CHEP Canada Inc. (2) .... Mississauga ON
CMC Electronics Inc. (2) .... Kanata ON
CMC Electronics Inc. (2) .... St-Laurent QC
Coca-Cola Bottling Company (2) .... Calgary AB
Communications Test Design, Inc. / CTDI (2) .... Oakville ON
Computing Devices Canada Ltd. / CDC (2) .... Calgary AB
Confluence Watersports Canada Inc. (2) .... Gananoque ON
CPUsed (2) .... Toronto ON
Dairyworld Foods Inc. (2) .... Brampton ON
DDK Apparel Inc. (2) .... Montréal QC
Decolin Inc. (2) .... Montréal QC
Dumex Medical (2) .... Toronto ON
DY 4 Systems Inc. (2) .... Kanata ON
Evertz Microsystems Ltd. (2) .... Burlington ON

Fiesta Barbeques Limited (2) .... Brampton ON
Fireplace Products International / FPI (2) .... Delta BC
Frost Fence & Wire Products Ltd. (2) .... Hamilton ON
GlaxoSmithKline (2) .... Mississauga ON
Global Thermoelectric Inc. (2) .... Calgary AB
Groupe Dynamite Inc. (2) .... Mount Royal QC
Groupe J.S. International (2) .... Montréal QC
H. Paulin & Co. Limited (2) .... Toronto ON
Heidelberg Canada (2) .... Toronto ON
Hunter Amenities International Ltd. (2) .... Burlington ON
IKO Industries Ltd. (2) .... Brampton ON
Ingram Micro Inc. (Canada) (2) .... Mississauga ON
Instantel Inc. (2) .... Kanata ON
Interhome Furniture (2) .... Markham ON
JDS Uniphase Corporation (2) .... Saanichton BC
Kaycan Ltd. (2) .... Pointe-Claire QC
Knoll North America Corporation (2) .... Toronto ON
Linamar Corporation, Eston Division (2) .... Guelph ON
Lockheed Martin Canada Inc. (2) .... Kanata ON
Maple Leaf Pork, Case Reddi Facilit (2) .... Stoney Creek ON
Maple Leaf Poultry (2) .... Toronto ON
Martin-Brower of Canada Co. (2) .... New Westminster BC
MEDIS Health & Pharmaceutical Servic (2) .... Mississauga ON
Milne & Craighead Inc. (2) .... Calgary AB
Ministry of Natural Resources, Ontario (F (2) .... Dryden ON
Mobilia Inc. (2) .... Pointe-Claire QC
Montage.dmc eBusiness Services (2) .... Ottawa ON
Nanowave Technologies Inc. (2) .... Toronto ON
Ontario Lottery and Gaming Corporation / (2) .... Toronto ON
Parasuco Jeans Inc. (2) .... St-Laurent QC
Parker Hannifin (Canada) Inc. (2) .... Grimsby ON
PBB Global Logistics (2) .... Richmond BC
Pet Valu Canada Inc. (2) .... Markham ON
PMC-Sierra, Inc. (2) .... Burnaby BC
Purdy's Chocolates (2) .... Vancouver BC
Quadra Chemicals Ltd. (2) .... Vaudreuil-Dorion QC
Rogers AT&T Wireless (2) .... Toronto ON
Rogers Cable Inc., Calgary Distribution (2) .... Calgary AB
Royal Group Technologies Inc. (2) .... Woodbridge ON
RSL COM Canada Inc. (2) .... Vancouver BC
Schneider Foods Inc. (2) .... Kitchener ON
Shopping Channel, The / TSC (2) .... Mississauga ON
Snap-On Tools of Canada Ltd. (2) .... Mississauga ON
Source Medical Corporation (2) .... Mississauga ON
Spirent Communications (2) .... Ottawa ON
Staples Business Depot Ltd. (2) .... Markham ON
Superior Cabinets Alberta Ltd. (2) .... Edmonton AB
Tiercon Industries Inc. (2) .... Stoney Creek ON
Tower Group International Canada Inc (2) .... Mississauga ON
Tower Group International Canada Inc. (2) .... Montréal QC
Tracer Industries Canada Ltd. (2) .... Edmonton AB
Trane Central Ontario (2) .... Toronto ON
Trillium Health Centre (2) .... Toronto ON
United Nations Children's Fund / UNICEF (2) .... Toronto ON
Van der Graaf Inc. (2) .... Brampton ON
Weishaupt Corporation (2) .... Mississauga ON
Wescam (2) .... Burlington ON
Westcan Wireless (2) .... Edmonton AB
Willson International Ltd. (2) .... Mississauga ON
Winpak Technologies Inc. (2) .... Toronto ON
Zenastra Photonics Inc. (2) .... Ottawa ON
AcceLight Networks (1) .... Nepean ON
Accent Labels Inc. (1) .... St-Laurent QC
ACL Services Ltd. (1) .... Vancouver BC
Advantex Marketing International Inc. (1) .... Toronto ON
AiT Corporation (1) .... Nepean ON
AlarmForce Industries Inc. (1) .... Toronto ON
Alberta Energy Company Ltd. / AEC (1) .... Calgary AB
Alberta Environment (1) .... Edmonton AB
Alberta Health and Wellness (1) .... Edmonton AB
Alberta Human Resources and Employment (1) .... Edmonton AB
Alberta Infrastructure & Transportation (1) .... Edmonton AB
Alcatel Canada Inc., Transport Automatio (1) .... Toronto ON
Alcoa Rexdale Packaging (1) .... Toronto ON
Algo Group Inc. (1) .... Montréal QC
Aliron Marketing Canada Inc. (1) .... Woodbridge ON
Allcan Electronic Distributors (1) .... Edmonton AB
Alltemp Sensors Inc. (1) .... Edmonton AB
Almag Aluminum Inc. (1) .... Brampton ON
Alphagraphics (1) .... Mississauga ON
AMEC (1) .... Vancouver BC
Amico - ISG (1) .... Burlington ON

LOGISTICS (Cont.)

Amram's Distributing Ltd. (1) .... Brampton ON
APW Enclosure Systems (1) .... Milton ON
Aramark Canada Ltd. (1) .... Toronto ON
ASA Alloys (1) .... Toronto ON
Ash City (1) .... Toronto ON
AstraZeneca (1) .... Mississauga ON
ATS Test Systems Inc. (1) .... Woodbridge ON
Aventis Pharma Inc. (1) .... Laval QC
Avon Engineering Ltd. (1) .... Waterdown ON
Aware Marketing Group (1) .... Toronto ON
B.C. Decker Inc. (1) .... Hamilton ON
Babco Sales Ltd. (1) .... Surrey BC
Bantrel Inc. (1) .... Calgary AB
Bariatrix International Inc. (1) .... Lachine QC
Bata Retail Canada (1) .... Toronto ON
Bazaar & Novelty (1) .... St. Catharines ON
BC Gas Utility Ltd. (1) .... Vancouver BC
Becker Group (1) .... Toronto ON
BECO Industries Ltd. (1) .... Anjou QC
Belbois Ltd. (1) .... Laval QC
Bell Helicopter Textron Canada (1) .... Mirabel QC
Bell Intrigna (1) .... Calgary AB
BMW Canada Inc. (1) .... Whitby ON
Bombardier Aerospace, Defense Services (1) .... Mirabel QC
Bragg Photonics Inc. (1) .... Dorval QC
Brenntag Canada Inc. (1) .... Toronto ON
Building Box, The (1) .... Markham ON
Burlington Technologies Inc., Burling (1) .... Burlington ON
C/S Construction Specialties Ltd. (1) .... Mississauga ON
C2 Media.com (1) .... Brantford ON
Cadbury Trebor Allan Inc. (1) .... Toronto ON
Cadbury Trebor Allan Inc. (1) .... Hamilton ON
Calgary, City of (1) .... Calgary AB
Canada Bread Company Ltd. (1) .... Edmonton AB
Canada Bread Company Ltd. (1) .... Concord ON
Canada Customs and Revenue Agency / CCRA (1) .... Ottawa ON
Canadian Broadcasting Corporation / CBC (1) .... Ottawa ON
Canadian General-Tower Ltd. (1) .... Cambridge ON
Canadian Global Foods Corporation (1) .... Toronto ON
Canadian Petcetera Limited Partnership (1) .... Delta BC
Canadian Survey Equipment Ltd. / Cansel (1) .... Burnaby BC
Canadian Tire Corporation Ltd. (1) .... Edmonton AB
Cangene Corporation (1) .... Winnipeg MB
CanRoof Corporation Inc. (1) .... Toronto ON
Capital Health, Royal Alexandra Hospita (1) .... Edmonton AB
Catena Networks (1) .... Kanata ON
CDA Industries Inc. (1) .... Pickering ON
Celestica Inc. (1) .... Toronto ON
CIBA Vision Sterile Manufacturing (1) .... Mississauga ON
CIMTEK Automation Systems (1) .... Burlington ON
Ciot Marble & Granite Inc. (1) .... Concord ON
Cirque du Soleil (1) .... Montréal QC
Classwave Wireless Inc. (1) .... Toronto ON
CML ATC Technologies Inc. (1) .... Hull QC
CML Emergency Services, Inc. (1) .... Hull QC
Cogeco Cable Inc. (1) .... Burlington ON
Cole Vision Canada, Inc. (1) .... Markham ON
Collections Andrade Inc. (1) .... Montréal QC
Collins & Aikman (1) .... Toronto ON
Columbia MBF (1) .... Mississauga ON
Commercial Spring and Tool Company L (1) .... Mississauga ON
Comstock Canada Ltd (1) .... Mississauga ON
Conair Consumer Products Inc. (1) .... Brampton ON
Consultronics Ltd. (1) .... Concord ON
Cowell Auto Group (1) .... Richmond BC
Creation Technologies Inc. (1) .... Mississauga ON
Crown Cork & Seal Canada Inc. (1) .... Concord ON
CTS of Canada Ltd. (1) .... Streetsville ON
Cummins Inc. (1) .... Toronto ON
Daito Precision Inc. (1) .... St-Laurent QC
Danier Leather Inc. (1) .... Toronto ON
Debiasi Group, The / DBG (1) .... Mississauga ON
Decor-Rest Furniture Ltd. (1) .... Woodbridge ON
Denso Manufacturing Canada, Inc. (1) .... Guelph ON
Department of Justice, Nova Scotia (Corp (1) .... Halifax NS
Dolico Printing (1) .... Ottawa ON
Dominion Colour Corporation (1) .... Toronto ON
Dresser Flow Control (1) .... Burlington ON
DRS Flight Safety and Communicati (1) .... Carleton Place ON
DSC Group of Companies (1) .... Concord ON
DuPont Canada Inc. (1) .... Mississauga ON
Dynamic Chocolates Inc. (1) .... Annacis Island BC
Dynamic Source Manufacturing Inc. (1) .... Calgary AB
Ecolab Ltd. (1) .... Mississauga ON
EFOS Corporation (1) .... Mississauga ON
Electro Sonic Inc. (1) .... Toronto ON
Electronics Boutique (1) .... Brampton ON
Emco Ltd. (1) .... Richmond BC
EMS Technologies Canada Ltd. (1) .... Ottawa ON
Ensil International (1) .... Markham ON
Excel Tech Ltd. / XLTEK (1) .... Oakville ON
EXI Wireless Systems Inc. (1) .... Richmond BC
Export Packers Company Ltd. (1) .... Brampton ON
F & K Mfg. Co. Limited (1) .... Toronto ON
Famous Players Inc. (1) .... Toronto ON
Faucher Industries Inc. (1) .... St-Leonard QC
Faurecia (1) .... Toronto ON
FCI Canada Inc. (1) .... Markham ON
FCX Specialty Valves (1) .... Mississauga ON
Federated Co-operatives Limited / FCL (1) .... Calgary AB
Federated Co-operatives Limited / FCL (1) .... Saskatoon SK
Fellfab Limited (1) .... Hamilton ON
Fernlea Flowers Ltd. (1) .... Delhi ON
Filtel Microwave Inc. (1) .... Vaudreuil-Dorion QC
Filtran Microcircuits Inc. (1) .... Ottawa ON
Fireco Inc. (1) .... Mississauga ON
First Air (1) .... Carp ON
Fluid Motion Technologies (1) .... Mississauga ON
Fluor Canada Ltd. (1) .... Calgary AB
Forzani Group Ltd., The (1) .... Calgary AB
Fritz Starber Inc. (1) .... Mississauga ON
fSONA Communications Corp. (1) .... Richmond BC
Fuji Photo Film Canada Inc. (1) .... Mississauga ON
Future Electronics Inc. (1) .... Pointe-Claire QC
G.E. Shnier Co. (1) .... Brampton ON
Gage Applied, Inc. (1) .... Lachine QC
GE Canada (1) .... Mississauga ON
GE Canada (1) .... Peterborough ON
GE Power Systems (1) .... Calgary AB
GE Power Systems (1) .... Guelph ON
Gear Centre Group of Companies, The (1) .... Edmonton AB
Gen-X Sports Inc. (1) .... Toronto ON
General Motors of Canada Ltd., Diesel Div (1) .... London ON
Genfoot Manufacturing (1) .... St-Laurent QC
Gennum Corporation (1) .... Burlington ON
Gentek Building Products Ltd. (1) .... Burlington ON
GFI Control Systems Inc. (1) .... Kitchener ON
Giffels Associates Limited (1) .... Toronto ON
Golden Boy Foods Inc. (1) .... Burnaby BC
Grant MacEwan College, Jasper Place Cam (1) .... Edmonton AB
Graybar Electric (Ontario) Ltd. (1) .... Kitchener ON
Great Atlantic & Pacific Co. of Canada L (1) .... Toronto ON
Grenville Management Services (1) .... Toronto ON
Greyhound Canada Transportation Corp. (1) .... Calgary AB
Grocery Gateway (1) .... Mississauga ON
GSI Lumonics Inc. (1) .... Kanata ON
Haliburton & White Group, Th (1) .... Dollard-des-Ormeaux QC
Hall of Names International Inc. (1) .... Kingston ON
Hamilton Hydro Inc. (1) .... Hamilton ON
Health Sciences Centre / HSC (1) .... Winnipeg MB
Heidelberg Canada (1) .... Mississauga ON
Henry Birks & Sons Inc. (1) .... Montréal QC
Henry Schein Arcona Inc. (1) .... St. Catharines ON
Herbon Naturals, Inc. (1) .... Richmond BC
Hershey Canada Inc. (1) .... Smith Falls ON
Hofland Ltd. (1) .... Mississauga ON
Honeywell IC (1) .... North Vancouver BC
Hush Puppies Canada (1) .... St-Laurent QC
Hymopack Ltd. (1) .... Toronto ON
IBM Canada Ltd. (1) .... Markham ON
ICP Global Technologies (1) .... Montréal QC
IKEA Calgary (1) .... Calgary AB
Ilco Unican Inc. (1) .... Montréal QC
Indeka Group, The (1) .... Oakville ON
Indigo Manufacturing Inc. (1) .... Markham ON
Inforetech Wireless Technology Inc. (1) .... Surrey BC
Innovator Electronic Assembly / IEA (1) .... Lachine QC
IPC Resistors Inc. (1) .... Mississauga ON
JDS Uniphase Corporation, Fiber-Optic Pr (1) .... Markham ON
JFB Technologies Inc. (1) .... Markham ON

LOGISTICS (Cont.)

Kawneer Company Canada Ltd. (1) ... Toronto ON
KCI Medical Canada, Inc. (1) ... Mississauga ON
Kelron Logistics (1) ... Surrey BC
Kingston General Hospital (1) ... Kingston ON
Kobe Interior Products Inc. (1) ... Burlington ON
Kohl & Frisch Limited (1) ... Concord ON
Kretschmar Inc. (1) ... Toronto ON
Kvaerner Process Systems / KPS (1) ... Calgary AB
Labatt Breweries Ontario (1) ... Toronto ON
Lanzarotta Wholesale Grocers Ltd. (1) ... Concord ON
Layfield Plastics Ltd. (1) ... Richmond BC
Lindor Inc. (1) ... Montréal QC
Liquidators Clearinghouse Inc. / LCI (1) ... Calgary AB
Liquor Distribution Branch, BC / LDB (1) ... Vancouver BC
Loblaw Companies Ltd. (1) ... Mississauga ON
Lowe-Martin Group, The (1) ... Ottawa ON
Main Knitting Inc. (1) ... Montréal QC
Maple Leaf Consumer Foods (1) ... Mississauga ON
Maple Leaf Poultry (1) ... Mississauga ON
March Networks Corporation (1) ... Kanata ON
Marks Supply Inc. (1) ... Kitchener ON
Matsu Manufacturing Inc. (1) ... Brampton ON
McCormick Canada Inc. (1) ... Mississauga ON
MDS Aero Support Corporation (1) ... Ottawa ON
MDS Nordion (1) ... Kanata ON
MedTec Marketing Limited (1) ... Burnaby BC
Mentor Engineering (1) ... Calgary AB
Mercedes-Benz Canada Inc. (1) ... Toronto ON
Meritor Suspension Systems Company (1) ... Milton ON
MetroPhotonics Inc. (1) ... Ottawa ON
Meubles Prestige Furniture (1) ... Orleans ON
Mevotech Inc. (1) ... Toronto ON
Micrologix Biotech Inc. (1) ... Vancouver BC
MicroSlate Inc. (1) ... Brossard QC
Minacs Worldwide Inc. (1) ... Richmond Hill ON
Ministry of Economic Development and Tra (1) ... Toronto ON
Ministry of Education / Ministry of Trai (1) ... Toronto ON
Ministry of Finance, BC (1) ... Victoria BC
Ministry of Forests, BC (Fort St. (1) ... Fort St. James BC
Ministry of Natural Resources, Ontario (F (1) ... Garson ON
Ministry of the Environment, Ontario (La (1) ... Toronto ON
Ministry of Transportation, Ontario (1) ... Thunder Bay ON
Mistahia Health Region (1) ... Grande Prairie AB
Mitchell Plastics Ltd. (1) ... Kitchener ON
Mitec Telecom Inc. (1) ... Pointe-Claire QC
Money's Mushrooms Ltd. (1) ... Campbellville ON
Montship Inc. (1) ... Mississauga ON
Mount Royal College (1) ... Calgary AB
Natrel Inc. (1) ... Toronto ON
NCR Canada Ltd. (1) ... Waterloo ON
NEPCAN Engineering Ltd. (1) ... Vancouver BC
Nestle Canada Inc. (1) ... Toronto ON
Nexen Inc. (1) ... Calgary AB
Nissin Transport (Canada) Inc. (1) ... Toronto ON
Norsat International Inc. (1) ... Burnaby BC
North Okanagan Health Region / NOHR (1) ... Armstrong BC
Novopharm Ltd. (1) ... Toronto ON
NPS Pharmaceuticals Inc. (1) ... Mississauga ON
NRB Inc. (1) ... Grimsby ON
NSI Communications (1) ... Pointe-Claire QC
Nuance Global Traders (Canada) Inc. (1) ... Richmond BC
Oakrun Farm Bakery Ltd. (1) ... Ancaster ON
Office Specialty (1) ... Toronto ON
Ontario Store Fixtures Inc. / OSF (1) ... Toronto ON
Optech Inc. (1) ... Toronto ON
Orion Bus Industries Ltd. (1) ... Mississauga ON
Overseas Express Consolidators Inc. / O (1) ... Montréal QC
P&H MinePro Services (1) ... Calgary AB
Pacific National Aquaculture (1) ... Victoria BC
Paging Network of Canada, Inc. / PageN (1) ... Vancouver BC
Palliser Furniture Ltd. (1) ... Airdrie AB
Panalpina Inc. (1) ... Mississauga ON
Parkhurst Knitwear (1) ... Toronto ON
Party Packagers (1) ... Toronto ON
Patella Manufacturing Inc. (1) ... Lasalle QC
Patheon Inc. (1) ... Toronto ON
Peregrine Systems, Inc. (1) ... Ottawa ON
PerkinElmer Optoelectronics Inc. (1) ... Vaudreuil QC
Petro-Canada (1) ... Calgary AB
Phantom Manufacturing (International) (1) ... Abbotsford BC
Phillips Petroleum Resources, Ltd. (1) ... Calgary AB
Piping Resources (1) ... Edmonton AB
Praxair Canada Inc. (1) ... Delta BC
Proco Machinery Inc. (1) ... Mississauga ON
Provincial Store Fixtures Ltd. (1) ... Mississauga ON
Psion Teklogix Inc. (1) ... Mississauga ON
Q-Media Services Corporation (1) ... Richmond BC
QLT Inc. (1) ... Vancouver BC
Quality Goods IMD Inc. (1) ... St-Laurent QC
Quebecor World Printpak (1) ... Calgary AB
Red Carpet Food Services (1) ... Stoney Creek ON
ReserveAmerica (1) ... Milton ON
Retail Ready Foods Inc. (1) ... Mississauga ON
Revolve Magnetic Bearings Inc. (1) ... Calgary AB
RexCan Circuits Inc. (1) ... Belleville ON
Rexel Canada Inc. (1) ... Burlington ON
Roe Logistics (1) ... Montréal QC
Rogers Cable Inc. (1) ... Saint John NB
Rogers Communications Inc. (1) ... Toronto ON
Roofmart Alberta Inc. (1) ... Calgary AB
Ropak Canada Inc. (1) ... Oakville ON
Royal Alliance Inc. (1) ... Woodbridge ON
Royal Bank Financial Group (1) ... Calgary AB
Russel Metals Inc. (1) ... New Westminister BC
Russell A. Farrow Limited (1) ... Ayr ON
S.A. Armstrong Ltd. (1) ... Toronto ON
San Francisco Group (1) ... Boucherville QC
Saputo Inc., Milk Division (1) ... Vancouver BC
Saskatoon District Health (1) ... Saskatoon SK
Schlumberger Canada Limited (1) ... Calgary AB
Schneider Foods Inc. (1) ... Mississauga ON
Scholastic Canada Ltd. (1) ... Markham ON
Scintrex Trace Corp. (1) ... Ottawa ON
Scott Paper Ltd. (1) ... Hull QC
Shared Services West, Regional Materials (1) ... Toronto ON
Shoppers Drug Mart (1) ... Toronto ON
Shopping Channel, The / TSC (1) ... Toronto ON
Siemens Automotive (1) ... London ON
Siemens Building Technologies Ltd., Cer (1) ... Richmond BC
Simon Fraser Health Region / SFH (1) ... New Westminster BC
Skjodt-Barrett Foods (1) ... Mississauga ON
Smart Technologies Inc. (1) ... Calgary AB
Smart Technologies Inc. (1) ... Stittsville ON
SNC-Lavalin Inc. (1) ... Montréal QC
SNC-Lavalin Inc., Chemicals & Petroleum (1) ... Calgary AB
Sobotec Ltd. (1) ... Hamilton ON
Solinet Systems Inc. (1) ... Ottawa ON
Spar Aerospace Limited (1) ... Edmonton AB
SS8 Networks Inc. (1) ... Ottawa ON
Stone & Webster Canada Limited (1) ... Toronto ON
Storkcraft Baby (1) ... Richmond BC
Summit Food Service Distributors Inc. (1) ... London ON
Suncor Energy Inc. (1) ... Calgary AB
Suncor Energy Inc., Oil Sands (1) ... Fort McMurray AB
Supercom Canada Ltd. (1) ... Markham ON
TELAV Audio Visual Services (1) ... Toronto ON
TELAV Audio Visual Services (1) ... Ottawa ON
Teldon International Inc. (1) ... Richmond BC
TelTech Assets.Com Ltd. (1) ... Calgary AB
Telus Mobility (1) ... Toronto ON
Thomas & Betts Limited (1) ... Iberville QC
Thorburn Equipment Inc. (1) ... Pointe-Claire QC
Tilley Endurables (1) ... Toronto ON
Tommy Hilfiger Canada Inc. (1) ... Montréal QC
Toromont CAT (1) ... Concord ON
Toromont Process Systems, Division of To (1) ... Calgary AB
Toshiba of Canada Limited (1) ... Markham ON
Trans Mountain Pipe Line Company Ltd. (1) ... Calgary AB
Trapeze Software Inc. (1) ... Mississauga ON
Trends International Corporation (1) ... Mississauga ON
Triple-C Inc. (1) ... Hamilton ON
Trophy Foods Inc. (1) ... Mississauga ON
Tube-Fab Ltd. (1) ... Mississauga ON
University of Calgary (1) ... Calgary AB
University of Toronto Press Inc. / UTP (1) ... Toronto ON
Valcom Limited (Ottawa) (1) ... Ottawa ON
Venetor Equipment Rental Inc. (1) ... Hamilton ON
Vestshell Inc. (1) ... Montréal QC
VIPswitch Inc. (1) ... Montréal QC
Visionwall Corporation (1) ... Edmonton AB
Vistek Ltd. (1) ... Toronto ON

LOGISTICS (Cont.)

Volvo Laval (1) .... Laval QC
Vopak Canada Ltd. (1) .... Toronto ON
Voyus Canada Inc. (1) .... Burnaby BC
VQuip Inc. (1) .... Burlington ON
Wajax Industries Limited (1) .... Mississauga ON
Wesco Distribution Canada Inc. (1) .... Markham ON
West Coast Apparel Inc. (1) .... Vancouver BC
Westfair Foods Ltd. (1) .... Burnaby BC
Weyerhaeuser Company Limited (1) ...... Edmonton AB
Willard Meats International Ltd. (1) .... Mississauga ON
Wilton Industries Canada Ltd. (1) .... Toronto ON
Windsor Casino Limited (1) .... Windsor ON
Wolfe Merchandising (1) .... Toronto ON
World Heart Corporation (1) .... Ottawa ON
XCELLSiS (1) .... Burnaby BC
Zircatec Precision Industries Inc. / Z (1) .... Port Hope ON

MANAGEMENT

See also: Consulting.

Bates Project Management Inc. (2 positions) .... Ottawa ON
Ministry of the Attorney General, Ontari (2) .... Toronto ON
Rockwell Automation Canada (2) .... Cambridge ON
Voyus Canada Inc. (2) .... Burnaby BC
Acklands-Grainger Inc. / AGI (1) .... Richmond Hill ON
Advanced Research Technologies Inc. / (1) .... St-Laurent QC
Alias / Wavefront (1) .... Toronto ON
Atlantis Systems International (1) .... Brampton ON
Canada Life Assurance Company (1) .... Toronto ON
CMC Electronics Inc. (1) .... St-Laurent QC
Cohoes Fashions Inc. (1) .... Montréal QC
Don Park Inc. (1) .... Toronto ON
EMS Technologies Canada Ltd (1) .... Ste-Anne-de-Bellevue QC
ENMAX Corporation (1) .... Calgary AB
Gilmore (1) .... Toronto ON
Gilmore Global Logistics Services / DocuL (1) .... Kanata ON
Great-West Life Assurance Company, The (1) .... Winnipeg MB
Hydro Ottawa (1) .... Ottawa ON
IBM Canada Ltd. (1) .... Markham ON
Institute of Health Economics / IHE (1) .... Edmonton AB
InterTAN, Inc. / RadioShack (1) .... Barrie ON
Jackman Manor (1) .... Aldergrove BC
Jo-Van Distributors Inc. (1) .... Toronto ON
Malaspina University-College, Nanaimo Ca (1) .... Nanaimo BC
Mark Anthony Group (1) .... Vancouver BC
McMaster University (1) .... Hamilton ON
Ministry of Community and Social Service (1) .... Toronto ON
Ministry of the Environment, Ontario (1) .... Toronto ON
Mobilia Inc. (1) .... Pointe-Claire QC
Mount Pleasant Group of Cemeteries (1) .... Toronto ON
Nedco (1) .... Richmond BC
Ontario Lottery and Gaming Corporation / (1) .... Toronto ON
Optech Inc. (1) .... Toronto ON
Panorama Business Views (1) .... Toronto ON
Pitney Bowes Management Services Canada (1) ...... Toronto ON
Raytheon Systems Canada Ltd. (1) .... Waterloo ON
ReserveAmerica (1) .... Milton ON
Shred-it (1) .... Oakville ON
Siemens Canada Ltd. (1) .... Mississauga ON
Simplot Canada Limited (1) .... Brandon MB
Sobeys Inc., Western Division (1) .... Edmonton AB
Southern Alberta Institute of Technology (1) .... Calgary AB
Superior Emergency Vehicles Ltd. (1) .... Red Deer AB
Thames Valley District School Board (1) .... London ON
Toronto Rehabilitation Institute (1) .... Toronto ON
Troy Manufacturing Ltd. (1) .... Brockville ON

MARKETING

See also: Sales, Direct Mktng., Advertising, Public Relations.

Research in Motion Limited / RIM (16 positions) .... Waterloo ON
Loyalty Group, The (10) .... Toronto ON
ATI Technologies Inc. (7) .... Thornhill ON

ENMAX Corporation (7) .... Calgary AB
DataMirror Corporation (6) .... Markham ON
Ministry of Economic Development and Tra (6) .... Toronto ON
Rogers Cable Inc. (6) .... Toronto ON
Solect Technology Group (6) .... Toronto ON
Corel Corporation (5) .... Ottawa ON
Med-Eng Systems Inc. (5) .... Ottawa ON
PrinterON Corporation (5) .... Kitchener ON
Rogers AT&T Wireless (5) .... Toronto ON
Sitraka Software Inc. (5) .... Toronto ON
Webplan Inc. (5) .... Ottawa ON
Fincentric Corp. (4) .... Richmond BC
LifeScan Canada Ltd. (4) .... Burnaby BC
Mitra Imaging Inc. (4) .... Waterloo ON
Procuron Inc. (4) .... Thornhill ON
Rogers Communications Inc. (4) .... Toronto ON
Ruffneck Heaters (4) .... Calgary AB
Sprint Canada Inc. (4) .... Toronto ON
ACNielsen Company of Canada (3) .... Markham ON
Aramark Canada Ltd. (3) .... Toronto ON
AT&T Canada (3) .... Toronto ON
Boulevard Media (Canada) Inc. / BMC (3) .... Vancouver BC
Centrepoint Technologies Inc. (3) .... Ottawa ON
CMC Electronics Inc. (3) .... St-Laurent QC
Convedia Corporation (3) .... Burnaby BC
CPI Plastics Group Ltd. (3) .... Mississauga ON
CreoScitex (3) .... Burnaby BC
Elcan Optical Technologies (3) .... Midland ON
GE Canada (3) .... Mississauga ON
Hummingbird Ltd. (3) .... Toronto ON
Intuit Canada Limited (3) .... Edmonton AB
March Networks Corporation (3) .... Kanata ON
MetaQuest Software (3) .... Montréal QC
MetroPhotonics Inc. (3) .... Ottawa ON
Northwood Technologies Inc. (3) .... Nepean ON
Ontario Lottery and Gaming Corporation / (3) .... Toronto ON
ReserveAmerica (3) .... Milton ON
S.A. Armstrong Ltd. (3) .... Toronto ON
Selkirk Financial Technologies, Inc. (3) .... Vancouver BC
Shoppers Drug Mart (3) .... Toronto ON
Sitraka Mobility (3) .... Toronto ON
Smart Technologies Inc. (3) .... Calgary AB
Spielo Gaming International (3) .... Dieppe NB
01 Communique Laboratory Inc. (2) .... Mississauga ON
ACD Systems (2) .... Saanichton BC
Advantex Marketing International Inc. (2) .... Toronto ON
Alberta Treasury Branches / ATB (2) .... Edmonton AB
AldrichPears Associates (2) .... Vancouver BC
Alliance Atlantis Communications Inc. (2) .... Toronto ON
Alterna Technologies Group Inc. (2) .... Calgary AB
BBM Bureau of Measurement (2) .... Toronto ON
Bell Intrigna (2) .... Calgary AB
Boehringer Ingelheim (Canada) Ltd. (2) .... Burlington ON
BTI Photonics Inc. (2) .... Ottawa ON
Burntsand Inc. (2) .... Vancouver BC
Cadillac Fairview Corporation Limited, T (2) .... Toronto ON
Calgary, City of (2) .... Calgary AB
Canada Life Assurance Company (2) .... Toronto ON
Cap Gemini Ernst & Young / CGEY (2) .... Toronto ON
Casino Niagara (2) .... Niagara Falls ON
Chemque Inc. (2) .... Toronto ON
Cimmetry Systems Inc. / CSI (2) .... St-Laurent QC
CIMTEK Automation Systems (2) .... Burlington ON
Civil Service Co-operative Credit Society (2) .... Ottawa ON
Class Software Solutions Ltd. (2) .... Burnaby BC
Club Monaco International (2) .... Toronto ON
Dairy Queen Canada Inc. (2) .... Burlington ON
EFA Software Services Ltd. (2) .... Calgary AB
Electro Sonic Inc. (2) .... Toronto ON
EMS Technologies Canada Ltd (2) .... Ste-Anne-de-Bellevue QC
Famous Players Inc. (2) .... Toronto ON
Federated Co-operatives Limited / FCL (2) .... Saskatoon SK
Fiera Foods Company (2) .... Toronto ON
Gage Applied, Inc. (2) .... Lachine QC
Ganz (2) .... Woodbridge ON
GE Syprotec Inc. (2) .... Pointe-Claire QC
George Brown College (2) .... Toronto ON
H.J. Heinz Company of Canada Ltd. (2) .... Toronto ON
IceFyre Semiconductor Inc. (2) .... Ottawa ON
Imaging Research Inc. (2) .... St. Catharines ON
Interactive Circuits and Systems Ltd. (2) .... Gloucester ON
INTRIA-HP (2) .... Toronto ON

For descriptions of the occupational categories used in this index, see page 458.

MARKETING (Cont.)

MARKETING (Cont.)

Impact Services (1) .... Toronto ON
In-Touch Survey Systems Inc. (1) .... Ottawa ON
Industrial-Alliance Pacific Life Insur (1) .... Vancouver BC
Inforetech Wireless Technology Inc. (1) .... Surrey BC
Infrastructures for Information, Inc. / (1) .... Toronto ON
Instantel Inc. (1) .... Kanata ON
InSystems Technologies, Inc. (1) .... Markham ON
Intellitactics Inc. (1) .... Kitchener ON
Irwin Toy Limited (1) .... Toronto ON
J. Walter Company Ltd. (1) .... Pointe-Claire QC
Jazz Monkey Media (1) .... Toronto ON
JDS Uniphase Corporation (1) .... Nepean ON
JVC Canada Inc. (1) .... Toronto ON
Kanotech Information Systems Ltd. (1) .... Edmonton AB
Kazootek Technologies (1) .... Vancouver BC
Kinsmen & Kinette Clubs of Canada (1) ...... Cambridge ON
Lanzarotta Wholesale Grocers Ltd. (1) .... Concord ON
Laura Canada (1) .... Toronto ON
Lenbrook (1) .... Pickering ON
Lifestyle Retirement Communities (1) .... Vancouver BC
Loewen Group Inc., The (1) .... Burnaby BC
Loewen Group Inc., The (1) .... Toronto ON
Lumenon (1) .... St-Laurent QC
Madvac Inc. (1) .... Longueuil QC
Manitoba Transportation & Government Se (1) .... Winnipeg MB
MapInfo Corporation (1) .... Toronto ON
Marchon Canada (1) .... Dorval QC
Matthew / Scott (1) .... Mississauga ON
Maxxam Analytics Inc. (1) .... Mississauga ON
McCormick Canada Inc. (1) .... London ON
McMaster University, Michael G. DeGroot (1) .... Hamilton ON
MedcomSoft Inc. (1) .... Toronto ON
Medisys Health Group Inc. (1) .... Toronto ON
Mercedes-Benz Canada Inc. (1) .... Toronto ON
Merisel Canada Inc. (1) .... Toronto ON
Metabo Canada Inc. (1) .... Mississauga ON
MIBRO Group, The (1) .... Toronto ON
Mikasa (1) .... Markham ON
Ministry of Consumer and Business Servic (1) .... Toronto ON
Ministry of Natural Resources, Onta (1) .... Peterborough ON
Mitec Telecom Inc. (1) .... Pointe-Claire QC
Mitsubishi Canada Ltd. (1) .... Vancouver BC
MKS Inc. (1) .... Waterloo ON
Mobilift (1) .... Calgary AB
Mount Pleasant Group of Cemeteries (1) .... Toronto ON
Mount Royal College (1) .... Calgary AB
MovieGoods (1) .... Calgary AB
National Bank of Greece / NBG (1) .... Montréal QC
New Automation Corporation / NAC (1) ...... Burlington ON
Nexmedia Technologies Inc. (1) .... Burnaby BC
Nextron Corporation (1) .... Calgary AB
Nortel Networks (1) .... Ottawa ON
Northern Alberta Institute of Technolog (1) ...... Edmonton AB
Novator Systems Ltd. (1) .... Toronto ON
Novopharm Ltd. (1) .... Toronto ON
Oakwood Associates (1) .... Calgary AB
Objexis Corporation (1) .... Montréal QC
Ontario Heritage Foundation, Corporate S (1) .... Toronto ON
Ontario Lottery and Gaming Corp (1) .... Sault Ste. Marie ON
Onvia.com (1) .... Vancouver BC
Optimal Robotics Corp. (1) .... Montréal QC
Ottawa, City of (1) .... Ottawa ON
Oxford Properties Group Inc. (1) .... Edmonton AB
P&H MinePro Services (1) .... Calgary AB
Paisley Products of Canada (1) .... Toronto ON
Pangaea Systems Inc. (1) .... Edmonton AB
Paradata Systems Inc. (1) .... Whistler BC
Patheon Inc. (1) .... Mississauga ON
PCsupport.com, Inc. (1) .... Burnaby BC
Pearson Peacekeeping Centre / PPC (1) ...... Clementsport NS
Penguin Books Canada Ltd. (1) .... Toronto ON
Peregrine Systems, Inc. (1) .... Ottawa ON
Phantom Manufacturing (International) (1) ...... Abbotsford BC
Phase Technology (1) .... Richmond BC
PhytoDerm Inc. (1) .... Montréal QC
Pizza Pizza Limited (1) .... Toronto ON
Please Mum (1) .... Vancouver BC
Positron Public Safety Systems Inc. (1) .... Montréal QC
Precidia Technologies (1) .... Kanata ON

PrimeWest Energy Trust (1) .... Calgary AB
Psion Teklogix Inc. (1) .... Mississauga ON
Public Service Commission of Canada, Al (1) .... Edmonton AB
PureEdge Solutions Inc. (1) .... Victoria BC
PyroGenesis Inc. (1) .... Montréal QC
Quake Technologies Inc. (1) .... Ottawa ON
QuestAir Technologies Inc. (1) .... Burnaby BC
Quick Link Communications Ltd. / QLC (1) .... Calgary AB
Radarsat International (1) .... Richmond BC
Radiant Communications (1) .... Vancouver BC
RAM Computer Group Inc. (1) .... Vaughan ON
Rational Software Corporation (1) .... Kanata ON
Resonance Photonics Inc. (1) .... Markham ON
Retail Ready Foods Inc. (1) .... Mississauga ON
Revolve Magnetic Bearings Inc. (1) .... Calgary AB
Rittal Systems Ltd. (1) .... Mississauga ON
RJL Packaging & Labelling Industries In (1) .... Montréal QC
RMH Teleservices International Inc. (1) .... Brantford ON
Roe Logistics (1) .... Montréal QC
RSL COM Canada Inc. (1) .... Vancouver BC
Ryerson Polytechnic University, School o (1) .... Toronto ON
Schneider Foods Inc. (1) .... Kitchener ON
SciCan (1) .... Toronto ON
Serca Foodservice Inc., Western Divisio (1) ...... Edmonton AB
ShawCor Ltd. (1) .... Toronto ON
Shirmax Fashions Ltd. (1) .... Montréal QC
Shopping Channel, The / TSC (1) .... Toronto ON
Sierra Wireless Inc. (1) .... Richmond BC
Silicon Video (1) .... Toronto ON
SMED International Inc. (1) .... Calgary AB
SNC-Lavalin Inc. (1) .... Edmonton AB
Solid Caddgroup Inc. (1) .... Markham ON
Solinst Canada Ltd. (1) .... Georgetown ON
Solvay Pharma Inc. (1) .... Toronto ON
Spin Master Toys (1) .... Toronto ON
SS8 Networks Inc. (1) .... Ottawa ON
SST (1) .... Waterloo ON
Stantec Consulting Ltd. (1) .... Vancouver BC
Stantec Geomatics Ltd. (1) .... Edmonton AB
Sun Life Financial (1) .... Toronto ON
Supercom Canada Ltd. (1) .... Markham ON
Synavant Inc. (1) .... Toronto ON
Taymor Industries (1) .... Delta BC
TDL Group Ltd., The (1) .... Oakville ON
Teldon International Inc. (1) .... Richmond BC
TELOS Technology Inc. (1) .... Richmond BC
Ten Star Financial Services / Ten Star (1) .... Waterdown ON
Tenaquip Ltd. (1) .... Ste-Anne-de-Bellevue QC
Thrive Media (1) .... Vancouver BC
TOA Canada Corporation (1) .... Mississauga ON
Top Producer Systems Inc. (1) .... Richmond BC
Trios College of Information Technol (1) .... Mississauga ON
Triversity Inc. (1) .... Toronto ON
University of Calgary (1) .... Calgary AB
URS Cole, Sherman (1) .... Thornhill ON
VHA Home HealthCare (1) .... Toronto ON
Virtual Prototypes Inc. / VPI (1) .... Montréal QC
Vitana Corporation (1) .... Ottawa ON
Vogue Brassiere Incorporated (1) .... Toronto ON
VoiceGenie.com (1) .... Toronto ON
Vopak Canada Ltd. (1) .... Toronto ON
Waterloo, City of (1) .... Waterloo ON
WaveMakers Research Inc. (1) .... Vancouver BC
WD-40 Products (Canada) Ltd. (1) .... Toronto ON
Web Krew Inc. (1) .... Toronto ON
Weber Marking Systems of Canada (1) .... Mississauga ON
Weekenders Canada Inc. (1) .... Richmond Hill ON
Welch & Company (1) .... Ottawa ON
WestBay Semiconductor Inc. (1) .... Vancouver BC
Westfair Foods Ltd. (1) .... Calgary AB
Westminster Savings Credit Union (1) .... New Westminster BC
White Spot Limited (1) .... Vancouver BC
Wi-LAN Inc. (1) .... Calgary AB
Wilfrid Laurier University (1) .... Waterloo ON
Wilton Industries Canada Ltd. (1) .... Toronto ON
Wind River Systems, Inc. (1) .... Calgary AB
Wysdom Inc. (1) .... Richmond Hill ON
Yamaha Motor Canada Ltd. (1) .... Toronto ON
Ziff Energy Group (1) .... Calgary AB
Zivex IT Utility Company (1) .... Kanata ON

For descriptions of the occupational categories used in this index, see page 458.

METALS

See also: Mining, Trades/Technicians, Automotive.

Alcan Primary Metal Group (5 positions) .... Kitimat BC
Linamar Corporation, Eston Division (5) .... Guelph ON
Spectra Aluminum Products Inc. (5) .... Woodbridge ON
Gerdau Courtice Steel Inc. (4) .... Cambridge ON
IPSCO Inc. (4) .... Regina SK
Kubes Steel Ltd. (4) .... Stoney Creek ON
Nitrex Metal Inc. (4) .... St-Laurent QC
Ancon Industries Inc. (3) .... Oshawa ON
Falconbridge Ltd., Sudbury Smelter (3) .... Falconbridge ON
George Kelk Corporation (3) .... Toronto ON
Inco Ltd., Manitoba Division (3) .... Thompson MB
Industrial Research and Development Inst (3) .... Midland ON
Iron Ore Company of Canada / IOC (3) .... Sept-Iles QC
Kubota Metal Corporation (3) .... Orillia ON
Lake Erie Steel Company (3) .... Nanticoke ON
Noranda Inc. (3) .... Pointe-Claire QC
Powertech Labs Inc. (3) .... Surrey BC
Salit Steel (3) .... Niagara Falls ON
Silex Design Inc. (3) .... Mississauga ON
Wolverine Ratcliffs Inc. (3) .... Fergus ON
Alliance Steel Corp. (2) .... Laval QC
ATCO Noise Management Ltd. (2) .... Calgary AB
Canam Steel Works (2) .... Calgary AB
Fisher & Ludlow (2) .... Burlington ON
Fluor Canada Ltd. (2) .... Calgary AB
Genfast Manufacturing Company (2) .... Brantford ON
GL&V / Dorr-Oliver Canada Inc. (2) .... Orillia ON
Global Thermoelectric Inc. (2) .... Calgary AB
Inco (2) .... Toronto ON
JP Metal America Inc. (2) .... Montréal QC
Liburdi Engineering Ltd. (2) .... Dundas ON
Linamar Corporation, Autocom Division (2) .... Guelph ON
Midland Steel Ltd. (2) .... Anjou QC
Russel Metals Inc. (2) .... Edmonton AB
Sanmina Enclosure Systems (2) .... Toronto ON
Syncrude Canada Ltd. (2) .... Fort McMurray AB
Titanium Ltd. (2) .... St-Laurent QC
Tubular Steel Inc. (2) .... Toronto ON
Velan Inc. (2) .... Montréal QC
Walters Inc. (2) .... Hamilton ON
A.G. Simpson Co. Limited (1) .... Cambridge ON
ABC Group Inc. (1) .... Toronto ON
Air Products Canada Ltd. (1) .... Brampton ON
Alberta Research Council / ARC (1) .... Edmonton AB
Alcoa Rexdale Packaging (1) .... Toronto ON
Alft (1) .... Hull QC
All New Manufacturing Inc. (1) .... Calgary AB
Amcan Castings Ltd. (1) .... Hamilton ON
Amico - ISG (1) .... Burlington ON
ASA Alloys (1) .... Toronto ON
Beavers Dental (1) .... Morrisburg ON
BF Goodrich Aerospace (1) .... Mississauga ON
Bodycote Ortech Inc. (1) .... Mississauga ON
Bradon Industries Ltd. / Hydra Rig Canad (1) .... Calgary AB
Budd Canada Inc. (1) .... Kitchener ON
C/S Construction Specialties Ltd. (1) .... Mississauga ON
Canam Manac Group Inc., The (1) .... Boucherville QC
Canron Construction Corp. (1) .... Toronto ON
Cellex Power Products Inc. (1) .... Richmond BC
Clayson Steel (1) .... Brampton ON
Cominco Ltd. (1) .... Trail BC
Commercial Spring and Tool Company L (1) .... Mississauga ON
Conestoga College of Applied Arts & Te (1) .... Kitchener ON
CWB Group (1) .... Mississauga ON
Duke Blakey, Inc. (1) .... Markham ON
Falconbridge Ltd. (1) .... Onaping ON
Flight Dynamics Corp. (1) .... St-Jean-sur-Richelieu QC
Flowserve Inc. (1) .... Woodbridge ON
Greening Donald Co. Ltd. (1) .... Orangeville ON
Haley Industries Ltd. (1) .... Haley ON
Halifax Shipyard Limited (1) .... Halifax NS
Hardt Equipment Manufacturing Inc. (1) .... Lachine QC
Honeywell IC (1) .... North Vancouver BC
Inco Ltd., Ontario Division (1) .... Copper Cliff ON
Kinectrics Inc. (1) .... Toronto ON
Makssteel Inc. (1) .... Mississauga ON
Ministry of Labour, Ontario (1) .... Toronto ON

MTU Maintenance Canada Ltd. (1) .... Richmond BC
National Research Council Canada, I (1) .... Boucherville QC
National Research Council Canada, Integra (1) .... London ON
National Steel Car Ltd. (1) .... Hamilton ON
PerkinElmer Optoelectronics Inc. (1) .... Vaudreuil QC
Pinacle Stainless Steel Inc. (1) .... Toronto ON
Pratt & Whitney Canada Corporation / P (1) .... Longueuil QC
Research in Motion Limited / RIM (1) .... Waterloo ON
S&C Electric Canada Ltd. (1) .... Toronto ON
Samuel, Son & Co., Ltd. (1) .... Mississauga ON
Schneider Electric (1) .... Toronto ON
Sherritt International Corp. (1) .... Fort Saskatchewan AB
Silex Inc. (1) .... Mississauga ON
SNC-Lavalin Inc., Chemicals & Petroleum (1) .... Calgary AB
Stackpole Limited, Automotive Gear D (1) .... Mississauga ON
Suncor Energy Inc., Oil Sands (1) .... Fort McMurray AB
Taylor Steel Inc. (1) .... Hamilton ON
Techmire Ltd. (1) .... Anjou QC
Thermadyne Canada (1) .... Oakville ON
Whitecourt Oil Corp. (1) .... Vaughan ON
Wilkinson Steel and Metals (1) .... Edmonton AB
Wurth Canada Limited (1) .... Mississauga ON
XCELLSiS (1) .... Burnaby BC
Zircatec Precision Industries Inc. / Z (1) .... Port Hope ON

MINING

See also: Geology/Geography, Metals, Oil & Gas, Engineering.

Albian Sands Energy Inc. (11 positions) .... Fort McMurray AB
Falconbridge Ltd. (7) .... Onaping ON
Inco Ltd., Manitoba Division (5) .... Thompson MB
Ministry of Energy and Mines, BC (5) .... Victoria BC
Fording Coal Limited, Fording River Oper (4) .... Elkford BC
Ministry of Labour, Ontario (3) .... Toronto ON
Nuna Logistics Ltd. (3) .... Yellowknife NT
Suncor Energy Inc., Oil Sands (3) .... Fort McMurray AB
Dome Mine (2) .... South Porcupine ON
Fluor Canada Ltd. (2) .... Calgary AB
Fording Coal Limited, Greenhills Operati (2) .... Elkford BC
Hatch Associates Ltd. (2) .... Sudbury ON
Hudson Bay Mining and Smelting Co., Lt (2) .... Flin Flon MB
Kinross Gold Corp., Timmins Operation (2) .... Schumacher ON
Lac de Gras Excavation Inc. (2) .... Yellowknife NT
Mansour Mining Inc. (2) .... Sudbury ON
Ministry of Labour, Ontario (2) .... London ON
Ministry of Labour, Ontario (Northern Re (2) .... Sudbury ON
Ministry of Northern Development and Min (2) .... Sudbury ON
Noranda Inc., Brunswick Mine (2) .... Bathurst NB
Syncrude Canada Ltd. (2) .... Fort McMurray AB
BHP Diamonds Inc. (1) .... Yellowknife NT
Cominco Ltd. (1) .... Trail BC
Inco Ltd. (1) .... Toronto ON
Inco Ltd., Ontario Division (1) .... Copper Cliff ON
Jacques Whitford Environment Ltd. (1) .... Calgary AB
Luscar Ltd. (1) .... Edson AB
Noranda Inc. (1) .... Pointe-Claire QC
P&H MinePro Services (1) .... Calgary AB
Public Service Commission of Canada, Al (1) .... Edmonton AB
Public Service Commission of Canada, Onta (1) .... Ottawa ON
Public Service Commission of Canada, Sask (1) .... Regina SK
Trivalence Mining Corporation (1) .... Vancouver BC

MULTIMEDIA

See also: Graphic Arts, Computing, Publishing/Media, Printing.

Radical Entertainment (26 positions) .... Vancouver BC
Spielo Gaming International (10) .... Dieppe NB
BitFlash Graphics, Inc. (9) .... Ottawa ON
PrinterON Corporation (8) .... Kitchener ON
Webplan Inc. (7) .... Ottawa ON
ATI Technologies Inc. (5) .... Thornhill ON
Filament Communications (5) .... Ottawa ON
March Networks Corporation (5) .... Kanata ON
Mindquake Software (5) .... Vancouver BC

MULTIMEDIA (Cont.)

TELAV Audio Visual Services (5) ... Lachine QC
Athabasca University (4) ... Athabasca AB
DigiGraphics (4) ... Kingston ON
ePALS Classroom Exchange (4) ... Ottawa ON
Rogers Media, Publishing (4) ... Toronto ON
TELAV Audio Visual Services (4) ... Ottawa ON
Advanced Micro Design (3) ... Edmonton AB
College of the North Atlantic, Step (3) ... Stephenville NF
CyberSurf Corporation (3) ... Calgary AB
Duocom Canada (3) ... Richmond Hill ON
Excite Canada Inc. (3) ... Toronto ON
Export Development Corporation / EDC (3) ... Ottawa ON
IBM Canada Ltd. (3) ... Markham ON
Inphinity Interactive Inc. (3) ... Vancouver BC
Intervisual Inc. (3) ... Calgary AB
Loyalty Group, The (3) ... Toronto ON
Lumic Electronics, Inc. (3) ... Nepean ON
Magma Communications Ltd. (3) ... Nepean ON
Nelvana Limited (3) ... Toronto ON
NetPCS (3) ... Kanata ON
NetPCS (3) ... Hull QC
New Media Innovation Centre / NewMIC (3) ... Vancouver BC
Pangaea Systems Inc. (3) ... Edmonton AB
Radiant Communications (3) ... Calgary AB
Red Caddy (3) ... Ottawa ON
Research in Motion Limited / RIM (3) ... Waterloo ON
TELAV Audio Visual Services (3) ... Toronto ON
TELAV Audio Visual Services (3) ... Montréal QC
ToonBoom Technologies (3) ... Montréal QC
Top Producer Systems Inc. (3) ... Richmond BC
TTG Systems Inc. (3) ... Edmonton AB
Valadeo Technologies Corp. (3) ... Toronto ON
Watchfire (3) ... Kanata ON
724 Solutions Inc. (2) ... Toronto ON
Alias / Wavefront (2) ... Toronto ON
Alliance Atlantis Communications Inc. (2) ... Toronto ON
Appareo Software Inc. (2) ... Burnaby BC
Arius3D Inc. (2) ... Mississauga ON
Artech Studios (2) ... Ottawa ON
Banff Centre, The (2) ... Banff AB
bitHeads, Inc. (2) ... Ottawa ON
BrandEra.com Inc. (2) ... Toronto ON
CaseWare International Inc. (2) ... Toronto ON
Catena Networks (2) ... Kanata ON
Center for Digital Imaging and Sound / C (2) ... Burnaby BC
Certified General Accountants Associat (2) ... Vancouver BC
Changepoint Corporation (2) ... Richmond Hill ON
Cognos Inc. (2) ... Ottawa ON
College of the Rockies (2) ... Cranbrook BC
Corel Corporation (2) ... Ottawa ON
Corus Entertainment Inc. (2) ... Toronto ON
Cquay Inc. (2) ... Calgary AB
DeepMetrix Corporation (2) ... Hull ON
Destiny Web Designs Inc. (2) ... Toronto ON
Dot Com Entertainment Group Inc. / DCEG (2) ... Oakville ON
Durham College (2) ... Oshawa ON
Infrastructures for Information, Inc. / (2) ... Toronto ON
inSITE Communications (2) ... Kingston ON
Interactive Media Group / IMG (2) ... Toronto ON
International Academy of Design and Techn (2) ... Ottawa ON
Kazootek Technologies (2) ... Vancouver BC
Kelly Phillips Productions Inc. (2) ... Montréal QC
Kids Can Press (2) ... Toronto ON
Kinaare Networks Canada Corporation (2) ... Mississauga ON
Management Board Secretariat (2) ... Toronto ON
Manitoba Finance (2) ... Winnipeg MB
McMillan & Associates (2) ... Ottawa ON
Media Wave Web Solutions (2) ... Ottawa ON
Merak Projects Ltd. (2) ... Calgary AB
Microtime Inc. (2) ... Ottawa ON
Ministry of the Environment, Ontario (2) ... Toronto ON
Novator Systems Ltd. (2) ... Toronto ON
Rogers iMedia (2) ... Toronto ON
Sharp's Audio-Visual Ltd. (2) ... Edmonton AB
Shopping Channel, The / TSC (2) ... Toronto ON
Silanis Technology Inc. (2) ... St-Laurent QC
Strategy First (2) ... Montréal QC
Technical University of British Columbia (2) ... Surrey BC
TELAV Audio Visual Services (2) ... Vancouver BC
Thrive Media (2) ... Vancouver BC
Trader.com (2) ... Edmonton AB
Videoscope (2) ... Toronto ON
Vistek Ltd. (2) ... Toronto ON
Weidmuller Ltd. (2) ... Markham ON
Worldprofit Inc. (2) ... Edmonton AB
01 Communique Laboratory Inc. (1) ... Mississauga ON
Accpac International Inc. (1) ... Richmond BC
ACD Systems (1) ... Saanichton BC
Adexa (1) ... Toronto ON
AIM Funds Management Inc. (1) ... Toronto ON
AiT Corporation (1) ... Ottawa ON
Alberta Community Development (1) ... Edmonton AB
Alberta Infrastructure & Transportation (1) ... Edmonton AB
Alberta Justice (1) ... Edmonton AB
ALNAV Platinum Group Inc. (1) ... Edmonton AB
Aludra Inc. (1) ... Toronto ON
AT&T Canada (1) ... Toronto ON
Audio Centre (1) ... St-Laurent QC
BC Gas Utility Ltd. (1) ... Vancouver BC
Benchmark Technologies Inc. (1) ... Vancouver BC
Beyond 20/20 Inc. (1) ... Ottawa ON
Bombardier Aerospace (1) ... Montréal QC
Boulevard Media (Canada) Inc. / BMC (1) ... Vancouver BC
Brampton, City of (1) ... Brampton ON
British Columbia Lottery Corporation (1) ... Kamloops BC
Burntsand Inc. (1) ... Vancouver BC
Bycast Media Systems Canada, Inc. (1) ... Vancouver BC
Canadian Forces Personnel Support Agency (1) ... Ottawa ON
Canadian Pharmacists Association / CPhA (1) ... Ottawa ON
CGI Group Inc. (1) ... Ottawa ON
Chancery Software Ltd. (1) ... Burnaby BC
Cinram International Inc. (1) ... Toronto ON
Cistel Technology Inc. (1) ... Nepean ON
CML Emergency Services, Inc. (1) ... Hull QC
Columbia House Canada (1) ... Toronto ON
Communications and Information Technology (1) ... Kanata ON
Control-F1 (1) ... Calgary AB
Coradiant Inc. (1) ... Montréal QC
CreoScitex (1) ... Burnaby BC
Cunningham & Lindsey Canada Ltd. (1) ... Hamilton ON
Danier Leather Inc. (1) ... Toronto ON
Databeacon Inc. (1) ... Ottawa ON
Delta Controls Inc. (1) ... Surrey BC
Dental Marketing Inc. (1) ... Vaughan ON
DevelopersNetwork.com Inc. (1) ... Toronto ON
Digital Accelerator Corporation (1) ... Vancouver BC
Douglas College (1) ... New Westminster BC
DSPA Software Inc. (1) ... Mississauga ON
Dynamic Mutual Funds (1) ... Toronto ON
E-smith, Inc. (1) ... Ottawa ON
EDM Products Inc. (1) ... Calgary AB
Empire Financial Group (1) ... Kingston ON
Empowertel Networks Inc. (1) ... Ottawa ON
Entero Corporation (1) ... Calgary AB
EPCOR Utilities Inc. (1) ... Edmonton AB
Excel Tech Ltd. / XLTEK (1) ... Oakville ON
Executive Needs Inc., The (1) ... Toronto ON
Exocom Group Inc., The (1) ... Ottawa ON
Ezenet Inc. (1) ... Toronto ON
Federation of Canadian Municipalities / F (1) ... Ottawa ON
Financial Services Commission of Ontario (1) ... Toronto ON
Fincentric Corp. (1) ... Richmond BC
FreeBalance Inc. (1) ... Ottawa ON
Frozen Pond Inc. (1) ... Toronto ON
Fuji Photo Film Canada Inc. (1) ... Mississauga ON
Gage Applied, Inc. (1) ... Lachine QC
George Brown College (1) ... Toronto ON
Global Crossing (1) ... Montréal QC
Grant MacEwan College (1) ... Edmonton AB
Grocery Gateway (1) ... Toronto ON
Group Telecom (1) ... Toronto ON
Harris Computer Systems (1) ... Nepean ON
Healthnet International Inc. (1) ... Vancouver BC
Hemera Technologies Inc. (1) ... Hull QC
Hewson Bridge and Smith Ltd. / HBS (1) ... Ottawa ON
Husky Injection Molding Systems Ltd. (1) ... Bolton ON
Ideas and Associates (1) ... Montréal QC
ImageWare Systems (1) ... Hull QC
Information Services Corporation of Saska (1) ... Regina SK
Intrawest Corporation (1) ... Vancouver BC
Ken Lewis Group Inc. (1) ... Markham ON

For descriptions of the occupational categories used in this index, see page 458.

MULTIMEDIA (Cont.)

Lakeland College (1) .... Vermilion AB
Law Society of Upper Canada, The / LSUC (1) .... Toronto ON
Legal Aid Ontario / LAO (1) .... Toronto ON
Lenbrook (1) .... Pickering ON
Linamar Corporation, Autocom Division (1) .... Guelph ON
Linamar Corporation, Eston Division (1) .... Guelph ON
Lockheed Martin Canada Inc. (1) .... Kanata ON
Lumenon (1) .... St-Laurent QC
Mastech Canada (1) .... Ottawa ON
Memoris, Inc. (1) .... Montréal QC
Mercury Filmworks (1) .... Vancouver BC
Merlin Creative Group Inc. (1) .... Calgary AB
MI Group, The (1) .... Mississauga ON
Microcell Connexions Inc. (1) .... Toronto ON
Millenium Biologix Inc. (1) .... Kingston ON
Ministry of Citizenship, Culture and Rec (1) .... Toronto ON
Ministry of Finance, Ontario (1) .... Toronto ON
Ministry of Finance, Ontario (1) .... Oshawa ON
Ministry of Health and Long-Term Care, On (1) .... London ON
Ministry of Health and Long-Term Care, O (1) .... Toronto ON
Ministry of the Environment, Ontario (Co (1) .... Toronto ON
Ministry of the Solicitor General, Ontar (1) .... Toronto ON
Ministry of Transportation, Ontario (1) .... Toronto ON
Ministry of Transportation, Ontar (1) .... St. Catharines ON
Mississauga, City of (1) .... Mississauga ON
Mold-Masters Ltd. (1) .... Georgetown ON
Montage.dmc eBusiness Services (1) .... Calgary AB
Mount Royal College (1) .... Calgary AB
Mount Sinai Hospital (1) .... Toronto ON
MuscleTech Research and Development (1) .... Mississauga ON
National Diamond Public Relations Ltd. (1) .... Calgary AB
National Grocers Company Limited / Lobla (1) .... Toronto ON
NCompass Labs (1) .... Vancouver BC
Net-Linx Americas, Inc. (1) .... Edmonton AB
NetMart Inc. (1) .... Montréal QC
New Brunswick Community College, Miram (1) .... Miramichi NB
NewHeights Software Corporation (1) .... Victoria BC
Nokia Products Ltd. (1) .... Richmond BC
Nova Scotia College of Art and Design / (1) .... Halifax NS
NTG Clarity Networks Inc. (1) .... Markham ON
Oakwood Associates (1) .... Calgary AB
Ontario Lottery and Gaming Corp (1) .... Sault Ste. Marie ON
Ontario March of Dimes (1) .... Toronto ON
Ontario Non-Profit Housing Association / (1) .... Toronto ON
Open Text Corporation (1) .... Waterloo ON
Optimal Robotics Corp. (1) .... Montréal QC
Overwaitea Food Group (1) .... Vancouver BC
PanelX.com / PanelX Technical Services (1) .... Oakville ON
Pangaea Systems Inc. (1) .... Calgary AB
Paradata Systems Inc. (1) .... Whistler BC
Peel District School Board (1) .... Mississauga ON
Penguin Books Canada Ltd. (1) .... Toronto ON
Pika Technologies Inc. (1) .... Kanata ON
Post Impressions Systems Inc. (1) .... Montréal QC
Procuron Inc. (1) .... Thornhill ON
Progestic International Inc. (1) .... Ottawa ON
Provance Technologies Inc. (1) .... Gatineau QC
Q-Media Services Corporation (1) .... Richmond BC
ReserveAmerica (1) .... Milton ON
Rittal Systems Ltd. (1) .... Mississauga ON
Rogers Cable Inc. (1) .... Toronto ON
Royal Bank Financial Group (1) .... Toronto ON
Ryerson Polytechnic University (1) .... Toronto ON
Savage Software (1) .... Vancouver BC
School District #60 (Peace River N (1) .... Fort St. John BC
SCP Science (1) .... Baie d'Urfe QC
Seljax International Inc. (1) .... Stony Plain AB
Senstar-Stellar Corporation (1) .... Carp ON
Shoppers Drug Mart (1) .... Toronto ON
Siemens Canada Ltd. (1) .... Mississauga ON
Sigem Inc. (1) .... Kanata ON
Sitraka Software Inc. (1) .... Toronto ON
Smart Technologies Inc. (1) .... Calgary AB
Solect Technology Group (1) .... Toronto ON
Sony Music Canada (1) .... Toronto ON
Stockscape.com Technologies Inc. (1) .... Vancouver BC
Stronco Audio-Visuals (1) .... Toronto ON
Systemcorp ALG Ltd. (1) .... Montréal QC
TAP Ventures, Inc. (1) .... Vancouver BC

Tarian Software Inc. (1) .... Ottawa ON
Telus Mobility (1) .... Toronto ON
TriAngulum Corporation (1) .... Calgary AB
University of Calgary (1) .... Calgary AB
University of Toronto at Scarborough / U (1) .... Toronto ON
Valcom Limited (Ottawa) (1) .... Ottawa ON
Vertical Builder (1) .... Calgary AB
VideoSpheres Inc. (1) .... Kanata ON
Vistek Ltd. (1) .... Calgary AB
Wajax Industries Limited (1) .... Mississauga ON
Web Krew Inc. (1) .... Toronto ON
Webstorm Media (1) .... Montréal QC
WorkDynamics Technologies Inc. (1) .... Ottawa ON
Xwave Solutions Inc. (1) .... Dorval QC
ZOX Technologies Inc. (1) .... Toronto ON

OIL & GAS
See also: Geology/Geography, Engineering, International, Trades/Technicians.

Suncor Energy Inc., Oil Sands (38 positions) ..... Fort McMurray AB
PanCanadian Petroleum Ltd. (25) .... Calgary AB
Alberta Energy Company Ltd. / AEC (24) .... Calgary AB
Delta Hudson Engineering Ltd. (24) .... Calgary AB
Shell Canada Limited (16) .... Calgary AB
Nexen Inc. (15) .... Calgary AB
Weatherford Canada Ltd. (15) .... Nisku AB
Alberta Energy Company Ltd. / AEC (14) .... Calgary AB
CoSyn Technology (14) .... Edmonton AB
Ryan Energy Technologies Inc. (14) .... Calgary AB
Tri Ocean Engineering Ltd. (13) .... Calgary AB
Anadarko Canada Corporation (12) .... Calgary AB
Kvaerner Process Systems / KPS (12) .... Calgary AB
VECO Canada Ltd. (12) .... Calgary AB
PrimeWest Energy Trust (11) .... Calgary AB
Suncor Energy Inc. (11) .... Calgary AB
Burlington Resources Canada Energy Ltd. (10) .... Calgary AB
Syncrude Canada Ltd. (10) .... Fort McMurray AB
VECO Canada Ltd. (10) .... Burnaby BC
Fluor Canada Ltd. (9) .... Calgary AB
Trans Mountain Pipe Line Company Ltd. (9) .... Calgary AB
AltaGas Services Inc. (8) .... Calgary AB
Colt Engineering Corporation (8) .... Calgary AB
Ensign Resource Service Group Inc. (8) .... Nisku AB
Equinox Engineering Ltd. (8) .... Calgary AB
Gemini Corporation (8) .... Calgary AB
Halliburton Canada Inc. (8) .... Nisku AB
Husky Oil Operations Ltd. (8) .... Calgary AB
Alberta Energy (7) .... Edmonton AB
Albian Sands Energy Inc. (7) .... Fort McMurray AB
Integrated Production Services Ltd. / IP (7) .... Calgary AB
Phoenix Technology Services LP (7) .... Calgary AB
Tartan Engineering Ltd. (7) .... Calgary AB
ACM Automation Inc. (6) .... Calgary AB
Bantrel Inc. (6) .... Edmonton AB
Colt Engineering Corporation (6) .... Edmonton AB
Pengrowth Management Ltd. / PML (6) .... Calgary AB
SNC-Lavalin Inc., Chemicals & Petroleum (6) .... Calgary AB
Calpine Canada Resources Ltd. (5) .... Calgary AB
Ensign Resource Service Group Inc. (5) .... Calgary AB
Newpark Drilling Fluids (5) .... Calgary AB
Propak Systems Ltd. (5) .... Airdrie AB
Rio Alto Exploration Ltd. (5) .... Calgary AB
Schlumberger Canada Limited (5) .... Calgary AB
ABB Inc. (4) .... Calgary AB
Alberta Resource Development (4) .... Edmonton AB
AMEC E&C Services (4) .... St. John's NF
Bantrel Inc. (4) .... Calgary AB
Dalen Drilling Services Ltd. (4) .... Airdrie AB
Engage Energy Canada, LP (4) .... Calgary AB
Fugro / SESL Geomatics Ltd. (4) .... Calgary AB
Kvaerner SNC-Lavalin Offshore / KSLO (4) .... Halifax NS
Oil and Gas Commission, BC (4) .... Victoria BC
Omni Directional Technologies Inc. (4) .... Calgary AB
Paradigm Geophysical (4) .... Calgary AB
Public Service Commission of Canada, Al (4) .... Edmonton AB
Technical Standards & Safety Authority / (4) .... Toronto ON
Union Gas Limited (4) .... Chatham ON
Alberta Energy and Utilities Board / EUB (3) .... Calgary AB

OIL & GAS (Cont.)

BJ Services Company Canada (3) .... Calgary AB
Bradon Industries Ltd. / Hydra Rig Canad (3) .... Calgary AB
Calfrac Well Services Ltd. (3) .... Calgary AB
Canada-Nova Scotia Offshore Petroleum Bo (3) .... Halifax NS
Canadian 88 Energy Corp. (3) .... Calgary AB
Cancoil Integrated Services Inc. (3) .... Calgary AB
Chevron Canada Ltd. (3) .... Vancouver BC
Enbridge Services (3) .... Markham ON
Enerflex Systems Ltd. (3) .... Calgary AB
ESTec Oilfield Inc. (3) .... Edmonton AB
Fekete Associates Inc. (3) .... Calgary AB
Flow Drilling Engineering Ltd. / FDEL (3) .... Calgary AB
Kvaerner SNC-Lavalin Offshore / KSLO (3) .... Mount Pearl NF
Meota Resources Corp. (3) .... Calgary AB
Millenia Resource Consulting (3) .... Calgary AB
Ministry of Energy and Mines, BC (3) .... Victoria BC
Nabors International Inc. (3) .... Calgary AB
NAL Resources Management Ltd. (3) .... Calgary AB
NeoCorr Engineering Ltd. (3) .... Calgary AB
Opsco Energy Industries Ltd. (3) .... Calgary AB
Saskatchewan Research Council / SRC (3) .... Saskatoon SK
SNC-Lavalin Inc. (3) .... Edmonton AB
Tundra Engineering Ltd. (3) .... Calgary AB
United Safety Ltd. (3) .... Calgary AB
University of Regina, Faculty of Engineer (3) .... Regina SK
Upside Engineering Ltd. (3) .... Calgary AB
XXL Engineering Ltd. (3) .... Calgary AB
Alberta Research Council / ARC (2) .... Edmonton AB
Apache Canada Ltd. (2) .... Calgary AB
Baytex Energy Ltd. (2) .... Calgary AB
BJ Pipeline Inspection Services (2) .... Calgary AB
Can-Am Surveys Ltd. (2) .... Calgary AB
CC Technologies Canada Ltd. (2) .... Calgary AB
Celsius Energy Resources Ltd. (2) .... Calgary AB
Challenger Geomatics Ltd. (2) .... Calgary AB
Colt Engineering Corporation (2) .... Markham ON
Computalog Ltd. (2) .... Edmonton AB
Computalog Ltd. (2) .... Calgary AB
Computer Sonics Systems Inc. / CSS (2) .... Calgary AB
Core Laboratories Canada Ltd. (2) .... Calgary AB
EFX Enerflex Systems Ltd. (2) .... Calgary AB
Encore Energy Inc. (2) .... Calgary AB
Enerchem International Inc. (2) .... Nisku AB
Energy Industries Inc. (2) .... Calgary AB
Enerline Restorations Inc. (2) .... Calgary AB
Enron Canada Corp. (2) .... Calgary AB
Harvard Energy (2) .... Calgary AB
Hitec Systems and Controls Inc. (2) .... Edmonton AB
Hitec Systems and Controls Inc. (2) .... Calgary AB
Hurricane Hydrocarbons Ltd. (2) .... Calgary AB
Imperial Oil Resources (2) .... Bonnyville AB
Kenonic Controls Ltd. (2) .... Calgary AB
Koch Petroleum Canada LP (2) .... Calgary AB
Landmark Graphics (2) .... Calgary AB
Macdonald Engineering Group Ltd. / MEG (2) .... Calgary AB
McElhanney Group Ltd., The (2) .... Vancouver BC
Merak Projects Ltd. (2) .... Calgary AB
Ministry of the Environment, Ontario (2) .... Toronto ON
Moody International Ltd. (2) .... Edmonton AB
National Oilwell, Downhole Tools Divisi (2) .... Edmonton AB
Northern Lights College / NLC (2) .... Dawson Creek BC
Paramount Resources Ltd. (2) .... Calgary AB
Passband Downhole Communications Inc. / (2) .... Calgary AB
Petro Plan Safety Ltd. (2) .... Calgary AB
Petro-Canada (2) .... Calgary AB
Plains Perforating Ltd. (2) .... Calgary AB
Polar Completions Engineering Inc. (2) .... Calgary AB
Precision Drilling Corporation (2) .... Calgary AB
QuestAir Technologies Inc. (2) .... Burnaby BC
Scott Land & Lease Ltd. (2) .... Calgary AB
Shaw Pipe Protection Ltd. (2) .... Calgary AB
Sproule Associates Limited (2) .... Calgary AB
Thermo Design Engineering Ltd. (2) .... Edmonton AB
TransAlta Corporation (2) .... Fort McMurray AB
Trican Well Service Ltd. (2) .... Calgary AB
UMA Engineering Ltd. (2) .... Calgary AB
United Oil & Gas Consulting Ltd. (2) .... Calgary AB
Ziff Energy Group (2) .... Calgary AB
Barton Instrument Systems Ltd. (1) .... Calgary AB

BC Gas Utility Ltd. (1) .... Vancouver BC
Bidell Equipment Inc. (1) .... Calgary AB
BJ Process & Pipeline Services (1) .... Edmonton AB
Cadastral Group Inc., The (1) .... Calgary AB
Calgary Co-operative Association Ltd. (1) .... Calgary AB
Can-Am Surveys Ltd. (1) .... Edmonton AB
CEF Technologies Ltd., Brittania Compres (1) .... Calgary AB
Chancellor Industrial Construction Ltd. (1) .... Nisku AB
Corridor Pipeline Limited (1) .... Edmonton AB
DBR Research Ltd. (1) .... Edmonton AB
Earth Tech Canada Inc. (1) .... Markham ON
Enbridge Pipelines Inc. (1) .... Edmonton AB
ENMAX Corporation (1) .... Calgary AB
ESBI Alberta Ltd. (1) .... Calgary AB
Excalibur-Gemini Group Ltd., The (1) .... Calgary AB
Flint Energy Services Ltd. (1) .... Sherwood Park AB
Fluor Constructors Canada Ltd. (1) .... Edmonton AB
Focus Corporation Ltd., The (1) .... Edmonton AB
Foster Wheeler Fired Heaters Ltd. (1) .... Calgary AB
Gas & Oil Accounting Ltd. (1) .... Calgary AB
Hanover Maloney (1) .... Calgary AB
Honeywell Ltd., Industrial Automation an (1) .... Calgary AB
Hyprotech Ltd. (1) .... Calgary AB
International Group Inc., The / IGI (1) .... Toronto ON
Jacques Whitford Environment Ltd. (1) .... Markham ON
Jiro Compression Ltd. (1) .... Stettler AB
Keyano College (1) .... Fort McMurray AB
Lincoln Technology Corporation (1) .... Calgary AB
Lockerbie Industra Inc. (1) .... New Westminster BC
Magic Span Fabricating Ltd. / MSF (1) .... Calgary AB
Matrikon Group (1) .... Edmonton AB
Medicine Hat, City of (1) .... Medicine Hat AB
Ministry of Employment and Investment, (1) .... Victoria BC
Ministry of Natural Resources, Ontario (1) .... London ON
Ministry of Natural Resources, O (1) .... South Porcupine ON
OIS-Fisher Inc. (1) .... St. John's NF
Parkvalley Consulting Ltd. (1) .... Calgary AB
Pason Systems Corp. (1) .... Calgary AB
Peacock Inc. (1) .... Edmonton AB
Peak Energy Services Ltd. (1) .... Calgary AB
Peloton Petroleum Software Solutions (1) .... Calgary AB
Penn West Petroleum Ltd. (1) .... Calgary AB
Phillips Petroleum Resources, Ltd. (1) .... Calgary AB
Piping Resources (1) .... Edmonton AB
Purcell Energy Ltd. (1) .... Calgary AB
Rockwell Automation Canada (1) .... Cambridge ON
Sanjel Corporation (1) .... Calgary AB
Shell Canada Limited (1) .... Fort Saskatchewan AB
Stantec Geomatics Ltd. (1) .... Edmonton AB
Sunoco Inc. (1) .... Toronto ON
Talisman Energy Inc. (1) .... Calgary AB
Williams Energy Canada Inc. (1) .... Calgary AB
Zed.i Solutions (1) .... Edmonton AB

OPERATIONS

See also: Logistics, Quality Control, Trades/Technicians.

Magna International Inc. (11 positions) .... Concord ON
Research in Motion Limited / RIM (6) .... Waterloo ON
Jungbunzlauer Canada Inc. (5) .... Port Colborne ON
Carpenter Canada Ltd. (4) .... Woodbridge ON
CMC Electronics Inc. (4) .... St-Laurent QC
CreoScitex (4) .... Burnaby BC
DSC Group of Companies (4) .... Toronto ON
Hitachi Canadian Industries Ltd. (4) .... Saskatoon SK
BC Hydro (3) .... Vancouver BC
BOC Canada Ltd. (3) .... Mississauga ON
Canada Bread Company Ltd. (3) .... Toronto ON
Creation Technologies Inc. (3) .... Burnaby BC
i-STAT Canada Ltd. (3) .... Kanata ON
IKO Industries Ltd. (3) .... Toronto ON
JDS Uniphase Corporation (3) .... Saanichton BC
MetroPhotonics Inc. (3) .... Ottawa ON
Nanowave Technologies Inc. (3) .... Toronto ON
New Automation Corporation / NAC (3) .... Burlington ON
Oakrun Farm Bakery Ltd. (3) .... Ancaster ON
Siemens Westinghouse (3) .... Hamilton ON
TransAlta Corporation (3) .... Calgary AB
Velan Inc. (3) .... Montréal QC

For descriptions of the occupational categories used in this index, see page 458.

OPERATIONS (Cont.)

OPERATIONS (Cont.)

Kohl & Frisch Limited (1) .... Calgary AB
Kraft Canada Inc., Cheese Operations (1) .... Ingleside ON
KristoFoam Industries Inc. (1) .... Concord ON
Lakeridge Health Corporation (1) .... Oshawa ON
Linamar Corporation, Eston Division (1) .... Guelph ON
Lockheed Martin Canada Inc. (1) .... Kanata ON
Lumenon (1) .... St-Laurent QC
Maple Leaf Pork (1) .... Brandon MB
Maple Leaf Pork, Case Reddi Facilit (1) .... Stoney Creek ON
Marks Supply Inc. (1) .... Kitchener ON
Matsu Manufacturing Inc. (1) .... Brampton ON
McCain Foods (Canada) (1) .... Coaldale AB
MDS Aero Support Corporation (1) .... Ottawa ON
Med-Eng Systems Inc. (1) .... Ottawa ON
MEDIS Health & Pharmaceutical Servic (1) .... Mississauga ON
Ministry of Community and Social Servic (1) .... Blenheim ON
Ministry of Labour, Ontario (1) .... London ON
Ministry of Labour, Ontario (1) .... Ottawa ON
Ministry of Labour, Ontario (Northern Re (1) .... Sudbury ON
Ministry of the Solicitor General, Ontar (1) .... Toronto ON
Ministry of Tourism, Culture and Recreat (1) .... Midland ON
Montage.dmc eBusiness Services (1) .... Ottawa ON
Mosaicwares Studio (1) .... Toronto ON
National Research Council Canada / NRC (1) .... Ottawa ON
Nemak (1) .... Windsor ON
Nextron Corporation (1) .... Calgary AB
Norcom / CDT (1) .... Kingston ON
Northern Alberta Institute of Technolog (1) .... Edmonton AB
NxtPhase Corporation (1) .... Vancouver BC
O'Hara Technologies Inc. (1) .... Richmond Hill ON
Ontario Clean Water Agency / OCWA (1) .... London ON
Ontario Clean Water Agency / OCWA (1) .... Kingston ON
Ontario College of Art and Design / OCAD (1) ...... Toronto ON
Ontario Power Generation (1) .... Toronto ON
Pacific Safety Products Inc. / PSP (1) .... Kelowna BC
Pentalift Equipment Corp. (1) .... Guelph ON
Poly-Pacific International Inc. (1) .... Edmonton AB
Prairie Malt Ltd. (1) .... Biggar SK
Private Recipes Ltd. (1) .... Brampton ON
Proceco Ltd. (1) .... Montréal QC
Procuron Inc. (1) .... Thornhill ON
Psion Teklogix Inc. (1) .... Mississauga ON
Public Service Commission of Canada, Al (1) .... Edmonton AB
Puratos Canada, Inc. (1) .... Mississauga ON
Purdy's Chocolates (1) .... Vancouver BC
Pure Technologies Inc. (1) .... Calgary AB
Ramcor Group (1) .... Flamborough ON
Resonance Photonics Inc. (1) .... Markham ON
RexCan Circuits Inc. (1) .... Belleville ON
Rockwell Automation Canada (1) .... Cambridge ON
Royal Group Technologies Inc. (1) .... Woodbridge ON
Russel Metals Inc. (1) .... New Westminister BC
S.A. Armstrong Ltd. (1) .... Toronto ON
Schneider Electric Services (1) .... Mississauga ON
Schneider Foods Inc. (1) .... Surrey BC
Schneider Foods Inc. (1) .... Port Perry ON
Senstar-Stellar Corporation (1) .... Carp ON
Shaw Pipe Protection Ltd. (1) .... Edmonton AB
ShawCor Ltd. (1) .... Toronto ON
Shopping Channel, The / TSC (1) .... Toronto ON
Sicht-Pack Hagner Inc. (1) .... St-Laurent QC
Siemens Dematic Ltd., Rapistan Divis (1) .... Mississauga ON
Sierra Wireless Inc. (1) .... Richmond BC
SKD Automotive Group (1) .... Milton ON
Sota Glazing Inc. (1) .... Brampton ON
SpaceBridge Networks Corporation (1) .... Hull QC
Stream International (1) .... Belleville ON
Supercom Canada Ltd. (1) .... Markham ON
Superior Emergency Vehicles Ltd. (1) .... Red Deer AB
Supreme Tooling Group (1) .... Toronto ON
Talon Systems Inc. (1) .... Mississauga ON
Targray Technology International I (1) .... Pointe-Claire QC
TELAV Audio Visual Services (1) .... Lachine QC
TelTech Assets.Com Ltd. (1) .... Calgary AB
Telus Integrated Communications (1) .... Toronto ON
Teraxion (1) .... Ste-Foy QC
Thales Optronics Canada Inc. (1) .... St-Laurent QC
Thomas & Betts Limited (1) .... Iberville QC

Trans Mountain Pipe Line Company Ltd. (1) .... Calgary AB
TransAlta Corporation, Sundance Generat (1) .... Duffield AB
Tropic Networks Inc. (1) .... Kanata ON
Ty-Crop Manufacturing Ltd. (1) .... Rosedale BC
UniFirst Canada Ltd. (1) .... Calgary AB
University of Regina (1) .... Regina SK
VA Tech Ferranti-Packard Transfor (1) .... St. Catharines ON
Vansco Electronics Ltd. (1) .... Winnipeg MB
Vestshell Inc. (1) .... Montréal QC
Viconics Electronics Inc. (1) .... St-Leonard QC
VIPswitch Inc. (1) .... Montréal QC
Visible Genetics Inc. (1) .... Toronto ON
Vopak Canada Ltd. (1) .... Toronto ON
Voyus Canada Inc. (1) .... Burnaby BC
VQuip Inc. (1) .... Burlington ON
Wavesat Telecom Inc. (1) .... St-Laurent QC
Weighpack Paxiom (1) .... Lachine QC
Westcoast Power Inc. (1) .... Calgary AB
Xantrex Technology Inc. (1) .... Burnaby BC
Zed.i Solutions (1) .... Edmonton AB

PACKAGING

See also: Graphic Arts, Printing, Trades/Technicians.

Apotex Inc. (9 positions) .... Toronto ON
GlaxoSmithKline (5) .... Mississauga ON
Patheon Inc. (5) .... Mississauga ON
Bonar Packaging Corp. (4) .... Burlington ON
Concord Confections Inc. (4) .... Concord ON
Patheon Inc. (4) .... Burlington ON
Zarpac Inc. (4) .... Oakville ON
Graham Packaging Canada (3) .... Burlington ON
Great Little Box Company Ltd., The (3) .... Vancouver BC
Multipak Ltd. (3) .... Mississauga ON
Taro Pharmaceuticals Inc. (3) .... Bramalea ON
Abbey Packaging Equipment Ltd. (2) .... Burlington ON
Belcor Industries Inc. (2) .... Richmond BC
Cadbury Trebor Allan Inc. (2) .... Toronto ON
Cadbury Trebor Allan Inc. (2) .... Hamilton ON
Heartland Shipping Supplies Inc. (2) .... Mississauga ON
Hunter Amenities International Ltd. (2) .... Burlington ON
Mead Packaging (Canada) Ltd. (2) .... Ajax ON
Neilson Dairy (2) .... Halton Hills ON
Norampac Inc., Concord Division (2) .... Concord ON
Pechiney Plastic Packaging (Canada) Inc (2) .... Brampton ON
Polytainers Inc. (2) .... Toronto ON
Shorewood Packaging Corporation (2) .... Toronto ON
Trillium Health Care Products (2) .... Brockville ON
Wentworth Mold Inc. (2) .... Hamilton ON
Winpak Technologies Inc. (2) .... Toronto ON
Astec Advanced Power Systems (1) .... St-Laurent QC
Atlantic Packaging Products Ltd. (1) .... Toronto ON
CanAmera Foods (1) .... Oakville ON
Co-Ex-Tec Industries (1) .... Concord ON
Cryovac Canada Inc. (1) .... Mississauga ON
Golden Boy Foods Inc. (1) .... Burnaby BC
Hershey Canada Inc. (1) .... Smith Falls ON
Korex Canada (1) .... Toronto ON
Labatt Breweries Ontario (1) .... Toronto ON
LiveWire Digital Imaging (1) .... Woodbridge ON
Maple Leaf Pork (1) .... Burlington ON
Merck Frosst Canada & Co. / Merck (1) .... Pointe-Claire QC
Metro Label Company Ltd. (1) .... Toronto ON
Nor Baker Inc. (1) .... Newmarket ON
Patheon Inc. (1) .... Toronto ON
Patheon Inc. (1) .... Fort Erie ON
RJL Packaging & Labelling Industries In (1) .... Montréal QC
Standard Paper Box (1) .... Mississauga ON
Talon Systems Inc. (1) .... Mississauga ON
Tiercon Industries Inc. (1) .... Stoney Creek ON
Trebor Allan Inc. (1) .... Hamilton ON
Tri-ad Graphic Communications Ltd. (1) .... Toronto ON
Trophy Foods Inc. (1) .... Mississauga ON
Weatherford / McAllister (1) .... Calgary AB
Weber Marking Systems of Canada (1) .... Mississauga ON
Weighpack Paxiom (1) .... Lachine QC
Wexxar Packaging Machinery Ltd. (1) .... Delta BC
Wrigley Canada Inc. (1) .... Toronto ON

For descriptions of the occupational categories used in this index, see page 458.

PHARMACEUTICAL

See also: Biotech/Biology, Health/Medical, Scientific.

PHARMACEUTICAL (Cont.)

Stratford General Hospital (1) .... Stratford ON
Syn X Pharma Inc. (1) .... Mississauga ON
Synsorb Biotech Inc. (1) .... Calgary AB
Thrifty Foods (1) .... Saanichton BC
Torcan Chemical Ltd. (1) .... Aurora ON
TorPharm (1) .... Toronto ON
University of Western Ontario, Faculty of (1) .... London ON
Varian Canada Inc. (1) .... Mississauga ON
Wal-Mart Canada Inc. (1) .... Mississauga ON
Whitby Mental Health Centre (1) .... Whitby ON

PLASTICS

See also: Operations, Engineering, Trades/Technicians.

ABC Group Inc. (26 positions) .... Toronto ON
Co-Ex-Tec Industries (7) .... Concord ON
CPI Plastics Group Ltd. (6) .... Mississauga ON
Polytainers Inc. (6) .... Toronto ON
Ottawa Mould Craft Ltd. (5) .... Ottawa ON
Supreme Tooling Group (5) .... Toronto ON
Wentworth Mold Inc. (5) .... Hamilton ON
Ropak Canada Inc. (4) .... Oakville ON
StackTeck Systems Inc. (4) .... Toronto ON
Comptec International Ltd. (3) .... Surrey BC
Garrtech Inc. (3) .... Stoney Creek ON
Nucon Systems Inc. (3) .... Markham ON
Becker Group (2) .... Toronto ON
Bonar Plastics (2) .... Lindsay ON
Brampton Engineering Inc. (2) .... Brampton ON
Canada Colors and Chemicals Ltd. / CCC (2) .... Toronto ON
Corma Inc. (2) .... Concord ON
Georgia-Pacific Canada, Consumer Product (2) .... Toronto ON
Horn Plastics Inc. (2) .... Whitby ON
Husky Injection Molding Systems Ltd. (2) .... Bolton ON
Husky Injection Molding Systems Ltd. (2) .... Bolton ON
Hymopack Ltd. (2) .... Toronto ON
Industrial Research and Development Inst (2) .... Midland ON
Komtech Inc. (2) .... Ottawa ON
Mitchell Plastics Ltd. (2) .... Kitchener ON
Research in Motion Limited / RIM (2) .... Waterloo ON
Ropak Canada Inc. (2) .... Annacis Island BC
Ryka Blow Molds Ltd. (2) .... Mississauga ON
ShawCor Ltd. (2) .... Toronto ON
SPM / United Plastics Group (2) .... Kirkland QC
Alberta Research Council / ARC (1) .... Edmonton AB
ATS Automation Tooling Systems Inc. (1) .... Cambridge ON
ATS Test Systems Inc. (1) .... Woodbridge ON
BNT Products (1) .... Mississauga ON
Brenntag Canada Inc. (1) .... Toronto ON
Canadian General-Tower Ltd. (1) .... Cambridge ON
Colgate-Palmolive Canada Inc. (1) .... Toronto ON
Collins & Aikman (1) .... Toronto ON
Duplium Corporation (1) .... Thornhill ON
Dynaplas Ltd. (1) .... Toronto ON
Laird Plastics (Canada) Inc. (1) .... Mississauga ON
M&R Plastics Inc. (1) .... Laval QC
Mold-Masters Ltd. (1) .... Georgetown ON
National Research Council Canada, I (1) .... Boucherville QC
Paradigm Electronics (1) .... Mississauga ON
Poly-Pacific International Inc. (1) .... Edmonton AB
Proco Machinery Inc. (1) .... Mississauga ON
Royal Group Technologies Inc. (1) .... Woodbridge ON
Shaw Pipe Protection Ltd. (1) .... Calgary AB
Sigem Inc. (1) .... Kanata ON
Tiercon Industries Inc. (1) .... Stoney Creek ON
Volex Canada Inc. (1) .... Kanata ON

PRINTING

*See also: Publishing/Media, Graphic Arts, Packaging, Trades/
Technicians.*

Heidelberg Canada (17 positions) .... Mississauga ON
Lowe-Martin Group, The (14) .... Ottawa ON

CreoScitex (9) .... Burnaby BC
Grenville Management Services (8) .... Toronto ON
Teldon International Inc. (6) .... Richmond BC
Baker Gurney & McLaren Press (4) .... Toronto ON
GHQ Imaging Inkjet Productions Ltd. (4) .... Toronto ON
Houghton Boston Printers (4) .... Saskatoon SK
Sundog Printing Ltd. (4) .... Calgary AB
Alden Print Management Inc. (3) .... Markham ON
Dollco Printing (3) .... Ottawa ON
Globel Direct Marketing (3) .... Richmond BC
Hamilton Web Printing (3) .... Stoney Creek ON
Polytainers Inc. (3) .... Toronto ON
Publishing Plus Ltd. (3) .... Ottawa ON
Alphagraphics (2) .... Mississauga ON
Canadian Bank Note Company, Ltd. (2) .... Ottawa ON
Central Reproductions (2) .... Mississauga ON
Gandalf Graphics (2) .... Toronto ON
Globel Direct Marketing (2) .... Calgary AB
Heidelberg Canada (2) .... Toronto ON
Hemlock Printers Ltd. (2) .... Burnaby BC
Metro Label Company Ltd. (2) .... Toronto ON
Minolta Business Equipment (Canada), Ltd (2) .... Markham ON
NEBS Business Products (2) .... Midland ON
Nisku Printers (1980) Ltd. (2) .... Nisku AB
Ronalds Printing (2) .... Calgary AB
Schiffenhaus Canada Inc. / SCI (2) .... Mississauga ON
Sun Chemical Ink Limited (2) .... Brampton ON
3M Canada Company (1) .... London ON
Baycrest Centre for Geriatric Care (1) .... Toronto ON
C2 Media.com (1) .... Brantford ON
Cameo Crafts Graphic Industries Ltd. (1) .... St-Laurent QC
Certified General Accountants Associat (1) .... Vancouver BC
Danka Canada Inc. (1) .... Brampton ON
Dominion Sample Ltd. (1) .... St-Leonard QC
Duplium Corporation (1) .... Thornhill ON
Heidelberg Canada (1) .... Richmond BC
Hewson Bridge and Smith Ltd. / HBS (1) .... Ottawa ON
IDMD Design & Manufacturing Inc. (1) .... Toronto ON
IKON Office Solutions (1) .... Vancouver BC
Ilco Unican Inc. (1) .... Montréal QC
Imaginex Inc. (1) .... Mississauga ON
Manitoba Justice / Culture, Heritage an (1) .... Winnipeg MB
Merisel Canada Inc. (1) .... Toronto ON
Ministry of Finance, Ontario (1) .... Oshawa ON
Ministry of Transportation, Ontar (1) .... St. Catharines ON
Minolta Business Equipment (Canada), Lt (1) .... Richmond BC
Minolta Business Equipment (Canada), (1) .... Gloucester ON
Multipak Ltd. (1) .... Mississauga ON
Multiple Sclerosis Society of Canada (1) .... Toronto ON
Noritsu Canada Ltd. (1) .... Mississauga ON
Pitney Bowes Management Services Canada (1) .... Toronto ON
Postal Promotions Limited (1) .... Toronto ON
Quebecor World Printpak (1) .... Calgary AB
Rogers Video (1) .... Richmond BC
Shirmax Fashions Ltd. (1) .... Montréal QC
Sony Music Canada (1) .... Toronto ON
Standard Life Assurance Company, The (1) .... Montréal QC
Stirling Print-All (1) .... Hamilton ON
Sun Life Financial (1) .... Toronto ON
Top Tape & Label Ltd. (1) .... Ancaster ON
Toronto Star Newspapers Ltd. (1) .... Toronto ON
Toronto Star Newspapers Ltd., Press C (1) .... Woodbridge ON
University of Toronto Press Inc. / UTP (1) .... Toronto ON
Wolfe Merchandising (1) .... Toronto ON

PUBLIC RELATIONS

See also: Advertising, Marketing, Govt./Nonprofit.

Ministry of the Environment, Ontario (6 positions) .... Toronto ON
Ministry of Finance, Ontario (5) .... Toronto ON
Calgary, City of (4) .... Calgary AB
Public Service Commission of Canada, Onta (4) .... Ottawa ON
Systemcorp ALG Ltd. (4) .... Montréal QC
AIC Ltd. (3) .... Burlington ON
Alberta Health and Wellness (3) .... Edmonton AB
Cabinet Office (3) .... Toronto ON
Ministry of Children and Family Develop (3) .... Victoria BC
Ministry of Health and Long-Term Care, O (3) .... Toronto ON
Ministry of Transportation, Ontario (3) .... Toronto ON

For descriptions of the occupational categories used in this index, see page 458.

PUBLIC RELATIONS (Cont.)

PUBLIC RELATIONS (Cont.)

Ontario Lottery and Gaming Corporation / (1) .... Toronto ON
Ontario Native Affairs Secretariat / ONA (1) .... Toronto ON
Ontario Non-Profit Housing Association / (1) .... Toronto ON
Ontario Teachers' Pension Plan Board (1) .... Toronto ON
Ottawa Regional Cancer Centre Foundation (1) .... Ottawa ON
Pika Technologies Inc. (1) .... Kanata ON
Precision Drilling Corporation (1) .... Calgary AB
PrimeWest Energy Trust (1) .... Calgary AB
PrinterON Corporation (1) .... Kitchener ON
Public Service Commission of Canada, Exec (1) .... Ottawa ON
Purolator Courier Ltd. (1) .... Mississauga ON
Quadrus Development Inc. (1) .... Calgary AB
Quake Technologies Inc. (1) .... Ottawa ON
Registered Nurses Association of Ontario (1) .... Toronto ON
Replicon Inc. (1) .... Calgary AB
Rogers Cable Inc. (1) .... Toronto ON
Rogers Cable Inc. (1) .... St. John's NF
Royal Bank Financial Group (1) .... Toronto ON
Royal Canadian Golf Association / RCGA (1) .... Oakville ON
Royal Canadian Mint / RCM (1) .... Ottawa ON
Royal Roads University (1) .... Victoria BC
Saskatchewan Liquor and Gaming Authority (1) .... Regina SK
SaskPower (1) .... Regina SK
Sault Area Hospitals (1) .... Sault Ste. Marie ON
Scarborough Community Care Access Centre (1) .... Toronto ON
Science Alberta Foundation (1) .... Calgary AB
Selkirk Financial Technologies, Inc. (1) .... Vancouver BC
Sir Mortimer B. Davis - Jewish General (1) .... Montréal QC
Sitraka Software Inc. (1) .... Toronto ON
Southern Alberta Institute of Technology (1) .... Calgary AB
Spirent Communications (1) .... Ottawa ON
Staples Business Depot Ltd. (1) .... Markham ON
Telus Corporation (1) .... Burnaby BC
TLC Laser Eye Centers (1) .... Mississauga ON
Tri-Media Marketing & Publicity Inc. (1) .... Welland ON
Trillium Health Centre (1) .... Toronto ON
Trivalence Mining Corporation (1) .... Vancouver BC
Union of Canadian Transportation Employee (1) .... Ottawa ON
United Nations Children's Fund / UNICEF (1) .... Toronto ON
United Way / Centraide Ottawa (1) .... Nepean ON
University of Guelph (1) .... Guelph ON
Upper Canada District School Board (1) .... Brockville ON
Valcom Limited (Ottawa) (1) .... Ottawa ON
Vancouver City Savings Credit Union / (1) .... Vancouver BC
Vancouver Community College / VCC (1) .... Vancouver BC
Vancouver / Richmond Health Board (1) .... Vancouver BC
VoiceGenie.com (1) .... Toronto ON
Watchfire (1) .... Kanata ON
Wyeth-Ayerst Canada Inc. (1) .... Toronto ON
Wysdom Inc. (1) .... Richmond Hill ON
Yee Hong Community Wellness Foundation (1) .... Toronto ON
YM - YWHA, Ben Weider Jewish Community (1) .... Montréal QC
York Region District School Board (1) .... Aurora ON

PUBLISHING/MEDIA

See also: Printing, Multimedia, Graphic Arts, Advertising.

Rogers Media, Publishing (17 positions) .... Toronto ON
Carswell (10) .... Toronto ON
Global Television Network Inc. (10) .... Toronto ON
Alliance Atlantis Communications Inc. (9) .... Toronto ON
NOWTV (7) .... Winnipeg MB
Rogers Media, Television (7) .... Toronto ON
Calgary Herald (5) .... Calgary AB
Corel Corporation (5) .... Ottawa ON
PrinterON Corporation (5) .... Kitchener ON
Research in Motion Limited / RIM (5) .... Waterloo ON
B.C. Decker Inc. (4) .... Hamilton ON
CBC / Radio Canada (4) .... Toronto ON
CroMedica Inc. (4) .... Ottawa ON
Fincentric Corp. (4) .... Richmond BC
Mount Royal College (4) .... Calgary AB
Patheon Inc. (4) .... Mississauga ON
Sitraka Software Inc. (4) .... Toronto ON
Alive Magazine (3) .... Burnaby BC

CDG Books Canada Inc. (3) .... Toronto ON
Gage Educational Publishing (3) .... Toronto ON
Irwin Publishing Ltd. (3) .... Toronto ON
McGraw-Hill Ryerson Ltd. (3) .... Whitby ON
Ministry of Labour, Ontario (3) .... Toronto ON
Ministry of Small Business, Tourism and (3) .... Burnaby BC
Mitra Imaging Inc. (3) .... Waterloo ON
MuscleMag International (3) .... Mississauga ON
National Book Service / NBS (3) .... Toronto ON
National Film Board of Canada / NFB (3) .... Montréal QC
NStein Technologies (3) .... Laval QC
Rogers Cable Inc. (3) .... Saint John NB
Scholastic Canada Ltd. (3) .... Markham ON
Shopping Channel, The / TSC (3) .... Mississauga ON
ACNielsen Company of Canada (2) .... Markham ON
Ailanthus Achievement Centre (2) .... Vancouver BC
Avid Media Inc. (2) .... Markham ON
Bell Intrigna (2) .... Calgary AB
Bombardier Aerospace, Defense Services (2) .... Mirabel QC
Canada Law Book Inc. (2) .... Aurora ON
Canadian Mass Media Inc. (2) .... Toronto ON
Canadian Pharmacists Association / CPhA (2) .... Ottawa ON
CH2M HILL Canada Ltd. (2) .... Toronto ON
CSA International (2) .... Toronto ON
Federation of Canadian Municipalities / F (2) .... Ottawa ON
Firefly Books Ltd. (2) .... Toronto ON
H.B. Fenn and Company Ltd. (2) .... Bolton ON
Inex Pharmaceuticals Corp. (2) .... Burnaby BC
IT / Net Consultants Inc. (2) .... Ottawa ON
Kelly Phillips Productions Inc. (2) .... Montréal QC
Kids Can Press (2) .... Toronto ON
Manitoba Justice / Culture, Heritage an (2) .... Winnipeg MB
Ministry of Transportation, Ontario (2) .... Toronto ON
MuscleTech Research and Development (2) .... Mississauga ON
Nelvana Limited (2) .... Toronto ON
Northwood Technologies Inc. (2) .... Nepean ON
OP Publishing Ltd. (2) .... Vancouver BC
Parkhurst Publishing Ltd. (2) .... Montréal QC
Patheon Inc. (2) .... Toronto ON
Pegasus Healthcare International (2) .... Montréal QC
Proceco Ltd. (2) .... Montréal QC
Progestic International Inc. (2) .... Ottawa ON
Publishing Plus Ltd. (2) .... Ottawa ON
Rational Software Corporation (2) .... Kanata ON
Rogers Cable Inc. (2) .... Toronto ON
Royal Bank Financial Group (2) .... Toronto ON
Savage Software (2) .... Vancouver BC
Spafax Canada Inc (2) .... Montréal QC
Spar Aerospace Limited (2) .... Edmonton AB
St. Paul Journal (2) .... St. Paul AB
Standard & Poor's (2) .... Toronto ON
Tribute Publishing (2) .... Toronto ON
TVOntario / TVO (2) .... Toronto ON
724 Solutions Inc. (1) .... Toronto ON
A.L.I. Technologies Inc. (1) .... Richmond BC
Acart Communications (1) .... Ottawa ON
AcceLight Networks (1) .... Nepean ON
Adexa (1) .... Toronto ON
Advanced Micro Design (1) .... Edmonton AB
Agile Systems Inc. (1) .... Waterloo ON
Alacris Inc. (1) .... Ottawa ON
Alberta Community Development (1) .... Edmonton AB
Alberta Finance (1) .... Edmonton AB
Alberta Learning (1) .... Edmonton AB
Applanix Corp. (1) .... Richmond Hill ON
Athabasca University (1) .... Athabasca AB
Atlantis Systems International (1) .... Brampton ON
Auditor General of Alberta (1) .... Edmonton AB
Automation Tooling Systems Inc. / ATS (1) .... Oakville ON
Axys Environmental Consulting Ltd. (1) .... Calgary AB
Azure Publishing Inc. (1) .... Toronto ON
Bell Intrigna (1) .... Vancouver BC
BitFlash Graphics, Inc. (1) .... Ottawa ON
British Columbia Institute of Technology (1) .... Burnaby BC
Brooks Automation Software Corporation (1) .... Richmond BC
Brunico Communications Inc. (1) .... Toronto ON
Butterworths Canada Ltd. (1) .... Markham ON
C-MAC Invotronics Inc. (1) .... Toronto ON
CAE Inc. (1) .... St-Laurent QC
Canadian Copyright Licensing Agency / CA (1) .... Toronto ON
Canadian Council on Health Services Accre (1) .... Ottawa ON

For descriptions of the occupational categories used in this index, see page 458.

PUBLISHING/MEDIA (Cont.)

Canadian Internet Registration Authority (1) ... Ottawa ON
Canadian Nurses Association / CNA (1) ... Ottawa ON
Catena Networks (1) ... Kanata ON
Cayenta Canada (1) ... Burnaby BC
Central Reproductions (1) ... Mississauga ON
Centrepoint Technologies Inc. (1) ... Ottawa ON
CH2M HILL Canada Ltd. (1) ... Calgary AB
Chalk Network, The (1) ... Burnaby BC
Chancery Software Ltd. (1) ... Burnaby BC
CINAR Animation (1) ... Montréal QC
Circuit Graphics Ltd. (1) ... Burnaby BC
CMC Electronics Inc. (1) ... St-Laurent QC
CMD Group (1) ... Toronto ON
Coley Pharmaceutical Group / CPG (1) ... Ottawa ON
Computalog Ltd. (1) ... Edmonton AB
Computing Devices Canada Ltd. / CDC (1) ... Calgary AB
Conestoga College of Applied Arts & Te (1) ... Kitchener ON
Coradiant Inc. (1) ... Montréal QC
Cquay Inc. (1) ... Calgary AB
CreoScitex (1) ... Burnaby BC
CTC Communications Corp. (1) ... Mississauga ON
CTF Systems Inc. (1) ... Port Coquitlam BC
CyberSurf Corporation (1) ... Calgary AB
DataMirror Corporation (1) ... Markham ON
DeepMetrix Corporation (1) ... Hull ON
Delta Controls Inc. (1) ... Surrey BC
Digital Dispatch Systems Inc. (1) ... Richmond BC
Doubleday Canada Ltd. (1) ... Toronto ON
E-Cruiter.com Inc. (1) ... Toronto ON
E-smith, Inc. (1) ... Ottawa ON
Education On-Line / EOL (1) ... Edmonton AB
EFOS Corporation (1) ... Mississauga ON
Electronics Workbench (1) ... Toronto ON
ePALS Classroom Exchange (1) ... Ottawa ON
Ernst & Young LLP (1) ... Ottawa ON
Evertz Microsystems Ltd. (1) ... Burlington ON
EXI Wireless Systems Inc. (1) ... Richmond BC
Flight Dynamics Corp. (1) ... St-Jean-sur-Richelieu QC
Fraser Institute, The (1) ... Vancouver BC
Gage Applied, Inc. (1) ... Lachine QC
Gandalf Graphics (1) ... Toronto ON
General Motors of Canada Ltd., Diesel Div (1) ... London ON
GeoMetrix Data Systems Inc. (1) ... Victoria BC
Grant MacEwan College (1) ... Edmonton AB
Grant MacEwan College, Jasper Place Cam (1) ... Edmonton AB
GSI Lumonics Inc., Telecom Optics Divisio (1) ... Nepean ON
Guthrie Phillips Group Inc. / GPG (1) ... Vancouver BC
Harcourt Canada Ltd. (1) ... Toronto ON
Horn and Associates (1) ... Concord ON
Hyprotech Ltd. (1) ... Calgary AB
i-STAT Canada Ltd. (1) ... Kanata ON
Inkra Networks Canada (1) ... Burnaby BC
Inphinity Interactive Inc. (1) ... Vancouver BC
InSystems Technologies, Inc. (1) ... Markham ON
Intellitactics Inc. (1) ... Kitchener ON
IT World Canada (1) ... Toronto ON
John Wiley & Sons, Inc. (1) ... Toronto ON
JuneWarren Publishing Ltd. (1) ... Calgary AB
Key Porter Books (1) ... Toronto ON
Lakeland College (1) ... Vermilion AB
Legislative Assembly of Ontario, Office (1) ... Toronto ON
Lethbridge Community College / LCC (1) ... Lethbridge AB
Linmor Technologies Inc. (1) ... Ottawa ON
Lovat Tunnel Equipment Inc. (1) ... Toronto ON
Management Board Secretariat (1) ... Toronto ON
Manitoba Labour & Immigration (1) ... Winnipeg MB
Manitoba Transportation & Government Se (1) ... Winnipeg MB
March Networks Corporation (1) ... Kanata ON
Matrikon Group (1) ... Edmonton AB
Maxim Group (1) ... Calgary AB
MDS Aero Support Corporation (1) ... Ottawa ON
MedcomSoft Inc. (1) ... Toronto ON
Mediagrif Interactive Technologies Inc (1) ... Longueuil QC
Mentor Engineering (1) ... Calgary AB
Merak Projects Ltd. (1) ... Calgary AB
Ministry of Education / Ministry of Trai (1) ... Toronto ON
Ministry of Finance, Ontario (1) ... Oshawa ON
Ministry of Health and Long-Term Care, O (1) ... Toronto ON
Ministry of the Attorney General, BC (V (1) ... Victoria BC
Ministry of the Environment, Ontario (1) ... Toronto ON
Ministry of the Environment, Ontario (Co (1) ... Toronto ON
MKS Inc. (1) ... Waterloo ON
MOSAID Technologies Inc. (1) ... Kanata ON
Nanowave Technologies Inc. (1) ... Toronto ON
National Research Council Canada / NRC (1) ... Ottawa ON
Net-Linx Americas, Inc. (1) ... Edmonton AB
NetPCS (1) ... Hull QC
NexInnovations (1) ... Mississauga ON
Nissan Canada Inc. (1) ... Mississauga ON
Nortel Networks (1) ... Ottawa ON
Northern Airborne Technology Ltd. / NAT (1) ... Kelowna BC
Northland Systems Training Inc. (1) ... Ottawa ON
Oerlikon Aerospace Inc. (1) ... St-Jean-sur-Richelieu QC
Okanagan University College / OUC (1) ... Kelowna BC
Ontario Clean Water Agency / OCWA (1) ... Toronto ON
Ontario Teachers' Pension Plan Board (1) ... Toronto ON
Open Learning Agency / OLA (1) ... Burnaby BC
Optech Inc. (1) ... Toronto ON
Optimal Robotics Corp. (1) ... Montréal QC
OZ Optics Ltd. (1) ... Carp ON
Paradata Systems Inc. (1) ... Whistler BC
Peloton Petroleum Software Solutions (1) ... Calgary AB
Penguin Books Canada Ltd. (1) ... Toronto ON
Pink Triangle Press (1) ... Toronto ON
POPstar Communications Canada, Inc. (1) ... Vancouver BC
Positron Public Safety Systems Inc. (1) ... Montréal QC
Prime Minister's Office (1) ... Ottawa ON
Proface Inde Electronics Inc. (1) ... Burnaby BC
Provance Technologies Inc. (1) ... Gatineau QC
Provincial Auditor of Ontario, Office of (1) ... Toronto ON
PureEdge Solutions Inc. (1) ... Victoria BC
QLT Inc. (1) ... Vancouver BC
Research in Motion Limited / RIM (1) ... Kanata ON
Rogers Cable Inc. (1) ... Richmond Hill ON
Rogers Cable Inc. (1) ... St. John's NF
Rogers Communications Inc. (1) ... Ottawa ON
Rogers iMedia (1) ... Toronto ON
Royal Canadian Golf Association / RCGA (1) ... Oakville ON
Saskatchewan Institute of Applied Scie (1) ... Saskatoon SK
SCP Science (1) ... Baie d'Urfe QC
Senstar-Stellar Corporation (1) ... Carp ON
Shana Corporation (1) ... Edmonton AB
Shopping Channel, The / TSC (1) ... Toronto ON
Silicon Access Networks Ltd. (1) ... Ottawa ON
Simon Fraser University (1) ... Burnaby BC
Sitraka Mobility (1) ... Toronto ON
SkillScape (1) ... Victoria BC
Smart Technologies Inc. (1) ... Calgary AB
Soft Tracks (1) ... Richmond BC
Solect Technology Group (1) ... Toronto ON
SpaceBridge Networks Corporation (1) ... Hull QC
SST (1) ... Waterloo ON
SureFire Commerce Inc. (1) ... Westmount QC
Tarian Software Inc. (1) ... Ottawa ON
Technical University of British Columbia (1) ... Surrey BC
Tellamon Photonic Networks Inc. (1) ... Ottawa ON
TELOS Technology Inc. (1) ... Richmond BC
Town Publishing Inc. (1) ... Hamilton ON
Trader.com (1) ... Edmonton AB
Transcontinental Media (1) ... Toronto ON
Tri-ad Graphic Communications Ltd. (1) ... Toronto ON
Trinity College School (1) ... Port Hope ON
TriVu Interactive Corporation (1) ... Mississauga ON
TTG Systems Inc. (1) ... Edmonton AB
University College of the Cariboo / UCC (1) ... Kamloops BC
Valadeo Technologies Corp. (1) ... Toronto ON
VIPswitch Inc. (1) ... Montréal QC
Vivonet Canada Inc. (1) ... Vancouver BC
Watchfire (1) ... Kanata ON
Wi-LAN Inc. (1) ... Calgary AB
William M. Mercer Limited (1) ... Ottawa ON
Xantrex Technology Inc. (1) ... Burnaby BC
Xillix Technologies Corp. (1) ... Richmond BC
Yotta Yotta Inc. (1) ... Edmonton AB
Zed.i Solutions (1) ... Calgary AB
Zenastra Photonics Inc. (1) ... Ottawa ON

PULP & PAPER

See also: Forestry, Printing, Engineering.

Sandwell Engineering Inc. (6 positions)	Vancouver BC
Celgar Pulp Company (5)	Castlegar BC
Pulp & Paper Research Institute of (4)	Pointe-Claire QC
Scott Paper Ltd. (4)	New Westminster BC
Western Pulp Limited Partnership, Por (4)	Port Alice BC
Abitibi-Consolidated Inc., Mackenzie R (3)	Mackenzie BC
Norske Skog Canada, Elk Falls Pri (3)	Campbell River BC
Scott Paper Ltd. (3)	Hull QC
Weyerhaeuser Company Limited (3)	Sturgeon Falls ON
Alberta Newsprint Company (2)	Whitecourt AB
Cariboo Pulp & Paper Company (2)	Quesnel BC
Casco Impregnated Papers Inc. (2)	Cobourg ON
Howe Sound Pulp and Paper Ltd. (2)	Port Mellon BC
Norampac Inc., Red Rock Division (2)	Red Rock ON
Slave Lake Pulp (2)	Slave Lake AB
St. Marys Paper Ltd. (2)	Sault Ste. Marie ON
Tencorr Packaging Inc. (2)	Toronto ON
Canpar Industries (1)	Grand Forks BC
College of the North Atlantic, Step (1)	Stephenville NF
Domtar Inc. (1)	Montréal QC
Domtar Inc., Communication Papers Divis (1)	Cornwall ON
Domtar Inc., Ottawa / Hull Mills (1)	Hull QC
E.B. Eddy Specialty Papers (1)	Espanola ON
Ellett Industries Ltd. (1)	Port Coquitlam BC
Honeywell IC (1)	North Vancouver BC
National Paper Goods (1)	Hamilton ON
Stothert Engineering Ltd. (1)	Vancouver BC
Tolko Industries Ltd. (1)	Vernon BC
Walsh Automation / Validation Technolog (1)	Montréal QC
Weyerhaeuser Company Limited (1)	Kamloops BC
Weyerhaeuser Company Limited, Dryden Mill (1)	Dryden ON

PURCHASING

See also: Logistics, Operations.

Bombardier Aerospace (11 positions)	Montréal QC
Procuron Inc. (7)	Thornhill ON
Delta Hudson Engineering Ltd. (6)	Calgary AB
Trillium Health Centre (6)	Toronto ON
CreoScitex (5)	Burnaby BC
OZ Optics Ltd. (5)	Carp ON
Westfair Foods Ltd. (5)	Calgary AB
Alberta Energy Company Ltd. / AEC (4)	Calgary AB
Creation Technologies Inc. (4)	Burnaby BC
Magna International Inc. (4)	Concord ON
MTU Maintenance Canada Ltd. (4)	Richmond BC
Nanowave Technologies Inc. (4)	Toronto ON
Research in Motion Limited / RIM (4)	Waterloo ON
Shared Services West, Regional Materials (4)	Toronto ON
Computing Devices Canada Ltd. / CDC (3)	Calgary AB
Computing Devices Canada Ltd. / CDC (3)	Ottawa ON
CPI Canada Inc. (3)	Georgetown ON
Dempsey Corporation (3)	Toronto ON
Electro Sonic Inc. (3)	Toronto ON
Fluor Canada Ltd. (3)	Calgary AB
Group Telecom (3)	Toronto ON
Lovat Tunnel Equipment Inc. (3)	Toronto ON
Management Board Secretariat (3)	Toronto ON
Manitoba Transportation & Government Se (3)	Winnipeg MB
MDS Aero Support Corporation (3)	Ottawa ON
NCR Canada Ltd. (3)	Waterloo ON
Orion Bus Industries Ltd. (3)	Mississauga ON
Rogers Communications Inc. (3)	Toronto ON
Shopping Channel, The / TSC (3)	Toronto ON
Staples Business Depot Ltd. (3)	Markham ON
Sun Life Financial (3)	Toronto ON
Suncor Energy Inc. (3)	Calgary AB
Suncor Energy Inc., Oil Sands (3)	Fort McMurray AB
Velan Inc. (3)	Montréal QC
Volvo Motor Graders (3)	Goderich ON
Zenastra Photonics Inc. (3)	Ottawa ON
Alberta Infrastructure & Transportation (2)	Edmonton AB
Alpha Technologies Ltd. (2)	Burnaby BC
Bombardier Aerospace, Regional Aircraft (2)	Toronto ON
Brampton, City of (2)	Brampton ON
Calea Ltd. (2)	Mississauga ON
Canadian Bank Note Company, Ltd. (2)	Ottawa ON
Cara Operations Ltd. (2)	Richmond BC
Casino Niagara (2)	Niagara Falls ON
Celestica Inc. (2)	Toronto ON
Cellex Power Products Inc. (2)	Richmond BC
Cognos Inc. (2)	Ottawa ON
DRS Flight Safety and Communicati (2)	Carleton Place ON
ENMAX Corporation (2)	Calgary AB
Ganz (2)	Woodbridge ON
GE Canada (2)	Mississauga ON
GFI Control Systems Inc. (2)	Kitchener ON
Global Thermoelectric Inc. (2)	Calgary AB
Growmark Inc. (2)	Mississauga ON
Hepcoe Credit Union Ltd. (2)	Toronto ON
Honda of Canada Manufacturing (2)	Alliston ON
Honeywell Inc. (2)	Montréal QC
Hunter Amenities International Ltd. (2)	Burlington ON
i-STAT Canada Ltd. (2)	Kanata ON
IBM Canada Ltd. (2)	Markham ON
IR Security & Safety (2)	Mississauga ON
JDS Uniphase Corporation (2)	Nepean ON
Kaycan Ltd. (2)	Pointe-Claire QC
Liftking Industries Inc. (2)	Woodbridge ON
Linamar Corporation, Eston Division (2)	Guelph ON
MacDonald Dettwiler Space and Advanced (2)	Brampton ON
Magna International Inc. (2)	Concord ON
MDS Nordion (2)	Kanata ON
Mitec Telecom Inc. (2)	Pointe-Claire QC
Oerlikon Aerospace Inc. (2)	St-Jean-sur-Richelieu QC
Ontario Pension Board (2)	Toronto ON
Open Text Corporation (2)	Waterloo ON
Orlick Industries Ltd. (2)	Hamilton ON
Patheon Inc. (2)	Mississauga ON
Peel, The Regional Municipality of (2)	Brampton ON
Psion Teklogix Inc. (2)	Mississauga ON
RAM Computer Group Inc. (2)	Vaughan ON
Royal Canadian Mint / RCM (2)	Ottawa ON
S.A. Armstrong Ltd. (2)	Toronto ON
Shoppers Drug Mart (2)	Toronto ON
Siemens Canada Ltd. (2)	Mississauga ON
Silex Inc. (2)	Mississauga ON
SpaceBridge Networks Corporation (2)	Hull QC
TELOS Technology Inc. (2)	Richmond BC
Tracer Industries Canada Ltd. (2)	Edmonton AB
Trapeze Software Inc. (2)	Mississauga ON
Triple-C Inc. (2)	Hamilton ON
Valcom Limited (Ottawa) (2)	Ottawa ON
Wescam (2)	Burlington ON
724 Solutions Inc. (1)	Toronto ON
A&B Sound Ltd. (1)	Vancouver BC
ABC Group Inc. (1)	Toronto ON
Accubid Systems Ltd. (1)	Toronto ON
Acres International Limited (1)	Castlegar BC
Advantech Advanced Microwave Technologies (1)	Dorval QC
Agile Systems Inc. (1)	Waterloo ON
Alberta Mental Health Board, Alberta Hosp (1)	Ponoka AB
Alcan Primary Metal Group (1)	Kitimat BC
All New Manufacturing Inc. (1)	Calgary AB
AMEC (1)	Vancouver BC
Apollo Microwaves Ltd. (1)	Pointe-Claire QC
Apotex Inc. (1)	Toronto ON
Aramark Canada Ltd. (1)	Toronto ON
AstraZeneca (1)	Mississauga ON
Audio Centre (1)	St-Laurent QC
Avianor Inc. (1)	Dorval QC
Baxter Corporation (1)	Alliston ON
Baycrest Centre for Geriatric Care (1)	Toronto ON
Bayer Inc. (1)	Toronto ON
Bazaar & Novelty (1)	St. Catharines ON
BC Biomedical Laboratories Ltd. (1)	Surrey BC
BC Rapid Transit Co. Ltd. / BCRTC (1)	Burnaby BC
Belbois Ltd. (1)	Laval QC
Bell Intrigna (1)	Edmonton AB
Bettis Canada Ltd. (1)	Edmonton AB
Bombardier Aerospace, Defense Services (1)	Mirabel QC
Bombardier Transport, Transit Systems (1)	Burnaby BC
Born Canada (1)	Calgary AB
BouClair Inc. (1)	Dorval QC
Brake Pro, Ltd. (1)	Concord ON
Brantford, Corporation of the City of (1)	Brantford ON

For descriptions of the occupational categories used in this index, see page 458.

PURCHASING (Cont.)

Bridge Brand Food Services Ltd. (1) ... Calgary AB
Bridgestone Firestone Canada Inc. / (1) ... Mississauga ON
Bulk Barn Foods Ltd. (1) ... Richmond Hill ON
C-MAC Industries Inc. (1) ... Kanata ON
C-MAC Invotronics Inc. (1) ... Toronto ON
C2 Media.com (1) ... Brantford ON
Caboodles Cosmetics (1) ... New Westminster BC
CAE Inc. (1) ... St-Laurent QC
CAE Machinery Ltd. (1) ... Vancouver BC
Calgary, City of (1) ... Calgary AB
Cameo Crafts Graphic Industries Ltd. (1) ... St-Laurent QC
Can-Eng Furnaces Ltd. (1) ... Niagara Falls ON
Canadian Wheat Board / CWB (1) ... Winnipeg MB
Capital Health, Royal Alexandra Hospita (1) ... Edmonton AB
Carewest (1) ... Calgary AB
Carrier Canada Ltd. (1) ... Mississauga ON
Cascade (1) ... Mississauga ON
CGU Group Canada Ltd. (1) ... Toronto ON
Christie Lites (1) ... Toronto ON
CIBA Vision Sterile Manufacturing (1) ... Mississauga ON
CIMTEK Automation Systems (1) ... Burlington ON
Civil Service Co-operative Credit Society (1) ... Ottawa ON
CMC Electronics Inc. (1) ... Kanata ON
CMC Electronics Inc. (1) ... St-Laurent QC
CML Emergency Services, Inc. (1) ... Hull QC
Colt Engineering Corporation (1) ... Calgary AB
Colt Engineering Corporation (1) ... Markham ON
Commercial Spring and Tool Company L (1) ... Mississauga ON
Comstock Canada Ltd. (1) ... Edmonton AB
Comstock Canada Ltd. (1) ... Burlington ON
Conestoga College of Applied Arts & Te (1) ... Kitchener ON
Cymbolic Sciences Inc. (1) ... Richmond BC
Dana Long Manufacturing Ltd. (1) ... Oakville ON
Dana Long Manufacturing Ltd. (1) ... Mississauga ON
Defence Construction Canada (1) ... Ottawa ON
DoALL Industrial Supplies (1) ... Toronto ON
Dominion Sample Ltd. (1) ... St-Leonard QC
Don Park Inc. (1) ... Toronto ON
Dorigo Systems Ltd. (1) ... Burnaby BC
DSC Group of Companies (1) ... Concord ON
DuPont Canada Inc. (1) ... Mississauga ON
DuPont Canada Inc. (1) ... Kingston ON
DY 4 Systems Inc. (1) ... Kanata ON
Edge Networks Corporation (1) ... Winnipeg MB
Elco Fine Foods Inc. (1) ... Richmond Hill ON
Ellett Industries Ltd. (1) ... Port Coquitlam BC
EPCOR Utilities Inc. (1) ... Edmonton AB
ESBI Alberta Ltd. (1) ... Calgary AB
Espial Group Inc. (1) ... Ottawa ON
Evans Consoles Inc. (1) ... Calgary AB
Export Packers Company Ltd. (1) ... Brampton ON
F & K Mfg. Co. Limited (1) ... Toronto ON
Falconbridge Ltd. (1) ... Toronto ON
Famous Players Inc. (1) ... Toronto ON
Fellfab Limited (1) ... Hamilton ON
Footner Forest Products Ltd. (1) ... High Level AB
Found Aircraft Canada Inc. (1) ... Parry Sound ON
Foxboro Canada Inc. (1) ... Dollard-des-Ormeaux QC
Frontier (1) ... Calgary AB
Fuji Photo Film Canada Inc. (1) ... Mississauga ON
GE Power Systems (1) ... Calgary AB
GE Power Systems (1) ... Guelph ON
Gear Centre Group of Companies, The (1) ... Edmonton AB
Gemini Corporation (1) ... Calgary AB
General Hydrogen / GH (1) ... Vancouver BC
George Brown College (1) ... Toronto ON
Giftcraft Ltd. (1) ... Brampton ON
GKO Engineering (1) ... Edmonton AB
Great Canadian Casinos Inc. (1) ... Richmond BC
Great-West Life Assurance Company, The (1) ... Winnipeg MB
GSI Lumonics Inc. (1) ... Kanata ON
GSI Lumonics Inc., Telecom Optics Divisio (1) ... Nepean ON
Halton Hills, Town of (1) ... Halton Hills ON
Hamilton Health Sciences Corporation, C (1) ... Hamilton ON
Hardt Equipment Manufacturing Inc. (1) ... Lachine QC
Henry Birks & Sons Inc. (1) ... Montréal QC
HFI Flooring Inc. (1) ... Calgary AB
Highland Equipment Ltd. (1) ... Toronto ON
Hofland Ltd. (1) ... Mississauga ON
Honeywell IC (1) ... North Vancouver BC
Hush Puppies Canada (1) ... St-Laurent QC
Hyprotech Ltd. (1) ... Calgary AB
Indigo Manufacturing Inc. (1) ... Markham ON
Information Services Corporation of Saska (1) ... Regina SK
Inland Group (1) ... Edmonton AB
Instantel Inc. (1) ... Kanata ON
International Plaza Hotel & Conference C (1) ... Toronto ON
IVL Technologies Ltd. (1) ... Victoria BC
JDS Uniphase Corporation, Fiber-Optic Pr (1) ... Markham ON
Keeweetinok Lakes Regional Health A (1) ... High Prairie AB
Kelowna, City of (1) ... Kelowna BC
Kids Can Press (1) ... Toronto ON
Kodak Canada Inc. (1) ... Toronto ON
KristoFoam Industries Inc. (1) ... Concord ON
Lafarge Construction Materials (1) ... Concord ON
Lakeland College (1) ... Vermilion AB
Leesta Industries Ltd. (1) ... Pointe-Claire QC
Liburdi Engineering Ltd. (1) ... Dundas ON
Linamar Corporation, Autocom Division (1) ... Guelph ON
Loadstar Dispatchers / Northern Industr (1) ... Edmonton AB
Loewen Group Inc., The (1) ... Toronto ON
LSG Sky Chefs (1) ... Mississauga ON
M&R Plastics Inc. (1) ... Laval QC
Madvac Inc. (1) ... Longueuil QC
Magic Span Fabricating Ltd. / MSF (1) ... Calgary AB
Maksteel Inc. (1) ... Mississauga ON
MapInfo Corporation (1) ... Toronto ON
Maple Leaf Consumer Foods (1) ... Mississauga ON
Marsan Foods Ltd. (1) ... Toronto ON
Master Flo Valve Inc. (1) ... Edmonton AB
Matsu Manufacturing Inc. (1) ... Brampton ON
McMaster University (1) ... Hamilton ON
Med-Eng Systems Inc. (1) ... Ottawa ON
Mentor Engineering (1) ... Calgary AB
Merisel Canada Inc. (1) ... Toronto ON
Merit Kitchens (1) ... Surrey BC
Ministry of Consumer and Business Servic (1) ... Toronto ON
Ministry of Correctional Services, Ontar (1) ... Toronto ON
Ministry of Correctional Services, Ontar (1) ... Toronto ON
Ministry of Health and Long-Term Care, O (1) ... Toronto ON
Mississauga, City of (1) ... Mississauga ON
Mobile Data Solutions Inc. / MDSI (1) ... Richmond BC
Modatek Systems (1) ... St. Thomas ON
Muir's Cartage Limited (1) ... Concord ON
NEPCAN Engineering Ltd. (1) ... Vancouver BC
Nexen Inc. (1) ... Calgary AB
NexInnovations (1) ... Mississauga ON
Nextrom Ltd. (1) ... Concord ON
Noranda Inc. (1) ... Pointe-Claire QC
Northern Elevator Ltd. (1) ... Toronto ON
Ontario College of Art and Design / OCAD (1) ... Toronto ON
Ontario Lottery and Gaming Corporation / (1) ... Toronto ON
OPIsystems Inc. (1) ... Calgary AB
Optech Inc. (1) ... Toronto ON
PACCAR Financial Services Ltd. (1) ... Mississauga ON
Palliser Furniture Ltd. (1) ... Airdrie AB
Paradigm Electronics (1) ... Mississauga ON
Patella Manufacturing Inc. (1) ... Lasalle QC
Patheon Inc. (1) ... Toronto ON
PC World (1) ... Toronto ON
Pengrowth Management Ltd. / PML (1) ... Calgary AB
Pet Valu Canada Inc. (1) ... Markham ON
Peter Kiewit Sons Co. Ltd. (1) ... Edmonton AB
Peterborough Regional Health Centre (1) ... Peterborough ON
Phoenix Hydraulics Group (1) ... Nisku AB
Plantech Control Systems Inc. (1) ... Vineland ON
Power Measurement Ltd. (1) ... Victoria BC
Prince George, City of (1) ... Prince George BC
Proceco Ltd. (1) ... Montréal QC
Professional Pharmaceutical Corp. (1) ... Lachine QC
PTI Group Inc. (1) ... Edmonton AB
Public Service Commission of Canada, Onta (1) ... Ottawa ON
Puratos Canada, Inc. (1) ... Mississauga ON
Purolator Courier Ltd. (1) ... Mississauga ON
Q-Tron Ltd. (1) ... Calgary AB
QLT Inc. (1) ... Vancouver BC
QuestAir Technologies Inc. (1) ... Burnaby BC
Raylo Chemicals Inc. (1) ... Edmonton AB
Raytheon Systems Canada Ltd. (1) ... Calgary AB
Raytheon Systems Canada Ltd. (1) ... Waterloo ON
Reber Inc. / R-2000 Inc. (1) ... Riviere-des-Prairies QC

PURCHASING (Cont.)

Ridgewood Industries (1) .... Cornwall ON
Robin Hood Multifoods Inc., Bick's Pla (1) .... Dunnville ON
Rogers AT&T Wireless (1) .... Toronto ON
Rogers Shared Services (1) .... Markham ON
Rogers Video (1) .... Richmond BC
RoundHeaven Communications Canada Inc. (1) ...... Vancouver BC
RSL COM Canada Inc. (1) .... Vancouver BC
Russel Metals Inc. (1) .... Mississauga ON
SanMar Canada (1) .... Richmond BC
Sanmina Enclosure Systems (1) .... Toronto ON
Schlumberger Completion Systems (1) .... Calgary AB
Scintrex Ltd. (1) .... Concord ON
Scintrex Trace Corp. (1) .... Ottawa ON
Senstar-Stellar Corporation (1) .... Carp ON
Shopping Channel, The / TSC (1) .... Mississauga ON
Siemens Automotive (1) .... London ON
Siemens Dematic Ltd., Rapistan Divis (1) .... Mississauga ON
Siemens Milltronics Process Instrum (1) .... Peterborough ON
Siemens Westinghouse (1) .... Hamilton ON
Smart Technologies Inc. (1) .... Stittsville ON
SNC-Lavalin Inc. (1) .... Edmonton AB
SNC-Lavalin Inc., Chemicals & Petroleum (1) .... Calgary AB
Sobeys Inc. (1) .... Mississauga ON
Sodexho Marriott Services Canada, Inc (1) .... Burlington ON
Solect Technology Group (1) .... Toronto ON
Solectron (1) .... Calgary AB
Sony Music Canada (1) .... Toronto ON
Sota Glazing Inc. (1) .... Brampton ON
Southern Alberta Institute of Technology (1) .... Calgary AB
Spirent Communications (1) .... Ottawa ON
Standard Paper Box (1) .... Mississauga ON
Stikeman Elliott (1) .... Toronto ON
Sun Life Financial (1) .... Montréal QC
Superior Emergency Vehicles Ltd. (1) .... Red Deer AB
Supreme Tooling Group (1) .... Toronto ON
Surface Mount Technology Centre Inc. / S (1) .... Markham ON
Swiss Herbal Remedies Ltd. (1) .... Richmond Hill ON
Sytek Enterprises Inc. (1) .... North Vancouver BC
Tantalus Systems Corp. (1) .... Burnaby BC
Technical University of British Columbia (1) .... Surrey BC
Technisonic Industries Limited (1) .... Mississauga ON
TELAV Audio Visual Services (1) .... Lachine QC
Tellamon Photonic Networks Inc. (1) .... Ottawa ON
Telus Mobility (1) .... Toronto ON
Tenaquip Ltd. (1) .... Ste-Anne-de-Bellevue QC
Therapist's Choice Medical Supplies Inc. (1) .... Toronto ON
Thomas & Betts Limited (1) .... Iberville QC
Thomson-CSF Optronique Canada Inc. (1) .... St-Laurent QC
Tilbury Cement Ltd. (1) .... Delta BC
Toromont CAT (1) .... Concord ON
Total Communications (1) .... Hamilton ON
TransAlta Corporation (1) .... Calgary AB
Tri-Ed Ltd. (1) .... Mississauga ON
VA Tech Ferranti-Packard Transfor (1) .... St. Catharines ON
Vancouver City Savings Credit Union / (1) .... Vancouver BC
Vancouver International Airport Authori (1) .... Richmond BC
Vancouver School Board / VSB (1) .... Vancouver BC
Vistek Ltd. (1) .... Toronto ON
VK Brunette Ltd. (1) .... New Westminster BC
Vogue Brassiere Incorporated (1) .... Toronto ON
Vopak Canada Ltd. (1) .... Edmonton AB
Walsh Automation / Validation Technolog (1) .... Montréal QC
Weatherford / McAllister (1) .... Calgary AB
Weighpack Paxiom (1) .... Lachine QC
West Park Healthcare Centre (1) .... Toronto ON
Wexxar Packaging Machinery Ltd. (1) .... Delta BC
Wheeltronic Ltd. (1) .... Mississauga ON
White Rose Home and Garden Centres (1) .... Unionville ON
Williams Energy Canada Inc. (1) .... Calgary AB
Windsor Casino Limited (1) .... Windsor ON
Winpak Technologies Inc. (1) .... Toronto ON
Winters Instruments (1) .... Toronto ON
Woodbine Entertainment Group (1) .... Toronto ON
Xantrex Technology Inc. (1) .... Burnaby BC
Yamaha Motor Canada Ltd. (1) .... Toronto ON

QUALITY CONTROL

See also: Actuarial, Logistics, Operations, Engineering.

Magna International Inc. (16 positions) .... Concord ON
Global Thermoelectric Inc. (6) .... Calgary AB
Research in Motion Limited / RIM (6) .... Waterloo ON
ABC Group Inc. (5) .... Toronto ON
Advantech Advanced Microwave Technologies (5) .... Dorval QC
Chemque Inc. (5) .... Toronto ON
CMC Electronics Inc. (5) .... St-Laurent QC
OZ Optics Ltd. (5) .... Carp ON
Wescam (5) .... Burlington ON
CIBA Vision Sterile Manufacturing (4) .... Mississauga ON
COM DEV International (4) .... Cambridge ON
EMS Technologies Canada Ltd (4) .... Ste-Anne-de-Bellevue QC
Mitec Telecom Inc. (4) .... Pointe-Claire QC
Optech Inc. (4) .... Toronto ON
Orlick Industries Ltd. (4) .... Hamilton ON
QuestAir Technologies Inc. (4) .... Burnaby BC
Taro Pharmaceuticals Inc. (4) .... Bramalea ON
Westport Innovations Inc. (4) .... Vancouver BC
Alpha Technologies Ltd. (3) .... Burnaby BC
BitFlash Graphics, Inc. (3) .... Ottawa ON
Concord Confections Inc. (3) .... Concord ON
Coretec Inc. (3) .... Toronto ON
DSC Group of Companies (3) .... Toronto ON
DY 4 Systems Inc. (3) .... Kanata ON
Dynacast Canada Inc. (3) .... Pointe-Claire QC
GlaxoSmithKline (3) .... Mississauga ON
International Group Inc., The / IGI (3) .... Toronto ON
JDS Uniphase Corporation (3) .... Saanichton BC
JDS Uniphase Corporation (3) .... Nepean ON
JDS Uniphase Corporation, Fiber-Optic Pr (3) .... Markham ON
Med-Eng Systems Inc. (3) .... Ottawa ON
QLT Inc. (3) .... Vancouver BC
Resonance Photonics Inc. (3) .... Markham ON
Sanmina Enclosure Systems (3) .... Toronto ON
Siemens Westinghouse (3) .... Hamilton ON
Tracer Industries Canada Ltd. (3) .... Edmonton AB
Wi-LAN Inc. (3) .... Calgary AB
Zenastra Photonics Inc. (3) .... Ottawa ON
Zircatec Precision Industries Inc. / Z (3) .... Port Hope ON
A.L.I. Technologies Inc. (2) .... Richmond BC
Alcatel Canada Inc., Transport Automatio (2) .... Toronto ON
Antomax Automotive Technologies (2) .... Mississauga ON
Baxter Corporation (2) .... Alliston ON
CAE Inc. (2) .... St-Laurent QC
Capital Metal Industries (2) .... Toronto ON
Cayenta Canada (2) .... Burnaby BC
Cellex Power Products Inc. (2) .... Richmond BC
Colgate-Palmolive Canada Inc. (2) .... Toronto ON
Commercial Spring and Tool Company L (2) .... Mississauga ON
Corrpro Canada, Inc. / Corrpower (2) .... Edmonton AB
CSA International (2) .... Toronto ON
CWB Group (2) .... Mississauga ON
Delta Controls Inc. (2) .... Surrey BC
Enersul Inc. (2) .... Calgary AB
Evans Consoles Inc. (2) .... Calgary AB
GE Power Systems (2) .... Calgary AB
GE Power Systems (2) .... Guelph ON
Janes Family Foods Ltd. (2) .... Toronto ON
Labatt Breweries Ontario (2) .... Toronto ON
Leitch Technology Corp. (2) .... Toronto ON
Linamar Corporation, Autocom Division (2) .... Guelph ON
Master Flo Valve Inc. (2) .... Edmonton AB
Matrikon Group (2) .... Edmonton AB
MetriCan Manufacturing Co. Inc. (2) .... Oakville ON
Ministry of Labour, Ontario (2) .... Toronto ON
Nanometrics Inc. (2) .... Kanata ON
Nanowave Technologies Inc. (2) .... Toronto ON
Patheon Inc. (2) .... Burlington ON
Patheon Inc. (2) .... Mississauga ON
PCL Constructors Inc. (2) .... Edmonton AB
PerkinElmer Optoelectronics Inc. (2) .... Vaudreuil QC
Pillsbury Canada Limited (2) .... Midland ON
Positron Public Safety Systems Inc. (2) .... Montréal QC
Productivity Improvement Center / PIC (2) .... Whitby ON
Psion Teklogix Inc. (2) .... Mississauga ON
Public Service Commission of Canada, Onta (2) .... Ottawa ON
Q-Tron Ltd. (2) .... Calgary AB

For descriptions of the occupational categories used in this index, see page 458.

QUALITY CONTROL (Cont.)

QJunction Technology Inc. (2) .... Waterloo ON
Royal Group Technologies Inc. (2) .... Woodbridge ON
S.A. Armstrong Ltd. (2) .... Toronto ON
Schneider Foods Inc. (2) .... Kitchener ON
Senstar-Stellar Corporation (2) .... Carp ON
Span Manufacturing Ltd. (2) .... Markham ON
Stream International (2) .... Belleville ON
Sulzer Mitroflow Corp. (2) .... Richmond BC
Sun Rich Fresh Foods Inc. (2) .... Richmond BC
Suncor Energy Inc., Oil Sands (2) .... Fort McMurray AB
Sytek Enterprises Inc. (2) .... North Vancouver BC
Toronto Transit Commission / TTC (2) .... Toronto ON
Tube-Fab Ltd. (2) .... Mississauga ON
Valcom Limited (Ottawa) (2) .... Ottawa ON
Visible Genetics Inc. (2) .... Toronto ON
Volex Canada Inc. (2) .... Kanata ON
Xcert International Inc. (2) .... Vancouver BC
Zed.i Solutions (2) .... Edmonton AB
Acceleron (1) .... St-Laurent QC
AcceLight Networks (1) .... Nepean ON
ACNielsen Company of Canada (1) .... Markham ON
Adexa (1) .... Toronto ON
Advanced Micro Design (1) .... Edmonton AB
Advanced Research Technologies Inc. / (1) .... St-Laurent QC
Agile Systems Inc. (1) .... Waterloo ON
Alacris Inc. (1) .... Ottawa ON
Alberta Agriculture, Food & Rural Devel (1) .... Edmonton AB
Alberta Cancer Board (1) .... Calgary AB
Alberta Mental Health Board, Alberta Hosp (1) .... Ponoka AB
All New Manufacturing Inc. (1) .... Calgary AB
Allied Clinical Research Inc. (1) .... Mississauga ON
Alltemp Sensors Inc. (1) .... Edmonton AB
Alumabrite Anodizing Ltd. (1) .... Hamilton ON
Amcan Castings Ltd. (1) .... Hamilton ON
Appareo Software Inc. (1) .... Burnaby BC
Appendix Technical Publishing Group (1) .... Ottawa ON
Astec Advanced Power Systems (1) .... St-Laurent QC
ATI Technologies Inc. (1) .... Thornhill ON
Atlantis Systems International (1) .... Brampton ON
Avianor Inc. (1) .... Dorval QC
BA Banknote Inc. (1) .... Ottawa ON
Babcock & Wilcox Canada (1) .... Cambridge ON
Ballard Power Systems Inc. (1) .... Burnaby BC
Becker Group (1) .... Toronto ON
Bell Helicopter Textron Canada (1) .... Mirabel QC
Biomira Inc. (1) .... Edmonton AB
bitHeads, Inc. (1) .... Ottawa ON
Blockade Systems Corporation (1) .... Toronto ON
Boeing Canada Technology Ltd., Arnprior (1) .... Arnprior ON
Bombardier Aerospace, Defense Services (1) .... Mirabel QC
Bombardier Aerospace, Regional Aircraft (1) .... Toronto ON
Bonar Plastics (1) .... Lindsay ON
Bragg Photonics Inc. (1) .... Dorval QC
Brenntag Canada Inc. (1) .... Toronto ON
Brown Applied Technology Inc. (1) .... Toronto ON
Burlington Technologies Inc., Burling (1) .... Burlington ON
Burlington Technologies Inc., Centenn (1) .... Burlington ON
Burntsand Inc. (1) .... Vancouver BC
C-MAC Industries Inc. (1) .... Cornwall ON
C-MAC Invotronics Inc. (1) .... London ON
Caledon, Town of (1) .... Caledon East ON
Canadian Blood Services / CBS (1) .... Ottawa ON
Canadian Cancer Society / CCS (1) .... Vancouver BC
Cangene Corporation (1) .... Winnipeg MB
CanRoof Corporation Inc. (1) .... Toronto ON
Central Park Lodges Ltd. (1) .... Calgary AB
Central Precast Inc. (1) .... Nepean ON
Chaps Group Inc. / CGS (1) .... Markham ON
CIMTEK Automation Systems (1) .... Burlington ON
Circle of Care (1) .... Toronto ON
Circuit Graphics Ltd. (1) .... Burnaby BC
Classwave Wireless Inc. (1) .... Toronto ON
CMC Electronics Inc. (1) .... Kanata ON
Co-Ex-Tec Industries (1) .... Concord ON
Coca-Cola Bottling Company (1) .... Calgary AB
Collins & Aikman (1) .... Toronto ON
Communications Test Design, Inc. / CTDI (1) .... Oakville ON
Community Care Access Centre of York R (1) .... Newmarket ON
Comptec International Ltd. (1) .... Surrey BC

Computer Sciences Corp. / CSC (1) .... Toronto ON
Conestoga-Rovers & Associates Limited / (1) .... Waterloo ON
Costco Wholesale Canada (1) .... Burnaby BC
Creation Technologies Inc. (1) .... Mississauga ON
Crown Cork & Seal Canada Inc. (1) .... Concord ON
CryoCath Technologies Inc. (1) .... Kirkland QC
CSA International (1) .... Edmonton AB
CTS of Canada Ltd. (1) .... Streetsville ON
Daito Precision Inc. (1) .... St-Laurent QC
Daminco Inc. (1) .... Oakville ON
Dare Foods Ltd. (1) .... Kitchener ON
David Brown Union Pumps (Canada) Ltd. (1) .... Burlington ON
Delta Hudson Engineering Ltd. (1) .... Calgary AB
Dempsey Corporation (1) .... Toronto ON
Dominion Spring Industries Corp. / D (1) .... Mississauga ON
Dorel Industries Inc. (1) .... Montréal QC
Dover Industries Ltd. (1) .... Burlington ON
Dresser Flow Control (1) .... Burlington ON
Dynaplas Ltd. (1) .... Toronto ON
EBA Engineering Consultants Ltd. (1) .... Edmonton AB
EFA Software Services Ltd. (1) .... Calgary AB
EFX Enerflex Systems Ltd. (1) .... Calgary AB
Electronics Manufacturing Group / EMG (1) .... Calgary AB
Elimetal Inc. (1) .... St-Laurent QC
Emanation Control Ltd. / EMCON (1) .... Nepean ON
Ensil International (1) .... Markham ON
FCI Canada Inc. (1) .... Markham ON
Fiera Foods Company (1) .... Toronto ON
Fifth Dimension Information Systems Inc (1) .... Edmonton AB
Filtel Microwave Inc. (1) .... Vaudreuil-Dorion QC
Fluid Motion Technologies (1) .... Mississauga ON
Frost Fence & Wire Products Ltd. (1) .... Hamilton ON
Full Circle Systems Inc. (1) .... Calgary AB
Ganz (1) .... Woodbridge ON
GE Canada (1) .... Mississauga ON
GE Glegg Water Technologies (1) .... Guelph ON
Gennum Corporation (1) .... Burlington ON
Gerdau Courtice Steel Inc. (1) .... Cambridge ON
Global Group, The (1) .... Toronto ON
Globel Direct Marketing (1) .... Richmond BC
Golden Boy Foods Inc. (1) .... Burnaby BC
Green Belting Industries Ltd. (1) .... Mississauga ON
H. Paulin & Co. Limited (1) .... Toronto ON
Hardt Equipment Manufacturing Inc. (1) .... Lachine QC
Hartford Fibres Ltd. (1) .... Kingston ON
Highwood Resources Ltd. (1) .... Calgary AB
Hitachi Canadian Industries Ltd. (1) .... Saskatoon SK
Hydrogenics Corporation (1) .... Mississauga ON
i-STAT Canada Ltd. (1) .... Kanata ON
iFire Technology Inc. (1) .... Toronto ON
IKO Industries Ltd. (1) .... Brampton ON
Indigo Manufacturing Inc. (1) .... Markham ON
Inex Pharmaceuticals Corp. (1) .... Burnaby BC
Inland Group (1) .... Edmonton AB
InphoGene BioCom Inc. (1) .... Burnaby BC
Instantel Inc. (1) .... Kanata ON
Intervisual Inc. (1) .... Calgary AB
Intuit GreenPoint (1) .... Calgary AB
Johnson & Johnson Medical Products (1) .... Markham ON
Kazootek Technologies (1) .... Vancouver BC
KCI Medical Canada, Inc. (1) .... Mississauga ON
Kretschmar Inc. (1) .... Toronto ON
KristoFoam Industries Inc. (1) .... Concord ON
LeBlanc Ltd. (1) .... Oakville ON
Linamar Corporation, Eston Division (1) .... Guelph ON
LNB Inc. (1) .... Toronto ON
Lockheed Martin Canada Inc. (1) .... Kanata ON
Lyreco Office Products (1) .... Toronto ON
M-Con Products Inc. (1) .... Carp ON
Macdonald Engineering Group Ltd. / MEG (1) .... Calgary AB
Magna International Inc. (1) .... Concord ON
Management Board Secretariat (1) .... Toronto ON
Maple Leaf Pork, Case Reddi Facilit (1) .... Stoney Creek ON
Mark IV Air Intake Systems (1) .... Montréal QC
MDS Aero Support Corporation (1) .... Ottawa ON
MedcomSoft Inc. (1) .... Toronto ON
Merak Projects Ltd. (1) .... Calgary AB
MessagingDirect Ltd. (1) .... Edmonton AB
Metro Tool and Die Ltd. / MTD (1) .... Mississauga ON
MetroPhotonics Inc. (1) .... Ottawa ON
Millenium Biologix Inc. (1) .... Kingston ON
Minacs Worldwide Inc. (1) .... Pickering ON

QUALITY CONTROL (Cont.)

Ministry of Health and Long-Term Care, O (1) .... Toronto ON
Molecular Mining Corporation (1) .... Kingston ON
NCR Canada Ltd. (1) .... Waterloo ON
Neilson Dairy (1) .... Halton Hills ON
Neilson Dairy (1) .... Ottawa ON
Nellcor Puritan Bennett (Melville) Ltd. (1) .... Ottawa ON
Net Safety Monitoring Inc. (1) .... Calgary AB
Newpark Drilling Fluids (1) .... Calgary AB
Nokia Products Ltd. (1) .... Ajax ON
Norcom Networks (1) .... Burnaby BC
Oakrun Farm Bakery Ltd. (1) .... Ancaster ON
OAO Technology Solutions / OAOT (1) .... Toronto ON
OIS-Fisher Inc. (1) .... St. John's NF
Ontario Power Generation (1) .... Toronto ON
Optotek Ltd. (1) .... Kanata ON
Orbital Technologies Inc. (1) .... Vancouver BC
Orion Bus Industries Ltd. (1) .... Mississauga ON
Paradata Systems Inc. (1) .... Whistler BC
Parkvalley Consulting Ltd. (1) .... Calgary AB
Pason Systems Corp. (1) .... Calgary AB
Phoenix Hydraulics Group (1) .... Nisku AB
Pika Technologies Inc. (1) .... Kanata ON
PPM 2000 Inc. (1) .... Edmonton AB
Prairie Malt Ltd. (1) .... Biggar SK
Praxair Canada Inc. (1) .... Delta BC
PricewaterhouseCoopers LLP (1) .... Hamilton ON
PrinterON Corporation (1) .... Kitchener ON
Provance Technologies Inc. (1) .... Gatineau QC
Provenance Systems Inc. (1) .... Ottawa ON
Quebecor World Printpak (1) .... Calgary AB
Ramco Electrical Consulting Ltd. (1) .... Calgary AB
Raytheon Systems Canada Ltd. (1) .... Waterloo ON
RexCan Circuits Inc. (1) .... Belleville ON
Ridgewood Industries (1) .... Cornwall ON
Rockwell Automation Canada (1) .... Cambridge ON
Rogers AT&T Wireless (1) .... Toronto ON
Rolls-Royce Canada Ltd. (1) .... Lachine QC
Royal Canadian Mint / RCM (1) .... Ottawa ON
Ruffneck Heaters (1) .... Calgary AB
Sagebrush Corporation (1) .... Edmonton AB
Saputo Inc. (1) .... St-Leonard QC
Sciemetric Instruments Inc. (1) .... Nepean ON
Scintrex Ltd. (1) .... Concord ON
Shaw Pipe Protection Ltd. (1) .... Edmonton AB
ShawCor Ltd. (1) .... Toronto ON
Silex Design Inc. (1) .... Mississauga ON
Silex Inc. (1) .... Mississauga ON
Sitraka Mobility (1) .... Toronto ON
Solectron (1) .... Calgary AB
South Lake Regional Health Centre (1) .... Newmarket ON
SpaceBridge Networks Corporation (1) .... Hull QC
Spectrum Signal Processing Inc. (1) .... Burnaby BC
SpeechWorks International, Inc. (1) .... Montréal QC
Stackpole Limited, Automotive Gear D (1) .... Mississauga ON
StackTeck Systems Inc. (1) .... Toronto ON
Standens Limited (1) .... Calgary AB
StockerYale Canada Inc. (1) .... Dollard-des-Ormeaux QC
Stone & Webster Canada Limited (1) .... Toronto ON
Storkcraft Baby (1) .... Richmond BC
Stuart Energy Systems (1) .... Mississauga ON
Summo Manufacturing (1) .... Burlington ON
Suncor Energy Inc. (1) .... Calgary AB
Swiss Herbal Remedies Ltd. (1) .... Richmond Hill ON
Talon Systems Inc. (1) .... Mississauga ON
Technisonic Industries Limited (1) .... Mississauga ON
Telesat Canada (1) .... Gloucester ON
Tellamon Photonic Networks Inc. (1) .... Ottawa ON
TELOS Technology Inc. (1) .... Richmond BC
Tiercon Industries Inc. (1) .... Stoney Creek ON
Timothy's World Coffee (1) .... Toronto ON
ToonBoom Technologies (1) .... Montréal QC
Trango Software Corporation (1) .... Richmond Hill ON
Tri Ocean Engineering Ltd. (1) .... Calgary AB
UMA Engineering Ltd. (1) .... Edmonton AB
Underwriters Adjustment Bureau Ltd. / UA (1) .... Toronto ON
Underwriters' Laboratories of Canada / U (1) .... Toronto ON
Viconics Electronics Inc. (1) .... St-Leonard QC
VideoSpheres Inc. (1) .... Kanata ON
VIPswitch Inc. (1) .... Montréal QC

Vogue Brassiere Incorporated (1) .... Toronto ON
Wardrop Engineering Inc. (1) .... Mississauga ON
Warren Shepell Consultants Corp. (1) .... Toronto ON
Watchfire (1) .... Kanata ON
Weatherford Canada Ltd. (1) .... Nisku AB
Welch & Company (1) .... Ottawa ON
Westfair Foods Ltd. (1) .... Calgary AB
Wheeltronic Ltd. (1) .... Mississauga ON
WorkDynamics Technologies Inc. (1) .... Ottawa ON
Wrigley Canada Inc. (1) .... Toronto ON
Xerox Canada, Supplies Development C (1) .... Mississauga ON
Xwave Solutions Inc. (1) .... Calgary AB
Xwave Solutions Inc. (1) .... Mississauga ON

REAL ESTATE

See also: Construction, Franchising, Architecture.

Ministry of Municipal Affairs and Housing (14 positions) Toronto ON
Management Board Secretariat (11) .... Toronto ON
Manitoba Transportation & Government Se (11) .... Winnipeg MB
Alberta Infrastructure & Transportation (9) .... Edmonton AB
Greenwin Property Management Inc. (8) .... Toronto ON
O&Y Enterprise (8) .... Toronto ON
Brookfield LePage Johnson Controls Facili (7) .... Ottawa ON
McElhanney Group Ltd., The (7) .... Vancouver BC
Peel, The Regional Municipality of (7) .... Brampton ON
Alberta Energy Company Ltd. / AEC (6) .... Calgary AB
Brookfield LePage Johnson Controls Facil (6) .... Markham ON
Mississauga, City of (6) .... Mississauga ON
Rogers Shared Services (6) .... Markham ON
Rohit Group, The (6) .... Edmonton AB
Apotex Inc. (5) .... Toronto ON
Ivanhoe Cambridge (5) .... Toronto ON
Public Service Commission of Canada, Onta (5) .... Ottawa ON
Sun Life Financial (5) .... Toronto ON
Brantford, Corporation of the City of (4) .... Brantford ON
Calgary, City of (4) .... Calgary AB
Manitoba Consumer & Corporate Affairs / (4) .... Winnipeg MB
Manitoba Intergovernmental Affairs (4) .... Winnipeg MB
Oxford Properties Group Inc. (4) .... Toronto ON
PrimeWest Energy Trust (4) .... Calgary AB
ProFac Facilities Management Services In (4) .... Toronto ON
Public Service Commission of Canada, Al (4) .... Edmonton AB
Standard Life Assurance Company, The (4) .... Montréal QC
Albi Homes Ltd. (3) .... Calgary AB
Angus Consulting Management Ltd. / ACML (3) .... Toronto ON
Bentall Corporation (3) .... Vancouver BC
Brookfield Properties Limited (3) .... Toronto ON
Commvesco Levinson-Viner Group / CLV Grou (3) .... Ottawa ON
Dundee Realty Management Corporation (3) .... Toronto ON
First Professional Management Inc. (3) .... Toronto ON
Group Telecom (3) .... Toronto ON
Jayman Master Builder (3) .... Edmonton AB
Kingston, Corporation of the City of (3) .... Kingston ON
Markham, Corporation of the Town of (3) .... Markham ON
Milton, Town of (3) .... Milton ON
Monarch Construction Ltd. (3) .... Toronto ON
Ontario College of Art and Design / OCAD (3) .... Toronto ON
Research in Motion Limited / RIM (3) .... Waterloo ON
Supportive Housing Coalition of Metropol (3) .... Toronto ON
Technical University of British Columbia (3) .... Surrey BC
UMA Engineering Ltd. (3) .... Edmonton AB
Alberta Community Development (2) .... Edmonton AB
Alberta Human Resources and Employment (2) .... Edmonton AB
Banff Centre, The (2) .... Banff AB
Beutel Goodman Real Estate Group Inc. (2) .... Toronto ON
Canada Mortgage and Housing Corporation / (2) .... Ottawa ON
Cara Operations Ltd., Harvey's Divis (2) .... Mississauga ON
Department of Municipal and Provincia (2) .... St. John's NF
Department of Works, Services and Tran (2) .... Goose Bay NF
Earth Tech Canada Inc. (2) .... Markham ON
Excel Homes Inc. (2) .... Calgary AB
Export Development Corporation / EDC (2) .... Ottawa ON
First Canadian Title Company (2) .... Mississauga ON
Focus Corporation Ltd., The (2) .... Edmonton AB
Industrial-Alliance Pacific Life Insur (2) .... Vancouver BC
Inex Pharmaceuticals Corp. (2) .... Burnaby BC
Information Services Corporation of Saska (2) .... Regina SK
Jacques Whitford Environment Ltd. (2) .... Burnaby BC

For descriptions of the occupational categories used in this index, see page 458.

REAL ESTATE (Cont.)

Larlyn Property Management Ltd. (2) .... London ON
Manitoba Family Services and Housing (2) .... Winnipeg MB
Ministry of Health and Long-Term Care, O (2) .... Toronto ON
Ministry of Social Development and Econ (2) .... Victoria BC
Morrison Homes (2) .... Calgary AB
New Brunswick Community College, Woods (2) .... Woodstock NB
O&Y CB Richard Ellis Facilities Manageme (2) .... Toronto ON
O&Y Enterprise (2) .... Vancouver BC
Okanagan University College / OUC (2) .... Kelowna BC
Ottawa Hospital, The (2) .... Ottawa ON
Ottawa Housing Corporation (2) .... Ottawa ON
Oxford Properties Group Inc. (2) .... Edmonton AB
PanCanadian Petroleum Ltd. (2) .... Calgary AB
Perimis Properties (2) .... Ottawa ON
Rogers Communications Inc. (2) .... Toronto ON
Royal Bank Financial Group (2) .... Toronto ON
Shane Homes (2) .... Calgary AB
Siemens Canada Ltd. (2) .... Mississauga ON
Stantec Consulting Ltd. (2) .... Concord ON
Staples Business Depot Ltd. (2) .... Markham ON
Steeves & Rozema Enterprises Ltd. (2) .... Sarnia ON
Sun Life Financial (2) .... Vancouver BC
Sun Life Financial (2) .... Montréal QC
TDL Group Ltd., The (2) .... Oakville ON
University of Calgary (2) .... Calgary AB
Urbandale Corporation (2) .... Ottawa ON
URS Cole, Sherman (2) .... Thornhill ON
Vancouver International Airport Authori (2) .... Richmond BC
Victoria Park Community Homes (2) .... Hamilton ON
Winnipeg, City of (Planning, Property a (2) .... Winnipeg MB
Abbotsford, City of (1) .... Abbotsford BC
ACNielsen Company of Canada (1) .... Markham ON
Alberta Energy Company Ltd. / AEC (1) .... Calgary AB
Alberta Infrastructure & Transportation (1) .... Edmonton AB
Alberta Sustainable Resource Developmen (1) .... Edmonton AB
Alberta Transportation (1) .... Edmonton AB
Aplin & Martin Consultants Ltd. (1) .... Surrey BC
Ashcroft Homes (1) .... Ottawa ON
AstraZeneca (1) .... Mississauga ON
Athabasca University (1) .... Athabasca AB
BA Banknote Inc. (1) .... Ottawa ON
Banff, Town of (1) .... Banff AB
Barrie, City of (1) .... Barrie ON
Baycrest Centre for Geriatric Care (1) .... Toronto ON
BC Rail Ltd. (1) .... North Vancouver BC
BC Transportation Financing Authority / (1) .... Victoria BC
Bell Intrigna (1) .... Calgary AB
Beverly Centre, The (1) .... Calgary AB
BJ Services Company Canada (1) .... Calgary AB
Black & McDonald Ltd. (1) .... Toronto ON
Brampton, City of (1) .... Brampton ON
British Columbia Assets & Land Corporat (1) .... Victoria BC
British Columbia Investment Management (1) .... Victoria BC
Brock University (1) .... St. Catharines ON
Building Box, The (1) .... Markham ON
Cadillac Fairview Corporation Limited, T (1) .... Toronto ON
Caledon, Town of (1) .... Caledon East ON
Calgary Airport Authority, The (1) .... Calgary AB
Calgary Board of Education, The (1) .... Calgary AB
Calpine Canada Resources Ltd. (1) .... Calgary AB
Canada Customs and Revenue Agency / CCRA (1) ..... Toronto ON
Canada Mortgage and Housing Corporation (1) .... Toronto ON
Canadian 88 Energy Corp. (1) .... Calgary AB
Canadian Bank Note Company, Ltd. (1) .... Ottawa ON
Canadian Blood Services / CBS (1) .... Ottawa ON
Canadian National Institute for the Blin (1) .... Toronto ON
Canadian Natural Resources Limited / CNR (1) .... Calgary AB
Canlight Group (1) .... Toronto ON
Centre for Addiction and Mental Health (1) .... Toronto ON
CentreCorp Management Services Ltd. (1) .... Markham ON
Cirque du Soleil (1) .... Montréal QC
Claridge Homes (1) .... Ottawa ON
Coast Plaza Suite Hotel, The (1) .... Vancouver BC
Columbia House Canada (1) .... Toronto ON
Corporate Research Group (1) .... Nepean ON
Creation Technologies Inc. (1) .... Burnaby BC
CreoScitex (1) .... Burnaby BC
David Schaeffer Engineering Ltd. (1) .... Markham ON
Deloitte & Touche (1) .... Toronto ON

Delta Pinnacle Hotel (1) .... Vancouver BC
Delta, The Corporation of (1) .... Delta BC
Department of Forest Resources & Agri (1) .... St. John's NF
Department of Health and Community Se (1) .... St. John's NF
Department of Human Resources, Nunavut (1) .... Igloolik NU
Department of Works, Services and Tra (1) .... St. John's NF
Dillon Consulting Ltd. (1) .... Toronto ON
DRS Flight Safety and Communicati (1) .... Carleton Place ON
Durham, The Regional Municipality of (1) .... Whitby ON
Emerald Lake Lodge (1) .... Field BC
EPCOR Utilities Inc. (1) .... Edmonton AB
Extendicare (Canada) Inc. (1) .... Markham ON
Federated Co-operatives Limited / FCL (1) .... Saskatoon SK
Financial Institutions Commission / FI (1) .... Vancouver BC
GE Capital Modular Space (1) .... Calgary AB
Gennum Corporation (1) .... Burlington ON
Georgian College (1) .... Barrie ON
Groupe Dynamite Inc. (1) .... Mount Royal QC
Guelph, City of (1) .... Guelph ON
Havergal College (1) .... Toronto ON
Hawthorne Homes (1) .... Calgary AB
Henderson Development (Canada) Ltd. (1) .... Vancouver BC
Holiday Inn Burlington (1) .... Burlington ON
Homestead Land Holdings Ltd. (1) .... Ottawa ON
Humane Society of Ottawa-Carleton / HSOC (1) .... Ottawa ON
Huron, County of (1) .... Goderich ON
IBM Canada Ltd. (1) .... Markham ON
iFire Technology Inc. (1) .... Toronto ON
IKO Industries Ltd. (1) .... Toronto ON
Jacques Whitford Environment Ltd. (1) .... Markham ON
Jacques Whitford Environment Ltd. (1) .... Ottawa ON
Jacques Whitford Environment Ltd. (1) .... Halifax NS
Jayman Master Builder (1) .... Calgary AB
JDS Uniphase Corporation (1) .... Saanichton BC
Jewish Community Centre of Greater Van (1) .... Vancouver BC
Kamloops, City of (1) .... Kamloops BC
Kawartha Lakes, Corporation of the City (1) .... Lindsay ON
Kerr Wood Leidal Associates Ltd. (1) .... North Vancouver BC
King's Health Centre (1) .... Toronto ON
Kingston General Hospital (1) .... Kingston ON
Kleinfeldt Consultants Limited (1) .... Mississauga ON
Langara Island Lodge (1) .... Richmond BC
Law Society of Upper Canada, The / LSUC (1) .... Toronto ON
Le Chateau (1) .... Mount Royal QC
Legislative Assembly of Ontario, Office (1) .... Toronto ON
Leisureworld Caregiving Centres (1) .... Markham ON
Lifestyle Retirement Communities (1) .... Mississauga ON
Lifestyle Retirement Communities, Forest (1) .... Toronto ON
Liquor Distribution Branch, BC / LDB (1) .... Vancouver BC
Loblaw Properties Ltd. / LPL (1) .... Toronto ON
Lockheed Martin Canada Inc. (1) .... Kanata ON
Louis Brier Home and Hospital (1) .... Vancouver BC
Loyalist College (1) .... Belleville ON
Manitoba Finance (1) .... Winnipeg MB
Manitoba Labour & Immigration (1) .... Winnipeg MB
Mayerthorpe Healthcare Centre (1) .... Mayerthorpe AB
McGill University Health Centre, Royal (1) .... Montréal QC
McMaster University (1) .... Hamilton ON
MDS Laboratories (1) .... Toronto ON
MDS Nordion (1) .... Kanata ON
MDS Pharma Services Inc. (1) .... St-Laurent QC
Medicine Hat, City of (1) .... Medicine Hat AB
Merisel Canada Inc. (1) .... Toronto ON
Metropolitan Hotel Toronto (1) .... Toronto ON
Ministry of Agriculture, Food and Rural A (1) .... Guelph ON
Ministry of Community and Social Service (1) .... Toronto ON
Ministry of Correctional Services, Ont (1) .... North Bay ON
Ministry of Health and Long-Term Care, (1) .... Kingston ON
Ministry of Labour, Ontario (1) .... Toronto ON
Ministry of Natural Resources, (1) .... Sault Ste. Marie ON
Ministry of Natural Resources, Ontario (1) .... Chapleau ON
Ministry of Natural Resources, Ontario (1) .... Hearst ON
Ministry of the Attorney General, BC (V (1) .... Victoria BC
Ministry of the Attorney General, Ontari (1) .... Toronto ON
Ministry of the Attorney General, Ontari (1) .... Toronto ON
Ministry of the Solicitor General, Ontari (1) .... Aylmer ON
Ministry of Tourism, Culture and Recreat (1) .... Toronto ON
Ministry of Transportation, Ontario (1) .... Thunder Bay ON
Ministry of Transportation, Ontario (1) .... New Liskeard ON
Ministry of Transportation, Ontario (1) .... London ON
Ministry of Transportation, Ontar (1) .... St. Catharines ON
Ministry of Transportation, Ontario (1) .... Kingston ON

REAL ESTATE (Cont.)

Mission, District of (1) .... Mission BC
Mission Services of Hamilton (1) .... Hamilton ON
Mistahia Health Region (1) .... Grande Prairie AB
Monit Management Ltd. (1) .... Montréal QC
Montreal Port Authority / MPA (1) .... Montréal QC
Mount Royal College (1) .... Calgary AB
Mount Sinai Hospital (1) .... Toronto ON
Mountain View County (1) .... Didsbury AB
MTU Maintenance Canada Ltd. (1) .... Richmond BC
National Trade Centre, The (1) .... Toronto ON
NAV Canada (1) .... Ottawa ON
NCE Resources Group Inc. (1) .... Calgary AB
Newmarket, Town of (1) .... Newmarket ON
Niagara, The Regional Municipality of (1) .... Thorold ON
NorQuest College (1) .... Edmonton AB
Nortel Networks (1) .... Ottawa ON
North Vancouver, The District of (1) .... North Vancouver BC
Northern Alberta Institute of Technolog (1) ...... Edmonton AB
O&Y Enterprise (1) .... Ottawa ON
Oakwood Retirement Communities Inc. (1) .... Kitchener ON
Object Technology International Inc. / OT (1) .... Ottawa ON
Okanagan Similkameen Health Region, Pe (1) .... Penticton BC
Ontario Heritage Foundation, Corporate S (1) .... Toronto ON
Ontario Lottery and Gaming Corporation / (1) .... Toronto ON
Ontario Power Generation (1) .... Toronto ON
Ottawa, City of (1) .... Ottawa ON
Participation House (1) .... Binbrook ON
Patheon Inc. (1) .... Toronto ON
Peerless Clothing Inc. (1) .... Montréal QC
Pet Valu Canada Inc. (1) .... Markham ON
Plaza Group, The (1) .... Baie d'Urfe QC
Polygon Interior Design Limited (1) .... Vancouver BC
Prince Edward, County of (1) .... Picton ON
Prince George, City of (1) .... Prince George BC
Procuron Inc. (1) .... Thornhill ON
Public Service Alliance of Canada / PSAC (1) .... Ottawa ON
Public Service Commission of Canada, BC (1) .... Victoria BC
Public Service Commission of Canada, B (1) .... Vancouver BC
Public Service Commission of Canada, (1) .... Yellowknife NT
Public Service Commission of Canada, Ont (1) .... Toronto ON
QuestAir Technologies Inc. (1) .... Burnaby BC
R.J. Burnside & Associates Ltd. (1) .... Brampton ON
R.V. Anderson Associates Limited (1) .... Toronto ON
Red Deer, City of (1) .... Red Deer AB
Regina, City of (1) .... Regina SK
Reitmans (Canada) Limited (1) .... Montréal QC
Research in Motion Limited / RIM (1) .... Kanata ON
Resorts of the Canadian Rockies Inc. / R (1) .... Calgary AB
Rice Brydone Ltd. (1) .... Toronto ON
Richmond, City of (1) .... Richmond BC
Rio Alto Exploration Ltd. (1) .... Calgary AB
RioCan Real Estate Investment Trust (1) .... Toronto ON
Rogers Communications Inc. (1) .... Toronto ON
Royal LePage Commercial Inc. (1) .... Toronto ON
Ruffneck Heaters (1) .... Calgary AB
Ryerson Polytechnic University (1) .... Toronto ON
Samson Canada Ltd. (1) .... Calgary AB
SAS Institute (Canada) Inc. (1) .... Toronto ON
School District #35 (Langley) (1) .... Langley BC
School District #36 (Surrey) (1) .... Surrey BC
School District #41 (Burnaby) (1) .... Burnaby BC
Scott Land & Lease Ltd. (1) .... Calgary AB
Seneca College of Applied Arts & Technol (1) .... Toronto ON
Sernas Group Inc., The (1) .... Whitby ON
Siemens Building Technologies Ltd. (1) .... Ottawa ON
Simon Fraser Health Region / SFH (1) .... New Westminster BC
SMED International Inc. (1) .... Calgary AB
Sobeys Inc., Western Division (1) .... Edmonton AB
Solinet Systems Inc. (1) .... Ottawa ON
Soloway Wright (1) .... Kingston ON
Spirent Communications (1) .... Ottawa ON
Spruce Grove, City of (1) .... Spruce Grove AB
St. Joseph's Health Centre (1) .... Toronto ON
Standens Limited (1) .... Calgary AB
Stantec Consulting Ltd. (1) .... Calgary AB
Stantec Consulting Ltd. (1) .... Hamilton ON
Starline Industries (1) .... Concord ON
Statesman Corporation (1) .... Calgary AB

Sterling Homes (1) .... Calgary AB
Stewart Title Guaranty Company (1) .... Toronto ON
STMicroelectronics (1) .... Nepean ON
Stream International (1) .... Belleville ON
Sturgeon County (1) .... Morinville AB
Surrey, City of (1) .... Surrey BC
TELOS Technology Inc. (1) .... Richmond BC
Toronto Catholic District School Board (1) .... Toronto ON
Toronto, City of (1) .... Toronto ON
Toronto Real Estate Board / TREB (1) .... Toronto ON
Toronto Star Newspapers Ltd., Press C (1) .... Woodbridge ON
TorPharm (1) .... Toronto ON
Trammell Crow Corporate Services Canada, (1) .... Toronto ON
TransAlta Corporation (1) .... Calgary AB
Trillium Health Centre (1) .... Toronto ON
Trow Consulting Engineers Ltd. (1) .... Brampton ON
University College of the Cariboo / UCC (1) .... Kamloops BC
University of Guelph (1) .... Guelph ON
University of Lethbridge (1) .... Lethbridge AB
Vancouver City Savings Credit Union / (1) .... Vancouver BC
Vancouver School Board / VSB (1) .... Vancouver BC
Westport Innovations Inc. (1) .... Vancouver BC
Whistler Blackcomb / Intrawest (1) .... Whistler BC
Whitby, Town of (1) .... Whitby ON
Winnipeg, City of (Public Works Departm (1) .... Winnipeg MB
YM - YWHA, Ben Weider Jewish Community (1) .... Montréal QC

RELIGIOUS

See also: Education.

Guelph General Hospital (2 positions) .... Guelph ON
Manitoba Justice / Culture, Heritage an (2) .... Winnipeg MB
Ministry of Correctional Services, Ontar (2) .... Toronto ON
Ministry of Correctional Services, Onta (2) .... Kingston ON
Ministry of the Attorney General, BC (2) .... Abbotsford BC
Providence Health Care, St. Paul's Hos (2) .... Vancouver BC
Brant Haldimand-Norfolk Catholic Distr (1) .... Brantford ON
Calgary Catholic School District (1) .... Calgary AB
Children's and Women's Health Centre o (1) .... Vancouver BC
Dufferin-Peel Catholic District Scho (1) .... Mississauga ON
Hotel Dieu Health Sciences Hospit (1) .... St. Catharines ON
Hotel Dieu Hospital (1) .... Cornwall ON
Hotel-Dieu Grace Hospital (1) .... Windsor ON
Humber River Regional Hospital, Finch Av (1) .... Toronto ON
King's University College, The (1) .... Edmonton AB
Manitoba Health, Selkirk Mental Health C (1) .... Selkirk MB
Ministry of Community and Social Service (1) .... Toronto ON
Ministry of Correctional Services, Ontari (1) .... London ON
Mount Royal College (1) .... Calgary AB
Mount Saint Vincent University (1) .... Halifax NS
Ottawa Hospital, The (1) .... Ottawa ON
Ottawa-Carleton Catholic School Board / O (1) .... Ottawa ON
Peterborough, Victoria, Northumberl (1) .... Peterborough ON
Providence Health Care, Mount St. Jose (1) .... Vancouver BC
Providence Health Care, St. Vincent's (1) .... Vancouver BC
Royal Victoria Hospital / RVH (1) .... Barrie ON
Sault Area Hospitals (1) .... Sault Ste. Marie ON
Simon Fraser Health Region, Burnaby Hosp (1) .... Burnaby BC
Simon Fraser Health Region / SFH (1) .... New Westminster BC
St. John's Rehabilitation Hospital (1) .... Toronto ON
St. Joseph's Health Care, Parkwood Hospit (1) .... London ON
United Synagogue Day School (1) .... Toronto ON
York Central Hospital (1) .... Richmond Hill ON

RETAIL

See also: Sales, Franchising, Apparel, Hospitality.

Chapters Inc. / Indigo Books & Music (17 positions) ..... Toronto ON
Shirmax Fashions Ltd. (10) .... Montréal QC
Groupe Dynamite Inc. (9) .... Mount Royal QC
Loblaw Companies Ltd. (8) .... Toronto ON
Shoppers Drug Mart (8) .... Toronto ON
Henry Birks & Sons Inc. (6) .... Montréal QC
Telus Mobility (6) .... Toronto ON
YM Inc. (6) .... Toronto ON
Collega for Aveda (5) .... Toronto ON

For descriptions of the occupational categories used in this index, see page 458.

RETAIL (Cont.)

RETAIL (Cont.)

Pepsi Bottling Group (Canada) (1) .... Mississauga ON
Pet Valu Canada Inc. (1) .... Markham ON
Please Mum (1) .... Vancouver BC
Premier Salons International (1) .... Markham ON
Providence Centre (1) .... Toronto ON
Public Service Commission, PEI (1) .... Charlottetown PE
Reebok Canada (1) .... Aurora ON
Reitmans (Canada) Limited (1) .... Montréal QC
Retail Ready Foods Inc. (1) .... Mississauga ON
RGO Office Products (1) .... Calgary AB
RJL Packaging & Labelling Industries In (1) .... Montréal QC
Rogers Cable Inc., Calgary Distribution (1) .... Calgary AB
Rooms International (1) .... Ottawa ON
Sen5es (1) .... Toronto ON
Shopping Channel, The / TSC (1) .... Toronto ON
Shopping Channel, The / TSC (1) .... Mississauga ON
Sobeys Inc. (1) .... Mississauga ON
TelTech Assets.Com Ltd. (1) .... Calgary AB
Tilley Endurables (1) .... Toronto ON
Timothy's World Coffee (1) .... Toronto ON
Trio Selection Inc. (1) .... Montréal QC
Trophy Foods Inc. (1) .... Mississauga ON
United Nations Children's Fund / UNICEF (1) .... Toronto ON
University of Western Ontario (1) .... London ON
Value Drug Mart Associates Ltd. (1) .... Edmonton AB
Value Village (1) .... Port Moody BC
Vistek Ltd. (1) .... Calgary AB
Vogue Brassiere Incorporated (1) .... Toronto ON
Westfair Foods Ltd. (1) .... Burnaby BC

SALES

See also: Marketing, Direct Mktng.

Research in Motion Limited / RIM (9 positions) .... Waterloo ON
Electro Sonic Inc. (8) .... Toronto ON
GE Canada (8) .... Mississauga ON
Minolta Business Equipment (Canada), Lt (8) .... Edmonton AB
Advantex Marketing International Inc. (6) .... Toronto ON
Brenntag Canada Inc. (6) .... Toronto ON
G&K Services (6) .... Ottawa ON
Radiant Communications (6) .... Calgary AB
Rockwell Automation Canada (6) .... Cambridge ON
Swiss Herbal Remedies Ltd. (6) .... Richmond Hill ON
Voyus Canada Inc. (6) .... Burnaby BC
ACD Systems (5) .... Saanichton BC
Acklands-Grainger Inc. / AGI (5) .... Richmond Hill ON
Air Products Canada Ltd. (5) .... Brampton ON
GBC Canada Inc. (5) .... Toronto ON
Integra Networks Corporation (5) .... Ottawa ON
Minolta Business Equipment (Canada), (5) .... Gloucester ON
Rittal Systems Ltd. (5) .... Mississauga ON
Webplan Inc. (5) .... Ottawa ON
AGFA (4) .... Toronto ON
Ainsworth Inc. (4) .... Toronto ON
Bird On a Wire Networks / BOAW (4) .... Mississauga ON
Ensil International (4) .... Markham ON
Fisher Scientific (4) .... Nepean ON
Future Electronics Inc. (4) .... Pointe-Claire QC
FutureLink (4) .... Toronto ON
Metasoft Systems Inc. (4) .... Vancouver BC
Pitney Bowes Management Services Canada (4) .... Toronto ON
Royal Doulton Company, The (4) .... Toronto ON
Shred-it (4) .... Oakville ON
Xerox Canada Ltd. (4) .... Toronto ON
A.R. Thomson Group (3) .... Edmonton AB
A.W. Miller Technical Sales (3) .... Mississauga ON
Advanced Motion and Controls Ltd. (3) .... Barrie ON
Brascon Architectural Products Inc. (3) .... Brampton ON
Carsen Group Inc. (3) .... Markham ON
Cintas Canada Ltd. (3) .... Mississauga ON
CyberSurf Corporation (3) .... Calgary AB
Dempsey Corporation (3) .... Toronto ON
Elco Fine Foods Inc. (3) .... Richmond Hill ON
EPCOR Utilities Inc. (3) .... Edmonton AB
Fincentric Corp. (3) .... Richmond BC

GE Capital Canada (3) .... Montréal QC
Husky Injection Molding Systems Ltd. (3) .... Bolton ON
Image Processing Systems Inc. / IPS (3) .... Markham ON
INTESYS Network Communications Ltd. (3) .... Toronto ON
MapInfo Corporation (3) .... Toronto ON
NCH Canada Inc. (3) .... Langley BC
Noritsu Canada Ltd. (3) .... Mississauga ON
NUHC Inc. (3) .... Woodbridge ON
Oracle Corporation Canada Inc. (3) .... Mississauga ON
OZ Optics Ltd. (3) .... Carp ON
Parker Hannifin (Canada) Inc. (3) .... Orillia ON
Poly-Pacific International Inc. (3) .... Edmonton AB
Procuron Inc. (3) .... Thornhill ON
Relizon Canada Inc. (3) .... Toronto ON
RGO Office Products (3) .... Calgary AB
Rogers Cable Inc. (3) .... Toronto ON
Rogers Cable Inc. (3) .... Richmond Hill ON
Rogers Communications Inc. (3) .... Ottawa ON
Shade-O-Matic (3) .... Toronto ON
Siemens Canada Ltd. (3) .... Mississauga ON
Silex Inc. (3) .... Mississauga ON
Snap-On Tools of Canada Ltd. (3) .... Mississauga ON
State Industrial Products (3) .... Mississauga ON
Systemcorp ALG Ltd. (3) .... Montréal QC
Telematic Controls Inc. (3) .... Calgary AB
Trends International Corporation (3) .... Mississauga ON
Vision2Hire Solutions (3) .... Vancouver BC
Wesco Distribution Canada Inc. (3) .... Edmonton AB
3M Canada Company (2) .... London ON
A. Berger Precision Ltd. (2) .... Brampton ON
Access Medical Inc. (2) .... Calgary AB
Accpac International Inc. (2) .... Richmond BC
Accpac International Inc. (2) .... Mississauga ON
ACNielsen Company of Canada (2) .... Markham ON
Active Health Management Inc. (2) .... Toronto ON
ADP Canada (2) .... Calgary AB
Advanced Business Interiors Inc. /ABI (2) .... Ottawa ON
AGF Management Ltd. (2) .... Toronto ON
Akinai (Calgary) Canada Inc. / ACI The I (2) .... Calgary AB
Alltemp Sensors Inc. (2) .... Edmonton AB
Alterna Technologies Group Inc. (2) .... Calgary AB
Aludra Inc. (2) .... Toronto ON
Amram's Distributing Ltd. (2) .... Brampton ON
ARK e-Tail Services Inc. (2) .... Toronto ON
Astound Inc. (2) .... Toronto ON
Bay St. Document Systems (2) .... Toronto ON
Beauty Systems Group (Canada) Inc. (2) .... Toronto ON
Bridge Brand Food Services Ltd. (2) .... Calgary AB
Burntsand Inc. (2) .... Toronto ON
Business Depot Ltd. / Staples (2) .... St. Catharines ON
Canada Colors and Chemicals Ltd. / CCC (2) .... Toronto ON
Canadian Linen and Uniform Services (2) .... Toronto ON
Canon Canada Inc. (2) .... Montréal QC
Caristrap International Inc. (2) .... Laval QC
Carlson Marketing Group Canada Ltd. / CM (2) .... Toronto ON
CB Engineering Ltd. (2) .... Calgary AB
Cedar Enterprise Solutions Inc. (2) .... Calgary AB
Charon Systems Inc. (2) .... Toronto ON
Clayson Steel (2) .... Brampton ON
Coinamatic Canada Inc. (2) .... Mississauga ON
Compugen Systems Ltd. (2) .... Mount Royal QC
Conec Corporation (2) .... Brampton ON
Convedia Corporation (2) .... Burnaby BC
Cooper Lighting (2) .... Mississauga ON
Coretec Inc. (2) .... Toronto ON
DataMirror Corporation (2) .... Markham ON
Delmar International Inc. (2) .... Lachine QC
Discover Communications Inc. (2) .... Brampton ON
Distican Inc. (2) .... Richmond Hill ON
E-Cruiter.com Inc. (2) .... Toronto ON
Ecolab Ltd. (2) .... Mississauga ON
Ecolab Ltd. (2) .... Mississauga ON
Energy Savings Corporation (2) .... Oakville ON
Festo Inc. (2) .... Mississauga ON
G.N. Johnston Equipment Co. Ltd. (2) .... Edmonton AB
GE Power Systems (2) .... Calgary AB
Gemini Positioning Systems Ltd. (2) .... Calgary AB
Gerrie Electric Wholesale Ltd. (2) .... Burlington ON
Global Star Software (2) .... Mississauga ON
Globel Direct Marketing (2) .... Richmond BC
Grand & Toy Ltd. (2) .... Edmonton AB
Grand & Toy Ltd. (2) .... Hamilton ON

For descriptions of the occupational categories used in this index, see page 458.

SALES (Cont.)

SALES (Cont.)

Coradiant Inc. (1) .... Montréal QC
Core Software Corp. (1) .... Nepean ON
Corel Corporation (1) .... Ottawa ON
CORPAV Presentation Group (1) .... Vancouver BC
Corporate Express (1) .... Calgary AB
Cowan Graphics Ltd. (1) .... Edmonton AB
CPUsed (1) .... Toronto ON
Cropac Equipment Ltd. (1) .... Oakville ON
Crown Wallpaper + Fabrics (1) .... Toronto ON
CSA International (1) .... Toronto ON
Cummins Inc. (1) .... Edmonton AB
CVDS Inc. (1) .... Pointe-Claire QC
Dairy Queen Canada Inc. (1) .... Burlington ON
Daminco Inc. (1) .... Oakville ON
Danka Canada Inc. (1) .... Brampton ON
Dare Foods Ltd. (1) .... Kitchener ON
Data Systems Marketing Inc. (1) .... Toronto ON
Decolin Inc. (1) .... Montréal QC
DeepMetrix Corporation (1) .... Hull ON
Delcon Development Group Ltd. (1) ...... Edmonton AB
Delphi Solutions Inc. (1) .... Markham ON
Delta Controls Inc. (1) .... Surrey BC
Descartes Systems Group (1) .... Waterloo ON
Destiny Web Designs Inc. (1) .... Toronto ON
Digital Dispatch Systems Inc. (1) .... Richmond BC
Diners Club International / enRoute (1) .... Montréal QC
DiverseyLever (1) .... Oakville ON
DMTI Spatial Inc. (1) .... Markham ON
Dominion Colour Corporation (1) .... Toronto ON
Dorel Industries Inc. (1) .... Montréal QC
DSC Group of Companies (1) .... Concord ON
Dura-Lite Heat Transfer Products Ltd. (1) ...... Calgary AB
Eagle Pump & Compressor Ltd. (1) .... Calgary AB
Edge Networks Corporation (1) .... Winnipeg MB
Edwards Systems Technology (1) ...... Owen Sound ON
EF Education (1) .... Toronto ON
Electronics Workbench (1) .... Toronto ON
Elimetal Inc. (1) .... St-Laurent QC
Ellett Industries Ltd. (1) .... Port Coquitlam BC
Elyps Dispatch Solutions (1) .... Burnaby BC
Emerald International Inc. (1) .... Toronto ON
Empowered Networks (1) .... Kanata ON
Enbridge Services (1) .... Markham ON
Enerchem International Inc. (1) .... Nisku AB
ENMAX Corporation (1) .... Calgary AB
Entretel Inc. (1) .... Oakville ON
Entrust Technologies Ltd. (1) .... Ottawa ON
Evans Consoles Inc. (1) .... Calgary AB
Evertz Microsystems Ltd. (1) .... Burlington ON
Excel Tech Ltd. / XLTEK (1) .... Oakville ON
Exocom Group Inc., The (1) .... Ottawa ON
Export Development Corporation / EDC (1) ...... Ottawa ON
Export Packers Company Ltd. (1) .... Brampton ON
Farm Business Consultants Inc. / FBC (1) ...... Calgary AB
FDM Software Ltd. (1) .... North Vancouver BC
Fernlea Flowers Ltd. (1) .... Delhi ON
Fireco Inc. (1) .... Mississauga ON
Fireplace Products International / FPI (1) .... Delta BC
First Cellular (1) .... Ottawa ON
Flowserve Inc. (1) .... St. Thomas ON
Fluor Canada Ltd. (1) .... Calgary AB
Focus Microwaves Inc. (1) .... St-Laurent QC
Focus on Health & Safety Inc. / FHS (1) .... Mississauga ON
Fonthill Lumber Ltd. (1) .... Fonthill ON
Forensic Technology Inc. (1) .... Cote St. Luc QC
Fourth R of Calgary Ltd., The (1) .... Calgary AB
Franklin Covey Canada, Ltd. (1) .... Cambridge ON
FreeBalance Inc. (1) .... Ottawa ON
Frozen Pond Inc. (1) .... Toronto ON
G.E. Shnier Co. (1) .... Brampton ON
G&K Work Wear (1) .... Mississauga ON
Gad Shaanan Design (1) .... Montréal QC
Ganz (1) .... Woodbridge ON
GE Capital Modular Space (1) .... Calgary AB
GE Lighting Canada (1) .... Oakville ON
GE Syprotec Inc. (1) .... Pointe-Claire QC
geoLOGIC Systems Ltd. (1) .... Calgary AB
GeoMetrix Data Systems Inc. (1) .... Victoria BC

George Kelk Corporation (1) .... Toronto ON
Giftcraft Ltd. (1) .... Brampton ON
Gilmore (1) .... Toronto ON
Global Group, The (1) .... Toronto ON
Global Thermoelectric Inc. (1) .... Calgary AB
Goldwell Cosmetics (Canada) Ltd. (1) .... Mississauga ON
Golf-Gig Management Systems Internationa (1) .... Calgary AB
Goodlife Foods (1) .... Calgary AB
Graybar Electric (Ontario) Ltd. (1) .... Kitchener ON
Green Lawn Care (1) .... Toronto ON
Halsall Associates Ltd. (1) .... Toronto ON
Hardt Equipment Manufacturing Inc. (1) ...... Lachine QC
Harris Computer Services (1) .... Mississauga ON
Hartford Fibres Ltd. (1) .... Kingston ON
Hayward Gordon Limited (1) .... Mississauga ON
Hemera Technologies Inc. (1) .... Hull QC
Henry Birks & Sons Inc. (1) .... Vancouver BC
Henry Birks & Sons Inc. (1) .... Montréal QC
Henry Schein Arcona Inc. (1) .... St. Catharines ON
Henry Technologies / Chil-Con Product (1) ...... Brantford ON
Herbon Naturals, Inc. (1) .... Richmond BC
HERO Industries Ltd. (1) .... Burnaby BC
Hewitt Equipment Ltd. (1) .... Pointe-Claire QC
Highland Equipment Ltd. (1) .... Toronto ON
Hitachi Canada, Ltd. (1) .... Mississauga ON
HMS Software (1) .... Pointe-Claire QC
Holland Chemical International (Canada) (1) ...... Calgary AB
Honeywell Ltd. (1) .... Burnaby BC
Honeywell Ltd. (1) .... Edmonton AB
Household Financial Corporation / HFC (1) ...... Edmonton AB
Household Financial Corporation / HFC (1) .... Toronto ON
Hummingbird Ltd. (1) .... Toronto ON
Hussmann Canada Inc. (1) .... Brantford ON
I-XL Industries Ltd. (1) .... Medicine Hat AB
i2 Technologies (1) .... Markham ON
ICAM Technologies Corp. (1) .... Pointe-Claire QC
ICP Global Technologies (1) .... Montréal QC
IDEC Canada, Ltd. (1) .... Mississauga ON
IKON Office Solutions (1) .... Vancouver BC
Imaging Research Inc. (1) .... St. Catharines ON
Imperial Tobacco Canada Limited (1) ...... Montréal QC
In-Touch Survey Systems Inc. (1) .... Ottawa ON
INA Canada Inc. (1) .... Oakville ON
InfoSpec Systems Inc. (1) .... Burnaby BC
ING Canada (1) .... Toronto ON
Innovator Electronic Assembly / IEA (1) ...... Lachine QC
Insight Canada Inc. (1) .... Montréal QC
Interfast Inc. (1) .... St-Laurent QC
International Datacasting Corporation / I (1) ...... Ottawa ON
International Datashare Corporation / ID (1) ...... Calgary AB
Intervisual Inc. (1) .... Calgary AB
Iris Power Engineering Inc. (1) .... Toronto ON
ITT Fluid Products Canada (1) .... Langley BC
ITT Fluid Products Canada (1) .... Guelph ON
J. Walter Company Ltd. (1) .... Pointe-Claire QC
Jamieson Laboratories Ltd. (1) .... Toronto ON
Jo-Van Distributors Inc. (1) .... Toronto ON
John Deere Credit Inc. (1) .... Burlington ON
Johnson & Johnson Consumer Products Inc (1) ...... Montréal QC
Johnson & Johnson Medical Products (1) ...... Markham ON
Kelron Logistics (1) .... Surrey BC
Ken Lewis Group Inc. (1) .... Markham ON
Kenwood Electronics Canada Inc. (1) .... Mississauga ON
Kestrel Data (Canada) Limited (1) .... Calgary AB
Klay Information Management Consulting L (1) ...... Calgary AB
Lanier Canada Inc. (1) .... Mississauga ON
Leitch Technology Corp. (1) .... Toronto ON
Lenbrook (1) .... Pickering ON
Logibro Inc. (1) .... Montréal QC
Logical Software Corporation (1) .... Burnaby BC
Lyreco Office Products (1) .... Toronto ON
M.B. Foster Associates Ltd. (1) .... Chesterville ON
M.R.S. Company Ltd. (1) .... Mississauga ON
M-Perial Display Inc. (1) .... Toronto ON
M3i Systems Inc. (1) .... Longueuil QC
Magma Communications Ltd. (1) .... Nepean ON
Magnokrom Inc. (1) .... Mississauga ON
Magnus Chemicals Ltd. (1) .... Boucherville QC
Maple Leaf Consumer Foods (1) .... Mississauga ON
Marks Supply Inc. (1) .... Kitchener ON
Mastech Canada (1) .... Mississauga ON
Matrikon Group (1) .... Edmonton AB

OCCUPATIONAL INDEX 555

SALES (Cont.)

Matthew / Scott (1) .... Mississauga ON
Maytag Canada (1) .... Burlington ON
MedcomSoft Inc. (1) .... Toronto ON
MemberWorks Canada Corporation (1) .... Montréal QC
Mentor Engineering (1) .... Calgary AB
Merit Kitchens (1) .... Surrey BC
Merriam School of Music (1) .... Oakville ON
Metcon Sales and Engineering Ltd. (1) .... Concord ON
Metro Tool and Die Ltd. / MTD (1) .... Mississauga ON
MicroAge (1) .... Nepean ON
Ministry of Economic Development and Tra (1) .... Toronto ON
Mitra Imaging Inc. (1) .... Waterloo ON
Mobilift (1) .... Calgary AB
Montage.dmc eBusiness Services (1) .... Nepean ON
Montage.dmc eBusiness Services (1) .... Ottawa ON
Moore Products Company (Canada) Inc. (1) .... Brampton ON
Motorola Canada Limited (1) .... Richmond Hill ON
Mount Pleasant Group of Cemeteries (1) .... Toronto ON
MovieGoods (1) .... Calgary AB
MPB Technologies Inc. (1) .... Pointe-Claire QC
MTU Maintenance Canada Ltd. (1) .... Richmond BC
Nabisco Ltd., Lakeshore Bakery (1) .... Toronto ON
Nanowave Technologies Inc. (1) .... Toronto ON
National Paper Goods (1) .... Hamilton ON
Nedco (1) .... Richmond BC
Net Safety Monitoring Inc. (1) .... Calgary AB
NetNation Communications, Inc. (1) .... Vancouver BC
NetPCS (1) .... Kanata ON
Nielsen Media Research (1) .... Markham ON
Nitrex Metal Inc. (1) .... St-Laurent QC
Northern Gifts Ltd. (1) .... Burnaby BC
Novator Systems Ltd. (1) .... Toronto ON
NPD Group Canada, Corp., The (1) .... Toronto ON
O'Brien Installations Ltd. (1) .... Stoney Creek ON
Ontario Lottery and Gaming Corporation / (1) .... Toronto ON
OPIsystems Inc. (1) .... Calgary AB
Optech Inc. (1) .... Toronto ON
Pacific Safety Products Inc. / PSP (1) .... Kelowna BC
Paisley Products of Canada (1) .... Toronto ON
Palliser Furniture Ltd. (1) .... Winnipeg MB
Pangaea Systems Inc. (1) .... Edmonton AB
Paradata Systems Inc. (1) .... Whistler BC
Parmalat Canada (1) .... Toronto ON
Peacock Inc. (1) .... Edmonton AB
Pentalift Equipment Corp. (1) .... Guelph ON
Phoenix Contact Ltd. (1) .... Mississauga ON
Piller Sausages & Delicatessens Ltd. (1) .... Waterloo ON
Porter-Cable Delta (1) .... Guelph ON
Praxair Canada Inc. (1) .... Delta BC
Premier Fasteners (1) .... Toronto ON
Priva Inc. (1) .... Montréal QC
Professional Pharmaceutical Corp. (1) .... Lachine QC
Profit Recovery Group Canada, Inc. / P (1) .... Cambridge ON
Progestic International Inc. (1) .... Ottawa ON
Protech Chemicals Ltd. (1) .... St-Laurent QC
Provance Technologies Inc. (1) .... Gatineau QC
Psion Teklogix Inc. (1) .... Mississauga ON
Q-Media Services Corporation (1) .... Richmond BC
QuestAir Technologies Inc. (1) .... Burnaby BC
Quick Link Communications Ltd. / QLC (1) .... Calgary AB
R. Carmichael Ltd. (1) .... Montréal QC
R.L. Brews Ltd. (1) .... Calgary AB
R. Nicholls Distributors Inc. (1) .... Longueuil QC
Radiant Communications (1) .... Vancouver BC
Ramcor Group (1) .... Flamborough ON
Rational Software Corporation (1) .... Kanata ON
Raylo Chemicals Inc. (1) .... Edmonton AB
Reebok Canada (1) .... Aurora ON
Replicon Inc. (1) .... Calgary AB
ReserveAmerica (1) .... Milton ON
Resonance Photonics Inc. (1) .... Markham ON
Retail Ready Foods Inc. (1) .... Mississauga ON
Rexel Canada Inc. (1) .... Burlington ON
Rich Products of Canada Ltd. (1) .... Fort Erie ON
Rogers AT&T Wireless (1) .... Burnaby BC
Rogers Cable Inc. (1) .... Toronto ON
Rogers Communications Inc. (1) .... Toronto ON
Rohde & Schwarz Canada Inc. (1) .... Kanata ON
RoomBlock Inc. (1) .... Toronto ON
RSL COM Canada Inc. (1) .... Vancouver BC
Ruffneck Heaters (1) .... Calgary AB
Russell A. Farrow Limited (1) .... Ayr ON
SafetySmart.com (1) .... Calgary AB
Sanmina Enclosure Systems (1) .... Toronto ON
Sanofi-Synthelabo Canada Inc. (1) .... Markham ON
SAS Institute (Canada) Inc. (1) .... Montréal QC
Schneider Electric Services (1) .... Mississauga ON
Schneider Foods Inc. (1) .... Surrey BC
SciCan (1) .... Toronto ON
Scintrex Trace Corp. (1) .... Ottawa ON
Scott Springfield Manufacturing Inc. (1) .... Calgary AB
Securicor Cash Services (1) .... Toronto ON
Seljax International Inc. (1) .... Stony Plain AB
Serca Foodservice Inc., Western Divisio (1) .... Edmonton AB
Seton (1) .... Richmond Hill ON
Shaben International Inc. (1) .... Edmonton AB
Shana Corporation (1) .... Edmonton AB
Sharp's Audio-Visual Ltd. (1) .... Edmonton AB
Shaw Pipe Protection Ltd. (1) .... Calgary AB
ShawCor Ltd. (1) .... Toronto ON
Shikatronics Inc. (1) .... La Prairie QC
Shopping Channel, The / TSC (1) .... Toronto ON
Siemens Building Technologies Ltd., Cer (1) .... Richmond BC
Siemens Canada Ltd., Medical Syste (1) .... Pointe-Claire QC
Siemens Westinghouse (1) .... Hamilton ON
Sifto Canada Inc. (1) .... Toronto ON
Sigma Systems Group Inc. (1) .... Toronto ON
SimplexGrinnell (1) .... Delta BC
Sitraka Mobility (1) .... Toronto ON
Skjodt-Barrett Foods (1) .... Mississauga ON
Skyway Business Machines (1) .... Mississauga ON
Solect Technology Group (1) .... Toronto ON
Sonitrol Security Systems (1) .... Mississauga ON
Speed-i-Com Inc. / SCI (1) .... Toronto ON
SpiderCache (1) .... Granville Island BC
Spielo Gaming International (1) .... Dieppe NB
Sprint Canada Inc. (1) .... Toronto ON
SSI Equipment Inc. (1) .... Burlington ON
Stockscape.com Technologies Inc. (1) .... Vancouver BC
StonCor Group (1) .... Delta BC
StonCor Group (1) .... Whitby ON
Strongco Equipment (1) .... Stittsville ON
Sundog Printing Ltd. (1) .... Calgary AB
Sunrise Assisted Living (1) .... Mississauga ON
Synopsys Inc. (1) .... Ottawa ON
SynreVoice Technologies Inc. (1) .... Markham ON
Targray Technology International I (1) .... Pointe-Claire QC
TaxSave Consultants Limited (1) .... Toronto ON
Taymor Industries (1) .... Delta BC
TELAV Audio Visual Services (1) .... Calgary AB
TELAV Audio Visual Services (1) .... Ottawa ON
TELAV Audio Visual Services (1) .... Lachine QC
TeleSpectrum Canada Inc. (1) .... Toronto ON
TelTech Assets.Com Ltd. (1) .... Calgary AB
TeraGo Networks Inc. (1) .... Calgary AB
Terrafix Geosynthetics Inc. (1) .... Toronto ON
Thermal Energy International Inc. (1) .... Nepean ON
Time iCR Inc. (1) .... Ottawa ON
TOA Canada Corporation (1) .... Mississauga ON
TOA Inc. (1) .... Toronto ON
Toronto MicroElectronics Inc. / TME (1) .... Mississauga ON
Toshiba Business Systems Inc. (1) .... Calgary AB
Toshiba of Canada Limited (1) .... Markham ON
Total Care Technologies Inc. (1) .... Kelowna BC
Tractel Ltd., Swingstage Division (1) .... Toronto ON
TriAngulum Corporation (1) .... Calgary AB
Trios College of Information Technol (1) .... Mississauga ON
TriVu Interactive Corporation (1) .... Mississauga ON
Trotter & Morton Technical Services Ltd. (1) .... Calgary AB
TrustMarque Canada Ltd. (1) .... St-Laurent QC
Trylon TSF (1) .... Elmira ON
Tyco Electronics Canada Ltd. (1) .... Markham ON
Uni-Ram Corporation Ltd. (1) .... Toronto ON
UniFirst Canada Ltd. (1) .... Edmonton AB
UniFirst Canada Ltd. (1) .... Calgary AB
United Nations Children's Fund / UNICEF (1) .... Toronto ON
USFilter / Wallace & Tiernan Products Ca (1) .... Markham ON
Van-Rob Stampings Inc. (1) .... Aurora ON
Vansco Electronics Ltd. (1) .... Winnipeg MB
Victorian Order of Nurses, Toronto-York (1) .... Markham ON
VideoSpheres Inc. (1) .... Kanata ON

SALES (Cont.)

Vitana Corporation (1) .... Ottawa ON
Volex Canada Inc. (1) .... Kanata ON
Vopak Canada Ltd. (1) .... Edmonton AB
W.I. Villager Ltd. / Marshlands Canada (1) .... Kingston ON
Wainbee Limited (1) .... Mississauga ON
Warner-Lambert Canada Inc. (1) .... Toronto ON
WD-40 Products (Canada) Ltd. (1) .... Toronto ON
Webstorm Media (1) .... Montréal QC
Weidmuller Ltd. (1) .... Markham ON
Westcan Wireless (1) .... Edmonton AB
Whitehall-Robins Inc. (1) .... Mississauga ON
Winpak Technologies Inc. (1) .... Toronto ON
Winters Instruments (1) .... Toronto ON
Wurth Canada Limited (1) .... Mississauga ON
Xebec Imaging Services Inc. (1) .... Ottawa ON
Xwave Solutions Inc. (1) .... Ottawa ON
Yaskawa Motoman Canada Ltd. (1) .... Mississauga ON
Yotta Yotta Inc. (1) .... Edmonton AB
Zenastra Photonics Inc. (1) .... Ottawa ON

SCIENTIFIC

See also: Biotech/Biology, Pharmaceutical, Health/Medical.

Origenix Technologies Inc. (8 positions) .... Laval QC
QLT Inc. (8) .... Vancouver BC
AnorMED Inc. (7) .... Langley BC
Public Service Commission of Canada, Onta (7) .... Ottawa ON
Public Service Commission of Canada, (7) .... Quebec City QC
SCP Science (7) .... Baie d'Urfe QC
Centre for Addiction and Mental Health (6) .... Toronto ON
Inex Pharmaceuticals Corp. (6) .... Burnaby BC
CANTEST Ltd. (5) .... Burnaby BC
ClinTrials BioResearch Ltd. / CTBR (5) .... Senneville QC
INO (5) .... Ste-Foy QC
Caprion Pharmaceuticals Inc. (4) .... Montréal QC
CreoScitex (4) .... Burnaby BC
Galian Photonics Inc. (4) .... Vancouver BC
McMaster University, Faculty of Health (4) .... Hamilton ON
Ministry of Agriculture, Food and Rural A (4) .... Guelph ON
Ministry of the Solicitor General, Ontar (4) .... Toronto ON
National Research Council Canada / NRC (4) .... Ottawa ON
Patheon Inc. (4) .... Mississauga ON
Public Service Commission of Canada, Al (4) .... Edmonton AB
Public Service Commission of Canada, BC (4) .... Victoria BC
Zenastra Photonics Inc. (4) .... Ottawa ON
Axelson BioPharma Research Inc. / ABR (3) .... Burnaby BC
Children's and Women's Health Centre o (3) .... Vancouver BC
Cytec Canada Inc. (3) .... Niagara Falls ON
General Paint Corp. (3) .... Vancouver BC
Hospital for Sick Children, The (3) .... Toronto ON
JR Laboratories Inc. (3) .... Burnaby BC
MethylGene Inc. (3) .... St-Laurent QC
Ministry of Agriculture, Food and Rural A (3) .... Guelph ON
Novopharm Ltd. (3) .... Toronto ON
Resonance Photonics Inc. (3) .... Markham ON
Sudbury Neutrino Observatory / SNO (3) .... Lively ON
University of Guelph (3) .... Guelph ON
Wyeth-Ayerst Canada Inc. (3) .... Toronto ON
Adherex Technologies Inc. (2) .... Ottawa ON
AGAT Laboratories (2) .... Calgary AB
Agrium Inc. (2) .... Redwater AB
Axys Group (2) .... Sidney BC
Brenntag Canada Inc. (2) .... Toronto ON
Canadian Sleep Institute / CSI (2) .... Calgary AB
Caro Research (2) .... Dorval QC
Carsen Group Inc. (2) .... Markham ON
Centre for Health Evaluation and Outco (2) .... Vancouver BC
Cytochroma Inc. (2) .... Kingston ON
Danapharm Clinical Research Inc. / DCRI (2) .... London ON
Department of National Defence, Headquart (2) .... Ottawa ON
Diabetogen Biosciences Inc. (2) .... London ON
Fluid Life Corp. (2) .... Edmonton AB
Forensic Technology Inc. (2) .... Cote St. Luc QC
Hamilton Regional Cancer Centre / HRCC (2) .... Hamilton ON

Intercorp Excelle Foods Inc. (2) .... Toronto ON
Intermap Technologies (2) .... Nepean ON
ITR Laboratories Canada Inc. (2) .... Baie d'Urfe QC
Jungbunzlauer Canada Inc. (2) .... Port Colborne ON
Kam Biotechnology Ltd. (2) .... Surrey BC
Lakehead University (2) .... Thunder Bay ON
Lumenon (2) .... St-Laurent QC
McGill University, Department of Pathol (2) .... Montréal QC
MDS Proteomics (2) .... Toronto ON
Memorial University of Newfoundland (2) .... St. John's NF
MetroPhotonics Inc. (2) .... Ottawa ON
Ministry of the Environment, Ontario (La (2) .... Toronto ON
Ministry of the Solicitor General, Ontar (2) .... Orillia ON
National Research Council Canada, Institu (2) .... Ottawa ON
NOVA Chemicals Corporation, Research and (2) .... Calgary AB
NPS Pharmaceuticals Inc. (2) .... Mississauga ON
Ontario Science Centre / OSC (2) .... Toronto ON
Public Service Commission of Canada, Ma (2) .... Winnipeg MB
School District #60 (Peace River N (2) .... Fort St. John BC
Scintrex Trace Corp. (2) .... Ottawa ON
Silliker Canada (2) .... Markham ON
Spectral Diagnostics Inc. (2) .... Toronto ON
Standards Council of Canada / SCC (2) .... Ottawa ON
Syn X Pharma Inc. (2) .... Mississauga ON
Torcan Chemical Ltd. (2) .... Aurora ON
University of Manitoba, Department of C (2) .... Winnipeg MB
University of Toronto, Department of Imm (2) .... Toronto ON
Varian Canada Inc. (2) .... Mississauga ON
Alberta Agriculture, Food & Rural Devel (1) .... Edmonton AB
Alberta Innovation & Science (1) .... Edmonton AB
Alberta Research Council / ARC (1) .... Edmonton AB
American Iron & Metal Company Inc. / AI (1) .... Montréal QC
Apotex Inc. (1) .... Toronto ON
Barringer Research (1) .... Mississauga ON
BASF Canada Inc. (1) .... Toronto ON
Baxter Corporation (1) .... Alliston ON
BC Cancer Agency (1) .... Vancouver BC
BC Research Inc. (1) .... Vancouver BC
Beckman Coulter Canada Inc. (1) .... Mississauga ON
BJ Pipeline Inspection Services (1) .... Calgary AB
Brock University (1) .... St. Catharines ON
Calgary, City of (1) .... Calgary AB
Canada Customs and Revenue Agency / CCRA (1) ..... Calgary AB
Canada Customs and Revenue Agency / CCRA (1) ..... Ottawa ON
Canadian Blood Services / CBS (1) .... Ottawa ON
Canadian Blood Services, Toronto Blood C (1) .... Toronto ON
Canadian Food Inspection Agency / CFIA (1) .... Nepean ON
Canadian Nuclear Safety Commission / CNSC (1) .... Ottawa ON
Cangene Corporation (1) .... Winnipeg MB
Casco Impregnated Papers Inc. (1) .... Cobourg ON
Chemque Inc. (1) .... Toronto ON
Cognis Canada Corporation (1) .... Mississauga ON
Coley Pharmaceutical Group / CPG (1) .... Ottawa ON
Concordia University College of Alberta (1) .... Edmonton AB
Cquay Inc. (1) .... Calgary AB
Cross Cancer Institute / CCI (1) .... Edmonton AB
CryoCath Technologies Inc. (1) .... Kirkland QC
Cryovac Canada Inc. (1) .... Mississauga ON
Dominion Colour Corporation (1) .... Toronto ON
DSI Datotech Systems Inc. (1) .... Vancouver BC
Dufferin-Peel Catholic District Scho (1) .... Mississauga ON
DuPont Canada Inc. (1) .... Mississauga ON
Enerchem International Inc. (1) .... Nisku AB
EXFO Electro-Optical Engineering Inc. (1) .... Vanier QC
Fiera Foods Company (1) .... Toronto ON
Gamma-Dynacare (1) .... Brampton ON
GE Syprotec Inc. (1) .... Pointe-Claire QC
Global Thermoelectric Inc. (1) .... Calgary AB
Golder Associates Ltd. (1) .... Calgary AB
Grant MacEwan College, Jasper Place Cam (1) .... Edmonton AB
Hydrogenics Corporation (1) .... Mississauga ON
Image Processing Systems Inc. / IPS (1) .... Markham ON
Inflazyme Pharmaceuticals Ltd. (1) .... Richmond BC
Infowave Software, Inc. (1) .... Burnaby BC
Innovus Research Inc. (1) .... Burlington ON
Jacques Whitford Environment Ltd. (1) .... Calgary AB
Kingston General Hospital, Radiation On (1) .... Kingston ON
Kvaerner Chemetics (1) .... Vancouver BC
Lakefield Research Limited (1) .... Lakefield ON
Langara College (1) .... Vancouver BC
Liponex Inc. (1) .... Ottawa ON
Lockheed Martin Canada Inc. (1) .... Kanata ON

SCIENTIFIC (Cont.)

London Regional Cancer Centre / LRCC (1) .... London ON
Lower Canada College (1) .... Montréal QC
Magnus Chemicals Ltd. (1) .... Boucherville QC
Malaspina University-College, Nanaimo Ca (1) .... Nanaimo BC
Maxxam Analytics Inc. (1) .... Mississauga ON
McMaster University (1) .... Hamilton ON
MDS Metro Laboratory Services (1) .... Burnaby BC
MDS Nordion (1) .... Vancouver BC
MDS Nordion (1) .... Kanata ON
Ministry of Transportation, Ontario (1) .... Toronto ON
National Research Council Canada, I (1) .... Boucherville QC
National Research Council Canada / NRC (1) .... Ottawa ON
National Research Council Canada / NRC (1) .... Ottawa ON
National Research Council Canada / NRC (1) .... Ottawa ON
North York General Hospital (1) .... Toronto ON
Ottawa Hospital, The (1) .... Ottawa ON
Peel, The Regional Municipality of (1) .... Brampton ON
PFB Corporation (1) .... Calgary AB
Phase Technology (1) .... Richmond BC
Philip Services Corporation / PSC (1) .... Burlington ON
Philips Analytical (1) .... Waterloo ON
Phoenix Contact Ltd. (1) .... Mississauga ON
Prescient NeuroPharma Inc. (1) .... Toronto ON
PSC Analytical Ltd. (1) .... Mississauga ON
Public Service Commission of Canada, B (1) .... Vancouver BC
Public Service Commission of Canada, Ont (1) .... Ottawa ON
Public Service Commission of Canada, Qu (1) .... Montréal QC
Queen's University, Cancer Research Lab (1) .... Kingston ON
Queen's University, National Cancer Ins (1) .... Kingston ON
Raylo Chemicals Inc. (1) .... Edmonton AB
Red Deer College (1) .... Red Deer AB
Regina Health District (1) .... Regina SK
Ryerson Polytechnic University (1) .... Toronto ON
SaskPower (1) .... Regina SK
Seacor Environmental Engineering Inc. (1) .... Richmond BC
SemBioSys Genetics Inc. (1) .... Calgary AB
ShawCor Ltd. (1) .... Toronto ON
StockerYale Canada Inc. (1) .... Dollard-des-Ormeaux QC
StockerYale Canada Inc. (1) .... St-Laurent QC
Suncor Energy Inc., Oil Sands (1) .... Fort McMurray AB
Sunnybrook & Women's College Health Scie (1) ...... Toronto ON
Swiss Herbal Remedies Ltd. (1) .... Richmond Hill ON
Syncrude Canada Ltd. (1) .... Fort McMurray AB
Synsorb Biotech Inc. (1) .... Calgary AB
Toronto Rehabilitation Institute (1) .... Toronto ON
TransAlta Corporation (1) .... Calgary AB
Underwriters' Laboratories of Canada / U (1) .... Toronto ON
University College of the Cariboo / UCC (1) .... Kamloops BC
University of British Columbia / UBC (1) .... Vancouver BC
University of Calgary (1) .... Calgary AB
University of New Brunswick, Facul (1) .... Saint John NB
University of Northern British Col (1) .... Prince George BC
University of Ottawa Heart Institute (1) .... Ottawa ON
University of Toronto, Faculty of Arts & (1) .... Toronto ON
University of Victoria (1) .... Victoria BC
University of Waterloo (1) .... Waterloo ON
Vancouver Hospital and Health Sciences (1) .... Vancouver BC
Vopak Canada Ltd. (1) .... Toronto ON
Weston Bakeries Ltd. (1) .... Toronto ON
York House School (1) .... Vancouver BC
York University (1) .... Toronto ON

TELECOM

See also: Engineering, Computing, Trades/Technicians.

Telus Mobility (88 positions) .... Toronto ON
Group Telecom (70) .... Toronto ON
EMS Technologies Canada Ltd (43) .... Ste-Anne-de-Bellevue QC
Research in Motion Limited / RIM (37) .... Kanata ON
Bell Intrigna (33) .... Calgary AB
Zenastra Photonics Inc. (33) .... Ottawa ON
Research in Motion Limited / RIM (32) .... Waterloo ON
MetroPhotonics Inc. (30) .... Ottawa ON
Rogers AT&T Wireless (29) .... Toronto ON
NSI Communications (28) .... Pointe-Claire QC
Siemens Canada Ltd., Telecom Innovation C (28) .... Kanata ON

Solinet Systems Inc. (28) .... Ottawa ON
Lantern Communications Canada Inc. (26) .... Ottawa ON
Wi-LAN Inc. (24) .... Calgary AB
Sedona Networks (23) .... Kanata ON
Edgeflow Inc. (22) .... Kanata ON
OZ Optics Ltd. (22) .... Carp ON
SpaceBridge Networks Corporation (21) .... Hull QC
Telus Integrated Communications (21) .... Toronto ON
IceFyre Semiconductor Inc. (19) .... Ottawa ON
Sprint Canada Inc. (19) .... Toronto ON
AcceLight Networks (18) .... Nepean ON
Tellamon Photonic Networks Inc. (18) .... Ottawa ON
TELOS Technology Inc. (17) .... Richmond BC
Nortel Networks (16) .... Ottawa ON
Telesat Canada (16) .... Gloucester ON
Ericsson Canada Inc. (15) .... Mount Royal QC
eWazo Technology Corporation (15) .... Victoria BC
Resonance Photonics Inc. (15) .... Markham ON
Unique Broadband Systems, Inc. / UBS (15) .... Concord ON
JDS Uniphase Corporation (14) .... Nepean ON
RSL COM Canada Inc. (14) .... Vancouver BC
Aastra Telecom (13) .... Calgary AB
Bell Intrigna (13) .... Edmonton AB
Telus Corporation (13) .... Burnaby BC
VIPswitch Inc. (13) .... Montréal QC
Computing Devices Canada Ltd. / CDC (12) .... Calgary AB
Northwood Technologies Inc. (12) .... Nepean ON
Sigma Systems Group Inc. (12) .... Toronto ON
Spectrum Signal Processing Inc. (12) .... Burnaby BC
Wavesat Telecom Inc. (12) .... St-Laurent QC
Norcom Networks (11) .... Burnaby BC
PMC-Sierra, Inc. (11) .... Burnaby BC
Rogers Cable Inc. (10) .... Toronto ON
Trillium Photonics (10) .... Ottawa ON
VoiceGenie.com (10) .... Toronto ON
Westcan Wireless (10) .... Edmonton AB
Consultronics Ltd. (9) .... Concord ON
fSONA Communications Corp. (9) .... Richmond BC
Public Service Commission of Canada, Onta (9) .... Ottawa ON
StockerYale Canada Inc. (9) .... Dollard-des-Ormeaux QC
SynchroPoint Wireless Inc. (9) .... Vancouver BC
BroadTel Canada (8) .... St-Laurent QC
Catena Networks (8) .... Kanata ON
Marconi Communications (8) .... Dorval QC
Performance Technologies, Inc. (8) .... Ottawa ON
Sierra Wireless Inc. (8) .... Richmond BC
Silicon Access Networks Ltd. (8) .... Ottawa ON
Tality Corp. (8) .... Ottawa ON
Bragg Photonics Inc. (7) .... Dorval QC
CMC Electronics Inc. (7) .... St-Laurent QC
Group Telecom (7) .... Calgary AB
Northland Systems Training Inc. (7) .... Ottawa ON
Pika Technologies Inc. (7) .... Kanata ON
Positron Public Safety Systems Inc. (7) .... Montréal QC
Sigem Inc. (7) .... Kanata ON
TRM Technologies, Inc. (7) .... Ottawa ON
Tropic Networks Inc. (7) .... Kanata ON
Trylon TSF (7) .... Elmira ON
Bell Intrigna (6) .... Vancouver BC
BTI Photonics Inc. (6) .... Ottawa ON
Digital Dispatch Systems Inc. (6) .... Richmond BC
Gennum Corporation (6) .... Burlington ON
GN NetTest (Canada) Inc., Networks Divis (6) .... Markham ON
Harris Corporation, Microwave Communicat (6) .... Calgary AB
Lumic Electronics, Inc. (6) .... Nepean ON
Microcell Connexions Inc. (6) .... Toronto ON
Mitec Telecom Inc. (6) .... Pointe-Claire QC
NetPCS (6) .... Kanata ON
Quick Link Communications Ltd. / QLC (6) .... Calgary AB
SS8 Networks Inc. (6) .... Ottawa ON
Vistar Telecommunications Inc. (6) .... Ottawa ON
Aastra Telecom (5) .... Concord ON
Avantas Networks Corp. (5) .... St-Laurent QC
Bell Mobility (5) .... Mississauga ON
BitFlash Graphics, Inc. (5) .... Ottawa ON
C1 Communications (5) .... Mississauga ON
CIMTEK Automation Systems (5) .... Burlington ON
CML Emergency Services, Inc. (5) .... Hull QC
Cogency Semiconductor Inc. (5) .... Kanata ON
Conex Business Systems Inc. (5) .... Edmonton AB
Futureway Communications Inc. (5) .... Richmond Hill ON
Global Crossing (5) .... Montréal QC

TELECOM (Cont.)

JDS Uniphase Corporation, Fiber-Optic Pr (5) .... Markham ON
Morrison Hershfield (5) .... Toronto ON
Network Design and Analysis / NDA Corpor (5) .... Markham ON
Novatel Wireless Technologies Ltd. (5) .... Calgary AB
PerkinElmer Optoelectronics Inc. (5) .... Vaudreuil QC
PMC-Sierra, Inc. (5) .... Kanata ON
Psion Teklogix Inc. (5) .... Mississauga ON
Quake Technologies Inc. (5) .... Ottawa ON
Rogers Cable Inc. (5) .... Toronto ON
Spirent Communications (5) .... Ottawa ON
Teraxion (5) .... Ste-Foy QC
724 Solutions Inc. (4) .... Toronto ON
Advantera Communications Inc. (4) .... Ottawa ON
Cap Gemini Ernst & Young / CGEY (4) .... Toronto ON
Circa Communications Ltd. (4) .... North Vancouver BC
Elcan Optical Technologies (4) .... Midland ON
Entourage Technology Solutions (4) .... Mississauga ON
Ericsson Communications Canada (4) .... Mississauga ON
Hyperchip (4) .... Montréal QC
Infowave Software, Inc. (4) .... Burnaby BC
Inkra Networks Canada (4) .... Burnaby BC
MegaSys Computer Technologies Ltd. (4) .... Calgary AB
Nokia Products Ltd. (4) .... Richmond BC
SNC-Lavalin Inc. (4) .... Montréal QC
Tantalus Systems Corp. (4) .... Burnaby BC
Toshiba Business Systems Inc. (4) .... Calgary AB
Trillium Digital Systems Canada, Ltd. (4) .... Burnaby BC
WestBay Semiconductor Inc. (4) .... Vancouver BC
Accord Communications (3) .... Calgary AB
Acterna Corporation (3) .... Burnaby BC
AT&T Canada (3) .... Toronto ON
ATI Technologies Inc. (3) .... Thornhill ON
Broadcom Corporation (3) .... Richmond BC
Centrepoint Technologies Inc. (3) .... Ottawa ON
COM DEV International (3) .... Cambridge ON
CSI Wireless Inc. (3) .... Calgary AB
Diablo Research Company (3) .... Richmond BC
Excite@Home Canada, Inc. (3) .... Toronto ON
Focus Microwaves Inc. (3) .... St-Laurent QC
Instantel Inc. (3) .... Kanata ON
Interalia Inc. (3) .... Calgary AB
International Datacasting Corporation / I (3) .... Ottawa ON
M/A-COM (3) .... Burnaby BC
Motorola Canada Limited (3) .... Richmond Hill ON
Nokia Products Ltd. (3) .... Ajax ON
Northwestel Inc. (3) .... Whitehorse YT
OMNEX Control Systems Inc. (3) .... Port Coquitlam BC
Ositech Communications Inc. (3) .... Guelph ON
Precidia Technologies (3) .... Kanata ON
Raytheon Systems Canada Ltd. (3) .... Waterloo ON
Rogers AT&T Wireless (3) .... Calgary AB
Rogers AT&T Wireless (3) .... Toronto ON
Rogers Communications Inc. (3) .... Toronto ON
Shaw Communications Inc. (3) .... Burnaby BC
SR Telecom Inc. (3) .... Kanata ON
SynreVoice Technologies Inc. (3) .... Markham ON
Tellabs TTG Inc. (3) .... Gloucester ON
Tellabs TTG Inc. (3) .... St-Laurent QC
TeraGo Networks Inc. (3) .... Calgary AB
Westfair Foods Ltd. (3) .... Calgary AB
Xwave Solutions Inc. (3) .... Dorval QC
ADP Canada (2) .... Toronto ON
Allcan Electronic Distributors (2) .... Edmonton AB
ATCO Electric (2) .... Edmonton AB
ATI Telecom International Co. (2) .... Edmonton AB
British Columbia Institute of Technology (2) .... Burnaby BC
C-MAC Industries Inc. (2) .... Kanata ON
Cadence Design Systems, Inc. (2) .... Ottawa ON
Calgary, City of (2) .... Calgary AB
Chromatic Software Inc. / CSI (2) .... Vancouver BC
CML Versatel Inc. (2) .... Hull QC
Cogeco Cable Inc. (2) .... Burlington ON
Cogency Semiconductor Inc. (2) .... Toronto ON
Coradiant Inc. (2) .... Montréal QC
Delphi Solutions Inc. (2) .... Calgary AB
Delphi Solutions Inc. (2) .... Markham ON
Empowered Networks (2) .... Kanata ON
Empowertel Networks Inc. (2) .... Ottawa ON
EMS Technologies Canada Ltd. (2) .... Ottawa ON
Enersource (2) .... Mississauga ON
Evertz Microsystems Ltd. (2) .... Burlington ON
EXI Wireless Systems Inc. (2) .... Richmond BC
Exocom Group Inc., The (2) .... Ottawa ON
Financial Institutions Commission / FI (2) .... Vancouver BC
Gage Applied, Inc. (2) .... Lachine QC
General Motors of Canada Ltd., Oshawa Tru (2) .... Oshawa ON
Group Telecom (2) .... Vancouver BC
H.H. Angus & Associates Ltd. (2) .... Toronto ON
IBM Canada Ltd. (2) .... Winnipeg MB
IBM Canada Ltd. (2) .... Markham ON
Intuit Canada Limited (2) .... Edmonton AB
Kinaare Networks Canada Corporation (2) .... Mississauga ON
Logibro Inc. (2) .... Montréal QC
Lumenon (2) .... St-Laurent QC
Matrikon Group (2) .... Edmonton AB
Maxim Morrison Hershfield Ltd. (2) .... Edmonton AB
Memoris, Inc. (2) .... Montréal QC
Minacs Worldwide Inc. (2) .... Richmond Hill ON
National Research Council Canada / NRC (2) .... Ottawa ON
Northern Alberta Institute of Technolog (2) .... Edmonton AB
NTG Clarity Networks Inc. (2) .... Markham ON
Ontario Lottery and Gaming Corporation / (2) .... Toronto ON
Paging Network of Canada, Inc. / PageNet (2) .... Toronto ON
Polycom Canada Inc. (2) .... North Vancouver BC
Potentia Telecom Power (2) .... Kanata ON
Precise Software Technologies Inc. (2) .... Nepean ON
PrinterON Corporation (2) .... Kitchener ON
Radiant Communications (2) .... Toronto ON
Redback Networks (2) .... Burnaby BC
Rogers AT&T Wireless (2) .... Burnaby BC
Rogers Shared Services (2) .... Markham ON
Royal Bank Financial Group (2) .... Toronto ON
SaskTel (2) .... Regina SK
SED Systems (2) .... Saskatoon SK
Shoppers Drug Mart (2) .... Toronto ON
Siemens Canada Ltd. (2) .... Mississauga ON
Simon Fraser University, School of Engin (2) .... Burnaby BC
Staples Business Depot Ltd. (2) .... Markham ON
Stream International (2) .... Belleville ON
Syndesis Limited (2) .... Ottawa ON
TierOne OSS Technologies Inc. (2) .... Mississauga ON
TransAlta Corporation (2) .... Calgary AB
Trylon - TSF (2) .... St-Lazare QC
Volex Canada Inc. (2) .... Kanata ON
Zucotto Wireless Inc. (2) .... Ottawa ON
360 Networks Inc. (2) .... Mississauga ON
Accpac International Inc. (1) .... Richmond BC
ACM Automation Inc. (1) .... Calgary AB
Advantech Advanced Microwave Technologies (1) .... Dorval QC
Agere Systems (1) .... Nepean ON
Ainsworth Inc. (1) .... Coquitlam BC
Ainsworth Inc. (1) .... Toronto ON
Alberta Environment (1) .... Edmonton AB
Algonquin College (1) .... Nepean ON
Altera Corp. (1) .... Nepean ON
AMEC E&C Services (1) .... St. John's NF
AT&T Canada (1) .... Toronto ON
Bantrel Inc. (1) .... Calgary AB
Bell Canada (1) .... Toronto ON
Bird On a Wire Networks / BOAW (1) .... Mississauga ON
bitHeads, Inc. (1) .... Ottawa ON
Boulevard Media (Canada) Inc. / BMC (1) .... Vancouver BC
Bracknell Telecom Services (1) .... Langley BC
Brampton, City of (1) .... Brampton ON
Brant Telephone Inc. (1) .... Burlington ON
Casino Niagara (1) .... Niagara Falls ON
Circadence Corporation (1) .... Toronto ON
CMP Design (1) .... Kanata ON
Coldswitch Technologies Inc. (1) .... Richmond BC
Com-Net Ericsson (1) .... Mississauga ON
Creation Technologies Inc. (1) .... Burnaby BC
Credit Valley Hospital, The (1) .... Mississauga ON
CVDS Inc. (1) .... Pointe-Claire QC
DMR Consulting Inc. (1) .... Calgary AB
DSC Group of Companies (1) .... Concord ON
Dynastream Technologies Inc. (1) .... Cochrane AB
Earth Tech Canada Inc. (1) .... Markham ON
Edge Networks Corporation (1) .... Winnipeg MB
EDS Innovations (1) .... Ottawa ON
English Montreal School Board / EMSB (1) .... Montréal QC

TELECOM (Cont.)

Enron Canada Corp. (1) .... Calgary AB
EXFO Electro-Optical Engineering Inc. (1) .... Vanier QC
Export Development Corporation / EDC (1) .... Ottawa ON
Extracomm Technologies Inc. (1) .... Toronto ON
Fidelity Investments Canada Limited (1) .... Toronto ON
Financial Services Commission of Ontario (1) .... Toronto ON
Fincentric Corp. (1) .... Richmond BC
Focus Business Solutions Inc. (1) .... Calgary AB
GE Canada (1) .... Mississauga ON
Geotech Communications Inc. (1) .... Brampton ON
Global Thermoelectric Inc. (1) .... Calgary AB
Globalstar / One Stop Wireless (1) .... Toronto ON
Greater Toronto Airports Authority / GTA (1) .... Toronto ON
Hatch Associates Ltd. (1) .... Mississauga ON
Hewlett-Packard (Canada) Ltd. (1) .... Mississauga ON
Hubbell Canada Inc. (1) .... Pickering ON
Huber + Suhner (Canada) Ltd. (1) .... Kanata ON
i-STAT Canada Ltd. (1) .... Kanata ON
IBI Group (1) .... Edmonton AB
Image Processing Systems Inc. / IPS (1) .... Markham ON
iMPath Networks Inc. (1) .... Nepean ON
INO (1) .... Ste-Foy QC
Intelcan Technosystems Inc. (1) .... Nepean ON
Interactive Media Group / IMG (1) .... Toronto ON
INTESYS Network Communications Ltd. (1) .... Toronto ON
IT Career Access Office, BC / ITCAO (1) .... Victoria BC
IVL Technologies Ltd. (1) .... Victoria BC
J & D Systems Inc. (1) .... Kitchener ON
JDS Uniphase Corporation (1) .... Saanichton BC
Kenonic Controls Ltd. (1) .... Calgary AB
Kvaerner SNC-Lavalin Offshore / KSLO (1) .... Mount Pearl NF
Kymata Canada Ltd. (1) .... Kanata ON
Mastech Canada (1) .... Ottawa ON
Mastech Canada (1) .... Montréal QC
Microcell Telecommunications Ltd. (1) .... Vancouver BC
Ministry of Health and Long-Term (1) .... Penetanguishene ON
Ministry of Health and Long-Term Care, O (1) .... Toronto ON
Ministry of Health and Ministry Respons (1) .... Victoria BC
Morrison Hershfield (1) .... Burnaby BC
Nanowave Technologies Inc. (1) .... Toronto ON
National Research Council Canada, Institu (1) .... Ottawa ON
National Research Council Canada / NRC (1) .... Ottawa ON
National Research Council Canada / NRC (1) .... Ottawa ON
Nedco (1) .... Richmond BC
NetMart Inc. (1) .... Montréal QC
NetPCS (1) .... Hull QC
Network Builders Inc. (1) .... Toronto ON
NICE Systems (1) .... Richmond BC
Northern Alberta Institute of Technolog (1) .... Edmonton AB
Novatel Inc. (1) .... Calgary AB
NRNS Inc. (1) .... Kanata ON
NxtPhase Corporation (1) .... Vancouver BC
OmniSales (1) .... Ottawa ON
Optotek Ltd. (1) .... Kanata ON
Quack.com (1) .... Waterloo ON
Radiant Communications (1) .... Calgary AB
Rocky Mountain Instruments Inc. / RMI (1) .... Edmonton AB
Rogers Cable Inc. (1) .... Kitchener ON
Rogers Cable Inc. (1) .... St. John's NF
Rogers Communications Inc. (1) .... Toronto ON
Rohde & Schwarz Canada Inc. (1) .... Kanata ON
RoundHeaven Communications Canada Inc. (1) .... Vancouver BC
Siemens Milltronics Process Instrum (1) .... Peterborough ON
SignalSoft Canada (1) .... Victoria BC
Sitraka Mobility (1) .... Toronto ON
Soft Tracks (1) .... Richmond BC
Solect Technology Group (1) .... Toronto ON
Southern Alberta Institute of Technology (1) .... Calgary AB
SpeechWorks International, Inc. (1) .... Montréal QC
Spielo Gaming International (1) .... Dieppe NB
St. Lawrence Seaway Management Co (1) .... St. Catharines ON
STMicroelectronics (1) .... Nepean ON
StockerYale Canada Inc. (1) .... St-Laurent QC
Sybridge Technologies Inc. (1) .... Nepean ON
Technical University of British Columbia (1) .... Surrey BC
Technisonic Industries Limited (1) .... Mississauga ON
TeleSpectrum Canada Inc. (1) .... Toronto ON
Thunder Bay, City of (1) .... Thunder Bay ON
Time iCR Inc. (1) .... Ottawa ON

Underwriters' Laboratories of Canada / U (1) .... Toronto ON
University Health Network, Shared Inform (1) .... Toronto ON
University of Calgary (1) .... Calgary AB
University of Northern British Col (1) .... Prince George BC
Valcom Limited (Ottawa) (1) .... Ottawa ON
Visions Electronics (1) .... Calgary AB
Voice Mobility Inc. (1) .... Richmond BC
Voyus Canada Inc. (1) .... Burnaby BC
WANN Connection Devices Inc. (1) .... Nepean ON
Xwave Solutions Inc. (1) .... Calgary AB
Zed.i Solutions (1) .... Calgary AB

TRADE SHOWS

See also: Marketing, Sales, Hospitality.

Exhibits International (5 positions) .... Toronto ON
Conference Board of Canada, The (4) .... Ottawa ON
OZ Optics Ltd. (4) .... Carp ON
Canadian Institute, The (3) .... Toronto ON
Canadian Intergovernmental Conference Sec (3) .... Ottawa ON
Marcus Evans (3) .... Toronto ON
TELAV Audio Visual Services (3) .... Toronto ON
AldrichPears Associates (2) .... Vancouver BC
Canadian Restaurant and Foodservices Ass (2) .... Toronto ON
INFONEX Inc. (2) .... Toronto ON
Institute for International Research (2) .... Toronto ON
Strategy Institute (2) .... Toronto ON
TELAV Audio Visual Services (2) .... Ottawa ON
Zucotto Wireless Inc. (2) .... Ottawa ON
Banff Centre, The (1) .... Banff AB
British Columbia Institute of Technology (1) .... Burnaby BC
Butterworths Canada Ltd. (1) .... Markham ON
Canadian Pharmacists Association / CPhA (1) .... Ottawa ON
Canadian Tourism Commission / CTC (1) .... Ottawa ON
CORPAV Presentation Group (1) .... Vancouver BC
Dental Marketing Inc. (1) .... Vaughan ON
Design + Communication Inc. (1) .... Montréal QC
Display Design Systems Ltd. (1) .... Edmonton AB
Fincentric Corp. (1) .... Richmond BC
Global Group, The (1) .... Toronto ON
Marcus Evans (1) .... Montréal QC
Ontario Science Centre / OSC (1) .... Toronto ON
PrinterON Corporation (1) .... Kitchener ON
Registered Nurses Association of Ontario (1) .... Toronto ON
Research in Motion Limited / RIM (1) .... Waterloo ON
Rogers Media, Publishing (1) .... Toronto ON
Scholarship Consultants of North Ame (1) .... Mississauga ON
Shoppers Drug Mart (1) .... Toronto ON
Stikeman Elliott (1) .... Toronto ON
Street Health (1) .... Toronto ON
TELAV Audio Visual Services (1) .... Calgary AB
Town Publishing Inc. (1) .... Hamilton ON
University Health Network / UHN (1) .... Toronto ON
University of Calgary (1) .... Calgary AB
University of New Brunswick / UNB (1) .... Fredericton NB
Videoscope (1) .... Toronto ON
Xwave Solutions Inc. (1) .... Ottawa ON

TRADES/TECHNICIANS

See also: Operations, Engineering.

Magna International Inc. (35 positions) .... Concord ON
Global Thermoelectric Inc. (16) .... Calgary AB
Orlick Industries Ltd. (12) .... Hamilton ON
Wescam (12) .... Burlington ON
Hydrogenics Corporation (11) .... Mississauga ON
Rockwell Automation Canada (11) .... Cambridge ON
Westport Innovations Inc. (11) .... Vancouver BC
Babcock & Wilcox Canada (10) .... Cambridge ON
Dynacast Canada Inc. (10) .... Pointe-Claire QC
QuestAir Technologies Inc. (10) .... Burnaby BC
Alberta Learning (9) .... Edmonton AB
Azurix North America (9) .... Hamilton ON
Northern Alberta Institute of Technolog (9) .... Edmonton AB
OZ Optics Ltd. (9) .... Carp ON
Cargill Foods (8) .... High River AB

TRADES/TECHNICIANS (Cont.)

ENMAX Corporation (8) .... Calgary AB
Liburdi Engineering Ltd. (8) .... Dundas ON
Ontario Power Generation (8) .... Toronto ON
BC Hydro (7) .... Vancouver BC
Evans Consoles Inc. (7) .... Calgary AB
Lovat Tunnel Equipment Inc. (7) .... Toronto ON
TransAlta Corporation (7) .... Calgary AB
Turbocor Inc. (7) .... Dorval QC
University of Calgary (7) .... Calgary AB
Advanced Motion and Controls Ltd. (6) .... Barrie ON
Alberta Infrastructure & Transportation (6) .... Edmonton AB
Almac Machine Works Ltd. (6) .... Edmonton AB
Apotex Inc. (6) .... Toronto ON
Budd Canada Inc. (6) .... Kitchener ON
Crescent Custom Yachts (6) .... Richmond BC
Ebco Technologies Inc. (6) .... Richmond BC
Gennum Corporation (6) .... Burlington ON
George Kelk Corporation (6) .... Toronto ON
MetroPhotonics Inc. (6) .... Ottawa ON
New Automation Corporation / NAC (6) .... Burlington ON
Optech Inc. (6) .... Toronto ON
Research in Motion Limited / RIM (6) .... Waterloo ON
Toronto Transit Commission / TTC (6) .... Toronto ON
A.W. Miller Technical Sales (5) .... Mississauga ON
Alberta Boilers Safety Association / AB (5) .... Edmonton AB
Albian Sands Energy Inc. (5) .... Fort McMurray AB
ATS Test Systems Inc. (5) .... Woodbridge ON
Bragg Photonics Inc. (5) .... Dorval QC
Can-Eng Furnaces Ltd. (5) .... Niagara Falls ON
CMC Electronics Inc. (5) .... St-Laurent QC
Cummins Inc. (5) .... Edmonton AB
Elcan Optical Technologies (5) .... Midland ON
Global Group, The (5) .... Toronto ON
Hershey Canada Inc. (5) .... Smith Falls ON
Ruffneck Heaters (5) .... Calgary AB
Schneider Foods Inc. (5) .... Kitchener ON
Siemens Westinghouse (5) .... Hamilton ON
Suncor Energy Inc., Oil Sands (5) .... Fort McMurray AB
Syncrude Canada Ltd. (5) .... Fort McMurray AB
Agile Systems Inc. (4) .... Waterloo ON
Aventis Pasteur Ltd. (4) .... Toronto ON
Burlington Technologies Inc., Burling (4) .... Burlington ON
Canada Brick Ltd. (4) .... Burlington ON
Carsen Group Inc. (4) .... Markham ON
IKO Industries Ltd. (4) .... Brampton ON
Instantel Inc. (4) .... Kanata ON
Mistahia Health Region (4) .... Grande Prairie AB
Naylor Group Inc. (4) .... Oakville ON
Noritsu Canada Ltd. (4) .... Mississauga ON
Northern Alberta Institute of Technolog (4) .... Edmonton AB
Optotek Ltd. (4) .... Kanata ON
Philips Engineering Ltd. (4) .... Burlington ON
Pro-Spec Inc. (4) .... Stoney Creek ON
Procor Ltd. (4) .... Oakville ON
QLT Inc. (4) .... Vancouver BC
Schneider Foods Inc. (4) .... Surrey BC
Sewer-Matic Services Inc. (4) .... Ottawa ON
Siemens Building Technologies Ltd., (4) .... Mississauga ON
Technical Standards & Safety Authority / (4) .... Toronto ON
TELAV Audio Visual Services (4) .... Lachine QC
Toromont CAT (4) .... Concord ON
Trebor Allan Inc. (4) .... Hamilton ON
Van-Rob Stampings Inc. (4) .... Aurora ON
Viconics Electronics Inc. (4) .... St-Leonard QC
Adams Manufacturing (3) .... Toronto ON
AiT Corporation (3) .... Ottawa ON
Alberta Infrastructure & Transportation (3) .... Edmonton AB
Amcan Castings Ltd. (3) .... Hamilton ON
Angus Consulting Management Ltd. / ACML (3) .... Toronto ON
Antomax Automotive Technologies (3) .... Mississauga ON
Bell & Howell Ltd. (3) .... Toronto ON
Bettis Canada Ltd. (3) .... Edmonton AB
C-MAC Invotronics Inc. (3) .... Toronto ON
Canadian General-Tower Ltd. (3) .... Cambridge ON
Cancable Inc. (3) .... Burlington ON
Cangene Corporation (3) .... Winnipeg MB
Carpenter Canada Ltd. (3) .... Woodbridge ON
CDA Industries Inc. (3) .... Pickering ON
Co-Ex-Tec Industries (3) .... Concord ON
Corlac Industries Ltd. (3) .... Lloydminster AB
Corridor Pipeline Limited (3) .... Edmonton AB
Creation Technologies Inc. (3) .... Burnaby BC
CWB Group (3) .... Mississauga ON
Department of Works, Services and Transpo (3) .... Gander NF
Dominion Spring Industries Corp. / D (3) .... Mississauga ON
Don Park Inc. (3) .... Toronto ON
DRS Flight Safety and Communicati (3) .... Carleton Place ON
DSC Group of Companies (3) .... Concord ON
E-One Moli Energy (Canada) Ltd. (3) .... Maple Ridge BC
Eagle Precision Technologies Inc. (3) .... Brantford ON
Edwards Systems Technology (3) .... Owen Sound ON
Electronics Manufacturing Group / EMG (3) .... Calgary AB
EPCOR Utilities Inc. (3) .... Edmonton AB
Excel Tech Ltd. / XLTEK (3) .... Oakville ON
Falconbridge Ltd. (3) .... Onaping ON
Flint Energy Services Ltd. (3) .... Red Deer AB
Fluor Constructors Canada Ltd. (3) .... Edmonton AB
Gienow Building Products Ltd. (3) .... Calgary AB
Golden Windows Ltd. (3) .... Kitchener ON
Grimsby Custom Tooling Ltd. (3) .... Stoney Creek ON
Haakon Industries (3) .... Kingston ON
Halton, The Regional Municipality of (3) .... Oakville ON
Hemosol Inc. (3) .... Toronto ON
Heroux Devtek, Magtron Division (3) .... Toronto ON
i-STAT Canada Ltd. (3) .... Kanata ON
Jungbunzlauer Canada Inc. (3) .... Port Colborne ON
Knoll North America Corporation (3) .... Toronto ON
Leitch Technology Corp. (3) .... Toronto ON
Linamar Corporation, Autocom Division (3) .... Guelph ON
Mania Technologie Canada Inc. (3) .... Toronto ON
Manitoba Transportation & Government Se (3) .... Winnipeg MB
MetriCan Manufacturing Co. Inc. (3) .... Oakville ON
Nienkamper (3) .... Toronto ON
Proceco Ltd. (3) .... Montréal QC
R.L. Brews Ltd. (3) .... Edmonton AB
Royal Group Technologies Inc. (3) .... Woodbridge ON
S.A. Armstrong Ltd. (3) .... Toronto ON
Scarborough Hospital, General Division (3) .... Toronto ON
Schneider Electric Services (3) .... Mississauga ON
School District #60 (Peace River N (3) .... Fort St. John BC
SCI Brockville Corp. (3) .... Brockville ON
Seyler Electric Ltd. (3) .... Orangeville ON
Siemens Canada Ltd. (3) .... Mississauga ON
Smurfit-MBI (3) .... Burlington ON
Stackpole Ltd., Engineered Products (3) .... Mississauga ON
StockerYale Canada Inc. (3) .... St-Laurent QC
Tennant Company (3) .... Mississauga ON
Thomson Technology Inc. (3) .... Langley BC
Unicco Facility Services (3) .... Napanee ON
VA Tech Ferranti-Packard Transfor (3) .... St. Catharines ON
Vancouver, City of (3) .... Vancouver BC
Velan Inc. (3) .... Montréal QC
Waterloo North Hydro Inc. (3) .... Waterloo ON
Wentworth Mold Inc. (3) .... Hamilton ON
Yachiyo of Ontario Manufacturing Inc. / Y (3) .... Barrie ON
Zenastra Photonics Inc. (3) .... Ottawa ON
ABC Group Inc. (2) .... Toronto ON
Akinai (Calgary) Canada Inc. / ACI The I (2) .... Calgary AB
AlarmForce Industries Inc. (2) .... Toronto ON
Alcan Primary Metal Group (2) .... Kitimat BC
Almag Aluminum Inc. (2) .... Brampton ON
AMEC Earth & Environmental Ltd. (2) .... Calgary AB
Anderson Water Systems Ltd. (2) .... Dundas ON
Arrow Speed Controls Ltd. (2) .... Vancouver BC
Artitalia Inc. (2) .... Montréal QC
Astec Advanced Power Systems (2) .... St-Laurent QC
Atlantis Systems International (2) .... Brampton ON
Atlas Cold Storage Canada Ltd. (2) .... Toronto ON
ATS Automation Tooling Systems Inc. (2) .... Cambridge ON
Audio Centre (2) .... Ottawa ON
Barton Instrument Systems Ltd. (2) .... Calgary AB
Baxter Corporation (2) .... Alliston ON
BJ Pipeline Inspection Services (2) .... Calgary AB
BJ Process & Pipeline Services (2) .... Edmonton AB
Black & McDonald Ltd. (2) .... Toronto ON
Bradford West Gwillimbury, Town of (2) .... Bradford ON
British Columbia Institute of Technology (2) .... Burnaby BC
Burlington Technologies Inc., Alumetco (2) .... Brantford ON
Burlington Technologies Inc., Centenn (2) .... Burlington ON
CAE Machinery Ltd. (2) .... Vancouver BC
Calgary, City of (2) .... Calgary AB

For descriptions of the occupational categories used in this index, see page 458.

TRADES/TECHNICIANS (Cont.)

Canada Bread Company Ltd. (2) .... Toronto ON
Canadian Gypsum Company / CGC Inc. (2) .... Hagersville ON
CanAmera Foods (2) .... Hamilton ON
Capital Metal Industries (2) .... Toronto ON
Cimetrix Solutions Inc. (2) .... Markham ON
CIMTEK Automation Systems (2) .... Burlington ON
CMC Engineering and Management Limited (2) .... Vancouver BC
College of the North Atlantic, Clare (2) .... Clarenville NF
Communications Test Design, Inc. / CTDI (2) .... Oakville ON
Conestoga College of Applied Arts & Te (2) .... Kitchener ON
Continental Electric Motor Services (No (2) .... Edmonton AB
CPI Canada Inc. (2) .... Georgetown ON
Cropac Equipment Ltd. (2) .... Oakville ON
Crown Cork & Seal Canada Inc. (2) .... Concord ON
Dairyworld Foods Inc. (2) .... Brampton ON
Daito Precision Inc. (2) .... St-Laurent QC
Diebold Company of Canada, The (2) .... Mississauga ON
Domtar Inc., Communication Papers Divis (2) .... Cornwall ON
DSM Biologics (2) .... Montréal QC
Dynamic Source Manufacturing Inc. (2) .... Calgary AB
Eaglewest Truck and Crane Inc. (2) .... Abbotsford BC
EDS Innovations (2) .... Mississauga ON
Electronics Workbench (2) .... Toronto ON
Elimetal Inc. (2) .... St-Laurent QC
EMS Technologies Canada Ltd (2) .... Ste-Anne-de-Bellevue QC
Enersource (2) .... Mississauga ON
Fairview College (2) .... Fairview AB
Faurecia (2) .... Toronto ON
Festo Inc. (2) .... Mississauga ON
Filtel Microwave Inc. (2) .... Vaudreuil-Dorion QC
Flight Dynamics Corp. (2) .... St-Jean-sur-Richelieu QC
Flowserve Inc. (2) .... St. Thomas ON
Fluor Canada Ltd. (2) .... Calgary AB
Frost Fence & Wire Products Ltd. (2) .... Hamilton ON
FTI Consulting, Inc. (2) .... Mississauga ON
Gage Applied, Inc. (2) .... Lachine QC
GE Power Services (2) .... Mississauga ON
General Hydrogen / GH (2) .... Vancouver BC
Geo-X Systems Ltd., Aram Division (2) .... Calgary AB
George Brown College (2) .... Toronto ON
Grande Prairie, City of (Transpor (2) .... Grande Prairie AB
Graphic Controls Canada Ltd. (2) .... Gananoque ON
Griffith Laboratories Ltd. (2) .... Toronto ON
H.H. Angus & Associates Ltd. (2) .... Toronto ON
Halton District School Board, The (2) .... Burlington ON
Hamilton Health Sciences Corporation, C (2) .... Hamilton ON
Hay River Community Health Board (2) .... Hay River NT
Honda of Canada Manufacturing (2) .... Alliston ON
Hunting Oilfield Services (2) .... Calgary AB
Hydro Ottawa (2) .... Ottawa ON
Ilco Unican Inc. (2) .... Montréal QC
Image Processing Systems Inc. / IPS (2) .... Markham ON
Imperial Oil Resources (2) .... Bonnyville AB
Indalex Aluminum Solutions Group (2) .... Mississauga ON
Industry Training & Apprenticeship Comm (2) .... Victoria BC
Inforetech Wireless Technology Inc. (2) .... Surrey BC
Intalite Ceiling Systems (2) .... St-Laurent QC
IPC Resistors Inc. (2) .... Mississauga ON
IPSCO Inc. (2) .... Regina SK
J & S Refrigeration Ltd. (2) .... St. Catharines ON
JDS Uniphase Corporation (2) .... Saanichton BC
JFB Technologies Inc. (2) .... Markham ON
Kinectrics Inc. (2) .... Toronto ON
Kraft Foods Canada (2) .... Cobourg ON
Larco Industrial Services Ltd. (2) .... Stoney Creek ON
LeBlanc Ltd. (2) .... Oakville ON
Leesta Industries Ltd. (2) .... Pointe-Claire QC
Lethbridge Community College / LCC (2) .... Lethbridge AB
Levi Strauss & Co. (Canada) Inc. (2) .... Brantford ON
Levitt-Safety (2) .... Oakville ON
Linamar Corporation, Eston Division (2) .... Guelph ON
Lockheed Martin Canada Inc. (2) .... Kanata ON
Lumenon (2) .... St-Laurent QC
Luscar Ltd. (2) .... Edson AB
Mamac Systems (Canada) Ltd. (2) .... Markham ON
Manitoba Transportation & Government Se (2) .... Winnipeg MB
Manitoba Transportation & Government S (2) .... Steinbach MB
Maple Leaf Consumer Foods (2) .... Toronto ON
McCain Foods (Canada) (2) .... Coaldale AB

McCoy Bros. Inc. (2) .... Edmonton AB
McGill University, Facilities Managemen (2) .... Montréal QC
Meritor Suspension Systems Company (2) .... Milton ON
Metcon Sales and Engineering Ltd. (2) .... Concord ON
Ministry of Health and Long-Term Car (2) .... Thunder Bay ON
Ministry of the Solicitor General, Ontar (2) .... Toronto ON
Minolta Business Equipment (Canada), Lt (2) .... Richmond BC
Mississauga, City of (2) .... Mississauga ON
Mitchell's Gourmet Foods Inc. (2) .... Saskatoon SK
Mitec Telecom Inc. (2) .... Pointe-Claire QC
Montreal Port Authority / MPA (2) .... Montréal QC
Montréal, Ville de (2) .... Montréal QC
National Research Council Canada / NRC (2) .... Ottawa ON
Nielsen Media Research (2) .... Markham ON
Northwest Territories Power Corporatio (2) .... Hay River NT
NRB Inc. (2) .... Grimsby ON
O&Y Enterprise (2) .... Ottawa ON
Oakrun Farm Bakery Ltd. (2) .... Ancaster ON
Oerlikon Aerospace Inc. (2) .... St-Jean-sur-Richelieu QC
Ontario Clean Water Agency / OCWA (2) .... London ON
Ontario Power Generation, Bruce Nuclear (2) .... Tiverton ON
Ontario Power Generation Inc., Ottawa an (2) .... Renfrew ON
OPIsystems Inc. (2) .... Calgary AB
Ottawa-Carleton District School Board / O (2) .... Nepean ON
Owens Corning Canada (2) .... Guelph ON
PanCanadian Petroleum Ltd. (2) .... Calgary AB
Par-Pak Ltd. (2) .... Brampton ON
Patella Manufacturing Inc. (2) .... Lasalle QC
PerkinElmer Optoelectronics Inc. (2) .... Vaudreuil QC
Philip Services Corporation / PSC (2) .... Burlington ON
Pitney Bowes of Canada Ltd. (2) .... Richmond BC
Plantech Control Systems Inc. (2) .... Vineland ON
Polytainers Inc. (2) .... Toronto ON
Powerlasers Ltd. (2) .... Concord ON
Powertech Labs Inc. (2) .... Surrey BC
PrimeWest Energy Trust (2) .... Calgary AB
Proco Machinery Inc. (2) .... Mississauga ON
Propak Systems Ltd. (2) .... Airdrie AB
Public Service Commission of Canada, Ont (2) .... Toronto ON
Public Service Commission, PEI (2) .... Charlottetown PE
Purolator Courier Ltd. (2) .... Toronto ON
Quickmill Inc. (2) .... Peterborough ON
Ramco Electrical Consulting Ltd. (2) .... Calgary AB
Raylo Chemicals Inc. (2) .... Edmonton AB
Raytheon Systems Canada Ltd. (2) .... Waterloo ON
Reber Inc. / R-2000 Inc. (2) .... Riviere-des-Prairies QC
RGO Office Products (2) .... Calgary AB
Ricoh / Savin Canada Inc. (2) .... Mississauga ON
Rittal Systems Ltd. (2) .... Mississauga ON
Robin Hood Multifoods Inc., Bick's Pla (2) .... Dunnville ON
Rogers Cable Inc. (2) .... Toronto ON
Rogers Cable Inc. (2) .... Richmond Hill ON
Ryan Energy Technologies Inc. (2) .... Calgary AB
Saskatchewan Institute of Applied Scie (2) .... Saskatoon SK
SaskPower (2) .... Regina SK
Satisfied Brake Products Inc. (2) .... Cornwall ON
Schlumberger Resource Management Ser (2) ...... Mississauga ON
Schneider Foods Inc. (2) .... Port Perry ON
Schneider Foods Inc. (2) .... Mississauga ON
Scintrex Trace Corp. (2) .... Ottawa ON
SecurityLink Ameritech (2) .... Ottawa ON
Shoppers Home Health Care (2) .... Hamilton ON
Siemens Building Technologies Ltd. (2) .... Ottawa ON
Siemens Building Technologies Ltd., Cer (2) .... Richmond BC
Siemens Milltronics Process Instrum (2) .... Peterborough ON
Siemens Technical Services (2) .... Hamilton ON
Silex Inc. (2) .... Mississauga ON
SimplexGrinnell (2) .... Delta BC
Snap-On Tools of Canada Ltd. (2) .... Mississauga ON
SNC-Lavalin Inc., Chemicals & Petroleum (2) .... Calgary AB
Solectron (2) .... Calgary AB
Southern Alberta Institute of Technology (2) .... Calgary AB
Southmount Cable Ltd. (2) .... Hamilton ON
SSI Equipment Inc. (2) .... Burlington ON
St. Lawrence Seaway Management Co (2) .... St. Catharines ON
Stackpole Limited, Automotive Gear D (2) .... Mississauga ON
Standard Paper Box (2) .... Belleville ON
Stanley Door Systems (2) .... Brampton ON
Steelcase Canada Ltd. (2) .... Markham ON
Steris Canada Inc. (2) .... Mississauga ON
Superior Cabinets Alberta Ltd. (2) .... Edmonton AB
Superior Propane Inc. (2) .... Smithville ON

TRADES/TECHNICIANS (Cont.)

Taro Pharmaceuticals Inc. (2) .... Bramalea ON
TECO Precision Inc. (2) .... St-Laurent QC
Tesma International Inc. (2) .... Maple ON
Textron Fastening Systems (2) .... Gananoque ON
Thermo Design Engineering Ltd. (2) .... Edmonton AB
Timothy's World Coffee (2) .... Toronto ON
Titanium Ltd. (2) .... St-Laurent QC
Toronto Zoo (2) .... Toronto ON
Toshiba of Canada Limited (2) .... Markham ON
Tracer Industries Canada Ltd. (2) .... Edmonton AB
Tri Ocean Engineering Ltd. (2) .... Calgary AB
TRIUMF Meson Research Facility (2) .... Vancouver BC
Triumph Tool Ltd. (2) .... Guelph ON
Trivalence Mining Corporation (2) .... Vancouver BC
Trylon TSF (2) .... Elmira ON
Tube-Fab Ltd. (2) .... Mississauga ON
University of Lethbridge (2) .... Lethbridge AB
Venetor Equipment Rental Inc. (2) .... Hamilton ON
Walsh Automation / Validation Technolog (2) .... Montréal QC
Whitby Mental Health Centre (2) .... Whitby ON
Williams Machinery Ltd. (2) .... Richmond BC
Woco Automotive Inc. (2) .... Concord ON
Wolverine Ratcliffs Inc. (2) .... Fergus ON
Xerox Canada, Supplies Development C (2) .... Mississauga ON
Yaskawa Motoman Canada Ltd. (2) .... Mississauga ON
York Central Hospital (2) .... Richmond Hill ON
Zed.i Solutions (2) .... Edmonton AB
A. Berger Precision Ltd. (1) .... Brampton ON
A.G. Simpson Co. Limited (1) .... Cambridge ON
Aavid Thermal Products (1) .... Woodbridge ON
Abba Parts and Service (1) .... Burlington ON
Acklands-Grainger Inc. / AGI (1) .... Richmond Hill ON
Acres International Limited (1) .... Oakville ON
ADGA Group Consultants Inc. (1) .... Ottawa ON
AEdifica (1) .... Montréal QC
Agrium Inc. (1) .... Redwater AB
Air Products Canada Ltd. (1) .... Brampton ON
Alberta Community Development (1) .... Edmonton AB
Alberta Energy Company Ltd. / AEC (1) .... Calgary AB
Alberta Justice (1) .... Edmonton AB
Alberta Sustainable Resource Developmen (1) .... Edmonton AB
Alft (1) .... Hull QC
AMEC (1) .... Vancouver BC
American Appraisal Canada, Inc. (1) .... Toronto ON
Andrew Canada Inc. (1) .... Whitby ON
Applanix Corp. (1) .... Richmond Hill ON
APW Enclosure Systems (1) .... Milton ON
Argus Technologies Ltd. (1) .... Burnaby BC
AstraZeneca (1) .... Mississauga ON
ATCO Electric (1) .... Edmonton AB
Atlantic Packaging Products Ltd. (1) .... Toronto ON
Audio Centre (1) .... St-Laurent QC
Automation Tooling Systems Inc. / ATS (1) .... Oakville ON
Avestin Inc. (1) .... Ottawa ON
Avon Engineering Ltd. (1) .... Waterdown ON
Axis Logistics Inc. (1) .... Milton ON
BA Banknote Inc. (1) .... Ottawa ON
Backyard Products Limited (1) .... Collingwood ON
Bariatrix International Inc. (1) .... Lachine QC
Bartle & Gibson Co. Ltd. (1) .... Port Coquitlam BC
Basic Technologies Corporation (1) .... Welland ON
Bath Fitter / Bain Magique (1) .... St-Eustache QC
BC Rapid Transit Co. Ltd. / BCRTC (1) .... Burnaby BC
BCL Magnetics (1) .... Burlington ON
BCS Associates Ltd. (1) .... Belleville ON
Beckman Coulter Canada Inc. (1) .... Mississauga ON
Bell Intrigna (1) .... Calgary AB
Berminghammer Foundation Equipment (1) .... Hamilton ON
Beta Machinery Analysis Ltd. (1) .... Calgary AB
BF Goodrich Aerospace (1) .... Mississauga ON
Bizerba Canada (1) .... Mississauga ON
Bloorview MacMillan Children's Centre, M (1) .... Toronto ON
Bodycote Ortech Inc. (1) .... Mississauga ON
Boiler Inspection & Insurance Company of (1) .... Toronto ON
Bombardier Aerospace (1) .... Montréal QC
Bombardier Inc., Completion Centre Montre (1) .... Dorval QC
Bombardier Transport, Transit Systems (1) .... Burnaby BC
Bomhoff Aerospace Corporation (1) .... St-Laurent QC
Bracknell Telecom Services (1) .... Langley BC
Bradon Industries Ltd. / Hydra Rig Canad (1) .... Calgary AB
Brandt Tractor Ltd. (1) .... Edmonton AB
Brant Community Healthcare System, Bra (1) .... Brantford ON
Brookfield LePage Johnson Controls Facil (1) .... Markham ON
Brooks, Town of (1) .... Brooks AB
Brown Applied Technology Inc. (1) .... Toronto ON
Burlington, City of (1) .... Burlington ON
C-MAC Industries Inc. (1) .... Kanata ON
C-Tech Ltd. (1) .... Cornwall ON
Cadbury Trebor Allan Inc. (1) .... Hamilton ON
Caledon, Town of (1) .... Caledon East ON
Cambridge Custom Tooling (1) .... Cambridge ON
Canadian Bank Note Company, Ltd. (1) .... Ottawa ON
Canadian Museum of Civilization Corporation (1) .... Hull QC
Canem-Harbour (1) .... Port Coquitlam BC
Canpar Industries (1) .... Grand Forks BC
Carrier Canada Ltd. (1) .... Edmonton AB
Carrier Canada Ltd. (1) .... Calgary AB
Cascade (1) .... Mississauga ON
CashCode (1) .... Concord ON
Casino Niagara (1) .... Niagara Falls ON
Catena Networks (1) .... Kanata ON
CB Engineering Ltd. (1) .... Calgary AB
CBCL Limited (1) .... Halifax NS
Cellex Power Products Inc. (1) .... Richmond BC
Central Precast Inc. (1) .... Nepean ON
Chem Systems Inc. (1) .... Burlington ON
Chemque Inc. (1) .... Toronto ON
Children's and Women's Health Centre o (1) .... Vancouver BC
Christie Lites (1) .... Toronto ON
CIBA Vision Sterile Manufacturing (1) .... Mississauga ON
Circuit Graphics Ltd. (1) .... Burnaby BC
Clifton Associates Ltd. (1) .... Calgary AB
CML Emergency Services, Inc. (1) .... Hull QC
CMP Design (1) .... Kanata ON
Coinamatic Canada Inc. (1) .... Mississauga ON
College of New Caledonia (1) .... Prince George BC
Collins & Aikman (1) .... Toronto ON
Columbia MBF (1) .... Mississauga ON
CompCanada Atlas (1) .... Edmonton AB
Computing Devices Canada Ltd. / CDC (1) .... Calgary AB
Computing Devices Canada Ltd. / CDC (1) .... Ottawa ON
Comstock Canada Ltd. (1) .... Edmonton AB
Comstock Canada Ltd (1) .... Mississauga ON
Conair Consumer Products Inc. (1) .... Brampton ON
Concord Confections Inc. (1) .... Concord ON
Coneco Equipment Inc. (1) .... Edmonton AB
Consultronics Ltd. (1) .... Concord ON
Corma Inc. (1) .... Concord ON
Corrpro Canada, Inc. / Corrpower (1) .... Edmonton AB
CryoCath Technologies Inc. (1) .... Kirkland QC
CTF Systems Inc. (1) .... Port Coquitlam BC
CTS of Canada Ltd. (1) .... Streetsville ON
Cytec Canada Inc. (1) .... Niagara Falls ON
Dailybread (1) .... Toronto ON
Daminco Inc. (1) .... Oakville ON
Dana Long Manufacturing Ltd. (1) .... Mississauga ON
Danka Canada Inc. (1) .... Brampton ON
DBR Research Ltd. (1) .... Edmonton AB
Debiasi Group, The / DBG (1) .... Mississauga ON
Debiasi Group, The / DBG (1) .... Mississauga ON
Delta Controls Inc. (1) .... Surrey BC
Deluxe Laboratories (1) .... Toronto ON
Denso Manufacturing Canada, Inc. (1) .... Guelph ON
Department of Human Resources, Nuna (1) .... Rankin Inlet NU
Department of Public Safety, NB (1) .... Fredericton NB
Department of Works, Services and Tr (1) .... Clarenville NF
Dimax Controls Inc. (1) .... Toronto ON
Domtar Inc., Ottawa / Hull Mills (1) .... Hull QC
Dorigo Systems Ltd. (1) .... Burnaby BC
Dresser Flow Control (1) .... Burlington ON
Ducks Unlimited Canada (1) .... Oak Hammock Marsh MB
Duocom Canada (1) .... Richmond Hill ON
Duplium Corporation (1) .... Thornhill ON
DuPont Canada Inc. (1) .... Kingston ON
Durham, The Regional Municipality of (1) .... Whitby ON
DY 4 Systems Inc. (1) .... Kanata ON
Dynapro (1) .... Annacis Island BC
E.S. Fox Ltd. (1) .... Niagara Falls ON
Earth Tech Canada Inc. (1) .... Markham ON
EBA Engineering Consultants Ltd. (1) .... Edmonton AB
Ecoplans Ltd. (1) .... Kitchener ON

For descriptions of the occupational categories used in this index, see page 458.

OCCUPATIONAL INDEX 563

TRADES/TECHNICIANS (Cont.)

Edmonton Catholic Schools (1) .... Edmonton AB
Edmonton Public Schools (1) .... Edmonton AB
EFX Enerflex Systems Ltd. (1) .... Calgary AB
Egan Visual (1) .... Woodbridge ON
Elyps Dispatch Solutions (1) .... Burnaby BC
EMC Group Ltd. (1) .... Concord ON
EMS Technologies Canada Ltd. (1) .... Ottawa ON
Energy Industries Inc. (1) .... Calgary AB
Epson Research and Development, Inc., (1) .... Vancouver BC
ESBI Alberta Ltd. (1) .... Calgary AB
Ethan Allen Home Interiors (1) .... Thornhill ON
Evertz Microsystems Ltd. (1) .... Burlington ON
F&P Manufacturing, Inc. (1) .... Tottenham ON
FCX Specialty Valves (1) .... Mississauga ON
Federation CJA (1) .... Montréal QC
Fellfab Limited (1) .... Hamilton ON
Finning (Canada) International Inc. (1) .... Edmonton AB
Fisher Scientific (1) .... Nepean ON
Flint Energy Services Ltd. (1) .... Edmonton AB
Flowserve Inc. (1) .... Woodbridge ON
Focus Microwaves Inc. (1) .... St-Laurent QC
Forensic Technology Inc. (1) .... Cote St. Luc QC
Frontier (1) .... Calgary AB
Fugro Airborne Surveys (1) .... Mississauga ON
Future Shop Ltd. (1) .... Mississauga ON
G-P Flakeboard Company (1) .... Bancroft ON
GE Syprotec Inc. (1) .... Pointe-Claire QC
General Equipment Ltd. (1) .... Vancouver BC
General Motors of Canada Ltd., Diesel Div (1) .... London ON
Genfast Manufacturing Company (1) .... Brantford ON
Georgian College (1) .... Barrie ON
GHQ Imaging Inkjet Productions Ltd. (1) .... Toronto ON
GKO Engineering (1) .... Edmonton AB
GlaxoSmithKline (1) .... Mississauga ON
Golden Mill Bakery (1) .... Hamilton ON
Graham Packaging Canada (1) .... Burlington ON
Graham Packaging Canada Ltd. (1) .... Mississauga ON
Grand & Toy Ltd. (1) .... Vaughan ON
H. Paulin & Co. Limited (1) .... Toronto ON
Haliburton & White Group, Th (1) .... Dollard-des-Ormeaux QC
Halifax Shipyard Limited (1) .... Halifax NS
Halton Hills, Town of (1) .... Halton Hills ON
Hamilton Hydro Inc. (1) .... Hamilton ON
Harris Computer Services (1) .... Mississauga ON
Heidelberg Canada (1) .... Mississauga ON
Henry Schein Arcona Inc. (1) .... St. Catharines ON
Hitachi Canada, Ltd. (1) .... Mississauga ON
Hitec Systems and Controls Inc. (1) .... Calgary AB
Honeywell Ltd. (1) .... Edmonton AB
Honeywell Ltd., Industrial Automation an (1) .... Calgary AB
Hudson Bay Mining and Smelting Co., Lt (1) .... Flin Flon MB
Hyd-Mech Group Ltd. (1) .... Woodstock ON
IDEC Canada, Ltd. (1) .... Mississauga ON
IDMD Design & Manufacturing Inc. (1) .... Toronto ON
iFire Technology Inc. (1) .... Toronto ON
iMPath Networks Inc. (1) .... Nepean ON
Inex Pharmaceuticals Corp. (1) .... Burnaby BC
InfoSpec Systems Inc. (1) .... Burnaby BC
Innovator Electronic Assembly / IEA (1) .... Lachine QC
Interactive Circuits and Systems Ltd. (1) .... Gloucester ON
Interautomation Inc. (1) .... Oakville ON
Intercon Security Ltd. (1) .... Toronto ON
Intergen Biomanufacturing Corporation (1) .... Toronto ON
International Group Inc., The / IGI (1) .... Toronto ON
International Utility Structures Inc. (1) .... Calgary AB
Iris Power Engineering Inc. (1) .... Toronto ON
IS2 Research Inc. (1) .... Nepean ON
ITT Fluid Products Canada (1) .... Guelph ON
J & J Display Sales Ltd. (1) .... Mississauga ON
Jacques Whitford Environment Ltd. (1) .... Ottawa ON
Jayne Industries Inc. (1) .... Stoney Creek ON
JDS Uniphase Corporation (1) .... Nepean ON
John Abbott College (1) .... Ste-Anne-de-Bellevue QC
Johnson & Johnson Medical Products (1) .... Markham ON
Joseph Brant Memorial Hospital (1) .... Burlington ON
JVC Canada Inc. (1) .... Toronto ON
KB Electronics Limited (1) .... Halifax NS
KCI Medical Canada, Inc. (1) .... Mississauga ON
Keyano College (1) .... Fort McMurray AB
Kinross Gold Corp., Timmins Operation (1) .... Schumacher ON
Kodak Canada Inc. (1) .... Toronto ON
Korex Canada (1) .... Toronto ON
Kubes Steel Ltd. (1) .... Stoney Creek ON
Lac de Gras Excavation Inc. (1) .... Yellowknife NT
Laird Plastics (Canada) Inc. (1) .... Mississauga ON
Langley, City of (1) .... Langley BC
Lanier Canada Inc. (1) .... Vancouver BC
Lanier Canada Inc. (1) .... Mississauga ON
Lantern Communications Canada Inc. (1) .... Ottawa ON
Laurysen Kitchens Ltd. (1) .... Stittsville ON
LensCrafters (1) .... Toronto ON
Lincoln Technology Corporation (1) .... Edmonton AB
Linear Transfer Systems Ltd. (1) .... Barrie ON
Lockerbie Industra Inc. (1) .... New Westminster BC
Lombard Canada Ltd. (1) .... Toronto ON
London, City of (1) .... London ON
London Health Sciences Centre / LHSC (1) .... London ON
London Hydro (1) .... London ON
Loyalist Township (1) .... Odessa ON
MacDonald Dettwiler & Associates Ltd. / (1) .... Richmond BC
Magna IV Engineering Ltd. (1) .... Edmonton AB
Manitoba Aboriginal & Northern Affairs (1) .... Winnipeg MB
Manitoba Justice / Culture, Heritage an (1) .... Winnipeg MB
Manitoba Labour & Immigration (1) .... Winnipeg MB
Manitoba Transportation & Government Ser (1) .... Dauphin MB
Manitoba Transportation & Gov (1) .... Portage la Prairie MB
Manitoba Transportation & Government Ser (1) .... Brandon MB
Mansour Mining Inc. (1) .... Sudbury ON
Maple Leaf Pork (1) .... Brandon MB
Maple Leaf Pork, Case Reddi Facilit (1) .... Stoney Creek ON
Maple Leaf Poultry (1) .... Toronto ON
Maple Lodge Farms Ltd. (1) .... Norval ON
Maple Reinders Inc. (1) .... Brampton ON
Maple Ridge, District of (1) .... Maple Ridge BC
March Networks Corporation (1) .... Kanata ON
Maritime Hydraulics (Canada) Ltd. (1) .... Calgary AB
Markham, Corporation of the Town of (1) .... Markham ON
Marsan Foods Ltd. (1) .... Toronto ON
Matrikon Group (1) .... Richmond BC
McCormick Rankin Corporation (1) .... Mississauga ON
McCrum's Office Furnishings (1) .... Calgary AB
McElhanney Group Ltd., The (1) .... Vancouver BC
McMaster University (1) .... Hamilton ON
Medicine Hat, City of (1) .... Medicine Hat AB
MedTec Marketing Limited (1) .... Burnaby BC
Mentor Engineering (1) .... Calgary AB
Merck Frosst Canada & Co. / Merck (1) .... Pointe-Claire QC
Metro Tool and Die Ltd. / MTD (1) .... Mississauga ON
Miele Ltd. (1) .... Richmond Hill ON
Ministry of Community and Social Service (1) .... Orillia ON
Ministry of Community and Social Service (1) .... Toronto ON
Ministry of Correctional Services, Ontar (1) .... Toronto ON
Ministry of Correctional Services, Onta (1) .... Kingston ON
Ministry of Education / Ministry of Trai (1) .... Toronto ON
Ministry of Small Business, Touris (1) .... Prince George BC
Ministry of Transportation, BC (1) .... Victoria BC
Ministry of Transportation, Ontario (1) .... Toronto ON
Minolta Business Equipment (Canada), Ltd (1) .... Markham ON
Minolta (Montreal) Inc. (1) .... St-Laurent QC
Mitel Corporation (1) .... Kanata ON
Moody International Ltd. (1) .... Edmonton AB
Moore Products Company (Canada) Inc. (1) .... Brampton ON
MOSAID Technologies Inc. (1) .... Kanata ON
Nabors International Inc. (1) .... Calgary AB
Nanometrics Inc. (1) .... Kanata ON
Nanowave Technologies Inc. (1) .... Toronto ON
National Paper Goods (1) .... Hamilton ON
National Research Council Canada, Institu (1) .... Ottawa ON
National Research Council Canada / NRC (1) .... Winnipeg MB
National Research Council Canada / NRC (1) .... Ottawa ON
National Research Council Canada / NRC (1) .... Ottawa ON
NAV Canada (1) .... Ottawa ON
Neilson Dairy (1) .... Ottawa ON
NEPCAN Engineering Ltd. (1) .... Vancouver BC
Net Safety Monitoring Inc. (1) .... Calgary AB
New Frontiers School Board (1) .... Chateauguay QC
Nextrom Ltd. (1) .... Concord ON
Niagara, The Regional Municipality of (1) .... Thorold ON
Nitrex Metal Inc. (1) .... St-Laurent QC
Noranda Inc. (1) .... Pointe-Claire QC
Nortel Networks (1) .... Ottawa ON

TRADES/TECHNICIANS (Cont.)

NSI Communications (1) ... Pointe-Claire QC
Nucon Systems Inc. (1) ... Markham ON
NxtPhase Corporation (1) ... Vancouver BC
O'Hara Technologies Inc. (1) ... Richmond Hill ON
Ottawa Hospital, The (1) ... Ottawa ON
Owen Sound, City of (1) ... Owen Sound ON
P&H MinePro Services (1) ... Calgary AB
Palfinger Inc. (1) ... Niagara Falls ON
Parmalat Canada (1) ... Toronto ON
Patheon Inc. (1) ... Toronto ON
Patheon Inc. (1) ... Mississauga ON
PCL Constructors Inc. (1) ... Edmonton AB
Peacock Inc. (1) ... Edmonton AB
Pechiney Plastic Packaging (Canada) Inc (1) ... Brampton ON
Peel Lumber (1) ... Milton ON
Peerless Clothing Inc. (1) ... Montréal QC
Peter Kiewit Sons Co. Ltd. (1) ... Edmonton AB
Peterborough Utilities Commission (1) ... Peterborough ON
Peto MacCallum Ltd. (1) ... Toronto ON
Philips Analytical (1) ... Waterloo ON
Phoenix Contact Ltd. (1) ... Mississauga ON
Phoenix Technology Services LP (1) ... Calgary AB
Pillsbury Canada Limited (1) ... Midland ON
Port Colborne, City of (1) ... Port Colborne ON
Power Measurement Ltd. (1) ... Victoria BC
Praxair Canada Inc. (1) ... Mississauga ON
Providence Health Care, Mount St. Jose (1) ... Vancouver BC
Provincial Store Fixtures Ltd. (1) ... Mississauga ON
Psion Teklogix Inc. (1) ... Mississauga ON
Public Service Commission of Canada, Al (1) ... Edmonton AB
Public Service Commission of Canada, B (1) ... Vancouver BC
Public Service Commission of Canada, Nov (1) ... Halifax NS
Public Service Commission of Canada, Qu (1) ... Montréal QC
Public Service Commission of Canada, (1) ... Quebec City QC
Pure Technologies Inc. (1) ... Calgary AB
Quaker Oats Company of Canada Limit (1) ... Peterborough ON
R.L. Brews Ltd. (1) ... Calgary AB
R.V. Anderson Associates Limited (1) ... Toronto ON
Ramada Plaza Hotel Harbourfront (1) ... Kingston ON
Rea International Inc. (1) ... Mississauga ON
Red Carpet Food Services (1) ... Stoney Creek ON
Red Deer College (1) ... Red Deer AB
Regina, City of (1) ... Regina SK
Regional Doors and Hardware (1) ... St. Catharines ON
RexCan Circuits Inc. (1) ... Belleville ON
Ridgewood Industries (1) ... Cornwall ON
Rivtow Marine Ltd. (1) ... Vancouver BC
Rocky Mountain Instruments Inc. / RMI (1) ... Edmonton AB
Rogers AT&T Wireless (1) ... Burnaby BC
Rogers Cable Inc. (1) ... Kitchener ON
Rogers Cable Inc. (1) ... Saint John NB
Ropak Canada Inc. (1) ... Oakville ON
Royal Canadian Mint / RCM (1) ... Ottawa ON
Samson Controls Inc. (1) ... Markham ON
Schlumberger Completion Systems (1) ... Calgary AB
Schneider Electric (1) ... Toronto ON
School District #06 (Rocky Mountain) (1) ... Kimberly BC
Sciemetric Instruments Inc. (1) ... Nepean ON
Scott Springfield Manufacturing Inc. (1) ... Calgary AB
Sedona Networks (1) ... Kanata ON
Selkirk College, Castlegar Campus (1) ... Castlegar BC
Semiconductor Insights Inc. (1) ... Kanata ON
Senstar-Stellar Corporation (1) ... Carp ON
Serco Facilities Management Inc. (1) ... Goose Bay NF
Shred-it (1) ... Oakville ON
Sicht-Pack Hagner Inc. (1) ... St-Laurent QC
Siemens Milltronics Process Instruments (1) ... Edmonton AB
SimplexGrinnell (1) ... Mississauga ON
Simplot Canada Limited (1) ... Brandon MB
Sky Eye America (1) ... Dorval QC
Skyway Business Machines (1) ... Mississauga ON
Solinet Systems Inc. (1) ... Ottawa ON
Span Manufacturing Ltd. (1) ... Markham ON
Spielo Gaming International (1) ... Dieppe NB
St. Joseph's Health Centre (1) ... Toronto ON
St. Lawrence College (1) ... Kingston ON
St. Peter's Health Services (1) ... Hamilton ON
Strongco Equipment (1) ... Stittsville ON
Sudbury Neutrino Observatory / SNO (1) ... Lively ON
Sulzer Mitroflow Corp. (1) ... Richmond BC
Sunnybrook & Women's College Health Scie (1) ... Toronto ON
Supreme Tooling Group (1) ... Toronto ON
Surrey, City of (1) ... Surrey BC
SWL Crane & Hoist 2000 Ltd. (1) ... Brampton ON
Symagery Microsystems Inc. (1) ... Kanata ON
Systemcorp ALG Ltd. (1) ... Montréal QC
Sytek Enterprises Inc. (1) ... North Vancouver BC
Talon Systems Inc. (1) ... Mississauga ON
Taylor Steel Inc. (1) ... Hamilton ON
Techmire Ltd. (1) ... Anjou QC
TELAV Audio Visual Services (1) ... Vancouver BC
TELAV Audio Visual Services (1) ... Toronto ON
Teldon International Inc. (1) ... Richmond BC
Tenaquip Ltd. (1) ... Ste-Anne-de-Bellevue QC
Teng & Associates Inc. (1) ... Mississauga ON
Testforce (1) ... St-Laurent QC
Tilbury Cement Ltd. (1) ... Delta BC
Tim Office Solutions (1) ... Toronto ON
TOA Canada Corporation (1) ... Mississauga ON
TOA Inc. (1) ... Toronto ON
Torcan Chemical Ltd. (1) ... Aurora ON
Toronto Catholic District School Board (1) ... Toronto ON
Toronto Star Newspapers Ltd., Press C (1) ... Woodbridge ON
TorPharm (1) ... Toronto ON
Totten Sims Hubicki Associates / TSH (1) ... Whitby ON
Trail Appliances Ltd. (1) ... Calgary AB
Trane Central Ontario (1) ... Toronto ON
TransAlta Corporation, Sundance Generat (1) ... Duffield AB
Tresco Industries (1) ... Calgary AB
Triathlon (1) ... Richmond BC
Trillium Health Centre (1) ... Toronto ON
Trillium Photonics (1) ... Ottawa ON
Trophy Foods Inc. (1) ... Mississauga ON
Trudell Medical International / TMI (1) ... London ON
Tubular Steel Inc. (1) ... Toronto ON
Underwriters' Laboratories of Canada / U (1) ... Toronto ON
Unisearch Associates Inc. (1) ... Concord ON
University of Alberta, Department of Ph (1) ... Edmonton AB
University of Guelph (1) ... Guelph ON
University of Toronto, Operations & Serv (1) ... Toronto ON
University of Waterloo (1) ... Waterloo ON
Valley City Manufacturing Company Limited (1) ... Dundas ON
Vancouver International Airport Authori (1) ... Richmond BC
Vansco Electronics Ltd. (1) ... Winnipeg MB
Vaughan, City of (1) ... Vaughan ON
Videoscope (1) ... Toronto ON
Volvo Motor Graders (1) ... Goderich ON
VQuip Inc. (1) ... Burlington ON
Vulcain Inc. (1) ... Delson QC
Wainbee Limited (1) ... Mississauga ON
Wajax Industries Limited (1) ... Edmonton AB
Walter Cumbria Engineering Ltd. / WCEL (1) ... Edmonton AB
WANN Connection Devices Inc. (1) ... Nepean ON
Wavesat Telecom Inc. (1) ... St-Laurent QC
Weidmuller Ltd. (1) ... Markham ON
Weishaupt Corporation (1) ... Mississauga ON
Wescast Industries Inc. (1) ... Brantford ON
Wesco Distribution Canada Inc. (1) ... Burnaby BC
Western Pulp Limited Partnership, Por (1) ... Port Alice BC
Westpower Equipment Ltd. (1) ... Calgary AB
Winpak Technologies Inc. (1) ... Toronto ON
Xantrex Technology Inc. (1) ... Burnaby BC
Xebec Imaging Services Inc. (1) ... Ottawa ON
Zed.i Solutions (1) ... Calgary AB

TRANSPORT

See also: Logistics, Operations, Aerospace, Automotive.

Alberta Infrastructure & Transportation (29 positions) Edmonton AB
Earth Tech Canada Inc. (27) ... Markham ON
Totten Sims Hubicki Associates / TSH (27) ... Whitby ON
Manitoba Transportation & Government Se (26) ... Winnipeg MB
Toronto Transit Commission / TTC (20) ... Toronto ON
Ministry of Transportation, Ontario (16) ... London ON
Ministry of Transportation, Ontario (16) ... Toronto ON
Ministry of Transportation, Ontar (15) ... St. Catharines ON
EBA Engineering Consultants Ltd. (14) ... Edmonton AB
Lea Consulting Ltd. (10) ... Toronto ON

For descriptions of the occupational categories used in this index, see page 458.

OCCUPATIONAL INDEX 565

TRANSPORT (Cont.)

Manitoba Transportation & Government Ser (10) .... Brandon MB
Ministry of Transportation, Ontario (10) .... Thunder Bay ON
Manitoba Transportation & Gov (9) .... Portage la Prairie MB
Ministry of Transportation, Ontario (9) .... North Bay ON
Ministry of Transportation, Ontario (9) .... Kingston ON
Calgary, City of (8) .... Calgary AB
Manitoba Highways & Transportation, Abo (8) .... Thompson MB
Manitoba Transportation & Government S (8) .... Steinbach MB
McElhanney Group Ltd., The (8) .... Vancouver BC
N.D. Lea Consultants Ltd. (8) .... Vancouver BC
Alberta Transportation (7) .... Edmonton AB
Manitoba Transportation & Government Ser (7) .... Dauphin MB
Ministry of Transportation, Ontario (7) .... New Liskeard ON
Mississauga, City of (7) .... Mississauga ON
Firm Transportation & Distribution Servi (6) .... Toronto ON
Giffels Associates Limited (6) .... Toronto ON
URS Cole, Sherman (6) .... Thornhill ON
AMEC Infrastructure Ltd. (5) .... Sherwood Park AB
Canarail Consultants Inc. (5) .... Montréal QC
ICS Courier Services (5) .... Mississauga ON
Marshall Macklin Monaghan Limited (5) .... Thornhill ON
Maxim Rentals and Leasing (5) .... Edmonton AB
Ministry of Transportation, BC (5) .... Nelson BC
Oshawa, City of (5) .... Oshawa ON
Public Service Commission of Canada, Onta (5) .... Ottawa ON
TCT Daily Motor Freight (5) .... Mississauga ON
Waterloo, The Regional Municipality of (5) .... Kitchener ON
Alberta Infrastructure & Transportation (4) .... Edmonton AB
BC Rapid Transit Co. Ltd. / BCRTC (4) .... Burnaby BC
Brantford, Corporation of the City of (4) .... Brantford ON
CH2M HILL Canada Ltd. (4) .... Toronto ON
Delcan Corporation (4) .... Niagara Falls ON
Dillon Consulting Ltd. (4) .... London ON
Dillon Consulting Ltd. (4) .... Toronto ON
GO Transit / Greater Toronto Transit Aut (4) .... Toronto ON
Guelph, City of (4) .... Guelph ON
Mackie Moving Systems (4) .... Oshawa ON
McCormick Rankin Corporation (4) .... Mississauga ON
Oerlikon Aerospace Inc. (4) .... St-Jean-sur-Richelieu QC
Public Service Commission of Canada, (4) .... Quebec City QC
Rosedale Transport Ltd. (4) .... Mississauga ON
Sandwell Engineering Inc. (4) .... Vancouver BC
Stantec Geomatics Ltd. (4) .... Edmonton AB
Stock Transportation Limited (4) .... Aurora ON
Surrey, City of (4) .... Surrey BC
Trow Consulting Engineers Ltd. (4) .... Brampton ON
United Parcel Service Canada Ltd. / UPS (4) .... Lachine QC
Vancouver, City of (4) .... Vancouver BC
Alcatel Canada Inc., Transport Automatio (3) .... Toronto ON
Atlas Cold Storage Canada Ltd. (3) .... Toronto ON
BC Transit (3) .... Victoria BC
Canadian Pacific Railway / CPR (3) .... Calgary AB
Clifton ND Lea Consulting Inc. (3) .... Calgary AB
Delcan Corporation (3) .... Toronto ON
Department of Works, Services and Tra (3) .... St. John's NF
IBI Group (3) .... Toronto ON
ICS Courier Services (3) .... Toronto ON
Kelowna, City of (3) .... Kelowna BC
Kingston, Corporation of the City of (3) .... Kingston ON
McCormick Rankin Corporation (3) .... Ottawa ON
Morrison Hershfield (3) .... Toronto ON
Muir's Cartage Limited (3) .... Concord ON
Oakville, Corporation of the Town of (3) .... Oakville ON
Overseas Express Consolidators Inc. / O (3) .... Montréal QC
Sewer-Matic Services Inc. (3) .... Ottawa ON
Shred-it (3) .... Oakville ON
TCT Logistics Inc. (3) .... Mississauga ON
TWF Logistics Group Inc. (3) .... Mississauga ON
United Parcel Service Canada Ltd. / UPS (3) .... Calgary AB
UPS Logistics Group Canada Limited (3) .... Oakville ON
York, The Regional Municipality of (3) .... Newmarket ON
ZTR Control Systems Inc. (3) .... London ON
Alberta Motor Association / AMA (2) .... Edmonton AB
Altruck International Truck Centres (2) .... Hamilton ON
AMEC (2) .... Vancouver BC
BC Rail Ltd. (2) .... North Vancouver BC
Bombardier Transportation (2) .... Toronto ON
Brampton, City of (2) .... Brampton ON
British Columbia Automobile Association (2) .... Burnaby BC
CAA Central Ontario (2) .... Thornhill ON
Canada 3000 Cargo Inc. (2) .... Mississauga ON
Carmanah Technologies Inc. (2) .... Victoria BC
Catholic District School Board of Eas (2) .... Kemptville ON
Climan Transport Services (2) .... Lachine QC
Con-Way Canada Express (2) .... Toronto ON
Con-Way Canada Express / Con-Way Tra (2) .... Mississauga ON
Conair Consumer Products Inc. (2) .... Brampton ON
Day & Ross Transportation Group, The (2) .... Hartland NB
Delcan Corporation (2) .... New Westminster BC
Delcan Corporation (2) .... London ON
Delcan Corporation (2) .... Gloucester ON
Department of Municipal and Provincia (2) .... St. John's NF
DHL International Express Ltd. (2) .... Calgary AB
Dibblee Construction Ltd. (2) .... Kingston ON
Direct Integrated Transporation (2) .... Edmonton AB
Direct Service Network Ltd. / DSN (2) .... Mississauga ON
Discount Car and Truck Rentals (2) .... Toronto ON
Eaglewest Truck and Crane Inc. (2) .... Abbotsford BC
Ecoplans Ltd. (2) .... Kitchener ON
Emery Worldwide (2) .... Mississauga ON
Fednav International Ltd. (2) .... Montréal QC
Fraser Surrey Docks Ltd. (2) .... Surrey BC
Hercules Inc. (2) .... Toronto ON
Highland Transport (2) .... Markham ON
Kent Line International Limited (2) .... Saint John NB
Loadstar Dispatchers / Northern Industr (2) .... Edmonton AB
Loomis Courier Service (2) .... Calgary AB
Manitoulin Transport (2) .... Gore Bay ON
Markham, Corporation of the Town of (2) .... Markham ON
Ministry of Transportation, Ontario (Dri (2) .... Toronto ON
National Car Rental (2) .... Toronto ON
Northern Star Trucking Ltd. (2) .... Toronto ON
Overseas Courier Service Ltd. / OCS (2) .... Mississauga ON
PHH Vehicle Management Services Inc. (2) .... Mississauga ON
Philip Services Corporation / PSC (2) .... Burlington ON
Purolator Courier Ltd. (2) .... Calgary AB
Purolator Courier Ltd. (2) .... Toronto ON
R.V. Anderson Associates Limited (2) .... Toronto ON
Reimer Express Lines Ltd. (2) .... Winnipeg MB
Ryder Transportation Services (2) .... Mississauga ON
Schneider National (2) .... Guelph ON
SMED International Inc. (2) .... Calgary AB
SNC-Lavalin Inc. (2) .... Vancouver BC
Sysco Food Services of Ontario (2) .... Peterborough ON
TDL Group Ltd., The (Distribution Centr (2) .... Oakville ON
Thrifty Car Rental (2) .... Richmond BC
Tower Group International Canada Inc. (2) .... Montréal QC
Trow Consulting Engineers Ltd. (2) .... London ON
UMA Engineering Ltd. (2) .... Burnaby BC
UMA Engineering Ltd. (2) .... Toronto ON
United Parcel Service Canada Ltd. / UPS (2) .... Delta BC
United Van Lines (Canada) Ltd. (2) .... Mississauga ON
Van-Kam Freightways Ltd. (2) .... Burnaby BC
Veri Transport Logistics (2) .... Exeter ON
Xtra Lease (2) .... Lachine QC
Acomarit Canada Inc. (1) .... Montréal QC
Acres International Limited (1) .... Vancouver BC
Acres International Limited (1) .... Oakville ON
AirIQ Inc. (1) .... Pickering ON
Ajax, Town of (1) .... Ajax ON
Akzo Nobel Coatings Ltd. (1) .... Toronto ON
Alberta Health and Wellness (1) .... Edmonton AB
Alberta Justice (1) .... Edmonton AB
ALNAV Platinum Group Inc. (1) .... Edmonton AB
ARI Financial Services Inc. (1) .... Mississauga ON
Armbro Construction Ltd. (1) .... Brampton ON
Atlas Van Lines (Canada) Ltd. (1) .... Oakville ON
Azurix North America (1) .... Hamilton ON
Bath Fitter / Bain Magique (1) .... St-Eustache QC
BC Hydro (1) .... Vancouver BC
BC Transportation Financing Authority / (1) .... Victoria BC
Bombardier Transport, Transit Systems (1) .... Burnaby BC
Bombardier Transportation (1) .... Kingston ON
Bot Construction Limited (1) .... Oakville ON
Bridge Brand Food Services Ltd. (1) .... Calgary AB
CAA South Central Ontario (1) .... Hamilton ON
Canadian Broadcasting Corporation / CBC (1) .... Ottawa ON
CH2M HILL Canada Ltd. (1) .... Calgary AB
Computing Devices Canada Ltd. / CDC (1) .... Ottawa ON
Dan Mulrooney Disposal Ltd. (1) .... Kingston ON

TRANSPORT (Cont.)

David Schaeffer Engineering Ltd. (1) .... Markham ON
Dennison Chevrolet Oldsmobile Ltd. (1) .... Richmond BC
Department of Human Resources, Nuna (1) .... Rankin Inlet NU
Department of Human Resources, Nunavut (1) .... Iqaluit NU
Department of Works, Services and Tr (1) .... Clarenville NF
DHL International Express Ltd. (1) .... Richmond BC
DHL International Express Ltd. (1) .... Nepean ON
Dillon Consulting Ltd. (1) .... Ottawa ON
Dillon Engineering Ltd. (1) .... Winnipeg MB
Durham, The Regional Municipality of (1) .... Whitby ON
Emerald International Inc. (1) .... Toronto ON
Enterprise Rent-A-Car (1) .... Nepean ON
Ethan Allen Home Interiors (1) .... Brampton ON
Fairview College (1) .... Fairview AB
Faucher Industries Inc. (1) .... St-Leonard QC
Federal Express Canada / FedEx (1) .... Mississauga ON
Federated Co-operatives Limited / FCL (1) .... Calgary AB
Federated Co-operatives Limited / FCL (1) .... Saskatoon SK
GE Capital Services / GECS (1) .... Mississauga ON
Grand & Toy Ltd. (1) .... Vaughan ON
Greater Toronto Airports Authority / GTA (1) .... Toronto ON
Greyhound Canada Transportation Corp. (1) .... Calgary AB
Haliburton & White Group, Th (1) .... Dollard-des-Ormeaux QC
Halifax Shipyard Limited (1) .... Halifax NS
Hamilton, City of (1) .... Hamilton ON
Hamilton Health Sciences Corporation, C (1) .... Hamilton ON
Hamilton-Wentworth, Regional Municipali (1) .... Hamilton ON
Hema-Quebec (1) .... St-Laurent QC
Hofland Ltd. (1) .... Mississauga ON
Hunter Amenities International Ltd. (1) .... Burlington ON
Huron, County of (1) .... Goderich ON
Inland Aggregates Ltd. (1) .... Calgary AB
ITT Fluid Products Canada (1) .... Langley BC
Justice Institute of BC / JIBC (1) .... New Westminster BC
Kelron Logistics (1) .... Surrey BC
Kitchener, City of (1) .... Kitchener ON
Kohl & Frisch Limited (1) .... Concord ON
Labatt Breweries Ontario (1) .... Toronto ON
Linamar Corporation, Autocom Division (1) .... Guelph ON
Linamar Corporation, Eston Division (1) .... Guelph ON
Lincoln, Town of (1) .... Beamsville ON
Lumsden Brothers Ltd. (1) .... Brantford ON
Magna International Inc. (1) .... Concord ON
Magna International Inc. (1) .... Concord ON
Management Board Secretariat (1) .... Toronto ON
Manitoba Transportation & Government Se (1) .... Winnipeg MB
Manitoba Transportation & Government Se (1) .... Thompson MB
Maxim Morrison Hershfield Ltd. (1) .... Calgary AB
Miller Waste Systems (1) .... Markham ON
Milton, Town of (1) .... Milton ON
Minacs Worldwide Inc. (1) .... Markham ON
Ministry of Finance, Ontario (1) .... Oshawa ON
Ministry of Forests, BC (Research Branc (1) .... Victoria BC
Ministry of Health and Long-Term (1) .... Penetanguishene ON
Ministry of Health and Long-Term Care, O (1) .... Toronto ON
Ministry of Northern Development and Min (1) .... Sudbury ON
Ministry of Transportation, BC (1) .... Victoria BC
Ministry of Water, Land and Air Protect (1) .... Victoria BC
Mobilia Inc. (1) .... Pointe-Claire QC
Money's Mushrooms Ltd. (1) .... Campbellville ON
Montship Inc. (1) .... Mississauga ON
Morrison Hershfield (1) .... Ottawa ON
New Brunswick Community College, Moncton (1) .... Moncton NB
North American Railway Steel Tie Corp. (1) .... Squamish BC
North Island College / NIC (1) .... Courtenay BC
Ocean Construction Supplies Ltd. (1) .... Vancouver BC
Ottawa-Carleton District School Board / O (1) .... Nepean ON
Ottawa-Carleton Transit Commission / OC T (1) .... Ottawa ON
Peel, The Regional Municipality of (1) .... Brampton ON
Plains Perforating Ltd. (1) .... Calgary AB
Praxair Canada Inc. (1) .... Delta BC
PTI Group Inc. (1) .... Edmonton AB
Public Service Commission of Canada, BC (1) .... Victoria BC
Public Service Commission of Canada, Ma (1) .... Winnipeg MB
Public Service Commission of Canada, Qu (1) .... Montréal QC
Public Service Commission of Canada, Sask (1) .... Regina SK
Ramcor Group (1) .... Flamborough ON
Recyclage Camco Inc. (1) .... Baie d'Urfe QC
Red Deer, City of (1) .... Red Deer AB

Regional Doors and Hardware (1) .... St. Catharines ON
Rivtow Marine Ltd. (1) .... Vancouver BC
Roe Logistics (1) .... Montréal QC
Roofmart Alberta Inc. (1) .... Calgary AB
Salit Steel (1) .... Niagara Falls ON
Saskatchewan Wheat Pool (1) .... Regina SK
Schneider Foods Inc. (1) .... Kitchener ON
Sheehan's Truck Centre Inc. (1) .... Burlington ON
Sonitrol Security Systems (1) .... Mississauga ON
Stantec Consulting Ltd. (1) .... Kitchener ON
Sunoco Inc. (1) .... Toronto ON
Teleflex (Canada) Ltd. (1) .... Richmond BC
Trail Appliances Ltd. (1) .... Calgary AB
TransAlta Corporation (1) .... Calgary AB
Transoft Solutions (1) .... Richmond BC
Travelers Leasing Corporation (1) .... Burnaby BC
UMA Engineering Ltd. (1) .... Edmonton AB
UMA Engineering Ltd. (1) .... Calgary AB
Vancouver International Airport Authori (1) .... Richmond BC
Velan Inc. (1) .... Montréal QC
Venetor Equipment Rental Inc. (1) .... Hamilton ON
Wardrop Engineering Inc. (1) .... Thunder Bay ON
Weldwood of Canada Limited (1) .... Vancouver BC
Westfair Foods Ltd. (1) .... Edmonton AB
Westfair Foods Ltd. (1) .... Calgary AB
Whistler, Resort Municipality of (1) .... Whistler BC
Whitehorse, City of (1) .... Whitehorse YT
Wilsonart Canada (1) .... Mississauga ON
Winnipeg, City of (Public Works Departm (1) .... Winnipeg MB
XCELLSiS (1) .... Burnaby BC
Zurich Canada (1) .... Toronto ON

For descriptions of the occupational categories used in this index, see page 458.

Geographic Index

GEOGRAPHIC INDEX

BRITISH COLUMBIA (Cont.)

BRITISH COLUMBIA (Cont.)

Richmond .... Ebco Technologies Inc. (8)
Richmond .... Nokia Products Ltd. (8)
Richmond .... Sulzer Mitroflow Corp. (8)
Richmond .... Accpac International Inc. (7)
Richmond .... Crescent Custom Yachts (7)
Richmond .... Nedco (7)
Richmond .... Raytheon Systems Canada Ltd. (7)
Richmond .... Richmond, City of (7)
Richmond .... Richmond Health Services (7)
Richmond .... Inflazyme Pharmaceuticals Ltd. (6)
Richmond .... Nuance Global Traders (Canada) Inc. (6)
Richmond .... Seacor Environmental Engineering Inc. (6)
Richmond ...... Siemens Building Technologies Ltd., Cerber (6)
Richmond .... Sun Rich Fresh Foods Inc. (6)
Richmond .... Williams Machinery Ltd. (6)
Richmond .... Xillix Technologies Corp. (6)
Richmond .... 3LOG Systems Inc. (5)
Richmond .... AeroInfo Systems Inc. (5)
Richmond .... Bird Construction Company (5)
Richmond .... Thrifty Car Rental (5)
Richmond .... Aten Advance Tech Inc. (4)
Richmond .... Cara Operations Ltd. (4)
Richmond .... Coldswitch Technologies Inc. (4)
Richmond .... Great Canadian Casinos Inc. (4)
Richmond .... Hudson General Aviation Services Inc. (4)
Richmond .... Keystone Environmental Ltd. (4)
Richmond .... Matrikon Group (4)
Richmond .... Richmond Honda (4)
Richmond .... Triathlon (4)
Richmond .... ACRO Aerospace Inc. (3)
Richmond .... Air Canada (3)
Richmond .... Broadcom Corporation (3)
Richmond .... Developmental Disabilities Association / D (3)
Richmond .... Diablo Research Company (3)
Richmond .... Fairmont Vancouver Airport (3)
Richmond .... Fields Stores (3)
Richmond .... Hayden Group, The (3)
Richmond .... Herbon Naturals, Inc. (3)
Richmond .... HMS Host (3)
Richmond .... Langara Island Lodge (3)
Richmond .... Mobile Data Solutions Inc. / MDSI (3)
Richmond .... MSAS Global Logistics (3)
Richmond .... Q-Media Services Corporation (3)
Richmond .... Transoft Solutions (3)
Richmond ...... Travel Underwriters Group of Companies, Th (3)
Richmond .... Belcor Industries Inc. (2)
Richmond .... British Columbia Pharmacy Association / BC (2)
Richmond .... Cadex Electronics Inc. (2)
Richmond .... Coast Capital Savings (2)
Richmond .... Dennison Chevrolet Oldsmobile Ltd. (2)
Richmond .... DHL International Express Ltd. (2)
Richmond .... Emco Ltd. (2)
Richmond .... Ensemble Systems Inc. (2)
Richmond .... Heidelberg Canada (2)
Richmond .... Kahn Zack Ehrlich Lithwick (2)
Richmond .... Lafarge Canada Inc. (2)
Richmond .... Lansdowne Dodge City Ltd. (2)
Richmond .... Layfield Plastics Ltd. (2)
Richmond .... Levelton Engineering Ltd. (2)
Richmond .... MacInnis Engineering Associates Ltd. / ME (2)
Richmond .... NICE Systems (2)
Richmond .... PBB Global Logistics (2)
Richmond .... Phase Technology (2)
Richmond .... Pitney Bowes of Canada Ltd. (2)
Richmond .... Radarsat International (2)
Richmond .... Richmond Suzuki Subaru (2)
Richmond .... SanMar Canada (2)
Richmond .... Storkcraft Baby (2)
Richmond .... Teleflex (Canada) Ltd. (2)
Richmond .... Terminal Forest Products Limited (2)
Richmond .... Trail Appliances Ltd. (2)
Richmond .... Voice Mobility Inc. (2)
Rosedale .... Ty-Crop Manufacturing Ltd. (3)
Saanichton .... ACD Systems (39)
Saanichton .... JDS Uniphase Corporation (24)
Saanichton .... Thrifty Foods (2)
Sardis .... Exel Canada (4)
Sechelt .... Sunshine Coast Community Health Council / S (2)
Shawnigan Lake .... Shawnigan Lake School (2)

Sidney .... Axys Group (4)
Sidney .... Greenlight Power Technologies, Inc. (3)
Smithers .... Ministry of Forests, BC (Prince Rupert Reg (3)
Smithers .... Homestake Canada Inc., Eskay Creek Mine (2)
Smithers .... Northgate Exploration Ltd., Kemess Mine (2)
Squamish .... North American Railway Steel Tie Corp. / N (2)
Surrey .... Technical University of British Columbia / T (34)
Surrey .... Surrey, City of (29)
Surrey .... Kwantlen University College (16)
Surrey .... Ministry of Children and Family Development, (11)
Surrey .... Powertech Labs Inc. (11)
Surrey .... School District #36 (Surrey) (11)
Surrey .... Delta Controls Inc. (10)
Surrey .... Inforetech Wireless Technology Inc. (10)
Surrey .... South Fraser Health Region / SFHR (7)
Surrey .... Schneider Foods Inc. (6)
Surrey .... Comptec International Ltd. (5)
Surrey .... ACR Systems Inc. (4)
Surrey .... Aplin & Martin Consultants Ltd. (4)
Surrey .... Babco Sales Ltd. (4)
Surrey .... BC Biomedical Laboratories Ltd. (4)
Surrey .... Kam Biotechnology Ltd. (4)
Surrey .... Fraser Surrey Docks Ltd. (3)
Surrey .... Kelron Logistics (3)
Surrey .... Merit Kitchens (3)
Surrey .... Southridge School (3)
Surrey .... Stantec Consulting Ltd. (3)
Surrey .... Surrey Metro Savings (3)
Surrey .... TRK Engineering Ltd. (3)
Surrey .... Hamilton, Duncan, Armstrong & Stewart (2)
Surrey .... Murchison, Thomson & Clarke (2)
Terrace .... North West Community Health Services Societ (2)
Terrace .... School District #82 (Coast Mountains) (2)
Terrace .... Talstra & Company (2)
Trail .... Cominco Ltd. (3)
Trail .... Kootenay Savings (2)
Vancouver .... Westport Innovations Inc. (68)
Vancouver .... McElhanney Group Ltd., The (57)
Vancouver .... Children's and Women's Health Centre of B (55)
Vancouver .... BC Hydro (54)
Vancouver .... QLT Inc. (52)
Vancouver .... Vancouver Hospital and Health Sciences Ce (38)
Vancouver .... Providence Health Care, St. Paul's Hospit (37)
Vancouver .... Vancouver / Richmond Health Board (28)
Vancouver .... Radical Entertainment (27)
Vancouver .... Sandwell Engineering Inc. (27)
Vancouver .... RSL COM Canada Inc. (26)
Vancouver .... Canadian Cancer Society / CCS (23)
Vancouver .... Liquor Distribution Branch, BC / LDB (21)
Vancouver .... Public Service Commission of Canada, BC / (21)
Vancouver ...... RoundHeaven Communications Canada Inc. (20)
Vancouver .... Boulevard Media (Canada) Inc. / BMC (19)
Vancouver .... General Hydrogen / GH (19)
Vancouver .... Industrial-Alliance Pacific Life Insuranc (19)
Vancouver .... Vancouver, City of (18)
Vancouver .... Westech Information Systems Inc. (18)
Vancouver .... SynchroPoint Wireless Inc. (17)
Vancouver .... Chromatic Software Inc. / CSI (16)
Vancouver .... Vancouver City Savings Credit Union / Van (14)
Vancouver .... Selkirk Financial Technologies, Inc. (13)
Vancouver .... Intrinsyc Software Inc. (12)
Vancouver .... NEPCAN Engineering Ltd. (12)
Vancouver .... Workers' Compensation Board of BC (12)
Vancouver .... AldrichPears Associates (11)
Vancouver .... AMEC (11)
Vancouver .... HSBC Bank Canada (11)
Vancouver .... Pacific Blue Cross / BC Life (11)
Vancouver .... Public Guardian and Trustee of British Co (11)
Vancouver .... Cue Datawest Ltd. (10)
Vancouver .... Intrawest Corporation (10)
Vancouver .... Kazootek Technologies (10)
Vancouver .... Mindquake Software (10)
Vancouver .... Overwaitea Food Group (10)
Vancouver .... Providence Health Care, St. Vincent's Hos (10)
Vancouver .... Financial Institutions Commission / FICOM (9)
Vancouver .... N.D. Lea Consultants Ltd. (9)
Vancouver .... University of British Columbia / UBC (9)
Vancouver .... Emily Carr Institute of Art and Design (8)
Vancouver .... General Paint Corp. (8)
Vancouver .... NCompass Labs (8)
Vancouver .... Purdy's Chocolates (8)
Vancouver .... QDesign Corporation (8)

BRITISH COLUMBIA (Cont.)

BRITISH COLUMBIA (Cont.)

Vancouver .... Enhanced Marketing Services Corp. / EMS (2)
Vancouver .... Fast + Epp (2)
Vancouver .... Forintek Canada Corp. (2)
Vancouver .... Great Canadian Railtour Company Ltd. (2)
Vancouver .... Group Telecom (2)
Vancouver .... Gulf and Fraser Credit Union (2)
Vancouver .... Henry Birks & Sons Inc. (2)
Vancouver .... Homeowner Protection Office (2)
Vancouver .... Hopping Kovach Grinnell (2)
Vancouver .... Hyatt Regency Vancouver (2)
Vancouver .... IKON Office Solutions (2)
Vancouver .... Kinetek Pharmaceuticals Inc. (2)
Vancouver .... Kvaerner Chemetics (2)
Vancouver .... Law Society of British Columbia, The (2)
Vancouver .... Legal Services Society (2)
Vancouver .... Little Mountain Residential Care & Housin (2)
Vancouver .... MDS Nordion (2)
Vancouver .... Mercedes-Benz Canada Inc. (2)
Vancouver .... Merrill Lynch Canada Inc. (2)
Vancouver .... Microcell Telecommunications Ltd. (2)
Vancouver .... Milestone's Grill and Bar (2)
Vancouver .... Ministry of Children and Family Developme (2)
Vancouver .... Multiple Sclerosis Society of Canada, Bri (2)
Vancouver .... Ocean Construction Supplies Ltd. (2)
Vancouver .... Onvia.com (2)
Vancouver .... Pacific Institute of Culinary Arts (2)
Vancouver .... Pacific Language Institute / PLI (2)
Vancouver .... ParaMed Home Health Care (2)
Vancouver .... ParaMed Home Health Care (2)
Vancouver .... Please Mum (2)
Vancouver .... Providence Health Care, Mount St. Joseph (2)
Vancouver .... RBC Insurance (2)
Vancouver .... RCI Capital Group Inc. (2)
Vancouver .... RLG International (2)
Vancouver .... Royal Arch Masonic Home (2)
Vancouver .... RSC Group, The (2)
Vancouver .... Saputo Inc., Milk Division (2)
Vancouver .... Scott Construction Ltd. (2)
Vancouver .... Semotus Systems Corporation (2)
Vancouver .... St. Paul's Hospital, Departments of Medic (2)
Vancouver .... Stikeman Elliot (2)
Vancouver .... Stockscape.com Technologies Inc. (2)
Vancouver .... Syncor Business Environments Ltd. (2)
Vancouver .... TAP Ventures, Inc. (2)
Vancouver .... Terra Group of Companies (2)
Vancouver .... THEmedia (2)
Vancouver .... Transcontinental Publications G.T. Inc. (2)
Vancouver .... University of British Columbia, Departme (2)
Vancouver .... University of British Columbia, Faculty o (2)
Vancouver .... University of British Columbia, Faculty (2)
Vancouver .... Vancouver General Hospital, Prostate Cent (2)
Vancouver .... Vancouver Resource Society (2)
Vancouver .... Victorian Order of Nurses / VON British C (2)
Vancouver .... Weldwood of Canada Limited (2)
Vancouver .... West Point Grey Academy (2)
Vancouver .... Westin Bayshore Resort & Marina, The (2)
Vanderhoof .... Ministry of Forests, BC (Vanderhoof Dist (3)
Vernon .... Progressive Solutions Inc. (3)
Vernon .... Tolko Industries Ltd. (3)
Vernon .... North Okanagan Health Region / NOHR (3)
Victoria .... Ministry of Health and Ministry Responsibl (49)
Victoria .... Ministry of Water, Land and Air Protection (48)
Victoria .... Ministry of Finance, BC (47)
Victoria .... IT Career Access Office, BC / ITCAO (43)
Victoria .... Ministry of Agriculture, Food and Fisherie (33)
Victoria .... Ministry of Children and Family Developmen (33)
Victoria .... Ministry of the Attorney General, BC (Vict (33)
Victoria .... Capital Health Region / CHR (25)
Victoria .... Ministry of Advanced Education, Training a (21)
Victoria .... Public Service Commission of Canada, BC / (18)
Victoria .... eWazo Technology Corporation (17)
Victoria .... Ministry of Energy and Mines, BC (15)
Victoria .... GeoMetrix Data Systems Inc. (12)
Victoria .... IVL Technologies Ltd. (12)
Victoria .... Ministry of Forests, BC (Research Branch) (12)
Victoria .... Public Service Employee Relations Commissi (11)
Victoria .... Royal Roads University (10)
Victoria .... Lodge at Broadmead, The (9)
Victoria .... NewHeights Software Corporation (9)

Victoria .... CroMedica Inc. (8)
Victoria .... Ministry of Social Development and Economi (8)
Victoria .... Oil and Gas Commission, BC (8)
Victoria .... BC Ferry Corporation (7)
Victoria .... British Columbia Investment Management Cor (7)
Victoria .... Carmanah Technologies Inc. (7)
Victoria .... PureEdge Solutions Inc. (7)
Victoria .... Forest Practices Board (6)
Victoria .... Islands Trust (6)
Victoria .... Lester B. Pearson College of the Pacific / (6)
Victoria .... Ministry of Employment and Investment, BC (6)
Victoria .... Royal British Columbia Museum (6)
Victoria .... SkillScape (6)
Victoria .... British Columbia Assets & Land Corporation (5)
Victoria .... Industry Training & Apprenticeship Commiss (5)
Victoria .... Pacific National Aquaculture (5)
Victoria .... BC Transit (4)
Victoria .... Information Science and Technology Agency, (4)
Victoria .... Ministry of Aboriginal Affairs, BC (4)
Victoria .... Ministry of Multiculturalism and Immigrati (4)
Victoria .... StressGen Biotechnologies Corp. (4)
Victoria .... British Columbia Pension Corporation (3)
Victoria .... Camosun College (3)
Victoria .... Ministry of Labour, BC (Workers' Compensat (3)
Victoria .... Ministry of Transportation, BC (3)
Victoria .... Office of the Auditor General, BC (Corpora (3)
Victoria .... Power Measurement Ltd. (3)
Victoria .... SignalSoft Canada (3)
Victoria .... University of Victoria (3)
Victoria .... Victoria, City of (3)
Victoria .... BC Transportation Financing Authority / BC (2)
Victoria .... Capital Regional District / CRD (2)
Victoria .... Environmental Assessment Office, BC (2)
Victoria .... Forest Renewal BC (2)
Victoria .... Ministry of Children and Family Developmen (2)
Victoria .... Ministry of Municipal Affairs, BC (2)
Victoria .... Oak Bay Lodge (2)
Victoria .... St. Michaels University School (2)
Whistler .... Paradata Systems Inc. (20)
Whistler .... Delta Whistler Resort (12)
Whistler .... Westin Resort & Spa, The (7)
Whistler .... Whistler Blackcomb / Intrawest (7)
Whistler .... Whistler, Resort Municipality of (4)
Williams Lake .... Ministry of Forests, BC (Cariboo Regi (3)

ALBERTA

Airdrie .... Propak Systems Ltd. (8 positions)
Airdrie .... Dalen Drilling Services Ltd. (4)
Airdrie .... Palliser Furniture Ltd. (2)
Athabasca .... Athabasca University (37)
Banff .... Banff Centre, The (19)
Banff .... Fairmont Banff Springs (6)
Banff .... Banff Mineral Springs Hospital (3)
Banff .... Banff, Town of (2)
Bonnyville .... Imperial Oil Resources (4)
Brooks .... Brooks, Town of (5)
Calgary .... University of Calgary (131)
Calgary .... Calgary, City of (106)
Calgary .... Global Thermoelectric Inc. (81)
Calgary .... Computing Devices Canada Ltd. / CDC (73)
Calgary .... Mount Royal College (66)
Calgary .... ENMAX Corporation (57)
Calgary .... PanCanadian Petroleum Ltd. (57)
Calgary .... Bell Intrigna (56)
Calgary .... Southern Alberta Institute of Technology / (53)
Calgary .... TransAlta Corporation (48)
Calgary .... Delta Hudson Engineering Ltd. (46)
Calgary .... Alberta Energy Company Ltd. / AEC (44)
Calgary .... Fluor Canada Ltd. (43)
Calgary .... Alberta Energy Company Ltd. / AEC (42)
Calgary .... Wi-LAN Inc. (38)
Calgary .... PrimeWest Energy Trust (31)
Calgary .... AltaGas Services Inc. (30)
Calgary .... Calgary Regional Health Authority / CRHA (30)
Calgary .... Shell Canada Limited (29)
Calgary .... Suncor Energy Inc. (29)
Calgary .... UMA Engineering Ltd. (29)
Calgary .... AMEC Earth & Environmental Ltd. (28)
Calgary .... Alterna Technologies Group Inc. (26)

ALBERTA (Cont.)

Calgary .... AIM Funds Management Inc. (4)
Calgary .... Akinai (Calgary) Canada Inc. / ACI The Imag (4)
Calgary .... Bank of Montreal, Harris Private Banking (T (4)
Calgary .... Barton Instrument Systems Ltd. (4)
Calgary .... Baytex Energy Ltd. (4)
Calgary .... Bidell Equipment Inc. (4)
Calgary .... Big Sisters and Big Brothers of Calgary and (4)
Calgary .... Calfrac Well Services Ltd. (4)
Calgary .... Calgary Board of Education, The (4)
Calgary .... Canada Bread Company Ltd. (4)
Calgary .... Canada Customs and Revenue Agency / CCRA (4)
Calgary .... Canadian Pacific Railway / CPR (4)
Calgary .... CB Engineering Ltd. (4)
Calgary .... Clifton Associates Ltd. (4)
Calgary .... Clifton ND Lea Consulting Inc. (4)
Calgary .... Con-Force Structures Ltd. (4)
Calgary .... DirectProtect (4)
Calgary .... Earth Signal Processing Ltd. (4)
Calgary .... Eastside Dodge (4)
Calgary .... Electronics Manufacturing Group / EMG (4)
Calgary .... Enerflex Systems Ltd. (4)
Calgary .... Enerline Restorations Inc. (4)
Calgary .... Excel Homes Inc. (4)
Calgary .... Federated Co-operatives Limited / FCL (4)
Calgary .... Fugro / SESL Geomatics Ltd. (4)
Calgary .... Gas & Oil Accounting Ltd. (4)
Calgary .... Golf-Gig Management Systems International I (4)
Calgary .... Goodlife Foods (4)
Calgary .... Graham Edmunds (4)
Calgary .... Hitec Systems and Controls Inc. (4)
Calgary .... International Datashare Corporation / IDC (4)
Calgary .... ISH Energy Ltd. (4)
Calgary .... Jaratech Business Solutions Corp. (4)
Calgary .... Koch Petroleum Canada LP (4)
Calgary .... LPI Communication Group Inc. (4)
Calgary .... Maxim Group (4)
Calgary .... Millenia Resource Consulting (4)
Calgary .... Morrison Homes (4)
Calgary .... Nabors International Inc. (4)
Calgary .... Novatel Inc. (4)
Calgary .... Oakwood Associates (4)
Calgary .... Omni Directional Technologies Inc. (4)
Calgary .... OPIsystems Inc. (4)
Calgary .... P&H MinePro Services (4)
Calgary .... Paramount Resources Ltd. (4)
Calgary .... Peace Hills General Insurance Company (4)
Calgary .... Penn West Petroleum Ltd. (4)
Calgary .... Petro-Canada (4)
Calgary .... PowerPlus Systems Corporation (4)
Calgary .... PricewaterhouseCoopers, Business Process Ou (4)
Calgary .... Q-Tron Ltd. (4)
Calgary .... Quebecor World Printpak (4)
Calgary .... Ramco Electrical Consulting Ltd. (4)
Calgary .... Rocky View No. 44, Municipal District of (4)
Calgary .... Sanjel Corporation (4)
Calgary .... Telematic Controls Inc. (4)
Calgary .... TenarisNetwork (4)
Calgary .... Toromont Process Systems, Division of Torom (4)
Calgary .... Trican Well Service Ltd. (4)
Calgary .... United Oil & Gas Consulting Ltd. (4)
Calgary .... Veritas GeoServices (4)
Calgary .... Watermark Advertising Design Ltd. (4)
Calgary .... Westpower Equipment Ltd. (4)
Calgary .... Zi Corporation of Canada Inc. (4)
Calgary .... Access Medical Inc. (3)
Calgary .... Accord Communications (3)
Calgary .... AGAT Laboratories (3)
Calgary .... Albi Homes Ltd. (3)
Calgary .... All New Manufacturing Inc. (3)
Calgary .... Allied Oil & Gas Corp. (3)
Calgary .... Associated Engineering Alberta Ltd. (3)
Calgary .... Beta Machinery Analysis Ltd. (3)
Calgary .... Born Canada (3)
Calgary .... Brisbin & Sentis Engineering Inc. (3)
Calgary .... Calgary Airport Authority, The (3)
Calgary .... Calgary Immigrant Aid Society (3)
Calgary .... Calgary Regional Health Authority / CRHA (3)
Calgary .... Canadian Imperial Bank of Commerce, CIBC We (3)
Calgary .... Canadian Sleep Institute / CSI (3)

Calgary .... Canadian Venture Exchange / CDNX (3)
Calgary .... Cancoil Integrated Services Inc. (3)
Calgary .... Catholic Family Service (3)
Calgary .... CDL Systems Ltd. (3)
Calgary .... Central Park Lodges Ltd. (3)
Calgary .... CGG Canada Services Ltd. (3)
Calgary .... CGU Group Canada Ltd. (3)
Calgary .... CompCanada Atlas (3)
Calgary .... Computalog Ltd. (3)
Calgary .... Corporate Express (3)
Calgary .... Crape Geomatics Corporation (3)
Calgary .... DeVry Institute of Technology (3)
Calgary .... Dominion Construction Company Inc. (3)
Calgary .... Dura-Lite Heat Transfer Products Ltd. (3)
Calgary .... Entero Corporation (3)
Calgary .... Excalibur-Gemini Group Ltd., The (3)
Calgary .... Farm Business Consultants Inc. / FBC (3)
Calgary .... Federated Insurance Company of Canada (3)
Calgary .... Flow Drilling Engineering Ltd. / FDEL (3)
Calgary .... Foster Wheeler Fired Heaters Ltd. (3)
Calgary .... Gibbs Gage Architects (3)
Calgary .... Hanover Maloney (3)
Calgary .... Harvard Energy (3)
Calgary .... HFI Flooring Inc. (3)
Calgary .... Holland Chemical International (Canada) / H (3)
Calgary .... Honeywell Ltd., Industrial Automation and C (3)
Calgary .... Hunting Oilfield Services (3)
Calgary .... Hurricane Hydrocarbons Ltd. (3)
Calgary .... Hutchinson Architects Inc. (3)
Calgary .... IKO Industries Ltd. (3)
Calgary .... ING Halifax (3)
Calgary .... Inland Aggregates Ltd. (3)
Calgary .... Interalia Inc. (3)
Calgary .... Investment Dealers Association of Canada / (3)
Calgary .... JuneWarren Publishing Ltd. (3)
Calgary .... K-LOR Contractors Services Ltd. (3)
Calgary .... Kasian Kennedy Architecture, Interior Desig (3)
Calgary .... Kingsway General Insurance Company (3)
Calgary .... Landmark Graphics (3)
Calgary .... LeBlond Partnership (3)
Calgary .... Ledcor Industries Ltd. (3)
Calgary .... Liquidators Clearinghouse Inc. / LCI (3)
Calgary .... M.H. Shaikh Professional Corporation (3)
Calgary .... Magic Span Fabricating Ltd. / MSF (3)
Calgary .... Maritime Hydraulics (Canada) Ltd. (3)
Calgary .... Martin Newby Consulting Ltd. (3)
Calgary .... Matrix Solutions Inc. (3)
Calgary .... Maxim Morrison Hershfield Ltd. (3)
Calgary .... Metafore Corporation (3)
Calgary .... Moss Fabrication Ltd. (3)
Calgary .... MovieGoods (3)
Calgary .... NeoCorr Engineering Ltd. (3)
Calgary .... Opsco Energy Industries Ltd. (3)
Calgary .... Petro Plan Safety Ltd. (3)
Calgary .... PFB Corporation (3)
Calgary .... Plains Perforating Ltd. (3)
Calgary .... Poon McKenzie Architects (3)
Calgary .... Precision Drilling Corporation (3)
Calgary .... Progressive Engineering Ltd. (3)
Calgary .... PsiNaptic Communications Inc. (3)
Calgary .... Purcell Energy Ltd. (3)
Calgary .... Resource Information Systems Inc. / RIS (3)
Calgary .... Rogers AT&T Wireless (3)
Calgary .... Rogers Cable Inc., Calgary Distribution Cen (3)
Calgary .... Rogers & Partners Securities Inc. (3)
Calgary .... SafetySmart.com (3)
Calgary .... Science Alberta Foundation (3)
Calgary .... Scott Land & Lease Ltd. (3)
Calgary .... Seacor Environmental Engineering Inc. (3)
Calgary .... Stikeman Elliott (3)
Calgary .... Talisman Energy Inc. (3)
Calgary .... Tresco Industries (3)
Calgary .... Tundra Engineering Ltd. (3)
Calgary .... United Parcel Service Canada Ltd. / UPS (3)
Calgary .... United Safety Ltd. (3)
Calgary .... Upside Engineering Ltd. (3)
Calgary .... Venture Communications Ltd. (3)
Calgary .... Vertefeuille Kassam (3)
Calgary .... Vocational and Rehabilitation Research Inst (3)
Calgary .... XXL Engineering Ltd. (3)
Calgary .... Ziff Energy Group (3)
Calgary .... Access International Automotive Ltd. (2)

ALBERTA (Cont.)

ALBERTA (Cont.)

Edmonton	Montage.dmc eBusiness Services	(17)
Edmonton	Bell Intrigna	(16)
Edmonton	Capital Health, Royal Alexandra Hospital	(16)
Edmonton	Northern Alberta Institute of Technology,	(16)
Edmonton	Westcan Wireless	(16)
Edmonton	Advanced Micro Design	(15)
Edmonton	Alberta Children's Services	(15)
Edmonton	Alberta Economic Development	(14)
Edmonton	Alberta Learning	(14)
Edmonton	CompuSoft Canada Inc.	(14)
Edmonton	Trader.com	(14)
Edmonton	Alberta Sustainable Resource Development	(13)
Edmonton	Shana Corporation	(13)
Edmonton	Alberta Corporate Services Centre	(12)
Edmonton	Alberta Mental Health Board, Alberta Hospi	(12)
Edmonton	Colt Engineering Corporation	(12)
Edmonton	SNC-Lavalin Inc.	(12)
Edmonton	Alberta Family and Social Services	(11)
Edmonton	Alberta Innovation & Science	(11)
Edmonton	Convergys Customer Management Canada Inc.	(11)
Edmonton	Intuit Canada Limited	(11)
Edmonton	Maxim Morrison Hershfield Ltd.	(11)
Edmonton	Pangaea Systems Inc.	(11)
Edmonton	Rocky Mountain Instruments Inc. / RMI	(11)
Edmonton	TTG Systems Inc.	(11)
Edmonton	Alberta Motor Association / AMA	(10)
Edmonton	Bettis Canada Ltd.	(10)
Edmonton	Cross Cancer Institute / CCI	(10)
Edmonton	Minolta Business Equipment (Canada), Ltd.	(10)
Edmonton	Alberta International and Intergovernmenta	(9)
Edmonton	Alberta Transportation	(9)
Edmonton	ATCO I-Tek	(9)
Edmonton	Bantrel Inc.	(9)
Edmonton	Capital City Savings	(9)
Edmonton	ING Western Union Insurance	(9)
Edmonton	MessagingDirect Ltd.	(9)
Edmonton	Sierra Systems	(9)
Edmonton	Alltemp Sensors Inc.	(8)
Edmonton	Almac Machine Works Ltd.	(8)
Edmonton	Capital Health, Glenrose Rehabilitation Ho	(8)
Edmonton	Caritas Health Group, Misericordia Communi	(8)
Edmonton	Graham Industrial Services Ltd.	(8)
Edmonton	NorQuest College	(8)
Edmonton	PCL Constructors Inc.	(8)
Edmonton	PTI Group Inc.	(8)
Edmonton	Wawanesa Mutual Insurance Company, The	(8)
Edmonton	Alberta Solicitor General	(7)
Edmonton	Canadian Western Bank	(7)
Edmonton	CGU Group Canada Ltd.	(7)
Edmonton	Cummins Inc.	(7)
Edmonton	Edmonton, City of	(7)
Edmonton	Poly-Pacific International Inc.	(7)
Edmonton	Raylo Chemicals Inc.	(7)
Edmonton	Rohit Group, The	(7)
Edmonton	Alberta Boilers Safety Association / ABSA	(6)
Edmonton	Alberta Research Council / ARC	(6)
Edmonton	Alberta Resource Development	(6)
Edmonton	All Weather Windows	(6)
Edmonton	ALNAV Platinum Group Inc.	(6)
Edmonton	CompCanada Atlas	(6)
Edmonton	Conex Business Systems Inc.	(6)
Edmonton	Focus Corporation Ltd., The	(6)
Edmonton	Maple Reinders Inc.	(6)
Edmonton	Sobeys Inc., Western Division	(6)
Edmonton	Superior Cabinets Alberta Ltd.	(6)
Edmonton	Alberta Alcohol and Drug Abuse Commission	(5)
Edmonton	Allcan Electronic Distributors	(5)
Edmonton	ATCO Power	(5)
Edmonton	Auditor General of Alberta	(5)
Edmonton	Chandos Construction Ltd.	(5)
Edmonton	Corrpro Canada, Inc. / Corrpower	(5)
Edmonton	Deloitte & Touche	(5)
Edmonton	Department of Justice, Alberta	(5)
Edmonton	Edmonton Catholic Schools	(5)
Edmonton	Edmonton Public Schools	(5)
Edmonton	Education On-Line / EOL	(5)
Edmonton	Enbridge Pipelines Inc.	(5)
Edmonton	Grocery People Ltd., The / TGP	(5)
Edmonton	Health Canada, Regional Nursing	(5)
Edmonton	Inland Group	(5)
Edmonton	Institute of Health Economics / IHE	(5)
Edmonton	Landmark Master Builder Inc.	(5)
Edmonton	Matrix Consulting Group Inc.	(5)
Edmonton	Maxim Rentals and Leasing	(5)
Edmonton	Moody International Ltd.	(5)
Edmonton	Stewart, Weir & Co. Ltd.	(5)
Edmonton	Thermo Design Engineering Ltd.	(5)
Edmonton	Walter Cumbria Engineering Ltd. / WCEL	(5)
Edmonton	Alberta Community Development	(4)
Edmonton	Alberta School Boards Association / ASBA	(4)
Edmonton	Alberta Teachers' Association / ATA	(4)
Edmonton	Alberta Treasury Branches / ATB	(4)
Edmonton	AMC Technologies Corp.	(4)
Edmonton	Associated Engineering Industrial Ltd.	(4)
Edmonton	Capital Health, Community Care and Public	(4)
Edmonton	Cohos Evamy Partners, The	(4)
Edmonton	Concordia University College of Alberta	(4)
Edmonton	Corridor Pipeline Limited	(4)
Edmonton	Edmonton Cellular	(4)
Edmonton	ESTec Oilfield Inc.	(4)
Edmonton	Fifth Dimension Information Systems Inc.	(4)
Edmonton	Fluor Constructors Canada Ltd.	(4)
Edmonton	Fountain Tire	(4)
Edmonton	Gear Centre Group of Companies, The	(4)
Edmonton	Geographic Dynamics Corp. / GDC	(4)
Edmonton	Good Samaritan Society, The	(4)
Edmonton	IBI Group	(4)
Edmonton	Industrial Evolution	(4)
Edmonton	Inland Cement Limited	(4)
Edmonton	Jayman Master Builder	(4)
Edmonton	King's University College, The	(4)
Edmonton	Laurentian Bank of Canada	(4)
Edmonton	Legal Aid Society of Alberta	(4)
Edmonton	Lincoln Technology Corporation	(4)
Edmonton	Maclab Hotels & Resorts	(4)
Edmonton	Magna IV Engineering Ltd.	(4)
Edmonton	Master Flo Valve Inc.	(4)
Edmonton	Medical Imaging Consultants	(4)
Edmonton	Oxford Properties Group Inc.	(4)
Edmonton	P.J. White Hardwoods Ltd.	(4)
Edmonton	Peter Kiewit Sons Co. Ltd.	(4)
Edmonton	Sagebrush Corporation	(4)
Edmonton	University of Alberta, Faculty of Nursing	(4)
Edmonton	Vopak Canada Ltd.	(4)
Edmonton	Workers' Compensation Board, Alberta	(4)
Edmonton	A.R. Thomson Group	(3)
Edmonton	Alberta College of Pharmacists	(3)
Edmonton	Alberta Securities Commission / ASC	(3)
Edmonton	ATCO Electric	(3)
Edmonton	Bird Construction Company	(3)
Edmonton	Bishop & McKenzie	(3)
Edmonton	BJ Process & Pipeline Services	(3)
Edmonton	Canadian Tire Corporation Ltd.	(3)
Edmonton	Capital Care Group, The	(3)
Edmonton	Caritas Health Group, Grey Nuns Community	(3)
Edmonton	Computalog Ltd.	(3)
Edmonton	Continental Electric Motor Services (North	(3)
Edmonton	DBR Research Ltd.	(3)
Edmonton	DCL Siemens Engineering Ltd.	(3)
Edmonton	Delcon Development Group Ltd.	(3)
Edmonton	Display Design Systems Ltd.	(3)
Edmonton	Edmonton Community Foundation	(3)
Edmonton	Family Centre, The	(3)
Edmonton	Ferguson Simek Clark / FSC	(3)
Edmonton	Flint Energy Services Ltd.	(3)
Edmonton	Fluid Life Corp.	(3)
Edmonton	Grant MacEwan College	(3)
Edmonton	Hitec Systems and Controls Inc.	(3)
Edmonton	Honeywell Ltd.	(3)
Edmonton	JuneWarren Publishing Ltd.	(3)
Edmonton	Kanotech Information Systems Ltd.	(3)
Edmonton	Land Data Technologies Inc. / LDT	(3)
Edmonton	LGS Group Inc.	(3)
Edmonton	Loadstar Dispatchers / Northern Industrial	(3)
Edmonton	Lockerbie & Hole Contracting Ltd.	(3)
Edmonton	MacLachlan & Mitchell Homes Inc.	(3)
Edmonton	Miller Thomson LLP	(3)
Edmonton	Ministry of Seniors, Alberta	(3)
Edmonton	Morningstar Air Express Inc.	(3)
Edmonton	Northwest Hydraulic Consultants Ltd. / NHC	(3)
Edmonton	Ogilvie LLP	(3)

ALBERTA (Cont.)

ALBERTA (Cont.)

St. Albert	CCI Industries Ltd. (4)
St. Albert	St. Albert, The City of (3)
St. Albert	Youville Home (3)
St. Paul	St. Paul Journal (2)
Stettler	Jiro Compression Ltd. (3)
Stony Plain	WestView Regional Health Authority / WR (4)
Stony Plain	Seljax International Inc. (3)
Vegreville	Vegreville Health Unit (2)
Vermilion	Lakeland College (11)
Westlock	Aspen Regional Health Authority No. 11 (3)
Wetaskiwin	Crossroads Regional Health Authority, Cr (3)
Whitecourt	Alberta Newsprint Company (2)

SASKATCHEWAN

Biggar	Prairie Malt Ltd. (2 positions)
Moose Jaw	Saskatchewan Institute of Applied Science (4)
Prince Albert	Saskatchewan Institute of Applied Sci (2)
Regina	Information Services Corporation of Saskatch (17)
Regina	Public Service Commission of Canada, Saskatc (15)
Regina	IPSCO Inc. (12)
Regina	Regina, City of (9)
Regina	University of Regina, Faculty of Engineering (8)
Regina	SaskTel (7)
Regina	Saskatchewan Liquor and Gaming Authority / S (6)
Regina	SaskPower (6)
Regina	University of Regina (6)
Regina	Farm Credit Canada / FCC (4)
Regina	Regina Health District (4)
Regina	Saskatchewan Post-Secondary Education and Sk (4)
Regina	Partners in Planning Financial Services Ltd. (3)
Regina	Saskatchewan Workers' Compensation Board / S (3)
Regina	University of Regina, Faculty of Education (3)
Regina	Kenroc Building Materials Co. Ltd. (2)
Regina	MacKenzie Art Gallery (2)
Regina	Saskatchewan Wheat Pool (2)
Regina	University of Regina, Language Institute (2)
Saskatoon	Saskatoon District Health (29)
Saskatoon	Saskatchewan Institute of Applied Science (9)
Saskatoon	Federated Co-operatives Limited / FCL (8)
Saskatoon	Hitachi Canadian Industries Ltd. (7)
Saskatoon	Correctional Service of Canada (5)
Saskatoon	Saskatchewan Research Council / SRC (5)
Saskatoon	Correctional Service of Canada (4)
Saskatoon	Houghton Boston Printers (4)
Saskatoon	University of Saskatchewan, College of Ed (4)
Saskatoon	SED Systems (3)
Saskatoon	Mitchell's Gourmet Foods Inc. (2)
Saskatoon	Saskatoon Credit Union (2)
Saskatoon	UMA Engineering Ltd. (2)

MANITOBA

Brandon	Manitoba Transportation & Govt Services (12 positions)
Brandon	Simplot Canada Limited (4)
Brandon	Brandon Regional Health Authority (3)
Brandon	Assiniboine Community College (2)
Brandon	Brandon University (2)
Brandon	Maple Leaf Pork (2)
Churchill	Churchill Regional Health Authority Inc. (3)
Dauphin	Manitoba Transportation & Government Servic (8)
Flin Flon	Hudson Bay Mining and Smelting Co., Ltd. (3)
Oak Hammock Marsh	Ducks Unlimited Canada (2)
Portage la Prairie	Manitoba Transportation & Govern (13)
Portage la Prairie	Manitoba Family Services and Hou (4)
Portage la Prairie	Manitoba Developmental Centre (5)
Selkirk	Manitoba Health, Selkirk Mental Health Cent (6)
Steinbach	Manitoba Transportation & Government Serv (10)
Swan River	Parkland Regional Health Authority (8)
Thompson	Manitoba Highways & Transportation, Aborig (10)
Thompson	Inco Ltd., Manitoba Division (8)
Thompson	Burntwood Regional Health Authority / BRHA (2)
Thompson	Manitoba Transportation & Government Servi (2)
Winnipeg	Manitoba Justice / Culture, Heritage and T (73)

Winnipeg	Manitoba Family Services and Housing (51)
Winnipeg	Manitoba Transportation & Government Servi (46)
Winnipeg	Manitoba Health (39)
Winnipeg	Manitoba Labour & Immigration (39)
Winnipeg	Manitoba Agriculture and Food (34)
Winnipeg	Manitoba Transportation & Government Servi (34)
Winnipeg	Manitoba Finance (32)
Winnipeg	Ceridian Canada Ltd. (27)
Winnipeg	Great-West Life Assurance Company, The (22)
Winnipeg	Public Service Commission of Canada, Manit (22)
Winnipeg	Vansco Electronics Ltd. (18)
Winnipeg	Manitoba Conservation (17)
Winnipeg	Manitoba Education, Training & Youth (17)
Winnipeg	Cangene Corporation (16)
Winnipeg	Manitoba Intergovernmental Affairs (15)
Winnipeg	Health Sciences Centre / HSC (10)
Winnipeg	NOWTV (10)
Winnipeg	Edge Networks Corporation (9)
Winnipeg	IBM Canada Ltd. (9)
Winnipeg	Manitoba Industry, Trades and Mines / ITM (9)
Winnipeg	Acres International Limited (7)
Winnipeg	Manitoba Consumer & Corporate Affairs / CC (7)
Winnipeg	Ship.com, Inc. (7)
Winnipeg	Canadian Wheat Board / CWB (6)
Winnipeg	Winnipeg, City of (Public Works Department (6)
Winnipeg	Winnipeg, City of (Water and Waste Departm (6)
Winnipeg	Manitoba Aboriginal & Northern Affairs (5)
Winnipeg	Manitoba Civil Service Commission (5)
Winnipeg	National Research Council Canada / NRC (5)
Winnipeg	Palliser Furniture Ltd. (5)
Winnipeg	UMA Engineering Ltd. (5)
Winnipeg	Winnipeg Regional Health Authority / WRHA (5)
Winnipeg	Agriculture and Agri-Food Canada (4)
Winnipeg	Canadian Grain Commission / CGC (4)
Winnipeg	Dillon Engineering Ltd. (4)
Winnipeg	Federated Insurance Company of Canada (4)
Winnipeg	Investors Group (4)
Winnipeg	Online Business Systems (4)
Winnipeg	Progestic International Inc. (4)
Winnipeg	Provincial Auditor's Office, Manitoba (4)
Winnipeg	St. Boniface General Hospital (4)
Winnipeg	Winnipeg, City of (Planning, Property and (4)
Winnipeg	Anishinaabe Mino-Ayaawin Inc. / AMA (3)
Winnipeg	Cargill Limited (3)
Winnipeg	North West Company, The (3)
Winnipeg	Optx Corporation (3)
Winnipeg	University of Manitoba, Department of Mech (3)
Winnipeg	University of Manitoba Libraries (3)
Winnipeg	Warehouse One (3)
Winnipeg	Manitoba Hydro (2)
Winnipeg	Manitoba Public Insurance (2)
Winnipeg	Mondetta Clothing Co. (2)
Winnipeg	Reimer Express Lines Ltd. (2)
Winnipeg	University of Manitoba, Department of Chem (2)

ONTARIO

Ajax	Rouge Valley Health System (5 positions)
Ajax	Nokia Products Ltd. (4)
Ajax	Pro-Bel Enterprises, Ltd. (4)
Ajax	Veridian Corporation (4)
Ajax	Ajax, Town of (3)
Ajax	Environmental Waste International / EWI (3)
Ajax	Messier-Dowty Inc. (3)
Ajax	Volkswagen Canada Inc. / VCI (3)
Ajax	Western Assurance Company (3)
Ajax	Mead Packaging (Canada) Ltd. (2)
Ajax	Siemens Canada Ltd., Production and Logistics (2)
Alliston	Honda of Canada Manufacturing (17)
Alliston	Baxter Corporation (8)
Ancaster	Oakrun Farm Bakery Ltd. (11)
Ancaster	Hamilton Region Conservation Authority (2)
Ancaster	Top Tape & Label Ltd. (2)
Arnprior	Boeing Canada Technology Ltd., Arnprior Di (3)
Ashton	Canadian Golf & Country Club, The (3)
Attawapiskat	Attawapiskat First Nation Education Au (2)
Aurora	York Region District School Board (20)
Aurora	York Catholic District School Board (9)
Aurora	Stock Transportation Limited (5)
Aurora	Van-Rob Stampings Inc. (5)

ONTARIO (Cont.)

ONTARIO (Cont.)

Burlington	David Brown Union Pumps (Canada) Ltd. (5)
Burlington	Halton Catholic District School Board (5)
Burlington	SIR Corp. (5)
Burlington	BCL Magnetics (4)
Burlington	Bonar Packaging Corp. (4)
Burlington	Canada Brick Ltd. (4)
Burlington	Cancable Inc. (4)
Burlington	Case Credit Ltd. / CNH Capital (4)
Burlington	Discovery Ford Sales (4)
Burlington	Fisher & Ludlow (4)
Burlington	Graham Packaging Canada (4)
Burlington	King Packaged Materials Company (4)
Burlington	Legato Systems (Canada) Inc. (4)
Burlington	Sibley & Associates Inc. (4)
Burlington	VQuip Inc. (4)
Burlington	ACI Automatic Cutting Inc. (3)
Burlington	Amico - ISG (3)
Burlington	Burlington Technologies Inc., Centennial (3)
Burlington	Cogeco Cable Inc. (3)
Burlington	CRS Robotics Corporation (3)
Burlington	Dresser Flow Control (3)
Burlington	Earth Energy Utility Corp. (3)
Burlington	Gerrie Electric Wholesale Ltd. (3)
Burlington	John Deere Credit Inc. (3)
Burlington	John Holland Chevrolet Oldsmobile Ltd. (3)
Burlington	Mitchell & Associates Consulting Enginee (3)
Burlington	Smurfit-MBI (3)
Burlington	SSI Equipment Inc. (3)
Burlington	Terrace Ford Lincoln Sales (3)
Burlington	7-Eleven Canada (2)
Burlington	Abba Parts and Service (2)
Burlington	Abbey Packaging Equipment Ltd. (2)
Burlington	Brant Telephone Inc. (2)
Burlington	Chem Systems Inc. (2)
Burlington	Comstock Canada Ltd. (2)
Burlington	Esslinger Foods Ltd. (2)
Burlington	Gentek Building Products Ltd. (2)
Burlington	Halton Adolescent Support Services (2)
Burlington	Kingsbury Canada Inc. (2)
Burlington	Kobe Interior Products Inc. (2)
Burlington	La-Z-Boy Furniture Galleries (2)
Burlington	Leggat Pontiac Buick Cadillac Ltd. (2)
Burlington	Maple Leaf Pork (2)
Burlington	Maytag Canada (2)
Burlington	Rexel Canada Inc. (2)
Burlington	Seldrum Corporation (2)
Burlington	Sniderman, Dykstra & Ford (2)
Burlington	Summo Manufacturing (2)
Caledon East	Caledon, Town of (7)
Cambridge	Rockwell Automation Canada (30)
Cambridge	Babcock & Wilcox Canada (19)
Cambridge	Cambridge Memorial Hospital / CMH (14)
Cambridge	ATS Automation Tooling Systems Inc. (12)
Cambridge	COM DEV International (11)
Cambridge	Canadian General-Tower Ltd. (7)
Cambridge	Trow Consulting Engineers Ltd. (7)
Cambridge	Profit Recovery Group Canada, Inc. / PRG (6)
Cambridge	Franklin Covey Canada, Ltd. (5)
Cambridge	Gerdau Courtice Steel Inc. (5)
Cambridge	Gore Mutual Insurance Company (5)
Cambridge	Arriscraft International Inc. (3)
Cambridge	Cambridge Public Library (3)
Cambridge	TravelActive.com Marketing Inc. (3)
Cambridge	A.G. Simpson Co. Limited (2)
Cambridge	Cambridge Custom Tooling (2)
Cambridge	Kinsmen & Kinette Clubs of Canada (2)
Cambridge	Pavey, Law (2)
Cambridge	Siemens Hearing Instruments Inc. (2)
Campbellville	Money's Mushrooms Ltd. (2)
Carleton Place	DRS Flight Safety and Communications (9)
Carp	OZ Optics Ltd. (106)
Carp	Senstar-Stellar Corporation (11)
Carp	First Air (5)
Carp	Morley Construction Inc. (3)
Carp	M-Con Products Inc. (2)
Chapleau	Ministry of Natural Resources, Ontario (4)
Chapleau	Chapleau Health Services (3)
Chatham	Prism Centre, The (7)
Chatham	Union Gas Limited (7)
Chatham	Chatham-Kent Health Alliance (2)
Chatham	Chatham-Kent, Municipality of (2)
Chesley	Bluewater District School Board (2)
Chesterville	M.B. Foster Associates Ltd. (2)
Cobourg	Arxx Building Products (4)
Cobourg	Kraft Foods Canada (4)
Cobourg	Casco Impregnated Papers Inc. (3)
Cochrane	Ministry of Natural Resources, Ontario (6)
Cochrane	Minto Counselling Centre (2)
Collingwood	Collingwood General & Marine Hospital / (9)
Collingwood	Backyard Products Limited (2)
Concord	Magna International Inc. (159)
Concord	DSC Group of Companies (33)
Concord	Unique Broadband Systems, Inc. / UBS (22)
Concord	Magna International Inc. (21)
Concord	Consultronics Ltd. (15)
Concord	Co-Ex-Tec Industries (13)
Concord	Kohl & Frisch Limited (11)
Concord	Concord Confections Inc. (10)
Concord	Toromont CAT (10)
Concord	Woco Automotive Inc. (8)
Concord	Aastra Telecom (7)
Concord	Atlas Corporation, The (7)
Concord	Crown Cork & Seal Canada Inc. (6)
Concord	Nextrom Ltd. (6)
Concord	RCP Inc. (6)
Concord	Corma Inc. (4)
Concord	EMC Group Ltd. (4)
Concord	Lafarge Construction Materials (4)
Concord	Muir's Cartage Limited (4)
Concord	WMA Securities of Canada Inc. (4)
Concord	Brake Pro, Ltd. (3)
Concord	CashCode (3)
Concord	Ciot Marble & Granite Inc. (3)
Concord	KristoFoam Industries Inc. (3)
Concord	Lanzarotta Wholesale Grocers Ltd. (3)
Concord	Metcon Sales and Engineering Inc. (3)
Concord	Powerlasers Ltd. (3)
Concord	Scintrex Ltd. (3)
Concord	Unisearch Associates Inc. (3)
Concord	AFGD Glass (2)
Concord	Canada Bread Company Ltd. (2)
Concord	Horn and Associates (2)
Concord	National Cheese Company Ltd. (2)
Concord	Norampac Inc., Concord Division (2)
Concord	Packaging Group, The (2)
Concord	Schaeffer & Associates Ltd. (2)
Concord	Speedy Auto & Window Glass (2)
Concord	Stantec Consulting Ltd. (2)
Concord	Starline Industries (2)
Copper Cliff	Inco Ltd., Ontario Division (3)
Cornwall	Cornwall General Hospital (8)
Cornwall	Ridgewood Industries (5)
Cornwall	C-MAC Industries Inc. (4)
Cornwall	C-Tech Ltd. (3)
Cornwall	Domtar Inc., Communication Papers Division (3)
Cornwall	Hotel Dieu Hospital (3)
Cornwall	Satisfied Brake Products Inc. (3)
Cornwall	Canadian Mental Health Association / CMHA (2)
Delhi	Fernlea Flowers Ltd. (3)
Dryden	Ministry of Natural Resources, Ontario (Fire (5)
Dryden	Weyerhaeuser Company Limited, Dryden Mill (5)
Dryden	Ministry of Natural Resources, Ontario (3)
Dryden	Northwestern Health Unit (2)
Dundas	Liburdi Engineering Ltd. (18)
Dundas	St. Joseph's Villa (4)
Dundas	Anderson Water Systems Ltd. (2)
Dundas	Valley City Manufacturing Company Limited (2)
Dunnville	Robin Hood Multifoods Inc., Bick's Plant (3)
Elginburg	Len Corcoran Excavating (3)
Elmira	Trylon TSF (10)
Espanola	E.B. Eddy Specialty Papers (2)
Exeter	Veri Transport Logistics (2)
Falconbridge	Falconbridge Ltd., Sudbury Smelter Bus (3)
Fergus	Wolverine Ratcliffs Inc. (6)
Flamborough	Ramcor Group (3)
Fonthill	Fonthill Lumber Ltd. (2)
Fort Erie	Irvin Aerospace Canada Ltd. (3)
Fort Erie	Patheon Inc. (3)
Fort Erie	Rich Products of Canada Ltd. (3)
Fort Frances	Ministry of Natural Resources, Ontario (6)
Fort Frances	Northwest Catholic District School Boa (2)

ONTARIO (Cont.)

ONTARIO (Cont.)

Kanata .... Rational Software Corporation (14)
Kanata .... Sigem Inc. (14)
Kanata .... Watchfire (14)
Kanata .... C-MAC Industries Inc. (13)
Kanata .... Cogency Semiconductor Inc. (13)
Kanata .... Symagery Microsystems Inc. (13)
Kanata .... Cloakware Corporation (12)
Kanata .... Nanometrics Inc. (12)
Kanata .... VideoSpheres Inc. (12)
Kanata .... MDS Nordion (9)
Kanata .... Tropic Networks Inc. (9)
Kanata .... Volex Canada Inc. (9)
Kanata .... KOM Inc. (6)
Kanata .... LSI Logic Corporation of Canada Inc. (6)
Kanata .... NRNS Inc. (6)
Kanata .... Optotek Ltd. (6)
Kanata .... PMC-Sierra, Inc. (6)
Kanata .... Precidia Technologies (6)
Kanata .... Communications and Information Technology On (5)
Kanata .... Empowered Networks (5)
Kanata .... Ottawa Senators Hockey Club (5)
Kanata .... Gilmore Global Logistics Services / DocuLink (4)
Kanata .... Modern Niagara Ottawa Inc. (4)
Kanata .... Robinson Consultants Inc. (4)
Kanata .... Semiconductor Insights Inc. (4)
Kanata .... CMP Design (3)
Kanata .... GSI Lumonics Inc. (3)
Kanata .... Ledcor Industries Ltd. (3)
Kanata .... Potentia Telecom Power (3)
Kanata .... Routes AstroEngineering Ltd. (3)
Kanata .... SR Telecom Inc. (3)
Kanata .... Zivex IT Utility Company (3)
Kanata .... Huber + Suhner (Canada) Ltd. (2)
Kanata .... Kanata Ford (2)
Kanata .... Kymata Canada Ltd. (2)
Kanata .... Mitel Corporation (2)
Kanata .... Rohde & Schwarz Canada Inc. (2)
Kanata .... Square Peg Communications Inc. / SPCI (2)
Kashechewan .... Hishkoonikun Education Authority (2)
Kemptville .... Ministry of Natural Resources, Ontario ((4)
Kemptville .... Catholic District School Board of Easter (3)
Kemptville .... North Grenville, Township of (2)
Kenora .... Ministry of Community and Social Services, O (5)
Kenora .... Ministry of Natural Resources, Ontario (3)
King City .... Country Day School, The (5)
Kingston .... Kingston General Hospital (41)
Kingston .... Ministry of Health and Long-Term Care, Ont (27)
Kingston .... Ministry of Health and Long-Term Care, Ont (16)
Kingston .... Ministry of Transportation, Ontario (14)
Kingston .... Kingston, Corporation of the City of (13)
Kingston .... Providence Continuing Care Centre / PCCC (11)
Kingston .... Empire Financial Group (10)
Kingston .... Hotel Dieu Hospital (10)
Kingston .... Ministry of Health and Long-Term Care, Ont (10)
Kingston .... Cytochroma Inc. (9)
Kingston .... Frontenac Children's Aid Society (9)
Kingston .... Ministry of Correctional Services, Ontario (9)
Kingston .... Kingston Regional Cancer Centre (8)
Kingston .... Millenium Biologix Inc. (7)
Kingston .... Correctional Service of Canada, Regional H (6)
Kingston .... DigiGraphics (6)
Kingston .... Hartford Fibres Ltd. (6)
Kingston .... KFL&A Community Care Access Centre (6)
Kingston .... Limestone District School Board (6)
Kingston .... Ministry of Health and Long-Term Care, Ont (6)
Kingston .... Molecular Mining Corporation (6)
Kingston .... All Care Health Services Ltd. (5)
Kingston .... Days Inn Kingston Hotel & Convention Centr (5)
Kingston .... Kingston Psychiatric Hospital (5)
Kingston .... Providence Continuing Care Centre / PCCC (5)
Kingston .... Victorian Order of Nurses / VON, Eastern L (5)
Kingston .... Bombardier Transportation (4)
Kingston .... Kingston Family YMCA (4)
Kingston .... Kingston Friendship Homes (4)
Kingston .... Queen's University, Faculty of Education (4)
Kingston .... St. Lawrence College (4)
Kingston .... Haakon Industries (3)
Kingston .... Hall of Names International Inc. (3)
Kingston .... inSITE Communications (3)

Kingston .... JL Richards & Associates Ltd. (3)
Kingston .... Kingston, Frontenac and Lennox & Addington (3)
Kingston .... Kingston General Hospital, Radiation Oncol (3)
Kingston .... Ministry of the Environment, Ontario (3)
Kingston .... Ontario March of Dimes (3)
Kingston .... ParaMed Home Health Care (3)
Kingston .... Queen's University, Cancer Research Labora (3)
Kingston .... Queen's University, Department of Human Re (3)
Kingston .... Queen's University, National Cancer Instit (3)
Kingston .... Ramada Plaza Hotel Harbourfront (3)
Kingston .... BDO Dunwoody LLP (2)
Kingston .... Canadian Microelectronics Corporation / CM (2)
Kingston .... Dan Mulrooney Disposal Ltd. (2)
Kingston .... Dibblee Construction Ltd. (2)
Kingston .... DuPont Canada Inc. (2)
Kingston .... Health Information Partnership, Eastern On (2)
Kingston .... John Howard Society of Canada (2)
Kingston .... Kelsey's International Inc. (2)
Kingston .... Kingston and District Immigrant Services / (2)
Kingston .... Norcom / CDT (2)
Kingston .... North Kingston Community Health Centre / N (2)
Kingston .... Ontario Clean Water Agency / OCWA (2)
Kingston .... Queen's University, Joseph S. Stauffer Lib (2)
Kingston .... Soloway Wright (2)
Kingston .... W.I. Villager Ltd. / Marshlands Canada (2)
Kirkland Lake .... Ministry of Natural Resources, Ontari (4)
Kitchener .... PrinterON Corporation (80)
Kitchener .... Schneider Foods Inc. (27)
Kitchener .... Grand River Hospital (24)
Kitchener .... Intellitactics Inc. (22)
Kitchener .... Waterloo, The Regional Municipality of (21)
Kitchener .... Conestoga College of Applied Arts & Techn (14)
Kitchener .... GFI Control Systems Inc. (12)
Kitchener .... St. Mary's General Hospital (12)
Kitchener .... Stantec Consulting Ltd. (9)
Kitchener .... Budd Canada Inc. (8)
Kitchener .... Oakwood Retirement Communities Inc. (7)
Kitchener .... Rogers Cable Inc. (6)
Kitchener .... Waterloo Catholic District School Board, (6)
Kitchener .... Ecoplans Ltd. (4)
Kitchener .... Dare Foods Ltd. (3)
Kitchener .... Golden Windows Ltd. (3)
Kitchener .... Huntington Society of Canada (3)
Kitchener .... Industrial & Financial Systems / IFS Nort (3)
Kitchener .... Kitchener, City of (3)
Kitchener .... Marks Supply Inc. (3)
Kitchener .... Mitchell Plastics Ltd. (3)
Kitchener .... Waterloo Region District School Board (3)
Kitchener .... Giffen Lee (2)
Kitchener .... Graybar Electric (Ontario) Ltd. (2)
Kitchener .... J & D Systems Inc. (2)
Lakefield .... Lakefield Research Limited (2)
Leamington .... Leamington District Memorial Hospital (3)
Lindsay .... Kawartha Lakes, Corporation of the City of (13)
Lindsay .... Bonar Plastics (3)
Lively .... Sudbury Neutrino Observatory / SNO (4)
London .... London Health Sciences Centre / LHSC (67)
London .... Ministry of Transportation, Ontario (24)
London .... London, City of (15)
London .... Siemens Automotive (13)
London .... Ministry of Correctional Services, Ontario ((11)
London .... Ministry of Health and Long-Term Care, Ontar (10)
London .... Ministry of the Environment, Ontario (London (10)
London .... Dillon Consulting Ltd. (9)
London .... Ministry of Labour, Ontario (8)
London .... Delcan Corporation (7)
London .... London Hydro (7)
London .... Ministry of Community and Social Services, O (7)
London .... 3M Canada Company (6)
London .... General Motors of Canada Ltd., Diesel Divisi (6)
London .... Trojan Technologies Inc. (6)
London .... Danapharm Clinical Research Inc. / DCRI (5)
London .... Diabetogen Biosciences Inc. (5)
London .... Ministry of Community and Social Services, O (5)
London .... National Research Council Canada, Integrated (5)
London .... Timberfield Roof Truss (5)
London .... Trow Consulting Engineers Ltd. (5)
London .... Middlesex-London Health Unit / MLHU (4)
London .... Ministry of Natural Resources, Ontario (4)
London .... St. Joseph's Health Care, Parkwood Hospital (4)
London .... University of Western Ontario, Department of (4)
London .... Fanshawe College (3)

ONTARIO (Cont.)

ONTARIO (Cont.)

Mississauga	Calea Ltd. (11)
Mississauga	CIBA Vision Sterile Manufacturing (11)
Mississauga	GE Capital Mortgage Insurance Canada (11)
Mississauga	Silex Design Inc. (11)
Mississauga	Tricom Technologies (11)
Mississauga	Wardrop Engineering Inc. (11)
Mississauga	CPI Plastics Group Ltd. (10)
Mississauga	Entourage Technology Solutions (10)
Mississauga	Kinaare Networks Canada Corporation (10)
Mississauga	Peel District School Board (10)
Mississauga	Winners Merchants Inc. (10)
Mississauga	01 Communique Laboratory Inc. (9)
Mississauga	A.W. Miller Technical Sales (9)
Mississauga	Diversicare Canada Management Services (9)
Mississauga	Edward Jones (9)
Mississauga	IPC Resistors Inc. (9)
Mississauga	Shopping Channel, The / TSC (9)
Mississauga	Trapeze Software Inc. (9)
Mississauga	Antomax Automotive Technologies (8)
Mississauga	C1 Communications (8)
Mississauga	Hofland Ltd. (8)
Mississauga	Ingram Micro Inc. (Canada) (8)
Mississauga	McCormick Rankin Corporation (8)
Mississauga	Orion Bus Industries Ltd. (8)
Mississauga	Stackpole Ltd., Engineered Products Div (8)
Mississauga	Wheeltronic Ltd. (8)
Mississauga	BOC Canada Ltd. (7)
Mississauga	Budget Car Rentals Toronto Ltd. (7)
Mississauga	Enersource (7)
Mississauga	G&K Work Wear (7)
Mississauga	KCI Medical Canada, Inc. (7)
Mississauga	Pallett Valo LLP (7)
Mississauga	Paradigm Electronics (7)
Mississauga	Primerica Financial Services (Canada) L (7)
Mississauga	Purolator Courier Ltd. (7)
Mississauga	Sobeys Inc. (7)
Mississauga	Toronto MicroElectronics Inc. / TME (7)
Mississauga	Tube-Fab Ltd. (7)
Mississauga	Atomic Energy of Canada Ltd. / AECL (6)
Mississauga	Bank of Montreal (6)
Mississauga	Baxter Healthcare Corporation (6)
Mississauga	C/S Construction Specialties Ltd. (6)
Mississauga	Coinamatic Canada Inc. (6)
Mississauga	Commercial Spring and Tool Company Ltd. (6)
Mississauga	CWB Group (6)
Mississauga	DuPont Canada Inc. (6)
Mississauga	EDS Innovations (6)
Mississauga	ESI Canada Inc. (6)
Mississauga	Focus on Health & Safety Inc. / FHS (6)
Mississauga	GE Capital Services / GECS (6)
Mississauga	Hatch Associates Ltd. (6)
Mississauga	Independent Rehabilitation Services Inc (6)
Mississauga	IR Security & Safety (6)
Mississauga	Kronos Computerized Time Systems (6)
Mississauga	Maple Leaf Consumer Foods (6)
Mississauga	MEDIS Health & Pharmaceutical Services (6)
Mississauga	Proco Machinery Inc. (6)
Mississauga	Schneider Electric Services (6)
Mississauga	Schneider Foods Inc. (6)
Mississauga	Siemens Dematic Ltd., Rapistan Division (6)
Mississauga	TCT Daily Motor Freight (6)
Mississauga	TCT Logistics Inc. (6)
Mississauga	Trophy Foods Inc. (6)
Mississauga	Xwave Solutions Inc. (6)
Mississauga	ADESA Canada Inc., Corporate Office (5)
Mississauga	Bell Mobility (5)
Mississauga	BNT Products (5)
Mississauga	Buchanan Associates (5)
Mississauga	Ceridian Canada Ltd. (5)
Mississauga	Columbia MBF (5)
Mississauga	Community Living Mississauga (5)
Mississauga	Dana Long Manufacturing Ltd. (5)
Mississauga	Darden Restaurants, Inc. (5)
Mississauga	Dominion Spring Industries Corp. / DSI (5)
Mississauga	DSPA Software Inc. (5)
Mississauga	Ecolab Ltd. (5)
Mississauga	Festo Inc. (5)
Mississauga	Fuji Photo Film Canada Inc. (5)
Mississauga	Grocery Gateway (5)
Mississauga	Hilti (Canada) Ltd. (5)
Mississauga	ICS Courier Services (5)
Mississauga	Maxxam Analytics Inc. (5)
Mississauga	MI Group, The (5)
Mississauga	Mobilia Inc. (5)
Mississauga	MuscleMag International (5)
Mississauga	PHH Vehicle Management Services Inc. (5)
Mississauga	RTO Enterprises Inc. (5)
Mississauga	Skyservice Airlines Inc. (5)
Mississauga	Supportive Housing in Peel Foundation, (5)
Mississauga	Talon Systems Inc. (5)
Mississauga	TLC Laser Eye Centers (5)
Mississauga	Trends International Corporation (5)
Mississauga	Trios College of Information Technology (5)
Mississauga	VitalAire Healthcare (5)
Mississauga	Weishaupt Corporation (5)
Mississauga	Wurth Canada Limited (5)
Mississauga	Xerox Canada, Supplies Development Cent (5)
Mississauga	Yaskawa Motoman Canada Ltd. (5)
Mississauga	Alphagraphics (4)
Mississauga	ARI Financial Services Inc. (4)
Mississauga	Arius3D Inc. (4)
Mississauga	Assure Health Management Inc. (4)
Mississauga	Beckman Coulter Canada Inc. (4)
Mississauga	Bizerba Canada (4)
Mississauga	Bodycote Ortech Inc. (4)
Mississauga	Canada 3000 Cargo Inc. (4)
Mississauga	Cara Operations Ltd., Harvey's Division (4)
Mississauga	Central Reproductions (4)
Mississauga	Cintas Canada Ltd. (4)
Mississauga	Computroniks Inc. (4)
Mississauga	CSB Systems Ltd. (4)
Mississauga	CTC Communications Corp. (4)
Mississauga	Debiasi Group, The / DBG (4)
Mississauga	Diversicare Canada Management Services, (4)
Mississauga	EFOS Corporation (4)
Mississauga	EMI Music Canada (4)
Mississauga	Ericsson Communications Canada (4)
Mississauga	FCX Specialty Valves (4)
Mississauga	FGI (4)
Mississauga	Fireco Inc. (4)
Mississauga	GE Power Services (4)
Mississauga	Global Star Software (4)
Mississauga	Goldwell Cosmetics (Canada) Ltd. (4)
Mississauga	Imaginex Inc. (4)
Mississauga	Innovative Cooling Dynamics / STT Techn (4)
Mississauga	La Senza Lingerie (4)
Mississauga	Ledcor Industries Ltd. (4)
Mississauga	Lifestyle Retirement Communities (4)
Mississauga	Maple Leaf Poultry (4)
Mississauga	Montage.dmc eBusiness Services (4)
Mississauga	Multipak Ltd. (4)
Mississauga	Oracle Corporation Canada Inc. (4)
Mississauga	Pennsylvania Life Insurance Company (4)
Mississauga	RBC Insurance (4)
Mississauga	Rea International Inc. (4)
Mississauga	Retail Ready Foods Inc. (4)
Mississauga	Rosedale Transport Ltd. (4)
Mississauga	Siemens Building Technologies Ltd., Lan (4)
Mississauga	Skylink Technologies Inc. (4)
Mississauga	Stackpole Limited, Automotive Gear Divi (4)
Mississauga	TOA Canada Corporation (4)
Mississauga	Wajax Industries Limited (4)
Mississauga	Weber Marking Systems of Canada (4)
Mississauga	Whitehall-Robins Inc. (4)
Mississauga	360 Networks Inc. (4)
Mississauga	Auto Sense (3)
Mississauga	BCE Emergis Inc., Assure Health Divisio (3)
Mississauga	BF Goodrich Aerospace (3)
Mississauga	Bio-Form Laboratories (3)
Mississauga	Bridgestone Firestone Canada Inc. / BFC (3)
Mississauga	Canadian Red Cross, Ontario Zone (3)
Mississauga	Care Plus (3)
Mississauga	Cascade (3)
Mississauga	Chalmers Suspensions International Inc. (3)
Mississauga	CHEP Canada Inc. (3)
Mississauga	Com-Net Ericsson (3)
Mississauga	Community Care Services Inc. (3)
Mississauga	Comstock Canada Ltd (3)
Mississauga	Con-Way Canada Express / Con-Way Transp (3)
Mississauga	Creation Technologies Inc. (3)
Mississauga	Debiasi Group, The / DBG (3)

ONTARIO (Cont.)

ONTARIO (Cont.)

ONTARIO (Cont.)

ONTARIO (Cont.)

ONTARIO (Cont.)

ONTARIO (Cont.)

Toronto	Rogers Media, Publishing	(49)
Toronto	CGU Group Canada Ltd.	(48)
Toronto	Sprint Canada Inc.	(47)
Toronto	Scarborough Hospital, General Division	(46)
Toronto	Ministry of Economic Development and Trade,	(45)
Toronto	Rogers Communications Inc.	(44)
Toronto	West Park Healthcare Centre	(44)
Toronto	Law Society of Upper Canada, The / LSUC	(43)
Toronto	Ministry of Finance, Ontario	(42)
Toronto	Ministry of Transportation, Ontario	(42)
Toronto	Rouge Valley Health System, Centenary Healt	(42)
Toronto	Solect Technology Group	(41)
Toronto	Toronto Transit Commission / TTC	(41)
Toronto	Ministry of Finance, Ontario	(39)
Toronto	Ministry of Labour, Ontario	(38)
Toronto	Canada Life Assurance Company	(37)
Toronto	North York General Hospital, General Divisi	(37)
Toronto	Toronto East General & Orthopaedic Hospital	(37)
Toronto	Ministry of Community and Social Services,	(35)
Toronto	St. Michael's Hospital	(35)
Toronto	Scarborough Hospital, Grace Division	(34)
Toronto	Shoppers Drug Mart	(34)
Toronto	Morrison Hershfield	(33)
Toronto	Public Service Commission of Canada, Ontari	(33)
Toronto	Aramark Canada Ltd.	(32)
Toronto	Rogers Cable Inc.	(32)
Toronto	George Brown College	(31)
Toronto	MedcomSoft Inc.	(31)
Toronto	Shopping Channel, The / TSC	(30)
Toronto	University Health Network / UHN	(30)
Toronto	Ontario Power Generation	(29)
Toronto	Bloorview MacMillan Children's Centre, MacM	(28)
Toronto	National Life Assurance Company of Canada	(28)
Toronto	Ontario Lottery and Gaming Corporation / OL	(28)
Toronto	Ryerson Polytechnic University	(28)
Toronto	Alliance Atlantis Communications Inc.	(27)
Toronto	Sigma Systems Group Inc.	(27)
Toronto	Telus Integrated Communications	(27)
Toronto	AGF Management Ltd.	(26)
Toronto	Centre for Addiction and Mental Health	(26)
Toronto	Ministry of Consumer and Business Services,	(26)
Toronto	Giffels Associates Limited	(25)
Toronto	Nanowave Technologies Inc.	(25)
Toronto	ADP Canada	(24)
Toronto	Carswell	(24)
Toronto	George Kelk Corporation	(24)
Toronto	Ministry of Citizenship, Culture and Recrea	(24)
Toronto	St. Joseph's Health Centre	(24)
Toronto	Ash City	(23)
Toronto	Celestica Inc.	(23)
Toronto	Financial Services Commission of Ontario /	(23)
Toronto	Riverdale Hospital, The	(23)
Toronto	Patheon Inc.	(22)
Toronto	Sitraka Mobility	(22)
Toronto	St. John's Rehabilitation Hospital	(22)
Toronto	Stone & Webster Canada Limited	(22)
Toronto	Electro Sonic Inc.	(21)
Toronto	Famous Players Inc.	(21)
Toronto	McCarthy Tetrault LLP	(21)
Toronto	Chapters Inc. / Indigo Books & Music	(20)
Toronto	Rogers Cable Inc.	(20)
Toronto	S.A. Armstrong Ltd.	(20)
Toronto	AT&T Canada	(19)
Toronto	CH2M HILL Canada Ltd.	(19)
Toronto	Children's Aid Society of Toronto	(19)
Toronto	Classwave Wireless Inc.	(19)
Toronto	CSA International	(19)
Toronto	Lombard Canada Ltd.	(19)
Toronto	Muki Baum Association	(19)
Toronto	SAS Institute (Canada) Inc.	(19)
Toronto	Alcatel Canada Inc., Transport Automation	(18)
Toronto	Computer Sciences Corp. / CSC	(18)
Toronto	INTRIA-HP	(18)
Toronto	William M. Mercer Limited	(18)
Toronto	Adexa	(17)
Toronto	Blockade Systems Corporation	(17)
Toronto	Cap Gemini Ernst & Young / CGEY	(17)
Toronto	Ontario Institute for Studies in Education	(17)
Toronto	Toronto, City of	(17)
Toronto	University Health Network / UHN	(17)
Toronto	Leitch Technology Corp.	(16)
Toronto	Ontario Science Centre / OSC	(16)
Toronto	Advantex Marketing International Inc.	(15)
Toronto	Grenville Management Services	(15)
Toronto	Havergal College	(15)
Toronto	Investment Dealers Association of Canada /	(15)
Toronto	Legislative Assembly of Ontario, Office of	(15)
Toronto	Ministry of the Attorney General, Ontario (	(15)
Toronto	Sunnybrook & Women's College Health Science	(15)
Toronto	VoiceGenie.com	(15)
Toronto	Brenntag Canada Inc.	(14)
Toronto	Canadian Institute for Health Information /	(14)
Toronto	CaseWare International Inc.	(14)
Toronto	Catholic Children's Aid Society of Toronto	(14)
Toronto	Club Monaco International	(14)
Toronto	DMC Inc.	(14)
Toronto	Dominion of Canada General Insurance Compan	(14)
Toronto	Global Television Network Inc.	(14)
Toronto	Hummingbird Ltd.	(14)
Toronto	Ministry of Community and Social Services,	(14)
Toronto	National Grocers Company Limited / Loblaws	(14)
Toronto	O&Y Enterprise	(14)
Toronto	Rogers Media, Television	(14)
Toronto	Stikeman Elliott	(14)
Toronto	Warren Shepell Consultants Corp.	(14)
Toronto	Chemque Inc.	(13)
Toronto	Franklin Templeton Investments	(13)
Toronto	Hewitt Associates	(13)
Toronto	Jewelstone Systems Inc. / JSI	(13)
Toronto	Kinark Child and Family Services	(13)
Toronto	Merisel Canada Inc.	(13)
Toronto	Nelvana Limited	(13)
Toronto	Ontario Teachers' Pension Plan Board	(13)
Toronto	Pizza Pizza Limited	(13)
Toronto	Polytainers Inc.	(13)
Toronto	Sony Music Canada	(13)
Toronto	Supreme Tooling Group	(13)
Toronto	United Nations Children's Fund / UNICEF Can	(13)
Toronto	Vistek Ltd.	(13)
Toronto	X.eye Inc.	(13)
Toronto	Baycrest Centre for Geriatric Care	(12)
Toronto	Collega for Aveda	(12)
Toronto	Discount Car and Truck Rentals	(12)
Toronto	DSC Group of Companies	(12)
Toronto	Excite@Home Canada, Inc.	(12)
Toronto	First Professional Management Inc.	(12)
Toronto	Global Group, The	(12)
Toronto	Greater Toronto Airports Authority / GTAA	(12)
Toronto	Greenwin Property Management Inc.	(12)
Toronto	H.H. Angus & Associates Ltd.	(12)
Toronto	Lea Consulting Ltd.	(12)
Toronto	Lovat Tunnel Equipment Inc.	(12)
Toronto	Ontario Municipal Employees Retirement Syst	(12)
Toronto	Percepta	(12)
Toronto	R.V. Anderson Associates Limited	(12)
Toronto	Scarborough Community Care Access Centre /	(12)
Toronto	Technical Standards & Safety Authority / TS	(12)
Toronto	Bombardier Aerospace, Regional Aircraft	(11)
Toronto	Cadillac Fairview Corporation Limited, The	(11)
Toronto	Canadian Depository for Securities Ltd. / C	(11)
Toronto	Citadel General Assurance Company, The	(11)
Toronto	Cogency Semiconductor Inc.	(11)
Toronto	College of Nurses of Ontario / CNO	(11)
Toronto	Hemosol Inc.	(11)
Toronto	Legal Aid Ontario / LAO	(11)
Toronto	MapInfo Corporation	(11)
Toronto	Mercedes-Benz Canada Inc.	(11)
Toronto	Miller Thomson LLP	(11)
Toronto	Ministry of the Solicitor General, Ontario	(11)
Toronto	Novopharm Ltd.	(11)
Toronto	OAO Technology Solutions / OAOT	(11)
Toronto	Sanmina Enclosure Systems	(11)
Toronto	ShawCor Ltd.	(11)
Toronto	Silicon Video	(11)
Toronto	Teleperformance Canada Inc. / TPCAN	(11)
Toronto	VFC Inc.	(11)
Toronto	Burntsand Inc.	(10)
Toronto	C-MAC Invotronics Inc.	(10)
Toronto	Cancer Care Ontario, Provincial Office / CC	(10)
Toronto	Centre for Addiction and Mental Health	(10)
Toronto	Dillon Consulting Ltd.	(10)

ONTARIO (Cont.)

Toronto .... Mania Technologie Canada Inc. (6)
Toronto .... Marcus Evans (6)
Toronto .... MDS Laboratories (6)
Toronto .... MDS Laboratories (6)
Toronto .... Metro Credit Union / MCU (6)
Toronto .... Ministry of Correctional Services, Ontario (6)
Toronto .... Ministry of Labour, Ontario (6)
Toronto .... Ministry of the Attorney General, Ontario ((6)
Toronto .... Ministry of the Attorney General, Ontario ((6)
Toronto .... Ministry of the Solicitor General, Ontario (6)
Toronto .... Natrel Inc. (6)
Toronto .... Nightingale Health Care Inc. (6)
Toronto .... Ontario Heritage Foundation, Corporate Serv (6)
Toronto .... Ontario March of Dimes (6)
Toronto .... Ontario Native Affairs Secretariat / ONAS (6)
Toronto .... Paging Network of Canada, Inc. / PageNet Ca (6)
Toronto .... Relizon Canada Inc. (6)
Toronto .... StackTeck Systems Inc. (6)
Toronto .... Sunoco Inc. (6)
Toronto .... Surrey Place Centre (6)
Toronto .... TAS Designbuild (6)
Toronto .... Tri-ad Graphic Communications Ltd. (6)
Toronto .... Underwriters' Laboratories of Canada / ULC (6)
Toronto .... University Health Network, Shared Informati (6)
Toronto .... University of Toronto, Professional Faculti (6)
Toronto .... Woodbine Entertainment Group (6)
Toronto .... Altera Corp. (5)
Toronto .... Arbor Memorial Services Inc. (5)
Toronto .... AT&T Canada (5)
Toronto .... Balmer Plaster Moulding Corporation of Amer (5)
Toronto .... Bartimaeus Inc. (5)
Toronto .... Bata Retail Canada (5)
Toronto .... BDO Dunwoody LLP (5)
Toronto .... Bell & Howell Ltd. (5)
Toronto .... Blaney McMurtry (5)
Toronto .... Boulevard Club, The (5)
Toronto .... BrandEra.com Inc. (5)
Toronto .... Brown Applied Technology Inc. (5)
Toronto .... Bulldog Group Inc., The (5)
Toronto .... Canada Bread Company Ltd. (5)
Toronto .... Canadian Bankers Association / CBA (5)
Toronto .... Canadian Institute, The (5)
Toronto .... Canadian Olympic Association / COA (5)
Toronto .... Cinram International Inc. (5)
Toronto .... Citibank Canada (5)
Toronto .... Corus Entertainment Inc. (5)
Toronto .... Cotton Ginny Ltd. (5)
Toronto .... Danier Leather Inc. (5)
Toronto .... Delcan Corporation (5)
Toronto .... Deloitte Consulting (5)
Toronto .... Destiny Web Designs Inc. (5)
Toronto .... DMR Consulting Inc. (5)
Toronto .... Dolce International (5)
Toronto .... Donahue Ernst & Young LLP (5)
Toronto .... Doubleday Canada Ltd. (5)
Toronto .... Downtown BMW (5)
Toronto .... DUCA Financial Services Credit Union Ltd. (5)
Toronto .... Faurecia (5)
Toronto .... GHQ Imaging Inkjet Productions Ltd. (5)
Toronto .... Glen Grove Suites (5)
Toronto .... GO Transit / Greater Toronto Transit Author (5)
Toronto .... Halsall Associates Ltd. (5)
Toronto .... Hong Fook Mental Health Association (5)
Toronto .... ICS Courier Services (5)
Toronto .... ING Bank of Canada / ING Direct (5)
Toronto .... Integrative Proteomics Inc. / IPI (5)
Toronto .... Intergen Biomanufacturing Corporation (5)
Toronto .... International Group Inc., The / IGI (5)
Toronto .... International Plaza Hotel & Conference Cent (5)
Toronto .... Judicial Appointments Advisory Committee (5)
Toronto .... JVC Canada Inc. (5)
Toronto .... Lang Michener (5)
Toronto .... Lifestyle Retirement Communities, Forest Hi (5)
Toronto .... Lyreco Office Products (5)
Toronto .... Maple Leaf Poultry (5)
Toronto .... Ministry of the Attorney General, Ontario (5)
Toronto .... Ministry of the Environment, Ontario (Envir (5)
Toronto .... Ministry of the Environment, Ontario (Labor (5)
Toronto .... Mount Pleasant Group of Cemeteries (5)

Toronto .... Nestle Canada Inc. (5)
Toronto .... Nienkamper (5)
Toronto .... North York Community Care Access Centre / N (5)
Toronto .... Oxford Properties Group Inc. (5)
Toronto .... Park Hyatt Toronto (5)
Toronto .... Penguin Books Canada Ltd. (5)
Toronto .... Prescient NeuroPharma Inc. (5)
Toronto .... Radiant Communications (5)
Toronto .... Red Carpet Food Services (5)
Toronto .... Registered Nurses Association of Ontario / (5)
Toronto .... Rekai Centre, The (5)
Toronto .... Rogers Communications Inc. (5)
Toronto .... Rogers iMedia (5)
Toronto .... Royal Doulton Company, The (5)
Toronto .... Royal Ontario Museum / ROM (5)
Toronto .... Royal & SunAlliance Canada (5)
Toronto .... Samtack (5)
Toronto .... Schneider Electric (5)
Toronto .... SCOR Canada Reinsurance Company (5)
Toronto .... State Street Canada (5)
Toronto .... Therapist's Choice Medical Supplies Inc. (5)
Toronto .... Toronto Catholic District School Board (5)
Toronto .... Underwriters Adjustment Bureau Ltd. / UAB (5)
Toronto .... University of Toronto at Scarborough / UTSC (5)
Toronto .... Upper Canada College, Preparatory School (5)
Toronto .... Upper Canada College, Upper School (5)
Toronto .... Videoscope (5)
Toronto .... Wilton Industries Canada Ltd. (5)
Toronto .... Winters Instruments (5)
Toronto .... Workplace Safety & Insurance Appeals Tribun (5)
Toronto .... Yee Hong Community Wellness Foundation (5)
Toronto .... Youthdale Treatment Centres (5)
Toronto .... Active Health Management Inc. (4)
Toronto .... Aisling Discoveries Child and Family Centre (4)
Toronto .... Alias / Wavefront (4)
Toronto .... ARIUS Research Inc. (4)
Toronto .... ASA Alloys (4)
Toronto .... Astound Inc. (4)
Toronto .... Atlantic Packaging Products Ltd. (4)
Toronto .... Axidata Inc. (4)
Toronto .... Baker Gurney & McLaren Press (4)
Toronto .... Bank of China (Canada) (4)
Toronto .... Bank of Montreal (4)
Toronto .... Bantrel Inc. (4)
Toronto .... Branksome Hall (4)
Toronto .... Cadbury Trebor Allan Inc. (4)
Toronto .... Canadian Cancer Society / CCS (4)
Toronto .... Canadian Copyright Licensing Agency / CANCO (4)
Toronto .... Canadian Global Foods Corporation (4)
Toronto .... Canadian Imperial Bank of Commerce, CIBC Te (4)
Toronto .... Canadian Imperial Bank of Commerce, Legal D (4)
Toronto .... Canadian Imperial Bank of Commerce, Nationa (4)
Toronto .... CanCare Health Services Inc. (4)
Toronto .... Cassels Brock & Blackwell LLP (4)
Toronto .... CDG Books Canada Inc. (4)
Toronto .... Charon Systems Inc. (4)
Toronto .... Christian Children's Fund of Canada / CCFC (4)
Toronto .... Clinidata (4)
Toronto .... CPUsed (4)
Toronto .... Crescent School (4)
Toronto .... Daedalian eSolutions (4)
Toronto .... DevelopersNetwork.com Inc. (4)
Toronto .... Dimax Controls Inc. (4)
Toronto .... Diversicare Canada Management Services, Roc (4)
Toronto .... EF Education (4)
Toronto .... Executive Needs Inc., The (4)
Toronto .... Experian (4)
Toronto .... Fraser Milner Casgrain LLP (4)
Toronto .... Gen-X Sports Inc. (4)
Toronto .... Geo Group, The (4)
Toronto .... Grant Emblems Ltd. (4)
Toronto .... Grocery Gateway (4)
Toronto .... Heenan Blaikie (4)
Toronto .... Heroux Devtek, Magtron Division (4)
Toronto .... Hertz Equipment Rental (4)
Toronto .... Highland Equipment Ltd. (4)
Toronto .... Hotel Inter-Continental Toronto (4)
Toronto .... HSBC Bank Canada (4)
Toronto .... Hymopack Ltd. (4)
Toronto .... Iacono Brown (4)
Toronto .... IBI Group (4)
Toronto .... Inco Ltd. (4)

ONTARIO (Cont.)

ONTARIO (Cont.)

Toronto	Kingsway College School (3)
Toronto	Kretschmar Inc. (3)
Toronto	Lancaster House (3)
Toronto	Lansing Buildall / Revy Home Centres Inc. (3)
Toronto	Leaside Group, Inc. (3)
Toronto	Leica Geosystems Ltd. (3)
Toronto	Loblaw Properties Ltd. / LPL (3)
Toronto	LOFT Community Services (3)
Toronto	Mann & Gahtan (3)
Toronto	Maple Leaf Consumer Foods (3)
Toronto	Maritime Life Assurance Company (3)
Toronto	Marsan Foods Ltd. (3)
Toronto	McData Corporation (3)
Toronto	Medisys Health Group Inc. (3)
Toronto	MetCap Living (3)
Toronto	Metro Label Company Ltd. (3)
Toronto	Mevotech Inc. (3)
Toronto	Ministry of Correctional Services, Ontario (3)
Toronto	Ministry of Finance, Ontario (3)
Toronto	Ministry of the Attorney General, Ontario ((3)
Toronto	Ministry of the Attorney General, Ontario ((3)
Toronto	Ministry of the Attorney General, Ontario ((3)
Toronto	Ministry of the Environment, Ontario (Commu (3)
Toronto	Ministry of the Environment, Ontario (Infor (3)
Toronto	Ministry of the Environment, Ontario (Integ (3)
Toronto	Ministry of Transportation, Ontario (Driver (3)
Toronto	Mmmuffins Canada Corp. (3)
Toronto	Morneau Sobeco (3)
Toronto	Multiple Sclerosis Society of Canada (3)
Toronto	Nissin Transport (Canada) Inc. (3)
Toronto	Northern Elevator Ltd. (3)
Toronto	Northern Star Trucking Ltd. (3)
Toronto	Nubase Technologies Inc. (3)
Toronto	Office Specialty (3)
Toronto	Old Mill, The (3)
Toronto	Ontario Bar Association / OBA (3)
Toronto	Ontario College of Pharmacists (3)
Toronto	Ontario Council of Alternative Businesses / (3)
Toronto	Ontario Store Fixtures Inc. / OSF (3)
Toronto	Oolagen Community Services (3)
Toronto	ORIX Financial Services Canada Ltd. / OFS C (3)
Toronto	Owens, Wright (3)
Toronto	Pace, Johnson (3)
Toronto	Parkhurst Knitwear (3)
Toronto	Party Packagers (3)
Toronto	PetsMart (3)
Toronto	Pilot Insurance Company, The (3)
Toronto	Preferred Health Care Inc. (3)
Toronto	Procter & Gamble Inc. (3)
Toronto	Professional Engineers Ontario / PEO (3)
Toronto	Provincial Auditor of Ontario, Office of th (3)
Toronto	RBC Dominion Securities Inc. (3)
Toronto	RBC Dominion Securities Inc. (3)
Toronto	Responsive Health Management (3)
Toronto	Rice Brydone Ltd. (3)
Toronto	Ricoh / Savin Canada Inc. (3)
Toronto	Ridout & Maybee LLP (3)
Toronto	RioCan Real Estate Investment Trust (3)
Toronto	RNG Group Inc. (3)
Toronto	Robins, Appleby & Taub (3)
Toronto	Ronco Protective Products (3)
Toronto	Royal St. George's College (3)
Toronto	Royal Ultraframe Ltd. (3)
Toronto	SciCan (3)
Toronto	Seneca College of Applied Arts & Technology (3)
Toronto	Shade-O-Matic (3)
Toronto	Signature Vacations Inc. (3)
Toronto	Smith Lyons LLP (3)
Toronto	Society of Energy Professionals, The (3)
Toronto	Spectrum Investment Management Ltd. (3)
Toronto	Spin Master Toys (3)
Toronto	St. Clement's School (3)
Toronto	Standard & Poor's (3)
Toronto	Staticon Ltd. (3)
Toronto	Stewart Title Guaranty Company (3)
Toronto	Street Health (3)
Toronto	Supportive Housing Coalition of Metropolita (3)
Toronto	Sutton Place Hotel, The (3)
Toronto	Terrafix Geosynthetics Inc. (3)
Toronto	THiiNC Information Management Inc. (3)
Toronto	Toronto Blue Jays Baseball Club (3)
Toronto	Toronto.com (3)
Toronto	Toronto Community Care Access Centre (3)
Toronto	Toronto Marriott Bloor Yorkville (3)
Toronto	Toronto Real Estate Board / TREB (3)
Toronto	TorPharm (3)
Toronto	Total Credit Recovery / TRC (3)
Toronto	Trammell Crow Corporate Services Canada, Lt (3)
Toronto	Transamerica Life Canada (3)
Toronto	Transcontinental Media (3)
Toronto	Tribute Publishing (3)
Toronto	Tubular Steel Inc. (3)
Toronto	Underwriters Adjustment Bureau Ltd. / UAB (3)
Toronto	Uni-Ram Corporation Ltd. (3)
Toronto	University Health Network, Medical Affairs (3)
Toronto	Value Village (3)
Toronto	Visible Genetics Inc. (3)
Toronto	Vocational Pathways Inc. (3)
Toronto	Warner Music Canada (3)
Toronto	Warner-Lambert Canada Inc. (3)
Toronto	Wexford Residence Inc., The (3)
Toronto	Workplace Safety & Insurance Board / WSIB (3)
Toronto	Wrigley Canada Inc. (3)
Toronto	York Community Services / YCS (3)
Toronto	York University (3)
Toronto	Yorktown Shelter for Women / Yorktown Child (3)
Toronto	Accubid Systems Ltd. (2)
Toronto	Alcoa Rexdale Packaging (2)
Toronto	Alfa Laval Canada (2)
Toronto	American Appraisal Canada, Inc. (2)
Toronto	Amore Sweets Corporation (2)
Toronto	Androcan Inc. (2)
Toronto	Azure Publishing Inc. (2)
Toronto	Bay St. Document Systems (2)
Toronto	Beutel Goodman Real Estate Group Inc. (2)
Toronto	Black, Sutherland, Crabbe LLP (2)
Toronto	Body Shop, The (2)
Toronto	Bombardier Transportation (2)
Toronto	BPA Group of Companies (2)
Toronto	BPA Group of Companies (2)
Toronto	Brans, Lehun, Baldwin (2)
Toronto	Brunico Communications Inc. (2)
Toronto	Cadesky and Associates (2)
Toronto	Canada 3000 Airlines Ltd. (2)
Toronto	Canadian Foundation on Compulsive Gambling (2)
Toronto	Canlight Group (2)
Toronto	Canron Construction Corp. (2)
Toronto	Carma Financial (2)
Toronto	CCH Canadian Ltd. (2)
Toronto	Central Park Lodges Ltd. (2)
Toronto	Central Toronto Community Health Centres / (2)
Toronto	Chappell Bushell Stewart (2)
Toronto	Cimco Refrigeration (2)
Toronto	Circle of Care (2)
Toronto	City Buick Pontiac Cadillac Ltd. (2)
Toronto	Clockwork.ca (2)
Toronto	Cognicase (2)
Toronto	College of Massage Therapists of Ontario / (2)
Toronto	Coltin International Group (2)
Toronto	Community AIDS Treatment Information Exchan (2)
Toronto	Community Care East York (2)
Toronto	Computer Workware Inc. (2)
Toronto	Con-Way Canada Express (2)
Toronto	Consulate General of Japan, The (2)
Toronto	Council of Ontario Universities / COU (2)
Toronto	Crestwood School (2)
Toronto	Crowne Plaza Toronto Centre (2)
Toronto	Cummins Inc. (2)
Toronto	D. Gary Gibson & Associates Rehabilitation (2)
Toronto	Days Inn (2)
Toronto	Dayton / Richmond Concrete Accessories (2)
Toronto	Devry, Smith & Frank (2)
Toronto	DoALL Industrial Supplies (2)
Toronto	East York Access Centre (2)
Toronto	Eli Lilly Canada Inc. (2)
Toronto	Emerald International Inc. (2)
Toronto	Enbridge Consumers Gas (2)
Toronto	ESRI Canada Inc. (2)
Toronto	F & K Mfg. Co. Limited (2)
Toronto	Falconer Charney Macklin (2)
Toronto	Fieldstone Day School / FDS (2)

ONTARIO (Cont.)

ONTARIO (Cont.)

Waterloo	Clarica Life Insurance Company (6)
Waterloo	NCR Canada Ltd. (6)
Waterloo	QJunction Technology Inc. (6)
Waterloo	Philips Analytical (5)
Waterloo	AEA Technology Engineering Software Ltd. / (4)
Waterloo	Waterloo, City of (4)
Waterloo	Waterloo North Hydro Inc. (4)
Waterloo	Equitable Life of Canada (3)
Waterloo	Bauer Industries Ltd. (2)
Waterloo	Lutherwood Community Opportunities Develop (2)
Waterloo	Manulife Financial Corporation (2)
Waterloo	Piller Sausages & Delicatessens Ltd. (2)
Waterloo	Wilfrid Laurier University (2)
Wawa	Ministry of Natural Resources, Ontario (6)
Welland	Tri-Media Marketing & Publicity Inc. (8)
Welland	Niagara College of Applied Arts & Technolog (3)
Welland	Basic Technologies Corporation (2)
Welland	Welland County General Hospital (2)
Whitby	Totten Sims Hubicki Associates / TSH (74)
Whitby	Durham, The Regional Municipality of (25)
Whitby	StonCor Group (14)
Whitby	Whitby Mental Health Centre (13)
Whitby	Patheon Inc. (7)
Whitby	Whitby, Town of (6)
Whitby	McGraw-Hill Ryerson Ltd. (5)
Whitby	Andrew Canada Inc. (4)
Whitby	Horn Plastics Inc. (4)
Whitby	Stonhard Ltd. (4)
Whitby	BMW Canada Inc. (3)
Whitby	Productivity Improvement Center / PIC (3)
Whitby	Sernas Group Inc., The (2)
Windsor	Hotel-Dieu Grace Hospital (17)
Windsor	Windsor Casino Limited (10)
Windsor	Allied Domecq, Spirits & Wine (7)
Windsor	Windsor Regional Hospital (7)
Windsor	Children's Rehabilitation Centre of Essex C (4)
Windsor	Child's Place, The (3)
Windsor	Nemak (3)
Windsor	DaimlerChrysler Canada Inc. (2)
Woodbridge	Ganz (28)
Woodbridge	Royal Group Technologies Inc. (16)
Woodbridge	ATS Test Systems Inc. (14)
Woodbridge	Soroc Technology Inc. (13)
Woodbridge	Carpenter Canada Ltd. (9)
Woodbridge	Pottruff & Smith Travel Insurance Broker (8)
Woodbridge	NUHC Inc. (5)
Woodbridge	Royal Building Systems (Cdn) Ltd. / RBS (5)
Woodbridge	Spectra Aluminum Products Inc. (5)
Woodbridge	Royal Alliance Inc. (4)
Woodbridge	Decor-Rest Furniture Ltd. (3)
Woodbridge	Toronto Star Newspapers Ltd., Press Cent (3)
Woodbridge	Aavid Thermal Products (2)
Woodbridge	Aliron Marketing Canada Inc. (2)
Woodbridge	Egan Visual (2)
Woodbridge	Flowserve Inc. (2)
Woodbridge	Liftking Industries Inc. (2)
Woodbridge	LiveWire Digital Imaging (2)
Woodstock	Hyd-Mech Group Ltd. (3)
Woodstock	Oxford, County of (2)

QUEBEC

Anjou	BECO Industries Ltd. (7 positions)
Anjou	Future Shop Ltd. (3)
Anjou	Hart Stores Inc. (3)
Anjou	Hartco Corporation (3)
Anjou	Midland Steel Ltd. (3)
Anjou	Techmire Ltd. (3)
Baie d'Urfe	SCP Science (14)
Baie d'Urfe	ITR Laboratories Canada Inc. (8)
Baie d'Urfe	Recyclage Camco Inc. (3)
Baie d'Urfe	Plaza Group, The (2)
Beaconsfield	Lester B. Pearson School Board (2)
Boucherville	San Francisco Group (18)
Boucherville	Canam Manac Group Inc., The (10)
Boucherville	National Research Council Canada, Indu (3)
Boucherville	Magnus Chemicals Ltd. (2)

Brossard	MicroSlate Inc. (6)
Brossard	Adacel Inc. (4)
Brossard	Linen Chest (4)
Chateauguay	New Frontiers School Board (5)
Chisasibi	Cree Board of Health and Social Services (7)
Cote St. Luc	Forensic Technology Inc. (17)
Cote St. Luc	Mount Sinai Hospital Centre (3)
Cote St. Luc	Griffith-McConnell Residence (2)
Cote St. Luc	Winners Merchants Inc. (2)
Delson	Vulcain (3)
Dollard-des-Ormeaux	StockerYale Canada Inc. (13)
Dollard-des-Ormeaux	Haliburton & White Group, The (3)
Dollard-des-Ormeaux	Foxboro Canada Inc. (2)
Dorval	Bragg Photonics Inc. (18)
Dorval	Marconi Communications (15)
Dorval	Xwave Solutions Inc. (12)
Dorval	Turbocor Inc. (10)
Dorval	BouClair Inc. (9)
Dorval	Matrox Electronic Systems Ltd. (9)
Dorval	Advantech Advanced Microwave Technologies, I (7)
Dorval	Bombardier Inc., Completion Centre Montreal (7)
Dorval	Innotech-Execaire Aviation Group, The (6)
Dorval	Novartis Pharmaceuticals Canada Inc. (6)
Dorval	USCO Logistics (5)
Dorval	AVS Technologies Inc. (3)
Dorval	Caro Research (3)
Dorval	Hilton Montreal Aeroport (3)
Dorval	Joseph Ribkoff Inc. (3)
Dorval	La Senza Lingerie (3)
Dorval	Marchon Canada (3)
Dorval	Sky Eye America (3)
Dorval	Avianor Inc. (2)
Dorval	Lumbermen's Underwriting Alliance (2)
Gatineau	Provance Technologies Inc. (19)
Hull	SpaceBridge Networks Corporation (32)
Hull	NetPCS (23)
Hull	CML Emergency Services, Inc. (12)
Hull	Hemera Technologies Inc. (11)
Hull	ImageWare Systems (7)
Hull	Alft (6)
Hull	Industry Canada (5)
Hull	Parks Canada Agency (4)
Hull	Scott Paper Ltd. (4)
Hull	CML ATC Technologies Inc. (3)
Hull	CML Versatel Inc. (3)
Hull	Canadian Museum of Civilization Corporation / (2)
Hull	Domtar Inc., Ottawa / Hull Mills (2)
Iberville	Thomas & Betts Limited (5)
Kirkland	Primetech Electronics Inc. (6)
Kirkland	Kuper Academy (4)
Kirkland	CryoCath Technologies Inc. (3)
Kirkland	SPM / United Plastics Group (2)
La Prairie	Shikatronics Inc. (2)
Lachine	Gage Applied, Inc. (27)
Lachine	TELAV Audio Visual Services (21)
Lachine	Rolls-Royce Canada Ltd. (14)
Lachine	Hardt Equipment Manufacturing Inc. (11)
Lachine	Delmar International Inc. (10)
Lachine	Professional Pharmaceutical Corp. (6)
Lachine	United Parcel Service Canada Ltd. / UPS (6)
Lachine	Berlex Canada Inc. (5)
Lachine	Weighpack Paxiom (4)
Lachine	Bariatrix International Inc. (3)
Lachine	Climan Transport Services (3)
Lachine	Innovator Electronic Assembly / IEA (3)
Lachine	Spinelli Lexus Toyota (3)
Lachine	Xtra Lease (3)
Lachine	ISB Group (2)
Lasalle	Patella Manufacturing Inc. (3)
Lasalle	Suss Woodcraft International (3)
Lasalle	Batts Canada Ltd. (2)
Laval	NStein Technologies (11)
Laval	Origenix Technologies Inc. (9)
Laval	Effigi Inc. (8)
Laval	Laura Canada (8)
Laval	Ailes de la Mode, Les (7)
Laval	Boulevard St-Martin Auto Inc. / BSM (5)
Laval	Parisella, Vincelli Associates Consulting Gro (5)
Laval	Belbois Ltd. (4)
Laval	Alliance Steel Corp. (3)
Laval	Business Depot Ltd. / Staples (3)
Laval	Volvo Laval (3)

QUEBEC (Cont.)

QUEBEC (Cont.)

Vaudreuil .... PerkinElmer Optoelectronics Inc. (18)
Vaudreuil .... Buckman Laboratories (2)
Vaudreuil-Dorion .... Filtel Microwave Inc. (6)
Vaudreuil-Dorion .... Quadra Chemicals Ltd. (4)
Verdun .... CLSC Verdun / Cote Saint-Paul (4)
Verdun .... RTP Pharma Inc. (2)
Westmount .... SureFire Commerce Inc. (32)
Westmount .... Rothenberg Group, The (5)
Westmount .... Stellate Systems (3)

NEW BRUNSWICK

Bathurst .... Noranda Inc., Brunswick Mine (3 positions)
Dieppe .... Spielo Gaming International (34)
Dieppe .... New Brunswick Community College, Dieppe Camp (3)
Fredericton .... Department of Health & Wellness, New Br (10)
Fredericton .... Department of Agriculture, Fisheries & (8)
Fredericton .... University of New Brunswick / UNB (7)
Fredericton .... Department of Public Safety, NB (6)
Fredericton .... SmartForce Corporation (5)
Fredericton .... Jacques Whitford Environment Ltd. (4)
Fredericton .... Department of Education, New Brunswick (3)
Fredericton .... Department of Finance, New Brunswick (3)
Fredericton .... Dillon Consulting Ltd. (3)
Fredericton .... University of New Brunswick, Department (3)
Hartland .... Day & Ross Transportation Group, The (3)
Miramichi .... New Brunswick Community College, Miramich (3)
Moncton .... Public Service Commission of Canada, New Br (22)
Moncton .... New Brunswick Community College, Moncton Ca (3)
Moncton .... Canadian Food Inspection Agency / CFIA (2)
Saint John .... Rogers Cable Inc. (7)
Saint John .... Atlantic Health Sciences Corporation / A (3)
Saint John .... Canada Customs and Revenue Agency, Saint (3)
Saint John .... New Brunswick Community College, Saint J (3)
Saint John .... University of New Brunswick, Faculty of (3)
Saint John .... Kent Line International Limited (2)
Saint John .... RMH Teleservices International Inc. (2)
Saint John .... University of New Brunswick, Faculty of (2)
St. Andrews .... New Brunswick Community College, St. An (2)
Woodstock .... New Brunswick Community College, Woodstoc (4)

NOVA SCOTIA

Antigonish .... St. Francis Xavier University (3 positions)
Clementsport .... Pearson Peacekeeping Centre / PPC (2)
Enfield .... IMP Group Ltd., Aerospace Division (21)
Enfield .... CanJet Airlines (11)
Enfield .... Air Nova / Air Canada Regional Inc. (2)
Halifax .... Queen Elizabeth II Health Sciences Centre / (17)
Halifax .... Keane Canada, Inc. (12)
Halifax .... Public Service Commission of Canada, Nova S (12)
Halifax .... Jacques Whitford Environment Ltd. (10)
Halifax .... Kvaerner SNC-Lavalin Offshore / KSLO (7)
Halifax .... Mount Saint Vincent University (7)
Halifax .... Department of Justice, Nova Scotia (Corpora (6)
Halifax .... MacDonald Dettwiler & Associates Ltd. / MDA (5)
Halifax .... Nova Scotia College of Art and Design / NSC (5)
Halifax .... Canada-Nova Scotia Offshore Petroleum Board (4)
Halifax .... CBCL Limited (4)
Halifax .... Dalhousie University, Faculty of Law (4)
Halifax .... Exocom Group Inc., The (4)
Halifax .... KB Electronics Limited (4)
Halifax .... Lockheed Martin Canada Inc. (4)
Halifax .... Halifax Shipyard Limited (3)
Halifax .... Rehabilitative Ergonomics Inc. (3)
Halifax .... Dalhousie University, Department of Civil E (2)
Halifax .... Dalhousie University, Faculty of Health Pro (2)
Stellarton .... Sobeys Canada Inc. (2)
Sydney .... Trakonic (4)
Wolfville .... Acadia University (5)
Wolfville .... Acadia University, Jodrey School of Compu (2)

PRINCE EDWARD ISLAND

Charlottetown .... Public Service Commission, PEI (60 positions)
Charlottetown .... Diagnostic Chemicals Limited / DCL (2)

NEWFOUNDLAND

Clarenville .... College of the North Atlantic (4 positions)
Clarenville .... Department of Works, Services and Transport (2)
Gander .... Department of Works, Services and Transport (5)
Goose Bay .... Department of Works, Services and Transport (2)
Goose Bay .... Serco Facilities Management Inc. (2)
Mount Pearl .... Kvaerner SNC-Lavalin Offshore / KSLO (4)
St. John's .... Department of Forest Resources & Agrifoods (28)
St. John's .... Department of Health and Community Services (24)
St. John's .... Department of Municipal and Provincial (24)
St. John's .... Public Service Commission of Canada, NF (22)
St. John's .... Department of Tourism, Culture and Recreation (12)
St. John's .... Department of Works, Services and Transport (9)
St. John's .... AMEC E&C Services (8)
St. John's .... Department of Fisheries & Aquaculture, NF (5)
St. John's .... Department of Executive Council, NF (4)
St. John's .... Rogers Cable Inc. (4)
St. John's .... Department of Environment, Newfoundland (3)
St. John's .... Danier Leather Inc. (2)
St. John's .... Department of Mines and Energy, Newfoundland (2)
St. John's .... Health Care Corporation of St. John's (2)
St. John's .... Memorial University of Newfoundland (2)
St. John's .... Newfoundland and Labrador Hydro Group (2)
St. John's .... OIS-Fisher Inc. (2)
Stephenville .... College of the North Atlantic, Stephenville(16)

YUKON

Whitehorse .... Yukon Public Service Commission (11 positions)
Whitehorse .... Public Service Commission of Canada, Yuk (9)
Whitehorse .... Northwestel Inc. (4)
Whitehorse .... Whitehorse, City of (2)
Whitehorse .... Yukon College (2)

NORTHWEST TERRITORIES

Fort Simpson .... Deh Cho Health and Social Services (3 positions)
Hay River .... Hay River Community Health Board (16)
Hay River .... Northwest Territories Power Corporation / (12)
Inuvik .... Beaufort-Delta Education Council (6)
Inuvik .... Inuvialuit Corporate Group (2)
Norman Wells .... Sahtu Divisional Education Council, Th (3)
Rae-Edzo .... Dogrib Community Services Board / DCSB (5)
Yellowknife .... Department of Health and Social Service (7)
Yellowknife .... Department of Executive, NWT (3)
Yellowknife .... Lac de Gras Excavation Inc. (3)
Yellowknife .... Nuna Logistics Ltd. (3)
Yellowknife .... Public Service Commission of Canada, NW (3)
Yellowknife .... Stanton Regional Health Board (3)
Yellowknife .... BHP Diamonds Inc. (2)
Yellowknife .... Explorer Hotel, The (2)
Yellowknife .... Raven Tours (2)
Yellowknife .... Yellowknife Catholic Schools (2)

NUNAVUT

Cambridge Bay ...... Department of Human Resources (4 positions)
Igloolik .... Department of Human Resources, Nunavut (4)
Iqaluit .... Department of Human Resources, Nunavut (38)
Rankin Inlet .... Department of Human Resources, Nunavut (17)

ACCOUNTING
ACTUARIAL
ADMINISTRATIVE
ADVERTISING
AEROSPACE
AGRICULTURE/FISHERIES
APPAREL
ARCHITECTURE
ARTS & CULTURE
AUTOMOTIVE
BANKING
BILINGUAL
BIOTECH/BIOLOGY
COMPUTING
CONSTRUCTION
CONSULTING
DESIGN
DIRECT MKTNG.
DISABLED
EDUCATION
ENGINEERING
ENVIRONMENTAL
FINANCE
FORESTRY
FRANCHISING
GEOLOGY/GEOGRAPHY
GOVT./NONPROFIT
GRAPHIC ARTS
HEALTH/MEDICAL
HOSPITALITY
HUMAN RESOURCE
INSURANCE
INTERNATIONAL
LAW
LIBRARIANS
LOGISTICS
MANAGEMENT
MARKETING
METALS
MINING
MULTIMEDIA
OIL & GAS
OPERATIONS
PACKAGING
PHARMACEUTICAL
PLASTICS
PRINTING
PUBLIC RELATIONS
PUBLISHING
PULP & PAPER
PURCHASING
QUALITY CONTROL
REAL ESTATE
RELIGIOUS
RETAIL
SALES
SCIENTIFIC
TELECOM
TRADE SHOWS
TRADES/TECHNICIANS
TRANSPORT

Also from the publishers of this directory...

Discover all the Canadian headhunters in your field

CANADIAN DIRECTORY OF SEARCH FIRMS (2002 EDITION)

Now in its 5th edition, the *Canadian Directory of Search Firms* is the most comprehensive guide to Canada's recruitment industry ever published. This directory lets you find all the headhunters who specialize in your field – over 2,500 firms and 4,200 recruitment professionals are profiled!

Firms are indexed by occupational specialty, city, level of position recruited and fee basis. None of the firms in this directory charges job-seekers a fee – all are paid by employer clients. Also includes a giant "Who's Who" index of Canada's recruitment industry.

This year's edition includes a detailed "how to" section on how to contact headhunters in your industry and more recruiter email addresses, occupational specialties and firm websites. Effortlessly bilingual. Trade paperback. 445 pages. ISBN 1-894450-04-3. **$49.95**

 Now also available on CD-ROM. Includes the full contents of the *Canadian Directory of Search Firms (2002 Edition)* in data format. Email your resume to all the headhunters in your field instantly! Sort and export records any way you like. PC/Mac. ISBN 1-894450-06-X. **$99.95**

*To order by credit card, call **1-800-361-2580** or (416) 964-6069. Credit card orders can also be faxed to (416) 964-3202. View sample pages and order online at **www.mediacorp2.com**. Sold at bookstores everywhere.*

Also from the publishers of this directory...

Find great employers that need people with your degree or diploma

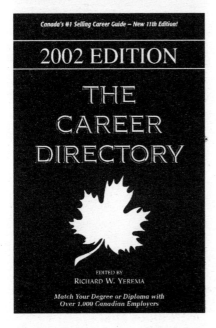

Canada's #1 Selling Career Guide – New 11th Edition!

2002 EDITION

THE CAREER DIRECTORY

EDITED BY
RICHARD W. YEREMA

Match Your Degree or Diploma with Over 1,000 Canadian Employers

THE CAREER DIRECTORY (2002 EDITION)

The Career Directory is Canada's all-time best-selling recruitment guide. This easy-to-use reference lets you match your degree or diploma with over 1,100 employers that need people with your educational qualifications.

The new 2002 edition is the biggest and best ever and features: **more employers** – over 1,100 great employers across Canada are profiled; **expanded indexing** – now has more index entries than ever before; **more "inside information"** on employers – our exclusive "star rating" system lets you know how fast each employer is growing; and **more academic fields** – over 300 university degree, college diploma and certificate programs are covered.

Each employer review provides valuable information on their operations, starting salaries, benefits, academic fields recruited and if summer or co-op jobs are offered. Plus you get full contact information, including HR contact names, email addresses, websites, fax and telephone numbers.

Find an employer that will let you make the most of your degree or diploma! The Career Directory is your key to the hidden job market! Trade paperback. 528 pages. ISBN 1-894450-07-8. **$29.95**

*To order by credit card, call **1-800-361-2580** or (416) 964-6069. Credit card orders can also be faxed to (416) 964-3202. View sample pages and order online at **www.mediacorp2.com**. Sold at bookstores everywhere.*

"A valuable reference guide for job seekers"
-THE TORONTO STAR

"It is easy-to-use, an excellent source, and is necessary for anyone who wants to break into the job market"
-THE UNDERGROUND, UNIV. OF TORONTO

"It can also help you determine whether a company is right for you even before you walk in the door"
-EYE ON TORONTO, CFTO - CTV

"The Career Directory is a user-friendly resource, easy to use and informative. It is an excellent career search resource"
-GUIDANCE & COUNSELLING MAGAZINE

"Helps one make sense of what occupations are available for what degrees, what prospective companies are actually looking for, and valuable contact names within various corporations"
-THE LEXICON, YORK UNIVERSITY

"The Career Directory is an affordable and essential book for job hunting and career planning in Canada"
-THE AQUINIAN, ST. THOMAS UNIVERSITY

"While written for new graduates seeking employment, it is useful for career-changers or students considering educational programs who want to foresee potential areas and types of employment. Also new Canadians with training from foreign institutions have found this book useful"
-CAREER ACTION NEWS, TORONTO CENTRE FOR CAREER ACTION

"Students intending to look for summer or full-time work later this year will find a valuable resource in The Career Directory"
-THE TORONTO STAR

"For those looking for that first job upon graduation or even a summer job, this book could prove invaluable"
-THE LANCE, UNIVERSITY OF WINDSOR

"Finding a job is the formidable hurdle facing university graduates and others these days....[The Career Directory] offer[s] information and advice that could help"
-THE STAR PHOENIX, SASKATOON

The #1 selling business book of the year...
THE GLOBE AND MAIL (4 JAN 2001)

"...a fountain of knowledge about Canadian workplaces, employers, workplace philosophies [and] perks"
-THE VANCOUVER SUN

"...these...companies are doing innovative things. They're really raising the bar."
-THE LONDON FREE PRESS

"...an updated guide on the best places to work"
-THE GLOBE AND MAIL

"Are you tired of the 9 to 5 grind? Probably not -- if you work for one of Canada's Top 100 Employers. ...Progressive companies north of the 49th parallel are going to extraordinary lengths to attract and retain quality employees."
-CHCH-TV, HAMILTON

"..showcase[s] the employers that are doing the most interesting things to attract and keep good employees"
-THE OTTAWA CITIZEN

"...a great way to find out which companies offer family-friendly benefits, such as job sharing and telecommuting, and which ones have earned the distinction of being named among the 10 best employers for women."
-CANADIAN LIVING

"...an interesting read which...bring[s] to light some innovative approaches to the workplace."
-KITCHENER-WATERLOO RECORD

"...[employers in this book recognize] that their employees have lives outside of work and they need time for those obligations."
-WINNIPEG FREE PRESS

"Canadian employers are going to extraordinary lengths to attract and retain quality employees."
-THE EDMONTON JOURNAL

"...profiles companies who do a lot for their employees."
-THE TORONTO SUN

"...rate[s] firms with the best working conditions, benefits and opportunities for advancement"
-THE OTTAWA SUN

"...the book will encourage other employers to create better workplaces and conditions for their workers."
-THE VANCOUVER PROVINCE

Also from the publishers of this directory...

Discover Canada's most amazing places to work

CANADA'S TOP 100 EMPLOYERS
(2002 EDITION)

The first edition of this book was a runaway best-seller — The Globe and Mail named it Canada's #1 selling business book last year.

The new 2002 edition is bigger and better — competition by employers to make this year's list was fierce! The result is an amazing group of employers that lead their industries in attracting and retaining employees. These companies and organizations offer truly exceptional employee benefits, working conditions and perks.

This year's list includes employers from every region of the country and every major industry. Before you apply for a new job anywhere, discover what Canada's top employers offer employees.

"...a fountain of knowledge about Canadian workplaces, employers, workplace philosophies [and] perks," says The Vancouver Sun. This book "showcase[s] the employers that are doing the most interesting things to attract and keep good employees" adds The Ottawa Citizen. Trade paperback. 334 pages. ISBN 1-894450-05-1. **$18.95**

*To order by credit card, call **1-800-361-2580** or (416) 964-6069. Credit card orders can also be faxed to (416) 964-3202. View sample pages and order online at **www.mediacorp2.com**. Sold at bookstores everywhere.*

603

Also from the publishers of this directory...

Get the contents of this directory in CD-ROM format

WHO'S HIRING 2002 – CD-ROM

If you liked the book, you'll love the CD-ROM! Now you can get the complete contents of the Who's Hiring 2002 in CD-ROM format.

The CD-ROM version provides you with the same great information as the print version, but also lets you:

- ✔ **Email your resume to all the employers** in your field quickly and efficiently.

- ✔ **Sort and export records** any way you like – there's no limit on how many records you can export.

- ✔ **Search for keywords** in over 5,000 firm descriptions and 50,000 job titles that are relevant to your job search (e.g. *Show me all employers providing "engineering consulting" services that recruit "Environmental Engineers"*).

- ✔ **Reverse-search** telephone and fax numbers, as well as email addresses.

The price of the CD-ROM edition is **$79.95** (book sold separately). PC/Mac compatible. Ontario residents add 8% PST. ISBN 1-894450-09-4

*To order by credit card, call **1-800-361-2580** or (416) 964-6069. Credit card orders can also be faxed to (416) 964-3202. Visit us online and order at **www.mediacorp2.com**.*

NOW ON CD-ROM

ACCOUNTING
ACTUARIAL
ADMINISTRATIVE
ADVERTISING
AEROSPACE
AGRICULTURE/FISHERIES
APPAREL
ARCHITECTURE
ARTS & CULTURE
AUTOMOTIVE
BANKING
BILINGUAL
BIOTECH/BIOLOGY
COMPUTING
CONSTRUCTION
CONSULTING
DESIGN
DIRECT MKTNG.
DISABLED
EDUCATION
ENGINEERING
ENVIRONMENTAL
FINANCE
FORESTRY
FRANCHISING
GEOLOGY/GEOGRAPHY
GOVT./NONPROFIT
GRAPHIC ARTS
HEALTH/MEDICAL
HOSPITALITY
HUMAN RESOURCE
INSURANCE
INTERNATIONAL
LAW
LIBRARIANS
LOGISTICS
MANAGEMENT
MARKETING
METALS
MINING
MULTIMEDIA
OIL & GAS
OPERATIONS
PACKAGING
PHARMACEUTICAL
PLASTICS
PRINTING
PUBLIC RELATIONS
PUBLISHING
PULP & PAPER
PURCHASING
QUALITY CONTROL
REAL ESTATE
RELIGIOUS
RETAIL
SALES
SCIENTIFIC
TELECOM
TRADE SHOWS
TRADES/TECHNICIANS
TRANSPORT

Also from the publishers of this directory...

See all the new jobs in your field every week

CANADA EMPLOYMENT WEEKLY

Every week, Canada Employment Weekly brings you over 1,000 of the best new job opportunities in the nation. No part-time, temporary, seasonal or agency jobs – just full-time careers with the companies and organziations that are succeeding in today's economy.

Our editors monitor recruitment at thousands of employers across Canada every week. Whenever a vacancy is announced in one of the occupations we track (see list at left), you'll read about it first in CEW. We do the legwork so you can spend your time applying for more and better positions.

In addition to leads on hundreds of unadvertised positions every week, you get valuable background information on employers that you won't see anywhere else. Best of all, 100% of the jobs in our paper are new every week – when you miss a single issue, you miss a lot!

All our subscriptions are sent via first-class mail to make sure each issue reaches you quickly. Subscription rates:

	Canada	USA	Overseas
12 issues (three months)	$55.80	$66.00	$103.50
50 issues (one year)	$232.50	$275.00	$431.25

Rates shown are in Canadian dollars. Canadian residents add 7% GST.

*To order by credit card, call **1-800-361-2580** or (416) 964-6069. Credit card orders can also be faxed to (416) 964-3202. View a sample issue and order online at **www.mediacorp2.com**. Sold at newsstands across Canada.*

Also from the publishers of this directory...

Get your copy of CEW before the ink is dry

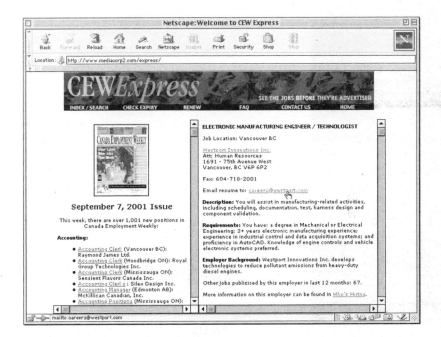

CEW*EXPRESS*

CEW*Express* is the fast online version of Canada Employment Weekly. It features exactly the same content as the newsprint edition, but offers the following advantages:

✔ **Instant Delivery.** A new issue is available to subscribers every Monday at 4:30 pm (Toronto time) — a full day before the paper appears on newsstands.

✔ **Searchable Text.** Job reports are searchable by keyword, so you can quickly find new opportunities in your field across different occupational categories.

✔ **Apply Faster.** Job listings include built-in links to employers' websites and recruiters' email addresses, so you can research hot prospects and apply for positions instantly.

✔ **Back Issues.** You can search the current week's issue plus the last three isssues.

Job reports in CEW*Express* are indexed under 61 major occupational categories, so you see all the vacancies in your field across Canada at once. And 100% of the positions are new every week, so you don't waste a moment reading outdated information.

A 12 week subscription to CEW*Express* costs only $49 plus tax, regardless of where you live. To subscribe, complete the online subscription form at:

http://www.mediacorp2.com

You'll receive a password that lets you access the site for the duration of your subscription.

ACCOUNTING
ACTUARIAL
ADMINISTRATIVE
ADVERTISING
AEROSPACE
AGRICULTURE/FISHERIES
APPAREL
ARCHITECTURE
ARTS & CULTURE
AUTOMOTIVE
BANKING
BILINGUAL
BIOTECH/BIOLOGY
COMPUTING
CONSTRUCTION
CONSULTING
DESIGN
DIRECT MKTNG.
DISABLED
EDUCATION
ENGINEERING
ENVIRONMENTAL
FINANCE
FORESTRY
FRANCHISING
GEOLOGY/GEOGRAPHY
GOVT./NONPROFIT
GRAPHIC ARTS
HEALTH/MEDICAL
HOSPITALITY
HUMAN RESOURCE
INSURANCE
INTERNATIONAL
LAW
LIBRARIANS
LOGISTICS
MANAGEMENT
MARKETING
METALS
MINING
MULTIMEDIA
OIL & GAS
OPERATIONS
PACKAGING
PHARMACEUTICAL
PLASTICS
PRINTING
PUBLIC RELATIONS
PUBLISHING
PULP & PAPER
PURCHASING
QUALITY CONTROL
REAL ESTATE
RELIGIOUS
RETAIL
SALES
SCIENTIFIC
TELECOM
TRADE SHOWS
TRADES/TECHNICIANS
TRANSPORT

Also from the publishers of this directory...

See all the jobs reported in your field in the past year

OUR INDUSTRY REPORT SERVICE

Each week we publish Industry Reports in 61 major occupations showing:

✔ **The Top 25 Employers in the field**, based on the number of new positions each employer created in the field in the past 12 months.

✔ **All the new job opportunities that have been reported across Canada in the field in the past year.** You get full details of each position, the qualifications required, salary offered (if publicized), background information on the employer, and full contact information (HR contact name, employer address, email, fax and website). We also show you the date the vacancy was first reported.

Industry Reports are available in printed or electronic (PDF or text) formats. Reports vary in length from 25 pages to over 400 pages for larger categories (such as Computing and Engineering).

Our Industry Reports are used by:

❑ **Job-seekers** who want to discover the top employers in their field and see complete details on all the positions publicized in their field in the past year.

❑ **Human Resource Managers** who want to learn the current qualifications, duties and salary levels (where publicized) that are being offered by other employers in their industry.

❑ **Headhunters and recruitment professionals** who have an outstanding candidate and need to know all the employers that could use this candidate's skills and qualifications.

The price for one Industry Report is **$59.95** and there is a 15% discount if you receive your report by email. Categories are updated every Tuesday.

*To order by credit card, call **1-800-361-2580** or (416) 964-6069. Credit card orders can also be faxed to (416) 964-3202. View sample a sample Industry Report and order online at **www.mediacorp2.com**.*

Comments & Changes Form

Please correct / add the following information in the next edition of *Who's Hiring*. We'll look into the matter you describe.

_____

_____

_____

_____

_____

_____

_____

_____

_____

_____

_____

_____

_____

NAME OF EMPLOYER

SUBMITTED BY (OPTIONAL)

DATE   TELEPHONE

Mail completed form to: Who's Hiring, c/o Mediacorp Canada Inc., 21 New Street, Toronto, ON M5R 1P7. Or fax to (416) 964-3202. You can also email corrections to: info@mediacorp2.com.

Order Form

This directory is sold at major bookstores across Canada. You can also order directly from the publisher:

- ❑ **Online.** Order securely online at http://www.mediacorp2.com.
- ❑ **Telephone.** To order by credit card, call 1-800-361-2580 or (416) 964-6069.
- ❑ **Fax.** Fax your credit card order to (416) 964-3202.
- ❑ **Mail.** Send this form and your cheque or money order (payable to "Mediacorp Canada Inc.") to the address below.

Total charges per copy ordered are:

Shipped to	Directory	Shipping	GST	Total
Canada	$34.95	$5.00	$2.80	$42.75
USA	34.95	9.95	0.00	34.90
Overseas	34.95	18.96	0.00	53.91

All orders are shipped on the same or next business day. Orders in Canada and the USA are shipped by Expressmail and delivered to you in three to four business days. Overseas shipments are sent by first classs airmail. FedEx delivery also available.

ORDER FORM

GST # 134051515

WHO'S HIRING 2002

Number of copies ordered: ☐

Method of Payment:
- ❑ Visa
- ❑ Amex
- ❑ MasterCard
- ❑ Cheque

NAME

ADDRESS

CITY   PROV.   POST. CODE

COUNTRY

TELEPHONE

CREDIT CARD NUMBER

EXPIRY DATE   /   SIGNATURE

Send or fax to

WHO'S HIRING 2002
21 NEW STREET, TORONTO, CANADA M5R 1P7
TEL. (416) 964-6069 • FAX (416) 964-3202
TO ORDER, CALL TOLL-FREE 1-800-361-2580
http://www.mediacorp2.com